# HUXFORD'S
# OLD
# BOOK
## VALUE GUIDE

**25,000 Listings of Old Books
with Current Values**

Eleventh
Edition

## COLLECTOR BOOKS

*A Division of Schroeder Publishing Co., Inc.*

The current values of this book should be used only as a guide. They are not intended to set prices, which vary from one section of the country to another. Auction prices as well as dealer prices vary and are affected by condition as well as demand. Neither the editors nor the publisher assumes responsibility for any losses that might be incurred as a result of consulting this guide.

SEARCHING FOR A PUBLISHER?

We are always looking for knowledgeable people considered to be experts within their fields. If you feel that there is a real need for a book on your collectible subject and have a large comprehensive collection, contact Collector Books.

**On the Cover:**

Habberton, John. *Our Country's Future.* 1891. International Pub. 1st. 8vo. ils. aeg. 694p. VG-. $50.00

Waugh, Ida. *Ideal Heads.* 1890. Sunshine Publishing Co. 1st. folio. 20 litho water-color engr. ftspc Jesse Wilcox Smith. aeg. F/G. from $150.00 to 400.00

Joseph Allen's Wife. *Samantha at the World's Fair.* 1893. Funk & Wagnalls. 1st. 8vo. ils Baron C. DeGrimm. 694p. VG. $60.00

DeGrazia, Ted. *ah ha Toro.* 1967. Northlands Pr. 1st. sgn author/ils. 4to. F/VG. $125.00

Crosby, Kathryn. *My Life With Bing.* 1983. Collage Press. ltd pre-publication edition. sgn. 4to. 355p. VG/G-. $40.00

Falls, C.B. *Mother Goose.* 1924. Doubleday Page. 1st. 4to. 96p. rpr. G+. from $150.00 to 170.00

Moore, Colleen. *Colleen Moore's Doll House.* 1979. Doubleday. 1st/2nd prt. inscr. 4to. 96p. xl. VG/G-. from $45.00 to 50.00

Hillerman, Tony. *The Ghostway.* 1985. Gollancz. 1st Eng. sgn bookplate. 12mo. 184p. AN/AN. from $65.00 to 100.00

London, Jack. *The Iron Heel.* Feb 1908. London. MacMillan. 16mo. 354p. G. from $150.00 to 200.00

Books featured on cover courtesy of
AL-PAC, Lamar Kelley
2625 E Southern Ave., C-120
Tempe, AZ 85282
602-831-3121 or fax 602-831-3193
alpac2625@aol.com

Editing and research: Linda Holycross
Cover design: Beth Summers

Collector Books
P.O. Box 3009
Paducah, Kentucky 42002 – 3009

Copyright © 1999 by Schroeder Publishing Co., Inc.

# INTRODUCTION

This book has been compiled to help both buyers and sellers. Two questions that we are asked most frequently are 'Can you tell me the value of my books?' and 'Where can I sell them?' *Huxford's Old Book Value Guide* will help answer both of these questions. Not only does this book place secondary market retail values (values that an interested party would be willing to pay to obtain possession of the book) on nearly 25,000 old books, it also lists scores of buyers along with the type of material each is interested in purchasing. These prices are taken from dealers' selling lists that have been issued within the past year. All of the listings are coded (A1, S7, etc.) before the price. This coding refers to a specific dealer's listing for that book. When two or more dealers have listed the same book, their codes will be listed alphabetically in the description line. Please refer to the section titled 'Booksellers' for codes.

If you were to sell your books to a dealer, you should expect to receive no more than 50% of the values listed in this book, unless the dealer has a specific buyer in mind for some of your material. In many cases, a dealer will pay less than 50% of retail for a book to stock.

Do not ask a dealer to evaluate your old books unless you intend to sell them to him. Most antiquarian book dealers in the larger cities will appraise your books and ephemera for a fee that ranges from a low of $10.00 per hour to $50.00 per hour (or more). If you have an extensive library of rare books, the $50.00-an-hour figure would be money well spent (assuming, of course, the appraiser to be qualified and honest).

*Huxford's Old Book Value Guide* places values on the more common holdings that many seem to accumulate. You will notice that the majority of the books listed are in the $10.00 to $40.00 range. Many such guides list only the rare, almost nonexistent books that the average person will never see. The format is very simple: listings are alphabetized first by the name of the author, translator, editor, or illustrator; if more than one book is listed for a particular author, each title is listed alphabetically under his or her name. When pseudonyms are known, names have been cross-referenced. (Please also see the section titled 'Pseudonyms' for additional information.) Dust jackets or wrappers are noted when present, and sizes (when given) are approximate. Condition is usually noted as well. (If condition is not stated, it is assumed to be very good.) Dates within parentheses indicate the copyright page dates while dates without parentheses are dates found on the title pages and/or are the actual publication dates.

Fine condition refers to books that are in perfect, as-issued condition with no defects. Books in near-fine condition are perfect, but not as crisp as those graded fine. Near-fine condition books show only a little wear from reading (such as very small marks on binding); but they still have no major defects. Books rated very good may show wear but must have no tears on pages, binding, or dust jacket (if issued). A rating of good applies to an average used book that has all of its pages and yet may have small tears and other defects. The term reading copy (some dealers also use 'poor') describes a book having major defects; however, its text must be complete. Ex-library books are always indicated as such; they may be found in any condition. This rule also applies to any Book Club edition. Some of our booksellers indicate intermediate grades with a + or ++, or VG-EX. We have endeavored to use the grade that best corresponded to the description of condition as given in each dealer's listing. If you want to check further on the condition of a specific book, please consult the bookseller indicated. Please note that the condition stated in the description is for the book and then the dust jacket. (Dust jackets on many modern first editions may account for up to 80% of their value.)

In the back of the book we have listed buyers of books and book-related material. When you correspond with these dealers, be sure to enclose a self-addressed, stamped envelope if you want a reply. Please do not send lists of books for an appraisal. If you wish to sell your books, quote the price that you want or negotiate price only on the items the buyer is interested in purchasing. When you list your books, do so by author, full title, publisher and place, date, and edition. Indicate condition, noting any defects on cover or contents.

When shipping your books, first wrap each book in paper such as brown kraft or a similar type of material. Never use newspaper for the inner wrap, since newsprint tends to rub off. (It may, however be used as a cushioning material within the outer carton.) Place your books in a sturdy corrugated box and use a good shipping tape to seal it. Tape reinforced with nylon string is preferable, as it will not tear. Books shipped by parcel post may be sent at a special fourth class book rate, which may be lower than regular parcel post zone rates.

# LISTING OF STANDARD ABBREVIATIONS

/ ...and, also, with, or indicates dual-title book
aeg......................................all edge gilt
Am......................................American
AN.........................................as new
AP ......proof, advance proof, advance uncorrected proof, or galley
ARC ....... advance reading or review copy
bdg.......................binding, bound
b&w............................black & white
bl...............................................blue
blk............................................black
BC.................any book club edition
brd.........................................boards
bstp.................................blindstamp
c.......................................copyright
ca...............................................circa
cb......................................cardboard
cbdg...........................comb binding
chip......................................chipped
clip............................clipped price
CMG.....Coward McCann Geoghegan
dbl............................................double
decor.................decoration, decorated
dk..............................................dark
dj....................................dust jacket
DIF..........................Donald I. Fine
DSP.......................Duell Sloan Pearce
dtd..........................................dated
E .................................east, eastern
edit............................................editor
ed ...........................................edition
emb.................embossed, embossing
Eng.....................England, English
ep...................................end pages
ERB............Edgar Rice Burroughs Inc.
ES.....................................errata slip
F ................................................fine
facs ....................................facsimile
ffe..........................front free endpaper
fld ..............................folding, folder
ftspc...................................frontispiece
FSC.........Farrar, Straus & Cudahy
FSG.................Farrar, Straus & Giroux
FSY ................Farrar, Straus & Young
fwd ....................................foreword
G .............................................good
GPO........Government Printing Office
gr ............................................green

gte......................................gilt top edge
HBJ.....Harcourt Brace Jovanovich, Inc.
HBW ................Harcourt Brace World
hc....................................hard cover
hist......................................history
HRW ...............Holt Rinehart Winston
ils..........................................illustrated
imp.................imprint, impression
intl..........................................initialed
inscr ...................................inscribed
Inst......................................Institute
Internat....................International
intro .................................introduction
LEC ............Limited Edition Club
lg...............................................large
Lib............................................library
lt................................................light
ltd ............................................limited
mc .......................................multicolor
mini...........................miniature book
MIT.........MA Institute of Technology
MOMA ........Museum of Modern Art
mtd......................................mounted
MTI ....................movie tie-in
Mus.....................................museum
N ..............................north, northern
NAL...............New American Library
Nat..........................................national
NEL ............New English Library
nd.............................................no date
ne...............................no edition given
NF...........................................near fine
NGS.......National Geographic Society
np........ no place given, no publisher stated
NYGS........New York Graphic Society
obl..........................................oblong
orig...............................................original
OUP .............Oxford University Press
p ...............................page, pages
pb...........................................paperback
pc................................................piece
pict.......................................pictorial
pl.............................plate, plates
Pr..............................................press
pref.......................................preface
pres .................................presentation
promo ...........................promotion
prt ............................print, printing
pub ..............publisher, publishing

rb ..........................................rebound
rem mk ......................remainder mark
repro ........................reproduction
rpl..........................................replaced
rpr...............................................repair
rpt .............................................reprint
RS...................................review slip
rstr ..........................................restored
S ...............................south, southern
S&S...................Simon & Schuster
sans ...............................none issued
sbdg ......................spiral binding
sc .............................................softcover
SF .........San Francisco, science fiction
sgn ................signature, signed
sm ..............................................small
sq ............................................square
stp ..........................stamp, stamped
supp ..........................supplement
swrp ...................shrink wrap
TB..........................................textbook
teg ............................top edge gilt
TLS........................typed letter signed
trans ..........................translated
TVTI ................................TV tie-in
U .....................................University
unp .....................................unpaged
UP....................uncorrected proof
VG....................................very good
W ...............................west, western
w/ ......with, indicates laid in material
wht.................................................white
wrp...................................wrappers
xl ...........................................ex-library
yel..........................................yellow
#d..........................................numbered
12mo......................about 7" tall
16mo............................6" to 7" tall
24mo.........................5" to 6" tall
32mo.........................4" to 5" tall
48mo ..............less than 4" tall
64mo.........................about 3" tall
sm 8vo.....................7½" to 8" tall
8vo....................................8" to 9" tall
sm 4to...............about 10" tall, quarto
4to .....................between 11" to 13" tall
folio................................13" or larger
elephant folio.................23" or larger
atlas folio ................................25"
double elephant folio ...larger than 25"

# ACKNOWLEDGMENTS

The editors and staff take this opportunity to express our sincere gratitude and appreciation to each business who has contributed their time and knowledge to help us. We believe the credibility of our book is greatly enhanced through their efforts. See the codes in the section called 'Booksellers' for their complete address and contact information. The 'Bookbuyers' section listing gives information concerning their specific genre interests.

A Tale of Two Sisters (A24)
A-Book-A-Brac Shop (A1)
Aard Books (A2)
Noreen Abbot Books (A3)
About Books (A4)
Adelson Sports (A5)
AL-PAC, Lamar Kelley (A8)
Alcott Books, Barbara Ruppert (A23)
Almark & Co.-Booksellers (A14)
American Botanist (A10)
An Uncommon Vision (A25)
Antiquarian Medical Books
   W. Bruce Frye (A13)
Antiquarian Books & Manuscripts
   James Tait Goodrich (G7)
Aplan Antiques & Art (A19)
Arnold's of Michigan
   Judith A. Herba (A16)
Artis Books (A17)
Aslan Books (A27)
Authors of the West (A18)
Avonlea Books Search Service (A7)
Beasley Books (B2)
Bela Luna Books (B3)
Between the Covers (B4)
Bicentennial Book Shop
   Vaughn & Michael Baber (B5)
Book & Tackle Shop
   Bernard Gordon (B14)
Book Baron (B9)
Book Broker (B10)
Book Corner, Michael Tennero (B11)
Book Treasures (B15)
Books of the Ages (B17)
Books Now & Then
   Dennis Patrick (B29)
Books West Southwest
   W. David Laird (B19)
The Bookseller, Inc.
   Frank & Andrea Klein (B18)
Bowie & Co. Booksellers, Inc. (B20)
Bromer Booksellers
   David & Anne Bromer (B24)
Brooks Books (B26)

Camelot Books (C1)
Chapel Hill Rare Books (C6)
Children's Book Adoption Agency (C8)
Steven Cieluch (C14)
Cinemage Books (C9)
Dad's Old Bookstore (D4)
Tom Davidson, Bookseller (D10)
Ursula Davidson (D1)
L. Clarice Davis (D2)
Dawson's Book Shop (D11)
Carol Docheff, Bookseller (D4)
Drusilla's Books (D6)
Eastside Books & Paper (E6)
Elder's Book Store (E4)
First Folio (F1)
Five Quail Books — West (F7)
Flo Silver Books (F3)
John Gach Fine & Rare Books (G1)
Galerie De Boicourt
   Eva W. Boicourt (G2)
Glo's Children's Series Books
   Gloria Stobbes (G6)
Grave Matters (G8)
Henry F. Hain III (H1)
Ken Hebenstreit, Bookseller (H11)
Susan Heller, Pages for Sages (H4)
Heritage Book Shop, Inc. (H5)
Murry Hudson (H9)
Hurley Books/Celtic Cross Books (H10)
Ilene Kayne (K2)
Jordan Gallery (J2)
Kenneth Karimole (K1)
Knollwood Books
   Lee & Peggy Price (K5)
Ken Lopez, Bookseller (L3)
Melvin Marcher, Bookseller (M4)
Marvelous Books
   Dorothy (Dede) Kern (M5)
Paul Melzer Fine & Rare Books (M9)
Meyer Boswell Books, Inc. (M11)
Mordida Books (M15)
My Book Heaven (M19)
My Bookhouse (M20)
MacDonnell Rare Books (M24)

Brian McMillan, Books (M21)
McGee's First Varieties (M22)
Monroe Stahr Books (M25)
Nerman's Books (N1)
Norris Books (N4)
Nutmeg Books (N2)
Oak Knoll Books (O10)
October Farm (O3)
David L. O'Neal
   Antiquarian Bookseller (O1)
The Old London Bookshop (O4)
K.C. & Jean C. Owings (O8)
Pandora's Books
   J. Grant Thiessen (P3)
R. Papinger, Baseball Books (P8)
Parmer Books (P4)
Parnassus Books (P5)
Quill & Brush
   Patricia & Allen Ahearn (Q1)
Kathleen Rais & Co. (R2)
Randall House, Pia Oliver (R3)
Jo Ann Reisler, Ltd. (R5)
Bill & Mimi Sachen (S1)
Stanley Schwartz (S3)
Second Harvest Books (S14)
Ellen Serxner (S13)
Snowy Egret Books (S15)
Stan Clark Military Books (S16)
Thomas Books (T2)
Thorn Books (T10)
Town's End Books
   John & Judy Townsend (T11)
Treasures From the Castle
   Connie Castle (T5)
Typographeum Bookshop (T9)
Vintage Books
   Nancy & David Haines (V3)
Volume I Books (V4)
Warren's Collector Books
   Warren Gillespie Jr. (W2)
Yesterday's Books (Y1)
Worldwide Antiquarian (W1)
Glenn Wiese (WF)

# A

A'BECKETT, Gilbert Abbott. *Comic Blackstone.* ca 1880. London. Bradbury Agnew. ils Cruikshank. 3-quarter morocco/marbled brd. VG. B20. $90.00

A'BECKETT, Gilbert Abbott. *Comic History of England.* nd. London. Bradbury Evans. 2 vol. 20 mc etchings/woodcuts. 3-quarter French levant. H4. $125.00

A.L.O.E.; see Tucker, Charlotte Maria.

AADLAND, Florence. *Big Love.* 1986. Warner. 1st thus. F/wrp. C9. $60.00

AAKER, David A. *Managing Brand Equity: Capitalizing on Value of Brand Name.* 1991. Macmillan. later prt. ils. F/dj. A2. $18.00

AAMSDEN, Charles Avery. *Prehistoric Southwesterners From Basketmaker to Pueblo.* 1949. LA. Southwest Mus. photos/ils/maps. 163p. VG/wrp. F7. $95.00

AARDEMA, Verna. *Bringing the Rain to Kapiti Plain.* 1981. NY. Dial. 1st. obl 4to. unp. NF/VG. T5. $25.00

AARDEMA, Verna. *Why Mosquitoes Buzz in People's Ears, a West African Tale.* (1975). NY. Dial. sm 4to. Caldecott Honor. bl cloth. G. T5. $15.00

AARON, Daniel. *Writers on the Left: Episodes in American Communism.* 1961. HBW. 1st. VG/dj. N2. $30.00

AARON, Henry. *Aaron, RF.* 1968. World. 1st. photos. F/dj. P8. $100.00

AARON, Henry. *I Had a Hammer: The Hank Aaron Story.* 1991. Harper Collins. 1st. sgn. F/dj. S9. $75.00

AARON & FADIMAN. *New Joys of Wine.* 1990 (1975). ils. 450p. VG/VG. E6. $17.00

ABBATE, Francesco. *American Art.* 1972. London. Octopus. ils. 158p. VG/dj. M10. $7.50

ABBATT, William. *Attack on Youngs' House (or Four Corners).* 1926. Tarrytown. 1/250. sgn. ils/rear fld map. 21p. O1. $85.00

ABBATT, William. *Battle of Pell's Point (or Pelham), October 18, 1776.* 1901. NY. self pub. 1st. 1/500. ils. G. M10. $50.00

ABBE, Cleveland. *Account of Progress in Meteorology & Allied Subjects...* 1883. GPO. 121p. xl. F/wrp. B14. $125.00

ABBE, Cleveland. *Account of Progress of Meteorology in 1884.* 1885. GPO. 176p. xl. wrp. B14. $200.00

ABBEY, Edward. *Back Roads of Arizona.* 1978. Northland. 1st. 168p. wrp. F7. $22.50

ABBEY, Edward. *Beyond the Wall: Essays From the Outside.* 1984. NY. HRW. 1st. NF/clip. A14. $87.50

ABBEY, Edward. *Cactus Country.* 1973. Time Life. 1st. 184p. VG. F7. $35.00

ABBEY, Edward. *Desert Images: American Landscape.* 1979. NY/London. HBJ. 1st. photos David Muench. NF/case. H4. $225.00

ABBEY, Edward. *Desert Solitaire.* 1988. Tucson, AZ. 1st. 255p. F/F. B19. $25.00

ABBEY, Edward. *Desert Solitaire: Season in the Wilderness.* 1968. McGraw Hill. 1st. 269p. F/NF. B20. $225.00

ABBEY, Edward. *Epitaph for a Desert Anarchist.* 1994. Atheneum. 1st. F/dj. T11. $25.00

ABBEY, Edward. *Fool's Progress: An Honest Novel.* 1988. Holt. 1st. NF/dj. A14. $52.50

ABBEY, Edward. *Fool's Progress: An Honest Novel.* 1988. NY. Holt. 1st. inscr/dtd 1988. NF/dj. S9. $300.00

ABBEY, Edward. *Good News.* 1980. Dutton. 1st. NF/F. B3. $125.00

ABBEY, Edward. *Hayduke Lives!* 1990. Boston. Little Brn. UP. F/wrp. B4. $125.00

ABBEY, Edward. *Monkey Wrench Gang.* 1975. Lippincott. 1st. NF/clip. A14. $122.50

ABBEY, J.R. *Travel in Aquatint & Lithography 1770-1860.* (1956-57). 2 vol in 1. rpt. 4to. 722p. F. A4. $295.00

ABBEY, Merrill. *Preaching to the Contemporary Mind.* 1963. Abingdon. 192p. VG/dj. B29. $7.00

ABBEY & MUENCH. *Desert Images: American Landscape.* 1987. Gallery Books. 3rd. ils. 239p. NF/NF. B19. $75.00

ABBOT, Anthony. *About the Murder of Geraldine Foster.* 1930. NY. Covici Friede. 1st. VG/rpr. M15. $200.00

ABBOT, I.A. *Laau Hawaii: Traditional Hawaiian Uses of Plants.* 1992. Bishop Mus. 173 photos. 163p. F/wrp. B1. $36.00

ABBOT, Willis J. *Panama & the Canal: Story of Its Achievement...* 1914. Dodd Mead. 1st. 468p. gilt bl cloth. NF. B20. $50.00

ABBOTT, Berenice. *World of Atget.* 1979. NY. Paragon. 1st thus. VG/glossy wrp. H4. $20.00

ABBOTT, E.C. *We Pointed Them North.* 1991. Lakeside Classic. 1st thus. teg. brn cloth. F/sans. T11. $30.00

ABBOTT, Eleanor Hallowell. *Molly Make-Believe.* 1910. NY. Century. 1st. ils Walter Title. VG. M20. $14.00

ABBOTT, G.F. *Songs of Modern Greece.* (1974). Athens. facs (CUP 1900 ed). Greek text. 243p. cloth. VG. Q2. $22.00

ABBOTT, George. *Brief Description of the Wold World...Empires & Kingdoms...* 1620. London. Marriot. 5th. 4to. unp. early 19th-C marbled brd. O1. $500.00

ABBOTT, Jacob. *Rollo on the Rhine (Rollo's Tour in Europe).* 1858. NY. John R Anderson. 12mo. lacks ffe. 218p. gilt brn cloth. VG. H4. $30.00

ABBOTT, Jacob. *Rollo's Tour in Europe: Rollo in London (#4).* 1869 (1858). NY. Sheldon. gr cloth. M20. $24.00

ABBOTT, Jane. *Angels May Weep.* 1937. Lippincott. 1st. F/NF. B4. $85.00

ABBOTT, John. *Scimitar.* 1992. NY. Crown. ARC/1st. F/ils wrp. A14. $21.00

ABBOTT, Katharine M. *Old Paths & Legends of the New England Border...* 1907. NY. Putnam. 1st. ils. 408p. G. M10. $35.00

ABBOTT, Katharine M. *Old Paths & Legends of the New England Border...* 1909 (1903). Putnam. rpt. 484p. gilt cloth. VG. O1. $30.00

ABBOTT, Keene. *Wine O' the Winds.* 1920. Garden City. 336p. G. G11. $8.00

ABBOTT, Lee K. *Strangers in Paradise.* 1987. Putnam. 1st. sgn/dtd 1994. NF/dj. R14. $50.00

ABBOTT, Lyman. *Henry Ward Beecher.* 1887. Hartford. Am Pub. 1st. gilt pict brn cloth. w/clip sgn. M24. $100.00

ABDALLA, A. *Sources for the History of Arabia.* U Riyadh. 2 vol. Eng/Arabic text. 44 pl/2 maps. cloth. dj/case. Q2. $132.50

ABDESSELM, Ahmed. *Ibn Khaldun et ses Lectures.* 1983. Paris. inscr. 127p. VG+. Q2. $33.00

ABDILL, George B. *Civil War Railroads.* (1961). Bonanza. rpt. 192p. VG. B10. $25.00

ABDILL, George B. *Civil War Railroads.* 1961. Seattle. Superior. 1st. photos. VG/dj. M20. $44.00

ABDUL, Raoul. *Blacks in Classical Music.* (1977). Dodd Mead. 1st. pres. F/dj. H4. $38.00

ABDULLAH, Achmed. *Bungalow on the Roof.* 1931. Mystery League. 1st. VG. N4. $25.00

ABEL, Ernest. *Ancient Views on Origins of Life.* 1973. Rutherford, NJ. 1st. 93p. dj. A13. $30.00

ABEL, Kenneth. *Bait.* 1994. Delacort. 1st. author's 1st book. F/F. H11. $30.00

ABEL, Robert. *Progress of a Fire.* 1985. S&S. 1st. 509p. VG/dj. R11. $15.00

ABEL & KALB. *Roots of Involvement: US in Asia 1784-1971.* 1972. Norton. 1st. 8vo. 336p. NF/dj. W2. $35.00

**ABELL, A.G.** *Skillful Housewife's Book or Complete Guide...* c 1846. NY. James Reed. 208p. E6. $30.00

**ABELL, Elizabeth.** *Westward, Westward, Westward.* 1958. Franklin Watts. G. A19. $25.00

**ABELL, Kathleen.** *King Orville & the Bullfrogs.* 1976. London. Faber. 1st. ils. 48p. F/dj. D4. $45.00

**ABELLAN, Jose Luis.** *Miguel de Unammuno a la luz de la Psicologia.* 1964. Madrid. Tecnos. 243p. prt stiff yel wrp/dj. G1. $30.00

**ABERCROMBIE, J.** *Inquiries Concerning Intellectual Powers...* 1835. Boston. old calf. G. S17. $35.00

**ABERNATHY, T.P.** *Burr Conspiracy.* 1954. NY. Oxford. 1st. 301p. VG/dj. M10. $20.00

**ABERNATHY, T.P.** *From Frontier to Plantation in Tennessee: A Study...* NC U. 1st. 14 maps. 392p. F. M4. $110.00

**ABORIGINES COMMITTEE MEETING.** *Some Account of Conduct of Religious Society of Friends...* 1844. London. Edward Marsh. 1st. 247p. detached covers/lacks backstrip/xl. V3. $135.00

**ABRAHAMS, Ethel Ewert.** *Frankturmalen und Schonschreiben.* 1980. Mennonite Pr. 1st. VG. R8. $40.00

**ABRAHAMS, Gerald.** *Technique in Chess.* 1961. London. Bell. 1st. ils. NF/clip. O4. $20.00

**ABRAHAMS, Harold.** *Extinct Medical Schools of Baltimore Maryland.* 1969. Baltimore. 1st. 332p. A13. $50.00

**ABRAHAMS, Peter.** *The Fan.* 1995. Warner. 1st. F/dj. P8. $15.00

**ABRAHAMS & STANSKY.** *Journey to the Frontier: Two Roads to Spanish Civil War.* 1966. Boston. 1st. dj. T9. $25.00

**ABRAMS, LeRoy.** *Flora of Los Angeles & Vicinity.* 1917. Stanford. 432p. B26. $50.00

**ABRAMSON, Harold A.** *Use of LSD in Psychotherapy & Alcoholism.* 1967. Bobbs Merrill. 1st trade. NF. B2. $45.00

**ABRAMSON, Harold A.** *Use of LSD in Psychotherapy.* 1960. NY. Josiah Macy Jr Found. 1st. G+. B2. $65.00

**ABRANSON, Erik.** *Shops of the High Seas.* 1976. NY. Crescent. 4to. 124p. NF/dj. M10. $12.50

**ABRAVENEL.** *Dialoghi di Amore, di Leone Hebreo Medico.* 1558. Venice. Giblio. 8vo. title device. quarter calf. R12. $750.00

**ABS, Michael.** *Physiology & Behavior of the Pigeon.* 1983. London. Academic. ils. 360p. laminated brd. G1. $65.00

**ABSE, Dannie.** *Fire in Heaven.* 1956. London. Hutchinson. 1st. VG/dj. H4. $50.00

**ABSHIRE, Richard.** *Dallas Deception.* 1992. NY. Morrow. 1st. F/F. H11. $20.00

**ABSHIRE, Richard.** *Turnaround Jack.* 1990. NY. Morrow. 1st. F/F. H11. $20.00

**ABU-IZZEDDIN, H. Said.** *Lebanon & Its Provinces: A Study by Governors...* 1963. Beirut. 8vo. ils/maps. 115p. cloth. VG. Q2. $20.00

**ABUJABER, Raouf Sa'd.** *Pioneers Over Jordan: Frontier of Settlement in Transjordan.* 1989. London. Tauris. 8 maps. 328p. cloth. F/dj. Q2. $40.00

**ACCADEMIA DEL CIMENTO.** *Saggi di Naturali Esperienze Fatte...* 1841. Florence. Tipografia Galileiana. 3 parts in 1. folio. K1. $300.00

**ACERRANO, Anthony J.** *Practical Hunter's Handbook.* 1978. NY. 1st. 246p. F/dj. A17. $10.00

**ACEVEDO LATORRE, Eduardo.** *Colombia: Trayectoria de un Pueblo.* 1976. Bogota. 4to. 73p. dj. F3. $15.00

**ACHDJIAN, Albert.** *Un Art Fondamental, le Tapis/Fundamental Art: The Rug.* 1949. Paris. Editions Self. 1st. folio. 296p. VG/stiff wrp/dj. W1. $65.00

**ACHEBE, Chinua.** *Christmas in Biafra & Other Poems.* 1973. Doubleday/Anchor. 1st. inscr. F. L3. $100.00

**ACHTEMEIER, Paul J.** *Harper's Bible Dictionary.* 1985. Harper. 1178p. VG. B29. $17.00

**ACKER, Kathy.** *Empire of the Senseless.* 1988. Grove. 1st. sgn. F/dj. O11. $30.00

**ACKER, Kathy.** *In Memoriam to Identity.* 1990. Grove Weidenfeld. 1st. sgn. F/dj. O11. $30.00

**ACKERLEY, J.R.** *EM Forster: A Portrait.* 1970. London. 1st. F/self wrp. L3. $30.00

**ACKERMAN, Diane.** *Natural History of the Senses.* 1990. Random. rem mk. 331p. VG/dj. A10. $25.00

**ACKERMAN, Forest J.** *Mr Monster's Movie Gold: Treasure-Trove...* 1981. Donning. 1st. photos. VG/wrp. C9. $90.00

**ACKERMAN, Irving C.** *Wire-Haired Fox Terrier.* 1928 (1927). NY. GH Watt. 1st. gilt brn cloth. M20. $35.00

**ACKERMAN, John.** *Mountain-Climbing Trains.* 1969. NY. Ives Washburn. 1st. 110p. reinforced cloth. F. D4. $25.00

**ACKERMAN, Karen.** *Song & Dance Man.* 1988. NY. Knopf. 1st. Caldecott Honor. AN/dj. T5. $45.00

**ACKROYD, Peter R.** *Exile & Restoration: A Study of Hebrew Thought...* (1968). Phil. Westminster. VG/dj. H10. $27.50

**ACKROYD, Peter.** *Chatterton.* 1978. Hammish Hamilton. 1st. F/F. B3. $60.00

**ACKROYD, Peter.** *First Light.* 1989. London. Hamish Hamilton. 1st. NF/VG. R14. $25.00

**ACKROYD & EVANS.** *Cambridge History of the Bible...* 1976. Cambridge. 649p. VG/wrp. B29. $19.00

**ACKWORTH, Robert.** *Dr Kildare: Assigned to Trouble.* 1963. Racine. TVTI. ils. VG. M20. $14.00

**ACKWORTH, Robert.** *Mary Winters, Student Nurse.* 1966. Avalon. 191p. xl. VG/dj. B36. $12.50

**ACOSTA SAIGNES, Miguel.** *Las Turas.* 1949. Caracas. 1st. 106p. wrp. F3. $10.00

**ACZEL, Amir D.** *Fermat's Last Theorem.* 1996. Four Walls Eight Windows. 1st. F/dj. M23. $40.00

**ADAIR, Dick.** *Dick Adair's Saigon: Sketches & Words From Artist's Journal.* 1971. NY Weatherhill. stated 1st. sm 4to. G/poor. R11. $15.00

**ADAIR & ADAIR.** *World Is Out.* 1978. New Glide/Dell. 1st. VG/wrp. C9. $25.00

**ADAM, Nicholas.** *Grammaire Italienne,... Precedee d'un Discours...* 1787. Paris. Chez l'Auteur. 223p. mottled calf. K1. $200.00

**ADAMS, Adrienne.** *Christmas Party.* 1978. Scribner. 1st. 32p. reinforced cloth. F/dj. D4. $45.00

**ADAMS, Alice.** *Families & Survivors.* 1974. Knopf. 1st. F/NF. M25. $45.00

**ADAMS, Alice.** *Southern Exposure.* 1995. Knopf. 1st. sgn. AN/dj. B30. $30.00

**ADAMS, Andy.** *Biff Brewster: Mystery of the Chinese Ring (#2).* 1960. Grosset Dunlap. VG/dj. M20. $14.00

**ADAMS, Andy.** *Log of a Cowboy.* 1903. Houghton Mifflin. 1st. 8vo. 387p. pict tan cloth. VG+. C6. $165.00

**ADAMS, Ansel.** *American Wilderness.* (1990). Boston/Toronto/London. Little Brn. stated 1st. folio. 107 photos. AN/NF. H4. $120.00

**ADAMS, Ansel.** *Camera.* 1980. NYGS. 1st. F/dj. T10. $35.00

**ADAMS, Ansel.** *Making a Photograph: An Introduction to Photography.* 1935. London. The Studio. 1st/2nd prt. 32 tipped-in pl. VG. M7. $175.00

**ADAMS, Ansel.** *Pageant of History in Northern California.* 1954. SF. Am Trust Co. cbdg/wrp. H4. $75.00

**ADAMS, Ansel.** *This Is the American Earth.* (1971). SF. Sierra Club. 5th prt. sgn. folio. 89p. F/VG. H4. $100.00

**ADAMS, Ansel.** *This Is the American Earth.* nd. Sierra Club/Ballantine. ARC. RS. NF/glossy wrp. w/2 5x7" Adams photos. H4. $300.00

**ADAMS, Ansel.** *Yosemite & the Range of Light.* 1979. NYGS. VG/dj. S5. $125.00

**ADAMS, Ansel.** *Yosemite & the Range of Light.* 1979. NYGS. obl folio. sgn pres/dtd 1979. 116 pl. maroon linen/bl cloth. dj. K1. $275.00

**ADAMS, Ansel.** *Yosemite & the Range of Light.* 1979. NYGS. 4th. obl folio. 28p+116 full-p b&w pl. bl cloth. F/VG. C6. $150.00

**ADAMS, Arthur.** *Quimby.* 1988. St Martin. 1st. F/NF. R11. $15.00

**ADAMS, Ben.** *Last Frontier: Short History of Alaska.* 1961. Hill Wang. 1st. VG/G. O1. $15.00

**ADAMS, Caroline.** *Prayer Book Pattern: A Consideration.* nd. Macmillan. 178p. H10. $15.00

**ADAMS, Carolyn.** *Stars Over Texas.* 1969. Naylor. 1st. 122p. F/dj. D4. $30.00

**ADAMS, Carolyn.** *Stars Over Texas.* 1969. Naylor. 1st. 8vo. F/VG. M5. $15.00

**ADAMS, Carsbie C.** *Space Flight: Satellites, Space Ships, Space Stations...* 1958. McGraw Hill. 8vo. ils. 373p. VG/dj. K5. $15.00

**ADAMS, Charles Francis.** *Antimomianism in the Colony of Massachusetts Bay 1636-1638.* 1894. Boston. Prince Soc. 1/250. 415+18p index. 3-quarter leather. H10. $125.00

**ADAMS, Charles Francis.** *Columbus & the Spanish Discovery of America: A Study...* 1892. Cambridge. John Wilson. rpt. sgn pres. wrp. O1. $65.00

**ADAMS, Charles Francis.** *Railroads: Their Origin & Problems.* 1878. Putnam. 1st. 12mo. inscr pres. 216p. O1. $115.00

**ADAMS, Charlotte.** *Four Seasons Cookbook.* 1971. NY. Ridge. ils. F/clip. A16. $15.00

**ADAMS, Charlotte.** *Singles' First Menu Cookbook.* 1975. Dodd Mead. G/dj. A16. $12.00

**ADAMS, Douglas.** *Dirk Gently's Holistic Detective Agency.* 1987. S&S. 1st. NF/dj. M20. $17.00

**ADAMS, Douglas.** *Hitchhiker's Guide to the Galaxy: A Trilogy in Four Parts.* 1986. London. Heinemann. 1st omnibus. NF/clip. A14. $21.00

**ADAMS, Douglas.** *Life, the Universe & Everything.* 1982. Harmony. 1st. NF/dj. M20. $27.00

**ADAMS, Douglas.** *Mostly Harmless.* 1992. London. Heinemann. 1st. VG+/dj. A14. $21.00

**ADAMS, Douglas.** *So Long, and Thanks for All the Fish.* 1984. London. Pan. 1st. NF/dj. A14. $28.00

**ADAMS, E. Charles.** *Origin & Development of Pueblo Katsina Cult.* 1991. Tucson, AZ. 1st. ils. 235p. NF/NF. B19. $35.00

**ADAMS, Emma Hildreth.** *To & Fro, Up & Down in Southern CA, OR & WA Territory...* 1888. Chicago. Cranston Stowe. 1st. 608p. gilt brn cloth. VG+. B20. $75.00

**ADAMS, Eustace L.** *Air Combat Stories for Boys: Wings of the Navy (#6).* 1936. Grosset Dunlap. lists 7 titles. VG/dj. M20. $30.00

**ADAMS, Eustace L.** *Andy Lane Flying Stories: Racing Around the World (#3).* 1928. Grosset Dunlap. lists to #12. VG/torn. M20. $27.00

**ADAMS, Frank Dawson.** *Birth & Development of Geological Sciences.* 1954. Dover. 1st thus. 506p. xl. VG. B14. $55.00

**ADAMS, Frederick B.** *Radical Literature in America...* 1939. Overbrook. 1st. 1/600. gilt red cloth. F. M24. $200.00

**ADAMS, Frederick.** *Conquest of the Tropics.* 1914. Doubleday. 1st. ils. 368p. gilt gr cloth. F3. $25.00

**ADAMS, George Matthew.** *Better Than Gold.* (1949). DSP. stated 1st. sgn. 8vo. VG/dj. H4. $25.00

**ADAMS, George Matthew.** *Just Among Friends.* 1928. Morrow. stated 1st. sgn pres. 8vo. 176p. VG. H4. $30.00

**ADAMS, Harold.** *Barbed Wire Noose.* 1987. Mysterious. 1st. F/dj. T2. $25.00

**ADAMS, Harold.** *Man Who Was Taller Than God.* 1992. NY. Walker. 1st. F/dj. T2. $25.00

**ADAMS, Henry.** *Democracy, a Novel.* nd. FSY. F/dj. H4. $15.00

**ADAMS, Henry.** *Education of Henry Adams.* 1942. LEC. 1st thus. 1/1500. ils/sgn Chamberlain. case. M17/Q1. $100.00

**ADAMS, Henry.** *Letters of Henry Adams (1858-1918).* (1930). Houghton Mifflin. 2 vol. MacDonald bdg. H4. $350.00

**ADAMS, I. William.** *Shibusawa; or, Passing of Old Japan.* 1906. Putnam. sm 8vo. 284p. gilt maroon cloth. K1. $50.00

**ADAMS, James Luther.** *Paul Tillich's Philosophy of Culture, Science & Religion.* 1965. Harper Row. 1st. 313p. VG/dj. H10. $20.00

**ADAMS, James Truslow.** *Adams Family.* (1930). Literary Guild. ils. G. M4. $10.00

**ADAMS, James Truslow.** *Adams Family.* 1930. Little Brn. 1st. ils. VG. H4. $15.00

**ADAMS, James Truslow.** *Provincial Society...History of American Life Vol III.* 1927. NY. ils. 347p. VG. M4. $20.00

**ADAMS, Joey.** *On the Road for Uncle Sam.* 1963. np. Bernard Geis. 1st. photos/map ep. 311p. VG/torn. R11. $20.00

**ADAMS, John Paul.** *Milton Caniff: Rembrandt of the Comic Strips.* 1946. McKay. 1st. ils. VG. C9. $90.00

**ADAMS, John Quincy.** *Wants of Man.* 1962. Worcester. St Onge. 1/950. 54p. aeg. full gr leather. B24. $125.00

**ADAMS, John.** *Treatise on Principles & Practice of Action of Ejectment...* 1821. NY. Stephen Gould. 8vo. 416p. full calf. H4. $250.00

**ADAMS, Joseph.** *Inquiry Into Laws of Different Epidemic Diseases...* 1809. London. For Johnson, Callow & Grace. 159p. gray brd/rb. uncut. B14. $450.00

**ADAMS, Joseph.** *Salmon & Trout Angling: Its Theory & Practice...* 1923. NY. Dutton. 1st Am. ils. 288p. VG/dj. H10. $50.00

**ADAMS, Judith A.** *American Amusement Park Industry: A History...* 1991. Boston. Twayne. 1st. photos. F/dj. A2. $20.00

**ADAMS, Judith Porter.** *Peacework: Oral Histories of Women Peace Activists.* 1990. Boston. Twayne. 1st. VG/G. V3. $12.00

**ADAMS, Laura.** *Norman Mailer: A Comprehensive Bibliography.* (1979). Metuchen, NJ. slim 8vo. 131p. F. H4. $15.00

**ADAMS, Marcia.** *Cooking From Quilt Country.* 1989. Potter. later ed. F/dj. R8. $15.00

**ADAMS, Maryline Poole.** *Mistletoe: Legends, Myths & Folk Lore.* 1984. Berkeley. Poole. mini. 1/100. sgn. prt letterpress/linocut ils. gr cloth. B24. $95.00

**ADAMS, Mortimer J.** *How To Read a Book: Art of Getting a Liberal Education.* (1972). S&S. 1st. 8vo. 426p. F/G. H4. $40.00

**ADAMS, Myron E.** *History & Achievements of Ft Sheridan Officer's Training...* 1920. Ft Sheridan. 4to. 487p. gilt cloth. H4. $35.00

**ADAMS, Nehemiah.** *Christ a Friend: Thirteen Discourses.* 1855. Boston. Jewett. 290p. H10. $12.50

**ADAMS, Paul L.** *Obsessive Children: Sociopsychiatric Study.* 1973. NY/London. Brunnr/Mazel & Butterworths. inscr pres. 289p. NF/dj. H4. $40.00

**ADAMS, Ramon F.** *Best of the American Cowboy.* (1957). Norman, OK. 1st. 289p. cloth. dj. D11. $40.00

**ADAMS, Ramon F.** *Rampaging Herd: A Bibliography of Books & Pamphlets...* 1982 (1959). Zubal. rpt. notes/index. 463p. AN. B19/E1/H10. $40.00

**ADAMS, Ramon F.** *Six-Guns & Saddle Leather.* 1982. Zubal. rpt of 1969 revised. 808p. F/F. B19. $40.00

**ADAMS, Randolph.** *British Head Quarters Map & Sketches.* 1928. Ann Arbor. Wm Clements Lib. ils. 144p. VG. B5. $45.00

**ADAMS, Richard C.** *Delaware Indian Legend & Story of Their Troubles.* 1899. WA, DC. 1st. ils. 72p. G. B18. $75.00

**ADAMS, Richard.** *Day Gone By.* 1990. London. Hutchinson. 1st. F/dj. R14. $30.00

**ADAMS, Richard.** *Grimm's Fairy Tales.* 1981. Kegan Paul. 1st. 18 mc pl. 128p. F/dj. D4. $75.00

**ADAMS, Richard.** *Iron Wolf & Other Stories.* 1980. Allen Lane. 1st. ils Yvonne Gilbert/Jennifer Campbell. F/F. B3. $40.00

**ADAMS, Richard.** *Maia.* 1984. Viking Penguin. 1st. NF/dj. A14. $42.00

**ADAMS, Richard.** *Prehistoric Mesoamerica.* (1977). Little Brn. 370p. F3. $20.00

**ADAMS, Richard.** *Shardik.* 1974. London. Allen Lane. 1st. inscr. author's 2nd novel. F/dj. B4. $350.00

**ADAMS, Richard.** *Shardik.* 1974. S&S. 1st. F/dj. P3. $25.00

**ADAMS, Richard.** *Shardik.* 1974. S&S. 1st Am. NF/VG. A14/N4. $21.00

**ADAMS, Richard.** *Traveller.* 1988. Knopf. 1st. F/dj. M23. $30.00

**ADAMS, Richard.** *Tyger Voyage.* 1976. Knopf. 1st Am. 8vo. 30p. NF/dj. D1. $45.00

**ADAMS, Samuel Hopkins.** *Great Amerian Fraud.* 1906. Collier. 1st. 146p. red cloth. NF. B20. $100.00

**ADAMS, Samuel Hopkins.** *Harvey Girls.* 1946. World. Forum Motion Picture ed. 8vo. 327p. red cloth. G+. F7. $30.00

**ADAMS, Stephen.** *Barbizon School & Origins of Impressionism.* 1994. London. Phaidon. 1st. ils. 240p. NF/dj. M10. $25.00

**ADAMS, William Howard.** *Eye of Thomas Jefferson.* 1976. Nat Gallery of Art. ils. 411p. w/guide to exhibition. VG. B10. $45.00

**ADAMS, William Mansfield.** *Tsunamis in the Pacific Ocean.* 1970. Honolulu. East-West Center Pr. 1st. VG/dj. N2. $20.00

**ADAMS & BEARD.** *Four Seasons Cookbook.* 1971. NY. Crescent. F/dj. V4. $15.00

**ADAMS & CARWARDINE.** *Last Chance To See.* 1990. Stoddard. 1st. VG/dj. P3. $25.00

**ADAMS & TAYLOR.** *Mont-Saint-Michel & Chartres.* 1957. LEC. 1st thus. 1/1500. photos/sgn Chamberlain. F/glassine/case. Q1. $150.00

**ADCOCK, F.E.** *Roman Art of War Under the Republic.* 1940. Cambridge, MA. 140p. teg. gilt device on cloth. VG+/dj. Q2. $36.50

**ADCOCK, Thomas.** *Sea of Green.* 1989. Mysterious. 1st. F/dj. M15. $65.00

**ADDAMS, Charles.** *Dear Dead Days.* 1959. NY. Putnam. 1st. VG/G. L1. $55.00

**ADDAMS, Charles.** *Homebodies.* 1954. S&S. 1st. VG/dj. L1. $45.00

**ADDAMS, Jane.** *Spirit of Youth & the City Streets.* 1909. Macmillan. 4th. xl. VG. A25. $15.00

**ADDAMS, Jane.** *Twenty Years at Hull House.* 1910. NY. Macmillan. 1st. 8vo. 462p+3p index. VG+/acetate wrp. H4. $50.00

**ADDINGTON, Sarah.** *Round the Year in Pudding Lane.* 1924. Little Brn. 1st. 8vo. 231p. G+. T5. $25.00

**ADDINGTON, Sarah.** *Tommy Tingle-Tangle.* 1927. Volland. ils Gertrude Kay. 39p. VG/pict wrp. D1. $50.00

**ADDISON, A.C.** *Romantic Story of the Mayflower Pilgrims.* 1911. London. Sir Isaac Pitman. 192p. teg. pict ep. B18. $17.50

**ADDISON, A.C.** *Romantic Story of the Puritan Fathers.* 1912. Boston. LC Page. 1st. 243p. teg. pict ep. VG. B18. $35.00

**ADDISON, Joseph.** *Works of...* 1811. London. 6 vol. marbled edges/ep. full brn leather. B30. $250.00

**ADDISON, STEELE & OTHERS.** *Spectator.* 1901. London/Boston. 8 vol. 1/200. 40 portraits+8 sketches w/tissue guards. F. H4. $2,500.00

**ADDISON, Thomas.** *Collection of Published Writings.* 1868. London. 1st. 242p. A13. $250.00

**ADELSON, Joseph.** *Handbook of Adolescent Psychology.* 1980. John Wiley. 2nd. 624p. bl cloth. VG/dj. G1. $75.00

**ADER, Robert.** *Psychoneuroimmunology.* 1991. Academic. 2nd revised/enlarged. 8vo. 1218p. prt blk cloth. G1. $100.00

**ADLEMAN, Robert H.** *Bloody Benders.* 1970. Stein Day. 1st. VG/dj. M20. $24.00

**ADLER, Bill.** *Motherhood: A Celebration.* 1987. Carroll Graf. 1st. F/F. H11. $20.00

**ADLER, Bill.** *Murder Game.* 1991. Caroll Graf. 1st. F/dj. N4. $22.50

**ADLER, Elmer.** *Informal Talk by Elmer Adler at University of Kansas...* 1953. Plantin. sq 8vo. 46p. VG/dj. H4. $40.00

**ADLER, Irene.** *I Remember Jimmy: Life & Times of Jimmy Durante.* 1980. NY. Arlington. 189p. VG/dj. C5. $15.00

**ADLER, Renata.** *Speedboat.* 1976. Random. 1st. author's 1st novel. NF/clip. A14. $35.00

**ADORNO, Rolena.** *Guaman Poma: Writing & Resistance in Colonial Peru.* 1991. Austin. 2nd. 189p. wrp. F3. $15.00

**AESOP.** *Aesop's Fables.* 1933. NY. LEC. 1/1500. sgn Bruce Rogers. 210p. teg. NF/case. H5. $250.00

**AESOP.** *Baby's Own Aesop.* 1886. London/NY. Warne. ils Walter Crane. 12mo. VG. D1. $275.00

**AESOP.** *Birds, the Beasts & the Bat.* 1983. np. Quail Hill. mini. 1/120. prt/sgn Rachel Barahal. tan laid-paper brd. B24. $65.00

**AESOP.** *Fables From Aesop.* 1966. OUP. 1st. ils JJ Grandville. bl cloth. VG. B27. $55.00

**AESOP.** *Fables of Aesop.* (1931). Three Sirens. edit WL Parker. ils Chas Bennett. teg. limp cloth. H4. $45.00

**AESOP.** *Fables of Aesop.* 1994. Gramercy. 1st. ils Edward Detmold. rem mk. F. B17. $17.50

**AESOP.** *Fables.* nd (1970s). facs 1912 ed. ils Rackham. VG/dj. M17. $15.00

**AESOP.** *Petit Fabuliste de la Jeunesse.* ca 1840. Paris. Presteau. mini. ils. aeg. ivory brd/red velvet. B24. $385.00

**AFLALO, F.G.** *Sketch of Natural History (Vertebrates) of British Islands.* 1898. Edinburgh. Blackwood. ils/photos. 498p. teg. VG. M12. $37.50

**AGAPIDA, Fra Antonio;** see Irving, Washington.

**AGASSIZ, Louis.** *Bibliographia Zoologiae et Geologiae...* 1968. NY. facs of 1848-54. 4 vol. A13. $150.00

**AGASSIZ & AGASSIZ.** *Journey in Brazil.* 1868. Ticknor Fields. 2nd. VG. A10. $145.00

**AGEE, Jon.** *Ellsworth.* 1983. NY. Pantheon. 1st. ils. 31p. F. D4. $25.00

**AGEE, Jonis.** *Strange Angels.* 1993. Ticknor Fields. 1st. sgn/dtd 1993. F/dj. R14. $35.00

**AGRAWALA, Vasudeva S.** *Indian Art.* 1965. Varanasi, India. Prithiva Prakashan. 1st. 389p. maroon cloth. VG/poor. F1. $35.00

**AGUIAR, Walter.** *Maya Land in Color.* 1978. Hastings. 1st. 32 mc pl. 96p. F3. $10.00

**AGUILAR, Grace.** *Home Influence: A Tale for Mothers & Daughters.* 1858. Boston. Hickling Swan & Brewer. VG/dj. M20. $14.00

**AGUILAR, Mila D.** *Comrade Is As Special As a Rice Seedling.* 1984. NY. Kitchin Table Women of Color. 1st. F/wrp. C6. $30.00

**AHEARN & AHEARN.** *Book Collecting: A Comprehensive Guide.* 1995. Putnam. 5500 entries. AN/dj. A27. $35.00

**AHLBERG & AHLBERG.** *Jolly Postman; or, Other People's Letters.* 1986. Little Brn. 1st Am. 16mo. unp. glossy brd. VG. T5. $30.00

**AHLBGERG, Hakon.** *Swedish Architecture in Twentieth Century.* 1925. Scribner. 152 pl+41p. VG/dj. F1. $225.00

**AHMAD, Ariz.** *History of Islamic Sicily.* 1975. Edinburgh. Islamic Surveys #10. 8vo. ils/map. 147p. VG/dj. Q1. $20.00

**AHTHOLOGY.** *Lord John 10.* 1988. Northridge. ARC. inscr. NF/wrp. L3. $450.00

**AICKMAN, Robert.** *Cold Hand in Mine.* nd. BC. F/dj. S18. $9.00

**AICKMAN, Robert.** *Model.* 1987. Arbor. 1st. NF/dj. S18. $25.00

**AICKMAN, Robert.** *Wine-Dark Sea.* 1988. Arbor. 1st. F/dj. M25. $15.00

**AIDALA, Thomas R.** *Hearst Castle, San Simeon.* 1981. Hudson Hills. 1st. photos Curtis Bruce. VG+/dj. C9. $90.00

**AIKEN, Conrad.** *Letter From Li Po & Other Poems.* 1955. OUP. 1st. F/G. M19. $25.00

**AIKEN, Conrad.** *Morning Song of Lord Zero.* 1963. OUP. 1st. inscr/dtd 1963. F/NF. O11. $90.00

**AIKEN, Conrad.** *Selected Letters of Conrad Aiken.* 1978. New Haven/London. Yale. 1st. 8vo. 350p. tan brd/brn cloth spine. F/clip. C6. $30.00

**AIKEN, George D.** *Pioneering With Wildflowers.* 1933. Putney, VT. self pub. 1st. 40 pl/index. 122p. VG. H10. $30.00

**AIKEN, Henry.** *National Sports of Great Britain.* 1903. London. Methuen. 12mo. mc pl. VG. O3. $38.00

**AIKEN, Joan.** *Cuckoo Tree.* 1971. Doubleday. 1st. ils Susan Obrant. VG+/dj. M5. $30.00

**AIKEN, Joan.** *Kingdom Under the Sea & Other Stories.* 1971. London. Cape. 1st. ils Pienkowski. F/dj. M5. $55.00

**AIKEN, Joan.** *Street.* 1978. Viking. 1st. VG/dj. M20. $24.00

**AIKEN, L.T.** *Donelson, Tennessee: Its History & Landmarks.* 1968. Nashville. photos. 366p. VG. M4. $35.00

**AIKIN, J.** *Aikin's Letters: A Father to His Son on Various Topics...* 1796. London. 2 vol. VG. S17. $100.00

**AINSLIE, Kathleen.** *Me & Catharine Susan.* nd (1902). London. Castell. 12mo. ils. unp. mc ils wrp w/silk cord. F1. $225.00

**AIYAR, S.P.** *Politics of Mass Violence in India.* 1967. Bombay. Manaktalas. 1st. VG/dj. N2. $15.00

**AKERS, Dwight.** *Drivers Up: Story of American Harness Racing.* 1938. Putnam. 1st. VG/fair. O3. $48.00

**AKIN, Emma E.** *Negro Boys & Girls.* 1938. OK City. Harlow Pub. 1st. G. B2. $65.00

**AKINDYNOS, Gregory.** *Letters of...* 1983. WA, DC. Dumbarton Oaks. trans Algela C Hero. 465p. H10. $50.00

**AKST, Daniel.** *St Burl's Obituary.* 1996. Denver. MacMurray Beck. 1st. F/dj. M23. $45.00

**AL-FARSY, Fouad.** *Modernity & Tradition: Saudi Equation.* 1990. London/NY. Kegan Paul. 337p. NF/dj. W1. $40.00

**ALBAUGH, William A.** *Confederate Arms.* 1957. Stackpole. VG. A19. $50.00

**ALBEE, Edward.** *Slumgullion Stew.* 1984. Dutton. 1st. sgn. F/dj. S9. $225.00

**ALBEE, Louis Rankin.** *Bartlett Collection: A List of Books on Angling, Fishes...* 1996 (1896). Mansfield, CT. Martino. rpt. 1/150. 1300 items. 180p. F. F1. $50.00

**ALBERS, Josef.** *Formulation: Articulation.* 1972. Abrams. 2 vol. 1/1000. sgn. 127 silkscreen prts. portfolio/case. B24. $1,000.00

**ALBERT, Arthur Lemuel.** *Fundamentals of Telephony.* 1943. London. 1st/3rd prt. ils. 374p. H6. $38.00

**ALBERT, G.D.** *Report of the Commission To Locate Side of Frontier Forts...* 1896. Harrisburg. 2 vol. 8 fld maps/25 dbl-p+40 full-p maps & plans. M4. $475.00

**ALBERT, James W.** *Through the Country of the Comanche Indians...* 1970. John Howell. 1st thus. 1/5000. 77p. beige cloth. F/VG. C6. $125.00

**ALBERT, Neil.** *Appointment in May.* 1996. Walker. 1st. AN/dj. N4. $25.00

**ALBERT, Neil.** *Burning March.* 1994. Dutton. 1st. F/F. H11. $40.00

**ALBERTS, Don E.** *Rebels on the Rio Grande: Civil War Journal...* 1993. Albuquerque. 1st. ils. 187p. F/stiff wrp. $25.00

**ALBERTS, Robert C.** *Good Provider: HJ Heinz & His 57 Varieties.* 1973. Houghton Mifflin. VG/dj. M20. $16.00

**ALBERTSON & PORTER.** *Romantic Record of Peter Francisco.* 1929. McClure. 103p. G+. B10. $95.00

**ALBRAND, Martha.** *Remembered Anger.* 1946. Little Brn. 2nd. G+/dj. P3. $10.00

**ALBRIGHT, H.** *New Orleans, Battle of the Bayous.* 1990. NY. 232p. F/dj. M4. $18.00

**ALBUS, Harry J.** *Mr Penny: Life of JC Penney in Story Form.* 1963. Eerdmans. 2nd. 89p. xl. H6. $32.00

**ALCOCK, Leslie.** *Was This Camelot? Excavations at Cadbury Castle 1966-1970.* 1972. Stein Day. 1st Am. sm 4to. VG/dj. N2. $15.00

**ALCOSSER, Murray.** *America in Bloom: Great American Gardens...* 1991. NY. photos. VG/dj. M17. $20.00

**ALCOTT, Louisa May.** *Aunt Jo's Scrap Bag... My Boys. Volume I.* 1872 (1871). Little Brn. 1st 1 vol. 12mo. ils. G+. M5. $110.00

**ALCOTT, Louisa May.** *Aunt Jo's Scrap-Bag.* 1929. Grosset Dunlap. ils. VG-. M17. $15.00

**ALCOTT, Louisa May.** *Flower Fables.* 1855. Boston. Geo Briggs. 1st. author's 1st book. 8vo. 182p. brn cloth. F. B24. $1,850.00

**ALCOTT, Louisa May.** *Jack & Jill.* 1903. Little Brn. 12mo. gilt brn cloth. VG. M7. $30.00

**ALCOTT, Louisa May.** *Jo's Boys. And How They Turned Out.* 1886. Boston. Roberts Bros. 1st/1st state. gilt brn cloth. M24. $45.00

**ALCOTT, Louisa May.** *Life, Letters & Journals.* 1889. Roberts. 1st/1st issue. edit ED Cheney. VG+. M5. $110.00

**ALCOTT, Louisa May.** *Little Women.* 1870 (1868). Roberts Bros. early (from 1st ed pl). gilt terra-cotta cloth. M24. $400.00

**ALCOTT, Louisa May.** *Louisa's Wonder Book.* 1975. Central MI U. 1st thus. sm 4to. 126p. brn cloth. NF/dj. T5. $25.00

**ALCOTT, Louisa May.** *Moods.* 1965. Boston. Loring. 1st/2nd prt. gilt terra-cotta cloth. M24. $150.00

**ALCOTT, Louisa May.** *Old-Fashioned Girl.* 1928. Phil. Winston. ils Clara Burd/4 pl. 342p. gilt bl cloth. NF. F1. $25.00

**ALCOTT, Louisa May.** *Three Proverb Stories.* (1870). Boston. Loring. 1st thus. gilt maroon cloth. M24. $75.00

**ALCOTT, Louisa May.** *Under the Lilacs.* 1934. Little Brn. cloth/pict label. VG/dj. M20. $22.00

**ALDEN, John Eliot.** *Rhode Island Imprints.* 1949. NY. Bowker. 1st. 665p. gilt bl cloth. F. F1. $95.00

**ALDEN, John Richard.** *General Gage in America.* 1948. LSG. 1st. 8vo. 313p. brn cloth. F/clip. C6. $50.00

**ALDEN, Paulette Bates.** *Feeding the Eagles.* 1988. St Paul. Graywolf. 1st. author's 1st book. F/dj. R14. $25.00

**ALDEN, Raymond MacDonald.** *Why the Chimes Rang & Other Stories.* 1945. Bobbs Merrill. 1st thus. ils. VG+/G. M5. $18.00

**ALDERMAN, Edwin Anderson.** *Woodrow Wilson: Memorial Address Delivered....* 1924. GPO. 88p. G. B10. $15.00

**ALDERSON, John.** *Some Useful Observations & Advices...* 1765. London. Luke Hinde. 1st. 12mo. 23p. unsewn pamphlet. V3. $75.00

**ALDIN, Cecil.** *Artist's Models.* 1930. London. HF & G Witherby. 1/310. sgn. 4to. 20 mc pl/tissue guards. teg. F/case. H5. $450.00

**ALDIN, Cecil.** *Dogs of Character.* 1927. Eyre Spottiswoode. 1/250. w/orig sgn sketch & TLS. Sangorski bdg. F. H5. $950.00

**ALDIN, Cecil.** *Farm Yard Puppies.* 1911. London. Henry Frowde/Hodder Stoughton. 4to. 12 pl. R5. $350.00

**ALDINGTON, Richard.** *Dream in the Luxembourg.* 1930. London. 1/308. sgn. T9. $50.00

**ALDINGTON, Richard.** *In Winter.* 1987. Typographeum. 1/100. ils/sgn Sylvia Nicolas O'Neill. T9. $50.00

**ALDINGTON, Richard.** *Lawrence of Arabia: A Biographical Enquiry.* 1955. Chicago. Regnery. 1st. 8vo. 448p. gilt bl cloth. G/fair. M7. $25.00

**ALDINGTON & DURRELL.** *Literary Lifelines, Correspondence.* 1981. NY. MacNiven Moore. 1st. T9. $18.00

**ALDIS, Mary.** *Plays for Small Stages.* 1915. Duffield. 105p. VG. C5. $12.50

**ALDISS, Brian W.** *And the Lurid Glare of the Comet.* 1986. Seattle. Serconia. 1st. sgn. F/NF. G10. $40.00

**ALDISS, Brian W.** *Barefoot in the Head.* 1970. Doubleday. 1st Am. rem mk. F/dj. M25. $25.00

**ALDISS, Brian W.** *Bury My Heart at WH Smith's.* 1990. Hodder Stoughton. 1st. F/dj. M23. $30.00

**ALDISS, Brian W.** *Dracula Unbound.* 1991. Harper Collins. 1st. rem mk. VG/dj. L1. $75.00

**ALDISS, Brian W.** *New Arrivals, Old Encounters.* 1979. Harper. 1st. VG/dj. S18. $7.00

**ALDISS, Brian W.** *Rude Awakening.* 1978. Weidenfeld Nicolson. 1st. VG/dj. P3. $25.00

**ALDREDGE & MCKEE.** *Timbertoes.* 1943. Chicago. revised. sgn. 123p. G+. B18. $37.50

**ALDRICH, Ann;** see Meaker, Marijane.

**ALDRICH, T.B.** *Still Water Tragedy.* 1880. Houghton Mifflin. 1st. VG. M20. $34.00

**ALDRIDGE, Alan.** *Gnole.* 1991. Heinemann. 1st. inscr. ils Miller/Willock. F/dj. T10. $50.00

**ALDRIDGE, Janet.** *Eight Rings on His Tail.* 1956. Viking. 1st. sgn. ils Kurt Wiese. VG/dj. M20. $30.00

**ALDRIDGE, Janet.** *Meadow Brook Girls Across the Country.* 1913. Phil. Altemus. 1st. ils. 251p. VG/dj. A25. $28.00

**ALDRIN & BARNES.** *Encounter With Tiber.* 1996. Warner. 1st sgn Aldrin. F/dj. O11. $50.00

**ALDRIN & MCCONNELL.** *Men From Earth.* 1989. Bantam. 1st. 312p. F/VG. K5. $20.00

**ALEXANDER, Bevin.** *Lost Victories: Military Genius of Stonewall Jackson.* 1992. NY. Holt. 1st. NF/clip. A14. $21.00

**ALEXANDER, C. Edward.** *Knowledge for Mother & Daughter.* 1961. Springfield, OH. Alexander Ent. 1st? ils/photos. 64p. VG+. A25. $15.00

**ALEXANDER, Charles.** *John McGraw.* 1988. Viking. photos. F/dj. P8. $20.00

**ALEXANDER, David.** *Murder Points a Finger.* 1953. Random. 1st. NF/dj. G8. $40.00

**ALEXANDER, David.** *Pennies From Hell.* 1960. Lippincott. 1st. VG/G+. G8. $25.00

**ALEXANDER, Edwin P.** *Civil War Railroads & More.* 1977. NY. 1st. ils. 166p. F/dj. E1. $50.00

**ALEXANDER, Edwin P.** *Collector's Book of the Locomotive.* nd. Bramhall. 2nd. VG/dj. P3. $25.00

**ALEXANDER, Fredrick Warren.** *Stratford Hall & the Lees Connected With Its History...* 1912. Oak Grove. 332p. B10. $75.00

**ALEXANDER, James W.** *Life of Archibald Alexander.* 1856. Phil. Presbyterian Brd of Pub. 563p. G+. B18. $37.50

**ALEXANDER, John.** *Conquest of the Air.* 1902. NY. 1st. 160p. pict cloth. G. B18. $75.00

**ALEXANDER, Kent.** *Count Down to Glory...* 1989. Los Angeles. Price Stern Sloan. 1st. ils. 185p. VG/dj. K5. $25.00

**ALEXANDER, L.M.** *Candy.* 1954. Dodd Mead. 1st. ils Rockwell Kent. red/wht cloth. VG. B27. $150.00

**ALEXANDER, Lloyd.** *First Two Lives of Lukas-Kasha.* 1978. Dutton. 1st (stated). sgn. 213p. rust cloth. NF/dj. T5. $45.00

**ALEXANDER, Lloyd.** *Fortune Tellers.* 1992. Dutton. 1st. ils TS Hyman. F/dj. M5. $25.00

**ALEXANDER, Lloyd.** *Illyrian Adventure.* 1986. Dutton. 1st. NF/VG. P2. $20.00

**ALEXANDER, Lloyd.** *Illyrian Adventure.* 1986. Dutton. 1st. 132p. F/dj. D4. $40.00

**ALEXANDER, Lloyd.** *Kestrel.* 1982. Dutton. 1st. 8vo. 244p. gr brd. VG/dj. T5. $25.00

**ALEXANDER, Lloyd.** *Marvelous Misadventures of Sebastian.* 1970. Dutton. 1st. 8vo. 204p. F/VG. T5. $30.00

**ALEXANDER, Lynne.** *Safe Houses.* 1985. Atheneum. 1st. F/F. H11. $20.00

**ALEXANDER, Michael.** *Discovering the New World.* (1976). NY. Harper. 1st Am. lg 4to. 224p. cloth. F3. $25.00

**ALEXANDER, Sue.** *Lila on the Landing.* 1987. Clarion. 1st. ils Ellen Eagle. NF/VG. B36. $13.00

**ALEXANDER, William.** *Historie des Femmes, Depuis la Plus Haute Antiquite...* 1791. Paris. Author & Briand. 4 vol. 8vo. quarter calf. R12. $400.00

**ALEXIE, Sherman.** *Lone Ranger & Tonto Fistfight in Heaven.* 1993. NY. Atlantic Monthly. 1st. F/dj. M23. $45.00

**ALEXIE, Sherman.** *Water Flowing Home.* 1996. Boise, ID. Limberlost. 1st trade. 1/400. sgn. F/wrp. O11. $65.00

**ALFORD, Violet.** *Peeps at English Folk-Dances.* 1923. London. Black. 1st. sm 8vo. 88p. red cloth. F. B20. $40.00

**ALFRED, H.J.** *Modern Angler.* 1898. London. Gill. new ed. ils. 196p. VG. A17. $40.00

**ALGER, Horatio.** *Slow & Sure.* nd. Chicago. Donohue. F. A19. $25.00

**ALGER, Horatio.** *Tattered Tom; or, Story of a Street Arab.* 1871. Boston. Loring. brn cloth. M20. $25.00

**ALGREN, Nelson.** *Last Carousel.* 1st. VG/dj. B30. $15.00

**ALGREN, Nelson.** *Man With the Golden Arm.* 1956. NY. Cardinal/Pocket. MTI. 2nd. VG/wrp. C9. $20.00

**ALGREN, Nelson.** *Walk on the Wild Side.* 1956. NY. Farrar. 1st. F/NF clip. B2. $50.00

**ALGREN, Nelson.** *Walk on the Wild Side.* 1956. NY. Farrar. 1st. VG/G. M19. $20.00

**ALGREN & DONOHUE.** *Conversations With Nelson Algren.* 1964. Hill Wang. 1st. F/NF. B2. $45.00

**ALIKI.** *Story of William Penn.* 1964. Prentice Hall. ils. unp. lg gr pict cloth. VG+/G. T5. $40.00

**ALINSKY, Saul.** *John L Lewis: An Unauthorized Biography.* 1949. Putnam. 1st. NF/dj. B2. $40.00

**ALKEN, Henry.** *National Sports of Great Britian.* 1903. London. Metheun. 12mo. 50 pl. VG. O3. $38.00

**ALKON, Paul K.** *Samuel Johnson & Moral Discipline.* 1967. Chicago. Northwestern. 1st. H13. $35.00

**ALKON & FOLKENFLIK.** *Pictures & Words. Papers Presented at Clark Library...1982.* 1984. LA. 118p. F/wrp. H13. $45.00

**ALLAN, John B.;** see Westlake, Donald E.

**ALLARD, William Albert.** *Vanishing Breed: Photographs of the Cowboy & the West.* 1982. Little Brn. photos. 144p. AN. J2. $135.00

**ALLARTON, G.** *Mysteries of Medical Life; or, Doctors & Their Doings.* 1856. London. 141p. VG. E6. $75.00

**ALLBEURY, Ted.** *All Our Tomorrows.* 1982. Mysterious. 1st. NF/VG. G8. $10.00

**ALLBEURY, Ted.** *All Our Tomorrows.* 1989. NY. 1st. VG/dj. T9. $8.00

**ALLBEURY, Ted.** *Children of Tender Years.* 1984. BEaufort. 1st Am. VG/G+. G8. $15.00

**ALLBEURY, Ted.** *Choice of Enemies.* 1972. St Martin. 1st. author's 1st novel. F/NF. M15. $100.00

**ALLBEURY, Ted.** *Where All the Girls Are Sweeter.* 1975. London. Peter Davies. 1st. F/dj. M15. $150.00

**ALLDAY, Elizabeth.** *Stefan Zweig.* 1972. Allen. 1st. 248p. VG. S14. $15.00

**ALLEN, Agnes.** *Story of the Book.* 1952. NY. Roy Pub. 1st Am. 8vo. 224p. cloth. dj. O10. $25.00

**ALLEN, Alice E.** *Rosemary.* Feb 1917. Boston. Page. 1st. Cozy Corner series. ils. 96p. VG. B36. $10.00

**ALLEN, Betsy;** *Connie Blair & serial pen name FOR* see Cavana, Betty.

**ALLEN, Charlotte Vale.** *Intimate Friends.* 1983. McClelland Stewart. 1st. sgn. NF/clip. A14. $21.00

**ALLEN, D.L.** *Michigan Fox Squirrel Management.* 1943. Lansing. Dept of Conservation. 1st. photos/maps. 404p. VG. A17. $27.50

**ALLEN, David D.** *Nature of Gambling.* 1952. Coward McCann. 1st. 249p. F/NF. B20. $25.00

**ALLEN, David O.** *India Ancient & Modern.* 1856. Boston. lg fld 1855 Hindostan map. 618p. emb cloth. NF. B14. $75.00

**ALLEN, David Rayvern.** *Early Books on Cricket.* 1987. London. 48 pl. 128p. F/F. A4. $75.00

**ALLEN, David Rayvern.** *Song for Cricket.* 1981. London. 4to. 219p. F/VG. A4. $65.00

**ALLEN, Dotaline.** *History of Nursing in Indiana.* 1950. Indianapolis. photos. VG. E6. $50.00

**ALLEN, Edward W.** *Mysterious Disappearance of Laperouse.* 1959. Tuttle. 1st. 8vo. 321p. NF/VG+. B20. $35.00

**ALLEN, Edward.** *Mustang Sally.* 1992. Norton. 1st. F/dj. R14. $30.00

**ALLEN, Everett S.** *Black Ships: Rumrunners of the Prohibition.* 1979. Boston. 1st. VG/dj. M17. $15.00

**ALLEN, F.** *Treatment of Kidney Diseases & High Blood Pressure, Part I.* 1925. Morristown, NY. Physiatric Inst. VG. E6. $18.00

**ALLEN, Frederick Lewis.** *Only Yesterday: Informal History of the Nineteen Twenties.* 1931. Bl Ribbon. G. A19. $25.00

**ALLEN, G.R.** *Butterfly & Angelfishes of the World. Vol 2.* 1985. Mentor, OH. 352p. F/dj. B1. $35.00

**ALLEN, Grant.** *Colour-Sense: Its Origin & Development.* 1879. Boston. Houghton Osgood. 1st Am. sm 8vo. gilt gr cloth. G. G1. $85.00

**ALLEN, Harris Stearns.** *Trail of Beauty.* 1940. SF. Allen. 1/100. sgn. w/orig watercolor by Wm Gaskin. F. B24. $100.00

**ALLEN, Henry T.** *Expedition to the Copper, Tanana & Koyukuk Rivers in 1885.* 1985. Anchorage. 96p. VG/wrp. A17. $10.00

**ALLEN, Hervey.** *Forest & the Fort.* 1943. Farrar Rhinehart. 1st. NF/VG. M15. $25.00

**ALLEN, Hervey.** *Israfel.* 1934. Farrar Rinehart. rpt (1-vol issue). ES. NF/dj. T11. $45.00

**ALLEN, Hervey.** *Toward the Morning.* 1948. Farrar Rinehart. 1st. sgn/dtd 1945. NF/VG. T11. $40.00

**ALLEN, Ida Bailey.** *Best Loved Recipes of the American People.* 1973. Doubleday. VG/dj. A16. $6.00

**ALLEN, Ida Bailey.** *Mrs Allen's Cook Book.* 1922. Sm Maynard. 3rd. thick 12mo. 756p. B11. $15.00

**ALLEN, Isabel.** *Circling Africa.* 1929. Boston. Marshall Jones. 1st. F/G. B11. $45.00

**ALLEN, James S.** *Negro Question.* 1936. NY. Internat. 1st. F/NF. B2. $45.00

**ALLEN, James S.** *Who Owns America?* 1946. NY. New Century. 1st. VG/wrp. B2. $30.00

**ALLEN, Leslie H.** *Bryan & Darrow at Dayton: Record & Documents...* 1925. NY. Arthur lee. gr cloth. M11. $125.00

**ALLEN, Lewis M.** *Printing With the Handpress...Definitive Manual...* 1969. Allen Pr. 1/140. 4to. 75p. full buckram. B24. $1,850.00

**ALLEN, Lois.** *Bear for Alice.* 1970. Hawthorn. 1st. ils Lois Allen. VG/dj. P2. $12.50

**ALLEN, Maury.** *Roger Maris: A Man for All Season.* 1986. DIF. 1st. F/dj. P8. $40.00

**ALLEN, P.** *Atlas of Atlases: Map Maker's Vision of the World.* 1992. NY. 1st. 300+ mc maps. F/rpr. M4. $65.00

**ALLEN, Raymond.** *Medical Education & the Changing Order.* 1946. NY. 1st. 142p. dj. A13. $20.00

**ALLEN, Richard Sanders.** *Covered Bridges of the Northeast.* 1957. Brattleboro, VT. Stephen Greene. 1st. 121p. VG/dj. B20. $35.00

**ALLEN, Steve.** *Murder in Vegas.* 1991. Zebra. 1st. F/NF. G8. $15.00

ALLEN, Thomas B. *Blue & the Gray.* 1992. NGS. photos Sam Abell. VG/dj. M17. $17.50

ALLEN, Tim. *Don't Stand Too Close to a Naked Man.* 1994. Hyperion. 1st. author's 1st book. F/F. H11. $25.00

ALLEN, Woody. *Four Films of Woody Allen...* 1982. Random. 2nd. ils. F/dj. C9. $42.00

ALLEN & ALLEN. *Liberated Traditionalism: Men & Women in Balance.* 1985. Multnomah. 217p. VG/dj. B29. $8.00

ALLEN & ALLEN. *NC Wyeth: Collected Paintings, Illustrations & Murals.* 1972. NY. Crown. 1st. ils. 225p. F/dj. O10. $100.00

ALLEN PRESS. *Allen Press Bibliography.* 1981. Greenbrae. 1st. 1/140 on handmade. 97p. w/TLS. F/case. B24. $1,150.00

ALLENDE, Isabel. *Eva Luna.* 1988. Knopf. 1st Am. F/F. D10. $40.00

ALLENDE, Isabel. *House of the Spirits.* 1985. NY. Knopf. 1st Am. F/F. D10. $75.00

ALLENDE, Isabel. *Infinite Plan.* 1993. Harper Collins. 1st Am. sgn. F/dj. O11. $30.00

ALLENDE, Isabel. *Of Love & Shadows.* 1987. Knopf. 1st Am. F/F. D10. $50.00

ALLENDE, Isabel. *Of Love & Shadows.* 1987. Knopf. 1st. sgn/dtd 1997. trans Margaret Sayers Peden. F/dj. R14. $90.00

ALLENDE, Isabel. *Stories of Eva Luna.* 1991. Atheneum. 1st. F/F. H11. $25.00

ALLENDE, Isabel. *Stories of Eva Luna.* 1991. Atheneum. 1st. sgn. trans Margaret Sayers Peden. F/F. B3/O11. $40.00

ALLEYNE, Margaret. *Story of Timothy Twitter.* 1966. London. Warne. 7th. sq 16mo. 44p. F/NF clip. C14. $18.00

ALLIBONE. *Critical Dictionary of English Literature...* 1965. 5 vol. VG. A4. $325.00

ALLINGHAM, Margery. *Allingham Case-Book.* 1969. Morrow. 1st Am. G+/dj. G8. $20.00

ALLINGHAM, Margery. *Mr Campion's Quarry.* 1970. Morrow. 1st Am. VG+. G8. $25.00

ALLINGHAM, Margery. *Mr Campion's Clowns.* 1967. London. Chatto Windus. Omnibus (3rd). F/dj. M15. $75.00

ALLINGHAM, Margery. *Mysterious Mr Campion.* 1963. London. Chatto Windus. 1st Onmibus. F/NF. M15. $75.00

ALLINGHAM, Margery. *Tether's End.* 1958. Doubleday. 1st. VG/dj. P3. $30.00

ALLIS, Oswald T. *Prophecy & the Church.* 1972. 339p. VG/wrp. B29. $8.00

ALLISON, Clyde; see Knowles, William.

ALLISON, Dorothy. *Bastard Out of Carolina.* 1992. Dutton. 1st. author's 1st novel. F/F. B4. $150.00

ALLISON, Dorothy. *Bastard Out of Carolina.* 1992. Dutton. 1st. F/NF. B3. $110.00

ALLISON, Pauline. *History of Eaton, CO.* 1963 (1942). Eaton, CO. rpt. VG. A19. $35.00

ALLISON & FRANK. *Kid Who Batted 1,000.* 1951. Doubleday. 1st. VG/G. P8. $25.00

ALLIX, Susan. *Flora: Words About Flowers From Sixteen Authors...* 1992. London. 1/26. ils/sgn Susan Allix. w/2 extra sgn ils. F/box. B24. $2,500.00

ALLOWAY, Lawrence. *Violent America: Movies 1946-1964.* 1971. MOMA. VG/wrp. C9. $36.00

ALLPORT, Gordon Willard. *Nature of Prejudice.* 1954. Cambridge. Addison-Wesley. 2nd. maroon cloth. G1. $25.00

ALLPORT, Gordon Willard. *Studies in Expressive Movement.* 1933. Macmillan. 12mo. inscr/sgn/dtd 1964. 269p. prt bl cloth. VG. G1. $100.00

ALLPORT, S. *Sermons in Stone: Stone Walls of New England & New York.* 1990. NY. 1st. ils. F/dj. M4. $30.00

ALLRED & DYKES. *Flat Top Ranch: Story of a Grassland Venture.* 1957. Norman, OK. 1st. 8vo. 232p. F/dj. B20. $35.00

ALLSOP, Kenneth. *Angry Decade.* 1958. London. 1st. dj. T9. $35.00

ALLSOPP, Fred W. *Albert Pike: A Biography.* 1928. Little Rock. Parke-Harper. 1st. 369p. cloth. D11. $60.00

ALLSOPP, Fred W. *Life Story of Albert Pike.* 1920. Parke-Harper News. 1st. ils. 130p. NF. B19. $65.00

ALMANAC. *London Almanack for the Year of Christ 1756.* (1755). London. Co of Stationers. mini. engraved/4-p panorama. aeg. Dutch gilt ep/silk. B24. $200.00

ALMANAC. *London Almanack for the Year of Christ 1791.* (1790). London. Co of Stationers. mini. ils moon phases/saint days/tidal info+panorama. B24. $375.00

ALMANAC. *London Almanack for the Year of Christ 1796* (1795). London. Co of Stationers. mini. chronology Eng monarchy from 1066. case. B24. $350.00

ALMANAC. *London Almanack for the Year of Christ 1812.* (1811). London. Co of Stationers. mini. red morocco/satin-lined silver filigree case. B24. $450.00

ALMANAC. *London Almanack for the Year of Christ 1813.* (1812). London. Co of Stationers. mini. 4p panorama Drury Lane Theatre. matching case. B24. $375.00

ALMANAC. *Miniature Almanack for the Year of Our Lord 1823.* 1823. Boston. Richardson & Lord/Prt JHA Frost. mini. 28p. F. B24. $85.00

ALMON, John. *Biographical, Literary & Political Anecdotes...* 1797. London. Longman Seeley. 3 vol. 1st. tall 8vo. VG. H13. $395.00

ALMOND, Gabriel A. *Political Development.* 1970. Little Brn. 1st. 8vo. VG/dj. A2. $12.50

ALMOND, Linda Stevens. *When Peter Rabbit Went A-Fishing.* 1923. Altemus. 1st? ils Margaret Campbell Hoopees. VG/dj. M5. $85.00

ALOE, Alfred. *Twelfth US Infantry 1798-1919: Its Story by Its Men.* 1919. US Infantry, NY. 1st. ils/rosters. 425p. VG. S16. $65.00

ALOTTA, Robert I. *Civil War Justice: Union Army Executions Under Lincoln.* 1989. Wht Mane Pub. 1st. F/dj. A14. $21.00

ALPHABET. *Animal & Train ABC.* ca 1908. London. Dean. ABC in 2 parts. ils. gilt gr cloth. NF. D1. $250.00

ALPHABET. *Apple Pie ABC.* 1897. McLoughlin. 4to. mc pict stiff paper wrp. R5. $200.00

ALPHABET. *Child's Illustrated Alphabet.* ca 1850. Phil. Keller & Bright. 8vo. 8p. bl prt wrp. R5. $175.00

ALPHABET. *Good Child's ABC.* ca 1910. Chicago. Donohue. 8vo. 8p. mc linen. R5. $40.00

ALPHABET. *Little Pet's Picture Alphabet.* ca 1865. McLoughlin. 12mo. pict self wrp. R5. $75.00

ALPHABET. *Mon Alphabet.* 1946. Paris. 12mo. French text. R5. $75.00

ALPHABET. *Playland.* ca 1950. London. Dean. 16p. mc pict covers. R5. $85.00

ALSBERG, John L. *Ancient Sculpture From Western Mexico.* 1968. Berkeley. Nicole Gallery. 1st. ils. cloth. F. B27. $145.00

ALSCHULER & HATTWICK. *Painting & Personality: A Study of Young Children.* 1947. Chicago. 2 vol. 8vo. ils/pl. red cloth. VG. G1. $75.00

ALSON, Lawrence. *Leave It to Beaver.* 1959. Golden. 1st. Little Golden #347. VG. R8. $25.00

ALTA. *Burn This & Memorize Yourself.* 1971. WA, NJ. Times Change. 1st. photos Ellen Shumsky. VG+. A25. $32.00

ALTHER, Lisa. *Bedrock.* 1990. Knopf. 1st. F/NF. T12. $35.00

**ALTHER, Lisa.** *Original Sins.* 1981. Knopf. 1st. F/NF. H11. $20.00

**ALTICK & LOUCKS.** *Browning's Roman Murder Story: A Reading of the Ring...* 1968. Chicago. VG/dj. B9. $15.00

**ALTIERI, James.** *Spearheaders: Personal History of Darby's Rangers.* 1979 (1960). WA. rpt. 325p. VG/dj. S16. $25.00

**ALTMAN, Stuart A.** *Social Communication Among Primates.* 1974. Chicago. 3rd. 293p. VG. S15. $15.00

**ALTROCCHI, Julia Cooley.** *Wolves Against the Moon.* 1957. Pageant Book Co. 572p. F/dj. A17. $25.00

**ALTSCHULE, Mark.** *Essays on Rise & Decline of Bedside Medicine.* 1989. Phil. 1st. 458p. A13. $30.00

**ALTSCHULER & GROSSVOGEL.** *Changing Channels.* 1992. Urbana. U IL. 214p. VG/dj. C5. $12.50

**ALTSHELER, Joseph.** *Great Sioux Trail.* 1924. NY. Appleton. VG/G. B5. $30.00

**ALTSHULER, Constance Wynn.** *Latest From Arizona! The Hesperian Letters, 1859-1861.* 1969. Arizona Hist Soc. 1st. fld map/index. 293p. F/NF. B19. $45.00

**ALVAREZ, A.** *Offshore: North Sea Journey.* 1986. Houghton Mifflin. 1st Am. 8vo. F/dj. A2. $12.00

**ALVERSON, Charles.** *Not Sleeping, Just Dead.* 1977. Houghton Mifflin. 1st. F/dj. P3. $13.00

**ALVES & SPELMAN.** *Near the Falls: Two Hundred Years of the Falls Church.* 1969. The Church. ils EPJ Beatty/photos Lee Briggs. 108p. VG/VG. B10. $30.00

**ALVORD, Clarence Walworth.** *Cohokia Records, 1778-1790. Vol 2.* 1907. Springfield, IL. IL State Hist Lib. ils 633p. B18. $37.50

**AMADI, Elechi.** *Great Ponds.* 1973. John Day. 1st. VG/dj. S13. $25.00

**AMADO, Jorge.** *Tereza Batista: Home From the Wars.* 1975. Knopf. 1st. F/NF. M19. $17.50

**AMADO, Jorge.** *Tieta.* 1979. Knopf. 1st Am. rem mk. NF/dj. A14. $17.50

**AMARAL, Anthony.** *How To Train Your Horse.* 1977. NY. Winchester. 1st. VG/dj. O3. $25.00

**AMARANT, Jules.** *Tall Baseball Stories.* 1948. Assn Pr. 1st. sgn. F/VG. P8. $150.00

**AMASON, H.H.** *History of Modern Art: Painting Sculpture, Architecture.* nd. Abrams. ils. VG/dj. M17. $30.00

**AMBER, John T.** *Gun Digest 1969.* 1968. Chicago. ils. 416p. VG/wrp. A17. $20.00

**AMBLER, Eric.** *Light of Day.* 1963. Knopf. 1st Am. F/VG. G8. $25.00

**AMBROSE, Stephen E.** *Crazy Horse & Custer.* 1975. Doubleday. 1st. quarter bl cloth. F/NF. T11. $100.00

**AMBROSE, Stephen E.** *Undaunted Courage: Meriwether Lewis, Thos Jefferson...* 1996. S&S. 511p. AN. J2. $225.00

**AMELIN, A.G.** *Theory of Fog Condensation.* 1967. Jerusalem, Israel. Program for Sci Trans. 2nd/revised. 8vo. VG/dj. A2. $18.00

**AMERICAN FEDERATION OF ARTS.** *101 Masterpieces of American Primitive Painting...* 1962. Doubleday. new ed. mc pl. 159p. cloth. VG/dj. D2. $35.00

**AMERICAN ORNITHOLOGISTS UNION.** *Checklist of North American Birds.* 1983. AOU. 6th. 877p. red cloth. F. S15. $25.00

**AMERICAN ORNITHOLOGISTS UNION.** *Checklist of North American Birds, Fourth Edition.* 1931. Lancaster, PA. 8vo. 526p. cloth. NF. C12. $50.00

**AMERICAN TECHNICAL SOCIETY.** *Cyclopedia of Mechanical Engineering.* 1908. Chicago. 391p. marbled edges. red bdg. H6. $65.00

**AMES, Lee J.** *Draw 50 Famous Cartoons.* 1979. Doubleday. ils. VG/dj. P12. $20.00

**AMES, Mary Ellis.** *Balanced Recipes.* 1933. Minnesota. Pillsbury. VG/special metal case. A16. $75.00

**AMES & CORRELL.** *Orchids of Guatemala.* 1952-53. Chicago. ils. 727p. B26. $85.00

**AMIET, Pierre.** *Art of the Ancient Near East.* 1980. NY. Abrams. ils/map/plans. 618p. cloth. AN/dj/mailing box. D2. $125.00

**AMIS, Kingsley.** *Crime of the Century.* 1987. Mysterious. 1st Am. NF/dj. G8. $15.00

**AMIS, Kingsley.** *Old Devils.* 1986. London. Hutchinson. 1st. NF/dj. A14. $28.00

**AMIS, Kingsley.** *Riverside Villas Murder.* 1973. HBJ. 1st. NF/NF. H11. $15.00

**AMIS, Martin.** *Einstein's Monsters.* 1987. NY. Harmony. 1st Am. sgn. rem mk. F/F. D10. $50.00

**AMIS, Martin.** *Information.* 1995. London. Cape. 1st. sgn. F/dj. O11. $35.00

**AMIS, Martin.** *Information.* 1995. NY. Harmony. 1st Am. sgn. F/dj. B20/R14. $45.00

**AMIS, Martin.** *Invasion of the Space Invaders: An Addict's Guide...* 1982. London. Hutchinson. 1st. sgn. intro Steven Spielberg. F/wrp. B4. $450.00

**AMIS, Martin.** *London Fields.* 1989. Harmony. 1st. sgn. F/F. B3/O11. $50.00

**AMIS, Martin.** *London Fields.* 1989. NY. Harmony. 1st Am. sgn. F/F. D10. $50.00

**AMIS, Martin.** *Moronic Inferno & Other Visits to America.* 1986. London. Cape. 1st. F/dj. B2. $35.00

**AMIS, Martin.** *Other People: A Mystery Story.* 1981. Viking. 1st Am. NF/G+. G8. $20.00

**AMIS, Martin.** *Rachel Papers.* 1974. Knopf. 1st Am. author's 1st book. F/dj. B4. $250.00

**AMIS, Martin.** *Rachel Papers.* 1974. Knopf. 1st Am. sgn. F/NF. D10. $200.00

**AMIS, Martin.** *Success.* 1987. Harmony. 1st Am. sgn. F/dj. O11. $45.00

**AMIS, Martin.** *Time's Arrow.* 1991. London. Cape. 1st. sgn. F/F. D10. $45.00

**AMIS, Martin.** *Time's Arrow.* 1991. NY. Harmony/Crown. 1st. sgn. F/dj. O11. $35.00

**AMIS, Martin.** *Time's Arrow; or, The Nature of the Offense.* 1991. NY. Harmony/Crown. 1st Am. F/dj. A14. $17.50

**AMMONS, A.R.** *Garbage.* 1993. Norton. 1st. sgn. F/dj. R5. $60.00

**AMORY & BRADLEE.** *Vanity Fair.* 1960. NY. Viking. 327p. VG. C5. $12.50

**AMOS, James.** *Memorial: Novel of the Vietnam War.* 1989. NY. Crown. 1st. F/dj. R11. $25.00

**AMOSS, B.** *Old Hasdrubal & Pirate.* 1971. Parents Magazine. 1st. F/sans. T12. $25.00

**AMRSTRONG, Florence A.** *Woman As Persons Under the Constitution.* 1944. WA. Nat Women's Party. 4p. wrp. M11. $25.00

**AMUNDSEN & ELLSWORTH.** *First Crossing of the Polar Sea.* 1927. NY. Doran. 1st. ils/maps. gilt bl cloth. VG. F1. $150.00

**AMUNDSEN & ELLSWORTH.** *Our Polar Flight.* 1925. NY. 1st. ffe removed. 373p. VG. B18. $95.00

**AN ANGLER.** *Salmonia: Of Days of Fly Fishing...Accounts of Habits...* 1970 (1828). Freshet. facs. 16mo. 273p. M/case. A17. $22.50

**ANAND, Valerie.** *Ruthless Yeoman: Bridges Over Time, Book II.* 1991. Headline. 1st. rem mk. F/clip. A14. $21.00

**ANATOLE, Ray;** see Weiss, Joe.

ANCKARSVARD, Karin. *Mysterious Schoolmaster*. 1959. Harcourt Brace. 1st Am. 8vo. 190p. G+/dj. T5. $25.00

ANCOURT, d'Abbe. *Lady's Preceptor; or, Letter to a Young Lady...* 1745. London. J Watts. 3rd. 8vo. 72p. plain wrp/cloth fld/case. K1. $450.00

ANDERS, Nedda Casson. *Chafing Dish Specialities*. 1954. Hearthside. G/dj. A16. $7.00

ANDERSCH, Martin. *Symbols, Signs, Letters*. 1989. NY. Design Pr. 1st. 255p. wht cloth/paper spine label. F/dj. F1. $75.00

ANDERSEN, Allen C. *Beagle As an Experimental Dog*. 1970. IA State. 1st. 616p. VG. A17. $30.00

ANDERSEN, Daren Born. *Alphabet in Five Acts*. 1993. Dial. 1st. obl 8vo. VG/dj. B17. $8.50

ANDERSEN, Hans Christian. *Bell & Other Tales*. 1967. Franklin, NH. Hillside. mini. 1/210. polished navy leather. B24. $110.00

ANDERSEN, Hans Christian. *Danish Fairy Legends & Tales*. 1846. London. Pickering. 1st Eng. 197p. half leather/marbled brd. F1. $450.00

ANDERSEN, Hans Christian. *Fairy Tales & Stories*. 1923 (1921). Macmillan. rpt. 8vo. ils Eric Pape. bl cloth. G+. T5. $15.00

ANDERSEN, Hans Christian. *Fairy Tales*. nd (1924). Hodder Stoughton. 1st trade. ils Kay Nielsen/12 mtd pl. NF. H5. $1,250.00

ANDERSEN, Hans Christian. *Fir Tree*. 1970. NY. Harper Row. 1st. 8vo. gr cloth/pict label. dj. R5. $75.00

ANDERSEN, Hans Christian. *Fire Eventyr (Four Fairy Tales)*. 1943. Hadersley (Denmark). KE Wulf. mini. ils. 20p. stiff wrp/prt dj. F. B24. $250.00

ANDERSEN, Hans Christian. *Little Mermaid*. 1939. Macmillan. 1st. ils Lathrop. unp. gilt cloth. VG/dj. D1. $295.00

ANDERSEN, Hans Christian. *Nightingale*. nd. Saxonville, MA. Picture Book Studio. ils Zwerger. F/NF. C14. $22.00

ANDERSEN, Hans Christian. *Princess & the Pea*. 1974. np. 1/40. 4to. ils/sgn Sarah Chamberlain. F/lt bl wrp. B24. $850.00

ANDERSEN, Hans Christian. *Snow Queen*. 1929. NY. 1/200. ils & sgn Katharine Beverley/Elizabeth Ellender. VG. B18. $150.00

ANDERSEN, Hans Christian. *Snow Queen*. 1972. Scribner. 1st thus. ils Marcia Brown. VG/dj. P2. $25.00

ANDERSEN, Hans Christian. *Snow Queen*. 1979. NY. 1st Am. adapted Naomi Lewis. ils Errol leCain. VG/dj. M17. $17.50

ANDERSEN, Hemming. *Historic Scientific Instruments in Denmark*. 1995. Copenhagen. Royal Danish Academy Sci & Letters. 446p. wrp. K5. $75.00

ANDERSON, A.W. *Coming of the Flowers*. ca 1950. NY. 267p. VG/dj. B26. $16.00

ANDERSON, A.W. *Coming of the Flowers*. nd. FSY. 1st Am? 12mo. VG/dj. A2. $16.00

ANDERSON, Alexander. *Autobiography of Early American Wood Engraver*. 1968. Trader's Pr/JR Levien. mini. 1/500. cloth-backed marbled brd. B24. $85.00

ANDERSON, Bernice G. *Topsy Turvy's Pigtails*. 1938 (1930). Chicago. Rand McNally. 8vo. ils Esther Friend. pict brd. G+. T5. $65.00

ANDERSON, Betty Baxter. *Nancy Blake, Copywriter*. 1942. NY. Cupples Leon. ils Roberta Paflin. VG/dj. M20. $16.00

ANDERSON, C.L.G. *Old Panama & Castilla del Oro*. 1914 (1911). Boston Page. 559p. teg. pict cloth. F3. $90.00

ANDERSON, C.W. *And So To Bed*. (1935). NY. 1st. unp. VG/dj. B18. $22.50

ANDERSON, C.W. *Black, Brown & Chestnut*. 1939. Macmillan. 2nd. G. A21. $40.00

ANDERSON, C.W. *Blaze Finds the Trail*. 1960. Macmillan. Childrens BC. VG/dj. A21. $30.00

ANDERSON, C.W. *Deep Through the Heart*. 1940. NY. Macmillan. 1st. ils. VG/dj. M20. $60.00

ANDERSON, C.W. *Tomorrow's Champion*. 1946. Macmillan. 1st. G. A21. $45.00

ANDERSON, Carol. *Violet Jacob: Diaries & Letters From India 1895-1900*. 1990. Edinburgh. Canongate. 1st. 213p. VG/dj. A25. $35.00

ANDERSON, Elaine. *University of Colorado Studies No 6*. 1968. Boulder, CO. G. A19. $25.00

ANDERSON, Eric M. *Critical Review of Literature on Puma*. 1983. CO Div Wildlife. 91p. F. S15. $9.00

ANDERSON, Florence Bennett. *Grandfather for Benjamin Franklin: True Story...* 1940. Boston. Meador. 1st. 462p. xl. fair. V3. $14.00

ANDERSON, Frank J. *Illustrated History of the Herbals*. 1977. NY. Columbia. ils/biblio/index. 270p. F. H10. $35.00

ANDERSON, Frank J. *Illustrated Treasury of Cultivated Flowers*. 1979. Crown. 50 full-p pl. AN/dj. A10. $40.00

ANDERSON, Frank J. *Latin Jive*. 1984. Spartanburg. Kitemaug. mini. 1/100. red cloth/paper chemise. B24. $50.00

ANDERSON, Gary Clayton. *Little Crow*. 1986. St. Paul, MN. MN Hist Soc. dj. A19. $25.00

ANDERSON, James Douglas. *Making the American Thoroughbred*. 1916. Norwood, MA. Plimpton. 1st. VG. O3. $135.00

ANDERSON, James H. *Life & Letters of Judge Thomas J Anderson & His Wife*. 1904. np. 1st. ils. 535p. G. B18. $22.50

ANDERSON, James L. *Cannibal: Photographic Audacity*. 1970. Sydney. Reed. VG/dj. S5. $25.00

ANDERSON, Ken. *Nessie & the Little Blind Boy of Loch Ness...* 1992. NH. Laughter. 1st. 1/1000. sgn. F/dj. C9. $90.00

ANDERSON, Ken. *Tom Hunter: Sophomore Pitcher*. 1947. Zondervan. 1st. VG/dj. P8. $25.00

ANDERSON, Kent. *Night Dogs*. 1998. Bantam. 1st thus. 1/1800. sgn. F/dj. R14. $50.00

ANDERSON, Kent. *Sympathy for the Devil*. 1987. Doubleday. ARC/1st. sgn. F/wrp. L3. $350.00

ANDERSON, Kent. *Sympathy for the Devil*. 1987. Doubleday. 1st. sgn. F/F. A14/D10. $140.00

ANDERSON, Kevin J. *X Files: Ground Zero*. 1995. Harper Collins. 1st. NF/dj. A14. $25.00

ANDERSON, Lauri. *Hunting Hemingway's Trout*. 1990. NY. Atheneum. 1st. author's 1st book. F/dj. R14. $30.00

ANDERSON, Maxwell. *Eve of St Mark: A Play in Two Acts*. 1942. Anderson House. 1st. VG/G. O4. $20.00

ANDERSON, Maxwell. *Wingless Victory: A Play in Three Acts*. 1936. Anderson House. 1st. 8vo. F/NF. B20. $135.00

ANDERSON, Nels. *Hobo*. 1923. Chicago. 1st. F. B2. $125.00

ANDERSON, Poul. *Infinite Voyage: Man's Future in Space*. 1969. NY. Crowell-Collier. ils. 160p. VG/dj. K5. $18.00

ANDERSON, Poul. *Operation Chaos*. 1971. Doubleday. 1st. F/NF. M23. $35.00

ANDERSON, Robert A. *Service for the Dead*. 1986. NY. Arbor. 1st. F/dj. R11. $35.00

ANDERSON, Sherwood. *Mid-American Chants*. 1918. NY/London. John Lane. 1st. yel cloth. VG. Q1. $125.00

ANDERSON, Sherwood. *Winesburg, Ohio*. 1978. NY. LEC. 1st thus. 1/1500. ils/sgn Ben Stahl. F/glassine. Q1. $125.00

ANDERSON, Warren R. *Owning Western History: Guide to Collecting Rare Documents*. 1993. Mtn Pr. 1st. ils/glossary. 118p. F/wrp. B19. $15.00

ANDERSON, William Marshall. *Adventures in the Rocky Mountains in 1834*. 1951. Am Turf Register. sc. F. A19. $40.00

ANDERSON & BOYD. *Fiasco: Real Story Behind...Energy Crisis*. 1983. NY. Times. 8vo. brd/cloth spine. VG/dj. W1. $22.00

ANDERSON & HANNA. *Micro Ways: Every Cook's Guide to Successful Microwaving*. 1990. Doubleday. G/VG. V4. $20.00

ANDERSON & KINZIE. *Little Magazine in America: Modern Documentary History*. 1978. 1st hc. ils. VG/dj. M17. $30.00

ANDERSON & PRONZINI. *Cambodia File*. 1981. Doubleday. 1st. NF/VG. R11. $30.00

ANDERSON & RASHIDIAN. *Iraq & the Continuing Middle East Crisis*. 1991. St Martin. 1st. 8vo. ils/tables. NF/dj. W1. $18.00

ANDERSON. *Manual on Bookselling*. 1969. Am Booksellers. 282p. VG. A4. $35.00

ANDERSSON & BEDOIRE. *Swedish Architecture, Drawings 1640-1970*. 1986. Stockholm. Byggforlaget/Swedish Mus Architecture. 1st. 257p. F/dj. O10. $55.00

ANDREAS-FRIEDRICH, Ruth. *Battleground Berlin, Diaries 1945-1948*. 1990. NY. 1st. trans A Boerresen. T9. $10.00

ANDREW, Prudence. *Sparkle From the Coal*. 1965. Putnam. 1st Am. 212p. NF/dj. D4. $35.00

ANDREW, W.P. *Memoir on the Euphrates Valley Route to India...* 1857. London. Allen. inscr ffe (lacks rear). 8vo. 2 lg fld maps. G. Q2. $530.00

ANDREWARTHA & BIRCH. *Distribution & Abundance of Animals*. 1982. Chicago. 275p. F. S15. $8.50

ANDREWARTHA & BIRCH. *Ecological Web: More on Distribution & Abundance of Animals*. 1986. U Chicago. 506p. F. S15. $12.00

ANDREWS, Charles M. *Colonial Background of the American Revolution*. 1931. New Haven. Yale. revised. 220p. gilt bl cloth. VG. S17. $20.00

ANDREWS, Edward D. *Community Industries of the Shakers*. 1933. Albany. U NY. ils/index. 322p. F/wrp. B14. $35.00

ANDREWS, Ella Matson. *Century of Fashions*. 1911. np. typed & watercolor by author+tipped-in pl. gilt decor leather/raised bands. B11. $2,500.00

ANDREWS, Henry. *Fossil Hunters: In Search of Ancient Plants*. 1980. Ithaca. 1st. 421p. A13. $20.00

ANDREWS, Jane. *Each & All: Seven Little Sisters Prove Their Sisterhood*. 1905. Ginn & Co. gray cloth. VG. B36. $17.50

ANDREWS, Kenneth R. *English Privateering Voyages to the West Indies 1588-1595*. 1959. Cambridge. Hakluyt Soc. 8vo. 9 pl/maps. F/dj. O1. $65.00

ANDREWS, Lori. *Black Power White Blood*. 1996. Pantheon. 1st. inscr. F/dj. T11. $30.00

ANDREWS, M. Carl. *No Higher Honor: Story of Mills E Godwin Jr.* (1970). Dietz. 207p. VG. B10. $25.00

ANDREWS, Mary Raymond S. *His Soul Goes Marching On*. 1922. Scribner. 1st. NF. T11. $12.00

ANDREWS, R.C. *Natural History of Asia, Vol I...* 1932. Am Mus Nat Hist. ils/fld pl/maps. 678p. VG+. M12. $750.00

ANDREWS, Ralph W. *Redwood Classic*. 1958. Seattle. photos. 174p. VG. B26. $24.00

ANDREWS, Roy Chapman. *Nature's Ways: How Nature Takes Care of Its Own*. 1951. NY. 206p. VG. A17. $15.00

ANDREWS, Roy Chapman. *On the Trail of Ancient Man*. 1926. Putnam. 58 photos/index. 376p. teg. gr cloth. K1. $85.00

ANDREWS, Tom. *On William Stafford: Worth of Local Things*. (1993). Ann Arbor. U MI. 1st. 281p. AN/dj. A18. $20.00

ANDREWS, W.D. *Swimming & Life-Saving*. 1889. Toronto. Wm Briggs. 1st. ils. 136p. gilt cloth. VG. B18. $45.00

ANDREWS, Wayne. *Architecture in New England*. 1973. Brattleboro. photos. VG/G. M17. $35.00

ANDRIST, Ralph. *Founding Fathers: George Washington...* 1972. NY. Newsweek. ils. 416p. VG/dj. M10. $18.50

ANDRIST, Ralph. *Long Death: Last Days of the Plains Indians*. 1964. Macmillan. 1st. VG/dj. L3. $50.00

ANDROS, Thomas. *Old Jersey Captive; or, Narrative of Captivity...* 1833. Boston. Wm Pierce. 1st. 80p. contemporary marbled paper/brd. B14. $175.00

ANG, Li. *Butcher's Wife*. 1986. SF. Northpoint. 1st Am. trans Goldblatt/Young. F/dj. D10. $40.00

ANGEL, Adriana. *Tiger's Milk: Women of Nicaragua*. 1987. NY. Seaver Books. 1st Am. 142p. dj. F3. $10.00

ANGELL, James Rowland. *Introduction to Psychology*. 1918. Henry Holt. 12mo. dk gray cloth. G. G1. $30.00

ANGELL, Roger. *Season Ticket*. 1988. Houghton Mifflin. 1st. F/dj. P8. $25.00

ANGELO, Valenti. *Com Amore: Valenti Angelo. A Biography 1971-1982*. 1992. SF. Linden Eds. 1/12. sgn. w/extra title p sgn James Linden. F. B24. $1,500.00

ANGELO, Valenti. *Golden Gate*. 1939. Viking. 1st. 8vo. 273p. VG+. C14. $12.00

ANGELO, Valenti. *Nino*. 1938. Viking/Jr Literary Guild. 1st thus. 244p. Newbery Honor. VG/G. P2. $18.00

ANGELOU, Maya. *On the Pulse of the Morning*. nd. Random. 1st hc. F/dj. B2. $35.00

ANGELOU, Maya. *On the Pulse of the Morning*. 1993. Random. 1st. F/burgundy wrp. O11. $35.00

ANGER, Kenneth. *Hollywood Babylon*. 1965. Assoc Proff Services. 1st Eng. F/wrp. C9. $90.00

ANGLE, Barbara. *Those That Mattered*. 1994. NY. Crown. 1st. author's 1st book. NF/F. H11. $15.00

ANGLE, Paul M. *Pictorial History of the Civil War Years*. 1967. NY. 1st. ils/photos. F/dj. E1. $40.00

ANGLE, Paul M. *Pioneers: Narrative of Noah Harris Letts & Thomas A Banning*. 1972. Lakeside Classic. ils. 290p. teg. F. B10/M10. $20.00

ANGLO, Michael. *Penny Dreadfuls & Other Victorian Horrors*. 1977. London. Jupiter. 1st. ils. F/dj. O4. $35.00

ANGLUND, Joan Walsh. *Almost a Rainbow*. 1980. Random. later. 12mo. gr cloth. AN/dj. R5. $100.00

ANGLUND, Joan Walsh. *Brave Cowboy*. (1959). Rand McNally. early ed. sq 12mo. red cloth. VG/G. T5. $35.00

ANGLUND, Joan Walsh. *Christmas Book*. 1983. Random. 2nd. 4to. sgn/drawing/pres on ffe. AN. R5. $100.00

ANGLUND, Joan Walsh. *Christmas Is a Time of Giving*. 1961. HBW. 1st. VG/G. P2. $18.00

ANGLUND, Joan Walsh. *In a Pumpkin Shell, a Mother Goose ABC*. 1960. Harcourt. 1st. F/VG+. M5. $105.00

**ANGLUND, Joan Walsh.** *Little Book of Love.* 1989. Random. 1st. 16mo. w/doll. AN/orig package. R5. $60.00

**ANGLUND, Joan Walsh.** *Love One Another.* 1981. Determined. 1st. 16mo. F/VG. M5. $20.00

**ANGLUND, Joan Walsh.** *Memories of the Heart.* 1984. Random. 4th. sgn/drawing/ pres on ffe. gilt cloth. R5. $85.00

**ANGLUND, Joan Walsh.** *Morning Is a Little Child.* 1969. HBW. 1st. ils JW Anguland. NF/G. P2. $25.00

**ANGLUND, Joan Walsh.** *Mother Goose Book.* 1991. HBJ. 1st. 12mo. AN/dj. R5. $75.00

**ANGLUND, Joan Walsh.** *Nibble Nibble Mousekin: A Tale of Hansel & Gretel.* 1962. NY. HBW. 1st thus. 8vo. gr brd. dj. R5. $75.00

**ANGLUND, Joan Walsh.** *See the Year.* 1984. Random. 1st. sgn on title p. mc pict brd. AN. R5. $75.00

**ANGLUND, Joan Walsh.** *Spring Is a New Beginning.* 1963. HBW. 1st. 16mo. unp. ils brd. F/F. C14. $22.00

**ANGLUND, Joan Walsh.** *What Color Is Love?* 1966. Harcourt. 1st. ils. NF/VG. M5. $20.00

**ANGOLIA, John.** *On the Field of Honor: History of Knight's Cross Bearers.* 1980. San Jose. 1st. photos. 368p. VG. S16. $40.00

**ANGUS, Ian.** *Paper Money.* 1974. St Mattin. 1st Am. 8vo. 128p. VG/dj. B11. $15.00

**ANIKIN, A.** *Gold: The Yellow Devil.* 1983. NY. International Pub. 1st Am. 12mo. VG/dj. A2. $15.00

**ANKENBRAND, Frank.** *Scroll of Birthday Haiku for Robert Massmann...* 1967. New Britain, CT. mini. 1/200 on Japanese Bokuryu. inscr Massmann. case. B24. $65.00

**ANNAN, David.** *Robot, the Mechanical Monster.* 1976. London. Lirrimer. 1st. ils. VG/wrp. C9. $36.00

**ANNEQUIN, Guy.** *Civilization of the Maya.* (1978). Geneva. Ferni. 1st Eng. photos/ils. 234p. F3. $20.00

**ANNIXTER & ANNIXTER.** *Year of the She Grizzly.* 1978. CMG. 1st. VG/G+. B36. $10.00

**ANNO.** *Anno's Sundial.* 1987. Philomel. popup. VG. B17. $20.00

**ANON.** *Come & Dine: Collection of Valuable Receipts...* 1872. VG. E6. $45.00

**ANON.** *Healing Art; or, Chapters on Medicine, Diseases, Remedies...* 1887. London. 2 vol. 1st. A13. $200.00

**ANON.** *Huntingdon Valley Hunt.* 1923. Willow Grove, PA. 12mo. 3 photos. 48p. VG. O3. $35.00

**ANON.** *Sex Truths: A Solution of Lost Youth, Lost Love...* nd. np. 1st? 36p. VG+/laminated self wrp. A25. $18.00

**ANON.** *Stories From Our Navy: Retold From St Nicholas.* 1929. NY. Century. 1st. sm 8vo. 195p. ils cloth. G. C14. $9.00

**ANON.** *Tricks of the Trade in Adulteration of Food & Physic.* 1856. London. VG. E6. $100.00

**ANONYMOUS MNEMONIC.** *Kings & Queens of England.* 1981. Poole. mini. 1/100. prt/binder Maryline Adams. 15p. decor brd. F. B24. $100.00

**ANSA, Tina McElroy.** *Ugly Ways.* 1993. harcourt Brace. 1st. G/dj. B30. $10.00

**ANSELL, Mary.** *Happy Garden.* 1912. London. Cassell. 224p. decor cloth. VG. A10. $18.00

**ANTHOLOGY.** *Brand Book Number Three, San Diego Corral of Westerners.* 1973. Arts & Crafts. 1/500. sgn 8 contributors. ils/photos. gilt gray cloth. VG+. F7. $125.00

**ANTHOLOGY.** *Circle of Nations.* 1993. Hillsboro, OR. Beyond Words Pub. 1st. sgn 3 contributors. F/dj. O11. $150.00

**ANTHOLOGY.** *Coming to Terms: American Plays & the Vietnam War.* 1985. NY. Theatre Communications Group. 1st hc/BC issue. VG/dj. R11. $15.00

**ANTHOLOGY.** *Naked Came the Manatee.* 1996. NY. Putnam. 1st. sgn 13 contributors. F/dj. M15. $200.00

**ANTHOLOGY.** *No Alibi: Celebration of Crime Writing.* 1995. Blakeney, Glos. Scorpion. 1/150. sgn all 27 contributors. F/dj. T2. $175.00

**ANTHOLOGY.** *Silver Scream.* 1988. Dark Harvest. 1/500. sgn all 19 contributors. F/dj/case. T2. $125.00

**ANTHOLOGY.** *Tower of Babel. An Anthology...* 1975. W Burke, VT. Janus. 1/110. ils/inscr VanVliet. 17 lithos/1 engraving. AN. B24. $1,500.00

**ANTHONY, Edgar Waterman.** *History of Mosaics.* 1935. Boston. Porter Sargent. 80 b&w pl. 333p. gilt blk cloth. F1. $35.00

**ANTHONY, Edward.** *Every Dog Has His Say.* 1947. Watson-Guptill. 1st. ils Morgan Dennis. NF/dj. A21. $95.00

**ANTHONY, Evelyn.** *Cardinal & the Queen.* 1968. Coward McCann. 1st. F/NF. M19. $25.00

**ANTHONY, Irvin.** *Paddle Wheels & Pistols.* 1929. Phil. Macrae Smith. 1st. 8vo. 329p. G. B11. $25.00

**ANTHONY, Katharine.** *Dolly Madison: Her Life & Times.* 1949. Doubleday. 1st. 426p. VG/clip. V3. $16.00

**ANTHONY, Katharine.** *Susan B Anthony: Her Personal History & Her Era.* 1954. Garden City. Doubleday. 1st. 521p. VG/torn. V3. $11.50

**ANTHONY, Patricia.** *Cold Allies.* 1993. HBJ. 2nd. author's 1st novel. AN/dj. M21. $10.00

**ANTHONY, Piers.** *Ghost.* 1986. NY. Tom Doherty. 1st. VG/dj. A23. $22.00

**ANTHONY, Piers.** *Juxtaposition.* 1982. Del Rey/Ballantine. 1st. Apprentice Adept #3. VG+/dj. A14. $17.50

**ANTHONY, Piers.** *On a Pale Horse.* 1983. Del Rey/Ballantine. 1st. Incantations of Immortality #1. VG+/dj. A14. $25.00

**ANTHONY, Piers.** *Shade of the Tree.* 1986. NY. Tom Doherty. 1st. F/dj. A23. $22.00

**ANTHONY, Piers.** *Split Infinity.* 1980. Del Rey/Ballantine. 1st. Apprentice Adept series #1. VG+/clip. A14. $22.00

**ANTHONY, Piers.** *Total Recall.* 1989. Morrow. 1st. F/NF. M25. $15.00

**ANTHONY, Piers.** *Unicorn Point.* 1989. Ace Putnam. 1st. 303p. AN/dj. M21. $15.00

**ANTHONY & CHILAND.** *Child in His Family: Perilous Development...* 1988. John Wiley. Allied Professionals Vol 8. 621p. VG/dj. G1. $60.00

**ANTONINUS, Brother.** *Robinson Jeffers: Fragments of an Older Fury.* 1968. np. Oyez. 1st. F/dj. A18. $20.00

**APGAR, A.C.** *Birds of the United States East of the Rocky Mountains.* 1898. NY. sm 8vo. ils. 415p. NF. C12. $36.00

**APOLLINAIRE, Guillaume.** *Firs.* 1950. Cummington. 1st. French-fld. F. M24. $45.00

**APOSTOL, Jane.** *South Pasadena, 1888-1988: A Centennial History.* 1988. S Pasadena Pub Lib. 1st. ils/index. 311p. F/NF. B19. $40.00

**APPEL, Alfred Jr.** *Signs of Life.* 1983. Knopf. 1st. VG/dj. S5. $27.50

**APPEL, Allen.** *Till the End of Time.* 1990. Doubleday. 1st. NF/dj. A14. $21.00

**APPIA, P.L.** *Ambulance Surgeon; or, Practical Observations...* 1862. Edinburgh. Blk. 266p. xl. G7. $395.00

**APPLEBY, John.** *Bad Summer.* 1958. Ives Washburn. 1st. VG. P3. $10.00

**APPLEMAN, Roy.** *Okinawa: Last Battle.* 1964. Rutland. 2nd. VG/dj. B5. $35.00

**APPLETON, George.** *Oxford Book of Prayer.* 1985. Oxford. 399p. VG/wrp. B29. $7.50

**APPLETON, Victor.** *Caves of Nuclear Fire.* 1956. Grosset Dunlap. VG/G. L4. $20.00

**APPLETON, Victor.** *Don Sturdy in Lion Land (#9).* 1929. Grosset Dunlap. lists 12 titles. VG/dj. M20. $50.00

**APPLETON, Victor.** *Movie Boys at the Big Fair (#16).* 1926. Garden City. VG/wrp. M20. $32.00

**APPLETON, Victor.** *Tom Swift & His Air Glider (#12).* 1912. Grosset Dunlap. lists 28 titles. VG/ragged edged dj. M20. $45.00

**APPLETON, Victor.** *Tom Swift & His Rocket Ship.* 1954. Grosset Dunlap. VG/G. L4. $20.00

**APPLETON, Victor.** *Tom Swift & the Captive Planetoid (#29).* 1967. Grosset Dunlap. 1st. lists to this title. VG. M20. $40.00

**APPLETON, Victor.** *Tom Swift Circling the Globe.* 1927. Grosset Dunlap. 1st. VG. T12. $20.00

**APSLEY, Lady.** *Bridleways Through History.* 1948. London. Hutchinson. 2nd/revised. VG/G. O3. $45.00

**APTHEKER, Herbert.** *Mission to Hanoi.* 1966. NY. Internat. sgn. photos. 128p. VG/wrp. R11. $30.00

**AQUILA, Richard.** *Wanted Dead or Alive: American West in Popular Culture.* 1996. U IL. 313p. AN. J2. $35.00

**AQUILEO PARRA.** *Memorias de Quileo Parra, Presidente de Colombia...1878.* 1912. Bogota. 474p. quarter leather. F3. $15.00

**AQUINAS.** *Basic Writings of Saint Thomas Aquinas.* 1945. Random. 2 vol. G. B29. $30.00

**ARAGON, Jane Chelsea.** *Major & the Mousehole Mice.* 1990. S&S. 1st. VG/dj. M20. $20.00

**ARBER, Agnes.** *Graminea: A Study of Cereal, Bamboo & Grass.* 1934. Cambridge. 480p. VG. A10. $45.00

**ARBER, Edward.** *Story of the Pilgrim Fathers, 1606-1623...* 1897. London. Ward Downey. 634p. VG. M10. $60.00

**ARBERRY, A.J.** *Aspects of Islamic Civilization As Depecited in Orig Texts.* 1971. Ann Arbor. U MI. 8vo. 409p. G/wrp. W1. $5.00

**ARBMAN, E.** *Ecstasy or Religious Trance...* 1963-1970. Stockholm. 3 vol. cloth. F. G1. $275.00

**ARBUTHNOT, Mary Hill.** *Children & Books.* 1947. Autographed 1st Ed bookplate. sgn. 640p. VG. A4. $95.00

**ARCH, Narziss.** *Uber den Willen.* 1910. Leipzig. Quelle Meyer. 24p. prt gr wrp. G1. $65.00

**ARCHAMBAULT & MARTIN.** *Beautiful Feast for the Big King Cat.* 1989. Harper Collins. 3rd. ils Bruce Degen. F/dj. V4. $10.00

**ARCHER, Jeffrey.** *First Among Equals.* 1984. Linden. 1st. F/VG+. M21. $10.00

**ARCHER, Jeffrey.** *Shall We Tell the President?* 1977. NY. Viking. 1st Am. sgn. NF/dj. A14. $32.00

**ARCHER, Kevin M.** *History of Santa Monica Fire Dept 1889-1989.* 1989. Visalia. self pub. 166p. silver stp fabricoid. D11. $35.00

**ARCHER, M.** *Natural History Drawings in the India Office Library.* 1962. London. 4to. ils. 116p. F/VG+. M12. $75.00

**ARCHER, William.** *Masks or Faces? Study in Psychology of Acting.* 1888. Longman Gr. sm 8vo. 232p. gr cloth. G1. $45.00

**ARCHIBALD, Joe.** *Easy Out.* 1963. MacRae SMith. 1st. F/VG. P8. $55.00

**ARCHIBALD, Joe.** *Full Count.* 1956. Macrae Smith. 1st. VG/dj. P8. $65.00

**ARCINIEGAS, German.** *Germans in the Conquest of America.* 1943. Macmillan. 1st. 217p. F3. $30.00

**ARCINIEGAS, German.** *Green Continent.* (1944). Knopf. 1st. 533p. F3. $15.00

**ARCTANDER, John W.** *Apostle of Alaska: Story of William Duncan of Metlakahtla.* 1909. Fleming Revell. 8vo. ils/map/photos. 395p. yel decor cloth. P4. $55.00

**ARDEN, William.** *3 Investigators: Mystery of the Moaning Cave.* 1973. Random. lists to Mystery of Monster Mtns. decor brd. VG. P3. $20.00

**ARDINGER, Richard.** *What Thou Lovest Well Remains.* 1986. Boise. Limberlost. 1st. 1/26 lettered. sgn 21 of 23 contributors. F/sans. L3. $575.00

**ARDIS.** *Guide to the Literature of Electrical & Electronics...* 1987. 697 entries. 190p. VG. A4. $85.00

**ARDIZZONE, Dony.** *Larabi's Ox.* 1992. Milkweed. 1st. F/wrp. R14. $25.00

**ARDIZZONE, Edward.** *Young Ardizzone.* 1970. Macmillan. 1st Am. ils Ardizzone. G/dj. P2. $35.00

**ARDIZZONE, Tony.** *Heart of the Order.* 1986. Holt. 1st. inscr/sgn twice. F/dj. P8. $45.00

**ARENDT, Erich.** *Colombia: Tierre de Soledades — Tierra del Fervor.* 1957. Leipzig. 4to. map/134 full-p pl. 19p text. F3. $15.00

**ARENDT & JASPERS.** *Correspondence 1926-69.* 1992. 1st. edit Kohler/Saner. trans R Kimber. T9. $28.00

**ARENDT & JASPERS.** *Essays in Understanding 1930-54.* 1994. NY. Kohn. 1st. T9. $28.00

**AREY, James A.** *Sky Pirates.* 1972. Scribner. 1st. 8vo. VG/dj. A2. $12.50

**ARGINTEAU, Judy.** *Movies of Alfred Hitchcock.* 1994. Minneapolis. Lerner. 80p. VG/dj. C5. $12.50

**ARKIN, Alan.** *Lemming Condition.* 1976. Harper Row. 1st. VG/dj. P2. $35.00

**ARKIN, Arthur M.** *Mind in Sleep: Psychology & Psychophysiology.* 1978. Hillsdale, NJ. Lawrence Earlbaum Assoc. gr cloth. VG. G1. $65.00

**ARKUSH & LEE.** *Land Without Ghosts: Chinese Impressions of America...* 1989. Berkeley. NF/dj. B9. $17.50

**ARMBRUSTER, Eugene L.** *Eastern District of Brooklyn With Illustrations & Maps.* 1912. NY. 205p. gr cloth. B14. $200.00

**ARMBRUSTER & TAYLOR.** *Astronaut Training.* 1990. NY. Franklin Watts. 8vo. 64p. F. K5. $10.00

**ARMER, Laura Adams.** *Forest Pool.* 1938. NY. 1st. 40p. VG. B18. $37.50

**ARMER, Laura Adams.** *Waterless Mountain.* 1981 (1931). McKay. rprt. 8vo. 212p. Newbery Award. bl cloth. NF/VG. T5. $20.00

**ARMES, Roy.** *Patterns of Realism.* 1971. Cranbury. 1st. dj. T9. $18.00

**ARMES, Roy.** *Third World Film Making & the West.* 1987. Berkeley. U CA. 381p. VG/wrp. C5. $12.50

**ARMITAGE, Merle.** *Accent on Life.* 1964. Ames, IA. 1st. ils. 386p. blk cloth. F1. $45.00

**ARMITAGE, Merle.** *Designed Books.* 1938. NY. Weyhe. 1st. F/stiff paper/card-covers. S9. $250.00

**ARMITAGE, Merle.** *Homage to the Santa Fe: Atchison Topeka & Santa Fe.* 1973. Manzanita. ils. 141p. NF/NF. B19. $35.00

**ARMOR, Samuel.** *History of Orange County, California...* 1921. LA. Hist Record Co. ils. 1669p. gilt pebbled cloth. D11. $200.00

**ARMOUR, Tommy.** *How To Play Your Best Golf All the Time.* 1953. S&S. 2nd. 151p. NF/VG. B20. $20.00

**ARMSTRONG, BUSBY & CARR.** *Reader's Hebrew-English Lexicon: Two Volumes in One...* 1984. Regency. 230p. VG/dj. B29. $23.00

ARMSTRONG, Charlotte. *Dream of Fair Woman.* 1966. Collins. 1st Eng. F/dj. M19. $17.50

ARMSTRONG, Charlotte. *Lemon in the Basket.* nd. BC. VG/dj. P3. $8.00

ARMSTRONG, Hamilton Fish. *Tito & Goliath.* 1951. London. Gollancz. 1st. 8vo. 318p. cloth. VG. W1. $20.00

ARMSTRONG, Leroy. *Pictorial Atlas Illustrating the Spanish-American War.* 1899. NY. Cram. ils/maps. 231p. pict cloth. G+. B18. $125.00

ARMSTRONG, Louis. *Satchmo: My Life in New Orleans.* 1954. Prentice Hall. 1st. 8vo. 240p. F/NF. B20. $45.00

ARMSTRONG, Margaret. *Murder in Stained Glass.* 1939. Random. 1st. VG. G8. $30.00

ARMSTRONG, Terence. *Russians in the Arctic.* 1958. Essential Books. photos/maps. VG/dj. M17. $20.00

ARMSTRONG, Walter P. *Count Joannes & Others.* 1981. Memphis. G/wrp. B30. $10.00

ARMSTRONG, Warren. *Atlantic Highway.* 1961. London. Harrap. 1st. 239p. F/dj. B20. $35.00

ARMSTRONG & DALGARNO. *Airglow & the Aurorae: Symposium Held at Belfast Sept 1955.* nd. London. pergamon. 420p. VG. K5. $75.00

ARNASON, Eleanor. *Woman of the Iron People.* 1991. Morrow. 1st. F/dj. M25. $25.00

ARNAZ, Desi. *Book.* 1976. Morrow. later prt. VG/dj. C9. $55.00

ARNO, Peter. *Whoops Dearie!* 1927. NY. S&S. 1st. sgn. 175p. NF/VG. B20. $200.00

ARNOLD, CHANNING & FROST. *American Egypt, a Record of Travel in Yucatan.* 1909. Doubleday Page. 1st Am. lg 8vo. 301p. gilt cloth. O1. $85.00

ARNOLD, Edwin. *Conversations With Erskine Caldwell.* 1988. U MS. 1st. Literary Conversations series. F/wrp. T11. $22.00

ARNOLD, Edwin. *Light of Asia.* 1926. Dodd Mead/Bodley Head. 1st. 1/3000. ils Hamzeh Carr. 177p. NF. B20. $60.00

ARNOLD, Eve. *Marilyn Monroe: An Appreciation.* 1987. Knopf. 1st. ils. F/dj. C9. $150.00

ARNOLD, Joseph. *Yearbook of the Dept of Agriculture.* 1908. GPO. 822p. brd. G+. A10. $28.00

ARNOLD, L. Eugene. *Childhood Stress.* 1990. John Wiley. 8vo. 603p. prt gray cloth. VG/dj. G1. $60.00

ARNOLD, Lloyd. *High on the Wild With Hemingway.* 1968. Caldwell. Caxton. 1st. F/dj. B5. $55.00

ARNOLD, M.S. *Colonial Arkansas, 1686-1804.* 1991. AR U. 1st. ils. 232p. F/dj. M4. $40.00

ARNOLD, Magda B. *Emotion & Personality.* 1960. Columbia. 2 vol. VG/dj. G1. $65.00

ARNOLD, Matthew. *Scholar Gipsy & Thyrsis.* 1910. London. Philip Warner. 1/100 on Japan vellum. ils/sgn WR Flint. teg. NF/case. H5. $500.00

ARNOLD, Oren. *Savage Son.* 1951. NM U. 1st. 273p. VG/G. B19. $10.00

ARNOLD, Oren. *Thunder in the Southwest.* 1952. Norman, OK. VG/dj. A19. $30.00

ARNOLD, Schuyler. *Wayside Marketing.* 1929. NY. DeLaMare. 123p. VG/dj. A10. $28.00

ARNOLD, Thurman W. *Bottlenecks of Business.* 1940. Reynal Hitchcock. cloth. M11. $50.00

ARNOLD, William Harris. *Ventures in Book Collecting.* 1923. NY. Scribner. 1st. ils. 356p. gilt blk cloth/gray brd. VG. F1. $25.00

ARNOLD & GROHMANN. *Islamic Book: Contribution to Its Art & History...* 1929. Leipzig. Pries. 1st. 1/375. 104 collotype pl. teg. cloth. VG. W1. $750.00

ARNOLD & HALE. *Hot Irons: Heraldry of the Range.* 1942. Macmillan. later prt. 273p. VG. B19. $20.00

ARNOW, Harriette. *Dollmaker.* 1954. Macmillan. true 1st. sgn. NF/clip. L3. $575.00

ARNSTEIN, Flora J. *Legacy of Hours.* 1927. Grabhorn. 1/250. 12mo. 61p. B20. $35.00

ARNTZEN & RAINWATER. *Guide to Literature of Art History.* 1980. Am Lib Assn. 4to 4037 references. 634p. F. A4. $85.00

ARONSON, T. *King in Love: King Edward VII's Mistresses.* 1988. Harper Row. 1st. F/NF. T12. $20.00

AROSENIUS, Erik. *Sagan om Fiskarpoijkarnas Resa Till det Underbara.* 1916. Stockholm. Hasse W Tullbergs Boktrycheri. 4to. 10 pl. beige brd. R5. $385.00

ARP, Halton. *Quasars, Redshifts & Controversies.* 1987. Berkeley. Interstellar Media. ils/photos/diagrams. 198p. F/dj. K5. $35.00

ARRIAGA & MARTINEZ. *Voyage of the Frigate Princesa to Southern CA in 1782...* 1982. Santa Barbara. Mission Archive. 1st. VG. O4. $20.00

ARROWSMITH, Joannem. *Tactica Sacra.* 1657. London. 1st. 8vo. 367+25p. Latin text. rb modern brn cloth. B11. $450.00

ARSENIS, Mylda L. *Dog Tales & Trimmings.* 1957. Howard Timmins. sgn. VG. A21. $20.00

ARTHUR, Ella Bentley. *My Husband Keeps Telling Me To Go To Hell.* 1954. Hanover. 1st. ils R Taylor. 79p. F/VG+. B20. $25.00

ARTHUR, R. *End of a Revolution.* 1965. NY. 1st. ils/maps. G/fair. M4. $13.00

ARTHUR, Robert. *Ghosts & More Ghosts.* 1963. Random. 1st/revised. VG/dj. B36. $10.00

ARTHUR, T.S. *Grappling With Monster; or, Curse & Cure of Strong Drink.* ca 1880. Phil. Edgewood. rpt. 320p. gilt bl cloth. B20. $50.00

ARTHUR & WITNEY. *Barn: A Vanishing Landmark in North America.* 1981. NY. Galahad. 256p. VG/dj. A10. $30.00

ARTHURS, Stanley. *American Historical Scene.* 1935. U PA. ils. leather spine. VG. M17. $75.00

ARTISS, Percy. *Market Gardening.* 1949. London. Collingridge. 2nd. 127p. VG. A10. $22.00

ARTLEY, GRAY & GRAY. *Tall Tales.* 1953. Scott Foresman. Reading for Independence #3. yel cloth. VG+. B36. $16.00

ARTLEY, GRAY & GRAY. *What Next.* 1952. Scott Foresman. Reading for Independence #2. aqua brd. VG. B36. $30.00

ARTOM, Guido. *Napoleon Is Dead in Russia: Extraordinary Story...* 1970. NY. 1st Am. 256p. VG/dj. S16. $20.00

ARTUSI, Pellegrino. *La Scienza in Cucine e l'Arte de Mangier Bene.* 1950. 573p. VG. E6. $35.00

ARTZIBASHEF, Michael. *War: A Play in Four Acts.* 1916. Knopf. 1st Am. 12mo. 73p+ads. VG. B20. $25.00

ARTZYBASHEFF, Boris. *Fairy Shoemaker.* 1928. NY. 1st. ils. 114p. VG. B18. $45.00

ASARO, Catherine. *Primary Inversion.* 1995. NY. Tor. 1st. sgn. author's 1st novel. F/dj. M23. $50.00

ASBURY, Herbert. *Golden Flood: Informal History of America's First Oil Field.* 1942. Knopf. thick 8vo. 324p. VG/dj. B20. $40.00

ASDELL, S.A. *Cattle Fertility & Sterility.* 1955. Little Brn. 1st. 227p. VG/dj. N2. $10.00

ASH, Edward. *Christian Profession of Society of Friends...* 1837. London. Arch. 1st. 12mo. 88p. worn/inner hinge broken. V3. $28.00

**ASH & DAY.** *Immortal Turpin, the Authentic History of...Highwayman.* 1948. London. Staples. M11. $50.00

**ASH & LAKE.** *Frog Raising for Pleasure & Profit & Other Bizarre Books.* 1985. London. Macmillan. 1st. 8vo. 180p. F/dj. B20. $35.00

**ASH.** *Subject Collections.* 1974. 4to. 908p. xl. VG. A4. $60.00

**ASHBAUGH, Don.** *Nevada's Turbulent Yesterday...a Study in Ghost Towns.* 1980. Westernlore. 5th. ils/index. 346p. F/F. B19. $20.00

**ASHBERY, John.** *Flow Chart.* 1991. Knopf. 1st. inscr/dtd 1996. F/dj. R14. $45.00

**ASHBERY, John.** *Three Madrigals.* 1968. NY. Poet's Pr. 1st. 1/162. sgn/#d. F/purple prt wrp. M24. $100.00

**ASHBROOK, Frank.** *Fur Farming for Profit.* 1951. Orange Judd. revised. 429p. dj. A17. $22.00

**ASHBURN, P.M.** *History of the Medical Department of the US Army.* 1929. Boston. 1st. 448p. A13. $100.00

**ASHE, Arthur.** *Off the Court.* 1981. NAL. 1st. 8vo. 230p. F/NF. B20. $75.00

**ASHE, Gordon;** see Creasey, John.

**ASHFORD, Daisy.** *Young Visitors; or, Mr Salteena's Plan.* 1919. Doran. 1st. ils. G. B27. $45.00

**ASHFORD, Jeffery.** *Conflict of Interests.* 1989. St Martin. 1st Am. VG-/dj. G8. $12.50

**ASHFORD, Jeffrey.** *Recipe for Murder.* 1980. Walker. F/dj. P3. $13.00

**ASHMORE & BAGGS.** *Mission to Hanoi: A Chronicle of Double-Dealing...* 1968. NY. Putnam. 1st. VG/dj. R11. $20.00

**ASHMUN, Margaret.** *Singing Swan: Account of Anna Seward...* 1968 (1930). NY. Greenwood. rpt. 8vo. 298p. gilt gr cloth. H13. $45.00

**ASHTON, Dore.** *Richard Lindner.* nd (1969). NY. Abrams. obl 4to. 217p. yel ep. gilt pict red cloth. F/NF. F1. $150.00

**ASHWAL, Stephen.** *Founders of Child Neurology.* 1990. SF. Norman. 124 biographical sketches. 935p. G7. $105.00

**ASIMOV, Isaac.** *Change!* 1981. Houghton Mifflin. 1st. 8vo. 201p. F/dj. W2. $30.00

**ASIMOV, Isaac.** *Earth Is Room Enough.* nd. BC. VG/dj. P3. $10.00

**ASIMOV, Isaac.** *Familiar Poems, Annotated.* 1977. Doubleday. 1st. VG/G. B30. $20.00

**ASIMOV, Isaac.** *Foundation's Edge.* 1982. Doubleday. 1st. VG+/clip. A14. $32.00

**ASIMOV, Isaac.** *Gods Themselves.* 1977. Norwalk, CT. Easton. reissue 1972 Doubleday 1st. aeg. leather. NF. A14. $35.00

**ASIMOV, Isaac.** *Gold.* 1995. Harper Prism. 1st. NF/dj. P3. $20.00

**ASIMOV, Isaac.** *Intelligent Man's Guide to Science.* 1960. Basic. 2 vol. 1st. 8vo. ils. bl cloth. VG/cse. B11. $45.00

**ASIMOV, Isaac.** *Nemesis.* 1989. Doubleday. 1st. AN/dj. M21. $20.00

**ASIMOV, Isaac.** *Opus 100.* 1969. Houghton Mifflin. 1st. F/NF clip. M19. $25.00

**ASIMOV, Isaac.** *Robots of Dawn.* 1983. Doubleday. 1st. VG+/clip. A14. $17.50

**ASIMOV, Isaac.** *Satellites in Outer Space.* 1960. Random. 1st. F/NF. B4. $125.00

**ASIMOV, Isaac.** *Sensuous Dirty Old Man.* 1971. NY. Walker. 1st/4th imp. VG/clip. A14. $14.00

**ASIMOV, Isaac.** *Sun Shines Bright.* 1981. Garden City. Doubleday. 1st. VG+/clip. A14. $17.50

**ASIMOV, Isaac.** *Visions of the Universe.* 1981. Montrose, CA. Cosmos Store. intro Carl Sagan. ils Iwasaki. F/VG. B11. $35.00

**ASIMOV, Issac.** *Fantastic Voyage II.* 1987. Doubleday. 1st. NF/VG+. S18. $10.00

**ASIMOV & SILVERBERG.** *Nightfall.* 1990. Doubleday. 1/750. sgns on limitation. NF/sans dj/VG+ case. A14. $70.00

**ASIMOV & SILVERBERG.** *Ugly Little Boy.* 1992. Doubleday. 1st. NF/dj. M23. $10.00

**ASINOF & BOUTON.** *Strike Zone.* 1994. Viking. 1st. sgn Bouton. F/dj. P8. $45.00

**ASKINS, Charles.** *Shotgunner's Book.* 1958. Stackpole. index/photos. 365p. VG/dj. A17. $15.00

**ASMUS, R.A.** *Horseshoes of Interest to Veterinarians.* 1946. Plant City, FL. Ken Kimbel. ils. 24p. VG. O3. $30.00

**ASPIN, Jehoshaphat.** *Naval & Military Exploits...Reign of George the Third...* 1820. London. Prt for Samuel Leigh by W Clowes. 2 vol. 1st. 12mo. VG. H5. $850.00

**ASPREY, Robert B.** *War in the Shadows.* 1975. NY. 2 vol. 1475p. dj. E1. $40.00

**ASQUITH, Cynthia.** *This Mortal Coil.* 1947. Arkham. 1st. VG/dj. B30. $50.00

**ASSOCIATED PRESS.** *Instant It Happened.* 1976. Abrams. folio. VG/dj. S5. $40.00

**ASSOCIATED PRESS.** *Moments in Time: 50 Years of Associated Press News Photos.* 1984. Gallery. VG/dj. S5. $20.00

**ASSOCIATION OF THE BAR.** *Lectures on Legal Topics.* 1929. Macmillan. gilt cloth. G. M11. $45.00

**ASSOULINE, Pierre.** *Gaston Gallimard: Half Century of French Publishing.* 1988 (1984). HBJ. 1st Am. 8vo. F/dj. A2. $15.00

**ASTON, George.** *Mostly About Trout.* 1921. London. 1st. 223p. VG. A17. $30.00

**ASTON, Pearl F.** *Everyone Can Paint Fabrics.* 1952. London/NY. Studio/Crowell. 1st. VG/dj. N2. $10.00

**ASTOR, Gerald.** *Disease Detectives: Deadly Medical Mysteries & People...* 1983. NY. 1st. 216p. A13. $20.00

**ASTOR, Mary.** *My Story.* nd. Doubleday. 1st. VG. T12. $10.00

**ASTRACHAN, Samuel.** *Malaparte in Jassy.* 1989. Wayne State. VG/dj. M17. $15.00

**ATCHISON, Stewart.** *Naturalist's Guide to Hiking the Grand Canyon.* 1985. Prentice Hall. ils. 172p. VG+. F7. $15.00

**ATCHISON, Stewart.** *Wilderness Called Grand Canyon.* 1991. Voyageur. ils/biblio. 128p. NF/NF. B19. $20.00

**ATCHISON & GRUBBS.** *Hiker's Guide to Arizona.* 1995. MT. 8vo. photos/maps. 237p. AN/stiff wrp. F7. $12.95

**ATCHITY, Kenneth John.** *Eterne in Mutabilitie: Unity of the Faerie Queene.* 1972. Archon. 1st. F/clip. N2. $10.00

**ATHAUS, J.** *On Paralysis, Neuralgia & Other Affections...* 1864. 3rd. VG. E6. $60.00

**ATHEARN, Robert G.** *Forts of the Upper Missouri.* 1967. Englewood Cliffs. 339p. F/dj. M4. $45.00

**ATHEARN, Robert G.** *High Country Empire.* 1960. McGraw Hill. F/dj. A19. $35.00

**ATHEARN, Robert G.** *Rebel of the Rockies: Denver & Rio Grande Western Railroad.* 1962. Yale. 1st. 8vo. 395p. F/NF. B20. $65.00

**ATHEARN, Robert G.** *Soldier in the West: Civil War Letters of Alfred L Hough.* 1957. Phil. 1st. ils. 250p. VG. E1. $50.00

**ATHEARN, Robert G.** *William Tecumseh Sherman & Settlement of the West.* 1956. Norman, OK. 1st. beige cloth. VG. A14. $14.00

**ATHELING, William;** see Blish, James.

**ATHERTON, Gertrude.** *Rulers of Kings.* 1904. Harper. 1st. VG. M20. $18.00

**ATHERTON, John.** *Fly & the Fish.* 1951. NY. Macmillan. 1st. 195p. G. H10. $100.00

**ATKESON & GOHS.** *Oregon.* 1968. Chas Belding. 1st. 188p. VG/dj. S14. $15.00

**ATKINS, Chet.** *Country Gentleman.* 1974. Chicago. 1st. VG/dj. B5. $20.00

**ATKINS, Meg Elizabeth.** *Samain.* 1977. London. Cassell. 1st. NF/dj. P3. $25.00

**ATKINSON, Brooks.** *Cleo for Short.* 1940. Howell Saskin. sgn. 31p. VG/dj. A21. $30.00

**ATKINSON, Frank B.** *Dynamic Dominion: Realignment & Rise...* (1992). Geo Mason U. 518p. VG/dj. B10. $22.50

**ATKINSON, James.** *Epitome of the Whole Art of Navigation...* 1782. London. Mount & Page. tables/tangents/secants. 336p. full leather. M10. $125.00

**ATKINSON, Jennifer McCabe.** *Eugene O'Neill, a Descriptive Bibliography.* 1974. Pittsburgh. 410p. gilt blk/bl cloth. F1. $60.00

**ATKINSON, Kate.** *Behind the Scenes at the Museum.* 1996. St Martin. 1st Am. NF/dj. M23. $20.00

**ATKINSON, Richard C.** *Stevens' Handbook of Experimental Psychology.* 1988 (1958). John Wiley. 2 vol. 2nd revised. prt maroon cloth. VG. G1. $125.00

**ATKINSON, Wilmer.** *Autobiography.* 1920. Phil. Atkinson. 375p. cloth. A10. $22.00

**ATLEE, Philip;** see Philips, James Atlee.

**ATTANASIO, A.A.** *Kingdom of the Grail.* 1992. NY. Harper Collins. 1st. F/dj. T10. $35.00

**ATTANASIO, A.A.** *Soltis.* 1994. Harper Collins. 1st. F/dj. A23. $35.00

**ATTANASIO & HENDERSON.** *Silent.* 1996. Tucson. McMillan. 1st. F/dj. M15. $30.00

**ATTENBOROUGH, Charles L.** *Law of Pawnbroking, With Pawnbrokers' Act...* 1897. London. 1st. brn cloth. M11. $125.00

**ATTENBOROUGH, David.** *Bridge to the Past.* 1961. NY. photos. 160p. VG/dj. S15. $12.00

**ATTENBOROUGH, Richard.** *In Search of Gandhi.* 1982. London. Bodley Head/ Piscatawa. 1st. inscr/dtd 1982. ils. F/dj. O11. $65.00

**ATTOE, David.** *Lion at the Door.* 1989. Little Brn. 1st. author's 1st novel. F/F. H11. $30.00

**ATWATER, Caleb.** *History of the State of Ohio, Natural & Civil.* (1838). Cincinnati. 2nd. 407p. full leather. B18. $150.00

**ATWATER, Richard.** *Secret History of Procopius.* 1927. Chicago. Pascal Covici. 1/760. sm 4to. 286p. gilt bl cloth. NF. F1. $50.00

**ATWOOD, Mae.** *In Rupert's Land: Memoirs of Walter Traill.* 1970. Toronto. McClelland Stewart. 1st. F/dj. A26. $25.00

**ATWOOD, Margaret.** *Barbed Lyres: Canadian Venomous Verse.* 1990. Porter. 1st. F/dj. T12. $30.00

**ATWOOD, Margaret.** *Bluebeard's Egg.* 1983. McClelland Stewart. 1st Canadian. NF/NF. B3. $40.00

**ATWOOD, Margaret.** *Cat's Eye.* 1988. Toronto. McClelland. 1st. F/dj. B3/T12. $40.00

**ATWOOD, Margaret.** *Dancing Girls.* 1977. Toronto. McClelland Stewart. 1st. F/F. D10. $50.00

**ATWOOD, Margaret.** *Journals of Susanna Moodie.* 1970. Toronto. OUP. 1st. sgn. F. O11. $125.00

**ATWOOD, Margaret.** *Lady Oracle.* 1976. McClelland Stewart. 1st Canadian. F/NF. B3. $125.00

**ATWOOD, Margaret.** *Life Before Man.* 1979. McClelland Stewart. 1st Canadian. NF/VG. B3. $40.00

**ATWOOD, Margaret.** *Murder in the Dark.* 1983. Toronto. Coach House. 1st. F. O11. $35.00

**ATWOOD, Margaret.** *Power Politics.* 1973. Harper Row. 1st Am. F/clip. L3. $75.00

**ATWOOD, Margaret.** *Robber Bride.* 1993. London. Bloomsbury. 1st Eng. sgn. F/dj. Q1. $60.00

**ATWOOD, Margaret.** *Robber Bride.* 1993. NY. Nan Talese. 1st Am trade. F/dj. A23. $25.00

**ATWOOD, Margaret.** *Surfacing.* 1972. Toronto. McClelland Stewart. inscr/dtd 1973. F/dj. B4. $300.00

**AUBERT, Roger.** *Concilium: Vol 27, Progress & Decline in History...* 1967. NY. Paulist. 1st Am. 8vo. VG/G. A2. $16.00

**AUBREY, Edmund.** *Sherlock Holmes in Dallas.* 1980. Dodd Mead. 1st. F/clip. N4. $30.00

**AUBRY, M.-P.** *Handbook of Cenozolic Calcareous Nannoplankton. Book 1.* 1984. NY. AMNH. Micropaleontology Handbook series. 266p. F. B1. $55.00

**AUCH, Mary Jane.** *Bird Dogs Can't Fly.* 1993. NY. 1st. 32p. F/dj. A17. $7.50

**AUCHINCLOSS, Louis.** *Diary of a Yuppie.* 1986. Franklin Lib. ltd. sgn. ils (not in trade). full leather. F. O1. $60.00

**AUCHINCLOSS, Louis.** *Watchfires.* 1982. Boston. Houghton Mifflin. 1st. gilt maroon cloth. F/NF. T11. $25.00

**AUDEMARS, Pierre.** *Now Dead Is Any Man.* 1980. Walker. F/dj. P3. $15.00

**AUDEN, W.H.** *About the House.* 1965. Random. 1st. VG/G. B30. $30.00

**AUDEN, W.H.** *Dance of Death.* 1933. London. Faber. 1st. 1/1200. G/dj. L3. $175.00

**AUDEN, W.H.** *For the Time Being.* 1944. Random. 1st. NF/G. L3. $125.00

**AUDEN, W.H.** *Homage to Clio.* 1960. Random. 1st. 1/5000. gilt half cloth. F/dj. M24. $50.00

**AUDEN, W.H.** *Nones.* 1951. Random. 1st. 1/4000. gilt half cloth. F/dj. M24. $50.00

**AUDEN, W.H.** *Nones.* 1952. London. 1st. dj. T9. $75.00

**AUDEN, W.H.** *Old Man's Road.* 1956. NY. Voyages. 1st. 1/50 (750 total). sgn. F/gray wrp. B24. $400.00

**AUDEN, W.H.** *Orators. An English Study.* (1922). London. Faber. 1st. author's 3rd book. cloth. F/dj. B24. $750.00

**AUDEN, W.H.** *Shield of Achilles.* 1955. Random. 1st. 1/4000. RS. half cloth. F/NF. M24. $75.00

**AUDEN, W.H.** *Some Poems.* 1940. London. Faber. 1st. NF/dj. B20. $100.00

**AUDEN, W.H.** *Spain.* 1937. London. 1st. stapled wrp. T9. $50.00

**AUDOT, L.** *La Cuisinere de la Campagne et de la Ville...* 1882 Paris. ils. 701p. G+. E6. $50.00

**AUDUBON, John James.** *Audubon Game Animals.* 1968. Hammond, IN/Maplewood, NJ. sgn. G. A19. $25.00

**AUDUBON, John James.** *Birds of America.* 1937. Macmillan. 1/2500. sm folio. gilt gr cloth/marbled brd. F/case. F1. $95.00

**AUEL, Jean M.** *Clan of the Cave Bear.* 1980. NY. Crown. 1st. F/dj. M19/S13/T11. $65.00

**AUEL, Jean M.** *Mammoth Hunters.* 1985. Crown. 1st. F/dj. H11. $25.00

**AUEL, Jean M.** *Mammoth Hunters.* 1985. Crown. 1st. NF/dj. L4. $20.00

**AUEL, Jean M.** *Mammoth Hunters.* 1985. Crown. 1st. sgn. NF/dj. S18. $45.00

**AUEL, Jean M.** *Plains of Passage.* 1990. NY. Crown. 1st. sgn. F/dj. Q1. $50.00

**AUEL, Jean M.** *Valley of Horses.* 1982. Crown. 1st. F/NF. M19. $15.00

**AUEL, Jean M.** *Valley of Horses.* 1982. Crown. 1st. sgn. F/dj. B35. $40.00

**AUGUSTINE.** *Confessions of St Augustine.* 1946. Everyman's Lib. trans EB Pusy. 352p. G/worn. B29. $7.00

**AUGUSTUS, Albert Jr.;** see Nuetzel, Charles.

**AULT, Phil.** *Whistles Round the Bend: Travel on America's Waterways.* 1982. Dodd Mead. F/dj. A19. $35.00

**AUNT FANNY.** *Fanny's Birth-Day, by Aunt Fanny.* 1866. Buffalo. Breed & Butler. mini. 64p. aeg. gilt bstp cloth. B24. $95.00

**AUNT FANNY.** *Fanny's Fair, by Aunt Fanny.* nd. Breed & Butler. mini. 63p. aeg. gilt bstp pub cloth. B24. $125.00

**AUNT FANNY.** *Fanny's Pic-Nic, by Aunt Fanny.* 1866. Buffalo. Breed & Butler. mini. 61p. gilt purple pub cloth. B24. $125.00

**AUSLANDER, Joseph.** *Five American Immortals.* 1940. Worcester. St Onge. mini. 1/475. w/5 tipped-in US commemorative stps. aeg. cloth. B24. $475.00

**AUSTEN, Jane.** *Pride & Prejudice.* 1894. London. Geo Allen. 1st thus. 1/275. 4to. 476p. Sangorski bdg. H5. $650.00

**AUSTER, Paul.** *African Trio by Georges Simenon.* 1979. NY. HBJ. 1st. F/F. B3. $75.00

**AUSTER, Paul.** *Leviathan.* 1992. Viking. 1st. sgn. F/dj. R14. $45.00

**AUSTIN, A.B.** *Angler's Anthology.* 1931. London. ils Norman Wilkinson. NF. M4. $50.00

**AUSTIN, Gabriel.** *Four Oaks Library.* 1957. Somerville, NJ. 1st. 1/1250. H13. $85.00

**AUSTIN, Mary.** *Land of Little Rain.* 1950. Houghton Mifflin. 1st thus. 132p. NF/dj. B20. $125.00

**AUSTIN, Mary.** *One-Smoke Stories.* 1934. Houghton Mifflin. 1st. 8vo. red-lettered gray cloth. F. R3. $65.00

**AUSTIN, Mary.** *Promised Land.* 1912. Houghton Mifflin. 1st. 373p. gilt bl cloth. VG. F1. $40.00

**AUSTIN, Mary.** *Room & Time Enough: Land of Mary Austin.* 1979. Northland. 1st. ils. 75p. F. B19. $35.00

**AUSTIN, O.L.** *Birds of Newfoundland Labrador.* 1932. Cambridge. 4to. fld map. 229p. cloth. NF. C12. $95.00

**AUSTIN & UEDA.** *Bamboo.* 1985. NY. Weatherhill. ils/biblio/index. 215p. VG/dj. H10. $35.00

**AUTOMOBILE QUARTERLY MAGAZINE.** *General Motors: The 1st 75 Years of Transportation Products.* 1983. Princeton Inst for Hist Research. 224p. H6. $45.00

**AUVIL, M.** *Covered Bridges of West Virginia: Past & Present.* 1977. Parsons. 3rd. sgn. F. M4. $25.00

**AVARY, Myrta.** *Dixie After the War.* 1906. ils. silvered/gilt cloth. VG. E6. $50.00

**AVEDON, Richard.** *Observations With Comments by Truman Capote.* 1959. S&S. 1st. folio. F/VG case. S9. $650.00

**AVEDON & CAPOTE.** *Observations.* 1959. NY. 1st. VG/G box. B5. $195.00

**AVENI, Anthony.** *Conversing With the Planets: How Science & Myth...* 1992. Time Books. 2nd. 255p. VG/VG. K5. $20.00

**AVERILL, Esther.** *Voyages of Jacques Cartier.* 1937. NY. Domino. 1st. F/G. M5. $75.00

**AVERY, Catherine B.** *New Century Handbook of Greek Art & Architecture.* 1972. Appleton Century. ils. 222p. cloth. VG/dj. D1. $15.00

**AVERY, G.** *Behold the Child: American Children & Their Books 1621-1922.* London. 1st. ils. 226p. F/dj. M4. $25.00

**AVERY, Gillian.** *Lost Railway.* 1980. London. Collins. 1st (stated). 8vo. 220p. VG/G. T5. $30.00

**AVERY, Thomas Eugene.** *Natural Resources Measurement.* 1975. McGraw Hill. 2nd. ils. 339p. G. H10. $17.50

**AVERY & BULL.** *Nineteenth Century Children, Heroes & Heroines...1780-1900.* 1965. London. Hodder Stoughton. 1st. ils. 260p. maroon cloth. VG/G. T5. $55.00

**AVIANUS.** *Fables.* 1993. Johns Hopkins. trans DR Slavitt. ils Neil Welliver. VG/dj. M17. $15.00

**AXELROD, Emmens.** *Exotic Tropical Fish.* 1981. TFH. ils/index. 650p. dj. A17. $16.50

**AXELROD & SCHULTZ.** *Handbook of Tropical Aquarium Fishes.* 1955. McGraw Hill. ne. 718p. VG. W2. $950.00

**AXFORD, Joseph Mack.** *Around the Campfires.* 1964. NY. 1st. inscr. 262p. G/dj. B18. $35.00

**AXTON, David;** see Koontz, Dean R.

**AYALA, Mitzi.** *Farmer's Cookbook: A Collection of Favorite Recipes...* 1981. Harbor. VG/dj. A16. $16.00

**AYE, Lillian.** *Iran Caboose.* 1952. Hollywood. House-Waarven. 8vo. 190p. cloth. VG/torn. W1. $18.00

**AYER, Jacqueline.** *Nadang & His Kite.* 1959. Harcourt Brace. 1st. ils Jacqueline Ayer. VG/dj. P2. $25.00

**AYMAR, Gordon C.** *Bird Flight.* 1938. NY. deluxe ed. 234p. VG/dj. A19. $17.50

**AYMARD, Andre.** *Le Premiers Rapports de Rome et de Confederation Achaienne.* 1938. Paris. 8vo. 438p. cloth. VG. Q2. $46.50

**AYRES, Atlee B.** *Mexican Architecture, Domestic, Civil & Ecclesiastical.* 1926. NY. Wm Helburn. folio. photos/ils/ftspc. gilt gr cloth. dj. K1. $200.00

**AYRES, E.C.** *Hour of the Manatee.* 1994. St Martin. 1st. NF/dj. G8. $25.00

**AZAROFF & BUERGER.** *Powder Method in X-Ray Crystallography.* 1958. McGraw Hill. 1st. ils. cloth. VG. B27. $30.00

**AZOY, A.C.M.** *Paul Revere's Horse.* 1949. Doubleday. 1st. VG. N2. $10.00

BAADE, Walter. *Evolution of Stars & Galaxies.* 1963. Cambridge. Harvard. 8vo. 321p. VG/dj. K5. $20.00

BAAR & HOWARD. *Polaris! Concept & Creation...Weapon.* 1960. Harcourt Brace. 8vo. 245p. VG/dj. K5. $25.00

BAARS & BUCHANAN. *Canyon Revisited. Rephotography of Grand Canyon 1923-1991.* 1994. Salt Lake City. photos. 168p. F. F7. $20.00

BAARS & MOLENAAR. *Geology of Canyonlands & Cataract Canyon.* 1971. np. 8vo. 99p. tan wrp. F7. $22.50

BAAS, J.H. *Outlines of the History of Medicine & Medical Profession.* 1889. NY. Vail. 1st Eng-language. 1173p. cloth. G7. $295.00

BAAS, Johann. *Outlines of History of Medicine & Medical Profession.* 1971. Huntington, NY. facs of 1889. 2 vol. 1st Eng trans. A13. $175.00

BAASKIN, John. *In Praise of Practical Fertilizer: Thoughts...* 1982. NY/London. Norton. 1st. F/NF. H4. $15.00

BABBITT, Bruce. *Grand Canyon: An Anthology...* nd. Northland. 1st. 8vo. 258p. VG/dj. F7. $65.00

BABBITT, Natalie. *Knee-Knock Rise.* 1978 (1970). FSG. 6th. sgn. Newbery Award. NF/NF. T5. $25.00

BABBITT, Natalie. *Tuck Everlasting.* 1975. FSG. 1st. 8vo. 139p. red cloth. VG+. T5. $35.00

BABCOCK, Havilah. *Education of Pretty Boy.* 1960. Holt. 1st. inscr. ils Arthur Fuller. NF/VG+. C15. $150.00

BABCOCK, Mary Kent Davey. *Christ Church, Salem Street, Boston: Old North Church...* (1940). self pub. ils. 271p. VG/G. M10. $15.00

BABCOCK, Philip H. *Falling Leaves.* 1937. Derrydale. 1/950. ils Aiden Ripley. NF. H4. $75.00

BABER, Lucy Harrison Miller. *Behind the Old Brick Wall: A Cemetery Story.* 1968. Lynchburg. Colonial Dames, Lynchburg Comm. 307p. VG/dj. B10. $45.00

BABSON, Marian. *Reel Murder.* 1986. St Martin. 1st Am. 180p. F/dj. D4. $30.00

BABSON, Marian. *Untimely Guest.* 1976. London. Collins Crime Club. 1st. F/dj. M15. $45.00

BABUN, Edward. *Varieties of Man.* 1969. Crowell-Collier. 2nd. 88p. F. D4. $20.00

BACALL, Lauren. *By Myself.* 1979. Knopf. 1st. 377p. VG/dj. P12. $15.00

BACALL, Lauren. *Now.* (1994). Knopf. 1st. sgn. F/dj. H4. $30.00

BACH, Richard. *Jonathan Livingston Seagull.* 1970. Macmillan. 1st. 93p. F/NF clip. B20. $150.00

BACH, Richard. *One.* 1988. Morrow. 1st. AN/dj. H4. $20.00

BACHELDER, Louise. *Dogs, Cats+Other Friends.* 1972. NY. Peter Pauper. ils Marian Morton. 62p. F/dj. D4. $20.00

BACHELLER, Irving. *Candle in the Wilderness: Tale of Beginning of New England.* (1930). Bobbs Merrill. 1st. 8vo. gilt gr cloth. F/NC Wyeth dj. R3. $65.00

BACHELLER, Irving. *Darrell of the Blessed Islands.* 1903. Boston. Lothrop. 1st. 8vo. 410p. dk red cloth. VG. C6. $40.00

BACHELLER, Irving. *Eben Holden's Last Day A-Fishing.* 1907. Harper. 1st. 12mo. gr cloth. F/dj. J3. $75.00

BACHELLER, Irving. *Keeping Up With Lizzie.* 1911. Harper. 1st. 12 pl. VG/dj. B11. $18.00

BACHELLER, Irving. *Keeping Up With Lizzie.* 1911. Harper. 1st. 8vo. 158p. F/NF. B20. $50.00

BACHELLER, Irving. *Keeping Up With Lizzie.* 1911. NY. Harper. 158p. G. $8.00

BACHELLER, Irving. *Keeping Up With William.* 1918. Bobbs Merrill. ils Gaar Williams. 115p. G. G11. $8.00

BACHELLER, Irving. *Light in the Clearing.* 1917. Bobbs Merrill. ils Arthur I Keller. 415p. G. G11. $10.00

BACHELLER, Irving. *Man for the Ages.* 1919. Bobbs Merrill. ils John Wolcott Adams. 416p. G. G11. $8.00

BACHELLER, Irving. *Story of a Passion.* 1917. E Aurora. Roycrofters. slim 16mo. 21p. VG/wrp. B11. $35.00

BACHELLER, Irving. *Vergilius.* 1904. NY. Harper. 279p. G. G11. $12.00

BACHELOR, John Calvin. *American Falls.* 1985. NY. Norton. 1st. quarter gr cloth/paper-covered brd. NF/dj. T11. $30.00

BACHMAN, Richard; see King, Steven.

BACKES, Clarus. *Growing Up Western.* 1990. Knopf. 1st. rem mk. NF/F. T11. $25.00

BACKHOUSE, James. *Life & Correspondence of Wm & Alice Ellis of Airton.* 1849. London. Chas Gilpin. 12mo. 298p. worn cloth. xl. V3. $24.00

BACKHOUSE, Janet. *John Scottowe's Alphabet Books.* 1974. Roxburghe Club/Scolar. folio. 28 fasc pl. gilt red morocco/cloth. F. K1. $275.00

BACON, Edwin M. *Literary Pilgrimages in New England: To Homes of Famous...* (1902). Silver Burdett. ARC. 8vo. 532p. VG. H4. $25.00

BACON, Edwin M. *Rambles Around Old Boston.* 1914. Little Brn. 1st. ils Lester G Hornby. 205p. VG. B18. $17.50

BACON, Francis. *Essay of Francis Bacon Lord Verulam.* 1913. Brentano. sm 4to. 235p. F/dj. G7. $95.00

BACON, Francis. *Essays or Counsels Civil & Moral & Wisdom of Ancients...* 1836. London. Pickering. sm 8vo. 350p. aeg. gilt burgandy morocco. G7. $145.00

BACON, Francis. *Essays.* 1906. London. Cambridge. 1/150. 8vo. parchment vellum/brd. worn. F1. $50.00

BACON, Francis. *Two Books of Francis Lord Verulam...* 1825. London. Pickering. fld tables. 402p. gilt paneled calf/raised bands. G7. $150.00

BACON, Lee. *Our Houseboat on the Nile.* 1902. Houghton Mifflin. ils Henry Bacon. 286p. xl. G. P12. $15.00

BACON, Margaret Hope. *One Woman's Passion for Peace & Freedom...Mildred S Olmsted.* 1993. Syracuse. 1st. 394p. AN/dj. V3. $22.00

BACON, Margaret Hope. *Quiet Rebels: Story of the Quakers in America.* 1985. Phil. New Soc Pub. 12mo. 239p. VG/wrp. V3. $10.00

BACON, Mrs. E.A. *Memoir of Rev Henry Bacon.* 1857. Boston. Tompkins. 8vo. brn cloth. VG. S17. $10.00

BACON, Roger. *Four Stumbling Blocks to Truth, by Anglican Mage R Bacon.* 1985. Dallas. Somesuch. mini. 1/250 (not for sale). fwd Stanley Marcus. pict brd. B24. $75.00

BACON. G.W. *Keeping Young & Well.* 1914. London. Fowler. 1st. 130p. VG+. A25. $20.00

BADE, William Frederic. *Life & Letters of John Muir.* 1923. Houghton Mifflin. 2 vol. 1st. gr cloth. F. B20. $325.00

BADER, Barbara. *American Picture Books From Noah's Ark to Beast Within.* 1976. Collier/Macmillan. 1st. 4to. 700 ils. 615p. F/NF. H4. $115.00

BADGER, Curtis J. *Eastern Shore: Pictorial History.* (1983). Donning. photos. VG/dj. B10. $40.00

BADSHA, Omar. *South Africa: Cordoned Heart: Essays...* 1986. Capetown. 1st. ils. 186p. NF/dj. W1. $20.00

BAEDEKER, Karl. *Baedeker's Greece.* 1894. 2nd. 12mo. 8 maps (1 fld)+18 plans. 376p. fair. H4. $86.00

**BAEDEKER, Karl.** *Baedeker's Lower Egypt.* 1895. 3rd. 12mo. 47 maps/plans+5 fld maps bdg-in. H4. $100.00

**BAEDEKER, Karl.** *London & Its Environs: Handbook for Travellers.* 1923. ne. 16mo. 72p+maps. VG. H4. $30.00

**BAEDEKER, Karl.** *Lower Egypt.* 1895. Leipsig. sm 8vo. ils/maps/plans. 293p. cloth. G+. Q2. $207.00

**BAEDEKER, Karl.** *Manuel de Conversation Pour le Voyaguer...* nd (1881). Leipzig. 8vo. 331p. cloth. G. Q2. $42.00

**BAEDEKER, Karl.** *Rhine From Rotterdam to Constance.* 1906. 6th revised. 52 maps (untorn fld map+29 plans). NF. H4. $25.00

**BAEDEKER, Karl.** *Switzerland & the Adjacent Portions of Italy, Savoy...* 1907. Baedeker. 22nd. 12mo. VG. B20. $40.00

**BAEDEKER, Karl.** *Switzerland & the Adjacent Portions of Italy...* 1905. London. Baedeker. 548p. G. M10. $15.00

**BAER, Dallas C.** *Messages of the Prophets to Their Day & Ours.* 1940. Pulpit. 152p. VG. B29. $11.50

**BAER, Helen G.** *Heart Is Like Heaven.* 1964. NY. 1st. NF/dj. M20. $30.00

**BAER & BANKMANN.** *Ancient Mexican Sculptures From Lukas Vischer Collection.* 1990. Basel. Wepf. 1st. German/Eng text. 179p. wrp. F3. $90.00

**BAERG, Harry J.** *How To Know the Western Trees.* 1955. Dubuque. 286p. tan cloth. F. B26. $14.00

**BAERWALD & MAHONEY.** *Story of Jewelry: Popular Account of Lure, Lore...* 1960. Abelard Schuman. 1st. 222p. F/NF. B20. $35.00

**BAEZ, Joan.** *And a Voice to Sing With: A Memoir.* 1987. NY. Summit. 1st. F/dj. T12. $40.00

**BAGBY, George.** *Evil Genius.* 1961. Crime Club. 1st. VG/dj. G8. $15.00

**BAGBY, George.** *Mysteriouser & Mysteriouser.* 1965. Crime Club. 1st. F/VG. M19. $17.50

**BAGNELL, Kenneth.** *Canadese: Portrait of Italian Canadians.* 1989. Macmillan. 1st. sgn. F/dj. T12. $12.00

**BAGSTER, Samuel.** *Management of Bees.* 1834. London. Bagster Pickering. 40 woodcuts. 244p. cloth. A10. $350.00

**BAHARI, Ebadollah.** *Bihzad: Master of Persian Painting.* 1996. London/NY. Tauris. folio. 272p. cloth. NF/dj. W1. $90.00

**BAILEY, Adrian.** *Taste of France.* (1983). Stewart Taabori Chang. photos Robert Freson. 288p. F/dj. H4. $35.00

**BAILEY, Alice Cooper.** *Kating Gander.* (1927). Joliet. Volland. 4th. ils MH Myers. 93p. pict brd. VG/box. T5. $65.00

**BAILEY, Alice Cooper.** *Katrina & Jan.* 1923. Volland. probable 1st. tall 8vo. pict brd. G+/AN box. T5. $65.00

**BAILEY, Anthony.** *Major Andre.* 1987. FSG. 1st. F/dj. T11. $45.00

**BAILEY, Carolyn Sherwin.** *Children of the Handicrafts.* 1935. Viking. 2nd. VG/G. R8. $30.00

**BAILEY, Carolyn Sherwin.** *From Moccasins to Wings: Stories of Our Travel Ways.* 1938. Milton Bradley. 1st. 8vo. ils Margaret Ayer. gray cloth. VG. T5. $12.00

**BAILEY, Carolyn Sherwin.** *Little Red Schoolhouse.* 1957. Viking. 1st. ils Dorothy Bayley Morse. red cloth. VG/dj. T5. $15.00

**BAILEY, Carolyn Sherwin.** *Pioneer Art in America.* 1944. Viking. 1st. ils Grace Paull. 221p. NF/VG+. D4. $45.00

**BAILEY, David.** *Naked Eye: Great Photographs of the Nude.* (1987). NY. Amphoto. 1st. photos. 191p. F/dj. H4. $60.00

**BAILEY, Emma.** *Sold to the Lady in the Green Hat.* 1962. Rutland. 228p. VG/dj. H7. $15.00

**BAILEY, F.M.** *Among the Birds in the Grand Canyon Country.* 1939. GPO. 8vo. 211p. gray-gr wrp. F7. $30.00

**BAILEY, F.M.** *Birds Recorded From the Santa Rita Mountains in South AZ.* 1923. Berkeley. lg 8vo. ils. 60p. F/wrp. C12. $15.00

**BAILEY, F.M.** *Comprehensive Catalogue of Queensland Plants.* 1909 (1890). Brisbane. 2nd. ils/pl. B1. $120.00

**BAILEY, Geoffrey.** *Conspirators.* 1960. NY. 1st. 306p. G/dj. E1. $25.00

**BAILEY, George W.** *Private Chapter of the War (1861-65).* 1880. St Louis. GI Jones. 271p. G+. B10. $100.00

**BAILEY, H.C.** *Mr Clunk's Text.* 1939. Doubleday Crime Club. 1st Am. F/NF. M15. $85.00

**BAILEY, J.O.** *Pilgrims Through Space & Time.* 1947. NY. Argus. VG/G. B9. $30.00

**BAILEY, James H.** *Pictures of the Past: Petersburg Seen by Simpsons 1819-95.* (1989). Ft Henry Branch, APVA. ils. 55p. VG. B10. $15.00

**BAILEY, Kenneth P.** *Ohio Company of Virginia.* 1939. Glendale. Arthur Clark. 1st. 5 maps. 374p. teg. G+. B18. $125.00

**BAILEY, L.H.** *Cyclopedia of American Horticulture.* 1904. Macmillan. 4 vol. VG. A10. $150.00

**BAILEY, L.H.** *Garden of Gourds.* 1937. NY. 1st. ils. 134p. dj. B26. $36.00

**BAILEY, L.H.** *Principles of Agriculture.* 1910. Macmillan. 16th. 336p. VG. A10. $28.00

**BAILEY, L.H.** *Standard Cyclopedia of Horticulture.* 1939. NY. 3 vol. index/photos. A17. $150.00

**BAILEY, Lee.** *Lee Bailey's Country Flowers.* (1985). NY. Potter. stated 1st. ils. 158p. F/dj. H4. $27.50

**BAILEY, Lee.** *Lee Bailey's Soup Meals: Main Event Soups...* (1989). 1st. photos. VG/dj. A16. $17.50

**BAILEY, Margaret.** *Boswell's Column, 1777-1783.* 1951. London. Wm Kimber. 1st. dj. H13. $85.00

**BAILEY, P.** *Oxford Book of London.* 1995. OUP. 1st. dj. T9. $18.00

**BAILEY, Paul.** *Jacob Hamblin, Bucskin Apostle.* 1961. Westernlore. sgn. 8vo. 408p. maroon cloth. VG/dj. F7. $55.00

**BAILEY, Paul.** *Walkara, Hawk of the Mountains.* 1954. Los Angeles. Westerlore. G/dj. A19. $45.00

**BAILEY, Pearl.** *Hurry Up, America, and Spit.* 1976. HBJ. 2nd. sgn. VG/NF. M20. $15.00

**BAILEY, Truman.** *Polynesian Venture.* 1939. Doubleday Doran. 1st. VG. N2. $12.00

**BAILEY, Vernon.** *Animal Life of the Carlsbad Cavern.* 1928. Baltimore. Williams & Wilkins. 1st. ils. 195p. F. B14. $45.00

**BAILEY, W.L.** *Our Own Birds: Familiar Natural History of Birds in US.* (1869). Phil. Lippincott. revised. ils. 265p. VG. M12. $37.50

**BAILEY & BISHOP.** *Notable Names in Medicine & Surgery.* 1959. Springfield. 3rd. 216p. A13. $100.00

**BAILEY & KNEBEL.** *Seven Days in May.* 1962. Harper Row. 1st. NF/G. M19. $17.50

**BAILEY & NIEDRACH.** *Pictorial Checklist of Colorado Birds.* 1967. Denver Mus Natural Hist. 1st. ils. 168p. F/VG. B20. $75.00

**BAILEY-KEMPLING, William.** *Poets Royal of England & Scotland.* 1908. Chatto Windus. 1/500 lg paper. sm 4to. 107p. 6 portrait pl. morocco. F. H5. $500.00

**BAILLIE, D.M.** *God Was in Christ: An Essay on Incarnation & Atonement.* 1948. Scribner. 230p. G. B29. $7.00

**BAILLIE, D.M.** *Out of Nazareth.* 1958. Scribner. 211p. VG/dj. B29. $8.50

**BAILLIE, G.H.** *Clocks & Watches. An Historical Bibliography. Vol I.* 1978. London. Holland. 414p. gilt beige linen. K1. $60.00

**BAIN, Alexander.** *John Stuart Mill, a Criticism: With Personal Recollections.* 1882. London. Longman Gr. 12mo. 201p. decor gr cloth. VG. G1. $125.00

**BAIN, Alexander.** *Practical Essays.* 1884. Longman Gr. 12mo. 338p. VG. G1. $75.00

**BAIN, David Howard.** *Aftershocks: Tale of Two Victims.* 1980. Methuen. 1st. 241p. VG/dj. R11. $16.00

**BAIN, Iain.** *Watercolours & Drawings of Thomas Bewick...* 1981. Cambridge, MA. MIT. 1 vol. 1st. ils. VG/case. M10. $95.00

**BAIN, J. Arthur.** *Life of Fridtjof Nansen: Scientist & Explorer...* 1897. London/ Sheffield. Simpkin/Bain. 3rd. 8vo. ils/ charts. B20. $100.00

**BAINBRIDGE, Beryl.** *Dressmaker.* 1973. Duckworth. true 1st. NF/dj. A24. $65.00

**BAINBRIDGE, John.** *Garbo.* 1955. Doubleday. 1st. photos. 256p. VG/G. A25. $15.00

**BAINTON, George.** *Art of Authorship. Literary Reminiscences...* 1890. London. James Clark. 1st. gilt bl decor cloth. NF. M24. $275.00

**BAINTON, Ronald H.** *Behold the Christ.* 1974. Harper. 224p. VG/worn. B29. $10.00

**BAIR, Deirdre.** *Biography of Anais Nin.* 1995. NY. 1st. dj. T9. $18.00

**BAIRD, Henry M.** *History of the Rise of the Huguenots of France.* 1900. Scribner. 2 vol. xl. VG. M10. $50.00

**BAIRD, Jane.** *Bombe Surprise a la Virgil Thompson.* 1992. Sausalito, CA. Feathered Serpent. mini. 1/75. sgn author/prt. B24. $65.00

**BAIRD, Robert.** *Transplanting Flowers; or, Memoirs of Mrs Rumpff...* 1839. NY. John S Taylor. 1st. inscr/dtd 1839. 159p. gr cloth. C6. $150.00

**BAIRD, Thomas.** *Smart Rats.* 1990. Harper Row. 1st. F/dj. D4. $25.00

**BAIRD & RIDGWAY.** *History of North American Birds...Land Birds.* (1874). Boston. 3 vol. 3rd. 64 chromolitho pl/593 woodcuts. NF. C12. $295.00

**BAIRNSFATHER, Bruce.** *From Mud to Mufti: With Old Bill on All Fronts.* 1919. NY/London. Putnam. ils/cartoons. VG. M17. $45.00

**BAKARICH, Sara Grace.** *Gunsmoke: True Story of Old Tombstone.* 1962. Gateway. 196p. wrp. B19. $15.00

**BAKELESS, John.** *Daniel Boone, Master of the Wilderness.* 1939. NY. 2nd. 480p. VG. B18. $19.50

**BAKELESS, John.** *Eyes of Discovery: Pageant of North America...* 1950. Lippincott. 1st. ils. 439p. VG. M10. $15.00

**BAKER, Arthur.** *Roman Alphabet.* 1976. Art Direction Book. 1st. 4to. cloth. dj. O10. $45.00

**BAKER, Betty.** *All-By-Herself.* 1980. Greenwillow. 1st. 8vo. 55p. NF. T5. $20.00

**BAKER, Betty.** *Save Sirrushany!* 1978. Macmillan. 1st. 134p. cloth. F/dj. D4. $35.00

**BAKER, Betty.** *Walk the World's Rim.* 1965. NY. Harper. 1st. 168p. pict brd. VG/dj. D4. $30.00

**BAKER, Brown.** *Story of Abraham Lincoln.* 1952. Grosset Dunlap. Signature Book series. 176p. VG. B36. $10.00

**BAKER, Carlos.** *Ernest Hemingway: A Life Story.* 1969. Scribner. 1st. sgn. G+/fair. B30. $45.00

**BAKER, Carroll.** *Baby Doll.* 1983. Arbor. 1st. sgn. ils. VG/dj. C9. $60.00

**BAKER, D.B.** *Explorers & Discoveries of the World.* 1993. Detroit. 4to. photos/maps. F. M4. $45.00

**BAKER, David.** *History of Manned Space Flight.* 1982. NY. Crown. 1st. lg 4to. ils. 544p. VG/dj. K5. $75.00

**BAKER, Don.** *Beyond Forgiveness: Healing Touch of Church Discipline.* 1984. Multnomah. 102p. VG/dj. B29. $7.00

**BAKER, Ernest A.** *History of the English Novel.* 1969. Barnes Noble. 11 vol. reissue+1 vol on modern literature. F/dj. B20. $250.00

**BAKER, George.** *Sad Sack.* 1944. S&S. 4th. 115 cartoons. VG/dj. C9. $42.00

**BAKER, J.H.** *Mary Todd Lincoln.* 1987. NY. 1st. ils. F/dj. M4. $25.00

**BAKER, Kevin.** *Sometimes You See It Coming.* 1993. Crown. 1st. F/dj. P8. $40.00

**BAKER, Laura Nelson.** *Children of the Wind & Pines.* 1967. Lippincott. 1st. ils Inez Storer. VG/dj. M20. $15.00

**BAKER, Lewis.** *Health & Beauty: Prescriptions & Advice.* nd (1920s). Dayton. self pub. 130p. VG. A25. $12.00

**BAKER, Margaret J.** *Hannibal & the Bears.* 1966. FSG. 1st Am. ils Walter Hodges. cloth. F/dj. B27. $55.00

**BAKER, Margaret J.** *Hannibal & the Bears.* 1966. FSG. 1st Am. 8vo. 115p. VG/dj. T5. $20.00

**BAKER, Michael.** *Our Three Selves: Life of Radclyffe Hall.* 1986. NY. Morrow. 1st Am. 386p. VG/dj. A25. $15.00

**BAKER, Nicholson.** *Room Temperature.* 1990. Grove Weidenfeld. 1st. author's 2nd book. F/dj. B2/B30/H11. $40.00

**BAKER, R. Robin.** *Human Navigation & the Sixth Sense.* 1981. S&S. 1st Am. VG/dj. N2. $7.50

**BAKER, R.H.** *Avifauna of Micronesia: Its Origin, Evolution...* 1951. Lawrence. 8vo. 16 maps. 359p. xl. NF. C12. $45.00

**BAKER, Ray Stannard.** *What Wilson Did at Paris.* 1919. Doubleday. 113p. G. B10. $8.00

**BAKER, Ray Stannard.** *Woodrow Wilson: Life & Letters.* 1927. Doubleday Page. 2 vol. 1st. VG. B10. $35.00

**BAKER, Russell.** *Good Times.* 1989. Morrow. 1st. sgn. F/dj. W2. $35.00

**BAKER, Samuel W.** *Wild Beasts & Their Ways: Reminiscences of Europe, Asia...* 1988. Prescott, AZ. 455p. leatherette. F. A17. $17.50

**BAKER, Susan.** *My First Murder.* 1989. NY. 1st. author's 1st novel. F/F. H11. $25.00

**BAKER, Susanne Devonshire.** *Artists of Alberta.* 1980. Edmonton. 1st Canadian. F/dj. T12. $40.00

**BAKER, Willard F.** *Bob Dexter & the Beacon Beach Mystery (#2).* 1925. Cupples Leon. lists 3 titles. VG/dj. M20. $25.00

**BAKER, William J.** *Jessie Owens: An American Life.* 1986. NY/London. photos. VG/dj. M17. $15.00

**BAKER, William King.** *John T Dorland.* 1898. London. Headley. G+. V3. $35.00

**BAKER & MURPHY.** *Handbook of Marine Science. Compounds of Marine Organisms.* 1981. 223p. F. B1. $65.00

**BAKER & TRAPHAGEN.** *Diagnosis & Treatment of Behavior-Problem Children.* 1935. Macmillan. 12mo. 383p. prt panelled crimson cloth. VG. G1. $35.00

**BAKER.** *Speech of Miss Polly Baker.* 1926. Cleveland. leather wrp. B18. $22.50

**BAKHIT, M.A.S.** *Ottoman Province of Damascus in 16th Century.* 1972. London. 3 maps. 314p. cloth. VG. Q2. $96.00

**BAKUZIS & HANSEN.** *Balsam Fir.* 1965. Minneapolis. 445p. VG/dj. B26. $45.00

**BALAKIAN, Peter.** *Theodore Roethke's Far Fields.* 1989. LSU. 1st. F/NF. L3. $30.00

**BALANCHINE, George.** *Complete Stories of the Great Ballets.* 1954. Doubleday. 1st. sgn. 615p. F/dj. B20. $100.00

**BALCH, Glenn.** *Indian Paint: Story of an Indian Pony.* 1942. Crowell. 1st. VG/G. O3. $25.00

**BALCH, Glenn.** *Midnight Colt.* 1952. Crowell. 2nd. sgn. ils Pers Crowell. VG. O3. $20.00

**BALCH, Glenn.** *White Ruff.* 1958. Grosset Dunlap. Famous Dog series. 235p. VG. B36. $15.00

**BALCH, Glenn.** *Wild Horse Tamer.* 1955. NY. Crowell. 1st. sgn pres. VG/G. O3. $30.00

**BALCHEN, Brent.** *Come North With Me: An Autobiography.* 1958. NY. 1st. inscr. VG/dj. B18. $45.00

**BALCOM, Mary G.** *Ghost Towns of Alaska.* 1970. Chicago. Adams. later. sgn. 84p. VG/wrp. P4. $16.00

**BALDACCI, David.** *Absolute Power.* 1986. Warner. 1st. F/dj. L1. $18.00

**BALDUCCI, Rita.** *Nutcracker.* 1991. Western Pub. 1st. ils Barbara Lanza. NF. B36. $4.25

**BALDWIN, C.H.** *Fifth Annual Report State Entomologist of Indiana.* 1912. Indianapolis. Burford. 324p. VG. A10. $25.00

**BALDWIN, Charles N.** *Universal Biographical Dictionary.* 1826. Richmond, VA. Normand White. 1st Am thus. 8vo. 444p. VG. C6. $225.00

**BALDWIN, Gordon C.** *Apache Indians: Raiders of the Southwest.* 1978. 4 Winds. 1st. ils/index. 221p. F/F. B19. $20.00

**BALDWIN, HANSON W.** *Battles Lost & Won.* 1966. NY. 1st. 532p. F/VG. E1. $40.00

**BALDWIN, J.** *Adjutant's Reports Grand Army.* 1887-97. Larami, WY. GAR Post No 1. hc. G. A19. $650.00

**BALDWIN, James Mark.** *Between Two Wars 1861-1921...* 1926. Boston. Stratford. 2 vol. ils/pl. panelled crimson cloth. VG. G1. $300.00

**BALDWIN, James Mark.** *Dictionary of Philosophy & Psychology...* 1960. Gloucester, MA. Peter SMith. 3 vol in 4. tan buckram. xl. G1. $200.00

**BALDWIN, James Mark.** *Elements of Psychology.* 1893. NY. Holt. 12mo. 372p+2p ads. brn cloth. G1. $65.00

**BALDWIN, James Mark.** *Fragments in Philosophy & Science, Being Collected Essays...* 1902. Scribner. 389p. panelled thatched crimson cloth. G. G1. $85.00

**BALDWIN, James Mark.** *Genetic Theory of Reality: Being Outcome of Genetic Logic...* 1915. Putnam/Knickerbocker. 335p. gr cloth. G1. $75.00

**BALDWIN, James Mark.** *Social & Ethical Interpretations in Mental Development...* 1897. Macmillan. 574p. pebbled crimson cloth. VG. G1. $150.00

**BALDWIN, James Mark.** *Thought & Things: A Study of Development & Meaning...* 1975. NY. Arno. 4 vol in 2. cream cloth. G1. $125.00

**BALDWIN, James.** *Another Country.* 1962. NY. Dial. 1st. F/dj. B2. $200.00

**BALDWIN, James.** *Blues for Mr Charlie.* 1964. Dial. ARC/1st. 8vo. 121p. RS. blk cloth. F/NF. C6. $200.00

**BALDWIN, James.** *Fire Next Time.* 1963. NY. Dial. 1st. VG/dj. S13. $16.00

**BALDWIN, James.** *Nobody Knows My Name.* 1961. Dial. 1st. F/VG. B2. $45.00

**BALDWIN, James.** *Rap on Race.* 1971. Lippincott. F/dj. A24. $70.00

**BALDWIN, James.** *School Reading by Grades, First Year.* 1897. NY. Am Book Co. G. M20. $14.00

**BALDWIN, James.** *Story of Roland.* 1930. Scribner. ils Peter Hurd. VG. M17. $35.00

**BALDWIN, Leland C.** *Whiskey Rebels.* 1939. Pittsburgh. 8vo. 326p. gr cloth. VG. C6. $60.00

**BALDWIN, May.** *Holly House & Ridges Row: A Tale of London Old & New.* 1908. Chambers. 1st. ils MV Wheelhouse. VG+. M5. $70.00

**BALFOUR, Lady Frances.** *Dr Elsie Inglis.* nd (1918). London. Hodder Stoughton. 1st. 253p. VG. w/ephemera. A25. $25.00

**BALFOUR, Michael.** *Royal Baby Book: For Prince & Princess of Wales.* 1981. London. Pan. 1st Eng. F/dj. T12. $45.00

**BALL, Alice E.** *Year With the Birds.* 1916. Gibbs/Van Vleck. 1st. sgn. ils RB Horsfall. 191p. gr cloth. NF. B20. $125.00

**BALL, Eustace Hale.** *Gaucho.* 1928. Grosset Dunlap. 1st photoplay. VG/dj. C9. $102.00

**BALL, Eve.** *In the Days of Victorio: Recollections...* 1970. Tucson, AZ. 1st. ils/notes/index. 222p. NF/VG+. B19. $55.00

**BALL, John.** *Johnny Get Your Gun.* 1969. Little Brn. later prt. G. P8. $25.00

**BALL, Larry D.** *United Marshals of NM & AZ Territories, 1846-1912.* (1978). Albuquerque. 1st. 315p. cloth. dj. D11. $60.00

**BALL, Zachary.** *Kep.* 1961. Holiday House. 1st. 207p. F/dj. D4. $30.00

**BALLANCE, Charles.** *Some Points in the Surgery of the Brain & Its Membranes.* 1907. London. 1st. 451p. A13. $500.00

**BALLANTINE, Bill.** *Wild Tigers & Tame Fleas.* nd (1958). NY. ils. VG/dj. M17. $20.00

**BALLARD, Ernest.** *Days in My Garden.* 1919. Cambridge. 195p. cloth. A10. $22.00

**BALLARD, H.C.** *Poems.* 1870. Chicago. Church Goodman Donnelly. 1st. 8vo. 164p. gr cloth. VG. C6. $60.00

**BALLARD, J.G.** *Crash.* 1973. FSG. 1st Am. 8vo. F/dj. S9. $150.00

**BALLARD, J.G.** *Empire of the Sun.* 1984. S&S. 1st. F/NF. M19. $17.50

**BALLARD, J.G.** *Kindness of Women.* 1991. NY. FSG. 1st Am. F/dj. T12. $25.00

**BALLARD, Mignon F.** *Minerva Cries Murder.* 1993. Carroll Graf. 1st. sgn. NF/VG. G8. $17.50

**BALLARD, Tod Hunter.** *Sheriff of Tombstone.* 1977. Doubleday. 1st. 187p. NF/NF. B19. $7.50

**BALLARIAN, Anna.** *Fabric Collage: Contemporary Stitchery & Applique.* 1976. Davis. 1st. F/sans. T12. $10.00

**BALLENTINE, George.** *Autobiography of an English Soldier in the US Army.* 1986. Lakeside Classic. 1st thus. edit WH Goetzmann. teg. brn cloth. F. T11. $30.00

**BALLIETT, Whitney.** *Dinosaurs in the Morning.* 1962. Phil. Lippincott. 1st. F/NF. B2. $75.00

**BALLIETT, Whitney.** *Dinosaurs in the Morning.* 1962. Phil/NY. 1st. VG/dj. M17. $40.00

**BALLIETT, Whitney.** *Sound of Surprise.* 1959. Dutton. 1st. author's 1st book. F/VG. B2. $75.00

**BALLINGER, James.** *Frederick Remington.* 1989. NY. ils/chronology/index. 160p. VG/dj. S16. $35.00

**BALLINGER, Raymond A.** *Lettering Art in Modern Use.* 1952. NY. Reinhold. 1st. 4to. 246p. F/NF. O10. $40.00

**BALLINGER, W.A.** *Rebellion.* 1967. Howard Baker. 1st. F/dj. P3. $15.00

**BALLOU, Marturin.** *Equatorial America.* 1900 (1892). Houghton Mifflin. 371p. xl. F3. $15.00

**BALLOU, Robert.** *World Bible.* 1944. Viking. 605p. VG/dj. B29. $7.50

**BALTHASAR, Juan Antonio.** *Juan Antonio Balthasar: Padre Visitador...1744-45.* 1957. AZ Pioneers Hist Soc. 1/600. 122p+1 fld facs & 1 pocket map. cloth. dj. D11. $40.00

**BALZLI & TENNER.** *Winter in the Wald (Winter in the Forest).* 1941. Zurich. Morgarten. 4to. limp brd. R5. $150.00

**BAMFORD, T.W.** *Practical Make-Up for the Stage.* 1959 (1940). London. Isaac Pitnam. 146p. VG. C5. $12.50

**BAMM, Peter.** *Early Sites of Christianity.* 1957. NY. photos. trans Stanley Godman. VG/dj. M17. $15.00

**BANARD & WOOD.** *Kembo: Little Girl of Africa.* 1928. NY. Friendship. 1st. Nursery series #1. 12mo. 60p+ads. NF/dj. B20. $65.00

**BANCROFT, Frederic.** *Slave-Trading in the Old South.* 1931. Baltimore. JH Hurst. 1st. lg 8vo. 415p. gilt purple cloth. F/dj. B29. $425.00

**BANCROFT, Joseph.** *Respiratory Function of the Blood, Part II Haemoglobin.* 1928. Cambridge. 2nd part of vol 2. 200p. cloth. NF. G7. $95.00

**BANCROFT, Laura.** *Babies in Birdland: A Fairy Tale.* 1911. Chicago. Reilly Britton. 1st thus. 8vo. 8 full-p mc pl. gr cloth. R5. $275.00

**BANDEL, Eugene.** *Frontier Life in the Army 1854-61.* 1932. Arthur H Clark. fld map. 33p. D11. $125.00

**BANDELIER, Adolf F.** *Delight Makers.* 1949. Dodd Mead. VG/dj. V4. $15.00

**BANDELIER, Adolph F.** *Contributions to History of Southwestern Portion of US.* 1890. John Wilson. 1st. fld map/notes. 206p. NF. B19. $150.00

**BANDELIER, Adolph F.** *Documentary History of Rio Grande Pueblos of NM.* 1910. np. Papers of School Am Archaeology #13. 28p. wrp. D11. $75.00

**BANDELIER, Adolph F.** *On Social Organization & Mode of Government... Mexicans.* 1879. Salem. inscr. wrp. D11. $50.00

**BANDELIER, Adolph F.** *Scientist on the Trail: Travel Letters of...* 1949. Quivira Soc. index. 132p. VG/sans. B19. $75.00

**BANERJI, Sara.** *Tea-Planter's Daughter.* 1988. London. Gollancz. 1st. NF/dj. A14. $28.00

**BANFIELD, A.W.F.** *Mammals of Canada.* 1977 (1974). U Toronto. F/VG. T12. $70.00

**BANGS, E. Geoffrey.** *Portals West: Folio of Late Nineteenth Century...* 1960. SF. CA Hist Soc. 1s1/1000. ils/photos. 87p. F/dj. B20. $75.00

**BANGS, John Kendrick.** *Bikey the Skicycle & Other Tales of Jimmieboy.* 1902. Riggs. 1st. ils Peter Newell. lacks ffe. VG. M5. $75.00

**BANGS, John Kendrick.** *House-Boat on the Styx.* 1896. Harper. 1st. 12mo. 172p+4p ads. gr cloth. VG. C6. $65.00

**BANGS, John Kendrick.** *Songs of Cheer.* 1910. Boston. Sherman French. 1st. 8vo. 64p. VG/dj. J3. $75.00

**BANHAM, Peter.** *Scenes in American Deserta.* 1982. Peregrine Smith. 1st. ils. 228p. NF/VG+. B19. $20.00

**BANKOFF, George.** *Story of Plastic Surgery.* 1952. London. 1st. 224p. A13. $100.00

**BANKS, Iain.** *Canal Dreams.* 1989. London. Macmillan. 1st. F/F. B3. $40.00

**BANKS, Iain.** *Player of Games.* 1988. London. Macmillan. 1st. F/dj. A24. $30.00

**BANKS, Iain.** *Walking on Grass.* 1985. London. Macmillan. 1st. NF/dj. A14. $88.00

**BANKS, Joanne Trautmann.** *Literature & Medicine, Vol 5: Use & Abuse Literary Concepts.* 1986. Johns Hopkins. 8vo. 185p. brd. F. C14. $15.00

**BANKS, Lynne Reid.** *Return of the Indian.* 1986. Doubleday. 1st. NF/dj. M25. $25.00

**BANKS, Russell.** *Affliction.* 1989. Harper Row. 1st. 8vo. 355p. F/dj. C6. $20.00

**BANKS, Russell.** *Affliction.* 1989. NY. Harper Row. 1st. sgn. F/dj. R14. $45.00

**BANKS, Russell.** *Athenea.* 1995. Knopf. 1st Am. sgn. F/dj. O11. $30.00

**BANKS, Russell.** *Book of Evidence.* (1989). Scribner. 1st Am. sgn. F/dj. O11. $40.00

**BANKS, Russell.** *Ghosts.* 1993. NY. Knopf. 1st. sgn. F/dj. O11. $35.00

**BANKS, Russell.** *Mefisto.* 1989. Boston. Godine. 1st Am. sgn. F/dj. O11. $45.00

**BANKS, Russell.** *Relationship of My Imprisonment.* 1983. Sun & Moon. 1st. F/dj. R14. $50.00

**BANKS, Russell.** *Sweet Hereafter.* 1991. Harper Collins. 1st. sgn. F/dj. O11. $45.00

**BANKS, T.H.** *Sir Gawain & the Green Knight.* 1929. NY. Crofts. 1st Am. gilt quarter cloth/brd. NF. M24. $45.00

**BANNERMAN, Helen.** *Little Black Sambo & the Baby Elephant.* 1925. Phil. Altemus. 1st. 12mo. pict label/cloth-backed brd. R5. $150.00

**BANNERMAN, Helen.** *Little Black Sambo.* ca 1920s. Chicago. Whitman. Just Right Books. ils C Shinn. 63+1p. bl cloth/label. D1. $400.00

**BANNERMAN, Helen.** *Little Black Sambo.* 1905. Reilly Britton. intro L Frank Baum. rb/orig spine. G+. M5. $225.00

**BANNERMAN, Helen.** *Story of Little Babaji.* 1996. Harper Collins. 1nd. ils/sgn Marcellino. F/dj. B17. $35.00

**BANNERMAN, Helen.** *Story of Little Black Sambo.* ca 1915. NY. Stokes. earpt rpt. 12mo. ils. 54p. ils brd/cloth spine. VG. B20. $300.00

**BANNERMAN, Helen.** *Story of Little Black Sambo.* 1919. Chicago. Donohue. sm 8vo. ils anon. red clth/pict label. G. D1. $200.00

**BANNERMAN, Helen.** *Story of Little Black Sambo: Animated Edition.* 1933. Garden City. 27 full-p ils by Wiese/animated AV Warren. dk bl cloth. R5. $850.00

**BANNERMAN & BANNERMAN.** *Birds of Cyprus.* 1958. London/Edinburgh. Oliver Boyd. 1st. ils Reid-Henry/Green. 384p. NF/clip. B20. $325.00

**BANNING, Kendall.** *Great Adventure.* 1926. NY. Marchbanks. 1st. 8vo. 44p. bl br/wht buckram spine. VG. C6. $40.00

**BANNING & HUGH.** *Six Horses.* 1930. NY. Century. G. O3. $35.00

**BANNISTER, Connie.** *Let's Face It.* (1954). Brn Bigelow. sc. 24mo. pict wrp. T5. $22.00

**BANNISTER, J.T.** *Survey of the Holy Land: Its Geography, History & Destiny...* nd. Bath. Binns Goodwin. ils/fld plan/maps. aeg. cloth. VG. Q2. $56.50

**BANNON, Laura.** *Famous Baby-Sitter.* 1960. Whitman. 1st. ils. 48p. F/VG+. D4. $35.00

**BANTA, R.E.** *Ohio.* 1949. Rinehart. 1st. ils Edward Shenton. VG/dj. M20. $50.00

**BANTOCK, Nick.** *Egyptian Jukebox.* 1993. Viking. 1st. rem mk. F/dj. B17. $15.00

**BANTOCK, Nick.** *Griffin & Sabine.* 1991. Chronicle. 1st prt. F/F. B3. $125.00

**BANTOCK, Nick.** *Runners, Sliders, Bouncers, Climbers...* 1992. Hyperion. 1st. obl 8vo. VG+. B17. $16.00

**BANTOCK, Nick.** *Solomon Grundi.* 1992. Viking. probable 1st. sm 16mo. rem mk. F. B17. $6.00

**BANTON, O.T.** *Decatur, Illinois: A Pictorial History.* 1983. Macon Co Hist Soc. VG. B9. $15.00

**BANVILLE, John.** *Athena.* 1995. London. Secker Warburg. 1st. NF/dj. A24. $35.00

**BANVILLE, John.** *Book of Evidence.* 1990. Scribner. 1st Am. sgn. F/dj. D10. $40.00

**BANVILLE, John.** *Ghosts.* 1993. Secker Warburg. 1st. F/F. B3. $40.00

**BARAGWANATH, A.K.** *Currier & Ives Favorites.* 1979. NY. Crown. 1st. 160p. F/dj. O10. $45.00

**BARAJAS & PEREZ.** *Manual de Identificacion de Arboles de Selva Baja Mediante.* 1990. Mexico. photos. 83p. sc. AN. B26. $32.00

**BARAKA, Amiri.** *Autobiography of Le Roi Jones.* 1977. Chicago. Lawrence Hill. 1st thus. inscr. F/wrp. R14. $40.00

**BARAKA, Amiri.** *Sidney Poet Heretical.* 1979. NY. 1st. inscr. NF/wrp. R14. $50.00

**BARASH, David P.** *Marmots: Social Behavior & Ecology.* 1989. Stanford. ils. 361p. F/dj. S15. $24.00

**BARATTA & BARATTA.** *Cooking for Jack.* 1996. NY. Pocket. F/dj. V4. $12.50

**BARBARY, James.** *Boer War.* 1969. Meredith. 1st. photos/map/index. 210p. VG/dj. S16. $35.00

**BARBE-MARBOIS, Francois.** *History of Louisiana.* 1830. Phil. Carey Lea. 1st Eng-language. 8vo. 524p. full calf. xl. C6. $250.00

**BARBEAU, Marius.** *Downfall of Temlaham.* 1928. Toronto. Macmillan. 8vo. ils. 253p. half cloth. NF/dj. P4. $165.00

**BARBEAU, Marius.** *Totem Poles. Two Volumes.* 1950. Ottawa. Nat Mus of Canada. blk cloth. P4. $150.00

**BARBER, Antonia.** *Mousehole Cat.* 1990. Macmillan. 1st. ils Nicola Bayley. F/VG+. M5. $30.00

**BARBER, Edwin A.** *American Glassware.* 1900. McKay. 1st. VG. M20. $27.00

**BARBER, Noel.** *Tanamera: Novel of Singapore.* 1981. Hodder Stoughton. 1st. NF/dj. A14. $21.00

**BARBER, Red.** *Walk in the Spirit.* 1969. Dial. 1st. VG/dj. P8. $40.00

**BARBER, Wiletta Ann.** *Drawback to Murder.* 1947. Scribner. 1st. G+. P3. $30.00

**BARBER & HOWE.** *Historical Collections of the State of New York.* 1841. NY. 1st. ils/map. full leather. VG. B18. $150.00

**BARBOSA & SCHULTZ.** *Insect Outbreaks.* 1987. Academic. 8vo. 578p. VG. S15. $30.00

**BARBOUR, Ambrose.** *Boz at Idleberg.* 1951. Lexington, KY. Bluegrass Bookshop. 1/200. sgn Townsend Barbour. NF. C6. $85.00

**BARBOUR, Hugh.** *Quakers in Puritan England.* 1964. New Haven. Yale. 1st. 8vo. 272p. VG/dj. R14. $45.00

**BARBOUR, Philip L.** *Jamestown Voyages Under the First Charter 1606-1609.* 1969. Cambridge. Hakluyt Soc. 8vo. 2 pl/6 maps. F/dj. O1. $100.00

**BARBOUR, Philip L.** *Three Worlds of Captain John Smith.* 1964. London. Macmillan. 1st. ils. 553p. VG/dj. M10. $18.50

**BARBOUR, Ralph H.** *Finkler's Field.* 1911. Appleton. 1st. VG/sans. P8. $60.00

**BARBOUR, Ralph H.** *Kingsford, Quarter.* 1910. NY. Century. 326p. G. G11. $15.00

**BARBOUR, Ralph H.** *Three Base Benson.* 1921. Appleton. 1st. G. P8. $50.00

**BARBOUR, Ralph H.** *Tod Hale on the Nine.* 1929. Dodd Mead. 1st. VG. P8. $65.00

**BARBOUR & ROBERTS.** *Early Quaker Writings.* 1973. Cedar Rapids, MI. Eerdmans. 622p. xl. V3. $50.00

**BARCLAY, Bill;** see Moorcock, Michael.

**BARCLAY, John.** *Selection From Letters & Papers of...* 1847. Phil. Longstreth. 1st Am. 328p. xl. V3. $18.00

**BARCLAY, Robert.** *Catechism & Confession of Faith...* 1752. Newport, RI. Prt James Franklin. 2nd. sm 8vo. contemporary bdg. O1. $750.00

**BARCLAY, Robert.** *Truth Triumphant Through Spiritual Warfare...* 1831. Phil. Benjamin Stanton. 3 vol. leather. G+. V3. $165.00

**BARCLAY, William.** *Ethics in a Permissive Society.* 1971. Harper. 223p. VG/dj. B29. $9.50

**BARCLAY, William.** *Jesus of Nazareth.* 1977. Collins World. 1st. VG/dj. C9. $48.00

**BARCLAY, William.** *Letters to the Philippians, Colossians & Thessalonians.* 1959. Westminster. 253p. VG/dj. B29. $6.50

**BARDI, P.M.** *Lasar Segall.* 1952. Sao Paulo. Museu De Sao Paulo. Italian text. sm 4to. ils. G/poor. F1. $40.00

**BARDIN, John Franklin.** *Last of Philip Banter.* 1947. Dodd Mead. 1st. VG/clip. M15. $75.00

**BAREA, Arturo.** *Forging of a Rebel.* 1972. London. trans I Barea. dj. T9. $25.00

**BARENHOLTZ, Edith F.** *George Brown Toy Sketchbook.* 1971. Princeton. Pyne. 1st. ils Geo Brown. 60p. NF/case. D1. $125.00

**BARER, Burl.** *Man Overboard: Counterfeit Resurrection of Phil Champagne.* 1994. Salt Lake City. 1st. F/dj. A23. $30.00

**BARER, Burl.** *Maverick.* 1994. Boston. Tuttle. 1st. 222p. VG/wrp. C5. $12.50

**BARFIELD, Owen.** *Owen Barfield on CS Lewis.* (1989). Wesleyan U. 1st Am. edit/intro GB Tennyson. AN/clip. A27. $20.00

**BARFIELD, Owen.** *Speaker's Meaning.* (1984). Wesleyan U. AN. A27. $13.00

**BARGER, E.L.** *Tractors & Their Power Units.* 1958. NY. Wiley. 2nd. 496p. cloth. A10. $25.00

**BARIO, Joanne.** *Fatal Dreams.* 1985. NY. Dial. 1st author's 1st book. F/F. H11. $30.00

**BARIS, Bonnie.** *Dance Words.* 1982. Shaker Heights, OH. Wind & Harlot. mini. 1/100. cloth. F. B24. $75.00

**BARKER, A.J.** *German Infantry Weapons of WWII.* 1969. NY. 1st. 76p. F/dj. E1. $25.00

**BARKER, B.U.** *Houses of the Revolution in Hanover, Massachusetts.* 1976. Hanover. photos/fld map. 151p. M4. $20.00

**BARKER, Charles A.** *Background of Revolution in Maryland.* 1940. New Haven. Yale. 1st. 8vo. 419p. red cloth. NF. C6. $75.00

**BARKER, Charles Francis.** *American Checker-Player.* 1880. Boston. De Wolfe. sm 8vo. 179p+32p. gilt gr cloth. VG. F1. $40.00

**BARKER, Cicely Mary.** *Flower Fairies of the Spring.* nd. London. Blackie. Tiny Tots. 24 mc pl. G. T12. $75.00

**BARKER, Cicely Mary.** *Old Rhymes for All Times.* 1993. Warne. 1st. 4to. ils. F/dj. B17. $15.00

**BARKER, Clive.** *Books of Blood: Volume II.* 1991. London. Macdonald. reissue. NF/dj. A14. $21.00

**BARKER, Clive.** *Cabal.* nd. BC. F/dj. S18. $10.00

**BARKER, Clive.** *Damnation Game.* 1987. Putnam. 1st. author's 1st novel. NF/dj. S18. $40.00

**BARKER, Clive.** *Everville.* 1994. Harper. 1st. F/dj. S18. $23.00

**BARKER, Clive.** *Everville: Second Book of the Art.* 1994. Harper Collins. 1/500. sgn on limitation. NF/case. A14. $105.00

**BARKER, Clive.** *Great & Secret Show.* 1989. Harper Row. 1st N Am of 1st Collins ed. VG+/dj. A14. $17.50

**BARKER, Clive.** *Imagica.* 1991. Harper Collins. ltd/1st Am. sgn on limitation. NF/case. A14. $105.00

**BARKER, Clive.** *Imagica.* 1991. Harper. 1st. F/dj. S18. $30.00

**BARKER, Clive.** *In the Flesh.* 1986. Poseidon. 1st. sgn. F/dj. T12. $75.00

**BARKER, Clive.** *Inhuman Condition.* 1986. Poseidon. 1st. F/dj. S18. $40.00

**BARKER, Clive.** *Inhuman Condition.* 1986. Poseidon. 1st. sgn. F/NF. B3. $75.00

**BARKER, Clive.** *Sacrament.* 1996. Harper Collins. 1st. NF/dj. L4. $16.00

BARKER, Clive. *Son of Celluloid.* 1991. Eclipse. 1st. AN. T12. $20.00

BARKER, Clive. *Tapping the Vein. Book One, Book Two & Book Three.* 1989-1990. Eclipse. 3 vol. F. C9. $60.00

BARKER, Clive. *Weaveworld.* 1987. London. Collins. 1st. sgn on title. NF/dj. A14. $70.00

BARKER, David. *Bukowski, the King of San Pedro.* 1985. Del Mar, CA. Tabula Rasa. mini. 1/250. Bukowski photo ftspc. 70p. tan cloth. B24. $95.00

BARKER, E. *When the Dogs Barked Treed.* 1946. Albuquerque. 1st. sgn. VG/dj. B5. $27.50

BARKER, F. *Olivers.* 1953. Phil. 1st. VG/dj. B5. $22.50

BARKER, James N. *Atlantic Souvenir: Christmas & New Year's Offering, 1828.* 1827. Phil. Lea Carey. 1st. gr-glazed prt brd. intact 5-panel box/2 labels. M24. $600.00

BARKER, Pat. *Ghost Road.* 1995. Dutton. 1st thus. Booker Award. F/dj. A23. $35.00

BARKER, Pat. *Union Street.* 1983. Putnam. 1st Am. F/NF. D10. $75.00

BARKER, Wayne. *Cryptanalysis of Single Columnar Transposition Cipher.* 1961. 1st. full leather. VG. E6. $25.00

BARKER & BUERKLE. *Bourbon Street Black: New Orleans Black Jazzman.* 1973. OUP. 1st. inscr Barker. VG/dj. B2. $100.00

BARKER & LEWIN. *Denver! An Insider's Look at the High, Wide & Handsome City.* 1972. Doubleday. VG/dj. V4. $12.50

BARKLEM, Jill. *Brambly Hedge Sea Story.* 1991. NY. Philomel. 1st Am. 16mo. wht glossy brd. F/dj. T5. $45.00

BARKLEM, Jill. *Brambly Hedge Summer Story.* 1980. Philomel. 10th. 16mo. unp. wht pict brd. NF/dj. T5. $32.00

BARKLEY, George H. *In Old Virginia.* ca 1950s. np. photos. 31p. VG. B10. $15.00

BARLOW, Joel. *Columbiad, a Poem.* 1807. Baltimore. Prt by Fry & Kammerer for Conrad. 4to. ils. 454p. w/sgn. O1. $375.00

BARNARD, Christian. *Night Season.* 1978. Prentice Hall. 1st. VG/dj. M20. $14.00

BARNARD, Robert. *Death & the Princess.* 1982. London. Collins Crime Club. sgn. F/clip. M15. $150.00

BARNARD, Robert. *Death of an Old Goat.* 1974. London. Collins Crime Club. F/dj. M15. $200.00

BARNARD, Robert. *Habit of Widowhood.* 1986. Scribner. 1st. F/dj. T12. $20.00

BARNARD & PEPPER. *Christiaan Barnard: One Life.* 1970. Macmillan. 1st Am. 8vo. 402p. NF/VG. C14. $20.00

BARNEBY, Rupert C. *Atlas of North American Astragalus. Parts I & II.* 1964. Bronx. 163 maps. 1188p. gr cloth. VG. B26. $140.00

BARNEBY, W. Henry. *Life & Labour in the Far, Far West...* 1884. London. Constable. 1st. fld map. 432p. fair. M10. $175.00

BARNES, C.E. *Kellogg, Charles; The Nature Singer, His Book.* 1930. Morgan Hill, CA. Pacific Science. 303p. cloth. VG. A10. $20.00

BARNES, Djuna. *Ryder.* 1928. Horace Livveright. 1st. VG. B2. $50.00

BARNES, F.A. *Canyon Country Geology for the Layman & Rockhound.* 1993. Wasatch. 8vo. 160p. VG. F7. $6.00

BARNES, F.A. *Utah Canyon Country.* 1986. UT Geog series. obl 4to. 117p. wrp. F7. $17.00

BARNES, Julian. *Cross Channel, Stories.* 1996. NY. 1st. dj. T9. $10.00

BARNES, Julian. *Talking It Over.* 1991. Knopf. 1st Canadian. NF/dj. S13. $10.00

BARNES, L.L. *Story of New London Academy, 1795-1945.* 1945. Forest, VA. Brd of Managers. 80p. VG. B10. $35.00

BARNES, Linda. *Cities of the Dead.* 1985. St Martin. 1st. sgn. F/dj. M15. $85.00

BARNES, Linda. *Snake Tattoo.* 1989. St Martin. 1st. VG/NF. N4. $25.00

BARNES, Linda. *Snapshot.* 1993. Delacorte. 1st. sgn. NF/dj. G8. $25.00

BARNES, R. Money. *Soldiers of London: Imperial Services Lib Vol VI.* 1963. London. Seeley. ils. 376p. VG/dj. S16. $40.00

BARNES, Ruth A. *I Hear America Singing. An Anthology of Folk Poetry.* (1937). Phil. Winston. 1st. ils Robert Lawson. 346p. beige cloth. R5. $150.00

BARNES, Trevor. *Midsummer's Night's Killing.* 1989. Morrow. 1st. F/dj. A23. $30.00

BARNET, Sylvan. *Classic Theatre: The Humanities in Drama.* 1975. Boston. Little Brn. 682p. VG/dj. C5. $12.50

BARNETT, Lincoln. *Treasure of Our Tongue: Story of English...* 1964. Knopf. 1st. 304p. G. P12. $7.00

BARNETT, Ruth. *They Weep on My Doorstep.* 1969. Halo. 1st. 8vo. 140p. F/prt wrp. B20. $25.00

BARNETT, Ted. *Gold Is Madness.* 1977. Golf Digest. F/NF. P12. $6.00

BARNHARDT, Wilton. *Gospel.* 1993. St Martin. 1st. F/dj. R14. $35.00

BARNHART, John Hendley. *Bibliography of John Kunkel Small.* 1935. NY. 1st. 15p. VG/wrp. M8. $45.00

BARNHOLTH, William I. *Hopocan (Capt Pipe) the Delaware Chieftain.* 1966. Summit Co Hist Soc. 19p. sbdg. B18. $20.00

BARNONIO, Giuseppe. *On Grafting in Animals: Degli Innesti Animali...* 1985. Boston Medical Lib. Bird & Bull. 87p. quarter gr morocco/pattern brd. AN. G7. $325.00

BARNUM, P.T. *Life of PT Barnum: Written by Himself.* 1855. NY. Redfield. 1st. author's 1st book. VG. Q1. $175.00

BAROJA, Pio. *Restlessness of Shanti Andia & Other Writings.* 1959. Ann Arbor. 2nd. trans Anthony Kerrigan. VG/dj. R11. $15.00

BARON, Randall. *Bridge Player's Dictionary.* VG. S1. $12.00

BARON & CARVER. *Bud Stewart: Michigan's Legendary Lure Maker.* 1990. Marceline, MO. 1st/ltd. ils/photos. 227p. AN. A17. $75.00

BARR, Alwyn. *Polignac's Texas Brigade.* 1964. TX. 1st. 72p. VG/wrp. S16. $75.00

BARR, E. Osmun. *Flying Men & Medicine: Effects of Flying Upon Human Body.* 1943. NY. 1st. xl. 254p. A13. $60.00

BARR, Nevada. *Ill Wind.* 1995. Putnam. 1st. F/F. H11. $25.00

BARR, Nevada. *Ill Wind.* 1995. Putnam. 1st. sgn. F/dj. G8. $35.00

BARR, Nevada. *Superior Death.* 1994. Putnam. 1st. NF/NF. H11. $30.00

BARR, Nevada. *Track of the Cat.* 1993. Putnam. 1st. F/dj. M15. $250.00

BARR, Roseanne. *My Life As a Woman.* Harper Row. NF/dj. A28. $10.00

BARR & SCHWARTZ. *My Sister Roseanne: True Story of Roseanne Arnold.* 1994. NY. Birch Lane. 1st. AN/dj. V4. $15.00

BARRAS DE ARAGON, Francisco. *Documentos Referentes a Mutis y Su Tiempo.* 1933. Madrid. 35p. VG/wrp. F3. $20.00

BARRE, Richard. *Bearing Secrets.* 1996. NY. Walker. 1st. sgn. F/dj. T2. $35.00

BARRE, Richard. *Bearing Secrets.* 1996. Walker. 1st author's 2nd novel. F/dj. N4. $25.00

BARRE, Richard. *Innocents.* 1995. NY. Walker. 1st. sgn. author's 1st novel. F/dj. T2. $50.00

**BARRETT, Andrea.** *Forms of Water.* 1993. Pocket. 1st. F/dj. O11. $25.00

**BARRETT, Andrea.** *Lucid Stars.* 1988. Delta Fiction. UP. author's 1st book. NF/wrp. O11. $35.00

**BARRETT, Andrea.** *Middle Kingdom.* 1995. NY. Pocket. 1st. F/dj. A23. $35.00

**BARRETT, Andrea.** *Secret Harmonies.* 1989. Delacorte. 1st. author's 2nd book. F/NF. B3. $40.00

**BARRETT, Andrea.** *Ship Fever.* 1996. Norton. 1st. F/dj. A23. $50.00

**BARRETT, C.K.** *Epistle to the Romans.* 1957. NY. Harper Row. VG/dj. M20. $25.00

**BARRETT, Ellen C.** *Baja California, 1535-1956.* 1957. 1/550. 4to. 2873 entries. 304p. NF. A4. $300.00

**BARRETT, John G.** *Sherman's March Through the Carolinas.* 1956. Chapel Hill. 8vo. 325p. VG/worn. C6. $40.00

**BARRETT, John.** *Bear Who Slept Through Christmas.* 1980. Childrens Pr. ils Rick Reinert. laminated brd. VG. B36. $11.00

**BARRETT, Lindsay.** *Song for Mumu.* 1974. WA. Howard U. 1st Am. assn/inscr to Walter Mosley. F/NF. D10. $45.00

**BARRETT, Marvin.** *Spare Days.* 1988. Arbor. 1st. F/dj. A23. $30.00

**BARRETT, Neal Jr.** *Hereafter Gang.* 1991. Ziesing. 1st. sgn. NF/F. S18. $50.00

**BARRETT, Neal Jr.** *Slightly Off Center.* 1992. Swan. 1st. sgn. intro JR Lansdale. F/wrp. S18. $35.00

**BARRETT, Peter.** *Great True Hunts.* 1967. Englewood Cliffs. index. 278p. xl. dj. A17. $17.50

**BARRETT & CAHN.** *Jazz Age.* 1959. Putnam. 1st. 4to. B2. $25.00

**BARRIE, James M.** *Admirable Crichton.* (1914). Hodder Stoughton. 1/500. ils/sgn Hugh Thomson. 234p. teg. F/case. H5. $800.00

**BARRIE, James M.** *Admirable Crichton.* 1914. Hodder Stoughton. 1st trade. pres. 20 mtd pl. F/case. B20. $600.00

**BARRIE, James M.** *Courage: Rectorial Address Delivered St Andrews U...* 1923 (1905). NY. Scribner. 16mo. 49p. VG+/G. C14. $7.00

**BARRIE, James M.** *Little White Bird.* 1902. London. Hodder Stoughton. 1st. 8vo. 312p. dk bl cloth. VG+. C6. $125.00

**BARRIE, James M.** *Peter Pan Animated Coloring Book.* 1943. Chicago. Derby Foods. obl 8vo. mc paper wrp/orig mailing envelope. R5. $275.00

**BARRIE, James M.** *Peter Pan in Kensington Gardens.* ca 1925. Hodder Stoughton. ils Rackham. gilt red cloth. VG. M20. $130.00

**BARRIE, James M.** *Peter Pan in Kensington Gardens.* 1906. London. Hodder Stoughton. ils Rackham. 125p. VG. H5. $1,250.00

**BARRIE, James M.** *Peter Pan in Kensington Gardens.* 1910. Hodder Stoughton. 7th Eng. ils Rackham/50 mtd mc pl. 125p text. gilt bdg. D1. $450.00

**BARRIE, James M.** *Quality Street.* nd. Hodder Stoughton. 1st trade. ils. lt bl cloth. VG. B27. $125.00

**BARRIE, James M.** *Tommy & Grizel.* 1900. Scribner. 1st. brn cloth. VG+. S13. $12.00

**BARRIE, James M.** *When a Man's Single: Tale of Literary Life.* 1888. Hodder Stoughton. 1st. gilt navy cloth. VG+. S13. $40.00

**BARRIE, James M.** *Window in Thrums.* 1889. Hodder Stoughton. 1st. VG. S13. $35.00

**BARRINGER, Edwin C.** *Story of Scrap.* 1947. Inst Scrap Iron & Steel. 8vo. 152p. F/VG. B20. $25.00

**BARRINGTON, E.J.W.** *Hormones & Evolution.* 1964. Krieger. 154p. cloth. A10. $10.00

**BARRINGTON, Mrs. Russell.** *Through Greece & Dalmatia: Diary of Impressions...* 1912. London. Black. ils. 263p. gilt purple cloth. NF. B20. $75.00

**BARRIS, Alex.** *Hollywood's Other Men.* 1975. NY. AS Barnes. 223p. VG/dj. C5. $12.50

**BARRON, Stephanie.** *Jane & the Man of the Cloth.* 1997. Bantam. 1st. sgn. F/dj. A23. $42.00

**BARRON, Stephanie.** *Jane & the Unpleasantness at Scargrave Manor.* 1996. Bantam. 1st. author's 1st novel. F/dj. N4. $40.00

**BARRON, Stephanie.** *Jane & the Unpleasantness at Scargrave Manor.* 1996. NY. Bantam. 1st. sgn. F/dj. A23. $48.00

**BARRON, T.A.** *Heartlight.* 1990. Philomel. 1st. F/F. B3. $25.00

**BARRON, T.A.** *Merlin Effect.* 1994. Phiomel. 1st. inscr/sgn twice. F/dj. T10. $65.00

**BARROW, Frances Elizabeth.** *Morsels of History, by Aunt Laura.* 1863. Buffalo. Breed & Butler. mini. 64p. aeg. gilt pub cloth. B24. $135.00

**BARROW & MUNDER.** *Joe Louis: 50 Years an American Hero.* 1988. McGraw Hill. 1st. photos. 270p. F/NF. R11. $17.00

**BARROWS, Marjorie.** *One Hundred Best Poems for Boys & Girls.* nd (c 1930). Racine. Whitman. early. 12mo. 125p. G. C14. $14.00

**BARROWS, Samuel J.** *Children's Courts in the United States.* 1904. GPO. 8vo. 80p. F/wrp. B14. $35.00

**BARROWS, Walter Bradford.** *Michigan Bird Life.* 1912. MI Agric College. photos/drawings. 822p. wrp/new spine label. A17. $45.00

**BARRY, HABBERTON & SUTPHEN.** *Runaway Flying-Machine & Other Stories...* 1910. NY. Harper. 1st. F/dj. B11. $150.00

**BARRY, Henry.** *I'll Be Seeing You.* 1952. Knopf. 1st. 8vo. 239p. VG+/dj. B20. $20.00

**BARRY, J.** *Strange Story of Harper's Ferry With Legends...* 1969. Shepherdstown. 200p. NF. M4. $15.00

**BARRY & KLINICKE.** *Centennial Bibliography of Orange County, CA.* 1989. Orange Co Hist Soc. 1/500. 339p. gilt cloth. D11. $50.00

**BARRYMORE, Ethel.** *Memories.* 1956. London. Hulton. 1st Eng. photos. VG/dj. C9. $24.00

**BARRYMORE, John.** *Confessions of an Actor.* 1926. Bobbs Merrill. 1st. VG. C9. $90.00

**BARSLEY, M.** *Orient Express.* 1967. NY. 1st. 204p. VG/dj. B5. $30.00

**BARSOCCHINI, Peter.** *Ghost.* 1989. Dutton. 1st. F/dj. T12. $25.00

**BARTECCHI, Carl E.** *Soc Trang: Vietnamese Odyssey.* 1980. Boulder, CO. Rocky Mtn Writers Guild. 8vo. photos. 181p. F/dj. R11. $40.00

**BARTH, Gunther.** *City People: Rise of Modern City Culture in 19th-C America.* 1980. NY. OUP. sgn. photos. VG/dj. M17. $20.00

**BARTH, John.** *Floating Opera.* 1956. Appleton Century Crofts. ARC/1st. author's 1st book. NF/dj. S9. $750.00

**BARTH, John.** *Friday Book.* 1984. NY. VG/dj. M17. $17.50

**BARTH, John.** *Lost in the Funhouse.* 1968. Doubleday. 1/250. sgn. F/case. Q1. $150.00

**BARTH, John.** *Lost in the Funhouse.* 1968. Doubleday. 1st. rem mk. VG/dj. L1. $45.00

**BARTH, John.** *Sabbatical.* 1982. NY. Putnam. 1st. NF/F. H11. $20.00

**BARTH, John.** *Skinny Annie Blues.* 1996. Kensington. 1st. sgn. F/dj. A24. $35.00

**BARTH, Karl.** *Ethics.* 1981. NY. Seabury. 534p. VG/G. H10. $35.00

BARTHEL, Thomas S. *Eighth Land: Polynesian Discovery & Settlement...* 1978 (1974). Honolulu. 1st Am. F/dj. A2. $22.50

BARTHELME, Donald. *Amateurs.* 1976. NY. 1st. dj. T9. $8.00

BARTHELME, Donald. *City Life.* 1968. FSG. 1st. F/dj. B30. $45.00

BARTHELME, Donald. *Come Back, Dr Caligari.* 1964. Little Brn. 1st. author's 1st book. xl. fair/G. B30. $50.00

BARTHELME, Donald. *Dead Father.* 1975. FSG. 1st. sgn. 8vo. 177p. blk cloth. NF/dj. C6. $50.00

BARTHELME, Donald. *Overnight to Many Distant Cities.* 1983. NY. Putnam. 1st. F/dj. H11. $30.00

BARTHELME, Donald. *Presents.* 1980. Dallas. Pressworks. 1/376. 4 tipped-in collages by author. 22p. F. F1. $75.00

BARTHELME, Frederick. *Brothers.* 1993. Viking. ARC. F/wrp. B30. $30.00

BARTHOLOMEW, Ed. *Western Hard-Cases; or, Gunfighers Named Smith.* 1960. Ruidoso. Frontier Book Co. sgn. 191p. cloth. dj. D11. $50.00

BARTHOLOMEW, Ed. *Wyatt Earp, 1848-1880: Untold Story.* 1963. Toyahvale. Frontier Book Co. 328p. cloth. D11. $60.00

BARTHOLOMEW, Mel. *Square Foot Gardening.* 1981. Emmaus. Rodale. 347p. VG/dj. A10. $18.00

BARTHOLOW, Robert. *Practical Treatise on Materia Medica & Therapeutics.* 1880. NY. Appleton. 595p. leather. G. H10. $40.00

BARTHORP, Michael. *North-Western Frontier, British Indian & Afghanistan...* 1982. Poole. 184p. VG/dj. S16. $35.00

BARTLETT, Elizabeth Ann. *Sarah Grimke: Letters on Quality of Sexes & Other Essays.* 1988. New Haven/London. Yale. 1st. 174p. VG/dj. V3. $14.00

BARTLETT, John. *Familiar Quotations.* 13th/Centennial. VG/G. M17. $20.00

BARTLETT, John. *Familiar Quotations.* 1891. Little Brn. 3-quarter leather/raised bands/maroon label. VG. S17. $30.00

BARTLETT, Lanier. *On the Old West Coast, Being Further Reminiscenses...* 1930. Morrow. ils. VG/dj. J2. $275.00

BARTLETT, Margaret Farrington. *Down the Mountain, a Book About Ever-Changing Soil.* 1963. NY. Young Scott. 1st. inscr. ils Rhys Caparn. F/dj. F1. $30.00

BARTLETT, N. Gray. *Mother Goose of '93.* 1893. Boston. Joseph Knight. VG. V4. $350.00

BARTLETT, Percy W. *Barrow Cadbury: A Memoir.* 1960. London. Bannisdale. 1st. 159p. VG/dj. V3. $16.00

BARTLETT, Richard D. *In Search of Reptiles & Amphibians.* 1988. Brill. 363p. F. S15. $12.00

BARTLETT, T.P. *Confessions of a Quack.* 1921. Oakland, CA. deMenezes & Sons. 1st. 144p. red cloth. B20. $35.00

BARTLETT, W.H. *Forty Days in the Desert.* ca 1850. London. Arthur Hall. 4th. 8vo. 206p. aeg. full red morocco. C6. $125.00

BARTLETT, W.H. *Jerusalem Revisited.* 1855. London. Arthur Hall/Virtue. 202p+fld panorama. morocco. VG. B5. $275.00

BARTLETT. *Nathaniel Tarn: Descriptive Bibliography.* 1987. 135p. F. A4. $135.00

BARTOLI, Pietro Santi. *Le Antiche Lucerne Sepolcrali Figurate.* 1691. Rome. Gio Fr Ancesco Buagni. 3 parts in 1. folio. calf. K1. $1,000.00

BARTOLI, Pietro Santi. *Raccolta die Varie Antichita e Lucerne Antiche...* ca 1690-1700. Rome. np. folio. 30 #d pl. contemporary vellum. K1. $500.00

BARTON, D. Plunket. *Story of the Inns of Court.* 1928. Boston. red cloth. M11. $45.00

BARTON, George A. *Archaeology & the Bible.* 1952. American. 745p. VG/torn. B29. $8.50

BARTON, LEWIS & WEISER. *Journey From Pennsylvania to Onondaga in 1743.* 1973. Barre, MA. Imp Soc. 1/1900. ils Nathan Goldstein. 132p. quarter leather. B18. $55.00

BARTON, May Hollis. *Barton Books for Girls: Little Miss Sunshine (#6).* 1928. Cupples Leon. VG/dj. M20. $25.00

BARTON, Richard Thomas. *Religious Doctrine & Medical Practice: A Handbook...* 1958. Springfield. CC Thomas. 1st. 8vo. 94p. F/NF. B20. $60.00

BARTRUM, Douglas. *Rhododendrons & Magnolias.* 1957. Lodnon. Garden BC. 176p. VG/dj. A10. $28.00

BARWICK, Garfield. *Administrative Features of Legislation on Restrictive Trade.* 1964. Canberra. Royal Inst Pub Admin. 47p. stapled wrp. M11. $35.00

BARZMAN, Ben. *Twinkle, Twinkle, Little Star.* nd. BC. VG/dj. P3. $8.00

BARZUN & TAYLOR. *Catalogue of Crime.* 1971. Harper Row. 1st. xl. VG/dj. M25. $35.00

BARZUN & TAYLOR. *Catalogue of Crime.* 1989. Harper Row. revised/enlarged. F/dj. M15. $85.00

BARZUN & TAYLOR. *Catalogue of Crime.* 1989. Harper Row. revised/enlarged. VG/dj. G8. $50.00

BAS, C. *Monografias de Zoologia Marina Vol 1...* 1986. Barcelona. 432p. NF. B1. $120.00

BASBANES, Nicholas A. *Gentle Madness.* (1995). NY. Holt. rpt. 584p. F/dj. O10. $35.00

BASBANES, Nicholas A. *Gentle Madness.* 1995. Holt. 1st. NF. B30. $50.00

BASBANES, Nicholas A. *Gentle Madness.* 1995. Holt. 1st. sgn. F/dj. M23. $100.00

BASCOM, H. Clay. *Requited; or, A Knight in Livery.* 1891. Troy, NY. HC Bascom. 1st. author's 1st/last book. 8vo. 390p. gilt gr cloth. B20. $75.00

BASE, Graeme. *Animalia.* 1987. Abrams. 1st. F/dj. M19. $17.50

BASHAM, A.L. *Origins & Development of Classical Hinduism.* 1989. Boston. edit KG Zysk. VG/dj. M17. $20.00

BASHLINE, L. James. *Eastern Trail.* 1972. Freshnet. 1st. 320p. dj. A17. $10.00

BASHLINE & SAULTS. *America's Great Outdoors: Ils Anthology...* 1976. NY. ils/index. dj. A17. $17.50

BASIE, Count. *Good Morning Blues: Autobiography of Count Basie.* 1986. Primus/DIF. 1st. NF/wrp. A14. $14.00

BASILE, Gloria Vitenza. *Jackal Helix: Global 2000 Trilogy: Book II.* 1984. NY. Pinnacle. 1st. VG/wrp. A14. $5.50

BASKIN, Leonard. *Ars Anatomica.* 1972. NY. 1/2500. sgn on justification. 13 pl. case. G7. $225.00

BASKIN, Leonard. *Hermaika. Twenty-Eight Drawings & Woodcut by Leonard Baskin.* 1986. Searsmont, ME. Eremite. 1/75 on wht Arches & bl Fabriano. w/extra sgn ils. AN. B24. $2,500.00

BASKIR & STRAUSS. *Chance & Circumstance: Draft, the War & Vietnam...* 1978. Knopf. 1st. ils/figures/tables/notes/index. NF/dj. R11. $20.00

BASS, Rick. *Deer Pasture.* 1985. TX A&M. 1st. sgn. author's 1st book. F/dj. A24. $250.00

BASS, Rick. *Ninemile Wolves.* 1992. Livingston. Clark City. 1st. sgn. F/F. B3. $75.00

BASS, Rick. *Platte River.* 1994. Houghton Mifflin. 1st. sgn. F/dj. O11. $35.00

**BASS, Rick.** *Watch.* 1989. NY. Norton. 1st. inscr. F/dj. M23. $50.00

**BASS, Rick.** *Wild to the Heart.* 1987. Stackpole. 1st. sgn. ils/sgn Elizabeth Hughes. F/F. B3. $225.00

**BASS, W.W.** *Grand Canyon in Poem & Picture.* 1941. private prt. 3rd. sgn. 12mo. 16p. wrp. F7. $100.00

**BASS, W.W.** *Rhymes & Jingles.* 1909. LA. JF Rowny. tall 8vo. 33p. tan wrp. F7. $175.00

**BASSETT, David L.** *Stereoscopic Atlas of the Human Anatomy: Central Nervous...* 1952. Portland. Sawyers. 4 vol+8 rells steroscopic views. F/box. G7. $175.00

**BASSETT, James.** *Commander Prince, USN.* 1971. NY. S&S. 2nd. bl cloth. NF. M15. $15.00

**BASSETT, John.** *Medical Reports of John Y Bassett, MD: Alabama Student.* 1941. Springfield. 1st. 62p. A13. $50.00

**BASSETT, Les.** *Frontier in Flames.* 1965. Toronto. Thomas Allen. 1st. F/NF. A26. $20.00

**BASSETT, Ronald.** *Tinfish Run.* 1977. Harper Row. 1st. F/NF clip. T11. $25.00

**BASSETT, Sara Ware.** *Flood Tide.* 1921. Boston. Little Brn. 328p. G. G11. $7.00

**BASSFORD, Amy O.** *Home-Thoughts From Afar, Letters of Thomas Moran...* 1967. E Hampton Free Lib. 8vo. 152p. gr cloth. dj. F7. $65.00

**BASTABLE, Bernard;** see Barnard, Robert.

**BATE, W. Jackson.** *Samuel Johnson.* 1977. HBJ. ils. dj. H13. $45.00

**BATE, W.N.** *Frontier Legend. Texas Finale of Capt William F Drannan.* 1954. New Bern, NC. Owen G Dunn Co. 1st. sgn. 68p. NF/wrp. C6. $35.00

**BATEMAN, Richard.** *Outer Coast.* 1985. Harcourt Brace. 1st. F/NF clip. T11. $30.00

**BATES, Carol Ann.** *Tales of the Elders: A Memory Book of Men & Women...* 1977. Chicago. Follett. VG/dj. V4. $15.00

**BATES, Elisha.** *Doctrines of Friends; or, Principles of Christian Religion.* 1893. London. Edward Hicks. 1st. 12mo. 277p. worn. V3. $12.00

**BATES, Joseph D.** *Fishing: An Encyclopedic Guide.* 1988. Gramercy. 3rd. photos/ils. 780p. F/dj. T11. $10.00

**BATES, Joseph D.** *Streamer Fly Tying & Fishing.* 1966. Stackpole. VG. A19. $25.00

**BATES, Joseph D.** *Streamer Fly Tying & Fishing.* 1966. Stackpole. 1st. 8 mc pl. 368p. NF/dj. A17. $50.00

**BATES, Katharine Lee.** *America the Beautiful & Other Poems.* 1911. NY. Crowell. 1st. 305p. teg. VG+. A25. $25.00

**BATES, Katharine Lee.** *American Literature.* 1898. Macmillan. 1st. photos. VG. A25. $15.00

**BATES, Marston.** *Land & Wildlife of South America.* (1968). NY. Time. 4to. ils. 200p. pict brd. F3. $10.00

**BATESON & LESLIE.** *Fairy Tale Palace.* 1996. St Martin. 1st. folio. F. B17. $15.00

**BATHELME, Frederick.** *Brothers.* 1993. NY. Viking. 1st. F/F. H11. $25.00

**BATTAILLE, Charles.** *Nouvelles Recherches sur la Phonation Memoire Presente...* 1861. Paris. Masson. 7 pl. 104p. new cloth. G. G7. $125.00

**BATTIE & COTTLE.** *Sotheby's Concise Encyclopedia of Glass.* 1991. Boston. Little Brn. 1st. ils/index. 208p. F/dj. P4. $60.00

**BATTISCOMBE, Georgina.** *Christina Rossetti: A Divided Life.* 1981. HRW. 1st Am. 8vo. cloth. F/dj. O10. $20.00

**BATTY & PARISH.** *Divided Union: Story of American Civil War.* 1987. Viking/Rainbird. 1st/2nd imp. rem mk. NF/dj. A14. $17.50

**BAUER, Bernhard A.** *Woman & Love.* 1934. NY. Dingwall Rock. 1st thus/2 vol ed. ils. VG+. A25. $40.00

**BAUER, Erwin.** *Bass in America.* 1955. S&S. 1st. ils. 137p. G. S14. $8.50

**BAUER, Erwin.** *Bear in Their World.* 1985. Outdoor Life. photos/biblio. 254p. F/dj. A17. $20.00

**BAUER, Erwin.** *Erwin Bauer's Bear in Their World.* 1990. Outdoor Life. AN/dj. A19. $25.00

**BAUER, Erwin.** *Fisherman's Digest: 8th Anniversary Deluxe Ed.* 1971. Northfield. 320p. wrp. A17. $15.00

**BAUER, Erwin.** *Outdoor Photography.* 1974 (1965). Dutton/Outdoor Life. 2nd revised. VG/dj. S5. $6.00

**BAUER, F.C.** *Illinois Soil Experiment Fields.* 1926. Urbana. 327p. wrp. A10. $20.00

**BAUER, John I.** *Revolution & Tradition in Modern American Art.* 1951. Cambridge. Harvard. ARC/1st. 170p. gr cloth. F/VG. F1. $65.00

**BAUER, K.J.** *Mexican War.* 1992. NE U. ils/maps. F. M4. $15.00

**BAUER, K.J.** *Surfboats & Horse Marines: US Navy Operations...* 1969. Annapolis. 1st. 291p. VG/dj. S15. $40.00

**BAUER, Max.** *Precious Stones: A Popular Account of Their Characters...* (1969). Rutland. Tuttle. 4to. 648p. red linen. K1. $85.00

**BAUER, Raymond A.** *New Man in Soviet Psychology.* 1952. Harvard. 1st. 229p. VG/dj. A2. $25.00

**BAUER & BOEREE.** *Battle of Arhem.* 1967. NY. 1st Am. 254p. G+/dj. B18. $17.50

**BAUM, L. Frank.** *Aunt Jane's Nieces at Work.* (1909). Reilly Lee. 4th. VG/G. B9. $75.00

**BAUM, L. Frank.** *Dorothy & the Wizard in Oz.* 1908?. Reilly Lee. bl bdg. A21. $75.00

**BAUM, L. Frank.** *Emerald City of Oz.* 1910?. Reilly Lee. ils John Neill. dk red bdg. VG. A21. $80.00

**BAUM, L. Frank.** *Father Goose, His Book.* ca 1910. Chicago. Donohue. 6th. ils Denslow. unp. VG/dj. D1. $425.00

**BAUM, L. Frank.** *Handy Mandy in Oz.* 1937. Chicago. Reilly Lee. 1st. ils JR Neill. red cloth/pict label. F/NF. F1. $500.00

**BAUM, L. Frank.** *Land of Oz.* 1931. Reilly Lee. ne. ils John Neill. G. T12. $75.00

**BAUM, L. Frank.** *Land of Oz.* 1961. Chicago. Reilly Lee. 1st thus. ils Dick Martin. mc pict brd. R5. $150.00

**BAUM, L. Frank.** *Life & Adventures of Santa Claus.* 1902. Bowen Merrill. 1st/1st state. ils MC Clark. 206p. red pict cloth. F. H5. $1,000.00

**BAUM, L. Frank.** *Lost Princess of Oz.* 1917. Chicago. Reilly Britton. 1st/1st state (w/ads). all edges yel. lt bl cloth/label. R5. $550.00

**BAUM, L. Frank.** *Mother Goose in Prose.* 1986. NY. Bounty. 1st thus. 8vo. teal brd. AN/dj. T5. $35.00

**BAUM, L. Frank.** *New Wonderland.* 1900. NY. Russell. 1st/1st issue. lg 4to. 16 mc pl. pict bdg. R5. $3,000.00

**BAUM, L. Frank.** *Ozma & the Little Wizard.* nd (1932). Reilly Lee/Jello. 1st Jello ed. ils paper bdg. B27. $195.00

**BAUM, L. Frank.** *Rinkitink in Oz.* 1935. Reilly Lee. ils JR Neill/12 mc pl. 314p. red cloth/label. NF/VG. D1. $400.00

**BAUM, L. Frank.** *Tick-Tok of Oz.* 1914. Chicago. Reilly Lee. ils JR Neill. gray cloth/pict label. VG. M20. $125.00

**BAUM, L. Frank.** *Wizard of Oz.* 1939. Grosset Dunlap. 1st thus. obl 8vo. ils Oskar Lebeck. R5. $75.00

**BAUM, L. Frank.** *Wizard of Oz.* 1944. Bobbs Merrill. ils Evelyn Copelman. VG. A21. $35.00

**BAUM, Vicki.** *Grand Opera.* 1947 (1942). London. Bles. F/G. T12. $10.00

**BAUM, Vicki.** *Hotel Berlin '43.* 1944. Doubleday Doran. 1st. VG/dj. M20. $15.00

**BAUM, Vicki.** *Weeping Wood.* 1943. Doubleday Doran. 531p. VG/dj. B18. $20.00

**BAUMANN, E.D.** *De Doktor en de Geneeskunde.* 1915. Amsterdam. 2 vol in 1. 1st. A13. $75.00

**BAUMGARDT, John.** *How To Prune Almost Everything.* 1968. Barrows. 192p. cloth. VG. A10. $12.00

**BAUMHOFF, Richard.** *Dammed Missouri Valley.* 1951. Knopf. G/dj. A19. $30.00

**BAUMLER, Ernst.** *In Search of the Magic Bullet: Great Adventures...* 1965. Thames Hudson. 1st. photos. 192p. VG/dj. S14. $8.00

**BAUR, John E.** *Dogs on the Frontier.* 1964. San Antonio. Naylor. cloth. dj. D11. $35.00

**BAUSANI, Alessandro.** *Persians From the Earliest Days to 20th Century.* 1975. London. Elek. ils/maps. 204p. cloth. F/dj. Q2. $20.00

**BAUSCH, Richard.** *Violence.* 1992. Houghton Mifflin. 1st. sgn. F/dj. M23. $25.00

**BAWDEN, Nina.** *Robbers.* 1989 (1989). Lee Shepard. 1st thus. 8vo. tan cloth spine/bl brd. F/dj. T5. $20.00

**BAWDEN & MCKITTERICK.** *Wallpapers.* 1989. Curwen. 1/40 deluxe. sgns. w/tipped-in specimens & extra portfolio. AN. B24. $1,750.00

**BAXT, George.** *Marlene Dietrich Murder Case.* 1993. St Martin. 1st. sgn. NF/VG. G8. $30.00

**BAXT, George.** *Parade of Cockeyed Creatures.* 1967. Random. 1st. VG/G+. G8. $25.00

**BAXT, George.** *Talking Pictures Murder Case.* 1990. St Martin. 1st. VG/dj. M20. $15.00

**BAXTER, Charles.** *First Light.* 1987. NY. Viking. 1st. sgn. F/dj. R14. $90.00

**BAXTER, Charles.** *First Light.* 1987. Viking. 1st. F/dj. A24/H11. $40.00

**BAXTER, Charles.** *Relative Stranger.* 1990. NY. Norton. 1st. F/F. B3. $35.00

**BAXTER, Charles.** *Shadow Play.* 1993. nY. Norton. ARC. F/wrp. M23. $30.00

**BAXTER, Charles.** *Through the Safety Net.* 1985. Viking. 1st. sgn. F/F. D10. $55.00

**BAXTER, George Owen;** see Faust, Frederick S.

**BAXTER, Richard.** *Saints' Everlasting Rest.* nd. NY. Am Tract Soc. 444p. half leather. H10. $20.00

**BAY, Kenneth E.** *How To Tie Fresh-Water Flies.* 1974. Winchester. 1st. photos. 152p. VG/dj. S14. $20.00

**BAYER, Henry G.** *Belgians: First Settlers in New York & in Middle States.* 1925. Devin-Adair. ils. 373p. VG. B18. $27.50

**BAYER, William.** *Great Movies.* 1973. Grosset Dunlap. 252p. VG/dj. C5. $12.50

**BAYER, William.** *Peregrine.* 1981. NY. Congdon Lattes. 1st. F/dj. A23. $38.00

**BAYLOR, Don.** *Don Baylor.* 1989. St Martin. 1st. inscr. F/dj. P8. $45.00

**BAYNES & MOSS.** *Byzantium: Introduction to East Roman Civilization.* 1948. Oxford. Clarendon. 8vo. 3 fld maps/48 pl. cloth. xl. VG. W1. $20.00

**BEACH, Belle.** *Riding & Driving for Women.* 1978. Croton-on-Hudson. Northland. facs. F/dj. O3. $45.00

**BEACH, Charles Amory.** *Air Service Boys Flying for France.* 1919. World Syndicate. VG/dj. M20. $15.00

**BEACH, Edward L.** *Dust on the Sea.* 1972. HRW. 3rd. 8vo. NF/dj. M7. $12.00

**BEACH, S.A.** *Apples of New York.* 1905. Albany. Lyon. 2 vol. 1st. ils/index. VG. H10. $200.00

**BEACH, Sylvia.** *Shakespeare & Company.* 1959. Harcourt Brace. 1st. 8vo. 220p. yel cloth. NF/dj. J3. $75.00

**BEACH, Sylvia.** *Ulysses in Paris.* 1956. Harcourt Brace. 1st. pict brd. F. M24. $200.00

**BEACH & NIEBUHR.** *Christian Ethics: Sources of the Living Tradition.* 1955. Ronald. 496p. VG/dj. B29. $12.00

**BEACHER, L.** *Contact Lens Technique: Textbook for Practitioners.* 1946. self pub. 4th. ils. VG. E6. $45.00

**BEADLE, J.H.** *Life in Utah; or, Mysteries & Crimes of Mormonism.* 1870. Phil. Nat Pub. 540p. gilt cloth. B18. $65.00

**BEAGLE, Peter S.** *Folk of the Air.* 1986. Ballantine. 1st. F/NF. M21. $14.00

**BEAGLEHOLE.** *Life of Capt James Cook.* 1974. Stanford. 50 pl/maps. 771p. NF/NF. A4. $95.00

**BEAHM, George.** *Stephen King Companion.* 1989. Andrews McMell. 1st. 1/1000. sgn. F/NF. P3. $35.00

**BEAHM, George.** *Stephen King Story.* 1991. Kansas City. Andrews McMell. 1st. VG/dj. L1. $50.00

**BEAL, Alvin C.** *Gladiolus & Its Culture.* 1927. Orange Judd. 1st. ils/index. 124p. H10. $17.50

**BEAL, F.E.L.** *Birds of California in Relation to Fruit Industry.* 1907 & 1910. GPO. USDA. 2 parts. 100p+96p. wrp. A10. $30.00

**BEALE & TUBERVILLE.** *History of the Ninth Virginia Calvary in War Between States.* 1899. Richmond, VA. BJ Johnson. 1st. 192p. gr cloth/rb. VG. M8. $2,500.00

**BEAMER, Esther K.** *Essence of Aspen.* 1976. Worcester. St Onge. mini. 1/1000. platinum edges. bl prt/silvered bl leather. B24. $75.00

**BEAMISH, Richard J.** *Boy's Story of Lindbergh: The Lone Eagle.* 1928. Phil. Winston. 8vo. photos. VG+. C14. $18.00

**BEAN, Amelia.** *Fancher Train.* 1958. NY. Doubleday. 1st. 8vo. 356p. brn/wht cloth. VG/dj. F7. $50.00

**BEAN, Ellis.** *Memoir of Col Ellis P Bean.* 1930. Dallas. BC of TX. 1st. 1/200. brn cloth-backed brd. F. w/promo. M24. $200.00

**BEAN, George E.** *Turkey's Southern Shore.* 1979. London. Benn. 2nd revised. ils/pl/map ep. 154p. cloth. VG/dj. Q2. $26.50

**BEAN, R. Bennett.** *Peopling of Virginia.* 1969 (1928). Crescendo Pub. rpt. photos/charts. 302p. B10. $45.00

**BEAN, R.B.** *Sir William Osler From His Bedside Teachings & Writings...* 1950. NY. Schuman. dj. G7. $75.00

**BEAN, Ruth.** *All-in-One Oven Meals.* 1952. Bramhall. G/dj. A16. $8.00

**BEAR, Fred.** *Field Notes.* 1993. Derrydale. photos. 288p. aeg. gilt leather. F. A17. $35.00

**BEAR, Greg.** *Eternity.* 1988. Warner. 1st. An/dj. M21. $15.00

**BEAR, Greg.** *Heads.* 1991. St Martin. 1st Am. sgn. F/dj. O11. $30.00

**BEAR, Greg.** *Moving Mars.* 1993. NY. Tor. 1st. sgn. F/dj. O11. $35.00

**BEARD, Alice.** *Mother Goose Movies in Eleven Reels.* 1917. NY. Stokes. 1st. lg 4to. 11 rhymes w/fld-over flaps. cloth. R5. $275.00

**BEARD, Charles A.** *American Government & Politics.* 1941 (1939). Macmillan. 8th. 8vo. xl. G. A2. $10.00

**BEARD, Charles A.** *Century of Progress.* 1933. Harper. 1st. gilt red brd. G. A28. $7.50

BEARD, Charles. *Reformation of 16th Century in Relation to Modern Thought...* 1927. London. Constable. 451p. G. H10. $22.50

BEARD, James. *New James Beard.* 1981. Knopf. 1st. hc. VG/dj. A16. $22.50

BEARD, John S. *Proteas of Tropical Africa.* 1992. Kenthurst, Australia. ils/maps/photos. 112p. AN. B26. $65.00

BEARD, Patten. *Twilight Tales.* 1934. Rand McNally. 1st. ils Ruth Caroline Eger. G. B11. $15.00

BEARD & BEARD. *America in Midpassage, Vol 1.* 1939. Macmillan. 1st. VG/dj. V4. $7.50

BEARDSLEY, Aubrey. *Early Work of Aubrey Beardsley.* 1920. London. John Lane. Bodley Head. 3rd. 157 pl. bl cloth. VG/dj. F1. $150.00

BEARDSLEY. *Hispano-Classical Translations ...1482-1699.* 1970. Duquesne. 187p. F/VG. A4. $135.00

BEASLEY, Frederick. *Search of Truth in Science of the Human Mind, Part First.* 1822. Phil. Potter. 561p. contemporary calf. VG. G1. $250.00

BEASLEY, H.M. *Beasley Versus Culbertson: Official...Record...Bridge Match.* ca 1933. VG. S1. $25.00

BEASLEY-MURRAY, G.R. *Jesus & the Kingdom of God.* 1986. Eerdmans. 446p. VG/dj. B29. $17.50

BEATH, Robert B. *Grand Army Blue-Book Containing Rules & Regulations...* 1884. Phil. 168p. gilt bl brd. H6. $42.00

BEATH, Warren Newton. *Death of James Dean: What Really Happened on Day He Crashed?* 1986. NY. Grove. 1st. F/dj. A14. $25.00

BEATIE, R.H. *Road to Manassas: Growth of Union Command...* 1961. Cooper Square. 1st. 285p. VG/dj. S16. $35.00

BEATON, M.C. *Death of a Hussy.* 1990. NY. 1st. F/NF. H11. $20.00

BEATTIE, Ann. *Burning House.* 1982. Random. 1st. F/NF. R14. $45.00

BEATTIE, Ann. *Chilly Scenes of Winter.* 1976. Doubleday. 1st. author's 1st novel. VG/dj. B30. $100.00

BEATTIE, Ann. *Falling in Place.* 1980. Random. 1st. author's 4th book. F/F. A24. $35.00

BEATTIE, Ann. *Spectacles.* 1985. NY. Ariel/Workman Pub. ils Winslow Pels. VG/dj. V4. $22.50

BEATTIE, Ann. *What Was Mine.* 1991. Random. 1st. sgn. F/dj. B30. $30.00

BEATTY, Bessie. *Red Heart of Russia.* 1918. NY. Century. 1st. photos. 480p. VG+. A25. $40.00

BEATTY, Jerome. *Matthew Loony & the Space Pirates.* 1972. Addison. 1st. ils Gahan Wilson. VG/dj. S18. $11.00

BEATTY, John. *Acolhuans: A Narrative of Sojourn & Adventure...* 1902. Columbus. 1st. ils. 423p. G. B18. $75.00

BEATTY & MARKS. *Precious Metals of Medicine.* 1975. Scribner. 1st. 8vo. 294p. F/NF. C14. $20.00

BEATY, John O. *Swords in the Dawn: Story of First Englishman.* 1937. Longman Gr. 1st Am. 12mo. 212p. NF. C14. $12.00

BEAUCHAMP, Loren; see Silverberg, Robert.

BEAUDRY, Evien C. *Puppy Stories.* 1934. Saalfield. ils Diana Thorne. VG. A21. $45.00

BEAULIEU, Victor-Levy. *Jack Kerouac: A Chicken Essay.* 1979. Toronto. Coach House. 2nd. NF/wrp. B2. $25.00

BEAUMON, Cyril W. *Design for the Ballet.* 1937. London. The Studio. ltd. 4to. ils. 152p. bl cloth. F1. $85.00

BEAUMONT, Arthur. *Artificial Manures.* 1946. Orange Judd. VG. V4. $30.00

BEAUMONT, BONNIE & MCLAUGH-LAN. *Qanat, Kariz & Khattara. Traditional Water Systems...* 1989. Wisbech. ils/figures/diagrams. 305p. VG/dj. Q2. $30.00

BEAURLINE, L.A. *Jonson & Elizabethan Comedy: Essays in Dramatic Rhetoric.* 1978. Huntington Lib. 1st. F/dj. O4. $20.00

BEAUS & MORALES. *Grand Canyon Geology.* 1990. Northern AZ Pr. 8vo. ils/photos/biblio/index. 518p. NF. F7. $24.00

BEBBINGTON, William. *Rogues Go Racing.* nd. Good & Betts. VG/dj. M20. $25.00

BECHDOLT, Frederick R. *When the West Was Young.* 1922. Century. 309p. VG. J2. $125.00

BECHET, Sidney. *Treat It Gentle.* 1960. Hill Wang. 1st. F/NF. B2. $50.00

BECHSTEIN, Ludwig. *Rabbit Catcher & Other Fairy Tales.* 1962. Macmillan. probable 1st. folio. VG. B17. $15.00

BECHTEREV, Vladimir M. *General Principles of Human Reflexology: An Intro...* 1933. London. Jarrolds. 1st Eng-language ed. 467P. bl buckram. VG. G1. $100.00

BECK, Doreen. *Book of Bottle Collecting.* 1953. Norton. 1st Am. VG/dj. M21. $15.00

BECK, Frank O. *Hobohemia.* 1956. Rindge, NH. Richard R Smith. 1st. F/VG. B2. $50.00

BECK, Theodric Romeyn. *Elements of Medical Jurisprudence.* 1829. London. 3rd. 640p. A13. $150.00

BECK, Ulrich. *Ecological Politics in an Age of Risk.* 1995. Polity Pr. trans from German. 216p. AN/dj. S15. $10.00

BECK & MASSMAN. *Rich Men, Single Women.* 1988. Delacorte. 1st. F/dj. A14. $17.50

BECKDOLT, Jack. *Mystery at Hurricane Hill.* 1951. Dutton. 1st. VG/dj. M20. $15.00

BECKER, Ethel A. *Treasury of Alaskana.* 1977. Bonanza. photos. VG/dj. A19. $25.00

BECKER, Stephen. *Blue Eyed Shan.* 1982. Random. 1st. F/G. T12. $20.00

BECKER & LINSCOTT. *Bedside Book of Famous French Stories.* 1945. Random. 1st. VG. T12. $15.00

BECKETT, Samuel. *Echo's Bones & Other Precipitates.* 1935. Europa. 1/327. F/wrp. B4. $1,000.00

BECKETT, Samuel. *Lessness.* 1970. London. Calder Boyars. 1st. 1/100. sgn. trans from French. F/case. L3. $500.00

BECKETT, Samuel. *Lost Ones.* 1984. New Overbrook. 1st revised. 1/250. 7 sgn prts. portfolio/box. AN. B24. $3,000.00

BECKFORD, Peter. *Thoughts on Hunting.* 1926. Methuen. 6th. ils. G. A21. $45.00

BECKFORD, Peter. *Thoughts Upon Hare & Fox Hunting in a Series of Letters...* 1932. NY. Cape/Ballou. 16 mc engravings. 327p. VG. H10. $50.00

BECKFORD, William. *Dreams, Waking Thoughts & Incidents...* 1971. Jeaneck. Fairleigh Dickinson. 1st. dj. H13. $65.00

BECKFORD, William. *Journal of William Beckford in Portugal & Spain 1787-1788.* 1955. NY. John Day. 1st Am. H13. $65.00

BECKFORD, William. *Life at Fonthill...* 1957. London. Hart Davis. ils. H13. $65.00

BECKFORD, William. *Recollections of Late Wm Beckford of Fonthill...* nd. Bath. facs. 1/750. H13. $65.00

BECKFORD, William. *William Beckford of Fonthill: Writer, Traveller...* 1960. Yale. F. H13. $65.00

BECKLAND, Eugene. *Physiological Mysteries & Revelations in Love, Courtship...* 1844. NY. Holland Glover. 12mo. 256p. Victorian cloth. G7. $45.00

BECKWITH, John. *Art of Constantinople: An Introduction to Byzantine Art...* 1961. London. Phaidon. 8vo. ils. 184p. cloth. G+/torn. Q2. $25.00

**BECKWITH & KNOX.** *Delta Force.* 1983. HBJ. 1st. photos. VG/dj. S14. $8.50

**BEDDALL, Barbara.** *Wallace & Bates in the Tropics.* (1969). Macmillan. 1st. 241p. dj. F3. $20.00

**BEDDARD, F.F.** *Natural History in Zoological Gardens...* 1905. London. Constable. ils/pl. 310p. VG. M12. $45.00

**BEDDIE.** *Bibliography of Capt James Cook, RN, FRS, Circumnavigator.* 1970. 2nd/revised. 4808 entries. VG/VG. A4. $200.00

**BEDDOES, Dick.** *Greatest Hockey Stories.* 1990. Macmillan. 1st Canadian. F/dj. T12. $20.00

**BEDELL, L. Frank.** *Shetland Pony.* 1959. Ames, IA. 1st. VG. O3. $40.00

**BEDFORD, Annie North.** *Susie's New Stove. Little Chef's Cookbook.* 1950. Little Golden. 1st A ed. 8vo. VG. M5. $40.00

**BEDFORD, Gunning S.** *Principles & Practice of Obstetrics.* 1862. NY. Wood. 100 wood engravings. 731p. cloth/rb spine. G7. $115.00

**BEDFORD, William.** *Catwalking.* 1993. London. Macmillan. 1st. NF/dj. A14. $28.00

**BEDICHEK, Roy.** *Adventures With a Texas Naturalist.* 1961. Austin, TX. VG/dj. A19. $25.00

**BEDINI, S.A.** *Thomas Jefferson: Statesman of Science.* 1990. NY. 1st. ils. 616p. F/dj. M4. $30.00

**BEE, Clair.** *Chip Hilton: A Pass & A Prayer.* (1951). Grosset Dunlap. not 1st. 216p. F/dj. H1. $15.00

**BEE, Robert L.** *Crosscurrents Along the Colorado. Impact of Government...* 1981. Tucson. 184p. pict wrp. F7. $15.00

**BEEBE, Charles William.** *Pheasants, Their Lives & Homes.* 1937. London. Robert Hale. 2 vol in 1. ils. G. H10. $75.00

**BEEBE, Lucius.** *Central Pacific & the Southern Pacific Railroads...* 1966. Howell North. Centennial ed. ils/photos/index. 631p. VG/poor. S16. $50.00

**BEEBE, William.** *Half Mile Down.* 1934. Harcourt Brace. 1st. 8vo. ils. VG/torn. B18. $22.50

**BEEBE, William.** *Half Mile Down.* 1934. NY. 1st. ils. 344p. F. B14. $35.00

**BEEBE & CLEGG.** *Mixed Train Daily: Book of Short-Line Railroads.* 1947. NY. sgns. VG/G. B30. $65.00

**BEECH & COLLEY.** *Cognitive Approaches to Reading.* 1987. Chichester. John Wiley. 315p. red brd. G1. $65.00

**BEECHER, Henry Ward.** *Norwood: Village Life in New England in 19th Century.* 1868. Scribner. 549p. G. S17. $10.00

**BEECHER.** *Miss Beecher's Domestic Receipt Book...* 1857 (1846). rb. E6. $75.00

**BEECKMAN, Ross.** *Last Woman.* 1909. NY. Watts. ils HC Christie. VG. M20. $15.00

**BEEDING, Francis.** *Death Walks in Eastrepps.* 1931. Mystery League. 1st. VG. N4. $27.50

**BEEDING, Francis.** *Eleven Were Brave.* 1941. NY. Harper. 1st Am. F/dj. B4. $150.00

**BEER, Thomas.** *Mauve Decade: American Life at End of 19th Century.* 1926. Knopf. 4th. G. P12. $6.00

**BEERBOHM, Max.** *Rosetti & His Circle.* 1922. London. Heinemann. 1st. 1/380. prt 1 side only/mtd ils. sgn. xl. B14. $195.00

**BEERY, Jesse.** *How I Trained My Trick Horse Charley.* nd. np. VG. O3. $18.00

**BEERY, Jesse.** *Illustrated Course in Horse Training.* 1944. Pleasant Hill. 8 booklets. VG. O3. $35.00

**BEETLE, Alan A.** *Distribution of the Native Grasses of California.* 1947. Berkeley. 184 distribution maps. VG. B26. $24.00

**BEETLES, Chris.** *Mabel Lucie Atwell.* 1988. Eng. Pavilion Books. 1st thus. 4to. 120p. F/heavy bl wrp. T5. $45.00

**BEGIEBING, Robert J.** *Strange Death of Mistress Coffin.* 1991. Algonquin. 1st. NF/dj. M20. $15.00

**BEHAN, Brendan.** *Hold Your Hour & Have Another.* 1963. Little Brn. 1st. F/VG. M19. $25.00

**BEHN, Harry.** *Faraway Lurs.* 1968 (1963). World. 8vo. 190p. red cloth. T5. $20.00

**BEHN, Jack.** *.45-70' Rifles.* (1956). Stackpole. 1st. inscr pres. ils. 137p. G/tattered. H10. $50.00

**BEHN, Noel.** *Seventh Silent Men.* 1984. Arbor. 1st. NF/dj. A14. $21.00

**BEHNKE, F.L.** *Natural History of Termites.* 1977. NY. Scribner. 8vo. ils. 118p. NF/VG. M12. $20.00

**BEHRENS, Elsa.** *Cooking the Spanish Way.* 1960. London. Spring Books. VG/dj. M20. $15.00

**BEHRENS, Helen Kindler.** *Diplomatic Dining.* 1974. NY Times. G/dj. A16. $12.50

**BEHRENS, June.** *Looking at Children.* 1977. Chicago. Adventures in Art series. 8vo. 31p. NF/VG. T5. $25.00

**BEHRMAN, S.N.** *Duveen.* 1951. Random. G/dj. A19. $25.00

**BEIFUSS, Joan.** *At the River I Stand.* 1st. sgn. VG. B30. $60.00

**BEILHARZ & LOPEZ.** *We Were 49ers! Chilean Accounts of California Gold Rush.* 1976. Pasadena, CA. Ward Ritchie. 1st. F/VG. O4. $15.00

**BEIM, Lorraine.** *Carol's Side of the Street.* 1951. World. ils Malman. VG/clip. B36. $6.50

**BELAYEV, Alexander.** *Amphibian.* nd. Moscow. Foreign Languages Pub House. 12mo. tan cloth. VG/worn. F1. $30.00

**BELDEN, Bauman L.** *Indian Peace Medals Issed in the United States.* 1966. Milford, CT. rpt of 1927. 1/350. 46p. VG/dj. B18. $65.00

**BELDEN, George P.** *Belden, the White Chief; or, Twelve Years Among Wild...* 1870. Cincinnati/NY. CF Vent. 1st. 8vo. ils. 513p. O1. $175.00

**BELFORD, Barbara.** *Violet.* 1990. NY. 1st. dj. T9. $12.00

**BELITT, Ben.** *Piedras del Cielo: Skystones. Poemas del Pablo Neruda.* 1981. Emanon. 1/60. sgn. 2 popups. bilingual text. Gray Parrot bdg. AN/dj/box. B24. $950.00

**BELKNAP, Buzz.** *Powell Centennial Grand Canyon River Guide.* 1973. Westwater Book. waterpoof ed. 8vo. VG/bl wrp. F7. $15.00

**BELKNAP, Charles E.** *History of the Michigan Organizations at Chickamauga...* 1863. Lansing, MI. Robert Smith. 2nd. G. V4. $100.00

**BELKNAP, D.P.** *Probate Law & Practice of California...* 1873. SF. Bancroft. 3rd. contemporary sheep. M11. $150.00

**BELL, A.N.** *Climatology & Mineral Waters of the United States...* 1885. NY. Wm Wood. 1st. lg 8vo. 386p. VG. B14. $75.00

**BELL, Anne Oliver.** *Diary of Virginia Woolf.* 1984. HBJ. 1st Am. NF/dj. W2. $30.00

**BELL, Anne Oliver.** *Diary of Virginia Woolf, Vol I: 1915-1919.* 1977. London. Hogarth. 1st. 356p. VG. M10. $15.00

**BELL, Charles.** *Anatomy of the Brain, Explained in Series of Engravings.* 1802. London. Longman Rees. 12 engraved pl (11 hand colored). brd/new rb/rpr. G7. $3,950.00

**BELL, Charles.** *Essays on the Anatomy of Expression in Painting.* 1984. Birmingham. facs of 1806 London. 4to. 186p. full leather. A13. $100.00

**BELL, Christine.** *Perez Family.* 1990. NY. Norton. 1st. author's 2nd novel. F/dj. B4. $75.00

BELL, Clare. *Ratha's Creature.* 1986. London. 1st. 8vo. VG/dj. M5. $40.00

BELL, Eric Temple. *Handmaiden of the Sciences.* 1937. Baltimore. Williams/Wilkins. 1st. 8vo. 216p. cloth. K5. $25.00

BELL, Gertrude. *Earlier Letters of Gertrude Bell.* 1937. London. Benn. 8vo. 347p. cloth. G. Q2. $41.50

BELL, H.W. *Baker-Street Studies.* 1934. London. Constable. 12mo. top edge gr. gilt brn coth. F. R3. $175.00

BELL, James P. *Our Quaker Friends of Ye Olden Times.* (1905). Lynchburg. JP Bell. ils. 287p. G. B10. $65.00

BELL, Jean K. *Tucky the Tiny Clown by Jean B Kell...* 1951. Asbury Park, NJ. Schuyler Pr. 14p. pict brd. R5. $250.00

BELL, Josephine. *Catalyst.* 1966. Macmillan. 1st Am. NF/dj. G8. $10.00

BELL, Josephine. *Double Doom.* 1957. Hodder Stoughton. 1st. G. G8. $10.00

BELL, Josephine. *Easy Prey.* 1959. Hodder Stoughton. 1st. VG/dj. G8. $30.00

BELL, Lilian. *As Seen by Me.* 1900. Harper. 306p. cloth. VG. W1. $28.00

BELL, Madison Smartt. *All Soul's Rising.* 1995. Pantheon. ltd. sgn tipped-in leaf. F/dj. R14. $35.00

BELL, Madison Smartt. *All Souls' Rising.* 1995. Pantheon. ARC. F. B4. $65.00

BELL, Madison Smartt. *Barking Man & Other Stories.* 1990. NY. Ticknor. 1st. F/F. H11. $30.00

BELL, Madison Smartt. *Doctor Sleep.* 1991. HBJ. 1st. inscr. NF/F. R14. $50.00

BELL, Madison Smartt. *Year of Silence.* 1987. Ticknor Fields. 1st. inscr. NF/VG. R14. $45.00

BELL, Quentin. *Virginia Woolf: Biography.* 1973. London. Hogarth. 2 vol. G. M10. $25.00

BELL, Richard. *Qur'an: Translated With Critial Re-Arrangement of Surahs.* 1939. Edinburgh. Clark. 2 vol. 8vo. cloth. VG. Q2. $36.50

BELL, Sam Hanna. *Theater in Ulster: A Survey of Dramatic Movement in Ulster.* 1981. Humanities. VG/dj. M17. $25.00

BELL, William Dixon. *Secret of Tibet.* 1938. Goldsmith. VG/dj. M20. $15.00

BELL & NATHAN. *Legal Hand-Book of Practical Laws & Procedure...* 1905. Grahamstown. Law Pub/African Book Co. red cloth/rb. xl. M11. $75.00

BELLAH, James Warner. *Ward 20.* 1946. Doubleday. 1st. VG/dj. M20. $38.00

BELLAIRS, George. *Death in the Wasteland.* 1964. London House. 1st. Edward Gorey cover. F/VG. M19. $17.50

BELLAMY, Edward. *Duke of Stockbridge: Romance of Shays' Rebellion.* 1962. Belknap. 1st thus. F/dj. N2. $15.00

BELLAS, R.C. *Mother of Exiles.* 1986. Baltimore. Xavier. mini. 1/250. dk gr cloth/gilt picture. B24. $45.00

BELLE, Pamela. *Lodestar.* 1987. Bodley Head. 1st. NF/dj. A14. $25.00

BELLER, Joe. *Cowboys & Indians: Characters in Oil & Bronze.* 1975. OK U. ils. F/dj. M4. $25.00

BELLESILES, M.A. *Revolutionary Outlaws: Ethan Allen...* 1993. VA U. 428p. F/dj. M4. $35.00

BELLINGHAUSEN, Thaddeus. *Voyage of Capt Bellinghausen to Antarctic Seas 1819-21.* 1945. London. Hakluyt Soc. 1st Eng-language. 8vo. ils/maps. 259p. bl cloth. F. O1. $300.00

BELLNER & WATERBURY. *Patrons & Clients in Mediterranean Societies.* 1977. London. Duckworth. 348p. cloth. VG/dj. Q2. $24.00

BELLOC, Hilaire. *Emerald of Catherine the Great.* 1926. London. Arrowsmith. 1st. NF/dj. M15. $250.00

BELLOC, Hilaire. *Missing Masterpiece.* 1929. Harper. 1st. NF. T12. $250.00

BELLOC, Hilarie. *Conversation With a Cat & Others.* 1931. London. Cassell. 1st. G. B27. $45.00

BELLONCI, Maria. *Private Renaissance.* 1989. Morrow. 1st Eng-language. F/dj. A14. $21.00

BELLOW, Saul. *Henderson the Rain King.* 1959. Viking. 1st. F/dj. S9. $250.00

BELLOW, Saul. *Herzog.* 1964. Weidenfeld Nicholson. 1st. NF/dj. B4. $125.00

BELLOW, Saul. *Humboldt's Gift.* 1975. Viking. 1st. F/dj. O11. $85.00

BELLOW, Saul. *Humboldt's Gift.* 1975. Viking. 1st. VG/dj. B30. $25.00

BELLOW, Saul. *More Die of Heartbreak.* 1987. Morrow. 1st. F/F. B3/H11. $25.00

BELLOW, Saul. *Mr Sammler's Planet.* 1970. Viking. 1st. F/NF. D10. $65.00

BELLOW, Saul. *Mr Sammler's Planet.* 1970. Viking. 1st. sgn. F/dj. O11. $140.00

BELLOW, Saul. *Recent American Fiction.* 1963. WA, DC. Lib of Congress. 1st. 12p. F/prt wrp. O11. $65.00

BELLOW, Saul. *Seize the Day.* 1956. Viking. 1st. VG+/dj. A24. $125.00

BELLOWS, A. *Philosophy of Eating.* 1873 (1870). VG. E6. $45.00

BELOT, Jean. *Les Oeuvres de M Jean Belot...* (1647). Rouen. Jacques Caillo. 2 parts in 1. woodcuts/lg fld pl. contemporary vellum. K1. $850.00

BELTING, Natalia. *Moon Was Tired of Walking on Air.* 1992. Houghton Mifflin. 1st. ils Will Hillenbrand. 48p. dj. F3. $15.00

BELVES, Pierre. *Decoupages 4.* 1948. Paris. Flammarion. sq 8vo. cutouts intact. stiff paper wrp. R5. $50.00

BEMBO, Pietro. *Il Primo (Second O) Volume Delle Lettere di M Pietro Bembo.* 1562. Venice. Girolamo Scotto. 2 vol in 1. 12mo. contemporary vellum. K1. $400.00

BEMELMANS, Ludwig. *Castle Number Nine.* 1937. Viking. 1st. VG/G. P2. $75.00

BEMELMANS, Ludwig. *Hansi.* 1934. NY. Viking. 1st. author's 1st book. pict brd/dj. R5. $485.00

BEMELMANS, Ludwig. *Madeline & the Gypsies.* 1959. NY. Viking. 1st. ils. 56p. F/VG. D1. $250.00

BEN-GURION, David. *Jews in Their Land.* 1974. Doubleday. 1st revised. ils. 351p. VG/dj. B5. $25.00

BENARDETE, Mair Jose. *Judeo-Spanish Ballads From New York.* 1981. Berkeley. U CA. 149p. G/dj. C5. $20.00

BENARY-ISBERT, Margot. *Blue Mystery.* 1957. Harcourt Brace. 1st. 8vo. 190p. red cloth. VG/G. T5. $22.00

BENAYOUN, Robert. *Look of Buster Keaton.* 1982. St Martin. 1st Am. F/NF. C9. $210.00

BENCHLEY, Nathaniel. *Beyond the Mists.* 1975. Harper Row. 1st. 8vo. cloth. F/VG. D4. $30.00

BENCHLEY, Peter. *Island.* 1979. Doubleday. 1st. F/NF. H11. $40.00

BENCHLEY, Peter. *Jaws.* 1974. Doubleday. 1st. VG/dj. M21. $30.00

BENCHLEY, Robert. *No Poems; or, Around the World Backwards & Sideways.* 1932. Harper. 1st. ils Gluyas Williams. NF/dj. B4. $475.00

BENDER, Carl B. *New Holland Grassland Manual.* 1962. New Holland, PA. 186p. VG. A10. $12.00

BENDER, Michael. *Waiting for Filippo, Life of Renaissance Architect.* 1995. Pavilion Books. 1st. 4to. F. B17. $20.00

**BENDER & MCCUEN.** *Indochina War: Why Our Policy Failed.* 1975. Anoka. Greenhaven. 122p. xl. wrp. R11. $10.00

**BENDFORD, Robert.** *Doctors in the Sky: Story of Aeor Medical Association.* 1955. Springfield. 1st. 326p. dj. A13. $50.00

**BENEDICT, David.** *General History of the Baptist Denomination...* 1850. NY. Colby. ils/index. 970p+ads. lacks spine. G. H10. $85.00

**BENEDICT, Howard.** *Quarter Century of Space Achievement.* 1984. Woodlands, TX. Pioneer Pub. 4to. 350p. VG/dj. K5. $40.00

**BENEDICT, Pinckney.** *Town Smokes.* 1987. Princeton. 1st. sgn. author's 1st book. F/wrp. M23. $75.00

**BENEDICTUS, David.** *Fourth of June.* 1962. London. 1st. dj. T9. $40.00

**BENEDIKT & WELLWARTH.** *Modern Spanish Theatre: Anthology of Plays.* 1968. NY. 1st. VG/dj. M17. $20.00

**BENET, Stephen Vincent.** *John Brown's Body.* 1928. Doubleday Doran. 1st. sgn. G+. B30. $20.00

**BENET, Stephen Vincent.** *John Brown's Body.* 1928. Doubleday Doran. 1st. 1/201. sgn. 8vo. 376p. F. w/TLS. H5. $500.00

**BENET, Stephen Vincent.** *John Brown's Body.* 1954 (1928). NY. Rinehart. rpt. cloth. NF. M8. $15.00

**BENFORD, Gregory.** *Across the Sea of Suns.* 1984. Timescape. 1st. rem mk. F/dj. M25. $25.00

**BENGIS, Ingrid.** *Combat in the Erogenous Zone.* 1972. Knopf. 1st. 8vo. 260p. VG/dj. B11. $15.00

**BENGTSON & KUZ.** *Photographic Atlas of Civil War Injuries.* 1966. Medical Staff Pr. ils. dj. G7. $125.00

**BENITEZ, Fernando.** *In the Magic Land of Peyote.* 1975. Austin, TX. 1st. F/NF. B2. $60.00

**BENJAMIN, Judah Philip.** *Speach of Hon JP Benjamin, of LA, on Rights of Secession...* 1860. WA, DC. Lemuel Towers. 1st. 16p. orig self-wrp. M8. $150.00

**BENJAMIN, L.T.** *History of American Psychology in Notes & News 1883-1945.* 1989. NY. Kraus. thick 8vo. 592p. gray buckram. F. G1. $75.00

**BENJAMIN, Mary A.** *Autographs: A Key to Collecting.* 1946. NY. RR Bowker. 1st. 8vo. 305p. F/NF. O10. $40.00

**BENKOVITZ, Miriam J.** *Frederick Rolfe: Baron Corvo.* 1977. NY. photos. VG/dj. M17. $25.00

**BENKOVITZ, Miriam J.** *Rolfe: A Biography.* 1977. NY. 1st. dj. T9. $25.00

**BENNEMAN, G.W.** *Wind & Tide: Homeward Bound.* 1891. NY. Powell. 1st. VG+. S13. $55.00

**BENNETT, Arnold.** *Lord Raingo.* 1926. NY. Geo Doran. 393p. G. G11. $15.00

**BENNETT, Arnold.** *Old Wives' Tale.* 1941. LEC. 2 vol. 1/1500. ils. gr cloth. dj/case. K1. $100.00

**BENNETT, Charles E.** *Quest for Glory.* 1991. U NC. 1st. F/dj. T11. $20.00

**BENNETT, Edna Mae.** *Turquoise & the Indian.* 1970. Chicago. Sage. F/dj. A19. $40.00

**BENNETT, Emmett.** *Pylos Tablets: Texts of the Inscriptions Found, 1939-1954.* 1955. Princeton. ils. 252p. cloth/orig covers bound in. VG. Q2. $46.50

**BENNETT, F.** *Monitor & the Navy Under Steam.* 1900. 28 pl. NF. E6. $45.00

**BENNETT, Geoffrey.** *Famous Harness Horses, Vol II, 1916-1931.* 1932. Welbeeson. 1/600. VG. A21. $500.00

**BENNETT, Ian.** *Rugs & Carpets of the World.* 1988. Secaucus, NJ. Wellfleet. 351p. NF/case. W1. $75.00

**BENNETT, Ira E.** *History of the Panama Canal, Its Construction & Builders.* 1915. WA, DC. Hist Pub. Builder's ed. 4to. 543p. VG. B11. $150.00

**BENNETT, John C.** *Christians & the State.* 1958. Scribner. 302p. VG/dj. B29. $11.50

**BENNETT, Lee.** *Elves, Fairies & Gnomes.* 1980. Knopf. 1st. obl 8vo. ils. VG/dj. B17. $25.00

**BENNETT, Margaret.** *From Baedeker to Worse: What My Guidebook Never Told Me.* 1968. Dodd Mead. 1st. VG/clip. M20. $15.00

**BENNETT, Paul A.** *Books & Printing: A Treasury for Typophiles.* 1951. NY/Cleveland. World. 1st. ils. 418p. F/dj. O10. $45.00

**BENNETT, Paul.** *Books & Printing: A Treasury for Typophiles.* 1951. Cleveland. World. 1st. 417p. gilt gray cloth. VG/dj. F1. $25.00

**BENNETT, Ralph.** *Ultra in the West: Normandy Campaign of 1944-45.* 1980. NY. BC. 336p. F/dj. J2. $10.00

**BENNETT, Rowena.** *Animal ABC.* 1935. Merrill. ils Milo Winter. pict paper wrp. R5. $75.00

**BENNETT, Wendell.** *Excavations at La Mata, Maracay, Venezuela.* 1937. NY. Am Mus Nat Hist. 1st. wrp. F3. $25.00

**BENNETT, Whitman.** *Practical Guide to American 19th-Century Color Plate Books.* 1949. NY. Bennett Book Studios. 132p. gilt red cloth. F1. $45.00

**BENNETT & CLARK.** *Art of Hungarian Cooking.* 1954. Doubleday. VG/G. V4. $15.00

**BENNY & BENNY.** *Sunday Nights at Seven.* 1990. Warner. 1st. F/dj. W2. $35.00

**BENSON, B.A.** *How to Live With a Parakeet.* 1959. NY. Messner. 1st. ils. VG/dj. A2. $15.00

**BENSON, Elizabeth.** *Conference on Chavin.* 1971. DC. 1st. ils/photos. 124p. F3. $30.00

**BENSON, Elizabeth.** *Conference on Olmec.* 1968. DC. 1st. ils/photos. 185p. F3. $45.00

**BENSON, Elizabeth.** *Maya World.* 1967. Crowell. 1st. 172p. VG. S14. $20.00

**BENSON, Robert.** *Great Winemakers of California.* 1977. Capra. 1st. ils. VG. B27. $35.00

**BENSON, Stella.** *Man Who Missed the Bus.* 1928. London. Elkin Mathews/Marrot. 1/530. sgn. brn brd. NF. R3. $30.00

**BENSON & DARROW.** *Manual of Southwestern Desert Trees & Shrubs.* 1944. Tucson. 411p. stiff wrp. F7. $32.50

**BENT, George P.** *Pioneer's Historical Sketches: Four Score & More Years...* nd. Chicago. ils. 381p. G/wrp. B18. $12.50

**BENT & ROSSUM.** *Police, Criminal Justice & Community.* 1976. Harper Row. 6th. rem mk. F. A2. $14.00

**BENTLEY, E.C.** *Clerihews Complete.* 1951. London. Werner Laurie. 1st. NF/cip. M15. $75.00

**BENTLEY.** *Blake Books: Annotated Catalogues of Wm Blake's Writings.* 1977. Oxford. 1091p. VG/dj. A4. $250.00

**BENTON, Frank.** *Cowboy Life on the Sidetrack: Being Extremely Humorous...* 1903. Western Stories Syndicate. assn sgn. VG. J2. $185.00

**BENTON, J.H.** *Book of Common Prayer: Its Origin & Growth.* 1910. Boston. private prt. gilt blk cloth/brn paper brd. G. F1. $25.00

**BENTON, Josephine M.** *John Woolman: Most Modern of Ancient Friends.* nd. Phil. Friends Central Bureau. 12mo. 62p. G. V3. $5.00

**BENTON, Mike.** *Illustrated History of Horror Comics.* 1991. Taylor. 1st. VG/dj. L1. $65.00

**BENY, Roloff.** *Persia: Bridge of Turquoise. Essay & Anthology...* 1975. NYGS. 1st. ils. 367p. VG/dj. W1. $160.00

**BENZONI, Juliette.** *Marianne & the Privateer.* 1972. NY. Putnam. 1st Am. trans from French by Anne Carter. NF/dj. A14. $17.50

**BERDOE, E.** *Origin & Growth of the Healing Art.* 1893. London. 1st. 509p. A13. $90.00

**BERENBERG, Ben Ross.** *Churkendoose.* 1974. NY. Wonder. ils D Cunningham. VG. B5. $25.00

**BERENDT, John.** *Midnight in the Garden of Good & Evil.* 1994. Random. 1st. sgn. F/NF. B2. $150.00

**BERENSON, Bernard.** *Passionate Sightseer: From Diaries 1947-56.* 1960. NY. photos. VG/G. M17. $17.50

**BERESFORD, Elisabeth.** *Vanishing Garden.* 1965. Funk Wagnall. 1st Am. ils Judith Valpy. VG/dj. M20. $22.00

**BERG, Elizabeth.** *Range of Motion.* 1995. NY. 1st/2nd prt. sgn. VG/dj. M17. $20.00

**BERGAUST, Erik.** *First Men in Space.* 1960. Putnam. ils. 47p. dj. K5. $20.00

**BERGAUST, Erik.** *Rocket City USA: From Huntsville, AL, to the Moon.* 1963. Macmillan. 1st. 216p. VG/dj. K5. $50.00

**BERGEN, Candice.** *Knock Wood.* 1984. NY. Linden. 1st. F/F. H11. $30.00

**BERGENGREN, Erik.** *Alfred Nobel: Man & His Work.* 1962. NY. Nelson. 1st Am. F/dj. A2. $25.00

**BERGER, John.** *Pig Earth.* 1979. London. Writers & Readers. 1st. F/dj. A14. $88.00

**BERGER, John.** *Pig Earth.* 1979. NY. Pantheon/ Random. 1st Am. NF/clip. A14. $17.50

**BERGER, John.** *Pig Earth.* 1979. NY. Pantheon/Random. 1st. F/dj. Q1. $25.00

**BERGER, Raoul.** *Executive Priviledge, a Constitutional Myth.* 1974. Harvard. G/dj. M11. $45.00

**BERGER, Stuart.** *Southampon Diet.* 1982. S&S. G/dj. A16. $6.00

**BERGERON, Victor.** *Trader Vic's Pacific Island Cookbook.* 1968. Doubleday. VG/G. A16. $15.00

**BERGGRAV, Eivind.** *Man & State.* 1951. Muhlenberg. 319p. VG/dj. B29. $10.50

**BERGH, P.** *Art of Ogden M Pleissner.* 1984. Boston. ils. 138p. F/dj. M4. $50.00

**BERGMAN, Andrew.** *James Cagney.* 1981. NY. Galahad. 156p. VG. C5. $12.50

**BERGMAN, Deborah.** *Southern Cross.* 1990. Putnam. 1st. F/dj. T12. $15.00

**BERGMAN, Peter G.** *Riddle of Gravitation.* 1968. Scribner. 1st. VG/dj. O4. $15.00

**BERGMAN, Ray.** *Trout.* 1952. Knopf. VG. A19. $25.00

**BERGMAN, Ray.** *With Fly, Plug & Bait.* 1947. Morrow. 1st. ils/index. 640p. VG/dj. H10. $50.00

**BERGMAN, Tamar.** *Boy From Over There.* 1988. Houghton Mifflin. 1st Am. 8vo. 180p. F/NF. C14. $16.00

**BERK, Ann.** *Laugh Lines.* 1989. NY. Random. 1st. G/dj. T12. $6.00

**BERK, Richard A.** *Social Impact of AIDS in the US.* nd (1988). Cambridge, MA. Abbot. 143p. cloth. F/dj. C14. $17.00

**BERKELEY, Henry J.** *Treatise on Mental Diseases, Based Upon Lecture Course...* 1899. NY. Appleton. ils/pl. 601p. quarter calf. VG. G7. $125.00

**BERKELEY, Henry Robinson.** *Four Years in the Confederate Artillery.* 1961. UNC. photos/maps. 156p. VG. B10. $75.00

**BERKELEY & BERKELEY.** *George William Featherstonhaugh, 1st US Gov Geologist.* 1988. tuscaloosa. 1st. 8vo. 357p. gilt gr cloth. P4. $40.00

**BERKNER, L.V.** *Manual on Rockets & Satellites.* 1958. London. Pergamon. 508p. cloth. xl. K5. $75.00

**BERKOUWER, G.C.** *Studies in Dogmatics, Man: Image of God.* 1978. Eerdmans. 375p. VG/dj. B29. $18.00

**BERKOWITZ, Henry J.** *Fire Eater: An Adventure Story.* 1941. Phil. Jewish Pub Soc. 1st. F/NF. B4. $150.00

**BERLAGE, Gai Ingham.** *Women in Baseball: Forgotten History.* 1994. Wesport. Praeger. 1st. VG/clip. M20. $35.00

**BERLE, Adolf A.** *Navigating the Rapids 1918-1971.* 1973. HBJ. 1st. 8vo. xl. G+/VG. A2. $10.00

**BERLIN, Sven.** *Jonah's Dream: Meditation on Fishing.* 1975. Los Altos. 1st. 126p. VG/dj. A17. $12.50

**BERLIN.** *Harvard Judaica Bookplates, a Catalogue...* 1986. Harvard. 4to. 295 ils. 339p. NF. A4. $95.00

**BERLITZ, Charles.** *Bermuda Triangle.* 1974. Doubleday. 1st. ils. 203p. NF. S14. $12.00

**BERLITZ, Charles.** *Bermuda Triangle.* 1974. Doubleday. 1st. NF/VG. H11. $20.00

**BERMAN, Louis.** *Religion Called Behaviorism.* 1927. Boni Liveright. 12mo. 153p. blk cloth/paper labels. NF/dj. H13. $65.00

**BERNADIN DE SAINT-PIERRE, J.H.** *Paul & Virginia.* 1888. London. Routledge. 1/800. ils Maurice Leloir. 208p. teg. deluxe bdg/wrp bdg in. F1. $350.00

**BERNARD, Art.** *Dog Days.* 1969. Caxton. 204p. F/dj. A17. $15.00

**BERNARD, Claude.** *La Science Experimentale.* 1878. Paris. Bailliere. 440p. quarter roan/marbled brd. xl. G7. $195.00

**BERNARD, Claude.** *Lecons sur les Effects de Substances Toxiques...* 1857. Paris. Bailliere. 488p. new cloth. xl. G7. $170.00

**BERNARD, Jacqueline.** *Journey Toward Freedom: Story of Sojourner Truth.* 1967. Norton. 2nd. xl. xl. V3. $10.00

**BERNARDI.** *Essai Sur Les Revolutions du Droit Francois.* 1785. Paris. Serviere. 8vo. calf. R12. $150.00

**BERNATOVA, Eva.** *Wonder Shoes.* 1990. FSG. 1st. ils Fiona Moodie. 24p. F/NF. C14. $14.00

**BERNEY, Esther S.** *Collector's Guide to Pressing Irons & Trivets.* 1977. Crown. 1st. 800+ photos. 182p. F/dj. H1. $85.00

**BERNHARD, Emery.** *Spotted Eagle & Black Crow, a Lakota Legend.* 1993. Holiday House. 1st. F/dj. B17. $12.50

**BERNHARD, Ruth.** *Gift of the Commonplace.* 1996. Carmel, CA. Woodrose. 1st. sgn. F/sans. O11. $120.00

**BERNHARDT, Sarah.** *Farewell American Tour of Mme Sarah Bernhardt...* 1891. NY. Rullman. 4to. parallel French/Eng text. orig prt wrp. R12. $85.00

**BERNHEIMER, Charles L.** *Rainbow Bridge. Circuling Navajo Mountain...* 1924. Doubleday Page. 1st. photos/maps. xl. VG. F7. $75.00

**BERNIER, O.** *Lafayette: Hero of Two Worlds.* 1983. NY. 1st. ils. F/rpr. M4. $15.00

**BERNSTEIN, Jeremy.** *Experiencing Science.* 1978. NY. 1st. 275p. A13. $17.50

**BERNSTEIN, Richard.** *Style Investing.* 1995. Wiley. 1st. 238p. NF/VG. W2. $65.00

**BERNSTEIN & KOBRIN.** *How the Sun Made a Promise & Kept It.* 1974. NY. 1st. ils Ed Heffeman. VG/dj. M17. $15.00

**BERRA, Yogi.** *Behind the Plate.* 1962. Argonaut. 1st. VG/dj. P8. $65.00

**BERRA, Yogi.** *It Ain't Over...* 1989. McGraw Hill. 1st. sgn. F/F. B3. $75.00

**BERRA, Yogi.** *Yogi.* 1961. Doubleday. 1st. sgn. VG/dj. P8. $65.00

**BERRIGAN, Daniel.** *Night Flight to Hanoi: War Diary With 11 Poems.* 1968. Macmillan. stated 1st. VG+/clip. R11. $25.00

**BERRIGAN & COLES.** *Geography of Faith: Conversations When Underground.* 1971. Boston. Beacon. 1st. NF/dj. R11. $35.00

**BERRY, Barbara.** *Look of Eagles.* 1973. BC. G. O3. $10.00

**BERRY, Carole.** *Death of a Difficult Woman.* 1994. Berkley. 1st. NF/dj. G8. $15.00

**BERRY, Carole.** *Island Girl.* 1991. St Martin. 1st. VG/dj. G8. $12.50

**BERRY, Don.** *Majority of Scoundrels: Informal History...* 1961. Harper. 1st. 432p. cloth. dj. D11. $60.00

**BERRY, Erick.** *Mom du Jos: Story of a Little Black Doll.* 1931. Doubleday Doran. 1st. 8vo. 116p. gold cloth. VG. T5. $65.00

**BERRY, Erik.** *Green Door to the Sea.* 1955. Viking. 1st. sgn. ils. Vg/dj. P2. $20.00

**BERRY, R.J.** *Inheritance & Natural History.* 1990. London. 350p. F/dj. S15. $12.00

**BERRY, Wendell.** *Part.* 1980. Northpoint. 1st. inscr/dtd 1994. F/NF. R14. $50.00

**BERRY, Wendell.** *Riverdure.* 1974. np. U CO. 1/100. sgn. F/Japanese-stitched wrp. B4. $350.00

**BERRY, Wendell.** *Sabbaths 1987.* 1991. Monterey, KY. Larkspur. 1/1000. sgn. F/sans. B3. $25.00

**BERRY, Wendell.** *Sayings & Doings.* 1975. Lexington. Gnomon. 1st. F/sans. L3. $45.00

**BERRY, Wendell.** *Wheel.* 1982. Northpoint. 1st. sgn. F/F. B3. $40.00

**BERRY, Wendell.** *Wheel.* 1982. SF. Northpoint. 1st. inscr/sgn. F/dj. L3. $100.00

**BERRYMAN, John.** *His Toy, His Dream.* 1st. VG/dj. B30. $27.50

**BERRYMAN, John.** *77 Dream Songs.* 1964. Farrar Straus. ARC/1st. gilt bl cloth. F/dj. w/pub card. M24. $150.00

**BERTON, Pierre.** *Great Lakes.* 1996. Toronto. 1st. photos Andre Gallant. F/dj. A26. $28.00

**BERTON, Pierre.** *Hollywood's Canada: Americanization of Our National Image.* 1975. Toronto. McClelland Stewart. 1st. NF/VG. A26. $30.00

**BERTON, Pierre.** *Klondike Fever: Life & Death of the Last Great Goldrush.* 1958. NY. Knopf. later prt. 8vo. 457p. blk cloth. P4. $30.00

**BERTON, Pierre.** *Klondike Quest: Photographic Essay, 1897-1899.* 1983. Toronto. McClelland Stewart. 1st. 240p. VG/NF. A26. $40.00

**BERTON, Pierre.** *My Country: The Remarkable Past.* 1976. McClelland. 1st Canadaian. NF/G. T12. $15.00

**BERTON, Pierre.** *Wild Frontier.* 1978. Toronto. McClelland Stewart. 1st. F/VG. A26. $15.00

**BERTON, Ralph.** *Remembering Bix.* 1974. Harper. 1st. F/dj. B2. $65.00

**BERTRAM, James G.** *Harvest of the Sea: Contribution to Natural & Economic...* 1865. London. ils. gr cloth. B14. $95.00

**BERTRAM, Werner.** *Royal Recluse: Memories of Ludwig II of Bavaria.* nd. Munich. photos. VG/dj. M17. $15.00

**BERTRAND, Louis.** *Le Mirage Oriental.* 1920. Paris. Perrin. 7th. 455p. VG. M7. $75.00

**BERTRAND & SOLBERT.** *Tactics & Duties for Trench Fighting.* 1918. NY. Putnam. 38 diagrams. 235p. dj. H6. $27.00

**BERWANGER, Eugene H.** *West & Reconstruction.* 1981. Chicago. IL U. AN/dj. A19. $25.00

**BESANT, Annie.** *Ancient Wisdom.* 1977 (1897). Adyar, India. Theosophical. 10th. 12mo. F/VG. A2. $10.00

**BESANT, Annie.** *Sketch of Theosophy.* 1951. Adyar, Madras, India. Theosophical Pub House. 1st. 23p. VG+/self wrp. A25. $20.00

**BESANT, Walter.** *Early London: Prehistoric, Roman, Saxon & Norman.* 1908. London. Blk. 4to. ils. 370p. full red leather. VG. M10. $50.00

**BESHOAR, Barron B.** *Hippocrates in a Red Vest.* 1973. Palo Alto, CA. Am West Pub. G/dj. A19. $35.00

**BESKOW, Elsa.** *Tale of the Wee Little Old Woman.* 1938. Harper. early ed. sq 4to. glassine dj. R5. $200.00

**BESSE, Joseph.** *Abstract of the Sufferings of People Called Quakers...* 1733. London. J Sowle. 3 vol. 12mo. xl. V3. $350.00

**BESSE, Joseph.** *Brief Account of Many of Prosecutions of...Quakers...* 1736. London. J Sowle. 1st. 12mo. 189p. missing covers/backstrip. V3. $150.00

**BESSEY, Ernst A.** *Morphology & Taxonomy of Fungi.* 1952 (1950). Phil. corrected ed. 791p. VG. B26. $30.00

**BESSIE, Alvah.** *Inquisition in Eden.* 1965. NY. Macmillan. VG/dj. V4. $35.00

**BESSIE, Alvah.** *Symbol.* 1966. Random. 1st. VG/dj. C9. $60.00

**BESTER, Alfred.** *Tender Loving Rage.* 1991. Tafford. 1st. F/dj. P3. $20.00

**BETHAM, Jeremy.** *Rationale of Judicial Evidence, Specially Applied...* 1995. Littleton. facsimile 1827 London. M11. $295.00

**BETHUNE, Thomas.** *Marvelous Musical Prodigy, Blind Tom, Negro Boy Pianist.* (1867). NY. French Wheat. 1st. NF/wrp. M24. $400.00

**BETJEMAN, John.** *Betjeman in Miniature.* 1976. Paisley, Scotland. Gleniffer. mini. 1/250. full leather/plastic box. B24. $95.00

**BETTEN, H.L.** *Upland Game Shooting.* 1940. Phil. 2nd. 450p. gilt cloth. A17. $20.00

**BETTENSON, Henry.** *Documents of the Christian Church.* 1947. Oxford. 457p. VG. B29. $6.00

**BETTER HOMES & GARDENS.** *New Cook Book.* 1968. Meredith. VG. A16. $12.00

**BETTS, Doris.** *Souls Raised From the Dead.* 1994. Knopf. 1st. 339p. F/dj. P12. $10.00

**BETTS, Ernest.** *Inside Pictures.* 1960. London. Cresset. 1st. VG/worn. M20. $22.00

**BETTS, Glynne Robinson.** *Writers in Residence: American Writers at Home.* 1981. Viking. 1st. quarter maroon cloth. F/NF. T11. $35.00

**BEUF, Ann H.** *Red Children in White America.* 1977. U PA. 1st. VG/dj. N2. $10.00

**BEVERIDGE, Albert J.** *Abraham Lincoln, 1809-1858.* Manuscript ed. 1/1000. 4 vol. VG. B18. $200.00

**BEVERIDGE, Albert J.** *Abraham Lincoln.* 1928. Houghton Mifflin. 2 vol. lg 8vo. gilt bl cloth. VG. S17. $17.50

**BEVERIDGE, Albert J.** *Life of John Marshall.* nd. 4 vol. 38 pl. G. A4. $35.00

**BEVIER, Robert S.** *History of 1st & 2nd Missouri Confederate Brigades...* 1878. St Louis. Bryan Brand. 1st. 4 pl. cloth. M8. $1,750.00

**BEY, Pilaff.** *Venus in the Kitchen; or, Love's Cookery Book.* 1953. Viking. 1st. ils Graham Greene. F/VG. M19. $35.00

**BEYER, Werner W.** *Keats — And the Daemon King.* 1947. OUP. 1st. VG/clip. O4. $20.00

**BEYER, William Gray.** *Minions of the Moon.* 1950. Gnome. 1st. VG/dj. M20. $32.00

**BIAGGI, V.** *Las Aves de Puerto Rico.* 1974 (1970). Puerto Rico. 2nd. lg 8vo. 64 full-p pl. 378p. gilt cloth. F/NF. C12. $65.00

**BIALK, Elisa.** *Tizz.* 1955. Chicago. 1st. G. O3. $18.00

**BIANCHI, John.** *Blue Steel & Gunleather.* 1978. N Hollywood, CA. Beinfeld. sgn. VG/dj. A19. $25.00

**BIANCHINI & CORBETTA.** *Complete Book of Fruits & Vegetables.* 1976. NY. 1st Am. VG/dj. B26. $40.00

**BIANCO, Margery.** *Bright Morning.* 1942. Viking. 1st. 8vo. 143p. VG. T5. $30.00

**BIANCO, Pamela.** *Paradise Square.* 1950. NY. Oxford. 1st. 8vo. 96p. VG/G+. T5. $65.00

**BIANCO, Pamela.** *Starlit Journey.* 1933. NY. 1st. ils. 46p. VG/dj. B18. $45.00

**BIBBY, G.** *Looking for Dilmun.* 1969. Knopf. ils. 383p. cloth. VG/dj. Q2. $24.00

**BIBLE COMMENTARY.** *Interpreter's Bible Commentary.* 1984. Abingdon. 12 vol. VG/dj. B29. $120.00

**BIBLE.** *Bible in Miniature, for Children. With 25 Engravings.* ca 1840. Lee Shepard. mini. lacks ffe. aeg. gilt purple cloth. B24. $175.00

**BIBLE.** *Book of Genesis.* 1970. Kentfield, CA. Allen. ils Blair Hughes-Stanton. cloth/case. B24. $400.00

**BIBLE.** *Book of Jonah. Taken From Authorized Version King James I.* 1926. Golden Cockerel. 1/175. sm 4to. 13 woodcuts. 15p. wht buckram. F. B24. $850.00

**BIBLE.** *Book of Jonah. Taken From Old Testament of King James...* 1960. NY. Hammer Creek. 1/40. ils Valenti Angelo. F/wrp/dj/chemise. B24. $425.00

**BIBLE.** *Book of Ruth.* 1947. LEC. 1/1950. ils Arthur Szyk. VG/case. D1. $225.00

**BIBLE.** *Canticum Canticorum (Song of Songs).* 1931. Weimer. Cranach. 1st thus. 1/200 Maillol-Kessler handmade. teg. F/box. M24. $2,250.00

**BIBLE.** *Cantique des Cantiques, Traduit en Francois...* 1694. Paris. Guillaume Desprez. 8vo. 558p. contemporary calf. K1. $375.00

**BIBLE.** *Ecclesiastes; or, The Preacher.* 1911. Houghton Mifflin. 1st. 1/335. gilt red brd. NF/torn glassine. M24. $200.00

**BIBLE.** *Four Gospels With the Acts of the Apostles.* 1844. Calcutta. Prt at Baptist Mission Pr. 336p. bl cloth. K1. $175.00

**BIBLE.** *Het Nieuwe Testament/Het Boek der Psalmen.* 1815 (1797). Dodrecht/ Amsterdam. 2 vol in 1. thick 16mo. full early calf/silver clasp. F1. $500.00

**BIBLE.** *Holy Bible, Containing the Old & New Testaments.* ca 1880. Spottiswoode. thick 4to. 6 mtd photos/2 maps. dbl-column text. aeg. wood box. H5. $950.00

**BIBLE.** *Holy Bible, Containing the Old & New Testaments.* 1974. Franklin Center, PA. Franklin Mint. ltd. thick 4to. 40 mc pl. sterling bdg. B11. $950.00

**BIBLE.** *Holy Bible, the King James Version.* 1983. Thomas Nelson. sm 8vo. 791p. VG. W2. $10.00

**BIBLE.** *Holy Bible Containing the Old & New Testaments.* 1911. Glascow. David Byrce. mini. 876p. full panel-stp roan/magnifying glass. NF. F1. $250.00

**BIBLE.** *Holy Bible.* 1911. London. Ballantyne. 3 vol. 8vo. ils/pl. full niger morocco. NF. H5. $450.00

**BIBLE.** *Holy Gospel According to Matthew, Mark, Luke, John.* 1962. Verona. 1/320. 4to. 372p. teg. morocco case. B24. $2,850.00

**BIBLE.** *Il Nuovo ed Eterno Testamento di Giesu Christo...* 1551. Lyon. np. 2 parts in 1. 16mo. ffe removed. contemporary vellum. K1. $750.00

**BIBLE.** *Living Bible, Holman Illustrated Edition.* 1973. Tyndale. 4th. sm 4to. 1226p. blk bdg. F. W2. $40.00

**BIBLE.** *New Testament MDXXVI.* 1954-55. Lexington, KY. Anvil. 4 vol. 1/300. ils Hammer. Charriere bdg. case. B24. $2,250.00

**BIBLE.** *Novum Testamentum.* 1763. Oxford. Clarendon. Greek text. lg 4to. 416p. contemporary red morocco/calf. K1. $850.00

**BIBLE.** *Proverb ia Salmonis...* 1748. Leyden. Johannem Luzac. 4to. lg vignettes. contemporary vellum. K1. $375.00

**BIBLE.** *Psalm Book.* 1978. Pownal, VT. Manson Hill. 1/175. sm 4to. ils Mark Livingston. buckram brd. F. B24. $850.00

**BIBLE.** *Psalms of Praise.* 1967. Flemington. St Teresa Pr. 1/100. sm 4to. 30p. F. B24. $750.00

**BIBLE.** *Samson & Delilah. From Book of Judges...* 1925. Golden Cockerel. 1/325. lg 8vo. 6 woodcuts/1 vignette by Robert Gibbings. F/dj. B24. $850.00

**BIBLE.** *Sermon on the Mount From Gospel According to Matthew.* 1995. np. Petrarch. 1st. 1/150. golden-orange cloth/vellum label. F. w/prt TLS. M24. $150.00

**BIBLE.** *Sermon on the Mount From Gospel of St Matthew...* 1973. Worcester. St Onge. mini. 1/1500. 55p. aeg. gilt red leather. B24. $50.00

**BIBLE.** *Song of Songs by Solomon.* 1985. Utrecht. Catharijne. mini. 1/155. ils sgn. gilt full vellum. B24. $150.00

**BIBLE.** *Song of Songs Which Is Solomon's. Authorized Version.* 1961. Chicago. Blk Cat. mini. 1/350. frenchfold. 34p. gilt wht leather. F. B24. $150.00

**BIBLE.** *Song of Songs.* 1925. Waltham, St Lawrence. Golden Cockerel. 1st thus. 1/750. ils Eric Gill. F. M24. $800.00

**BIBLE.** *Ten Commandments.* 1971. Los Angeles. Bela Blau. mini. Hebrew/Eng text. gilt brn leather. F. B24. $85.00

**BIBLE.** *Visualized Bible.* 1985. Tyndale. KJV. 1149p. VG. B29. $13.00

**BIBLE.** *Voice of the Prophets. Messianic Prophecies.* 1970. Flemington, NJ. St Teresa Pr. 1/125 on handmade. sm 4to. 33p. F. B24. $650.00

**BIBLE.** *Young Readers Bible.* 1971. Abingdon. RSV. 871p. VG. B29. $10.00

**BICK, Edgar.** *Source Book of Orthopaedics.* 1948. Baltimore. 2nd. lib buckram. xl. A13. $85.00

**BICKEL, Alexander M.** *Morality of Consent.* 1975. New Haven. Yale. 1st. VG/dj. M20. $20.00

**BICKENHEUSER, Fred.** *Tiffin Glassmasters.* 1979. Glassmasters Pub. 1st. sgn. 103p. VG/ils wrp. H1. $25.00

**BICKHAM, Jack M.** *38 Most Common Fiction Writing Mistakes.* 1992. Writer's Digest Books. 1st. 8vo. 117p. F. W2. $15.00

**BICKLEY, Francis.** *Adventures of Harlequin.* 1923. London. Sewyn Blount. 1st. 8vo. 119p. Sangorski Sutcliffe bdg. F/case. H5. $750.00

**BIDDLE, George.** *Green Island.* 1930. Coward McCAnn. ils. 177p. lt gr cloth. VG/G. F1. $100.00

**BIDDLE, Nicholas.** *Nicholas Biddle in Greece: Journals & Letters of 1806.* 1993. Penn State. 8vo. F/dj. A2. $20.00

**BIDDLE, Perry.** *Abingdon Hospital Visitation Manual.* 1988. Abingdon. 205p. leatherette. VG. B29. $9.50

**BIDERMANAS, Izis.** *Paris des Reves.* 1950. Lausanne. Eds Clairefontaine. 1st. 4to. NF/dj. S9. $125.00

**BIERCE, Ambrose.** *Cynic's Word Book.* 1906. Doubleday Page. 1st. 8vo. 233p. teg. olive cloth. NF. H5. $275.00

**BIERCE, Ambrose.** *My Favorite Murder.* 1916. NY. Guido Bruno. 1st separate. stapled wrp. M24. $150.00

**BIERCE, L.V.** *Historical Reminiscences of Summit County.* 1854. Akron. 1st. 157p. G. B18. $225.00

**BIERDS, Linda.** *Flights of the Harvest-Mare.* 1985. Boise. Ahsahta. 1st. sgn. F. O11. $30.00

**BIERDS, Linda.** *Stillness, the Dancing.* 1988. NY. Holt. 1st. sgn. F. O11. $30.00

**BIERRING, Walter.** *One Hundred Years of Iowa Medicine.* 1958. IA City. 1st. 116p. $20.00

**BIGELOW, Jacob.** *Natural Disease, Illustrated in Various Discourses & Essays.* 1854. Boston. 1st. 391p. A13. $225.00

**BIGELOW, John Jr.** *On the Bloody Trail of Geronimo.* 1958. LA. Westernlore. 1/750. 237p. emb cloth. dj. D11. $40.00

**BIGELOW, John Mason.** *Death Is an Early Riser.* 1940. Scribner. 1st. VG. G8. $10.00

**BIGELOW, John.** *Memoir of Life & Public Service of John Chas Fremont.* 1856. Derby Jackson. 1st. 8vo. 480p. gilt cloth. VG. O1. $75.00

**BIGELOW, John.** *Supreme Court & the Electoral Commission: An Open Letter...* 1903. NY. Knickerbocker. pres. prt sewn wrp. M11. $75.00

**BIGGER, Ruby Vaughan.** *My Miss Nancy: Nancy Astor's Virginia Mammy...* 1924. Macon. JW Burke. inscr. 45p. G. B10. $275.00

**BIGGERS, Earl Derr.** *Agony Column.* 1916. Bobbs Merrill. 194p. G. G11. $20.00

**BIGGERS, Earl Derr.** *Behind That Curtain.* (1928). Grosset Dunlap. rpt. VG/dj. M19. $15.00

**BIGGERS, Earl Derr.** *Love Insurance.* (1914). Grosset Dunlap. rpt. 402p. G+. P12. $15.00

**BIGGERS, Earl Derr.** *Love Insurance.* 1914. Toronto. McLeod Allen. 1st Canadian? 402p. G. G11. $15.00

**BIGGERS, Earl Derr.** *Seven Keys to Baldpate.* 1913. Bobbs Merrill. lacks ftspc/torn title p. G11. $15.00

**BIGGINS, John.** *Emperor's Coloured Coat.* 1992. London. Secker Warberg. 1st. F/NF. T11. $125.00

**BIGGINS, John.** *Two-Headed Eagle.* 1995. NY. St Martin. 1st. NF/NF. M15. $35.00

**BILL, James A.** *Eagle & the Lion.* 1988. Yale. 520p. NF/dj. W1. $24.00

**BILLIAS, G.A.** *General Glover & His Marblehead Mariners.* 1960. NY. 1st. ils/maps. 243p. NF/VG. M4. $35.00

**BILLINGS, John D.** *Hardtack & Coffee.* 1960. Lakeside Classic. 1st thus. teg. NF. T11. $35.00

**BILLINGS, William.** *Continental Harmony: Containing a Number of Anthems, Fuges.* 1961. Harvard. facs 1974 vol. VG/dj. M17. $30.00

**BILLINGS & HURD.** *Hospitals, Dispensaries & Nursing.* 1984. NY. facs of 1894. 719p. A13. $125.00

**BILLINGTON, Ray Allen.** *Genesis of the Frontier Thesis: A Study...* 1971. Huntington Lib. 1st. notes/index/biblio. 315p. F. B19. $20.00

**BILLYBOY.** *Barbie: Her Life & Times.* 1987. Crown. 1st. VG/dj. M20. $38.00

**BIMBA, Anthony.** *Molly Maguires: True Story of Labor's Martyred Pioneers...* 1932. NY. Internat Pub. VG/fair. V4. $15.00

**BIMSON, Walter.** *West & Walter Bimson.* 1971. AZ. 1st. 223p. F/dj. E1. $65.00

**BINDER, Otto.** *Jets & Rockets: A Golden Learn-About Book.* 1961. NY. Golden. 4to. 48p. juvenile. K5. $8.00

**BINDING, Tim.** *Perfect Execution.* 1996. London. Picador. 1st. author's 2nd novel. F/dj. T2. $35.00

**BINET, Alfred.** *L'Annee Psychologique Neuvieme Annee.* 1903. Paris. Reinwald Schliecher. 666p. contemporary bdg. G1. $65.00

**BINET, Alfred.** *Les Revelations de l'Ecriture d'Apres und Controle...* 1906. Paris. Felix Alcan. ils. 260p. contemporary bdg. G1. $100.00

**BINET & FERE.** *Animal Magnetism.* 1993. NY. Classics of Psychiatry & Behavioral Sciences Lib. G1. $65.00

**BINET & HENRI.** *La Fatique Intellectuelle.* 1898. Paris. Reinwald Schleicher. 338p. pub gr cloth. VG. G1. $125.00

**BINET & SIMON.** *Development of Intelligence in Children.* 1916. Baltimore. Wms Wilkins. portrait ftspc. 336p. panelled bl cloth. VG. G1. $125.00

**BINGER, C.A.L.** *Personality in Arterial Hypertension.* 1945. NY. Psychosomatic Medicine Monographs. 1st. 8vo. NF/G+. C14. $15.00

**BINGHAM, Barry H.** *Horseman's Handbook/Barns & Related Equipment.* 1972. Blacksburg. VPI. ils. VG/wrp. O3. $25.00

**BINGHAM, Caleb.** *Hunters; or, Sufferings of Hugh & Francis in the Wilderness.* 1953 (1814). Hanover. Dartmouth. facs. woodcuts. VG. M17. $15.00

**BINGHAM, Hiram.** *Across South America.* (1911). Houghton Mifflin. ils/maps. 405p. gilt gr cloth. F3. $45.00

**BINGHAM, Hiram.** *Lost City of the Incas.* 1948. NY. 1st. ils/index. 263p. VG/G. B5. $35.00

**BINGHAM, Hiram.** *Lost City of the Incas.* 1962 (1948). NY. DSP. 7th. 263p. map ep. F3. $25.00

**BINGHAM, Rebecca.** *Alphabet Salmagundi.* 1988. Hyattsville, MD. Rebecca Pr. 1/200. sgn. red/gilt stp gr cloth. B24. $75.00

**BINGHAM, Rebecca.** *Flirtations.* 1984. Hyattsville, MD. Rebecca Pr. mini. 1/200. sgn. mauve silk damask. B24. $125.00

**BINGHAM, Rebecca.** *Mammon & Archer/Springtime a la Carte/Last Leaf by O Henry.* 1988. Hyattsville. Rebecca Pr. mini. 3 vol. 1/200. sgn. cut-away case. B24. $150.00

**BINGHAM, Rebecca.** *Quo'pourri.* 1989. Hyattsville, MD. Rebecca Pr. mini. 1/15 (75 total). sgn. lilac brd. B24. $225.00

**BINHEIM, Max.** *Women of the West: A Series of Biographical Sketches...* 1928. LA. Pub Pr. 223p. gilt cloth. D11. $50.00

**BINSTOCK, Louis.** *Power of Maturity.* 1969. Hawrthorne Books. 1st. 8vo. 179p. NF/VG. W2. $10.00

**BINYON, T.J.** *Murder Will Out: Detective in Fiction.* 1989. OUP. ils. VG. M17. $17.50

**BIRD, Harrison.** *Attack on Quebec: American Invasion of Canada 1775-1776.* 1968. OUP. 1st. F/dj. M15. $40.00

**BIRD, Isabella L.** *Lady's Life in the Rocky Mountains.* 1960. Norman, OK. 1st. 252p. VG. B18. $35.00

**BIRD, Michael S.** *Ontario Fraktur: Pennsylvania-German Folk Art Tradition...* 1977. MF Feheley. 1st. VG/dj. R8. $50.00

**BIRD, Sarah.** *Boyfriend School.* 1989. Doubleday. 1st. author's 3rd book. F/F. B3. $60.00

**BIRGE & BIRGE.** *Inland Lakes of Wisconsin: The Plankton...* 1922. Madison. ils/charts/diagrams. 222p. A17. $25.00

**BIRKBECK, Morris.** *Notes on a Journey in America From Coast of Virginia...* 1819. Phil. M Carey. 2nd. 8vo. full calf/blk spine label. VG. F1. $200.00

**BIRKERTS, Sven.** *American Energies: Essays on Fiction.* 1992. NY. VG/dj. M17. $15.00

**BIRLEY, Anthony.** *Marcus Aurelius: A Biography.* 1987. Yale. revised. ils. VG/dj. M17. $25.00

**BIRMINGHAM, Stephen.** *Jacqueline Bouvier Kennedy Onassis.* 1978. Grosset Dunlap. 1st. sm 4to. 241p. NF/VG. W2. $25.00

**BIRMINGHAM, Stephen.** *Real Lace: America's Irish Rich.* 1973. Harper Row. 1st. photos. 322p. VG/dj. S14. $20.00

**BIRMINGHAM, Stephen.** *Shades of Fortune.* 1989. Little Brn. 1st. NF/dj. M20. $15.00

**BIRNEY & CHOATE.** *Seventy-Five Years of Mammalogy 1919-1994.* 1994. Am Soc Mammalogists. Special Pub #11. 433p. F/dj. S15. $30.00

**BISCOTTI.** *Bibliography of Am Sporting Books, 1926-1985.* 1977. 1/1000. 5000 entries. 582p. F/case. A4. $75.00

**BISHIR & BROWN.** *Architects & Builders in North Carolina...* 1990. Chapel Hill. F/dj. V4. $35.00

**BISHOP, Amasa S.** *Project Sherwood: US Program in Controlled Fusion.* 1958. Reading, MA. Adisson-Wesley. 1st. 8vo. 216p. VG/dj. K5. $15.00

**BISHOP, Claire Huchet.** *Pancakes-Paris.* 1947. Viking. 1st. ils Georges Schreiber. 1948 Newbery Honor. VG. T5. $35.00

**BISHOP, George.** *New England Judged by the Spirit of the Lord.* 1885. Phil. Thos Wm Stuckey. 482p. V3. $60.00

**BISHOP, J.** *Day Lincoln Was Shot.* 1955. NY. 1st. ils. 304p. G. M4. $15.00

**BISHOP, John.** *Joyce's Book of the Dark: Finnegan's Wake.* 1986. WI U. VG/dj. M17. $35.00

**BISHOP, Michael.** *Brittle Innings.* 1994. NY. Bantam. 1st. F/F. H11. $20.00

**BISHOP, Michael.** *Count Geiger's Blues.* 1992. NY. Tor. 1st. F/NF. H11. $20.00

**BISHOP, Michael.** *Unicorn Mountain.* 1988. NY. Arbor/Morrow. 1st. NF/dj. M23. $35.00

**BISHOP, William A.** *Winged Warfare.* 1975. Folkestone, Eng. Bailey Swinfen. 1st? 8vo. 281p. VG/dj. M7. $42.50

**BISHOP & DAVIES.** *Railways & War Before 1918.* 1972. NY. 1st Am. 154p. F/dj. E1. $25.00

**BISHOP & DESMOND.** *Background to Evolution in Africa.* 1967. Chicago. hc. VG/dj. B9. $35.00

**BISKIND, Peter.** *Seeing Is Believing.* 1983. Pantheon. 1st. VG/dj. L1. $55.00

**BISSON, Terry.** *Talking Man.* 1986. NY. Arbor. 1st. sgn/dtd. F/dj. G10. $35.00

**BISSON, Terry.** *Voyage to the Red Planet.* 1990. NY. Morrow. 1st. sgn. F/dj. M23. $35.00

**BITTNER, Herbert.** *Kaethe Kollwitz.* 1964. NY. Yoseloff. 4th. 147 pl. VG/dj. F1. $35.00

**BIVINS, John.** *Moravian Potters.* 1972. Chapel Hill. 300p. VG. B18. $45.00

**BIXBY, W.** *Connecticut: A New Guide.* 1974. NY. 386p. F/dj. M4. $25.00

**BJORK, Kenneth O.** *West of the Great Divide: Norwegian Migration...1847-1893.* 1958. Northfield. Norwegian-Am Hist Assn. 671p. bl cloth. P4. $75.00

**BJORNSTAD, Edith.** *Wings in Waiting: History of IA Methodist Hospital.* 1952. Des Moines, IA. 1st. 238p. A13. $20.00

**BLACK, Arthur.** *Old Black Magic.* 1989. Stoddart. 1st. F/NF. P3. $30.00

**BLACK, Campbell.** *Wanting.* nd. BC. F/NF. S18. $5.00

**BLACK, Mary Martin.** *Summerfield Farm.* 1951. Viking. 1st. ils Wesley Dennis. VG/dj. M20. $35.00

**BLACK, Matthew.** *Aramaic Approach to the Gospels & Acts.* 1967. Oxford. 359p. VG/dj. B29. $19.00

**BLACK, Robert C.** *Railroads of the Confederacy.* (1952). UNC. 360p. VG/G. B10. $75.00

**BLACK & LE FAYE.** *Jane Austen Cookbook.* 1995. Chicago Review. 1st. F/dj. V4. $25.00

**BLACK & ROELKER.** *Rhode Island Chaplain in the Revolution: Letters...* 1949. Providence. RI Soc of Cincinnati. sm 8vo. 82p. F. B14. $55.00

**BLACKBURN, Benjamin.** *Trees & Shrubs in Eastern North America.* 1952. NY. 358p. map ep. VG. B26. $20.00

**BLACKBURN, John.** *Scent of New-Mown Hay.* 1958. Mill Morrow. 1st Am. NF/dj. M21. $35.00

**BLACKBURN, Julia.** *Emperor's Last Island: Journey to St Helena.* 1991. NY. 1st. VG/dj. M17. $15.00

**BLACKBURN, Paul.** *In, On or About the Premises.* 1968. London. Cape Goliard. 1/750 (7750 total). F/dj. L3. $55.00

**BLACKBURN, Tom.** *Jolly Rogers: Story of Tom Blackburn & Navy...* 1989. NY. Orion. 1st. photos/roster/index. 270p. F/dj. S16. $24.00

**BLACKER, J.F.** *ABC of Collecting Old Continental Pottery.* 1913. London. Stanley Paul. 315p. gilt brn cloth. VG. F1. $25.00

**BLACKER, William.** *Essay on Improvement to Be Made in Cultivation of Sm Farms.* 1837. Dublin. Hardy Walker. 5th. 90p. wrp. A10. $45.00

**BLACKFORD, Susan Leigh.** *Memoir: Chapter One in Life in & out of the Army...* 1959. percy. rpt of 1894 JP Bell. VG. B10. $35.00

**BLACKMAN, Honor.** *Honor Blackman's Book of Self-Defense.* 1965. Andre Deutsch. VG/dj. P3. $75.00

**BLACKMORE, R.D.** *Slain by the Doones.* 1895. Dodd Mead. 1st Am/later issue. VG. M20. $22.00

**BLACKMUR, R.P.** *Second World.* 1942. Cummington. 1st. 1/300. blk cloth. F/tattered glassine dj. M24. $75.00

**BLACKSHEAR.** *Wisconsin Authors & Their Books, 1836-1975.* 4to. 660p. VG. A4. $95.00

**BLACKSTOCK, Harvey.** *Bitter Humour: About Dope, Safe Cracking & Prisons.* 1967. Toronto. Burns & MacEacheron. 1st. F/NF. A26. $40.00

**BLACKSTONE, William.** *Commentaries on Laws of England in Four Books, 4th Edition.* 1770. Oxford. Clarendon. 4th. 4to. contemporary calf. M11. $3,500.00

**BLACKWEIDER, Richard E.** *Monograph of the West Indian Beetles of Family Stapylinidae.* 1943. Smithsonian. 658p. NF. S15. $30.00

**BLACKWOOD, Andrew.** *From the Rock to the Gates of Hell.* 1968. Baker. 127p. VG/dj. B29. $8.00

**BLADES, William F.** *Fishing Flies & Fly Tying: American Insects...* 1962. Stackpole. enlarged 2nd. ils. 319p. VG. A17. $45.00

**BLAINE, John.** *Rick Brant: Flying Stingraee.* 1963. Grosset Dunlap. 176p. xl. VG-. B36. $40.00

**BLAINE, John.** *Rick Brant: Rocket's Shadow (#1).* nd. Grosset Dunlap. VG/dj. P3. $8.00

**BLAINE, Marge.** *Terrible Thing That Happened at Our House.* 1975. Parent's Magazine. 4to. unp. VG. T5. $25.00

**BLAIR, Clay Jr.** *Silent Victory.* 1975. Lippincott. F/dj. A19. $25.00

**BLAIR, John.** *History of Medicine in the University of St Andrews.* 1987. Edinburgh. 1st. 416p. dj. A13. $45.00

**BLAIR, Laurence.** *Garden Clinic.* 1942. Macmillan. 146p. VG/dj. A10. $15.00

**BLAIR, Walter.** *Mark Twain's West.* 1985. Lakeside Classic. 1st thus. teg. F. T11. $30.00

**BLAIR, Walter.** *Mike Fink.* 1933. Holt. G. A19. $60.00

**BLAKE, E.V.** *Arctic Experiences Containing Capt Geo E Tyson...* 1874. NY. ils/map. 486p. new cloth. M4. $65.00

**BLAKE, Henry.** *Talking With Horses.* 1976. NY. Dutton. 1st Am/2nd prt. VG/dj. O3. $15.00

**BLAKE, John.** *Public Health in the Town of Boston 1630-1822.* 1959. Cambridge. 1st. 278p. dj. A13. $45.00

**BLAKE, William.** *Auguries of Innocence.* 1968. NY. Grossman. 1st trade. F/box. M24. $65.00

**BLAKE, William.** *Beams. Selections From William Blake.* 1964. Berkeley. Peacock. mini. 1/300. bl prt/gray wrp. B24. $40.00

**BLAKE, William.** *Songs of Innocence & Experience With Other Poems.* 1866. London. Pickering. 1st. 12mo. brn cloth/paper spine label. R3. $450.00

**BLAKE, William.** *Songs of Innocence.* 1955. London. Trianon. ltd. 1/1600. VG/marbled case. 8vo. ils. case. B11. $450.00

**BLAKER, Richard.** *Jefferson Secret.* 1929. Doubleday Doran. 1st. VG/dj. M15/M17. $65.00

**BLAKEWAY, Claire.** *Jacques Prevert.* 1990. Rutherford. Fairleigh Dickinson. 218p. VG/dj. C5. $15.00

**BLAKEY, Robert.** *Angling; or, How to Angle & Where to Go.* 1860s. London/NY. Routledge. 12mo. 188p. fair. H10. $35.00

**BLAKSLEY, J.** *Travels, Trips & Trots.* 1904. London. Keliher. 2nd. 8vo. ils. teg. VG. W1. $45.00

**BLANCHAN, Neltje.** *American Flower Garden.* 1909. NY. 1/1050. teg. VG. B18. $125.00

**BLANCHARD, Alrene.** *Bear & Henry.* 1987. Barrons. 1st. 4to. ils Jean Claverie. F/dj. M5. $20.00

**BLANCHARD, Ken.** *One Minute Manager.* 1981. Blanchard-Johnson. 1st. VG/dj. P3. $10.00

**BLANCHARD & PEACOCK.** *Navigation, a 3-D Exploration.* 1992ard.. Orchard Books. 1st. obl 8vo. popups. VG. B17. $15.00

**BLANCHARD & WELLMAN.** *Life & Times of Sir Archie 1805-1833.* 1958. Chapel Hill. UNC. 1st. VG/G. O3. $45.00

**BLANCK, Jacob.** *Bibliography of American Literature. Vol 7.* 1983. New Haven. Yale. 1st. gilt blk cloth. NF. F1. $100.00

**BLANCK & WINSHIP.** *Bibliography of American Literature, Vol 9.* 1991. Yale. 4to. ils. 522p. F. A4. $165.00

**BLANCK.** *Bibliography of American Literature.* 1957-1991. Yale. 9 vol. 4to. ils. vol 1-6 xl. F. A4. $1,195.00

**BLAND, Jane Cooper.** *Currier & Ives: A Manual for Collectors.* 1931. Doubleday Doran. ils/checklist. 349p. tan cloth. F. P4. $150.00

**BLANDING, Don.** *Pilot Bails Out.* 1943. 1st. inscr. F/VG. M19. $15.00

**BLANKENSHIP, W.D.** *Brotherly Love.* 1981. Arbor. 1st. F/dj. T12. $50.00

**BLANKENSHIP, W.D.** *Leavenworth Irregulars.* 1974. Bobbs Merrill. stated 1st. 264p. dj. R11. $60.00

**BLANTON, Richard.** *Ancient Mesoamerica: Comparison of Change in 3 Regions.* (1992). Cambridge. 300p. wrp. F3. $20.00

**BLASDALE, Walter A.** *Cultivated Species of Primula.* 1948. Berkeley. 284p. VG/dj. B26. $45.00

**BLASSINGAME, W.** *Live From the Devil.* 1949. Garden City. 1st. VG/VG. B5. $20.00

**BLATT, Sidney J.** *Continuity & Change in Art: Development Modes...* 1984. Lawrence Erlbaum. pres. ils. 411p. VG/dj. G1. $50.00

**BLATTY, William Peter.** *Exorcist.* 1971. Harper Row. 1st. VG/G. L1. $60.00

**BLATTY, William Peter.** *I'll Tell Them I Remember You.* 1973. Norton. 1st. F/dj. A24. $35.00

**BLATTY, William Peter.** *Legion.* 1983. S&S. 1st. xl. G/VG. S18. $4.00

**BLATTY, William Peter.** *Ninth Configuration.* 1978. Harper. 1st. VG/dj. S18. $15.00

**BLAUNER, Peter.** *Slow Motion Riot.* 1991. Morrow. 1st. author's 1st book. F/dj. S18. $35.00

**BLAZICEK, O.J.** *Skreta's Family Portrait of Dionysio Miseroni.* 1964. London. Spring. Vg/dj. B11. $15.00

**BLAZIER, George.** *Cutler Collection of Letters & Documents 1748-1925.* 1962-63. Marietta, OH. ils. 102p. VG. B18. $25.00

**BLESER, Carol.** *Secret & Sacred: Diaries of James Henry Hammond...* 1988. Oxford. 342p. F/F. B10. $15.00

**BLINN, Carol.** *Out West: A Poem on Paste.* 1988. Easthampton. Warwick. 1/30. sgn. 4to. french-fold. F/paper chemise/box. B24. $550.00

**BLISH, James.** *Issue at Hand, 2nd Edition.* 1973. Advent. F/dj. P3. $20.00

**BLISH, James.** *More Issues at Hand.* 1974. Advent. F/dj. P3. $20.00

**BLISH, James.** *Tale That Wags the God.* 1987. Advent. 1st. F/dj. P3. $20.00

**BLISS, Carey S.** *Jusius Firmicus Maternus & the Aldine Edition...* 1981. LA. Kenneth Karmiole. 1/164 (includes org leaf from 1499 ed). gray cloth. F. F1. $475.00

**BLITZ, Marcia.** *Donald Duck.* 1979. NY. Harmony. 1st. F/dj. C9. $102.00

**BLIVEN, Bruce.** *Mirror for Greatness: Six Americans.* 1975. McGraw Hill. 1st. 251p. VG/dj. V3. $15.00

**BLOCH, Iwan.** *Sexual Life of Our Time: Complete Encyclopedia...* 1937. NY. Falstaff. 1st thus. 790p. VG+. A25. $20.00

**BLOCH, Joshua.** *Of Making Many Books: An Annotated List...* 1953. 339p. NF. A4. $95.00

**BLOCH, Robert.** *Eight Million Ways To Die.* 1982. Arbor. 1st. F/dj. M15. $425.00

**BLOCH, Robert.** *Jekyll Legacy.* 1990. NY. Tor. 1st. sgn. F/dj. A24. $35.00

**BLOCH, Robert.** *Lori.* 1989. NY. Tor. 1st. sgn. F/dj. T2. $40.00

**BLOCH, Robert.** *Lori.* 1989. Tor. 1st. F/dj. M21. $15.00

**BLOCH, Robert.** *Monsters in Our Midst.* 1993. Tor. 1st. F/clip. S18. $20.00

**BLOCH, Robert.** *Psycho House.* 1990. NY. Tor. 1st. sgn. F/dj. T2. $35.00

**BLOCH, Robert.** *Psycho House.* 1990. Tor. 1st. NF/dj. G8. $10.00

**BLOCH, Robert.** *Psycho II.* 1982. Binghamton. Whispers. 1st. 1/750. sgn. F/dj/case. M15. $75.00

**BLOCH, Robert.** *Psycho II.* 1982. Warner. 1st. sgn. F/wrp. C9. $60.00

**BLOCH, Robert.** *Psycho II.* 1982. Whispers. 1st. F/dj. N4. $40.00

**BLOCH, Robert.** *Psycho.* 1959. S&S. 1st. inscr Janet Leigh on ffe. w/sgn slip. G/dj. L1. $2,500.00

**BLOCH, Robert.** *Screams.* 1989. Underwood Miller. 1st. 1/300. sgn. F/dj/case. M15. $125.00

**BLOCH, Robert.** *Unholy Trinity: Three Novels of Suspense.* 1986. Santa Cruz. Scream. 1st combined. sgn bookplate. F/dj. T2. $50.00

**BLOCH & GEIS.** *Man, Crime & Society: Forms of Criminal Behavior.* 1966 (1962). Random. 5th. 8vo. G+/VG+. A2. $11.00

**BLOCHMAN, Lawrence G.** *Dr Squibb: Life & Times of a Rugged Idealist.* 1958. S&S. 2nd. 371p. G+. V3. $10.00

**BLOCK, Eugene B.** *Great Train Robberies of the West.* Coward McCa. nn. 317p. G/dj. J2. $50.00

**BLOCK, Lawrence.** *Ariel.* 1980. NY. Arbor. 1st. VG/dj. M21. $15.00

**BLOCK, Lawrence.** *Burglar in the Library.* 1997. London. No Exit. 1st (precedes Am). F/dj. M15. $55.00

**BLOCK, Lawrence.** *Burglar Who Traded Ted Williams.* 1994. NY. Dutton. 1st. F/dj. M15. $35.00

**BLOCK, Lawrence.** *Dance at the Slaughterhouse.* 1991. Morrow. 1st. sgn. F/dj. D10. $40.00

**BLOCK, Lawrence.** *Devil Knows You're Dead.* 1993. Morrow. 1st. sgn. F/dj. N4. $35.00

**BLOCK, Lawrence.** *In the Midst of Death.* 1995. Delavan, WI. G&G Books. 1st Am hc. 1/500. sgn. F/dj. M15. $65.00

BLOCK, Lawrence. *Like a Lamb to Slaughter.* 1984. Arbor. 1st. sgn. VG+/clip. A14. $42.00

BLOCK, Lawrence. *Long Line of Dead Men.* 1994. Morrow. 1st. sgn. F/dj. D10. $30.00

BLOCK, Lawrence. *Random Walk: A Novel for a New Age.* 1988. NY. Tor. 1st. sgn. NF/clip. A14. $25.00

BLOCK, Lawrence. *Sins of the Fathers.* 1992. Dark Harvest. 1/400. sgn. intro/sgn Stephen King. AN/box. T12. $120.00

BLOCK, Lawrence. *Sins of the Fathers.* 1992. Dark Harvest. 1st hc. F/dj. T2. $25.00

BLOCK, Lawrence. *Ticket to the Boneyard.* 1990. Wm Morrow. 1st. NF/VG. L4. $15.00

BLOCK, Lawrence. *Ticket to the Boneyard.* 1990. Morrow. 1st. F/F. H11. $25.00

BLOCK, Lawrence. *Ticket to the Boneyard.* 1990. Morrow. 1st. sgn. F/dj. S18. $30.00

BLOCK, Lawrence. *Time to Murder & Create.* 1993. Dk Harvest. 1st Am hc. 1/300. sgn Block/Kellerman. F/dj/case. M15. $125.00

BLOCK, Lawrence. *Triumph of Evil.* 1972. Hodder Stoughton. 1st Eng. VG+/dj. A14. $52.50

BLOCK, Lawrence. *Walk Among the Tombstones.* 1992. Morrow. 1st. F/F. H11. $30.00

BLOCK, Lawrence. *Walk Among the Tombstones.* 1992. NY. Morrow. 1st. sgn. F/dj. L3/M15. $45.00

BLOCK, Lawrence. *When the Sacred Gin Mill Closes.* 1986. NY. Arbor. 1st. sgn. F/dj. A23. $46.00

BLOCK, Thomas H. *Orbit.* 1982. NY. Coward. 1st. F/NF. H11. $20.00

BLOCK. *Women in American Music: A Bibliography...* 1979. 5024 entries. 338p. F. A4. $35.00

BLOETSCHER, Virginia Chase. *Indians of the Cuyahoga Valley.* 1987. Akron. 2nd. 111p. VG/wrp. B18. $17.50

BLOM, Benjamin. *New York Photographs 1850-1950.* 1982. Dutton. folio. VG/dj. S5. $95.00

BLOMBERG, Rolf. *Buried Gold & Anacondas.* (1959). London. Geo Allen. 1st. ils/fld maps. 144p. F3. $25.00

BLOMBERY & MALONEY. *Proteacea of the Sydney Region.* 1992. Kenthurst, Australia. 215 mc photos. AN. B26. $38.00

BLOMFIELD & INIGO. *Formal Garden in England.* 1892. London. Macmillan. 2nd. ils. 249p. wht cloth. VG. F1. $95.00

BLOND, Georges. *Death of Hitler's Germany.* 1954. Macmillan. 1st. 302p. VG/dj. S16. $17.50

BLOND, Georges. *Elephants.* 1961. NY. 1st. photos. 181p. F/dj. A17. $15.00

BLOOM, Alan. *Hardy Plants of Distinction.* 1965. London. photos. VG/dj. B26. $22.50

BLOOM, Alan. *Plantsman's Perspective.* 1987. London. Collins. 154p. cloth. VG/dj. A10. $15.00

BLOOM, Amy. *Come to Me.* 1993. Harper Collins. 1st. sgn. author's 1st book. F/dj. O11. $45.00

BLOOM, Amy. *Love Invents Us.* 1997. Random. 1st. sgn. F/dj. O11. $30.00

BLOOM, Harold. *Dr Samuel Johnson & James Boswell.* 1986. NY. Chelsea. 1st. tall 8vo. 280p. F/dj. H13. $65.00

BLOOM, Harold. *Thomas Pynchon.* 1986. Chelsea. 1st. 8vo. F/dj. S9. $35.00

BLOOMSTER, Edgar L. *Sailing & Small Craft Down the Ages.* 1940. US Naval Inst. 1st. 1/700. sgn/#d. leather spine. R8. $65.00

BLOT, Pierre. *Handbook of Practical Cookery for Ladies & Professional...* 1868 (1867). sm 4to. 525p. G+. E6. $75.00

BLOTNER, Joseph. *Selected Letters of William Faulkner.* 1977. London. Scholar. 1st. 8vo. 488p. burgundy cloth. NF/dj. H4. $30.00

BLOTNER, Joseph. *Uncollected Stories of William Faulkner.* 1979. Franklin Lib. 1st/ltd. leather. F. M21. $75.00

BLOWER, James M. *Northern Ohio Traction Revisited.* ca 1970. Akron. 1st. 181p. VG. B18. $38.50

BLUM & BLUM. *Dangerous Hour: Lore & Culture of Crisis & Mystery...* 1970. London. Chatto Windus. 410p. cloth. VG/torn. Q2. $36.50

BLUME, Judy. *Freckle Juice.* 1972 (1971). Four Winds. 2nd. 8vo. 40p. VG-/torn. T5. $15.00

BLUME, Judy. *Superfudge.* 1980. Dutton. 1st. 8vo. VG/dj. B17. $25.00

BLUMENTHAL, Walter Hart. *Book Gluttons & Book Gourmets.* 1962. Chicago. Blk Cat. mini. 1/300. 84p. aeg. gilt gr leather. F. B24. $135.00

BLUND, Wilfrid. *Persian Spring.* 1957. London. Barrie. ils/map/32 pl. 252p. cloth. VG/dj. Q2. $20.00

BLUNDEN, Edmund. *Retreat.* 1928. London. Cobden Sanderson. 1st trade. inscr to poet JR Anderson/dtd 1935. NF/dj. J3. $150.00

BLUNDEN, Edmund. *To Themis.* 1931. Beaumond. 1/406. as issued. T9. $65.00

BLUNT, Charles P. *Patrick Henry: Henry Country Years (1779-1784).* (1976). Womack. 72p. xl. B10. $12.00

BLUNT, Wilfrid. *Complete Naturalist: A Life of Linnaeus.* 1971. NY. ils. 256p. VG/dj. B26. $30.00

BLUNT, Wilfrid. *Tulipomania.* 1950. London. Penguin. 1st. 16 mc pl. VG/dj. A10. $30.00

BLY, Robert. *Loving a Woman in Two Worlds.* 1985. Garden City. Dial. 1st. VG/F. B3. $20.00

BLY, Robert. *Teeth Mother Naked at Last.* (1970). City Lights. 2nd/revised/1st thus. 16mo. Poet series #26. VG/wrp. R11. $17.00

BLY, Robert. *This Tree Will Be Here for a Thousand Years.* 1979. Harper Row. UP. sgn. NF/wrp. R14. $90.00

BLY & RAY. *Poetry Reading Against the Vietnam War.* 1966. Madison. Sixties Pr/Am Writers Against Vietnam War. 1st. NF/wrp. R11. $70.00

BLYTHE, Ronald. *Pleasures of Diaries: Four Centuries of Private Writing.* 1989. NY. Pantheon. 1st Am. 388p. F/dj. O10. $25.00

BLYTON, Enid. *Circus of Adventure.* 1953. St Martin. 1st Am. 8vo. 316p. VG/dj. T5. $30.00

BLYTON, Enid. *Five Go Down to the Sea.* 1953. London. Brockhampton. 1st thus. 8vo. ils Eileen Soper. red brd. VG/G+. T5. $20.00

BLYTON, Enid. *Five Go Down to the Sea.* 1961. Reilly Lee. 1st Am. ils Frank Aloise. VG/dj. M5. $22.00

BLYTON, Enid. *Ring O'Bells Mystery.* 1951. Collins. 1st. ils Gilbert Dunlop. VG. M5. $25.00

BLYTON, Enid. *Secret Seven & the Case of the Music Lover.* 1972. Chicago. Childrens Book Pr. ils Tom Dunnington. 125p. VG. B36. $8.00

BLYTON, Enid. *Shock for the Secret Seven.* 1961. Brockhamtpon. 1st. ils Burgess Sharrocks. NF/VG. M5. $38.00

BLYTON, Enid. *Tales of Robin Hood.* nd. London. Geo Newnes Ltd. 12mo. 128p. red cloth. VG. T5. $25.00

BLYTON, Enid. *Wishing-Chair Again.* 1950. London. George Newnes. 1st. 8vo. 192p. red cloth. T5. $40.00

BOARD, John. *Horse & Pencil.* 1950. London. Christopher Johnson. 1st. VG/dj. O3. $48.00

BOARDMAN, Samuel. *Climate, Soil, Physical Resources...of the State of Maine.* 1884. GPO. 60p. VG/wrp. A10. $15.00

**BOAS, Franz.** *Kathlamet Texts.* 1901. WA. Bur Am Ethnology. 3-quarter leather/raised bands. VG. S17. $90.00

**BOAS & POWELL.** *Introduction to Handbook of American Indian Languages.* 1970. Lincoln, NE. 3rd Bison Book. 8vo. 221p. VG/wrp. F7. $5.00

**BOASE, T.S.R.** *St Francis of Assisi.* 1968. IN U. ils Arthur Boyd. VG/dj. M17. $15.00

**BOATNER, Mark M.** *Civil War Dictionary.* (1959). David McKay. rpt. 974p. VG. B10. $35.00

**BOATRIGHT, Mody C.** *Mexican Border Ballads & Other Lore.* 1946. Austin. TX Folklore Soc. 1st. 34p. VG. A18. $40.00

**BOBART, H.H.** *Basketwork Through the Ages.* nd (1936). OUP. rpt. 8vo. 176p. gilt bl cloth. NF/dj. H1. $48.00

**BOCCACCIO, Giovanni.** *Decameron.* 1982. Berkeley. U CA. 3 vol. 1st thus. trans John Payne. F/case. F1. $65.00

**BOCCACCIO, Giovanni.** *Della Geneologia de Gli Dei...* 1606. Venice. Lucio Spineda. 4to. 268p. contemporary vellum. K1. $275.00

**BOCHAROV, Gennady.** *Russian Roulette: Afghanistan Through Russian Eyes.* 1990. Harper Collins. 187p. NF/dj. W1. $18.00

**BOCKMUEHL, Markus.** *This Jesus: Martyr, Lord, Messiah.* 1994. IVP. 242p. F/wrp. B29. $8.50

**BODE, C.** *Maryland: A Bicentennial History.* 1978. NY. photos/map. F/dj. M4. $15.00

**BODENHEIM, Maxwell.** *Replenishing Jessica.* 1925. Boni Liveright. 1st. NF/dj. Q1. $150.00

**BODEY, Donald.** *FNG.* 1985. Viking. 1st. author's 1st novel. NF/NF. R11. $40.00

**BODGER, Joan.** *How the Heather Looks: A Joyous Journey...* 1966 (1965). NY. Viking. 2nd. 8vo. 276p. beige/olive cloth. T5. $40.00

**BODMER, B.P.** *Armature of Conquest: Spanish Accounts of Discovery...* 1973. Stanford. 2 vol. NF. M10. $15.00

**BOEGEHOLD, Betty.** *Hurray for Pippa!* 1980. Knopf. 1st. ils Cyndy Szekers. NF. M5. $25.00

**BOEHIKE & CHAPLIN.** *Fishes of the Bahamas & Adjacent Tropical Waters.* 1970. Academy Nat Sci of Phil. 1st/2nd prt. 771p. VG. S15. $140.00

**BOESEN & BOJE.** *Old Danish Silver.* 1949. Copenhagen. Hassing. 496 photos. silvered blk cloth. VG/dj. F1. $100.00

**BOESSENECKER, John.** *Lawman: Life & Times of Harry Morse.* nd. ils/maps/photos. 384p. VG/dj. E1. $30.00

**BOETTICHER, Wolfgang.** *Robert Schuman: Einfuhrung in Petsonlichkeit und Werk.* 1941. Berlin. 4to. 688p. quarter leather/vellum. VG. S5. $125.00

**BOGAN, Louis.** *Body of This Death.* 1923. McBride. 1st. quarter linen/brd/paper label. F/tattered. M24. $125.00

**BOGARDE, Dirk.** *Orderly Man.* 1983. Knopf. 1st. photos. VG/dj. C9. $25.00

**BOGLE, Donald.** *Brown Sugar.* 1980. Harmony. 1st. VG/dj. C9. $60.00

**BOGNER, Norman.** *Madonna Complex.* 1968. Coward. 1st. F/F. H11. $30.00

**BOHATTA-MORPURGO, Ida.** *Adventures of Mr Pipweasel.* 1934. Munich. Art Institutes/Mueller. 1st Eng. 8vo. gr cloth. dj. R5. $100.00

**BOHJALIAN, Christopher.** *Killing in the Real World.* 1988. St Martin. 1st. sgn. author's 1st book. F/dj. B30. $70.00

**BOHJALIAN, Christopher.** *Past the Bleachers.* 1992. Carroll Graf. 1st. F/dj. P8. $12.50

**BOHN, Thomas W.** *Light & Shadows: A History of Motion Pictures.* 1987. Mtn View. Mayfield. 3rd. 427p. VG/wrp. C5. $12.50

**BOHNE, P.W.** *Highlights in History of American Whaling.* 1968. Rosemead, CA. Bookhaven. mini. 1/500. ils. gray mottled brd/gilt leather. F. B24. $95.00

**BOHUN, William.** *Declarations & Pleadings in Most Unusual Actions...* 1743. London. Henry Lintot/Samuel Birt. 2nd. modern speckled calf. M11. $850.00

**BOHUN, William.** *Institutio Legalis; or, Introduction to Study...Laws of Eng.* 1713. London. Nutt/Isaac Cleave. modern quarter speckled calf/box. M11. $450.00

**BOK, Edward W.** *Man From Maine.* 1923. Scribner. 1st. ils. 278p. VG. S14. $17.50

**BOKUSHI, Suzuki.** *Snow Country Tales: Life in the Other Japan.* 1986. Weatherhill. 1st. 343p. AN/dj. A17. $15.00

**BOLAND, D.J.** *Eucalyptus Seed.* 1980. Canberra. ils/photos. 191p. dj. B26. $32.50

**BOLESLAVSKY, Richard.** *Acting the First Lessons.* 1949. NY. Theatre Arts Books. 134p. VG/dj. C5. $12.50

**BOLL, Heinrich.** *Group Portrait With Lady.* 1973. McGraw Hill. VG/G. L4. $16.00

**BOLLER, Henry A.** *Among the Indians: Eight Years in the Far West.* 1959. Chicago. Lakeside Classic. 461p. bl cloth. NF. P4. $40.00

**BOLLES, Frank.** *Land of the Lingering Snow: Chronicles of a Stroller...* 1891. Boston. 12mo. 234p. gilt cloth. VG. A17. $15.00

**BOLLIGER, Max.** *Eine Zwergengeschichte.* 1983. Bohem. 1st. sgn. VG. B17. $20.00

**BOLTE, J. Willard.** *Backyard Farmer.* 1914. Chicago. Forbes. 1st. 238p. VG. A10. $25.00

**BOLTON, Charles Knowles.** *Private Soldier Under Washington.* 1976. Williamstown. ils. 258p. Vg/dj. B18. $22.50

**BOLTON, Ethel Stanwood.** *American Wax Portraits.* 1929. Boston. 1/550. photos. VG/VG case. M17. $60.00

**BOLTON, Henry E.** *Anza's California Expeditions. Five Volumes.* 1930. Berkeley. 5 vol. 8vo. ils/14 maps/106 pl/47 facs. bl cloth. P4. $850.00

**BOLTON, Herbert E.** *Coronado: Knight of Pueblos & Plains.* 1949. Whittlesey. 491p. blk cloth. VG/dj. F7. $40.00

**BOLTON, Herbert E.** *Pageant in the Wilderness. Story of Escalante Expedition...* 1950. UT State Hist Soc. ils/maps. 265p. cloth. NF. D11. $100.00

**BOLTON, Herbert E.** *Pageant in the Wilderness. Story of Escalante Expedition...* 1951. Salt Lake City. ils/rear pocket map. maroon fabrikoid. VG+. F7. $75.00

**BOLTON, Richard.** *Weathered Texture Workshop.* 1984. Watson Guptill. 4th. blk cloth. F/clip. T11. $25.00

**BOMBAUGH, Charles Carroll.** *Gleanings From the Harvest-Fields of Literature...* 1870. Baltimore. T Newton Kurtz. 12mo. gilt bl cloth. R3. $35.00

**BONAPARTE, Napoleon.** *Courier Extraordinaire Envoye par Bounaparte...* 1797. Paris. Leguay. 4to. 4p (fld). R12. $75.00

**BONAPARTE, Napoleon.** *New Letters of Napoleon I Ommited From Edition Pub Under...* 1897. Appleton. trans Lady Mary Loyd. sm 8vo. 380p. gilt top. VG. H1. $27.50

**BOND, Allen.** *When the Hopkins Came to Baltimore.* 1927. Baltimore. 1st. 84p. A13. $30.00

**BOND, Jules J.** *Rice & Pasta Cuisine I Love.* 1978. Leon Amiel. 1st. photos. VG/dj. S14. $7.00

**BOND, Michael.** *Paddingdon at Work.* 1967. Houghton Mifflin. 1st. 12mo. ils Peggy Fortnum. VG/clip. C14. $22.00

**BOND, Michael.** *Paddington at Large.* 1963. Houghton Mifflin. 2nd. ils Peggy Fortnum. 128p. VG/clip. C14. $15.00

**BOND, Michael.** *Thursday Ahoy!* 1969. London. Harrap. 1st Eng. 8vo. 134p. maroon brd. VG/G. T5. $30.00

**BOND, Mrs. Oresmus B.** *Cavalry Life in Tent & Field.* 1894. NY. Selwin Tait. 1st. 376p. gilt pict cloth. D11. $50.00

**BOND, Octavia Zollicoffer.** *Old Tales Retold; or, Perils & Adventures of TN Pioneers.* 1906. Nashville. brn cloth. VG. B30. $50.00

**BOND, Thomas E.T.** *Wild Flowers of the Ceylon Hills.* 1953. London. 1st. ils. B26. $42.50

**BOND, W.H.** *Eighteenth Century Studies in Honor of Donald F Hyde.* 1970. NY. Spiral. 1st. 1/1650. tall 4to. 424p. linen brd. F/box. H13. $95.00

**BOND.** *Comprehensive Bibliography on Operations Research.* 1958. 4to. 200p. xl. VG. A4. $45.00

**BONDY, Louis W.** *Miniature Books: Their History From the Beginnings...* 1981. London. Shepard. 1st. ils. gilt red cloth. F/dj. F1. $75.00

**BONES, Jim Jr.** *Texas West of the Pecos.* 1981. TX A&M. 1st. ils. 136p. F/F. B19. $25.00

**BONHOEFFER, Dietrich.** *Act of Being.* 1961. Harper Row. 1st Am. 192p. H10. $20.00

**BONILLA & PARRILLA.** *Puerto Rico: Supervivencia y Liberacion.* 1971. Rio Pedras. Ediciones Liberia Internacional. 1st. VG. N2. $10.00

**BONN-BYRNE, Brian Oswald.** *Ireland: The Rock Whence I Was Hewn.* 1929. Little Brn. M11. $20.00

**BONNER, John T.** *Evolution of Culture in Animals.* 1989. Princeton. ils. 204p. F. S15. $8.00

**BONNER, M.G.** *Base Stealer.* 1951. Knopf. 1st. VG/G. P8. $35.00

**BONNER, Mary Graham.** *365 Bedtime Stories.* 1987. Derrydale. 1st thus. 302p. cloth. F/VG+. C14. $8.00

**BONNER, Raymond.** *At the Hand of Man: Peril & Hope for Africa's Wildlife.* 1993. Knopf. 322p. VG/NF. S15. $10.00

**BONNER, Willard Hallam.** *Pirate Laureate: Life & Legends of Captain Kidd.* 1947. Rutgers. VG/dj. M17. $25.00

**BONNEY, T.G.** *Story of Our Planet.* 1902 (1893). London. Cassell. 8vo. ils. 592p. cloth. K5. $30.00

**BONSAL, Stephen.** *Edward Fitzgerald Beale: Pioneer in Path of Empire 1822...* 1912. Putnam. 1st. ils. 312p. teg. D11. $150.00

**BONWICK, James.** *Egyptian Belief & Modern Thought.* 1956. Indian Hills. Falcon's Wing. VG. D2. $20.00

**BOONE, J. Allen.** *Letters to Strongheart.* 1945. Prentice Hall. 9th. inscr/sgn. NF/case. A21. $75.00

**BOONE & CROCKETT CLUB.** *North American Big Game.* 1971. Pittsburgh. 1st. 403p. dj. A17/B5. $50.00

**BOONE & CROCKETT CLUB.** *Records of North American Big Game.* 1981. 8th vol in series. 1st. 409p. F/dj. M4. $25.00

**BOONE & CROCKETT CLUB.** *19th Big Game Awards 1983-1985.* 1986. Dumfries. 170 photos. 410p. F/dj. A17. $30.00

**BOONE & GRUNSKA.** *Hack.* 1978. Highland. 1st. F/VG. P8. $85.00

**BOOTE, Richard.** *Historical Treatise of Action or Suit of Law...* 1795. London. Strahan/Woodfall. contemporary calf/rb. M11. $650.00

**BOOTH, Christopher B.** *House of Rogues.* 1923. Chelsea. 1st. VG. G8. $20.00

**BOOTH, Harris.** *Aeroplane Performance Calculations.* 1921. EP Dutton. 1st. 207p. NF. H7. $20.00

**BOOTHBY, Guy.** *Kidnapped President.* 1902. London. Ward Lock. 1st. VG. M15. $75.00

**BOR, N.L.** *Grasses of Burma, Ceylon, India & Pakistan.* 1960. Oxford. ils. 767p. VG/dj. B26. $65.00

**BORA, S.J.** *Variability of Rhinanthus Serotinus.* 1972. Groningen. inscr. ils/tables. 158p. sc. B26. $22.50

**BORD & BORD.** *Ancient Mysteries of Britain.* 1986. Salem House. 1st. ils. F/dj. T10. $45.00

**BORDEAUX, H.** *Guynemer: Knight of the Air.* 1918. Yale. 1st. xl. VG. E6. $75.00

**BORDEAUX, William J.** *Custer's Conqueror.* nd. Smith. VG. A19. $250.00

**BORDEN, Mary.** *Flamingo.* 1927. Doubleday Doran. 1st. F/dj. B4. $350.00

**BORDEN, Mary.** *You, the Jury & a Novel.* 1952. NY. Longman Gr. worn. M11. $15.00

**BORDEN, W.** *Use of the Rontgen Ray by the Medical Dept of US Army...* 1900. GPO. 1st. 4to. 98p. VG. E6. $350.00

**BORDON, Mrs. John.** *Cruise of the Northern Light, Explorations & Hunting...* 1928. Macmillan. 1st. 317p. gilt bl cloth. VG. F1. $40.00

**BOREIN, Edward.** *Borein's West.* 1952. Santa Barbara, CA. Schauer Prt Studio. ils. F. A19. $125.00

**BORGES, Jorge Luis.** *Congress.* 1974. London. Enitharmon. 1st. 1/50 (300 total). sgn author/trans. F/dj. L3. $850.00

**BORGESON & JADERQUIST.** *Sports & Classic Cars.* 1955. Bonanza. rpt. ils. VG/G. P8. $25.00

**BORISOVA & STERNIN.** *Russian Art Nouveau.* 1988. NY. Rizzoli. 1st Eng-language. 400p. gilt blk cloth. F/NF. F1. $85.00

**BORLAND, Hal.** *This Hill, This Valley.* 1957. S&S. 1st. ils Peter Marks. 315p. tan cloth. VG/dj. F1. $20.00

**BORN, Wolfgang.** *American Landscape Painting: An Interpretation.* 1948. Yale. ils. 228p. cloth. VG. D2. $35.00

**BOROWITZ, Albert.** *Innocence & Arsenic: Studies in Crime & Literature.* 1977. Harper Row. 1st. 170p. F/dj. O10. $25.00

**BORROR, Donald J.** *Dictionary of Word Roots & Combining Forms.* 1960. Mountain View, CA. 137p. sc. VG. B26. $15.00

**BORSKI & MILLER.** *Jolly Tailor. And Other Tales Translated From Polish.* 1964. NY. ils Kazimir Klepacki. VG. M17. $22.50

**BORST, Ronald V.** *Graven Images.* 1992. Grove. 1st. VG/dj. L1. $50.00

**BORYCZKA & CARY.** *No Strength Without Union: Illustrated History...* 1982. np. OH Hist Soc. VG/dj. V4. $45.00

**BOSHER, Kate Langley.** *How It Happened.* 1914. NY. Harper. 1st. 164p. G. H11. $8.00

**BOSHER, Kate Langley.** *Mary Cary, Frequently Martha.* 1910. NY. Harper. 1st. 168p. VG. G11. $8.00

**BOSK, Charles L.** *All God's Mistakes: Genetic Counseling Pediatric Hospital.* 1992. Chicago. 1st. 195p. F/dj. C14. $15.00

**BOSQUI, Edward.** *Memoirs of Edward Bosqui.* 1952. Oakland, CA. Grabhorn. 1/350. ils. 182p. blk cloth/spine label. K1. $125.00

**BOSSE, Malcolm.** *Vast Memory of Love.* 1992. NY. 1st. VG/dj. M17. $17.50

**BOSTOCK & RILEY.** *Natural History of Pliny, Translated... Vol III.* 1965. London. Bohn. sm 8vo. decor cloth. VG+. M12. $37.50

**BOSTON, L.M.** *Fossil Snake.* 1976. Atheneum. 1st Am. 8vo. 53p. tan cloth. F/dj. T5. $30.00

**BOSTON, Lucy M.** *Perverse & Foolish: A Memoir of Childhood & Youth.* 1979. Atheneum. 1st Am. 8vo. 140p. F/dj. T5. $35.00

**BOSTON, Richard.** *Osbert: Portrait of Osbert Lancaster.* 1989. London. 1st. ils. VG/dj. M17. $17.50

**BOSWELL, Hazel.** *French Canada.* 1938. Viking. 1st. 16mo. 83p. beige cloth. NF/dj. D1. $75.00

BOSWELL, James. *Boswell in Search of a Wife, 1766-1769.* 1956. McGraw Hill. 1st thus. 390p. gilt bl cloth. F1. $40.00

BOSWELL, James. *Boswell's Life of Johnson.* ca 1920. NY. Bigelow. 6 vol. 8vo. bl cloth. C6. $95.00

BOSWELL, James. *Boswell's Life of Johnson.* 1891. NY. Harper. 6 vol. edit George Birkbeck Hill. Lauriat morocco. F1. $495.00

BOSWELL, James. *Dorando, a Spanish Tale.* 1930. London. Elkin Mathews. sm 8vo. 1/600. 44p. VG. H13. $95.00

BOSWELL, James. *Journal of Tour to Herbrides With Samuel Johnson, LLD.* 1785. Dublin. Wht, Byrone & Cash. 1st Dublin. tall 8vo. 524p. H13. $795.00

BOSWELL, James. *Journal of Tour to Herbrides With Samuel Johnson, LLD.* 1807. London. Cadell Davies. 4th. tall 8vo. 460p. polished calf. H13. $395.00

BOSWELL, James. *Journey of a Tour to Corsica.* 1951. London. Williams Norgate. blk cloth. dj. H13. $45.00

BOSWELL, James. *Letters of James Boswell.* 1924. Clarendon. 2 vol. 1st. tall 8vo. red cloth. F. H13. $175.00

BOSWELL, James. *Life of Samuel Johnson, LLD.* 1925. London. Dent. 3 vol. ils Herbert Railton. cloth. H13. $165.00

BOSWELL, James. *Life of Samuel Johnson, LLD.* 1931. London. OUP. 2 vol. sm 8vo. gilt cloth. VG. H13. $65.00

BOSWELL, James. *Life of Samuel Johnson, LLD.* 1938. Curwen. 3 vol. 1/1500. 1st. tan cloth. H13. $275.00

BOSWELL, James. *Life of Samuel Johnson, LLD.* 1993. London. Folio Soc. 2 vol. gilt brn linen/red label. AN/case. H13. $295.00

BOSWELL, James. *Life of Samuel Johnson, LLD...* 1791. London. Henry Baldwin for Chas Dilly. 2 vol. 1st. F. H13. $6,800.00

BOSWELL, James. *Life of Samuel Johnson, LLD: Temple Bar Edition.* 1922. Doubleday Page. 10 vol. lg 8vo. pl/facs. brd/vellum spines. H13. $395.00

BOSWELL, James. *Life of Samuel Johnson.* 1952. Random/Modern Lib. 1st. tall 16mo. 559p. F/VG. H1. $12.00

BOSWELL, James. *Utrecht Verse.* 1985. Utrecht. Buchelius. mini. 1/60. blk wrp/paper label. B24. $85.00

BOSWELL, Robert. *Crooked Hearts.* 1987. Knopf. 1st. sgn/dtd 1997. author's 2nd book. F/F. B3. $65.00

BOSWELL, Robert. *Dancing in the Movies.* 1986. Iowa City, IA. 1st. sgn. author's 1st book. F/dj. O11. $125.00

BOSWELL, Robert. *Living To Be 100: Stories.* 1994. Knopf. 1st. sgn. F/dj. O11. $25.00

BOSWELL, Robert. *Mystery Ride.* 1993. Knopf. 1st. F/dj. T11. $15.00

BOSWELL, Robert. *Mystery Ride.* 1993. Knopf. 1st. sgn. F/dj. O11. $35.00

BOSWELL, Thomas. *Heart of the Order.* 1989. Doubleday. 1st. F/F. B3. $15.00

BOSWORTH, C.E. *Iran & Islam: In Memory of Late Vladimir Minorsky.* 1971. Edinburgh. 18 pl/ils/map. 574p. VG/dj. Q2. $30.00

BOSWORTH, Louise Marion. *Living Wage of Women Workers: A Study of Incomes...* May 1911. Phil. Am Academy Political & Social Sci. 90p. VG+/wrp. A25. $50.00

BOSWORTH, Newton. *Hochelaga Depicta; or, New Picture of Montreal...* 1846. Montreal. RWS Mackay. 8vo. 22 fld ils/fld map. 284p+27p addenda. purple cloth. O1. $375.00

BOTIN, B.A. *Civil War Treasury of Tales, Legends & Folklore.* 1981. Promotory. 1st thus. ils Warren Chappell. NF/dj. A14. $17.50

BOTTOMS, David. *Any Cold Jordan.* 1987. Atlanta. Peachtree. 1st. author's 1st novel. NF/dj. H11. $25.00

BOTTOMS, David. *Easter Weekend.* 1990. Houghton Mifflin. 1st. sgn. F/dj. R14. $50.00

BOTWELL, Jean. *Dancing Princess.* 1965. HBW. 1st. 190p. cloth. F/NF. D4. $30.00

BOUCAUT, James Penn. *Arab: Horse of the Future.* 1905. London. Gay & Bird. 1st. G. O3. $195.00

BOUCHER, Anthony. *Exeunt Murderers: Best Mystery Stories of Anthony Boucher.* 1983. S IL U. 1st. F/dj. M15. $45.00

BOUCHER, Jean. *Sermons de la Simvlee Conversation...* 1594. Ivxte Paris. Chaudiere. thick 8vo. quarter calf. R12. $800.00

BOUCHER, Sharon. *Teddy Bear of Bumpkin Hollow.* 1956 (1948). Rand McNally. Elf Book. 8vo. unp. pict brd. G+. T5. $30.00

BOUDET, Jacques. *Man & Beast: A Visual History.* 1964. NY. 1st Am. ils/photos. 295p. F/dj. A17. $27.50

BOULDING, Elise. *My Part in the Quaker Adventure.* 1953. Phil. Friends Central Bureau. 8vo. 96p. G/wrp. V3. $12.00

BOULENGER, E.G. *British Angler's Natural History.* 1946. London. Collins. 8vo. ils/pl. 48p. F/VG. M12. $10.00

BOULESTIN, X.M. *Finer Cooking or Dishes for Parties.* 1937. NY. OUP. 12mo. 198p. VG. B11. $25.00

BOULLE, Pierre. *My Own River Kwai.* 1967. NY. 1st. trans X Fielding. dj. T9. $18.00

BOURDILLON, T.F. *Forest Trees of Travancore.* 1976 (1908). Dehra Dun. rpt. photos. 456p. AN. B26. $22.00

BOURDON, David. *Warhol.* 1989. NY. Abrams. ils. 432p. silvered whit cloth. NF/VG. F1. $40.00

BOURGEAU, Art. *Exploring the World of Wolves.* 1983. Scribner. 1st. F/dj. T11. $75.00

BOURGEAU, Art. *Seduction.* 1988. DIF. 1st. F/dj. G8/Q1. $20.00

BOURGEAU, Art. *Seduction.* 1988. DIF. 1st. sgn. F/dj. Y1. $30.00

BOURGEAU, Art. *Wolfman.* 1989. DIF. 1st. F/NF. M21. $15.00

BOURKE-WHITE, Margaret. *Halfway to Freedom.* 1949. NY. S&S. 1st. 8vo. VG/NF. S9. $100.00

BOURKE-WHITE, Margaret. *Shooting the Russian War.* 1942. S&S. 1st. F/NF. B2. $65.00

BOURLIERE, Francois. *Natural History of Mammals.* 1955. London. 363p. A13. $15.00

BOURNE, Eulalia. *Blue Colt.* 1979. Northland. ils. 103p. NF/NF. B19. $15.00

BOURNE, Miriam Anne. *First Family: George Washington & His Intimate Relations.* (1982). Norton. 1st. ils. VG/dj. B10. $25.00

BOURNE, Miriam Anne. *Nature Journal: A Monthly Guide to Wildlife.* 1990. WA, DC. Starwood. 1st. 8vo. decor brd. F. M7. $18.00

BOURNE, R. *Red King's Rebellion: Racial Politics in New Eng 1675-78.* 1990. NY. 1st. ils/map. NF/rpr. M4. $20.00

BOURNE, Russell. *View From Front Street.* 1989. NY. 1st. ils. 282p. F/dj. A17. $20.00

BOURNE, William. *Regiment for the Sea & Other Writings on Navigation...* 1963. Cambridge. Hakluyt Soc. ils/fld map. 464p. pict bl cloth. dj. K1. $45.00

BOURTIER, S.H. *Murder's Burning.* Random. 1st. NF/VG. G8. $15.00

BOUSSARD, Leon. *Le Secret du Colonel Lawrence.* 1941. Paris. Mont-Louis Clermont Ferrand. 1st. 124p. G/VG. M7. $60.00

BOUSSINGAULT, J.B. *Rural Economy.* 1860. NY. Saxton. 507p. VG. A10. $20.00

**BOUTELL, Charles.** *Monumental Brasses & Slabs: Historical & Descriptive Notice.* 1847. London. Geo Bell. 1st. ftspc/ils. later morocco. C6. $125.00

**BOUTON, Jim.** *Ball Four.* 1993. Barnes Noble. 1st thus. sgn. F/dj. C15. $18.00

**BOUVIER, E.L.** *Psychic Life of Insects.* 1922. NY. Century. 1st Eng-language. 12mo. trans LO Howard. 377p. G1. $45.00

**BOUWSMA, William J.** *John Calvin: Sixteenth-Century Portrait.* 1988. OUP. ils/index. 310p. F/dj. H10. $35.00

**BOVA, Ben.** *Dueling Machine.* 1969. HRW. 1st. sgn/dtd. F/clip. G10. $45.00

**BOVA, Ben.** *Flight of Exiles.* 1972. NY. Dutton. 1st. sgn. VG+/clip. A14. $25.00

**BOVA, Ben.** *Millenium: Novel About People & Politics in Year 1999.* 1976. London. Macdonald & Jane's. 1st. sgn. VG+/dj. A14. $17.50

**BOVA, Ben.** *Voyagers.* 1981. Doubleday. 1st. sgn. VG+/clip. A14. $28.00

**BOVA & POGUE.** *Trikon Deception.* 1992. NY. Tom Doherty. 1st. F/dj. A23. $30.00

**BOVA & PREISS.** *First Contact: Search for Extraterrestrial Intelligence.* 1990. NY. NAL. 1st. VG/dj. N2. $10.00

**BOVET, Pierre.** *Fighting Instinct.* 1923. Dodd Mead. 1st Am. trans John Young/Thos Greig. xl. VG. G1. $30.00

**BOWDEN, Charles.** *Desierto.* 1991. Norton. 1st. F/dj. R14. $35.00

**BOWDEN, Charles.** *Frog Mountain Blues.* 1987. Tucson. U AZ. 1st. photos Jack Dykinga. F/dj. R14. $50.00

**BOWDEN, William H.** *Printing on Vellum.* 1994. Islip. 1/100. wrp. T9. $32.00

**BOWDITCH, N.I.** *History of the Massachusetts General Hospital.* 1851. Boston. 1st. lacks 2 pl. 442p. xl. A13. $150.00

**BOWE, Richard J.** *Historical Album of Colorado.* 1959. Denver. ils sgn. G. A19. $30.00

**BOWEN, Ashley.** *Journals of Ashley Bowen (1728-1813).* 1973. Salem, MA. Peabody Mus of Salem. sgn pres. 326p. gilt cloth. F/dj. O1. $50.00

**BOWEN, Elizabeth.** *Joining Charles.* 1929. London. Constable. 1st. 8vo. 216p. red cloth. VG. J3. $275.00

**BOWEN, Elizabeth.** *Seven Winters, Memories of a Dublin Childhood...* 1962. NY. Knopf. 1st. 273p. gilt gr cloth. NF/dj. F1. $30.00

**BOWEN, Frank C.** *From Carrack to Clipper: Book of Sailing Ship Models.* 1948. London. Halton. 66 pl. 74p. G. M10. $16.50

**BOWEN, J.J.** *Strategy of Robet E Lee.* 1914. Neale. 256p. G. B10. $85.00

**BOWEN, Marshal E.** *Utah People in the Nevada Desert: Homestead & Community...* 1994. UT State. 1st. ils/index. 134p. F/F. B19. $17.50

**BOWEN, Michael.** *Can't Miss.* 1987. Harper Row. 1st. F/dj. P8. $25.00

**BOWEN, Michael.** *Faithfully Executed.* 1992. NY. St Martin. 1st. F/dj. A23. $30.00

**BOWEN, Peter.** *Imperial Kelly.* 1992. NY. Crown. 1st. F/dj. M15. $40.00

**BOWEN, Robert Sidney.** *Big Inning.* 1955. Lee Shepard. 1st. VG/dj. P8. $60.00

**BOWEN, Robert Sidney.** *Infield Flash.* 1969. Lee Shepard. 1st. VG/dj. P8. $35.00

**BOWEN, Robert Sidney.** *Infield Spark.* 1954. Lee Shepard. 1st. VG/dj. P8. $60.00

**BOWEN, Robert Sidney.** *Lightning Southpaw.* 1967. Lee Shepard. 1st. VG/dj. P8. $50.00

**BOWEN, Robert Sidney.** *Player - Manager.* 1949. Lee Shepard. 1st. VG. P8. $10.00

**BOWEN, Robert Sidney.** *Red Randall in the Allutians.* 1945. Grosset Dunlap. 1st. NF/VG. B36. $13.00

**BOWEN & JUX.** *Afro-Arabian Geology: A Kenematic View.* 1987. London. Chapman Hall. 295p. 8vo. ils brd. F. B1. $42.50

**BOWEN & REEVES.** *Legends: Art of Richard Stone Reeves.* 1989. Birmingham. Oxmoor. 1st. obl folio. F/VG/mailing box. O3. $150.00

**BOWEN & VON MECK.** *Beloved Friend.* 1937. NY. Random. 484p. G. C5. $15.00

**BOWEN-ROWLANDS, Ernest.** *Seventy-Two Years at the Bar, a Memoir...* 1924. London. Macmillan. orig crimson cloth. M11. $65.00

**BOWER, Barbara.** *Worzel Gummidge: Scarecrow of Scatterbrook Farm.* 1947. Putnam. ils Ursula Koering. xl. G+. B36. $16.00

**BOWER, F.O.** *Origin of a Land Flora.* 1908. London. Macmillan. 1st. 8vo. ils. gilt gr cloth. NF. C12. $75.00

**BOWER, F.O.** *Primitive Land Plants Also Known as the Archegoniatae.* 1935. London. Macmillan. 1st. 8vo. ils. 658p. gilt gr cloth. VG. C12. $75.00

**BOWERS, Claude G.** *Tragic Era.* 1929. Houghton Mifflin. 1st. 8vo. 567p. blk cloth. VG. S17. $10.00

**BOWERS, John.** *University & Medicine: Past, Present & Tomorrow.* 1977. NY. 1st. 239p. dj. A13. $40.00

**BOWES, Anne LaBastille.** *Bird Kingdom of the Mayas.* 1967. Van Nostrand. 1st. 80p. dj. F3. $15.00

**BOWLBY, John.** *Charles Darwin: A New Life.* 1990. NY. ils. VG/dj. M17. $15.00

**BOWLES, Ella Shannon.** *Let Me Show You New Hampshire.* 1938. Knopf. ils/fld maps. orange cloth. F/dj. B14. $95.00

**BOWLES, Paul.** *Let It Come Down.* 1952. Random. 1st. VG/dj. C9. $120.00

**BOWLES, Paul.** *Little Stone.* 1950. London. Lehmann. 1st. author's 2nd book. F/dj. O11. $350.00

**BOWLES, Paul.** *Next to Nothing: Collected Poems 1926-1977.* 1981. Blk Sparrow. 1st 1/500. F/dj. L3. $55.00

**BOWLES, Paul.** *Scenes.* 1968. Blk Sparrow. 1st. 1/50 (300 total). sgn. F. L3. $1,000.00

**BOWLES, Paul.** *Spider's House.* 1955. Random. 1st Am. F/dj. B4. $350.00

**BOWLES, Samuel.** *Across the Continent: Summer's Journey to Rocky Mountains...* 1866. NY. Hurd Houghton. later ed. 8vo. fld map. 452p. terra-cotta cloth. VG. O1. $100.00

**BOWMAN, Allen.** *Morale of the American Revolutionary Army.* 1943. WA, DC. 160p. VG/wrp. B18. $45.00

**BOWMAN, David.** *Let the Dog Drive.* 1992. NY U. 1st. sgn. author's 1st book. F/dj. O11. $110.00

**BOWMAN, Hank W.** *Famous Guns From Famous Collections.* 1957. NY. 143p. dj. A17. $12.50

**BOWMAN, Isaiah.** *Desert Trails of Atacama.* 1924. Am Geog Soc. 1st. lg 8vo. 362p. gray cloth/gilt labels. B11. $35.00

**BOWMAN, John S.** *Civil War Almanac.* 1983. NY. 1st. ils/index. 400p. F/stiff wrp. E1. $15.00

**BOWMAN, Larry G.** *Captive Americans: Prisoners During the American Revolution.* 1976. Athens, OH. 1st. F/dj. M15. $20.00

**BOWMAN, R.I.** *Morphological Differentiation Adaptation Galapagos Finches.* 1961. U CA. ils/photos. 302p. xl. NF. C12. $35.00

**BOWMAN & LA MARCA.** *Pleasures of the Porch: Ideas for Gracious Outdoor Living.* 1997. Rizoli. folio. photos. F/dj. A28. $16.00

**BOWMAN & ZOSS.** *Pictorial History of Baseball.* 1986. Gallery. sm folio. 240p. VG/dj. B11. $20.00

**BOWNELL & IRELAND.** *Everyday Living.* 1935. Rand McNally. 1st. ils Martha E Miller. 218p. VG+. A25. $20.00

**BOWSER, F.P.** *African Slave in Colonial Peru 1524-1650.* 1974. Stanford. 1st. ils. F/dj. M4. $22.00

**BOYD, Brendan.** *Blue Ruin.* 1991. Norton. 1st. F/dj. P8. $25.00

**BOYD, Eva Jolene.** *Old Overland Stagecoaching.* 1993. Plano. Republic of TX Pr. 1st. 200p. F. O3. $12.00

**BOYD, G.A.** *Elias Boudinot: Patriot & Statesman 1740-1821.* 1952. Princeton. 1st. ils. 312p. NF. M4. $25.00

**BOYD, James.** *Drums.* 1925. Scribner. 1st. VG. T11. $45.00

**BOYD, James.** *Long Hunt.* 1930. Scribner. 8vo. 376p. F/case. C6. $95.00

**BOYD, L.A.** *Coast of Northeast Greenland With Hydrographic Studies...* 1948. Am Geog Soc Pub #30. 5 panoramas/7 fld maps. 339p. VG. M4. $55.00

**BOYD, Thomas.** *Light-Horse Harry Lee.* 1931. Scribner. 1st. 359p. VG/dj. B10. $35.00

**BOYD, Thomas.** *Mad Anthony Wayne.* 1929. Scribner. 1st. xl. VG. M10. $12.50

**BOYD, William Kenneth.** *Story of Durham.* 1925. Durham, NC. 1st. 8vo. 345p. bl cloth. VG. C6. $85.00

**BOYD, William.** *Brazzaville Beach.* 1991. Morrow. 1st. F/F. B3. $30.00

**BOYD, William.** *Good Man in Africa.* 1981. Morrow. 1st Am. F/dj. M25. $40.00

**BOYD, William.** *New Confessions.* 1987. Hamish Hamilton. true 1st. F/dj. D10. $40.00

**BOYD, William.** *New Confessions.* 1988. Morrow. 1st Am. NF/dj. R14. $25.00

**BOYD, William.** *On the Yankee Station.* 1984. NY. Morrow. 1st. NF/dj. R11. $30.00

**BOYD & BOYD.** *Greentown in Color.* 1969. Converse, IL. self pub. 1st. tall 8vo. cbdg. VG. H1. $45.00

**BOYD & BOYD.** *Greentown.* 1972. Wallace Homestead. 4th. ils. sbdg. 618p. VG/dj. H1. $22.50

**BOYDEN, Stephen.** *Western Civilization in Biological Perspective.* 1992. Clarendon. 370p. AN/wrp. S15. $15.00

**BOYER, Mary G.** *Arizona in Literature: A Collection of Best Writings...* 1934. Arthur H Clark. 1st. index. 574p. VG. B19. $45.00

**BOYER, Rick.** *Billingsgate Shoal.* 1982. Houghton Mifflin. 1st. F/rpr. M15. $85.00

**BOYER, Rick.** *Penny Ferry.* 1984. Houghton Mifflin. 1st. F/F. H11. $35.00

**BOYER, Rick.** *Whale's Footprints.* 1988. Houghton Mifflin. 1st. F/dj. A14. $25.00

**BOYLAN, Clare.** *Last Resorts.* 1986. Summit. 1st. F/dj. A23. $32.00

**BOYLAN, Eleanor.** *Working Murder.* 1989. Holt. 1st. VG+/NF. G8. $20.00

**BOYLAN, Grace Duffie.** *Our Little Eskimo Kiddies.* 1901. Hurst. 1st. lg 8vo. ils Ike Morgan. VG. M5. $35.00

**BOYLE, Alistair.** *Con.* 1996. Santa Barbara. Knoll. 1st. F/dj. A23. $36.00

**BOYLE, Andrew.** *Trenchard: Man of Vision.* 1962. London. Collins. 1st. 768p. gilt red-orange cloth. NF/NF clear plastic. M7. $35.00

**BOYLE, Frederick.** *About Orchids.* 1893. London. Chapman Hall. 1st. 8vo. ils. 250p. VG. C6. $200.00

**BOYLE, Kay.** *Gentlemen I Address You Privately.* 1933. Smith Haas. 1st. VG/dj. A24. $150.00

**BOYLE, Kay.** *Words That Must Somehow Be Said: Selected Essays of...* 1985. Northpoint. 1st. 262p. VG/dj. A25. $20.00

**BOYLE, T. Coraghessan.** *Budding Prospects.* 1984. NY. Viking. ARC. sgn. F/F. D10. $135.00

**BOYLE, T. Coraghessan.** *Budding Prospects.* 1984. Viking. 1st. NF/NF. R14. $75.00

**BOYLE, T. Coraghessan.** *Budding Prospects.* 1984. Viking. 1st. sgn. F/dj. O11. $85.00

**BOYLE, T. Coraghessan.** *Descent of Man.* 1979. Little Brn. 1st. inscr to sister. rpr front hinge. NF/dj. B4. $2,500.00

**BOYLE, T. Coraghessan.** *Descent of Man.* 1980. London. Gollancz. 1st. sgn. author's 1st book. F/NF. O11. $65.00

**BOYLE, T. Coraghessan.** *East Is East.* 1990. Viking. 1st. sgn. F/clip. O11. $45.00

**BOYLE, T. Coraghessan.** *If the River Was Whiskey.* 1989. Viking Penguin. 1st. sgn. F/dj. O11. $45.00

**BOYLE, T. Coraghessan.** *If the River Was Whiskey.* 1989. Viking. 1st. NF/dj. M23. $25.00

**BOYLE, T. Coraghessan.** *Road to Wellville.* 1993. Viking. 1st. F/dj. A23. $30.00

**BOYLE, T. Coraghessan.** *Road to Wellville.* 1993. Viking. 1st. sgn. F/dj. O11. $45.00

**BOYLE, T. Coraghessan.** *Tortilla Curtain.* 1995. Viking. 1st. sgn/dtd 1995. F/dj. R14. $45.00

**BOYLE, T. Coraghessan.** *World's End.* 1987. Viking. 1st. sgn. F/dj. O11. $65.00

**BOYLES & BOYLES.** *Homesteaders.* 1909. McClurg. G. A19. $25.00

**BOYNTON, H.V.** *Dedication of Chickamauga & Chattanooga Nat Military Park.* 1986. GPO. 374p. 3-quarter leather. B18. $37.50

**BRACELAND, Francis.** *Institute of Living: Hartford Retreat, 1822-1972.* 1972. Hartford. 1st. 242p. A13. $20.00

**BRACKEN, Arnold C.** *Dream of Troy.* 1974. Lipscomb. 1st. ils. cloth. VG/dj. W1. $22.00

**BRACKEN, C.P.** *Roman Ring.* 1968. London. Cassell. 1st. F/dj. M17. $65.00

**BRACKENRIDGE, H.M.** *Recollections of Persons & Places in the West.* 1834. Phil. 1st. 244p. rb. B18. $95.00

**BRACKENRIDGE, H.M.** *Views of Louisiana; Containing Geogrphical, Statistical...* 1817. Baltimore. Schaeffer & Maund. 12mo. 324p. contemporary sheep. K1. $375.00

**BRACKENRIDGE, Hugh Henry.** *Law Miscellanies: Containing Intro to Study of Law...* 1814. Phil. P Byrne. sheep. working copy. M11. $150.00

**BRADBURY, Edward P.;** see Moorcock, Michael.

**BRADBURY, Ray.** *Death Is a Lonely Business.* 1985. Knopf. 1st. VG/NF. B30. $35.00

**BRADBURY, Ray.** *Graveyard for Lunatics: Another Tale of Two Cities.* 1990. Knopf. 1st. sgn. F/dj. M25. $45.00

**BRADBURY, Ray.** *Green Shadows, White Whale.* 1992. Knopf. 1st. ils Edward Sorel. NF/dj. A14. $17.50

**BRADBURY, Ray.** *Haunted Computer & the Android Pope.* 1981. Knopf. 1st. NF/VG. B30. $45.00

**BRADBURY, Ray.** *Haunted Computer & the Android Pope.* 1981. NY. Knopf. 1st. sgn/dtd 1996. F/dj. R14. $60.00

**BRADBURY, Ray.** *I Sing the Body Electric.* nd. BC. NF/VG. S18. $5.00

**BRADBURY, Ray.** *New Biblical Texts, by Ray Bradbury.* 1985. Santa Ana. Gold Stein. mini. 1st. 1/75. sgn Bradbury/D'Ambrosio. F/case. B24. $450.00

**BRADBURY, Ray.** *Stories of Ray Bradbury.* 1980. Knopf. 1st. VG+/clip. A14. $42.00

**BRADBURY, Ray.** *Where Robot Mice & Robot Men Run Round in Robot Towns.* 1977. Knopf. 1st. NF/NF. B30. $40.00

**BRADBURY, Ray.** *Yestermorrow: Obvious Answers to Impossible Futures...* 1991. Capra. 1st. NF/dj. B30. $25.00

**BRADDON, Russell.** *Joan Sutherland.* 1962. London. Collins. 256p. G. C5. $17.50

**BRADEN, Charles S.** *Religious Aspects of the Conquest of Mexico.* 1930. Durham. Duke U. 1st. 344p. cloth. dj. D11. $50.00

**BRADEN, Charles S.** *World's Religions: A Short History.* 1939. Abingdon-Cokesbury. 256p. VG. B29. $8.50

**BRADEN, James A.** *Trail of the Seneca.* 1936. Akron. Saalfield. 12mo. G/VG. A2. $8.00

**BRADFIELD, Scott.** *Dream of the Wolf: Stories.* 1990. Knopf. 1st Am. VG+/dj. A14. $21.00

**BRADFIELD, Scott.** *History of Luminous Motion.* 1989. London. Bloomsbury. 1st. NF/dj. A14. $35.00

**BRADFIELD, Scott.** *Secret Life of Houses.* 1988. London. Unwin Hyman. 1st. sgn. NF/dj. A14. $42.00

**BRADFIELD, Scott.** *What's Wrong With America?* 1994. St Martin. 1st Am. sgn. F/dj. R14. $35.00

**BRADFORD, Barbara Taylor.** *Women in His Life.* 1990. Random. 1st. F/dj. T12. $35.00

**BRADFORD, Duncan.** *Wonders of the Heavens, Being Popular View of Astronomy...* 1837. Boston. Am Stationers. lg 4to. 371p. K7. $300.00

**BRADFORD, Erle.** *Christopher Columbus.* 1973. London. Michael Joseph. 1st. ils. 288p. VG/dj. M10. $28.50

**BRADFORD, Erle.** *Mediterranean: Portrait of a Sea.* 1971. NY. photos. VG/dj. M17. $20.00

**BRADFORD, Ned.** *Battles & Leaders of the Civil War: One-Volume Edition...* 1956. Appleton Century Crofts. 1st. VG/VG-. A14. $14.00

**BRADFORD, Perry.** *Born With the Blues.* 1965. NY. Oak. ARC? F/NF. w/promo material. B2. $125.00

**BRADFORD, Roark.** *How Come Christmas.* 1948. NY. Harper. VG/dj. B5. $20.00

**BRADFORD, Roark.** *This Side of Jordan.* 1929. Harper. 1st. inscr. B30. $22.50

**BRADFORD, William.** *Of Plymouth Plantation 1620-1647.* 1952. NY. 1st. VG/G. M17. $30.00

**BRADLEY, Glenn D.** *Story of the Pony Express.* 1914. Chicago. 2nd. 175p. VG. B18. $22.50

**BRADLEY, John.** *Love & Obits.* 1992. Holt. 1st. F/dj. R14. $30.00

**BRADLEY, Marion Zimmer.** *Heritage of Hastur.* 1977. Boston. Gregg. 1st hc. VG/sans. B11. $75.00

**BRADLEY, Marion Zimmer.** *Mists of Avalon.* 1982. NY. Knopf. 1st. VG/dj. B11. $200.00

**BRADLEY, Michael.** *Communion in Solitude.* 1975. Scrimshaw. 1st. 96p. dj. F3. $15.00

**BRADLEY, Van Allen.** *Book Collector's Handbook of Values, 1976-1977.* 1975. Putnam. 2nd. thick 8vo. 536p. F/NF. O10. $55.00

**BRADLEY, Van Allen.** *Book Collector's Handbook of Values, 1981-83 Edition.* 1982. 4th. 654p. 20,000 entries. F/NF. A4. $95.00

**BRADLEY, Van Allen.** *More Gold in Your Attic.* 1961. NY. Fleet Pub. 1st. 8vo. 415p. cloth. F/dj. O10. $30.00

**BRADLEY, Will.** *Delectable Art of Printing: Called Also Printer Man's Joy...* 1905. Boston. Am Type Founders Co. 1st. tan wrp. M24. $600.00

**BRADNER, Enos.** *Northwest Angling.* 1950. NY. ils/photos/index. 239p. VG/dj. A17. $20.00

**BRADSHAW, Gillian.** *Hawk of May.* 1980. S&S. 1st. author's 1st book. F/dj. M21. $30.00

**BRADSHAW, S.D.** *Ecophysiology of Desert Reptiles.* 1986. Academic. 324p. F. S15. $12.50

**BRADSHAW, Sidney Ernest.** *On Southern Poetry Prior to 1860.* 1900. Richmond, VA. 1st. 162p. xl. VG. M8. $45.00

**BRADY, Charles.** *Seven Games in October.* 1979. Little Brn. 1st. F/VG. P8. $25.00

**BRADY, Cyrus Townsend.** *American Fights & Fighters.* 1900. McClure Philips. G. A19. $40.00

**BRADY, Cyrus Townsend.** *Border Fights & Fighters: Stories of the Pioneers...* 1902. NY. McClure Phillips. 1st. ils/maps. 382p. VG. H7. $45.00

**BRADY, Cyrus Townsend.** *Island of Surprise.* McClurg. 1st. ils Walter Tittle. F. M19. $25.00

**BRADY, Cyrus Townsend.** *Recollections of a Missionary in Great West.* 1901. NY. 200p. VG. B5. $30.00

**BRADY, Edward Foster.** *Memoir of Edward Foster Brady...* 1839. London. Harvey Darton. 1st. 12mo. 166p. V3. $30.00

**BRADY, Frank.** *Boswell's Political Career.* 1965. New Haven/London. 1st. 8vo. 200p. cloth. dj. H13. $65.00

**BRADY, John.** *Good Life.* 1994. Toronto. Harper Collins. 1st. sgn. F/dj. A14. $28.00

**BRADY, John.** *Stone of the Heart.* 1988. Toronto. Collins. 1st. author's 1st book. NF/VG. A14. $21.00

**BRADY, Maureen.** *Give Me Your Good Ear.* 1979. NY. Spinsters. 1st. 235p. VG+. A25. $15.00

**BRADY, Virginia.** *Kittens & Cat Book.* 1960. McGraw Hill. 1st. ils Nitsa Savramis. sbdg. VG. M5. $55.00

**BRADY, William.** *Kedge-Anchor; or, Young Sailor's Assistant.* 1854. NY. 7th. ils. M17. $75.00

**BRADY & DANZIGER.** *Great Biographer, 1789-1795.* 1989. McGraw Hill. ils. AN/dj. H13. $85.00

**BRAGG, Melvin.** *Laurence Olivier.* 1984. St Martin. 1st Am. photos. NF/F. W2. $35.00

**BRAGG, Melvyn.** *Richard Burton: A Life.* 1989. Little Brn. 1st Am. NF. W2. $25.00

**BRAIN, Russell.** *Diseases of the Nervous System.* 1952. London. Oxford. 4th/2nd imp. 1002p. NF. C14. $22.00

**BRAINERD, Thomas.** *Life of John Brainerd.* 1865. Phil. Presbyterian Pub Comm. 1st. 492p. aeg. B18. $45.00

**BRAKEFIELD, Tom.** *Hunting Big-Game Trophies: A North American Guide.* 1976. Outdoor Life. 446p. F/dj. A17. $15.00

**BRAM, Christopher.** *Father of Frankenstein.* 1995. Dutton. 1st. F/dj. C9. $36.00

**BRAMBLETT, Claud A.** *Patterns of Primate Behavior.* 1976. Palo Alto. ils. 320p. VG. S15. $12.00

**BRAMS, Stanley H.** *Remembrances of Things Past.* 1975. Detroit. Trends. 1st. inscr. 92p. F. B18. $19.50

**BRANCH, Hettye Wallace.** *Story of 80 John: Biography of Respected Negro Ranchmen...* 1960. Greenwich. VG/dj. J2. $95.00

**BRAND, Eirck D.** *Band Instrument Repairing Manual.* 1946. self pub. 198p. VG. S5. $15.00

**BRAND, John.** *Observations on Popular Antiquities...* 1810. London. Baynes. 424p. 3-quarter leather. VG. M10. $175.00

**BRAND, Max;** see Faust, Fredrick S.

**BRAND, Millen.** *Local Lives: Poems About the Pennsylvania Dutch.* 1975. Potter. 1st. VG/G+. R8. $10.00

**BRANDEIS, Madeline.** *Little Indian Weaver.* 1928. Grosset Dunlap. 8vo. 134p. bl brd. pict dj. F7. $38.00

**BRANDEIS, Madeline.** *Little Tom of England.* 1925. Grosset Dunlap. F/G. M19. $17.50

**BRANDER, Michael.** *Complete Guide to Horsemanship.* 1971. Scribner. 1st Am. F/NF clip. C15. $15.00

**BRANDER, Michael.** *Hunting & Shooting From Earliest Times to Present Day.* 1971. NY. 255p. VG. A17. $20.00

**BRANDO & LINDSEY.** *Brando: Songs My Mother Taught Me.* 1994. Random. 1st. VG/dj. V4. $12.50

**BRANDON, Heather.** *Casualties: Death in Vietnam, Anguish & Survival in America.* 1984. St Martin. 1st. photos. F/dj. R11. $30.00

**BRANDON, Jay.** *Fade the Heat.* 1990. Pocket. 1st. NF/dj. S18. $15.00

**BRANDON, Jay.** *Predators Waltz.* 1989. St Martin. 1st. author's 1st hc. F/NF. S18. $27.00

**BRANDON, William.** *Last Americans: Indian in American Culture.* 1974. McGraw Hill. VG/dj. A19. $30.00

**BRANDT, Bill.** *Behind the Camera.* 1985. NY. Aperture. 1st. F/dj. S9. $85.00

**BRANDT, Herbert.** *Alaska Bird Trails.* 1943. Cleveland. lg 8vo. ils Allan Brooks/E Kalmbach. 464p. NF. C12. $220.00

**BRANDT, Johanna.** *Grape Cure.* 1950. Harmony Centre. 191p. VG/dj. A10. $26.00

**BRANDT, John C.** *Introduction to the Solar Wind.* 1970. SF. Freeman. 1st. lg 8vo. 199p. VG/dj. K5. $30.00

**BRANDT, Sebastian.** *Shyp of Fooles.* 1982 (1509). Seal Harbor, ME. High Loft. 1/50 (150 total). w/portfolio. box. B24. $1,150.00

**BRANDT & GUMMERE.** *Byways & Boulevards in & About Historic Philadelphia.* 1925. Phil. Corn Exchange Nat Bank. 320p. G+. B18. $12.50

**BRANN, W.C.** *Best of Brann, the Iconoclast.* 1967. Waco. Texian. 1st. cloth. F/dj. M24. $25.00

**BRANON, Bill.** *Devil's Hole.* 1995. Harper. 1st. sgn. F/dj. S18. $35.00

**BRANON, Bill.** *Let Us Prey.* 1994. Harper. 1st. author's 1st novel. sgn. F/dj. S18. $40.00

**BRANSON, Ann.** *Journal of Ann Branson.* 1892. Phil. Wm Pile. 408p. xl. fair. V3. $25.00

**BRANSTON, Brian.** *Lost Gods of England.* 1974. OUP. ils. VG/dj. M17. $35.00

**BRANSTON, Frank.** *Sergeant Ritchie's Conscience.* 1978. St Martin. 1st Am. VG/dj. G8. $15.00

**BRANT, Irving.** *Impeachment, Trials & Errors.* 1974. Knopf. M11. $35.00

**BRANT, Irving.** *James Madison, Secretary of State 1800-1809.* 1953. Indianapolis. 1st. ils. 533p. VG/fair. M4. $30.00

**BRANT, Irving.** *James Madison: Father of the Constitution, 1787-1800.* 1950. Indianapolis. 1st. ils. 520p. gilt red cloth. F. H3. $40.00

**BRASHLER, William.** *Bingo Long Traveling All Stars.* 1973. Harper Row. 1st. F/VG. P8. $50.00

**BRASHLER, William.** *Don: Life & Death of San Giancana.* 1977. NY. Harper. 1st. VG/dj. B5. $20.00

**BRASSAI.** *Paris Years.* 1995. NY. 1st. trans T Bent. dj. T9. $15.00

**BRAUDE, Ann.** *Radical Spirits: Spiritualism & Women's Rights...* 1989. Boston. Beacon. 1st. rem mk. VG/dj. V3. $12.00

**BRAUDY, Susan.** *This Crazy Thing Called Love.* nd. BC. VG/dj. P3. $10.00

**BRAUDY, Susan.** *What the Movies Made Me Do.* 1985. Knopf. 1st. VG/dj. C9. $24.00

**BRAUER, Jerald C.** *Lively Experiment Continued.* 1987. Mercer. VG/dj. M17. $15.00

**BRAUN, Lilian Jackson.** *Cat Who Sniffed Blue.* 1988. Putnam. 1st. sgn. F/dj. B2. $65.00

**BRAUTIGAN, Richard.** *Confederate General From Big Sur.* 1964. Castle. VG/dj. S13. $10.00

**BRAUTIGAN, Richard.** *Dreaming of Babylon: A Private Eye Novel 1942.* 1977. Delacorte/Lawrence. 1st. VG+/dj. A14. $28.00

**BRAUTIGAN, Richard.** *Galilee Hitch-Hiker.* 1966. SF. Cranium. 1st/2nd issue. 1/700. F. L3. $375.00

**BRAUTIGAN, Richard.** *In Watermelon Sugar.* 1968. SF. Four Seasons. 1st. sgn/dtd 1968. F. L3. $1,000.00

**BRAUTIGAN, Richard.** *Pill Versus the Springmill Mine Disaster.* 1981. Blk Sparrow. 1st. 1/500. F/dj. L3. $55.00

**BRAUTIGAN, Richard.** *Rommel Drives on Deep Into Egypt.* 1970. Delacorte/Lawrence. 1st. F/NF. O11. $150.00

**BRAUTIGAN, Richard.** *Sombrero Fallout: A Japanese Novel.* 1976. S&S. 1st. F/dj. B30/H11. $50.00

**BRAUTIGAN, Richard.** *Sombrero Fallout: A Japanese Novel.* 1976. S&S. 1st. rem mk. VG+/dj. A14. $25.00

**BRAUTIGAN, Richard.** *Tokyo-Montana Express.* 1980. NY. Delacorte. 1st. F/F. B2. $40.00

**BRAUTIGAN, Richard.** *Tokyo-Montana Express.* 1981. London. Cape. 1st. F/dj. A24. $30.00

**BRAUTIGAN, Richard.** *Trout Fishing in America/Pill Vs Springmill.../Watermelon...* 1969. Delacorte. 1st Omnibus/1st trade hc. VG+/dj. A14. $175.00

**BRAUTIGAN, Richard.** *Willard & His Bowling Trophies: A Perverse Mystery.* 1975. S&S. 1st. F/dj. B4. $85.00

**BRAUTIGAN, Richard.** *Willard & His Bowling Trophies: A Perverse Mystery.* 1975. S&S. 1st. 1st. VG/dj. B30. $50.00

**BRAVERMAN, J.B.S.** *Citrus Products.* 1949. NY. Interscience. 424p. VG/dj. A10. $25.00

**BRAVERMAN, Kate.** *Milk Run.* 1977. Momentum. 1st. author's 1st book. VG/wrp. M19. $45.00

**BRAVERMAN, Kate.** *Squandering the Blue.* 1990. Ballantine. 1st. NF/dj. S18. $14.00

**BRAZER, Esther Stevens.** *Early American Decoration.* 1947. Pond-Ekberg. 2nd/memorial ed. ils. VG. R8. $50.00

**BRAZER, Esther Stevens.** *Early American Decoration: Comprehensive Treatise...* 1961. Springfield. 4th. ils. VG/dj. M17. $25.00

**BRAZIER, Mary A.B.** *Bibliography of Electroencephalography 1875-1948.* 1950. Internat Fed EEG & Clinical Neurophysio. 178p. xl. G7. $75.00

**BREAKENRIDGE, William M.** *Helldorado: Bringing the Law to the Mesquite.* 1982. RR Donnelley. Lakeside Classics #80. ils/notes/index. 454p. F. B19. $25.00

**BREAN, Herbert.** *Traces of Merrilee.* 1966. Morrow. 1st. VG-/G. G8. $12.50

**BRECHT, Bertolt.** *Seven Plays.* 1961. NY. Grove. 1st. F/NF. B2. $30.00

**BRECKENRIDGE, Gerald.** *Radio Boys Rescue the Lost Alaska Expedition.* 1922. AL Burt. 227p. tan pict cloth. P4. $65.00

**BRECKENRIDGE, Sean.** *Yuppie Scum.* 1993. NY. 1st. author's 1st book. F/F. H11. $25.00

**BREDES, Don.** *Muldoon.* 1982. HRW. 1st. author's 2nd book. F/dj. M25. $15.00

**BREED & ROAT.** *Geology of the Grand Canyon.* 1974. Flagstaff/Grand Canyon. 1st. 8vo. stiff pict wrp. VG/dj. F7. $32.50

**BREEN, Jon L.** *Gathering Place.* 1984. NY. Walker. 1st. F/dj. M15. $45.00

**BREEN, Quirinus.** *Christianity & Humanism.* 1968. Eerdmans. 283p. VG/dj. B29. $10.50

**BREESKIN, Adelyn D.** *Milton Avery.* 1970. NYGS. 1st. 4to. VG+. S13. $15.00

**BREIHAN, Carl.** *Complete & Authentic Life of Jesse James.* 1953. NY. Fell. 1st. ils/index. 287p. VG/dj. B5. $20.00

**BREIHAN, Carl.** *Day Jesse James Was Killed.* 1961. NY. Fell. 1st sgn pres. 235p. G. B5. $30.00

**BREIHAN, Carl.** *Outlaws of the Old West.* nd. Bonanza. VG/dj. A19. $25.00

**BREIHAN, Carl.** *Younger Brothers.* 1961. San Antonio. Naylor. 1st. ils. 260p. G/dj. B5. $25.00

**BREMMER, James.** *Canadian Record of Performance Etc Jersey Cattle.* 1947. Toronto. Canadian Jersey Cattle Club. 512p. VG. A10. $20.00

**BRENAN, Gerald.** *Personal Record.* 1975. NY. 1st. dj. T9. $25.00

**BREND, Gavin.** *My Dear Mr Holmes.* 1951. London. Geo Allen. 1st. F/clip. M15. $65.00

**BRENNAN, Joseph Payne.** *Stories of Darkness & Dread.* 1973. Arkham. 1st. VG/G+. L1. $75.00

**BRENNAN, Louis A.** *American Dawn: New Model of American Prehistory.* 1970. Macmillan. 1st. 8vo. VG/F. A2. $12.00

**BRENNAN, Louis A.** *No Stone Unturned: An Almanac of North American Prehistory.* 1960 (1959). London. Gollancz. 1st. ils. F/dj. A2. $15.00

**BRENNAN, W.A.** *Tobacco Leaves: Being Book of Facts for Smokers.* 1915. Menasha, WI. Geo Banta. 1st/1st issue. brn cloth. B14. $150.00

**BRENNER, Anita.** *Wind That Swept Mexico.* 1971. Austin. new ed. 310p. dj. F3. $30.00

**BRENT-DYER, Elinor.** *Chalet School & the Lintons.* (1952). London. Chambers Ltd. rpt. 8vo. 319p. gr brd. VG. T5. $20.00

**BRETT, George Sidney.** *History of Psychology, Vol II: Medieval & Early Modern...* 1921. Allen Unwin/Macmillan. 394p. VG. G1. $75.00

**BRETT, Jan.** *Twelve Days of Christmas.* 1990. Putnam. 1st. mini. F. M5. $8.00

**BRETT, Lily.** *What God Wants.* 1991. Birch Lane. 1st. F/dj. S13. $10.00

**BRETT, Simon.** *Christmas Crimes at Puzzle Manor.* 1991. Delacorte. 1st. F/dj. T12. $20.00

**BRETT, Simon.** *Mrs, Presumed Dead.* 1988. London. Macmillan. 1st. sgn. F/dj. A14. $28.00

**BRETT & BROWN.** *London Bookshop: Pictorial Record.* 1977. Pinner. 1st. dj. T9. $25.00

**BRETTSCHNEIDER & CALITRI.** *Goliath Head.* (1972). NY. Crown. 1st. 8vo. 346p. F/NF. H4. $20.00

**BREWER, Reginald.** *Delightful Diversion: Whys & Wherefores of Book Collecting.* 1935. NY. Macmillan. 1st. sgn. 320p. gray cloth. NF/dj. F1. $50.00

**BREWER, S.M.** *Design for a Gentleman.* 1963. London. Chapman Hall. 1st. gilt red cloth. dj. H13. $35.00

**BREWSTER, William.** *Concord River: Sketches From the Journals of...* 1937. Harvard. 1st. ils Frank Benson. 259p. VG/partial. A17. $45.00

**BREWTON & BREWTON.** *Christmas Bells Are Ringing.* 1951. Macmillan. 1st. xl. G. B36. $15.00

**BRIAN, Nancy.** *River to Rim: Guide to Place Names Along Colorado River...* 1992. Earthquest. 8vo. sgn. 176p. AN. F7. $15.00

**BRICE, Marshall M.** *Stonewall Brigade Band.* 1967. McClure. 213p. VG. B10. $40.00

**BRICK, John.** *Raid.* 1960. DSP. 184p. xl. VG. B36. $7.00

**BRIDGEMAN, P.H.** *Tree Surgery.* 1979. Pomfret, VT. photos/diagrams. 144p. VG/dj. B26. $22.50

**BRIDGES, Ann.** *Alphonse Mucha: Complete Graphic Works.* 1980. 1st. 4to. 163 pl. 192p. F/NF. A4. $85.00

**BRIDGES, E. Lucas.** *Uttermost Part of the World.* 1948. London. 1st. ils. 558p. NF. B14. $45.00

**BRIDGES, Robert.** *Growth of Love.* 1913. Portland, ME. Mosher. 1st thus. 1/450. quarter decor brd. M24. $65.00

**BRIDGES, Robert.** *New Verse.* 1925. Clarendon. 1st. 1/100. sgn/#d. full wht parchment. F/VG. M24. $250.00

**BRIDGES & TILTMAN.** *Master Minds of Modern Science.* 1940 (1930). London. Harrap. new/revised. 278p. cloth. K5. $25.00

**BRIDGETT, T.E.** *History of the Holy Eucharist in Great Britain.* 1908. London. Burns Oates. 4to. 324p. VG. M10. $95.00

**BRIDGMAN, Betty.** *Lullaby for Eggs, a Poem.* 1955. Macmillan. 1st. 8vo. aqua cloth. VG/G. T5. $35.00

**BRIDGMAN, L.J.** *From Maine to California With the Kewts.* 1902. NY. Dodge. 1st. 4to. cloth. R5. $125.00

**BRIER.** *Egyptian Mummies: Unraveling the Secrets of Ancient Art.* 1994. 120 photos. 352p. F/NF. A4. $35.00

**BRIGGS, Joe Bob.** *Cosmic Wisdom of Joe Bob Briggs.* 1990. Random. 1st. F/F. H11. $25.00

**BRIGGS, Joe Bob.** *Joe Bob Goes to the Drive-In.* 1987. Dell. 1st. intro Stephen King. VG/wrp. S18. $15.00

**BRIGGS, Kenneth A.** *Holy Siege: Year That Shook Catholic America.* 1992. Harper Collins. 1st. photos. F/dj. A2. $13.00

**BRIGGS, S.** *Essays, Humor & Poems of Nathaniel Ames, Father & Son...* 1891. Cleveland. ils/map. 490p. VG. M4. $70.00

**BRIGHAM, Arthur A.** *Progressive Poultry Culture.* 1912. Cedar Rapids. Torch. 4th. 293p. VG. A10. $25.00

**BRIGHAM, Clarence S.** *History & Bibliography of American Newspapers 1690-1820.* 1947. Am Antiquarian Soc. 2 vol. 4to. VG. A4. $325.00

**BRIGHAM, Clarence S.** *Paul Revere's Engravings.* 1954. Am Antiquarian Soc. 1st. ils. NF/VG. T11. $125.00

**BRILL, Toni.** *Date With a Dead Doctor.* 1991. St Martin. 1st Am. NF/VG. G8. $12.50

**BRILLAT-SAVARIN, Jean A.** *Handbook of Dining, Corpulency & Leanness...* 1865. NY. E6. $110.00

**BRILLAT-SAVARIN, Jean A.** *Physiology of Taste; or, Meditations on Transcendental...* 1949. NY. LEC. 1/1500. lg 8vo. 471p. quarter pigskin/paper brd. F/case. H5. $250.00

**BRIMM, Charles.** *Medicine in the Bible, the Pentateuch, Torah.* 1936. NY. 1st. 384p. A13. $250.00

**BRIN, David.** *Postman.* 1985. Bantam. 1st. F/NF. M21. $30.00

**BRING & WAYEMBERGH.** *Japanese Gardens.* 1981. NY. 214p. sc. F. B26. $22.50

**BRININSTOOL, E.A.** *Fighting Indian Warriors: True Tales of Wild Frontiers.* 1953. Harrisburg. Stackpole. revised. F/F. E1. $60.00

**BRININSTOOL, E.A.** *Fighting Indian Warriors: True Tales of Wild Frontiers.* 1953. Harrisburg. Stackpole. VG/dj. A19. $35.00

**BRININSTOOL, E.A.** *Trail Dust of a Maverick.* 1914. Dodd Mead. 1st. photos. 249p. wht stp cloth/label. D11. $100.00

**BRINK, Andre.** *Wall of the Plague.* 1984. Summit. 1st Am. sgn. NF/dj. D10. $45.00

**BRINK, Carol Ryrie.** *Magical Melons: More Stories About Caddie Woodlawn.* 1964 (1944). Macmillan. 12th. 8vo. gray cloth. F/dj. T5. $30.00

**BRINK, Carol.** *Twin Cities.* 1961. Macmillan. 1st. photos. 197p. VG/dj. S14. $12.00

**BRINKLEY, David.** *Washington Goes to War.* 1988. Knopf. 286p. VG/dj. P12/S14. $10.00

**BRINKLEY, William.** *Ninety & Nine.* 1966. Doubleday. 1st. VG/dj. T11. $20.00

**BRINNIN, John Malcolm.** *Sway of the Grand Saloon: Social History of North Atlantic.* 1971. NY. 1st. ils. VG/dj. M17. $25.00

**BRINTON, Howard.** *Divine-Human Society.* nd. Wallingford, PA. Pendle Hill. 12mo. 107p. xl. V3. $10.00

**BRION, Patrick.** *Tex Avery.* 1986. Germany. Schuller, Verlagsgesellschaft. 1st. ils/fld ils. F/F. C9. $180.00

**BRION, Patrick.** *Tom & Jerry: Definitive Guide to Their Animated Adventures.* 1990 (1987). Harmony. 1st Am. ils. F/dj. A2. $30.00

**BRISLEY, Joyce L.** *Milly-Molly-Mandy Stories.* 1930 (1928). NY. Geo Sully. 4th. 8vo. 96p. beige cloth. VG. T5. $25.00

**BRISSOT, Jeane-Pierre.** *Commerce of America With Europe...* 1795. NY. Swords. sm 8vo. ftspc portrait. cloth. R12. $175.00

**BRISTER, Bob.** *Shotgunning: The Art & the Science.* 1977. Winchester. 3rd. 321p. F/dj. A17. $15.00

**BRISTOL, Roger P.** *Supplement to Charles Evans' American Bibliography.* 1970. Charlottesville. 1st. AN. F1. $50.00

**BRISTOW, J.** *Oxford Book of Adventure Stories.* 1995. OUP. 1st. dj. T9. $15.00

**BRITE, Poppy Z.** *Lost Souls.* Oct 1992. NY. Abyss. 1st. VG/dj. L1. $55.00

**BRITE, Poppy Z.** *Lost Souls.* 1992. Delacorte. 1st. author's 1st book. AN/dj. S18. $40.00

**BRITE, Poppy Z.** *Lost Souls.* 1992. NY. Delacorte. 1st. sgn. author's 1st novel. NF/dj. M21. $30.00

**BRITISH MUSEUM LIBRARY.** *Catalogue of Books, Manuscripts, Maps & Drawings...* nd. rpt (1903-40). 8 vol in 4. 120,000 entries. F. A4. $250.00

**BRITISH MUSEUM LIBRARY.** *German Incunabula in the British Museum.* 1975. NY. Hacker Art Books. rpt. folio. intro Stanley Morrison. cream buckram. F. M24. $125.00

**BRITTAN, Samuel Byron.** *Man & His Relations: Ils Influence of Mind on Body...* 1865. NY. Cotton W Bean. 1st/later issue. 578p. panelled pebbled cloth. G1. $85.00

**BRITTON, Christopher.** *Paybacks.* 1985. DIF. 1st. NF/dj. R11. $30.00

**BRITTON, John.** *Architectural Antiquities of Great Britian.* 1807-1826. Longman Hurst Rees. 5 vol. 1st. ils Le Kew. quarter gr peppled morocco. F1. $850.00

**BRITTON, Nan.** *President's Daughter.* 1927. NY. ils. 399p. VG/dj. B18. $25.00

**BROADFOOT, Barry.** *10 Lost Years 1929-1939: Memories of Canadians...* 1973. Toronto. Doubleday. 1st. F/VG. A26. $12.00

**BROADFOOT, Tom.** *Civil War Books: A Priced Checklist With Advice.* 1990. 3rd. 571p. F. A4. $50.00

**BROBECK, Florence.** *Chafing Dish Cookery.* nd. NY. Barrows Co. G/dj. A16. $10.00

**BROBECK, Florence.** *Cook It in a Casserole.* 1943. Am Book/Stratford. G. A16. $10.00

**BROBECK, John.** *History of the American Physiological Soc: First Century...* 1987. Bethesda. 1st. 533p. wrp. A13. $35.00

**BROCH, Hermann.** *Spell.* 1987. FSG. 1st Am. trans. F/dj. S18. $30.00

**BROCK, Alan St. H.** *History of Fireworks.* 1949. London. Harrap. 1st. 8 mc pl. gilt bl cloth. NF/G. F1. $85.00

**BROCK, Darryl.** *If I Never Get Back.* 1990. NY. Crown. 1st. Nf/dj. A14. $28.00

**BROCK, Emma.** *High in the Mountains.* 1938. Whitman. 1st. gr cloth/pict label. VG. T5. $30.00

**BROCK, Emma.** *Kristie & the Colt.* 1949. Knopf. 1st. ils. Vg/dj. P2. $25.00

**BROCK, Emma.** *One Little Indian Boy.* 1932. KNopf. 1st. G. P12. $15.00

**BROCK, Emma.** *Present for Auntie & Too Fast for John.* 1940. Knopf. ils. VG/G. P12. $20.00

**BROCK, Emma.** *Then Came Adventure.* 1941. Knopf. 1st. VG/dj. P2. $20.00

**BROCK, R.A.** *Miscellaneous Papers, 1672-1865.* 1887. The Society. 374p. cloth. B10. $85.00

**BROCK, Robert K.** *Archibald Cary of Ampthill: Wheelhorse of the Revolution.* (1937). Garrett Massie. 183p. G. B10. $20.00

**BROCK, Robert K.** *Archibald Cary of Ampthill: Wheelhorse of the Revolution.* 1937. Richmond, VA. Garrett Massie. 1st. 183p. VG/dj. M10. $25.00

**BROCKMAN, H.A.N.** *Caliph of Fonthill.* 1956. London. Werner Laurie. 1st. ils/map/ep. dj. H13. $65.00

**BRODER, Patricia Janis.** *Great Paintings of the Old West.* 1979. Abbeville. VG/dj. A21. $45.00

**BRODER, Patricia Janis.** *Hopi Painting: The World of the Hopis.* 1978. Dutton. VG/dj. A19. $75.00

**BRODEUR, Paul.** *Stunt Man.* 1970. Atheneum. 1st. F/NF. H11. $35.00

**BRODIE, F.M.** *Devil Drives: Life of Sir Richard Burton.* 1967. NY. photos/maps. VG/fair. M4. $25.00

**BRODSKY & WEISS.** *Cleopatra Papers: A Private Correspondence.* 1963. S&S. 1st. VG/dj. C9. $25.00

**BROMFIELD, Louis.** *It Takes All Kinds.* 1939. NY. 1st. inscr. 690p. G. B18. $15.00

**BROMFIELD, Louis.** *Modern Hero.* 1932. NY. 1st. VG/G. B5. $30.00

**BROMFIELD, Louis.** *Out of the Earth.* 1950. Harper. 1st. 305p. VG/fair. H1. $16.00

**BROMLEY.** *Clockmakers Library, Catalogue of Books & Manuscripts...* 1977. 4to. 52 pl/1077 entries. F/F. A4. $65.00

**BRONK, William.** *Living Instead.* 1991. Northpoint. 1st. F/dj. R14. $25.00

**BRONSON, P.** *Bombardiers.* 1995. Random. 1st. F/dj. R14. $30.00

**BRONTE, Charlotte.** *Life & Works of Charlotte Bronte & Her Sisters.* 1883. London. 7 vol. half leather/marlbed brd. F. B30. $300.00

**BRONTE, Charlotte.** *Professor.* 1857. London. Smith Elder. 1st/1st bdg/1st catalog. gilt purple cloth. M24. $1,500.00

**BRONTE, Emily.** *Wuthering Heights.* 1943. Random. ils Eichenberg. 213p. VG. C14. $16.00

**BRONTE & MCMAHON.** *Vittles & Vice: Extraordinary Guide to What's Cooking...* 1952. Chicago. VG/dj. V4. $20.00

**BROOK, Stephen.** *Bibliography of the Gehenna Press.* 1976. Northampton. JP Dwyer. 1st. 1/400. gilt red cloth. F. M24. $100.00

**BROOKE, Hindle.** *America's Wooden Age: Aspects of Its Early Technology.* 1975. Tarrytown. Sleepy Hollow Restorations. 1st. 218p. VG/dj. B5. $25.00

**BROOKE, L. Leslie.** *Freddy Plays Football.* 1949. Knopf. 1st. 8vo. ils Kurt Wiese. gray cloth. dj. R5. $385.00

**BROOKE, L. Leslie.** *Ring O' Roses: A Nursery Rhyme Picture Book.* 1922. London. Warne. 4to. pict cloth. dj. R5. $150.00

**BROOKE, Rupert.** *Lithuania, a Play.* 1935. London. 1st. T9. $45.00

**BROOKE, Rupert.** *1914 & Other Poems.* 1915. Doubleday Page. 1st. 1/87. teg. half navy morocco. F. B24. $1,500.00

**BROOKMAN, Lester G.** *Nineteenth Century Postage Stamps of the United States.* 1947. NY, NY. HL Linquist. 2 vol. 4to. gr cloth. dj. S5. $125.00

**BROOKNER, Anita.** *Debut.* 1981. NY. Linden. 1st. author's 1st novel. F/NF. A24. $40.00

**BROOKNER, Anita.** *Fraud.* 1992. Random. 1st. NF/dj. H11. $15.00

**BROOKNER, Anita.** *Jacques-Louis David.* 1980. NY. 1st. ils. VG/dj. M17. $75.00

**BROOKS, Charles E.** *Nymph Fishing for Larger Trout.* 1976. Crown. VG. A19. $30.00

**BROOKS, Cleanth.** *Percy Letters: Correspondence of T Percy & Wm Shenstone.* 1977. New Haven. Yale. 1st. VG. H13. $45.00

**BROOKS, E.S.** *Historic Girls: Stories of Girls Who Influenced History...* 1887. NY. 1st. 225p. VG. B18. $17.50

**BROOKS, F.T.** *Imperial Botanical Conference 1924.* 1925. Cambridge. 390p. cloth. VG. A10. $25.00

**BROOKS, Gwendolyn.** *Aloneness.* 1971. Detroit. Broadside. 1st. NF/wrp. B2. $65.00

**BROOKS, Gwendolyn.** *Blacks.* 1991. Chicago. 3rd World. 5th. inscr. 512p. VG. B2. $30.00

**BROOKS, Gwendolyn.** *Report From Part One.* 1972. Detroit. Broadside. 1st. F/plain brn dj. B2. $40.00

**BROOKS, H.** *Diagnostic Methods: A Guide for History...* 1923 (1916). VG. E6. $15.00

**BROOKS, Joe.** *Complete Guide to Fishing Across North America.* 1966. Outdoor Life. ils/index. 613p. VG/dj. A17. $15.00

**BROOKS, Joe.** *Trout Fishing.* 1972. Harper Row. ils/pl. VG. A19. $25.00

**BROOKS, Juanita.** *Mountain Meadows Massacre.* 1962 (1950). np. 1st thus. ils/photos. red cloth. VG+. F7. $40.00

**BROOKS, Juanita.** *On the Ragged Edge. Life & Times of Dudley Leavitt.* 1973. UT State Hist Soc. 8vo. 175p. VG/dj. F7. $37.50

**BROOKS, Loretta E.** *Along the Hudson.* 1959. NY. Exposition. 1st. sm 8vo. 44p. gr cloth. G/dj. M7. $35.00

**BROOKS, Noah.** *Boys of Fairport.* 1919. Scribner. rpt. G+. P8. $200.00

**BROOKS, Noah.** *Our Baseball Club.* 1884. Dutton. intro Henry Chadwick. 1st baseball novel. emb brd. P8. $500.00

**BROOKS, Owen.** *Inheritance.* 1980. HRW. 1st. VG/dj. L1. $35.00

**BROOKS, Patrica.** *Meals That Can Wait.* 1970. Gramercy. G/dj. A16. $10.00

**BROOKS, R.R.** *Serpentine & Its Vegetation: A Multidisciplineary Approach.* 1987. Diosorides. 454p. F/dj. S15. $15.00

**BROOKS, Richard.** *Boiling Point.* 1947. Harper. 1st. NF/VG+. B4. $150.00

**BROOKS, Richard.** *Brix Foxhole.* 1945. Harper. 1st. NF/VG+. B4. $125.00

**BROOKS, Stewart.** *McBurney's Point: Story of Appendicitis.* 1969. London. 1st. 168p. A13. $60.00

**BROOKS, Terry.** *Magic Kingdom for Sale - Sold!* 1986. Del Rey/Ballantine. 1st. VG+/dj. A14. $17.50

**BROOKS, Terry.** *Sword of Shannara.* 1972. Random. 1st. author's 1st book. ils Hildebrandt. VG+/dj. A14. $175.00

**BROOKS, Terry.** *Wizard at Large.* 1988. Del Rey/Ballantine. 1st. Magic Kingdom of Landover #3. NF/clip. A14. $25.00

**BROOKS, Van Wyck.** *New England: Indian Summer.* 1940. Dutton. 1st. 1/997. sgn/#d. cloth-backed brd/labine. F/glassine/box. M24. $150.00

**BROOKS, Virginia Field Walton.** *Screed of Safari Scribe.* 1947. Memphis. inscr. VG+/wrp. B30. $27.50

**BROOKS, Walter R.** *Freddy Goes to Florida.* 1960. Knopf. rpt. ils Kurt Weise. VG. P12. $60.00

**BROONZY, Big Bill.** *Big Bill Blues.* 1955. NY/London. Grove/Cassell. 1st US issue. NF/dj. B2. $65.00

**BROPHY, Frank Cullen.** *Arizona Sketch Book.* 1952. Phoenix, AZ. 1st. ils/map ep. 310p. VG/dj. B18. $22.50

**BROSNAN, John.** *Horror People.* 1976. St Martin. 1st. VG/G. L1. $35.00

**BROSNAN, John.** *James Bond in the Cinema.* 1972. S Brunswick. AS Barnes. 1st Am. F/dj. M15. $50.00

**BROTHERSON, J.H.F.** *Observations on Early Public Health Movement in Scotland.* 1952. London. 1st. 119p. A13. $40.00

**BROUGH, Bennet H.** *Treatise on Mine Surveying.* 1888. London. Griffin. 302p. red cloth. F. B14. $35.00

**BROUGHAM, Henry Lord.** *Historical Sketches of Statesmen Who Flourished...* 1839. Phil. Lea Blanchard. 2 vol. 1st Am. emb purple muslin/labels. M24. $125.00

**BROUGHAM, Henry Lord.** *Historical Sketches of Statesmen...Time of George III.* 1839-1843. London. Chas Knight. 3 vol. ils/portraits. half brn leather/tan cloth. F1. $300.00

**BROUN, Hob.** *Inner Tube.* 1985. Knopf. 1st. F/dj. M25. $15.00

**BROWER, David.** *Wilderness: America's Living Heritage.* 1962 (1961). Sierra Club. VG/dj. S5. $8.00

**BROWER, Keith H.** *Contemporary Latin American Fiction: Annotated Bibliography.* 1989. 236p. F. A4. $40.00

**BROWER, Kenneth.** *Micronesia: Island Wilderness.* 1973. Friends of the Earth. VG/dj. R8. $20.00

**BROWN, Alexander Crosby.** *Dismal Swamp Canal.* 1967. Norfolk Co Hist Soc. ils/photos/maps. VG. B10. $20.00

**BROWN, Alfred.** *Old Masterpieces in Surgery: A Collection of Thoughts...* 1928. Omaha. private prt. ils. 263p. brd. G7. $125.00

**BROWN, Alfred.** *Old Masterpieces in Surgery: A Collection of Thoughts...* 1928. Omaha. private prt. 1st. sgn. 263p. A13. $350.00

**BROWN, Alice.** *Early American Herb Recipes.* 1966. Tuttle. 1st. 4to. 174p. F/F. E6. $45.00

**BROWN, Anthony C.** *Secret Life of Sir Stewart Graham Menzies...* 1987. Macmillan. 1st. ils. 830p. VG/dj. S14. $12.00

**BROWN, Arthur.** *Eleventh Hour.* 1940. Fundamental Truth. 159p. VG. B29. $8.00

**BROWN, B. Frank.** *Crotons of the World.* 1995. Valkaria, FL. photos. AN. B26. $40.00

**BROWN, Buster.** *Semolina Grumbles.* (1949). London. Collins. 8vo. 96p. orange cloth. G+/dj. T5. $25.00

**BROWN, C.M.** *Benjamin Stillman: Life in the Young Republic.* 1989. Princeton. ils. 377p. F/dj. M4. $30.00

**BROWN, CAROTHERS & JOHNSON.** *Grand Canyon Birds.* 1987. Tucson. sm 8vo. 320p. AN. F7. $22.50

**BROWN, Christopher Nicholas.** *Holmes.* 1978. NY. Home Planet. 1st. inscr. F/stapled wrp. L3. $35.00

**BROWN, Christy.** *Poems.* 1973. Stein Day. 1st. F/G. A23. $30.00

**BROWN, Dale.** *Day of the Cheetah.* 1989. NY. 1st. F/dj. T12. $30.00

**BROWN, Dale.** *Flight of the Old Dog.* 1987. DIF. 1st. author's 1st book. NF/dj. H11. $30.00

**BROWN, Dale.** *Flight of the Old Dog.* 1987. DIF. 1st. F/dj. N4. $40.00

**BROWN, Dale.** *Silver Town.* 1988. DIF. 1st. 349p. NF/dj. M21. $25.00

**BROWN, Dee.** *Bury My Heart at Wounded Knee.* 1970. Barrie Jenkins. 1st. map/photos. VG/dj. J2. $125.00

**BROWN, Dee.** *Creek Mary's Blood.* 1980. NY. HRW. 1st. NF/dj. T11. $25.00

**BROWN, Dee.** *Fort Phil Kearny: An American Saga.* 1962. Putnam. ils/map ep. 251p. VG. J2. $70.00

**BROWN, Dee.** *Hear That Lonesome Whistle Blow.* 1977. NY. 1st. photos/map ep. F/dj. M4. $25.00

**BROWN, Dee.** *Wondrous Times on the Frontier.* 1991. Little Rock. August House. 1st. F/F. B3. $20.00

**BROWN, Douglas Summers.** *Historical & Biographical Sketches of Greensville...* 1968. Riparian Woman's Club. 2nd. ils. 439p. VG/dj. B10. $50.00

**BROWN, E.K.** *Willa Cather: A Critical Biography.* 1943. NY. Knopf. 1st. ils WA Dwiggins. 351p. gr cloth. VG/fair. F1. $25.00

**BROWN, Eric.** *Time-Lapsed Man & Other Stories.* 1990. Birmingham. Drunken Dragon. 1st hc. author's 1st book. F/dj. T2. $30.00

**BROWN, Eve.** *Plaza Cookbook.* 1972. Prentice Hall. G/dj. A16. $30.00

**BROWN, Fredric.** *Happy Ending.* 1990. Missoula. McMillan. 1st. F/dj. T2. $45.00

**BROWN, Fredric.** *Martians Go Home.* 1955. Dutton. 1st. NF/dj. M15. $400.00

**BROWN, Fredric.** *Screaming Mimi.* 1949. Dutton. 1st. F/dj. M15. $400.00

**BROWN, Fredric.** *What Mad Universe.* 1978. SF. Pennyfarthing. rpt. inscr by author's widow. F/dj. M15. $65.00

**BROWN, Fredric.** *4 Novels.* 1983. London. Zomba. Omnibus. M15. $75.00

**BROWN, G.G.** *Literary History of Spain.* 1972. London. Benn. 1st Eng. NF/dj. O4. $10.00

**BROWN, G.I.** *Introduction to Electronic Theories of Organic Chemistry.* 1958. Longman Gr. 1st. cloth. VG. B27. $15.00

**BROWN, G.I.** *Simple Guide to Modern Valency Theory.* 1953. Longman Gr. 1st. cloth. VG. B27. $20.00

**BROWN, Giles T.** *Ships That Sail No More: Marine Transportation 1910-1940.* 1966. Lexington. 1st. 8vo. 287p. bl cloth. VG/dj. P4. $40.00

**BROWN, Harry.** *Walk in the Sun.* 1944. Knopf. 1st. 187p. VG. H1. $12.50

**BROWN, Helen E.** *West Coast Cook Book.* 1952. Little Brn. G. A16. $15.00

**BROWN, Helen Gurley.** *Having It All.* 1982. S&S. BC. NF/VG. W2. $15.00

**BROWN, Henry Collins.** *Fifth Avenue Old & New 1824-1924.* 1924. 5th Ave Assn. 1st. VG. P3. $45.00

**BROWN, Henry Collins.** *Old Yonkers 1646-1922: A Page of History.* 1922. NY. Valentine's Manual. mini. photos. 192p. bl flexible cloth. VG. F1. $75.00

**BROWN, James.** *Moroccan.* 1993. Lococo-Mulder. 1st. 4to. wrp. B2. $50.00

**BROWN, Joe David.** *Addie Pray.* 1971. S&S. 1st. VG/dj. C9. $30.00

**BROWN, John Gregory.** *Decorations in a Ruined Cemetery.* 1994. Houghton Mifflin. 1st. author's 1st book. F/dj. R14. $60.00

**BROWN, John Mason.** *Daniel Boone: Opening of the Wilderness.* 1952. Random. Landmark series. VG/dj. B36. $13.00

**BROWN, John.** *Two Against the Amazon.* 1953. Dutton. 1st. maps. 247p. dj. F3. $20.00

**BROWN, Larry.** *Big Bad Love.* 1989. Algonquin. 1st. F/F. B3. $30.00

**BROWN, Larry.** *Dirty Work.* 1989. Algonquin. 1st. F/F. H11. $30.00

**BROWN, Larry.** *Dirty Work.* 1989. Algonquin. 1st. sgn. author's 2nd book. F/dj. B3/R14. $35.00

**BROWN, Larry.** *Facing the Music.* 1988. Algonquin. 1st. F/dj. D10. $125.00

**BROWN, Lawrason.** *Rules for Recovery From Pulmonary Tuberculosis...* 1923. 4th. VG. E6. $15.00

**BROWN, Leslie.** *Africa: A Natural History.* 1965. NY. Random. ils/photos/map. 299p. gilt cloth. NF/VG. M12. $37.50

**BROWN, Mabel.** *Neuropsychiatry & the War: A Bibliography...* 1918. NY. 2 vol. 1st. wrp. A13. $75.00

**BROWN, Marcia.** *Child's Good Night Book.* 1943. NY. Wm R Scott Inc. 1st. 12mo. pict brd. dj. R5. $150.00

**BROWN, Marcia.** *Cinderella.* 1954. Scribner. 1st. 4to. 1955 Caldecott Honor. dj. R5. $1,500.00

**BROWN, Marcia.** *Country Noisy Book.* 1940. NY. Wm R Scott Inc. early ed. ils Leonard Weisgard. pict brd. dj. R5. $125.00

**BROWN, Marcia.** *Dick Whittington & His Cat.* 1950. NY. Scribner. 1st. sgn pres. 1951 Caldecott Honor. pict gray cloth. R5. $250.00

**BROWN, Marcia.** *Felice.* 1958. Scribner. 1st. 4to. gray pict cloth. dj. R5. $135.00

**BROWN, Marcia.** *Little Cowboy.* 1948. NY. Wm R Scott Inc. 1st. ils Esphyr Slobodkina. pict brd. dj. R5. $225.00

**BROWN, Marcia.** *Lotus Seed, Children, Pictures & Books.* 1986. Scribner. 1st. 8vo. red brd. NF/VG. T5. $35.00

**BROWN, Marcia.** *Noisy Book.* 1939. NY. Wm R Scott Inc. early ed. 8vo. ils Leonard Weisgard. mc dj. R5. $125.00

**BROWN, Marcia.** *Noon Balloon.* 1952. NY. Harper. 1st. ils Leonard Weisgard. pict brd. dj. R5. $150.00

**BROWN, Marcia.** *Winter Noisy Book.* 1947. Harper. early ed. 8vo. pict brd. dj. R5. $125.00

**BROWN, Margaret Wise.** *Baby Animals.* 1941. Random. 1st. ils Mary Cameron. VG/fair. M5. $45.00

**BROWN, Margaret Wise.** *House of a Hundred Windows.* 1945. Harper. 1st. lg 4to. VG. M5. $15.00

**BROWN, Margaret Wise.** *On Christmas Eve.* 1985. Harper. rpt. ils Beni Montresor. VG. B17. $8.50

**BROWN, Margaret Wise.** *Shhhhhhh...Bang, a Whispering Book.* 1943. Harper. 1st. 4to. unp. G. T5. $30.00

**BROWN, Margaret Wise.** *Sneakers, Seven Stories About a Cat.* (1955). Wm R Scott Inc. possible 1st. 144p. brn cloth. G+. T5. $25.00

**BROWN, Marion.** *Pickles & Preserves.* 1960. NY. Avenel. G/dj. A16. $15.00

**BROWN, Marvin L.** *Baroness von Riedesdel & the American Revolution.* 1965. UNC. 222p. VG/dj. B10. $15.00

**BROWN, Michael.** *Pandemonium: Further Explorations Into Worlds Clive Barker.* 1991. Eclipse. 1st. F/sans. T12. $75.00

**BROWN, Miriam Jones.** *Friends School Haverford 1885-1985.* 1985. Exton, PA. Schiffer. 128p. VG. V3. $16.00

**BROWN, Olympia.** *Acquaintances, Old & New, Among Reformers.* nd. 1st. sgn. G. V4. $125.00

**BROWN, Paul.** *Daffy Taffy.* 1955. Scribner. 1st/A. sm 4to. unp. rust pict cloth. xl. VG. T5. $30.00

**BROWN, Paul.** *Fire a Mascot.* 1939. Scribner. 1st. xl. VG. A21. $75.00

**BROWN, Paul.** *Pony Farm.* 1948. Scribner. 1st. VG/dj. A21. $55.00

**BROWN, Paul.** *War Paint.* 1936. Scribner. xl. G. A21. $75.00

**BROWN, R.A.** *One Hundred Horse-Drawn Carriages.* 1977. Colchester, Eng. ils. 56p. VG. O3. $18.00

**BROWN, Rita Mae.** *High Hearts.* 1986. Bantam. 1st. F/dj. B3/T12. $40.00

**BROWN, Rita Mae.** *In Her Day.* 1976. Plainfield, VT. Daughters Inc. 1st. 196p. VG+. A25. $28.00

**BROWN, Rita Mae.** *Plain Brown Rapper.* 1976. Oakland. Diana. 1st. author's 2nd book. ils Sue Sellars. NF/wrp. B4. $150.00

**BROWN, Rita Mae.** *Six of One.* 1978. Harper Row. 1st. sgn. F/NF clip. A24. $55.00

**BROWN, Rita Mae.** *Six of One.* 1978. NY. Harper Row. 1st. 8vo. 310p. dj. P4. $20.00

**BROWN, Rita Mae.** *Wish You Were Here.* 1990. NY. Bantam. 1st. F/clip. A23. $32.00

**BROWN, Rosellen.** *Before & After.* 1992. FSG. ARC. F/dj. A23. $32.00

**BROWN, Susan.** *Book of 40 Puddings.* 1882. Scribner. 1st. G+. E6/T10. $100.00

**BROWN, Susan.** *Mrs Gilpin's Frugalities: Remnants & 200 Ways Using Them.* 1883. obl 8vo. G+. E6. $100.00

**BROWN, Thomas.** *Lectures on Philosophy of the Human Mind.* 1828. Hallowell, MA. Glazier. 2 vol. contemporary mottled calf. xl. G1. $50.00

**BROWN, Thomas.** *Observations on Zoonomia of Erasmus Darwin, MD.* 1798. London. 560p. rb modern cloth. G1. $285.00

**BROWN, Thomas.** *Taxidermist's Manual.* 1885. Orange Judd. 115p. cloth. VG. A10. $50.00

**BROWN, W. Sorley.** *Life & Genius of TWH Crosland.* 1928. London. Palmer. 1st. ils. 490p. gilt bl cloth. F1. $45.00

**BROWN, Wesley.** *Tragic Magic.* 1978. Random. 1st. author's 1st book. F/F. H11. $35.00

**BROWN, William F.** *Field Trials.* 1982. San Diego. revised. 239p. F/dj. A17. $12.00

**BROWN & CRISTIE.** *Bibliography of British History 1789-1851.* 1977. 4782 entries. 793p. F/F. A4. $95.00

**BROWN & GIBSON.** *Biogeography.* 1983. St Louis. ils. 643p. B26. $45.00

**BROWNE, Anthony.** *King Kong.* 1994. Atlanta. Turner. 92p. VG/dj. C5. $12.50

**BROWNE, Charles F.** *Artemus Ward: His Travels.* 1865. NY. Carleton. 1st/1st state. gilt deep purple cloth. F. M24. $125.00

**BROWNE, Corinne.** *Casualty: Memoir of Love & War.* 1981. Norton. 1st. NF/dj. R11. $25.00

**BROWNE, Gerald A.** *Hot Siberian.* 1989. Arbor/Morrow. 1st. VG/dj. P3. $20.00

**BROWNE, Lewis.** *Graphic Bible.* Dec 1939. Macmillan. not 1st. lg map. F/G. P12. $12.00

**BROWNE, Lewis.** *Wisdom of Israel.* 1945. Modern Lib. 748p. VG/dj. B29. $13.50

**BROWNE, Ray B.** *Spirit of Australia: Crime Fiction of Arthur W Upfield.* 1988. Bowling Green. 1st. F/dj. M15. $50.00

**BROWNE, Thomas.** *Religio Medici Together With a Letter to a Friend...* 1981. Birmingham. facs of 1845 London. 388p. full leather. A13. $60.00

**BROWNE, Thomas.** *Religio Medici.* 1898. London. Geo Bell. 1/500. 187p. wht cloth/vellum spine. F1. $75.00

**BROWNELL, Henry H.** *War-Lyrics & Other Poems.* 1866 (1865). Boston. 243p. VG. E6. $25.00

**BROWNING, E.B.** *Essay on Mind, With Other Poems.* 1826. London. James Duncan. 1st/mixed states. modern drab brd. M24. $1,250.00

**BROWNING, E.B.** *Prometheus Bound & Other Poems.* 1851. NY. CS Francis. 1st Am. aeg. gilt purple-brn cloth. F. M24. $1,650.00

**BROWNING, Norma Lee.** *Joe Maddy of Interlochen.* 1963. Chicago. Regnery. VG/dj. A28. $11.00

**BROWNING, Robert.** *Men & Women.* 1908. Hammersmith. Doves. 2 vol. 1st thus. 1/250. full limp vellum. F. M24. $1,850.00

**BROWNING, Robert.** *Pied Piper of Hamelin.* (1937). Rand McNally. later ed. 56p. VG. B18. $35.00

**BROWNLIE & LOCKLEY.** *Secrets of Natural New Zealand.* 1987. Aukland. ils. 176p. F/dj. S15. $22.00

**BRUCCOLI, Matthew J.** *James Gould Cozzens: A Descriptive Bibliography.* 1981. U Pittsburgh. ils. 207p. F. A4. $85.00

**BRUCCOLI, Matthew J.** *Nelson Algren: A Descriptive Bibliography.* 1985. U Pittsburgh. 185p. gilt bl cloth. F. F1. $50.00

**BRUCCOLI, Matthew J.** *Ross MacDonald/Kenneth Millar: Descriptive Bibliography.* 1983. U Pittsburgh. 1st. F/sans. M15. $85.00

**BRUCE, Dickson Jr.** *Violence & Culture in the Antebellum South.* 1979. Austin. 322p. VG/dj. S16. $20.00

**BRUCE, Edward C.** *Century: Its Fruits & Festival.* 1877. Lippincott. 252p. gilt cloth. G. B18. $45.00

**BRUCE, F.F.** *Book of the Acts.* 1954. Eerdmans. 555p. VG/dj. B29. $15.00

**BRUCE, F.F.** *English Bible: History of Translations.* 1961. OUP. 1st Am. 234p. VG/dj. H10. $37.50

**BRUCE, John Goodall.** *Bruce Family Descending From George Bruce (1650-1715).* 1977. Goodall. 195p. VG. B10. $65.00

**BRUCE, Leo.** *Murder in Miniature: Short Stories of Leo Bruce.* 1992. Chicago. Academy Chicago. 1st Am. F/NF. M15. $35.00

**BRUCE, Lorne.** *Free Books for All: Public Library Movement in Ontario...* 1994. Toronto. Dundurn. 1st. sgn. AN. A26. $45.00

**BRUCE, Robert V.** *Launching of Modern American Science 1846-1876.* 1987. Cornell. 446p. AN. A10. $18.00

**BRUCE, Robert.** *Fighting Norths & Pawnee Scouts.* 1932. Lincoln, NE. NE State Hist Soc. sgn. F. A19. $60.00

**BRUCE, Wallace.** *Rip Van Winkle's Keg.* ca 1890s. NY. Bryant Literary Union. keg shape w/31" scene-ils strip. R5. $750.00

**BRUCKER & WATSON.** *Longest Cave.* 1976. Knopf. 1st. VG/dj. O4. $20.00

**BRUCKER & WATSON.** *Longest Cave.* 1976. NY. 1st. photos/map. 315p. F/dj. M4. $25.00

**BRUEDERLIN, Max.** *Geoscientific Studies & Potential of Natural Environment.* 1975. Deutsche UNESCO. 25 papers/separate map. 312p. NF. S15. $10.00

**BRUES, Charles T.** *Insects, Food & Ecology.* 1972. Dover. rpt. ils. 466p. stiff wrp. S15. $10.00

**BRUNAS, Michael.** *Universal Horrors.* 1990. NY. McFarland Jefferson. 1st. VG/sans. L1. $85.00

**BRUNDAGE, Burr.** *Empire of the Inca.* (1969). Norman. 2nd. 396p. dj. F3. $20.00

**BRUNDAGE, Burr.** *Lords of Cuzco.* (1967). Norman. 458p. dj. F3. $30.00

**BRUNDAGE, Frances.** *What Happened To Tommy.* 1921. Rochester, NY. Stecher Lithographic. 4to. mc pict paper wrp. R5. $85.00

**BRUNN, H.O.** *Story of the Original Dixieland Jazz Band.* 1960. Baton Rouge. LSU. 1st. F/NF. B2. $75.00

**BRUNNER, Emil.** *Christian Doctrine of Creation & Redemption.* 1974. Westminster. 386p. VG/dj. B29. $14.50

**BRUNO, Anthony.** *Bad Business.* 1991. Delacorte. 1st. sgn. Gibbons/Tozzi #4. F/dj. R8. $20.00

**BRUNS, Roger A.** *Damndest Radical: Life & World of Ben Reitman...* 1987. Urbana, IL. 1st. photos. F/dj. A2. $15.00

**BRUNSWIK, Egon.** *Wahrnehmug und Gegendstandswelt...* 1934. Franz Deuticke. author's 1st book German text. prt yel wrp. G1. $75.00

**BRUSH, Frederic.** *Alleghenians.* 1940. NY. Blackshaw. 1st. VG/G. B5. $35.00

**BRYAN, Ashley.** *Beat the Story-Drum, Pum-Pum.* 1980. Atheneum. 1st. F/dj. V4. $25.00

**BRYAN, Ashley.** *Cat's Purr.* (1985). Atheneum. 1st/3rd prt. inscr/dtd 1989. 42p. F/NF. T5. $30.00

**BRYAN, Howard.** *Robbers, Rogues & Ruffians.* 1991. Santa Fe, NM. Clear Light. AN/dj. A19. $25.00

**BRYAN, J.** *Sword Over the Mantel.* 1960. McGraw Hill. 123p. G/fair. B10. $30.00

**BRYAN, William Cullen.** *Letters From the East.* 1869. NY. Putnam. 256p. cloth. VG. W1. $30.00

**BRYAN, William S.** *Our Islands & Their People.* 1899. NY. Thompson. 2 vol. 1st. folio. VG. E6. $75.00

**BRYANT, Billy.** *Children of Ol' Man River: Life & Times of Showboat Trouper.* 1988. Chicago. Lakeside Classic. photos. 354p. F. M4. $20.00

**BRYANT, Edward.** *Fetish.* 1991. Axolotl. 1/300. sgn. AN/dj. M21. $35.00

**BRYANT, Florence C.** *Memories of a Country Girl.* 1988. Vantage. 1st. ils. 191p. VG/dj. B10. $15.00

**BRYANT, George.** *Transactions Wisconsin State Agricultural Society 1880.* 1881. Madison. Atwood. 500p. VG. A10. $15.00

**BRYANT, Jennifer Fisher.** *Lucretia Mott: Guiding Light.* 1996. Grand Rapids, MI. Eerdmans. 1st. 182p. VG/dj. V3. $15.00

**BRYANT, John.** *Health & the Developing World.* 1978. Ithaca. 345p. wrp. A13. $15.00

**BRYANT, Sara Cone.** *Best Stories to Tell Children.* 1912 (1905). Houghton Mifflin. 16 pl. gilt cloth. G+. T5. $30.00

**BRYANT, Sara Cone.** *Epaminondas & His Auntie.* 1938. Houghton Mifflin. 1st. 8vo. 16p. tan brd. pict dj. R5. $150.00

**BRYANT, Will.** *Escape From Sonora.* 1973. Random. 1st. F/F. H11. $30.00

**BRYANT, Will.** *Escape From Sonora.* 1973. Random. 1st. 307p. VG/VG. B19. $10.00

**BRYCE, James.** *Impressions of South Africa.* 1898. NY. Century. 2nd. 8vo. 3 fld maps. cloth. xl. VG. W1. $15.00

**BRYDEN, H. Anderson.** *Gun & Camera in South America.* 1988. Prescott, AZ. photos/map. 535p. leatherette. F. A17. $20.00

**BRYON, May.** *Jack-A-Dandy: Tale of the Vain Jackdaw.* nd (1920s). London. Hodder Stoughton. sm 8vo. 48p. VG-. T5. $22.00

**BRYSON, W. Hamilton.** *Legal Education in Virginia 1779-1979.* 1982. Charlottesville. U VA. M11. $50.00

**BUARQUE, Chico.** *Turbulence.* 1992. Pantheon. 1st. F/F. H11. $20.00

**BUCHAN, Elizabeth.** *Beatrix Potter.* (1987). London. Hamish Hamilton. rpt. NF. T5. $25.00

**BUCHAN, John.** *King's Grace.* 1935. Hodder Stoughton. 1st. 1/500. sgn/#d. full vellum brd. fld box/label. M24. $225.00

**BUCHANAN, A. Russell.** *David S Terry of California.* 1956. San Marino, CA. 1st. NF/G. O4. $15.00

**BUCHANAN, Edna.** *Contents Under Pressure.* 1992. Hyperion. 1st. NF/dj. M21. $20.00

**BUCHANAN, Edna.** *Never Let Them See You Cry.* 1992. Random. 1st. F/dj. N4. $30.00

**BUCHANAN, Robert.** *North Coast & Other Poems.* 1868. London. Routledge. 1st. ils. full calf/raised bands. VG. S17. $40.00

**BUCHANAN, Zetton.** *In the Hands of the Arabs.* (1921). London. Hodder Stoughton. 8vo. 15 pl. 239p. cloth. VG. Q2. $86.00

**BUCHANAN & BUCHANAN.** *Bacteriology.* 1936. Macmillan. 532p. VG. A10. $15.00

**BUCHANAN & MURRAY.** *Charlatan.* 1895. Chicago. F Tennyson Neely. 1st Am. F. M15. $100.00

**BUCHMANN & NABHAN.** *Forgotten Pollinators.* 1966. WA, DC. Island Pr. 292p. AN/dj. A10. $25.00

**BUCK, Alfred A.** *Health & Disease in Four Peruvian Villages...* 1968. Johns Hopkins. 1st. 8vo. VG/dj. A2. $20.00

**BUCK, William J.** *William Penn in America; or, Account of His Life...* 1888. Phil. self pub. 1st. 424p. VG. V3. $60.00

**BUCKAN, William.** *Domestic Medicine; or, Treatise on Prevention & Cure...* 1784. Phil. Cruikshank. 540p. contemporary calf. G7. $175.00

**BUCKHARDT, Rudy.** *Mobile Homes.* 1979. Calais. Z Pr. 1/26 lettered. sgn. F/dj. w/orig prt. S9. $450.00

**BUCKINGHAM, Nash.** *Blood Lines.* (1947). 1st. VG/G. B30. $75.00

**BUCKINGHAM, Nash.** *De Shootinest Gent'man.* 1992. Derrydale. 1/2500. fwd Harold Sheldon. 240p. aeg. F. A17. $25.00

**BUCKLEY, Amelia King.** *Keeneland Assoc Library.* 1958. U KY. VG/dj. A21. $45.00

**BUCKLEY, Christopher.** *Wet Work.* 1991. Knopf. 1st. 275p. VG/dj. P12. $8.00

**BUCKLEY, Gial Lumet.** *Hornes: An American Family.* 1986. Knopf. 1st. xl. VG/dj. P12. $15.00

**BUCKLEY, Holland.** *Scottish Terrier.* 1913. London. Dog World. photos. 89p. VG. A17. $25.00

**BUCKLEY, James M.** *History of Methodism in the United States.* 1897. NY. 1 vol. ils. marbled brd/burgundy decor spine. VG. B30. $75.00

**BUCKLEY, Michael J.** *Day at the Farm.* 1937. np. JH Nash. 4to. 12p. brn cloth. dj. K1. $50.00

**BUCKLEY, William F.** *Atlantic High: A Celebration.* 1982. Doubleday. 1st. photos. 266p. VG/dj. S14. $9.00

**BUCKLEY, William F.** *Temptation of Wilfred Malachey.* 1985. Workman. 1st. 8vo. 45p. F/F. C14. $18.00

**BUDGE, E.A. Wallis.** *Book of the Dead.* 1960. New Hyde Park, NY. U Books. 1st thus. F/VG. A2. $20.00

**BUDGE, E.A. Wallis.** *Tutankhamen: Amenism, Atenism & Egyptian Monotheism...* NY. Bell. rpt. ils/pl/index. 160p. cloth. F/dj. D2. $15.00

**BUDGE, Frances Anne.** *Isaac Sharp: Apostle of the Nineteenth Century.* 1898. London. Headley. 12mo. 297p. VG. V3. $17.00

**BUDIANSKY, Stephen.** *Nature of Horses.* 1997. NY. Free Pr. 1st. sm 4to. F/dj. O3. $25.00

**BUECHNER, Frederick.** *Faces of Jesus.* 1974. Riverwood. 1st. 4to. 918p. F. W2. $175.00

**BUECHNER, Frederick.** *Return of Ansel Gibbs.* 1958. Knopf. 1st. sgn/dtd 1994. NF/VG. R14. $50.00

**BUECHNER, Frederick.** *Wishful Thinking: A Theological ABC.* 1973. Harper. 100p. G. B29. $9.00

**BUEHRER, Beverley Bare.** *Boris Karloff: A Bio-Bibliography.* 1993. Westport. Greenwood. 283p. VG. C5. $15.00

**BUEL, Ronald A.** *Dead End: Automobile in Mass Tansportation.* 1972. Prentice Hall. 8vo. G+/VG. A2. $11.00

**BUELL, Augustus.** *William Penn As Founder of Two Commonwealths.* 1904. NY. Appleton. 368p. G+. V3. $22.00

**BUENKER, John D.** *Immigration & Ethnicity: A Guide to Information Sources.* 1977. 1468 entries. 317p. xl. VG. A4. $50.00

**BUFF & BUFF.** *Kobi: A Boy of Switzerland.* 1939. Viking. 1st. 4to. 128p. VG/dj. T5. $30.00

**BUFFUM & MARSHALL.** *From Mexican Days to the Gold Rush.* 1993. Lakeside Classic. 1st thus. teg. brn cloth. F. T11. $25.00

**BUHLER, Curt F.** *Early Books & Manuscripts: 40 Years of Research.* 1973. Grolier/Pierpont Morgan. ltd ed. 1/510. 20 pl. 662p. blk cloth. K1. $100.00

**BUHLER, Karl.** *Abriss der Geistigen Entwicklung des Kindes.* 1925. Quelle Meyer. 2nd revised. German text. 152p. G1. $35.00

**BUKOWSKI, Charles.** *Bring Me Your Love.* 1983. Santa Barbara. 1/26 (376 total). sgn. ils/sgn R Crumb. AN. B24. $400.00

**BUKOWSKI, Charles.** *Going Modern.* nd. Freemont. Ruddy Duck. 1/500. F/wrp. R14. $50.00

**BUKOWSKI, Charles.** *Poems & Drawings/Epos, a Quarterly of Poetry.* 1962. Crescent City, FL. Epos. 1st. F/yel wrp. M24. $100.00

**BUKOWSKI, Charles.** *Scarlet.* 1976. Santa Barbara. Blk Sparrow. 1/150. sgn/#d. F/chipped acetate dj. B2. $250.00

**BUKOWSKI, Charles.** *Screams From the Balcony (Selected Letters 1960-70).* 1993. Santa Rosa. Blk Sparrow. 1/600. sgn. F. B9. $100.00

**BUKOWSKI, Charles.** *War All the Time. Poems 1981-1984.* 1984. Blk Sparrow. 1/400. sgn/#d. F/F. B2. $200.00

**BULKIN & LARKIN.** *Amazon Poetry: An Anthology...* 1975. Brooklyn. Out & Out Books. 1st. 110p. VG/self wrp. A25. $20.00

**BULL, William Perkins.** *From Medicine Man to Medical Man: A Record of a Century...* 1934. Toronto. 1/875. sgn twice. G7. $95.00

**BULLA, Cyde Robert.** *Viking Adventure.* (1963). NY. Crowell. Weekly Reader BC. 8vo. pict brd. G+. T5. $15.00

**BULLEN & PROUT.** *Yachting: How to Sail & Manage a Small Modern Yacht.* 1930. Glasgow. 2nd. ils. VG. M17. $25.00

**BULLER, A.H.** *Essays on Wheat.* 1919. Macmillan. 339p. cloth. VG. A10. $50.00

**BULLER, Walter Lawry.** *Birds of New Zealand.* 1979. new ed. ils. F/dj/case. B30. $45.00

**BULLIET, C.J.** *Significant Moderns & Their Pictures.* 1936. London. Allen Unwin. 1st. 199p. mc fabric w/gr titles. NF. F1. $50.00

**BULLOCK, Alan.** *Hitler & Stalin: Parallel Lives.* 1992. NY. 1st. photos. VG/dj. M17. $25.00

**BULLOCK, Helen.** *Williamsburg Art of Cookery...* 1966. Williamsburg, VA. G+. A16. $10.00

**BUMILLER, Elizabeth.** *May You Be the Mother of a Hundred Sons...* 1990. Random. not 1st. VG/dj. N2. $10.00

**BUMP, Darrow.** *Ruffed Grouse: Its History, Propagation, Management.* 1978. NY State Conserv Dept. 1/950, ils/index. F. A17. $85.00

**BUMP, Orlando F.** *Law & Practice in Bankruptcy, Practice in Bankruptcy...* 1872. Baker Voorhis. sheep. M11. $250.00

**BUNGE, Carlos-Octavio.** *Principles de Psychologie Individuelle et Sociale.* 1903. Paris. Felix Alcan. 1st Frenc-language. 12mo. 256p. G. G1. $30.00

**BUNNELL, Lafayette Houghton.** *Discovery of the Yosemite & Indian War of 1851.* (1880). Chicago. Fleming Revell. 1st. inscr. ils. 331p. gilt cloth. D11. $450.00

**BUNSON, Maggie.** *Faith in Paradise: A Century & Half of Roman Catholic...* 1977. St Paul. Daughters of St Paul. 256p. NF/dj. P4. $25.00

**BUNTING, Eve.** *In the Haunted House.* 1990. Clarion. 1st. ils Susan Meddaugh. F/VG. P2. $12.50

**BUNYAN, John.** *Pilgrim's Progress From This World to That Which Is to Come.* 1895. London. John C Nimmo. ils Wm Strang. 379p. half brn crushed morocco. VG. F1. $250.00

**BUNYAN, John.** *Pilgrim's Progress From This World to That Which Is to Come.* 1938. NY. Rae D Henkle. Special Anniversary ed. ils Wm Strang. 379p. F. B14. $55.00

**BUOL, S.W.** *Soil Genesis & Classification.* 1973. Ames, IA. 360p. cloth. VG. A10. $20.00

**BURANELLI, Vincent.** *King & the Quaker: Study of William Penn & James II.* 1962. Phil. U PA. 1st. 241p. xl. dj. V3. $11.00

**BURANELLI, Vincent.** *Trial of Peter Zenger.* 1957. NY. University. 1st. VG/dj. S13. $15.00

**BURBANK, P.N.** *Diderot: A Critical Biography.* 1992. NY. 1st. ils. VG/dj. M17. $20.00

**BURCH, John P.** *Charles W Quantrell: True History of His Guerrilla Warfare.* 1923. Vega, TX. self pub. ils. 266p. VG. B10. $45.00

**BURCH, Mark.** *Road Game: A Summer's Tale.* 1986. Vanguard. 1st. author's 1st novel. F/VG. P8. $45.00

**BURCHETT, Wilfred.** *Mekong Upstream.* 1957. Hanoi. Red River Pub. 1st. photos/fld map. VG/self wrp. R11. $75.00

**BURCK, Jacob.** *Hunger & Revolt: Cartoons by Burck.* nd. NY. Daily Worker. VG. V4. $100.00

**BURDETTE, Robert J.** *Rise & Fall of the Mustache & Other Hawk-Eyetems.* 1877. Burlington, IA. Burlington. 1st. Ils RW Wallis. 8vo. 328p. gilt cloth. K1. $75.00

**BURDICK & LEDERER.** *Sarkhan.* 1965. McGraw Hill. 1st. VG/dj. R11. $25.00

**BURDIN & DUBOIS.** *Histoire Academique de Magnetisme Animal Accompagnee...* 1841. Paris/London. Bailliere. 651p. contemporary bdg. G1. $250.00

**BURGESS, Alan.** *Longest Tunnel.* 1990. GRove Weidenfeld. 1st. 289p. gr cloth. F/dj. M7. $25.00

**BURGESS, Anthony.** *Any Old Iron.* 1989. Random. 1st. F/dj. T10. $35.00

**BURGESS, Anthony.** *Dead Man in Deptford.* 1995. NY. 1st thus. dj. T9. $12.00

**BURGESS, Anthony.** *Earthly Powers.* 1980. NY. 1st. dj. T9. $20.00

**BURGESS, Anthony.** *Kingdom of the Wicked.* 1985. Franklin Lib. 1st. sgn. maroon 'reconstituted' leather. F. M24. $45.00

**BURGESS, Anthony.** *Long Trip to Teatime.* 1976. Dempsey & Squires. F/dj. P3. $15.00

**BURGESS, Anthony.** *Long Trip to Teatime.* 1976. Stonehill. 1st. VG/dj. S13. $12.00

**BURGESS, Anthony.** *On Going to Bed.* 1982. Abbeville. 1st. VG/F. B30. $40.00

**BURGESS, Anthony.** *This Man & Music.* 1983. NY. 1st. VG/dj. M17. $15.00

**BURGESS, Dorothy.** *Dream & Deed: Story of Katharine Lee Bates.* 1952. Norman, OK. 1st. photos. 241p. VG/dj. A25. $20.00

**BURGESS, Gelett.** *Miniature Purple Cow.* 1966. Pasadena. Dawson. mini. ils Grant Dahlstrom. Bela Blau bdg. B24. $100.00

**BURGESS, R.H.** *This Was Chesapeake Bay.* 1963. Cornell Maritime. 1st. 4to. ils/map. 310p. F/dj. M4. $22.00

**BURGESS, Thornton W.** *Adventures of Jimmy Skunk.* 1918. Little Brn. 1st. 12mo. pict cloth. R5. $100.00

**BURGESS, Thornton W.** *Adventures of Ol' Mistah Buzzard.* 1931 (1919). Little Brn. Bedtime Story Book. ils Harrison Cady. gray cloth. VG. M5. $35.00

**BURGESS, Thornton W.** *Adventures of Old Man Coyote.* (1916). Toronto. 1st Canadian. F/sans. T12. $150.00

**BURGESS, Thornton W.** *Adventures of Poor Mrs Quack.* (1917). Grosset Dunlap. 8vo. 189p. G+. T5. $18.00

**BURGESS, Thornton W.** *Adventures of Poor Mrs Quack.* 1917. Little Brn. 1st. ils Harrison Cady. 12mo. pict cloth. R5. $100.00

**BURGESS, Thornton W.** *Adventures of Reddy Fox.* 1946. Little Brn. Bedtime Story series. ils/inscr Harrison Cady. VG/dj. D1. $185.00

**BURGESS, Thornton W.** *Animal World of Thornton Burgess.* 1961. Platt Munk. rpt. 8vo. ils Cady. VG/G. B17. $25.00

**BURGESS, Thornton W.** *Burgess Bird Book for Children.* nd. Little Brn. decor brd. NF. P3. $35.00

**BURGESS, Thornton W.** *Burgess Flower Book for Children.* 1923. Little Brn. 1st. 8vo. blk cloth. G+. T5. $50.00

**BURGESS, Thornton W.** *Buster Bear's Twins.* 1923. Little Brn. 1st. ils Harrison Cady. dk bl cloth/pict label. R5. $150.00

**BURGESS, Thornton W.** *Mother West Wind How Stories.* (1916). Grosset Dunlap. 8vo. ils Harrison Cady. bl brd. G+. T5. $15.00

**BURGESS, Thornton W.** *Mother West Wind How Stories.* 1916. Little Brn. 1st. ils Harrison Cady. G. M5. $65.00

**BURGLON, Nora.** *Children of the Soil.* 1933 (1932). Doubleday Doran. 1st thus. 1933 Newbery Honor. yel cloth. G+. T5. $35.00

**BURK, Bruce.** *Waterfowl Studies for the Decoy Maker, Collector, Hunter...* 1977. Winchester. 2nd. 700 photos. 254p. F. A19. $30.00

**BURKARD, W.E.** *Builders for Good Health.* 1946. Chicago. Lyons Carnahan. 1st. ils. 318p. VG+. A25. $20.00

**BURKARD, W.E.** *Good Health Is Fun.* 1946. Chicago. Lyons Carnahan. 1st. ils. 295p. VG+. A25. $20.00

**BURKE, Alan Dennis.** *Dead Wrong.* 1990. NY. 1st. F/dj. H11. $20.00

**BURKE, Alan Dennis.** *Driven to Murder.* 1986. Atlantic Monthly. 1st. F/dj. P3. $16.00

**BURKE, Charles T.** *Puritans at Bay: War Against King Philip & Squaw Sachems.* 1967. NY. ils. VG. M17. $15.00

**BURKE, Edmund.** *On Conciliation With the Colonies & Other Papers...* 1975. LEC/Stinehour. 1/200. ils/sgn Lynd Ward. 268p. F. H13. $195.00

**BURKE, Edmund.** *Philosophical Inquiry Into Origin of Our Ideas...* 1810. London. Thomas Tegg. sm 8vo. 172p. pub brd. H13. $125.00

**BURKE, Fred.** *Clive Barker, Illustrator.* 1984. Bison. 1/750. sgn. AN/dj. T12. $150.00

**BURKE, James Lee.** *Black Cherry Blues.* 1989. Little Brn. 1st. F/dj. C15. $85.00

**BURKE, James Lee.** *Black Cherry Blues.* 1989. Little Brn. 1st. 8vo. Dave Robicheaux series. NF/dj. S9. $75.00

**BURKE, James Lee.** *Burning Angel.* 1995. Hyperion. 1st. sm 4to. F/dj. W2. $30.00

**BURKE, James Lee.** *Burning Angel.* 1995. NY. Hyperion. 1st. sgn. F/dj. A23/M15. $45.00

**BURKE, James Lee.** *Cadillac Jukebox.* 1996. Hyperion. 1st. F/dj. A23. $42.00

**BURKE, James Lee.** *Cadillac Jukebox.* 1996. Hyperion/Trice. 1st. 1/175. sgn. F/sans/case. T2. $150.00

**BURKE, James Lee.** *Cadillac Jukebox.* 1996. London. Orion. 1st Eng. sgn. F/dj. T2. $50.00

**BURKE, James Lee.** *Cimarron Rose.* 1997. London. Orion. 1st (precedes Am). F/dj. M15. $75.00

**BURKE, James Lee.** *Convict & Other Stories.* 1995. London. Orion. 1st Eng. 1/500. NF/dj. A14. $63.00

**BURKE, James Lee.** *Dixie City Jam.* 1994. London. Orion. 1st. F/dj. M15. $45.00

**BURKE, James Lee.** *Heaven's Prisoners.* 1988. Holt. 1st. F/dj. M15. $165.00

**BURKE, James Lee.** *Heaven's Prisoners.* 1988. NY. Holt. 1st. NF/dj. A14. $122.50

**BURKE, James Lee.** *In the Electric Mist With Confederate Dead.* 1993. Hyperion. 1st. sgn. F/dj. A23. $60.00

**BURKE, James Lee.** *In the Electric Mist With Confederate Dead.* 1993. NY. Hyperion. 1st. F/dj. M15. $50.00

**BURKE, James Lee.** *Morning for Flamingos.* 1990. Little Brn. 1st. inscr. F/dj. M15. $100.00

**BURKE, James Lee.** *Neon Rain.* 1987. NY. Holt. 1st. sgn. 1st Dave Robicheaux. F/dj. T2. $225.00

**BURKE, James Lee.** *Neon Rain.* 1989. Mysterious/Hutchinson. 1st thus. sgn on title. NF/ils wrp as issued. A14. $175.00

**BURKE, James Lee.** *Stained White Radiance.* 1992. NY. Hyperion. 1st. sgn. F/F. O11. $45.00

**BURKE, James Lee.** *Sunset Limited.* 1998. NY. Doubleday. 1st. sgn. F/dj. M15. $45.00

**BURKE, James Lee.** *Two For Texas.* 1992. Huntington Beach. James Cahill. 1st hc. 1/400. sgn. F/case. M15. $250.00

**BURKE, James Lee.** *Winter Light.* 1992. Huntington Beach. James Cahill. 1st hc. 1/300. sgn. F/sans. M15. $135.00

**BURKE, Jan.** *Hocus.* 1997. S&S. 1st. sgn. F/dj. A23. $35.00

**BURKE, John N.** *Mozart & His Music.* 1959. NY. 1st. VG/dj. M17. $25.00

**BURKE, John.** *Origins of the Science of Crystals.* 1966. Berkeley. 198p. A13. $25.00

**BURKE, Ken.** *Trees.* 1982. Mt Vernon, VA. ils. 144p. F. B26. $15.00

**BURKE, Richard E.** *Senator (Ted Kennedy).* 1992. St Martin. 1st. F/dj. T11. $5.00

**BURKE, Thomas.** *Go, Lovely Rose.* 1931. Brooklyn, NY. Sephra Lib. 1/110. sgn. VG. M17. $20.00

**BURKERT, Nancy Ekholm.** *Valentine & Orson.* 1989. FSG. 1st. F/VG. M5. $40.00

**BURKETT, Charles William.** *History of Ohio Agriculture.* 1900. Concord, NH. 211p. G. B18. $25.00

**BURKHALTER, Lois Wood.** *Marion Koogler McNay.* 1968. San Antonio. McNay Art Inst. inscr. F. 19. $50.00

**BURL, Aubrey.** *Stone Circles of the British Isles.* 1976. Yale. 1st. 36 pl/50 text figures. F/dj. T10. $75.00

**BURLAND, Brian.** *Stephen Dacatur: The Devil & the Endymion.* 1975. London. Allen Unwin. 1st. inscr. F/NF. T11. $35.00

**BURLAND, Cottie.** *Aztecs: Gods & Fates in Ancient Mexico.* (1980). NY. Galahad. 1st thus. 4to. 128p. dj. F3. $15.00

**BURLEIGH, Thomas D.** *Georgia Birds.* 1958. Norman. 1st. ils. 746p. VG/clip. B18. $55.00

**BURLEY, W.J.** *Death in Willow Pattern.* 1969. London. Gollancz. 1st. F/dj. M15. $85.00

**BURLEY, W.J.** *Wycliffe & the Scapegoat.* 1979. Doubleday. 1st Am. NF/VG. N4. $20.00

**BURLEY, W.J.** *Wycliffe's Wild Goose Chase.* 1982. Crime Club. 1st Am. VG/dj. G8. $17.50

**BURN, Barbara.** *North American Birds.* 1984. Bonanza. 1st. photos. 96p. F/VG. S14. $15.00

**BURN, Robert S.** *Hints for Farmers.* 1860. London. Routledge. 171p. xl. A10. $25.00

**BURNABY, Fred.** *On Horseback Through Asia Minor.* 1877. London. Sampson Low. 1st. G. O3. $65.00

BURNARD, Bonnie. *Casino & Other Stories.* 1994. Harper Collins. 1st. author's 2nd book. F/dj. H11. $40.00

BURNBULL, Colin M. *Mountain People.* 1972. S&S. 1st. 8vo. ils/maps. VG/dj. W1. $16.00

BURNE-JONES, Edward. *Creation.* 1981. Tarzana, CA. mini. 1/100. hand-colored/sgn Barbara Raheb. gilt blk morocco. B24. $200.00

BURNER, W.J. *Mozart: Man & His Works.* 1938. Knopf. 1st. 8vo. 464p. G. S14. $15.00

BURNET, F.M. *Integrity of the Body: A Discussion of Modern Immunological.* 1962. Cambridge. 1st. 189p. A13. $25.00

BURNETT, E.K. *Inlaid Stone & Bone Artifacts From Southern California.* 1944. NY. 71 ils. 60p. NF. M4. $45.00

BURNETT, Frances H. *Little Princess.* 1963. Harper Collins. late rpt/new format. ils Tasha Tudor. rem mk. F/dj. B17. $15.00

BURNETT, Frances H. *Secret Garden.* 1962. Harper. rpt. 8vo. rem mk. F/dj. B17. $15.00

BURNETT, Frances Hodgson. *Editha's Burglar..* (1888). Boston. Dana Estes. 12mo. 66p. red cloth. G+. T5. $25.00

BURNETT, Frances Hodgson. *Land of the Blue Flower.* 1909. NY. mc ftspc. VG. M17. $20.00

BURNETT, Frances Hodgson. *Little Lord Fauntleroy.* 1889. London. Warne. 16th. sq 8vo. 269p. ils RB Birch. aeg. Bayntum bdg. F. H5. $250.00

BURNETT, Frances Hodgson. *Little Princess.* 1963. Lippincott. 1st thus. ils Tasha Tudor. VG/G. M5. $150.00

BURNETT, Frances Hodgson. *Lost Prince.* 1915. Century. 1st. ils ML Bower. VG. B27. $55.00

BURNETT, Frances Hodgson. *Sara Crewe; or, What Happened at Miss Minchin's.* 1981. London. Methuen. 1st Eng. 79p. emb mauve brd. F/NF. T5. $35.00

BURNETT, Frances Hodgson. *Secret Garden: A Thrushwood Book.* 1938. Grosset Dunlap. VG. B36. $6.00

BURNETT, I. Compton. *Pastors & Masters: A Study.* 1925. London. Heath Cranton. 126p. VG/dj. M10. $75.00

BURNETT, John. *Autobiography of the Working Class...Vol II, 1900-1945.* 1987. NY U. 1113 annotated entries. 447p. NF. A4. $45.00

BURNETT, W.R. *Goodhues of Sinking Creek.* 1934. NY. 1st. ils JJ Lankes. quarter cloth. VG/dj. B18. $27.50

BURNETT, W.R. *Romelle.* 1946. NY. Knopf. 1st. F/NF. M15. $85.00

BURNETT, W.R. *Underdog.* 1957. Knopf. 1st. F/clip. M15. $75.00

BURNETT, W.R. *Vanity Row.* 1952. Knopf. 1st. F/VG. B4. $150.00

BURNETT, Whit. *Two Bottles of Relish.* 1943. NY. Dial. 1st. VG/dj. M21. $30.00

BURNEY, Charles. *Account of Musical Performances in Westminster-Abbey...* 1785. London. Payne Robinson. lg 4to. 8 full-p pl. quarter calf (weak). R12. $450.00

BURNEY, Charles. *Burney's Musical Tours in Europe.* 1959. OUP. 2 vol. 1st. tall 8vo. F/dj. H13. $195.00

BURNEY, Charles. *General History of Music, From Earliest Ages...* 1776-1789. London. Prt for Author. 4 vol. 1st. tall 8vo. gilt brd. H13. $1,895.00

BURNEY, Eliza P. *Memoir & Correspondence of Eliza P Burney.* 1884. Lippincott. 12mo. 377p. xl. V3. $19.00

BURNEY, Fanny. *Camilla; or, A Picture of Youth.* 1802. London. Payne/Cadell. 5 vol. sm 8vo. rb/gray linen spines/red labels. H13. $495.00

BURNEY, Fanny. *Cecilia; or, Memoirs of an Heiress.* nd (1825). London. JF Dove. 2 vol. 480p+extra engraved titles/ftspc. morocco. H13. $295.00

BURNEY, Fanny. *Evelina; or, History of Young Lady's Introduction to World.* 1779. London. Lowndes. 3 vol. 8vo. tree calf. F. H13. $495.00

BURNHAM, Eleanor Waring. *Justin Morgan: Romantic History of a Horse.* 1911. NY. Shakespeare. 1st. 160p. VG. O3. $95.00

BURNHAM, Frederick Russell. *Taking Chances.* 1994. Wolfe. photos/facs. 293p. F. A17. $20.00

BURNHAM, Frederick. *Scouting on Two Continents.* 1928. Doubleday. ils. 370p. VG/dj. B5. $37.50

BURNS, Eric. *Joy of Books.* 1995. Prometheus. 1st. F/dj. M23. $20.00

BURNS, James J. *Educational History of Ohio.* 1905. Columbus. 756p. rb. VG. B18. $95.00

BURNS, James MacGregor. *Crosswinds of Freedom.* 1989. Knopf. 1st trade. sm 4to. 864p. NF/F. W2. $45.00

BURNS, John. *Anatomy of the Gravid Uterus.* 1908. Boston. Cushing. 1st Am. pl. 248p. G7. $175.00

BURNS, John. *Principles of Midwifery Including Diseases of Women...* 1835 (1831). 8vo. 12 pl. worn leather/marlbed brd. G+. E6. $85.00

BURNS, John. *Principles of Midwifery Including Diseases of Women...* 1837. NY. CS Francis. 12 pl/1 fld leaf. 806p. full sheep. fair. G7. $125.00

BURNS, Olive Ann. *Cold Sassy Tree.* 1984. NY. VG/dj. M17. $30.00

BURNS, Rex. *Killing Zone.* 1988. NY. Viking Penguin. 1st. F/clip. A14. $17.50

BURNS, Robert. *Complete Writings of Robert Burns. In Ten Volumes.* 1926-1927. Boston. Houghton Mifflin. 10 vol. 1/1000. rose cloth over brn emb brd. K1. $350.00

BURNS, Robert. *Cottar's Saturday Night.* (1890). London. Marcus Ward. ils. 22p. VG. M10. $32.50

BURNS, Robert. *Poetical Works.* 1808. Alnwick. Catnach & Davison. 2 vol. 1st. 12mo. tree calf. F1. $600.00

BURNS, Stanley B. *Forgotten Marriage: Painted Tintype & Decorated Frame...* 1995. NY. Burns. 1st. ils. 213p. F/dj. S9. $75.00

BURNS, Tex; see L'Amour, Louis.

BURNS, Walter Noble. *One Way Ride.* 1931. Doubleday. 1st? 313p. VG/dj. B5. $37.50

BURR, Anna R. *Weir Mitchell, His Life & Letters.* 1929. NY. 1st. 424p. A13. $50.00

BURR, Frank A. *Life of General Philip Sheridan.* 1888. Providence. Reid. 1st. ils. pict bdg. VG. E6. $30.00

BURRAGE, A.M. *Intruders: New Weird Tales.* 1995. Chester. Ash-Tree. 1st. 1/500. 26 stories. F/dj. T2. $45.00

BURRIDGE, W. *New Physiological Psychology.* 1933. London. Arnold. 12mo. gilt bl cloth. G1. $30.00

BURROUGHS, Edgar Rice. *Beasts of Tarzan.* 1917. AL Burt. VG. P3. $35.00

BURROUGHS, Edgar Rice. *Carson of Venus.* 1939. Tarzana. ERB. 1st. F/dj. L3. $750.00

BURROUGHS, Edgar Rice. *Jungles of Tarzan.* 1921. Grosset Dunlap. 1st thus. red-brn cloth. G+. M21. $40.00

BURROUGHS, Edgar Rice. *Land That Time Forgot.* nd. Doubleday BC. VG/dj. M21. $10.00

BURROUGHS, Edgar Rice. *Llana of Gathol.* 1948. Tarzana. ERB. 1st. F/NF. B2. $150.00

BURROUGHS, Edgar Rice. *Monster Men.* 1929. Chicago. McClurg. 1st. 304p. sm 8vo. tan cloth. VG. H1. $145.00

BURROUGHS, Edgar Rice. *Pellucidar.* Grosset Dunlap. later prt. sm 8vo. 322p. G/dj. H1. $15.00

BURROUGHS, Edgar Rice. *Tarzan, Lord of the Jungle.* 1943. Grosset Dunlap. F/NF. M19. $35.00

BURROUGHS, Edgar Rice. *Tarzan & the Foreign Legion.* 1947. Tarzana. ERB. 1st. F/dj. B2. $150.00

BURROUGHS, Edgar Rice. *Tarzan & the Jewels of Opar.* 1912. McClurg. 2nd. VG. P3. $90.00

BURROUGHS, Edgar Rice. *Tarzan of the Apes.* 1914. Chicago. McClurg. 1st (Old Eng imp on copyright). 8vo. ils Arting. F. H5. $1,750.00

BURROUGHS, Edgar Rice. *Tarzan of the Apes.* 1915. AL Burt. sm 8vo. 400p. gr cloth. G/dj. H1. $30.00

BURROUGHS, Edgar Rice. *Tarzan Twins.* 1927. Joliet. PF Volland. 6th. ils Douglas Grant. ils brd. mc pict dj. R5. $385.00

BURROUGHS, John Rolfe. *Where the Old West Stayed Young.* 1962. Morrow. ils/brands. 376p. VG. J2. $145.00

BURROUGHS, William S. *Adding Machine.* 1986. Seaver. 1st. F/F. B3. $40.00

BURROUGHS, William S. *Cat Inside.* 1992. Viking. 1st trade. ils Brion Gysin. F/sans. B30. $35.00

BURROUGHS, William S. *Cities of the Red Night.* 1981. HRW. 1st. F/dj. Q1. $35.00

BURROUGHS, William S. *Cobble Stone Gardens.* 1976. Cherry Valley, NY. 1st. 1/50. sgn. F. B4. $350.00

BURROUGHS, William S. *Ghost of a Chance Serpent's Tale.* 1995. Hight Risk Books. 1st trade. F/sans. B30. $35.00

BURROUGHS, William S. *Last Words of Dutch Schultz.* 1976. Viking. 1st Am. inscr/dtd 1996. F/NF. R14. $125.00

BURROUGHS, William S. *Last Words of Dutch Schultz.* 1981. NY. Seaver. 1st thus. VG/wrp. C9. $25.00

BURROUGHS, William S. *My Education: Book of Dreams.* 1995. Viking. 1st. F/dj. B30. $45.00

BURROUGHS, William S. *Place of Dead Roses.* 1983. HRW. 1st. NF/NF. B3. $55.00

BURROUGHS, William S. *Seven Deadly Sins.* nd. NY. Lococo-Mulder. ltd. 4to. F/sans. B2. $100.00

BURROUGHS, William S. *Ticket That Exploded.* 1967. NY. Grove. 1st Am. sgn/dtd 1995. NF/dj. R14. $250.00

BURROUGHS, William S. *Ticket That Exploded.* 1967. NY. Grove. 1st. VG/dj. B30. $90.00

BURROUGHS, William S. *Tornado Alley.* 1989. Cherry Valley. 1st hc. F/sans. B30. $85.00

BURROUGHS & LANSDALE. *Tarzan: The Lost Adventure.* 1995. Dark Horse. 1st. sgn Lansdale. AN/dj. S18. $45.00

BURROWS, Millar. *Outline of Biblical Theology.* 1946. Westminster. 380p. VG/dj. B29. $10.50

BURROWS, William E. *Exploring Space.* 1990. Random. 1st. 502p. NF/F. W2. $35.00

BURRUS, Ernest J. *Kino & the Cartography of Northwestern New Spain.* 1965. Tucson. AZ Pioneers Hist Soc. 1/750. folio. maps. F. P4. $450.00

BURRUS, Ernest J. *Wenceslaus Linck's Reports & Letters, 1762-1778.* 1967. Dawson's Book Shop. 1st. ils/notes. 94p. F/sans. B19. $27.50

BURSTYN, Joan N. *Past & Promise: Lives of New Jersey Women.* 1997. Syracuse. 4to. 468p. VG/wrp. V3. $18.00

BURT, Nathaniel. *Perennial Philadelphians: Anatomy of American Aristocracy.* 1963. Little Brn. 1st. VG/dj. V3. $16.50

BURTON, Anthony. *National Trust Guide to Our Industrial Past.* 1983. London. Geo Philip. ils. 240p. VG/dj. M10. $12.50

BURTON, Asa. *Essays on Some of First Principles of Metaphysicks...* 1824. Mirror Office. 414p. contemporary calf. G1. $185.00

BURTON, Bill. *Sportsman's Encyclopedia.* 1971. NY. 638p. VG/dj. A17. $17.50

BURTON, Ernest DeWitt. *Syntax of the Moods & Tenses in New Testament Greek.* 1978. Kregel. 215p. VG. B29. $10.50

BURTON, Gabrielle. *Heartbreak Hotel.* 1986. Scribner. 1st. F/F. A23. $35.00

BURTON, Gabrielle. *Heartbreak Hotel.* 1986. Scribner. 1st. F/NF. B3. $25.00

BURTON, Gabrielle. *I'm Running Away From Home But I'm Not Allowed...* nd (1976). Pittsburgh. Know Inc. 1st. ils Diane Footlick. F/NF. B4. $150.00

BURTON, John Hill. *Book-Hunter...* 1882. Edinburgh. Blackwood. later ed/lg paper. 8vo. 427p. later bl cloth. G. C6. $85.00

BURTON, Maurice. *Shell: Natural History of Britain.* 1970. London. lg 8vo. 479p. VG/dj. S15. $16.00

BURTON, Michael C. *John Henry Faulk.* 1993. Eakin. 1st. NF. W2. $20.00

BURTON, Richard F. *Arabian Nights.* 1935. Bl Ribbon. VG. M21. $15.00

BURTON, Richard F. *Zanzibar: City, Island & Coast.* 1872. London. 2 vol. 1st. ils/maps. scarce leather bdg. VG. H3. $500.00

BURTON, Richard. *Memorial Day.* 1897. Boston. Copeland Day. 1st. 12mo. 73p. brn cloth. VG. C6. $40.00

BURTON, Robert. *Anatomy of Melancholy: What It Is, Causes...* 1898. new ed. G+. E6. $35.00

BURTON, Robert. *Anatomy of Melancholy: What It Is, Kinds...* 1879. London. Democritus. 747p. full leather. gilt bl calf. B18. $75.00

BURTON, Robert. *Anatomy of Melancholy: What It Is...* 1925. London. Nonesuch. 2 vol. volio. ils E McKnight Kauffer. vellum brd. G7. $175.00

BURTON, Robert. *Martyrs in Flames; or, History of Popery.* 1729. London. Bettesworth. 3rd. 188p+1 leaf ads. full calf. F1. $300.00

BURTON, Virginia Lee. *Choo Choo: Story of Little Engine Who Ran Away.* 1937. Houghton Mifflin. later prt. sgn pres. 4to. orange pict cloth. pict dj. $150.00

BURTON, Virginia Lee. *Katy & the Big Snow.* 1943. Houghton Mifflin. 1st. sgn pres. pict cloth. R5. $150.00

BURTON, Virginia Lee. *Maybelle the Cable Car.* 1952. Boston. Houghton Mifflin. 1st. sq 4to. pict dj. R5. $150.00

BURUMA, Ian. *Playing the Game.* 1991. Farrar. 1st. F/F. H11. $15.00

BUSCAGLIA, Leo. *Love.* 1972. Thorofare, NJ. Chas B Slack. 1st. NF/VG+. B4. $150.00

BUSCH, Frederick. *Absent Friends.* 1989. Knopf. 1st. F/NF. R14/S18. $25.00

BUSCH, Frederick. *Girls.* 1997. Crown. 1st. AN/dj. S18. $17.00

BUSCH, Frederick. *I Wanted a Year Without a Fall.* 1971. London. Calder Boyars. 1/1000. sgn. F/dj. R14. $90.00

BUSCH, Frederick. *Sometimes I Live in the Country.* 1986. Godine. 1st. inscr. NF/dj. S13. $18.00

BUSCH, Frederick. *War Babies.* 1989. New Directions. 1st. F/dj. R14. $25.00

BUSCH, Moritz. *Travels Between the Hudson & the Mississippi, 1851-1852.* 1971. Lexington, KY. 1st. trans/edit NH Binger. 295p. VG/dj. B18. $12.50

BUSCH, Wilhelm. *Das Grosse Wilhelm Busch Hausbuch: Ein Heiteres Album...* 1984. Munich, Germany. 380-394 thousand. lg 4to. 623p. F/NF. C14. $35.00

BUSCH, Wilhelm. *Schnaken & Schnurren (Joking & Joking).* nd. Munchen. Braun & Schneider. 2 vol. later prt. 4to. R5. $100.00

BUSCHKE & CUTLER. *Cancer: Its Diagnosis & Treatment.* 1938. Phil. Saunders. 1st. tall 8vo. 757p. NF. C14. $60.00

BUSCHOR, Ernst. *Phidias der Mensch.* 1948. Munich. Bruckmann. ils. 142p. brd. D2. $40.00

BUSH, Lee. *Euclid Beach Is Closed for the Season.* 1977. Cleveland. 2nd. ils/index. 331p. VG/dj. B5. $35.00

BUSHNELL, Clyde. *La Carrera Politica y Militar de Juan Alvarez.* (1988). Mexico. 1st. 291p. wrp. F3. $15.00

BUSHONG, Millard K. *Old Jube: Biography of General Jubal A Early.* 1990. Wht Mane Pub. 1st/5th imp. F/dj. A14. $17.50

BUSIA, Akosua. *Seasons of Beento Blackburd.* 1996. Boston. Little Brn. 1st. sgn. author's 1st book. F/dj. O11. $20.00

BUTCHART, Harvey. *Grand Canyon Treks III.* 1985. La Siesta. photos/maps/index. 72p. VG. F7. $7.00

BUTCHER, David. *Stanbrook Abbey Press 1956-1990.* 1992. Whittington. 1/17 on Oasis goatskin. teg. w/ephemera. F/box. B24. $2,250.00

BUTLER, Charles. *Historical Memoirs of English, Irish & Scottish Catholics...* 1822. London. John Murray. 4 vol. full calf/raised bands. VG. S17. $200.00

BUTLER, F. *Wine & Wine Lands of the World.* 1926. London. 1st. photos. VG. E6. $40.00

BUTLER, Gwendoline. *Coffin & the Paper Man.* 1990. St Martin. 1st/2nd prt. F/dj. A23. $30.00

BUTLER, Gwendoline. *Dull Dead.* 1962. Walker. 1st. F/VG. M19. $35.00

BUTLER, Jack. *Jack's Skillet.* 1997. Algonquin. 1st. sgn. F/dj. M23. $40.00

BUTLER, Jack. *Nightshade.* 1989. Atlantic. 1st. NF/F. H11. $15.00

BUTLER, John. *Electro Therapeutics & Electro Surgery.* 1878. NY. College Homeopathic Medicine. 1st. ils. NF. E6. $150.00

BUTLER, Robert Olen. *Alleys of Eden.* 1981. Horizon. 1st. sgn. author's 1st book. F/NF. A24. $150.00

BUTLER, Robert Olen. *Deep Green Sea.* 1997. Holt. 1st. sgn. F/dj. R14. $40.00

BUTLER, Robert Olen. *Good Scent From a Strange Mountain.* 1992. Holt. 1st. sgn. rem mk. F/NF. R14. $90.00

BUTLER, Robert Olen. *On Distant Ground.* 1995. Knopf. 1st. rem mk. VG/dj. B30. $50.00

BUTLER, Robert Olen. *Sun Dogs.* 1982. Horizon. 1st. sgn. author's 2nd book. F/F. B3. $150.00

BUTLER, Robert Olen. *They Whisper.* 1994. Holt. later prt. inscr/dtd 1994. F/dj. S13. $20.00

BUTLER, Robert Olen. *Wabash.* 1987. Knopf. 1st. sgn. F/F. B3. $60.00

BUTLER, Robert Olen. *Wabash.* 1994. Holt. 1st thus. sgn. F/dj. M23. $50.00

BUTLER, W.J. *Fort Smith, Past & Present.* 1972. Ft Smith. 208p. F. M4. $30.00

BUTLER, William E. *Soviet Union & Law of the Sea.* 1971. Johns Hopkins. G/dj. M11. $45.00

BUTTERFIELD, H. *Christianity & History.* (1950). NY. Scribner. 146p. H10. $15.00

BUTTERFIELD, Roger. *Saturday Evening Post Treasury.* 1954. S&S. 1st. photos. 544p. G. S14. $15.00

BUTTERFIELD, W.H. *Making Fences, Walls & Hedges.* 1914. NY. McBride. 1st. 12mo. G. H10. $15.00

BUTTERWORTH, Bill. *Arable Management.* 1980. London. Northwood. 238p. VG. A10. $15.00

BUTTERWORTH, Hazekiah. *Zigzag Journeys in Northern Lands: Rhine to the Arctic.* 1884. Boston. 320p. G. B18. $22.50

BUTTERWORTH, W.F. *Stock Car Racer.* 1966. Norton. 3rd. VG. B36. $13.00

BUTTREE, Julia M. *Rhythm of the Redman.* 1930. NY. Barnes. VG. A19. $50.00

BUTTRICK, George. *Parables of Jesus.* 1928. Harper. 174p. G. B29. $9.00

BUTTS, D. Gregory Claiborne. *From Saddle to City by Buggy, Boat & Railway.* 1920s. np. photos. VG. B10. $25.00

BUXBAUM, Benjamin. *Benjamin Franklin, a Reference Guide 1907-1983.* 1988. 804p. F. A4. $65.00

BYARS, Betsy. *After the Goat Man.* 1974. Viking. 1st. 126p. yel pict brd. VG/G. T5. $25.00

BYARS, Betsy. *Summer of the Swans.* (1970). Viking. 3rd. 8vo. 1971 Newbery Honor. 142p. VG/G. T5. $25.00

BYATT, A.S. *Possession.* 1990. Random. 1st. NF/VG+. S13. $35.00

BYE, R. *Vanishing Depot.* 1973. Wynewoood, PA. 1st. 113p. VG/dj. B5. $40.00

BYINGTON, Eloise. *Wishbone Children.* 1934. Whitman. 1st. ils. VG+/dj. M5. $35.00

BYNUM, W.F. *Science & the Practice of Medicine in the 19th Century.* 1994. NY. 1st. 283p. wrp. A13. $20.00

BYRD, Max. *London Transformed: Images of the City in 18th Century.* 1978. New Haven. Yale. 1st. VG. H13. $45.00

BYRD, Richard E. *Discovery: Story of 2nd Byrd Antarctic Expedition.* 1935. NY. 1st. photos/index. 405p. G. S16. $25.00

BYRD, Richard E. *Discovery: Story of 2nd Byrd Antarctic Expedition.* 1935. NY. Putnam. 1/500. sgn. 8vo. 405p. half bl cloth/parchment brd. F/glassine/case. H5. $450.00

BYRD, Richard E. *Little America: Aerial Exploration in the Antarctic...* 1930. NY. 1st. photos/maps. VG. s16. $35.00

BYRD, Richard E. *Little America: Aerial Exploration in the Antarctic...* 1930. Putnam. 1/1000. Author's Autograph ed. 8vo. 436p. F/glassine/box. H5. $500.00

BYRD, Richard E. *Skyward.* 1981. Lakeside Classic. 1st thus. teg. brn cloth. F/sans. T11. $25.00

BYRNE, D. *Hangman's House.* 1926. NY/London. Century. 1st Am/lg paper sgn. 1/345. ils JR Flanagan. 466p. VG. F1. $40.00

BYRNE, John A. *Whiz Kids.* 1993. Doubleday. 1st. F/dj. H11. $20.00

BYRNE, Muriel St. Clare. *Lisle Letters.* 1981. Chicago. 6 vol. VG. M10. $150.00

BYRNE, Oliver. *Dictionary of Machines, Mechanics, Engine-Work... Vol II.* 1851. NY. Appleton. 4to. 960p. half leather. K5. $50.00

BYWATER, H. *Strange Intelligence: Memoirs of Naval Secret Service.* 1931. 1st Am. map. xl. G+. E6. $30.00

**CABANIS, P.J.G.** *Rapports du Physique et du Moral de l'Homme.* 1802. Paris. Crapart Caille et Ravier. 2 vol. 8vo. modern buckram. G1. $750.00

**CABELL, James Branch.** *Cream of the Jest: Comedy of Evasions.* 1927. NY. McBride. 1st ils. ils Pape/intro Harold Ward. James MacDonald bdg. H4. $125.00

**CABELL, James Branch.** *Jurgen.* 1923. NY. McBride. 1st ils. ils Ray F Coyle. gte. 3-quarter turquoise morocco. H4. $175.00

**CABELL, James Branch.** *Line of Love.* 1905. Harper. 1st. 8vo. 10 Howard Pyle pl. 291p. NF. B20. $85.00

**CABELL, James Branch.** *Line of Love.* 1905. Harper. 1st. ils Howard Pyle. VG. S13. $55.00

**CABELL, James Branch.** *Smirt: An Urban Nightmare.* 1934. McBride. 1st. F/NF. B4. $150.00

**CABELL, James Branch.** *Special Delivery: Packet of Reptiles.* 1933. NY. McBride. 1st. 272p. G. M10. $20.00

**CABELL, James Branch.** *Taboo: A Legend Retold From the Dirghic...* 1921. NY. McBride. 1st. 1/820. NF/dj. Q1. $125.00

**CABELL & HANNA.** *St Johns: Parade of Diversities.* 1943. NY. Rivers of Am. ils/map. 342p. NF. M4. $18.00

**CABLE, G.W.** *Old Creole Days.* 1879. Scribner. 1st/1st prt. inscr/dtd. gilt turquoise cloth. gilt morocco case. M24. $225.00

**CABLE, G.W.** *Old Creole Days.* 1897. NY. McBride. author's 1st book. ils Albert Herter. F-. H4. $200.00

**CABOT, Richard C.** *Case Histories in Medicine: Diagnosis, Prognosis...* 1912 (1911). ils. VG. E6. $18.00

**CACKLER, Christian.** *Recollections of an Old Settler...* 1992 (1874). Kent. rpt. ils. 52p. wrp. B18. $10.00

**CADBURY, Henry J.** *Jesus What Manner of Man.* 1947. Macmillan. 1st. 12mo. 123p. G/dj. V3. $22.00

**CADBURY, Henry J.** *Peril of Modernizing Jesus.* 1937. Macmillan. 1st. 12mo. 216p. G/dj. V3. $15.00

**CADISCH, J.** *Geologie der Schweizer Alpen.* 1953. Wepf Verlag. 1st. ils. VG. B27. $45.00

**CADNUM, Michael.** *Ghostwright.* 1992. Carroll Graf. 1st. AN/dj. M21. $25.00

**CADWALLADER, Priscilla.** *Memoir of Priscilla Cadwallader.* 1864. Phil. Ellwood Zell. 2nd. 16mo. 141p. loose cover/detached backstrip. V3. $16.00

**CADY, Jack.** *Man Who Could Make Things Vanish.* 1983. Arbor. 1st. NF/VG. M21. $25.00

**CADY, Jack.** *Well.* 1980. Arbor. 1st. NF/dj. S18. $36.00

**CAESALPINO, Dorolle M.** *Caesalpin Questions Peripateticinnes.* 1929. Paris. 240p. later cloth. G7. $35.00

**CAESAR, Gene.** *King of the Mountain Men: Life of Jim Bridger.* 1961. Dutton. 1st. photos. 317p. NF/VG. T11. $60.00

**CAESAR, Irving.** *Sing a Song of Safety.* 1937. NY. self pub. 1st. ils Rose O'Neill. sbdg. B20. $125.00

**CAFAGNA, Albert C.** *Child Nurturance.* 1982. NY. Plenum. 3 vol. 274p. VG. G1. $65.00

**CAGE, James C.** *Maxon Scout.* 1968. San Antonio. map. 25p. E1. $18.00

**CAHN, Matthew Alan.** *Environmental Deceptions.* 1995. NY. 179p. NF/wrp. S15. $6.00

**CAHN, Sammy.** *Songwriter's Rhyming Dictionary.* (1983). Facts on File. 1st. sgn pres. 162p. F/dj. H4. $100.00

**CAIANELLO, E.R.** *Physics of Cognitive Processes.* 1986. NY. World Scientific. 463p. prt gr laminated brd. G1. $75.00

**CAIDIN, Martin.** *Red Star in Space.* 1963. NY. Crowell Collier. 8vo. 280p. VG/dj. K5. $40.00

**CAIDIN, Martin.** *Rockets & Missiles: Past & Future.* 1954. McBride. lg 8vo. 208p. dj. K5. $40.00

**CAILLOU, Alan.** *Alien Virus.* 1957. Davies. 1st Eng. VG/dj. G8. $25.00

**CAIN, James M.** *Cain Times Three.* 1969. Knopf. 1st Collected. VG/dj. S18. $5.00

**CAIN, James M.** *Cloud Nine.* 1984. Mysterious. 1st. F/F. B3. $50.00

**CAIN, James M.** *Enchanted Isle.* 1985. Mysterious. 1st. F/F. B3. $40.00

**CAIN, James M.** *Mignon.* 1962. NY. Dial. presumed 1st. VG/dj. M21. $15.00

**CAIN, James M.** *Past All Dishonor/Postman Always Rings Twice.* 1946. Fiction BC. VG/G. L4. $15.00

**CAIN, James M.** *Rainbow's End.* 1975. NY. Mason Charter. 1st inscr. VG/NF. B4. $350.00

**CAIN, James M.** *Serenade.* 1937. KNopf. 1st. author's 2nd novel. VG/dj. A24. $175.00

**CAIN, Michael.** *Louise Nevelson.* 1989. NY. Chelsea. 1st. F/sans. H4. $13.00

**CAIN, Paul.** *Seven Slayers.* 1987. LA. Blood & Guts. 1st hc. 1/250. intro/sgn WF Nolan. F/dj. M15. $45.00

**CAINE, Lou S.** *North American Fresh-Water Sport Fish.* 1949. NY. 1st. 212p. VG. A17. $15.00

**CAINE, Michael.** *What's It All About?* 1992. Turtle Bay. 1st Am. sgn. F/dj. O11. $45.00

**CAINE, William.** *Glutton's Mirror.* 1926. Adelphi. 1st. 88p. blk cloth/orange spine letters. NF. B20. $75.00

**CAIRNS, Bob.** *Comeback Kids.* 1989. St Martin. 1st. F/VG. P8. $15.00

**CAIRNS, Bob.** *Pen Men.* 1992. St Martin. 1st. VG+/dj. P8. $12.50

**CALABRO, Marian.** *Operation Grizzly Bear.* 1989. NY. 118p. F/dj. S15. $8.50

**CALDECOTT, Randolph R.** *Randolph Caldecott's Picture Book, No 2.* nd. London/NY. Warne. early. xl. VG. H4. $25.00

**CALDER, Alexander.** *Animal Sketching.* 1926. Pelham, NY. Bridgeman. 1st. F/dj. B4. $400.00

**CALDER, Alexander.** *Derriere le Miroir.* 1973. France. Maeght. 1/150. sgn. folio. 28p+limitation. 5 lithos. loose in fld. H4. $1,800.00

**CALDER, Richard.** *Dead Girls.* 1992. London. Collins. 1st. AN/dj. M21. $30.00

**CALDER, Richard.** *Dead Girls.* 1995. St Martin. 1st. author's 1st book. F/dj. M23. $20.00

**CALDERONE, Mary S.** *Human Sexuality & the Quaker Conscience.* 1973. Phil. Friends General Conference. 12mo. 22p. VG/wrp. V3. $5.00

**CALDWELL, Bill.** *Islands of Maine: Where America Really Began.* 1981. Portland. 1st. sgn. F/dj. M4. $18.00

**CALDWELL, Erskine.** *Jenny by Nature.* 1961. FSC. 1st. VG/dj. B30. $40.00

**CALDWELL, Erskine.** *Journeyman.* 1935. Viking. 1st. 1/1475. inscr. lt buff paper. red cloth. case. B24. $285.00

**CALDWELL, Erskine.** *Miss Mamma Aimee.* 1967. NAL. 1st. F/NF. A24. $40.00

**CALDWELL, Erskine.** *Molly Cottontail.* 1958. Little Brn. 1st. ils Wm Sharp. VG/dj. M5. $45.00

**CALDWELL, Erskine.** *Place Called Estherville.* 1950. London. Falcon. marked To Be Sold Continent of Europe Only. NF/wrp/dj. H4. $30.00

**CALDWELL, Erskine.** *Stories of Life North & South.* 1983. Dodd Mead. 1st. F/dj. M19. $17.50

**CALDWELL, Erskine.** *Tragic Ground.* (1944). DSP. 1st. VG/dj. H4. $15.00

**CALDWELL, Erskine.** *We Are the Living.* 1933. Viking. 1st. inscr. author's 2nd book. F/NF. B4. $450.00

**CALDWELL, Frank.** *Wolf, the Storm Leader.* 1953. NY. Dodd Mead. new/enlarged. 8vo. bl cloth. P4. $42.00

**CALDWELL, George W.** *Ghost Stories of the California Missions.* 1939. Hollywood, CA. self pub. 1st. red cloth. VG/dj. O4. $15.00

**CALDWELL, Irene.** *Helps by the Way.* 1935. London. Faith Pr. 1st. 16mo. VG/dj. B11. $18.00

**CALDWELL, Robert Graham.** *Red Hannah: Delaware's Whipping Post.* 1947. U PA. 1st. 144p. F/NF. B20. $35.00

**CALDWELL, Taylor.** *Captains & Kings.* 1972. Doubleday. 1st. NF/G. L4. $25.00

**CALDWELL, Taylor.** *Captains & Kings.* 1972. Doubleday. 1st. sgn. VG/dj. B30. $40.00

**CALDWELL, Taylor.** *Romance of Atlantis.* 1975. NY. Morrow. 1st. 285p. VG/dj. A25. $12.00

**CALDWELL & STERN.** *I, Judas.* 1977. Atheneum. 1st. NF/dj. A14. $28.00

**CALHOUN, Frances Boyd.** *Miss Minerva & William Green Hill.* 1903. Reilly Lee. 54th. ils. VG/dj. M20. $35.00

**CALHOUN, George M.** *Growth of Criminal Law in Ancient Greece.* 1927. Berkeley. 1st. 8vo. 149p. gilt bl cloth. F. B20. $30.00

**CALHOUN, John C.** *Works of...* 1968. Russell. facs of 1851-56. 6 vol. xl. VG. B10. $125.00

**CALHOUN, Mary.** *Cross-Country Cat.* 1979. Morrow. 1st. ils Erick Ingraham. F/G. H4. $25.00

**CALHOUN, Mary.** *High-Wire Henry.* 1991. NY. Morrow. 1st. 40p. F/dj. D4. $20.00

**CALHOUN & DELAMERE.** *Working Bibliography of Greek Law.* 1927. Harvard. maroon cloth. M11. $85.00

**CALICOTT, J. Baird.** *In Defense of Land Ethic: Essays Environmental Philosophy.* 1989. NY State. 325p. NF. S15. $6.00

**CALIFANO, Joseph A. Jr.** *Student Revolution: Global Confrontation.* 1970. NY. Norton. 2nd. F/dj. A2. $12.00

**CALIFORNIA BENCH & BAR.** *Los Angeles Bench & Bar, Centennial Edition 1949-1950.* 1950. Wilson & Sons. photos. 300+p. cloth. M11. $75.00

**CALIFORNIA STATE FORESTRY.** *Handbook of Forest Protection.* 1918. Sacramento. 106p. VG. A10. $50.00

**CALISHER, Hortense.** *Herself.* 1972. Arbor. 8vo. 401p. H4. $20.00

**CALISHER, Hortense.** *In the Absense of Angels: Stories.* 1951. Little Brn. 1st. 8vo. 243p. NF/dj. B20. $40.00

**CALKINS, Ernest Elmo.** *They Broke the Prairie: Being Some Account of Settlement...* 1937. Scribner. 1st. 8vo. 451p. F/NF. B20. $35.00

**CALKINS, Frank.** *Rocky Mountain Warden.* 1970. NY. 1st. ils. 266p. F/dj. A17. $10.00

**CALKINS, John.** *History of the 347th Machine Gun Battalion...* ca 1920. Horwinski Co. 1st. 140p. VG. S16. $95.00

**CALKINS, Mary Whiton.** *First Book in Psychology.* 1910 (1909). Macmillan. new/enlarged ed/1st prt. 12mo. ils. 419p. NF. C14. $25.00

**CALKINS, R.H.** *High Tide: Drama & Tragedy of Seattle's Waterfront.* 1952. Seattle. Marine Digest Pub. 1st. 356p. NF/dj. B20. $35.00

**CALLAHAN, Harry M.** *Ansel Adams in Color.* (1993). Little Brn. 1st. edit Schaefer/Stillman. AN/dj. H4. $30.00

**CALLAHAN, Harry M.** *Color 1941-1980.* 1980. Providence. Matrix Pub. 1st. folio. sgn. F/case. w/photo. S9. $200.00

**CALLEN, Larry.** *Dashiel & the Night.* 1981. NY. Dutton. 1st. 32p. F/dj. D4. $20.00

**CALLERY & MOSIMANN.** *Tradition of Bookbinding in 20th Century...* 1979. Pittsburgh. VG. H4. $10.00

**CALLIET.** *Manuel Bibliographique des Sciences...* nd. 3 vol. 1/100. rpt. 11,648 entries. A4. $175.00

**CALLISON, Brian.** *Act of War.* 1977. Dutton. 1st Am. quarter yel cloth/paper-covered brd. F/dj. T11. $45.00

**CALLISON, Brian.** *Flock of Ships.* 1970. Putnam. 1st Am. author's 1st book. NF/dj. T11. $60.00

**CALLOW, Philip.** *From Noon to Starry Night: Life of Walt Whitman.* 1992. Chicago. Dee. 1st. 394p. NF/dj. M10. $22.50

**CALLOW, Philip.** *Lost Earth: Life of Cezanne.* 1995. Chicago. Ivan R Dee. F/dj. B9. $17.50

**CALLOW, Phillip.** *Vincent Van Gogh: A Life.* 1990. London. 1st. dj. T9. $22.00

**CALLOW, Simon.** *Charles Laughton: Difficult Actor.* 1987. NY. photos. VG/dj. M17. $15.00

**CALLOWAY, Cab.** *New Cab Calloway's Hepsters Dictionary.* 1944. self pub. 16p. F/self wrp. B2. $600.00

**CALVERLEY, Eleanor T.** *My Arabian Days & Nights: Medical Missionary in Old Kuwait.* 1958. Crowell. 1st. sm 8vo. 182p. VG/torn. W1. $20.00

**CALVERT, H.R.** *Astronomy: Globes, Orreries & Other Models.* 1967. London. HMSO for The Science Mus. 48p. VG. K5. $20.00

**CALVERT, Patricia.** *Hadder Maccoll.* 1985. Scribner. 1st. NF/dj. B36. $8.00

**CALVIN, Ross.** *Difficult Loves.* (1984. HBJ. 1st Am. trans Weaver/Colquhoun/Wright. F/NF. H4. $20.00

**CALVIN, Ross.** *Sky Determines.* (1948). Albuquerque. 8vo. 333p. F/G. H4. $30.00

**CALVIN, William H.** *River That Flows Uphill.* 1986. Macmillan. 1st. bl brd. dj. F7. $40.00

**CALVIN & GAZENKO.** *Foundations of Space Biology & Medicine.* 1975. NASA/Nauka. 3 vol in 4. VG/dj. K5. $120.00

**CALVINO, Italo.** *Baron in the Trees.* 1959. Random. 1st Am. F/NF. O11. $200.00

**CALVINO, Italo.** *Castle of Crossed Destinies.* 1977. NY. stated 1st. trans Wm Weaver. VG/VG. M17. $45.00

**CALVINO, Italo.** *Difficult Loves.* (1984). HBJ. 1st Am. F/NF. H4. $20.00

**CALVOCORESSI & WINT.** *Total War: Story of World War II.* 1980. Pantheon. 1st. VG/F. V4. $10.00

**CAMBRIDGE, Ada.** *Humble Enterprise.* 1896. Appleton. VG. M20. $15.00

**CAMBRIDGE, Richard.** *Works...* 1803. London. Cadell Davies. 1st. tall/wide 4to. 16 pl. early morocco. H13. $450.00

**CAMERON, Carey.** *Daddy Boy.* 1989. Algonquin. 1st. F/F. H11. $30.00

**CAMERON, Eleanor.** *Mysterious Christmas Shell.* 1961. Little Brn. 1st. NF/dj. M21. $20.00

**CAMERON, Ian.** *Impossible Dream: Building of Panama Canal.* 1971. Morrow. ils/maps/line drawings/ep maps. VG/dj. B11. $20.00

**CAMERON, Ian.** *To the Ends of the Earth...* 1980. Dutton. 1st. 4to. 288p. F/dj. B20. $25.00

**CAMERON, James R.** *Motion Picture With Sound.* 1929. Cameron. sgn. cloth. VG. C5. $180.00

**CAMERON, James.** *Witness.* 1966. London. Gollancz. 1st. VG/dj. R11. $30.00

**CAMERON, Malcolm E.** *Pterygium Throughout the World.* 1965. Springfield. Chas Thomas. 1st. 188p. NF. C14. $25.00

**CAMERON, N.** *Face of China As Seen by Photographers & Travelers 1860...* 1978. Phil. obl 4to. photos. 159p. F/dj. M4. $45.00

**CAMERON, Peter.** *One Way or Another.* 1986. Harper Row. 1st. F/F. D10. $45.00

**CAMERON, Roderick.** *Shells.* 1972. London. ils. 100p. NF/dj. S15. $9.00

**CAMMIDGE.** *Plain Cookery Receipts for Use in York (England)...* 1893. 34p. G. E6. $30.00

**CAMMON, Betsey Johnson.** *Island Memoir: Personal History of Anderson & McNeil...* 1969. Puyallup, WA. Valley. 2nd. sm 4to. 225p. F/NF. B20. $35.00

**CAMP, Joe.** *Underdog.* 1993. Atlanta. Longstreet. 230p. VG/dj. C5. $12.50

**CAMP, John;** see Sandford, John.

**CAMP & WAGNER.** *Plains & the Rockies: Bibliography of Original Narratives...* 1953. Columbus. 3rd/revised. cloth/recased. VG+. M8. $150.00

**CAMPA, Arthur L.** *Treasure of the Sangre de Cristos.* 1963. OK U. 1st. red cloth. F/dj. T10. $35.00

**CAMPBELL, A.B.** *When I Was in Patagonia.* (1953). London. Christopher Johnson. 1st. 202p. G. F3. $15.00

**CAMPBELL, Agnes H.** *Peacock Fables.* 1964-67. Berkeley. Peacock. mini. 3 vol. 1/600. bl prt. prt wrp. B24. $95.00

**CAMPBELL, Albert.** *Pacific Wagon Roads: Letter From Secretary of Interior...* 1859. WA. 125p. extracted. J2. $625.00

**CAMPBELL, Alexander.** *Milennial Harbinger.* 1856. Bethany, VA. 4th Series. 722p. 3-quarter leather. G. B5. $40.00

**CAMPBELL, Bebe Moore.** *Brothers & Sisters.* 1994. NY. Putnam. 1st. sgn. F/dj. O11. $35.00

**CAMPBELL, Bebe Moore.** *Singing in the Comeback Choir.* 1998. Putnam. 1st. sgn. F/F. O11. $30.00

**CAMPBELL, Bebe Moore.** *Successful Women, Angry Men.* 1986. Random. 1st. sgn. author's 1st book. F/dj. O11. $100.00

**CAMPBELL, Bebe Moore.** *Sweet Summer.* 1989. NY. Putnam. 1st. sgn. F/dj. O11. $45.00

**CAMPBELL, Bryn.** *Exploring Photography.* 1978. NY. Hudson Hills. 1st Am. VG. S5. $15.00

**CAMPBELL, C.** *Delusion & Belief.* 1926. 1st. 79p. VG. E6. $18.00

**CAMPBELL, David G.** *Crystal Desert: Summers in Antarctica.* 1992. Houghton Mifflin. 308p. F/wrp. S15. $9.00

**CAMPBELL, Elizabeth.** *Encyclopedia of World Cookery.* 1968. London. Hamlyn. G/dj. A16. $15.00

**CAMPBELL, G.G.** *History of Nova Scotia.* 1948. Toronto. Ryerson. 1st. 288p. VG/dj. B18. $17.50

**CAMPBELL, G.R.** *Jaws Too! Natural History of Crocodilians...* 1985. Ft Myers. Sutherland. 4to. photos/ils. 267p. F/VG+. M12. $30.00

**CAMPBELL, Harlan.** *Monkey on a Chain.* 1993. Doubleday. 1st. author's 1st novel. F/dj. R11. $30.00

**CAMPBELL, James.** *Bombing of Nuremberg.* 1974. Garden City. 1st. 193p. VG/dj. B18. $22.50

**CAMPBELL, James.** *Exiled in Paris.* 1995. NY. Olympia. 1st. dj. T9. $18.00

**CAMPBELL, James.** *Talking at the Gates: Life of James Baldwin.* 1991. Viking. 1st. ils. 306p. F/dj. S14. $10.00

**CAMPBELL, John Lord.** *Lives of the Chief Justices of England...* 1857-58. John Murray. 3 vol. polished calf. M11. $850.00

**CAMPBELL, John Lord.** *Lives of the Lord Chancellors & Keepers of Great Seal...* 1846. London. 7 vol. 2nd. full leather/marbled edges & ep. F. B30. $425.00

**CAMPBELL, John Lord.** *Lives of the Lord Chancellors & Keepers of Great Seal...* 1847-1869. London. John Murray. 8 vol. teg. 3-quarter tan morocco. M11. $1,250.00

**CAMPBELL, Joseph.** *Masks of God: Occidental Mythology...* 1976. Penguin. 4 vol. VG/wrp. B29. $25.00

**CAMPBELL, Julie.** *Ginny Gordon & the Disappearing Candlesticks.* 1948. Whitman. VG/dj. M20. $15.00

**CAMPBELL, Lang.** *Rig-Ma-Role Picture Land.* 1925. Newark. Chas Graham. lg 4to. pict brd. pict mc dj. R5. $150.00

**CAMPBELL, Mary Mason.** *Betty Crocker's Kitchen Gardens.* 1971. NY. Universal. 1st. ils Tasha Tudor. VG/clip. M20. $65.00

**CAMPBELL, Ramsey.** *Ancient Images.* 1989. Scribner. 1st Am. F/dj. S18. $25.00

**CAMPBELL, Ramsey.** *Dark Companions.* 1982. Macmillan. 1st. VG/dj. L1. $80.00

**CAMPBELL, Ramsey.** *Doll Who Ate His Mother.* 1976. Bobbs Merrill. 1st. author's 1st novel. F/dj. M21. $100.00

**CAMPBELL, Ramsey.** *Face That Must Die.* 1983. Scream. 1st. 1/100. sgn. VG/case. L1. $400.00

**CAMPBELL, Ramsey.** *Face That Must Die.* 1984. Scream. 2nd. intro Robert Bloch/ils JK Potter. F/NF. S18. $37.00

**CAMPBELL, Ramsey.** *Incarnate.* 1983. Macmillan. 1st. F/NF. N4. $40.00

**CAMPBELL, Ramsey.** *Night of the Claw.* 1983. St Martin. 1st. NF/dj. S18. $34.00

**CAMPBELL, Ramsey.** *Parasite.* 1980. Macmillan. 1st. VG/G. L1. $50.00

**CAMPBELL, Reau.** *Mexico: Tours Through the Egypt of the New World.* 1890. NY. Crawford. 88p. wrp. F3. $25.00

**CAMPBELL, Robert.** *Boneyards.* 1992. Pocket. 1st. F/F. H11. $20.00

**CAMPBELL, Robert.** *In a Pig's Eye.* 1991. Pocket. 1st. F/dj. N4. $20.00

**CAMPBELL, Thomas.** *Pleasures of Hope, With Other Poems...* 1826. London. Longman. New ed. 144p. red morocco. NF. B20. $90.00

**CAMPBELL, William T.** *Big Beverage.* 1952. Tupper & Love. 1st. 8vo. 429p. decor tan cloth. VG/dj. B20. $35.00

**CAMPBELL & HUNT.** *KC Irving: Art of the Industrialist.* 1973. Toronto. McClelland Stewart. 1st. F/G clip. A26. $15.00

**CAMPION, Frank.** *AMA & US Health Policy Since 1940.* 1984. Chicago. 1st. 603p. A13. $40.00

**CAMUS, Albert.** *Caligula & 3 Other Plays.* 1958. Knopf. 1st. VG/dj. B30. $32.50

**CAMUS, Albert.** *Fall.* 1957. NY. Knopf. 1st Am. gilt quarter cloth. F/dj. M24. $40.00

**CAMUS, Albert.** *Fall.* 1966. Kentfield, CA. Allen. 1/140. ils Lewis Allen. brd. B24. $500.00

**CAMUS, Albert.** *Possesed.* 1960. Knopf. 1st. VG/dj. B30. $32.50

**CAMUS, Albert.** *Speech of Acceptance Upon Award of the Nobel Prize.* 1958. NY. Knopf. 1st Am. F/prt wrp. w/Knopf copy. M24. $85.00

**CANADAY, John.** *Lives of the Painters.* 1969. Norton. 4 vol. 1st. VG/case. M20. $45.00

**CANBY, Courtlandt.** *History of Rockets & Space.* 1963. Hawthorn. 4to. ils. 112p. VG/dj. K5. $15.00

**CANBY, Henry Seidel.** *Brandywine.* (1941). Farrar Rhinehart. rpt. 8vo. 285p. F/dj. O10. $30.00

**CANBY, Henry Seidel.** *Thoreau.* 1939. Houghton Mifflin. 1st. 8vo. ils NC Wyeth. gilt red buckram. F/dj. R3. $85.00

**CANCIAN, Frank.** *Another Place.* 1974. Scrimshaw. 1st. 95p. wrp. F3. $15.00

**CANCIAN, Frank.** *Change & Uncertainty in a Peasant Economy.* 1972. Stanford. 1st. 208p. dj. F3. $20.00

**CANDLER, Edmund.** *Long Road to Baghdad.* 1919. London. Cassell. 2 vol. ils/pl/maps. 311p. decor cloth. VG. Q2. $80.00

**CANEMAKER, John.** *Felix: Twisted Tale of the World's Most Famous Cat.* 1991. Pantheon. 1st. F/NF. P3. $30.00

**CANETTI, F.** *Crowds & Power.* 1962. NY. 1st. VG/dj. B5. $25.00

**CANIFF, William.** *Manual of Practice Surgery, Based on Pathology...* 1866. Phil. Lindsay Blakiston. 402p. cloth/rb spine. G7. $495.00

**CANIN, Ethan.** *Blue River.* 1991. Houghton Mifflin. 1st. F/dj. M19. $17.50

**CANNADINE, David.** *Pleasures of the Past: Reflections on Queens, Kings...* 1989. NY. 1st. ils. VG/dj. M17. $17.50

**CANNELL, Dorothy.** *How to Murder Your Mother-in-Law.* 1994. Bantam. 1st. F/F. H11. $20.00

**CANNING, Victor.** *Crimson Chalace.* 1978. NY. Morrow. 1st Am. 479p. wht brd/gilt red cloth spine. F/dj. F1. $20.00

**CANNON, Walter Bradford.** *Bodily Changes in Pain, Hunger, Fear & Rage...* 1989. Birmingham. Classics of Psychiatry & Behavioral Sciences Lib. G1. $65.00

**CANNON, Walter Bradford.** *Bodily Changes in Pain, Hunger & Rage.* 1915. Appleton. sm 8vo. 311p. ruled russet cloth. VG. G1. $100.00

**CANOT, Theodore.** *Adventures of an African Slaver.* 1928. Garden City. VG. M20. $25.00

**CANSDALE, George.** *All the Animals of the Bible Lands.* 1970. Zondervan. 1st. 8vo. ils. 272p. VG/dj. W1. $22.00

**CANTOR, Eddy.** *Caught Shott: Saga of Wailing Wall Street.* 1929. Toronto. Musson. NF/G. T12. $30.00

**CANTOR, Gilbert M.** *Barnes Foundation Reality Vs Myth.* 1963. Phil. Chilton. G/dj. A19. $30.00

**CANTOR, Louis.** *Wheelin' on Beale.* 1992. Pharos. 1st. sgn. F/dj. B30. $25.00

**CANTOR & SWANN.** *Cranks Recipe Book.* 1982. London. Dent. VG. V4. $15.00

**CANTOS, Jack.** *Werewolf Family.* 1980. Houghton Mifflin. 1st. VG/dj. L1. $40.00

**CANTY, Kevin.** *Stranger in This World.* 1994. Doubleday. 1st. author's 1st book. F/dj. M23. $40.00

**CAPA & CORNELL.** *Farewell to Eden.* 1964. Harper Row. 1st. photos. VG/dj. M20. $22.00

**CAPEK, Karl.** *Nine Fairy Tales. And One More Thrown in for Good Measure.* 1990. Northwestern U. VG/dj. M17. $20.00

**CAPERTON, Helena Lefroy.** *Social Register of Virginia.* 1951. Garrett Massie. 246p. VG. B10. $8.00

**CAPLAN, Lincoln.** *Tenth Justice, Solicitor General & Rule of Law.* 1987. Knopf. M11. $35.00

**CAPOTE, Truman.** *Breakfast at Tiffany's: A Short Novel & 3 Short Stories.* 1958. Random. 1st. inscr. G/fair. B30. $85.00

**CAPOTE, Truman.** *Christmas Memory.* (1966). Random. later prt. VG/dj. C9. $48.00

**CAPOTE, Truman.** *Christmas Memory.* 1966. Random. 1st. 1/600. sgn. gr cloth. red case. B24. $300.00

**CAPOTE, Truman.** *Grass Harp.* 1951. Random. 1st. NF/VG clip. B20. $85.00

**CAPOTE, Truman.** *In Cold Blood.* nd. BC. RS. F/dj. S18. $12.00

**CAPOTE, Truman.** *In Cold Blood.* 1965. NY. Random. 1st. F/dj. Q1. $150.00

**CAPOTE, Truman.** *Music for Chameleons.* 1980. Random. 1st. F/NF. H11. $35.00

**CAPOTE, Truman.** *Thanksgiving Visitor.* 1968. Random. 1st. AN/VG case. B30. $50.00

**CAPPS & MOFFIT.** *Geology & Mineral Resources of the Nizina District...* 1911. GPO. 8vo. 111p. xl. wrp. B14. $25.00

**CAPRA, Frank.** *Name Above the Title.* 1971. Macmillan. 1st. VG/dj. C9. $30.00

**CAPRARA, Giovanni.** *Complete Encyclopedia of Space Satellites...* 1986. Portland House. 450+ photos/diagrams. 219p. VG/dj. K5. $30.00

**CAPSTICK, Peter H.** *Death in the Long Grass.* 1977. St Martin. 1st. VG/dj. B5. $30.00

**CAPSTICK, Peter H.** *Death in the Silent Places.* 1981. NY. 3rd. 258p. dj. A17. $15.00

**CAPSTICK, Peter H.** *Last Ivory Hunter.* 1988. St Martin. AN/dj. A19. $30.00

**CAPUTO, Philip.** *DelCorso's Gallery.* 1983. HRW. 1st. author's 3rd book. F/F. A24. $32.50

**CAPUTO, Philip.** *DelCorso's Gallery.* 1983. HRW. ARC/1st. VG/wrp. B30. $25.00

**CAPUTO, Philip.** *DelCorso's Gallery.* 1983. NY. Holt. 1st. F/NF. H11. $30.00

**CAPUTO, Philip.** *Horn of Africa.* 1980. HRW. 1st. author's 1st novel. F/NF. H11. $35.00

**CAPUTO, Philip.** *Horn of Africa.* 1980. HRW. 1st. NF/dj. A14. $28.00

**CAPUTO, Philip.** *Means of Escape: Memoirs of Disasters of War.* 1991. Harper Collins. ARC/1st. sgn. NF/wrp. Q1. $50.00

**CARAS, Roger A.** *Dangerous to Man: Wild Animals, a Definitive Study...* 1964. Phil. 1st. 433p. F/dj. A17. $17.50

**CARAS, Roger A.** *Monarch of Deadman's Bay: Life & Death of a Kodiak Bear.* 1969. Boston. 1st. ils. 185p. VG/dj. A17. $10.00

**CARAS & FOSTER.** *Venomous Animals & Poisonous Plants.* 1994. Houghton MIfflin. Peterson Field Guide series. ils. AN. S15. $12.00

**CARAWAN & CARAWAN.** *We Shall Overcome!: Songs of Southern Freedom Movement.* 1963. NY. Oak Pub. 1st. VG/trade pb dj. V4. $30.00

**CARD, Orson Scott.** *Abyss.* 1989. Legend/Century. 1st hc. sgn. NF/dj. A14. $42.00

**CARD, Orson Scott.** *Abyss.* 1989. London. Legend/Century. 1st. F/dj. M21. $35.00

**CARD, Orson Scott.** *Ender's Game.* 1985. NY. Tor. 1st. VG/NF. A24. $300.00

**CARD, Orson Scott.** *Lost Boys.* 1992. Harper Collins. 1st. F/dj. N4. $30.00

**CARD, Orson Scott.** *Red Prophet.* 1988. NY. Tor. 1st. sgn. F/dj. M23. $50.00

**CARD, Orson Scott.** *Seventh Son.* 1987. NY. Tor. 1st. sgn. F/dj. M23. $55.00

**CARD, Orson Scott.** *Seventh Son.* 1987. Tor. 1st. F/dj. M21. $40.00

**CARD, Orson Scott.** *Ships of Earth.* 1994. NY. Tom Doherty. VG/dj. B9. $15.00

**CARD, Orson Scott.** *Songmaster.* 1980. NY. Dial. 1st. VG/dj. M21. $75.00

**CARD, Orson Scott.** *Speaker for the Dead.* 1986. Tor. 1st. sgn. VG+/clip. A14. $122.50

**CARD, Orson Scott.** *Speaker for the Dead.* 1986. Tor. 1st. VG+/clip. A14. $70.00

**CARD, Orson Scott.** *Xenocide.* 1991. NY. Tor. 1st. sgn. NF/clip. A14. $25.00

**CARD & HENDERSON.** *Farm Poultry Production.* 1940. Danville. Interstate. 245p. VG. A10. $10.00

**CARDOZO, Benjamin N.** *Law & Literature & Other Essays & Addresses.* 1931. Harcourt Brace. bl cloth. M11. $50.00

**CARDOZO, Benjamin N.** *Nature of the Judicial Process.* 1937. Yale. 8th. cloth. M11. $45.00

**CAREY, Arthur A.** *Memoirs of a Murder Man.* 1930. Doubleday Doran. 1st. VG. P3. $20.00

**CAREY, Bernice.** *Three Widows.* 1952. Doubleday Crime Club. 1st. F/NF. B4. $100.00

**CAREY, Charles.** *Van Suyden Sapphires.* 1905. Dodd Mead. 1st. VG. M15. $45.00

**CAREY, M.V.** *Mystery of the Singing Serpent.* 1972. Random. Alfred Hitchcock & 3 Investigators #17. VG. M20. $18.00

**CAREY, Peter.** *Bliss.* 1982. Harper Row. 1st Am. sgn. F/clip. O11. $45.00

**CAREY, Peter.** *Oscar & Lucinda.* 1988. Harper Row. 1st Am. NF/dj. R14. $30.00

**CAREY, Peter.** *Tax Inspector.* 1992. Knopf. 1st Am trade. sgn. F/dj. O11. $30.00

**CAREY, Peter.** *Unusual Life of Tristan Smith.* 1995. Knopf. 1st Am. sgn. F/dj. B30. $35.00

**CAREY, Robert D.** *Vanished Frontier.* 1929. np. sc. G. A19. $25.00

**CAREY, Rosa Nouchette.** *Our Bessie.* nd. NY. Federal Book. 331p. G. G11. $7.00

**CARHART, Alfreda Post.** *Masoud the Bedouin.* 1915. NY. Missionary Edu Movement of US/Canada. 1st. 249p. F. M7. $30.00

**CARHART, Edith Beebe.** *History of Bellingham, WA.* 1926. Bellingham. Argonaut. 1/500. sm 8vo. 100p. gr cloth. H1. $75.00

**CARKEET, David.** *Error of Our Ways.* 1997. NY. Holt. 1st. F/dj. A14. $21.00

**CARLBERG, G.** *Thirty Years in China 1905-1935.* 1937. np. ils/maps. 230p. NF. M4. $15.00

**CARLETON, George W.** *Our Artist in Cuba: Fifty Drawings on Wood.* 1865. NY. Carleton. 12mo. gilt maroon cloth. F1. $175.00

**CARLETON, James Henry.** *Mountain Meadows Massacre.* 1995. Arthur H Clark. 8vo. 39p. red wrp. F7. $15.00

**CARLISLE, Bill.** *Bill Carlisle, Lone Bandit.* 1946. Pasadena, CA. 1st. 220p. map ep. G. B18. $35.00

**CARLISLE, Henry.** *Voyage to the First of December.* 1972. Putnam. BC. rpt. gray cloth. F/NF. T11. $15.00

**CARLSON, Dick.** *Women in San Diego: History in Photographs.* 1978. San Diego. 1st thus. 34p. brn buckram. F. B20. $25.00

**CARLSON, Esther.** *Moon Over the Back Fence.* 1947. Doubleday. 1st. VG/dj. P2. $25.00

**CARLSON, George.** *Fun for Juniors.* 1941. Platt Munk. ils. VG/dj. M20. $15.00

**CARLSON, John Roy.** *Cairo to Damascus.* 1951. Knopf. 1st. ils. VG/tattered dj. W1. $18.00

**CARLSON, Lorentz.** *Here Come the Littles.* 1984. Scholastic. VG. M20. $15.00

**CARLSON, Natalie Savage.** *Jean-Claude's Island.* (1963). Harper Row. early ed. 8vo. 148p. VG/G. T5. $30.00

**CARLSON, Natalie Savage.** *Talking Cat & Other Stories of French Canada.* 1952. Harper. 1st. G/dj. V4. $15.00

**CARLSON, Raymond.** *Gallery of Western Paintings.* 1951. McGraw Hill. 1st. 85p. red cloth. F/G. B20. $50.00

**CARLYLE, John.** *Dante's Divine Comedy: Inferno, a Literal Prose Trans.* 1876. NY. Harper. 375p. F. B14. $35.00

**CARLYLE, Thomas.** *Collectanea Thomas Carlyle 1821-1855.* 1903. Canton, PA. Kirgate. 1st. 8vo. 142p. gr cloth/paper spine label. C6. $65.00

**CARLYLE, Thomas.** *Sartor Resartus: Life & Opeinions of Her Teufelsdrickh...* 1931. London. LEC. 1st thus. 1/1500. NF/VG case. C6. $150.00

**CARMAN, W.Y.** *History of Firearms From Earliest Times to 1914.* 1955. St Martin. 1st Am. 8vo. 207p. NF/VG+. B20. $45.00

**CARMER, Carl.** *Dark Trees to the Wind: Cycle of York State Years.* 1949. NY. Wm Sloane. 1st. sgn pres. 8vo. 370p. F/NF. B20. $50.00

**CARMICHAEL, Bill.** *Incredible Collectors, Weird Antiques & Odd Hobbies.* 1971. Prentice Hall. 1st. 4to. 282p. NF/VG. B20. $25.00

**CARMICHAEL, Harry;** see Creasey, John.

**CARMICHAEL, Hoagy.** *Stardust Road.* 1946. NY. Rinehart. 1st. VG/G. B5. $40.00

**CARMICHAEL, John P.** *My Greatest Day in Baseball.* 1963. Grosset Dunlap. ils. VG/dj. B36. $6.00

**CARMICHAEL, Orton H.** *Shadow on the Dial.* 1915. NY. Abingdon. VG. B9. $15.00

**CARMICHAEL, Stokely.** *Stokely Speaks: Black Power to Pan-Africanism.* 1971. NY. Random. 1st. F/dj. B2. $65.00

**CARNEGIE, Andrew.** *Edwin M Stanton: An Address by..., on Stanton Memorial...* 1906. Doubleday Page. 1st. prt wrp. M8. $45.00

**CARNEGIE, Andrew.** *Empire of Business.* 1902. Doubleday Page. 1st. VG. B4. $75.00

**CARNEGIE, Andrew.** *Our Coaching Trip: Brighton to Inverness.* 1882. NY. private prt. Prt for Private Circulation. 1st. pres. VG. O3. $265.00

**CARNER-RIBALTA, J.** *Els Catalans en la Descoberta I Colonitzacio...* 1947. Mexico City. Biblioteca Catalana. 133p. prt wrp. D11. $30.00

**CARNOY, Alan.** *Democracia Si! A Way to Win the Cold War.* 1962. Vantage. 1st. photos. F/dj. R11. $15.00

**CARO, Dennis.** *Devine War.* 1986. Arbor. 1st. F/dj. M25. $15.00

**CARO, Robert A.** *Power Broker.* 1974. Knopf. BC. 1246p. VG/dj. P12. $10.00

**CARO, Robert A.** *Years of Lyndon Johnson, Vol 1: Path to Power.* 1982. Knopf. 1st. photos. 882p. VG. S14. $10.00

**CARPENTER, Alfred B.F.** *Blocking of Zeebrugge.* 1922. London. 1st. 298p. VG. B18. $35.00

**CARPENTER, Don.** *From a Distant Place.* 1988. Northpoint. 1st. F/dj. M23. $20.00

**CARPENTER, E.** *An Unknown People.* 1897. London. 31p. VG. E6. $50.00

**CARPENTER, Edmund.** *Oh, What a Blow That Phantom Gave Me!* 1973. HRW. 1st. 8vo. 192p. F/NF. B20. $25.00

**CARPENTER, Edwin H.** *Early Cemeteries of the City of Los Angeles.* 1973. Dawson's Book Shop. 1/300. ils. 49p. pict brd/cloth spine. D11. $50.00

**CARPENTER, Edwin H.** *Printers & Publishers in Southern California.* 1964. La Siesta. 1st. inscr. ils/index. 48p. F. B19. $45.00

**CARPENTER, Frances.** *Our Little Friends of the Netherlands: Dirk & Dientje.* nd (1935). np. Am Book Co. ils Curtiss Sprague. 201p. brd. C14. $12.00

**CARPENTER, Frances.** *South American Wonder Tales.* 1969. Chicago. Follett. 1st. 191p. dj. F3. $15.00

**CARPENTER, Frank.** *Mexico.* (1924). Doubleday. ils/map/index. 285p. F3. $15.00

**CARPENTER, Harry A.** *Adventures in Science With Jane & Paul.* 1953. Boston. Allyn Bacon. new ed. ils/photos. VG+. A25. $18.00

**CARPENTER, Humphrey.** *Geniuses Together: American Writers in Paris in the 1920s.* 1988. Boston. 1st. dj. T9. $18,000.00

**CARPENTER, Kenneth E.** *Books & Society in History: Papers of Assn of College...* 1983. NY. Bowker. 1st. 8vo. 254p. F/dj. O10. $45.00

**CARPENTER, Rhys.** *Sculpture of the Nike Temple Parapet.* 1929. Harvard. ils/figures. 83p. cloth. VG/dj. Q2. $40.00

**CARPENTER, William Benjamin.** *Nature & Man: Essays Scientific & Philosophical.* 1889. NY. Appleton. 1st Am. 12mo. 483p. panelled pebbled mauve cloth. NF. G1. $100.00

**CARPENTER, William Benjamin.** *On the Use & Abuse of Alcoholic Liquors, in Health...* 1851. Boston. Temperance Soc/Crosby Nichols. 1st thus. 264p. NF. G1. $100.00

**CARPOZI, George Jr.** *Gary Cooper Story.* 1970. Arlington. 1st. photos. VG/dj. C9. $25.00

**CARR, Archie.** *Handbook of Turtles.* 1952. Cornell. 1st. G+. R8. $55.00

**CARR, Caleb.** *Alienist.* 1994. Random. 1st. F/dj. B4. $85.00

**CARR, Edward Hallett.** *What Is History? A Distinguished Historian Seeks...* 1993. Knopf. 3rd. 209p. VG/dj. P12. $12.00

**CARR, John Dickson.** *Dark of the Moon.* 1967. Harper Row. 1st. VG/dj. G8. $45.00

**CARR, John Dickson.** *Ghosts' High Noon.* 1969. Harper Row. 1st. VG/dj. G8. $55.00

**CARR, John Dickson.** *Life of Sir Arthur Conan Doyle.* Barnes Noble. rpt. Nf/dj. G8. $20.00

**CARR, John Dickson.** *Skeleton in the Clock.* 1948. NY. Morrow. 1st. F/dj. M15. $125.00

**CARR, John Dickson.** *Witch of the Low Tide.* 1961. Harper. 1st. VG/dj. T8. $45.00

**CARR, Philippa;** see Hibbert, Eleanor Alice.

**CARR, Terry.** *Ides of Tomorror: Original Science Fiction Tales of Horror.* 1976. Little Brn. 1st. VG/dj. M20. $15.00

**CARR, Terry.** *Universe 3.* 1973. Random. 1st. F/dj. A23. $36.00

**CARR & CHACE.** *America Invulnerable: Quest for Absolute Security...* 1988. Summit Books. 1st. F/dj. O11. $40.00

**CARR & CHACE.** *Angel of Darkness.* 1977. Random. 1st trade. sgn. F/dj. O11. $35.00

**CARRARA, Umbertino.** *Columbus Carmen Epicum.* 1730. Augsburg. Mathiae Wolff. 8vo. 330p. maroon paneled calf. K1. $300.00

**CARRASCO, David.** *To Change Place: Aztec Ceremonial Landscapes.* (1991). Niwot. 1st. ils. 254p. dj. F3. $30.00

**CARRASCO & MOCTEZUMA.** *Moctezuma's Mexico: Visions of the Aztec World.* (1992). Niwot. 1st. 4to. 188p. dj. F3. $45.00

**CARRERE, Emmanuel.** *Mustache.* 1988. Scribner. 1st. F/dj. A23. $30.00

**CARRICK, Alice Van Leer.** *Collector's Luck in England.* 1926. Little Brn. VG. M20. $45.00

**CARRIER, Robert.** *Connoisseur's Cookbook.* 1965. NY. ils. VG/G. M17. $17.50

**CARRIER, Robert.** *Cooking for You.* (1973). Viking. 1st. Vg/dj. A16. $17.50

**CARRIGHER, Sally.** *Twilight Seas. A Blue Whale's Journey.* 1975. NY. 2nd. ils Peter Parnall. F/VG. S15. $12.00

**CARRINGTON, Edith.** *Nobody's Business.* ca 1890. NY. Dutton. ils Etheline Dell. 192p. lt pk cloth. NF. B20. $40.00

**CARRINGTON, Margaret I.** *Absaraka.* 1950. Lakeside Classic. 1st thus. edit Quaife. fld map. teg. red cloth. VG. T11. $38.00

**CARRINGTON, Noel.** *Popular Art in Britain.* 1945. King penguin. lacks ffe. VG. P3. $10.00

**CARRINGTON, Richard.** *Great National Parks of the World.* 1967. Random. photos. VG/dj. A19. $35.00

**CARRINGTON, Wirt Johnson.** *History of Halifax County, V.A.* 1969 (1924). Regional Pub. 535p. VG. B10. $35.00

**CARRITHERS, T.W.** *How to Put on a Horse Show.* 1971. S Brunswick. Barnes. 1st. VG/G. O3. $10.00

**CARROLL, David.** *Matinee Idols.* 1972. NY. Arbor. 159p. VG/dj. C5. $12.50

**CARROLL, James.** *Fault Lines.* 1980. Little Brn. 1st. sgn. rem mk. NF/dj. R11. $45.00

**CARROLL, James.** *Madonna Red.* 1976. Little Brn. 1st. author's 1st book. F/VG. M19. $25.00

**CARROLL, James.** *Mortal Friends.* 1978. Little Brn. 1st. author's 2nd book. NF/dj. S18. $30.00

**CARROLL, John M.** *Black Military Experience in the American West.* 1971. Liveright. sgn. ils. VG/dj. J2. $425.00

**CARROLL, John M.** *Black Military Experience in the American West.* 1971. NY. 1st. 428p. NF/dj. E1. $225.00

**CARROLL, John M.** *Custer Autograph Album.* ils/index. 200p. cloth. dj. E1. $25.00

**CARROLL, John M.** *Custer: From the Civil War to Little Big Horn.* 1981. Bryan, TX. sbdg. VG. E1. $50.00

**CARROLL, Jonathan.** *Black Cocktail.* 1991. St Martin. 1st Am. NF/dj. M23. $20.00

**CARROLL, Jonathan.** *Child Across the Sky.* 1989. Century. ltd. 1/250. sgn. gray cloth. F/box. B30. $75.00

**CARROLL, Jonathan.** *Outside the Dog Museum.* 1991. NY. Doubleday. 1st Am. F/dj. A14/M23. $21.00

**CARROLL, Jonathan.** *Voice of Our Shadow.* 1983. Viking. 1st. NF/dj. B30. $100.00

**CARROLL, Lewis.** *Alice in Wonderland.* ca 1955. Whitman. ils Roberta Paflin. 284p. VG. B36. $6.00

**CARROLL, Lewis.** *Alice in Wonderland.* 1978. Austin. Amistad. mini/#d (not stated). ils/marbled ep. 40p. hand-bdg. F. B24. $125.00

**CARROLL, Lewis.** *Alice in Wonderland.* 1979. Japan. Walt Disney Prod. Japanese text. VG+/sans? C9. $60.00

**CARROLL, Lewis.** *Alice in Wonderland/Through the Looking-Glass.* ca 1940. Paris. Minia. 2 vol. ils Tenniel. full leather/raised bands. box. R5. $275.00

**CARROLL, Lewis.** *Alice's Adventures in Wonderland W/Cut-out Pictures...* 1917. NY. Cupples Leon. 1st thus. ils Julia Greene/helen Pettes. pict brd. R5. $585.00

**CARROLL, Lewis.** *Alice's Adventures in Wonderland.* 1984. London. Macmillan. facs. ils Tenniel. 192p. VG. M10. $16.50

**CARROLL, Lewis.** *Alice's Adventures in Wonderland.* 1987. Knopf. ils. 143p. VG/dj. P12. $25.00

**CARROLL, Lewis.** *Alice's Adventures in Wonderland/Through the Looking Glass.* 1866 & 1872. London. Macmillan. 2 vol. 1st/1st issue points. ils Tenniel. full morocco. F. B24. $8,500.00

**CARROLL, Lewis.** *Alice's Adventures in Wonderland/Through the Looking Glass.* 1911. London. Macmillan. 1st thus. 8vo. all edges tinted. gilt red cloth. R5. $250.00

**CARROLL, Lewis.** *Alice's Adventures in Wonderland/Through the Looking Glass.* 1989. Choice Pub. 3rd. 8vo. 188p. F. W2. $30.00

**CARROLL, Lewis.** *Alice's Adventures in Wonderland/Through the Looking Glass.* 1993. Folio Soc. 2 vol. ils Tenniel. VG/VG case. M17. $30.00

**CARROLL, Lewis.** *Hunting of the Snark.* 1876. London. Macmillan. 1st. 1/100 special red cloth. 83p. F/blk cloth case. H5. $2,250.00

**CARROLL, Lewis.** *Jaberwocky.* nd. Rosemead, CA. Bookhaven. mini. 1/300. ils/glossary Bohne. marbled brd/leather. B24. $75.00

CARROLL, Lewis. *Jaberwocky.* 1986. Berkeley. Poole. mini. 1/99. ils/prt/sgn MP Adams+wood Jacob's ladder. B24. $350.00

CARROLL, Lewis. *Pig-Tale.* 1975. Little Brn. 1st. lg 8vo. gilt brn cloth. F/G. M7. $28.00

CARROLL, Lewis. *Through the Looking Glass & What Alice Found There.* ca 1929. Phil. Altemus. 16mo. red cloth backed purple brd. dj. R5. $185.00

CARROLL, Lewis. *Through the Looking Glass in Words of One Syllable.* 1908. Chicago. Saalfield. 1st thus. 8vo. 110+2p ads. pict gr cloth. F. C6. $50.00

CARROLL, Lewis. *Through the Looking Glass.* 1905. NY. Stokes. 1st thus. 8vo. purple-gray cloth. R5. $175.00

CARROLL, Lewis. *Useful & Instructive Poetry.* 1954. London. Bles. 1st. VG/acetate dj. Q1. $125.00

CARROLL, Lewis. *Useful & Instructive Poetry.* 1954. Macmillan. 1st. ils. 45p. VG/G. T5. $55.00

CARROLL, Lewis. *Verses From Alice.* 1944. London. Collins. 1st thus. ils GL Sherwood. unp. gilt bl cloth. VG/dj. D1. $225.00

CARROLL & HAGGARD. *Three New Mexico Chronicles...* 1942. Quivira. 1/557. VG. A4. $275.00

CARRUTH, Hayden. *Asphalt Georgics.* 1985. New Directions. 1st. sgn. F/dj. O11. $50.00

CARRUTH, Hayden. *Collected Longer Poems.* 1993. Copper Canyon. sgn. F/dj. O11. $50.00

CARRUTH, Hayden. *Collected Shorter Poems 1946-1911.* 1992. Port Townsent, WA. Copper Canyon. 1st. sgn. F/dj. O11. $70.00

CARRUTH, Hayden. *Sleeping Beauty.* 1982. Harper Row. 1st. F/dj. O3. $30.00

CARRUTHERS, Zilpha. *Path of the Gopatis.* 1926. Nat Dairy Council. ils Jessie Gillespie. 100p. VG+/worn. B20. $40.00

CARSON, Gerald. *Old Country Store.* 1954. OUP. F/dj. H6. $45.00

CARSON, Gerald. *One for a Man, Two for a Horse.* 1961. Bramhall. ils/photos. 128p. H6. $38.00

CARSON, James. *Saddle Boys in the Grand Canyon.* 1913. Cupples Leon. lists 5 titles. VG/dj. M20. $30.00

CARSON, Rachel. *Sea Around Us.* 1980. LEC. 1/200. photos/sgn Alfred Eisenstadt. 254p. F/case. B24. $250.00

CARSON, Rachel. *Silent Spring.* 1961. Houghton Mifflin. 1st. 8vo. 368p. gilt gr cloth. F/NF. J3. $200.00

CARSON, Robert. *Waterfront Writers: Literature of Work.* 1979. Harper Row. 1st. VG/dj. N2. $10.00

CARSWELL, Catherine. *Savage Pilgrimage.* 1932. London. 1st. inscr. T9. $50.00

CARTER, Angela. *Shadow Dance.* 1966. London. Heinemann. true 1st. author's 1st book. NF/VG. A24. $185.00

CARTER, C.F. *Wedding Day in Literature & Art...* 1906. Dodd Mead. 1st. 8vo. 294p. gilt bl cloth. NF. B20. $40.00

CARTER, Elizabeth. *All the Works of Epictetus.* 1758. London. A Miller. 2nd. polished calf/raised bands. H13. $485.00

CARTER, Elizabeth. *Memoirs of the Life of Mrs Elizabeth Carter.* 1809. Boston. Greenleaf. 1st Am. tall 8vo. full polished calf. H13. $245.00

CARTER, Henry. *Yellow Fever: Epidemiological & Historical Study...* 1931. Baltimore. 1st. 308p. xl. A13. $90.00

CARTER, Jimmy. *Always a Reckoning.* 1995. Time Books. 1st. sgn. F/dj. O11. $40.00

CARTER, Jimmy. *Blood of Abraham.* 1985. Houghton Mifflin. 1st. sgn. F/dj. O11. $75.00

CARTER, Jimmy. *Blood of Abraham: Insights to the Middle East.* 1985. Boston. Houghton Mifflin. 8vo. 6 maps. NF/dj. W1. $18.00

CARTER, Jimmy. *Little Baby Snoogle-Fleejer.* 1995. NY. Times Books. 1st. sgn. ils Amy Carter. F/dj. O11. $60.00

CARTER, Jimmy. *Living Faith.* 1996. Times Books. 1st. sgn. F/dj. O11. $40.00

CARTER, Jimmy. *Outdoor Journal.* 1988. NY. Bantam. 1st. sgn. F/dj. O11. $95.00

CARTER, Jimmy. *Talking Peace: Vision for the Next Generation.* 1993. Dutton Children's Book. ARC/1st. F/pict wrp. Q1. $40.00

CARTER, John. *ABC for Book Collectors.* 1992. Knopf. 5th. 450 definitions. NF/dj. A27. $15.00

CARTER, Lin. *Dreams From R'Lyeh.* 1975. Arkham. 1st. 1/3152. F/dj. T2. $45.00

CARTER, Mary Randolph. *American Junk.* 1994. Viking. folio. photos. VG/dj. A28. $16.00

CARTER, Peter. *Children of the Book.* 1982. OUP. 1st. 271p. F/dj. D4. $35.00

CARTER, Polly. *Harriet Tubman.* 1990. NJ. Silver. 1st. 8vo. ils Brian Pinkney. F. C14. $12.00

CARTER, Robert. *Coast of New England: New Edition of Summer Cruise...* 1969. Somersworth. ils. store stp. VG/dj. M17. $15.00

CARTER, Russell Gordon. *Singing Dog.* 1931. Penn Pub. ils Bessie Crawford Watson. G. A21. $24.00

CARTER, Russell Gordon. *White Plume of Navarre.* (1928). Volland. 2nd. 191p. gr cloth/pict label. G. T5. $45.00

CARTER, Samuel III. *Blaze of Glory: Fight for New Orleans 1814-1815.* 1971. NY. 1st. ils/map. F/G. M4. $30.00

CARTER, Samuel III. *Cherokee Sunset: A Nation Betrayed.* 1976. Doubleday. F/dj. A19. $25.00

CARTER, Vincent O. *Bern Book: Record of a Voyage of the Mind.* 1973. NY. John Day. VG/dj. B9. $15.00

CARTER, Winifred. *Dr Johnson's Dear Mistress, Mrs Hester Thrale.* 1950. Philosophical Lib. 1st. 8vo. gilt blk linen. VG. H13. $35.00

CARTER & CARTER. *Everything to Gain: Making the Most of Rest of Your Life.* 1987. Random. 1st. AN/F. V4. $10.00

CARTER & KENERLEY. *Concern.* 1972. Western Yearly Meeting. 12mo. 107p. VG/wrp. V3. $7.00

CARTER & POLLARD. *Enquiry Into Nature of Certain 19th-C Pamphlets.* 1934. London/NY. Constable/Scribner. 1st. maroon cloth. F/dj. M24. $350.00

CARTERETTE & FRIEDMAN. *Handbook of Perception Vol I.* 1974. NY. Academic. 431p. panelled brn cloth. VG/dj. G1. $65.00

CARTHY, J.D. *Animal Navigation.* 1956. NY. ils. 151p. VG/dj. S15. $15.00

CARTIER, John O. *Modern Deer Hunter.* 1976. NY. ils/index. 310p. dj. A17. $12.00

CARTIER-BRESSON, Henri. *Henri Cartier-Bresson, Photographer.* 1979. NYGS. 1st. F/NF. B2. $100.00

CARTIER-BRESSON, Henri. *Henri Cartier-Bresson, Photographer.* 1979. NYGS. 1st. thick 4to. ils. F/F. S9. $150.00

CARTLAND, Fernando G. *Southern Heroes; or, Friends in War Time.* 1895. Cambridge. Riverside. 1st. 480p. V3. $85.00

CARTWRIGHT, Julia. *Bright Remembrance. Diaries of Julia Cartwright.* 1989. Weidenfeld Nicolson. 1st. F/dj. A23. $35.00

**CARUS, Carl Gustav.** *Physis: Zur Geschichte des Leiblichen Lebens.* 1851. Stuttgart. GB Scheitlin. German text. 496p. contemporary bdg. G1. $185.00

**CARUTHERS, William.** *Loafing Along Death Valley Trails...* 1951. Ontario, CA. Death Valley Pub. 1st. VG/sans. O4. $15.00

**CARVER, Jeffrey A.** *Rapture Effect.* 1987. Tor. 1st. RS. F/dj. P3. $20.00

**CARVER, Raymond.** *At Night the Salmon Move.* 1976. Santa Barbara. Capra. 1st. 1/100. sgn. F/NF. L3. $750.00

**CARVER, Raymond.** *Cathedral.* 1983. NY. Knopf. 1st. F/F. D10/R14. $100.00

**CARVER, Raymond.** *Early for the Dance.* 1986. Concord. Ewert. 1st. 1/136. sgn. F/sans. L3. $250.00

**CARVER, Raymond.** *New Path to the Waterfall.* 1989. Atlantic Monthly. 1st. ils Tess Gallagher. F/NF. B3. $50.00

**CARVER, Raymond.** *Painter & the Fish.* 1988. Concord. Ewert. 1st. 1/74. sgn/#d. F. L3. $175.00

**CARVER, Raymond.** *What We Talk About When We Talk About Love.* 1981. NY. Knopf. 1st. sgn. 2nd story collection. F/dj. S9. $450.00

**CARVER, Raymond.** *Where I'm Calling From.* 1988. Atlantic Monthly. 1st. NF/dj. A24. $40.00

**CARVER, Raymond.** *Where Water Comes Together With Other Water.* 1985. Random. 1st. F/F. D10. $75.00

**CARWILE, Howard H.** *Speaking From Byrdland.* (1960). Lyle Stewart. 157p. VG. B10. $50.00

**CARY, James.** *Tanks & Armor in Modern Warfare.* 1966. NY. 1st. ils. VG/dj. B18. $22.50

**CARY, Lorene.** *Price of a Child.* 1995. Knopf. 1st. F/dj. M23. $40.00

**CARY & WARMINGTON.** *Ancient Explorers.* 1929. London. Methuen. ils/fld maps. 270p. cloth. G+. Q2. $23.50

**CASADA, James A.** *Biobibliographical Study.* 1990. Boston. 1st. dj. T9. $10.00

**CASADA, James A.** *Sir Richard F Burton: A Bibliographical Study.* 1990. Boston. Hall. 1st Am. 8vo. F/sans. A2. $25.00

**CASANOVA, Jacques.** *Memoirs of...* 1922. London. private prt. 2 vol. 1st thus. 8vo. wht buckram. VG/dj. C6. $75.00

**CASANOVA, Jacques.** *Memoirs of...* 1925. Aventuros. 12 vol. 1/1000. ils Rockwell Kent. blk cloth. F/dj. F1. $600.00

**CASEBIER, Dennis G.** *Camp Beale's Spring & Hualpai Indians.* 1980. Tales of Mojave Road. 8vo. 240p. emb brn buckram. NF. F7. $42.50

**CASEBIER, Dennis G.** *Camp Rock Spring, California.* 1973. Tales of Mojave Road. 130p. VG+. F7. $22.50

**CASELLA, Dolores.** *World of Breads.* 1966. NY. David Wht Co. G/dj. A16. $8.00

**CASEY, John.** *American Romance.* 1977. Atheneum. 1st. F/F. D10. $85.00

**CASEY, John.** *Testimony & Demeanor.* 1979. Knopf. 1st. F/F. D10. $55.00

**CASEY, T.A.** *Corneal Grafting.* nd (1972). London. Butterworths. 1st. 8vo. 340p. F/dj. C14. $28.00

**CASEY & DOUGLAS.** *Lackawana Story.* 1951. NY. 1st. 223p. VG/G. B5. $30.00

**CASH, J.H.** *Working the Homestake.* 1973. IA U. 1st. photos. F/dj. M4. $25.00

**CASH, Johnny.** *Man in White.* 1986. Harper Row. 1st. NF/clip. A14. $21.00

**CASKEY, L.D.** *Geometry of Greek Vases: Attic Vases in Mus of Fine Arts...* 1922. Mus of Fine Arts. 1st. ils. w/prospectus. B27. $275.00

**CASO, Alfonso.** *Aztecs: People of the Sun.* 1958. Norman. ARC/1st. ils. beige cloth. F/dj. T10. $125.00

**CASPARY, Vera.** *Bedelia.* 1945. London. Eyre Spottiswoode. 1st. F/dj. M14. $75.00

**CASSANDRA, Knye;** see Disch, Thomas.

**CASSEDAY, Ben.** *History of Louisville.* 1852. Louisville. Hull & Bro. 1st. 8vo. fld map. 255+39p ads. brn cloth. C6. $150.00

**CASSEDY, James H.** *American Medicine & Statistical Thinking 1800-1860.* 1984. Cambridge. 1st. 306p. dj. A13. $40.00

**CASSELS, Lavender.** *Struggle for the Ottoman Empire 1717-1740.* 1967. NY. Crowell. 226p. VG. W1. $22.00

**CASSIDY, James.** *Family Guide to the Bible.* 1984. Readers Digest. 832p. VG/dj. B29. $16.00

**CASSILL, R.V.** *Norton Anthology of Short Fiction.* 1978. Norton. 1st. NF/wrp. S13. $8.00

**CASSIN, John.** *Illustrations of Birds in California, Texas, Oregon...* 1991. TX State Hist Assn. 1/250. 50 mc pl. 298p. F/case. B20. $175.00

**CASSINI, Oleg.** *Thousand Days of Magic: Dressing Jacqueline Kennedy...* 1995. NY. Rizzoli. F/dj. B9. $30.00

**CASSIODORUS.** *Psalterii Davidici Expositio.* 1519. Paris. Petit. sm folio. woodcut. vellum/rb. lib stp. R12. $675.00

**CASSON, Lionel.** *Ancient Mariners, Seafarers & Sea Fighters...* 1991. Princeton. 2nd. ils. VG/dj. M17. $22.50

**CASSON, Stanley.** *Some Modern Sculptors.* 1928. OUP. 1st. ils. 119p. gilt bl cloth. F1. $40.00

**CASTANEDA, Carlos.** *Separate Reality.* (1971). NY. 1st. 317p. dj. F3. $20.00

**CASTANEDA, Carlos.** *Tales of Power.* 1974. S&S. 1st. 207p. dj. F3. $20.00

**CASTEL, Albert.** *William Clarke Quantill: His Life & Times.* 1962. NY. Fell. 1st. VG/dj. B5. $40.00

**CASTIGLIONI, Arturo.** *History of Medicine.* 1941. NY. 1st. 1013p. A13. $175.00

**CASTILLO & GARCIA.** *Cesar Chavez: A Triumph of Spirit.* 1995. Norman, OK. AN/dj. V4. $22.50

**CASTLE, Charles.** *Oliver Messel: A Biography.* 1986. NY. 1st. fwd John Gielgud. dj. T9. $15.00

**CASTLE, Egerton.** *Young April.* 1907. Grosset Dunlap. photoplay. sm 8vo. 452p. VG. H1. $15.00

**CASTLEMAN, Riva.** *Century of Artists Books.* 1994. NY. MOMA. 1st. lg 4to. 264p. AN/dj. J3. $55.00

**CASTLEMAN & SUTTON.** *Massachusetts General Hospital 1955-1980.* 1983. Boston. 1st. 410p. A13. $30.00

**CATAK, Ladislaus.** *Cactus Guide.* 1956. Van Nostrand. 1st. 6-line inscr. 144p. NF. B14. $40.00

**CATESBY, Mark.** *Natural History of Carolina, Florida & Bahama Islands...* 1974. Savannah, GA. Beehive. facs (3rd/London 1771). 1/500. 50 pl. 107p. AN/box. C6. $900.00

**CATHER, Willa.** *April Twilights.* 1903. Boston. Gorham. 1st. author's 1st book. gray brd/labels. F. M24. $1,650.00

**CATHER, Willa.** *Death Comes for the Archbishop.* 1927. NY. Knopf. 1/175. sgn. marbled brd/cloth spine. case. D11. $500.00

**CATHER, Willa.** *Novels & Stories of Willa Cather.* 1937-1941. Houghton Mifflin. 13 vol. Autograph ed. 1/950. ils. F/dj. H5. $4,000.00

**CATHER, Willa.** *Old Beauty & Others.* 1948. Knopf. 1st. NF/VG. A24. $50.00

**CATHER, Willa.** *Shadows on the Rock.* 1931. Knopf. 1st. 1/619. sgn. 280p. marbled cloth/leather spine. F1. $375.00

CATHER, Willa. *Shadows on the Rock*. 1931. Knopf. 1st. 8vo. 280p. VG+/dj. B20. $75.00

CATHER, Willa. *Troll Garden*. 1905. McClure. 1st/2nd bdg. gilt red cloth. F. M24. $450.00

CATO & VITIELLO. *Joyce Images*. nd. Norton. folio. AN/dj/swrp. A28. $35.00

CATON, Edward. *Ballet Class*. 1961. London. Harrap. 126p. G/dj. C5. $12.50

CATTERMOLE, E.G. *Famous Frontiersman, Pioneers & Scouts...* 1883. Chicago. Coburn Newman. 1st. 540p. G+. B18. $95.00

CATTON, Bruce. *American Heritage Picture History of the Civil War*. 1960. NY. ils/index. F/dj. E1. $45.00

CATTON, Bruce. *Bibliography of the American Civil War*. 1962. NY/PA Co. ARC. 18p. stiff wrp. B10. $10.00

CATTON, Bruce. *Coming Fury: Centennial History of the Civil War. Vol 1*. 1961. Doubleday. 1st. NF/clip. A14. $21.00

CATTON, Bruce. *Gettysburg: Final Fury*. 1974. Doubleday. 2nd. 4to. ils/maps. VG/dj/case. S17. $8.00

CATTON, Bruce. *Grant Moves South*. nd. Little Brn. rpt. NF/dj. A14. $28.00

CATTON, Bruce. *Grant Takes Command*. 1969. Little Brn. 1st. NF/clip. A14. $35.00

CATTON, Bruce. *Mr Lincoln's Army*. 1962. NY. 1st. index/biblio. 363p. NF/dj. E1. $30.00

CATTON, Bruce. *Never Call Retreat: Centennial History of Civil War*. 1965. NY. stated 1st. 555p. F/VG. E1. $35.00

CATTON, Bruce. *Waiting for the Morning Train: An American Boyhood*. 1972. Doubleday. 1st. photos. 260p. F/dj. Y1. $25.00

CAUCCI & NASTASI. *Hatches: A Complete Guide to Fishing Hatches...* 1975. NY. 1st. 320p. NF/dj. A17. $45.00

CAUDILL, Rebecca. *Happy Little Family*. 1947. Winston/Literary Guild. 1st. 8vo. 116p. gilt burgundy bdg. VG. T5. $25.00

CAUDILL, Rebecca. *Schoolhouse in the Woods*. 1949. Winston. 1st. 8vo. 120p. gr cloth. VG. T5. $20.00

CAUDILL, Rebecca. *Tree of Freedom*. 1949. Viking/Jr Literary Guild. 1st thus. 8vo. 279p. gilt gr cloth. VG/G. T5. $30.00

CAUDILL, Rebecca. *Up & Down the River*. 1951. Winston/Jr Literary Guild. 1st thus. 8vo. VG. T5. $20.00

CAUDWELL, Irene. *Damien of Molokai, 1840-1889*. 1932. NY. 203p. gilt red cloth. VG. H3. $35.00

CAUGHEY, John Walton. *American West, Frontier & Region*. 1969. Ward Ritchie. 287p. VG/dj. J2. $75.00

CAUGHEY & CAUGHEY. *California Heritage*. 1962. Ward Ritchie. 1st. NF/dj. T10. $35.00

CAULFIELD, Patricia. *Everglades*. 1970. Sierra Club. edit Paul Brooks. VG. S5. $20.00

CAUNITZ, William J. *Exceptional Clearance*. 1991. Crown. 1st. F/dj. G8. $12.50

CAUNITZ, William J. *One Police Plaza*. 1984. 1st. author's 1st book. F/VG. M19. $17.50

CAUNITZ, William J. *Suspects*. 1986. NY. Crown. 1st. NF/F. R14. $30.00

CAUSTON, Richard. *Nichiren Shoshu Buddhism: A Popular Introduction...* 1989. SF. 1st. VG/dj. M17. $25.00

CAUTE, David. *Joseph Losey: A Revenge on Life*. 1994. OUP. 1st. VG/dj. C9. $36.00

CAUZ, Louis. *Baseball's Back in Town*. 1977. Canada. Controlled Media (CMC). 1st. lg format. VG/dj. P8. $125.00

CAVAICK, Wemyss. *Uprooted Heather: Story of the Selkirk Settlers*. 1967. Vancouver. Mitchell. 1st. F/NF. A26. $20.00

CAVALLERO CARRANCO, Juan. *Pearl Hunters in Gulf of California, 1668: Summary Report...* 1966. Dawson's Book Shop. 1st. 91p. VG/sans. B19. $40.00

CAVANA, Betty. *Connie Blair: Clue in Blue (#1)*. 1948. Grosset Dunlap. lists to #2. VG/dj. M20. $15.00

CAVANA, Betty. *Connie Blair: Clue in Blue*. (1948). Grosset Dunlap. 8vo. 216p. brn brd. G+. T5. $15.00

CAVANA, Betty. *Connie Blair: Puzzle in Purple*. (1948). Grosset Dunlap. 8vo. 216p. brn brd. G+. T5. $15.00

CAVANNA, Betty. *Going on Sixteen*. 1956. Westminster. ne. 220p. VG/dj. B36. $20.00

CAVANNA, Betty. *Spice Island Mystery*. 1969. Morrow. 1st. VG/dj. P2. $20.00

CAVAZZA, Elisabeth. *Don Finimondone Calabrian Sketches*. 1892. NY. CL Webster. ftspc ils Dan Beard. VG. B14. $55.00

CAVE, Hugh B. *Disciples of Dread*. Sept 1988. NY. Tor. 1st. VG/G+. L1. $35.00

CAVE, Roderick. *Private Press*. 1983. NY/London. Bowker. 2nd. 8vo.389p. gilt rust cloth. F/dj. F1. $65.00

CAWTHORN & MOORCOCK. *Fantasy: The 100 Best Books*. 1988. 216p. F/F. A4. $30.00

CAXTON, William. *History of Reynard the Foxe*. 1892. Hammersmith. Kelmscott. 1/300 on paper. 4to. limp vellum w/ribbon ties. B24. $35.00

CAXTON, William. *Subtyl Historyes & Fables of Esope. Translated...* 1930. Grabhorn. 1/175. 8vo. ils Valenti Angelo. full red morocco. F. B24. $1,000.00

CEBULASH, Mel. *Ruth Marini: World Series Star*. 1985. Lerner. 1st. F/dj. P8. $20.00

CECIL, David. *Two Quiet Lives*. 1948. London. 1st. dj. T9. $20.00

CECIL, Henry. *Daughters in Law*. 1961. Michael Joseph. 1st Eng. VG/G. G8. $20.00

CECIL, Henry. *Ways & Means*. 1952. London. 1st. dj. T9. $30.00

CECIL, Robert. *Hitler's War Machine*. 1975. Secaucus, NJ. rpt. 248p. F/dj. E1. $30.00

CECILLIA, Madame. *Spiritual Gleanings for Marian Sodalists*. 1913. London. Longman Gr. 216p. VG. H10. $15.00

CEDAR & TORREY. *Joel: The Potter's Son*. 1954. Abingdon. VG/dj. V4. $15.00

CELIZ. *Diary of the Alarcon Expedition Into Texas 1718-1719*. 1935. Quivira Soc. 1/600. 10 pl/2 maps. NF. A4. $275.00

CERAM, C.W. *First American: Story of North American Archaeology*. 1971. HBJ. 1st. VG/dj. R11. $27.00

CERF, Bennett. *Great Modern Short Stories*. 1942. Random. 1st. NF/sans. S18. $25.00

CERF, Bennett. *Three Famous Murder Novels*. 1941. Modern Lib. VG/dj. P3. $30.00

CERF & ERSKINE. *At Random: Reminiscences of Bennett Cerf*. 1977. NY. Random. 1st. lg 8vo. 306p. dj. O10. $25.00

CERNUSCHI, Henri. *Nomisma; or, Legal Tender*. 1877. Appleton. 1st Am. 8vo. 157p. brn cloth. VG+. B20. $75.00

CERVE, Wishar. *Lemuria: Lost Continent of the Pacific*. 1980 (1931). rpt. 275p. dj. F3. $15.00

CHABON, Michael. *Model World & Other Stories*. 1991. Morrow. 1st. sgn. F/F. B3. $40.00

CHABON, Michael. *Mysteries of Pittsburgh*. 1988. Morrow. 1st. author's 1st novel. F/dj. C9/M23. $30.00

**CHABON, Michael.** *Wonder Boys.* 1995. NY. Villard. 1st. sgn/dtd 1995. F/dj. R14. $45.00

**CHACKO, David.** *Black Chamber.* 1988. NY. 1st. F/dj. T12. $20.00

**CHACKO, David.** *White Gamma.* 1988. NY. 1st. F/F. H11. $20.00

**CHADOURNE, Marc.** *China.* 1932. Covici Friede. 1st. Am. ils Miguel Covarrubias. 308p. NF/dj. B20. $125.00

**CHADWICK, Lester.** *Batting to Win.* 1911. Cupples Leon. 1st. lacks title p. G. P8. $25.00

**CHADWICK & SUTTON.** *Tropical Rain Forest: Leeds Symposium.* 1984. Leeds, Eng. Leeds Philosophical & Literature. 1st. 8vo. F/VG. A2. $30.00

**CHAFEE, Zechariah Jr.** *Cases on Equitable Remedies, Interpleader, Bills of Peace...* 1938. Cambridge. Langdell Hall. M11. $65.00

**CHAFFEE, Allen.** *Sitka the Snow Baby.* 1934. McLoughlin. ils Peter DaRu. VG/dj. M20. $20.00

**CHAFFETZ, David.** *Journey Through Afganistan: A Memorial.* 1981. Chicago. Regnery. sgn pres. 254p. NF/dj. W1. $20.00

**CHAFFIN, Lorah B.** *Sons of the West.* 1941. Caxton. 284p. VG/dj. J2. $98.00

**CHAI, Chen Kang.** *Taiwan Aborigines: A Genetic Study of Tribal Variations.* 1967. Cambridge. Harvard. 1st. VG/dj. N2. $22.50

**CHALKER & OWINGS.** *Science-Fantasy Publishers: Critical & Bibliographic Hist.* 1991. 3rd. 4to. 772p. F. A4. $250.00

**CHALMER, Patrick.** *Kenneth Graham: Life, Letters & Unpublished Work.* 1933. London. Methuen. 1st. ils/photos. bl cloth. VG. D1. $125.00

**CHALMERS, Mary.** *Easter Parade.* 1988. Harper Row. 1st. sm 4to. unp. F. C14. $12.00

**CHALMERS, Stephen.** *Whispering Ghost.* 1939. NY. Caxton. VG/dj. M21. $15.00

**CHALMERS, Thomas.** *Memoir of the Life & Writings...William Hanna.* 1850-51. NY. Harper. 3 vol. 1st Am. G/old lib labels. H10. $65.00

**CHAMBERLAIN, E.R.** *Marguerite of Navarre.* 1974. 1st. VG/dj. M17. $17.50

**CHAMBERLAIN, N.H.** *Samuel Sewall & the World He Lived In.* 1897. Boston. ils. w/promo pamphlet. M17. $40.00

**CHAMBERLAIN, Narcissa.** *Omelette Book.* 1971. Knopf. 1st. VG/dj. P12. $15.00

**CHAMBERLAIN, R.H.** *Early Loading Tools & Bullet Molds.* 1988. Union City, TN. Pioneer. sgn. AN. A19. $25.00

**CHAMBERLAIN, Samuel.** *Etched in Sunlight: Fifty Years in the Graphic Arts.* 1968. Boston Pub Lib. 1st. ils. 227p. gilt bl cloth. F1. $50.00

**CHAMBERLAIN, Samuel.** *Fair Is Our Land.* 1946 (1942). Hastings. 7th. VG. S5. $12.00

**CHAMBERLAIN, Sarah.** *Wood Engravings by...* ca 1979. Easthampton, MA. Chamberlain. 1/10 boxed sets of 48 sgn prts. AN/box. B24. $125.00

**CHAMBERLAIN & CHAMBERLAIN.** *Chamberlain Calendar of French Cooking.* 1958. Hastings. 1st. sbdg. VG. V4. $7.50

**CHAMBERLIN, Harry D.** *Training Hunters, Jumpers & Hacks.* 1937. NY. Derrydale. 1st. 1/1250. 329p. VG. H10. $45.00

**CHAMBERLIN, Roy Bullard.** *Winners.* 1933. Abingdon. 1st. F/dj. B20. $15.00

**CHAMBERS, Anne.** *Practical Guide to Marbling Paper.* 1986. Thames Hudson. 1st. ils. 88p. cloth. F/dj. O10. $35.00

**CHAMBERS, Lenoir.** *Stonewall Jackson.* 1959. Morrow. 2 vol. 1st. NF/box. B10. $110.00

**CHAMBERS, Oswald.** *My Utmost for His Highest.* (1994). Discovery House. 1st. AN/dj. A27. $17.00

**CHAMBERS, Oswald.** *Prayer: A Holy Occupation.* 1992. Discovery House. AN/dj. A27. $13.00

**CHAMBERS, Robert W.** *Drums of Aulone.* 1927. NY. Appleton. 1st. 348p. G. G11. $15.00

**CHAMBERS, Robert.** *Vestiges of the Natural History of Creation...* 1969. NY. facs of 1844. 390p. A13. $25.00

**CHAMBERS & SHANK.** *Salt-Water & Printer's Ink: Norfolk & Its Newspaper...* 1967. UNC. sgns. ils. 418p. VG/G. B10. $35.00

**CHAMICH (CHAMICHIN), Michael.** *History of Armenia.* 1827. Calcutta. 2 vol. ils/fld pl. 3-quarter leather. B5. $195.00

**CHAMPE, John L.** *Ash Hollow Cave.* 1946. Lincoln, NE. sc. F. A19. $25.00

**CHAMPION, Larry S.** *Essential Shakespeare: Annotated Bibliography...* 1986. Boston. GK Hall. 477p. F. A4. $45.00

**CHAMPION, Richard.** *Considerations on Present Situation of Great Britain...* 1784. London. Stockdale. 2nd. rb. VG. M10. $85.00

**CHAMPLIM, John Denison.** *Orations, Addresses & Speeches of Chauncey M Depew.* 1910. NY. private prt. 8 vol. ils. VG. A4. $165.00

**CHAMPLIN, Harry.** *Brilliance-Gradation-Sharpness With Miniature Camera.* 1938. Camara Craft Pub. 1st. VG. S5. $10.00

**CHAMPLIN, P.** *Raphael Pumpelly: Gentleman Geologist of Gilded Age.* 1994le. AL U. 1st. 273p. F/dj. M4. $25.00

**CHANCE, J.B.** *Mexican War Journal of Captain Franklin Smith.* 1991. MS U. 1st. F/dj. M4. $35.00

**CHANCELLOR, E. Beresford.** *Literary Diversions.* 1925. London. Dulau. 1st. 8vo. 180p. bl cloth. VG/dj. C6. $35.00

**CHANCELLOR, John.** *Charles Darwin.* 1973. Taplinger. 238p. cloth. VG. A10. $15.00

**CHANCELLOR, John.** *Murder Syndicate.* 1949. London. Eldon. 1st. F/dj. M15. $45.00

**CHANCELLOR, John.** *Peril & Promise.* 1990. Harper Row. 1st trade. sm 4to. 176p. F/dj. W2. $35.00

**CHANDLER, A. Bertram.** *Up to the Sky in Ships.* 1982. NESFA. 1st. F/dj. P3. $20.00

**CHANDLER, Ann C.** *Pan the Piper & Other Marvelous Tales.* 1923. Harper. 1st. ils. 234p. gilt bl cloth. VG. D1. $40.00

**CHANDLER, Asa.** *Hookworm Disease: Its Distribution, Biology, Epidemiology...* 1929. Macmillan. 1st. 494p. VG/dj. N2. $45.00

**CHANDLER, Edna Walker.** *Missing Mitt.* 1955. Ginn. 1st. VG. P8. $25.00

**CHANDLER, John Greene.** *Remarkable History of Chicken Little.* 1979. Boston. Bromer. mini. 1/85. hand-calligraphed Janet Hobbes. marbled brd. F. B24. $125.00

**CHANDLER, R.** *Travels in Asia Minor 1764-1765.* 1971. London. abridged from 1825 ed. ils. 253p. VG/frayed. M4. $35.00

**CHANDLER, Raymond.** *Antaeus. English Summer, a Gothic Romance.* 1976. Tangier. Ecco. 8vo. ils Edward Gorey. F/NF gr lettered pk wrp. R3. $10.00

**CHANDLER, Raymond.** *Big Sleep.* 1946. Cleveland/NY. World. 1st thus. VG. M21. $25.00

**CHANDLER, Raymond.** *Big Sleep.* 1986. SF. 1/425. ils/sgn Lou Stoumen. 249p. litho Plexiglas bdg. F1. $525.00

**CHANDLER, Raymond.** *Big Sleep.* 1989. Northpoint. 1st thus. NF/dj. S13. $20.00

CHANDLER, Raymond. *Killer in the Rain.* 1964. Houghton Mifflin. 1st Am. F/VG+. C15. $150.00

CHANDLER, Raymond. *Long Goodbye.* 1954. Houghton Mifflin. 1st Am. VG/clip. M15. $275.00

CHANDLER, Raymond. *Playback.* (1958). London. Hamish Mailton. 1st. 8vo. silvered red cloth. F/dj. R3. $125.00

CHANDLER, Raymond. *Raymond Chandler's Unknown Thriller: Screenplay of Playback.* 1985. NY. intro RB Parker. VG/dj. M17. $20.00

CHANDLER, Raymond. *Raymond Chandler Speaking.* 1962. London. Hamish Hamilton. 1st (precedes Am). F/NF. M15. $100.00

CHANDLER, Raymond. *Smell of Fear.* 1965. London. Hamish Hamilton. 1st. F/NF. M15. $300.00

CHANDLER & PARKER. *Poodle Springs.* 1989. Putnam. 1st. F/dj. R8. $9.00

CHANDOHA, Walter. *How to Photograph Cats, Dogs & Other Animals.* 1973. NY. Crown. 1st. sm 4to. VG/G. O3. $28.00

CHANG & CHANG. *Encyclopedia of Chinese Food & Cooking.* 1970. NY. Crown. 8vo. F/VG rpr. B11. $15.00

CHANIN & CHANIN. *This Land These Voices: A Different View of AZ History...* 1977. Flagstaff. Northland. VG/dj. V4. $25.00

CHANNING, William Ellery. *Selected Writings: Edited by David Robinson.* (1985). NY. Paulist. 1st. 310p. F/dj. H10. $16.50

CHANOFF & VAN TOAI. *Portrait of the Enemy.* 1986. Random. 1st. F/dj. R11. $30.00

CHANUTE, Octave. *Progress in Flying Machines.* 1976. Long Beach, CA. facs of 1894. VG/dj. B18. $45.00

CHANZANOF, William. *Welch's Grape Juice From Corporation to Co-Operative.* 1977. Syracuse. 407p. VG/dj. A10. $42.00

CHAPEL, Charles Edward. *Art of Shooting.* 1960. NY. 424p. VG/dj. A17/P12. $15.00

CHAPEL, Charles Edward. *Guns of the Old West.* 1961. Coward McCann. 1st. sm 4to. 306p. VG/dj. B20. $40.00

CHAPELL, Fred. *Farewell, I'm Bound to Leave You.* 1996. NY. Picador. 1st. sgn. F/dj. M23. $30.00

CHAPELLE, Howard I. *History of American Sailing Ships.* 1935. NY. Norton. 1st trade. lg 8vo. 400p. cream cloth. VG. B11. $75.00

CHAPELLE, Howard I. *National Watercraft Collection.* 1960. Mus of Hist/Tech of US Nat Mus. photos. G+. M17. $25.00

CHAPIN, A.B. *Puritanism Not Genuine Protestantism.* 1847. Stanford/Swords. 16mo. 226p. brn cloth. ex-Sunday school book. G. S17. $10.00

CHAPIN, Anna Alice. *Everyday Fairy Book.* ca 1930. London. Coker. later prt. ils JW Smith. 159p. red cloth/wht brd. H5. $450.00

CHAPIN, Anna Alice. *Konigskinder: The Royal Children.* 1911. London. Harper. 276p. xl. G. C5. $12.50

CHAPIN, Theodore. *Structure & Stratigraphy of Gravina & Revillagigedo Islands.* 1918. US Geol Soc. pl/maps. 19p. VG/wrp. H7. $15.00

CHAPLIN, Arnold. *Harveian Oration on Medicine in Century Before Harvey.* 1922. London. 1st. 28p. A13. $25.00

CHAPLIN, Arnold. *St Helena Who's Who; or, Directory of the Island...* 1919. NY. Dutton. 1st Am on handmade. 257p. VG. H10. $50.00

CHAPLIN, F.K. *Effects of the Reformation on Ideals of Life & Conduct.* 1927. Cambridge. Heffer. 167p. H10. $20.00

CHAPLIN, R.E. *Study of Animal Bones From Archaeological Sites.* 1971. London. Seminar. VG/dj. M20. $30.00

CHAPMAN, Alex. *Begin's Israel, Murbarak's Egypt.* 1983. London. Allen. 1st. 8vo. ils. NF/dj. W1. $18.00

CHAPMAN, Allen. *Radio Boys' First Wireless.* (1922). Grosset Dunlap. later ed. 216p. bl cloth. VG/dj. H1. $12.00

CHAPMAN, Berlin Basil. *Otoes & Missourias.* 1965. Times Journal. F. A19. $60.00

CHAPMAN, Ervin S. *Particeps Criminis: Story of a California Rabbit Drive.* 1910. Fleming Revell. 1st. 8vo. 107p. tan cloth. B20. $30.00

CHAPMAN, F.M. *Camps & Cruises of an Ornithologist.* 1908. NY. Scribner. 1st. 250 photos. 432p. gilt pict cloth. NF. C12. $48.00

CHAPMAN, Frank. *Life in an Air Castle.* 1938. NY. Appleton. 1st. 250p. xl. F3. $20.00

CHAPMAN, I.A. *History of Wyoming With Appendix...* 1971. Cottonport. rpt (1830). 209p. NF. M4. $35.00

CHAPMAN, James B. *Terminology of Holiness.* 1947. Beacon Hill. 112p. VG. B29. $8.00

CHAPMAN, Keith. *Military Air Transport Operations.* 1989. London. 1st. ils. VG. B18. $25.00

CHAPMAN, Lee; see Bradley, Marion Zimmer.

CHAPMAN, R.W. *Johnson: Prose & Poetry. With Boswell's Character...* 1934. Oxford. Clarendon. 8vo. 195p. gilt blk linen. VG. H13. $85.00

CHAPMAN, R.W. *Johnsonian & Other Essays & Reviews.* 1953. Clarendon. 1st. H13. $65.00

CHAPMAN, R.W. *Portrait of a Scholar & Other Essays...* 1922. OUP. inscr. H13. $95.00

CHAPMAN, Raymond. *Victorian Debate: English Literature & Society 1832-1901.* 1968. NY. Literature & Society series. VG/dj. M17. $15.00

CHAPMAN, V.J. *Coastal Vegetation.* 1976. Oxford. 2nd. ils. 292p. B26. $40.00

CHAPMAN, Walker. *Golden Dream.* 1967. Bobbs Merrill. 1st. 436p. xl. dj. F3. $10.00

CHAPMAN & WRAY. *Christmas Trees for Pleasure & Profit.* 1979 (1957). New Brunswick, NJ. 2nd. ils. 212p. VG/dj. B26. $15.00

CHAPONE, Hester. *Miscellanies in Prose & Verse.* 1775. London. Dilly. 1st. sm 8vo. 178p. tree calf. H13. $295.00

CHAPPELL, Fred. *Brighten the Corner Where You Are.* 1989. St Martin. 1st. G/dj. B30. $20.00

CHAPPELL, George S. *Basket of Poses.* 1924. Boni. 1st. ils Hogarth (pseud Rockwell Kent). 109p. F/NF. B20. $300.00

CHAPPELL & HOOPER. *Radio Audience Measurement.* 1944. Stephen Daye. 1st. 8vo. 246p. NF/VG+. B20. $60.00

CHAPUT, Don. *Virgil Earp: Western Peace Officer.* 1994. Affiliate Writers of Am. ils/maps. 255p. J2. $40.00

CHARBONNEAUX, Jean. *La Sculpture Grecque Classique.* 1942. Lausanne. La Guild du Livre. 2nd. French text. VG. D2. $35.00

CHARCOT, J.M. *Clinical Lectures on Senile & Chronic Diseases...* 1881. London. New Sydenham Soc. 6 pl. 307p. xl. G7. $135.00

CHARCOT, J.M. *Lectures on Localisation of Cerebral & Spinal Diseases...* 1883. London. New Sydenham Soc. 341p. cloth. G7. $250.00

CHARGAFF, Erwin. *Heraclitean Fire, Sketches From a Life Before Nature.* 1978. NY. 1st. 252p. dj. A13. $25.00

CHARLES, John. *Contrivance of Collegiation.* 1955. London. 1st. 24p. A13. $15.00

CHARLES, Robert H. *Roundabout Turn.* 1930. London. 1/65. ils/sgn Leslie Brooks. cloth. VG. B18. $95.00

CHARLESTON, Robert J. *Masterpieces of Glass: A World History of Corning Museum.* 1980. NY. Abrams. 1st. photos. VG/dj. M17. $60.00

**CHARLESWORTH, James H.** *Old Testament Pseudepigrapha...* 1983-85. Doubleday. 2 vol. biblios/index. VG/dj. H10. $85.00

**CHARLOT, Jean.** *Art From the Mayans to Disney.* 1939. NY. Sheed Ward. 285p. dj. D11. $50.00

**CHARLOTT, DODD & PAYAR.** *Charlot Murals in Georgia.* 1947. Athens. 1st. 1/2500. VG/dj. B5. $45.00

**CHARNAS, Suzy McKee.** *Dorthea Dreams.* 1986. Arbor. 1st. F/dj. M25. $25.00

**CHARNAS, Suzy McKee.** *Furies.* 1994. NY. Tor. 1st. sgn. F/dj. G10. $32.00

**CHARNEY, Mark J.** *Barry Hannah.* 1992. Twayne. 1st. US Authors series. F/dj. T11. $20.00

**CHARTERIS, Evan.** *Life & Letters of Sir Edmund Gosse.* 1931. London. ils. 539p. VG. A4. $85.00

**CHARTERIS, Leslie.** *Call for the Saint.* 1948. Doubleday Crime Club. 1st Am. F/NF. B4. $150.00

**CHARTERIS, Leslie.** *First Saint Omnibus.* 1939. Hodder Stoughton. 1st. F/VG. M15. $350.00

**CHARTERIS, Leslie.** *Saint Annual 1979.* 1978. Cheshire. Stafford Pemberton. 1st. lg format. F/sans. M15. $65.00

**CHARTERIS, Leslie.** *Senor Saint.* 1959. London. Hodder Stoughton. 1st Eng. F/dj. M15. $65.00

**CHARTERS & KUNSTADT.** *Jazz: History of the NY Scene.* 1962. Doubleday. 1st. NF/dj. B2. $50.00

**CHARYK, John C.** *Little White Schoolhouse: Volume I.* 1973. Prairie Books. 3rd. F/G. A26. $15.00

**CHARYN, Jerome.** *Eisenhower, My Eisenhower.* 1971. HRW. 1st. F/dj. M25. $25.00

**CHARYN, Jerome.** *War Cries Over Avenue C.* 1985. DIF. 1st. F/dj. R14. $30.00

**CHARYN, Jerome.** *7th Babe.* 1979. Arbor. 1st. F/VG. P8. $150.00

**CHASE, Don M.** *Jedediah Strong Smith: He Opened the West...* 1958. 40p. VG/wrp. J2. $40.00

**CHASE, Ernest Dudley.** *Romance of the Greeting Cards...* 1956. Chicago. 1st. ils. 247p. VG/fair. M10. $30.00

**CHASE, Harold S.** *Hope Ranch: A Rambling Record.* 1963. Santa Barbara Hist Soc. 121p. cloth. D11. $50.00

**CHASE, Ilka.** *Around the World & Other Places.* 1970. Doubleday. 1st. 8vo. 300p. map ep. B11. $15.00

**CHASE, Joan.** *Bonneville Blue.* 1991. FSG. 1st. F/dj. R14. $30.00

**CHASE, Pliny Earle.** *Elements of Meteorology for Schools & Households.* 1884. Phil. Porter Coates. sm 8vo. 128p. decor cloth. VG. K5. $85.00

**CHASE, R.** *Ungeared Mind.* 1926 (1918). ils. VG. E6. $45.00

**CHASE, Salmon Portland.** *Authentic Speeches of SP Chase, Secretary of Treasury...* 1863. WA. WH Moore. 1st. 36p. wrp. M8. $65.00

**CHASE-RIBOUND, Barbara.** *Valide: Novel of the Harem.* 1986. NY. Morrow. 1st. NF/VG. A14. $21.00

**CHASIN, Helen.** *Coming Close & Other Poems.* 1968. Yale. ARC/1st. cloth. VG/dj. L3. $55.00

**CHATEAUBRIAND.** *Voyages en Amerique, en France, et en Italie.* 1830. paris. Lefevre et Ladvocat. 2 vol. tall 8vo. calf. R12. $150.00

**CHATHAM, Russell.** *Angler's Coast.* 1990. Clark City. 1st. photos. F/dj. T11. $70.00

**CHATHAM, Russell.** *Silent Seasons.* 1988. Clark City. 1st. sgn/dtd 1990. F/wrp/dj. T11. $125.00

**CHATTERTON, Pauline.** *Coordinated Crafts for the Home.* 1980. Richard Marek. 1st. 4to. 208p. VG/dj. S14. $10.00

**CHATWIN, Bruce.** *Songlines.* 1987. Franklin Lib. true 1st Am (precedes trade). sgn. 8vo. 294p. leather. B20. $175.00

**CHAUCER, Geoffrey.** *Canterbury Tales.* 1934. Covici Friede. 1st trade. ils. tan cloth. VG. B27. $100.00

**CHAUCER, Geoffrey.** *Geoffrey Chaucer's ABC.* 1967. SF. Grabhorn-Hoyem. 1st. 1/1000. decor brd. w/prospectus. M24. $45.00

**CHAUCER, Geoffrey.** *Works of Geoffrey Chaucer.* 1928-29. Oxford. Shakespeare Head. 8 vol. 1/375. 4to. ils Lynton Lamb. F. B24. $2,000.00

**CHAUCER, Geoffrey.** *Works of...Now Newly Imprinted.* 1896. Hammersmith. Kelmscott. 1/438. 87 engravings Burke-Jones. 556p. F/special box. B24. $55,000.00

**CHAUNITZ, William J.** *Exceptional Clearance.* 1991. Crown. 1st. F/F. H11. $25.00

**CHAUNITZ, William J.** *One Police Plaza.* 1984. Crown. 1st. author's 1st book. F/F. H11. $40.00

**CHAUNITZ, William J.** *Suspects.* 1986. NY. Crown. 1st. NF/F. H11. $30.00

**CHAUVOLS, Louis.** *William Harvey: His Life & Times, His Discoveries...* 1961. London. 1st. 271p. A13. $20.00

**CHAVALIER, Maurice.** *I Remember It Well.* 1970. Macmillan. 1st. 221p. F/VG. S14. $10.00

**CHAYEFSKY, Paddy.** *Altered States.* 1978. Harper Row. BC. VG/dj. B30/C9. $20.00

**CHAYEFSKY, Paddy.** *Goddess.* 1958. S&S. 1st. VG/dj. C9. $60.00

**CHAYEFSKY, Paddy.** *Middle of the Night.* 1957. Random. 1st. F/clip. B4. $185.00

**CHAYEFSKY, Paddy.** *Passion of Josef D.* 1964. Random. 1st. F/NF. B4. $175.00

**CHEATHAM & GRISWOLD.** *Cases & Materials on Conflict of Laws. Second Edition.* 1941. Chicago. Foundation. bl buckram. M11. $50.00

**CHEESMAN, Evelyn.** *Islands Near the Sun: Off the Beaten Track...* 1927. London. Witherby. 1st. ils/photos. 304p. VG/dj. A25. $40.00

**CHEEVER, Benjamin.** *Letters of John Cheever.* 1989. London. Cape. 1st. VG/dj. P3. $25.00

**CHEEVER, John.** *Brigadier & the Golf Widow.* 1964. Harper Row. 1st. NF/clip. D10. $55.00

**CHEEVER, John.** *Expelled.* 1988. LA. Sylvester Orphanos. 1st/ltd. sgn Cheever/Updike/Cowley/Chappell. F/case. L3. $350.00

**CHEEVER, John.** *Stories of John Cheever.* 1978. Knopf. 1st. F/F. D10. $60.00

**CHEEVER, John.** *World of Apples.* 1973. Knopf. 1st. F/dj. B30. $30.00

**CHEKE, John.** *Pronvntialione Graecae...* 1555. Basle. Episcopius. 8vo. prt device on title. gilt calf. R12. $975.00

**CHENEY, Margaret.** *Coed Killer.* 1976. NY. Walker. 1st. VG/dj. B5. $25.00

**CHENEY, Warren.** *Challenge.* 1906. Bobbs Merrill. ils NC Wyeth. 386p. G. G11. $10.00

**CHENEY, William.** *Types in Cases of William Cheney. 1961 Type Specimen Book.* 1961. Dawson. mini. 1/139 total. sgn. 40p. blk leather. F. B24. $100.00

**CHERN, Margaret Booth.** *New Complete Newfoundland.* 1987. Howell Book House. 2nd/10th prt. 287p. F. A17. $10.00

**CHERNEV, Irving.** *Chessboard Magic! Collection of 160 Brilliant Chest Endings.* 1943. NY. Chess Review. 1st. 12mo. 162p. G. B11. $18.00

**CHERNEV & HARKNESS.** *Invitation to Chess.* 1945. S&S. 8vo. 224p. G/dj. B11. $15.00

**CHERNEV & REINFELD.** *Fireside Book of Chess.* 1949. NY. S&S. 1st. 8vo. 400p. red cloth. B11. $15.00

**CHERNS, Albert.** *Quality of Working Life & the Kibbutz Experience...* 1980. Norwood. G. V4. $25.00

**CHERRINGTON, Ernest H.** *Anti-Saloon League Year Book 1909.* 1909. Columbus, OH. Anti-Saloon League. 1st. photos. 256p. VG. A25. $25.00

**CHERRY, Joe H.** *Molecular Biology of Plants.* 1973. NY. ils. 204p. dj. B26. $30.00

**CHERRY, P.P.** *Portage Path.* 1911. Akron. fld map. 106p. B18. $45.00

**CHERRYH, C.J.** *Cyteen.* 1988. NY. Warner. 1st. F/dj. M21. $50.00

**CHESBRO, George C.** *Bleeding in the Eye of a Brainstorm.* 1995. S&S. 1st. rem mk. F/dj. A14. $21.00

**CHESBRO, George C.** *Fear in Yesterday's Rings.* 1991. Mysterious. 1st. F/F. H11. $20.00

**CHESBRO, George C.** *Fear in Yesterday's Rings.* 1991. Mysterious. 1st. sgn. F/dj. T2. $30.00

**CHESBRO, George C.** *Shadow of a Broken Man.* 1977. S&S. 1st. F/dj. B4. $85.00

**CHESBRO, George C.** *Two Songs This Archangel Sings.* 1986. Atheneum. 1st. F/clip. A14. $28.00

**CHESBRO, George C.** *Veil.* 1986. Mysterious. 1st. sgn. NF/dj. G8. $35.00

**CHESELDEN, William.** *Anatomy of the Human Body, XI Edition.* 1778. London. Rivington. 40 pl by Vandergrucht. contemporary calf. G7. $135.00

**CHESELDEN, William.** *Anatomy of the Human Body. VIII Edition.* 1756. London. Hitch Dodsley. 40 copper pl by Vandergrucht. contemporary calf. G7. $250.00

**CHESHIRE, Leone.** *Computing Diagrams for Tetrachoric Correlation Coefficient.* 1933. Chicago. obl 4to. unp. stiff gr wrp. G1. $30.00

**CHESLER, Phyllis.** *Woman & Madness.* 1972. Doubleday. 1st. photos. 360p. VG. S14. $8.00

**CHESLEY, Larry.** *Seven Years in Hanoi: POW Tells His Story.* 1973. Salt Lake City. Bookcraft. stated 1st. sgn pres. dj. R11. $45.00

**CHESNUTT, Charles W.** *House Behind the Cedars.* 1900. Houghton Mifflin. 1st. gr pict cloth. M24. $275.00

**CHESTERFIELD, Earl of.** *Letters to His Son on Art of Becoming a Man of the World...* 1917. NY. 2 vol. uncut/unopened. teg. 3-quarter brn leather. VG. H3. $80.00

**CHESTERFIELD, Lord.** *Chesterfield's Correspondence With Various Ladies...* (1930). London. Fanfrolico. 1st. 1/480. bstp cloth. H13. $165.00

**CHESTERTON, G.K.** *Ballad of the White Horse.* 1911. NY. 1st. T9. $45.00

**CHESTERTON, G.K.** *Brave New Family: GK Chesterton on Men & Women...* (1990). Ignatius. 1st Am. AN/wrp. A27. $13.00

**CHESTERTON, G.K.** *Charles Dickens: A Critical Study.* 1911. NY. Dodd Mead. 300p. G. H10. $20.00

**CHESTERTON, G.K.** *Collected Works of...,* *Vol I, Heretics, Orthodoxy...* (1986). Ignatius. 1st Am. edit/intro/notes David Dooley. 397p. AN/dj. A27. $30.00

**CHESTERTON, G.K.** *Coloured Lands.* 1938. NY. Sheed Ward. 1st Am. ils. gr cloth. VG/dj. F1. $50.00

**CHESTERTON, G.K.** *Everlasting Man.* (1993). Ignatius. 1st thus. AN/wrp. A27. $13.00

**CHESTERTON, G.K.** *Father Brown of the Church of Rome: Selected Mystery...* (1996). Ignatius. 1st Am. 20 stories. AN/dj. A27. $18.00

**CHESTERTON, G.K.** *George Bernard Shaw.* 1909. London. Lane. 1st Am. VG. B27. $45.00

**CHESTERTON, G.K.** *Orthodoxy.* (1944). Harold Shaw. 1st thus. fwd Philip Yancey. AN/dj. A27. $15.00

**CHESTERTON, G.K.** *Secret of Father Brown.* 1927. London. 1st. T9. $50.00

**CHESTNUT, James Jr.** *Relations of the States: Speach of Hon James Chestnut Jr...* 1860. Baltimore. John Murphy. 1st. 24p. wrp. M8. $125.00

**CHESTNUT, Mary M.** *Diary From Dixie.* 1950. Houghton Mifflin. 8vo. 572p. bl cloth. VG. S17. $12.50

**CHESTNUT, Mary.** *Mary Chestnut's Civil War.* 1981. Yale. 1st. NF/VG. A4. $65.00

**CHETWODE, Penelope.** *Two Middle-Aged Ladies in Andalusia.* 1963. London. John Murray. VG/G. O3. $18.00

**CHEUSE, Alan.** *Tennessee Waltz.* 1990. Salt Lake City. Gibbs Smith. 1st. inscr/dtd 1990. F. R14. $35.00

**CHEYNEY, Peter.** *Stars Are Dark.* 1943. London. Collins. 1st. VG/dj. M15. $45.00

**CHICKERING & GARDNER.** *Ballads & Songs of Southern Michigan.* 1939. Ann Arbor. 1st. F/NF. B2. $100.00

**CHIDLEY, J.J.** *Miniature Toastmaster.* ca 1840. London. Chidley. mini. 139p. dk bl glazed wrp. B24. $150.00

**CHILD, Julia.** *Mastering the Art of French Cooking.* 1967. Knopf. 14th. 684p. G+. P12. $10.00

**CHILD, Lydia Maria.** *American Frugal Housewife, Dedicated to Those...* 1842 (1835). 130p. G+. E6. $75.00

**CHILD, Lydia Maria.** *Appeal in Favor of That Class of Americans Called Africans.* 1833. Boston. Allen Ticknor. 1st. contemporary 3-quarter brn calf/marbled brd. M24. $1,250.00

**CHILD, Lydia Maria.** *Isaac T Hopper: A True Life.* 1881. Dodd Mead. new ed. 12mo. 493p. V3. $22.50

**CHILD, Theodore.** *Spanish-American Republics.* 1891. NY. Harper. 1st. 150 maps/ils. 444p. xl. F3. $25.00

**CHILD & YNTEMA.** *Julia Child & More Company.* 1979. Knopf. 1st. ils. VG/dj. B27. $45.00

**CHILD STUDY ASSOCIATION OF AM.** *Read Me More Stories.* (1951). NY. Crowell. 9th. 8vo. ils. 166p. VG/G. T5. $25.00

**CHILDRESS, Mark.** *Crazy in Alabama.* 1993. NY. Putnam. UP. sgn. F/wrp. M23. $100.00

**CHILDRESS, Mark.** *Tender.* 1990. Harmony. 1st. inscr. F/dj. B30. $40.00

**CHILDRESS, Mark.** *V for Victor.* 1989. Knopf. 1st. sgn. author's 2nd book. F/dj. R14. $50.00

**CHILDS, Henry E.** *Where Birders Go in Southern California: Locality Guide...* 1990. Audubon Soc. sgn. sbdg. VG. A28. $11.00

**CHILDS, Herbert.** *American Genius: Life of Ernest Orlando Lawrence.* 1968. NY. 1st. sgn pres. ils. 576p. VG/dj. B18. $195.00

**CHILDS, Marilyn C.** *Men Behind the Morgan Horse.* 1979. Leominster. sgn. F. O3. $395.00

**CHILDS, Marilyn C.** *Training Your Colt to Ride & Drive.* 1969. Van Nostrand. 1st/2nd prt. VG/dj. O3. $25.00

**CHILTON, John.** *Who's Who of Jazz: Storyville to Swing Street.* 1978. Time-Life. 1st Am. blk cloth. F/sans. A14. $21.00

**CHIN, Hoong F.** *Malaysian Flowers in Colour.* 1982 (1977). Kuala Lumpur. ils. 172p. VG/dj. B26. $20.00

**CHINDAHL, George L.** *History of the Circus in America.* 1959. Caxton. 279p. Vg/dj. S5. $60.00

CHINN, Walter Neal. *Autobiography of...His Relatives & Friends.* 1976. Fredricksburg. photos. 167p. VG. B10. $25.00

CHINWEIZU. *Energy Crisis.* 1978. NY. NOK Pub. 1st. inscr. F/dj. L3. $45.00

CHIPMAN, Donald E. *Nuno de Guzman & Province of Panuco in New Spain 1518-33.* 1967. Clark. 1st. ils/index. 322p. NF/sans. B19. $40.00

CHIPMAN, N. *Tragedy of Andersonville: Trial of Capt Henry Wirz...* 1911. self pub. lg 8vo. VG. E6. $125.00

CHIPPERFIELD, Jimmy. *My Wild Life.* 1976. Putnam. 1st Am. 219p. VG/dj. S5. $25.00

CHIRAGIAN, Achavir. *La Dette de Sang.* 1984. Bruxelles, Belgium. 2nd. lg 16mo. 335p. NF. M7. $27.50

CHIROL, Valentine. *Fifty Years in a Changing World.* 1928. Harcourt Brace. 351p. cloth. G+. Q2. $30.00

CHISHOLM, Ruari. *Ladysmith.* 1979. London. Osprey. 1st. 224p. VG/dj. M10. $15.00

CHITTENDEN, Hiram Martin. *American Fur Trade of the Far West.* 1935. Pr of Pioneers. 2 vol. ils/map. VG. J2. $450.00

CHITTENDEN, Hiram Martin. *History of American Fur Trade of Far West.* 1954. Academic. 2 vol. VG. J2. $195.00

CHOATE, Mark. *Nazis in the Pineywoods.* 1989. Best of E TX. 1st. sm 4to. 150p. F/dj. W2. $20.00

CHOLET, Bert. *All American Art of Cartooning.* 1944. Higgins Ink Co. 4th. VG/wrp. C9. $60.00

CHOMSKY, Carol. *Acquisition of Syntax in Children From 5 to 10.* 1969. MIT. 1st. 8vo. 126p. F/NF. C14. $22.00

CHORAO, Kay. *Baby's Story Book.* 1985. Dutton. 1st. 4to. 64p. NF/clip. C14. $20.00

CHORLEY, E. Clowes. *Men & Movements in the American Episcopal Church.* 1950. NY. Scribner. 501p. G/dj. H10. $45.00

CHORLEY, Richard. *Spatial Analysis in Geomorphology.* 1972. Harper Row. 1st. cloth. B27. $35.00

CHOTZINOFF, Samuel. *Toscanini: An Intimate Portrait.* 1956. Knopf. 148p. G. C5. $12.50

CHRISTENSEN, Erwin O. *Early American Wood Carving.* 1952. Cleveland/NY. World. 1st. ils. VG/dj. D2. $25.00

CHRISTENSEN, Erwin O. *Index of American Design.* 1950. Macmillan. 1st. 229p. cloth. VG. D2/F1. $35.00

CHRISTESON & CHRISTESON. *Wild Animal Stories.* 1935. Whitman. 1st. ils. 157p. F. B20. $85.00

CHRISTIAN, William A. *Moving Crucifixes in Modern Spain.* 1992. Princeton. 1st. ils. F/dj. A2. $25.00

CHRISTIANSEN, Reider T. *Folkways of Norway.* 1964. Chicago. VG/clip. B9. $15.00

CHRISTIE, Agatha. *Akhnaton.* 1973. Dodd Mead. 1st. F/VG. M19. $17.50

CHRISTIE, Agatha. *By the Pricking of My Thumbs.* 1968. London. Collins. 1st. F/dj. T10. $75.00

CHRISTIE, Agatha. *Caribbean Mystery.* 1964. Collins. 1st. NF/dj. M25. $35.00

CHRISTIE, Agatha. *Cat Among the Pigeons.* 1959. London. Collins Crime Club. 1st. VG+/clip. A14. $35.00

CHRISTIE, Agatha. *Clocks.* 1963. London. Collins Crime Club. 1st. VG/dj. A14. $28.00

CHRISTIE, Agatha. *Clocks.* 1964. Dodd Mead. 1st. F/NF. M19. $65.00

CHRISTIE, Agatha. *Come Tell Me How You Live.* 1946. London. Collins. 1st. F/VG. M15. $250.00

CHRISTIE, Agatha. *Curtain.* 1975. Collins Crime Club. 1st. NF/dj. M25. $25.00

CHRISTIE, Agatha. *Curtain.* 1975. Dodd Mead. 1st? 238p. F/NF. M7. $15.00

CHRISTIE, Agatha. *Elephants Can Remember.* 1972. Collins. 1st. F/NF. M25. $25.00

CHRISTIE, Agatha. *Elephants Can Remember.* 1972. Dodd Mead. 1st Am. F/clip. T10. $50.00

CHRISTIE, Agatha. *Endless Night.* 1967. Dodd Mead. 1st Am. VG/dj. M20. $37.00

CHRISTIE, Agatha. *Hound of Death & Other Stories.* 1933. London. Odhams. 1st. F/F. B4. $1,200.00

CHRISTIE, Agatha. *Hound of Death & Other Stories.* 1933. London. Odhams. 1st. NF/dj. M15. $450.00

CHRISTIE, Agatha. *Man in the Brown Suit.* 1924. Dodd Mead. 1st Am. G+. C15. $100.00

CHRISTIE, Agatha. *Mirror Crack'd From Side to Side.* 1962. London. Collins Crime Club. VG+/dj. A14. $87.50

CHRISTIE, Agatha. *Miss Marple's Final Cases.* 1979. Collins. 1st. VG/dj. P3. $18.00

CHRISTIE, Agatha. *Murder of Roger Ackroyd.* 1926. Dodd Mead. 4th. VG/dj. P3. $30.00

CHRISTIE, Agatha. *Mystery of the Blue Train.* 1928. Dodd Mead. 1st Am. 8vo. 306p. F/dj. J3. $1,500.00

CHRISTIE, Agatha. *Pocket Full of Rye.* 1957. Collins Crime Club. rpt. NF/VG. P3. $30.00

CHRISTIE, Agatha. *Postern of Fate.* 1973. Dodd Mead. 1st? 8vo. 310p. patterned paper brd/red cloth spine. F/NF. M7. $19.00

CHRISTIE, Agatha. *Sleeping Murder: Miss Marple's Last Case.* 1976. London. Collins. 1st. F/dj. T12. $40.00

CHRISTIE, Agatha. *Third Girl.* 1966. London. Collins. Crime Club. 1st. F/NF. N4. $50.00

CHRISTIE, Agatha. *Third Girl.* 1967. Dodd Mead. 1st. VG/dj. P3. $20.00

CHRISTIE, O.F. *Johnson on the Essayist: His Opinions on Men, Morals...* 1924. London. Grant Richards. VG. H13. $45.00

CHRISTOPHER, Matt. *Baseball Pals.* 1956. Little Brn. 1st. VG/G. P8. $25.00

CHRISTOPHER, Matt. *Look Who's Playing First Base.* 1971. Little Brn. 1st. VG/G. P8. $20.00

CHRISTY, E.V.A. *Cross-Saddle & Side-Saddle: Modern Riding...* nd (1932). Lippincott. 1st Am. G. O3. $65.00

CHRISTY, E.V.A. *Modern Side-Saddle Riding.* 1985. Mt Holly, NJ. ISSO. 1/600 (facs of 1907 revised). VG. O3. $25.00

CHUBB, Thomas C. *Dante & His World.* (1966). Little Brn. 1st. 831p. H10. $20.00

CHUIKOV, Vasili. *Fall of Berlin.* 1968. HRW. 1st. maps. 261p. VG/dj. S16. $25.00

CHURCH, Peggy Pond. *Familiar Journey.* (1936). Santa Fe. Writers Eds. 49 poems. NF/dj. A18. $20.00

CHURCH, Peggy Pond. *House at Otowi Bridge: Story of Edith Warner...* 1966. NM U. 3rd. 143p. VG/NF. B19. $25.00

CHURCH, Thomas. *History of the Great Indian War: Old French & Indian Wars...* ca 1850. NY. H Dayton. later prt. 360p. bstp cloth. B18. $45.00

CHURCH OF ENGLAND. *Book of Common Prayer.* 1664-1665. Cambridge. John Field. 2 parts in 1. 12mo. dbl-column text. contemporary bdg. K1. $350.00

CHURCHILL, Randolph S. *Winston S Churchill, Vol I: Youth 1874-1900.* 1966. Houghton Mifflin. 1st. sm 4to. 614p. NF/VG. W2. $1,200.00

CHURCHILL, Robert. *How to Shoot: Some Lessons in Science of Shot Gun Shooting.* 1932 (1930). London. 3rd. photos. VG. A17. $30.00

**CHURCHILL, Winston S.** *Address of the Right Honorable Winston Churchill...1943.* 1943. GPO. 1st. F/prt wrp. M24. $200.00

**CHURCHILL, Winston S.** *Blood, Sweat & Tears.* 1941. Putnam. 1st Am. 8vo. 462p. NF/G. W2. $95.00

**CHURCHILL, Winston S.** *Closing the Ring: Second World War.* 1951. Houghton Mifflin. BC. VG/dj. A28. $8.50

**CHURCHILL, Winston S.** *Crossing.* 1904. NY. Macmillan. 1st. 598p. G. G11. $8.00

**CHURCHILL, Winston S.** *Dwelling Place of Light.* 1917. NY. Macmillan. 1st. 462p. G. G11. $8.00

**CHURCHILL, Winston S.** *Far Country.* 1915. NY. Macmillan. 1st. 509p. G. G11. $8.00

**CHURCHILL, Winston S.** *History of the English-Speaking Peoples.* 1956. London. Cassell. 4 vol. 1st. 8vo. maps. Bayntum bdg. F. H5. $950.00

**CHURCHILL, Winston S.** *Lord Randolph Churchill.* 1906. NY. Macmillan. 2 vol. 1st Am. teg. gilt red cloth. NF. B20. $400.00

**CHURCHILL, Winston S.** *Mr Crewe's Career.* 1908. Macmillan. 1st. 498p. G. G11. $8.00

**CHURCHILL, Winston S.** *Painting As a Pastime.* 1950. NY. Whittlesey. 1st Am. 20 mc pl. gr cloth. dj. B14. $45.00

**CHURCHILL, Winston S.** *Second World War/Gathering Storm/Finest Hour...* 1948-1953. Houghton Mifflin. 6 vol. 1st Am. 8vo. gilt red cloth. NF. W2. $2,400.00

**CHUTE, Carolyn.** *Beans.* 1985. Chatto Windus. 1st. F/dj. A23. $45.00

**CHUTE, Carolyn.** *Letourneau's Used Auto Parts.* 1988. NY. Ticknor. 1st. NF/dj. H11. $10.00

**CHUTE, Marchette.** *Shakespeare of London.* 1949. Dutton. 397p. VG. C5. $12.50

**CHUTE, Marchette.** *Stories From Shakespeare.* 1956. Cleveland. World. 1/975. buckram. B18. $25.00

**CHUTKOW, Paul.** *Depardieu.* 1994. Knopf. 351p. VG/dj. C5. $12.50

**CHYET, Stanley F.** *Lopez of Newport.* 1970. Detroit. 1st. 246p. F/VG. B18. $19.50

**CIARDI, J.** *Selected Letters of John Ciardi.* 1991. U AR. 1st. VG/dj. M17. $25.00

**CINTRON, Lola.** *Goddess of the Bullring.* (1960). Bobbs Merrill. 1st. 349p. dj. F3. $25.00

**CIRKER & CIRKER.** *Dictionary of American Portraits.* 1968. NY. Dover. 1st/4th prt. catalogs 4000+ portraits. VG+/fair. F1. $100.00

**CISCO, Walter Brian.** *States Rights Gist: South Carolina General of Civil War.* 1991. Wht Mane Pub. 1st. F/dj. A14. $21.00

**CISNEROS, Sandra.** *Woman Hollering Creek.* 1991. NY. Random. 1st. sgn/dtd 1998. F/dj. R14. $75.00

**CITINO, David.** *Letter of Columbus, by...,* with Monotypes by Anthony Rice. 1990. Logan Elm. 1/30. sgns. 4to. 28 monotypes. sewn flax-paper wrp/case. B24. $1,200.00

**CLAFLIN, Mary B.** *Personal Recollections of John G Whittier.* 1893. NY. Crowell. 1st. 16mo. 95p. V3. $15.00

**CLAGETT, Marshall.** *Science of Mechanics in the Middle Ages.* 1959. Madison, WI. 1st. 711p. A13. $45.00

**CLAIBORNE, Herbert A.** *Comments on Virginia Brickwork Before 1800.* 1957. Walpole Soc. ils/photos. 47p. VG. B10. $50.00

**CLAIBORNE & FRANEY.** *Cooking With Craig Claiborne & Pierre Franey.* 1983. NY. Times. xl. VG/G. V4. $12.50

**CLAIR, Maxine.** *Rattlebone.* 1994. FSG. 1st. F/dj. H11. $30.00

**CLAIRBORNE, Craig.** *NY Times Cookbook.* 1961. Harper Row. G. A16. $9.00

**CLAIRE, William.** *Literature in Medicine. Vol 3: Physician As Writer.* 1984. Albany. 1st. 168p. A13. $30.00

**CLANCY, Tom.** *Cardinal of the Kremlin.* 1988. NY. Putnam. 1st. F/F. H11. $35.00

**CLANCY, Tom.** *Cardinal of the Kremlin.* 1988. Putnam. 1st. VG/VG. B3/L4. $20.00

**CLANCY, Tom.** *Clear & Present Danger.* 1989. NY. Putnam. 1st. NF/F. H11. $25.00

**CLANCY, Tom.** *Debt of Honor.* 1994. Putnam. 2nd. NF/NF. L4. $20.00

**CLANCY, Tom.** *Hunt for Red October.* 1984. Taiwan. piracy ed. 8vo. author's 1st book. VG/NF. S9. $125.00

**CLANCY, Tom.** *Patriot Games.* 1987. Putnam. 1st. NF/dj. L4. $35.00

**CLANCY, Tom.** *Red Storm Rising.* 1986. NY. Putnam. 1st. author's 2nd book. NF/F. H11. $50.00

**CLANCY, Tom.** *Red Storm Rising.* 1986. Putnam. F/NF. L4. $55.00

**CLANCY, Tom.** *Without Remorse.* 1993. Putnam. VG/G+. L4. $20.00

**CLAPESATTLE, Helen.** *Doctors Mayo.* nd (1941). Minneapolis. 2nd. 8vo. 822p. VG. C14. $10.00

**CLAPHAM & CONSTABLE.** *As Nature Intended: Pictorial History of the Nude...* 1982. Heinemann Quixote. 1st. VG/wrp. C9. $48.00

**CLAPP, Elizabeth Fisk.** *Maryland Gardens & Houses.* (1938). Garden Clubs of MD. 1st. photos/maps. 133p. G. B10. $25.00

**CLAPPERTON, Hugh.** *Journal of Second Expedition Into Interior of Africa...* 1829. London. rpr fld map. 355p. marbled edges/ep. leather/cloth. M4. $350.00

**CLARE, George.** *Last Waltz in Vienna: Rise & Destruction of a Family.* 1980. NY. VG/dj. M17. $15.00

**CLARE, Helen.** *Five Dolls & Their Friends.* 1968. Prentice Hall. 1st. 8vo. 120p. gold cloth. VG/G. T5. $55.00

**CLARE, John.** *Shepherd's Calendar.* 1964. OUP. 1st thus. 139p. gilt brn cloth. F/dj. F1. $40.00

**CLARIDGE, Richard.** *Tractatus Hierographicus; or, Treatise of Holy Scriptures.* 1878. NY. Stephen Wood. 2nd Am. 12mo. 171p. VG. V3. $35.00

**CLARK, A.R.** *Geodesy.* 1880. Oxford. Clarendon. ils. 356p. VG. B14. $75.00

**CLARK, Allen C.** *Greenleaf & Law in the Federal City.* 1901. WF Roberts. ils. 355p. VG. B10. $65.00

**CLARK, Alonzo.** *Lectures on Diseases of the Heart.* 1884. Birmingham Medical Lib. 1st. VG. E6. $45.00

**CLARK, Ann Nolan.** *In My Mother's House.* 1941. Viking. 1st. 4to. 1942 Caldecott Honor. 56p. pict dj. R5. $150.00

**CLARK, Ann Nolan.** *Looking-for-Something.* 1952. Viking. 1st. ils Leo Politi. aqua-gr cloth/pict label. mc dj. R5. $150.00

**CLARK, Ann Nolan.** *Secret of the Andes.* 1952. NY. Viking. 1st. sgn. 1953 Newbery Award. mc dj. R5. $300.00

**CLARK, Anna.** *Struggle for the Breeches: Gender & Making of British...* 1995. Berkeley. 1st. F/dj. V4. $17.50

**CLARK, Carol.** *Thomas Moran, Watercolors of the American West...* 1980. U TX. photos. F. J2. $145.00

**CLARK, Douglas.** *Performance.* 1985. London. Gollancz. 1st. F/dj. A14. $28.00

**CLARK, Elmer T.** *Small Sects of America.* 1937. Nashville. Cokesbury. 8vo. 311p. VG. H7. $20.00

**CLARK, George Rogers.** *Sketch of His Campaign in Illinois in 1778-1779...* 1907. Cincinnati. Robert Clarke. 101p. gilt bl cloth. VG. S17. $40.00

**CLARK, Hazel.** *Fibres to Fabrics: Techniques & Projects for Handspinners.* 1985. BT Batsford. 1st. sm 4to. 136p. NF/dj. S15. $15.00

**CLARK, J. Max.** *Colonial Days.* 1902. Denver, CO. Smith-Brooks Co Pub. VG. A19. $125.00

**CLARK, J. Reuben.** *Memorandum on the Monroe Doctrine.* 1930. GPO. 238p. prt sewn wrp. M11. $45.00

**CLARK, James L.** *Good Hunting.* 1966. Norman, OK. G/dj. A19. $35.00

**CLARK, Joseph I.C.** *Japan at First Hand: Her Islands, Their People...* 1918. Dodd Mead. 1st. 8vo. ils. brn brd. B11. $35.00

**CLARK, Kenneth.** *Animals & Men.* 1977. NY. 240p. dj. A17. $17.50

**CLARK, Kenneth.** *Another Part of the Wood: A Self-Portrait.* 1974. London. 1st. F/dj. T9. $18.00

**CLARK, Kenneth.** *Civilization: A Personal View.* 1970. Harper Row. 1st. photos. 359p. VG/dj. S14. $17.50

**CLARK, Kenneth.** *Leonardo Da Vinci.* 1988. NY. revised. VG/dj. M17. $20.00

**CLARK, Kenneth.** *Masterpieces of 50 Centuries: Metropolitan Museum of Art.* 1970. NY. 1st. dj. T9. $25.00

**CLARK, Kenneth.** *Romantic Rebellion.* (1973). Harper Row. 1st Am. 366p. 278p. F/dj. H1/M17. $20.00

**CLARK, Mary Higgins.** *Cry in the Night.* 1983. London. Collins. 1st. F/F. B3. $20.00

**CLARK, Mary Higgins.** *Stillwatch.* 1984. S&S. 1st. rem mk. NF/F. H11. $25.00

**CLARK, Mary Higgins.** *Stranger Is Watching.* 1977. S&S. 1st. F/dj. M15. $45.00

**CLARK, Paul.** *Pioneer Microbiologist of America.* 1961. Madison. 369p. A13. $50.00

**CLARK, Philip.** *Soviet Manned Space Program: Ils History of Men...* 1988. NY. Orion. 4to. ils. 192p. F/dj. K5. $30.00

**CLARK, Roland.** *Roland Clark's Etchings.* 1990. Derrydale. Lyon. 1/2500. ils. leatherette. aeg. F. A17. $30.00

**CLARK, Ronald.** *Man Who Broke Purple: Life of Colonel William F Friedman.* 1977. Boston. 1st. ils. 271p. NF/VG. E1. $25.00

**CLARK, Thomas D.** *Kentucky.* 1942. Farrar Rhinehart. Rivers of Am series. G. A19. $25.00

**CLARK, Tom.** *Who Is Sylvia?* 1979. Berkeley. Bl Wind. 1st. author's 1st book. F/VG clip. B3. $20.00

**CLARK, Virginia.** *Grand Canyon Country.* 1986. W Trail Pub. 8vo. 143p. stiff pict wrp. F7. $10.00

**CLARK, Walter H.** *Psychology of Religion.* 1963. Macmillan. 485p. G. B29. $8.50

**CLARK, Walter Van Tilburg.** *Strange Hunting.* 1985. Reno. 1st ltd. 1/115 (100 for sale). 22p. AN/sans. A18. $125.00

**CLARK, Walter Van Tilburg.** *Track of the Cat.* (1949). Random. 1st. 8vo. teal cloth. F/dj. R3. $100.00

**CLARK, Walter Van Tilburg.** *Watchful Gods & Other Stories.* (1950). NY. Random. 1st. 8vo. top edge red. white-lettered bl cloth. F/NF. R3. $100.00

**CLARK, William Bell.** *Naval Documents of the American Revolution.* 1964-1976. GPO. 7 vol. dk bl cloth. F to NF/sans. T11. $300.00

**CLARK & NEWCOMB.** *Georgie Clark: Thirty Years of River Running.* nd. SF. 4to. 165p. stiff mc wrp. F7. $75.00

**CLARKE, Anna.** *Cabin 3033.* 1986. Crime Club. 1st. F/dj. P3. $13.00

**CLARKE, Anna.** *Deathless & the Dead.* 1976. Collins Crime Club. 1st. NF/VG. P3. $25.00

**CLARKE, Arthur C.** *Exploration of Space.* (1951). NY. ils. VG/dj. M17. $15.00

**CLARKE, Arthur C.** *Fountains of Paradise.* 1988. Norwalk, CT. Easton. 1st thus. ils Bob Eggleton. aeg. leather. NF. A14. $32.00

**CLARKE, Arthur C.** *Imperial Earth.* 1976. HBJ. 1st. VG/dj. P3. $15.00

**CLARKE, Arthur C.** *Indian Ocean Adventure.* 1961. Harper Row. ils Mike Wilson. 107p. reinforced cloth. NF. D4. $25.00

**CLARKE, Arthur C.** *Profiles of the Future.* 1984. NY. Holt. 1st. F/F. H11. $30.00

**CLARKE, Arthur C.** *Report on Planet Three.* 1973 (1972). London. Gollancz. 2nd. 249p. xl. dj. K5. $12.00

**CLARKE, Arthur C.** *Songs of Distant Earth.* 1986. Ballantine. 1st. F/F. H11. $35.00

**CLARKE, Arthur C.** *Tales From the White Hart.* 1970. HBW. 1st hc. NF/VG. A14. $70.00

**CLARKE, Arthur C.** *Tales From the White Hart.* 1970. HBW. 1st. VG/dj. P3. $50.00

**CLARKE, Arthur C.** *Voices Across the Sea.* 1958. London. Muller. 1st. NF/dj. A14. $35.00

**CLARKE, Arthur C.** *2010: Odyssey Two.* 1982. Del Rey. 1st. NF/dj. P3. $30.00

**CLARKE, Arthur Miller.** *From Grove to Cove to Grove: Brief History...* 1962. np. photos. prt fabricoid. D11. $40.00

**CLARKE, Basil.** *Mental Disorder in Earlier Britain.* 1975. Cardiff, Wales. 1st. 335p. A13. $50.00

**CLARKE, C.** *Nepenthes of Borneo.* 1997. Koto Kinabalu. 122 mc photos. 207p. F. C12. $100.00

**CLARKE, Charles G.** *Early Film Making in Los Angeles.* 1976. Dawson's Book Shop. photos. 59p. pict brd/cloth spine. D11. $50.00

**CLARKE, Charles G.** *Professional Cinematography.* 1964. Hollywood. ils. F/sans. C9. $60.00

**CLARKE, Covington.** *Mystery Flight of Q2.* 1932. Reilly Lee. 1st. NF/dj. M19. $25.00

**CLARKE, Dwight L.** *Stephen Watts Kearny, Soldier of the West.* 1961. Norman, OK. 1st. 448p. cloth. dj. D11. $65.00

**CLARKE, Dwight L.** *William Tecumseh Sherman: Gold Rush Banker...* 1969. SF. CA Hist Soc. 1st. NF/dj. A14. $25.00

**CLARKE, J. Harold.** *Small Fruits for Your Home Garden.* 1958. Doubleday BC. 372p. VG/dj. A10. $15.00

**CLARKE, Peyton Neale.** *Old King William Homes & Families.* 1897. Morton. photos. 211p. VG. B10. $200.00

**CLARKE, Robert.** *Information Wanted With Reference to Early Settlers...* 1870. Robert Clarke. 11p. wrp. B18. $45.00

**CLARKE, Sue.** *Foxhunter Champions.* 1988. Birmingham. Lequs. 1st. VG/dj. O3. $22.00

**CLARKE & DEWHURST.** *Illustrated History of Brain Function.* 1972. Oxford. lg 4to. pres. 154p. VG/dj. G7. $150.00

**CLARKE & O'MALLEY.** *Human Brain & Spinal Cord, a Historical Study...* 1996. Norman. 2nd/revised. 1/750. 951p. dj. G7. $195.00

**CLARKSON, Ewan.** *Halic: Story of a Gray Seal.* 1970. Dutton. 1st. ils Richard Ciffari. G/dj. P2. $15.00

**CLARKSON, L.** *Buttercup's Visit to Little Stay At Home.* 1881. Dutton. revised/enlarged. sm 4to. 40p. ils paper brd. VG+. B20. $250.00

**CLARKSON, Thomas.** *Portraiture of Quakerism, Taken From View of Moral Education.* 1870. Indianapolis. Merrill Field. 8vo. 511p. VG. V3. $40.00

**CLARY, F.** *Color Bearer.* 1864. Am Tract. 16mo. 108p. VG. E6. $25.00

**CLAUDIANUS, Claudius.** *Claudiani Quae Exstant.* 1650. Leiden. Ex Officina Elzeviriana. 2 vol in 1. 1st thus. 16mo. xl. C6. $150.00

**CLAVELL, James.** *Children's Story.* 1981. Delacorte. 1st. F/VG. B3. $20.00

**CLAVELL, James.** *Children's Story.* 1981. Delacorte. 1st. NF/dj. S13. $15.00

**CLAVELL, James.** *Noble House.* 1981. Delacorte. 1st. F/NF. H11. $35.00

**CLAVELL, James.** *Whirlwind.* 1981. Delacorte. 1st. NF/dj. P3/T12. $35.00

**CLAVELL, James.** *Whirlwind.* 1986. Morrow. 1st. sm 4to. 1147p. F/dj. W2. $50.00

**CLAVELL, James.** *Whirlwind.* 1986. Morrow. 1st. 8vo. 1147p. VG/dj. W1. $16.00

**CLAYDEN, Arthur W.** *Cloud Studies.* 1925 (1905). London. John Murray. 2nd/revised. ils. 200p. G/dj. K5. $24.00

**CLAYSON, Alan.** *Ringo Starr.* 1991. London. Sidgwick Jackson. 282p. G/dj. C5. $15.00

**CLAYTON, H. Helm.** *Solar Activity & Long-Period Weather Changes.* 1926. Smithsonian. lg 8vo. xl. K5. $15.00

**CLEARY, Beverly.** *Dr Mr Henshaw.* 1983. Morrow. 1st. ils/sgn Zelinsky. 1983 Newberry Honor. 134p. NF/dj. T5. $55.00

**CLEARY, Beverly.** *Ramona Forever.* 1984. Morrow. 1st. 8vo. 182p. orange brd/cloth spine. VG/dj. T5. $25.00

**CLEARY, Beverly.** *Ramona Quimby, Age 8.* 1981. Morrow. 1st. ils Alan Tiegreen. 190p. NF/VG. T5. $28.00

**CLEATOR, P.E.** *Rockets Through Space: Dawn of Interplanatary Travel.* 1936. NY. S&S. 1st. xl. tattered dj. K5. $125.00

**CLEAVER, Eldridge.** *Eldridge Cleaver.* 1969. Ramparts/Random. 1st. F/dj. A24. $40.00

**CLEAVER & CLEAVER.** *Hazel Rye.* 1983. Lippincott. 1st. F/dj. V4. $20.00

**CLEAVES, F.** *Old Tippecanoe: William Henry Harrison & His Time.* 1986. Norwalk. Easton. ils/maps. 422p. gilt leather. M4. $35.00

**CLELAND, Charles E.** *Prehistoric Animal Ecology & Ethnozoology in Great Lakes...* 1966. U MI. 294p. VG. S15. $12.00

**CLELAND, Robert Glass.** *Cattle on a Thousand Hills: Southern California 1850-70.* 1941. Huntington Lib. 1st. VG. O4. $40.00

**CLELAND, Robert Glass.** *Irvine Ranch of Orange County.* 1952. San Marino, CA. Huntington Lib. 1st. VG/sans. O4. $25.00

**CLELAND, Robert Glass.** *Mormon Chronicle: Diaries of John D Lee: 1848-1876.* 1955. Huntington Lib. VG. F7. $155.00

**CLEMENS, Dale P.** *Fiberglass Rod Making.* 1976. Winchester. 4th. 189p. F/dj. A17. $15.00

**CLEMENS, Samuel L.** *Adventures of Huckleberry Finn.* 1885. NY. Chas Webster. 1st/2nd prt (3 text changes). gilt gr cloth. M24. $600.00

**CLEMENS, Samuel L.** *Adventures of Huckleberry Finn.* 1948. Grosset Dunlap. 8vo. ils Donald McKay. 373p. VG. W2. $80.00

**CLEMENS, Samuel L.** *Adventures of Tom Sawyer.* 1936. NY. Heritage Rpts. ils Norman Rockwell. 284p. NF. W2. $200.00

**CLEMENS, Samuel L.** *American Claimant.* 1892. NY. 1st. ils. 227p. xl on rear ep only. VG. B18. $95.00

**CLEMENS, Samuel L.** *Eve's Diary.* 1906. London/NY. 1st. ils Lester Ralph. 109p. pict cloth. VG. B18. $95.00

**CLEMENS, Samuel L.** *Extract From Captain Stormfield's Visit to Heaven.* 1909. Harper. 1st. red pict cloth. M24. $85.00

**CLEMENS, Samuel L.** *Gilded Age.* 1873. Hartford/Cincinnati. Am Pub. 1st (all early states present). gilt blk cloth. M24. $1,500.00

**CLEMENS, Samuel L.** *Gilded Age: Tale of Today, Vol I.* 1901. Harper. ne. inscr/sgn. 8vo. 350p. VG. W2. $275.00

**CLEMENS, Samuel L.** *How to Tell a Story & Other Essays.* 1897. NY. Harper. 1st. gilt red decor cloth. F/fragment dj. M24. $1,250.00

**CLEMENS, Samuel L.** *Jumping Frog. In English, Then in French, Then Clawed Back.* 1986. Evanston, IL. mini. 1/225. ftspc Robert Wahlgren. gilt gr cloth. B24. $125.00

**CLEMENS, Samuel L.** *Life on the Mississippi.* 1883. Boston. Osgood. 1st/2nd issue (no ils on p441). 624p. VG. H7. $225.00

**CLEMENS, Samuel L.** *Life on the Mississippi.* 1883. Boston. Osgood. 1st/2nd state. gilt pict brn cloth. F. M24. $375.00

**CLEMENS, Samuel L.** *Luck, by Mark Twain.* 1984. Evanston, IL. mini. 1/199. ils RJ Wahlgren. 50p. teg. gold cloth brd. B24. $95.00

**CLEMENS, Samuel L.** *Man That Corrupted Hadleyburg.* 1900. London. Chatto Windus. 1st Eng. gilt yel-orange pict cloth. M24. $200.00

**CLEMENS, Samuel L.** *Mark Twain Compliments the President's Wife.* 1984. Bromer. mini. 1/50 (200 total). hand colored. Blumenthal bdg. B24. $350.00

**CLEMENS, Samuel L.** *Mark Twain in Nevada.* 1927. NV Branch Am Assn U Women. 1st separate. VG/wrp. M24. $75.00

**CLEMENS, Samuel L.** *Mark Twain on Simplified Spelling.* 1906. NY. Simplified Spelling Brd. 1st/2nd state (broken type). M24. $450.00

**CLEMENS, Samuel L.** *Mark Twain's (Burlesque) Autobiography & First Romance.* 1871. NY. Sheldon. 1st/1st state. prt wrp. M24. $225.00

**CLEMENS, Samuel L.** *Mark Twain's Autobiography.* 1924. Harper. 2 vol. 1st. teg. gilt bl cloth. F/NF. M24. $250.00

**CLEMENS, Samuel L.** *Mark Twain's Notebook.* 1935. NY. Harper. 1st/1st prt. edit AB Paine. gilt bl cloth. F/dj. M24. $200.00

**CLEMENS, Samuel L.** *Mark Twain's Speeches.* 1910. NY. Harper. 1st/1st state. gilt red cloth. F. M24. $150.00

**CLEMENS, Samuel L.** *Mark Twain-Howells Letters.* 1960. Cambridge. 2 vol. 1st. blk cloth. F/NF. M24. $150.00

**CLEMENS, Samuel L.** *Merry Tales.* 1892. NY. Webster. 1st/1st state. gilt olive cloth. NF. M24. $150.00

**CLEMENS, Samuel L.** *New War-Scare.* 1981. Santa Barbara. Neville. 1/100. edit James Pepper. ils TW Williams. AN. R3. $90.00

**CLEMENS, Samuel L.** *Prince & the Pauper.* 1906. Harper. inscr/sgn. 8vo. 315p. G. W2. $1,800.00

**CLEMENS, Samuel L.** *Prince & the Pauper.* 1937. Winston. 1st thus. ils. gilt red cloth. VG. M5. $28.00

**CLEMENS, Samuel L.** *Pudd'nhead Wilson & Those Extraordinary Twins.* 1899. Harper. 8vo. 324p. NF. W2. $300.00

**CLEMENS, Samuel L.** *Report From Paradise.* 1952. Harper. 8vo. ils Chas Locke. bl brd/cream cloth. NF/dj. R3. $40.00

**CLEMENS, Samuel L.** *Roughing It.* 1892. Hartford, CT. Am Pub Co. early. 591p. cloth. VG. M8. $45.00

**CLEMENS, Samuel L.** *Tom Sawyer Detective & Other Stories.* 1924. Grosset Dunlap. ne. sm 8vo. 217p. VG/dj. W2. $45.00

**CLEMENS, Samuel L.** *Tom Sawyer.* 1946. Grosset Dunlap. VG/G. L4. $35.00

**CLEMENS, Samuel L.** *Tragedy of Pudd'nhead Wilson: And the Comedy...* 1894. Hartford. Am Pub. 1st/earliest state (sheets bulking...). NF. Q1. $600.00

**CLEMENS, Samuel L.** *Tramp Abroad.* 1880. Hartford. Am Pub. 1st/early issue. 328 ils. brn cloth. VG. A24. $500.00

**CLEMENS, Samuel L.** *1601; or, Conversation at Social Fireside...* 1962. Chicago. mini. 1/100 (400 total). aeg. gilt red leather. F. B24. $225.00

**CLEMENS, Virginia Phelps.** *Horse in Your Backyard.* 1991. NY. Prentice Hall. 1st. VG/dj. O3. $25.00

**CLEMENT, Aeron.** *Cold Moons.* 1989. Delacorte. 1st Am. F/dj. T10. $35.00

**CLEMENT, J.** *Noble Deeds of American Woman.* 1852. Buffalo. Derby. later prt. 480p. bstp cloth. B18. $25.00

**CLEMENT, Maud Carter.** *History of Pittsylvania County, Virginia.* 1929. JP Bell. 1st. ils/maps. 340p. VG. B10. $125.00

**CLEMENT, Maude Carter.** *Frontiers Along the Upper Roanoke River, 1740-76.* (1964). JP Bell. ils/map. 77p. VG. B10. $35.00

**CLEMENTS, Frederic E.** *Dynamics of Vegetation...* 1949. NY. Wilson. 1st. 296p. VG. B26/H10. $27.50

**CLEMENTS, James B.** *History of Irwin County.* 1932. Atlanta. 1st. ils. 539p. cloth. VG. M8. $250.00

**CLEMENTS, LOMASK & MACMILLAN.** *American Tradition: A Classic Guide to Regional Cooking.* 1989. London. Advanced Marketing Services. F/VG. V4. $25.00

**CLEMENTS, Mark A.** *Land of Nod.* 1995. DIF. 1st. inscr. F/NF. N4. $35.00

**CLEMONS, Harry.** *University of Virginia Library 1825-1950...* 1954. Charlottesville, VA. U VA Lib. 1st. ils. 229p. cloth. VG. M8. $35.00

**CLEMONS, V.M.** *History of Searcy County, Arkansas & Its People.* 1987. Marshall. 1st. 1/1000. photos/map ep. 252p. F. M4. $45.00

**CLENENTS & MORTON.** *Long Long Age.* 1985. Lilliput. mini. 1/55. hand-colored ils. teg. dk red morocco/sterling clasp. B24. $350.00

**CLEUGH, James.** *Secret Enemy: Story of a Disease (Syphilis).* 1954. NY. 1st. 273p. A13. $25.00

**CLEVELAND, Patience.** *Lion Is Busy.* 1963. NY. Atlantis. 39p. G. C5. $12.50

**CLEVELAND, Ray L.** *Ancient South Arabian Necropolis.* 1965. Johns Hopkins. ils/fld plan/index. cloth. VG/dj. D2. $50.00

**CLEVELAND, Reginald M.** *American Fledges Wings: History of Guggenheim Fund...* (1942). NY. 1/750. ils/map ep. 224p. dj. B18. $125.00

**CLIFFORD, Clark.** *Counsel to the President: A Memoir.* 1991. Random. 1st. 709p. NF/F. W2. $35.00

**CLIFFORD, James L.** *Dictionary Johnson: The Middle Years.* 1979. McGraw Hill. 1st. F/dj. H13. $85.00

**CLIFFORD, James L.** *Dr Campbell's Diary of a Visit to England in 1775.* 1947. Cambridge. 1st. intro SC Roberts. H13. $65.00

**CLIFFORD, James L.** *Hester Lynch Piozzi (Mrs Thrale).* 1941. OUP. 1st. 8 pl/portrait ftspc. H13. $125.00

**CLIFFORD, James L.** *Young Sam Johnson.* 1955. McGraw Hill. 1st. ils. dj. H13. $65.00

**CLIFFORD & GREENE.** *Samuel Johnson: Survey & Bibliography of Critical Studies.* 1970. Minneapolis, NM. 1st. F/F. H13. $95.00

**CLIFFORD & GREENE.** *Samuel Johnson: Survey & Bibliography of Critical Studies.* 1970. U MN. 349p. F/VG. A4. $85.00

**CLIFT, G.G.** *Remember the Raisin.* 1961. Frankfort. 1st. VG/G. B5. $40.00

**CLIFTON, Bud;** see Stacton, David.

**CLIFTON, E. Marston.** *Sketches of Some Booksellers of Time of Samuel Johnson.* 1972. Clifton. Kelley. 9 portrait pl. VG. H13. $35.00

**CLIFTON, Lucille.** *My Brother Fine With Me.* 1975. NY. 1st. ils Moneta Barnett. VG/dj. M17. $15.00

**CLIFTON, Oliver Lee.** *Campfire Boys at Silver Fox Farm.* 1924. Barse Hopkins. ils Chas Wrenn. xl. VG. P12. $12.00

**CLINE, C. Terry.** *Damon.* 1975. Putnam. 1st. author's 1st book. NF/NF. S18. $35.00

**CLINE, Howard.** *Mexico: Revolution to Evolution, 1940-1960.* 1962. London. Oxford. 1st. 375p. F3. $15.00

**CLINE, Platt.** *They Came to the Mountain: Story of Flagstaff's Beginnings.* 1986. Flagstaff. 4th. 8vo. blk cloth. 364p. F/dj. F7. $25.00

**CLINEBELL, Howard.** *Contemporary Growth Therapies.* 1981. Abingdon. 304p. VG/dj. B29. $9.00

**CLINGMAN, Thomas Lanier.** *Speech of Hon Thomas L Clingman, of NC...1860.* 1860. WA. Congressional Globe Office. 1st. 16mo. wrp. M8. $75.00

**CLINTON, George.** *Public Papers of George Clinton, 1st Governor or NY.* 1899. NY. 6 vol. fld maps. NY state seal on cover. B18. $125.00

**CLINTON-BADDELEY, V.C.** *No Case for the Police.* 1970. London. Gollancz. 1st. F/VG. M15. $45.00

**CLISE, Michael.** *Ophelia's World.* 1984. Clarkson Potter. 1st. ils Burns Marsha. F/VG+. P2. $50.00

**CLISSOLD, Stephen.** *Barbary Slaves.* 1977. London. Elek. ils/maps/pl. cloth. dj. Q2. $24.00

**CLOUD, B.** *Business of Newspapers on the Western Frontier.* 1992. NE U. 1st. 255p. F/dj. M4. $20.00

**CLOUGH & QUARMBY.** *Public Library Service for Ethnic Minorities...* 1978. London. Lib Assn. 1st. 8vo. 369p. F/dj. O10. $25.00

**CLOVER, Samuel Travers.** *On Special Assignment.* 1965. Argonaut. F. A19. $25.00

**CLOWES, Edith.** *Maksim Gorky: A Reference Guide.* 65037. 263p. F. A4. $35.00

**CLOWES, William.** *Hymns Ancient & Modern, for Use in Services of the Church.* ca 1895. London. Clowes. mini. India tissue. 862p. aeg. simulated ivory bdg. B24. $225.00

**CLUTE, Nelson.** *Our Ferns in Their Haunts.* 1901. NY. Stokes. 332p. VG. A10. $48.00

**CLUTTON-BROCK, T.H.** *Evolution of Parental Care.* 1991. Princeton. 352p. F. S15. $8.00

**CLYMER, Eleanor.** *Belinda's New Spring Hat.* 1969. Franklin Watts. 1st. 32p. VG. C14. $7.00

**CLYMER, Eleanor.** *House on the Mountain.* 1971. Dutton. 1st. ils Leo Carty. VG/dj. P2. $15.00

**CLYMER, Floyd.** *Album of Historical Steam Traction Engines & Threshing...* 1959. Bonanza. photos/drawings/charts. VG/dj. H6. $55.00

**CLYNE, Dougls.** *Anchorage on the Costa Brava.* 1957. Christopher Douglas. 1st. VG/dj. P2. $10.00

**CLYNES, Michael;** see Doherty, P.C.

**COALE, Samuel.** *Anthony Burgess.* 1981. NY. VG/dj. M17. $15.00

**COATES, B.J.** *Birds of Papua New Guinea.* 1985-1990. Queensland. Aderley. 2 vol. 493 mc photos/362 distribution maps. F/dj. C12. $285.00

**COATES, Christopher.** *Tropical Fish for a Private Aquarium.* 1933. NY. 1st. photos. 226p. G. A17. $15.00

**COATS, Alice M.** *Garden Shrubs & Their Histories.* 1965 (1964). NY. 1st Am. 416p. dj. B26. $35.00

**COATS, Peter.** *House & Garden Book of English Gardens.* 1988. Boston. 1st. dj. T9. $18.00

**COATSWORTH, Elizabeth.** *Alice-All-By-Herself.* 1937 (1937). Macmillan. 2nd. 181p. VG/torn. T5. $30.00

**COATSWORTH, Elizabeth.** *Bess & the Spinx.* 1967. Macmillan. stated 1st. xl. VG. B36. $15.00

**COATSWORTH, Elizabeth.** *Cat Who Went to Heaven.* 1958. Macmillan. 1st. ils Lynd Ward. rust-brn cloth. mc dj. R5. $125.00

**COATSWORTH, Elizabeth.** *Children Come Running.* 1960. Golden. 1st. NF/dj. S13. $10.00

**COATSWORTH, Elizabeth.** *Dog From Nowhere.* 1958. Row Peterson. 1st. ils Don Sibley. F/VG. P2. $25.00

**COATSWORTH, Elizabeth.** *Forgotten Island.* (1942). Grosset Dunlap. ils. 66p. G+. T5. $25.00

**COATSWORTH, Elizabeth.** *Pika & the Roses.* 1959. Pantheon. 1st. sq 8vo. tan pict brd. VG. T5. $15.00

**COBB, Belton.** *Like a Guilty Thing.* 1959. NY. British Book Centre. 1st Am. F/NF. B4. $75.00

**COBB, Betty Reynolds.** *Little Boy Black & Other Sketches.* 1926. Macon, GA. JW Burke. 1st. 172p. gray cloth. NF. B20. $75.00

**COBB, Edwin L.** *No Cease Fires: War on Poverty in Roanoke Valley.* (1984). Seven Locks. 176p. F/F. B10. $20.00

**COBB, Humphrey.** *Paths of Glory.* 1935. Viking. 1st. NF/VG. S13. $55.00

**COBB, Irvin S.** *Those Times & These.* 1917. Doran. 1st. VG+/dj. S13. $25.00

**COBB, Ty.** *My Life in Baseball: The True Record.* 1961. Doubleday. 1st. NF/dj. B4. $85.00

**COBB, Ty.** *My Life in Baseball: The True Record.* 1961. Doubleday. 1st. photos. VG+/dj. P8. $75.00

**COBB, William.** *Walk Through Fire.* 1992. NY. Morrow. 1st. F/dj. R14. $25.00

**COBB & JONES.** *Voices of the French Revolution.* 1988. Topsfield. dj. T9. $25.00

**COBBETT, James Paul.** *Ride of Eight Hundred Miles in France.* 1824. London. Cobbett. 8vo. w/4p pub list. R12. $100.00 ˉ

**COBBETT, William.** *Cobbett's Country Book.* 1975. Schocken. 216p. VG/dj. A10. $22.00

**COBDEN-SANDERSON, T.J.** *Ideal Book; or, Book Beautiful: A Tract of Calligraphy...* 1900. Hammersmith. Doves. 1st. 1/300. gilt limp vellum. F. M24. $750.00

**COBER, Alan E.** *Cober's Choice.* 1979. Dutton. 1st. ils. dj. B27. $45.00

**COBLENTZ, Stanton A.** *Demons, Witch Doctors & Modern Man.* 1965. NY. Yoseloff. 1st. 8vo. G/dj. A2. $12.00

**COBLENTZ, Stanton A.** *Long Road to Humanity.* 1959. NY. Yoseloff. 1st. 8vo. VG/dj. A2. $14.00

**COBLENTZ, Stanton A.** *Militant Dissenters.* 1970. S Brunswick. Barnes. 1st. 8vo. VG/dj. A2. $12.00

**COCHRAN, Doris M.** *Herpetology of Hispaniola.* 1941. Smithsonian. 387p. VG. S15. $40.00

**COCHRAN, R.** *Vance Randolph: An Ozark Life.* 1985. IL U. 1st. 284p. F/dj. M4. $25.00

**COCHRAN, William C.** *Western Reserve & the Fugitive Slave Law, a Prelude...* 1920. Cleveland. Western Reserve Hist Soc Pub #101. 235p. B18. $37.50

**COCHRANE, G.R.** *Flowers & Plants of Victoria & Tasmania.* 1980 (1968). Sydney. revised. photos. 176p. VG/dj. B26. $55.00

**COCKBURN, George.** *Robin Hood.* 1925. Winston. ils. 352p. VG. B36. $10.00

**COCKBURN, James.** *Review of General & Particular Causes...Disorders...Friends.* 1829. Phil. Philip Price. 1st. 12mo. 281p. ES. leather. G. V3. $25.00

**COCKBURN & CURRAN.** *Speeches of the Right Honorable John Philpot Curran...* 1808. Dublin. Stockdale & Sons. diced calf. M11. $650.00

**COCKERELL, Sydney.** *Some German Woodcuts of the Fifteenth Century.* 1897. Hammersmith. 1/225. 4to. 35 woodcuts. 14p. linen-backed bl brd. F. B24. $3,000.00

**COCKRANE, J.A.** *Dr Johnson's Printer: Life of Wm Strahan.* 1964. Cambridge. Harvard. 1st. VG/dj. H13. $85.00

**COCKRILL, W. Ross.** *Husbandry & Health of the Domestic Buffalo.* 1974. Rome. ils. 993p. VG/dj. S15. $15.00

**COCTEAU, Jean.** *Opium: Diary of a Cure.* 1957. London. Peter Owen Ltd. 1st. VG/dj. C9. $90.00

**COCTEAU, Jean.** *Paris Album.* 1956. London. WH Allen. 1st. ils. VG/dj. C9. $42.00

**CODRESCU, Andrei.** *Blood Counters.* 1995. NY. 1st. dj. T9. $10.00

**CODY, Liza.** *Rift.* 1988. London. Collins Crime Club. 1st. F/dj. M15. $45.00

**CODY, Robin.** *Ricochet River.* 1992. Knopf. 1st. sgn. F/dj. O11. $20.00

**CODY & INMAN.** *Great Salt Lake Trail.* 1966. Ross Haines. rpt. 1/1500. 219p. F/sans. B19. $25.00

**COE, George W.** *Frontier Fighter: Autobiography of George W Coe.* 1984. Lakeside Classic. 1st thus. edit Nunis. teg. brn cloth. F. T11. $25.00

**COE, Michael.** *Maya.* (1986). NY. Thames Hudson. 3rd. 190p. F3. $15.00

**COE, Michael.** *Mexico.* 1962. NY. Praeger. 1st. ils/maps. 245p. dj. F3. $25.00

**COE, Wesley R.** *Papers From the Harriman Alaska Expedition. XX: Nemerteans.* 1901. WA Acad Sci. 13 full-p pl. 84+26p. G/thick wrp. H7. $35.00

**COEL, Margaret.** *Dead End.* 1997. Mission Viejo. ASAP. 1st. 1/150. sgns. F/sans. M15. $50.00

**COELHO, George.** *Coping & Adaptation.* 1974. NY. Basic Books. 454p. bl cloth. VG/dj. G1. $35.00

**COETZEE, J.M.** *Age of Iron.* 1990. Random. 1st Am. NF/F. R14. $25.00

**COETZEE, J.M.** *From the Heart of the Country.* 1977. Harper Row. 1st. VG/G. B30. $25.00

**COETZEE, J.M.** *Life & Times of Michael K.* 1984. NY. Viking. 1st. F/NF. M23. $20.00

**COFFEY, Brian;** see Koontz, Dean R.

**COFFEY, Walter.** *Productive Sheep Husbandry.* 1918. Lippincott. 479p. VG. A10. $20.00

**COFFIN, Author B.** *Robinson Jeffers: Poet of Inumanism.* (1971). Madison. U WI. 1st. F/NF. A18. $25.00

**COFFIN, Charles C.** *Boys of '76.* 1876. Harper. 8vo. gilt bl cloth. VG. S17. $15.00

**COFFIN, Charles C.** *Drum-Beat of the Nation.* 1988. Harper. 8vo. 478p. bl cloth. VG. S17. $15.00

**COFFIN, Marian Cruger.** *Trees & Shrubs for Landscape Effects.* 1940. NY. photos. 169p. VG/dj. B26. $25.00

**COFFIN, William Sloane.** *Once to Every Man.* 1977. NY. Atheneum. 1st. NF/VG. R11. $25.00

**COFFIN & HOLDEN.** *Brick Architecture of the Colonial Period in MD & VA.* 1919. Architectural Book Pub. 118 pl. G. B10. $200.00

**COFFMAN, Ralph J.** *Coleridge's Library: Bibliography of Books...* 1987. 4to. 301p. F. A4. $85.00

**COHEN, Daniel.** *Hiram Bingham & the Dream of Gold.* (1984). NY. Evans. 1st. 182p. VG/dj. F3. $15.00

**COHEN, I.B.** *Science & Founding Fathers: Science in Political Thought...* 1995. NY. 1st. ils. 368p. F/dj. M4. $25.00

**COHEN, Isidor.** *Historical Sketches & Sidelights of Miami Florida.* 1925. Miami. private prt. revised. 12mo. 213p. gilt navy brd. B11. $50.00

**COHEN, Jon.** *Max Lakeman & the Beautiful Stranger.* 1990. NY. Warner. 1st. F/F. H11. $20.00

**COHEN, Leonard.** *Parasites of Heaven.* 1966. McClelland Stewart. 1st. NF/wrp. R14. $40.00

**COHEN, Leonard.** *Stranger Music.* 1993. NY. Pantheon. 1st. sgn. F/dj. Q1. $75.00

**COHEN, Michael.** *Pathless Way.* 1984. Madison. 1st. 408p. xl. VG/dj. A10. $20.00

**COHEN, Morton.** *Rudyard Kipling to Rider Haggard: Record of a Friendship.* 1965. London. Hutchinson. 1st. VG/dj. M10. $12.50

**COHEN, S.** *Images of the Spanish-American War, April-August.* 1898. Missoula. ils/photos. 293p. F. M4. $40.00

**COHEN, Stan.** *Historic Sites of West Virginia: A Pictorial Guide.* 1981. Pictorial Histories. 2nd. ils/maps. 240p. VG. B10. $10.00

**COHEN, Stan.** *Homestead & Warm Springs Valley of Virginia: Pict Heritage.* (1984). Pict Histories Pub. 4th. ils/maps. 96p. VG. B10. $6.00

**COHEN, Wilfred R.** *Wave Crest: Glass of CF Monroe.* 1987. Collector Books. 1st. sgn. 236p. gilt bl brd. F/plastic. H1. $125.00

**COHEN & ROSS.** *Handbook of Clinical Psychobiology & Pathology.* 1983. WA, DC. Hemisphere. 2 vol. cloth. G1. $65.00

**COHEN-DE RICCI.** *Guide de l'Amateur de Livres a Gravures du XVIII Siecle.* nd. rpt. 1/150. ils. 5000 entries. F. A4. $90.00

**COHN, Albert M.** *George Cruikshank: A Catalogue Raisonne...1806-1877.* 1996. Staten Is. Martino. rpt (1924). 1/150. 2114 entries. AN. F1. $75.00

**COHN, Art.** *Michael Todd's Around the World in 80 Days Almanac.* 1956. Random. 71p. VG. C5. $12.50

**COKE, Edward.** *Complete Copy-Holder; Being a Learned Discourse...* 1673-1909. London. M11. $500.00

**COKE, Edward.** *Fourth Part of the Institutes of Laws of England...* 1648. London. Prt by Flesher, Lee & Pakeman. contemporary calf. G. M11. $850.00

**COKE, Richard.** *Heart of the Middle East.* 1926. London. Butterworth. 8vo. ils/pl/maps. cloth. G. Q2. $36.50

**COLAM, Lance.** *Death Treasure of the Khmers.* 1939. Stanley Paul. 1st. ils. 256p. G. S14. $17.50

**COLBORNE, Robert.** *Plain English Dispensatory: Containing Natural History...* 1753. London. H Kent. 348+18p index+ES. recent 3-quarter calf. VG. G7. $250.00

**COLBY, George.** *Horseman's Friend.* 1866. Gettsyburg. Wible. 16mo. 30p. brd. fair. O3. $65.00

**COLBY & VAN DEN BERGHE.** *Ixil Country: A Plural Society in Highland Guatemala.* 1969. Berkeley. 1st. 218p. dj. F3. $25.00

**COLDEN, Cadwallader.** *History of the Five Indian Nations of Canada...* 1902. NY. New Amsterdam. 2 vol. 12mo. fld map. gray cloth. B20. $75.00

**COLE, Bill.** *John Coltrane.* 1976. Schirmer. 1st. F/NF. B2. $65.00

**COLE, Howard N.** *Heraldry in War.* 1950. Aldershot. Wellington. 3rd. NF/G. B9. $65.00

**COLE, Natalie Robinson.** *Children's Art From Deep Down Inside.* 1966. John Day. 1st. photos. NF/VG. S13. $20.00

**COLE, William.** *Cat-Hater's Handbook.* 1963. Dial. 1st. ils Tomi Ungerer. VG/dj. P2. $30.00

**COLE, William.** *Oh, What Nonsense.* 1966. Viking. 1st. 8vo. ils Tomi Ungerer. VG/G. B17. $10.00

**COLE & EDWARDS.** *Grand Slam: 13 Great Short Stories About Bridge.* 1975. Putnam. VG. S1. $12.00

**COLEGATE, Isabel.** *Shooting Party.* 1981. Viking. 1st. F/F. H11. $30.00

**COLEMAN, J. Winston Jr.** *Bibliography of Writings of J Winston Coleman Jr.* 1953. Lexington, KY. 1st. 19p. VG/wrp. M8. $75.00

**COLEMAN, Jane Candia.** *Doc Holliday's Woman.* 1995. NY. Warner. 1st. F/dj. T11. $30.00

**COLEMAN, Jim.** *Covering the World of Quarter Horses...Directory...* nd. Ft Worth. 4to. photos. 183p. VG. O3. $65.00

**COLEMAN, Jonathan.** *At Mother's Request: A True Story of Money, Murder...* 1985. Atheneum. VG/dj. A28. $12.50

**COLEMAN, Ray.** *Man Who Made the Beatles.* 1989. NY. McGraw Hill. 1st. VG/dj. B5. $20.00

**COLEMAN, W.** *Collection of Facts & Documents...* 1972 (1804). rpt. 238p. F. M4. $20.00

**COLERIDGE, Ernest Hartley.** *Life & Correspondence of John Duke Lord Coleridge...* 1904. Appleton. 2 vol. 1st Am. lg 8vo. gilt maroon cloth. B20. $75.00

**COLERIDGE, Henry Nelson.** *Six Months in the West Indies in 1825.* 1832. London. John Murray. 3rd. 12mo. fld map ftspc. half calf/marbled sides. F1. $125.00

**COLERIDGE, Samuel Taylor.** *Poetical Works of...Edited With Biographical Intro...* 1893. London. Macmillan. 8vo. 659p. 3-quarter brn morocco. VG+. B20. $90.00

**COLERIDGE, Samuel Taylor.** *Rime of the Ancient Mariner.* (1910). NY. Crowell. 1st Am. lg 4to. ils Pogany. blk cloth. R5. $500.00

**COLERIDGE, Samuel Taylor.** *Zapolya: Christmas Tale in Two Parts...* 1817. London. Prt for Rest Fenner. 1st. 8vo. 128p. later bdg. F. H5. $1,100.00

**COLES, Manning.** *Night Train to Paris.* 1952. Crime Club. 1st Am. VG/G-. G8. $20.00

**COLES, Manning.** *Nothing to Declare.* 1960. Crime Club. 1st Am. VG/G. G8. $30.00

**COLFER, Enid.** *Cucumber: Story of a Siamese Cat.* 1961. Thomas Nelson. 1st. tall 8vo. 98p. F/NF clip. C14. $17.00

**COLINVAUX, Paul.** *Why Big Fierce Animals Are Rare.* 1978. Princeton. 256p. VG/dj. S15. $12.50

**COLLARD, Cyril.** *Savage Nights.* 1993. London. Rodarmor. 1st. dj. T9. $10.00

**COLLENUCCIO, Pandolfo.** *Dell'Istoria del Regno di Napoli...* 1771. Naples. Giovanni Gravier. 3 vol. 4to. contemporary vellum. K1. $300.00

**COLLES, H.C.** *Grove's Dictionary of Music & Musicians.* 1944. NY. Macmillan. 6 vol. 3rd. gilt gr cloth. VG. F1. $150.00

**COLLIDGE, Louis A.** *Ulysses S Grant, Vol I.* 1924. Houghton Mifflin. 3rd. 12mo. VG. A2. $10.00

**COLLIER, Andrew.** *Socialist Reasoning: An Inquiry Into Political Philosophy...* 1990. London. Pluto. F/dj. V4. $20.00

**COLLIER, George A.** *Socialists of Rural Andalusia...* 1987. Stanford. 1st. 8vo. F/dj. A2. $25.00

**COLLIER, Jane.** *Essay on Art of Ingeniously Tormenting; With Proper Rules...* 1753. London. A Millar. 1st. 8vo. 234p. H13. $285.00

**COLLIER, Richard.** *House Called Memory.* 1961. Dutton. 1st Am. 8vo. 190p. NF/dj. W2. $25.00

**COLLIN & COLLIN.** *Pleasures of Seafood...* 1976. HRW. 1st. VG/dj. V4. $15.00

**COLLINGS, Ellsworth.** *101 Ranch.* 1938. Norman. 2nd. ils. 250p. VG/dj. B5. $45.00

**COLLINS, A.S.** *Authorship in the Days of Johnson.* 1929. Doubleday. 1st. blk cloth. VG. H13. $85.00

**COLLINS, Carvel.** *Erskine Caldwell's Men & Women.* nd. Boston. 1st. VG/dj. M21. $40.00

**COLLINS, Dean.** *Our Garden Book.* 1941. Binfords Mort. 1st. ils. 190p. G. S14. $17.50

**COLLINS, G.N.** *Mango in Porto Rico.* 1903. WA, DC. photos. 36p. wrp. B26. $30.00

**COLLINS, H.B.** *Aleutian Islands: Their People & Natural History.* Feb 1945. Smithsonian. ils. 131p. NF/wrp. M12. $25.00

**COLLINS, H.B.** *Prehistoric Art of the Alaskan Eskimo.* 1929. WA. 52p. VG. M4. $18.00

**COLLINS, Herbert Ridgeway.** *Presidents on Wheels: Complete Collection of Carriages...* nd. Bonanza. ils. VG/dj. M17. $20.00

**COLLINS, Jackie.** *Rock Star.* 1988. S&S. 1st. sm 4to. 511p. F/dj. W2. $35.00

**COLLINS, Joan.** *Past Imperfect: An Autobiography.* 1984. S&S. 8vo. 358p. F. W2. $20.00

**COLLINS, John S.** *My Experiences in the West.* 1970. Lakeside Classic. ils. 252p. NF. M10. $20.00

**COLLINS, John S.** *My Experiences in the West.* 1970. Lakeside Classic. 1st thus. teg. dk brn cloth. F/sans. T11. $25.00

**COLLINS, John.** *Two Forgers.* 1992. New Castle. 1st/1st prt. gilt cloth. AN/dj. M24. $50.00

**COLLINS, Nancy A.** *Dark Love.* nd. BC. VG/dj. P3. $10.00

**COLLINS, Nancy.** *Midnight Blue: Sonia Blue Collection.* 1995. Stone Mountain, GA. White Wolf. VG/dj. M21. $20.00

**COLLINS, Philip.** *Smokerama: Classic Tobacco Accoutrments.* 1992. Chronicle. 1st. obl 8vo. 124p. VG/dj. S14. $12.00

**COLLINS, Stephen.** *Eye Contact.* 1994. Bantam. 1st. author's 1st book. NF/dj. S18. $30.00

**COLLINS & DAVIS.** *Medieval Book of Seasons.* 1992. NY. 1st Am. ils. VG/dj. M17. $20.00

**COLLINS & LA PIERRE.** *O Jerusalem!* 1972. S&S. 1st. 8vo. ils/map ep. cloth. NF/dj. W1. $18.00

**COLLINS & LEE.** *Black Portrait of an African Journey.* 1971. Grand Rapids. Eerdmans. 1st. sgn. NF. w/ephemera. B2. $125.00

**COLLIS, John Stewart.** *Christopher Columbus.* 1977. NY. VG/dj. M17. $20.00

**COLLIS, Louise.** *Soldier in Paradise: Life of Capt John Stedman, 1744-1797.* 1966. Harcourt Brace. 1st Am. 231p. VG+. F3. $20.00

**COLLODI, Carlo.** *Adventures of Pinocchio.* nd. NY. Macmillan. 3rd. ils Attilio Mussino. trans from Italian. 404p. VG. D1. $225.00

**COLLODI, Carlo.** *Pinocchio's Adventures in Wonderland.* 1898. Boston. John Marsh. 1st. 12mo. gilt bl cloth/floral brd. M5. $275.00

**COLLODI, Carlo.** *Pinocchio: Adventures of a Marionette.* 1904. Ginn. ils Chas Copeland/trans WS Cramp. VG/pict label. M17. $20.00

**COLLODI, Carlo.** *Pinocchio: Story of a Puppet.* ca 1920s (1914). Lippincott. 1st/9th prt. ils Maria Kirk. red cloth. G. B27. $45.00

**COLLODI, Carlo.** *Pinocchio: Story of a Puppet.* April 1919. Lippincott. 4th. ils. VG. B36. $22.00

**COLLODI, Carlo.** *Story of a Puppet; or, Adventures of Pinocchio.* 1892. London. Cassell. 1st Am. sm 8vo. 232p. ils. off-wht cloth. F/clamshell case. H5. $5,000.00

**COLLODI, Carlo.** *Walt Disney's Version of Pinocchio.* 1939. NY. Random. 1st. VG/sans. C9. $150.00

**COLMAN, Andrew M.** *Companion Encyclopedia of Psychology.* 1994. London. Routledge. 2 vol. prt bl brd. VG. G1. $125.00

**COLMER, Michael.** *Whalebone to See Through: History of Body Packaging...* 1980. AS Barnes. 1st Am. VG/wrp. C9. $60.00

**COLOPHON.** *Annual of Bookmaking.* 1938. NY. Colophon. 4to. ils/pl/photos. unp (400p). beige cloth. K1. $60.00

**COLOR LIBRARY BOOKS, LTD.** *Colorado River, Picture Book to Remember Her By.* 1985. Crescent. 4to. 64p. wht cloth. VG/dj. F7. $7.50

**COLTER, Cyrus.** *Hippodrome.* 1973. Chicago. Swallow. 1st. xl. VG/clip. B9. $20.00

**COLTON, Harold S.** *Black Sand, Prehistory in Northern Arizona.* 1960. U NM. 1st. 8vo. ils. 132p. cloth. F. F7. $60.00

**COLTON, Matthew.** *Frank Armstrong, Captain of the Nine.* 1913. Hurst. 1st. VG. P8. $25.00

**COLUM, Padraic.** *Adventures of Odysseus & the Tale of Troy.* 1918. Macmillan. 1st. 8vo. ils Willy Pogany. 254p. rust cloth. VG. T5. $55.00

**COLUM, Padraic.** *Balloon: A Comedy in Four Acts.* 1929. NY. 1st. VG. M17. $15.00

**COLUM, Padraic.** *Big Tree of Bunlahy.* 1933. NY. ils Jack Yeats. 166p. VG. B18. $37.50

**COLUM, Padraic.** *Frenzied Prince, Being Heroic Stories of Ancient Ireland.* 1943. McKay. 1st. ils Willy Pogany. NF/VG. C15. $65.00

**COLUM, Padraic.** *Golden Fleece & Heroes Who Lived Before Achilles.* 1936 (1921). Macmillan. 8vo. ils Willy Pogany. 1922 Newbery Honor. VG-. t5. $35.00

**COLUM, Padraic.** *Voyager: Legends & History of Atlantic Discovery.* 1925. Macmillan. 1st. ils Winfred Jones. 188p. VG/worn. D1. $50.00

**COLUMBUS, Christopher.** *La Carta de Colon.* 1958. Madrid. Graficas Yagues. ils facs. 152p. pseudo-morocco brn cloth. K1. $100.00

**COLVER, Anne.** *Bread-and-Butter Journey.* 1970. HRW. 1st. 8vo. 101p. tan pict brd. NF/VG. T5. $35.00

**COLWIN, Laurie.** *Big Storm Knocked It Over.* 1993. Harper. 1st. NF/dj. S13. $10.00

**COMBE, George.** *Constitution of Man Considered in Relation Eternal Objects.* 1829. Boston. Carter Hendee. 1st Am. 12mo. rb. NF. G1. $85.00

**COMBIER, Cyprien.** *Voyage au Golfe de Californie.* (1864). Paris. Bertrand. fld map of Sonora. 544p. modern cloth/orig wrp bdg in. D11. $250.00

**COMBS, Harry.** *Brules.* 1994. Delacorte. 1st. F/dj. T11. $25.00

**COMBS, Loula Long.** *My Revelation.* 1947. Lee's Summit. Longview. sgn pres. VG/fair. O3. $225.00

**COMETTI, Elizabeth.** *American Journals of Lt John Enys.* 1976. Syracuse. 1st. 377p. VG/dj. S16. $26.50

**COMFORT, Alex.** *Tetarch.* 1981. Wildwood House. 1st. NF/VG. P3. $25.00

**COMFORT, Will Lexington.** *Last Ditch.* 1916. NY. Doran. 1st. 360p. G. G11. $10.00

**COMINI, Alessandra.** *Fantastic Art of Vienna.* 1978. Knopf. 40 pl+31p. gilt maroon cloth. F/NF. F1. $45.00

**COMMAGER, Henry S.** *Second St Nicholas Anthology.* 1950. Random. 1st. 8vo. 586p. gilt gr/red brd. NF. C14. $17.00

**COMMAGER, Henry S.** *Spirit of 'Seventy-Six.* 1958. Bobbs Merrill. 2 vol. 1st. F/dj. T11. $40.00

**COMOR, Andri-Paul.** *La Legion Etrangere.* 1992. Paris. Presses Universitaires de France. 126p. F. M7. $24.00

COMPTON, William David. *Where No Man Has Gone Before: A History...* 1989. NASA. 415p. G/wrp. K5. $40.00

COMPTON-BURNETT, I. *Manservant & Maidservant.* 1947. London. Gollancz. 1st. 243p. VG. M10. $25.00

COMSTOCK, Elizabeth L. *Life & Letters & Elizabeth Comstock.* 1895. London. Headley. 12mo. 511p. xl. V3. $15.00

COMSTOCK, George F. *Let Us Reason Together.* 186?. np. 1st. wrp. M8. $85.00

CONANT, Roger. *Mercer's Belles: Journal of a Reporter.* 1960. U WA. 1st. 8vo. 190p. F/dj. B20. $45.00

CONARELLI DELLA ROVERE. *La Philis de Sciro...* 1707. Bruxelles. Antoine Claudinot. 2 vol in 1. 12mo. contemporary bdg. K1. $175.00

CONAWAY, James. *Memphis Afternoons.* 1993. Houghton Mifflin. 1st. sgn. VG/dj. B30. $35.00

CONCOLORCORVO. *El Lazarillo: A Guide for Inexperienced Travelers...* 1965. Bloomington. IU. 1st Eng trans. unbound proof/wrp/dj. F3. $35.00

CONDON, George E. *Cleveland: Prodigy of the Western Reserve.* 1979. Tulsa, OK. ils. 240p+68p business biographies. VG/dj. B18. $30.00

CONDON, John F. *Jafsie Tells All!* (1926). NY. Jonathan Lee. 238p. lacks ffe. G. B18. $37.50

CONDON, Richard. *Infinity of Mirrors.* 1964. Random. 1st. F/NF. H11. $30.00

CONDON, Richard. *Prizzi's Family.* 1986. Putnam. 1st. F/NF. T12. $20.00

CONDON, Richard. *Prizzi's Honor.* 1982. NY. CMG. 1st. NF/clip. A14. $25.00

CONDON & GEHMAN. *Eddie Condon's Treasury of Jazz.* 1956. Dial. 1st. VG/dj. B2. $35.00

CONE & SNYDER. *Mastering Microwave Cooking.* 1986. S&S. 1st. VG/dj. V4. $12.50

CONE & SNYDER. *Microwave Entertaining.* 1989. S&S. 1st. photos. 319p. VG/dj. S14. $12.00

CONGDON, H.W. *Old Vermont Houses.* 1940. Brattleboro. 1st. 125 photos. 190p. VG/dj. B5. $30.00

CONGRESSIONAL CLUB. *Congressional Club Cookbook.* 1970. 8th. 606p. VG. E6. $18.00

CONGREVE, William. *Comedies.* 1895. Chicago. Stone Kimball. 2 vol. Eng Classics series. teg. tan cloth. F. F1. $75.00

CONGREVE, William. *Details of the Rocket System...* 1970. Ottawa. Mus Rstr Service. new ed. 1/850. leather. VG. K5. $75.00

CONKLIN, Edmund S. *Principles of Abnormal Psychology.* 1927. Holt. 457p. VG/tattered. G1. $28.50

CONKLIN, John E. *Art Crime.* 1994. Westport, CT. VG/dj. M17. $12.50

CONKLING, Margaret C. *Memoirs of the Mother & Wife of Washington.* 1851. Auburn. new/revised/enlarged. 248p. G. B18. $22.50

CONLEY & SORENSEN. *Staggering Steeple: Story of Alcoholism & Churches.* 1971. Pilgrim Pr. 1st. 8vo. VG/dj. A2. $16.00

CONLIN, Mary Lou. *Simon Perkins of the Western Reserve.* 1968. Cleveland. Western Reserve Hist Soc. 215p. VG/dj. B18. $15.00

CONNAUGHTON, Shane. *Run of the Country.* 1992. St Martin. 1st. F/dj. M23. $25.00

CONNELL, Evan S. *Alchymist's Journal.* 1991. Northpoint. 1st. F/dj. R14. $25.00

CONNELL, Evan S. *Mrs Bridge.* 1959. Viking. 1st. F/NF. B4. $450.00

CONNELLEY, William E. *Collections of the Kansas State Historical Society...* 1918. Topeka, KS. 896p. F/case. E1. $150.00

CONNELLEY, William E. *Doniphan's Expedition & Conquest of New Mexico & California.* 1907. Topeka, KS. 1st. ils/fld maps. 670p. E1. $200.00

CONNELLEY, William E. *War With Mexico, 1846-1847; Doniphan's Expedition...* 1907. Topeka. self pub. ils/2 fld maps. 670p. gilt cloth. D11. $150.00

CONNELLY, Marc. *Souvenir From Qam.* 1965. Holt. 1st. F/F. H11. $30.00

CONNELLY, Michael. *Black Echo.* 1992. Little Brn. 1st. sgn. author's 1st novel. F/dj. T2. $100.00

CONNELLY, Michael. *Black Ice.* 1993. Little Brn. 1st. F/dj. N4. $50.00

CONNELLY, Michael. *Blood Work.* 1997. Tucson. McMillan. 1st. 1/300. sgn. F/dj/case. M15. $200.00

CONNELLY, Michael. *Blood Work.* 1998. Little Brn. 1st. AN/dj. S18. $40.00

CONNELLY, Michael. *Last Coyote.* 1995. little Brn. 1st. sgn. F/dj. M15. $60.00

CONNELLY, Michael. *Trunk Music.* 1997. Little Brn. 1st. sgn. AN/dj. S18. $46.00

CONNELLY, Michael. *Trunk Music.* 1997. Little Brn. 1st. sgn. VG/dj. G8. $20.00

CONNER, Daniel Ellis. *Joseph Reddeford Walker & Arizona Adventure.* 1956. Norman. 1st. ils. 364p. VG/dj. B18. $27.50

CONNER & STANNARD. *Comeback.* 1987. St Martin. 1st. photos. 239p. VG/dj. S14. $9.00

CONNETT, Eugene V. *Duck Decoys...Make Them...Paint Them...Rig Them.* 1953. NY. 3rd. 116p. ils. dj. A17. $45.00

CONNOLD, Edward T. *British Vegetable Galls: Introduction to Their Study.* 1902. NY. Dutton. ils/index. 312p. xl. G. H10. $95.00

CONNOLLY, Cyril. *Condemned Playground.* 1946. Macmillan. 1st. gilt rust cloth. F/dj. M24. $100.00

CONNOLLY, Cyril. *Modern Movement: 100 Key Books From England...1880-1950.* 1965. London. Hamish Hamilton. 1st. silvered bl brd. F/NF. M24. $200.00

CONNOLLY, Cyril. *Modern Movement: 100 Key Books From England...1880-1950.* 1966. NY. Atheneum. 1st Am. gilt blk cloth. F/NF. M24. $100.00

CONNOLLY, Cyril. *Romantic Friendship: Letters to Noel Blakiston.* 1975. London. 1st. dj. T9. $25.00

CONNOR, C.L. *Art & Miracles in Medieval Byzantium: Crypt at Hosios...* 1991. Princeton. ils/pl. 132p. cloth. F/dj. Q2. $62.00

CONNOR, D. Russell. *Record of a Legend...Benny Goodman.* 1984. Let's Dance. 1st. 4to. F/F. B2. $100.00

CONNOR, Jeff. *Stephen King Goes to Hollywood.* 1987. NAL. AN/sans. T12. $20.00

CONNOR, Ralph. *Prospector.* 1904. NY. Revell. 1st. 401p. G+. G11. $15.00

CONOT, Robert E. *Justice at Nuremberg: First Comprehensive Dramatic Account.* 1983. Harper Row. photos/notes/biblio/index. 593p. VG/dj. S16. $25.00

CONQUIST, Arthur. *Integrated System of Classification of Flowering Plants.* 1981. NY. 200+ pl. 1262p. F/dj. B26. $125.00

CONRAD, Annie Gilliam. *Street Above the Steps.* 1954. McClure. 1st. 51p. VG. B10. $8.00

CONRAD, Barnaby. *Gates of Fear.* (1957). NY. Crowell. 1st. 4to. 337p. dj. F3. $20.00

CONRAD, Barnaby. *How to Fight a Bull.* 1968. Doubleday. 1st. 224p. dj. F3. $20.00

CONRAD, Howard L. *Uncle Dick Wootton.* 1980. Time Life. ils. aeg. leatherette. F/sans. B19. $20.00

CONRAD, Joseph. *Almayer's Folly.* 1895. London. Fisher Unwin. 1st/1st issue. author's 1st book. teg. gr cloth. M24. $1,650.00

**CONRAD, Joseph.** *Arrow of Gold.* 1919. Doubleday Page. 1st/2nd issue (credentials/who). bl brd. NF. M25. $45.00

**CONRAD, Joseph.** *Dover Patrol: A Tribute.* 1922. Canterbury, Eng. Goulden. 1st. 1/75. F/wrp/chemise/case. B24. $475.00

**CONRAD, Joseph.** *Falk.* 1903. NY. McClure Phillips. 1st Am. gilt bl cloth. M24. $150.00

**CONRAD, Joseph.** *Letters From Conrad 1895 to 1924.* 1928. Bloomsbury. Nonesuch. 1/925 on Arches. 335p. VG. F1. $150.00

**CONRAD, Joseph.** *Notes on My Books.* 1921. Doubleday Page. 1st. 1/250. sgn. 178p. teg. NF. H5. $450.00

**CONRAD, Joseph.** *Secret Agent, a Simple Tale.* 1907. Methuen. 1st. w/40p ads dtd 1907. gilt red cloth. NF. B24. $1,350.00

**CONRAD, Joseph.** *Secret Agent.* 1907. NY. Harper. 1st Am. VG. M15. $100.00

**CONRAD, Joseph.** *Secret Agent.* 1923. London. Werner Laurie. 1st. 1/1000. sgn. NF/VG. L3. $500.00

**CONRAD, Joseph.** *Secret Agent: Drama in Four Acts.* 1921. Canterbury, Eng. 1st. 1/52 or 53. F/wrp. B24. $2,750.00

**CONRAD, Joseph.** *Tales of Hearsay.* 1925. Doubleday. 1st Am. NF/dj. J3. $80.00

**CONRAD, Joseph.** *Tales of Hearsay.* 1925. London. Fisher Unwin. 1st Eng. 288p. gilt gr cloth. VG/dj. J3. $175.00

**CONRAD, Joseph.** *Under Western Eyes.* 1911. NY. Harper. 1st Am. gilt bl cloth. NF. B20. $100.00

**CONRAD, Joseph.** *Youth & Two Other Stories.* 1903. McClure Phillips. 1st Am. gilt gr cloth. M24. $150.00

**CONRAD & SELZNICK.** *Doll Face Has a Party.* 1994. Harper Collins. 1st. F/dj. V4. $12.50

**CONRAN, John.** *Journal of Life & Gospel Labours of John Conran...* 1852. Phil. Longstreth. 12mo. 248p. V3. $32.00

**CONROY, Frank.** *Body & Soul.* 1993. Houghton Mifflin. 1st. F/F. H11. $25.00

**CONROY, Frank.** *Midair.* 1985. NY. Dutton. 1st. NF/F. H11. $25.00

**CONROY, Pat.** *Beach Music.* 1995. Doubleday. 1st. F/dj. T12. $70.00

**CONROY, Pat.** *Beach Music.* 1995. Doubleday. 1st. sgn. VG/dj. B30. $60.00

**CONROY, Pat.** *Prince of Tides.* 1986. Houghton Mifflin. 1st. NF/dj. B30. $60.00

**CONROY, Pat.** *Prince of Tides.* 1986. Houghton Mifflin. 1st. sgn. F/dj. S18. $75.00

**CONROY, Pat.** *The Water Is Wide.* 1972. Houghton Mifflin. 1st. author's 2nd book. NF/VG. B4. $300.00

**CONROY, Richard Timothy.** *Mr Smithson's Bones.* 1993. St Martin. 1st. F/dj. N4. $25.00

**CONROY, Richard Timothy.** *Mr Smithson's Bones.* 1993. St Martin. 1st. VG/dj. G8. $15.00

**CONSTANTINE, K.C.** *Man Who Liked Slow Tomatoes.* 1992. Boston. Godine. 1st. F/clip. M15. $100.00

**CONSUMER GUIDE EDITORS.** *Ferrari: Sports Racing & Road Cars.* (1982). NY. Beekman. ils. 255p. F/dj. H4. $40.00

**CONTENAU, Georges.** *L'Art de L'Asie Occidentale Ancienne.* 1928. Paris/Bruxelles. ils/map. VG. Q2. $30.00

**CONTENTO & GREENBERG.** *Index to Crime & Mystery Anthologies.* 1991. 4to. 750p. F. A4. $95.00

**CONWAY, James.** *Napa: Story of an American Eden.* 1990. Houghton Mifflin. 1st. map ep. VG/dj. A28. $12.50

**CONWAY & RICCI.** *Films of Marilyn Monroe.* 1964. Citadel. 1st. VG/dj. C9. $60.00

**CONZATTI, Casiano.** *Flora Taxonomica Mexicana. Vol 1 & Vol 2.* 1946 & 1947. Mexico. ils. 377p. stiff wrp. B26. $150.00

**COOK, Blanche Wiesen.** *Declassified Eisenhower.* 1981. Doubleday. 1st. 432p. NF/F. W2. $35.00

**COOK, Fannie.** *Mrs Palmer's Honey.* 1946. Doubleday. 1st. inscr. F/NF. B2. $75.00

**COOK, Frederic A.** *Through the First Antarctic Night 1898-1899.* 1980. Montreal. McGill-Queen's U. rpt of 1900 1st. VG+. P4. $95.00

**COOK, Harold.** *Decline of the Old Medical Regime in Stuart London.* 1986. Ithaca. 1st. 310p. dj. A13. $27.50

**COOK, James.** *Journals of Captain James Cook on His Voyages of Discovery.* 1968-1974. Cambridge. 6 vol. ils/fld pl/58 charts. 8vo. gilt bl cloth. F/NF. F1. $1,250.00

**COOK, Olive.** *Movement in Two Dimensions.* 1963. London. Hutchinson. 1st. VG/dj. C9. $102.00

**COOK, R.L.** *Soil Management for Conservation & Production.* 1962. NY. Wiley. 527p. VG. A10. $20.00

**COOK, Robin.** *Godplayer.* 1983. London. Macmillan. 1st. VG/VG. B3. $10.00

**COOK, Robin.** *Harmful Intent.* 1990. Putnam. 1st. F/dj. T12. $25.00

**COOK, Roy J.** *One Hundred & One Famous Poems.* 1929. Cable Co Book Div. revised. ils. VG. W2. $45.00

**COOK, Thomas H.** *Breakhart Hill.* 1995. Bantam. 1st. F/NF. S18. $20.00

**COOK, Thomas H.** *Evidence of Blood.* 1991. Putnam. 1st. F/NF. S18. $25.00

**COOK, William.** *Wen, Botany & the Mexican Hat: Adventures of 1st Women...* 1987. Callisto Books. 1st. stiff wrp. F7. $15.00

**COOKE, Alistair.** *Alistair Cooke's America.* 1973. Knopf. 1st. NF/VG. P12. $20.00

**COOKE, David C.** *My Best Murder Story.* 1955. Merlin. 1st. VG/G. N4. $20.00

**COOKE, David.** *Enterprise: Greatest of the Flat-Tops.* 1963. NY. photos/index. 128p. VG/dj. S16. $30.00

**COOKE, John Esten.** *Stonewall Jackson & the Old Stonewall Brigade.* (1954). U VA. 76p. VG. B10. $50.00

**COOKE, John Esten.** *Wearing of the Gray: Being Personal Portraits...* 1959. IN U. 1st thus. 8vo. 572p. NF/dj. B20. $45.00

**COOKE, Josiah.** *Credentials of Science: Warrant of Faith.* 1893. NY. 2nd. 324p. A13. $35.00

**COOKE, Michael.** *Ancient Curse of the Baskervilles.* 1984. Bloomington. Gaslight. 1st thus. F/sans. T2. $12.00

**COOKE, Philip St. George.** *Scenes & Adventures in the Army; or, Romance...* 1859. Phil. Lindsay Blakiston. missing ffe. 432p. cloth. D11. $100.00

**COOKRIDGE, E.H.** *Baron of Arizona.* 1967. John Day. 1st. ils. 304p. dj. B19. $15.00

**COOKSON, Arthur G.** *From Harrow to Hawk.* 1978. Vantage. 1st. inscr/sgn. F/NF. A26. $20.00

**COOKSON, Catherine.** *Tinker's Girl.* 1994. London. Bantam. 1st. NF/dj. A14. $14.00

**COOLEY, Leland Frederi.** *Run for Home.* 1958. Garden City. Doubleday. 1st. VG/dj. T11. $20.00

**COOLIDGE, Dane.** *Fighting Men of the West.* 1932. Dutton. sgn. 343p. G/dj. J2. $60.00

**COOLIDGE, Dane.** *Gun-Smoke.* (1928). Grosset Dunlap. 231p. blk stp cloth. w/photo. D11. $50.00

**COOLIDGE, Olivia.** *Marathon Looks on the Sea.* 1967. Boston. Houghton Mifflin. 1st. 248p. F/NF. D4. $45.00

**COOLING, Benjamin Franklin.** *Jubal Early's Raid on Washington 1864.* 1989. Baltimore, MD. Nautical/Aviation Pub. 1st. F/dj. A14. $21.00

**COOLING & OWEN.** *Mr Lincoln's Forts: A Guide to Civil War Defenses of WA.* 1988. Wht Mane Pub. 1st. F/ils wrp. A14. $14.00

**COOMARASWAMY, Amanda.** *Buddha & the Gospel of Buddhism.* 1916. NY. 1st. ils. 370p. VG. B5. $40.00

**COOMBES, Allen J.** *Dictionary of Plant Names.* 1993 (1985). Portland. AN. B26. $11.00

**COOMES, David.** *Dorothy L Sayers: Careless Rage for Life.* (1992). Lion. 1st Am. ils/notes/index. AN/dj. A27. $20.00

**COON, Carleton S.** *Hunting Peoples.* 1981. NY. Lyons. 1st. 414p. wrp. A17. $12.50

**COON, Nelson.** *Using Plants for Healing.* 1979. Emmaus, PA. Rodale. F+/dj. A19. $25.00

**COON, Nelson.** *Using Plants for Healing.* 1979. Rodale. 272p. VG/dj. A10. $12.00

**COONEY, Barbara.** *American Folk Songs for Christmas by Ruth Seeger.* 1953. Doubleday. 1st. xl. VG/dj. B17. $10.00

**COONEY, Barbara.** *Little Juggler.* 1961. Hastings. 1st. 47p. reinforced cloth. F/dj. D4. $60.00

**COONEY, Barbara.** *Only Opal, Diary of a Young Girl.* 1994. Philomel. 1st. 4to. VG/dj. B17. $15.00

**COONEY, Barbara.** *Snow Birthday.* 1955. FSC. 1st. obl 4to. lt bl cloth. mc dj. R5. $85.00

**COONEY, Ellen.** *All the Way Home.* 1984. Putnam. 1st. rem mk. F/VG. P8. $20.00

**COONTS, Stephen.** *Flight of the Intruder.* 1986. Annapolis. 1st. author's 1st book. NF/F. H11. $25.00

**COOPER, Astley.** *Anatomy & Surgical Treatment of Inguinal...Hernia.* 1804. London. T Cox. atlas portfolio. 11 pl/legend leaves. 60p. G7. $1,495.00

**COOPER, Bransby B.** *Surgical Essays: Result of Clinical Observations...* 1843. London. 4 pl. brd. G7. $195.00

**COOPER, Dennis.** *Try.* 1994. Grove. 1st. F/NF. R14. $25.00

**COOPER, Dennis.** *Wrong.* 1992. Grove Weidenfeld. 1st. F/F. H11. $25.00

**COOPER, Douglas.** *Work of Graham Sutherland.* 1962. London. Humphries. 2nd. tall 4to. wht paper brd. F1. $75.00

**COOPER, Henry S.F.** *Search for Life on Mars.* 1980. HRW. 1st. 8vo. 254p. VG/dj. K5. $15.00

**COOPER, Henry S.F.** *Thirteen: Flight That Failed.* 1973. NY. Dial. 8vo. 199p. VG/dj. K5. $50.00

**COOPER, J. California.** *Some Soul to Keep.* 1987. St Martin. 1st. sgn. author's 3rd book. F/VG+. A24. $35.00

**COOPER, James A.** *Sheila.* 1922 (1921). Cleveland. Internat Fiction Lib. rpt. Vg/dj. A2. $10.00

**COOPER, James Fenimore.** *Complete Works...* late 19th C. 10 vol. 4to. gilt gr cloth. G. S17. $35.00

**COOPER, James Fenimore.** *Deerslayer; or, First War-Path.* 1929. Scribner. 1st ils ed. ils NC Wyeth. sq 8vo. 462p. Riviere bdg. F. H5. $450.00

**COOPER, James Fenimore.** *Last of the Mohicans.* 1836. London. 16mo. full gr polished calf. VG. S17. $65.00

**COOPER, James Fenimore.** *Last of the Mohicans.* 1946. Scribner. later prt. NF/dj. T11. $45.00

**COOPER, Jilly.** *Araminta's Wedding or a Fortune Secured: Country House...* 1993. London. Methuen. 1st. ils Sue Macartney-Shape. NF/dj. A14. $21.00

**COOPER, John C.** *Right to Fly: Study in Air Power.* 1947. Holt. gr cloth. G. M11. $45.00

**COOPER, John R.** *College League Mystery.* 1953. Garden City. 1st. G. P8. $5.00

**COOPER, John R.** *Mel Martin: Mystery at the Ball Park.* 1947. Cupples Leon. 1st. G. P8. $10.00

**COOPER, Natasha.** *Poison Flowers.* 1992. NY. Crown. 1st Am. VG/dj. G8. $15.00

**COOPER, Page.** *Pat's Harmony.* 1952. World. VG/dj. A21. $20.00

**COOPER, Paul L.** *Archeological Investigations in Heart Butte Reservoir Area.* 1958. GPO. 8vo. 40p. F/prt wrp. P4. $20.00

**COOPER, Samuel.** *Daniel Wheeler's Voyage of Life.* 1945. Mt Holly, NJ. 12mo. 48p. G/wrp. V3. $9.00

**COOPER, Susan R.** *Houston in the Rearview Mirror.* 1990. St Martin. 1st. sgn. F/dj. A24. $125.00

**COOPER, Susan.** *Grey King.* 1975. NY. Atheneum. 1st. ils Michael Heslop. gray-gr cloth. mc dj. R5. $110.00

**COOPER, Susan.** *Jethro & the Jumbie.* 1979. Atheneum. 1st. sgn. ils/sgn Ashley Bryan. 28p. cloth. F/dj. D4. $65.00

**COOTE, Colin R.** *Sir Winston Churchill: Self-Portrait...* 1954. London. Eyre Spottiswoode. 304p. VG/fair. M10. $16.50

**COOVELIS, Mark.** *Gloria.* 1994. Pocket. 1st. sgn. F/dj. R14. $45.00

**COOVER, Robert.** *Universal Baseball Association.* 1968. Random. 1st. F/VG. P8. $125.00

**COPE, Oliver.** *Man, Mind & Medicine: The Doctor's Education...* nd (1968). Lippincott. possible 1st. 8vo. 144p. F/VG. C14. $15.00

**COPE, Zachary.** *Royal College of Surgeons of England: A History.* 1959. London. 1st. 360p. A13. $60.00

**COPELAND, Edwin B.** *Coco-Nut.* 1914. London. ils. 212p. VG/dj. B26. $60.00

**COPELAND, William.** *Five Hours From Isfahan.* 1975. Putnam. 1st. F/F. H11. $25.00

**COPEMAN, Edward.** *Collection of Cases of Apoplexy...* 1845. London. Churchill. 205p. purple Victorian cloth. G7. $250.00

**COPEMAN, W.S.C.** *Doctors & Disease in Tudor Times.* 1960. London. 186p. A13. $80.00

**COPEMAN, W.S.C.** *Short History of Gout & Rheumatic Diseases.* 1964. Berkeley. 1st. 236p. A13. $75.00

**COPLON, Jeff.** *Gold Buckle: Grand Obsession of Rodeo Bull Riders.* 1995. Harper Collins. 1st. ils. 275p. AN. B19. $10.00

**COPPARD, A.E.** *Nixey's Harlequin: Ten Tales.* 1931. London. Cape. 1st. VG/dj. V4. $65.00

**COPPER, Basil.** *Exploits of Solar Pons.* 1993. Minneapolis. Fedogan Bremer. 1st. F/dj. T2. $25.00

**COPPER, Basil.** *House of the Wolf.* 1983. Arkham. 1st. VG/dj. L1. $70.00

**COPPER, Basil.** *Necropolis: A Novel of Gothic Mystery.* 1980. Arkham. 1st. G/VG. B30. $50.00

**COPPOLA, Eleanor.** *Notes.* 1979. S&S. 1st. VG/dj. R11. $15.00

**COPWAY, G.** *Ojibway Conquest: Tale of the Northwest...* 1850. Putnam. 1st Am. 12mo. 91p. complete. H4. $100.00

**CORBELL, Carole.** *In the Wings.* 1997. Stoddard. 1st Canadian/true 1st. author's 2nd novel. F/F. B3. $40.00

**CORBETT, A.** *Poultry Yard & Market.* 1877. NY. Orange Judd. 96p. cloth. A10. $30.00

**CORBETT, Jim.** *Man-Eaters of Kumaon.* 1946. NY. Oxford. 1st Am. BC. dj. A17. $12.50

**CORBETT, Jim.** *Man-Eaters of Kumaon.* 1946. OUP. 1st Am. NF/VG. A14. $17.50

**CORBETT, Scott.** *Baseball Trick.* 1965. Little Brn. later prt. VG/dj. P8. $20.00

**CORBETT, Scott.** *Steady Freddie.* 1970. Dutton. 1st. ils Lawrence Beall Smith. VG/dj. B36. $13.00

**CORBETT, W.J.** *Song of Pentecost.* 1983. Dutton. stated 1st. VG/dj. B36. $15.00

**CORBETT & CORBETT.** *French Cooking in Old Detroit Since 1701.* 1951. Detroit. Wayne U. sbdg. G. V4. $12.50

**CORBETT & CORBETT.** *French Cooking in Old Detroit Since 1701.* 1951. Wayne U. ils. VG. E6. $25.00

**CORBETT.** *Representing Feminity: Middle-Class Subjectivity...* 1992. Oxford. 248p. F/F. A4. $40.00

**CORBIN, Steven.** *Hundred Days From Now.* 1994. Boston. Alyson. 1st. F/dj. C9. $30.00

**CORBITT, Helen.** *Helen Corbitt Cooks for Company.* 1974. Houghton Mifflin. 1st. VG. A16. $10.00

**CORCORAN, Brewer.** *Barbarian.* 1917. Page. 1st. G. P8. $35.00

**CORDAN, Wolfgang.** *Secret of the Forest: On the Track of Maya Temples.* 1963. London. Gollancz. 1st. photos. 163p. dj. F3. $25.00

**CORDRY & CORDRY.** *Mexican Indian Costumes.* 1968. U TX. 1st. ils/pl/figures/6 maps. gilt red cloth. F/dj. T10. $300.00

**CORE, Earl L.** *Vegetation of West Virginia.* 1966. Parsons, WV. ils. 217p. VG/dj. B26. $22.50

**CORE, Sue.** *Ravelings From a Panama Tapestry.* 1933. Dobbs Ferry. ils EA Richards. VG. M17. $15.00

**CORELLI, Marie.** *Master Christian.* 1900. NY. Dodd Mead. 1st. 604p. G+. G11. $20.00

**COREN, Michael.** *Gilbert: Man Who Was GK Chesterton.* (1990). Paragon. 1st Am. photos/biblio/index. F/dj. A27. $15.00

**COREN, Michael.** *Man Who Created Narnia: Story of CS Lewis.* (1996). Eerdmans. 1st Am. photos/chronology/index. AN/dj. A27. $22.00

**CORLE, Edwin.** *Desert Country.* 1941. DSP. 2nd. 8vo. 357p. red cloth. VG. F7. $25.00

**CORLE, Edwin.** *Gila: River of the Southwest.* 1951. Rinehart. 1st. ils/index. 402p. NF/VG. B19. $40.00

**CORMAN, Avery.** *Kramer Versus Kramer.* 1977. NY. Random. 1st. F/NF. R14. $25.00

**CORMAN, Avery.** *Old Neighborhood.* 1980. S&S/Linden. 1st. NF/VG. A14. $21.00

**CORMAN, H.E.** *Phrenological Analysis of Harry Crouse.* 1914. Coburn, PA. 10p. B18. $125.00

**CORMIER, Robert.** *Chocolate War.* 1974. Pantheon. 1st. 8vo. 253p. brn brd. T5. $30.00

**CORN, Alfred.** *Contemporary Writers on the New Testament.* 1990. Viking. 361p. VG/dj. B29. $9.50

**CORN, Wanda A.** *Art of Andrew Wyeth.* 1973. NYGS. 1st. ils. 176p. F/VG. T11. $50.00

**CORNELIUS, Asher L.** *Cross-Examination of Witness, Rules, Principles & Ils.* 1929. Bobbs Merrill. gilt maroon cloth. G. M11. $75.00

**CORNELL, John J.** *Principles of the Religious Society of Friends...* 1896. Baltimore. Isaac Walker. 1st. 12mo. 45p. VG. V3. $16.00

**CORNFORD, Frances.** *Autumn Midnight.* 1923. London. Poetry Bookshop. 1st. ils Eric Gill. 23p. brn prt wrp. F1. $295.00

**CORNFORD, Frances.** *Travelling Home & Other Poems.* 1948. London. 1st. inscr. dj. T9. $65.00

**CORNING, Howard McKinley.** *This Earth & Another Country: New & Selected Poems.* (1969). Portland. Tall Pine Imp. 1st. wrp. A18. $10.00

**CORNISH, Nellie.** *Miss Aunt Nellie: Autobiography of Nellie Cornish.* 1964. U WA. 1st. VG/G. P2. $15.00

**CORNS & SPARKE.** *Bibliography of Unfinished Books in Eng Language.* 1969. 271p. F. A4. $45.00

**CORNWALL, J. Spencer.** *Century of Singing: Salt Lake Mormon Tabernacle Choir.* 1958. Desert Book. 1st. ils. 426p. VG/dj. w/sgn card. S14. $15.00

**CORNWELL, Bernard.** *Battle Flag.* 1995. Harper Collins. 1st. F/dj. T11. $15.00

**CORNWELL, Bernard.** *Rebel.* 1993. Harper Collins. 1st Eng. F/NF clip. T11. $40.00

**CORNWELL, Bernard.** *Redcoat.* 1988. NY. Viking. 1st AM. F/dj. M23. $35.00

**CORNWELL, Bernard.** *Sharpe's Devil.* 1992. Harper Collins. 1st. F/dj. T11. $25.00

**CORNWELL, Bernard.** *Sharpe's Eagle: Richard Sharpe & Talavera Campaign...* 1981. Viking. 1st Am. VG+/dj. A14. $35.00

**CORNWELL, Patricia D.** *All That Remains.* 1992. NY. Scribner. 1st Am. sgn. F/dj. B3/M15. $75.00

**CORNWELL, Patricia D.** *All That Remains.* 1992. NY. Scribner. 1st Am. VG+/dj. A14. $42.00

**CORNWELL, Patricia D.** *All That Remains.* 1992. Scribner. 1st. F/F. H11. $50.00

**CORNWELL, Patricia D.** *Body Farm.* 1994. Scribner. ARC. sgn. F/dj. A23. $75.00

**CORNWELL, Patricia D.** *Body Farm.* 1994. Scribner. 1st. NF/dj. A14. $22.00

**CORNWELL, Patricia D.** *Cruel & Unusual.* 1993. NY. Scribner. 1st. F/dj. A23/H11/N4. $30.00

**CORNWELL, Patricia D.** *From Potter's Field.* 1995. Scribner. 1st. F/F. H11. $20.00

**CORNWELL, Patricia D.** *From Potter's Field.* 1995. Scribner. 1st. NF/dj. A14. $17.50

**CORNWELL, Patricia D.** *Hornets Nest.* 1996. Putnam. 1st. sgn. NF/F. S18. $35.00

**CORNWELL, Patricia D.** *Postmortem.* 1990. NY. Scribner. 1st. Scarpetta #1. F/dj. M15. $950.00

**CORNWELL, Patricia D.** *Time for Remembering: Ruth Bell Graham Story.* 1983. Harper Row. 1st. author's 1st book. F/VG. C15. $100.00

**CORONITI & HUGHES.** *Planetary Electrodynamics...* 1969. NY. Gordon Breach. 2 vol. 8vo. ils. cloth. xl. K5. $60.00

**CORPI, Lucha.** *Eulogy for a Brown Angel.* 1992. Houston. Arte Publico. ARC/1st. F/NF. A24. $30.00

**CORRELL & CORRELL.** *Aquatic & Wetland Plants of Southwestern United States.* 1972. WA, DC. EPA ed. ils. 1777p. VG. B26. $130.00

**CORRELL & GOSDEN.** *All About Amos 'n' Andy & Their Creators.* 1930. Rand McNally. 2nd. F/VG. C9. $150.00

**CORRIGAN, Douglas.** *That's My Story.* 1938. NY. 1st. VG. B5. $27.50

**CORSE, Carita Doggett.** *Key to the Golden Islands.* 1931. Chapel Hill. 1/212. sgn. 16 full-p ils. 165p. gilt cloth. F. O1. $75.00

**CORSER, H.P.** *Totem Lore & Land of the Totem.* 1930s. Nugget Shop. ils. 100p. VG+. B19. $45.00

**CORSETTI, Achille.** *La Intelligenza Degli Animali Bruti...* 1890. Roma. Industriale. 598p. later cloth. G1. $85.00

**CORSO, Gregory.** *Gasoline.* 1958. City Lights. 1st. Pocket Poet #8. intro Allen Ginsberg. wrp. M24. $75.00

**CORSON, Juliet.** *Miss Corson's Practical American Cookery & Household...* 1886 (1885). E6. $65.00

**CORSON, William.** *Betrayal.* 1968. NY. 3rd. 317p. VG/dj. E1. $25.00

**CORTAZAR, Julio.** *Manual for Manuel.* 1978. Pantheon. 1st. F/F. H11. $40.00

**CORTAZZI, Hugh.** *Isles of Gold, Antique Maps of Japan.* nd. 4to. ils/90 maps. 196p. F/F. A4. $85.00

**CORTRIGHT, David.** *Soldiers in Revolt: American Military Today.* 1975. Anchor/ Doubleday. 1st. 8vo. VG/dj. R11. $25.00

**CORWIN, Norman.** *Date With Sandburg.* 1981. Northridge, CA. Santa Susana. mini. 1/100. sgn. 20p. full buckram. B24. $85.00

**CORY, J. Campbell.** *Cartoonist's Art.* 1912. Chicago. Tumbo. 4to. ils wrp. F1. $75.00

**COSARELLI, Kate.** *Living Color.* 1987. NAL. 1st. NF/dj. A14. $21.00

**COSBY, Bill.** *Fatherhood.* 1986. Doubleday. 1st. F/dj. T12. $20.00

**COSTAIN, Thomas B.** *Tontine.* 1955. Doubleday. 2 vol. 1st. ils Herbert Ryman. NF/dj. A14. $52.50

**COSTAIN, Thomas B.** *Tontine.* 1956. London. Collins. 1st Eng. VG/dj. M19. $17.50

**COSTELLO, Charles G.** *Symptoms of Psychopathology: A Handbook.* 1970. John Wiley. heavy 8vo. 679p. VG/dj. G1. $65.00

**COTLER, Amy.** *My Little House Cookbook.* 1995. Harper Collins. 1st. AN/F. V4. $12.50

**COTTON, John.** *Keyes of the Kingdom of Heaven, Power Therof...* 1843. Boston. Tappan Dennet. rpt (1644 London). 8vo. 108p. cloth. NF. O1. $45.00

**COTTON DES HOUSSAYES.** *Des Devoirs et des Qualites du Bibliothecaire.* 1839. Paris. 4to. prt wrp. R12. $150.00

**COTTRELL, Leonard.** *Lost Cities.* 1957. Rinehart. 1st. 24 pl. VG/dj. W1. $20.00

**COUGHLIN, William J.** *Twelve Apostles.* 1984. Putnam. 1st. NF/dj. S13. $12.00

**COULSON, Thomas.** *Mata Hari, Courtesan & Spy.* 1932. Bl Ribbon. MTI. VG+. C15. $20.00

**COULTER, John.** *Fundamentals of Plant-Breeding.* 1914. Appleton. 347p. VG. A10. $25.00

**COULTER, Stanley.** *Catalogue of Flowering Plants & of Ferns & Their Allies...* 1901. np. 525p. new brn buckram. VG. B26. $50.00

**COUNSELMAN, Mary Elizabeth.** *Half in Shadow.* 1978. Arkham. 1st collection. VG/dj. L1. $35.00

**COUNTRYMAN, Vern.** *Douglas (Wm O Douglas) Opinions.* 1977. Random. VG/dj. M11. $45.00

**COUPS, Plenty.** *Famous American Indians.* 1944. Chicago. Groves. 1st. F/NF. B9. $65.00

**COURLANDER, H.** *Drum & the Hoe.* 1960. Berkeley. 1st. ils. 371p. VG/G. B5. $30.00

**COURLANDER & HERZOG.** *Cow-Tail Switch & Other West African Stories.* nd. HRW. ils Madye Lee Chastain. xl. VG/dj. P12. $16.00

**COURTER, Gay.** *Beansprout Book.* 1973. S&S. stiff paper. VG. A10. $8.50

**COURTNEY, William P.** *Dodsley's Collection of Poetry.* 1968. NY. Franklin. rpt. 8vo. 157p. gilt red cloth. H13. $45.00

**COURTNEY & SMITH.** *Bibliography of Samuel Johnson.* 1925. Clarendon. 1st ils. 1/350. 35 pl. 186p. VG. A4. $250.00

**COURVILLE, Cyril B.** *Cerebral Palsy: A Brief Introduction to Its History...* 1954. LA. San Lucas Pr. 80p. G7. $65.00

**COUSIN, Jean.** *L'Art de Dessiner Augmente de Plusieurs Figures...* (1802). Paris. Chas Jourbert. 32 full-p woodcuts+pl w/skeleton figures. 72p. G7. $1,750.00

**COUSINS, Norman.** *Albert Schweitzer's Mission: Healing & Peace.* 1985. Norton. 1st. VG/dj. R8. $12.50

**COUSINS & RILEY.** *Colonial Architecture of Salem.* 1919. Little Brn. 1st. tall 8vo. half brn cloth/brn brd. VG. F1. $75.00

**COUSTEAU, J.** *Whale.* 1972. NY. 1st Am. 304p. F/dj. A17. $10.00

**COUTANT, Charles G.** *History of Wyoming From Earliest Known Discoveries Vol I.* 1899. Laramie, WY. Chaplin. 2 vol. 1st. thick 8vo. 712p. cloth/leather spine. G. O1. $275.00

**COVINGTON, Dennis.** *Salvation on Sand Mountain.* 1994. Reading, MA. Addison Wesley. 1st. F/dj. M23. $40.00

**COVINGTON, Michael.** *Negative.* 1993. Viking. 1st. author's 1st book. AN/dj. S18. $27.00

**COWAN, Robert Ernest.** *Bibliographical Notes on Early California.* 1905. GPO. sgn Holliday. prt wrp. D11. $30.00

**COWAN, Robert Ernest.** *Bibliography of the History of California 1510-1930.* nd. 3 vol in 1. 1/500. 830p. VG. A4. $75.00

**COWAN, Robert Ernest.** *Biography of the History of California 1510-1930.* 1933. SF. John Henry Nash. 3 vol. w/sgn card. P4. $595.00

**COWAN, Robert Ernest.** *Norton I, Emperor of the United States & Protector Mexico.* 1923. CA Hist Soc. inscr. 12p. prt wrp. D11. $30.00

**COWAN, Sam K.** *Sergeant York & His People.* 1922. NY. 1st. ils. 282p. VG. B18. $45.00

**COWAN, T.W.** *Honey Bee: Its Natural History, Anatomy & Physiology.* 1890. London. Hutchinson. 2nd. ils. 220p+ads. VG. M12. $25.00

**COWARD, Noel.** *Present Laughter.* 1946. Doubleday. 1st. VG/dj. A24. $30.00

**COWART, Jack.** *Roy Lichtenstein 1970-1980.* 1981. NY. Hudson Hills. 4to. 100 b&w ils/67 mc pl. 175p. wht cloth. F/NF. H4. $70.00

**COWIE, Peter.** *World Cinema: Diary of a Day.* 1995. Woodstock. Overlook. 416p. VG/dj. C5. $15.00

**COWIE & GUMMER.** *Christian Calendar.* 1974. Merriam. VG/dj. B29. $11.00

**COWLES, Fleur.** *Friends & Memories.* 1975. London. 1st. sgn. photos. VG/dj. M17. $20.00

**COWLEY, Malcolm.** *Faulkner-Cowley File: Letters & Memories, 1944-1962.* 1966. Viking. 1st. G/dj. B30. $35.00

**COWLEY & SMITH.** *Books That Changed Our Minds.* 1939. NY. Kelmscott. 1st. 285p. cloth. F/dj. O10. $25.00

**COWPER, Richard.** *Custodians & Other Stories.* 1976. London. Gollancz. 1st. AN/dj. M21. $40.00

**COWPER, William.** *John Gilpin's Ride.* 1982. Evanston, IL. mini. ils Ward Schori. 52p. gilt blk leather. B24. $125.00

**COX, A.B.** *Jugged Journalism.* 1925. London. Herbert Jenkins. 1st. VG+. M21. $40.00

**COX, Donald W.** *Space Race: From Sputnik to Apollo...And Beyond!* 1962. Phil. Chilton. sgn. 393p. VG/dj. K5. $35.00

**COX, E.H.M.** *Plant Hunting in China.* 1961 (1945). London. Oldbourne. ils/maps. 230p. VG. B26. $40.00

**COX, E.H.M.** *Plant Hunting in China: A History of Botanical Exploration.* 1945. London. Scientific Book Guild. 8vo. ils/maps. decor bfd. NF. C12. $85.00

**COX, Edward G.** *Reference Guide to the Literature of Travel...* nd. 1/350. rpt. 1754p. F. A4. $185.00

**COX, Harvey.** *Religion in the Secular City.* 1984. S&S. 1st. 304p. VG/torn. B29. $8.50

**COX, James.** *Biblical Preaching: Expositor's Treasury.* 1983. Westminster. 372p. VG/worn. B29. $11.50

**COX, James.** *My Native Land: The United States...* 1895. St Louis. Blair. 1st. ils. bl cloth. VG. Q1. $60.00

**COX, Joseph A.** *Recluse of Herald Square: Mystery of Ida E Wood.* 1964. Macmillan. 1st. VG. N2. $10.00

**COX, Joseph.** *Crop Production & Soil Management.* 1925. NY. Wiley. 516p. cloth. VG. A10. $15.00

**COX, Mary L.** *History of Hale County Texas.* 1937. Plainview. sgn. 230p. VG. J2. $245.00

**COX, Morris.** *Four Seasons. Impression of Spring, Summer, Autumn & Winter.* 1965-66. London. Gogmagog. 1/100. 4 vol (each sgn). pict brd. F. B24. $3,250.00

**COX, Morris.** *From a London Suburb. Poems by Morris Cox.* 1975. London. Gogmagog. 1/24. sgn. 4 full-size intaglio pl on Mingei. F. B24. $750.00

**COX, Morris.** *Web of Nature. Printbook Illustrating a Principle.* 1964. London. Gogmagog. 1/50 on Japan. w/29 emb offset prts. F/case. B24. $950.00

**COX, Morris.** *Winter Trees, a Pictorial Study.* 1977. London. Gogmagog. 1/25. sgn. 8vo. frenchfold. w/TLS. F. B24. $1,350.00

**COX, Nellie Iverson.** *Harsh Land & Proud: Saga of the Arizona Strip.* 1982. Las Vegas. 4to. 358p. brn fabricoid. NF. F7. $90.00

**COX, Nellie Iverson.** *Sky High & Canyon Deep. Ballads & Legends of AZ Strip...* 1988. Utah. 8vo. RS. AN/tan wrp. F7. $12.95

**COX, Palmer.** *Another Brownie Book.* (1890). NY. Century. thin 8vo. pictorial brd. Frederic Remington's copy. NF. R3. $150.00

**COX, Palmer.** *Brownies.* 1962. Franklin, NH. Hillside. mini. 1/375. 54p. cloth-backed pict brd. B24. $85.00

**COX, Palmer.** *Brownies: Their Book.* (1915). Eau Claire, WI. Hale. 144p. G. B18. $27.50

**COX, Palmer.** *Frolic on Wheels.* 1895. Hubbard. 1st. ils. VG. M5. $75.00

**COX, Palmer.** *Queer People With Wings & Stings.* 1888. Phil. Hubbard. G. M20. $52.00

**COX, Palmer.** *That Stanley!* 1878. NY. Art Prt Est. 1st. ils. 64p. rb. F1. $75.00

**COX, Peter A.** *Dwarf Rhododendrons.* 1973. NY. Macmillan. ils/index. 296p. VG/G. H10. $20.00

**COX, Samuel Sullivan.** *Miscegenation or Almagamation: Fate of Freedman...1864.* 1864. WA, DC. Constitutional Union. 1st. dbl-column text. 11p. wrp. M8. $150.00

**COX, Samuel Sullivan.** *Speech of..., of OH, on Joint Resolution Explanatory...1864.* 1864. WA, DC. Gibson. 1st. 16p. wrp. M8. $45.00

**COX & TAYLOR.** *Primulas for Garden & Greenhouse.* 1947 (1928). Oxford. Dulau. ils. 86p. VG. A10. $20.00

**COXE, George Harmon.** *Impetuous Mistress.* 1958. Knopf. 1st. VG/dj. N4. $25.00

**COXE, George Harmon.** *With Intent to Kill.* 1964. Knopf. BC. 180p. F/VG. P12. $8.00

**COYLE, Harold.** *Savage Wilderness.* 1977. NY. S&S. 1st. F/dj. T11. $25.00

**COZZENS, James Gould.** *Ask Me Tomorrow.* 1940. Harcourt Brace. 1st. F/VG clip. F/VG clip. B4. $150.00

**COZZENS, Peter.** *Darkest Hours of the War.* 1997. U NC. ils. VG/dj. M17. $15.00

**COZZENS, Peter.** *Shipwreck of Their Hopes: Battles for Chattanooga.* 1994. Urbana. ils/maps. 515p. VG/dj. S16. $25.00

**CRABTREE, Adam.** *Animal Magnetism, Early Hypnotism & Psychical Reasearch...* 1988. NY. Kraus. thick 8vo. 522p. prt gray buckram. G1. $125.00

**CRABTREE, Helen.** *Saddle Seat Equitation.* 1970. Doubleday. 1st/3rd prt. VG/fair. O3. $15.00

**CRACROFT, Sophia.** *Lady Franklin Visits Sitka, Alaska 1870...* 1981. Anchorage. AK Hist Soc. 134p. gray cloth. P4. $75.00

**CRADDOCK, Harry.** *Savoy Cocktail Book.* 1930. NY. Richard R Smith. 1st Am. 8vo. 287p. Sangorski bdg. F. H5. $650.00

**CRADDOCK, Patricia B.** *Edward Gibbon: A Reference Guide.* 1987. 525p. F. A4. $55.00

**CRAIG, Gordon A.** *Politics of the Unpolitical: German Writers & Problem...* 1995. OUP. 1st Am. 8vo. F/dj. A2. $20.00

**CRAIG, John.** *All GODS Children.* 1975. Morrow. 1st. VG/dj. P8. $35.00

**CRAIG, Michel William.** *General Edward Hand: Winter Doctor.* 1984. Rock Ford Found. 1st. F/sans? T11. $25.00

**CRAIG, Patricia.** *Oxford Book of English Detective Stories.* 1990. Oxford. 1st. F/NF. G8. $10.00

**CRAIGE, John H.** *Black Bagdad: Arabian Nights Adventure...* 1933. NY. VG/G. M17. $20.00

**CRAIGHEAD & CRAIGHEAD.** *Hawks in the Hand: Adventures in Photography & Falconry.* nd. np. orig prt. 57 photos. 290p. pict cloth. NF/dj. C12. $145.00

**CRAIS, Robert.** *Free Fall.* 1993. Bantam. 1st. F/dj. M23. $30.00

**CRAIS, Robert.** *Lullaby Town.* 1992. NY. Bantam. 1st. sgn. F/dj. M15. $350.00

**CRAIS, Robert.** *Monkey's Raincoat.* 1989. London. Piakus. 1st hc. sgn. F/dj. M15. $250.00

**CRAIS, Robert.** *Monkey's Raincoat.* 1993. Doubleday. 1st Am. NF/dj. M21. $100.00

**CRAIS, Robert.** *Stalking the Angel.* 1989. Bantam. 1st. F/dj. M15/M23. $45.00

**CRAIS, Robert.** *Stalking the Angel.* 1989. Bantam. 1st. sgn. F/dj. D10. $75.00

**CRAM, Ralph Adams.** *Church Building: A Study of Principles of Architecture...* 1924. Boston. Marshall Jones. 3rd. 345p. gilt cloth. D2. $35.00

**CRAMER, Richard B.** *What It Takes. The Way to the White House.* 1992. Random. 1st. sm 4to. 1047p. F/dj. W2. $60.00

**CRAMPTON, C. Gregory.** *Outline History of Glen Canyon Region, 1776-1922.* 1959. Salt Lake City. Glen Canyon Series 9. 60 photos/map. 137p. VG. F7. $37.50

**CRAMPTON, C. Gregory.** *Zunis of Cigola.* 1977. Salt Lake City, UT. F/dj. A19. $45.00

**CRAN, Marion.** *Garden of Experience.* 1920. London. Jenkins. 4th. 316p. cloth. VG. A10. $20.00

**CRANE, Cheryl.** *Detour: A Hollywood Story.* nd. BC. VG/dj. P3. $8.00

**CRANE, Frances.** *Cinnamon Murder.* 1946. Random. 1st. NF/VG. H11. $30.00

**CRANE, Frances.** *Coral Princess Murders.* 1954. Random. 1st. F/dj. M15. $50.00

**CRANE, Frances.** *Shocking Pink Hat.* 1946. Random. 1st. F/NF. M15. $50.00

**CRANE, Katharine Elizabeth.** *Blair House: Past & Present, an Account of Its Life...* 1945. US Dept of State. ils. VG/case. B10. $25.00

**CRANE, Leo.** *Desert Drums: Pueblo Indians of New Mexico 1540-1928.* 1972. Rio Grande. ils/index. 407p. VG/sans. B19. $20.00

**CRANE, Leo.** *Indians of the Enchanted Desert.* 1925. Little Brn. 1st. F/VG+. B20. $150.00

**CRANE, Stephen.** *Little Regiment & Other Episodes of American Civil War.* 1896. NY. 1st/1st issue. 196p. G. B18. $125.00

CRANE, Stephen. *Monster & Other Stories.* 1899. Harper. 1st. xl. VG. B18. $175.00

CRANE, Stephen. *Open Boat & Other Stories.* 1898. Doubleday McClure. 1st/state B bdg (no sequence). silvered gr cloth. M24. $250.00

CRANE, Stephen. *Red Badge of Courage.* 1896. NY. Appleton. 2nd. decor tan cloth. VG. T11. $145.00

CRANE, Stephen. *Red Badge of Courage.* 1931. Random. 1/980. ils Valenti Angelo. 142p. VG/dj. F1. $200.00

CRANE, Stephen. *Three Stories of Peacetime.* 1965. Kingsport. 1/1250. intro Matthew Bruccoli. VG. M17. $30.00

CRANE, Walter. *Baby's Bouquet.* (1878). Routledge. 1st. 8vo. G. M5. $85.00

CRANE, Walter. *Flower Wedding.* 1905. London. Cassell. 1st. 40 mc ils on French-fld leaves. gr brd. F. H5. $325.00

CRANE & DRESSES. *Masque of Days.* 1901. London. Cassell. 1st. ils Walter Crane. unp. pict brd. VG. D1. $325.00

CRAVEN, Avery Odell. *Soil Exhaustion As a Factor in Agricultural History...* 1925. IL U. 179p. stiff paper. B10. $45.00

CRAVEN, Thomas. *Treasury of American Prints.* 1939. S&S. sbdg. blk cloth/bl brd/paper label. F/G dj/case. F1. $50.00

CRAVER & MARGO. *Tom Lea.* 1995. TX Western Pr. 1st. ils. F/F. T11. $40.00

CRAWFORD, Christina. *Mommie Dearest.* 1978. Morrow. BC. F/NF. W2. $15.00

CRAWFORD, F. Marion. *Diva's Ruby.* 1908. Macmillan. 1st. ils JM Flagg. gilt gr cloth. VG+. S13. $12.00

CRAWFORD, F. Marion. *Rules of the South: Sicily, Calabria, Malta.* 1901. NY. Macmillan. 2 vol. xl. G. M10. $10.00

CRAWFORD, I.M. *Art of the Wandjina: Aboriginal Cave Paintings in Kimberley.* 1968. Melbourne. OUP. 1st. 8vo. 144p. VG/dj. B11. $85.00

CRAWFORD, M.D.C. *Heritage of Cotton: Fibre of Two Worlds & Many Ages.* 1924. Grosset Dunlap. early rpt. 244p. gilt floral pattern cloth. VG+. B20. $35.00

CRAWFORD, M.H. *Methods & Theories of Anthropological Genetics.* 1973. U NM. 1st. 509p. dj. F3. $15.00

CRAWFORD, MacDermot. *Madame deLafayette & Her Family.* 1907. NY. James Pott. 1st. ils. 358p. VG. S17. $12.50

CRAWFORD, Mary C. *Romance of Old New England Rooftrees.* 1922. Boston. 390p. G. M4. $18.00

CRAWHALL, Joseph. *Compleatest Angling Booke.* 1970. Freshet. facs of 1881. mould-made Nideggen paper. F/case. A17. $27.50

CRAYDER, Teresa. *Sudden Fame.* 1966. Macmillan. stated 1st. VG/dj. B36. $11.00

CREAMER, Robert. *Baseball in '41.* 1991. Viking. 1st. photos. F/dj. P8. $30.00

CREAMER, Robert. *Lugosi: Man Behind the Cape.* 1976. Chicago. Regnery. 1st. VG/dj. L1. $600.00

CREASEY, John. *Crime-Haters.* nd. BC. VG/dj. P3. $8.00

CREASEY, John. *Dissemblers.* 1967. Scribner. 1st. F/F. H11. $30.00

CREASEY, John. *Executioners.* 1967. Scribner. 1st. NF/dj. N4. $20.00

CREASEY, John. *Gideon's Fog.* 1974. Harper Row. 1st. F/dj. M19. $15.00

CREASEY, John. *Make-Up for the Toff.* 1967. Walker. 1st. VG/dj. M19. $15.00

CREASEY, John. *Policeman's Dread.* 1962. London. 1st. VG/dj. M17. $30.00

CREEKMORE, B.B. *Knoxville.* 1979. TN U. 3rd expanded. 333p. F/dj. M4. $17.00

CREELEY, Robert. *Day Book.* 1972. Scribner. 1st. sgn. F/NF. O11. $65.00

CREELEY, Robert. *Four Poems From a Form of Women.* 1959. NY. private prt. 1st. 1/300. bl prt wrp. M24. $125.00

CREELEY, Robert. *Hello: Journal, February 29-May 3, 1976.* 1978. New Directions. 1st. sgn. F/dj. O11. $75.00

CREELEY, Robert. *Island.* 1963. Scribner. 1st. author's 1st novel. VG/dj. R11. $40.00

CREELEY, Robert. *Pieces.* 1969. Scribner. 1st. sgn. RS. F/dj. Q1. $25.00

CREELEY, Robert. *Robert Creeley Reads.* 1967. London. Turret/Calder & Boyars. 1st. sgn. O11. $90.00

CREIGHTON, Don. *Little League Old-Timers.* 1967. Steck-Vaughn. 1st. VG/dj. P8. $20.00

CREIGHTON, Margaret S. *Rites & Passages: Experience of American Whaling 1830-70.* 1995. Cambridge. 1st. ils. 233p. bl cloth. P4. $55.00

CREMER, Jan. *I Jan Cremer.* 1965. London. 1st. trans Wyngaard/Trocchi. dj. T9. $15.00

CRESPI, Camilla T. *Trouble With a Bad Fit.* 1996. Harper Collins. 1st. VG/dj. R8. $15.00

CRESPI, Camilla T. *Trouble With Thin Ice.* 1993. Harper. 3rd. rem mk. VG/dj. R8. $10.00

CRESPI & GAY. *170 Cats.* 1939. NY. Random. 1st. obl 4to. mc pict dj. R5. $135.00

CRESSEY, James. *Max the Mouse.* 1979. Prentice Hall. 1st Am. ils Tamasin Cole. VG/dj. P2. $12.50

CRESSWELL, Beatrice. *Royal Progress of King Pepito.* 1960s. Merrimack. 8vo. ils Greenaway. VG/dj. B17. $15.00

CRESSWELL, Helen. *Secret World of Polly Flint.* (1982). Macmillan. 1st Am. ils Shirley Felt. 176p. orange brd. F/NF. T5. $30.00

CREWDSON, Isaac. *Water Baptism, an Ordinance of Christ.* 1837. London. Darton Holborn Hill. 1st. 12mo. 31p. disbound. V3. $40.00

CREWS, Donald. *Bicycle Race.* 1985. NY. Greenwillow. 1st. unp. F/dj. D4. $35.00

CREWS, Donald. *Freight Train.* 1978. NY. Greenwillow. 1st. obl 4to. 1979 Caldecott Honor. pict brd. R5. $110.00

CREWS, Donald. *Truck.* 1980. NY. Greenwillow. 1st. VG/dj. B5. $25.00

CREWS, Harry. *All We Need of Hell.* 1987. Harper Row. 1st. F/NF. B3. $50.00

CREWS, Harry. *Blood & Grits.* 1979. Harper Row. 1st. F/F. B4. $100.00

CREWS, Harry. *Blood & Grits.* 1979. Harper Row. 1st. F/NF. O11. $70.00

CREWS, Harry. *Body.* 1990. Poseidon. ARC/1st. F/F. w/pub promo materials. O11. $70.00

CREWS, Harry. *Body.* 1990. Poseidon. 1st. F/dj. C9. $25.00

CREWS, Harry. *Gypsy's Curse.* 1974. Knopf. 1st. inscr. NF/dj. R14. $225.00

CREWS, Harry. *Hawk Is Dying.* 1973. Knopf. 1st. sgn. F/dj. B4. $250.00

CREWS, Harry. *Knockout Artist.* 1988. Harper Row. 1st. F/F. D10. $35.00

CREWS, Harry. *Knockout Artist.* 1988. Harper Row. 1st. NF/dj. A14. $25.00

CREWS, Harry. *Where Does One Go When There's No Place Left to Go?* 1998. Blood & Guts. 1/400. sgn/#d. as issued. B30. $100.00

CRICHTON, Michael. *Airframe.* 1996. Knopf. 1st. 8vo. F/dj. W2. $25.00

**CRICHTON, Michael.** *Binary.* 1972. Knopf. 1st. F/F. M15. $145.00

**CRICHTON, Michael.** *Binary.* 1972. Knopf. 1st. NF/NF. M19. $75.00

**CRICHTON, Michael.** *Case of Need.* 1993. Dutton. 1st thus. 8vo. 319p. F/dj. W2. $25.00

**CRICHTON, Michael.** *Congo.* 1980. Knopf. 1st. F/NF. M15. $45.00

**CRICHTON, Michael.** *Disclosure.* 1994. Knopf. 1st. sgn. F/dj. M25. $60.00

**CRICHTON, Michael.** *Disclosure.* 1994. Knopf. 399p. VG/dj. P12. $15.00

**CRICHTON, Michael.** *Five Patients.* 1970. Knopf. 1st. VG/F. H11. $50.00

**CRICHTON, Michael.** *Great Train Robbery.* 1975. Knopf. F. A19. $25.00

**CRICHTON, Michael.** *Great Train Robbery.* 1975. Knopf. 1st. VG/F clip. H11. $35.00

**CRICHTON, Michael.** *Jurassic Park.* 1990. Knopf. 1st. F/dj. A24. $60.00

**CRICHTON, Michael.** *Jurassic Park. Special Gift Edition.* 1993. Knopf. gift ed. autopen sgn. 12 dinosaur pl. F/F/acetate dj. C9. $60.00

**CRICHTON, Michael.** *Lost World.* 1995. Knopf. 1st. F/NF. S18. $20.00

**CRICHTON, Michael.** *Rising Sun.* 1992. Knopf. 1st. F/dj. N4. $35.00

**CRICHTON, Michael.** *Terminal Man.* 1972. Knopf. 1st. F/NF. B3. $50.00

**CRICHTON, Michael.** *Terminal Man.* 1972. Knopf. 1st. NF/dj. S13. $22.00

**CRICHTON, Michael.** *Terminal Man.* 1972. Knopf. 1st. VG/NF. M23. $15.00

**CRIDER, Bill.** *Booked for a Hanging.* 1992. St Martin. 1st. sgn. F/dj. T2. $25.00

**CRIDER, Bill.** *Shotgun Saturday Night.* 1987. Walker. 1st. sgn. author's 2nd book. F/dj. A24. $40.00

**CRIDER, Bill.** *Texas Capitol Murders.* 1992. St Martin. 1st. F/dj. A23. $35.00

**CRIDLAND, Robert B.** *Practical Landscape Gardening.* 1926. NY. De La Mare. 2nd/6th prt. 276p. gilt gr cloth. F1. $25.00

**CRILE, George.** *Mechanistic View of War & Peace.* 1915. NY. 1st. 104p. A13. $40.00

**CRISCOM, L.** *Distribution of Bird-Life in Guatemala...* 1932. NY. 8vo. 439p. F/wrp. C12. $120.00

**CRISP, Olga.** *Studies in Russian Economy Before 1914.* 1976. London. Macmillan. 1st. F/dj. B11. $15.00

**CRISP, Stephen.** *Epistle to Friends Concerning the Present...* 1797. London. James Phillips. 10th. 12mo. 32p. V3. $55.00

**CRISP, Stephen.** *Memorable Account of the Christian Experiences...* 1694. London. T Sowle. 536 of 543p. rb/lt worn leather. V3. $200.00

**CRISPIN, Edmund.** *Best Tales of Terror.* 1962. London. Faber. 1st. NF/dj. M15. $45.00

**CRITCHELY, MacDonald.** *Parietal Lobes.* 1953. London. Arnold. 480p. lib buckram. G7. $150.00

**CROCKER, Betty.** *Betty Crocker's Cookbook.* 1970. Golden. looseleaf. VG. A16. $15.00

**CROCKER, Betty.** *Betty Crocker's Cookery Book.* 1963. 4th. sbdg. VG. E6. $15.00

**CROCKER, Betty.** *Betty Crocker's Picture Cookbook.* 1950. General Mills. 1st. VG. W2. $40.00

**CROCKER, William.** *Canela (Eastern Timira). I: Ethnographic Introduction.* 1990. Smithsonian. 1st. 4to. 487p. wrp. F3. $30.00

**CROCKER, William.** *Growth of Plants.* 1948. Reinhold. 450p. VG. A10. $20.00

**CROCKETT, James.** *Perennials.* 1972. Time Life. 160p. VG. A10. $18.00

**CROCKETT, S.R.** *Sir Toady Crusoe.* 1905. Stokes. 1st. 356p. cloth. G. C14. $12.00

**CROFT-COOKE, Rupert.** *Exotic Food.* 1971. Herder. G/dj. A16. $20.00

**CROFTS, Freeman Wills.** *Anything to Declare?* 1957. London. Hodder Stoughton. 1st. VG/dj. M15. $100.00

**CROFTS, Freeman Wills.** *Purple Sickle Murders.* 1929. Harper. 1st Am. G. N4. $25.00

**CROFUTT, G.A.** *Crofutt's New Overland Tourist & Pacific Coast Guide...* 1878. Chicago. Overland. 8vo. dbl columns/full-p pl. 321p. gr cloth. O1. $120.00

**CROIL, James.** *Steam Navigation: Its Relation to Commerce of Canada & US.* 1973 (1898). Wm Briggs. Coles Canadian Collection. F/pict wrp. A26. $15.00

**CROLY, George.** *Tarry Thou-Till-I-Come.* 1901. NY. 1st. ils Thulstrup. 588p. gilt dk red cloth. VG. H3. $40.00

**CROMBIE, Deborah.** *All Shall Be Well.* 1994. NY. Scribner. 1st. sgn. F/dj. T2. $35.00

**CROMIE, Robert.** *Great Chicago Fire.* 1958. McGraw Hill. 1/110. sgn. NF/VG+. B20. $45.00

**CROMIE & PINKSTON.** *Dillinger: Short Violent Life.* 1962. NY. McGraw Hill. 1st. 266p. VG/dj. B5. $25.00

**CROMPTON, Anne Eliot.** *Gawain & Lady Green.* 1997. DIF. 1st. F/dj. T10. $40.00

**CROMPTON, Anne Eliot.** *Snow Pony.* 1991. NY. Holt. 1st. F/dj. O3. $20.00

**CRONIN, A.J.** *Green Years.* 1945. Little Brn. 347p. VG. W2. $20.00

**CRONIN, Edward W.** *Arun: Natural History of the World's Deepest Valley.* 1979. Houghton Mifflin. 236p. F/VG. S15. $9.00

**CRONIN, Francis D.** *Under the Southern Cross: Sage of the American Division.* 1951. WA. Combat Forces. 1st. 432p. VG. S16. $95.00

**CRONIN, Justin.** *Short History of the Long Ball.* 1990. Council Oak. 1st. F/dj. P8. $15.00

**CRONIN, Vincent.** *Paris on the Eve 1900-1914.* 1989. London. 1st. dj. T9. $18.00

**CRONKHITE, Daniel.** *Recollections of a Young Desert Rat: Impressions of NV...* 1972. Sagebrush. 1st. 102p. F/VG. B19. $45.00

**CRONKITE, Walter.** *Reporter's Life.* 1996. NY. Knopf. 1st. sgn bookplate. F/dj. A23. $42.00

**CRONLEY, Jay.** *Screwballs.* 1980. Doubleday. 1st. F/VG. P8. $60.00

**CROOK, George.** *General George Crook: His Autobiography.* 1946. Norman, OK. 1st. 326p. cloth. dj. D11. $50.00

**CROOKSHANK, F.G.** *Epidemiological Essays.* 1931. NY. 1st. 136p. A13. $50.00

**CROSBY, Alexander.** *Old Greenwood, Pathfinder of the West.* 1967. Talisman. 1st. 144p. VG. J2. $75.00

**CROSBY, Alexander.** *Steamboat Up the Colorado...1857-1858.* 1965. Little Brn. 1st. ils Bjorklund. VG/dj. F7. $32.50

**CROSBY, Caresse.** *Graven Images.* 1926. Houghton Mifflin. 1st. F/clip. B4. $850.00

**CROSBY, Percy.** *Skippy.* 1929. Grosset Dunlap. ils. VG/dj. A21. $50.00

**CROSFIELD, Domini.** *Dances of Greece.* 1948. NY. Chanticleer. ils. 40p. gray cloth. NF/dj. B14. $40.00

**CROSLAND, T.W.H.** *Five Notions.* 1903. London. Grant Richards. 1st. teg. gilt maroon cloth. F. M24. $60.00

**CROSS, Amanda.** *Question of Max.* 1976. Knopf. 1st. NF/dj. M25. $25.00

**CROSS, Amanda.** *Theban Mysteries.* 1971. Knopf. 1st. F/NF. M25. $30.00

**CROSS, Peter.** *Knight in Medieval England.* 1996. Stroud, Eng. F/dj. O3. $25.00

**CROSS, Wilbur L.** *Thanksgiving Day Proclamations of His Excellency...* 1963. Worcester. St Onge. mini. 1/1000. portrait ftspc. 56p. gilt bl leather. B24. $35.00

**CROSS & MOORE.** *Atlas of Mercury.* 1977. NY. Crown. ils/photos. 48p. VG/dj. K5. $25.00

**CROSSMAN, Carl L.** *China Trade, Export Furniture, Silver & Other Objects.* 1972. Princeton. Pyne. 1st. ils. 275p. gilt bl cloth. F/NF. F1. $100.00

**CROTHERS, Samuel McChord.** *Children of Dickens.* 1933. Scribner. ils JW Smith. VG. M17. $65.00

**CROTZ, Keith.** *Ewaniana: Writings of Joe & Nesta Ewan.* 1989. Chillicothe. Am Botanist. 67p. VG/dj. A10. $25.00

**CROUCH, Benny.** *Cullen Montgomery Baker: Reconstruction Desperado.* nd. np. ils/maps. 190p. VG/dj. E1. $35.00

**CROUCH, Brodie.** *Jornada del Muerto: Pageant in the Desert.* 1989. AH Clark. 1st. notes/index/map. 219p. F. B19. $20.00

**CROUGH, B.** *Jornada del Muerto: Pageant of the Desert.* 1989. Spokane. 1/750. 219p. F/dj. M4. $40.00

**CROUTIER, Alev.** *Taking the Waters: Spirit, Art, Sensuality.* 1992. NY. 224p. A13. $40.00

**CROW DOG, Mary.** *Lakota Woman.* 1990. Grove Weidenfeld. 1st. photos. NF/dj. R14. $35.00

**CROWE, Cameron.** *Fast Times at Ridgemont High.* 1981. S&S. 1st. F/dj. B4. $150.00

**CROWE, Philip K.** *Sport Is Where You Find It.* 1953. NY. 1st. sgn. ils Paul Brown. 189p. VG. A17. $30.00

**CROWELL, Grace Noll.** *Lifted Lamp.* 1942. Harper. 1st. sm 8vo. 55p. VG/dj. W2. $10.00

**CROWL, Philip.** *Campaign in the Marianas: US Army in WWII, War in Pacific.* 1985. WA. fld mc maps/photos/index. 505p. VG. S16. $35.00

**CROWLEY, John.** *Love & Sleep.* 1994. NY. Bantam. 1st. sgn. F/dj. M23. $50.00

**CROWLEY, Mary Catherine.** *Heroine of the Strait.* 1902. Boston. Little Brn. 1st. 373p. G. G11. $8.00

**CROWN, Lawrence.** *Marilyn at Twentieth Century Fox.* 1987. London. Planet Books/WH Allen. 1st. VG/dj. A14. $17.50

**CROWTHER, James Arnold.** *Ions, Electrons & Ionizing Radiations.* 1924. Longman Gr. 4th. ils. 328p. cloth. K5. $50.00

**CROWTHER, Samuel.** *Romance & Rise of the American Tropics.* 1929. Doubleday. 1st. 390p. F3. $15.00

**CROY, Homer.** *Jesse James Was My Neighbor.* 1949. NY. DSP. 4th. 313p. VG/dj. B5. $30.00

**CROY, Homer.** *Last of the Great Outlaws, Cole Younger.* 1956. NY. DSP. 1st. ils/index. VG/dj. B5. $25.00

**CROY, Homer.** *Wheels West.* 1953. Hastings. 8vo. 242p. VG/dj. P4. $30.00

**CRUICKSHANK, Alan D.** *Wings in the Wilderness.* 1947. NY. 1st. 125 full-p photos. 260p. VG/dj. A17. $17.50

**CRUIKSHANK, George.** *Points of Humour.* 1823-24. London. Baldwin. 2 parts in 1 vol. 1st. sgn Riviere. 20 pl. 19th-C calf. M24. $500.00

**CRUIKSHANK, Percy.** *Frog That Would a Wooing Go.* ca 1840. London. Read. 12mo. pict stiff paper wrp. R5. $275.00

**CRUM, Gertrude.** *World of Menus & Recipes.* 1970. Bobbs Merrill. G/dj. A16. $6.50

**CRUM, Laura.** *Cutter.* 1994. St Martin. 1st. author's 1st novel. F/F. H11. $25.00

**CRUM, Laura.** *Hoofprints.* 1996. St Martin. 1st. VG/dj. O3. $25.00

**CRUMB, R.** *Yum Yum Book: Oggie & the Beanstalk.* 1975. SF. Scrimshaw. 1st. 8vo. ils. 144p. F/dj. R3. $60.00

**CRUMLEY, James.** *Bordersnakes.* 1996. Mysterious. 1st. sgn. F/dj. A23/M15. $45.00

**CRUMLEY, James.** *Collection.* 1991. London. Picador. Omnibus. F/dj. M15. $85.00

**CRUMLEY, James.** *Dancing Bear.* 1983. Random. 1st. sgn. F/dj. M15. $125.00

**CRUMLEY, James.** *Last Good Kiss.* 1978. Random. 1st. rem mk. F/dj. D10. $85.00

**CRUMLEY, James.** *Mexican Duck Tree.* 1994. London. Picador. 1st. sgn. F/dj. A23. $48.00

**CRUMLEY, James.** *Mexican Pig Bandit.* 1998. Mission Viejo. ASAP. 1st. 1/300. sgns. F/as issued. M15. $60.00

**CRUMLEY, James.** *Mexican Tree Duck.* 1993. Mysterious. 1st. sgn. F/dj. M15. $45.00

**CRUMLEY, James.** *One to Count Cadence.* 1969. Random. 1st. sgn. author's 1st book. F/NF. B3. $250.00

**CRUMLEY, James.** *Pigeon Shoot.* 1987. Santa Barbara. 1st. 1/350. sgn. F/sans. M15. $135.00

**CRUMP, Irving.** *Our Movie Makers.* 1940. Dodd Mead. photos. VG/dj. C9. $90.00

**CRUSE, Amy.** *Englishman & His Books in the Early Nineteenth Century.* ca 1930s. NY. Crowell. 1st Am. 301p. cloth. F/dj. O10. $55.00

**CRUXENT & ROUSE.** *Arqueologia Cronologica de Venezuela.* 1961. Pan Union Panamericana. 2 vol. ils/maps. wrp. F3. $30.00

**CRYSLER, M.A.** *Collected Works on Botany & Plant Anatomy.* 1904-1944. various places. contains 21 offprints. lg 8vo. 350+p. early cloth. NF. C12. $48.00

**CUBITT & JOYCE.** *Dies ist Namibia.* 1992. Capetown, RSA. Struik. 1st. ils/map. 160p. NF/dj. W1. $35.00

**CUDAHY, Brian J.** *Change at Park Street Under: Story of Boston's Subways.* 1972. Brattleboro. photos. VG/dj. M17. $30.00

**CUDDON, J.A.** *Penguin Book of Ghost Stories.* 1991. Bloomsbury. F/dj. P3. $20.00

**CUDDON, J.A.** *Penguin Book of Horror Stories.* 1991. Bloomsbury. 2nd. F/dj. P3. $20.00

**CUDDY & SCOTT.** *British Columbia in Books, Annotated Bibliography.* 1974. Vancouver. 4to. 152p. VG/wrp. A4. $65.00

**CULBERT, T. Patrick.** *Lost Civilization: Story of the Classic Maya.* 1974. Harper Row. 123p. wrp. F3. $20.00

**CULHANE, John.** *Walt Disney's Fantasia.* 1987. NY. Abradale. rpt. F/dj. C9. $30.00

**CULLEN, Countee.** *Copper Sun.* 1927. NY. Harper. 1st. NF. B2. $125.00

**CULLEN, W.** *First Lines in Practice of Physic, Vol II.* 1784. Edinburgh. 455p. rb. E6. $100.00

**CULLUM, Grove.** *Selection & Training of the Polo Pony.* 1934. NY. Scribner. 1st/A ed. G. O3. $65.00

**CULPEPPER, N.** *Herbal Legacy.* 1986. Lilliput. mini. 1/250. hand-colored ils. teg. gilt brn full morocco. B24. $185.00

**CULVER, Timothy;** see Westlake, Donald E.

**CUMBERLAND, Charles.** *Mexican Revolution: Constitutionalist Years.* 1972. Austin. U TX. 1st. photos/biblio/index. 449p. F3. $20.00

**CUMBERLAND, Richard.** *Jew; or, Benevolent Hebrew. A Comedy.* 1795. Cork. Harris. 12mo. wrp. R12. $175.00

**CUMBERLAND, Richard.** *Memoirs...Written by Himself...* 1806. London. Lackington Allen Co/Temple of Muses. 2 vol in 1. 1st. H13. $295.00

**CUMMING, C.F.** *Granite Grags of California.* 1886. Edinburgh/London. Blackwood. 8vo. 384p+rear pocket map. NF. O1. $200.00

CUMMING, Primrose. *Wednesday Pony.* (1939). London. Blackie. ils Stanley Lloyd. 190p. red brd. T5. $25.00

CUMMING, Roualeyn Gordon. *Five Years of a Hunter's Life in the Interior of S Africa...* 1851. NY. Harper. 2 vol. 8vo. lacks ffe. G-. H7. $75.00

CUMMING & RANKIN. *Fate of a Nation: American Revolution...* 1975. London. Phaidon. 4to. 352p. gilt gr cloth. F/NF. F1. $35.00

CUMMINGS, Byron. *First Inhabitants of AZ & Southwest.* 1953. Tucson. Cummins Pub. 8vo. 251p. VG/dj. F7. $85.00

CUMMINGS, Byron. *Indians I Have Known.* 1952. Tucson. AZ Silhouettes. 8vo. photos. dj. F7. $55.00

CUMMINGS, E.E. *EIMI (I Am).* 1933. Covici Friede. 1st. 1/1381. sgn. F/dj. B24. $675.00

CUMMINGS, E.E. *Poems.* 1958. Harcourt Brace. 1st. tall 8vo. brn brd/blk cloth spine. F. F1. $25.00

CUMMINGS, E.E. *Puella Mae.* Golden Eagle. 1st. ils. VG+/dj. B30. $30.00

CUMMINGS, E.E. *Santa Claus.* 1974. Paris. Eds de l'Herne. 1/75 on d'Arches. Ils Calder. 41p. w/9 orig etchings. F. H5. $5,000.00

CUMMINGS, E.E. *ViVa.* 1931. Horace Liveright. 1st. 1/95. sgn. F/case. B24. $950.00

CUMMINGS, Primrose. *Chestnut Filly.* 1940. Mill Co INc. ils Stanley Lloyd. VG. A21. $45.00

CUMMINGS & MCFARLAND. *Federal Justice: Chapters in History of Justice...* 1937. Macmillan. 1st. lg 8vo. 576p. gilt red cloth. B20. $25.00

CUMMINS, Clessie. *My Days With the Diesel.* 1967. Phil. 1st. VG/dj. B5. $40.00

CUMMINS, Julia H. *My Garden Comes of Age.* 1926. Macmillan. 1st. photos. 180p. VG. A25. $20.00

CUMMINS, Maureen. *Aureole to Zingaresca: An Exotic Alphabet Book.* 1994. Center for Books Arts. 1/60. marked Artist Copy. M/prt wrp/cloth case. B24. $950.00

CUMMINS, Maureen. *Phantasies of a Love Thief. Eleventh-Century Sanskrit Poem.* 1994. NY. Inanna. 1/30. sgn. obl 4to. frenchfold. w/10 proof sheets. AN. B24. $1,250.00

CUMMINS, Maureen. *Song of Songs. Tale of Two Lovers & One City.* 1990. Covelo, CA. 1/25. sgn. w/9 orig drawings & sgn note. F/box. B24. $1,250.00

CUNARD, Nancy. *Brave Poet: Indomitable Rebel.* 1968. Phil. 1st. edit H Ford. T9. $35.00

CUNARD, Nancy. *Nous Gens d'Espagne.* 1949. Perpignan. self pub. 1/500. sgn. VG/wrp. B2. $85.00

CUNEO, John. *Air Weapon, 1914-1916.* 1947. Harrisburg. 1st. ils. 503p. VG/dj. B18. $175.00

CUNNINGHAM, Carol. *Alphabet Alfresco.* (1985). Mill Valley, CA. Sunflower. mini. 1/85. sgn. cloth prt w/ducks. F. B24. $75.00

CUNNINGHAM, Carol. *Woven Winds.* 1987. Mill Valley, CA. Sunflower. mini. 1/40. sgn. mc silk over brd. B24. $125.00

CUNNINGHAM, Imogen. *After Ninety.* 1977. Seattle. U WA. 1st. F/NF. B20. $75.00

CUNNINGHAM, J. Morgan; see Westlake, Donald E.

CUNNINGHAM, Jere. *Visitor.* 1978. St Martin. 1st. author's 2nd book. NF/VG+. S18. $40.00

CUNNINGHAM, John. *Quakers From Their Origin Till Present Time...* 1868. Edinburgh. John Menzies. 12mo. 334p. V3. $25.00

CUNNINGHAM, Julia. *Maybe, a Mole.* 1974. Pantheon. 1st. ils Cyndy Szekeres. F/G. M5. $20.00

CUNNINGHAM, Julia. *Mouse Called Junction.* 1980. Pantheon. 1st. obl 8vo. ils Michael Hague. bl brd. NF/VG. T5. $45.00

CUNNINGHAM, Marion. *Fannie Farmer Baking Book.* 1996. Random. 1st. sm 4to. 624p. F/NF. W2. $60.00

CUNNINGHAM, Michael. *Flesh & Blood.* 1995. FSG. 1st. author's 2nd book. F/dj. R14. $30.00

CUNNINGHAM, Michael. *Home at the End of the World.* 1990. FSG. 1st. sgn. F/dj. O11. $45.00

CUNNINGHAM, Michael. *Home at the End of the World.* 1990. FSG. 1st. NF/F. H11. $25.00

CUNNINGHAM, N.E. *In Pursuit of the Life of Thomas Jefferson.* 1987. LA U. 1st. ils. 414p. F/dj. M4. $25.00

CUNNINGHAM, N.E. *Jeffersonian Republicans in Power: Party Operations...* (1963). UNC. 318p. VG/dj. B10. $35.00

CUNNINGHAM, Peter. *Story of Nell Gwyn: And Sayings of Charles the Second.* 1852. London. Bradbury Evans. 1st. ils. 212p. Kaufmann bdg. F1. $200.00

CUPPLES, Mrs. George. *Life of Miss Dollikins.* ca 1860s. London. Nelson. obl 16mo. ils/sgn R Patterson. R5. $350.00

CURLEY, Thomas. *Samuel Johnson & the Age of Travel.* 1976. Athens, GA. 1st. dj. H13. $45.00

CURRENT, Richard. *Encyclopedia of the Confederacy: Definitive Source Book...* 1993. NY. 4 vol. ils/index. VG. S16. $175.00

CURREY, L.W. *Science Fiction & Fantasy Authors, a Bibliography...* 1979. identifies 1st eds of 216 authors. 600p. F. A4. $250.00

CURREY, Richard. *Fatal Light.* 1988. Dutton. 1st. author's 1st book. NF/dj. A24. $40.00

CURREY, Richard. *Fatal Light.* 1988. NY. Dutton. 1st. NF/dj. R11. $17.00

CURRIE, Ellen. *Moses Supposes.* 1994. S&S. 1st. F/dj. M23. $20.00

CURRIER & TILTON. *Bibliography of Oliver Wendell Holmes.* 1953. NY. 1st. 708p. A13. $100.00

CURRY, Robert A. *Bahamian Lore.* 1930. Paris. 2nd. 1/1030. unp. VG/dj. B18. $22.50

CURRY, W.L. *History of Jerome Township, Union County, Ohio.* 1913. Columbus. 1st. inscr. photos/ils. 205p. G. B18. $150.00

CURTIS, G.T. *Life of Daniel Webster.* 1870. NY. Appleton. 2 vol. 2nd. 3-quarter leather/raised bands. VG. S17. $65.00

CURTIS, Joseph H. *Life of Campestrils Ulm, Oldest Inhabitant of Boston Common.* 1910. Boston. ils/maps. 88p. bl brd. B26. $38.00

CURTIS, Laura A. *Elusive Daniel Defoe.* 1984. London/NY. Vision/Barnes Noble. 1st. 8vo. F/dj. A2. $14.00

CURTIS, Paul A. *Guns & Gunning.* 1941. Outdoor Life. special ed. 384p. NF. A17. $17.50

CURTIS, Thomas Quinn. *Von Stroheim.* 1971. FSG. 1st. VG/dj. C9. $55.00

CURTIS, Tony. *Kid Andrew Cody & Julie Sparrow.* 1977. Doubleday. 1st. VG/dj. C9. $25.00

CURWEN, Henry Darcy. *Johnson Sampler.* 1963. Harvard. 1st. dj. H13. $75.00

CURWOOD, James Oliver. *Alaskan.* 1923. NY. Cosmopolitan. 1st. 326p. VG. G11. $20.00

CURWOOD, James Oliver. *Flaming Forest.* 1921. NY. Cosmopolitan. 1st. 296p. VG. G11. $10.00

CURWOOD, James Oliver. *Gentleman of Courage.* 1924. NY. Cosmopolitan. 1st. 342p. G. G11. $15.00

CURWOOD, James Oliver. *Valley of Silent Men.* 1920. NY. Cosmopolitan. 1st. 298p. VG. G11. $15.00

CURZON, Julian. *Great Cyclone at St Louis & E St Louis, May 27, 1896...* 1896. St Louis. Cyclone Pub. 8vo. photos. 416p. K5. $80.00

CUSHING, Frank H. *My Adventures in Zuni.* 1967. Palmer Lake, CO. Filter. rpt. AN. A19. $30.00

CUSHING, Frank H. *Nation of the Willows.* 1965-83. Northland. rpt. 8vo. gr brd. NF/dj. F7. $45.00

CUSHING, Harvey. *Bio-Biography of Andreas Vesalius.* 1943. NY. Schuman. 1/800. ils. 228p. quarter morocco/linen. G7. $495.00

CUSHING, Harvey. *Consecratio Medici & Other Papers.* 1929. Boston. 1st/3rd prt. 276p. A13. $90.00

CUSHING, Harvey. *From a Surgeon's Journal.* 1936. Boston. 1st/later prt. 534p. A13. $40.00

CUSHING, Harvey. *Life of Sir William Osler.* 1925. Oxford. 2 vol. 1st/1st issue. bl cloth. G7. $145.00

CUSHING, Harvey. *Pituitary Body & Its Disorders. Clinical States...* 1912. Phil. 2nd imp. 341p. cloth. G7. $495.00

CUSHING, Harvey. *Studies in Intracranial Physiology & Surgery...* 1926. OUP. stiff prt wrp. G7. $495.00

CUSHING, Harvey. *Tumors of Nervus Acusticus & Syndrome of Cerebellopontine...* 1917. Phil. Saunders. 296p. cloth. VG. G7. $495.00

CUSHING & EISENHARDT. *Meningiomas: Their Classification, Regional Behaviour...* 1938. Springfield. Thomas. lg royal 8vo. 685 figures. 785p. NF/dj. G7. $1,395.00

CUSHMAN, Dan. *Great North Trail.* 1966. NY. McGraw Hill. 1st. 8vo. 384p. bl cloth. P4. $30.00

CUSHMAN, Henry Wyles. *Historical & Biographical Genealogy of the Cushmans...* 1855. Boston. Little Brn. 1st. 666p. G. B5. $95.00

CUSHMAN, Mary. *Missionary Doctor: Story of 20 Years in Africa.* 1944. 2nd. photos. VG/dj. E6. $18.00

CUSSLER, Clive. *Cyclops.* 1986. S&S. 1st. F/F. B3. $45.00

CUSSLER, Clive. *Night Probe!* 1981. Bantam. 1st. F/VG+. C15. $40.00

CUSSLER, Clive. *Raise the Titanic!* 1976. Viking. 1st. sgn. F/dj. M15. $145.00

CUSSLER, Clive. *Vixen 03.* 1978. Viking. 1st. sgn. F/F. P3/T2. $35.00

CUSSLER, Clive. *Vixen 03.* 1978. Viking. 1st. VG/dj. S13. $18.00

CUSTER, Elizabeth B. *Follow the Guidon.* 1890. Harper. 1st. 8vo. 341p. cloth. NF. O1. $75.00

CUSTER, George. *My Life on the Plains.* 1952. Lakeside Classic. edit Milo Milton Quaife. xl. G. V4. $22.50

CUTAK, Ladislaus. *Cactus Guide.* 1956. Van Nostrand. 1st. 144p. NF/dj. B14. $40.00

CUTLER, C.C. *Greyhounds of the Sea: Story of American Clipper Ship.* 1984. Annapolis. 3rd. photos/plans. 688p. F/dj. M4. $35.00

CUTRER, T.W. *Ben McCulloch & the Frontier Military Tradition.* 1993. NC U. 1st. ils/maps. 402p. F/dj. M4. $30.00

CUTRIGHT, Paul Russell. *Lewis & Clark: Pioneering Naturalists.* 1969. Urbana. 1st. VG/dj. B5. $75.00

CUTTER, E. *Contribution to Treatment of Uterine Versions & Flexions.* 1876. 2nd. ils. VG. E6. $35.00

CUTTER, Elizabeth. *Trends in Plant Morphogenesis.* 1967. London. Longman. 329p. Vg/dj. A10. $20.00

CYWIN, Allen. *Agricultural Pollution of Great Lakes Basin.* 1971. WA. EPA. 94p. VG/wrp. A10. $12.00

CZOLOWSKI, T. *Toronto Calling.* 1976. Olympiad. F/dj. T12. $8.00

CZWIKLITZER, Christopher. *Picasso's Posters.* (1970-71). Random. 1st Am. folio. 365p+chronological catalogu. F/dj. F1. $250.00

# D

**D'AGAPEYEFF, A.** *Codes & Ciphers, Compass Book.* nd. London. F/F. E6. $12.00

**D'AMBROSIO, Charles.** *Point.* 1995. Boston. Little Brn. 1st. sgn. F/dj. O11. $40.00

**D'AMBROSIO, Charles.** *Point.* 1995. Little Brn. 1st. F/dj. M23. $20.00

**D'AMBROSIO, Joseph.** *In the Small Garden of Gloria Stuart.* 1986. LA. 1/50. sgn. 64p. 2/2 sgn serigraphs. gold kid. F/clamshell box. B24. $750.00

**D'AMBROSIO, Joseph.** *Krome, a Further Experience.* 1971. np. 1/100. sgn. 8vo. silkscreen prts. silver leather. F. B24. $850.00

**D'AMBROSIO, Joseph.** *Land of the Inca.* 1985. Mill Valley, CA. mini. 1/25 (85 total). sgn/prt C Cunningham. 3-D bdg/case. B24. $325.00

**D'AMBROSIO, Joseph.** *Windjammers.* 1988. Lorson's Books & Prts. 1/21. sgn suite of 15 etchings. F/Box. B24. $850.00

**D'AULAIRE, Ingri.** *Magic Meadow.* 1958. Doubleday. 1st. cloth-backed ils brd. mc dj. R5. $185.00

**D'AULAIRE & D'AULAIRE.** *George Washington.* 1936. Doubleday. 1st. tall 4to. ils. VG. D1. $45.00

**D'AULAIRE & D'AULAIRE.** *Wings for Per.* 1944. Doubleday Doran. 1st. ils. unp. bl cloth. VG/torn. D1. $85.00

**D'AULAIRE & PARIN.** *Abraham Lincoln.* 1942. NY. Doubleday. later prt. folio. ils. F/dj. H4. $45.00

**D'AULAIRE & PARIN.** *Book of Greek Myths.* nd (1962). Doubleday. early (pre-ISBN). 192p. G+. C14. $18.00

**D'AULAIRE & PARIN.** *Leif the Lucky.* (1941). Doubleday. New Ed. xl. NF/dj. H4. $24.00

**D'AULAIRE & PARIN.** *Leif the Lucky.* 1941. Doubleday Doran. 1st. 4to. mc dj. R5. $200.00

**D'AULAIRE & PARIN.** *Lord's Prayer.* 1934. Doubleday Doran. 1st. lg 4to. pict brd/pict dj/glassine dj. R5. $175.00

**D'AULAIRE & PARIN.** *Trolls Garden.* 1972. Doubleday. 2nd. ils. 62p. F/dj. H4. $30.00

**D'AUVERGNE.** *Aresta Amorum, Cum Erudita Benedicti Curtii Symphoriani...* 1544. Paris. Chas Langelier. 8vo. 211p. contemporary vellum. K1. $750.00

**D'EMILIO & FREEDMAN.** *Intimate Matters: History of Sexuality in America.* 1988. Harper Row. 1st. photos. 428p. VG/dj. A25. $22.00

**D'ESSEN, Lorrain.** *Kangaroos in the Kitchen: Story of Animal Talent Scouts.* 1959. McKay. 1st. photos. VG/clip. A25. $20.00

**DABNEY, R.L.** *Life & Campaigns of Lt-Gen Thomas J Jackson...* 1976 (1865). Harrisburg, VA. Sprinkle Pub. reissue. gray cloth. NF. A14. $21.00

**DABNEY, Virginius.** *Patriots: American Revolution, Generation of Genius.* 1975. NY. Atheneum. 1st. ils. 248p. NF/dj. M10. $22.50

**DACEY, Philip.** *Gerard Manley Hopkins Meets Walt Whitman in Heaven...* 1982. Great Barrington, MA. Penmaen. 1/300. ils Michael McCurdy. F/dj. F1. $50.00

**DADANT, C.P.** *First Lessons in Beekeeping.* 1938. Am Bee Journal. revised. ils. 127p. VG. S14. $15.00

**DAGGETT, David.** *Count the Cost: Address to People of CT...* 1804. Hartford. Hudson Goodwin. 1st. 8vo. half modern morocco. NF. O1. $300.00

**DAHL, Roald.** *Ah, Sweet Mystery of Life.* 1990. Knopf. 1st. ils John Lawrence. F/F. B3. $25.00

**DAHL, Roald.** *BFG.* 1982. FSG. ltd. 1/300. sgn. bl cloth. case. R5. $585.00

**DAHL, Roald.** *Boy: Tales of Childhood.* 1984. NY. FSG. 1st Am. 8vo. pict dj. R5. $75.00

**DAHL, Roald.** *Minipins.* 1991. London. Cape. 1st. ils Patrick Benson. F/F. B3. $45.00

**DAHL, Roald.** *My Uncle Oswald.* 1979. London. Michael Joseph. 1st. F/F. B3. $85.00

**DAHL, Roald.** *My Uncle Oswald.* 1979. London. Michael Joseph. 1st. VG/NF clip. A14. $21.00

**DAHL, Roald.** *Switch Bitch.* 1974. Knopf. 1st. F/dj. M21. $35.00

**DAHL, Roald.** *Two Fables.* 1986. FSG. 1st. ils Grahame Dean. F/VG clip. B30. $20.00

**DAHL, Roald.** *Witches.* 1983. FSG. 1st. ils Quentin Blake. 202p. VG/dj. D1. $35.00

**DAHL, Tessa.** *Working for Love.* 1989. Delacorte. 1st. F/F. B3. $15.00

**DAICHES, David.** *Critical Approaches to Literature.* 1956. Prentice Hall. 1st. VG/G. O4. $15.00

**DAIKEN, Leslie.** *Children's Toys Throughout the Ages.* (1980). London. Spring. ils. 207p. VG. M10. $15.00

**DAILEY, Janet.** *Great Alone.* 1986. NY. Poseidon. rem mk. VG/dj. P4. $25.00

**DAINOW, Joseph.** *Essays on Civil Law of Obligations.* 1969. LSU. G/dj. M11. $45.00

**DAKIN, Janet Wilder.** *Jeffy's Journal: Raising a Morgan Horse.* 1990. NY. Stephen Gr/Pelham. 1st. F/dj. O3. $15.00

**DALBY, Richard.** *Golden Age of Children's Book Illustration.* 1991. Michael O'Mara. 1st. F/dj. P3. $35.00

**DALBY, Richard.** *Tales of Witchcraft.* 1994. Castle. F/NF. P3. $18.00

**DALE, Alzina Stone.** *Dorothy L Sayers: Centenary Celebration.* (1993). Walker. 1st Am. 15 essays. ANd/j. A27. $19.00

**DALE, Alzina Stone.** *Maker & Craftsman: Story of Dorothy L Sayers.* 1978. Grand Rapids. ils. VG/dj. M17. $25.00

**DALE, Alzina Stone.** *Maker & Craftsman: Story of Dorothy L Sayers.* 1992. Harold Shaw. 1st. AN/wrp. A27. $12.00

**DALE, Edward Everett.** *Cattle Range Industry: Ranching of Great Plains...* 1960. Norman, OK. new ed/1st prt. 207p. cloth. dj. D11. $35.00

**DALE, Henry.** *Adventures in Physiology With Excursions Autopharmacology.* 1965. London. 652p. A13. $30.00

**DALE, Paul.** *70 North to 50 South.* 1969. Englewood Cliffs. 1st. ils/maps. 370p. VG/dj. B5. $35.00

**DALE, Philip.** *Medical Biographies: Ailments of 33 Famous Persons.* 1952. Norman, OK. 1st. 259p. A13. $40.00

**DALEY, Robert.** *Faint Cold Fear.* 1990. Little Brn. 1st. NF/dj. G8. $12.50

**DALEY, Robert.** *Prince of the City.* 1978. Boston. Houghton Mifflin. 1st. F/NF. H11. $35.00

**DALEY, Robert.** *Year of the Dragon.* 1981. NY. S&S. 1st. F/F. H11. $25.00

**DALEY, Rosie.** *In the Kitchen With Rosie: Oprah's Favorite Recipes.* 1994. Knopf. 8th. photos. 129p. VG/dj. P12. $7.00

**DALGAIRNS.** *Practice of Cookery Adapted to Business of Every Day Life...* 1830. Boston. 396p. rb. G+. E6. $200.00

**DALGLIESH, Alice.** *Courage of Sarah Noble.* 1954. Scribner. 1st. ils Leonard Weisgard. F/G. P2. $35.00

**DALI, Salvador.** *Hidden Faces.* 1944. Dial. 1st Am. 8vo. 413p. NF/VG+. B20. $75.00

**DALI, Salvador.** *Les Diners de Gala.* 1973. NY. VG/dj. B30. $65.00

**DALLAS, A.J.** *Reports of Cases Ruled & Adjudged in Courts in PA...* 1889. NY. Banks & Bros. 4 vol. full sheep. M11. $450.00

**DALLAS, Rita.** *Kennedy Case.* 1973. Putnam. 8vo. 352p. NF/VG. W2. $25.00

**DALLAS, Sandra.** *Persian Pickle Club.* 1995. St Martin. 1st. F/dj. M23. $20.00

**DALMAIS, Anne-Marie.** *And May the Best Animal Win!* 1986. Golden. 1st A ed. ils Doris Susan Smith. VG. M5. $10.00

**DALMAIS, Anne-Marie.** *Best Bedtime Stories of Mother Pig.* 1989. Derrydale. 1st Am. sm 4to. 29p. NF. C14. $12.00

**DALPHIN & WILLIAMS.** *Junior Classics, Vol 1: Fairy Tales & Fables.* 1956. PF Collier. 54th prt. 8vo. 358p. NF. W2. $35.00

**DALPHIN & WILLIAMS.** *Junior Classics, Vol 5: Stories That Never Grow Old.* 1956. PF Collier. 54th prt. 8vo. 391p. NF. W2. $135.00

**DALRYMPLE, Bryon W.** *Modern Book of the Black Bass.* 1972. Winchester. 1st. ils. 206p. VG/dj. S14. $10.00

**DALRYMPLE, Byron W.** *How to Rig & Fish Natural Baits.* 1976. Outdoor Life. 165p. ils/index. F/dj. A17. $10.00

**DALRYMPLE, Margaret Fisher.** *Merchant of Manchac: Letterbooks...1768-1790.* 1978. LSU. 451p. NF/dj. M10. $27.50

**DALTON, David.** *Rolling Stones: First Twenty Years.* 1981. Knopf. 192p. G+. P12. $20.00

**DALTON, John C.** *History of the College of Physicians & Surgeons...NY...* 1888. NY. 208p. xl. G7. $75.00

**DALY, Maureen.** *Patrick Visits the Farm.* 1959. Dodd Mead. 1st. ils Ellie Simmons. VG/dj. P2. $25.00

**DAMAS, David.** *Handbook of North American Indians Volume 5: Arctic.* 1984. Smithsonian. 829p. F. A17. $30.00

**DAMJAN, Mischa.** *December's Travels.* 1986. NY. Dial. 1st. 32p. F/dj. D4. $30.00

**DAMON, Valerie Hubbard.** *Grindle Lamfoon & the Procurnious Fleekers.* 1978. Star. 1st. sgn. ils Valerie. VG/dj. M20. $25.00

**DAMS, Jeanne M.** *Body in the Transept.* 1995. NY. Walker. 1st. F/dj. M23. $50.00

**DANA, Edward Salisbury.** *Minerals & How to Study Them...* (1895). NY. John Wiley. 2nd revised. 390p. gilt cloth. K5. $45.00

**DANCE, Helen Oakley.** *Stormy Monday: T-Bone Walker Story.* 1987. LSU. 1st. F/NF. B2. $45.00

**DANCER, Rex.** *Bad Girl Blues.* 1994. S&S. 1st. author's 1st book. F/F. H11. $25.00

**DANDY, Walter J.** *Intracranial Arterial Aneurysms.* 1947. Ithaca. 3rd. 5 fld charts. 146p. G7. $295.00

**DANE, Clemence.** *Babyons.* 1934. Doubleday Doran. rpt. 378p. VG/dj. M21. $30.00

**DANIEL, Dorothy.** *Cut & Engraved Glass 1771-1905.* (1950). Barrows. 6th. sm 4to. 441p. F/dj. H1. $75.00

**DANIEL, William Barker.** *Rural Sports/Supplement.* 1801-1813. London. Bunny Gold. 3 vol. ils/44 fine steel engravings. rb. F1. $875.00

**DANIELL, Rosemary.** *Fatal Flowers.* 1980. HRW. 1st. NF/dj. M23. $20.00

**DANIELL, Rosemary.** *Sexual Tour of the Deep South: Poems by Rosemary Daniell.* 1975. HRW. 1st. sc. 97p. VG+. A25. $12.00

**DANIELL & DANIELL.** *Picturesque Voyage to India by Way of China.* 1910. London. Thos Davidson. 1st. 50 aquatints. half gr morocco/5 raised bands. K1. $7,500.00

**DANIELS, Bruce C.** *Puritans at Play: Leisure & Recreation...* 1995. St Martin. 1st. VG/G. M10. $15.00

**DANIELS, Bruce C.** *Town & Country: Essays on Structure of Local Governments...* 1978. Wesleyan U. 1st. 279p. NF/dj. M10. $22.50

**DANIELS, G.H.** *American Science in the Age of Jackson.* 1994. AL U. 282p. F. M4. $15.00

**DANIELS, Jonathan.** *Mosby: Gray Ghost of the Confederacy.* (1959). Lippincott. 1st. ils Albert Orbaan. 122p. F/VG. B10. $25.00

**DANIELS, Josephus.** *Life of Woodrow Wilson 1856-1924.* 1924. 8vo. ils. 381p. gilt bl cloth. VG. S17. $7.00

**DANIELS, Les.** *Silver Skull.* 1979. Scribner. 1st. VG/G. L1. $60.00

**DANIELS, Les.** *Yellow Fog.* 1986. Donald Grant. 1st. sgn. Don Sebastian Villanueva #4. VG/dj. L1. $50.00

**DANN, Jack.** *Future Power.* 1976. Random. 1st. NF/VG. P3. $15.00

**DANN, John C.** *Nagle Journal.* 1988. Weidenfeld Nicholson. 1st. half cloth. F. T11. $60.00

**DANN, John C.** *Revolution Remembered: Eyewitness Accounts of the War...* 1980. Chicago. 1st. 446p. xl. VG/dj. M10. $25.00

**DANNENFELDT, Karl H.** *Leonard Rauwolf: 16th-Century Physician, Botanist...* 1968. Cambridge, MA. ils. 321p. F/dj. B26. $22.50

**DANSEREAU, Pierre.** *Biogeography: An Ecological Perspective.* 1957. Ronald. 394p. VG/dj. A10. $25.00

**DANTE, Alighieri.** *Divine Comedy.* 1969. Grossman. 3 vol. 1st thus. ils Baskin. tan linen/brn brd. F/VG. O4. $150.00

**DANTE, Alighieri.** *Stone Beloved.* 1986. Austin. Kairos. 1/150. ils Peter Nickel. silvered vellum/gray brd. F/case. F1. $400.00

**DANTE, Alighieri.** *Vision; or, Hell, Purgatory & Paradise.* 1883. Boston. trans HF Cary. VG. M17. $17.50

**DANTICAT, Edwidge.** *Breath, Eyes, Memory.* 1994. Soho. 1st. author's 1st book. F/dj. A24. $65.00

**DANTICAT, Edwidge.** *Krik? Krak!* 1995. NY. Soho. 1st. sgn. author's 2nd book. F/dj. R14. $65.00

**DANTON.** *Index to Festschriften in Librarianship.* 1970. 472p. VG. A4. $150.00

**DANVERS, Dennis.** *Wilderness.* 1991. NY. Poseidon. 1st. F/dj. R14. $30.00

**DANZ, Louis.** *Psychologist Looks at Art.* 1937. Longman Gr. 21 pl. VG/dj. G1. $38.00

**DARDIS, Tom.** *Keaton, the Man Who Wouldn't Lie Down.* 1980. Penguin. 1st. VG/wrp. C9. $48.00

**DARE, Ann.** *Clockwatchers' Cookbook.* 1973. Hamlyn. G/dj. A16. $9.00

**DARINGTON, Edgar B.P.** *Circus Boys Across the Continent.* 1911. Saalfield. lists 5 titles. VG/dj. M20. $20.00

**DARLING, W.** *Bankrupt Bookseller.* 1947. Edinburgh. Robert Grant. Collected Vol. 8vo. 351p. NF/VG. H4. $35.00

**DARLING & DARLING.** *Bird.* 1962. Boston. 2nd. ils/index. 261p. VG/dj. A17. $10.00

**DARLINGTON, C.D.** *Chromosome Botany & Origin of Cultivated Plants.* 1963. London. Aleen. 231p. VG/dj. A10. $20.00

**DARLINGTON, William.** *Memorials of John Bartram & Humphry Marshall.* 1967. NY. facs of 1849. 585p. F/dj. B26. $65.00

**DARLOWE & MOULE.** *Historical Catalogue of Prt Eds of Holy Scripture... 1903-1911.* 4 vol 1/350. 2341p/5 indexes. F. A4. $250.00

**DARNTON, Robert.** *Business of Enlightenment.* 1979. Harvard. ils. VG/dj. M17. $30.00

**DARROW, Clarence.** *Story of My Life.* 1932. Scribner. 1st/A. H4. $30.00

**DARROW, Clarence.** *Verdicts of the Court of Chicago.* 1963. Quadrangle. 1st. 8vo. 448p. VG+. H4. $10.00

**DARTON, F.J. Harvey.** *Children's Books in England, Five Centuries of Social Life.* 1932. Cambridge. 1st. 359p. gilt gr cloth. VG/G. F1. $100.00

**DARTON, F.J. Harvey.** *Children's Books in England.* 1960. Cambridge. 2nd. intro Kathleen Lines. 367p. xl. dj. H4. $16.00

**DARTON, N.H.** *Story of the Grand Canyon of Arizona: A Popular Ils Account.* 1922. Kansas City. Fred Harvey. 5th. sm 8vo. 80p. VG/stiff wrp. F7. $35.00

**DARTT, Robert L.** *GA Henty: A Bibliography.* 1971. 201p. F/NF. A4. $150.00

**DARWIN, Bernard.** *Golf Between Two Wars.* 1985. Chatto Windus. Classics of Golf series. 8vo. 227p. NF. H4. $35.00

**DARWIN, Charles Robert.** *Descent of Man & Selection in Relation to Sex.* 1971. LEC/Griffin. pref Ashley Montagu/ils Fritz Kredel. 362p. F. g1. $125.00

**DARWIN, Charles Robert.** *Expression of Emotions in Man & Animals.* 1872. London. John Murray. 7 heliotype pl/21 text ils. 374p. emb gr cloth. G1. $575.00

**DARWIN, Charles Robert.** *Expressions of Emotions in Man & Animals.* 1872. London. John Murray. 1st/1st issue. 374p. gr cloth. VG. G7. $995.00

**DARWIN, Charles Robert.** *Illustrated Origin of Species...Abridged by RE Leakey.* 1979. Hill Wang. 1st Am. sm 4to. 240p. F/dj. W2. $500.00

**DARWIN, Charles Robert.** *Insectivorous Plants.* 1895 (1875). NY. 30 text woodcuts. 462p. red leather/marbled brd. B26. $75.00

**DARWIN, Charles Robert.** *Journal of Researches Into Natural History & Geology...* 1952 (1839). NY. Hafner. rpt. 8vo. 16 pl/map ep. 629p. gilt brn cloth. VG. H4. $40.00

**DARWIN, Charles Robert.** *Journal of Researches Into Natural History & Geology...* 1957. NY. Heritage. ils. 489p. F/VG case. M12. $45.00

**DARWIN, Charles Robert.** *Life & Letters of Chas Darwin...Seventh Thousand Revised.* 1888 (1887). London. John Murray. 3 vol. 3rd revised/2nd prt. gilt gray-gr cloth. G1. $150.00

**DARWIN, Charles Robert.** *Life & Letters of...* 1897. NY. Appleton. 2 vol. edit Francis Darwin. VG. H4. $75.00

**DARWIN, Charles Robert.** *On the Origin of Species by Means of Natural Selection.* 1963. Heritage. ils Paul Landacre. 470p. case. A13. $80.00

**DARWIN, Charles Robert.** *On the Origin of the Species...Facsimile of 1st Edition.* 1964. Harvard. 8vo. 513p. F. W2. $30.00

**DARWIN, George Howard.** *Tides & Kindred Phenomena in Solar System.* 1898. NY. gr cloth. VG. B14. $75.00

**DARY, David A.** *Buffalo Book.* 1974. Chicago. 1st. ils. 374p. VG/NF. S15. $30.00

**DAS, P.K.** *Monsoons.* 1972. St Martin. ils/figures. 162p. VG/dj. K5. $30.00

**DASENT, G.W.** *East of the Sun, West of the Moon.* (1921). McKay. 8 full-p Edna Cooke pl. 289p. gr cloth. VG. B20. $45.00

**DATER, Judy.** *Imogen Cunningham: Portrait.* 1979. NYGS. 1st. sgn. NF/clip. S9. $125.00

**DAUBE, David.** *Collected Studies in Roman Law, Herausgegeben...* 1991. Frankfurt. Vittorio Klostermann. 2 vol. 78 essays. M11. $205.00

**DAUGHERTY, James.** *Bold Dragoon & Other Ghostly Tales.* 1942. Knopf. 5th. sgn pres. 8vo. orange cloth. pict dj. R5. $75.00

**DAUGHERTY, James.** *Lincoln's Gettysburg Address.* 1947. Whitman. 1st. lg 4to. 16 full-p ils. bl textured cloth. pict dj. R5. $100.00

**DAUZET, Marceline.** *One Happy Day.* 1939. Akron. Saalfield. ils Janet Laura Scott. VG. M20. $30.00

**DAVENPORT, Cyril.** *Beautiful Books.* (1929). London. Metheun. 1st. sq 8vo. 110p. H4. $22.00

**DAVENPORT, Guy.** *Ecologues: Eight Stories.* 1981. SF. ils Roy Behrens. VG/dj. M17. $20.00

**DAVENPORT, L.** *Bride's Cookbook.* 1908. 1st. 12 tabs on title. E6. $95.00

**DAVENPORT, Marcia.** *Mozart.* 1932. Scribner. 1st Am. NF/VG. W2. $125.00

**DAVENPORT, Steward.** *Carribbean Cavalier.* 1957. Dutton. 1st. VG/dj. L1. $15.00

**DAVENPORT, W.A.** *Art of the Gawain: Poet.* 1978. London. 1st. gr cloth. F/dj. T10. $45.00

**DAVENTRY, Leonard.** *Man of Double Deed.* 1965. Doubleday. VG/dj. P3. $20.00

**DAVID, Catherine.** *Simone Signoret.* 1993. Woodstock. Overlook. 213p. VG/dj. C5. $15.00

**DAVID, Peter.** *Star Trek: Next Generation: Imzadi.* 1992. S&S. 1st. F/dj. T12. $20.00

**DAVID, Robert.** *Malcolm Campbell, Sheriff.* 1932. Casper. Wyomingana. 1st. fair. V4. $110.00

**DAVID & VAN GRONINGEN.** *Papyrological Primer.* 1946. Leyden. 6 pl/2 maps. 168p. bl cloth. Q2. $30.00

**DAVIDS, Arlette.** *Flowers: Rock Plants. Drawn by Arlette Davids...* (1939). London/Paris/NY. Hyperion. 1st. folio. 40 mc pl. VG. H10. $75.00

**DAVIDSON, Diane Mott.** *Grilling Season.* 1997. Bantam. 1st. sgn. F/dj. A23. $38.00

**DAVIDSON, Diane Mott.** *Main Corpse.* 1996. NY. Bantam. 1st. F/dj. A23. $36.00

**DAVIDSON, Donald.** *Outland Paper.* 1924. Houghton Mifflin. 1st. F. L3. $250.00

**DAVIDSON, Donald.** *Tennessee: New River: Civil War to TVA.* 1948. Rinehart. 1st. 8vo. 377p. NF/dj. B20. $65.00

**DAVIDSON, George.** *Identification of Sir Francis Drake's Anchorage...* 1890. CA Hist Soc. inscr to WH Davis. 13 fld maps. 58p. prt wrp. D11. $50.00

**DAVIDSON, Harold G.** *Edward Borein, Cowboy Artist: Life & Works of...* 1974. Doubleday. 1st. 189p. gr buckram. AEG. F/case. B20. $450.00

**DAVIDSON, Harold G.** *Jimmy Swinnerton, the Artist & His Works.* 1985. Hearst Books. 1st. 8vo. 160p. VG/dj. F7. $50.00

**DAVIDSON, Orlando.** *Deadeyes: Story of the 96th Infantry Division.* 1974. WA. 1st. 310p. VG. S16. $75.00

**DAVIDSON, T.G.** *Speech of TG Davidson in House of Representatives...1859.* 1860. WA. Thos McGill. 1st. 15p. wrp. M8. $45.00

**DAVIE, M.** *Titanic: Life & Death of a Legend.* 1987. NY. 1st. VG/dj. B5. $40.00

**DAVIES, Arthur L.** *Sketches, Scholars & Scandals of a Quiet College Town.* 1975. Toronto. Dent. 1st. F/G. A26. $12.00

**DAVIES, C.M.** *Fun, Ancient & Modern.* 1878. London. Tinsley Bros. 2 vol. 1st. gilt bl cloth. B20. $300.00

**DAVIES, Horton.** *Christian Worship, Its History & Meaning.* 1957. NY. Abington. 128p. G. H10. $17.50

**DAVIES, J.** *Inkeeper's & Butler's Guide; or, Directory...Wines...* 1811. 14th. 199p. VG. E6. $225.00

**DAVIES, Jennifer.** *Victorian Kitchen.* 1889. London. 1st. 4to. mc woodcuts. F/F. E6. $25.00

**DAVIES, John.** *Legend of Hoby Baker.* 1966. Boston. 1st. ils. B14. $75.00

**DAVIES, Randall.** *English Society of the 18th Century in Contemporary Art.* 1907. London. Seeley. 4to. ils. xl. VG. H13. $35.00

**DAVIES, Rhys.** *Stars, World & the Women.* 1930. London. 1/550. sgn. VG+. A15. $60.00

**DAVIES, Richard.** *Photographs by a Russian Writer, Leonid Andreyev.* 1989. Thames Hudson. VG/dj. S5. $22.50

**DAVIES, Robertson.** *Introduction to 21st Toronto Antiquarian Book Fair.* 1993. Letters & Coach House. 1/100. sgn. F/wrp. B2. $200.00

**DAVIES, Robertson.** *Lyre of Orpheus.* 1988. Viking. 1/150. sgn/#d. decor brd. F/glassine. D10. $145.00

**DAVIES, Robertson.** *Lyre of Orpheus.* 1989. Viking. 1st. VG/F. B30. $25.00

**DAVIES, Robertson.** *Murther & Walking Spirits.* 1991. NY. 1st. VG/dj. M17. $15.00

**DAVIES, Robertson.** *Rebel Angels.* 1981. Macmillan. 1st Canadian. VG/G. B30. $40.00

**DAVIES, Robertson.** *Rebel Angels.* 1981. NY. 1st. VG/dj. M17. $25.00

**DAVIES, Robertson.** *Rebel Angels.* 1981. Toronto, Canada. Macmillan. 1st. VG/VG. M21. $45.00

**DAVIES, Robertson.** *Renown at Stratford: A Record of Shakespeare Festival...* 1953. Clark Irwin. 1st Canadian. ils Grant MacDonald. VG/G. B30. $60.00

**DAVIES, Russell.** *Ronald Searle: A Biography.* 1990. London. 4to. 192p. F/F. A4. $85.00

**DAVIES, Valentine.** *Miracle on 34th Street.* 1947. Harcourt Brace. 1st. sm 8vo. 120p. stp red cloth. F/clip. H5. $300.00

**DAVIES & KEELER.** *Bibliography of British History, Stuart Period.* 1970. Oxford. 2nd/revised. 4350 entries. 769p. F/F. A4. $95.00

**DAVINE, David.** *Hadrian's Wall: Study of the NW Frontier of Rome.* 1969. Boston. 1st Am. 244p. VG/dj. B18. $22.50

**DAVIS, Albert Belisle.** *Marquis at Bay.* 1992. Baton Rouge. 1st. F/dj. A23. $34.00

**DAVIS, Alec.** *Package & Print: Development of a Container & Label Design.* 1968. Clarkson Potter. 1st Am. 4to. ils. 112p. cloth. F/dj. O10. $65.00

**DAVIS, Bailey Fulton.** *Amherst County, Virginia, Courthouse Miniatures...* nd. typscript bdg in lib buckram. G. B10. $65.00

**DAVIS, Ben.** *Strange Angel.* 1991. San Antonio. Corona. 1st. F/dj. A23. $30.00

**DAVIS, Bertram.** *Johnson Before Boswell.* 1960. Yale. 1st. dj. H13. $65.00

**DAVIS, Bertram.** *Proof of Eminence: Life of Sir John Hawkins.* 1973. Bloomington, IN. IU. 1st. dj. H13. $65.00

**DAVIS, Burke.** *Cowpens-Guilford Courthouse Campaign.* 1962. Lippincott. 1st. 208p. F/dj. H1. $17.50

**DAVIS, Charles G.** *Ship Model Builder's Assistant.* 1977 (1926). Edward Sweetman. VG. M20. $15.00

**DAVIS, Charles G.** *Ship Models, How to Build Them.* 1925. Salem, MA. Marine Research Soc. 139p. gilt bl cloth. F1. $75.00

**DAVIS, Charles G.** *Ships of the Past.* 1929. Salem. Marine Research Soc. 1st. VG. w/AL & ad brochure. M20. $100.00

**DAVIS, Charles.** *Marine & Fresh-Water Plankton.* 1955. MI State. VG. S15. $12.00

**DAVIS, Christopher.** *Philadelphia.* 1993. NY. Bantam. 1st. F/dj. A23. $35.00

**DAVIS, Clyde.** *Eyes of Boyhood.* 1953. Lippincott. 1st. 323p. F/dj. D4. $35.00

**DAVIS, Daphne.** *Stars!* 1983. NY. Stewart Tabori Chang. 277p. VG/dj. C5. $25.00

**DAVIS, Deering.** *American Cow Pony.* 1962. Van Nostrand. 1st. NF/dj. A21. $45.00

**DAVIS, Duke.** *Flashlights From Mountain & Plain.* 1911. Pentecostal Union. 1st. 266p. gilt red cloth. VG+. B20. $65.00

**DAVIS, Eliza Timberlake.** *Wills & Administrations of Surry County, VA 1671-1750.* 1980 (1955). Genealogical Pub. rpt. 184p. F. B10. $25.00

**DAVIS, Ellis A.** *Davis' New Commercial Encyclopedia of WA, OR & ID.* 1990. Berkeley/Seatle. folio. photos/fld map. 190p. red cloth. B20. $175.00

**DAVIS, Frank Marshall.** *47th Street.* 1948. Prairie City. Decker. 1st. VG/dj. B2. $275.00

**DAVIS, Garrett.** *On the Exchange of Prisoners: Speech of..., Dec 15, 1863.* 1863. WA, DC. L Towers. 1st. dbl-column text. 15p. wrp. M8. $75.00

**DAVIS, Garrett.** *Speech of..., of Kentucky...January 1864.* 1864. WA, DC. L Towers. 1st. 31p. wrp. M8. $75.00

**DAVIS, H.L.** *Proud Riders.* (1942). Harper. 1st. F/VG. A18. $100.00

**DAVIS, Harriet Eager.** *Elmira: Girl Who Loved Edgar Allan Poe.* 1966. Houghton Mifflin. 1st. 137p. VG/dj. M21. $20.00

**DAVIS, Howard Charles.** *Murder Starts From Fishguard.* 1966. London. John Long. 1st. NF/dj. M15. $45.00

**DAVIS, Howell.** *South American Handbook.* 1939. London. 694p. gilt red cloth. F3. $10.00

**DAVIS, J.E.** *Ye Sylvan Archer, May 1927 to Dec 1943.* 1993. Derrydale. 7 vol. 1/1250. sgn Glenn St Charles. F. A17. $150.00

**DAVIS, James D.** *History of the City of Memphis.* 1972 (1873). facs. F/dj. B30. $60.00

**DAVIS, Jefferson.** *Short History of the Confederate States of America.* 1890. Belford Co. 1 vol complete. ils. 505p. gray cloth. G. S17. $27.50

**DAVIS, John J.** *Evangelical Ethics: Issues Facing the Church Today.* 1985. Presb/Reford. 299p. VG/dj. B29. $11.50

**DAVIS, John P.** *Let Us Build a National Negro Congress.* 1935. WA. Sponsor Nat Negro Congress. NF/wrp. B2. $25.00

**DAVIS, Laina R.** *Melody, Mutton Bone & Sam.* 1950. Doubleday. ils Paul Brown. VG/dj. A21. $75.00

**DAVIS, Lindsey.** *Dying Light in Corduba.* 1996. Mysterious. ARC. F/dj. A23. $25.00

**DAVIS, Lindsey.** *Iron Hand of Mars.* 1993. NY. Crown. 1st Am. sgn. F/dj. T2. $35.00

**DAVIS, Lindsey.** *Last Act in Palmyra.* 1996. Mysterious. 1st Am. VG/dj. M17. $15.00

**DAVIS, Lindsey.** *Silver Pigs.* 1989. London. Sidgwick Jackson. 1st. F/NF. M15. $600.00

**DAVIS, Lindsey.** *Silver Pigs.* 1989. NY. Crown. 1st Am. sgn. author's 1st novel. F/dj. T2. $65.00

**DAVIS, Lindsey.** *Three Hands in the Fountain.* 1997. London. Century. 1st. sgn. F/dj. M15. $55.00

**DAVIS, Lindsey.** *Time to Depart.* 1995. London. Century. 1st. F/dj. M15. $60.00

**DAVIS, Margaret G.** *Madison Country, Virginia: A Revised History.* (1977). Bell. Brd Supervisors. ils. 332p. VG. B10. $35.00

**DAVIS, Matthew L.** *Memoirs of Aaron Burr.* 1858. Harper. 696p. G. B18. $35.00

**DAVIS, Norma.** *Trade Winds Cookery: Tropical Recipes for All America.* 1956. Richmond. self pub. sbdg. VG. E6. $25.00

**DAVIS, Patti.** *Way I See It.* 1992. Putnam. 1st. F/dj. P12. $8.00

**DAVIS, Paxton.** *Battle of New Market.* (1963). Little Brn. 1st. 145p. F/F. B10. $25.00

**DAVIS, Richard Harding.** *Captain Macklin.* 1902. NY. Scribner. 1st. 329p. G. G11. $10.00

**DAVIS, Richard Harding.** *Captain Macklin: His Memoirs.* 1909. Scribner. rpt. 328p. gilt red cloth. F3. $10.00

**DAVIS, Richard Harding.** *Gallegher & Other Stories.* 1919. Scribner. intro EL Burlingame. sm 8vo. 306p. VG. W2. $25.00

DAVIS, Richard Harding. *Notes of a War Correspondent.* (1912). NY. later prt. 263p. VG. E1. $25.00

DAVIS, Richard Harding. *Once Upon a Time.* 1910. NY. Scribner. 1st. 280p. G+. G11. $15.00

DAVIS, Richard Harding. *Ranch Life in Texas.* 1984. Austin, TX. Jenkins. 1st separate. 1/450. 16p. NF/wrp. M8. $45.00

DAVIS, Richard Harding. *Ranson's Folly.* 1902. NY. Scribner. 1st. 345p. VG. G1. $8.00

DAVIS, Richard Harding. *Texas Delineated: Some Disconnected Views From the Past.* 1971. Austin, TX. Pemberton. 1st. 26p. VG/wrp. M8. $38.00

DAVIS, Richard Harding. *Van Bibber & Others.* 1892. NY. Harper. 1st. 249p. G. G11. $25.00

DAVIS, Skeeter. *Bus Fare to Kentucky.* 1993. NY. Birch Lane. 338p. G/dj. C5. $12.50

DAVIS, Val. *Track of the Scorpion.* 1996. St Martin. 1st. F/dj. M23. $40.00

DAVIS, W.H. *History of Doylestown, Old & New.* 1905. Doylestown, PA. 373p. VG. B18. $65.00

DAVIS, W.H. *100 Greatest Golf Courses. And Then Some.* 1982. revised. photos. VG/dj. M17. $20.00

DAVIS, Wade. *Serpent & the Rainbow.* 1985. S&S. 1st. F/VG. L4. $25.00

DAVIS, William C. *Battle at Bull Run: A History of 1st Major Campaign...* 1977. NY. BC. 298p. F/dj. E1. $30.00

DAVIS, William C. *Battle at Bull Run: A History...* 1977. Garden City. 1st. 298p. VG/clip. B18. $15.00

DAVIS, William C. *Jefferson Davis: The Man & His Hour.* 1991. NY. Harper Collins. 1st. NF/dj. A14. $17.50

DAVIS, William C. *Touched by Fire: Photographic Portrait of Civil War I & II.* 1986. Boston. 2 vol. 1st. F/dj. E1. $95.00

DAVIS & HEYWOOD. *Principles of Angiosperm Taxonomy.* 1965. Princeton. Van Nostrand. 558p. VG/dj. A10. $30.00

DAVIS & HEYWOOD. *Principles of Angiosperm Taxonomy.* 1967 (1963). Edinburgh. 3 fld charts. 558p. VG. B26. $36.00

DAVIS & MIDDLEMAS. *Colored Glass.* 1974. London. Hamlyn Pub. 2nd. 4to. NF/dj. M21. $35.00

DAVISON, Grace L. *Gates of Memory.* 1955. Santa Ynez. 1st. inscr. VG/dj. O4. $20.00

DAVISON, Peter. *Walking the Boundaries.* 1974. Atheneum. 1st. inscr. F/NF. L3. $45.00

DAVY, G. Burton. *Saga of the Rockies.* nd. Manchester, NH. Cummings. 8vo. 14 pl. 39p. gilt 2-tone cloth. F. O1. $300.00

DAWISHA, A.I. *Egypt in the Arab World.* 1976. London. Macmillan. ils/figures. 234p. VG. Q2. $30.00

DAWKINS, R.M. *Monks of Athos.* 1936. London. Allen Unwin. ils/fld map. 408p. G+. Q2. $92.00

DAWN, Marva J. *Reaching Out Without Dumbing Down: A Theology...* 1995. Eerdmans. 316p. F/wrp. B29. $9.00

DAWSON, Carol. *Waking Spell.* 1992. Algonquin. 1st. author's 1st book. F/dj. O11. $35.00

DAWSON, Christopher. *Mongol Mission: Narratives & Letters...* 1955. NY. Sheed Ward. ils/tables. 246p. VG/torn. Q2. $36.50

DAWSON, Elmer. *Buck's Winning Hit.* 1930. Grosset Dunlap. 1st. G. P8. $12.50

DAWSON, Emma Frances. *Gracious Visitation.* 1921. BC of CA. 1/300. 8vo. gilt red cloth. NF. R3. $50.00

DAWSON, Fielding. *Great Day for a Ballgame.* 1973. Bobbs Merrill. 1st. F/VG. P8. $45.00

DAWSON, Fielding. *Three Penny Lane.* 1981. Blk Sparrow. 1/250. sgn. NF/mylar dj. B9. $35.00

DAWSON, Fielding. *Virginia Dare: Stories 1976-1981.* 1985. Blk Sparrow. 1st. VG. B9. $15.00

DAWSON, George Francis. *Life & Services of Gen John A Logan, Soldier & Statesman.* 1884. National Tribune. 467p. B19. $95.00

DAWSON, Grace. *California.* 1939. Macmillan. 1st. VG/G. P2. $15.00

DAWSON, Jean. *Boys & Girls of Garden City.* 1914. Boston. Ginn. 1st. photos. 346p. VG+. A25. $18.00

DAWSON, John. *Complete Guide to Prints & Printmaking...* 1981. NY. Excalibur. 1st Am. 4to. 192p. cloth. F/dj. O10. $35.00

DAWSON, William Leon. *Birds of California, a Complete, Scientific & Popular...* 1940. NY. Devin Adair. 4 vol. Format DeLuxe. sgn. 1400 ils. F/dj/case. F1. $650.00

DAWSON & KENNEDY-SKIPTON. *Elizabethan Handwriting, 1500-1650, a Manual.* 1966. NY. Norton. 1st. ils. 130p. cloth. F/dj. O10. $55.00

DAY, A. Grove. *Adventures of the Pacific.* 1969. Meredith. 1st. NF/NF. H11. $30.00

DAY, Alexandra. *Carl's Christmas Day.* 1996. FSG. 4th. VG. B36. $10.00

DAY, Clarence. *Crow's Nest.* 1921. Knopf. 1st author's 2nd book. F/NF. B20. $150.00

DAY, Clarence. *God & My Father.* 1932. Knopf. 1st. photos. NF/dj. S13. $20.00

DAY, Clarence. *Scenes From the Mesozoic.* 1935. New Haven. Yale. 1st. ils. NF/VG. L3. $65.00

DAY, Deforest. *August Ice.* 1990. NY. SMP. 1st. author's 1st book. F/F. H11. $30.00

DAY, Deforest. *Cold Killing.* 1990. NY. Carroll Graf. 1st. F/F. H11. $20.00

DAY, Dianne. *Fire & Fog.* 1996. Doubleday. 1st. F/dj. G8/T2. $25.00

DAY, H. Kellogg. *About 97 Years & a Day.* 1980. Vantage. 1st. photos. 204p. VG/dj. B18. $17.50

DAY, James. *Six Flags of Texas.* 1968. Waco. 1st. mc pl. 138p. VG/dj. S16. $45.00

DAY, Jeremiah. *Inquiry Respecting the Self-Determining Power of Will...* 1838. New Haven. Herrick Noyes. inscr pres. 200p. emb brn cloth. VG. G1. $135.00

DAY, Richard. *Summer Landmark.* 1947. Macmillan. 1st. 106p. F/dj. D4. $35.00

DAY, Robert. *All Out of the Sack Race!* 1945. Random. unp. G. C5. $12.50

DAY, Thomas. *History of Sandford & Merton.* 1845. New Haven. Babcock. 222p. emb cloth. VG. F1. $45.00

DAY & KEYES. *Tax Documents from Theadelphia, Papyri of 2nd Century AD.* 1956. NY. Columbia. gilt blk cloth. M11. $85.00

DAY-LEWIS, Sean. *Bulleid Last Giant of Steam.* 1964. London. 1st. 300p. VG/dj. B5. $25.00

DAYTON, Dorothy. *Epic of Alexandra.* 1979. Winston-Salem. JF Blair. ARC/1st. ils Virginia Ingram. VG/dj. M20. $40.00

DAZZI, Romano. *Self-Development in Drawing...* 1928. Putnam/Knickerbocker. 99 pl. 281p. pebbled blk cloth. VG. G1. $50.00

DE ALARCON, Pedron. *Three-Cornered Hat.* 1959. LA. LEC. 1st thus. 1/1500. ils/sgn Roger Duvoisin. F/glassine/F case. Q1. $75.00

DE ANDRADE, Carlos Drummond. *Travelling in the Family.* 1986. Random. UP/1st. trans Bishop/Rabassa. F/wrp. L3. $30.00

DE ANDREA, William L. *Five O'Clock Lightning.* 1982. St Martin. BC. F/VG. P8. $10.00

DE ANGELI, Marguerite. *Elin's Amerika.* 1941. Doubleday Doran. 1st. sq 8vo. unp. beige cloth. T5. $25.00

**DE ANGELI, Marguerite.** *Prayers & Graces for Small Children.* 1941. Grosset Dunlap. early. 8vo. VG/dj. B17. $30.00

**DE ANGELI, Marguerite.** *Skippack School.* 1939. Doubleday. 1st. ils. xl. VG/dj. D1. $120.00

**DE ANGELI, Marguerite.** *Ted & Nina Go to the Grocery Store.* 1935. Doubleday Doran. 1st. obl 8vo. mc pict brd. mc pict dj. R5. $250.00

**DE ANGELI, Marguerite.** *Ted & Nina Have a Happy Rainy Day.* 1936. Doubleday Doran. possible 1st. obl 24mo. gray buckram. reading copy. T5. $45.00

**DE ANGELI, Marguerite.** *Up the Hill.* 1942. Doubleday Doran. 1st. sq 4to. tan cloth. mc dj. R5. $75.00

**DE ANGELI, Marguerite.** *Yonie Wondernose.* 1944. Doubleday Doran. 1st. 4to. dj. R5. $85.00

**DE ARMOND, R.N.** *Founding of Juneau.* 1967. Juneau. Centennial ed. inscr. ils/photos/map. wrp. P4. $40.00

**DE BAETS, Maurice.** *Apostle of Alaska: Life of Most Reverend Chas John Seghers.* 1943. St Anthony Guild. 8vo. 282p. gilt gr cloth. VG/dj. P4. $45.00

**DE BALZAC, Honore.** *Physiology of Marriage; or, Meditations of Eclectic...* 1924. NY. Boni. 1/1000. 4to. linen spine/paper title label/brd. VG. F1. $50.00

**DE BEAUMONT, Edouard.** *Sword & Womankind: Being Informative History...* 1929. NY. Panurge. 1/1000. VG. M20. $18.00

**DE BEAUMONT, Marguerite.** *Way of the Horse.* 1953. London. Hurst Blackett. 1st. VG/G. O3. $25.00

**DE BEAUVOIR, Simone.** *Prime of Life.* 1962. Cleveland. World. VG/dj. M20. $15.00

**DE BEER, G.R.** *Development of the Vertebrate Skull.* 1937. Oxford. Clarendon. 143 pl. 522p. cloth. G7. $95.00

**DE BEER, Gavin.** *Sciences Were Never at War.* 1960. London. 1st. 279p. A13. $30.00

**DE BERARDINIS, Olivia.** *Let Them Eat Cheesecake: Art of Olivia.* 1993. Ozone Productions. ils. VG/dj. M17. $25.00

**DE BERNIERES, Louis.** *Corelli's Mandolin.* 1994. Pantheon. ARC. sgn. F. O11. $45.00

**DE BERNIERES, Louis.** *Senor Vivo & the Coca Lord.* 1991. Morrow. 1st Am. F/dj. M23. $25.00

**DE BERNIERES, Louis.** *Senor Vivo & the Coca Lord.* 1991. Morrow. 1st. sgn. F/dj. O11. $50.00

**DE BERNIERES, Louis.** *War of Don Emmanuel's Nether Parts.* 1991. Morrow. 1st. author's 1st book. F/NF. B3. $75.00

**DE BESAULT, L.** *President Trujillo, Dominican Republic.* 1941. Santiago. ils. 509p. VG/G. B5. $17.50

**DE BLASIS, Celeste.** *Graveyard Peaches.* 1991. St Martin. 1st. F/NF. P3. $18.00

**DE BLASIS, Celeste.** *Swan's Chance.* 1985. NY. Bantam. 1st/3rd imp. NF/VG. A14. $14.00

**DE BOLD, Joseph W.** *Happening Worlds of John Brunner.* 1975. Kennikat. 1st. F/dj. P3. $20.00

**DE BOODT, Anselmus Boetius.** *Gemmarum et Lapidum Historia.* 1647. Leyden. Johannis Marie. 2 fld tables/woodcuts. 576p. old calf. K1. $1,250.00

**DE BOUGAINVILLE, Louis A.** *Voyage Round the World...1766-1769.* 1772. London. Prt for J Nourse. 1st Eng-language. 5 fld charts. 476p. P4. $6,000.00

**DE BOURRIENNE, Louis A.F.** *Memoirs of Napoleon Bonaparte.* 1891. Scribner. 4 vol. gilt bl cloth. VG. S17. $25.00

**DE BRAY, Lys.** *Art of Botanical Illustration.* 1997 (1989). Bromley, Kent. ils. 192p. sc. B26. $26.00

**DE BRUNHOFF, Jean.** *Babar & Father Christmas.* 1940. NY. Random. 1st Am. sm folio. mc pict dj. R5. $400.00

**DE BRUNHOFF, Jean.** *Babar & His Children.* (1938). Random. 66th. F/sans. T12. $17.00

**DE BRUNHOFF, Jean.** *Babar the King.* 1935. NY. H Smith/R Haas. 1st Am. Babar #3. folio. 47p. VG. D1. $700.00

**DE BRUNHOFF, Laurent.** *Babar's Little Girl.* 1987. Random. 1st. 4to. unp. NF. C14. $16.00

**DE CALLATAY, Vincent.** *Atlas of the Sky.* 1958. London. Macmillan. trans Harold Spences Jones. 157p. G. K5. $35.00

**DE CAMP, L. Sprague.** *Castle of Iron.* 1950. Gnome. 1st. 224p. VG/dj. B18. $27.50

**DE CAMP, L. Sprague.** *Honorable Barbarian.* 1989. Del Rey. 1st. VG/dj. M20. $22.00

**DE CAMP, L. Sprague.** *Lovecraft: A Biography.* 1975. Doubleday. 1st. VG/dj. J3. $45.00

**DE CAMP & LEY.** *Lands Beyond.* 1952. Rinehart. 1st thus. 214p. F3. $15.00

**DE CAMPOS, D. Redig.** *Art Treasures of the Vatican.* 1975. Prentice Hall. 1st Am. VG/dj. M20. $32.00

**DE CARDONA, Nicolas.** *Geographic & Hydographic Descriptions of Many...Seas...* 1974. Dawson's Book Shop. Baja CA Travel series #35. ils/notes. 111p. NF. B19. $40.00

**DE CARLO, Yvonne.** *Yvonne.* 1987. St Martin. 1st. VG/dj. C9. $30.00

**DE CASTRO, V.A.** *Second NY Infantry at the Mexican Border.* 1916. Schenetady. G+. E6. $45.00

**DE CERVANTES SAAVEDRA, Miguel.** *Adventures of Don Quixote.* nd. London/Melbourne. Ward Lock. ils Harry Theaker. 344p. F/NF. D4. $50.00

**DE CERVANTES SAAVEDRA, Miguel.** *Adventures of Don Quixote.* 1928. Houghton Mifflin. 1st. ils Herman Bacharach. VG. M19. $25.00

**DE CERVANTES SAAVEDRA, Miguel.** *History & Adventures of Renowned Don Quixote de la Mancha...* (1794). London. Alex Hogg. 1 vol ed. folio. 12 copper pl. contemporary calf. K1. $175.00

**DE CERVANTES SAAVEDRA, Miguel.** *History & Adventures of the Renowned Don Quixote.* nd (1797). London. C Cooke. Pocket ed. 5 vol. 12mo. 15 pl. NF. H5. $400.00

**DE CHAMBRUN, Marquis Adolphe.** *Impressions of Lincoln & the Civil War.* 1952. NY. Random. 1st. 175p. VG/dj. S17. $7.50

**DE CHASTELLUX, Marquis.** *Travels in North America in Years 1780, 1781 & 1782.* 1963. Inst Early Am Hist. 2 vol. ils. VG. M17. $45.00

**DE CONDILLAC, Etienne Bonnot.** *Condillac's Treatise on Sensations.* 1930. London. Favil. 1st Eng-language/British issue. 250p. NF. G1. $75.00

**DE DIENES, Andre.** *Marilyn Mon Amour: Private Album of Andre deDienes...* 1985. St Martin. VG/dj. S5. $75.00

**DE DIENES, Andre.** *Nude Pattern.* 1958. Bodley Head. 1st. photos. NF/dj. S9. $150.00

**DE FIERRO BLANCO, Antonio.** *Journey of the Flame.* 1933. Houghton Mifflin. 1st. gilt blk cloth. VG/dj. T10. $75.00

**DE FOE, Daniel.** *Life & Strange Surprising Adventures of Robinson Crusoe...* nd. Dutton. ils JA Symington. teg. pict gray cloth. F1. $30.00

**DE FOE, Daniel.** *Robinson Crusoe.* 1920. Cosmopolitan. 1st thus. ils NC Wyeth. red cloth/pict pl. VG+. M5. $155.00

**DE FOE, Daniel.** *Robinson Crusoe.* 1968. Franklin Watts. 1st Am thus. ils Ardizzone. VG/G. P2. $25.00

**DE FONTENELLE, Bernard.** *Elements de la Geometrie de l'Infini.* 1727. Paris. L'Imprimerie Royale. 1st. 1 fld engraved pl. 548p. K1. $1,000.00

**DE FRANCA, Isabella.** *Journal of a Visit to Maderia & Portugal (1853-1854).* 1970. Portugal. Junta Geral. 4to. 270p. VG/dj. B11. $75.00

**DE GAURY, Gerald.** *Arabia Phoenix.* 1947 (1946). London. Harrap. ils/map ep. cloth. G+. Q2. $26.50

**DE GAURY, Gerald.** *Arabia Phoenix: Account of Visit to Ibn Saud...* 1946. London/Sydney. 1st. 8vo. sgn. 169p. cloth. VG. W1. $45.00

**DE GEREZ, Toni.** *Louhi: Witch of North Farm, a Story From Finland...* 1986. NY. ils Barbara Cooney. VG. M17. $15.00

**DE GRAFFENRIED, Thomas.** *DeGraffenried Family Scrap Book: 1191-1956.* 1958. U VA. ils/photos. 267p. B10. $45.00

**DE GREGORIO, George.** *Joe DiMaggio.* 1983. Scarborough. 1st. VG/dj. P8. $35.00

**DE GROOT, Roy A.** *Feasts for All Seasons.* 1966. Knopf. VG/dj. A16. $12.00

**DE GROOT, Roy A.** *Revolutionizing French Cooking.* 1976. McGraw Hill. 1st. NF. W2. $30.00

**DE GROOT & VOSTMAN.** *Sailing Ships: Prints by Dutch Masters, 16th to 19th C.* 1980. Viking. 1st. 284p. F/dj. B20. $50.00

**DE GRUMMOND, Jan Lucas.** *Renato Beluche: Smuggler, Privateer & Patriot.* 1983. LA State U. 1st. 300p. dj. F3. $20.00

**DE GUEVARA, Antonio.** *Libro Llamado Menosprecio de Corte y Albanca de Aldea.* 1591. Lyon. Jean de Tournes. sm 8vo. 552p. contemporary vellum. K1. $1,200.00

**DE HALSALLE, Henry.** *Romance of Modern First Editions.* 1931. Lippincott. 192p. gilt rose cloth. VG. F1. $15.00

**DE HARTOG, Jan.** *Children: A Personal Record for the Use of Adoptive Parents.* 1969. Atheneum. 1st. 265p. VG/G. V3. $15.00

**DE HARTOG, Jan.** *Commodore.* 1986. Harper Row. ARC/1st. lt bl cloth. w/promo materials. F/dj. T11. $35.00

**DE HARTOG, Jan.** *Distant Shore.* 1952. Harper. 1st. author's 2nd book. NF/VG. H11. $25.00

**DE HAURAANE, Ernest Duv.** *Frenchman in Lincoln's America, Vol I.* 1974. Lakeside Classic. 1st thus. teg. dk bl cloth. F/sans. T11. $35.00

**DE HAVEN, Tom.** *Jersey Luck.* 1980. Harper Row. 1st. sgn/dtd 1987. NF/dj. R14. $45.00

**DE HURST.** *How Women Should Ride.* 1892. Harper. 1st. VG. O3. $95.00

**DE KRUIF, Paul.** *Hunger Fighters.* 1928. NY. Harcourt Brace. 1st. ils Zadig. VG+/dj. B20. $20.00

**DE KRUIF, Paul.** *Kaiser Wakes the Doctors.* 1943. NY. 1st. 158p. A13. $25.00

**DE LA BEDOYERE, Michael.** *Future of Catholic Christianity.* (1966). Phil. Lippincott. 313p. H10. $15.00

**DE LA MARE, Walter.** *Bells & Grass.* 1943. Viking. 1st. ils Dorothy Lathrop. VG/dj. D1. $35.00

**DE LA MARE, Walter.** *Down-A Down-Derry.* 1922. London. Constable. 1st. ils Lathrop. 190p. dk bl cloth. VG. D1. $100.00

**DE LA MARE, Walter.** *Eight Tales.* 1971. Arkham. 1st. 1/2992. VG/VG. L1. $45.00

**DE LA MARE, Walter.** *Listeners & Other Poems.* 1927. London. Constable. 1st ils. 80p. F/dj. B20. $85.00

**DE LA MARE, Walter.** *Motley & Other Poems.* 1927. London. Constable. 1st ils. 70p. F/dj. B20. $85.00

**DE LA MARE, Walter.** *Mr Bumps & His Monkey.* 1942. Winston. 1st. ils DP Lathrop. 69p. mc dj. R5. $225.00

**DE LA MARE, Walter.** *Peacock Pie.* 1961. Knopf. 8vo. ils Barbara Cooney. VG. B17. $12.50

**DE LA MARE, Walter.** *Peacock Pie.* 1989. Holt. 1st. ils Louise Brierley. F/dj. B17. $12.50

**DE LA MARE, Walter.** *Penny a Day.* 1960. Knopf. 1st thus. ils Paul Kennedy. 209p. NF/VG. T5. $25.00

**DE LA MARE, Walter.** *Winged Chariot & Other Poems.* 1951. NY. Viking. 1st Am. 160p. gilt maroon cloth. F1. $50.00

**DE LA METTRIE, Julien Ofray.** *Man a Machine.* 1993. NY. Classics of Psychiatry & Behavioral Sciences Lib. 216p. G1. $65.00

**DE LA ROCHE, Mazo.** *Portrait of a Dog.* 1930. Little Brn. 1st. ils Morgan Dennis. VG. A21. $45.00

**DE LA TORRE, Lillian.** *Dr Samuel Johnson, Detector...* 1946. NY. Knopf. 1st. sm 8vo. rpr dj. H13. $45.00

**DE LACLOS, Choderlos.** *Les Liaisons Dangereuses.* 1929. Blk Sun. 1/1000. 14 pl. trans Dowson. NF/wrp/glassine/wht cloth case. H5. $850.00

**DE LAMARTINE, A.** *History of the French Revolution of 1848.* 1849. Boston. Phillips Sampson. stated 1st Am. 12mo. VG. A2. $140.00

**DE LANGE & GOLDSMITH.** *Theories of Evolution.* 1912. NY. 1st Eng trans rpt. 352p. A13. $25.00

**DE LARMINAT, Max-Henri.** *Sky Blue: Kandinsky (An Art Play Book).* 1990. NY. Abrams. NF. H4. $37.50

**DE LE PIERRE, Octavo.** *Rose: Its Cultivation, Use & Symbolic Meaning in Antiquity.* 1856. London. Smith Elder. 1/100 (2nd state). pk brd. very scarce. A10. $300.00

**DE LEON, Arnoldo.** *Tejano Community 1836-1900.* 1982. Albuquerque. F/dj. V4. $17.50

**DE LEON, Josefina V.** *Mexican Cook Book Devoted to American Homes.* 1977. Spanish/Eng text. VG/wrp. A16. $25.00

**DE LEON, T.C.** *South Songs...* 1866. NY. Blelock. 153p. VG. S16. $95.00

**DE LILLO, Don.** *Amazons.* 1980. HRW. 1st. F/VG+. B30. $37.50

**DE LILLO, Don.** *Day Room.* 1987. Knopf. 1st. F/dj. A24. $50.00

**DE LILLO, Don.** *Libra.* 1988. Viking. 1st. F/NF. H11. $30.00

**DE LILLO, Don.** *Players.* 1977. Knopf. 1st. NF/VG. B3. $90.00

**DE LILLO, Don.** *Ratner's Star.* 1976. Knopf. 1st. inscr. author's 4th novel. F/dj. B4. $275.00

**DE LILLO, Don.** *White Noise.* 1985. Viking. 1st. F/dj. B4. $125.00

**DE LISLE, Leconte.** *Midi.* 1977. Newark, VT. Janus. 1/75. bilingual text. ils VanVliet. natural linen. F/case. B24. $850.00

**DE MARCO, Angelus A.** *Rome & the Vernacular.* 1961. Westminster, MD. Newman. 8vo. Vg/dj. A2. $20.00

**DE MARIA, Robert.** *Johnson's Dictionary & Language of Learning.* 1986. Oxford. Clarendon. 1st. F/dj. H13. $65.00

**DE MARIA, Robert.** *Life of Samuel Johnson.* 1993. Oxford. Blackwell. 1st. F/dj. H13. $75.00

**DE MARIA, Robert.** *To Be a King: Novel About Christopher Marlowe.* 1976. Bobbs Merrill. 1st. NF/dj. A14. $25.00

**DE MARINIS, Rick.** *Lovely Monster: Adventures of Claude Raines & Dr Tellenbeck.* 1975. S&S. 1st. F/NF. R14. $50.00

**DE MARINIS, Rick.** *Lovely Monster: Adventures of Claude Rains...* 1975. S&S. 1st. rem mk. VG/dj. A14. $21.00

**DE MAUPASSANT, Guy.** *La Maison Tellier.* 1933. Paris. Vollard. 1/305. ils after Edgar Degas. teg. morocco-trimmed case. B24. $1,850.00

**DE MEDICI, Lorenza.** *Italy: The Beautiful Cookbook.* 1988. Intercontinental Pub. 1st. folio. 256p. F/dj. W2. $60.00

**DE MEDINA, Pedro.** *Libro de la Verdad...* 1570. Alcala deHenares. Andres deAngulo. folio. contemporary limp vellum. K1. $1,250.00

**DE MEDINA Y ORMAECHEA, A.A.** *La Legislacion Penal de los Pueblos Latinos.* 1899. Mexico. Tipofraffa Oficina Timbre. 54 dbl-fld leaves. 40p. F3. $125.00

**DE MEJO, Oscar.** *There's a Hand in the Sky.* 1983. Pantheon. 1st. VG/dj. B9. $20.00

**DE MERE, Antoine Gombaud.** *Les Oeuvres.* 1692. Amsterdam. Mortier. 2 vol in 1. 1st collected ed. 8vo. ils. vellum. R12. $225.00

**DE MEYER, Adolph.** *Singular Elegance: Photographs of Baron Adolpf DeMeyer.* 1994. Chronicle. folio. phhotos. brn cloth. NF/dj. A28. $45.00

**DE MILLE, Agnes.** *Dance to the Piper.* 1952. Little Brn. 1st. VG/dj. C9. $36.00

**DE MIRABEAU, Gabriel Riqueti.** *Erotika Biblion.* 1783. Rome (Neuchatel). De l'Imprimerie du Vatican. 8vo. 192p. mottled calf. K1. $450.00

**DE MONOU, Rene.** *La Pratique Du Chevalier ou l'Exercice de Monter a Cheval...* 1651. Paris. Guillaume Loyson/JB Loyson. 4to. ils/engravings. 245p. K1. $1,000.00

**DE MONTAIGNE, Michel.** *Essays.* nd. NY. trans Chas Cotton. 3-quarter brn leather. VG. M17. $40.00

**DE MONTAIGNE, Michel.** *Montaigne's Essays.* 1931. London. Nonesuch. 2 vol. 1/1375. teg. Riviere bdg. F. H5. $750.00

**DE MONTOYA, Juan.** *New Mexico in 1602, Juan deMontoya's Relation to Discovery.* s1938. Quivira. 1/550. 12 pl. 155p. NF. A4. $275.00

**DE MONVEL, Roger Boutet.** *Le Bon Anglais. Images de Guy Arnoux.* ca 1917. Paris. Devambez. obl 12mo. 12 pochoir woodcuts. woodcut wrp. K1. $100.00

**DE MONVEL, Roger Boutet.** *Nos Freres d'Amerique. Images de Guy Arnoux.* ca 1918. Paris. Devambez. obl 12mo. 12 pochoir woodcuts. woodcut wrp. K1. $100.00

**DE NADAILLAC, Marquis.** *Pre-Historic America.* 1893 (1884). NY. Putnam. 219 ils/index. 566p. teg. gilt pict bdg. F3. $75.00

**DE NOLHAC, Pierre.** *Marie Antoinette.* 1905. London. 3-quarter bl leather/bl cloth brd. VG M17. $50.00

**DE OLIVARES, Jose.** *Our Islands & Their People Seen With Camera & Pencil.* (1899). ND Thompson. Vol 1 of 2 only. 384p. G. H1. $37.50

**DE OVIEDO Y VALDES, G.F.** *Conquest & Settlement of the Island of Boriquen...* 1975. Avon. LEC. 1/2000. ils/sgn Delano. 143p. F/dj/case. P4. $150.00

**DE PORTE, Michael V.** *Nightmares & Hobbyhorses.* 1974. Huntington Lib. 1st. F/NF clip. O4. $15.00

**DE POUGY, Liane.** *My Blue Notebooks.* 1979. NY. 1st. trans Diana Athill. VG/dj. M17. $17.50

**DE PROFT, Melanie.** *American Family Cookbook.* 1971. Doubleday. 1st. 800p. VG. S14. $20.00

**DE QUINCEY, Thomas.** *Diary of Thomas De Quincey, 1803.* 1927. Payson Clarke. 1/1500. 252p. gilt brn buckram. VG/G. F1. $50.00

**DE REAUMUR, R.A.F.** *Natural History of Ants.* 1926. Knopf. 8vo. ils. 280p. F/VG. M12. $45.00

**DE REGNIERS, Beatrice Schenk.** *Week in the Life of Best Friends & Other Poems...* 1986. Atheneum. 1st. 47p. lavender cloth. F/NF. T5. $30.00

**DE RELY, Jehan.** *L'Ordre Tenv et Garde en L'Assemblee des Trois Estats...* 1558. Paris. Galliot de Pre. 8vo. prt device at end. vellum. R12. $650.00

**DE ROCOLES, Jean Baptiste.** *Les Imposteurs Insignes.* 1683. Amsterdam. thick 12mo. 16 full-p portraits. calf. R12. $575.00

**DE ROSIER, Arthur H.** *Removal of the Choctaw Indians.* 1970. U TN. ARC. 208p. RS. F/NF. B20. $45.00

**DE ROUGEMONT, Denis.** *Devil's Share.* 1945. Pantheon. 221p. VG. B29. $15.00

**DE SADE, Marquis.** *Dialogue Between a Priest & a Dying Man.* 1925. Chicago. Pascal Covici. 1/650. 4to. 52p. teg. blk cloth. NF/VG. F1. $45.00

**DE SAINT-EXUPERY, Antoine.** *Le Petit Prince.* 1946. Boston. French text. ils/notes. VG. M17. $17.50

**DE SAINT-EXUPERY, Antoine.** *Little Prince...* 1943. NY. Reynal Hitchcock. 1st Am. ils. 91p. lt brn cloth. NF/clip. H5. $600.00

**DE SAINT-EXUPERY, Antoine.** *Night Flight.* 1932. NY. Century. 1st Am. sm 8vo. trans Stuart Gilbert. gilt bl cloth. NF/dj. H5. $250.00

**DE SEGUR, Madame.** *Happy Surprises.* 1929. Whitman. 1st. 8vo. ils. VG. M5. $20.00

**DE SEGUR, Philip.** *History of Expedition to Russia...Napoleon in Year 1812.* 1825. Phil. Littell. 1st. 8vo. 546p. 3-quarter leather. w/fld map. B11. $450.00

**DE SIRCA, Vittorio.** *Bicycle Theif.* 1968. S&S. 1st. F/wrp. C9. $36.00

**DE SITTER, L.U.** *Structural Geology.* 1956. McGraw Hill. 1st. ils. VG. B27. $40.00

**DE SOUZA, Baretto.** *Advanced Equitation.* 1926. Dutton. G. O3. $20.00

**DE ST. JORRE, John.** *Venus Bound: Erotic Voyage of Olympia Press & Its Writers.* 1994. NY. 1st. dj. T9. $15.00

**DE TREVINO, Elizabeth.** *Casilda of the Rising Moon: A Tale of Magic & Faith...* 1967. FSG. 1st. 8vo. xl. G+. T5. $12.00

**DE VAULT & JOHNSON.** *Informer: Confessions of an Ex-Terrorist.* 1982. Toronto. Fleet. 1st Canadian. F/dj. T12. $10.00

**DE VEGA, Carpio.** *Arcadia, Prosas, y Versos...* ca 1700. Barcelona. aeg. 284p. gilt red morocco. K1. $1,250.00

**DE VERA, Jose Maria.** *Educational Television in Japan.* 1967. Sophia U/Chas Tuttle. 1st. 140p. VG/clip. N2. $12.50

**DE VILAMIL, R.** *Resistance of Air.* 1917. London. 1st. ils. 192p. xl. B18. $35.00

**DE VIRVILLE, Davy.** *Histoire de la Botanique en France.* 1954. Paris. Soc Ed D'en. 394p. wrp/clamshell box. A10. $75.00

**DE VOLTAIRE, Francois Maria;** see Voltaire.

**DE VORE, Irven, Ed.** *Primate Behavior: Field Studies of Monkeys & Apes.* 1965. NY. biblio/index/photos. F/dj. A17. $17.50

**DE VOTO, Bernard.** *Across the Wide Missouri.* 1947. Houghton Mifflin. G/rpr. A19. $35.00

**DE VOTO, Bernard.** *Year of Decision 1846.* nd (1943). Houghton Mifflin. rpt. NF/VG. A14. $21.00

**DE VRIES, Peter.** *Reuben, Reuben.* 1964. Little Brn. 1st. NF/dj. A14. $25.00

**DE VRIES, Peter.** *Sauce for the Goose.* 1981. Little Brn. 1st. rem mk. NF/dj. R14. $25.00

**DE VRIES, Peter.** *Slouching Towards Kalamazoo.* 1983. Little Brn. 1st/4th imp. rem mk. NF/dj. A14. $15.00

**DE WALL, Frans.** *Chimpanzee Politics: Power & Sex Among Apes.* 1982. Harper Row. 1st Am. VG/dj. N2. $10.00

**DE WALL, Guilelmus.** *De Spina Bifida. Dissertatio Inauguralis Pathologico...* 1847. Berolinia. Typis B Schlesinger. gilt gr morocco/rb. G7. $250.00

**DE WEERD, Harvey.** *President Wilson Fights His War.* 1968. NY. 1st. 457p. E1. $40.00

**DE WOLFF, J.H.** *Pawnee Bill: His Experience & Adventures on Western Plains.* 1902. np. Pawnee Bill's Historic Wild West Co. 1st. 108p. D11. $125.00

**DE ZAYAS, F.G.** *Law & Philosophy of Zakat.* 1960. Damascus. 1/1000. 2 fld tables. 420p. VG. Q2. $40.00

**DE ZEMBLER, Charles.** *Once Over Lightly.* 1939. NY. 1st. ils. NF/dj. S13. $18.00

**DE ZOUCHE, Dorothy E.** *Rodean School 1885-1955.* 1955. private prt. 1st. photos/fld ils. 225p. VG. H7. $10.00

**DE ZUMARRAGA, Juan.** *Colleccion de Documentos Ineditos Relativos...* 1884. Madrid. Hernandez. 556p. modern tree sheep/red & olive calf labels. K1. $100.00

**DEACHMAN, T.** *Auto Bio Chemic Treatment.* 1922. self pub. 1st. VG. E6. $65.00

**DEAK, Gloria.** *Picturing America, 1497-1899; Prints, Maps & Drawings...* 1988. Princeton. 2 vol. ils. F/F. A4. $395.00

**DEAN, Abner.** *Come As You Are.* 1952. S&S. 1st. 4to. VG/dj. N2. $8.50

**DEAN, Amber.** *Dead Man's Float.* 1944. Crime Club. F/dj. P3. $15.00

**DEAN, Amber.** *Wrap It Up.* nd. Collins. VG. P3. $15.00

**DEAN, D.M.** *Breaking Trail: Hudson Stuck of Texas & Alaska.* 1988. OH U. 1st. photos/map. 344p. F/dj. M4. $30.00

**DEAN, Elizabeth Lippincott.** *Dolly Madison: Nation's Hostess.* 1928. Lee Shepard. 250p. pict label. V3. $14.00

**DEAN, Graham M.** *Herb Kent: West Point Cadet.* 1936. Goldsmith. 250p. red bdg. VG. B36. $8.00

**DEANE, Elsie.** *Mother Goose Picture Book With Rhymes.* (1939). NY. Samuel Gabriel. 4to. wine-red cloth/pict label. mc dj. R5. $125.00

**DEANE, Norman;** see Creasey, John.

**DEANE, Seamus.** *Reading in the Dark.* 1996. London. 1st. dj. T9. $65.00

**DEAR, Ian.** *America's Cup: Informal History.* 1980. NY. Dodd Mead. 1st. VG/dj. P4. $30.00

**DEARDEN, Seton.** *Arabian Knight: Study of Sir Richard Burton.* 1953. London. Barker. revised. 8vo. ils/map ep. 256p. cloth. VG/dj. Q2. $30.00

**DEARMENT, Bob.** *Alias Frank Canton.* ils/index. 402p. dj. E1. $30.00

**DEAS, Michael J.** *Portraits & Daguerreotypes of Edgar Allan Poe.* 1989. VA U. 1st. 198p. VG. B10. $15.00

**DEAVER, Jeffery.** *Maidens Grave.* 1994. Viking. 1st. sgn. An/dj. S18. $35.00

**DEAVER, Jeffery.** *Praying for Sleep.* 1993. Viking. 1st. sgn. F/F. S18. $45.00

**DEAVER, Jeffrey.** *Maiden's Grave.* 1995. Viking. 1st. VG/dj. R8. $11.00

**DEBS, Eugene V.** *Debs: His Life, Writings & Speeches.* 1908. Girard, KS. The Appeal to Reason. 1st. VG. V4. $100.00

**DECKER, Duane.** *Fast Man on a Pivot.* 1951. Morrow. later prt. VG/dj. P8. $65.00

**DEDERA, Don.** *Little War of Our Own: Pleasant Valley Feud Revisited.* 1988. Northland. ils/notes/index. 308p. F/wrp. B19. $20.00

**DEE, Ed.** *14 Peck Slip.* 1994. NY. Warner. 1st. author's 1st book. F/F. H11. $40.00

**DEE, Jonathan.** *Lover of History.* 1990. Ticknor Fields. 1st. author's 1st book. F/dj. A24. $25.00

**DEEPING, Warwick.** *Doomsday.* 1927. Knopf. 1st. 8vo. 367p. fair. S14. $7.00

**DEERE, John.** *Corny Cornpicker Finds a Home.* 1959. John Deere. 1st. 8vo. F. M5. $75.00

**DEERING, Freemont B.** *Border Boys on the Trail (#1).* 1911. AL Burt. VG/dj. M20. $30.00

**DEFORD, Frank.** *Casey on the Loose.* 1989. Viking. 1st. F/dj. P8. $10.00

**DEFORD, Frank.** *Cut 'n' Run.* 1973. Viking. 1st. author's 1st novel. NF/F. H11. $20.00

**DEFOREST, J.A.** *Volunteer's Adventure: Union Captain's Record of Civil War.* 1946. Yale. 2nd. F/VG. E6. $20.00

**DEGENER, Otto.** *Plants of Hawaii National Parks.* 1945 (1930). Ann Arbor. ils/pl. 312p. sc. B26. $16.00

**DEGENERES, Ellen.** *My Point...And I Do Have One.* 1995. Bantam. NF/dj. A28. $10.00

**DEGENHARDT, Richard K.** *Belleek: Complete Collectors Guide & Ils Reference.* 1993. Radnor, PA. Wallace Homestead. ils. NF/dj. M10. $60.00

**DEHN, Paul.** *Quake, Quake, Quake.* 1961. S&S. 1st. 8vo. 110p. yel cloth. NF/dj. J3. $70.00

**DEIDER, Antonio.** *Dissertatio Medica de Morbis Venereis...* 1742. London. Palmer. 129p. contemporary calf/rb. G7. $150.00

**DEIGHTON, Barbara.** *Little Learning.* 1988. Quartet. 1st Eng. F/dj. G8. $25.00

**DEIGHTON, Len.** *Battle of Britain.* 1980. London. Cape. 1st. 224p. bl cloth. F/dj. M7. $45.00

**DEIGHTON, Len.** *Berlin Game.* 1983. Hutchinson. 1st. F/NF. B3. $30.00

**DEIGHTON, Len.** *Berlin Game.* 1984. Knopf. 1st. 8vo. 345p. NF/VG+. S14. $12.50

**DEIGHTON, Len.** *Billion Dollar Brain.* 1966. London. Cape. 1st Eng. VG+/VG. A14. $52.50

**DEIGHTON, Len.** *Close-Up.* 1972. Atheneum. 1st. F/F. H11. $30.00

**DEIGHTON, Len.** *Funeral in Berlin: Secret File No 3.* 1964. London. Cape. 1st. VG+/clip. A14. $87.50

**DEIGHTON, Len.** *Goodbye Mickey Mouse.* 1982. London. Hutchinson. 1st. F/NF clip. B3. $40.00

**DEIGHTON, Len.** *Horse Under Water: Secret File No 2.* 1963. London. Cape. 1st/2nd issue (blk ep). VG/dj. A14. $70.00

**DEIGHTON, Len.** *London Match.* 1985. London. Hutchinson. 1st. F/F. B3. $40.00

**DEIGHTON, Len.** *London Match.* 1986. Knopf. 1st. 8vo. 407p. NF/VG. S14. $12.50

**DEIGHTON, Len.** *Spy Hook.* 1988. Knopf. 1st. 8vo. 292p. F/NF. S14. $11.00

**DEIGHTON, Len.** *Spy Line.* 1989. Knopf. 1st. NF/F. H11. $10.00

**DEIGHTON, Len.** *Spy Line.* 1989. London. Hutchinson. 1st. F/F. B3. $30.00

**DEIGHTON, Len.** *Spy Sinker.* 1990. NY. Harper Collins. ARC. F/dj. A23. $30.00

**DEIGHTON, Len.** *SS-GB.* 1979. Knopf. 1st Am. F/VG. N4. $20.00

**DEIGHTON, Len.** *Yesterday's Spy.* 1975. London. Cape. 1st. NF/F. B3. $75.00

**DEIN, Erling.** *Sct Hans Hospital Roskilde, Denmark 1816-1966...* 1966. Copenhagen. Munksgaard. apparent 1st. 259p. xl. NF. C14. $22.00

**DEISSMANN, Adolf.** *Bible Studies.* 1979. Alpha. rpt (1923 T&T Clark). 384p. VG. B29. $28.00

**DEISSMANN, Adolf.** *Light From the Ancient East.* 1980. Baker. 535p. VG/wrp. B29. $14.50

**DEJONG, Meindert.** *Horse Came Running.* 1970. Macmillan. 1st. ils Paul Sagsoorian. xl. B36. $10.00

**DEKEL, Efraim.** *Shai: Exploits of Hagana Intelligence.* 1959. Yoseloff. 1st. 8vo. 369p. VG. W1. $20.00

**DEKNATEL, Frederick B.** *Edvard Munch.* 1950. NY. MOMA. 8vo. ils. 120p. G/dj. F1. $20.00

**DEKOBRA, Maurice.** *Wings of Desire.* 1925. Macaulay. 1st. pict cloth. VG. N2. $10.00

**DEL GAUDIO, Sybil.** *Dressing the Part: Sternberg, Dietrich & Costume.* 1993. London. Fairleigh Dickinson. 95p. VG/dj. C5. $12.50

**DEL PLAINE, Carlos.** *Son of Orizaba: Memoirs of Childhood in Mexico.* 1954. NY. Exposition. 1st. 62p. dj. F3. $15.00

**DEL REY, Lester.** *Early Del Rey.* 1975. Doubleday. 1st. F/VG. M19. $17.50

**DEL RIO, Amelia Martinez.** *Sun, the Moon & the Rabbit.* 1935. NY. Sheed Ward. pub proof. obl 4to. R5. $275.00

**DEL VECCHIO, John M.** *For the Sake of All Living Things.* 1990. Bantam. 1st. NF/dj. R11/R14. $25.00

**DEL VECCHIO, John M.** *For the Sake of All Living Things.* 1990. Bantam. 1st. 790p. VG/dj. S16. $22.50

**DEL VECCHIO, John M.** *13th Valley.* 1982. Toronto. Bantam. 1st Canadian. F/F. B3. $75.00

**DELAHAYE, G.** *Pamela Learns to Ride.* 1968. Hart. 1st. ils Marcel Marlier. F/VG. M5. $30.00

**DELAND, Margaret.** *Dr Lavendar's People.* 1903. NY. Harper. 1st. 370p. G. G11. $8.00

**DELAND, Margaret.** *Kays.* 1926. Harper. 1/250. sgn pub. decor brn cloth. VG. S13. $25.00

**DELAND, Margaret.** *New Friends in Old Chester.* (1924). NY/London. Harper. 1st. 12mo. 272p. gilt red cloth. VG/dj. J3. $100.00

**DELAND, Margaret.** *Vehement Flame.* 1922. Harper. 1st. inscr. 378p. red cloth. NF/dj. J3. $100.00

**DELANY, Paul.** *Neo-Pagans, Friendship & Love in Rupert Brooke Circle.* 1987. London. 1st. dj. T9. $25.00

**DELANY, Samuel R.** *Bridge of Lost Desire.* 1987. Arbor. 1st. F/dj. M25. $15.00

**DELANY, Samuel R.** *They Fly at Ciron.* 1995. NY. Tor. 1st thus. sgn. F/dj. C9. $48.00

**DELANY & HEARTH.** *Delany Sisters Book of Everyday Wisdom.* 1994. NY. Kodansha. AN/dj. V4. $10.00

**DELAPORTE, Francois.** *History of Yellow Fever: An Essay...* 1991. Cambridge. 1st. 181p. A13. $35.00

**DELAUNEY, Charles.** *Jazz Parody.* 1948. London. ils/photos. 110p. VG/dj. B5. $35.00

**DELDERFIELD, R.F.** *All Over the Town.* 1947. Hodder Stoughton. 1st. author's 1st novel. NF/dj. A14. $17.50

**DELDERFIELD, R.F.** *Seven Men of Gascony.* 1949. Bobbs Merrill. 1st. NF/dj. A14. $42.00

**DELDERFIELD, R.F.** *Seven Men of Gascony.* 1973. S&S. 1st. F/NF clip. T11. $25.00

**DELDERFIELD, R.F.** *Stop at a Winner.* 1978. S&S. 1st Am. VG+/dj. A14. $17.50

**DELDERFIELD, R.F.** *Too Few Drums.* 1964. S&S. 1st. NF/VG. T11. $20.00

**DELGADILLO, Daniel.** *Atlas Geographico de la Republica Mexicana, Atlas General.* May 22 1910. Mexico City. Edicion Centenario. 31 full-p pl. 76p. ES. VG. B14. $275.00

**DELINSKY, Barbara.** *For My Daughters.* 1994. NY. Harper Collins. 1st. F/dj. T12. $35.00

**DELITZSCH, Franz Julius.** *System der Biblischen Psychologie.* 1861 (1855). Dorffling Franke. 2nd revised/enlarged. German text. 500p. VG. G1. $100.00

**DELL, Anthony.** *Llama Land: East & West of the Andeas in Peru.* 1927. NY. Doran. 8vo. 248p. red cloth. NF. O1. $75.00

**DELLACHIESA, Carolyn.** *Pinocchio Under the Sea.* 1913. Macmillan. 1st. ils Florence Wilde. VG. B5. $40.00

**DELLENBAUGH, Frederick S.** *Breaking the Wilderness.* 1905. Putnam. 1st. 360p. pict cloth. D11. $100.00

**DELLENBAUGH, Frederick S.** *Canyon Voyage: Narrative of the 2nd Powell Expedition...* 1908. NY. Putnam. 1st. ils/maps. 277p. pict cloth. D11. $100.00

**DELLENBAUGH, Frederick S.** *Canyon Voyage: Narrative of the 2nd Powell Expedition...* 1926. Yale. gilt bl cloth. VG. F7. $75.00

**DELLENBAUGH, Frederick S.** *Romance of the Colorado River...* 1902. Putnam. 8vo. 213p. VG. F7. $110.00

**DELLENBAUGH, Frederick S.** *Romance of the Colorado River: Story of Its Discovery.* 1982. Time Life. ils/index. 399p. F/sans. B19. $20.00

**DELORIA, Ella.** *Speaking of Indians.* (1944). Friendship. 163p. VG/wrp. B18. $45.00

**DELORIA, Vine Jr.** *Custer Died for Your Sins.* 1969. Macmidllan. 1st. sgn. F/VG. B3. $75.00

**DELORIA, Vine Jr.** *Custer Died for Your Sins.* 1969. Macmillan. 1st. VG/dj. R8. $45.00

**DEMBNER, S.** *Arthur & William E Massee: Modern Circulation Methods.* 1968. McGraw Hill. 1st. 4to. cloth. F/dj. O10. $15.00

**DEMBO, L.S.** *Confucian Odes of Ezra Pound.* 1963. U CA. 1st. rem mk. VG/clip. O4. $20.00

**DEMENT'EV & GLADKOV.** *Birds of the Soviet Union.* 1966-1968. Jerusalem. 6 vol. 13 pl/683 maps/848 figures. 4989p. NF. C12. $425.00

**DEMIJOHN, Thomas;** see Disch, Thomas.

**DEMING, Henry Champion.** *Speech of..., Delivered February 27th, 1864.* 1864. WA, DC. Gibson. 1st. 16p. wrp. M8. $85.00

**DEMING, Richard.** *American Spies: Real Life Stories of Undercover Agents...* 1960. Whitman. ils Leonard Vosburgh. 210p. NF. B36. $10.00

**DEMOOR, Jean.** *Die Anormalen Kinder und Ihre Behandlung in Haus und Schule.* 1901. Altenburg. Druck/Oskar Bonde. German text. 292p. modern line. G1. $100.00

**DENG, Francis Mading.** *Tradition & Modernization, a Challenge for Law...* 1971. Yale. G/dj. M11. $45.00

**DENHARDT, Robert M.** *Foundation Sires of the American Quarter Horse.* 1977. OK U. 2nd. NF/dj. A21. $45.00

**DENING, Greg.** *Mr Bligh's Bad Language: Passion, Power & Theater...* 1992. Cambridge. ils. VG/dj. M17. $27.50

**DENIS, Michaela.** *Leopard on My Lap.* 1955. Messner. 1st. 8vo. 254p. F/NF. B20. $30.00

**DENISE, Christopher.** *Fool of the World & the Flying Ship.* 1994. Philomel. 1st. F/dj. B17. $12.50

**DENISON, George Burlingame.** *Record of the Descendants of Samuel Denison...* 1884. Muscatine, IA. 72p. G. S5. $35.00

**DENLINGER, Milo.** *Complete Dachshund.* 1947. Denlinger. 1st. Ils Edwin McGargee. NF. A21. $45.00

**DENNIE, Charles.** *History of Syphilis.* 1962. Springfield. 1st. 137p. A13. $50.00

**DENNIE, James.** *Remarks on Judge Thacher's Sentence in Case...* 1841. Boston. Dutton Wentworth. orig stabbed wrp. M11. $75.00

**DENNIS, Jerry.** *Place on the Water: An Angler's Reflections on Home.* 1993. NY. 2nd. ils Glenn Wolf. 224p. F/dj. A17. $15.00

**DENNIS, Morgan.** *Morgan Dennis Dog Book.* 1946. Viking. 1st. ils. NF/dj. A21. $75.00

**DENNIS, Morgan.** *Purebreds.* 1954. Winston. 1st. VG. A21. $45.00

**DENNY, Arthur H.** *Pioneer Days on Puget Sound.* 1965. Fairfield. Ye Galleon. 8vo. 83p. B20. $50.00

**DENNY, George H.** *Dread Fishwish & Other Tales.* 1975. Freshet. 222p. F/dj. A17. $15.00

**DENNY & INGRAM.** *Complete Encyclopedia of Vegetables & Vegetarian Cooking.* 1997. NY. Anness. VG/dj. V4. $45.00

**DENON, Vivant.** *Travels in Lower & Upper Egypt During Campaigns Bonaparte.* 1804. London. R Taylor. 2 vol in 1. rb modern gr calf/gr cloth. K1. $250.00

**DENONN, Lester E.** *Wit & Wisdom of Oliver Wendell Holmes: Father & Son.* 1953. Boston. Beacon. 1st. 116p. gr cloth. F/dj. B14. $25.00

**DENSLOW, W.W.** *Billy Bounce.* 1913. Chicago. Donohue. 1st prt after 1906 1st. 279p. gr cloth. VG. F1. $300.00

**DENSLOW, W.W.** *Simple Simon.* (1904). Dillingham. 1st thus. 4to. stiff paper bdg. R5. $225.00

**DENSMORE, Frances.** *Music of Santo Domingo Pueblo, New Mexico.* 1938. SW Mus. 1st. ils. 186p. NF. B19. $50.00

**DENSMORE, Frances.** *Yuman & Yaqui Music.* 1932. GPO. 1st. ils/nots. 216p. wrp. B19. $45.00

**DENTAL SCHOOL OF HARVARD.** *75th Anniversary of the Founding: A Record...* 1944. Harvard. 1st. 8vo. 52p. gilt cloth. C14. $32.00

**DENTON, Bradley.** *Buddy Holly Is Alive & Well on Ganymede.* 1991. Morrow. 1st. author's 2nd book. NF/dj. R14. $25.00

**DENVER & TOBIER.** *Take Me Home: An Autobiography.* 1994. Harmony. 1st. ils. 262p. VG/dj. S14. $11.00

**DEPEW, Albert N.** *Gunner Depew.* 1918. Chicago. Reilly Britton. 1st? sm 8vo. 312p. gilt bl cloth. VG+. M7. $35.00

**DERBY, W.P.** *Bearing Arms in the 27th MA Regiment Volunteer Infantry...* 1883. 1st. 8 pl/maps. VG. E6. $150.00

**DERBYSHIRE, John.** *Seeing Calvin Coolidge in a Dream.* 1996. St Martin. 1st. author's 1st novel. F/dj. A23/M23. $40.00

**DERHAM, William.** *Astro-Theology; or, Demonstration of Being & Attributes...* 1743. np. 6th/corrected. sm 4to. 3 fld copper pl. contemporary polished calf. H13. $245.00

**DERLETH, August.** *Boy's Way.* 1947. Stanton Lee. 1st. 8vo. 109p. bl cloth. NF/dj. J3. $250.00

**DERLETH, August.** *Chronicles of Solar Pons.* 1973. Arkham. 1st. collects 10 stories. F/dj. T2. $25.00

**DERLETH, August.** *Countryman's Journal.* 1963. DSP. 1st. NF/VG. P3. $25.00

**DERLETH, August.** *Fire & Sleet & Candlelight.* 1961. Arkham. 1st. VG/dj. B30. $125.00

**DERLETH, August.** *Harrigan's File.* 1975. Sauk City. 1st. F/dj. T10. $40.00

**DERLETH, August.** *In Re: Sherlock Holmes.* 1945. Mycroft Moran. 1st. NF/dj. J3. $175.00

**DERLETH, August.** *Mr George & Other Odd Persons.* 1963. Arkham. 1st. VG/dj. P3. $30.00

**DERLETH, August.** *Night Side.* 1947t. Rinehart. 1st. NF/VG. M19. $35.00

**DERLETH, August.** *Three Problems for Solar Pons.* 1952. Mycroft Moran. 1/996. 8vo. 112p. gilt stp cloth. F/dj. J3. $275.00

**DERLETH, August.** *Village Daybook: A Sac Prairie Journal.* 1947. Pelligrini Cudahy. 1st. VG. P3. $20.00

**DEROCHES, Catherine F.** *La Puce De Mme Desroches.* 1872. Paris. Librairie des Bibliophiles. sm 8vo. B20. $275.00

**DERR, Mark.** *Frontiersman.* 1993. Morrow. 1st. gilt bdg. F/dj. T11. $15.00

**DERRYDALE.** *Decade of American Sporting Books & Prints 1927-1937.* Derrydale. ltd. 1/950. VG. A21. $250.00

**DESCHIN, Jacob.** *Canon Photography: A Working Manual...* 1957. Camera Craft. 1st. VG/dj. S5. $10.00

**DESMOND, Alice Curtis.** *Feathers, Story of a Rhea.* 1940. Macmillan. 1st. ils Wilfred Bronson. VG/G. P2. $15.00

**DESMOND, Alice Curtis.** *George Washington's Mother.* 1961. Dodd Mead. 1st. VG/dj. w/TLS. T11. $30.00

**DESORMEAUX.** *Histoire de Louis deBourbon, Secod du Nom, Prince de Conde.* 1766-1768. Paris. Saillant, Veuve Duchesne, Desaint. 4 vol. fld pl. calf. R12. $250.00

**DESROCHES-NOBLECOURT, C.** *Life & Death of a Pharaoh: Tutankhamen.* 1963. NYGS. photos FL Kenett. 312p. cloth. dj. D2. $25.00

**DETMOLD & DUGDALE.** *Book of Baby Birds.* ca 1920. Hodder Stoughton. mc pl. 120p. NF. B20. $250.00

**DETT, R. Nathaniel.** *Religious Folk-Songs of the Negro.* 1927. Hampton Inst. 1st. F. B2. $125.00

**DEUEL, Leo.** *Conquistadors Without Swords.* 1967. St Martin. 1st. 647p. dj. F3. $25.00

**DEUTSCH, Felix.** *Psychosomatic Concept in Psychoanalysis.* 1953. Internat U Pr. 1st. 8vo. 182p. xl. NF. C14. $15.00

**DEVAMBEZ, Pierre.** *Greek Sculpture.* 1961. NY. Tudor. photos Robert Deschames. unp. cloth. dj. D2. $20.00

**DEVERDUN, Alfred.** *True Mexico: Mexico-Tenochtitlan.* 1938. Menasha, WI. Geo Banta. 1st. sgn. 304p. tattered dj. F3. $35.00

**DEVINE, Dominic.** *Devil at Your Elbow.* 1966. London. Collins Crime Club. 1st. F/NF. M15. $65.00

**DEVINE, Laurie.** *Nile.* 1983. London. Andre Deutsch. 1st. NF/clip. A14. $25.00

**DEVIVIER, W.** *Christian Apologetics: A Rational Exposition...* 1924. NY. Wagner. 2 vol. index. xl. G. H10. $37.50

**DEVLIN & DEVLIN.** *How Fletcher Was Hatched!* 1969. Parents Magazine. 1st? sm 4to. VG. M5. $12.00

**DEWEES, W.** *Treatise on Diseases of Females.* 1847 (1827). 12 pl. full leather. E6. $125.00

**DEWEY, John.** *Psychology.* 1887. NY. Harper. author's 1st book. pebbled mauve cloth. NF. G1. $300.00

**DEWSBURY, Donald A.** *Comparative Psychology in 20th Century.* 1984. Stroudsburg, PA. Hutchinson Ross. 411p. pebbled prt gr fabricoid. G1. $65.00

**DEWSBURY, Donald A.** *Mammalian Sexual Behavior.* 1981. Hutchinson Ross. 382p. F. S15. $36.00

**DEXTER, Colin.** *As Good As Gold.* 1994. London. Kodak. 1st appearance. F/wrp. M15. $45.00

**DEXTER, Colin.** *Death Is Now My Neighbour.* 1996. London. Macmillan. 1st. sgn. F/dj. M15. $65.00

**DEXTER, Colin.** *Jewel That Was Ours.* 1991. Bristol. Scorpion. 1st. 1/150. sgn. special bdg. F/acetate dj. M15. $250.00

**DEXTER, Colin.** *Jewel That Was Ours.* 1991. NY. Crown. 1st. F/F. B3. $45.00

**DEXTER, Colin.** *Last Seen Wearing.* 1976. St Martin. 1st Am. F/NF. M15. $500.00

**DEXTER, Colin.** *Morse's Greatest Mystery & Other Stories.* 1993. London. Macmillan. 1st Eng. F/dj. T12. $22.00

**DEXTER, Colin.** *Morse's Greatest Mystery.* 1993. NY. Crown. 1st. F/dj. A23. $32.00

**DEXTER, Colin.** *Neighbourhood Watch.* 1993. Richmond. Moorhouse Sorenson. 1st. sgn. F. M15. $250.00

**DEXTER, Colin.** *Neighbourhood Watch.* 1993. Richmond. Moorhouse. 1st. F/wrp. Q1. $100.00

**DEXTER, Colin.** *Secret of Annexe 3.* 1986. London. Macmillan. 1st. F/NF. M15. $325.00

**DEXTER, Colin.** *Way Through the Woods.* 1992. Bristol. Scorpion. 1st. 1/150. sgn/#d. F/acetate dj. M15. $200.00

**DEXTER, Pete.** *Deadwood.* 1986. Random. 1st. inscr/dtd 1989. NF/F. R14. $50.00

**DEXTER, Pete.** *Paperboy.* 1995. Random. 1st. F/F. H11. $25.00

**DEXTER, Pete.** *Paperboy.* 1995. Random. 1st. sgn. F/dj. Q1. $50.00

**DEXTER, Pete.** *Paris Trout.* 1988. Random. 1st. NF/F. H11. $25.00

**DEXTER, Peter.** *Deadwood.* 1986. Random. 1st. NF/dj. T11. $25.00

**DEXTER, W.W.** *Texas: Imperial State of America With Her Diadem of Cities.* (1903). St Louis. TX World Fair Comm. unp. decor cloth. B18. $48.00

**DI FILIPPO, Paul.** *Ribofunk.* 1996. Four Walls Eight Windows. 1st. F/NF. M23. $25.00

**DI FILIPPO, Paul.** *Steampunk Trilogy.* 1995. Four Walls Eight Windows. 1st. F/F. H11. $30.00

**DI FUSCO, John.** *Tracers.* 1986. Hill Wang. 1st. F/dj. R11. $50.00

**DI MAGGIO, Joe.** *Lucky to Be a Yankee.* 1946. Field. 1st. photos. VG/dj. P8. $200.00

**DI MONA, Joseph.** *Last Man at Arlington.* 1973. NY. Fields. 1st. NF/F. H11. $20.00

**DIAMANT, L.** *Chaining the Hudson: Fight for the River in Am Revolution.* 1989. NY. ils/map. F/dj. M4. $25.00

**DIAMOND, Solomon.** *Roots of Psychology: Sourcebook in History of Ideas.* 1977. NY. Basic. thick 8vo. 781p. russet cloth. VG/dj. G1. $65.00

**DIAZ, Junot.** *Drown.* 1996. Riverhead. 1st. author's 1st book. F/dj. R14. $25.00

**DIAZ DEL CASTILLO, Bernal.** *Memoirs of the Conquistador Bernal Diaz Del Castillo...* 1844. London. Hatchard. 2 vol. trans JI Lockhart. stp cloth. D11. $200.00

**DIBBLE, R.F.** *John L Sullivan: An Intimate Narrative.* 1925. Little Brn. 1st. ils/photos. 209p. gr cloth. NF. B20. $40.00

**DIBDIN, Michael.** *Cabal.* 1993. NY. Doubleday Crime. 1st Am. sgn. F/dj. O11. $30.00

**DIBDIN, Michael.** *Dark Specter.* 1995. Pantheon. ARC/1st Am. F/wrp. S18. $30.00

**DIBDIN, Michael.** *Dead Lagoon.* 1995. Pantheon. 1st Am. sgn. RS. F/dj. O11. $30.00

**DIBDIN, Michael.** *Dying of the Light.* 1993. London. Faber. 1st. F/dj. M15. $50.00

**DIBDIN, Michael.** *Dying of the Light.* 1994. Pantheon. 1st. sgn. F/dj. O11. $25.00

**DIBDIN, Michael.** *Vendetta.* 1990. London. Faber. 1st. NF/dj. A14. $70.00

**DIBDIN, Michael.** *Vendetta.* 1991. Doubleday. 1st Am. F/dj. N4. $25.00

**DIBDIN, Michael.** *Vendetta.* 1991. Doubleday. 1st. sgn. F/dj. O11. $30.00

**DIBNER, Martin.** *Admiral.* 1967. Doubleday. BC. NF/VG. T11. $10.00

**DIBNER & RUBIEN.** *Concepts, Critiques & Commments: Wide & Varied.* 1976. NY. Dibner/Rubien. ils/pl. 334p. gilt brn cloth. cloth case. K1. $60.00

**DICK, Erma Biesel.** *Old House: Holiday & Party Cookbook.* (1969). Cowles. 1st. ils. VG/dj. A16. $25.00

**DICK, J. Harrison.** *Sweet Peas for Profit: Cultivation, Under Glass & Outdoors.* 1914. NY. De La Mare. 1st. ils. 147p. VG. H10. $15.00

**DICK, Philip K.** *Beyond Lies the Wub: Volume One of Collected Stories of...* 1988. London. Gollancz. 1st Eng. 25 stories. F/dj. T2. $30.00

**DICK, Philip K.** *Crack in Space.* 1989. Surrey. Severn. 1st hc. F/dj. T2. $35.00

**DICK, Philip K.** *Man in the High Castle.* nd. BC. VG/dj. P3. $10.00

**DICK, Philip K.** *Our Friends From Frolix 8.* 1989. Middlesex. Kinnell. 1st Eng hc. F/dj. T2. $30.00

**DICK, Philip K.** *Scanner Darkly.* 1977. Doubleday. 2nd. rem mk. F/dj. P3. $25.00

**DICK, William B.** *Dick's Games of Patience; or, Solitaire With Cards.* 1884. NY. Dick & Fitzgerald. revised/enlarged. 154p+ads. gilt brn cloth. B20. $50.00

**DICK & JANE READER.** *Before We Read Developmental Activities for Pre-Reading...* 1937. Scott Foresman. student ed. obl 4to. 42p. R5. $175.00

**DICK & JANE READER.** *Before We Read Developmental Activities for Pre-Reading...* 1937. Scott Foresman. teacher ed. obl 4to. mc wrp/mailing envelope+order info. R5. $475.00

**DICK & JANE READER.** *Before We Read.* 1962. Scott Foresman. sc workbook. unused. AN/wrp. A23. $90.00

**DICK & JANE READER.** *Friends & Neighbors.* 1941. Scott Foresman. VG. A23. $80.00

**DICK & JANE READER.** *Friends Old & New.* 1964 (1963). Scott Foresman. 2nd/part 1. 5th. 8vo. 240p. school stp. pict cloth. T5. $30.00

**DICK & JANE READER.** *Fun Wherever We Are.* 1962. Scott Foresman. 3rd pre-primer. school stamp. VG/wrp. A23. $50.00

**DICK & JANE READER.** *Fun Wherever We Are.* 1962. Scott Foresman. 79p. xl. VG/wrp. B36. $40.00

**DICK & JANE READER.** *Fun With Our Family.* 1962. Scott Foresman. 2nd pre-primer. VG/wrp. A23. $60.00

**DICK & JANE READER.** *Fun With Our Friends.* 1962. Scott Foresman. teacher ed. school stp. VG. A23. $50.00

**DICK & JANE READER.** *Fun With Our Friends.* 1962. Scott Foresman. 1st in series. yel ils brd. xl. VG. B36. $36.00

**DICK & JANE READER.** *Guess Who.* 1951. Scott Foresman. school stp. G/wrp. A23. $45.00

**DICK & JANE READER.** *Guess Who.* 1956. Scott Foresman. school stp. G. A23. $40.00

**DICK & JANE READER.** *Guide to Accompany Guess Who.* 1962. Scott Foresman. VG. A23. $80.00

**DICK & JANE READER.** *Guidebook for the Basic Primer Fun With Dick & Jane.* (1940). Scott Foresman teacher ed. 8vo. 192p+162p. R5. $275.00

**DICK & JANE READER.** *More Friends & Neighbors.* 1946. Scott Foresman. school stp. G. A23. $20.00

**DICK & JANE READER.** *More Friends Old & New.* 1963. Scott Foresman. teacher ed. school stp. VG. A23. $50.00

**DICK & JANE READER.** *More Fun With Our Friends.* 1962. Scott Foresman. teacher ed. school stp. G. A23. $40.00

**DICK & JANE READER.** *More Streets & Roads.* 1946. Scott Foresman. school stp. G. A23. $20.00

**DICK & JANE READER.** *New Days & Deeds.* (1962). Scott Foresman. 8vo. ils. 320p. olive cloth. xl. VG. T5. $35.00

**DICK & JANE READER.** *New Friends & Neighbors.* 1956. Scott Foresman. school stp. G. A23. $40.00

**DICK & JANE READER.** *New Fun With Dick & Jane.* 1956. Scott Foresman. 1st. school stp. VG. A23. $90.00

**DICK & JANE READER.** *New Guess Who.* 1962. Scott Foresman. school stp. VG. A23. $70.00

**DICK & JANE READER.** *New More Friends & Neighbors.* (1956). Scott Foresman. 2nd grade/2nd primer. 7th. 240p. gold pict cloth. VG. T5. $45.00

**DICK & JANE READER.** *New More Friends & Neighbors.* 1956. Scott Foresman. previous owner's name on ffe. VG. A23. $45.00

**DICK & JANE READER.** *New Our Friends.* 1956. Scott Foresman. school stp. F. A23. $120.00

**DICK & JANE READER.** *New Our Friends.* 1956. Scott Foresman. school stp. G. A23. $40.00

**DICK & JANE READER.** *New We Come & Go.* 1951. Scott Foresman. F/wrp. A23. $175.00

**DICK & JANE READER.** *New We Look & See.* 1952. Scott Foresman. New Cathedral Basic Readers. F/wrp. A23. $150.00

**DICK & JANE READER.** *New We Work & Play.* 1951. Scott Foresman. F/wrp. A23. $175.00

**DICK & JANE READER.** *New We Work & Play.* 1952. Scott Foresman. Cathedral ed. 64p. VG/wrp. B36. $50.00

**DICK & JANE READER.** *Our New Friends.* 1946-47. Scott Foresman. student ed. 8vo. 191p. bl pict cloth. R5. $150.00

**DICK & JANE READER.** *Sally, Dick & Jane. The New Basic Readers.* 1962. Scott Foresman. sm sticker w/student's name. VG/wrp. A23. $75.00

**DICK & JANE READER.** *Sally Does It.* 1940. Appleton Century. ils Robb Beebe. 8vo. F/VG. M5. $85.00

**DICK & JANE READER.** *Think-and-Do Book For Use With More Fun With Our Friends.* 1962. Scott Foresman. sc workbook. unused. AN/wrp. A23. $60.00

**DICK & JANE READER.** *Think-and-Do Book to Accompany Guess Who.* 1951. Scott Foresman. sc workbook. unused. AN/wrp. A23. $110.00

**DICK & JANE READER.** *Think-and-Do Book to Accompany New Fun With Dick & Jane.* 1956. Scott Foresman. sc workbook. unused. AN/wrp. A23. $125.00

**DICK & JANE READER.** *We Talk, Spell & Write, Book 1-1, Basic Language Program.* 1956. Scott Foresman. ils. F. B17. $85.00

**DICKASON, Christie.** *Indochine: Epic Novel of Vietnam.* 1987. Villard/Random. Special Readers ed of 1st Am. NF/ils wrp. A14. $14.00

**DICKASON, David Howard.** *Daring Young Men: Story of American Pre-Raphaelites.* 1970. NY. Benj Blom. ils/notes/index. NF. D2. $25.00

**DICKASON, Olive Patricia.** *Indian Arts in Canada.* 1972. Ottawa. Dept Indian Affairs & Northern Development. 138p. P4. $85.00

**DICKENS, Charles.** *American Notes for General Circulation.* 1842. London. Chapman Hall. 2 vol. 1st/1st issue (no intro). gilt cloth. F. B24. $1,500.00

**DICKENS, Charles.** *Chimes.* (1913). Hodder Stoughton. 1st thus. ils Hugh Thomson. 137p. red cloth. F/box. H5. $450.00

**DICKENS, Charles.** *Christmas Carol.* 1995. Harcourt Brace. lg 8vo. F. B36. $22.00

**DICKENS, Charles.** *David Copperfield.* 1980. Franklin Lib. ils Paul Degen. 803p. VG. B36. $20.00

**DICKENS, Charles.** *Dicken's Stories About Children.* 1929. Winston. 8vo. 274p. VG. W2. $30.00

**DICKENS, Charles.** *Doctor Marigold's Perscriptions.* 1865. London. Chapman Hall. 1st. VG/bl prt wrp. w/ad of Our Mutual Friend. M24. $85.00

**DICKENS, Charles.** *Great Expectations.* 1861. NY. James G Gregory. 2 vol. 1st Am/1st issue. contemporary bdg. VG. M24. $1,750.00

**DICKENS, Charles.** *Great Expectations.* 1861. Phil. TB Peterson. 1st ils ed. 16mo. 523p. gilt blk cloth. M24. $250.00

**DICKENS, Charles.** *Life & Adventures of Martin Chuzzlewit.* 1844. Chapman Hall. 1st. 1st. 40 etched pl. Bayntum bdg. aeg. F. H5. $750.00

**DICKENS, Charles.** *Life of Our Lord.* 1934. London. Assoc Newspapers. 1st. sm 4to. 128p. gilt maroon cloth. F/VG. H1. $65.00

**DICKENS, Charles.** *Life of Our Lord.* 1934. St Martin. 1st Am. F/VG. M19. $35.00

**DICKENS, Charles.** *Little Dorritt.* 1857. Phil. TB Peterson. 1st Am. gilt blk cloth. NF. M24. $450.00

**DICKENS, Charles.** *Mr Pickwick's Christmas.* (1906). NY. Platt Peck. 149p. VG. B18. $30.00

**DICKENS, Charles.** *Mystery of Edwin Drood.* 1870. London. 1st (from parts, bdg w/covers+ads). 3-quarter leather. M17. $300.00

**DICKENS, Charles.** *No Thoroughfare.* 1867. London. 1st. F/bl prt wrp. M24. $165.00

**DICKENS, Charles.** *Old Lamps for New Ones & Other Sketches & Essays...* 1897. NY. New Amsterdam Book. 1st. orig maroon decor cloth. RS. NF. M24. $200.00

**DICKENS, Charles.** *Our Mutual Friend.* 1886. London. Chapman Hall. 2 vol. 1st/unrecorded rem issue. gr cloth. VG. M24. $300.00

**DICKENS, Charles.** *Posthumous Papers of the Pickwick Club.* 1844. Dodd Mead. ils. 687p. 3-quarter morocco. F. F1. $125.00

**DICKENS, Charles.** *Works...* 1891-1894. London. Chapman Hall. 14 vol. ils Cruikshank/Stone/etc. half morocco. F1. $895.00

**DICKENS, Homer.** *Films of Marlene Dietrich.* 1968. Citadel. 1st. ils. VG/dj. C9. $48.00

**DICKENS, Monica.** *Great Escape.* 1971. London. Kaye Ward. 1st. Early Bird series. F/dj. D4. $20.00

**DICKERSON, Albert Inskip.** *Selected Writings.* 1974. Dartmouth. 1st. 8vo. F/dj. A2. $15.00

**DICKEY, Christopher.** *Expats: Travels in Arabia, From Tripoli to Teheran.* 1990. Atlantic Monthly. 1st. 228p. NF/dj. W1. $20.00

**DICKEY, Christopher.** *With the Contras: A Reporter in Wilds of Nicaragua.* 1985. S&S. 1st. 327p. dj. F3. $10.00

**DICKEY, Herbert.** *Misadventures of a Tropical Medico.* 1929. Dodd Mead. 1st. 304p. F3. $20.00

**DICKEY, James.** *Bronwen, the Traw & the Shape-Shifter.* 1986. HBJ. 1st. ils Richard Jesse Watson. rem mk. NF/F. B3. $20.00

**DICKEY, James.** *Puella.* 1982. Doubleday. 1st. sgn. F/dj. B30. $55.00

**DICKEY, James.** *To the White Sea.* 1993. Houghton Mifflin. 1st. inscr. NF/dj. R14. $60.00

**DICKEY, James.** *Tucky the Hunter.* 1978. Crown. 1st. NF. C14. $16.00

**DICKEY, James.** *Zodiac.* 1976. Doubleday. 1st. NF/dj. w/inscr card. J3. $40.00

**DICKEY, Page.** *Breaking Ground: Portraits of Ten Garden Designers.* 1997. NY. Artisan. 1st. folio. ils/index. 207p. F/dj. H10. $37.50

**DICKEY & KERKSIS.** *Field Artillery Projectiles of the Civil War 1861-65.* 1968. Atlanta. Phoenix. 1st. 1/500 #d. ils. 307p. M8. $150.00

**DICKEY & VAN ROSSEM.** *Birds of El Salavdor.* 1938. Chicago. Field Nat Hist Mus. lg 8vo. ils/photos. 609p. VG/wrp. C12. $130.00

**DICKIE, Edgar Primrose.** *God Is Light.* 1954. Scribner. 261p. VG/torn. B29. $13.00

**DICKINSON, Charles.** *With or Without.* 1987. Knopf. 1st. NF/F. R14. $30.00

**DICKINSON, Emily.** *Further Poems of Emily Dickinson.* 1929. Little Brn. only/2nd prt/lg paper. 1/465. teg/ribbon mk. VG/case. J3. $400.00

**DICKINSON, Emily.** *Further Poems of Emily Dickinson.* 1929. Little Brn. 1st. 8vo. 208p. teg. dk gr cloth. NF/dj. H5. $250.00

**DICKINSON, Peter.** *Healer.* 1983. NY. Delacorte. 1st Am. 184p. F/dj. D4. $40.00

**DICKINSON, Peter.** *Merlin Dreams.* 1988. Delacorte. 1st. ils Alan Lee. F/dj. B17. $25.00

**DICKINSON, Peter.** *Perfect Gallows.* 1988. Pantheon. F/G+. L4. $12.00

**DICKINSON, Peter.** *Play Dead.* 1992. Mysterious. 1st Am. rem mk. F/dj. N4. $15.00

**DICKINSON & DOWD.** *Winter Picnic: Story of 4 Months' Outing...* 1888. Holt. 1st. 265p. yel-orange cloth. B20. $65.00

**DICKSON, Carter;** see Carr, John Dickson.

**DICKSON, Gordon R.** *Star Road.* 1975. Robert Hale. 1st. VG/dj. P3. $15.00

**DICKSON, L.E.** *New First Course in Theory of Equations.* 1939. John Wiley. 14th prt. bl cloth. VG. B27. $20.00

**DICKSON & HOLMES.** *Practical Horticulture for the Pacific Slope.* 1927. SF. ils/photos. 343p. B26. $20.00

**DIDION, Joan.** *Miami.* 1987. S&S. 1st. inscr/dtd 1994. rem mk. F/dj. R14. $45.00

**DIDION, Joan.** *Play It As It Lays.* 1970. FSG. 1st. inscr/dtd 1992. VG/dj. R14. $50.00

**DIDION, Joan.** *Play It As It Lays.* 1970. FSG. 1st. VG/dj. C9. $36.00

**DIDION, Joan.** *Slouching Towards Bethlehem.* 1968. FSG. 1st. author's 2nd book. F/sbdg wrp. L3. $750.00

**DIEDERICH, B.** *Al Burt Into Graham Green: Papa Doc.* 1969. NY. 1st. VG/dj. B5. $17.50

**DIEHL, Charles.** *Byzantium: Greatness & Decline.* 1957. Rutgers. 1st. ils. cloth. VG/dj. W1. $22.00

**DIEHL, Edith.** *Bookbinding: Its Background & Technique.* 1946. Rhinehart. 2 vol. ils. gilt blk cloth. pub case/prt label. F1/K1. $150.00

**DIEHL, Edith.** *Bookbinding: Its Background & Technique.* 1946. Rinehart. 2 vol. 1st. 8vo. cloth. VG. P2. $90.00

**DIEHL, Gaston.** *Fauves.* 1975. NY. Abrams. ils. 4to. tan cloth. F/dj. F1. $75.00

**DIEHL, William.** *Chameleon.* 1981. Random. 1st. author's 2nd novel. NF/dj. S18. $30.00

**DIEHL, William.** *Hooligans.* 1984. Villard. 1st. F/F. H11. $25.00

**DIEHL, William.** *Thai Horse.* 1987. NY. Villard. 1st. F/F. H11. $25.00

**DIEKE, G.H.** *Ladybeetles of the Genus Epilachna in Asia, Europe...* 1947. Smithsonian. 183p. VG. S15. $15.00

**DIERKS, J.C.** *Leap to Arms: Curan Campaign of 1898.* 1970. Phil. 1st. F/dj. M4. $18.00

**DIETRICH, Marlene.** *Marlene Dietrich's ABC.* 1962. Doubleday. BC. VG/dj. C9. $25.00

**DIETRICH, William.** *Final Forest.* 1992. S&S. 1st. sm 4to. 303p. F/dj. W2. $30.00

**DIETZ, Howard.** *Dancing in the Dark.* 1974. Quadrangle/NY Times. 1st. inscr. 370p. NF/dj. B20. $150.00

**DIGBY, Kenelm.** *Discours Fait en une Celebre Assemblee.* 1669. Paris. Thos Jolly. 12mo. 91+4p. contemporary calf. G7. $650.00

**DIGBY, Kenelm.** *Private Memoirs...Written by Himself...* 1827-1828. London. Saunders Otley. 1st. 328+48p. contemporary full polished calf. G7. $495.00

**DIKTY, Alan S.** *Boy's Book Collector.* nd. Starmount. F. P3. $75.00

**DILENSCHNEIDER, Robert L.** *Power & Influence.* 1990. Prentice Hall. 1st. 8vo. 258p. F/dj. W2. $30.00

**DILLARD, Annie.** *American Childhood.* 1987. Harper Row. 1st. F/NF. M23. $25.00

**DILLARD, Annie.** *American Childhood.* 1987. Harper Row. 1st. sgn. F/dj. T11. $40.00

**DILLARD, Annie.** *American Childhood.* 1987. Harper Row. ltd. 1/250. sgn. F/case. B3. $100.00

**DILLARD, Annie.** *Encounters With Chinese Writers.* 1984. Wesleyan U. 1st. F/VG. B30. $20.00

**DILLARD, Annie.** *Holy the Firm.* 1977. Harper Row. 1st. NF/F. B3. $50.00

**DILLARD, Annie.** *Living.* 1992. Harper Collins. F/dj. V4. $15.00

**DILLARD, Annie.** *Writing Life.* 1989. Harper Row. 1st. F/dj. M23. $20.00

**DILLEN, Frederick G.** *Hero.* 1994. Steerforth. 1st. author's 1st novel. F/dj. R14. $35.00

**DILLEY, Arthur Urbane.** *Oriental Rugs & Carpets: A Comprehensive Study.* 1931. NY/London. Scribner. 1st. 4to. 79 pl. 303p. VG. W1. $125.00

**DILLON, Brian.** *Salinas de los Nueve Cerros, Guatemala.* 1977. NY. Ballena. 1st. 94p. wrp. F3. $20.00

**DILLON, Helen.** *Garden Artistry: Secrets of Planting & Designing...* 1995. Macmillan. 1st. ils/biblio. 190p. F/VG. H10. $25.00

**DILLON, Julia L.** *Blossom Circle of the Year in Southern Gardens.* 1922. NY. photos. 201p. VG/dj. B26. $25.00

**DILLON, Richard.** *Burnt-Out Fires.* 1973. Englewood Cliffs. Prentice Hall. F/dj. A19. $25.00

**DILLWYN, George.** *Occasional Reflections, Offered Principally Use Schools.* 1815. Burlington, NJ. David Allinson. 1st. 12mo. 206p. leather. V3. $25.00

**DIMBLEBY, Jonathan.** *Palestinians.* 1979. London/Melbourne/NY. Quartet. 1st. ils. 256p. VG/dj. W1. $25.00

**DIMITRI, Ivan.** *Flight to Everywhere.* 1944. NY. Whittlesey. 4to. ils. 240p. VG/fair. B11. $20.00

**DINE, Jim.** *Apocalypse: Revelation of Saint John the Divine.* 1982. SF. Arion. 1/150. sgns Dine/prt Andrew Hoyem. oak brd/pigskin. AN. B24. $4,000.00

**DINESEN, Isak.** *Anecdotes of Destiny.* 1958. Random. 1st. NF/dj. B30. $50.00

**DINESEN, Isak.** *Ehrengard.* 1963. Random. 1st. NF/dj. B30. $35.00

**DINESEN, Isak.** *Shadow on the Grass.* 1960. Michael Joseph. 1st Eng. F/NF. M19. $45.00

**DINESEN, Isak.** *Shadows on the Grass.* 1960. London. Michael Joseph. 1st. VG/dj. T9. $40.00

**DINESEN, Isak.** *Shadows on the Grass.* 1961. Random. 1st Am. 8vo. ils. 152p. VG. B11. $20.00

**DINGWALL, Eric J.** *Some Human Oddities: Studies in the Queer...* 1962. Hyde Park, NY. University Books. 1st. 198p. F/VG+. B20. $25.00

**DIPPIE, Brian W.** *Charles M Russell: Word Painter, Letters 1887-1926.* 1993. Abrams. photos. AN. J2. $110.00

**DIRINGER, David.** *Illuminated Book: Its History & Production.* 1967. 4to. 514p. 270p. F/F. A4. $350.00

**DIRKS & HAUSMANN.** *Germany in Color.* nd. NY. Studio/Crowell. lg 4to. red cloth. H4. $20.00

**DIRVIN, Joseph I.** *Louise de Marillac: Of the Ladies & Daughters of Charity.* 1970. NY. 1st. VG/dj. M17. $20.00

**DISCH, Thomas M.** *Businessman.* 1984. Harper Row. 1st. F/NF. M21. $30.00

**DISCH, Thomas M.** *Fun With Your New Head.* 1971. Doubleday. 1st Am. rem mk. F/dj. B2. $25.00

**DISCH, Thomas M.** *Priest.* 1994. Knopf. 1st. F. S18. $7.00

**DISCH, Thomas M.** *The MD.* 1991. Knopf. 1st. F/F. H11. $35.00

**DISNEY STUDIOS.** *Adventures of Mickey Mouse, Book 2.* 1932. Phil. McKay. early. sm 8vo. VG. D1. $400.00

**DISNEY STUDIOS.** *Baby Weems.* 1941. Doubleday Doran. 1st. 4to. lg bl cloth. mc pict dj. R5. $485.00

**DISNEY STUDIOS.** *Cold Blooded Penguin.* 1946. Little Golden Book D2. 24p. red mk on cover. K2. $20.00

**DISNEY STUDIOS.** *Darby O'Gill.* Little Golden Book D81. A ed. K2. $8.00

**DISNEY STUDIOS.** *Davy Crockett's Keelboat Race.* Little Golden Book D47. A ed. K2. $22.00

**DISNEY STUDIOS.** *Donald Duck in America on Parade.* Little Golden Book D131. 2nd. VG. K2. $10.00

**DISNEY STUDIOS.** *Donald Duck.* 1935. Racine. Whitman. 1st (1st Donald Duck). folio. VG/wrp. H5. $1,250.00

**DISNEY STUDIOS.** *Donald Duck.* 1978. Abbeville. 1st. sm folio. 195p. NF. B20. $85.00

**DISNEY STUDIOS.** *Dopey He Don't Talk None.* 1938. Racine. Whitman. 1st. 12p. mc paper wrp. R5. $275.00

**DISNEY STUDIOS.** *Elmer Elephant.* 1936. Australia. Photogravures Ltd. 12p booklet. G. C9. $60.00

**DISNEY STUDIOS.** *Jungle Book.* Little Golden Book D120. A ed. K2. $14.00

**DISNEY STUDIOS.** *Les Trois Petits Cochons (The Three Little Pigs).* 1936. Paris. Hachette. 4to. 3 dbl-p popups. mc brd/mc dj. R5. $800.00

**DISNEY STUDIOS.** *Mary Poppins: A Jolly Holiday.* Little Golden Book D112. A ed. K2. $9.00

**DISNEY STUDIOS.** *Mickey Mouse, the Miracle Maker.* nd. Whitman. 24mo, 96p. VG. D1. $50.00

**DISNEY STUDIOS.** *Mickey Mouse Goes Christmas Shopping.* Little Golden Book D33. A ed. K2. $22.00

**DISNEY STUDIOS.** *Mickey Mouse Medley.* ca 1950. London. Dean. mc ils. 16p. mc pict bdg. file copy. R5. $100.00

**DISNEY STUDIOS.** *Mickey Mouse Picnic.* Little Golden Book D15. A ed. bend in corner. K2. $24.00

**DISNEY STUDIOS.** *Mickey Mouse Story Book Album.* 1978 (1931). David McKay. 1st thus. ils. F/dj. P2. $25.00

**DISNEY STUDIOS.** *Mickey Mouse.* 1978. Abbeville. 1st. 11 stories. 204p. F/dj. B20. $85.00

**DISNEY STUDIOS.** *Mother Goose.* Little Golden Book D79 A ed. K2. $15.00

**DISNEY STUDIOS.** *Pete's Dragon.* Little Golden Book D137. 1st. VG. K2. $10.00

**DISNEY STUDIOS.** *Robin Hood.* Little Golden Book D126. 1st. VG. K2. $12.00

**DISNEY STUDIOS.** *Sleeping Beauty & the Good Fairies.* Little Golden Book D71. B ed. K2. $20.00

**DISNEY STUDIOS.** *Snow White & the Seven Dwarfs.* 1937. NY. Harper. 1st. lg 4to. mc ils. 80p. mc dj. R5. $250.00

**DISNEY STUDIOS.** *Stories From Fantasia.* (1940). Random. 1st thus. 4to. mc pict brd. mc pict dj. R5. $300.00

**DISNEY STUDIOS.** *The Pop-Up Silly Symphonies.* (1933). Bl Ribbon. 4 popups. mc pict brd/dj. R5. $1,200.00

**DISNEY STUDIOS.** *Three Little Wolves.* 1937. prt on linen-like paper. VG+. C9. $102.00

**DISNEY STUDIOS.** *Thumper.* Little Golden Book D119. A ed. K2. $20.00

**DISNEY STUDIOS.** *Walt Disney's Mickey Mouse Cookbook.* c 1975. Golden. 92p. VG. E6. $20.00

**DISNEY STUDIOS.** *Walt Disney's Pinocchio Picture Book.* 1940. Whitman. lg 4to shapebook. mc pict wrp. R5. $150.00

**DISSTON, Harry.** *Beginning Polo.* 1973. S Brunswick. Barnes. 1st. VG/G. O3. $35.00

**DITKA, Mike.** *Ditka.* 1986. Bonus Books. 1st. 8vo. 271p. F/dj. W2. $25.00

**DITMARS, Raymond L.** *Reptile Book.* 1908. Doubleday Page. ils. 472p. VG. M7. $25.00

**DITMARS, Raymond L.** *Reptiles of the World.* 1941. NY. revised. 321p. VG. A17. $15.00

**DITMARS, Raymond L.** *Thrills of a Naturalist's Quest.* 1932. NY. ils. 268p. VG. S15. $10.00

**DITZEL, Paul C.** *Fire Engines & Firefighters.* 1976. Crown. 1st. ils. 256p. F/clip. T11. $36.00

**DIX, Morgan.** *Lectures on the First Prayer Book of King Edward VI.* 1881. NY. Young. 1st. 103p. G/wrp. H10. $45.00

**DIXON, Edward H.** *Scenes in the Practice of a New York Surgeon.* 1855. De Witt/Davenport. 1st. thick 8vo. 407p. bl cloth. G+. B20. $75.00

**DIXON, Franklin W.** *Hardy Boys: Clue of the Broken Blade (#21).* (1942). Grosset Dunlap. later prt. 218p. VG. B36. $8.00

**DIXON, Franklin W.** *South of the Border.* nd. Grosset Dunlap. VG/dj. P3. $15.00

**DIXON, Franklin W.** *Ted Scott: Rescued in the Clouds (#2).* nd. Grosset Dunlap. VG/dj. P3. $15.00

**DIXON, Hepworth.** *John Howard & the Prison: World of Europe.* 1852. Webster, MA. 442. gilt cloth. VG. B14. $75.00

**DIXON, Roger.** *Noah II.* 1975. Harwood-Smart. F/VG clip. P3. $15.00

**DIXON, Thomas.** *Birth of a Nation.* 1915. Grosset Dunlap. MTI. VG/dj. C9. $180.00

**DIXON, Thomas.** *Life Worth Living: A Personal Experience.* 1910 (1905). Doubleday Page. rpt. 140p. lt gr ils cloth. B20. $25.00

**DIXON, Wheeler Wiston.** *Films of Reginald LeBorg: Interviews, Essays & Filmography.* 1992. Metuchen Scarecrow. 175p. VG. C5. $15.00

**DIXON, William Hepworth.** *Personal History of Lord Bacon.* 1861. Leipzig. Tauchnitz. 3-quarter brn leather/marbled brd. M17. $20.00

**DIXON, Winifred Hawkridge.** *Westward Hoboes: Ups & Downs of Frontier Motoring.* 1922. Scribner. ils/map ep. 377p. VG. F7. $50.00

**DIXON & GODRICH.** *Blues & Gospel Records 1902-1942.* 1963. np. 1st. NF. B2. $150.00

**DOANE, Michael.** *Legends of Jesse Dark.* 1984. Knopf. 1st. author's 1st novel. F/dj. M19. $17.50

**DOBELL, Clifford.** *Antony Van Leeuwenhoek & His Little Animals.* 1958. NY. Russell. 435p. VG/dj. A10. $25.00

**DOBIE, J. Frank.** *Frontier Tales of White Mustang.* 1979. Dallas. Somesuch. mini. 1/395. prt/sgn David Holman. cream leather. B24. $95.00

**DOBKIN, Alix.** *Alix Dobkin's Adventures in Women's Music.* 1979. NY. Tomato. 1st. ils/photos. 70p. AN. A25. $25.00

**DOBKIN, Marjorie Housepian.** *Making of a Feminist: Early Journals & Letters of MC Thomas.* 1979. Kent State. 314p. wrp. V3. $11.00

**DOBKINS & HENDRICKS.** *Winnie Ruth Judd: Trunk Murders.* 1973. Grosset Dunlap. 1st. ils. 248p. NF/VG. B19. $15.00

**DOBLHOFER, Ernst.** *Voices in Stone: Decipherment of Ancient Scripts & Writings.* 1961. Viking. 1st. 8vo. 327p. NF/dj. W1. $12.00

**DOBSON, Austin.** *Miscellanies.* 1898. Dodd Mead. sm 8vo. H13. $45.00

**DOBSON, B.A.** *Principles of Carding Cotton: Manufacture of Card Wire...* 1892. Bolton. revised/enlarged. ils. 91p. G. B18. $45.00

**DOBSON, James C.** *Straight Talk.* 1991. World. 1st. sm 4to. 237p. F/dj. W2. $30.00

**DOBYNS, Stephen.** *Cold Dog Soup.* 1985. Viking. 1st. NF/NF. H11. $30.00

**DOBYNS, Stephen.** *Dancer With One Leg.* 1983. NY. Dutton. 1st. sgn. NF/VG. R14. $40.00

**DOBYNS, Stephen.** *Saratoga Bestiary.* 1988. Viking Penguin. 1st. NF/clip. A14. $21.00

**DOBYNS, Stephen.** *Saratoga Snapper.* 1986. Viking Penguin. 1st. NF/dj. A14. $28.00

**DOBYNS & EULER.** *Ghost Dance of 1889 Among Pai Indians of Northwestern AZ.* 1967. Prescott College. 8vo. photos/index. gray cloth. dj. F7. $55.00

**DOBYNS & EULER.** *Havasupai People.* 1971. Phoenix. Northland. Indian Tribal series. sgn. 72p. stiff wrp. F7. $25.00

**DOCKSTADER, Frederick J.** *American Indian in Graduate Studies...* 1973. NY. 2nd. 362p. VG. M8. $45.00

**DOCTOROW, E.L.** *American Anthem.* 1982. NY. Tabori Chang. 1st. sgn. ils JC Suares. F/sans. R14. $100.00

**DOCTOROW, E.L.** *Book of Daniel.* 1971. Random. 1st. sgn. F/F. D10. $135.00

**DOCTOROW, E.L.** *Jack London, Hemingway & the Constitution.* 1993. Random. 1st. F/dj. A24. $20.00

**DOCTOROW, E.L.** *Lives of the Poets.* 1984. Random. 1st. F/F. H11. $25.00

**DOCTOROW, E.L.** *Lives of the Poets.* 1984. Random. 1st. sgn. F/F. D10. $60.00

**DOCTOROW, E.L.** *Loon Lake.* 1980. Random. 1st. inscr. F/dj. R14. $40.00

**DOCTOROW, E.L.** *Ragtime.* 1975. Random. 1st. F/NF. H11. $40.00

**DOCTOROW, E.L.** *World's Fair.* (1985). Random. 3rd. F/VG. L4. $10.00

**DOCTOROW, E.L.** *World's Fair.* 1985. Random. 1st. Nat Book Award. F/dj. A24/H11. $30.00

**DOCTOROW, E.L.** *World's Fair.* 1985. Random. 1st. sgn. F/F. D10. $60.00

**DOCTOROW, E.L.** *World's Fair.* 1985. Random. 1st. sgn. NF/dj. B30/R14. $45.00

**DODD, William.** *Hymns of Callimachus, Translated From the Greek...* 1755. London. 1st. 4to. 212p. H13. $395.00

**DODD, William.** *Sisters; or, History of Lucy & Caroline Sanson.* 1791. London. Harrison. 2 vol in 1. sm 4to. 169p. recent morocco. H13. $285.00

**DODD, William.** *Thoughts in Prison, in Five Parts...* 1793. London. Dilly. 4th. sm 12mo. full polished calf. H13. $295.00

**DODGE, Bertha S.** *Potatoes & People.* 1970. Boston. 1st. 190p. VG/dj. B26. $15.00

**DODGE, Ernest.** *New England & the South Seas.* 1965. Cambridge. 1st. 216p. gr cloth. F/dj. P4. $40.00

**DODGE, Mary A.** *Gail Hamilton's Life in Letters.* 1901. Lee Shepard. 2 vol. 1st. 8vo. VG. A2. $50.00

**DODGE, Mary Mapes.** *Hans Brinker; or, The Silver Skates, Accompanied by...* nd (ca 1920). Phil. Macrae Smith. 7th. VG/dj. w/orig Cooke watercolor. B4. $1,000.00

**DODGE, Mary Mapes.** *Hans Brinker; or, The Silver Skates.* 1917. Phil. McKay. 1st thus. ils Maginel Wright Enright. 345p. gray cloth. F/NF. B20. $150.00

**DODGE, Mary Mapes.** *Hans Brinker; or, The Silver Skates.* 1932. NY. Garden City. ils NC Wyeth/Peter Hurd. 305p. NF. F1. $25.00

**DODGE, Richard Irving.** *Our Wild Indians: 33 Years' Personal Experience...* 1885. Hartford. 653p. G+. B18. $95.00

**DODGE & DODGE.** *Making Miniatures in 1/12 Scale.* 1991. UK. photos/diagrams. VG/dj. M17. $15.00

**DODGE & RATNER.** *Baking With Jim Dodge.* 1991. S&S. 1st. F/dj. V4. $25.00

**DODGSON, Campbell.** *Old French Colour Prints.* 1924. London. Halton Truscott. 1/1250. NF. B20. $85.00

**DODSLEY, Robert.** *Collection of Poems by Several Hands.* 1775. London. Dodsley. 6 vol. sm 8vo. full polished mottled calf. H13. $295.00

**DODSLEY, Robert.** *Toy-Shop: A Dramatick Satire.* 1735. London. Prt for Lawton Gulliver at Homer's Head. 5th. 46p. B14. $95.00

**DOERFLINGER, Thomas M.** *Vigorous Spirit of Enterprise: Merchants & Economic...* 1986. Norton. VG. M10. $12.50

**DOERR, Harriet.** *Consider This, Senora.* 1993. Harcourt Brace. 1st. inscr/dtd 1995. F/dj. R14. $60.00

**DOERR, Harriet.** *Stones for Ibarra.* 1984. Viking. 1st. author's 1st novel. F/dj. B4. $85.00

**DOERR, Harriet.** *Stones for Ibarra.* 1985. London. Deutsch. 1st. author's 1st book. F/F. B3. $50.00

**DOERR, Harriet.** *Tiger in the Grass.* 1995. Viking. ARC. sgn/dtd 1997. F/dj. R14. $65.00

**DOESTOEVKSKY, Fyodor.** *Notebooks for Crime & Punishment.* 1967. Chicago. hc. VG/dj. B9. $15.00

**DOHERTY, P.C.** *Ancient Evil.* 1995. St Martin. 1st Am. NF/dj. G8. $20.00

**DOHERTY, P.C.** *White Rose Murders: Being 1st Journal of Sir Roger Shallot.* 1991. London. Headline. 1st. F/clip. A14. $42.00

**DOHERTY, Robert W.** *Hicksite Separation: Sociological Analysis...* 1967. Rutgers. 157p. VG/G. V3. $25.00

**DOHERTY & DOHERTY.** *Lawn Tennis.* 1903. NY. Baker Taylor. 1st Am. photos. NF. Q1. $75.00

**DOIG, Ivan.** *Bucking the Sun.* 1996. S&S. 1st. F/dj. O11/R14. $25.00

**DOIG, Ivan.** *English Creek.* 1984. Atheneum. 1st. sgn. F/NF. O11. $55.00

**DOIG, Ivan.** *Heart Earth.* 1993. NY. Atheneum. 1st. sgn. F/dj. R14. $40.00

**DOIG, Ivan.** *Ride With Me, Mariah Montana.* 1990. Atheneum. 1st. sgn. F/dj. O11. $40.00

**DOIG, Ivan.** *This House of Sky.* 1978. Harcourt Brace. 1st. inscr. 314p. F/NF. B20. $225.00

**DOIG, Ivan.** *Winter Brothers, a Season at the Edge of America.* 1980. HBJ. 1st. F/VG. B3. $45.00

**DOLAN, J.R.** *Yankee Peddlers of Early America.* 1965. NY. ils. 270p. F/dj. M4. $22.00

**DOLAN & SILVER.** *William Crawford Gorgas: Warrior in White.* 1968. Dodd Mead. 1st. 8vo. 269p. VG/G. S14. $8.00

**DOLCI, Danilo.** *Man Who Plays Alone.* 1968. Pantheon. 1st Am. 8vo. VG/dj. A2. $12.50

**DOLINGER, Glenna Louise.** *Dr Thomas Walker, Father of Kentucky.* 1950. private prt. fld map. VG. B10. $35.00

**DOLINGER, Jane.** *Inca Gold: Find It If You Can. Touch It If You Dare...* 1968. Chicago. Regnery. 1st. photos. 189p. dj. F3. $15.00

**DOLLARD, John.** *Caste & Class in a Southern Town.* 1937. OUP. 502p. blk cloth. VG. G1. $75.00

**DOLLARD, John.** *Victory Over Fear.* 1942. Reynal Hitchcock. thick 12mo. inscr. 213p+3p. gray cloth. G1. $75.00

**DOLNICK, Amy.** *Between Deep Valley & the Great World: Maud Hart Lovelace...* 1993. Twin Cities. Betsy-Tacy Soc. 1st. 38p. S14. $8.00

**DOLPH, Jack.** *Hot Tip.* 1951. Doubleday Crime Club. 1st. VG/dj. M15. $35.00

**DOLPH, Jack.** *Murder Is Mutual.* 1948. NY. Morrow. 1st. F/VG. M15. $40.00

**DOLSON, H.** *Great Oildorado: Gaudy & Turbulent Years of 1st Oil Rush...* 1959. NY. ils/maps. 406p. NF. M4. $23.00

**DOMENECHE, Abbe.** *Seven Years' Residence in Great Deserts of North America.* 1860. London. Longman Gr. 2 vol. 1st. 58 full-p litho/fld map. red morocco. D11. $600.00

**DOMES, Jurgen.** *China After the Cultural Revolution.* 1977 (1975). Berkeley. 1st Am. 8vo. F/dj. A2. $25.00

**DOMINICK, Mabel A.** *Bible & Historical Design: A Perspective...* 1961 (1936). Plimpton. 9th. ils. F/VG. A2. $12.00

**DONAHEY, Mary Dickerson.** *Down Spider Web Lane.* 1909. Barse Hopkins. 1st. 130p. bl cloth/paper label. NF. B20. $75.00

**DONAHEY, William.** *Teenie Weenie Neighbors.* (1945). Whittlesey House. 1st. 8vo. mc pict brd. R5. $175.00

**DONAHUE, M. Patricia.** *Nursing, the Finest Art: Ils History.* 1985. St Louis. 1st. 4to. 504p. A13. $75.00

**DONALD, David.** *Charles Sumner & the Rights of Man.* 1970. Knopf. 1st. NF/VG. A14. $28.00

**DONALDSON, Alfred L.** *History of the Adirondacks, Vol 1.* 1977. Harrison. Harbor Hill. maps/photos. 383p. F/dj. A17. $25.00

**DONALDSON, D.J.** *New Orleans Requiem.* 1994. St Martin. 1st. sgn. F/VG. B30. $30.00

**DONALDSON, D.J.** *No Mardi Gras for the Dead.* 1992. St Martin. 1st. NF/VG. A14. $42.00

**DONALDSON, Henry Herbert.** *Growth of the Brain.* 1895. London. Walter Scott Ltd/ Scribner. 1st. 12mo. 374p. cloth. xl. G1. $65.00

**DONALDSON, J.** *Real Pretend.* 1992. Checkerboard. 1st. obl 8vo. F/dj. B17. $45.00

**DONALDSON, Stephen R.** *Gap Into Conflict: The Real Story.* 1991. NY. Bantam. 1st Am trade. sgn. F/NF. G10. $27.00

**DONALDSON, Stephen R.** *Gilden-Fire.* 1983. London. Collins. 1st thus. ils Peter Goodfellow. VG+/dj. A14. $17.50

**DONALDSON, Stephen R.** *Mirror of Her Dreams.* 1986. Ballantine/Del Rey. 1st. sm 4to. 642p. F. H11/W2. $25.00

**DONALDSON, Stephen R.** *One Tree.* 1982. Del Rey/Ballantine. 1st. Chronicles of Thomas Covenant #2. VG+/dj. A14. $21.00

**DONALDSON, Thomas.** *George Catlin Indian Gallery in the US National Museum.* 1887. GPO. thick 8vo. 144 #d maps/pl. 939p. cloth. O1. $300.00

**DONALDSON & ROYCE.** *Affair to Remember: My Life With Cary Grant.* 1989. Putnam. 1st. F/dj. T12. $20.00

**DONIA & FINE.** *Bosnia & Hercegovina: Tradition Betrayed.* 1994. Columbia. 2nd. ils. F/dj. A2. $18.00

**DONLEAVY, J.P.** *Destinies of Darcy Dancer.* 1978. London. 1st. dj. T9. $28.00

**DONLEAVY, J.P.** *Ginger Man.* 1955. Paris. Olympia. Traveller's Companion #7/1st. author's 1st book. VG. A24. $500.00

**DONLEAVY, J.P.** *Lelia: Further in the Destinies of Darcy Dancer, Gentleman.* 1983. Franklin Center, PA. 1st. sgn. brn 'reconstituted' leather. F. M24. $45.00

**DONNELLY, Elfie.** *Offbeat Friends.* 1982. Crown. 1st Am. 119p. NF/clip. C14. $14.00

**DONNELLY, Liza.** *Dinosaurs' Halloween.* 1987. Scholastic. 1st. sq 8vo. unp. NF/NF. T5. $30.00

**DONNELLY, Ralph W.** *Confederate States Marine Corps: Rebel Leathernecks.* 1989. Wht Mane Pub. 1st. NF/dj. A14. $21.00

**DONOGHUE, Denis.** *Lover of Strange Souls.* 1995. NY. 1st. dj. T9. $15.00

**DONOHUE, Phil.** *Donohue: My Own Story.* 1979. S&S. 1st. sgn. NF/VG. W2. $30.00

**DONOSO, Jose.** *House in the Country.* 1984. London. Allen Lane. 1st. NF/dj. A14. $21.00

**DONOVAN, Dick.** *Chronicles of Michael Danevitch.* 1897. London. Chatto Windus. 1st. silvered bl cloth. NF. M15. $100.00

**DONOVAN, Dick.** *In the Face of Night.* 1908. London. John Long. 1st. dk bl pict cloth. VG. M15. $100.00

**DONOVAN, Frank.** *Unlucky Hero.* 1963. NY. 1st. 179p. VG/dj. E1. $25.00

**DONOVAN, Professor.** *US Army Physical Exercises Revised...* (1902). Street Smith. sm 8vo. 130p. VG. H1. $12.00

**DONOVAN, Robert J.** *Tumultuous Years.* 1982. Norton. 1st. sm 4to. 444p. VG/F. W2. $25.00

**DONOVAN & MURDOCH.** *Game of Golf & the Printed Word 1566-1985.* 1987. Endicott, NY. Castalio. 658p. gilt gr cloth. F1. $35.00

**DOOLIN, William.** *Wayfarers in Medicine.* 1949. London. 1st. 284p. A13. $30.00

**DOOLING, Richard.** *White Man's Grave.* 1994. FSG. 1st. F/dj. M23. $25.00

**DOOLITTLE, Jerome.** *Body Scissors.* 1990. Pocket. 1st. F/NF. H11. $20.00

**DOOLITTLE, Jerome.** *Bombing Officer.* 1982. Dutton. 1st. F/dj. R11. $25.00

**DOOLITTLE, Jerome.** *Strangle Hold.* 1991. Pocket. 1st. F/F. H11. $25.00

**DOOLY, William G.** *Great Weapons of World War II.* 1969. Bonanza. rpt. ils. VG. E1. $35.00

**DOPAGNE, Jacques.** *Dali.* 1974. Leon Amiel. 1st. VG/dj. P3. $15.00

**DORAN, Dave.** *Highway of Hunger: Story of America's Homeless Youth.* 1933. Workers Lib/Young Worker. 1st. VG/wrp. B2. $30.00

**DORAN, Geroge H.** *Chronicles of Barabbas, 1884-1934; Further Chronicles...* 1952. NY. Rinehart. rpt. 8vo. 446p. F/dj. O10. $25.00

**DORBON-AINE.** *Bibliotheca Esoterica, Catalogue Annote et Illustre...* nd. 6707 entries. 662p. F. A4. $75.00

**DORF, Philip.** *Liberty Hyde Bailey.* 1956. Ithaca. 1st. ils. AN/dj. B26. $22.50

**DORFLES, Gillo.** *Kitsch: World of Bad Taste.* 1973. Bell. photos. VG/dj. C9. $60.00

**DORIAN, Edith.** *Ask Dr Christmas.* 1951. Whittlesey. 1st. ils Nora Unwin. VG/dj. M5. $28.00

**DORLAND, W.A. Newman.** *American Pocket Medical Dictionary.* 1916. Phil. Saunders. 9th. 691p. leatherette wrp. C14. $14.00

**DORN, Edward.** *Geography.* (1968). London. Fulcrum. 1st Eng. F/VG. A18. $35.00

**DORN, Edward.** *Gunslinger, Book II.* 1969. Blk Sparrow. 1st ltd. 1/250. sgn. cloth. F/dj. A18. $60.00

**DORN, Edward.** *Gunslinger, Book III.* 1972. West Newbury, MA. 1st. lg format. 40p. stiff cb. A18. $20.00

**DORN, Edward.** *North Atlantic Turbine.* (1967). London. Fulcrum. 1st Eng. map ep. F/VG. A18. $35.00

**DORNBUSCH, Charles E.** *Military Bibliography of the Civil War.* 1961-72. NY Public Lib. 3 vol in 9. 1st. VG. M8. $250.00

**DORNBUSCH, Charles E.** *Military Bibliography of the Civil War. Volume 2.* 1967. NY. 1st. VG/prt wrp. M8. $45.00

**DORR, Frank I.** *Hayseed & Sawdust.* 1934. Boston. Wormsted Smith. 8vo. ils. 228p. red brd. VG. B11. $25.00

**DORRIE, Doris.** *Love, Pain & the Whole Damn Thing.* 1989. Knopf. 1st Am. F/dj. C9. $25.00

**DORRIS, Michael.** *Broken Cord.* 1989. Harper Row. 1st. F/F. B3. $40.00

**DORRIS, Michael.** *Broken Cord.* 1989. Harper Row. 1st. sgn. NF/NF. R14. $75.00

**DORRIS, Michael.** *Sees Behind Trees.* 1996. NY. Hyperion. 1st. sgn. author's 3rd children's book. F/dj. O11. $35.00

**DORRIS, Michael.** *Yellow Raft in Blue Water.* 1987. Holt. 1st. inscr./sgn. author's 1st book. F/dj. B4. $150.00

**DORRIS, Michael.** *Yellow Raft in Blue Water.* 1987. NY. Holt. 2nd. sgn. NF/dj. S13. $40.00

**DORRIS, Michael.** *Yellow Raft in Blue Water.* 1988. London. Hamish Hamilton. 1st. sgn. RS. F/dj. L1. $125.00

**DORRIS & ERDRICH.** *Crown of Columbus.* 1991. Harper Collins. 1st. sgn. F/F. B3. $60.00

**DORSEY, F.** *Master of the Mississippi.* 1941. Boston. 1st. VG/G. B5. $45.00

**DORSHEIMER, William.** *Life & Public Services of Hon Grover Cleveland...* 1884. Russell Henderson. 8vo. 575p. bl cloth. G. S17. $7.50

**DORSON, Richard.** *America Begins.* 1950. Pantheon. 438p. AN/dj. A10. $18.00

**DORST, Jean.** *Before Nature Dies.* 1970. Houghton Mifflin. 1st. ils. 352p. xl. VG. S14. $8.00

**DORST, Jean.** *South America and Central America: A Natural History.* 1967. Random. 1st. 298p. VG/dj. M12. $30.00

**DOS PASSOS, John.** *Garbage Man: A Parade With Shouting.* 1926. Harper. 1st. 1/1000. 1st state bdg. NF/dj. Q1. $200.00

**DOS PASSOS, John.** *Grand Design.* 1949. Houghton Mifflin. 1st. VG/VG. H11. $40.00

**DOS PASSOS, John.** *Midcentury.* 1961. Andre Deutsch. VG/G. M19. $17.50

**DOS PASSOS, John.** *Number One.* 1943. Houghton Mifflin. 1st. NF/VG. A24. $60.00

**DOS PASSOS, John.** *Pushcart at the Curb.* 1922. Doran. 1st. 1/1313. VG. D10. $75.00

**DOS PASSOS, John.** *State of the Nation.* 1944. Houghton Mifflin. 1st. inscr. NF/dj. L3. $550.00

**DOS PASSOS, John.** *USA: The 42nd Parallel, Nineteen Nineteen, The Big Money.* 1946. Houghton Mifflin. 3 vol. 1st ils ed. 1/365. sgn. off-wht buckram. case. H5. $450.00

**DOSKOW, Ambrose.** *Historic Opinions of the United States Supreme Court.* 1935. NY. Vanguard. blk cloth. M11. $250.00

**DOSS, James.** *Shaman's Bones.* 1997. NY. Avon. 1st. sgn. F/dj. A23. $45.00

**DOSS, James.** *Shaman Sings.* 1994. St Martin. 1st. F/dj. M23. $35.00

**DOSSICK.** *Doctoral Research at the School of Education, NY U...* 1972. 4336 entries. 250p. VG. A4. $45.00

**DOTI & SCHWEIKART.** *Banking in the American West...* 1991. Norman, OK. 1st. F/dj. V4. $20.00

**DOTY, Robert.** *Photography in America.* 1974. Random. 1st. 4to. 255p. VG/NF. B20. $35.00

**DOUGHERTY, James.** *Secret Happiness of Marilyn Monroe.* 1976. Playboy. 1st thus. photos. VG/wrp. C9. $90.00

**DOUGHERTY, Raymond Philip.** *Records From Erech: Time of Nabonidus.* 1920. OUP/Yale. ils/84 pl. 47p. cloth. VG+. Q2. $20.00

**DOUGHTY, Robert A.** *Breaking Point: Sedan & the Fall of France, 1940.* 1990. Hamden, CT. 1st. maps. F/dj. A2. $25.00

**DOUGLAS, Amanda M.** *Kathie's Aunt Ruth.* 1912. Lee Shepard. ils C Howard. 257p. VG. P12. $25.00

**DOUGLAS, Amanda M.** *Red House Children's Vacation.* 1914. Lee Shepard. 1st. 8vo. VG. M5. $10.00

**DOUGLAS, Byrd.** *Steamboatin' on the Cumberland.* 1961. Nashville. TN Book Co. ils. 407p. gray cloth. F1. $25.00

**DOUGLAS, Carole Nelson.** *Good Night, Mr Holmes.* 1990. NY. Tor. ARC/1st. F/wrp. T2. $15.00

**DOUGLAS, Drake.** *Horrors!* 1989. Woodstock, NY. Overlook. 1st. 418p. F/NF. M21. $20.00

**DOUGLAS, Henry Kyd.** *I Rode With Stonewall: War Experiences...* nd. Chapel Hill. 1st/12th imp. NF/clip. A14. $28.00

**DOUGLAS, J.D.** *Twentieth Century Dictionary of Christian Biography.* 1995. 439p. F/F. A4. $45.00

**DOUGLAS, Lloyd C.** *Big Fisherman.* 1959. Random. unp. VG. C5. $12.50

**DOUGLAS, Lloyd C.** *Magnificent Obsession.* 1929. Grosset Dunlap. ne. 330p. VG. W2. $25.00

**DOUGLAS, Staff-Captain.** *George Fox, the Red Hot Quaker.* nd. London. Internat Headquarters. 16mo. 110p. xl. V3. $11.00

**DOUGLAS, Stephen Arnold.** *Admission of Kansas Under Wyandott Constitution...1860.* 1860. WA. Lemuel Towers. 1st. dbl-column text. 8p. VG. M8. $85.00

**DOUGLAS, William O.** *Democracy's Manifesto: Counter Plan for Free Society.* 1962. Doubleday. 1st. VG/dj. B9. $15.00

**DOUGLAS, William O.** *Farewell to Texas, a Vanishing Wilderness.* 1967. NY. McGraw Hill. 1st. G/dj. M11. $65.00

**DOUGLAS, William O.** *Go East, Young Man: The Early Years.* 1974. Random. 1st. ils. 493p. VG/dj. S14. $10.00

**DOUGLAS, William O.** *Go East, Young Man: The Early Years.* 1974. Random. 1st. inscr/sgn. VG/dj. M11. $150.00

**DOUGLAS, William O.** *My Wilderness: The Pacific West.* 1960. Doubleday. sgn Frances Lee Jaques. 206p. VG. J2. $40.00

**DOUGLAS, William O.** *My Wilderness: The Pacific West.* 1960. Garden City. Doubleday. F/dj. A19/P2. $25.00

**DOUGLAS, William O.** *Russian Journey.* 1956. Doubleday. 1st. ils. 255p. G/dj. S14. $5.00

**DOUGLASS, Barbara.** *Good as New.* 1982. Lee Shepard. 1st Am. sm 4to. wht pict brd. VG/G+. T5. $30.00

**DOUGLASS, Ben.** *History of Wayne County, Ohio.* 1878. Indianapolis. ils. 868p. G. B18. $125.00

**DOUGLASS, P.F.** *Story of German Methodism: Biography of Immigrant Soul.* 1939. Cincinnati. 294p+64p appendix. VG/poor. M4. $20.00

**DOUMAS, C.** *Thera & the Aegean World: Papers Presented...* 1978-80. London. 2 vol. ils/fld amps. cloth. VG/dj. Q2. $75.00

**DOURNOVO, Lydia A.** *Armenian Miniatures.* 1961. Abrams. 1st. thick 4to. 181+7p. F/NF. O10. $115.00

**DOVE, Rita.** *Darker Face of the Earth.* 1994. Brownsville. Storyline. 1/250+26 lettered. sgn. F/sans. R14. $150.00

**DOVEREN & THOMAS.** *De Bonte Droom van het Circus.* nd. Het Netherlands, Zuiv. Uitgave. 1st Dutch. ils. cloth. VG. B27. $150.00

**DOW, George Francis.** *Slave Ships & Slaving.* 1927. Salem. 1st. 349p. G. B5. $100.00

**DOW, George Francis.** *Slave Ships & Slaving.* 1968. Cambridge. Cornell Maritime. 386p. blk cloth. F/dj. B14. $35.00

**DOW, Lorenzo.** *History of Cosmopolite; or, 4 Vols of Lorenzo Dow's Journal.* 1848. VA. Joshua Martin. 720p. G+. B18. $75.00

**DOWD, James Patrick.** *Custer Lives.* 1982. Ye Galleon. F/dj. A19. $35.00

**DOWD & SPENDER.** *Serious Business.* 1937. Country Life/Scribner. 1st. sm folio. 150p. F/VG. B20. $85.00

**DOWDEY, Clifford.** *Death of a Nation: Story of Lee & His Men at Gettysburg.* (1958). Knopf. 1st. 383p. VG/dj. B10. $35.00

**DOWELL, Coleman.** *Silver Swanne.* 1983. NY. Grenfell. 1/115. sgn. Claudia Cohen bdg. F. F1. $175.00

**DOWLING, Noel T.** *Cases on Constitutional Law.* 1950. Foundation Pr. M11. $25.00

**DOWLING, William C.** *Language & Logos in Boswell's Life of Johnson.* 1981. Princeton. 1st. dj. H13. $45.00

**DOWMAN, Keith.** *Masters of Enchantment: Lives & Legends of Mahasiddhas.* 1988. Rochester, VT. ils Robert Beers. VG/dj. M17. $25.00

**DOWNER, Jane.** *Happy Dieter.* 1974. Regional Ent. G. A16. $10.00

**DOWNES, Stephen.** *New Compleat Angler.* 1984. London. Orbis. 4to. ils. NF/dj. M10. $16.50

**DOWNEY, Bill.** *Tom Bass, Black Horseman.* 1975. St Louis. Saddle & Bridle. 1st. F/dj. B2. $40.00

**DOWNEY, F.** *Texas & the War With Mexico.* 1961. Am Heritage Jr Lib. 1st. ils. 153p. NF. M4. $20.00

**DOWNING, A.J.** *Architecture of Country Houses...* 1854. NY. Appleton. 320 ils. 484p. G. H10. $185.00

**DOWNING, A.J.** *Rural Essays.* 1857. NY. Leavitt Allen. ils. teg. quarter gre morocco. VG. F1. $275.00

**DOWNING, Elliot R.** *Naturalist in the Great Lakes Region.* 1922. Chicago. 2nd. 328p. VG. A17. $20.00

**DOWNING, G.** *Massage Book.* 1972. Esalen Inst. 4to. VG/G. E6. $15.00

**DOWNING & PAPAS.** *Tales of the Hodja.* 1966. OUP. 1st thus. VG/dj. V4. $25.00

**DOWNING & SCULLY.** *Architectural Heritage of Newport, RI, 1640-1915.* 1967. NY. 2nd. photos. VG/dj. M17. $30.00

**DOYLE, Arthur Conan.** *Adventures of Sherlock Holmes.* 1892. NY. 1st/later prt. VG. M17. $40.00

**DOYLE, Arthur Conan.** *Adventures of Sherlock Holmes.* 1965. Racine, WI. Golden. ils Jo Polenso. 249p. VG. B36. $10.00

**DOYLE, Arthur Conan.** *Adventures of Sherlock Holmes/Memoirs of Sherlock Holmes.* 1892 & 1894. London. Geo Newnes. 2 vol. 1st. w/sgn calling card. full bl morocco. F. F1. $1,650.00

**DOYLE, Arthur Conan.** *Complete Sherlock Holmes Vol I.* nd. Doubleday Doran. A Conan Doyle Memorial ed. red stp blk cloth. VG. M21. $15.00

**DOYLE, Arthur Conan.** *Conan Doyle Stories.* (1960). Platt Munk. 8vo. 494p. gilt cloth. VG/dj. M7. $20.00

**DOYLE, Arthur Conan.** *Croxley Master.* (1925). NY. Doran. 1st Am. VG/dj. M15. $125.00

**DOYLE, Arthur Conan.** *Great Boer War.* nd. London. Thos Nelson. 575p. gilt bl cloth. VG. M7. $35.00

**DOYLE, Arthur Conan.** *Great Britain & the Next War.* 1914. Boston. Sm Maynard. 1st Am/1st book ed. crown 8vo. 48p. NF/glassine dj. J3. $350.00

**DOYLE, Arthur Conan.** *Hound of the Baskervilles.* 1902. McClure Phillips. 1st Am. G. P3. $100.00

**DOYLE, Arthur Conan.** *Hound of the Baskervilles.* 1968. Whitman. VG. P3. $12.00

**DOYLE, Arthur Conan.** *Lost World.* (1912). Hodder Stoughton/Doran. 1st Am. ils Joseph Clement Coll. 309p. tan cloth. H1. $50.00

**DOYLE, Arthur Conan.** *Rodney Stone.* 1896. NY. Appleton. gilt decor brd. G. V4. $25.00

**DOYLE, Arthur Conan.** *Rufugees.* 1899. Harper. ils. G+. G8. $12.50

**DOYLE, Arthur Conan.** *Sign of Four.* 1893. London. Geo Newnes. 3rd. gilt red cloth. NF. M15. $375.00

**DOYLE, Arthur Conan.** *Stories for Boys.* ca 1938. Cupples Leon. 1st. ils. VG+. S18. $15.00

**DOYLE, Arthur Conan.** *Study in Scarlet.* 1985. Peerage. VG/dj. P3. $20.00

**DOYLE, Arthur Conan.** *Three of Them.* 1923. London. Murray. 1st. 12mo. F/dj. J3. $75.00

**DOYLE, Arthur Conan.** *Tragedy of the Korosko.* 1898. London. Smith Elder. 1st. 8vo. 326p. gilt maroon cloth. VG+. B20. $250.00

**DOYLE, Roddy.** *Paddy Clarke Ha Ha Ha.* 1993. NY. Viking. 1st Am. sgn. F/dj. O11. $85.00

**DOYLE, Roddy.** *Van.* 1992. Viking Penguin. 1st Am. sgn. F/dj. O11. $75.00

**DOYLE, Roddy.** *Woman Who Walked Into Doors.* 1996. London. Cape. 1st. sgn. F/dj. O11. $65.00

**DOYLE, Roddy.** *Woman Who Walked Into Doors.* 1996. Viking. 1st. 8vo. sgn. F/dj. S9. $40.00

**DOYLE, William B.** *Centennial History of Summit County, Ohio.* 1908. Chicago. 1st. 1115p. aeg. rb buckram. VG. B18. $95.00

**DOYLE & STEWART.** *Stand in the Door: Wartime History...* 1988. Williamstown. 1st. ils/maps/index. 428p. VG/dj. S16. $40.00

**DOZOIS, Gardner.** *Slow Dancing Through Time.* 1990. Kansas City, MO. 1st. 1/374. sgn. AN/dj. M21. $45.00

**DR. A;** see Asimov, Isaac.

**DRABKIN, I.E.** *Caelius Aurelianus: On Acute Diseases & Chronic Diseases.* 1950. Chicago. 1019p. NF/worn. G7. $95.00

**DRACHMAN, Virginia.** *Hospital With a Heart: Women Doctors & Paradox...* 1984. Ithaca. 1st. 258p. A13. $40.00

**DRAGO, H.S.** *Canal Days in America: History & Romance of Old Towpath...* 1972. NY. ils. 311p. NF/dj. M4. $60.00

**DRAKE, Benjamin.** *Life of Tecumseh & His Brother the Prophet...* 1852. Cincinnati. 235p. G. B18. $65.00

**DRAKE, Charles D.** *Labour Law, Third Edition.* 1981. London. Sweet Maxwell. 278p. prt sewn wrp. M11. $15.00

**DRAKE, Daniel.** *Pioneer Life in Kentucky.* 1948. NY. 1st. 257p. A13. $50.00

**DRAKE, Daniel.** *Systematic Treatise, Historical, Etiological & Practical...* 1854. Lippincott Grambo. 2nd series. 878p. sheep. G7. $995.00

**DRAKE, Lea Bodine.** *This Tilting Dust.* 1955. Francestown, NH. Golden Quill. 1st. 61p. gilt brn/textured cloth. F/dj. F1. $50.00

**DRAKE, Samuel Adams.** *Historic Fields & Mansions of Middlesex.* 1874. Boston. Osgood. 21 pl (not in later ed). 442p. gilt cloth. B18. $45.00

**DRAKE, Samuel G.** *Book of the Indians of North America: Comprising Details...* 1833. Boston. Josiah Drake. 8vo. ils/vignettes. contemporary calf. VG. O1. $85.00

**DRANNAN, W.F.** *Capt WF Drannan, Chief of Scouts...* 1910. Chicago. Thos W Jackson. 1st. ils. 407p. cloth. D11. $75.00

**DRANNAN, W.F.** *Thirty One Years on the Plains & in the Mountains...* 1899. Chicago. Rhodes McClure. 1st. ils. 586p. poor. M10. $100.00

**DREADSTONE, Carl;** see Campbell, Ramsey.

**DREISER, Theodore.** *Chains.* 1927. NY. Boni Liveright. 1st. 1/440. sgn. 425p. 3-quarter gr morocco. NF. H5. $200.00

**DREISER, Theodore.** *Epitaph, a Poem.* 1929. NY. Heron. 1/700 (1100 total) on Keiyo Kami. sgn. F/case. F1. $150.00

**DREISER, Theodore.** *Hand of the Potter.* 1918. NY. Boni Liveright. 1st. F. B2. $100.00

**DRENNAN, Georgia T.** *Everblooming Roses for the Outdoor Garden of the Amateur.* 1912. NY. ils/photos. 250p. tan cloth. B26. $32.50

**DREW, J.M.** *Farm Blacksmithing.* 1907. St Paul. Webb. VG. O3. $65.00

**DREW, Thomas.** *John Brown Invasion: An Authentic History of Harper's Ferry.* 1860. Boston. James Campbell. 1st. M24. $450.00

**DREYER, Peter.** *Gardner Touched With Genius: Life of Luther Burbank.* 1975. CMG. 1st. ils/biblio/index. 322p. VG. H10. $20.00

**DRIGGS, Howard R.** *Westward America.* 1942. Putnam/American Trails. Autograph ed. pres. sgn/ils Jackson. F/glassine/case. B20. $750.00

**DRIGGS & LEWINE.** *Black Beauty, White Heat.* 1982. Morrow. 1st. 4to. F/dj. B2. $200.00

**DRIMMER, F.** *Until You Are Dead: Book of Executions in America.* 1990. NY. ARC/1st. photos. 280p. F/dj. M4. $30.00

**DRIMMER, Frederick.** *Very Special People.* 1973. Amjon. 1st. NF/VG. S18. $20.00

**DRINKER, Cecil K.** *Psychiatric Research: Papers Read at Dedication...1946.* 1947. Cambridge. Harvard. 1st. ils. 113p. VG. C14. $20.00

**DRINKLE, Ruth Wolfley.** *Heritage of Architecture & Arts.* (1994). Fairfield Heritage Assn. 2nd/revised. 186p. pict brd. VG/dj. B18. $25.00

**DRINKWATER, John.** *Life & Adventures of Carl Laemmle.* 1931. London. Heinemann. 1st. photos. VG/dj. C9. $150.00

**DROBISCH, Moritz Wilhelm.** *Empirische Psychologie nach Naturwissenschaftlicher Methode.* 1842. Leipzig. Leopold Voss. German text. 356p. patterned paper brd. VG. G1. $150.00

**DROSCHER, Vitus B.** *They Love & Kill.* 1976. NY. ils. VG/dj. M17. $20.00

**DRUCKER, Mary J.** *Rubber Industry in Ohio.* 1937. Occupational Study 1. 1st. 76p. prt wrp. B18. $25.00

**DRUCKER, Philip.** *Native Brotherhoods: Modern International Organizations.* 1958. GPO. BAE Bulletin #168. 8vo. 194p. olive cloth. NF. P4. $45.00

**DRUETT, Joan.** *She Was a Sister Sailor: Whaling Journals of Mary Brewster.* 1992. Mystic Seaport Mus. 1st. 449p. AN/dj. P4. $40.00

**DRUMMOND, Henry.** *Natural Law in the Spiritual World.* nd. Altemus. 371p. VG/case. B29. $20.00

**DRUMMOND, Henry.** *Tropical Africa.* 1888. NY. Humboldt. woodcuts. 68p. VG. H7. $12.50

**DRUMMOND, Walter;** see Silverberg, Robert.

**DRURY, A.W.** *History of the Church of the United Brethern in Christ.* 1931. United Brethern. revised. 832p. VG. R8. $15.00

**DRURY, Allen.** *Decision.* 1983. Doubleday. VG/dj. P3. $15.00

**DRURY, Allen.** *Decision.* 1983. Franklin Lib. ltd 1st. sgn. gr leather. F. A24. $40.00

**DRURY, Allen.** *Preserve & Protect.* 1968. Doubleday. 1st. G/dj. A28. $10.00

**DRURY, Clifford Merrill.** *California Imprints, 1846-1876.* 1970. self pub. bibliography of 1099 titles. 220p. cloth. D11. $60.00

**DRURY, Heber.** *Useful Plants of India.* 1985 (1873). Dehra Dun. 2nd/rpt. 512p. dj. B26. $15.00

**DRURY, Tom.** *End of Vandalism.* 1994. Houghton Mifflin. 1st. F/dj. A24. $40.00

**DRUSE, Ken.** *Collector's Garden: Designing With Extraordinary Plants.* 1996. NY. Clarkson Potter. ils/index. 248p. VG/dj. H10. $25.00

**DRUSE, Ken.** *Natural Shade Garden.* 1992. NY. Clarkson Potter. 4to. 238p. VG/dj. H10. $22.50

**DRYDEN, John.** *All For Love; or, World Well Lost.* 1931. Westminster. Stourton. 1/158. 97p. VG+. F1. $200.00

**DRYDEN, John.** *Fables: Ornamented With Engravings...* 1797. London. Bensley. lg paper ed. tall/wide folio. 241p. full tree calf. H13. $595.00

**DRYDENK, James.** *Poultry Breeding & Management.* 1928. Orange Judd. 402p. cloth. VG. A10. $20.00

**DTLENSCHNEIDER, Robert L.** *Power & Influence.* 1990. Prentice Hall. 1st. 8vo. 258p. F/dj. W2. $30.00

**DU BOIS, W.E.B.** *Darkwater.* 1920. Harcourt. 1st. VG. B2. $175.00

**DU BOIS, William Pene.** *Gentleman Bear.* 1985. FSG. ARC. 4to. unbdg (no brd). mc dj w/all internal sigs. R5. $85.00

**DU BOIS, William Pene.** *Gentleman Bear.* 1985. FSG. 1st. F/NF. T11. $30.00

**DU BOIS, William Pene.** *Giant.* 1954. NY. Viking. 1st. 8vo. mc dj. R5. $85.00

**DU BOIS, William Pene.** *Peter Graves.* 1950. Viking/Jr Literary Guild. 1st thus. ils. VG/dj. P2. $30.00

**DU BOIS, William Pene.** *Twenty-One Balloons.* 1947. Viking. 1st. ils. 180p. VG. D1. $35.00

**DU BOIS, William Pene.** *Twenty-One Balloons.* 1949. Robert Hale. 1st Eng. VG+/dj. P2. $25.00

**DU BOSE, Heyward.** *Mamba's Daughters: A Novel of Charleston.* 1929. NY. Literary Guild. 311p. deckle edged/ils ep. H6. $34.00

**DU CHAILLU, Paul.** *Explorations & Adventures in Equatorial Africa.* 1861. NY. Harper. 1st Am. ils. 531p. 3-quarter leather. H7. $100.00

**DU CHAILLU, Paul.** *My Apingi Kingdom: With Life in the Great Sahara.* 1871. NY. Harper. 2nd. 8vo. ils. xl. W1. $30.00

**DU CHAILLU, Paul.** *My Apingi Kingdom: With Life in the Great Sahara.* 1928. NY. 263p. VG. A17. $17.50

**DU LAURENS, Honore.** *Vera et Simplex Narratio Colloqvii Inter Viros...* 1593. Paris. Morel. 8vo. vellum. R12. $300.00

**DU MAURIER, Daphne.** *Don't Look Now.* 1971. Doubleday. 1st. VG/dj. B30. $75.00

**DU MAURIER, Daphne.** *Don't Look Now.* 1971. Doubleday. 1st. xl. VG/dj. S18. $7.00

**DU MAURIER, Daphne.** *Echoes From the Macabre.* 1976 (1952). Doubleday. 1st Am/revised. VG/dj. G8. $20.00

**DU MAURIER, Daphne.** *House on the Stand.* 1969. Doubleday. 1st. NF/dj. S18. $40.00

**DU MAURIER, Daphne.** *Hungry Hill.* 1943. Doubledy. 1st. VG+. S18. $8.00

**DU MAURIER, Daphne.** *Jamaica Inn.* 1945. Triangle. rpt. pub sgn. VG/dj. S18. $15.00

**DU MAURIER, Daphne.** *Kiss Me Again, Stranger.* 1952. Doubleday. 1st. ils. VG+. S18. $5.00

**DU MAURIER, Daphne.** *Lifetime Burning.* 1982. Random. 1st. inscr. F/dj. B30. $35.00

DU MAURIER, Daphne. *Rock Cried Out.* 1979. HBJ. 1st. sgn. F/dj. B30. $30.00

DU MAURIER, Daphne. *Winding Stair: Sir Francis Bacon, His Rise & Fall.* 1977. Doubleday. 1st Am. VG/dj. P3. $20.00

DU MAURIER, George. *Trilby.* 1894. NY. Harper. 1st Am. 464p. G. G11. $10.00

DU MAURIER & QUILLER-COUCH. *Castle Dor.* 1962. Doubleday. 1st Am. VG/dj. T10. $65.00

DU MONT, John S. *Custer Battle Guns.* 1974. Ft Collins, CO. Old Army. F/dj. A19. $75.00

DU RYER, Andre. *L'Alcoran de Mahomet...* 1649. Paris. Sommaville. thick 12mo. vellum. R12. $275.00

DU SHANE, Helen. *Baja California Travels of Charles Russell Orcutt.* 1971. Dawson's Book Shop. 1/500. ils/notes. 77p. VG+/sans. B19. $25.00

DUANE, Diane. *Doore Into Sunset: Volume Three of Tale of the Five.* 1993. NY. Tor. 1st. F/dj. A14. $17.50

DUANE, O.B. *Discovering Art: Mucha.* 1996. London. Brockhampton. F/dj. B9. $15.00

DUBOIS, Henry Leopold. *History of a French Dagger...* 1828. London. Duckworth. 2 vol. 8vo. subscriber list. brd. R12. $125.00

DUBUS, Andre. *Broken Vessels.* 1991. Boston. Godine. 1st. sgn. F/dj. R14. $60.00

DUBUS, Andre. *Dancing After Hours.* 1996. Knopf. 1st. sgn. 14 stories. F/dj. R14/S9. $50.00

DUBUS, Andre. *Finding a Girl in America.* 1980. Boston. Godine. 1st. sgn. 8vo. NF/dj. S9. $125.00

DUBUS, Andre. *Voices From the Moon.* 1984. Boston. Godine. 1st. F/F. B3. $35.00

DUBUS, Andre. *Voices From the Moon.* 1984. Boston. Godine. 1st. sgn. F/dj. R13. $50.00

DUCASSE, Isadore. *Maldoror (Les Chants de Maldoror).* 1943. np. New Directions. 8vo. F/case. B2. $85.00

DUCHE, Jacob. *Duty of Standing Fast in Our Spiritual & Temporal Liberties.* 1775. Phil/London. Evans. 1st Eng. 8vo. 19th-C marbled brd. O1. $225.00

DUCKER, James H. *Men of Steel Rails, Workers on Atchison, Topeka & Santa Fe.* (1983). Lincoln. ils. 220p. F/dj. B18. $17.50

DUCKWORTH, Paul. *Experimental & Trick Photography.* 1964. Universal Photo Books. 2nd. VG. C9. $30.00

DUDEN, Gottfired. *Report on Journey to Western States of North America.* 1980. Columbia, MO. rpt. 372p. VG/dj. B5. $30.00

DUDGEON, Piers. *Garden Planner.* 1981. London. BPS. 4to. ils. 247p. NF/dj. M10. $12.50

DUDLEY, A.T. *Phillips Exeter: Great Year.* 1907. Lee Shepard. 1st. VG. P8. $30.00

DUDLEY, A.T. *Phillips Exeter: With Mask & Mitt (#4)).* 1906. Lee Shepard. 1st. VG+. P8. $35.00

DUDLEY, Mary. *Life of..., Including Account of Her Religious Engagements.* 1842. Phil. Nathan Kite. 2nd Am. 12mo. 293p. full leather. xl. V3. $32.00

DUDLEY & WILLIAMS. *Mr Popper's Penguins.* 1993. Little Brn. 1st. 4to. popups. VG. B17. $14.00

DUDYCHA, George J. *Psychology for Law Enforcement Officers.* 1955. Springfield, IL. Chas Thomas. thick 8vo. 404p. NF/dj. G1. $38.50

DUE, Tananarive. *Between.* 1995. Harper Collins. 1st. author's 1st book. F/F. H11. $25.00

DUERRENMATT, Friedrich. *Quarry.* 1962. Greenwich, CT. 1st Am. VG/dj. B4. $85.00

DUFF, Annis. *Bequest of Wings: A Family's Pleasures With Books.* 1944. NY. Viking. 1st. 207p. cloth. F/dj. O10. $12.50

DUFF, E. Gordon. *Dialogue or Communing Between Wise King Solomon...* 1892. London. Lawrence Bullen. 8vo. gilt cloth. VG. F1. $25.00

DUFF GORDON, Lady Lucie. *Narratives of Remarkable Criminal Trials...* 1846. London. John Murray. later? G. M11. $250.00

DUFFIELD, Kenneth G. *Four Little Pigs Didn't Have a Mother.* 1919. Altemus. Wee Book for Wee Folks. ils K Duffield. 60p+ads. VG. D1. $12.50

DUFFY, Brian. *Head Count.* 1991. NY. Putnam. 1st. author's 1st novel. F/F. H11. $15.00

DUFFY, John. *Tulane University Medical Center: 150 Years of Medicine.* 1984. Baton Rouge. 1st. 253p. A13. $27.50

DUFFY, Margaret. *Murder of Crows.* 1987. NY. SMP. 1st. author's 1st book. F/F. H11. $20.00

DUFFY & GESCHWIND. *Dyslexia: A Neuroscientific Approach to Clinical Evaluation.* 1985. Little Brn. ARC. 8vo. 223p. F. C14. $35.00

DUFRESNE, John. *Lethe, Cupid, Time & Love.* 1994. Canada. LeBow. 1/150. sgn. F/wrp. B3. $60.00

DUFRESNE, John. *Love Warps the Mind a Little.* 1997. Norton. 1st. sgn. F/dj. R14. $45.00

DUFRESNE, John. *Way That Water Enters Stone.* 1991. Norton. 1st. 1/5000. sgn. F/dj. R14. $150.00

DUGGAN, Alfred. *Little Emperors.* 1953. Coward McCann. 1st. F/dj. T10. $35.00

DUGGAR, B.M. *Fungus Diseases of Plants.* 1909. Boston. 508p. tan cloth. B26. $21.00

DUGGAR, B.M. *Proceedings of the Internat Congress Plant Sciences.* 1929. Menasha, WI. Banta. 2 vol. cloth. A10. $40.00

DUGGER, Ronnie. *On Reagan: The Man & His Presidency.* 1983. McGraw Hill. 1st. sm 4to. NF/F. W2. $30.00

DUGMORE, A. Radclyffe. *Romance of the Newfoundland Caribou.* 1913. Phil. 1st. 181p. VG. A17. $50.00

DUGMORE, A. Radclyffe. *Wonderland of Big Game, Being Account of Two Trips...* 1925. London. Arrowsmith. 1st. 8 monochrome maps. 288p. G. H7. $60.00

DUHEME, Jacqueline. *Birthdays.* 1966. Determined. ils. 16p. brd. F/NF. D4. $35.00

DUKE, Alton. *When the Colorado River Quit the Ocean.* 1974. Yuma. Southwest Prt. 1st. 122p. gr paper over brd. VG/dj. F7. $50.00

DUKE, Donald. *Water Trails West.* 1978. Doubleday. 1st. VG/dj. P3. $20.00

DUKE, Harvey. *Superior Quality Hall China: A Guide for Collectors.* 1977. ELO Book. 1st. 8vo. ils. 100p. G+/glossy wrp. w/price guide. H1. $20.00

DUKE, Marc. *DuPonts.* 1976. Dutton. 1st. F/NF. W2. $40.00

DUKE OF BEDFORD. *Science & Fruit Growing.* 1919. London. Macmillan. 330p. cloth. VG. A10. $55.00

DULAC, Edmund. *Lyrics Pathetic & Humorous From A to Z.* 1908. London. Warne. 1st. 4to. 24 mc pl. off-wht cloth/gray-gr pict brd. H5. $750.00

DULAC, Edmund. *Stories From the Arabian Nights.* 1920s. Doran. rpt. 16 mc pl. VG. B17. $85.00

DULL, Mrs. S.R. *Southern Cooking.* 1972 (1928). Grosset Dunlap. VG/dj. A16. $12.50

DULL, P. *Battle History of Imperial Japanese Navy 1941-45.* 1982 (1978). lg 8vo. F/F. E6. $15.00

DUMAS, Alexandre. *Adventures in Algeria.* 1959. Phil. Chilton. 1st Am. F/dj. O4. $25.00

**DUMAS, Alexandre.** *Celebrated Crimes Vol 5.* 1910. Collier. VG. P3. $20.00

**DUMAS, Alexandre.** *Love & Liberty.* nd. London. Stanley Paul. 1st Eng. trans RS GArnett. NF/G. O4. $25.00

**DUMAS, Alexandre.** *Marguerite de Valois & Chicot, the Jester.* (1893). Collier. Works of Alexandre Dumas #5. VG. P3. $35.00

**DUMBARTON, Oaks.** *Death & Afterlife in Pre-Columbian America.* 1975. DC. 1st. 196p. F3. $45.00

**DUMBARTON, Oaks.** *Emblem & State in the Classic Maya Lowlands.* 1976. DC. 1st. photos. 204p. F3. $45.00

**DUMONT, Frank.** *Witmark Amateur Minstrel Guide & Burnt Cork Encyclopedia.* (1899). Chicago. Witmark. 168p. pict cloth. G+. B18. $75.00

**DUN, John.** *No New Frontiers: 11 Stories Inspired by Arizona Sunshine.* 1938. Roycrofters. 1st. 175p. VG/sans. B19. $20.00

**DUNATHAN, Clint.** *Century Book 1863-1963.* 1963. self put. photos/maps. dj. A17. $20.00

**DUNAWAY, David King.** *Aldous Huxley Recollected, an Oral History.* 1995. NY. 1st. dj. T9. $10.00

**DUNBAR, Anthony P.** *Against the Grain: Southern Radicals & Prophets 1929-1959.* 1982. Charlottesville, VA. 2nd. AN/dj. V4. $30.00

**DUNBAR, Elizabeth.** *Talcott Williams, Gentleman of Fourth Estate.* 1936. Columbia. VG. N2. $10.00

**DUNBAR, Paul Laurance.** *Love of Landry.* 1900. NY. Dodd Mead. 1st. G. G11. $50.00

**DUNBAR, R.I.** *Reproductive Decisions: Economic Analysis of Gelada Baboon.* 1984. Princeton. 265p. F/wrp. S15. $7.00

**DUNBAR, Sophie.** *Behind Eclaire's Doors.* 1993. NY. SMP. 1st. author's 1st book. F/F. H11. $25.00

**DUNBAR, Tony.** *Crooked Man.* 1994. Putnam. 1st. author's 1st novel. NF/F. H11. $20.00

**DUNCAN, Andrew.** *Medical & Philosophical Commentaries by Society Physicians.* 1795. Phil. 10 vol. mixed ed. full leather. VG. E6. $750.00

**DUNCAN, David Douglas.** *Goodbye Picasso.* nd (1974). NY. Grosset Dunlap. 4to. thick-grained cloth. NF/VG. F1. $50.00

**DUNCAN, David Douglas.** *Self-Portrait: USA.* 1969. Abrams. VG/dj. S5. $37.00

**DUNCAN, David James.** *River Teeth.* 1995. Doubleday. 1st. F/dj. M23. $35.00

**DUNCAN, Dayton.** *Out West.* 1987. NY. Viking. 1st. F/F. H11. $25.00

**DUNCAN, MERKER & RITCHIE.** *Bruce Rogers: A Panel Discussion...* 1981. SF. BC of CA. 1st. 1/650. gilt brn cloth. dj. M24. $75.00

**DUNCAN, Robert L.** *Fire Storm.* 1978. NY. Morrow. 1st. NF/F. H11. $15.00

**DUNCAN, Robert.** *Serpent's Mask.* 1989. St Martin. 1st. F/dj. S18. $24.00

**DUNCAN, Thomas D.** *Recollections of..., a Confederate Soldier.* 1922. Nashville. McQuiddy. 1st/only. sm 4to. 213p. F/prt wrp. C6. $275.00

**DUNCAN & JAMES.** *Introduction to British Lichens.* 1970. Arbroath. 292p. F/dj. B26. $27.50

**DUNDES, Alan.** *Study of Folklore.* (1965). Berkeley. ils. VG. M17. $20.00

**DUNGLISON, Robley.** *History of Medicine From Earliest Ages...* 1872. Phil. 1st. 287p. A13. $50.00

**DUNHAM, Katherine.** *Journey to Accompong.* 1946. Holt. 1st. F/VG. B2. $40.00

**DUNHAM, Sam C.** *Goldsmith of Nome & Other Verse.* 1901. WA, DC. Neale. 1st. 80p. H7. $20.00

**DUNLAP, Knight.** *Religion: Its Functions in Human Life.* 1946. McGraw Hill. 362p. emb red cloth. G1. $50.00

**DUNLAP, Susan.** *Death & Taxes.* 1992. Delacorte. 1st. sgn. NF/dj. G8. $25.00

**DUNLAP, Thomas R.** *Saving America's Wildlife.* 1988. Princeton. 222p. NF/dj. S15. $12.00

**DUNLOP, Ian.** *Degas.* 1979. NY. Harper. 1st Am. 240p. VG/dj. B11. $30.00

**DUNLOP, Richard.** *Doctors of the American Frontier.* 1965. NY. 1st. 228p. dj. A13. $40.00

**DUNN, Arthur Wallace.** *Gridiron Nights.* 1915. NY. 1st. 371p. VG. B5. $45.00

**DUNN, Dorothy.** *Plains Indian Sketch Books of Zo-Tom & Howling Wolf.* 1969. Northland. 1st. ils. NF/VG+. B19. $75.00

**DUNN, J.P.** *Massacres of the Mountains.* 1958. NY. facs. ils/index. 669p. VG/dj. E1. $40.00

**DUNN, James Taylor.** *St Croix.* 1965. NY. 1st. Rivers of Am series. ils Gerald Hazzard. 309p. VG. B18. $22.50

**DUNN, Katherine.** *Geek Love.* 1989. Knopf. 1st. sgn. F/dj. M19. $65.00

**DUNN, Katherine.** *Truck.* 1971. Harper Row. 1st. NF/dj. B3. $150.00

**DUNN, L.C.** *Heredity & Variation: Continuity & Change in Living World.* 1934. NY. U Soc. 1st. photos/ils. 120p. VG+. A25. $10.00

**DUNN, Peter M.** *First Vietnam War.* 1985. Hurst. photos/map/bibliography/index. 392p. VG/dj. S16. $25.00

**DUNN & TROXELL.** *By the Roadside.* 1928. Evanston. Row Peterson. 4th. ils Nell Hukle. 256p. VG+. A25. $12.00

**DUNNE, John Gregory.** *Dutch Shea, Jr.* 1982. S&S. 1st. F/clip. Q1. $25.00

**DUNNETT, Alastair M.** *Alistair Maclean Introduces Scotland.* 1972. Andre Deutsch. 1st. NF/dj. P3. $30.00

**DUNNETT, Dorothy.** *Dolly & the Nanny Bird.* 1982. Knopf. 1st Am. VG+/dj. A14. $21.00

**DUNNETT, Dorothy.** *Moroccan Traffic.* 1991. London. Chatto Windus. 1st. VG+/dj. A14. $17.50

**DUNNETT, Dorothy.** *Niccolo Rising: House of Niccolo Book One.* 1986. London. Michael Joseph. 1st. NF/dj. A14. $22.00

**DUNNETT, Dorothy.** *Ringed Castle: Lymond Chronicles, Volume Five.* 1971. London. Cassell. 1st. VG+/VG. A14. $140.00

**DUNNETT, Dorothy.** *Spring of the Ram: House of Niccolo, Book Two.* 1987. London. Michael Joseph. 1st. VG+/dj. A14. $22.00

**DUNNING, John.** *Booked to Die.* 1992. Scribner. 1st. F/dj. B2. $600.00

**DUNNING, John.** *Booked to Die.* 1992. Scribner. 1st. sgn. F/F. B3. $750.00

**DUNNING, John.** *Booked to Die.* 1993. London. Allison Busby. 1st/PBO. sgn. F. B3. $50.00

**DUNNING, John.** *Bookman's Wake.* 1995. NY. Scribner. 1st. sgn. F/dj. M15. $75.00

**DUNNING, John.** *Bookman's Wake.* 1995. Scribner. 1st. F/F. H11. $45.00

**DUNNING, John.** *Tune in Yesterday: Ultimate Encyclopedia...* 1976. Prentice Hall. 1st. author's 1st book. F/VG. B2. $100.00

**DUNNINGTON, George A.** *History & Progress of the Country of Marion, West Virginia.* 1880. Fairmont, WV. Dunnington. 12mo. 162p. gilt emb brn cloth. VG. F1. $150.00

**DUNTHORNE, Gordon.** *Flower & Fruit Prints of 18th & Early 19th Centuries...* 1938. 1/2500. sm folio. 75 pl. 289p. VG. A4. $450.00

**DUPIN, Andre Marie Jean J.** *Prospectus des Lettres sur la Profession d'Avocat...* 1818. Paris. disbound/untrimmed. M11. $250.00

**DUPIN, Jacques.** *Miro.* (1962). Abrams. ils/46 pl. 596p. blk cloth. NF/dj. F1. $175.00

**DUPLAIX, Georges.** *Pee-Gloo.* 1935. Harper. 1st. ils. VG. D1. $200.00

**DUPLAIX & SIMON.** *World Guide to Mammals.* 1976. NY. ils/maps. 283p. F/dj. A17. $17.50

**DUPUY, Trevor N.** *Military Life of Genghis, Kahn of Khans.* 1969. NY. 1st. ils. 131p. VG/VG. B18. $15.00

**DUPUY, Trevor N.** *Military Life of Genghis, Khan of Khans.* 1969. Franklin Watts. 1st. F/NF. M19. $25.00

**DUPUY, William Atherton.** *Baron of the Colorados.* 1940. Naylor. 1st. 177p. VG/VG. B19. $30.00

**DUPUY & HAYES.** *Military History of World War I: Volume 5.* 1967. NY. Watts. 1st. 109p. F/NF. D4. $20.00

**DURAND, Loup.** *Daddy.* 1988. NY. Villard. 1st. F/F. H11. $20.00

**DURAND, Loup.** *Jaquar.* 1990. NY. Villard. 1st. F/F. H11. $25.00

**DURANT, John.** *Dodgers.* 1948. Hastings. 1st. ils. VG. P8. $50.00

**DURANT & RICE.** *Come Out Fighting: Pictorial History of the Ring.* 1946. NY. Essential/DSP. 1st. 4to. F/VG+. B4. $150.00

**DURDEN, Charles.** *Fifth Law of Hawkins.* 1990. NY. St Martin. 1st. F/dj. R11. $15.00

**DURHAM, Philip.** *Down These Mean Streets a Man Must Go.* (1963). Chapel Hill. 1st. 8vo. gilt gray cloth. F/dj. R3. $60.00

**DURIEZ, Colin.** *CS Lewis Handbook.* (1994). Baker. 1st Am. AN/wrp. A27. $10.00

**DURRANT, MEACOCK & WHIT- WORTH.** *Machine Printing.* 1973. NY. Hastings. 1st Am. 8vo. 245p. cloth. F/dj. O10. $35.00

**DURRANT, Tom.** *Camellia Story.* 1982. Auckland. special ed. inscr. photos/ils. F/case. B26. $50.00

**DURRELL, Alexis.** *Crockery Cooking.* 1975. Weathervane. G/dj. A16. $8.00

**DURRELL, Lawrence.** *Acte: A Play.* 1965. London. Faber. 1st. 8vo. 76p. F/VG. M7. $35.00

**DURRELL, Lawrence.** *Antrobus Competer.* 1985. London. 1st. dj. T9. $20.00

**DURRELL, Lawrence.** *Black Book.* 1938. Paris. Obelisk. 1st. G/wrp. B2. $250.00

**DURRELL, Lawrence.** *Blue Thirst.* 1975. Santa Barbara. Capra. 1st. 56p. F/wrp. M7. $30.00

**DURRELL, Lawrence.** *Clea.* 1960. London. Faber. 1st. VG/VG. T9. $60.00

**DURRELL, Lawrence.** *Clea.* 1960. London. Faber. 1st. Alexandria Quartet #4. NF/VG. A24. $75.00

**DURRELL, Lawrence.** *Constance or Solitary Practices.* 1982. Viking. 1st. NF/dj. S13. $12.00

**DURRELL, Lawrence.** *Justine.* 1957. Dutton. 1st Am. 8vo. 253p. red/blk cloth. VG/dj. J3. $75.00

**DURRELL, Lawrence.** *Livia or Buried Alive.* 1978. London. 1st. F/dj. T12. $100.00

**DURRELL, Lawrence.** *Monsieur; or, The Prince of Darkness.* 1974. London. Faber. 1st. 8vo. 295p. F/dj. M7. $45.00

**DURRELL, Lawrence.** *Nunquam.* 1970. London. Faber. 1st. NF/dj. A14. $35.00

**DURRELL, Lawrence.** *Nunquam: A Novel.* 1970. NY. Dutton. 319p. F/NF. A4. $25.00

**DUSENBERY, B.M.** *Moment to Memory of General Andrew Jackson.* 1846. Nashua. 1st. full calf. VG. S17. $50.00

**DUSTIN, F.** *Custer Tragedy: Events Leading Up To & Following...* 1987 (1939). El Segundo. rpt. 1/200. 3 fld maps/photos. F. M4. $85.00

**DUTCHER, R. Adams.** *Introduction to Agricultural Biochemistry.* 1951. NY. Wiley. 502p. VG/dj. A10. $12.00

**DUTTON, Bertha.** *Sun Father's Way: Kiva Murals of Kuaua.* 1963. U NM. 100+ photos. 237p. VG/dj. J2. $95.00

**DUTTON, Clarence E.** *Tertiary History of the Grand Canon District.* 1882. GPO. monograph only. rstr brn buckram. VG+. F7. $500.00

**DUTTON, M.K.** *Historical Sketch of Bookbinding as an Art.* 1926. Norwood. Holliston Mills. 144p. teg. gilt red cloth. VG. F1. $35.00

**DUVAL, Mathias.** *Artistic Anatomy.* 1886. London. 2nd. 324p. A13. $90.00

**DUVEEN.** *Bibliotheca Alchemica et Chemica, Annotated Catalog...* nd. rpt. 1/150. 16 pl/2000 entries. F. A4. $85.00

**DUVOISIN, Roger.** *A for the Ark.* 1952. Lee Shepard. 1st. 4to. mc pict brd. R5. $150.00

**DWIGGINS, W.A.** *Layout in Advertising.* 1928. Harper. 1st. 8vo. 200p. cloth. VG/dj. B20. $50.00

**DWIGHT, T.** *Frozen Sections of a Child.* 1881. 1st. 4to. 15 pl. 66p. VG. E6. $125.00

**DWIGHT, Theodore W.** *Trial by Impeachment.* (1967). Phil. Am Law Register. 26p. disbound. lacks rear wrp. M11. $65.00

**DWYER, Deanna;** see Koontz, Dean R.

**DWYER, K.R.;** see Koontz, Dean R.

**DYBEK, Stuart.** *Childhood & Other Neighborhoods.* 1980. NY. Viking. 1st. sgn. author's 1st book. F/NF clip. O11. $20.00

**DYE, E.E.** *Conquest: True Story of Lewis & Clark.* 1936. NY. 10th. ils. 448p. VG. B5. $17.50

**DYER, Anthony.** *Classic African Animals: Big Five.* 1973. Winchester. ltd. 1/375. sgn/#d. VG/case. B30. $400.00

**DYER, Mary M.** *Portraiture of Shakerism.* 1822. New Hampshire. full leather. G. B30. $50.00

**DYER & FRASER.** *Rocking Chair: An American Institution.* 1928. NY. Century. 1st. 8vo. 124p. brn cloth. NF. B20. $65.00

**DYKES, Jeff.** *Fifty Great Western Illustrators, a Bibliographic Checklist.* (1975). Northland. 1st. 457p. VG/dj. B18. $65.00

**DYKSTRA, C.A.** *Colorado River Development & Related Problems.* 1930. Am Academy Political/Social Sci. 8vo. red brd. F7. $30.00

**DYKSTRATA, Lenny.** *Nails.* 1987. Doubleday. 1st. F/VG. P8. $30.00

**DYNES.** *Encyclopedia of Homosexuality.* 1990. St James. 2 vol. 4to. F. A4. $95.00

**DZIEMIANOWICZ, Stefan R.** *Weird Tales.* 1988. Bonanza. 1st thus. G/dj. L1. $35.00

EAGAN, Jennifer. *Invisible Circus.* 1995. Doubleday. 1st. F/dj. M23. $25.00

EAGAN, Lesley. *Dream Apart.* nd. BC. VG/dj. P3. $8.00

EAGAN, Lesley. *In the Death of a Man.* 1970. Harper. 1st. VG/dj. G8. $17.50

EAGLETON, Wells P. *Brain Abscess: Its Surgical Pathology...* 1922. Macmillan. 297p. xl. G7. $125.00

EAMES, G.T. *Horse to Remember.* 1947. Messner. 1st. ils Paul Brn. VG/dj. A21. $50.00

EAMES, H. *Winners Lose All: Dr Cook & Theft of North Pole.* 1973. Boston. photos/map. 346p. NF/dj. M4. $20.00

EAMES. *Eames Design: Work of Office of Chas & Ray Eames.* (1989). NY. Abrams. 4to. ils/photos. 456p. blk cloth. F/dj. K1. $75.00

EARHART, Amelia. *Last Flight.* Nov 1937. NY. 8vo. 229p. map ep. gilt red cloth. VG. B14. $75.00

EARHART, Amelia. *20 Hours, 40 Minutes: Our Flight in Friendship.* 1928. Grosset Dunlap. rpt. ils. 314p. VG. B18. $32.50

EARL, Guy Chaffee. *Indian Legends & Songs.* 1980. np. 1/500. 79p. NF/sans. B19. $25.00

EARL, John Prescott. *School Team in Camp.* 1909. Penn. 1st. VG. P8. $45.00

EARL, Stephen. *Hills of the Boasting Woman.* 1963. London. Readers Union. ils/biblio. 160p. dj. F3. $15.00

EARLANSON, Eileen W. *Cytological Conditions & Evidences for Hybridity...Roses.* 1929. np. inscr. ils/maps/pl. wrp. B26. $12.50

EARLE, J. *Chirurgical Works of Percival Pott.* 1891. 1st Am. lg 8vo. 14 pl. full leather. G+. E6. $450.00

EARLE, Olive. *Lampshades: How to Make Them.* 1921. Dodd Mead. 1st. tall 8vo. 102p. bl cloth. B20. $85.00

EARLE, Pliny. *History Description & Statistics of Bloomingdale Asylum...* 1848. NY. Egbert Hovey King. ftspc of Asylum. rb. G7. $350.00

EARLEY, Tony. *Here We Are in Paradise.* 1994. Little Brn. 1st. author's 1st book. F/dj. R14. $35.00

EARLEY, Tony. *Here We Are in Paradise.* 1994. Little Brn. 1st. author's 1st book. F/dj. A24. $45.00

EARLY, Gerald. *Daughters: On Family & Fatherhood.* 1994. Addison Wesley. 1st. F/dj. R14. $25.00

EARLY, Jack. *Creative Kind of Killer.* 1984. Franklin Watts. 1st. F/dj. A23. $32.00

EARLY Jubal Anderson. *Lieutenant General Jubal Anderson...* 1912. Lippincott. 1st. 496p. NF. M8. $375.00

EASSON & ESSICK. *William Blake: Book Illustrator, Bibliography & Catalogue...* 1972. 66 pl. 72p. VG/wrp. A4. $95.00

EAST, Ben. *Danger!* 1970. Outdoor Life/Dutton. 1st. ils Tom Beecham. VG/dj. M20. $25.00

EAST, Charles. *Civil War Diary of Sarah Morgan.* 1991. Athens, GA. U GA. 1st. F/dj. A14. $25.00

EASTBURN, Robert. *Dangers & Sufferings of Robert Eastburn.* 1904. Cleveland. Burroughs. 1/27 on Imperial Japanese vellum. 76p. B18. $150.00

EASTLAKE, William. *Bamboo Bed.* 1971. NY. Zebra. 1st. VG/wrp. R11. $17.00

EASTLAKE, William. *Castle Keep.* 1965. NY. S&S. 1st. VG/dj. L1. $50.00

EASTLAKE, William. *Child's Garden of Verses for the Revolution.* 1970. NY. Grove. 1st. VG/dj. B30/R11. $30.00

EASTLAKE, William. *Dancers in the Scalp House.* 1975. Viking. 1st. F/NF clip. B3. $75.00

EASTMAN, Charles Eastman. *Soul of the Indian.* 1911. Boston. 1st. 170p. VG. B18. $45.00

EASTMAN, E.R. *Not With Dreams.* 1954. NY. Greenberg. 1st. sgn bookplate. NF/VG. T11. $10.00

EASTMAN, E.R. *Walking the Broad Highway.* 1956. Chicago. Am Agriculturist. 211p. VG. A10. $18.00

EASTMAN, Edwin. *Seven & Nine Years Among the Camanches (sic) & Apaches...* 1873. Jersey City. Johnson. 1st. 8vo. 307p. brn cloth. VG. B20. $100.00

EASTMAN, P.D. *Cat in the Hat Beginner Book Dictionary.* 1964. Random. F/sans. T12. $25.00

EASTON, MOTTRAM & PARTRIDGE. *Three Personal Records of War.* 1929. London. 1/100. sgns. T9. $85.00

EASTON, Pheobe Jane. *Marbling: A History & Bibliography.* 1983. Dawson's Bookshop. 1st. sgn. 190p. beige linen/inlaid marbled paper. F. B20. $250.00

EASTWOOD, Alice. *Handbook of the Trees of California.* 1905. SF. 57 pl. 86p. new buckram. rare. B26. $120.00

EATON, A.H. *Beauty Behind Barbed Wire.* 1952. NY. ils/index. 209p. VG/fair. B5. $60.00

EATON, Mary. *Cook & Housekeeper's Complete & Universal Dictionary...* 1823 (1822). ils. 493p. half leather/marbled brd. E6. $250.00

EAUCLAIRE, Sally. *Cat in Photography.* 1990. Boston. photos. VG/dj. M17. $15.00

EAVENSON, Howard N. *Coal Through the Ages.* 1935. NY. AIME. 1st. sm 8vo. 123p. gilt red cloth. VG+. B20. $25.00

EBAN, Eleanor F. *War in the Cradle of the World. Mesopotamia.* 1918. London. Hodder Stoughton. ils/pl. 312p. cloth. G. Q2. $46.50

EBERHART, A.G. *Everything About Dogs.* 1902. Camp Dennison, OH. Eberhart Kennels. stated 2nd. 8vo. 282p. purple cloth. B20. $35.00

EBERHART, Mignon G. *Bayou Road.* 1979. NY. Random. 1st. F/F. H11. $20.00

EBERHART, Mignon G. *Danger Money.* 1974. Random. F/NF. N4. $25.00

EBERHART, Mignon G. *Nine O'Clock Tide.* 1977. Random. 1st. F/F. H11. $20.00

EBERHART, Richard. *Collected Poems 1930-1976.* 1976. NY. Oxford. 1st. inscr/dtd 1984. VG/dj. R14. $75.00

EBERLE, Irmengarde. *Picture Stories for Children (A Rebus).* 1984. Delacorte. 1st thus. 98p. F/NF. C14. $20.00

EBERSOLE, Barbara. *Fletcher Martin.* 1954. Gainesville, FL. 1st. 4to. 51p. F/VG+. B20. $60.00

EBIN, David. *Drug Experience.* 1961. Orion. 1st. VG/dj. R8. $40.00

EBSEN, Buddy. *Other Side of Oz.* 1993. Newport Beach. Donovan. 285p. VG/dj. C5. $15.00

EBY & FLEMING. *Case of the Malevolent Twin.* 1946. Dutton. 1st. G+. G8. $12.50

ECCLES, Marjorie. *Cast a Cold Eye.* 1988. NY. Crime Club. 1st. F/F. H11. $40.00

ECHEVERRIAL & WILKIE. *French Image of America, a Chronological...Bibliography...* 1994. 1601 entries. NF. A4. $160.00

ECK, Joe. *Elements of Garden Design.* 1996. NY. Holt. 1st. ils/index. 164p. F/dj. H10. $17.50

ECKBO, Garrett. *Landscape for Living.* 1950. NY. 1st. photos/plans. 262p. VG/dj. B26. $40.00

ECKBO, Garrett. *Urban Landscape Design.* 1964. McGraw Hill. 4to. ils. gr cloth. VG. F1. $35.00

**ECKENRODE, H.J.** *Jefferson Davis: President of the South.* 1923. Macmillan. 1st. 371p. G+. B10. $25.00

**ECKENRODE, Hamilton James.** *George B McClellan, the Man Who Saved the Union.* 1941. Chapel Hill. U NC. 1st. 296p. cloth. VG. M8. $45.00

**ECKER, Alexander.** *Cebral Convolutions of Man Represented...* 1873. NY. Appleton. 1st Am. 87p. cloth. G7. $150.00

**ECKERT, Allan W.** *Dreaming Tree.* 1968. Little Brn. 1st. decor cloth. F/NF. T11. $75.00

**ECKERT, Allan W.** *Great Auk.* 1963. Little Brn. 1st. NF/VG. T11. $75.00

**ECKERT, Allan W.** *Incident at Hawk's Hill.* 1971. Little Brn. rpt. sgn. VG/G. B17. $22.50

**ECKERT, Allan W.** *Johnny Logan, Shawnee Spy.* 1983. Little Brn. 1st. NF/dj. T11. $70.00

**ECKERT, Allan W.** *Owls of North America (North of Mexico).* 1974. Doubleday. 1/250. sgn author/aritst. 278p. F/case. B20. $300.00

**ECKERT, Allan W.** *Sorrow in Our Heart: Life of Tecumseh.* 1992. NY. 1st. F/dj. T11. $40.00

**ECKERT, Allan W.** *Twilight of Empire.* 1988. Little Brn. 1st. Winning of Am #6. rem mk. NF/dj. T11. $40.00

**ECKERT, Allan W.** *Wild Season.* 1967. Little Brn. ils Karl Karalus. 244p. F/NF. D4. $30.00

**ECKERT, Allan W.** *Wilderness Empire.* 1980. Little Brn. 1st. inscr. G/dj. V4. $40.00

**ECKSTEIN, Gustav.** *Body Has a Head.* 1970. NY. 1st. 799p. dj. A13. $20.00

**ECKSTEIN, Gustav.** *Everyday Miracle.* 1965. Harper Row. ils Kevin McIntyre. 146p. F/NF. D4. $25.00

**ECKSTEIN, Yechiel.** *What Christians Should Know About Jews & Judaism.* 1984. Word. 336p. VG/dj. B29. $11.00

**ECO, Umberto.** *Foucault's Pendulum.* 1989. HBJ. 1st Am. F/dj. N4. $30.00

**ECO, Umberto.** *How to Travel With a Salmon & Other Essays.* 1994. NY. 1st. trans Wm Weaver. VG/dj. M17. $15.00

**ECO, Umberto.** *Island of the Day Before.* 1995. Harcourt. ARC. F/wrp. B2. $50.00

**ECO, Umberto.** *Postcript to the Name of the Rose.* 1984. HBJ. 1st. F/dj. M21/T12. $30.00

**ECO, Umberto.** *Search for the Perfect Language.* 1995. Oxford/Cambridge. VG+/dj. M17. $17.50

**ECOBICHON & W.** *Environment la Tobacco Smoke.* 1989. Lexington Books. 1st. 389p. VG. N2. $15.00

**EDDICOTT, Wendell.** *Adventures With Rod & Harpoon Along Florida Keys.* 1925. Stokes. ils. NF. B14. $75.00

**EDDINGS, David.** *Diamond Throne.* 1989. Del Rey/Ballantine. 1st. NF/clip. A14. $28.00

**EDDINGS, David.** *Queen of Sorcery.* 1983. London. Century. 1st hc. Belgariad #2. NF/dj. A14. $175.00

**EDDINGS, David.** *Ruby Knight.* 1991. Del Rey/Ballantine. 1st. Elenium #2. NF/dj. A14. $17.50

**EDDINGS, David.** *Sorceress of Darshiva.* 1989. Ballantine. 1st. F/F. B3. $20.00

**EDDINGTON, A.S.** *Nature of the Physical World.* 1929 (1928). Cambridge. 4th. 361p. cloth. G. K5. $25.00

**EDDY, Clyde.** *Down the World's Most Dangerous River.* 1929. Stokes. photos. 293p. VG/dj. F7. $210.00

**EDDY, Daniel C.** *Europe: Its Scenes & Society.* 1859. Bradley Dayton. 11th. S17. $10.00

**EDDY, John A.** *New Sun: Solar Results From Skylab.* 1979. NASA. SP-402. 4to. 198p. VG. K5. $35.00

**EDDY, Mary Baker.** *Christ & Christmas.* 1897. Christian Science Pub. 12mo. 59p. aeg. limp leather/ribbon marker. H4. $175.00

**EDDY, Mary Baker.** *Retrospection & Introspection.* 1899. Boston. 15th thousand. 130p. aeg. VG. B14. $35.00

**EDDY, Mary Baker.** *What Christmas Means to Me & Other Christmas Messages.* 1949. Boston. 50p. gr cloth. AN/dj. B14. $25.00

**EDE, Charles.** *Art of the Book.* 1951. London. The Studio. 4to. ils. gilt gr cloth. F/dj. F1. $80.00

**EDEL, Edmond.** *Silvia: Tragedia de Una Morfinomania (Coleccion Pompadour).* nd. Madrid. 12mo. 193p. VG/wrp. H4. $30.00

**EDEL, Leon.** *James Joyce: The Last Journey.* (1947). NY. Gotham Book Mart. 1st. quarter bl cloth/prt brd. NF. M24. $65.00

**EDEL & RAY.** *Henry James & HG Wells: Record of Their Friendship...* 1958. Urbana, IL. ARC. 8vo. 272p. RS. F/worn. H4. $20.00

**EDELMAN, Bernard.** *Ownership of the Image, Elements for Marxist Theory of Law.* 1979. Routledge/Kegan Paul. M11. $45.00

**EDELMAN & GRODNICK.** *Ideal Cheese Book.* 1986. NY. Harper Row. F/VG. V4. $12.50

**EDENS, Cooper.** *ABC of Fashionable Animals.* 1989. Gr Tiger. 1st. 55p. F/sans. D4. $30.00

**EDENS, Cooper.** *Santa Cow Island Edens.* 1994. Gr Tiger/S&S. 1st. ils. VG. B36. $15.00

**EDERER, Bernard Francis.** *Birch Coulie.* 1957. Exposition. G. w/sgn letter. A19. $30.00

**EDGERTON, Clyde.** *Floatplane Notebooks.* 1988. London. Viking. ARC. F/F. B3. $15.00

**EDGERTON, Clyde.** *In Memory of Junior.* 1992. Algonquin. 1st. sgn. NF/dj. B30. $22.00

**EDGERTON, Clyde.** *Raney.* 1985. Chapel Hill. 1st. author's 1st book. inscr/dtd 1985. F/dj. L3. $500.00

**EDGERTON, Clyde.** *Redeye.* 1995. Chapel Hill. 1st. sgn. F/dj. B20. $35.00

**EDGERTON, Clyde.** *Walking Across Egypt.* 1986. Algonquin. 1st. sgn. F/F. B3. $75.00

**EDGERTON, Clyde.** *Walking Across Egypt.* 1987. Algonquin. 1st. sgn. NF/dj. M23. $50.00

**EDGERTON, Clyde.** *Walking Across Egypt.* 1988. Jonathan Cape. 1st. sgn. F/VG. B30. $45.00

**EDGERTON, Clyde.** *Where Trouble Sleeps.* 1997. Algonquin. 1st. F/dj. M23. $25.00

**EDGERTON, Jesse.** *New Quakerism.* 1900. Columbiana, OH. Wilbur Union. 12mo. 12p. wrp. V3. $12.00

**EDGERTON, Leslie H.** *Death of Tarpons.* 1996. Denton, TX. 1st. author's 1st book. F/F. H11. $40.00

**EDGERTON & GERMESCHAUSEN.** *Mercury Arc As Actinic Stroboscopic Light Source.* 1933. Cambridge. F/wrp. B14. $55.00

**EDIE, George.** *Art of English Shooting.* 1993. SF. Arion. 1st thus. 1/250. gilt quarter brn morocco. F/case. M24. $100.00

**EDINBOROUGH, Arnold.** *Festivals of Canada.* 1981. Lester/Orpen Dennys. 1st. VG/dj. P3. $20.00

**EDINGER, Ludwig.** *Twelve Lectures on Structure of Central Nervous System...* 1891. Phil. Davis. 230p. cloth. G. G7. $75.00

**EDINGER, William.** *Samuel Johnson & Poetic Style.* 1977. Chicago. 1st. VG/dj. H13. $45.00

**EDLIN, Herbert L.** *Know Your Broadleaves.* 1973 (1968). London. 166 pl. 143p. sc. B26. $12.50

**EDMINSTER, Frank C.** *American Game Birds of Field & Forest.* 1954. NY. Scribner. 1st. VG/clip. H4. $35.00

**EDMINSTER, Frank C.** *Ruffled Grouse.* 1947. Macmillan. G/dj. A19. $30.00

**EDMONDS, Harry.** *Secret Voyage.* 1946. Mac Donald. VG. P3. $10.00

**EDMONDS, Walter.** *Beaver Valley.* 1971. Little Brn. 1st. ils Leslie Morrill. VG/dj. T11. $55.00

**EDMONDS, Walter.** *Chad Hanna.* (1940). Little Brn. 1st. NF/VG. T11. $50.00

**EDMONDS, Walter.** *Drums Along the Mohawk.* (1936). Little Brn. 64th prt. gilt cloth. F/dj. T11. $45.00

**EDMONDS, Walter.** *Drums Along the Mohawk.* 1936. Little Brn. 1st. NF/VG 1st state. B3. $110.00

**EDMONDS, Walter.** *In the Hands of the Senecas.* 1947. Little Brn. 1st. NF/dj. T11. $55.00

**EDMONDS, Walter.** *Three Stalwarts.* 1962. Little Brn. 1st thus. NF/clip. T11. $40.00

**EDMONDS & MIMURA.** *Paramount Pictures & People Who Made Them.* 1980. San Diego. AS Barnes. 1st. 4to. 272p. VG/dj. B11. $15.00

**EDMONDSON, G.W.** *From Epworth to London With John Wesley...* (1890). Cincinnati/Chicago. obl 4to. gilt violet cloth. VG. B14. $60.00

**EDMONSON, Munro.** *Ancient Furniture of the Itzas: Book of Chilam Balm...* 1982. Austin. U TX. 1st. 220p. dj. F3. $50.00

**EDMUNDSON, William.** *Journal of Life, Travels, Sufferings & Labour of Love...* 1774. London. Mary Hinde. 2nd. 12mo. 371p. worn leather/broken hinge. V3. $110.00

**EDSON, Newell W.** *Choosing a Home Partner.* 1926. NY. Assoc Pr. 1st. VG+. A25. $20.00

**EDWARD, Oliver.** *Talking of Books.* 1957. London. Heinemann. 1st. 8vo. 306p. F/dj. O10. $15.00

**EDWARDES & MASTERS.** *Cradle of Erotica.* 1966. NY. 1st. VG/dj. B5. $25.00

**EDWARDS, A. Cecil.** *Persian Carpet: Survey of Carpet-Weaving Industry of Persia.* 1975. London. Duckworth. 4th. 384p. NF/dj. W1. $90.00

**EDWARDS, A. Herbage.** *Paris Through the Attic.* 1922 (1918). Dutton. 4th. 12mo. VG/dj. A2. $20.00

**EDWARDS, Anne.** *Early Reagan: Rise to Power.* 1987. Morrow. 1st. F/VG. T12. $100.00

**EDWARDS, Anne.** *Road to Tara: Life of Margaret Mitchell.* 1983. NY/New Haven. 1st. photos. VG/dj. M17. $15.00

**EDWARDS, Anne.** *Survivors.* 1968. NY. HRW. 1st. F/dj. A23. $40.00

**EDWARDS, Bill.** *Millersburg, the Queen of Carnival Glass.* (1982). Collector Books. 8vo. 132p. VG/glossy wrp. H1. $30.00

**EDWARDS, Bryan.** *Historical Survey of French Colony in Island of ST Domingo.* 1797. London. John Stockdale. 4to. lg fld map/tables. 248p. contemporary tree calf. K1. $600.00

**EDWARDS, Clayton.** *Treasury of Heroes & Heroines: Record of High Endurance...* 1920. Hampton. ils Choate/Cooke. VG. M19. $25.00

**EDWARDS, Corwin D.** *Price Discrimination Law, a Review of Experience.* 1959. Brookings Inst. private xl. M11. $35.00

**EDWARDS, E.I.** *Desert Voices: Descriptive Bibliography.* 1958. LA. Westernlore. 1st. 1/500. VG/dj. O4. $75.00

**EDWARDS, George Wharton.** *Vanishing Towers & Chimes of Flanders.* 1916. Phil. Penn. special ltd ed. 1/35 on Italian handmade. F/case. H5. $600.00

**EDWARDS, Harry Stillwell.** *Eneas Africanus.* 1930. Dallas. BC of TX. 1st. 1/300. batik brd/label. F/NF box. M24. $100.00

**EDWARDS, I.E.S.** *Tutanchamum Das Grab und Seine Schatze.* 1977. 4to. German text. 256p. VG/dj. B11. $18.00

**EDWARDS, Isabel M.** *Glove Making.* (1946). NY/Chicago. Pitman. later prt. 12mo. 90p. VG. H4. $25.00

**EDWARDS, John O.** *Peroxide Reaction Mechanisms.* 1962. NY. Interscience. 8vo. 245p. VG/dj. K5. $60.00

**EDWARDS, Jonathan.** *Great Christian Doctrine of Original Sin Defended...* 1761. London. Re-Prt for G Keith/J Johnson. 1st Eng. 8vo. VG. O1. $400.00

**EDWARDS, Jonathan.** *Life of Rev David Brainerd...* nd. NY. Am Tract Soc. Evangelical Family Lib #7. half leather. H10. $35.00

**EDWARDS, Leo.** *Jerry Todd, Editor-In-Grief.* (1930). Grosset Dunlap. VG/dj. H4. $60.00

**EDWARDS, Leo.** *Jerry Todd & the Bob-Tailed Elephant.* (1929). Grosset Dunlap. later ed of 3rd format. sm 8vo. 235p. pict ep. NF/dj. H1. $20.00

**EDWARDS, Leo.** *Jerry Todd & the Purring Egg.* 1926. Grosset Dunlap. 1st. sm 8vo. 213p. red cloth. G/dj. H1. $18.00

**EDWARDS, Leo.** *Jerry Todd & the Talking Frog.* 1925. Grosset Dunlap. 1st. sm 8vo. 226p. red cloth. G/dj. H1. $20.00

**EDWARDS, Leo.** *Jerry Todd & the Waltzing Hen.* (1925). Grosset Dunlap. VG/dj. H4. $30.00

**EDWARDS, Leo.** *Jerry Todd's Cuckoo Camp.* 1940. Grosset Dunlap. 1st of 3rd format. sm 8vo. 216p. VG. H1. $25.00

**EDWARDS, Leo.** *Jerry Todd's Poodle Parlor.* 1938. Grosset Dunlap. VG/dj. H4. $85.00

**EDWARDS, Leo.** *Jerry Todd: Buffalo Bill Bath Tub.* (1937). Grosset Dunlap. 1st of 3rd format. sm 8vo. 232p. pict ep. F/VG. H1. $25.00

**EDWARDS, Leo.** *Poppy Ott: Poppy Ott & Co, Inferior Decorators.* 1937. Grosset Dunlap. 1st/2nd format. sm 8vo. 210p. red cloth. F/VG. H1. $18.00

**EDWARDS, Leo.** *Poppy Ott: Poppy Ott & the Freckled Goldfish.* 1928. Grosset Dunlap. 1st. 269p. red cloth. G/VG. H1. $15.00

**EDWARDS, Leo.** *Poppy Ott: Poppy Ott & the Prancing Pancake.* 1930. Grosset Dunlap. 1st. sm 8vo. 298p. red cloth. NF/dj. H1. $25.00

**EDWARDS, Leo.** *Poppy Ott: Poppy Ott's Pedigreed Pickles.* 1927. Grosset Dunlap. 1st. 243p. sm 8vo. red cloth. H1. $12.00

**EDWARDS, Leo.** *Poppy Ott: The Monkey's Paw.* 1938. Grosset Dunlap. 1st. sm 8vo. 214p. red cloth. VG/G. H1. $30.00

**EDWARDS, Lionel.** *Huntsmen Past & Present.* 1929. London. Eyre Spottiswoode. 1st. sm 4to. VG/G. O3. $125.00

**EDWARDS, Peter.** *Blood Brothers: How Canada's Most Powerful Mafia...* 1990. Toronto. Key Porter. 1st. inscr/sgn. NF/VG. A26. $35.00

**EDWARDS, R.B.** *Reason & Religion: Introduction to Philosophy of Religion.* 1972. HBJ. 386p. G. B29. $11.00

**EDWARDS & TERRY.** *Governor's Mansion of the Palmetto State.* 1978. Columbia. 1st. inscr/dtd 1978. G/VG. V4. $17.50

**EDWARDS & ZANETTA.** *Stardust: David Bowie Story.* (1986). McGraw Hill. 8vo. photos. 433p. F/NF. H4. $10.00

**EDWARDS-YEARWOOD, Grace.** *In the Shadow of the Peacock.* 1988. McGraw Hill. 1st. F/F. D10. $40.00

**EEKELAAR & KATZ.** *Marriage & Cohabitation in Contemporary Societies.* 1980. Toronto. Butterworth. 1st. VG. B27. $12.00

**EELLS & O'DAY.** *High Times Hard Times.* 1981. Putnam. 1st. F/F. B2. $45.00

**EEMANS, M.** *L'Art Vivant en Belgique.* 1972. Bruxelles. 68 tipped-in mc pl/index. 208p. cloth. NF/dj. D2. $75.00

EFFINGER, George Alec. *What Entrophy Means to Me.* 1972. Doubleday. 1st. NF/NF. P3. $15.00

EGAMI, Tomo. *Typical Japanese Cooking.* 1959. Tokyo. Shibata. 1st. ils. VG. N2. $10.00

EGAN, Ferol. *Sand in a Whirlwind.* 1972. Doubleday. F/dj. A19. $40.00

EGEJURU, Phanuel Akubueze. *Towards African Literary Independence: A Dialogue...* 1980. Westport. Greenwood. 1st. 173p. R11. $17.00

EGERTON, Thomas. *Speech of the Lord Chancellor of England...* 1609. London. later blk morocco. M11. $650.00

EGGLESTON, George Cary. *History of the Confederate War: Its Causes & Conduct...* 1910. NY. Sturgis Walton. 2 vol. 1st. cloth. NF. M8. $350.00

EGGLESTON, William. *Democratic Forest.* 1989. Doubleday. 1st Am. F/dj. C9. $90.00

EGGLESTON & SEELYE. *Tecumseh & the Shawnee Prophet.* 1878. Dodd Mead. 1st. lg map. 332p. gilt cloth. D11. $60.00

EGLOFF, Fred. *El Paso Lawman.* ltd. ils/biblio/index. 141p. AN/dj. E1. $17.00

EHLE, John. *Last One Home.* 1984. Harper. 1st. NF/dj. S13. $10.00

EHRENBURG, Ilya. *Thaw.* 1955. Chicago. Regnery. 1st. 8vo. G/dj. B11. $15.00

EHRENFELD & MACK. *Chamelon Variant.* 1980. NY. Dial. 1st. F/F. H11. $25.00

EHRENFIELD, David. *Beginning Again: People & Nature in the New Millenium.* 1993. OUP. 216p. AN. S15. $6.00

EHRENSTEIN & REED. *Rock on Film.* 1982. NY. Delilah. 75 photos. VG/wrp. C9. $36.00

EHRLICH, Gretel. *Arctic Heart: A Poem Cycle.* 1992. Santa Barbara. Capra. 1st. sgn. F. O11. $25.00

EHRLICH, Gretel. *Drinking Dry Clouds.* 1991. Santa Barbara. Capra. 1st. F/wrp. R14. $25.00

EHRLICH, Gretel. *Islands, the Universe, Home.* 1991. Viking. 1st. sgn. F/dj. O11. $40.00

EHRLICH, Gretel. *Match to the Heart.* 1994. Pantheon. ARC. sgn. F/wrp/NF case. B4. $65.00

EHRLICH, Louise. *Baptism of Desire: Poems.* 1989. Harper Row. 1st. sgn. F/dj. O11. $35.00

EHRLICH, Louise. *Jacklight.* 1990. London. Sphere. 1st. sgn. F. O11. $35.00

EHRLICH & EHRLICH. *Population, Resources & Environment.* 1970. Freeman. 1st. 383p. VG. S15. $10.00

EHRLICHMAN, John. *Witness to Power.* 1982. S&S. 1st. f/dj. W2. $30.00

EICHLER, Alfred. *Death of an Ad Man.* 1954. Abelard-Schuman. VG/dj. P3. $15.00

EICKELMAN, Dale F. *Middle East: Anthropological Approach.* 1981. NJ. Prentice Hall. inscr. ils/figures. 336p. G/wrp. Q2. $15.00

EICKHOFF, Randy Lee. *Fourth Horseman.* 1998. NY. Tom Doherty Assoc. 1st. gilt blk bdg. F/dj. T11. $22.00

EIFERT, Virginia. *Delta Queen: Story of a Steamboat.* 1960. Dodd Mead. 1st. 242p. F/dj. B18. $22.50

EIGHNER, Lars. *Travels With Lizabeth.* 1993. St Martin. 1st. F/dj. R14. $60.00

EINARSEN, Arthur S. *Pronghorn Antelope & Its Management.* 1948. Wildlife Management Inst. 2nd. ils. 238p. F/dj. S15. $30.00

EINHARD THE FRANK. *Life of Charlemagne.* 1970. Folio Soc. NF/case. P3. $20.00

EINSTEIN, Charles. *Willie Mays: Coast to Coast Giant.* 1963. Putnam. 1st. photos. VG. P8. $20.00

EISELEY, Loren. *Fox at the Wood's Edge.* 1990. NY. Holt. 1st. 517p. gray cloth. F/dj. T11. $45.00

EISELEY, Loren. *Innocent Assassins.* 1973. Scribner. 1st. ils Laszlo Kubinyi. NF/NF. B3. $35.00

EISELEY, Loren. *Night Country.* 1971. Scribner. 1st. VG/dj. M19. $17.50

EISEN, Gustavus A. *Portraits of Washington.* 1932. Hamilton. vol 1 only. 323p. VG. B10. $85.00

EISENBERG, D. *Meyer Laskey, Mogul of the Mob.* 1979. NY. Paddington. 1st. 346p. VG/dj. B5. $25.00

EISENBERG, Larry. *Best Laid Schemes.* 1971. Macmillan. 1st. F/dj. P3. $20.00

EISENBERG & TAYLOR. *Ultimate Fishing Book.* 1991. NY. ils. F/dj. A17. $30.00

EISENHOWER, Dwight D. *At Ease: Stories I Tell to Friends.* 1967. Doubleday. ne. sm 4to. 400p. NF/VG. W2. $40.00

EISENHOWER, Dwight D. *Crusade in Europe.* 1948. Doubleday. 1st. 559p. F/dj. H1. $20.00

EISENHOWER, Dwight D. *Mandate for Change: White House Years 1953-1956.* 1963. Doubleday. 1st. sm 4to. 650p. VG/dj. S14. $12.00

EISENSTADT, Jill. *Kiss Out.* 1991. Knopf. 1st. NF/F. R14. $25.00

EISENSTAEDT, Alfred. *Eisenstaedt's Album: Fifty Years of Friends & Acquaintances.* 1976. Viking. 1st. VG/dj. C9. $90.00

EISENSTAEDT, Alfred. *Eisenstaedt's Guide to Photography.* 1978. Viking. VG/dj. S5. $16.00

EISENSTAEDT, Alfred. *Eisenstaedt's Guide to Photography.* 1978. Viking. 1st. ils. F/VG. P12. $25.00

EISENSTEIN, Phyllis. *Born to Exile.* 1978. Arkham. VG/blocked price. L1. $35.00

EISLER, Steven. *Space Wars, Worlds & Weapons.* 1979. Crescent. F/dj. P3. $6.00

EITELJORG, Harrison. *Treasures of the American West.* 1981. Balance House. 172p. VG/dj. J2. $65.00

EITNER, Walter H. *Walt Whitman's Western Jaunt.* (1981). Lawrence. Regents Pr of KS. 1st. photos/index. AN/dj. A18. $20.00

EKBAUM, Arthur. *Destruction of Independent Farming in East Europe.* 1949. Stockholm. Estonian Infor Centre. 59p. A10. $15.00

EKMAN, Gosta. *Essays in Psychology Dedicated to David Katz.* 1951. Uppsala. Almqvist Wiksells. 283p. stiff cream wrp. G1. $45.00

ELDER, Art. *Blue Streak & Doctor Medusa.* nd. Whitman. VG. P3. $13.00

ELDER, W. *Biography of Elisha Kent Kane.* 1858. Phil. 4 pl. 416p. new cloth. M4. $60.00

ELDERFIELD, John. *Matisse in the Collection of the Museum of Modern Art.* 1978. MOMA. ils/fld ils. gilt linen cloth. F/VG. F1. $35.00

ELDRIDGE, Charlotte. *Godey Lady Doll.* 1953. Hastings. 1st. ils. VG+/G. M5. $12.00

ELFLANDSSON, Galad. *Black Wolf.* 1979. Grant. 1st. 1/1000. VG/G+. L1. $45.00

ELFONT, Edna A. *Roar of Thunder, Whisper of Wind: Portrait of MI Waterfalls.* 1993 (1984). E Lansing, MI. Thunder Bay. 4to. F/wrp. A2. $12.00

ELIOT, Charles W. *American Historical Documents 1000-1904.* 1969. Harvard Classics. 62nd. VG. P3. $20.00

ELIOT, Charles W. *Harvard Classics Five Foot Shelf of Books Vol 38...* nd (1910). NY. Collier. 418p. NF. C14. $15.00

**ELIOT, George.** *Adam Bede.* 1859. NY. Harper. 1st Am. gilt brn cloth. M24. $100.00

**ELIOT, George.** *Felix Holt: The Radical.* 1883. John B Alden. fair. P3. $12.00

**ELIOT, Jane.** *History of the Western Railroads.* 1995. Crescent. photos. AN. J2. $35.00

**ELIOT, Marc.** *Kato Kaelin: Whole Truth.* 1995. Harper Collins. 1st. 8vo. 270p. AN/F. H4. $10.00

**ELIOT, Porter.** *In Wilderness Is the Preservation of the World.* 1962. Sierra Club. 107p. VG/dj. A10. $25.00

**ELIOT, T.S.** *Cocktail Party.* 1950. HBW. 189p. VG. C5. $12.50

**ELIOT, T.S.** *Cocktail Party.* 1950. Harcourt Brace. 1st. F/NF. L3. $85.00

**ELIOT, T.S.** *Confidential Clerk.* 1954. Harcourt Brace. 1st Am. NF/VG. L3. $45.00

**ELIOT, T.S.** *Confidential Clerk.* 1954. London. Faber. 1st issue. NF/1st issue. L3. $125.00

**ELIOT, T.S.** *Cultivation of Christmas Trees.* 1956. London. Faber. 1st. 1/10140. F/prt wrp/envelope. M24. $50.00

**ELIOT, T.S.** *Cultivation of Christmas Trees.* 1956. NY. Farrar Straus. 1st Am. 1/3pict brd. F. M24. $35.00

**ELIOT, T.S.** *Elder Statesman.* 1959. London. Faber. 1st. F/dj. L3. $75.00

**ELIOT, T.S.** *Ezra Pound: His Metric & Poetry.* 1917. Knopf. 1st. 1/1000. author's 2nd book. gilt pk brd. M24. $300.00

**ELIOT, T.S.** *Homage to John Dryden.* 1924. London. Hogarth. 1st. 1/2000. NF/prt wrp. M24. $125.00

**ELIOT, T.S.** *Literature of Politics.* 1955. London. Conservative Political Centre. 1st. 1/6160. F/prt wrp. M24. $65.00

**ELIOT, T.S.** *Little Gidding.* 1942. London. Faber. 1st. NF/hand-sewn brn wrp. Q1. $150.00

**ELIOT, T.S.** *Poems 1909-1925.* nd. NY/Chicago. 1st Am. VG. M17. $35.00

**ELIOT, T.S.** *What Is a Classic?* 1945. London. Faber. 1st. F/prt wrp. M24. $200.00

**ELIOT, Willard A.** *Forest Trees of the Pacific Coast.* 1948 (1938). NY. revised. 565p. B26. $32.50

**ELKIN, Stanley.** *Mrs Ted Bliss.* 1995. NY. Hyperion. 1/1500. sgn. author's final novel. maroon cloth. F/sans. A24. $70.00

**ELKINS, Aaron.** *Icy Clutches.* 1990. Mysterious. 1st. F/dj. M19. $15.00

**ELKINS, Aaron.** *Murder in the Queen's Armies.* 1985. Walker. 1st. inscr/dtd 1988. F/dj. A24. $200.00

**ELKINS, Aaron.** *Old Bones.* 1987. Mysterious. 1st. F/dj. M15. $95.00

**ELKINS, Aaron.** *Old Bones.* 1987. Mysterious. 1st. NF/dj. A14. $70.00

**ELLER, E.M.** *Chesapeake Bay in the American Revolution.* 1981. Century. 1st. ils. 600p. F/dj. M4. $40.00

**ELLIN, Stanley.** *Dark Fantasitic.* (1983). Mysterious. 1/250. sgn. blk-lettered blk cloth. F/box. R3. $60.00

**ELLIN, Stanley.** *Luxembourg Run.* 1977. Random. 1st. VG/dj. N4. $20.00

**ELLIN, Stanley.** *Specialty of the House & Other Stories.* 1979. Mysterious. 1st. 1/250. sgn/#d. F/NF. A24. $85.00

**ELLINGTON & DANCE.** *Duke Ellington in Person: An Intimate Memoir...* 1978. Houghton Mifflin. 1st. 8vo. 236p. F/NF. B20. $45.00

**ELLIOT, E.D.** *Training Gun Dogs to Retrieve.* 1952. NY. Field & Stream Outdoor series. 1st. VG/dj. M17. $15.00

**ELLIOT, William.** *Coming to Terms With Life.* 1944. John Knox. sgn. 142p. G. B29. $13.50

**ELLIOTT, Eugene Clinton.** *History of Variety: Vaudeville in Seattle...to 1914.* 1944. Seattle. 1/500. 85p. F/stiff brn wrp. B20. $65.00

**ELLIOTT, Francis Perry.** *Haunted Pajamas.* 1911. Bobbs Merrill. 1st. G. W2. $20.00

**ELLIOTT, Franklin R.** *Elliott's Fruit Book; or, American Fruit Grower's Guide...* 1858. NY. Moore. ils/index. 503p. fair. H10. $65.00

**ELLIOTT, James.** *Cold Cold Heart.* 1994. Delacorte. 1st. F/F. H11. $25.00

**ELLIOTT, James.** *Transport to Disaster.* 1962. NY. 1st. VG/dj. B5. $20.00

**ELLIOTT, Lawrence.** *Daniel Boone: Long Hunter.* 1977. London. Allen Unwin. 1st. 242p. VG/dj. B18. $15.00

**ELLIOTT & HOBBS.** *Gasoline Automobile.* 1915. NY/London. 1st. 8vo. gr cloth. F. B14. $55.00

**ELLIS, A.F.** *Adventuring in the Coral Seas.* 1937. Sydney. 2nd. photos. 264p. VG. M12. $50.00

**ELLIS, Bret Easton.** *Less Than Zero.* 1985. S&S. 1st. author's 1st novel. F/dj. R14. $75.00

**ELLIS, Carleton.** *Chemistry of Synthetic Resins. Vol II.* 1935. Reinhold. tall 8vo. VG. H1. $16.00

**ELLIS, Constance Dimock.** *Magnificent Enterprise: A Chronicle of Vassar College.* 1961. Poughkeepsie. Vassar. 1st. ils. 138p. VG+. A25. $30.00

**ELLIS, Edward S.** *Dewey & Other Naval Commanders.* 1900. 1st. 15 muc pl. VG. E6. $25.00

**ELLIS, Edward S.** *Life & Times of Col Daniel Boone.* 1884. Porter Coats. Alta ed. 269+16p pub book list. decor brd. VG. B36. $35.00

**ELLIS, Edward S.** *Path in the Ravine.* 1895. Phil. Coates. 319p. G. G11. $15.00

**ELLIS, Edward S.** *Young Scout: Story of a West Point Lieutenant.* 1895. NY. 275p. pict cloth. E1. $40.00

**ELLIS, Frederick D.** *Tragedy of the Lusitania.* 1915. np. ils. 320p. VG. B18. $22.50

**ELLIS, George E.** *Oration Delivered at Charleston, MA on 17th of June, 1841.* 1841. Boston. Crosby. 1st. 8vo. 72p. prt wrp. O1. $65.00

**ELLIS, Havelock.** *Chapman.* 1934. Bloomsbury. Nonesuch. tall 8vo. 147p. Curwen bdg. F/worn case. F1. $150.00

**ELLIS, Havelock.** *Studies in Psychology of Sex.* 1928. Phil. FA Davis. 7 vol. various prt. brn cloth. G1. $150.00

**ELLIS, Jerry.** *Bareback! One Man's Journey Along Pony Express Trail.* 1993. Delacorte. 1st. F/dj. O3. $25.00

**ELLIS, Jerry.** *Walking the Trail: One Man's Journey Along Cherokee Trail.* 1991. Delacorte. 1st. VG/dj. N2. $10.00

**ELLIS, John B.** *Sights & Secrets of the National Capital.* 1869. US Pub Co. ils. 512p. VG. B10. $20.00

**ELLIS, John Tracy.** *Catholic Bishops: A Memoir.* 1983. Wilmington, DE. Michael Glazier. 1st. 182p. VG/dj. N2. $10.00

**ELLIS, Mel.** *Eagle to the Wind.* 1978. HRW. 1st. F/dj. P2. $12.50

**ELLIS, Norman.** *Instrumentation & Arranging for Radio & Dance Orchestra.* 1937. Schirmer. 193p. G. S5. $35.00

**ELLIS, SEEBOHM & SYKES.** *At Home With Books: How Booklovers Live With...Libraries.* 1995. NY. Carol Southern. 1st/later prt. 248p. F/dj. O10. $50.00

**ELLIS, William T.** *Billy Sunday: Man & His Message.* 1914. U Book/Bible House. Authorized ed. 8vo. 451p. dk bl cloth. VG. S17. $10.00

**ELLIS, William.** *Journal of William Ellis: Narrative of Tour of Hawaii...* 1963 (1825). rpt. ils/fld map. F. M4. $20.00

**ELLIS & KELLER.** *History of the German People.* 1916. 15 vol. 1/1500. leather. VG. A4. $95.00

**ELLISON, Douglas.** *David Lant: The Vanished Outlaw.* 1988. Aberdeen, SD. Midstates. sgn. F/dj. A19. $45.00

**ELLISON, Harlan.** *Again, Dangerous Visions.* nd. BC. VG/dj. S18. $8.00

**ELLISON, Harlan.** *Angry Candy.* 1988. Houghton Mifflin. 1st. F/dj. M25. $25.00

**ELLISON, Harlan.** *Deathbird Stories.* 1975. Harper. 1st. inscr. NF/F. S18. $55.00

**ELLISON, Harlan.** *Mefisto in Onyx.* 1993. Ziesing. 1/1000. sgn. ils/sgn Frank Miller. NF/case. M19. $60.00

**ELLISON, Harlan.** *Shatterday.* 1980. Houghton Mifflin. 1st. F/VG. M19. $45.00

**ELLISON, Harlan.** *Stalking the Nightmare.* 1982. Phantasia. 1st. 1/700. sgn. VG/case. L1. $175.00

**ELLISON, James Whitfield.** *Summer After the War.* 1972. Dodd Mead. 1st. F/price blocked. R11. $35.00

**ELLISON, Mary.** *Support for Secession: Lancashire & American Civil War.* 1972. Chicago. 259p. NF/dj. M10. $15.00

**ELLISON, Ralph.** *Shadow & Act.* 1964. Random. 1st. F/NF. B2. $200.00

**ELLISON, Rhoda Coleman.** *Check List of Alabama Imprints 1807-1870.* 1946. U AL. 1st. 151p. NF/stiff prt wrp. M8. $45.00

**ELLISON, Virginia H.** *Pooh Party Book.* 1971. Dutton. 1st. ils Shepard. cloth. F/dj. B27. $55.00

**ELLISON, Viriginia H.** *Pooh Cookbook.* nd (c1969). Dutton. ils EH Shepard. 120p. VG. C14. $14.00

**ELLISON & PRICE.** *Life & Adventures in CA of Don Agustin Janssens 1834-1856.* 1953. Huntington Lib. sgn Price. 165p. dj. P4. $30.00

**ELLROY, James.** *Big Nowhere.* 1988. Mysterious. 1st trade. F/dj. R14. $25.00

**ELLROY, James.** *Big Nowhere.* 1988. Mysterious. 1st. VG/dj. G8. $17.50

**ELLROY, James.** *Big Nowhere.* 1988. Ultramarine. 1st. 1/350. sgn. F/case. M15. $125.00

**ELLROY, James.** *My Dark Places.* 1996. Knopf. ARC/1st. sgn. NF/F. w/review material. B30. $50.00

**ELLROY, James.** *Suicide Hill.* 1986. Mysterious. 1st. inscr. F/dj. M15. $100.00

**ELLROY, James.** *White Jazz.* 1992. Knopf. 1st. NF/dj. G8. $25.00

**ELLROY, James.** *White Jazz.* 1992. Knopf. 1st. sgn. F/dj. R14. $45.00

**ELLSBERG, Edward.** *Hell on Ice: Saga of the Jeanette.* 1938. Dodd Mead. 1st. 8vo. 42p. bl cloth. G. P4. $30.00

**ELLSWORTH, J. Lewis.** *57th Annual Report Massachusetts State Board of Agriculture.* 1910. Boston. Wright. 357p+257p. VG. A10. $15.00

**ELLSWORTH, Lincoln.** *Beyond Horizons.* 1983. NY. BC. ils. 403p. VG/dj. B18. $45.00

**ELLSWORTH, Lyman R.** *Guys on Ice.* 1952. NY. McKay. later prt. 8vo. 277p. P4. $25.00

**ELLSWORTH, M.S.** *Mormon Odyssey: Story of Ida Hunt Udall, Plural Wife.* 1992. IL U. 1st. 296p. F/dj. M4. $20.00

**ELLWANGER, H.B.** *Rose: A Treatise on Cultivation, History, Family...* 1908 (1882). NY. revised. 310p. gilt bdg. B26. $30.00

**ELLWOOD, Thomas.** *History of Life of Thomas Ellwood...* 1855. Manchester. John Harrison. 6th. 12mo. 307p. G+. V3. $35.00

**ELMAN, Robert.** *Atlantic Flyway.* 1972. NY. 250 photos. 200 p. F/dj. A17. $35.00

**ELMORE, James Buchanan.** *Twenty-Five Years in Jackville.* 1904. Alamo, IN. self pub. ils. 215p. G. B18. $27.50

**ELMSLIE, Kenward.** *Girl Machine.* 1971. Angel Hair. 1st. 1/500. sgn. F/stapled wrp. L3. $45.00

**ELMSLIE, Kenward.** *I Trust the Wrong People.* 1966. NY. Chappell. 1st. inscr. NF. L3. $35.00

**ELON, AMOS.** *Timetable.* 1980. Doubleday. VG/dj. P3. $15.00

**ELOSEGI, Joseba.** *Quiero Morir por Algo.* 1977. Barcelona. Plaza Janes. 1st. VG/clip. N2. $10.00

**ELSHTAIN & TOBIAS.** *Women, Militarism & War.* 1990. Rowman Littlefield. 1st. F. R8. $15.00

**ELSON, Marilyn.** *Duffy on the Farm.* 1984. Golden. 1st A ed. folio. VG. M5. $12.00

**ELSON & GRAY.** *Elson-Gray Basic Readers, Book Three.* 1936. Scott Foresman. 2nd. 337p. xl. VG. B36. $35.00

**ELSTER, John.** *Local Justice in America.* 1995. NY. Russell Sage. 1st. VG/dj. N2. $12.50

**ELTING, John R.** *Amateurs, to Arms: Military History of War of 1812.* 1995. NY. Da Capo. 353p. VG. M10. $12.50

**ELTON, Ben.** *Popcorn.* 1996. London. S&S. 1st. F/dj. M15. $100.00

**ELVERSON, Virginia T.** *Cooking Legacy.* 1975. NY. Walker. G/dj. A16. $15.00

**ELY, David.** *Mr Nicholas.* 1974. Putnam. 1st. rem mk. F/NF. B2. $25.00

**ELY, Lawrence D.** *Space Science for the Layman.* 1967. Springfield, IL. Chas C Thomas. ils. 200p. dj. xl. K5. $20.00

**ELY, Scott.** *Starlight.* 1987. NY. Weidenfeld Nickolson. 1st. F/F. H11/R11. $30.00

**EMBERSON, F.G.** *Mark Twain's Vocabulary: A General Survey.* 1935. Columbia. U MO Studies. 1st. NF/prt wrp. M24. $100.00

**EMERICK, Richard G.** *Man of the Canyon: Old Indian Remembers His Life.* 1992. Northern Lights. 8vo. 170p. dj. F7. $22.50

**EMERSON, Alice B.** *Betty Gordon at Boarding School (#4).* 1921. Cupples Leon. lists 8 titles. VG/ragged edged dj. M20. $20.00

**EMERSON, Alice B.** *Ruth Fielding at Briarwood Hall.* 1913. NY. Cupples Leon. 1st. ils. 204p. VG+. A25. $20.00

**EMERSON, Dorothy.** *Among the Mescalero Apaches: Story of Father Albert Braum.* 1973. Tucson, AZ. ils. 224p. NF/NF. B19. $25.00

**EMERSON, Earl.** *Yellow Dog Party.* 1991. Morrow. 1st. F/F. H11/N4. $25.00

**EMERSON, Edwin Jr.** *History of the 19th Century: Year by Year, Vol I.* ca 1900. VG/sans. S18. $5.00

**EMERSON, Elizabeth H.** *Walter C Woodward: Friend on the Frontier, a Biography.* 1952. np. 12mo. 316p. xl. V3. $15.00

**EMERSON, Jill;** see Block, Lawrence.

**EMERSON, L.O.** *Golden Wreath: Choice Collection of Favorite Melodies...* 1956. Boston. Oliver Ditson. 240p. G. C5. $12.50

**EMERSON, Ralph Waldo.** *Essays of Ralph Waldo Emerson.* 1924. LEC. 1/1500. prt/sgn John Henry Nash. cloth. VG. F1. $65.00

**EMERSON, Ralph Waldo.** *Essays.* 1906. Hammersmith. Doves. 1/25 on vellum. sm 4to. 311p. F/case. H5. $4,000.00

**EMERSON, Ralph Waldo.** *Friendship.* 1939. Worcester. St Onge. mini. 1/950. aeg. Sangorski/Sutcliffe bl bdg (scarce). B24. $575.00

**EMERSON, Ralph Waldo.** *Method of Nature: Oration Delivered Before Soc of Adelphi.* 1841. Boston. Samuel Simpkins. 1st. 1/500. stitched (as issued). M24. $650.00

**EMERSON, Ralph Waldo.** *Napoleon.* ca 1920. Cincinnati/NY. Jennings Graham/Eaton Mains. 12mo. 45p. cloth. VG. W1. $10.00

**EMERSON, Ralph Waldo.** *Nature: Addresses & Lectures.* 1849. Boston/Cambridge. James Munroe. 1st/A bdg (no priority). gilt blk cloth. M24. $375.00

**EMERSON, Ralph Waldo.** *Representative Men.* 1850. Boston. Phillips Sampson. 1st/1st prt/1st bdg. gilt blk cloth. NF. M24. $400.00

**EMERSON, Ralph Waldo.** *Western Journey With Mr Emerson.* 1884. Little Brn. 1st. sm 4to. NF/dj. J3. $600.00

**EMERTON, Norma.** *Scientific Reinterpretation of Form.* 1984. Ithaca. 1st. 318p. A13. $25.00

**EMERY, R.G.** *High Inside.* 1948. MacRae Smith. later prt. VG/dj. P8. $65.00

**EMME, Eugene M.** *Aeronautics & Astronautics...* 1961. NASA. 8vo. 240p. gilt cloth. VG. K5. $25.00

**EMMETT, Chris.** *Texas Camel Tales.* 1932. San Antonio. Naylor. 1st. sgn. 8vo. 275p. VG/dj. w/pre-pub subscriber list. B11. $875.00

**EMPSON, William.** *Seven Types of Ambiguity.* 1930. London. 1st. dj. T9. $85.00

**EMRICH, Duncan.** *It's an Old Wild West Custom.* 1949. Vanguard. 1st. Am Customs series. NF/G. T11. $20.00

**ENDE, Michael.** *Never Ending Story.* 1983. Doubleday. 1st. ils. red/gr prt. VG/dj. B5. $50.00

**ENDORE, Guy.** *Werewolf in Paris.* 1933. Grosset Dunlap. G. L1. $50.00

**ENDRES, Ernest.** *Day With the Gnomes (Little Mother Stories).* ca 1910. London. Nister. 16mo. mc ils. cloth-backed brd. R5. $135.00

**ENG, Steve.** *Jimmy Buffett.* 1996. St Martin. 1st. F/dj. T11. $25.00

**ENGDAHL, Sylvia Louise.** *Planet-Girded Suns: Man's View of Other Solar Systems.* 1974. Atheneum. 1st. NF/VG. O4. $15.00

**ENGEBRETSON, Pat.** *History of Butte County, South Dakota, 1988.* 1989. Dallas, TX. Curtis Media. F. A19. $125.00

**ENGEL, Alan.** *Variant.* 1988. DIF. 1st. F/NF. M21. $15.00

**ENGEL, George.** *Fainting: Physiological & Psychological Considerations.* 1950. Springfield, IL. Chas Thomas. 1st. 141p. NF. C14. $18.00

**ENGEL, Marion.** *Bear.* 1976. Toronto. 1st Canadian. sgn. F/dj. T12. $90.00

**ENGELMAN & JOY.** *Two Hundred Years of Military Medicine.* 1975. Ft Detrick. 1st. 56p. wrp. A13. $15.00

**ENGER, L.L.** *Sinner's League.* 1994. Penzler (S&S). 1st. F/dj. P8. $15.00

**ENGERS, Joe.** *Great Book of Wildfowl Decoys.* 1990. Thunder Bay. folio. 300 photos. 320p. F/VG. A4. $55.00

**ENGLE, Paul.** *Golden Child.* 1962. Dutton. 1st. ils. cloth. VG. B27. $45.00

**ENGLE, William H.** *State of the Accounts of the County Lieutenants...1777-1789.* 1896. PA. CM Busch. 3 vol. teg. half leather/marbled brd. B18. $125.00

**ENGLEBERT, Omer.** *Last of the Conquistadors: Junipero Serra.* 1956. NY. Harcourt Brace. 1st. trans from French. VG. O4. $15.00

**ENGLISH, Barbara.** *War for a Persian Lady.* 1971. Houghton Mifflin. VG/dj. M20. $22.00

**ENGLISH, John.** *Kindergarten Soldier-Military Thought of Lawrence of Arabia.* 1985. Toronto. Royal Canadian Military Inst. yearbook. NF/wrp. M7. $22.50

**ENNIS, Michael.** *Duchess of Milan.* 1992. NY. Viking. 1st. NF/NF. H11. $15.00

**ENRIGHT, D.J.** *Ill at Ease: Writers on Ailments.* 1989. London. 365p. A13. $30.00

**ENROTH, Ronald.** *Churches That Abuse.* 1992. Zondervan. 231p. VG/dj. B29. $8.00

**ENSIGN, Georgianne.** *Great Beginnings: Opening Lines of Great Novels.* 1993. 256p. F/F. A4. $25.00

**ENSIGN, Georgianne.** *Great Endings: Closing Lines of Great Novels.* 1995. ils. 276p. F/F. A4. $25.00

**ENYEART, James L.** *Jerry N Uelsmann: Twenty-Five Years, a Retrospective.* 1982. NYGS. 1st. photos. VG/dj. M17. $50.00

**EPHRON, Nora.** *Scribble Scribble.* 1978. Knopf. 1st. NF/dj. A24. $25.00

**EPLING, Carl.** *Californian Salvias.* 1938. St Louis. ils. VG/wrp. B26. $42.50

**EPPLE, Anne Orth.** *Field Guide to Plants of Arizona.* 1995. Mesa. ils. 347p. sc. AN. B26. $25.00

**EPPS, John.** *Life of John Walker, MD.* 1832. London. Whittaker Treacher. 342p. quarter roan/marbled brd. G7. $135.00

**EPSTEIN, Daniel Mark.** *No Vacancies in Hell.* 1973. NY. Liveright. ARC/1st. inscr/dtd 1977. F/NF. L3. $40.00

**EPSTEIN, Daniel Mark.** *Young Men's Gold.* 1978. Woodstock. Overlook. 1st. inscr. F/dj. L3. $45.00

**EPSTEIN & VALENTINO.** *Those Lips, Those Eyes.* 1992. NY. Birch Lane. unp. VG/dj. C5. $15.00

**ERDOES, Richard.** *Picture History of Rome.* 1965. Macmillan. 1st. ils. 60p. cloth. F/torn. D4. $35.00

**ERDOES & ORTIZ.** *American Indian Myths & Legends.* 1984. Pantheon. NF/wrp. B9. $15.00

**ERDRICH, Louise.** *Antelope Wife.* 1998. Harper Flamingo. ARC/UP. F. B30. $25.00

**ERDRICH, Louise.** *Baptism of Desire.* 1989. Harper Row. 1st. sgn. F/F. D10. $50.00

**ERDRICH, Louise.** *Beet Queen.* 1986. NY. Holt. 1st. sgn. F/F. D10/R14. $50.00

**ERDRICH, Louise.** *Beet Queen.* 1986. NY. Holt. 1st. F/F. H11/M25. $25.00

**ERDRICH, Louise.** *Blue Jay's Dance.* 1995. Harper Collins. 1st. sgn. F/dj. R14. $40.00

**ERDRICH, Louise.** *Jacklight.* 1984. HRW. 1st. sgn. F/wrp. D10. $195.00

**ERDRICH, Louise.** *Love Medicine.* 1984. HRW. 1st. F/NF. D10. $125.00

**ERDRICH, Louise.** *Tales of Burning Love.* 1996. Harper Collins. ARC. F/wrp. R14. $40.00

**ERDRICH, Louise.** *Tracks.* 1988. Holt. 1st. 226p. F/NF. B19. $10.00

**ERDRICH, Louise.** *Tracks.* 1988. NY. Holt. ARC. sgn. F/F. D10. $50.00

**ERENS, Patricia.** *Films of Shirley MacLane.* 1978. NY. AS Barnes. 202p. VG/dj. D4. $35.00

**ERHARDT, Walter.** *Hemerocallis.* 1992. Portland. photos. 160p. AN/dj. B26. $30.00

**ERHLICH & ERHLICH.** *Population, Resources, Environment: Issues in Human Ecology.* 1970. WH Freeman. 1st. 383p. VG. S15. $10.00

**ERICKSON, Erik H.** *Gandhi's Truth: On the Origins of Militant Nonviolence.* 1969. Norton. 1st. VG/clip. N2. $10.00

**ERICKSON, Steve.** *Arc d'X.* 1993. Poseidon. 1st. sgn. F/dj. R14. $45.00

**ERICKSON, Steve.** *Days Between Stations.* 1985. Poseidon. 1st. sgn. rem mk. F/dj. R14. $75.00

**ERICSON, Eric E.** *Guide to Colored Steuben Glass 1903-1933. Book 2.* 1965. self pub. 1st. 10 pl. 162p. stiff wrp. H1. $28.00

**ERNSBERGER, George.** *Mountain King.* 1978. Morrow. 1st. F/F. H11. $45.00

**ERSHOFF, Peter.** *Little Magic Horse.* 1942. Macmillan. 1st thus. ils Vera Bock. VG/G. P2. $35.00

**ERSKINE, Jim.** *Bert & Susie's Messy Tale.* 1979. Crown. 1st. 24mo. unp. F/NF. C14. $14.00

**ERSKINE, John.** *Helen Retires: An Opera in Three Acts.* 1934. Bobbs Merrill. 1st. 8vo. 107p. VG/dj. B20. $40.00

**ERSKINE, John.** *Institute of Law of Scotland. A New Edition...* 1871. Edinburgh. 2 vol. maroon buckram. M11. $350.00

**ERSKINE, Margaret.** *Dead by Now.* 1953. Crime Club. 1st Am. VG/G. G8. $25.00

**ERSKINE, Payne.** *Harper & the King's Horse.* 1905. Chicago. Bl Sky Pr. 1/500. ils SK Smith. gilt maroon cloth. F1. $100.00

**ERVIN, Keith.** *Fragile Majesty.* 1989. Seattle. 272p. VG. S15. $7.50

**ESAREY, Logan.** *Indiana Home.* 1954. Bloomington. IU. 1/1550. ils Franklin Booth/Bruce Rogers. F/VG case. F1. $50.00

**ESBACH, Lloyd Arthur.** *Tyrant of Time.* 1955. Fantasy. 1st. Donald Grant bdg. F/dj. P3. $20.00

**ESCOFFIER, A.** *Escoffier Cook Book.* 1941. Crown. BC. G/dj. A16. $12.00

**ESCOFFIER, A.** *Kochkunst Fuhrer: Le Guide Culinaire, Deutsche...* 1904. Frankfurt. 806p. emb leather. VG. E6. $225.00

**ESCOFFIER, A.** *L'Aire-Memoire Culinaire.* 1919. Paris. 360p. G+. E6. $50.00

**ESDAILE, Arundell.** *Autolycus' Pack & Other Light Wares...* 1940. London. Grafton. 1st. H13. $65.00

**ESHBACH, Lloyd Arthur.** *Over My Shoulder: Reflections on a Science Fiction Era.* 1983. Oswald Train. 1st. sgn. NF/dj. P3. $30.00

**ESIN, Emel.** *Mecca the Blessed: Madinah the Radiant.* 1963. NY. Crown. 1st. 4to. 222p. VG. W1. $50.00

**ESKELUNG, Karl.** *Vagabond Fever: A Gay Journey in Land of Andes.* 1954. Chicago. Rand McNally. 1st. 240p. dj. F3. $15.00

**ESKENAZI, Gerald.** *Lip.* 1993. Morrow. 1st. F/VG+. P8. $20.00

**ESPY, Hilda.** *Another World: Central America.* 1970. Viking. 1st. 311p. dj. F3. $15.00

**ESQUIVEL, Laura.** *Like Water for Chocolate.* 1992. Doubleday. 1st Am. F/dj. O11. $65.00

**ESSOE & LEE.** *Cecil B DeMille: Man & His Pictures.* 1970. NY. Castle. rpt. ils. VG/dj. C9. $25.00

**ESTERGREEN, M. Morgan.** *Kit Carson: Portrait in Courage.* 1962. OK U. 1st. ils. 320p. D11. $50.00

**ESTLEMAN, Loren D.** *City of Widows.* 1991. NY. Forge. 1st. F/dj. A23. $32.00

**ESTLEMAN, Loren D.** *Kill Zone.* 1984. Mysterious. 1st. F/NF. M23. $30.00

**ESTLEMAN, Loren D.** *Lady Yesterday.* 1987. Houghton Mifflin. 1st. F/F. B3. $25.00

**ESZTERHAS, Joe.** *Nark!* 1974. Straight Arrow. 1st. NF/VG. M19. $25.00

**ESZTERHAS & ROBERTS.** *Thirteen Seconds: Confrontation at Kent State.* 1970. Dodd Mead. sgns. 308p. VG/dj. B18. $27.50

**ETCHECOPAR & HUE.** *Birds of North Africa From Canary Islands to Red Sea.* 1967. Edinburgh. 1st Eng-language. ils/24 mc pl. 612p. cloth. NF/dj. C12. $85.00

**ETCHISON, Dennis.** *California Gothic.* 1995. Dreamhaven. 1st ltd. 1/750. sgn. ils JK Potter. AN/dj. S18. $39.00

**ETCHISON, Dennis.** *Cutting Edge.* 1986. Doubleday. 1st. F/NF. S18. $25.00

**ETCHISON, Dennis.** *Shadow Man.* 1993. Dell. 1st. sgn. F/dj. S18. $30.00

**ETHERIDGE, Kenneth.** *Viola, Furgy, Bobbi & Me.* 1989. Holiday House. 1st. F/VG. P8. $12.50

**ETS, Marie Hall.** *Mister Penny.* 1935. Viking. 1st. obl 12mo. 48p. VG. D1. $150.00

**ETTENBERG, Eugene M.** *Type for Books & Advertising.* 1947. Van Nostrand. 1st. 4to. 160p. cloth. F/NF. O10. $35.00

**ETTINGER, Markus.** *Psychologie und Ethik des Antisemitismus im Altherthum...* 1891. Wien. Gottlieb's Buchhandlung. 29p. prt yel wrp. G1. $125.00

**ETTLESON, Abraham.** *Lewis Carroll's Through the Looking Glass Decoded.* 1966. NY. Philosophical Lib. 84p. F/VG. A4. $125.00

**EUBANK, H. Ragland.** *Authentic Guide Book of Historic Northern Neck of Virginia.* 1934. Whittet Shepperson. ils/map. 108p. G+. B10. $25.00

**EUBANK, Keith.** *Summit at Teheran: Untold Story.* 1985. Morrow. 1st. sm 4to. 528p. NF/F. W2. $45.00

**EUGENIDES, Jeffrey.** *Virgin Suicides.* 1993. NY. FSG. 1st. author's 1st book. F/F. H11. $50.00

**EULER, Robert C.** *Southern Paiute Ethnohistory.* 1966. Glen Canyon series 28. 8vo. 139p. stiff brn wrp. F7. $30.00

**EUNSON, Robert.** *Pearl King: Story of Fabulous Mikimoto.* 1955. NY. Greenberg. 1st. 8vo. 243p. VG+/dj. B20. $20.00

**EURIPEDES.** *Alcestis.* 1930. London. 1/260. trans/sgn Aldington. T9. $45.00

**EVAN, Joe.** *Biographical Dictionary of Rocky Mountain Naturalists.* 1981. Utrecht. 253p. cloth. AN. A10. $50.00

**EVANOFF, Vlad.** *Hunting Secrets of the Experts.* 1964. NY. photos. 251p. F/dj. A17. $12.50

**EVANOVICH, Janet.** *One for the Money.* 1994. Scribner. 1st. sgn. F/dj. M15. $100.00

**EVANS, Alwen.** *Short Illustrated Guide to the Anophelines...* 1927. London. Liverpool School Tropical Medicine #3. 79p. VG. S15. $5.00

**EVANS, E.P.** *Criminal Prosecution & Capital Punishment of Animals.* 1906. London. Heinemann. later cloth. VG. M11. $250.00

**EVANS, Edna.** *Tales From the Grand Canyon, Some True, Some Tall.* 1985. Northland. stiff pict wrp. F7. $13.00

**EVANS, Eli N.** *Judah P Benjamin: Jewish Confederate.* 1988. Free/Macmillan. 1st. NF/dj. A14. $28.00

**EVANS, Eli N.** *Provincials: Personal History of Jew in the South.* 1973. Atheneum. 2nd. 369p. VG/G. B10. $35.00

**EVANS, Emory G.** *Thomas Nelson & the Revolution in Virginia.* (1978). Bicentennial Comm. 57p. wrp. B10. $15.00

**EVANS, Henry.** *Botanical Prints.* 1977. SF. ils/pl/linocuts. VG/tattered. B26. $32.50

**EVANS, J. Warren.** *Horse.* 1977. WH Freeman. 1st. tall 8vo. 766p. F. H1. $12.00

**EVANS, Joan.** *Flowering of the Middle Ages.* 1966. McGraw Hill. 1st. ils/index. VG/dj. B5. $37.50

**EVANS, Lawton B.** *Trail Blazers: Pioneers of the Northwest.* 1925. Springfield. Milton Bradley. 1st. NF/VG. T11. $35.00

**EVANS, Richard.** *McEnroe: Rage for Perfection.* 1982. S&S. 1st. photos. 192p. NF/VG. S14. $8.00

**EVANS, Thomas.** *Old Ballads. Historical & Narrative...* 1784. London. T Evans. 1st collected. 4 vol. sm 8vo. full tree calf. H13. $495.00

**EVANS, Walker.** *Walker Evans at Work.* 1982. Harper Row. 1st. 745p. NF/dj. S9. $125.00

**EVANS, Walker.** *Walker Evans.* 1971. MOMA. 1st. 192p. NF/VG+. T11. $40.00

**EVANS, Walker.** *Walker Evans.* 1971. NY. MOMA. sq 4to. ils. 189p. VG/dj. F1. $25.00

**EVANS, William Bacon.** *Jonathan Evans & His Time 1759-1839...* 1959. Boston. Christopher. 1st. 192p. VG. V3. $25.00

**EVANS & EVANS.** *Piety Promoted in Collection of Dying Sayings...Quakers...* 1854. Phil. Friends Book Store. new/completed ed. 4 vol. leather. V3. $125.00

**EVELYN, John.** *Memoirs for My Grand-Son.* 1926. Bloomsbury. Nonesuch. 1st thus. 1/1250. emb limp vellum. F/tissue dj/box. M24. $85.00

**EVENSON, Brian.** *Altmann's Tongue.* 1994. Knopf. AP. author's 1st book. NF/prt wrp. S9. $25.00

**EVEREST, Allan S.** *Rum Across the Border: Prohibition Era in Northern NY.* 1976. Syracuse. 1st. photos. VG/dj. M17. $15.00

**EVERETT, David.** *Common Sense in Dishabile; or, Farmer's Monitor.* 1799. Worcester, MA. Thomas. 1st in book form. 12mo. 120p. later leather. O1. $200.00

**EVERETT, Edward.** *Eulogy on Life & Character of John Quincy Adams...* 1848. Boston. Dutton Wentworth. 8vo. inscr. 71p. VG/bl wrp. B14. $750.00

**EVERETT, Edward.** *Life of George Washington.* 1860. Sheldon. 348p. VG. B10. $35.00

**EVERETT, M.** *Natural History of Owls.* 1977. London. photos. 156p. F/VG. M12. $20.00

**EVERETT, Percival.** *Suder.* 1983. Viking. 1st. F/VG. P8. $25.00

**EVERETT, Percival.** *Walk Me to the Distance.* 1985. Ticknor Fields. 1st. sgn. F/dj. R11. $50.00

**EVERETT, Percival.** *Zulus.* 1990. Sag Harbor. Permanent. 1st. F/dj. R14. $40.00

**EVERETT, William.** *Double Play.* 1874 (1870). Lee Shepard. VG. P8. $225.00

**EVERS, Crabbe.** *Duffy House: Fear in Fenway (#4).* 1993. Morrow. 1st. sgn. F/dj. P8. $75.00

**EVERS, Crabbe.** *Duffy House: Fear in Fenway (#4).* 1993. NY. Morrow. 1st. F/F. H11. $20.00

**EVERS, Crabbe.** *Duffy House: Tigers Burning (#5).* 1994. Morrow. 1st. F/dj. P8. $15.00

**EVERSON, David.** *Suicide Squeeze.* 1991. St Martin. 1st. F/dj. P8. $12.50

**EVERSON, William.** *Hollywood Bedlam.* 1994. NY. Carol. 253p. VG/wrp. C5. $12.50

**EVERSON, William.** *Man Who Writes.* 1980. Northridge, CA. Shadows. 1st. 1/26. sgn. gr cloth/morocco. AN/case. B24. $750.00

**EVERSON, William.** *Masks of Drought.* 1980. Blk Sparrow. 1/500. 92p. F. F1. $45.00

**EVERSON, William.** *Novum Psalterium Pii XII.* 1955. LA. Everson. 1/20 (48 total). maroon gilt cloth. w/ephemera. F/case. B24. $5,000.00

**EVERSON, William.** *Residual Years.* 1948. New Directions. 1st/expanded. VG/G. L3. $65.00

**EVERSON, William.** *Single Source.* 1966. Berkeley. Oyez. 1/1000. F/NF. w/prospectus. L3. $75.00

**EWAN, Joseph.** *Synopsis of the North American Species of Delphinium.* 1945. Boulder. ils/photos. 190p. B26. $50.00

**EWEING, Juliana Horatia.** *Mary's Meadow & Other Tales of Fields & Flowers.* 1915. London. ils MV Wheelhouse. VG. M17. $25.00

**EWEING, Juliana Horatia.** *Story of a Short Life.* ca 1910. Little Brn. sm 8vo. 130p+ads. pict cloth. NF. B20. $25.00

**EWELL, Alice Maude.** *Virginia Scene; or, Life in Old Prince.* (1931). JP Bell. ils. 228p. VG. B10. $65.00

**EWELL & HUNT.** *Sharpening the Combat Edge: Use of Analysis...* 1974. WA. Dept of Army. 1st. 8vo. ils/charts/tables/appendix. F. R11. $25.00

**EWERS, John C.** *Artists of the Old West.* 1965. Garden City. 1st. ils. 240p. E1. $75.00

**EWING & EWING.** *Ewing Genealogy With Cognate Branches.* (1919). np. 185p. G. S5. $75.00

**EXLEY, Frederick.** *Fan's Notes.* 1968. Harper. 1st. NF/dj. B4. $275.00

**EXMAN, Eugene.** *House of Harper, One Hundred Fifty Years of Publishing.* 1967. Harper Row. 1st. 8vo. 236p. F/dj. O1. $25.00

**EXNER, Friedrich.** *Die Psychologie der Hegelschen Schule.* 1842 & 1844. Friedrich Fleischer. 2 vol in 1. German text. G. G1. $175.00

**EXPILLY, Claude.** *Histoire Dv Chevalier Bayard.* 1650. Grenoble. Nicolas. 8vo. calf. R12. $475.00

**EYLER, John.** *Victorian Social Medicine: Ideas & Methods of Wm Farr.* 1979. Baltimore. 1st. 262p. dj. A13. $30.00

**EYLES, Allen.** *Cary Grant Film Album.* 1971. London. Ian Allen. 1st. VG/sans. C9. $30.00

**EYLES, Allen.** *James Stewart.* 1984. Stein Day. 1st. sm 4to. 264p. NF/dj. W2. $30.00

**EYLES, Desmond.** *Doulton Lambeth Wares.* 1975. London. Hutchinson. 1st. 4to. 179p. gilt bl cloth. VG/dj. H1. $125.00

**EYLIE, Francis E.** *Tides & Pull of the Moon.* 1979. Brattleboro. ils. VG/dj. M17. $15.00

**EYSENCK, Hans Jurgen.** *Encyclopedia of Psychology.* 1972. Herder. 3 vol. 1st Am. 8vo. gray cloth. G1. $125.00

**EZELL, John S.** *New Democracy in America: Travels of Francisco deMiranda...* 1963. Norman, OK. 1st. trans JP Wood. 217p. NF/VG. B20. $20.00

**FAAS & HUGHES.** *Ted Hughes: Unaccommodated Universe...* 1980. Blk Sparrow. ltd trade. 1/750. sgns. 8vo. 225p. taupe brd/quarter cloth. F/wrp. H4. $50.00

**FABER, Doris.** *Life of Lorena Hickok...* 1980. Morrow. 1st. ils. 384p. VG/dj. S14. $15.00

**FABER, Petrus.** *Agnosticon... Sive de re Athletica Ludisque...* 1595. Lyon. Thos Soubron. 4to. 684p. old sheep/rb. K1. $750.00

**FABER DU FAUR.** *German Baroque Literature, a Catalogue...* nd. rpt. 2 vol in 1. ils/2375 entries. 741p. F. A4. $95.00

**FABIAN, Stephen.** *Fantasy by Fabian.* 1978. de la Ree. 1st. NF/dj. P3. $60.00

**FABRE, D.G.** *Beyond the River of the Dead.* 1963. London. Travel BC. 191p. F3. $15.00

**FABRE, J.H.** *Heavens.* ca 1925. Lippincott. trans EE Fournier D'Albe. 336p. K5. $30.00

**FABRE, J.H.** *Life of the Spider.* 1916 (1912). Dodd Mead. VG. M20. $25.00

**FABYAN, Robert.** *New Chronicles of England & France.* 1811. London. Rivington. edit Henry Ellis. 723p. 3-quarter dk gr morocco. F1. $275.00

**FAGAN, Brian M.** *Great Journey: Peopling of Ancient America.* 1987. London. Thames Hudson. ils. 288p. NF/dj. M10. $22.50

**FAGAN, Brian M.** *Journey From Eden: Peopling of Our World.* 1990. London. ils/photos. VG/dj. M17. $12.50

**FAGAN, Brian M.** *Kingdom of Gold, Kingdom of Jade.* 1991. NY. Thames Hudson. 1st. 240p. dj. F3. $25.00

**FAGET, Max.** *Manned Space Flight.* 1965. HRW. 8vo. ils. 176p. VG/wrp. K5. $20.00

**FAIR, A.A.; see Gardner, Erle Stanley.**

**FAIR, Jeff.** *Great American Bear.* 1990. Minocqua. photos Lynn Rogers. 192p. F/dj. A17. $20.00

**FAIRBAIRN, A.M.** *Place of Christ in Modern Theology.* 1893. NY. Scribner. 556p. G. H10. $17.50

**FAIRBAIRNS, Zoe.** *Stand We at Last.* 1983. Houghton Mifflin. 1st. VG/dj. M20. $15.00

**FAIRCHILD, David.** *World Was My Garden: Travels of a Plant Explorer.* 1938. Scribner. 8vo. 497p. VG. H4. $40.00

**FAIRCHILD, Lee M.** *Complete Book of the Gladiolus.* 1953. NY. ils/drawings. VG/dj. B26. $16.00

**FAIRCHILD, T.B.** *History of Town of Cuyahoga Falls, Summit Co, OH.* 1876. Cleveland. 1st. stiff wrp/case. B18. $95.00

**FAIRCHILD, William.** *Catsigns.* 1981. NY. Clarkson Potter. 1st Am. 96p. F/dj. D4. $25.00

**FAIRCHILD & HAYWARD.** *Now That You Know: What Every Parent Should Know...* 1979. HBJ. 1st. 227p. VG/dj. A25. $15.00

**FAIRFAX, John.** *Zuihitsu: Poetic Journal.* 1996. Francestown. Typographeum. 1/100. dj. T9. $30.00

**FAIRFAX-BLAKEBOROUGH, J.** *Analysis of Turf; or, Duties & Difficulties Racing...* 1927. Lonon. Philip Allan. 8vo. 321p. 3-quarter leather/stained cloth sides. H4. $35.00

**FAIRLESS, Michael.** *Roadmender.* 1902. Duckworth. New ed. ils EW Waite. 121p. gilt gr cloth. NF. B20. $30.00

**FAIRLIE, Gerard.** *Bulldog Drummond Attacks.* 1939. London. Hodder Stoughton. 1st. NF/dj. M15. $400.00

**FAITH, Nicholas.** *Winemasters: Story Behind the Glory & Scandal of Bordeaux.* 1978. NY. 1st. ils. VG/dj. M17. $20.00

**FALCONER, Elizabeth.** *Owl & the Pussycat.* 1993. Ideals. 1st. 4to. popups. F. B17. $10.00

**FALCONER, Thomas.** *Letters & Notes on the Texan Santa Fe Expedition, 1841-42.* 1930. Dauber & Pine Bookshops. 159p. D11. $75.00

**FALES, William E.S.** *Brooklyn's Guardians: A Record of the Faithful...* 1887. Brooklyn. self pub. 1st. thick 8vo. 517p. gilt blk morocco. VG+. B20. $175.00

**FALK, Peter H.** *Print Price Index '93 (1991-1992 Auction Season).* 1992. Sound View. thick 4to. 1470p. F. A4. $95.00

**FALL, Bernard.** *Street Without Joy.* 1961. Stackpole. 1st/2nd prt. VG. R11. $75.00

**FALL, Ralph Emmett.** *Historical Record of Bowling Green.* 1970. Tidewater Weeklies. photos/map. 94p. VG. B10. $25.00

**FALLACI, Oriana.** *Limelighters.* 1967. Michael Joseph. 1st. VG/dj. C9. $30.00

**FALLIS, Gregory S.** *Lightning in the Blood.* 1993. St Martin. 1st. F/F. H11. $25.00

**FALLOWELL, Duncan.** *One Hot Summer in St Petersburg.* 1994. London. Cape. 1st. NF/dj. A14. $35.00

**FALLOWS & KNIGHTTON.** *Companion to Medieval & Renaissance Music.* 1992. NY. 1st. dj. T9. $20.00

**FALLS, DeWitt Clinton.** *History 7th Regiment 1889-1922.* 1948. VG. w/ephmera. E6. $50.00

**FALLWELL, Marshall Jr.** *Allen Tate: A Bibliography.* 1969. NY. Davis Lewis. F/NF. H4. $25.00

**FALS-BORDA, Orlando.** *Peasant Society in the Colombian Andes.* 1962. Gainesville. 1st. indix/biblio/glossary. 277p. dj. F3. $15.00

**FAMILY CIRCLE.** *Family Circle Cookbook.* 1992. S&S. VG. A16. $10.00

**FAMILY CIRCLE.** *Family Circle Favorite Recipes Cookbook.* 1977. IL. Paramount. G/dj. A16. $8.00

**FANE, Julian.** *Cautionary Tales for Women.* 1988. London. Hamish Hamilton. 1st. F/dj. A14. $28.00

**FANNES, C.** *Birds of the St Croix River Valley: Minnesota & Wisconsin.* 1981. N Am Fauna #73. 8vo. ils. 196p. F/wrp. C12. $30.00

**FANNING, Edmund.** *Voyages to the South Seas, Indian & Pacific Oceans...* 1970 (1938). Gregg. rpt. 8vo. 324p. beige cloth. P4. $32.50

**FANNING, J.T.** *Practical Treatise on Water-Suppy Engineering...* 1877. 1st. 619p. A13. $100.00

**FANNING, Louis A.** *Betrayal in Vietnam.* 1976. New Rochelle. Arlington. 1st. ils/map. VG/dj. R11. $15.00

**FANNING, Pete.** *Great Crimes of the West.* 1929. SF. self pub. 1st. 292p. gr cloth. NF. B20. $65.00

**FANTA, John.** *Full Life.* 1952. Boston. Little Brn. 1st. pres/assn copy/dtd 1956. VG/VG+. S9. $1,500.00

**FARAGHER, J.M.** *Daniel Boone: Life & Legend of American Pioneer.* 1992. NY. 1st. ils. 429p. F/dj. M4. $30.00

**FARB, Peter.** *Face of North America: Natural History of a Continent.* 1963. NY. 316p. F/dj. A17. $10.00

**FARBER, Laurence.** *Doctors' Legacy: Selection of Physicians' Letters 1721-1954.* 1955. NY. 1st. 267p. A13. $40.00

**FARBER, Norma.** *How the Hibernators Came to Bethlehem.* 1980. NY. Walker. 1st thus. sgn pres. bl cloth. mc dj. R5. $60.00

**FARBER, Norma.** *Up the Down Elevator.* nd (c 1979). Reading, MA. Addison-Wesley. 1st. 12mo. unp. F/VG. C14. $12.00

**FARHI, Moris.** *Last of Days, a Novel.* 1983. NY. Crown. 1st. 8vo. map ep. 538p. VG/dj. W1. $18.00

**FARIS, John T.** *Seeing the Middle West.* 1923. Lippincott. 1st. 254p. teg. brn cloth. F. B20. $50.00

**FARIS, John T.** *Seeing the Sunny South.* 1921. Lippincott. 8vo. 320p. VG+. H4. $15.00

**FARJEON, Eleanor.** *Children's Bells.* 1960. Walck. 1st Am. ils Peggy Fortnum. VG/dj. P2. $35.00

**FARJEON, Eleanor.** *Eleanor Farjeon's Poems for Children.* 1951 (1926). Lippincott. 4th. 8vo. 236p. bl cloth. G/tattered. T5. $25.00

**FARJEON, Eleanor.** *One Foot in Fairyland.* 1938. Stokes. 1st. ils Robert Lawson. 8vo. dk bl cloth. dj. R5. $175.00

**FARLEY, Carol.** *Loosen Your Ears.* 1977. NY. Atheneum. 1st. 214p. F/dj. D4. $25.00

**FARLEY, James A.** *Behind the Ballots: Personal History of a Politician.* 1938. Harcourt Brace. 2nd. 8vo. VG+. A2. $12.50

**FARLEY, James A.** *Jim Farley's Story: The Roosevelt Years.* 1948. McGraw Hill. 2nd. inscr/dtd pres. NF. H4. $11.00

**FARLEY, Joseph Pearson.** *West Point in the Early Sixties With Incidents of the War.* 1902. Troy, NY. Pafraets. 1st. inscr/sgn. 201p. VG. S16. $85.00

**FARLEY, Walter.** *Black Stallion Returns.* 1945. Random. 9th. VG/dj. A21. $40.00

**FARLEY, Walter.** *Black Stallion's Filly.* 1952. Random. 1st. NF/dj. A21. $65.00

**FARLEY, Walter.** *Black Stallion's Legend.* 1983. Random. 1st. VG/dj. A21. $35.00

**FARLEY, Walter.** *Black Stallion.* 1941. Random. 18th prt. VG/dj. A21. $45.00

**FARLEY, Walter.** *Island Stallion.* nd. Random. 13th prt. ils Keith Ward. cream brd. VG. B36. $10.00

**FARLIE, Gerard.** *Deadline for Macall.* 1956. Mill. 1st Am. G+/dj. G8. $25.00

**FARM JOURNAL.** *Farm Journal's Freezing & Canning Cookbook.* 1963. Doubleday. G/dj. A16. $6.00

**FARMER, Bernard J.** *Gentle Art of Book Collecting.* 1950. Thorsons. 1st. VG/G. P3. $25.00

**FARMER, Fannie Merritt.** *Book of Good Dinners.* 1914 (1905). Dodge. lg 8vo. 259p. F/wrp. E6. $35.00

**FARMER, Frances.** *Will There Really Be a Tomorrow?* 1972. NY. 1st. VG/dj. B5. $25.00

**FARMER, John David.** *Ensor.* 1976. Braziller. 50 mc pl. 48p. VG/stiff wrp. D2. $35.00

**FARMER, Philip Jose.** *Grand Adventure.* 1984. Berkley. 1/325. sgn. gilt maroon cloth. F/sans dj/case. A24. $85.00

**FARMER, Philip Jose.** *Magic Labyrinth.* 1980. Berkley Putnam. 1st. F/dj. P3. $35.00

**FARMER, William C.** *Ordnance Field Guide: Restricted.* 1945. Military Service Pub. 3 vol. 1st. G. S16. $150.00

**FARNAM, Henry W.** *Chapters in History of Social Legislation in US to 1860.* 1938. Carnegie Inst of WA. edit Clive Day. M11. $75.00

**FARNHAM, Albert B.** *Home Tanning & Leather Making Guide.* 1922. Columbus, OH. 178p. VG. H6. $30.00

**FARNHAM, Mateel Howe.** *Rebellion.* 1927. NY. Dodd. 1st. F/VG+. B4. $100.00

**FARNOL, Jeffrey.** *Broad Highway.* 1912. Little Brn. ils CE Brock. VG. M19. $25.00

**FARNOL, Jeffrey.** *Money Moon.* 1911. Dodd Mead. ils Arthur Keller. NF. M19. $35.00

**FAROVA, Anna.** *Sudek.* 1995. Prague. Torst. 1st. folio. Czech text. photos. F/dj/cb case. S9. $350.00

**FARQUHAR, Francis P.** *Books of the Colorado River & the Grand Canyon...* 1953. Dawson. 1st. sm 8vo. red cloth/paper label. VG+. F7. $27.50

**FARQUHAR, J.B.** *Farquhar's Official Directory of Bedford County, PA.* 1879. Bedford, PA. 116p. quarter cloth. B18. $25.00

**FARR, Finis.** *Margaret Mitchell of Atlanta.* 1965. Morrow. 1st. tall 8vo. 244p. xl. G. H1. $15.00

**FARRAR, Emmie Ferguson.** *Old Virginia Houses: Mobiack Bay Country.* 1955. Hastings. sgn. photos. 189p. F/F. B10. $45.00

**FARRAR, F.A.** *Old Greek Nature Stories.* 1910. London. Harrap. 256p. NF. B20. $85.00

**FARRAR, S.D.** *Housekeeper, With Recipes for Cooking & Preparing Food...* 1872. 1st. 288p. G+. E6. $45.00

**FARRAR & HINES.** *Old Virginia Houses: The Mountain Empire.* (1978). Delmar. photos. 189p. F/F. B10. $65.00

**FARRELL, Gillian B.** *Alibi for an Actress.* 1992. NY. Pocket. 1st. author's 1st book. F/F. H11. $25.00

**FARRELL, James Gordon.** *Singapore Grip.* 1979. Knopf. 1st Am. sm 4to. 432p. NF/VG. W2. $30.00

**FARRELL, James T.** *Bernard Clare.* 1946. Vanguard. 1st. NF/dj. S13. $15.00

**FARRELL, James T.** *Fate of Writing in America.* 1946. New Directions. 1st. F/orange prt wrp. M24. $35.00

**FARRELL, James T.** *My Baseball Diary.* 1957. Barnes. 1st. VG/G. P8. $40.00

**FARRELL, James T.** *Olive & Mary Anne.* 1977. Stonehill. 1st. F/dj. M19. $17.50

**FARRELLY, David.** *Book of Bamboo.* 1984. SF. ils. 340p. VG/dj. B26. $45.00

**FARRER, Reginald.** *My Rock-Garden.* 1911. London. Arnold. 4th. 8vo. ils. 303p. gray-gr cloth. B20. $45.00

**FARRINGTON, E.I.** *Ernest H Wilson, Plant Hunter. With List...* 1931. Boston. 1st. 34 pl. 197p. NF/VG. C12. $50.00

**FARRINGTON, S. Kip.** *Atlantic Game Fishing.* 1937. NY. 1st. intro Hemingway. ils/pl. gilt blk cloth. VG. H3. $90.00

**FARRIS, John.** *Fiends.* 1990. Dark Harvest. 1/500. ils/sgn Phil Parks. AN/box. T12. $75.00

**FARRIS, John.** *Fury.* 1993. Severn House. 1st hc/Eng. F/dj. L4. $30.00

**FARRIS, John.** *King Windom.* 1967. Trident. 1st. author's 3rd book. F/dj. M25. $60.00

**FARRIS, John.** *Scare Tactics.* 1988. NY. Tor. 1st. VG/dj. P3. $18.00

**FARRIS, John.** *Scare Tactics.* 1988. Tor. 1st. AN/dj. S18. $30.00

**FARRIS, John.** *Son of the Endless Night.* 1985. BC. NF/VG. S18. $4.00

**FARRIS, John.** *Uninvited.* 1985. nd. BC. NF/dj. S18. $7.00

**FARROW, John.** *Story of Thomas More.* 1954. NY. ils. VG/dj. M17. $17.50

**FARROW, W. Milton.** *How I Became a Crack Shot: With Hints to Beginners.* 1980. Prescott, AZ. Wolf. facs of 1882. 204p. leatherette. F. A17. $10.00

**FARSHLER, Earl R.** *Riding & Training.* 1959. Van Nostrand. 2nd. VG/dj. M20. $17.00

**FARSON, Daniel.** *Man Who Wrote Dracula.* 1975. London. Michael Joseph. 1st Eng. VG/dj. L1. $125.00

**FARSON, Robert H.** *Cape Cod Railroads: Including Martha's Vineyard & Nantucket.* 1993. Yarmouth Port, MA. ils. VG/dj. M17. $40.00

**FARWELL, Byron.** *Great Anglo-Boer War.* 1976. Harper Row. 1st. 494p. biblio/index. VG/dj. S16. $20.00

**FASCO, Rudolph.** *In Quest of the Zohar.* 1990. Little Great Whale. 255p. F/dj. D4. $25.00

**FAST, Howard.** *Moses, Prince of Egypt.* 1958. Crown. ne. 303p. VG. W2. $40.00

**FAST, Howard.** *Sylvia.* 1992. Birch Lane. 1st thus. F/VG. P3. $20.00

**FAST, Irene.** *Gender Identity: A Differentiation Model.* 1984. Hillsdale, NJ. Lawrence Erlbaum. 1st. 189p. F. C14. $15.00

**FAST, Julius.** *Model for Murder.* 1956. NY. Rinehart. 1st. F/dj. M15. $45.00

**FASTLICHT, Samuel.** *Bibliografia Odontologica Mexicana.* 1954. La Presa Medica Mexicana. pres. half sheep/linen brd/paper wrp bdg-in. F. G7. $295.00

**FAULK, Andre.** *Visa Pour l'Arabie.* 1958. Paris. Gallimard. 3rd. 257p. VG. M7. $55.00

**FAULK, John Henry.** *Uncensored John Henry Faulk.* 1985. TX Monthly. 1st. sm 4to. 164p. NF/F. W2. $25.00

**FAULK, Odie B.** *Crimson Desert: Indian Wars of the American Southwest.* 1974. Oxford. 1st. ils/index. 237p. VG/G. B19. $20.00

**FAULK, Odie B.** *Destiny Road. Gila Trail & Opening of the Southwest.* 1973. Oxford. 8vo. 232p. brn cloth. VG/dj. F7/M20. $30.00

**FAULK, Odie B.** *Geronimo Campaign.* 1969. Oxford. 1st. F/NF. B9. $35.00

**FAULK, Odie B.** *Land of Many Frontiers: History of American Southwest.* 1968. Oxford. 1st. 8vo. 358p. dj. F7. $35.00

**FAULK, Odie B.** *Making of a Great Merchant: Raymond A Young & TG&Y Stores.* 1980. OK City. OK Heritage Assn/Western Heritage. 284p. AN. dj. H6. $42.00

**FAULKNER, Georgene.** *Christmas Stories.* 1916. Chicago. Daughaday. 1st. ils Frederic Richardson. dk gr cloth. dj. R5. $275.00

**FAULKNER, Nancy.** *Great Reckoning.* 1970. Dutton. 216p. F/dj. D4. $25.00

**FAULKNER, Robert Kenneth.** *Jurisprudence of John Marshall.* 1968. Princeton. VG/dj. M11. $75.00

**FAULKNER, William.** *As I Lay Dying.* 1967. Modern Lib. 1st thus. F/VG. B3. $20.00

**FAULKNER, William.** *Big Woods.* 1955. NY. 1st. F. B5. $70.00

**FAULKNER, William.** *Collected Stories of...* 1943. Random. BC. gray cloth. VG. H4. $10.00

**FAULKNER, William.** *Collected Stories of...* 1950. Random. 1st issue (The on spine). NF/dj. B4. $300.00

**FAULKNER, William.** *Country Lawyer & Other Stories for the Screen.* 1987. U MS. 1st. F/dj. C9. $55.00

**FAULKNER, William.** *Early Prose & Poetry.* 1962. Atlantic/Little Brn. 1st. VG/dj. B30. $75.00

**FAULKNER, William.** *Essays, Speeches & Public Letters.* (1965). Random. 1st. 8vo. 233p. F/dj. H4. $50.00

**FAULKNER, William.** *Green Bough.* 1933. NY. Smith Haas. 1st. ils Lynd Ward. VG/dj. L3. $450.00

**FAULKNER, William.** *Green Bough.* 1933. Smith Haas. ltd. 1/360. sgn. tan cloth. NF/sans. B4. $1,200.00

**FAULKNER, William.** *Green Bough.* 1933. Smith Haas. 1st. 8vo. ils Lynd Ward. gilt gr cloth. NF/dj. R3. $500.00

**FAULKNER, William.** *Helen: Courtship & Mississippi Poems.* (1981). Tulane/ Yoknapatawpha. 1st trade. ES. AN/dj. H4. $35.00

**FAULKNER, William.** *Intruder in the Dust.* 1948. Random. 1st. F/NF. B4. $225.00

**FAULKNER, William.** *Intruder in the Dust.* 1948. Random. 1st. VG. H4. $35.00

**FAULKNER, William.** *Jealousy & Episode.* 1955. Faulkner Studies. 1/500. VG/sans. B30. $300.00

**FAULKNER, William.** *Knight's Gambit.* 1949. Random. 1st (not stated). top edge bl. red V-cloth. NF/VG. B30. $225.00

**FAULKNER, William.** *Light in August.* Oct 1932. Smith Haas. 1st. aeg. rb Sangorski/Sutcliffe. B30. $775.00

**FAULKNER, William.** *Mansion.* 1959. Random. 1st. 8vo. NF/dj. S9. $125.00

**FAULKNER, William.** *Mansion.* 1959. Random. 1st. 8vo. 436p. F/F. M24. $150.00

**FAULKNER, William.** *Mayday.* (1978). Notre Dame/London. 1st trade. F/dj. H4. $25.00

**FAULKNER, William.** *Mirror of Chartres Street.* (1953). Minneapolis. Faulkner Studies. 1/1000. NF/dj. H4. $200.00

**FAULKNER, William.** *Mississippi Poems.* 1979. Yoknapatawpha. ARC. 1/125. intro/sgn Joseph Blotner. VG/wht wrp. B30. $200.00

**FAULKNER, William.** *Reivers.* (1962). NY. Random. 1st trade. w/o BOMC bstp. NF/VG+. H4. $50.00

**FAULKNER, William.** *Reivers: A Reminiscence.* 1962. London. Chatto Windus. 1st Eng. NF/dj. A14. $70.00

**FAULKNER, William.** *Requiem fur Eine Nonne (Requiem for a Nun).* (1961). Berlin. Deutsch Buch-Gemeinschaft. 8vo. 272p. F. H4. $100.00

**FAULKNER, William.** *Salmagundi.* 1932. Casanova. 1/525. F/G box. B30. $550.00

**FAULKNER, William.** *Selected Letters of...* 1977. Random. 1st trade. edit Joseph Blotner. VG/G. B30. $75.00

**FAULKNER, William.** *Sherwood Anderson & Other Famous Creoles.* 1926. New Orleans. Pelican Bookshop. 1st/1st issue. 1/250. gr brd/label. M24. $2,250.00

**FAULKNER, William.** *Soldier's Pay.* 1926. Boni Liveright. 1st. author's 1st full-length book. VG. A24. $500.00

**FAULKNER, William.** *These 13: Stories.* 1931. NY. Cape Smith. 1/299. sgn. 8vo. VG/plain tissue wrp/sans case/box. B20. $2,500.00

**FAULKNER, William.** *These 13: Stories.* 1931. NY. Cape Smith. 1st. NF/dj. B24. $825.00

**FAULKNER, William.** *Uncollected Stories of William Faulkner.* 1979. Random. 1st. NF/VG. S13. $30.00

**FAULKNER, William.** *Uncollected Stories of...* 1980. Chatto Windus. 1st. VG/F. B30. $50.00

**FAULKNER, William.** *Wishing Tree.* 1964. NY. Random. 1/500. ils Don Bolognese. F/F. K3. $200.00

**FAULKNER, William.** *Wishing Tree.* 1964. Random. 1/500 #d. ils Don Bolognese. F/NF. H4. $175.00

**FAULKS, Sebastian.** *Birdsong.* 1996. Random. ARC. F/NF. B30. $35.00

**FAUST, Frederick S.** *Killers.* 1931. NY. Macaulay. 1st. F/VG. M15. $325.00

**FAUST, Frederick S.** *Max Brand's Best Poems: Verses From Master of Popular Prose.* 1992. Santa Barbara. Fifthian. 1st/Centennial ed. RS. AN/dj. A18. $30.00

**FAUST, Frederick S.** *Mountain Riders.* 1946. Dodd Mead. 1st. F/NF. M15. $150.00

**FAUST, Frederick S.** *Red Devil of the Range.* 1934. NY. Macaulay. 1st. VG/dj. M15. $250.00

**FAUST, Frederick S.** *Stolen Stallion.* 1945. Dodd Mead. 1st. F/NF. M15. $150.00

**FAUST, Joan Lee.** *Book of Vegetable Gardening, The New York Times.* 1975. Quadrangle/NY Times. 1st. photos/ils. 282p. NF/G. S14. $9.00

**FAUST, Joan Lee.** *New York Times Book of Houseplants.* 1973. NY Times. ils Allianora Rosse. 274p. VG/G. P12. $8.00

**FAUST, Ron.** *Fugitive Moon.* 1995. Forge. 1st. F/dj. P8. $25.00

**FAVOUR, Alpheus H.** *Old Bill Williams, Mountain Man.* 1936. Chapel Hill. 1st. ils. 229p. dj. D11. $75.00

**FAWCETT, Claire Hallard.** *We Fell in Love With the Circus.* 1949. Lindquist. 1st. 198p. VG/dj. S5. $20.00

**FAWCETT, Howard.** *Citrus Diseases & Their Control.* 1936. McGraw Hill. 2nd. 656p. cloth. VG. A10. $20.00

**FAWCETT, P.H.** *Lost Trails, Lost Cities.* 1953. Funk Wagnall. 1st. 332p. dj. F3. $25.00

**FAWKES, Francis.** *Argonautics of Apolloniius Rhodius.* 1780. London. Dodsley. 4 books in 1. revised/corrected. full calf. H4. $65.00

**FAY, Frank.** *How to Be Poor.* 1945. Prentice Hall. ils James Montgomery Flagg. 172p. VG. C5. $12.50

**FEARING, Daniel B.** *Check List of Books on Angling, Fish, Fisheries...* 1995. Mansfield, CT. Martino. rpt. 1/150. 138p. gilt gr cloth. F. F1. $55.00

**FEATHER & GITLER.** *Encyclopedia of Jazz in the Seventies.* 1976. Horizon. 1st. NF/dj. A14. $21.00

**FEATHERSTONE, Donald.** *Bowmen of England: Story of the English Longbow.* 1968. NY. 1st Am. 200p. F/dj. A17. $30.00

**FECHNER, Gustav Theodor.** *Die Drei Motive und Grunde des Glaubens.* 1863. Druck/Breitkopf Hartel. German text. 256p. gr cloth. VG. G1. $275.00

**FECHNER, Gustav Theodor.** *Uber Einige Verhaltnisse des Binocularen Sehens.* 1860. S Hirzel. German text. 563p. prt tan wrp. G1. $175.00

**FEDER, Norman.** *American Indian Art.* nd. Abrams. lg 4to. 407p. F/NF. C15. $100.00

**FEDER, Norman.** *American Indian Art.* 1983. Harrison House/Abrams. 4to. 446p. gilt red cloth. F/dj. F1. $95.00

**FEDER, Norman.** *American Indian Art.* 1995. Abradale. photos. VG/dj. M17. $40.00

**FEDER & JOESTEN.** *Weland Story.* 1954. McKay. 1st. VG/dj. B5. $20.00

**FEE, John G.** *Autobiography of...* 1891. Chicago. 1st. 211p. B18. $35.00

**FEEGEL, John R.** *Malpractice.* 1981. NY. NAL. 1st. F/F. H11. $15.00

**FEHL, Fred.** *On Broadway, Performance Photographs.* 1978. TX U. photos. VG/dj. C9. $36.00

**FEHLER, Gene.** *Center Field Grasses.* 1991. McFarland. 1st. VG/sans. P8. $25.00

**FEIFFER, Jules.** *Carnal Knowledge.* 1971. FSG. 1st. NF/dj. B4. $150.00

**FEIKEMA, Feike;** see Manfred, Frederick.

**FEIN, Harry H.** *Gems of Hebrew Verse: Poems for Young People.* nd (c 1940). Boston. Humphries. apparent 1st. 12mo. NF/G. C14. $15.00

**FEINBERG, Abraham.** *Rabbi Feinberg's Hanoi Diary.* 1968. Don Mills. Longmans Canada. intro Linus Pauling. 258p. NF/VG. R11. $75.00

**FEINBERG, Ellen O.** *Following the Milky Way: Pilgrimage Across Spain.* 1989. IA State. 1st. photos. 308p. VG/dj. S14. $12.00

**FEINBERG, Leslie.** *Stone Butch Blues.* 1993. Ithaca. Firebrand. 1st. inscr. photos. 301p. VG+. A25. $18.00

**FEININGER, Andreas.** *Complete Photographer.* 1970 (1965). Prentice Hall. 8th. VG/dj. S5. $15.00

**FEININGER, Andreas.** *Darkroom Techniques. Vol 2.* 1974. Garden City. Amphoto. VG/dj. S5. $12.00

**FEINSTEIN, John.** *Forever's Team.* 1989. Villard. 1st. sm 4to. 375p. F/dj. W2. $30.00

**FEIS, Herbert.** *Europe: the World's Banker, 1870-1914...* 1971 (1930). Augustus M Kelley. VG. S5. $15.00

**FEIST, Raymond.** *Darkness at Stehanon.* 1986. Doubleday. 1st. F/VG. M19. $15.00

**FEIST, Raymond.** *Faerie Tale.* 1988. Doubleday. 1st. F/F. H11. $30.00

**FEIST, Raymond.** *Silverthorn.* 1985. Doubleday. 1st. F/VG. M19. $25.00

**FELDMAN, Eddy S.** *Art of Street Lighting in Los Angeles.* 1972. Dawson's Book Shop. photos. 55p. pict brd. D11. $50.00

**FELIBIEN, Jean Francois.** *Recueil Historique de la Vie et des Ouvrages...* 1690. Paris. Louis Lucas. 4to. index. contemporary calf. K1. $450.00

**FELLER, Bob.** *How to Pitch.* 1948. NY. 1st. VG/fair. B5. $20.00

**FELLER, Bob.** *Now Pitching Bob Feller.* 1990. Birch Lane. later prt. sgn. photos. F/dj. P8. $45.00

**FELLINI, Federico.** *Federico Fellini: Early Screenplays...* 1971. Grossman. 1st. F/dj. C9. $60.00

**FELLOWS & FREEMAN.** *This Way to the Big Show: Life of Dexter Fellows.* 1936. Viking. 1st. 362p. NF/worn. B20. $50.00

**FELLOWS & FREEMAN.** *This Way to the Big Show: Life of Dexter Fellows.* 1938 (1936). Halcyon House. 4th. ils. G. A2. $15.00

**FENAROLI, Luigi.** *Flora Della Alpi.* 1955. Milan. ils. 369p. NF/dj. B26. $66.00

**FENGER, Christian.** *Collected Works of...* 1912. Phil. 2 vol. 1st. A13. $150.00

**FENNELL, J.H.** *Natural History of British & Foreign Quadrupeds...* 1841. London. Thomas. ils. 556p. contemporary bdg. M12. $60.00

**FENNEMAN, N.M.** *On the Lake of the Southeastern Wisconsin.* 1902. Madison. WI Nat Hist & Geol Survey. 178p. G. A17. $27.50

**FENSKA, Richard R.** *Tree Experts Manual.* 1947 (1943). NY. ils. 192p. dj. $20.00

**FENTON & FENTON.** *Fossil Book: Record of Prehistoric Life.* 1958. Doubleday. ils. 482p. VG/dj. K5. $20.00

**FERBER, Edna.** *American Beauty.* 1931. Doubleday. 1st. VG. L4. $12.00

**FERBER, Edna.** *Showboat.* 1926. Doubleday. 1st. VG. T12. $40.00

**FERBER, Edna.** *Showboat.* 1926. Garden City. Doubleday Page. 1st. VG/dj. Q1. $75.00

**FERE, Charles.** *Sensation et Mouvement: Etudes Experimentales...* 1877. Paris. Bailliere. 1st/later issue. 164p+ads dtd 1892. prt gr wrp. G1. $150.00

**FERGUSON, Bruce.** *Shadow of His Wings.* 1987. Arbor. 1st. F/dj. M21. $12.00

**FERGUSON, Don.** *Lion King.* 1994. Walt Disney. 94p. VG. C5. $12.50

**FERGUSON, Douglas C.** *Moths of American North of Mexico.* 1978. London. 9 pl. 110p. F. S15. $33.00

**FERGUSON, James.** *Ferguson's Astronomy, Explained Upon Sir Isaac Newton...* 1811 (1756). Edinburgh. Ballantyne. 2 vol. enlarged ed. 22 pl. leather. K5. $550.00

**FERGUSON, John.** *Bibliotheca Chemica.* 1954. London. Derek Vershoyle. 2 vol. rpt. tan cloth. F1. $165.00

**FERGUSON, Mary.** *China Medical Board & Peking Union Medical College.* 1970. NY. 263p. A13. $40.00

**FERGUSSON, Erna.** *Dancing Gods.* 1957. Albuquerque. rpt. G/dj. A19. $45.00

**FERGUSSON, Erna.** *Venezuela.* 1939. Knopf. 1st. 346p. VG. F3. $10.00

**FERLINGHETTI, Lawrence.** *Back Roads to Far Towns After Basho.* 1970. np. 1st. VG/F wrp. L3. $100.00

**FERLINGHETTI, Lawrence.** *Como eu Costumava Dizer.* 1972. Lisbon. Publicacoes Dom Quixote. 108p. G+/wrp. R11. $15.00

**FERLINGHETTI, Lawrence.** *Coney Island of the Mind.* 1968. New Directions. 1st. F/case. R11. $60.00

**FERLINGHETTI, Lawrence.** *Her.* 1966. London. MacGibbon Kee. 1st Eng. author's 1st/only novel. NF/dj. L3. $45.00

**FERLINGHETTI, Lawrence.** *Love in the Days of Rage.* 1988. Bodley Head. 1st. VG/VG. B3. $20.00

**FERLINGHETTI, Lawrence.** *Starting From San Francisco.* 1961. New Directions. 1st. sgn/dtd 1994. F/sans. R14. $75.00

**FERLINGHETTI & PETERS.** *Literary San Francisco: A Pictorial History...* 1980. City Lights/Harper Row. 1st. ils. VG/dj. R11. $35.00

**FERLITA & MAY.** *Parables of Lina Wertmuller.* 1977. Paulist. 1st. inscr. 104p. F/wrp. C9. $36.00

**FERM, Vergilius.** *Protestant Credo.* 1953. Philosophical Lib. 241p. VG. B29. $10.00

**FERMI, Laura.** *Atoms for the World.* 1957. Chicago. VG/dj. B9. $15.00

**FERMOR, Patrick Leigh.** *Roumeli: Travels to Northern Greece.* 1966. Harper Row. 1st. 16 pl/map ep. 248p. VG/dj. W1. $18.00

**FERN, Alan M.** *Word & Image.* 1968. MOMA. sq 4to. 160p. VG/dj. F1. $50.00

**FERN & KAPLIN.** *Viewpoints: Library of Congress Selection Pict Treasures.* nd. NY. Arno. rpt. obl 4to. 223p. cloth. F/dj. O1. $45.00

**FERNANDEZ, Don Felipe.** *New Practical Grammar of Spanish Languages...* 1800. London. 2nd. 8vo. 383p. contemporary calf. VG. W1. $25.00

**FERNIE, F.** *Dry-Fishing in Border Waters.* 1912. London. Blk. 1st. photos. 136p. gilt cloth. VG. A17. $35.00

**FERRANDINO, Joseph.** *Firefight.* 1987. NY. Soho. 1st. F/dj. R11/R14. $25.00

**FERRARS, E.X.** *Beware of the Dog. A Virginia & Felix Mystery.* 1992. Doubleday. 1st. F/dj. A23. $30.00

**FERRARS, E.X.** *Cup & the Lip.* 1975. London. Collins Crime Club. 1st. NF/dj. G8. $25.00

**FERRARS, E.X.** *Doubly Dead.* 1963. Doubleday Crime Club. 1st. 8vo. 186p. F/dj. H1. $20.00

**FERRER DE VALDECEBRO, Andres.** *Govierno General, Moral, y Politico...* 1696. Barcelona. Thomas Loriente. 4to. ils/woodcuts/index. 432p. VG. K1. $1,750.00

**FERRIER, David.** *Functions of the Brain.* 1886. NY. Putnam. 2nd Am. 498p. rb cloth. G1. $475.00

**FERRIGNO, Robert.** *Horse Latitudes.* 1990. Morrow. 1st. author's 1st book. rem mk. NF/dj. S18. $25.00

**FERRIL, Thomas Hornsby.** *New & Selected Poems.* 1952. Harper. G/dj. A19. $25.00

**FERRIS, Benjamin.** *History of Original Settlements on the Delaware...* 1846. Wilson Heald. 1st. 8vo. 312p+rear pocket map. later half navy morocco. O1. $2,000.00

**FERRIS, James Cody.** *X Bar X Boys at Nugget Camp (#6).* 1928. Grosset Dunlap. 1st. lists 5 titles. VG/dj. M20. $25.00

**FERRIS, Robert.** *Soldier & Brave: Historic Places Assoc With Indian Affairs.* 1971. WA, DC. new ed. ils/maps. 453p. F. E1. $50.00

**FERRIS, Timothy.** *Galaxies.* 1980. SF. Sierra. 1st. ils/photos. VG/VG. K5. $75.00

**FERRIS, W.A.** *Life in the Rocky Mountains, a Diary of Wanderings...* 1940. Old West Pub. 1st. fld map. 365p. VG. J2. $495.00

**FESSENDEN, Thomas Green.** *Democracy Unveiled; or, Tyranny Stripped of Garb...* 1805. Prt by David Carlisle for Author. 2nd. 8vo. 220p. O1. $200.00

**FESSENDEN, Thomas Green.** *Register of Arts; or, Compendious View...Inventions.* 1808. Phil. Conrad. 8vo. 404p. xl. K5. $150.00

**FETHERLING, Doug.** *Five Lives of Ben Hecht.* 1977. Toronto. Lester Orpen. 1st. 8vo. 228p. F/NF. B20. $15.00

**FETHERLING, Doug.** *Wheeling, an Ils History.* 1983. Woodland Mills. Windsor. 1st. 114p. F/dj. B18. $12.50

**FETZ, Ingrid.** *Valentine Box.* 1966. Crowell. 4th. ils Maud Hart Lovelace. xl. VG/dj. B17. $25.00

**FEUCHTWANGER, L.** *Fermented Liquors: Brewing, Distilling, Rectifying...* 1858. 1st. xl. G+. E6. $110.00

**FEUER, Leon I.** *Jewish Literature Since the Bible.* 1957. Am Hebrew Congregation. Book One. 297p. VG. B29. $8.50

**FEUER, Lewis.** *Einstein & the Generations of Science.* 1974. NY. 1st. 374p. A13. $17.50

**FEUERLICHT, Roberta.** *Desperate Act.* 1968. NY. McGraw Hill. 1st. 176p. F/dj. D4. $25.00

**FEUILLET, Octave.** *Story of Mr Punch.* 1929. Dutton. 1st. ils Hader/trans JH Gable. orange cloth. dj. R5. $85.00

**FEWKES, Jesse Walter.** *Archeological Expedition to Arizona in 1895.* 1971. Rio Grande. Report Bureau Am Ethnology #17. 4to. pict ep. brd. VG. F7. $55.00

**FEYNMAN, Richard P.** *QED: Strange Theory of Light & Matter.* 1985. Princeton. 1st. diagrams. VG/dj. M17. $20.00

**FICHTE, Johann Gottlieb.** *Reden an die Deutshce Nation.* 1808. Berlin. Realschulbuchhandlung. 8vo. quarter calf. R12. $750.00

**FIEDLER, Leslie A.** *Waiting for the End.* 1964. Stein Day. 1st. VG/dj. N2. $10.00

**FIELD, Edward Salisbury.** *Six-Cylinder Courtship.* 1907. McBride. 1st. gr cloth/pict insert. VG+. S13. $15.00

**FIELD, Edward.** *Stand Up, Friend, With Me.* 1963. NY. Grove. 1st. inscr. F/NF. L3. $65.00

**FIELD, Eugene.** *Auto-Analysis.* 1901. NY. HM Caldwell. 37p. lacks ffe. G11. $10.00

**FIELD, Eugene.** *Lullaby Book.* 1963. Evanston, IL. Schori. mini. 1/600. sgn. 58p. aeg. full bl morocco. B24. $175.00

**FIELD, Eugene.** *Poems of Childhood.* 1904. Scribner. 1st thus. 4to. 199p. Riviere bdg. F. H5. $350.00

**FIELD, Eugene.** *Poems of Childhood.* 1904. Scribner. 1st. 4to. teg. blk cloth/pict label. D1/R5. $175.00

**FIELD, Henry M.** *From Egypt to Japan.* 1890. Scribner. 16th. teg. cloth. VG. W1. $20.00

**FIELD, Michael.** *Fair Rosamund.* 1897. London. Hacon Ricketts. 1/210. paper brd/paper spine label. F1. $200.00

**FIELD, Michael.** *Julia Domna.* 1903. London. Hacon Ricketts. 1/240. ostrich pattern paper/paper spine label. F1. $125.00

**FIELD, Rachel.** *All This, & Heaven Too.* 1938. Macmillan. 1st. 594p. NF/worn. B20. $75.00

**FIELD, Rachel.** *All Through the Night.* 1940. Macmillan. 1st. less than 16mo. VG/dj. B17. $25.00

**FIELD, Robert D.** *Art of Walt Disney.* 1943. Macmillan. 237 b&w+59 pl. VG+. C9. $480.00

**FIELD, Ross.** *Years Out.* 1973. Knopf. 1st. inscr. F/dj. L3. $50.00

**FIELD, Roswell.** *Bondage of Ballinger.* 1903. Chicago. Revell. 1st. 8vo. gilt gr cloth. w/2p assn letter. R3. $100.00

**FIELD, Roswell.** *In Sunflower Land: Stories of God's Own Country.* 1892. Chicago. FJ Schulte. 1st. inscr. author's 1st book. teg. chemise/case. w/2 AL. R3 $100.00

**FIELD, Roswell.** *Little Miss Dee.* 1904. Chicago. Revell. 1st. 8vo. gilt gr cloth. NF. R3. $30.00

**FIELD, Sara Bard.** *Barabbas: Dramatic Narrative.* 1932. NY. Boni. 1st. inscr/sgn. VG/dj. A18. $40.00

**FIELD & MILLER.** *Boys & Girls Film Book.* 1948. Great Britain. Burke Pub. revised. VG. C9. $48.00

**FIELD & PEDERSON.** *To See Ourselves.* 1937. Macmillan. 1st. gr cloth. VG/dj. B4. $125.00

**FIELD & SPITTAL.** *Reader's Guide to the Place-Names of United Kingdom.* 1990. thousands of entries/maps. 363p. F/NF. A4. $45.00

**FIELD-MARSHAL, Lord Roberts.** *Forty-One Years in India.* 1897. London. Bentley. 2 vol. VG. B9. $100.00

**FIELDER, M.** *Treasure of Homestake Gold.* 1970. Aberdeen. 478p. NF. M4. $35.00

**FIELDING, Helen.** *Cause Celeb.* 1994. London. Picador/Pan. 1st. author's 1st book. F/dj. A14. $35.00

**FIELDING, Henry.** *History of Adventures of Joseph Andrews & His Friend Adams.* 1768. London. Millar Cadell. 2 vol. 8th/revised/corrected. polished calf. H13. $325.00

**FIELDING, Henry.** *History of Tom Jones, a Foundling.* 1823. London. Samuel Richards. 4 vol. quarter blk calf. VG/cloth case. F1. $300.00

**FIELDING, Henry.** *Works...* 1813. London. Dent. 12 vol. teg. half olive levant/marbled brd. VG+. F1. $500.00

**FIELDING, Howard.** *Straight Crooks.* 1927. Chelsea. 1st. VG. G8. $20.00

**FIELDING, Raymond.** *Technological History of Motion Pictures & Television.* 1967. U CA. 1st. F/dj. C9. $90.00

**FIELDS, James T.** *Boston Book.* 1850. Boston. Ticknor Reed Fields. 1st. purple cloth. F. M24. $150.00

**FIELDS, Mrs. James T.** *Whittier: Notes of His Life & His Friendships.* 1893. Harper. 1st. 16mo. 103p. VG. V3. $12.00

**FIELDS, W.C.** *Fields for President.* 1940. Dodd Mead. 1st. ils O Soglow. VG/NF. B4. $450.00

**FIELDS & FIELDS.** *From the Bowery to Broadway.* 1993. NY. Oxford. 1st hc. photos. 552p. VG/dj. C5. $25.00

**FIELDS.** *Proceedings of International Mathematical Congress.* 1928. Toronto. 2 vol. pres to Thomas A Edison. thick 4to. NF. A4. $1,250.00

**FIGES, Eva.** *Little Eden: A Child at War.* 1978. NY. 1st. dj. T9. $12.00

**FIJNJE VAN SALVERDA, J.G.W.** *Aerial Navigation.* 1894. NY. 1st. 209p. VG. B18. $75.00

**FILDES, Valerie.** *Breasts, Bottles & Babies.* 1986. Edinburgh. 1st. 462p. A13. $50.00

**FILIPPINI, A.** *100 Ways of Cooking Eggs.* 1892. 1st. obl 8vo. VG. E6. $30.00

**FILLER, Louis.** *Unknown Edwin Markham: His Mystery & Significance.* (1966). Yellow Springs, OH. Antioch. 1st. AN/sans? A18. $15.00

**FILLIPPINI, A.** *25 Years With Delmonicos: The Table, How to Buy Food...* 1889. 1st. lg 8vo. recipes+120p menues. 432p. E6. $75.00

**FILLIS, James.** *Breaking & Riding.* 1902. London. Hurst Blackett. VG. O3. $145.00

**FILLIS, James.** *Principes de Dressage et d'Equitation.* 1890. Paris. Marpon et Flammarion. 1st. French text. half leather. O3. $125.00

**FINCH, Christopher.** *Art of Walt Disney.* 1973. Abrams. 1st. NF/VG+. T11. $100.00

**FINCH, Christopher.** *Art of Walt Disney: From Mickey Mouse to Magic Kingdom.* nd (c 1975). Abrams. New Concise NAL ed. 4to. 160p. F/NF. C14. $25.00

**FINCH, Frank.** *Los Angeles Dodgers.* 1977. Jordan. 1st. F/VG. P8. $25.00

**FINCH, Robert.** *Story of Minor League Baseball.* 1953. Nat Ass Prof BB Leagues. 1st. photos/stats/records. VG/sans. P8. $200.00

**FINCHER, Terry.** *Creative Techniques in Photo-Journalism.* 1980. Lippincott/Crowell. 1st. photos. 168p. VG/dj. S14. $7.50

**FINDLAY, Alexander George.** *Directory for Navigation of the North Pacific Ocean...* nd. London. RH Laurie. 3rd. ils/maps. 1315p. D11. $300.00

**FINDLAY, Hugh.** *Garden Making & Keeping.* 1932. Doubleday. 252p. cloth. VG. A10. $22.00

**FINDLEY, James S.** *Bats: Community Perspective.* 1993. Cambridge. 167p. F/dj. S15. $17.00

**FINE, Anne.** *Killjoy.* 1987. Mysterious. 1st. F/F. H11. $20.00

**FINGER, Charles J.** *Frontier Ballads.* 1927. Doubleday Page. 1st. ils Paul Honore. VG. A18. $20.00

**FINGER, Charles J.** *Romantic Rascals.* 1927. McBride. 1st. ils Paul Honore. F. C15. $20.00

**FINGERMAN, M.** *Control of Chromatophores.* 1963. NY. 184p. F. S15. $15.00

**FINLASON, W.F.** *Reeves' History of the English Law, From Time of the Romans.* 1880. Phil. M Murphy, Law Bookseller. 5 vol. brn pebbled cloth. VG. M11. $250.00

**FINLAY, Ian.** *Scottish Gold & Silver Work.* 1956. London. Chatto Windus. 1st. lg 8vo. VG/dj. B11. $65.00

**FINLAY, Roger T.** *Adventures on Strange Islands.* nd. Chicago. Goldsmith. ils. VG/dj. B36. $16.00

**FINLAY, Virgil.** *Third Book of Virgil Finlay.* 1979. de la Ree. 1st. NF/dj. P3. $65.00

**FINLAYSON, Ann.** *Champions at Bat: Three Power Hitters.* 1970. Garrard. ils. lt gr cloth. VG. B36. $10.00

**FINNE, K.N.** *Igor Sikorsky: The Russian Years.* (1987). England. 1st. ils. 223p. VG/dj. B18. $25.00

**FINNEY, Charles G.** *Circus of Doctor Lao.* 1948. London. Gray Walls. 1st. VG/G clip. L1. $125.00

**FINNEY, Charles G.** *Circus of Doctor Lao.* 1984. Newark. Janus. 1/150. sgns Finney/ils Claire VanVliet. AN/box. B24. $1,850.00

**FINNEY, Jack.** *Assault on a Queen.* 1959. S&S. 1st. F/NF. B2. $65.00

**FINNEY, Jack.** *From Time to Time.* 1995. S&S. 1st. F/NF. S18. $15.00

**FINNEY, Jack.** *Woodrow Wilson Dime.* 1968. S&S. 1st. F/F. B2. $60.00

**FINNEY, Jack.** *5 Against the House.* 1954. London. Eyre Spottiswoode. 1st. F/NF. M15. $125.00

**FINSTEAD, Suzanne.** *Heir Not Apparent.* 1984. TX Monthly. 1st. VG/dj. W2. $20.00

**FIRBANK, Ronald.** *Inclinations.* 1916. London. Grant Richards. 1st. lacks ffe. VG/dj. Q1. $200.00

**FIRBANK, Ronald.** *Prancing Nigger.* 1924. Brentano. 1st. VG/partial. S13. $30.00

**FIREBRACE, Aylmer.** *Fire Service Memories.* 1949. London. Andrew Melrose. 1st. 299p. NF/F. B20. $35.00

**FIROR, John.** *Changing Atmosphere: A Global Challenge.* 1990. New Haven. Yale. 1st. 8vo. 145p. K5. $12.00

**FIRSOFF, Val A.** *Old Moon & the New.* 1970. South Brunswick, NJ. AS Barnes. ils/pl. 286p. VG/dj. K5. $20.00

**FISCHER, D.H.** *Albion's Seed: Four British Folkways in America.* 1989. NY. ils. VG/dj. M17. $30.00

**FISCHER, D.H.** *Albion's Seed: Four British Folkways in America.* 1989. OUP. ils/maps. 946p. NF/dj. M4. $35.00

**FISCHER, James A.** *Priests: Images, Ideals & Changing Roles.* 1987. Dodd Mead. 1st. 8vo. F/dj. A2. $12.50

**FISH, Chet.** *Outdoor Life Bear Book.* 1984. Outdoor Life. 4th. photos. 407p. F/dj. A19. $17.50

**FISH, Robert L.** *Incredible Sherlock Holmes.* 1966. S&S. 1st. inscr. F/NF. M15. $150.00

**FISH & ROTHBLATT.** *Handy Death.* 1973. S&S. 1st. rem mk. F/VG. P8. $40.00

**FISHBEIN, Morris.** *Bibliography of Infantile Paralysis 1789-1944.* 1946. Phil. 1st. 672p. A13. $60.00

**FISHBEIN, Morris.** *Doctors & Specialists.* 1930. Bobbs Merrill. 1st. ils. VG. E6. $15.00

**FISHBEIN, Morris.** *Fads & Quackery in Healing, an Analysis of the Foibles...* 1932. NY. 1st. 382p. A13. $70.00

**FISHBEIN, Seymour L.** *Grand Canyon Country: Its Majesty & Its Love.* 1991. NGS. lg 8vo. 197p. brn cloth. VG/dj. F7. $20.00

**FISHEL, Wesley R.** *Vietnam: Anatomy of a Conflict.* 1968. FE Peacock Pub. 879p. F/VG. R11. $40.00

**FISHER, A. Hugh.** *Frolics With Uncle Yule.* 1928. Hale Cushman. 1st. 4to. ils. NF/VG. S13. $18.00

**FISHER, Aileen.** *My Cat Has Eyes of Sapphire Blue.* 1973. NY. Crowell. 1st ils Marie Angel. 24p. beige cloth. VG/dj. D1. $50.00

**FISHER, Carrie.** *Surrender the Pink.* 1990. S&S. 1st. sgn. VG/dj. C9. $42.00

**FISHER, Clay.** *Tall Men.* 1954. Houghton Mifflin. 1st. 8vo. xl. VG/dj. S9. $30.00

**FISHER, Clive.** *Life & Times.* 1996. NY. 1st. dj. T9. $15.00

**FISHER, Douglas A.** *Steel Serves the Nation 1901-1951.* 1956. NY. ils ep. 227p. VG. B18. $15.00

**FISHER, George P.** *Out of the Woods: Romance of Camp Life.* 1896. Chicago. McClurg. 1st. 12mo. 270p. gr cloth. NF/dj. J3. $75.00

**FISHER, George.** *Instructor, or American Young Man's Best Companion...* 1794. Walpole, NH. Isiah Thomas/David Carlisle. 8vo. 384p. later bdg. O1. $300.00

**FISHER, GERBERG & WOLIN.** *Art of Cartooning: Seventy-Five Years...* 1975. NY. Scribner. 1st. folio. 224p. F/dj. B20. $20.00

**FISHER, Harrison.** *American Beauties.* nd. Grosset Dunlap. decor E Stetson Crawford/21 Fisher ils. G. A21. $350.00

**FISHER, Hugh Dunn.** *Gun & the Gospel. Early Kansas & Chaplain Fisher.* 1902. KS City. Hudson-Kimberly Pub. 4th. ils. 347p. cloth. VG. M8. $150.00

**FISHER, Irving.** *Noble Experiment.* 1930. NY. Alcohol Info Comm. 2nd. 12mo. 492p. VG. B11. $50.00

**FISHER, James.** *Wildlife in Danger.* 1969. Viking. 368p. NF/dj. S15. $12.00

**FISHER, James.** *World of Birds.* nd. Doubleday. ils. G/dj. A19. $25.00

**FISHER, John.** *Defensio Regie Assertionis Contra Babylonica...* 1525. Cologne. Quentell. 8vo. calf/rb. R12. $1,275.00

**FISHER, John.** *Magic of Lewis Carroll.* 1973. S&S. VG/dj. M20. $30.00

**FISHER, John.** *Reform & Insurrection in Bourbon, New Granada & Peru.* 1990. LSU. s1st. 356p. dj. F3. $20.00

**FISHER, Leonard Everett.** *Alphabet Art, Thirteen ABCs from Around the World.* 1978. Four Winds. 1st. xl. VG/VG. B17. $6.50

**FISHER, Leonard Everett.** *Printers: Colonial American Craftsmen.* 1965. NY. Franklin Watts. 1st. ils. cloth. F/NF. O10. $25.00

**FISHER, M.F.K.** *Alice B Toklas Cook Book.* 1984. Harper Row. 1st thus. 8vo. 288p. gr cloth. F/dj. J3. $90.00

**FISHER, M.F.K.** *Alphabet for Gourmets.* 1949. NY. 1st. ils Marvin Bileck. VG/G. M17. $50.00

**FISHER, M.F.K.** *Not Now, But Now.* 1947. Viking. 1st. 8vo. gr cloth. VG/dj. J3. $150.00

**FISHER, M.F.K.** *Sister Age.* 1983. Knopf. 1st. F/F. B3. $40.00

**FISHER, M.L.** *Albatross of Midway Island.* 1974 (1970). Carbondale, IL. photos/maps. 156p. cloth. F/dj. C12. $15.00

**FISHER, M.L.** *Albatross of Midway Island: Natural History of Laysan...* 1970. Carbondale. S IL U. ils/photos/2 maps. 156p. NF/G+. M12. $15.00

**FISHER, Majorie.** *Food & Flowers for Informal Entertaining.* 1965. Hearthside. G/dj. A16. $10.00

**FISHER, Reginald.** *Way of the Cross: New Mexico Version.* 1943. School of Am Research. 1st. ils. 35p. NF. B19. $100.00

**FISHER, Sara Carolyn.** *Process of Generalizing Abstraction & Its Product...* 1916. Psychological Review. 3 fld pl/1 fld table. 213p. VG/brn wrp. G1. $40.00

**FISHER, Vardis.** *Children of God: An American Epic.* 1939. NY. Harper. 1st. 769p. VG/dj. D11. $75.00

**FISHER, Vardis.** *Sonnets to an Imaginary Madonna.* nd. Opal Laurel Holmes. 1st rpt. author's 1st book. AN/dj. A18. $25.00

**FISHER, Vardis.** *Tale of Valor: Novel of Lewis & Clark Expedition.* 1958. Doubleday. 1st. 8vo. 456p. AN/dj. H1. $35.00

**FISHER & HOLMES.** *Gold Rushes & Mining Camps of Early American West.* 1968. Caxton. 1st. AN. J2. $65.00

**FISHER & JONES.** *Wheats of Commerce: Commercial Wheat Classes.* 1937. London. 55p. VG/wrp. A10. $26.00

**FISHER & LOCKLEY.** *Sea-Birds: An Introduction to Natural History...* 1954. Boston. photos. VG/G. M17. $25.00

**FISK, Erma J.** *Peacocks of Baboquivari.* 1983. Norton. ils. 283p. NF/NF. B19. $20.00

**FISK, Wilbur.** *Hard Marching Every Day: Civil War Letters of...1861-65.* 1992. U KS. edit Rosenblatt. fwd Reid Mitchell. VG/dj. M17. $20.00

**FISKE, John.** *American Revolution.* 1898. Houghton Mifflin. 8vo. ils/maps. 403p. cloth. F. O1. $35.00

**FISKE, John.** *American Revolution.* 1919. Boston. 2 vol in 1. G. M4. $15.00

**FISKE, John.** *Darwinism & Other Essays.* 1896. Boston. 2nd. 374p. A13. $35.00

**FISKE, Willard.** *Chess Tales & Chess Miscellanies.* 1912. Longman Gr. 1st. 8vo. 427p. gilt maroon cloth. VG+. B20. $75.00

**FITCH, George.** *Sizing Up Uncle Sam: Vestpocket Essays...* 1914. NY. Stokes. 1st. sm 8vo. 238p. blk cloth/pict label. VG+. B20. $25.00

**FITCH, H.S.** *Home Ranges, Territories & Seasonal Movements...* 1958. Lawrence, KS. 1/50. ils/pl. 326p. F/wrp. M12. $37.50

**FITCH, Samuel S.** *Functions of the Lungs & Cure of Pulmonary Consumption.* 1859 (1856). G+. E6. $65.00

**FITCH, Samuel S.** *Six Lectures on Uses of the Lungs.* 1847. Carlisle. 324p. wrp. A10. $35.00

**FITT, Mary.** *Night-Watchman's Friend.* 1953. London. Macdonald. 1st. F/NF. M15. $45.00

**FITZGERALD, A. Ernest.** *High Priests of Waste.* 1972. Norton. 1st. inscr. F/dj. A2. $20.00

**FITZGERALD, A. Ernest.** *Pentagonists: An Insider's View of Waste, Mismanagement...* 1989. Houghton Mifflin. 1st. F/dj. A2. $15.00

**FITZGERALD, Ed.** *Ballplayer.* 1957. Barnes. 1st. VG/G. P8. $20.00

**FITZGERALD, Ed.** *College Slugger.* 1950. Barnes. 1st. VG. P8. $20.00

**FITZGERALD, Ed.** *Nickel an Inch, a Memoir.* 1985. NY. Atheneum. 1st. 310p. cloth. F/dj. O10. $20.00

**FITZGERALD, Ed.** *Turning Point.* 1948. Barnes. 1st. VG/VG. P8. $75.00

**FITZGERALD, Edward.** *Rubaiyat of Omar Khayyam.* 1943. Jamaica. mini. 24 full-p ils. 112p. gilt gr vinyl cloth/box. B24. $250.00

**FITZGERALD, Emily McCorkle.** *Army Doctor's Wife on the Frontier: Letters...1874-1878.* 1962. Pittsburgh. 1st. 8vo. photos. 352p. bl cloth. P4. $55.00

**FITZGERALD, F. Scott.** *Afternoon of an Author.* 1st trade (after Princeton ltd). VG/dj. B30. $50.00

**FITZGERALD, F. Scott.** *All the Sad Young Men.* 1926. Scribner. 1st. VG. H4. $150.00

**FITZGERALD, F. Scott.** *All the Sad Young Men.* 1926. Scribner. 1st. 8vo. 267p. dk gr cloth. NF/dj. H5. $2,000.00

**FITZGERALD, F. Scott.** *All the Sad Young Men.* 1926. Scribner. 1st/1st prt. 1/10100. gilt gr cloth. F. M24. $200.00

**FITZGERALD, F. Scott.** *Dear Scott/Dear Max: Fitzgerald-Perkins Correspondence.* 1971. Scribner. 8vo. 282p. VG/dj. P4. $25.00

**FITZGERALD, F. Scott.** *Flappers & Philosophers.* 1920. NY. Scribner. 1st/1st prt. bl-gr cloth. NF. M24. $225.00

**FITZGERALD, F. Scott.** *Golden Moment: Novels of...* 1970. U IL. VG/dj. M17. $15.00

**FITZGERALD, F. Scott.** *Great Gatsby.* 1984. SF. Arion. 1/400. ils/sgn Michael Graves. w/2 extra ils. AN/box. B24. $1,250.00

**FITZGERALD, F. Scott.** *Love in the Night.* 1994. NY. Clarkson Potter. 1st separate Am. bl pict brd/ribbon ties. F/sans. Q1. $35.00

**FITZGERALD, F. Scott.** *Mystery of the Raymond Mortgage.* 1960. Random. 1st. 1/750. F/bl prt wrp. M24. $275.00

**FITZGERALD, F. Scott.** *Preface to This Side of Paradise.* 1975. IA City. Windover. 1st. 1/150. gray cloth/label. M24. $200.00

**FITZGERALD, F. Scott.** *This Side of Paradise.* 1920. Scribner. 1st/1st prt. gilt gr cloth. F. M24. $675.00

**FITZGERALD, Ken.** *Weathervanes & Whirligigs.* 1967. Clarkson Potter. 1st. VG/dj. O3. $35.00

**FITZGERALD, Oscar P.** *Three Centuries of American Furniture.* 1982. Gramercy. rpt. ils. VG/dj. R8. $15.00

**FITZGERALD, Penelope.** *Knox Brothers.* 1977. NY. 1st. photos. VG/dj. M17. $20.00

**FITZGERALD, Percy.** *Boswell's Autobiography.* 1912. London. Chatto Windus. 1st. VG. H13. $45.00

**FITZGERALD, Percy.** *Life, Letters & Writings of Charles Lamb.* 1895. Phil. Lippincott. 6 vol. Temple ed. 3-quarter leather. VG. S17. $225.00

**FITZGERALD, Zelda.** *Collected Writings.* 1991. Scribner. 1st. thick 8vo. 480p. F/dj. J3. $35.00

**FITZHUGH, Bill.** *Pest Control.* 1997. NY. Avon. 1st. author's 1st novel. F/dj. T2. $30.00

**FITZSIMMONS, Cortland.** *Death on the Diamond.* 1934. Grosset Dunlap. rpt. VG/dj. P8. $40.00

**FITZSIMONS, M.A.** *Empire by Treaty.* 1964. Notre Dame. 1st. 235p. NF/VG clip. M7. $32.50

**FIXEL, Rowland W.** *Law of Aviation.* 1927. Albany. Matthew Bender. 1st. maroon cloth. M11. $250.00

**FLACK, Marjorie.** *I See a Kitty.* 1943. Garden City. very early/possible 1st. ils Hilma Larsson. VG/dj. B17. $35.00

**FLAGG, John H.** *Lyrics of New England & Other Poems.* 1909. Cedar Rapids. Torch. sgn. thin 8vo. 3-quarter tan leather/gr cloth. VG. S17. $25.00

**FLAMINI, Roland.** *Scarlett, Rhett & a Cast of Thousands...* 1976. Macmillan. 2nd. 100 photos. VG/dj. C9. $78.00

**FLANAGAN, Thomas.** *End of the Hunt.* 1994. Dutton. 1st. VG/dj. M17. $15.00

**FLANAGAN, Thomas.** *Year of the French.* 1979. HRW. 1st. NF/dj. T11. $25.00

**FLAUBERT, Gustave.** *Salammbo: Story of Ancient Carthage.* 1930. NY. Brn House. 1/800. 4to. ils Alexander King. Riviere bdg. F/case. H5. $1,500.00

**FLAVELL, A.J.** *TE Lawrence: Legend & Man.* 1988. Oxford. Bodleian Lib. 113p. AN. M7. $25.00

**FLAVELL, George F.** *Log of the Panthon: Account of 1896 River Voyage...* 1987. Boulder. Pruett. 8vo. 107p. VG+. F7. $15.00

**FLAVELL, M. Kay.** *George Grosz: A Biography.* 1988. Yale. ils. VG/dj. M17. $30.00

**FLAWN, Louis.** *Gardening With Cloches.* 1957. London. Gifford. 202p. VG/dj. A10. $28.00

**FLECK, G. Peter.** *Mask of Religion.* 1980. Buffalo. 2nd. sgn. VG/dj. M17. $17.50

**FLEET, Betsy.** *Green Mount After the War: Correspondence of...* (1978). U VA. photos. VG/fair. B10. $15.00

**FLEET, H.** *Concise Natural History of New Zealand.* 1986. Auckland. Heinemann. ils/photos/map. 275p. VG. M12. $22.50

**FLEET, W.H.** *How I Came to Be Governor of the Island of Cacona.* 1989. SF. Arion. 1st. ils. 1/325. quarter cloth. F. M24. $100.00

**FLEISCHER, Richard.** *Just Tell Me When to Cry.* 1993. Carroll Graf. 349p. VG/dj. C5. $12.50

**FLEISCHMAN, Harry.** *Norman Thomas: A Biography.* 1964. Norton. 2nd. sgn. VG/G. V4. $40.00

**FLEISCHMAN, J.** *Art of Blending & Compounding Liquors & Wines.* 1885. 1st. VG. E6. $40.00

**FLEISCHMAN, Paul.** *Bull Run.* (1993). Harper Collins. 1st. ils. 104p. VG/dj. B10. $15.00

**FLEISCHMAN, Sid.** *Jim Ugly.* 1992. Greenwillow. stated 1st. VG/dj. B36. $22.00

**FLEITMANN, Lida L.** *Comments on Hacks & Hunters.* 1921. Scribner. ils. VG. A21. $40.00

**FLEMING, Anne.** *Death & Deconstruction.* 1995. St Martin. 1st Am. sm 8vo. O10. $20.00

**FLEMING, Archibald Lang.** *Archibald the Arctic.* 1956. Appleton Century Crofts. 1st. ils. F/dj. T10. $25.00

**FLEMING, Berry.** *Lucinderella.* 1967. John Day. 1st. F/dj. T12. $30.00

**FLEMING, G.** *Modern Horseshoeing: A Practical Work...* 1904. Chicago. Ogilvie. VG. O3. $45.00

**FLEMING, G.** *Practical Horseshoeing With Twenty-Nine Illustrations.* 1872. NY. Appleton. 1st Am. VG. O3. $85.00

**FLEMING, G.** *Roaring in Horses: Its History, Nature, Causes...* 1889. London. Belliere Tindall Cox. 1st. xl. VG. O3. $45.00

**FLEMING, Ian.** *Casino Royale.* 1954. Macmillan. 1st Am. author's 1st book. gr cloth. F/dj. H5. $750.00

**FLEMING, Ian.** *Chitty Chitty Bang Bang!* 1968. Random. 1st. adapted for beginning readers. F. M15. $75.00

**FLEMING, Ian.** *Gilt-Edged Bonds.* 1961. Macmillan. 1st thus. VG/dj. B11. $45.00

**FLEMING, Ian.** *Jamaica.* 1973. London. Deutsch. 1st. map ep. VG/dj. B11. $15.00

**FLEMING, Ian.** *Man With the Golden Gun.* 1965. London. Cape. 1st. F/dj. M15. $100.00

**FLEMING, Ian.** *Man With the Golden Gun.* 1965. London. Cape. 1st. NF/F. B3. $85.00

**FLEMING, Ian.** *Man With the Golden Gun.* 1965. NAL. 1st. F/NF clip. B3. $25.00

**FLEMING, Ian.** *Octopussy & the Living Daylights.* 1966. London. Cape. 1st. F/clip. M15. $45.00

**FLEMING, Ian.** *Octopussy & the Living Daylights.* 1966. NAL. 2nd. ils. NF/VG. S18. $6.00

**FLEMING, Ian.** *On Her Majesty's Secret Service.* 1963. London. Cape. 1st. F/dj. M15. $200.00

**FLEMING, Ian.** *Spy Who Loved Me.* 1962. London. Cape. 1st. F/dj. M15. $175.00

**FLEMING, Ian.** *Thunderball.* 1961. London. Cape. 1st. F/dj. M15. $275.00

**FLEMING, Theodore H.** *Short-Tailed Fruit Bat.* 1988. U Chicago. 365p. F/dj. S15. $30.00

**FLEMING, Thomas.** *Liberty!* 1997. Viking. 1st. sgn. F/dj. T11. $75.00

**FLEMING, Thomas.** *New Jersey: Bicentennial History.* 1977. NY. 1st. photos/maps. 214p. F/dj. M4. $15.00

**FLEMING, Thomas.** *Now We Are Enemies.* 1960. St Martin. 1st. quarter blk cloth/red-paper covered brd. F/VG. T11. $50.00

**FLEMING, Thomas.** *Over There.* 1992. Harper Collins. 1st. sgn. NF/dj. T11. $30.00

**FLEMING, Thomas.** *Remember the Morning.* 1997. NY. Forge. 1st. sgn. F/dj. T11. $35.00

**FLETCHER, Colin.** *Thousand-Mile Summer: Desert & High Sierra.* 1964. Howell-North. 1st. photos. VG/dj. S14. $11.00

**FLETCHER, Ernest.** *Wayward Horseman.* 1958. Sage. 217p. VG. J2. $60.00

**FLETCHER, H.L.V.** *Rose Antholgy.* 1963. London. ils Wm McLaren. 256p. VG/dj. B26. $25.00

**FLETCHER, Inglis.** *Lusty Wind for Carolina.* 1944. Bobbs Merrill. 1st. VG/dj. M21. $25.00

**FLETCHER, Inglis.** *Roanoke Hundred.* 1948. Bobbs Merrill. 1st. sgn. VG. B11. $50.00

**FLETCHER, J.M.** *Proceedings of Dorset Natural History...Vols 52 & 54.* 1931 & 1933. Dorchester. private prt. 2 vol. ils/fld map. NF. M12. $30.00

**FLETCHER, J.S.** *South Foreland Murder.* 1930. Knopf. 1st Am. VG. G8. $17.50

**FLETCHER, John Gould.** *XXIV Elegies.* 1953. Santa Fe. Writers Eds. 1st. 1/400. sgn. VG. L3. $60.00

**FLETCHER, L.** *Introduction to Study of Meteorites...* 1896. London. 96p. xl Harvard U. F. B14. $55.00

**FLETCHER, Margaret.** *Sketches of Life & Character in Hungary.* 1892. London/NY. Sonnenschein/Macmillan. 1st. 12mo. 248p. xl. VG. W1. $28.00

**FLETCHER, S.W.** *How to Make a Fruit Garden...* 1906. Doubleday Page. 1st. ils. 283p. G. H10. $30.00

**FLETCHER, S.W.** *Pennsylvania Agriculture & Country Life.* 1955 & 1971. Harrisburg. 2 vol. ils. F/dj. M4. $55.00

**FLEXNER, Abraham.** *Medical Education: A Comparative Study.* 1925. NY. 1st. 334p. A13. $125.00

**FLEXNER, James Thomas.** *Double Adventure of John Singleton Copley.* 1969. Boston. ils. VG/dj. M17. $15.00

**FLEXNER, James Thomas.** *George Washington: Anguish & Farewell.* 1972. Boston. 1st. ils. VG/dj. M17. $27.50

**FLEXNER, James Thomas.** *Wilder Image: Painting of America's Native School...* 1962. Little Brn. 1st. 407p. VG/dj. D2. $40.00

**FLEXNER & THOMAS.** *William Henry Welch & the Heroic Age of American Medicine.* 1941. Viking. 1st. 539p. NF. C14. $17.00

**FLICK, Art.** *Master Fly-Tying Guide.* 1972. NY. photos. 207p. VG/dj. A17. $35.00

**FLICK, Art.** *Streamside Guide to Naturals & Their Imitations.* 1947. NY. Putnam. 1st. 12mo. 110p. VG/fair. H10. $75.00

**FLINT, A.** *Treatise on Principles & Practice of Medicine.* 1873. 4th. full leather. VG. E6. $45.00

**FLINT, KOSTIN & KUZNETSOV.** *Birds of the USSR Including Eastern Europe...* 1991. Norwalk, CT. Easton. special ed. ils/pl/maps. 353p. full leather. F. C12. $60.00

**FLINT, Timothy.** *Recollections of the Last Ten Years in Valley of MS.* 1968. Carbondale, IL. 1st thus. 343p. VG/dj. B18. $35.00

**FLINT & RIMINGTON.** *1983 BBC2 Television Tournament Grand Slam...* VG. S1. $10.00

**FLIPPO, Chet.** *Your Cheatin' Heart.* 1981. NY. 1st. VG/dj. B5. $30.00

**FLOOD, Richard.** *Fighting Southpaw.* 1949. Houghton Mifflin. probable 1st. VG. P8. $35.00

**FLORES, Moncayo, Jose.** *Derecho Agrario Boliviano, Doctrina, Exposicion...* 1956. La Paz. Don Bosco. 397p. prt sewn wrp. M11. $25.00

**FLORESCU, Radu.** *In Search of Frankenstein.* 1975. NYGS. 1st. rem mk. VG/G+. L1. $75.00

**FLORESCU & MCNALLY.** *Dracula: Biography of Vlad the Impaler.* 1973. NY. Hawthorn. 1st. VG/dj. L1. $75.00

**FLORESCU & MCNALLY.** *Dracula: Prince of Many Faces.* 1989. Little Brn. 1st. AN/dj. M21. $40.00

**FLORESCU & MCNALLY.** *Essential Dracula.* 1978. NY. Mayflower. VG/G clip. L1. $55.00

**FLORIN, Lambert.** *Western Wagon Wheels.* nd. Bonanza. 1st thus. sm 4to. NF/dj. M21. $20.00

**FLORIS, Maria.** *Bakery Cakes & Simple Confectionery.* 1968. Bonanza. G/dj. A16. $20.00

**FLORNEY, Bertram.** *World of the Inca.* 1956. Vanguard. 1st. 212p. dj. F3. $20.00

**FLORY, Jane.** *Mr Snitzel's Cookies.* 1950. Rand McNally. 1st. 16mo. VG. M5. $12.00

**FLOWER, B.O.** *Whittier: Prophet, Seer & Man With Portrait.* 1896. Boston. Arena. 1st. 160p+ads. fair. V3. $14.00

**FLOWERS, Arthur.** *Another Good Loving Blues.* 1993. Viking. 1st. VG/dj. B30. $25.00

**FLOWERS, Arthur.** *De Mojo Blues: De Quest of High John deConqueror.* 1985. Dutton. 1st. F/dj. R11. $45.00

**FLOYD, Olive.** *Phebe Anna Thorne, Quakeress, 1828-1909.* 1958. Rye, NY. private prt. 1st. 12mo. 80p. VG. V3. $16.00

**FLOYER, Philip.** *Proctor's Practice in the Ecclesiastical Courts...* 1744. London. 1st. contemporary calf. M11. $650.00

**FLUSFEDER, D.L.** *Man Kills Woman.* 1993. FSG. 1st. F/dj. A23. $30.00

**FLYNN, Don.** *Suitcase in Berlin.* 1989. NY. Walker. 1st. NF/F. H11. $15.00

**FLYNN, Lucine Hansz.** *Antique & Deadly.* 1988. NY. Walker. 1st. author's 1st mystery. F/F. H11. $20.00

**FODER & GARRETT.** *Psychology of Language: Introduction to Psycholinguistics...* 1974. McGraw Hill. 537p. prt blk cloth. G1. $65.00

**FODOR, Laszlo.** *Argentina.* 1941. Hastings. 1st. 23p. dj. F3. $15.00

**FOEHL & HARGREAVES.** *Story of Logging: The White Pine in Saginaw Valley.* 1964. Bay City. Red Key. ils/reading list/photos. 70p. A17. $30.00

**FOGG, H.G. Witham.** *Creating a Luxury Garden.* 1975. Edinburgh. 160p. VG/dj. A10. $16.00

**FOGG, William Perry.** *Land of the Arabian Nights: Being Travels Through Egypt...* 1875. Chicago/NY. 1st. ils. 350p. VG. W1. $85.00

**FOLEY, Daniel J.** *Flowering World of Chinese Wilson.* 1969. London. 1st. ils. 334p. gr florals on blk cloth. F/VG clip. H3. $35.00

**FOLEY, Rae.** *Death & Mr Potter.* 1955. Dodd Mead. 1st. VG/G. G8. $35.00

**FOLEY & LORD.** *Easter Garland: Vivid Tapestry of Customs, Traditions...* 1963. Chilton. 1st. ils CE Bowd. cloth. VG+. B27. $55.00

**FOLLETT, Helen.** *Islands on Guard.* 1943. NY. photos. VG. M17. $15.00

**FOLLETT, Ken.** *Key to Rebecca.* 1980. Morrow. 1st. F/VG clip. N4. $25.00

**FOLLETT, Ken.** *Pillars of the Earth.* 1989. NY. 1st. VG/dj. M17. $15.00

**FOLLETT, Ken.** *Storm Island.* 1978. London. Macdonald/James. 1st. F/dj. M15. $400.00

**FOLSOM, Merrill.** *More Great American Mansions & Their Stories.* 1962. Hastings. photos. VG/dj. M17. $17.50

**FOLTZ, Charles Steinman.** *Surgeon of the Seas: Adventurous Life of Jonathan Foltz...* 1931. Bobbs Merrill. 1st. 351p. cloth. VG. M8. $65.00

**FONDA, Jane.** *Cooking for Healthy Living.* 1996. Turner. 1st. 240p. F/dj. W2. $35.00

**FONDILLER, Harvey.** *Best of Popular Photography.* 1979. Ziff-Davis. 1st. ils. 392p. VG/dj. S14. $20.00

**FONER & MAHONEY.** *House Divided: America in the Age of Lincoln.* 1990. Chicago Hist Soc. 1st. ils. 179p. NF/dj. M10. $32.50

**FONES, Alfred C.** *Mouth Hygiene: A Text-Book for Dental Hygienists.* 1934. Lea Febiger. 4th. 372p. NF. C14. $20.00

**FONTAINE, Andre.** *History of the Cold War From Korean War to Present.* 1969. NY. Pantheon. 1st. VG/dj. N2. $10.00

**FONTAINE, Joan.** *No Bed of Roses, an Autobiography.* 1978. NY. Morrow. 2nd. inscr. photos. VG/dj. C9. $90.00

**FONTENELLE, Bernard.** *Plurality of Worlds.* 1929. London. Nonesuch. 1/1600. sm 8vo. full limp vellum/leather thongs. F1. $40.00

**FOOTE, Samuel.** *Dramatic Works, To Which Is Prefixed a Life of the Author.* 1781 & 1795. London. Lowndes Bladon. 2 vol. thick 8vo. full mottled calf. H13. $325.00

**FOOTE, Shelby.** *Civil War: Fort Sumter to Perryville/Fredericksburg to...* nd. BC. 3 vol. ils/index. VG. E1. $100.00

**FOOTE, Shelby.** *September, September.* 1977. Random. 1st. F/dj. B30. $110.00

**FOOTE, Shelby.** *View of History.* 1981. Palaemon. 1st. 1/140. sgn. F/as issued. B30. $200.00

**FOOTNER, Hulbert.** *Murder of a Bad Man.* 1936. NY. Harper. 1st Am. VG/dj. M15. $60.00

**FORBES, Allan.** *Our Garden Friends the Bugs.* 1962. NY. Exposition. 1st. 190p. VG/dj. A10. $15.00

**FORBES, Allan.** *Taverns & Stagecoaches of New England.* 1953. Boston. Rand. sc. A19. $30.00

**FORBES, Allan.** *Towns of New England & Old England, Ireland & Scotland.* 1921. Putnam. 2 vol. teg. gilt cloth. VG. B18. $65.00

**FORBES, Edgar Allen.** *Land of the White Helmet. Light & Shadows Across Africa.* 1910. NY/London. Revell. 8vo. 356p. xl. VG. W1. $24.00

**FORBES, Esther.** *Johnny Tremain.* (1943). Houghton Mifflin. 27th. gr cloth. F/VG. T11. $30.00

**FORBES, Esther.** *Rainbow in the Road.* 1954. Houghton Mifflin. 1st. NF/VG. P2. $15.00

**FORBES, Reginald D.** *Woodlands for Profit & Pleasure.* 1971. WA, DC. ils/tables. sc. VG. B26. $15.00

**FORBUSH, E.H.** *Birds of Massachusetts & Other New England States...* 1925. MA Dept Agriculture. 481p. cloth. VG. B1. $75.00

**FORBUSH & MAY.** *Natural History of the Birds of Eastern & Central N Am.* 1939. Houghton Mifflin. 97 mc pl. 554p. NF/dj. A17. $30.00

**FORCE, Peter.** *American Archives: Fourth Series. Vol III.* 1840. 2010p. 3-quarter leather. G. B18. $95.00

**FORD, Alla T.** *Infinitely Yours.* 1969. Hong Kong. Ford. 1/700. sgn. 22p. gilt red cloth. F. B24. $50.00

**FORD, Alla T.** *Joy of Collecting Children's Books.* 1968. Hong Kong. Ford. mini. 1/500. sgn. gilt red cloth. F. B24. $90.00

**FORD, G.M.** *Bum's Rush.* 1997. NY. Walker. 1st. sgn. F/dj. A23. $45.00

**FORD, G.M.** *Cast in Stone.* 1996. NY. Walker. 1st. sgn. F/dj. A23. $45.00

**FORD, Gerald.** *Time to Heal.* 1979. Harper Row. 1st. sgn. G/dj. B30. $75.00

**FORD, Herbert.** *No Guns on Their Shoulders.* 1968. Nashville. Southern Pub. 144p. F/VG. R11. $50.00

**FORD, James A.** *Judge of Men.* 1968. Hodder Stoughton. NF/dj. P3. $7.00

**FORD, Jesse Hill.** *Feast of St Barnabas.* 1969. Atlantic/Little Brn. 1st. VG/dj. B30. $25.00

**FORD, Jesse Hill.** *Raider.* 1975. Atlantic/ Little Brn. 1st. sgn. G/dj. B30. $55.00

**FORD, Leslie.** *Woman in Black.* 1947. SCribner. 1st. VG/G. N4. $20.00

**FORD, Paul Leicester.** *True George Washington.* 1897 (1896). Lippincott. 4th. ils. teg. 319p. VG. B10. $15.00

**FORD, R. Clyde.** *Sandy MacDonald's Man: Tale of Mackinaw Fur Trade.* 1929. Lansing. 207p. cloth. A17. $17.50

**FORD, Richard.** *Communist.* 1987. Derry Koontz. 1/200 (240 total). sgn. F/wrp. R14. $175.00

**FORD, Richard.** *Granta Book of the American Short Story.* 1992. NY/London. Granta/Viking. ARC. contributor sgns. F/dj. D10. $110.00

**FORD, Richard.** *Independence Day.* 1995. Knopf. 1st. F/dj. B4. $100.00

**FORD, Richard.** *Independence Day.* 1995. Knopf. 1st. sgn. F/dj. M23. $125.00

**FORD, Richard.** *Independence Day.* 1995. Little Brn. 1st Canadian. F/dj. A23. $50.00

**FORD, Richard.** *Rock Springs.* 1987. NY. Atlantic Monthly. 1st. F/dj. B30/Q1. $50.00

**FORD, Richard.** *Wildlife.* 1990. Atlantic Monthly. 1st. sgn. F/dj. R14. $45.00

**FORD, Richard.** *Wildlife.* 1990. Atlantic Monthly. 1st. sgn. rem mk. VG/dj. B30. $35.00

**FORD, Tennessee Ernie.** *Tennessee Ernie Ford's Book of Favorite Hymns.* 1962. Bramhall. 130p. F/NF. P12. $12.00

**FORD, Thomas.** *History of Illinois.* 1945. Lakeside Classic. 1st thus. edit Quaife. teg. red cloth. NF/sans. T11. $25.00

**FORD & FORD.** *Good Morning.* 1926. Dearborn, MI. 1st. VG. T12. $55.00

**FORD & GANNES.** *War in Africa.* 1935. Workers Lib. 1st. NF/wrp. B2. $25.00

**FORD & LANG.** *Fighting Southpaw.* 1962. Argonaut. 1st. VG/G. P8. $25.00

**FOREL, August.** *Die Sexuelle Frage: Eine Naturwissenschaftliche...* 1805. Munchen. Ernst Reinhardt. thick 8vo. German text. 587p. leather-backed brd. G1. $185.00

**FOREL, Auguste Henri.** *Social World of the Ants Compared With That of Men.* 1929. NY. Boni. 2 vol. 1st Eng-language. thick 8vo. 24 pl/138 ils. cloth. G1. $350.00

**FOREMAN, Grant.** *Indians & Pioneers: Story of American Southwest Before 1830.* 1930. New Haven. Yale. 1st. ils. 327p. cloth. D11. $75.00

**FOREMAN, Michael.** *Images of the Past: Photographic Review of Winchester...* 1980. Winchester-Frederick Co Hist Soc. 144p. VG/dj. B10. $45.00

**FOREMAN, Michael.** *Mother Goose.* 1991. HBJ. 1st. obl 8vo. ils. VG/dj. B17. $16.00

**FOREMAN, Michael.** *Panda & the Bushfire.* 1986. Prentice Hall. 1st. 4to. F/dj. B17. $15.00

**FORESTER, C.S.** *Admiral Hornbower in the West Indies.* 1958. Little Brn. 1st. NF/VG. T11. $50.00

**FORESTER, C.S.** *Barbary Pirates.* 1953. Random. VG/dj. B36. $8.50

**FORESTER, C.S.** *Bedchamber Mystery.* 1944. Toronto. Reginald Saunders. NF/VG. T11. $180.00

**FORESTER, C.S.** *Captain From Connecticut.* 1941. Little Brn. 1st. NF/VG. T11. $65.00

**FORESTER, C.S.** *Captain From Connecticut.* 1941. Little Brn. 1st. VG. L4. $10.00

**FORESTER, C.S.** *Captain Horatio Hornblower.* 1939. Little Brn. 1st. ils NC Wyeth. VG/case. A14. $22.00

**FORESTER, C.S.** *Commodore Hornblower.* 1945. London. 1st. VG/dj. T9. $50.00

**FORESTER, C.S.** *Commodore Hornblower.* 1945. Toronto. Reginald Saunders. 1st Canadian. VG. A14. $15.00

**FORESTER, C.S.** *Flying Colours.* 1939. Little Brn. 1st Am. bl cloth. VG+/VG. T11. $350.00

**FORESTER, C.S.** *Good Shepherd.* 1955. Little Brn. ARC. RS. VG/poor. B30. $20.00

**FORESTER, C.S.** *Good Shepherd.* 1955. Little Brn. 1st Am. NF/dj. B2. $40.00

**FORESTER, C.S.** *Good Shepherd.* 1955. London. Michael Joseph. 1st. blk cloth. NF/VG+. T11. $65.00

**FORESTER, C.S.** *Gun.* 1933. Little Brn. 1st. 1/2000. decor cloth. VG+. T11. $155.00

**FORESTER, C.S.** *Hornblower & the Atropos.* 1953. London. Michael Joseph. 1st Eng. NF/VG. T11. $100.00

**FORESTER, C.S.** *Hornblower Companion.* 1964. Boston. 1st. dj. T9. $30.00

**FORESTER, C.S.** *Hornblower During the Crisis.* 1967. Little Brn. 1st. VG/dj. B30. $75.00

**FORESTER, C.S.** *Lord Hornblower.* 1946. Little Brn. 1st. NF/G+ clip. T11. $35.00

**FORESTER, C.S.** *Man in the Yellow Raft.* 1969. Little Brn. ARC. RS. VG/dj. B30. $60.00

**FORESTER, C.S.** *Napoleon & His Court.* 1924. London. Methuen. 1st/1st issue (ads dtd 3/24). variant gr cloth. NF/dj. B4. $1,500.00

**FORESTER, C.S.** *Naval War of 1812.* 1957. London. Michael Joseph. 1st. 1/7500. dk bl cloth. F/NF. T11. $130.00

**FORESTER, C.S.** *Nightmare.* 1954. Little Brn. 1st. gray cloth. F/NF. T11. $60.00

**FORESTER, C.S.** *Poo-Poo & the Dragons.* 1942. Little Brn. 1st. 8vo. gr cloth. dj. R5. $350.00

**FORESTER, C.S.** *Randall & the River of Time.* 1950. London. Michael Joseph. 1st. blk cloth. F/clip. T11. $115.00

**FORESTER, C.S.** *Ship of the Line.* 1938. Toronto. Saunders. 1st Canadian. bl cloth. VG. A14. $22.00

**FORESTER, C.S.** *Ship.* 1943. Boston. 1st. VG/fair. B5. $30.00

**FORESTER, C.S.** *To the Indies.* 1940. Little Brn. 1st. VG/dj. T11. $85.00

**FORESTER, Frank.** *Warwick Woodlands.* 1990. Derrydale. 1/2500. aeg. gilt leather. F. A17. $25.00

**FORGUE, Norman W.** *One Hundred Proverbs Adapted From the Japanese.* 1960. Chicago. Blk Cat. mini. 1/17 (300 total). 28p. deep maroon skiver leather. F. B24. $225.00

**FORMA, Warren.** *They Were Ragtime.* 1976. Grosset Dunlap. ils/250 photos. A19. $30.00

**FORMAN, Henry Chandlee.** *Tidewater Maryland Architecture & Gardens.* c 1956. Bonanza. 208p. decor ep. VG/clip. P4. $35.00

**FORMAN, Michael.** *Land of Dreams.* 1982. HRW. 1st Am. 32p. F/dj. D4. $30.00

**FORREST, Earle R.** *Missions & Pueblos of the Old Southwest.* 1929. Arthur H Clark. 1st. photos. 386p. teg. bl cloth. NF. P4. $215.00

**FORREST, Elizabeth Chabot.** *Daylight Moon.* 1937. NY. Stokes. 2nd. 8vo. map ep. beige cloth. P4. $25.00

**FORREST & HILL.** *Lone War Trail of the Apache Kid.* 1947. Trail's End. 1st. ils/index. 143p. VG. B19. $40.00

**FORRESTER, Victoria.** *Latch Against the Wind.* 1985. Atheneum. 1st. 48p. F/dj. D4. $25.00

**FORSEE, Aylesa.** *William Henry Jackson, Pioneer Photographer of the West.* 1964. Viking. photos. 205p. VG. J2. $70.00

**FORSHAW, J.M.** *Australian Parrots.* 1969. Wynnewood, PA. 1st Am. 70 tipped-in mc photos/maps. 306p. cloth. NF/dj. C12. $200.00

**FORSTER, E.M.** *Aspects of the Novel.* 1927. Harcourt Brace. reissue. sm 8vo. 250p. F/dj. O1. $30.00

**FORSTER, E.M.** *Passage to India.* 1924. London. Edward Arnold. 1st. NF/dj. B24. $1,000.00

**FORSTER & SANDWEISS.** *Denizens of the Desert.* 1988. Albuquerque. F. A19. $30.00

**FORSYTH, Cecil.** *Orchestration.* 1947. Macmillan. 2nd. 530p. G. S5. $15.00

**FORSYTH, Frederick.** *Day of the Jackal.* 1971. Viking. 1st. F/VG. M19. $17.50

**FORSYTH, Frederick.** *Day of the Jackal.* 1971. Viking. 1st. VG/clip. S13. $15.00

**FORSYTH, Frederick.** *Day of the Jackal.* 1971. London. 1st. VG/dj. T9. $65.00

**FORSYTH, Frederick.** *Fourth Protocol.* 1984. Viking. 1st Am. VG/dj. N4. $20.00

**FORSYTH, Frederick.** *Odessa File.* 1972. NY. Viking. 1st. NF/NF clip. H11. $25.00

**FORSYTH, Frederick.** *Shepherd.* 1976. NY. Viking. 1st. F/NF. M23. $25.00

**FORSYTH, Friedrich.** *Dogs of War.* 1974. London. 1st. VG/dj. T9. $35.00

**FORTESCUE, John.** *Difference Bewteen an Absolute & Ltd Monarchy...* 1719. London. Bowyer. 8vo. ils. contemporary paneled calf. R12. $450.00

**FORTIER, Samuel.** *Use of Water in Irrigation.* 1916. McGraw Hill. 325p. VG. A10. $20.00

**FORTLAGE, Karl.** *Acht Psychologischen Vortatge.* 1869. Hermann Dufft. German text. 348p. contemporary bdg. G1. $85.00

**FORTUINE, Robert.** *Chills & Fever. Health & Disease in Early History of Alaska.* 1989. U AK. inscr. 8vo. gray cloth. NF/dj. P4. $45.00

**FORTY & FORTY.** *Bovington Tank Collection.* 1992. Southampton, Eng. Ensign. 1st. 127p. F. M7. $25.00

**FOSHAY, Ella M.** *Audubon, John James.* 1997. Abrams. 55 mc pl. maroon cloth. AN/dj. A28. $40.00

**FOSHAY, Ella M.** *Mr Luman Reed's Picture Gallery.* 1990. Abrams. ils. VG/dj. M17. $40.00

**FOSHAY, Ella M.** *Reflections of Nature: Flowers in American Art.* 1984. NY. 1st. ils. VG/dj. M17. $30.00

**FOSS, Gerald D.** *Three Centuries of Freemasonry in New Hampshire.* 1972. Concord. sgn. ils. VG/dj. M17. $30.00

**FOSTER, Adriance S.** *Practical Plant Anatomy.* 1950. Van Nostrand. 2nd. biblio/index. 228p. G. H10. $25.00

**FOSTER, Alan Dean.** *Day of the Dissonance.* 1984. Phantasia. 1st/ltd. 1/375. F/dj/case. P3. $40.00

**FOSTER, Alan Dean.** *Moment of the Magician.* 1984. Phantasia. 1st/ltd. 1/375. F/dj/case. P3. $40.00

**FOSTER, Alan Dean.** *Star Wars: Splinter of the Mind's Eye.* nd. BC. VG/dj. P3. $8.00

**FOSTER, B.F.** *Concise Treatise on Commercial Book-Keeping...* 1839. Boston. Perkins Marvin. 3rd. 194+17p. G. H7. $15.00

**FOSTER, Coram.** *Rear Admiral Byrd & the Polar Expeditions.* 1930. NY. AL Burt. 1st. 8vo. bl cloth. P4. $30.00

**FOSTER, Elon.** *6000 Sermon Illustrations.* 1953. BAker. 704p. G. B29. $11.00

**FOSTER, H. Lincoln.** *Rock Gardening: Guide to Alpines & Other Wildflowers...* 1968. Bonanza. ils/biblio/index. 449p. VG/worn. H10. $20.00

**FOSTER, J.J.** *Chats on Old Miniatures.* 1908. NY. mc ftspc. ils. 3-quarter bl leather/marbled brd. VG. M17. $50.00

**FOSTER, J.W.** *Pre-Historic Races of the United States of America.* 1873. Chicago. SC Griggs. 415p. gilt gr cloth. G7. $125.00

**FOSTER, O'Kane.** *In the Night Did I Sing.* 1942. Scribner. 1st. NF/VG. B9. $85.00

**FOSTER, Pearl Byrd.** *Classic American Cooking.* 1983. S&S. G/dj. A16. $15.00

**FOSTER, Richard.** *Prayer: Finding the Heart's True Home.* 1992. Harper. notes/index. AN/dj. A27. $15.00

**FOSTER, W. Bert.** *In Alaskan Waters.* 1910. Phil. Penn. 363p. lt bl cloth. P4. $30.00

**FOSTER, William H.** *New England Grouse Shooting.* 1970 (1941). NY. rpt. ils. fwd Bruette. F/dj. A17. $60.00

**FOSTER & SMITH.** *Devotional Classics: Selected Reading...* (1993. Harper. AN/wrp. A27. $15.00

**FOSTER & TRELL.** *Prince Valiant in the Days of King Arthur.* (1951). NY. ils. 128p. VG/dj. B18. $35.00

**FOTHERGILL, Samuel.** *Ten Discourses Delivered Extempore...Quakers...1767-1770.* 1806. Phil. B Johnson. 16mo. 220p. worn full leather. V3. $45.00

**FOURNIER, Pierre Simon.** *Manual Typographique.* 1764-1766. Paris. Fournier. 2 vol. 8vo. 21 fld/double-p pl. full brn morocco. R12. $8,750.00

**FOWKE, Gerard.** *Archaeological History of Ohio, Mound Builders...* ca 1902. Columbus. ils/maps. 760p. G. B18. $75.00

**FOWLER, Connie May.** *River of Hidden Dreams.* 1993. Putnam. 1st. F/dj. M23. $25.00

**FOWLER, Connie May.** *Sugar Cage.* 1992. NY. Putnam. 1st. sgn. F/dj. M23. $40.00

**FOWLER, Don D.** *Photographed All the Best Scenery: Jack Hiller's Diary...* 1973. Salt Lake City. 2nd. obl 8vo. 225p. wht cloth. dj. F7. $40.00

**FOWLER, Don D.** *Western Photographs of John K Hillers: Myself in the Water.* 1989. Smithsonian. VG/dj. J2. $75.00

**FOWLER, Earlene.** *Fool's Puzzle.* 1994. Berkley. 1st. F/dj. M23. $40.00

**FOWLER, Gene.** *Good Night, Sweet Prince.* 1945. Phil. Blakiston. 474p. G/dj. C5. $12.50

**FOWLER, Guy.** *Dawn Patrol.* 1930. Grosset Dunlap. MTI/true 1st. F/VG+. B4. $350.00

**FOWLER, H.W.** *Dictionary of Modern English Usage.* 1926. London. Humphrey Milford. 1st. VG. Q1. $250.00

**FOWLER, Harlan D.** *Three Caravans to Yuma.* 1980. Glendale, CA. Arthur H Clark. F. A19. $55.00

**FOWLER, Karen Joy.** *Sarah Canary.* 1991. NY. Holt. 1st. F/dj. M25. $45.00

**FOWLER, Russell.** *Operating Room & the Patient.* 1906. Phil. 1st. ils. 172p. A13. $300.00

**FOWLER, W.M.** *Baron of Beacon Hill: Biography of John Hancock.* 1980. Boston. 1st. ils. 366p. F/dj. M4. $30.00

**FOWLER & FOWLER.** *Concise Oxford Dictionary of Current English.* 1919. Oxford. Clarendon. 8vo. Riviere bdg. NF. H5. $150.00

**FOWLES, John.** *Aristos: Self-Portrait in Ideas.* 1964. Little Brn. 1st. author's 2nd book. NF/VG. J3. $150.00

**FOWLES, John.** *Collector.* 1963. Little Brn. ARC/1st Am. author's 1st book. NF/lt yel prt wrp. M24. $275.00

**FOWLES, John.** *Collector.* 1963. Little Brn. 1st. author's 1st book. NF/VG. J3. $130.00

**FOWLES, John.** *French Lieutenant's Woman.* 1969. London. Cape. 1st. 8vo. top edge brn. gilt brn cloth. F/dj. R3. $185.00

**FOWLES, John.** *Introduction: Remembering Cruikshank.* 1964. Princeton. 1st offprt. less than 50. sgn. F/wrp. L3. $450.00

**FOWLES, John.** *Maggot.* 1985. Boston. Little Brn. 1st. F/NF. H11. $20.00

**FOWLES, John.** *Of Memories & Magpies.* 1983. Austin. Tom Taylor. 1st. 1/200. AN/French-fld wrp. w/Christmas greeting. M24. $125.00

**FOWLKES, Martha.** *Behind Every Successful Man: Wives of Medicine & Academe.* 1980. NY. 1st. 223p. A13. $40.00

**FOX, Charles Donald.** *Little Robinson Crusoe, a New Crusoe Story...* 1925. NYC. 1st. ils. 168p. VG/dj. B18. $50.00

**FOX, Charles Philip.** *Ticket to the Circus: Pictorial History of Ringlings.* 1969. Bramahll. 184p. VG/dj. O3/S5. $25.00

**FOX, Daniel.** *Power & Illness: Failure & Future of American Health Policy.* 1993. Berkeley. 1st. 183p. A13. $30.00

**FOX, Dottie.** *Below the Rim: One Woman's Adventures in the Grand Canyon.* nd. Snowmass, CO. sgn. 98p. VG+/stiff wrp. F7. $15.00

**FOX, George.** *Journal of George Fox.* 1948. London. Dent. 12mo. 359p. G. V3. $12.00

**FOX, George.** *Journal of George Fox.* 1952. Cambridge. 12mo. 379p. VG. V3. $35.00

**FOX, George.** *Warlord's Hill.* 1982. Times Books. 1st. VG/dj. N4. $17.50

**FOX, Helen M.** *Years in My Herb Garden.* 1953. BC. photos/plans. VG/dj. B26. $11.00

**FOX, John Jr.** *Blue-Grass & Rhodendrom.* 1901. Scribner. 1st. 12mo. 294p. dk brn cloth. VG. J3. $95.00

**FOX, John Jr.** *Little Sheperd of Kingdom Come.* (1903). Grosset Dunlap. later prt. 404p. VG. B36. $16.00

**FOX, John Jr.** *Little Shepherd of Kingdom Come.* 1906. Scribner. VG. S18. $12.00

**FOX, John Jr.** *Little Shepherd of Kingdom Come.* 1931. Scribner. 1st thus. ils NC Wyeth. 322p. VG. D1. $200.00

**FOX, John Jr.** *Trail of the Lonesome Pine.* 1908. Scribner. 1st. 422p. G. G11. $15.00

**FOX, Michael W.** *Supercat: Raising the Perfect Feline Companion.* 1990. NY. Howell. VG/dj. O3. $6.00

**FOX, Paula.** *One-Eyed Cat.* 1984. Bradbury. 1st. 8vo. 216p. F/NF. T5. $30.00

**FOX, Robert.** *Antarctica & the South Atlantic: Discovery, Development...* 1985. London. 1st. 8vo. 336p. VG/dj. P4. $27.50

**FOX, Sally.** *Medieval Woman: Illustrated Book of Days.* 1985. Toronto. 1st Canadian. F/sans. T12. $15.00

**FOX, Siv Cedering.** *Mother Is.* 1975. Stein Day. 1st. inscr/dtd 1975. F/dj. L3. $55.00

**FOX, Uffa.** *Racing Cruising & Design.* 1938. Scribner. 340p. G+. B5. $95.00

**FOX, Warwick.** *Toward a Transpersonal Ecology.* 1995. SUNY. 390p. VG/wrp. S15. $5.00

**FOX, William Price.** *Dr Golf.* 1963. Phil. 1st. ils Chas Rodriques. ils gr brd. VG. B14. $45.00

**FOX & GATES.** *What Is Your Dog Saying?* 1977. CMG. sgn Fox. VG/G. O3. $25.00

**FOX-SHEINWOLD, Patricia.** *Gone But Not Forgotten.* 1971. NY. Bell. 219p. VG/dj. C5. $12.50

**FOXX, Aleister.** *Harm's Way.* 1992. NY. SMP. 1st. F/F. H11. $15.00

**FOXX, Jack;** see Pronzini, Bill.

**FRACASTORO, Girolamo.** *Opera Omnia, in Unum Proxime Post Illius Mortem Collecta...* 1574. Venice. Apud Juntas. 2nd. 4to. ils/woodcuts. 213p. 18th-C half vellum. K1. $850.00

**FRAIPONT, J.** *Collections Zoologiques du Baron Edm De Selys Longchamps...* 1910. Bruzelles. Hayez. sm folio. 2 mc pl. 130p. VG/wrp. C12. $75.00

**FRALEY, Tobin.** *Carnival Animal.* 1984. Zephyr. 2nd. obl 4to. 127p. F/NF. C15. $20.00

**FRALEY, Tobin.** *Great American Carousel: A Century of Master Craftmanship.* 1994. SF. Chronicle. 1st. ils. 132p. F/dj. O3. $18.00

**FRANCATELLI, C.** *Modern Cook: Practical Guide to Culinary Art.* 1880 (1846). lg 8vo. 560p. VG. E6. $75.00

**FRANCE, Anatole.** *Gods Are A-Thirst.* 1942. London. Nonesuch. ils Jean Oberle. 205p. VG/case. F1. $20.00

**FRANCE, Anatole.** *Gods Are A-Thirst.* 1942. London. Nonesuch. lg 8vo. 205p. decor brd. F/NF case. M7. $35.00

**FRANCE, Anatole.** *In All France: Children in Town & Country.* 1930. Whitman. 1st. Young-Heart Book. VG. B27. $45.00

**FRANCE, Anatole.** *Nos Enfants.* nd. Paris. Librairie Hachette. 4to.ils DeMonvel. cloth-backed brd. R5. $125.00

**FRANCE, Anatole.** *Penguin Island.* 1927. Bodley Head. 16th. lacks ffe. VG. P3. $18.00

**FRANCIS, Clare.** *Night Sky.* 1984. NY. Morrow. 1st. F/F. H11. $20.00

**FRANCIS, Daniel.** *Discovery of the North: Exploration of Canada's Arctic.* 1986. Edmonton. Hurtig Pub Ltd. 224p. F/dj. P4. $35.00

**FRANCIS, Dick.** *Across the Board.* 1975. Harper Row. 1st thus. VG/dj. A24. $35.00

**FRANCIS, Dick.** *Banker.* 1982. London. Michael Joseph. 1st. F/dj. M15. $65.00

**FRANCIS, Dick.** *Bolt.* 1986. London. Michael Joseph. 1st. sgn. F/dj. M15. $85.00

**FRANCIS, Dick.** *Bolt.* 1986. Putnam. 1st Am. NF/dj. G8. $12.50

**FRANCIS, Dick.** *Bonecrack.* 1972. Harper. 1st Am. NF/dj. N4. $60.00

**FRANCIS, Dick.** *Break In.* 1985. London. Michael Joseph. 1st. F/NF clip. B3. $50.00

**FRANCIS, Dick.** *Come to Grief.* 1995. London. Michael Joseph. 1st. F/dj. M15. $55.00

**FRANCIS, Dick.** *Comeback.* 1991. London. Michael Joseph. 1st. F/F. B3. $50.00

**FRANCIS, Dick.** *Decider.* 1993. Putnam. 1st Am. VG/dj. O3. $15.00

**FRANCIS, Dick.** *Edge.* 1988. Putnam. 1st. F/dj. T12. $45.00

**FRANCIS, Dick.** *Enquiry.* 1969. London. Michael Joseph. 1st. F/dj. M15. $250.00

**FRANCIS, Dick.** *Hot Money.* 1987. London. Michael Joseph. 1st. F/dj. M15. $45.00

**FRANCIS, Dick.** *Knock Down.* 1974. London. Michael Joseph. 1st. F/dj. M15. $125.00

**FRANCIS, Dick.** *Longshot.* 1990. Michael Joseph. 1st. F/NF. B3. $30.00

**FRANCIS, Dick.** *Odds Against.* 1965. London. Michael Joseph. 1st. F/dj. M15. $500.00

**FRANCIS, Dick.** *Proof.* 1984. London. Michael Joseph. 1st. F/dj. M15. $50.00

**FRANCIS, Dick.** *Reflex.* 1981. Putnam. 1st Am. sgn. F/dj. B2. $60.00

**FRANCIS, Dick.** *Risk.* 1977. London. Michael Joseph. 1st. F/dj. M15. $100.00

**FRANCIS, Dick.** *Smokescreen.* 1972. London. Michael Joseph. 1st. F/dj. M15. $125.00

**FRANCIS, Dick.** *Straight.* 1989. Putnam. 1st Am. NF/dj. G8. $15.00

**FRANCIS, Dick.** *To the Hilt.* 1996. London. Michael Joseph. 1st. F/dj. M15. $55.00

**FRANCIS, Dick.** *Trial Run.* 1978. Harper. 1st Am. F/NF. M25. $15.00

**FRANCIS, Dick.** *Twice Shy.* 1981. London. Michael Joseph. 1st. F/F. B3. $75.00

**FRANCIS, Dick.** *Whip Hand.* 1979. Harper Row. 1st Am. VG/dj. O3. $45.00

**FRANCIS, Dick.** *Whip Hand.* 1979. London. Michael Joseph. 1st. F/F. M15. $75.00

**FRANCIS, Dick.** *Whip Hand.* 1979. London. Michael Joseph. 1st. F/NF. A24. $60.00

**FRANCIS, John W.** *Old New York; or, Reminiscences of Past Sixty Years.* 1866. NY. WJ Widdleton. 8vo. portrait ftspc. 400p. terra-cotta cloth. NF. O1. $75.00

**FRANCIS, Richard.** *Arabian Nights Entertainments...* 1954. NY. Crowell. For Members of LEC. 4 vol. 1/1500. ils Szyk. F/case. H5. $300.00

**FRANCIS, Ronald D.** *Migrant Crime in Australia.* 1981. U Queensland. 1st. VG/dj. N2. $9.00

**FRANCIS, Valentine Mott.** *Thesis on Hospital Hygiene.* 1859. NY. 1st. 217p. A13. $350.00

**FRANCK, Harry.** *Lure of Alaska.* 1939. NY. Stokes. 8vo. 306p. beige cloth. VG/dj. P4. $38.00

**FRANCK, Harry.** *Vagabonding Down the Andes.* 1917. NY. Century. 1st. 612p. teg. F3. $20.00

**FRANCK & SCHNEIDER.** *Wunder des Schneeschuhs: Ein System des Richtigen...* 1925. Hamburg. Gebruder Enoch. 2 vol. ils/photos. bl cloth. case. D2. $270.00

**FRANCL, Joseph.** *Overland Journey of Joseph Francl.* 1968. SF. Wm Wreden. 1/540. ils Patricia Oberhaus. 55p. F. P4. $95.00

**FRANCOISE, Seignobosc.** *In Gay Paris.* 1956. NY. Scribner. 1st. 4to. striped cloth. mc dj. R5. $150.00

**FRANCOME & MACGREGOR.** *Declared Dead.* 1988. London. Headline. 1st. F/dj. T2. $45.00

**FRANCOME & MACGREGOR.** *Eavesdropper.* 1986. London. MacDonald. 1st sgn Francome. F/dj. T2. $60.00

**FRANK, Alan.** *Horror Film Handbook.* 1982. Barnes Noble. 1st. VG/dj. C9. $36.00

**FRANK, Louis.** *Medical History of Milwaukee 1834-1914.* 1915. Milwaukee. 1st. 271p. xl. A13. $100.00

**FRANK, Morrey.** *Every Young Man's Dream.* 1984. Silverback. 1st. F/VG. P8. $45.00

**FRANKFORT, Ellen.** *Voice: Life at the Village Voice.* 1976. Morrow. 1st. 8vo. cloth. F/dj. O10. $15.00

**FRANKFURTER, Felix.** *Case of Sacco & Vanzetti.* 1927. Boston. Little Brn. 1st. 118p. yel cloth. AN/yel dj. B14. $150.00

**FRANKLIN, Benjamin.** *Advice to Young Man on Choosing a Mistress, 1745.* (1982). Berkeley. Poole. mini. 1/130. prt/designer/sgn MP Adams. F. B24. $95.00

**FRANKLIN, Benjamin.** *Benjamin Franklin's Letter on Taking an Older Woman...* 1983. Manteno, IL. Bronte. mini. 1/50. hand-colored ils. pink/bl marbled brd. B24. $125.00

**FRANKLIN, Benjamin.** *Benjamin Franklin: Biography in His Own Words.* 1972. NY. ils. 416p. F/dj. M4. $27.00

**FRANKLIN, Benjamin.** *Porposals Relating to Education of Youth in Pennsylvania.* 1931. Phil. U PA. facs. 8vo. intro Wm Pepper. NF. O1. $30.00

**FRANKLIN, Benjamin.** *Works of the Late Dr Benjamin Franklin...* 1793. London. Robinson. 2 vol. 2nd. 8vo. gilt tree calf/rb spine labels. NF. O1. $400.00

**FRANKLIN, Colin.** *Private Presses.* 1969. Chester Springs, PA. Dudour. gilt ochre cloth. F/VG+. F1. $60.00

**FRANKLIN, Eugene.** *Bold House Murders.* 1973. Stein Day. 1st. sm 8vo. cloth. F/dj. O10. $25.00

**FRANKLIN, Jay.** *Rat Race.* 1940. FPCI. 1st. VG/dj. P3. $35.00

**FRANKLIN, John Hope.** *Militant South, 1800-1861.* 1956. Cambridge. 1st. 317p. Vg/dj. B18. $37.50

**FRANKLIN, Wayne.** *Discoverers, Explorers, Settlers.* 1979. Chicago. 1st. 8vo. gr cloth. NF/dj. P4. $25.00

**FRANKLIN, Wayne.** *Discoverers, Explorers, Settlers: Diligent Writers...* 1989. Chicago. later. 252p. VG/wrp. M10. $15.00

**FRANKS & LAMBERT.** *Early California Oil, Photographic History, 1865-1940.* 1985. College Sta. TX A&M. 1st. 4to. 243p. blk cloth. F/dj. P4/T10. $35.00

**FRANTZ, Joe B.** *Driskill Hotel.* 1973. Austin. Encino. 1st. F/clear acetate as issued. A24. $40.00

**FRANZ, Joseph.** *Star Fleet Technical Manual.* 1975. Ballantine. 1st. NF/red wrp. F1. $45.00

**FRANZ & PISMIS.** *Observational Parameters & Dynamical Evolution...* 1977. Mexico City. 4to. 216p. G/wrp. K5. $25.00

**FRANZEN, Bill.** *Hearing From Wayne.* 1988. Knopf. 1st. F/dj. M25. $35.00

**FRASER, Anthea.** *Island-in-Waiting.* 1979. St Martin. 1st. VG/dj. P3. $10.00

**FRASER, Antonia.** *Love Letters.* 1989. London. 1st thus. dj. T9. $22.00

**FRASER, Antonia.** *Warrior Queens.* 1989. NY. Knopf. 1st Am. ils. F/dj. T10. $25.00

**FRASER, Antonia.** *Weaker Vessel.* 1984. Knopf. 1st Am. NF/VG. P3. $20.00

**FRASER, C. Lovat.** *Book of Simple Toys.* 1982. Bryn Mawr. 1st thus. 1/1000. ils. unp. cloth. F/sans. D4. $95.00

**FRASER, George MacDonald.** *Flash for Freedom!* 1972. Knopf. 1st Am. VG+/dj. A14. $35.00

**FRASER, George MacDonald.** *Flashman & the Angel of the Lord.* 1994. Knopf. 1st. F/dj. T11. $40.00

**FRASER, George MacDonald.** *Flashman & the Dragon.* 1986. NY. Knopf. 1st. F/dj. T11. $35.00

**FRASER, George MacDonald.** *Flashman & the Redskins (#7).* 1982. Knopf. 1st Am. NF/dj. T11. $35.00

**FRASER, George MacDonald.** *Flashman at the Charge: From Flashman Papers 1854-1855.* 1973. London. Barrie Jenkins. 1st. VG+/VG. A14. $70.00

**FRASER, George MacDonald.** *Flashman's Lady.* 1977. London. Barrie Jenkins. 1st. F/dj. M15. $125.00

**FRASER, George MacDonald.** *Flashman.* 1969. NY. World. 1st. NF/F. T11. $85.00

**FRASER, George MacDonald.** *Flashman: From the Flashman Papers 1839-1842.* 1969. London. Jenkins. 1st. VG+/dj. A14. $122.50

**FRASER, George MacDonald.** *General Danced at Dawn.* 1973. Knopf. 1st Am. F/clip. T11. $100.00

**FRASER, George MacDonald.** *Pyrates.* 1984. Knopf. 1st Am. F/dj. T11. $25.00

**FRASER, George MacDonald.** *Royal Flash.* 1970. London. Barrie Jenkins. 1st. F/dj. M15. $200.00

**FRASER, George MacDonald.** *Royal Flash: From the Flashman Papers 1842-43 & 1847-48.* 1976. London. Barrie Jenkins. 1st/2nd imp. VG+/clip. A14. $22.00

**FRASER, Hugh.** *Handy Book of Ornamental Conifers & Rhododendrons...* 1875. Edinburgh. 292p. xl. B26. $30.00

**FRASER, James.** *Who Steals My Name?* 1976. Crime Club. 1st Am. VG/G. G8. $15.00

**FRASER & FRASER.** *Seven Years on the Pacific Slope.* 1914. Dodd Mead. 1st. photos. xl. VG. S14. $40.00

**FRASSANITO, William A.** *Grant & Lee: Virginia Campaigns 1864-1865.* 1983. Scribner. 1st. NF/clip. A14. $25.00

**FRAXEDAS, J. Joaquin.** *Lonely Crossing of Juan Cabera.* 1993. St Martin. 1st. F/dj. R14. $35.00

**FRAYN, Michael.** *Landing on the Sun.* 1991. NY. 1st. dj. T9. $10.00

**FRAYNE, Trent.** *Northern Dancer & Friends.* 1969. NY. Funk Wagnall. VG. O3. $20.00

**FRAZER, Robert W.** *Forts & Supplies: Role of the Army in Economy of SW...* 1983. NM U. 1st. 253p. F/F. B19. $30.00

**FRAZER, Robert W.** *Forts of the West.* (1965). Norman, OK. 1st. 246p. F/VG. E1. $60.00

**FRAZER, Robert W.** *Mansfield on the Condition of Western Forts 1853-1854.* 1963. Norman, OK. 1st. ils. 254p. E1. $55.00

**FRAZER & FRAZER.** *Pasha the Pom: Story of a Little Dog.* 1937. London. Blackie. 1st. 12mo. 117p. G. C14. $22.00

**FRAZIER, Charles.** *Cold Mountain.* 1997. Atlantic Monthly. 1st. author's 1st book. F/dj. A24/Y1. $200.00

**FRAZIER, Charles.** *Cold Mountain.* 1997. Sceptre. 1st Eng. sgn. F/wrp. B30. $150.00

**FRAZIER, Ian.** *Dating Your Mom.* 1986. FSG. 1st. F/dj. M23. $30.00

**FRAZIER, Ian.** *Great Plains.* 1989. FSG. F/dj. A19. $25.00

**FRAZIER, Ian.** *Great Plains.* 1989. FSG. 1st. 8vo. 290p. VG/dj. B11. $15.00

**FRAZIER, Robert Caine;** see Creasey, John.

**FREDE, Richard.** *Secret Circus.* 1967. Random. 1st. F/F. H11. $25.00

**FREDERICK, J.V.** *Ben Holladay: Stagecoach King.* 1940. Glendale, CA. Arthur H Clark. F/dj. A19. $250.00

**FREDERICK, William.** *100 Great Garden Plants.* 1975. Knopf. 214p. VG/dj. A10. $18.00

**FREDERICKSON, A.D.** *Ad Orientem.* 1889. London. WH Allen. 1st. 25 mc litho pl/2 maps. teg. gilt crimson cloth. VG. C12. $235.00

FREDRICKSON & STEWART. *Film Annual 1992.* 1992. Aliso Viejo Companion. 336p. VG/wrp. C5. $12.50

FREDRIKSSON, Kristine. *American Rodeo, From Buffalo Bill to Big Business.* 1985. TX A&M. 1st. photos. 255p. F. J2. $42.00

FREE, James Lamb. *Training Your Retriever.* 1968. Coward McCann. 3rd. photos. brn cloth. G. A28. $10.00

FREEDMAN, Robert O. *Soviet Jewry in the Decisive Decade 1971-80.* 1984. Durham. Duke. F/sans. B9. $12.50

FREEDMAN, Russell. *Lincoln: A Photobiography.* 1987. NY. Clarion. 1st. 4to. 1988 Newberry. AN/dj. R5. $100.00

FREEDMAN, Russell. *Wendell Berry.* 1997. Lexington. U KY. 1st. 1/400. Author copy. gilt red cloth. F. S9. $45.00

FREEHAND, Julianna. *Seafaring Legacy: Photographs, Diaries, Letters...* 1981. NY. Random. 1st. obl 4to. 209p. NF/dj. P4. $38.00

FREELING, Nicolas. *Arlette.* 1981. Pantheon. 1st Am. NF/dj. G8. $12.50

FREELING, Nicolas. *Aupres de ma Blonde.* 1972. Harper. 1st Am. NF/clip. M25. $25.00

FREELING, Nicolas. *Kitchen.* 1970. NY. 1st Am. ils Gail Garraty. VG/dj. M17. $20.00

FREELING, Nicolas. *Lovely Ladies.* 1971. Harper. 1st Am. VG+/dj. M25. $15.00

FREELING, Nicolas. *Not as Far as Velma.* 1989. Deutsch. 1st Eng. NF/dj. G8. $20.00

FREELING, Nicolas. *One More River.* 1988. London. Little Brn. 1st. F/dj. M15. $45.00

FREELING, Nicolas. *You Who Know.* 1994. Mysterious. 1st Am. VG/dj. G8. $12.50

FREEMAN, Bud. *You Don't Look Like a Musician.* 1974. Detroit. Balamp. 1st. sgn. F/dj. B2. $100.00

FREEMAN, Douglas Southall. *Last Parade.* 1932. Richmond, VA. Whittet Shepperson. 1/500. 20 leaves/ftspc/mtd pl. M8. $650.00

FREEMAN, Douglas Southall. *Lee of Virginia.* (1958). Scribner. later prt. 243p. VG/VG. B10. $35.00

FREEMAN, Douglas Southall. *RE Lee: A Biography.* 1935. NY. ils. VG. M17. $100.00

FREEMAN, Douglas Southall. *Washington: A Biography. Vol 2, Young Washington.* 1948. Scribner. 1st. 464p. VG. B10. $25.00

FREEMAN, James Dillet. *Once Upon a Christmas.* 1978. Unity Books. 1st. sm 4to. 173p. NF. W2. $20.00

FREEMAN, Lewis R. *Colorado River, Yesterday, To-Day & Tomorrow.* 1923. NY. 1st. 451p. bl cloth. VG. F7. $50.00

FREEMAN, Lewis R. *Down the Yellowstone.* 1922. NY. 1st. photos. 282p. NF. A17. $40.00

FREEMAN, Lewis R. *Waterways on Westward Wandering.* 1927. NY. 1st. photos. VG. M17. $25.00

FREEMAN, Mae Blacker. *Fun With Cooking.* 1947. NY. Random. ils. 29p. red glazed brd. VG/G. F1. $50.00

FREEMAN, Margaret B. *Unicorn Tapestries.* 1976. MOMA. photos. VG/dj. M17. $37.50

FREEMAN, Mary Eleanor Wilkins. *Yates Pride: A Romance.* 1912. NY/London. Harper. 1st. 16mo. 65p. brn cloth. F/dj. J3. $125.00

FREEMAN, R. Austin. *Dr Thorndyke's Crime File.* 1941. Dodd Mead. 1st. G. N4. $45.00

FREEMAN, R. Austin. *For the Defense: Dr Thorndyke.* 1934. Dodd Mead. 1st Am. F/VG. M15. $175.00

FREEMAN, R. Austin. *Savant's Vendetta.* 1920. London. C Arthur Pearson. 1st Eng. VG/dj. M15. $1,350.00

FREEMAN, R.B. *Works of Charles Darwin: Annotated Bibliographical Handlist.* 1977. Kent Dawson. revised/enlarged. 235p. NF. M12. $95.00

FREEMAN, R.B. *Works of Charles Darwin: Annotated Bibliographical Handlist.* 1977. London. 2nd. 235p. VG. A13. $65.00

FREEMAN, Roger A. *Mustang at War.* 1974. Doubleday. lg 8vo. 160p. maroon paper brd. VG. M7. $10.00

FREEMAN, Samuel. *Town Officer; or, Power & Duty of Selectmen...* 1805. Boston. contemporary sheep. M11. $75.00

FREEMAN, Susan Tax. *Neighbors: Social Contact in a Castilian Hamlet.* 1970. Chicago. F/NF. B9. $15.00

FREEMANTLE & HASKELL. *Two Views of Gettysburg.* 1964. Lakeside Classic. 1st thus. teg. NF/sans. T11. $40.00

FREETH & WINSTONE. *Explorers of Arabia From Renaissance to Victorian Era.* 1978. NY. Holmes Meier. ils/maps. 308p. cloth. VG/dj. Q2. $24.00

FREMANTLE, Anne. *Great Ages of Western Philosophy.* 1957. Houghton Mifflin. 6 vol. VG/case. M20. $30.00

FREMONT, Jessie Benton. *Year of American Travel.* 1960. SF. Plantin/BC of CA. 1/450. 121p. half cloth/decor brd. P4. $95.00

FREMONT, John Charles. *Exploring Expedition to Rocky Mountains, OR & CA.* 1851. Buffalo. Geo Derby. 456p. bstp cloth. B18. $25.00

FREMONT, John Charles. *Narratives of Exploration & Adventure.* 1957. NY. Longman Gr. rpt. 532p. dk bl cloth. P4. $40.00

FRENCH, Hannah D. *Bookbinding in Early America, Seven Essays on Mathers...* 1986. Worcester. Am Antiquarian Soc. 1st. gilt rust cloth. F/dj. M24. $50.00

FRENCH, Joseph Lewis. *Sagas of the Seas.* 1924. NY. Dial. 1st. NF/VG. T11. $35.00

FRENCH, L.H. *Nome Nuggets. Some of the Experiences of a Party of Gold...* 1901. NY. Montross Clarke Emmons. 1st. 8vo. cloth. P4. $125.00

FRENCH, L.H. *Seward's Land of Gold: Five Season's Experience...* nd (1905). NY. Montross Clarke Emmons. 1st. 101p. G. A17. $75.00

FRENCH, Nicci. *Memory Game.* 1997. London. Heinemann. 1st. author's 1st novel. F/dj. M15. $85.00

FRENCH, Patrick. *Younghusband: Last Great Imperial Adventurer.* 1994. NY. ils. VG/dj. M17. $15.00

FRENCH, Peter. *Philosophers in Wonderland.* 1975. Llewellyn. 1st. ils. fair/dj. B27. $25.00

FRENCH, R.K. *History & Virtues of Cyder.* 1982. NY. ils. VG/dj. M17. $25.00

FRENCH, William. *Some Recollections of Western Ranchman, NM, 1883-1899.* 1928. Stokes. 283p. VG. J2. $625.00

FRERE-COOK, G. *Decorative Arts of the Mariner.* 1966. London. photos/maps. F/dj. M4. $55.00

FRESHNEY, R.I. *Animal Cell Culture: A Practical Approach.* 1986. Oxford. IRL Pr. 8vo. 248p. F. B1. $40.00

FREUCHEN, Peter. *Law of Larion.* c 1952. McGraw Hill. 8vo. 313p. blk cloth. VG/dj. P4. $30.00

FREUCHENS, Peter. *Book of the Eskimos.* 1961. Cleveland. World. VG/dj. A19. $35.00

FREUD, Sigmund. *Das Unbehagen in der Kultur.* 1930. Wien/Leipzig. Internationaler Psychoanalytischer. German text. 12mo. G1. $85.00

FREUD, Sigmund. *Die Zukunft Einer Illusion.* 1927. Leipzig/Wien/Zurich. Internationaler Psychoanalytischer. sm 8vo. 91p. F. G1. $175.00

FREUD, Sigmund. *Group Psychology & Analysis of the Ego.* 1921. London. Internat Psycho-Analytical Pr. 1st. 134p. gr cloth. G1. $150.00

**FREUD, Sigmund.** *History of the Psychoanalytic Movement.* 1917. NY. Nervous & Mental Disease Pub. 1st Am. tan wrp. M24. $300.00

**FREUD, Sigmund.** *Interpretation of Dreams.* 1921. London. intro AA Brill. VG. M17. $15.00

**FREUD, Sigmund.** *Interpretation of Dreams.* 1960. Basic. 1st. ils. F/dj. P12. $15.00

**FREUD, Sigmund.** *Origins of Psychoanalysis: Letters to Wilhelm Fliess...* 1954. Basic Books. 1st. 8vo. 486p. VG/G. C14. $25.00

**FREUND & ULICH.** *Religion & the Public Schools, the Legal Issue...* 1965. Cambridge. VG. M11. $50.00

**FREWIN, Leslie.** *Dietrich.* 1967. Stein Day. ne. VG. W2. $15.00

**FRIED, John J.** *Life Along the San Andreas Fault.* 1973. Saturday Review. 1st. sgn. NF/dj. O4. $15.00

**FRIEDERICI, Georg.** *Scalping in America.* 1907. GPO. 8vo. disbound. P4. $16.50

**FRIEDLANDER, Max J.** *From Van Eyck to Bruegel: Early Netherlandish Painting.* 1956. Phaidon. ils. VG/dj. M17. $35.00

**FRIEDLANDER, Walter.** *Mannerism & Anti-Mannerism in Italian Painting.* 1957. Cornell. ils. VG/G. M17. $17.50

**FRIEDLANDER & ROSENBERG.** *Paintings of Lucas Cranach.* 1978. Secaucus. Wellfleet. 162p+434 monochrome pl. gilt blk cloth. F/dj. F1. $65.00

**FRIEDMAN, Jake.** *Common Sense Candy Teacher.* 1915 (1911). VG. E6. $60.00

**FRIEDMAN, Kinky.** *Case of Lone Star.* 1987. Morrow. 1st. F/dj. M15. $55.00

**FRIEDMAN, Kinky.** *Elvis, Jesus & Coca-Cola.* 1993. S&S. 1st. sgn. F/dj. A24. $35.00

**FRIEDMAN, Kinky.** *Frequent Flyer.* 1989. Morrow. 1st. sgn. F/F. B3. $40.00

**FRIEDMAN, Kinky.** *Musical Chairs.* 1991. Morrow. 1st. inscr. F/dj. M15. $100.00

**FRIEDMAN, Kinky.** *When the Cat's Away.* 1988. Beech Tree. 1st. author's 1st book. F/dj. N4. $35.00

**FRIEDMAN, Mickey.** *Venetian Mask.* 1987. Scribner. 1st. F/F. H11. $20.00

**FRIEDMAN, Milton.** *Tax Limitation, Inflation & the Role of Government.* 1978. Fisheer Inst. 110p. VG. S5. $15.00

**FRIEDMAN, Philip.** *Reasonable Doubt.* 1990. NY. DIF. 1st. F/F. H11. $20.00

**FRIEDMAN, Reuben.** *History of Dermatology in Philadelphia.* 1955. NY. 556p. A13. $65.00

**FRIEDMAN, Ruth.** *Portrait of Jewish Life, Fredericksburg, Virginia 1860-1986.* (1986). self pub. photos. 100p. VG. B10. $25.00

**FRIEDMAN, Steven G.** *History of Vascular Surgery.* 1989. NY. ils. 223p. F/VG. A4. $65.00

**FRIEDMANN, H.** *Natural-History Background of Camouflage.* 1942. WA. Smithsonian. ils/pl. VG+/wrp. M12. $10.00

**FRIEDRICH, Carl Joachim.** *Philosophy of Law in Historical Perspective.* 1958. Chicago U. VG/dj. M11. $45.00

**FRIEDRICH, Otto.** *End of the World, a History.* 1982. CMG. ne. 384p. VG/NF. W2. $25.00

**FRIEDRICH, Otto.** *Olympia: Paris in the Age of Manet.* 1992. NY. Harper Collins. rem mk. VG/dj. B9. $15.00

**FRIEDWALD, Will.** *Jazz Singing: America's Great Voices From Bessie Smith...* 1990. NY. 1st. VG/dj. M17. $25.00

**FRIENDLICH, Dick.** *Pinch Hitter.* 1964. Westminster. 1st. VG/G. P8. $30.00

**FRIENDLY, Alfred.** *Beaufort of the Admiralty: Life of Sir Frances Beaufort...* 1977. NY. 1st. ils. VG/dj. M17. $27.50

**FRIES, Adelaide L.** *Records of the Moravians in North Carolina, Vol 8 1823-37.* 1954. Raleigh. NC Hist Soc. lg 8vo. gilt maroon cloth. VG. M7. $40.00

**FRIES & WEST.** *Chemical Warfare.* 1921. NY. 445p. A13. $100.00

**FRIESEN, Victor Carl.** *Spirit of Huckleberry: Sensuousness in Henry Thoreau...* 1984. U Alberta. 1st. F/dj. P3. $20.00

**FRIGGE, Karli.** *Landschapjes.* nd. np. obl 8vo. handwritten intro. 12 marbled papers tipped-in. 30p. F. B24. $950.00

**FRIGGE, Karli.** *Marbled Landscapes. Decorated Papers. Volume I.* 1989. Buren, Netherlands. Fritz Kniuf. 1/99. sgn. obl 4to. F/glassine. B24. $600.00

**FRIGGE, Karli.** *Marbled Plants. Decorated Papers. Volume II.* 1989. Buren, Netherlands. Fritz Kniuf. Dutch/Eng text. 6 marbled papers. F/dj. B24. $750.00

**FRIGGE, Karli.** *Marmer Proeven (Marbled Proofs).* 1985. Delft, Holland. tall 4to. sgn. 218 mtd samples. natural leather. F. B24. $1,500.00

**FRIGNET, Ernest.** *La Californie: Historie des Progres de l'un des Etat-Unis...* 1867. Paris. Schlesinger. Deuxieme ed. fld map. 479p. prt wrp. D11. $150.00

**FRIIS & SHELBY.** *United States Polar Exploration.* 1970. Athens. OH U. 199p. map ep. bl cloth. P4. $45.00

**FRIMMER, Steven.** *Dead Matter.* 1982. HRW. 1st. 220p. F/dj. O10. $35.00

**FRINGS, Ketti.** *Look Homeward, Angel.* 1958. Scribner. 1st. F/dj. B4. $150.00

**FRINK, Maurice.** *Cow Country Cavalcade: 80 Years of WY Stock Growers...* 1954. Old West Pub. 243p. VG/dj. J2. $75.00

**FRINK, Maurice.** *Photographer on an Army Mule.* 1965. Norman, OK. 2nd. ils. 151p. E1. $40.00

**FRITZ, Samuel.** *Journal of the Travels & Labours of Father Samuel Fritz.* 1922. London. Hakluyt. 2nd Series #LI. 8vo. 164p. bl cloth. P4. $135.00

**FRITZ & WILLIAMS.** *Triumph of Culture: 18th-Century Perspectives.* 1972. Toronto. 1st. VG/dj. N2. $12.50

**FROESCHELS, Emil.** *Selected Papers of Emil Froeschels, 1940-1964.* 1964. Amsterdam. North-Holland Pub. pres. 232p. stiff gray wrp. G1. $45.00

**FROILAND, S.G.** *Natural History of the Black Hills.* 1982. Sioux Falls. Center West Studies. ils/fld map. 175p. VG+. M12. $17.50

**FROME, David.** *Strange Death of Martin Green.* 1931. Doubleday Crime Club. 1st. F/dj. M15. $150.00

**FRONTINUS, Sextus Julius.** *Water Supply of the City of Rome.* 1973. New Eng Water Works Assn. photos. trans Clemens Herschel. VG. M17. $40.00

**FROST, David.** *I Gave Them a Sword: Behind the Scenes of Nixon Interviews.* 1978. Morrow. 1st. sm 4to. 320p. NF/G. W2. $20.00

**FROST, Edwin Brant.** *Astronomer's Life.* 1933. Houghton Mifflin. 8vo. 300p. G/dj. K5. $50.00

**FROST, John.** *Indian Wars of the United States...* 1859. NY. CM Saxton. ils. 300p. bstp cloth. G+. B18. $45.00

**FROST, Mark.** *Six Messiahs.* 1995. Morrow. 1st. F/dj. G8. $25.00

**FROST, O.W.** *Tales of Eskimo Alaska.* 1971. AK Methodist U. 8vo. 91p. red cloth. P4. $20.00

**FROST, Robert.** *A Boy's Will.* 1915. Holt. 1st Am/later issue. author's 1st book. VG. L3. $375.00

**FROST, Robert.** *Masque of Reason.* 1945. NY. Henry Holt. 1st trade. inscr/dtd 1945. 23p. navy cloth. F/dj. J3. $275.00

**FROST, Robert.** *Selected Prose of...* 1966. HRW. 1st. VG/clip. B30. $50.00

**FROST, S. Annie.** *Godey's Lady's Book, Receipts & Household Hints.* 1870. Phil. 1st. 454p. VG. E6. $50.00

**FROST, Thomas.** *Circus Life & Circus Celebrities.* 1881. London. Chatto Windus. 328p. VG. S5. $125.00

**FROST & RONALDS.** *Catalogue of Books & Papers Relating to Electricity...* nd. rpt. 1/150. 13,000 entries. 579p. F. A4. $85.00

**FROTHINGHAM, A.L.** *Roman Cities in Italy & Dalmatia.* 1910. NY. Sturgis Walton. 1st. xl. G+. A2. $25.00

**FRUM, Linda.** *News Makers: Behind Cameras With Canada's Top TV Journalist.* 1990. Toronto. 1st. F/dj. T12. $15.00

**FRY, Christopher.** *Curtmangle.* 1961. OUP. 99p. VG/dj. C5. $12.50

**FRY, Christopher.** *Firstborn.* 1950 (1946). OUP. 101p. VG. C5. $12.50

**FRY, John.** *Select Poems, Containing Religious Epistles...* 1805. Stanford. Daniel Lawrence. 12mo. 224p. leather. V3. $50.00

**FRY, Rosalie K.** *Matelot, Little Sailor of Brittany.* 1958. Dutton. 1st. 8vo. ils. VG/G. M5. $38.00

**FRY & WHITE.** *Big Trees.* 1930. Stanford. 1st. ils. 114p. map ep. cloth. B26. $16.00

**FRYATT, H.N.** *Agriculture: Its Essentials & Non-Essentials...* 1854. NY. Magagno. 57p. A10. $25.00

**FRYE, Northrop.** *Words With Power.* 1990. 1st. VG/dj. M17. $15.00

**FRYER, Jane Eayre.** *Easy Steps in Cooking for Big & Little Girls...* 1912. pre-1st (no imp). VG. E6. $175.00

**FRYER, Jane Eayre.** *Mary Frances Cookbook.* 1912. John Winston. ils Hays/Boyer. 175p. bl cloth/paper label. VG. D1. $160.00

**FRYER, Jane Eayre.** *Mary Frances Cookbook.* 1912. Phil. Winston. 1st. ils MG Hays/JA Boyer. 175p. dk bl cloth/label. VG/dj. R5. $285.00

**FRYER, Jane Eayre.** *Mary Frances Housekeeper.* 1914. Phil. Winston. 1st. all paper dolls present/unmarked. VG. B5. $135.00

**FUCHS, Eduard.** *Honore Daumier Lithographien: 1861-1872.* nd (1920). Munich. Albert Langen. folio. ils. gilt brn paper/yel cloth. VG. F1. $100.00

**FUCHS, Ernest.** *Text-Book of Ophthalmology.* 1896. NY. Appleton. ils. 788p. half morocco. G7. $175.00

**FUCHS, Ernst.** *Ernst Fuchs: Der Feuerfuchs.* 1988. Frankfurt. Umschau. sgn pres. ils/pl/photos. 287p. gilt purple cloth. D2. $350.00

**FUENTES, Carlos.** *Buried Mirror.* 1992. Houghton Mifflin. 1st. 399p. dj. F3. $30.00

**FUENTES, Carlos.** *Constancia & Other Stories for the Virgins.* 1990. FSG. 1st. trans Thos Christensen. F/dj. R14. $25.00

**FUENTES, Carlos.** *Old Gringo.* 1986. London. Deutsch. ARC. F/NF. B3. $25.00

**FUENTES, Carlos.** *Terra Nostra.* 1976. FSG. ARC/1st. inscr. F/dj. L3. $500.00

**FUERTES & OSGOOD.** *Artist & Naturalist in Ethiopia.* 1936. NY. 1st. lg 8vo. 249p. gilt cloth. NF. C12. $185.00

**FUESS, Claude M.** *Life of Caleb Cushing.* 1923. Harcourt Brace. 2 vol. 1000p. cloth. VG. A10. $50.00

**FULANAN.** *Marsh Arab Haji Rikkan.* 1928. Phil. 1st. ils/map. 320p. VG. B5. $25.00

**FULBECKE, William.** *Direction or Preparative to the Study of Law...* 1987. Aldershot. Wildwood. facs of 1829. 252p. prt sewn wrp. M11. $45.00

**FULLBROOK, Earl.** *Red Cross in Iowa.* 1922. IA City. 2 vol. A13. $30.00

**FULLER, Andrew.** *Memoirs of the Late Rev Samuel Pearce...in India, 1793.* nd. NY. Am Tract Soc. 288p. G. H10. $25.00

**FULLER, C.E.** *Firearms of the Confederacy: Shoulder Arms, Pistols...* 1944. Huntington, WV. 1st. 333p. orig cloth. NF/dj. M8. $350.00

**FULLER, George W.** *History of Pacific Northwest.* 1931. NY. Knopf. sgn. 38 pl/fld map. 383p. bl cloth. P4. $135.00

**FULLER, Jack.** *Fragments.* 1984. Morrow. 1st. F/dj. R11. $30.00

**FULLER, Joseph J.** *Master of Desolation. Reminiscences of Capt Joseph J Fuller.* 1980. Mystic. 1st. 8vo. 349p. gilt bl cloth. F/dj. P4. $30.00

**FULLER, Roger;** see Tracy, Don.

**FULLERTON, Alexander.** *Publisher.* 1971. NY. Putnam. 1st Am. 254p. F/dj. O10. $30.00

**FULLERTON, Hugh.** *Jimmy Kirkland & the Plot for a Pennant.* 1915. Winston. 1st. VG. P8. $35.00

**FULLERTON, Hugh.** *Jimmy Kirkland of the Shasta Boys Team.* 1915. Winston. later prt. 1st of series. VG/G. P8. $75.00

**FULLERTON, Mary.** *Table, Home & Health: Household & Culinary Topics.* 1892. 1st. lg 8vo. ils/recipes/menus. 792p. VG. E6. $60.00

**FULTON, FOWKE & JOHNSTON.** *Folk Songs of Canada: Comprehensive Collection...* 1975. Waterloo Music Co. 5th. VG/wrp. A26. $15.00

**FULTON, James.** *Peach Culture.* 1870. Orange Judd. 190p. beveled brd. VG. A10. $35.00

**FULTON, James.** *Peach Culture.* 1905 (1889). NY. revised/enlarged. ils. 204p. VG. B26. $36.00

**FULTON, John F.** *Aviation Medicine in Its Preventive Aspects, Hist Survey.* 1948. London. 1st. 174p. A13. $150.00

**FULTON, John F.** *Bibliography of Honourable Robert Boyle.* 1932. Oxford. 1st separate. inscr. 172p. wrp. G7. $175.00

**FULTON, John F.** *Great Medical Biographers: A Study in Humanism.* 1951. Phil. UP Pr. inscr pres/dtd 1960. ils. cloth. 107p. G. G7. $175.00

**FULTON, John F.** *Harvey Cushing: A Biography.* 1946. Springfield. 754p. xl. G7. $50.00

**FULTON, John F.** *Selected Readings in History of Physiology.* 1930. Springfield. 1st. 317p. A13. $100.00

**FULTON, John F.** *Sign of Babinski: Study of Evolution of Cortical Dominance.* 1932. Springfield. Thomas. 165p. NF/dj. G7. $95.00

**FULTON, John.** *Palestine: The Holy Land.* 1900. Phil. Winston. ils/16 full-p maps. 527p. teg. VG. W1. $45.00

**FURBANK, P.N.** *Diderot: A Critical Biography.* 1992. NY. 1st. ils. VG/dj. M17. $20.00

**FURLONGE, Geoffrey.** *Palestine, My Country. Story of Musa Alami.* 1969. London. Murray. 8vo. ils/3 full-p maps. 242p. VG. W1. $16.00

**FURMAN, Laura.** *Glass House.* 1980. Viking. 1st. F/dj. A23. $32.00

**FURNAS & FURNAS.** *Man, Bread & Destiny: Story of Man's Food.* 1938. London. 1st. 364p. A13. $45.00

**FURNEAUX, Patrick.** *Arts of the Eskimo: Prints.* 1974. Signum Oxford. NF/VG. P3. $75.00

**FURNEAUX, R.** *Krakatoa.* 1964. Englewood Cliffs. photos/map. 224p. NF. M4. $18.00

**FURST, Alan.** *Shadow Trade.* 1983. Delacorte. 1st. NF/NF. H11. $15.00

**FURST & FURST.** *North American Indian Art.* c 1982. Rizzoli. photos. 236p. gilt rust cloth. P4. $65.00

**FURSTENBERG.** *Das Franzosiche Buch in Achtzehnten Jahrhundert Empirezeit.* 1929. Weimar. 4to. 433p. VG. A4. $195.00

**FUSSELL, Paul.** *Abroad: British Literary Travelling Between the Wars.* 1980. NY. Oxford. 1st. inscr. F/dj. B4. $150.00

**FUSSELL, Paul.** *Doing Battle, Making of a Skeptic.* 1996. Boston. 1st. dj. T9. $15.00

**FUSSELL, Paul.** *Samuel Johnson & the Life of Writing.* 1971. HBJ. 1st. dj. H13. $65.00

**FUTCH, Ovid L.** *History of Andersonville Prison.* 1968. Gainsville, FL. 1st. VG/clip. A14. $25.00

**FUXA & YOSHINORI.** *Epizootiology of Insect Diseases.* 1987. John Wiley. 555p. F/dj. S15. $20.00

**FYFE, Thomas Alexander.** *Who's Who in Dickens.* 1971. Haskell. VG. P3. $75.00

**FYFIELD, Frances.** *Shadow Play.* 1993. Pantheon. 1st. sgn. F/dj. B2. $30.00

**FYNN, A.J.** *American Indian As Product of Environment.* 1907. Boston. Little Brn. 1st. ils. 275p. VG. B5. $65.00

# G

GABEREAU, Vicki. *This Won't Hurt a Bit.* 1987. Toronto. Collins. 1st Canadian. F/dj. T12. $20.00

GABLE, Kathleen. *Clark Gable, a Personal Portrait.* 1961. Prentice Hall. 1st. VG/dj. C9. $36.00

GABORIAU, Emile. *Count's Millions.* 1913. NY. Scribner. 391p. G+. G11. $10.00

GABRIEL, Kathryn. *Marietta Wethrill: Reflections on Life With Navajos...* 1992. Boulder. Johnson Books. 8vo. 241p. VG/dj. F7. $20.00

GABRIELSON & LINCOLN. *Birds of Alaska.* 1959. Harrisburg/WA. Stackpole/Wildlife Management Inst. ils. 922p. VG/dj. P4. $350.00

GADDIS, William. *Carpenter's Gothic.* 1985. Viking. 1st. F/F. D10. $45.00

GADDIS, William. *Carpenter's Gothic.* 1985. Viking. 1st. NF/F. A24. $30.00

GADDIS, William. *Frolic of His Own.* 1994. NY. Poseidon. 2nd. 586p. F/dj. P4. $25.00

GADDIS, William. *Recognitions.* 1962. London. MacGibbon Kee. 1st. VG/dj. B2. $125.00

GADOL, Peter. *Mystery Roast.* 1993. NY. Morrow. 1st. F/dj. M23. $25.00

GADOW, Hans. *Wanderings of Animals.* 1913. Cambridge. 1st. 17 maps. 150p. red cloth. NF. B20. $50.00

GAEBELEIN, Frank E. *Christian, Arts & Truth: Regaining the Vision of Greatness.* 1985. Multnomah. 261p. VG/dj. B29. $7.50

GAER, Joseph. *First Round: Story of the CIO Political Action Committee.* 1944. DSP. 1/1000. VG+. B2. $35.00

GAFF & GAFF. *Adventures on Western Frontier: Major General John Gibbon.* 1994. IN U. 1st. 256p. F/dj. M4. $27.00

GAG, Wanda. *Funny Thing.* 1929. Coward McCann. 1st. author's 2nd children's book. 32p. yel brd. VG. D1. $325.00

GAG, Wanda. *Growing Pains.* 1940. Coward McCann. 1st. 8vo. 179p. beige cloth. VG/dj. D1. $150.00

GAG, Wanda. *Nothing at All.* 1941. Coward McCann. 1st. obl 4to. orange brd. mc dj. R5. $485.00

GAGE, Nicholas. *Bourlotas Fortune.* 1975. NY. Holt. 1st. NF/NF. H11. $20.00

GAGE, Nicholas. *Place for Us: Eleni's Children in America.* 1989. Houghton Mifflin. 8vo. ils. NF/dj. W1. $18.00

GAGE, Wilson. *Big Blue Island.* 1966. World. 3rd. tall 8vo. 121p. NF/VG clip. C14. $8.00

GAINES, Ernest J. *In My Father's House.* 1978. Knopf. 1st. F/NF. B3. $150.00

GAINES, Ernest J. *Lesson Before Dying.* 1994. Knopf. 4th. 256p. F/dj. P12. $12.00

GAINES & SWAN. *Weeds of Eastern Washington & Adjacent Areas.* 1972. Davenport, WA. Camp-Na-Bor-Lee Assn. 349p. VG. A10. $30.00

GAITSKILL, Mary. *Bad Behavior.* 1988. Poseidon. 1st. F/dj. D10. $45.00

GAITSKILL, Mary. *Bad Behavior.* 1989. London. Hodder Stoughton. 1st Eng. author's 1st book. F/dj. R14. $30.00

GAITSKILL, Mary. *Two Girls, Fat & Thin.* 1991. Poseidon. 1st. sgn. F/F. D10. $40.00

GALBRAITH, John Kenneth. *Age of Uncertainty.* 1977. Houghon Mifflin. 1st. F/NF. T12. $50.00

GALBRAITH, John Kenneth. *Great Crash of 1929.* 1988. Boston. VG/dj. M17. $12.50

GALBREATH, Charles B. *History of Ohio.* 1925. Chicago. 5 vol. ils. 4to. xl. B18. $65.00

GALDONE, Paul. *Hans in Luck.* 1979. NY. 1st. ils. VG+. M5. $15.00

GALDONE, Paul. *Teeny-Tiny Woman: A Ghost Story.* 1984. Clarion. 1st. sm 8vo. unp. NF/dj. T5. $30.00

GALDSTON, Iago. *Behind the Sulfa Drugs: A Short History of Chemotherapy.* 1943. NY. 1st. 174p. A13. $40.00

GALE, Robert L. *Plots & Characters in Works of Mark Twain.* 1973. Hamden. Archon. 2 vol. 1st. gilt gr cloth. xl. F. M24. $100.00

GALEN. *On the Natural Faculties.* 1915. London. 1st of Brock trans. 339p. A13. $100.00

GALEWITZ & WINSLOW. *Fontaine Fox's Toonerville Trolley.* 1972. Weathervane. 2nd. ils. VG/dj. C9. $42.00

GALINDO, Sergio. *Precipice (El Bordo).* 1969. Austin/London. 8vo. 185p. gray cloth. P4. $15.00

GALLAGHER, Elaine. *Candidly Caine.* 1992. NY. Robson Books. 318p. VG/dj. C5. $12.50

GALLAGHER, Gary W. *Fighting for the Confederacy: Personal Recollections...* 1989. Chapel Hill. 1st. NF/dj. A14. $25.00

GALLAGHER, Gary W. *Lee the Soldier.* 1996. U NE. ils. VG/dj. M17. $25.00

GALLAGHER, Nancy. *Medicine & Power in Tunisia, 1780-1900.* 1983. Cambridge. 1st. 145p. dj. A13. $30.00

GALLAGHER, Stephen. *Oktober.* 1989. Tor. 1st. NF/dj. P3. $25.00

GALLANT, Mavis. *Overhead in a Balloon: Twelve Stories of Paris.* 1985. Random. 1st. NF/dj. S13. $10.00

GALLANT, Roy A. *Exploring Mars.* 1956. Garden City. stated 1st. ils. VG/G. A2. $20.00

GALLAWAY, B.P. *Dark Corner of the Confederacy...* 1968. Dubuque, IA. 1st. 188p. VG/stiff wrp. E1. $95.00

GALLENKAMP, Charles. *Maya: The Riddle & Rediscovery of a Lost Civilization.* 1985. NY. Viking. 3rd. 235p. AN/dj. P4. $23.00

GALLICO, Paul. *Day Jean-Pierre Joined the Circus.* 1970. NY. Watts. 1st Am. 74p. F/dj. D4. $30.00

GALLICO, Paul. *Man Who Was Magic.* 1966. Doubleday. 1st. 203p. VG/dj. M21. $15.00

GALLICO, Paul. *Mrs 'Arris Goes to Paris.* (1958). Doubleday. early. 16mo. 157p. NF/VG+. C14. $10.00

GALLICO, Paul. *Poseidon Adventure.* 1969. NY. Coward. 1st. F/NF clip. H11. $40.00

GALLUCCI & GALLUCCI. *James E Birch, a Sacramento Chapter in History...* 1958. Sacramento. 1/500. 34p. F. P4. $45.00

GALLUP, J. *Outlines of an Arrangement of Medical Nosology...* 1831. 2nd. G. E6. $195.00

GALSTON, Clarence G. *Behind the Judicial Curtain.* 1959. Barrington. pres. cloth. M11. $45.00

GALSWORTHY, John. *Addresses in America.* 1919. NY. 1st. bl cloth. G/dj. J3. $75.00

GALSWORTHY, John. *Author & Critic.* 1933. NY. House of Books. 1st. 1/300. gilt blk cloth. F. M24. $45.00

GALSWORTHY, John. *Forsythe Saga.* 1922. London. Hutchinson. 1st. teg/silk ribbon. flexible maroon leather. F. M24. $300.00

GALSWORTHY, John. *Maid in Waiting.* 1931. London. Heinemann. 1/525. 349p. VG. M10. $65.00

GALSWORTHY, John. *Plays of John Galsworthy.* 1929. London. Dickworth. 1150p. quarter gr crushed morocco/marbled sides. F1. $65.00

GALSWORTHY, John. *Silver Spoon.* (1926). London. 1st trade. F/NF. J3. $50.00

**GALSWORTHY, John.** *Swan Song.* 1928. London. 1st. F/NF. J3. $50.00

**GALTON, Francis.** *Finger Prints.* 1892. London. Macmillan. 216p. ruled mauve cloth. G1. $750.00

**GALTON, Francis.** *Hereditary Genius: An Inquiry Into Its Laws & Consequences.* 1869. London. Macmillan. 390p. panelled mauve cloth. xl. G1. $750.00

**GALVEZ.** *Instructions for Governing the Interior Provinces New Spain.* 1951. Quivira. 1/500. NF. A4. $275.00

**GALVIN, J.R.** *Minute Men, First Fight: Myths & Realities...* 1989. WA. ils. 247p. F/dj. M4. $20.00

**GALVIN, Thomas A.** *Father Baker & His Lady of Victory Charities.* 1925. Buffalo Catholic Pub. 1st? 8vo. VG. A2. $15.00

**GAMBADO, Geoffrey.** *Academy for Grown Horsemen.* 1929. Dickinson. ltd. 1/500. A21. $95.00

**GAMBLE, C.F. Snowden.** *Story of a North Sea Air Station...* 1928. London. Oxford. 1st. ils. 446p. G+. B18. $450.00

**GAMBRELL, Herbert.** *Anson Jones: Last President of Texas.* 1948. Doubleday. 1st. 8vo. 462p. F/dj. B20. $35.00

**GAMBRILL & MACKENZIE.** *Sporting Stables & Kennels.* 1935. London. Eyre Spottiswoode. 1/200. 4to. G. O3. $165.00

**GAMIO, Manuel.** *Introduccion, Sintesis y Conclusiones de la Obra...* 1922. Mexico. Secretaria de Educacion Publica. maroon cloth. VG. P4. $65.00

**GAMMON, John K.** *Overcoming Obstacles in Environmental Policymaking.* 1994. SUNY. 250p. NF/wrp. S15. $5.00

**GAMMONS, Peter.** *Beyond the Sixth Game.* 1985. Houghton Mifflin. 1st. F/VG. P8. $25.00

**GAMOW, George.** *Creation of the Universe.* 1952. Viking. 1st. VG/torn. K5. $12.00

**GANCEL.** *Gancel's Culinary Encyclopedia of Modern Cooking.* 1920. 8000+ recipes/300 articles. 511p. VG. E6. $60.00

**GANGOLY, O.C.** *Indian Terra-Cotta Art.* 1959. NY. Wittenborn. photos Amiya Tarafdar. 76p. tan cloth. VG. F1. $75.00

**GANN, Ernest K.** *Gentlemen of Adventure.* 1984. NY. Arbor. 1st. NF/F. H11. $25.00

**GANN, Thomas W.F.** *Maya Indians of Southern Yucatan & Northern Honduras.* 1918. GPO. Bur Ethnology Bulletin 64. 8vo. 146p. P4. $50.00

**GANNETT, Henry.** *Forest Reserves of the United States.* 1900. WA, DC. 5 double-p maps/rear pocket map. wrp. B26. $40.00

**GAPE, A.T.** *Vegetation of the District of Minbu in Upper Burma.* 1978 (1904). Dehra Dun. rpt. 141p. AN. B26. $12.50

**GARAGIOLA, Joe.** *Baseball Is a Funny Game.* 1960. Lippincott. 12th. gr-lettered orange brd. VG/G. A28. $13.00

**GARAVAGLIA & WORMAN.** *Firearms of the American West, Vol II.* 500+ photos/index. 413p. AN/dj. J2. $60.00

**GARAVAGLIA & WORMAN.** *Firearms of the American West 1803-1894.* 1998. U CO. 2 vol. sgns. AN/dj. J2. $185.00

**GARBER, Angus G.** *Hoops!* 1992. NY. Mallard. 128p. VG/dj. B11. $15.00

**GARBER, Joseph R.** *Vertical Run.* 1995. Bantam. 1st. F/F. H11. $30.00

**GARBO, Norman.** *Movement.* 1969. Morrow. 1st. NF/VG. R11. $25.00

**GARBO, Norman.** *Spy.* 1980. NY. Norton. 1st. F/F. H11. $15.00

**GARCES, Francisco.** *On the Trail of the Spanish Pioneer: Diary...* 1900. Harper. 2 vol. 1st. ils/fld map. B19. $300.00

**GARCES, Francisco.** *Record of Travels in Arizona & California 1775-1776.* 1965. SF. John Howell. 1/1250. 4to. ils/maps. 113p. VG+. F7. $75.00

**GARCIA MARQUEZ, Gabriel;** see Marquez, Gabriel Garcia.

**GARCIA-AGUILERA, Carolina.** *Bloody Shame.* 1997. Putnam. 1st. sgn. F/dj. A23. $42.00

**GARD, R. Max.** *End of the Morgan Raid.* 1963. Lisbon, OH. ils. 22p. wrp. B18. $12.50

**GARD, Wayne.** *Great Buffalo Hunt.* 1959. Knopf. VG. A19. $35.00

**GARD, Wayne.** *Great Buffalo Hunt.* 1960. NY. ils. VG/poor. S15. $15.00

**GARDAM, Jane.** *Bilgewater.* 1976. London. Hamish Hamilton. NF/NF. B3. $75.00

**GARDEN, JF.** *Bugaboos.* 1987. Revelstroke. 1st. 156p. F/dj. A17. $25.00

**GARDENER, John.** *For Special Services.* 1982. London. Cape. 1st Eng. F/NF. M19. $25.00

**GARDENER, John.** *Licence Renewed.* 1981. London. Cape. 1st. F/clip. B3. $65.00

**GARDENER & HEIDER.** *Gardens of War: Life & Death in New Guinea Stone Age.* 1968. NY. 4to. 184p. F/dj. M4. $15.00

**GARDENIER, Andrew.** *Successful Stockman & Manual of Husbandry.* 1899. Springfield, MA. King. 634p. cloth. A10. $18.00

**GARDENSHIRE, Samuel M.** *Long Arm.* 1906. NY. Harper. 1st. pict brd. F. M15. $125.00

**GARDINER, A.G.** *Life of George Cadbury.* 1923. London. Cassell. 324p. xl. V3. $26.00

**GARDINER & WALKER.** *Raymond Chandler Speaking.* 1977. Houghton Mifflin. 1st. VG-/G+. G8. $35.00

**GARDNER, Alan.** *Six Day Week.* 1966. Coward McCann. 1st Am. VG/dj. P3. $15.00

**GARDNER, Brian.** *Mafeking: A Victorian Legend.* 1967. HBW. 1st Am. 246p. VG/dj. S16. $35.00

**GARDNER, Erle Stanley.** *Bigger They Come.* 1939. Morrow. 1st. VG. H4. $45.00

**GARDNER, Erle Stanley.** *Case of the Blonde Bonanza.* 1962. Black. 1st thus. NF/dj. S13. $10.00

**GARDNER, Erle Stanley.** *Case of the Daring Decoy.* 1957. Morrow. 1st. F/NF. M15. $45.00

**GARDNER, Erle Stanley.** *Case of the Green-Eyed Sister.* 1953. Morrow. 1st. 12mo. VG-/dj. M21. $30.00

**GARDNER, Erle Stanley.** *Case of the Lazy Lover.* 1947. Morrow. 1st. VG+/dj. A24. $60.00

**GARDNER, Erle Stanley.** *Case of the Phantom Fortune.* 1964. Morrow. 1st. F/dj. M15. $45.00

**GARDNER, Erle Stanley.** *Case of the Shapely Shadow: A Perry Mason Mystery.* 1960. NY. WJ Black. BC. VG/dj. B9. $15.00

**GARDNER, Erle Stanley.** *Case of the Substitute Face.* 1938. Morrow. 1st. F/NF. M15. $350.00

**GARDNER, Erle Stanley.** *Case of the Vagabond Virgin.* 1948. Morrow. 1st. F/G. M19. $45.00

**GARDNER, Erle Stanley.** *DA Calls a Turn.* 1944. Morrow. 1st. 12mo. store stps. G+/dj. M21. $45.00

**GARDNER, Erle Stanley.** *Double or Quits.* 1946. Triangle. 1st thus. VG/dj. P3. $18.00

**GARDNER, Erle Stanley.** *Mexico's Magic Square.* 1968. NY. 1st. inscr. 205p. VG/dj. B18. $35.00

**GARDNER, Erle Stanley.** *Neighborhood Frontiers: Desert Country, Puget Sound...* 1954. Morrow. 1st. ils. 272p. NF/VG. B19. $25.00

**GARDNER, Erle Stanley.** *Shills Can't Cash Chips.* 1961. 1st. VG/G. M19. $17.50

**GARDNER, J. Anthony.** *Iraq-Iran War, a Bibliography.* 1989. 140p. F. A4. $35.00

**GARDNER, Jani.** *Let's Celebrate.* 1969. Hawthorn. 1st. G/fair. A16. $10.00

**GARDNER, John.** *Child's Bestiary.* 1977. Knopf. 1st. F/NF. L3. $65.00

**GARDNER, John.** *Complete State of Death Objects.* 1969. Viking. 1st. NF/dj. S13. $12.00

**GARDNER, John.** *Death Is Forever.* 1992. Putnam. 1st Am. NF/dj. G8. $12.50

**GARDNER, John.** *Freddy's Book.* 1980. Knopf. 1st. sgn. NF/dj. R14. $90.00

**GARDNER, John.** *Freddy's Book.* 1980. NY. 1st. VG/dj. M17. $15.00

**GARDNER, John.** *Icebreaker.* 1983. Hodder Stoughton. 1st. sgn. 250p. F/NF. B20. $45.00

**GARDNER, John.** *In the Suicide Mountains.* 1977. Knopf. 1st. ils Joe Servello. F/NF. A24. $50.00

**GARDNER, John.** *In the Suicide Mountains.* 1977. Knopf. 1st. 159p. 8vo. VG/G. C14. $17.00

**GARDNER, John.** *In the Suicide Mountains.* 1980. Houghton Mifflin. 1st. ils Joe Servello. NF/wrp. R14. $20.00

**GARDNER, John.** *Mickelsson's Ghosts.* 1982. Knopf. 1st. ils Joel Gardner. rem mk. NF/dj. A14. $21.00

**GARDNER, John.** *Nickel Mountain.* 1973. Knopf. 1st. author's 6th novel. VG/VG. B30. $40.00

**GARDNER, John.** *Nobody Lives Forever.* 1986. Putnam. 1st Am. NF/VG+. G8. $15.00

**GARDNER, John.** *Secret Generations.* 1985. London. Heinemann. 1st. sgn. F/dj. A24. $30.00

**GARDNER, John.** *Stillness.* 1986. Knopf. 1st. NF/dj. A24. $30.00

**GARDNER, Martin.** *Ambidextrous Universe.* 1964. Basic Books. ils John Mackey. 294p. xl. NF/F. W2. $25.00

**GARDNER, Miriam;** see Bradley, Marion Zimmer.

**GARDNER, Nancy.** *Peace, O River.* 1986. FSG. 1st. 246p. F/dj. D4. $25.00

**GARDNER, Raymond Hatfield.** *Old West, Adventures of Arizona Bill.* 1944. Naylor. 315p. VG. J2. $90.00

**GARDNER, Richard A.** *MBD: Family Book About Minimal Brain Dysfunction.* 1973. NY. Aronson. 1st. ils. F/dj. A2. $15.00

**GARDNER, Virginia.** *Rosenberg Story.* 1954. Masses/Mainstream. 1st. VG/dj. E6. $75.00

**GARDNER, Will.** *Coffin Saga.* 1949. Whaling Mus Pub. sgn. photos. VG/dj. M17. $50.00

**GARDNER, Will.** *Three Bricks & Three Brothers: Story of Nantucket Whale-Oil.* 1958. Cambridge. Riverside. 1st. sgn. VG. V3. $20.00

**GARDNER & NYE.** *Wizard of Oz & Who He Was.* 1957. E Lansing, MI. 1st. 208p. ochre cloth. F/dj. F1. $75.00

**GARDNER-SHARP, Abbie.** *History of the Spirit Lake Massacre & Captivity of...* 1885. IA Prt Co. rb in orig cover. G. A19. $150.00

**GARFIELD, Brian.** *Paladin.* 1979. S&S. 1st. NF/clip. A14. $21.00

**GARFIELD, Leon.** *King in the Garden.* 1985. Lee Shepard. 1st Am. 4to. unp. VG. C14. $11.00

**GARFIELD & FORREST.** *Wolf & the Raven: Totem Poles of Southeastern Alaska.* 1977. Seattle/London. later prt. ils. 148p. wrp. P4. $12.50

**GARIS, Howard R.** *Adventures of Uncle Wiggily.* (1924). Newark. Chas Graham. 1st. 4to. red brd/pict label. R5. $225.00

**GARIS, Howard R.** *Uncle Wiggily's Holidays.* (1922). Newark. Chas Graham. 8vo. silver lettered bl cloth/pict label. R5. $85.00

**GARIS, Howard R.** *Uncle Wiggily's Snow Man.* (1922). Newark. Chas Graham. 8vo. silver lettered gr cloth/pict label. R5. $85.00

**GARLAND, Albert.** *Infantry in Vietnam.* 1967. Ft Benning. Infantry Magazine. 1st. ils. 409p. NF/VG. R11. $40.00

**GARLAND, Hamlin.** *Daughter of the Middle Border.* 1921. Grosset Dunlap. VG/dj. A19. $30.00

**GARLAND, Hamlin.** *Son of the Middle Border.* 1923. Macmillan. G/dj. A19. $25.00

**GARLAND, James A.** *Private Stable: Its Establishment, Management, Appointments.* 1903. Little Brn. ils/photos. VG. A21. $550.00

**GARLAND, Joseph E.** *Great Pattillo.* 1966. Little Brn. 1st. F/VG. T11. $35.00

**GARLAND, Kenneth W.** *Development of the Guided Missile.* 1954. London. Iliffe. 2nd. 292p. G/dj. K5. $40.00

**GARMAN, Alice.** *Adlai Stevenson's Veto 1949.* 1971. Amsterdam. mini. 1/250. sgn. gilt brn leather. B24. $175.00

**GARNER, Alan.** *Bag of Moonshine.* 1986. NY. Delacorte. 1st Am. F/dj. T10. $50.00

**GARNER, Bess Adams.** *Mexico: Notes in the Margin.* 1937. Boston. Houghton Mifflin. 1st. 8vo. 163p. beige cloth. P4. $35.00

**GARNER, Bess Adams.** *Windows in an Old Adobe.* 1939. Progress Bulletin. 1st. sgn. photos. 246p. VG. S14. $50.00

**GARNER, Elvira.** *Ezekiel.* 1937. Holt. 1st. lg 8vo. VG. M5. $78.00

**GARNER, Helen.** *Honour & Other People's Children.* 1982. Seaview. 1st Am. F/dj. M25. $15.00

**GARNER, Wightman W.** *Production of Tobacco.* 1951. NY. Blakiston. revised 1st. ils/biblio. 520p. G+. H10. $30.00

**GARNER & STRATTON.** *Domestic Architecture of England During Tudor Period.* (1929). Scribner. 2 vol. folio. 210 pl. red cloth. dj. K1. $300.00

**GARNER & STRATTON.** *Domestic Architecture of England During Tudor Period.* 1939. London. Batsford. 2 vol. 2nd/revised. 210 pl. red cloth. NF/dj/glassine. F1. $600.00

**GARNETT, A. Campbell.** *Mind in Action: A Study of Motives & Values.* 1932. Appleton. 12mo. 226p. prt blk cloth. xl. VG. G1. $22.50

**GARNETT, Eve.** *Holiday at the Dew Drop Inn: One End Street Story.* 1962. London. 1st Eng. ils. VG/dj. M17. $22.50

**GARNETT, Louisa A.** *Muffin Shop.* 1908. Rand McNally. 1st. ils Hope Dunlap. 80p. VG. D1. $150.00

**GARNETT, Porter.** *Papers of the San Francisco Committee of 1851. I & II.* 1910. Berkeley. F/prt wrp. P4. $65.00

**GARON, Paul.** *Devil's Son-in-Law: Story of Peetie Wheatstraw...* 1971. London. Studio Vista. F/wrp. B2. $25.00

**GARRARD, Lewis H.** *Yah-To-Yah & the Taos Trail; or, Prairie Travel...* (1955). Norman, OK. 1st thus. 298p. F/VG+. B18. $37.50

**GARRATY, John Arthur.** *Silas Wright.* 1949. Columbia. pres. M11. $50.00

**GARRETT, George.** *Abraham's Knife.* 1961. Chapel Hill. 1st. inscr. VG/fair. L3. $85.00

**GARRETT, Richard.** *Atlantic Disasters: The Titanic & Other Victims...* 1986. London. Buchan Enright. 1st. 286p. F/dj. B20. $30.00

**GARRIOTT, Edward B.** *Cold Waves & Frosts in the United States.* 1906. GPO. 328 mc charts. xl. K5. $45.00

**GARRISON, F.G.** *History of Medicine... Fourth Edition.* 1960. Phil. Saunders. later rpt. G7. $45.00

**GARRISON, Jim.** *Heritage of Stone.* 1970. NY. Putnam. 2nd. 253p. VG/dj. B5. $30.00

**GARRISON, William Lloyd.** *Selections From the Writings & Speeches of...* 1852. Boston. Wallcut. 1st. 8vo. 416p. gilt cloth. NF+. O1. $125.00

**GARRISON & MORTON.** *Morton's Medical Bibliography, Fifth Edition...* 1991. Scholar Pr. 1243p. G7. $145.00

**GARRITY, John.** *Golf, a 3D Exploration.* 1996. Viking. 1st. 4to. popup. F. B17. $15.00

**GARST, Shannon.** *Scotty Allan, King of the Dog-Team Drivers.* 1946. NY. Messner. 2nd. 8vo. tan cloth. P4. $22.00

**GARSTIN, Crosbie.** *Samuel Kelly: An Eighteenth-Century Seaman.* 1925. NY. Stokes. 1st. 320p. gilt cloth. P4. $60.00

**GARTON, Ray.** *Lot Lizards.* 1991. Ziesing. 1st. F/dj. N4. $45.00

**GARVER, Thomas H.** *George Tooker.* 1985. Clarkson Potter. 1st. 144p. F/dj. B20. $50.00

**GARVEY & WICK.** *Arts of the French Book 1900-1965.* 1967. Dallas. S Methodist U. ils. 120p. stiff wrp. F1. $40.00

**GARWOOD, D.** *Crossroads of America: Story of Kansas City.* 1948. NY. 1st. ils. 331p. VG. M4. $18.00

**GARY, Romain.** *Europa.* 1978. NY. 1st. trans B Bray/author. dj. T9. $8.00

**GASCOIGNE, Bamber.** *Christians.* 1977. Morrow. 1st. sm 4to. 304p. F/VG. S14. $17.50

**GASH, Jonathan.** *Gold by Gemini.* 1978. Harper. 1st. F/VG. M19. $45.00

**GASH, Jonathan.** *Great California Game.* 1991. St Martin. 1st Am. inscr/dtd 1991. F/dj. R14. $40.00

**GASH, Jonathan.** *Judas Pair.* 1977. London. Collins Crime Club. 1st. Lovejoy #1. F/dj. M15. $600.00

**GASH, Jonathan.** *Sleepers of Erin.* 1983. London. Collins Crime Club. 1st. F/dj. M15. $200.00

**GASH, Jonathan.** *Very Last Gambado.* 1990. St Martin. 1st. sgn. NF/dj. B3. $25.00

**GASK, Arthur.** *Silent Dead.* 1950. Herbert Jenkins. 1st. VG. P3. $25.00

**GASKELL, Philip.** *New Introduction to Bibliography.* 1995. Winchester. St Paul's Bibliographies. 438p. prt sewn wrp. M11. $30.00

**GASPEY, Terry W.** *Not a Tame Lion: Spiritual Legacy of CS Lewis.* (1996). Highland Books. 1st Am. AN/dj. A27. $15.00

**GASQUE & MARTIN.** *Apostolic History & the Gospel.* 1970. Paternost. 378p. VG/dj. B29. $19.50

**GASS, Patrick.** *Gass's Journal of the Louis & Clark Expedition.* 1904. Chicago. McClurg. 8vo. 7 pl. 298p. 3-quarter leather/orange cloth. VG. B11. $450.00

**GASS, William H.** *Fiction & the Figures of Life.* 1970. Knopf. 1st. sgn. NF/dj. R14. $75.00

**GASS, William H.** *In the Heart of the Country.* 1968. Harper Row. 1st. author's 2nd book. F/dj. O11. $160.00

**GASS, William H.** *Omensetter's Luck.* 1967. London. Collins. 1st. 8vo. author's 1st book. NF/dj. S9. $175.00

**GASS, William H.** *Willie Masters' Lonesome Wife.* 1971. NY. Knopf. 1st thus. F/dj. Q1. $40.00

**GASS, William H.** *World Within the World.* 1978. Knopf. 1st. sgn. VG/dj. R14. $65.00

**GASSNER & NICHOLS.** *Best Film Plays of 1943-1944.* 1945. Crown. 1st. VG. C9. $72.00

**GAST, Ross H.** *Contentious Consul: A Biography of John Coffin Jones.* 1976. LA. Dawson. sgn. 8vo. 212p. gr cloth. NF. P4. $65.00

**GASTON, Edwin W. Jr.** *Early Novel of the Southwest.* 1961. NM U. 1st. 318p. cloth. dj. D11. $35.00

**GATE, Ethel May.** *Tales From the Enchanted Islands.* 1926. yale. 1st. ils Lathrop. VG/dj. B17. $85.00

**GATES, Betsey.** *Colton Letters: Civil War Period 1861-1865.* 1993. Scottsdale, AZ. McLane Pub. 1st. F/dj. A14. $28.00

**GATES, H.L.** *Devil's Lady.* 1933. NY. Macaulay. 1st. F/VG. M15. $65.00

**GATES, Henry Louis.** *Black Male: Representations of Masculinity...* 1994. NY. Whitney Mus Am Art. 1st. sgn. F. O11. $25.00

**GATIN, C.L.** *Dictionaire Aide-Memoire de Botanique.* 1924. Paris. ils/map. 847p. gray cloth. B26. $95.00

**GATTY, Horatis K.F.** *Juliana Horatia Ewing & Her Books.* 1887. London. SPCK. sm 8vo. prt brd. F1. $25.00

**GAUCH, Patricia Lee.** *This Time, Tempe Wick?* (1974). CMG. 4th. 8vo. 43p. gold cloth. NF/VG. T5. $25.00

**GAUNT, William.** *Impressionists.* 1970. Thames Hudson. 1st. NF/VG. P3. $100.00

**GAUTIER & PANASSIE.** *Guide to Jazz.* 1956. Boston. 1st. VG/dj. B5. $40.00

**GAVIN, D. Antonio.** *Master-Key to Popery in Five Parts.* 1822. Hagerstown, MD. 1st thus. 8vo. 297p. full cheep. C6. $200.00

**GAY, Carl W.** *Productive Horse Husbandry.* 1932. Lippincott. 4th. index. 335p. F. A17. $15.00

**GAY, John.** *Trivia; or, Art of Walking the Streets of London.* 1922. London. O'Connor. intro WH Williams. 92p. teg. gilt wht cloth. F1. $65.00

**GAY, Zhenya.** *Bits & Pieces.* 1958. Viking. 1st. 8vo. ils. VG. M5. $10.00

**GAYLIN, Willard.** *Partial Justice, Study of Bias in Sentencing.* 1974. Knopf. M11. $25.00

**GAYLOR, Annie Laurie.** *Women Without Superstition: No Gods, No Masters...* 1930. Freedom From Religion Found. ils. VG/dj. M17. $40.00

**GAYLORD, Isabella.** *Cooking With an Accent. Herb Grower's Cookbook.* 1963. Branford. 8vo. 149p. VG/G+. B11. $15.00

**GEATZ, E.** *Moment of Madness: People Vs Jack Ruby.* 1968. NY. 1st. VG/dj. B5. $25.00

**GEBAUER, Phyllis.** *Pagan Blessing.* 1979. Viking. 1st. F/NF. M21. $25.00

**GECKLE, E.** *Plaster of Paris Technic.* 1948 (1945). VG/dj. E6. $20.00

**GEDDES, Patrick.** *Life & Work of Sir Jagadis C Bose...* 1920. Longman Gr. 9 pl/26 text ils. pub bl-gray cloth. G. G1. $85.00

**GEDDES & GROSSET.** *Robin Hood & His Merry Men.* 1996. Longmeadow. 1st. sm 8vo. 160p. F/dj. W2. $20.00

**GEER, Andrews.** *Reckless: Pride of the Marines.* 1955. Dutton. 1st. G/fair. w/ephemera. O3. $28.00

**GEER, John James.** *Beyond the Lines or a Yankee Prisoner Loose in Dixie.* 1864 (1863). VG. E6. $75.00

**GEERTZ & LOMATUWAY'MA.** *Children of Cottonwood: Piety & Ceremonialism in Hopi...* 1987. NE U. 1st. ils/notes/index. 412p. F/sans. B19. $35.00

**GEFFEN, Alice M.** *Food Festival.* 1986. Pantheon. G/wrp. A16. $6.00

**GEHRS, John H.** *Agricultural Nature Study.* 1929. NY. Am Book. 184p. cloth. A10. $15.00

**GEIGER, George.** *Profiles in Salt-Water Angling.* 1973. Prentice Hall. 1st. ils. 479p. VG/dj. B11. $18.00

**GEIGER, Jennifer.** *See-Me-Learn Toys.* 1988. Sedgewood. 1st. NF/dj. S13. $12.00

**GEIGER, Maynard.** *Palou's Life of Fray Junipero Serra.* 1955. WA, DC. Academy of Am Franciscan Hist. 547p. bl cloth. NF. P4. $95.00

**GEIGER & WAKEMAN.** *Trail to California.* 1945. New Haven. Yale. 266p. VG/dj. P4. $55.00

**GEILKIE, Cunningham.** *Hours With the Bible.* 1988. Alden. 6 vol. VG. B29. $30.00

**GEIS, Bernard.** *Picture Story of Leo Tolstoy's War & Peace.* 1956. Fell. 1st. photos. NF/VG clip. S13. $18.00

**GEISEL, Theodore Seuss.** *Bartholomew & the Oobleck.* 1977 (1949). Random. 4to. unp. NF. C14. $16.00

**GEISEL, Theodore Seuss.** *Dr Seuss's Sleep Book.* (1962). NY. Random. 1st. 4to. mc pict brd. mc pict dj. R5. $475.00

**GEISEL, Theodore Seuss.** *Happy Birthday to You!* (1959). NY. Random. 1st. 4to. md pict brd. mc dj. w/sgn tipped in. R5. $750.00

**GEISEL, Theodore Seuss.** *How the Grinch Stole Christmas.* 1957. Random. possible 1st. ils. xl. G. B36. $35.00

**GEISEL, Theodore Seuss.** *I Had Trouble in Getting to Solla Sollew.* (1965). NY. Random. 1st. 4to. ils brd. mc dj. R5. $475.00

**GEISEL, Theodore Seuss.** *If I Ran the Zoo.* 1964. HRW. stated 1st. 8vo. 46p. NF/$3.50 dj. D1. $250.00

**GEISEL, Theodore Seuss.** *Marvin K Mooney Will You Please Go Now.* (1972). NY. Random. 1st. 8vo. pict prt. mc pict dj. R5. $200.00

**GEISEL, Theodore Seuss.** *More Boners.* 1931. NY. Viking. 1st. 12mo. blk lettered dk gr cloth. pict dj. R5. $350.00

**GEISEL, Theodore Seuss.** *Oh, the Places You'll Go!* 1990. NY. Random. 1st. 4to. VG/dj. D1. $50.00

**GEISEL, Theodore Seuss.** *One Fish Two Fish Red Fish Blue Fish.* 1960. Random. 1st. sm 4to. 63p. VG/dj. D1. $500.00

**GEISEL, Theodore Seuss.** *Seven Lady Godivas.* (1939). NY. Random. 1st. 4to. maroon decor beige cloth. mc dj. R5. $400.00

**GEISEL, Theodore Seuss.** *Six by Seuss: A Treasury of Dr Seuss Classics.* 1991. Random. 3rd. 4to. 345p. F. W2. $240.00

**GEIST, Valerius.** *Mule Deer County.* 1990. Minocqua, WI. North Word. photos Michael Francis. VG/dj. M17. $22.50

**GELATT, R.** *Fabulous Phonograph.* 1955. Phil. 1st. VG/dj. B5. $45.00

**GELB, Alan.** *Most Likely to Succeed.* 1990. Dutton. 1st. VG/dj. A28. $11.00

**GELB, N.** *Jonathan Carver's Travels Through America 1766-1768...* 1993. NY. ils/map. 245p. F. M4. $15.00

**GELB & GELB.** *O'Neill.* 1962. NY. Harper. 1st. ils/index. 970p. beige cloth. F/F. B9. $20.00

**GELDERMAN, Carol.** *Louis Auchincloss: A Writer's Life.* 1993. NY. Crown. 1st. NF/dj. A28. $13.00

**GELLERT, Hugo.** *Comrade Gulliver.* 1935. Putnam. 1st. VG. B2. $50.00

**GEMMILL & JONES.** *Pharmacology at the University of Virginia...* 1966. U VA. ils. 134p. VG. B10. $12.00

**GENDERS, Roy.** *Colour All the Year Round...* 1961. St Martin. BC. 287p. VG/worn. H10. $10.00

**GENDERS, Roy.** *Greenhouse for Pleasure & Profit.* 1955. London. Mus. 189p. VG/dj. A10. $20.00

**GENDERS, Roy.** *Handbook of Hardy Border Plants.* 1957. London. ils/photos. 296p. VG/dj. B26. $17.50

**GENDERS, Roy.** *Miniature Roses.* 1960. London. Blandford. 104p. xl. dj. A10. $15.00

**GENDERS, Roy.** *Polyanthus.* 1963. London. Faber for Garden BC. 231p. VG/dj. A10. $22.00

**GENERAL FOODS CORPORATION.** *All About Home Baking.* 1933. G. A16. $10.00

**GENET, Jean.** *Querrelle.* 1974. Grove. 1st Am. VG/dj. C9. $42.00

**GENEVOIX, Maurice.** *Last Hunt.* 1940. Random. 1st. 281p. F/VG. D4. $45.00

**GENG, Vernonica.** *Love Trouble Is My Business.* 1988. Harper Row. 1st. NF/F. B3. $15.00

**GENT, Peter.** *Franchise.* 1983. Villard. 1st. xl. VG/dj. S18. $8.00

**GENT, Peter.** *Texas Celebrity Turkey Trot.* 1978. Morrow. 1st. F/F. H11. $30.00

**GENTHE, Arnold.** *Book of the Dance.* 1920. Boston. Internat. 1st thus. photos. NF. S9. $150.00

**GENTHE, Arnold.** *Old Chinatown: Book of Pictures by...* 1913. NY. Kennerley. 91 photo pl. 210p. blk cloth. K1. $200.00

**GENTICORE & HEAD.** *Ontario's History in Maps.* 1984. Toronto/Buffalo/London. 1st ltd. 1/500. F/NF. P4. $400.00

**GENTILLET.** *Discours, Svr Les Moyens de Bien Govverner...* 1576. Geneva. Stoer? 8vo. fine title device. vellum. R12. $1,250.00

**GENTRY, Curt.** *Last Days of the Late, Great State of California.* 1968. Putnam. 1st. 8vo. 382p. VG. S14. $8.00

**GEORGE, Carol V.R.** *God's Salesman, Norman Vincent Peale & Power...* 1993. OUP. 1st. sm 4to. 271p. NF/F. W2. $30.00

**GEORGE, Elizabeth.** *For the Sake of Elena.* 1992. NY. Putnam. 1st. F/dj. A24. $25.00

**GEORGE, Henry.** *History of the 3rd, 7th, 8th & 12th Kentucky CSA.* 1911. Louisville, KY. CT Dearing Prt Co. 1st. 193p. NF. M8. $850.00

**GEORGE, Henry.** *Land Question, What It Involves...* 1912 (1891). Doubleday Page. 151p. G. S5. $12.00

**GEORGE, Henry.** *Perplexed Philosopher: Examination of Mr Herbert Spencer...* 1892. Chas Webster. 319p. G. S5. $20.00

**GEORGE, Henry.** *Science of Political Economy.* 1898 (1897). Doubleday McClure. 545p. VG. S5. $35.00

**GEORGE, Jean Craighead.** *Julie of the Wolves.* 1972. Harper. 1st. 8vo. 1973 Newbery. ils brd. F/dj. R5. $200.00

**GEORGE, Jean Craighead.** *Moon of the Moles.* 1969. Crowell. 1st. sgn. ils Robert Levering. 39p. cloth. F/NF. D4. $45.00

**GEORGE, Nelson.** *Blackface: Reflections on African-Americans & the Movies.* 1994. Harper Collins. 1st. 28 photos. VG/dj. C9. $24.00

**GEORGE, Nelson.** *Death of Rhythm & Blues.* 1988. Pantheon/Random. ARC. RS. F/clip. A14. $25.00

**GEORGE, Sara.** *Acid Drop.* 1975. Atheneum. 1st. F/dj. B4. $85.00

**GERARD, Max.** *Dali.* 1968. Abrams. ils/fld pl. NF/gilt & ils foil dj. F1. $100.00

**GERARD, Philip.** *Hatteras Light.* 1986. Scribner. 1st. author's 1st book. 246p. F/dj. W2. $30.00

**GERGMAN, Ingmar.** *Scenes From a Marriage.* 1974. Pantheon. 1st Am. VG/dj. M20. $22.00

**GERHARD, Peter.** *Pirates in Baja, CA.* 1963. Tlapalan. 1/500. 11p. wrp. P4. $49.00

**GERHARD, Peter.** *Pirates on the West Coast of New Spain, 1575-1742.* 1960. Glendale. Arthur H Clark. 274p. burgandy cloth. P4. $125.00

**GERHARD, Peter.** *Southwestern Frontier of New Spain.* 1993. OK U. 219p. F. M$. $18.00

**GERHARD, William Wood.** *Diagnosis, Pathology & Treatment of Diseases of Chest.* 1850. Phil. Barrington Haswell. 3rd. 8vo. 351p. C14. $45.00

**GERHARD, William.** *Preliminary Report on System of Sewage Disposal...* 1887. Albany. Argus. 15p. VG/wrp. A10. $20.00

**GERHARDI, William.** *Futility: A Novel on Russian Themes.* 1923. Duffield. 1st Am. 8vo. intro Edith Wharton. 256p. F/NF. J3. $250.00

**GERLACH, Rex.** *Fly Fishing for Rainbows.* 1988. Stackpole. 1st. sgn. 222p. AN/dj. A17. $30.00

**GERMAN, William.** *Doctors Anonymous: Story of Laboratory Medicine.* 1944. Garden City. 300p. A13. $20.00

**GERNER, Ken.** *Red Dreams.* 1978. Copper Canyon Pr. 1st. inscr to poet Linda Gregg. F/wrp. L3. $45.00

**GERNSHEIM, Helmut.** *Incunabula of British Photographic Literature...* 1984. ils/1261 entries. 159p. F/F. A4. $95.00

**GERRY, Mary S.** *Willie's Voyage to India: A True Story for Fannie...* 1857. Boston. ils. VG. M17. $40.00

**GERSHAW, F.W.** *Short Grass Area: Brief History of Southern Alberta.* (c 1955). np. sgn. gilt red cloth. A26. $25.00

**GERSHEIM & GERSHEIM.** *Alvin Langdon Coburn, Photographer: An Autobiography.* 1966. London. Faber. 1st. 4to. 144p. NF/VG. B20. $65.00

**GERSHON, Freddie.** *Sweetie Baby Cookie Honey.* 1986. Arbor. 1st. F/dj. T12. $25.00

**GERSTACKER, Frederich.** *Arkansas Backwoods.* 1991. MO U. 1st. ils. 253p. F/dj. M4. $25.00

**GERSTACKER, Frederich.** *How a Bride Was Won; or, A Chase Across the Pampas.* 1869 (1868). NY. Appleton. 274p. F3. $45.00

**GERSTACKER, Frederich.** *Wild Sports in the Far West.* nd. NY. JW Lovell. 396p. dk bl emb cloth/rb. P4. $125.00

**GERSTACKER, Frederich.** *Wild Sports in the Far West.* 1881. JW Lovell. ils. 396p. G. B19. $25.00

**GERSTACKER, Frederich.** *Wild Sports of the Far West: Narrative of German Wanderer...* 1968 (1854). Duke U. rpt. ils. 409p. F/dj. M4. $50.00

**GERSTEIN, Mordicai.** *Mountains of Tibet.* 1987. Harper Row. 1st. 32p. NF/dj. D4. $35.00

**GESELL, Arnold.** *How a Baby Grows: Story in Pictures.* 1945. Harper. 800+ photos. VG/dj. G1. $50.00

**GETHERS, Peter.** *Cat Abroad: Further Adventures of Norton...* 1993. NY. Crown. 1st. VG/dj. O3. $15.00

**GETLEIN, Frank.** *Harry Jackson. Monograph.* 1969. NY. Kennedy Galleries. 1/300. sgn/#d. w/sgn etching. boxed. B5. $75.00

**GETTINGS, Fred.** *Book of the Hand: Ils History of Palmistry.* 1967. London. 1st/2nd prt. 217p. dj. A13. $50.00

**GETTY, J. Paul.** *Golden Age.* 1968. S&S. ne. G. W2. $15.00

**GEVITZ, Norman.** *DO's Osteopathic Medicine in America.* 1982. Baltimore. 1st. 183p. A13. $37.50

**GHALIOUNGUI, Paul.** *Magic & Medical Science in Ancient Egypt.* 1963. London. 1st. 189p. A13. $85.00

**GHANEM, Shukri M.** *OPEC: Rise & Fall of an Exclusive Club.* 1985. London/NY/Sydney. KPI. 8vo. tables. 233p. NF/dj. W1. $18.00

**GHIRSHMAN, Roman.** *Arts of Ancient Iran From Its Origins to Time of Alexander.* 1964. Golden. 1st. trans Stuart Gilbert/James Emmons. 590 pl. NF/dj. D2. $135.00

**GHIRSHMAN, Roman.** *Arts of Ancient Iran From Its Origins to Time of Alexander.* 1964. NY. Golden. 1st. ils/maps/diagrams. 440p. VG/dj. W1. $125.00

**GIBB, Andrew Dewar.** *Trial of Motor Car Accident Cases, a Guide...* 1938. London. Sweet Maxwell. 2nd. M11. $50.00

**GIBBENS, Byrd.** *This Is a Strange Country: Letters of Westering Family...* 1988. Albuquerque. 1st. 8vo. 438p. brn cloth. AN/dj. P4. $30.00

**GIBBERD, Frederick.** *Town Design.* 1959. NY. Praeger. 1st Am. ils. VG/dj. F1. $100.00

**GIBBON, Edward.** *This History of the Decline & Fall of Roman Empire.* 1820. London. Rivington. 12 vol. New ed. 2 fold maps. half calf/marbled sides. F1. $950.00

**GIBBON & SMART.** *Rock & Pop Super Stars.* 1983. NY. Crescent. G/dj. C5. $12.50

**GIBBONS, H.A.** *Introduction to World Politics.* 1922. NY. Century. 1st. 595p. G. A2. $12.50

**GIBBONS, Kaye.** *Charms for the Easy Life.* 1993. Putnam. 1st. sgn. F/dj. B30. $45.00

**GIBBONS, Kaye.** *Cure for Dreams.* 1991. Algonquin. ARC. sgn. F/wrp. B3. $65.00

**GIBBONS, Kaye.** *Cure for Dreams.* 1991. Algonquin. 1st. F/F. D10. $35.00

**GIBBONS, Kaye.** *Cure for Dreams.* 1991. Algonquin. 1st. sgn. F/dj. A24. $45.00

**GIBBONS, Kaye.** *Ellen Foster.* 1987. Algonquin. UP. author's 1st book. F/prt beige wrp. B3. $175.00

**GIBBONS, Kaye.** *Ellen Foster.* 1987. Algonquin. 1st. author's 1st book. F/NF. A24. $95.00

**GIBBONS, Kaye.** *Ellen Foster.* 1987. Algonquin. 1st. F/F. D10. $125.00

**GIBBONS, Kaye.** *Ellen Foster.* 1988. Jonathan Cape. 1st. author's 1st book. F/F. w/sgn bookplate. B30. $75.00

**GIBBONS, Kaye.** *Sights Unseen.* 1995. Putnam. 1st. sgn. F/dj. O11. $30.00

**GIBBONS, Kaye.** *Virtuous Woman.* 1989. Algonquin. 1st. author's 2nd novel. F/dj. O11. $65.00

**GIBBONS, Martin.** *Identifying Palms.* 1993. Seacaucus. ils. 80p. AN/dj. B26. $8.00

**GIBBONS, William.** *Review & Refutation of Some Opprobrious Charges...* 1847. Phil. TE Champan. 12mo. 185p. ES. leather. V3. $25.00

**GIBBS, A.** *Peruvian & Bolivian Guano.* 1844. London. Ridgway. 95p. VG. A10. $30.00

**GIBBS, James A.** *Pacific Graveyard.* 1964. Portland. Binfords & Mort. 3rd. 296p. red cloth. VG/dj. P4. $35.00

**GIBBS, Jim.** *Disaster Log of Ships.* 1971. Seattle. Superior. 1st. 4to. 176p. P4. $40.00

**GIBBS, Jim.** *Pacific Square-Riggers.* 1969. Seattle. Superior. 1st. sm 4to. 122p. P4. $35.00

**GIBBS, Jim.** *Pacific Square-Riggers: Pictorial History...* 1977. Bonanza. rpt. sm 4to. 192p. VG/dj. S14. $20.00

**GIBBS, Jim.** *West Coast Windjammers in Story & Pictures.* 1968. NY. Bonanza. 4to. 188p. VG/dj. P4. $30.00

**GIBBS, Wolcott.** *Bird Life at the Pole.* 1931. Morrow. 1st. sm 8vo. 171p. NF/dj. B20. $90.00

**GIBRAN, Kahlil.** *Prophet.* 1971. Knopf. ils. VG/G. P12. $12.00

**GIBRAN, Kahlil.** *Tears & Laughter.* 1949. Philosophical. trans from Arabic by AR Ferris/edit ML Wolf. 94p. VG. W2. $15.00

**GIBSON, Alexander.** *Radcliffe Infirmary.* 1926. London. 1st. 316p. A13. $50.00

**GIBSON, Arrell Morgan.** *America's Exiles: Indian Colonization of Oklahoma.* 1976. OK Hist Soc. ils. 155p. F. M4. $15.00

**GIBSON, Arrell Morgan.** *Journal of the West With Special Issue of Ranching...* 1975. U OK. ils. VG/wrp. J2. $125.00

**GIBSON, G.A.** *Physician's Art: Attempt to Expand John Locke's Fragment...* 1933. Oxford. 1st. 237p. A13. $50.00

**GIBSON, George Rutledge.** *Journal of a Soldier Under Kearny & Doniphan.* 1935. Arthur H Clark. 371p. teg. D11. $100.00

**GIBSON, Margaret.** *Butterfly Ward.* 1980. Vanguard. 1st. F/dj. Q1. $30.00

**GIBSON, Margaret.** *Considering Her Condition.* 1978. Vanguard. 1st. F/NF. R11. $40.00

**GIBSON, Walter.** *Boat.* 1953. Houghton. 1st. ils John Groth. VG/dj. S13. $20.00

**GIBSON, Walter.** *Magic Explained.* 1949. Perma. 1st. VG+. M21. $25.00

**GIBSON, William.** *British Contributions to Medical Science.* 1971. London. 302p. A13. $60.00

**GIBSON, William.** *Miracle Worker.* 1976. Knopf. 131p. VG/dj. C5. $12.50

**GIBSON, William.** *New Treatise on Diseases of Horses.* 1751. London. Millar. 264p. ils ftspc/32 copper pl. contemporary calf. K1. $850.00

**GIDAL, Peter.** *Andy Warhol: Films & Paintings.* 1971. Studio Vista/Dutton. 1st. VG/wrp. C9. $60.00

**GIDDINGS, J.L.** *Ancient Men of the Arctic.* 1967. NY. Knopf. 1st. 8vo. 391p. VG/dj. P4. $35.00

**GIDDINGS, J.L.** *Kobuck River People.* 1961. College. Studies of Northern Peoples #1. 159p. F. P4. $38.50

**GIDDINGS, Joshua R.** *Exiles of Florida; or, Crimes Committed...* 1858. Columbus. ils. 338p. B18. $195.00

**GIDE, Andre.** *Counterfeiters.* 1928. London. 1st. trans D Bussy. fair/dj. T9. $45.00

**GIDE, Andre.** *Two Legends: Oedipus & Theseus.* 1950. Knopf. 1st Borzio/1st trans in Eng. 115p. VG+/dj. F1. $35.00

**GIDEON, Hieromonk.** *Round the World Voyage of Hieromonk Gideon, 1803-1809.* 1989. Kingston/Fairbanks. Limestone. inscr. 8vo. 184p. map ep. P4. $55.00

**GIERACH, John.** *Another Lousy Day in Paradise.* 1996. NY. S&S. 1st. F/dj. T11. $35.00

**GIESLER, Jerry.** *Jerry Giesler Story As Told to Pete Martin.* 1960. S&S. 1st. 341p. dj. D11. $35.00

**GIFFORD, Barry.** *Day at the Races: Education of a Racetracker.* 1988. NY. VG/dj. M17. $15.00

**GIFFORD, Barry.** *Landscape With Traveler: Pillow Book of Frances Reeves.* 1980. NY. Dutton. 1st. sgn. F/NF. B20. $75.00

**GIFFORD, Barry.** *Sailor's Holiday.* 1991. Random. 1st. rem mk. NF/dj. B3. $20.00

**GIFFORD, Barry.** *Wild at Heart: Story of Sailor & Lula.* 1990. Grove Weidenfeld. 1st. F/dj. C9. $30.00

**GIFFORD, Tom.** *Anglers & Muscle Heads.* 1960. NY. 1st. VG/G. B5. $30.00

**GIFFORE, Denis.** *Pictorial History of Horror Movies.* 1973. Hamlyn. 2nd. VG/dj. L1. $60.00

**GIGER, H.R.** *HR Giger Posterbook.* 1991. Taschen. 1st. folio. French/German/Eng text. F. C9. $42.00

**GIHON, John H.** *Geary & Kansas...* 1857. Phil. 348p. B18. $35.00

**GIKEY, Elliot Howard.** *Ohio Hundred Year Book.* 1901. Columbus. 773p. G. B18. $25.00

**GILB, Dagoberto.** *Last Known Residence of Mickey Acuna.* 1994. Grove. 1st. sgn. F/dj. O11. $20.00

**GILB, Dagoberto.** *Winners on the Pass Line & Other Stories.* 1985. El Paso. Cinco Puntos. 1st. sgn. author's 1st book. F/wrp. B3. $175.00

**GILBAR, Steven.** *Open Door: When Writers First Learned to Read.* 1989. Boston. VG/dj. M17. $17.50

**GILBERT, A.W.** *Potato.* 1917. Macmillan. Rural Science series. 12mo. 16 pl. 318p. B1. $45.00

**GILBERT, B. Miles.** *Avian Osteology.* 1981. Laramie, WY. sc. VG. A19. $45.00

**GILBERT, B. Miles.** *Mammalian Osteology.* 1980. Laramie, WY. sgn. sc. G. A19. $35.00

**GILBERT, Bill.** *Trailblazers.* Time Life. photos. VG. J2. $45.00

**GILBERT, C.E.** *Two Presidents.* 1973. San Antonio. 85p. F/dj. E1. $25.00

**GILBERT, Dorothy Lloyd.** *Guilford: Quaker College.* 1937. Greensboro, NC. 359p. xl. V3. $15.00

**GILBERT, Helen Earle.** *Go-To-Sleep Book.* 1936. Rand McNally. 1st. ils Keith Ward. VG. M5. $20.00

**GILBERT, Humphrey.** *Voyages & Colonising Enterprises of...* 1940. London. Hakluyt. 2 vol. 8vo. ils/intro/notes/index. P4. $295.00

**GILBERT, John.** *Tigress.* 1987. London. 1st. VG/dj. M17. $25.00

**GILBERT, Michael.** *After the Fine Weather.* 1963. Hodder Stoughton. 1st Eng. VG/G. G8. $40.00

**GILBERT, Michael.** *Flash Point.* 1974. London. Hodder Stoughton. 1st. F/dj. M15. $50.00

**GILBERT, Sarah.** *Dixie Riggs.* 1991. Warner. 1st. F/dj. M25. $35.00

**GILBERT, Sarah.** *Summer Gloves.* 1993. NY. Warner. rem mk. P4. $19.00

**GILBERT & SULLIVAN.** *Authentic Libretti of the Operas.* 1939. NY. 157p. G. C5. $12.50

**GILBRETH, Frank B.** *Of Whales & Women: One Man's View of Nantucket History.* 1956. Crowell. 1st. ils Donald McKay. NF/dj. B4. $85.00

**GILCHRIST, Ellen.** *Age of Miracles.* 1995. Little Brn. 1st. F/dj. R14. $25.00

**GILCHRIST, Ellen.** *Anna Papers.* 1988. Little Brn. 1st. F/F. D10. $50.00

**GILCHRIST, Ellen.** *Annunciation.* 1983. Little Brn. 1st. F/F. D10. $65.00

**GILCHRIST, Ellen.** *Courts of Love. Stories.* 1996. Boston. Little Brn. 1st. 8vo. 288p. F/dj. P4. $30.00

**GILCHRIST, Ellen.** *Falling Through Space.* 1987. Boston. Little Brn. 1st. VG/dj. B5. $25.00

**GILCHRIST, Ellen.** *Land Surveyor's Daughter.* 1979. Fayetteville. Lost Roads. 1st. sgn. F/wrp. B4. $600.00

**GILCHRIST, Ellen.** *Light Can Be Both Wave & Particle.* 1989. Little Brn. 1st. F/dj. R14. $25.00

**GILCHRIST, Ellen.** *Net of Jewels.* 1992. Little Brn. 1st. NF/dj. B30. $20.00

**GILCHRIST, Ellen.** *Victory Over Japan.* 1984. Little Brn. 1st. F/F. D10. $65.00

**GILCHRIST, Ellen.** *Victory Over Japan.* 1984. Little Brn. 1st. F/NF. H11. $45.00

**GILDER, William H.** *Ice-Pack & Tundra.* 1883. NY. Scribner. 8vo. 2 maps/1 fld map. 344p. gilt bdg. P4. $250.00

**GILES, Robert H.** *Ecology of Small Forested Watershed Treated...* (1970). Wildlife Monographs #24. 81p. NF/wrp. S15. $7.00

**GILI, Philida.** *Nutcracker.* 1992. Harper Collins. 1st. popups. VG. B17. $16.00

**GILI, Philida.** *Sleeping Beauty.* 1995. Harper Festival. 1st. 8vo. VG. B17. $12.50

**GILKEY, Landon.** *Religion & the Scientific Future.* 1970. Harper. 193p. VG/dj. B29. $8.00

**GILL, Anton.** *Dance Between Flames: Berlin Between the Wars.* 1993. NY. photos. VG/dj. M17. $15.00

**GILL, Bartholomew.** *Death of an Ardent Bibliophile.* 1995. Morrow. 1st. F/dj. M23. $20.00

**GILL, Brendan.** *Happy Times.* 1973. HBJ. 1st. photos Jerome Zerbe. VG/dj. C9. $48.00

**GILL, Eric.** *Engravings of...* 1983. Wellingborough. Skelton. 2 vol+portfolio. 1/85 (1425). F/case. B24. $1,500.00

**GILL, Eric.** *Four Gospels of the Lord Jesus Christ.* 1988. Wellingborough. Skelton. 1/80 (600 total). Zaehnsdorf bdg. w/prospectus & proof. B24. $950.00

**GILL, Patrick;** see Creasey, John.

**GILL & FINLAYSON.** *Colonial Virginia.* (1973). Nelson. 2nd. ils. 176p. F/G. B10. $8.50

**GILL & HEALY.** *Shrubs & Vines for Northeastern Wildlife.* 1974. Upper Darby, PA. ils. 180p. wrp. B26. $15.00

**GILLELAN, Howard G.** *Complete Book of Bow & Arrow.* 1994. Derrydale. 1/1250. 320p. aeg. gilt leather. F. A17. $22.00

**GILLES, Ray.** *Rayquiem: Cartoons.* nd. Mechelen. Belgian text. unp. G/dj. C5. $12.50

**GILLESPIE, W.M.** *Treatise on Land-Surveying: Comprising Theory...* 1873. NY. Appleton. 424p. G. H10. $15.00

**GILLESPIE & MECHLING.** *American Wildlife in Symbol & Story.* 1987. U TN. 1st. 251p. AN/dj. S15. $12.00

**GILLETT, James B.** *Six Years With the Texas Rangers.* 1943. Lakeside Classic. 1st thus. edit Quaife. teg. VG/sans. T11. $65.00

**GILLETTE & ZIEMANN.** *White House Cookbook: Comprehensive Cyclopedia of Info...* 1919 (1887). sm 4to. 619p. VG. E6. $50.00

**GILLHAM, Charles E.** *Raw North.* 1947. NY. AS Barnes. 8vo. 275p. map ep. bl cloth. VG. P4. $25.00

**GILLIAM & PALMER.** *Face of San Francisco.* 1960. Doubleday. ils. tan brd/red spine. G/dj. A28. $18.00

**GILLIARD, E. Thomas.** *Living Birds of the World: 1500 Species Described.* 1958. NY. ils. 400 p. VG/dj. A17. $22.50

**GILLIARD & LE CROY.** *Birds of the Victor Emanuel & Hindenberg Mountains...* 1961. NY. lg 8vo. ils/map. 86p. VG+/wrp. C12. $32.00

**GILLILAND, Cary.** *Sylloge of US Holdings in National Numismatic Collection...* 1992. Smithsonian. 1st. ils. F. M4. $60.00

**GILLIN, John Lewis.** *Taming the Criminal, Adventures in Penology.* 1931. NY. Macmillan. crimson cloth. VG. M11. $65.00

**GILLIS, Jackson.** *Chain Saw.* 1988. St Martin. 1st. author's 2nd book. F/F. H11. $20.00

**GILLIS, William R.** *Goldrush Days With Mark Twain.* 1930. NY. Boni. 1st. gilt gr cloth. VG/dj. M24. $100.00

**GILLISS, James Melville.** *US Naval Astronomical Expedition to Southern Hemisphere.* 1855. WA. Nicholson. 2 vol. 1st. 4to. ils. modern bdg. P4. $450.00

**GILLON, E.V.** *Early New England Gravestone Rubbings.* 1966. NY. 4to. G. M4. $15.00

**GILMER, Walker.** *Horace Liveright: Publisher of the Twenties.* 1970. NY. David Lewis. 1st. VG/dj. M17. $17.50

**GILMOR, Elizabeth.** *William Gilmor-Sarah Hanna 1778...* 1932. Wooster, OH. ils. 238p. VG. B18. $45.00

**GILMOR, Frances.** *Traders to the Navajos: Story of the Wetherills of Kayenta.* 1934. Houghton Mifflin. 8vo. 265p. orange cloth. VG/G+. F7. $45.00

**GILMORE, Mikal.** *Shot in the Heart.* 1994. Doubleday. 1st. F/case. B4. $75.00

**GILMOUR, David.** *How Boys See Girls.* 1991. Random. 1st. F/dj. R14. $25.00

**GILMOUR, Pat.** *Lasting Impressions. Lithography As Art.* 1988. London. Alexandria. 1st. gilt bdg. F/dj. P4. $60.00

**GILPATRIC, Guy.** *Gentleman & the Walrus Mustache.* 1939. Dodd Mead. 3rd. NF/clip. T11. $35.00

**GILPATRIC, Guy.** *Glencannon Meets Tugboat Annie.* 1950. Harper. 1st. NF/VG. T11. $70.00

**GILSVIK, Bob.** *Complete Book of Trapping.* 1976. Radnor, PA. Chilton. G/dj. A19. $25.00

**GINCANO, John.** *White-Washed Elephant.* 1936. Grosset Dunlap. ils Kay Hunter. 25p. VG/dj. D4. $35.00

**GINGER, Ray.** *Bending Cross, a Biography of Eugene Victor Debs.* 1949. New Brunswick. Rutgers. dj. M11. $35.00

**GINGRICH, Arnold.** *Fishing in Print: Guided Tour Through 5 Centuries...* 1974. NY. Winchester. 1st. 344p. VG/dj. H10. $50.00

**GINGRICH, Arnold.** *Toys of a Lifetime.* 1966. NY. Knopf. 1st. 370p. VG/dj. H10. $35.00

**GINSBERG, Allen.** *Allen Verbatim: Lectures on Poetry, Politics, Consciousness.* 1974. McGraw Hill. 1st. edit Gordon Ball. VG/dj. R11. $45.00

**GINSBERG, Allen.** *Cosmopolitan Greetings: Poems, 1986-1992.* 1994. Harper Collins. 1st. sgn. F/dj. O11. $55.00

**GINSBERG, Allen.** *Iron Horse.* 1974. City Lights. 1st. sgn w/corrections to text. F. O11. $85.00

**GINSBERG, Allen.** *Journals: Mid-Fifties 1954-1958.* 1995. Harper Collins. 1st. F/dj. R14. $25.00

**GINSBURG, Isaac.** *Western Atlantic Scorpion Fishes.* 1953. Smithsonian. 103p. NF. S15. $10.00

**GINZBERG, Louis.** *Legends of the Jews.* 1909. Jewish Pub Soc of Am. 1st. 8vo. 424p. G. H1. $20.00

**GIOVANNI, Nikki.** *Gemini.* 1971. Bobbs Merrill. 1st. F/NF. L3. $150.00

**GIOVANNI, Nikki.** *Selected Poems of Nikki Giovanni.* 1996. Morrow. 1st. F/dj. R14. $30.00

**GIOVANNI & WALKER.** *Poetic Equation.* 1974. WA, DC. Howard U. 1st. sgn Giovanni. F/VG. L3. $75.00

**GIOVANNITTI, Len.** *Man Who Won the Medal of Honor.* 1973. Random. 1st. F/NF. B4. $85.00

**GIOVINAZZO, Buddy.** *Life Is Hot in Cracktown.* 1993. NY. Thunder. 1st. author's 1st book. F/F. H11. $30.00

**GIPE, George.** *Canary Island Quickstep.* 1977. Crowell. 1nd. F/VG. T12. $20.00

**GIPSON, Fred.** *Fabulous Empire.* 1946. Boston. 1st. 411p. VG. B5. $25.00

**GIPSON, Lawrence.** *Coming of the Revolution 1763-1775.* 1954. Harper. 1st. ils. 287p. VG/dj. S17. $10.00

**GIPSON, Morrell.** *Surprise Doll.* (1949). Wonder/Grosset Dunlap. 8vo. ils Steffie Lerch. pict glossy brd. VG+. T5. $65.00

**GIRARDI, Robert.** *Madeleine's Ghost.* 1995. Delacorte. 1st. F/dj. A23. $40.00

**GIRARDI, Robert.** *Pirate's Daughter.* 1997. Delacorte. 1st. sgn. F/dj. A23. $46.00

**GIRARDI, Robert.** *Vaporetto 13.* 1997. Delacorte. 1st. AN/dj. S18. $20.00

**GIRAUDOUX, Jean.** *Ondine.* 1954. RAndom. 1st. NF/VG. A24. $30.00

**GIRODIAS, Maurice.** *Best of Olympia.* 1966. London. Olympia/New Eng. 1st. Traveller's Companion series #107. NF. B2. $35.00

**GIROU, Jean.** *Carcassonne: It's City-It's Crown.* 1930. Grenoble B Arthaud. 8vo. photos. VG+/dj. M21. $40.00

**GIROUX, E.X.** *Death for a Double.* 1990. St Martin. 1st. rem mk. F/dj. A23. $30.00

GIROUX, Henry A. *Pedagogy & Hope Theory, Culture & Schooling.* 1997. Westview. 1st. VG/dj. N2. $10.00

GIRSHAM & THOMAS. *Burma Jack.* 1971. Norton. 1st. 156p. tan cloth. VG/dj. M7. $28.50

GISH, Lillian. *Dorothy & Lillian Gish.* 1973. Scribner. 1st. inscr. 800+photos. F/VG. C9. $210.00

GISSING, George. *Sins of the Fathers & Other Tales.* 1924. Chicago. Covici. 1st. 1/550. 124p. G. F1. $35.00

GITTLEMAN, John L. *Carnivore Behavior, Ecology & Evolution.* 1989. Cornell. 19 separately authored papers. 620p. F. S15. $15.00

GIUDICE, Gaspare. *Piranello: A Biography.* 1975. OUP. 1st Am. F/dj. A2. $20.00

GIUSTINIANI, Michele. *Lettere Memorabili.* 1669. Rome. Nicol'Angelo Tinass. narrow 12mo. 2 pl. 584p. aeg. contemporary morocco. K1. $250.00

GLANZ. *German Jew in America: Annotated Bibliography.* 1969. 4to. 2527 entries. 208p. A4. $35.00

GLASER, Lynn. *America on Paper, First Hundred Years.* 1989. Phil. Assoc Antiquaries. ils. gilt brn cloth. F/dj. F1. $50.00

GLASER & WORSTER. *Ruby: An Ordinary Woman.* 1995. Faber. 1st. sgns. F/dj. T11. $35.00

GLASS, Bentley. *Survey of Biological Progress.* 1957. Academic. VG. S5. $15.00

GLASS, Philip. *Music by Philip Glass.* 1987. Harper Row. 1st. inscr. F/clip. O11. $60.00

GLASS-GRAY, Charles. *Off at Sunrise: Overland Journal of...* 1976. San Marino, CA. Huntington Lib. 1st. F/dj. O4. $25.00

GLASSCOCK, Lucille. *Texas Wildcatter.* 1952. San Antonio. 1st. sgn pres. VG/G. B5. $20.00

GLASSE, Hannah. *Art of Cookery Made Plain & Easy.* 1751. London. 4th. polished calf/raised bands. lacks ftspc. E6. $450.00

GLASSER, Ronald. *365 Days.* 1971. NY. Braziller. 1st. 292p. VG/clip. R11. $15.00

GLASSMAN, Judith. *Year in Music.* 1979. NY. Columbia. 184p. G/dj. C5. $12.50

GLAZIER, Willard. *Down the Great River.* 1891. Phil. ils/fld map. 443p+63p appendix. pict cloth. VG. B18. $27.50

GLEASON, Duncan. *Islands & Ports of California.* 1958. NY. Devon Adair. 200p. lt bl cloth. VG. P4. $20.00

GLEASON, Duncan. *Islands of California: Their History, Romance...* 1951. Los Angeles. Sea Pub. 1st. inscr. ils. NF/G. O4. $30.00

GLEASON, Ralph J. *Jam Session.* 1958. Putnam. 1st. inscr. F/VG. B2. $85.00

GLEASON & GLEASON. *Beloved Sister: Letters of James Henry Gleason 1841-59.* 1978. Arthur H Clark. 1st. VG/dj. O4. $15.00

GLEASON & VETSCH. *Cozy Book of Mother Goose.* 1926. Racine. Whitman. 16mo. bl-gray brd. mc pict dj. R5. $110.00

GLEBE, Iris Webb. *Earl of Dublin.* 1988. McNaughton Gunn. 1st. photos. VG/dj. P8. $100.00

GLENDINNING, Victoria. *Suppressed Cry: Life & Death of a Quaker Daughter.* 1969. London. Kegan Paul. 1st. 120p. VG/clip. V3. $17.50

GLICK, Allen. *Winter's Coming, Winter's Gone.* 1984. Pinnacle. 1st trade. NF/dj. R11. $22.00

GLICKMAN, Jay L. *Yellow-Green Vaseline!: A Guide to the Magic Glass.* 1991. Antique Pub. 1st. 32 mc pl. 111p. VG+. w/guide. H1. $25.00

GLIMCHER & GLIMCHER. *Je Suis le Cahier: Sketchbooks of Picasso.* 1986. Atlantic Monthly. 1st. ils. 349p. VG/dj. N2. $30.00

GLINES, Carroll V. *Doolittle's Tokyo Raiders.* 1964. Van Nostrand Reinhold. rpt. sgn. 8vo. 447p. w/sgn photo. VG/dj. B11. $1,250.00

GLUBB, John Bagot. *Short History of the Arab Peoples.* 1969. Hodder Stoughton. 43 maps/14 tables. 318p. cloth. VG/dj. Q2. $20.00

GLUBB, John Bagot. *Story of the Arab Legion.* 1948. Hodder Stoughton. 1st. 8vo. ils/maps. 371p. VG. W1. $40.00

GLUBOK, Shirley. *Art of Ancient Greece.* 1963. NY. Atheneum. 1st. inscr. sm 4to. 48p. VG/torn. T5. $35.00

GLUCKMAN, Max. *Politics, Law & Ritual in Tribal Society...* 1968. Chicago. Aldine. VG/dj. M11. $50.00

GNOLI, Domenico. *Orestes; or, The Art of Smiling.* 1961. S&S. 1st. 4to. ils. NF/VG. S13. $45.00

GOAD & HAMMOND. *Scientist on Trail: Travel Letters of AF Bandelier...* 1949. Quivira. 1/500. 154p. NF. A4. $300.00

GOBLE, Paul. *Iktomi & the Ducks: A Plains Indian Story.* 1990. Orchard. 1st. ils. NF/dj. M5. $12.00

GODARD, Andre. *Art of Iran.* 1965. NY. Prager. 179 pl/maps. 320p. cloth. NF/dj. D2. $65.00

GODBEER, R. *Devil's Dominion: Magic & Religion in Early New England.* 1992. Cambridge. 1st. 253p. F/dj. M4. $18.00

GODBEY, A.H. *Stanley in Africa: Paladin of Nineteenth Century.* 1892. Mercantile Pub/Adv. rpt. poor. P3. $10.00

GODDARD, Anthea. *Vienna Pursuit.* 1976. Walker. NF/dj. P3. $8.00

GODDARD, Paul E. *Anatomy, Physiology & Pathology of the Human Teeth...* 1844. Phil. Carey Hart. 30 full-p pl. 227p. new cloth. G7. $395.00

GODDARD, Robert H. *Rocket Development: Liquid-Fuel Rocket Research 1929-41.* 1948. Prentice Hall. 8vo. 291p. cloth. xl. VG/dj. K5. $250.00

GODDARD, Robert. *Closed Circle.* 1993. Poseidon. ARC/1st. F/dj. S18. $27.00

GODDEN, Rumer. *Four Dolls, Impunity Jane, The Fairy Doll, Holly & Candy...* 1983. Greenwillow. 1st Am. sm 4to. 137p. F/VG. T5. $45.00

GODDEN, Rumer. *In Noah's Ark.* 1949. NY. 61p. VG. S15. $10.00

GODDEN, Rumer. *In This House of Brede.* 1969. Viking. 1st. 376p. VG/dj. A25. $15.00

GODDEN, Rumer. *Mouse House.* 1957. Viking. 1st. 8vo. ils Adrienne Adams. 63p. G+/fair. T5. $35.00

GODDEN & GODDEN. *Mercy, Pity, Peace & Love: Stories.* 1989. NY. 1st. VG/dj. M17. $20.00

GODEY & HALE. *Lady's Book.* 1869. Phil. Louis Godey. 8vo. pl (some fld). 522p. blk leather spine/raised bands. G. D1. $200.00

GODFREY, Henry. *Your El Salvador Guide.* 1968. Funk Wagnall. 1st. 168p. F3. $10.00

GODFREY, Henry. *Your Yucatan Guide.* 1967. Funk Wagnall. 1st. ils/maps. 196p. F3. $15.00

GODFREY, Thomas. *Murder at the Opera.* 1989. Mysterious. 1st. VG/dj. M20. $15.00

GODFREY & WOOTEN. *Aquatic & Wetland Plants of Southeastern United States.* 1979. Athens. Monocotyledons. 712p. F. B26. $46.00

GODSELL, Philip H. *Arctic Trader.* 1946. Toronto. Macmillan. later revised. 8vo. gray cloth. VG/dj. P4. $35.00

GODWIN, Rick. *Exposing Witchcraft in the Church.* 1997. Creation House. 169p. VG. B29. $9.00

GODWIN, William. *Enquirer.* 1797. London. Robinson. lg 8vo. cloth. R12. $575.00

**GOERCH, Carl.** *Ocracoke.* 1964. Winston/Salem. JF Blair. 8vo. ils. 223p. VG/dj. B11. $15.00

**GOERKE, Heinz.** *Linnaeus.* 1973 (1966). NY. ils. trans from German. VG+/dj. B26. $30.00

**GOERNER, Fred.** *Search for Amelia Earhart.* 1966. Garden City. Doubleday. stated 1st. 326p. bl cloth. P4. $25.00

**GOETSCHIUS, Percy.** *Material Used in Musical Composition: System of Harmony.* 1941. Schirmer. 265p. G. S5. $20.00

**GOETZ, Charles E.** *Prophet With Honor: Fred Tuttle Colter Story.* 1965. Phoenix. sgn. ils/map. 91p. brn simulated leathr. VG+. F7. $30.00

**GOETZMANN, William H.** *Army Exploration in American West 1803-1863.* 1959. New Haven. Yale. 1st. ils/facs pocket maps. VG. B18. $125.00

**GOETZMANN, William H.** *Explorations & Empire: Explorer & Scientist...* 1993. NY. ils/maps. F/dj. M4. $30.00

**GOETZMANN, William H.** *New Lands, New Man: America & Second Great Age of Discovery.* 1986. NY. Viking. ils/map ep. 528p. half cloth. AN/dj. P4. $25.00

**GOETZMANN, William H.** *New Lands, New Man: America & Second Great Age of Discovery.* 1986. Viking. ils. VG/dj. M17. $15.00

**GOETZMANN & WILLIAMS.** *Atlas of North American Exploration...* 1992. 4to. 90 portraits/100 mc maps. 224p. F/F. A4. $35.00

**GOFF, May.** *Household Cyclopedia of Hints for Modern Homes...* 1871. Detroit Free Pr. 2nd. 644p. VG. E6. $75.00

**GOFF & MCCAFFREE.** *Century in the Saddle: 100-Year Story of Colorado...* 1967. Johnson Pub. 365p. AN. J2. $135.00

**GOFFE, Jules.** *Le Livre du Cuisine.* 1877 (1867). Paris. ils. rb. VG. E6. $200.00

**GOGARTY, Oliver St. John.** *James Augustine Joyce.* 1949. Dallas. Times Herald. 1st. 1/1050. buff prt wrp. M24. $65.00

**GOH, Poh Seng.** *If We Dream Too Long.* 1972. Singapore. Island Pr. inscr. 177p. NF/dj. R11. $40.00

**GOHM, D.C.** *Antique Maps of Europe, the Americas, West Indies...* 1972. 4to. 128p. F/NF. A4. $55.00

**GOHM, D.C.** *Maps & Prints for Pleasure & Investment.* 1978. 2nd revised. ils. 211p. F/F. A4. $35.00

**GOLDBERG, Hank M.** *Prosecution Responds: OJ Simpson Trial Prosecutor...* 1996. Birch Lane. 1st. photos. VG/dj. S14. $12.00

**GOLDBERG, Lee.** *Television Series Revivals.* 1993. McFarland. 196p. VG. C5. $12.50

**GOLDEN, Arthur.** *Memoirs of a Geisha.* 1997. NY. Knopf. 1st. author's 1st novel. F/dj. T2. $75.00

**GOLDENSON, Robert M.** *Longman Dictionary of Psychology & Psychiatry.* 1984. London. Walter D Glanze Book. lg 8vo. 815p. blk cloth. dj. G1. $85.00

**GOLDER, F.A.** *Bering's Voyages: An Account of Efforts of Russians...* 1935. NY. Am Geog Soc. 2 vol. 2nd. 12mo. fld maps/photos. NF. P4. $250.00

**GOLDER, F.A.** *Father Herman: Alaska's Saint.* 1968. SF. Orthodox Christian Books & Icons Group. 66p. F. P4. $40.00

**GOLDFLUSS, Howard E.** *Judgment.* 1986. NY. DIF. 1st. author's 1st book. F/F. H11. $40.00

**GOLDFRANK, Esther S.** *Artist of Isleta Paintings in Pueblo Society.* 1967. Smithsonian. 227p. gilt bl cloth. P4. $50.00

**GOLDFRANK, Esther S.** *Notes on an Undirected Life: One Anthropologist Tells It.* 1978. Queens College. 1st. ils. 244p. NF. B19. $40.00

**GOLDING, Arthur.** *Icarus. Out of Ovid's Metamorphoses. Done Into Eng by...* (1983). np. Wind & Harlot. mini. 1/27. frenchfold. woodcut. tan brd/prt label. B24. $175.00

**GOLDING, Louis.** *Good-Bye to Ithaca.* 1958. Yoseloff. 8vo. ils/maps. cloth. VG/dj. W1. $20.00

**GOLDING, Louis.** *In the Steps of Moses the Conqueror.* nd (1938). London. Rich Cowan. 1st. 366p. NF. M7. $20.00

**GOLDING, Louis.** *Luigi of Catanzaro.* 1926. London. Archer. 1st. 1/100. sgn. VG/custom fld. M15. $350.00

**GOLDING, William.** *Double Tongue.* 1995. NY. 1st. dj. T9. $12.00

**GOLDING, William.** *Free Fall.* 1960. Harcourt Brace. 1st Am. F/VG+. B4. $150.00

**GOLDING, William.** *Paper Men.* 1984. NY. FSG. 1st. F/F. H11. $20.00

**GOLDING, William.** *Rights of Passage.* 1980. 1st. Booker Prize. F/dj. M19. $12.50

**GOLDING, William.** *Scorpion God.* 1971. Harcourt. 1st. NF/VG. S13. $12.00

**GOLDMAN, Emma.** *Living My Life.* 1931. Knopf. 2 vol. G+/dj. B2. $300.00

**GOLDMAN, Emma.** *Social Significance of the Modern Drama.* (1914). Boston. Richard D Badger. sm 8vo. 316p. tan cloth. K1. $275.00

**GOLDMAN, Francisco.** *Long Night of White Chickens.* 1992. NY. Atlantic. 1st. F/dj. M23. $50.00

**GOLDMAN, James.** *Myself As Witness.* 1979. Random. VG/dj. A28. $13.00

**GOLDMAN, Morris.** *Flourescent Antibody Methods.* 1968. Academic. 303p. xl. G. S5. $12.00

**GOLDMAN, William.** *Edged Weapons.* 1985. London. Granada. 1st. F/NF. A24. $25.00

**GOLDMAN, William.** *Marathon Man.* 1974. Delacorte. 1st. F/dj. B2. $35.00

**GOLDMAN, William.** *Marathon Man.* 1974. Delacorte. 1st. VG/dj. P3. $30.00

**GOLDMAN, William.** *Tinsel.* 1979. Delacorte. 1st. F/NF. S18. $35.00

**GOLDMAN, William.** *Wigger.* 1974. HBJ. 1st. ils Errol LeCain. F/dj. B4. $250.00

**GOLDMARK, Josephine.** *Fatigue & Efficiency: A Study in Industry.* 1912. Charities Pub Comm of Russell Sage Foundation. 3rd. sgn. H1. $30.00

**GOLDMSITH, Oliver.** *Citizen of the World; or, Letters From Chinese Philosopher.* 1792. London. Vernor Otridge. 2 vol. sm 8vo. full mottled calf/blk leather labels. H13. $295.00

**GOLDMSITH, Oliver.** *Life of Richard Nash of Bath, Esq.* 1762. London. Newbery Frederick. 1st. ftspc. 234p. full calf. H13. $495.00

**GOLDMSITH, Oliver.** *Poems for Young Ladies, in Three Parts, Educational...* 1785. London. E Johnson. tall 12mo. 276p. early calf/new leather label. H13. $295.00

**GOLDMSITH, Oliver.** *Traveller, a Poem.* 1770. London. Carman Newberry. 4to. 23p. blk crushed morocco. H13. $395.00

**GOLDSCHMIDT, Walter.** *Sebei Law.* 1967. Berkeley. M11. $35.00

**GOLDSMID, Edmund.** *Pretty Gentleman; or, Softness of Manners Vindicated...* 1885. Edinburgh. private prt. 1/275 for subscribers. 12mo. 32p. H13. $95.00

**GOLDSMITH, Barbara.** *Johnson Versus Johnson.* 1987. Knopf. 1st. 285p. VG/dj. P12. $10.00

**GOLDSMITH, Margaret.** *Christina of Sweden: A Psychological Biography.* 1935. Doubleday Doran. 1st. 308p. VG+. A25. $15.00

**GOLDSMITH, Oliver.** *Deserted Village.* 1802. London. Harper. 1st. 4to. 120p. teg. gilt red cloth. NF. H13. $85.00

**GOLDSMITH, Oliver.** *Deserted Village.* 1912. Boston. Bibliophile Soc. 1/469. ils/sgn WHW Bicknell. full polished calf/case. H13. $165.00

**GOLDSMITH, Oliver.** *Essays, 1765.* 1970. Menston. Scholar. facs. sm 8vo. F. H13. $35.00

**GOLDSMITH, Oliver.** *History of Little Goody Two Shoes.* 1925. Macmillan. 16mo. ils Alice Woodward. 91p. VG. D1. $35.00

**GOLDSMITH, Oliver.** *Retaliation: A Poem Including Epithets...* 1929. Westport. Ellis/Georgian Pr. 1/435. folio. salmon brd/label. H13. $95.00

**GOLDSMITH, Oliver.** *She Stoops to Conquer; or, The Mistakes of a Night.* 1912. London. Hodder Stoughton. 1st thus. 1/350. ils/sgn Hugh Thomson. H13. $395.00

**GOLDSMITH, Oliver.** *Vicar of Wakefield.* 1914. London. Constable. 1/500. ils/sgn EJ Sullivan. 344p. NF/cloth clamshell case. H5. $850.00

**GOLDSMITH, Oliver.** *Works of...* 1854. London. John Murray. 4 vol. edit Peter Cunningham. quarter gr moocco. F1. $350.00

**GOLDSMITH, Oliver.** *Works of...* 1854. London. John Murray. 4 vol. teg. Tout red morocco/silk markers. NF. H5. $500.00

**GOLDSMITH, Olivia.** *First Wives Club.* 1992. Poseidon. 1st. author's 1st book. F/dj. A24. $30.00

**GOLDSMITH, Olivia.** *Flavor of the Month.* 1993. NY. Poseidon. 1st. 8vo. 698p. NF/dj. P4. $20.00

**GOLDSTEIN, Irving.** *Trial Technique, Third Printing.* 1935. Chicago. Callaghan. maroon buckram. M11. $85.00

**GOLDSTEIN, Kurt.** *After Effects of Brain Injuries in War...* 1942. NY. Grune Stratton. 244p. cloth. G7. $55.00

**GOLDSTEIN, Philip.** *Genetics Is Easy: Handbook of Information.* 1955. NY. Lantern. VG. O3. $25.00

**GOLDSTEIN, Rebecca.** *Mazel: A Novel.* 1995. NY. Viking. 1st. 8vo. 357p. half cloth. F/dj. P4. $24.00

**GOLDSTEIN, William N.** *Introduction to the Borderline Conditions.* 1985. Northvale, NJ. Jason Aronson. 1st. 8vo. 241p. F. C14. $15.00

**GOLDSTEIN & ZORNOW.** *Screen Image of Youth: Movies About Children & Adolescents.* 1980. Scarecrow. 1st. sgn Goldstein. F. C9. $30.00

**GOLDSTROM, John.** *Narrative History of Aviation.* 1930. NY. 1st. ils. 319p. VG. B18. $45.00

**GOLDWATER, Barry M.** *Conscience of a Conservative.* 1960. Sheperdsville, KY. Victor Pub. sgn inscr pres. 124p. dj. K1. $100.00

**GOLDWATER, Barry M.** *Delightful Journey Down the Green & Colorado Rivers.* 1970. AZ Hist Found. 1/100. deluxe ed. sgn. rust cloth/leather spine. case/photo. F7. $295.00

**GOLDWATER & TREVES.** *Artists on Art From the XIV to XX Century...* 1947. NY. Pantheon. 2nd revised. ils. 500p. G7. $75.00

**GOLDWYN, Robert M.** *Beyond Appearance: Reflections of a Plastic Surgeon.* 1986. Dodd Mead. 1st. 229p. NF/clip. C14. $15.00

**GOLL, Yvan.** *Four Poems of the Occult.* 1962. Allen Pr. 5 vol. 1/130. folio. ils. F/loose in wrp/chemise/case. B24. $2,000.00

**GOLOWANJUK, Jascha.** *My Golden Road From Samarkand.* 1993. London. Quartet Books. reissue (1958 1st Eng). NF/dj. A14. $21.00

**GOMBRICH, E.H.** *Image & the Eye: Further Studies in Psychology...* 1982. Cornell. ils. VG/dj. M17. $30.00

**GOMBROWICZ, Witold.** *Pornografia.* 1966 (1960). Grove. 1st Am. 12mo. F/VG. A2. $20.00

**GONDOR, Emery J.** *You Are...Puzzle Book for Children.* 1937. Modern Age. 1st. ils EJ Gondor/49 picture puzzles. VG/dj. D1. $135.00

**GONZALEZ-GERTH, Miguel.** *Ruben Dario Centennial Studies.* 1972. Austin. 120p. dj. F3. $10.00

**GOOCH, Fanny Chambers.** *Face to Face With the Mexicans.* 1887. NY. Ford Howard Hulbert. ils. 584p. pict cloth. D11. $100.00

**GOOD, Arthur.** *Magical Experiments; or, Science in Play.* 1894. Phil. ils. trans Curwen/Waters. 329p. cloth. B18. $32.50

**GOOD, Edward.** *Book of Affinity. By Moysheh Oyved.* 1933. London. Heinemann. 1/525. 7 mtd pl. 112p. aeg. blk cloth. pub box. K1. $300.00

**GOOD, Gregory.** *Earth, the Heavens & the Carnegie Instit of Washington.* 1994. Am Geophysical Union. 4to. 252p. K5. $42.00

**GOOD, John Mason.** *Book of Nature.* 1831. NY. from London ed. 467p. full calf. A17. $20.00

**GOODALL, Daphne Machin.** *Flight of the East Prussian Horses.* 1973. Arco. VG/dj. O3. $35.00

**GOODALL, John S.** *Edwardian Christmas.* 1978. Atheneum. 1st Am. obl 8vo. VG/dj. B17. $30.00

**GOODALL, JOHNSON & PHILIPPI.** *Lasaves de Chile. Su Concocimiento y sus Costumbres.* 1946 & 1951. Buenos Aires. Platt Establecimientos Graficos SA. 2 vol. P4. $195.00

**GOODCHILD, George.** *Follow McLean.* 1961. Jarrolds. 1st Eng. VG/dj. G8. $30.00

**GOODCHILD, George.** *Monster of Grammont.* 1930. Mystery League. 1st. F/VG. M19. $25.00

**GOODCHILD, George.** *Q33.* (1933). London. Odhams. 1st. F/NF. M15. $50.00

**GOODE, John.** *Recollections of a Lifetime.* 1906. Neale. 266p. B10. $50.00

**GOODE, Paul R.** *United States Soldiers' Home: A History.* 1957. Richmond, VA. private rpt. 1st hc. sgn. 288p. VG. S16. $35.00

**GOODFRIEND.** *Published Diaries & Letters of American Women...* 1987. 244p. F. A4. $45.00

**GOODHART, A.L.** *English Law & the Moral Law.* 1953. London. Stevens. G/dj. M11. $65.00

**GOODISON, Nicholas.** *English Barometers, 1680-1860.* 1968. NY. Clarkson Potter. ils. 353p. VG/dj. K5. $100.00

**GOODKIND, Terry.** *Wizard's First Rule.* 1994. NY. Tor. 1st. NF/F. H11. $30.00

**GOODLANDER, C.W.** *Memoirs & Recollections of CW Goodlander of Early Ft Scott.* 1900. Monitor Prt. 1st. ils. 147p. NF. B19. $50.00

**GOODLOE, Daniel R.** *Southern Platform; or, Manual of Southern Sentiment...* 1858. Boston. Jewett. 8vo. dbl-column text. bl prt wrp. O1. $65.00

**GOODMAN, David Michael.** *Western Panorama 1849-1875: Travels, Writings...* 1966. Clark. 1st. ils/notes/index. 326p. NF/brn wrp. B19. $45.00

**GOODMAN, Eric.** *In Days of Awe.* 1991. Knopf. 1st. F/dj. P8. $12.50

**GOODMAN, Jack.** *Fireside Book of Dog Stories.* 1943. S&S. ils Cecil Aldin. VG/dj. A21. $35.00

**GOODMAN, Mary Ellen.** *Race Awareness in Young Children.* 1952. Cambridge. Addison Wesley. 1st. VG/dj. N2. $12.50

**GOODMAN, Paul.** *Break-Up of Our Camp/Ceremonial/Facts of Life.* 1978. Blk Sparrow. 3 vol. 1/200. NF. B9. $125.00

**GOODMAN, Paul.** *Hawkweed.* 1967. Random. 1st. 185p. gilt brn cloth. F/VG. F1. $17.50

**GOODMAN, Richard M.** *Planning for a Healthy Baby.* 1986. OUP. 1st. F/NF. S13. $10.00

**GOODRICH, Lloyd.** *Edward Hopper.* nd (1978?). Abrams lg obl 4to. 300 ils. 306p. F/dj. C15. $125.00

**GOODRICH, Lloyd.** *Winslow Homer.* 1959. NY. Great Am Artists. VG/dj. M17. $15.00

**GOODRICH & NEESE.** *Uinta Basin Flora.* 1986. Ogden. ils. 320p. sc. B26. $25.00

**GOODRUM, Charles A.** *Dewey Decimated.* (1977). Crown. 1st. 8vo. gr-lettered orange cloth spine/blk brd. dj. R3. $35.00

**GOODSPEED, D.J.** *German Wars 1914-1945.* 1977. Boston. 1st. VG/dj. M17. $20.00

**GOODWIN, Brian.** *How the Leopard Changed Its Spots...* 1994. NY. ils. VG/dj. M17. $15.00

**GOODWIN, Doris Kearns.** *Fitzgeralds & Kennedys.* 1987. S&S. BC. 8vo. 932p. F/dj. W2. $25.00

**GOODWIN, J.R.** *Twenty Feet From Glory.* 1970. Morgantown. photos. 209p. F/dj. M4. $30.00

**GOODWIN, John C.** *Insanity & the Criminal.* 1923. London. Hutchinson. 1st. 320p. gilt bl cloth. VG+. B20. $45.00

**GOODWIN, John.** *Idols & the Prey: Novel of Haiti.* 1953. Harper. 1st. F/VG. B4. $85.00

**GOODWYN, Frank.** *Poems About the West.* 1976. Pioneer Am Soc. ils. VG. J2. $25.00

**GOOLD-ADAMS, Richard.** *Middle East Journey.* 1947. London. Murray. 8vo. ils/pl/dbl-p map. 195p. cloth. VG. Q2. $20.00

**GORBACHEV, Mikhail.** *At the Summit.* 1988. NY. 1st. NF/dj. T12. $20.00

**GORD, G.M.** *Cast in Stone.* 1996. NY. Walker. 1st. sgn GM Ford. F/dj. T2. $35.00

**GORD, G.M.** *Who in Hell Is Wanda Fuca?* 1995. NY. Walker. 1st. sgn. author's 1st novel. F/2 djs. T20. $150.00

**GORDEEVA, Ekaterina.** *My Sergi.* 1996. Warner. 1st. sgn. F/dj. T11. $60.00

**GORDIMER, Nadine.** *Black Interpreters: Notes on African Writing.* 1973. Johannesburg. Ravan. South African ed/PBO/true 1st. NF/wrp. B3. $75.00

**GORDIMER, Nadine.** *Jump & Other Stories.* 1991. FSG. 1st Am. sgn. F/F. D10. $50.00

**GORDIMER, Nadine.** *My Son's Story.* 1990. FSG. 1st Am. sgn. F/F. D10. $50.00

**GORDON, Alison.** *Dead Pull Hitter.* 1988. St Martin. 1st Am. F/VG. P8. $15.00

**GORDON, Alison.** *Grave's Retreat.* 1989. Doubleday. 1st. F/VG. P8. $25.00

**GORDON, Alison.** *Night Game.* 1992. McClelland Stewart. 1st. F/dj. P8. $22.50

**GORDON, Alison.** *Safe at Home.* 1990. McClelland Stewart. 1st. F/dj. P8. $25.00

**GORDON, Anthony.** *Russian Ballet, Camera Studies.* 1939. London. Geoffrey Bles. 1st. 96 tipped-in pl. gilt bl cloth. VG. F1. $200.00

**GORDON, Armistead C.** *Jefferson Davis.* 1918. Scribner. 1st. inscr. 329p. VG. B10. $50.00

**GORDON, Barbara.** *I'm Dancing As Fast As I Can.* 1979. Harper Row. later prt. VG/dj. C9. $36.00

**GORDON, Caroline.** *Malefactors.* 1956. Harcourt Brace. 1st. inscr. NF. B4. $300.00

**GORDON, Dixie.** *How Sweet It Is: Story of Dixie Crystals & Savannah Foods.* 1992. Savannah Foods. 109p. H6. $30.00

**GORDON, Elizabeth.** *Really So Stories.* 1924. Volland. 1st. 8vo. 96p. G. B11. $25.00

**GORDON, Jan.** *Modern French Painters.* 1939. London. Bodley Head. 3rd. ils. tan cloth. VG. F1. $25.00

**GORDON, John.** *Borzoi.* 1974. Arco. VG/dj. A21. $20.00

**GORDON, Martin.** *Gordon's Print Price Annual 1994.* 1994. thick 4to. 35,000 prints sold at auction. NF. A4. $125.00

**GORDON, Mary McDougall.** *Overland to California With the Pioneer Line.* 1985. Stanford. 2nd. 247p. rust cloth. F. M4/P4. $30.00

**GORDON, Mary.** *Final Payments.* 1978. Random. 1st. sgn. author's 1st book. NF/dj. R14. $75.00

**GORDON, Patricia.** *Boy Jones.* 1943. Viking. 1st. 158p. F/dj. D4. $30.00

**GORDON, Stewart.** *Gunswift.* 1956. Avalon. 1st. F/dj. M25. $25.00

**GORDON, W.J.** *Round About the North Pole.* 1907. NY. Dutton. 1st Am. 294p. bl cloth. P4. $50.00

**GORDON & GORDON.** *Our Son Pablo.* 1946. McGraw Hill. 2nd. 235p. F3. $15.00

**GORDON & GORDON.** *Race for the Golden Tide.* 1983. 1st. inscr. F/VG. M19. $17.50

**GORDON & GORDON.** *That Darn Cat (Undercover Cat).* 1973. Doubleday. MTI. photos. VG/G. O3. $18.00

**GORE, Al.** *Earth in the Balance: Ecology & the Human Spirit.* 1992. Houghton Mifflin. F/dj. S15. $5.00

**GORENSTEIN, Shirley.** *Not Forever on Earth.* 1975. Scribner. 1st. ils/index. 153p. dj. F3. $15.00

**GORES, Joe.** *Contract Null & Void.* 1995. Mysterious. 1st. NF/dj. G8. $20.00

**GORES, Joe.** *Dead Man.* 1993. Mysterious. 1st. F/dj. N4. $25.00

**GORES, Joe.** *Gone, No Forwarding.* 1978. NY. Random. 1st. F/dj. M15. $75.00

**GOREY, Edward.** *Doubtful Guest.* 1957. Doubleday. 1st. ils. yel cloth. NF/clip. J3. $200.00

**GOREY, Edward.** *QRV, by Edward Gorey.* 1989. Boston. Bromer. mini. 1/85. ils/sgn Gorey (29 hand-colored ils). F/case. B24. $350.00

**GOREY, Edward.** *Water Flowers.* 1st. sgn. 64p. gr/blk bdg. VG/dj. P12. $120.00

**GOREY, Edward.** *Willowdale Handcar.* 1979. Dodd Mead. 1st. 16mo. unp. F/dj. D1. $25.00

**GORGES, Raymond.** *Ernest Harold Baynes: Naturalist & Crusader.* 1928. Houghton Mifflin. photos. VG. S15. $10.00

**GORHAM, Charles O.** *Gilded Hearse.* 1948. NY. Creative Age. 1st. 8vo. 246p. F/dj. O10. $10.00

**GORKI, Maxim.** *Bystander.* 1930. NY. Literary Guild. 729p. VG. F1. $25.00

**GORKY, Maxim.** *Reminiscences of Leonid Andreyev.* 1928. NY. Crosby Gaige. 12mo. 85p. paper brd/cloth spine. B20. $25.00

**GORMAN, Ed.** *Cry of Shadows.* 1990. St Martin. 1st. F/VG. S18. $28.00

**GORMAN, Ed.** *Predators.* nd. BC. F/dj. P3. $10.00

**GORMAN, Ed.** *Prisoners & Other Stories.* 1992. Baltimore. CD Pub. 1st. sgn. 22 stories. F/dj. T2. $30.00

**GORMAN, Ed.** *Several Deaths Later.* 1988. St Martin. 1st. sgn. F/dj. T2. $25.00

**GORMAN & GREENBERG.** *Invitation to Murder.* 1991. Dark Harvest. 1/400. sgn all contributors. F/dj/case. B2. $125.00

**GORNY, Hein.** *Ein Hundebuch.* 1951. Munchen. 2nd. photos Gaudissin/text Graf Wolf. 120p. VG. A17. $25.00

**GORRA, Michael.** *English Novel at Mid-Century.* 1990. NY. VG/dj. M17. $15.00

**GORSE, Golden.** *Moorland Mousie.* 1930. Jr Literary Guild. ils Lionel Edwards. G/dj. A21. $45.00

**GORZALES DAVILA, Francisco.** *Ancient Cultures of Mexico.* 1968. Mexico. INAH. 80p. wrp. F3. $10.00

**GOSHEN, Charles.** *Documentary History of Psychiatry.* 1967. NY. 1st. 904p. A13. $50.00

**GOSLING, F.G.** *Before Freud: Neurasthenia & the American Medical Community.* 1987. Chicago. 1st. 192p. dj. A13. $300.00

**GOSNELL, Harpur Allen.** *Before the Mast in the Clippers...1856-1860.* 1937. NY. Derrydale. 1/950. tall 8vo. red cloth. NF. P4. $225.00

**GOSNER, Kenneth L.** *Field Guide to the Atlantic Seashore.* 1978. Houghton Mifflin. 329p. NF/VG. S15. $12.50

**GOSS, Helen Rocca.** *California White Cap Murders: Episode in Vigilantism.* 1969. Santa Barbara. Kennedy. 1st. sgn. 132p. red cloth. AN. P4. $40.00

**GOSS, John.** *Mapping of North America.* 1990. Secaucus. Wellfleet. 85 maps. 184p. NF/dj. P4. $75.00

**GOSS, Michael.** *Poltergeists: Annotated Bibliography of Works...* 1979. 1111 entries. 351p. F. A4. $55.00

**GOSS, N.S.** *History of the Birds of Kansas.* 1891. Topeka. lg 8vo. 35 pl. 692p. NF. C12. $110.00

**GOSSE, P.H.** *Monuments of Ancient Egypt.* 1847. London. SPCK. ils. gr stp cloth. G. Q2. $47.00

**GOSSE, P.H.** *Romance of Natural History.* 1862. Boston. Gould. 8vo. 372p. VG+. M12. $75.00

**GOSSE, P.H.** *Romance of Natural History.* 1902. NY. AL Burt. 348p. cloth. VG. M12. $25.00

**GOSWAMI, Amit.** *Self-Aware Universe: How Consciousness Creates...* 1993. NY. Putnam. 1st. VG/dj. N2. $10.00

**GOTO, Seikichiro.** *Book of Handcrafted Paper.* 1984. Tokyo. Kodansha. 1/290. tipped-in ils/samples. box w/clasps & pub box. B24. $950.00

**GOTO, Seikichiro.** *Japanese Paper & Papermaking.* 1958 & 1960. Bijutsu-shuppansa-sha. 2 vol. ils/samples. F/Oriental-style wrp. B24. $2,250.00

**GOTO, Seikichiro.** *Japanese Paper Wagami-Inden.* 1957. Bijutsu-shuppansa-sha. 1/150. ils/samples. AN/paper wrp/chemise. B24. $125.00

**GOTTFRIED, Robert.** *Black Death: Natural & Human Disaster in Medieval Europe.* 1983. NY. 1st. 203p. dj. A13. $45.00

**GOTTLEIB, A.** *Peyote & Other Phycoactive Cacti: How to Use...* 1977. 16p. wrp. E6. $22.00

**GOUDGE, Eileen.** *Such Devoted Sisters.* 1992. NY. Viking. UP/1st. NF/wrp. Q1. $35.00

**GOUDGE, Elizabeth.** *Rosemary Tree.* (1956). Coward McCann. 8vo. 381p. red cloth. VG/G. T5. $25.00

**GOUDIE, Andrew.** *Human Impact on the Natural Environment.* 1992. Blackwell. 3rd. 388p. F/wrp. S15. $11.00

**GOUGH, Barry M.** *To the Pacific & Arctic With Beechey...* 1973. Cambridge. Hakluyt. 1st. 2nd Series #143. 8vo. bl cloth. P4. $45.00

**GOUGH, John.** *History of the People Called Quakers...* 1790. Dublin. Robert Jackson. 4 vol. 1st. 12mo. leather. V3. $175.00

**GOUGH, Kathleen.** *Ten Times More Beautiful: Rebuilding of Vietnam.* 1978. NY. Monthly Review. 1st Am. photos. F/NF. R11. $40.00

**GOUGH, Laurence.** *Hot Shots.* 1989. Viking. 1st. F/dj. N4. $15.00

**GOUGH, Robert.** *Highbush Blueberry & Its Management.* 1994. NY. Food Products. 272p. AN. A10. $28.00

**GOULART, Ron.** *Even the Butler Was Poor.* 1990. NY. Walker. 1st. F/F. H11. $20.00

**GOULD, A.A.** *Naturalist's Library...* ca 1846-48. NY. Kearny. ils/index. 879p. fair. H10. $47.50

**GOULD, Ed.** *Entertaining Canadians.* 1988. Victoria. Cappis. 323p. VG/dj. C5. $15.00

**GOULD, Ed.** *Ralph Edwards of Lonesome Lake.* 1979. Saanichton, BC. Hancock. 1st. AN/dj. A26. $30.00

**GOULD, Frank W.** *Common Texas Grasses.* 1978. College Sta. 1st. ils. 267p. sc. B26. $15.00

**GOULD, George Milbry.** *Righthandedness & Lefthandedness...Writing Posture...* 1908. Lippincott. 12mo. 210p. gr cloth. G1. $65.00

**GOULD, George.** *Borderland Studies: Miscellaneous Addresses & Essays...* 1896. Phil. 1st. inscr. 24 essays. 384p. A13. $50.00

**GOULD, J.** *Hummingbirds.* 1990. Secaucus, NJ. Wellfleet. 2 vol. facs. folio. ils. 76p. F. C12. $100.00

**GOULD, John.** *Monstrous Depravity.* 1963. Morrow. G/dj. A16. $10.00

**GOULD, Laurence McKinley.** *Cold: Record of Antarctic Sledge Journey.* 1932. NY. Brewer Warren Putnam. 1st. ils/index. 275p. VG. B5. $35.00

**GOULD, Laurence McKinley.** *Cold: Record of Antarctic Sledge Journey.* 1984. Carleton College. ltd. 213p. NF/dj. P4. $75.00

**GOULD, Lois.** *Medusa's Gift.* 1991. Knopf. 1st. F/dj. R14. $25.00

**GOULD, Stephen Jay.** *Flamingo's Smile.* 1985. NOrton. 1st. ils. NF. S15. $7.00

**GOULD & PYLE.** *Anomalies & Curiosities of Medicine...* 1901. Phil. Saunders. 295 ils/12 pl. 968p. xl. G7. $125.00

**GOULD & PYLE.** *Anomalies & Curiousities of Medicine.* 1962. NY. ils/index. 968p. VG/G. B5. $30.00

**GOULDEN, Joseph C.** *Benchwarmers, Private World of Powerful Federal Judges.* 1974. NY. Weybright Talley. 2nd. VG/dj. M11. $25.00

**GOURGEAU, Art.** *Wolfman.* 1989. DIF. 1st. F/dj. M21. $15.00

**GOURLAY, Logan.** *Olivier.* 1973. London. Weidenfeld Nicolson. 208p. VG/dj. C5. $12.50

**GOURLAY, Logan.** *Olivier.* 1974. Stein Day. 1st. VG/dj. C9. $25.00

**GOURMET MAGAZINE.** *Best of Gourmet.* 1992. VG/dj. A16. $17.50

**GOVERNMENT PRINTING OFFICE.** *Handbook of American Indians North of Mexico.* 1907. Bureau Am Ethnology. 2 vol. A19. $250.00

**GOVERNMENT PRINTING OFFICE.** *Manual for Army Cooks. Pub by Authority of Secretary War...* 1896. GPO. 306p. full leather. E6. $65.00

**GOVERNMENT PRINTING OFFICE.** *Organization & Status of Missouri Troops...Civil War.* 1902. 1st. 1/100. 336p. half cloth/leather. M8. $350.00

**GOVERNMENT PRINTING OFFICE.** *War of Rebellion: Official Records...April 16-July 31, 1861.* 1880. WA. G. A19. $75.00

**GOWER, Charlotte.** *Northern & Southern Affiliations of Antillean Culture.* 1927. Menasha, WI. Am Anthro Assoc Memoirs #35. wrp. F3. $30.00

**GOWERS, William Richard.** *Diagnosis of Diseases of the Brain & Spinal Cord.* 1885. NY. Wm Wood. 293p. Wood lib bdg. G. G7. $150.00

**GOWERS, William Richard.** *Epilepsy & Other Chronic Convulsive Disorders.* nd (1885). NY. Wood. 255p. Wood lib bdg. G7. $135.00

**GOYEN, William.** *Come, the Restorer.* 1974. Doubleday. 1st. F/clip. M25. $25.00

**GRABAR, Andre.** *Byzantine Painting.* 1953. Geneva. Skira. ils/map. 200p. cloth. VG. Q2. $58.00

**GRABER, Ralph.** *Baseball Reader.* 1951. Barnes. 1st. VG/G. P8. $30.00

GRACE, Sherrill. *Swinging the Maelstrom: New Perspectives...* 1992. McGill-Queen. 1st. F. P3. $25.00

GRADY, James. *Rivers of Darkness.* 1991. NY. Warner. 1st. F/F. H11. $25.00

GRADY, James. *Six Days of the Condor.* 1974. NY. Norton. 1st. MTI. F/dj. M15. $125.00

GRAE, Carmarin. *Paz.* 1984. Chicago. Blazon. 1st. 326p. VG+. A25. $10.00

GRAF, J.H. *Litteratur de Landesvermessung: Katalog Kartensammlungen...* 1998. Mansfield, Centre, CT. Martino. 4 parts in 1. rpt. 1/150. gilt cloth. F1. $95.00

GRAFTON, Sue. *A Is for Alibi.* 1982. HRW. 1st. sgn. F/dj. D10. $1,200.00

GRAFTON, Sue. *B Is for Burglar.* 1986. London. Macmillan. 1st Eng. inscr. F/NF. M15. $200.00

GRAFTON, Sue. *C Is for Corpse.* 1986. NY. Holt. AP. NF/wrp. A14. $105.00

GRAFTON, Sue. *D Is for Deadbeat.* 1987. Holt. 1st. F/dj. D10. $300.00

GRAFTON, Sue. *D Is for Deadbeat.* 1987. NY. Holt. 1st. sgn. F/dj. M15. $350.00

GRAFTON, Sue. *E Is for Evidence.* 1988. Holt. 1st. F/dj. D10. $165.00

GRAFTON, Sue. *F Is for Fugitive.* 1989. NY. Holt. 1st. F/dj. M15. $75.00

GRAFTON, Sue. *F Is for Fugitive.* 1989. NY. Holt. 1st. NF/dj. A14. $70.00

GRAFTON, Sue. *G Is for Gumshoe.* 1990. NY. Holt. 1st. NF/dj. A14. $32.00

GRAFTON, Sue. *H Is for Homicide.* 1991. Holt. 1st. sgn. F/dj. M25. $45.00

GRAFTON, Sue. *H Is for Homicide.* 1991. Holt. 1st. VG+/dj. S13. $10.00

GRAFTON, Sue. *I Is for Innocent.* 1992. Holt. 1st. F/dj. N4. $30.00

GRAFTON, Sue. *I Is for Innocent.* 1992. NY. Holt. 1st. sgn. F/dj. M15. $45.00

GRAFTON, Sue. *J Is for Judgement.* 1993. NY. Holt. 1st. F/F. B30. $50.00

GRAFTON, Sue. *J Is for Judgment.* 1993. Holt. 1st. VG/dj. R8. $12.50

GRAFTON, Sue. *K Is for Killer.* 1994. Holt. 1st. 284p. F/dj. W2. $40.00

GRAFTON, Sue. *K Is for Killer.* 1994. NY. Holt. 1st. sgn. F/F. B30. $50.00

GRAFTON, Sue. *L Is for Lawless.* 1995. Holt. 1st. sgn. F/dj. B30. $50.00

GRAHAM, Alberta Powell. *Great Band of America.* 1951. NY. Thos Nelson. 185p. G/dj. C5. $12.50

GRAHAM, Angus. *Golden Grindstone: Adventures of George M Mitchell.* 1935. Phil. 1st Am. 8vo. ils. 304p. yel/beige cloth. P4. $75.00

GRAHAM, Anne Dunbar. *Bird in My Bed.* 1971. Taplinger. VG/dj. A28. $16.00

GRAHAM, Anthony. *Death Business.* 1967. Boardman. 1st. VG/dj. P3. $25.00

GRAHAM, Benjamin. *Security Analysis.* 1962. NY. 4th. NF/dj. B5. $150.00

GRAHAM, Bessie. *Bookman's Manual. A Guide to Literature.* 1921. NY. RR Bowker. VG. B2. $25.00

GRAHAM, Frank Jr. *Casey Stengel.* 1958. John Day. 1st. photos. VG/G. P8. $45.00

GRAHAM, Gerald G. *Canada Film Technology, 1896-1986.* 1989. Newark. U DE. 272p. VG/dj. C5. $20.00

GRAHAM, Harry. *Group of Scottish Women.* 1908. Duffield. 1st. ils. 343p. VG+. A25. $50.00

GRAHAM, James; see Patterson, Henry.

GRAHAM, John Alexander. *Aldeburg Cezanne.* nd. BC. F/dj. P3. $8.00

GRAHAM, John Alexander. *Babe Ruth Caught in a Snowstorm.* 1973. Houghton Mifflin. 1st. F/VG. P8. $75.00

GRAHAM, Lloyd. *Deceptions & Myths of the Bible.* 1975. NY. University Books. 484p. VG/G. H10. $17.50

GRAHAM, Margaret. *Swing Shift.* 1951. NY. Citadel. 1st. F/NF. B2. $40.00

GRAHAM, R.B. Cunninghame. *Jose Antonio Paez.* 1970 (1929). NY. Cooper Square. rpt. ils/rear fld map. 328p. F3. $20.00

GRAHAM, R.B. Cunninghame. *North American Sketches of RB Cunninghame.* 1986. U AL. 8vo. 145p. gr cloth. P4. $20.00

GRAHAM, Sheilah. *Garden of Allah.* 1970. NY. Crown. 1st. F/NF. H11. $40.00

GRAHAM, Shirley. *There Was Once a Slave... Heroic Story of Frederick Douglas.* 1947. Messner. 1st. 8vo. 310p. G. H1. $16.00

GRAHAM, Tim. *Royal Review.* 1984. London. Michael Joseph. 1st Eng. F. T12. $40.00

GRAHAM, W.A. *Custer Myth.* 1953. Bonanza/Crown. B rpt. ils. VG/dj. A2. $16.00

GRAHAM, Walter. *Beginnings of English Literary Periodicals: A Study...* 1926. OUP. 5 pl. 102p. VG. A4. $85.00

GRAHAM, Winston. *Black Moon: Novel of Cornwall 1794-1795.* 1973. London. Collins. 1st. VG+/NF clip. A14. $32.00

GRAHAM, Winston. *Four Swans: Novel of Cornwall 1795-1797.* 1976. London. Collins. 1st. VG+/VG. A14. $22.00

GRAHAM, Winston. *Loving Cup: A Novel of Cornwall 1813-1815.* 1984. London. Collins. 1st. VG+/dj. A14. $28.00

GRAHAM, Winston. *Miller's Dance: Novel of Cornwall 1812-1813.* 1982. London. Collins. 1st. VG+/dj. A14. $28.00

GRAHAM, Winston. *Spanish Armadas.* 1972. Doubleday. 1st. ils. 288p. VG/dj. S14. $12.00

GRAHAM, Winston. *Spanish Armadas.* 1972. London. Collins. ARC/1st. RS. VG+/clip. A14. $32.00

GRAHAM & HEMMING. *Tales of the Iron Road.* 1990. Paragon. 1st. sm 4to. 222p. F/dj. W2. $35.00

GRAHAM & TELEK. *Leaf Protein Concentrates.* 1983. Westport. 844p. cloth. F. B1. $125.00

GRAHAME, Kenneth. *Dream Days.* 1930. Dodd Mead. 1st Am. ils EH Shepard. VG/dj. A21. $50.00

GRAHAME, Kenneth. *Reluctant Dragon.* 1983. NY. 1st. ils Michael Hague. VG/dj. M17. $15.00

GRAHAME, Kenneth. *River Bank From Wind in the Willows.* 1977. Scribner. 1st. ils Adrienne Adams. F/VG+. M5. $35.00

GRAHAME, Kenneth. *Wind in the Willows.* 1913. Scribner. 1st thus. 8vo. ils Paul Bransom. teg. bl ribbed cloth. R5. $300.00

GRAHAME, Kenneth. *Wind in the Willows.* 1951. London. Methuen. 1/500. ils Rackham/12 mtd mc pl. Sangorski bdg. F. H5. $2,250.00

GRAHN, Judy. *True to Life Adventure Stories: Volume One.* 1978. Oakland. Diana. 224p. sc. VG+. A25. $15.00

GRAINGE, M. *Handbook of Plants With Pest-Control Properties.* 1988. NY. ils. 470p. B26. $41.00

GRAMATKY, Hardie. *Hercules: Story of an Old-Fashioned Fire Engine.* 1940. Putnam. 1st. 4to. red cloth. dj. R5. $110.00

GRANBERG, Wilber. *People of the Maguey.* 1970. NY. Praeger. 1st. 160p. dj. F3. $15.00

**GRAND, Gordon.** *Silver Horn.* 1932. Derrydale. 1st. 1/950. VG. O3. $275.00

**GRAND, Gordon.** *Southborough Fox.* 1939. Derrydale. 1/1450. sgn. ils Eleanor Iselin Mason. 239p. gilt red cloth. F. F1. $50.00

**GRAND, P.M.** *Prehistoric Art: Paleolithic Painting & Sculpture.* 1967. NYGS. ils/maps/pl. 103p. cloth. VG/dj. D2. $25.00

**GRAND ARMY OF THE REPUBLIC.** *Services for Use of the Grand Army of the Republic...* Oct 1884. Toledo, OH. 64p. maroon bdg. H6. $26.00

**GRANGER, Ann.** *Say It With Poison.* nd. St Martin. 2nd. VG/dj. P3. $17.00

**GRANGER, Bill.** *Drover & the Designated Hitter.* 1994. Morrow. 1st. F/dj. P8. $25.00

**GRANGER, Bill.** *Zurich Numbers.* 1984. Crown. 1st. F/NF. N4. $25.00

**GRANIT, Ragnar.** *Receptors & Sensory Perception: A Discussion of Aims...* 1955. Yale. 370p. bl-gray cloth. VG/dj. G1. $65.00

**GRANIT, Ragnar.** *Receptors & Sensory Perception: A Discussion of Aims...* 1955. Yale. 370p. xl. VG. S5. $25.00

**GRANOVETTER, Matthew.** *Bridge Team Murders.* 1992. Ballston Lake. Granovetter. 1st. F/dj. M15. $45.00

**GRANT, Blanche C.** *Taos Indians.* 1976. Rio Grande. ils/notes/index. 132p. NF. B19. $15.00

**GRANT, Campbell.** *Rock Paintings of the Chumash.* 1993. Santa Barbara 4to. ils/figures/pl. 163p. tan cloth. VG/dj. P4. $125.00

**GRANT, Charles.** *Best of Shadows.* Oct 1988. Doubleday. 1st. rem mk. VG/dj. L1. $40.00

**GRANT, Charles.** *Jackals.* 1994. NY. Forge. 1st. F/dj. M23. $20.00

**GRANT, Charles.** *Night Visions 2.* 1985. Dark Harvest. 1st. sgn. F/dj. T12. $85.00

**GRANT, Douglas.** *Cock Lane Ghost.* 1965. NY. Macmillan. 1st. 8vo. 117p. wht linen. VG. H13. $65.00

**GRANT, Joseph D.** *Redwoods & Reminiscences.* 1973. SF. early photos. 216p. rust cloth. NF. P4. $60.00

**GRANT, Judith Skelton.** *Enthusiasms of Robertson Davies.* 1990. Viking. 1st. rem mk. F/dj. P3. $18.00

**GRANT, Linda.** *Love Nor Money.* 1991. Scribner. 1st. F/dj. G8. $20.00

**GRANT, Linda.** *Woman's Place.* 1994. Scribner. 1st. NF/dj. G8. $20.00

**GRANT, Maxwell.** *Norgil: More Tales of Prestidgitection.* 1979. Mysterious. 1st. NF/dj. G8. $35.00

**GRANT, Michael.** *Classical Greeks.* 1989. Scribner. 1st. F/dj. P3. $27.00

**GRANT, Michael.** *Visible Past: Recent Archaeological Discoveries...* 1990. NY. ils. VG/dj. M17. $17.50

**GRANT, Mrs. G. Forsyth.** *Hero of Crampton School.* nd. Edinburgh. WP Nimmo, Hay & Mitchell. 176p. loose ftspc. G11. $7.50

**GRANT, Peter.** *Surgical Arena.* 1993. Newmark Pub. 1st. NF/dj. A28. $12.00

**GRANT, Robert M.** *Historical Introduction to the New Testament.* 1963. Harper Row. 448p. VG/dj. H10. $22.50

**GRANT, Robert.** *Jack Hall; or, School Days of an American Boy.* 1890. Jordan Marsh. later prt. VG. P8. $75.00

**GRANT, Robert.** *Undercurrent.* 1904. Scribner. 1st. ils FC Yohn. 480p. G. G11. $8.00

**GRANT, Stephanie.** *Passion of Alice.* 1995. Boston. Houghton Mifflin. 1st. 260p. F/dj. P4. $25.00

**GRANT, Ulysses S.** *Personal Memoirs of...* 1886. NY. Webster. 2 vol. 1st. gr cloth/shoulder straps. VG. S17. $80.00

**GRANT, Vernon.** *Tinker Tim the Toy Maker.* 1934. Whitman. 1st. ils. 29p. VG/dj. D1. $200.00

**GRANZOTTO, Gianni.** *Christopher Columbus: Dream & the Obsession.* 1985. Doubleday BC. 8vo. 300p. half cloth. AN/dj. P4. $15.00

**GRAS, Norman.** *History of Agriculture in Europe & America.* 1946. NY. Crofts. 2nd. 496p. cloth. VG. A10. $20.00

**GRASS, Gunter.** *Dog Years.* 1963. HBW. 1st. G/dj. B30. $25.00

**GRASS, Gunter.** *Tin Drum.* 1963. HBJ. 1st. author's 1st novel. VG+/dj. A24. $50.00

**GRATTON, John.** *Journal of Life of Ancient Servant of Christ...* 1805. Stanford, NY. Daniel Lawrence. 16mo. 224p. full leather. V3. $28.00

**GRAU, Shirley Ann.** *Condor Passes.* 1971. Knopf. 1st. F/dj. M21. $20.00

**GRAU, Shirley Ann.** *Nine Women.* 1986. Franklin Lib. ltd. sgn. ils Anthony Russo. leather. VG+. C9. $60.00

**GRAU, Shirley Ann.** *Nine Women: Stories.* 1985. Knopf. 1st. 8vo. 204p. rem mk. VG/dj. S14. $10.00

**GRAUER, Neil A.** *Remember Laughter: A Life of James Thurber.* 1995. Lincoln/London. U NE. 204p. F/dj. P4. $25.00

**GRAVER, Elizabeth.** *Have You Seen Me?* 1991. Pittsburgh. 1st. author's 1st book. F/F. B3. $35.00

**GRAVES, Clifford M.** *Brand Book Number Eight: San Diego Corral of Westerners.* 1987. The Corral. 1st. ils. 263p. NF/sans. B19. $50.00

**GRAVES, J.A.** *California Memories 1857-1930.* 1930. Times-Mirror. 1st. VG. O4. $20.00

**GRAVES, J.A.** *My Seventy Years in California 1857-1927.* 1927. Los Angels. Times-Mirror. 1st. VG. O4. $20.00

**GRAVES, J.A.** *Out of Doors: California & Oregon.* 1912. LA. Grafton. inscr. 122p. brd. P4. $75.00

**GRAVES, John.** *Goodbye to a River.* 1960. Knopf. 1st. ils Russell Waterhouse. F/dj. B4. $175.00

**GRAVES, John.** *Goodbye to a River: A Narrative.* 1961. Knopf. 4th. 306p. NF/VG. B19. $20.00

**GRAVES, Robert.** *Anger of Achilles.* 1959. Doubleday. 1st. ils Ronald Searle. F/dj. Q1. $75.00

**GRAVES, Robert.** *Lawrence & the Arabian Adventure.* 1928. Doubleday Doran. ils/23 pl/map ep. 400p. cloth. VG. Q2. $33.00

**GRAVES, Robert.** *Sergeant Lamb's America.* 1940. Random. 1st Am. F/VG. T11. $125.00

**GRAVES, Robert.** *Transformations of Lucius, Otherwise Known as Golden Ass.* 1950. Hammondsworth, Middlesex. Penguin. 1/2000. teg. 298p. F/NF/case. B20. $125.00

**GRAY, A.** *1982 Janine.* 1984. Viking. 1st Am. author's 2nd novel. F/dj. A24. $35.00

**GRAY, A.W.** *Man Offside.* 1991. Dutton. 1st. VG/dj. P3. $20.00

**GRAY, Albert Zabriskie.** *Land & the Life: Sketches & Studies in Palestine.* 1876. NY. Randolph. 1st. sm 8vo. ils. xl. VG. W1. $55.00

**GRAY, Asa.** *How Plants Grow.* 1858. NY/Chicago. Ivison Blakeman. ils. sm 8vo. gr pict brd. B14. $55.00

**GRAY, Cecil.** *Predicaments; or, Music & the Future.* 1936. OUP. 298p. xl. G. C5. $12.50

**GRAY, Charles Glass.** *Off at Sunrise: Overland Journal of Charles Glass Gray.* 1976. San Marino. Huntington Lib. 1st. 8vo. 186p. bl cloth. AN/dj. P4. $25.00

**GRAY, Charles Wright.** *Gray Dogs: An Anthology of Stories About Them.* 1925. Garden City. VG/dj. A21. $20.00

**GRAY, Charles Wright.** *Hosses.* 1937. Sun Dial. VG/dj. A21. $30.00

**GRAY, Elizabeth Janet.** *Adam of the Road.* 1942. Viking. 1st. sgn. ils Robert Lawson. 1942 Newbery. mc dj. R5. $375.00

**GRAY, Franicine du Plessix.** *Rage & Fire: Life of Louise Colet, Pioneer Feminist...* 1994. NY. sgn. ils. VG/dj. M17. $20.00

**GRAY, G.R.** *Catalogue of British Birds in Collection British Museum.* 1863. London. 8vo. 247+8p ads. gilt brn pebble cloth. VG. C12. $95.00

**GRAY, Henry.** *Anatomy of the Human Body. 26th Edition...* 1955. Phil. Lea Febiger. 1202 ils. 1480p. cloth. G7. $295.00

**GRAY, James.** *Boozie: Impact of Whiskey on the Prairie West.* 1972. Macmillan. 243p. VG/dj. J2. $75.00

**GRAY, Muriel.** *Trickster.* 1995. Doubleday. 1st Am. author's 1st book. NF/F. S18. $30.00

**GRAY, P.N.** *From the Peace to the Fraser: Newly Discovered...* 1994. Boone & Crockett. 1st. photos/maps. 400p. F/dj. M4. $60.00

**GRAY, POOLEY & WALCOTT.** *Paths & Pathfinders.* 1946. Scott Foresman. 528p. xl. VG. B36. $20.00

**GRAY, POOLEY & WALCOTT.** *Wonders & Workers, Basic Reader.* 1946. Scott Foresman. 8th-grade reader. 544p. VG+. B36. $20.00

**GRAY, Simon.** *Butley.* 1971. London. Methuen. 1st. F/dj. B4. $175.00

**GRAY, Thomas.** *Elegy in a Country Churchyard & Other Poems.* 1904. David Bryce. mini. ils. 384p. limp brn suede w/yapp edges. F. B24. $85.00

**GRAY, Thomas.** *Elegy Written in a Country Churchyard.* 1929. Audubon, NJ. LW Washburn. mini. 1/64. 17p. gilt bl morocco. B24. $275.00

**GRAY, Thomas.** *Elegy Written in a Country Churchyard.* 1960. Worcester. St Onge. mini. 1/1000. aeg. gilt calf. B24. $125.00

**GRAY, Thomas.** *Odes of Mr Gray.* 1757. Strawberry Hill. 1st/1st issue. wide 4to. uncut/rare half-title present. H13. $2,250.00

**GRAY, Thomas.** *Poems & Letters.* 1879. Chiswick. 1st thus. ils/pres Eton. 415p. Riviere bdg. H13. $195.00

**GRAY & OSBORNE.** *Elvis Altas: Journey Through Elvis Presley's America.* 1996. NY. Holt. F/dj. B9. $17.50

**GRAYBILL, Florence Curtis.** *Edwin Sheriff Curtis: Visions of a Vanishing Race.* 1976. NY. Crowell. 1st. 303p. NF/dj. B20. $135.00

**GRAYSON, Richard.** *I Brake for Delmore Schwartz.* 1982. Zephyr. 1/25. sgn. ils Girard Mabe. NF/dj. S13. $20.00

**GRAZULIS, Thomas P.** *Significant Tornadoes, 1880-1989.* 1991. St Johnsbury, VT. Environmental Films. 4to. 526p. VG/wrp. K5. $100.00

**GREAT BRITIAN WAR OFFICE.** *List of All the Officers of the Army.* 1779. London. War Office. aeg. gilt straight-grain red morocco. K1. $450.00

**GRECO, Antonella.** *La Cappella di Nicculo V del Beato Angelico.* 1980. Rome. Instituto Poligrafico Zecca Stato. ils. 91p. cloth. F. D2. $85.00

**GREELEY, Aldophus W.** *Handbook of Alaska: Its Resources, Products...* 1925. NY. Scribner. 3rd. 8vo. ils/maps. 330p. P4. $35.00

**GREELEY, Aldophus W.** *Report on Proceedings of US Expedition to Lady Franklin Bay.* 1888. GPO. 2 vol. 4to. blk cloth. P4. $500.00

**GREELEY, Andrew M.** *Gold Game.* 1986. Warner. 1st. NF/dj. P3. $20.00

**GREELEY, Andrew M.** *Magic Cup.* 1979. McGraw Hill. 1st. F/dj. T10. $100.00

**GREELEY, R. Gordon.** *Art & Science of Horseshoeing.* 1970. Phil. Lippincott. 1st. VG/G. O3. $25.00

**GREEN, Anna Katharine.** *Chief Legatee.* 1916. Dodd Mead. 1st. VG. P3. $50.00

**GREEN, Anne Bosworth.** *Dipper Hill.* 1925. NY. Century. VG. O3. $25.00

**GREEN, Ben K.** *Biography of the Tennessee Walking Horse.* 1960. Pantheon. 1st. VG. O3. $95.00

**GREEN, Ben K.** *Color of Horses.* 1991. Northland. 4to. 127p. VG. O3. $35.00

**GREEN, Ben K.** *Horse Conformation as to Soundness & Performance.* 1981. Flagstaff. Northland. revised. VG/dj. O3. $25.00

**GREEN, Ben K.** *Horse Tradin'.* 1967. NY. 1st. VG/dj. B5. $50.00

**GREEN, Ben K.** *Last Trail Drive Through Downtown Dallas.* 1971. Northland. 1/100. half leather. F/case. J2. $1,200.00

**GREEN, Ben K.** *Wild Cow Tales in Thirteen Stories...* 1969. Knopf. 1st. xl. VG/G. P12. $30.00

**GREEN, Bernard R.** *Building for Library of Congress.* 1898. GPO. removed. 13 pl. VG. P4. $18.00

**GREEN, Donald E.** *Panhandle Pioneer: Henry C Hitch, His Ranch & His Family.* 1980. Norman. 1st/2nd prt. 294p. AN/dj. P4. $25.00

**GREEN, Elizabeth A.H.** *Modern Conductor.* 1961. Prentice Hall. 9th. 8vo. F/VG+. A2. $14.00

**GREEN, George Dawes.** *Caveman's Valentine.* 1994. NY. Warner. 1st. F/F. H11. $50.00

**GREEN, George Dawes.** *Caveman's Valentine.* 1994. NY. Warner. 1st. sgn. F/dj. M15. $65.00

**GREEN, Gerald.** *American Prophet.* 1977. Doubleday. 1st. 323p. NF/VG. B19. $20.00

**GREEN, Harvey.** *Uncertainty of Everyday Life 1915-1945.* 1992. 1st. photos. VG/dj. M17. $20.00

**GREEN, Horace.** *General Grant's Last Stand: A Biography.* 1936. Scribner. 1st. 334p. cloth. NF/dj. M8. $125.00

**GREEN, Jane.** *Gift-Giver's Cookbook.* 1971. S&S. G/dj. A16. $6.00

**GREEN, John Richard.** *Conquest of England.* 1899. London. Macmillan. 2 vol in 1. 8vo. aeg. full red morocco. F1. $200.00

**GREEN, Judith.** *Laughing Souls: Days of the Dead in Oaxaca, Mexico.* 1969. San Diego. 1st. 27p. wrp. F3. $10.00

**GREEN, Kate.** *Night Angel.* 1989. Delacorte. 1st. F/NF. N4. $17.50

**GREEN, Michele.** *Dream at the End of the World: Paul Bowles...* 1991. Harper Collins. 1st. F/dj. R11. $20.00

**GREEN, Peter.** *Beyond the Wild Wood: World of Kenneth Grahame.* 1983. NY. photos. VG/dj. M17. $20.00

**GREEN, Peter.** *Kenneth Grahame, a Biography.* 1959. Cleveland. World. 1st. 400p. gilt bl cloth. NF/dj. F1. $50.00

**GREEN, Peter.** *Kenneth Grahame, a Biography.* 1959. World. 1st. 400p. bl cloth. VG/dj. D1. $45.00

**GREEN, Raleigh.** *Genealogical & Historical Notes on Culpeper County, VA.* 1964 (1900). Regional Pub. VG/dj. B10. $45.00

**GREEN, Richard Lancelyn.** *Bibliography of A Conan Doyle.* 1983. Clarendon. 1st. ils. 712p. AN/dj/mailer. J3. $1,500.00

**GREEN, Richard Lancelyn.** *Sherlock Holmes Letters.* 1986. U IA. 1st. F/dj. P3. $40.00

**GREEN, W.E.** *Green Family.* 1930. np. hc typescript. S5. $35.00

**GREEN & MARTIN.** *Oz Scrapbook.* 1977. Random. 1st. 182p. F/dj. B20. $50.00

**GREENAN, Russell H.** *Nightmare.* 1970. Random. 1st. sgn. VG/dj. B30. $20.00

**GREENAWAY, Kate.** *A Apple Pie.* (1886). London. Routledge. 1st (Schuster 1c). obl 4to. gilt bl cloth. R5. $475.00

**GREENAWAY, Kate.** *Almanack for 1926.* London. Warne. 1st. all edges yel. blk cloth. prt glassine dj. R5. $225.00

**GREENAWAY, Kate.** *Day in a Child's Life.* nd. London. Warne. ils. 24p. glazed brd/gr cloth spine. F1. $45.00

**GREENAWAY, Kate.** *Fairy Gifts.* (1882). Dutton. 2nd Am. 8vo. 128p+16p ads. R5. $125.00

**GREENAWAY, Kate.** *Little Ann & Other Poems, by Jane & Ann Taylor.* 1882. London. Routledge. inscr/dtd 1883. Frederick Locker bookplate. F/box. B24. $9,500.00

**GREENAWAY, Kate.** *Poor Nelly, Polly & Joe.* ca 1893. Cassell. VG. M19. $35.00

**GREENAWAY, Kate.** *Queen of the Pirate Isle.* (1886). London. Chatto Windus. 1st/1st issue (Schuster 1a). 8vo. red edges. F. R5. $225.00

**GREENAWAY, Kate.** *Under the Window: Pictures & Rhymes for Children.* ca 1920. London. Warne. sm 4to. 56p. wht cloth. NF. B20. $90.00

**GREENBERG, Eric Rolfe.** *Celebrant.* 1983. Everest House. 1st. F/VG. P8. $125.00

**GREENBERG, Jonathan.** *Staking a Claim: Jake Simmons Jr...* 1990. NY. photos. VG/dj. M17. $17.50

**GREENBERG, Julie T.** *Duplicate Decisions: A Club Director's Guide for Ruling...* 1982. 1st. VG/wrp. S1. $8.00

**GREENBERG, Martin.** *Holmes for the Holidays.* 1996. Berkley. 1st. F/dj. P3. $22.00

**GREENBERG, Martin.** *New Adventures of Sherlock Holmes.* 1980. Carroll Graf. Centennial ed. AN/dj. T12. $35.00

**GREENBERG, Martin.** *On the Diamond.* 1987. Bonanza. 1st. F/VG. P8. $10.00

**GREENBERG & GREENBERG.** *Whiskey in the Kitchen.* 1968. Weathervane. G/dj. A16. $12.00

**GREENBERG & SARRANTONIO.** *100 Hair-Raising Little Horror Stories.* Barnes Nobel. 1st. F/dj. S18. $8.50

**GREENBURG, Grayce.** *Dachshund.* 1955. Judy Pub Co. VG. A21. $30.00

**GREENE, Bob.** *All Summer Long.* 1993. Doubleday. 1st. sgn. F/dj. B30. $25.00

**GREENE, Bob.** *Homecoming: When the Soldiers Returned From Vietnam.* 1989. NY. Putnam. 1st. NF/dj. R11. $20.00

**GREENE, Donald.** *Politics of Samuel Johnson.* 1960. Yale. 1st. VG. H13. $85.00

**GREENE, Donald.** *Samuel Johnson's Library, an Annotated Guide.* 1975. Victorica, BC. U Victoria. 128p. wrp. H13. $65.00

**GREENE, Donald.** *Samuel Johnson.* 1984. OUP. edit Frank Kermode. dj. H13. $85.00

**GREENE, E.B.** *Foundations of American Nationality.* 1968. NY. rpt. F/dj. M4. $30.00

**GREENE, E.R.** *Birds of Georgia: Preliminary Checklist & Bibliography...* 1945. Athens. 8vo. ils/map. 111p. NF. C12. $40.00

**GREENE, Felix.** *Vietnam! Vietnam!* 1966. Palo Alto. Fulton. 2nd. VG. C9. $90.00

**GREENE, Frederick D.** *Armenian Massacres; or, Sword of Mohammed...* nd (1896). np (Phil). 100+ engravings/photos. 512p. marbled foredge. F. H3. $125.00

**GREENE, Graham.** *Complaisant Lover.* 1961. Viking. 1st Am. NF/VG. A24. $45.00

**GREENE, Graham.** *England Made Me.* 1935. Doubleday Doran. 1st Am. 305p. VG+/dj. B20. $500.00

**GREENE, Graham.** *Getting to Know the General.* 1984. London. Bodley Head. 1st. F/F. B3. $75.00

**GREENE, Graham.** *Human Factor.* 1978. Sydney. Bodley Head. 1st. NF/dj. A24. $45.00

**GREENE, Graham.** *In Search of a Character: Two African Journals.* 1961. London. Bodley Head. 1st. VG+/dj. A14. $52.50

**GREENE, Graham.** *In Search of a Character: Two African Journals.* 1961. NY. Viking. 1st. 1/600. gilt quarter gr cloth. F/acetate dj. M24. $150.00

**GREENE, Graham.** *Labyrinthine Ways.* 1940. NY. Viking. 1st Am/1st state (2p transposed). yel cloth. dj. M24. $1,250.00

**GREENE, Graham.** *Little Steamroller.* 1974. Doubleday. 1st. xl. F/VG+. P2. $25.00

**GREENE, Graham.** *Loser Takes All.* 1955. London. 1st. VG. M17. $30.00

**GREENE, Graham.** *Loser Takes All.* 1955. London. Heinemann. 1st. F/NF. B2. $125.00

**GREENE, Graham.** *Monsignor Quixote.* 1982. London. Bodley Head. 1st. F/F. B3. $60.00

**GREENE, Graham.** *Our Man in Havana.* 1958. London. Heinemann. 1st. VG+/dj. A14. $70.00

**GREENE, Graham.** *Our Man in Havana.* 1958. Viking. 1st. F/VG. M19. $35.00

**GREENE, Graham.** *Quiet American.* 1989. London. Bodley Head. Collected ed. new intro. NF/dj. A14. $17.50

**GREENE, Graham.** *Sense of Reality.* 1963. NY. Viking. 1st Am. F/VG clip. A24. $45.00

**GREENE, Graham.** *Travels With My Aunt.* 1970. Viking. 1st Am. VG/dj. C9. $30.00

**GREENE, Graham.** *Ways of Escape.* 1980. S&S. UP/1st Am. F/yel prt wrp. Q1. $75.00

**GREENE, Hugh.** *Cosmopolitan Crimes: Foreign Rivals of Sherlock Holmes.* 1972. NY. Pantheon. 1st Am. F/VG. T2. $25.00

**GREENE, Jerome A.** *Slim Buttes, 1876.* 1982. Norman. U OK. 1st. ils/maps. F/dj. T10. $35.00

**GREENE, Jonathan H.** *Desperado in Arizona, 1858-1860...* 1964. Stagecoach. 1/700. ils. 89p. F/F. B19. $35.00

**GREENE & GREENE.** *Victorian Villainies: Four Classic Victorian Tales.* 1984. Viking. 1st thus. VG/dj. M17. $25.00

**GREENE & LOMASK.** *Vanguard: A History.* 1971. Smithsonian. sm 4to. 308p. VG/dj. K5. $80.00

**GREENEWALT, C.H.** *Hummingbirds.* 1960. NY. 1st. 69 tipped-in photos. 250p. F/NF. C12. $95.00

**GREENFIELD, J. Godwin.** *Atlas of Muscle Pathology in Deuromuscular Diseases.* 1957. Edinburgh/London. Livingstone. 1st. ils. 104p. VG. N2. $8.50

**GREENFIELD, Jeff.** *Television, the First Fifty Years.* 1977. Abrams. 1st. photos. F/dj. C9. $60.00

**GREENHAW, Wayne.** *Making of a Hero: Story of Lt William Calley Jr.* 1971. Louisville. Touchstone. 1st. maps. 226p. F/NF. R11. $30.00

**GREENHILL, G.** *Dynamics of Mechanical Flight.* 1912. London. 1st. ils. 121p. VG. B18. $25.00

**GREENLEAF, Stephen.** *Beyond Blame.* 1986. Villard. 1st. VG/dj. G8. $15.00

**GREENLEAF, Stephen.** *Blood Type.* 1992. NY. Morrow. 1st. F/F. H11. $20.00

**GREENLEAF, Stephen.** *Southern Cross.* 1993. Morrow. 1st. NF/dj. G8. $15.00

**GREENWALD, Harold.** *Call Girl: Social & Psychoanalytic Study.* 1958. Ballantine. 1st. F/VG+. B4. $100.00

**GREENWALT, Emmett.** *Point Loma Community in California, 1897-1942.* 1955. Berkeley. ils/photos/index. 236p. VG/dj. P4. $75.00

**GREENWOOD, Frederick.** *Imagination in Dreams & Their Study.* 1894. London. Macmillan. 198p+16p catalog. gr cloth. G1. $75.00

**GREENWOOD, J.** *Wild Sports of the World: A Boy's Book of Natural History.* 1862. London. Beeton. ils/maps. pict gold cloth. VG. M12. $175.00

**GREENWOOD, John.** *Mosley by Moonlight.* 1984. Walker. 1st Am. NF/dj. G8. $20.00

**GREENWOOD, Marianne.** *Tattooed Heart of Livingston.* 1965. Stein Day. 1st. 187p. dj. F3. $20.00

**GREENWOOD, William Henry.** *Steel & Iron.* 1884. London. Cassell. 2nd. ils/diagrams. 536p. VG. B14. $75.00

**GREER, George Cabell.** *Early Virginia Immigrants, 1623-1666.* 1960 (1912). Genealogical Pub. rpt. 376p. VG. B10. $35.00

**GREER, Germaine.** *Change: Women, Aging & the Menopause.* 1992. Knopf. 1st. sm 4to. 422p. VG/dj. S14. $10.00

**GREER, Germaine.** *Female Eunuch.* 1970. London. MacGibbon Kee. UP. VG+/brn butcher paper wrp. B4. $300.00

**GREER, Germaine.** *Obstacle Race: Fortunes of Women Painters & Their Work.* 1979. NY. 1st. ils. VG/G. M17. $25.00

**GREER, Robert O.** *Devil's Hatband.* 1996. Mysterious. 1st. F/dj. M23. $35.00

**GREGG, Andy.** *Drums of Yesterday.* 1968. Santa Fe. 1st. 40p. F/stiff wrp. E1. $30.00

**GREGG, Kate L.** *Road to Santa Fe: Journals & Diaries of George C Sibley...* 1952. NM U. 1st. 280p. cloth. dj. D11. $45.00

**GREGOIRE, Henri-Baptiste.** *Rapport Sur La Bibliographie.* 1794. Paris. Quiber-Pallissaux. 8vo. caption title. stitched. R12. $375.00

**GREGORICH, Barbara.** *She's On First.* 1987. Contemporary. 1st. VG/dj. P8. $40.00

**GREGORY, Dick.** *Dick Gregory's Bible Tales.* 1974. Stein Day. 1st. F/NF. B2. $25.00

**GREGORY, Herbert E.** *Physical & Commercial Geography Colored Maps...* 1940. Boston. Ginn. xl. F. b14. $55.00

**GREGORY, Lady.** *Book of Saints & Wonders Put Down Here...* 1906. Dundrum. Dun Emer. 1st. 1/200. F/orig glassine. B24. $475.00

**GREGORY, Lady.** *Kincora: A Drama in Three Acts.* 1905. NY. John Quinn. 1st Am. 1/50. sgn. F/gray wrp. B24. $850.00

**GREGORY, R.W.** *Farm Business Management.* 1951. Lippincott. 546p. VG. A10. $10.00

**GREGORY, Sinda.** *Private Investigations: Novels of Dashiell Hammett.* 1985. SIU. 1st. F/dj. G8. $25.00

**GREGORY, Stephen.** *Cormorant.* 1986. London. Heinemann. 1st Eng. VG/dj. L1. $40.00

**GREGORY, Stephen.** *Woodwitch.* 1988. St Martin. 1st. NF/dj. S13. $12.00

**GREGORY, Valiska.** *Terribly Wonderful, a Mr Poggle & Scamp Book.* 1986. Macmillan. 1st. NF/dj. M5. $9.00

**GREGORY & SPERIGLIO.** *Crypt 33: Saga of Marilyn Monroe: The Final Word.* 1993. NY. Birch Lane/Carol Pub Group. 1st. F/dj. A14/P3. $21.00

**GREGOTTI, Vittorio.** *New Directions in Italian Architecture.* 1968. Brazillier. 1st. sm 4to. 128p. NF/VG. S14. $13.00

**GREIG, J.Y.T.** *Psychology of Laughter & Comedy.* 1923. London. Allen Unwin. 304p. ruled bl-gray cloth. VG. G1. $45.00

**GRENDON, Stephen;** see Derleth, August.

**GRENIER, Roger.** *Years in Ambush.* 1960. Knopf. 1st. F/NF. T12. $20.00

**GRENVILLE, T.N.E.** *Population Dynamics.* 1972. Academic. 445p. xl. VG. S5. $15.00

**GRESHAM, Douglas H.** *Lenten Lands: My Childhood With Joy Davidman & CS Lewis.* (1988). Macmillan. 1st Am. photos/index. AN/dj. A27. $15.00

**GRESHAM, Grits.** *Complete Book of Bass Fishing.* 1966. Outdoor Life. photos/ils. 264p. F/dj. A17. $12.50

**GRESHAM, Grits.** *Complete Wildfowler.* 1973. Winchester. 294p. cloth. A17. $12.50

**GRESHAM, Matilda McGrain.** *Life of Walter Quintin Gresham, 1832-1895.* 1919. Rand McNally. 2 vol. 1st. ils. xl. cloth. M8. $150.00

**GRESHAM, William Lindsay.** *Monster Midway.* 1953. Rinehart. 1st. G/dj. L1. $25.00

**GRESS, Edmund G.** *Dash Through Europe With Snapshots by the Way.* 1923. NY. Oswald. 1st. F/NF. O10. $30.00

**GREVILLE, Fulke.** *Life of the Renowned Sir Philip Sidney.* 1652. London. Seile. sm 8vo. calf. R12. $650.00

**GREY, C.G.** *Luftwaffe.* 1964. London. Faber. G. A19. $25.00

**GREY, Lita.** *My Life With Chaplin.* 1966. Bernard Geis. 1st. 8vo. 325p. red cloth. P4. $35.00

**GREY, Richard.** *Memoria Technica; or, New Method Artificial Memory...* 1790. London. Prt Chas King. sm 8vo. 119p. contemporary panelled calf. G. G1. $150.00

**GREY, Zane.** *Border Legion.* 1944. NY. Black. cream/red bdg. VG. B11. $15.00

**GREY, Zane.** *Fighting Caravans.* 1929. Toronto. Musson. 1st. G. T12. $50.00

**GREY, Zane.** *Fugitive Trail.* 1957. Harper. 1st. 8vo. 215p. F/VG+. B20. $75.00

**GREY, Zane.** *Last of the Plainsmen.* 1911. NY. Grosset Dunlap. A19. $25.00

**GREY, Zane.** *Nevada.* 1928. Harper. 1st. tan cloth. VG. S13. $10.00

**GREY, Zane.** *Redheaded Outfield & Other Stories.* 1948. Grosset Dunlap. rpt. F/VG. P8. $40.00

**GREY, Zane.** *Reef Girl.* 1977. NY. Harper. 1st. VG/dj. B5. $40.00

**GREY, Zane.** *Roping Lions in the Grand Canyon.* nd. Grosset Dunlap. rpt. owner dtd 1924. 190p. orange cloth. pict dj. F7. $22.50

**GREY, Zane.** *Tales of Lonely Trails.* 1922. Harper. 8vo. ils. 394p. VG. F7. $37.50

**GREY, Zane.** *Tales of Southern Rivers.* 1924. NY. Harper. 1st. 249p. F. B11. $100.00

**GREY, Zane.** *Under the Tonto Rim.* 1926. Harper. 1st. 8vo. blk-lettered gr cloth. F/dj. R3. $275.00

**GREY, Zane.** *Young Pitcher.* 1939. Grosset Dunlap. rpt. VG/G. P8. $20.00

**GREY, Zane.** *Zane Grey: The Man & His Work.* 1928. NY. Harper. ils. 56p. gilt leatherette. D11. $50.00

**GREY OWL.** *Pilgrims of the Wild: His Classic Autobiography.* (1973). Toronto. Macmillan. rpt. wrp. A26. $15.00

**GREYER, Siegfried.** *Battleships & Battle Cruisers, 1905-1970.* 1974. Doubleday. sm 4to. ils. 480p. F/VG. H1. $24.00

**GREYSON, Richard I.** *Development of Flowers.* 1994. NY. ils. 314p. AN. B26. $50.00

**GRIERSON, J.M.** *Records of the Scottish Volunteer Force 1859-1908.* 1972. London. 47 mc pl. F/dj. M4. $65.00

**GRIERSON, John.** *I Remember Lindbergh.* 1977. HBJ. 1st. F/dj. T11. $15.00

**GRIFFEN, Jeff.** *Poodle Book.* 1968. Doubleday. VG. A21. $20.00

**GRIFFIN, Charles C.** *Latin America: A Guide to Historical Literature.* 1971. U TX. 4to. 7087 entries. 730p. F/F. A4. $95.00

**GRIFFIN, Harold.** *Alaska & the Canadian Northwest.* 1944. NY. Norton. 8 pl/dbl-face map. 221p. lacks ffe. VG/dj. P4. $20.00

**GRIFFIN, Peter.** *Less Than a Treason: Hemingway in Paris.* 1990. OUP. photos. VG/dj. M17. $15.00

**GRIFFIN, W.E.B.** *Counterattack.* 1990. NY. Putnam. 1st. Corps series #3. NF/dj. A14. $22.00

**GRIFFIN, W.E.B.** *Lieutenants: Brotherhood of War, Book I.* nd. NY. Jove. 1st Am/BC. VG/dj. A14. $15.00

**GRIFFIN, W.E.B.** *New Breed: Brotherhood of War, Book VII.* 1987. Putnam. 1st. VG+/dj. A14. $22.00

**GRIFFIS, W.E.** *Mikado's Empire.* 1876. Harper. ils. 645p. gilt brn cloth. VG. B20. $75.00

**GRIFFITH, John.** *Journal of Life, Travels & Labours in Work of...* 1780. Phil. Crukshank. 12mo. 426+112p. leather. V3. $80.00

**GRIFFITHS, Julia.** *Autographs for Freedom.* 1854. Auburn. Alden Beardsley. 309p. B18. $65.00

**GRIGG, E.R.N.** *Biologic Relativity.* 1967. Chicago. 1st. 257p. A13. $25.00

**GRIGG, J.R.** *Dear Jean: History of a Family...* 1993. Springdale. photos. F. M4. $20.00

**GRIGGS, Robert F.** *Valley of Ten Thousand Smokes.* 1922. WA. NGS. ils/9 maps. gilt bl cloth. AN/as issued. B14. $60.00

**GRIME, W.C.** *Birds of the Pymatuning Region.* 1952. Harrisburg, PA. PA Game Comm. 8vo. 90 photos/maps. 224p. NF/wrp. C12. $25.00

**GRIMES, Martha.** *Five Bells & Bladebone.* 1987. Little Brn. 1st. NF/dj. G8. $20.00

**GRIMES, Martha.** *I Am the Only Footman.* 1986. Little Brn. 1st. F/clip. B3. $45.00

**GRIMES, Martha.** *Old Contemptibles.* 1991. Little Brn. 1st. F/dj. T12. $45.00

**GRIMES, Tom.** *Season's End.* 1992. Little Brn. 1st. F/dj. P8. $12.50

**GRIMES, Tom.** *Stone of the Heart.* 1990. Four Walls Eight Windows. 1st. F/VG. P8. $30.00

**GRIMM & GRIMM.** *Beauty & the Beast.* 1984. Morro Bay, CA. Tabula Rasa. mini. 1/300. 48p. gilt brn leather. B24. $50.00

**GRIMM & GRIMM.** *Drei Marchen.* ca 1910. Mainz. Jos Scholz. 1st combined. German text. ils Julius Diez. obl 4to. dj. R5. $585.00

**GRIMM & GRIMM.** *Grimm's Fairy Stories.* 1922. Cupples Leon. ils Gruelle. A21. $80.00

**GRIMM & GRIMM.** *Grimm's Fairy Tales.* 1909. Doubleday Page. 1st. ils Rackham. olive brd. G. S13. $16.00

**GRIMM & GRIMM.** *Hansel & Gretel.* 1980. Dial. 1st. lg 4to. ils Susan Jeffers. mc pict dj. R5. $100.00

**GRIMM & GRIMM.** *Hansel y Grethel.* 1948. Argentina. Codex. ils Chikie/4 tab-activated full-p moveables. brd. R5. $100.00

**GRIMM & GRIMM.** *King Grisly-Beard.* 1973. FSG. 1st. ils Sendak. glazed brd. VG. D1. $45.00

**GRIMM & GRIMM.** *Rapunzel.* 1984. Morro Bay, CA. Tabula Rasa. mini. 1/300. marbled brd/gilt bl leather. B24. $50.00

**GRIMSHAW, Anne.** *Horse: A Bibliography of British Books 1851-1976.* 1982. 1/1000. sgn. 3226 entries. 508p. F/F. A4. $125.00

**GRINDAL, Richard.** *Whiskey Murders.* 1987. Walker. 1st Am. NF/dj. G8. $15.00

**GRINNELL, David;** see Wollheim, Don.

**GRINNELL & MILLER.** *Distribution of Birds of California.* 1944. Berkeley. 1st. Pacific Coast Avifauna #27. cloth. VG. C12. $63.00

**GRINNELL & STORER.** *Animal Life in the Yosemite: An Account of Mammals, Birds...* 1924. Berkeley. U CA. F. B20. $200.00

**GRINSPOON, Lester.** *Cocaine: Drug & Its Social Evolution.* 1976. NY. 1st. 308p. A13. $25.00

**GRIPPANDO, James.** *Pardon.* 1994. Harper Collins. 1st. F/F. H11. $20.00

**GRISCOM, J.** *Uses & Abuses of Air.* 1850 (1849). ils/pl. VG. E6. $275.00

**GRISCOM & SNYDER.** *Birds of Massachusetts: Annotated & Revised Check List.* 1955. Salem. 1st. 8vo. 295p. cloth. F. C12. $30.00

**GRISELL, Robert.** *Messereschmitt, BF109.* 1980. London. Janes. 1st. ils. 48p. brd. VG. M10. $10.00

**GRISFIELD, J.W.** *Colorado Desert.* 1862. GPO. 26p. stapled prt wrp. D11. $75.00

**GRISHAM, John.** *Chamber.* 1994. Doubleday. 1st. NF/F. S18. $18.00

**GRISHAM, John.** *Chamber.* 1994. Doubleday. 1st. sgn. F/dj. B30/L3. $50.00

**GRISHAM, John.** *Chamber.* 1994. Doubleday. 1st. VG/dj. A28. $15.00

**GRISHAM, John.** *Client.* 1993. Doubleday. ltd 1st. sm 4to. 422p. F/dj. W2. $150.00

**GRISHAM, John.** *Firm.* 1991. Doubleday. 1st. NF/dj. M19. $100.00

**GRISHAM, John.** *Pelican Brief.* 1992. Doubleday. 1st. F/F. N4. $50.00

**GRISHAM, John.** *Pelican Brief.* 1992. Doubleday. 1st. F/NF. H11. $45.00

**GRISHAM, John.** *Pelican Brief.* 1993. Doubleday. ltd. sgn. leather case. B30. $300.00

**GRISHAM, John.** *Rainmaker.* 1995. Doubleday. 1st. F/dj. S18. $15.00

**GRISHAM, John.** *Runaway Jury.* 1996. Doubleday. 1st. sgn. F/dj. B30. $35.00

**GRISHAM, John.** *Street Lawyer.* 1998. Doubleday. 1st. sgn. F/dj. R14. $50.00

**GRISMER, R.L.** *Mexico por Automovil.* 1938. Macmillan. 1st. 141p. map ep. pict cloth. F3. $10.00

**GRISWOLD, Mac.** *Pleasures of the Garden: Images From the NY MOMA.* 1987. NY. Abrams. 160p. AN/dj. A10. $25.00

**GRISWOLD & WELLER.** *Golden Age of American Gardens...1890-1940.* 1991. Abrams. 1st. ils/index. 408p. F/dj. H10. $48.00

**GRIZZARD & SMITH.** *Glory Glory.* 1981. Atlanta. 1st. VG/dj. B5. $35.00

**GROB, Gerald.** *Inner World of American Psychiatry 1890-1940...* 1985. New Brunswick, NJ. 1st. 310p. dj. A13. $35.00

**GROHMANN, Will.** *Paul Klee.* nd (1955). Abrams. ils+catalogue of works. blk cloth. VG/dj. F1. $100.00

**GROHMANN, Will.** *Paul Klee.* 1965. Buchergilde Gutenberg. 4th. German text. ils. VG/G. R8. $60.00

**GROMIE, William.** *Secrets of the Seas.* 1971. Reader's Digest. 1st. ils. 192p. F/G. S14. $8.00

**GROOM, Winston.** *Better Times Than These.* 1978. Summit. 1st. NF/clip. D10. $65.00

**GROOM, Winston.** *Forrest Gump.* 1986. Doubleday. 1st. F/F. D10. $225.00

**GROOM, Winston.** *Forrest Gump.* 1986. Doubleday. 1st. NF/F. B2. $150.00

**GROOM, Winston.** *Shrouds of Glory.* 1995. Atlantic Monthly. 1st. NF/dj. M23. $20.00

**GROOS, Karl.** *Die Spiele der Menschen.* 1899. Jena. Gustav Fischer. 538p. later brn buckram. G1. $75.00

**GROPP, Louis Oliver.** *House Beautiful: Decorating Style.* 1992. NY. Hearst. F/dj. B9. $17.50

**GROSE, Francis.** *Olio: Being a Collection of Essays...* 1792. London. Hooper. 1st. 8vo. 321p. marbled brd/recent calf spine. H13. $295.00

**GROSECLOSE, Elgin.** *Ararat.* 1939. NY. Carrick Evans. 1st. 8vo. 482p. cloth. VG. W1. $18.00

**GROSS, Edward.** *Top Gun: Films of Tom Cruise.* 1990. Las Vegas. Pioneer. 144p. VG/wrp. C5. $12.50

**GROSS, Harvey.** *Contrived Corridor: History & Fatality in Modern Literature.* 1971. U MI. 1st. NF/dj. O4. $15.00

**GROSS, Joel.** *Sarah.* 1987. Morrow. 1st. F/F. H11. $25.00

**GROSS, Joel.** *Spirit in the Flesh.* 1986. Dutton. 1st. F/dj. T12. $25.00

**GROSS, Leslie.** *Housewives' Guide to Antiques.* 1959. Exposition. 1st. ils. 180p. VG/G. S14. $10.00

**GROSS, Milton.** *Yankee Doodles.* 1948. House of Kent. 1st. photos. VG/G. P8. $15.00

**GROSS, Samuel D.** *History of American Medical Literature from 1776 to Present.* 1972. NY. facs of 1876. A13. $60.00

**GROSS, Samuel D.** *System of Surgery.* 1872. Phil. 2 vol. 8vo. ils. full sheep. xl. G7. $175.00

**GROSS, William B.** *From San Diego, CA to Washington DC...* (1916). San Diego. 2-p map/ils. 57p. ils wrp. D11. $250.00

**GROSS & WEDEMAR.** *What's This?* 1936. London. Harrap. 1st. sm 8vo. 94p. NF/VG+. B20. $150.00

**GROSSER, Morton.** *Fabulous Fifty.* 1990. Atheneum. 1st. F/VG+. P8. $20.00

**GROSSINGER, Richard.** *Temple of Baseball.* 1985. North Atlantic. 1st. F/VG. P8. $30.00

**GROSSMAN, Anne Chotzinof.** *Lobscouse & Spotted Dog.* 1997. NY. Norton. 1st. F/NF. T11. $25.00

**GROSSMAN, Lionel.** *Men & Masks: A Study of Moliere.* 1963. Baltimore. Johns Hopkins. 310p. VG/dj. C5. $12.50

**GROSSMAN & GROSSMAN.** *Chinese Kosher Cookbook.* 1964. VG. E6. $12.00

**GROSSMAN & GROSSMAN.** *Kosher Cookbook Trilogy.* 1965. F/F. E6. $15.00

**GROSZ, George.** *Little Yeas & a Big No: Autobiography of...* 1946. NY. Dial. ils. 343p. blk cloth. VG. F1. $40.00

**GROTE, George.** *History of Greece.* 1859. NY. 12 vol. half brn leather/marbled brd. F. B30. $375.00

**GROTE, George.** *History of Greece.* 1872. London. 10 vol. 4th. half brn leather/marbled brd. VG. B30. $200.00

**GROTE, L.R.** *Medizin in der Gegenwart in Selbstdarstellungen.* 1927. Leipzig. Felix Meiner. photos. 251p. gray linen. G1. $175.00

**GROTIUS, Hugo.** *Freedom of the Seas; or, Right Which Belongs to Dutch...* 1916. NY. OUP. 1st Eng trans. modern sheep. M11. $150.00

**GROUSSET, R.** *Empire of the Steppes: History of Central Asia.* 1970. Rutgers. 687p. NF. M4. $25.00

**GROUT, Donald Jay.** *History of Western Music.* 1980. Norton. 3rd. ils. 849p. VG/dj. S14. $15.00

**GROVE, David C.** *Chalcatzingo: Excavations on the Olmec Frontier.* 1984. NY. Thames Hudson. 1st Am. ils/notes/chronology. 184p. VG/dj. P4. $35.00

**GROVE, Fred.** *Running Horses.* 1980. Doubleday. 1st. VG/G. O3. $25.00

**GROVER, Eulalie Osgood.** *Overall Boys.* (1905). Chicago. ils Bertha Corbett. 123p. VG. B18. $37.50

**GROVER, Paula K.** *White Boys & River Girls.* 1995. Chapel Hill. Algonquin. 1st. 225p. NF/dj. P4. $25.00

**GROVES, J. Walton.** *Edible & Poisonous Mushrooms of Canada.* 1962. Ottawa. Canada Dept Agric. 298p. VG/dj. A10. $28.00

**GROVES, William Henry.** *Rational Memory.* 1912. NY. Cosmopolitan. 2nd. 12mo. 172p. prt panelled gr cloth. VG. G1. $37.50

**GRUBB, Davis.** *Night of the Hunter.* 1953. Harper. Advance pres. sgn. VG/sans. B30. $200.00

**GRUBB, Davis.** *Voices of Glory.* 1962. Scribner. 1st. F/NF. B2. $35.00

**GRUBE, Ernst J.** *World of Islam.* ca 1966. McGraw Hill. 1st. Landmarks of World's Art. 176p. NF/dj. W1. $35.00

**GRUDIN, Robert.** *Time & Art of Living.* 1982. SF. VG/dj. M17. $17.50

**GRUELLE, Johnny.** *Johnny Gruelle's Golden Book.* 1925. Chicago. ils. VG. M17. $27.50

**GRUELLE, Johnny.** *My Very Own Fairy Stories.* 1949. NY. Gruelle. 8vo. unp. VG/dj. D1. $125.00

**GRUELLE, Johnny.** *Raggedy Andy Goes Sailing.* 1943. McLoughlin. Westfield Classics. ils Justin C Gruelle. ils brd. dj. R5. $100.00

**GRUELLE, Johnny.** *Raggedy Ann & Andy & the Camel With Wrinkled Knees.* (1924). Joliet. Volland. 19th. 8vo. ils brd. pict box. R5. $250.00

**GRUELLE, Johnny.** *Raggedy Ann in the Deep Woods.* (1930). Joliet. Volland. 1st. 8vo. pict box. R5. $400.00

**GRUELLE, Johnny.** *Raggedy Ann's Lucky Pennies.* 1932. Donohue. 8vo. ils. 94p. VG/dj. D1. $125.00

**GRUELLE, Johnny.** *Raggedy Ann's Magical Wishes.* 1928. Chicago. Donohue. 8vo. ils. 95p. pict brd. VG/dj. D1. $125.00

**GRUELLE, Johnny.** *Raggedy Ann's Wishing Pebble.* 1925. Donohue. 1st thus. F/dj. S9. $300.00

**GRUENFELD, Lee.** *Irreparable Harm.* 1993. NY. Warner. 1st. author's 1st book. F/F. H11. $25.00

**GRUENING, Ernest.** *Battle for Alaska Statehood.* 1967. U AK. inscr. 8vo. blk cloth. NF/VG. P4. $30.00

**GRUMMOND, J.L.** *Baratarians & the Battle of New Orleans.* 1961. LA U. 1st. 180p. F/dj. M4. $35.00

**GRUNDY, Isabel.** *Samuel Johnson & the Scale of Greatness.* 1986. Leicester. 1st. F/dj. H13. $65.00

**GRUNES, Barbara.** *Lunch & Brunch Cookbook.* 1985. Ideal. G/dj. A16. $8.00

**GRUNSKY, Carl Ewald.** *Stockton Boyhood: Being Reminiscences of...From 1855-1877.* 1959. Friends Bancroft Lib. 1/800. 154p. gr cloth. F. P4. $65.00

**GRUTER, Margaret.** *Law & the Mind, Biological Origins of Human Behavior.* 1991. Sage Pub. 157p. prt wrp. M11. $25.00

**GRUZINSKI, Serge.** *Painting the Conquest.* 1992. France. Flammerion. 1st. 239p. dj. F3. $65.00

**GRZIMEK, H.C.B.** *Grzimek's Animal Life Encyclopedia. Vol 3.* 1972. Van Nostrand. 541p. F/dj. B1. $60.00

**GRZIMEK & GRZIMEK.** *Serengeti Shall Not Die.* 1961. NY. 1st Am. 344p. F. S15. $13.50

**GRZYBOWSKI, Kazimierz.** *Soviet Legal Institutions, Doctrines & Social Functions.* 1962. Ann Arbor. M11. $35.00

**GUALINO, Lorenzo.** *Storia Medica Dei Romani Pontefici.* 1934. Torino. 1st. 589p. quarter leather. A13. $100.00

**GUARESCHI, Giovanni.** *House That Nimo Built.* 1953. London. Frenaye. 1st. dj. T9. $15.00

GUBBINS, Flora Irene. *Grass on the Downs & Other Poems.* 1947. MI. James. 3rd. 12mo. 75p. gr cloth. B11. $15.00

GUENEE, Bernard. *Between Church & State: Lives of Four French Prelates...* 1987. Chicago. NF/dj. B9. $35.00

GUENTHER, Konrad. *Naturalist in Brazil.* 1931. Houghton Mifflin. 400p. VG. A10. $37.50

GUEST, C.Z. *First Garden.* 1987. McGraw Hill. 1st. lg 8vo. 141p. F/dj. P12. $75.00

GUEST, Edgar A. *Heap O' Living.* 1916. Chicago. Reilly Lee. 192p. VG/G. G11. $10.00

GUEST, Edgar A. *It Can Be Done.* 1938. Chicago. Reilly Lee. 204p. VG/G. G11. $10.00

GUEST, Jack A. *Longest Mile.* (1962). Toronto. Allen. 1st. NF/dj. A26. $30.00

GUEST, Judith. *Ordinary People.* 1976. Viking. 1st. author's 1st book. NF/NF. H11. $25.00

GUGGENHEIM, Peggy. *Out of This Century Confessions of an Art Addict.* 1979. NY. Universe. 1st. fwd Gore Vidal. ils. 396p. VG/dj. A25/M17. $20.00

GUIARD, Emile. *La Trepanation Cranienne Chez Les Neolithiques...* 1930. Paris. Masson. 13 pl of trephination skulls. 126p. G7. $175.00

GUIGUET, C.J. *Ecological Study of Goose Island, British Columbia...* 1953. Victoria, BC. lg 8vo. ils. 78p. VG/wrp. C12. $27.00

GUILD, Curtis. *Abroad Again; or, Fresh Foray in Foreign Lands.* 1879. Boston/NY. Lee Shepard/Dillingham. sm 8vo. 474p. VG. W1. $18.00

GUILD, Curtis. *Over the Ocean.* 1884. Lee Shepard. 558p. VG. S17. $7.50

GUILD, Marion Pelton. *Selected Poems of Katharine Lee Bates.* 1930. Houghton Mifflin. 1st. 230p. VG+. A25. $22.00

GUILLAUME, Paul. *La Psychologie des Singes.* 1941. Paris. 1st separate. ils. 335p. prt gr wrp. G1. $28.50

GUILLEMIN, Amedee. *Le Ciel: Notions d'Astronomie a l'Usage des Gens du Monde...* 1866 (1864). Paris. Hatchette. 3rd. 4to. ils/pl. 632p. half leather. K5. $250.00

GUILLEN, Michael. *Five Equations That Changed the World.* 1995. NY. Hyperion. 8vo. 277p. VG/dj. P4. $15.00

GUINEY, Corinne. *Beauty & the Beast. Classic Fairytale Retold...* 1982. Berkeley. Wild Hare. mini. 1/100. 30p. marbled brd. B24. $125.00

GUINNESS, Alec. *Blessings in Disguise.* 1986. Knopf. 1st Am. sm 4to. 238p. NF/F. W2. $20.00

GUINNESS, Alex. *Blessings in Disguise.* 1986. London. Hamish Hamilton. 1st/7th imp. 242p. F/clip. M7. $32.50

GUINNESS & SEEL. *No God But God: Breaking With Idols of Our Age.* 1992. Moody. 223p. F/wrp. B29. $8.00

GUION, Lady. *Exemplary Life of Pious Lady Guion...* 1804. Phil. Crukshank. 503p. leather. V3. $60.00

GULLION, Gordon. *Grouse of the North Shore.* 1984. Oshkosh. Willowcreek. 144p. F. A17. $40.00

GULLION, Gordon. *Grouse of the North Shore.* 1984. Oshkosh. Willowcreek. 144p. F. A17. $40.00

GUMMERMAN, Jay. *We Find Ourselves in Moontown.* 1989. Knopf. 1st. author's 1st book. F/dj. R14. $35.00

GUMMERMAN, Jay. *We Find Ourselves in Moontown.* 1989. Knopf. 1st. sgn. F/dj. B4. $85.00

GUNDELL, H. *Herb Gundell's Complete Guide to Rocky Mountain Gardening.* 1985. Dallas. 500+ mc photos. sc. VG. B26. $12.50

GUNN, Alexander. *Hermitage-Zoar Notebook & Letters of...* 1902. NY. 2 vol. 1/296 on handmade. full morocco. F/chemise/case. B18. $295.00

GUNN, James. *End of the Dreams.* 1975. Scribner. 1st. F/dj. M25. $15.00

GUNN, Peter. *Vernon Lee, Violet Paget, 1856-1935.* 1964. OUP. 1st. ils. gilt salmon cloth/cream brd. NF/VG. F1. $30.00

GUNN & GUNN. *Tegucigalpa, Honduras.* 1966. Tegucigalpa. 1st. 332p. dj. F3. $25.00

GUNTER, Pete A. *Big Thicket...* 1993. U N TX. ils/maps. 229p. F/wrp. S15. $7.00

GUNTHART, Lotte. *Linger Golden Light.* 1984. Pittsburgh. Hunt Botanical Inst. 250p. A10. $25.00

GUNTHER, John. *Death Be Not Proud.* 1949. Harper. 1st. NF/VG. T11. $40.00

GUNTHER, John. *Inside South America.* 1967. Harper Row. 1st. 8vo. 610p. F. W2. $350.00

GUNTHER, Max. *Doom Wind.* 1986. Contemporary. 1st. NF/dj. S13. $10.00

GURALNICK, Peter. *Searching for Robert Johnson.* 1989. Dutton. 1st. F/dj. B2. $75.00

GURDJIAN, E.S. *Head Injury From Antiquity to the Present...* 1973. Springfield. 139p. AN/dj. G7. $75.00

GURDJIEFF, G.I. *Meetings With Remarkable Men.* 1963. Dutton. 1st. F/NF. B2. $50.00

GURGANUS, Allan. *Oldest Living Confederate Widow Tells All.* 1989. Knopf. 1st. F/dj. A23/B20. $50.00

GURGANUS, Allan. *Plays Well With Others.* 1997. Knopf. 1st. sgn. F/dj. O11. $30.00

GURGANUS, Allan. *White People.* 1991. Knopf. 1st. F/F. B3. $20.00

GURGANUS, Allan. *White People.* 1991. Knopf. 1st. sgn. F/dj. O11. $25.00

GURNER, A. Logan. *Diseases of the Nose, Throat & Ear...* 1927. NY. Wood. 440p. cloth. G7. $95.00

GURNEY, Alan. *Below the Convergence: Voyages Toward Antarctica 1699-1839.* 1997. NY/London. Norton. 1st. 8vo. ils/maps/index. 315p. AN/dj. P4. $28.00

GURNEY, Gene. *Walk in Space: Story of Project Gemini.* 1967. Random. 8vo. ils. 185p. G. K5. $10.00

GURNEY, Joseph John. *Baptism & Supper: Disuse of Typical Rites of Worship of God.* 1873. Phil. Lewis. 12mo. 96p. V3. $35.00

GURNEY, Joseph John. *Essay on Habitual Exercise of Love to God.* nd. Am Tract Soc. 16mo. 242p. leather. G. V3. $32.00

GURNEY, Joseph John. *Four Lectures on Evidences of Christianity.* 1859. Longstreth. 2nd. 12mo. 176p. G. V3. $22.00

GURNEY, Joseph John. *Observations of Religious Pecularities of Society Friends.* 1832. Phil. Nathan Kite. 2nd Am. 331p. G. V3. $50.00

GURR, David. *Troika.* 1979. NY. Methuen. 1st. author's 1st book. F/NF wht dj. H11. $25.00

GUSSOW, Mel. *Don't Say Yes Until I Finish Talking.* 1971. Doubleday. 318p. VG/dj. C5. $12.50

GUSSOW & ODELL. *Mushrooms & Toadstools: An Account of More Common...* 1927. Ottawa. Minister of Agric. 1st. 4to. 274p. gilt gr cloth. VG+. B20. $75.00

GUSTAFSON, A.F. *Conservation of the Soil.* 1937. McGraw Hill. ils/index. 312p. xl. VG. H10. $15.00

GUSTAV VON BERG, Baron. *From Kapuvar to California, 1893...* 1979. SF. BC of CA. 1/500. 73p. P4. $75.00

GUTCHEON, Beth. *Still Missing.* 1981. Putnam. 1st. F/NF. H11. $15.00

GUTERSON, David. *Country Ahead of Us, the Country Behind.* 1989. NY. Harper. 1st. F/dj. B4. $250.00

**GUTERSON, David.** *Family Matters: Why Homeschooling Makes Sense.* 1992. HBJ. 1st. F/dj. A24/O11. $35.00

**GUTERSON, David.** *Snow Falling on Cedars.* 1994. Harcourt Brace. 1st. sgn. F/dj. B30/O11. $150.00

**GUTHERIE, Douglas.** *History of Medicine.* 1946. Phil. 1st Am. 448p. A13. $50.00

**GUTHERIE, Sally R.** *Jonathan, a Celebrated Club...* 1995. LA. Jonathan Club. ils. 129p. gilt cloth. D11. $40.00

**GUTHORN, Peter J.** *Sea Bright Skiff & Other New Jersey Shore Boats.* 1971. Rutgers. VG/G. R8. $35.00

**GUTHRIE, A.B.** *Big Sky.* 1947. Sloane. early prt. VG/dj. S13. $35.00

**GUTHRIE, A.B.** *Genuine Article.* 1977. Houghton Mifflin. 1st. NF/VG. G8. $35.00

**GUTHRIE, A.B.** *Murder in the Cotswolds.* 1989. Houghton Mifflin. 1st. F/dj. N4. $15.00

**GUTHRIE, A.B.** *Playing Catch-Up.* 1985. Houghton Mifflin. 1st. F/NF. A23. $25.00

**GUTHRIE, A.B.** *These Thousand Hills.* 1956. Houghton Mifflin. 1st. red-orange cloth. NF/VG. T11. $40.00

**GUTHRIE, A.B.** *These Thousand Hills.* 1956. Houghton Mifflin. 1st. 8vo. F/dj. S9. $50.00

**GUTTMAN.** *Concordance to Standard Edition Psychological Works Freud.* 1984. NY. Internat U Pr. 6 vol. thick 4to. NF. A4. $350.00

**GUTTRIDGE, Leonard.** *Icebound: The Jeannette Expedition's Quest for North Pole.* 1986. Annapolis. 2nd/corrected. 8vo. 357p. brn cloth. AN/dj. P4. $29.00

**GUY, Guy Gavriel.** *Song for Arbonne.* 1992. NY. Crown. 1st Am. F/dj. A23. $32.00

**GUY, William A.** *Principles of Forensic Medicine.* 1845. Harper. 1st Am. thick 8vo. 711p. full brn calf. B20. $300.00

**GUYLFORDE, Richard.** *Pylgrymage of Sir Richard Guylforde to Holy Land AD 1506.* 1851. London. Camden Soc 1st series #51. sm 4to. ils/table. cloth. VG. Q2. $64.00

**GWALTNEY, John Langston.** *Drylongso: A Self-Portrait of Black America.* 1981. NY. Vantage. 1st. NF/wrp. R11. $10.00

**GWYNN, S.** *Mungo Park & Quest of the Niger.* 1935. NY. 1st. ils/maps/index. 269p. VG/fair. B5. $30.00

**GYGAX, Gary.** *Players Handbook.* 1978. TSR Dungeons & Dragons. decor brd. VG. P3. $20.00

**GYSIN, Brion.** *Process.* 1987. Overlook. 1st thus. fwd Robert Palmer. VG/dj. R11. $25.00

# H

HAARLEM, J.F. Ostervald. *Evangile de Notre Seigneur Jesus Christ Selon St Matthiew...* 1900. Haarlem. Enschede. mini. gilt bstp brn pub cloth/WM Stone case. F. B24. $275.00

HAAS, Ernst. *Himalayan Pilgrimage.* 1978. Studio Book. photos. VG/dj. M17. $50.00

HAAS, Robert. *Sun Under Wood.* 1996. NY. Ecco. 1st. sgn/dtd 1998. F/dj. R14. $40.00

HABBERTON, John. *Trif & Trixy.* 1897. Altemus. 16mo. 241p. red cloth. T5. $15.00

HABENSTEIN & LAMERS. *History of American Funeral Directing.* 1956. Milwaukee. ils/77 pl. 636p. NF/dj. M4. $65.00

HABERLAND, Wolfgang. *Art of North America.* 1968. NY. Greystone. revised. 60 mc pl. 257p. P4. $35.00

HABERLEIN, E.F. *Amateur Trainer Multum in Parvo.* 1943. McPherson, KS. 38th. ils/index. 139p. G/wrp. A17. $12.50

HACHIYA. *Hiroshima Diary: Journal of a Japanese Physician...1945.* 1955. U NC. 249p. VG/VG. A4. $65.00

HACK, John T. *Prehistoric Coal Mining in Jeddito Valley, Arizona.* 1942. Peabody Mus. 5 pl/10 ils. F/wrp. B14. $55.00

HACKER, Leonard. *Cinematic Design.* 1931. Am Photographic Pub. 1st. 12 b&w+pl. F. C9. $150.00

HACKETT, Alice Payne. *Fifty Years of Best Sellers 1895-1945.* 1945. NY. RR Bowker. 1st. 8vo. F/NF. O10. $17.50

HACKETT, Brian. *Planting Design.* 1979. NY. ils/photos. VG. B26. $17.50

HACKETT, George Stuart. *Joint Ligament Relaxation Treated by Fibro-Osseous...* 1956. Springfield. Chas Thomas. 1st. 8vo. 97p. F/NF. C14. $30.00

HACKETT, Walter. *Swans of Ballycastle.* 1954. Ariel. 1st. lg 8vo. ils Bettina. F/G. M5. $25.00

HACKL, Alfons. *Fred Astaire & His Work.* 1970. Austria Internat. 1st. photos. VG/sans. C9. $60.00

HACSKAYLO, Edward. *Mycorrhizae.* 1971. GPO. 255p. cloth. VG. A10. $30.00

HADDAM, Jane. *Stillness in Bethlehem.* 1992. Bantam. 1st. sgn. Gregor Demarkian series. VG/dj. R8. $25.00

HADDOX, John. *Antonio Caso: Philosopher of Mexico.* 1971. Austin. 1st. 128p. dj. F3. $20.00

HADER & HADER. *Friendly Phoebe.* 1953. Macmillan. 1st. ils. VG+. M5. $11.00

HADER & HADER. *Hansel & Gretel.* 1927. Macmillan. 1st. sq 12mo. pict brd. dj. R5. $200.00

HADER & HADER. *Little Antelope.* 1962. Macmillan. 1st. VG/G. P2. $30.00

HADER & HADER. *Midget & Bridget.* 1934. Macmillan. 1st. VG. D1. $40.00

HADFIELD, A.M. *Time to Finish the Game.* 1964. London. Phoenix House. 1st. 8vo. VG/dj. A2. $10.00

HADINGHAM, Evan. *Fighting Triplanes.* 1969. Macmillan. 1st Am. 240p. VG/torn. S16. $35.00

HADLEY, Martha E. *Diary of Martha E Hadley.* 1969. Mt Dora. Loren S Hadley. fld map/photos. 210p. cbdg. P4. $125.00

HAFEN, Leroy R. *Mountain Men & Fur Trade of the Far West...Volume IX.* 1972. Arthur H Clark. 8vo. 420p. P4. $65.00

HAFEN, Leroy R. *Mountain Men & the Fur Trade in the Far West...* 1965-1972. Arthur Clark. 10 vol. inscr 1st vol. ils/maps. F/plain dj. P4. $275.00

HAFEN, Leroy R. *Overland Mail, 1849-1869...* 1926. Arthur H Clark. fld map. 361p. cloth. D11. $200.00

HAFEN, Lyman. *Flood Street to Fenway.* 1987. Put Place. 1st. inscr Hurst. photos. F/VG. P8. $75.00

HAFEN & HAFEN. *Fort Laramie & the Pageant of the West 1834-1890.* 1984. Lincoln, NE. 1st Bison. 427p. F/stiff wrp. E1. $15.00

HAFEN & HAFEN. *Handcarts to Zion: Story of Unique Western Migration...* 1960. Arthur H Clark. Pioneers ed. 8vo. 328p. brn cloth. dj. F7. $85.00

HAFEN & HAFEN. *Old Spanish Trail: Santa Fe to Los Angeles...* 1954. Clark. ils/map. 369p. VG. J2. $225.00

HAFEN & YOUNG. *Ft Laramie & the Pageant of the West 1834-1890.* 1938. Clark. 429p. VG. J2. $250.00

HAFTMANN, HENTZEN & LIEBER-MAN. *German Art of the Twentieth Century.* 1957. MOMA. ils. VG/dj. M17. $25.00

HAGBERG, David. *Crossfire.* 1991. NY. Tor. 1st. VG/dj. A28. $12.00

HAGEDORN, Hermann. *Roosevelt in the Bad Lands.* 1921. Houghton Mifflin. 1st. 491p. VG. B18. $25.00

HAGER, Jean. *Night Walker.* 1990. St Martin. 1st. sgn. F/dj. T2. $55.00

HAGER, Jean. *Ravenmocker.* 1992. Mysterious. 1st. sgn. F/dj. T2. $30.00

HAGER, Jean. *Redbird's Cry.* 1994. Mysterious. 1st. F/F. H11. $30.00

HAGER, Jean. *Seven Black Stones.* 1995. Mysterious. 1st. sgn. Molly Bearpaw #3. F/dj. A24. $27.50

HAGERMAN, Edward. *American Civil War & Origins of Modern Warfare: Ideas...* 1988. Bloomington, IN. IU. 1st. F/dj. A14. $35.00

HAGGARD, H. Rider. *Finished.* 1917. London. Ward Lock. 1st. 12mo. 320p. gr cloth. VG. M21. $45.00

HAGGARD, H. Rider. *When the World Shook.* 1919. London. Cassell. 1st. 12mo. 347p. brn cloth. VG. M21. $75.00

HAGGARD, Howard W. *Mystery, Magic & Medicine: Rise of Medicine...* 1933. Doubleday Doran. 1st. VG. E6. $15.00

HAGGARD, William. *Yesterday's Enemy.* 1976. Eng. 1st. F/dj. M19. $17.50

HAGGER, Mary. *Extracts From Memoranda of Mary Hagger, Ashford, Kent.* 1841. London. Harvey Darton. 1st. 12mo. 108p. V3. $18.00

HAGOOD, Richard. *Ryder Truck Lines: First Half Century.* 1982. Lake City, FL. ils/biblio. 283p. dj. H6. $28.00

HAGSTRUM, Jean H. *Samuel Johnson's Literary Criticism.* 1968. Chicago. dj. H13. $45.00

HAGUE, Harlan. *Road to California...* 1848. Glendale, CA. ils. 325p. VG. B18. $50.00

HAGUE, Michael. *Alphabears.* 1984. Holt. 1st. 4to. VG/dj. B17. $20.00

HAGUE, Michael. *Beauty & the Beast.* 1983. HRW. 1st. 4to. VG/dj. B17. $25.00

HAGUE, Michael. *Cinderella & Other Tales From Perrault.* 1989. Holt. 1st. sgn. F/F. B3. $35.00

HAGUE, Michael. *Cinderella & Other Tales From Perrault.* 1989. Holt. 1st. 4to. F/dj. B17. $20.00

HAGUE, Michael. *Family Christmas Treasury.* 1995. Holt. 1st. lg 8vo. red leather-type brd. NF. B36. $16.00

HAGUE, Michael. *Legend of the Veery Bird.* 1985. HBJ. 1st. sgn. F/dj. B17. $65.00

HAGUE, Michael. *Little Women.* 1993. Holt. 1st. 12mo. F/F/box. B17. $20.00

HAGUE, Michael. *Perfect Present.* 1996. Morrow. 1st. sgn. F/dj. B17. $35.00

HAGUE, Michael. *Reluctant Dragon.* 1983. Holt. 1st. 4to. F/dj. $30.00

**HAGUE, Michael.** *Twinkle, Twinkle, Little Star.* 1992. Morrow. 1st. sgn. F/dj. B17. $35.00

**HAGUE, Michael.** *We Wish You a Merry Christmas.* 1990. Holt. 1st. F/dj. M5. $10.00

**HAHN, Emily.** *Degree of Prudery.* 1950. NY. 1st. ils. 340p. VG/F. H13. $45.00

**HAHN, Emily.** *Love Conquers Nothing.* 1959. London. Dobson. 1st. F/VG. B3. $10.00

**HAHN, Emily.** *Mabel: Biography of Mabel Dodge Luhan.* 1977. Boston, MA. Houghton Mifflin. G/dj. A19. $30.00

**HAIBLUM, Isidore.** *Wilk Are Among Us.* 1975. Doubleday. 1st. VG/dj. P3. $15.00

**HAIG-BROWN, Roderick L.** *Return to the River.* 1941. Morrow. 1st. ils Charles DeFeo. 248p. F/VG+. B20. $100.00

**HAIG-BROWN, Roderick L.** *Western Angler: Account of Pacific Salmon & Western Trout.* 1939. Derrydale. 1/950. 2 vol. 43 pl/fld chart/fld map. F. H5. $850.00

**HAIG-BROWN, Roderick L.** *Whale People.* 1962. London. Collins. 184p. VG/clip. P4. $25.00

**HAIGHT, W.R.** *Annual Canadian Catalogue of Books, Second Supplement...* 1904. Toronto. 1/500. 66p. cloth. A4. $65.00

**HAILE, Bernard.** *Waterway: Navajo Ceremonial Myth Told by Black Mustache...* 1979. Mus N AZ Pr. American Tribal Relations. Eng/Navaho text. 152p. P4. $95.00

**HAILEY, Arthur.** *Wheels.* 1971. Doubleday. 1st. NF/G. L4. $45.00

**HAINAUX, Rene.** *State Design Throughout the World Since 1935.* (1956). NY. Theatre Arts Books. 200p. dj. K1. $100.00

**HAINES, Francis.** *Appaloosa.* 1963. Carter. Special ed. NF/dj. A21. $75.00

**HAINES, Francis.** *Buffalo.* 1970. Crowell. 1st. ils. F/dj. M4. $30.00

**HAINES, H.H.** *Trees, Shrubs & Economic Herbs of the Southern Circle...* 1984 (1916). Dehra Dun. rpt. 384p. AN/dj. B26. $12.50

**HAINING, Peter.** *Ghouls.* 1971. Stein Day. 1st. VG/G. L1. $45.00

**HAINING, Peter.** *Movie Monsters.* 1988. Severn. 1st. xl. VG/dj. L1. $25.00

**HAINING, Peter.** *Nightmare Reader.* 1973. Doubleday. 1st. xl. VG/dj. S18. $8.00

**HAINING, Peter.** *Sherlock Holmes Scrapbook.* 1986. Crescent. 1st thus. 4to. F/dj. M21. $30.00

**HAINING, Peter.** *Vampire.* 1985. Severn. 1st hc. VG/dj. L1. $45.00

**HAIRSTON, L. Beatrice.** *Brief History of Danville, Virginia, 1728-1954.* (1955). Dietz. sgn. ils. 138p. VG/G. B10. $65.00

**HALAAS, David Fridtjof.** *Boom Town Newspapers: Journalism on Rocky Mountain Mining...* 1981. U NM. photos/map/index. 146p. gray cloth. dj. P4. $30.00

**HALACY, D.S.** *Father of Supersonic Flight.* (1965). NY. Messner. 2nd. 192p. cloth. F/dj. D4. $20.00

**HALAS & MANVELL.** *Art in Movement: New Directions in Animation.* 1970. Hastings. 1st. ils. VG/dj. C9. $90.00

**HALBERSTAM, David.** *Noblest Roman.* 1961. Houghton Mifflin. 1st. F/dj. B4. $250.00

**HALBERSTAM, David.** *October 1964.* 1994. Villard. 1st. sgn. 380p. F/dj. B20. $30.00

**HALDANE, J.S.** *New Physiology & Other Addresses.* 1919. London. 1st. 156p. A13. $75.00

**HALDEMAN-JULIUS, E.** *Outline of Bunk: Including Admirations of a Debunker.* 1929. Boston. Stratford. 1st. sgn. VG. N2. $45.00

**HALDERMAN, Joe.** *Mindbridge.* 1976. St Martin. 1st. sgn. F/NF. G10. $32.00

**HALDERMAN, Joe.** *Tool of the Trade.* 1987. Morrow. 1st. sgn. F/dj. G10. $30.00

**HALE, Edward Everett.** *Man Without a Country.* nc (1960). Franklin Watts. Ils LE Fisher. 53p. VG/dj. C14. $8.00

**HALE, Matthew.** *Human Science & Social Order: Hugo Munsterberg...* 1980. Phil. 1st. 239p. A13. $30.00

**HALE, Sarah.** *Ladies New Book of Cookery for Private Families...* 1852. 1st. 474p. rb. E6. $75.00

**HALE & HALE.** *Flight Through Mexico.* 1893 (1886). Boston. ils. 301p. gilt pict cloth. F3. $35.00

**HALECKI, O.** *History of Poland.* 1992. Barnes Noble. New ed. F/dj. B9. $15.00

**HALES, Peter B.** *William Henry Jackson & Transformation of Am Landscape.* 1988. Temple U. ils. 355p. VG/dj. J2. $275.00

**HALETT & LAING.** *Dictionary of Anonymous & Pseudonymous English Literature.* nd. 7 vol. revised/enlarged. 60,000 entries. scarce. A4. $895.00

**HALEY, Alex.** *Different Kind of Christmas.* 1988. Doubleday. 1st. 8vo. 101p. wht linen. F/clip. J3. $75.00

**HALEY, Alex.** *Roots.* 1976. Doubleday. 1st. F/F. B2. $100.00

**HALEY, Alex.** *Roots.* 1976. Doubleday. 1st. inscr. G+/dj. O4. $180.00

**HALEY, Andrew G.** *Rocketry & Space Exploration.* 1958. Van Nostrand. ils. 334p. cloth. K5. $40.00

**HALEY, Earl.** *Revolt on the Painted Desert.* 1952. House-Warven. 1st. 376p. F. B19. $15.00

**HALEY, J. Evetts.** *Charles Goodnight, Cowman & Plainsman.* 1936. Houghton Mifflin. 1st. 485p. D11. $125.00

**HALEY, Jacquetta.** *Pleasure Grounds, AJ Downing & Montgomery Place.* 1988. Tarrytown. Sleepy Hollow. 96p. VG/dj. A10. $25.00

**HALEY, James L.** *Apaches: History & Culture Portrait.* 1981. Doubleday. 1st. ils/notes/index. 453p. NF/NF. B19. $35.00

**HALEY, John L.** *Buffalo War.* 1976. BC. ils/index. 290p. VG/dj. E1. $30.00

**HALEY, Neale.** *How to Teach Group Riding.* 1970. S Brunswick. Barnes. VG/G. O3. $26.00

**HALEY, Nelson Cole.** *Whale Hunt: Narrative of a Voyage.* 1948. NY. Ives Washburn. 304p. map ep. cloth. VG. P4. $40.00

**HALL, A.D.** *Feeding of Crops & Stock.* 1911. Dutton. 298p. VG. A10. $18.00

**HALL, Adam;** see Trevor, Elleston.

**HALL, Angelo.** *Astronomer's Wife: Biography of Angeline Hall.* 1908. Baltimore. Nunn. 8vo. 129p. VG. K5. $100.00

**HALL, Angus.** *Signs of Things to Come.* 1975. Danbury. F. P3. $10.00

**HALL, Ansel Franklin.** *General Report on Rainbow Bridge-Monument Valley Expedition.* 1934. Berkeley. 8vo. 32p. stiff gray wrp. F7. $75.00

**HALL, Basil.** *Extracts From a Journal Written on Coasts of Chili, Peru...* 1824. Edinburgh. Archibald Constable. 2 vol. 2nd. half calf. P4. $265.00

**HALL, Basil.** *Great Polyglot Bibles, With a Leaf...* 1966. SF. BC of CA. 1/400. loose in prt wrp. cloth clamshell box. B24. $450.00

**HALL, Basil.** *Great Polyglot Bibles Including a Leaf Complutensian...* 1966. BC of CA. 1/400. pres. F/clamshell case. B20. $650.00

**HALL, Charles Francis.** *Arctic Researches & Life Among the Esquimaux...1860-1862.* 1865. NY. Harper. 1st. fld map. 595p. 3-quarter marbled bdg. P4. $550.00

**HALL, Charles Francis.** *Life With the Esquimaux: A Narrative of Arctic Experience...* 1970. Rutland. Tuttle. 547p. dk red cloth. P4. $95.00

**HALL, Christopher Webber.** *Geography & Geology of Minnesota, Vol 1.* 1903. Minneapolis. HW WIlson. ils/photos. xl. VG. B14. $75.00

**HALL, Clayton Colman.** *Narratives of Early Maryland, 1633-1684.* 1910. Scribner. 8vo. fld ftspc/2 full-p pl. cloth. F. O1. $35.00

**HALL, David.** *Record Book.* 1948. NY. Oliver Durrell. 1394p. G/dj. C5. $12.50

**HALL, Donald.** *Oxford Book of Children's Verse in America.* 1985. OUP. VG/dj. M17. $15.00

**HALL, Donald.** *Season's at Eagle Pond.* 1987. Ticknor Fields. 1st. F/case. B3. $45.00

**HALL, Donald.** *Without.* 1998. Houghton Mifflin. 1st. sgn. F/as issued. R14. $35.00

**HALL, Edwin.** *Sweynheym & Pannartz & Origins of Printing in Italy.* 1991. Bird & Bull. 1/275. 8vo. ils. burgandy morocco. cloth case. K1. $450.00

**HALL, Granville Stanley.** *Adolescence...* 1916. NY. Appleton. 2 vol. heavy 8vo. red cloth. G. G1. $85.00

**HALL, Granville Stanley.** *Adolescence: Its Psychology & Relations to Physiology...* 1904. NY. Appleton. 2 vol. ruled red cloth. G1. $150.00

**HALL, Henry Marion.** *Gathering of Shore Birds.* 1960. Bramhall. 242p. xl. G. S5. $20.00

**HALL, J.K.** *One Hundred Years of American Psychiatry.* 1947. NY. 1st/2nd prt. 649p. xl. A13. $75.00

**HALL, James W.** *Bones of Coral.* nd. BC. F/dj. S18. $8.00

**HALL, James W.** *Bones of Coral.* 1991. Knopf. ARC. sgn. author's 4th book. F/wrp. B3. $45.00

**HALL, James W.** *False Statements.* 1986. Pittsburgh. Carnegie-Mellon U. 1st. sgn. F/sans. M15. $65.00

**HALL, James W.** *Gone Wild.* 1995. Delacorte. 1st. F/dj. S18. $24.00

**HALL, James W.** *Mean High Tide.* 1994. Delacorte. ARC. NF. M19. $15.00

**HALL, James W.** *Tropical Freeze.* 1989. NY. Norton. 1st. F/F. B3. $35.00

**HALL, James.** *Essay on the Origin, History & Principles...Architecture.* 1813. Edinburgh. folio. 60 pl. 74p. teg. quarter leather. F1. $650.00

**HALL, Jim.** *False Statements.* 1986. Carnegie-Mellon. 1st. sgn. F/dj. L3. $150.00

**HALL, Leland.** *Salah & His American.* 1935. Knopf. ils Maitland DeGogoriza. 199p. G+. P12. $20.00

**HALL, Marguerite.** *Public Health Statistics.* 1942. NY. 1st. 408p. A13. $25.00

**HALL, Marshall.** *On the Reflex Function of the Medulla Oblongata...* 1833. extracted rpt. tall 4to. contemporary calf/rb. G7. $595.00

**HALL, Melvin.** *Journey to the End of an Era: An Informal Autobiography.* 1947. Scribner. 1st. 8vo. 438p. cloth. VG/dj. W1. $26.00

**HALL, Robert deZouche.** *Bibliography on Vernacular Architecture.* 1972. Newton Abbot. 1st. 8vo. 191p. F/dj. O10. $40.00

**HALL, Sharlot M.** *Cactus & Pine: Songs of the Southwest.* 1989. Sharlot Hall Mus. 3rd. 251p. F/F. B19. $20.00

**HALL, Sharlot M.** *Sharlot Hall on the Arizona Strip: A Diary...* 1975. Northland. 1st. 97p. NF/NF. B19. $25.00

**HALL, Thomas.** *Sourcebook in Animal Biology.* 1951. NY. 1st. 716p. A13. $50.00

**HALL, Wade.** *Smiling Phoenix, Southern Humor From 1865-1914.* 1965. Gainesville, FL. 1st. inscr. 375p. F/dj. F1. $40.00

**HALL, William.** *Irrigation Development History, Customs, Laws...* 1886. Sacramento. Supt State Prt. russet cloth. M11. $250.00

**HALL & MAXWELL.** *Passion for Freedom: Life of Sharlot Hall.* 1982. Tucson. U AZ. 8vo. ils. brn cloth. F/VG. F7. $35.00

**HALLE, Louis J.** *Storm Petrel & the Owl of Athena.* 1970. Princeton. 1st. cloth. VG. B27. $25.00

**HALLENBECK, Cleve.** *Alvar Nunez Cabeza de Vaca: Journey & Route...1534-1536.* 1940. Arthur H Clark. 8vo. 326p. dk bl cloth. NF. P4. $350.00

**HALLENBECK & WILLIAMS.** *Legends of the Spanish Southwest.* 1938. Glendale. 1st. 342p. teg. bl cloth. w/prospectus. NF. P4. $250.00

**HALLIBURTON, Richard.** *New Worlds to Conquer.* (1929). Bobbs Merrill. ils. 368p. F3. $15.00

**HALLIDAY, Brett.** *Murder Is My Business.* 1945. Dodd Mead. 1st. F/dj. M15. $55.00

**HALLIMAN, Timothy.** *Incinerator.* 1992. Morrow. 1st. NF/dj. G8. $17.50

**HALLINAN, Timothy.** *Everything But the Squeal.* 1990. NAL. 1st. NF/dj. G8. $12.50

**HALLIWELL, Leo B.** *Light in the Jungle.* 1959. McKay. 1st. ils. 269p. VG. S14. $7.00

**HALLIWELL, Leslie.** *Mountain of Dreams: Golden Years of Paramount Pictures.* 1976. Stonehill. 1st. VG/dj. C9. $48.00

**HALLOCK, Charles.** *Fishing Tourist: Angler's Guide & Reference Book.* 1873. Harper. 1st. 239p. xl. H10. $45.00

**HALLOCK, Charles.** *Sportsman's Gazetteer & General Guide.* 1877. Forest Stream. ils/2 fld maps/index. cloth. lacks rear pocket map. H10. $65.00

**HALLOWELL, A. Irving.** *Contributions to Anthropology: Selected Papers of...* 1976. Chicago. 1st. 8vo. F/dj. A2. $40.00

**HALLOWELL, Tommy.** *Duel of the Diamond.* 1990. Viking. 1st. F/dj. P8. $10.00

**HALPER, Albert.** *Chicago Crime Book.* 1967. World. 1st. VG/dj. P3. $20.00

**HALPERIN, Joan Ungersma.** *Felix Feneon: Aesthete & Anarchist...* 1988. Yale. 1st. ils. 425p. VG/dj. S14. $17.50

**HALPERN, Daniel.** *Foreign Neon.* 1991. Knopf. 1st. F/dj. M23. $25.00

**HALPERN, Daniel.** *Life Among Others.* 1978. NY. Viking. 1st. inscr. F/dj. L3. $40.00

**HALPERT, Sam.** *When We Talk About Raymond Carver.* 1991. Gibbs Smith. 1st. 5 contributors sgn. F/dj. O11. $125.00

**HALSE, Albert O.** *Architectural Rendering: Techniques of Contemporary...* 1972. McGraw Hill. NF/dj. B9. $25.00

**HALSEY, R.T. Haines.** *Pictures of Early New York on Dark Blue Staffordshire...* 1899. Dodd Mead. 3 vol. 1/30 on Imperial Japon. w/extra suite pl. box. B24. $5,000.00

**HALSEY & TOWER.** *Homes of Our Ancestors.* nd. New England. rpt. ils. 302p. VG/dj. M21. $30.00

**HALSEY & TOWER.** *Homes of Our Ancestors.* 1925. Doubleday Page. 1st. 302p. quarter cloth. VG/dj. B18. $22.50

**HALSTEAD, M.** *Story of Cuba: Her Struggles for Liberty...* 1898. 6th. pict bdg. VG. E6. $20.00

**HALSTEAD, Ward C.** *Brain & Intelligence: A Quantitative Study of Frontal Lobes.* 1947. Chicago. 1st. 206p. G. C14. $17.00

**HALYBURTON, James D.** *Decisions of Hon James D Halyburton...* 1864. Richmond. Ritchie & Dunnavant. 1st/only. 8vo. 14p. prt self wrp. C6. $95.00

**HAMBIDGE, G.** *Soils & Men: Yearbook of Agriculture 1938.* 1938. GPO. 1232p. w/fld pocket map. A10. $30.00

**HAMBURGER, Jean.** *Discovering the Individual: Fascinating Journey...* 1978. Norton. 1st Am. 125p. F/NF. C14. $16.00

**HAMER, Malcolm.** *Shadows on the Green.* 1994. London. Headline. 1st. F/dj. M15. $45.00

**HAMER, Malcolm.** *Sudden Death.* 1991. London. Headline. 1st. sgn. F/dj. M15. $45.00

**HAMILL, Pete.** *Flesh & Bone.* 1977. Random. 1st. VG/NF. S18. $15.00

**HAMILL, Peter.** *Flesh & Blood.* 1977. Random. 1st. F/F. H11. $30.00

**HAMILTON, C.M.** *19th-C Mormon Architecture & City Planning.* 1995. OUP. 1st. 203p. F/dj. M4. $35.00

**HAMILTON, Charles.** *Great Forgers & Famous Fakes: Manuscript Forgers of Am...* 1980. ils. 286p. VG/VG. A4. $45.00

**HAMILTON, Charles.** *In Search of Shakespeare: A Reconnaissance Into Life...* 1985. 286p. VG/wrp. A4. $45.00

**HAMILTON, Dorothy.** *Rosalie.* 1977. Herald. 1st. ils Undada. NF/sans. P2. $8.00

**HAMILTON, E.** *Rainbow & Speedy.* 1959. Barnes. ils Lionel Edwards. VG/dj. A21. $35.00

**HAMILTON, E.P.** *French & Indian Wars: Story of Battles & Forts...* 1962. NY. 1st. 318p. NF. M4. $20.00

**HAMILTON, Elisabeth B.** *Reginald Birch: His Book.* 1939. Harcourt Brace. 1st. 280p. red cloth. VG/dj. D4/T5. $35.00

**HAMILTON, Franklin;** see Silverberg, Robert.

**HAMILTON, G.H.** *Art & Architecture of Russia.* 1954. Harmondsworth. Pelican History of Art series. 8vo. ils. 320p. VG/dj. Q2. $43.00

**HAMILTON, Henry Raymond.** *Epic of Chicago.* 1932. 365p. NF. A4. $35.00

**HAMILTON, J.G. DeRoulhac.** *Three Centuries of Southern Records, 1607-1907.* ca 1944. np. 1st thus. NF/wrp. M8. $27.50

**HAMILTON, J.P.** *Travels Through the Interior Provinces of Columbia.* 1827. London. John Murray. 2 vol. 1st. half morocco/5 raised bands. P4. $495.00

**HAMILTON, James.** *Arthur Rackham: A Biography.* 1990. Little Brn. 4to. ils. 199p. F/F. A4. $65.00

**HAMILTON, Jane.** *Book of Ruth.* 1988. Ticknor Fields. ARC. 8vo. author's 1st book. w/promo material. F/dj. S9. $350.00

**HAMILTON, Jane.** *Book of Ruth.* 1988. Ticknor Fields. 1st. NF/dj. D10. $135.00

**HAMILTON, Joyce.** *White Water: Colorado Jet Boats Expedition 1960.* 1963. New Zealand. Caxton. 1st. 8vo. 44 pl. 259p. blk/wht cloth. dj. F7. $80.00

**HAMILTON, Michael P.** *Vietnam War: Christian Perspectives.* 1967. Grand Rapids. Eerdmans. 140p. stp. VG. R11. $25.00

**HAMILTON, Milton.** *Country Printer.* 1936. Columbia. 373p. F. A4. $95.00

**HAMILTON, P.J.** *Colonial Mobile: A Story of Southwestern History.* 1910. Boston. 1st revised. 594p. VG. B5. $65.00

**HAMILTON, Richard.** *20,000 Alarms.* 1975. Playboy. 1st. VG+/dj. T11. $30.00

**HAMILTON, Robert.** *Progress of Society.* 1969 (1936). Augustus Kelley. rpt. VG. S5. $15.00

**HAMILTON, Vernon.** *Cognitive Structures & Processes of Human Motivation...* 1983. Chichester, Eng. John Wiley. 352p. gr fabricoid. VG/dj. G1. $65.00

**HAMILTON, Virginia.** *MC Higgins, the Great.* 1974. Macmillan. 1st. 8vo. 1975 Newbery. brn cloth. dj. R5. $400.00

**HAMILTON, W.J.** *Weasels of New York: Their Natural History...* 1933. Notre Dame. 8vo. 344p. VG+/wrp. B20. $35.00

**HAMILTON, W.T.** *My Sixty Years on the Plains...* 1960. Norman. 1st. 184p. VG/dj. B18. $22.50

**HAMILTON, Walter.** *Parodies of the Works of English & American Authors...* 1885. London. Reeves Turner. 6 vol. 1st. gilt gr pebbled cloth. F. M24. $650.00

**HAMMETT, Dashiell.** *Battle of the Aleutians...a Graphic History 1942-1943.* 1943. GPO. 1st. ils. F/b&w prt bl wrp. R3. $175.00

**HAMMETT, Dashiell.** *Creeps by Night.* 1931. John Day. VG. L1. $45.00

**HAMMETT, Dashiell.** *Dain Curse.* nd. Grosset Dunlap. rpt. F/dj. M15. $135.00

**HAMMETT, Dashiell.** *Dashiell Hammett Omnibus.* 1950. London. Cassell. Omnibus (5 novels+4 short stories). F/VG. M15. $200.00

**HAMMETT, Dashiell.** *Maltese Falcon.* 1987. Franklin Lib. NF. G8. $20.00

**HAMMETT, Dashiell.** *Thin Man.* nd. Grosset Dunlap. rprt. F/dj. M15. $100.00

**HAMMIL, Joel.** *Limbo.* 1980. Arbor. 1st. VG/dj. P3. $13.00

**HAMMOND, Dorothy.** *Confusing Collectibles: A Guide to Identification...* 1969. Leon, IA. 1st. 221p. F/VG. H1. $48.00

**HAMMOND, George P.** *Alexander Barclay, Mountain Man, From London Corsetier...* 1976. Old West Pub. 246p. 3 rear pocket maps. VG. J2. $350.00

**HAMMOND, George P.** *Noticias de California.* 1958. SF. BC of CA. 1/400. 53p. NF. P4. $125.00

**HAMMOND, S.H.** *Wild Northern Scenes; or, Sporting Adventures...* 1857. NY. Derby Jackson. 1st. 341p. G. H10. $45.00

**HAMMOND & HOUSEHOLDER.** *Intro to Statistical Method...* 1962. Knopf. 1st. bl cloth. B27. $15.00

**HAMMOND & MORGAN.** *Guide to the Manuscript Collections of Bancroft Lib.* 1963-1972. Berkeley. U CA. 2 vol. 1st. cloth. dj. D11. $125.00

**HAMNER, Laura V.** *Short Grass & Longhorns.* 1943. U OK. 269p. G/dj. J2. $145.00

**HAMPE, Theodore.** *Crime & Punishment in Germany As Illustrated by Nuremberg...* 1929. EP Dutton. 1st Am. 8vo. 175p. gr cloth. NF. B20. $40.00

**HAMSUN, Knut.** *Call of Life.* (1962). Ellington, CT. mini. 1/350. frenchfold. marbled brd. B24. $75.00

**HANAUER, Elsie.** *Old West: People & Places.* 1969. Cranbury, NJ. 1st. ils. 169p. E1. $30.00

**HANCE, Robert A.** *Destination Earth II.* 1977. Vantage. VG/dj. P3. $10.00

**HANCOCK, H. Irving.** *Japanese Physical Training.* 1904. Putnam. later prt. ils. orange cloth. VG+/dj. J3. $75.00

**HANCOCK, Natalie Morris.** *Peterpuck.* 1933. Oxford. Basil Blackwood. 1st. sgn. 95p. heavy cloth. NF. D4. $65.00

**HANCOCK, Thomas.** *Principles of Peace Exemplified...1798.* 1830. Providence. HH Brown. 16mo. 215p. xl. V3. $28.00

**HAND, Douglas.** *Gone Whaling: A Search for Orcas in Northwest Waters.* 1994. NY. S&S. 1st. 233p. rem mk. F/dj. P4. $20.00

**HAND, Richard A.** *Bookman's Guide to the Indians of the Americas...* 1989. London. Scarecrow. 1st. 8vo. 750p. tan cloth. F/sans. P4. $125.00

**HAND, Sherman.** *Colors in Carnival Glass. Book 4.* 1972. self pub. 1st. 8vo. ils. 100p. sbdg. VG/glossy wrp. H1. $37.50

**HAND, Thomas.** *Guenon on Milch Cows.* 1883. Orange Judd. 131p. cloth. VG. A10. $20.00

**HANDFORTH, Thomas.** *Mei Li.* (1938). Doubleday. early rpt. Caldecott Honor. VG/G. T5. $55.00

**HANDLEMAN, Howard.** *Bridge to Victory.* 1943. NY. Random. 1st. 8vo. 275p. map ep. dk bl cloth. VG/remnant. P4. $35.00

**HANDLER, Milton.** *Cases & Other Materials on Trade Regulation.* 1937. Chicago. Foundation. bl buckram. M11. $75.00

**HANDLIN, Oscar.** *Harvard Guide to American History.* 1963. Cambridge. 1st. 689p. NF/VG. M8. $35.00

**HANES, Bailey C.** *Bill Doolin, Outlaw.* 1968. Norman. 1st thus. VG/clip. B18. $20.00

**HANES, Peggy.** *Emigrant Trails in the Black Rock Desert.* 1980. Reno. Bureau Land Management. ils/tables/maps. F. P4. $40.00

**HANFF, Helene.** *Duchess of Bloomsbury Street.* 1977. London. Andre Deutsch. 1st Eng/2nd imp. NF/clip. A14. $25.00

**HANFF, Helene.** *84, Charing Cross Road.* 1970. Grossman. 1st/4th imp. NF/VG clip. A14. $21.00

**HANHAM.** *Bibliography of British History, 1851-1914.* 1976. Oxford. 10,829 entries. F/F. A4. $95.00

**HANKE, Lewis.** *Spanish Struggle for Justice in Conquest of America.* 1959. U PA. 2nd. 217p. dj. F3. $25.00

**HANLEY, James.** *Another World.* 1972. London. 1st. dj. T9. $30.00

**HANLEY & LUCIA.** *Owyee Trails, West's Forgotten Corner.* 1974. Caxton. ils/map ep. VG. J2. $30.00

**HANNA, Archibald.** *American Book of Great Adventures of the Old West.* 1969. Am Heritage. 384p. VG/dj. J2. $40.00

**HANNA, Edward B.** *Whitechapel Horrors.* 1992. Carroll Graf. 1st. F/F. H11. $25.00

**HANNA, Warren L.** *Life & Times of James Willard Schultz (Apikuni).* 1986. U OK. 1st. F/dj. T11. $35.00

**HANNA, Warren L.** *Lost Harbor: Controversy Over Drake's CA Anchorage.* 1979. Berkeley. 1st. inscr. 8vo. 439p. map ep. bl cloth. F/dj. P4. $45.00

**HANNAH, Barry.** *Bats Out of Hell.* 1993. Houghton Mifflin. 1st. F/dj. M23. $40.00

**HANNAH, Barry.** *He, Jack!* 1987. Paris. Olivier Orban. 1st French. sgn. F/wrp. R14. $35.00

**HANNAH, Barry.** *Tennis Handsome.* 1983. Knopf. 1st. F/NF. R11. $20.00

**HANNOCK, Ralph.** *Rainbow Republics: Central America.* 1947. Coward McCann. 1st. fld rear pocket map. F3. $25.00

**HANNON, Ezra;** see Hunter, Evan.

**HANNON, Leslie F.** *Discoverers: Seafaring Men Who First Touched Coasts...* 1971. Toronto. McClelland Stewart. 1st. F/NF. A26. $20.00

**HANNUM, Alberta.** *Paint the Wind.* 1958. Viking. 1st. ils Beatien Yazz. F/dj. T10. $40.00

**HANNUM, Alberta.** *Spin a Silver Dollar.* 1970. Viking. ils. 173p. VG/VG. B19/P4. $20.00

**HANO, Arnold.** *Big Out.* 1951. Barnes. 1st. VG/dj. P8. $50.00

**HANSARD, Luke.** *Auto-Biography.* 1991. London. Prt Hist Soc. 1st trade. gilt gr cloth. M24. $25.00

**HANSEN, Alvin H.** *Fiscal Policy: Business Cycles.* 1969 (1941). Norton. 462p. G. S5. $12.00

**HANSEN, Erik Fosnes.** *Psalm at Journey's End.* 1996. FSG. 1st Am. F/dj. M23. $40.00

**HANSEN, Hans Jurgen.** *Art & the Seafarer.* 1968. Viking. possible 1st. ils/photos. 296p. NF/VG. T11. $65.00

**HANSEN, J.W.F.** *Beyond the Cherubim.* 1964. Vantage. 1st. 224p. VG/fair. B10. $50.00

**HANSEN, Joseph.** *Fadeout.* 1970. Harper Row. 1st. sgn. F/VG. C15. $45.00

**HANSEN, Joseph.** *Gravedigger.* 1982. Holt. 1st. F/dj. M25. $15.00

**HANSEN, Joseph.** *Job's Year.* 1983. Holt. 1st. NF/dj. M25. $15.00

**HANSEN, Joseph.** *Nightwork.* 1984. HRW. 1st. F/dj. M19. $15.00

**HANSEN, Joseph.** *Skinflick.* 1979. Holt. 1st. F/dj. M25. $25.00

**HANSEN, Joseph.** *Steps Going Down.* Foul Play. 1st. F/VG. M19. $15.00

**HANSEN, Robert P.** *Back to the Wall.* 1957. Morrow. 1st. VG/dj. G8. $20.00

**HANSEN, Ron.** *Assassination of Jesse James by the Coward Robert Ford.* 1983. NY. Knopf. 1st. rem mk. F/F clip. H11. $35.00

**HANSEN, Ron.** *Assassination of Jesse James by the Coward Robert Ford.* 1984. London. Souvenir. 1st. F/dj. B4. $75.00

**HANSEN, Ron.** *Assassination of Jessie James by the Coward Robert Ford.* 1983. Knopf. 1st. F/F. D10. $75.00

**HANSEN, Ron.** *Atticus.* 1996. Harper Collins. 1st. sgn. F/dj. O11. $35.00

**HANSEN, Ron.** *Desperadoes.* 1979. Knopf. 1st. sgn. author's 1st book. F/F. D10. $175.00

**HANSEN, Ron.** *Mariette in Ectasy.* 1991. Harper Collins. 1st. F/F. D10. $45.00

**HANSEN, Ron.** *Nebraska.* 1989. Atlantic Monthly. 1st. F/NF. D10. $50.00

**HANSEN, Ron.** *Nebraska.* 1991. Omaha. Abattoir. 1/500. sgn. ils Karen Kunc. F/prt brn wrp. O11. $120.00

**HANSEN, Woodrow James.** *Search for Authority in California.* 1960. Oakland. 1/750. 192p. gr cloth. F. P4. $35.00

**HANSON, Charles E. Jr.** *Northwest Gun.* 1992. Chadron, NE. Mus of Fur Trade. rpt. VG. A19. $25.00

**HANSON, June Andrea.** *Winter of the Owl.* 1980. Macmillan. 1st. VG/dj. O3. $22.00

**HANSON, Kenneth O.** *Distance Anywhere.* (1967). Seattle. 1st. F/NF. A18. $25.00

**HANSON & JONES.** *Biogeochemistry of Blue, Snow & Ross's Geese.* 1976. S IL. 281p. VG. S5. $25.00

**HANUSCH, Ignaz Johann.** *Handbuch der Erfahrungs-Seelenlehre in Philosofisches...* 1820. Wien. Gedruckt/Carl Gerold. sm 8vo. 365p. G1. $17,150.00

**HAPPEL, Margaret.** *Ladies' Home Journal Handbook of Holiday Cuisine.* 1970. Downe Pub. G/dj. A16. $6.00

**HARAN, Menahem.** *Temples & Temple Service in Ancient Israel.* 1985. Eisenbrauns. 394p. VG. B29. $21.00

**HARASZTHY, Arpad.** *Wine-Making in California.* 1978. SF. BC of CA. 1/600. 69p. F/dj. P4. $95.00

**HARBISON, W.A.** *Dream Maker.* 1992. NY. Walker. 1st. F/F. H11. $25.00

**HARBORD, James G.** *Leaves From a War Diary.* 1925. NY. 2nd. 407p. VG. E1. $35.00

**HARDACRE, Val.** *Woodland Nuggets of Gold.* 1968. NY. 1st. ils. 304p. G/dj. B18. $22.50

**HARDEMAN, Nicholas.** *Wilderness Calling: Hardmen Family in American Westward...* 1977. Knoxville. bibliography/notes. 357p. AN/dj. P4. $35.00

**HARDEMAN, Nicholas.** *Wilderness Calling: Hardmen Family in American Westward...* 1977. Knoxville. 1st. 356p. VG/dj. S16. $25.00

**HARDIN, Charles.** *Politics of Agriculture.* 1952. Glencoe. Free Pr. 282p. VG/dj. A10. $15.00

**HARDING, Bertita.** *Magic Fire.* 1953. Bobbs Merrill. 451p. G/dj. C5. $12.50

**HARDING & LINDEMANN.** *Bibliography of Composition & Rhetoric.* (1991). Carbondale/Edwardsville. S IL U. 4to. 1798 entries. 192p. NF. H4. $35.00

**HARDING & WENTZ.** *Copybook From the Hand of Agustin V Zamorano.* 1974. LA. Zamorano Club. 1/250. F. P4. $95.00

**HARDMAN, Frederick.** *Scenes & Adventures in Central America.* 1852. Edinburgh. Blackwood. 298p. marbled blind-stp cloth. D11. $50.00

**HARDWICK, Michael.** *Complete Guide to Sherlock Holmes.* 1986. St Martin. 1st Am. NF/dj. P3. $25.00

**HARDWICK, Michael.** *Revenge of the Hound.* 1987. NY. Villard. 1st. F/F. H11. $25.00

**HARDWICK & HARDWICK.** *Dicken's England.* 1970. S Brunswick/NY. AS Barnes. 1st. 172p. F/dj. O10. $25.00

**HARDWICK & HARDWICK.** *Literary Journey: Visits to Homes of Great Writers.* 1968. NY. AS Barnes. 1st. sm 4to. 102p. cloth. F/dj. O10. $20.00

**HARDY, Allison.** *Wild Bill Hickok: King of the Gun-Fighters.* 1943. Girard, KS. Haldeman-Julius. sc. G. A19. $35.00

**HARDY, M.J.** *Lockheed Constellation.* 1973. NY. ils. 128p. F/VG. B18. $37.50

**HARDY, Max.** *Two Over One Game Force.* 1990s. revised/expaned/updated. VG/wrp. S1. $8.00

**HARDY, Phil.** *Western.* 1983. NY. Morrow. 1st. photos. F/dj. C9. $90.00

**HARDY, Thomas.** *Dynasts.* 1904-06-08. London. Macmillan. 3 vol. 1st. gilt gr cloth. VG. M24. $450.00

**HARDY, Thomas.** *Jude the Obscure.* 1993. Folio Soc. 2nd. ils Peter Reddick. VG/case. M17. $25.00

**HARDY, Thomas.** *Selected Poems of Thomas Hardy.* 1921. London. Warner. 1/1025 on handmade Riccardi. Sangorski bdg. F/case. H5. $400.00

**HARDY, Thomas.** *Two on a Tower.* 1905. NY. Harper. 8vo. 333p. gilt cloth. VG. K5. $35.00

**HARDY, William.** *Guide to Art Nouveau Style.* 1986. ils/index. 128p. dj. O8. $12.50

**HARDY & HENNIKER.** *Spectre of the Real/In Scarlet in Gray.* 1896. Boston/ London. Roberts Bros/John Lane. 1st. gilt brick cloth. F. M24. $275.00

**HARDYMENT, Christina.** *Home Comfort: History of Domestic Arrangements.* 1992. UK. ils/photos. M17. $30.00

**HARE, Cyril.** *Best Detective Stories of Cyril Hare.* 1959. London. Faber. 1st. F/dj. M15. $85.00

**HARE, Cyril.** *With a Bare Bodkin.* 1946. London. Faber. 1st. VG/dj. M15. $75.00

**HARFIELD, Alan.** *Pigeon to Packhorse: Illustrated Story of Animals...* 1989. Chippenham. Picton. 1st. ils. VG/dj. O3. $38.00

**HARGRAVE, C.P.** *History of Playing Cards & Bibliography of Cards & Gaming.* 1930. Houghton Mifflin. sm folio. 31 mc pl/78p bibliography. 492p. VG. A4. $450.00

**HARING, Douglas.** *Land of Gods & Earthquakes.* 1929. Columbia U. 1st. 8vo. 203p. NF/VG. B20. $30.00

**HARJO, Joy.** *Woman Who Fell From the Sky.* 1994. NY. Norton. 1st. sgn. F/clip. O11. $40.00

**HARK, A.** *Hex Marks the Spot: Pennsylvania Dutch Country.* 1938. Phil. 316p. G. M4. $12.00

**HARKEY, Ira.** *Pioneer Bush Pilot.* 1974. Seattle. 1st. VG/dj. B5. $50.00

**HARKINS, Philip.** *Double Play.* 1951. Holiday House. 1st. G+. P8. $15.00

**HARKINS, Philip.** *Southpaw From San Francisco.* 1948. Morrow. 1st. G+. P8. $20.00

**HARKNESS, Peter.** *Modern Garden Roses.* 1988. Chester, CT. 108 photos. 144p. AN/dj. B26. $17.50

**HARLAN, George H.** *San Francisco Bay Ferry Boats.* 1967. Howell-North. 1st. 4to. 195p. NF/G+. S14. $25.00

**HARLAN, Jack.** *Plant Scientists & What They Do.* 1964. NY. Watts. 1st. 181p. F/NF. D4. $20.00

**HARLAND, Marian.** *Common Sense in the Household: A Manual...* 1871. 1st. 556p. half leather. G+. E6. $90.00

**HARLEMAN, Ann.** *Bitter Lake.* 1996. S Methodist U. 1st. sgn. VG/dj. M17. $15.00

**HARLOW, Neal.** *Maps of San Francisco Bay.* 1950. SF. BC of CA. facs. 1/300. 201p. F. A4. $110.00

**HARLOW, Neal.** *Maps of the Pueblo Lands of San Diego.* 1987. LA. Dawson. 1/375. sgn. 80 maps. 244p. VG+. P4. $225.00

**HARLOW, V.T.** *Colonising Expeditions to West Indies & Guiana 1623-1667.* 1925. London. Hakluyt Soc. 8vo. 262p. cloth. F. O1. $75.00

**HARLOW, W.S.** *Duties of Sheriffs & Constables...* 1907. SF. Bancroft-Whitney Co. buckram. M11. $75.00

**HARMAN, Fred.** *Great West in Paintings by Fred Harmen, Cowboy Artist.* 1969. Castle Books. 186p. VG. J2. $70.00

**HARMER, Paul.** *Muck Soils of Michigan.* 1941. E Lansing. Agriculture Experiment Sta. 128p. VG. A10. $22.00

**HARMETZ, Aljean.** *Round Up the Usual Suspects.* 1992. Hyperion. 1st. 402p. VG/dj. C5. $15.00

**HARMON, A.W.** *Base Hit.* 1970. Lippincott. 1st. F/VG. P8. $40.00

**HARMON, Nolan.** *Famous Case of Myra Clark Gaines.* 1946. LSU. gr cloth. M11. $65.00

**HARMSEN, Tyrus G.** *Forty Years of Book Collecting.* 1985. LA. Tiger. 1/150. unp. NF. P4. $25.00

**HARNSBERGER, Caroline Thomas.** *Mark Twain & the Birds.* 1984. Evanston, IL. Schori. mini. 1/239 prt letterpress. 55p. bl cloth/metal pl. B24. $110.00

**HARNWELL, Gaylord P.** *Principles of Electricity & Electromagnetism.* 1949 (1938). McGraw Hill. 2nd. ils. 670p. VG+. A25. $15.00

**HARPENDING, Asbury.** *Great Diamond Hoax & Other Stirring Incidents...* (1958). Norman, OK. 1st thus. 211p. VG/dj. B18. $37.50

**HARPER, Harry.** *Evolution of the Flying Machine.* nd (1930s). Phil. ils. 288p. xl. G. B18. $45.00

**HARPER, Henry H.** *Journey in Southeastern Mexico...* 1910. Boston. self pub. 100p. chemise/case. D11. $100.00

**HARPER, Henry H.** *Story of a Nephrectomy: True History of Semi-Tragic Episode.* 1927. Norwood, MA. Plimpton. 1st. 8vo. 57p. bl cloth/cream spine. F/case. B20. $75.00

**HARPER, Merritt.** *Animal Husbandry for Schools.* 1918. Macmillan. 409p. cloth. G. A10. $15.00

**HARPER, Wilhelmina.** *Dog Show: Selection of Favorite Dog Stories.* 1950. Houghton Mifflin. 1st. ils. cloth/label. VG. B27. $55.00

**HARPER, Wilhelmina.** *Flying Hoofs.* 1939. Houghton Mifflin. ils Paul Brown. VG/dj. A21. $50.00

**HARPER, Wilhelmina.** *Little Book of Necessary Ballads.* 1930. Harper. 86p. cloth. NF. D4. $40.00

**HARPER, Wilhemina.** *Selfish Giant & Other Stories.* 1935. McKay. 1st. ils Kate Seredy. F/VG. M5. $145.00

**HARPUR, B.** *Impossible Victory: Account of Battle for Po River.* 1981. 1st Am. VG/dj. E6. $13.00

**HARRAP, George C.** *Love Lyrics From Five Centuries.* nd. NY. Crowell. lg 8vo. ils. teg. bl cloth. F/dj. F1. $50.00

**HARRINGTON, Burton.** *Essentials of Poster Design.* (1925). Poster Advertising Assn. lg 8vo. ils/pl. 134p. brn cloth. K1. $125.00

**HARRINGTON, J.C.** *Archaeology & Historical Society.* 1965. Nashville. Am Assn for State & Local Hist. ils. 53p. VG/wrp. P4. $16.00

**HARRINGTON, James.** *Oceana & Other Works...Collected, Methodiz'd, Review'd...* 1737. London. Prt for A Miller. 2nd. contemporary calf. M11. $450.00

**HARRINGTON, John P.** *Ethnography of the Tewa Indians.* 1916. GPO. 29th Annual Report Bureau Am Ethnology. olive cloth. P4. $150.00

**HARRINGTON, John P.** *Tobacco Among the Karuk Indians of California.* 1932. GPO. 1st. Bureau Ethnology Bulletin #94. 284p. VG/wrp. P4. $48.50

**HARRINGTON, John.** *Metamorphosis of Ajax, a New Discourse on a Stale Subject...* 1927. London. Fanfrolico. 1/454. tall 8vo. lt gray brd. F1. $150.00

**HARRINGTON, Kent.** *Dia De Los Muertos.* 1997. Tucson. McMillan. 1st. sgn. F/dj. M15. $35.00

**HARRINGTON, Mark Raymond.** *Southwest Museum Papers. Number Eight. Gypsum Cave, NV...* 1963 (1933). Highland Park. rpt. 197p. F/prt wrp. P4. $25.00

**HARRINGTON, Rebie.** *Cinderella Takes a Holiday in the Northland.* 1937. Fleming Revell. 8vo. 269p. bl cloth. P4. $35.00

**HARRINGTON, William.** *Cromwell File.* 1986. St Martin. 1st. NF/VG. N4. $17.50

**HARRIOT, Thomas.** *Briefe & True Report of the New Found Land of Virginia.* 1972 (1590). Dover. rpt. 91p. VG. B10. $10.00

**HARRIS, Benjamin Butler.** *Gila Trail: Texas Argonauts & CA Gold Rush.* 1960. Norman, OK. 175p. cloth. dj. D11. $35.00

**HARRIS, Burton H.** *Progress in Pediatric Trauma.* 1985. Boston. New Eng Medical Center. 4to. 161p. NF. C14. $18.00

**HARRIS, Charlaine.** *Real Murders.* 1990. NY. Walker. 1st. F/dj. A23. $30.00

**HARRIS, Christie.** *Once Upon a Totem.* 1967. NY. Atheneum. later prt. 8vo. 148p. P4. $25.00

**HARRIS, Dean.** *By Path & Trail.* 1908. Chicago Newspaper Union. 1st. 225p. cloth. D11. $25.00

**HARRIS, Dorothy Joan.** *House Mouse.* 1973. NY. Warne. 1st. sgn pres. lt bl cloth/brn vignette. dj. R5. $60.00

**HARRIS, F.S.** *Sugar-Beet in America.* 1919. NY. Macmillan. 1st. 342p. xl. G. H10. $17.50

**HARRIS, Frank.** *Man Shakespeare.* 1909. NY. Boni. 422p. VG. C5. $12.50

**HARRIS, Frank.** *My Reminiscences as a Cowboy.* 1930. Boni. 1st. ils. 217p. VG/wrp. B19. $65.00

**HARRIS, George.** *Iraq: Its People, Society & Culture.* 1958. New Haven, CT. Survey of World Culture #3. 5 maps. 350p. cloth. VG/dj. Q2. $36.50

**HARRIS, Henry.** *California's Medical Story.* 1932. Grabhorn. 8vo. 24 photo pl. 422p. yel cloth. K1. $50.00

**HARRIS, J.R.** *Anglers Entomology.* 1966. NY. Barnes. VG/dj. A19. $45.00

**HARRIS, Jed.** *Watchman, What of the Night.* 1963. Doubleday. 154p. VG/dj. C5. $12.50

**HARRIS, Jessie W.** *Everyday Foods.* 1939. Houghton Mifflin. G. A16. $10.00

**HARRIS, Joel Chandler.** *Daddy Jake the Runaway & Other Stories.* 1889. NY. Century. 1st. 4to. 145p. G. D1. $200.00

**HARRIS, Joel Chandler.** *Gabriel Tolliver.* 1902. McClure Phillips. 1st. gilt red cloth. VG. S13. $30.00

**HARRIS, Joel Chandler.** *Jump on Over!* 1989. HBJ. 1st. RS. F/dj. D4. $45.00

**HARRIS, Joel Chandler.** *Little Mr Thimblefinger.* 1894. Houghton Mifflin. ils Oliver Herford. G. A21. $75.00

**HARRIS, Joel Chandler.** *Tales of the Home Folks in Peace & War.* 1898. Houghton Mifflin. 1st. 417p. lg gr cloth. VG+. B20. $125.00

**HARRIS, Joel Chandler.** *Uncle Remus, His Songs & Sayings.* 1881. NY. Appleton. 1st/3rd state. 12mo. 8 pl/ils. 231+6p ads. leather. B11. $575.00

**HARRIS, Joel Chandler.** *Uncle Remus & the Little Boy.* 1910. Sm Maynard. 1st. ils JM Conde. 172p. VG. B27. $275.00

**HARRIS, Joel Chandler.** *Uncle Remus-His Songs & Sayings/Folk-Lore of Old Plantation.* 1881. NY. Appleton. 1st/3rd state (presumptuous on last line p9). sgn. F1. $800.00

**HARRIS, John H.** *Dawn in Darkest Africa.* 1912. London. Smith Elder. 1st. photos/fld map. 304p. gilt red cloth. xl. H7. $35.00

**HARRIS, John.** *Covenant With Death.* 1961. London. 1st. VG+/VG. A14. $42.00

**HARRIS, John.** *Old Trade of Killing.* 1966. NY. Morrow. 1st. NF/dj. A14. $32.00

**HARRIS, John.** *Spring of Malice.* 1962. London. Hutchinson. 1st. VG+/clip. A14. $42.00

**HARRIS, Julie.** *Longest Winter.* 1995. NY. St Martin. 8vo. 306p. half cloth. F/dj. P4. $24.00

**HARRIS, Larry.** *Bridge Director's Companion.* 3rd/revised. VG/wrp. S1. $15.00

**HARRIS, M.** *Aurelian or Natural History of English Insects...* 1986 (1766). Middlesex. Newnes. rpt. ils. 104p. F. M12. $20.00

**HARRIS, Malcolm.** *Old New Kent County: Some Accounts of Planters...* 1977. West Point. 2 vol. VG. B10. $100.00

**HARRIS, Marilyn.** *Night Games.* 1987. Doubleday. 1st. VG/NF. S18. $15.00

**HARRIS, Mark.** *Band the Drum Slowly.* 1956. Knopf. 1st. inscr. VG/G. P8. $250.00

**HARRIS, Mark.** *Diamond.* 1994. DIF. 1st. AN/dj. P8. $22.50

**HARRIS, Mark.** *Heart of Boswell.* 1981. McGraw Hill. 1st. tall 8vo. F/dj. H13. $55.00

**HARRIS, Mark.** *Mark the Glove Boy.* 1964. Macmillan. 1st. F/NF. M25. $25.00

**HARRIS, Mark.** *Short Work of It: Selected Writings.* 1979. U Pittsburgh. 1st. sgn. F/dj. P8. $45.00

**HARRIS, Mark.** *Southpaw.* 1953. Bobbs Merrill. 1st. G/dj. P8. $175.00

**HARRIS, Mark.** *Ticket for a Seamstitch.* 1957. Knopf. 1st. VG/dj. P8. $65.00

**HARRIS, Mark.** *Trumpet of the World.* 1946. Reynal Hitchcock. 1st. author's 1st book. G+/dj. B30. $60.00

**HARRIS, Miriam Coles.** *Missy.* 1980. NY. GW Carleton. 412p. G+. G11. $8.00

**HARRIS, Nathaniel.** *Life & Works of Dali.* 1994. Chelsea. ARC. 12mo. NF/dj. A28. $15.00

**HARRIS, Robert.** *Enigma.* 1995. Random. 1st. F/F. H11. $15.00

**HARRIS, Robert.** *Enigma.* 1995. Random. 1st. NF/F. S18. $12.00

**HARRIS, Sheldon.** *Blues Who's Who.* 1979. New Rochelle. Arlington House. NF/dj. B2. $125.00

**HARRIS, Thistle Y.** *Wild Flowers of Australia.* 1952. Sydney. Angus. 3rd. 206p. VG/dj. A10. $35.00

**HARRIS, Thomas.** *Black Sunday.* 1975. Putnam. 1st. F/NF. T2. $100.00

**HARRIS, Thomas.** *Red Dragon.* 1981. NY. Putnam. 1st. NF/clip. M21. $30.00

**HARRIS, Thomas.** *Red Dragon.* 1981. Putnam. 1st. F/NF. S18. $40.00

**HARRIS, Thomas.** *Silence of the Lambs.* 1988. St Martin. 1st. F/F. B3/T12. $100.00

**HARRIS & HARRIS.** *Eldon House: 5 Women's Views of the 19th Century.* 1994. Toronto. Champlain Soc. 1st. 8vo. 517p. red cloth. F. P4. $125.00

**HARRIS & THADDEUS.** *Treatise on Some Insects Injurious to Vegetation.* 1883. NY. Orange Judd. 8vo. 640p. 3-quarter leather/raised bands. P4. $250.00

**HARRISON, Anthony H.** *Swinburne's Medievalism.* 1988. Baton Rouge. LSU. 1st. gr cloth. F/dj. T10. $25.00

**HARRISON, C.R.** *Ornamental Conifers.* 1975. NY. Macmillan. 1st. ils/index. 224p. VG. H10. $25.00

**HARRISON, Caroline Rives.** *Historic Guide: Richmond & the James River.* (1955). Cussons. 7th. photos/maps. 41p. VG. B10. $5.00

**HARRISON, Chip;** see Block, Lawrence.

**HARRISON, David.** *Footsteps in the Sand.* 1959. London. Benn. ils/map. 453p. cloth. VG/rpr dj. Q2. $57.00

**HARRISON, Dick.** *Unnamed Country: Struggle for Canadian Prairie Fiction.* 1977. U Alberta. 1st. VG. P3. $10.00

**HARRISON, Edith Ogden.** *Enchanted House & Other Fairy Stories.* 1913. McClurg. 1st. ils Frederick Richardson. F/fair. M5. $95.00

**HARRISON, Edith.** *Below the Equator.* 1918. Chicago. McClurg. 1st. 288p. gilt red cloth. F3. $20.00

**HARRISON, Elizabeth.** *Study of Child-Nature From the Kindergarten Standpoint.* 1895 (1890). Chicago Kindergarten College. 11th. 207p. VG+. A25. $25.00

**HARRISON, Fairfax.** *Aris Sonis Focisque...The Harrisons of Skimino...* 1910. private prt. 413p. B10. $250.00

**HARRISON, Fairfax.** *Equine FFV's.* 1928. Richmond. private prt. 1st/ltd. VG. O3. $295.00

**HARRISON, Fairfax.** *Landmarks of Old Prince William: Study of Origins...* (1964). Chesapeake Book Co. 2 vol. rpt. 724p. VG. B10. $65.00

**HARRISON, Florence.** *Rhyme of a Run & Other Verse.* ca 1910. London. Blackie. 1st. 4to. 18 tipped-in pl. pict cloth. R5. $400.00

**HARRISON, Harry.** *Return to Eden.* 1988. Bantam. 1st trade. F/NF. M21. $20.00

**HARRISON, Harry.** *West of Eden.* 1984. Granada. 1st. sgn. F/dj. M21. $35.00

**HARRISON, Jamie.** *Edge of the Crazies.* 1995. Hyperion. 1st. sgn. author's 1st novel. F/dj. T2. $40.00

**HARRISON, Jim.** *Dalva.* 1988. Dutton. 1st. F/dj. A24. $30.00

**HARRISON, Jim.** *Dalva.* 1988. Dutton. 1st. F/NF. H11. $25.00

**HARRISON, Jim.** *Julip.* 1994. Boston. Houghton Mifflin. 1st. sgn. F/dj. R14. $75.00

**HARRISON, Jim.** *Julip.* 1994. Houghton Mifflin. 1st. F/dj. B30. $22.50

**HARRISON, Jim.** *Just Before Dark.* 1991. Livingston. Clark City. 1/250. sgn. F/case. B3. $150.00

**HARRISON, Jim.** *Legends of the Fall.* 1979. Delacorte. 1st trade after 3-vol boxed & ltd. F/F. D10. $85.00

**HARRISON, Jim.** *Legends of the Fall.* 1980. London. Collins. 1st Eng. F/dj. Q1. $75.00

**HARRISON, Jim.** *Selected & New Poems.* 1982. Delacorte/Seymour. 1st. 1/250. sgn. F/case. L3. $250.00

**HARRISON, Jim.** *Sundog.* 1984. Dutton. 1st. sgn. NF/VG. R14. $60.00

**HARRISON, Jim.** *Woman Lit by Fireflies.* 1991. Weidenfeld Nicolson. 1st Eng. sgn. F/dj. R14. $45.00

**HARRISON, Katherine.** *Kiss.* 1997. Random. 1st. F/dj. R14. $35.00

**HARRISON, Katherine.** *Thicker Than Water.* 1991. Random. 1st. author's 1st novel. F/dj. R14. $40.00

**HARRISON, Laura Soulliere.** *Architecture in the Parks, National Historic Landmark...* 1986. GPO. Nat Park Service, 482p. stiff wht wrp. F7. $37.50

**HARRISON, Michael.** *Study in Surmise: Making of Sherlock Holmes.* 1984. Bloomington. Gaslight. 1st. F/dj. M15. $65.00

**HARRISON, Paul W.** *Doctor in Arabia.* 1943. Lodnon. Hale. 7 pl/map. 285p. cloth. G. Q2. $26.00

**HARRISON, Payne.** *Storming Intrepid.* 1989. NY. Crown. 1st. author's 1st book. F/F. H11. $30.00

**HARRISON, Payne.** *Thunder of Erebus.* 1991. Crown. 1st. F/dj. A23/H11. $25.00

**HARRISON, Richard E.** *Handbook of Bulbs & Perennials for Southern Hemisphere.* 1971 (1953). Palmerston North, NZ. revised 3rd. photos. 282p. dj. B26. $27.50

**HARRISON, Whit;** see Whittington, Harry.

**HARRISON, William.** *Roller Ball Murder.* 1974. NY. Morrow. 1st. F/dj. B4. $150.00

**HARRISON, William.** *Savannah Blue.* 1981. Marek. 1st. F/F. H11. $25.00

**HARROD-EAGLES, Cynthia.** *Orchestrated Death.* 1992. Scribner. 1st Am. NF/dj. N4. $25.00

**HARROLD, Charles F.** *John Henry Newman: Expository & Critical Study of His Mind.* 1945. London/NY/Toronto. VG/G. M17. $15.00

**HARROW, Benjamin.** *Casimir Funk: Pioneer in Vitamins & Hormones.* 1955. Dodd Mead. 1st. pres. F/VG+. B20. $20.00

**HARSCH, Rick.** *Driftless Zone.* 1997. S Royalton, VG. Steerforth. 1st. F/dj. M23. $20.00

**HARSHBERGER, John W.** *Botanists of Philadelpha & Their Work.* 1899. Phil. ils. 457p. gilt bl cloth. VG. B26. $275.00

**HARSTING, Jessie.** *Stephen King at the Movies.* 1986. NY. Starlog. 1st. F/wrp. C9. $60.00

**HART, Carolyn G.** *Christie Caper.* 1991. NY. Bantam. 1st. sgn. F/dj. T2. $30.00

**HART, Carolyn G.** *Dead Man's Island.* 1993. NY. Bantam. 1st. sgn. F/dj. A23. $35.00

**HART, Carolyn G.** *Death in Lover's Lane.* 1997. NY. Avon. 1st. sgn. F/dj. A23. $35.00

**HART, Carolyn G.** *Scandal in Fair Haven.* 1994. NY. Bantam. 1st. sgn. F/dj. A23. $35.00

**HART, Carolyn G.** *Southern Ghost.* 1995. NY. Bantam. 1st. F/dj. A23. $32.00

**HART, Edward.** *Shire Horses.* 1983. London. Batsford. 1st. VG/dj. O3. $38.00

**HART, Frank J.** *Speed Boy.* 1938. Lakewood House. 1st. VG/G. P8. $150.00

**HART, Helen.** *Mary Lee at Washington.* 1918. Whitman. ils. 215p. G/dj. P12. $15.00

**HART, Herbert M.** *Pioneer Forts of the West.* 1967. Seattle. Superior. 1st. 192p. VG/dj. B18. $27.50

**HART, Jerome.** *Levantine Log-Book.* 1905. Longman Gr. 36 pl. 404p. decor cloth. G. Q2. $30.00

**HART, Philip.** *Golden Lure.* 1934. Saalfield. VG/dj. M19. $17.50

**HART, Robert A.** *Eccentric Tradition: American Diplomacy in Far East.* 1976. Scribner. 1st. ils. F/VG. A2. $15.00

**HART, Scott.** *Washington at War: 1941-1945.* 1970. Englewood Cliffs. 1st. ils. 296p. F/dj. E1. $30.00

**HART, William S.** *My Life East & West.* 1994. Lakeside Classic. 1st thus. teg. brn cloth. F/sans. M4/T11. $25.00

**HART, William S.** *My Life East & West.* 1994. Lakeside Classic. 12mo. ils. brn cloth. VG. B11. $15.00

**HART-CORELL, Belle.** *Footprints: A History of General Claire L Chennault...* 1983. np. Belle Oliver Hart-Corell. inscr. 63p. VG/dj. B18. $27.50

**HART-DAVIS, Rupert.** *Power of Chance: A Table of Memory.* 1991. London. 1st. dj. T9. $40.00

**HARTE, Bret.** *Complete Poetical Works.* 1886. London. Chatto Windus. 1st Eng collected. 324p. VG. A18. $35.00

**HARTE, Bret.** *Poems.* 1871. Boston. Fields Osgood. 1st. VG+. A18. $100.00

**HARTE, Bret.** *Queen of the Pirate Isle.* 1955. London. Warne. ils Greenaway. 64p. tan cloth. F/dj. F1. $50.00

**HARTE, Bret.** *Works of...* ca 1916. NY. Collier. 25 vol. 8vo. gilt gr cloth. B20. $75.00

**HARTLAND, Michael.** *Third Betrayal.* 1986. London. Hodder Stoughton. 1st. F/dj. M15. $65.00

**HARTLEY, C.B.** *Life of Daniel Boone: Founder of Kentucky.* nd. NY. 385p. G. M4. $15.00

**HARTLEY, Harold.** *Studies in the History of Chemistry.* 1971. Oxford. 1st. 243p. A13. $40.00

**HARTLEY, L.P.** *Eustace & Hilda.* 1958. British Book Centre. 1st Am. F/NF. M19. $17.50

**HARTLEY, R.A.** *History & Bibliography of Boxing Books.* ca 1980s. 4to. 359p. F/F. A4. $95.00

**HARTMANN, L.** *Story of Cham D'Asile, As Told by Two of the Colonists.* 1937. Dallas, BC of TX. 1st Eng-language. 1/300. gilt gr cloth. F/box. M24. $275.00

**HARTMANN, Sadakichi.** *Last Thirty Days of Christ.* 1920. private prt. 1/3000. 110p. gilt blk cloth. K1. $150.00

**HARTOV, Steven.** *Heat of Ramadan.* 1992. HBJ. 1st. author's 1st book. bstp on title p. NF/F. H11. $15.00

**HARTUNG, E.J.** *Astronomical Objects for Southern Telescopes...* 1968. Cambridge. 8vo. 238p. xl. dj. K5. $40.00

**HARTWIG, G.** *Workers Under the Ground; or, Mines & Mining.* 1893. London. Longman Gr. 126p. red cloth. F1. $95.00

**HARTZOG, H.S.** *Triumphs of Medicine.* 1927. Garden City. 1st. 317p. A13. $25.00

**HARVEY, A. McGehee.** *Research & Discovery in Medicine...Johns Hopkins.* 1981. Baltimore. 1st. 322p. dj. A13. $40.00

**HARVEY, Anne.** *Shades of Green.* 1992. NY. ils. 192p. F/dj. S15. $12.50

**HARVEY, Brian.** *Race Into Space: Soviet Space Programme.* 1988. Chichester, UK. Ellis Horwood. 4to. 381p. VG. K5. $35.00

**HARVEY, Byron III.** *Ritual in Pueblo Art: Hopi Life in Hopi Painting.* 1970. Mus of Am Indians. ils/biblio. 174p. NF/wrp. B19. $35.00

**HARVEY, Henry.** *History of the Shawnee Indians.* 1977. Millwood, NY. rpt of 1855. 316p. B18. $20.00

**HARVEY, John.** *Ghosts of Chance.* 1992. London. Smith/Doorstop. 1st. F/stiff wrp. M15. $65.00

**HARVEY, John.** *Lonely Hearts.* 1989. NY. Holt. 1st Am. sgn. author's 1st novel. F/dj. T2. $45.00

**HARVEY, John.** *Rough Treatment.* 1990. London. Viking. 1st. F/dj. M15. $75.00

**HARVEY, John.** *Rough Treatment.* 1990. NY. Holt. 1st Am. sgn. F/dj. T2. $30.00

**HARVEY, John.** *Victorian Novelists & Their Illustrators.* 1971. NY. University. 1st. photos. VG/dj. S13. $30.00

**HARVEY, Oscar J.** *History of Wilkes-Barre.* 1909. Wilkes-Barre. Raeder. 4 vol. ils. cloth. B18. $195.00

**HARVEY, Peggy.** *Great Recipes From the World's Greatest Cooks.* 1964. Gramercy. VG/dj. A16. $10.00

**HARVEY, Samuel.** *History of Hemostasis.* 1929. NY. 1st. 128p. A13. $50.00

**HARVEY, Stephen.** *Directed by Vincente Minnelli.* 1989. Harper Row. 315p. VG/wrp. C5. $15.00

**HARVEY, William.** *Circulation of the Blood & Other Writings. Translated...* 1977. London. 236p. xl. A13. $35.00

**HARVEY, William.** *De Motu Locali Animalium, 1627.* 1959. Cambridge. ltd. 4to. 163p. dj. A13. $100.00

**HARVEY, William.** *Movement of the Heart & Blood in Animals.* 1957. Springfield. ltd. trans KJ Franklin. 209p. A13. $60.00

**HARVEY & HUCKEL.** *American Indians: First Families of the Southwest.* 1920. Kansas City. 2nd. sm folio. w/mc sketch. G+. F7. $70.00

**HARWOOD, Lee.** *White Room.* 1968. London. Fulcrum. 1st. 1/100. sgn. F/acetate. L3. $65.00

**HASKELL, Daniel C.** *Tentative Check-List of Early European Railway Literature...* 1955. Boston. Harvard Graduate School of Business. M11. $75.00

**HASKELL, P.T.** *Insect Sounds.* 1961. Quadrangle. inscr/dtd 1962. F/dj. B14. $55.00

**HASKETT.** *Bibliography of American Immigration History.* 1978. rpt. 403p. F. A4. $60.00

**HASKINS, George Lee.** *Law & Authority in Early Massachusetts, a Study...* 1960. Macmillan. M11. $50.00

**HASLAM, John.** *Observations on Madness & Melancholy...* 1809. London. J Callow. enlarged. 345p. brd. VG. G7. $495.00

**HASS, Hans.** *Manta: Under the Red Sea With Spear & Camera.* 1953. Chicago. 1st. 278p. map ep. F/dj. A17. $15.00

**HASSALL, Arthur.** *Life of Napoleon.* 1911. Little Brn. 1st. 8vo. 321p. cloth. VG. W1. $25.00

**HASSALL, Joan.** *Wood Engravings of Joan Hassall.* 1960. London. OUP. 1st. 12mo. ils. gilt blk cloth. NF/VG. F1. $60.00

**HASSELBACH & REISS.** *Fuher-Ex: Memoirs of a Former Neo-Nazi.* 1996. NY. 1st. dj. T9. $10.00

**HASSETT, William D.** *Off the Record With FDR 1942-1945.* 1960. London. photos. VG/dj. M17. $15.00

**HASSLER, Jon.** *Staggerford.* 1977. Atheneum. 1st. F/NF. D10. $85.00

**HASSRICK, Peter H.** *Artists of the American Frontier: The Way West.* 1988. Promontory. new prt. ils. F. A19. $35.00

**HASSRICK, Peter H.** *Frederick Remington: Paintings, Drawings & Sculpture...* (1973). NY. Abrams. 218p. VG/dj. B18. $45.00

**HASSRICK, Royal B.** *Sioux: Life & Customs of a Warrior Society.* 1975. Norman, OK. VG/dj. A19. $25.00

**HASTINGS, George T.** *Trees of Santa Monica.* 1956. Santa Monica, CA. 1st. VG. O4. $25.00

**HASTINGS, Viscount.** *Golden Octopus. Legends of South Seas.* nd. Dutton. 1st Am. 1/1040. F/dj. A15. $75.00

**HATA & IZAWA.** *Japanese Naval Aces & Fighter Unites in WWII.* 1989. Annapolis. Naval Inst. 1st. 8vo. 442p. VG/dj. B11. $50.00

**HATCH, Elvin.** *Theories of Man & Culture.* 1973. NY/London. Columbia. 2nd. 8vo. 384p. P4. $25.00

**HATCH, P.L.** *Notes on the Birds of Minnesota.* 1892. Minneapolis. Geol/Nat Hist Survey of MN Report #1. 8vo. cloth. NF. C12. $90.00

HATCH, Robert McConniell. *Major John Andre: A Gallant in Spy's Clothing.* 1986. Houghton Mifflin. 1st. ils. VG/dj. M17. $25.00

HATCH & SLOANE. *Little Book of Bells.* 1964. NY 1st. ils. 85p. bl cloth. F/dj. H3. $75.00

HATCHER, J.B. *Bone Hunters in Patagonia.* 1985. Woodbridge. Oxbow. rpt. 8vo. brn cloth. AN. P4. $30.00

HATCHER, Julian S. *Book of the Garland.* 1948. Infantry Journal. 1st. sm 4to. 292p. VG. S14. $40.00

HATCHER, Julian S. *Hatcher's Notebook.* 1962. Stackpole. expanded ed. VG/dj. A19. $35.00

HATOUM, Milton. *Tree of the South Heaven.* 1994. NY. Atheneum. 1st Eng-language. trans Ellen Watson. F/dj. A23. $30.00

HATTERAS, Owen; see Mencken, H.L.

HATTON, Richard G. *Handbook of Plant & Floral Ornament.* 1960. NY. ils. 539p. sc. B26. $15.00

HAUCK, Louise Platt. *Little Doctor.* 1936. NY. Penn. 305p. bl cloth. VG. B36. $10.00

HAUGHTON, Percy D. *How to Watch & Understand Football.* 1922. Boston. Marshall Jones. ils. 48p. VG/wrp. B14. $20.00

HAUGLAND, Vern. *Eagle Squadrons: Yanks in RAF 1940-42.* 1979. NY. 1st. photos. VG/dj. M17. $22.50

HAUROWITZ, Felix. *Progress in Biochemistry.* 1950. S Karger. 393p. xl. G. S5. $20.00

HAURY, Emil W. *Kivas of the Tusayan Ruin.* 1931. Globe, AZ. 8vo. ils. 26p. wrp. F7. $65.00

HAUSHALTER, William M. *Mrs Eddy Purloins From Hegel.* 1936. Boston. Beachamp. 126p+16p ms facs. bl cloth. xl. K1. $75.00

HAUSWALD, Carol. *Letters From the Tribe (1967-1977).* 1979. Lombard, IL. Stone Circle. 1st. sgn. F/dj. B2. $25.00

HAUTMAN, Pete. *Drawing Dead.* 1993. S&S. 1st. F/dj. A23. $60.00

HAUTMAN, Pete. *Drawing Dead.* 1993. S&S. 1st. sgn. F/dj. R14. $75.00

HAUTMAN, Pete. *Moral Nuts.* 1996. S&S. 1st. sgn. F/dj. A23. $42.00

HAVEILL, Adrian. *Last Mogul.* 1992. NY. St Martin. 1st. 8vo. 302p. half cloth. P4. $30.00

HAVEL, Vaclav. *Open Letters, Selected Writings.* 1991. NY. 1st. edit P Wilson. dj. T9. $15.00

HAVIARAS, Stratis. *Heroic Age.* 1984. S&S. 1st. 352p. brn cloth. rem mk. NF/clip. J3. $50.00

HAVIARAS, Stratis. *When the Tree Sings.* 1979. S&S. 1st. inscr/dtd 1979. F/NF. L3. $75.00

HAVILAND, Virginia. *William Penn: Founder & Friend.* 1952. NY. Abingdon. 128p. VG. V3. $9.00

HAWES, Charles Boardman. *Dark Frigate.* (1971). Little Brn. 8th. 8vo. yel cloth/blk spine. VG. T5. $20.00

HAWES, Elizabeth. *Fashion Is Spinach.* 1938. Random. 3rd. 337p. decor ep. VG+. A25. $30.00

HAWES, Lloyd. *Dedham Pottery & Earlier Robertson's Chelsea Potteries...* 1968. Dedham Hist Soc. ils. 52p. linen cloth. NF. B14. $145.00

HAWGOOD, John A. *America's Western Frontiers: Story of Explorers...* 1967. Knopf. ils/photos. 440p. VG. J2. $35.00

HAWKE, David. *Transaction of Free Men: Birth & Course of Declaration...* (1980). NY. Da Capo. 282p. VG. M10. $12.50

HAWKEN, Paul. *Ecology of Commerce: A Declaration of Sustainability.* 1993. Harper Collins. 250p. NF/dj. S15. $10.00

HAWKES, Alex D. *Orchids: Their Botany & Culture.* 1961. Harper Row. 1st. 297p. VG/G. H10. $30.00

HAWKES, Alex D. *World of Vegetable Cookery.* 1984. S&S. G. A16. $6.00

HAWKES, John. *Adventures in the Alaskan Skin Trade.* 1985. NY. S&S. 1st. rem mk. VG/dj. P4. $25.00

HAWKES, John. *Cannibal.* 1949. New Directions. 1st. sgn. author's 1st book. 223p. NF/dj. B20. $275.00

HAWKES, John. *Sweet William.* 1993. S&S. 1st. sgn. F/dj. R14. $50.00

HAWKES, John. *Travesty.* 1976. Chatto Windus. 1st Eng. sgn. NF/VG. R14. $45.00

HAWKES, John. *Whistlejacket.* 1988. NY. 1st. VG/dj. M17. $17.50

HAWKES, John. *Whistlejacket.* 1989. London. Secker Warburg. 1st. VG/G. O3. $25.00

HAWKESWORTH, John. *Adventurer.* 1788. Dublin. J Moore. 4 vols. new/corrected. tall 12mo. tree calf. H13. $325.00

HAWKINS, Arthur. *Cook It Quick.* 1971. NY. Avenel. G/dj. A16. $10.00

HAWKINS, Hanson. *Flyways: Pioneering Waterfowl Management in North America.* 1984. WA. USDI. ils/maps. 517p. F. A17. $20.00

HAWKINS, John. *Life of Samuel Johnson.* 1787. Dublin. Chamberlain. 1st Dublin. tall 8vo. 533p. uncut/rb 3-quarter leather. H13. $395.00

HAWKINS, Richard. *Observations of Sir Richard Hawkins.* 1933. London. 1/475. ils/maps. half vellum/bl cloth. P4. $250.00

HAWKINS & ZIMRING. *Pursuit of Criminal Justice...* 1984. Chicago. M11. $45.00

HAWLEY, Ellis W. *Herbert Hoover As Secretary of Commerce: Studies...* 1981. Iowa City. 1st. 8vo. 263p. VG/dj. V3. $20.00

HAWLEY, Mabel C. *Four Little Blossoms at Brookside Farm.* (1920). Cupples Leon. later prt. ils red cloth. VG. B36. $8.00

HAWLEY, Walter. *Oriental Rugs, Antique & Modern.* 1933. NY/London/Toronto. Lane/Lane/Bell Cockburn. 1st. ils/maps. teg. cloth. W1. $45.00

HAWS, Duncan. *Ships & the Sea: A Chronological Review.* 1985. London. Chancellor. rpt. 4to. NF/VG. P4. $20.00

HAWTHORN, Audrey. *Kwakiutl Art.* 1994. Seattle/Vancouver. 4to. 272p. NF. P4. $55.00

HAWTHORNE, Hildegarde. *Life of Thomas Paine.* 1949. Longmans. 1st. VG/dj. W2. $15.00

HAWTHORNE, Hildegarde. *Old Seaport Towns of New England.* 1916. Dodd Mead. 1st. 8v9. 312p. G. B11. $15.00

HAWTHORNE, Nathaniel. *Complete Works...* 1892. Boston. 13 vol. half brn leather/marbled brd. F. B30. $425.00

HAWTHORNE, Nathaniel. *Life of Franklin Pierce.* 1852. Ticknor Reed Fields. 1st. rb w/orig spine. Q1. $175.00

HAWTHORNE, Nathaniel. *Mosses From an Old Manse.* 1846. NY. Wiley Putnam. 2 vol in 1 (as issued). 1st. blk cloth. F. M24. $850.00

HAWTHORNE, Nathaniel. *Scarlet Letter.* nd (1926). Grosset Dunlap. MTI. F/VG. B4. $125.00

HAWTHORNE, Nathaniel. *Tanglewood Tales.* 1913. Rand McNally. Windemere ed. ils Milo Winter. 283p. gr cloth. VG. M7. $30.00

HAWTHORNE, Nathaniel. *Tanglewood Tales.* 1918. Hodder Stoughton. 1st trade. 4to. 244p. aeg. F/case. H5. $600.00

HAWTHORNE, Nathaniel. *Tanglewood Tales.* 1921. Phil. Penn Pub. 1st thus. ils V Sterrett. 261p. bl cloth/pict label. VG. D1. $285.00

HAWTHORNE, Nathaniel. *Wonder Book for Girls & Boys.* 1910 (1892). Houghton Mifflin. rpt. ils Walter Crane. 210p. VG+. B20. $100.00

HAWTHORNE, Nathaniel. *Wonder Book of Tanglewood Tales for Girls & Boys.* 1913. Duffield. ils Parrish. 4to. 358p. teg. Sangorski bdg. NF. H5. $350.00

**HAWTHORNE, Nathaniel.** *Wonder Book.* (1922). Doubleday Doran. 8vo. 206p. maroon cloth. T5. $70.00

**HAY, Elizabeth.** *Sambo Sahib: Story of Helen Bannerman.* 1981. Edinburgh. Paul Harris. 1st Eng. 194p. gilt red cloth. VG/dj. D1. $75.00

**HAY, John.** *Pike County Ballads.* 1871. Boston. Osgood. xl. fair. V4. $100.00

**HAY, William Howard.** *New Health Era.* 1934. NY. Hay System. 1st/5th prt. cloth. VG. M8. $45.00

**HAYASHI, Takashi.** *Olfaction & Taste II.* 1967. Oxford. Pergamon. heavy 8vo. 835p. VG/tattered. G1. $85.00

**HAYCOCK, Ernest.** *Long Storm.* 1946. Little Brn. VG. L4. $8.00

**HAYCOX, Ernest.** *Rough Air.* 1934. Doubleday Doran. 1st. F/F. B4. $400.00

**HAYDEN, A. Eustace.** *Biography of the Gods.* 1941. macmillan. 1st. 8vo. F/VG. A2. $25.00

**HAYDEN, Dorothea Hoaglin.** *These Pioneers.* 1938. LA. self pub. 1st. VG/sans. O4. $20.00

**HAYDEN, Tom.** *Love of Possession Is a Disease With Them.* 1972. HRW. 1st. 134p. VG/clip. R11. $15.00

**HAYDEN & WAKE.** *Bonnie & Clyde Book.* 1972. S&S. 1st. VG/dj. C9. $60.00

**HAYE, M. Horace.** *Veterinary Notes for Horse Owners...* 1987. S&S. 17th/revised. ils/index. 740p. F/dj. H10. $27.50

**HAYES, Benjamin.** *Pioneer Notes From Diaries of Judge Benjamin Hayes...* 1929. LA. private prt. 307p. gilt cloth. D11. $150.00

**HAYES, Billy.** *Midnight Express.* 1977. Dutton. 1st. F/NF. M23. $20.00

**HAYES, Florence.** *Arctic Gateway.* 1940. NY. Friendship. dbl-p map/phtos. P4. $20.00

**HAYES, Gordon.** *Antarctica, a Treatise on Southern Continent.* 1928. London. Richards. 1st. lg 8vo. 448p. bl cloth. F. O1. $20.00

**HAYES, Harold T.P.** *Dark Romance of Diane Fossey.* 1990. S&S. 1st. F/dj. T11. $25.00

**HAYES, Helen.** *On Reflection: An Autobiography.* 1968. Evans. 1st. sgn. VG/dj. B30. $45.00

**HAYES, Isaac I.** *Arctic Boat Journey.* 1860. Boston. Brn Taggard Chase. 1st. lacks 1 map. rb. P4. $45.00

**HAYES, Isaac I.** *Open Polar Sea: Narrative of Voyage of Discovery...* 1867. NY. ils/maps. 454p. new cloth. M4. $65.00

**HAYES, John E.R.** *Invention: Its Attributes & Definition.* 1942. Cambridge. Addison-Wesley. M11. $75.00

**HAYES, Joseph.** *Ways of Darkness.* 1986. Morrow. 1st. F/dj. A23. $35.00

**HAYES, M. Horace.** *Stable Management & Excercise.* 1974. NY. Arco. VG/dj. O3. $18.00

**HAYES, Rutherford B.** *Diary of a President.* 1964. David McKay. 1st. 8vo. 329p. F/VG. H1. $40.00

**HAYES, William.** *Genetics of Bacteria & Their Viruses.* 1965. Wiley. 740p. xl. S5. $15.00

**HAYES & GARRISON.** *Key to Important Woody Plants of East Oregon & Washington.* 1960. WA, DC. ils. 227p. maroon cloth. F. B26. $24.00

**HAYGOOD, Atticus G.** *New South: Gratitude, Amendement, Hope...* 1880. Oxford. 16p. G. B10. $75.00

**HAYGOOD, T.M.** *Henry William Ravenel 1814-1887.* 1987. AL U. 204p. F/dj. M4. $25.00

**HAYLEY, William.** *Philosophical, Historical & Moral Essay on Old Maids.* 1785. London. 3 vol. 1st. tall 8vo. 3-quarter calf/marbled brd. H13. $495.00

**HAYMAN, Ronald.** *Proust: A Biography.* 1990. NY. 1st. dj. T9. $25.00

**HAYNES, David.** *Live at Five.* 1996. Minneapolis. Milkweed. 1st. F/dj. O11. $30.00

**HAYNES, David.** *Right by My Side.* 1993. Minneapolis. New Rivers. 1st. 1/2500. author's 1st book. NF. O11. $35.00

**HAYNES, David.** *Somebody Else's Mama.* 1995. Milkweed. 1st. sgn. author's 2nd book. F/dj. A24. $60.00

**HAYNES, Roy.** *Hungarian Game.* 1973. S&S. 1st. author's 1st book. H11. $20.00

**HAYNES, Sybille.** *Land of the Chimaera: Archeological Excursion in SW Turkey.* 1974. Chatto Windus. ils. 159p. cloth. VG/dj. Q2. $30.00

**HAYS, Denys.** *Age of the Renaissance.* 1968. McGraw Hill. VG/dj. M20. $45.00

**HAYS, Helen Ashe.** *Little Maryland Garden.* 1909. NY. ils. 201p. NF. B26. $37.50

**HAYS, P.** *Electricity & Methods of Employment in Removing...* 1889. 1st. ils. xl. VG. E6. $85.00

**HAYTER, Sparkle.** *Nice Girls Finish Last.* 1996. Viking. 1st. sgn. F/dj. R14. $45.00

**HAYTHORNTHWAITE, Philip.** *Uniforms of the Civil War.* 1990. Sterling Pub. 1st Am. F/wrp. A14. $14.00

**HAYWARD, A.** *Vital Magnetic Cure & Exposition of Vital Magnetism...* 1873 (1871). VG. E6. $65.00

**HAYWARD & THOMSON.** *Journal of William Tully: Medical Student at Dartmouth...* 1977. Science Hist Pub. 1st. 88p. VG. M10. $20.00

**HAYWARD & WALSH.** *Walt Disney's the Shaggy Dog.* 1959. Golden. 1st. Little Golden Book #D82. VG. R8. $12.00

**HAYWOOD, A.** *Autobiography, Letters & Literary Remains.* 1861. London. Longman. 2 vol. 1st/revised. 8vo. VG. H13. $295.00

**HAYWOOD, Carolyn.** *Halloween Treats.* 1981. Morrow. 1st. 8vo. 175p. orange brd. NF/VG. T5. $25.00

**HAYWOOD, Gar Anthony.** *Not Long for This World.* 1990. St Martin. 1st. F/NF. M23. $40.00

**HAZAN, Marcella.** *Marcella's Italian Kitchen.* 1986. Knopf. BC. photos. NF/dj. P12. $20.00

**HAZARD, Caroline.** *Nailer Tom's Diary: The Journal of Thomas B Hazard.* 1930. Boxton, MA. Merrymount. 1/400. VG. A19. $200.00

**HAZARD, Caroline.** *Thomas Hazard, Son of Robert Called College Tom...* 1893. Houghton Mifflin. 1st. G+. V3. $40.00

**HAZARD, Rowland G.** *Language: Its Connection With Present Condition & Future.* 1836. Providence, RI. Marshall Brn. 12mo. 153p. G1. $125.00

**HAZELGROVE, William Elliot.** *Tobacco Sticks.* 1995. Chicago. Pantonne. 1st. sgn. NF/dj. M23. $30.00

**HAZELTON, Joseph Powers.** *Scouts, Spies & Heros of the Great Civil War.* 1892. NJ. Star Pub. lg 8vo. ils. 512p. rb gray cloth/blk label. VG. S17. $27.50

**HAZEN, A.T.** *Catalogue of Horace Walpole's Literature.* Yale. 3 vol. 4to. ils. F/F. A4. $95.00

**HAZEN, Barbara Shook.** *It Isn't Fair!: A Book About Sibling Rivalry.* 1986. Golden Book. 1st. ils Carolyn Bracken. unp. NF. C14. $8.00

**HAZEN, Robert M.** *Breakthrough: Race for the Superconductor.* 1988. NY. Summit. 1st. 8vo. ils. 271p. half cloth. F/dj. P4. $20.00

**HAZEN, William E.** *Readings in Population & Community Ecology.* 1964. Saunders. 338p. xl. S5. $15.00

**HAZEN & TREFIL.** *Science Matters: Achieving Scientific Literacy.* 1991. Doubleday. 294p. F/VG. S15. $10.00

**HAZLETON, Lesley.** *Where Mountains Roar: Personal Report From Sinai...* 1980. HRW. 222p. VG/dj. B29. $9.00

**HEACOX, Cecil E.** *Complete Brown Trout.* 1974. Winchester. 1st. ils. F/dj. T11. $55.00

**HEAD, Henry.** *Aphasia & Kindred Disorders of Speech.* 1926. Cambridge. 2 vol. 4to. xl. bl lib buckram. G1. $125.00

**HEAD, Henry.** *Aphasia & Kindred Disorders of Speech.* 1926. Cambridge. 2 vol. 4to. gr cloth. VG. G7. $395.00

**HEAD, Henry.** *Studies in Neurology.* 1920. London/Oxford. Frowde/Hodder Stoughton. 2 vol. heavy 4to. xl. G1. $300.00

**HEAD, Henry.** *Studies in Neurology.* 1920. OUP. 2 vol. 4to. cloth. VG. G7. $350.00

**HEAD, Michael G.** *Foot Regiments of the Imperial Guard.* 1973. Almark. 1st. 124p. VG/stiff wrp. S16. $35.00

**HEAD, Michael G.** *French Napoleonic Artillery.* 1970. London. Almark. 1st. 72p. ils. VG/stiff wrp. S16. $25.00

**HEAD, Michael G.** *French Napoleonic Lancer Regiments.* 1971. Almark. 1st. 72p. VG/stiff wrp. S16. $35.00

**HEADINGTON, Christopher.** *Sweet Sleep: A Collection of Lullabies, Poems...* 1989. Potter. 1st. obl 8vo. ils. VG/dj. B17. $12.50

**HEADLAND, Helen.** *Swedish Nightingale: Biography of Jenny Lind.* 1940. Rock Island, IL. ils. VG. w/sgn note. M17. $20.00

**HEADLEY, Victor.** *Yardie.* 1992. NY. Atlantic. 1st. F/F. H11. $25.00

**HEADSPETH, William C.** *Masterful Maneuver: Retreat to Dan, Important Link...* (1976). S Boston, VA. 1st. ils. 40p. NF. M8. $85.00

**HEADSTROM, Richard.** *Nature in Miniature.* 1968. Knopf. 412p. VG. P12. $8.00

**HEADSTROM, Richard.** *Nature in Miniature.* 1968. NY. 412p. VG/dj. A17. $15.00

**HEAGNEY, H.J.** *Behold This Heart: Story of St Margaret Mary Alacoque.* 1947. NY. Kenedy. 1st. 347p. xl. G. H10. $15.00

**HEAL, Edith.** *Robin Hood.* 1928. Rand McNally. 1st thus. ils Dan Content. VG. M5. $55.00

**HEALD, Edward Thornton.** *History of Stark County, a Digest...* 1963. Canton. 1st. ils. 183p. wrp. B18. $20.00

**HEALD, Tim.** *Brought to Book.* 1988. NY. DDCC. 1st. F/NF. H11. $25.00

**HEALEY, B.J.** *Plant Hunters.* 1975. NY. ils/photos. F/dj. B26. $30.00

**HEALEY, Pepper Mainwaring.** *You & Your Pony.* 1977. S Brunswick. Barnes. 1st. 4to. VG/G. O3. $35.00

**HEALY, Jeremiah.** *Staked Goat.* 1986. Harper Row. 1st. F/F. H11/R11. $30.00

**HEALY, William.** *Reconstructing Behavior in Youth: A Study...* 1929. Knopf. ARC. 325p. prt bl cloth. RS. G1. $35.00

**HEANEY, Howell J.** *Thirty Years of Bird & Bull, a Bibliography 1958-88.* 1988. Newtown. Bird & Bull. 1/300. complete suite/samples. AN/portfolio/box. B24. $400.00

**HEANEY, Seamus.** *Door Into Dark.* 1969. Oxford. 1st. F/F. B2. $200.00

**HEANEY, Seamus.** *From the Republic of Conscience.* 1985. Dublin. Amnesty Internat. 1/2000. ils John Behan. F/wrp. r14. $75.00

**HEANEY, Seamus.** *Government of the Tongue: Selected Prose 1978-1987.* 1989. FSG. 1st Am. F/dj. O11. $30.00

**HEANEY, Seamus.** *Place & Displacement.* 1984. np. 1st. F/stapled wrp/dj. L3. $65.00

**HEANEY, Seamus.** *Selected Poems 1966-1987.* 1990. FSG. 1st. F/dj. O11. $35.00

**HEAPS, Willard A.** *Riots USA 1765-1970.* 1970 (1966). Seabury. revised. xl. G/VG. A2. $10.00

**HEARD, H.F.** *Taste of Honey.* 1941. NY. Vanguard. 1st. F/VG. M15. $150.00

**HEARN, C.G.** *Capture of New Orleans 1862.* 1995. LSU. 1st. 292p. F/dj. M4. $25.00

**HEARN, Lafcadio.** *Chita: Memory of Last Island.* 1889. NY. Harper. 1st. gilt tan decor cloth. F. M24. $275.00

**HEARN, Lafcadio.** *Tales of the East.* 1952. Rodale. 1st thus. NF/VG case. S13. $20.00

**HEARNE, R.P.** *Luftkrieg.* 1909. Berlin. Hofbuchhandlung. 1st. 8vo. German text. 255p+1p ad. B11. $450.00

**HEARNE, Samuel.** *Journey From Prince of Wales' Fort in Hudson Bay...* 1968. Amsterdam/NY. facs. 8 pl/maps. 458p. AN. P4. $125.00

**HEARNE, Vicki.** *White German Shepherd.* 1988. Atlantic Monthly. 1st. NF/F. R14. $25.00

**HEAT-MOON, William Least.** *Blue Highways.* 1982. Atlantic/Little Brn. 1st. NF/VG. H11. $55.00

**HEATH, Royton E.** *Collectors' Alpines.* 1964. London. 1st. photos. 527p. VG/dj. B26. $52.50

**HEATH-STUBBS, John.** *Watchman's Flute.* 1978. Manchester. 1st. sgn. wrp. T9. $20.00

**HEATTER, Maida.** *Maida Heatter's Book of Great Cookies.* 1977. Knopf. 1st. 277p. VG/dj. P12. $15.00

**HEBERDEN, William.** *Commentaries on History & Cure of Diseases.* 1982. Birmingham. facs of 1802 London. 483p. full leather. A13. $50.00

**HECHT, Ben.** *Erik Dorn.* 1921. Putnam. 1st. inscr. G-. B2. $50.00

**HECHT, Robert A.** *Oliver LaFarge & the American Indian: A Biography.* 1991. Scarecrow. 1st. ils/notes/index. 370p. F/sans. B19. $25.00

**HECKER, W.R.** *Auriculas & Primroses.* 1971. Branford. 216p. AN/dj. A10. $15.00

**HECKSCHER, August.** *Public Happiness.* 1962. Atheneum. 1st. VG. N2. $10.00

**HECKSCHER & ROBINSON.** *When LaGuardia Was Mayor: New York's Legendary Years.* 1978. Norton. 1st. VG/clip. N2. $10.00

**HEDGE, Levi.** *Elements of Logick; or, Summary of General Principles...* 1827. Boston. Hillard Gray. 1st. VG. V4. $100.00

**HEDGES, Peter.** *What's Eating Gilbert Grape.* 1991. Poseidon. 1st. F/dj. C9. $30.00

**HEDGPETH, Joel.** *Treatise on Marine Ecology & Paleoecology, Vol I.* 1957. Geol Soc of Am. Memoir 67. 1296p. maroon cloth. xl. VG. S15. $35.00

**HEDGPETH & REED.** *Art of Tom Lovell: Invitation to History.* 1993. Greenwich. ils. F. J2. $75.00

**HEDIN & HOLTHAUS.** *Great Land: Reflections on Alaska.* 1994. Tucson/London. U AZ. 1st. map. 317p. AN/dj. P4. $38.00

**HEFLEY & HEFLEY.** *No Time for Tombstones: Life & Death in Vietnamese Jungle.* 1974. Harrisburg. Christian Pub. 1st. F/NF. R11. $25.00

**HEGELER & HEGELER.** *ABZ of Love.* 1963. NY. Medical Pr. facs. ils. VG/dj. B11. $15.00

**HEGEMANN, Elizabeth Compton.** *Navaho Trading Days.* 1966. U NM. photos. 388p. gray cloth. dj. F7. $85.00

**HEGI, Ursula.** *Floating in My Mother's Palm.* 1990. Poseidon. 1st. NF/F. H11. $50.00

**HEGI, Ursula.** *Salt Dancers.* 1995. S&S. 1st. F/dj. M23. $20.00

**HEGNER, Robert.** *Big Fleas Have Little Fleas; or, Who's Who Among Protozoa.* 1938. Baltimore. Williams Wilkins. 1st. 4to. 285p. VG+/dj. B20. $50.00

**HEIDEL, William.** *Hippocratic Medicine, Its Spirit & Method.* 1941. NY. 1st. 149p. A13. $50.00

**HEILNER, Van Campen.** *Our American Game Birds.* 1941. NY. ils Lynn Bogue Hunt. 178p. red cloth. VG. H3. $60.00

**HEIM, Scott.** *Mysterious Skin.* 1995. Harper Collins. ARC/1st. F/dj. w/photo. C9. $42.00

**HEIN, Hilde.** *Exploratorium: Museum As Laboratory.* 1990. Smithsonian. 1st. VG/dj. N2. $7.50

**HEINEMANN, Larry.** *Paco's Story.* 1987. London. Faber. UP. F/wrp/trade dj. R14. $35.00

**HEINEMANN, Larry.** *Paco's Story.* 1987. London. Faber. 1st. F/F. B3. $30.00

**HEINIGER, H.A.** *Grand Canyon.* 1975 (1971). WA, DC. Luce. 1st Am. photos. VG/dj. A2. $30.00

**HEINIGER & HEINIGER.** *Great Book of Jewels.* 1974. NYGS. 1st Am. lg folio. ils. 316p. F. B20. $85.00

**HEINLEIN, Robert A.** *Job: A Comedy of Justice.* 1984. Ballantine. 1st. 376p. F/dj. M21. $25.00

**HEINLEIN, Robert A.** *Revolt in 2100.* 1953. Shasta. 1st. F/NF. P3. $500.00

**HEINLEIN, Robert A.** *Stranger in a Strange Land.* nd. BC. 1961 Hugo Award. VG/dj. P3. $15.00

**HEINLEIN, Robert A.** *Stranger in a Strange Land.* 1991. Ace Putnam. 1st. F/dj. P3. $30.00

**HEINLEIN, Robert A.** *Time for the Stars.* 1956. Scribner. 1st. 244p. F/NF. B20. $200.00

**HEINS, Henry Hardy.** *Golden Anniversary Bibliography of Edgar Rice Burroughs.* 1964. Donald Grant. 1/1000. 418p. F/worn. A4. $450.00

**HEINTZ, Caroline Lee.** *Aunt Patty's Scrap Bag.* 1872. Peterson. ils Darley. 322p. VG. P12. $30.00

**HEINTZ, William F.** *San Francisco's Mayors: 1850-1880.* 1974. Woodside. Gilbert Richrds. 1st. 4to. yel cloth. VG/dj. P4. $25.00

**HEISENBERG, W.** *Nuclear Physics.* 1953. NY. Philosophical Lib. 8vo. 224p. VG/dj. K5. $25.00

**HEISKELL, Charles.** *100 Books on Hollywood & the Movies.* 1993. LA. Book Collectors. 1/500. patterned wrp w/flaps. D11. $40.00

**HEITMAN, F.B.** *Historical Register of the United States Army...* 1890. Nat Tribune. sm 4to. 890p. full leather. G. H1. $65.00

**HEIZER, Robert F.** *Destruction of California Indians.* 1974. Peregrine Smith. 8vo. 321p. VG/dj. P4. $48.00

**HEIZER, Robert F.** *Languages, Territories & Names of California Indian Tribes.* 1966. LA/Berkeley. U CA. 5 maps. NF/dj. P4. $65.00

**HEIZER, Robert F.** *Sources of Stones Used in Prehistoric Mesoamerican Sites.* 1976. Ramona. Ballena. rpt. 103p. wrp. F3. $20.00

**HEKKIG, Johanna M.** *Pigtails.* 1937. NY. Stokes. 1st. ils Molly Castle. VG/dj. D1. $60.00

**HELBERT, Clifford L.** *Ecce Littera. Volume I.* 1987. Milwaukee. mini. ltd. 30p+fld dbl-sided panorama. gr brd. B24. $85.00

**HELD, Peter;** see Vance, Jack.

**HELENIAK & HEWITT.** *Confederate High Command & Related Topics...* 1990. Wht Mane Pub. 1st. NF/dj. A14. $21.00

**HELL, Richard.** *Go Now.* 1996. NY. Scribner. 1st. sgn. author's 1st novel. F/dj. O11. $30.00

**HELLE, Andre.** *French Toys.* 1915. Paris. L'Avenir Feminin. 8vo. stiff paper wrp/pict dj. R5. $200.00

**HELLEBRAND, Nancy.** *Londoners: Photographs.* 1974. London. Humphries. 1st. 48p. NF. B20. $35.00

**HELLENGA, Robert.** *Sixteen Pleasures.* 1994. NY. Soho. 1st. 8vo. 327p. AN/dj. P4. $25.00

**HELLENTHAL, J.A.** *Alaskan Melodrama.* 1936. Liveright. 1st. photos/maps. 312p. G. S14. $20.00

**HELLER, H.L.** *Sourdough Sagas: Journals, Memoirs, Tales & Recollections...* 1967. Cleveland. 1st. photos. F/dj. M4. $28.00

**HELLER, John.** *Of Mice, Men & Molecules.* 1960. NY. 1st. 176p. A13. $25.00

**HELLER, Joseph.** *Catch-22.* 1961. Taiwan. piracy. 8vo. gr cloth/brd. F/NF. S9. $125.00

**HELLER, Joseph.** *Catch-22.* 1994. S&S. Commemorative. 1/750. sgn/#d. F/case/swrp. R14. $150.00

**HELLER, Joseph.** *Closing Time.* 1994. NY. 1/750. sgn. case. T9. $60.00

**HELLER, Joseph.** *Closing Time.* 1994. S&S. 1st. sgn. F/dj. R14. $40.00

**HELLER, Joseph.** *Good As Gold.* 1979. S&S. 1st. sgn. VG/dj. B30. $50.00

**HELLER, Joseph.** *Now & Then.* 1988. NY. Knopf. 1st. sgn. F/dj. R14. $45.00

**HELLER, Joseph.** *Picture This.* 1988. Putnam. 1st. F/dj. T12. $25.00

**HELLER, Joseph.** *Something Happened.* 1974. Knopf. 1st. sgn. VG/dj. B30. $50.00

**HELLER, Mark A.** *Palestinian State: Implications for Israel.* 1983. Harvard. 1st. 11 full-p maps. 190p. VG/dj. W1. $18.00

**HELLER, Michael.** *Accidental Center.* 1972. Fremont. Sumac. 1st. 1/100. sgn/inscr to poet Cid Corman. VG/NF. L3. $85.00

**HELLER, Morris.** *American Hunting & Fishing Books...Bibliography 1800-1970.* 1997. ils. 216p. F/F. A4. $75.00

**HELLER, Reinhold.** *Hildegard Auer, a Yearning for Art.* 1987. Millwood, NY. Assoc Faculty Pr. 214p. linen cloth. F1. $45.00

**HELLER & SCOTT.** *Alaska Dietary Survey, 1956-1961.* nd. Anchorage. US Dept Health Edu Welfare. 281p. wrp. P4. $28.00

**HELLMAN, Ethel L.** *Blizzards of South Dakota.* 1970. Millboro, SD. self pub. G. A19. $30.00

**HELLMAN, Lillian.** *Scoundrel Time.* 1976. Little Brn. 1st/ltd. tall 8vo. 155p. gr-beige cloth. NF. J3. $150.00

**HELLMAN, Lillian.** *Watch on the Rhine.* 1941. NY. World. 170p. VG. C5. $12.50

**HELLYER, A.G.** *English Gardens Open to the Public.* 1956. London. Country Life. 4to. 160p. VG/dj. A10. $28.00

**HELMAN, Isidore Stanislas H.** *Faits Memorables des Empereurs de la Chine...* (1788). Paris. Chez l'Auteur. 4to. 24 copper pl/24 leaves. rose paper brd. uncut. K1. $1,000.00

**HELMER, William.** *Gun That Made the Twenties Roar.* 1969. Macmillan. 1st. ils/index. 286p. VG/dj. B5. $35.00

**HELMERICKS, Bud.** *Arctic Bush Pilot.* 1956. Boston. Little Brn. 180p. red cloth. P4. $22.00

**HELMERICKS, Constance.** *Australian Adventure.* 1971. Prentice Hall. 357p. NF/F. W2. $30.00

**HELMES, Anthony Zachariah.** *Travels From Buenos Ayres, by Potosi, to Lima...* 1807 (1806). London. Richard Phillips. 2nd Eng trans. 8vo. half leather/marbled brd. NF. P4. $250.00

**HELMS, Mary.** *Middle America: Culture...* 1975. Prentice Hall. 1st. 367p. dj. F3. $30.00

**HELMS, Randel.** *Tolkien's World.* 1974. Houghton Mifflin. 1st. VG/dj. P3. $25.00

**HELPRIN, Mark.** *Dove of the East.* 1975. NY. Knopf. 1st. author's 1st book. F/NF. B2. $50.00

**HELPRIN, Mark.** *Swan Lake.* 1989. Boston. Ariel. 1st. ils Chris Van Allsburg. F/dj. R14. $40.00

**HELPRIN, Mark.** *Winter's Tale.* 1983. HBJ. 1st. F/dj. M23. $50.00

**HELPRIN, Mark.** *Winter's Tale.* 1983. HBJ. 1st. NF/NF. R14. $45.00

**HELVETIUS, Claude Adrien.** *De L'Esprit.* 1776 (1758). Amsterdam/Leipsick. 2 vol. later ed. 12mo. contemporary calf. G1. $185.00

**HELVETIUS, Claude Adrien.** *De L'Esprit; or, Essays on the Mind...* 1759. London. Prt for Trans. 1st Eng-language. 4to. 331p. G. G1. $875.00

**HELWEG-LARSEN, Kjeld.** *Columbus Never Came.* 1964. London. Jarrolds. 2nd. inscr. 240p. dj. F3. $20.00

**HEMANS, Felicia.** *Breaking Waves Dashed High.* 1879. Lee Shepard. ils LB Humphrey. VG. P12. $60.00

**HEMINGWAY, Ernest.** *Across the River & Into the Trees.* 1950. NY. 1st. VG. M17. $40.00

**HEMINGWAY, Ernest.** *Across the River & Into the Trees.* 1950. Scribner. 1st state (yel letters on dj spine). NF/VG clip. A24. $250.00

**HEMINGWAY, Ernest.** *Complete Short Stories of... The Finca Vigia Edition.* 1987. Scribner. F/F. D10. $50.00

**HEMINGWAY, Ernest.** *Farewell to Arms.* 1929. London. Cape. 1st. VG. B5. $125.00

**HEMINGWAY, Ernest.** *For Whom the Bell Tolls.* 1940. Scribner. 1st. thick 8vo. 471p. NF/VG+ 1st issue. B20. $375.00

**HEMINGWAY, Ernest.** *Garden of Eden.* 1986. Scribner. 1st. F/dj. R14. $50.00

**HEMINGWAY, Ernest.** *God Rest You Merry Gentlemen.* 1933. NY. House of Books. 1st. 1/300. NF. Q1. $1,250.00

**HEMINGWAY, Ernest.** *In Our Time.* 1930. Scribner. 1st thus. author's 2nd book. blk cloth/gold labels. NF. M24. $100.00

**HEMINGWAY, Ernest.** *Men Without Women.* 1927. Scribner. 1st state. blk cloth/gold labels. VG+. S13. $125.00

**HEMINGWAY, Ernest.** *Men Without Women.* 1955. London. VG/G. M17. $25.00

**HEMINGWAY, Ernest.** *Old Man & the Sea.* 1952. Hamburg. Rowohlt. 1st German. VG/dj. B5. $125.00

**HEMINGWAY, Ernest.** *Old Man & the Sea.* 1954 (1952). NY. Scribner. VG/F. T12. $40.00

**HEMINGWAY, Ernest.** *Sun Also Rises.* 1926. Scribner. 1st/1st prt/1st issue. blk cloth/gold labels. M24. $500.00

**HEMINGWAY, Ernest.** *Torrents of Spring.* 1926. Scribner. 1st. F/dj. B24. $4,500.00

**HEMINGWAY, Ernest.** *Torrents of Spring.* 1932. Paris. Crosby Continental. rpt. English text. VG/wrp. B2. $150.00

**HEMMING, John.** *Search for El Dorado.* 1978. London. Michael Joseph. 1st. 4to. 223p. F3. $25.00

**HEMMINGER, Jane M.** *Recipes of Madison County.* 1995. Oxmoor. 1st. F/dj. W2. $35.00

**HEMPEL, J.** *Homeopathic Domestic Physician.* 1846. 1st. 24mo. 180p. G+. E6. $30.00

**HEMPHILL, Paul.** *Long Gone.* 1979. Viking. 1st. inscr. VG/dj. P8. $50.00

**HEMPSTONE, Smith.** *Tract of Time.* 1966. Houghton Mifflin. 3rd. VG/dj. R11. $15.00

**HENDERSON, Andrew.** *Field Guide to the Palms of the Americas.* 1995. Princeton. ils/maps. 376p. sc. AN. B26. $30.00

**HENDERSON, Andrew.** *Palms of the Amazon.* 1995. NY. OUP. 1st. ils/index. 362p. xl. VG. H10. $75.00

**HENDERSON, David.** *Men & Wales at Scammon's Lagoon.* 1972. LA. Dawson. 1/700. Baja CA Travel Series 29. 313p. gray cloth. P4. $165.00

**HENDERSON, G.F.R.** *Civil War: A Soldier's View.* 1958. U Chicago. VG. M17. $17.50

**HENDERSON, I.F.** *Dictionary of Scientific Terms.* 1960. Van Nostrand. 7th. 8vo. 595p. F. B11. $18.00

**HENDERSON, James.** *Frigates: Account of Lighter Warships of Napoleonic Wars...* 1994. London. ils. VG/dj. M17. $25.00

**HENDERSON, John B.** *Cruise of the Tomas Barrera.* 1916. Putnam. 8vo. 320p. F. P4. $50.00

**HENDERSON, LeGrand.** *How Baseball Began in Brooklyn.* 1958. Abingdon. 1st. VG. P8. $20.00

**HENDERSON, Peter.** *Campaign of Chaos...1776: In the Jaws of a Juggernaut...* 1975. Haworth. 1st ltd. ils/index. 1140p. VG/dj. S16. $30.00

**HENDERSON, Peter.** *Gardening for Profit.* 1893. Orange Judd. revised. 376p. cloth. VG. A10. $28.00

**HENDERSON, Peter.** *Practical Floriculture.* 1900. Orange Judd. 325p. cloth. VG. A10. $25.00

**HENDERSON, Randall.** *On Desert Trails: Today & Yesterday.* 1941. Westernlore. 1st. 8vo. 357p. gray cloth. dj. F7. $50.00

**HENDERSON, Randall.** *Sun, Sand & Solitude: Vignettes From Notebook...* 1968. Westernlore. 1st. 8vo tan cloth. VG/dj. F7. $40.00

**HENDERSON, Richard.** *Racing-Cruiser.* 1970. Reilly Lee. NF/dj. B9. $15.00

**HENDERSON, Robert W.** *Early American Sport: A Check-List of Books...* 1953. NY. Barnes. 12 pl/index. 234p. G. H10. $65.00

**HENDERSON, W.** *Common Sense in the Kitchen: A Treatise on Art of Cooking...* nd. np. 337+58p. G. E6. $95.00

**HENDERSON, W.** *Modern Domestic Cookery & Useful Receipt Book.* 1844. ils/5 steel pl. 360p+61p recipes. VG. E6. $175.00

**HENDERSON, Zenna.** *People: No Different Flesh.* 1967. Doubleday. 1st Am. VG/dj. B11. $200.00

**HENDRICK, Basil.** *North Mexican Frontier.* 1971. Carbondale. 1st. 255p. dj. F3. $20.00

**HENDRICKS, George D.** *Bad Man of the West.* 1970. San Antonio, TX. Naylor. F/dj. A19. $35.00

**HENDRICKS, Vicki.** *Miami Purity.* 1995. Pantheon. 1st. sgn. VG/dj. B30. $22.50

**HENDRIE, Laura.** *Stygo.* 1994. Aspen. MacMurray Beck. 1st. F/dj. M23. $25.00

**HENDRY, James B.** *Small World of Khanh Hau: Study of Economic Life...* 1964. Chicago. Aldine. 312p. VG/clip. R11. $35.00

**HENFREY, Arthur.** *Vegetation of Europe: Its Conditions & Causes.* 1852. London. Voorst. 387p. cloth. VG. A10. $40.00

**HENFREY, Colin.** *Through Indian Eyes.* 1965. Holt. 1st Am. 286p. F3. $20.00

**HENIE, Sonja.** *Wings on My Feet.* 1940. NY. 1st. sgn. G/dj. B5. $45.00

**HENLE, Fritz.** *Fritz Henle's Rollei.* 1950. Hastings. 1st. photos. VG+/dj. S9. $75.00

**HENNECKE-SCHNEEMELCHER.** *New Testament Apocrypha.* 1963. Westminster. 2 vol. VG. B29. $60.00

**HENNESSY, Max.** *Back to Battle.* 1980. NY. 1st. VG/dj. M17. $15.00

**HENNESSY, Max.** *Dangerous Years.* 1977. NY. Atheneum. 1st Am. F/NF. T11. $35.00

**HENNESSY, Max.** *Soldier of the Queen.* 1980. Atheneum. 1st Am. F/NF. T11. $45.00

**HENRICHSEN, Margaret.** *Seven Steeples.* 1953. Boston. Houghton Mifflin. 1st. sgn. ils Wm Bass. VG/dj. A25. $15.00

**HENRY, John Frazier.** *Early Maritime Artists of Pacific Northwest Coast 1741-1841.* 1984. Vancouver/Toronto. Douglas McIntyre. 4to. ils. 240p. blk cloth. NF. P4. $65.00

**HENRY, John Joseph.** *Accurate & Interesting Account of Hardships & Sufferings...* 1812. Lancaster. 1st. full calf. B18. $295.00

**HENRY, Marguerite.** *Album of Horses.* 1951. Chicago. Rand McNally. 1st/A. 4to. 113p. VG+/G+. T5. $40.00

**HENRY, Marguerite.** *Album of Horses. Illustrated by Wesley Dennis.* 1959. Chicago. Rand McNally. 4to. VG/G. O3. $35.00

**HENRY, Marguerite.** *Birds at Home.* 1942. Donohue. ils Jacob B Abbott. NF. A17. $20.00

**HENRY, Marguerite.** *Born to Trot.* 1950. Rand McNally. 1st. sgn. ils Wesley Dennis. VG/G. O3. $95.00

**HENRY, Marguerite.** *Brighty of the Grand Canyon.* 1953. Chicago. Rand McNally. 1st. VG/G. F7. $40.00

**HENRY, Marguerite.** *Cinnabar: The One O'Clock Fox.* 1956. Rand McNally. 1st. ils Wesley Dennis. VG/G. O3. $68.00

**HENRY, Marguerite.** *Justin Morgan Had a Horse.* nd. Grosset Dunlap. VG/G. O3. $15.00

**HENRY, Marguerite.** *Justin Morgan Had a Horse.* 1947 (1945). Wilcox Follett. 3rd. 1946 Newbery Honor. 88p. beige brd. G+. T5. $45.00

**HENRY, Marguerite.** *King of the Wind.* (1948). Rand McNally. 1st. 4to. 1949 Newbery. gilt red cloth. dj. R5. $150.00

**HENRY, Marguerite.** *San Domingo.* 1972. Rand McNally. 1st. ils Robert Lougheed. VG/dj. A21. $45.00

**HENRY, Marguerite.** *Sea Star: Orphan of Chincoteague.* 1949. Rand McNally. 1st. ils Wesley Dennis. VG/dj. A21. $55.00

**HENRY, Marguerite.** *White Stallion of Lipizza.* 1964. Rand McNally. 1st. ils Wesley Dennis. VG/G. O3. $65.00

**HENRY, Matthew.** *Henry's Exposition: Exposition of Old & New Testament.* 1836. Phil. 6 vol/complete. 1st Am. old calf. G. S17. $120.00

**HENRY, O.** *Cabbages & Kings.* 1904. NY. McClure Phillis. 1st. prt cloth. VG. H4. $150.00

**HENRY, O.** *O Henry Stories.* (1962). Platt Munk. 8vo. 479p. VG/worn. H4. $20.00

**HENRY, O.** *Postscripts.* 1923. Harper. 1st. VG/clip. B4. $400.00

**HENRY, O.** *Sixes & Sevens.* 1911. Doubleday Page. 1st. 8vo. red cloth. G. J3. $75.00

**HENRY, O.** *Tales of O Henry: Sixty-Two Stories.* 1993. Barnes Noble. VG/dj. B11. $15.00

**HENRY, O.** *Voice of the City & Other Stories.* 1935. LEC. 1/1500. ils/sgn George Grosz. 221p. F/glassine/case. B20. $350.00

**HENRY, Sue.** *Murder on the Iditarod Trail.* 1991. Atalantic Monthly. 1st. F/dj. M15. $250.00

**HENRY, Thomas R.** *Strangest Things in the World...* 1958. WA. 200p. dj. A17. $10.00

**HENRY, Walter.** *Events of a Military Life: Being Recollections...* 1843. London. Pickering. 2 vol. revised 2nd. half morocco. G7. $495.00

**HENRY, Will.** *Alias Butch Cassidy.* 1967. Random. 1st. 209p. cloth. dj. D11. $40.00

**HENRY, Will.** *I, Tom Horn, Last Will & Testament of the Old West.* 1975. Lippincott. 339p. VG. J2. $275.00

**HENRY, Will.** *Last Warparth.* 1966. NY. Random. 1st. NF/NF. T11. $80.00

**HENRY, Will.** *Maheo's Children.* 1968. Phil. Chilton. 1st. gray cloth. F/clip. T11. $80.00

**HENRY, Will.** *To Follow a Flag.* 1953. Random. 1st. NF/VG. T11. $65.00

**HENRY, William A.** *Visions of America: How We Saw the 1984 Election.* 1985. Atlantic Monthly. 1st. 8vo. F/VG. A2. $12.50

**HENRY, William.** *Elements of Experimental Chemistry.* 1817. Phil. Webster. 4th (from 7th London). 656p. K5. $125.00

**HENRY & ZILBOORG.** *History of Medical Psychology.* (1941). NY. Norton. 8vo. 505p. F/G. H4. $35.00

**HENRY II (King of France).** *Epistola...ad Amplissimos Sacri Imperii Ordines.* 1553. Paris. Chas Estienne. 4to. Estienne title device. stitched. R12. $300.00

**HENRY II (King of France).** *Ordonnances...sur les Plainctes & Doleances Faictes...* 1629. Paris. Estienne Mettayer Prevost. 2 works in 1. calf. R12. $975.00

**HENRY IV (King of France).** *Recueil des Lettres Missives de Henry IV.* 1843-1876. Paris. Imprimerie Royale. 9 vol. lg 4to. facs letters. orig brd. R12. $850.00

**HENSHALL, James A.** *Book of Black Bass.* 1978. Montgomery. facs of 1881. 463p. gilt cloth. F. A17. $30.00

**HENSHAW, Julia W.** *Wild Flowers of the North American Mountains.* 1917 (1915). NY. ils/pl. 383p. VG. B26. $36.00

**HENSLOW, T. Geoffrey.** *Garden Instruction.* 1940. London. Quality. 1st. 324p. cloth. VG. A10. $25.00

**HENSON, Matthew A.** *Negro Explorer at the North Pole.* 1912. NY. Stokes. 1st. 8vo. photos. 200p. bl cloth. P4. $750.00

**HENTOFF & MCCARTHY.** *Jazz.* 1959. Rinehart. 1st. F/NF. B2. $35.00

**HENTY, G.A.** *Through Russian Snows.* 1895. NY. Scribner. 1st. VG+. T11. $45.00

**HENTY, G.A.** *With Clive in India.* nd. Grosset Dunlap. VG/dj. P3. $20.00

**HEPBURN, Katherine.** *Making of 'The African Queen'...* 1987. NY. Knopf. 1st. F/dj. C9. $25.00

**HEPBURN, Katherine.** *Me. Stories of My Life.* 1991. Knopf. 1st. F/dj. T11/W2. $35.00

**HEPPENHEIMER, T.A.** *Toward Distant Suns.* 1979. Stackpole. ils/diagrams. 256p. VG/dj. K5. $16.00

**HEPPER, F.N.** *Wild African Herbaria of Isert & Thonning.* 1976. Kew. ils/maps. 227p. VG/dj. B26. $30.00

**HERBART, Johann Friedrich.** *Science of Education.* 1977. WA, DC. U Pub of Am. lg 8vo. brn fabricoid. G1. $65.00

**HERBART, Johann Friedrich.** *Text-Book in Psychology.* 1977. WA, DC. U Pub of Am. lg 8vo. 200p. brn fabricoid. G1. $65.00

**HERBART, Johann Friedrich.** *Text-Book in Psychology: An Attempt to Fund Science...* 1891. NY. Appleton. 1st Eng-language. 12mo. 200p. prt gr cloth. VG. G1. $250.00

**HERBERT, A.P.** *Independent Member.* 1951. Doubleday. 1st Am. 8vo. VG/dj. A2. $15.00

**HERBERT, Charles.** *Relic of the Revolution...* 1847. Boston. 1st. 18mo. 258p. NF. O1. $125.00

**HERBERT, Frank.** *Chapterhouse: Dune.* 1985. Putnam. 1st. inscr. F/dj. O11. $50.00

**HERBERT, Frank.** *Chapterhouse: Dune.* 1985. Putnam. 1st. 464p. F/NF. M21. $15.00

**HERBERT, Frank.** *Dosadi Experiment.* 1977. Putnam. 1st. sgn. F/NF. O11. $60.00

**HERBERT, Frank.** *Eye.* 1985. Masterworks. ils Jim Burns. 328p. F. W2. $15.00

**HERBERT, James.** *Moon.* 1985. Crown. 1st Am. F/dj. S18. $40.00

**HERBERT, James.** *Sepulchre.* 1987. London. Hodder Stoughton. 1st. F/dj. M21. $30.00

**HERBERT, W.** *Antiquities of Inns of Court & Chancery... Sketches...* 1804. London. Vernor & Hood. 1st. 8vo. 377p. full mottled calf. VG. B20. $350.00

**HERBERT & RANSOM.** *Ascension Factor.* 1991. Putnam. 1st. F/F. T12. $25.00

**HERBST, Josephine.** *New Green World.* 1954. Hastings. 272p. cloth. VG. A10. $38.00

**HERDEG, Walter.** *Film & TV Graphics 2.* 1976. Graphics Pr. Eng/German/Frech text. VG. C9. $90.00

**HERGESHEIMER, Joseph.** *San Cristobal de la Habana.* 1927. Knopf. photos. 255p. dj. F3. $20.00

**HERGESHEIMER, Joseph.** *Traill by Armes.* 1929. London. Elkin Mathews. 1st. 1/530. sgn. Woburn Books #17. xl. VG/dj. J3. $125.00

**HERIHY, James Leo.** *Midnight Cowboy.* 1965. S&S. 1st. VG/VG clip. R14. $50.00

**HERITEAU & VIETTE.** *American Horticultural Society Flower Finder.* 1992. NY. S&S. 1st. ils/index. 300p. VG/dj. H10. $32.50

**HERKLOTS, G.A.C.** *Hong Kong Birds.* 1953. Hong Kong. ils AM Hughs. 333p. F/VG. C12. $46.00

**HERLIHY, James Leo.** *All Fall Down.* 1960. Dutton. 1st. inscr. NF/dj. B4. $150.00

**HERM, Gerhard.** *Celts.* 1977. St Martin. 1st. F/G. P3. $18.00

**HERMAN, O.** *Recensio Critica Automatica of Doctrine Bird-Migration.* 1905. Budapest. Eng text. fld map. 74p. VG. C12. $35.00

**HERMAN, Samuel W.** *Hell on the Border.* 1953. Ft Smith, AR. Border Pub. sc. G. A19. $35.00

**HERMAN & ORTZEN.** *Peoples, Seas & Ships.* 1967. Putnam. VG/dj. B9. $25.00

**HERMANN, Paul.** *Conquest by Man.* 1954. Harper. 1st. 455p. dj. F3. $15.00

**HERMANN, Paul.** *Great Age of Discovery.* 1956. Harper. 8vo. 507p. VG/worn. P4. $25.00

**HERMES, Margaret.** *Phoenix Next.* 1981. Chicago. 1st. author's 1st book. F/F. H11. $25.00

**HERNDON, Booton.** *Great Land.* 1971. NY. Weybright Talley. 8vo. 241p. dk bl cloth. VG/dj. P4. $25.00

**HERNDON, Venable.** *James Dean: A Short Life.* 1974. Doubleday. 1st. NF/clip. A14. $25.00

**HERNDON, Venable.** *James Dean: A Short Life.* 1974. London. Futura. VG/dj. P3. $30.00

**HERNER, Charles.** *Arizona Rough Riders.* 1970. Tucson, AZ. 1st. ils/notes/index. 275p. F/NF. B19. $50.00

**HEROLD, J. Christopher.** *Joan, Maid of France.* 1952. NY. 1st. ils Frederick Chapman. VG/G. M17. $15.00

**HERR, John K.** *Story of the US Cavalry 1775-1942.* 1953. Little Brn. A19. $45.00

**HERRE, Albert W.C.T.** *Lichen Flora of the Santa Cruz Peninsula, California.* 1910. WA, DC. 243p. new buckram. B26. $45.00

**HERRESHOFF, L. Francis.** *Captain Nat Herreshoff: His Life & Yachts He Designed.* 1974. NY. photos. VG/dj. M17. $30.00

**HERRICK, Christine.** *Chafing Dish Supper.* 1906 (1894). E6. $45.00

**HERRICK, James.** *Short History of Cardiology.* 1942. Springfield. 1st. sgn. 258p. xl. A13. $150.00

**HERRIGEL, Eugen.** *Zen & the Art of Archery.* 1953. Pantheon. 1st. NF/dj. B2. $40.00

**HERRIN, Lamar.** *Rio Loja Ringmaster.* 1977. Viking. 1st. VG/dj. P8. $50.00

**HERRINGER, Robert.** *Geschichte der Medizinschen Abbildung...* 1967. Munchen Heinz Moos. ils. 179p. dj. G7. $125.00

**HERRON, Don.** *Dark Barbarian: Writings of Robert E Howard.* 1984. Greenwood. ils. 261p. F. A4. $45.00

**HERRON, Don.** *Sarim.* 1971. Austin. Jenlins Pub. 1/400. sgn. NF. F1. $25.00

**HERRON, Shaun.** *Bird in Last Year's Nest.* 1974. ARC. F/NF. M19. $25.00

**HERSCHEL, William.** *Scientific Papers of Sir William Herschel...* 1912. London. Royal Soc/ Royal Astronomical Soc. 2 vol. K5. $1,200.00

**HERSEY, John.** *Hiroshima.* 1946. Knopf. 1st. VG/dj. H10. $12.00

**HERSEY, John.** *Hiroshima.* 1946. Knopf. 1st. 118p. VG. P12. $6.00

**HERSEY, John.** *Life Sketches.* 1989. Knopf. 1st. F/dj. T11. $12.00

**HERSEY, John.** *Under the Eye of the Storm.* 1967. Knopf. 1st. inscr/dtd 1967. F/NF clip. O11. $65.00

**HERSEY, John.** *Wall.* 1967. NY. Modern Lib. 1st. rem mk. NF/dj. S13. $38.00

**HERSEY, John.** *Walnut Door.* 1977. Knopf. 1st. F/NF. A24. $25.00

**HERSEY, John.** *Walnut Door.* 1977. Knopf. ARC/UP/1st. NF/orange prt wrp. M24. $30.00

**HERSH, Seymour.** *My Lai 4: Report on the Massacre & Its Aftermath.* 1970. Random. 1st. 210p. F/NF. R11. $30.00

**HERSHLAG, Z.Y.** *Turkey: An Economy in Transition.* (1958?). The Hague. inscr. 340p. simulated leather. VG/dj. Q2. $28.00

**HERTOG, J.P.** *Strength of Materials.* 1961 (1949). Dover. 1st. VG/wrp. B27. $10.00

**HERVE, Henri.** *Revue de l'Aeronautique.* 1892. Paris. Masson. ils/pl. 132p. G+. B18. $195.00

**HERVEY, Henry.** *Series of Lectures on Old Testament Miracles.* 1844. Springfield, OH. 301p. G. B18. $45.00

**HERZIG, Alison.** *Boonville Bombers.* 1991. Viking. 1st. F/dj. P8. $10.00

**HERZOG, Arthur.** *IQ83.* 1978. S&S. 1st. VG/dj. P3. $15.00

**HERZSTEIN, Robert E.** *Henry R Luce: A Political Portrait of the Man...* 1994. Scribner. 1st. photos. F/dj. A28. $16.00

**HESELTINE, Marjorie.** *Basic Book Book.* 1947. Riverside. A16. $10.00

**HESKI, Thomas M.** *Little Shadow Catcher.* 1978. Superior. 1st. inscr. 175p. VG/dj. J2. $110.00

**HESS, Albert G.** *Chasing the Dragon.* 1965. North-Holland. 1st. VG/dj. R8. $45.00

**HESS, Earl J.** *Liberty, Virtue & Progress: Northerners & Their War...* 1988. NY U. 1st. F/wrp. A14. $10.50

**HESSE, Herman.** *Autobiographical Writings.* 1972. London. 1st. trans D Lindley. edit T Ziolkowski. dj. T9. $25.00

**HESSELTINE, William Best.** *Civil War Prisons: A Study in War Psychology.* 1930. Columbus. OH State. 1st. 290p. cloth. NF/dj. M8. $250.00

**HESTON, Charlton.** *Actor's Life: Journals 1956-1976.* 1978. Dutton. 1st. lg 8vo. 482p. F/dj. B20. $30.00

**HETERINGTON, A.L.** *Early Ceramic Wares of China.* 1922. NY. Scribner. 100 pl. 160p. tan cloth. VG+. F1. $150.00

**HEUER, Kenneth.** *Men of Other Planets.* 1951. NY. Pellegrini Cudahy. ils. 160p. K5. $20.00

**HEUMAN, William.** *Little League Champs.* 1953. Lippincott. 1st. VG. P8. $17.50

**HEUREUX, Bill.** *Hockey: An All Star Sports Book.* 1972. Follett. 2nd. VG/dj. B36. $11.00

**HEUVELMANS, Bernard.** *In the Wake of the Sea-Serpents.* 1968. NY. Zoological UFOs. ils. 645p. VG. S15. $18.00

**HEUVELMANS, Bernard.** *On Track of the Unknown Animals.* 1959. NY. 1st. VG/VG. B5. $30.00

**HEWARD, Constance.** *Ameliaranne Camps Out.* nd. Phil. ils SB Pearse. VG. M17. $27.50

**HEWARD, Constance.** *Ameliaranne Camps Out.* 1939. London. Harrap. 1st. 58p. VG/dj. D4. $45.00

HEWAT, Alan. *Lady's Time*. 1985. Harper Row. 1st. F/NF. M25. $25.00

HEWES, Agnes Danforth. *Boy of the Lost Crusade*. nd. 14th. ils Gustaf Tenggren. VG/dj. M17. $15.00

HEWETT, Edgar L. *Ancient Andean Life*. 1939. Bobbs Merrill. 1st. 8vo. ils/fld map. 336p. bl cloth. VG+. P4. $60.00

HEWETT, Edgar L. *Ancient Life in Mexico & Central America*. 1936. Bobbs Merrill. 1st. 8vo. map ep. bl cloth. P4. $75.00

HEWETT, Edgar L. *Chaco Canyon & Its Monuments*. 1936. Albuquerque. 1st. ils. 234p. G. B5. $30.00

HEWETT, Edgar L. *Pajarito Plateau & Its Ancient Poeple*. 1938. NM U. 1st. ils/11 pl. cloth. dj. D11. $50.00

HEWETT & MAUZY. *Landmarks of New Mexico*. 1940. NM U. 1st. 200p. cloth. dj. D11. $40.00

HEWITT, E.J. *Sand & Water Culture Methods Used Study of Plant Nutrition*. 1952. E Malling. Kent. 241p. dj. A10. $20.00

HEWITT, Jean. *Family Circle Quick Menu Cookbook*. 1975. NY Times. G/dj. A16. $10.00

HEWITT, Lawrence Lee. *Port Hudson: Confederate Bastion on the Mississippi*. 1987. LSU. 1st. NF/dj. A14. $21.00

HEWITT, R. *Bird Malaria*. 1940. John Hopkins. 1st. 8vo. gilt cloth. F. C12. $45.00

HEWITT, R.H. *Notes by the Way: Memoranda of a Journey Across the Plains*. 1955. Seattle. McCaffrey. Olympia ed. 8vo. 79p. pk cloth. F. B20. $25.00

HEWITT, Richard. *Physician-Writer's Book: Tricks of the Trade...* 1957. Phil. 1st. 417p. A13. $25.00

HEWLETT, Sylvia Ann. *Lesser Life: Myth of Women's Liberation in America*. 1986. NY. 1st. sgn pres. ils. 461p. F/VG. H3. $30.00

HEY, William. *Treatise on the Puerperal Fever: Illustrated by Cases...* 1817. Phil. Carey & Sons. 1st Am. 234p. brd/paper spine. NF. G7. $395.00

HEYER, Carol. *Beauty & the Beast*. 1989. Ideals. 1st. sgn. 32p. F/dj. D4. $30.00

HEYER, Georgette. *Civil Contract*. 1961. NY. 1st Am. VG. M17. $15.00

HEYER, Georgette. *Death in the Stocks*. 1970. Dutton. 1st Am. VG/clip. S13. $14.00

HEYER, Georgette. *Grand Sophy*. (1950). Putnam. later prt. 8vo. gilt turquoise cloth. VG. H1. $10.00

HEYERDAHL, Thor. *Ra Expositions*. 1971. Doubleday. 1st. sgn. VG/G. B30. $100.00

HEYERDAHL, Thor. *Tigris Expedition: In Search of Our Beginnings*. 1981. Doubleday. 1st. 8vo. ils/map ep. 349p. NF/dj. W1. $22.00

HEYLINGER, William. *Bartley, Freshman Pitcher*. 1911. Appleton. 1st. G+. P8. $65.00

HEYLINGER, William. *Bean-Ball Bill & Other Stories*. 1930. Grosset Dunlap. 1st. VG. P8. $40.00

HEYLINGER, William. *Loser's End*. 1937. Goldsmith. 1st. rem mk. G+. P8. $12.50

HEYM, Stefan. *Wandering Jew*. 1984. HRW. 1st Am. F/dj. M25. $25.00

HEYMAN, Max L. *Prudent Soldier*. 1959. Glendale, CA. 418p. F. E1. $125.00

HEYMAN & MEAD. *Family*. (1965). Macmillan. photos. full yel linen. NF. H4. $10.00

HEYWOOD, V.H. *Modern Methods in Plant Taxonomy*. 1968. London. ils. 312p. dj. B26. $25.00

HIAASEN, Carl. *Double Whammy*. 1987. Putnam. 1st. rem mk. NF/dj. B2. $50.00

HIAASEN, Carl. *Lucky You*. 1977. Knopf. 1st. sgn. F/dj. R14. $40.00

HIAASEN, Carl. *Lucky You*. 1997. New Orleans. BE Trice. 1st. 1/150. sgn. special bdg. F/sans dj/F case. M15. $150.00

HIAASEN, Carl. *Native Tongue*. 1991. Knopf. 1st. sgn. F/F. B3/M15. $60.00

HIAASEN, Carl. *Native Tongue*. 1991. Knopf. 1st. VG/dj. B30. $35.00

HIAASEN, Carl. *Stormy Weather*. 1995. Knopf. 1st. F/dj. R14. $25.00

HIAASEN, Carl. *Strip Tease*. 1993. Knopf. 1st. sgn. F/NF. B3. $40.00

HIAASEN, Carl. *Strip Tease*. 1993. Knopf. 1st. F/dj. R14. $35.00

HIAASEN, Carl. *Tourist Season*. 1986. Putnam. 1st. VG+/dj. B30. $115.00

HIAASEN & MONTALBANO. *Trap Line*. 1993. London. Severn. 1st. sgn Hiaasen. F/F. B3. $125.00

HIBBEN, Thomas. *Sons of Vulcan: Story of Metals*. 1940. Phil. Lippincott. VG/fair. O3. $25.00

HIBBERT, Christopher. *Personal History of Samuel Johnson*. 1971. London. Longman. H13. $45.00

HIBBERT, Christopher. *Popes*. 1982. Stonehenge. 1st. Treasures of World series. 176p. NF. S14. $19.00

HIBBERT, Christopher. *Redcoats & Rebels: War for America 1770-1781*. 1990. London. 375p. F/dj. M4. $20.00

HIBBERT, Christopher. *Wolfe at Quebec*. 1959. Cleveland. 1st. 194p. VG/dj. B18. $17.50

HIBBERT, Eleanor Alice. *Bastard King*. 1974. Robert Hale. 1st. F/VG. M19. $17.50

HIBBERT, Eleanor Alice. *Bride of Pendorric*. 1963. London. Collins. 1st. VG/dj. A14. $15.00

HIBBERT, Eleanor Alice. *Captive*. 1989. Doubleday. 1st. F/dj. T12. $20.00

HIBBERT, Eleanor Alice. *Daughter of Deceit*. nd. BC. VG/dj. P3. $8.00

HIBBERT, Eleanor Alice. *Demon Lover*. nd. BC. VG/dj. P3. $8.00

HIBBERT, Eleanor Alice. *Flaunting, Extravagant Queen*. 1957. London. Robert Hale. 1st. VG+/VG. A14. $25.00

HIBBERT, Eleanor Alice. *Goldsmith's Wife*. 1950. London. Robert Hale. 1st. VG+/clip. A14. $42.00

HIBBERT, Eleanor Alice. *Indescretions of the Queen*. 1970. London. Robert Hale. 1st. Georgian Saga #8. VG+/dj. A14. $22.00

HIBBERT, Eleanor Alice. *Lament for a Lost Lover*. 1977. Harper Collins. 1st. VG+/clip. A14. $21.00

HIBBERT, Eleanor Alice. *Legend of the Seventh Virgin*. 1965. London. Collins. 1st. VG/clip. A14. $15.00

HIBBERT, Eleanor Alice. *Lion Triumphant*. 1974. Putnam. 1st. NF/VG. M19. $17.50

HIBBERT, Eleanor Alice. *Louis the Well-Beloved*. 1959. London. Robert Hale. 1st. VG/dj. A14. $25.00

HIBBERT, Eleanor Alice. *Love-Child*. 1978. London. Collins. 1st. NF/dj. A14. $25.00

HIBBERT, Eleanor Alice. *Love-Child*. 1978. NY. Putnam. 1st. VG/dj. M20. $15.00

HIBBERT, Eleanor Alice. *Miracle at St Bruno's*. 1972. London. Collins. 1st. VG+/clip. A14. $25.00

HIBBERT, Eleanor Alice. *Mistress of Mellyn*. 1961. London. Collins. 1st. VG+/dj. A14. $28.00

HIBBERT, Eleanor Alice. *Regent's Daughter*. 1971. London. Robert Hale. 1st. Georgian Saga #9. VG+/dj. A14. $25.00

HIBBERT, Eleanor Alice. *Shivering Sands*. 1969. London. Collins. 1st. NF/clip. A14. $22.00

HIBBERT, Eleanor Alice. *Sun in Splendor*. 1983. Putnam. 1st. F/NF. M19. $17.50

**HICHBORN, William.** *Trip of the Ancients: A Memoir of Events...* 1897. Maiden, MA. photos. VG. M17. $15.00

**HICHCOCK, Alfred.** *Grave Suspicions.* 1984. Dial. 1st. VG/dj. P3. $15.00

**HICKEL, Walter J.** *Who Owns America?* 1971. Prentice Hall. 8vo. 328p. wht cloth. F/VG. P4. $20.00

**HICKEY, D.R.** *War of 1812: Forgotten Conflict.* 1989. IL U. ils/maps. 457p. NF/dj. M4. $27.00

**HICKMAN & ROBERTS.** *Forever Dobie.* 1994. Birch Lane. 301p. VG/dj. C5. $12.50

**HICKOCK, Laurens Persius.** *Rational Psychology; or, Subjective Idea & Objective Law...* 1849. Auburn. Derby Miller. 717p. emb Victorian cloth. VG. G1. $375.00

**HICKS, Edward.** *Letters of Elias Hicks: Including Also Observations...* 1861. Phil. TE Chapman. 240p. G+. V3. $65.00

**HICKS, Edward.** *Memoirs of Life & Religious Labors of Edward Hicks...* 1851. Phil. Merrihew Thompson. 12mo. 365p. V3. $125.00

**HICKS, Edward.** *Six Queries Proposed to Elias Hicks...* 1830. NY. Wm Mercein. 1st. 12mo. disbound. G+. V3. $40.00

**HICKS, Elias.** *Journal of Life & Religious Labours of Elias Hicks.* 1832. NY. Isaac Hopper. 451p. full leather. G. B18. $45.00

**HICKS, J.R.** *Contribution to the Theory of the Trade Cycle.* 1961 (1950). Oxford. 201p. xl. VG. S5. $12.00

**HICKS, John Edward.** *Adventures of a Tramp Printer 1888-1890.* 1950. Kansas City. 1st. 285p. VG/G. B5. $25.00

**HICKS & HICKS.** *Quaker: Being a Series of Sermons, Vol I.* 1827. Phil. MTC Gould. 300p. no covers/missing title p. V3. $25.00

**HIEB, Louis A.** *Tony Hillerman: A Bibliography.* 1990. Tucson. Gigantic Hound. 1st. sgn. F/sans. M15. $45.00

**HIEMSTRA, Marvin R.** *26 Compliments, by Marvin R Hiemstra.* 1991. Juniper Von Phitzer. mini. 1/100. sgn author/prt. aeg. maroon bdg. B24. $85.00

**HIGDON, Hal.** *Last Series.* 1974. Dutton. 1st. F/dj. P8. $30.00

**HIGDON, Hal.** *Union Vs Dr Mudd.* 1964. Chicago. 1st. sgn. VG/dj. B5. $30.00

**HIGGINBOTHAM, Don.** *Atlas of the American Revolution.* 1974. Rand McNally. 50 period maps. 217p. F/clip. T11. $125.00

**HIGGINBOTHAM, Don.** *War of American Independence: Military Attitudes...* 1971. NY. 1st. photos/index. VG/dj. S16. $40.00

**HIGGINS, Charlotte M.** *Angel Children; or, Stories From Cloud-Land* 1855 (1854). Boston. Philips. 134p. red cloth. F1. $85.00

**HIGGINS, Ethel B.** *Type Localitis of Vascular Plants in San Diego County, CA.* 1959. SF. map. 60p. wrp. B26. $20.00

**HIGGINS, George V.** *Cogan's Trade.* 1974. Knopf. 1st. F/dj. N4. $25.00

**HIGGINS, George V.** *Digger's Game.* 1973. NY. Knopf. 1st. author's 2nd book. NF/NF. H11. $25.00

**HIGGINS, George V.** *Patriot Game.* 1982. Knopf. 1st. sgn. NF/VG. R14. $35.00

**HIGGINS, George V.** *Rat of Fire.* 1981. Knopf. 1st. sgn. NF/VG. R14. $40.00

**HIGGINS, George V.** *Rat of Fire.* 1981. NY. 1st. VG/dj. M17. $15.00

**HIGGINS, George V.** *Victories.* 1991. Andre Deutsch. 1st. F/dj. P8. $25.00

**HIGGINS, Jack.** *Cold Harbor.* 1990. S&S. 1st. F/dj. M21. $15.00

**HIGGINS, Jack.** *Confessional.* 1985. Stein Day. 1st. F/VG+. N4. $15.00

**HIGGINS, Jack.** *Eye of the Storm.* 1992. London. Chapman. 1st. F/dj. M15. $45.00

**HIGGINS, Jack.** *Night of the Fox.* 1986. S&S. F/VG. L4. $15.00

**HIGGINS, Jack.** *Prayer for the Dying.* 1973. London. Collins. 1st. F/NF. M15. $75.00

**HIGGINS, Jack.** *President's Daughter.* 1997. London. Michael Joseph. 1st. F/dj. M15. $45.00

**HIGGINS, Jack.** *Valhalla Exchange.* 1977. London. Hutchinson. 1st. F/dj. M15. $75.00

**HIGGINS, W.M.** *Earth: Its Physical Condition & Most Remarkable Phenomena.* ca 1870. London. Blackwood. 6th. 392p. cloth. G. K5. $40.00

**HIGGINS & SORRENTINO.** *Handbook of Motivation & Cognition: Foundations...* 1990. NY. Guilford. heavy 8vo. 621p. VG/dj. G1. $65.00

**HIGGINSON, A. Henry.** *British & American Sporting Authors.* 1951. Hutchinson. ils. VG/dj. A21. $225.00

**HIGGINSON, Ella.** *Alaska, the Great Country.* 1919. Macmillan. revised. 8vo. stp Property US Army. VG. H7. $12.50

**HIGGINSON, Thomas Wentworth.** *Outdoor Papers.* 1886. Lee Shepard. P12. $20.00

**HIGGS, L.** *Bahamian Cookbook: Recipes by Ladies of Nassau.* 1965. 123p. wrp. E6. $12.00

**HIGH, Mongique Raphel.** *Encore.* 1981. Delacorte. 1st. 578p. F. W2. $25.00

**HIGHAM, Charles.** *Bette.* 1981. NY. Macmillan. 316p. VG/dj. C5. $12.50

**HIGHAM, Charles.** *Marlene: Life of Marlene Dietrich.* 1977. NY. Norton. 319p. VG/dj. C5. $12.50

**HIGHSMITH, Patricia.** *Boy Who Followed Ripley.* 1980. London. Heinemann. 1st. F/dj. M15. $50.00

**HIGHSMITH, Patricia.** *Mermaids on the Golf Course.* 1985. London. Heinemann. 1st. F/clip. A24. $20.00

**HIGHSMITH, Patricia.** *Mermaids on the Golf Course.* 1988. Penzler. 1st. F/dj. R8. $9.00

**HIGHSMITH, Patricia.** *Ripley Under Water.* 1992. NY. 1st. VG/dj. M17. $15.00

**HIGHSMITH, Patricia.** *This Sweet Sickness.* 1961. London. Heinemann. 1st Eng. VG/clip. M15. $65.00

**HIGHWATER, Jamake.** *Ceremony of Innocence.* 1985. Harper Row. 1st. F/F. D10. $40.00

**HIGHWATER, Jamake.** *Ceremony of Innocence.* 1985. Harper Row. 1st. Ghost Horse Cycle #2. F/VG clip. A24. $30.00

**HIGHWATER, Jamake.** *Journey to the Sky.* 1978. Crowell. 1st. F/dj. D10. $50.00

**HIGHWATER, Jamake.** *Legend Days.* 1984. Harper Row. 1st. F/NF. D10. $40.00

**HIGHWATER, Jamake.** *Many Smokes, Many Moons.* 1978. Lippincott. 1st. F/clip. D10. $60.00

**HIGHWATER, Jamake.** *Native Land.* 1986. Little Brn. 1st. F/F. D10. $35.00

**HIGHWATER, Jamake.** *Shadow Show.* 1986. NY. Alfred van der Marck. 1st. maroon brd. F/NF. D10. $35.00

**HIGHWATER, Jamake.** *Sun, He Dies.* 1980. Lippincott/Crowell. 1st. F/VG. B3. $30.00

**HIGHWATER, Jamake.** *Sun, He Dies.* 1980. Lippincott/Crowell. 1st. NF/F. D10. $35.00

**HIGINBOTHAM, John D.** *When the West Was Young: Historical Reminiscences...* 1933. Toronto. Ryerson. 1st. 1/500. sgn. 328p. teg. gr cloth. VG. C6. $150.00

**HIGONNET, Margaret Randolph.** *Behind the Lines: Gender & Two World Wars.* 1987. Yale. 1st. 8vo. F/dj. A2. $18.00

**HIJUELOS, Oscar.** *Fourteen Sisters of Emilio Montez O'Brien.* 1993. FSG. F/dj. B9. $15.00

**HIJUELOS, Oscar.** *Fourteen Sisters of Emilio Montez O'Brien.* 1993. FSG. 1st. sgn. F/dj. D10. $40.00

**HIJUELOS, Oscar.** *Mambo King Plays Songs of Love.* 1989. FSG. 1st. F/F. H11. $45.00

**HIJUELOS, Oscar.** *Mambo Kings Play Songs of Love.* 1989. FSG. 1st. VG+/dj. B30. $25.00

**HILDEBRANDT, Greg.** *Dragons.* 1994. Little Brn. 1st. folio. popups/engineer Keith Moseley. F. B17. $15.00

**HILDEBRANDT, Hans.** *Zeppelin-Denkmal Fuer das Deutche Volk.* nd (1920s). Stuttgart. lg 4to. German text. ils. 388p. gilt blk cloth. B11. $750.00

**HILDEBRANDT, Rita & Tim.** *Merlin & the Dragons of Atlantis.* 1983. Bobbs Merrill. 1st. ils. F/dj. T10. $175.00

**HILDESCHEIMER, Wolfgang.** *Collected Stories.* 1987. NY. trans Neugroschel. VG/dj. M17. $15.00

**HILDICK, E.W.** *Manhattan Is Missing.* 1969. Doubleday. 1st. 8vo. 239p. bl cloth. NF/VG. T5. $35.00

**HILDRETH, Richard.** *Atrocious Judges: Lives of Judges Infamous As Tools...* 1856. NY. Miller Orton Mulligan. cloth. M11. $150.00

**HILDRETH, S.P.** *Memoirs of the Early Pioneer Settlers of Ohio...* 1854. Cincinnati. 2nd. 539p. B18. $125.00

**HILEN, Andrew.** *Diary of Clara Crowninshield.* 1956. U WA. 1st. NF/dj. O4. $25.00

**HILGARTNER, Beth.** *Necklace of Fallen Stars.* 1979. Little Brn. 1st. 8vo. 209p. VG/dj. T5. $55.00

**HILL, Aaron.** *King Henry the Fifth; or, Conquest of France...* 1723. London. W Chetwood. 1st. sm 8vo. rb/new ep. R3. $70.00

**HILL, Benjamin L.** *Lectures on American Eclectic System of Surgery.* 1850. Cincinnati. Phillips. 100 ils. 671p. sheep. G7. $175.00

**HILL, Eileen.** *Candle Shop Mystery.* 1967. Whitman. ils. 192p. VG/dj. B36. $7.50

**HILL, Eileen.** *Robin Kane: Mystery of the Phantom.* 1966. Whitman. ils. 192p. VG. B36. $7.00

**HILL, Frederick Trevor.** *Lincoln, the Lawyer.* 1906. NY. Century. 1st. ils. 332p. VG. B5. $40.00

**HILL, George Birkbeck.** *Johnsonian Miscellanies.* 1897. Harper. 2 vol. 1st Am. 8vo. teg/uncut. gilt bl cloth. H13. $265.00

**HILL, George Birkbeck.** *Talks About Autographs.* 1896. Houghton Mifflin. 1st. 25 pl. VG. H13. $65.00

**HILL, George W.** *New Theory of Jupiter & Saturn: Astronomical Papers...* 1890. WA, DC. Navy Dept/Bureau of Equipment. 4to. 576p. cloth. K5. $75.00

**HILL, Grace Livingston.** *Bright Arrows.* 1946. Lippincott. 1st. 247p. dk bl cloth. G+. B36. $9.00

**HILL, Hamlin.** *Mark Twain & Elisha Bliss.* (1964). Columbia, MO. U MO. 1st. gilt brn cloth. F/dj. M24. $85.00

**HILL, Janet McKenzie.** *Up-to-Date Waitress.* 1906. 1st. 52 photos. VG+. E6. $60.00

**HILL, John;** see Koontz, Dean R.

**HILL, Joseph F.** *History of Warner's Ranch & Its Environs.* 1927. private prt. 1/1000. 221p. VG. F7. $100.00

**HILL, Margaret Livingston.** *Children's Lamp.* 1932. McKay. 1st. ils Walter Stewart. unp. bl cloth/pict label. F. F1. $150.00

**HILL, Michael Garibaldi.** *Edward Randolph & the American Colonies, 1676-1703.* (1960). UNC. ARC. 241p. VG/dj. B10. $25.00

**HILL, Pati.** *Pit & the Century Plant.* 1956. London. Gollancz. 276p. VG/dj. A10. $18.00

**HILL, Porter.** *War Chest.* 1988. NY. Walker. 1st Am. rem mk. NF/dj. T11. $20.00

**HILL, R.B.** *Hanta Yo.* 1979. Garden City. 834p. NF/dj. M4. $18.00

**HILL, Reginald.** *Fairly Dangerous Thing.* 1972. Foul Play. 1st Am. VG/dj. G8. $35.00

**HILL, Reginald.** *Fell of Dark.* 1971. London. Collins Crime Club. 1st. author's 2nd mystery. F/dj. M15. $300.00

**HILL, Reginald.** *No Man's Land.* 1985. London. Collins. 1st. inscr. F/dj. M15. $50.00

**HILL, Reginald.** *Very Good Hater.* 1974. Foul Play. 1st Am. NF/dj. G8. $25.00

**HILL, Sara Jane F.** *Mrs Hill's Journal: Civil War Reminiscences.* 1980. Lakeside Classic. 1st thus. teg. dk brn cloth. NF/sans. T11. $25.00

**HILL, William.** *California Trail: Yesterday & Today.* 1986. Boulder, CO. Pruett Pub. AN/dj. A19. $35.00

**HILL & LYE.** *Weymouth at War: Ron Hill's Story of Vessel My Girl.* 1990. Dorset. 1st. 8vo. 76p. gilt brd. F/dj. M7. $15.00

**HILL & MUDIE.** *Letters of Lenin.* 1937. Harcourt Brace. 1st Am. G. V4. $15.00

**HILLARD, E.B.** *Last Men of the Revolution.* 1968. Barre. rpt. F/dj. M4. $15.00

**HILLBURN, Samuel M.** *Gaines Sensei: Missionary to Hiroshima.* 1936. Kobe. Friend-Sha. 1st. photos. hand-made paper/hand-sewn bdg. 175p. VG+. A25. $40.00

**HILLER, E.** *Calendar of Cakes, Fillings & Frosting. 365 Recipes.* ca 1915. Volland. ils/ribbon ties. VG/narrow 4to wrp. E6. $45.00

**HILLERMAN, Tony.** *Blessingway.* 1970. London. Macmillan. 1st. F/NF. M15. $450.00

**HILLERMAN, Tony.** *Coyote Waits.* 1990. Harper Row. 1st. F/dj. R14. $30.00

**HILLERMAN, Tony.** *Coyote.* 1993. Oslo, Norway. Aschehoung. 1st Norwegian. sgn. F/NF. A24. $50.00

**HILLERMAN, Tony.** *Dark Wind.* 1982. Harper Row. 1st. inscr. F/dj. L3. $375.00

**HILLERMAN, Tony.** *Dark Wind.* 1982. Harper Row. 1st. VG+/dj. A14. $140.00

**HILLERMAN, Tony.** *Fallen Man.* 1997. London. Michael Joseph. 1st. F/dj. M15. $45.00

**HILLERMAN, Tony.** *Fly on the Wall.* 1990. Armchair Detective. 1/100. sgn on limitation. burgandy cloth. NF/case. A14. $87.50

**HILLERMAN, Tony.** *Ghostway.* 1984. San Diego. McMillan. 1st. 1/300. sgn. F/dj. M15. $600.00

**HILLERMAN, Tony.** *Ghostway.* 1985. Harper Row. 1st. F/VG. M19. $75.00

**HILLERMAN, Tony.** *Ghostway.* 1985. London. Gollancz. 1st. NF/dj. A14. $42.00

**HILLERMAN, Tony.** *Skinwalkers.* 1986. Harper Row. 1st. sgn. F/F/case. B3. $350.00

**HILLERMAN, Tony.** *Skinwalkers.* 1986. NY. Harper Row. 1st. F/dj. M15. $75.00

**HILLERMAN, Tony.** *Skinwalkers.* 1988. London. Michael Joseph. 1st. F/clip. A24. $50.00

**HILLERMAN, Tony.** *Spell of New Mexico.* 1976. Albuquerque. U NM. 1st. F/clip. M15. $150.00

**HILLERMAN, Tony.** *Talking God.* 1989. Harper Row. 1st. F/dj. M19. $35.00

**HILLERMAN, Tony.** *Talking Mysteries: Conversation With Tony Hillerman.* 1991. U NM. 3rd. F/dj. P3. $18.00

**HILLERMAN, Tony.** *Thief of Time.* 1988. Harper Row. 1st. F/dj. D10. $45.00

**HILLERMAN, Tony.** *Thief of Time.* 1988. Harper Row. 1st. sgn. F/dj. M15. $75.00

**HILLERMAN, Tony.** *Words, Weather & Wolfmen.* 1989. Gallup. Southwesterner Books. 1st. 1/350. sgns. F/dj. M15. $150.00

**HILLES, Frederick W.** *Age of Johnson: Essays Presented to Chauncy Brewster Tinker.* 1964 (1949). Yale. rpt. dj. H13. $85.00

**HILLES, Frederick W.** *Literary Career of Sir Joshua Reynolds.* 1936. Cambridge. 1st. ils. 318p. VG. H13. $85.00

**HILLES, Frederick W.** *Literary Career of Sir Joshua Reynolds.* 1967 (1936). CT. Archon. rpt. H13. $55.00

**HILLES, Frederick W.** *New Light on Dr Johnson: Essays...* 1959. Yale. 1st. inscr. H13. $125.00

**HILLES, Frederick W.** *Portraits by Sir Joshua...* 1952. Yale. 3rd in series. 11 pl. 224p. VG. A4. $45.00

**HILLHOUSE, James.** *Propositions for Amending Constitution of United States...* 1808. WA. 1st. 8vo. F/stiched self wrp. O1. $225.00

**HILLIER, Bevis.** *Cartoons & Caricatures.* 1976. NY/London. Studio Vista/Dutton. 1st. VG/wrp. C9. $48.00

**HILLIER, J.** *Art of the Japanese Book.* 1987. London. 2 vol. 225 mc pl. F/dj/case. M4. $350.00

**HILLIER, J.R.** *Japanese Drawings From the 17th Through 19th Century.* 1965. NY. ils. VG/dj. M17. $20.00

**HILLIS, Newell Dwight.** *Quest of John Chapman.* 1904. NY. 349p. G. B18. $32.50

**HILLS, A.W.D.** *Heat & Mass Transfer in Process Metallurgy.* 1967. London. Inst Mining. 1st. 8vo. F/VG. A2. $40.00

**HILLS, George Morgan.** *History of the Church in Burlington, NJ...* 1876. Trenton, NJ. Wm Sharp. 1st. V3. $28.00

**HILLS, John Waller.** *History of Fly Fishing for Trout.* 1971. Rockville Center, NY. Freshet. F/box. A19. $35.00

**HILLS, Lawrence D.** *Alpines Without a Garden.* 1953. London. photos/ils. 192p. B26. $25.00

**HILTON, James.** *Goodbye, Mr Chips.* 1935. Little Brn. 1st. inscr. ils. gr cloth. VG/dj. J3. $100.00

**HILTON, John Buxton.** *Asking Price.* 1983. London. Collins Crime Club. 1st. F/NF. M15. $40.00

**HILTON, John Buxton.** *Death in Midwinter.* 1969. London. Cassell. 1st. inscr. author's 2nd mystery. F/dj. M15. $75.00

**HILTON, John.** *Notes on Some Developmental & Functional Relations...* 1855. London. Churchill. 93p. VG. G7. $395.00

**HILTON, R. Greer.** *Voices of the Southwest: Book of Texan Verse.* 1923. Macmillan. 1st. VG+. A18. $15.00

**HIMES, Chester.** *Case of Rape.* 1980. NY. Targ. 1st. 1/350. sgn. F/tissue dj. M15. $150.00

**HIMES, Chester.** *Case of Rape.* 1984. Howard U. 1st thus. F/dj. A24. $25.00

**HIMES, Chester.** *End of the Primitive.* 1990. London. Allison Busby. 1st complete. F/NF. A24. $50.00

**HIMES, Chester.** *If He Hollers Let Him Go.* 1947. London. Falcon. 1st Eng. author's 1st novel. F/NF. M15. $300.00

**HIMMELFARB, Gertrude.** *On Looking Into the Abyss: Untimely Thoughts on Culture...* 1994. NY. VG/dj. M17. $15.00

**HIND, Arthur.** *Catalogue of Rembrandt's Etchings...* 1923. London. Vol 1 (of 2) only. ils. VG. A4. $175.00

**HINDE, Thomas.** *Games of Chance.* 1965. Vanguard. 1st. F/G. T12. $30.00

**HINDMARSH, W.A.** *Magnetism & the Cosmos.* 1967. NY. Am Elsevier. 1st. ils. 8vo. VG/dj. A2. $15.00

**HINE, Robert F.** *William Andrew Spalding: Los Angeles Newspaperman.* ca 1961. San Marino, CA. Huntington Lib. 1st. F/dj. O4. $15.00

**HINE, Robert V.** *Soldier in the West: Letters of Theodore Talbot...* 1972. Norman, OK. 1st. ils/noste. 210p. E1. $35.00

**HINES, C.O.** *Upper Atmosphere in Motion.* 1974. WA, DC. Am Geophysical Union. 1027p. cloth. VG. K5. $30.00

**HINES, Jack.** *Minstrel of the Yukon.* 1948. NY. Greenberg. 2nd. 8vo. 231p. VG. H7. $15.00

**HINES, S.** *I Remember Laura.* 1994. Nelson. 1st. 8vo. VG/dj. B17. $16.50

**HINKLE, Thomas.** *Bugle.* 1939. Grosset Dunlap. VG/dj. A21. $20.00

**HINKLEY, Julian Wisner.** *Narrative of Service With Third Wisconsin Infantry.* 1912. WI Hist Comm. 1st. 1/250. 197p. VG. S16. $125.00

**HINKS, Peter.** *Victorian Jewelry: Complete Compendium...* 1996. London. Studio. rpt. F/dj. B9. $35.00

**HINMAN, Wilbur S.** *Corporal Si Klegg & His Pard: How They Talked, Lived...* 1888 (1887). 705p. VG. E6. $30.00

**HINSHAW, David.** *Rufus Jones, Master Quaker.* (1951). NY. Putnam. ils/biblio/ index. 306p. xl. G. H10. $17.50

**HINTON, Alan.** *Shells of New Guinea & the Central Indo-Pacific.* 1975. Hong Kong. rpt. 44 full-p mc pl. 94p. VG/dj. S15. $24.00

**HIORNS, Arthur H.** *Mixed Metals or Metallic Alloys.* 1890. London. Macmillan. 384p. xl. F. B14. $75.00

**HIPKINS, A.J.** *Musical Instruments: Historic, Rare & Unique...* 1945. London. Black. sm folio. ils Wm Gibb. 124p. burgundy cloth. K1. $200.00

**HIPPOCRATES.** *Aphorism of Hippocrates: With Trans Into Latin & English...* 1982. Birmingham. facs of 1822 London. 314p. leather. A13. $95.00

**HIPPOCRATES.** *On Intercourse & Pregnancy: An English Translation...* 1952. NY. 1st Eng trans. 128p. A13. $100.00

**HIRD, Frank.** *HM Stanley: Being the Authorized Life of Sir HM Stanley.* ca 1935. London. Stanley Paul. 8vo. 16 pl. 320p. VG/dj. W1. $22.00

**HIRSCH, Bob.** *Arizona Roamin' — 25 Easy Arizona Trips...* 1979. Rock Along Pub. 8vo. 96p. VG. F7. $4.50

**HIRSCHHORN, Richard.** *Target Mayflower.* 1977. HBJ. 1st. quarter cloth. NF/dj. T11. $15.00

**HIRSCHMANN, Fred.** *Portrait of Arizona.* 1990. Graphic Arts Center. 4to. 80p. stiff wrp. F7. $129.50

**HIRSCHMANN, Ira A.** *Life Line to a Promised Land.* 1946. Vanguard. 3rd. sgn/dtd. G/dj. A2. $12.00

**HIRSHBERG, Al.** *What's the Matter With the Red Sox?* 1973. Dodd Mead. 1st. photos. F/dj. P8. $40.00

**HIRSHSON, Stanley P.** *Lion of the Lord: Biography of Brigham Young.* 1969. Knopf. ils/notes/biblio. 391p. G. H10. $25.00

**HIRST, Stephen.** *Life in a Narrow Place: Havasupal of Grand Canyon.* 1976. McKay. 1st. tall 8vo. 302p. yel cloth. dj. F7. $45.00

**HIRST, Stephen.** *Wavsuw 'Baaja: People of the Blue-Green Water.* 1985. Supai, AZ. 8vo. 259p. bl-gr brd. pict dj. F7. $45.00

**HISCOCK, Ira B.** *Ways to Community Health Education.* 1940 (1939). OUP. 2nd. ils. F/VG. A2. $30.00

**HISCOE, H.B.** *Appalachian Passage.* 1991. GA U. 1st. 321p. F/dj. M4. $18.00

**HISS, Tony.** *Laughing Last.* 1977. Houghton Mifflin. 1st. F/G. B2. $25.00

**HITCHCOCK, A.S.** *Methods of Descriptive Systematic Botany.* 1925. NY. ils. 216p. B26. $25.00

**HITCHCOCK, Alfred.** *Best of Mystery.* nd. Galahad. 2nd. VG/dj. P3. $10.00

**HITCHCOCK, Alfred.** *Daring Detectives.* 1969. Random. VG/dj. P3. $20.00

**HITCHCOCK, Alfred.** *Stories That Scared Even Me.* nd. BC. VG/dj. P3. $10.00

**HITCHCOCK & STANDLEY.** *Flora of the District of Columbia & Vicinity.* 1919. GPO. 327p. VG. A10. $45.00

**HITCHENS, Dolores.** *Nets to Catch the Wind (Widows Won't Wait).* 1952. Crime Club. 1st. VG. P3. $20.00

**HITCHENS & HITCHENS.** *Grudge.* 1963. Doubleday Crime Club. 1st. 8vo. 185p. F/dj. H1. $25.00

**HITCHMAN, Janet.** *Such a Strange Lady.* 1975. NEL. 1st Eng. VG/dj. G8. $30.00

**HITE, Molly.** *Breach of Immunity.* 1992. NY. SMP. 1st. author's 2nd novel. F/F. H11. $25.00

**HITTI, Philip K.** *Arabs: Short History.* 1943. Princeton. 224p. cloth. VG. Q2. $24.00

**HITTI, Philip K.** *History of the Arabs: From Earliest Times to Present.* 1958. London. Macmillan. ils/21 maps. 822p. cloth. VG. Q2. $60.00

**HITTI, Philip K.** *Near East in History: 5000-Year Story.* 1961. Van Nostrand. 1st. ils. 574p. VG/torn. W1. $30.00

**HJORTSBERG, William.** *Falling Angel.* 1978. HBJ. 1st. F/dj. M21. $75.00

**HJORTSBERG, William.** *Gray Matters.* nd. S&S. 2nd. F/dj. P3. $10.00

**HJORTSBERG, William.** *Gray Matters.* 1971. S&S. 1st. sgn. F/NF. B2. $50.00

**HJORTSBERG, William.** *Nevermore.* 1994. Atlantic. 1st. F/F. H11/S18. $25.00

**HOAGLAND, Edward.** *Courage of Turtles.* 1970. NY. Random. 1st. inscr. F/dj. L3. $300.00

**HOBAN, Russell.** *Kleinzeit.* 1974. NY. Viking. 1st Am. NF/dj. A14. $25.00

**HOBAN, Russell.** *Lion of Boaz-Jachin & Jachin-Boaz.* 1973. Stein Day. 1st. F/F. D10. $50.00

**HOBAN, Russell.** *Story of Hester Mouse, Who Became a Writer.* 1965. Norton. 1st. 8vo. 48p. gr cloth. NF/VG. T5. $40.00

**HOBART, John H.** *Quaker by Convincement: Spiritual Autobiography.* 1951. NY. McKay. 12mo. 227p. G/worn. V3. $22.00

**HOBART, Lois.** *Mexican Mural.* 1963. NY. Harcourt Brace. 1st. 224p. F3. $10.00

**HOBBS, James.** *Wild Life in the Far West...* 1873. Hartford. Wiley Waterman Eaton. 2nd. 483p. gilt cloth. D11. $225.00

**HOBBS, William Herbert.** *Peary.* 1936. Macmillan. 1st. lg 8vo. 502p. F/NF. B20. $75.00

**HOBERMAN, Mary Ann.** *Cozy Book.* 1982. Viking. 1st. ils Tony Chen. VG. M5. $10.00

**HOBSON, Anthony.** *Apollo & Pegasus: An Enquiry Into Formation & Dispersal...* 1975. Amsterdam. Van Heusden. 1st. 1/250. sgn. gilt bl cloth. F/dj. w/TLS. M24. $225.00

**HOBSON, Anthony.** *Great Libraries.* 1970. NY. Putnam. lg 4to. 320p. VG/VG. A4. $145.00

**HOBSON, Anthony.** *Great Libraries.* 1970. NY. Putnam. 1st Am. 4to. 320p. F/dj. O10. $200.00

**HOBSON, Archie.** *Remembering America, a Sampler of WPA American Guide...* 1985. Columbia. 1st. 391p. F/dj. O10. $25.00

**HOBSON, Laura Z.** *Laura Z, a Life.* 1983. Arbor. 1st. VG/dj. B11. $18.00

**HOBSON, Linda Whitney.** *Walker Percy: Comprehensive Descriptive Bibliography.* 1988. New Orleans. Faust. 1st. 8vo. intro Walker percy. 115p. F/sans. S9. $35.00

**HOCH, Edward D.** *Diagnosis: Impossible, Problems of Dr Sam Hawthorne.* 1996. Norfolk. Crippen Landru. 1st. 1/300. sgn. F/dj. T2. $50.00

**HOCHHUTH, Rolf.** *Deputy.* 1964. NY. Grove. 352p. xl. dj. C5. $12.50

**HOCKING, William Ernest.** *Meaning of Immortality in Human Experience...* 1957. Harper. 263p. VG/dj. H10. $20.00

**HOCKNEY, David.** *Cameraworks.* 1984. Knopf. 1st. ils. NF. S14. $75.00

**HOCKNEY, David.** *72 Drawings.* 1971. Viking. 1st. inscr. VG/dj. B4. $250.00

**HODEL, Donald R.** *Chamedorea Palms.* 1992. np. ils. photos. 350p. AN/dj. B26. $45.00

**HODEL & WRIGHT.** *Enter the Lion: Posthumous Memoir of Mycroft Holmes.* 1979. Dent. 1st Eng. VG/dj. G8. $30.00

**HODGE, Charles.** *Systematic Theology. Vol II.* 1946. Eerdmans. 782p. G. B29. $12.00

**HODGE, Frederick Webb.** *Handbook of American Indians North of Mexico.* 1907. GPO. 2 vol. 8vo. ils/fld map. cloth. O1. $150.00

**HODGE, Frederick Webb.** *History of Hawikuh, New Mexico...* 1937. LA. Hodge Pub Fund/Mus of Am Indian. 1/1000. w/ephemera. K1. $125.00

**HODGE & SMITH.** *Economies & Politics in the Aztec Realm.* 1994. NY. Inst Mesoamerican Studies. 1st. 478p. wrp. F3. $25.00

**HODGES, George.** *William Penn.* 1929. Houghton Mifflin. 16mo. 140p. VG. V3. $15.00

**HODGES, John C.** *Library of Wm Congreve.* 1955. NY Public Lib. 4to. 119p. F. A4. $65.00

**HODGES, Margaret.** *Saint George & the Dragon.* 1984. Little Brn. 1st. obl 4to. 1985 Caldecott. 32p. F/F. B17. $75.00

**HODGES, Peter R.** *Temples of Dreams.* 1994. Great Britain. SR Publications. 82p. F/wrp. C9. $55.00

**HODGETTS, E.A. Brayley.** *Life of Catherine the Great of Russia.* 1914. NY. ils. VG. M17. $17.50

**HODGETTS, E.A. Brayley.** *Vidocq: Master of Crime.* 1928. London. Selwyn Blount. 1st. 8vo. 319p. gilt gr cloth. VG+. B20. $50.00

**HODGKIN, Thomas.** *Trail of Our Faith & Other Papers.* 1911. London. Macmillan. 1st. V3. $18.50

**HODGMAN, Carolyn S.** *How Santa Filled the Christmas Stockings.* 1916. Rochester, NY. Stecher Lithograph Co. ils WF Stecher. stiff bdg. R5. $110.00

**HODGSON & PAINE.** *Fast & Easy Needlepoint.* 1978. Doubleday. 3rd. ils. 96p. VG/dj. S14. $8.00

**HODNETT, E.** *English Woodcuts 1480-1535.* 1973. OUP. rpt. 200 fscs woodcuts. 483p+82p additions/corrections. F. M4. $125.00

**HOEG, Peter.** *Smilla's Sense of Snow.* 1993. FSG. 1st Am. F/dj. M15. $50.00

**HOEG, Peter.** *Smilla's Sense of Snow.* 1993. FSG. 1st. NF/F. H11. $40.00

**HOEG, Peter.** *Smilla's Sense of Snow.* 1993. FSG. 1st. VG/dj. N4. $30.00

**HOEHLING, A.A.** *Damn the Torpedoes!: Naval Incidents of Civil War.* 1989. Winston-Salem, NC. John F Blair. 1st. F/dj. A14. $25.00

**HOEHLING, A.A.** *Great War at Sea: History of Naval Action 1914-1918.* 1965. NY. 1st. ils/maps. VG/dj. E1. $35.00

**HOEHLING & HOEHLING.** *Day Richmond Died.* (1981). AS Barnes. 2nd. 270p. rem mk. dj. B10. $25.00

**HOFF, Arne.** *Dutch Firearms.* 1978. London. 1st. ils. VG/dj. S16. $75.00

**HOFF, Syd.** *Slugger Sol's Slump.* 1979. Windmill. 1st. F. P8. $15.00

**HOFFDING, H.** *Psychologie in Umrissen auf Grundlage der Erfahrung.* 1887. Leipzig. Fru's Verlag. 1st German-language. 463p. G1. $65.00

**HOFFECKER, Carol E.** *Delaware: A Bicentennial History.* 1977. NY. Norton. 1st. 8vo. cloth. F/dj. O10. $25.00

**HOFFERT, Sylvia.** *Private Matters: American Attitudes Toward Childbearing...* 1989. Chicago. 1st. 229p. A13. $30.00

**HOFFMAN, Alice.** *Illumination Night.* 1987. Putnam. 1st. F/dj. M19. $15.00

**HOFFMAN, Alice.** *Practical Magic.* 1995. NY. Putnam. 1st. F/dj. A24. $20.00

**HOFFMAN, Alice.** *Property Of.* 1977. FSG. 1st. F/F. B3. $150.00

**HOFFMAN, Alice.** *Seventh Heaven.* 1990. NY. Putnam. 1st. F/F. w/promo card. R14. $35.00

**HOFFMAN, Alice.** *Seventh Heaven.* 1990. Putnam. 1st. sgn. NF/dj. B30. $40.00

**HOFFMAN, Alice.** *Turtle Moon.* 1992. Putnam. 1st. F/dj. B4. $45.00

**HOFFMAN, Charles Fenno.** *Winter in the West.* 1966. np. 2 vol. rpt (1835). VG. B18. $19.50

**HOFFMAN, Daniel.** *City of Satisfactions.* 1963. Oxford. 1st. F/NF clip. R14. $30.00

**HOFFMAN, Hans.** *Theology of Reinhold Neibuhr.* 1956. NY. 1st. VG/G. B5. $20.00

**HOFFMAN, John.** *Hank Sauer.* 1953. Barnes. 1st. VG/dj. P8. $75.00

**HOFFMAN, Malvina.** *Sculpture Inside & Out.* 1939. NY. Norton. 1st. photos. 300p. VG+/VG. A25. $30.00

**HOFFMAN, W.** *Camp, Court & Seige: Narrative of Personal Adventure...* 1877. 1st. xl. VG. E6. $20.00

**HOFFMANN, E.T.** *Nutcracker.* 1984. Crown. 1/250. ils/sgn Sendak. 102p. AN/case/orig litho. D1. $1,200.00

**HOFFMANN, Heinrich.** *Slovenly Peter (Der Struwwelpeter).* 1935. NY. LEC. 1/1500. 1st thus. trans Mark Twain. VG/case. D1. $500.00

**HOFFMANN, Heinrich.** *Struwwelpeter & Other Stories.* 1904. McLoughlin. 4to. cloth-backed mc pict brd. R5. $875.00

**HOFFMANN, Heinrich.** *Struwwelpeter.* ca 1960s. London. Blackie. 24p. pict brd. VG/dj. D1. $40.00

**HOFFMEISTER, Donald F.** *Mammals of the Grand Canyon.* 1971. U IL. ils/index. 183p. VG/dj. F7. $27.50

**HOFFNUNG, Gerard.** *Ho-Ho Hoffnung.* 1959. Harper. 1st. 4to. F/clip. C15. $25.00

**HOGAN, Chuck.** *Standoff.* 1995. Doubleday. 1st. F/F. H11. $25.00

**HOGAN, Inez.** *Nappy Has a New Friend.* 1947. Scott Foresman. school ed. 8vo. cloth. VG. M5. $45.00

**HOGAN, Inez.** *Nappy Is a Cowboy.* 1949. Dutton. 1st. 12mo. pict brd. dj. R5. $85.00

**HOGARTH, D.G.** *Nearer East.* 1905. London. Frowde. 8vo. ils/fld maps. 296p. G+. Q2. $63.00

**HOGG, Ian V.** *Complete Illustrated Encyclopedia of World's Firearms.* 1978. NY. ils. 320p. F/dj. A17. $30.00

**HOGG, Ian V.** *History of Fortification.* 1981. NY. ils. F/dj. M4. $45.00

**HOGG, Ian V.** *Israeli War Machine.* 1983. Chartwell. 1st Am. 4to. 192p. VG/dj. B11. $15.00

**HOGGMANN, Detlef.** *Playing Card: Illustrated History.* 1973. NYGS. ils/pl/footnotes/index. 96p. cloth. NF/dj. D2. $125.00

**HOGNER, Nils.** *Dynamite: The Wild Stallion.* 1953. NY. Aladdin. VG/fair. O3. $22.00

**HOGROGIAN, Nonny.** *One Fine Day.* 1971. Macmillan. 1st. sgn. 1972 Caldecott. yel cloth. dj. R5. $300.00

**HOGSTRAND, Olle.** *Gambler.* 1973. Pantheon. 1st Am. VG/G. O3. $25.00

**HOGUE, Charles L.** *Latin American Insects & Entomology.* 1993. U CA. photos. 536p. F/dj. S15. $22.00

**HOHMANN & KELLEY.** *EF Schmidt's Investigations of Salado Sites in Arizona...* 1988. Flagstaff. Mus N AZ Bulletin 56. F/wrp. M12. $17.50

**HOIG, Stan.** *Jesse Chisholm: Ambassador of the Plains.* 1991. CO U. 1st. ils. 226p. F/F. B19. $25.00

**HOKE, Helen.** *Major & the Kitten.* 1941. Franklin Watts. ils Diana Thorne. G. A21. $35.00

**HOKE, Helen.** *Mr Sweeney.* 1940. Henry Holt. 1st. VG/G. P2. $15.00

**HOLBERG, Ludvig.** *Nicolai Klimii Iter Svbterranevm Novam Tellvris Theoriam.* 1745. Copenhagen/Leipzig. Mengel. 8vo. 6 pl. pub list at end. vellum. R12. $425.00

**HOLBROOK, M.** *Hygiene of the Brain & Nerves & Cure of Nervousness...* 1879 (1878). VG. E6. $50.00

**HOLBROOK, Richard.** *Centennial of the 7th Regiment.* 1906. sm folio. VG. E6. $50.00

**HOLBROOK, Richard.** *Handbook of Co K 7th Regiment 107 Infantry NYNG.* 1940. 1st. lg 8vo. VG. E6. $40.00

**HOLBROOK, Stewart H.** *America's Ethan Allen.* 1949. Houghton Mifflin. 1st. ils/assn/sgn pres Lynd Ward. red cloth. mc pict dj. R5. $150.00

**HOLBROOK, Stewart H.** *Columbia.* 1956. NY. Rivers of Am. F. M4. $18.00

**HOLBROOK, Stewart H.** *Ethan Allen.* 1940. Macmillan. 1st. 283p. VG/poor. S17. $10.00

**HOLBROOK, Stewart H.** *Old Post Road: Story of the Boston Post Road.* 1962. McGraw Hill. 1st. 8vo. 273p. AN/dj. H1. $35.00

**HOLBROOK, Stewart H.** *Old Post Road: Story of the Boston Post Road.* 1962. NY. Am Trail series. 273p. F/dj. M4. $30.00

**HOLDEN, Craig.** *River Sorrow.* 1994. Delacorte. 1st. F/clip. H11. $30.00

**HOLDSTOCK, Robert.** *Earthwind.* 1977. London. Faber. 1st. author's 2nd book. F/dj. A24. $30.00

**HOLDSTOCK, Robert.** *Eye Among the Blind.* 1976. London. Faber. 1st. sgn. author's 1st book. F/dj. A24. $50.00

**HOLLAND, Cecelia.** *Great Maria.* 1974. Knopf. 1st. 8vo. 519p. F/dj. W2. $25.00

**HOLLAND, Marion.** *Big Ball of String.* (1958). Random BC. sm 4to. ils. 64p. VG. T5. $25.00

**HOLLAND, Ray P.** *Shotgunning in the Uplands.* 1945. NY. 2nd. ils. VG. M17. $20.00

**HOLLAND, Rupert Sargent.** *Historic Railroads.* 1927. Phil. ils. 343p. G. B18. $22.50

**HOLLAND, Rupert Sargent.** *Historic Ships.* 1926. Phil. Macrae Smith. 1st. 8vo. 390p. F/fair box. B11. $50.00

**HOLLAND, Steve.** *Mushroom Jungle: History of Postwar Paperback Publishing.* 1993. Westbury, Wiltshire. Zero. 1st. F/stiff wrp. M15. $45.00

**HOLLAND, Tom.** *Lord of the Dead.* 1995. Pocket. 1st. VG/dj. L1. $35.00

**HOLLANDER, Bernard.** *Brain, Mind & External Signs of Intelligence.* 1931. Allen Unwin. 47 half-tones. 288p. navy cloth. NF/dj. G1. $75.00

**HOLLANDER, Bernard.** *Mental Functions of the Brain: An Investigation...* 1901. Putnam. pres. 38 pl. 512p. panelled gr cloth. G. G1. $100.00

**HOLLANDER, E.** *Plastic und Medizin.* 1912. Enke. 576p. new cloth. G7. $125.00

**HOLLANDER, John.** *Head of the Bed.* 1974. Boston. Godine. 1st. sgn. VG/sans. R14. $35.00

**HOLLANDER, Nicole.** *Mercy, It's the Revolution & I'm in My Bathrobe.* 1982. St Martin. 1st. sgn. F/wrp. B2. $35.00

**HOLLANDER, Xaviera.** *Xaviera's Supersex.* 1976. NY. New American. lg 8vo. ils. 223p. VG/dj. B11. $15.00

**HOLLENBERG, Norman K.** *Management of Hypertension: Multifactorial Approach.* 1987. Springfield, NJ. 1st. 178p. F/dj. C14. $30.00

**HOLLEY, Val.** *James Dean: The Biography.* 1915. NY. 1st. dj. T9. $15.00

**HOLLICK, Frederick.** *Male Generative Organs in Health & Disease...* 1842. NY. TM Strong. 452p. emb cloth. VG. B14. $45.00

**HOLLIDAY, C.W.** *Valley of Youth.* 1948. Caldwell. Caxton. 1st. sgn. photos. 357p. F/dj. A17. $25.00

**HOLLIDAY, Michael;** see Creasey, John.

**HOLLING, Holling Clancy.** *Paddle-to-the-Sea.* 1941. Houghton Mifflin. 1st. 4to. 1942 Caldecott. beige cloth. R5. $150.00

**HOLLISS & SIBLEY.** *Disney Studio Story.* 1988. NY. Crown. 1st. volio. 256p. F/dj. B20. $75.00

**HOLLISS & SIBLEY.** *Snow White & the Seven Dwarfs & Making of Classic Film.* 1987. S&S. 1st. ils. F/dj. C9. $90.00

**HOLLISTER, Mrs.** *Mrs Hollister's Domestic Receipt Book For Cooking...* 1857. Hartford. self pub. rb. 96p. G+. E6. $125.00

**HOLLON, W. Eugene.** *Lost Pathfinder: Zebulon Montgomery Pike.* 1949. Norman, OK. 1st. 240p. cloth. dj. D11. $40.00

**HOLLOWAY, Carroll C.** *Texas Gun Lore.* 1951. San Antonio, TX. Naylor. G. A19. $35.00

**HOLLYN, Lynn.** *Lynn Hollyn's Christmas Toyland.* 1985. Knopf. 1st. VG/G. P12. $18.00

**HOLM, Bill.** *Northwest Coast Indian Art: Analysis of Form.* 1978. Vancouver. Douglas McIntyre. later prt. 115p. VG/dj. P4. $35.00

**HOLMBERG, Rita.** *Farm Journal's Greatest Dishes From the Oven.* 1977. S&S. G/dj. A16. $7.00

**HOLME, Bryan.** *Advertising: Reflections of a Century.* 1982. Viking. 1st. 324p. F/dj. B20. $45.00

**HOLME, Bryan.** *Enchanted World Pictures to Grow Up With.* 1979. OUP. 1st. NF/dj. S13. $10.00

**HOLME, Bryan.** *Kate Greenaway Book.* 1976. Viking. 1st. F/NF. T11. $18.00

**HOLME, Charles.** *Pen, Pencil & Chalk: Series of Drawings...* 1911. London. The Studio. 1st. ils. G. B27. $95.00

**HOLMES, Beth.** *Whipping Boy.* 1978. Merek. 1st. VG/dj. S18. $10.00

**HOLMES, Charles M.** *Principles & Practice of Horse-Shoeing.* 1949. Leeds. Farriers Journal. VG. O3. $40.00

**HOLMES, E. Burton.** *Burton Holmes Travelogues With Illustrations... Vol 6.* 1908. McClure. 8vo. photos. 335p. VG. F7. $60.00

**HOLMES, Efner Tudor.** *Deer in the Hollow.* 1993. Philomel. 1st. 4to. ils Tudor. rem mk. VG. B17. $15.00

**HOLMES, Gordon.** *National Hospital Queens Square 1860-1948.* 1954. Edinburgh. 1st. 98p. A13. $50.00

**HOLMES, Joseph.** *Canyons of the Colorado.* 1996. Chronicle Books. 4to. brn cloth. AN/dj. F7. $40.00

**HOLMES, L. Seale.** *Holmes Handbook & Catalogue of Canada & British N America.* May 1945. 2nd. VG/dj. M17. $25.00

**HOLMES, Maurice G.** *From New Spain by Sea to the Californias, 1519-1668.* 1963. Arthur H Clark. fld map. 307p. cloth. D11. $75.00

**HOLMES, Oliver Wendell.** *Autocrat of the Breakfast-Table.* 1858. Boston. Phillips Sampson. pebbled cloth. G7. $175.00

**HOLMES, Oliver Wendell.** *Before the Curfew & Other Poems, Chiefly Occasional.* 1888. Boston. 1st. 110p. A13. $50.00

**HOLMES, Oliver Wendell.** *Dissertation of Acute Pericarditis.* 1937. Boston. 1st. 12mo. 39p. full vellum. A13. $75.00

**HOLMES, Oliver Wendell.** *Elsie Venner: Romance of Destiny.* 1861. Ticknor Fields. 2 vol. 1st. Victorian cloth. G. G7. $125.00

**HOLMES, Oliver Wendell.** *Homeopathy & Its Kindred Delusions.* 1842. Boston. 1st. 72p. brd. VG. A13. $175.00

**HOLMES, Oliver Wendell.** *Mechanism in Thought & Morals: An Address...* 1871. Boston. Osgood. 12mo. 105p. ochre cloth. VG. G1. $125.00

**HOLMES, Oliver Wendell.** *Medical Essays: 1842-1882.* 1899. Boston. 445p. A13. $60.00

**HOLMES, Oliver Wendell.** *Olive Wendell Holmes Yearbook.* 1894. Houghton Mifflin. 1st thus. 12mo. 220p. gilt gr cloth. VG/dj. J3. $160.00

**HOLMES, Oliver Wendell.** *Over the Teacups.* 1891. Houghton Mifflin. 1st/1st issue (no price on ad leaf). 319p. teg. G7. $125.00

**HOLMES, Oliver Wendell.** *Professor at the Breakfast Table.* 1860. Ticknor Fields. 1st/1st issue. 410p. brn pebbled cloth. VG. G7. $125.00

**HOLMES, Richard.** *Coleridge, Early Visions.* 1989. Viking. 1st Am. 443p. F/NF. A4. $35.00

**HOLMES & ROHRBACH.** *Stagecoach East: Stagecoach Days in East...* 1983. WA. 1st. ils. 220p. F/dj. M4. $25.00

**HOLT, E. Emmett.** *Diseases of Infancy & Childhood.* 1899. NY. Appleton. 1st/later issue. ils. 117p. 3-quarter calf. G7. $195.00

**HOLT, Edwin Bissell.** *Concept of Consciousness.* 1914. London. Geo Allen. 1st Eng. pres. 344p. prt gr cloth. G1. $85.00

**HOLT, Guy.** *Jurgen & the Law, a Statement With Exhibits...* 1923. NY. McBride. 1/1080. M11. $125.00

**HOLT, L.** *Care & Feeding of Children.* 1900 (1894). enlarged. VG. E6. $30.00

**HOLT, Samuel;** see Westlake, Donald E.

**HOLT, Stephen.** *Phantom Roan.* 1949. Longman Gr. ils Pers Crowell. VG/G. B36. $20.00

**HOLT, Stephen.** *Whistling Stallion.* nd. Grosset Dunlap. Famous Horse Stories series. VG. O3. $15.00

**HOLT, Stephen.** *Wild Palomino: Stallion of the Prairies.* nd. Grosset Dunlap. Famous Horse Stories series. G. O3. $10.00

**HOLT, Victoria;** see Hibbert, Eleanor Alice.

**HOLT & QUINN.** *Star Mothers.* 1988. S&S. 308p. VG/dj. C5. $17.50

**HOLTON, Isaac.** *New Granada: Twenty Months in the Andes.* 1967. Carbondale. 1st thus. 223p. edit/intro CH Gardiner. dj. F3. $15.00

**HOLTON, Thomas.** *International Peace Court, Design for a Move From State...* 1970. The Hague. Martinus Nijhoff. 111p. prt sewn wrp. M11. $45.00

**HOLTZAPFFEL, Charles.** *Printing Apparatus for Use of Amateurs.* 1971. Pinner. 1st. edit Chambers/Mosley. T9. $25.00

**HOLTZMAN, Jerome.** *Fielder's Choice.* 1979. HBJ. later prt. VG/dj. P8. $15.00

**HOLWAY, John.** *Voices From the Great Black Baseball Leagues.* 1975. Dodd Mead. 1st. photos/stats. F/VG. P8. $125.00

**HOLZER, Erika.** *Eye for an Eye.* 1993. NY. Tor. 1st. F/F. H11. $30.00

**HOLZWORTH, John M.** *Twin Grizzles of Admiralty Island.* 1932. Phil. Lippincott. 4th. 8vo. ils. 250p. VG/dj. P4. $25.00

**HOMANS, John.** *Textbook of Surgery: Compiled From Lectures...* 1932. Springfield. Chas Thomas. enlarged/revised. 1231p. G. C14. $15.00

**HOME, Jessie.** *Happiest Christmas.* 1955. Racine, WI. Whitman. ils Irma Wilde. VG+. B36. $7.00

**HOMEL, David.** *Rat Palms.* 1992. Harper Collins. 1st. AN/dj. P8. $20.00

**HOMER.** *Commentary on Homer's Odyssey, Volume I.* 1988. Oxford. Clarendon. 1st Eng. sm 8vo. maroon brd. F/dj. M7. $45.00

**HOMER.** *Illustrated Odyssey.* 1980. London. 1st thus. intro J Hawkes. trans EV Rieu. dj. T9. $20.00

**HOMER.** *Song of Demeter & Persephone, Homeric Hymn.* (1902). Chicago. Ralph Fletcher Seymour. sm 12mo. 54p. blk cloth. K1. $100.00

**HOMEWOOD, Harry.** *Final Harbor.* 1980. McGraw Hill. 1st. F/NF. T11. $25.00

**HONEA, Charla.** *Reader's Companion to Crossing the Threshold of Hope.* 1994. Paraclete. 232p. F/dj. B29. $10.00

**HONES, Diana Wynne.** *Homeward Bounders.* 1981. NY. Greenwillow. 1st Am. sgn. 224p. F/NF. D4. $55.00

**HONEYMAN, A. VanDoren.** *Bright Days in Sunny Lands.* 1904. Plainfield, NJ. self pub. 1st. sgn pres. 30 pl. 420p. cloth. VG. W1. $30.00

**HONGXUN, Yang.** *Classical Gardens of China.* 1982. Van Nostrand Reinhold. 1st. ils/index. 128p. VG/dj. H10. $27.50

**HONIG, Donald.** *Baseball When the Grass Was Real.* 1975. Coward McCann. 1st. photos. VG/G. P8. $30.00

**HONIG, Donald.** *Last Man Out.* 1993. Dutton. ARC. F/dj. P8. $25.00

**HONIG, Donald.** *Plot to Kill Jackie Robinson.* 1992. Dutton. 1st. F/dj. P8. $15.00

**HONNESS, Elizabeth.** *Flight of Fancy.* 1941. Oxford. 1st. ils Pelagie Doane. unp. VG. C14. $8.00

**HONORE, Tony.** *Tribonian.* 1978. London. Duckworth. 314p. cloth. VG/dj. Q2. $26.50

**HOOD, Miriam.** *Gunboat Diplomacy.* 1977. NY. Barnes. 1st Am. 202p. dj. F3. $15.00

**HOOD, Robert E.** *12 at War: Great Photographers Under Fire.* 1967. Putnam. 159p. ils brd. NF/sans. R11. $40.00

**HOOD, Thomas.** *Hood's Own: First & Second Series.* 1839 & 1861. London. AH Baily. 2 vol. teg. Riviere full red morocco/raised bands. F. B20. $500.00

**HOOD'S SARSAPIRELLA.** *Hood's Practical Cookbook for the Average Household.* 1897. 1st. 16mo. 351p. VG. E6. $20.00

**HOOK, Donald D.** *Madmen of History.* 1976. Jonathan David. VG/dj. P3. $18.00

**HOOK, F.A.** *Merchant Adventurers 1914-1918.* 1920. London. Blk. 1st. sm 8vo. 320p. gilt bl cloth. VG. M7. $60.00

**HOOKER, Worthington.** *Child's Book of Nature: 3 Parts in 1.* 1880. NY. 12mo. ils. G. A17. $20.00

**HOOKER, Worthington.** *Natural History: For the Use of Schools & Families.* (1888). Harper. 8vo. ils/engravings. 382p. quarter leather/cloth. VG. M12. $20.00

**HOOKER, Worthington.** *Natural History: For the Use of Schools & Families.* 1864. NY. 382p. G. A17. $15.00

**HOOPER, Walter.** *CS Lewis: Bibliography.* 1991. Aidan Mackey. 1st. sgn Mackey. AN/wrp. A27. $12.50

**HOOPER, Walter.** *CS Lewis: Companion & Guide.* 1996. Harper Collins. 1st. 940p. AN/dj. A27. $40.00

**HOOPES, Chad L.** *What Makes a Man: Annie E Kennedy & John Bidwell Letters...* 1973. Fresno, CA. Valley Pub. 1st. F/NF. O4. $25.00

**HOOPES, Donelson F.** *American Watercolor Painting.* 1977. Watson Guptill. 1st. ils/biographies. 208p. F/dj. D2. $70.00

**HOORMAN, Ferdinand.** *Rivals on the Ridge.* 1930. NY. Frederick Pustet. 1st. NF/dj. M15. $65.00

**HOOTON, Earnest Albert.** *Up From the Ape.* 1946. Macmillan. revised. 788p. xl. G. S5. $15.00

**HOOVER, Herbert.** *American Epic: Vol IV: Guns Cease Killing...* 1964. Chigago. Regnery. 1st. 322p. VG/dj. V3. $18.00

**HOOVER, Herbert.** *Think of the Next Generation.* 1949. Stanford. 1st. sgn. F/stapled as issued. M24. $200.00

**HOPE, Bob.** *Bob Hope's Own Story: Have Tux, Will Travel.* 1954. S&S. 308p. VG/dj. C5. $17.50

**HOPE, Bob.** *Five Women I Love.* 1966. Doubleday. 1st. 255p. F. W2. $15.00

**HOPE, Brian;** see Creasey, John.

**HOPE, Christopher.** *Hottentot Room.* 1987. NY. 1st. dj. T9. $10.00

**HOPE, Laura Lee.** *Bobbsey Twins at School.* 1912. Grosset Dunlap. gr cloth/pict label. VG/G. P12. $12.00

**HOPE, Laura Lee.** *Bobbsey Twins at Sugar Maple Hill.* 1946. Grosset Dunlap. ne. sm 8vo. 210p. VG. W2. $15.00

**HOPE, Laura Lee.** *Story of the Bold Tin Soldier.* 1920. Grosset & Dunlap. ils Harry L Smith. 120p. bl bdg. G. P12. $8.00

**HOPKINS, Albert A.** *Home-Made Beverages: Manufacture of Non-Alcholic...* 1919. Scientific American. 2nd. VG/G+. E6. $30.00

**HOPKINS, Andrea.** *Book of Courtly Love.* 1994. SF. Harper. 1st Am. AN/dj. T10. $16.00

**HOPKINS, Andrea.** *Chronicles of King Arthur.* 1994. Viking STudio. 1st Am. F/dj. T10. $25.00

**HOPKINS, Anthony.** *Music All Around Me.* 1967. London. Leslie Frewin. 217p. G/dj. C5. $12.50

**HOPKINS, Clark.** *Discovery of Dura-Europas.* 1979. Yale. ils/maps. 309p. cloth. xl. G/dj. Q2. $30.00

**HOPKINS, Ernest Jerome.** *What Happened in the Mooney Case?* 1932. NY. Brewer Warren Putnam. 1st. inscr Mooney. VG. B2. $300.00

**HOPKINS, J. Castell.** *Canadian Annual Review of Public Affairs: 1916.* (1917). Toronto. Annual Review Pub. 929p. half morocco/marbled brd. A26. $65.00

**HOPKINS, Lee Bennett.** *To Look at Any Thing.* 1978. HBJ. 1st. VG/dj. S5. $8.00

**HOPKINS, Mary Alden.** *Dr Johnson's Lichfield.* 1952. Hastings. 1st. inscr. dj. H13. $45.00

**HOPKINS, Robert.** *Darwin's South America.* 1969. John Day. 1st. 224p. dj. F3. $20.00

**HOPKINS, Samuel.** *Puritans & Queen Elizabeth...* (1875). NY. Randolph. 3 vol. G. H10. $95.00

**HOPKINS, Tighe.** *Wards of the State.* 1913. London. Herbert & Daniel. 1st. 8vo. 340p. gilt maroon cloth. VG. B20. $30.00

**HOPKINS, William John.** *She Blows! And Sparm at That!* 1922. Houghton Mifflin. 1st. ils Clifford W Ashley. bl cloth. R3. $35.00

**HOPPER, James.** *Coming Back With the Spitball.* 1914. Harper. 1st. F/VG. P8. $175.00

**HOPPER, Vincent F.** *Chaucer's Canterbury Tales.* 1970. Barron Edu Series. revised/enlarged. sm 8vo. 530p. NF. W2. $15.00

**HOPPS, Walter.** *Jacob Kainen.* 1993. Thames Hudson. rem mk. NF/wrp. H4. $22.00

**HORAN, James D.** *Across the Cimarron.* 1956. Bonanza. F/dj. A19. $30.00

**HORAN, James D.** *Confederate Agent: Discovery in History.* 1954. NY. Crown. 1st. pumpkin cloth. VG. A14. $14.00

**HORAN, James D.** *Desperate Women.* 1952. NY. Putnam. 1st. VG/dj. B5. $20.00

**HORAN, James D.** *Of America East & West: Selections From Writings of...* 1984. FSG. 1st. NF/clip. A14. $17.50

**HORAN, James D.** *Outlaws.* ils/photos/index. 312p. AN. E1. $20.00

**HORAN, James D.** *Pinkertons: Detective Dynasty That Made History.* 1968. Bonanza. F/dj. A19. $25.00

**HORATIUS FLACCUS, Quintus.** *Carmina Alcaica.* 1903. Chelsea. Ashenden. 1st thus. 1/150 on Japanese vellum. F. M24. $1,250.00

**HORGAN, Paul.** *Approaches to Writing.* 1973. FSG. 1st. NF/dj. T11. $25.00

**HORGAN, Paul.** *Centuries of Santa Fe.* 1956. Dutton. 1st. 363p. map ep. VG/dj. B18. $22.50

**HORGAN, Paul.** *Great River: Rio Grande in North American History.* 1954. Rinehart. 1st. ils/maps. NF/NF case. B19. $65.00

**HORGAN, Paul.** *Heroic Triad: Essays in Social Energies...* 1970. HRW. 1st. 256p. NF/VG. B19. $200.00

**HORGAN, Paul.** *Lamy of Santa Fe.* 1975. FSG. 1st. F/NF. A24. $50.00

**HORGAN, Paul.** *Main Line West.* 1936. NY. Harper. 1st. sgn. author's 4th book. F/VG+. A24. $300.00

**HORGAN, Paul.** *Of America East & West: Selections From Writings of...* 1982. FSG. 1st. 393p. F/F. B19. $25.00

**HORGAN & HURD.** *Return of the Weed.* 1936. NY. Harper. 1/350. sgns. NF. B2. $350.00

**HORLER, Sydney.** *Curse of Doone.* 1930. Mystery League. 1st Am. VG. G8. $10.00

**HORN, Barbar Lee.** *Joseph Papp: A Bio-Biography.* 1992. NY. Greenwood. 409p. VG. C5. $20.00

**HORN, Calvin.** *New Mexico's Troubled Years...* 1963. Horn & Wallace. 1st. ils. 239p. NF/VG. B19. $25.00

**HORN, Maurice.** *Comics of the American West.* 1977. Winchester. G/dj. A19. $25.00

**HORN & WALLACE.** *Confederate Victories in the Southwest: Prelude to Defeat.* 1961. Albuquerque. Horn Wallace. 1/1000. 201p. cloth. dj. D11. $100.00

**HORNADAY, William T.** *Camp-Fires in the Canadian Rockies.* 1906. Scribner. 1st. ils/maps/index. 353p. rpr bdg. B19. $60.00

**HORNADAY, William T.** *Minds & Manners of Wild Animals.* 1922. Scribner. xl. G. A19. $25.00

**HORNADAY, William T.** *Official Guide Book, NY Zoological Park.* 1938. NY Zoological Soc. 24th/Komodo Dragon ed. sm 8vo. 224p. VG. H1. $18.00

**HORNADAY, William T.** *Wild Life Conservation.* 1914. Yale. 1st. ils. 240p. gilt cloth. xl. A17. $25.00

**HORNBY, Nick.** *High Fidelity.* 1995. Riverhead. 1st. author's 1st novel. F/F. H11. $20.00

**HORNER, Charles F.** *Great Men & Famous Women.* 1894. NY. Selmar Hess. 8 vol. 4to. gilt brn cloth. VG. S17. $45.00

**HORNER, Charles F.** *Life of James Redpath.* 1926. NY/NJ. Barse Hopkins. 1st. gr watered-silk bdg/labels. NF. M24. $65.00

**HORNER, K.O.** *Birds of Bahrain: Selected Breeding & Migrant Birds.* 1989. Brahrain Nat Hist Soc. private prt. 4to. 50p. VG. C12. $30.00

**HORNIBROK, F.A.** *Culture of the Abdomen: Ritual of Health...* 1933. NY. Doubleday Doran. early rpt. ils/fld chart. 113p. VG+/dj. B20. $25.00

**HORNOT, Antoine.** *Anecdotes Americaines, ou Histoire Abregee des Principaux...* 1776. Paris. Vincent. 8vo. calf. R12. $200.00

**HORNUNG, C.P.** *Way It Was in the USA: Pictorial Panorama of America...* 1987. OUP. ils. 363p. F. M$. $20.00

**HOROWITZ, I.A.** *Chess: Games to Remember.* 1972. NY. McKay. 1st. NF/VG. O4. $20.00

**HOROWITZ, I.A.** *Golden Treasury of Chess.* 1969. NY. Galahad. 8vo. ils. 185+5p index. VG/dj. B11. $15.00

**HOROWITZ, Norman H.** *To Utopia & Back: Search for Life in Solar System.* 1986. NY. WH Freeman. 1st. 168p. VG/dj. K5. $20.00

**HORRICKS, Raymond.** *Count Basie & His Orchestra.* 1957. London. Gollancz. 1st. F/dj. B2. $50.00

**HORRICKS, Raymond.** *Dizzy Gillespie & the Be-Bop Revolution.* 1984. Spellmount/ Hippocrene. 1st. ils brd. NF/sans. A14. $10.50

**HORSMAN, R.** *War of 1812.* 1969. NY. 1st. 286p. NF/dj. M4. $28.00

**HORSTING, Jessica.** *Midnight Graffiti.* 1992. Warner. 1st. F/VG. S18. $15.00

**HORT, Mrs. Alfred.** *Via Nicaragua: A Sketch of Travel.* 1987. Conway, NH. La Tienda. facs 1887 London. 267p. F3. $25.00

**HORTON, Lydiard Heneage W.** *Dream Problem & the Mechanism of Thought...* 1926. Phil. Cartesian Research Soc. 2 vol. 3rd. bl cloth. G1. $100.00

**HORWITZ, E.L.** *Mountain People, Mountain Crafts.* 1974. NY. 143p. VG. M4. $10.00

**HORWITZ, Larry Wolfe.** *Over 101 Uses for a Dead Husband, an Owner's Manual.* 1994. Hallmark. 1st. lg 8vo. VG. M7. $24.00

**HOSACK, David.** *Observations on Vision. Communicated by George Pearson.* 1794. rpt. pres. 3 fld pl. marbled wrp/emb stp on title. G7. $495.00

**HOSEN, Frederick E.** *Rifle, Blanket & Kettle: Selected Indian Treaties & Laws.* 1985. McFarland. 1st. index. B19. $185.00

**HOSKING & NEWBERRY.** *Art of Bird Photography.* 1948 (1944). London. Country Life. revised. VG/dj. A17/S5. $8.00

**HOSKINS, Katherine.** *Penetential Primer.* 1945. Cummington. 1st. 1/330. F/deep violet wrp/wrp-around band. M24. $60.00

**HOSMER, James K.** *Color Guard: Being a Corporal's Notes...* 1864. Boston. Walker Wise. 1st. 244p. G. M10. $32.50

**HOTCHKISS, Brian D.** *Noble Beasts: Animals in Art.* 1994. Little Brn/Bullfinch. 1st. sq 4to. VG/dj. O3. $25.00

**HOTCHNER, A.E.** *Papa Hemingway: A Personal Memoir.* 1966. Random. ne. 8vo. 304p. VG. W2. $45.00

**HOTCHNER, A.E.** *Sophia, Living & Loving, Her Own Story.* 1979. Morrow. 1st. sm 4to. 256p. NF/dj. W2. $30.00

**HOTMAN, Francois.** *Francogallia.* 1586. Frankfurt. Wechel. 8vo. title device. quarter calf. R12. $975.00

**HOTMAN, Francois.** *Memoires de Messire Caspar de Colligny.* 1665. Paris. Barbin. 12mo. calf. R12. $250.00

**HOTTES, Alfred C.** *Book of Shrubs.* 1928. NY. photos. VG. M17. $15.00

**HOUCK, James.** *Soybeans & Their Products.* 1972. Minneapolis, MN. 294p. dj. A10. $18.00

**HOUDINI.** *Miracle Mongers & Their Methods.* 1920. NY. Dutton. 1st. NF. Q1. $125.00

**HOUGEN, Richard T.** *Cooking With Hougen.* 1960. NY. Abingdon. G/dj. A16. $7.00

**HOUGH, Emerson.** *Mississippi Bubble.* 1902. Bowen Merrill. 2nd. 452p. loose ftspc. G11. $15.00

**HOUGH, Emerson.** *Purchase Price.* 1919. Bobbs Merrill. 415p. G. G11. $18.00

**HOUGH, Emerson.** *Story of the Cowboy.* 1897. NY. Appleton. 1st. ils. 349p. cloth. D11. $50.00

**HOUGH, Emerson.** *Story of the Outlaw.* 1907. NY. Outing. 1st/1st issue. 15 pl. 401p. pict cloth. B18. $75.00

**HOUGH, Emerson.** *54-40 or Fight.* 1909. Bobbs Merrill. ils Arthur Keller. 402p. weak front hinge. G11. $15.00

HOUGH, H.B. *Mostly on Martha's Vineyard: A Personal Record.* 1975. NY. 1st. 289p. VG/dj. M4. $10.00

HOUGH, Richard. *Buller's Dreadnought.* 1982. NY. Morrow. 1st Am. VG/NF. T11. $30.00

HOUGH, Richard. *Captain Bligh & Mr Christian: Men & the Mutiny.* 1973. NY. 1st. ils. VG/dj. M17. $22.50

HOUGH, Richard. *Fight of the Few.* 1980. Morrow. 1st. F/F. H11. $30.00

HOUGH, Romeyn Beck. *Handbook of the Trees of Northern States...* 1947. NY. rpt. photos/range maps. cloth. VG. B26. $25.00

HOUGH, Romeyn Beck. *Handbook of the Trees of the Northern States & Canada...* (1907). Harper. ils/ads/index. 470p. G. H10. $45.00

HOUNIHAN. *Hounihan's Baker's & Confectioner's Guide & Treasure...* 1877. Staunton. self pub. 13 mc pl. G+. E6. $85.00

HOURANI, Albert. *History of the Arab People.* 1991. Cambridge. 1st. 8vo. ils/maps. NF/dj. Q2/W1. $30.00

HOURANI, George Faldo. *Arab Seafaring in the India Ocean in Ancient & Medieval...* 1951. Princeton. 1st. ils/maps. 131p. cloth. VG/dj. Q2. $33.00

HOUSE, Home D. *Wildflowers...* 1935. Macmillan. 4to. 362p. VG. H10. $65.00

HOUSE, Julius T. *John G. Neihardt: Man & Poet.* 1920. Wayne, NE. FH Jones. 1st. ftspc. F. A18. $25.00

HOUSEHOLD, Geoffrey. *Sending.* 1980. Little Brn. 1st Am. VG/dj. M21. $15.00

HOUSEMAN, A.E. *Complete Poems.* 1959. Holt. Centennial/1st prt. F. T10. $50.00

HOUSEMAN, A.E. *Last Poems.* 1944. London. Grant Richards. 2nd? 64p. gilt brn cloth. VG. M7. $30.00

HOUSEMAN, A.E. *Manuscript Poems of...* 1955. U MN. 1st. ils. F/VG. T10. $75.00

HOUSEMAN, A.E. *More Poems.* 1936. Knopf. 1st Am. gilt bl brd. F/clip. T10. $100.00

HOUSER, Caroline. *Dionysos & His Circle: Ancient Through Modern.* 1980. Fogg Art Mus. sgn. ils/glossary. 125p. D2. $30.00

HOUSEWRIGHT, David. *Penance.* 1995. Woodstock. Countryman. 1st. sgn. F/dj. M15. $85.00

HOUSMAN, Laurence. *Arabian Nights.* 1921. Phil. Penn. ils Virginia Sterrett/16 pl & tissue guards. VG. D1. $385.00

HOUSMAN, Laurence. *Cynthia.* 1947. London. 1/500. sgn. T9. $25.00

HOUSTON, James. *Running West.* 1989. NY. Crown. 1st. NF/clip. T11. $25.00

HOUSTON, S.D. *Maya Glyphs.* 1990. Berkley. 2nd. 4to. wrp. F3. $15.00

HOWARD, Alfred. *Lord Chesterfield's Letters, Sentences & Maxims.* nd. Phil. Porter Coates. 10th Am. sm 24mo. gr cloth. VG. M7. $25.00

HOWARD, Cecil. *Pizarro & the Conquest of Peru.* 1968. Harper. Am Heritage Pub. 2nd. 153p. F3. $15.00

HOWARD, Clark. *Arm.* 1967. LA. Sherbourne. 1st. F/F. H11. $40.00

HOWARD, Denis. *New South Wales System.* 1970. VG/wrp. S1. $10.00

HOWARD, Donald S. *WPA & Federal Relief Policy.* 1943. NY. Russell Sage. xl. B2. $75.00

HOWARD, Helen Addison. *War Chief Joseph.* 1941. Caldwell, ID. 2nd. 368p. E1. $35.00

HOWARD, J.H. *Story of the Spoilt Piggy (Dame Dingle's Linen).* 1867. McLoughlin. 8vo. pict linen bdg. R5. $135.00

HOWARD, James L. *Seth Harding, Mariner: Naval Picture of the Revolution.* 1930. New Haven. 8vo. 301p. bl cloth. VG. S17. $15.00

HOWARD, John. *Edict of the Grand Duke of Tuscany, for Reform Criminal...* 1789. Warrington. Prt by W Eyres. xl Harvard. modern quarter calf. M11. $450.00

HOWARD, Maureen. *Facts of Life.* 1978. Little Brn. 1st. NF/dj. S13. $12.00

HOWARD, Maureen. *Natural History.* 1992. Norton. 1st. 393p. F/NF. S15. $10.00

HOWARD, Robert E. *Black Vulmea's Vengence.* 1976. Donald Grant. 1st. VG/dj. L1. $40.00

HOWARD, Robert E. *Worms of the Earth.* 1974. Donald Grant. 1st. VG/dj. L1. $55.00

HOWARD, Robert West. *Great Iron Trail: Story of 1st Transcontinental Railroad.* 1962. Putnam. 376p. VG/dj. J2. $45.00

HOWARD, Ruth Leslie. *Quite Remarkable Father.* 1959. Harcourt Brace. 1st Am. VG/dj. C9. $30.00

HOWARD, Sanford. *Seventh Annual Report State Board Agriculture of Michigan.* 1868. Lansing. Kerr. 490p. cloth. VG. A10. $30.00

HOWARD, Thomas. *CS Lewis: Man of Letters, a Reading of His Fiction.* (1987). Ignatius. 1st Am. wrp. A27. $12.00

HOWARD, Thomas. *Novels of Charles Williams.* (1991). Ignatius. 1st. AN/wrp. A27. $15.00

HOWARD, Walter L. *Luther Burbank: Victim of Hero Worship.* 1945-46. Waltham, MA. 208p. wrp. B26. $35.00

HOWARD & TEMPLETON. *Human Spatial Orientation.* 1966. John Wiley. 533p. gr cloth. VG/dj. G1. $65.00

HOWARTH, David. *Desert King: Life of Ibn Saud.* 1964. Collins. 8vo. 11 pl. 252p. cloth. VG/dj. Q2. $20.00

HOWARTH, David. *Sledge Patrol.* 1957. NY. 1st. photos. VG/dj. M17. $15.00

HOWAY, Frederic W. *Voyages of the Colombia to the Northwest Coast 1787-1790.* 1990. OR Hist Soc. 518p. F/dj. M4. $45.00

HOWAY, Frederic W. *Voyages of the Columbia to the Northwest Coast 1787-1790...* 1941. MA Hist Soc. VG. w/pres card. P4. $225.00

HOWE, G. Melvyn. *Man, Environment & Disease in Britain.* 1972. NY. 1st. 285p. dj. A13. $50.00

HOWE, J. *Excessive Venery, Masturbation & Continence: Etiology...* 1884 (1883). G+. E6. $65.00

HOWE, James Virgil. *Modern Gunsmith: A Guide for the Amateur & Professional...* 1941. Funk Wagnall. 2 vol. 4th. w/supplement. NF. B19. $200.00

HOWE, Julia Ward. *Reminiscences 1819-1899...* 1900. Boston. Houghton Mifflin. 8vo. 465p. tan cloth. F. B14. $55.00

HOWE, Lucien. *Bibliography of Hereditary Eye Defects.* 1928. Cambridge. 58p. wrp. A13. $40.00

HOWE, Mark DeWolfe. *Harvard Volunteers in Europe: Personal Records...* 1916. Cambridge. Harvard. 1st. 12mo. 263p. gilt cloth. VG. C14. $22.00

HOWE, Mark DeWolfe. *Holmes-Laski Letters: Correspondence of Mr Justice Holmes...* 1953. Harvard. 2 vol. cloth. xl. M11. $100.00

HOWE, Mark DeWolfe. *Justice Oliver Wendell Holmes, Shaping Years 1841-1870.* 1957. Cambridge. pres. bl cloth. M11. $65.00

HOWE, Walter. *Mining Guild of New Spain & Its Tribunal General.* 1968 (1949). NY. Greenwood. rpt. 534p. F3. $30.00

HOWE & MATHEWS. *American Clipper Ships 1833-1858.* 1967. Argosy Antiquarian. 2 vol. ils. F/case. P4. $125.00

HOWE & STURTEVANT. *Birds of Rhode Island.* 1899. Middleton(?), RI. private prt. annotated list/ils. 111p. VG. C12. $65.00

**HOWELL, A.H.** *Birds of Alabama.* 1924. Montgomery, AL. ils. 384p. NF. C12. $50.00

**HOWELL, John Thomas.** *Marin Flora: Manual of Flowering Plants & Ferns...* 1949. U CA. 1st. inscr. dj. O4. $20.00

**HOWELL & WHITE.** *Working Together.* 1952. Comm Baptist Women of VA. 105p. VG. B10. $25.00

**HOWELLS, W.D.** *Garroters.* 1898. NY. later prt. sgn. Blk & White series. 90p. decor cloth. B18. $37.50

**HOWES, Isaiah C.** *Jane, Be Good.* 1928. Macmillan. 1st. ils. 155p. NF/VG. B20. $40.00

**HOWES, Wright.** *USiana, 1650-1950: A Selective Bibliography...* nd. rpt of 2nd. 1/150. 11620 entries. F. A4. $65.00

**HOWEY, W. Oldfield.** *Cat in the Mysteries of Magic & Religion.* 1956. NY. Castle. 1st Am. 254p. NF/clip. B20. $40.00

**HOWLAND, E.** *American Economical Housekeeper & Family Receipt Book.* 1849. rb. G+. E6. $95.00

**HOWLAND, E.** *New England Economical Housekeeper.* 1846 (1845). G+. E6. $150.00

**HOWSON, Gerald.** *Burgoyne of Saratoga: A Biography.* 1979. Times. 360p. VG/dj. S17. $15.00

**HOY, Ken.** *Strange Scavenging Creatures.* 1994. Ideals. 1st. 5 popups. F. B17. $12.50

**HOYLE, Fred.** *Of Men & Galaxies.* 1964. Seattle. 8vo. 73p. VG/dj. K5. $14.00

**HOYT, Edwin P.** *Damdest Yankees: Ethan Allen & His Clan.* 1976. Brattleboro, VT. 1st. ils/map ep. VG/dj. B18. $12.50

**HOYT, Edwin P.** *Damdest Yankees: Ethan Allen & His Clan.* 1976. Brattleboro. 1st. ils. 262p. F/dj. M4. $35.00

**HOYT, Edwin P.** *From the Turtle to the Nautilus: Story of Submarines.* 1963. Boston/Toronto. ils C Greer. VG. M17. $15.00

**HOYT, Edwin P.** *Jumbos & Jackasses, a Popular History of Political Wars.* 1960. Doubleday. VG/dj. M11. $25.00

**HOYT, Elizabeth.** *Play Days.* nd (c 1909). Boston/Chicago. WA Wilde. Happy Hour series. 12mo. 96p. fair. C14. $10.00

**HOYT, Henry E.** *Frontier Doctor.* 1929. Houghton Mifflin. 1st. inscr. 260p. cloth. D11. $50.00

**HOYT, Mary Finch.** *American Women of the Space Age.* 1966. Atheneum. 1st. 88p. xl. VG. A25. $12.00

**HOYT, Richard.** *Darwin's Secret: Novel of the Amazon.* 1989. Doubleday. 1st. F/dj. T12. $22.00

**HOYT, Richard.** *Japanese Game.* 1995. Forge. 1st. F/dj. P8. $20.00

**HOYT, Richard.** *Manna Enzyme.* 1982. Morrow. 1st. NF/VG+. N4. $20.00

**HOYT, Richard.** *Marimba.* 1992. Tor. 1st. NF/dj. N4. $15.00

**HOYT, Richard.** *Siege.* 1987. Tor. 1st. F/F. H11. $25.00

**HOYT, Sherman.** *Memoirs.* 1950. NY. 1st. photos. VG. M17. $17.50

**HOYT, W.G.** *Studies of Relations of Rainfall & Run-Off in the US.* 1936. GPO. 301p. xl. F. B14. $55.00

**HOYT & GRAY.** *At Home Hanna.* 1956. Scott Foresman. 71p. ils cloth brd. VG. B36. $22.00

**HOYT & GRAY.** *In the Neighborhood Hanna.* 1965. Scott Foresman. 192p. VG. B36. $22.00

**HSIA, R. Po-Chia.** *Myth of Ritual Murder: Jews & Magic in Reformation Germany.* 1988. New Haven. Yale. M11. $45.00

**HUARTE, Juan.** *Essame de Gli Ingengni de gl'Huomini...* 1586. Venetia. Presso Aldo. 367p. early 19th-C bdg. G1. $385.00

**HUBBARD, Charles D.** *Old New England Village: People, Ways...* 1947. Portland, ME. ils. VG. M17. $20.00

**HUBBARD, Douglas.** *In Old Virginia City.* 1966. Ginn & Co. ils Ed Vella. unp. gray cloth. VG. B36. $8.00

**HUBBARD, Earl R.** *My Seventeen Years With the Pioneers.* nd. np. G. A19. $30.00

**HUBBARD, Elbert.** *Little Journeys to Homes of Great Philosphers. Book 1.* 1904. E Aurora. ils. VG. M17. $25.00

**HUBBARD, Elbert.** *Philosophy of Elbert Hubbard.* 1916. Roycrofters. 1/9982. sgn by son. VG. M17. $30.00

**HUBBARD, G.D.** *Geologic Atlas of the United States, Columbus Folio.* 1915. WA. 1st. 3 fld maps/fld pl. 116p. G. B18. $45.00

**HUBBARD, J. Niles.** *Sketches of Border Adventures...of Major Moses VanCampen.* 1893. Fillmore. JNO S Minard. ils. 337p. quarter leather. fair. B18. $35.00

**HUBBARD, John.** *Rudiments of Geography: Being Concise Description...* 1814. Barnard, VT. contemporary bdg. B14. $125.00

**HUBBARD, L. Ron.** *Dianetics.* 1950. NY. 1st. VG/fair. B5. $75.00

**HUBBARD, L. Ron.** *Slaves of Sleep.* 1948. Shasta. 1st. Hannes Bok cover art. F/NF. B9/P3. $400.00

**HUBBARD, Margaret Ann.** *Murder Takes the Veil.* 1950. Bruce. 2nd. VG/dj. P3. $15.00

**HUBBARD, Margaret Ann.** *Sister Simon's Murder Case.* 1959. Bruce. NF/dj. P3. $15.00

**HUBBARD, Margaret Ann.** *Step Softly on My Grave.* 1966. Bruce. 1st. NF/dj. P3. $18.00

**HUBBELL, Jay B.** *South in American Literature 1607-1900.* 1954. Durham. 1st. 987p. NF/VG. M8. $45.00

**HUBBLE, Edwin.** *Observational Approach to Cosmology.* 1937. Oxford. Clarendon. 8vo. ils/pl. 68p. VG. K5. $75.00

**HUBER, Raphael M.** *St Anthony of Padua: Doctor of the Church Universal...* 1948. Milwaukee. VG/G. M17. $15.00

**HUBER, Richard.** *Dragons. A Universal Myth.* 1983. Austin. Amistad. mini. ils. 40p. quarter cloth/ils brd. F. B24. $100.00

**HUBIN, Allen J.** *Best Detective Stories of the Year, 1974: 28th Annual.* 1974. Dutton. 1st. NF/dj. P3. $30.00

**HUBIN, Allen J.** *Best Detective Stories of the Year 1972.* 1972. Dutton. 2nd. VG/dj. P3. $20.00

**HUBIN, Allen J.** *Best Detective Stories 1971.* 1971. Dutton. 2nd. xl. VG/dj. P3. $8.00

**HUBIN, Allen J.** *Bibliography of Crime Fiction, 1749-1975...* 1979. Dutton. thick 4to. 712p. A4. $95.00

**HUDDLESTON, L.E.** *Origins of the American Indians: European Concepts...* 1967. Austin. 179p. F/dj. M4. $35.00

**HUDSON, Bell.** *Billy the Kid: Most Hated, Most Loved Outlaw...* 1949. Hustler. 1st. 52p. VG/wrp. B19. $35.00

**HUDSON, Derek.** *Lewis Carroll.* 1954. London. Constable. 1st. 354p. VG. M10. $15.00

**HUDSON, Mary W.** *Esther the Gentile.* 1888. Topeka. Crane. 167p. gilt cloth. D11. $60.00

**HUDSON, Robert.** *Disease & Its Control: Shaping of Modern Thought.* 1983. Westport, CT. 1st. 259p. A13. $40.00

**HUDSON, W.H.** *Birds of La Plata.* 1920. Dent/Dutton. Lg Paper ed. 2 vol. 1st trade. 22 pl. gilt gr cloth. F. B20. $300.00

**HUDSON, W.H.** *Purple Land.* 1929. Duckworth. 1st thus. purple cloth. VG. S13. $15.00

**HUFF, Mary Nancy.** *Robert Penn Warren: A Bibliography.* 1968. NY. David Lewis. 1st. 171p. 2-tone cloth. NF/dj. O10. $20.00

**HUFF, Russell.** *Companion to Wings of War II.* 1987. Sarasota. 1st. ils. 105p. VG/wrp. S16. $22.00

**HUFF, Theodore.** *Charlie Chaplin.* 1951. Henry Schuman. 1st. VG/dj. C9. $72.00

**HUFFMAN, Morna M.** *Lutheranism Takes Root in Settlement of Pennsylvania...* 1982. self pub. 1st. 191p. VG. S14. $12.00

**HUFFORD, Grace Thompson.** *My Poetry Book, an Anthology of Modern Verse...* ca 1930s. Chicago. Winston. hc. ils/inscr Willy Pogany. VG. B9. $75.00

**HUGGINS, Nathan Irvin.** *Black Odyssey.* 1977. Pantheon. 1st. F/dj. B2/M23. $30.00

**HUGGLER, Tom.** *Grouse of North America.* 1990. Minocqua, WI. 1st. 1/4000. photos. AN/dj. A17. $45.00

**HUGHES, Arthur.** *History of Cytology.* 1959. NY. 1st. 158p. A13. $50.00

**HUGHES, Colin;** see Creasey, John.

**HUGHES, David.** *But for Bunter.* 1985. London. Heinemann. 1st. NF/dj. A14. $28.00

**HUGHES, David.** *Star of Bethlehem: Astronomer's Confirmation.* 1979. Walker. 1st. F/VG. O4. $15.00

**HUGHES, Dean.** *Angel Park All Stars: Winning Streak (#3).* 1990. Knopf. F. P8. $6.00

**HUGHES, Dorothy B.** *Ride the Pink Horse.* 1946. DSP. 1st. F/clip. m15. $75.00

**HUGHES, Frieda.** *Getting Rid of Aunt Edna.* 1986. Harper Row. 1st. ils Ed Levine. xl. VG/clip. B36. $16.00

**HUGHES, Glenn.** *Academe: Book of Characters.* 1952. Seattle. U WA Bookstore. 1st. VG/wrp. A18. $10.00

**HUGHES, Hatcher.** *Hell-Bent For Heaven: A Play in Three Acts.* 1924. NY. Harper. 1st. NF/dj. Q1. $200.00

**HUGHES, Howard.** *Hell's Angels Press Book.* nd (1930). np (Hollywood, CA). ils. 32p. VG. B18. $95.00

**HUGHES, J. Donald.** *Story of Man at Grand Canyon.* 1967. GCNHA. 1st. 195p. cloth. VG+. F7. $35.00

**HUGHES, Langston.** *Simple Speaks His Mind.* 1950. S&S. 1st. F/NF. B2. $200.00

**HUGHES, Langston.** *Ways of White Folks.* 1934. NY. Knopf. 1st. orange cloth. VG. A24. $100.00

**HUGHES, R. Kent.** *Disciplines of a Godly Man.* 1995. Crossway. New ed. study questions. 288p. VG/dj. B29. $10.00

**HUGHES, Richard.** *High Wind in Jamaica.* 1929. Chatto Windus. 1/150. sgn. teg. NF. B20. $200.00

**HUGHES, Shirley.** *Alfie Gives a Hand.* 1983. Lee Shepard. 1st Am. sm 8vo. wht brd/lib bdg. F/dj. T5. $30.00

**HUGHES, Sukey.** *Washi: The World of Japanese Paper.* 1978. Kodansha Internat. 1st. 360p. NF/VG+. B20. $125.00

**HUGHES, Ted.** *Football.* 1995. Alton. Prospero Poets. 1st. sgn Hughs/ils Chris Battye. F/F. R14. $85.00

**HUGHES, Ted.** *Moon-Whales.* 1976. Viking. ARC/1st. RS. F/NF. w/photo. L3. $65.00

**HUGHES, Ted.** *Moortown.* 1979. London. Faber. 1st. ils Hughes/Baskin. ES. NF/F. R14. $65.00

**HUGHES, Ted.** *Season Songs.* 1975. Viking. 1st. F/dj. O11. $40.00

**HUGHES, Thomas.** *Little History of St Andrews Parish...Early...Farming...* 1889. Charleston Bridge Co. 12p. A10. $30.00

**HUGHES, Thomas.** *Tom Brown's School Days.* 1985. Dent. VG/dj. P3. $15.00

**HUGHES, Virginia.** *Peggy Lane Theater Stories: Peggy Finds the Theater.* 1966. Grosset Dunlap. ils Sergio Leone. 174p. VG. B36. $10.00

**HUGO, Hermannus.** *Pia Desideria, Tribus Libris Comprehensa...* 1740. Antwerp. Joannem Baptistam Verdussen. 12mo. 416p. old calf. K1. $350.00

**HUIE, William Bradford.** *Americanization of Emily.* 1959. Dutton. 1st. NF/dj. B4. $125.00

**HUIE, William Bradford.** *Klansman.* 1967. Delacorte. 1st. F/VG. M19. $17.50

**HUISMAN, Denis.** *Encyclopedie de la Psychologie.* 1962. Paris. Fernand Nathan. folio. ils/mc pl. 250p. emb leather. VG/dj. G1. $125.00

**HULBERT, Archer Butler.** *Old National Road: Chapter of American Expansion.* 1901. Columbus. ils. xl. G. B18. $37.50

**HULBERT, Archer Butler.** *Portage Paths: Keys to the Continent.* 1903. Cleveland. Arthur Clark. ils. 194p. teg. G+. B18. $37.50

**HULETT, G.D.** *Textbook of Principles of Osteopathy.* 1903. Kirksville, MO. 1st. 366p. A13. $75.00

**HULL, Clark Leonard.** *Aptitude Testing.* 1928. Yonkers-on-Hudson, NY. World. 12mo. 535p. red cloth. VG. G1. $65.00

**HULL, Clark Leonard.** *Hypnosis & Suggestibility: An Experimental Approach.* 1933. Appleton Century. 416p. emb blk cloth. F/dj. G1. $125.00

**HULL, D.W.** *Astrological Orig of Jeho-Vah-God of Old & New Testaments.* 1872. Chicago. Birney Hand. 1st. 8vo. 39p. pk wrp. C6. $40.00

**HULRLBURT, Allen.** *Layout, the Design of the Printed Page.* 1978. Watson Guptill. rpt. sm 4to. cloth. F/dj. O10. $35.00

**HULTEN, Eric.** *Flora of Alaska & Neighboring Territories.* 1981 (1968). Stanford. 4to. 1008p. VG/dj. B26. $80.00

**HULTON, P.** *Work of Jacques la Moyne de Morges: Hugenot Artist...* 1977. British Mus/ Huguenot Soc. 2 vol. F/NF case. M4. $165.00

**HUME, Christopher.** *From the Wild: Portfolios of N Am Finest Wildlife Artists.* 1987. North Word. ils. VG/dj. M17. $30.00

**HUME, David.** *History of England.* 1863. Little Brn. 6 vol. 8vo. gilt brn cloth. S17. $40.00

**HUME, Edgar E.** *Victories of Army Medicine: Scientific Accomplishments...* 1943. Phil. 1st. 250p. A13. $40.00

**HUME, H. Harold.** *Azaleas. Kinds & Culture.* 1949 (1948). NY. 2nd. 199p. VG/dj. B26. $20.00

**HUME, H. Harold.** *Camellias in America.* 1955. Harrisburg. McFarland. revised. 422p. AN. A10. $75.00

**HUME, H. Harold.** *Citrus Fruits & Their Culture.* 1904. Jacksonville. 1st. ils. 597p. VG. B5. $65.00

**HUMES, Edward.** *Mississippi Mud: True Story From Corner of Deep South.* 1994. S&S. 1st. inscr/dtd 1994. NF/dj. B30. $30.00

**HUMM, Maggie.** *Annotated Critical Bibliography of Feminist Criticism.* 1987. GK Hall. 900 entries. 251p. F/F. A4. $45.00

**HUMPHREY, Grace.** *Story of the Williams.* 1926. Phil. Penn Pub. 1st. 224p. G. V3. $24.00

**HUMPHREY, Robert R.** *90 Years & 535 Miles: Vegetation Changes...* 1987. NM U. 1st. ils. 448p. F/F. B19. $25.00

**HUMPHREY, William.** *Home From the Hill.* 1958. Knopf. 1st. NF/dj. D10. $60.00

**HUMPHREY, William.** *Ordways.* 1964. Knopf. 1st. F/dj. D10. $50.00

**HUMPHREY, William.** *Proud Flesh.* 1973. Knopf. 1st. sgn. F/F. D10. $65.00

**HUMPHREY, Zephine.** *Cactus Forest.* 1938. Dutton. 1st. 245p. G. B19. $20.00

**HUMPHREY, Zephine.** *God & Company.* 1953. Harper. 1st. 12mo. 128p. G/dj. B11. $15.00

**HUMPHREYS, F.** *Manual of Specific Homeopathy Administration of Medicine...* self pub. VG. E6. $18.00

**HUMPHREYS, John O.** *American Racetracks & Contemporary Racing Art.* 1966. S Bend. 1st. ils/index. 240p. xl. G. A17. $20.00

**HUMPHREYS, Robin A.** *Evolution of Modern Latin America.* 1973. Cooper Sq Pub. 8vo. 196p. VG. P4. $18.00

**HUMPHREYS, Travers.** *Book of Trials.* 1953. London. Heinemann. 2nd. G. M11. $65.00

**HUNEVEN, Michelle.** *Round Rock.* 1997. NY. Knopf. 1st. sgn. author's 1st book. F/dj. R14. $45.00

**HUNGERFORD, Edward.** *Story of the Baltimore & Ohio Railroad 1827-1927.* 1928. NY. 2 vol. 1st. ils/map ep. G. B18. $45.00

**HUNSBERGER, W.** *Franconia Mennonites in American Wars.* 1951. self pub. VG. E6. $20.00

**HUNT, Aurora.** *Major General James Henry Carleton, 1814-1873.* 1958. Glendale. Arthur H Clark. ils. 390p. cloth. D11. $75.00

**HUNT, Carrles Cummins.** *Genealogical History of Robert & Abigail Pancoast Hunt...* 1906. np. 202p. G. S5. $50.00

**HUNT, Frazier.** *MacArthur & the War Against Japan.* 1944. Scribner. G. A19. $35.00

**HUNT, Frazier.** *Tragic Days of Billy the Kid.* 1956. NY. Hastings. G/dj. A19. $30.00

**HUNT, Irene.** *Lottery Rose.* 1976. Scribner. 1st. 8vo. maroon cloth. F/NF. T5. $30.00

**HUNT, Kyle;** see Creasey, John.

**HUNT, Mabel Leigh.** *Lucinda, a Little Girl of 1860.* 1934. NY. 1st. inscr. 233p. VG/dj. B18. $37.50

**HUNT, Marsha.** *Free.* 1992. Dutton. 1st. AN/dj. B30. $45.00

**HUNT, Marsha.** *Joy.* 1990. Dutton. 1st. author's 1st book. rem mk. F/AN. B30. $60.00

**HUNT, N. Clemmons.** *Poetry of Other Lands.* nd (1883). Porter Coates. VG. M17. $20.00

**HUNT, Rockwell D.** *Fifteen Decisive Events of California History.* 1959. LA. Hist Soc S CA. 1st. F/sans. O4. $25.00

**HUNT, Thomas H.** *Ghost Trails to California.* 1974. Am West Pub. 1st. ils/maps. 290p. NF/clip. B19. $20.00

**HUNT, W. Ben.** *Indian Silversmithing.* 1960. Milwaukee. Bruce. 1st. ils/index. 160p. VG. B5. $30.00

**HUNT, William R.** *To Stand at the Pole: Dr Cook-Admiral Peary...* 1981. Stein Day. 8vo. 288p. half cloth. P4. $20.00

**HUNT & ROSSI.** *Art of the Old West: From Collection of Gilcrease Institute.* 1981. promotory. rpt. 236p. NF/dj. B19. $40.00

**HUNT & THOMPSON.** *North to the Horizon: Arctic Doctor & Hunter 1913-1917.* 1980. Camden. 117p. F/dj. A17. $20.00

**HUNTER, Dard.** *Chinese Ceremonial Paper: A Monograph...* 1937. Chillicothe. Mtn House. 1/125. sgn/#d. 6 fld pl/2 samples/2 collotypes. F/case. B24. $8,500.00

**HUNTER, Dard.** *Old Papermaking in China & Japan.* 1932. Chillicothe. Mtn House. 1/200. sgn. tipped-in ils/samples. w/portfolio. case. B24. $3,850.00

**HUNTER, Dard.** *Papermaking in Southern Siam.* 1936. Chillicothe. Mtn House. 1/115 on handmade. assn inscr. ils/samples. F. B24. $6,500.00

**HUNTER, Evan.** *Ax.* 1964. S&S. 1st. F/dj. M15. $165.00

**HUNTER, Evan.** *Doors.* 1975. Stein Day. 1st. NF/clip. A14. $28.00

**HUNTER, Evan.** *Downtown.* 1991. Morrow. 1st. F/F. H11. $15.00

**HUNTER, Evan.** *Far From the Sea.* 1983. Atheneum. 1st. F/F. H11. $35.00

**HUNTER, Evan.** *Poison.* 1987. NY. Arbor. 1st. F/dj. M15. $45.00

**HUNTER, Evan.** *Tricks.* 1987. NY. Arbor. 1st. F/F. H11. $20.00

**HUNTER, Fred.** *Presence of Mind.* 1994. NY. Walker. 1st. sgn. author's 1st novel. F/dj. T2. $25.00

**HUNTER, Jack D.** *Expendable Spy.* 1965. Dutton. 1st. F/NF. H11. $30.00

**HUNTER, James Davison.** *Culture Wars: Struggle to Define America.* 1990. Basic. 416p. VG/wrp. B29. $8.50

**HUNTER, John.** *Treatise on the Blood, Inflammation & Gun-Shot Wounds.* 1982. Birmingham. facs of 1794. 575p. full leather. A13. $100.00

**HUNTER, Lillie Mae.** *Moving Finger.* 1956. Plains Prt. ils. 171p. VG. J2. $80.00

**HUNTER, Mollie.** *Furl of Fairy Wind.* 1978. Harper Row. 1st. 8vo. ils/sgn Stephen Gammell. VG/dj. B17. $25.00

**HUNTER, Stephen.** *Black Light.* 1996. Doubleday. 1st. NF/F. H11. $15.00

**HUNTER, Stephen.** *Black Light.* 1996. Doubleday. 1st. sgn. F/dj. S18. $45.00

**HUNTER, Stephen.** *Day Before Midnight.* 1989. NY. Bantam. 1st. VG/F. H11. $35.00

**HUNTER, Stephen.** *Dirty White Boys.* 1994. Random. 1st. NF/F. H11. $30.00

**HUNTER, Stephen.** *Time to Hunt.* 1998. Doubleday. 1st. sgn. F/dj. S18. $40.00

**HUNTER, Stephen.** *Violent Screen.* 1995. Bancroft. 1st. sgn. F/dj. S18. $45.00

**HUNTER, William A.** *Forts on the Pennsylvania Frontier, 1753-1758.* 1960. PA Historical Mus Comm. tall 8vo. 596p. gilt bdg. NF. H1. $30.00

**HUNTER, William.** *Hunter's Lectures on Anatomy.* 1972. Amsterdam. Elsevier. facs. thick 4to. G7. $95.00

**HUNTER & ROSE.** *Album of Gun-Fighers.* 1951. Rose/Hunter Pub. 236p. VG/dj. J2. $575.00

**HUNTFORD, Roland.** *Amundsen Photographs.* 1987. NY. index. 199p. F/dj. A17. $30.00

**HUNTINGTON & MCCLELLAND.** *History of the Ohio Canals.* 1905. Columbus. OH Archeological & Hist Soc. VG. B18. $150.00

**HUNTLEY, Thomas.** *Buckets & Leaves.* 1992. NY. Vantage. 2nd. 203p. silvered burgundy cloth. P4. $16.00

**HURD, Edith Thacher.** *Mother Kangaroo.* 1976. boston. 1st. ils Clement Hurd. VG/dj. M17. $30.00

**HURD, Michael.** *Orchestra.* 1980. Facts on File. 224p. G/dj. C5. $12.50

**HURST, Arthur.** *Time Has Come.* 1947. London. 1st. 42p. A13. $25.00

**HURST, E.K.** *Biographical Sketch of Amariah Brigham, MD...* 1858. Utica. McClure. 2nd. 123p. cloth. G7. $175.00

**HURST, Fanny.** *Anatomy of Me.* 1958. Doubleday. 1st. NF/G. T12. $10.00

**HURST, Jack.** *Nathan Bedford Forrest.* 1993. Knopf. 1st. F/dj. M23. $35.00

**HURST, Jack.** *Nathan Bedford Forrest: A Biography.* 1993. Knopf. 1st. NF/dj. A14. $17.50

**HURST, James Willard.** *Law & Social Process in United States History.* 1960. Ann Arbor. MI Law School. bl cloth. M11. $65.00

**HURT, R.D.** *Ohio Frontier: Crucible of the Old Northwest 1720-1830.* 1996. IN U. 1st. ils/map. F/dj. M4. $25.00

HURT, Zuelia Ann. *Country Samplers.* 1984. Birm. Oxmoor. 1st. 128p. VG/dj. B11. $15.00

HUSBAND, Joseph. *Story of the Pullman Car.* 1917. McClurg. 1st. sm 8vo. 161p. gilt gr cloth. B20. $75.00

HUSEMAN, Ben W. *Wild River, Timeless Canyon.* 1995. U AZ. obl 4to. ils/maps/map ep. gilt tan cloth. dj. F7. $70.00

HUSSAK, Eugen. *Determination of Rock-Forming Minerals.* 1886. NY. Wiley. 103 woodcuts. 233p. xl. NF. B14. $125.00

HUSSEY, J.M. *Storia del Mondo Medievale. Vol III. L'Impero Bizantino.* 1978. Italy. Garzanti. ils/fld pl/map. 902p. VG/dj. Q2. $75.00

HUSSEY, John A. *Voyage of the Raccoon: A Secret Journal...1813-1814.* 1958. SF. Taylor. ils. half morocco. w/prospectus. P4. $250.00

HUSSEY, Samuel F. *Brief Examination of Asa Rand's Book 'Word in Season'...* 1821. Salem. Cushing. 16mo. 237p. quarter calf. xl. V3. $50.00

HUSTON, A.B. *Historical Sketch of Farmers' College.* ca 1905. Students Assn. ils 175p. G. B18. $37.50

HUSTON, Paul Griswold. *Around an Old Homestead.* 1906. Cincinnati. 362p. pict cloth. B18. $35.00

HUSTON, Shaun. *Breeding Ground.* 1985. London. Allen. 1st. NF/dj. A14. $25.00

HUSTON, Shaun. *Deadheads.* 1993. London. Little Brn. 1st. NF/dj. A14. $21.00

HUSTON, Shaun. *Relics.* 1991. London. Macdonald. 1st hc. NF/dj. A14. $21.00

HUSTON, Shaun. *Shadows.* 1985. London. Allen. 1st. NF/dj. A14. $28.00

HUSTVEDT & KLINGBERG. *Warning Drum: The British Home Front Faces Napoleon...* 1944. U CA. 297p. F/NF. A4. $225.00

HUTCHESON, Francis. *Inquiry Into Original of Our Ideas of Beauty & Virtue...* 1726. London. Darby. 2nd revised/enlarged. 304p. contemporary calf. G1. $450.00

HUTCHESON, T.B. *Production of Field Corps.* 1936. McGraw Hill. 445p. VG. A10. $20.00

HUTCHINS, Fred L. *What Happened in Memphis.* 1965. Kingsport, TN. w/TLS. VG. B30. $50.00

HUTCHINSON, Robert A. *Off the Books: Citibank & World's Biggest Money Game.* 1986. Morrow. 1st. 8vo. F/dj. A2. $15.00

HUTCHINSON, Robert W. *Advanced Text-Book of Magnetism & Electricity, Vol I & II.* 1927. London. WB Clive/U Tutorial. ils. xl. VG. B14. $125.00

HUTCHINSON, W.H. *World, the Work & the West of WHD Koerner.* 1978. U OK. ils/photos. 243p. VG/dj. J2. $110.00

HUTCHINSON, W.J. *Road Accidents & Sketching.* (1927). London. Police Review. official 1st. 32p. stiff cloth brd. M11. $35.00

HUTCHINSON & RACHAL. *Papers of James Madison, Vol 6: Jan 1-April 30, 1783.* 1969. Chicago. ils. 545p. NF/VG. M10. $16.50

HUTCHISON, E.H. *Violent Truce: Military Observer Looks at Arab-Israeli...* 1956. Devin Adair. 8vo. 199p. VG/dj. W1. $16.00

HUTTON, Harold. *Doc Middleton: Life & Legends of Notorious Plains Outlaw.* 1980. Sage Books. 2nd. ils/map ep. 290p. NF/NF. B19. $15.00

HUTTON, Laurence. *Edwin Booth.* 1893. Harper. Harper B&W series. lg 32mo. 59p. wht cloth. VG. M7. $24.00

HUTTON, Paul Andrew. *Custer Reader.* 1992. Lincoln. photos/biblio/index. 585p. VG/dj. S16. $28.50

HUTTON, Paul Andrew. *Soldiers West: Biographies From Military Frontier.* 1987. U NE. ils/maps. 276p. VG. J2. $65.00

HUXLEY, Aldous. *Art of Seeing.* 1943. Canada. Macmillan. 1st. VG/fair. P3. $30.00

HUXLEY, Aldous. *Art of Seeing.* 1943. London. 1st. dj. T9. $18.00

HUXLEY, Aldous. *Brave New World.* 1932. London. Chatto Windus. 1st. 306p. gilt bl cloth. NF/VG. H5. $1,500.00

HUXLEY, Aldous. *Crows of Pearblossom.* (1967). NY. Random. Weekly Reader BC. 8vo. unp. VG. T5. $17.00

HUXLEY, Aldous. *Defeat of Youth.* 1918. Oxford. Blackwell. 1st. 1/250. NF/gr decor stiff yapped wrp. M24. $225.00

HUXLEY, Aldous. *Devils of Loudun.* 1952. Harper. 1st. VG. P3. $40.00

HUXLEY, Aldous. *Genius & the Goddess.* 1955. Harper. 1st Am. xl. VG/dj. M25. $15.00

HUXLEY, Aldous. *Proper Studies.* 1928. Doubleday Doran. 1st Am. VG/dj. B4. $200.00

HUXLEY, Anthony. *Plant & Planet.* 1974. Readers Union. 428p. F/VG. S15. $10.00

HUXLEY, Elspeth. *Livingstone & His African Journeys.* 1974. NY. photos/ils. VG/dj. M17. $20.00

HUXLEY, Elspeth. *Whipsnade: Captive Breeding for Survival.* 1981. London. Collins. 1st. VG/clip. N2. $10.00

HUXLEY, Judith. *Judith Huxley's Table for Eight: Recipes & Menus...* 1984. Morrow. VG/G. A16. $10.00

HUXLEY, Julian. *From an Antique Land: Ancient & Modern in Middle East.* 1961. London. Parrish. 8vo. 66 pl/maps. cloth. VG/torn. W1. $14.00

HUXLEY, Thomas Henry. *Evidence as to Man's Place in Nature.* 1863. NY. 1st Am. G+. A15. $100.00

HUYGEN, Will. *Book of the Sandman/Alphabet of Sleep.* 1989. NY. Abrams. 1st. obl 8vo. 121p. AN/NF. T5. $30.00

HUYGEN, Will. *Gnomes.* 1977. Abrams. 4to. ils Poortvliet. 212p. F/dj. C14/T11. $25.00

HUYSMANS, J.K. *Grunewald: The Paintings.* (1958). NY. ils. VG/dj. M17. $30.00

HYAMS, Edward. *History of Gardens & Gardening.* 1971. London. Dent. 345p. VG/dj. A10. $60.00

HYAMS, Edward. *Irish Gardens.* 1967. London. MacDonald. 160p. VG/dj. A10. $45.00

HYAMS, Edward. *Ornamental Shrubs for Temperate Zone Gardens.* 1965-67. London. 6 vol. ils. VG/djs. B26. $45.00

HYAMS & ORDISH. *Last of the Incas: Rise & Fall of an American Empire.* 1963. S&S. 1st. 294p. dj. F3. $25.00

HYDE, Christopher. *Week Down in Devon: A History...* 1976. Rednor. Chilton. 1st. VG/dj. O3. $25.00

HYDE, Dayton O. *Yamsi: Heartwarming Journal of One Year on Wilderness Ranch.* 1971. Dial. 1st. ils. 318p. VG/dj. P12/S14. $12.50

HYDE, George E. *Life of George Bent: Written From His Letters.* (1968). Norman, OK. 389p. dj. D11. $45.00

HYDE, Mary. *Thrales of Streatham Park.* 1977. Harvard. 1st. lg 8vo. ils. F/dj. H13. $65.00

HYDE, Philip. *Navajo Wildlands: As Long As the Rivers Shall Run.* 1967. Sierra Club. VG/rpr. S5. $40.00

HYDE & LEYDET. *Last Redwoods: Photographs & Story of Vanishing...* 1963. Sierra Club. 1st. ils/fld map. VG/G. B19. $45.00

HYDER, Clyde Kenneth. *Snow of Kansas.* 1954. U KS. 296p. G. S5. $20.00

HYER, Richard. *Riceburner.* 1986. NY. Scribner. 1st. F/NF. R11. $15.00

**HYGINUS, Gaius Julius.** *Poeticon Astonomicon.* 1985. Greenbrae, CA. Allen. 1/140. trans Livingston/Smith. pict linen. case. B24. $350.00

**HYLAND, Ann.** *Medieval War Horse From Byzantium to the Crusades.* 1994. London. Grange/Sutton. F/dj. O3. $25.00

**HYMAN, Charles J.** *Astronautics Dictionary: German-English, English-German.* 1968. NY. Consultants Bureau. 237p. VG/dj. K5. $18.00

**HYMAN, Dick.** *It's the Law.* 1936. Doubleday Doran. 1st. ils Otto Soglow. 120p. F/VG+. B20. $50.00

**HYMAN, Susan.** *Edward Lear's Birds.* 1980. Wellfleet. folio. 90p. 96p. F/F. A4. $65.00

**HYMAN, Tom.** *Prussian Blue.* 1991. Viking. 1st. F/dj. T12. $35.00

**HYMAN & THORPE.** *Laura: Tales of the Diamond.* 1991. Woodford. 1st. AN/dj. P8. $30.00

**HYMAN & TRACHTENBERG.** *Architecture: From Prehistory to Post-Modernism.* 1986. Abrams. 1st. photos. 606p. F/dj. S14. $55.00

**HYND, Alan.** *Defenders of the Damned...* 1960. NY. AS Barnes. M11. $50.00

**HYND, Noel.** *Giants of the Polo Grounds.* 1988. Doubleday. 1st. photos. VG/dj. P8. $35.00

**HYNE, C.J. Cutcliffe.** *Kate Meredith, Financier.* 1906. NY. Authors & Newspapers Assn. Schipper/Block's Peoria ed. G11. $15.00

**HYSMANS, J.K.** *Down There (La Bas).* 1924. NY. Boni. 1st Am. trans Keene Wallis. 318p. purple cloth. dj. K1. $125.00

I

IACOCCA & NOVAK. *Iacocca.* 1984. Bantam. 1st/14th prt. F/NF. T12. $15.00

IANNA, Philip A. *Proceedings of the Fourth Astrometric Conference.* 1971. Charlottesville, VA. 4to. 305p. G/wrp. K5. $25.00

IARUSSO, Marilyn. *Stories.* 1977. NY Public Lib. 7th. 93p. F/wrp. D4. $20.00

ICARDI, Aldo. *American Master Spy.* 1954. Stalwart Ent. 1st. VG/G. E6. $25.00

ICHIKAWA, Satomi. *Suzette & Nicholas in the Garden.* 1986. St Martin. 1st Am. 29p. F/sans. D4. $25.00

ICKIKAWA, Satomi. *Child's Book of Seasons.* 1976. NY. 1st Am. ils. VG. M5. $12.00

IDEL, Albert E. *Great Blizzard.* 1948. Holt. BC. VG/G. P8. $30.00

IGLAUER, Edith. *Strangers Next Door.* 1991. Harbour. 1st. VG/dj. N2. $10.00

IGNATIUS, David. *Siro.* 1991. NY. FSG. 1st. F/F. H11. $35.00

ILES, Frances. *Malice Aforethought. Story of Commonplace Crime.* 1931. Gollancz. 1st. 12mo. orange cloth. R3. $125.00

ILES, Greg. *Black Cross.* 1995. Dutton. 1st. F/NF. N4. $35.00

ILIFF, Flora Gregg. *People of the Blue Water.* 1954. Harper. 1st. 271p. bl cloth. VG/G. F7. $27.50

ILLINGWORTH, Frank. *Highway to the North.* 1955. NY. Philosophical Lib. 8vo. ils/fld map. 293p. VG/dj. P4. $20.00

ILLINGWORTH, Frank. *North of the Circle.* 1951. Philsophical Lib. 8vo. 253p. VG. P4. $25.00

ILLSON, Willard Rouse. *Harrod's Old Fort, 1791.* 1929. KY Hist Soc. 1st. 12p. B10. $25.00

IMAIDA, Isao. *Old Enemy, New Friend.* 1979. Tokyo. Hoshino. mini. 1/150. Japanese/ Eng text. #d/inset gold pl. leather. B24. $300.00

IMBER, Jonathan. *Abortion & the Private Practice of Medicine.* 1986. New Haven. 1st. 164p. A13. $30.00

IMBERDIS, J. *Papyrus, or the Craft of Paper.* 1961. Bird & Bull. 1/113. 8vo. 36p. buff prt brd. F. B24. $750.00

IMHOLTE, John Quinn. *First Volunteers: History of 1st MN Volunteer Regiment...* 1963. Minneapolis. Ross & Haines. 1st. NF/clip. A14. $28.00

IMPEY, John. *New Instructor Clericalis, Stating the Authority...* 1786. London. 2nd. contemporary mottled calf. M11. $450.00

IMPEY, Rose. *Letter to Santa Claus.* Nov 1989. Delacorte. 1st. ils Sue Porter. VG+. B36. $9.00

INAYAT KHAN, Hazrat. *Sufi Message of Hazrat Inayat Khan. Vol XI: Philosophy...* 1964. London. Barrie Rockliff. 8vo. 259p. VG/tattered. W1. $18.00

INDIANA YEARLY MEETING. *Discipline of Society of Friends of IN Yearly Meeting 1838.* 1939. Cincinnati. A Pugh. 12mo. 97p. worn leather. V3. $35.00

INESCO, Eugene. *Story Number 3 for Children Over Three Years of Age.* 1971. NY. Harlin Quist. 1st Am. F/dj. C9. $42.00

INGALLS, Fay. *Valley Road: Story of Virginia Hot Springs.* 1949. Cleveland. World. 2nd. F/NF. B20. $12.50

INGE, William. *Come Back, Little Sheba.* 1950. NY. Random. 1st. author's 1st book. F/clip. Q1. $200.00

INGERSOLL, Ernest. *Country Cousins: Short Studies in Natural History of US.* 1884. NY. Harper. 1st. 252p. gilt bl cloth. VG+. B20. $45.00

INGERSOLL, Ernest. *Dragons & Dragon Lore.* 1928. Payson Clarke. 1st. ils. paper brd/blk cloth spine. VG+. B20. $75.00

INGERSOLL, Ernest. *Silver Caves.* 1900. Dodd Mead. 1st. 8vo. 216p. NF/dj. J3. $75.00

INGERSOLL, Robert Green. *Complete Lectures of...* nd. Chicago. J Regan. 411p. reading copy. H1. $12.00

INGLIS, Andrew F. *Behind the Tube.* 1990. Boston. Focal. 527p. VG. C5. $20.00

INGLIS, Brian. *History of Medicine.* 1965. Cleveland. 1st. 196p. dj. A13. $50.00

INGLIS & WEST. *Alternative Health Guide.* 1983. Knopf. 1st Am. 352p. VG/dj. P12. $12.00

INGOLD, Ernest. *House in Mallorca.* 1950. SF. Paul Elder. 48p. patterned cloth. D11. $50.00

INGOLDSBY, Thomas. *Jackdaw of Rheims.* 1913. London. ils Chas Folkard. G. M17. $20.00

INGRAM, Rex Llopis. *Mars in the House of Death.* 1939. Knopf. 1st. VG/dj. C9. $78.00

INGRAMS, Richard. *Dr Johnson by Mrs Thrale: Anecdotes in Their Orig Form.* 1984. Chatto Windus/Hogarth. 1st. F/dj. H13. $55.00

INGSTAD, Helge. *Nunamiut: Among Alaska's Inland Eskimos.* 1954. Norton. 1st. photos. 303p. VG. S14. $17.50

INMAN, Arthur Crew. *Inman Diary.* 1985. Cambridge. Harvard. 2 vol. 1st. gilt bl cloth. F/case/pub wrp band. F1. $35.00

INMAN, Henry. *Stories of the Old Santa Fe Trail.* 1881. Kansas City, MO. Ramsey Millett Hudson. 1st. 8vo. ils. 287p. cloth. O1. $150.00

INNES, Hammond. *Conquistadors.* 1970 (1969). NY. Knopf. rpt. 8vo. 336p. red cloth. dj. F7. $25.00

INNES, Hammond. *Wreck of the Mary Deare.* 1956. Knopf. 1st Am. VG/G. L4. $22.00

INNES, Lowell. *Pittsburgh Glass 1797-1891.* 1976. Houghton Mifflin. 1st. 4to. 522p. blk cloth. VG/dj. H1. $175.00

INNES, Michael. *Hare Sitting Up.* 1959. London. Gollancz. 1st. F/VG. M15. $40.00

INNES, Michael. *Honeybath's Heaven.* 1977. London. Gollancz. 1st. F/dj. C15. $25.00

INNIS & INNIS. *Gold in the Blue Ridge: Story of the Beale Treasure.* 1973. WA. ils/maps. F/dj. M4. $28.00

INSKIP, Eleanor. *Colorado River Through Glen Canyon Before Lake Powell.* 1995. Inskip Ink. 8vo. photos. stiff pict wrp. F7. $25.00

INSKIPP & INSKIPP. *Guide to the Birds of Nepal.* 1985. New Delhi. ils/figures. 392p. cloth. VG. C12. $20.00

INTERNATION BRIDGE ASSOC. *Bridge Writer's Choice 1964: Their Favorite hands.* VG. S1. $10.00

IOESCO, Eugene. *Story Number 1.* 1968. Harlan Quist. 1st. ils Etienne Delessert. NF/dj. D4. $55.00

IOONS, Walter. *Diamond Dreams.* 1995. Little Brn. 1st. F/dj. P8. $40.00

IPCAR, Dahlov. *Brown Cow Farm.* (1959). Doubleday. early ed. 42p. brd. F/dj. D4. $30.00

IRBY, Kenneth. *Relation.* 1970. Blk Sparrow. 1st. 1/26 (201 total). sgn/lettered. F/dj. w/ils. L3. $125.00

IREDALE, Tom. *Birds of New Guinea.* 1956. Melbourne. Georgian House. 2 vol. 1st. 35 mc pl/fld map. teg. NF. B20. $375.00

IRELAND, Alexander Jr. *Book-Lover's Enchiridion.* 1884. London. Simpkin Marshall. 4th. 8vo. 492p. gilt bl cloth. VG. H4. $30.00

IRIS, Scharmel. *Spanish Earth.* (1964). Chicago. Ralph Fletcher Seymour. inscr/sgn. gilt bl linen. F/NF. H4. $75.00

IRONS, W.V. *Water Resources of the Upper Colorado River Basin.* 1964. GPO. 1036p. A10. $25.00

IRVIN & RILEY. *Nice Guys Finish First: Autobiography of Monte Irvin.* 1996. Carroll Graf. 1st. 8vo. photos. F/dj. A2. $15.00

**IRVINE, Robert.** *Gone to Glory.* 1990. St Martin. 1st. F/dj. P8. $50.00

**IRVING, Blanche M.** *Five Deer on Loco Mountain Road: People & Places...* 1982. Sunstone. 1st. sgn. ils. 64p. F/sans. B19. $20.00

**IRVING, Clifford.** *Final Argument.* 1993. S&S. 1st. F/NF. T12. $20.00

**IRVING, Frederick.** *Safe Deliverance.* 1942. Boston. 1st. 308p. A13. $25.00

**IRVING, John.** *Cider House Rules.* 1985. Franklin Lib. ltd 1st. sgn. aeg. full leather. F. Q1. $250.00

**IRVING, John.** *Cider House Rules.* 1985. Morrow. 1st. F/F. H11. $35.00

**IRVING, John.** *Cider House Rules.* 1985. Morrow. 1st. NF/dj. S18. $25.00

**IRVING, John.** *Cider House Rules.* 1985. NY. Morrow. 1st. 1/795. sgn. teg. gilt quarter linen. F/dj/box. M24. $125.00

**IRVING, John.** *Hotel New Hampshire.* 1981. Dutton. 1st. F/dj. B30. $30.00

**IRVING, John.** *Prayer for Owen Meany.* 1989. Morrow. 1st/ltd. 543p. F/dj. W2. $35.00

**IRVING, John.** *Prayer for Owen Meany.* 1989. Toronto. Dennys. 1st Canadian. NF/F. H11. $35.00

**IRVING, John.** *Widow for One Year.* 1998. Unicycle. 1/1200. sgn/#d. special leather. AN. B30. $160.00

**IRVING, John.** *World According to Garp.* 1978. Dutton. 1st. author's 4th novel. gilt quarter cloth. F/dj. M24. $125.00

**IRVING, Pierre.** *Life & Letters of Washington Irving.* 1883. Putnam. 3 vol. Memorial ed. 1/300. ils/tissue guards. VG. H4. $60.00

**IRVING, Washington.** *Astoria; or, Anecdotes of an Enterprise Beyond Rocky Mtns.* 1836. Carey Lee Blanchard. 2 vol. 1st/2nd state. ils/fld map. B18. $150.00

**IRVING, Washington.** *Astoria; or, Anecdotes of an Enterprise Beyond Rocky Mtns.* 1964. U OK. 556p. VG/dj. J2. $95.00

**IRVING, Washington.** *Chronicle of Conquest of Granada.* 1829. Phil. Lea Carey. 2 vol. sm format prt. 8vo. full calf. H4. $125.00

**IRVING, Washington.** *History of New York From the Beginning of the World...* 1820. London. John Murray. 1st Eng. 8vo. 520p. maroon morocco. O1. $225.00

**IRVING, Washington.** *Knickerbocker's History of New York.* 1894. Putnam. 2 vol. Van Twiller ed. 8vo. Ils EW Kemble. stp wht cloth. VG. H4. $100.00

**IRVING, Washington.** *Life of George Washington.* 1975. Tarrytown. 1st. ils/maps. F/dj. M4. $35.00

**IRVING, Washington.** *Oliver Goldsmith, a Biography.* 1872. Phil. Lippincott. 8vo. 427p. teg. cloth. w/facs letter. VG. H13. $175.00

**IRVING, Washington.** *Rip Van Winkle & Legend of Sleepy Hollow.* 1974. ils Felix OC Darley. VG/dj. M17. $20.00

**IRVING, Washington.** *Rip Van Winkle.* (1921). Phil. McKay. 1st. ils NC Wyeth. teg. dk brn cloth/label. R5. $275.00

**IRVING, Washington.** *Rip Van Winkle.* 1951. Ithaca. Abbe. 1/275. ils Elfriede Abbe. F. H4. $450.00

**IRVING, Washington.** *Rip Van Winkle.* 1993. Creative Eds. probable 1st. folio. VG/dj. B17. $15.00

**IRVING, Washington.** *Rip Van Winkle: Legend of the Kaatskill Mountains.* 1879. NY. Putnam. Prt for Henry L Hinton. ils/4 mtd photos. 32p. gr cloth. F1. $175.00

**IRVING, Washington.** *Rip Van Winkle: Legend of the Kaatskill Mountains.* 1923. Lippincott. 7th. ils Edna Cook. VG. T12. $30.00

**IRVING, Washington.** *Tales of Alhambra.* nd. Granada, Spain. red leather. M17. $15.00

**IRVING, Washington.** *Wolfert's Roost & Other Papers, Now First Collected.* 1855. Putnam. 12mo. 384p+12p ads. pict olive cloth. VG. K1. $50.00

**IRVING, Washington.** *Wolfert's Roost & Other Papers.* 1855. NY. Putnam. 1st/1st prt/1st bdg. gilt gr cloth. NF. M24. $100.00

**IRWIN, Constance.** *Fair Gods & Stone Faces.* 1963. St Martin. 1st. 346p. dj. F3. $25.00

**IRWIN, David.** *Alone Across the Top of the World.* 1935. Winston. 1st. 8vo. 254p. G. S14. $20.00

**IRWIN, Frank.** *Herbal Woodcuts & Legends.* 1971. Tilton, NH. Hillside. mini. 1/250. sgn/#d. 56p. pink pict cloth. B24. $95.00

**IRWIN, Inez Haynes.** *Maida's Little Island.* 1939. Grosset Dunlap. VG/dj. M20. $20.00

**IRWIN, Jim.** *To Rule the Night: Discovery Voyage of Astronaut...* (1973). Phil/NY. inscr pres. F/VG. H4. $200.00

**IRWIN, Wallace.** *Letters of a Japanese Schoolboy.* 1909. Doubleday Page. 1st. cream cloth. F. M24. $50.00

**IRWIN, Will.** *House That Shadows Built.* 1928. Doubleday Doran. 1st. F/VG. C9. $115.00

**ISAACS, Arnold R.** *Without Honor: Defeat in Vietnam & Cambodia.* 1983. Johns Hopkins. 1st. ils/photos/maps. 559p. VG/dj. R11. $15.00

**ISAACS, Susan.** *Magic Hour.* 1991. Harper Collins. 1st. F/dj. T12. $15.00

**ISAACS, Susan.** *Shining Through.* 1988. Harper Row. 1st. sgn. NF/dj. B30. $25.00

**ISCHLONDSKY, Naum Efimovich.** *Neuropsyche und Himrind.* 1930. Berlin. Urban & Schwarzenberg. 2 vol. buckram. G1. $75.00

**ISEMAN, John W.** *Aviation Manual: A Practical Handbook.* 1930. NY. Popular Science. 1st. 698p. G+. B18. $47.50

**ISHERWOOD, Christopher.** *Diaries 1939-60.* 1996. London. 1st. edit K Bucknell. dj. T9. $35.00

**ISHERWOOD, Christopher.** *Down There on a Visit.* 1962. S&S. 1st. VG/G. B30. $25.00

**ISHERWOOD, Christopher.** *Memorial: Portrait of a Family.* 1946. Norfolk. 1st. dj. T9. $65.00

**ISHERWOOD, Christopher.** *People One Ought to Know.* 1982. London. Macmillan. 1st. unp. brd. F/dj. D4. $35.00

**ISHERWOOD, Christopher.** *Prater Violet.* 1946. London. Methuen. 1st. NF/dj. A24/T9. $50.00

**ISHIGURO, Kazuo.** *Remains of the Day.* 1986. NY. Knopf. 1st Am. F/dj. C9. $90.00

**ISHIGURO, Kazuo.** *Remains of the Day.* 1989. London. Faber. 1st. 8vo. F/dj. S9. $200.00

**ISLAS, Arturo.** *Migrant Souls.* 1990. NY. Morrow. 1st. F/F. H11. $20.00

**ISOCRATES.** *Orationes et Epistolae...* (1549). Venice. Petrus Nicolinus Sabiensis. Greek text. 276p. K1. $750.00

**ISOCRATES.** *Orationes et Epistolae...* 1553. Paris. Michaelis Vascosani. 8vo. 510p+42p. old vellum. K1. $450.00

**ISRAEL, Lee.** *Estee Lauder: Beyond the Magic.* 1985. Macmillan. 1st. NF/dj. W2. $30.00

**ISSLER, Anne Roller.** *Stevenson at Silverado.* 1974. Valley Pub. revised/3rd prt. F/wrp. W2. $15.00

**ISTVAN, Kafer.** *Az Egyetemi Nyomda Negyszza Eve.* (1977). Magyar. Helikon. 4to. Hungarian text. ils. 247p+index. F/dj. H4. $75.00

**ITIX, Charles.** *Looking Good: A Guide for Men.* 1977. Hawthorn. later prt. photos Bruce Weber. VG/dj. C9. $60.00

**IVANOFF, Pierre.** *Monuments of Civilization: Maya.* 1973. Grosset Dunlap. 2nd. 191p. dj. F3. $40.00

**IVANOV-KHOLODNYI & NIKOL'SKII.** *Sun & the Ionosphere: Short-Wave Solar Radiation...* 1972. Jerusalem. Israel Program for Scientific Trans. 366p. xl. K5. $15.00

**IVERSON, Peter.** *When Indians Became Cowboys: Native Peoples & Cattle...* 1994. U OK. photos. 266p. AN. J2. $45.00

**IVES, A.G.L.** *British Hospitals.* 1948. London. 1st. 50p. A13. $20.00

**IVES, George.** *Bibliography of Oliver Wendell Holmes.* 1907. Houghton Mifflin. 1/530. 337p. F1. $65.00

**IVES, J. Moss.** *Ark & the Dove: Beginning of Civil & Religious Liberties...* 1936. London. ils. VG/G. M17. $20.00

**IVES, Morgan;** see Bradley, Marion Zimmer.

**IVINS, William M.** *Prints & Books: Informal Papers.* 1926. Cambridge. 8vo. 'Withdrawn' on ffe. 375p. H4. $20.00

**IVY, A.C.** *Observations on Krebiozen in the Treatment of Cancer.* 1956. Chicago. Regnery. 1st. 88p. F/worn. N2. $12.50

**IWASAKI, Chihiro.** *Momoko & the Pretty Bird.* 1973. Follett. 1st. ils. F/NF. M5. $15.00

**IZANT, Grace Goulder.** *This Is Ohio.* (1953). Cleveland/NY. World. 1st. inscr/dtd pres. 264p. w/business card. H4. $20.00

**IZQUIERDO, Jose.** *La Primera Casa de las Ciencias en Mexico...* 1958. Mexico City. 1st. inscr. 271p. dj. A13. $40.00

**IZZARD, Bob.** *Adobe Walls Wars: Fascinating Yet True Story...* 1993. TX. 1st. maps. 116p. stiff wrp. E1. $30.00

**IZZEDDIN, Nejla.** *Arab World: Past, Present & Future.* 1953. Chicago. Regnery. 1st. 8vo. ils. 412p. cloth. VG. W1. $25.00

**IZZI, Eugene.** *Booster.* 1989. St Martin. 1st. F/dj. A23. $30.00

**IZZI, Eugene.** *Invasions.* 1990. NY. Bantam. 1st. F/dj. B2/H11. $30.00

**IZZI, Eugene.** *Prowlers.* 1991. Bantam. 1st. F/F. H11. $30.00

JAAP, Rowena. *Adventures of Rowena & Wonderful Jam & Jelly Factory.* 1987. Stanley. 1st. ils Deborah G Rogers. VG+. M5. $20.00

JABBER, Fuad A. *International Documents on Palestine 1967.* 1970. Beriut. Inst for Palestine Studies. 748p. VG. M7. $135.00

JABLOKOV, Alexander. *Deeper Sea.* 1992. AvoNova Morrow. 1st. F/dj. P3. $22.00

JABLOKOV, Alexander. *River of Dust.* 1996. AvoNova Morrow. 1st. F/dj. P3. $22.00

JABLONSKI, Stanley. *Russian-English Medical Dictionary.* 1958. NY. 1st. 423p. A13. $45.00

JABLONSKI & STEWART. *Gershwin Years.* 1958. Doubleday. 1st. ils. VG/dj. C9. $60.00

JACK, Ellen E. *Fate of a Fairy; or, 27 Years in the Far West.* 1910. Chicago. WB Conkey. 1st. 8vo. 213p. red cloth/pict label. NF. B20. $100.00

JACK, Ian. *English Literature 1815-1832.* 1963. Clarendon. 1st. VG/sans. O4. $20.00

JACK, Marian. *Story of Bulgy Billy.* 1926. Whitman. 16mo. dk brn lettered bl-gray brd. mc pict dj. R5. $100.00

JACKINSON, Alexander. *Barnum-Cinderella World of Publishing.* 1971. NY. Impact. 1st. 8vo. 353p. cloth. F/dj. O10. $25.00

JACKISCH, Philip. *Modern Winemaking.* 1991. Cornell. 4th. ils. VG/dj. M17. $15.00

JACKLIN, Tony. *Jacklin: Champion's Own Story.* 1970. NY. 1st. photos. VG/dj. M17. $15.00

JACKSON, A.T. *Mills of Yesterday.* 1971. TX W Pr. 1st. ils. 103p. NF/sans. B19. $15.00

JACKSON, Benjamin Daydon. *Anatomy of Bibliomania Vol 2.* 1931. Scribner. 8vo. 434p. gr cloth. xl. H4. $20.00

JACKSON, Benjamin Daydon. *Glossary of Botanic Terms With Derivation & Accent.* (1965). London. Duckworth. 4th. 8vo. 481p. VG. H4. $20.00

JACKSON, C. Paul. *Clown at Second Base.* 1952. Crowell. 1st. VG/G. P8. $45.00

JACKSON, C. Paul. *Little Leaguer's 1st Uniform.* 1952. Crowell. 1st. VG. P8. $20.00

JACKSON, C. Paul. *Pee Wee Cook of the Midget League.* 1964. Hastings. 1st. F/VG. P8. $30.00

JACKSON, C. Paul. *Rookie Catcher With the Atlantic Braves.* 1966. Hastings. 1st. VG/G. P8. $30.00

JACKSON, C. Paul. *Rose Bowl All-American.* 1949. NY. Crowell. VG/dj. M20. $30.00

JACKSON, C. Paul. *Second Time Around Rookie.* 1968. Hastings. 1st. VG/dj. P8. $30.00

JACKSON, C. Paul. *Two Boys & a Soap Box Derby.* 1958. Hastings. ils. 118p. xl. VG. B36. $9.00

JACKSON, Carlton. *Hattie: Life of Hattie McDaniel.* 1990. Madison Books. 1st. photos. VG/dj. C9. $36.00

JACKSON, Carlton. *Zane Grey.* 1973. Boston. 1st. VG. B5. $35.00

JACKSON, Cary. *Midget League Catcher Jackson.* 1966. Follett. 1st. ils George Mocniak. 139p. xl. G+. B36. $12.00

JACKSON, Cary. *Shorty at Shortstop.* 1951. Wilcox Follet. 1st. VG. P8. $20.00

JACKSON, Charles T. *Massachusetts Medical College: Dr Jackson's Remarks.* 1847. A13. $100.00

JACKSON, Charles. *Lost Weekend.* 1944. Farrar Rhinehart. 1st. F/VG. B4. $150.00

JACKSON, Clarence S. *Picture Maker of the Old West.* Bonanza. rpt. VG/dj. S5. $22.50

JACKSON, Clarence S. *Picture Maker of the Old West.* 1947. Scribner. 308p. VG. J2. $165.00

JACKSON, Harry. *Lost Way Bronze Casting.* 1972. Flagstaff. Northland. 1st. sgn. ils. 127p. VG/dj. B5. $45.00

JACKSON, Helen Hunt. *Ramona: A Story.* 1900. Boston. Little Brn. Monterey ed. 2 vol. decor bl cloth. P4. $195.00

JACKSON, Henry. *Mr Jackson's Mushrooms.* 1979. Ottawa. Nat'l Mus Canada. mc pl. 161p. F/dj. A17. $35.00

JACKSON, Holbrook. *Anatomy of Bibliomania Vol 2.* 1931. Scribner. 8vo. 434p. gr cloth. H4. $20.00

JACKSON, Holbrook. *Bibliophile's Almanack for 1927.* 1927. London. Fleuron. 1st/ltd. 1/325. 8vo. 68p. buckram. H4. $70.00

JACKSON, Holbrook. *Bookman's Pleasure.* 1947. Farrar Straus. 1st Am. 264p. VG+. H4. $15.00

JACKSON, Holbrook. *Books About Books: Anatomy of Bibliomania.* (1981). NY. Avenel. 8vo. 668p. VG/dj. H4. $20.00

JACKSON, Holbrook. *Dreamers of Dreams: Rise & Fall of 19th-C Idealism.* (1948). London. Faber. 1st. 8vo. 283p. gilt red-brn cloth. VG. H4. $18.00

JACKSON, Holbrook. *Fear of Books.* 1932. Soncino/Scribner. 1/2000. VG. H4. $65.00

JACKSON, Holbrook. *Printing of Books.* 1938. London. Cassell. 1st. half brn morocco/marbled brd. NF. F1. $195.00

JACKSON, Jack. *Mapping Texas & the Gulf Coast...* 1990. TX A&M. 4to. 17 maps. 103p. F/F. A4. $30.00

JACKSON, James E. *Revolutionary Tracings: In World Politics...* 1974. NY. Internat Pub. 1st. sgn pres. NF/dj. R11. $30.00

JACKSON, John A. *Blind Pig.* 1978. NY. Random. 1st. F/dj. M15. $250.00

JACKSON, John A. *Dead Folks.* 1996. Atlantic Monthly. 1st. sgn. F/NF. O11. $25.00

JACKSON, John A. *Deadman.* 1994. Atlantic Monthly. 1st. F/dj. M15. $45.00

JACKSON, John A. *Deadman.* 1994. Atlantic Monthly. 1st. sgn. F/dj. O11. $35.00

JACKSON, John A. *Grootka.* 1990. Woodstock. Countryman. 1st. inscr. F/dj. M15. $125.00

JACKSON, John A. *Hit on the House.* 1993. Atlantic Monthly. 1st. inscr/dtd 1993. F/dj. O11. $40.00

JACKSON, John C. *Shadow of the Tetons.* 1993. Mtn Pr. 1st. gray cloth. F/dj. T11. $25.00

JACKSON, John G. *Introduction to African Civilizations.* 1970. NY. U Books. 1st. 384p. cloth. VG. W1. $18.00

JACKSON, John Hughlings. *Selected Writings of...* 1958 (1931). London. Staples. 2 vol. tall 8vo. gr cloth. G1. $275.00

JACKSON, John J. *Cases of Disease on Nervous System in Patients...* 1868. London. Churchill. rpt. 22p. prt wrp/newly recased. G7. $195.00

JACKSON, Joseph Henry. *Bad Company: California State Robbers.* 1949. Harcourt Brace. 1st. 346p. VG/dj. B5. $20.00

JACKSON, Joseph Henry. *Gold Rush Album.* 1949. Scribner. 1st. ils. 239p. NF/G+. B19. $30.00

JACKSON, Joseph Henry. *Mexican Interrlude.* 1973. G&D. new/revised. 346p. map ep. F3. $15.00

JACKSON, Mary V. *Engines of Instruction, Mischief & Magic...* 1989. Lincoln, NE. U NE. 1st. 304p. F/dj. B20. $25.00

JACKSON, Mason. *Pictorial Press: Its Origin & Progress.* (1969). Burt Franklin. rpt. 8vo. 362p. AN/sans. H4. $25.00

JACKSON, Michael. *Moon Walk.* 1988. Doubleday. 1st. ils/fld pl. VG/dj. C9. $36.00

**JACKSON, Mick.** *Underground Man.* 1997. London. Picador. 1st. 8vo. F/dj. S9. $35.00

**JACKSON, Peter.** *St George & the Dragon.* 1972. London. Pollocks Toy Theatres. 1st thus. ils. brd. B27. $45.00

**JACKSON, Radway.** *Concise Dictionary of Artists' Signatures.* (1981). NY. Alpine Fine Arts/Landmark. 224p. F/dj. H4. $65.00

**JACKSON, Reggie.** *Reggie: Autobiography of Reggie Jackson.* 1984. Villard. 1st. sgn. 333p. F/dj. B20. $50.00

**JACKSON, Robert B.** *Let's Go Yaz.* 1968. Walck. 1st. VG+. P8. $25.00

**JACKSON, Sheldon G.** *Quaker Preachers on the Prairies: Life & Times of...* 1985. Glendora, CA. Citrus. 140p. AN. V3. $14.00

**JACKSON, Shirley.** *Famous Sally.* 1966. Harlan Quist. 1st. 46p. F/worn. D4. $45.00

**JACKSON, Shirley.** *Haunting of Hill House.* 1959. Viking. 1st. F/NF. B4. $600.00

**JACKSON, Shirley.** *Haunting of Hill House.* 1963. London. Four Square. 1st thus. 190p. VG+/wrp. H4. $6.50

**JACKSON, W. Turrentine.** *Treasure Hill: Portrait of a Silver Mining Camp.* 1963. Tucson, AZ. 1st. ils/index. 245p. NF/G. B19. $25.00

**JACKSON, W. Turrentine.** *Wells Fargo & Co in Idaho Territory.* 1984. Boise. ID State Hist Soc. 120p. VG. B18. $19.50

**JACKSON, Wilfrid Scarborough.** *Nine Points of the Law.* 1903. London. John Lane. 1st. F. M15. $125.00

**JACKSON, William Alexander.** *Records of a Bibliographer.* 1967. Cambridge, MA. Belknap. 1st. gilt blk cloth. F/dj. T10. $35.00

**JACKSON, William Henry.** *Time Exposure.* 1940. Putnam. 2nd. ils. 341p. VG/dj. B5. $55.00

**JACKSON & JACKSON.** *High School Backstop.* 1963. Whittlesey. later prt. xl. G/dj. P8. $8.00

**JACOB, Giles.** *Compleat Sportsman, in Three Parts...* 1718. London. Nutt Gossing. 12mo. 152+4p. contemporary calf. K1. $400.00

**JACOB, Giles.** *New Law-Dictionary: Containing Intrepretation & Definition.* 1736. London. Nutt Gosling. contemporary panelled calf. M11. $450.00

**JACOBS, Flora Gill.** *Doll House Mystery.* 1958. Coward McCann. 11th. inscr/dtd 1990. NF/dj. C14. $18.00

**JACOBS, Flora Gill.** *History of Dolls' Houses.* 1954. London. Cassell. 1st. 320p. NF/VG. D4. $65.00

**JACOBS, Flora Gill.** *History of Dolls' Houses.* 1965. NY. Scribner. 1st thus. ils. 342p. NF/dj. B20. $75.00

**JACOBS, Frances E.** *Finger Plays & Action Rhymes.* 1941. Lee Shepard. 1st. ils Lura/Courtney Owen. VG+/G. M5. $55.00

**JACOBS, Joseph.** *Book of Wonder Voyages.* 1986. London. David Nutt. ils John D Batten. tan cloth. F1. $100.00

**JACOBS, Joseph.** *Buried Moon.* 1969. NY. Bradbury. 1st. ils Susan Jeffers. NF/dj. D4. $45.00

**JACOBS, Joseph.** *Coo-My-Dove, My Dear.* 1976. Atheneum. 1st. 32p. cloth. VG. D4. $25.00

**JACOBS, Joseph.** *Indian Fairy Tales.* 1892. London. David Nutt. 1st. ils John D Batten. VG. M5. $75.00

**JACOBS, Lou Jr.** *Amphoto Guide to Lighting.* 1981 (1979). Amphoto. 2nd. sc. VG. S5. $5.00

**JACOBS, P.H.** *Poultry Doctor.* 1908. Phil. Boericke. 88p. cloth. VG. A10. $25.00

**JACOBS, Peter.** *Journal of...Jacobs, Indian Wesleyan Missionary...* 1858. NY. Prt for Author. 8vo. 96p. xl. O1. $125.00

**JACOBS, Phil.** *Planet Earth.* 1989. S&S. 1st. engineer Paul Willgress. F. B17. $15.00

**JACOBS, W.W.** *Master of Craft.* 1900. London. 1st. ils. dj. T9. $50.00

**JACOBS & TUCKER.** *War of 1812: Compact History.* 1969. NY. 1st. 224p. F/dj. M4. $22.00

**JACOBS-BOND, Carrie.** *Tales of Little Dogs.* 1921. Volland. 29th. 12mo. ils K Dodge. G. D1. $40.00

**JACOBSEN, T.** *Treasures of Darkness, a History of Mesopotamian Religion.* 1976. Yale. ils. 273p. VG/dj. Q2. $24.00

**JACOBSON, Timothy.** *Making Medical Doctors: Science & Medicine at Vanderbilt...* 1987. Tuscaloosa, AL. 1st. 349p. dj. A13. $30.00

**JACOBY, George W.** *Unsound Mind & the Law, a Presentaion...* 1918. Funk Wagnall. M11. $75.00

**JACOBY, Oswald.** *On Poker.* 1954. NY. revised. VG/G. M17. $15.00

**JACOPETTI, Alexandra.** *Native Funk & Flash: Emerging Folk Art.* 1974. Scrimshaw. 1st. obl 8vo. 112p. G/wrp. S14. $30.00

**JACQUEMARD, Simonne.** *Night Watchman.* 1964. HRW. 1st. VG/clip. P3. $13.00

**JACQUES-GARVEY, Amy.** *Philiosophy & Opinions of Marcus Garvey.* 1992. Atheneum. F/glossy wrp. H4. $12.00

**JAEGER, J.C.** *Introduction to the Laplace Transform.* 1949. London. 1st. bl brd. VG. B27. $12.00

**JAEGER, Oscar R.** *Great Grand Canyon Adventure: A Narrative...* 1932. Dubuque, IA. 8vo. 196p. yel cloth. VG+. F7. $135.00

**JAFFE, Hans L.C.** *20,000 Years of World Painting: Comprehensive Hist Survey...* (1967). NY. Abrams. folio. 418p. NF/worn. H4. $25.00

**JAFFE, Michael.** *Van Dyck's Antwerp Sketchbook.* 1966. London. Macdonald. 2 vol. ils/pl. NF/dj. D2. $145.00

**JAFFE, Sherril.** *Scars Make Your Body More Interesting.* 1975. LA. Blk Sparrow. 1st. 1/200. sgn. F/NF. L3. $35.00

**JAFFE, Sherril.** *This Flower Only Blooms Every Hundred Years.* 1979. Blk Sparrow. 1/26 lettered. sgn/orig drawing. NF/mylar. B9. $65.00

**JAFFEE, Annette Williams.** *Adult Education.* 1981. Ontario Pr. 1st. sgn. NF/dj. S13. $20.00

**JAFFEE, Michael Grant.** *Dance Real Slow.* 1996. FSG. 1st. author's 1st book. F/dj. T12. $50.00

**JAFFERY, Sheldon.** *Horror & Unpleasantries: A Biographical History...* (1983). Bowling Green State U. 2nd. pres. author's 1st book. 144p. F/VG. H4. $45.00

**JAFFRE, Jody.** *Horse of a Different Killer.* 1995. NY. Fawcett Columbine. 1st. VG/dj. O3. $30.00

**JAGENDORF, M.** *Fold Wines, Cordials & Brandies.* 1963. 2nd. lg 8vo. F/F. E6. $12.00

**JAGENDORF, M.** *New England Bean-Pot: American Folk Stories to Read...* nd (1948). Vanguard. 1st. 272p. G+. C14. $15.00

**JAGENDORF, M.** *Penny Puppets, Penny Theatre & Penny Plays.* 1941. Bobbs Merrill. 1st. 190p. VG. C14. $12.00

**JAHN, Michael.** *Murder at the Museum of Natural History.* 1994. St Martin. 1st. F/NF. N4. $20.00

**JAHODA, G.** *Florida: Bicentennial History.* 1976. NY. 1st. photos. F/dj. M4. $15.00

**JAHODA, Gustav.** *Psychology of Superstition.* 1974. NY. Aronson. 8vo. 158p. F. H4. $20.00

**JAKES, John.** *California Gold.* 1989. Random. 1st. F/dj. T12. $25.00

**JAKES, John.** *California Gold.* 1989. Random. 1st. sm 4to. 658p. VG/dj. S14. $9.50

**JAKES, John.** *Holiday for Havoc.* 1991. Armchair Detective. 1st Am. 1/100. sgn. F/case. A24. $45.00

**JAKUBOWSKI, Maxim.** *New Crimes 2.* 1991. Carroll Graff. 1st. AN/dj. S18. $20.00

**JALOVEC, Karel.** *German & Australian Violin-Makers.* 1967. London. Paul Hamlyn. sm volio. 439p. F/NF. B20. $250.00

**JAM, Teddy.** *Night Cars.* 1988. Franklin Watts. 1st. F/clip. M5. $18.00

**JAMES, Bill C.** *Buck Chadborn, Border Lawman.* photos. 68p. F. E1. $35.00

**JAMES, Bill C.** *Sheriff AJ Royal, Ft Stockton, Texas.* 1984. Ltd. G. A19. $45.00

**JAMES, Bill.** *Politics of Glory.* 1994. Macmillan. 1st. VG/dj. P8. $15.00

**JAMES, Clive.** *Brillant Creatures.* 1983. London. 1st. dj. T9. $28.00

**JAMES, Croake.** *Curiosities of Law & Lawyers.* 1883. Albany/NY. Banks. 1st. lg 8vo. 514p. gilt brn cloth. NF. B20. $60.00

**JAMES, Donald.** *Monstrum.* Villard. ARC/1st. F/wrp. S18. $30.00

**JAMES, E.O.** *From Cave to Cathedral: Temples & Shrines of Prehistoric...* 1965. NY. Praeger. NF/VG. B9. $30.00

**JAMES, George Wharton.** *Arizona, the Wonderland: History of Ancient Cliff...* 1917. Page. 1st. ils/index. 478p. VG. B19. $125.00

**JAMES, George Wharton.** *Arizona, the Wonderland.* 1920. Boston. Page. 8vo. 478p. teg. gilt brn cloth. VG. F7. $85.00

**JAMES, George Wharton.** *California Romantic & Beautiful.* 1909. Boston. Page. 5th. 72 photos. 433p. VG. B5. $30.00

**JAMES, George Wharton.** *Grand Canyon of Arizona: How to See It.* 1910. Little Brn. 12mo. gilt gr cloth. NF. F7. $65.00

**JAMES, George Wharton.** *Heroes of California.* 1910. Little Brn. 1st. ils. 515p. bdg variant. D11. $60.00

**JAMES, George Wharton.** *In & Around the Grand Canyon.* 1900. Pasadena ed. 1/500. sgn/#d. lg 8vo. 3-quarter leather. VG. F7. $375.00

**JAMES, George Wharton.** *Indian Basketry & How to Make Baskets.* 1903. NY. Henry Malkan. G. A19. $135.00

**JAMES, George Wharton.** *Indian Blankets & Their Makers.* 1937. Tudor. F. A19. $150.00

**JAMES, George Wharton.** *Indian Blankets & Their Makers.* 1974. Rio Grande. 3rd. ils/index. 213p. AN. B19. $20.00

**JAMES, George Wharton.** *Living the Radiant Life: A Personal Narrative.* 1917. Pasadena. Radiant Life. 291p. gilt cloth. D11. $35.00

**JAMES, George Wharton.** *What the White Race May Learn From the Indian.* 1908. Chicago. Forbes. 1st. lg 8vo. 269p. gilt red cloth. VG+. B20. $225.00

**JAMES, Harry C.** *Cahuilla Indians: Men Called Master.* 1960. Westernlore. 1st. ils Don Perceval. 185p. NF/NF. B19. $40.00

**JAMES, Harry C.** *Ovada, an Indian Boy of the Grand Canyon.* 1969. Ward Ritchie. 8vo. ils Don Perceval. VG/G. F7. $40.00

**JAMES, Henry.** *Awkward Age.* 1899. London. Heinemann. 1st/1st prt/1st bdg. 1/2000. bl cloth w/4 iris. VG. M24. $150.00

**JAMES, Henry.** *Beast in the Jungle.* 1963. Allen. 1/130. ils Hughes-Stanton. brd. B24. $500.00

**JAMES, Henry.** *International Episode.* 1879. Harper. 1st/1st state. 3-quarter tan cloth/rb. VG/prt wrp. $650.00

**JAMES, Henry.** *Little Tour in France.* 1900. London. Heinemann. 1st Eng. teg. gray cloth. NF. M24. $150.00

**JAMES, Henry.** *Novels & Tales of...* 1907-1917. Scribner. 26 vol. teg. gilt maroon cloth. B20. $1,250.00

**JAMES, Henry.** *Reverberator.* 1888. London/NY. Macmillan. 1st Am. 1/500. sm 8vo. 229p. gilt bl cloth. G+. B20. $100.00

**JAMES, Henry.** *Small Boy & Others.* 1913. London. Macmillan. 1st/1st issue. 1/1000. inscr/dtd. F. B24. $3,850.00

**JAMES, Henry.** *Small Boy & Others.* 1913. Scribner. 1st/1st issue. gilt olive-gray sateen cloth. F/dj. M24. $600.00

**JAMES, Henry.** *Transatlantic Sketches.* 1875. Boston. Osgood. 1st. 1/1578. 401p. gr cloth. F. B24. $750.00

**JAMES, Henry.** *Travelling Companions.* 1919. Boni Liveright. 1st. VG. M20. $32.00

**JAMES, Henry.** *Washington Square.* 1881. Harper. 1st. ils George duMaurier. xl. VG. S13. $75.00

**JAMES, Henry.** *Washington Square.* 1881. NY. Harper. 1st. gilt olive pict cloth. xl. G. M24. $85.00

**JAMES, John.** *Lords of the Loon.* 1972. St Martin. 1st. F/NF. S18. $25.00

**JAMES, Lawrence.** *Golden Warrior.* 1993. Paragon. 1st. 406p. blk cloth/brn paper brd. F/dj. M7. $35.00

**JAMES, Lawrence.** *Savage Wars: British Campaigns in Africa 1870-1920.* 1985. St Martin. 1st. 297p. VG/dj. S16. $22.50

**JAMES, Lawrence.** *Savage Wars: British Campaigns of Africa 1870-1920.* 1985. St Martin. 1st. 8vo. 297p. F/dj. M7. $35.00

**JAMES, M.R.** *Collected Ghost Stories.* 1994. Wordsworth Classics. F/NF. L4. $12.00

**JAMES, Margaret.** *Black Glass.* (1981). Collector Books. 8vo. 80p. VG/glossy wrp. H1. $25.00

**JAMES, P.D.** *Certain Justice.* 1997. London. Faber. 1st. sgn. F/dj. M15. $65.00

**JAMES, P.D.** *Children of Men.* 1993. Knopf. 1st. 241p. VG/dj. S14. $12.00

**JAMES, P.D.** *Death of an Expert Witness.* 1977. London. Faber. 1st. F/dj. M15. $200.00

**JAMES, P.D.** *Devices & Desires.* 1990. Knopf. 1st Am trade. sgn. F/F. M25. $35.00

**JAMES, P.D.** *Devices & Desires.* 1990. Knopf. 1st Am trade. sgn. F/VG. C9. $30.00

**JAMES, P.D.** *Original Sin.* 1994. London. 1st. dj. T9. $40.00

**JAMES, P.D.** *Original Sin.* 1995. Knopf. 1st. sgn. VG/VG. A23. $40.00

**JAMES, P.D.** *Skull Beneath the Skin.* 1982. London. Faber. 1st. F/dj. M15. $100.00

**JAMES, P.D.** *Skull Beneath the Skin.* 1982. Scribner. 1st Am. sgn. F/dj. D10. $60.00

**JAMES, P.D.** *Skull Beneath the Skin.* 1982. Scribner. 1st. F/clip. H11. $35.00

**JAMES, P.D.** *Taste for Death.* 1986. Knopf. 1st Am. F/dj. M23. $25.00

**JAMES, P.D.** *Taste for Death.* 1986. Knopf. 1st. VG/clip. B3. $20.00

**JAMES, Peter N.** *Soviet Conquest From Space.* 1974. New Rochelle, NY. Arlington. 8vo. 256p. VG/dj. K5. $25.00

**JAMES, Peter.** *Possession.* 1988. Doubleday. 1st Am. NF/dj. N4. $25.00

**JAMES, Peter.** *Sweet Heart.* 1990. St Martin. 1st Am. F/dj. S18. $18.00

**JAMES, Rian.** *Dining in NY.* 1930. 1st. VG. E6. $15.00

**JAMES, Will.** *Drifting Cowboy.* 1925. Scribner. 1st. author's 2nd book. 241p. VG. O1. $100.00

**JAMES, Will.** *Lone Cowboy.* 1930. Scribner. 1st. VG/dj. A21. $75.00

**JAMES, Will.** *Sand.* 1929. Grosset Dunlap. VG/damaged. A21. $20.00

**JAMES, Will.** *Scorpion: A Good Bad Horse.* 1936. Scribner. 1st. RS. NF/dj. B20. $325.00

**JAMES, William.** *Collected Essays & Reviews.* 1920. Longman Gr. 516p. panelled gr cloth. VG. G1. $65.00

**JAMES, William.** *Letters of...; Edited by Henry James.* 1920. Atlantic Monthly. 2 vol. 1st trade/early prt. bl cloth. VG. G1. $65.00

**JAMES, William.** *Principles of Psychology.* 1890. Holt. 2 vol. 1st/3rd prt. assn copy. rb red buckram. G1. $450.00

**JAMES, William.** *Principles of Psychology.* 1890. NY. Holt. 2 vol. 1st (Psy-Chology hypenated in ads). solander cases. G1. $18.50

**JAMES, William.** *Principles of Psychology.* 1950. NY. facs of 1890. 2 vol in 1. A13. $35.00

**JAMES, William.** *Principles of Psychology.* 1988. Birmingham. Classics of Psychiatry & Behavioral Sciences Lib. 2 vol. G1. $100.00

**JAMES, William.** *Varieties of Religious Experience: A Study in Human Nature.* 1992. NY. Classics of Psychiatry & Behavioral Sciences Lib. F. G1. $75.00

**JAMES & SWANSON.** *By a Woman's Hand: A Guide to Mystery Fiction...* 1994. profiles 262 writers. 254p. F. A4. $35.00

**JAMISON, Martin.** *Idi Amin & Uganda: Annotated Bibliography.* 1992. Westport, CT. Greenwood. 1st. 8vo. 145p. VG. W1. $20.00

**JAMMER, Max.** *Concepts of Mass in Classical & Modern Physics.* 1961. Harvard. 1st. 8vo. 230p. VG/dj. H1. $30.00

**JAMMER, Max.** *Concepts of Space: History of Theories of Space...* 1954. Harvard. 8vo. 196p. quarter cloth/brd. xl. K5. $25.00

**JANCE, J.A.** *Hour of the Hunter.* 1991. Ballantine. 1st. 370p. orange brd/yel cloth spine. NF/clip. J3. $25.00

**JANCE, J.A.** *Hour of the Hunter.* 1991. Morrow. 1st. sgn. F/NF. A23. $40.00

**JANCE, J.A.** *More Perfect Union.* 1992. London. Severn. 1st hc. F/NF. A24. $30.00

**JANCE, J.A.** *Name Withheld.* 1996. Morrow. 1st. sgn. F/dj. A23. $40.00

**JANCE, J.A.** *Tombstone Courage.* 1994. Morrow. 1st. F/dj. P3. $20.00

**JANE, Cecil.** *Journal of Christopher Columbus.* 1989. NY. Bonanza. ils. 227p. VG/dj. M10. $12.50

**JANE, Fred T.** *Jane's All the World Aircraft 1913.* 1969. NY. Arco. 248p. VG/dj. B18. $45.00

**JANET, Pierre.** *Psychological Healing: Historical & Clinical Study.* 1925. Macmillan. 2 vol. 1st Eng-language/Am issue. brn cloth. G1. $285.00

**JANICK, Jules.** *Horticultural Reviews. Vol 1.* 1979. Westport. B26. $20.00

**JANNEY, Samuel M.** *Conversations on Religious Subjects Between Father...* 1860. Phil. Friends Book Assn. 16mo. 216p. cloth. V3. $12.00

**JANNEY, Samuel M.** *Life of William Penn With Selections From Correspondence...* 1852. Phil. Lippincott Grambo. 2nd revised. 576p+ads. rb. VG. V3. $45.00

**JANNEY, Samuel M.** *Life of William Penn With Selections From Correspondence...* 1882. Phil. Friends Book Assn. 6th revised. 12mo. 591p. V3. $25.00

**JANNEY, Samuel M.** *Peace Principles Exemplified in Early History of PA.* 1876. Phil. Friends Book Assn. 16mo. 169p. G. V3. $20.00

**JANOVY, John.** *Fields of Friendly Strife.* 1987. NY. Viking. 1st. rem mk. F/dj. T11. $15.00

**JANOWITZ, Tama.** *American Dad.* 1981. NY. Putnam. 1st. store sticker on rear flap. F/F. H11. $65.00

**JANOWITZ, Tama.** *By the Shores of Gitchee Gumee.* 1996. NY. Crown. ARC/1st. F/dj. S9. $40.00

**JANOWITZ, Tama.** *Cannibal in Manhattan.* 1987. Crown. 1st. F/dj. S13. $10.00

**JANSON, Thor.** *Land of Green Lightning.* 1994. Pomegranate. 1st. obl 4to. wrp. F3. $25.00

**JANSON, W.H.** *History of Art, Fourth Edition.* 1991. Abrams. F/dj. P3. $50.00

**JANSSEN, Han.** *De Geschiedenis van de Speelkaart.* nd. Dutch/Eng text. 356p. F/F. A4. $125.00

**JANUS, Christopher G.** *Search for Peking Man.* 1975. Macmillan. 1st. F/NF. M23. $25.00

**JARDEN, Mary Louise.** *Young Brontes: Charlotte & Emily, Branwell & Anne.* 1944. NY. ils Helen Sewell. VG/dj. M17. $20.00

**JARDETZKY, Wenceslas S.** *Theories of Figures of Celestial Bodies.* 1958. NY. Interscience. 8vo. 186p. VG/dj. K5. $28.00

**JARDINE, Lisa.** *Erasmus, Man of Letters...* 1993. Princeton. 1st. ils. VG/dj. M17. $25.00

**JARES, Joe.** *Whatever Happened to Gorgeous George.* 1974. Englewood Cliffs. 1st. VG/dj. B5. $25.00

**JARRATT, Vernon.** *Eat Italian Once a Week.* 1967. Bonanza. G/dj. A16. $7.00

**JARRELL, Randall.** *Fly by Night.* 1976. FSG. 1st. ils/sgn/dtd Maurice Sendak. silvered blk cloth. dj. R5. $200.00

**JARRELL, Randall.** *Pictures From an Institution.* 1954. Eng. 1st. F/G. M19. $17.50

**JARVIS, C.S.** *Scattered Shots.* 1942. London. Murray. 1st. 148p. G/dj. C5. $12.50

**JASTROW, Joseph.** *Fact & Fable in Psychology.* 1901. Boston. Houghton Mifflin. 1st/late issue. 375p. G. G1. $38.00

**JASTROW, Joseph.** *Sanity First: Art of Sensible Living.* 1935. NY. Greenberg. 312p. gray cloth. VG. G1. $30.00

**JASTROW, Joseph.** *Subconscious.* 1906. London/NY. Constable/Houghton Mifflin. 1st Eng. 549p. G. G1. $65.00

**JAXGUR, Joseph.** *Birth of Marilyn.* 1991. St Martin. ARC/1st. F/dj. w/promo material. C9. $102.00

**JAY, WIlliam.** *Review of Causes & Consequences of the Mexican War.* 1849. Boston. Mussey. 333p. cloth. D11. $100.00

**JEAL, Tim.** *Boy-Man.* 1990. NY. 1st. AN/as issued. T9. $18.00

**JEANES & MUENCH.** *Grand Canyon Hike.* 1962. Follett. 4to. photos. dj. F7. $12.50

**JEBB, Samuel.** *Life of Robert Earl of Leicester, Favorite of Queen...* 1727. London. Woodman Lyon. 8vo. engr ftspc. calf. R12. $225.00

**JECKYLL, Gertrude.** *Some English Gardens.* 1905. London. 3rd. ils Elgood. 130p. teg. gilt cloth. B26. $185.00

**JEFFERS, Robinson.** *Be Angry at the Sun.* 1941. Random. 1/100. sgn. 156p. marbled brd/gilt tan spine. NF. F1. $400.00

**JEFFERS, Robinson.** *Women at Point Sur.* 1927. Liveright. 1st. F/NF. B4. $350.00

**JEFFERS, Susan.** *Brother Eagle, Sister Sky.* 1991. Dial. 1st. folio. VG/dj. B17. $25.00

**JEFFERSON, Mary Armstrong.** *Homes & Buildings in Amelia County, Virginia.* 1964. self pub. photos/map ep. 160p. VG. B10. $45.00

**JEFFERSON, Thomas.** *Jefferson's Notes on the State of Virginia...* 1800. Baltimore. Pechin. 1st. 8vo. ils/charts/maps/fld table. later bdg. O1. $575.00

**JEFFERSON, Thomas.** *President Jefferson Writes Capt Lewis Letter of Instruction.* 1986. np. Minikin. mini. 1/150. ils Max Marbles. cloth-backed marbled brd. F. B24. $125.00

JEFFERSON, Thomas. *Summary View of the Rights of British America.* 1976. Caxton. facs. 40p. VG. M10. $15.00

JEFFERSON, Thomas. *Thomas Jefferson on Science & Freedom. Letter to Student...* 1964. Worcester. St Onge. mini. 1/1000. portrait ftspc. gilt dk gr leather. B24. $85.00

JEFFERSON-BROWN, M.J. *Daffodil: Its History, Varieties & Cultivation.* 1951. London. ils/maps. VG. B26. $35.00

JEFFREY, Edward C. *Comparative Anatomy & Phylogeny of the Coniferales. Part I.* 1903. Boston. ils. wrp. lB26. $30.00

JEFFREY, J.R. *Converting the West: Biography of Narcissa Whitman.* 1991. OK U. 1st. 239p. F/dj. M4. $20.00

JEFFRIES, Roderic. *River Patrol.* 1968. Harper Row. 206p. F. D4. $25.00

JELLICOE, J. *Grand Fleet, 1914-1916.* 1919. Doran. 1st. ils/plans/diagrams. VG. E6. $45.00

JEN, Gish. *Mona in the Promised Land.* 1996. Knopf. 1st. F/dj. R14. $25.00

JEN, Gish. *Typical American.* 1991. Houghton Mifflin. 1st. inscr/dtd 1991. author's 1st book. F/dj. R14. $75.00

JENIKE, Michael A. *Geriatric Psychiatry & Psychopharmacology...* 1989. Chicago. Year Book Medical Pub. 1st. 398p. F. C14. $15.00

JENKINS, Dan. *Baja Oklahoma.* 1981. Atheneum. 1st. NF/dj. M23. $15.00

JENKINS, Dan. *Limo.* 1976. Atheneum. 1st. sgn. F/NF. A24. $35.00

JENKINS, Dan. *Semi-Tough.* 1972. Atheneum. 1st. VG+/NF. H11. $15.00

JENKINS, Elizabeth. *Mystery of King Arthur.* 1975. CMG. 1st. VG/dj. P3. $20.00

JENKINS, Hester Donaldson. *Educational Ambassador to Near East...Mary Mills Patrick...* 1925. NY. Revell. 1st. photos. 426p. VG+. A25. $25.00

JENKINS, Jerry. *Rookie.* 1991. Wolgemuth Hyatt. 1st. F/dj. P8. $12.50

JENKINS, John H. *Future of Books.* 1982. Austin, TX. 1st. 13p. VG/prt wrp. M8. $28.00

JENKINS, Olaf P. *Geologic Guidebook of San Francisco Bay Counties...* 1951. CA Dept Nat Resources. 1st. ils/maps. 392p. NF. S14. $30.00

JENKINS, Olaf P. *Mother Load Country: Geologic Guidebook Along Hwy 49...* 1948. CA Dept Nat Resources. 1st. ils/maps. 164p. VG. S14. $50.00

JENKINS, Peter. *Walk Across America.* 1979. Morrow. 1st. F/NF. M23. $25.00

JENKINS, Will F. *Last Spaceship.* 1949. NY. Frederick Fell. 1st. NF/dj. B20. $50.00

JENKINS, Will F. *Murder in the USA.* 1946. Crown. 1st. VG. P3. $35.00

JENKINSON, Charles. *Discourse on Conduct of Government of Great Britain...* 1794. London. Debrett. 8vo. disbound. R12. $125.00

JENKINSON, Michael. *Wild Rivers of North America.* 1981. EP Dutton. 2nd. 409p. VG+/wrp. F7. $12.00

JENKINSON, Michael. *Wilderness Rivers of America.* 1981. Abrams. 1st. 280p. F/case. A17. $30.00

JENKS, Edward. *History of Politics.* 1918 (1900). Dutton. 5th. 12mo. G. A2. $10.00

JENKS, Geroge C. *Double Curve Dam, the Pitcher Detective.* ca 1950s. Dime Novel Club. VG. P8. $12.50

JENKS, James. *Complete Cook, Teaching Art of Cookery in All Branches.* 1768. London. 364p. rb. VG. E6. $300.00

JENNER, William. *Lectures & Essays on Fevers & Diptheria 1849-1879.* 1893. Macmillan. 581p. cloth. G7. $25.00

JENNESS, Diamond. *Indians of Canada.* 1934. Ottawa. Nat Mus of Canada. 8vo. ils. gilt cloth. F. O1. $85.00

JENNESS, Mary. *Twelve Negro Americans.* 1936. Friendship. 1st. VG/wrp. B2. $35.00

JENNINGS, Dana Close. *Days of Steam & Glory.* 1968. Aberdeen, SC. ils. 95p. H6. $25.00

JENNINGS, Dean; see Fox, Gardner F.

JENNINGS, Gary. *Treasure of the Superstition Mountains.* 1973. NY. 1st. ils/maps. VG/dj. B5. $25.00

JENNINGS, J.D. *Prehistory of North America.* 1989. Mtn View. ils. 365p. F. M4. $20.00

JENNINGS, John. *Gentleman Ranker.* 1942. Reynal Hitchcock. 1st. bl linen. NF/VG. T11. $25.00

JENNINGS, John. *Salem Frigate.* 1946. NY. Doubleday. 1st. NF/VG. T11. $25.00

JENNINGS, John. *Shadow & the Glory.* 1943. NY. Reynal Hitchcock. 1st. NF/VG. T11. $25.00

JENNINGS, Maureen. *Except the Dying.* 1997. St Martin. 1st. sgn. author's 1st novel. F/dj. T2. $75.00

JENNINGS, N.A. *Texas Ranger.* 1992. Lakeside Classic. 1st thus. teg. brn bdg. F/sans/swrp. T11. $35.00

JENNINGS, Preston. *Book of Trout Flies. Containing List of Most Important...* 1972. NY. Crown. ils. 190p. VG/dj. B11. $18.00

JENNINGS, Renz L. *Boy From Taylor.* 1977. np. 1st. ils. 378p. NF/NF. B19. $45.00

JENNINGS & NORBECK. *Prehistoric Man in the New World.* 1965. Chicago. VG/dj. B9. $25.00

JENSEN, Oliver. *America & Russia: Century & Half of Dramatic Encounters.* 1962. NY. S&S. 1st. F/dj. B11. $12.50

JENSEN, Oliver. *America's Yesterdays: Images of Our Lost Past Destroyed...* 1978. S&S. photos. 352p. cloth. F/dj. D2. $40.00

JENSEN, Paul M. *Boris Karloff & His Films.* 1974. NY. Barnes/Tantivy. 1st. F/dj. C9. $48.00

JENSON, Robert W. *America's Theologian: A Recommendation of Jonathan Edwards.* 1988. OUP. VG/dj. M17. $20.00

JEPSON, Willis L. *Synopsis of North American Godetias.* 1907. Berkeley. ils. wrp. B26. $35.00

JEPSON, Willis L. *Vegetation of the Summit of Mt St Helena.* 1899. Berkeley. rpt. pl. VG/wrp. B26. $27.50

JEREMIAS, Joachim. *Jerusalem in the Times of Jesus.* 1977. Fortress. 405p. VG/wrp. B29. $8.50

JERGER, Joseph J. *Systems Preliminary Design.* 1960. Van Nostrand. 8vo. 625p. VG. K5. $50.00

JEROME, Owen Fox. *Murder at Avalon Arms.* 1931. Clode. 1st. VG. G8. $20.00

JERROLD, Walter. *Mother Goose's Nursery Rhymes.* (1909). NY. Dodge. 1st Am. ils Hassall. 364p. gilt pict cloth. R5. $150.00

JESCHKE, Susan. *Rima & Zeppo.* 1976. Windmill/Dutton. 1st. 32p. cloth. F/dj. D4. $25.00

JESSE, Edward. *Favorite Haunts & Rural Studies...* 1847. London. John Murray. 1st. ils. VG+. B20. $85.00

JETER, Goetze. *Strikers.* 1937. Stokes. 1st. F/NF. B2. $60.00

JETT & HYDE. *Navajo Wildlands: As Long As Rivers Shall Run.* 1967. Sierra Club. 1st. folio. brn cloth. VG/dj. F7. $95.00

JEVONS, W. Stanley. *Logic.* 1876. London. Macmillan. 2nd. VG. T12. $30.00

JEWELL, Nancy. *Calf, Goodnight.* 1973. Harper Row. 1st. RS. F/dj. D4. $35.00

**JEWELL, Nancy.** *Family Under the Moon.* 1976. Harper Row. 1st. obl 16mo. 32p. NF/G+. T5. $35.00

**JEWETT, Sara Orne.** *Tory Lover.* 1901. Houghton Mifflin. 1st. 8vo. gilt bl cloth. VG+. M5. $75.00

**JEWETT, Sarah Orne.** *Lady Ferry.* 1950. Colby College. 1st separate. sm 8vo. 61p. VG/dj. J3. $150.00

**JEWETT, Sarah Orne.** *White Heron: And Other Stories.* 1886. Houghton Mifflin. 1st. gilt gr cloth. VG. Q1. $175.00

**JEYNS, Soame.** *View of the Internal Evidence of the Christian Religion.* 1793. Boston. Andrews. lg 12mo. 162p. marbled paper wrp/ribbon ties. H13. $195.00

**JHABVALA, R. Prawer.** *Amrita: A Novel.* 1956. NY. Norton. ARC/1st Am. 8vo. RS. F/dj. S9. $175.00

**JIGMEI, N.N.** *Tibet.* 1981. NY. ils/photos. 296p. F/dj. M4. $20.00

**JILLSON, Joyce.** *Real Women Don't Pump Gas.* 1982. Pocket. ils Lee Lorenz. 91p. VG. P12. $6.00

**JILLSON, Joyce.** *Real Women Don't Pump Gas.* 1982. Pocket. 1st. F/dj. T12. $15.00

**JOB, Herbert K.** *Sport of Bird Study.* 1908. Outing. 1st. ils. cloth. VG. B27. $35.00

**JODOROWSKY, Alexandro.** *El Topo: A Book of the Film.* 1971. Douglas Books. 1st. F/dj. C9. $72.00

**JOHANNSEN, Albert.** *Phiz: Illustrations From the Novels of Chas Dickens.* 1956. Chicago. obl 4to. ils. 422p. VG. A4. $350.00

**JOHANNSEN, N.** *Neglected Point in Connection With Crises.* 1971 (1902). Augustus Kelley. 194p. VG. S5. $15.00

**JOHN, B.** *Libby: Sketches & Journals of Libby Beaman...* 1987. Tulsa. ils. 201p. F. M4. $22.00

**JOHN, Tommy.** *Tommy John Story.* 1978. Revell. 1st. sgn. photos. F/dj. P8. $35.00

**JOHN OF SALISBURY.** *Policraticvs.* 1595. Leyden. Plantin. 8vo. overlapping vellum. R12. $875.00

**JOHNGARD, P.A.** *Crane Music: Natural History of American Cranes.* 1991. Smithsonian. 8vo. ils/maps. 136p. F/dj. M12. $20.00

**JOHNS, Rowland.** *Our Friend the Cocker Spaniel.* 1932. NY. photo ftspc. VG/dj. A17. $15.00

**JOHNS, Rowland.** *Rowland Johns Book.* 1947. Methuen. 3rd. ils. NF/dj. A21. $40.00

**JOHNSGARD, P.** *Waterfowl: Their Biology & Natural History.* 1968. np. NF. M12. $25.00

**JOHNSON, A.F.** *Selected Essays on Books & Printing.* 1970. Amsterdam. Van Gendt. 1st. sm folio. maroon cloth. M24. $125.00

**JOHNSON, A.T.** *Rhodendrons, Azaleas, Magnolias, Camellias & Ornamental...* 1948. London. ils. VG/dj. B26. $14.00

**JOHNSON, Adrian.** *America Explored: Cartographical History of Exploration...* 1974. Viking. 1st. ils. 252p. VG/dj. B18. $50.00

**JOHNSON, B.P.** *Transactions of New York State Agricultural Society.* 1860. cloth. VG. A10. $35.00

**JOHNSON, C.** *When Mother Lets Us Cook.* 1908. 1st. ils. VG+. E6. $45.00

**JOHNSON, Charlene R.** *Florida Thoroughbred.* 1993. Gainsville. U FL. 1st. F/dj. O3. $39.00

**JOHNSON, Charles A.** *Denver's Mayor Speer.* 1969. Denver Bighorn Books. 1st. ils. F/dj. A2. $15.00

**JOHNSON, Charles.** *Middle Passage.* 1990. Atheneum. 1st. F/dj. D10. $95.00

**JOHNSON, Charles.** *Sorcerer's Apprentice.* 1986. Atheneum. 1st. F/dj. A10. $50.00

**JOHNSON, Clinton.** *Fraudulent California Land Grants.* 1926. np. Clinton Johnson. ils. 24p. prt wrp. D11. $50.00

**JOHNSON, Crockett.** *Blue Ribbon Puppies.* 1958. Harper. 1st. 12mo. gray cloth. pict dj. R5. $125.00

**JOHNSON, Crockett.** *What Will Walter Be?* 1964. HRW. 1st. ils Crockett Johnson. G/dj. P2. $15.00

**JOHNSON, Curt.** *Artillery.* 1976. London. Octopus. ils. 144p. VG/dj. M10. $8.50

**JOHNSON, Denis.** *Angels.* 1983. Chatto Windus. 1st Eng. inscr/dtd 1992. author's 1st novel. F/dj. R14. $85.00

**JOHNSON, Denis.** *Fiskadoro.* 1985. Chatto Windus. 1st. F/NF clip. B3. $60.00

**JOHNSON, Denis.** *Jesus' Son.* 1992. FSG. 1st. F/dj. M23. $40.00

**JOHNSON, Denis.** *Stars at Noon.* 1986. Knopf. 1st. F/NF. B3. $40.00

**JOHNSON, Denis.** *Stars at Noon.* 1986. Knopf. 1st. sgn. F/dj. R14. $85.00

**JOHNSON, Derek.** *Plants of the Western Boreal Forest & Aspen Parkland.* 1995. Edmonton, Alberta. 800 photos/900 line drawings, 392p. sc. AN. B26. $25.00

**JOHNSON, Diane.** *Dashiell Hammett: A Life.* 1983. Random. AP. 8vo. F/yel wrp. R3. $40.00

**JOHNSON, Diane.** *Lesser Lives: True History of the First Mrs Meredith...* 1972. NY. 1st. ils. VG. M17. $15.00

**JOHNSON, Don.** *Hummers, Knucklers & Slow Curves.* 1991. IL U. 1st. 84 poems. AN/dj. P8. $30.00

**JOHNSON, Dorothy M.** *Bloody Bozeman: Perilous Trail to Montana's Gold.* 1971. McGraw Hill. 1st. VG/dj. M20. $40.00

**JOHNSON, Edward.** *Domestic Practice of Hydropathy.* 1858. London. 5th. 524p. A13. $65.00

**JOHNSON, Elizabeth Goodwin.** *Piano Lady's Dream.* nd. Boston/NY. ils Arthur Antolini. VG. M17. $20.00

**JOHNSON, Franklin A.** *One More Hill.* 1949. NY. 1st. maps. 181p. G. B18. $125.00

**JOHNSON, Harmer.** *Guide to the Arts of the Americas.* 1992. NY. Rizzoli. 1st. 4to. 240p. gilt brn cloth. P4. $45.00

**JOHNSON, Harry R.** *Water Resources of Antelope Valley, California.* 1911. GPO. 2 fld maps/1 fld pocket map/7 full-p ils. 92p. D11. $50.00

**JOHNSON, Haynes.** *Bay of Pigs.* 1964. NY. Norton. BC. 8vo. 368p. F/VG+. M7. $15.00

**JOHNSON, Howard A.** *Global Odyssey: Episcopalian's Encounter...* (1963). Harper Row. 1st. 448p. VG. H10. $17.50

**JOHNSON, Hugh.** *International Book of Trees.* 1973. NY. ils. 288p. VG/dj. B26. $42.50

**JOHNSON, James W.** *Advances in Chemoreception.* 1970. Appleton Crofts. 412p. xl. VG. S5. $15.00

**JOHNSON, James Weldon.** *God's Trombones.* 1929. London. Allen Unwin. 1st. NF. B2. $75.00

**JOHNSON, James Weldon.** *Saint Peter Relates an Incident.* 1935. NY. Viking. 1st trade. 8vo. gilt blk cloth. NF/dj. J3. $450.00

**JOHNSON, Josephine.** *Seven Houses.* 1973. NY. 1st. sgn. VG/fair. B5. $25.00

**JOHNSON, L.F.** *Famous Kentucky Tragedies & Trials...* 1916. Louisville. Baldwin Law Book Co. gilt bl cloth. G. M11. $85.00

**JOHNSON, Laurence A.** *Over the Counter & on the Shelf.* 1961. Bonanza. lg 8vo. 140p. VG/dj. M7. $20.00

**JOHNSON, Loyal R.** *How to Landscape Your Grounds.* 1945 (1941). NY. ils/plans. 221p. VG/dj. B26. $20.00

JOHNSON, Lyndon Baines. *Vantage Point.* 1971. HRW. 1st. sgn. 636p. F/dj. W2. $150.00

JOHNSON, Margaret S. *Red Joker.* 1950. Morrow. 1st. 8vo. 95p. cloth. G. C14. $6.00

JOHNSON, Martin. *Cannibal Land: Adventures With a Camera in New Hebrides.* 1929. Boston. 191p. blk cloth. B14. $40.00

JOHNSON, Martin. *Lion: African Adventure With the King of Beasts.* 1929. NY. 1st. ils/fld map. 281p. NF. A17. $30.00

JOHNSON, Martin. *Lion: African Adventure With the King of Beasts.* 1929. NY/London. Putnam. 1st. tall 8vo. 281p. VG. W1. $20.00

JOHNSON, Mary Elizabeth. *Pillows: Designs, Patterns & Projects.* 1978. Oxmoor. 1st. 4to. 192p. NF. S14. $5.00

JOHNSON, Newton A. *James Addison Reavis & the Peralta Grant...* 1942. np. 1st. 120p. NF/wrp. B19. $20.00

JOHNSON, Owen. *Hummingbird.* 1917 (1910). Baker Taylor. later prt. F. P8. $45.00

JOHNSON, Owen. *Varmit.* 1910. Baker Taylor. 3rd. G+. P8. $40.00

JOHNSON, Philip. *Glass House.* 1993. NY. Pantheon. 1st. NF/dj. P4. $45.00

JOHNSON, Robert Underwood. *Remembered Yesterdays.* 1923. Little Brn. 1st. gilt olive-brn cloth. dj. M24. $100.00

JOHNSON, Rossiter. *Clash of Nations: Causes & Consequences.* 1914. Thos Nelson. 1st. ils. 340p. G. S14. $25.00

JOHNSON, Rossiter. *Story of a Great Conflict: History of War of Secession...* 1894 (1888). Bryan, Taylor. 2nd. photos/maps. 604p. VG. B10. $45.00

JOHNSON, Roy P. *Jacob Horner of the Seventh Cavalry, Vol 16, No 2.* 1949. State Hist Soc of ND. sc. G. A19. $30.00

JOHNSON, Samuel. *Conjugal Fidelity.* 1929. Mill House. 1st. 1/30. F/hand-made paper wrp. M24. $100.00

JOHNSON, Samuel. *Dictionary of the English Language; in Which Words...* 1819. Phil. James Maxwell. 2 vol. 1st Am from 11th London. marbled brd. H13. $1,950.00

JOHNSON, Samuel. *Harleian Miscellany; or, Collection of Scarce & Curious...* 1744-46. London. Osborne. 8 vol. tall 4to. subscriber list ea vol. VG. H13. $2,250.00

JOHNSON, Samuel. *Harleian Miscellany: An Entertaining Selection.* 1924. London. Cecil Palmer. 1st thus. tall 8vo. 272p. red cloth. H13. $65.00

JOHNSON, Samuel. *Johnson & Queeney, Letters From...to Queeney Thrale...* 1932. London. Cassell/Curwood. 1st. 1/500. tall 8vo. marbled cloth/red leather label. H13. $95.00

JOHNSON, Samuel. *Journey to the Western Islands of Scotland.* 1775. London. Strahan Cadell. 1st/1st issue (12-line errata). H13. $759.00

JOHNSON, Samuel. *Letters of Samuel Johnson/Mrs Thrale's Letters to Him.* 1952. Clerendon. 3 vol. 1st. tall 8vo. maroon linen. NF. H13. $295.00

JOHNSON, Samuel. *Lives of the Most Eminent English Poets...* 1790-1791. London. Rivington. 4 vol. tall 8vo. polished calf. H13. $385.00

JOHNSON, Samuel. *Poems.* 1941. Oxford. Clarendon. 1st. edit DN Smith/EL McAdam. VG. H13. $65.00

JOHNSON, Samuel. *Poetical Works. Complete in 1 Volume, New Edition.* 1785. London. Osborne Griffin. sm 8vo. half-titles present. early calf/leather label. H13. $295.00

JOHNSON, Samuel. *Prayers & Meditations, Composed by Dr Johnson...* 1807. London. Cadell Davis. 4th. tall 8vo. 230p. F. H13. $295.00

JOHNSON, Samuel. *Prayers Composed by Dr Samuel Johnson.* 1937. Mt Vernon. Golden Eagle. Archetype Deluxe Ed. 1/418. case. H13. $95.00

JOHNSON, Samuel. *Prayers.* 1947. London. Shenval. edit Elton Trueblood. 12mo. 99p. H13. $35.00

JOHNSON, Samuel. *Preface to Shakespeare.* 1985. Bristol. facs (1778). intro PJ Smallwood. 8vo. F. H13. $45.00

JOHNSON, Samuel. *Prince of Abissina: A Tale.* 1759. London. Dodsley. 2 vol. 2nd. 12mo. full polished calf. H13. $595.00

JOHNSON, Samuel. *Rambler.* 1800. London. 3 vol. 24mo. old calf/blk labels. VG. S17. $100.00

JOHNSON, Samuel. *Rasselas.* 1819. London. McLean. 197p. red pebbled morocco/red leather label. H13. $195.00

JOHNSON, Samuel. *RB Adam Library Relating to Dr Samuel Johnson & His Era.* 1929. OUP. 3 vol. 1st. 1/500. tall 4to. ils/vignettes. uncut. H13. $985.00

JOHNSON, Samuel. *Selected Essays.* 1889. London. Dent. 2 vol. edit George Birkbeck Hill/ils Herbert Railton. VG. H13. $95.00

JOHNSON, Samuel. *Selected Poetry & Prose.* 1977. Berkeley. 1st. 8vo. edit Frank Brady/WK Winsatt. 642p. F/acetate. H13. $85.00

JOHNSON, Samuel. *Some Unpublished Letters to & From Dr Johnson.* 1932. Manchester. sm 4to. 55p+4p ads. uncut/unopened/wrp/dj. H13. $65.00

JOHNSON, Samuel. *Vulture.* 1970. Boston. Godine. 1/3000. ils/sgn Lance Hidy. F/wrp. H13. $45.00

JOHNSON, Samuel. *Works, With an Essay on His Life & Genius...* 1835. NY. Geo Dearborn. 2 vol. 1st complete Am. thick 4to. sgn pres Murphy. H13. $450.00

JOHNSON, Stephen. *History of Cardiac Surgery 1896-1955.* 1970. Baltimore. 1st. 201p. dj. A13. $100.00

JOHNSON, Thomas C. *Inventory of the Winchester Repeating Arms Company.* 1991. Lynham Sayce. AP. 1/500. pub inscr. blk cloth. F. T11. $175.00

JOHNSON, Warren. *Muddling Toward Frugality.* 1978. Sierra Club. 1st. 252p. F/dj. A17. $15.00

JOHNSON, Willis Fletcher. *Fumigation Methods: Treatise for Farmers, Fruit Growers...* 1920. Orange Judd. 313p. AN. A10. $18.00

JOHNSON, Willis Fletcher. *History of the Johnstown Flood.* 1889. Edgewood. 1st. ils. 518p. VG. B14/S14. $40.00

JOHNSON, Willis Fletcher. *Life of Wm Tecumseh Sherman: Late Retired General, USA.* 1891. Edgewood Pub. 1st. intro OO Howard. gilt navy cloth. G+. A14. $21.00

JOHNSON & JOHNSON. *Distance Riding: From Start to Finish.* 1976. Houghton Mifflin. G/dj. O3. $15.00

JOHNSON & JOHNSON. *Yankee's Wander World: Circling the Globe...* 1949. NY. Norton. 1st. sgns. ils. 277p. VG. B11. $35.00

JOHNSON & KIOKEMEISTER. *Calculus.* 1959. Allyn Bacon. 1st. gray cloth. VG. B27. $15.00

JOHNSON & MALONE. *Dictionary of American Biography.* 1929-1944. 22 vol. 4to. 15,000 entries. VG. A4. $995.00

JOHNSON & SMITH. *Megatectonics of Continents & Oceans.* 1970. Rutgers. 1st. cloth. VG. B27. $30.00

JOHNSTON, Abraham Robinson. *Marching With the Army of the West, 1846-1848.* 1936. Glendale. Arthur H Clark. Southwest Hist series IV. ftspc/fld map. 368p. cloth. D11. $100.00

JOHNSTON, Alexander Keith. *School Atlas of Astronomy...* 1877. Edinburgh. Johnston. new/enlarged. 21 dbl-p mc pl. VG. K5. $225.00

**JOHNSTON, Angus James.** *Virginia Railroads in the Civil War.* (1961). UNC. ARC. 336p. w/pub photo. VG/VG. B10. $45.00

**JOHNSTON, Annie Fellows.** *Little Colonel, Maid of Honor.* 1948. Boston. Page. ils EB Barry. VG/dj. M20. $35.00

**JOHNSTON, Annie Fellows.** *Little Colonel.* 1896. Joseph Night. 1st/2nd issue. gilt red cloth. VG. M5. $70.00

**JOHNSTON, Annie Fellows.** *Road of the Loving Heart.* 1922. Boston. Page. 1st. 77p. gr cloth. NF. B20. $40.00

**JOHNSTON, Carol.** *Thomas Wolfe, a Descriptive Bibliography.* 1987. Pittsburgh. 295p. gilt bl cloth. F. F1. $50.00

**JOHNSTON, Denis Foster.** *Analysis of Sources of Information on Population of Navaho.* 1966. GPO. 1st. 226p. F. B19. $25.00

**JOHNSTON, Edward.** *Decoration & Its Uses.* 1991. Double Elephant. 1st. F/dj. P3. $22.00

**JOHNSTON, Edward.** *Writing & Illuminating & Lettering.* 1980. London. Pitman Taplinger. 439p. G+. M10. $8.50

**JOHNSTON, James Ambler.** *Echoes of 1861-1961.* 1971. Richmond. private prt. 1st. ils/maps/pl. 111p. cloth. M8. $125.00

**JOHNSTON, James R.** *Accoutrements.* nd. np. 4to. photos. 211p. VG. O3. $30.00

**JOHNSTON, Joseph Eggleston.** *Narrative of Military Operations: Anthology of Urban Fear.* 1874. Appleton. 1st. 602p. half leather. M8. $350.00

**JOHNSTON, Paul.** *Body Politic.* 1997. London. Hodder Stoughton. 1st. F/dj. M15. $100.00

**JOHNSTON, Terry C.** *Cry of the Hawk.* 1992of the. NY. Bantam. 1st. quarter bl cloth. F/dj. T11. $30.00

**JOHNSTON, Terry C.** *Winter Rain.* 1993. NY. Bantam. 1st. F/dj. T11. $30.00

**JOHNSTONE, Paul.** *Sea-Craft of Prehistory.* 1980. Harvard. ils VG/dj. M17. $35.00

**JOHNSTONE, Paul.** *Seafarers & Sea Fighters of Mediterranean in Ancient Times.* 1991. Princeton. 2nd. ils. VG/dj. M17. $22.50

**JOINER, D.L.** *Ladybird Book of British Railway Locomotives.* 1958. Wills Hepworth. 1st. 16mo. 51p. NF/VG. S14. $13.00

**JOLINE, Adrian H.** *Meditations of an Autograph Collector.* 1901. NY. Harper. 1st. 316p. teg. half red morocco. VG. F1. $75.00

**JOLLEY, Harley E.** *Blue Ridge Parkway.* (1969). TN U. 172p. VG. B10. $10.00

**JOLY, J. Swift.** *Stone & Calculus Disease of the Urinary Organs.* 1929. CV Mosby. 1st Am. 189p. cloth. VG. B27. $25.00

**JOLY, John.** *Surface History of Earth.* 1925. Clarendon. 1st. xl. VG. B14. $125.00

**JONES, Antony Armstrong.** *Snowdon: Photographic Autobiography.* 1979. Times. 1st. photos. 239p. NF/VG. S14. $27.50

**JONES, Benjamin.** *Co-Operative Production.* 1962 (1894). Austustus Kelley. rpt. 839p. VG. S5. $15.00

**JONES, Brian.** *Practical Astronomer.* 1990. S&S. ils. 160p. VG/torn. K5. $15.00

**JONES, Charles.** *Look to the Mountain Top.* 1972. Jose, CA. Gousha. G/dj. A19. $25.00

**JONES, Christopher.** *Deciphering Maya Hieroglyphs.* 1984. Phil U Mus. 2nd. sbdg. F3. $25.00

**JONES, David.** *Palms in Australia.* 1993 (1984). Chatswood, NSW. 2nd. 278p. AN/dj. B26. $40.00

**JONES, Diana Wynne.** *Everard's Ride.* 1995. Framingham. NESFA. 1st. 1/815. F/dj. T2. $25.00

**JONES, Diana Wynne.** *Minor Arcana.* 1996. London. Gollancz. 1st. 7 stories. F/dj. T2. $35.00

**JONES, Diana Wynne.** *Power of Three.* 1977. Greenwillow. 1st. 250p. gold brd/pub lib bdg. VG/G. T5. $45.00

**JONES, Diana Wynne.** *Spellcoats.* 1979. NY. Atheneum. 1st Am. 8vo. 250p. olive cloth. NF/dj. T5. $35.00

**JONES, Douglas C.** *Barefoot Brigade.* 1981. HRW. 1st. F/dj. T11. $30.00

**JONES, Douglas C.** *Come Winter.* 1989. NY. Holt. ARC/1st. w/promo material. F/dj. T11. $35.00

**JONES, Douglas C.** *Court-Martial of George Armstrong Custer.* 1976. Scribner. 1st. 8vo. 291p. B20/S16. $25.00

**JONES, Douglas C.** *Roman.* 1986. NY. Holt. 1st. NF/dj. T11. $20.00

**JONES, Ellen.** *Fatal Crown.* 1991. S&S. 1st. inscr. F/dj. M19. $17.50

**JONES, Ernest.** *Life & Works of Sigmund Freud.* 1953. NY. 3 vol. VG/dj. B30. $60.00

**JONES, Fred.** *Farm Gas Engines & Tractors.* 1963. McGraw Hill. 4th. 518p. cloth. VG+. A10. $35.00

**JONES, G. Wayman.** *Alias Mr Death.* 1932. NY. Fiction League. 1st. VG/dj. M15. $45.00

**JONES, Gayl.** *White Rat.* 1977. Random. 1st. short stories. F/NF. A24. $50.00

**JONES, Gwyneth.** *North Wind.* 1996. NY. Tor. 1st. F/dj. M23. $25.00

**JONES, H. Spencer.** *Worlds Without End.* 1935. London. English U. 1st. 8vo. ils. 262p. K5. $25.00

**JONES, Henry M.** *Ships of Kingston 'Good-Bye, Fare Ye Well.'* 1926. Plymouth, MA. ils. G+. M17. $35.00

**JONES, Howard Mumford.** *Pursuit of Happiness.* 1953. Cambridge. Harvard. VG/dj. M11. $65.00

**JONES, Idwal.** *China Boy.* (1936). LA. Primavera. 1/1000. red suede. D11. $100.00

**JONES, Idwal.** *High Bonnet.* 1947. London. Heinemann. 1st. 154p. D11. $50.00

**JONES, Idwal.** *Vineyard.* 1942. DSP. 1st. 279p. D11. $75.00

**JONES, Ira (Taffy).** *Tiger Squadron: Story of 74 Squadron, RAF, in 2 World Wars.* 1955. London. Allen. rpt. 8vo. 295p. VG/dj. B11. $45.00

**JONES, J. Mervyn.** *British Nationality Law & Practice.* 1948. Oxford. bl cloth. M11. $50.00

**JONES, J.K.** *Mammals of the Northern Great Plains.* 1983. U NE. 376p. F/dj. S15. $21.00

**JONES, Jack Colvard.** *Circulatory System of Insects.* 1977. Springfield. ils. 255p. VG/dj. S15. $20.00

**JONES, James A.** *Courts by Day From 'The Evening News.'* nd. Sampson Low Marston. 1st. 8vo. VG/dj. A2. $35.00

**JONES, James.** *From Here to Eternity.* 1st. author's 1st book. VG/dj. B30. $100.00

**JONES, James.** *Go to the Widow-Maker.* 1967. Delacorte. 1st. 618p. F/VG. H1. $28.00

**JONES, James.** *Merry Month of May.* 1971. Delacorte. 1st. VG/dj. S18. $10.00

**JONES, James.** *Pistol.* 1958. Scribner. 1st. VG/dj. B30. $30.00

**JONES, James.** *Some Came Running.* 1957. Scribner. 1st. VG/dj. B30. $75.00

**JONES, James.** *Thin Red Line.* 1962. NY. 1st. NF/dj. T9. $45.00

**JONES, James.** *Thin Red Line.* 1962. Scribner. 1st. VG/clip. A14. $28.00

**JONES, James.** *Touch of Danger.* 1973. Doubleday. 1st. 8vo. gilt burgundy cloth. F/dj. R3. $50.00

**JONES, James.** *Whistle.* 1978. Delacorte. 1st. F/NF. T12. $35.00

**JONES, John Beauchamp.** *Rebel War Clerk's Diary at Confederate States Capital.* 1866. Lippincott. 2 vol in 1. 1st. cloth. M8. $450.00

**JONES, Ken.** *Destroyer Squadron 12: Arleigh Burke's Force.* 1956. Phil. Chilton. 1st. maps/index. 283p. VG/dj. B5. $32.50

**JONES, Lloyd.** *US Fighters: 1925-1980s.* 1975. Fallbrook. photos/diagrams. 322p. VG/dj. S16. $45.00

**JONES, Louise Seymour.** *Human Side of Bookplates.* 1952. Ward Ritchie. 2nd. ils. 158p. gilt cloth. F1. $65.00

**JONES, Madison.** *Buried Land.* 1963. Second Chance. 1st. sgn. F/dj. B30. $20.00

**JONES, Mary Stevens.** *18th-Century Perspective: Culpeper County.* 1976. Culpeper Hist Soc. photos. 150p. G+. B10. $25.00

**JONES, Rufus.** *Church's Debt to Heretics.* ca 1924. Doran. 12mo. 256p. V3. $20.00

**JONES, Rufus.** *Eternal Gospel.* 1938. Macmillan. 1st. 235p. G/dj. V3. $21.00

**JONES, Rufus.** *George Fox, an Autobiography.* 1919. Phil. Ferris Leach. 12mo. 584p. G. V3. $14.00

**JONES, Rufus.** *New Quest.* 1928. Macmillan. 1st. 12mo. 202p. xl. V3. $12.00

**JONES, Rufus.** *Quakerism: Spiritual Movement.* 1963. Phil Yearly Meeting. 205p. VG/dj. V3. $25.00

**JONES, Rufus.** *Re-Thinking Religious Liberalism.* 1935. Boston. Beacon. 26p. V3. $20.00

**JONES, Rufus.** *Remnant.* 1920. London. Swarthmore. 1st. V3. $22.00

**JONES, Rufus.** *Some Exponents of Mystical Religion.* 1930. Abingdon. 12mo. 237p. V3. $22.00

**JONES, Scott E.** *Soldier Boy.* 1995. St Martin. 1st. author's 1st book. F/NF. S18. $30.00

**JONES, Shirley.** *Five Flowers for My Father.* 1990. S Croydon. Red Hen. 1/40. sgn. 7 sgn mezzotints. AN/box. B24. $750.00

**JONES, Shirley.** *Greek Dance.* 1980. London. 1/40. 5 full-p etchings. loose/as issued. F/paper folder/box. B24. $550.00

**JONES, Shirley.** *Same Sun.* 1978. np. 1/25. sgn. 9 sgn etchings/9 poems. loose. AN/F box. B24. $650.00

**JONES, Shirley.** *Scop Hwilom Sang (Sometimes a Poet Sang).* 1983. London. 1/25 (50 total). 7 etchings. bdg/sgn Denise Lubett. brn goatskin. F/box. B24. $3,000.00

**JONES, Stephen.** *Horror: 100 Best Books.* 1990. Carroll Graf. 1st. VG/wrp. L1. $20.00

**JONES, Stephen.** *Shadows in Eden: Clive Barker.* 1991. Underwood Miller. 1/500. sgn. AN/box. T12. $125.00

**JONES, T.** *Hawaii Book: Story of Our Island Paradise.* 1961. Chicago. ils. VG/G. M17. $20.00

**JONES, Terry L.** *Lee's Tigers: Louisiana Infantry in Army of Northern VA.* 1987. Baton Rouge. LSU. 1st/3rd imp. NF/dj. A14. $25.00

**JONES, Thelma.** *Once Upon a Lake: A History of Lake Minnetonka...* 1957. Ross Haines. 1st. ils. 285p. A17. $17.50

**JONES, Tim.** *Last Great Race: Iditarod Sled Dog Race.* 1982. Seattle. ils/map ep. 266p. F/dj. A17. $15.00

**JONES, U.J.** *History of the Early Settlement of the Juniata Valley.* 1940. Harrisburg. rpt (1889). 440p. map ep. VG+. B18. $45.00

**JONES, Virgil Carrington.** *Eight Hours Before Richmond.* 1957. NY. Holt. 1st. NF/VG clip. A14. $21.00

**JONES, Virgil Carrington.** *Ranger Mosby.* 1944. UNC. 3rd. 347p. VG. B10. $35.00

**JONES, W. Mac.** *Douglas Register Being a Detailed Record of Births...* 1928. JW Ferguson. 412p. VG. B10. $125.00

**JONES, Walter.** *Sandbar.* 1982. Casper, WY. Basco Inc. AN. A19. $30.00

**JONES & JONES.** *Ithaca Sojourners.* 1980. Gainesville, FL. Old Mariners. slim 8vo. 70p. VG. B11. $18.00

**JONES & NEWMAN.** *Horror: 100 Best Books.* 1988. Carroll Graf. 1st Am. VG/dj. L1. $35.00

**JONES-NORTH, Jacquelyn Y.** *Czechoslovakian Perfume Bottles & Boudoir Accessories.* 1990. Antique Pub. 1st. 4to. 128p. F. w/price guide. H1. $48.00

**JONG, Erica.** *How to Save Your Own Life.* 1977. HRW. 1st. F/dj. B4. $65.00

**JONG, Erica.** *Loveroot.* 1975. HRW. ARC/1st. inscr/dtd 1977. F/NF. L3. $75.00

**JONG, Erica.** *Loveroot.* 1975. HRW. 1st. F/dj. R14. $35.00

**JONSON, Ben.** *Volpone; or, The Foxe.* 1898. London. Leonard Smithers. 1/100 (1000 total). w/extra ils. B24. $2,750.00

**JONSSON, Reidar.** *My Life as a Dog.* 1990. FSG. 1st Am. F/dj. C9. $30.00

**JORAVSKY, David.** *Russian Psychology: A Critical History.* 1989. Oxford. Blackwell. heavy 8vo. Blk cloth. VG/dj. G1. $65.00

**JORDAN, Barbara.** *Barbara Jordan: A Self-Portrait.* 1979. Doubleday. 1st. sgn Jordan/Hearon. F/NF. A24. $100.00

**JORDAN, Bill.** *No Second Place Winner.* 1977. Shreveport, LA. 7th. 114p. dj. A17. $25.00

**JORDAN, Cornelia Jane M.** *Flowers of Hope & Memory: A Collection of Poems.* 1861. Richmond. A Morris. 1st (Confederate imp). 330p. cloth. M8. $650.00

**JORDAN, E.L.** *Hammond's Nature Atlas of America.* 1952. NY. ils/maps. 256p. VG/dj. A17. $17.50

**JORDAN, Joe.** *Bluegrass Horse Country.* 1940. Lexington. Transylvania. 1st trade. sgn. G. O3. $65.00

**JORDAN, Neil.** *Neil Jordan Reader.* 1993. NY. Vintage. 1st. F/wrp. C9. $48.00

**JORDAN, Neil.** *Night in Tunisia.* 1979. London. Writers & Readers Pub. 1st UK. F/NF. D10. $100.00

**JORDAN, Pat.** *Cheat.* 1984. Villard. 1st. F/VG. P8. $30.00

**JORDAN, Philip.** *Peoples' Health: History of Public Health in Minnesota...* 1953. St Paul. 1st. 524p. A13. $25.00

**JORDAN, Richard.** *Journal of the Life & Religious Labors of Richard Jordan...* 1829. Friends Book Store. 16mo. 172p. leather. V3. $32.00

**JORDAN, Robert.** *Fires of Heaven.* 1993. Tor. 1st. NF/dj. M21. $15.00

**JORDAN, Robert.** *Shadow Rising.* 1992. NY. Tor. 1st. F/F. H11. $35.00

**JORDAN, Ted.** *Norma Jean: My Secret Life With Marilyn Monroe.* 1989. NY. Morrow. 1st. F/dj. A14. $21.00

**JORDAN, Terry G.** *North American Cattle-Ranching Frontiers.* 1988. NM U. ils/biblio. 320p. AN/wrp. B19. $15.00

**JORDANOFF, Assen.** *Man Behind the Flight.* (1942). NY. 1st. 276p. VG/dj. B18. $45.00

**JORGENSON, Nels Leroy.** *Dave Palmer's Diamond Mystery.* 1954. Cupples Leon. 1st. VG. P8. $10.00

**JORROCKS, John.** *Private Stable: Establishment, Management & Appointments.* 1899. Boston. Little Brn. 1st. G. O3. $350.00

**JOSCELYN, Archie.** *Golden Bowl.* 1931. Internat Fiction Lib. VG/fair. P3. $25.00

**JOSEPH, Benjamin M.** *Besieged Bedfellows: Israel & the Land of Apartheid.* 1988. NY/London/Westport. Greenwood. 1st. 8vo. 174p. F. W1. $20.00

**JOSEPH, Mark.** *Typhoon.* 1991. S&S. 1st. sm 4to. 300p. F/dj. W2. $30.00

**JOSEPH, Michael.** *Charles, the Story of a Friendship.* 1952. NY. Prentice Hall. 1st Am. 110p. NF/dj. D4. $35.00

**JOSEPHUS, Flavius.** *Historien und B Discher Geschichten...* 1569. Frankfurt. Raben/ Feyrabend/Erden. 3 parts in 1. woodcuts. G. K1. $1,500.00

**JOSEPHY, Alvin M.** *American Heritage Book of Indians.* 1961. NY. ils/maps. VG/case. S16. $30.00

**JOSEPHY, Alvin M.** *American Heritage June 1976.* 1976. American Heritage. VG. P3. $10.00

**JOSEPHY, Alvin M.** *Now That the Buffalo's Gone: Study of Today's Am Indians.* 1982. NY. 1st. 300p. F/dj. M4. $25.00

**JOSLIN, Sesyle.** *Baby Elephant's Baby Book.* 1964. HBW. 1st. ils Weisgard. unp. NF/VG. C14. $20.00

**JOSS, John.** *Sierra, Sierra.* 1977. Los Altos. Soaring. 1st. inscr. NF/dj. R11. $125.00

**JOUHANDEAU, Marcel.** *Petit Bestiaire.* 1944. Librairie Gallimard. 1/330. 8 etchings by Laurencin. bdg/sgn Claes. AN/wrp. B24. $6,000.00

**JOYCE, James.** *Anna Livia Plurabelle: Fragment of Work in Progress.* 1930. London. Faber. 1st. Criterion Miscellany #15. VG. Q1. $200.00

**JOYCE, James.** *Epiphanies.* 1956. Buffalo. 1st. 1/550. F. L3. $350.00

**JOYCE, James.** *Finnegans Wake.* 1939. London/NY. Faber/Viking. 1/425. sgn/#d. 628p. teg. red cloth. NF. B20. $6,500.00

**JOYCE, James.** *Giacomo Joyce.* 1968. NY. Viking. 1st trade. F/dj. Q1. $30.00

**JUDA, L.** *Wise Old Man: Turkish Tales of Nasreddin Hodja.* nd (c1963). Edinburgh. Thomas Nelson. probable 1st. ils Theobald. NF/VG. C14. $18.00

**JUDD, Bob.** *Monza.* 1992. NY. Morrow. 1st. F/F. H11. $25.00

**JUDD, Charles Hubbard.** *Psychology: General Introduction.* 1907. Scribner. thick 12mo. 389p. gr cloth. VG. G1. $35.00

**JUDD, W.W.** *Birds of Albany County.* 1907. Albany, NY. private prt. 1/300. sgn. gilt cloth. F. C12. $110.00

**JUDSON, Clara I.** *Child Life Cook Book.* 1929. Rand McNally. ils w/silhouettes. glazed brd. NF/dj. D1. $60.00

**JUDSON, Phoebe Goodell.** *Pioneer's Search for an Ideal Home: A Book...* 1966. WA State Hist Soc. 1st thus. 207p. gilt bl cloth. NF. B20. $50.00

**JUDSON & JUDSON.** *Let's Go to Colombia.* 1949. Harper. 1st. 332p. dj. F3. $15.00

**JUGAKU, Bunsho.** *Bibliographical Study of Wm Blake's Note-Book.* 1971. ils. 175p. F. A4. $35.00

**JUKES, Thomas H.** *Molecules & Evolution.* 1966. Columbia. 285p. xl. VG. S5. $20.00

**JULIAN & PHILLIPS.** *Other Woman: Life of Violet Trefusis.* 1976. Boston. 1st. ils. VG/G. M17. $25.00

**JULIEN, Catherine.** *Hatunqolla: View of Inca Rule From Lake Titicaca Region.* 1983. Berkeley. 1st. 286p. wrp. F3. $25.00

**JULL, Morley A.** *Successful Poultry Management.* 1943. McGraw Hill. 2nd. ils/fld mc pl. VG. H10. $17.50

**JUNG, C.G.** *Psychological Types or Psychology of Individuation.* 1923. NY/London. Calssic First Ed. 654p. G. B14. $95.00

**JUNG, C.G.** *Psychology & Alchemy.* 1953. NY. 1st Eng trans. 563p. A13. $100.00

**JUNGE, Mark.** *JE Stimson, Photographer of the West.* 1985. U NE. 1st. photos. AN/clip. J2. $125.00

**JUNGER, Ernst.** *Details of Time.* 1995. NY. 1st. trans Neugroschel. edit Hervier. dj. T9. $10.00

**JUNIUS (STAT NOMINIS UMBRA).** *Letters.* 1801. London. Prt by T Bensley for Vernor & Hood. 2 vol. tall 8vo. H13. $350.00

**JUST, Ward.** *To What End: Report From Vietnam.* 1968. Houghton Mifflin. 3rd. 209p. NF/dj. R11. $20.00

**JUSTICE, Donald.** *Donald Justice Reader.* 1991. Middlebury College. 1st. VG/dj. M17. $15.00

**JUSTICE, Hilda.** *Life & Ancestry of Warner Mifflin.* 1905. Ferris Leach. 1st. 240p. backstrip mostly gone/detached covers. V3. $25.00

**JUSTINIANUS I.** *Instututionum Libri...* 1647. venice. Guerilios. sm 12mo. 444p. contemporary vellum. K1. $85.00

**JUSTIS, May.** *Big Log Mountain.* 1958. Henry Holt. stated 1st. 184p. xl. VG. B36. $16.00

**JUSTIS, May.** *House in No End Hollow.* 1938. Doubleday Doran. stated 1st. ils Erick Berry. orange cloth. xl. B36. $30.00

**JUVENALIS, D. Junii.** *Junii Juvenalis Aquinatis Satyrae.* 1685. Zyliana. thick 8vo. Latin text. 980+68p index. full leather. B11. $425.00

# K

KADANS, Joseph M. *Encyclopedia of Fruits, Vegetables, Nuts & Seeds...* 1973. W Nyack, NY. Parker. 8vo. 215p. F/NF. H4. $15.00

KADREY, Richard. *Kamikaze L'Amour.* 1995. St Martin. 1st. F/dj. M23. $25.00

KADREY, Richard. *Metrophage (A Romance of the Future).* 1988. London. Gollancz. 1st. author's 1st novel. F/dj. T2. $25.00

KAEL, Pauline. *State of Art.* 1985. Dutton. 1st. VG/dj. C9. $36.00

KAEL, Pauline. *Taking It All In.* 1984. NY. Holt. 1st. 8vo. 525p. F/NF. B20. $50.00

KAESE, Harold. *Boston Braves.* 1948. Putnam. 1st. photos. F/VG+. P8. $100.00

KAFKA, Franz. *Amerika.* nd (1940). Norfolk, CT. New Directions. 1st Am. F/NF. B4. $400.00

KAFKA, Franz. *Amerika. Preface by Klaus Mann. Trans by Edwin Muir.* 1946. New Directions. 1st thus. 8vo. 277p. VG. H4. $22.00

KAFKA, Franz. *Conversation With the Supplicant.* 1971. West Burke, VT. Janus. 1/100. ils/sgn Claire VanVliet. w/ephemera. F/box. B24. $1,500.00

KAFKA, Franz. *Der Kubelreiter. The Bucket Rider.* 1972. Newark, VT. Janus. 1/100. ils/sgn Jerome Kaplan. German text. F/box. B24. $550.00

KAFKA, Franz. *Metamorphosis.* 1946. Vanguard. 1st Am thus. 8vo. 98p. G. H4. $17.50

KAFKA, Franz. *Trial.* 1956. Modern Lib. 1st. NF/VG+. S13. $12.00

KAFKA, Gustav. *Handbuch der Vergleichenden Psychologie.* 1922. Ernst Reinhardt. 3 vol. heavy 8vo. G1. $100.00

KAGAN, Elaine. *Blue Heaven.* 1996. Knopf. 1st. 351p. F/dj. P12. $10.00

KAGAN, Solomon. *Jewish Medicine.* 1952. Boston. 1st. 575p. xl. A13. $200.00

KAGANOVICH, A.L. *Splendours of Leningrad.* 1969. NY. photos Gerard Bertin. trans James Hogarth. VG/dj. M17. $20.00

KAHLER, Heinz. *Art of Rome & Her Empire.* 1964. Greystone. ils. 256p. VG/dj. B29. $16.00

KAHN, David. *Hitler's Spies.* 1978. NY. Macmillan. 1st. thick 8vo. 671p. NF/dj. B20. $30.00

KAHN, E.J. *Voice of the American Phenomenon.* 1947. Harper. 1st. photos. VG/dj. B5. $25.00

KAHN, Michael A. *Canaan Legacy.* 1988. Lynx. 1st. sm 4to. 385p. F/dj. W2. $30.00

KAHN, Roger. *Boys of Summer.* 1972. Harper Row. 1st. VG/dj. P8. $35.00

KAHN, Roger. *Joe & Marilyn: A Memory of Love.* 1986. Morrow. 1st. NF/dj. A14. $22.00

KAHO, Noel. *Monopoly Investigation.* 1938. Randsell Inc. gilt crimson cloth. M11. $65.00

KAINS, Josephine; see Goulart, Ron.

KAINS, M.G. *Grow Your Own Fruit.* 1940. NY. 1st. photos. VG/dj. M17. $15.00

KAIR & MOYNAHAN. *Ace Powell Book: Etching Catalogue Volume II.* 1978. Cheney, WA. Art of Northwest. 1/150. 110p. brn buckram. F/case. B20. $125.00

KAJENCKI, Francis C. *Star on Many a Battlefield: Brevet Brigadier Gen J Karge...* 1980. Farileigh Dickinson U. 1st. NF/clip. A14. $25.00

KAKONIS, Tom. *Criss Cross.* 1990. NY. SMP. 1st. F/NF. H11. $25.00

KAKONIS, Tom. *Michigan Roll.* 1988. NY. St Martin. 1st. author's 1st book. F/F. H11. $50.00

KAKU, Michio. *Hyperspace: Scientific Odyssey Through Parallel Universes...* 1994. OUP. 8vo. 359p+index. AN/dj. H4. $16.00

KALAIDJIAN, Walter. *Languages of Liberation.* 1989. NY. Columbia. 8vo. 263p. red cloth. F/dj. H4. $15.00

KALFATOVIC, Mary C. *New Deal Fine Arts Project: A Bibliography 1933-1992.* 1994. Greenwood. 725p. VG. A4. $95.00

KALINOWSKY, Lothar B. *Shock Treatments, Psychosurgery & Other Somatic Treatments.* 1952. NY. Grune Stratton. 2nd revised. 8vo. 396p. G. C14. $17.00

KALINSKY, George. *New York Mets: Photographic History.* 1995. Macmillan. 1st. photos. F/dj. P8. $27.50

KALLIR, Otto. *Grandma Moses.* 1973. Abrams. ils. VG/dj. B9. $45.00

KALMAN, Maria. *Max in Hollywood, Baby.* 1992. NY. Viking. 1st. sm 4to. F/F. C14. $22.00

KALMAN, Maria. *Sayonara, Mrs Kackleman.* 1989. Viking. 1st. sm 4to. unp. NF/NF clip. C14. $18.00

KALOGRIDIS, Jeanne. *Covenant With the Vampire.* 1994. Delacorte. 1st. VG/dj. L1. $45.00

KALTENBORN, H.V. *I Broadcast the Crisis.* 1938. Random. 1st. 8vo. 359p. NF/VG. B20. $45.00

KAMAN, Maira. *Hey Willy, See the Pyramids.* (1988). Viking. Kestrel. 1st. 4to. F/dj. H4. $25.00

KAMEN-KAYE, Dorothy. *Speaking of Venezuela.* 1947. Caracas. 1st. 247p. dj. F3. $15.00

KAMINISKI, Thomas. *Early Career of Samuel Johnson.* 1987. OUP. 1st. dj. H13. $45.00

KAMINSKY, Stuart M. *Bullet for a Star.* 1977. St Martin. 1st. author's 1st book. F/NF. C15. $100.00

KAMINSKY, Stuart M. *Exercise in Terror.* 1985. St Martin. 1st. F/NF. B2. $35.00

KAMINSKY, Stuart M. *Man Who Walked Like a Bear.* 1990. Scribner. 1st. sgn. F/dj. B2. $35.00

KAMINSKY, Stuart M. *Never Cross a Vampire.* 1980. St Martin. 1st. F/dj. C15. $85.00

KAMINSKY, Stuart M. *Never Cross a Vampire.* 1980. St Martin. 1st. sgn. VG/dj. L1. $125.00

KAMINSKY, Stuart M. *When the Dark Man Calls.* 1983. St Martin. 1st. F/NF. M23. $25.00

KAMINSKY, Stuart M. *You Bet Your Life.* 1978. St Martin. 1st. F/dj. C15. $100.00

KAMM, Minnie Watson. *Fifth Pitcher Book.* 1948. Grosse Point Farms, MI. self pub. 1st. 207p. sbdg. VG. H1. $32.50

KAMM, Minnie Watson. *First Two Hundred Pattern Glass Pitchers.* 1970. Kamm Pub. 5th/4th prt. 8vo. 138p. VG/heavy wrp/plastic dj. H1. $26.00

KAMMAN, Madeleine. *Dinner Against the Clock.* 1973. NY. Atheneum. BC. G/dj. A16. $6.00

KAMMAN, Madeleine. *Making of a Cook.* 1971. Weathervane. BC. AN/dj. A16. $6.00

KAMMEN, Robert. *Soldiers Falling Into Camp: Battles at Rosebud...* 1992. London. Tonson. maps. 240p. F/F. A4. $35.00

KAMSTRA, Jerry. *Frisco Kid.* 1975. Harper Row. 1st. 8vo. VG/clip. R11. $25.00

KANE, Annie. *Golden Sunset; or, Homeless Blind Girl.* 1864. Baltimore. JW Bond. gilt brn cloth. G+. H4. $8.00

KANE, Elisha Kent. *Arctic Explorations.* 1996. Lakeside Classics. 1st thus. teg. brn bdg. F. T11. $30.00

KANE, Elisha Kent. *Arctic Explorations: 2nd Grinnell Expedition...* 1856. Phil. 2 vol. 300+ engravings. brn cloth. G. B30. $75.00

KANE, Elisha Kent. *Gongorism & the Golden Age: A Study...* 1928. Chapel Hill. 1st. 8vo. ils. 275p. gilt blk cloth. B20. $40.00

KANE, Elisha Kent. *US Grinnell Expedition in Search of Sir John Franklin.* 1854. Harper. 8vo. 11 pl/3 maps. 522p. VG. O1. $100.00

**KANE, Harnett T.** *Bride of Fortune.* 1948. Doubleday. stated 1st. 8vo. 301p. dj. H4. $10.00

**KANE, Harnett T.** *Spies for the Blue & Gray: A Composite Biography...* 1954. Hanover. 1st. sgn. NF/VG. A14. $28.00

**KANE, Henry.** *Until You Are Dead.* 1951. Inner Sanctum. 1st. F/VG. M19. $25.00

**KANE, Mary.** *Bibliography of the Works of Fiske Kimball.* 1959. U VA. inscr/edit Nichols. 67p. VG. B10. $15.00

**KANE, Sean.** *Spenser's Moral Allegory.* (1989). Toronto. 8vo. 237p. F/dj. H4. $30.00

**KANEKO, Jiro.** *Clinical Biochemistry of Domestic Animals.* 1980. NY. Academic. 3rd. VG. O3. $22.00

**KANIN, Garson.** *Moviola.* 1979. S&S. 1st. sgn. VG/dj. C9. $48.00

**KANITZ, Walter.** *White Kepi.* 1956. Regency. 1st. 8vo. red cloth. VG+. M7. $20.00

**KANIUK, Yoram.** *Confessions of a Good Arab, a Novel.* 1988. NY. Braziller. 1st. 215p. VG/dj. W1. $18.00

**KANOWITZ, Leo.** *Poem Is a Four-Letter Word.* 1970. Lawrence. Coronado. 280p. prt wrp. M11. $45.00

**KANT, Immanuel.** *Anthropologie in Pragmatischer Hinsicht.* 1798. Konigsburg. Friedrich Nicolovius. 334p. contemporary bdg. G1. $750.00

**KANTOR, MacKinlay.** *Andersonville.* 1955. Cleveland. World. 1st. NF/VG. A14. $28.00

**KANTOR, MacKinlay.** *Diversey.* 1928. Coward McCann. 1st. author's 1st book. red cloth. VG/G. J3. $150.00

**KANTOR, MacKinlay.** *Work of Saint Francis.* 1958. Cleveland. World. 1st. 109p. F/dj. D4. $45.00

**KAO, John.** *Jamming.* 1996. Harper Collins. 1st. sgn. 204p. F/dj. W2. $25.00

**KAPLAN, Barbara B.** *Land & Heritage in the Virginia Tidewater: A History...* (1993). King & Queen Hist Soc. 1st. 279p. VG. B10. $45.00

**KAPLAN, Helen Singer.** *Sexual Aversion, Sexual Phobias & Panic Disorder.* 1987. NY. Brunner/Malzel. 1st. 158p. F/dj. C14. $20.00

**KAPLAN, Howard.** *Chopin Express.* 1978. Dutton. 1st. author's 2nd book. F/F. H11. $25.00

**KAPLAN, John.** *Trial of Jack Ruby.* 1966. NY/London. Macmillan. 2nd. 8vo. 392p. F/dj. H4. $12.50

**KAPLAN, John.** *Trial of Jack Ruby.* 1965. Macmillan. 1st. 392p. VG/dj. B5. $25.00

**KAPLAN, Moise N.** *Big Game Angler's Paradise.* 1937. Liveright. 1st. 8vo. 400p. gilt bl cloth. VG+. B20. $65.00

**KAPLAN, Morton A.** *Dissent & the State in Peace & War...* 1970. NY. Dunellen. 1st. 8vo. VG/dj. A2. $15.00

**KAPLAN, Philip.** *Making of a Collector: Laukhuff's of Cleveland.* 1990. Akron. N OH Bibliophilic Soc. 1/350. H4. $20.00

**KAPLAN & PIKELNER.** *Interstellar Medium.* 1970. Boston. Harvard. 1st Am. ils. 465p. VG/dj. A2. $20.00

**KAPOS, Martha.** *Post-Impressionists: A Retrospective.* 1973. NY. Beaux Arts Eds. lg 4to. ils. 380p+index. AN/dj. H4. $45.00

**KAPP, Edmond X.** *Reflections: A Second Series of Drawings.* 1922. London. Cape. 1/50. sgn. 24 tipped-in pl. gilt wht cloth. F1. $40.00

**KAPPEL, P.** *New England Gallery.* 1966. Boston. 1st. ils. 150p. F/dj. M4. $50.00

**KAPRALOV, Yuri.** *Castle Dubrava.* 1982. Dutton. 1st. VG/dj. L1. $40.00

**KARASEK, Oldrich.** *Symfonie, Golden Prague Symphony.* 1988. Edito Suprophon. F/VG+. B9. $15.00

**KARASZ, Ilonka.** *Twelve Days of Christmas.* 1949. Harper. 1st. NF/VG. H4. $25.00

**KAREN, Ruth.** *Song of the Quail: Wonderous World of the Maya.* 1972. Four Winds. 222p. dj. F3. $15.00

**KARETNIKOVA & STEINMETZ.** *Mexico According to Einstein.* 1991. Albuquerque. 1st. 4to. 200p. F3. $25.00

**KARIG, Walter.** *Don't Tread on Me.* 1954. Rinehart. 1st. VG/dj. T11. $25.00

**KARL, Frederick R.** *Contemporary English Novel.* (1962). FSC. 1st. 304p. xl. dj. H4. $15.00

**KARLIN, PAQUET & ROTTMANN.** *Free Fire Zone: Short Stories by Vietnam Veterans.* 1973. Coventry, CT. Casualty Pr. 208p. VG/wrp. R11. $85.00

**KARLIN, Wayne.** *Lost Armies.* 1988. NY. Holt. 1st. F/dj. R11. $30.00

**KARLIN & LESSARD.** *Theoretical Studies on Sex Ratio Evolution.* 1986. Princeton. 313p. F/dj. S15. $10.00

**KARLSEN, C.F.** *Devil in the Shape of a Woman: Witchcraft...* 1987. NY. 360p. F/dj. M4. $18.00

**KARMER, Edward E.** *Dark Destiny.* 1994. White Wolf. 1st. NF/F. S18. $20.00

**KARNES, Thomas.** *Failure of Union: Central America, 1824-1960.* 1961. Chapel Hill. 1st. 277p. xl. F3. $15.00

**KARNOW, Stanley.** *Vietnam: History. First Complete Account of Vietnam at War.* 1983. NY. 1st. 750p. rem mk. F/dj. E1. $45.00

**KAROLEVITZ, Robert F.** *Doctors of the Old West: Pictorial History of Medicine...* 1967. Superior. 1st. 192p. F/dj. B20. $40.00

**KARR, Mary.** *Devil's Tour.* 1993. New Directions. 1st. sgn. F. O11. $45.00

**KARSH, Yousef.** *Karsh & Fisher See Canada.* 1960. Toronto. Thomas Allen. NF/VG. A26. $20.00

**KARSH, Yousuf.** *Karsh: American Legends.* 1992. Little Brn. 1st. F/dj. Q1. $60.00

**KARSTEN, Mia C.** *Old Company's Garden at the Cape & Its Superintendents.* 1951. Cape Town. 188p. VG/partial dj. B26. $40.00

**KARWOWSKI & YATES.** *Advances in Industrial Orgonomics & Saftey III.* 1991. London. Taylor Francis. heavy 8vo. 952p. prt brd. F. G1. $125.00

**KASANIN, J.S.** *Language & Thought in Schizophrenia: Collected Papers...* 1944. Berkley/LA. 1st. 12mo. 133p. gr cloth. NF. C14. $25.00

**KASDAN, Sara.** *Mazel Tov Y'All.* 1968. Vanguard. G/dj. A16. $15.00

**KASIMATIS, A.N.** *Wine Grape Varieties in San Joaquin Valley.* 1972. np. ils/photos. sc. B26. $17.50

**KASMINOFF, Ross.** *Sentry.* 1995. Crown. 1st. F/F. H11. $25.00

**KASTELAN, Jure.** *Split.* 1964. Beograd. Jugoslavija. 1st. 4to. 96 pl. cloth. VG. W1. $18.00

**KASTENMEIR, Robert W.** *Vietnam Hearings: Voices From the Grassroots.* 1966. Doubleday. 1st. VG/price blocked wrp. R11. $25.00

**KASTLE, Herbert.** *Edward Berner Is Alive Again!* 1975. Prentice Hall. 1st. VG/dj. P3. $20.00

**KASTNER, Erich.** *Emil & the Detectives, Tans by May Masse.* 1930 (1929). Doubleday. 8vo. ils Walter Trier. 224p. NF/dj. T5. $30.00

**KASTNER, Erich.** *Simpletons.* (1957). NY. Messner. 1st thus. 4to. red cloth. dj. R5. $75.00

**KATICIC & NOVAK.** *Two Thousand Years of Writing in Croatia.* 1989. Zagreb. photos. 180p. NF/VG. A4. $65.00

**KATKOV, George.** *Trial of Bukharin.* 1969. Stein Day. G/dj. M11. $45.00

**KATSAINOS, George M.** *Syphilis & Its Accomplices in Mischief...* nd (1922). NYC. private prt. 455p. VG. C14. $50.00

**KATZ, Bobbi.** *Upside Down & Inside Out: Poems for All Your Pockets.* 1973. Franklin Watts. 1st. sq 12mo. F/VG. C14. $15.00

**KATZ, David.** *Studien zur Kinderpsychologie.* 1913. Leipzig. Quelle & Meyer. 86p. prt gray wrp. G1. $75.00

**KATZ, Friedrich.** *Ancient American Civilizations.* 1972. NY. Praeger. 1st. 386p. dj. F3. $30.00

**KATZ, Samuel.** *Days of Fire: Secret History of Irgun Zvai Leumi...* 1968. NY. photos. VG/dj. M17. $15.00

**KATZ, William Loren.** *Black West: Documentary & Pictorial History.* 1971. Doubleday. 3rd. NF/dj. B20. $45.00

**KATZ & KATZ.** *Conversations With Children.* 1936. Kegan Paul Trench. 1st English-language. 318p. bl cloth. VG/dj. G1. $50.00

**KATZENBACH & KATZENBACH.** *Practical Book of American Wallpaper.* 1951. Lippincott. 1st. sm folio. 142p. F/dj. B20. $100.00

**KAUFELT, David.** *Fat Boy Murders.* 1993. Pocket. 1st. F/dj. A23. $30.00

**KAUFELT, David.** *Silver Rose.* 1983. Macmillan. 1st. F/dj. P3. $25.00

**KAUFFELD, Carl.** *Snakes & Snake Hunting.* 1957. NY. 266p. dj. A17. $9.50

**KAUFFMAN, Christopher J.** *Tradition & Transformation in Catholic Culture.* (1988). Macmillan. ils/index. 366p. VG/dj. H10. $22.50

**KAUFFMAN, Russell.** *Chihuahua.* 1952. Judy. 1st. ils/photos. 158p. VG/dj. A17. $15.00

**KAUFMAN, Lewis.** *Moe Berg: Athelete, Scholar, Spy.* 1974. Little Brn. 1st. photos. F/VG. P8. $55.00

**KAUFMAN, Sue.** *Diary of a Mad Housewife.* 1967. Random. 1st. author's 3rd novel. F/VG. A24. $40.00

**KAUFMAN, William I.** *Catholic Cookbook.* 1965. Citadel. 1st. ils. 296p. VG/case. B11. $35.00

**KAUFMAN, William I.** *Champagne.* 1973. NY. ils. VG/dj. M17. $25.00

**KAUFMAN & KAY.** *G Is for Grafton.* 1997. Holt. 1st. F/dj. G8. $25.00

**KAUFMAN & RYSKIND.** *Night at the Opera.* 1973. NY. Viking. 3rd. VG/rpr wrp. C9. $36.00

**KAVALER, Lucy.** *Astors: A Family Chronicle of Pomp & Power.* 1966. NY. 2nd. photos. VG/dj. M17. $15.00

**KAVAN, Anna.** *Julia & the Bazooka & Other Stories.* 1975. Knopf. 1st Am. F/dj. A23. $40.00

**KAVANAGH, Dan;** see Barnes, Julian.

**KAVANAGH, Marcus.** *Criminal & His Allies.* 1928. Indianapolis. Bobbs Merrill. cloth. M11. $35.00

**KAVANAGH, Marcus.** *You Be the Judge.* 1929. Chicago. Argus. M11. $35.00

**KAWABATA, Yasunari.** *House of the Sleeping Beauties & Other Stories.* 1969. London. Quadriga. 1st. red cloth brd. F/dj. D10. $65.00

**KAWABATA, Yasunari.** *House of the Sleeping Beauties.* 1969. Kodansha Internat Ltd. 1st Am. 149p. F/NF. B20. $30.00

**KAYE, M.M.** *Death in Cyprus.* 1984. St Martin. 1st Am. F/dj. A23. $25.00

**KAYE, M.M.** *Trade Wind.* 1981. St Martin. 1st. NF/dj. M21. $20.00

**KAYSEN, Susanna.** *Girl Interrupted.* 1993. Turtle Bay. UP. F/wrp. R14. $40.00

**KAZAN, Elia.** *Assassins.* 1972. Stein Day. 1st. RS. VG/dj. S18. $15.00

**KAZAN, Elia.** *Elia Kazan: A Life.* 1988. Knopf. 1st. 848p. F/NF. P12. $10.00

**KAZAN, Elia.** *Understudy.* 1975. Stein Day. 1st. sgn. VG/dj. B30. $40.00

**KAZANTZAKIS, Nikos.** *Christopher Columbus.* 1972. Kentfield, CA. Allen. 1/140. wrp/cloth box. B24. $450.00

**KAZZIHA, Walid W.** *Revolutionary Transformation in the Arab World...* 1975. London/Tonbridge. 1st. 118p. cloth. NF/dj. W1. $18.00

**KEANE, Molly.** *Queen Lear.* 1988. Dutton. 1st Am. F/F. B3. $30.00

**KEARNEY, Julian;** see Goulart, Ron.

**KEARNEY, T.H.** *Report on Botanical Survey of Dismal Swamp Region.* 1901. WA. 13 pl/40 figures/2 maps. new cloth. NF. C12. $75.00

**KEARSE, Amalya.** *Bridge Conventions Complete.* revised/expanded through Jan 1984. VG/wrp. S1. $12.00

**KEARY, Annie.** *Heroes of Asgard.* 1979. Mayflower. F/dj. P3. $25.00

**KEATING, Bern.** *Famous American Explorers.* 1972. Chicago. Rand McNally. 1st. VG+. M10. $7.50

**KEATING, Bern.** *Mighty Mississippi.* 1971. WA, DC. NGS. 1st. 8vo. ils. 200p. F/VG. B11. $15.00

**KEATING, Bern.** *Northwest Passage: From the Mathew to the Manhattan...* 1970. Chicago/NY/SF. photos. VG/dj. M17. $22.50

**KEATING, Edward.** *Story of Labor: 33 Years on Rail Workers' Fighting Front.* 1953. WA, DC. 1st. 305p. VG/dj. B18. $17.50

**KEATING, H.R.F.** *Bedside Companion to Crime.* 1989. Mysterious. 1st. sgn. F/dj. M19. $25.00

**KEATING, H.R.F.** *Death & the Visiting Fireman.* 1973. Doubleday. 1st Am. sgn. NF/dj. M25. $35.00

**KEATING, H.R.F.** *Death of a Fat God.* 1963. Collins Crime Club. 1st Eng. F/VG. M19. $45.00

**KEATING, H.R.F.** *Murder Must Appetize.* 1981. Mysterious/Lemon Tree. 1st revised. 1/250. F/case. P3. $45.00

**KEATING, H.R.F.** *Underside.* 1974. Macmillan. 1st. F/dj. T12. $30.00

**KEATING, H.R.F.** *Writing Crime Fiction.* 1986. NY. 1st. VG/dj. M17. $15.00

**KEATING, Lawrence A.** *Fleet Admiral: Story of William F Halsey.* nd. Phil, PA. VG/dj. A19. $25.00

**KEATING, Michline.** *Bachelor's Heyday.* 1933. NY. Alfred King. 1st. F/dj. B4. $200.00

**KEATING, William.** *By Laws: Philadelphia Society for Promoting Agriculture.* ca 1819. Phil. Soc. disbound. A10. $20.00

**KEATING & KEATING.** *Florida.* 1972. Chicago. Rand McNally. 1st. NF/VG. B9. $20.00

**KEATINGE, Maurice.** *True History of the Conquest of Mexico.* 1927 (1800). NY. McBride. rpt 1st 1800 London. 562p. cloth. F3. $25.00

**KEATON, Buster.** *My Wonderful World of Slapstick.* 1960. Doubleday. VG/dj. C9. $108.00

**KEATON, Diane.** *Reservations.* 1980. Knopf. 1st. photos. VG+/wrp. C9. $36.00

**KEATS, Ezra Jack.** *Letter to Amy.* 1968. Harper Row. possible 1st. 32p. F/dj. D4. $25.00

**KEATS, Ezra Jack.** *Snowy Day.* 1966 (1962). Viking. 8th. obl 8vo. Caldecott Honor. bl-gray pict cloth. G. T5. $15.00

**KEATS, John.** *Eve of St Agnes.* 1896. River Forest, IL. Auvergne. 1/65. 8vo. inscr. gilt red cloth. F. B24. $4,000.00

**KEELE, Kenneth D.** *Evolution of Clinical Methods in Medicine.* 1963. Springfield. Chas Thomas. 1st. 115p. VG. C14. $18.00

**KEELER, Mary Frear.** *Sir Francis Drake's West Indian Voyage 1585-1586.* 1981. London. Hakluyt Soc. 8vo. 20 maps/pl. 358p. cloth. F/dj. O1. $65.00

**KEELY, Charles.** *Old Greenwood: Story of Caleb Greenwood, Trapper...* 1936. Western Prt Co. 1/350. sgn pres. 128p. VG/dj. J2. $395.00

**KEENE, Carolyn.** *Nancy Drew Cookbook.* 1973. Grosset Dunlap. G. A16. $20.00

**KEEPING, Charles.** *Willie's Fire-Engine.* 1980. NY. OUP. 1st Am. 32p. F/sans. D4. $45.00

**KEESHAN, Bob.** *Growing Up Happy.* 1989. Doubleday. 1st. F/dj. S13. $10.00

**KEIFITZ, Norman.** *Sensation.* 1975. Atheneum. 1st. F/dj. P8. $25.00

**KEIL & DILITZSECH.** *Commentary on the Old Testament.* 1977. Eerdmans. 10 vol. VG. B29. $120.00

**KEILHOLZ, F.J.** *Year's Progress in Solving Farm Problems of Illinois.* 1929. Urbana. 270p. VG. A10. $15.00

**KEILLIN, David.** *History of Cell Respiration & Cytochrome.* 1966. Cambridge. 1st. 416p. A13. $100.00

**KEILLOR, Garrison.** *Lake Wobegone Days.* 1985. Viking. 1st. author's 2nd book. F/NF. R14. $45.00

**KEILLOR, Garrison.** *Lake Wobegone Days.* 1985. Viking. 1st. inscr. F/dj. B30. $50.00

**KEILLOR, Garrison.** *Sandy Bottom Orchestra.* 1996. Hyperion. 1st. F/clip. T11. $30.00

**KEILLOR, Garrison.** *WLT: A Radio Romance.* 1991. NY. Viking. 1st. F/dj. T12. $20.00

**KEITH, Agnes Newton.** *Children of Allah Between the Sea & Sahara.* 1966. Little Brn/Atlantic. 1st Am. 8vo. ils. 467p. VG/dj. W1. $18.00

**KEITH, Arthur.** *Autobiography: Philosophical.* 1950. NY. ils. VG. M17. $40.00

**KEITH, Arthur.** *Darwinism & What It Implies.* 1928. London. 1st. 56p. A13. $45.00

**KEITH, E.C.** *Gun for Company.* 1937. Country Life. 1st. 202p. xl. M10. $5.00

**KEITH, Elmer.** *Guns & Ammo for Big Game Hunting.* 1965. Los Angeles. 384p. VG/dj. A17. $50.00

**KEITH, Elmer.** *Hell, I Was There.* 1979. Los Angeles. Petersen. revised. 308p. dj. A17. $40.00

**KEITH, Harold.** *Rifles for Watie.* 1957. Crowell. 1st. 8vo. 1958 Newbery Honor. 332p. VG/G. T5. $45.00

**KEITH, Lloyd B.** *Wildlife's Ten-Year Cycle.* 1962. U WI. 201p. xl. VG. S5. $12.00

**KELBER, Werner H.** *Kingdom in Mark: A New Place & a New Time.* 1974. Fortress. 173p. VG. B29. $14.50

**KELBER & SCHLESINGER.** *Union Printers & Controlled Automation.* 1967. NY. Free Pr. 1st. 8vo. 300p. F/dj. O10. $35.00

**KELEMEN, Pal.** *Medieval American Art.* 1956. Macmillan. 1 vol ed. 414p. silvered blk cloth. F1. $40.00

**KELLAND, Clarence Budington.** *Catty Atkins, Financier.* 1923. Harper. 1st. sm 8vo. ils WW Clarke. 247p. VG/G. H1. $25.00

**KELLAND, Clarence Budington.** *Mark Tidd in Business.* (1915). Harper. sm 8vo. ils WW Clark. G/dj. H1. $16.00

**KELLAR, Kenneth.** *Seth Bullock: Frontier Marshal.* 1972. Aberdeen, SD. N Plains. dj. A19. $75.00

**KELLAWAY, Deborah.** *Irises & Other Flowers. Watercolors by Elizabeth Blackadder.* 1994. NY. Abrams. 102p. F/dj. H10. $15.00

**KELLER, George.** *Here, Keller Train This.* 1961. Random. 2nd. VG/dj. S5. $20.00

**KELLER, H.A.** *Yesterday's Sin: A Nudist Novel.* 1934. NY. Macaulay. 1st. F/VG. B4. $100.00

**KELLER, Helen.** *Optimism.* 1903. Crowell. 1st. G. M19. $45.00

**KELLER, Ila.** *Batik: Art & Craft.* 1969. Rutland. Tuttle. sq 8vo. 75p. VG/dj. B11. $15.00

**KELLER, John E.** *Krispin's Fair.* 1976. Little Brn. 1st. 12mo. unp. NF/dj. C14. $18.00

**KELLER, Werner.** *Bible as History: Confirmation of the Book of Books.* 1956. NY. Morrow. 1st. ils. VG/dj. W1. $8.00

**KELLERMAN, Jonathan.** *Butcher's Theater.* 1986. Bantam. 1st. F/NF. N4. $35.00

**KELLERMAN, Jonathan.** *Time Bomb.* 1990. NY. Bantam. 1st. F/NF. H11. $20.00

**KELLERMAN, Jonathan.** *Web.* 1996. Bantam. 1st. NF/dj. S18. $13.00

**KELLETT, Jocelyn.** *Hawthorn Parsonage: Home of the Brontes.* 1977. Bronte Soc. VG/VG. M17. $30.00

**KELLEY, Emmett.** *Clown: My Life in Tatters & Smiles.* 1954. Prentice Hall. 271p. G/dj. S5. $65.00

**KELLEY, Ethel M.** *When I Was Little.* 1915. Chicago. Rand McNally. ils Maud Hunt Squire. 96p. VG. M10. $40.00

**KELLEY, Joseph J. Jr.** *Life & Times in Colonial Philadelphia.* 1973. Stackpole. 256p. VG/dj. V3. $15.00

**KELLEY, Kate.** *Election Day: An American Holiday, an American History.* 1991. NY. ils. VG/dj. M17. $15.00

**KELLEY, Kitty.** *Elizabeth Taylor: Last Star.* 1981. NY. S&S. 1st. NF. T12. $8.00

**KELLEY, Kitty.** *His Way: Unauthorized Biography of Frank Sinatra.* 1984. Bantam. 1st. F/dj. T12. $20.00

**KELLEY, Kitty.** *Nancy Reagan: Unauthorized Biography.* 1991. S&S. 1st. photos. 603p. VG/dj. S14. $12.00

**KELLEY & WRIGHT.** *Riding Instructor's Manual.* 1975. Garden City. Doubleday. ils. VG/dj. O3. $25.00

**KELLY, Fred.** *One Thing Leads to Another.* 1936. Houghton Mifflin. photos Margaret Bourke-White. VG. S5. $15.00

**KELLY, Howard A.** *Cyclopedia of American Medical Biography...* 1912. Phil. Saunders. 2 vol. 8vo. cloth. VG. G7. $150.00

**KELLY, J.B.** *Arabia, the Gulf & the West.* 1980. NY. Basic. 1st Am. 8vo. 5 maps. 530p. xl. VG. W1. $30.00

**KELLY, Josephine.** *Dark Shepard.* 1967. Paterson. 1st. ils. VG/dj. M17. $15.00

**KELLY, L.V.** *Range Men: Story of the Ranchers & Indians of Alberta.* (1980). Toronto. Coles. rpt. F/wrp. A26. $15.00

**KELLY, Lawrence C.** *Navajo Roundup: Selected Correspondence of Kit Carson...* 1970. Pruett. 1st. ils/notes/index. 192p. NF/clip. B19. $25.00

**KELLY, Luther S.** *Yellowstone Kelly: Memoirs of...* 1926. New Haven. 1st. ils/fld map. 268p. VG/dj. B18. $125.00

**KELLY, Robert.** *Congs I-XXX.* 1968. Cambridge. Pym-Randall. 1st. 1/400. sgn. F/NF. L3. $85.00

**KELLY, Robert.** *Loom.* 1975. Blk Sparrow. 1/50. sgn/handwritten illumination. NF/torn mylar. B9. $100.00

**KELLY, Robert.** *Scorpions.* 1969. London. Calder Boyars. 1st Eng. F/clip. L3. $35.00

**KELLY, Susan B.** *Hope Against Hope.* 1991. Scribner. 1st. F/F. H11. $25.00

**KELLY, Susan B.** *Hope Will Answer.* 1993. Scribner. 1st. F/F. H11. $25.00

**KELLY, Walt.** *Jack Acid Society Black Book.* 1962. S&S. 1st. NF/wrp. C15. $60.00

**KELLY & ROBINSON.** *Season of Dreams.* 1992. Voyageur. 1st. photos. F/VG. P8. $30.00

**KELMAN, James.** *Greymound for Breakfast.* 1987. FSG. 1st Am. NF/dj. M25. $35.00

**KELSEY, Harry.** *Juan Rodriguez Cabrillo.* 1986. Huntington Lib. 1st. ils/notes/index. 261p. F/F. B19. $30.00

**KELSEY, Rayner Wickersham.** *Friends & the Indians 1655-1917.* 1917. Phil. Assoc Executive Comm of Friends on Indian Affairs. V3. $65.00

**KELTON, Elmer.** *Art of Frank McCarthy.* 1992. NY. 1st. fld pl. 160p. VG/dj. S16. $40.00

**KELTON, Elmer.** *Art of James Bama.* 1993. Bantam. photos. 160p. AN. J2. $60.00

**KEMAL, Yashar.** *Wind From the Plain, a Novel.* 1969. Dodd Mead. 1st Am. 286p. xl. VG/dj. W1. $18.00

**KEMBLE, Edward W.** *Blackberries & Their Adventures.* 1897. London. Kegan Paul. 1st Eng. 16 full-p pl. pict brd. R5. $850.00

**KEMBLE, James.** *Idols & Invalids.* 1936. Garden City. 328p. A13. $40.00

**KEMELMAN, Harry.** *Day the Rabbi Resigned.* 1992. FAwcett. 1st. F/dj. G8. $15.00

**KEMELMAN, Harry.** *Someday the Rabbi Will Leave.* 1985. Morrow. 1st. NF/dj. G8. $15.00

**KEMELMAN, Harry.** *Thursday the Rabbi Walked Out.* 1978. Putnam. 1st. F/dj. T12. $35.00

**KEMELMAN, Harry.** *Wednesday the Rabbi Got Wet.* 1976. Morrow. 1st. NF/clip. N4. $15.00

**KEMP, Peter.** *Great Age of Sail.* 1986. Facts on File. 1st. 127p. red cloth. F/dj. T11. $50.00

**KEMP, Sam.** *Black Frontiers: Pioneer Adventures With Cecil Rhodes...* 1931. NY. Brewer Warren Putnam. 1st. 278p. map ep. F. H7. $20.00

**KENAMORE, Clair.** *From Vauquois Hill to Exermont: History...* 1919. Guard Pub. 1st. ils/maps. 435p. VG. S16. $75.00

**KENDALL, George W.** *Narrative of Expedition Across Great South-Western Prairies.* 1845. London. David Bogue. 2 vol in 1. 1st 1-vol ed. fld map. gilt cloth. D11. $75.00

**KENDALL, John.** *Letters on Religious Subjects...2 Vols in One.* 1831. Phil. Thomas Kite. 16mo. 176+178p. full leather. VG. V3. $25.00

**KENDRICK, Grace.** *Mouth-Blown Bottle.* (1968). Fallon, NV. self pub. 200p. yel cloth. F/dj. H1. $35.00

**KENDRICK & TATTERSALL.** *Hand-Woven Carpets, Oriental & European.* 1922. London. Benn. 2 vol. 1/1000. 4to. 205 pl. VG. W1. $360.00

**KENEALLY, Thomas.** *Family Madness.* 1986. S&S. 1st Am. rem mk. F/dj. R14. $25.00

**KENEALLY, Thomas.** *Family Madness.* 1986. Toronto. Dennys. 1st Canadian. sgn. NF/F. B3. $40.00

**KENEALY, Maurice Edward.** *Tichorne Tragedy.* 1913. London. Griffiths. 1st. 368p. gilt red cloth. VG. B20. $125.00

**KENNAN, George.** *Salton Sea: Account of Harriman's Flight...* 1917. Macmillan. 8vo. photos. bl cloth. VG. F7. $80.00

**KENNAN, George.** *Tragedy of the Pelee: A Narrative of Personal Experience...* 1902. NY. Outlook. 1st. 8vo. 257p. gilt brn cloth. VG+. B20. $90.00

**KENNAWAY, James.** *Some Gorgeous Accident.* 1967. 1st. NF/dj. M19. $14.00

**KENNEDY, Donald.** *From Cell to Organism: Readings From Scientific American.* 1967. Freeman. 256p. xl. VG. S5. $12.00

**KENNEDY, E.** *General John B Woodward: Biography/Memoir.* 1897. De Vinne. VG. E6. $35.00

**KENNEDY, Edward M.** *Eulogy to US Senator Robert F Kennedy by His Brother...* (1968). Worcester. St Onge. mini. 1/2000. portrait ftspc. 27p. aeg. gilt dk gr leather. B24. $85.00

**KENNEDY, Elijah R.** *Contest for California in 1861...* 1912. Houghton Mifflin. 1st. ils. 361p. gilt cloth. D11. $75.00

**KENNEDY, Gregory P.** *Vengeance Weapon 2.* 1983. Smithsonian. ils/photos. 87p. VG/wrp. K5. $25.00

**KENNEDY, John F.** *Burden & the Glory.* 1964. Harper Row. BC. 8vo. sgn. 293p. F/NF. W2. $350.00

**KENNEDY, John F.** *Inaugural Address of...* nd. Worcester. Onge. mini. 1st (no seal). tipped-in JFK ftspc. gilt bl leather. B24. $80.00

**KENNEDY, John F.** *Inaugural Address of...* nd. Worcester. St Onge. mini. 2nd (w/seal). tipped-in JFK ftspc. gilt bl leather. B24. $50.00

**KENNEDY, John F.** *Profiles in Courage.* 1961. Harper. Inaugural ed. sgn. 266p. NF. W2. $450.00

**KENNEDY, John F.** *To Turn the Tide.* 1962. NY. Harper. 1st. F/dj. Q1. $125.00

**KENNEDY, John F.** *Why England Slept.* 1940. NY. 1st. red pict cloth. B14. $150.00

**KENNEDY, Leigh.** *Journal of Nicholas the American.* 1987. London. Cape. 1st. 208p. AN/dj. M21. $35.00

**KENNEDY, Lucy.** *Sunlit Field.* 1950. Crown. 1st. G+. P8. $15.00

**KENNEDY, Michael S.** *Cowboys & Cattlemen.* 1964. NY. Hastings House. 364p. VG/dj. B18. $22.50

**KENNEDY, Michael S.** *Red Man's West.* 1965. NY. 1st. ils. 342p. F/VG. E1. $45.00

**KENNEDY, Moorhead.** *Ayatollah in the Cathedral: Reflections of a Hostage.* 1986. NY. Hill Wang. 1st Am. sgn pres. 8vo. 241p. NF/dj. W1. $20.00

**KENNEDY, Richard.** *Amy's Eyes.* 1985. Harper Row. 1st. 437p. cloth. F/dj. D4. $35.00

**KENNEDY, Roger G.** *Rediscovering America.* 1990. Boston. ils/photos. VG/dj. M17. $17.50

**KENNEDY, Sylvia.** *See Ourzazate & Die: Travels Through Morocco.* 1992. Scribner. 1st. ils/map. 342p. NF/dj. W1. $18.00

**KENNEDY, William.** *Billy Phelans' Greatest Game.* 1978. Viking. 1st. VG/dj. B5. $50.00

**KENNEDY, William.** *Quinn's Book.* 1988. London. Cape. 1st. sgn. F/NF. B3. $35.00

**KENNER, Hugh.** *Mazes.* 1989. SF. Northpoint. 1st. F/dj. O4. $15.00

**KENNERLY, David Hume.** *Shooter.* 1979. NY. Newsweek Books. 1st. 272p. NF/dj. R11. $40.00

**KENNY, H.A.** *Cape Ann, Cape America.* 1971. Phil. 294p. NF/G. M4. $18.00

**KENNY, H.A.** *Cape Ann: Cape America.* 1971. Phil. Lippincott. 2nd. ils. VG/dj. A2. $14.00

**KENRICK, V.** *Horses in Japan.* 1964. London. 1st. ils. 196p. F/dj. M4. $13.00

**KENT, Alexander.** *Command a King's Ship.* 1973. London. Hutchinson. 1st Eng. sgn. NF/dj. T11. $185.00

**KENT, Alexander.** *Command a King's Ship.* 1974. NY. Putnam. 1st Am. NF/VG. T11. $50.00

**KENT, Alexander.** *Enemy in Sight.* 1970. Putnam. 1st Am. sgn. VG+/VG. A14. $63.00

**KENT, Alexander.** *Flag Captain.* 1971. Putnam. 1st Am. VG+/VG-. A14. $28.00

**KENT, Alexander.** *Form Line of Battle!* 1969. Putnam. 1st Am. VG+/dj. A14. $70.00

**KENT, Alexander.** *Inshore Squadron.* 1978. London. Hutchinson. 1st. NF/dj. T11. $65.00

**KENT, Alexander.** *Stand Into Danger.* 1981. NY. Putnam. 1st. navy cloth. F/NF. T11. $60.00

**KENT, Alexander.** *Success to the Brave.* 1983. London. 1st. VG/dj. M17. $30.00

**KENT, Alexander.** *To Glory We Steer.* 1968. Putnam. 1st. NF/VG. T11. $115.00

**KENT, Henry Watston.** *What I Am Pleased to Call My Education.* 1949. NY. Grolier. 208p. gilt bl cloth. F1. $25.00

**KENT, James.** *Commentaries on American Law. Twelfth Edition.* 1989. Littleton. Fred Rothman. 4 vol. facs of 12th. M11. $295.00

**KENT, John.** *Elizabeth Fry.* 1963. NY. Arco. 1st Am. 144p. G+. V3. $14.00

**KENT, Rockwell.** *After Long Years.* 1968. Ausable Forks, NY. Asgaard. 1/200. sgn. 21p. gilt brn cloth. F1. $375.00

**KENT, Rockwell.** *Canterbury Tales of Geoffrey Chaucer.* 1930. Covici-Friede. 2 vol. 1/75 (999 total). sgn. w/duplicate ils. teg. pigskin. B24. $4,500.00

**KENT, Rockwell.** *Salamina.* 1935. Harcourt Brace. ils. VG. J2. $125.00

**KENYON, F.W.** *Consuming Flame: Story of George Eliot.* 1970. Dodd Mead. 1st. NF/dlip. O4. $15.00

**KERBER, Linda K.** *Women of the Republic: Intellect & Ideology...* 1986. NY. Norton. ils. 304p. VG. M10. $10.00

**KERMODE, Frank.** *Continuities.* nd. Random. 1st. F/dj. O4. $10.00

**KERN, Gregory;** see Tubb, E.C.

**KERN, Marna Elyea.** *Complete Book of Handcrafted Paper.* 1980. CMG. 1st. 8vo. lacks ffe. F/dj. O10. $25.00

**KERNAN, Michael.** *Lost Diaries of Frans Hals.* 1993. St Martin. 1st. author's 1st book. F/F. B3. $30.00

**KERNBERG, Otto.** *Borderline Conditions & Pathological Narcissim.* 1997. Northvale. Aronson. NF/wrp. B9. $15.00

**KEROUAC, Jack.** *Heaven & Other Poems.* 1977. Bolinas. Grey Fox. 1st wrp prt. F. R11. $25.00

**KEROUAC, Jack.** *On the Road.* 1957. Viking. 1st. F/2nd prt dj. Q1. $750.00

**KEROUAC, Jack.** *On the Road.* 1957. Viking. 1st. VG/dj. B4. $1,250.00

**KERR, Alvin.** *Family Cookbook: French.* 1973. NY. Ridge. G/dj. A16. $15.00

**KERR, Ben;** see Ard, William (Thomas).

**KERR, Graham.** *Complete Galloping Gourmet Cookbook.* 1979. Grosset Dunlap. 1st. NF. W2. $45.00

**KERR, Jean.** *Penny Candy.* 1970. Doubleday. 1st. NF/dj. M25. $25.00

**KERR, Philip.** *German Requiem.* 1991. London. Viking. 1st. F/dj. M15. $50.00

**KERR, Philip.** *Gridiron.* 1995. London. Chatto Windus. 1st. F/dj. M15. $50.00

**KERR, Philip.** *March Violets.* 1989. London. Viking. 1st. F/dj. M15. $250.00

**KERR, Robert Pollok.** *Land of Holy Light: Book of Travel Through Bible Countries.* 1891. Richmond, VA. Presbytarian Comm. 1st. 8vo. map/pl. VG. W1. $65.00

**KERR, Walter.** *Silent Clowns.* 1975. Knopf. 2nd. VG/dj. C9. $60.00

**KERRIGAN, John;** see Kessler, Leo.

**KERSAUDY, Francois.** *Churchill & deGaulle.* 1982. Atheneum. 1st Am. sm 4to. NF/F. W2. $40.00

**KERSHAW, Alister.** *Empty Rooms.* 1990. Francestown. Typographeum. 1/75. dj. T9. $30.00

**KERSTING, Rudolf.** *White World: Life & Adventures Within Arctic Circle...* 1902. NY. Scribner. 1st. 8vo. 386p. G+. B20. $125.00

**KERTESZ, Andre.** *J'aime Paris.* 1974. NY. Grossman. 1st. 200+ photos. NF/dj. S9. $150.00

**KESAVAN, Mukul.** *Looking Through Glass.* 1995. Chatto Windus. 1st. author's 1st book. F/dj. A14. $28.00

**KESEY, Ken.** *Demon Box.* 1986. Viking. 1st. F/dj. S9. $45.00

**KESEY, Ken.** *Demon Box.* 1986. Viking. 1st. sgn. F/dj. O11. $65.00

**KESEY, Ken.** *Further Inquiry.* 1990. Viking. 1st. sgn. F/dj. R14. $60.00

**KESEY, Ken.** *Sailor Song.* 1992. Viking. 1st. sgn. F/dj. O11. $50.00

**KESEY, Ken.** *Sometimes a Great Notion.* 1964. Viking. 1st. F/dj. S9. $300.00

**KESSEL, Dmitri.** *Splendors of Christendom.* 1964. Lausanne. Edita. 1st. VG/dj. B5. $37.50

**KESSLER, A.D.** *Fortune at Your Feet.* 1981. HBJ. 1st. sm 4to. 282p. F/dj. W2. $25.00

**KESSLER, Leo.** *Slaughter at Salerno: Wotan 2.* 1985. London. Macdonald. 1st. VG/dj. A14. $17.50

**KESSLER, Leo.** *Slaughter Ground.* 1982. London. Macdonald. 1st hc. VG/dj. A14. $17.50

**KESSLER, Leo.** *Watchdog.* 1984. London. Hutchinson. 1st. VG+/dj. A14. $17.50

**KETCHUM, Hank.** *Dennis the Menace.* 1952. Holt. 1st author's 1st book. VG+. S13. $15.00

**KETCHUM, Richard.** *Decisive Day: Battle for Bunker Hill.* 1974. Doubleday. 272p. VG/clip. S17. $7.50

**KETCHUM, Richard.** *Will Rogers: The Man & His Times.* 1973. Am Heritage. 1st. sm 4to. quarter leather. F/sans/case. T11. $40.00

**KETTLE, John.** *Big Generation.* (1980). Toronto. McClelland Stewart. F/NF. A26. $20.00

**KEVORKIAN, Jack.** *Story of Dissection.* nd. NY. Philosophical Lib. 80p. G7. $45.00

**KEY, Francis Scott.** *Poems of the Late Francis Scott Key.* 1857. NY. Robert Carter. 1st/B bdg (no sequence). gilt brn cloth. VG. M24. $200.00

**KEYES, Frances Parkinson.** *Dinner at Antoine's.* 1947. NY. Messner. 1st. NF. T12. $10.00

**KEYES, Frances Parkinson.** *Land of Stones & Saints.* 1957. NY. ils. VG/dj. M17. $15.00

**KEYES, Josa.** *Teddy Bear Story.* 1985. Gallery Books. 1st. photos. F/VG. M5. $15.00

**KEYNES, Geoffrey.** *Bibliography of Sir Thomas Browne.* 1968. Oxford. 2nd. 293p. dj. A13. $200.00

**KEYNES, Geoffrey.** *Gates of Memory.* 1981. OUP. 1st. 8vo. 428p. VG/dj. S14. $17.50

**KEYNES, Geoffrey.** *Personality of William Harvey: Linacre Lecture.* 1949. Cambridge. 48p. NF/dj. G7. $65.00

**KEYNES, Geoffrey.** *Watch of Nightingales.* 1981. London. 1/400. dj. T9. $50.00

**KEYNES, John Maynard.** *Revision of Treaty Being Sequel to Economic Consequences...* 1922. Harcourt Brace. 242p+pub catalog. G. S5. $25.00

**KHADDURI, Majid.** *Independent Iraq: Study in Politics Since 1932.* 1951. OUP. 8vo. 291p+pocket map. cloth. VG/dj. Q2. $46.50

**KHATCHATURIAN, K.A.** *Teatralno-Dekoratsionnoie Iskusstvo Sovietskoi Armenii.* 1979. Moskva. Izobraziltelnote Iskusstvo. 1st. sq 8vo. 135p. F. M7. $50.00

**KHAYAT, M.** *Food From the Arab World.* 1965. Beirut. VG/G. E6. $22.00

**KHAYYAM, Omar.** *Rubaiyat of Omar Khayyam.* 1940. NY. Heritage. ils Szyk. VG. B9. $25.00

**KHAYYAM, Omar.** *Rubbaiyat of Omar Khayyam.* 1904. London. Routledge. 8vo. ils after Gilbert James. 160p. teg. NF/clamshell case. H5. $3,000.00

**KHLEBNIKOV, Velimir.** *King of Time: Poems, Fictions & Visions of the Future.* 1985. Harvard. ils. VG/dj. M17. $25.00

**KIDD, John.** *On the Adaptation of External Nature to Physical Condition.* 1833. London. Pickering. 375p. contemporary bl cloth. G1. $135.00

**KIDD, Mary M.** *Cape Peninsula.* 1983. Claremont, RSA. ils. 239p. sc. F. B26. $25.00

**KIDDER, Tracy.** *Among Schoolchildren.* 1989. Houghton Mifflin. 1st. F/dj. R14. $25.00

**KIDDER, Tracy.** *Old Friends.* 1993. Houghton Mifflin. 1st. F/NF. H11. $15.00

**KIDNEY, Walter C.** *Winchester: Limestone, Sycamores & Architecture.* (1977). Preservation of Hist Winchester Inc. 120p. VG/dj. B10. $45.00

**KIEFER, Middleton.** *Pax.* 1958. Random. 1st. NF/dj. R11. $20.00

**KIELL, Norman.** *Blood Brothers: Siblings as Writers.* 1983. NY. ils. VG/dj. M17. $25.00

**KIELTY, Bernadine.** *Marie Antoinette.* 1955. Random. ils Douglas Gorsline. VG/dj. w/sgn letter. B36. $22.00

**KIEMAN & MOORE.** *First Fiction: An Anthology of 1st Published Stories...* 1994. 1st. intro Jane Smiley. VG/dj. M17. $20.00

**KIENZLE, William X.** *Rosary Murders.* 1979. Andrews McMeel. 1st. VG/dj. G8. $30.00

**KIENZLE, William X.** *Shadow of Death.* 1983. Andrews McMeel. 1st. VG/NF. G8. $10.00

**KIERAN, John.** *Introduction to Nature.* 1966. NY. 223p. VG/dj. A17. $15.00

**KIERKEGAARD, Rod.** *Shooting Stars.* 1987. Catalan Communications. 1st. ils. VG. C9. $60.00

**KIES.** *Occult in the Western World, Annotated Bibliography.* 1986. 890 entries. 244p. F. A4. $65.00

**KIESER, Paul W.** *Our Martyred Presidents.* 1965. Franklin, NH. Hillside. mini. 1/500. JFK US postage stp ftspc. gilt leather. B24. $200.00

**KIETHLEY, George.** *Donnor Party.* 1972. NY. Braziller. 1st. VG/dj. O4. $15.00

**KIGER, Robert.** *Kate Greenaway: Catalogue of Exhibition...* 1980. Pittsburgh. Hunt. 106p. cloth. VG. A10. $35.00

**KIHLMAN, B.A.** *Actions of Chemicals on Dividing Cells.* 1966. Prentice Hall. 260p. xl. VG. S5. $12.00

**KIJEWSKI, Karen.** *Copy Kat.* 1992. Doubleday. 1st. F/dj. B2. $50.00

**KIJEWSKI, Karen.** *Kat Scratch Fever.* 1997. Putnam. ARC. F/wrp. B30. $20.00

**KIJEWSKI, Karen.** *Katwalk.* 1989. St Martin. 1st. author's 1st novel. F/dj. M15. $250.00

**KIJEWSKI, Karen.** *Wild Kat.* 1994. Doubleday. 1st. F/F. H11. $25.00

**KILBOURN, John.** *Ohio Gazetteer; or, Topographical Dictionary...* 1833. Columbus. 512p. full leather. B18. $135.00

**KILBOURN, William.** *Pipeline: Trans Canada & Great Debate...* (1970). Toronto. Clarke Irwin. 1st. F/NF. A26. $15.00

**KILGO & WILKINS.** *Collector's Guide to Anchor Hocking's Fire King Glassware.* 1991. K&W Collectibles. 1st. photos. NF. S14. $10.00

**KILIAN, Crawford.** *Icequake.* 1979. Douglas & McIntyre. 1st. NF/dj. P3. $30.00

**KILMER, Joyce.** *Trees.* 1924. Doran. 1st. ils. F/VG. M5. $55.00

**KILMER, Nicholas.** *Harmony in Flesh & Black.* 1995. NY. Holt. 1st. sgn. author's 1st novel. F/dj. T2. $25.00

**KILMER, Nicholas.** *Man With a Squirrel.* 1996. NY. Holt. 1st. sgn. F/dj. T2. $20.00

**KILNER, Colleen Browne.** *La-La Man in Music Land.* 1927. Lee Shepard. 1st. 4to. wine-red pict cloth. pict dj. R5. $75.00

**KILNER, W.** *Compendium of Modern Pharmacy & Druggist Formulary.* 1888. 686p. leather brd. G+. E6. $30.00

**KILZER, Louis C.** *Churchill's Deception: Dark Secret That Destroyed Nazi...* 1994. S&S. 1st. 335p. NF/dj. M10. $27.50

**KIMBALL, Caleb.** *Awakened Sinner Directed.* 1853. Boston. Benj Perkins. 12th. 16mo. brn cloth. VG. S17. $5.00

**KIMBALL, Fiske.** *Thomas Jefferson, Architect: Original Designs...* 1968. De Cappo. facs of 1916. ils/pl. 205p. VG/fair. B10. $500.00

**KIMBALL, William R.** *Vietnam: The Other Side of Glory.* 1987. Canton. Daring Books. 336p. NF/VG. R11. $22.00

**KIMBER, Benjamin.** *Grand Canyon Deeps.* 1960. Roadrunner Guidebooks & Research. 4to. stiff wrp. F7. $30.00

**KIMBLE, George H.T.** *Our American Weather.* 1961 (1955). Bloomington, IN. IU. rpt. 322p. VG. K5. $10.00

**KIMMEL & SEGALOFF.** *Love Stories: Hollywood's Most Romantic Movies.* 1992. NY. Longmeadow. 1st. 174p. VG/dj. C5. $12.50

**KINAHAN, Sonia.** *Gardening With Trees.* 1990. London. ils/pl. 153p. AN. B26. $12.50

**KINCADE, Wynn.** *Vicky Loring: Career for Vicky.* 1962. Golden. 1st. ils Mel Crawford. VG. B36. $10.00

**KINCAID, Jamaica.** *Annie John.* 1985. FSG. 1st. F/dj. D10. $60.00

**KINCAID, Jamaica.** *Autobiography of My Mother.* 1996. FSG. ARC. F/wrp. w/promo material. B30. $20.00

**KINCAID, Jamaica.** *Lucy.* 1990. FSG. 1st. sgn. F/F. D10/R14. $50.00

**KINCAID, Jamaica.** *Lucy.* 1990. FSG. 1st. F/dj. A24/B3. $35.00

**KINCAID, R.L.** *Wilderness Road.* 1947. Indianapolis. Am Trails series. ils/map. 392p. G. M4. $20.00

**KINDIG, Joseph.** *Philadelphia Chair, 1685-1785.* (1978). Hist Soc of York Co. 8vo. unp (108p). gilt stiff wrp. H1. $25.00

**KINERT, Reed.** *Little Helicopter.* 1947. Macmillan. possible 1st. unp. VG/clip. C14. $15.00

**KING, B.B.** *BB King Songbook: Black & Blue.* nd. Lincolnwood. Gibsonn. 1st. VG/wrp. B2. $30.00

**KING, Benjamin.** *Bullet for Stonewall: A Novel.* 1990. Gretna, LA. Pelican. 1st. F/dj. A14. $21.00

**KING, Bucky.** *Big Horn Polo: History of Polo in the Big Horn.* 1987. Sheridan. sgn. 69p. VG. O3. $45.00

**KING, Charles W.** *Natural History of Precious Stones & Precious Metals.* 1870. London. Bell Dandy. ils. 364p. emb gr cloth. F. B14. $75.00

**KING, Charles.** *Mama's Boy.* 1992. Pocket. 1st. author's 1st book. F/dj. S18. $40.00

**KING, Charles.** *Trooper Ross & Signal Butte.* 1895. Phil. Lippincott. G. A19. $45.00

**KING, Charles.** *Under Fire.* 1895. Phil, PA. Lippincott. G. A19. $30.00

**KING, David S.** *Mountain Meadows Massacre: Search for Perspective.* 1970. WA. Great Western series 8. 1/250. sgn. 8vo. orange brd. F7. $50.00

**KING, Dorothy N.** *Take the Children.* 1945. NY. Morrow. 1st. ils Dorothy King/6 moveables. VG. D1. $120.00

KING, Elmer R. *Handbook of Historical Landmarks of California.* 1938. LA. private prt. 1st. VG. O4. $15.00

KING, Florence. *Southern Ladies & Gentlemen.* 1975. NY. Stein Day. 1st. F/NF. B4. $125.00

KING, George S. *Last Slaver.* 1933. NY. Putnam. 1st. NF/dj. B4. $250.00

KING, Henry C. *History of the Telescope.* 1955. Cambridge, MA. Sky. sm 4to. 456p. cloth. G. K5. $150.00

KING, Joseph A. *Winter of Entrapment: New Look at the Donner Party.* 1992. Toronto. PD Meany. 1st. ils. F/dj. T10. $36.00

KING, Larry L. *One-Eyed Man.* 1966. NAL. 1st. F/dj. Q1. $75.00

KING, Laurie R. *Beekeeper's Apprentice.* 1994. St Martin. 1st. F/dj. M15. $350.00

KING, Laurie R. *Grave Talent.* NY. St Martin. 1st/5th imp. sgn. NF/dj. A14. $21.00

KING, Laurie R. *Grave Talent.* 1995. Harper Collins. 1st Eng. author's 1st book. F/dj. A24. $90.00

KING, Laurie R. *Monstrous Regiment of Women.* 1995. St Martin. 1st. sgn. NF/dj. A14. $32.00

KING, Laurie R. *To Play the Fool.* 1995. St Martin. 1st. sgn. VG+/dj. A14. $32.00

KING, LAWTON & FOWLE. *People's Guide to Dakota, the Land of Promise.* 1882. Milwaukee. sc. G. A19. $300.00

KING, Lester C. *Morphology of the Earth: A Study & Synthesis...* 1962. NY. Hafner. 699p. pocket maps. xl. NF. B14. $75.00

KING, Lester. *Road to Medical Enlightenment, 1650-1695.* 1970. NY. 1st. 209p. A13. $45.00

KING, Martin Luther Jr. *I Have a Dream.* 1993. Harper Collins. 1st. F/dj. R14. $25.00

KING, Martin Luther Jr. *Why Can't We Wait.* 1964. Harper Row. 1st. VG/dj. B30. $100.00

KING, Moses. *King's Handbook of New York City.* 1892. Boston. Moses King. 889 ils. 928p. decor cloth. D2. $160.00

KING, Stephen. *Carrie.* 1974. Doubleday. 1st. F/dj. T12. $700.00

KING, Stephen. *Christine.* 1983. NY. Viking. 1st. VG/dj. L1/P3. $60.00

KING, Stephen. *Cujo.* 1981. Viking. 1st. F/dj. H11. $55.00

KING, Stephen. *Danse Macabre.* 1981. Everest. 1st. F/dj. P3. $100.00

KING, Stephen. *Dark Half.* 1989. NY. Viking. 1st. VG/dj. L1. $35.00

KING, Stephen. *Dead Zone.* 1979. NY. Viking. 1st. author's 6th book. VG/dj. L1. $150.00

KING, Stephen. *Different Seasons.* 1982. Viking. 1st. VG+/clip. A14. $42.00

KING, Stephen. *Dolores Clairborne.* 1993. Viking. 1st. F/dj. H11/T12. $35.00

KING, Stephen. *Firestarter.* 1980. NY. Viking. 1st. VG+/clip. A14. $52.50

KING, Stephen. *Insomnia.* 1994. Viking. 1st. AN/dj. S18. $25.00

KING, Stephen. *It.* 1986. Viking. 1st. F/dj. N4. $35.00

KING, Stephen. *It.* 1986. Viking. 1st. G/VG. L4. $15.00

KING, Stephen. *Misery.* 1987. Viking. 1st. F/dj. H11. $40.00

KING, Stephen. *Misery.* 1987. Viking. 1st. VG/dj. L4. $25.00

KING, Stephen. *Needful Things.* 1991. Viking. 1st. VG/dj. L4. $15.00

KING, Stephen. *Nightmares & Dreamscapes.* 1993. Viking. 1st. AN/dj. T12. $75.00

KING, Stephen. *Nightmares in the Sky.* 1988. Viking. 1st. F/dj. S18. $30.00

KING, Stephen. *Nightmares in the Sky.* 1988. Viking. 128p. VG/dj. A10. $20.00

KING, Stephen. *Pet Sematary.* 1983. Doubleday. 1st. NF/dj. M21. $30.00

KING, Stephen. *Regulators.* 1996. Dutton. 1st. AN/dj. S18. $25.00

KING, Stephen. *Rose Madder.* 1995. Viking. 1st. F/dj. T12. $50.00

KING, Stephen. *Selected From Carrie.* 1992. Literacy Volunteers of NY. 1st. NF/wrp. M25. $15.00

KING, Stephen. *Shining.* 1977. Doubleday. 1st. F/dj. T12. $200.00

KING, Stephen. *Skeleton Crew.* 1985. Putnam. 1st. NF/clip. A14. $32.00

KING, Stephen. *Skeleton Crew.* 1985. Viking. 1st. VG/dj. L4. $25.00

KING, Stephen. *Stand.* 1978. Doubleday. 1st (date code T39 on p823). VG+/clip. A14. $210.00

KING, Stephen. *Stand.* 1990. NY. MacDonald. 5th. sgn. gilt & red-stp blk brd. F/dj. R3. $165.00

KING, Stephen. *Talisman.* 1984. Viking. 1st. VG/G. L4. $20.00

KING, Stephen. *Thinner.* 1984. NAL. 1st. F/dj. M25. $60.00

KING, Stephen. *Thinner.* 1984. NAL. 1st. NF/dj. A14/H4. $52.50

KING, Stephen. *Tommyknockers.* 1987. Putnam. 1st. F/NF. N4. $35.00

KING, Stephen. *Tommyknockers.* 1987. Putnam. 1st. VG/NF. M21. $20.00

KING, Tabitha. *Caretakers.* 1983. Macmillan. 1st. F/dj. T12. $25.00

KING, Tabitha. *Small World.* 1981. Macmillan. 1st. sgn bookplate. F/dj. T12. $40.00

KING, Tabitha. *Trap.* 1985. Macmillan. F/dj. L4. $15.00

KING, Thomson. *Consilidated of Baltimore, 1816-1950: A History...* 1950. Consolidated. photos/photo ep. 335p. VG. B10. $35.00

KING, Ursula. *Women & Spirituality: Voices of Protest & Promises.* 1989. NY. New Amsterdam. 1st. 273p. VG/dj. A25. $18.00

KING, W. *Story of the Spanish-American War & Revolt in Philippines.* 1900 (1898). NY. obl folio. 4 pl. VG. E6. $150.00

KING, Willard L. *Melville Weston Fuller, Chief Justice of US 1888-1910.* 1950. Macmillan. G/dj. M11. $45.00

KING & WINKS. *Crimes of the Scene.* 1997. St Martin. 1st. sgn. F/dj. G8. $25.00

KING JOHN. *Magna Carta of King John AD 1215.* 1965. Worcester. St Onge. mini. 1/1250. 70p. aeg. gilt beige leather. B24. $75.00

KING-SMITH, Dick. *Harry's Mad.* 1984. NY. Crown. 1st Am. 8vo. 123p. rem mk. VG/dj. T5. $45.00

KINGHORNE & LAMON. *How to Select the Laying Hen.* 1931. Orange Judd. 1st. 124p. VG/G. H10. $15.00

KINGMAN, Lee. *Pierre Pidgeon.* 1943. WI. EM Hale. ils Arnold Edwin Bare. 43p. xl. G. P12. $6.00

KINGSBERRY, A. *Akron Negro Directory.* nd (1940). np. 128p. G. B18. $125.00

KINGSBURY, Noel. *New Perennial Garden.* 1996. Holt. 1st. ils/index. 160p. VG/dj. H10. $30.00

**KINGSLEY, Charles.** *Water Babies.* 1916. Dodd Mead. 1st. ils JW Smith/12 mc pl. 362p. gilt gr cloth. VG. H5. $650.00

**KINGSLEY, Charles.** *Westward Ho!* 1920. Scribner. 1st. ils NC Wyeth. blk cloth/pict label. mc dj. R5. $485.00

**KINGSLEY, Charles.** *Westward Ho!* 1936. Scribner. ils NC Wyeth. VG. M17. $65.00

**KINGSLEY, Charles.** *Works of...* 1893. London. 13 vol. bl-gr half leather/marbled brd. F. B30. $300.00

**KINGSLEY, Florence Morse.** *Transfiguration of Miss Philura.* 1901. Funk Wagnalls. 1st Am. sgn Margaret Armstrong. 81p. NF/dj. J3. $125.00

**KINGSMILL, Hugh.** *Johnson Without Boswell: Contemporary Portrait...* 1941. NY. VG. M17. $20.00

**KINGSMILL, Hugh.** *Samuel Johnson.* nd (1938?). London. Barker. VG. H13. $15.00

**KINGSOLVER, Barbara.** *Animal Dreams.* 1990. Harper Row. 1st. F/dj. O11. $40.00

**KINGSOLVER, Barbara.** *Animal Dreams.* 1990. Harper Row. 1st. sgn. F/F. D10. $50.00

**KINGSOLVER, Barbara.** *Another America.* 1992. Seattle. Seal Pr. 1st. 1/1700. F/dj. O11. $50.00

**KINGSOLVER, Barbara.** *Bean Trees.* 1989. London. Virago. 1st Eng. F/dj. R14. $75.00

**KINGSOLVER, Barbara.** *Holding the Line: Women in Great Arizona Mine Strike 1983.* 1989. Cornell. ILR Pr. 1/816. sgn. F/sans. B3. $150.00

**KINGSOLVER, Barbara.** *Pigs in Heaven.* 1993. Harper Collins. 1st. sgn. F/dj. O11. $40.00

**KINGSTON, Charles.** *Judges & the Judged.* 1926. NY. Dodd Mead. 1st Am. 267p. red cloth. B20. $25.00

**KINGSTON, Maxine Hong.** *Tripmaster Monkey: His Fake Book.* 1989. Knopf. 1st. NF/dj. R14. $30.00

**KINNELL, Galway.** *Black Light.* 1966. Houghton Mifflin. 1st. G+/VG. B30. $37.50

**KINNELL, Galway.** *Imperfect Thirst.* 1994. Houghton Mifflin. 1st. F/dj. O11. $25.00

**KINROSS, Lord.** *Ataturk: Rebirth of a Nation.* 1965. London. Weidenfeld Nicolson. ils/pl/maps. 542p. VG/torn. Q2. $36.50

**KINROSS, Lord.** *Hagia Sophia: History of Constantinople.* 1972. NY. Newsweek. 1st. ils. 172p. VG/dj. W1. $28.00

**KINSELLA, W.P.** *Box Socials.* 1991. Ballantine. 1st Am. sgn. F/dj. P8. $75.00

**KINSELLA, W.P.** *Box Socials.* 1991. Ballantine. 1st. F/dj. B4. $45.00

**KINSELLA, W.P.** *Box Socials.* 1991. Toronto. Collins. 1st. F/F. B3. $40.00

**KINSELLA, W.P.** *Dance Me Outside.* 1977. Boston. Godine. 1st. F/F. B3. $60.00

**KINSELLA, W.P.** *Further Adventures of Slugger McBatt.* 1988. Houghton Mifflin. 1st. inscr. F/dj. P8. $65.00

**KINSELLA, W.P.** *Iowa Baseball Confederacy.* 1986. Houghton Mifflin. 1st. NF/dj. M19. $17.50

**KINSELLA, W.P.** *Iowa Baseball Confederacy.* 1986. Houghton Mifflin. 1st. sgn. F/VG+. P8. $85.00

**KINSELLA, W.P.** *Red Wolf, Red Wolf.* 1987. Ontario. Collins. 1st. sgn. F/dj. R14. $50.00

**KINSELLA, W.P.** *Shoeless Joe.* 1982. Houghton Mifflin. 1st. F/VG. P8. $125.00

**KINSELLA, W.P.** *Two Spirits Soar.* 1990. Stoddart. 1st Canadian. F/NF. T11. $75.00

**KINSEY, Patricia Fuller.** *Albert the Albert.* 1968. Funk Wagnall. 1st. ils Zena Bernstein. F/dj. M5. $12.00

**KINSMILL, Hugh.** *Johnson Without Boswell.* 1941. Knopf. dj. H13. $35.00

**KINZER, W.P.** *Catalogue of High-Bred Trotting Stock.* 1886. Wooster, OH. 22p. wrp. B18. $20.00

**KIP, William Ingraham.** *Early Days of My Episcopate.* 1954. Oakland. Biobooks. 1/500. purple/gray cloth. P4. $35.00

**KIPLING, Rudyard.** *Barrack-Room Ballads & Other Verses.* 1892. London. 1st. T9. $65.00

**KIPLING, Rudyard.** *Captains Courageous.* 1957. Nelson Doubleday. Jr Deluxe Eds. 8vo. 224p. NF. W2. $75.00

**KIPLING, Rudyard.** *Choice of Kipling's Prose.* 1987. London. VG/dj. M17. $17.50

**KIPLING, Rudyard.** *Five Nations.* 1903. London. Methuen. 1st. L3/T9. $65.00

**KIPLING, Rudyard.** *Fringes of the Fleet.* 1915. NY. cream bdg. VG. M17. $20.00

**KIPLING, Rudyard.** *History of England.* 1911. Oxford. 1st. 15 mc pl. VG+. B27. $175.00

**KIPLING, Rudyard.** *Jungle Book.* 1894. NY. 1st Am. gilt gr cloth. VG. B14. $75.00

**KIPLING, Rudyard.** *Many Inventions.* 1893. London. Macmillan. 1st. 8vo. gilt bl cloth. NF/gr 3-quarter morocco case. R3. $125.00

**KIPLING, Rudyard.** *Poems 1886-1929.* 3 vol (2 only present). ltd ed. 1/525. sgn. lib pocket remnant. NF. B30. $550.00

**KIPLING, Rudyard.** *Rudyard Kipling's Verse, Inclusive Edition.* 1937. Doubleday Page. 1st. contemporary full red morocco. M24. $150.00

**KIPLING, Rudyard.** *Two Jungle Books.* 1925. Doubleday Page. 1st. ils Lockwood. red cloth. G. B27. $75.00

**KIPP, J.B.** *Colorado River.* June 1950. LA. Muir Dawson. 12mo. brd. VG. F7. $175.00

**KIRBY, James P.** *Selected Articles on Criminal Justice.* 1926. Wilson. M11. $45.00

**KIRBY-SMITH, H.T.** *US Observatories: A Directory & Travel Guide...* 1976. NY. Van Nostrand. 2nd. 173p. xl. K5. $16.00

**KIRCHOFF, M.J.** *Baranof Island: Illustrated History.* 1990. Juneau. 1st. 1/1000. 193p. F/dj. M4. $20.00

**KIRK, George.** *Middle East in the War: Survey of International Affairs...* 1952. OUP. ils/maps. 511p. cloth. VG/rpr. Q2. $58.00

**KIRK, Paul.** *Great Dismal Swamp.* 1979. Charlottesville. 1st. 427p. VG/dj. B5. $30.00

**KIRK, Russell.** *Creature of the Twilight: His Memorials.* 1966. Fleet. 1st. VG/dj. B30. $20.00

**KIRK, Russell.** *Princess of All Lands.* 1979. Arkham. 1st. F/dj. M21. $45.00

**KIRK & KLOTZ.** *Faulkner's People: Complete Guide & Index to Characters...* (19630. LA. U CA. 1st. 8vo. 354p. F/NF. H4. $45.00

**KIRK & TILNEY-BASSETT.** *Plastids: Their Chemistry, Structure, Growth & Inheritance.* 1967. London. WH Freeman. lg 8vo. 608p. dj. B1. $250.00

**KIRKBRIDE, Alec Seath.** *Crackle of Thorns: Experiences in Middle East.* 1956. London. Murray. 1st. 201p. NF/VG+. M7. $75.00

**KIRKHAM, E. Kay.** *Research in American Genealogy.* 1956. Desert Book. 447p. G. S5. $15.00

**KIRKLAND, John.** *Modern Baker: Confectionery & Caterer.* 1924 (1907). London. 4 vol. 100 pl/250 text ils. VG. E6. $125.00

**KIRKWOOD, Edith Brown.** *Animal Children.* (1913). Volland. 28th. 8vo. ils MT Ross. 96p. pict brd. R5. $100.00

**KIRKWOOD, James.** *There Must Be a Pony!* 1960. Little Brn. 1st. author's 1st book. VG/VG- clip. A14. $35.00

**KIRSCH & MURPHY.** *West of the West.* 1967. Dutton. 1st. F/dj. O4. $20.00

**KIRST, Hans Hellmut.** *Forward, Gunner Asch!* 1956. Little Brn. 1st Am. trans Robert Kee. VG+/VG. A14. $28.00

**KIRST, Hans Hellmut.** *Last Stop Camp 7.* 1969. NY. 1st. dj. T9. $15.00

**KIRST, Hans Hellmut.** *Night of the Generals.* 1963. London. Collins. 1st Eng. trans JM Brownjohn. VG+/clip. A14. $22.00

**KIRST, Hans Hellmut.** *Party Games.* 1980. London. 1st. trans JM Brownjohn. F. T9. $18.00

**KIRST, Hans Hellmut.** *What Became of Gunner Asch.* 1964. London. Collins. 1st Am. trans from German by JM Brownjohn. VG+/dj. A14. $22.00

**KIRSTEN, Lincoln.** *Dance: A Short History of Classic Theatrical Dancing.* 1935. NY. Putnam. bl cloth. VG. B14. $100.00

**KIRZNER, Israel M.** *Classics in Austrian Economics: A Sampling...* 1995. Wm Pickering. 3 vol. index. VG. S5. $75.00

**KISMARIC & SHAWCROSS.** *Forced Out: Agony of the Refugee in Our Time.* 1989. Human Rights Watch. 1st. folio. 192p. VG/wrp. S14. $10.00

**KISSEL, Howard.** *David Merrick.* 1993. NY. Applause. 565p. VG/dj. C5. $12.50

**KISSINGER, Henry A.** *Nuclear Weapons & Foreign Policy.* 1957. Harper for Council Foreign Relations. inscr. F/G. B4. $650.00

**KISSINGER, Henry A.** *Years of Upheaval.* 1982. Little Brn. 1st. NF/G. W2. $75.00

**KITAMURA & ISHIZU.** *Garden Plants in Japan.* 1963. Tokyo. photos. 266p. VG. B26. $45.00

**KITCHEL, Denison.** *Too Grave a Risk, the Connally Amendment Issue.* 1963. NY. Morrow. M11. $35.00

**KITELEY, Brian.** *I Know Many Songs But I Cannot Sing.* 1996. S&S. 1st. F/dj. A24. $20.00

**KITSON, C.H.** *Studies in Fugue.* 1922. Oxford. Clarendon. 104p. G. C5. $12.50

**KITTO, H.D.F.** *In the Mountains of Greece.* 1933. London. Methuen. 8vo. 3 pl/1 map. 150p. cloth. VG/dj. Q2. $58.00

**KITTON, Frederic G.** *Dickensiana: A Bibliography of Literature...* 1971. rpt. 544p. F. A4. $35.00

**KITTON, Frederic G.** *Novels of Charles Dickens: A Bibliography & Sketch.* (1897). 1st/Am issue. 245p. VG. A4. $75.00

**KITTREDGE, Mary.** *Dead & Gone.* 1989. Walker. 1st. F/NF. G8. $30.00

**KITTREDGE, Mary.** *Walking Dead Man.* 1992. St Martin. 1st. NF/dj. G8. $20.00

**KITTREDGE, William.** *Hole in the Sky.* 1992. Knopf. 1st. inscr/dtd. F/dj. S9. $75.00

**KITTRIEGE, Henry C.** *Cape Cod: Its People & Their History.* 1930. Boston. 1st. pict cloth. B14. $65.00

**KIZZIA, T.** *Wake of an Unseen Object: Among Native Cultures Bush Alaska.* 1991. NY. 1st. 278p. F/dj. M4. $25.00

**KLAMKIN, Charles.** *Weathervanes: History, Manufacture & Design...* 1973. NY. Hawthorn. 1st. 4to. VG/G. O3. $45.00

**KLAMKIN, Marian.** *Collector's Guide to Depression Glass.* 1973. Hawthorn. 1st. ils. 225p. VG/dj. H1. $45.00

**KLANN & MARTIN.** *Jehovah of the Watchtower.* 1953. NY. 1st. 125p. VG/dj. B5. $45.00

**KLAPTHOR, M.** *First Ladies Cookbook: Favorite Recipes of All Presidents.* 1966. photos. VG/G+. E6. $20.00

**KLASS, David.** *Different Season.* 1988. Lodestar (Dutton). 1st. F/dj. P8. $25.00

**KLASS, Philip J.** *Secret Sentries in Space.* 1971. Random. 236p. VG/clip, K5. $25.00

**KLAUSNER, Joseph.** *Messianic Idea in Israel...* 1955. Macmillan. 1st Am. 543p. G. H10. $30.00

**KLAUSNER, Joseph.** *Messianic Idea in Israel...* 1955. NY. 1st. VG/dj. B5. $40.00

**KLAVAN, Andrew.** *Don't Say a Word.* 1991. Pocket. 1st. F/NF. S18. $30.00

**KLAVAN, Andrew.** *Don't Say a Word.* 1991. Pocket. 1st. VG/dj. P3. $20.00

**KLAVAN, Andrew.** *True Crime.* 1995. Crown. 1st. F/dj. S18. $25.00

**KLAW & LANSDALE.** *Weird Business.* MOJO. 1st. sgn. F/dj. S18. $50.00

**KLEES, F.** *Pennsylvania Dutch.* 1950. NY. 1st. VG/G. B5. $25.00

**KLEIN, Clayton.** *Cold Summer Wind.* 1983. Wilderness House. 277p. F/dj. A17. $15.00

**KLEIN, Norma.** *My Life As a Body.* 1987. Knopf. 1st. 8vo. 247p. F. W2. $20.00

**KLEIN, Norma.** *Naomi in the Middle.* 1974. NY. 1st. ils Leigh Grant. VG/dj. M17. $15.00

**KLEIN, Randolph Shiplet.** *Portrait of Early American Family: Shippens of PA...* 1975. U PA. 1st. 373p. VG/dj. V3. $15.00

**KLEINICK, Robert.** *Das Dorf (The Village).* 1926. Oldenburg. Gerhard Staling. tall 16mo. 12-panel panorama. R5. $400.00

**KLEINMAN, Sonny.** *Staying at the Top: Life of a CEO.* 1986. NY. NAL. 1st. F/dj. T12. $20.00

**KLEMENT, Al.** *Rustlin' Along the Brazos.* 1980. NY. Vantage. 1st. inscr. F/VG+. T11. $45.00

**KLEMIN, Diana.** *Illustrated Book: Its Art & Craft.* nd. Bramhall. 4to. ils. wht cloth. NF/dj. F1. $20.00

**KLEVER, H.L.** *Erskine Caldwell: A Biography.* 1993. U TN. 1st. xl. VG/dj. T11. $35.00

**KLICKMANN, Flora.** *Flower-Patch Garden Book.* 1933. London. 1st. 332p. lavender cloth. VG. B26. $15.00

**KLIEMAN, Aaron S.** *Foundations of British Policy in Arab World.* 1970. Johns Hopkins. 1st. 322p. F/VG. M7. $60.00

**KLIMA, Ivan.** *Love & Garbage.* 1991. NY. Knopf. 1st Am. sgn. F/dj. O11. $50.00

**KLIMA, Ivan.** *My Golden Trades.* 1994. Scribner. UP. sgn. F. O11. $45.00

**KLIMA, Ivan.** *Waiting for the Dark, Waiting for the Light.* 1995. Grove. 1st Am. sgn. F/dj. O11. $40.00

**KLINCK, Richard E.** *Land of Room Enough & Time Enough.* 1953. U NM. 1st. 135p. map ep. F7. $35.00

**KLINE, Morris.** *Mathematics & the Physical World.* 1959. NY. Crowell. 8vo. 482p. VG/dj. K5. $25.00

**KLINKOWITZ, Jerome.** *Donald Barthelme: A Comprehensive Bibliography.* 1977. Hamden. Archon/Shoe String. 1st. F/NF. B2. $25.00

**KLINKOWITZ, Jerry.** *Short Season & Other Stories.* 1988. Johns Hopkins. 1st. F/VG. P8. $20.00

**KLIPPART, John.** *Wheat Plant.* 1860. Cincinnati. Moore. 706p. leather spine/cloth brd. A10. $50.00

**KLIX & HAGENDORF.** *Human Memory & Cognitive Abilities...* 1986. Amsterdam. North-Holland. 2 vol. 8vo. prt gr cloth. VG. G1. $100.00

**KLOPFER, Peter H.** *Behavioral Aspects of Ecology.* 1962. Prentice Hall. 1st. F. B14. $55.00

**KLOPFER, Peter H.** *Behaviorial Aspects of Ecology.* 1962. Prentice Hall. 171p. xl. VG. S5. $12.00

**KLOSE, Norma Cline.** *Benny: Biography of a Horse.* 1966. Lee Shepard. 2nd. xl. G. B36. $8.00

KLOSE & MCCOMBS. *Typhoon Shipments.* 1974. Norton. 1st. VG/dj. R11. $25.00

KLOSS, William. *Samuel FB Morse.* 1988. ilindex. 160p. dj. O8. $18.50

KLUCHEVSKY, V.O. *Course in Russian History: The 17th Century.* 1968. Chicago. Quadrangle. F/clip. B9. $15.00

KLUCKHOHN, Clyde. *Navajo Witchcraft.* nd (1944). Boston. Beacon. ltd. 8vo. 254p. dj. F7. $75.00

KLUCKHOHN, Clyde. *Ramah Navaho.* 1966. GPO. 8vo. stiff wrp. F7. $17.50

KLUCKHOHN, Clyde. *To the Foot of the Rainbow: A Tale of 25 Hundred Miles...* 1980. Rio Grande. ils/maps/index. 280p. NF/sans. B19. $25.00

KLUTE, Jeanette. *Woodland Portraits.* 1954. Boston. 1st. photos. VG. M17. $25.00

KNAFLA, Louis. *Law & Justice in New Land: Essays in Western Canada...* (1986)Calga. ry. Carswell. 1st. AN/wrp. A26. $20.00

KNAPP, Joseph G. *Seeds That Grew.* 1960. Hinsdale. Anderson. 1st. ils/charts. NF/G. P12. $15.00

KNAPPEN, Theodore M. *Wings of War, an Account...* 1920. NY. 1st. photos. 289p. VG. B18. $47.50

KNEBEL, Feltcher. *Crossing the Berlin.* 1981. Doubleday. 1st. NF/dj. S13. $10.00

KNEELAND, George. *Commercialized Prostitution in New York City.* 1913. NY. 1st. 334p. A13. $50.00

KNIGHT, Adam; see Lariar, Lawrence.

KNIGHT, Alanna. *Deadly Beloved.* 1989. St Martin. 1st Am. NF/dj. G8. $15.00

KNIGHT, Alanna. *Enter Second Murderer.* 1988. St Martin. 1st Am. VG/G. G8. $12.50

KNIGHT, Charles. *Old England: Pictorial Museum of Recal, Ecclesiastical...* 1854. London. Sangster Fletcher. 2 vol in 1. ils/pl. aeg. morocco. K1. $300.00

KNIGHT, Clayton. *War Birds: Diary of an Unknown Aviator.* 1926. NY. 1st. ils. VG. E6. $30.00

KNIGHT, Damon. *Best From Orbit.* 1975. Putnam. 1st. xl. VG/dj. S18. $5.00

KNIGHT, Damon. *Creating Short Fiction.* 1981. Cincinnati. Writers Digest. 1st. VG/G. N2. $10.00

KNIGHT, David. *Farquharson's Physique: And What It Did to His Mind.* 1971. Hodder Stoughton. 1st. author's 1st book. NF/clip. A14. $28.00

KNIGHT, Ellis Cornelia. *Dinarbas, a Tale: Being a Continuation of Rasselas...* 1793. London. Dilley. 3rd. 8vo. 336p. tree calf. VG. H13. $295.00

KNIGHT, Eric. *Flying Yorkshireman.* 1938. Harper. 1st. 273p. VG/G. M21. $25.00

KNIGHT, Eric. *Lassie Come Home.* 1943. HRW. ilsils DL Baldridge. 239p. orange/tan cloth. xl. B36. $10.00

KNIGHT, John Alden. *Field Book of Fresh-Water Angling.* 1944. Putnam. 1st. 12mo. 207p. G/G-. H10. $22.50

KNIGHT, John Alden. *Theory & Technique of Fresh-Water Angling.* 1940. Harcourt Brace. ils. VG/G. R8. $35.00

KNIGHT, Kathleen Moore. *Death Goes to a Reunion.* 1952. Crime Club. 1st. VG/G. G8. $25.00

KNIGHT, Kathleen Moore. *Port of Seven Strangers.* nd. Crime Club. rpt. VG/G+. G8. $15.00

KNIGHT, Kathleen Moore. *Port of Seven Strangers.* 1945. Doubleday Crime Club. 1st. VG/dj. R8. $10.00

KNIGHT, Kathleen Moore. *Trouble at Turkey Hill.* 1946. Crime Club. 1st. G+. G8. $12.50

KNIGHT, Ruth Adams. *Stand by for the Ladies!: Distaff Side of Radio.* 1939. Coward McCann. 1st. ils Eileen Evans. 179p. G+. A25. $12.00

KNIGHT, Ruth Adams. *Valiant Comrades.* 1943. Doubleday Doran. 1st. ils. VG. A21. $30.00

KNIGHT, Walter B. *3000 Illustrations for Christian Service.* 1950. Eerdmans. 745p. G. B29. $7.50

KNIGHT & KNIGHT. *Plane Crash!* nd. Chilton. 2nd. VG/dj. M21. $20.00

KNIGHTLY, Philip. *First Casualty. From Crimea to Vietnam.* 1975. NY. 1st. 465p. F/VG. E1. $35.00

KNIGIN & ZIMILES. *Contemporary Lithographic Workshop Around the World.* 1974. Van Nostrand. 1st. sm folio. 318p. F/dj. O10. $50.00

KNIPE, Emilie Benson. *Story of Old Ironsides.* 1928. Dodd Mead. 1st. NF. T11. $65.00

KNOLL & MCFADDEN. *War Crimes & the American Conscience.* 1970. HRW. 1st. Nf/VG. R11. $30.00

KNOPF, Mildred O. *Around the World Cookbook for Young People.* 1966. NY. Knopf. 1st. G/dj. A16. $10.00

KNOPF & KNOPF. *Food of Italy: How to Prepare It.* 1964. Knopf. 397p. G+. P12. $12.00

KNOWER, Daniel. *Adventures of a Forty-Niner: An Historic Decription...* 1894. Albany. Weed Parsons. 1st. 12mo. 200p. gilt cloth. F. O1. $85.00

KNOWLES, David. *Secrets of the Camera Obscura.* 1994. SF. Chronicle. 1st. F/dj. M23. $35.00

KNOWLES, John. *Indian Summer.* 1966. Secker Warburg. 1st thus. NF/dj. S13. $18.00

KNOWLES, John. *Indian Summer: A Novel.* 1966. NY. Random. 1st. 8vo. F/dj. S9. $45.00

KNOWLES, John. *Separate Peace.* 1960. Macmillan. ARC/1st. F/clip. S9. $375.00

KNOWLES, Joseph. *Alone in the Wilderness.* 1913. Boston. 1st. 295p. VG. B18. $40.00

KNOWLES & WHEELWRIGHT. *Travels in New England.* 1989. NY. ils. 160p. F/dj. M4. $20.00

KNOWLTON, F.H. *Jurassic Flora of Cape Lisburne, Alaska.* 1914. US Geol Survey. 4 pl. 16p. VG/wrp. H7. $12.50

KNOX, Bill. *Crossfire Killings.* 1986. London. Century. 1st. F/dj. M15. $45.00

KNOX, Bill. *Draw Batons!* 1973. London. John Long. 1st. F/dj. M15. $50.00

KNOX, Calvin; see Silverberg, Robert.

KNOX, R. *Works of EH Shepard.* 1980. Schocken Books. 1st. 300+ils. 256p. brn cloth. VG/dj. D1. $65.00

KNOX, Robert. *Manual of Artistic Anatomy for Use of Sculptors, Painters...* 1832. London. Renshaw. ils. 175p. patterned brd/new recased. G7. $75.00

KNOX, Thomas W. *Lives of James G Blaine & John A Logan...* 1884. Hartford. 1st. 502p. brn cloth. G. S17. $7.50

KNYSTAUTAS, Algirdas. *Natural History of the USSR.* 1987. McGraw Hill. 4to. ils/photos. 224p. F/dj. B1. $38.50

KNYSTAUTAS, Algirdas. *Natural History of the USSR.* 1987. NY. 1st Am. 224p. VG/dj. A17. $25.00

KOBLER, John. *Afternoon in the Attic.* ca 1950. Dodd Mead. 1st thus. VG/dj. L1. $45.00

KOCH, Ed. *Fishing the Midge.* 1972. Rockville Centre, NY. F. A19. $25.00

KOCH, Robert. *Louis Tiffany's Glass, Bronzes, Lamps.* (1971). NY. Crown. 2nd. 208p. F/dj. H1. $65.00

**KOCH, Sigmund.** *Psychology: Study of a Science.* 1959-1963. McGraw Hill. 6 vol. heavy 8vo. prt gr cloth. G1. $250.00

**KOCH, Theodore W.** *More Tales for Bibliophiles.* 1965. Chicago. Blk Cat. mini. 3 vol. 1/125 (200 total). leather/case. B24. $325.00

**KOCHER, Paul H.** *Master of Middle-Earth.* 1972. Houghton Mifflin. 1st. F/dj. P3. $30.00

**KOCHKUNST.** *Illustrite Halbonatschrift for Hotel, Restaurant...* 1901. Frankfurt. 3 bdg vol. VG. E6. $95.00

**KOEBEL, W.** *Central America.* 1925. London. Fisher Unwin. 3rd. 382p. F3. $20.00

**KOEHLER, Horst.** *Das Bunte Blumenbuch, Straucher und Baume Unserer Garten.* 1958. Gutersloh. ils. 381p. VG/dj. B26. $9.00

**KOEHLER, Sylvester Rosa.** *Original Etchings by American Artists.* 1883. London/Paris/NY. Cassell. 1st. 20 full-p etchings. brn morocco/cloth. B20. $1,000.00

**KOEHLER, William R.** *Koehler Method of Open Obedience for Ring, Home & Field.* (1970). Macmillan. rpt. AN. A28. $11.00

**KOERNER, Joseph Leo.** *Caspar David Friedrich & Subject of Landscape.* 1990. Yale. ils. VG/dj. M17. $50.00

**KOESTLER, Arthur.** *Thirteenth Tribe: Khazar Empire & Its Heritage.* 1976. Random. 1st. 8vo. 255p. NF/dj. W1. $22.00

**KOESTLER & KOESTLER.** *Stranger on the Square.* 1984. London. 1st. edit H Harris. dj. T9. $15.00

**KOFFKA, Kurt.** *Zur Analyse der Vorstellunge und Ihrer Gesetze.* 1912. Leipzig. Quelle & Meyer. 392p. contemporary bdg. G1. $175.00

**KOGAN, Herman.** *Long White Line: Story of Abbott Laboratories.* 1963. NY. 1st. 309p. A13. $20.00

**KOGOS, Fred.** *Dictionary of Yiddish Slang & Idioms.* 1967. NY. Citadel. 1st. F/F. H11. $25.00

**KOHLER, Wolfgang.** *Intelligenzprufungen und Menschenaffen.* 1921. Berlin. Julius Springer. 2nd revised. tall 8vo. prt buff wrp. G1. $125.00

**KOHLER, Wolfgang.** *Place a Value in World of Facts.* 1938. Liveright. 418p. panelled bl cloth. G1. $75.00

**KOHNKE, Helmut.** *Soil Physics.* 1968. McGraw Hill. 224p. xl. VG. S5. $15.00

**KOKONIS, Tom.** *Criss Cross.* 1990. St Martin. 1st. sgn. F/dj. N4. $40.00

**KOLLER, Larry.** *Treasury of Angling.* 1963. NY. photos George Silk. F/VG. B30. $25.00

**KOLLER, Larry.** *Treasury of Angling.* 1963. NY. photos George Silk. 252p. VG. A17. $20.00

**KOLLER, Larry.** *Treasury of Hunting.* 1965. NY. ils. 251p. VG/dj. A17. $15.00

**KOLLWITZ, Kaethe.** *Kaethe Kollwitz.* 1946. NY. H Bittner. 1st. ils. 70 pl. VG+/dj. A25. $85.00

**KOLODIN, Irving.** *New Guide to Recorded Music.* 1947. Garden City. Doubleday. 382p. G. C5. $12.50

**KOLPACK, Ronald L.** *Biological & Oceanographical Survey of Santa Barbara...* 1971. U S CA. Sea Grant Pub #2. 476p. VG. S15. $20.00

**KOLPAS, Norman.** *Cup of Coffee: From Plantation to Pot...* 1993. Grove. 1st. ils. 144p. F/dj. H10. $15.00

**KOMROFF, Manuel.** *Thomas Jefferson.* 1966. NY. Messner. 191p. G. M10. $7.50

**KONIGSBURG, E.L.** *About the B'nai Bagels.* 1969. Atheneum. later prt. VG/dj. P8. $12.50

**KOONTZ, Dean R.** *After the Last Race.* 1974. NY. Atheneum. 1st. VG+/clip. A14. $175.00

**KOONTZ, Dean R.** *Bad Place.* 1990. NY. Putnam. 1st. sgn. VG/dj. L1. $100.00

**KOONTZ, Dean R.** *Bad Place.* 1990. Putnam. 1st. NF/dj. N4. $22.50

**KOONTZ, Dean R.** *Blood Risks.* 1973. Bobbs Merrill. 1st. VG+/dj. A14. $175.00

**KOONTZ, Dean R.** *Cold Fire.* 1991. NY. Putnam. 1st/ltd. 1/750. sgn/#d. F/dj/case. G10. $140.00

**KOONTZ, Dean R.** *Cold Fire.* 1991. Putnam. 1st trade. AN/dj. M21. $20.00

**KOONTZ, Dean R.** *Dark Rivers of the Heart.* 1994. Knopf. ARC. F/pict wrp. B3. $50.00

**KOONTZ, Dean R.** *Dark Rivers of the Heart.* 1994. Knopf. 1st. 487p. F/dj. P12. $15.00

**KOONTZ, Dean R.** *Dark Rivers of the Heart.* 1994. Knopf. 1st. sgn. AN/dj. S18. $40.00

**KOONTZ, Dean R.** *Face of Fear.* nd. BC. sgn. NF/dj. S18. $25.00

**KOONTZ, Dean R.** *Face of Fear.* 1977. Bobbs Merrill. 1st. F/NF. M15. $200.00

**KOONTZ, Dean R.** *Flesh in the Furnace.* 1972. Bantam. 1st. NF/wrp. A14. $28.00

**KOONTZ, Dean R.** *Hideaway.* 1992. Putnam. 1st. F/F. H11. $35.00

**KOONTZ, Dean R.** *Intensity.* 1996. Knopf. NF/dj. P12. $12.50

**KOONTZ, Dean R.** *Lightning.* 1988. Putnam. 1st. sgn. VG/dj. L1. $100.00

**KOONTZ, Dean R.** *Midnight.* 1989. Putnam. 1st. VG/dj. L1. $45.00

**KOONTZ, Dean R.** *Phantoms.* 1983. Putnam. 3rd. sgn. NF/dj. S18. $50.00

**KOONTZ, Dean R.** *Shattered.* 1973. Random. 1st. VG+/VG. A14. $105.00

**KOONTZ, Dean R.** *Surrounded.* 1974. Bobbs Merrill. 1st. VG+/VG. A14. $105.00

**KOPAL, Zdenek.** *New Photographic Atlas of the Moon.* 1971. Taplinger. 4to. 311p. VG/dj. K5. $75.00

**KOPAL, Zdenek.** *Realm of the Terrestrial Planets.* 1979. NY. Wiley/Halsted. 8vo. 223p. VG/dj. B11. $17.50

**KOPP & KOPP.** *Southwest: A Contemporary Anthology.* 1977. Red Earth. 1st. 418p. VG/wrp. B19. $15.00

**KORDA, Michael.** *Immortals.* 1992. Poseidon. 1st trade. F/dj. T12. $25.00

**KORDA, Michael.** *Wordly Gods.* 1982. NY. Random. 1st. F/dj. A23. $32.00

**KORN, Bertram Wallace.** *American Jewry & the Civil War.* 1951. Jewish Pub Soc. photos. 331p. xl. VG. B10. $65.00

**KORNBLATT, Joyce Reiser.** *Nothing to Do With Love.* 1981. NY. Viking. ARC/1st. author's 1st book. F/dj. S13. $20.00

**KORNS & MORGAN.** *West From Fort Bridger: Pioneering of Immigrant Trails...* 1994. UT State. 1st. ils. 328p. B19. $30.00

**KORSHIN, Paul.** *Johnson After 200 Years.* 1986. PA U. 1st. VG/dj. H13. $85.00

**KORSHIN, Paul.** *Widening Circle: Essays on Circulation of Literature...* 1976. Phil. 1st. dj. H13. $45.00

**KOSAK, Carl.** *Man Who Liked to Look at Himself.* 1986. Hodder Stoughton. 1st. new afterword by author. NF/dj. A14. $21.00

**KOSHTOYANTS, K.S.** *Essays on History of Physiology in Russia.* 1964. Am Psychological Assn. 320p. ils. prt gr cloth. G1. $85.00

**KOSINSKI, Jerzy.** *Devil Tree.* 1973. HBJ. 1st. sgn. F/dj. M25. $45.00

**KOSINSKI, Jerzy.** *Future Is Ours, Comrade.* 1960. Doubleday. 1st. author's 1st book. F/NF. B2. $175.00

**KOSINSKI, Jerzy.** *Future Is Ours, Comrade: Conversations With the Russians.* 1960. London. Bodley Head. 1st Eng. possible rem mk. VG/fair. V4. $225.00

**KOSINSKI, Jerzy.** *Hermit of 69th Street.* 1988. Holt. 1st. NF/dj. S13. $9.00

**KOTHARI, D.S.** *Nuclear Exposions & Their Effects.* 1958. Delhi, India. 276p. dj. A13. $75.00

**KOTZWINKLE, William.** *Doctor Rat.* 1976. Knopf. 1st. NF/F. B3. $40.00

**KOTZWINKLE, William.** *Game of Thirty: A Novel.* 1994. Boston. Houghton Mifflin. ARC/1st. NF/wrp. Q1. $45.00

**KOTZWINKLE, William.** *Jack in the Box.* 1980. Putnam. 1st. sgn. F/dj. D10. $50.00

**KOTZWINKLE, William.** *Midnight Examiner.* 1989. Houghton Mifflin. 1st. sgn/dtd 1989. F/dj. R14. $45.00

**KOTZWINKLE, William.** *Queen of Swords.* 1984. Putnam. ARC. sgn. F/dj. D10. $50.00

**KOTZWINKLE, William.** *Trouble in Bugland.* 1983. Godine. 1st. ils Joe Servello. F/NF. M19. $35.00

**KOURNAKOFF, Sergei N.** *Russia's Fighting Forces.* 1942. NY. Internat. 2nd. sgn. VG+. B2. $75.00

**KOUTSIKAS, Costas.** *Engravings of Chios.* 1994. Akritas Pub. 2 vol. ils/fld panorama. cloth. VG/dj. Q2. $207.00

**KOVACS, I.** *Some Methodological Achievements of Hungarian Hybrid...* 1970. Budapest. Kiado. 385p. dj. A10. $35.00

**KOZIEK, Josef.** *Pohadka Lesa.* 1929. Prague. Statni Nakladateslstvi. 4to. cloth. R5. $200.00

**KOZLOWSKI, T.T.** *Shedding of Plant Parts.* 1973. Academic. 560p. xl. VG. S5. $30.00

**KRAEMER, Hendrik.** *Theology of the Laity.* 1958. Westminster. 191p. G/dj. B29. $8.00

**KRAEMER, Henry.** *Applied & Economic Botany.* 1916. Phil. self pub. 2nd. 822p. A17. $20.00

**KRAENZEL, Carl Frederick.** *Great Plains in Transition.* 1955. Norman, OK. 1st. 428p. cloth. dj. D11. $35.00

**KRAKEL, Dean.** *Adventures in Western Art.* 1977. Lowell. 1st. ils. 377p. NF/VG. B19. $75.00

**KRAKEL, Dean.** *James Boren: A Study in Discipline.* 1968. Northland. ils/photos. 59p. VG. J2. $60.00

**KRAMER, Aaron.** *Tune of the Calliope: Poems & Drawings of New York.* 1958. NY/London. 1/500 (Subscriber ed). sgns. 107p. F/VG+. B20. $125.00

**KRAMER, Edith.** *Art As Therapy With Children.* 1971. Schocken. 1st. ils. NF/dj. S13. $15.00

**KRAMER, Frank R.** *Voices in the Valley...* 1964. Madison, WI. 1st. 300p. VG/dj. B18. $15.00

**KRAMER, J.J.** *Last of the Grand Hotels.* 1978. Van Nostrand Reinhold. F/dj. A19. $35.00

**KRAMER, Jack.** *300 Extraordinary Plants for Home & Garden.* 1994. NY. Abbeville. 1st. 227p. VG/dj. H10. $35.00

**KRAMER & ZUKOR.** *Public Is Never Wrong: My Fifty Years in Motion Pictures.* 1954. London. Cassell. 1st. VG/dj. C9. $60.00

**KRANTZ, Judith.** *Scruples.* 1978. Crown. author's 1st book. 474p. NF/dj. W2. $50.00

**KRAUS, H.P.** *Nineteenth Catalogue.* nd. NY. Kraus. 4to. tipped-in pl. gilt wht cloth. VG. F1. $50.00

**KRAUS, Karl.** *Worte in Versen III: Der Horerin.* 1918. Leipzig. Schriften Karl Kraus. NF. B2. $150.00

**KRAUS, Robert.** *First Robin.* nd (c 1965). Harper Row. 48mo. unp. C14. $8.00

**KRAUS, Robert.** *Good Mousekeeper.* 1977. Windmill/Dutton. 1st. sm 4to. ils Hilary Knight. yel cloth. F/NF. T5. $45.00

**KRAUS & KRAUS.** *Gothic Choirstalls of Spain.* 1986. London. Kegan Paul. 1st. ils. F/dj. T10. $35.00

**KRAUS & KRAUS.** *Hidden Worlds of Misericords.* 1975. NY. photos. F/dj. M4. $50.00

**KRAUSE, Herbert.** *Thresher.* 1974. Sioux Falls, SD. Brevet. rpt. F. A19. $25.00

**KRAUSS, Ruth.** *How to Make an Earthquake.* 1954. NY. Harper. 1st. 8vo. dj. R5. $100.00

**KRAUSS, Stephen.** *Encyclopaedic Handbook of Medical Psychology.* 1976. London. Butterworths. 4to. 585p. prt maroon cloth. VG/tattered. G1. $65.00

**KRAVITZ, Bob.** *Mile High Madness.* 1994. Times. 1st. photos. F/dj. P8. $20.00

**KRAVITZ, Nathaniel L.** *3,000 Years of Hebrew Literature.* 1972. 586p. F/F. A4. $20.00

**KREBS, Charles J.** *Ecology: Experimental Analysis of Distribution & Abundance.* 1978. Harper Row. 2nd. VG. S15. $10.00

**KREDEL, Fritz.** *Andromache: A Tragedy.* 1986. Lexington, KY. Anvil. 1/7 (500 total). hand-color by Carolyn Hammer. AN/case. B24. $1,350.00

**KREEFT, Peter.** *Knowing the Truth of God's Love.* 1988. Servant Books. 208p. VG. B29. $6.50

**KREHBIEL, H.E.** *Afro-American Folksongs.* nd. NY. Schirmer. 3rd. F. B2. $75.00

**KREIDER, Claude M.** *Bamboo Rod & How to Build It.* 1951. Macmillan. 1st. ils. 140p. VG. H10. $100.00

**KREIG, Margaret B.** *Green Medicine: Search for Plants That Heal...* 1964. Chicago. 2nd. ils. 462p. VG/dj. B26. $20.00

**KREISLER, Fritz.** *Four Weeks in the Trenches.* 1915. Boston. 1st. ils. 86p. VG/dj. B18. $25.00

**KREISS, Nancy.** *Alien Light.* 1988. Arbor. 1st. F/dj. M25. $15.00

**KREMENTZ, Jill.** *How It Feels When a Parent Dies.* 1981. Knopf. 1st. VG/dj. S13. $12.00

**KREMPIN, Jack.** *Palms & Cycads Around the World.* 1993 (1990). Broadbeach Waters. revised. 695p. AN. B26. $50.00

**KRESGE, Stanley S.** *SS Kresge Story.* 1979. Racine, WI. Western Pub. photos/chronology. 373p. gilt red bdg. H6. $38.00

**KRESS, Nancy.** *Aliens of Earth.* 1993. Arkham. 1st. 18 stories. F/dj. T2. $22.00

**KRESS, Nancy.** *Dancing on Air.* 1997. SF. Tachyon. 1st. 1/26 lettered. sgn. F/dj/case. T2. $60.00

**KRESS, Nancy.** *Golden Grove.* 1984. Bluejay. 1st. F/dj. T2. $20.00

**KRESSLER, Edward.** *Flannery O'Connor & the Language of Apocalypse.* 1986. Princeton. 163p. VG. B29. $13.50

**KRETSCHMER, Ernst.** *Geniale Menschen.* 1931 (1929). Berlin. Julius Springer. 2nd. 43p portrait pl. 259p. prt bl cloth. G1. $65.00

**KRETSCHMER, Ernst.** *Physique & Character: An Investigation of Nature...* 1925. Harcourt Brace. 1st Am (prt on British sheets). 266p. gr cloth. G1. $75.00

**KREY, Otto.** *Ships Cook & Baker.* 1944 (1942). Cornell. Maritime. VG. E6. $20.00

**KRICK, Robert Kenneth.** *Neale Books: An Annotated Bibliography.* 1977. Dayton. 1st. 234p. cloth. NF. M8. $35.00

**KRICKEBERG, Walter.** *Pre-Columbian American Religion.* 1968. London. 1st Eng. 365p. dj. F3. $35.00

**KRIEG, Margaret.** *Green Medicine: Search for Plants That Heal.* 1964. Chicago. Rand. 1st. 462p. VG/dj. A10. $20.00

**KRIEGER, Louis C.C.** *Mushroom Handbook.* 1967 (1936). Dover. 560p. VG. S5. $20.00

**KRISHTALKA, L.** *Dinosaur Plots & Other Intrigues in Natural History.* 1989. Morrow. ils/photos. 316p. F/dj. M12. $17.50

**KRIST, Gary.** *Garden State.* 1989. HBJ. 1st. F/NF. R14. $90.00

**KRISTOFFERSEN, Eva.** *Bee in Her Bonnet.* 1944. Crowell. 1st. 12mo. 168p. VG/G. C14. $18.00

**KROMBEIN, K.V.** *Catalog of the Hymenoptera in America North of Mexico.* 1979. Smithsonian. 3 vol. 4to. cloth. B1. $200.00

**KRONBY, Madelaine.** *Secret in My Pocket.* 1977. McClelland Stewart. 1st Canadian. sgn. NF/sans. T12. $20.00

**KRONENBERGER, Louis.** *Cavalcade of Comedy.* 1953. NY. S&S. 1st. NF. T12. $60.00

**KRONENBERGER, Louis.** *Extraordinary Mr Wilkes.* 1974. Doubleday. 1st. gilt blk linen brd/gr linen spine. dj. H13. $35.00

**KRONENBERGER, Louis.** *Kings & Desparate Men: Life in 18th-Century England.* 1942. Knopf. 1st. gilt maroon bdg. VG/G+. P12. $20.00

**KRONFELD, Peter C.** *Human Eye in Anatomical Transparencies.* 1944. Bausch Lomb. 1st/2nd prt. 99p. NF. C14. $35.00

**KRONICK, David.** *Literature of the Life Sciences.* 1985. Phil. 1st. 219p. A13. $25.00

**KROPOTKIN, Peter Alexeivich.** *Anarchism: Its Philosophy & Ideal.* 1908. London. Freedom Office. 8vo. caption title+ad at end. stitched. R12. $125.00

**KRUEGER, Carl.** *Wings of the Tiger.* 1966. NY. Fell. 3rd. VG/dj. R11. $30.00

**KRUEGER, Walter.** *From Down Under to Nippon: Story of Sixth Army in WWII.* 1953. WA, DC. 1st. 393p. NF/dj. E1. $35.00

**KRUGER, Mary.** *Death on the Cliff Walk.* 1994. NY. Kensington. 1st. author's 1st book. F/F. H11. $25.00

**KRUGER, Paul.** *If the Shroud Fits.* 1969. S&S. 1st. F/VG. M19. $17.50

**KRUGER, T.J.** *Trees, Shrubs & Climbers.* 1981. Bethal. ils. 570p. F. B26. $75.00

**KRUMBEIN & SLOSS.** *Stratigraphy & Sedimentation.* 1951. Freeman. 1st. ils/charts. cloth. VG. B27. $30.00

**KRUMBHAAR, E.B.** *Pathology.* 1937. NY. 1st. 206p. xl. A13. $40.00

**KRUMGOLD, Joseph.** *...And Now Miguel.* (1953). NY. Crowell. 1st. ils Jean Charlot. 1954 Newbery. dj. R5. $200.00

**KRUMMEL, D.W.** *Bibliographical Handbook of American Music.* 1987. U IL. 700 entries. 280p. F. A4. $35.00

**KRUMMEL & SADIE.** *Music Printing & Publishing.* 1990. London/NY. Norton. ils/biographical dictionary/64p glossary. F/F. A4. $50.00

**KRUPP, E.C.** *In Search of Ancient Astronomies.* 1978. Doubleday. 8vo. 300p. VG/dj. K5. $30.00

**KRUSKA, Dennis G.** *Sierra Nevada Big Trees.* 1985. Los Angeles. ils. 63p. linen. AN. B26. $15.00

**KRUTCH, Joseph Wood.** *Grand Canyon: Today & All Its Yesterdays.* 1958. Sloane. 1st. 276p. NF/VG. B19. $25.00

**KRUTCH & PORTER.** *Baja California & the Geography of Hope.* 1967. Sierra Club. 1st. photos. F/dj. M4. $60.00

**KRUTILLA, John V.** *Natural Environments.* 1972. Johns Hopkins. 352p. xl. VG. S5. $20.00

**KRYTHE, Maymie R.** *Sampler of American Songs.* 1969. Harper Row. 1st. F/dj. P12. $9.00

**KRYZHANOVSKII, O.L.** *Lepidopterous Fauna of the USSR & Adjacent Countries.* 1988. Smithsonian. 8vo. ils. cloth. F/dj. B1. $48.00

**KUBASTA, Voitech.** *How Columbus Discovered America.* 1960. London. Bancroft. tall 4to. mc ils/dbl-p popup. moveable wheel on bdg. R5. $250.00

**KUBASTA, Voitech.** *Tournament.* 1961. London. Bancroft. lg 4to. dbl-p popup castle. stiff paper wrp. R5. $300.00

**KUBITSCHEK, H.E.** *Introduction to Research With Continuous Cultures.* 1970. Prentice Hall. 195p. xl. VG. S5. $12.00

**KUBLER, George.** *Era of Charles Mahon Stereotypes 1750-1825.* 1938. NY. 1st. ils. 120p. G. B5. $22.50

**KUBLER, George.** *Mexican Architecture of the 16th Century.* 1948. New Haven. Yale. 2 vol. photos/ils/plans. cloth. D11. $100.00

**KUCK & TONGG.** *Modern Tropical Garden: Its Design, Plant Materials...* 1955. Honolulu. ils. 250p. B26. $35.00

**KUGLER, Harold.** *Arc Welding Lessons for School & Farm Shop.* 1965. Cleveland. Lincoln Arc Welding. 343p. VG. A10. $18.00

**KUH, Charlotte.** *Motorman.* 1929. Macmillan. Happy Hour Books. 1st. ils Kurt Wiese. NF/dj. B27. $150.00

**KUHLKEN, Ken.** *Loud Adios.* 1991. NY. SMP. 1st. F/F. H11. $40.00

**KUHLMAN, Katheryn.** *God Can Do It Again.* 1969. Prentice Hall. 256p. G. B29. $9.00

**KUHN, Charles L.** *German Expressionism & Abstract Art: The Harvard Collection.* 1957. Harvard. ils. VG/dj. M17. $40.00

**KULPE, Oswald.** *Grundiss der Psychologie auf Experimenteller Grundlage...* 1893. Leipzig. Wilhelm Engelmann. heavy 8vo. 478p. NF. G1. $550.00

**KULPE, Oswald.** *Vorlesungen uber Psychologie.* 1922 (1919). Leipzig. Hirzel. 2nd enlarged. 340p. prt brn cloth. G. G1. $25.00

**KUMIN, Maxine.** *Microscope.* 1984 (1968). NY. Harper Row. 1st thus. 12mo. ils Arnold Lobel. F/VG. T5. $25.00

**KUMIN, Maxine.** *Why Can't We Live Together Like Civilized Human Beings?* 1982. NY. Viking. UP. F/wrp. w/promo notice. R14. $45.00

**KUMLIEN, L.L.** *Friendly Evergreens.* 1946. Dundee, IL. ils/index. VG. A17. $17.50

**KUMLIEN, L.L.** *Hill's Book of Evergreens.* 1939 (1936). Dundee, IL. 2nd. 304p. VG. B26. $22.50

**KUMMER, Frederic Arnold.** *Courage Over the Andes.* nd (1940). Phil/NY. Winston/Jr Lit Guild. 8vo. 251p. NF. C14. $6.00

**KUMMER, Frederic Arnold.** *Song of Sixpence.* 1913. Franklin Watts. 1st. VG. P3. $15.00

**KUMMER, Hans.** *Social Organization of Hamadryas Baboons: A Field Study.* 1968. Chicago. 189p. F/dj. S15. $27.00

**KUMMER, Hans.** *Social Organization of Hamadryas Baboons: A Field Study.* 1968. Chicago. 189p. xl. VG. S5. $20.00

**KUNDERA, Milan.** *Immortality.* 1991. Grove Weidenfeld. 1st. F/dj. M23. $30.00

**KUNDERA, Milan.** *Joke.* 1982. Harper Row. 1st Am. NF/dj. A24. $35.00

**KUNDERA, Milan.** *Unbearable Lightness of Being.* 1984. Harper Row. 1st Am. ils. VG/dj. C9. $42.00

**KUNDERA, Milan.** *Unbearable Lightness of Being.* 1984. Harper Row. 1st. trans from Czech. F/dj. A24. $60.00

**KUNDERA, Milan.** *Zert.* 1967. Prague. Zatva. 1st. sgn. author's 1st book. VG/dj. L3. $750.00

**KUNHARDT, Philip B.** *Eisenstaedt's Celebrity Portraits.* 1984. NY. Greenwich. unp. VG/dj. C5. $15.00

**KUNHARDT, Philip B.** *New Birth of Freedom: Lincoln at Gettysburg.* 1983. Little Brn. 1st. F/clip. A14. $25.00

**KUNITZ, Stanley.** *Wellfleet Whale & Companion Poems.* 1983. NY. Sheep Meadow. 1st deluxe. F. O11. $35.00

**KUNITZ & LEVY.** *Navajo Aging: Transition From Family to Instutional Support.* 1991. AZ U. 1st. sgn Levy. 181p. F/sans. B19. $20.00

**KUNKEL, G.** *Plants for Human Consumption.* 1984. Koenigstein. ils. 393p. F. B26. $70.00

**KUPFERBERG, Herbert.** *Amadeus: Mozart Mosaic.* 1987. UK. ils. VG/dj. M17. $17.50

**KURALT, Charles.** *Life on the Road.* 1990. Putnam. 1st. F/2 djs. T11. $15.00

**KURATOMI, Chizuko.** *Mr Bear & the Robbers.* 1970. NY. Dial. 1st. 24p. cloth. F/dj. D4. $35.00

**KURELEK, William.** *Prairie Boy's Winter: Paintings & Story.* 1973. Boston. 2nd. ils. VG/dj. M17. $20.00

**KURLAND, Philip B.** *Supreme Court Review 1967.* 1967. Chicago U. cloth. M11. $35.00

**KURUTZ, Gary F.** *California Gold Rush, Descriptive Bibliography of Books...* 1997. BC of CA. 1/1000. 33 pl. 801p. F. A4. $150.00

**KURZ, R.F.** *Journal of Rudolph Friederich Kurz...* 1937. BAE Bulletin 115. 48 pl. 382p. VG. M4. $45.00

**KURZWEIL, Allen.** *Case of Curiosities.* 1992. HBJ. 1st. NF/dj. M25. $35.00

**KURZWELL, Allen.** *Case of Curiosities.* 1992. HBJ. ARC. author's 1st novel. NF/wrp. B3. $30.00

**KUSHNER, Ellen.** *Thomas the Rhymer.* 1990. NY. Morrow. 1st. F/dj. M21. $30.00

**KUSKIN, Karla.** *Philharmonic Gets Dressed.* nd. Harper Row. unp. F/VG clip. C14. $8.00

**KYBALOVA, Ludmilla.** *Carpets of the Orient.* 1970. London/NY. Hamlyn. 2nd. ils/pl. 57p. cloth. VG/dj. W1. $20.00

**KYLE, Duncan.** *Exit.* 1993. Harper Collins. 1st. F/dj. T12. $25.00

**KYLE, Elizabeth.** *Holly Hotel: A Mystery.* 1947 (1945). Houghton Mifflin. 8vo. ils Nora Unwin. 298p. bl cloth. G+. T5. $25.00

**KYRRIS, Costas P.** *Tourkia kai Valkania.* 1986. Athens. 357p. VG. Q2. $26.50

L'AMOUR, Louis. *Bendigo Shafter.* 1979. Dutton. 1st. VG/dj. R8. $60.00

L'AMOUR, Louis. *Education of a Wandering Man.* 1989. NY. Bantam. 1st. NF/NF. B3. $15.00

L'AMOUR, Louis. *Fair Blows the Wind.* 1978. Dutton. 1st. F/clip. B2. $100.00

L'AMOUR, Louis. *Jubal Sackett.* 1985. Bantam. 1st. NF/F. H11. $55.00

L'AMOUR, Louis. *Sackett's Land.* 1974. Saturday Review/Dutton. 1st. 8vo. F/dj. S9. $250.00

L'AMOUR, Louis. *Smoke From the Altar.* (1990). Bantam. 1st thus. AN/dj. A18. $15.00

L'ENGLE, Madeleine. *And Both Were Young.* 1949. Lee Sheperd. 1st. VG/dj. B4. $450.00

L'ENGLE, Madeleine. *Glimpses of Grace. Daily Thoughts & Reflections.* (1996). Harper. 366 entries. AN/dj. A27. $18.00

L'ENGLE, Madeleine. *Other Side of the Sun.* 1971 (1971). FSG. 3rd. 8vo. 344p. blk cloth. NF/VG. T5. $25.00

L'EPINE. *Fortress of Fear. Story Classics.* 1953. Emmaus, PA. ils Gustave Dore. trans Tom Hood. VG/VG case. M17. $20.00

L'HAMMEDIEU, Dorothy K. *Bow-Bow Stories.* 1937. Platt Munk. ils AO Scott. A21. $40.00

L'HERTIER DE BRUTELLE, C.-L. *Sertum Anglicum.* 1963 (1788). Pitsburgh. Hunt Botanical. facs. 34 full-p pl. B1. $40.00

L'HEUREUX, John. *Rubics for a Revolution.* 1967. Macmillan. 1st. sgn. author's 2nd book. NF/dj. R14. $55.00

L'MOMOND, C.F. *De Viris Illustribus Urbis Romae: A Romulo ad Augustum.* 1821. NY. w/dictionary by James Hardie. leather. M17. $15.00

LA FARGE, Oliver. *Pictorial History of the American Indian.* 1956. Crown. 1st. 4to. NF/dj. S18. $35.00

LA FARGE, Phyllis. *Christmas Adventure.* 1974. HRW. 1st. VG/dj. B36. $11.00

LA FEMINA, James. *They Still Play Baseball on the Moon.* 1994. Cosmo. 1/250. sgn. AN. P8. $20.00

LA FONTAINE. *Fables of La Fontaine.* (1890). NY. Cassell. ils Gustave Dore. 175p. G+. B5. $35.00

LA FONTAINE. *Fables of La Fontaine.* 1940. NY. Harper. 1st. ils Andre Helle/trans MW Brown. 39p. VG. D1. $100.00

LA FONTAINE. *La Fontaine's Tales: Imitated in English Verse.* 1814. London. private prt. 2 vol. 12mo. 65 pl. teg. gilt full brn morocco. F. R3. $400.00

LA FONTAINE. *Trois Fables, de La Fontaine.* 1965. Pasadena. mini. ils Cheney. French text. 21p. full limp vellum. B24. $150.00

LA GUARDIA, Robert. *Wonderful World of TV Soap Operas.* 1974. Ballantine. 2nd. VG. C9. $30.00

LA PLANTE, Lynda. *Bella Mafia.* 1990. London. Sidgwick Jackson. 1st. F/dj. T12. $45.00

LA ROSA INC. *101 Ways to Prepare Macaroni.* 1937. 16mo. suede wrp. E6. $10.00

LA RUE PERRINE, A.M. *Letters Concerning Plan of Salvation As Addressed...* 1816. NY. 12mo. 236p. contemporary sheep. G. S17. $25.00

LA TROBE-BATEMAN, Lee. *Florida Trucking for Beginners.* 1913. DeLand. Painter. 205p. cloth. VG. A10. $22.00

LA WALL, Charles H. *Four Thousand Years of Pharmacy: An Outline of Pharmacy...* 1927. Lippincott. 3rd imp. thick 8vo. gilt red cloth. H7. $30.00

LACEY, Margaret. *Silent Friends: Quaker Quilt.* 1994. Urbana, IL. Stormline. 2nd. 108p. VG/dj. V3. $12.00

LACEY, Robert. *Little Man.* 1991. Little Brn. 1st. F/dj. L4. $22.00

LACK, David. *Darwin's Finches: An Essay on General Biological Theory...* 1968 (1947). Peter Smith. rpt. 204p. F. S15. $12.00

LACKSCHEWITZ, Klaus. *Vascular Plants of West-Central Montana...Guidebook.* 1991. Ogden. ils. 648p. VG. B26. $40.00

LACOMBE, Jacques. *Abrege Chronologique de l'Histoire du Nord...* 1762. Paris. Jean-Thomas Herissant. 2 vol. sm 8vo. mottled calf. K1. $250.00

LACOUR, Gene. *Globes of Llarum.* 1980. Doubleday. 1st. F/dj. T12. $15.00

LACOUR, Pierre. *Manufacture of Liquors, Wines & Cordials...* (1863). NY. Dick & Fitzgerald. 312p. gilt blind-stp blk cloth. G. H7. $35.00

LACY, Allen. *Glory of Roses.* 1990. NY. Stewart Tabori Chang. 1st. ils/biblio/index. 239p. F/dj. H10. $27.50

LACY, Leslie Alexander. *Rise & Fall of a Proper Negro: An Autobiography.* 1970. Macmillan. 1st. NF/dj. R11. $17.00

LADD, Elizabeth. *Mystery for Meg.* 1962. Wm Morrow. 1st. 8vo. 189p. bl cloth. VG/dj. T5. $30.00

LADD, George Trumbull. *Elements of Physiological Psychology.* 1887. Scribner. ils. 696p. emb olive cloth. VG. G1. $85.00

LADD, George Trumbull. *Philosophy of Mind: An Essay...* 1895. Scribner. 414p. panelled olive cloth. G1. $75.00

LADD, George Trumbull. *Psychology Descriptive & Explanatory: A Treatise...* 1894. Scribner. heavy 8vo. 676p. panelled olive cloth. G1. $65.00

LADD, Harry S. *Treatise on Marine Ecology & Paleocology. Vol 2.* 1963 (1957). WA. Geol Soc of Am. 1077p. xl. S15. $35.00

LADD, Horatio. *History of the War With Mexico.* (1883). Dodd Mead. 1st. 328p. gilt cloth. D11. $75.00

LADD, William J. *Ladd's Discount Book, Double Indexed Edition.* 1887. NY. Sargent. 1st. gr cloth. VG. S13. $35.00

LADD & LADD. *Portland Glass: Legacy of a Glass House Down East.* 1992. Collector Books. 1st. 191p. ils brd. F. H1. $45.00

LADIES HOME JOURNAL. *Dessert Cookbook.* 1964. Doubleday. G/dj. A16. $15.00

LADNER, Mildred. *OC Seltzer, Painter of the Old West.* 1979. U OK. 224p. VG. J2. $115.00

LADNER, Mildred. *William de la Montagne Cary.* 1984. U OK. 1st. Gilcrease-OK series. F/dj. T11. $50.00

LADURIE, Emmanuel Le Roy. *Carnival in Romans.* 1979. NY. 1st. trans M Feeney. dj. T9. $20.00

LADY OF CHARLESTON. *Carolina Housewife; or, House & Home by Lady of Charleston.* 1847. Charleston. 1st. 192p. rb. fair. E6. $150.00

LAFAYETTE. *Memoirs of General LaFayette...* 1825. Hartford. Barber Robinson. 8vo. 3 pl. calf. R12. $150.00

LAFFERTY, R.A. *Does Anyone Else Have Something to Add?* 1974. Scribner. 1st. F/dj. P3. $20.00

LAFFERTY, R.A. *Space Chantey.* 1976. Dobson. 1st. F/dj. P3. $40.00

LAFITAU, Joseph Francois. *De Zeden der Wilden van Amerika...* 1731. Gravenhage. Gerard Vander Poel. 2 vol in 1. folio. contemporary bdg. K1. $3,000.00

**LAFRAMBOISE, Leon.** *History of Combat Support Branches: Branch of Service...* 1977. Steelville. 1st. 239p. VG. S16. $28.50

**LAGERKVIST, Par.** *Holy Land.* 1966. Random. 1st Am. F/dj. B4. $85.00

**LAGUARDIA, Robert.** *Red Tempestuous: Life of Susan Hayward.* 1985. Macmillan. 1st. VG/dj. W2. $25.00

**LAIDLAW, Brett.** *Three Nights in the Heart of the Earth.* 1988. NY. Norton. 1st. F/F. H11. $25.00

**LAIT, Jack.** *Big House.* 1930. Grosset Dunlap. MTI. NF/fair. M19. $35.00

**LAKE, Nancy.** *Daily Dinners: Collection of 366 Distinct Menus...* 1892. London. VG. E6. $30.00

**LAKE, Nancy.** *Menus Made Easy; or, How to Order Dinner...* ca 1887. 3rd. E6. $40.00

**LAKE & OULTMAN.** *Eusebius: Ecclesiastical History.* 1980. Harvard. 2 vol. VG. B29. $24.00

**LAKE & WRIGHT.** *Bibliography of Archery.* 1994. Derrydale. 1/1250. 5000 entries. 501p. F. A4. $125.00

**LAKELA, Ogla.** *Flora of Northeastern Minnesota.* 1965. Minneapolis. ils/maps. 541p. VG. B26. $55.00

**LALICKI, Barbara.** *If There Were Dreams to Sell.* 1984. NY. 1st. ils Margot Tomes. 32p. F/dj. D4. $25.00

**LALLY, Kevin.** *Wilder Times: Life of Billy Wilder.* 1996. Holt. 1st. sm 4to. 496p. F/dj. W2. $40.00

**LAM & SHATZ.** *Development of the Visual System...* 1991. Cambridge. MIT. 1st. 299p. F/VG. C14. $30.00

**LAMANTIA, Philip.** *Ekstasis.* 1959. San Francisco. Auerhahn. 1st. wrp. B2. $75.00

**LAMAR.** *Reader's Encyclopedia of the American West.* 1977. Crowell. 1316p. F/NF. A4. $75.00

**LAMB, Albert.** *Presbyterian Hospital & the Columbia-Presbyterian Medical...* 1955. NY. 1st. 495p. A13. $50.00

**LAMB, Charles.** *Witches & Other Night Fears.* 1968. Dawson. mini. 1/125. ils Wallace Nethery. 52p. full blk leather. B24. $125.00

**LAMB, Charles.** *Works...* 1818. London. Ollier. 2 vol. 1st/1st issue (ads dtd 1818). 12mo. teg. F1. $850.00

**LAMB, Dana S.** *Bright Salmon & Brown Trout.* 1996. Meadow Run. 1st. yel/gr cloth. F/sans/case. T11. $60.00

**LAMB, Frank H.** *Book of Broadleaf Trees: Story...* 1939. NY. 1st. ils/map ep. 367p. VG. B26. $32.50

**LAMB, Frederick.** *Forty Years in the Old Bailey.* 1913. London. Stevens. 1st. thick 8vo. 356p. B20. $40.00

**LAMB, Harold.** *Crusades: Iron Men & Saints.* 1930. Doubleday Doran. 1st. 8vo. 368p. cloth. VG. W1. $18.00

**LAMB, Hugh.** *Victorian Nightmares.* 1977. Taplinger. 1st Am. VG/dj. L1. $35.00

**LAMB, Martha.** *History of the City of New York.* 1877. NY. AS Barnes. 2 vol. ils. B5. $210.00

**LAMB, Samuel H.** *Woody Plants of the Southwest: Field Guide...* 1975. Santa Fe. 4to. sc. AN. B26. $13.00

**LAMB, Wally.** *She's Come Undone.* 1992. NY. Pocket. 1st. NF/F. H11. $35.00

**LAMB, Wally.** *She's Come Undone.* 1992. NY. Pocket. 1st. F/F. B3. $60.00

**LAMBARD, William.** *Eirenarcha; or, Office of the Justices of the Peace.* 1581. London. Bynnemann. 1st. contemporary calf. M11. $3,500.00

**LAMBDIN, Dewey.** *For King & Country.* 1994. DIF. Omnibus/1st thus. F/wrp. T11. $45.00

**LAMBDIN, Dewey.** *HMS Cockerel.* 1995. DIF. 1st. NF/clip. A14. $22.00

**LAMBDIN, Dewey.** *King's Coat.* 1989. DIF. 1st. Alan Lewrie #1. NF/F. T11. $185.00

**LAMBDIN, Dewey.** *King's Coat.* 1989. DIF. 1st. author's 1st book. VG+/dj. A14. $52.50

**LAMBDIN, Dewey.** *King's Commission.* 1991. DIF. 1st. Alan Lewrie #3. F/dj. T11. $95.00

**LAMBERT, Gavin.** *Dangerous Edge.* 1976. Grossman. 1st. VG/dj. P3. $30.00

**LAMBERT, Harold B.** *Dakota Territory Songs.* nd. Dakota Music Co. sc. G. A19. $25.00

**LAMBERT, Janet.** *Little Miss Atlas.* (1949). Dutton. 190p. VG. B36. $20.00

**LAMBERT, Janet.** *Star Dream.* 1951. Dutton. 1st. 8vo. VG/G. M5. $35.00

**LAMBERT, Janet.** *Star Spangled Summer.* 1941. Grosset Dunlap. ils Sandra James. G. B36. $11.00

**LAMBORN, L.L.** *American Carnation Culture.* 1901 (1885). Alliance, OH. 4th. 174p. B26. $22.50

**LAMBOT, Isobel.** *Identity Trap.* 1978. London. Hale. 1st. F/dj. M15. $45.00

**LAMBRECHT, Bernhard.** *New Style of Confectionary.* ca 1933. London/Glasgow. Maclaren. 1st Eng. 4to. 132p. coarse tan cloth. NF. B20. $250.00

**LAMEY, H.Y.** *Memories of Nat H Jones: An Insurance Man.* 1900. Spectator. 273p. gr cloth. VG. B20. $45.00

**LAMON & LEE.** *Poultry Feeds & Feeding.* 1929. Orange Judd. 247p. VG. A10. $18.00

**LAMOTT, Anne.** *All New People.* 1989. SF. Northpoint. 1st. sgn. F/dj. B4. $85.00

**LAMOTT, Anne.** *Crooked Little Heart.* 1997. Pantheon. 1st. sgn. F/dj. R14. $40.00

**LAMOTT, Anne.** *Hard Laughter.* 1980. Viking. 1st. author's 1st book. F/dj. T10. $75.00

**LAMOTT, Anne.** *Hard Laughter.* 1989. London. Boyars. 1st. 1/650. author's 1st book. F/F. B3. $100.00

**LAMOTTE, Jeanne deSaint-Remy.** *Memoirs...Containing Compleat Justification of Conduct...* 1798. London. Ridgway for Author. 8vo. sgn. gilt calf. R12. $200.00

**LAMPKIN, Richard H.** *Naked Eye Stars: Catalogued by Constellation...* 1972 (1962). Edinburgh. Gall Inglis. 2nd. 8vo. 46p. VG/wrp. K5. $10.00

**LAMPORT, Felicia.** *Scrap Irony.* 1961. Houghton Mifflin. 1st. ils Edward Gorey. F/NF. C15. $25.00

**LANCASTER, O.** *Human Body: Short Account of Anatomical Arrangement...* tall narrow folio. VG. E6. $45.00

**LANCASTER, Robert A.** *Historic Virgnia Homes & Churches.* 1915. Lippincott. 1st. 527p. G. B26. $150.00

**LANCTOT, G.** *Canada & the American Revolution 1774-1783.* 1967. Harvard. 321p. F/dj. M4. $30.00

**LAND, Myrick.** *Fine Art of Literary Mayhem: A Lively Account...* 1963. HRW. 1st. 8vo. 242p. cloth. F/dj. O10. $37.50

**LANDE, Lawrence M.** *Psalms: Intimate & Familiar.* 1945. Toronto. Musson. 1st. F/NF. T12. $30.00

**LANDE.** *Lawrence Lande Collection of Canadiana...a Bibliography.* 1965. 1/950. sgn/#d. folio. fld maps/2328 entries. 339p. pigskin. NF/VG case. A4. $400.00

**LANDER, Frederick West.** *Maps & Reports of the Ft Kearney, South Pass...* 1861. WA. House Representatives. 39p. removed. VG. J2. $95.00

**LANDOIS, L.** *Text-Book of Human Physiology...* 1887. Phil. Blakiston. 922p. xl. B14. $75.00

**LANDON, Margaret.** *Anna & the King of Siam.* 1944. NY. John Day. 1st. ils Margaret Ayers. F/NF clip. B4. $175.00

**LANDSTROM, Bjorn.** *Columbus: Story of Don Critobal Colon...* 1967. Macmillan. ils/maps. 207p. dj. D2. $55.00

**LANE, Alfred.** *Report State Board of Geological Survey of Michigan 1906.* 1907. Lansing. Wynkoop. fld ils/maps/charts. 300p. G. A10. $35.00

**LANE, Edward.** *Thousand & One Nights.* 1889. London. Chatto Windus. 3 vol. 8vo. gilt gr cloth. VG. H5. $250.00

**LANE, Ferdinand C.** *Mysterious Sea.* 1947. Doubleday. 345p. NF. B14. $24.00

**LANE, Franklin.** *Letters of Franklin Lane.* 1922. Houghton Mifflin. 1st. ils. F. A2. $20.00

**LANE, Jack C.** *Armed Progressive General Leonard Wood.* 1978. San Rafael. 1st. ils/notes. 329p. F/dj. E1. $50.00

**LANE, John.** *Against Information.* 1995. New Native. 1st. 1/500. sgn. F/sans. L3. $35.00

**LANE, Margaret.** *Biography of a Phenomenon.* (1938). London. 1st. inscr Hugh Walpole. frayed dj. T9. $45.00

**LANE, Margaret.** *Samuel Johnson & His World.* 1975. Harper. ils/map ep. F/dj. H13. $65.00

**LANE, Mark.** *Rush to Judgement.* 1966. NY. 1st. VG/dj. B5. $25.00

**LANE, Thomas A.** *America on Trial: War for Vietnam.* 1971. New Rochelle, NY. Arlington. 1st. F/VG. A2. $20.00

**LANES, Selma G.** *Art of Maurice Sendak.* 1980. Abrams. 1st. ils Sendak. 278p. F. D1. $150.00

**LANG, Allen Kim.** *Wild & Outside.* 1965. Chilton. 1st. VG/dj. P8. $75.00

**LANG, Andrew.** *Angling Sketches.* 1891. London. 2nd. ils. 176p. gilt cloth. VG. A17. $45.00

**LANG, Andrew.** *Animal Story Book.* 1896. London. Longman Gr. ils HJ Ford. 400p. aeg. gilt lion on dk bl cloth. A24. $150.00

**LANG, Andrew.** *Chronicles of Pantouflia.* 1981. Godine. 1st thus. ils Jeanne Tithering. F/NF. P2. $15.00

**LANG, Andrew.** *Cock Lane & Common-Sense.* (1894). Longman Gr. 8vo. 357+24p ads. gilt red cloth. VG. D1. $125.00

**LANG, Andrew.** *Letters to Dead Authors.* 1893. Scribner. 12mo. 253p. VG. F1. $20.00

**LANG, Andrew.** *Monk of Fife.* 1898. Longman. 7th. G+. P3. $25.00

**LANG, Andrew.** *Oxford.* 1916. London. Seeley Service. 1/355. 223p. VG. M10. $48.50

**LANG, Andrew.** *True Story Book.* (1893). Longman Gr. 2nd. 337p. aeg. bl brd. VG. D1. $85.00

**LANG, Daniel.** *Casualties of War.* 1969. McGraw Hill. 1st. 121p. VG/wrp. R11. $40.00

**LANG, H. Jack.** *Wit & Wisdom of Abraham Lincoln...* (1941). Greenburg. inscr. 265p. VG/dj. B10. $50.00

**LANG, John.** *Land of the Golden Trade: West Africa.* ca 1900. NY. Stokes. 8vo. ils/2 maps. 315p. VG (lacks 1 pl). H7. $12.50

**LANG, John.** *Land of the Golden Trade: West Africa.* ca 1915. London. Jack. 8vo. 315p. gr cloth. B20. $65.00

**LANG, Mrs. Andrew.** *Strange Story Book.* 1913. London. Longman Gr. 12 mc pl/ils HJ Ford. 313p. teg. 3-quarter morocco. B20. $150.00

**LANGDELL, C.C.** *Summary of Equity Pleading.* 1883. Cambridge. Chas Sever. 2nd. brn cloth. M11. $250.00

**LANGDON-BROWN, Walter.** *Thus We Are Men.* 1939. London. Paul Trench. 1st/2nd prt. VG. B27. $45.00

**LANGE, John;** see Crichton, Michael.

**LANGE, Oliver.** *Vandenberg.* 1971. Stein Day. VG/dj. P3. $15.00

**LANGFORD, Walter.** *Legends of Baseball.* 1987. Diamond. 1st. F/sans. P8. $30.00

**LANGGUTH, A.J.** *Noise of War: Ceasar, Pompey, Octavian & Struggle for Rome.* 1994. NY. ils. VG/dj. M17. $20.00

**LANGHEIN, Eric.** *Jefferson Davis, Patriot: Biography 1808-1865.* 1962. Vantage. 1st. NF/VG. A14. $21.00

**LANGHORNE, Dr.** *Fables of Flora.* 1804. Longworth. 9 full-p copper engravings. 70p. full leather. A10. $125.00

**LANGLEY, L.L.** *Contraception, Benchmark Papers in Human Physiology.* 1973. Stroudsburg, PA. 1st. 500p. A13. $50.00

**LANGLEY, Samuel Pierpont.** *Langley Memoir on Mechanical Flight.* 1911. Smithsonian. edit Chas Manly. ils. gilt gr cloth. VG. B11. $850.00

**LANGSTAFF, J. Brett.** *From Now to Adam: Peter Tompkins' Adventures in Bible.* 1928. Harper. 1st. 28 mc pl. gilt cloth. VG. B27. $65.00

**LANGSTAFF, John.** *Saint George & the Dragon: A Mummer's Play.* 1973. NY. Antheneum. 1st. sgn/dtd 1990. 8vo. NF/clip. C14. $25.00

**LANGSTON, Wallace R.** *Historical Record of the One Hundred 36th Anti-Aircraft...* 1945. Belgium. DeVoss-Van Kleef Ltd. 1st. 277p. VG. S16. $75.00

**LANGTON, Jane.** *Dark Nantucket Noon.* 1975. NY. Harper. 1st. F/dj. M15. $100.00

**LANGTON, Jane.** *Good & Dead.* 1986. NY. St Martin. 1st. F/dj. M15. $35.00

**LANGTON, Jane.** *Murder at the Gardner.* 1988. St Martin. 1st. VG/dj. G8. $35.00

**LANHAM, Uri.** *Bone Hunters.* 1973. Columbia. 1st. 8vo. 285p. brn cloth. dj. F7. $40.00

**LANIER, Sidney.** *Poems of Sidney Lanier.* 1906. Scribner. sm 8vo. 260p. VG. H1. $27.50

**LANIER, Sterling E.** *War for the Lot: A Tale of Fantasy & Terror.* 1969. Follett. 1st. ils. NF/VG+. S13. $25.00

**LANKES, J.J.** *Woodcut Manual.* ca 1935. NY. Crown. rpt. ils. 122p. lt tan cloth. B20. $40.00

**LANKS, Herbert C.** *By Pan American Highway Through South America.* 1942. NY. Appleton. 1st. 4to. xl. F3. $10.00

**LANKS, Herbert C.** *Highway to Alaska.* 1944. Appleton Century. 1st. photos. 200p. VG. H7. $20.00

**LANNER & LANNER.** *Pinon Pine: Natural & Cultural History.* 1981. Reno, NV. 8vo. 208p. F/dj. M12. $20.00

**LANNING, John.** *Pedro de la Torre: Doctor to Conquerors.* 1974. LSU. 1st. 145p. dj. F3. $25.00

**LANNING, John.** *18th-Century Enlightenment in U of San Carlos of Guatemala.* 1956. Ithaca. Cornell. 1st. 372p. F3. $20.00

**LANNING & LANNING.** *Texas Cowboys: Memories of Early Days.* 1984. TX A&M. ARC. photos. AN. J2. $125.00

**LANSDALE, Joe R.** *Act of Love.* 1989. London. Kinnell. 1st hc. VG/dj. L1. $50.00

**LANSDALE, Joe R.** *Act of Love.* 1989. London. Kinnell. 1st. sgn. author's 1st novel. AN/dj. S18. $80.00

**LANSDALE, Joe R.** *Bad Chili.* 1997. Mojo. 1/500. author's personal copy. ils John Picacio. AN/dj. S18. $65.00

**LANSDALE, Joe R.** *By Bizarre Hands.* 1989. Ziesing. 1st. sgn. An/dj. S18. $45.00

**LANSDALE, Joe R.** *Cold in July.* 1989. Zeising. 1st. sgn. F/dj. S18. $55.00

**LANSDALE, Joe R.** *Dead in the West.* 1990. London. Kinnell. 1st hc/1st UK. sgn. AN/dj. S18. $50.00

**LANSDALE, Joe R.** *Drive-In.* 1989. London. Kinnell. 1st hc/1st UK. sgn. AN/dj. S18. $55.00

**LANSDALE, Joe R.** *Magic Wagon.* 1988. Chivers. 1st. sgn. F/sans. S18. $100.00

**LANSDALE, Joe R.** *Mucho Mojo.* 1994. Mysterious. 1st. sgn. F/dj. S18. $45.00

**LANSDALE, Joe R.** *Razored Saddles.* 1989. Dark Harvest. 1st trade. sgn. AN/dj. M21. $40.00

**LANSDALE, Joe R.** *Savage Season.* 1990. Ziesing. 1st. sgn. F/dj. S18. $60.00

**LANSDALE, Joe R.** *Two Bear Mambo.* 1995. Mysterious. 1st. sgn. F/dj. S18. $35.00

**LANSDALE, Joe R.** *Writer of the Purple Sage.* 1994. Cemetray. 1st. 1/500. ils/sgn Mark A Nelson. AN/case. S18. $100.00

**LANSDALE & LANSDALE.** *Dark at Heart.* 1992. Dark Harvest. 1st. sgn. S18. $40.00

**LAPP, Ralph E.** *Man & Space: Next Decade.* nd. London. Scientific BC. 183p. K5. $13.00

**LAQUEUR, Walter Z.** *Communism & Nationalism in the Middle East.* 1956. London. RKP. 8vo. 362p. VG/dj. Q2. $33.00

**LARDNER, Dyonysius.** *Railway Economy: A Treatise...* 1850. NY. Harper. 142p. bstp cloth. G. B18. $125.00

**LARDNER, Ring.** *Love With a Smile.* 1933. Scribner. 1st. VG. P8. $175.00

**LARDNER, Ring.** *Ring Around the Bases.* 1992. Scribner. 1st. edit Matthew Brucolli. F/VG. P8. $27.50

**LARDNER, Ring.** *Say It With Oil.* 1923. NY. Doran. 1st. NF/dj. B2. $125.00

**LARDNER, Ring.** *Treat 'Em Rough.* 1918. Bobbs Merrill. 1st. G. P8. $65.00

**LARDNER, Ring.** *You Know Me Al.* 1925. Scribner. rpt. VG/G. P8. $45.00

**LARIAR, Lawrence.** *Win, Place & Die!* 1953. NY. Appleton Century. 1st. F/dj. M15. $45.00

**LARKIN, David.** *Art of Nancy Ekholm Burkert.* 1977. Peacock/Bantam. 1st. ils. F/wrp. M5. $30.00

**LARKIN, Margaret.** *Seven Shares in a Gold Mine.* 1960. London. Readers Union. ils. 213p. F3. $15.00

**LARKIN COMPANY.** *Good Things to Eat & How to Prepare Them.* c 1906. Buffalo, NY. ils. 70p. H6. $54.00

**LARKIN COMPANY.** *Good Things to Eat & How to Prepare Them.* 1908 (1907). 71p. flexible bdg. E6. $25.00

**LARMOTH, Jeanine.** *Murder on the Menu: Food & Drink in English Mystery Novel.* 1972. Scribner. 1st. VG/dj. P3. $25.00

**LAROM, Henry V.** *Mountain Pony: Story of the Wyoming Rockies.* 1946. Grosset Dunlap. VG/dj. B36. $13.00

**LARSEN, Larry.** *Mastering Largemouth Bass.* 1989. N Am Fishing Club. 1st. photos. 261p. VG. S14. $10.00

**LARSON, Edward.** *Trail & Error: American Controversy Over Creation...* 1985. NY. 1st. A13. $25.00

**LARSON, Kerry C.** *Whitman's Drama of Consensus.* 1988. Chicago. 1st. 269p. VG. M10. $18.50

**LARSON, Orvin.** *American Infidel: Robert G Ingersoll: A Biography.* 1962. Citadel. 1st. ils. 316p. VG/dj. B18. $15.00

**LARSON, T.A.** *Wyoming: Bicentennial History.* 1977. NY. photos/maps. 198p. F/dj. M4. $15.00

**LASCELLES, Mary.** *Jane Austen & Her Art.* 1954. OUP. gilt bl cloth. F/fair. F1. $35.00

**LASHLEY, Karl Spencer.** *Neuropsychology of Lashley: Selected Papers...* 1960. McGraw Hill. prt red cloth. VG/dj. G1. $75.00

**LASHNER, William.** *Hostile Witness.* 1995. Harper Collins. 1st. NF/NF. H11. $15.00

**LASORDA, Tommy.** *Artful Dodger.* 1985. Arbor. 1st. F/dj. P8. $25.00

**LASSNER, Jacob.** *Topography of Baghdad in the Early Middle Ages.* 1970. Detroit. Wayne State. 8 maps. 324p. quarter cloth/brd. VG/dj. Q2. $55.00

**LASSWELL, Harold Dwight.** *World Politics & Personal Insecurity.* 1935. McGraw Hill. 308p. blk cloth. G1. $65.00

**LATHAM, Hiram.** *Trans-Missouri Stock Raisings, Pasture Lands of N Am...* 1966. Old West Pub. 1st ltd. ils. VG. J2. $55.00

**LATHAM, Jean Lee.** *Carry on Bowditch.* 1955. Houghton Mifflin. 1st. sgn. 1958 Newbery. dk gr cloth. dj. R5. $300.00

**LATHBURY, Mary A.** *Idyls of the Months.* 1885. NY. Routledge. 4to. aeg. gray cloth. NF. B20. $375.00

**LATHEM, Emma.** *Ashes to Ashes.* 1971. Inner Sanctum. 1st. F/VG. M19. $17.50

**LATHEM, Emma.** *Going for the Gold.* 1981. S&S. 1st. F/dj. C15. $15.00

**LATHEM, Emma.** *Murder to Go.* 1969. S&S. 1st. F/dj. A23. $38.00

**LATHEM, Emma.** *Sweet & Low.* 1974. S&S. 1st. F/dj. A23. $34.00

**LATHROP, Dorothy P.** *Colt From Moon Mountain.* 1941. NY. 1st. 60p. unp. VG/dj. B18. $125.00

**LATHROP, Dorothy P.** *Hide & Go Seek.* 1938. Macmillan. 1st. teal cloth. mc dj. R5. $100.00

**LATHROP, Dorothy P.** *Presents for Lupe.* 1940. Macmillan. 1st. lg 4to. orange cloth. mc dj. R5. $110.00

**LATHROP, George Parsons.** *Study of Hawthorne.* 1876. Boston. Osgood. 1st. 1/2000. prt terra-cotta cloth. M24. $150.00

**LATTA, Frank.** *Handbook of Yokuts Indians.* (1977). Santa Cruz. Bear State Books. revised. ils. 765p. gilt cloth. D11. $100.00

**LAUCK, W.J.** *Political & Industrial Democracy, 1776-1926.* 1926. Funk Wagnall. 374p. VG. S5. $20.00

**LAUDE, G.A.** *Kansas Shorthorns.* 1920. Iola, KS. 1st. ils. 647p. B18. $45.00

**LAUFER, Berthold.** *Insect-Musicians & Cricket Champions of China.* 1927. Chicago. Field Mus. 1st. 8vo. 27p. VG+/prt wrp. B20. $45.00

**LAUFER, Berthold.** *Ostrich Egg-Shell Cups of Mesopotamia & Ostrich...* 1926. Field Mus Nat Hist. 9 pl. 50p. F/wrp. S15. $4.00

**LAUGHLIN, Clara E.** *Stories of Author's Loves.* 1902. Lippincott. 2 vol. 1st. gilt bl cloth. B20. $50.00

**LAUGHLIN, James.** *New Directions 12.* 1950. New Directions. 1st. 556p. NF/VG. R11. $35.00

**LAUGHLIN, James.** *Some Natural Things.* 1945. New Directions. 1st. F/VG. L3. $45.00

**LAURANCE & WOOD.** *Visual Optics & Sight Testing.* 1936. London. School of Optics. 4th. 458p. ES. cloth. VG. C14. $15.00

**LAURGAARD, Rachel Kelly.** *Patty Reed's Doll.* 1961. Caxton. 1st/3rd prt. ils Elizabeth S Michael. F. B27. $45.00

**LAUT, Agnes C.** *Blazed Trail of the Old Frontier.* 1926. McBride. 1st trade. ils after CM Russell/1 fld map. 271p. VG. B18. $95.00

**LAUT, Agnes C.** *Through Our Unknown Southwest.* 1925. NY. McBride. 5th. 8vo. gilt blk cloth. G+. F7. $22.50

**LAVATER, John.** *Essays on Physignomy.* 1797. London. trans from last Paris ed. ils. half red leather. VG. E6. $495.00

LAVAYSEE, M. *Statistical, Commercial & Political Description Venezuela.* 1969. Westport, CT. Negro U. rpt (1820 London). 479p. F3. $20.00

LAVENDER, David. *Let Me Be Free: Nez Perce Tragedy.* 1992. Harper Collins. AN/dj. A19. $30.00

LAVENDER, David. *River Runners of the Grand Canyon.* 1986. Tucson. 2nd. sm 4to. 147p. bl cloth. VG. F7. $35.00

LAVER, James. *Costume in the Theater.* 1964. Hill Wang. 8vo. ils. 212p. VG/dj. B20. $25.00

LAVER, James. *Stitch in Time; or, Pride Prevents a Fall.* 1927. London. Nonesuch. 1/1525. 4to. stiff wrp. F1. $20.00

LAVERY, Brian. *Nelson's Navy: Ships, Men & Organization 1793-1815.* 1997. Annapolis. Naval Inst. rpt. gilt gray cloth. F/dj. T11. $75.00

LAVINE, Emanuel H. *Gimme; or, How Politicians Get Rich.* 1931. Vanguard. 1st. 298p. VG+/dj. B20. $50.00

LAVINIA, R. *Donkey Detectives Davis.* 1955. Doubleday. ils. 220p. VG/dj. B36. $13.00

LAW, James. *Farmer's Veterinary Adviser.* 1880. Ithaca. self pub. 426p. cloth. A10. $10.00

LAW & LUTHER. *Rommel: Narrative & Pictorial History.* 1980. San Jose. 1st. 368p. VG. S16. $35.00

LAWDER, Douglas. *Trolling.* 1977. Boston. Little Brn. 1st. inscr. F/wrp. L3. $30.00

LAWES, Lewis E. *Meet the Murderer.* 1940. Harper. 1st. 8vo. 339p. F/NF. B20. $40.00

LAWING, N.N. *Alaska Nellie.* 1990. Lawing. photos/map. 202p. F. M4. $13.00

LAWRENCE, A.W. *Greek Architecture.* 1957. Harmondsworth, Eng. Penguin Ltd. 327p. NF. M7. $60.00

LAWRENCE, A.W. *TE Lawrence by His Friends.* 1954. London. Cape. New ed (2nd). gilt maroon buckram. NF/clip. M7. $65.00

LAWRENCE, D.H. *Collected Letters of...* 1962. Viking. 2 vol. 1st. gilt blk cloth. F/dj/case. F1. $55.00

LAWRENCE, D.H. *Complete Plays of...* 1965. Viking. 1st. VG/dj. B30. $45.00

LAWRENCE, D.H. *Etruscan Places.* 1932. London. 1st. photos. A15. $60.00

LAWRENCE, D.H. *Glad Ghosts.* 1926. London. Ernest Benn. 1st. 1/500. F/wrp. B2. $350.00

LAWRENCE, D.H. *Man Who Died.* 1931. London. 1st. partial dj. T9. $85.00

LAWRENCE, D.H. *Mornings in Mexico.* 1927. Knopf. 4th. VG/$2.50 dj price. S13. $35.00

LAWRENCE, D.H. *Pansies.* 1929. Knopf. 1st Am. F/G+. B4. $400.00

LAWRENCE, D.H. *Plumed Serpent.* 1926. London. 1st. VG. A15. $75.00

LAWRENCE, D.H. *Selected Letters.* 1958. FSG. 1st. VG/dj. B30. $35.00

LAWRENCE, D.H. *Selected Literary Criticism.* 1956. Viking. 1st. VG/dj. B30. $30.00

LAWRENCE, D.H. *Story of Doctor Manente.* 1929. Florence. Oironi. 1st. sgn/trans Lawrence. VG/wrp. L3. $650.00

LAWRENCE, D.H. *Tortises. Six Poems by...* 1983. Chelonidae. 1/10 (300). ils/sgn AJ Robinson. red goatskin. F/box. B24. $3,000.00

LAWRENCE, D.H. *Women in Love.* 1920. NY. private prt. 1/1250. VG. A15. $275.00

LAWRENCE, David Herbert. *Man Who Died.* 1992. Yolla Bolly. 1/30 (130). sgn Baskin/Fowles. w/extra suite prts. complete. AN. B24. $3,650.00

LAWRENCE, David. *Supreme Court; or, Political Puppets?* 1937. Appleton Century. M11. $35.00

LAWRENCE, Elizabeth Atwood. *His Very Silence Speaks.* 1989. Detroit, MI. Wayne State. AN/dj. A19. $30.00

LAWRENCE, George. *Adanson: Bicentennial of Michal Adanson's Families...* 1963 & 1965. Pittsburgh. Hunt. 2 vol. AN. A10. $55.00

LAWRENCE, George. *Catalog of the 2nd International Exhibition Botanical Art...* 1968. Pittsburgh. ils. 267p. F. B26. $15.00

LAWRENCE, George. *Taxonomy of Vascular Plants.* 1951. Macmillan. 1st. 823p. G. H10. $45.00

LAWRENCE, Liza. *Vistas at Eagle's Nest.* nd. Fredericksburg. photos. VG. B10. $15.00

LAWRENCE, Martha C. *Murder in Scorpio.* 1995. NY. St Martin. 1st. sgn. F/dj. A23. $36.00

LAWRENCE, Miriam B. *Flowers & Plants on United States Postage Stamps.* 1970. E Greenwich, RI. River's Edge Studio. mini. 1/500. 45p. stiff gr wrp. B24. $150.00

LAWRENCE, R. deTreville. *Jefferson & Wine. Vol III.* 1976. Plains, VA. sgn. ils. beige linen. F. B26. $20.00

LAWRENCE, Rae. *Satisfaction.* 1987. Poseidon. 1st. F/dj. T12. $15.00

LAWRENCE, Robert. *Lohengrin.* 1938. Grosset Dunlap. ils Alexandre Serebriakoff. VG. D4. $20.00

LAWRENCE, Starling. *Legacies.* 1996. FSG. 1st. F/dj. M23. $20.00

LAWRENCE, T.E. *Letters of...* 1939. Doubleday Doran. 1st. edit David Garnett. 16 pl/4 maps. 896p. VG. W1. $30.00

LAWRENCE, T.E. *Mint.* 1955. Doubleday. 1st thus. 1/1000. #d. F/NF case. M7. $125.00

LAWRENCE, T.E. *Odyssey of Homer.* 1932. OUP. 1st. 1st Am trade. VG/sans. L3. $65.00

LAWRENCE, T.E. *Revolt in the Desert.* 1927. NY. Doran. 1st Am. ils/1 fld map. 335p. cloth. VG. W1. $18.00

LAWRENCE, T.E. *Seven Pillars of Wisdom.* 1935. Garden City. 1st Am. VG. L3. $85.00

LAWRENCE, T.E. *TE Lawrence by His Friends.* 1937. London. Cape. 1st. F. L3. $75.00

LAWRENCE, T.E. *TE Lawrence: Selected Letters.* 1989. NY. Norton. 1st Am. F/dj. Q1. $35.00

LAWRENCE, William R. *Extracts From Diary & Correspondence of Late Amos Lawrence.* 1855. Gould Lincoln. 369p. G. S17. $8.50

LAWSON, J. Gilchrist. *Greatest Thoughts About the Bible.* 1918. Standard. 205p. VG. B29. $7.50

LAWSON, Robert. *Captain Kidd's Cat.* 1956. Little Brn. 4th. 8vo. 152p. NF/tattered. C14. $18.00

LAWSON, Robert. *Dick Whittington & His Cat.* 1949. LEC. 1/2500. sgn Lawson/Jean Hersholt (edit). tall 4to. orange cloth. R5. $150.00

LAWSON, Robert. *I Discover Columbus.* 1941. Little Brn. 1st. 8vo. turquoise cloth. pict dj. R5. $150.00

LAWSON, Robert. *Mr Wilmer.* 1945. Boston. Little Brn. 1st. 8vo. yel cloth. mc pict dj. R5. $125.00

LAWSON, Robert. *Rabbit Hill.* 1944. Viking. 1st. ils. decor cloth. G. T11. $20.00

LAWSON, Robert. *Smeller Martin.* 1950. Viking. 1st. 8vo. gr cloth. mc pict dj. R5. $125.00

LAWSON, Robert. *Tough Winter.* 1954. Viking. 1st. 8vo. bl cloth. VG/dj. D1. $60.00

LAWSON, Robert. *Tough Winter.* 1954. Viking. 1st. 8vo. gray-bl cloth. F/mc dj. R5. $150.00

LAWTON, A.T. *Window in the Sky: Astronomy From Beyond...* 1979. NY. Pergamon. 1st Am. 8vo. F/dj. A2. $15.00

LAYCOCK, George. *Alien Animals: Story of Imported Wildlife.* 1966. Nat Hist Pr. photos. 240p. VG/dj. S15. $10.00

**LAYCOCK, George.** *Wild Bears...Grizzly, Brown & Black Bears.* 1980. Outdoor Life. ils/biblio/index. 272p. F. A17. $25.00

**LAYLANDER, O.J.** *Whittlings.* 1928. Cedar Rapids. Torch. sgn. 174p. dk gr cloth. F/NF/case. F1. $25.00

**LAYMAN, Lloyd.** *Fire Fighting Tactics.* 1967. Boston. Natl Fire Protection Assn. ils/photos. VG+. H7. $15.00

**LAYMON, Richard.** *Bite.* 1996. London. Headline. 1st. sgn. F/dj. T2. $45.00

**LAYMON, Richard.** *Flesh.* 1987. London. WH Allen. 1st. sgn. F/dj. T2. $100.00

**LAYMON, Richard.** *In the Dark.* 1994. London. Headline. 1st. sgn. F/dj. T2. $50.00

**LAYMON, Richard.** *Midnight's Lair.* 1993. St Martin. 1st. F/dj. P3. $20.00

**LAYNE, McAvoy.** *How Audie Murphy Died in Vietnam.* 1973. Doubleday/Anchor. wrp. R11. $60.00

**LAYTON, T.A.** *Wine & Food Society's Guide to Cheese & Cheese Cookery.* 1967. Cleveland Wine & Food. 1st Am. VG/G. A2. $15.00

**LAZAREV, V.N.** *Novgorodian Icon Painting.* 1969. Moscow. Iskusstvo. Russian/Eng texts. 76 mc pl. dj. D2. $70.00

**LAZARUS, Richard.** *Letters From Colombia.* 1984. Cincinnati. 1st. photos. 130p. F3. $10.00

**LAZELL, J.D.** *Wildlife of the Florida Keys: A Natural History.* 1989. WA Island. ils. 253p. F/wrp. M12. $22.50

**LAZZARO, G. DiSan.** *Homage to Henri Matisse.* 1970. NY. Tudor. Special issue. 4to. w/orig linocut. F. F1. $100.00

**LE BLANC, Georgette.** *Blue Bird for Children.* 1914. Silver Burdett. 182p. VG. B18. $35.00

**Le BRITTON, John.** *Britton (on Laws of England). The Second Edition...* 1640. London. xl-Newberry Lib. modern 3-quarter morocco. M11. $850.00

**LE CAIN, Errol.** *White Cat.* 1973. NY. Bradbury. 1st Am. 32p. VG/dj. D4. $45.00

**LE CARRE, John.** *Honourable Schoolboy.* 1977. Knopf. 1st. NF/NF. H11. $25.00

**LE CARRE, John.** *Incongruous Spy.* 1963. NY. Walker. 1st Omnibus. VG+/VG clip. A14. $21.00

**LE CARRE, John.** *Little Drummer Girl.* 1983. Knopf. 1st. F/F. H11. $45.00

**LE CARRE, John.** *Little Drummer Girl.* 1983. London. Hodder Stoughton. 1st. sgn. F/dj. M15. $150.00

**LE CARRE, John.** *Looking-Glass War.* 1965. London. Heinemann. 1st. NF/clip. A14. $105.00

**LE CARRE, John.** *Naive & Sentimental Lover.* 1971. Hodder Stoughton. 1st. NF/clip. A14. $70.00

**LE CARRE, John.** *Night Manager.* 1993. Knopf. 1st. F/F. H11. $20.00

**LE CARRE, John.** *Our Game.* 1995. Hodder Stoughton. 1st. 1/about 1000. NF/dj. A14. $280.00

**LE CARRE, John.** *Our Game.* 1995. Knopf. 1st trade. 302p. F/dj. W2. $30.00

**LE CARRE, John.** *Perfect Spy.* 1986. Knopf. 1st. F/NF. H11. $20.00

**LE CARRE, John.** *Russia House.* 1989. Knopf. 1st. NF/F. H11. $25.00

**LE CARRE, John.** *Russia House.* 1989. London Ltd Ed. 1st. 1/250. sgn. special bdg. F/glassine. M15. $200.00

**LE CARRE, John.** *Russia House.* 1989. London. 1st. sgn. dj. T9. $75.00

**LE CARRE, John.** *Secret Pilgrim.* 1991. Viking. 1st. F/F. H11. $35.00

**LE CARRE, John.** *Small Town in Germany.* 1968. Coward McCann. 1st Am. F/dj. C15. $45.00

**LE CARRE, John.** *Small Town in Germany.* 1968. Coward McCann. 1st Am. VG/dj. M20. $27.00

**LE CARRE, John.** *Small Town in Germany.* 1968. Coward McCann. 1st. NF/NF. H11. $30.00

**LE CARRE, John.** *Small Town in Germany.* 1968. London. Heinemann. 1st issue (plain rear dj panel prt 30s net). VG+/dj. A14. $87.50

**LE CARRE, John.** *Smiley's People.* 1980. Knopf. 1st Am. F/dj. N4. $30.00

**LE CARRE, John.** *Spy Who Came in From the Cold.* 1964. Coward McCann. 1st. NF/VG. H11. $25.00

**LE CARRE, John.** *Tailor of Panama.* 1996. Hodder Stoughton. 1st. sgn. NF/dj. A14. $70.00

**LE CARRE, John.** *Tailor of Panama.* 1996. London. Hodder Stoughton. 1st. sgn. F/dj. M15. $100.00

**LE CARRE, John.** *Tinker, Tailor, Soldier, Spy.* 1974. London. Hodder Stoughton. 1st. F/clip. M15. $100.00

**LE CARRE, John.** *Tinker, Taylor, Soldier, Spy.* 1974. Knopf. 1st. 355p. F/dj. D4. $50.00

**LE CONTE, Joseph N.** *High Sierra of California.* 1907. Am Alpine Club. ils/fld map. 16p. prt wrp. D11. $150.00

**LE CORBEAU, Adrien.** *Forest Giant.* 1924. London. Cape. 1st. trans TE Lawrence. 158p. G/poor. M7. $50.00

**LE CORBUSIER.** *Towards a New Architecture.* ca 1928. NY. Brewer Warren. 1st Am. lg 8vo. 290p. peach cloth. K1. $200.00

**LE FLEMING, Christopher.** *Peter Rabbit Music Books, Book II: 6 Easy Duets.* 1935. London. J&W Chester. ils/fwd Beatrix Potter. VG. M20. $125.00

**LE GALLIENNE, Richard.** *Love Letters of the King.* 1901. Little Brn. 1st. 8vo. 282+2p ads. gilt gr cloth. NF. J3. $50.00

**LE GALLIENNE, Richard.** *Old Country House.* 1902. Harper. 144p. leather spine. A10. $25.00

**LE GALLIENNE, Richard.** *Romance of Zion Chapel.* 1898. Bodley Head. 3rd. sgn. 297p. blk cloth. F1. $45.00

**LE GEAR.** *List of Geographical Atlases in Lib of Congress...* nd. Vols 5-9. 1/150. 2805p. F. A4. $325.00

**LE GEAR.** *United States Atlases: A List of Atlases...* nd. 2 vol in 1. 1/150. rpt. 767p. F. A4. $85.00

**LE GUIN, Ursula K.** *Dispossessed.* 1986. Easton. 1st thus. 1/300. AN. M21. $40.00

**LE GUIN, Ursula K.** *Fisherman of the Inland Sea.* 1994. Harper Prism. 1st. sgn. F/dj. R14. $35.00

**LE GUIN, Ursula K.** *Malafrena.* 1979. Putnam. 1st. F/dj. A24. $30.00

**LE GUIN, Ursula K.** *Searoad: Chronicles of Klatsand.* 1991. Harper Collins. 1st. sgn. F/dj. R14. $35.00

**LE MAY, Alan.** *One of Us Is a Murderer.* 1930. Crime Club. VG. P3. $20.00

**LE MAY, Alan.** *Searchers.* 1954. NY. Harper. 1st. 8vo. 272p. F/NF. B20. $200.00

**LE PRAT, Therese.** *Le Masque et l'Humain.* 1959. Paris. La Combe. 1st. VG/dj. S9. $175.00

**LE QUEUX, William.** *Bond of Black.* 1899. London. FV White. 1st. VG. M15. $135.00

**LE ROY, Mervyn.** *It Takes More Than Talent.* 1953. Knopf. 1st. VG/dj. C9. $42.00

**LEA, F.A.** *Tragic Philosopher: A Study of Friedrich Nietzsche.* 1957. NY. Philosophical Lib. VG/dj. M17. $17.50

**LEA, Homer.** *Valor of Ignorance.* Aug 1943. Harper. not 1st. 249p. F/G. H1. $12.00

**LEA, R.G.** *History of the Practice of Medicine in Prince Edward Island.* 1964. Prince Edward Island. 1st. 112p. A13. $45.00

**LEA, Reba Fitzpatrick.** *Belfield Fitzpatricks & Elim Colemans: History & Genealogy.* 1958. Lynchburg. Brn Morrison. ils/charts. 469p. VG. B10. $50.00

**LEA, Tom.** *Brave Bulls.* 1949. Little Brn. ARC/1st. RS. F/dj. S9. $150.00

**LEA, Tom.** *Hands of Cantu.* 1964. Little Brn. 1st. w/sgn leaf. F/NF. B2. $100.00

**LEA, Tom.** *Hands of Cantu.* 1964. Little Brn. 1st. yel cloth. F/VG clip. T11. $45.00

**LEA, Tom.** *King Ranch.* 1957. Boston. Little Brn. 2 vol. 838p. pict ep. VG/case. B18. $75.00

**LEA, Tom.** *Old Mount Franklin.* (1968). El Paso Electric Co. 1/150 (450 total). prt/sgn Carl Hertzog. cloth. D11. $100.00

**LEAB, Daniel J.** *From Sambo to Superspade: Black Experience...* 1975. Boston. inscr. photos. 301p. F. B14. $55.00

**LEACH, Brownie.** *Kentucky Derby Diamond Jubilee, 1875-1949.* 1949. NY. 1st. 192p. F. A17. $25.00

**LEACH, D.E.** *Northern Colonial Frontier 1607-1763.* 1966. NY. ils/map. F. M4. $25.00

**LEACH, David G.** *Rhododendrons of the World & How to Grow Them.* 1961. NY. 544p. F/torn. B26. $60.00

**LEACH, Linda York.** *Indian Miniature Paintings & Drawings.* 1986. Cleveland Mus Art/IU. ils/pl. 324p. cloth. F/dj. D2. $75.00

**LEACOCK, Stephen.** *Moonbeams From the Larger Lunacy.* 1915. NY. John Lane. 1st. 282p. G. G11. $15.00

**LEACOCK, Stephen.** *Other People's Money.* nd. Royal Trust Co. later prt. NF. A26. $50.00

**LEADBEATER, Mary.** *Memoirs & Letters of Richard & Elizabeth Shackleton...* 1823. NY. Samuel Wood. 12mo. 318p. xl. G. V3. $40.00

**LEAF, Munro.** *Arithmetic Can Be Fun.* 1949. Lippincott. 1st stated. ils. VG. M5. $10.00

**LEAF, Munro.** *Lucky You.* 1955. Lippincott. 1st. 4to. 48p. red cloth. dj. R5. $125.00

**LEAF, Munro.** *Madeline & the Bad Hat.* 1956. NY. Viking. 1/985. sm folio. 54p. gr cloth. R5. $485.00

**LEAF, Munro.** *Madeline & the Gypsies.* 1959. Viking. 1st. 4to. gr cloth. pict dj. R5. $375.00

**LEAF, Munro.** *Noodle.* 1937. Stokes. 1st. sgn ffe. obl 4to. tan cloth. R5. $300.00

**LEAF, Munro.** *Turnabout.* 1967. Lippincott. 1st. 8vo. sgn pres w/drawing. yel cloth. dj. R5. $275.00

**LEAF, Munro.** *War-Time Handbook for Young Americans.* 1942. Stokes. 1st. 64p. red cloth. VG+. B20. $35.00

**LEAF, Munro.** *Wee Gillis.* 1938. Viking. 1st. sgn. ils Robert Lawson. Scotch plaid brd. dj. R5. $175.00

**LEAKEY, L.S.** *Animals in Africa.* 1956. London. Harvill. VG. A19. $30.00

**LEAMING, Barbara.** *Bette Davis.* 1992. NY. S&S. 397p. VG/dj. C5. $12.50

**LEAMING, Thomas.** *Philadelphia Lawyer in London Courts.* 1911. NY. Holt. 1st. 8vo. 199p. gilt red cloth. B20. $30.00

**LEAR, Edward.** *Dong With a Luminous Nose.* 1969. NY. Young Scott Books. 1st thus. ils/sgn Edward Gorey. unp. mauve cloth. F/dj. J3. $75.00

**LEAR, Edward.** *History of Four Little Children Who Went Round the World.* 1967. Harlin Quist. 1st thus. ils Stanley Mack. VG/G. P2. $15.00

**LEAR, Edward.** *Jumblies.* (1969). NY. Adama Books. ils Edward Gorey. unp. NF. T5. $25.00

**LEAR, Edward.** *Nonsense ABCs.* 1931. Rand McNally. 12mo. ils. VG. M10. $9.50

**LEAR, Edward.** *Nonsense Songs.* nd. London/NY. Warne. later prt. ils Leslie Brooke. aeg. pict cloth. VG. B18. $45.00

**LEAR, Edward.** *Pelican Chorus & Other Nonsense Verses.* 1899?. London. Warne. 1st. 8vo. all edges orange. pict brd. R5. $250.00

**LEAR, Peter;** see Lovesey, Peter.

**LEARSI, R.** *Jews of America: A History.* 1954. Cleveland. 382p. G/poor. M4. $10.00

**LEARY, Timothy.** *Interpersonal Diagnosis of Personality...* 1957. NY. Ronald. 1st. NF/dj. B4. $450.00

**LEARY, Timothy.** *Mindmirror.* 1986. San Mateo, CA. Electronic Arts. inscr. w/17p manual+disk. O11. $125.00

**LEARY, Timothy.** *Politics of Ecstasy.* 1968. Putnam. 1st. 8vo. NF/dj. S9. $175.00

**LEARY, Timothy.** *Psychedelic Experience: A Manual...* 1964. U Books. VG. R8. $110.00

**LEARY, William M.** *Aviation's Golden Age.* 1989. Iowa City. 1st. ils. 201p. VG. B18. $25.00

**LEASOR, James.** *War at the Top.* 1959. Michael Joseph. 1st. VG/dj. P3. $30.00

**LEAVITT, David.** *Equal Affections.* 1989. Weidenfeld Nicolson. 1st. sgn. F/dj. R14. $45.00

**LEAVITT, David.** *Lost Language of Cranes.* 1986. Knopf. 1st. author's 1st novel. F/dj. O11. $40.00

**LEAVITT, David.** *Lost Language of Cranes.* 1986. Knopf. 1st. inscr. VG/dj. C9. $90.00

**LEAVITT, David.** *While England Sleeps.* 1993. Viking. 1st. F/dj. O11. $60.00

**LEAVITT, Nancy.** *Road Alphabet.* 1993. Stillwater, ME. mini. 1/26. calligraphic bdg manuscript+panorama. 14p. B24. $150.00

**LEAVY, Herbert.** *Successful Small Farms.* 1978. Farmington, MI. 188p. A10. $22.00

**LEBLANC, Maurice.** *Golden Triangle: Return of Arsene Lupin.* 1917. NY. 1st Am. NF. M15. $85.00

**LEBOYER, Frederick.** *Birth Without Violence.* 1975. Knopf. 2nd. 115p. VG. P12. $10.00

**LECHNER & LECHNER.** *World of Salt Shakers.* 1982. Collector Books. 2nd. 52 mc pl. 127p. glossy wrp. H1. $30.00

**LECKIE, William H.** *Buffalo Soldiers: A Narrative of Negro Calvary in West.* 1967. Norman, OK. 3rd. 290p. E1. $35.00

**LECKY, E.** *Story of Jack the Cat.* 1890. NY. Thomas Nelson. 12mo. all edges red. pict brd. R5. $100.00

**LECOURT, Dominique.** *Proletarian Science? Case of Lysenko.* 1977. NY. 1st Eng trans. 165p. A13. $25.00

**LECZOWSKI, George.** *Middle East in World Affairs.* 1952. NY. Cornell. 8 maps. 459p. cloth. VG/torn. Q2. $36.50

**LEDERMAN, Leon.** *God Particle: If the Universe Is the Answer...* 1993. Boston. VG/dj. M17. $15.00

**LEE, Brian North.** *Early Printed Book Labels.* 1976. London. 1st. dj. T9. $28.00

**LEE, Cazenove Gardner Jr.** *Lee Chronicle: Studies of Early Generations of Lees of VA.* 1957. NY U. ils. 411p. VG. B10. $75.00

**LEE, Chang-Rae.** *Native Speaker.* 1995. NY. Riverhead. 1st. author's 1st book. PEN/Hemingway Award. F/dj. R14. $40.00

**LEE, Gus.** *China Boy.* 1991. Dutton. 1st. sgn. F/F. B3. $50.00

**LEE, Gypsy Rose.** *Mother Finds a Body.* 1945. World. 312p. G. P12. $10.00

**LEE, Harper.** *To Kill a Mocking Bird: 35th-Anniversary Edition.* 1995. Harper Collins. 1st thus/later prt. sgn. F/dj. Q1. $375.00

**LEE, J.** *Fighter Facts & Fallacies.* 1943 (1942). G/dj. E6. $12.00

**LEE, James Ward.** *Classics of Texas Fiction.* 1987. E-Heart. 1st. 197p. F/VG. A4. $95.00

**LEE, Jay M.** *Artilleryman.* 1920. Kansas City, MO. 1st. ils. 359p. B18. $150.00

**LEE, Jennette.** *Uncle William: Man Who Was Shif'less.* 1908. Century. ils. 298p. VG. P12. $10.00

**LEE, Judith Yaross.** *Garrison Keillor, a Voice of America.* 1991. U MS. 1st. 230p. F/dj. T11. $35.00

**LEE, Laurel.** *Mourning Into Dancing.* 1982. Dutton. 1st. gilt bl cloth. VG/dj. P12. $10.00

**LEE, Laurie.** *Illustrated Cider With Rosie.* 1984. London. 1st. sgn. dj. T9. $65.00

**LEE, Li-Young.** *Winged Seed.* 1995. S&S. 1st. sgn. F/dj. O11. $20.00

**LEE, Lilian.** *Farewell to My Concubine.* 1993. NY. Morrow. 1st. F/dj. H11. $25.00

**LEE, Linsey.** *Edible Wild Plants of Martha's Vineyard.* 1975. Martha's Vineyard. ils/recipes/index. 88p. sc. B26. $12.50

**LEE, Mabel Barbee.** *Cripple Creek Days.* 1959. Doubleday. VG/dj. A19. $30.00

**LEE, Marshall.** *Books of Our Time, 1951.* 1951. NY. OUP. ils. 120p. VG. M10. $12.50

**LEE, Mary Catherine.** *Quaker Girl of Nantucket.* 1917. Houghton Mifflin. xl. G+. P12. $15.00

**LEE, Melicent Humason.** *Marcos: A Mountain Boy of Mexico.* 1937. Whitman Jr Pr Book. ils Hader. 80p. G-. P12. $12.00

**LEE, Mrs. N.K.M.** *Cook's Own Book.* 1972. Arno. G/dj. A16. $10.00

**LEE, Nell Moore.** *Patriot Above Profit: Portrait of Thomas Nelson, Jr...* 1988. Rutledge Hill. 1st. photos/maps/index. 640p. VG/dj. S16. $27.50

**LEE, Powder River Jack.** *Stampede & Tales of the Far West.* (1938). Greensburg. private prt. 8vo. 154p. G. P4. $25.00

**LEE, Powder River Jack.** *Stampede & Tales of the Far West.* nd. Standardized Pr. sgn. ils/photos. VG. J2. $125.00

**LEE, Raymond.** *Not So Dumb: Animals in the Movies.* 1970. Castle. 238p. VG/G. P12. $10.00

**LEE, Richard M.** *General Lee's City: An Illustrated Guide...* 1987. EMP PUb. 1st. NF/wrp. A14. $10.50

**LEE, Robert.** *Lectures on the Theory & Practice of Midwifery.* 1844. Phil. 1st. lg 8vo. 544p+catalog of medical books. full leather. E6. $75.00

**LEE, Sherman E.** *History of Far Eastern Art.* 1964. Prentice Hall. ils. VG/dj. M17. $40.00

**LEE, Stan.** *You Don't Say.* 1963. Non-Pariel Pub. ils. G+. P12. $10.00

**LEE, Vernon.** *In Praise of Old Gardens.* 1912. Portland, ME. Mosher. F/dj/case. H7. $85.00

**LEE, Vincent.** *Chanasuyu: Ruins of the Inca Vilcabamba.* 1989. Wilson, WY. 1st. sgn. 108p. wrp. F3. $25.00

**LEE, Vincent.** *Investigations in Bolivia.* 1992. Wilson, WY. 1st. sgn. 105p. wrp. F3. $25.00

**LEE, W.S.** *Green Mountains of Vermont.* 1955. NY. 1st. photos. 318p. F/torn. M4. $25.00

**LEE, W.S.** *Sierra.* NY. Putnam.. 1st. ils Edward Sanborn. 1st. VG/dj. O4. $15.00

**LEE, Wayne C.** *Bat Masterson.* 1960. Whitman. ils Adam Szwejkowski. 282p. VG. P12. $10.00

**LEE, Wayne C.** *Slugging Backstop.* 1957. Dodd Mead. 1st. VG/dj. P8. $65.00

**LEE, William;** see Burroughs, William S.

**LEE & VAN HECKE.** *Gangsters & Hoodlums: The Underworld in the Cinema.* 1971. AS Barnes. 1st. 264p. NF/dj. B20. $25.00

**LEEBRON, Fred G.** *Out West.* 1996. Doubleday. 1st. author's 1st book. F/F. H11. $25.00

**LEEMANN-VAN ELCK.** *Die Zurcherische Buchillustration Von Den Anfangen...* 1952. Zurich. 1/850. 4to. ils. 253p. VG. A4. $165.00

**LEEMING, Joseph.** *Papercraft: How to Make Toys, Favors & Useful Articles.* 1949. Lippincott. 1st. ils. VG. M5. $10.00

**LEEN, Edward.** *Holy Ghost & His Work in Souls.* 1939. Sheed Ward. 341p. G. H10. $15.00

**LEES, Gene.** *Waiting for Dizzy.* 1991. NY. OUP. 1st. F/dj. Q1. $30.00

**LEFCOURT, Peter.** *Dreyfus Affair.* 1992. Random. later prt. F/dj. P8. $10.00

**LEFEBURE, V.** *Riddle of the Rhine.* 1921. London. VG. E6. $12.00

**LEFEVRE, Edwin.** *Man Who Won.* 1970. Enkhuizen, Holland. mini. ils JR Levien. 61p. cloth/prt spine label. F. B24. $150.00

**LEFEVRE, Felicite.** *Clock, the Mouse & the Red Hen: An Old Tale Retold.* nd. Phil. Macrae Smith. 15th prt. unp. G. C14. $14.00

**LEFFINGWELL, William Bruce.** *Art of Wing Shooting: Practical Treatise...* 1895. Rand McNally. 1st. ils. 190+40P. red cloth. NF. H7. $95.00

**LEGLER, Henry Eduard.** *Walt Whitman: Yesterday & Today.* 1916. Chicago. Bros of Book. 1st. 1/600 on Fabriano. 8vo. 72p. NF/dj. J3. $125.00

**LEHANE, Dennis.** *Drink Before the War.* 1994. Harcourt Brace. 1st. F/NF. M23. $45.00

**LEHANE, Dennis.** *Sacred.* 1997. Morrow. 1st. sgn. F/dj. A23. $40.00

**LEHANE, Dennis.** *Take My Hand.* 1996. Morrow. 1st. sgn. F/dj. A23. $42.00

**LEHMAN, Anthony L.** *Paul Landacre: A Life & a Legacy.* 1983. Dawson's Book Shop. 198p. cloth. D11. $150.00

**LEHMAN, David.** *Perfect Murder: Study in Detection; a Guide...* 1989. NY. VG/dj. M17. $15.00

**LEHMAN, Rosamund.** *Orion. Vol II.* 1945. London. Nicholson Watson. 1st. 8vo. gilt red buckram. F. M7. $35.00

**LEHMANN, Lotte.** *Midway in Song.* 1938. Bobbs Merrill. 250p. xl. G. C5. $12.50

**LEHMANN, V.W.** *Forgotten Legions: Sheep in the Rio Grande Plain of TX.* 1969. TX Western. 1st trade. ils/notes/index. 226p. NF/VG. B19. $45.00

**LEHMERT, Donald J.** *River Basin Survey Papers No 7. Archeological Investigation.* 1954. GPO. map/fld chart. 190p. VG. S5. $22.00

**LEHNER, Ernst.** *Alphabets & Ornaments.* 1952. NY/Cleveland. World. 1st. 4to. 256p. F/dj. O10. $65.00

**LEHRER, Jim.** *Kick the Can.* 1988. Putnam. 1st. F/NF. M23. $20.00

**LEIB, Franklin Allen.** *Fire Arrow.* 1988. Presidio. F/NF. P3. $20.00

**LEIBER, Fritz.** *Specter Is Haunting Texas.* 1969. Walker. 1st. G/dj. L1. $65.00

**LEIBERMAN, Herbert.** *Night Call From a Distant Time Zone.* 1982. NY. Crown. 1st. F/F. H11. $25.00

**LEIBERMAN, Herbert.** *Sandman, Sleep.* 1993. NY. SMP. 1st. F/F. H11. $20.00

**LEIBY, James.** *Charity & Correction in New Jersey: A History...* 1967. New Brunswick. VG/dj. M11. $45.00

**LEICHTENTRITT, Hugo.** *Serge Koussevitzky.* 1947. Cambridge. Harvard. 199p. G. C5. $12.50

**LEICHTER, Howard.** *Comparative Approach to Policy Analysis: Health Care...* 1979. London. 1st. 326p. A13. $30.00

**LEIGH, Clara.** *Glimpses of South America: A Log.* 1924. Chicago. Ye Cloister Print Shop. 1st. 62p. F3. $15.00

**LEIGH, E.G.** *Adaption & Diversity: Natural History & Mathematics...* 1971. Freeman. 8vo. ils/photos. decor cloth. F. M12. $15.00

**LEIGH, Janet.** *Psycho: Behind the Scenes of the Classic Thriller.* 1995. Harmony. 1st. sgn. VG/dj. L1. $50.00

**LEIGH FERMOR, Patrick.** *Between the Woods & the Water.* 1986. London. 1st. sgn. dj. T9. $75.00

**LEIGHTON, Clare.** *Four Hedges: A Gardener's Chronicle.* 1935. NY. Macmillan. 1st. VG/dj. B5. $27.50

**LEIGHTON, Clare.** *Sometime — Never.* 1939. Macmillan. 1st. tall 8vo. 178p. VG/dj. J3. $95.00

**LEIGHTON, Clare.** *Tempestuous Petticoat: The Story.* 1947. Rinehart. 1st. 8vo. 272p. lime-gr cloth. VG/dj. J3. $75.00

**LEIGHTON, Margaret.** *Canyon Castaways.* 1966. FSG. 1st. VG/dj. B36. $22.00

**LEIGHTON & LEIGHTON.** *Navaho Door: Introduction to Navaho Life.* 1945. Harvard. 2nd. ils. 149p. NF. B19. $30.00

**LEIMBACH, Marti.** *Diving Young.* 1990. Doubleday. 1st. author's 1st book. F/F. H11. $20.00

**LEINHARD, L.G.** *Nectar From Below: Technique of Locating Underground Water.* 1977. NY. Vantage. 1st. ils. 35p. VG/dj. H10. $15.00

**LEINSTER, Murray;** see Jenkins, Will F.

**LEITHAUSER, Brad.** *Hence.* 1989. Knopf. 1st. NF/dj. M21. $20.00

**LEITHAUSER, Joachim.** *World Beyond the Horizon.* 1955. Knopf. 1st. 412p. dj. F3. $20.00

**LEITNER, Irving A.** *Pear Shaped Hill.* 1960. Golden. 1st A ed. 8vo. ils. VG+/tattered. M5. $12.00

**LEITNER, Konradi.** *Hypnotism for Professionals.* 1953. STravon. 1st. G/dj. R8. $15.00

**LEJEUNE, Anthony.** *CA Lejeune Film Reader.* 1991. Manchester. Carcanet. 365p. VG/dj. C5. $20.00

**LEJEUNE, Anthony.** *Strange & Private War.* 1987. Crime Club. 1st. VG/dj. P3. $15.00

**LEKSELL, Lars.** *Stereotaxis & Radiosurgery.* 1971. Springfield. Thomas. 69p. dj. G7. $125.00

**LELAND, Christopher T.** *Mrs Randall.* 1987. Houghton Mifflin. 1st. F/F. H11. $15.00

**LELCHUCK, Alan.** *On Home Ground.* 1987. Gulliver. 1st. F/VG+. P8. $20.00

**LEMAITRE, Jules.** *On the Margins of Old Books.* 1929. Coward McCann. 1/265. tall 8vo. 322p. F. F1. $50.00

**LEMAITRE DE RUFFIEU, Francois.** *Handbook of Riding Essentials.* 1987. Harper Row. 1st/2nd prt. VG/dj. O3. $25.00

**LEMANN, Nancy.** *Lives of the Saints.* 1985. Knopf. 1st. F/F. H11. $30.00

**LEMARCHAND, Elizabeth.** *Alibi for a Corpse.* 1969. London. Hart Davis. 1st. F/clip. M15. $45.00

**LEMARCHAND, Elizabeth.** *Change for the Worse.* 1980. London. Piatkus. 1st. F/dj. M15. $45.00

**LEMARCHAND, Elizabeth.** *Death of an Old Girl.* 1967. Walker. 1st Am. VG/NF. G8. $15.00

**LEMARCHAND, Elizabeth.** *Glade Manor Murder.* 1988. Walker. 1st Am. F/dj. G8. $22.50

**LEMCKE, Gisine.** *European & American Cookery.* 1895. 1st. 609p. E6. $60.00

**LEMON, Lee T.** *Partial Critics.* 1965. OUP. 1st. NF/VG. O4. $10.00

**LEMON, Mark.** *Legends of Number Nip.* 1864. London. Macmillan. 1st. sm 8vo. teg. yel calf. G. S17. $50.00

**LEMONOFIDES, Dino.** *British Cavalry Standards.* 1971. London. Almark. 1st. ils/pl. VG/stiff wrp. S16. $17.50

**LEMPIERE, W.** *Popular Lectures on Study of Natural History...* (1830). London. Whittaker Treacher. 2nd. 8vo. quarter leather. VG+. M12. $95.00

**LENCZOWSKI, George.** *Middle East in World Affairs.* 1953. NY. Cornell. 2nd. 8 maps. 459p. VG. W1. $18.00

**LENHOFF & LENHOFF.** *Hydra & the Birth of Experimental Biology-1744...* 1986. Pacific Grove. Boxwood pr. 280p. VG. A17. $30.00

**LENNON, John.** *Skywrighting by Word of Mouth, Including Ballad...* 1986. NY. Harper. 1st. AN/dj. B14. $60.00

**LENNOX, Charlotte Ramsey.** *Female Quixote; or, Adventures of Arabella...* 1810. London. 2 vol. new ed. 12mo. full tan calf. H13. $395.00

**LENNOX, Charlotte Ramsey.** *Memoirs for History of Madame deMaintenon & the Last Age.* 1757. London. 5 vol. 1st. 12mo. full early speckled calf. H13. $595.00

**LENNOX, John.** *Margaret Laurence.* 1993. McClelland Stewart. 1st. NF/VG. P3. $40.00

**LENS, Sidney.** *Forging of the American Empire: From Revolution to Vietnam.* 1971. NY. Crowell. 1st. 462p. NF/dj. R11. $22.00

**LENSKI, Lois.** *Blue Ridge Billy.* (1946). Lippincott. 1st. 8vo. aqua cloth. pict dj. R5. $110.00

**LENSKI, Lois.** *Little Airplane.* 1938. OUP. 1st. sq 8vo. beige cloth. VG. D1. $60.00

**LENSKI, Lois.** *Little Engine That Could.* 1941. Book House for Children. 24mo. mc pict paper wrp. R5. $45.00

**LENSKI, Lois.** *My Friend the Cow.* 1952 (1946). Chicago. Nat Dairy Council. unp. VG/wrp. T5. $55.00

**LENSKI, Lois.** *Strawberry Girl.* (1945). Lippincott. 3rd. 8vo. 1946 Newbery. dk gr cloth. mc pict dj. R5. $125.00

**LENT, John A.** *Comic Art in Africa, Asia, Australia & Latin America...* 1996. ils/6506 entries. F. A4. $70.00

**LENT, John A.** *Comic Art of Europe: Internat Comprehensive Bibliography.* 1994. 8809 entries. 684p. F. A4. $75.00

**LENTZ, Harold B.** *Cinderella & Other Tales.* (1933). Bl Ribbon. thick 4to. 4 popups. pict brd. mc pict dj. R5. $650.00

**LENTZ, Harris M. III.** *Science Fiction, Horror & Fantasy: Film & Television...* 1983. Jefferson McFarland. 1374p. VG/dj. C5. $30.00

**LENTZ, Perry.** *Falling Hills.* 1967. NY. Scribner. 1st. NF/dj. A14. $21.00

**LENZ, Hans.** *El Papel Indigena Mexicano: Historia & Supervivencia.* 1948. Mexico City. Rafael Leora y Chavez. 300+ils & 11 samples. F. B24. $1,250.00

**LENZ, Lee W.** *Marcus E Jones: Western Geologist, Mining Engineer...* 1986. Claremont, CA. ils. 486p. F/dj. B26. $30.00

**LEON, Donna.** *Acqua Alta.* 1996. Harper Collins. 1st. NF/dj. G8. $25.00

**LEON, Donna.** *Death at La Fenice.* 1992. NY. Harper Collins. 1st. author's 1st novel. F/dj. T2. $30.00

**LEONARD, Burgess.** *Stretch Bolton Comes Back.* 1958. Lippincott. 1st. VG/dj. P8. $40.00

**LEONARD, Elisabeth Anne.** *Into Darkness Peering: Race & Color in the Fantastic.* 1997. Greenwood. 1st. F/sans. P3. $58.00

**LEONARD, Elmore.** *Bandits.* 1987. Arbor. 1st trade. F/F. B3. $30.00

**LEONARD, Elmore.** *Bandits.* 1987. Arbor. 1st. NF/dj. N4/T12. $28.00

**LEONARD, Elmore.** *Bandits.* 1987. Mysterious. 1st. 1/26. sgn/lettered. special bdg. F/case. M15. $65.00

**LEONARD, Elmore.** *Big Bounce.* 1989. NY. Armchair Detective. 1st Am hc. F/dj. M15. $45.00

**LEONARD, Elmore.** *Cat Chaser.* 1982. Arbor. 1st. NF/VG. B3. $40.00

**LEONARD, Elmore.** *City Primeval. High Noon in Detroit.* 1980. NY. Arbor. 1st. F/NF. Q1. $60.00

**LEONARD, Elmore.** *City Primeval. High Noon in Detroit.* 1980. NY. Arbor. 1st. sgn. F/dj. D10. $75.00

**LEONARD, Elmore.** *Cuba Libra.* 1998. Delacorte. 1st. sgn. F/dj. R14. $45.00

**LEONARD, Elmore.** *Freaky Deaky.* 1988. NY. Arbor/Morrow. UP/1st. F/prt wrp. M15. $100.00

**LEONARD, Elmore.** *Get Shorty.* 1990. Delacorte. 1st. sgn. F/dj. D10. $40.00

**LEONARD, Elmore.** *Get Shorty.* 1990. NY. Delacorte. 1st. F/dj. T12. $35.00

**LEONARD, Elmore.** *Glitz.* (1985). Mysterious. 1st trade. 4to. silvered bl cloth. gray ep. F/box. R3. $40.00

**LEONARD, Elmore.** *Glitz.* 1985. Arbor. 1st unltd. 8vo. 251p. F/NF. W2. $25.00

**LEONARD, Elmore.** *Killshot.* 1989. Arbor. 1st. sgn. F/dj. A24. $40.00

**LEONARD, Elmore.** *La Brava.* 1983. Arbor. ARC. w/photo. F/F. B3. $60.00

**LEONARD, Elmore.** *La Brava.* 1983. NY. Arbor. 1st. F/dj. B2. $25.00

**LEONARD, Elmore.** *Maximum Bob.* 1991. Delacorte. 1st. sgn. F/dj. D10. $35.00

**LEONARD, Elmore.** *Pronto.* 1993. Delacorte. 1st. sgn. F/dj. D10. $35.00

**LEONARD, Elmore.** *Pronto.* 1993. Delacorte. 1st. VG/dj. R8. $11.00

**LEONARD, Elmore.** *Riding the Rap.* 1995. Delacorte. 1st. VG/dj. R8. $11.50

**LEONARD, Elmore.** *Stick.* 1983. NY. Arbor. 1st. F/dj. M15. $65.00

**LEONARD, Elmore.** *Touch.* 1987. Arbor. 1st. 245p. NF/dj. M21. $15.00

**LEONARD, Elmore.** *Unknown Man No 89.* 1977. London. Secker Warburg. 1st. F/dj. M15. $150.00

**LEONARD, Fred.** *Guide to the History of Physical Education.* 1923. Phil. 1st. 361p. A13. $75.00

**LEONARD, J. Edson.** *Flies.* 1950. NY. Barnes. VG. A19. $35.00

**LEONARD, Jonathan.** *Ancient America.* 1967. NY. Time. 1st. 192p. F3. $15.00

**LEONARD, Thomas C.** *Above the Battle: War-Making in America...* NY. photos/notes. F/dj. E1. $25.00

**LEONARD, Zenas.** *Narrative of the Adventures of Zenas Leonard.* 1934. Lakeside Classic. 1st thus. edit Quaife. fld map. teg. NF/sans. T11. $45.00

**LEONARD.** *Spanish Approach to Pensacola, 1689-1693.* 1939. Quivira. 1/550. fld map. 340p. VG. A4. $300.00

**LEOPARDI, Giacomo.** *Poesie.* 1901. Firenze. mini. all edges red. gilt limp blk leather. F. B24. $135.00

**LEOPOLD, Aldo.** *Sound County Almanac & Sketches Here & There.* 1950. OUP. 2nd. 226p. VG. A10. $20.00

**LEPOUTRE & SIENKO.** *Solutions Metal-Ammoniac Properties Physicohimiques.* 1964. Benjamin. 1st. cloth. VG. B27. $25.00

**LEPPMANN, Wolfgang.** *Rilke: A Life.* 1984. NY. 1st. photos. VG/dj. M17. $25.00

**LEPRINCE-RINQUET, Louis.** *Cosmic Rays.* 1950. Prentice Hall. 1st. VG/dj. O4. $15.00

**LERNER, Abe.** *Assault on the Book: Critique of Fine Printing...* 1979. North Hills. Bird & Bull. 1st. 1/200. F/prt wrp. M24. $35.00

**LERNER, Alan Jay.** *Brigadoon.* 1947. Coward McCann. 1st. F/NF. B4. $500.00

**LERNER, Alan Jay.** *My Fair Lady.* 1956. NY. Warner. unp. VG. C5. $12.50

**LERNER, Ira.** *Mexican Jewry in the Land of the Aztecs: A Guide.* 1963. Mexico. 2nd. 252p. wrp. F3. $20.00

**LERNER & LOEWE.** *Camelot.* 1961. Random. 1st. NF/dj. T10. $150.00

**LEROY, Mervyn.** *It Takes More Than Talent.* 1953. Knopf. 1st. sgn. NF/dj. M25. $60.00

**LESAGE, Alain Rene.** *Adventures of Gil Blas of Santillane.* 1937. LEC. 2 vol. 1/1500. ils/sgn John Austen. gray over bl cloth. K1. $100.00

**LESBERG, Sandy.** *Great Classic Recipes of Europe.* 1972. Prentice Hall. G/dj. A16. $20.00

**LESCARBOT, Marc.** *Nova Francia: A Description of Acadia, 1606.* (1928). NY. 1st thus. ils. 346p. G. B18. $22.50

**LESLEY, Craig.** *River Song.* 1989. Houghton Mifflin. 1st. sgn. F/NF. B3. $75.00

**LESLEY, Craig.** *Winterkill.* 1984. Boston. Houghton Mifflin. 1st. F/dj. D10. $125.00

**LESLEY, L.B.** *Uncle Sam's Camels: Journal of May Humphreys Stacy...* 1929. Harvard. sgn. 208p. xl. lib bdg. F. M4. $55.00

**LESLEY, Lewis Burt.** *Uncle Tom's Camels: Journal of May Humphreys Stacy...* 1929. Cambridge. Harvard. 1st. fld map. 298p. cloth. F/dj. D11. $75.00

**LESLIE, E.** *Directions for Cookery in Its Various Banches.* 1840 (1837). quarter leather. E6. $100.00

**LESLIE, E.** *Receipts for Pastry, Cake, Sweetmeats.* 1835 (1827). G. E6. $95.00

**LESLIE, Frank.** *Report on Fine Arts.* 1868. GPO. folio. pres. prt purple wrp. R12. $225.00

**LESLIE, Jacques.** *Mark: War Correspondent's Memoir of Vietnam & Cambodia.* 1995. Four Walls Eight Windows. 1st. ils/map ep. 305p. F/dj. R11. $17.00

**LESLIE, Warren.** *Starrs of Texas.* 1978. S&S. 1st. 8vo. 511p. NF/G. W2. $20.00

**LESQUEREUX, Leo.** *Contributions to Fossil Flora of Western Territories.* 1878. GPO. 64 pl. 366p. VG. A10. $125.00

**LESS, Willis T.** *Stories in Stone, Telling of Some of the Wonderlands...* 1927. NY. Van Nostrand. 3rd/corrected. 236p. VG. F7. $40.00

**LESSING, Doris.** *Children of Violence.* 1966. S&S. 1st. VG/dj. M19. $17.50

**LESSING, Doris.** *Good Terrorist.* 1985. London. Cape. 1st. F/dj. Q1. $35.00

**LESSING, Erich.** *Discoverers of Space: A Pictorial Narration.* 1969. ils. VG/dj. M17. $20.00

**LESTER, Charles Edward.** *Life of Sam Houston.* 1855. NY. Derby. ils/maps. 402p. cloth/leather spine label. NF. O1. $100.00

**LESTER, Julius.** *All Is Well: An Autobiography.* 1976. Morrow. 1st. 319p. VG/dj. R11. $20.00

**LESTER, Julius.** *Knee-High Man & Other Tales.* 1972. Dial. 1st. ils Ralph Pinto. VG/dj. B17. $25.00

**LESTER, R.M.** *Weather Prediction.* ca 1941. London. Hutchinson. new/revised. 8vo. 132p. VG/dj. K5. $22.00

**LETCHWORTH, Thomas.** *Twelve Discourses, Delivered Chiefly at the Meeting-House...* 1794. Salem. Thos Cushing. 248p. brd. V3. $110.00

**LETCHWORTH, W.** *Insane in Foreign Countries.* 1889. 1st. 20 pl. VG. E6. $175.00

**LETHEM, Jonathan.** *Amnesia Moon.* 1995. Harcourt Brace. 1st. author's 2nd book. F/F. H11. $30.00

**LETHEM, Jonathan.** *As She Climbed Across the Table.* 1997. Doubleday. 1st. sgn. F/dj. O11. $30.00

**LETHEM, Jonathan.** *Gun, With Occasional Music.* 1994. Harcourt Brace. 1st. sgn. F/dj. M15. $65.00

**LETHEM, Jonathan.** *Wall of the Sky, Wall of the Eye.* 1996. Harcourt Brace. 1st. F/dj. A23. $36.00

**LETTERHOUSE, Marie Elisabeth.** *Francis A Drexel Family.* 1938. Sisters of Blessed Sacrament. 418p. VG. S5. $25.00

**LETTS, Billie.** *Where the Heart Is.* 1995. NY. Warner. 1st. sgn. author's 1st novel. F/dj. M23. $40.00

**LETTWICH, Richard N.** *Price System & Resource Allocation.* 1973 (1955). Dryden. 5th. VG. S5. $15.00

**LEVERTOV, Denise.** *Life in the Forest.* 1978. New Directions. 1/150. sgn. F/pub case. O11. $125.00

**LEVI, Giulio A.** *Il Comico.* 1913. Genova. AF Formiggini. 134p. prt gray wrp. G. G1. $50.00

**LEVI, Peter.** *Johnson's Journey to the Western Island of Scotland...* 1990. London. Folio Soc. lg 8vo. F/case. H13. $225.00

**LEVIN, Alexandra Lee.** *Szolds of Lombard Street, a Baltimore Family, 1859-1909.* 1960. Phil. 1st. 412p. VG/dj. B18. $9.50

**LEVIN, Ira.** *Boys From Brazil.* 1976. Random. 1st. VG/NF. R14. $40.00

**LEVIN, Ira.** *Boys From Brazil.* 1976. S&S. 1st. NF/dj. S18. $45.00

**LEVIN, Ira.** *Deathtrap.* 1979. Random. 1st. F/NF. S18. $25.00

**LEVIN, Ira.** *No Time for Sergeants.* 1956. Random. 1st/MTI. VG/dj. A24. $35.00

**LEVIN, Ira.** *Rosemary's Baby.* 1967. Random. 1st. VG/G+. B30. $75.00

**LEVIN, Ira.** *Rosemary's Baby.* 1967. Random. 1st. VG/clip. B11. $50.00

**LEVIN, Ira.** *This Perfect Day.* 1970. Random. 1st. NF/dj. A14. $42.00

**LEVIN, Jennifer.** *Water Dancer.* 1982. Poseidon. 1st. author's 1st book. F/NF. M19. $17.50

**LEVIN, Meyer.** *If I Forget Thee: Picture Story of Modern Palestine.* 1947. Viking. 1st. sm 4to. 143p. G/dj. H1. $22.50

**LEVIN, Michael.** *Settling the Score.* 1989. S&S. 1st. F/F. H11. $20.00

**LEVINE, Isaac Don.** *Mitchell, Pioneer of Air Power.* 1943. DSP. 1st. 8vo. 420p. G. B11. $15.00

**LEVINE, Leo.** *Ford: Dust & the Glory.* 1969. NY. VG/dj. B5. $70.00

**LEVINE, Paul.** *Slashback.* 1995. Morrow. 1st. F/F. H11. $15.00

**LEVINE, Philip.** *Simple Truth.* 1994. Knopf. 1st. F/dj. O11. $30.00

**LEVINE, Philip.** *Walk With Tom Jefferson.* 1988. Knopf. 1st. sgn. F/NF. O11. $55.00

**LEVINE, Philip.** *What Work Is.* 1991. Knopf. 1st. F/F. O11. $30.00

**LEVINE, Sol.** *Appointment in the Sky.* 1963. Walker. sgn. fwd LB Johnson. 214p. F/NF. W2. $30.00

**LEVINSON-LESSING, V.F.** *Hermitage, Leningrad: Baroque & Rococo Masters.* 1965. London. Hamlyn. ils/pl. VG/fair. M10. $25.00

**LEVISON, J.J.** *Home Book of Trees & Shrubs.* 1949. NY. enlarged. 524p. cloth. G. A17. $16.50

**LEVITAN, Kalman L.** *Miniature Books Relating to Postage Stamps.* 1983. Skokie. Blk Cat. mini. 2 vol. intro RE Massmann. gilt red leather. F. B24. $125.00

**LEVITAN, Kalman L.** *Tongues of Flame.* 1989. Palm Beach Gardens. Kaycee. mini. 1/200. 65p. dk bl bdg. B24. $45.00

**LEVITH.** *Fiddlers in Fiction.* 1979. ils. 219p. F. A4. $25.00

**LEVITSKY, Ronald.** *Wisdom of Serpents.* 1992. Scribner. 1st. F/dj. A23. $25.00

**LEVITT, Helen.** *Mexico City.* 1997. Norton. 1/200. sgn. ils. 144p. special bdg. F/case. K1. $150.00

**LEVON, Fred.** *Manx Cat.* 1970. NAL. 1st. VG/dj. G8. $10.00

**LEVY, David Mordecai.** *Studies in Sibling Rivalry.* 1937. Am Othopsychiatric Assn. tall 8vo. 96p. prt blk cloth. G. G1. $28.50

**LEVY, Jerrold E.** *Hand Trembling, Frenzy Witchcraft & Moth Madness.* 1988. Tucson, AZ. 1st. 196p. F/F. B19. $25.00

**LEVY, Lester S.** *Give Me Yesterday: American History in Song, 1890-1920.* 1975. Norman, OK. U OK. 1st. F/dj. B20. $35.00

**LEVY, Reuben.** *Baghdad Chronicle.* 1929. Cambridge. 8vo. ils. 279p. cloth. VG. Q2. $80.00

**LEWANSKI.** *Subject Collections in European Libraries: A Directory...* 1965. Bowker. 829p. VG. A4. $45.00

**LEWES, George Henry.** *Physiology of Common Life.* 1873. Appleton. 2 vol. 12mo. G. G1. $65.00

**LEWIN, Kurt.** *Der Begriff der Genese in Physik, Biologie...* 1922. Berlin. Julius Springer. 240p. prt cream wrp. VG. G1. $75.00

**LEWIN, Kurt.** *Vorsatz Wille und Bedurfnis.* 1926. Berlin. Julius Springer. assn. 92p. contemporary bdg. G1. $100.00

**LEWIS, Alfred Henry.** *Wolfville Nights.* (1902). NY. Stokes. 1st/1st issue. 8vo. gilt blk cloth. F/box. R3. $50.00

**LEWIS, Alfred Henry.** *Wolfville.* (1897). NY. Stokes. 1st. 8vo. ils Remington. gilt red cloth. chemise/case. R3. $75.00

**LEWIS, Arthur H.** *Children's Party.* 1972. Trident. 1st. VG/dj. P3. $25.00

**LEWIS, Arthur H.** *Copper Beeches.* 1971. Trident. 1st. VG/dj. G8. $35.00

**LEWIS, Arthur H.** *Copper Beeches.* 1971. Trident. 1st. xl. VG/dj. P3. $20.00

**LEWIS, Berkeley R.** *Notes on Ammunition of the American Civil War.* 1959. Am Ordnance Assn. unp. VG. B10. $25.00

**LEWIS, Bernard.** *Jews of Islam.* 1984. London. RKP. ils/pl. 245p. VG/dj. Q2. $24.00

**LEWIS, C.D.** *Otterbury Incident.* 1949. NY. Viking. 1st Am. 148p. F/dj. D4. $65.00

**LEWIS, C.D.** *Otterbury Incident.* 1949. Viking. 1st Am. VG/dj. P2. $35.00

**LEWIS, C.S.** *All My Road Before Me: Diary of CS Lewis, 1922-1927.* 1991. HBJ. 1st Am. photos/index. AN/dj. A27. $25.00

**LEWIS, C.S.** *Chronicles of Narnia.* (1994). Harper Collins. 4 vol. ils Pauline Baynes. AN/dj/box. A17. $105.00

**LEWIS, C.S.** *Chronicles of Narnia.* 1950-56. Macmillan. 1st Am. 7 vol. VG to F/dj. A27. $3,250.00

**LEWIS, C.S.** *Chronicles of Narnia.* 1955-56. Bodley Head. 1st Eng. 7 vol. VG to F/dj (1 facs). A27. $10,000.00

**LEWIS, C.S.** *Four Loves.* (1988). Harcourt Brace. Classic Ed. An/dj. A27. $18.00

**LEWIS, C.S.** *Great Divorce.* 1946. Macmillan. 1st Am. NF/dj. Q1. $125.00

**LEWIS, C.S.** *Grief Observed.* (1989). Harper Row. Gift ed. fwd Madeleine L'Engle. AN/dj. A27. $13.00

**LEWIS, C.S.** *Letters of CS Lewis.* (1933). Harcourt Brace. 1st revised/enlarged/Harvest Orig. AN/wrp. A27. $15.00

**LEWIS, C.S.** *Mere Christianity.* (1952). Macmillan. AN/dj. A27. $15.00

**LEWIS, C.S.** *Quotable Lewis: Encyclopedia Selection of Quotes...* (1989). Tyndale. photos/biblio/index. 651p. AN/dj. A27. $20.00

**LEWIS, C.S.** *Readings for Meditaion & Reflection.* (1992). Harper. AN/wrp. A27. $12.00

**LEWIS, C.S.** *Riddle of Joy.* (1989). Eerdmans. edit MacDonald/Tadie. AN. A27. $15.00

**LEWIS, C.S.** *Screwtape Letters.* (1990). Barbour. Christian Lib series. lg type. AN/sans. A27. $12.50

**LEWIS, C.S.** *Space Trilogy.* (1996). Scribner. Classics Ed. 3 vol. AN/dj. A27. $67.00

**LEWIS, C.S.** *Surprised by Joy: Shape of My Early Life.* (1984). HBJ. AN/dj. A27. $15.00

**LEWIS, C.S.** *Voyage of the Dawn Treader.* 1960. Macmillan. 1st. ils Pauline Baynes. 210p. VG/dj. B27. $150.00

**LEWIS, Clara.** *I Love Spring.* 1965. Little Brn. 1st. 28p. F/NF. D4. $25.00

**LEWIS, Deborah;** see Grant, Charles.

**LEWIS, Elizabeth Foreman.** *Ho-Ming, Girl of China.* 1934. Winston. ils Kurt Wiese. orange cloth. xl. VG. B36. $13.00

**LEWIS, Emily H.** *Wo'Wakita Reservation Recollections.* 1980. Lake Mills, IA. Graphic. ltd. G/dj. A19. $30.00

**LEWIS, George E.** *Indiana Company, 1763-1798...* 1941. Clark. VG. J2. $235.00

**LEWIS, Gregg.** *Power of a Promise Kept.* 1995. Focus on Family. 13 stories. 186p. VG. B29. $8.00

**LEWIS, Harlan.** *Chromosone Numbers of California Delphiniums.* 1951. St Louis. ils. wrp. B26. $9.00

**LEWIS, Harry.** *Making Money From Hens.* 1919. Lippincott. 217p. VG. A10. $20.00

**LEWIS, Heather.** *House Rules.* 1994. Doubleday/Talese. 1st. author's 1st book. F/dj. R14. $30.00

**LEWIS, J. Patrick.** *Earth Verses & Water Rhymes.* 1991. NY. Atheneum. 1st. sgn. 32p. F/dj. D4. $30.00

**LEWIS, Jack.** *Guns & Guerrillas.* 1966. N Hollywood. Challenge. VG/wrp. R11. $40.00

**LEWIS, Janet.** *Wife of Martin Guerre.* 1941. SF. Cold Pr. 1st thus. 1/300. sgn. NF/dj. J3. $300.00

**LEWIS, Jim.** *Sister.* 1993. St Paul. Graywolf. 1st. sgn. author's 1st book. F/dj. w/pub card. R14. $50.00

**LEWIS, John Frederick.** *History of an Old Phil Land Title.* 1934. Phil. np. 1st. 273p. xl. B18. $45.00

**LEWIS, John Taylor.** *Ole Master's Cedar Grove: Story of a Virginia Plantation.* 1957. private prt. sgn. photos. G+. B10. $35.00

**LEWIS, Lloyd.** *Sherman, Fighting Prophet.* 1932. Harcourt Brace. 1st. 690p. cloth. NF. M8. $45.00

**LEWIS, Lloyd.** *Sherman, Fighting Prophet.* 1932. NY. 1st. ils/maps. 690p. G. B18. $17.50

**LEWIS, Lorna.** *Puppy & the Cat.* 1940. Grosset Dunlap. 1st. sq 4to. ils. VG/G. M5. $38.00

**LEWIS, Norman.** *World, the World: Memoirs of a Legendary Traveler.* 1987. NY. 1st. VG/dj. M17. $15.00

**LEWIS, Oscar.** *George Davidson: Pioneer West Coast Scientist.* 1954. Berkeley/LA. 8vo. index/chronology/list pub. 146p. VG/clip. P4. $85.00

**LEWIS, Oscar.** *Life in a Mexican Village: Tepoztlan Restudied.* 1951. Urbana, IL. 2nd. ils Alberto Beltran. 512p. F3. $15.00

**LEWIS, Oscar.** *Pedro Martinez: A Mexican Peasant & His Family.* 1964. Random. 1st. 507p. dj. F3. $15.00

**LEWIS, Richard.** *Miracles: Poems by Children of English-Speaking World.* 1966. S&S. 1st. sq 12mo. 214p. F/NF. C14. $22.00

**LEWIS, Richard.** *There Are Two Lives: Poems of Children of Japan.* 1970. S&S. 1st. sm 8vo. 96p. F/NF clip. C14. $14.00

**LEWIS, Roy Harley.** *Manuscript Murders.* 1982. St Martin. 1st Am. VG/G. G8. $20.00

**LEWIS, Roy Harley.** *Where Agents Fear to Tread.* 1984. St Martin. 1st Am. NF/dj. G8. $17.50

**LEWIS, Sinclair.** *Ann Vickers.* 1933. Grosset Dunlap. MTI. F/NF. B4. $125.00

**LEWIS, Sinclair.** *Ann Vickers.* 1933. NY. 1st. VG/dj. S18. $60.00

**LEWIS, Sinclair.** *Cass Timberline.* 1945. Random. 1st. 390p. NF/dj. B20. $35.00

**LEWIS, Sinclair.** *Dodsworth.* 1929. NY. Harcourt Brace. 1st. 8vo. 377p. VG+. B20. $45.00

**LEWIS, Sinclair.** *Gideon Planish.* 1943. Random. 1st. VG/dj. S13. $15.00

**LEWIS, Sinclair.** *It Can't Happen Here.* 1935. Doubleday Doran. 1st. inscr. NF/dj. B4. $950.00

**LEWIS, Sinclair.** *It Can't Happen Here.* 1935. Doubleday Doran. 1st. xl. G. G11. $35.00

**LEWIS, Thomas.** *Guns of Cedar Creek.* 1989. NY. Harper Row. 1st. F/dj. A14. $25.00

**LEWIS, Thomas.** *Medicine Men: Oglala Sioux Ceremony & Healing.* 1990. Lincoln, NE. AN/dj. A19. $25.00

**LEWIS, Tom.** *Storied New Mexico: Annotated Bibliography of Novels...* 1919. NM U. 1st. sgn. 224p. F/F. B19. $20.00

**LEWIS, William Draper.** *Great American Lawyers, Lives & Influence of Judges...* 1907-1909. Phil. Winston. 8 vol. 1/1000. gilt 3-quarter calf. M11. $450.00

**LEWIS, Wilmarth S.** *Three Tours Through London...1797.* 1941. New Haven. Yale. 1st. 8vo. 135p. gray cloth/paper labels. H13. $95.00

**LEWIS, Wyndham.** *Journey Into Barbary, Morocco Writings & Drawings.* 1983. Blk Sparrow. 1/226. sgn. VG/mylar. B9. $35.00

**LEWIS & ROSENBLUM.** *Effect of the Infant on Its Caregiver...* 1974. NY. Wiley. Interscience Pub. 264p. prt aqua cloth. VG/dj. G1. $65.00

**LEWIS & SILVER.** *Great Balls of Fire: Uncensored Story of Jerry Lee Lewis.* 1982. St Martin. ils. 373p. VG. P12. $5.00

**LEY, Willy.** *Space Pilots.* 1957. Poughkeepsie, NY. Guild. 4to. 44p. pict brd. K5. $18.00

**LEYBURN, J.** *Haitian People.* 1941. New Haven. 1st. 342p. VG/dj. B5. $22.50

**LEYDET, Francois.** *Coyote: Defiant Songdog of the West.* 1988. U OK. revised. VG/dj. R8. $15.00

**LEYDET, Francois.** *Grand Canyon: Time & the River Flowing.* 1964. Sierra club. VG/dj. S5. $35.00

**LEYDET, Francois.** *Tomorrow's Wilderness.* 1963. Sierra Club. photos Ansel Adams. F/dj. A17. $15.00

**LEYHAUSEN, Paul.** *Verhaltensstudien an Katzen.* 1956. Berlin/Hamburg. Paul Parey. ils. 120p. prt pict wrp. VG. G1. $50.00

**LEYSON, Burr W.** *Man, Rockets & Space.* 1954. Dutton. 1st. VG/dj. K5. $40.00

**LI ZHISUI.** *Private Life of Chairman Mao.* (1994). Random. 1st. 8vo. 682p. F/dj. H4. $20.00

**LIANG, Yen.** *Tommy & Dee-Dee.* 1953. Oxford. 1st. ils. F/VG. M5. $28.00

**LIBBEY, H.W.** *Libbey's Indian Medical Infirmary.* 1860. Cleveland. Nevins. 24p. prt blk wrp. B18. $125.00

**LIBBY, Bill.** *Fred Lynn: Young Star.* 1977. Putnam. 1st. F/dj. P8. $30.00

**LIBEN, Lynn S.** *Deaf Children: Developmental Perspectives.* 1978. Academic. pres. G1. $38.00

**LIBERMAN, Alexander.** *Marlene: An Intimate Photographic Memoir.* (1992). Random. 1st. photos. 120p. F/dj. H4. $15.00

**LIBRADO, Fernando.** *Breath of the Sun: Life in Early California...* 1979. Banning. Malki Mus. 178p. cloth. dj. D11. $35.00

**LICHINE, Alexis.** *Guide to the Wines & Vineyards of France.* 1979. Knopf. 1st/2nd prt. sm 4to. 449p. F/dj. W2. $45.00

**LICHTEN, Frances.** *Folk Art of Rural Pennsylvania.* (1946). Scribner. later prt. 4to. 276p. VG. H1. $35.00

**LICHTENBERG & LORRAH.** *Channel's Destiny.* 1982. Doubleday. 1st. sgns. F/dj. G10. $25.00

**LIDDELL, E.G.T.** *Discovery of Reflexes.* 1960. Oxford. 1st. 174p. A13. $100.00

**LIDDLE, Peter H.** *Airman's War 1914-1918.* 1987. Poole, Eng. Blandford. ils/notes/index. 226p. VG/dj. S16. $25.00

**LIDELL, Sally.** *Sotheby's Art at Auction 1987-1988.* 1988. NY. ils. VG/dj. M17. $35.00

**LIEB, Fred.** *Boston Red Sox.* 1947. Putnam. 1st. photos. VG+/G+. P8. $85.00

**LIEB, Fred.** *Connie Mack: Grand Old Man of Baseball.* 1945. Putnam. 1st. NF/VG. B4. $65.00

**LIEB, Fred.** *Philadelphia Phillies.* 1953. Putnam. 1st. photos. VG+/G+. P8. $275.00

**LIEB, Fred.** *Pittsburgh Pirates.* 1948. Putnam. 1st. photos. VG. P8. $100.00

**LIEBENSON, Harold A.** *You, the Expert Witness.* 1962. Mendelein, IL. Callaghan. 1st. NF/sand. O4. $20.00

**LIEBER, Arthur.** *You Can Be a Printer.* 1976. Lee Shepard. 1st. 8vo. 128p. F/dj. O10. $17.50

**LIEBER, Francis.** *Final Report & Address of the President.* 1866. NY. Loyal Pub Soc. 13p. stabbed prt wrp. M11. $45.00

**LIEBERMAN, Herbert.** *City of the Dead.* 1976. S&S. 1st. xl. VG/NF. S18. $4.00

**LIEBERMAN, William S.** *Drawings From the Kroller-Muller National Museum, Otterlo.* 1973. MOMA. 90p. NF/wrp. H4. $12.00

**LIEBERT, Herman W.** *Dr Johnson's First Book. An Account of Variant Issues...* 1950. Yale. 1/150. 8vo. 8p. heavy paper wrp. H13. $85.00

**LIEBERT, Herman W.** *Johnson's Last Literary Project: An Account...* 1948. New Haven. self pub. 1/200. sm 8vo. F/heavy bl paper wrp. H13. $85.00

**LIEBKNECHT, Wilhelm.** *Speeches of Wilhelm Liebknecht.* 1928. NY. Internat Voices of Revolt series. F. B2. $35.00

**LIEBMAN, Marcel.** *Russian Revolution.* 1970. Random. 1st Am. ils. VG/dj. A2. $17.50

**LIFE MAGAZINE EDITORS.** *Life Book of Christmas.* 1963. NY. Time. 3 vol. 4to. VG. H4. $18.00

**LIFSHEY, Earl.** *Housewares Story: History of American Housewares Industry.* 1973. Chicago. Nat Housewares Mfg Assn. 1st/only. F/NF. B9. $20.00

**LIFTON, Robert.** *Home From the War: Vietnam Veterans...* 1973. S&S. 1st. 478p. NF/dj. R11. $25.00

**LIFTON, Robert.** *Nazi Doctors: Medical Killing & Psychology of Genocide.* 1986. NY. 1st. 561p. A13. $35.00

**LIGGETT, Carr.** *Rowfant Rhymes: Definitive Laurete Anthology...* (1972). Cleveland Rofant. 8vo. 71p. full cloth. H4. $45.00

**LIGHTBODY, Andy.** *Submarines Hunter/Killer 7 Boomers.* 1990. Beekman. 1st. pres. 192p. VG/dj. S16. $20.00

**LIGHTFOOT, Robert Henry.** *History & Interpretation in the Gospels.* nd. Harper. 236p. G. H10. $17.50

**LIGHTON, Conrad.** *Cape Floral Kingdon.* 1973. Cape Town. 221p. VG/dj. B26. $30.00

**LIGON, J.S.** *New Mexico Birds & Where to Find Them.* 1961. Albuquerque, NM. 1st. ils Kalmbach/Brooks. 360p. NF/dj. C12. $70.00

**LIGOTTI, Thomas.** *Grimscribe: His Lives & Works.* 1991. Carroll Graf. 1st. sgn. F/dj. S18. $45.00

**LIGOTTI, Thomas.** *Noctuary.* 1994. Carrol Graf. 1st. F/dj. B30. $20.00

**LILIENTHAL, Otto.** *Der Vogelflug.* 1910. Munchen. Oldenbourg. 2nd. 8 fld charts. 186p. B18. $175.00

**LILIUS, Aleko.** *Turbulent Tangier.* 1956. London. Elek. 8vo. 179p. cloth. VG. W1. $18.00

**LILLY, Lambert.** *History of the Middle States Ils by Tales...* 1854. Boston. Ticknor Fields. 167p. bstp cloth. B18. $17.50

**LIMOJON DE SAINT DIDIER, A.T.** *La Ville et la Republique de Venise.* 1680. Paris. Claude Barbin. 12mo. 504p. contemporary mottled calf. K1. $475.00

**LIMON, Graciela.** *Memories of Ana Calderon.* 1994. Arte Publico. 1st. sgn. F/dj. M19. $17.50

**LIN, Hazel.** *Moon Vow.* 1958. NY. 1st. sgn pres in Eng/Chinese. 312p. gr cloth. VG/clip. H3. $45.00

**LINCOLN, Abraham.** *Abraham Lincoln, Selections From His Writings.* 1950. Worcester. St Onge. mini. 1/1500. 76p. aeg. Sangorski/Sutcliffe bdg. B24. $275.00

**LINCOLN, Abraham.** *Gettysburg Address of Abraham Lincoln.* 1961. SF. Dawson/Cheney. mini. 1/100. gilt full red leather. F. B24. $175.00

**LINCOLN, Abraham.** *Gettysburg Address of Abraham Lincoln.* 1963. Los Angeles. Dawson. mini. Centennial ed. 1/1000. Blau bdg. F. B24. $65.00

**LINCOLN, Abraham.** *Life & Public Service of General Zachary Taylor.* 1922. Houghton Mifflin. 1st. 1/435. quarter linen/marbled brd. tissue dj/box. M24. $100.00

**LINCOLN, Abraham.** *Lincoln's Gettysburg Address: Pictorial Interpretation...* (1947). Chicago. Whitman. 2nd. ils. F/VG. H4. $30.00

**LINCOLN, D.** *Mrs Lincoln's Boston Cookbook: What to Do...* 1895 (1883). 536p. VG. E6. $40.00

**LINCOLN, F.C.** *Migration of American Birds.* 1939. NY. 1st. ils LA Fuertes. 189p. F. C12. $20.00

**LINCOLN, Joseph C.** *Bradshaws of Harniss.* 1944. Appleton Century. later prt. VG. H4. $12.00

**LINCOLN, Joseph C.** *Cape Cod Ballads.* 1902. Trenton. Albert Brandt. 1st. 198p. F. B5. $70.00

**LINCOLN, Joseph C.** *Christmas Days.* 1938. NY. Coward McCann. 1st. ils Harold Brett. VG+. H4. $16.00

**LINCOLN, Joseph C.** *Shavings.* 1918. Appleton. 1st. ils HM Brett. VG/dj. S13. $15.00

**LINDBERGH, Anne Morrow.** *Bring Me a Unicorn: Diaries & Letters of...1922-1928.* 1972. HBJ. NF. H4. $10.00

**LINDBERGH, Anne Morrow.** *Hour of Gold, Hour of Lead.* 1973. HBJ. rpt. NF/dj. T11. $8.00

**LINDBERGH, Anne Morrow.** *North to the Orient.* 1935. NY. Harcourt Brace. 1st. 8vo. 255p. xl. VG. W2. $65.00

**LINDBERGH, Charles A.** *Of Flight & Life.* 1948. Scribner. 1st. F/NF. B4. $100.00

**LINDBERGH, Charles A.** *Spirit of Saint Louis.* 1953. Scribner. 1st. 8vo. 562p. pict ep. H4. $12.00

**LINDBERGH, Charles A.** *We.* 1927. Putnam. 1st. 1/1000. sgn. 308p. gilt brd. F/glassine/box. B18. $2,500.00

**LINDE, Shirley Motter.** *Airline Stewardess Handbook.* 1968. Minneapolis. Careers Research. 1st. 126p. sc. VG+. A25. $15.00

**LINDEGREN, Erik.** *ABC of Lettering & Printing Types.* 1980. NY. Greenwich. rpt/3 vol in 1. 348p. F/NF. O10. $65.00

**LINDELL HART, Adrian.** *Strange Company.* 1953. Weidenfeld Nicolson. 1st. 8vo. 211p. VG/G. M7. $55.00

**LINDEN, J.** *Manual of Exanthematic Method of Cure.* 1906 (1878). VG. E6. $45.00

**LINDER, Leslie.** *History of the Tale of Peter Rabbit.* 1976. London. Warne. 1st. sm 4to. 63p. NF. T5. $65.00

**LINDER, Leslie.** *History of Writings of Beatrix Potter...* 1971 (1971). London. Warne. 2nd. sm 4to. 446p. NF/dj. T5. $120.00

**LINDERMAN, Frank.** *Indian Old-Man Stories.* 1920. Scribner. 1st. ils CM Russell. VG. B5. $125.00

**LINDIP, Edmund.** *Hubert the Traveling Hippopotamus.* 1961. Little Brn. 1st. ils Jane Carson. VG/dj. P2. $16.00

**LINDLAHR, Anna.** *Lindlahr Vegetarian Cook Book & ABC of Natural Dietetics.* 1922. Chicago. Lindlahr. 15th. VG. B9. $15.00

**LINDMAN, Maj.** *Flicka, Ricka, Dicka & Their New Friend.* 1942. Chicago. Whitman. 1st Am. 4to. tan cloth/pict label. pict dj. R5. $200.00

**LINDMAN, Maj.** *Snipp, Snapp, Snurr & the Gingerbread.* 1932. Whitman. 1st Am. 4to. dk orange cloth/pict label. R5. $150.00

**LINDNER, Buller.** *Pike: An In-Fisherman Handbook of Strategies.* 1983. Brainerd. ils. 245p. VG/dj. A17. $15.00

**LINDNER, Gustav Adolf.** *Lehrbuch der Empirischen Psychologie...* 1875 (1858). Wien. Carl Gerold's Sohn. 4th revised. ms 8vo. 232p. G. G1. $125.00

**LINDNER, Gustav Adolf.** *Manual of Empirical Psychology As Inductive Science...* 1889. Boston. DC Heath. 1st Eng-language. 274p. russet cloth. G1. $85.00

**LINDQUIST, Jennie D.** *Little Silver House.* (1959). Harper. possible 1st. 8vo. 213p. bl-gr cloth. VG/G. T5. $40.00

**LINDSAY, A.D.** *Modern Democratic State, Vol I.* 1945 (1943). London. OUP. 3rd. 12mo. F/dj. A2. $10.00

**LINDSAY, Cynthia.** *Dear Boris: Life of William Henry Pratt, aka Boris Karloff.* 1975. Knopf. 1st. VG/dj. C9. $60.00

**LINDSAY, David.** *English Poetry 1700-1780.* 1974. London. Dent. notes/biblio/short biogs. F/dj. H13. $25.00

**LINDSAY, Howard.** *Prescott Proposals.* 1954. Random. 1st. NF/dj. A24. $20.00

**LINDSAY, Jack.** *Time to Live.* 1946. London. 1st. dj. T9. $45.00

**LINDSAY, Merrill.** *Kentucky Rifle.* 1972. NY. Arma. 1st. inscr pres. 77 mc pl. unp. VG/dj. H10. $75.00

**LINDSAY, Merrill.** *One Hundred Great Guns: Illustrated History of Firearms.* 1968. London. Blandford. 1st. ils. 379p. VG. M10. $50.00

**LINDSAY, Michael.** *Unknown War: North China 1937-1945.* 1975. Bergstrom Boyle. 1st. ils. NF/clip. B20. $35.00

**LINDSAY, Paul.** *Witness to the Truth.* 1992. Random. 1st. author's 1st book. F/NF. H11. $25.00

**LINDSAY, Vachel.** *Every Soul Is a Circus.* 1929. Macmillan. 1st. ils Lindsay/George Richards. F. A18. $30.00

**LINDSAY, Vachel.** *Springfield Town Is Butterfly Town.* 1969. Kent State. 1st. unp. F/dj. D4. $125.00

**LINDSEY, Bessie M.** *American Historical Glass.* 1967. Tuttle. 2nd. tall 8vo. 541p. F/dj. H1. $40.00

**LINDSEY, David L.** *Body of Truth.* 1992. Doubleday. 1st. sgn. F/dj. A24. $30.00

**LINDSEY, David L.** *Cold Mind.* 1983. Harper Row. 1st. F/NF. H11. $35.00

**LINDSEY, David L.** *Heat From Another Sun.* 1984. Harper Row. 1st. F/F. H11/N4. $30.00

**LINDSEY, Robert.** *Gathering of Saints.* 1988. S&S. AN/dj. A19. $30.00

**LINDSLEY, A.** *Sketches of an Excursion to Southern Alaska.* 1965. Seattle. Shorey. facs. 73p. P4. $15.00

**LINDUSKA, Joseph.** *Waterfowl Tomorrow.* 1964. USDI. 770p. VG. A17. $15.00

**LINDWORSKY, Johannes.** *Der Willie: Seine Erscheinung und Seine Beherrschung...* 1923. Leipzig. Johann Ambrosius Barth. 3rd revised. 282p. G1. $25.00

**LINE, David.** *Screaming High.* 1985. Little Brn. 1st Am. Not for Resale stp. VG/dj. R11. $15.00

**LINE, Les.** *Audubon Society Book of Insects.* 1983. NY. 156 full-p photos. 264p. F/dj. S15. $30.00

**LINE & LINE.** *Grand Canyon Love Story: A True Living Adventure.* 1984. Leather Stocking Books. 8vo. 300p. stiff wrp. F7. $17.50

**LINFORD, Velma.** *Wyoming, Frontier State.* 1947. Old West Pub. ils/maps/photos. VG. J2. $50.00

**LINGEMAN, R.** *Small Town America: Narrative History.* 1980. NY. 547p. F/dj. M4. $25.00

**LINGENFELTER, R.E.** *First Through the Grand Canyon.* 1958. Dawson. 1/300. 12mo. 119p. VG. F7. $225.00

**LINGENFELTER, R.E.** *Steamboats on the Colorado River, 1852-1916.* 1978. Tucson. U AZ. 195p. VG/G. F7. $60.00

**LININGTON, Elizabeth.** *Date With Death.* 1966. Harper Row. 1st. xl. VG/dj. P3. $8.00

**LINKE, Franz.** *Die Luftschiffahrt von Montgolfier bis Zeppelin...* 1910. Berlin. Alfred Schall. 1st. German text. 8vo. 378+2p. gilt bl cloth. B11. $450.00

**LINKE, Lilo.** *People of the Amazon.* 1965. London. Adventurers CLub. 189p. dj. F3. $20.00

**LINKLATER, Eric.** *Voyage of the Challenger.* 1972. Doubleday. 288p. VG. A10. $35.00

**LINN, James Weber.** *James Keeley, Newspaperman.* 1937. Bobbs Merrill. 1st. 8vo. 286p. VG+. B20. $20.00

**LINN, John J.** *Reminiscenes of Fifty Years in Texas.* 1935. Steck Co. 8vo. 369p. brn cloth. VG+. B20. $25.00

**LINNETT, J.W.** *Wave Mechanics & Valency.* 1970. Metheun. 1st. VG. B27. $25.00

**LINSDAY, David.** *Mercy.* 1990. Doubleday. 1st. xl. VG/dj. S18. $7.00

**LINSKY & STRAUS.** *Social Stress in the United States...* 1986. Dover, MA. Auburn House. 1st. ils. F/dj. A2. $20.00

**LINTHURST, Randolph.** *Journal of Leo Smith.* 1976. Atams. F. P8. $45.00

**LINTON, Irwin H.** *Lawyer Examines the Bible: Introduction to Christian...* 1943. WA Wilds Co. 1st. 8vo. 300p. F/dj. H1. $18.00

**LINTON, W.J.** *Poetry of America: Selections From 100 American Poets...* 1878. London. Geo Bell. 1st. gilt gr cloth. M24. $225.00

**LIONARDO, Alessandro.** *Dialogi...Della Inventione Poetica.* 1554. Venice. Pietrasanta. 4to. prt device on title. gilt calf/rb. R12. $550.00

**LIPKIND, William.** *Little Tiny Rooster.* nd (c 1960). HBW. 4to. unp. VG. C14. $14.00

**LIPMAN, Jean.** *American Primitive Painting.* 1942. London/NY. OUP. 1st. ils/bibliography. 172p. VG/dj. D2. $40.00

**LIPOWITZ & WEINER.** *Rarities in American Cut Glass.* (1975). Houston, TX. Collectors House of Books. 294p. AN/sealed swrp. H1. $75.00

**LIPPS, Theodor.** *Grundtatsachen des Seelenlebens.* 1883. Bonn. Max Cohen. 709p. contemporary bdg. G1. $65.00

**LIPSCOMB, F. Martin.** *Diseases of Old Age.* 1932. London. Bailliere Tindall & Cox. 1st. 472p. VG. B14. $45.00

**LIPSIUS, Justus.** *Monita et Exempla Politica.* 1630. Amsterdam. Guiljelmum Blaeuw. 16mo. 238p. contemporary vellum. K1. $200.00

**LIPSYTE, Robert.** *Jack & Jill.* 1982. Harper Row. 1st. F/VG. P8. $12.50

**LISCOMB, F. Martin.** *Diseases of Old Age.* 1932. London. Bailliere. 1st. 472p. VG. B14. $45.00

**LISH, Gordon.** *Dear Mr Capote.* 1983. Holt Rinehart. 1st. F/dj. A23. $32.00

**LISTER, Joseph.** *Collected Papers of Joseph, Baron Lister.* 1979. Birmingham. facs of 1909. 2 vol. full leather. A13. $175.00

**LISTER & LISTER.** *Those Who Came Before.* 1983. SW Parks/Monuments. 1st. photos. 184p. VG. S14. $16.00

**LISTON, Robert A.** *Pueblo Surrender.* 1988. Evans. 1st. NF/VG. P3. $19.00

**LITCHFIELD, P.W.** *Autumn Leaves: Reflections of an Industrial Lieutenant.* 1945. Cleveland. 1st. 8vo. 125p. F/NF. B20. $100.00

**LITCHFIELD, Sarah.** *Hello Alaska.* 1945. Whitman. 1st. 32p. VG. D4. $25.00

**LITTAUER, Vladimir.** *Be a Better Horseman.* 1941. Derrydale. 1st. 1/1500. G. O3. $65.00

**LITTAUER, Vladimir.** *Boots & Saddles Riding School 1927-1937.* nd. NYC. 64p. VG. O3. $85.00

**LITTAUER, Vladimir.** *Schooling Your Horse.* 1974. NY. Arco. VG/G. O3. $20.00

**LITTELL, Robert.** *Amateur.* 1981. S&S. 1st. F/dj. A23. $32.00

**LITTELL, Robert.** *Sweet Reason.* 1974. Houghton Mifflin. 1st. F/NF. B4. $85.00

**LITTLE, Elbert L.** *Checklist of Native & Naturlized Trees of United States.* 1953. WA, DC. 472p. cloth. B26. $17.50

**LITTLE, James A.** *Jacob Hamblin: Narrative of His Personal Experience...* 1881. Salt Lake City. 12mo. 144p. bl cloth. F7. $160.00

**LITTLE, Nina Fletcher.** *Abby Aldrich Rockefeller Folk Art Collection...* 1957. Boston. Little Brn. 1st. 164 mc pl. 402p. F/case. D2. $65.00

**LITTLE, William.** *Oxford Universal Dictionary: On Historic Principals.* 1955. OUP. revised CT Onions. VG. M17. $35.00

**LITTLE & WADSWORTH.** *Common Trees of Puerto Rico & the Virgin Islands.* 1964. USDA. lg 8vo. 548p. cloth. VG. B1. $68.00

**LITTLEFIELD, Bill.** *Prospect.* 1989. Houghton Mifflin. ARC. author's 1st book. F/wrp. w/letter. M25. $35.00

**LITTLEFIELD, Bill.** *Prospect.* 1989. Houghton Mifflin. 1st. F/dj. A23. $32.00

**LITTLEJOHN, David.** *Dr Johnson: His Life in Letters.* 1965. NY. Prentice Hall. 1st. dj. H13. $45.00

**LIU, Aimee E.** *Cloud Mountain.* 1997. NY. Warner. 1st. sgn bookplate. F/dj. S9. $30.00

**LIVELY, Penelope.** *Heat Wave.* 1996. Harper Collins. 1st. sgn. F/dj. R14. $45.00

**LIVELY, Penelope.** *Moon Tiger.* 1988. Grove. UP. sgn. F/prt wrp. B3. $60.00

**LIVELY, Penelope.** *Passing On.* 1990. Grove Weidenfeld. 1st. sgn. F/F. B3. $30.00

**LIVERSIDGE, Douglas.** *Prince Charles: Monarch in the Making.* 1975. London. 1st Eng. F/dj. T12. $35.00

**LIVINGSTON, A.D.** *Fishing for Bass: Modern Tactics & Tackle.* 1974. Lippincott. 1st. ils/index. 256p. VG/dj. A17. $12.50

**LIVINGSTON, Armstrong.** *Doublecross.* 1929. Internat Fiction Lib. VG/dj. P3. $35.00

**LIVINGSTON, Armstrong.** *Night of Crime.* 1938. Sovereign. 1st. G. P3. $25.00

**LIVINGSTON, Bernard.** *Their Turf: America's Horsey Set...* 1973. NY. Arbor. VG/VG. O3. $15.00

**LIVINGSTON, Edward.** *Answer to Mr Jefferson's Justification of His Conduct...* 1813. Phil. Wm Fry. 1st. xl. V4. $300.00

**LIVINGSTON, Harold.** *Ride a Tiger.* 1987. Morrow. 1st. F/dj. A23. $40.00

**LIVINGSTON, Myra Cohn.** *Poems for Mothers.* 1988. Holiday House. 1st. 32p. NF/dj. C14. $15.00

**LIVINGSTON, Nancy.** *Fatality at Bath & Wells.* 1986. NY. St Martin. 1st. F/F. H11. $20.00

**LIVINGSTON & LANSDOWNE.** *Birds of the Northern Forest.* 1966. Houghton Mifflin. 4to. 247p. bl cloth. F/VG. M7. $50.00

**LIVINGSTONE, David.** *Livingstone's Travel & Researches in South Africa...* 1858. Phil. Bradley. 1st. 8vo. 440p. cloth. G. W1. $35.00

**LIVINGSTONE, William.** *Livingstone's History of the Republican Party.* 1900. Detroit. self pub. 2 vol. G. V4. $140.00

**LIZARS, John.** *System of Practical Surgery With Numerous Explanatory Plate.* 1938-1839. Edinburgh. WH Lizars. 42 pl. scarce. G7. $895.00

**LIZARS & MACFARLANE.** *In the Days of the Canada Company: Story of Settlement...* 1896. Toronto. 1st. ils. 494p. decor cloth. G. B18. $125.00

**LLEWELLYN, Sam.** *Deadeye.* 1991. NY. Summit. 1st Am. F/F. T11. $20.00

**LLEWELLYN, Sam.** *Sea Story.* 1987. St Martin. 1st. F/NF. H11. $20.00

**LLEWELLYN, Sam.** *Small Parts in History.* 1985. London. 1st. ils. VG/dj. M17. $40.00

**LLEWELWN, Richard.** *None But the Lonely Heart.* 1943. Macmillan. 2nd. G/poor. L4. $15.00

**LLOYD, Ann.** *Good Guys, Bad Guys.* 1983. Orbis Great Movies. 1st. NF/dj. P3. $15.00

**LLOYD, Ann.** *Wild & Young.* 1983. Orbis Great Movies. 1st. VG/dj. P3. $15.00

**LLOYD, Charles.** *Human Reproduction & Sexual Behavior.* 1964. Lee Febiger. ils/photos. 564p. VG. P12. $6.00

**LLOYD, John Uri.** *Etidorpha; or, End of the Earth.* 1895. Cincinnati. self pub. 1st. inscr. gilt gr cloth. NF. B2. $350.00

**LLOYD, John Uri.** *Red-Head.* 1903. Dodd Mead. 1st pres inscr. 8vo. 208p. gr cloth. F. B20. $60.00

**LLOYD, Ruth.** *Explorations in Psychoneuro-immunology.* 1987. Orlando. Seminars in Psychiatry series. 8vo. F. C14. $25.00

**LLOYD-JONES, D. Martyn.** *Studies in the Sermon on the Mount.* 1950. Eerdmans. 2 vol. VG/dj. B29. $21.00

**LLYWELYN, Morgan.** *Last Prince of Iceland.* 1992. Morrow. 1st. NF/dj. S13. $12.00

**LLYWELYN, Morgan.** *Silverlight.* 1996. NY. Baen. 1st. F/dj. A23. $32.00

**LO PINTO, M.** *New York Cookbook.* 1952. VG. E6. $12.00

**LOBANOV-ROSTOVSKY, A.** *Grinding Mill: Reminiscences of War & Revolution...* 1935. Macmillan. 1st Am. 12mo. F/VG. A2. $50.00

**LOBEL, Arnold.** *Book of Pigericks.* 1983. Harper Row. 1st. ils Arnold Lobel. VG/NF. P2. $20.00

**LOBEL, Arnold.** *Fables.* 1980. Harper Row. 1st. NF/VG. M5. $40.00

**LOBEL, Arnold.** *Frog & Toad Together.* 1973 (1972). Harper Row. 2nd. 64p. F/NF. C14. $14.00

**LOBEL, Arnold.** *Mouse Soup.* nd (1977). NY. Harper Row. I Can Read Book. stated 1st. 64p. VG/G clip. C14. $15.00

**LOCHHEAD, Marion.** *Battle of the Birds & Other Celtic Tales.* 1981. Edinburgh. Mercat. 1st. 148p. F/dj. D4. $35.00

**LOCHTE, Dick.** *Blue Bayou.* 1992. S&S. 1st. F/F. H11. $35.00

**LOCHTE, Dick.** *Laughing Dog.* 1988. 1st. VG/dj. M17. $17.50

**LOCHTE, Dick.** *Sleeping Dog.* 1985. Arbor. 1st. F/NF. H11. $40.00

**LOCKE, David R.;** see Nasby, Petroleum.

**LOCKE, E.** *Three Years in Camp & Hospital.* 1871 (1870). rb/orig spine/new ep. VG. E6. $50.00

**LOCKE, John.** *Abridgement of Mr Locke's Essay Human Understanding.* 1731 (1696). London. Knapton. 4th/corrected. 12mo. VG. G1. $225.00

**LOCKE, John.** *Treatise on Conduct of the Understanding.* 1828. Boston. 24mo. polished leather. VG. S17. $40.00

**LOCKE & LOCKE.** *Locke Art Glass, a Guide for Collectors.* 1987. Dover. 4to. 64p. glossy wrp. H1. $19.00

**LOCKER, Thomas.** *Family Farm.* 1988. NY. Dial. 1st. 32p. F/dj. D4. $25.00

**LOCKRIDGE, Kenneth.** *New England Town: First Hundred Years: Dedham, Mass.* 1970. Norton. 208p. VG. M10. $12.50

**LOCKRIDGE, Ross.** *Raintree County.* 1948. Houghton Mifflin. 1st. F/NF clip. B2. $150.00

**LOCKRIDGE, Ross.** *Raintree County.* 1948. Houghton Mifflin. 1st. sgn. F/VG. B4. $1,500.00

**LOCKWOOD, Frank C.** *Apache Indians.* 1938. Macmillan. 1st. ils/notes. 348p. VG. B19. $35.00

**LOCKWOOD, Frank C.** *Arizona Characters.* 1928. Times-Mirror. 1st. ils. 230p. VG. B19. $45.00

**LOCKWOOD, Frank C.** *Pioneer Days in Arizona: From Spanish Occupation...* 1932. Macmillan. 1st. ils/index. 387p. G. B19. $30.00

**LOCKWOOD, Frank C.** *Pioneer Days in Arizona: From Spanish Occupation...* 1932. Macmillan. 8vo. 387p. rb/new ep. VG+. F7. $70.00

**LOCKWOOD, George B.** *New Harmony Movement.* 1905. NY. Appleton. 1st. 8vo. 404+4p. VG. H7. $35.00

**LOCKWOOD & PAGE.** *Tucson: The Old Pueblo.* nd. Phoenix. 1st. inscr Lockwood. 94p. G. B18. $65.00

**LOCKYER, Herbert.** *Cameos of Prophecy; or, Are These the Last Days?* 1942. Zondervan. 128p. VG/worn. B29. $9.50

**LOCKYER, Herbert.** *Holy Spirit of God.* 1981. Thos NElson. 246p. VG/dj. B29. $11.00

**LOCKYER, J. Norman.** *Spectroscope & Its Applications.* 1873. London. Macmillan. sm 8vo. 117p. G. K5. $70.00

**LOCY, William.** *Story of Biology.* 1925. NY. 1st. ils. 495p. A13. $45.00

**LODGE, Henry Cabot.** *Story of the Revolution.* 1903. Scribner. 604p. G. S17. $10.00

**LOEB, Evelyn.** *Festive Desert Cookery.* 1969. Peter Pauper. G/dj. A16. $8.00

**LOEB, Jacques.** *Dynamics of Living Matter.* 1906. Macmillan. ils. panelled thatched blk cloth. G1. $85.00

**LOEB, Jacques.** *Organism as a Whole From Physiochemical Viewpoint.* 1916. Putnam. 379p. gr cloth. VG. G1. $65.00

**LOESENER, Thomas.** *Monographia Aquifoliacearum.* 1901 & 1908. Halle, Karras. 2 vol. ils/fld maps. 3-quarter maroon leather. A10. $90.00

**LOEWENTHAL, Max.** *Life & Soul: Outlines of Future Theoretical Physiology...* 1934. Allen Unwin. ils/pl. 291p. ochre cloth. NF/dj. G1. $60.00

**LOEWINSOHN, Ron.** *Watermelons.* 1959. NY. Totem. 1st. 1/1000. sgn. F/wrp. R14. $55.00

**LOFTING, Hugh.** *Doctor Dolittle & the Green Canary.* 1950. Lippincott. 1st thus. 276p. yel brd. VG/dj. D1. $85.00

**LOFTING, Hugh.** *Doctor Dolittle's Circus.* 1924. NY. 1st. inscr. ils. 379p. G. B18. $225.00

**LOFTING, Hugh.** *Doctor Dolittle's Return.* 1933. NY. Stokes. 1st. 8vo. orange cloth/pict label. mc dj. R5. $250.00

**LOFTING, Hugh.** *Story of Mr Tubbs.* 1923. NY. ils. 91p. G. B18. $35.00

**LOFTS, Norah.** *Domestic Life in England.* 1976. Doubleday. 1st. F/VG. P3. $25.00

**LOFTS, Norah.** *Scent of Cloves.* 1957. Doubleday. 1st. F/NF. M19. $15.00

**LOFTUS, Richard J.** *Nationalism in Modern Anglo-Irish Poetry.* 1964. U WI. 1st thus. VG/dj. O4. $15.00

**LOFTUS & MCINTYRE.** *Valhalla's Wake: IRA, M16 & Assassination of Young American.* 1989. Atlantic Monthly. 1st. VG/dj. N2. $10.00

**LOGAN, Herschel C.** *Drummer Boy of Shiloh.* 1986. Ampersand. mini. 1/100. 20p. gray brd/cloth. AN. B24. $95.00

**LOGAN, Herschel C.** *Little Portraits of Famous Americans.* 1973. Santa Ana. Dawson. mini. 1/250. sgn. 32 portraits. Bela Blau bdg. AN. B24. $110.00

**LOGAN, Herschel C.** *Lost & Found, a Teddy Bear.* 1983. Santa Ana, CA. Log-Anne. mini. sgn. frenchfold. pict label/cloth. yel dj. B24. $95.00

**LOGAN, Kate Virginia Cox.** *My Confederate Girlhood: The Memoirs of...* 1932. Garrett Massie. 1st. photos. 150p. G/poor. B10. $75.00

**LOGAN, Margaret.** *CAT Caper.* 1990. Walker. 1st. VG/dj. R8. $10.00

**LOGAN, Margaret.** *Deathhampton Summer.* 1988. Walker. 1st. NF/dj. G8. $20.00

**LOGGINS & LOGGINS.** *Unimaginable Life.* 1997. Avon. 1st. 8vo. 379p. F/dj. W2. $30.00

**LOGSDON, Tom.** *Your Guide to Investing in Space Exploration.* 1988. NY. Crown. sm 4to. 256p. VG/dj. K5. $22.00

**LOGUE, Christopher.** *Ode to the Dodo: Poems From 1953 to 1978.* 1981. London. Cape. 1st Eng. F/dj. T12. $25.00

**LOHF & SHEEHY.** *Sherwood Anderson: A Bibliography.* 1973. ils. 125p. F. A4. $85.00

**LOHMEYER & MCPHARLIN.** *Recollections of Cleveland & Detroit.* 1948. np. Golden Anniversary Souvenir. 77p. B18. $17.50

**LOMAS, Charlotte Rider.** *Garden Whimseys.* 1923. NY. 171p. VG. B26. $15.00

**LOMAX, Alan.** *Mister Jelly Roll.* nd. Grove. rpt. VG. B2. $25.00

**LOMAX, Alan.** *Rainbow Sign.* 1959. Duell. 1st. F/NF. B2. $40.00

**LOMAX, John Sr.** *Cow Camps & Cattle Herds.* 1967. Austin. Encino. 1/750. sgn/#d. ils WD Wittliff. F/acetate cover. A24. $85.00

**LOMAX, Louis E.** *Thailand: The War That Is, the War That Will Be.* 1967. Random. 1st. map/appendices. VG/dj. R11. $40.00

**LOMBE, Henry.** *Exhortation Given Forth at Requirings of Lord...* 1694. London. T Sowle. 1st. 7p. unbdg pamphlet. V3. $125.00

**LOMMEL, Eugene.** *Nature of Light...* 1875. London. Henry S King. ils. 356p. cloth. G. K5. $30.00

**LONDON, A.** *Complete American-Jewish Cookbook.* 1971 (1952). 3500 kosher recipes. F/VG. E6. $15.00

**LONDON, Champion.** *Our Hawaii.* 1917. NY. Macmillan. 1st. 345p. VG. B5. $115.00

**LONDON, Jack.** *Abysmal Brute.* 1913. NY. 1st. 169p. VG. B18. $95.00

**LONDON, Jack.** *Before Adam.* 1907. Macmillan. ils Chas Livingston Bull. 242p. brn linen. K1. $100.00

**LONDON, Jack.** *Best Short Stories of...* 1953. NY. 1st thus. S18. $5.00

**LONDON, Jack.** *God of His Fathers.* 1901. NY. McClure Phillips. 1st. gilt bl cloth. lacks ffe o/w F. M24. $275.00

**LONDON, Jack.** *John Barleycorn.* 1913. Grosset Dunlap. G. A19. $40.00

**LONDON, Jack.** *Little Lady of the Big House.* 1916. Macmillan. 1st. 8vo. 392p. stp bl cloth. VG+/NF. B20. $150.00

**LONDON, Jack.** *Revolution.* 1910. Macmillan. 1st. 8vo. 309p. maroon cloth. NF. B20. $385.00

**LONDON, Jack.** *Star Rover.* 1917. NY. Grosset. ils. VG/dj. B5. $45.00

**LONDON YEARLY MEETING.** *Rules of Discipline of Religious Society of Friends...* 1834. London. Darton Harvey. 3rd. 4to. 335p. G. V3. $60.00

**LONG, David.** *Blue Spruce.* 1995. Scribner. 1st. sgn. F/dj. O11. $30.00

**LONG, Frank Belknap.** *Hounds of Tindalos.* 1946. Arkahm. 1st. F/NF. B9. $150.00

**LONG, Frank Belknap.** *Rim of the Unknown.* 1972. Arkham. 1st. VG/dj. B30. $40.00

**LONG, James W.** *Essential Guide to Prescription Drugs.* 1988. Harper. 5th. 8vo. 994p. F/dj. W2. $65.00

**LONG, Jeff.** *Duel of Eagles.* 1990. NY. Morrow. BC. 431p. dj. F3. $10.00

**LONG, John Luther.** *War; or, What Happens When One Loves One's Enemy.* (1913). Bobbs Merrill. 1st. ils NC Wyeth. gilt red cloth. F. R3. $90.00

**LONG, Lyda Belknap;** see Long, Frank Belknap.

**LONG, Margaret.** *Santa Fe Trail: Following Old Historic Pioneer Trails...* (1954). Denver. Kistler Stationary Co. 281p. cloth. dj. D11. $75.00

**LONG, Max.** *Lava Flow Murders.* 1940. Lippincott. 1st. F/dj. M15. $150.00

**LONG, Philip S.** *Dreams, Dust & Depression.* 1972. Calgary. Cypress. 1st. sgn. F/VG. A26. $30.00

**LONG, S.** *Account of Expedition From Pittsburgh to Rocky Mountains...* 1972. Imp Soc. 1/1950. 547p. F/NF case. M4. $75.00

**LONG, William H.** *Apparatus for Measuring Metabolism & Activity in Animals.* 1939. Ann Arbor. U MI School Forestry & Conservation #5. 35p. S5. $7.00

**LONG, William J.** *Wilderness Ways.* 1900. Boston. Ginn. ils Copeland. pict cloth. G. A17. $12.50

**LONGACRE, Edward G.** *Mounted Raids of the Civil War.* 1975. Cranbury, NJ. 1st. 348p. F/dj. E1. $45.00

**LONGFELLOW, Henry Wadsworth.** *Christus.* 1872. Boston. Osgood. 3 vol. 1st. gilt wine cloth. VG. M24. $350.00

**LONGFELLOW, Henry Wadsworth.** *Courtship of Miles Standish & Other Poems.* 1859. Ticknor Fields. 1st/3rd prt. aeg. gilt tan cloth. M24. $150.00

**LONGFELLOW, Henry Wadsworth.** *Evangeline.* 1848. Boston. Wm Ticknor. 1st lg paper. 1/50. private pres. yel brd/label. M24. $4,500.00

**LONGFELLOW, Henry Wadsworth.** *Evangeline.* 1909. Reilly Britton. 1st thus. ils JR Neill. cloth. VG. B27. $55.00

**LONGFELLOW, Henry Wadsworth.** *New-England Tragedies.* 1868. Ticknor Fields. 1st. gr cloth brd. VG. Q1. $125.00

**LONGFELLOW, Henry Wadsworth.** *Poets & Poetry of Europe.* 1845. Phil. Carey Hart. 1st/2nd prt. F. M24. $300.00

**LONGFELLOW, Henry Wadsworth.** *Song of Hiawatha.* 1891. Houghton Mifflin. 1st. ils Remington. teg. marbled ep. F. H5. $450.00

**LONGFELLOW, Henry Wadsworth.** *Song of Hiawatha.* 1898. Chicago. Geo M Hill. Minnehaha ed. VG. A19. $25.00

**LONGFORD, Elizabeth.** *Elizabeth.* 1983. Toronto. Musson. 1st. F. T12. $35.00

**LONGFORD, Elizabeth.** *Winston Churchill: A Pictorial Life Story.* 1974. 1st Am. VG/dj. M17. $15.00

**LONGRIGG, S.H.** *Four Centuries of Modern Iraq.* 1968. Farnborough. Gregg. 4 pl/5 maps/genealogy table. 378p. cloth. VG/dj. Q2. $47.00

**LONGSTREET, Stephen.** *Masts to Spear the Stars.* 1967. Doubleday. 1st. olive drab cloth. F/NF. T11. $30.00

**LONGSTREET, Stephen.** *War Cries on Horseback.* 1970. NY. BC. 335p. E1. $25.00

**LONGSTREET & LONGSTREET.** *Salute to American Cooking.* 1968. Hawthorn. G/dj. A16. $8.00

**LONGUEVILLE, Peter.** *English Hermit; or, Unparalleled Sufferings...* 1786. London. Harrison. 8vo. 2 full-p pl. cloth. R12. $150.00

**LONSDALES, Roger.** *Charles Burney, a Literary Biography.* 1965. Clarendon. 1st. dj. H13. $45.00

**LONSTEIN & MARINO.** *Compleat Sinatra.* 1970. Ellenville. Compleat Pub. 1st. sm 4to. F/dj. B2. $85.00

**LOO, Miriam B.** *Loo's Family Favorites Cookbook.* 1977. Current. G/wrp. A16. $6.00

**LOOMIS, Elias.** *Introduction to Practical Astronomy.* 1860. NY. Harper. 497p. calf. w/catalog. B14. $150.00

**LOOMIS, Elias.** *Treatise on Algebra.* 1846. Harper. 1st. 346+6p. full leather. VG. H7. $20.00

**LOOMIS, F.A.** *As Long as Life: Memoirs of...Mary Canaga Rowland...* 1994. Seattle. Storm Peak. 1st. photos. 177p. AN. A25. $12.00

**LOOMIS, Noel M.** *Texan-Santa Fe Pioneers.* 1958. Norman, OK. 1st. fld map. cloth. dj. D11. $35.00

**LOOS, Anita.** *Kiss Hollywood Goodbye.* 1974. Viking. F/VG. L4. $12.00

**LOPEZ, Barry Holstun.** *About This Life.* 1988. Knopf. 1st. sgn. F/dj. R14. $40.00

**LOPEZ, Barry Holstun.** *Arctic Dreams.* 1986. Scribner. 1st. F/F. B3. $60.00

**LOPEZ, Barry Holstun.** *Arctic Dreams.* 1986. Scribner. 1st. sgn. F/dj. O11. $75.00

**LOPEZ, Barry Holstun.** *Crossing Open Ground.* 1988. Scribner. 1st. sgn. F/dj. O11. $55.00

**LOPEZ, Barry Holstun.** *Crow & Weasel.* 1990. SF. Northpoint. 1st. sgn. 1st issue bdg. F/dj. O11. $85.00

**LOPEZ, Barry Holstun.** *Crown & Weasel.* 1990. Toronto. Random. 1st Canadian. sgn. ils Tom Pohrt. F/dj. R14. $45.00

**LOPEZ, Barry Holstun.** *Desert Notes.* 1976. Andrews McMeel. 1st. NF/dj. M23. $200.00

**LOPEZ, Barry Holstun.** *Lessons From the Wolverine.* 1997. Athens, GA. 1st. sgn. F/dj. O11. $35.00

**LOPEZ, Barry Holstun.** *Of Wolves & Men.* 1978. Scribner. 1st. sgn. F/NF. O11. $175.00

**LOPEZ, Barry Holstun.** *Rediscovery of North America.* 1990. KY U. 1st. NF/VG. B19. $10.00

**LOPEZ, Barry Holstun.** *River Notes.* 1979. Kansas City. Andrews McMeel. 1st. sgn. F/clip. O11. $95.00

**LOPEZ, Barry Holstun.** *Winter Count.* 1981. Scribner. 1st. sgn. F/NF. O11. $95.00

**LOPEZ, Steve.** *Third & Indiana.* 1994. NY. Viking. 1st. author's 1st book. F/dj. R14. $30.00

**LORAC, E.C.R.** *And Then Put Out the Light.* 1949. Crime Club. 1st. VG/G. G8. $30.00

**LORAC, E.C.R.** *Murder on a Monument.* 1958. London. Collins Crime Club. 1st. F/clip. M15. $75.00

**LORAIN, John.** *Nature & Reason, Harmonized in Practice of Husbandry.* 1825. Phil. Carey Lea. 563p. full leather. B18. $45.00

**LORAND, Arnold.** *Old Age Deferred: Causes of Old Age & Its Postponement...* 1926. Phil. FA Davis. 6th. 500p. gr cloth. F. B14. $40.00

**LORANT, Stefan.** *New World: First Pictures of America...* 1946. NY. Duell Sloan. 1st. 292p. F3. $50.00

**LORCA, Federico Garcia.** *Three Tragedies.* 1947. New Directions. 1st thus. NF/VG. S13. $40.00

**LORCH, Robert S.** *Democratic Process & Administrative Law.* 1969. Wayne State. M11. $35.00

**LORD, Bette Bao.** *In the Year of the Boar & Jackie Robinson.* 1984. Harper Row. later prt. VG/dj. P8. $20.00

**LORD, John.** *Beacon Lights of History.* 1883. NY. Fords Howard Hulbert. 8 vol. 8vo. dk red cloth. G. S17. $15.00

**LORD, John.** *Maharajas.* 1971. NY. Random. 1st. ils/map ep. 241p. cloth. NF/dj. W1. $18.00

**LORD, Sheldon;** see Block, Lawrence.

**LORD, Walter.** *Time to Stand.* 1961. NY. 1st. VG/dj. B5. $17.50

**LORENZ, Alfred Lawrence.** *Hugh Gaine, a Colonial Printer...* 1972. Carbondale. S IL U. 1st. 192p. cloth. F/dj. O10. $35.00

**LORENZ, Otto.** *Art Nouveau.* nd. Germany. Artbook Internat. F/dj. B11. $22.50

**LORENZ, Tom.** *Guys Like Us.* 1980. Viking. 1st. F/VG. P8. $25.00

**LORIMER, Joyce.** *English & Irish Settlement on the River Amazon 1550-1646.* 1989. London. Hakluyt Soc. 1st. 8vo. 10 maps. 499p. cloth. dj. O1. $45.00

**LORIMER, Norma.** *By the Waters of Egypt.* 1914. NY. Brentano. 12mo. 314p. xl. B11. $20.00

**LORING, J. Alden.** *African Adventure Stories.* 1914. NY. Scribner. 1st. 301p. VG. H7. $30.00

**LORING, Roxamond B.** *Decorated Book Papers: Being Account of Their Designs...* 1952. Cambridge. 2nd. pl. blk cloth. dj. B14. $50.00

**LORIOUX, Felix.** *Le Buffon des Enfants. Ill-Les Oiseaux Exotiques.* (1948). Paris. Marcus. 1st. sq 4to. mc pict brd. R5. $300.00

**LORISTON-CLARKE, Jennie.** *Complete Guide to Dressage.* 1987. Phil. Running Pr. 1st Am. VG/dj. O3. $25.00

**LOTT, Arnold.** *Most Dangerous Sea: US Navy in Mine Warfare WWII.* 1959. Annapolis. 1st. ils. 332p. VG/G. B5. $50.00

**LOTZ, Jim.** *Mounties: History of Royal Canadian Mounted Police.* 1984. Greenwich, CT. Royce (Bison Books). 1st. photos. 160p. F/dj. A26. $15.00

**LOTZE, Hermann.** *Metaphysic in Three Books: Ontology, Cosmology & Psychology.* 1928. Cambridge. 284p. NF/dj. G1. $65.00

**LOTZE, Rudolf Hermann.** *Medizinische Psychologie oder Physiologie der Seele.* 1852. Leipzig. Weidmann'sche Buchhandlung. 632p. pub bdg. G1. $750.00

**LOUGHERY, John.** *Alias SS Van Dine.* 1992. Scribner. 1st. F/dj. N4. $20.00

**LOUGHNEY, A.M.** *Normal Weight Correct Eating.* 1919. Seattle. 1st. sm 4to. 172p. VG/stiff wrp. B20. $35.00

**LOUGHRAN, Peter.** *Third Beast.* 1990. Scarborough. 1st. F/NF. S18. $20.00

**LOUIS, P.C.A.** *Pathological Researches on Phthisis.* 1836. Boston. blk cloth. G. B14. $95.00

**LOUNSBERRY, Alice.** *Guide to the Wild Flowers.* nd. NY. 4th. ils. VG. M17. $20.00

**LOUNSBERRY, Alice.** *Southern Wind Flowers & Trees.* 1901. NY. Stokes. 1st. ils/index. 570p. G. H10. $25.00

**LOUSTAU-LALANNE, P.** *Land Birds of the Grantic Islands of the Seychelles.* 1962. Seychelles. 32p. gr cloth/orig wrp bound in. NF. C12. $35.00

**LOUYS, Pierre.** *Collected Tales of...* 1930. Chicago. Argus. 1st. 1/2000. 16 full-p ils. F/dj/case. B20. $100.00

**LOVE, John F.** *McDonald's Behind the Arches.* 1986. Bantam. 1st. VG/dj. P3. $12.00

**LOVE & ROBINSON.** *Hot Monogamy.* 1994. Dutton. 1st. 8vo. 310p. F/dj. W2. $30.00

**LOVECRAFT, H.P.** *Dark Brotherhood.* 1966. Arkham. 1st. 1/3460. F/NF. M21. $125.00

**LOVEJOY, David S.** *Rhode Island Politics & the American Revolution 1760-1776.* 1969. RI. fld map. 256p. dj. B18. $9.50

**LOVEJOY & LOVEJOY.** *Memoir of Rev Elijah P Lovejoy...* 1838. NY. Taylor. 8vo. brd/paper spine. R12. $275.00

**LOVELL, Jim.** *Lost Moon.* 1994. Houghton Mifflin. 1st. F/dj. M23. $40.00

**LOVELL & LOVELL.** *Discovering the Universe.* 1963. Harper Row. 4to. 136p. VG/dj. K5. $10.00

**LOVESEY, Peter.** *Last Detective.* 1991. Doubleday. 1st. F/dj. M23. $30.00

**LOVETT, Sarah.** *Dangerous Attachments.* 1995. Villard. 1st. sgn. author's 1st book. F/dj. A23. $40.00

**LOVING, Nancy S.** *Go the Distance: Complete Resource of Endurance Horses.* 1977. N Pomfret. Trafalgar. 1st. VG. O3. $25.00

**LOW, A.M.** *Adrift in the Stratosphere.* nd. Peal. G+/dj. P3. $18.00

**LOW, A.M.** *Woodrow Wilson: An Interpretation.* 1918. Little Brn. 1st. 291p. VG. B10. $15.00

**LOW & SCHIEBER.** *Applied Solid State Physics.* 1970. NY. Plenum. 244p. NF/dj. M10. $8.50

**LOWE, C.M.** *Changing Pictures.* ca 1900. London. Nister. 4to. 6 dbl half-wheel moveable pl. F. R5. $1,500.00

**LOWE, David Garrard.** *Stanford White's New York.* 1992. NY. 1st. photos. VG/dj. M17. $25.00

**LOWE, John.** *Medical Missions: Their Place & Power.* 1886. London. 1st. 292p. A13. $75.00

**LOWE, Percival G.** *Five Years a Dragoon ('49 to '54).* 1965. OK U. 1st thus. ils/notes/index. 336p. VG/dj. B19. $25.00

**LOWE, Samuel E.** *New Story of Peter Rabbit.* 1926. Whitman. 1st. 16mo. ils Allan Wright. blk/turquoise pict brd. mc pict dj. R5. $100.00

**LOWELL, A. Lawrence.** *Government & Parties in Continental Europe, Vol 1.* 1897 (1896). Houghton Mifflin. 2nd. 8vo. VG. A2. $15.00

**LOWELL, Amy.** *Some Imagist Poets, an Anthology.* 1915. Boston. 1st. wrp. T9. $145.00

**LOWELL, James Russell.** *Conservations on Some of the Old Poets.* 1893. McKay. 1st. VG/sans. O4. $15.00

**LOWELL, James Russell.** *Courtin'.* 1874. Boston. Osgood. 1st. ils Winslow Homer. gilt gr cloth. M24. $300.00

**LOWELL, James Russell.** *Last Poems.* 1895. Houghton Mifflin. 1st. 16mo. 47p. dk gr cloth. VG+/dj. J3. $175.00

**LOWELL, James Russell.** *Works...* 1890. Houghton Mifflin. Standard Lib ed. 10 vol. teg. quarter morocco. F1. $600.00

**LOWELL, James Russell.** *Writings of...* 1890. Boston. 11 vol. half brn leather/marbled brd. VG+. B30. $400.00

**LOWELL, Michele.** *Your Purebred Kitten: A Buyer's Guide.* 1995. NY. Holt/Owl Book. 1st. F/dj. O3. $15.00

**LOWELL, Percival.** *Evolution of Worlds.* 1909. Macmillan. 1st. 8vo. ils/pl. 262p. cloth. K5. $100.00

**LOWMAN, Al.** *Printer at the Pass: Work of Carl Hertzog.* 1972. San Antonio. Inst Texan Cultures. 1st. gilt bdg. F. M24. $125.00

**LOWNSBERY, Eloise.** *Marta the Doll.* nd (c 1946). Longman Gr. 1st. ils Marya Werten. 118p. G. C14. $10.00

**LOWRIE, Donald A.** *Rebellious Prophet: Life of Nicolai Berdyaev.* 1960. Harper. 310p. VG/G. H10. $17.50

**LOWRY, Martha.** *Floral Art for America.* 1964. NY. Barrows. 191p. VG/dj. A10. $20.00

**LOWRY, Robert.** *Journey Out: Three Stories.* 1945. Cincinnati. Little Man. 1/300. sgn. F. B2. $75.00

**LOWRY, Timothy.** *And Brave Men, Too.* 1985. NY. Crown. 1st. 246p. NF/dj. R11. $25.00

**LOWTHER & WORTHINGTON.** *Encyclopedia of Practical Horticulture: A Reference System.* 1914. N Yakima. 2037p. VG. B26. $135.00

**LOY, Mina.** *Lost Lunar Baedeker.* 1996. NY. 1st. VG/dj. M17. $15.00

**LUBBOCK, Basil.** *Nitrite Clippers.* 1932. Boston. 1st. ils/index. 159p. VG. B5. $95.00

**LUBBOCK, Basil.** *Western Ocean Packets.* 1925. Boston. photos. VG. M17. $32.50

**LUCAS, E.L.** *Art Books: A Basic Bibliography on Fine Arts.* 1968. NYGS. 245p. F. A4. $65.00

**LUCAS, June Richardson.** *Children of France & the Red Cross.* 1918. NY. 1st. sgn. 193p. A13. $75.00

**LUCAS, Robert Irwin.** *Tarentum Pattern Glass.* 1981. self pub. 1st. 422p. ES. F/dj. H1. $27.50

**LUCAS & SYNGE.** *ICUN Plant Red Data Book.* 1980 (1978). Morges, Switzerland. 540p. VG/dj. B26. $30.00

**LUCE, J.V.** *End of Atlantis.* 1973. London. BCA. ils. 224p. cloth. VG/dj. Q2. $20.00

**LUCE, Philip A.** *Road to Revolution: Communist Guerilla Warfare in US.* 1967. San Diego. Viewpoint. 1st? 12mo. F/wrp. A2. $7.50

**LUCE, R. Duncan.** *Individual Choice Behavior: A Theoretical Analysis.* 1959. John Wiley. 1st. 153p. NF/VG. C14. $25.00

**LUCHETTI, Cathy.** *Woman of the West.* 1982. Antelope Island. 240p. VG/dj. J2. $155.00

**LUCIA, Victor O.** *Modern Gnathological Concepts.* 1961. St Louis. CV Mosby. 1st. tall 8vo. 610p. NF. C14. $55.00

**LUCIANO, Ron.** *Umpire Strikes Back.* 1982. Bantam. 1st. F/VG. P8. $25.00

**LUCIE-SMITH, Edward.** *Art of the 1930s: Age of Anxiety.* 1985. NY. 1st. ils. VG/G. M17. $30.00

**LUDLUM, Robert.** *Aquitaine Progression.* 1984. Random. 1st. F/F. H11. $35.00

**LUDLUM, Robert.** *Bourne Ultimatium.* 1990. NY. Random. 1st. F/dj. T12. $35.00

**LUDLUM, Robert.** *Chancellor Manuscript.* 1977. NY. Dial. 1st. NF/NF. H11. $35.00

**LUDLUM, Robert.** *Cry of the Halidon.* 1974. Delacorte. 1st. F/NF. H11. $70.00

**LUDLUM, Robert.** *Holycroft Covenant.* 1978. NY. Marek. 1st. VG/NF. H11. $35.00

**LUDLUM, Robert.** *Matlock Paper.* 1973. Dial. 1st. NF/dj. N4. $55.00

**LUDLUM, Robert.** *Rhinemann Exchange.* 1974. Dial. 1st. F/NF. H11. $35.00

**LUDLUM, Robert.** *Scarlatti Inheritance.* 1971. World. 1st. VG/fair acetate dj. N4. $75.00

**LUDOLF, Hiob.** *Lexicon Aethiopico-Latinum... Accessit Authoris...* 1661. London. Roycroft. 3 parts in 1. full tan calf. K1. $1,500.00

**LUDWIG.** *Maxfield Parrish.* 1973. 4to. 111 ils/64 mc pl/1900 entries. NF/NF. A4. $125.00

**LUGINBUHL & SKIFF.** *Observing Handbook & Catalogue of Deep-Sky Objects.* 1990. Cambridge. charts/tables/figures. 352p. VG. K5. $50.00

**LUHAN, Mabel Dodge.** *Una & Robin.* 1976. Berkeley. Friends of Bancroft Lib. 1st. photos. 36p. F. A18. $40.00

**LUKACH, Joan M.** *Hilla Rebay: In Search of the Spirit in Art.* 1983. Braziller. 1st. photos. 366p. VG/dj. S14. $12.00

**LUKE, Thomas;** see Masterton, Graham.

**LUMHOLTZ, Carl.** *New Trails in Mexico: An Account...* 1912. Scribner. 1st. ils/fld maps. 411p. gilt cloth. D11. $100.00

**LUMHOLTZ, Carl.** *Unknown Mexico: A Record of 5 Years' Exploration...* 1902. Scribner. 2 vol. 1st. maps. cloth. D11. $150.00

**LUMLEY, Brian.** *Last Aerie.* 1993. Tor. 1st. F/dj. S18. $23.00

**LUMMIS, Charles F.** *Flowers of Our Lost Romance.* 1929. Houghton Mifflin. 1st. decor gold cloth. VG/sans. O4. $60.00

**LUMMIS, Charles F.** *My Friend Will.* 1961. Cultural Assets Pr. 3rd. 12mo. photos. 51p. stiff wrp. F7. $10.00

**LUMMIS, Charles F.** *Tramp Across the Continent.* 1892. Scribner. 1st. 270p. marbled brd. D11. $100.00

**LUMMIS, Charles F.** *Tramp Across the Continent.* 1917 (1892). Scribner. 270p. gr pict cloth. VG. F7. $40.00

**LUND, Morten.** *Skier's World.* nd. Random. 1st. sm 4to. 252p. G/dj. S14. $8.50

**LUNDBERG, Ferdinand.** *Rich & the Super-Rich.* 1969. NY. Lyle Stuart. VG. A19. $25.00

**LUNN, Henry.** *Aegean Civilizations.* 1925. London. Benn. 1st. 8vo. G. W1. $20.00

**LUNNY.** *Early Maps of North America.* 1961. NJ Hist Soc. 26 full-p maps. 48p. NF. A4. $65.00

**LUNT, James.** *Hussein of Jordan: Searching for a Just & Lasting Peace.* 1989. NY. Morrow. 1st. 278p. cloth. VG/dj. W1. $20.00

**LUPICA, Mike.** *Dead Air.* 1986. Villard. 1st. VG/dj. R8. $12.00

**LUPICA, Mike.** *Limited Partner.* 1990. Villard. 1st. F/F. P8. $45.00

**LUPOFF, Richard A.** *Circumpolar.* 1984. Timescape. 1st. F/dj. P3. $20.00

**LUPOFF, Richard A.** *Comic Book Killer.* 1988. Offspring. ltd. sgn. F/case. w/Gangsters at War comic. M19. $35.00

**LUPOFF, Richard A.** *Countersolar!* 1987. Arbor. 1st. F/dj. P8. $15.00

**LUPOFF, Richard A.** *Ova Hamlet Papers.* 1979. Pennyfarthing. 1st. sgn. VG/wrp. M19. $17.50

**LUPOFF, Richard A.** *Space War Blues.* 1980. Gregg. F/sans. P3. $15.00

**LUPOFF, Richard A.** *Sword of the Demon.* 1977. Harper Row. 1st. F/dj. P3. $18.00

**LURIA, Alexander R.** *Neuropsychology of Memory.* 1976. WA, DC. Winston/Wiley. 372p. rose cloth. VG/dj. G1. $75.00

**LURIE, Alison.** *Don't Tell the Grown-Ups: Subversive Children's Literature.* 1990. Little Brn. 1st. 8vo. 229p. F/NF. C14. $16.00

**LURIE, Alison.** *Foreign Affairs.* 1984. Franklin Lib. ltd. sgn. full leather. F. A24. $40.00

**LURIE, Alison.** *Women & Ghosts.* 1994. NY. Nan A Talese. 1st Am. F/dj. A23. $32.00

**LUSIS, Andy.** *Astronomy & Astronautics: Enthusiast's Guide...* 1986. Facts on File. 8vo. 292p. K5. $25.00

**LUSTBADER, Eric.** *Floating City: A Nicholas Linnear Novel.* 1994. Pocket. 1st thus. VG/dj. A28. $12.00

**LUSTGARTEN, Edgar.** *One More Unfortunate.* 1947. Scribner. 1st Am. VG/G+. C15. $25.00

**LUTES, Della.** *Bridge Food For Bridge Fans.* 1932. Boston. Barrows. VG. V4. $120.00

**LUTHER, Martin.** *Accents in Luther's Theology.* 1967. Concordia. edit Heino Kadai. 272p. G/wrp. B29. $7.50

**LUTHER, Martin.** *Eine Heer. Predigt Widder den Turchen.* 1529. Wittenberg. Schirlentz. 4to. title decor att to Cranach. quarter calf. R12. $1,250.00

**LUTHER, T.** *High Spots of Custer & Battle of Little Big Horn Literature.* 1967. Kansas City, MO. Posse of Westerners. sgn. F. A19. $100.00

**LUTHER & LUTHER.** *Governors of Virginia, 1776-1974.* 1974. Eastern Shore News. photos. 124p. VG/dj. B10. $12.00

**LUTZ, Alma.** *Susan B Anthony: Rebel, Crusader, Humanitarian.* 1959. Boston. Beacon. 1st. 340p. G/clip. V3. $14.00

**LUTZ, F.E.** *Prince George-Hopewell Story.* 1957. Richmond. 314p. G. M4. $18.00

**LUTZ, F.E.** *Prince George-Hopewell Story.* 1957. Wm Byrd. photos/map ep. 314p. VG. B10. $50.00

**LUTZ, John.** *Better Mousetraps.* 1988. St Martin. 1st. F/dj. C15. $18.00

**LUTZ, John.** *Diamond Eyes.* 1990. St Martin. 1st. VG/dj. G8. $15.00

**LUTZ, John.** *Lazarus Man.* 1979. Morrow. 1st. sgn. NF/VG. G8. $17.50

**LUTZ, John.** *Spark.* 1993. Holt. 1st. F/NF. G8. $20.00

**LUVAAS, William.** *Going Under.* 1994. NY. Putnam. 1st. sgn. F/dj. R14. $35.00

**LUVAAS & NELSON.** *US Army War College Guide to Battles of Chancellorsville...* 1988. Carlisle, PA. S Mtn Pr. 1st. F/dj. A14. $25.00

**LUXENBERG, Stan.** *Roadside Empires: How Chains Franchised America.* 1985. NY. Viking/Penguin. 1st. index. 313p. F/dj. H6. $38.00

**LYELL, Charles.** *Second Visit to the United States of North America.* 1849. Harper. 1st Am. 8vo. gilt blk cloth. O1. $450.00

**LYLE, Mel.** *Power Boy Adventure: Mystery of the Flying Skeleton.* 1964. Racine. 1st. F. T12. $8.00

**LYLE, Mel.** *Power Boys Adventure: Mystery of the Vanishing Lady.* 1967. Whitman. 1st. ils. VG/dj. B36. $8.00

**LYMAN, Chester S.** *Around the Horn to Sandwich Islands & California 1845-1850.* 1924. New Haven. Yale. 16 pl. map ep. VG. P4. $125.00

**LYMAN, George D.** *John Marsh Lyman, Pioneer.* 1931. Chautauqua. 1st. ils/map ep. 394p. VG+. B19. $50.00

**LYMAN, George D.** *Ralston's Ring: California Plunders the Comstock Lode.* 1937. Scribner. 1st. photos. 368p. VG/dj. S14. $25.00

**LYMAN, H.** *Insomnia & Other Disorders of Sleep.* 1885. 1st. VG. E6. $75.00

**LYNAM, Robert.** *British Essayists; With Prefaces Biographical, Historical...* 1827. London. JF Dove. 30 vol. 12mo. portraits. full bl polished calf/raised bands. R3. $4,000.00

**LYNCH, D.T.** *Epoch & Man: Martin Van Buren & His Times.* 1971. Port WA. 2 vol. ils. NF. M4. $42.00

**LYNCH, James.** *With Stevenson to California.* 1954. Oakland. Biobooks. 1/500. map. 57p. gr cloth. NF. B20. $35.00

**LYNCH, Kathleen M.** *Jacob Tonson.* 1971. Knoxville. U TN. F/dj. H13. $65.00

**LYNCH, Kenneth.** *Garden Ornaments.* 1974. Canterbury, CT. 768p. VG. A10. $35.00

**LYNCH, Kenneth.** *Sundials.* 1971. Canterbury, CT. 128p. VG. A10. $45.00

**LYND, Robert.** *Dr Johnson & Company.* 1928. Doubleday. 1st. gilt bl cloth. H13. $15.00

**LYNDS, Dennis.** *Falling Man.* 1970. Random. 1st. F/F. H11. $30.00

**LYNE, Pat.** *Shrouded in Mist.* 1984. Leominster, Eng. 1st. VG/G. O3. $65.00

**LYNN, Jack.** *Factory.* 1982. Harper Row. 1st. F/F. H11. $20.00

**LYNN, Janet.** *Peace + Love.* 1973. Creation House. 1st. 1/50,000. F/G. T12. $12.00

**LYNN, Margaret.** *Mrs Maitland's Affair.* 1963. Doubleday Crime Club. 1st. 238p. F/dj. H1. $9.00

**LYON, Danny.** *Bikeriders.* 1997. Santa Fe. Twin Palms. 1/26 lettered. sgn. F/pub case. S9. $350.00

**LYON, Peter.** *Wild, Wild West.* 1969. Funk Wagnall. VG/dj. A19. $30.00

**LYONS, A. Neil.** *Moby Lane.* 1916. Bodley Head. 1st. VG. w/Alexander Woolcott sgn letter about book. S13. $25.00

**LYONS, Arthur.** *Blue Sense.* 1991. Mysterious. 1st. F/dj. P3. $20.00

**LYONS, Arthur.** *Dead Are Discreet.* 1974. Mason Lipscomb. 1st. F/dj. T10. $100.00

**LYONS, Arthur.** *Hard Trade.* 1981. HRW. 1st. F/VG. P3. $25.00

**LYONS, Dorothy.** *Bluegrass Champion.* nd. Grosset Dunlap. Famous Horse Stories series. G. O3. $15.00

**LYONS, Dorothy.** *Bluegrass Champion.* 1949. Grosset Dunlap. VG/dj. A21. $35.00

**LYONS, Dorothy.** *Bright Wampum.* 1958. Harcourt Brace. 1st. VG/G. O3. $48.00

**LYONS, Dorothy.** *Copper Khan.* 1950. Harcourt Brace. 1st. VG/G. O3. $48.00

**LYONS, Dorothy.** *Golden Sovereign.* 1947. Harcourt Brace. VG/G. O3. $40.00

**LYONS, Dorothy.** *Midnight Moon.* 1946. Harcourt Brace. VG/G. O3. $40.00

**LYONS, Dorothy.** *Pedigree Unknown.* 1973. HBJ. pict brd. VG. O3. $25.00

**LYONS, Dorothy.** *Pedigree Unknown.* 1973. HBJ. 1st. VG/dj. A21. $45.00

**LYONS, Dorothy.** *Red Embers.* 1948. NY. Harcourt Brace. 1st. VG/G. O3. $48.00

**LYONS, Dorothy.** *Silver Birch.* 1939. Harcourt Brace. 1st. VG. O3. $30.00

**LYONS & LYONS.** *Someone Is Killing the Great Chefs of America.* 1993. Little Brn. 1st. VG/dj. B11. $15.00

**LYONS & LYONS.** *Someone Is Killing the Great Chefs of Europe.* 1976. HBJ. 1st (B in letter string). F/VG. P12. $18.00

**LYONS & PETRUCELLI.** *Die Geschichte der Medizin im Spiegel der Kunst.* 1980. Cologne. 1st German. 615p. dj. A13. $150.00

**LYSAGHT, A.M.** *Joseph Banks in Newfoundland & Labrador.* 1766. Berkeley. 512p. VG/dj. A10. $150.00

**LYTLE, Horace.** *How to Train Your Bird Dog.* 1934. Hochwalt. 224p. pict cloth. G. A17. $12.50

**LYTTLETON, Raymond A.** *Modern Universe.* 1956. Harper. later prt. ils. VG/dj. A2. $15.00

**LYTTON, Harold.** *Last of the Saxon Kings.* 1898. London. red half leather/marbled brd. F. B30. $45.00

**M'CLINTOCK, Francis Leopold.** *Narrative of Discovery of Fate of Sir John Franklin...* (1972). Edmonton. Hurtig. 1st thus. 3 maps/facs. NF/dj. A26. $65.00

**M'CLINTOCK, Francis Leopold.** *Voyage of the Fox in the Arctic Seas: A Narrative...* 1860. Boston. Ticknor Fields. 1st Am. 14 pl/4 maps. O1. $75.00

**M'CLUNG, John A.** *Sketches of Western Adventure...* 1838. James. rpt of 1836. ils/notes. 318p. B19. $50.00

**M'COSH, James.** *Method of the Divine Government, Physical & Moral.* 1867. NY. Robert Carter. 8th. 549p. G. H10. $25.00

**M'DIARMID, J.** *Sketches From Nature.* 1830. Edinburgh. Oliver & Boyd. VG. M12. $95.00

**M'HENRY, John.** *Ejectment Law of Maryland: Embracing...* 1822. Frederick-Town. Herald Pr by John P Thomson. modern quarter calf. M11. $250.00

**MABEY, Richard.** *Flowers of the Kew: 350 Years of Paintings...* 1989. NY. Atheneum. 1st. ils/biblio/index. 208p. F/dj. H10. $22.50

**MABEY, Richard.** *Flowers of the Kew: 350 Years of Paintings...* 1989. NY. Atheneum. 1st. ils. VG/dj. M17. $30.00

**MABIE, Peter.** *A to Z Book.* 1929. Whitman. 4to. NF/pict wrp. D1. $60.00

**MABIE, Peter.** *Toy Shop Parade.* 1930. Racine. Whitman. 4to. mc pict wrp. R5. $60.00

**MABLY.** *Des Droites et Des Devoirs Du Citoyen.* 1789. Kehl. 8vo. calf. R12. $250.00

**MACADAMS, Lewis.** *Poetry Room.* 1971. Harper Row. ARC/1st. inscr/dtd 1975, F/dj. L3. $75.00

**MACAFFEE, Robert B.** *History of the Late War in the Western Country...* 1816. Lexington. Worsley Smith. 1st. 8vo. aeg. Riviere bdg. F. O1. $1,200.00

**MACARDLE, Dorothy.** *Uninvited.* 1942. Literary Guild of Am. 8vo. 342p. VG/dj. H1. $19.00

**MACARTNEY, Carol.** *Easy Stages of Cook Book.* 1972. London. Octopus. G/dj. A16. $15.00

**MACAULAY, David.** *Black & White.* 1990. Houghton Mifflin. 1st. 1991 Caldecott. mc pict dj. R5. $110.00

**MACAULAY, David.** *Way Things Work.* 1988. Boston. 1st. 384p. VG+. C14. $17.00

**MACAULAY, Rose.** *Letters to a Friend, 1950-1952.* 1962. NY. 1st Am. edit C Babington-Smith. VG/dj. M17. $15.00

**MACAULAY, Thomas Babington.** *History of England From Accession of James 2.* 1856. NY. Harper. 2 vol. leather. VG. V4. $150.00

**MACAULEY, Rose.** *Pleasure of Ruins.* 1964. Thames Hudson. 1st. ils/index. 286p. VG/dj. B5. $37.50

**MACAULEY, Thomas Babinton.** *Critical & Historical Essays.* 1874. Longman Gr. 8vo. 850p. 3-quarter calf. H13. $45.00

**MACBETH, George.** *Anna's Book.* 1983. London. 1st. dj. T9. $8.00

**MACBETH, George.** *Noah's Journey.* 1966. NY. Viking. 1st. obl 4to. NF/sans. L3. $75.00

**MACBETH, George.** *Samurai.* 1975. HBJ. 1st. author's 1st novel. VG/F. H11. $15.00

**MACBETH, George.** *Seven Witches.* 1978. HBJ. 1st. inscr. F/NF. L3. $50.00

**MACCANN & PERRY.** *New Film Index.* 1975. Dutton. 522p. VG/dj. C5. $15.00

**MACDONALD, Betty.** *Anybody Can Do Anything.* 1950. Phil. 1st. VG/dj. B5. $22.50

**MACDONALD, Betty.** *Mrs Piggle-Wiggle's Magic.* (1957). Lippincott. 8vo. 126p. gr brd. G+. T5. $12.00

**MACDONALD, Betty.** *Onions in the Stew.* 1955. Phil. 1st. VG/VG. B5. $20.00

**MACDONALD, Betty.** *Plague & I.* 1948. Lippincott. 1st. sgn. VG/dj. B20. $50.00

**MACDONALD, D.** *Velvet Claw: Natural History of the Carnivores.* 1992. London. BBC. ils/photos. 256p. F/VG+. M12. $30.00

**MACDONALD, Duncan B.** *Development of Muslim Theology, Jurisprudence...* 1903. NY. Scribner. 386p. cloth. VG+. Q2. $53.00

**MACDONALD, George.** *At the Back of the North Wind.* 1919. Phil. 1st. ils JW Smith. gilt tan cloth. VG+. B20. $175.00

**MACDONALD, George.** *Expression of Character: Letters of...* 1994. Eerdmans. 1st. edit/pref GE Sadler. AN/dj. A27. $20.00

**MACDONALD, George.** *Golden Key.* 1976. FSG. 8vo. 86p. bl brd. F/dj. D1. $75.00

**MACDONALD, George.** *Heart of George MacDonald.* (1994). Harold Shaw. 1st. edit/intro Rolland Hein. AN/dj. A27. $24.00

**MACDONALD, George.** *Light Princess.* 1969. NY. FSG. 1st. ils Maurice Sendak. 110p. xl. G. G11. $15.00

**MACDONALD, George.** *Pincess & the Goblin.* (1920). Phil. McKay. Newbery Classic reissue. 263p. VG+. D4. $55.00

**MACDONALD, George.** *Princess & the Goblin.* 1920. Phil. McKay. rpt. 8vo. VG/dj. M21. $95.00

**MACDONALD, John D.** *Barrier Island.* 1986. Knopf. 1st. F/dj. A23. $32.00

**MACDONALD, John D.** *Bright Orange for the Shroud.* 1972. Phil. Lippincott. 1st Am hc. VG/dj. M15. $125.00

**MACDONALD, John D.** *Cinnamon Skin.* 1982. Harper Row. 1st. F/NF. H11. $30.00

**MACDONALD, John D.** *Empty Copper Sea.* 1978. Lippincott. 1st. store stp on bottom edges. F/NF. H11. $40.00

**MACDONALD, John D.** *Empty Copper Sea.* 1978. Lippincott. 1st. VG/VG. B3. $20.00

**MACDONALD, John D.** *Free Fall in Crimson.* 1981. Harper Row. 1st. F/NF. A23. $30.00

**MACDONALD, John D.** *Girl in the Plain Brown Wrapper.* 1973. Lippincott. 1st Am. hc. F/NF. M15. $125.00

**MACDONALD, John D.** *Good Old Stuff.* 1982. Harper Row. 1st. F/F. H11. $30.00

**MACDONALD, John D.** *Green Ripper.* 1979. Lippincott. 1st. NF/F. H11. $25.00

**MACDONALD, John D.** *Green Ripper.* 1979. Lippincott. 1st. VG/NF. M23. $15.00

**MACDONALD, John D.** *Lonely Silver Rain.* 1985. Knopf. 232p. NF/dj. H11/P12. $15.00

**MACDONALD, John D.** *One Fearful Yellow Eye.* 1977. Phil. Lippincott. 1st Am hc. NF/dj. M15. $100.00

**MACDONALD, John D.** *One More Sunday.* 1984. Knopf. 1st. NF/NF. H11. $15.00

**MACDONALD, John D.** *Please Write for Details.* 1959. S&S. 1st. 8vo. F/dj. S9. $150.00

**MACDONALD, John D.** *Quick Red Fox.* 1964. Phil. Lippincott. 1st Am hc. F/NF. M15. $400.00

**MACDONALD, John D.** *Scarlet Ruse.* 1980. NY. Lippincott Crowell. 1st Am hc. F/dj. M15. $125.00

**MACDONALD, John D.** *Three for McGee.* 1967. Doubleday. Omnibus. F/NF. M15. $300.00

**MACDONALD, John D.** *You Live Once.* 1976. London. Hale. 1st hc. F/dj. M15. $75.00

**MACDONALD, John Ross;** see Millar, Kenneth.

**MACDONALD, Kim.** *Light Meals Including Cold Dishes & Outdoor Cooking.* 1971. Crescent. G/dj. A16. $10.00

**MACDONALD, Margaret.** *Storyteller's Sourcebook, a Subject, Title & Motif Index...* 1982. 836p. VG. A4. $75.00

**MACDONALD, Ross;** see Millar, Kenneth.

**MACDONOGH, Giles.** *Brillat-Savarin: Judge & His Stomach.* 1992. Chicago. VG/dj. M17. $27.50

**MACELTREE, Wilmer W.** *Along the Western Brandywine.* 1912. np. 2nd. 199p. teg. gilt cloth. B18. $45.00

**MACELTREE, Wilmer W.** *Down the Eastern & Up the Black Brandywine.* 1912. np. 2nd. sgn. 176p. teg. gilt cloth. B18. $45.00

**MACEWEN, William.** *Pyogenic Infective Diseases of the Brain & Spinal Cord.* 1893. Glasgow. Maclehose. 2nd. 688p. quarter sheep/marbled brd. G7. $695.00

**MACFADDEN, Bernard.** *Hair Culture: Rational Methods for Growing Hair...* 1922. NY. Physical Culture. 1st. 199p. bl cloth. VG+. B20. $20.00

**MACFADDEN, Bernard.** *Hair Culture: Rational Methods for Growing Hair...* 1929. NY. self pub. ils. VG. H7. $14.00

**MACFADDEN, Harry Alexander.** *Rambles in the Far West.* 1906. Hollidaysburg, PA. 1st. 42 pl. 278p. gilt gr cloth. F. H7. $50.00

**MACFALL, Haldane.** *Book of Lovat Claud Fraser.* 1923. London. Dent. 184p. VG/dj. D4. $225.00

**MACFARLANE, David.** *Come From Away.* 1991. London. Scribner. 1st Eng. F/dj. A23. $40.00

**MACFARLANE, Iris.** *Mouth of the Night.* 1976. NY. Macmillan. 1st Am. ils. F/NF. D4. $30.00

**MACGINITIE, Nettie.** *Marine Mollusca of Point Barrow, AK.* 1959. Smithsonian. 27 pl. P4. $45.00

**MACGREGOR, J.G.** *North-West of Sixteen.* (1968). Edmonton. Hurtig. 1st. xl. VG/NF. A26. $15.00

**MACH, Ernst.** *Erkenntnis und Irrtum: Skizzen zur Psychologie...* 1905. Leipzig. Johann Ambrosius Bath. tall 8vo. 461p. G. G1. $350.00

**MACHEN, Arthur.** *Ornaments in Jade.* 1924. NY. Knopf. 1st. 1/1000. sgn/#d. F/glassine/case. Q1. $150.00

**MACHETANZ & MACHETANZ.** *Robbie & the Sled Dog Race.* 1964. Scribner. juvenile. VG/clip. P4. $25.00

**MACHIAVELLI, Niccolo.** *Historiae Florentinae.* 1610. Strasbourg. Zetzner. 8vo. portrait. brd. R12. $500.00

**MACINNES, Helen.** *Cloak of Darkness.* 1982. HBJ. 1st. VG/dj. G8. $10.00

**MACINNES, Helen.** *Prelude to Terror.* 1978. HBJ. 1st. VG-/G+. G8. $7.50

**MACK, Burton L.** *Mack & Christian Origins: A Myth of Innocence.* 1988. Fortress. 432p. VG. B29. $13.50

**MACK, Connie.** *My 66 Years in the Big Leagues.* 1950. Winston. 1st. VG/G. C15. $50.00

**MACKAIL, John W.** *Biblia Innocentium, Being Story of God's Children...* 1892. Hammersmith. Kelmscott. 1st thus. 1/200. gilt limp vellum/gr silk ties. M24. $600.00

**MACKAY, Charles.** *Extraordinary Popular Delusions & Madness of Crowds.* 1954. LC Page. 724p. G. B29. $19.50

**MACKAY, Charles.** *Life & Liberty in America; or, Sketches of a Tour in US...* 1859. NY. Harper. 1st Am. 8vo. 10 pl. cloth. O1. $85.00

**MACKAY, Constance D'Arcy.** *Plays of the Pioneers.* 1976 (1915). NY. Core Collection Books. 158p. xl. VG. C5. $12.50

**MACKAY, James.** *Allan Pinkerton: First Private Eye.* ils/index. 256p. dj. E1. $28.00

**MACKAY, John.** *Good Shooting.* 1960. NY. sgn. photos. 138p. F. A17. $17.50

**MACKAY-SMITH, Alexander.** *Race Horses of America 1832-1872: Portraits...Edward Troye.* 1981. Saratoga Springs. Nat Mus Racing. 1/1500. sgn/#d/ils. VG. O3. $125.00

**MACKEEVER, Frank C.** *Native & Naturalized Plants of Nantucket.* 1968. Amherst. 132p. VG/dj. B26. $17.50

**MACKEN, Walter.** *Flight of the Doves.* 1968. Macmillan. 1st. F/VG. M5. $45.00

**MACKENZIE, Alexander.** *Alexander Mackenzie's Voyage to Pacific Ocean in 1793.* 1967. NY. 384p. VG/dj. B18. $17.50

**MACKENZIE, Alexander.** *Alexander Mackenzie's Voyage to the Pacific Ocean.* 1931. Lakeside Classic. 1st thus. edit Quaife. teg. VG. T11. $50.00

**MACKENZIE, Compton.** *Rival Monster.* 1952. London. 1st. inscr. dj. T9. $50.00

**MACKENZIE, Donald A.** *Teutonic Myth & Legend.* 1934. NY. Wm Wise. 1st. ils. gilt bl cloth. F/dj. T10. $75.00

**MACKENZIE, Jeanne.** *Victorian Courtship.* 1979. OUP. 1st Am. 146p. F/NF. D4. $30.00

**MACKIE, Richard J.** *Range Ecology & Relations of Mule Deer, Elk & Cattle...* (1970). Wildlife Monographs #20. 79p. F/wrp. S15. $7.00

**MACKIN, Bill.** *Cowboy & Gunfighter Collectibles: Photographic Encyclopedia.* 1989. Mtn Pr. ils. 172p. NF/wrp. B19. $10.00

**MACKINTOSH, H.R.** *Doctrine of the Person of Jesus Christ.* 1912. T&T Clark. 540p. fair. B29. $9.50

**MACKINTOSH, N.J.** *Psychology of Animal Learning.* 1974. London. Academic. 730p. panelled ochre cloth. VG/dj. G1. $60.00

**MACKLIN, Herbert W.** *Brasses of England.* 1907. Dutton. 1st Am. 336p. VG. H10. $45.00

**MACKSEY, Kenneth.** *Partisans of Europe in Second World War.* 1975. NY. 1st. ils. 271p. VG/dj. B18. $15.00

**MACLACHLAN, Colin.** *Criminal Justice in 18th-Century Mexico: A Study...* 1974. Berkeley. 1st. dj. F3. $30.00

**MACLAINE, Shirley.** *Dancing in the Light.* 1985. Bantam. 1st. 421p. G. W2. $20.00

**MACLAY, John.** *Mindwarps.* 1991. Dreamhouse. 1st. 1/500. sgn. AN/sans. S18. $30.00

**MACLAY, John.** *Other Engagements.* 1987. Dreamhouse. 1st. 1/1000. sgn. AN/sans. S18. $25.00

**MACLAY, John.** *Voices From the Night.* 1994. Baltimore. Maclay. 1st. 1/75. sgn. F/case. G10/M21. $55.00

**MACLEAN, Alistair.** *Athabasca.* 1980. London. 1st. dj. T9. $15.00

**MACLEAN, Alistair.** *Captain Cook.* 1972. Doubleday. 1st Am. VG/dj. M20. $32.00

**MACLEAN, Alistair.** *Caravan to Vaccares.* 1970. Collins. 1st. VG/dj. P3. $25.00

**MACLEAN, Alistair.** *HMS Ulysses.* 1955. London. Collins. 1st. author's 1st book. red cloth. F/VG. T11. $95.00

**MACLEAN, Alistair.** *Lawrence of Arabia.* 1962. Random. 1st. beige buckram. F/VG. M7. $40.00

**MACLEAN, Alistair.** *Lonely Sea.* 1986. Doubleday. 1st. quarter gr cloth. F/NF. T11. $35.00

**MACLEAN, Alistair.** *Puppet on a Chain.* 1969. Doubleday. 1st Am. NF/VG. N4. $25.00

**MACLEAN, Alistair.** *River of Death.* 1981. London. 1st. dj. T9. $12.00

**MACLEAN, Alistair.** *Seawitch.* 1977. Doubleday. 1st Am. F/NF. N4. $25.00

**MACLEAN, Andrew.** *RB Bennett: Prime Minister of Canada.* (1934). Toronto. Excelsior. 1st. sgn/#d. VG/G. A26. $25.00

**MACLEAN, Virginia.** *Much Entertainment: A Visual & Culinary Record...* 1973. NY. ils. VG/dj. M17. $20.00

**MACLEISH, Archibald.** *America Was Promises.* 1939. DSP. 1st. silvered bl cloth. F/NF. T10. $75.00

**MACLEISH, Archibald.** *Free Man's Books.* 1942. Mt Vernon. Peter Pauper. 1st. quarter red cloth. F/glassine dj. M24. $35.00

**MACLEISH, Archibald.** *Poetry & Experience.* 1961. Houghton Mifflin. 1st. gilt gray cloth. F/NF. T10. $75.00

**MACLENNAN, Hugh.** *Rivers of Canada.* 1974. Toronto. ils. VG/dj. M17. $20.00

**MACLEOD, Charlotte.** *Had She But Known.* 1994. Mysterious. 1st. F/dj. P3. $25.00

**MACLEOD, Charlotte.** *Owl Too Many. A Peter Shandy Mystery.* 1991. Mysterious. 1st. sgn. F/NF. A23. $36.00

**MACLEOD, Charlotte.** *Rest You Merry.* 1978. Doubleday Crime Club. 1st. F/dj. M15. $100.00

**MACLEOD, Charlotte.** *Silver Ghost.* 1988. Mysterious. 1st. NF/NF. A23. $30.00

**MACLEOD, Norman.** *We Thank You All the Time.* 1941. Prairie City, IL. Pr of James A Decker. 1st. F/VG. A18. $40.00

**MACMAHON, Henry.** *Ten Commandments.* 1924. Grosset Dunlap. MTI. 12 scenes. NF. C15. $65.00

**MACMICHAEL, William.** *Gold-Headed Cane.* 1827. London. 1st. 179p. quarter leather/marbled brd. A13. $600.00

**MACMICHAEL, William.** *Gold-Headed Cane. Second Edition.* 1828. London. Murray. 267p. recent quarter calf/marbled brd. G7. $125.00

**MACMICHAEL, William.** *Lives of British Physicians.* 1830. London. Murray. 267p. recent quarter calf/marbled brd. G7. $95.00

**MACMILLAN, Terry.** *Mama.* 1987. Houghton Mifflin. 1st. sgn. author's 1st book. F/NF. B2. $300.00

**MACMULLEN, Jerry.** *Star of India: Log of an Iron Ship.* 1961. Howell-North. 8vo. map ep. tan cloth. VG/dj. P4. $35.00

**MACNEICE, Louis.** *Springboard.* 1945. Random. 1st. NF/dj. A24. $40.00

**MACNEIL, Duncan.** *Charge of Cowardice.* 1978. St Martin. 1st. gilt gr cloth. F/NF. T11. $70.00

**MACNEIL, Duncan.** *Cunningham's Revenge.* 1985. NY. Walker. 1st Am. F/dj. T11. $35.00

**MACNEIL, Duncan.** *Sadhu on the Mountain Peak.* 1973. St Martin. 1st Am. F/dj. T11. $50.00

**MACNUTT, Francis Augustus.** *Bartholomew de Las Caas: His Life...* 1909. Arthur H Clark. 472p. gilt brd. D11. $175.00

**MACNUTT, Francis Augustus.** *Fernando Cortes: His Five Letters of Relation to Chas V.* 1908. Arthur H Clark. 2 vol. 1/750. gilt cloth. D11. $225.00

**MACPHAIL, Andrew.** *Three Persons.* 1929. NY/Montreal. Louis Carrier. 1st. 346p. gilt bl cloth. VG. M7. $45.00

**MACPHERSON, James.** *Fingal: An Ancient Epic Poem in 6 Books...* 1762. London. Becket DeHondt. 2nd (same year as 1st). tall 4to. 270p. polished calf. H13. $375.00

**MACPHERSON, Malcolm C.** *Time Bomb: Fermi, Heisenberg & Race for Atomic Bomb.* 1986. NY. photos. VG/dj. M17. $15.00

**MACPHERSON, Rett.** *Family Skeletons.* 1997. St Martin. 1st. F/dj. A23. $40.00

**MACQUITTY, Betty.** *Victory Over Pain: Morton's Discovery of Anaesthesia.* 1969. NY. 1st. 208p. dj. A13. $35.00

**MACRAE, Eleanor Harris.** *William Diuquid of Buckingham County Virginia.* (1970s). self pub. 271p. mechanically reproduced. VG. B10. $65.00

**MACSHANE, Frank.** *Life of Raymond Chandler.* nd. Dutton. 1st. VG/dj. G8. $20.00

**MACVEY, John W.** *Alone in the Universe?* 1963. Macmillan. 1st. xl. K5. $15.00

**MADDEN, Betty I.** *Art, Crafts & Architecture in Early Illinois.* 1974. IL State Mus. ils. 297p. cloth. F/dj. D2. $45.00

**MADDEN, Henry Miller.** *Xantus: Hungarian Naturalist in Pioneer West.* 1949. Books of the West. 1st. ils/notes/biblio. 312p. NF. B19. $50.00

**MADDEN, John.** *One Size Doesn't Fit All.* 1988. Villard. 1st. sgn. F/dj. M19. $17.50

**MADDOX, Tony.** *Noah's Ark, a Pop-Up Playbook.* 1994. Heinemann. 1st. folio. engineer Arlie Apte. F. B17. $15.00

**MADDUX, Vernon R.** *John Hittson: Cattle King on the TX & CO Frontier.* 1994. CO U. 1st. ils/index. 214p. AN. B19. $20.00

**MADIGAN, Thomas F.** *Word Shadows of the Great: Lure of Autograph Collecting.* 1930. Stokes. inscr. 300p. cloth. D11. $40.00

**MADIS, George.** *Winchester Book.* 1961. Dallas, TX. self pub. sgn. AN. A19. $50.00

**MADISON, Charles.** *Irving to Irving: Author-Publisher Relations 1800-1974.* 1974. Bowker. 1st. 8vo. VG/dj. A2. $20.00

**MADISON, Charles.** *Jewish Publishing in America: Impact on Jewish Writing...* 1976. NY. Sanhedrin. 1st. 8vo. 294p. F/dj. O10. $25.00

**MADISON, Charles.** *Owl Among Colophons: Henry Holt As Publisher & Editor.* 1966. HRW. 1st. pres. 198p. cloth. F/dj. P1. $17.50

**MADISON, Janet.** *Sweethearts Always, Poems of Love.* 1906. Reilly Britton. 1st. ils H Putnam Hall. VG. M5. $110.00

**MADISON, Larry.** *Trout River.* 1988. Abrams. 1st. inscr. bl 4to. photos. 167p. F/dj. T11. $45.00

**MADONNA.** *Sex.* Prepared for Quebec. few French-text p. aluminum bdg. AN/foil wrp. A4. $85.00

**MADSON, John.** *Stories From Under the Sky.* 1961. IA State. 1st. 205p. F/G. A17. $17.50

**MAFFEI, Jarquis Scipio.** *Compleat History of Ancient Amphitheatres...* 1730. London. Noorthouck. 1st. 8vo. 15 pl (10 fld). 412p. contemporary calf. W1. $450.00

**MAGALINI, Sergio.** *Dictionary of Medical Syndromes.* 1971. Phil. 591p. A13. $75.00

**MAGATH, Thomas B.** *Medicolegal Necropsy, a Symposium...* 1934. Baltimore. Williams Wilkins. M11. $50.00

**MAGEE, Harvey White.** *Story of My Life.* (1926). NY. Boyd. sgn. sm 8vo. 138p. gilt maroon cloth. K1. $50.00

**MAGILL, Frank N.** *Masterpieces of Christian Literature in Summary Form.* 1963. Salem. 2 vol. VG/dj. B29. $26.00

**MAGINNIS, Arthur J.** *Atlantic Ferry: Its Ships, Men & Working.* 1892. London. Whittaker. sm 8vo. 304p. gilt bl cloth. VG+. B20. $150.00

**MAGISTRALE, Tony.** *Landscape of Fear: Stephen King's American Gothic.* 1988. Bowling Green. Popular. 1st. AN/dj. T12. $45.00

**MAGNER, D.** *Magner's Standard Horse & Stock Book.* 1908 (1903). Saalfield. 1756 ils+17 pl. 1181p. gilt stp bdg. VG. H1. $40.00

**MAGNUSON, James.** *Rundown.* 1977. Dial. 1st. F/dj. P8. $40.00

**MAGORIAN, Michelle.** *Back Home.* 1984. Harper Row. 1st. 375p. F/dj. D4. $30.00

**MAGRIEL, Paul.** *Backgammon.* 1976. NY. 1st. VG/dj. B5. $60.00

**MAGUIRE, A.** *Dinosaur Pop-Up ABC.* 1995. Little Simon. 1st. ils Dick Dudley. F. B17. $14.00

**MAGUIRE, Gregory.** *Wicked: Life & Times of the Wicked Witch of the West.* 1995. Harper Collins. 1st. VG/dj. B30. $22.50

**MAHAFFY, J.P.** *Rambles & Studies in Greece.* ca 1900. Phil. Winston. ils/fld map. 535p. gilt bl cloth. VG+. H7. $17.50

**MAHAN, A.T.** *Great Commanders: Admiral Farragut.* 1892. NY. Appleton. 1/1000. lg paper ed. 333p. 2-tone gold cloth. P4. $350.00

**MAHAN, A.T.** *Influence of Sea Power Upon History 1660-1783.* 1894. Little Brn. 7th. gilt bl cloth. G. S17. $30.00

**MAHAN, A.T.** *Life of Nelson: Embodiment of Sea Power of Great Britain.* 1897. Little Brn. 2 vol. gilt bdg. VG. S17. $80.00

**MAHAN, A.T.** *Sea Power in Its Relation to War of 1812.* 1969. NY. 2 vol. ils. F. M4. $45.00

**MAHARAJAH OF COOCH BEHAR.** *Thirty-Seven Years of Big Game Shooting in Cooch Behar...* 1993. Prescott, AZ. ltd facs of 1808. 8vo. aeg. leatherette. F. A17. $45.00

**MAHFOUZ, Naguib.** *Palace of Desire.* 1991. Doubleday. 1st Am. Cairo Trilogy #2. F/dj. A24. $30.00

**MAHLER, Donald A.** *Dyspenea.* 1990. Mt Kisco, NY. Futura. 1st. 8vo. F/sans. A2. $30.00

**MAHONEY, Dan.** *Detective First Grade.* 1993. NY. SMP. 1st. F/F. H11. $25.00

**MAHONEY, Rosemary.** *Early Arrival of Dreams.* 1990. Fawcett Columbine. 1st. author's 1st book. F/F. B3. $40.00

**MAIDEN, Cecil.** *Borrowed Crown.* 1968. Viking. 1st. 223p. F/dj. D4. $35.00

**MAILER, Norman.** *American Dream.* Dial. 1st. VG/dj. B30. $50.00

**MAILER, Norman.** *Armies of the Night.* 1968. NAL. 1st. VG/clip. B30. $25.00

**MAILER, Norman.** *Existential Errands.* 1972. Boston. 1st. VG/dj. M17. $25.00

**MAILER, Norman.** *Gospel According to the Son.* 1997. Random. 1st. sgn. F/dj. R14. $60.00

**MAILER, Norman.** *Harlot's Ghost.* 1991. NY. Random. 1st. sgn. F/dj. R14. $65.00

**MAILER, Norman.** *Picasso.* 1995. Atlantic Monthly. 1st. sgn. F/dj. R14. $75.00

**MAILER, Norman.** *Presidential Papers.* 1963. NY. Putnam. 1st. VG/dj. B30. $30.00

**MAILER, Norman.** *White Negro: Superficial Reflections on the Hipster.* 1957. SF. City Lights. 1st/later state. (75¢ price). wrp. R11. $20.00

**MAILING, Arthur.** *Schroeder's Game.* 1977. Harper Row. 1st. xl. VG/dj. P3. $5.00

**MAILLOL, Aristide.** *Dialogues des Courtisanes.* 1948. Paris. Mourlot. 1/275. 35 lithos. 94p. full vellum wrp/chemise/case. B24. $1,500.00

**MAILLOL, Aristide.** *Eclogues of Vergil. In the Original Latin...* 1927. London. Cranach. 1/200 (264 total). 42 ils. bl brd. F/chemise/case. B24. $2,500.00

**MAILS, Thomas E.** *Cherokee People: Story of Cherokees From Earliest Origins...* 1992. Council Oaks. 1st trade. 1/100. sgn. ils/index. 368p. F. B19. $100.00

**MAILS, Thomas E.** *Pueblo Children of the Earth Mother.* 1983. Doubleday. 2 vol. 1st. ils/notes/index. AN/dj/case. P4. $150.00

**MAILS, Thomas E.** *Secret Native American Pathways.* 1988. Tulsa, OK. Council Oak Books. F. A19. $25.00

**MAIMBOURG, Louis.** *Histoire de Pontificat de S Gregoire le Grand.* 1686. Paris. Claude Barbin. 1st. 4to. ils. contemporary sheep. K1. $200.00

**MAINE, Henry Summer.** *Popular Government. Sixth Edition.* 1918. London. John Murray. gr cloth. M11. $35.00

**MAIR, C.** *Through the Mackenzie Basin: A Narrative of Athabasca...* 1908. Toronto. W Briggs. ils. 494p. VG+. M12. $175.00

**MAIR, George B.** *Miss Turquoise.* 1965. Random. 1st. F/NF. H11. $20.00

**MAIRINGER, Franz.** *Horses Are Made to Be Horses.* 1990. NY. Howell. VG/fair. O3. $30.00

**MAISEL, Albert.** *Harmone Quest.* 1965. NY. 1st. 262p. dj. A13. $20.00

**MAISKY, Ivan.** *Memoirs of a Soviet Ambassador: The War, 1939-1943.* 1968 (1965). Scribner. 1st Am. VG/dj. A2. $12.50

**MAITLAND, Alan.** *Favourite Scary Stories From Graveside.* 1996. Viking. 1st Canadian. F/dj. P3. $25.00

**MAITLAND, Frederic William.** *Life & Letters of Leslie Stephen.* 1906. London. Duckworth. 3-quarter morocco. M11. $250.00

**MAITLAND, Frederic William.** *Records of the Parliament Holden at Westminster...* 1893. London. Eyre Spottiswoode. roan-backed brd. M11. $250.00

**MAITLAND, Frederic William.** *Township & Borough, Being Ford Lectures...1897.* 1898. Cambridge. 2nd in series. M11. $150.00

**MAITLAND, Lester J.** *Knights of the Air.* 1929. Garden City. 1st. ils. 338p. G. B18. $75.00

**MAITLAND & POLLOCK.** *History of English Law, Before the Time of Edward I...* 1895. Cambridge. 1st Am. 2 vol. gilt bl cloth. M11. $450.00

**MAJNO, Guido.** *Healing Hand: Man & Wound in the Ancient World.* 1977. Harcourt Brace. 2nd. ils. 571p. dj. G7. $45.00

**MAJOR, Charles.** *Dorothy Vernon of Haddon Hall.* 1902. Macmillan. ils HC Christy. 369p. weak hinges. G11. $10.00

**MAJOR, Harlan.** *Fishing Behind the Eight Ball.* 1952. Harrisburg. 1st. photos. 254p. F/dj. A17. $12.50

**MAJOR, Ralph A.** *Classic Descriptions of Disease With Biographical Sketches.* 1932. Springfield. pres. 630p. G7. $150.00

**MAJOR, Ralph A.** *History of Medicine.* 1954. Springfield. 2 vol. dj. G7. $145.00

**MAJORS, Alexander.** *Seventy Years on the Frontier...Memoirs...* 1893. Rand McNally. 1st. 325p. gilt cloth. D11. $75.00

**MAJUMDAR, Margaret A.** *Althusser & the End of Leninism?* 1995. London. Pluto. 1st. 8vo. VG. A2. $40.00

**MAKEMSON, Maud.** *Book of the Jaguar Priest.* 1951. NY. Henry Schuman. 1st. 238p. dj. F3. $45.00

**MAKOWSKY, Veronica A.** *Caroline Gordon: A Biography.* 1989. OUP. 1st. 8vo. F/dj. A2. $13.00

**MAKTARI, A.M.A.** *Water Rights & Irrigation Practices in Lahj...* 1971. Cambridge. Oriental Pub #21. 2 maps. 202p. cloth. VG. Q2. $36.50

**MALAMUD, Bernard.** *Fixer.* 1966. Farrar STraus. 1st. F/dj. Q1. $75.00

**MALAMUD, Bernard.** *Idiots First.* (1963). Farrar Straus. 1st/1st prt. 8vo. red ep. gray brd/blk cloth spine. dj. R3. $65.00

**MALAMUD, Bernard.** *Natural.* 1952. Harcourt Brace. 1st. MTI. F/VG+. P8. $2,500.00

**MALAMUD, Bernard.** *Pictures of Fidelman.* 1969. FSG. 1st. NF/dj. R14. $35.00

**MALAMUD, Bernard.** *Rembrandt's Hat.* 1973. FSG. 1st. NF/dj. R14. $35.00

**MALAMUD, Bernard.** *Tenants.* 1971. FSG. 1st. F/F. H11. $40.00

**MALAN.** *Gustave Dore: Adrift on Dreams of Splendor...Bibliography.* 1995. 4to. ils. 352p. F/F. A4. $40.00

**MALCOLM, C.A.** *Diary of George Sandy.* 1943. Edinburgh. Constable. 69p. wrp. M11. $75.00

**MALCOLM, Janet.** *Journalist & the Murderer.* 1990. Knopf. 1st. 8vo. 162p. NF/VG. S14. $10.00

**MALCOLM, John.** *Godwin Sideboard.* 1984. London. Collins Crime Club. 1st. sgn. F/dj. M15. $100.00

**MALCOLM, John.** *Sheep, Goats & Soap.* 1991. London. Collins Crime Club. 1st. F/dj. M15. $45.00

**MALCOLMSON, Anne.** *William Clake: An Introduction.* 1967. NY. 1st. ils. VG/dj. M17. $27.50

**MALCOLMSON, David.** *London: The Dog Who Made the Team.* 1963. DSP. 1st. inscr by London's ownder. VG/G. P8. $40.00

**MALLARY, Peter T.** *Houses of New England.* 1984. Thames Hudson. 1st. photos. 208p. NF/VG. S14. $15.00

**MALLET, Beatrice.** *ABC.* ca 1950. England. Birn Bros Ltd. 4to. stiff linenized paper. R5. $65.00

**MALLET-JORIS, Francoise.** *Witches.* 1970. FSG. later. G/dj. L1. $12.50

**MALLOCH, Archibald.** *Finch & Baines: A 17th-C Friendship.* 1917. Cambridge. 8 pl/ftspc. 89p. G7. $95.00

**MALLOCK, W.H.** *On Life & Death, by Lucretius.* 1976. Skokie. Blk Cat. mini. 1/249. ils Calvin Brazelton. 51p. gilt blk leather. F. B24. $75.00

**MALONE, Dumas.** *Story of the Declaration of Independence.* 1954. Oxford. 1st. 282p. VG/G. B10. $25.00

**MALONE, H.T.** *Cherokees of the Old South: People in Transition.* 1956. GA U. 1st. 238p. F/dj. M4. $35.00

**MALONEY, Tom.** *US Camera 1957.* nd. US Camera/DSP. G/VG. S5. $20.00

**MALORY, Thomas.** *Birth, Life & Acts of King Arthur, of His Noble Knights...* 1927. London. Dent. 3rd. 1/1600. lg 4to. ils Beardsley. teg. F. H5. $950.00

**MALORY, Thomas.** *Boy's King Arthur.* 1936. Scribner. ils NC Wyeth. VG. M17. $65.00

**MALOS, Ellen.** *Politics of Housework.* 1980. London. Allison Busby. 1st. VG/dj. N2. $10.00

**MALOUF, David.** *Conversations at Curlow Creek.* 1996. Chatto Windus. 1st. sgn. F/dj. O11. $40.00

**MALOUF, David.** *Harland's Half Acre.* 1984. Knopf. 1st Am. sgn. F/dj. O11. $45.00

**MALOUF, David.** *Remembering Babylon.* 1993. London. Chatto Windus. 1st. sgn. F/dj. O11. $40.00

**MALOUF, David.** *Remembering Babylon.* 1993. Sydney. Chatto Windus/Random. 1st Australian. F/dj. Q1. $45.00

**MALOUF, David.** *Selected Poems.* 1991. North Ryde, NSW. Angus Robertson. 1st. sgn. F. O11. $35.00

**MALPASS, Eric.** *At the Height of the Moon.* 1967. London. Heinemann. 1st. NF/VG. A14. $28.00

**MALRAUX, Andre.** *Anti-Memoirs.* 1968. NY. 1st. trans T Kilmartin. dj. T9. $20.00

**MALRAUX, Andre.** *Days of Wrath.* 1936. Random. 1st. NF/dj. T10. $100.00

**MAMET, David.** *Some Freaks.* 1989. NY. Viking. 1st. F/dj. R14. $40.00

**MAMET, David.** *Warm & Cold.* 1988. NY. Grove. 1st. ils Donald Sultan. F/dj. A24. $30.00

**MAMOT, Patricio.** *Filipino Physicians in America.* 1981. Indianapolis. 278p. A13. $50.00

**MANCHESTER, Herbert.** *Diamond Match Co: A Century of Service...1835-1935.* c 1935. Diamond Match Co. 108p. gilt brn stiff bdg. H6. $68.00

**MANCHESTER, Herbert.** *William Armstrong Fairburn: A Factor in Human Progress.* c 1940. NY. Blanchard. 162p. H6. $44.00

**MANCHESTER, William.** *American Caesar: Douglas MacArthur, 1880-1964.* 1978. Boston. Little Brn. inscr/sgn author/Gene Autry. F/dj. A19. $50.00

**MANDELA, Nelson.** *Long Walk to Freedom.* 1994. Little Brn. 1st. F/dj. A24. $25.00

**MANDERINO, John.** *Sam & His Brother Len.* 1994. Chicago. 1st. author's 1st book. F/F. H11. $40.00

**MANDERS, Olga Sarah.** *Mrs Manders' Cook Book.* 1968. Viking. G/dj. A16. $15.00

**MANDERSON, C.** *Twin Seven Shooters.* 1902. 8vo. 54p. gilt bdg. VG. E6. $70.00

**MANELI, Mieczyslaw.** *War of the Vanquished.* 1971. Harper Row. 1st. trans Maria deGorey. VG/clip. R11. $20.00

**MANFRED, Frederick.** *No Fun on Sunday.* 1990. Norman, OK. 1st. F/dj. P8. $20.00

**MANFRED, Frederick.** *Scarlet Plume.* 1964. Trident. sgn. F/dj. A19. $45.00

**MANFRED, Frederick.** *Wind Blows Free.* 1979. Sioux Falls, SD. Center for Western Studies. VG/dj. A19. $30.00

**MANJO, G.** *Healing Hand, Man & Wound in Ancient World.* 1975. Harvard. 1st. is. 571p. VG/G. E6. $35.00

**MANKIEWICA & WELLES.** *Citizen Kane Book: Shooting Script.* 1971. Little Brn. 1st. VG+. B9. $15.00

**MANLEY, Cyril C.** *Decorative Victorian Glass.* 1981. Van Nostrand Reinhold. 1st Am. 128p. VG. H1. $85.00

**MANLEY, Seon.** *My Heart's in Greenwich Village.* 1969. NY. Funk Wagnall. 1st. ils. 221p. VG/VG. A25. $18.00

**MANLY, H.P.** *Electric & Oxy-Acetylene Welding.* 1941. Chicago. Drake. VG/dj. B9. $15.00

**MANLY, Peter L.** *20-CM Schmidt-Cassegrain Telescope.* 1994. Cambridge. photos/diagrams. 265p. F/dj. K5. $35.00

**MANN, Arthur.** *Baseball Confidential.* 1951. NY. 1st. VG/dj. B5. $20.00

**MANN, Arthur.** *Decline & Fall of NY Yankees.* 1967. NY. 1st. VG/dj. B5. $17.50

**MANN, C. Riborg.** *Manual of Advanced Optics.* 1902. Chicago. Scott Foresman. 1st. 196p. cloth. G. K5. $35.00

**MANN, Heinrich.** *Small Town Tyrant.* 1944. NY. Creative Age. 1st Am. F/VG+. B4. $250.00

**MANN, Leonard.** *Murder in Sydney.* 1937. London. Cape. 1st. VG/dj. M15. $100.00

**MANN, May.** *Elvis & the Colonel.* 1977. Drake. VG/dj. P3. $20.00

**MANN, Patricia.** *Systematics of Flowering Plants.* 1952. London. ils. 307p. dj. B26. $17.50

**MANN, Philip.** *Eve of the Queen.* 1983. NY. Arbor. 1st. F/F. H11. $40.00

**MANN, Thomas.** *Joseph the Provider.* 1944. Knopf. 1st. VG/dj. M25. $35.00

**MANN, Zane.** *Fair Winds & Far Places.* 1978. Minneapolis. Dillon. 1st. 8vo. 272p. VG/dj. B11. $15.00

**MANN & TRAIN.** *Social England: A Record of Progress of People...* 1902-1904. London. 6 vol. ils. gilt brn cloth. B14. $200.00

**MANNING-SANDERS, Ruth.** *Book of Ghosts & Goblins.* 1978 (1968). London. Methuen. rpt. turquoise brd. NF/dj. T5. $25.00

**MANNING-SANDERS, Ruth.** *Book of Magic Animals.* 1975. Dutton. 1st. 8vo. 127p. bl cloth. VG/G. T5. $25.00

**MANNINGER, Vilmos.** *Der Entwickelungsgang der Antiseptic und Aseptic.* 1904. Breslau. 1st. 168p. xl. A13. $75.00

**MANOIL, A.** *Psychologie Experimentale en Italie...* 1938. Paris. Felix Alcan. 489p. prt gr wrp/cloth drop box. G1. $65.00

**MANON, J.K.** *War of 1812.* 1972. FL U. ils/maps. 476p. F/dj. M4. $35.00

**MANSEL, Henry Longueville.** *Philosophy of the Conditioned.* 1866. London. Strahan. 12mo. panelled pebbled brn cloth. G1. $125.00

**MANSFIELD, J.B.** *History of the Great Lakes.* 1972. Cleveland. Freshwater. 2 vol. facs of 1899. gilt cloth. A17. $195.00

**MANSFIELD, Justine.** *True Tales of Kidnappings...* 1932. NY. 1st. 8vo. 272p. F/NF. B20. $60.00

**MANSFIELD, Katherine.** *Garden Party: And Other Stories.* 1939. London. Verona. 1/1200. ils/sgn Marie Laurencin. 16 lithos. 315p. NF/dj. B24. $3,500.00

**MANSO, Peter.** *Mailer: His Life & Times.* 1985. S&S. 1st. F/dj. T12. $20.00

**MANSUELLI, Guido A.** *Galleria Degli Uffizi: Le Sculpture.* 1958 & 1961. Rome. Instituto Poligrafico Stato. 2 vol. ils. cloth. NF. D2. $175.00

**MANTLE, Mickey.** *Mick.* 1985. Doubleday. 1st. sgn. 248p. NF/VG+. B20. $100.00

**MANTLE, Mickey.** *Mickey Mantle Story.* 1953. Holt. 1st. VG+. P8. $75.00

**MANTLE, Mickey.** *My Favorite Summer 1956.* 1991. Doubleday. 1st. sgn. F/dj. S9. $275.00

**MANUZIO, Aldo the Younger.** *Eleganze.* 1558. Venice. Paul Manutius. 8vo. Aldine Anchor on title. gilt calf. R12. $750.00

**MANUZIO, Aldo the Younger.** *Le Attioni Di Castruccio Castacane de Gli Antelminelli.* 1590. Rome. Heirs of Gigliotti. 4to. portrait. vellum. R12. $850.00

**MANZ & SCHICKTANZ.** *Puppchens Himmelsreise (Dolly's Trip to Heaven).* 1927. Leipzig. Edwin Freyer. 1st. 4to. 12 full-p pl. R5. $300.00

**MAPP, Alf J.** *Frock Coats & Epaulets.* (1963). Yoseloff. 501p. VG/VG. B10. $50.00

**MAPP, Alf J.** *Virginia Experiment: Old Dominion's Role...1607-1781.* 1974 (1957). Open Court. 2nd revised. 577p. VG. B10. $15.00

**MAPP, Edward.** *Blacks in American Films: Today & Yesterday.* 1972. Metuchen, NJ. ils. 378p. silvered brd. F. B14. $35.00

**MAPPIN, G.F.** *Bigger & Better Roses.* 1936. NY. ils/photos. 155p. B26. $16.00

**MAPPLETHORPE, Robert.** *Black Book.* 1996. Boston. Miniature Eds. 1st thus. wrp. T9. $12.00

**MAPPLETHORPE, Robert.** *Some Women.* 1989. Boston. Bullfinch. 1st. 86 portraits. F/NF. C9. $120.00

**MAQUARRIE, John.** *Principles of Christian Theology.* 1977. Scribner. 2nd. 544p. VG/wrp. B29. $7.00

**MARA, Bernard;** see Moore, Brian.

**MARACLE, Lee.** *Bobbi Lee: Indian Rebel.* 1990. Toronto. Women's Pr. 1st. AN/wrp. A26. $25.00

**MARBERRY, M.M.** *Splendid Poseur: Joaquin Miller, American Poet.* (1953). NY. Crowell. 1st. VG/dj. A18. $20.00

**MARBLE, Annie Russell.** *Builders & Books: Romance of American History & Literature.* 1931. NY. Appleton. 1st. ils. 353p. F/dj. O1. $10.00

**MARBLE, Annie Russell.** *Pen Names & Personalities.* 1930. Appleton. 1st. 8vo. 255p. F/dj. O10. $40.00

**MARCH, John.** *Reports; or, New Cases; Taken in...Years King Charles I.* 1675. London. Prt for Samuel Heyrick. contemporary sheep. M11. $250.00

**MARCH-PENNEY, John.** *Japanese Flower Arrangement: Ikebana.* 1969. London. Hamlyn. 4to. ils. 141p. VG/dj. M10. $10.00

**MARCILLY, A.** *Paul et Virginie, by Jacques-Henri Bernardin de St Pierre.* ca 1835. Paris. Didot Freres. 6 full-p ils/vignette. rose cloth/leather label. B24. $150.00

**MARCOSSON, Isaac F.** *African Adventure.* 1921. NY. John Lane. 1st. 8vo. 288p. red cloth. B11. $25.00

**MARCOSSON, Isaac F.** *Black Golconda: Romance of Petroleum.* 1924. Harper. 1st. 8vo. 369p. B11. $35.00

**MARCUS, Joyce.** *Inscriptions of Calakmul.* 1987. Ann Arbor. 1st. 4to. 205p. wrp. F3. $25.00

**MARCUS, Stanley.** *Book Club of Texas.* 1989. Dallas. DeGolyer Lib. 1/100. sgn. marbled brd/cloth spine. F/as issued. A24. $125.00

**MARCUS, Stanley.** *Quest for the Best.* 1979. Viking. mini. 1/850. 228p. dj. AN. B24. $175.00

**MARCY, R.B.** *Thirty Years of Army Life on the Border...Indians Nomads...* 1866. Harper. ils. 442p. VG. J2. $285.00

**MARDER, Tod A.** *Critical Edge: Controversy in Recent American Architecture.* 1985. MIT. 1st. 4to. VG/dj. A2. $20.00

**MARGIL, Antonio.** *Nothingness Itself: Selected Writings.* 1976. Chicago. photos. VG/dj. M17. $20.00

**MARGOLIN, Philip.** *Gone, But Not Forgotten.* 1993. Doubleday. 1st. F/dj. S18. $20.00

**MARGOLIN, Phillip.** *After Dark.* 1995. Doubleday. 1st. F/dj. R8. $12.00

**MARGOLIS, John D.** *Joseph Wood Krutch: A Writer's Life.* 1980. TN U. 1st. ils/notes/index. 254p. F/NF. B19. $25.00

**MARGOTTA, Roberto.** *Story of Medicine.* 1968. NY. 1st. 319p. dj. A13. $50.00

**MARGULIES, Stan.** *Spartacus.* 1960. NY. Bryna. unp. VG. C5. $12.50

**MARIE, Pierre.** *Lectures on Diseases of the Spinal Cord.* 1895. London. New Sydenham Soc. 244 woodcuts. 511p. G7. $150.00

**MARIL, Nadja.** *Runaway Molly Midnight: Artist's Cat.* 1980. Owings Mills, MD. Stemmer House. 1st. 8vo. 25p. F. C14. $8.00

**MARINO, Josef.** *Hi! Ho! Pinocchio!* 1940. Reilly Lee. 1st. 4to. ils Wm Donahey. 127p. bl cloth/label. mc dj. R5. $100.00

**MARINOS & MARINOS.** *Plants of the Alpine Tundra.* 1981. np. ils/photos. 64p. sbdg. B26. $11.00

**MARIO, Thomas.** *Midnight Cookbook.* 1971. Chicago. Cowles. G/dj. A16. $7.00

**MARITAIN, Jacques.** *Integral Humanism: Temporal & Spiritual Problems...* 1968. NY. Scribner. 308p. G/dj. H10. $20.00

**MARITAIN, Raissa.** *Arbre Patriarche/ Patriarch Tree.* 1965. Worcester. Stanbrook. 1/550 on Barcham Green's Etham paper. F/dj/case. B2. $125.00

**MARK, Hans.** *Space Station: A Personal Journey.* 1987. Durham, NC. Duke. 8vo. 264p. F/dj. K5. $15.00

**MARK, Mary Ellen.** *Ward 81.* 1979. NY. S&S. 1st thus. obl 8vo. VG/wrp. S9. $75.00

**MARKBY, William.** *Introduction to Hindu & Mahommedan Law...* 1906. Oxford. Clarendon. brn cloth. M11. $85.00

**MARKHAM, Beryl.** *Splendid Outcast: African Stories.* 1987. SF. Northpoint. 1st. sm 8vo. 193p. F/dj. Q1. $35.00

**MARKHAM, Edwin.** *Shoes of Happiness & Other Poems.* 1916 (1913). Doubleday Page. sgn. VG. M20. $30.00

**MARKLAND, George.** *Pteryplegia; or, Art of Shooting-Flying.* 1931. Derrydale. 1st thus. 1/300. complete set/blank wrp. F. M24. $150.00

**MARKMAN & MARKMAN.** *Flayed Gods: Mesoamerican Mythological Tradition.* 1992. Harper. 1st. 456p. xl. dj. F3. $15.00

**MARKS, J.;** see Highwater, Jamake.

**MARKS, Paul Mitchell.** *And Die in the West.* nd. ils/maps. 480p. F/wrp. E1. $18.00

**MARKS, Paula Mitchell.** *And Die in the West.* 1989. Morrow. 1st. map ep. VG. J2. $225.00

**MARKS, Stuart A.** *Southern Hunting in Black & White: Nature, History...* 1991. Princeton. 1st. 327p. AN/dj. A17. $15.00

**MARKS-HIGHWATER, J.;** see Highwater, Jamake.

**MARLOWE, Amy Bell.** *Frances of the Ranges.* 1915. Grosset Dunlap. VG/dj. M20. $35.00

**MARLOWE, G.E.** *Churches of Old New England: Their Architecture...* 1947. NY. 1st. photos. 222p. VG. M4. $17.00

**MARLOWE, Hugh;** see Patterson, Henry.

**MARLOWE, Jeffrey.** *Stephen Foster: Fifteen Favorite Songs...* 1942. Boston Music Co. ils Hauman. 63p. G. B10. $25.00

**MARLOWE, Kenneth.** *Mr Madam: Confessions of a Male Madam.* 1964. LA. Sherbourne. 1st. 8vo. 246p. F/dj. B20. $25.00

**MARMELSZADT, Willard.** *Musical Sons of Aesculapius.* 1946. NY. 1st. sgn. 116p. A13. $225.00

**MARNHAM, Patrick.** *Road to Katmandu.* 1971. Putnam. 1st. F/dj. A23. $35.00

**MARON, Margaret.** *Bootlegger's Daughter.* Mysterious. 2nd. sgn. NF/dj. G8. $20.00

**MARON, Margaret.** *Fugitive Colors.* 1995. Mysterious. 1st. F/dj. A23. $34.00

**MARON, Margaret.** *Killer Market.* 1997. Mysterious. ARC. F/dj. A23. $30.00

**MARON, Margaret.** *Shooting at Loons.* 1994. Mysterious. 1st. F/dj. N4. $25.00

**MARON, Margaret.** *Up Jumps the Devil.* 1996. Mysterious. ARC. F/dj. A23. $20.00

**MARPLE, Alice.** *Iowa Authors & Their Works.* 1918. Des Moines. 367p. xl. VG. A4. $60.00

**MARQUEZ, Gabriel Garcia.** *Chronicle of a Death Foretold.* 1983. Knopf. ist. F/F. D10. $45.00

**MARQUEZ, Gabriel Garcia.** *Chronicle of a Death Foretold.* 1983. Knopf. 1st. F/NF. B2. $30.00

**MARQUEZ, Gabriel Garcia.** *Clandestine in Chile.* 1989. London. Granta. 1st. F/F. B3. $40.00

**MARQUEZ, Gabriel Garcia.** *General in His Labyrinth.* 1990. NY. 1st. F/dj. B30. $25.00

**MARQUEZ, Gabriel Garcia.** *Innocent Erendira & Other Stories.* 1978. Harper Row. 1st. F/F. B30. $60.00

**MARQUEZ, Gabriel Garcia.** *Love in the Time of Cholera.* 1988. NY. Knopf. 1st. F/dj. A23/D10. $50.00

**MARQUEZ, Gabriel Garcia.** *Love in the Time of Cholera.* 1988. NY. Knopf. 1st. NF/clip. H11. $30.00

**MARQUEZ, Gabriel Garcia.** *News of a Kidnapping.* 1997. Knopf. 1st. F/dj. S13. $12.00

**MARQUEZ, Gabriel Garcia.** *Story of a Ship-Wrecked Sailor.* 1986. NY. Knopf. 1st Am. F/VG+. C9. $25.00

**MARQUIS, Donald M.** *Finding Buddy Bolden: First Man of Jazz.* 1978. Goshen. Pinchpenny. F/wrp. B2. $35.00

**MARQUIS, Thomas.** *Custer Cavalry & Crows.* 1975. Ft Collins. F. A19. $75.00

**MARR, John W.** *Data on Mountain Environments: I Front Range. 16 Sites.* 1967. U CO. 110p. xl. VG. S5. $12.00

**MARR, John W.** *Ecosystems of the East Slope of Front Range in Colorado.* 1967. U CO. Studies in Biology #8. 134p. VG/wrp. S15. $12.00

**MARRACK, J.R.** *Chemistry of Antigens & Antibodies.* 1939. London. Medical Research. revised. ils. 194p. VG. A25. $15.00

**MARRIC, J.J.;** see Creasey, John.

**MARRIOT, Alice.** *Dequoyah, Leader of the Cherokees.* 1956. Random. ils Bob Riger. NF/VG. B36. $11.00

**MARRIOTT, Alice.** *Hell on Horses & Women.* 1953. OK U. ils. 290p. F/dj. M4. $22.00

**MARRIOTT, Alice.** *Valley Below.* 1949. OK U. 1st. ils. F/VG. M4. $40.00

**MARRYAT, Frederick.** *Poor Jack.* 1840. London. Longman. ils. 384p. later 19th-C gr calf. K1. $85.00

**MARS-JONES, Adam.** *Monopolies of Loss.* 1993. Knopf. 1st. sgn. F/dj. O11. $25.00

**MARS-JONES, Adam.** *Monopolies of Loss.* 1993. Knopf. 1st. 250p. F/dj. P12. $18.00

**MARS-JONES, Adam.** *Waters of Thirst.* 1994. Knopf. 1st Am. sgn. RS. F/dj. O11. $30.00

**MARSH, F.E.** *Fully Furnished: Christian Worker's Equipment.* 1973. Kregel. 390p. VG/dj. B29. $9.00

**MARSH, Ngaio.** *Death at the Bar.* 1940. Boston. 1st. VG/G. M17. $30.00

**MARSH, Ngaio.** *Died in the Wool.* 1945. Toronto. Collins. 1st Canadian. VG/dj. A14. $28.00

**MARSH, Ngaio.** *Hand in Glove.* 1962. London. Collins Crime Club. 1st. VG+/dj. A14. $35.00

**MARSH, Ngaio.** *Off With His Head.* 1957. London. Collins Crime Club. 1st. F/dj. M15. $45.00

**MARSH, Ngaio.** *Singing in the Shrouds.* 1958. London. Collins Crime Club. 1st. VG+/dj. A14. $35.00

**MARSH, Norman S.** *Rule of Law in a Free Society, a Report...* 1959. Geneva. Internat Comm of Jurists. bl cloth. M11. $45.00

**MARSH, U. Bowdoin.** *Bowdoin Family in the United States.* 1982. private prt. photos. 228p. VG. B10. $45.00

**MARSH, William Jr.** *Our President Herbert Hoover.* 1930. New Milford, CT. Wm/Chas Marsh. G+. V3. $12.00

**MARSHALL, A.J.** *Bower-Birds: Their Displays & Breeding Cycles.* 1954. Oxford. lg 8vo. ils. 212p. cloth. NF/dj. C12. $75.00

**MARSHALL, A.J.** *Darwin & Huxley in Australia.* 1970. Sydney. 142p. VG/dj. B26. $25.00

**MARSHALL, Anne.** *Day Before Cookbook.* 1973. Octopus. G/dj. A16. $8.00

**MARSHALL, Don B.** *California Shipwrecks.* 1978. Seattle. Superior. 1st. 4to. 171p. VG/dj. P4. $40.00

**MARSHALL, Edison.** *Pagan King.* 1959. Doubleday. 1st. F/NF. M19. $17.50

**MARSHALL, Frances Ireland.** *Magic Inc. Year Book 1967-1968.* 1968. Chicago. Magic Inc. sgn. 112p. VG/wrp. B11. $25.00

**MARSHALL, Henry Rutgers.** *Consciousness.* 1909. Macmillan. thick 8vo. 685p. bl cloth. VG. G1. $65.00

**MARSHALL, Henry Rutgers.** *Instinct & Reason: An Essay...* 1898. Macmillan. heavy 8vo. 574p. pebbled ruled russet cloth. xl. VG. G1. $65.00

**MARSHALL, J.** *American Bastille: History of Illegal Arrests...* 1875 (1869). 728p. full leather. VG. E6. $25.00

**MARSHALL, James.** *Santa Fe: Railroad That Built an Empire.* 1945. Random. 1st. ils/maps. 465p. remnant dj. B19. $45.00

**MARSHALL, Mel.** *Delectable Egg & How to Cook It.* 1968. Trident. 1st. G/dj. A16. $15.00

**MARSHALL, Mel.** *How to Make Your Own Lures & Flies.* 1976. Outdoor Life. 186p. F/dj. A17. $15.00

**MARSHALL, N.B.** *Aspects of Marine Zoology.* 1967. Academic. 270p. xl. VG. S5. $12.00

**MARSHALL, Nina L.** *Mosses & Lichens.* 1910. Doubleday Page. 327p. teg. VG. M7. $35.00

**MARSHALL, Nina L.** *Mushroom Book: A Popular Guide to Identification & Study...* 1919. Doubleday Page. 64 mc pl. VG. B11. $40.00

**MARSHALL, Paule.** *Daughters: A Novel.* 1991. Atheneum. 1st. sgn. F/dj. R14. $40.00

**MARSHALL, Paule.** *Daughters: A Novel.* 1991. NY. Atheneum. 1st. F/dj. Q1. $35.00

**MARSHALL, Robert.** *Arctic Wilderness.* 1956. Berkeley. 1st. 171p. VG/dj. B5. $35.00

**MARSHALL, S.L.** *Ambush: Battle of Day Tieng.* 1969. NY. Cowles. 1st. photos/ sketches/glossary. VG/dj. R11. $35.00

**MARSHALL, S.L.** *Crimsoned Prairie.* 1972. Scribner. inscr. F/dj. A19. $60.00

**MARSHALL, William.** *Nightmare Syndrome.* 1997. Mysterious. ARC. F/dj. A23. $25.00

**MARSTEN, Richard;** see Hunter, Evan.

**MARSTON, Edward.** *Merry Devils.* 1989. St Martin. 1st. F/dj. A23. $30.00

**MARSTON, Muktuk.** *Men of the Tundra. Alaska Eskimos at War.* 1972. NY. October House. 2nd. inscr. VG/dj. P4. $45.00

**MARSZALEK, John F.** *Sherman: Soldier's Passion for Order.* 1993. Free/Macmillan. 1st. F/dj. A14. $25.00

**MARTENE, Edmond.** *Voyage Litteraire de Deux Religieux Benedictins...* 1717-1724. Paris. Delaulne. 3 vol. ils/pl/fld plan. mottled calf. xl. K1. $450.00

**MARTENS & SISSON.** *Jack London First Editions.* 1979. Oakland. Star Rover. 1st. lt bl pict cloth. F/glassine. M24. $150.00

**MARTIGNONI, Margaret.** *Ils Treasury of Children's Literature.* nd (1955). Grosset Dunlap. prt from new pl. sm 4to. 512p. F/VG+ case. C14. $25.00

**MARTIN, A.E.** *Curious Crime.* 1952. Crime Club. 1st. VG/dj. G8. $25.00

**MARTIN, Allana.** *Death of a Healing Woman.* 1996. St Martin. 1st. F/dj. M23. $35.00

**MARTIN, Bill Jr.** *Wizard.* 1970. HRW. 1st? ils Sal Murdocca. F. M5. $12.00

**MARTIN, Bill.** *Tatty Mae & Catty Mae.* 1970. HRW. 1st. ils Aldren Watson. F. M5. $12.00

**MARTIN, Billy.** *Billyball.* 1987. Doubleday. 1st. F/dj. P8. $150.00

**MARTIN, Charles L.** *Sketch of Sam Bass, the Bandit.* (19560. Norman, OK. 1st thus. 166p. VG/dj. B18. $35.00

**MARTIN, David.** *Beginning of Sorrows.* 1998. Vintage. rpt/1st. sgn. F/wrp. S18. $15.00

**MARTIN, David.** *Bring Me Children.* 1993. Random. 1st. sgn/dtd. F/dj. S18. $45.00

**MARTIN, David.** *Confederate Monuments at Gettysburg...* 1986. Hightstown. ils/fld map. 297p. VG. S16. $25.00

**MARTIN, David.** *Crying Heart Tattoo.* 1982. HRW. 1st. F/dj. T12. $20.00

**MARTIN, David.** *Crying Heart Tattoo.* 1982. HRW. 1st. sgn/dtd. author's 2nd book. F/dj. S18. $90.00

**MARTIN, David.** *Cul-de-Sac.* 1997. Villard. 1st. sgn/dtd. AN/dj. S18. $35.00

**MARTIN, David.** *Final Harbor.* 1984. HRW. 1st. sgn/dtd. AN/dj. S18. $75.00

**MARTIN, David.** *Lie to Me.* 1990. Random. 1st. inscr/dtd. F/dj. S18. $48.00

**MARTIN, David.** *Spiegel the Cat.* 1971. Clarkson Potter. 1st Am. ils Roy Mckie. VG/dj. P2. $20.00

**MARTIN, David.** *Tap, Tap.* 1994. Random. 1st. sgn/dtd. AN/dj. S18. $38.00

**MARTIN, Del.** *Battered Wives.* 1976. SF. Gilde. 1st. 269p. VG. A25. $15.00

**MARTIN, Dick.** *Visitors From Oz.* 1960. Reilly Lee. 1st. sgn pres/dtd 1960. mc pict brd. pict dj. R5. $600.00

**MARTIN, Douglas D.** *Arizona Chronology: Territorial Years, 1846-1912.* 1963. Tucson, AZ. 1st. 72p. NF/wrp. B19. $25.00

**MARTIN, Douglas D.** *Lamp in the Desert: Story of U of Arizona.* 1960. Tucson, AZ. 1st. ils/index. 304p. VG/NF. B19. $20.00

**MARTIN, Douglas D.** *Silver, Sex & Six-Guns: Tombstone Saga...* 1962. Tombstone Epitaph. ils. 62p. NF. B19. $35.00

**MARTIN, Douglas D.** *Yuma Crossing.* 1954. U NM. 1st. 8vo. 243p. yel cloth. gr dj. F7. $30.00

**MARTIN, Edward Winslow.** *Secrets of a Great City...New York City.* 1868. Phil. Nat Pub. 1st. 8vo. ils/fld pl. 522+10p ads. O1. $85.00

**MARTIN, Edwin C.** *Our Own Weather...* 1913. Harper. 1st. 8vo. 281p. ils cloth. K5. $20.00

**MARTIN, Geoffrey.** *Modern Soap & Detergent Industry.* 1931. NY. Van Nostrand. 2 vol. 8vo. fld pl. brn cloth. B20. $85.00

**MARTIN, George R.R.** *Armageddon Rag.* 1983. Poseidon. 1st. F/NF. T12. $30.00

**MARTIN, George R.R.** *Fever Dreams.* nd. BC. NF/VG. S18. $8.00

**MARTIN, George R.R.** *Fever Dreams.* 1982. Poseidon. 1st. VG/dj. L1. $65.00

**MARTIN, George R.R.** *Tuf Voyaging.* 1986. Baen. 1st. AN/dj. S18. $20.00

**MARTIN, George R.R.** *Voyaging.* 1986. Baen. 1st. F/NF. M21. $15.00

**MARTIN, George W.** *Transactions of the Kansas State Historical Soc 1905-1906.* 1906. Topeka. State Prt Office. Vol 4 only. 654p. B18. $25.00

**MARTIN, Harry Edwin.** *Tents of Grace, a Tragedy & Four Short Stories.* 1910. Cincinnati. 1st. 98p. fair. B18. $25.00

**MARTIN, Helen Reimensnyder.** *Sabina: Story of the Amish.* 1905. NY. Century. 233p. G+. G11. $8.00

**MARTIN, Henri.** *Popular History of France.* 1877. Boston. 3 vol. ils. dk gr cloth. VG. B30. $50.00

**MARTIN, Henry Byam.** *Polynesian Journal.* 1981. Salem, MA. 1st. ils. VG/dj. M17. $17.50

**MARTIN, Isaac.** *Journal of Life, Travels, Labours & Religious Exercises...* 1834. Phil. Wm P Gibbons. 1st. 12mo. 160p. G+. V3. $26.00

**MARTIN, J. Wallis.** *Likeness in Stone.* 1977. London. Hodder Stoughton. 1st. NF/dj. M15. $250.00

**MARTIN, J.P.** *Private Yankee Doodle, Being Narrative of Adventures...* 1962. Boston. 1st. 305p. F/dj. M4. $28.00

**MARTIN, Jack;** see Etchison, Dennis.

**MARTIN, John.** *America Dancing.* 1936. NY. Dodge. ARC/1st. photos Thomas Bouchard. NF/dj. S9. $175.00

**MARTIN, John.** *Letter to the Earl of Lauderdale...* 1793. London. J Ridgway. later ornate gr calf. M11. $450.00

**MARTIN, Joseph Plumb.** *Yankee Doodle Boy.* 1995. NY. Holiday. 1st thus. F/dj. T11. $12.00

**MARTIN, Judith.** *Miss Manners' Guide to Rearing Perfect Children.* 1984. Atheneum. 1st. F/dj. S13. $12.00

**MARTIN, L.** *Intellectural Conquest of Peru.* 1968. NY. Fordham. 1st. 194p. dj. F3. $20.00

**MARTIN, L.C.** *Optical Measuring Instruments: Their Construction...* 1924. London. Blackie. ils/photos/diagrams. cloth. xl. K5. $45.00

**MARTIN, Laura C.** *Garden Flower Folklore.* 1987. Chester, CT. 273p. AN/dj. B26. $18.00

**MARTIN, Lawrence.** *George Washington Atlas.* 1932. US George Washington Bicentennial Comm. 49 pl/85 maps. B10. $150.00

**MARTIN, Lester.** *This Is the Poodle.* 1960. TFH Pub. VG/dj. A21. $20.00

**MARTIN, Malachi.** *King of Kings.* 1980. S&S. 1st. NF/F. H11. $20.00

**MARTIN, Newell.** *Spincach & Zweiback: The Writings.* 1993. Millbrook, NY. VG/dj. M17. $15.00

**MARTIN, Percy.** *Mexico's Treasure House (Guanajuato).* 1906. NY. Cheltenham. 1st. 259p. gilt red cloth. F3. $55.00

**MARTIN, Robert Bernard.** *With Friends Possessed: Life of Edward Fitzgerald.* 1985. NY. 1st Am. VG/dj. M17. $17.50

**MARTIN, Robert K.** *Hero, Captain & Stranger: Male Friendship, Social Critique.* 1986. U NM. 144p. VG. M10. $12.50

**MARTIN, Robert L.** *Paradox of the Liar.* 1970. Yale. 1st. VG/dj. N2. $15.00

**MARTIN, Russell.** *Cowboy: Enduring Myth of the Wild West.* 1983. Stewart Tabori. photos. 432p. AN. J2. $245.00

**MARTIN, Valerie.** *Consolation of Nature.* 1988. Houghton Mifflin. 1st. F/dj. A23. $34.00

**MARTIN & MARTIN.** *Brave Little Indian.* 1951. Winston. 1st. ils Charlene Bisch. VG. M5. $25.00

**MARTIN & MARTIN.** *Lightning: A Cowboy's Colt.* 1948. Tell-Well Pr. 4to. VG/dj. O3. $25.00

**MARTIN & MARTIN.** *Martins of Gunbarrel.* 1959. Caxton. sgn. VG/dj. A19. $35.00

**MARTIN & MARTIN.** *Silver Stallion.* 1949. Tell-Well Pr. sm 4to. VG/dj. O3. $22.00

**MARTIN & NELSON.** *Boy: A Photographic Essay.* 1964. 400+ photos. 232p. F/VG. A4. $85.00

**MARTIN & STRAIGHT.** *Index to Michigan Geology 1823-1955.* 1956. MI Dept Conser. 461p. VG. A17. $45.00

**MARTINEAU, Harriet.** *Traditions of Palestine.* 1839. Boston. Wm Crosby. 138p. emb blk cloth. VG. B14. $50.00

**MARTINEZ, Buck.** *From Worst to First: Toronto Blue Jays in 1985.* 1985. Funk Wagnall. 1st Canadian. F. T12. $25.00

**MARTINEZ, Jose Longinos.** *Journal of Jose Longinos Martinez.* 1961. John Howell/L Kennedy. 1/1000. ils/3 fld maps. 114p. gilt gr cloth. F. K1. $35.00

**MARTINEZ, Patrick.** *Observer's Guide to Astronomy, Vol I.* 1994 (1987). Cambridge. trans Storm Dunlop. VG. K5. $20.00

**MARTINI, Steve.** *Compelling Evidence.* 1992. Putnam. 1st. F/dj. A23. $30.00

**MARTINS, Richard.** *Cinch.* 1986. Villard. 1st. F/F. H11. $20.00

**MARTZ, John.** *Central America: Crisis & Challenge.* 1959. Chapel Hill. 1st. index. 356p. F3. $20.00

**MARTZOLFF, Clement L.** *Fifty Stories From Ohio History.* 1921. Columbus. 254p. G. B18. $17.50

**MARX, Groucho.** *Groucho Letters.* 1967. S&S. 1st. photos. NF/dj. J3. $75.00

**MARX, Karl.** *Theories of Social Value, Part 2 (Vol 4 of Capital).* nd. Moscow. Progress Pub. F. V4. $150.00

**MARZOLLO, Jean.** *Teddy Bear Book.* 1989. Dial. 1st. ils Schweninger. F/VG. M5. $18.00

**MASEFIELD, John.** *Conway: From Her Foundation to the Present Day.* 1933. NY. ils. VG. M17. $17.50

**MASEFIELD, John.** *Taking of the Gry.* 1934. Macmillan. 1st. NF/VG. T11. $45.00

**MASEREEL, Frans.** *Passionate Journey: Novel in 165 Woodcuts.* 1948. NY. Lear. 1st Am. 8vo. 187p. NF/clip. B20. $125.00

**MASHBURN, J.H.** *Murder & Witchcraft in England, 1550-1640.* 1971. OK U. inscr/sgn. 287p. F/dj. M4. $45.00

**MASO, Carole.** *Art Lover.* 1990. Northpoint. 1st. F/F. B3. $25.00

**MASON, A. Hughlett.** *Journal of Chas Mason & Jeremiah Dixon.* 1969. Am Philosophical Soc. 231p. VG/G. B10. $75.00

**MASON, A.E.W.** *Four Feathers.* ca 1930. London. Thos Nelson. 12mo. 379p. G. M7. $25.00

**MASON, A.E.W.** *House in Lordship.* 1946. Dodd Mead. xl. VG. P3. $10.00

**MASON, A.E.W.** *Sapphire.* 1933. Hodder Stoughton. 1st. VG. P3. $45.00

**MASON, Anne.** *War Against Chaos.* 1988. Hamish Hamilton. 1st. NF/dj. P3. $22.00

**MASON, Bobbie Ann.** *Feather Crowns.* 1993. Harper. 1st. sgn. F/dj. S13. $20.00

**MASON, Bobbie Ann.** *In Country.* 1985. Harper Row. 1st. F/dj. A23. $36.00

**MASON, Bobbie Ann.** *In Country.* 1986. Chatto Windus. 1st. F/F. B3. $30.00

**MASON, Bobbie Ann.** *Love Life.* 1989. Harper Row. 1st. F/F. H11. $20.00

**MASON, Bobbie Ann.** *Midnight Magic. Selected Stories.* 1998. Hopewell. 1st. sgn. F/dj. R14. $45.00

**MASON, Bobbie Ann.** *Shiloah & Other Stories.* 1982. Harper. UP. inscr. author's 1st fiction book. F/wrp. B4. $350.00

**MASON, Bobbie Ann.** *Spence+Lila.* 1988. Harper Row. 1st. ils LaNelle Mason. F/dj. A23. $32.00

**MASON, F. Van Wyck.** *Armored Giants.* 1980. Little Brn. 1st. F/VG. T11. $15.00

**MASON, F. Van Wyck.** *Brimstone Club.* 1971. Little Brn. 1st. F/NF. T11. $20.00

**MASON, F. Van Wyck.** *High Command.* 1984. NY. Morrow. 1st. F/dj. T11. $20.00

**MASON, F. Van Wyck.** *Our Valiant Few.* 1971. Little Brn. 1st. NF/VG. T11. $25.00

**MASON, F. Van Wyck.** *Winter at Valley Forge.* 1953. Random. ils Harper Johnson. 190p. G+. B36. $6.50

**MASON, F. Van Wyck.** *Young Titan.* 1959. Doubleday. 1st. NF/clip. T11. $35.00

**MASON, Gene W.** *Minus Three.* 1970. Englewood Cliffs. 1st. F/dj. B20. $25.00

**MASON, Herbert.** *Rise of the Luftwaffe 1918-1940.* 1973. NY. 1st. biblio/index. 402p. VG/dj. S16. $25.00

**MASON, John.** *Self-Knowledge: A Treatise...* 1769 (1745). London. James Buckland. 8th. 12mo. 228p. VG. G1. $150.00

**MASON, Lisa.** *Arachne.* 1990. NY. Morrow. 1st. F/dj. G10. $20.00

**MASON, Mary Ann.** *From Father's Property to Children's Rights...* 1994. Columbia. VG/dj. M11. $27.50

**MASON, Mary.** *Young Housewife's Counsellor & Friend With Directions...* 1871. 1st. 380p. G+. E6. $70.00

**MASON, Miriam E.** *Benjamin Lucky.* 1956. Macmillan. 1st. ils Vee Guthrie. F/VG. M5. $18.00

**MASON, Otis T.** *Basket-Work of the North American Aborigines.* 1890. GPO. 1st separate. ils. D11. $75.00

**MASON, Susanna.** *Selections From Letters & Manuscripts of Late Susanna Mason.* 1836. Phil. Rackliff Jones. 1st. 12mo. 312p. G. V3. $45.00

**MASON, Theodore K.** *South Pole Ponies.* 1979. Dodd Mead. 1st. VG. O3. $22.00

**MASON, Walt.** *Uncle Walt: Poet Philosopher.* 1911. Chicago. Adams. 2nd. 8vo. 189p. pict brn cloth. F/rpr. C6. $200.00

**MASON-BAHR, Philip.** *Synopsis of Tropical Medicine.* 1943. Baltimore. Williams & Wilkins. apparent 1st Am. ils. 224p. NF. C14. $20.00

**MASPERO, Gaston.** *Passing of the Empires 850 BC to 330 BC.* 1900. NY. Appleton. 1st Am. ils/pl/maps. 824p. cloth. VG. W1. $55.00

**MASSEY, Vincent.** *Speaking of Canada.* (1959). Toronto. Macmillan. 2nd. inscr/sgn. F/NF. A26. $25.00

**MASSIE, Robert K.** *Dreadnought: Britain, Germany & Coming of Great War.* 1991. NY. Random. 1st. ils. 1007p. NF/dj. M10. $30.00

**MASSIE, Robert K.** *Peter the Great: His Life & World.* 1981. Knopf. 6th. silvered blk bdg. VG/G. P12. $12.00

**MASSMANN, Robert E.** *Adventures of the Flighty Old Woman.* 1966. New Britain, CT. mini. 1/500. 12p. prt wrp/yel prt paper sleeve. B24. $65.00

**MASSMANN, Robert E.** *Bibliomidgets of Achille J St Onge: A Memorial...* 1979. New Britain. St Onge. mini. 1/1000. 84p. red gilt-stp leatherette/chemise. B24. $50.00

**MASSMANN, Robert E.** *Der Winzige Struwwelpeter.* 1982. New Britain. mini. 1/300. sgn author/ils. 14p. pict label/gr leatherette/case. B24. $75.00

**MASSMANN, Robert E.** *How the Art of Printing Was Invented: A Bibliofantasy.* nd. Anton Bohm/Massmann. mini. 1/400. 44p. red prt buff wrp. B24. $95.00

**MASSMANN, Robert E.** *Mark Twain Turnover...Mark Twain & Devil/Advice for Good...* 1972. New Britain, CT. mini. 1/250. 2-sided book w/center popup. leatherette/case. B24. $200.00

**MASSMANN, Robert E.** *REM Magic Nursery Rhymes.* 1977. New Britain, CT. mini. 1/500. 28p. gr leatherette/paper label. paper chemise. B24. $95.00

**MASSMANN, Robert E.** *Vatican Peep.* 1985. Sudbury, MA. Kurbel. mini. 1/300. fld peep-show Dome of St Peter. AN. B24. $175.00

**MASSON, Jeffery Mousaieff.** *Dogs Never Lie About Love: Reflections...* 1997. NY. Crown. 1st. F/dj. T12. $35.00

**MASSON & MCCARTHY.** *When Elephants Weep: Emotional Lives of Animals.* 1995. Delacorte. 1st. F/sans. T12. $35.00

**MAST, Gerald.** *Short History of the Movies.* 1986. NY. 4th. xl. T9. $6.00

**MASTAI & MASTAI.** *Stars & Stripes: American Flag As Art...* 1973. NY. photos. F/dj. M4. $60.00

**MASTEN, A.H.** *Story of Adirondac.* 1968. Syracuse. ils. 199p. F/dj. M4. $25.00

**MASTERS, Edgar Lee.** *Lincoln the Man.* 1931. Dodd Mead. 1st. 520p. VG. B10. $15.00

**MASTERS, Edgar Lee.** *Sangamon.* 1942. NY. 1st. ils Lynd Ward. VG/G. B5. $35.00

**MASTERS, Joseph.** *Stories of the Far West: Heroic Tales of Last Frontier.* 1935. Ginn. 297p. VG. J2. $45.00

**MASTERTON, Graham.** *Scare Care.* 1989. NY. Tor. 1st. NF/dj. M21. $17.50

**MASTERTON, Graham.** *Sweetman Curve.* 1990. London. Severn. 1st hc. F/dj. G10. $27.50

**MASUROVSKY, B.** *Sherbets, Water Ices & Modern Soda Fountain Operation.* 1933. VG. E6. $30.00

**MATERA, Lia.** *Face Value.* 1994. S&S. 1st. sgn. F/dj. G8. $25.00

**MATES, Benson.** *Stoic Logic.* 1961. Berkeley. 2nd/1st wrp trade. 12mo. 148p. VG. H1. $10.00

**MATHER, Berkeley.** *Spy for a Spy.* 1968. Scribner. 1st. F/F. H11. $35.00

**MATHER, Cotton.** *Cotton Mather on Witchcraft Being the Wonders...* 1974. NY. 172p. NF/dj. M4. $15.00

**MATHER, Cotton.** *Essays to Do Good: Addressed to All Christians...* 1808. Boston. Lincoln Edmands. 8vo. 148p. contemporary calf. F. O1. $125.00

**MATHER, Eleanore Price.** *Pendle Hill: Quaker Experiment in Education & Community.* 1980. Wallingford, PA. Pendle Hill. 12mo. 118p. VG/dj. V3. $16.00

**MATHER, Helen.** *Light Horsekeeping: How to Get a Horse & How to Keep It.* 1970. Dutton. 1st. F/NF. T12. $25.00

**MATHERS, E. Powys.** *Red Wise.* 1926. Golden Cockerel. 1st. 1/500. ils Robert Gibbings. NF/dj. Q1. $150.00

**MATHES, Valerie Sherer.** *Helen Hunt Jackson & Her Indian Reform Legacy.* 1990. Austin. U TX. 1st. 8vo. 235p. AN/dj. P4. $28.00

**MATHES, W. Michael.** *Capture of Santa Ana, Cabo San Lucas, Nove 1587...* 1969. Dawson's Book Shop. 1st. ils/fld map. 59p. B19. $15.00

**MATHES, W. Michael.** *Spanish Approaches to the Island of California 1628-1632.* 1975. SF. BC of CA. 1/400. tall 8vo. facs map. beige pict brd/label. F. K1. $60.00

**MATHESON, Richard.** *Created By.* 1993. Bantam. 1st. author's 1st novel. AN/dj. S18. $35.00

**MATHESON, Richard.** *Earthbound.* 1994. Tor. 1st Am. F/dj. N4. $20.00

**MATHESON, Richard.** *Now You See It...* 1995. Tor. 1st. sgn. F/dj. S18. $50.00

**MATHESON, Richard.** *7 Steps to Midnight.* 1993. NY. Forge. 1st. AN/dj. T12. $35.00

**MATHEWS, John Joseph.** *Osages: Children of the Middle Waters.* 1961. Norman, OK. G/dj. A19. $45.00

**MATHEWSON, Christy.** *Catcher Craig.* 1915. Grosset Dunlap. rpt. VG. P8. $30.00

**MATHEWSON, Christy.** *Pitcher Pollack.* 1914. Dodd Mead. 1st. 1st in series. VG. P8. $65.00

**MATHEWSON, Christy.** *Pitching in a Pinch.* 1977. Stein Day. rpt. photos. F/VG. P8. $45.00

**MATHEWSON, R. Duncan.** *Treasure of the Atocha.* 1986. Dutton. 1st. 8vo. 160p. VG/dj. B11. $35.00

**MATISSE, Henri.** *Poemes de Charles d'Orleans.* 1950. Teriade. 1/1230. 54 mc sgn lithos. loose. stiff wrp/glassine/case. B24. $2,250.00

**MATISSE.** *Jazz.* 1983. folio. ils. 156p. F/F/VG cb case. A4. $265.00

**MATOS MOCTEZUMA, Eduardo.** *Great Temple of the Aztecs.* 1988. Thames Hudson. 1st. 192p. dj. F3. $35.00

**MATSCHAT, Cecile.** *Seven Grass Huts.* 1939. NY. ils. 281p. F3. $10.00

**MATTESON, Stefanie.** *Murder on High.* 1994. NY. Berkley Crime Club. 1st. F/dj. A23. $32.00

**MATTHEW, D.J.A.** *Norman Conquest.* 1966. Stocken. 1st Am. 8vo. F/dj. A2. $15.00

**MATTHEWS, Courtland W.** *After Many Winds.* (1974). Matthews. 1st. wrp. AN. A18. $10.00

**MATTHEWS, Greg.** *Heart of the Country.* 1986. NY. Norton. 1st. author's 2nd book. F/NF. H11. $25.00

**MATTHEWS, J.W.** *New Zealand Trees.* 1956 (1951). Wellington. 2nd. ils. VG/dj. B26. $16.00

**MATTHEWS, John Carter.** *Richard Henry Lee.* (1978). Bicentennial Comm. photos. 86p. VG. B10. $12.00

**MATTHEWS, Leslie G.** *Antiques of Pharmacy.* 1971. London. Bell. 1st. 120p. xl. G/dj. H1. $30.00

**MATTHEWS & MATTHEWS.** *Arthurian Book of Days.* 1990. Macmillan. 1st. F/dj. T10. $30.00

**MATTHEWS & MATTHEWS.** *Encyclopedia of Celtic Wisdom.* 1994. Rockport, MA. Element. 1st Am. F/dj. T10. $35.00

**MATTHIESSEN, Francis Otto.** *Sarah Orne Jewett.* 1929. Houghton Mifflin. 1st. 8vo. 160p. gr cloth. VG/dj. J3. $75.00

**MATTHIESSEN, Peter.** *African Silences.* 1991. Random. 1st. F/dj. A23. $50.00

**MATTHIESSEN, Peter.** *Baikal.* 1992. London. Thames Hudson. 1st. photos Boyd Norton. F/NF. B3. $50.00

**MATTHIESSEN, Peter.** *Blue Meridian.* 1995. London. Harvill. 1st. sgn. F/dj. R14. $45.00

**MATTHIESSEN, Peter.** *Cloud Forest: A Chronicle of South American Wilderness.* 1961. NY. 1st. ils. 280p. VG/dj. B14. $35.00

**MATTHIESSEN, Peter.** *In the Spirit of Crazy Horse.* 1983. Viking. UP/1st. sgn. F/NF. L3. $450.00

**MATTHIESSEN, Peter.** *Indian Country.* 1984. NY. Viking. 1st. sgn. NF/NF. R14. $100.00

**MATTHIESSEN, Peter.** *Nine-Headed Dragon River. Zen Journals 1969-1982.* 1986. Boston. Shambala. 1st. sgn. F/dj. R14. $100.00

**MATTHIESSEN, Peter.** *On the River Styx & Other Stories.* 1986. Random. true 1st. sgn. F/F. B3. $60.00

**MATTHIESSEN, Peter.** *On the River Styx & Other Stories.* 1989. SF. Sierra BC. 1st. sgn. RS. F/dj. O11. $90.00

**MATTHIESSEN, Peter.** *Oomingmak: Expedition to Musk Ox Island in Bering Sea.* 1967. Hastings. 1st. sgn. photos. ils brd. F/F. B3. $100.00

**MATTHIESSEN, Peter.** *Peter Matthiessen.* (?). Twayne. 1st. US Authors series. F/NF. T11. $45.00

**MATTHIESSEN, Peter.** *Race Rock.* 1954. NY. Harper. 1st. author's 1st book. 306p. VG+/worn. B20. $225.00

**MATTHIESSEN, Peter.** *Sand Rivers.* 1981. NY. Viking. 1st. sgn. F/NF. R14. $90.00

**MATTHIESSEN, Peter.** *Shore Birds of North America.* 1967. NY. 1st. ils Robert Vertity Clem. 270p. off-wht buckram. F/VG. H3. $225.00

**MATTHIESSEN, Peter.** *Snow Leopard.* 1978. Viking. 1st trade. NF/NF. B3. $50.00

**MATTHIESSEN, Peter.** *Snow Leopard.* 1978. Viking. 1st trade. 338p. VG/dj. H7. $17.50

**MATTHIESSEN, Peter.** *Under the Mountain Wall.* 1962. Viking. BC. 1st. sgn. NF/VG clip. R14. $125.00

**MATTISON, Alice.** *Field of Stars.* 1992. NY. Morrow. 1st. NF/dj. M23. $15.00

**MATTISON, Alice.** *Field of Stars.* 1992. NY. Morrow. 1st. sgn. author's 1st book. F/dj. R14. $40.00

**MAUDSLAY & MAUDSLAY.** *Glimpse at Guatemala & Some Notes...* 1992 (1899). Flo Silver. rpt. 60 pl/index/plans/fld map. 289p. F3. $40.00

**MAUGHAM, Robin.** *Servant.* 1949. Harcourt Brace. 1st Am. thin 8vo. 62p. F/NF. B20. $35.00

**MAUGHAM, W. Somerset.** *Ashenden.* 1947. Tower. 1st thus. G+/dj. L4. $35.00

**MAUGHAM, W. Somerset.** *Cakes & Ale.* 1930. Garden City. 308p. G. G11. $20.00

**MAUGHAM, W. Somerset.** *Christmas Holiday.* 1939. Doubleday Doran. 1st Am. 8vo. 314p. blk cloth. F/dj. H5. $200.00

**MAUGHAM, W. Somerset.** *France at War.* (1940). London. Heinemann. sgn pres. 12mo. rb gr cloth. F/wrp. R3. $135.00

**MAUGHAM, W. Somerset.** *My South Sea Island.* 1964. Chicago. mini. 1st book ed. 1/199. frenchfold. gilt gr leather. F. B24. $150.00

**MAUGHAM, W. Somerset.** *Ten Novels & Their Authors.* (1954). London. Heinemann. ARC. 8vo. F/wrp. R3. $175.00

**MAUGHAM, W. Somerset.** *Writer's Point of View.* 1951. London. Cambridge. 1st. F/stiff wrp/clip dj. B4. $150.00

**MAULE, Joshua.** *Transactions & Changes in Society of Friends...* 1886. Lippincott. 1st. 384p. VG. V3. $25.00

**MAULE, Tex.** *Beatty of the Yankees.* 1963. McKay. 1st. 2nd in series. VG/dj. P8. $40.00

**MAUNDER & MAUNDER.** *Heavens & Their Story.* 1910 (1908). London. Chas Kelly. 2nd. photos. 357p. gilt leather. K5. $30.00

**MAURICE, Frederick.** *Robert E Lee, the Soldier.* 1925. Boston. maps. VG. M17. $25.00

**MAUROIS, Andre.** *Country of 36 Thousand Wishes.* 1930. Appleton. 1st Am. trans from French. 66p. VG. D1. $75.00

**MAUROIS, Andre.** *My Latin American Diary.* 1953. London. Falcon. 1st. 89p. dj. F3. $15.00

**MAUSLAY, A.P.** *Biologia Centrali-Americana or Contribution of Knowledge...* 1974. 6 vol. rpt. ils/pl/figures. F. M4. $225.00

**MAVOR, James.** *Voyage to Atlantis.* 1969. Putnam. 1st. 320p. dj. F3. $15.00

**MAVOR, William.** *Historical Account of Most Celebrated Voyages, Travels...* 1802-1803. Phil. Bradford. 24 vol. 1st Am. 16mo. tree calf. G. W1. $420.00

**MAVROGORDATO, John.** *Digenes Akrites.* 1956. Oxford. Clarendon. 8vo. 273p. cloth. VG/dj. Q2. $92.00

**MAWSON, Timothy.** *Garden Room: Bringing Nature Indoors.* 1994. NY. Clarkson Potter. 1st. ils Ivan Teresstchenko. F/dj. H10. $22.50

**MAX-MULLER, Friedrich.** *Science of Thought.* 1887. Longman Gr. thick 8vo. 664p+32p catalog. gr cloth. G. G1. $85.00

**MAXES, Anna.** *Dead to Rights.* 1994. St Martin. 1st. F/dj. A23. $32.00

**MAXWELL, A.E.** *Gatsby's Vineyard.* 1987. Doubleday. 1st. F/dj. M15. $45.00

**MAXWELL, A.E.** *King of Nothing. A Fiddler Mystery.* 1992. Villard. 1st. NF/NF. A23. $25.00

**MAXWELL, Albert Ernest.** *Experimental Design in Psychology & Medical Sciences.* 1958. Methuen. 1st. 8vo. 147p. NF. C14. $15.00

**MAXWELL, Margaret F.** *Passion for Freedom: Life of Sharlot Hall.* 1982. Tucson, AZ. 1st. ils/notes/index. 235p. F/F. B19. $40.00

**MAXWELL, R. Carl.** *Genealogy & History of Alexander Maxwell of 1804-1883...* 1967. Farmville Herald. photos. mechanically repro typescript. 3-ring binder. B10. $75.00

**MAXWELL, Thomas.** *Suspense Is Killing Me.* 1990. Mysterious. 1st. F/F. H11. $15.00

**MAXWELL, William.** *Ancestors.* 1971. NY. Knopf. 1st. sgn. NF/VG clip. R14. $90.00

**MAXWELL, William.** *Outermost Dream.* 1989. NY. Knopf. 1st. F/dj. Q1. $35.00

**MAXWELL, William.** *VA Historical Register & Literary Advisor, Vol 1 & Vol 2.* 1948 & 1949. MacFarlane Fergusson. half leather/marbled brd. B10. $150.00

**MAY, Earl Chapin.** *Principo to Wheeling, 1715-1945.* 1945. NY. 1st. ils/map ep. 335p. VG. B18. $20.00

**MAY, John.** *Ani Ani, Kai Kai: Bush Foods, Local Markets & Culinary Arts.* 1988 (1982). New South Wales. VG. E6. $35.00

**MAY, Robert L.** *Rudolph, the Red-Nosed Reindeer.* 1963. Evanston, IL. Schori. mini. ltd. sgn Schori. aeg. red morocco. B24. $150.00

**MAY, Robert.** *Rudolph, the Red-Nosed Reindeer.* 1963. Evanston, IL. sgn author/pub. aeg. gilt red leather. F. R5. $200.00

**MAY, Robin.** *Gold Rushes: From California to the Klondike.* 1977. London. Wm Luscombe. 1st. sm 4to. ils. F/dj. O4. $20.00

**MAY, Sophie.** *Dotty Dimple Out West.* 1910. Lee Shepard. ils. G+. P12. $10.00

**MAYER, Brantz.** *Captain Canot; or, Twenty Years of an African Slaver.* 1854. NY. Appleton. fair. V4. $185.00

**MAYER, Charles.** *Hoodoo, Voodoo & Bugaboo.* 1939. Dallas, TX. Century Feature Syndicate. 1st. 98p. F/NF. B20. $125.00

**MAYER, Dorothy.** *Tina Mina.* 1930. Houghton Mifflin. 1st. ils Robert Nathan. 103p. VG/dj. B20. $300.00

**MAYER, Felix.** *Die Strukter des Traumes.* 1937. Haag. Martinus Nijhoff. thin 8vo. 55p. prt gray wrp. VG. G1. $35.00

**MAYER, Marianna.** *Carlo Collodi's Pinocchio.* 1981. Four Winds. 1st. 8vo. 122p. F/VG. C14. $17.00

**MAYER, Mercer.** *Little Monsters.* 1978. Golden. 1st. 4to. VG+. M5. $18.00

**MAYER, S.L.** *Hitler's Wartime Picture Magazine. Signal.* 1977. Prentice Hall. 3rd. red cloth. F/dj. M7. $25.00

**MAYER & RILEY.** *Public Domain, Private Dominion: A History...* 1985. Sierra Club. 1st. 8vo. VG/dj. A2. $15.00

**MAYERSON, Evelyn Wilde.** *Sanjo.* 1979. Lippincott. 1st. 8vo. 274p. NF/dj. W2. $20.00

**MAYES, Vernon O.** *Nanise: A Navajo Herbal.* 1989. Tsaile, AZ. Navajo Comm College. sc. F. A19. $25.00

**MAYES, Willie.** *Danger in Centerfield.* 1963. Argonaut. 1st. VG/dj. P8. $75.00

**MAYFIELD, H.** *Kirtland's Warbler.* 1960. Bloomfield Hills, MI. 8vo. 242p. decor cloth. NF. C12. $55.00

**MAYFIELD, Julian.** *Grant Parade.* 1961. NY. Vanguard. 1st. F/NF. B2. $40.00

**MAYHEW, Edward.** *Blaine's Outlines of the Veterinary Art...* 1854. Longman Brn. 669p. half leather/marbled brd. G. O3. $68.00

**MAYLE, Peter.** *Acquired Tastes.* 1992. NY. 1st. dj. T9. $15.00

**MAYLE, Peter.** *Year in Province/Toujours Provence.* 1992. NY. 2 vol. 1st. ils J Clancey. case. T9. $28.00

**MAYNARD, Joyce.** *To Die For.* 1992. Dutton. 1st. F/dj. T12. $25.00

**MAYNARD, Kenneth.** *Lieutenant Lamb.* 1984. NY. St Martin. ARC/1st. Mathew Lamb #1. w/promo materials. F/NF. T11. $45.00

**MAYNARD, Samuel T.** *Successful Fruit Culture.* 1911 (1905). NY. ils. 274p. cloth. B26. $20.00

**MAYNE, Richard.** *Community of Europe.* 1963. Norton. M11. $25.00

**MAYO, Bernard.** *Jefferson Himself: Personal Narrative of Many-Sided...* 1942. Houghton Mifflin. 1st. sm 4to. 384p. VG. S14. $23.00

**MAYO, C.M.** *Sky Over El Nido.* 1995. Athens. U GA. 1st. F/dj. M23. $35.00

**MAYO, Jim;** see L'Amour, Louis.

**MAYONE DIAS, Eduardo.** *Cantares de Alem-Mar.* 1982. Coimbre. Ordem. 1/1000. 4to. 223p. wrp. F3. $10.00

**MAYOR, A. Hyatt.** *Prints & People: Social History of Printed Pictures.* 1971. Metro Mus of Art. 1st. sm 4to. ils. F/dj. O10. $58.00

**MAYOR, Archer.** *Scent of Evil.* 1992. NY. Mysterious. 1st. F/dj. M15. $45.00

**MAYOR, Susan.** *Collecting Fans.* 1980. Christies Internat Collectors. photos. VG/dj. M17. $22.50

**MAYR, E.** *List of New Guinea Birds...* 1941. NY. ils/fld map. VG/wrp. C12. $68.00

**MAYR & PROVINE.** *Evolutionary Synthesis: Perspectives on Unification Biology.* 1980. Cambridge. 1st. 487p. A13. $35.00

**MAYS, Willie.** *Born to Play Ball.* 1955. Putnam. 1st. VG. P8. $45.00

**MAZUR, Gail.** *Nightfire.* 1978. Boston. Godine. 1st. inscr. G/sans. L3. $25.00

**MAZZANOVICH, Anton.** *Trailing Geronimo.* 1931. NY. 3rd. ils. 322p. VG/dj. B18. $50.00

**MCADAM, E.L.** *Dr Johnson & the English Law.* 1951. Syracuse. 1st. VG. H13. $65.00

**MCADAM & MILNE.** *Johnson's Dictionary: A Modern Selection.* 1963. Pantheon. 2nd. 8vo. 465p. cloth. VG/F. H13. $65.00

**MCADIE, Alexander G.** *Climatology of California.* 1903. WA, DC. GPO. ils/pl. cloth. G. K5. $45.00

**MCAFEE, John P.** *Slow Walk in a Sad Rain.* 1993. NY. Warner. 1st. F/F. H11. $30.00

**MCALEER, John.** *Rex Stout: A Biography.* 1977. Boston. Little Brn. 1st. 621p. VG/dj. V3. $22.00

**MCAULAY, L.** *Battle of the Bismark Sea.* ils/map. 226p. VG/dj. S16. $20.00

**MCAULEY, Mary.** *Germany in Wartime.* 1917. 1st. ils. G+. E6. $20.00

**MCAULEY, Paul J.** *Four Hundred Billion Stars.* 1988. London. Gollancz. 1st. author's 1st novel. F/dj. M21. $40.00

**MCAULEY, Paul J.** *Pasquale's Angel.* 1994. London. 1st. dj. T9. $10.00

**MCBAIN, Ed;** see Hunter, Evan.

**MCBRIDE, H.W.** *Rifleman Went to War.* 1987. Mt Ida. 398p. F/G. M4. $25.00

**MCCABE, James D.** *Our Young Folks Abroad. Adventures of Four American Boys...* 1886 (1881). Lippincott. 312p. rust-red cloth. NF. B20. $50.00

**MCCABE, John.** *Cagney: A Biography.* 1997. Knopf. ARC/1st. 8vo. F/dj. w/pub slip & fld poster. S9. $35.00

**MCCAFFREY, Anne.** *All the Weyrs of Pern.* 1991. Del Rey. 1st. F/dj. T10. $25.00

**MCCAFFREY, Anne.** *Coelura.* 1983. Undersood Miller. 1st. ils Kevin Eugene Johnson. VG+/dj. A14. $32.00

**MCCAFFREY, Anne.** *Killashandra.* 1985. NY. Del Rey. 1st. 303p. F/dj. D4. $30.00

**MCCAFFREY, Anne.** *Moreta: Dragonlady of Pern.* 1983. Del Rey/Ballantine. 1st. VG+/dj. A14. $22.00

**MCCAFFREY, Anne.** *White Dragon.* 1978. Del Rey/Ballantine. 1st. Dragonriders of Pern #2. VG+/clip. A14. $52.50

**MCCAFFREY, Donald W.** *Golden Age of Sound Comedy.* 1973. London. Tantivy Pr. 208p. VG/dj. C5. $12.50

**MCCAIG, Donald.** *Man Who Made the Devil Glad.* 1986. NY. Crown. 1st. F/F. H11/M23. $20.00

**MCCALL, Anthony;** see Kane, Henry.

**MCCALL MAGAZINE EDITORS.** *McCall's Big Book of Dollhouses & Miniatures.* 1983. Chilton. 1st. ils/ 286p. VG/dj. S14. $20.00

**MCCALLA, William C.** *Wild Flowers of Western Canada.* 1920. Toronto. photos. 132p. gilt cloth. B26. $17.50

**MCCALLUM, Ian.** *Architecture USA.* 1959. NY. 1st. photos. VG/dj. M17. $50.00

**MCCALLUM, John.** *Tiger Wore Spikes.* 1956. Barnes. 1st. photos/stats/index. G+. P8. $30.00

**MCCAMMON, Robert R.** *Bethany's Sin.* 1989. London. Kinnell. 1st hc. F/dj. M25. $35.00

**MCCAMMON, Robert R.** *Bethany's Sin.* 1989. London. Kinnell. 1st hc. sgn on title. NF/dj. A14. $52.50

**MCCAMMON, Robert R.** *Blue World.* 1989. London. Grafton. 1st Eng. VG/dj. L1. $100.00

**MCCAMMON, Robert R.** *Boy's Life.* 1991. Pocket. 1st. F/dj. N4. $35.00

**MCCAMMON, Robert R.** *Boys Life.* 1991. Pocket. 1st. sgn. F/dj. S18. $50.00

**MCCAMMON, Robert R.** *Gone South.* 1992. Pocket. 1st. AN/dj. S18. $25.00

**MCCAMMON, Robert R.** *Mine.* 1990. NY. Pocket. 1st. F/F. H11. $30.00

**MCCAMMON, Robert R.** *Mystery Walk.* 1983. NY. Holt. 1st. F/NF. H11. $60.00

**MCCAMMON, Robert R.** *Night Boat.* 1990. London. Kinnell. 1st hc NF/dj. A14. $35.00

**MCCAMMON, Robert R.** *Night Visions 8.* 1990. Dark Harvest. 1st. NF/dj. M21. $25.00

**MCCAMMON, Robert R.** *Swan Song.* 1989. Dark Harvest. 1/650. sgn. ils/sgn Chas Lang. AN/box. T12. $150.00

**MCCAMMON, Robert R.** *They Thirst.* 1991. Dark Harvest. 1st. VG/dj. L1. $50.00

**MCCAMMON, Robert R.** *Usher's Passing.* 1984. HRW. 1st. NF/dj. S18. $45.00

**MCCAMMON, Robert R.** *Wolf's Hour.* 1989. London. Grafton. 1st Eng hc. VG/dj. L1. $100.00

**MCCANN, Colum.** *Fishing the Slow-Black RIver.* 1994. London. Phoenix House. 1st. author's 1st book. F/dj. A24. $135.00

**MCCANN & RANDOLPH.** *Ozark Folklore, an Annotated Bibliography.* 1987. U MO. 2 vol. 4100 entries. F/F. A4. $125.00

**MCCARRY, Charles.** *Bride of the Wilderness.* 1988. NAL. 1st. quarter maroon cloth. F/clip. T11. $20.00

**MCCARRY, Charles.** *Last Supper.* 1983. Dutton. 1st. F/F. H11. $20.00

**MCCARRY, Charles.** *Tears of Autumn.* 1975. London. Hutchinson. 1st. VG/clip. R11. $35.00

**MCCARRY, Charles.** *Tears of Autumn.* 1975. NY. Saturday Review. 1st. NF/NF. H11. $25.00

**MCCARTHY, Albert.** *Big Band Jazz.* 1974. NY. 1st. VG/dj. B5. $45.00

**MCCARTHY, Albert.** *Dance Band Era: Dancing Decades From Ragtime to Swing...* 1982. Chilton. 176p+index. F/VG. B20. $25.00

**MCCARTHY, Charles H.** *Lincoln's Plan of Reconstruction.* 1901. McClure Phillips. 1st. G. B10. $90.00

**MCCARTHY, Cormac.** *All the Pretty Horses.* 1992. Knopf. 1st. VG/G+. L1. $50.00

**MCCARTHY, Cormac.** *All the Pretty Horses.* 1992. London. Picador. 1st. F/dj. O11. $150.00

**MCCARTHY, Cormac.** *All the Pretty Horses.* 1992. NY. Knopf. 1st. sgn. Nat Book Award/Nat Book Critics Cir Award. NF/2nd dj. A24. $350.00

**MCCARTHY, Cormac.** *Blood Meridian.* 1985. Random. 1st. F/dj. B4. $800.00

**MCCARTHY, Cormac.** *Child of God.* 1973. Random. 1st. NF/dj. B2. $600.00

**MCCARTHY, Cormac.** *Crossing.* 1994. Knopf. 1st. NF/dj. B30. $35.00

**MCCARTHY, Cormac.** *Crossing.* 1994. Knopf. 1st. 1/1000. sgn. F/dj. M25. $250.00

**MCCARTHY, Cormac.** *Crossing.* 1994. London. Picador. 1st. F/dj. O11. $30.00

**MCCARTHY, Elaine Clark.** *Falconer.* 1996. London. Hutchinson. 1st. author's 1st book. F/dj. A14. $21.00

**MCCARTHY, Joe.** *McCarthyism: Fight for America.* 1952. NY. Devin Adair. 1st. 4to. photos. 104p. VG. B14. $40.00

**MCCARTHY, Justin.** *Muslims & Minorities: Population of Ottoman Anatolia...* 1983. NY U. 248p. cloth. VG. Q2. $47.00

**MCCARTHY, Mary.** *Company She Keeps.* 1942. S&S. 1st. sgn Vincent Starrett. VG/dj. S13. $25.00

**MCCARTHY, Mary.** *Hanoi.* 1968. London. Weidenfeld Nicolson. 1st. 138p. NF/dj. R11. $40.00

**MCCARTHY, Mary.** *Oasis.* 1949. NY. Random. 1st. 181p. NF/dj. B20. $165.00

**MCCARTHY, William.** *Hester Thrale Piozzi: Portrait of a Liteary Woman.* 1985. Chapel Hill. 1st. 8vo. 306p. AN/dj. H13. $75.00

**MCCARTNEY, John.** *Story of a Great Horse.* 1902. Indianapolis. 1st. sgn pres. B5. $45.00

**MCCARTNEY & OKKELBERG.** *Papers of the Michigan Academy of Science, Arts & Letters...* 1930. Ann Arbor. 493p. gilt cloth. F. A17. $25.00

**MCCARTY, John L.** *Maverick Town: Story of Old Tascosa.* 1946. Norman. OK U. 2nd. 8vo. 277p. VG/dj. P4. $40.00

**MCCARTY, Tom.** *Tom McCarthy's Own Story.* 1986. Hamilton, MT. Rocky Mtn House. sgn. sc. F. w/ephemera. A19. $75.00

**MCCASLAND, David.** *Oswald Chambers: Abandoned to God: Life Story of the Author.* (1993). Discovery. photos/biblio/index. AN/dj. A27. $20.00

**MCCHRISTIAN, Douglas C.** *US Army in the West 1870-1880.* 1995. U OK. 1st. photos. 315p. J2. $85.00

**MCCLANE, A.J.** *American Angler.* 1954. Holt. 1st. F/VG clip. T11. $25.00

**MCCLANE, A.J.** *McClane's New Standard Fishing Encyclopedia.* 1974. HRW. 1st. 4to. 1156p. F/NF clip. T11. $55.00

**MCCLELLAN, Henry Brainerd.** *Life & Campaigns of Major-Genral JEB Stuart...* 1885. Houghton Mifflin. 1st. 7 fld maps. 468p. half leather. M8. $1,250.00

**MCCLELLAN, J.** *Regional Anatomy in Its Relation to Medicine & Surgery.* 1891. 2 vol. 4to. 97 mc pl. VG. E6. $250.00

**MCCLELLAN, John L.** *Crime Without Punishment.* 1962. DSP. 1st. VG/dj. N2. $10.00

**MCCLELLAND, Doug.** *Golden Age of B Movies.* 1978. NY. Bonanza. 216p. VG. C5. $12.50

**MCCLOSKEY, Robert.** *Lentil.* 1940. Viking. 1st. author's 1st book. red-lettered gray cloth. dj. R5. $475.00

**MCCLOSKEY, Robert.** *Make Way for Ducklings.* 1942 (1941). NY. Viking. 3rd. sgn. Caldecott. brn cloth. mc pict dj. R5. $375.00

**MCCLOSKEY, Robert.** *Time of Wonder.* (1957). Viking. 1st. 4to. 1958 Caldecott. dk bl cloth. mc pict dj. R5. $750.00

**MCCLUNG, Robert M.** *Vulcan: Story of a Bald Eagle.* 1955. Morrow. 1st. ils McClung. yel cloth. VG. B36. $11.00

**MCCLURE, James.** *Caterpillar.* 1973. Harper Row. 1st Am. author's 2nd book. F/NF. A24. $30.00

**MCCLURE, James.** *Four & Twenty Virgins.* 1973. London. Gollancz. 1st. F/dj. M15. $150.00

**MCCLURE, James.** *Son Dog.* 1991. Mysterious. ARC/1st. 1/500. sgn. NF/wrp. N4. $30.00

**MCCLURE, Michael.** *Gargoyle Cartoons.* 1971. NY. Delacorte. 1st trade. inscr. photos. NF/dj. L3. $85.00

**MCCLURE, Michael.** *Gorf.* 1976. New Directions. 1st. F/dj. L3. $35.00

**MCCLURE, Michael.** *Gorf.* 1976. New Directions. 1st. sgn/dtd 1994. NF/VG. R14. $45.00

**MCCLUSKEY, John.** *Mr America's Last Season Blues.* 1983. LSU. 1st. F/dj. R11. $15.00

**MCCONKEY, Harriet B.** *Dakota War Whoop.* 1965. Lakeside Classic. 1st thus. teg. w/pub card. NF. T11. $42.00

**MCCONNEL, J.L.** *Western Characters; or, Types of Border Life...* 1853. Refield. 1st. 378p. G-. B18. $45.00

**MCCONNEL & ROSS.** *Our Family's Starbuck Ancestry.* 1963. Mt Vernon, OH. cbdg/sc. G. S5. $25.00

**MCCONNELL, Francis John.** *Christlike God.* (1927). Abington. 12mo. 275p. F. H1. $5.00

**MCCONNELL, Malcolm.** *Into the Mouth of the Cat: Story of Lance Sijan...* 1985. NY. Norton. 1st. 253p. F/NF. R11. $25.00

**MCCOOL, J.M.** *Cooling Off.* 1984. Boston. Little Brn. 1st. author's 1st book. F/F. H11. $20.00

**MCCORD, David.** *Notes From Four Cities.* 1969. Worcester. St Onge. mini. 1/1500. aeg. gilt stp brn leather. B24. $35.00

**MCCORKLE, Jill.** *Carolina Moon.* 1996. Chapel Hill. 1st. 8vo. 260p. NF/dj. P4. $25.00

**MCCORKLE, Jill.** *Ferris Beach.* 1990. Algonquin. 1st. sgn. F/dj. A24. $47.50

**MCCORKLE, Jill.** *Tending to Virginia.* 1987. Algonquin. 1st. rem mk. NF/NF. B3. $20.00

**MCCORMAC, Billy M.** *Aurora & Airglow.* 1967. NY. Reinhold. 8vo. 689p. xl. K5. $50.00

**MCCORMAC, Billy M.** *Radiating Atmosphere.* 1971. NY. Springer. sm 4to. 455p. xl. K5. $30.00

**MCCORMACK, Eric.** *Paradise Motel.* 1989. Markham. Viking. 1st. F/F. H11. $15.00

**MCCORMICK, Patricia.** *Lady Bullfighter.* (1954). Holt. 1st. photos/ils. 209p. dj. F3. $12.50

**MCCORMICK, Robert R.** *War Without Grant.* 1950. NY. Bond Wheelwright. 1st. VG/G. A14. $14.00

**MCCORMICK, Wilfred.** *Bronc Burnett: Big Ninth (#10).* 1958. Grosset Dunlap. rpt. VG/dj. P8. $25.00

**MCCORMICK, Wilfred.** *Bronc Burnett: Fielder's Choice (#3).* 1949. Putnam. 1st. VG+. P8. $30.00

**MCCORMICK, Wilfred.** *Bronc Burnett: The Three Two Pitch (#1).* 1948. Putnam. 1st. VG/dj. P8. $45.00

**MCCORMICK, Wilfred.** *Rocky McCune: Hot Corner (#2).* 1958. McKay. 1st. F/VG. P8. $75.00

**MCCOSH, James.** *Emotions.* 1880. Scribner. 12mo. 255p. ruled gr cloth. VG. G1. $75.00

**MCCOURT, Frank.** *Angela's Ashes: A Memoir.* 1996. Scribner. 1st. sgn. AN/dj. B4. $400.00

**MCCOY, Drew R.** *Last of the Fathers: James Madison...* 1996. Cambridge. 386p. VG/wrp. M10. $16.50

**MCCOY, Horace.** *Black Box Thrillers: 4 Novels by Horace McCoy.* 1983. London. Zomba. 1st combined. F/dj. T2. $30.00

**MCCOY, John Pleasant.** *Swing the Big-Eyed Rabbit.* 1944. Blakiston/Dutton. 1st. 283p. F/NF. B20. $20.00

**MCCOY, Joseph G.** *Historic Sketches of Cattle Trade of the West & Southwest.* 1951. Columbus. rpt. ils. 427p. B18. $35.00

**MCCOY, Lois.** *Late Bloomer.* 1980. Harper Row. 1st. 8vo. 225p. NF/VG. W2. $20.00

**MCCOY, Maureen.** *Divining Blood.* 1992. Poseiden. 1st. F/F. H11. $20.00

**MCCRACKEN, Elizabeth.** *Giant's House.* 1996. Dial. 1st. F/dj. O11. $40.00

**MCCRACKEN, Elizabeth.** *Here's Your Hat What's Your Hurry.* 1993. NY. Turtle Bay. 1st. F/dj. O11. $100.00

**MCCRACKEN, Harold.** *Charles M Russell Book.* 1957. Doubleday. rpt. ils. 236p. NF/poor. T11. $40.00

**MCCRACKEN, Harold.** *Frederick Remington's Own West: Great Western Artist...* 1960. NY. Dial. ils. VG/torn. J2. $28.00

**MCCRACKEN, Harold.** *George Catlin & the Old Frontier.* nd. Bonanza. F/dj. A19. $35.00

**MCCRACKEN, Harold.** *George Catlin & the Old Frontier.* 1959. NY. Dial. 1st trade. 216p. VG/dj. P4. $75.00

**MCCRACKEN, Harold.** *Sentinal of the Snow Peaks: Story of the Alaskan Wild.* (1945). Phil. Lippincott. 1st. 151p. bl cloth. P4. $18.00

**MCCRUMB, Sharyn.** *Missing Susan.* 1991. Ballantine. 1st. sgn. 266p. blk brd/blk spine. NF/dj. J3. $35.00

**MCCRUMB, Sharyn.** *She Walks These Hills.* 1994. NY. Scribner. 1st. sgn. F/dj. M23. $50.00

**MCCRUMB, Sharyn.** *Zombies of the Gene Pool.* 1992. S&S. 1st. F/dj. D10. $45.00

**MCCUE, Andy.** *Baseball by the Book.* 1991. Wm Brn. 1st. AN/sans. P8. $25.00

**MCCUE, George.** *Octagon: Being an Account of Famous Washington Residence...* 1976. AIA Found. 101p. VG. B10. $15.00

**MCCULLAGH, James.** *Solar Greenhouse Book.* 1978. Emmaus. Rodale. 328p. VG/dj. A10. $18.00

**MCCULLERS, Carson.** *Heart Is a Lonely Hunter.* 1940. Houghton Mifflin. 1st. NF/VG clip. B4. $650.00

**MCCULLERS, Carson.** *Member of the Wedding.* 1946. New Directions. 118p. VG. C5. $12.50

**MCCULLERS, Carson.** *Member of the Wedding: A Play.* 1951. New Directions. 1st. 8vo. brn cloth. NF/VG. S9. $150.00

**MCCULLERS, Carson.** *Sweet as a Pickle & Clean as a Pig.* 1964. Houghton Mifflin. 1st. ils Rolf Gerald. F/NF clip. B4. $200.00

**MCCULLOUGH, Andrew.** *Rough Cut.* 1976. NY. Morrow. 1st. F/NF. H11. $20.00

**MCCULLOUGH, Colleen.** *First Man in Rome.* 1990. Morrow. 1st. sm 4to. 896p. F/dj. W2. $30.00

**MCCULLOUGH, Colleen.** *Ladies of Missalonghi.* 1987. Harper. 1st. NF/dj. H10. $7.00

**MCCULLOUGH, Colleen.** *Thorn Birds.* 1977. Harper Row. 1st. NF/VG. M19. $15.00

**MCCULLOUGH, David Willis.** *Think on Death.* 1991. Viking. 1st. F/dj. G8. $12.50

**MCCULLY, Helen.** *Cooking With Helen McCully Beside You.* 1970. Random. BC. G/dj. A16. $8.00

**MCCULLY & RICHARDSON.** *Picasso: A Life, Volume 1 1881-1906.* 1991. NY. 1st. dj. T9. $30.00

**MCCUTCHAN, Philip.** *Apprentice to the Sea.* 1995. St Martin. 1st Am. F/dj. T11. $30.00

**MCCUTCHAN, Philip.** *Cameron & the Kaiserhof.* 1984. London. Barker. 1st. NF/dj. A14. $28.00

**MCCUTCHAN, Philip.** *Cameron Comes Through.* 1980. London. Barker. 1st. NF/dj. A14. $35.00

**MCCUTCHAN, Philip.** *Cameron in Command.* 1983. London. Barker. 1st. NF/dj. A14. $28.00

**MCCUTCHAN, Philip.** *Cameron's Crossing.* 1993. St Martin. 1st Am. Cameron #12. F/NF. T11. $35.00

**MCCUTCHAN, Philip.** *Convoy of Fear.* 1990. St Martin. 1st Am. F/dj. T11. $25.00

**MCCUTCHAN, Philip.** *Halfhyde on the Amazon.* 1988. St Martin. 1st Am. F/NF. T11. $35.00

**MCCUTCHAN, Philip.** *Halfhyde Outward Bound.* 1983. St Martin. 1st Am. NF/VG. T11. $30.00

**MCCUTCHAN, Philip.** *Tom Chatto: Apprentice.* 1995. London. Weidenfeld Nicolson. 1st. F/dj. T11. $50.00

MCCUTCHEON, George Barr. *Cowardice Court*. 1907. Dodd Mead. ils Harrison Fisher. 140p. G. G11. $12.00

MCCUTCHEON, George Barr. *Graustark: Story of a Love Behind a Throne*. 1901. Chicago. Herbert Stone. 1st. VG. N2. $65.00

MCCUTCHEON, George Barr. *Jane Cable*. 1906. NY. Dodd Mead. 1st. ils Harrison Fisher. 336p. G. G11. $10.00

MCCUTCHEON, George Barr. *Mr Bingle*. 1915. Dodd Mead. 1st. ils James Montgomery Flagg. 357p. G. G11. $8.00

MCDANIEL, Bruce W. *Desert: God's Crucible*. 1926. Gorham. ils 118p. NF/NF. B19. $30.00

MCDANIEL, Ethel Hittle. *Contribution of Society of Friends to Education in Indiana*. 1939. IN Hist Soc. 1st. 8vo. 113p. VG. V3. $20.00

MCDANIEL, Ruel. *Vinegarroon*. 1936. Kingsport, TN. Southern Pub. F. A19. $65.00

MCDERMOTT, John D. *Forlorn Hope*. 1978. Boise, ID. ID State hist Soc. F. A19. $65.00

MCDEVITT, Jack. *Standard Candles*. 1996. SF. Tachyon. 1st. 1/100. sgn. ils/sgn Michael Dashow. F/dj. T2. $40.00

MCDONALD, Elvin. *Handbook for Greenhouse Gardeners*. 1966. Irvington-On-Hudson. 92p. VG. B26. $7.50

MCDONALD, Gregory. *Fletch, Too*. 1986. Warner. 1st. F/dj. N4. $25.00

MCDONALD, Gregory. *Flynn's In*. 1985. 1st Eng. F/NF. M19. $17.50

MCDONALD, H.D. *Theories of Revelation: An Historical Study 1700-1960*. 1979. Baker. VG/wrp. B29. $13.00

MCDONALD, T.H. *Exploring the Northwest Territory: Sir Alexander Mackenzie*. 1966. Norman, OK. 1st. 133p. F/torn. B20. $45.00

MCDONALD, Walter. *Caliban in Blue & Other Poems*. 1976. Texas Tech. 1st. NF. R11. $20.00

MCDONOUGH, Nancy. *Garden Sass: Catalog of Arkansas Folkways*. 1975. NY. photos. 319p. F/dj. M4. $18.00

MCDOUGAL, A. *Secret of Sucessful Restaurants*. 1929. 1st. VG. E6. $25.00

MCDOUGALL, John. *Pathfinding on Plain & Prairie: Stirring Scenes of Life...* 1971 (1898). Toronto. Coles. facs. F/wrp. A26. $20.00

MCDOUGALL, W.B. *Grand Canyon Wild Flowers*. 1964. Northland. 8vo. 259p. gilt gr cloth. NF. F7. $22.50

MCDOUGALL, W.B. *Plant Ecology*. 1931. Lea Febiger. 338p. xl. G. S5. $15.00

MCDOUGALL, Walter A. *Heavens & the Earth: A Political History...* 1985. NY. Basic. 1st. ils/cartoons. 555p. K5. $25.00

MCDOUGALL, William. *Outline of Psychology*. 1924. Scribner. 456p. brn cloth. xl. G1. $30.00

MCDOWELL, Frank. *Plastic Surgery*. 1987. Austin, TX. 329p. A13. $125.00

MCDOWELL, Michael. *Toplin*. 1987. Scream. 1/250. sgn. ils/sgn Harry O Morris. AN/box. T12. $125.00

MCELROY, Susan Chernak. *Animals as Teachers & Healers*. 1997. Ballantine. 1st. 8vo. 253p. F/dj. S14. $10.00

MCEWAN, Ian. *Black Dogs*. 1992. London. Cape. 1st. sgn. F/dj. O11. $35.00

MCEWAN, Ian. *Cement Garden*. 1978. S&S. 1st Am. NF/VG clip. R14. $50.00

MCEWAN, Ian. *Cement Garden*. 1978. S&S. 1st Am. sgn. author's 1st novel. F/F. D10. $60.00

MCEWAN, Ian. *Imitation Game & Other Plays*. 1982. Houghton Mifflin. 1st Am. sgn. F/clip. D10. $60.00

MCEWAN, Ian. *Innocent*. 1990. Doubleday. 1st. F/F. H11. $30.00

MCEWAN, Ian. *Innocent*. 1990. Lester. 1st Canadian. AN/dj. S18. $25.00

MCEWEN, Inez Puckett. *So This Is Ranching*. 1948. Caxton. 1/1000. sgn. 270p. red cloth. VG+. B20. $50.00

MCFARLAND, Dennis. *Face at the Window*. 1997. Broadway. 1st. sgn. F/dj. R14. $35.00

MCFARLAND, Dennis. *Music Room*. 1990. Houghton Mifflin. 1st. author's 1st book. NF/F. H11. $40.00

MCFARLAND, J. Horace. *My Growing Garden*. 1915. NY. ils/pl. 216p. VG. B26. $30.00

MCFARLANE, L.R.C. *Eighty Years With Horses*. 1973. Wellington, NZ. Reed. 1st. VG/G. O3. $18.00

MCFEE, William. *Harbourmaster*. 1931. Doubleday. 1st. 1/377. sgn. NF. J3. $70.00

MCGAHERN, John. *Collected Stories*. 1993. Knopf. 1st Am. sgn. F/dj. M25. $60.00

MCGAHERN, John. *Collected Stories*. 1993. NY. Knopf. 1st. VG/dj. M17. $20.00

MCGAIG, Donald. *Nop's Trials*. 1984. NY. Crown. 1st. NF/F. M23. $25.00

MCGAUGHEY, Neil. *And Then There Were Ten*. 1995. Scribner. 1st. F/dj. N4. $25.00

MCGAUGHEY, Neil. *Otherwise Known as Murder*. 1994. NY. Scribner. 1st. F/dj. M23. $35.00

MCGEE, D.H. *Famous Signers of the Declaration*. 1955. NY. inscr/sgn. 307p. F/dj. M4. $20.00

MCGEE, J. Vernon. *Revelation*. 1980. Thru the Bible. 3 vol. VG/wrp. B29. $7.00

MCGEE, J. Vernon. *Through the Bible With J Vernon McGee*. 1981. Thos Nelson. 5 vol. hc. VG. B29. $70.00

MCGINLEY, Patrick. *Goosefoot*. 1982. NY. Dutton. 1st Am. F/dj. Q1. $35.00

MCGINNIS, R.A. *Beet-Sugar Technology*. 1951. NY. Reinhold. 574p. cloth. VG. A10. $22.00

MCGINNISS, Joe. *Blind Faith*. 1989. Putnam. 1st. 381p. F/NF. W2. $35.00

MCGINTY, Billy. *Old West: As Written in Words of...* 1937. np. sgn pres. 108p. VG/stiff pict wrp. J2. $1,375.00

MCGIVERN, William P. *Summitt*. 1982. NY. Arbor. 1st. F/NF. H11. $15.00

MCGOVERN, George. *Grassroots*. 1977. NY. Random. inscr. VG/dj. A19. $35.00

MCGOVERN, John. *Golden Censer; or, Duties of Today & Hopes of Future*. 1888. Chicago. Union. VG. B9. $20.00

MCGOWAN, Carl. *Organization of Judicial Power in the United States*. 1969. Northwestern. VG/dj. M11. $45.00

MCGOWAN, Harold. *Another World for Christmas*. 1984. Central Islip, NY. Metaprobe Inst. 1st. VG/dj. M21. $15.00

MCGRADY, Mike. *Dove in Vietnam*. 1968. Funk Wagnall. 245p. NF/dj. R11. $25.00

MCGRATH, Patrick. *Grotesque*. 1989. Poseidon. 1st. F/dj. M23. $20.00

MCGRATH, Patrick. *Spider*. 1990. Poseidon. 1st. F/dj. M23. $10.00

MCGREGOR, Miriam. *Weeds in My Garden*. (1986). Lorson's Books & Prts. mini. 1/50 (175 total). sgn. w/extra proof set. B24. $275.00

MCGRILLIS, John O.C. *Printer's Abecedarium*. 1974. Boston. Godine. 1st. 8vo. unp. F/dj. O10. $25.00

MCGUANE, Thomas. *Keep the Change*. 1989. Houghton Mifflin. 1/150. sgn. F/case. B3. $150.00

**MCGUANE, Thomas.** *Nothing But Blue Skies.* 1992. Houghton Mifflin. 1/300 special bdg. sgn. F/case. B2. $125.00

**MCGUANE, Thomas.** *Nothing But Blue Skies.* 1992. Houghton Mifflin. 1st. sgn. F/dj. R14. $45.00

**MCGUANE, Thomas.** *Panama.* 1978. FSG. 1st. sgn/dtd 1998. NF/F. R14. $55.00

**MCGUANE, Thomas.** *Something to Be Desired.* 1985. London. Secker Warburg. 1st Eng. sgn/dtd 1998. F/dj. R14. $35.00

**MCGUANE, Thomas.** *To Skin a Cat.* 1986. Dutton. 1st. F/dj. Q1. $45.00

**MCGUANE, Thomas.** *To Skin a Cat.* 1987. Secker Warburg. 1st. sgn. F/F. B3. $40.00

**MCGUANE, Thomas.** *92 in the Shade.* 1972. London. Collins. 1st. F/VG. B3. $75.00

**MCGUANE, Thomas.** *92 in the Shade.* 1973. NY. FSG. 1st. F/dj. O11. $140.00

**MCGUIRE, Bob.** *Black Bears: Technical & Hunting Guide Book.* 1983. Blountville, TN. 1st. sgn. 189p. VG. A19. $15.00

**MCHARGUE, Georgess.** *Horseman's World.* 1981. Delacorte. 1st. VG/dj. O3. $22.00

**MCHATTON-RIPLEY.** *From Flag to Flag: Woman's Adventures in the South...* 1889 (1888). xl. VG. E6. $65.00

**MCHUGH, Heather.** *Dangers.* 1977. Houghton Mifflin. 1st. inscr. F/dj. L3. $40.00

**MCHUGH, Maureen F.** *China Mountain Zhang.* 1992. NY. Tor. 1st. author's 1st novel. F/NF. G10. $35.00

**MCINERNEY, Jay.** *Ransom.* 1985. Vintage Contemporaries. ARC. F/wrp. R14. $40.00

**MCINTYRE, Judith W.** *Common Loon: Spirit of Northern Lakes.* 1989. NM U. 2nd. ils+33 1/3-rpm record. F/dj. A17. $20.00

**MCINTYRE, Nancy.** *It's a Picnic!* 1969. Viking. G/dj. A16. $15.00

**MCINTYRE, Ruth A.** *Debts Hopeful & Desperate: Financing Plymouth Colony.* 1963. Plymouth Plantation. 1st? sgn. 8vo. w/inscr postcard. F/dj. A2. $17.50

**MCISSAC, F.J.** *Tony Sarg Marionette Book.* 1921. NY. BW Huebsch. 1st. 12mo. 58p. pict brd. NF. D1. $85.00

**MCIVER.** *Cookery & Pastry as Taught & Practiced by Mrs McIver...* 1789. London. new ed. 264p. orig full leather. E6. $275.00

**MCKAY, George.** *Bibliography of Robert Bridges.* 1933. Columbia. 1st. 1/550. teg. gilt quarter gr cloth. F. M24. $125.00

**MCKAY, R.H.** *Little Pills: An Army Story.* 1918. Pittsburg, KS. Pittsburg Headlight. 127p. cloth. D11. $100.00

**MCKAY, Robert.** *Under the Trapeze.* 1989. Cincinnati. Brass Ring. 516p. S5. $10.00

**MCKAY.** *American Book Auction Catalogues, 1713-1934, a Union List.* 1967. ils. 592p. NF. A4. $150.00

**MCKEAN, Hugh F.** *Lost Treasures of Louis Comfort Tiffany.* 1980. Doubleday. 1st. 4to. 304p. NF/plastic. H1. $90.00

**MCKEARIN & MCKEARIN.** *American Glass.* (1941). Crown. 3rd. 622p. VG/G. H1. $40.00

**MCKEARIN & MCKEARIN.** *American Glass.* 1959. NY. Crown. ils/photos. F/dj. A19. $35.00

**MCKEE, Edwin D.** *Ancient Landscapes of the Grand Canyon Region.* 1931. Lockwood-Hazel. 1st. ils Russell Hastings. VG/dj. F7. $55.00

**MCKEE, Edwin D.** *Environment & History of Toroweap & Kaibab Formations...* 1938. WA, DC. fld/pl. 268p. xl. F7. $75.00

**MCKEE, Russell.** *Last West: History of the Great Plains of North America.* 1974. Crowell. ils/maps/photos. VG/dj. J2. $40.00

**MCKEEVER, William.** *Farm Boys & Girls.* 1913. Macmillan. 326p. cloth. A10. $15.00

**MCKELVEY, Jean T.** *Changing Law of Fair Representation.* 1985. Ithaca. ILR Pr. M11. $35.00

**MCKENDRY, Maxime.** *Seven Centuries Cookbook.* 1973. McGraw Hill. G/dj. A16. $25.00

**MCKENNA, Richard.** *Left-Handed Monkey Wrench.* 1984. Annapolis. Naval Inst. 1st. half red-orange cloth. F/NF. T11. $80.00

**MCKENNA, Richard.** *Sand Pebbles.* 1962. NY. Harper Row. 1st. red cloth. NF/VG. T11. $65.00

**MCKENNA, Rollie.** *Portrait of Dylan: A Photographer's Memoir.* 1982. Owings Mills, MD. 1st. photos. VG/dj. M17. $37.50

**MCKENNA, Stephen.** *Datchley Inheritance.* 1930. Dodd Mead. 1st. G+. G8. $15.00

**MCKENZIE, D.F.** *Stationers's Company Apprentices, 1701-1800.* 1978. Oxford. Bibliographical Soc. 1st. quarter cloth. F. M24. $50.00

**MCKENZIE, John L.** *Two-Edged Sword.* 1956. Bruce. 317p. VG/dj. B19. $9.50

**MCKEON, John J.** *Serpent's Crown.* 1991. Walker. 1st. author's 1st book. F/F. H11. $20.00

**MCKEOWN, Martha Ferguson.** *Alaska Silver.* 1951. NY. Macmillan. 2nd. 274p. dj. P4. $23.00

**MCKILLIP, Patricia.** *Moon & the Face.* 1985. Atheneum. 1st. 146p. cloth. F/dj. D4. $45.00

**MCKINLEY, Robin.** *Hero & the Crown.* 1985. Greenwillow. 1st. F/dj. M25. $45.00

**MCKINLEY, Robin.** *Outlaws of Sherwood.* 1988. Greenwillow. 1st. F/dj. M25. $25.00

**MCKINLEY, William.** *Speeches & Addresses of...* 1894. NY. Appleton. ils. 664p. B18. $27.50

**MCKINNEY, E.L.** *King of Indoor Sports.* 1963. Chicago. Petit Oiseau. mini. 1/50. 21p. bl brd. B24. $175.00

**MCKINNEY, William M.** *Treatise on the Law of Fellow-Servants...* 1890. Northport. Edward Thompson. sheep. M11. $75.00

**MCKINNEY-WHETSTONE,** Diane. *Tumbling.* 1996. Morrow. 1st. author's 1st book. F/F. H11. $20.00

**MCKINNON, Allan.** *Assignments in Iraq.* 1960. Crime Club. 1st. F/VG. M19. $17.50

**MCKINNON, Harold R.** *Higher Law, an Address...* 1946. Berkeley. Gillick. 17p. prt stapled wrp. M11. $25.00

**MCKINSTRY, Bruce L.** *California Gold Rush Overland Diary of Byron N McKinstry...* 1975. Arthur H Clark. 401p. cloth. dj. D11. $45.00

**MCKITTERICK, David.** *Stanley Morison & DB Updike: Selected Correspondence.* 1979. NY. Moretus. 1st. 8vo. F/dj. O10. $30.00

**MCKITTERICK, Molly.** *Medium Is Murder.* 1992. NY. St. Martin. 1st. author's 1st book. NF/F. H11. $20.00

**MCLANATHAN, Richard K.B.** *Ship Models.* 1957. Mus Fine Arts. ils. 20p. VG. M10. $10.00

**MCLANATHAN, Richard.** *Gilbert Stuart.* 1986. ils/index. 159p. dj. O8. $18.50

**MCLANATHAN, Robert.** *Brandywine Heritage.* 1971. NYGS. 1st. ils. VG+/wrp. S13. $18.00

**MCLAURIN, John J.** *Sketches in Crude Oil: Some Accidents & Incidents...* 1898. Harrisburg. 2nd. ils. 452p. B18. $45.00

**MCLEAN, Allan Campbell.** *Glasshouse.* 1968. HBW. 1st. F/NF. H11. $35.00

**MCLEAN, Rauri.** *Victorian Publisher's Book-Bindings in Paper.* 1983. London. Gordon Fraser. 1st. 112p. F/glassine. F1. $120.00

**MCLEAN, Ruari.** *Typographers on Type: Illustrated Anthology...* 1995. NY. Norton. 1st. tall 8vo. F/dj. O10. $27.00

**MCLENNAN, Rob.** *Growing Proteas.* 1993. Kenhurst, Australia. photos. sc. AN. B26. $14.00

**MCLEOD, Alexander.** *Pigtails & Gold Dust.* 1947. Caxton. 1st. VG/sans. O4. $35.00

**MCLEOD, James Richard.** *Theodore Roethke: A Manuscript Checklist.* (1971). Kent State. 1st. index. F/sans. A18. $25.00

**MCLEOD, W.** *Geography of Palestine; or, The Holy Land...* 1854. London. map ftspc. G. M17. $25.00

**MCLINTIC, Guthrie.** *Me & Kit.* 1955. Little Brn. 1st. 341p. F/NF. B20. $90.00

**MCLINTOCK, F.L.** *Narrative of Discovery of Fate of Sir John Franklin...* 1859. London. Murray. 3 fld maps/2 pocket maps. 403p. rb. NF. M4. $400.00

**MCLINTON, Katherine Morrison.** *Collecting American Glass.* (1950). Granmercy. 2nd. sm 8vo. 64p. F/VG plastic. H1. $22.50

**MCLOUGHLIN, Denis.** *Wild & Woolly: An Encyclopedia of the Old West.* 1975. Barnes Noble. 2500 entries. VG/dj. A4. $65.00

**MCLOUGHLIN BROTHERS.** *Around the World in an Automobile.* 1907. obl 4to. mc pict stiff brd. R5. $300.00

**MCLOUGHLIN BROTHERS.** *Childhood Heroes. Stories of Robinson Crusoe...* 1889. 4to. mc pict brd. R5. $150.00

**MCLOUGHLIN BROTHERS.** *Circus Sports.* 1897. 12-panel hinged panorama. cloth. R5. $450.00

**MCLOUGHLIN BROTHERS.** *Death & Burial of Cock Robin.* nd. Springfield, MA. 8vo. 6p. linen. VG. T5. $85.00

**MCLOUGHLIN BROTHERS.** *Good Natured Boy. Young America Series.* ca 1865. 24mo. mc pict self cover. R5. $100.00

**MCLOUGHLIN BROTHERS.** *History of Goody Two-Shoes. Uncle Frank's Series.* ca 1865. 16mo. mc pict paper wrp. R5. $200.00

**MCLOUGHLIN BROTHERS.** *Hop O' My Thumb. Little Delights.* ca 1875. 16mo. mc pict self covers. R5. $65.00

**MCLOUGHLIN BROTHERS.** *Little Goody Two-Shoes. Miss Merryheart's Series.* ca 1860. tall 8vo. rose pict paper wrp. R5. $200.00

**MCLOUGHLIN BROTHERS.** *Little Rooster & the Ugly Duckling.* 1900. McLoughlin Bros. 4to. mc pict wrp. R5. $90.00

**MCLOUGHLIN BROTHERS.** *Little Tom Tucker. Aunt Jenny's Musical Series.* ca 1865. tall 8vo. mc pict paper wrp. R5. $300.00

**MCLOUGHLIN BROTHERS.** *Nursery Songs. Grandmother Goose's Series.* ca 1882. 8vo. mc pict covers. R5. $85.00

**MCLOUGHLIN BROTHERS.** *Old Woman & Her Pig.* (1890). Little Pig series. unp. G/wrp. D1. $40.00

**MCLOUGHLIN BROTHERS.** *Puss in Boots. Father's Series.* ca 1865. 12mo. mc pict self cover. R5. $65.00

**MCLOUGHLIN BROTHERS.** *Rip Van Winkle.* ca 1880. NY. Picture Book series. ils thomas Nast. VG. D1. $285.00

**MCLOUGHLIN BROTHERS.** *Story (History) of Tom Thumb. Familiar Series.* ca 1879. 8vo. mc pict paper wrp. R5. $75.00

**MCLOUGHLIN BROTHERS.** *Three Little Pigs. Nursery Series.* 1905. 4to. mc pict paper wrp. R5. $75.00

**MCLUHAN, Marshall.** *Culture Is Our Business.* (1970). McGraw Hill. 3rd. ils. F/dj. A26. $35.00

**MCMAHON, Jo.** *Deenie Folks & Friends of Theirs.* (1925). Volland. 1st (so stated). ils John Gee. 8vo. ils brd/pub box. R5. $200.00

**MCMEEKIN, Clark.** *Old Kentucky Country.* 1957. DSP. 1st. 214p. VG/fair. B10. $45.00

**MCMEEKIN, Isabel McLennan.** *Kentucky Derby Winner.* 1949. Grosset Dunlap. later prt. bl tweed brd. G+. B36. $9.00

**MCMICHAEL, Robert.** *One Man's Obsession.* 1986. Prentice Hall. 1st. rem mk. VG/dj. N2. $12.50

**MCMILLAN, Terry.** *Disappearing Acts.* 1990. London. Cape. 1st. author's 2nd book. F/dj. O11. $40.00

**MCMILLAN, Terry.** *How Stella Got Her Groove Back.* 1996. Viking. 1st. sgn. F/dj. B30. $55.00

**MCMILLAN, Terry.** *Mama.* 1987. Houghton Mifflin. 1st. author's 1st book. F/NF. B3. $350.00

**MCMILLAN, Terry.** *Waiting to Exhale.* 1992. NY. Viking. 1st. NF/dj. R14. $40.00

**MCMILLAN, Terry.** *Waiting to Exhale.* 1992. Viking Penguin. 1st. sgn+sgn bookplate. F/dj. O11. $60.00

**MCMURRY, Richard M.** *John Bell Hood & War for Southern Independence.* 1982. Lexington. 239p. VG/dj. S16. $35.00

**MCMURRY, Richard M.** *Road Past Kennesaw: Atlanta Campaign 1864.* 1972. US Dept Interior. 1st. ils. 72p. NF. S14. $15.00

**MCMURTRIE, Douglas C.** *Bibliography of Mississippi Imprints 1798-1830.* 1945. Beauvoir Community, MS. 1st. 168p. cloth. NF. M8. $150.00

**MCMURTRIE, Douglas C.** *Note on P Joseph Forster: Pioneer Alabama Printer.* 1943. Harrisburg, MS. 1st. VG/wrp. M8. $75.00

**MCMURTRIE, Douglas C.** *Pioneer Printer of New Orleans.* 1930. Chicago. 1st. 1/250. 17p. VG/wrp. M8. $65.00

**MCMURTRIE, Douglas C.** *Pioneer Printing in North Carolina.* 1932. Springfield, IL. 1st. 1/200. 4p. VG/wrp. M8. $75.00

**MCMURTRIE, Douglas C.** *Preliminary Short-title Check List of Books...1784-1860.* 1937. Jacksonville. 1st. 15p. VG/wrp. M8. $75.00

**MCMURTRY, Larry.** *All My Friends Are Going to Be Strangers.* 1972. S&S. 1st. sgn. F/dj. Q1. $300.00

**MCMURTRY, Larry.** *Anything for Billy.* 1988. S&S. 1st. sgn. F/F. B3. $60.00

**MCMURTRY, Larry.** *Buffalo Girls.* 1990. S&S. 1st. sgn. F/F. B3. $50.00

**MCMURTRY, Larry.** *Buffalo Girls.* 1990. S&S. 1st. VG/dj. J2. $40.00

**MCMURTRY, Larry.** *Evening Star.* 1992. S&S. 1st. NF/F. H11. $20.00

**MCMURTRY, Larry.** *Last Picture Show.* 1966. NY. Dial. 1st/1st prt. cream cloth. F/dj. M24. $600.00

**MCMURTRY, Larry.** *Lonesome Dove.* 1985. S&S. 1st. F/dj. T11. $200.00

**MCMURTRY, Larry.** *Lonesome Dove.* 1985. S&S. 1st. sgn. NF/dj. B30. $325.00

**MCMURTRY, Larry.** *Some Can Whistle.* 1989. NY. S&S. 1st. F/dj. J3. $35.00

**MCMURTRY, Larry.** *Somebody's Darling.* 1978. S&S. 1st. F/dj. Q1. $60.00

**MCMURTRY, Larry.** *Somebody's Darling.* 1978. S&S. 1st. rem mk. F/dj. M19. $45.00

**MCMURTRY, Larry.** *Splendors & Miseries of Being an Author-Bookseller.* 1995. ABAA. 1st. 1/750. 12p. VG/wrp. N2. $35.00

**MCMURTRY, Larry.** *Streets of Loredo.* 1993. NY. S&S. 1st. F/dj. Q1. $35.00

**MCMURTRY, Larry.** *Terms of Endearment.* 1975. S&S. 1st. inscr/sgn. NF/dj. S9. $350.00

**MCMURTRY, Larry.** *Terms of Endearment.* 1975. S&S. 1st. NF/dj. D10. $75.00

**MCMURTRY, Larry.** *Terms of Endearment.* 1975. S&S. 1st. sgn. F/NF. O11. $175.00

**MCMURTRY, Larry.** *Texasville.* 1987. S&S. 1st. rem mk. F/NF. H11. $15.00

**MCMURTRY, Larry.** *Zeke & Ned.* 1997. NY. S&S. ARC/1st. w/promo materials. F/dj. T11. $35.00

**MCMURTRY & OSSANA.** *Pretty Boy Floyd: A Novel.* 1994. S&S. 1st. sgns. 444p. F/dj. B20. $40.00

**MCNALLY, Raymond T.** *Clutch of Vampires.* 1974. NYGS. 1st. VG/G+. L1. $75.00

**MCNALLY, Raymond T.** *In Search of Dracula.* 1972. NYGS. 1st. G/dj. L1. $75.00

**MCNALLY, Tom.** *Fisherman's Bible.* 1976. Chicago. 1st. photos/ils. 444p. F/dj. A17. $20.00

**MCNALLY & MCNALLY.** *This Is Mexico.* 1947. Dodd Mead. 1st. 4to. 216p. dj. F3. $15.00

**MCNAMARA, Eugene.** *Interior Landscape: Literary Criticism of Marshall McLuhan.* 1969. McGraw Hill. stated 1st. VG/dj. N2. $10.00

**MCNAMARA, Joseph D.** *Fatal Command.* 1987. Arbor. 1st. NF/NF. H11. $15.00

**MCNAMEE, Eoin.** *Resurrection Man.* 1995. NY. Picador. 1st. F/dj. M23. $40.00

**MCNAMEE, Thomas.** *Grizzly Bear.* 1985. NY. ils. 308p. F/dj. S15. $18.00

**MCNARY, Kyle.** *Ted 'Double Duty' Radcliffe.* 1994. McNary. 1st. sgn. photos. AN/wrp. P8. $40.00

**MCNEER, Mary.** *California Gold Rush.* 1950. Random. ils Lynd Ward. VG/G. B36. $16.00

**MCNEER, May.** *Golden Flash.* 1947. Viking. 1st. 227p. VG+. D4. $45.00

**MCNEER, May.** *Wolf of Lambs.* 1967. Houghton Mifflin. 1st. ils Lynd Ward. mc pict cloth. dj. R5. $50.00

**MCNEIL, Helen.** *Emily Dickinson.* 1986. London. Virgo. 208p. VG/wrp. M10. $10.00

**MCNEIL, John.** *Spy Game.* 1980. NY. Coward McCann. 1st. author's 2nd book. F/F. H11. $25.00

**MCNEILL, Elizabeth.** *Nine & a Half Weeks: A Memoir of a Love Affair.* 1978. Dutton. 1st. F/dj. B4. $150.00

**MCNEILL, William.** *Plagues & Peoples.* 1976. Garden City, NY. 1st. 369p. A13. $30.00

**MCNICHOLS, Charles.** *Crazy Weather.* 1944. Macmillan. 1st. 195p. F/NF. D4. $30.00

**MCNIGHT, W.J.** *Pioneer Outline History of Northwestern Pennsylvania.* 1905. Lippincott. inscr/dtd 1915. ils. emb flyleaf. F. V4. $200.00

**MCNITT, Frank.** *Indian Traders.* 1962. Norman, OK. 1st. 8vo. red cloth. dj. F7. $75.00

**MCNULTY, Faith.** *Mouse & Tim.* 1978. Harper Row. 1st. sm 4to. 48p. NF/VG. T5. $35.00

**MCORMICK, Leander J.** *Fishing Around the World.* 1937. NY. photos. 307p. G. A17. $15.00

**MCPHAUL, Jack.** *Johnny Torrid, First of the Gang Lords.* 1970. New Rochelle. Arlington House. 1st. ils. 489p. VG/G. B5. $25.00

**MCPHEE, John.** *Coming Into the Country.* 1977. NY. FSG. 1st. F/NF. B3. $75.00

**MCPHEE, John.** *Deltoid Pumpkin Seed.* 1973. FSG. 1st. sgn. NF/dj. R14. $100.00

**MCPHEE, John.** *Encounters With the Archdruid.* 1971. FSG. 1st. 8vo. 245p. brn cloth. dj. F7. $65.00

**MCPHEE, John.** *Giving Good Weight.* 1979. Farrar Straus. 1st. F/dj. H11/Q1. $30.00

**MCPHEE, John.** *Headmaster: Boyden of Deerfield.* 1966. Farrar Strauss. 1st. 149p. VG/dj. B5. $65.00

**MCPHEE, John.** *In Suspect Terrain.* 1983. FSG. 1st. F/NF clip. H11. $35.00

**MCPHEE, John.** *Levels of the Game.* 1969. FSG. 1st. F/NF clip. B2. $65.00

**MCPHEE, John.** *Levels of the Game.* 1969. FSG. 1st. F/NF. B3. $85.00

**MCPHEE, John.** *Looking for a Ship.* 1990. FSG. 1st. F/dj. R14. $25.00

**MCPHEE, John.** *Outcroppings.* 1988. Gibbs Smith. 1st. photos Tom Till. 130p. F/F. B19. $35.00

**MCPHEE, John.** *Sense of Where You Are.* 1965. FSG. 1st. author's 1st book. F/G+. B4. $250.00

**MCPHEE, John.** *Wimbledon, a Celebration.* 1972. NY. Viking. 1st. ils Alfred Eisenstaedt. VG/dj. R14. $65.00

**MCPHEE, John.** *Wimbledon, a Celebration.* 1972. Viking. 1st. photos Alfred Eisenstaedt. F/VG. B3. $125.00

**MCPHERSON, Flora.** *Watchman Against the World: Story of Norman McLeod...* 1962. London. Robert Hale. 1st. VG/clip. N2. $12.50

**MCPHERSON, William.** *To the Sargasso Sea.* 1978. S&S. 1st. F/F. H11. $20.00

**MCQUEEN, Cyrus B.** *Field Guide to Peat Mosses of Boreal North America.* 1990. U New Eng. 138p. F. S15. $7.00

**MCQUINN, Donald E.** *Targets.* 1980. Macmillan. 1st. sgn. F/NF. R11. $45.00

**MCREYNOLDS, Robert.** *Thirty Years on the Frontier.* 1906. Colorado Springs, CO. El Paso Pub. G. A19. $95.00

**MCSHERRY, Frank Jr.** *Nightmares in Dixie.* 1987. Little Rock, AR. August House. 1st. VG/dj. L1. $35.00

**MCSHERRY, Frank.** *Baseball 3,000.* 1981. Elsevier/Nelson. 1st. F/VG. P8. $65.00

**MCSPADDEN, J. Walker.** *Animals of the World.* 1947. Garden City. G. A19. $30.00

**MCSWEENY, Bill.** *Impossible Dream.* 1968. Coward McCann. 1st. VG/dj. P8. $45.00

**MCSWIGAN, Marie.** *Five on a Merry-Go-Round.* 1943. Dutton. stated 1st. red cloth. xl. VG. B36. $22.00

**MCVITTIE, G.C.** *Fact & Theory in Cosmology.* 1961. NY. Macmillan. 8vo. 190p. VG/dj. K5. $16.00

**MCWATTERS, George S.** *Knots United; or, Ways & By-Ways Hidden Life Am Detectives.* 1871. Hartford. early rpt. 665p. G+. B18. $37.50

**MCWHINNIE, R.E.** *Those Good Years at Wyoming U.* 1966. Laramie, WY. F/dj. A19. $25.00

**MCWILLIAM, Candia.** *Debatable Land.* 1994. London. Bloomsbury. 1st. F/NF. A24. $35.00

**MCWILLIAMS, Carey.** *Ill Fares the Land.* 1942. Little Brn. ARC. 8vo. RS. NF/dj. S9. $125.00

**MEACHAM, Ellis K.** *East Indianman.* 1976. Boston. Little Brn. 1st. gilt bl cloth. F/VG. T11. $85.00

**MEACHAM, Ellis K.** *On the Company's Service.* 1976. Little Brn. 1st. Percival Merewether #2. F/NF. T11. $75.00

**MEAD, Cary Hoge.** *Wings Over the World: Life of George Jackson Mead.* 1971. Wauwatosa. 1st. 314p. VG/dj. B18. $25.00

**MEAD, Margaret.** *Culture & Commitment: A Study of the Generation Gap.* 1970. NY Nat Hist/Doubleday. sm 8vo. 91p. F/dj. H4. $12.50

**MEADE, Martha L.** *Recipes From the Old South.* 1961. Bramhall. G/dj. A16. $12.00

**MEADE, Mrs. L.T.** *Sweet Girl Graduate.* 1891. London. Cassell. 1st. 288p. G11. $12.00

**MEADE, Robert Douthat.** *Judah P Benjamin: Confederate Statesman.* 1943. Oxford. ils/photos. VG/G. B10. $60.00

**MEADE, Robert Douthat.** *Patrick Henry: Practical Revolutionary.* (1969). Lippincott. 531p. VG/VG. B10. $35.00

**MEADE, William.** *Old Churches & Families of Virginia.* nd. Lippincott. 2 vol. G. B10. $135.00

**MEADER, Herman Lee.** *Motor Goose Rhymes for Motor Ganders.* 1905. NY. Grafton. 12mo. 112p. orange paper brd/pict label. NF. H4. $35.00

**MEADOW, Ben.** *Faces: Narrative History of Portrait in Photography.* 1977. NYGS. 1st. VG. S5. $70.00

**MEADOWCROFT, Enid LaMonte.** *Gift of the River.* 1937. Crowell. 1st. ils Katherine Dewey. G/dj. P2. $20.00

**MEADOWCROFT, Enid LaMonte.** *Story of Davy Crockett.* 1952. Grosset Dunlap. lists to Story of Geo Washington. 178p. rem mk. VG. B36. $8.00

**MEAGHER, John R.** *RCA Television Pict-O-Guide.* 1949. Harrison, NJ. RCA Television. 3 vol. 1st. obl 12mo. sbdg. F. B20. $50.00

**MEAKIN, Budgett.** *Moors: A Comprehensive Description.* 1902. London. Sonnenschein. 8vo. 503p. gilt gr cloth. NF. H4. $100.00

**MEALY & MEALY.** *Sing for Joy: A Songbook for Young Children.* 1961. CT. Seabury. 1st. ils Karla Kuskin. 138p. G+. T5. $20.00

**MEANS, Florence Crannell.** *It Takes All Kinds.* 1964. Houghton Mifflin. 1st. 8vo. 234p. F/dj. w/TLS & photos. H4. $75.00

**MEANS, James.** *Aeronautical Annual 1895.* 1895 (1894). Boston. 172p. wrp. B18. $195.00

**MEANS, Philip Ainsworth.** *Ancient Civilizations of the Andes.* 1931. Scribner. 1st. 586p. F3. $45.00

**MEANS, Russell.** *Where White Men Fear to Tread.* 1995. St Martin. 1st. sgn. F/dj. O11. $50.00

**MEANY, Edmond S.** *Mt Rainier: A Record of Exploration.* 1957. Binfords & Mort. rpt. 8vo. 325p. F/VG+. B20. $40.00

**MEANY, Tom.** *Baseball's Greatest Pickers.* 1951. Barnes. 1st. photos. F/G. P8. $20.00

**MEANY, Tom.** *Stan Musial: The Man.* 1951. Barnes. 1st. G+/clip. P8. $50.00

**MEBANE, John.** *Collecting Brides' Baskets & Other Glass Fancies.* (1976). Wallace-Homestead. ne. 174p. VG/glossy wrp. H1. $45.00

**MEBANE, Mary E.** *Mary: An Autobiography.* 1981. Viking. 1st. F/dj. B2. $25.00

**MECH, L. David.** *Way of the Wolf.* 1991. Stillwater, MN. Voyageur. AN/dj. A19. $25.00

**MECH, L. David.** *Wolf: Ecology & Behavior of an Endangered Species.* 1970. Am Mus Natural Hist. 1st. 384p. VG/dj. S15. $24.00

**MECH, L. David.** *Wolves of Isle Royale.* 1966. WA. ils. 210p. VG. S15. $15.00

**MEDAWAR, Peter.** *Pluto's Republic.* 1982. OUP. 351p. VG/dj. A10. $30.00

**MEDLEY & PARGELLIS.** *Bibliography of British History, 18th Century 1714-1789.* 1951. 4558 entries. 668p. NF. A4. $95.00

**MEDLOCK, J.L.** *When Swallows Fly Home: Tale of Life in Old Center.* 1976. OK City. photos. 172p. F. M4. $16.00

**MEDVEDEV, Zhoras A.** *Rise & Fall of TD Lysenko.* 1969. Columbia. 3rd. VG/dj. A2. $12.50

**MEDVEDEV, Zhores A.** *Medvedev Papers.* 1971 (1970). Macmillan/St Martin. 1st thus. 8vo. F/dj. A2. $15.00

**MEDVEDEV, Zhores A.** *Soviet Agriculture.* 1987. NY. Norton. 1st. 464p. VG/dj. H10. $20.00

**MEDVEL, V.** *History of Endoctrinology.* 1982. Boston. 1st. 913p. A13. $100.00

**MEDVEL & THORNTON.** *Royal Hospital of St Bartholomew 1123-1973.* 1974. London. 1st. 423p. A13. $60.00

**MEE, Charles L.** *End of Order: Versailles 1919.* 1980. Dutton. 1st. 301p. NF/dj. M7. $30.00

**MEE, Charles L.** *Ohio Gang: World of Warren G Harding.* 1981. NY. 1st. ils. 248p. VG/dj. B18. $12.50

**MEEK, M.R.D.** *This Blessed Plot.* 1991. Scribner. 1st. F/F. H11. $25.00

**MEEK, S.P.** *Gustav.* 1940. Knopf/Borzoi Books. VG. A21. $30.00

**MEEK, S.P.** *Jerry: The Adventures of an Army Dog.* 1942. NY. Appleton Century. ils Clinton Balmer. VG/dj. A21. $40.00

**MEEK, S.P.** *Omar: A State Police Dog.* 1953. Knopf. 1st. rb. VG. P12. $15.00

**MEEKER, Arthur.** *Prairie Avenue.* 1949. Knopf. BC. NF/VG. H4. $10.00

**MEEKER, Ezra.** *Pioneer Reminiscenes of Puget Sound: A Tragedy of Leshi.* 1905. Lowman Hanford. 1st. 8vo. 555p. bl cloth. VG+. B20. $135.00

**MEEN & TUSHINGHAM.** *Crown Jewels of Iran.* 1974. Toronto/Buffalo. U Toronto. 2nd. folio. ils. 159p. VG. W1. $65.00

**MEERLOO, Joost A.M.** *Dance: From Ritual to Rock & Roll, Ballet to Ballroom.* 1960. Phil/NY. ils/photos. VG/G. M17. $15.00

**MEESE, Edwin III.** *With Reagan.* 1992. Regnery Gateway. 1st. sgn. F/F. W2. $35.00

**MEGARGEE, Edwin.** *Horses.* 1946. Messner. 1st. obl 4to. ils. VG. H4. $20.00

**MEGGENDORFER, Lothar.** *Im Zirkus.* ca 1880s. Germany. 4to. 6-panel panorama w/4 3-level popup scenes. complete. B24. $1,750.00

**MEGGENDORFER, Lothar.** *Neue Thierbilder (New Livestock Picture Book).* ca 1890. Munchen. Braun und Schneider. 6th. tall 4to. 8 tab moveables. R5. $1,200.00

**MEHRING, Walter.** *Lost Library: Autobiography of a Culture.* (1951). Bobbs Merrill. 1st. 8vo. 290p. NF/VG. H4. $35.00

**MEIGS, Cornelia.** *Clearing Weather.* 1928. Little Brn. 1st. ils Frank Dobias. 312p. G/fair. G11. $10.00

**MEIGS, Cornelia.** *Critical History of Children's Literature.* (1969). London. Macmillan. revised. 8vo. 708p. xl. VG/dj. H4. $25.00

**MEIGS, Cornelia.** *Wind in the Chimney.* 1934. NY. Macmillan. 1st. 144p. VG. D4. $35.00

**MEIGS, John.** *Cowboy in American Prints.* 1972. Sage. xl. VG/dj. A21. $45.00

**MEIGS, Peveril.** *Dominican Mission Frontier of Lower California.* 1935. U CA. 1st. photos/maps. VG. S14. $75.00

**MEIJERING, Piet.** *Signed With Their Honor: Air Chivalry During Two World Wars.* 1988. NY. 1st. photos/biblio/index. VG/dj. S16. $25.00

**MEILACH, D.Z.** *Creating Art From Anything...* 1968. Reilly Lee. ils/pl. 119p. cloth. dj. D2. $25.00

**MEISSNER, Bill.** *Hitting Into the Wind.* 1994. Random. 1st. F/dj. P8. $15.00

**MELANSON, Philip H.** *Spy Saga: Lee Harvey Oswald & US Intelligence.* 1990. Praeger. 1st. VG/dj. N2. $12.50

**MELBER, Jehuda Hermann.** *Cohen's Philosophy of Judaism.* (1968). NY. Jonathan. 8vo. 593p. NF/VG. H4. $18.50

**MELE, Pietro Francesco.** *Roma.* nd. Edizioni Mediterranee. VG/dj. S5. $10.00

**MELLAART, James.** *Catal Huyuk: Neolithic Town in Anatolia.* 1967. McGraw Hill. 1st. ils/pl. 232p. cloth. NF/dj. W1. $40.00

**MELLAART, James.** *Earliest Civilizations of the Near East.* 1965. McGraw Hill. 143p. VG. D2. $15.00

**MELLAART, James.** *Neolithic of the Near East.* 1975. Scribner. 300p. VG/wrp. B29. $11.50

**MELLAN & MELLAN.** *Removing Spots & Stains.* 1959. NY. Chemical Pub Co. xl. VG. H4. $10.00

**MELLEN, Joan.** *Privilege: Enigma of Sasha Bruce.* (1982). Dial. BC. photos. 306p. VG/dj. B10. $10.00

**MELLERSH, H.E.L.** *Destruction of Knossos: Rise & Fall of Minoan Crete.* 1993. VG/dj. M17. $15.00

**MELLIN, Jeanne.** *Horses Across the Ages.* 1954. Dutton. 1st. obl 4to. G. O3. $45.00

**MELLY, George.** *Don't Tell Sybil: Intimate Memoir of ELT Mesens.* 1997. Heinemann. 1st. F/dj. P3. $35.00

**MELMOTH, William Henry.** *Works of Homer, Including New & Complete Eds of Iliad...* ca 1780. London. Alex Hogg. 1st. tall 4to. Root bdg. H13. $950.00

**MELODY, Michael E.** *Apaches: Critical Bibliography.* 1977. IN U. 1st. 86p. VG+. B19. $10.00

**MELONEY, William Brown.** *Rush to the Sun.* 1937. Farrar. 1st. sgn. VG/dj. S13. $20.00

**MELTZER, Milton.** *American Revolutionaries: History in Their Own Words...* 1987. NY. Crowell. 1st. 210p. F/NF clip. C14. $14.00

**MELVILLE, Herman.** *Billy Budd Sailor, an Insider Narrative.* 1987. Married Mettle. 1/185. ils Deborah Alterman. 104p. aeg. Glaister bdg. AN/box. B24. $2,000.00

**MELVILLE, Herman.** *Confidence Man.* 1857. NY. Dix Edwards. 1st issue (Miller & Holman listed as prt). NF. B4. $6,500.00

**MELVILLE, Herman.** *Moby Dick.* 1926. NY. Modern Lib. 1st thus. 566p. brn leatherette. G. B14. $25.00

**MELVILLE, Herman.** *Moby Dick.* 1930. NY. Random. 1st trade. ils Rockwell Kent. H4. $30.00

**MELVILLE, Herman.** *Omoo: Narrative of Adventures in South Seas.* 1847. London. 1st (precedes Am). map. brn leather. M17. $600.00

**MELVILLE, Herman.** *Refugee.* 1865. Phil. Peterson. 1st thus. gilt red cloth. NF. M24. $350.00

**MELVILLE, James.** *Chrysanthemum Chain.* 1982. St Martin. 1st Am. VG/dj. C15/G8. $20.00

**MELVILLE, James.** *Go Gently, Gaijin.* nd. St Martin. 1st Am. VG/dj. G8. $20.00

**MELVILLE, Jennie.** *Making Good Blood.* 1989. St Martin. 1st Am. NF/dj. G8. $15.00

**MELVILLE, Jennie.** *Morbid Kitchen.* 1996. St Martin. 1st Am. NF/dj. G8. $20.00

**MELVILLE, Jennie.** *Windsor Red.* 1988. St Martin. 1st Am. F/dj. G8. $15.00

**MELVILLE, Lewis.** *Life & Letters of Tobias Smollett.* 1927. Houghton Mifflin. VG. H4. $15.00

**MELVIN, A. Gordon.** *Seashell Parade: Fascinating Facts, Pictures & Stories.* 1973. Tuttle. 1st. ils. F/dj. A2. $22.50

**MEMLING, Carl.** *Maverick.* 1959. 1st. Little Golden Book #354. VG. R8. $15.00

**MEMMO, Andrea.** *Sua Eccellenza il Signor Andrea Memmo...* 1787. Venice. Antonio Zatta. lg 4to. 40p. marbled thin brd. K1. $250.00

**MENCKEN, H.L.** *Bathtub Hoax & Other Blasts & Bravos...* 1958. Knopf. 1st. VG. H4. $20.00

**MENCKEN, H.L.** *Bathtub Hoax & Other Blasts & Bravos...* 1958. NY. Knopf. 1st. 286p. F/NF. B20. $40.00

**MENCKEN, H.L.** *Days of HL Mencken: Three Volumes in One...* (1947). Dorset. 8vo. F/dj. H4. $25.00

**MENCKEN, H.L.** *In Defence of Women.* 1927. NY. 10th. VG. M17. $20.00

**MENDELSOHN, Felix.** *Superbaby.* 1969. Nash. 1st. F/VG. P8. $85.00

**MENDELSOHN, Jane.** *I Was Amelia Earhart: A Novel.* 1996. Knopf. 1st. author's 1st novel. F/dj. O11. $40.00

**MENDELSOHN, Oscar A.** *Dictionary of Drink & Drinking.* 1965. Hawthorn. 1st Am. VG. B9. $20.00

**MENDELSSOHN.** *South African Bibliography.* nd. 2 vol. 1/175. 10,000 entries. F. A4. $150.00

**MENDENHALL, Walter C.** *Geology of the Central Copper River Region, Alaska.* 1905. US Geol Survey. 1st. 20 pl/11 figures/9 maps+3 fld pocket. 133+4p. wrp. H7. $65.00

**MENGE & SHIMRAK.** *Civil War Notebook of Daniel Chisholm: A Chronicle...* 1989. Orion. 1st. F/dj. A14. $17.50

**MENGER, Matt J.** *In the Valley of the Mekong.* 1970. Patterson. St Anthony's Guild. 1st hc. VG/dj. R11. $30.00

**MENHENNET, Alan.** *Order & Freedom: German Literature & Society 1720-1805.* 1973. NY. 1st. VG/dj. M17. $17.50

**MENNINGER, Edwin A.** *Flowering Trees of the World.* 1962. NY. ils/photos. 336p. dj. B26. $90.00

**MENNINGER, Edwin A.** *Seaside Plants of the World.* 1964. NY. ils/photos. VG/dj. B26. $52.50

**MENOTTI, G.C.** *Last Savage.* 1964. NYGS. 1st. 48p. NF/VG. D4. $35.00

**MENPES, Mortimer.** *Whistler as I Knew Him.* 1904. London. Blk. ils. 153p. 3-quarter bl calf/cloth. VG+. B20. $175.00

**MENSING, J.P.M.** *De Bepaalde Straffen in Het Hanbalietische Recht...* 1936. Leiden. Brill. 8vo. 157p. VG+. Q2. $58.00

**MENTZEL, Christian.** *Kurtze Chinesische Chronologia Order Zeitregister...* 1696. Berlin. Johann Michael R. sm 4to. 2 tables. modern calf. K1. $650.00

**MENZIES, E.G.** *Millstone Valley.* 1969. Rutgers. ils. 308p. NF/G. M4. $30.00

**MEPISASHVILE & TSINTSADZE.** *Arts of Ancient Georgia.* 1979. London. ils/plans. 310p. cloth. VG/dj. Q2. $75.00

**MERCANTANTE, Anthony S.** *Zoo of the Gods: Animals in Myth, Legend & Fable.* 1974. NY. 1st. ils. VG/dj. M17. $22.50

**MERCER, Judy.** *Fast Forward.* 1995. Pocket. 1st. F/F. H11. $25.00

**MERCHANT, Paul;** see Ellison, Harlan.

**MERCHANT, R.A.** *Man & Beast.* 1968. Macmillan. 1st. ils. VG/dj. A2. $12.00

**MERCIA, Leonard S.** *Raising Poultry the Modern Way.* 1980. VT. Garden Way. 220p. VG. A10. $6.00

**MEREDITH, Robert.** *Around the World on Sixty Dollars.* 1895. Chicago. Laird Lee. 1st. dk olive cloth. G+. M21. $20.00

**MEREDITH, Robert.** *Around the World on Sixty Dollars.* 1901. Chicago. Thompson Thomas. sm 8vo. ils. 372p. cloth. VG. W1. $22.00

**MEREDITH, Roy.** *Mr Lincoln's Camera Man: Mathew B Brady.* 1974. Dover. 2nd revised. 350 photos. NF/wrp. A14/H11. $21.00

**MEREDITH, William.** *Hazard, the Painter.* 1975. Knopf. 1st trade. F/dj. L3. $35.00

**MEREDITH, William.** *Wreck of the Thresher.* 1964. NY. Knopf. 1st. inscr/sgn. F/NF. L3. $75.00

**MEREDITH & MEREDITH.** *Mr Lincoln's Military Railroads: Pictorial History...* 1979. NY. 1st. photos. VG/dj. M17. $40.00

**MERIWETHER, Lee.** *Tramp Trip: How to See Europe on Fifty Cents a Day.* 1887. Harper. 276p. gilt maroon cloth. G+. P12. $35.00

**MERK, Frederick.** *History of the Westward Movement.* 1978. Knopf. VG/dj. A19. $35.00

**MERLEN, Michel.** *Poemes Arraches.* 1982. Caen. 1st. 1/300. 80p. sgn Antonio bdg/onlaid wood/suede. wrp/case/chemise. J3. $1,350.00

**MERRIAM, Eve.** *After Nora Slammed the Door: American Women in the 1960s...* 1964. Cleveland. World. 1st. 236p. VG/dj. A25. $18.00

**MERRIAM, Robert L.** *History of John Russell Cutler Co 1833-1936.* 1976. Greenfield, MA. Bete. ils. F/dj. A19. $40.00

**MERRILL, Flora.** *Flush of Wimpole Street & Broadway.* 1933. McBride. 3rd. ils Edwina. VG. A21. $50.00

**MERRILL, James M.** *William Tecumseh Sherman.* 1971. Rand McNally. 1st. NF/dj. A14. $25.00

**MERRILL, James.** *Seraglio.* 1957. Knopf. 1st. NF/VG. R14. $75.00

**MERRIMAN, Roger Bigelow.** *Suleiman the Magnificent, 1520-1566.* 1966. NY. Cooper Sq. ils. 325p. cloth. VG. Q2. $40.00

**MERRINGTON, M.** *Custer Story.* 1950. NY, NY. Devin Adair. F. A19. $45.00

**MERRINGTON, M.** *Custer Story: Life & Letters of Gen A Custer & His Wife...* 1994. rpt. 15 photos. F/NF. A4. $25.00

**MERRITT, Elizabeth.** *Old Wye Church, Talbot County, MD, 1694-1954.* 1954. MD Hist Soc. 42p. VG. B10. $8.00

**MERRITT, Percival.** *Marginalia: Comprising Some Extracts...* 1925. Harvard. 1st. 9 ils. patterned cloth. H13. $145.00

**MERSHON, W.B.** *Recollections of My 50 Years Hunting & Fishing.* 1923. Boston. Stratford. ils. 259p. VG. B18. $75.00

**MERTON, Thomas.** *Hidden Ground of Love.* 1985. FSG. 1st. F/F. B3. $30.00

**MERTON, Thomas.** *Mystics & Zen Masters.* 1967. Farrar. 1st. F/dj. B2. $25.00

**MERTZ, Barbara Gross.** *Ammie, Come Home.* 1968. Meredith. 1st. F/dj. C15. $50.00

**MERTZ, Barbara Gross.** *Copenhagen Connection.* 1982. Congdon Lattes. 1st. F/dj. M15. $45.00

**MERTZ, Barbara Gross.** *Hippopotamus Pool.* 1996. Warner. 1st. sgn. NF/dj. G8. $25.00

**MERTZ, Barbara Gross.** *Last Camel Died at Noon.* (1991). NY. Warner. 1st. sgn. NF/dj. A23. $36.00

**MERTZ, Barbara Gross.** *Naked Once More.* 1989. NY. Warner. 1st. F/F. H11. $25.00

**MERTZ, Barbara Gross.** *Sea King's Daughter.* 1975. Dodd Mead. 1st. F/dj. M15. $65.00

**MERTZ, Barbara Gross.** *Vanish With the Rose.* 1992. S&S. 1st. sgn. NF/dj. G8. $22.50

**MERWIN, W.S.** *Animae.* 1969. SF. Kayak. 1st. 1/1200. sgn. ils Lynn Schroeder. F. O11. $65.00

**MERWIN, W.S.** *Dancing Bears.* 1954. New Haven. Yale. 1st. sgn. F/NF. O11. $265.00

**MERWIN, W.S.** *Green With Beasts.* 1956. London. Hart Davis. 1st. sgn. author's 3rd book. F/dj/band & bulletin. O11. $200.00

**MERWIN, W.S.** *Regions of Memory: Uncollected Prose 1949-82.* 1987. U IL. 1st. sgn. F/dj. O11. $55.00

**MERWIN, W.S.** *Robert the Devil.* 1981. Windhover. 1/310. sgn. 11 hand-colored engravings. 45p. full linen/case. B24. $950.00

**MERYMAN, Richard.** *Andrew Wyeth.* 1968. Boston. Houghton Mifflin. 1st. obl folio. 165 mc pl. brn over tan cloth. dj. K1. $150.00

**MESEY-THOMPSON, R.F.** *Fishing Catechism.* 1905. London. Arnold. 1st. 227p. gilt cloth. NF. A17. $25.00

**MESSERSCHMIDT, Jim.** *Trial of Leonard Peltier.* 1983. Boston. S End Pr. F. A19. $25.00

**MESSICK, H.** *King's Mountain: Epic of Blue Ridge Mountain Men...* 1976. Boston. 1st. inscr. F/dj. M4. $25.00

**METAXES & RAGLIN.** *Birthday ABC.* 1995. S&S. 2nd. ils. rem mk. F/dj. B17. $10.00

**METCALF, C.L.** *Destructive & Useful Insects: Their Habits & Control.* 1939 (1928). NY. 2nd. 981p. B26. $20.00

**METCALF, Z.P.** *General Catalog of Homoptera. Fascicili VI Cicadelloidea.* 1964. USDA. 348p. xl. VG. S5. $15.00

**METCALFE-SHAW, Gertrude E.** *English Caravanners in the Wild West...* 1926. London. Blackwood. ils. 400p. D11. $40.00

**METCHNIKOFF, Elie.** *Prolongation of Life: Optimistic Studies.* 1908. NY. trans PC Mitchell. ils. 343p. B14. $75.00

**METEYARD, Eliza.** *Group of Englishmen: Being Records of Younger Wedgwoods...* 1871. London. brn polished sheepskin. VG. B14. $200.00

**METIVIER, Don A.** *Metivier on Saratoga, Glens Falls, Lake George...* 1993. Champaign, IL. Sagamore. 1st. 8vo. photos. F/dj. A2. $12.00

**METRAUX, Alfred.** *History of the Incas.* 1969. Pantheon. 1st Am. 205p. F3. $20.00

**METZ, Alice Hulett.** *Early American Pattern Glass.* 1958. self pub. 1st. sgn. wide 8vo. 241p. sbdg. H1. $35.00

**METZ, Leon Clair.** *John Selman: Texas Gunfighter.* 1966. Hastings. 1st. ils/index. 254p. VG/dj. B5. $25.00

**METZ, Leon Clair.** *Shooters.* 1976. El Paso. Mangan. 1st. ils. 300p. VG/dj. B5. $25.00

**METZ, Robert.** *CBS: Reflections in a Bloodshot Eye.* 1975. Playboy. 1st. VG/dj. P3. $18.00

**METZLER, Paul.** *Tennis Styles & Stylists.* 1970. Macmillan. 1st. 175 photos. F/dj. C15. $18.00

**MEYER, Adolphe.** *Eggs in 1,000 Ways.* 1917. narrow 8vo. full leather. VG. E6. $60.00

**MEYER, Nicholas.** *Canary Trainer.* 1993. Norton. 1st. AN/dj. N4. $20.00

**MEYER, Nicholas.** *Target Practice.* 1974. HBJ. 1st. F/dj. M25. $45.00

**MEYER, Nicholas.** *West End Horror.* 1976. Dutton. 1st. F/F. H11. $20.00

**MEYER, William R.** *Film Buff's Catalog.* 1978. Arlington House. 432p. VG. C5. $12.50

**MEYERS, Annette.** *Big Killing.* 1989. Bantam. 1st. author's 1st book. F/F. H11. $30.00

**MEYERS, Jeffrey.** *Robert Frost: A Biography.* 1996. London. Constable. 1st. VG/dj. M10. $26.50

**MEYERS, William H.** *Sketches of California & Hawaii by...Gunner, USN...* 1970. SF. BC of CA. 1/450. folio. ils. open-weave linen/spine label. F. B20. $275.00

**MEYNELL, Alice.** *Wares of Autolycus: Selected Literary Essays of...* 1965. London. OUP. 1st. F/VG. O4. $15.00

**MEYNELL, Laurence.** *Fatal Flaw.* 1973. Macmillan. 1st Eng. VG/dj. G8. $12.50

**MEYNELL, Viola.** *Letters of JM Barrie.* 1947. Scribner. 1st. 311p. cloth. F/dj. O10. $20.00

**MICHAEL, Bryan;** see Moore, Brian.

**MICHAEL, Judith.** *Tangled Web.* 1994. S&S. 1st. F/dj. W2. $25.00

**MICHAEL, M.A.** *Traveller's Quest: Original Contributions...* 1950. London. Wm Hodge. 1st. 8vo. F/VG. A2. $30.00

**MICHAELS, Barbara;** see Mertz, Barbara Gross.

**MICHALOWSKI, Kazimierz.** *Art of Ancient Egypt.* nd (1969). NY. Abrams. ils/charts/maps. cloth. D2. $90.00

**MICHALS, Duane.** *Changements.* 1981. Paris. Herscher. 1st. inscr. F/dj. B4. $200.00

**MICHEELS, Peter A.** *Heat: Fire Investigators & Their War on Arson & Murder.* 1991. St Martin. 1st. 8vo. F/dj. A2. $12.00

**MICHEL, Pierre.** *James Gould Cozzens: Annotated Checklist.* 1971. Kent State. 123p. VG. A4. $35.00

**MICHELL, John.** *Who Wrote Shakespeare?* 1996. ils. 272p. F/F. A4. $25.00

**MICHENER, Charles D.** *Social Behavior of the Bees.* 1974. Harvard. Belknap. 1st. 404p. A17/S14. $20.00

**MICHENER, E.** *Manual of Weeds; or, The Weed Exterminator.* 1872. Phil. King Baird. 148p. cloth. A10. $40.00

**MICHENER, James A.** *Centennial.* 1974. Random. 1st. VG+/clip. A14. $42.00

**MICHENER, James A.** *Centennial.* 1974. Random. 1st. 1/500. #d/sgn. 909p. dk bl cloth. F/case. H5. $300.00

**MICHENER, James A.** *Chesapeake.* 1978. Random. 1st. NF/F. H11. $30.00

**MICHENER, James A.** *Drifters.* 1971. Random. 1st. NF/dj. A24. $60.00

**MICHENER, James A.** *Eagle & the Raven.* 1990. Austin, TX. State House. 1st. sgn. F/dj. B3. $45.00

**MICHENER, James A.** *Eagle & the Raven.* 1990. Austin. State House. 1st/1st issue (no accent on Yucatan on ffe). F/dj. Q1. $40.00

**MICHENER, James A.** *Floating World.* 1954. NY. 1st. VG/dj. B5. $105.00

**MICHENER, James A.** *Floating World.* 1954. Random. 1st. author's 7th book. NF/VG. T11. $250.00

**MICHENER, James A.** *Hawaii.* 1959. Random. 1st. VG/G. B5. $50.00

**MICHENER, James A.** *Hawaii.* 1959. Random. 1st. 1/400. sgn. 937p. gilt brn cloth. F/case. H5. $600.00

**MICHENER, James A.** *Hawaii.* 1959. Random. 1st. 8vo. NF/dj. S9. $150.00

**MICHENER, James A.** *James A Michener's Writer's Notebook.* 1992. Random. Literary Guild. rpt. 182p. F/dj. T11. $45.00

**MICHENER, James A.** *Kent State: What Happened & Why.* 1971. NY. Random. 1st. VG+/dj. A14. $52.50

**MICHENER, James A.** *Mexico.* 1992. NY. Random. 1st. 625p. map ep. half cloth. VG/dj. P4. $25.00

**MICHENER, James A.** *Modern Japanese Print. An Appreciation.* 1962. Rutland/Tokyo. Tuttle. 1/475 (510 total). sgn. 10 woodblock prts. wood case. B24. $2,250.00

**MICHENER, James A.** *Presidential Lottery: Reckless Gamble in Our Electoral...* 1969. Random. 1st. NF/dj. A14. $52.50

**MICHENER, James A.** *Sayonara.* 1954. Random. 1st. VG+/dj. S13. $45.00

**MICHENER, James A.** *Six Days in Havana.* 1989. Austin, TX. 1st. F/F. B3. $40.00

**MICHENER, James A.** *Source.* 1965. Random. 1st. VG. S13. $15.00

**MICHENER, James A.** *Tales of the South Pacific.* 1947. Macmillan. 1st. author's 1st fiction. F/VG+. B4. $2,500.00

**MICHENER, James A.** *Tales of the South Pacific.* 1947. NY. 1st. VG. A14. $140.00

**MICHENER, James A.** *World Is My Home.* 1992. Random. 1st. quater cloth. F/dj. T11. $25.00

**MICHENER & MICHENER.** *American Social Insects.* 1951. Van Nostrand. 267p. VG/dj. A10. $15.00

**MICHOTTE, Albert Edward.** *La Preception de la Causalite.* 1946. Louvian. Pub Universitaires de Louvain. tall 8vo. 296p. G1. $45.00

**MICKLE, Isaac.** *Gentleman of Much Promise: Diary of Isaac Mickle.* 1977. U PA. 2 vol. quarter cloth. F/case. B18. $27.50

**MICKLE, Shelley Fraser.** *Queen of October.* 1989. Chapel Hill. 1st. author's 1st book. VG+/F. B30. $20.00

**MICKLE, Shelley Fraser.** *Queen of October.* 1989. Chapel Hill. 1st. inscr. author's 1st book. F/dj. B30. $50.00

**MICKLER, Ernest Matthew.** *White Trash Cooking.* (1986). Ten Speed. 12th. 134p. sbdg. VG. H1. $15.00

**MICKLISH, Rita.** *Sugar Bee.* 1972. Delacorte. 1st. pres sticker. F/NF. D4. $30.00

**MICQUELLUS, Johannes Lodoicus.** *Avreliae Vrbis Memorabilis ab Anglis Obsidio...* 1560. Paris. Wechel. 8vo. gilt morocco. R12. $1,275.00

**MIDDLECOFF, Cary.** *Golf Doctor.* 1950. NY. 1st. inscr. VG. B30. $15.00

**MIDDLEKAUFF, R.** *Glorious Cause: American Revolution 1763-1789.* 1982. Oxford. 1st. ils/maps. F/dj. M4. $25.00

**MIDDLETON, Faith.** *Goodness of Ordinary People.* 1996. Crown. 1st. F/dj. T11. $25.00

**MIDDLETON, R. Hunter.** *Cherryburn Prints I & II.* 1973. Chicago. Cherryburn. 2 folio portfolios. sgns. handmade wrp/box. B24. $2,750.00

**MIDDLETON, Richard.** *Ghost Ship.* 1926. Aries. 1st thus. 1/300. inscr Laurence Gomme. VG+. M21. $125.00

**MIDDLETON, W.E. Knowles.** *History of the Theories of Rain...* 1965. London. Oldbourne. 8vo. 222p. VG/dj. K5. $35.00

**MIDDLETON, W.E. Knowles.** *Invention of the Meteorological Instruments.* 1969. Baltimore. 1st. 362p. A13. $45.00

**MIDDLETON, William D.** *Interurban Era.* 1978. Milwaukee. ils. 432p. F/VG+. B18. $65.00

**MIELCHE, Hakon.** *Lands of Aladdin.* 1955. London. Hodge. ils/pl. cloth. VG+/dj. Q2. $30.00

**MIERS, Earl.** *Monkey Shines.* 1952. World. 1st. VG/dj. P8. $30.00

**MIETES, A.T.** *Energy Metabolism.* 1968. FA Davis. 186p. xl. VG. S5. $9.00

**MIKESH, Robert C.** *Japan's World War II Balloon Attacks on North America.* 1978. Smithsonian. 3rd. photos. VG/wrp. M17. $20.00

**MILAN, Victor.** *Cybernetic Shogun.* 1990. Morrow. 1st. F/dj. M25. $15.00

**MILBURN, Frank.** *Polo: Emperor of Games.* 1994. NY. Knopf. 1st. F/dj. O3. $25.00

**MILBURN, Frank.** *Sheltered Lives.* 1986. Doubleday. 1st. rem mk. NF/dj. R11. $15.00

**MILBURN, Matthew.** *Report on Experiments With Guano, Prize Essay.* 1845. London. Simpkin. 18p. VG/wrp. A10. $30.00

**MILES, Alexander.** *Edinburgh School of Surgery Before Lister.* 1918. London. 1st. 220p. A13. $30.00

**MILES, Bebe.** *Bluebells & Bittersweet.* 1969. NY. ils. 168p. F/dj. B26. $22.00

**MILES, Charles.** *Indian & Eskimo Artifacts of North America.* 1963. Am Legacy Pr. AN/dj. A19. $50.00

**MILES, Henry Downes.** *English Country Life.* ca 1860. London. McKenzie. 52 engravings. 524p. half leather. H1. $250.00

**MILES, Keith;** see Tralins, Bob.

**MILES, Manly.** *Stock-Breeding: Practical Treatise...* 1879. NY. Appleton. 1st. G. O3. $20.00

**MILES & MILES.** *Insect Pests of Glasshouse Crops.* 1948. London. Lockwood. 200p. cloth. VG. A10. $22.00

**MILFORD, Louis.** *Memoir; or, Cursory Glance at My Different Travels.* 1956. Lakeside Classic. 1st thus. teg. dk bl cloth. NF. T11. $25.00

**MILL, John Stuart.** *Autobiography.* 1873. London. Longman Gr. sm 4to. list of author's works at end. cloth. R12. $375.00

**MILL, John Stuart.** *Examination of Sir Wm Hamilton's Philosophy...* 1865. Boston. Spencer. 2 vol. 1st Am. 12mo. panelled mauve cloth. NF. G1. $200.00

**MILLAIS, J.G.** *Newfoundland & Its Untrodden Ways.* 1967. Abercrombie Fitch. rpt. 340p. F/torn. M4. $30.00

**MILLAR, John F.** *American Ships of the Colonial & Revolutionary Periods.* 1978. NY. Norton. 1st. ils. 356p. VG/dj. M10. $45.00

**MILLAR, Kenneth.** *Black Money.* 1966. NY. Knopf. 1st. NF/dj. M15. $250.00

**MILLAR, Kenneth.** *Blue City.* 1947. Knopf. 1st. 8vo. top edge bl. bl-stp red cloth. F/fragile. R3. $250.00

**MILLAR, Kenneth.** *Blue Hammer.* 1976. Knopf. 1st. NF/dj. M21. $35.00

**MILLAR, Kenneth.** *Lew Archer: Private Investigator.* 1977. Mysterious. 1st. 1/250. sgn. F/dj/case. M15. $300.00

**MILLAR, Kenneth.** *Self-Portrait: Ceaselessly Into the Past.* 1981. Capra. 1/250. sgn MacDonald/Eudora Welty. gilt blk morocco. F. R3. $90.00

**MILLAR, Kenneth.** *Sleeping Beauty.* 1973. Knopf. 1st. VG/dj. S18. $15.00

**MILLAR, Margaret.** *Beyond This Point Are Monsters.* nd. Random. AP. sgn. 8vo. wrp. R3. $75.00

**MILLAR, Margaret.** *Vanish in an Instant.* (1952). Random. 1st/1st prt. sgn. 8vo. gilt gray brd. F/NF. R3. $125.00

**MILLARD, H.** *Treatise on Bright's Disease of the Kidneys.* 1886. 1st. 8vo. ils. VG. E6. $55.00

**MILLARD, S.T.** *Goblets.* 1956. Topeka. Central Pr. 7. 177 pl. unp. VG. H1. $22.50

**MILLARD, S.T.** *Opaque Glass.* (1941). Topeka, KS. Central Pr. 3rd. 8vo. 325 pl. unp. G. H1. $65.00

**MILLAY, Edna St Vincent.** *Princess Marries the Page.* 1932. Harper. 1st. ils. cloth/brd. G. B27. $25.00

**MILLAY, Edna St. Vincent.** *Huntsman, What Quarry?* 1939. NY/London. Harper. 1st. F/NF. M19. $25.00

**MILLAY, Edna St. Vincent.** *Mine the Harvest.* 1954. Harper. 1st. 8vo. 140p. VG/dj. H1. $30.00

**MILLAY, Edna St. Vincent.** *Renascence & Other Poems.* 1917. NY. Mitchell Kennerley. 1st. author's 1st book. NF/G. L3. $125.00

**MILLER, Agnes.** *Colfax Bookplate.* 1926. NY. Century. 1st. author's 1st book. cloth. F/dj. O10. $45.00

**MILLER, Alec.** *Stone & Marble Carving.* 1948. Berkeley. 1st. 120p. VG/dj. B5. $30.00

**MILLER, Alice Duer.** *Cinderella in Verse.* 1943. Coward McCann. 1st. 64p. brd. VG/dj. D4. $25.00

**MILLER, Alice Duer.** *I Have Loved England.* 1941. Putnam. 4th. photos. gilt bl cloth. VG/G. M7. $25.00

**MILLER, Arthur.** *After the Fall.* 1964. Viking. 1/499 (999 total). sgn. F/glassine/case. D10. $245.00

**MILLER, Arthur.** *Creation of the World & Other Business.* 1973. NY. Viking. 1st. NF/clip. A24. $30.00

**MILLER, Arthur.** *Death of a Salesman.* 1949. Viking. 139p. VG. C5. $12.50

**MILLER, Arthur.** *Death of a Salesman.* 1981. Viking. special ils ed. sgn. NF/dj. R14. $60.00

**MILLER, Arthur.** *Focus.* 1945. Reynal Hitchcock. 1st. 8vo. F/NF. S9. $375.00

**MILLER, Arthur.** *Timeblends: A Life.* 1987. NY. Grove. 1st. 8vo. rem mk. NF/VG. O4. $20.00

**MILLER, Arthur.** *Tropic of Cancer.* 1961. NY. Grove. 1st thus. intro Karl Shapiro. VG/dj. R14. $40.00

**MILLER, D.A.** *Captain Jack Crawford: Buckskin Poet, Scout & Showman.* 1993. NM U. 1st. ils. 363p. F/dj. M4. $25.00

**MILLER, Dan B.** *Erskine Caldwell: Journey From Tobacco Road.* 1995. Knopf. 1st. 459p. F/NF. T11. $40.00

**MILLER, David E.** *Hole-in-the-Rock: An Epic...* 1959. Salt Lake City. 1st. sm 4to. 229p. VG. F7. $55.00

**MILLER, Edgar S.** *Milling Studies: A Survey of the Flour Milling Process.* 1928. Chicago. Nat Miller. 224p. cloth. VG. A10. $42.50

**MILLER, F.H.** *Memorial Album of Revolutionary Soldiers.* 1958. Crete. ils. 406p. F. M4. $25.00

**MILLER, Francis Trevelyan.** *Photographic History of the Civil War.* 1911. 10 vol. bl cloth. VG. E6. $225.00

**MILLER, Francis Trevelyan.** *Photographic History of the Civil War.* 1912. NY. Review of Reviews. 10 vol. 2nd. cloth. F. M8. $650.00

**MILLER, Frank B.** *Diary Comes to Life.* nd (1953?). np (PA?). self pub. 78p. imitation leather. B18. $95.00

**MILLER, Genevieve.** *Adoption of Inoculation for Smallpox in England & France.* 1957. Phil. 1st. 355p. A13. $50.00

**MILLER, Helen Hill.** *Case for Liberty.* 1965. Chapel Hill. VG/dj. M11. $65.00

**MILLER, Henry.** *Black Spring.* 1963. Grove. 1st Am (after Obelisk of 1938). VG/dj. B30. $45.00

**MILLER, Henry.** *Dear, Dear Brenda.* 1986. Morrow. 1st. edit GS Sindell. quarter gray cloth. F/dj. T11. $20.00

**MILLER, Henry.** *Letters of Henry Miller & Wallace Fowlie.* 1975. Grove. 1st. F/dj. M19. $17.50

**MILLER, Henry.** *Tropic of Capricorn.* 1939. Paris. Obelisk. 1st/1st issue (ES dtd 1939). variant bdg. F/self wrp. B4. $2,000.00

**MILLER, J. Hillis.** *Illustration.* 1992. Harvard. ils. VG/dj. M17. $20.00

**MILLER, J.P.** *Skook.* 1984. Warner. 1st. VG/dj. L1. $25.00

**MILLER, James.** *Passion of Michel Foucault.* 1993. NY. 1st. dj. T9. $18.00

**MILLER, Joaquin.** *Building of the City Beautiful.* 1905. Albert Brandt. 1st complete. NF. M19. $45.00

**MILLER, Joaquin.** *His California Diary Beginning in 1855 & Ending in 1857.* 1936. Seattle. Dogwood. 1/700. 8vo. 106p. beige cloth. F. B20. $35.00

**MILLER, John A.** *Cutdown.* 1997. Pocket. 1st. sgn. F/dj. M23. $35.00

**MILLER, John A.** *Jackson Street & Other Soldier Stories.* 1995. Berkeley, CA. 1st. sgn. F/dj. M23. $45.00

**MILLER, Jonathan.** *Body in Question.* 1978. NY. 1st. 352p. A13. $45.00

**MILLER, Katherine.** *Five Plays From Shakespeare.* 1964. Houghton Mifflin. ne. sm 4to. 236p. NF/G. W2. $60.00

**MILLER, Ken.** *Open All Night.* 1995. Woodstock. Overlook. 1st. F/dj. S9. $75.00

**MILLER, Lawrence M.** *American Spirit: Visions of a New Corporate Culture.* 1984. Morrow. 1st. VG/clip. P3. $15.00

**MILLER, Lee G.** *Story of Ernie Pyle.* 1950. Viking. ils. 439p. VG/dj. P12. $8.00

**MILLER, Lillian B.** *In Pursuit of Fame: Rembrandt Peale, 1779-1860.* 1992. Nat Portrait Gallery. 1st. VG/dj. R8. $35.00

**MILLER, Mark F.** *Dear Old Roanoke: A Sesquicentennial Portrait.* 1992. Mercer. photos. 330p. VG/box. B10. $35.00

**MILLER, Mark.** *Wine: A Gentleman's Game.* 1984. Harper Row. 1st. ils. VG/dj. M17. $20.00

**MILLER, Merle.** *What Happened.* 1972. Harper Row. 1st. NF/NF. H11. $15.00

**MILLER, Nathan.** *Sea of Glory: Naval History of American Revolution.* 1974. Annapolis. biblio/index. 558p. VG/dj. S16. $27.50

**MILLER, Nory.** *Helmut Jahn.* (1986). NY. Rizzoli. sgn pres Helmut Jahn. sq 4to. 264p. silvered rust cloth. K1. $100.00

**MILLER, Olive Beaupre.** *My Book House.* 1953. Chicago. Book House for Children. 12 vol. NF. V4. $175.00

**MILLER, Olive Beaupre.** *Picturesque Tale of Progress.* 1953. Chicago. Book House for Children. 9 vol. NF. V4. $150.00

**MILLER, Orson K.** *Mushrooms of North America.* nd. Dutton. VG/dj. B9. $25.00

**MILLER, Paul Eduard.** *Esquire's Jazz Book.* 1944. Smith Durrell. 1st. 8vo. 230p. NF/VG. B20. $50.00

**MILLER, Rex.** *St Louis Blues.* 1995. Maclay. 1st. 1/500. sgn. AN/sans/cover. S18. $50.00

**MILLER, Rick.** *Train Robbing Bunch.* 1983. Creative. 1st trade. ils. 175p. AN. B10. $10.00

**MILLER, Robert.** *Boy Day.* 1938. Portland. Falmouth. 1st. sgn/dtd 1943. 8vo. 93p. dj. B20. $20.00

**MILLER, Ruth.** *Saul Bellow: Biography of the Imagination.* 1991. NY. 1st. VG/VG. M17. $15.00

**MILLER, Sally M.** *Flawed Liberation: Socialism & Feminism.* 1981. Westport. Greenwood. 1st. photos. 211p. VG/dj. A25. $15.00

**MILLER, Sue.** *Family Pictures.* 1990. Harper Row. 1st. sgn. F/NF. B3. $35.00

**MILLER, Sue.** *Good Mother.* 1986. Harper Row. 1st. author's 1st book. F/NF. B3. $50.00

**MILLER, Sue.** *Good Mother.* 1986. Harper Row. 1st. author's 1st book. NF/dj. R14. $40.00

**MILLER, Walter M.** *Canticle for Leibowitz.* 1959. Lippincott. 1st. F/NF. B2. $600.00

**MILLER, William J.** *Training of an Army: Camp Curtin & North's Civil War.* 1990. Wht Mane Pub. 1st. F/dj. A14. $21.00

**MILLER, William.** *Ottoman Empire & Its Successors 1801-1927.* 1936. Cambridge. 8vo. ils/5 maps. 644p. cloth. VG. Q2. $40.00

**MILLER & MILLER.** *New Martinsville Glass Story.* 1972. Richardson Pub. 1st. sgns. catalog rpts/photos. w/price guide. H1. $45.00

**MILLER & MORATH.** *Chinese Encounter.* 1979. FSG. 1st. 8vo. 255p. VG/dj. B11. $15.00

**MILLER & NIN.** *Literate Passion: Letters 1932-53.* 1987. NY. 1st. edit G Stuhlmann. dj. T9. $18.00

**MILLET, Gabriel.** *L'Ecole Grecque Dans l'Architecuture Byzantine.* 1916. Paris. Leroux. ils/figures. 328p. quarter vellum/brd. VG. Q2. $290.00

**MILLET, Kate.** *Basement.* 1979. S&S. 1st. rem mk. VG/dj. R14. $25.00

**MILLETT, Kate.** *Sita.* 1977. FSG. 1st. sgn. 322p. VG/dj. A25. $18.00

**MILLETT, Meryn.** *Native Trees of Australia.* 1971. Melbourne. 165 photos. VG/dj. B26. $18.00

**MILLGRAM, Abraham Ezra.** *Great Jewish Ideas.* 1966. B'nai B'rith. 352p. G/dj. B29. $9.00

**MILLHAUSER, Steven.** *Barnum Museum.* 1990. NY. Poseidon. 1st. F/F. B3. $45.00

**MILLHAUSER, Steven.** *Barnum Museum.* 1990. Poseidon. 1st. VG/dj. B30. $25.00

**MILLHAUSER, Steven.** *Barnum Museum.* 1990. Poseidon. ARC. author's 5th book. RS/pub promo material. F/dj. B4. $150.00

**MILLHAUSER, Steven.** *In the Penny Arcade.* 1986. Knopf. 1st. author's 3rd book. F/NF. B3. $50.00

**MILLHAUSER, Steven.** *Little Kingdoms.* 1993. NY. Poseidon. 1st. rem mk. NF/dj. R14. $30.00

**MILLHAUSER, Steven.** *Portrait of a Romantic.* 1977. Knopf. 1st. sgn. rem mk. VG+/dj. B30. $75.00

**MILLIKAN, Robert A.** *Science & the New Civilization.* 1930. Scribner. 1st. 194p. VG+. A25. $20.00

**MILLON, Theodore.** *Handbook of Clinical Health Psychology.* 1982. NY. Plenum. heavy 8vo. 608p. prt gr cloth. VG. G1. $65.00

**MILLS, Charles.** *Choice.* 1943. Macmillan. 1st. inscr. VG/dj. S13. $35.00

**MILLS, Charles.** *Harvest of Barren Regrets: Army Career...FW Benteen...* 1985. Clark. ils. VG. J2. $295.00

**MILLS, James.** *Underground Empire.* 1986. Doubleday. 1st. sgn. 1165p. NF/dj. W2. $40.00

**MILLS & MOYER.** *Shock & Hypotension: Pathogenesis & Treatment...* nd (1956). NY. Grune & Stratton. 1st. sm 4to. 718p. VG/dj. C14. $20.00

**MILLSON, Larry.** *Ballpark Figures.* 1987. Toronto. McClelland Stewart. 1st. F/VG+. P8. $45.00

**MILNE, A.A.** *Chloe Marr.* 1946. Dutton. 1st Am. 8vo. VG/G. A2. $12.00

**MILNE, A.A.** *Christopher Robin Birthday Book.* 1930. London. Methuen. 1st. ils Shepard. VG. B14. $300.00

**MILNE, A.A.** *Fourteen Songs From When We Were Very Young.* 1925. Dutton. ils EH Shepard. A21. $60.00

**MILNE, A.A.** *House at Pooh Corner.* (1928). London. Methuen. 1st. 12mo. ils EH Shepard. teg. gilt salmon cloth. dj. R5. $750.00

**MILNE, A.A.** *Hums of Pooh.* 1929. London. Methuen. 1st. lg 4to. ils EH Shepard. beige cloth/prt brd. F/dj. H5. $350.00

**MILNE, A.A.** *King's Breakfast.* 1925. London. Shepard. 1st. dj. T9. $45.00

**MILNE, A.A.** *Nalle Pu (Winnie the Pooh).* 1969. Stockholm. ils Shepard. VG. M17. $30.00

**MILNE, A.A.** *Now We Are Six.* (1927). Dutton. 1/200. sgn Milne/Shepard. ils bl paper brd/cloth spine. dj/box. R5. $2,000.00

**MILNE, A.A.** *Now We Are Six.* 1927. London. Methuen. 1st. aeg. bl leather. F/box. B4. $1,500.00

**MILNE, A.A.** *Now We Are Six.* 1927. London. Methuen. 1st. ils Ernest Shepard. teg. gilt maroon cloth. D1. $350.00

**MILNE, A.A.** *Toad of Toad Hall.* (1929). London. Methuen. 1st. 8vo. teg. silvered bl cloth. prt dj. R5. $250.00

**MILNE, A.A.** *When We Were Very Young.* 1950. Dutton. 8vo. VG/dj. B17. $25.00

**MILNE, A.A.** *Winnie Ille Pu: A Latin Version of Winnie the Pooh.* 1961. NY. ils Shepard. trans Alexander Lenard. VG/dj. M17. $17.50

**MILNE, A.A.** *Winnie the Pooh.* (1926). London. Meuthuen. 1st. 12mo. teg. gilt gr cloth. R5. $600.00

**MILNE, A.A.** *Winnie the Pooh.* 1955 (1926). Dutton. 1st. ils Ernest Shepard. G. M5. $10.00

**MILNE, J.G.** *Greek Coinage.* 1931. Oxford. Clarendon. 12 pl. 131p. cloth. G. Q2. $20.00

**MILNE & MILNE.** *Insect Worlds.* 1980. NY. 274p. F/NF. S15. $10.00

**MILNE & MILNE.** *Nature of Life.* 1972. NY. ils. 208p. F/dj. A17. $20.00

**MILNER, Mordaunt.** *Godolphin Arabian: Story of the Matchem Line.* 1990. London. Allen. 1st. O3. $25.00

**MILNES, R.M.** *Life, Letters & Literary Remains of John Keats.* 1848. Putnam. 2 vol. 1st Am. gilt gr cloth. M24. $165.00

**MILON & PETTER.** *Fauna of Madagascar, XXXV: Oiseaux.* 1973. Tananarive/Paris. French text. ils. 263p. NF. C12. $80.00

**MILOSZ, Czeslaw.** *Land of Ulro.* 1984. NY. FSG. 1st Am. trans from Polish. F/dj. A24. $35.00

**MILTHORPE & MOORBY.** *Introduction to Crop Physiology.* 1974. Cambridge. 202p. xl. VG. S5. $12.00

**MILTON, James.** *Police.* 1984. NY. Gallery. unp. G. C5. $12.50

**MILTON, John.** *Areopargitica: A Speech of Mr John Milton...* 1907. Hammersmith. Doves. 1/300 (325 total) on Batchelor. 73p. F/case. H5. $850.00

**MILTON, John.** *Histoire Entiere & Veritable Dv Procez de Charles Stuart...* 1650. London. JG. 3 parts in 1. sm 8vo. vellum. R12. $375.00

**MILTON, John.** *Poetical Works.* 1799-1804. London. 4 vol in 2. leather. A15. $60.00

**MINARIK, E.H.** *Father Bear Comes Home.* 1959. Harper. 1st. ils Sendak. VG+. M5. $25.00

**MINCHIN, C.O.** *Sea Fishing.* 1911. London. Blk. 1st. F. B9. $85.00

**MINDELEFF & STEVENSON.** *Study of Pueblo Architecture, Sand Paiting of Navajos.* 1891. GPO. 4to. 298p. olive cloth. VG. P4. $210.00

**MINGUS, Charles.** *Beneath the Underdog.* 1971. Knopf. 1st. NF/dj. B2. $50.00

**MINOR, Thomas.** *Diary of Thomas Minor, Stonington, CT, 1653 to 1684.* 1899. New London. 221p. VG. M4. $45.00

**MINOT, Charles S.** *Bibliography of Vertebrate Embryology.* 1893. Boston. 1st. 128p. A13. $75.00

**MINOT, Stephen.** *Ghost Images.* 1979. Harper Row. 1st. author's 3rd book. NF/VG. R14. $25.00

**MINOT, Susan.** *Folly.* 1992. Seymour Lawrence. 1st. inscr. NF/dj. S13. $15.00

**MIRABEAU, Count of.** *Memoirs of the Courts of Europe.* 1910. Collier. 9 vol (not complete). 8vo. bl cloth. G. S17. $15.00

**MIRABEAU.** *Memoire a Consulter et Consultation Pour Mme Mirabeau.* 1783. Aix. Mouret. 4to. caption title. wrp. R12. $225.00

**MIRABEAU.** *Sur La Liberte de la Presse, Imite de l'Anglois, De Milton.* 1789. London. 8vo. stitched. R12. $575.00

**MIROV, N.T.** *Genus Pinus.* 1967. NY. 602p. VG. B26. $145.00

**MIRSKY, Reba Paeff.** *Mozart.* 1960. Chicago. Follet. ils WT Mars. VG/dj. M17. $25.00

**MISHIMA, Yukio.** *Decay of the Angel.* 1974. Knopf. 1st Am. NF/dj. M25. $25.00

**MISHIMA, Yukio.** *Spring Snow.* 1972. Knopf. 1st Am. NF/clip. M25. $25.00

**MISHIMA, Yukio.** *Temple of Dawn.* 1973. Knopf. 1st Am. Sea of Fertility #3. F/dj. A24. $50.00

**MISS READ;** see Saint, Dora Jessie.

**MISTRY, R.** *Swimming Lessons.* 1989. Houghton Mifflin. 1st. F/F. B3. $30.00

**MITCHARD, Jacquelyn.** *Deep End of the Ocean.* 1996. Viking. 1st. author's 1st novel. recommended by Oprah Winfrey. F/F. H11. $60.00

**MITCHEL, O.M.** *Planetary & Stellar Worlds.* 1868. NY. 3-quarter leather/marbled brd/bands/blk labels. VG. S17. $40.00

**MITCHELL, Donald.** *Wet Days at Edgewood.* 1865. Scribner. 324p. A10. $45.00

**MITCHELL, Edwin Valentine.** *It's an Old State Pennsylvania Custom.* 1947. Bonanza. rpt. Am Customs series. gr cloth. NF/VG. T11. $25.00

**MITCHELL, Edwin Valentine.** *Morocco Bound: Adrift Among Books.* 1929. Farrar Rhinehart. 1st/2nd prt. 232p. cloth. F/dj. O10. $25.00

**MITCHELL, Ehrman B.** *MFH: Ponies for Young People.* 1960. Van Nostrand. VG/fair. O3. $12.00

**MITCHELL, Gladys.** *Death of a Delft Blue.* 1964. London. Michael Joseph. 1st. F/dj. M15. $85.00

**MITCHELL, J.** *Luchow's German CG.* 1964 (1952). VG/VG. E6. $12.00

**MITCHELL, J.B.** *Discipline & Bayonets: Armies...American Revolution.* 1967. NY. maps. 223p. F/dj. M4. $20.00

**MITCHELL, Jan.** *Cooking a la Longchamps.* 1964. Doubleday. 1st. G/dj. A16. $20.00

**MITCHELL, John K.** *Remote Consequences of Injuries of Nerves & Treatment.* 1895. Phil. Lea Bros. ils. B14. $300.00

**MITCHELL, Joni.** *Complete Poems & Lyrics.* 1997. NY. Crown. 1st. F/dj. R14. $35.00

**MITCHELL, Julian.** *Undiscovered Country.* 1969. Grove. 1st. VG/dj. B30. $20.00

**MITCHELL, Juliet.** *Woman's Estate.* 1971. Pantheon. 1st. F/F. H11. $35.00

**MITCHELL, M.H.** *Passenger Pigeon in Ontario.* 1935. Toronto. lg 8vo. ils/maps. 181p. NF. C12. $160.00

**MITCHELL, Margaret.** *Gone With the Wind.* May 1936. Macmillan. 1st/1st issue. sgn on inserted leaf. 8vo. teg. Sangorski bdg. NF. H5. $2,500.00

**MITCHELL, Margaret.** *Gone With the Wind.* 1936. Macmillan. 2nd issue (June 1936). gray cloth. VG. B20. $85.00

**MITCHELL, Margaret.** *Margaret Mitchell & Her Novel, Gone With the Wind.* 1936. NY. Macmillan. 1st (promo pamphlet). F/pict wrp. M24. $300.00

**MITCHELL, S. Weir.** *Comfort of the Hills & Other Poems. Second Edition.* 1911. NY. Century. inscr. 98p. cloth. G7. $395.00

**MITCHELL, S. Weir.** *Injuries of Nerves & Their Consequences.* 1872. Lippincott. 1st. 377p. cloth. VG. G7. $895.00

**MITCHELL, S. Weir.** *Madeira Party.* 1975. Sacramento. Corti Bros. 1/1000. VG. M17. $50.00

**MITCHELL, S. Weir.** *Mr Kris Kingle: A Christmas Tale...* 1904. Phil. Geo Jacobs. ils Clyde O Deland. 105p. gr cloth. G. G7. $275.00

**MITCHELL, S. Weir.** *Mr Kris Kringle.* 1893. Phil. Geo W Jacobs. 1st. 8vo. 48p. NF. H5. $250.00

**MITCHELL, S. Weir.** *Red City: Hist Novel 2nd Administration Pres Washington.* 1922. Century. 8vo. 421p. G. S17. $6.00

**MITCHELL, Sidney Alexander.** *SZ Mitchell & the Electrical Industry.* 1960. FSC. 1st. VG. N2. $10.00

**MITCHELL, Stephen.** *Parables & Portraits.* 1990. Harper Row. 1st. F/dj. R14. $25.00

**MITCHELL & WILLIAMS.** *Way of the Explorer: Apollo Astronaut's Journey...* 1996. NY. Putnam. 1st. 230p. F/dj. K5. $20.00

**MITCHELL-HEDGES, F.A.** *Danger My Ally.* 1954. Little Brn. 1st Am. 278p. VG/dj. H7. $20.00

**MITCHELL-HEDGES, F.A.** *Danger My Ally.* 1954. London. Elek Books. 1st. 255p. F/dj. F3. $35.00

**MITCHISON, Naomi.** *Blood of the Martyrs.* 1948. McGraw Hill. 375p. G. W2. $30.00

**MITFORD, Jessica.** *Faces of Philip.* 1984. NY. 1st. dj. T9. $12.00

**MITFORD, Jessica.** *Grace Had an English Heart.* 1988. NY. 1st. dj. T9. $12.00

**MITFORD, Nancy.** *Blessing.* 1951. London. 1st. dj. T9. $35.00

**MITFORD, Nancy.** *Don't Tell Alfred.* 1960. London. 1st. dj. T9. $18.00

**MITFORD, Nancy.** *Talent to Annoy, Essays.* 1987. NY. 1st. edit C Mosley. dj. T9. $15.00

**MITSUMASA, Anno.** *Anno's Twice Told Tales/Fisherman & His Wife/4 Clever Bros.* 1993. Philomel. 1st. 4to. F/dj. B17. $17.50

**MIX, Paul E.** *Life & Legend of Tom Mix.* 1972. Barnes. VG/dj. P3. $23.00

**MIYAO, Shigeo.** *Twelve Months in Edo.* nd. np (Iseya). mini. Japanese text on pastel papers. Oriental-sewn wrp. B24. $100.00

**MODIN, Yuri.** *My Five Cambridge Friends.* 1994. NY. 1st. trans Roberts/intro Leitch. dj. T9. $12.00

**MOE, Richard.** *Last Full Measure: Life & Death of 1st MN Volunteers.* 1993. NY. ils. VG/dj. M17. $17.50

**MOELLER & MOELLER.** *Oregon Trail: Photographic Journey.* 1985. Beautiful America. 1st. ils. 144p. VG/dj. S14. $20.00

**MOESCHLER, V.** *Virginia Cookery.* 1930. self pub. 115p. VG. E6. $30.00

**MOFFAT, Robert.** *Missionary Labours & Scenes in Southern Africa.* 1842. London. John Snow. 3rd thousand. 16 pl/fld map. later(?) cloth. VG. H7. $85.00

**MOFFATT, James.** *Everyman's Life of Jesus.* 1925. Doran. 242p. VG. B29. $10.00

**MOFFIT, Fred H.** *Headwater Regions of Gulkana & Susitna Rivers, AK...* 1912. GPO. US Geol Survey Bulletin 498. 8vo. fld map. 82p. P4. $15.00

**MOGENSEN, Jan.** *Teddy in the Undersea Kingdom.* 1985. Stevens. 1st. ils. NF. M5. $12.00

**MOHR, Nancy L.** *Lady Blows a Horn.* 1995. Unionville, PA. Sevynmore. 1st. sgn. VG/dj. O3. $25.00

**MOHR, Nicolas.** *Excursion Through America.* 1973. Lakeside Classic. 1st thus. 2 fld maps. teg. NF. T11. $40.00

**MOHR, R.H.** *Mettlach Steins Including Plaques, Beakers & Punch Bowls...* (1966). Mohr Pub. revised. 8vo. ils. 110p. w/price guide. H1. $30.00

**MOHUN, Barry.** *Compilation of Warehouse Laws & Decisions. Second Edition.* 1914. Chicago. Nickerson Collins. buckram. M11. $50.00

**MOLDENKE, Harold N.** *American Wild Flowers.* 1949. NY. photos. 453p. F. B26. $17.50

**MOLES, Robert N.** *Definition & Rule in Legal Theory...* 1987. Oxford. VG/dj. M11. $45.00

**MOLEY, Raymond.** *Our Criminal Courts.* 1930. Minton Balch. M11. $75.00

**MOLL, Albert.** *Hypnotism.* 1895. London/NY. 3rd. edit Havelock Ellis. 410p. VG. B14. $55.00

**MOLLOY, Paul.** *Pennant for the Kremlin.* 1964. Doubleday. 1st. inscr. VG/dj. P8. $35.00

**MOLSEED, Elwood.** *Genus Trigidia (Iridaceae) of Mexico & Central America.* 1970. Berkeley. ils. 127p. wrp. B26. $15.00

**MOMADAY, N. Scott.** *Ancient Child.* 1989. NY. Doubleday. 1st. sgn. author's 1st novel. F/NF. A24. $50.00

**MOMADAY, N. Scott.** *House Made of Dawn.* 1968. NY. Harper. 1st. F/dj. B4. $450.00

**MOMADAY, N. Scott.** *In the Presence of the Sun: Stories & Poems 1961-1991.* 1992. St Martin. 8vo. 1/241. sgn. 145p. F/case. from $110 to $125.00

**MOMADAY, N. Scott.** *Way to Rainy Mountain.* 1969. NM U. ils Al Momaday. 88p. NF/rpr. M4. $20.00

**MONACHAN, John;** see Burnett, W.R.

**MONAGHAN, Frank.** *French Travelers in the United States, 1765-1932...* 1961. NY. Antiquarian Pr. 1/750. 130p. cloth. D11. $50.00

**MONAGHAN, Hanna Darlington.** *Dear George: George Fox, Man & Prophet.* 1970. Phil. Franklin. 298p. VG/dj. V3. $25.00

**MONAGHAN, Jay.** *Book of the American West.* 1963. NY. Messner. 1st. 4to. 607p. VG. O3. $35.00

**MONAGHAN, Jay.** *Civil War on the Western Border.* 1955. Bonanza. 454p. NF/dj. E1. $35.00

**MONAGHAN, Jay.** *Last of the Bad Men: Legend of Tom Horn.* (1946). Indianapolis. later prt. 293p. VG/dj. B18. $22.50

**MONAGHAN, Tom.** *Pizza Tiger.* 1986. Random. ils. 346p. dj. H6. $24.00

**MONAHAN, Bret.** *Book of Common Dread.* July 1993. St Martin. 1st. VG/dj. L1. $35.00

**MONATOWA, M.** *Polish Cooking.* 1960. London. VG/G+. E6. $15.00

**MONBIOT, George.** *Amazon Watershed: New Environmental Investigation.* 1991. London. 276p. F/NF. S15. $10.00

**MONCKTON, C.A.W.** *Taming New Guinea: Some Experiences...* 1921. John Lane. 1st Am. ils/map. G. A2. $50.00

**MONCREIFFE, Iain.** *Royal Highness. Ancestry of a Royal Child.* 1982. London. Hamilton. 1st. lg 8vo. VG/dj. B11. $15.00

**MONETT, Paul.** *Half-Way Home.* 1991. NY. Crown. 1st. sgn. NF/dj. C9. $120.00

**MONEYHON & ROBERT.** *Portraits of Conflict: Photographic History of Louisiana.* 1990. 1st. photos. 355p. F. M4. $30.00

**MONFREDO, Miriam Grace.** *Blackwater Spirits.* 1995. St Martin. 1st. F/dj. T2. $30.00

**MONFREDO, Miriam Grace.** *North Star Conspiracy.* 1993. St Martin. 1st. sgn. F/dj. T2. $35.00

**MONIG, Christopher.** *Abra-Cadaver.* 1958. Dutton. 1st. VG/dj. M19. $17.50

**MONK, George S.** *Light: Principles & Experiments.* 1937. McGraw Hill. 1st. G. K5. $30.00

**MONK, Samuel H.** *Sublime: Study of Critical Theories in XVII Century England.* 1935. NY. Mod Lang Assn. inscr. VG. H13. $95.00

**MONKMAN, Noel.** *From Queensland to the Great Barrier Reef.* 1958. NY. 1st. 182p. F/VG clip. H3. $30.00

**MONRO, Donald.** *Praelectiones Medicae Ex Cronii Instituto, Annis 1774...* 1776. London. Gul Hay. 1st. 199+4p+ES+ad leaf. rb. G7. $795.00

**MONRO, Thomas.** *Physician as Man of Letters, Science & Action.* 1933. Glasgow. 1st. 212p. A13. $90.00

**MONROE, James.** *View of the Conduct of the Executive in Foreign Affairs...* 1797. Phil. Benjamin Franklin Bache. 407p. rebound. B10. $200.00

**MONROE, Marilyn.** *My Story.* 1974. Stein Day. 1st. NF/VG. M19. $17.50

**MONSARRAT, Nicholas.** *Fair Day's Work.* 1964. London. Cassell. 1st. bl cloth. NF/VG. T11. $20.00

**MONSARRAT, Nicholas.** *Ship That Died of Shame & Other Stories.* 1974. NY. Wm Sloane. 1st. VG/dj. T11. $10.00

**MONSMAN, G.** *Olive Schreiner's Fiction: Landscape & Power.* 1991. rpt. ils. F/dj. M4. $15.00

**MONTAGU, Elizabeth.** *Essay on Writings & Genius of Shakespeare...* 1772. London. Dilly. 3rd. tall 8vo. 288p. H13. $295.00

**MONTAGUE, John.** *Bitter Harvest: An Anthology...* 1989. NY. 1st. VG/dj. M17. $25.00

**MONTECINO, Marcel.** *Crosskiller.* 1988. Arbor. 1st. author's 1st book. xl. VG/dj. S18. $6.00

**MONTELEONE, Thomas F.** *Borderlands 2.* 1991. Baltimore. Borderlands. 1st/ltd hc. 1/750. sgn all 22 contributors. F/dj/case. G10. $55.00

**MONTES DA OCA, T.** *Hummingbirds & Orchids in Mexico.* 1963. Mexico. ltd. 60 full-p pl. 34p. cloth. G/dj. C12. $35.00

**MONTESQUIEU.** *Spirit of Laws.* 1802. Worcester. Isaiah Thomas. 2 vol. 8vo. calf. R12. $750.00

**MONTESSORI, Maria.** *Pedagogical Anthropology.* 1913. NY. Stokes. 1st Eng-language. 508p. panelled bl cloth. xl. G1. $75.00

**MONTEVECCHI & TUCK.** *Newfoundland Birds: Exploitation, Study & Conservation.* 1987. Cambridge. 273p. cloth. F. C12. $20.00

**MONTGOMERY, Elizabeth Rider.** *Mystery of Edison Brown.* 1960. Scott Foresman. 1st. ils Betty Beeby. 218p. VG. B36. $13.00

**MONTGOMERY, Field Marshall.** *Normandy to the Baltic: 21st Army Group.* 1948. Hougthon Mifflin. 1st. F/NF. B9. $50.00

**MONTGOMERY, James.** *Gleanings From Pious Authors: Comprising the Wheatsheaf...* 1859. Phil. Longstreth. new ed. 466p. VG. A10. $35.00

**MONTGOMERY, Lucy Maude.** *Emily of New Moon.* 1934. Toronto. McClelland Stewart. 1st. xl. NF/G. T12. $50.00

**MONTGOMERY, Richard G.** *Pechuck: Lorne Knight's Adventure in the Arctic.* 1932. Dodd Mead. inscr. 8vo. 219p. VG/dj. P4. $65.00

**MONTGOMERY, Robert.** *Sacco-Vanzetti: Murder & Myth.* 1960. Devin Adair. 1st. F/VG. B2. $35.00

**MONTGOMERY, Rutherford.** *Big Red: A Wild Stallion.* 1971. Caldwell. Caxton. 1st. F/dj. O3. $38.00

**MONTGOMERY, Rutherford.** *Big Red: A Wild Stallion.* 1971. Caxton. 1st. ils Pers Crowell. VG/dj. A21. $35.00

**MONTGOMERY, Rutherford.** *Golden Stallion's Revenge.* nd. Grosset Dunlap. Famous Horse Stories series. G. O3. $12.00

**MONTGOMERY, Rutherford.** *Golden Stallion's Victory.* nd. Grosset Dunlap. Famous Horse Stories series. VG. O3. $12.00

**MONTGOMERY, Rutherford.** *Golden Stallion's Victory.* 1956. Grosset Dunlap. ils Geo Giguere. VG/dj. A21. $20.00

**MONTGOMERY, Rutherford.** *Golden Stallion to the Rescue.* 1954. Little Brn. 1st. VG. O3. $35.00

**MONTGOMERY, Rutherford.** *Midnight: Wild Stallion of the West.* (1940). Grosset Dunlap. ils Jacob Bates. 275p. VG. B36. $18.00

**MONTGOMERY, Rutherford.** *Tim's Mountain.* 1959. Cleveland. World. 1st. 12mo. 219p. F/NF. C14. $14.00

**MONTGOMERY, Rutherford.** *Walt Disney's Cougar: Fact-Fiction Nature Story.* 1961. Golden. ils Robert Magnusen. VG. B36. $13.00

**MONTGOMERY, Zachary.** *Poison Fountain...Wherein the Terrible Growth of Crime...* 1878. SF. self pub. emb cloth. M11. $75.00

**MONTROSS, Lynn.** *United States Marines: Pictorial History.* 1959. NY. Rinehart. 1st. sm 4to. gr paper brd/blk cloth spine. VG/dj. M7. $25.00

**MONTROSS, Lynn.** *War Through the Ages.* 1946. Harper. revised/enlarged. 1007p. gilt cloth. G/dj. M7. $17.50

**MONZERT, L.** *Independent Liquorist; or, Art of Preparing Coridals...* 1866. VG. E6. $65.00

**MOODIE, J.W.D.** *Ten Years in South Africa...* 1835. London. Bentley. 2 vol. ils/pl. gilt 19th-C bl calf. K1. $400.00

**MOODY, Bill.** *Death of a Tenor Man.* 1995. NY Walker. 1st. F/dj. M23. $40.00

**MOODY, Ralph.** *Old Trails West: Stories of the Trails That Made a Nation.* 1963. Promontory. ils/maps. 318p. VG. J2. $40.00

**MOODY, Ralph.** *Stagecoach West: Story of Frontier Express Lines...* 1967. Crowell. 1st. 341p. map ep. VG. J2. $50.00

**MOODY, Richard.** *Kit Carson & the Wild Frontier.* 1955. Random. 5th. Landmark #53. ils Galli. 184p. VG. B36. $9.00

**MOODY, Rick.** *Ice Storm.* 1994. Little Brn. 1st. F/dj. B30. $25.00

**MOODY, Susan.** *Penny Saving.* 1990. Michael Joseph. 1st. author's 1st novel. lF/dj. T2. $30.00

**MOOG, Vianna.** *Bandeirantes & Pioneers.* (1964). Braziller. 1st. 316p. dj. F3. $25.00

**MOON, James H.** *Why Friends (Quakers) Do Not Baptize With Water.* 1909. Fallsington. JH Moon. 16mo. 70p+ad. worn. V3. $15.00

**MOONEY, J.** *Myths of the Cherokees/Sacred Formulas of Cherokees.* 1982. rpt. ils. F/dj. M4. $40.00

**MOONEY, Michael M.** *Hindenburg.* 1972. NY. Dodd Mead. 1st. 8vo. 278p. F/VG. B20. $20.00

**MOORCOCK, Michael.** *Mother London.* 1989. Harmony. 1st Am. NF/dj. M21. $15.00

**MOORE, Alexander.** *Life Cycles in Atchalan: Diverse Careers...* 1973. NY. Teachers College. 1st. ils. 220p. wrp. F3. $15.00

**MOORE, Alma.** *Grasses, Earth's Green Wealth.* 1960. Macmillan. 150p. VG/dj. A10. $16.00

**MOORE, Anne Carroll.** *Century of Kate Greenaway.* 1946. NY/London. Warne. 8vo. ils. VG/glassine. D1. $85.00

**MOORE, Anne Carroll.** *Three Owls: Book About Children's Books...* 1925. Macmillan. 1st. VG. P3. $85.00

**MOORE, Arthur K.** *Contestable Concepts of Literary Theory.* 1973. LSU. 240p. VG/dj. M10. $6.50

**MOORE, Brian.** *Answer From Limbo.* 1962. Atlantic/Little Brn. 1st. sgn. F/NF clip. D10. $75.00

**MOORE, Brian.** *Black Robe.* 1985. Dutton. 1st Am. F/dj. Q1. $40.00

**MOORE, Brian.** *Catholics.* 1973. HRW. ARC. sgn. F/clip. D10. $60.00

**MOORE, Brian.** *Color of Blood.* 1990. Dutton. 1st. F/F. H11. $20.00

**MOORE, Brian.** *Fergus.* 1970. HRW. 1st. F/NF. D10. $50.00

**MOORE, Brian.** *Lies of Silence.* 1990. Doubleday. 1st. F/F. H11. $20.00

**MOORE, Brian.** *Lies of Silence.* 1990. London. 1st. sgn. F/dj. T9. $45.00

**MOORE, Brian.** *Revolution Script.* 1971. HRW. 1st. sgn. F/F. D10. $65.00

**MOORE, Brian.** *Temptation of Eileen Hughes.* 1981. FSG. 1st. sgn. F/F. D10. $50.00

**MOORE, C.L.** *Black God's Shadow.* 1977. Donald Grant. 1st. VG/dj. L1. $40.00

**MOORE, Carman.** *Somebody's Angel Child: Story of Bessie Smith.* 1969. Crowell. 1st. F/NF. B2. $45.00

**MOORE, Christopher.** *Practical Demon-Keeping.* 1992. St Martin. 1st. F/dj. G10/H11. $32.00

**MOORE, Clement C.** *Night Before Christmas (Moving Picture Books).* ca 1915. NY. Sully Kleinteich. 4to. cloth-backed pict brd. R5. $450.00

**MOORE, Clement C.** *Night Before Christmas.* (1931). Phil. Lippincott. 1st Am. ils Rackham. gr cloth/pict label. R5. $150.00

**MOORE, Clement C.** *Night Before Christmas.* (1949). S&S/Little Golden. 4th. ils Corinne Malvern. 28p. brd. VG. D4. $15.00

**MOORE, Clement C.** *Night Before Christmas.* (1962). Worcester. St Onge. mini. 1/1200. ils Tasha Tudor. aeg. red cloth. B24. $95.00

**MOORE, Clement C.** *Night Before Christmas.* ca 1910. Donohue. 4to. pict covers mtd on linen. R5. $175.00

**MOORE, Clement C.** *Twas the Night Before Christmas.* 1937. Chicago. Merrill. lg 4to. mc pict wrp. R5. $85.00

**MOORE, E.W.** *Natchez Under-the-Hill.* 1958. Natchez. 1st. inscr. ils. 131p. F/dj. M4. $23.00

**MOORE, Elaine T.** *Winning Your Spurs.* 1953-54. Bramhall. 1st. ils Paul Brown. VG/dj. A21. $40.00

**MOORE, Evelyn.** *Sanoccho: Stories & Sketches of Panama.* 1947. Panama. Star & Herald. 2nd. 214p. pict cloth. F3. $25.00

**MOORE, G.** *Missouri Controversey 1819-1821.* nd. Lexington, KY. 1st. 383p. VG/dj. B5. $30.00

**MOORE, Harry Estill.** *Tornadoes Over Texas: A Study of Waco & San Angelo...* 1958. Austin. ils. 334p. dj. K5. $35.00

**MOORE, J.** *Old Family Receipts.* 1929. NY. self pub. 102p. VG. E6. $30.00

**MOORE, James Tice.** *Two Paths to the New South: Virginia Debt Controversy...* (1974). U KY. maps. 167p. VG/dj. B10. $45.00

**MOORE, John M.** *South Today.* 1916. Missionary Ed Movement. photos. 251p. VG. B10. $15.00

**MOORE, John M.** *Who Is Who in Arizona.* 1958. np. 1st. 288p. NF/sans. B19. $35.00

**MOORE, John.** *Cabildo in Peru Under the Bourbons.* 1966. Durham. Duke. 1st. 275p. dj. F3. $20.00

**MOORE, Julia.** *Sweet Singer of Michigan.* 1928. Chicago. Pascal Covici. 158p. decor brd. VG/dj. B18. $37.50

**MOORE, Lorrie.** *Anagrams.* 1986. Knopf. 1st. author's 2nd novel. F/dj. D10. $75.00

**MOORE, Lorrie.** *I Know Some Things: Stories About Childhood...* 1992. Boston. Faber. 1st. 2 contributors sgn. F/dj. O11. $35.00

**MOORE, Lorrie.** *Self-Help.* 1985. Knopf. 1st. author's 1st book. F/dj. D10. $160.00

**MOORE, Norman.** *History of Study of Medicine in British Isles.* 1908. Oxford. 1st. 202p. A13. $100.00

**MOORE, Patrick.** *Astronomy of Birr Castle.* 1971. London. Mitchell Beazley. 8vo. 81p. xl. K5. $50.00

**MOORE, Patrick.** *Earth Satellites.* 1956. Norton. 8vo. 157p. K5. $20.00

**MOORE, Patrick.** *Guide to the Planets.* 1954. Norton. 1st Am. ils/pl. 254p. VG/dj. K5. $25.00

**MOORE, Patrick.** *Survey of the Moon.* 1963. Norton. 8vo. 333p. VG/dj. K5. $30.00

**MOORE, Patrick.** *Watchers of the Stars.* 1973. Putnam. 1st. NF/dj. O4. $20.00

**MOORE, Peter C.** *Disarming the Secular Gods: How to Talk...* 1989. IVP. 223p. VG/wrp. B29. $8.00

**MOORE, Robin.** *Country Team.* 1967. NY. Crown. 1st. F/dj. R11. $30.00

**MOORE, Robin.** *Green Berets.* 1965. 1st. VG/G. E6. $12.00

**MOORE, Ruth.** *Niels Bohr: Man, His Science & the World They Changed.* 1966. NY. Knopf. 1st. 436p. orange cloth. P4. $45.00

**MOORE, S.H.** *Moore's Standard Directory & Reference Book Elyria, OH.* 1909. SH Moore. 171p. G+. B18. $25.00

**MOORE, Suzanne.** *Jabberwocky, by Lewis Carroll.* 1986. Ashfield, MA. triangular panorama. handwritten. 44p. F/blk silk box. B24. $950.00

**MOORE & SEED.** *Ecology of Rocky Coasts.* 1986. Columbia. photos. 467p. AN/dj. S15. $30.00

**MOORE & VERMILYEA.** *Thayer's 'Casey at the Bat.'* 1994. McFarland. 1st. F/sans. P8. $22.50

**MOORE-LANDECKER, Elizabeth.** *Fundamentals of the Fungi.* 1972. Prentice Hall. 482p. xl. VG. S5. $35.00

**MOOREHEAD, Warren King.** *Etowah Papers, I, II, III, IV.* 1932. Yale. sm 4to. 178p. gr cloth. K1. $50.00

**MOOREHOUSE, Alfred C.** *Triumph of the Alphabet, a History of Writing.* 1953. NY. Henry Schuman. 1st. 8vo. 223p. cloth. F/dj. O10. $45.00

**MOORHEAD, Alan.** *March to Tunis.* 1967. Harper. 1st. 592p. VG/dj. M7. $25.00

**MOORHOUSE, G.** *India Britannica.* 1983. NY. 1st Am. 288p. F/dj. M4. $20.00

**MOORMAN, Fay.** *My Heart Turns Back: Childhood Memories of Rural Virginia...* (1964). Exposition. 1st. 124p. VG/G. B10. $18.00

**MOORMAN, L.J.** *Pioneer Doctor.* 1951. OK U. photos. 252p. F/dj. M4. $15.00

**MOORMAN, Lewis.** *Tuberculosis & Genius.* 1940. Chicago. 1st. 272p. A13. $60.00

**MORAND, Anne.** *Prints of Thomas Moran in Thomas Gilcrease Institute...* 1986. Gilcrease Mus. sm 4to. 255p. cloth. F7. $60.00

**MORANTZ-SANCHEZ, Regina.** *Sympathy & Science, Women Physicians in American Medicine.* 1985. NY. 1st. 464p. dj. A13. $35.00

**MORAVIA, Alberto.** *Wayward Life.* 1960. Secker Warburg. 1st. 12mo. VG/dj. A2. $15.00

**MORAVIA, Alberto.** *Which Tribe Do You Belong To?* 1974 (1972). FSG. 1st Am. 8vo. F/dj. A2. $12.50

**MORE, Hannah.** *Structures on Modern System of Female Education.* 1799. London. Strahan for Dadell Davies. 2 vol. 6th. full flame calf. H13. $295.00

**MOREAU, R.E.** *Bird Faunas of Africa & Its Islands.* 1966. London. Academic. lg 8vo. ils/pl/maps. 424p. NF/dj. C12. $80.00

**MOREL, C.** *Le Cerveau sa Topographie Anatomique.* 1880. Paris. Berger-Levrault. 17 engraved pl. 48p. G7. $250.00

**MOREL, J.** *Progressive Catering: A Comprehensive Treatment of Food...* 1952. London. 4 vol. 1st. ils/700 photos/pl. pebbled royal bl brd. VG. E6. $125.00

**MORELLA, Joe.** *Films of World War II.* (1973). Seacaus, NJ. Citadel. 1st. 254p. VG/dj. M7. $20.00

**MORENO, Francisco Jose.** *Between Faith & Reason: An Approach...* 1977. NY. NY U. inscr. 133p. tan cloth. G1. $28.50

**MORENO, H.J.** *Moreno's Dictionary of Spanish Names: CA Cities & Towns.* 1916. San Luis Obispo, CA. 1st. VG. O4. $25.00

**MOREY, Walts.** *Scrub Dog of Alaska.* 1971. NY. 1st Am. inscr. 8vo. 212p. bl cloth. VG/dj. P4. $30.00

**MORFI, Fray Juan Agustin.** *History of Texas, 1673-1779.* 1935. Quivira. 2 vol. 1/500. ils/fld maps. F. A4. $650.00

**MORGAN, Barbara.** *Barbara Morgan.* 1972. photos. VG/dj. M17. $25.00

**MORGAN, Barbara.** *Martha Graham.* 1941. DSP. 1st. 4to. VG. S9. $60.00

**MORGAN, Charlotte E.** *Origin & History of the New York Employing Printers Assn...* 1930. NY. Columbia. 1st. 8vo. cloth. F/NF. O10. $35.00

**MORGAN, Conway Lloyd.** *Animal Behaviour.* 1900. London. Longman Gr. sm 8vo. 334p+32p ads. panelled bl buckram. G1. $85.00

**MORGAN, Conway Lloyd.** *Introduction to Comparative Psychology.* 1894. London. Walter Scott Ltd. 12mo. 382p+18p ads. emb crimson cloth. G1. $250.00

**MORGAN, Dale L.** *West of William H Ashley.* 1964. Rosenstock. ltd ed. VG. J2. $850.00

**MORGAN, Dan.** *Complete Baseball Joke Book.* 1953. Stravon. 1st. VG/dj. P8. $50.00

**MORGAN, Dan.** *Rising in the West: True Story of an Oakie Family...* 1992. Knopf. stated 1st. photos. NF/dj. P12. $15.00

**MORGAN, DeWolfe.** *Before Homer: Boy's Story of the Earliest Greeks.* 1938. Longman Gr. 1st. 261p. VG. C14. $10.00

**MORGAN, Glenn G.** *Soviet Administrative Legality...* 1962. Stanford. M11. $35.00

**MORGAN, J.W.** *California Impressions, an Englishman's Travels...* 1990. Northridge. Santa Susana. 1/200. sgn edit. beige cloth/label. F. K1. $50.00

MORGAN, James M. *Jackson-Hope & Society of Cincinnati Medals...* 1979. McClure. 276p. VG/G. B10. $65.00

MORGAN, Janet. *Agatha Christie: A Biography.* 1985. Knopf. 3rd. NF/dj. P3. $18.00

MORGAN, L.H. *American Beaver & His Works.* 1868. Lippincott. 1st. 8vo. 330p. red cloth. B1. $235.00

MORGAN, Lewis Henry. *American Beaver & His Works.* 1868. Lippincott. 23 fld pl/fld map. 330p. panelled mauve cloth. G1. $650.00

MORGAN, Marlo. *Mutant Message Down Under.* 1994. Harper Collins. 1st trade. F/dj. B30. $30.00

MORGAN, Richard E. *Supreme Court & Religion.* 1972. Free Pr. G. M11. $45.00

MORGAN, Robert. *Blue Valleys.* 1989. Peachtree. 1st. F/dj. M23. $35.00

MORGAN, Robin. *Monster.* 1972. Random. 1st. inscr/dtd 1972. F/NF. L3. $45.00

MORGAN, Ted. *Maugham: A Biography.* 1980. S&S. 1st. F/NF clip. P3. $25.00

MORGAN & MORGAN. *South on the Sound: Ils History of Tacoma & Pierce Co.* 1984. Woodland Hills, CA. Windsor. 1st. sgn. 199p. F/dj. B20. $25.00

MORGANSTEIN, Gary. *Take Me Out to the Ballgame.* 1980. St Martin. 1st. F/dj. P8. $35.00

MORGENSTERN, L. *Esthetiques d'Orient et d'Occident.* 1937. Paris. Leroux. 25 pl. 282p. VG. Q2. $36.50

MORGENSTERN, Oskar. *On Accuracy of Economic Observations.* 1965 (1963). Princeton. 322p. xl. VG. S5. $20.00

MORIS, Edita. *Love to Vietnam.* 1968. NY. Monthly Review. 92p. NF/dj. R11. $40.00

MORISON, Samuel Eliot. *Maritime History of Massachusetts 1783-1860.* 1921. Houghton Mifflin. 1/385. 401p. bl brd/blk cloth spine. VG/case. B11. $475.00

MORISON, Samuel Eliot. *Maritime History of Massachusetts 1783-1860.* 1941. Boston. ils. 421p. F. M4. $25.00

MORISON, Samuel Eliot. *Samuel DeChamplain: Father of New France.* 1972. Boston. 1st. ils. 299p. VG/dj. B5. $25.00

MORISON, Samuel Eliot. *Supplement & General Index: Vol 15, History of US...* 1962. Boston. photos. VG/dj. M17. $45.00

MORISON, Samuel Eliot. *Victory in the Pacific 1945.* 1960. Boston. photos/maps. VG/dj. M17. $17.50

MORISON & MORISON. *New Hampshire: A Bicentennial History.* 1976. NY. 1st. photos/map. 209p. F/dj. M4. $15.00

MORLAND, Nigel. *Outline of Sexual Criminology.* 1967. NY. Hart. M11. $35.00

MORLEY, Christopher. *Middle Kingdom: Poems 1929-1944.* 1944. Harcourt Brace. 1st. VG/dj. B30. $22.50

MORLEY, Christopher. *Where the Blue Begins.* 1922. Phil. Lippincott. rpt. ils Rackham. 227p. NF/worn. B20. $100.00

MORLEY, Felix. *Gumption Island: A Fantasy of Coexistence.* 1956. Caxton. 1st. F/NF. M19. $25.00

MORLEY, Patricia. *Kurelek: A Biography.* 1986. Toronto. Macmillan. 1st. F/dj. A26. $20.00

MORREL, M.M. *Young Hickory: Life of President James K Polk.* 1949. NY. 1st. inscr. 381p. NF/dj. M4. $30.00

MORRELL, David. *Blood Oath.* 1982. NY. St Martin. ARC/1st. RS. F/dj. M15. $90.00

MORRELL, David. *Desperate Measures.* 1994. Warner. 1st. F/dj. S18. $22.00

MORRELL, David. *First Blood.* 1990. Armchair Detective. rpt. AN/dj. S18. $10.00

MORRELL, David. *League of Night & Fog.* 1987. Dutton. 1st. F/dj. S18. $30.00

MORRELL, David. *League of Night & Fog.* 1987. Dutton. 1st. VG/NF. H11. $10.00

MORRELL, Thomas. *Abridgement of Ainsworth's Dictionary English & Latin.* 1825. Phil. 1030p. old calf. G. S17. $35.00

MORRIS, Anna Van Rensselaer. *Apple Woman of the Klickitat.* 1918. Duffield. 1st. sm 8vo. 271p. VG. S14. $30.00

MORRIS, Charles. *Life of Queen Victoria & Story of Her Reign.* 1901. WE Schull. 574p. dk red cloth. VG. S17. $10.00

MORRIS, Desmond. *Mammals: Guide to the Living Species.* 1965. NY. ils. 448p. VG. S15. $10.00

MORRIS, Earl H. *Temple of the Warriors.* 1931. Scribner. ils. 251p. G+. B18. $35.00

MORRIS, F.O. *Natural History of Nests & Eggs of British Birds.* 1896. London. Nimmo. 4th revised. ils. gilt cloth. NF. M12. $350.00

MORRIS, George Ford. *Portraitures of Horses.* 1952. Shrewsbury. Fordacre Studios. 1st. obl folio. ils. VG. O3. $595.00

MORRIS, George Ford. *Portraitures of Horses.* 1952. Shrewsbury. Fordacre Studios. 1st/only. obl folio. VG/fair. O3. $645.00

MORRIS, Gregory L. *Talking Up a Storm: Voices of the New West.* 1994. Lincoln. U NE. 1st. sgn 3 contributors. F/dj. O11. $50.00

MORRIS, Henry. *Bird & Bull Number 13.* 1972. North Hills. Bird & Bull. 1st. 1/140. quarter parchment/paper brd. F. M24. $450.00

MORRIS, Henry. *Onmibus.* 1967. North Hills. Bird & Bull. 1/500. 8vo. Sangorski Sutcliffe bdg. w/prospectus. B24. $400.00

MORRIS, Henry. *Paper Maker: A Survey of Lesser-Known Hand Paper Mills...* 1974. North Hills. Bird & Bull. 1/175. sm 4to. 128p. w/prospectus. F. B24. $1,000.00

MORRIS, Holly. *Different Angle: Fly Fishing Stories by Women.* 1995. Seattle. Seal Pr. 1st. sgn. F/dj. O11. $65.00

MORRIS, Jan. *Locations.* 1992. Oxford. 1st. dj. T9. $15.00

MORRIS, Jan. *Manhattan '45.* 1987. NY. Oxford. 1st. F/F. H11. $30.00

MORRIS, Jan. *Pleasures of a Tangled Life.* 1989. London. 1st. dj. T9. $15.00

MORRIS, Joseph. *Reminiscences of Joseph Morris, Being a Brief History...* 1899. Mt Gilead, OH. Sentinel Prt House. 2nd. 12mo. 212p. VG. V3. $30.00

MORRIS, Mark. *Mark Morris.* 1993. FSG. 1st. sgn. F/dj. O11. $75.00

MORRIS, Myrtle M. *Joseph & Philena (Elton) Fellows: Their Ancestry...* nd (1940). np. inscr. ils. 404p. VG. B18. $37.50

MORRIS, Percy A. *Field Guide to Shells of Atlantic & Gulf Coasts...* 1973. Houghton Mifflin. 3rd. photos. VG/wrp. S15. $5.00

MORRIS, Peter. *Modelling Cognition.* 1987. John Wiley. 309p. brn brd. G1. $75.00

MORRIS, Roy. *Sheridan: Life & Wars of General Phil Sheridan.* 1992. NY. Crown. 1st. F/dj. A14. $30.00

MORRIS, William. *Address Delivered by...* 1898. London. Chiswick. 1st. quarter linen/prt brd. F. M24. $400.00

MORRIS, William. *Aims of Art.* 1887. London. Doves Bindery. sq 16mo. 39p. full brn morocco. F. H5. $1,500.00

MORRIS, William. *Love Is Enough, or Freeing of Pharamond: A Morality.* 1897. Hammersmith. Kelmscott. 1/300. 4to. ils Edward Bourne-Jones. F/box. B24. $3,000.00

MORRIS, William. *Story of Cupid & Psyche.* 1974. London/Cambridge. Clover Hill. 1/130 deluxe. complete. F/box. B24. $2,000.00

MORRIS, Willie. *Always Stand in Against the Curve.* 1983. Yoknapatawpha. 6 autobiographical essays. sgn. F/VG. P8. $75.00

MORRIS, Willie. *Good Old Boy.* 1971. NY. Harper. 1st. VG/dj. B5. $25.00

MORRIS, Willie. *My Dog Skip.* 1995. Random. 1/500. sgn. 122p. F/case. B20. $50.00

MORRIS, Willie. *My Dog Skip.* 1995. Random. 1st. F/dj. M23. $15.00

MORRIS, Willie. *North Toward Home.* 1967. Houghton Mifflin. 1st. F/NF. B4. $150.00

MORRIS, Willie. *Prayer for the Opening of the Little League Season.* 1993. Northtowne Prts. F. P8. $150.00

MORRIS, Wright. *Cause of Wonder.* 1963. Atheneum. 1st. VG/dj. B30. $35.00

MORRIS, Wright. *Ceremony in Lone Tree.* 1960. Atheneum. 1st. VG/dj. B30. $45.00

MORRIS, Wright. *God's Country & My People.* 1968. NY. 1st. VG/dj. B5. $75.00

MORRIS, Wright. *Home Place.* 1948. Scribner. 1st. author's 1st book to feature photos. F/dj. B4. $300.00

MORRIS, Wright. *Inhabitants.* 1946. Scribner. 1st. 4to. 112p. olive cloth. dj. K1. $150.00

MORRIS, Wright. *Life.* 1973. Harper. 1st. inscr. F/NF. B4. $150.00

MORRIS, Wright. *Man & Boy.* 1951. Knopf. 1st/2nd prt. 212p. VG. S14. $25.00

MORRIS, Wright. *Plains Song.* 1980. Harper Row. 1st. NF/dj. B30. $20.00

MORRIS, Wright. *Solo.* 1983. Harper Row. 1st. F/dj. M23. $25.00

MORRIS & RASKIN. *Lawrence of Arabia: 30th Anniversary Pictorial History.* 1992. NY. Anchor/Doubleday. 1st. lg 8vo. 237p. F/pict wrp. M7. $45.00

MORRISON, A.J. *Travels in Virginia in Revolutionary Times.* (1922). Bell. 138p. VG/dj. B10. $65.00

MORRISON, Anne Hendry. *Women & Their Careers: A Study of 306 Women in Business...* 1934. NY. Nat Federation of Business & Professional Women. VG. A25. $20.00

MORRISON, Ben Y. *Street & Highway Planting.* nd (1913). Sacramento. 119p. wrp. B26. $22.50

MORRISON, E.M. *Isle of Wight County, 1608-1907.* 1957 (1907). APVA. rpt. photos. 72p. VG. B10. $15.00

MORRISON, J.H. *Streams in the Desert: Picture of Life in Livingstonia.* 1969. NY. Negro U. rpt. sm 8vo. 7 pl. 174p. VG. W1. $18.00

MORRISON, James K. *Consumer Approach to Community Psychology.* 1979. Nelson Hall. 1st. VG/dj. N2. $10.00

MORRISON, Jim. *American Night: Vol 2.* 1990. NY. Villard. 1st. F/F. B3. $20.00

MORRISON, Toni. *Beloved.* 1987. Knopf. 1st. F/F. from $60 to $75.00

MORRISON, Toni. *Jazz.* 1992. Knopf. stated 2nd. gilt blk bdg. VG/dj. P12. $20.00

MORRISON, Toni. *Jazz.* 1992. Knopf. 1st. F/F. B2/B3. $40.00

MORRISON, Toni. *Jazz.* 1992. Knopf. 1st. sgn. F/clip. D10. $75.00

MORRISON, Toni. *Playing in the Dark. Whiteness & the Literary Imagination.* 1992. Harvard. 1st. F/dj. D10. $65.00

MORRISON, Toni. *Song of Solomon.* 1977. Knopf. 1st. sgn. F/F. D10. $300.00

MORRISON, Toni. *Song of Solomon.* 1977. Taiwan. pirated ed. sgn. F/dj. D10. $100.00

MORRISON, Toni. *Tar Baby.* 1981. Knopf. 1st. F/NF. B2. $60.00

MORRISON, Toni. *Tar Baby.* 1981. Knopf. 1st. gilt wht cloth. F/VG. P12. $50.00

MORRISON, Toni. *Tar Baby.* 1981. Knopf. 1st. sgn. F/clip. D10. $165.00

MORRISON, Tony. *Pathways to the Gods.* 1978. Harper. 1st. 208p. dj. F3. $20.00

MORRISON, W. Douglas. *Juvenile Offenders.* 1898. NY. Appleton. Authorized ed. 317p. teg. 3-quarter brn morocco. B20. $50.00

MORRISON & OWEN. *Planetary System.* 1996 (1988). Reading, MA. Addison-Wesley. 2nd. ils. 570p. F. K5. $30.00

MORROW, Bradford. *Come Sunday.* 1985. Weidenfeld Nicholson. 1st. sgn. F/F. B3/O11. $50.00

MORROW, Bradford. *Trinity Fields.* 1995. NY. Viking. 1st. sgn. F/dj. O11. $35.00

MORROW, Elizabeth. *Shannon.* 1941. Macmillan. 1st. 12mo. ils Helen Torrey. VG+/G. M5. $20.00

MORROW, James. *City of Truth.* 1992. St Martin. 1st. sgn/dtd. F/dj. G10. $27.00

MORROW, James. *Only Begotten Daughter.* 1990. Morrow. 1st. sgn/dtd. F/dj. G10. $67.00

MORROW, James. *This Is the Way the World Ends.* 1986. NY. Holt. 1st. sgn. VG/NF. B3. $40.00

MORSE, Benjamin, M.D.; see Block, Lawrence.

MORSE, Edward S. *Glimpses of China & Chinese Homes.* 1902. Boston. ils. VG. M17. $100.00

MORSE, Edwin W. *America in the War: Vanguard of American Volunteers...* 1919. Scribner. 1st. photos. 281p. VG+. A25. $15.00

MORSE, O.A. *Vindication of Claim of MW Ball...* 1867. NY. MW Dodd. 1st. inscr MW Ball. gilt gr cloth. M24. $125.00

MORSE, Samuel French. *All in a Suitcase.* 1966. Little Brn. 1st. obl 8vo. pict cloth. dj. R5. $85.00

MORSON, Ian. *Falconer's Crusade.* 1994. London. Gollancz. 1st. author's 1st novel. F/dj. T2. $30.00

MORSON, Ian. *Psalm for Falconer.* 1997. St Martin. 1st Am. F/dj. G8. $20.00

MORTENSEN, William. *Pictorial Lighting.* 1935. Camera Craft. 1st. 4to. ES. NF/VG. S9. $100.00

MORTENSEN, William. *Pictorial Lighting.* 1948. Camera Craft. 2nd. VG. S5. $15.00

MORTIMER, John. *Like Men Betrayed.* 1953. London. Collins. 1st. author's 4th book. VG/dj. A24. $40.00

MORTIMER, Ruth. *Italian Sixteenth-Century Books.* 1974. Cambridge. Harvard. 2 vol. 1st. gilt rust cloth. F. M24. $400.00

MORTON, H. *Genito-Urinary Diseases & Syphillis.* 1903 (1902). ils/pl. 521p. VG. E6. $25.00

MORTON, James F. *Exempting the Churches.* 1916. NY. Truth Seeker. 1st. F/wrp. B2. $60.00

MORTON, Martha. *Her Lord & Master.* ca 1900. NY. RF FEnno. ils HC Christy/Esther MacNamara. 475p. G11. $10.00

MORTON, Rosalie Slaughter. *Doctor's Holiday in Iran.* 1940. Funk Wagnall. 1st. 8vo. 15 pl. xl. VG. W1. $18.00

MOSBY, Henry S. *Wildlife Investigational Techniques.* 1965. Ann Arbor. Wildlife Soc. 2nd. 419p. cloth. A17. $20.00

MOSEL, Arlene. *Funny Little Woman.* (1972). Dutton. 1st. ils Blair Lent. 1973 Caldecott. pict dj. R5. $150.00

MOSELEY, Benjamin. *Commentaries on the Lues Bovilla; or, Cow Pox...* 1806. London. Longman Gr. 184p. orig sugar brd/no label. G7. $495.00

MOSELEY, Michael. *Chan Chan: Andean Desert City.* 1982. Albuquerque. 1st. 373p. dj. F3. $30.00

MOSER, Barry. *Fall of Camelot Portfolio.* ca 1986. W Hatfield. Pennyroyal. 1/85. inscr. 33 sgn prts. purple cloth/label. F/box. B24. $950.00

MOSER, Barry. *Thirteen Botanical Wood Engravings.* 1974. Easthampton. Pennyroyal. 1/100. unbound suite sgn prts. F/tan wrp. B24. $575.00

MOSER, Hans Joachim. *Heinrich Schutz: His Life & Work.* 1957 (1939). Concordia Pub House. 16 pl. 740p. VG/dj. S5. $30.00

MOSES, Irene E. Phillips. *Rhythmic Action Plays & Dance.* 1928. Springfield, MA. Milton Bradley. 4to. 164p. VG. B11. $15.00

MOSGROVE, George Dallas. *Kentucky Cavaliers in Dixie...* 1895. Louisville. Currier-Journal Job Prt. 265p. cloth. M8. $850.00

MOSLER, Hermann. *Judicial Protection Against the Executive. Two Volumes.* 1969. Oceana Pub. 2 vol. M11. $65.00

MOSLEY, Leonard. *Gideon Goes to War: Story of Wingate.* 1955. London. Barker. 1st. 256p. gilt red buckram. F/VG. M7. $42.50

MOSLEY, Walter. *Black Betty.* 1994. NY. Norton. 1st. F/dj. M15. $45.00

MOSLEY, Walter. *Gone Fishin'.* 1997. Baltimore. Blk Classic. 1st. F/dj. B9. $15.00

MOSLEY, Walter. *Gone Fishin'.* 1997. Baltimore. Blk Classic. 1st. sgn. F/dj. M15. $50.00

MOSLEY, Walter. *Little Yellow Dog.* 1996. Norton. 1st. VG/dj. G8. $15.00

MOSLEY, Walter. *Red Death.* 1991. Norton. 1st. sgn. F/dj. D10. $65.00

MOSLEY, Walter. *Red Death.* 1991. NY. Norton. 1st. F/dj. A24/M15. $50.00

MOSLEY, Walter. *White Butterfly.* 1992. Norton. 1st. sgn. F/dj. D10. $125.00

MOSS, Pete. *How to Ride & Train the Western Horse.* 1967. Pleasant Hill. Beery School of Horsemanship. 7 booklets. VG. O3. $35.00

MOSS, S. *Natural History of the Antarctic Peninsula.* 1988. NY. Columbia. ils/maps. 208p. NF/dj. M12. $37.50

MOSTEL, Zero. *Zero Mostel's Book of Villians.* 1976. Doubleday. 1st. VG/wrp. C9. $48.00

MOTHER GOOSE. *Mother Goose.* ca 1890. London. Nister. obl 8vo. shapebook. 14p. stiff paper covers. R5. $125.00

MOTHER GOOSE. *Mother Goose.* ca 1910. Donohue. 8vo. 8p. mc linen. R5. $40.00

MOTLEY, John Lothrop. *History of the United Netherlands.* 1874. Harper. 4 vol. gilt brn cloth. xl. VG. S17. $40.00

MOTLEY, John Lothrop. *Rise of the Dutch Republic.* 1859. NY. 3 vol. full leather/marbled edges. F. B30. $150.00

MOTLEY, Willard. *Knock on Any Door.* 1947. Appleton Century Crofts. 1st. 504p. VG/dj. R11. $20.00

MOTT, Bessie Q. *American Woman & Her Bank.* 1929. Doubleday Doran. 1st. 12mo. 252p. bl cloth. NF/dj. J3. $65.00

MOTT, Maria. *Short Account of Life & Last Ilness of Maria Mott...* 1848. NY. Egbert Hovey King. 1st. 16mo. 41p. G+. V3. $15.00

MOTT. *History of American Magazines, Vol I (1743-1850).* 1956. Cambridge, MA. F. P13. $75.00

MOTT. *History of American Magazines, Vol I-V.* 1968 (1968). Cambridge, MA. 5 vol. F/djs. P13. $425.00

MOTT. *History of American Magazines, Vol II (1850-1865).* 1956. Cambridge, MA. F. P13. $75.00

MOTT. *History of American Magazines, Vol IV (1885-1905).* 1956. Cambridge, MA. VG+. P13. $100.00

MOTTELAY. *Bibliographical History of Electricity & Magnetism.* nd. rpt. 1/300. 593p. F. A4. $75.00

MOTTRAM, R.H. *Apple Disdained.* 1928. London. 1st. 1/530. sgn. drab brd. VG/dj. J3. $75.00

MOULE, C.F.D. *Origin of Christology.* 1980. Cambridge. 187p. VG/wrp. B29. $14.50

MOULIN, Fred. *Orchids in Australia.* 1958. Luasanne. photos. 149p. VG/dj. B26. $26.00

MOUNT, Robert. *Scrimshaw History.* 1986. Morrow Bay, CA. Tabula Rasa. mini. 1/100. sgn. ivory/bl leather. box. B24. $150.00

MOURAD, Kenize. *Regards From a Dead Princess, a Novel of Life.* 1989. Arcade/Little Brn. 1st Am. 562p. NF/dj. W1. $18.00

MOURELLE, Don Francisco A. *Voyage of the Sonora: From 1775 Journal of...* 1987. Ye Galleon. ltd reissue. 1/301. F/sans. B19. $20.00

MOWAT, Farley. *Black Joke.* 1963. Little Brn. 1st Am. VG/dj. T11. $50.00

MOWAT, Farley. *Born Naked.* 1993. Key Porter. 1st. F/dj. P3. $30.00

MOWAT, Farley. *Born Naked.* 1994. Houghton Mifflin. 1st. F/dj. T11. $25.00

MOWAT, Farley. *Curse of the Viking Grave.* 1966. Little Brn. 1st. F/clip. T11. $45.00

MOWAT, Farley. *My Discovery of America.* 1985. Toronto. McClelland Stewart. 1st Canadian. F/clip. B3. $75.00

MOWAT, Farley. *My Father's Son: Memories of War & Peace.* 1992. Toronto. Key Porter. 1st. sgn twice. F/dj. A26. $40.00

MOWAT, Farley. *Never Cry Wolf.* 1963. McClelland Stewart. 1st Canadian. F/NF (only 1 of 2). T12. $90.00

MOWAT, Farley. *Snow Walker.* 1975. Toronto. McClelland Stewart. 1st. F/F. A26. $30.00

MOWAT, Farley. *Tundra.* 1973. Toronto. McClelland Stewart. 1st. F/dj. A26. $35.00

MOWAT, Farley. *Virunga: Passion of Diane Fossey.* 1987. McClelland Stewart. 1st. VG. P3. $25.00

MOWAT, Farley. *West Viking: Ancient Norse in Greenland & North America.* 1965. Boston/Toronto. 1st. VG/dj. M17. $22.50

MOWBRAY, J.P. *Conquering of Kate.* 1903. Doubleday Page. 1st. 315p. G+. G11. $8.00

MOWRY, George D. *Another Look at the Twentieth-Century South.* (1973). LSU. 90 p. VG/VG. B10. $10.00

MOWRY, Jess. *Way Past Cool.* 1992. FSG. 1st. F/F. H11. $20.00

MOXLEY, Verna. *Wind 'Til Sundown.* 1954. Caldwell, ID. Caxton. AN/dj. A19. $25.00

MOYES, Patricia. *Murder Fantastical.* 1967. HRW. 1st Am. F/NF. C15. $20.00

MOYNAHAN & TROMP. *West of Sandy Ingersoll.* 1974. Art of Northwest. 1/100. 93p. F/dj. w/orig sketch. B20. $125.00

MOZART, Leopold. *Grundliche Violinschule.* 1770. Augsburg. Lotter. 4to. 3 full-p pl/fld table. modern calf. R12. $2,250.00

MUDIAM, Prithvi Ram. *India & the Middle East.* 1994. London/NY. British Academic. 1st. 8vo. 232p. VG. W1. $16.00

MUENSCHER, Walter Conrad. *Aquatic Plants of the United States.* 1944. Ithaca, NY. Comstock. ils/index. 374p. VG. H10. $22.50

MUHLBACH, Louise. *Berlin & Sans-Souci. Vol 3.* 1967. PF Collier. 1st. 8vo. 497p. NF. W2. $115.00

MUHLBACH, Louise. *Marie Antoinette & Her Son.* 1867. PF Collier. 1st. 8vo. 566p. NF. W2. $195.00

MUHLBACH, Louise. *Napoleon & Blucher. Vol 9.* 1893. PF Collier. 8vo. 607p. VG. W2. $225.00

MUIR, Augustus. *Shadow on the Left.* 1928. Bobbs Merrill. 1st Am. VG/dj. M15. $50.00

MUIR, John. *Climb the Mountains.* 1965. Pasadena. Glen Dawson. mini. 1/40. Bela Blau bdg. F. B24. $225.00

**MUIR, John.** *Gentle Wilderness: Sierra, Nevada.* 1968 (1967). Sierra Club/ Ballantine. 3rd. photos Richard Kauffman. VG/dj. S5. $15.00

**MUIR, John.** *Notes on My Journeying in California's Northern Mountains.* 1975. Ashland, OR. 72p. wrp. A17. $15.00

**MUIR, John.** *Stickeen.* 1909. Houghton Mifflin. tan cloth. P4. $195.00

**MUIR, John.** *Thousand-Mile Walk to the Gulf.* 1916. Houghton Mifflin. 1st. 8vo. ils. 220p. teg. gr cloth. F. B20. $250.00

**MULDER, M.E.** *Green Ray or Green Flash (Rayon Vert), At Rise...of Sun.* 1922. The Hague. VanStockum Zoon. sm 4to. 141p. G/wrp. K5. $100.00

**MULDOON, Paul.** *Faber Book of Contemporary Irish Poetry.* 1986. London. 1st. dj. T9. $20.00

**MULFORD, Clarence E.** *Bar-20 Days.* 1911. AC McClurg. 1st. ils Maynard Dixon. 412p. decor brn cloth. G+. B20. $35.00

**MULFORD, Clarence E.** *Corson of the JC.* 1927. Doubleday Page. 1st. VG. M25. $25.00

**MULLAN, Bob.** *Are Mothers Really Necessary?* 1987. Weidenfeld Nicolson. 1st Am. 8vo. 210p. F. W2. $25.00

**MULLER, Gulli Lindh.** *Introduction to Medical Science.* 1944. Phil. Saunders. 2nd. 8vo. 454p. NF. C14. $10.00

**MULLER, J.** *Invasion of America: Fact Story...* 1916 (1915). VG/fair. E6. $18.00

**MULLER, Marcia.** *Cheshire Cat's Eye.* 1983. St Martin. 1st. F/dj. M15. $200.00

**MULLER, Marcia.** *Shape of Dread.* 1989. Mysterious. 1st. sgn. NF/dj. G8. $30.00

**MULLER, Marcia.** *Trophies & Dead Things.* 1990. Mysterious. 1st. 8vo. 266p. beige brd. F/dj. J3. $35.00

**MULLINS, Lisa C.** *Early Architecture in the South.* (1987). Nat Hist Soc. 236p. VG. B10. $35.00

**MUMEY, Nolie.** *James Pierson Beckwourth 1856-1866.* 1957. Denver, CO. Old West Pub. inscr. F. A19. $200.00

**MUMEY, Nolie.** *1958 Brand Book of the Denver Westerners.* 1959. Boulder, CO. Johnson Pub. ltd. F. A19. $75.00

**MUMFORD, F.B.** *Breeding of Animals.* 1922. Macmillan. 310p. cloth. A10. $12.00

**MUMFORD, James.** *Narrative of Surgery: A Historical Sketch.* 1906. Phil. 1st. 983p. A13. $50.00

**MUMFORD, Lewis.** *Herman Melville.* 1929. Literary Guild of Am. sm 8vo. ils. 377p. gilt bl brd. VG/G+. M7. $20.00

**MUMFORD, Lewis.** *Man as Interpreter.* 1950. NY. Harcourt Brace. 1st. decor brd. F/clip. M24. $35.00

**MUMFORD, Lewis.** *South in Architecture.* 1967. DeCapo. rpt of 1941. 147p. xl. VG. B10. $15.00

**MUNBY, A.N.L.** *Portrait of an Obsession: Life of Sir Thomas Philipps...* 1967. Putnam. 1st Am. 8vo. 278p. NF/VG. O10. $35.00

**MUNDAY, Albert H.** *Eyes of the Army & Navy.* (1917). NY. 226p. G+. B18. $37.50

**MUNN, Charles Clark.** *Uncle Terry: Story of the Maine Coast.* 1901. Lee Shepard. ils Helena Higginbotham. G+. P12. $6.00

**MUNN, Norman L.** *Psychological Development: An Introduction...* 1938. Houghton Mifflin. 1st. 482p. prt gr cloth. G1. $65.00

**MUNNINGS, Alfred.** *Ballads & Poems.* 1957. London. Mus Pr. 1st trade. G. O3. $30.00

**MUNRO, Alice.** *Friends of My Youth.* 1990. Toronto. McClelland Stewart. 1st. F/NF clip. O11. $25.00

**MUNRO, Alice.** *Moon of Jupiter.* 1983. Knopf. 1st Am. F/NF. M25. $25.00

**MUNRO, Alice.** *Open Secrets.* 1994. NY. Knopf. 1st Am. F/dj. O11. $25.00

**MUNRO, Alice.** *Progress of Love.* 1986. Knopf. 1st Am. F/dj. O11. $30.00

**MUNRO, Alice.** *Progress of Love.* 1986. Toronto. McClelland Stewart. 1st Canadian. F/F. B3. $50.00

**MUNROE, Enid.** *Artist in the Garden: Guide to Creative & Natural Planting.* 1994. NY. Holt. 262p. F/dj. H10. $25.00

**MUNROE, Kurk.** *Fur-Seal's Tooth: Story of Alaskan Adventure.* 1894. NY/London. Harper. VG. P4. $45.00

**MUNROE, Ruth L.** *Schools of Psychoanalytic Thought: An Exposition, Critique.* 1955. NY. Dryden. 1st. lg 8vo. 670p. VG/dj. C14. $18.00

**MUNSON, Edward L.** *Theory & Practice of Military Hygiene.* 1901. NY. Wm Wood. 1st. ils. 971p. NF. E6. $65.00

**MUNSON, Ronald.** *Nothing Human.* 1991. Pocket. 1st. F/F. H11. $25.00

**MUNSTERBERG, Hugo.** *Die Willenshandlung: Beitrag zur Physiologischen...* 1888. JCB Mohr (Paul Siebeck). author's 1st book. 163p. contemporary bdg. xl. G1. $125.00

**MUNSTERBERG, Hugo.** *On the Witness Stand: Essays on Psychology & Crime.* 1908. McClure. 12mo. 269p. prt brn cloth. F. G1. $85.00

**MUNTHE, Axel.** *Vagaries.* 1898. London. 1st. T9. $60.00

**MUNTING, Roger.** *Hedges & Hurtles: A Special & Economic History...* 1987. London. Allen. 1st. VG/dj. O3. $25.00

**MUNZ, Philip A.** *Revision of the Genus Fuchsia (Onagraceae).* 1943. SF. 137p. B26. $27.50

**MURAKAMI, Haruki.** *Hard-Boiled Wonderland/End of the World.* 1991. NY. Kodansha. 1st. F/dj. M23. $25.00

**MURASAKI, Lady.** *Sacred Tree: Being Second Part of Tale of the Genji.* 1926. Houghton Mifflin. 1st Am. trans Arthur Waley. F/VG+. B4. $125.00

**MURATORI, Lodovico Antonio.** *Della Forza Della Fantasia Umana.* 1779 (1740). Venezia. Giovanni Gatti. 6th. 207p. later brd. G1. $175.00

**MURAVIN, Victor.** *Diary of Vikenty Angarov.* 1978. Newsweek Books. 1st Am. 8vo. F/dj. A2. $10.00

**MURCHIE, Guy.** *Song of the Sky.* 1954. Houghton Mifflin. ils. NF. S15. $10.00

**MURCHISON, Carl.** *Handbook of General Experimental Psychology.* 1934. Worcester, MA. Clark U. thick 8vo. 1125p. emb red cloth. VG. G1. $60.00

**MURDOCH, Iris.** *Bell.* 1984. London. Chatto Windus. Collected ed. rem mk. NF/clip. A14. $14.00

**MURDOCH, Iris.** *Existentialists & Mystics.* nd. Birmingham. 1/100. sgn. dj. T9. $100.00

**MURDOCH, Iris.** *Offical Rose.* 1962. NY. 1st. dj. T9. $25.00

**MURDOCH, Iris.** *Red & the Green.* 1965. London. Chatto Windus. 1st. VG+/dj. A14. $35.00

**MURDOCH, Iris.** *Red & the Green.* 1965. Viking. 1st. VG/dj. B11. $35.00

**MURDOCH, Iris.** *Unicorn.* 1963. London. Chatto Windus. 1st. VG+/dj. A14. $52.50

**MURDOCH, Iris.** *Unofficial Rose.* 1962. London. Chatto Windus. 1st. VG/dj. A14. $28.00

**MURDOCK, Eugene C.** *Mighty Casey All-American.* 1984. Greenwood. 1st. F. P8. $25.00

**MURDOCK, Harold.** *Earl Percy Dines Abroad.* 1924. Houghton Mifflin. 1st. tall 4to. 46p. VG. H13. $95.00

**MURIE, A.** *Naturalist in Alaska.* 1961. NY. photos/drawings. F/dj. M4. $18.00

**MURLE, Adolph.** *Wolves of Mt McKinley.* 1971 (1944). WA. 1st. 238p. VG. S15. $9.00

**MURLOCK, Dinah.** *Little Lame Prince & His Travelling Cloak.* 1937. Rand McNally. later prt. 128p. G. B18. $22.50

**MURLOCK, Dinah.** *Little Lame Prince & His Travelling Cloak...* 1909. Chicago. Rand McNally. ils Hope Dunlap. 121p. gilt gr cloth. VG+. B20. $50.00

**MURLOCK, Miss;** see Murlock, Dinah.

**MURPHY, Arthur.** *Works of Cornelius Tacitus.* 1805. London. Stockdale. 8 vol. tall 8vo. fld maps. uncut. H13. $495.00

**MURPHY, Earl.** *Water Purity: Study of Legal Control of Natural Resources.* 1961. Madison. 1st. 212p. dj. A13. $25.00

**MURPHY, Jim.** *Boys' War: Confederate & Union Soldiers Talk...* 1990. Clarion. 1st. photos. 110p. NF. P12. $20.00

**MURPHY, Margaret Deeds.** *Fondue, Chafing Dish & Casserole Cookery.* 1969. Hawthorne. G/dj. A16. $15.00

**MURPHY, Marguerite.** *Borrowed Alibi.* 1961. Avalon. 1st. xl. VG/G. G8. $12.50

**MURPHY, Robert Cushman.** *Bird Islands of Peru.* 1925. Putnam. 1st. xl. F3. $20.00

**MURPHY, Robert Cushman.** *Loggood for Grace: Whaling Brig Daisy 1912-1913.* 1947. Macmillan. 1st. 8vo. 290p. F/VG+. B20. $45.00

**MURPHY, Robert Cushman.** *Oceanic Birds of South America.* 1936. NY. 2 vol. ils after FL Jacques. gr cloth. F/case. B30. $50.00

**MURPHY, Sophia.** *Mitford Family Album.* 1985. London. 1st. photos. VG/dj. M17. $30.00

**MURPHY, Thomas D.** *Seven Wonderlands of the American West.* 1925. LC Page. 1st. 352p. VG. J2. $85.00

**MURRAY, A.H. Hallam.** *Sketches on the Old Road Through France to Florence.* 1906. Dutton. 2nd. 8vo. VG. A2. $40.00

**MURRAY, Albert.** *South to a Very Old Place.* 1971. McGraw Hill. 1st. VG/fair. B30. $20.00

**MURRAY, Beatrice;** see Posner, Richard.

**MURRAY, Frank.** *Beekeeper's Craft.* 1985. Lilliput. mini. 1st. 12 hand-colored ils. prt/sgn Armstrong. gr morocco. B24. $185.00

**MURRAY, Henry Alexander.** *Endeavors in Psychology: Selections...* 1981. Harper Row. 1st. 8vo. F/F. A2. $20.00

**MURRAY, Henry Alexander.** *Explorations in Personality.* 1938. NY. Oxford. heavy 8vo. 761p. red cloth. G1. $75.00

**MURRAY, J.** *System of Materia Medica.* 1821 (1815). 2 vol. full leather. VG. E6. $175.00

**MURRAY, James C.** *Spanish Chronicles of the Indies: Sixteenth Century.* 1994. NY. Twayne. 1st. 8vo. 188p. gr cloth. F/dj. P4. $25.00

**MURRAY, Janet.** *Traditional Scots Recipes: With Fine Feeling for Food.* 1972. Bramhall. G/dj. A16. $10.00

**MURRAY, John Fisher.** *Picturesque Tour of the River Thames in Its Western Course.* 1845. London. Henry G Bohn. 1st. 8vo. 356p. gr cloth. F. H5. $450.00

**MURRAY, Kenneth.** *Down to Earth: People of Appalachia...* (1974). Appalachia Consortium Pr. photos. 128p. VG. B10. $15.00

**MURRAY, Marian.** *Circus! From Rome to Ringling.* 1956. NY. Appleton Century Crofts. ils. 352p. O3/S5. $40.00

**MURRAY, Melvin L.** *Fostoria, Ohio Glass II.* 1992. self pub. 1st. 184p. AN/glossy wrp. H1. $45.00

**MURRAY, Ruth S.** *Valiant for the Truth; or, Some Memorials of George Fox...* 1883. NY. Burr. 12mo. 232p. cloth. G. V3. $20.00

**MURRAY, Sean.** *Ireland's Fight for Freedom & the Irish in the USA.* 1934. NY. Irish Workers Club/Workers Lib. NF/wrp. B2. $50.00

**MURRAY, William.** *Tip on a Dead Crab.* 1984. Viking. 1st. inscr/sgn twice. F/dj. D10. $75.00

**MURRY, MCBRIDE & WINTER.** *Black Adolescence, Current Issues & Annotated Bibliography.* 1990. Boston. GK Hall. 167p. F. A4. $35.00

**MURTZ, Harold A.** *Gun Digest Book of Exploded Firearms Drawings.* 1974. Northfield, IL. Digest Books. 1st. ils. F. A2. $20.00

**MUSCATINE, Doris.** *Book of California Wine.* 1984. U CA/Sotheby's. 1st. ils. 616p. VG/dj. S14. $30.00

**MUSE, Maude.** *Psychology for Nurses: A Text Book.* 1931 (1930). ils. VG. E6. $20.00

**MUSEUM OF MODERN ART.** *Life in Photography: Edward Steichen.* 1963. Doubleday. VG/dj. S5. $40.00

**MUSGRAVE, Clifford.** *Life in Brighton From Earliest Times to Present.* 1970. Archon. 1st. VG/dj. P3. $30.00

**MUSICK, John R.** *Hawaii...Our New Possessions.* 1898. NY/London. Funk Wagnall. 534p. red cloth. P4. $200.00

**MUSICK, John R.** *Stories of Missouri.* 1897. Am Book Co. 288p. gilt cloth. G. B18. $19.50

**MUSICK, Phil.** *Who Was Roberta?* 1974. Doubleday. 1st. VG/dj. P8. $85.00

**MUSIL. Alois.** *Middle Euphrates: A Topographical Itinerary.* 1927. NY. Oriental Studies #3. ils/2 pocket maps. 426p. cloth. G. Q2. $298.00

**MUSSOLINI, Benito.** *Cardinal's Mistress.* 1928. NY. Boni. 1st Am. NF/VG. B4. $125.00

**MUTSCHLER, Felix E.** *River Runner's Guide to the Canyons of Green & Colorado...* 1969. Denver. Powell Society Ltd. 8vo. 79p. VG+. F7. $12.50

**MUZZEY, David Saville.** *Thomas Jefferson.* 1918. Scribner. 1st. 319p. VG. B10. $25.00

**MYERS, Frederick William H.** *Human Personality & Its Survival of Bodily Death.* 1920 (1903). Longman Gr. 2 vol. 1st Am/6th prt. panelled navy cloth. G1. $100.00

**MYERS, Jeffrey.** *TE Lawrence: A Bibliography.* 1974. NY/London. Garland. 48p. cloth. VG. Q2. $27.00

**MYERS, John L.** *Arizona Governors, 1912-1990.* 1989. Heritage Pub. 1st. ils/index. 206p. NF/NF. B19. $20.00

**MYERS, Robert J.** *Cross of Frankenstein.* 1975. Lippincott. 1st. rem mk. VG/G. L1. $75.00

**MYERS, Tamar.** *Parsley, Sage, Rosemary & Crime.* 1995. Doubleday. 1st. inscr. F/dj. M23. $20.00

**MYERS & MYERS.** *Life & Nature Under the Tropics; or, Sketches of Travels...* 1871. NY. Appleton. 1st. 8vo. 330p. cloth. VG. O1. $150.00

**MYERS & SWETT.** *Trolleys to the Surf: Story of LA Pacific Railway.* 1976. Glendale. Interurbans. 1st. ils. 208p. cloth. dj. D11. $50.00

**MYKEL, A.W.** *Windchime Legacy.* 1980. St Martin. 1st. author's 1st book. NF/dj. A14. $42.00

**MYRER, Anton.** *Last Convertible.* 1978. Putnam. 1st. NF/clip. A14. $17.50

**MYRER, Anton.** *Violent Shore.* 1962. Little Brn. 1st. 503p. AN/VG. H1. $15.00

**MYRES, J. Arthur.** *Masters of Medicine: Historical Sketch of College...* 1968. St Louis. 1st. 921p. A13. $45.00

**MYRES, Sandra L.** *Westering Women & the Frontier Experience 1800-1915.* 1982. U NM. 1st. VG/dj. R8. $16.00

**MYRICK, David.** *Determined Mrs Rindge & Her Legendary Railroad...* 1996. Ventura Hist Soc. 53p. wrp. D11. $10.00

**MYRICK, Herbert.** *Turkeys & How to Grow Them.* 1912. Orange Judd. ils/index. 159p. xl. G. H10. $17.50

**MYRICK, Herbert.** *Turkeys & How to Grow Them: A Treatise...* (1918). NY. Judd. 12mo. ils. 159p+ads. VG+. M12. $50.00

**NABOKOV, Vladimir.** *Bend Sinister.* 1947. NY. Holt. 1st. VG/dj. A24. $175.00

**NABOKOV, Vladimir.** *Enchanter.* 1986. NY. Putnam. 1st. sgn. F/NF. A24. $85.00

**NABOKOV, Vladimir.** *Laughter in the Dark.* 1960. New Directions. 1st. VG/dj. B30. $25.00

**NABOKOV, Vladimir.** *Nabokov's Quartet.* 1966. NY. Phaedra. 1st. F/NF. B3. $75.00

**NABOKOV, Vladimir.** *Transparent Things.* 1972. McGraw Hill. 1st. NF/VG. B30. $25.00

**NABUCO, Carolina.** *Life of Joaquinn Nabuco.* 1950. Stanford. 8vo. 373p. map ep. bl cloth. VG/dj. P4. $35.00

**NADER, Ralph.** *Unsafe at Any Speed: Designed-In Dangers...Automobile.* 1965. NY. Grossman. 4th. inscr. NF/VG. B4. $150.00

**NADOLNY, Sten.** *Discovery of Slowness.* 1987. NY. Viking. 1st Am. F/dj. T11. $20.00

**NAEF.** *Collection of Alfred Stieglitz.* 1978. MOMA. ils/photos/pl. 544p. xl. A4. $75.00

**NAETHER, Carl A.** *Book of the Pigeon.* 1939. Phil. McKay. 1st. 8vo. VG/fair. A2. $25.00

**NAIPAUL, V.S.** *Among the Believers: An Islamic Journey.* 1981. NY. Knopf. 1st trade. 430p. VG. W1. $18.00

**NAIPAUL, V.S.** *Bend in the River.* 1979. Knopf. 1st Am. F/dj. A24. $55.00

**NAIPAUL, V.S.** *Guerrillas.* 1975. Knopf. 1st Am/2nd prt. G/dj. P12. $8.00

**NAIPAUL, V.S.** *Way in the World.* 1984. Knopf. 1st. VG/dj. M17. $17.50

**NAIR, P. Thankappan.** *Peacock: National Bird of India.* 1977. Calcutta. Firma KLM Private Ltd. 1st. 304p. VG/dj. N2. $25.00

**NAISBITT, John.** *Global Paradox.* 1994. Morrow. 1st. sm 4to. 394p. F/dj. W2. $35.00

**NAITUM, Duane.** *Songs From the Storyteller's Stone.* 1994. Seattle. Duane Niatum. sgn. F/bl ils wrp. O11. $35.00

**NAKAMURA, Gen.** *Kamisuki Mura Kodani.* 1970. Japan. 1/200. 50 prts w/105 extra leaves of samples. F/chemise. B24. $950.00

**NAKAYAMA, Shigeru.** *History of Japanese Astronomy: Chinese Background...* 1969. Cambridge. 8vo. 329p. VG/dj. K5. $45.00

**NALBANDOV, A.V.** *Reproductive Physiology.* 1964. Freeman. 2nd. 316p. xl. G. S5. $12.00

**NANCE, C. Roger.** *Archaeology of La Calsada.* 1992. Austin. U TX. 8vo. 234p. F/dj. P4. $45.00

**NANCY, Ted L.** *Letters From a Nut.* 1997. Avon. 1st. unp. NF/dj. W2. $35.00

**NANSEN, Fridtjof.** *Farthest North: Being Record of a Voyage of Exploration...* 1898. Harper. Popular ed. 679p. NF. B20. $85.00

**NANSEN, Fridtjof.** *In Northern Mists. Vol 1.* 1911. NY. Stokes. 1st. 384p. VG. B5. $95.00

**NAPIER, Robina.** *Johnsoniana: Anecdotes of Late Samuel Johnson, LLD...* 1884. London. Geo Bell. 1st. tan linen. H13. $145.00

**NAPIER, Simon.** *Back Woods Blues.* 1968. Blues Unlimited. 1st. NF/wrp. B2. $50.00

**NARANJO & ORSTEIN.** *On the Psychology of Meditation.* 1971. NY. VG/VG. M17. $40.00

**NASH, D.W.** *Pharoah of the Exodus.* 1863. London. JR Smith. 1st. 8vo. ftspc. 319p. gilt dk gr cloth. NF. H5. $200.00

**NASH, F.O.H.** *Kattie of the Balkans.* 1931. London/NY. 1st. F/dj. B20. $35.00

**NASH, Gerald D.** *American West Transformed: Impact of Second World War.* 1985. IN U. 1st. 8vo. 304p. F/dj. B20. $15.00

**NASH, Jay Robert.** *Look for the Woman.* 1981. Evans. 1st. photos. VG/dj. C9. $30.00

**NASH, Joseph.** *Mansions of England in the Olden Time.* 1912. London. Heinemann. New ed. 104 full-p pl. gilt red cloth. B20. $85.00

**NASH, N. Richard.** *Cry Macho.* 1975. Delacorte. 1st. NF/F. T12. $15.00

**NASH, Ogden.** *Good Intentions.* 1942. Little Brn. 1st. 8vo. 180p. F/NF. B20. $50.00

**NASH, Paul W.** *Gilded Fly: Short Stories.* 1993. Typographeum. 1/100. ils EL James. dj. T9. $35.00

**NASH, PUGACH & TOMASSON.** *Social Security: First Half Century.* 1988. Albuquerque. 1st. F/NF. N2. $15.00

**NASH & OFFEN.** *Dillinger, Dead or Alive.* 1970. Chicago. Regnery. 1st. ils. 204p. VG/dj. B5. $30.00

**NASHIF, Huda.** *Pre-School Education in the Arab World.* 1985. London/Sydney/Dover. Croom Helm. 1st. 8vo. 204p. NF/dj. W1. $18.00

**NASMITH, George G.** *Timothy Eaton.* 1923. McClelland Stewart. 1st. VG. P3. $35.00

**NASMYTH, Spike.** *2355 Days: A POW's Story.* 1991. NY. Orion. 1st. photos. 264p. F/dj. R11. $15.00

**NASTICK, Sharon.** *Mr Radgast Makes an Unexpected Journey.* 1981. NY. Crowell. 1st. 85p. F/dj. D4. $20.00

**NATHAN, Robert.** *Dunkirk: A Ballad.* 1942. Knopf. 1st. 8vo. 7p. VG/wrp. B20. $50.00

**NATHAN, Robert.** *Enchanted Voyage.* 1936. Knopf. 1st. 8vo. 187p. NF/dj. B20. $75.00

**NATHAN, Robert.** *Selected Poems.* 1935. Knopf. 1st. 38p. gilt bl cloth/paper label. F/dj. F1. $40.00

**NATHAN, Robert.** *Winter Tide: Sonnets & Poems.* 1940. Knopf. 1st. 1/2500. 54p. F/dj. B20. $50.00

**NATIONAL GEOGRAPHIC SOCIETY.** *Mountain Worlds.* 1988. WA. 1st. sq 4to. 320p. F/dj. M4. $30.00

**NAUDE, Gabriel.** *Instructions Concerning Erecting a Library...* 1903. Houghton Mifflin. 1/419. 12mo. 160p. quarter tan calf/marbled brd. F/case. H5. $200.00

**NAUEN, Elinor.** *Diamonds Are a Girl's Best Friend.* 1994. Faber. 1st. AN/dj. P8. $25.00

**NAUGLE & SHERRY.** *Concordance to the Poems of Samuel Johnson.* 1973. Ithaca. Cornell. 1st. Eng/Latin text. F. H13. $45.00

**NAUMANN, Rudolf.** *Architectur Kleinasiens.* 1971. Tubingen. Wasmuth. ils/maps/2 pocket maps. 508p. cloth. VG/case. Q2. $75.00

**NAUMOFF, Lawrence.** *Night of the Weeping Women.* 1988. Atlantic Monthly. 1st. author's 1st book. rem mk. NF/F. B3. $35.00

**NAUMOFF, Lawrence.** *Silk Hope.* 1994. Harcourt. 1st. F/F. H11. $20.00

**NAUMOV, N.P.** *Ecology of Animals.* 1972. U IL. 650p. xl. VG. S5. $75.00

**NAUS, Burt.** *Visionary Leadership.* 1992. Josse Bass. 1st. sm 4to. 237p. F/dj. W2. $20.00

**NAVA, Michael.** *How Town.* 1990. Harper Row. 1st. NF/dj. G8. $12.50

**NAVE, Orville.** *Nave's Topical Bible.* 1970. Moody. 1464p. VG. B29. $13.00

**NAVRATILOVA & VECSEY.** *Martina.* 1985. Knopf. 4th. photos. 287p. VG/dj. P12. $8.00

**NAWWAB, Ismail I.** *Aramco & Its World, Arabia & the Middle East.* 1918. Saudi Arabia. Aramco. 2nd. 4to. 275p. VG/dj. B11. $25.00

**NAWWAB, Ismail.** *Aramco & Its World: Arabia & the Middle East.* 1918. Saudi Arabia. Aramco. 2nd. F/dj. B9. $20.00

**NAYLOR, Gloria.** *Bailey's Cafe.* 1992. HBJ. 1st. sgn. F/dj. M25. $50.00

**NAYLOR, Gloria.** *Linden Hills.* 1985. Ticknor Fields. 1st. F/dj. A24/H11. $45.00

NAYLOR, Gloria. *Mama Day*. 1988. Ticknor. 1st. F/clip. H11. $35.00

NAYLOR, Gloria. *Women of Brewster Place*. 1982. Viking. 1st. author's 1st book. NF/NF. B3. $300.00

NAYLOR, James Ball. *In the Days of St Clair*. 1908. Saalfield. ils. 420p. decor cloth. VG. B18. $19.50

NAYLOR, James Ball. *Ralph Marlowe*. 1901. Akron. 4th. 412p. G. B18. $15.00

NAYLOR, Maria. *Authentic Indian Designs*. 1975. Dover. ils. G. A19. $25.00

NEAL, Larry. *Hoodoo Hollerin' Bebop Ghosts*. 1974. WA, DC. Howard U. 1st. inscr/dtd 1975. F/NF. L3. $40.00

NEARING, Scott. *Twilight of Empire*. 1930. Vanguard. 1st. VG. B2. $25.00

NEBENZAHL, Kenneth. *Bibliography of Printed Battle Plans...1775-1795*. 1975. Chicago. NF/dj. M10. $22.50

NEBLETTE, C.B. *Photography: Its Principles & Practice*. 1943. London. Chapman Hall. 4th/rpt. 8vo. ils. 865p. G. K5. $50.00

NECKER, C. *Natural History of Cats*. 1970. Barnes. 8vo. ils. 326p. NF/G. M12. $22.50

NEE, Watchman. *Spiritual Man*. 1969. Christian Fellowship. 3 vol. VG/wrp. B29. $12.50

NEEDHAM, Joseph. *Science, Religion & Reality*. 1955. NY. 355p. A13. $40.00

NEEDHAM, Richard. *Wit & Wisdom of Richard Needham*. 1977. Edmonton. Hurtig. 1st. sgn. NF/wrp. A26. $10.00

NEELY, Barbara. *Blanche Among the Talented Tenth*. 1994. St Martin. 1st. F/dj. C9. $30.00

NEELY, Richard. *Madness of the Heart*. 1976. NY. Crowell. 1st. NF/F. H11. $25.00

NEELY, Robert D. *Laws of Dickens & Their Clerks*. 1938. Boston. Christopher Pub. red cloth. M11. $65.00

NEERGAARD, Ebbe. *Story of Danish Film*. 1963. Denmark. Danish Inst. photos. VG/wrp. C9. $48.00

NEF, Karl. *Outline of History of Music*. 1964 (1935). NY. Columbia. 2nd. 400p. VG/glassine. C5. $12.50

NEFF, Terry A. *Proud Heritage: 2 Centuries of American Art...* 1987. Chicago. ils. VG/dj. M17. $40.00

NEFFLEN, John. *Method of Increasing the Yield of the Milch-Cow*. 1853. Phil. Rogers. fld pl. 54p. A10. $45.00

NEFZAWI, Shaykh. *Perfumed Garden*. 1964. NY. Castle. trans Sir Richard Burton. 128p. VG/dj. W1. $18.00

NEHRBASS, Richard. *Perfect Death for Hollywood*. 1991. Harper Collins. 1st. F/F. H11. $25.00

NEIDELMAN, Edna H. *American's Lincoln: From the Hearts of Many Poets*. (1966). Pageant. 135p. VG/dj. B10. $15.00

NEIDER, Charles. *Great West*. Bonanza. rpt. ils. 457p. VG/dj. B19. $20.00

NEIDER, Charles. *Great West*. 1958. Coward McCann. ils/map ep. VG/dj. J2. $68.00

NEIHARDT, John G. *Black Elk Speaks*. 1932. NY. Morrow. 1st. 280p. G+. B5. $75.00

NEIHARDT, John G. *Poetic Values: Their Reality & Our Need of Them*. 1925. Macmillan. 1st. F. A18. $40.00

NEIHARDT, John G. *Sixth Grandfather: Black Elk's Teachings*. 1984. Lincoln, NE. VG/dj. A19. $25.00

NEIHARDT, John G. *Song of Hugh Glass*. 1915. Macmillan. 1st. F. A18. $50.00

NEIHARDT, John G. *Splendid Wayfaring: Story of Exploits...Jedediah Smith...* 1924. NY. later prt. 290p. B18. $37.50

NEIL, M. *Calendar of Dinners With 615 Recipes Including Story Crisco*. 1919 (1913). G+. E6. $13.00

NEILL, John. *Outlines of the Arteries With Short Description*. 1945. Phil. Barrington. pres. 6 hand-colored pl. 30p. VG. G7. $95.00

NEILL, John. *Outlines of the Veins & Lymphatics With Short Descriptions*. 1847. 1st. ils. VG. E6. $125.00

NEIMAN, LeRoy. *Horses*. 1979. Abrams. sgn pres/dtd. ils. 350p. D2. $395.00

NELSON, Albert F.J.H. *There Is Life on Mars*. 1956. NY. Citadel. 8vo. 152p. VG/dj. K5. $30.00

NELSON, Arty. *Technicolor Pulp*. 1995. NY. Warner. 1st. author's 1st book. F/F. H11. $30.00

NELSON, B. *Galapagos: Islands of Birds*. 1968. NY. 338p. cloth. F/dj. C12. $35.00

NELSON, Donald A. *Television Antennas: Design, Construction, Installation...* 1951. Indianapolis. Howard Sams. 8vo. VG/wrp. A2. $14.00

NELSON, Gil. *Trees of Florida*. 1994. Sarasota. ils. 352p. sc. AN. B26. $20.00

NELSON, Miles. *Personal Recollections of General Nelson Miles*. 1897. Chicago. Werner. F. A19. $350.00

NELSON, Nancy. *Any Time, Any Place, Any River*. 1991. Flagstaff. Red Lake Books. 1st. 8vo. 83p. stiff wrp. F7. $10.00

NELSON, Robert L. *Partners With Power, Social Transformation of Lg Law Firm*. 1988. Berkeley. M11. $35.00

NELSON, Thomas Jr. *Letters of..., Governor of Virginia*. 1874. Richmond. 1st. 1/500. later cloth. VG. M8. $250.00

NELSON, William E. *Americanization of the Common Law...1760-1830*. 1975. Cambridge. Harvard. M11. $35.00

NELSON, Willie. *Autobiography: Willie*. 1988. S&S. 334p. G/dj. C5. $12.50

NEMEC, David. *Beer & Whisky League*. 1994. NY. Lyons Burford. 1st. F/dj. G10. $18.00

NEPOS, Cornelius. *Quae Extant*. 1684. Leyden. Jacobi Hackii. 16mo. 306p. contemporary vellum. K1. $100.00

NERUDA, Pablo. *Extravagaria*. 1974. NY. Farrar. 1st Am. F/dj. B2. $35.00

NERUDA, Pablo. *Ode to Typography*. 1977. Labyrinth Eds. 1/100. tall 4to. frenchfold. AN/gray marbled wrp/chemise. B24. $950.00

NESBIT, E. *Daphne in Fitzroy Street*. 1909. Doubleday Page. 1st. red cloth/label. VG/dj. B27. $150.00

NESBIT, William. *How to Hunt With the Camera*. 1926. NY. 337p. VG. A17. $30.00

NESBITT, Alexander. *Lettering: History & Technique of Lettering as Design*. 1950. Prentice Hall. 1st. 4to. 300p. F/dj. O10. $30.00

NESMITH, J.H. *Soldiers Manual*. 1963. Washington. 73p. VG. S16. $25.00

NESMITH, Robert I. *Dig for Pirate Treasure*. 1958. Bonanza. 8vo. 302p. VG/dj. B11. $18.00

NESSELL, C.W. *Restless Spirit*. 1963. Minneapolis, MN. 112p. wht cloth. H6. $24.00

NESTLE, Joan. *Restricted Country*. 1987. Ithaca. Firebrand. 1st. sgn. 189p. VG+. A25. $20.00

NETHERTON & NETHERTON. *Fairfax County in Virginia: Pictorial History*. (1986). Donning. photos. 216p. VG/VG. B10. $35.00

NEUBERGER, Max. *Essays in the History of Medicine*. 1930. NY. 1/300. 210p. A13. $50.00

NEUBERGER, Max. *History of Medicine. Vol 1*. 1910. London. Frowde. 1st. 4to. G7. $150.00

NEUGEBAUER, O. *Astronomy & History: Selected Essays*. 1983. Springer-Verlag. ils. 538p. VG/wrp. K5. $40.00

**NEUGEBOREN, Jay.** *Listen Ruben Fontanez.* 1968. Houghton. 1st. VG/dj. S13. $12.00

**NEUGEBOREN, Jay.** *Stolen Jew.* 1981. HRW. 1st. F/dj. T12. $45.00

**NEUMANN, Robert.** *Passion: Six Literary Marriages.* 1932. Harcourt Brace. 1st Am. 8vo. 213p. F/dj. B20. $25.00

**NEUNZIG, H.H.** *Moths of America North of Mexico...* 1990. lg 8vo. ils/pl. 165p. NF. B1. $40.00

**NEUSTADT, Egon.** *Lamps of Tiffany.* (1970). Fairfield. folio. 224p. F/clip. H1. $200.00

**NEVE, J.L.** *Churches & Sects of Christendom.* 1944. Lutheran. 509p. G. B29. $13.50

**NEVEROV, Howard.** *Federigo; or, The Power of Love.* 1954. Atlantic/Little Brn. 1st. NF/VG. L3. $55.00

**NEVILLE, Dorothy.** *Carr P Collins, Man on the Move.* 1963. Dallas, TX. Park Pr. inscr/sgn Collins. 185p. F. W2. $20.00

**NEVILLE, Emily Cheney.** *Fogerty.* 1969. Harper Row. early ed. 182p. cloth. F/dj. D4. $30.00

**NEVIN, David.** *Mexican War.* 1979. Time-Life Old West. 1st. maps. 240p. F. M4. $20.00

**NEVIN, David.** *1812.* 1996. NY. Tom Doherty. 1st. bl cloth. F/dj. T11. $25.00

**NEVINS, A.** *Polk: Diary of a President 1845-1849...* 1952. NY. 512p. NF/poor. M4. $30.00

**NEVINS, Francis M. Jr.** *120-Hour Clock.* 1986. NY. Walker. 1st. F/NF. A23. $25.00

**NEVINSON, Henry W.** *More Changes, More Chances.* ca 1925. NY. Harcourt Brace. 1st. ils. 427p. VG. W1. $45.00

**NEVIUS, Laird.** *Discovery of Modern Anaesthesia.* 1894. NY. 1st. 112p. A13. $250.00

**NEW ENGLAND YEARLY MEETING.** *Faith & Practice of New England Yearly Meeting...* 1950. Cambridge, MA. 12mo. 158p. wrp. V3. $4.00

**NEW ENGLAND YEARLY MEETING.** *Rules of Discipline of Yearly Meeting Held on Rhode Island.* 1840. New Bedford. Lindsey. 156p. worn leather. V3. $16.00

**NEW YORK YEARLY MEETING.** *Book of Discipline of New York Yearly Meeting...* 1930. Knickerbocker. revised. 24mo. 93p. VG. V3. $15.00

**NEWBERRY, Clare Turlay.** *Barkis.* 1938. Harper. 1st. 12mo. 30p. VG/dj. D1. $150.00

**NEWBERRY, Clare Turlay.** *Marshmallow.* 1942. Harper. 1st. lg 4to. pict dj. R5. $150.00

**NEWBOLT, Frank.** *Etchings of Van Dyck.* 1906. London. Newnes/Scribner. ils/pl. cloth spine/brd. D2. $45.00

**NEWBOUND & NEWBOUND.** *Southern Potteries, Inc. Blue Ridge Dinnerware.* 1980. Collector Books. 1st. 8vo. 120p. VG/stiff wrp. H1. $16.00

**NEWCOMB, Harvey.** *Negro Pew: Being an Inquiry Concerning Propriety...* 1837. Boston. Knapp. 1st. 8vo. 108p. O1. $200.00

**NEWCOMB, Rexford.** *Old Mission Churches & Historic Houses of California.* 1925. Phil. Lippincott. 1st. ils. 363p. cloth. D11. $100.00

**NEWELL, R.C.** *Biology of Intertidal Animals.* 1970. Am Elsevier. 555p. xl. G. S5. $50.00

**NEWELL, William Wells.** *Games & Songs of American Children.* 1883. Harper. 1st. 242p. beige cloth. VG. B20. $150.00

**NEWELL & SMITH.** *Mighty MO: The USS Missouri.* 1969. NY. Bonanza. 3rd. sm 4to. bl cloth. NF/dj. M7. $20.00

**NEWHAFER, Richard.** *No More Bugles in the Sky.* 1966. NAL. stated 1st. VG/dj. R11. $60.00

**NEWHALL, Nancy.** *Elequent Light.* 1963. SF. Sierra Club. 1st. photos. F/dj. T10. $150.00

**NEWHALL & NEWHALL.** *Master of Photography.* 1958. Braziller. VG/dj. S5. $25.00

**NEWHAN, Ross.** *California Angels.* 1982. S&S. 1st. sgn Gene Autry. F/dj. P8. $100.00

**NEWMAN, Christopher.** *Dead End Game.* 1994. Putnam. 1st. F/dj. P8. $15.00

**NEWMAN, Daisy.** *I Take Thee, Serenity.* 1982. Houghton Mifflin. BC. 314p. VG/dj. V3. $9.50

**NEWMAN, Daisy.** *Procession of Friends: Quakers in America.* 1972. Doubleday. 1st. 460p. xl. dj. V3. $18.00

**NEWMAN, G.F.** *Sir, You Bastard.* 1970. S&S. 1st. F/F. H11. $30.00

**NEWMAN, John Henry.** *Apologia pro Vita Sua...* 1931. Macmillan. Modern Readers series. 1st. 380p. G/dj. H10. $17.50

**NEWMAN, Katherine S.** *Declining Fortunes.* 1993. Harper Collins. 1st. sm 4to. 257p. F/dj. W2. $35.00

**NEWMAN, Kim.** *Anno Dracula.* 1992. London. S&S. 1st. sgn label on title p. F/dj. M15. $150.00

**NEWMAN, Kim.** *Anno Dracula.* 1993. Carroll Graff. 1st Am. F/dj. S18. $40.00

**NEWMAN, Ralph.** *Abraham Lincoln's Last Full Measure of Devotion.* 1981. Chicago. Monastery Hill. mini. 1/299. sgn. gilt bl leather/case. B24. $200.00

**NEWMAN, Ralph.** *Lincoln for the Ages.* 1960. Doubleday. 1st. 519p. gray cloth. F/VG. F1. $25.00

**NEWMAN, Ralph.** *Man & Nature, Selected Essays of Giorgio Del Vecchio.* 1969. Notre Dame. cloth. M11. $45.00

**NEWMAN, Ralph.** *Selective Checklist of Carl Sandburg's Writings.* 1952. Chicago. 1st thus/offprt. 1/500. NF. M8. $28.00

**NEWQUIST, Roy.** *Conversations With Joan Crawford.* 1980. Citadel. 1st. NF/dj. T12. $15.00

**NEWSOM, Samuel.** *Dwarfed Tree Manual for Westerners.* 1964 (1960). Tokyo. 5th. ils. 133p. VG/dj. B26. $20.00

**NEWTON, A. Edward.** *Bibliography & Pseudo-Bibliography.* 1936. Phil. U PA. 2nd. VG/G. B5. $27.50

**NEWTON, A. Edward.** *Dr Johnson, a Play.* 1923. Boston. Atlantic Monthly. 1st. ils. H13. $45.00

**NEWTON, A. Edward.** *Rare Books, Original Drawings, Autograph Letters of...* 1941. Parke-Bernet Galleries. 4 vol. sm 4to. F/dj as issued. O10. $135.00

**NEYHART, Louise A.** *Henry's Lincoln.* 1958 (1945). Holiday House. 1st thus. ils Chas Banks Wilson. F/fair. M5. $10.00

**NGUYEN, Thai.** *Is South Vietnam Viable?* 1962. Manila. Carmelo & Bauermann. 314p. VG. R11. $75.00

**NIATUM, Duane.** *Ascending Red Cedar Moon.* 1973. NY. Harper Row. ARC/1st. inscr. F/dj. L3. $125.00

**NIBLACK, Albert P.** *Coast Indians of Southern Alaska & N British Columbia...* 1887. GPO. 100+ pl/fld charts. 161p. brn cloth. VG. O1. $75.00

**NICHOL, B.P.** *Once: A Lullaby.* 1986. Greenwillow. 1st. obl 8vo. unp. F/dj. T5. $30.00

**NICHOLLS, Phillip.** *Hemeopathy & the Medical Profession.* 1988. London. 1st. 298p. A13. $30.00

**NICHOLS, Anne.** *Abie's Irish Rose.* 1929. Grosset Dunlap. MTI. F/NF. B4. $100.00

**NICHOLS, John.** *American Blood.* 1987. NY. Holt. 1st. inscr. F/dj. B2. $45.00

**NICHOLS, John.** *Fragile Beauty: John Nichols' Milagro Country...* 1987. Gibbs Smith. 1st. ils. 146p. NF/dj/swrp. B19. $30.00

**NICHOLS, John.** *Ghost in the Music.* 1979. Holt. 1st. inscr/dtd 1987. F/dj. M25. $35.00

**NICHOLS, John.** *Ghost in the Music.* 1979. NY. Holt. 1st. NF/F. H11. $30.00

**NICHOLS, John.** *Magic Journey.* 1978. HRW. 1st. F/NF. B4. $375.00

**NICHOLS, John.** *Minor Lives: A Collection of Biographies...* 1971. Harvard. 1st. portrait ftspc. 367p. gilt bl cloth. F/dj. H13. $95.00

**NICHOLS, John.** *Nirvana Blues.* 1981. HRW. 1st. F/dj. T12. $85.00

**NICHOLS, Leigh;** see Koontz, Dean R.

**NICHOLS, P.** *Cancer: Its Proper Treatment: Value of Escharotics...* 1941. VG. E6. $18.00

**NICHOLS, R.F.** *Franklin Pierce: Young Hickory of the Granite Hills.* 1958. Penn State. ils. 625p. NF. M4. $40.00

**NICHOLS & O'NEAL.** *Architecture in Virginia, 1776-1959: Old Dominion's...* (1958). VA Mus Fine Arts. unp. sbdg. VG. B10. $25.00

**NICHOLSON, William S.** *Historic Homes & Churches of Virginia's Eastern Shore.* (1984). Atlantic. ils/photos. 176p. VG/VG. B10. $45.00

**NICKERSON, Jane.** *Florida Cookbook.* 1973. Gainsville, FL. 1st. VG/dj. A16. $12.00

**NICKLAUS, Jack.** *My 55 Ways to Lower Your Golf Score.* 1964. S&S. 1st. ils. NF/dj. P12. $12.00

**NICOL, D.M.** *Immortal Emperor: Life & Legend of Constantine Palaiologus.* 1992. Cambridge. 12 pl. 148p. cloth. VG/dj. Q2. $26.50

**NICOLSON, Harold.** *Paul Verlaine.* 1921. Boston. 1st Am. author's 1st book. G/dj. Q1. $175.00

**NICOLSON, Nigel.** *Flight of the Mind/Question of Things Happening...* 1975 & 1976. London. Hogarth. 2 vol. 1st. VG/dj. M10. $50.00

**NIEBUHR, Rheinhold.** *Nature & Destiny of Man: A Christian Interpretation...* 1941-43. Scribner. 2 vol. 1st Am. G. H10. $35.00

**NIEKRO & NIEKRO.** *Knuckleballs.* 1986. Freundlich. 1st. F/dj. P8. $25.00

**NIELSEN, Helen.** *After Midnight.* 1966. Gollancz. 1st Eng. VG/G. G8. $17.50

**NIELSEN, Helen.** *Fifth Caller.* 1959. Morrow. 1st. VG/dj. G8. $15.00

**NIELSEN, Kay.** *In Powder & Crinoline Fairy Tales.* 1913. Hodder Stoughton. 1st. lg 4to. teg. glassine dj/pub box. R5. $2,000.00

**NIETHAMMER, Carolyn.** *Daughters of the Earth.* 1977. Macmillan. F/dj. A19. $25.00

**NIGHBERT, David.** *Strikezone.* 1989. St Martin. 1st. F/dj. P8. $25.00

**NIGHTINGALE, Gay.** *Growing Cyclamen.* 1982. Portland. ils/photos. F/dj. B26. $20.00

**NIJINSKA & RAWLINSON.** *Bronislava Nijinska: Early Memoirs.* 1981. HRW. 1st. F/dj. T12. $60.00

**NIKOLSKII, George V.** *Theory of Fish Populatin Dynamics.* 1969. Oliver Boyd. 323p. xl. VG. S5. $25.00

**NILES, Blair.** *Colombia: Land of Miracles.* 1924. NY. Century. 1st. 389p. cloth. dj. F3. $15.00

**NIMS, John Frederick.** *Iron Pastoral.* 1947. NY. Wm Sloane. 1st. inscr. author's 1st book. F/dj. B2. $35.00

**NIMS-SMITH, Dwight L.** *Photographer & the River, 1889-90.* 1967. Santa Fe. 1st. 1/600. 12mo. VG/dj. F7. $100.00

**NIN, Anais.** *Henry & June.* 1986. HBJ. 1st. F/NF. B3. $20.00

**NIRVANA.** *Chocolate Making: Comprehensive Treatise.* ca 1920s?. London. 16mo. photos/ads. 167p. VG. E6. $35.00

**NISBET, H.B.** *Herder & the Philosophy & History of Science.* 1970. Cambridge. 1st. 358p. A13. $25.00

**NISSEN, Claus.** *Die Botanische Buchillustration, Ihre Geschichte...* nd. 2 vol in 1. 1/225. 4to. 2387 entries. F. A4. $250.00

**NISWANDER, Adam.** *Charm.* 1993. Phoenix. Integra. 1st. sgn. author's 1st novel. F/dj. T2. $25.00

**NIVEN, J.** *Martin Van Buren: Romantic Age of American Politics.* 1983. OUP. 1st. ils. F/dj. M4. $35.00

**NIVEN & POURNELLE.** *Football.* 1985. Ballantine. 1st. F/dj. S13. $15.00

**NIXON, Alan.** *Attack on Vienna.* 1972. St Martin. 1st. F/dj. P3. $13.00

**NIXON, Alan.** *Item 7.* 1970. S&S. 1st. F/dj. P3. $13.00

**NIXON, Cornelia.** *Now You See It.* 1991. Boston. Little Brn. 1st. author's 1st book. F/dj. H11. $20.00

**NIXON, John Lowery.** *Dark & Deadly Pool.* 1987. Delacorte. 2nd. G+/dj. B36. $8.00

**NIXON, N.F.** *Subliminal Perception: Nature of a Controversy.* 1917. London. McGraw Hill. 362p. NF/dj. G1. $88.00

**NIXON, Pat.** *Century of Medicine in San Antonio.* 1936. San Antonio. 1st. 405p. A13. $65.00

**NIXON, Paul.** *Warath.* 1987. Kenthurst, NSW. photos. 80p. F. B26. $27.50

**NIXON, Richard M.** *Inaugural Address of...,  President of the United States.* (1969). Worcester. St Onge. 1/1500. photo ftspc. 44p. aeg. gilt bl leather. B24. $30.00

**NIXON, Richard M.** *Real War.* 1980. NY. Warner. 341p. map ep. F/NF. R11. $17.00

**NIXON, Richard M.** *Six Crises.* 1962. Doubleday. 1st. inscr. 8vo. 460p. VG+/dj. B20. $250.00

**NOAKES, Aubry.** *Sportsmen in a Landscape.* 1994. Lippincott. 1st Am. VG/dj. O3. $45.00

**NOAKES, Vivien.** *Edward Lear, a Biography.* 1986. 4to. ils/60 mc pl. 216p. F/F. A4. $95.00

**NOAKES, Vivien.** *Painter Edward Lear.* 1991. Newton Abbot. 1st. dj. T9. $20.00

**NOBLE, Daniel.** *Brain & Its Physiology...* 1995. NY. Classics of Neurology/Neurosurgery Lib. sm 8vo. G1. $65.00

**NOBLE, Lorraine.** *Four-Star Scripts: Actual Shooting Scripts...* 1936. Doubleday Doran. 1st. VG+. C9. $60.00

**NOBLE, Peter.** *Fabulous Orson Welles.* 1956. Hutchinson. 1st. photos. VG/clip. C9. $180.00

**NOBLE-IVES, Sarah.** *Story of Teddy the Bear.* ca 1923. Springfield, MA. lg 4to. 6 full-p mc pl. pict brd. R5. $225.00

**NOCK, O.** *World Atlas of Railways.* 1983. NY. Bonanza. rpt. VG/dj. B9. $20.00

**NOEL, Lucie.** *James Joyce & Paul L Leon.* 1950. Gotham Book Mart. 1st. F/bl prt wrp. M24. $125.00

**NOEL, Theophilus.** *Autobiography & Reminiscences of Theophilus Noel.* 1904. Noel. 348p. gilt cloth. D11. $225.00

**NOEL-BAKER, F.** *Spy Web.* 1955. 1st. intro Philbrick. F/G+. E6. $15.00

**NOFI, Albert A.** *Opening Guns: Ft Sumter to Bull Run...Vol I.* 1988. Gallery/WH Smith. 1st. NF/dj. A14. $14.00

**NOGUCHI, Yone.** *American Diary of a Japanese Girl. By Miss Glory.* 1902. NY. Stokes. lg 8vo. ils. woven bamboo spine/prt brd. K1. $150.00

**NOGUCHI, Yone.** *Selected Poems of...* 1921. Four Seas/Elkin Mathews. 1st Am. teg. NF/case. Q1. $250.00

**NOHL, J.** *Black Death: A Chronicle of the Plague.* 1924. NY. ils/index. 284p. VG. B5. $35.00

**NOLAN, Keith William.** *Battle for Hue: Tet, 1968.* 1983. Novato. Presidio Pr. 201p. NF/VG. R11. $15.00

**NOLAN, Liam.** *Small Man of Nanataki.* 1966. Dutton. 1st. sm 8vo. 162p. NF/VG. W2. $10.00

**NOLAN, William A.** *Making of a Surgeon.* 1970. NY. Random. 1st. 8vo. VG/dj. A2. $8.50

**NOLAN, William A.** *Making of a Surgeon.* 1970. Random. BC. 8vo. F/dj. A2. $8.50

**NOLAN, William A.** *Surgeon's World.* 1972. Random. 1st. 8vo. 366p. NF/VG. C14. $15.00

**NOLAN, William F.** *Hammett: A Life at the Edge.* 1983. Congdon Weed. 1st. VG/dj. P3. $17.00

**NOLAN, William F.** *McQueen.* 1984. Congdon Weed. 1st. NF/dj. T11. $10.00

**NOLL, Mark A.** *Scandal of the Evangelical Mind.* 1994. IVP. 274p. VG/dj. B29. $12.50

**NOON, Jeff.** *Pollen.* 1996. NY. Crown. 1st. F/F. H11. $30.00

**NOON, Jeff.** *Vurt.* 1995. NY. Crown. 1st Am. author's 1st book. F/dj. A24/H11. $30.00

**NORDANG, Bruno.** *Patagonia Year.* 1938. Knopf. 1st Am. 253p. dj. F3. $20.00

**NORDHOFF, Charles.** *California: For Health, Pleasure & Residence.* 1873. Harper. 255p. pict cloth. B18. $65.00

**NORDHOFF, Charles.** *Communistic Societies of the United States.* 1875. Harper. 1st. B2. $150.00

**NORDHOFF, Charles.** *Communistic Societies of the United States.* 1962 (1875). rpt. ils/map. 439p. F/dj. M4. $50.00

**NORDHOFF, Charles.** *History of Playing Cards.* 1977. Buffalo. Hillside. 1/250. hand-colored ils. 48p. orange pict cloth. B24. $95.00

**NORDHOFF, Charles.** *Peninsular California: Some Account of the Climate...* 1888. NY. Harper. 1st. ils/maps. 130p. D11. $100.00

**NORDYKE, Lewis.** *John Wesley Hardin: Texas Gunman.* 1957. Morrow. 1st. 278p. VG/dj. B5. $25.00

**NORFLEET, Frank J.** *Norfleet: Actual Experiences of a Texas Rancher's...Chase...* 1924. Sugar Land, TX. 8vo. ils. cloth. VG. O1. $65.00

**NORGAARD, Erik.** *With Love to You: History of the Erotic Postcard.* 1969. Clarkson Potter. 1st Am. ils. 120p. pict brd. B18. $20.00

**NORMAN, Charles.** *Hornbeam Tree & Other Poems.* 1988. Holt. 1st. ils Ted Rand. F/dj. D4. $25.00

**NORMAN, Howard.** *Bird Artist.* 1994. FSG. 1st. F/dj. R14. $45.00

**NORMAN, Howard.** *Bird Artist.* 1994. London. Faber. true 1st. 8vo. F/dj. S9. $85.00

**NORMAN, Howard.** *How Glooskap Outwits the Ice Giants.* 1989. Little Brn. 1st. ils Michael McCurdy. VG/NF. A24. $45.00

**NORMAN, Howard.** *Kiss in the Hotel Joseph Conrad & Other Stories.* 1989. NY. Summit. 1st. author's 1st collection short fiction. F/dj. O11. $50.00

**NORMAN, Howard.** *Northern Lights.* 1987. Summit. 1st. author's 1st book. NF/NF. B3. $175.00

**NORMAN, Howard.** *Who-Paddled-Backward-With Trout.* 1987. Little Brn. 1st. F/dj. O11. $100.00

**NORMAN, John.** *Medicine in the Ghetto.* 1969. NY. 1st. 333p. A13. $50.00

**NORMAN, Rick.** *Fielder's Choice.* 1991. August. 1st. sgn. F/dj. P8. $45.00

**NORRIE, Ian.** *Traveller's Guide to Celebration of London.* 1984. NY. Historical Times. 1st Am. 8vo. 217p. F. B11. $15.00

**NORRIS, Charles.** *Bread.* 1923. Dutton. 1st. inscr. G. M19. $25.00

**NORRIS, Frank.** *McTeague: A Story of San Francisco.* 1899. Doubleday McClure. 1st/2nd issue. wht stp red cloth. F. M24. $300.00

**NORRIS, Joel.** *Serial Killers.* 1988. NY. Dolphin. 1st. F/dj. A23. $30.00

**NORRIS, Kathleen.** *Belle-Mere.* 1931. Doubleday. 1st. F/NF. B2. $50.00

**NORRIS, Kathleen.** *Certain People of Importance.* 1922. Doubleday. 1st. F/dj. B2. $75.00

**NORRIS, Kathleen.** *Little Ships.* 1925. Doubleday. 1st. F/dj. B2. $40.00

**NORRIS, Kathleen.** *Red Silence.* 1929. Doubleday. 1st. F/dj. B2. $60.00

**NORRIS, Kenneth S.** *Hawaiian Spinner Dolphin.* 1994. CA U. 408p. F/dj. S15. $30.00

**NORRIS & WASHINGTON.** *Last of the Scottsboro Boys.* 1979. NY. 1st. 281p. VG/dj. B5. $20.00

**NORTH, Andrew;** see Norton, Andre.

**NORTH, Anthony;** see Koontz, Dean R.

**NORTH, Arthur Walbridge.** *Camp & Camino in Lower California: A Record...* 1910. Baker Taylor. 1st. ils/index. 346p. VG+. B19. $45.00

**NORTH, Darian.** *Criminal Seduction.* 1993. Dutton. 1st. author's 1st book. NF/F. H11. $25.00

**NORTH, Dick.** *Lost Patrol.* 1978. Alaska Northwest. 1st. ils. 138p. VG. S14. $10.00

**NORTH, Francis.** *Lord Keeper's Speech to Mr Serjeant Saunders...* 1682. London. modern 3-quarter calf/marbled brd. M11. $450.00

**NORTH, Mary Remsen.** *Down the Colorado River, by a Lone Girl Scout.* 1930. Putnam. 1st. 8vo. orange cloth. VG/dj. F7. $75.00

**NORTH, Sterling.** *Abe Lincoln: Log Cabin to White House.* 1956. Random. 5th. Landmark Book #61. VG/dj. P12. $15.00

**NORTHEND, Mary Harrod.** *Historic Doorways of Old Salem.* 1926. Houghton Mifflin. 1st. photos. 96p. gilt cloth. B18. $22.50

**NORTHROP, Henry Davenport.** *Indian Horrors; or, Massacres by Red Men...* ca 1900. Phil. Nat Pub. ils/woodcuts. 600p. gilt emb bdg. H6. $68.00

**NORTHROP, N.B.** *Pioneer History of Medina County.* 1972. Portland, IN. rpt of 1861. 224p. VG. B18. $55.00

**NORTHUMBERLAND, Eighth Duke.** *Shadow of the Moor.* 1990. Stocksfield. Spredden. 12mo. 69p. VG/dj. O3. $25.00

**NORTON, Alice;** see Norton, Andre.

**NORTON, Andre.** *Brother to Shadows.* 1993. Morrow. 1st. lF/dj. T10. $30.00

**NORTON, Andre.** *Dread Companion.* 1970. HBJ. 1st. F/dj. T10. $75.00

**NORTON, Andre.** *Gate of the Cat.* 1987. Ace. 1st. F/dj. T10. $45.00

**NORTON, Andre.** *Imperial Lady.* 1989. NY. Tor. 1st. F/dj. A24. $20.00

**NORTON, Andre.** *Iron Cage.* 1974. Viking. 1st. F/NF. G10. $36.50

**NORTON, Andre.** *Jargoon Pard.* 1974. NY. Atheneum. 1st. NF/dj. M21. $30.00

**NORTON, Andre.** *Plague Ship.* 1956. Gnome. 1st. blk-lettered gray cloth. F/dj. T10. $250.00

**NORTON, Bettina A.** *Edwin Whitefield, 19th-Century North American Scenery.* 1977. Barre Pub. 1st. ils. 158p. G+. B18. $17.50

**NORTON, Charles Eliot.** *Historical Studies of Church Buildings in Middle Ages.* 1880. NY. Harper. 1st. 331p. G. H10. $45.00

**NORTON, Charles.** *Handbook of Florida.* 1892. NY. Longmans. 49 maps/plans/fld map. 392p. VG. B14. $55.00

**NORTON, J.E.** *Bibliography of Works of Edward Gibbon.* 1970. 272p. F. A4. $45.00

**NORTON, Mary.** *Borrowers.* 1991. HBJ. 1st. ils Michael Hague. F/dj. B17. $20.00

**NORWICH, John Julius.** *Sahara.* 1968. Weybright Talley. ils/pl. 240p. NF/dj. W1. $30.00

**NOSSITER, Bernard D.** *Fat Years & Lean: American Economy Since Roosevelt.* 1990. Harper Row. 1st. 271p. VG. S5. $12.00

**NOTESTEIN, Lucy Lilian.** *Wooster of the Miffle West.* 1937. London. Yale. 1st. ils. 333p. VG/dj. B18. $22.50

**NOTESTEIN, Wallace.** *English People on Eve of Colonization 1603-1630.* 1954. Harper. 1st. ils. 302p. VG/dj. S17. $10.00

**NOTT, C.** *Sketches of the War: Series of Letters...* 1865 (1863). G+. E6. $65.00

**NOTTINGHAM, Stratton.** *Wills & Administrations of Accomack County, VA 1663-1800.* 1973. Polyanthos. 494p. VG. B10. $50.00

**NOURSE, Alan.** *Fourth Horseman.* 1983. Harper Row. 1st. F/dj. T12. $25.00

**NOURSE, J.E.** *Narrative of the Second Arctic Expedition...* 1879. WA. 12 text maps/lg fld map mtd on cloth. 644p. new cloth. M4. $165.00

**NOVA, Craig.** *Incandescence.* 1979. Harper. 1st. F/dj. M25. $25.00

**NOVAK, Joseph;** see Kosinski, Jerzy.

**NOVLE, Joan Russell.** *Recollection of Virginia Woolf.* 1972. London. Peter Owen. 1st. 207p. VG/dj. M10. $12.50

**NOVOMEYSKY, M.A.** *Given to Salt: Struggle for the Dead Sea Concession.* 1958. London. Parrish. ils. 286p. cloth. VG/dj. Q2. $26.50

**NOWLIN, William.** *Bark Covered House; or, Back in the Woods Again...* 1876. Detroit. Prt for Author. 12mo. 250p. dk brn cloth. K1. $1,250.00

**NOWOSIELSKI, Sophie.** *Memoirs of a Woman Solider: In the Hurricane of War.* 1929. photos. VG. E6. $25.00

**NOYCE, Wilfrid.** *South Col: A Personal Story of Ascent of Everest.* 1955. Wm Sloane. 1st. F/VG. M19. $17.50

**NOYES, Alfred.** *Pageant of Letters.* 1940. NY. Sheed Ward. 1st. 8vo. 356p. cloth. F/dj. O10. $25.00

**NOYES, Stanley.** *Shadowbox.* 1970. Macmillan. 1st. F/NF. H11. $15.00

**NOYES, William.** *Wood & Forest.* 1912. Peoria. 2nd. 294p. B26. $35.00

**NUGENT, Beth.** *Live Girls.* 1996. Knopf. 1st. rem mk. F/sans. R14. $25.00

**NULAND, Sherwin.** *Doctors: Biography of Medicine.* 1988. NY. 1st. 519p. A13. $30.00

**NUNN, Kem.** *Pomona Queen.* 1992. NY. Pocket. 1st. F/NF. B3. $20.00

**NURSE, H.A.** *Poultry Houses, Coops & Equipment.* 1914. St Paul. Webb. 96p. VG/wrp. A10. $20.00

**NUSBAUM, Deric.** *Deric With the Indians.* 1927. Putnam. 1st. sm 8vo. G. C14. $10.00

**NUSEIBEH, Hazem Zaki.** *Palestine & the United Nations.* 1981. NY/London/Melbourne. 1st. 8vo. 200p. cloth. NF/dj. W1. $18.00

**NUSSER, Richard.** *Walking After Midnight.* 1989. NY. Villard. 1st. F/F. H11. $20.00

**NUTT, Katherine F.** *Gold, Guns & Grass: South Park & Fairplay, Colorado...* 1983. Flagstaff. 1st. ils/map/biblio. F/wrp. B19. $12.50

**NUTTALL, T.** *Popular Handbook of the Birds of the United States & Canada.* 1903 (1891). Boston. revised/annotated. 2 vol in 1. xl. VG. C12. $42.00

**NUTTING, Anthony.** *Arabs: Narrative History From Mohammed to Present.* 1964. NY. Potter. 1st Am. tall 8vo. 13 maps/charts. 424p. VG/dj. W1. $28.00

**NUTTING, Anthony.** *Gordon, Martyr & Misfit.* 1967. London. Rpt Soc. 2nd. gilt simulated leather. VG. M7. $25.00

**NUTTING, Wallace.** *Clock Book.* 1934 (1924). Garden City. 8vo. 312p. gilt tan cloth. F. B20. $60.00

**NUTTING, Wallace.** *Virginia Beautiful.* (1935). Garden City. later ed. 300+ photos. 262p. VG+/dj. H7. $30.00

**NUTTING, Wallace.** *Virginia Beautiful.* 1930. Framingham, MA. sgn. photos. 306p. VG. B18. $25.00

**NYE, Bud.** *Stay Loose.* 1959. Doubleday. 1st. VG/G. P8. $30.00

**NYE, Nelson.** *Champions of the Quarter Tracks.* 1959. Coward McCann. 1st. VG/fair. O3. $85.00

**NYE, Nelson.** *Horse Thieves.* 1987. Evans. 1st. 179p. F/F. B19. $15.00

**NYE, Nelson.** *Your Western Horse.* 1968. AS Barnes. 3rd. VG/dj. A21. $35.00

**NYE, Robert.** *Merlin.* 1979. Putnam. 1st Am. 215p. gilt blk cloth. F/dj. F1. $25.00

**NYLANDER, J.C.** *Our Own Snug Fireside: Images of New England Home...1860.* 1993. NY. 1st. ils. VG/dj. M17. $25.00

**NYLANDER, J.C.** *Our Own Snug Fireside: Images of New England Home...1860.* 1993. NY. 1st. ils. 317p. F/dj. M4. $30.00

O'BALLANCE, Edgar. *Arab Guerilla Power 1967-1972.* 1974. London. Faber. ils/map. 246p. cloth. VG+/dj. Q2. $15.00

O'BRIAN, Conor Cruise. *God Land: Reflections on Religion & Nationalism.* 1988. Harvard. F/VG. B9. $15.00

O'BRIAN, Patrick. *Adieux: A Farewell to Sartre.* 1984. Pantheon. 1st. F/dj. Q1. $50.00

O'BRIAN, Patrick. *Desolation Island.* 1979. NY. Stein Day. 1st Am. Aubry-Maturin #5. F/dj. T11. $275.00

O'BRIAN, Patrick. *Golden Ocean.* 1957. NY. John Day. 1st Am. NF/dj. T11. $650.00

O'BRIAN, Patrick. *HMS Surprise.* 1973. Phil. Lippincott. 1st Am. Aubrey-Maturin #3. NF/dj. T11. $275.00

O'BRIAN, Patrick. *Master & Commander.* 1969. Phil. Lippincott. 1st Am. Aubrey-Maturn #1. NF/VG. T11. $475.00

O'BRIAN, Patrick. *Master & Commander.* 1969. Phil/NY. Lippincott. 1st. F/clip. B4. $1,250.00

O'BRIAN, Patrick. *Master & Commander.* 1970. London. Collins. 1st. VG/dj. L3. $1,250.00

O'BRIAN, Patrick. *Picasso: A Biography.* 1976. NY. VG/dj. M17. $50.00

O'BRIAN, Patrick. *Post Captain.* 1972. Phil. Lippincott. 1st Am. Aubrey-Maturin #2. bl cloth. F/VG. T11. $600.00

O'BRIAN, Patrick. *Rendezvous.* 1994. NY. Norton. 1st. F/dj. T11. $35.00

O'BRIAN, Patrick. *Thirteen Gun Salute.* 1991. NY. Norton. 1st Am. Aubry-Maturin #13. F/dj. T11. $75.00

O'BRIAN, Patrick. *Wine-Dark Sea.* 1993. NY. Norton. 1st Am. Aubury-Maturin #16. F/dj. T11. $50.00

O'BRIEN, Darcy. *Margaret in Hollywood.* 1991. Morrow. 1st. rem mk. F/NF. H11. $15.00

O'BRIEN, Frederick. *White Shadows in the South Seas.* 1920. NY. photos. 3-quarter dk red leather/brn brd. VG. M17. $50.00

O'BRIEN, Geoffrey. *Hardboiled America: Lurid Years of Paperbacks.* 1981. Van Nostrand Reinhold. 1st. F/wrp. C9. $42.00

O'BRIEN, Jack. *Return of Silver Chief.* 1943. John Winston. ils Kurt Wiese. VG/dj. A21. $20.00

O'BRIEN, Kate. *Romance of English Literature.* (1944). Hastings. 8vo. 324p. orange cloth. H4. $14.00

O'BRIEN, M.A. *New English-Russian & Russian-English Dictionary.* 1944. NY. Dover. 12mo. 366p. navy cloth. H4. $11.00

O'BRIEN, Marian Maeve. *Collector's Guide to Dollhouses & Dollhouse Miniatures.* 1974. NY. Hawthorn. 4to. 273p. B9/H4. $16.00

O'BRIEN, Mildred Jackson. *Rug & Carpet Book.* 1951. McGraw Hill. 1nd. 8vo. NF/VG clip. H4. $20.00

O'BRIEN, P.J. *Will Rogers: Ambassador of Good Will...* 1935. Winston. 1st. ils. VG/dj. C9. $30.00

O'BRIEN, Pat. *Wind at My Back.* 1964. Doubleday. 1st. NF/VG. M19. $35.00

O'BRIEN, Sharon. *American Indian Tribal Governments.* 1989. U OK. 1st. sm 4to. 349p. VG. S14. $20.00

O'BRIEN, Tim. *Going After Cacciato.* 1978. Delacorte. 1st. F/dj. B4. $400.00

O'BRIEN, Tim. *Going After Cacciato.* 1978. London. Cape. 1st. F/NF. B3. $125.00

O'BRIEN, Tim. *If I Die in the Combat Zone.* 1973. London. Calder Boyars. 1st Eng. author's 1st book. F/dj. Q1. $200.00

O'BRIEN, Tim. *In the Lake of the Woods.* 1994. Houghton Mifflin. 1st. sgn. Q1. $50.00

O'BRIEN, Tim. *In the Lake of the Woods.* 1994. Houghton Mifflin. 1st. F/F. H11. $40.00

O'BRIEN, Tim. *Nuclear Age.* 1985. Knopf. 1st. F/F. H11. $35.00

O'BRIEN, Tim. *Nuclear Age.* 1985. Knopf. 1st. sgn. F/F. A24. $65.00

O'BRIEN, Tim. *Nuclear Age.* 1985. Knopf. 1st. sgn. rem mk. F/dj. B2. $50.00

O'BRIEN, Tim. *Speaking of Courage.* 1980. Santa Barbara. Neville. 1/300. sgn. F/sans. B9. $100.00

O'BRIEN & SAYERS. *Sinatra Sessions, 1939-1980.* 1980. Dallas. Sinatra Soc. 1st. w/TLS. B2. $35.00

O'CALLAHAN, Joseph T. *I Was Chaplain on the Franklin (bound w/3 other titles).* (1957). Garden City, NY. Catholic Family BC. 8vo. 311p. F/dj. H4. $35.00

O'CASEY, Sean. *Drums of Father Ned: Mickrocosm of Ireland.* 1960. Macmillan. 209p. F/wrp. H4. $15.00

O'CHEL, Shaemas. *It Never Could Happen; or, The Second American Revolution.* 1932. NY. Coventry. 1st. 191p. VG. N2. $50.00

O'CLERY, Helen. *Queens, Queens, Queens.* 1965. NY. Watts. 1st. 195p. cloth. F/dj. D4. $30.00

O'CONNELL, Carol. *Mallory's Oracle.* 1994. Putnam. 1st. author's 1st book. F/F. H11. $30.00

O'CONNELL, Carol. *Man Who Cast Two Shadows.* 1995. Putnam. 1st. F/F. H11. $30.00

O'CONNELL, Carol. *Man Who Lied to Women.* 1995. London. Hutchinson. 1st (precedes Am). F/dj. M15. $100.00

O'CONNELL, Charles. *Victor Books of Symphonies.* 1948. S&S. 556p. G. C5. $12.50

O'CONNELL, Jack. *Box Nine.* 1992. Mysterious. 1st. sgn. VG/dj. M17. $20.00

O'CONNELL, Jack. *Wireless.* 1993. Mysterious. 1st. F/F. H11. $25.00

O'CONNELL, Nicholas. *At the Field's End: Interviews With 20 Pacific NW Writers.* 1987. Seattle. Madrona Pub. 1st. sgn 7 contributors. F/dj. O11. $125.00

O'CONNOR, Edwin. *I Was Dancing.* 1964. Atlantic/Little Brn. 1st. F/NF. A24. $35.00

O'CONNOR, Edwin. *Oracle.* 1951. Harper. 1st. F/NF. B4. $175.00

O'CONNOR, Eileen. *Flexing for Ballet.* 1950. NY. Dance Magazine. unp. G. C5. $12.50

O'CONNOR, Flannery. *Everything That Rises Must Converge.* 1965. NY. 1st. F/VG. B30. $150.00

O'CONNOR, Flannery. *Habit of Being.* (1979). FSG. 1st. 8vo. 617p. H4. $30.00

O'CONNOR, Flannery. *Home of the Brave.* 1981. NY. Albondocani. 1st. 1/200. F/marbled paper wrp. Q1. $200.00

O'CONNOR, Flannery. *Violent Bear It Away.* 1960. FSC. 1st. NF/dj. B30. $250.00

O'CONNOR, Flannery. *Wise Blood.* 1952. Harcourt Brace. 1st. yel brd. F/NF. M24. $1,250.00

O'CONNOR, Frank. *Shakespeare's Progress.* (1960). World. 8vo. 191p. NF/dbl dj. H4. $30.00

O'CONNOR, Jack. *Big Game Animals of North America.* (1961). Dutton/Outdoor Life. 20 mc pl. NF. H4. $25.00

O'CONNOR, Jack. *Big Game Animals of North America.* 1964. Dutton. 3rd. G. B11. $25.00

O'CONNOR, Jack. *Complete Book of Rifles & Shotguns.* 1966. Outdoor Life. revised/uptd. 477p. F/dj. A17. $17.50

O'CONNOR, Jack. *Rifle Book.* 1964. Knopf. 2nd/revised. 8vo. 332p. NF. H4. $20.00

O'CONNOR, Jack. *Shotgun Book.* 1965. Knopf. 1st. lg 8vo. 332p. F/F. B20. $50.00

O'CONNOR, Jack. *Shotgun Book.* 1965. NY. Knopf. 1st. 332p. F/VG. H10. $35.00

**O'CONNOR, John E.** *William Paterson, Lawyer & Statesman 1745-1806.* 1979. Rutgers. VG/dj. M11. $50.00

**O'CONNOR, Richard.** *Bat Masterson: Biography...* 1957. Doubleday. VG. J2. $50.00

**O'CONNOR, Richard.** *Guns of Chickamauga: A Novel.* 1955. Doubleday. 1st. NF/dj. A14. $25.00

**O'CONNOR, Richard.** *Johnstown, the Day the Dam Broke.* 1957. Lippincott. 1st. 8vo. 255p. AN/dj. H1. $22.50

**O'CONNOR, Richard.** *Wild Bill Hickock.* 1959. Doubleday. 1st. VG/dj. B5. $20.00

**O'CONNOR, Robert.** *Buffalo Soldiers.* 1993. Knopf. 1st. rem mk. F/dj. B2. $100.00

**O'CONOR, A.P.** *Forty Years With Fighting Cocks.* 1929. Goshen. private prt. 327p. NF. M4. $100.00

**O'DELL, Scott.** *Amethyst Ring.* 1983. Houghton Mifflin. 1st. 212p. F/dj. D4. $30.00

**O'DELL, Scott.** *Treasure of Topo-El-Bampo.* 1972. Houghton Mifflin. 1st. 8vo. 48p. F/VG. C14. $18.00

**O'DONNELL, Elliott.** *Werewolves.* 1965. Longview. 1st thus. lg 8vo. 292p. NF/VG. B20. $40.00

**O'DONNELL, Mabel.** *New Friendly Village: Alice & Jerry Basic Reader.* 1948 (1936). Row Peterson. sm 8vo. ils Hoopes. 256p. bl cloth. VG. T5. $45.00

**O'DONNELL, Peter.** *Dead Man's Handle.* 1985. London. Souvenir. 1st. sgn. F/dj. M15. $90.00

**O'DONNELL, Peter.** *I, Lucifer.* 1967. London. Souvenir. 1st. F/clip. M15. $135.00

**O'DONNELL, Peter.** *Xanadu Talisman.* 1981. London. Souvenir. 1st. F/dj. M15. $100.00

**O'DONNELL & TRAVOLTA.** *Making It in Hollywood.* 1995. Naperville. Sourcebooks. 248p. VG/dj. C5. $12.50

**O'DWYER, E.J.** *Thomas Frognall Dibdin, Bibliographer & Bibliomaniac...* 1967. Pinner. Private Lib Assn. 1st. 1/1400. 8vo. 45p. F/dj. O10. $45.00

**O'FLAHERTY, Joseph S.** *Those Powerful Years: South Coast & Los Angeles 1887-1917.* 1978. Exposition. 1st. F/dj. O4. $15.00

**O'FLAHERTY, Liam.** *Mr Gilhooley.* 1926. London. Cape. 1st. NF/VG. B9. $75.00

**O'GORMAN, Hubert J.** *Lawyers & Matrimonial Cases: A Study...* 1963. NY. Free Pr. VG/dj. M11. $45.00

**O'GORMAN, James F.** *Aspects of American Printmaking 1800-1950.* 1988. Syracuse. 1st. obl 8vo. 245p. F/dj. O10. $45.00

**O'HARA, John.** *Elizabeth Appleton.* (1963). NY. Random. 1st/1st prt. 8vo. top edge bl. bl cloth. dj. R3. $20.00

**O'HARA, John.** *From the Terrace.* 1958. Random. 1st. F/NF. B4. $85.00

**O'HARA, John.** *Hat on the Bed.* (1963). NY. Random. 1st/1st prt. 8vo. bl-stp gr cloth. dj. R3. $20.00

**O'HARA, John.** *Lovey Childs: A Philadelphian's Story.* 1969. Random. 1st. F/dj. D10. $50.00

**O'HARA, John.** *Lovey Childs: A Philadelphian's Story.* 1973. Random. 1st. NF/VG. R14. $35.00

**O'HARA, John.** *Ourselves to Know.* 1960. Random. 1st. 8vo. sgn. 408p. NF/VG. W2. $250.00

**O'HARA, John.** *Stories of Venial Sin From Pipe Night.* 1952. NY. Avon. 1st. digest size. F/wrp. B4. $50.00

**O'HARA, John.** *Time Element & Other Stories.* 1972. Random. 1st. NF/VG. S13. $10.00

**O'HARA, Mary.** *Novel-in-the-Making.* 1954. NY. McKay. 1st. 244p. cloth. F/dj. O10. $10.00

**O'HARA, Mary.** *Wyoming Summer.* 1963. Doubleday. 1st. VG/dj. S13. $20.00

**O'HEARN, Joseph C.** *New England Fishing Schooners.* 1947. Milwaukee. photos. sbdg. VG. M17. $30.00

**O'HOGAIN, Daithi.** *Myth, Legend & Romance: Encyclopedia of Irish...* 1991. Prentice Hall. 1st. NF/dj. B9. $50.00

**O'KANE, Richard H.** *Clear the Bridge!* 1977. NY. Rand McNally. 1st. VG/dj. B5. $37.50

**O'KANE, Walter Collins.** *Intimate Desert.* 1969. Tucson, AZ. 1st. ils/species list. 143p. F. B19. $10.00

**O'KEEFFE, Georgia.** *Georgia O'Keeffe by Georgia O'Keeffe.* 1976. Studio Book. 1/175. sgn. 108 mc pl+separate fld of 16 pl & photo. F. D2. $2,200.00

**O'KEEFFE, Georgia.** *Georgia O'Keeffe.* 1976. Viking. 1st. folio. 108 pl. cloth. F/VG. C15. $125.00

**O'KEEFFE, Georgia.** *Georgia O'Keeffe: A Studio Book.* 1978. NY. Viking. 2nd prt. ils/100 pl. VG/dj. A25. $75.00

**O'MALLEY, Martin.** *Gross Misconduct: Life of Spinner Spencer.* 1988. NY. Viking. 1st. NF/VG. T12. $15.00

**O'MALLEY, Patrick.** *Affair of the Blue Pig.* 1965. NY. MS Mill. 1st. 159p. cloth. F/dj. O10. $30.00

**O'MALLEY & SAUNDERS.** *Leonardo da Vinci on the Human Body.* 1952. NY. Schuman. tall 4to. ils. 506p. NF. G7. $125.00

**O'MARA, Michael.** *Dogs. Ten Etchings.* 1976. LA. Peggy Christian. mini. 1/75. each prt sgn. loose as issued/portfolio. B24. $200.00

**O'NAN, Stewart.** *Snow Angels.* 1994. Doubleday. UP. author's 1st novel. F/wrp. R14. $125.00

**O'NEAL, Bill.** *Encyclopedia of Western Gun Fighters.* 1979. Norman, OK. 1st. ils. 386p. VG/dj. B5. $30.00

**O'NEAL, Bill.** *Henry Brown: The Outlaw Marshal.* 1980. College Sta. Creative. inscr. F. A19. $35.00

**O'NEAL, Bill.** *Texas League.* 1987. Eakin. 1st. F/VG. P8. $45.00

**O'NEAL, Cora.** *Gardens & Homes of Mexico.* 1947. Dallas. Banks. 2nd. 221p. VG/dj. A10. $50.00

**O'NEAL, Mary Lee Strickland.** *Why Did You Start Without Me?* 1975. San Antonio. Naylor. 1st. inscr/dtd 1975. F/dj. B9. $75.00

**O'NEAL, William B.** *Jefferson's Fine Arts Library for University of Virginia...* (1956). U VA. 53p. B10. $10.00

**O'NEAL & WEEKS.** *Work of William Lawrence Bottomley in Richmond.* (1985). U VA. 1st. sgn. 262p. VG/VG. B10. $125.00

**O'NEIL, Timothy.** *Shades of Gray.* 1987. Viking. 1st. xl. VG/NF. S18. $5.00

**O'NEIL & WULF.** *I Was Right on Time.* 1996. S&S. UP. VG+/wrp. P8. $15.00

**O'NEILL, Dennis J.** *Whale of a Territory: Story of Bill O'Neill.* 1966. NY. 1st. sgn. 249p. VG/dj. B18. $22.50

**O'NEILL, Eugene.** *All God's Chillun Got Wings & Welded.* 1924. Boni Liveright. 1st. NF/dj. Q1. $175.00

**O'NEILL, Eugene.** *All God's Chillun Got Wings & Welded.* 1924. Boni Liveright. 1st. sgn. F/NF. B4. $1,350.00

**O'NEILL, Eugene.** *Dynamo.* 1929. Liveright. ltd. 1/775. sgn/#d. bl paper brd. VG+/case. A24. $200.00

**O'NEILL, Eugene.** *Dynamo.* 1929. Liveright. 1/775. sgn. mottled bl brd. F/spider-web case. B2. $350.00

**O'NEILL, Eugene.** *Last Will & Testament of Extremely Distinguised Dog.* 1972. Worcester. St Onge. mini. 1/1000. 26p. gilt tan leather. B24. $85.00

**O'NEILL, Eugene.** *Marco Millins.* 1927. Boni Liveright. 1st. F/dj. B4. $450.00

**O'NEILL, Tip.** *Man of the House.* 1987. Random. 1st. VG. W2. $20.00

**O'REILLY, Montagu.** *Who Has Been Tampering With These Pianos?* 1948. New Directions. NF/wrp. B2. $45.00

**O'REILLY, Victor.** *Games of the Hangman.* 1991. Grove Weidenfeld. 1st. F/NF. H11. $25.00

**O'ROURKE, Frank.** *Flashing Spikes.* 1948. Barnes. 1st. VG. P8. $25.00

**O'ROURKE, Frank.** *Greatest Victory & Other Baseball Stories.* 1950. Barnes. 1st. VG. P8. $30.00

**O'ROURKE, Frank.** *Heavenly World Series & Other Baseball Stories.* 1952. NY. Barnes. 1st. VG/clip. B4. $150.00

**O'ROURKE, Frank.** *Never Come Back.* 1952. Barnes. 1st. VG+. P8. $25.00

**O'ROURKE, Frank.** *Nine Good Men.* 1952. Barnes. 1st. VG/dj. P8. $65.00

**O'ROURKE, P.J.** *Give War a Chance.* 1952. London. Pan. 1st Eng. F/NF. T12. $20.00

**O'ROURKE, P.J.** *Parliament of Whores.* 1991. Atlantic Monthly. 1st. inscr. 8vo. 233p. F/dj. B20. $20.00

**O'ROURKE, William.** *Notts: A Striking Novel.* 1996. NY. Marlowe. 1st. F/F. H11. $25.00

**O'SHAUGHNESSY, Edith.** *Diplomat's Wife in Mexico.* 1916. NY. Harper. 1st. 356p. F3. $15.00

**O'SHEA, Sean;** see Tralins, Bob.

**O'TOOKE, Peter.** *Loitering With Intent: The Apprentice.* 1996. NY. Hyperion. 1st. F/dj. B9. $15.00

**O'TOOLE, G.J.A.** *Honorable Treachery: History of US Intelligence...* 1991. Atlantic Monthly. BC. ils. F/dj. A2. $10.00

**O'TOOLE, G.J.A.** *Honorable Treachery: History of US Intelligence...* 1991. Atlantic Monthly. 1st. ils. NF/VG. S14. $15.00

**O.J. PORTER & COMPANY.** *Accelerated Traffic Test at Stockton Airfield...* 1949. Dept Army Corps Eng. 1st. ils/photos/charts. cloth. VG. B27. $65.00

**OAKENFULL, J.C.** *Brazil in 1910.* 1910. Devonport, Eng. self pub. 1st. photos/2 fld maps. 280p. VG. H7. $12.50

**OAKES, Maud.** *Two Crosses of Todos Santos.* 1951. NY. Pantheon. Bolligen series. 1st. 274p. F3. $75.00

**OAKES, Vanya.** *Footprints of the Dragon.* 1953. Winston. 3rd. inscr/sgn on half title. ils Tyrus Wong. cloth. VG. B27. $45.00

**OAKLEY, Graham.** *Henry's Quest.* 1986. Atheneum. 1st. obl 8vo. VG/dj. B17. $15.00

**OAKLEY, Imogen Brashear.** *Awake, America! And Other Verse.* 1934. Phil. Macrae Smith. 8vo. sgn. 74p. VG. B11. $40.00

**OAKLEY, Violet.** *Holy Experiment: Our Heritage From William Penn 1644-1944.* 1951. Phil. Cogleas Studio. 2nd. 1/1000. sgn. 164p. V3. $60.00

**OAKS, Gladys.** *Ten Little Pets Come Home.* 1945. World. 1st. ils. VG. M5. $10.00

**OASLEY, A.S.** *Calligraphy & Palaeography: Essays Presented...* 1966. NY. October House. 1st Am. sm 4to. 287p. cloth. F/NF. O10. $55.00

**OATES, Joyce Carol.** *Angel Fire.* 1973. Baton Rouge. LSU. 1st. inscr pres/dtd 1973. NF. Q1. $50.00

**OATES, Joyce Carol.** *Angel of Light.* 1981. NY. Dutton. 1st. NF/clip. G10. $15.00

**OATES, Joyce Carol.** *By the North Gate.* 1963. Vanguard. 1st. sgn. author's 1st book. F/NF. L3. $450.00

**OATES, Joyce Carol.** *Childhood.* 1977. Vanguard. 1st. inscr. NF/wht dj. R14. $45.00

**OATES, Joyce Carol.** *Cupid & Psyche: A Short Story.* 1970. NY. Algondocani. 1st. 1/26. sgn/lettered. inscr/dtd 1970. F/mailer. Q1. $250.00

**OATES, Joyce Carol.** *Garden of Earthly Delights.* 1967. NY. Vanguard. 1st. F/dj. B4. $200.00

**OATES, Joyce Carol.** *Goddess & Other Women.* 1974. Vanguard. 1st. sgn. NF/VG. R14. $60.00

**OATES, Joyce Carol.** *Lives of the Poet.* 1987. NY. S&S. 1st. rem mk. VG/dj. L1. $35.00

**OATES, Joyce Carol.** *Lives of the Twins by Rosamond Smith.* 1987. S&S. 1st. F/dj. J3. $75.00

**OATES, Joyce Carol.** *Mysteries of Winterhurn.* 1984. Dutton. 1st. NF/F. S18. $30.00

**OATES, Joyce Carol.** *Mysteries of Winterhurn.* 1984. Franklin Lib. 1st. sgn. full leather. F. B3. $100.00

**OATES, Joyce Carol.** *Night-Side.* 1977. Vanguard. 1st. sgn. F/NF. S9. $100.00

**OATES, Joyce Carol.** *Night-Side.* 1977. Vanguard. 1st. sgn. VG/dj. L1. $85.00

**OATES, Joyce Carol.** *Solstice.* 1985. Dutton. 1st. F/dj. A23. $30.00

**OATES, Joyce Carol.** *Soul/Mate.* 1989. Dutton. 1st. xl. VG/NF. S18. $7.00

**OATES, Joyce Carol.** *Soul/Mate.* 1989. NY. Dutton. 1st. VG/dj. L1. $30.00

**OATES, Joyce Carol.** *Unholy Loves.* 1977. Vanguard. 1st. NF/dj. S9. $45.00

**OATES, Joyce Carol.** *Where Is Here?* 1992. Ecco. 1st. sgn. F/dj. S13. $30.00

**OATES, Joyce Carol.** *Zombie.* 1995. Dutton. 1st. inscr. F/dj. R14. $40.00

**OATES, Wayne.** *Revelation of God in Human Suffering.* 1959. Westminster. 143p. VG/dj. B29. $7.50

**OATTS, L.B.** *Highland Light Infantry...Famous Regiments Series.* 1969. Leo Cooper. 1st. photos. 113p. VG. S16. $35.00

**OBER, Frederick A.** *Camps in the Caribees: Adventures...* 1880. Boston. Lee Shepard. 1st. ils. 366p. gilt bdg. VG. H7. $65.00

**OBER, Frederick A.** *Travels in Mexico & Life Among the Mexicans.* (1887). Boston. Estes Lauriat. revised. ils. 732p. F3. $65.00

**OBERDORFER, Don.** *Tet!* 1971. Doubleday. 1st. photos. 385p. VG/dj. R11. $40.00

**OBERHOLSER, Harry C.** *Bird Life of Louisiana.* 1938. New Orleans. Dept Conservation. inscr pres. 8vo. 834p. VG. H4. $75.00

**OBERTH, Hermann.** *Moon Car.* 1959. NY. Harper. 1st Am. trans Willy Ley. 98p. K5. $50.00

**OBEYESEKERE, Gananath.** *Apotheosis of Captain Cook, European Mythmaking...* 1992. Princeton/Bishop Mus. 1st. 268p. F/F. A4. $65.00

**OBEYESEKERE, Gananath.** *Apotheosis of Captain Cook, European Mythmaking...* 1992. Princeton/Bishop Mus. 1st. 8vo. ils/notes/index. 251p. blk cloth. VG. P4. $45.00

**OBOLENSKY, Dimitri.** *Byzantine Commonwealth: Eastern Europe 500-1453.* 1971. NY. Praeger. ils/64 pl/10 maps. 445p. cloth. VG. Q2. $43.00

**OBOLER, Arch.** *Night of the Auk.* 1958. Horizon. 1st. 8vo. 180p. F/VG+. B20. $45.00

**OBRAZTSOV, Sergei.** *My Profession.* 1960. Soviet Union Foreign Lang. 1st Eng. F. C9. $42.00

**OBREGON, Mauricio.** *Argonauts to Astronauts: Unconventional History...* 1980. Harper. 1st. 205p. dj. F3. $15.00

**OBREGON.** *Columbus Papers, Barcelona Letter of 1493...* 1991. obl 4to. 93p. F/case. A4. $95.00

**OCHS, Sidney.** *Elements of Neurophysiology.* 1965. Wiley. 621p. xl. VG. S5. $15.00

**OCKLEY, Simon.** *History of the Saracens.* 1847. London. Henry Bohn. 4th. 8vo. 512p. gr cloth. H4. $50.00

**ODEN, Thomas C.** *Requiem: Lament in Three Movements.* 1995. Abingdon. F/dj. B29. $9.00

**ODENS, Peter.** *Desert Trackers.* 1975. Yuma, AZ. G. A19. $25.00

**ODETS, Clifford.** *Three Plays.* 1935. Covici friede. 1st. NF. B2. $65.00

**ODLER, Daniel.** *Cannibal Kiss.* 1989. Random. 1st. F/F. H11. $20.00

**ODUM & PIGEON.** *Tropical Rain Forest: A Study...* 1970. US Atomic Energy Comm. ils/photos. 1000p. VG. S15. $75.00

**OE, Kenzaburo.** *Silent Cry.* 1974. NY. Kodansha Internat/USA Ltd. 1st Am. F/clip. O11. $50.00

**OEHLER, C.M.** *Great Sioux Uprising.* 1959. OUP. sgn pres. ils/maps. 272p. VG/dj. J2. $80.00

**OEHSER, Paul H.** *National Geographic Society Research Reports.* NGS. ils. 399p. VG/dj. S15. $12.00

**OEHSER, Paul H.** *Sons of Science.* 1949. NY. Schuman. 220p. cloth. VG. A10. $25.00

**OEMLER, Marie Conway.** *Johnny Reb: A Story of South Carolina.* (1929). NY/London. Century. 1st/2nd prt. 433p. cloth. NF/dj. M8. $65.00

**OESTERLEN, F.** *Medical Logic.* 1855. London. 1st Eng trans. 437p. xl. A13. $75.00

**OESTERLEY & ROBINSON.** *Hebrew Religion: Its Origin & Development.* 1944. SPCK. 488p. G. B29. $10.00

**OFFIONG, Daniel A.** *Imperialism & Dependency: Obstacles to African Development.* 1982 (1980). Pantheon. 1st Am. 8vo. VG/dj. A2. $20.00

**OFFUTT, Chris.** *Good Brother.* 1997. S&S. ARC. sgn. author's 3rd book. F/pict wrp. R14. $45.00

**OFFUTT, Chris.** *Same River Twice.* 1993. NY. S&S. 1st. sgn. F/dj. M23. $65.00

**OGDEN, Charles Kay.** *Meaning of Psychology.* 1926. Harper. 4 half-tones/14 text ils. xl. G1. $30.00

**OGDEN, E.C.** *Broad-Leaved Species of Potamogeton of North America...* 1943. np. ils/maps. 138p. wrp. B26. $36.00

**OGDEN, Robert Morris.** *Hearing...* 1924. Harcourt Brace. ils. 351p. bl cloth. VG. G1. $35.00

**OGDEN, Samuel.** *Step-By-Step to Organic Vegetable Growing.* 1972. Emmaus. Rodale. 3rd. 182p. VG/dj. A10. $20.00

**OGG, Oscar.** *Alphabet Source Book.* 1947. NY. Dover. rpt. 199p. cloth. F/dj. O10. $55.00

**OGG, Oscar.** *26 Letters.* 1948. NY. Crowell. 1st. ils. 254p. F/NF. O10. $25.00

**OGILVIE FLOUR MILLS.** *Ogilvie's French-Canadian Cookbook.* ca 1910. Montreal/ Winnipeg. 134p. VG/flexible stiff later wrp. E6. $40.00

**OGLE, Nathaniel.** *Memoirs of Monkeys...* 1825. London. Whittaker. 1st. 152p. later-styel brn quarter calf. F. B20. $375.00

**OGLESBY, Ray T.** *River Ecology & Man.* 1972. Academic. 465p. xl. VG. S5. $15.00

**OHIO YEARLY MEETING.** *Discipline of the Society of Friends of OH Yearly Meeting...* 1839. Mt Pleasant, OH. Enoch Harris. 16mo. 116p. worn leather. V3. $45.00

**OKKONEN, Mark.** *Baseball Memories 1950-1959.* 1993. Sterling. 1st. F/dj. P8. $35.00

**OKRI, Ben.** *Astonishing Gods.* 1995. Little Brn. 1st Canadian. F/dj. A14. $28.00

**OKRI, Ben.** *Incidents at the Shrine.* 1986. London. Heinemann. 1st. author's 3rd book. F/dj. A24. $45.00

**OLCOTT, Antony.** *May Day in Magadan.* 1983. Bantam. 1st. 8vo. 317p. F/NF. W2. $25.00

**OLCOTT, Henry S.** *Agricultural Lectures.* 1860. NY. 1st. inscr Asa Gray/dtd 1861. 186p. VG. B14. $70.00

**OLCOTT, Henry S.** *Outlines of the First Course of Yale Agriculture Lectures.* 1860. NY. 1st. 186p. VG. B14. $70.00

**OLDER, Fremont.** *California Missions & Their Romances.* 1945. NY. photos. VG. M17. $15.00

**OLDER, Julia.** *Menus a'Trois.* 1987. NY. Stephen Greene. G/dj. A16. $10.00

**OLDFELD, Peter.** *Alchemy Murder.* 1929. Washburn. 1st. VG/dj. N4. $22.50

**OLDS, Bruce.** *Raising Holy Hell.* 1995. NY. Holt. 1st. sgn. F/dj. R14. $35.00

**OLEKSIW, Susan.** *Murder in Mellingham.* 1993. Scribner. 1st. F/dj. R8. $12.00

**OLFERS, Sibylle V.** *When the Root Children Wake Up.* 1939. NY. Stokes. 8 full-p mc pl. blk lettered gr cloth/mc label. dj. R5. $375.00

**OLIVA, Tony.** *Tony O!* 1973. Hawthorn. 1st. photos. VG/dj. P8. $100.00

**OLIVER, M.** *Cooking Is Child's Play.* 1965. 1st Am. Eng/French text. ils. VG. E6. $20.00

**OLIVER, Paul.** *Conversation With the Blues.* 1965. London. Cassell. 1st. F/NF. B2. $125.00

**OLIVER, Peter.** *New Chronicle of the Compleat Angler.* 1936. NY/London. Paisley. 1st. ils/index. VG. H10. $110.00

**OLIVER, Raymond.** *La Cuisine.* 1969. Tudor. G/dj. A16. $30.00

**OLLARD, Richard.** *Clarendon & His Friends.* 1988. NY. 1st. ils. VG/dj. M17. $15.00

**OLMSTEAD, Frederick Law.** *Cotton Kingdom: A Selection.* 1971. NY. edit David Freeman Hawke. VG/dj. M17. $25.00

**OLMSTEAD, Robert.** *Trail of Heart's Blood Wherever We Go.* 1990. Random. 1st. F/F B3. $25.00

**OLSEN, Herb.** *Painting Children in Watercolor.* 1960. Bonanza. 1st thus. ils. VG/dj. B5. $18.00

**OLSEN, Jack.** *Predator.* 1991. Delacorte. 8vo. 366p. F/NF. W2. $25.00

**OLSHAN, Joseph.** *Warmer Season.* 1987. McGraw Hill. 1st. author's 2nd book. F/dj. R14. $35.00

**OLSON, Albert.** *Picture Painting for Young Artists.* 1906. Chicago. Thompson Thomas. 1st. ils. VG. D1. $65.00

**OLSON, Charles.** *Mayan Letters.* 1953. Divers. F/wrp. B2. $200.00

**OLSON, John.** *John Olson's Book of the Rifle.* 1974. JP O'Hara. 1st. ils. 255p. VG/G. S14. $12.00

**OLSON, Toby.** *Dorit in Lesbos.* 1990. Linden. 1st. sgn/dtd 1997. F/dj. R14. $40.00

**OLSON & SILVA.** *Dead End: City Limits: Anthology of Urban Fear.* 1991. NY. St Martin. 1st. F/dj. G10. $15.00

**OMAN.** *Seafaring Nation.* 1979. London. Ministry Information/Culture. ils/maps. 196p. VG/dj. Q2. $47.00

**OMARR, Sydney.** *Cooking With Astrology.* 1970. NY. World. VG/dj. A16. $7.00

**OMWAKE, John.** *Conestoga Six-Horse Bell Teams of Eastern Pennsylvania.* 1930. Cincinnati. Pub John Omwake for Private Distribution. 1st. sgn pres. O3. $195.00

**OMWAKE, John.** *Conestoga Six-Horse Bell Teams of Eastern Pennsylvania.* 1930. Cincinnati. 2nd. inscr. 163p. VG. B18. $95.00

**ONDAATJE, Michael.** *Coming Through Slaughter.* 1976. Norton. 1st. NF/clip. B30. $60.00

**ONDAATJE, Michael.** *English Patient.* 1992. Knopf. 1st Am. F/dj. B4. $150.00

**ONDAATJE, Michael.** *In the Skin of a Lion.* 1987. NY. 1st. VG/dj. M17. $30.00

**OPIE & OPIE.** *I Saw Esau. Schoolchild's Pocket Book.* (1992). Candlewick. 1/350. sgn. 8vo. dk gr brd/pict label. case/label. R5. $450.00

**OPLER, Morris E.** *Grenville Goodwin Among Western Apaches: Letters...* 1973. Tucson, AZ. 1st. ils/index. F/NF. B19. $25.00

**OPPEN, Mary.** *Meaning a Life: An Autobiography.* 1978. Santa Barbara. Blk Sparrow. ltd. 1/26. sgn. NF/mylar. B9. $50.00

**OPPENHEIM, E. Phillips.** *Harvey Garrard's Game.* 1926. Little Brn. 1st. VG/dj. S13. $18.00

**OPPENHEIM, E. Phillips.** *New Tenant.* 1912. Collier. 2nd. 8vo. G. B20. $18.00

**OPPENHEIM, E. Phillips.** *Spy Paramount.* 1936. Little Brn. 1st. VG. B20. $15.00

**OPPENHEIMER, Heinrich.** *Medical & Allied Topics in Latin Poetry.* 1928. London. 1st. 445p. A13. $100.00

**OPPENHEIMER, Jerry.** *Barbara Walters: Unauthorized Biography.* 1990. St Martin. 1st. F/dj. T11. $10.00

**OPPENHEIMER, Joel.** *Wrong Season.* 1973. Bobbs Merrill. 1st. VG+/G+. P8. $40.00

**OPTIC, Oliver.** *Undivided Nation.* 1899. Lee Shepard. 1st. 482p. F. H1. $20.00

**ORCZY, Baroness.** *Eldorado: Story of the Scarlet Pimpernel.* nd. Hodder Stoughton. ne. F. T12. $60.00

**ORDE, A.J.** *Death & the Dogwalker.* 1990. Doubleday. 1st. author's 2nd book. F/NF. H11. $15.00

**ORDE, A.J.** *Little Neighborhood Murder.* 1989. Doubleday. 1st. NF/dj. G8. $30.00

**ORDISH, Geroge.** *Living American House.* nd. np. ils. 320p. F/dj. S15. $8.50

**ORDWAY & WAKEFORD.** *Conquering the Sun's Empire.* 1968. Dutton. 2nd. 128p. dj. K5. $20.00

**ORE, Rebecca.** *Alien Bootlegger & Other Stories.* 1993. NY. Tor. 1st. F/NF. G10. $15.00

**OREN, Dan A.** *Joining the Club: History of Jews & Yale.* 1985. New Haven. Yale. 1st. 8vo. VG/dj. A2. $20.00

**ORFIELD, Didrick.** *Uncle Didrick's Stories.* 1954. MN Pub Co. revised. sgn. 96p. VG/worn. D4. $30.00

**ORGA, I.** *Portrait of a Turkish Family.* 1950. Macmillan. 306p. decor cloth. VG. Q2. $24.00

**ORGAIN, Kate Alma.** *Southern Authors in Poetry & Prose.* 1908. Neale Pub. 1st. 233p. cloth. VG. M8. $85.00

**ORGEL, Doris.** *Merry Merry February.* 1977. Parents Magazine. 1st. 4to. nonsense rhymes. VG. M5. $12.00

**ORITA, Zenji.** *I-Boat Captain.* 1976. Canoga Park, CA. Major Books. 8vo. 317p. VG/dj. B11. $35.00

**ORLANDO, Guido.** *Confessions of a Scoundrel.* 1954. Winston. 1st. VG/dj. N2. $10.00

**ORLEAN, Susan.** *Saturday Night.* 1990. Knopf. 1st. 8vo. 258p. NF/dj. S14. $90.00

**ORLEANS, Leo A.** *Science in Contemporary China.* 1980. Stanford. 1st. ils. F/dj. A2. $20.00

**ORLOVITZ, Gil.** *Concerning Man.* 1947. Banyan. 1/350. inscr/dtd 1947. F/dj. B4. $350.00

**ORMOND, Clyde.** *Hunting in the Northwest.* 1948. Knopf. 1st. 8vo. 274p. VG+/dj. B20. $45.00

**ORMOND, Clyde.** *Hunting Our Medium-Size Game.* 1958. Stackpole. 219p. dj. A17. $10.00

**ORNE.** *Language of the Foreign Book Trade...* 1976. 3rd. 26,000 entries. 343p. NF. A4. $125.00

**OROZCO, Alfredo Torres.** *La Conciliacion Sindical en Espana.* 1962. Madrid. 266p. prt sewn wrp. M11. $35.00

**ORR & ORR.** *Wildflowers of Western America.* 1981 (1974). NY. 270p. VG/dj. B26. $25.00

**ORTHWEIN, Edith Hall.** *Petals of Love for Thee.* 1904. Dodge Pub. 1st. lg 8vo. 64p. NF. B20. $75.00

**ORTIZ, Elisabeth Lambert.** *Complete Book of Caribbean Cooking.* 1973. Evans. G/dj. A16. $10.00

**ORTIZ, Elizabeth Lambert.** *Complete Book of Caribbean Cooking.* 1973. BC. VG/VG. E6. $12.00

**ORTIZ, Simon.** *After & Before the Lightning.* 1994. Tucson, AZ. 1st. F/F. B3. $40.00

**ORTON, Helen Fuller.** *Mystery in the Old Cave.* 1950. Lippincott. 1st. 8vo. ils Robert Doremus. 121p. VG. T5. $12.00

**ORWELL, George.** *Animal Farm.* 1946. Harcourt Brace. 1st Am. VG/dj. M25. $75.00

**ORWELL, George.** *Coming Up for Air.* 1950. Harcourt Brace. 1st Am. F/NF. A24. $70.00

**ORWELL, George.** *Nineteen Eighty-Four.* 1949. Harcourt Brace. ARC/1st. NF/maroon prt buff wrp. M24. $650.00

**ORWELL, George.** *Nineteen Eighty-Four.* 1949. Harcourt Brace. 1st. NF. B3. $100.00

**OSBORN, Albert S.** *Mind of the Juror as Judge of the Facts...* 1938. Albany. Boyd Prt. dk maroon cloth. M11. $150.00

**OSBORN, Herbert.** *Fragments of Entomological History...* 1937. Columbus. A13. $45.00

**OSBORN, John Jay.** *Paper Chase.* 1971. Houghton Mifflin. 1st. F/clip. B4. $300.00

**OSBORN, Paul.** *Point of No Return.* 1952. Random. 1st. F/VG. A24. $35.00

**OSBORNE, Charles.** *Life & Crimes of Agatha Christie.* 1984. Agatha Christie Mystery Collection. VG/dj. P3. $20.00

**OSBORNE, H.** *Oxford Companion of Art.* 1970. NY. 1st. dj. T9. $22.00

**OSBORNE, John.** *Look Back in Anger.* 1957. London. Faber. 1st Eng. NF/dj. Q1. $100.00

**OSBORNE, Walter D.** *Quarter Horse.* 1967. Grosset Dunlap. VG/dj. O3. $25.00

**OSGOOD, Henry O.** *So This Is Jazz.* 1926. Little Brn. 1st. 258p. VG/dj. B20. $150.00

**OSIER & WOZNIAK.** *Century of Serial Publications in Psychology 1850-1950...* 1984. NY. Kraus. 806p. gray buckram. G1. $75.00

**OSLER, William.** *Concise History of Medicine.* 1919. Baltimore. 1st. 66p. xl. A13. $100.00

**OSLER, William.** *Evolution of Modern Medicine.* 1982. Birmingham. facs of 1921. 243p. full leather. A13. $75.00

**OSLER, William.** *Principles & Practice of Medicine.* 1892. NY. Appleton. 1st/2nd issue. linen brd/quarter calf spine. VG. G7. $595.00

**OSLER, William.** *Principles & Practice of Medicine.* 1893. NY. Appleton. 1st/later issue. 1079p+ads. 3-quarter sheep/rb spine. G7. $250.00

**OSLER, William.** *Science & Immortality.* 1905. Boston. 1st/rpt. 12mo. 54p. A13. $60.00

**OSLEY, A.S.** *Luminario, Introduction to Italian Writing Books...* 1972. Nieukoop. Miland Pub. 1st. sm volio. gray linen. F/NF. M24. $100.00

**OSLEY, A.S.** *Scribes & Sources.* 1980. Boston. Godine. 1st Am. NF/dj. O4. $25.00

**OSOFSKY, Joy D.** *Handbook of Infant Development...* 1979. John Wiley. Personality Processes series. 8vo. 954p. VG/dj. G1. $75.00

**OSSENDOWSKI, Ferdinand.** *Fire of Desert Folk: Account of Journey Through Morocco.* 1926. NY. Dutton. 1st. 8vo. 354p. xl. VG. W1. $8.00

**OSTENSO, Martha.** *Wild Geese.* 1925. Dodd Mead. 6th. 356p. VG. W2. $30.00

**OSTER, Jerry.** *Saint Mike.* 1987. Harper Row. 1st. F/dj. T12. $20.00

**OSTERGAARD, Vilhelm.** *Tycho Brahe.* 1907 (1895). Copenhagen. Glydendalske Boghandel Nordisk Forlag. 273p. VG. K5. $40.00

**OSTRANDER, Sheila.** *Festive Food Decoration.* 1969. Gramercy. G/dj. A16. $7.00

**OSTROGORSKY, George.** *History of the Byzantine State.* 1957. Rutgers. 1st Am. maps. 548p. AN/dj. H1. $48.00

**OSTROGORSKY, George.** *History of the Byzantine State.* 1957. Rutgers. 1st Am. 41 pl/map ep. 548p. VG. W1. $20.00

**OSTROW, Joanna.** *...In the Highlands Since Time Immemorial.* 1970. Knopf. 1st. author's 1st book. F/NF. H11. $30.00

**OSWALT, Wendell H.** *Mission of Change in Alaska: Eskimos & Moravians...* 1963. San Marino. Huntington Lib. 8vo. 170p. gr cloth. NF/dj. P4. $40.00

**OTERO, Miguel Antonio.** *My Life on the Frontier, 1864-1882: Incidents & Characters.* 1935. Pr of Pioneers. 1st. index. 293p. VG/G. B19. $175.00

**OTIS, James.** *Toby Tyler; or, Ten Weeks With a Circus.* (1967). Grosset Dunlap. Companion Lib. sm 8vo. 183p. G+. T5. $10.00

**OTSWALD, Hans.** *Zille's Vermaechtnis.* 1930. Berlin. Paule Franke. ils. 464p. orange cloth. D2. $40.00

**OTT, Frederick W.** *Films of Carole Lombard.* 1972. Citadel. 2nd. VG/wrp. C9. $30.00

**OTT, Ludwig.** *Fundamentals of Catholic Dogma.* 1964. Herder. 544p. VG/dj. B29. $15.50

**OTTESEN, Carole.** *Native Plant Primer.* 1995. Harmony. 1st. ils/biblio/index. 354p. F/dj. H10. $35.00

**OTTO, Martha Potter.** *Ohio's Prehistoric Peoples.* 1980. Columbus. OH Hist Soc. 75p. VG/pict wrp. B18. $12.50

**OTTO, Whitney.** *How to Make an American Quilt.* 1991. NY. Villard. 1st. F/F. B3. $100.00

**OTTO, Whitney.** *Now You See Her.* 1994. NY. Villard. 1st. author's 2nd book. NF/F. H11. $25.00

**OTWAY, Howard.** *Evangelist.* 1954. NY. Harper. 1st. F/VG. H11. $40.00

**OUELLETTE, Pierre.** *Deus Machine.* 1994. Villard. 1st/stated thus. AN/dj. A28. $11.50

**OUIDA.** *Works of...* 1892. London. 30 vol. half leather/marbled brd. F. B30. $350.00

**OULTON, Walley Chamberlain.** *Wonderful Story-Teller.* 1797. Boston. Bumstead. 8vo. calf. R12. $125.00

**OUSTALET, M.E.** *Revision de Queloques Especes d'Oiseaux de la Chine...* 1901. Paris. sm folio. ils. 27p. new cloth. C12. $95.00

**OUTDOOR LIFE.** *Story of American Hunting & Firearms.* 1959. NY. 172p. VG/case. A17. $25.00

**OUTHWAITE, Grenbry.** *Enchanted Forest.* 1921. London. Black. 1/500. sgn. 15 mtd mc pl/15 b&w ils. gilt wht pict cloth. R5. $3,500.00

**OUTLAND, Charles F.** *Mines, Murders & Grizzlies: Tales of California...* 1986. Ventura Hist Soc. revised. ils/notes/index. 151p. NF/NF. B19. $25.00

**OUTLAND, Charles F.** *Sespe Gunsmoke: Epic Case of Rancher Versus Squatters.* 1991. Ventura Hist Soc. 1st. ils/notes/index. 181p. F/F. B19. $30.00

**OVER & THOMAS.** *Birds of South Dakota.* 1902. Vermillion, SD. 8vo. ils. 142p. NF/wrp. C12. $30.00

**OVERMIER & SENIOR.** *Books & Manuscripts of the Bakken.* 1992. ils. 6000+entries. 525p. F. A4. $85.00

**OVERSTREET, Anne E.** *Books, Pamphlets & Reprints of Willard Rouse Jillson...* 1954. Dearborn. 1st. NF/prt wrp. M8. $75.00

**OVERTON, Grant.** *American Nights Entertainment.* 1923. Scribner. 1st. 12mo. 386p. gr cloth/gold labels. NF/dj. J3. $50.00

**OVERTON, Robert.** *Chase Around the World.* 1900. London. Warne. 1st. NF. M15. $125.00

**OVINGTON, Ray.** *Sportsman Artists Game Bag.* 1989. Clinton, NJ. Amwell. ltd. sgn. ils. F/box. A19. $65.00

**OVINGTON, Ray.** *Tactics on Trout.* 1969. Knopf. 1st. ils/index. 327p. F/dj. A17. $15.00

**OWEN, Catherine.** *Choice Cookery: Not for Those Seeking Economy.* 1889. 1st. VG. E6. $85.00

**OWEN, Frank.** *Murder for the Millions.* 1946. Fell. 1st. NF/VG. N4. $30.00

**OWEN, Howard.** *Littlejohn.* 1993. NY. Villard. 1st thus. F/dj. M23. $40.00

**OWEN-SMITH, R.N.** *Megaherbivores: Influence of Very Large Body Size...* 1992. Cambridge. 369p. F/wrp. S15. $18.50

**OWENS, Harry J.** *Scandalous Adventures of Reynard the Fox.* 1945. Knopf. 1st. sgn on ep. cloth/brd. F. B27. $75.00

**OWENS, Hubert B.** *Georgia's Planting Prelate.* 1945. Athens. 1/100. cloth. dj. B26. $30.00

**OWENS, L.T.** *JH Mason, 1875-1951, Scholar, Printer.* 1976. London. Frederick Muller. 1st. gilt bl cloth. F/dj. M24. $50.00

**OWENS, L.T.** *JH Mason, 1875-1951, Scholar, Printer.* 1976. London. 1st. VG/dj. T9. $15.00

**OWENS, Robert Dale.** *Wrong of Slavery. Right of Emancipation...* 1864. Lippincott. VG+. B2. $100.00

**OWENS, William A.** *Slave Mutiny, Revolt on the Schooner Amistad.* 1953. NY. 1st. 312p. VG/dj. B18. $25.00

**OWNER, Collison.** *King Crime: An English Study of America's Greatest Problem.* 1932. NY. Holt. 1st Am. 8vo. 275p. NF/VG. B20. $30.00

**OXENBURY, Helen.** *Tom & Pippo Go for a Walk.* 1988. Aladdin. 1st. ils. VG+. M5. $10.00

**OXNAM, Robert B.** *Cinnabar.* 1989. NY. SMP. 1st. author's 1st novel. F/F. H11. $25.00

**OXNARD, Charles E.** *Order of Man.* 1983. Hong Kong. ils. 366p. F. S15. $12.00

**OZIAS, Blake.** *All About Wine.* 1973. Crowell. 1st revised. photos/maps. 144p. VG/G. S14. $5.00

**OZICK, Cynthia.** *Cannibal Galaxy.* 1983. NY. Knopf. 1st. F/dj. A24. $25.00

**OZICK, Cynthia.** *Trust.* 1966. NAL. 1st. F/NF. B4. $675.00

P

PACE, Tom. *Fisherman's Luck.* 1971. Harper Row. 1st. 246p. G/torn. H10. $15.00

PACHE, Rene. *Inspiration & Authority of Scripture.* 1969. Sheffield. 349p. F/wrp. B29. $9.00

PACHELLA & WITTEN. *Alchemy & the Occult: A Catalogue of Manuscripts...* 1977. Yale. 2 vol. sm folio. F/case. A4. $350.00

PACK, J. *Man Who Burned Washington: Admiral Sir Geo Cockburn...* 1987. Emsworth. 1st. ils. 288p. F/dj. M4. $20.00

PACKARD, Francis. *History of Medicine in the United States.* 1963. NY. facs of 1931. 2 vol. 1323p. A13. $250.00

PACKARD, Francis. *Some Account of the Pennsylvania Hospital...* 1938. Phil. 1st. 133p. A13. $75.00

PADDEN, R.C. *Hummingbird & the Hawk.* 1967. Columbus, OH. 1st. 319p. dj. F3. $30.00

PADDLEFORD, C. *Best in American Cooking.* 1970 (1960). abridged. VG. E6. $20.00

PADEN, Irene. *Wake of the Prairie Schooner.* 1943. Macmillan. 8vo. ils. 514p. red cloth. B11. $40.00

PADEREWSKI, Ignace Jan. *Paderewski Memoirs.* 1938. NY. Scribner. 1st. 8vo. 404p. VG. B11. $15.00

PADGETT, Abigail. *Child of Silence.* 1993. Mysterious. 1st. rem mk. F/dj. M23. $30.00

PADGETT, Abigail. *Turtle Baby.* 1995. Mysterious. 1st. F/dj. M23. $20.00

PADGETT, Lewis. *Gnome There Was.* 1950. S&S. 1st. VG. T12. $80.00

PADILLA, Herberto. *Self-Portrait of the Other: A Memoir.* 1990. FSG. 1st. 8vo. F/dj. A2. $13.00

PADOVER, Saul K. *Experiment in Germany: Story of Am Intelligence Officer.* 1946. DSP. 400p. tan cloth. VG/dj. G1. $50.00

PADOVER, Saul K. *World of the Founding Fathers: New Bicentennial Edition.* 1977. S Brunswick. Barnes. 553p. NF/dj. M10. $15.00

PAGE, Charles N. *Feathered Pets: A Treatise on Food, Breeding, Care...* 1898. Des Moines. self pub. 142p. VG. A17. $25.00

PAGE, Jake. *Pastorale, a Natural History of Sorts.* 1985. Norton. 1st. ils WH Gibson. NF/F. B3. $50.00

PAGE, Joseph A. *Revolution That Never Was: Northeast Brazil 1955-1964.* 1972. Grossman. 1st. 8vo. VG/dj. A2. $15.00

PAGE, Marco. *Reclining Figure.* 1952. Random. 1st. NF/VG. M19. $25.00

PAGE, Norman. *Dickens Chronology.* 1988. genealogical table. 164p. F/F. A4. $45.00

PAGE, Norman. *Dr Johnson Chronology.* 1990. 151p. F/NF. A4. $40.00

PAGE, Norman. *Interviews & Recollections.* 1987. NJ. Barnes Noble. dj. H13. $35.00

PAGE, Patti. *Once Upon a Dream: A Personal Chat With All Teenagers.* 1960. Bobbs Merrill. 1st. F/NF. B4. $85.00

PAGE, Russell. *Education of a Golfer.* 1983. NY. ils. VG/dj. M17. $30.00

PAGE, Thomas Nelson. *John Marvel, Assistant.* 1909. NY. Scribner. 1st. ils James Montgomery Flagg. G. G11. $12.00

PAGE, Thomas Nelson. *Old Dominion: Her Making & Her Manners.* 1908. Scribner. 1st. 8vo. F. M5. $25.00

PAGE, Thomas Nelson. *Old Gentleman of the Black Stock.* 1901. Scribner. 1st. ils HC Christy. gilt turquoise brd. VG. S13. $10.00

PAGE, Thomas Nelson. *Robert E Lee: Man & Soldier.* 1911. NY. Scribner. 1st. lg 8vo. 734p. gilt maroon cloth. B20. $50.00

PAGE & PAGE. *Evolution of Stars: How They Form, Age & Die.* 1968 (1968). NY. Macmillan. 2nd. 8vo. 334p. VG/dj. K5. $25.00

PAGE & THORNTON. *Apollo-Soyuz Experiments in Space.* 1977. NASA. set of 9 booklets. K5. $90.00

PAGET, Guy. *Sporting Pictures of England.* 1946. London. Collins. 2nd. ils. VG/G. O3. $25.00

PAGET, John. *Paradoxes & Puzzles: Historical, Judicial & Literary.* 1874. Edinburgh/London. Blackwood. 1st. 472p. rust cloth. NF. B20. $75.00

PAGET, R.L. *Cap & Gown, Third Series.* 1903. Boston. LC Page. 1st. gream pict cloth (no college arms). F. M24. $200.00

PAGNEL, Camille. *Geschichte Scanderbeg's Oder Turken & Christen...* 1856. Tubingen. 8vo. in Gothic script. 409p. cloth. VG. Q2. $257.00

PAIGE, Leroy Satchel. *Maybe I'll Pitch Forever.* 1962. Garden City. 1st. VG/G. B5. $45.00

PAIGE, Leroy Satchel. *Pitchin' Man.* 1948. Clevland News. 1st. VG/wrp. P8. $35.00

PAIGE, Richard; see Koontz, Dean R.

PAIGE & SWIFT. *Elements of Linear Algebra.* 1961. Ginn. 1st. gray cloth. VG. B27. $20.00

PAINE, Albert Bigelow. *How Mr Rabbit Lost His Tail.* April 1915. Harper. 1st/2nd prt. 12mo. 102p. VG. B27. $45.00

PAINE, Martyn. *Discourse on the Soul & Instinct...* 1849 (1848). NY. EH Fletcher. 2nd/enlarged. emb Victorian cloth. G1. $85.00

PAINE, Thomas. *Genuine Trial of Thomas Paine...Rights of Man.* 1793. London. Jordan. 8vo. ftspc portrait. calf. R12. $350.00

PAINE, Thomas. *Life & Writings of... Edited & Annotated...* 1915. NY. Vincent Parke. Centenary Memorial Ed. 10 vol. G. H10. $165.00

PAINE, Thomas. *Writings of...* 1793. Albany. Prt by Chas/Geo Webster. 1st Am. later bdg. O1. $500.00

PAINE & SOPER. *Art & Architecture of Japan.* 1955. Pentuin. photos. VG. M17. $30.00

PAISLEY, Keith. *Protected Cultivation, Modern Management.* 1962. London. Pearson. 215p. VG/dj. A10. $32.00

PAKENHAM, T. *Scramble for Africa 1876-1912.* 1991. NY. ils. 738p. F/dj. M4. $30.00

PALECEK, L. *Magic Grove.* 1985. NY. Picture Book Studio. ils Josef Palecek. 42p. F/dj. D4. $25.00

PALEY, Grace. *Little Disturbances of Man.* 1959. Doubleday. 1st. author's 1st book. VG/dj. A24. $135.00

PALEY, Grace. *Little Disturbances of Man.* 1959. Doubleday. 1st. sgn. author's 1st book. F/NF. B4. $350.00

PALEY, William. *Miscellaneous Works of...* 1821. London. 4 vol. 3-quarter old calf/marbled brd. S17. $125.00

PALGRAVE, William G. *Personal Narrative of a Year's Journey Through...Arabia.* 1868. London. Macmillan. 8vo. ils/fld map/fld plans. 421p. cloth. VG. Q2. $86.00

PALIN, Michael. *Hemingway's Chair.* 1995. London. Methuen. 1st. author's 1st novel. F/NF. A24. $35.00

PALLIS, Marietta. *Tableaux in Greek History.* 1952. London. MacLehose. folio. ils. 160p. G/wrp. M10. $50.00

PALLISER, Charles. *Quincunx.* 1990. Ballantine. 1st. author's 1st book. NF/dj. S13. $10.00

PALLISER, Charles. *Quincunx.* 1990. Ballantine. 1st. F/dj. T12. $30.00

PALLOTTINO, Massimo. *Meaning of Archaeology.* 1968. Abrams. 1st Am. lg 4to. 350p. F/NF. B20. $35.00

PALMATARY, H.C. *Archaeology of the Lower Tapajos Valley, Brazil.* 1960. Am Philos Soc. ils/maps. NF. M4. $25.00

**PALMER, Alonzo B.** *Diarrhoea & Dysentery: Modern Views on Their Pathology...* 1887. 1st. VG. E6. $75.00

**PALMER, Arnold.** *Arnold Palmer's Complete Book of Putting.* 1986. Atheneum. 1st. F/dj. C15. $14.00

**PALMER, E.L.** *Fieldbook of Natural History.* 1949. NY. ils. 664p. VG+. M12. $27.50

**PALMER, Frederick.** *Clark of the Ohio.* 1929. Dodd Mead. VG. A19. $35.00

**PALMER, Frederick.** *Over the Pass.* 1912. NY. Scribner. 1st. 438p. G. G11. $12.00

**PALMER, Howard.** *Real Baseball Story.* 1953. Pageant. 1st. VG. P8. $135.00

**PALMER, Joe E.** *Old Baseball Scouts & His Players.* 1987. Remlap. 1st. F/wrp. P8. $25.00

**PALMER, Laura.** *Shrapnel in the Heart: Letters & Remembrances...* 1987. Random. 1st. F/NF. R11. $17.00

**PALMER, Marjorie.** *1918-1923. German Hyperinflation.* 1967. Palmer, NY. Trader's Pr. mini. 1/2500 (400 destroyed). ils/maps/charts. F. B24. $160.00

**PALMER, Ralph S.** *Maine Birds.* July 1949. Cambridge. 1st. 656p. gilt gr cloth. F. B14. $75.00

**PALMER, Robin.** *Wings of the Morning: Verses From the Bible.* 1968. NY. Walck. 1st. 8vo. unp. NF/VG. C14. $8.00

**PALMER, Stuart.** *Rook Takes Knight.* 1968. Random. 1st. F/clip. M15. $35.00

**PALMER, William J.** *Court Vs the People, a Study...* 1969. Chicago. Chas Hallberg. G/worn. M11. $45.00

**PALOS, Stephan.** *Chinese Art of Healing.* 1971. NY. 1st. 235p. xl. A13. $20.00

**PALWICK, Susan.** *Flying in Place.* 1992. NY. Tor. 1st. F/dj. G10. $20.00

**PAMUK, Orhan.** *New Life.* 1997. FSG. 1st. sgn. F/dj. O11. $45.00

**PANASSIE, Hughues.** *Hot Jazz.* 1934. NY. Witmark. 1st. F/NF. B2. $200.00

**PANASSIE, Hughues.** *Real Jazz.* 1942. Smith Durrell. 1st. F/NF. B2. $85.00

**PANCAKE, Breece D'J.** *Storis of D'J Pancake.* 1983. Little Brn. 1st. author's 1st/only book. NF/dj. Q1. $25.00

**PANCOAST, Henry S.** *English Prose & Verse, From Beowulf to Stevenson.* 1915. Holt. sm 4to. 816p. NF. W2. $75.00

**PANCOAST & VANDERBECK.** *Beautiful Womanhood: Guide to Mental & Physical Development.* 1904. Chicago. ils. VG. M17. $35.00

**PANICH & TRULSSON.** *Desert Southweast Gardens.* 1990. NY. 245p. VG/dj. B26. $42.50

**PANNEKOEK, A.** *History of Astronomy.* 1961. NY. Interscience. 8vo. 521p. VG/dj. K5. $40.00

**PANSHIN, Alexei.** *Heinlein in Dimension.* 1974. Advent. 4th. F/dj. P3. $20.00

**PAPAYANIS, Nicholas.** *Coachmen of 19th-Century Paris.* 1993. Baton Rouge. LSU. 1st. F/dj. O3. $25.00

**PAPAZOGLOU, Orania.** *Sanctity.* 1986. Crown. 1st. author's 3rd novel. F/dj. N4. $30.00

**PAPE, Dorothy.** *Captives of the Mighty: Christ & the Japanese Enigma.* 1959. Chicago. Moody. NF/VG. B9. $15.00

**PAPE, Frank C.** *Book of Psalms.* 1912. London. Hutchinson. 1/150. sgn. 282p. half bl morocco/marbled brd. F. B24. $550.00

**PARACELSUS.** *Four Treaties of Theophrastus von Hohenheim...* 1941. Baltimore. 1st. 256p. A13. $100.00

**PARADIS, Marjorie.** *Mr DeLuca's Horse.* 1966. Atheneum. ils Judith Brown. xl. B36. $13.00

**PARAMOURE, Anne.** *Complete Miniature Schnauzer.* 1959. Denlinger. 528p. VG. A17. $12.50

**PARETSKY, Sara.** *Bitter Medicine.* 1987. Morrow. 1st. F/dj. D10. $75.00

**PARETSKY, Sara.** *Blood Shot.* 1988. Delacorte. 1st. F/dj. M19. $35.00

**PARETSKY, Sara.** *Blood Shot.* 1988. Delacorte. 1st. F/NF. A23. $25.00

**PARETSKY, Sara.** *Blood Shot.* 1988. Delacorte. 1st. sgn. F/dj. T2. $45.00

**PARETSKY, Sara.** *Burn Marks.* 1990. Delacorte. 1st. F/dj. N4. $30.00

**PARFIELD, Peter.** *Titanic & the Californian.* 1966. NY. John Day. 1st. ils/index. 318p. G+. B5. $50.00

**PARFIT, J.T.** *Among the Druzes of Lebanon & Bashan.* 1917. London. Hunter Longhurst. 8vo. ils. 252p. cloth. VG. Q2. $52.00

**PARGETER, Edith Mary.** *City of Gold & Shadows.* 1974. Morrow. 1st. VG/NF. C15. $50.00

**PARGETER, Edith Mary.** *Confession of Brother Haluin.* 1988. Mysterious. 1st. NF/dj. G8. $15.00

**PARGETER, Edith Mary.** *Dead Man's Ransom.* 1984. London. Macmillan. 1st. Cadfael #9. F/dj. M15. $175.00

**PARGETER, Edith Mary.** *Excellent Mystery.* 1985. London. Macmillan. 1st. Cadfael #11. F/dj. M15. $150.00

**PARGETER, Edith Mary.** *Fallen Into the Pit.* 1991. Mysterious. 1st. F/dj. A23. $32.00

**PARGETER, Edith Mary.** *Holy Thief.* 1993. Mysterious. 1st Am. NF/dj. A23. $25.00

**PARGETER, Edith Mary.** *Monk's-hood.* 1980. London. Macmillan. 1st. Cadfael #3. F/dj. M15. $400.00

**PARGETER, Edith Mary.** *Never Pick Up Hitch-Hikers.* 1976. London. Macmillan. 1st. F/dj. M15. $350.00

**PARGETER, Edith Mary.** *Potter's Field.* 1989. London. Headline. 1st. F/NF. B3. $40.00

**PARGETER, Edith Mary.** *Rare Benedictine: Advent of Brother Cadfael.* 1989. Mysterious. 1st. ils Clifford Harper. F/NF. M19. $17.50

**PARGETER, Edity Mary.** *Black is the Color of My True Love's Heart.* 1967. London. Collins Crime Club. 1st. F/clip. M15. $200.00

**PARINI, Jay.** *Anthracite Country.* 1982. Random. 1st. F/F. B2. $45.00

**PARINI, Jay.** *Patch Boys.* 1986. Holt. 1st. author's 2nd novel. F/NF. R14. $30.00

**PARIS, Edmond.** *Genocide in Satellite Croatia, 1941-1945.* 1962. Chicago. Balkan Affairs. NF/dj. B9. $30.00

**PARISH, Edmund.** *Hallucinations & Illusions: A Study...* 1897. London. Walter Scott Ltd. 1st Eng-language. 12mo. 390p. emb crimson cloth. G1. $75.00

**PARISH, Peggy.** *Amelia Bedelia & the Surprise Shower.* nd (1966). Harper Row. I Can Read Book. 8vo. 64p. VG+/fair. C14. $6.00

**PARISH, Peggy.** *Play Ball, Amelia Bedelia.* 1972. Harper Row. 1st. F/dj. P8. $12.50

**PARISH, Roberta.** *Plants of Southern Interior British Columbia.* 1996. Vancouver. photos/ils. 463p. AN. B26. $25.00

**PARISH, S.B.** *Catalogue of Plants Collected in the Salton Sink.* 1913. WA, DC. inscr. fld map. wrp. B26. $27.50

**PARK, Bertram.** *World of Roses.* 1962. NY. ils. unp. VG+/dj. B26. $16.00

**PARKER, Al.** *Baseball Giant Killer.* 1976. Nortex. 1st. F/VG+. P8. $100.00

**PARKER, Dorothy.** *Collected Short Stories of Dorothy Parker.* 1942. Modern Lib. later prt. inscr/dtd 1953. F/VG+ clip. B4. $375.00

**PARKER, Dorothy.** *Here Lies: Collected Stories of Dorothy Parker.* 1939. NY. Literary Guild. 1st thus? sgn Dorothy Thompson. 362p. VG/clip. A25. $50.00

**PARKER, Dorothy.** *Ladies of the Corridor.* 1954. NY. 1st. VG. B5. $50.00

**PARKER, Eric.** *Lonsdale Library of Hounds & Dogs, Vol XIII.* 1932. Sealley. 100 ils. VG. A21. $65.00

**PARKER, Franklin.** *Central American Republics.* 1971. London. Oxford. 2 fld maps. 348p. F3. $20.00

**PARKER, James Reed.** *Pleasure Was All Mine.* 1946. NY. Current. 1st. sm 8vo. 214p. NF/dj. B20. $20.00

**PARKER, Kathleen.** *We Won Today.* 1977. Doubleday. 1st. F/VG. P8. $35.00

**PARKER, Robert B.** *All Our Yesterdays.* 1994. Delacorte. 1st. F/dj. A23. $30.00

**PARKER, Robert B.** *Catskill Eagle.* 1985. Delacorte. 1st. NF/NF. A23. $30.00

**PARKER, Robert B.** *Crimson Joy.* 1988. Delacorte. 1st. F/dj. R14. $25.00

**PARKER, Robert B.** *Early Autumn.* 1981. Delacorte. 1st. NF/dj. M21. $40.00

**PARKER, Robert B.** *Introduction to Raymond Chandler's Unknown Thriller...* 1985. NY. Mysterious. 1st. F/wrp. M15. $200.00

**PARKER, Robert B.** *Love & Glory.* 1983. Delacorte. 1st. F/dj. A20. $30.00

**PARKER, Robert B.** *Pastime.* 1991. Putnam. 1st. F/dj. G8. $15.00

**PARKER, Robert B.** *Pastime.* 1991. Putnam. 1st. 1/150. sgn. F/case. M15. $135.00

**PARKER, Robert B.** *Promised Land.* 1976. Boston. Houghton Mifflin. 1st. sgn. F/dj. M15. $150.00

**PARKER, Robert B.** *Sudden Mischief.* 1998. Putnam. 1st. sgn. F/dj. M15. $40.00

**PARKER, Robert B.** *Thin Air.* 1995. Putnam. 1st. G+/NF. G8. $15.00

**PARKER, Robert B.** *Valediction.* 1984. Delacorte Lawrence. 1st. F/dj. M15. $35.00

**PARKER, Robert B.** *Widening Gyre.* 1983. Delacorte. 1st. F/F. T2. $45.00

**PARKER, Robert B.** *Wilderness.* 1979. Delacorte Lawrence. 1st. F/dj. M15. $85.00

**PARKER, Samuel.** *Journal of Exploring Tour Beyond Rocky Mountains...* 1842. Ithaca. 3rd. 408p. gilt blk cloth. G (lacks map). H7. $50.00

**PARKER, T. Jefferson.** *Laguna Heat.* 1985. NY. St Martin. 1st. F/NF. H11. $50.00

**PARKER, T. Jefferson.** *Laguna Heat.* 1985. St Martin. 1st. author's 1st novel. VG/dj. w/promo letter. R14. $35.00

**PARKER, T. Jefferson.** *Little Saigon.* 1988. NY. St Martin. 1st. F/F. H11. $30.00

**PARKER, T. Jefferson.** *Little Saigon.* 1988. St Martin. 1st. sgn. F/dj. A23. $42.00

**PARKER, T. Jefferson.** *Pacific Beat.* 1991. St Martin. 1st. F/dj. A23. $36.00

**PARKER, T. Jefferson.** *Pacific Beat.* 1991. St Martin. 1st. NF/dj. R11. $13.00

**PARKER, Ulla Hyde.** *Cousin Beatie.* 1981. Eng. Warne. 1st. sm 8vo. 40p. F/dj. T5. $55.00

**PARKER, Wayne.** *Bridewell Site.* ca 1982. Crosbyton. Crosby Co Pioneer Memorial. sgn. cbdg. VG. P4. $25.00

**PARKER, Willie J.** *Halt I'm A Federal Game Warden.* 1977. Nashville. 1st. 210p. dj. B5. $25.00

**PARKER & SMITH.** *Scene Design & Stage Lighting, Third Edition.* 1974. HRW. 597p. VG. M10. $7.50

**PARKES, Henry.** *History of Mexico.* 1960. Boston. Houghton Mifflin. 3rd. 458p. dj. F3. $15.00

**PARKINSON, C. Northcoate.** *Dead Reckoning.* 1978. Houghton Mifflin. 1st Am. F/NF clip. T11. $40.00

**PARKINSON, C. Northcoate.** *Dead Reckoning.* 1978. Houghton Mifflin. 1st. F/dj. A23. $42.00

**PARKINSON, C. Northcoate.** *Fireship.* 1975. Houghton Mifflin. 1st Am. Delancey #2. bl cloth. F/NF. T11. $30.00

**PARKINSON, C. Northcoate.** *Life & Times of Horatio Hornblower.* 1970. Little Brn. 1st. NF/VG. T11. $70.00

**PARKINSON, C. Northcoate.** *Touch & Go.* 1977. Houghton Mifflin. 1st Am. F/dj. T11. $50.00

**PARKINSON, John.** *Garden of Pleasant Flowers.* 1976. Dover. 627p. VG/dj. A10. $50.00

**PARKINSON, Norman.** *Sisters Under the Skin.* 1979 (1978). St Martin. 1st Am. VG/dj. S5. $25.00

**PARKINSON, Norman.** *Would You Let Your Daughter.* 1985. NY. Grove. 1st Am. ils. VG/clip. C9. $90.00

**PARKINSON, Norman.** *Would You Let Your Daughter.* 1985. NY. Grove. 1st Am. VG/clip. C9. $90.00

**PARKMAN, Francis.** *Montcalm & Wolfe.* (1984). Toronto. Viking BC. 1st thus. F/NF. A26. $30.00

**PARKMAN, Francis.** *Montcalm & Wolfe.* 1984. NY. Atheneum. ils. 590p. VG/dj. M10. $18.50

**PARKMAN, Francis.** *Oregon Trail.* 1892. Little Brn. 1st. ils Remington. 411p. half brn morocco. F. H5. $450.00

**PARKMAN, Francis.** *Works of...* 1902. Little Brn. 17 vol. Frontenac ed. teg. bl cloth/paper spine label. F. B20. $650.00

**PARKS, George Bruner.** *Richard Hakluyt & the English Voyages.* 1928. NY. Am Geog Soc. 1st. 8vo. ils/maps. 289p. NF. O1. $85.00

**PARKS, Gordon.** *Choice of Weapons.* 1966. Harper Row. 1st. VG/dj. R11. $35.00

**PARKS, Gordon.** *Gordon Parks: Poet & His Camera.* 1968. Viking/Studio. VG/dj. S5. $50.00

**PARKS, Gordon.** *Learning Tree.* 1963. Harper Row. 1st. inscr/dtd. F/NF. D10. $140.00

**PARKS, Gordon.** *Learning Tree.* 1963. Harper Row. 1st. NF/VG. S13. $38.00

**PARKS, Tim.** *Family Planning.* 1989. Grove Weidenfeld. 1st. F/dj. A23. $34.00

**PARKS, Tim.** *Home Thoughts.* 1987. NY. Grove. 1st. F/dj. A23. $34.00

**PARKS, Tim.** *Italian Neighbors.* 1992. Grove Weidenfeld. 1st. F/dj. A23. $34.00

**PARKS, Tim.** *Loving Roger.* 1986. London. Heinemann. 1st. F/dj. A23. $50.00

**PARKS, Tim.** *Tongues of Flame.* 1985. London. Heinemann. 1st. author's 1st novel. F/NF. A24. $75.00

**PARKS, Tim.** *Tongues of Flame.* 1986. NY. Grove. 1st. author's 1st book. F/dj. A23. $50.00

**PARLIN, S.W.** *American Trotter: A Treatise on His Origin, History...* 1905. Boston. Am Horse Breeder. 1st. 319p. G. B18. $50.00

**PARLOA, Maria.** *Miss Parloa's Kitchen Companion: A Guide...* 1887. 20th. 966p. E6. $45.00

**PARLOA, Maria.** *Miss Parloa's New Cook Book & Marketing Guide.* 1880. 1st. 430p. VG. E6. $75.00

**PARLOA, Maria.** *Miss Parloa's Young Housekeeper Designed...Beginners.* 1894 (1893). 404p. VG. E6. $50.00

**PARMELEE & MACDONALD.** *Bird of West-Central Ellesmere Island & Adjacent Areas.* 1960. Ottawa. Nat Mus Canada Bull #169. 10 photos. 103p. NF/wrp. C12. $28.00

**PARMET, Herbert S.** *Eisenhower & the American Crusades.* 1972. NY. 1st. photos. VG/dj. M17. $15.00

**PARRINGTON, V.L.** *Connecticut Wits.* 1969. NY. 514p. G/wrp. M4. $10.00

**PARRISH, Anne D.** *Knee High to a Grasshopper.* 1923. Macmillan. 1st. ils. 208p. orange cloth. VG. D1. $75.00

**PARRISH, Anne D.** *Story of Appleby Capple.* 1950. Harper. 1st? ils. VG. M5. $22.00

**PARRISH, Louis.** *Cooking as Therapy.* 1975. Arbor. G/dj. A16. $6.00

**PARRISH, Maxfield.** *Maxfield Parrish Pop-Up Book.* 1994. Pomegranate. 1st. obl 8vo. popups. VG+. B17. $16.00

**PARRISH, Michael E.** *Anxious Decades: America in Prosperity & Depression...* 1992. NY. ils. VG/dj. M17. $20.00

**PARRISH, Randall.** *Last Voyage of the Donna Isabel.* 1908. Chicago. McClurg. 1st. sm 8vo. 367p. VG. M7. $20.00

**PARRISH, Randall.** *My Lady of the North.* 1904. Chicago. McClurg. 1st. 362p. weak hinges. G11. $8.00

**PARRISH, T. Michael.** *Richard Taylor: Soldier Prince of Dixie.* 1992. U NC. 1st. F/dj. A14. $28.00

**PARRISH & PARRISH.** *Dream Coach.* 1924. Macmillan. 1st. 8vo. bl cloth. VG. M5. $60.00

**PARRISH & WILLINGHAM.** *Confederate Imprints: A Bibliography of Southern Pub...* (1987). Jenkins Foster. sgn Parrish. 991p. AN. B10. $135.00

**PARROT, Andre.** *Flood & Noah's Ark.* 1955. London. SCM Pr. Studies in Biblical Archaeology #1. 8vo. ils. 76p. dj. Q2. $13.50

**PARROT, Andre.** *Sumer: Dawn of Art.* 1961. Golden. ils/photos/maps/glossary. 446p. cloth. NF/dj. D2. $85.00

**PARRY, J.H.** *Discovery of South America.* 1979. Taplinger. 1st. 320p. dj. F3. $35.00

**PARRY, John S.** *Extra-Uterine Pregnancy: Its Causes, Species...* 1876. Phil. Lea. 276p. cloth. G7. $195.00

**PARSONS, C.W.** *British Antarctic (Terra Nova) Expedition, 1910.* 1934. London. British Mus. ils. VG/wrp. M12. $25.00

**PARSONS, Frances Theodora.** *According to Season: Talks About Flowers...* 1902. NY. Scribner. ils/index. VG. H10. $20.00

**PARSONS, Frances Theodora.** *How to Know the Ferns...* 1900. NY. Scribner. ils/index. G. H10. $15.00

**PARSONS, Geoffrey.** *Stream of History (Volumes III & IV).* 1929. Scribner. 2 vol (of 4). 1st trade. 8vo. bl cloth. F. R3. $75.00

**PARSONS, John E.** *Henry Derirnger's Pocket Pistol.* 1952. NY. Morrow. ils. 255p. VG/dj. B18. $35.00

**PARSONS, John E.** *Peacemaker & Its Rivals.* 1950. Morrow. G/dj. A19. $45.00

**PARSONS, John Herbert.** *Introduction to Study of Colour Vision.* 1915. Putnam. 308p. gr cloth. Am issue bdg. G1. $65.00

**PARSONS, Leonard.** *Influence of Harvey & His Contemporaries on Paediatrics.* 1950. London. 1st. 23p. A13. $25.00

**PARSONS, Usher.** *Directions for Making Anatomical Preparations...* 1831. Phil. Carey Lea. 4 pl. 316p+ads. full sheep. G7. $135.00

**PARTON, James.** *General Jackson...Great Commanders Series.* 1892. Appleton. 1st/lg paper issue. 1/1000. map/index. 332p. VG. S16. $125.00

**PARTRIDGE, Anthony.** *Golden Web.* 1911. Little Brn. 1st. ils Wm Kirkpatrick. 339p. G. G11. $8.00

**PASLEY, Virginia.** *In Celebration of Food.* 1974. S&S. 1st. G/dj. A16. $17.50

**PASOLINI, Pier Paolo.** *Letters 1940-54.* 1992. London. 1st. trans S Hood. edit N Naldini. dj. T9. $18.00

**PASQUARIELLO, Donald D.** *Conversations With Andrew Greeley.* 1988. Quinlan. 1st. NF/dj. P3. $20.00

**PASTON, George.** *Little Memoirs of the 18th Century.* 1901. NY. Dutton. 2nd. gilt blk cloth. VG. H13. $65.00

**PASTON, George.** *Social Caricature in the 18th Century.* 1905. London. Methuen. tall folio. ils. 144p. teg. gilt bl cloth. H13. $345.00

**PASTON & QUENNELL.** *To Lord Byron.* 1939. Scribner. 12 pl. 275p. VG/dj. B11. $40.00

**PATCHEN, Kenneth.** *Dark Kingdom.* 1942. NY. Harris Givens. 1st. inscr. author's 4th book. F. L3. $250.00

**PATCHEN, Kenneth.** *First Will & Testament.* (1948). NY. Padell. 1st thus/reissue. sgn. NF/VG clip. L3. $150.00

**PATCHEN, Kenneth.** *First Will & Testament.* 1939. New Directions. 1st. 1/800. author's 2nd book. F/NF. L3. $450.00

**PATCHEN, Kenneth.** *Memoirs of a Shy Pornographer.* 1948. London. Grey Walls. 1st. NF/dj. L3. $75.00

**PATCHEN, Kenneth.** *Orchards, Thrones & Caravans.* 1953. SF. Prt Workshop. 1st. 1/120. sgn. vellum issue. F/NF/clamshell box. L3. $750.00

**PATCHEN, Kenneth.** *Red Wine & Yellow Hair.* 1949. New Directions. 1st. 1/2000. inscr. VG/dj. L3. $375.00

**PATCHEN, Kenneth.** *See You in the Morning.* 1949. London. Grey Walls. 1st. VG/NF. L3. $100.00

**PATCHEN, Kenneth.** *There's Love All Day: Poems by California's Kenneth Patchen.* (1970). Hallmark Eds. 1st. ils Tom diGrazia. F/VG. A18. $20.00

**PATER, Walter.** *Appreciations With Essay on Style.* 1889. London. 442p. gilt cloth. VG. B14. $75.00

**PATER, Walter.** *Greek Studies: Series of Essays.* 1895. London. Macmillan. 1st. photo ftspc. bl cloth. F. B14. $75.00

**PATER, Walter.** *Plato & Platonism: A Series of Lectures.* 1893. London. Macmillan. 1st. bl cloth. VG. B14. $65.00

**PATER, Walter.** *Renaissance: Studies in Art & Poetry.* 1907. NY. 3-quarter leather/maroon brd. VG. M17. $20.00

**PATERNAK, Boris.** *Safe Conduct: Early Autobiography & Other Works...* 1959. London. Elek. 1st. 8vo. F/dj. A2. $25.00

**PATERSON, Katherine.** *Jacob Have I Loved.* 1980. NY. Crowell. 1st. 8vo. 1981 Newbery. gilt cloth. mc pict dj. R5. $100.00

**PATERSON, Nathaniel.** *Manse Garden.* 1838. Glasgow. Collins. 262p. VG. A10. $75.00

**PATERSON, W. Romaine.** *Nemesis of Nations: Studies in History.* 1907. NY. Putnam. 1st. 8vo. 348p. cloth. G. W1. $20.00

**PATERSON, W.P.** *Rule of Faith.* nd. Revell. 468p. VG. B29. $9.50

**PATERSON, Wilma.** *Fountain of Gardens: Plants & Herbs of the Bible.* (1992). Overlook. ils/biblio/index. 160p. VG/dj. H10. $52.00

**PATMORE, Derek.** *Star & the Crescent: Anthology of Modern Turkish Poetry.* 1946 (1945). London. Constable. rpt. 50p. VG. Q2. $20.00

**PATON, Alan.** *For You Departed: A Memoir.* 1969. Scribner. 1st. sm 8vo. 156p. F/clip. B20. $20.00

**PATON, Alan.** *Too Late the Phalarope.* 1953. Scribner. 1st Am. sgn. NF/VG. R14. $90.00

**PATRICK, Vincent.** *Pope of Greenwich Village.* 1979. NY. Seaview. 1st. author's 1st book. NF/NF. H11. $15.00

PATRIDGE, Norman. *Bad Intentions.* 1996. Burton. Subterranean. 1st. 1/500. sgn. F/dj. T2. $40.00

PATRIDGE, Norman. *Spyder.* 1995. Burton. Subterranean. 1st. 1/500. sgn. F/wrp. T2. $12.00

PATROUCH, Joseph F. *Science Fiction of Isaac Asimov.* 1974. Doubleday. VG/dj. P3. $22.00

PATTEN, Bernard. *Systems Analysis & Simulation in Ecology. Vol 1.* 1971. Academic. 607p. xl. VG. S5. $35.00

PATTEN, Marguerite. *Cakes & Baking.* 1972. Hamlyn Pub. G/dj. A16. $15.00

PATTEN, Marguerite. *Fish, Meat, Poultry & Game.* 1970. NY. Hamlyn. G/dj. A16. $20.00

PATTEN, Marguerite. *Made a Menu Book.* 1965. London. Hamlyn. G/dj. A16. $10.00

PATTERSON, Edmund DeWitt. *Yankee Rebel in the Civil War Journal of...* 1966. U NC. 1st. ils. 207p. cloth. NF/VG. M8. $65.00

PATTERSON, Harry. *To Catch a King.* 1979. Stein Day. 1st Am. F/NF. P3. $25.00

PATTERSON, J.B. *Life of Ma-ka-Tai-Me-She-Kia-Kiak or Black Hawk...* 1834. Boston. 2nd. 12mo. 155p. VG. H7. $120.00

PATTERSON, James. *Along Came a Spider.* 1993. Little Brn. ARC. sgn. F/dj. A23. $35.00

PATTERSON, James. *Black Market.* 1986. S&S. rem mk. F/F. H11. $20.00

PATTERSON, James. *Hide & Seek.* 1996. Little Brn. 1st. sgn. F/dj. A23. $42.00

PATTERSON, James. *Hide & Seek.* 1996. Little Brn. 1st. VG/dj. R8. $12.00

PATTERSON, James. *Jack & Jill.* 1996. Boston. Little Brn. 1st. sgn. F/dj. A23. $42.00

PATTERSON, James. *Jack & Jill.* 1996. Little Brn. 1st. NF/F. S18. $13.00

PATTERSON, James. *Kiss the Girls.* 1995. Little Brn. F/F. T12. $45.00

PATTERSON, James. *Midnight Club.* 1989. Boston. Little Brn. 1st. sgn. F/dj. A23. $48.00

PATTERSON, James. *Miracle on the 17th Green.* 1996. Boston. Little Brn. 1st. sgn. F/dj. A23. $38.00

PATTERSON, Lillie. *Lumberjacks of the North Woods.* 1967. Garrard. 8vo. 96p. xl. VG. W2. $15.00

PATTERSON, Richard North. *Degree of Guilt.* 1993. Knopf. 1st. F/F. H11. $30.00

PATTERSON, Richard North. *Degree of Guilt.* 1993. Knopf. 1st. NF/F. S18. $25.00

PATTERSON, Richard North. *Eyes of a Child.* 1995. Knopf 1st. 594p. F/dj. P12. $12.00

PATTERSON, Richard North. *Final Judgment.* 1995. NY. Knopf. ARC. F/dj. A23. $34.00

PATTERSON, Richard North. *Lasko Tangent.* 1979. NY. Norton. 1st. F/dj. M15. $275.00

PATTERSON, Richard North. *Silent Witness.* 1996. Knopf. 1st. F/dj. S18. $18.00

PATTIE-FLINT, Timothy. *Personal Narrative of James O Pattie of Kentucky.* Christmas 1930. Lakeside Pr/RR Donnelley. 428p. red cloth. VG. F7. $40.00

PATTISON, Iain. *John McFadyean: Great British Veterinarian.* 1981. London/NY. JA Allen. 1st. VG/dj. N2. $10.00

PAUL, Barbara. *But He Was Already Dead When I Got There.* 1985. Scribner. 1st. NF/dj. G8. $15.00

PAUL, Barbara. *He Huffed & He Puffed.* 1989. Scribner. 1st Eng. NF/dj. G8. $20.00

PAUL, Charlotte. *Minding Our Own Business.* 1955. Random. 1st. sgn. 8vo. 310p. NF/dj. B20. $20.00

PAUL, Elliot. *My Old Kentucky Home.* 1949. Random. 1st. NF/VG. T11. $35.00

PAUL, Hermann. *Principles of History of Language.* 1889. Macmillan. 2nd/1st Eng-language. 512p. ruled brn cloth. VG. G1. $85.00

PAUL, John II. *Crossing the Threshold of Hope.* 1994. Knopf. 1st Am. VG/dj. B11. $15.00

PAUL, Rodman Wilson. *Mining Frontiers of the Far West 1848-1880.* 1974. Albuquerque. 2nd. 236p. VG/wrp. P4. $30.00

PAUL, S. *Economical Cookbook.* 1905. 1st. ils. VG. E6. $30.00

PAUL II, John. *Crossing the Threshold of Hope.* 1994. Knopf. 1st/4th prt. inscr. 8vo. 244p. F/dj. W2. $45.00

PAULHAN, Frederic. *L'Activite Mentale et les Elements de l'Esprit.* 1889. Paris. Bailliere. thick 8vo. 588p. later cloth. G1. $75.00

PAULHAN, Frederic. *Laws of Feeling.* 1930. Harcourt Brace. 1st Am/prt on British sheets. 213p. gr cloth. G1. $45.00

PAULI, Hertha. *Silent Night: Story of a Song.* 1943. Knopf. 1st. gilt bl bdg. 84p. G/dj. P12. $25.00

PAULI, Hertha. *St Nicholas' Travels.* 1945. Houghton Mifflin. 1st. 8vo. F/VG. M5. $32.00

PAULIN, Tom. *Faber Book of Vernacular Verse.* 1990. London. 1st. dj. T9. $15.00

PAULL, Mrs. George A. *Prince Dimple & His Everyday Doings. Told for Little Ones.* 1890. Anson Randolph. 8vo. ils. gilt bl cloth. M5. $55.00

PAULSEN, Gary. *Murphy.* 1985. NY. Walker. 1st. F/F. B3. $30.00

PAUPERT, Jean-Marie. *What Is the Gospel?* 1962. NY. Hawthorn. 1st. 8vo. VG/dj. A2. $15.00

PAVAROTTI, Luciano. *Pavarotti: My Own Story.* 1981. Doubleday. ne. F. W2. $20.00

PAVLOV, Ivan Petrovich. *Conditioned Reflexes: An Investigation...* 1927. Oxford/ Humphrey Milford. 1st Eng-language. lg 8vo. 430p. pebbled blk cloth. G1. $200.00

PAVLOV, Ivan Petrovich. *Die Arbeit der Verdauungsdrusen.* 1898. Wiesbaden. Bergmann. 199p. VG. G7. $1,500.00

PAVLOV, Ivan Petrovich. *Die Physiologie der Hochsten.* 1932. Tivoli. Arti Grefiche Aldo Chicca. 18p. prt brn wrp. rare. G1. $150.00

PAVLOV, Ivan Petrovich. *Lectures on Conditioned Reflexes...* 1982 (1941). NY. Internat Pub. 3rd Eng-language. trans/inscr Jenkins. 414p. blk cloth. G1. $75.00

PAVLOV, Ivan Petrovich. *Lectures on Conditioned Reflexes...* 1991. Birmingham. Classics of Psychiatry & Behavioral Sciences Lib. 2 vol. G1. $100.00

PAVLOV, Ivan Petrovich. *Selected Works.* 1955. Moscow. 1st. 654p. A13. $100.00

PAVLOV, Ivan Petrovich. *Work of the Digestive Glands. A Facsimile of 1st Russian...* 1982. Birmingham. 1st thus. full leather. A13. $100.00

PAVLOV, Ivan Petrovich. *Work of the Digestive Glands. Lectures by...* 1902. London. Griffin. 196p. red cloth. VG. G7. $495.00

PAVLOV, Ivan Petrovich. *Works of the Digestive Glands.* 1910 (1902). London. Griffin. 2nd Eng-language. 266p. xl. G1. $200.00

PAWEL, Ernst. *Labyrinth of Exile: Life of Theodor Herzl.* 1989. FSG. 1st. VG/dj. N2. $10.00

PAWLETT, Nathaniel Mason. *Louisa County Road Orders 1742-48.* 1975. VA Hwy & Transp Council. 57p. sbdg. xl. VG. B10. $25.00

PAXSON, Frederic L. *History of the American Frontier 1763-1893.* 1924. Houghton Mifflin. 1st. ils/11 maps. 598p. VG. B18. $35.00

PAXTON, Harry. *Whiz Kids.* 1950. McKay. 1st. photos. VG/G. P8. $250.00

PAXTON, Mary. *River Gold.* 1928. Bobbs Merrill. 1st. 8vo. VG+/fair. M5. $15.00

PAYNE, Alan; see Jakes, John.

PAYNE, David. *Ruin Creek.* 1993. Doubleday. 1st. F/dj. R14. $40.00

PAYNE, Josephine Balfour. *Once There Was Olga.* 1944. Putnam. 1st. ils. VG. M5. $15.00

PAYNE, Robert. *Dream & the Tomb: History of the Crusades.* 1984. NY. 1st. ils. VG/dj. M17. $17.50

PAYNE, Robert. *Lost Treasures of the Mediterranean World.* 1962. NY. Thos Nelson. 1st. sm 4to. ils. NF/dj. W1. $28.00

PAYNE, Roger. *Among Whales.* 1995. NY. 1st. ils. 431p. F/dj. S15. $18.00

PAYNE, Roger. *Extracts From the Diary of Roger Payne.* 1929. NY. Harbor. 1/525. brn brd/paper label. F. F1. $45.00

PAYNE, Stephen. *Where the Rockies Ride Herd.* 1965. Sage. F/dj. A19. $45.00

PAYNE, Theodore. *Life on the Modjeska Ranch in the Gay Nineties.* 1962. self pub. 1st. F/dj. O4. $15.00

PAZ, Octavio. *Conjunctions & Disjunctions.* 1974. NY. 1st Am. trans Helen R Lane. VG/dj. M17. $17.50

PAZ, Octavio. *Double Flame: Love & Eroticism.* 1995. Harcourt Brace. rem mk. F/dj. B9. $15.00

PAZ, Octavio. *Other Voice.* 1991. HBJ. 1st. F/dj. M23. $20.00

PAZ, U. *Birds of Israel.* 1987. Lexington, MA. lg 8vo. photos. 264p. NF. C12. $60.00

PAZZI, Roberto. *Searching for the Emperor.* 1988. NY. 1st. F/dj. A23. $36.00

PEABODY, J.B. *John Adams: Biography in His Own Words.* (1973). NY. Newsweek. Founding Father series. 4to. 208p. bl cloth. H4. $10.00

PEABODY, J.B. *John Adams: Biography in His Own Words.* 1973. NY. 2 vol. deluxe ed. ils. padded leatherette. NF/dj. M4. $20.00

PEABODY, Robert. *Hospital Sketches.* 1916. Boston. 1st. 91p. A13. $45.00

PEACOCK, Doug. *Baja!* 1991. Boston. Bullfinch. 1st. F/F. B3. $50.00

PEACOCK, Howard. *Nature of Texas.* 1990. TX A&M. 80 mc photos. 124p. F/dj. S15. $10.00

PEALE, Mrs. Norman Vincent. *Adventure of Being a Housewife.* 1971. Guideposts. ne. F/NF. W2. $20.00

PEARCE, John Ed. *Colonel: Captivating Biography of Dynamic Founder Fast Food.* 1982. NY. Doubleday. 1st. fwd JY Brown. 225p. F/NF. H6. $28.00

PEARCE, Philippa. *Battle of Bubble & Squeak.* 1978. London. Andre Deutsch. 88p. F/dj. D4. $35.00

PEARCE, T.M. *Cartoon Guide of New Mexico.* 1939. JJ Augustin. 1st. ils/index. 107p. G. B19. $10.00

PEARL, Cyril. *Youth's Book on the Mind...* 1847. Portland, ME. Hyde Lord Duren/E French. revised. 12mo. VG. G1. $50.00

PEARLMAN, Moshe. *Digging Up the Bible.* 1980. Morrow. 240p. VG/torn. B29. $12.50

PEARS, Ian. *Titian Committee.* 1991. London. Gollancz. 1st. F/dj. M15. $65.00

PEARSE, A.S. *Animal Ecology.* 1939. McGraw Hill. 2nd. xl. VG. S5. $12.00

PEARSE, Eleanor H.D. *Florida's Vanishing Era From Journals of Young Girl.* (1947). np. photos. 75p. quarter cloth. B18. $27.50

PEARSE, R. *Three Years in the Levant.* 1949. London. Macmillan. 8vo. 294p. cloth. G+. Q2. $24.00

PEARSON, Anthony. *Great Case of Tithes Truly Stated...* 1730. London. J Sowle. 1st. 12mo. 292p. worn leather. V3. $95.00

PEARSON, Edmund. *Queer Books.* 1928. Doubleday. 1st. 8vo. 298p. F/dj. O10. $40.00

PEARSON, Edmund. *Trial of Lizzie Borden.* 1937. Doubleday Doran. 1st. ils. 433p. VG. B18. $35.00

PEARSON, Francis Calhoun. *Sparks Among the Ashes.* 1873. Lippincott. 1st. 327p. VG+. A25. $35.00

PEARSON, Haydn. *Country Flavor Cookbook.* 1962. Bramhall. 222p. VG/dj. A16. $7.50

PEARSON, Hesketh. *Johnson & Boswell: Story of Their Lives.* 1958. Harper. 1st. 8vo. 390p. F/dj. H13. $45.00

PEARSON, Howard A. *Lectures on Diseases of Children.* ca 1986. np. 8vo. 186p. NF/wrp. C14. $10.00

PEARSON, John. *James Bond: The Authorized Biography of 007.* 1973. NY. Morrow. 1st Am. F/dj. M15. $45.00

PEARSON, John. *James Bond: The Authorized Biography of 007.* 1973. NY. Morrow. 1st Am. VG/dj. G8. $25.00

PEARSON, John. *Wildlife & Safari in Kenya.* ca 1970. Nairobi. E African Pub House. 384p. VG. A17. $20.00

PEARSON, Michener. *Special Report on Diseases of Horses.* 1911. WA. USDA. revised 1st. index. 614p. F. A17. $15.00

PEARSON, Ridley. *Never Look Back.* 1985. St Martin. 1st. sgn. F/dj. M15. $125.00

PEARSON, Ridley. *Seizing of Yankee Green Mall.* 1987. St Martin. 1st. sgn. author's 3rd book. F/NF. B3. $65.00

PEARSON, T.R. *Call & Response.* 1989. NY. Linden. 1st. F/NF. R14. $30.00

PEARSON, T.R. *Last of How It Was.* 1987. Linden. 1st. F/dj. D10. $45.00

PEARSON, T.R. *Off for the Sweet Hereafter.* 1986. Linden. 1st. author's 2nd book. F/dj. D10. $45.00

PEARSON, T.R. *Short History of a Small Place.* 1985. Linden. 1st. author's 1st book. VG/dj. B30. $25.00

PEARSON, T.R. *Short History of a Small Place.* 1985. NY. Linden. 1st. F/NF. D10. $60.00

PEARSON & SHAW. *Live Extension Companion.* 1984. Warner. 1st. sm 4to. 430p. F/dj. W2. $35.00

PEARY, Danny. *Cult Movies 3: Fifty More of the Classics...* 1988. NY. Delta. ils. VG/wrp. C9. $36.00

PEARY, Josephine Diebitsch. *Snow Baby.* 1901. NY. 7th. 84p. VG. B18. $50.00

PEASE, T.C. *Frontier State 1818-1848.* 1987. IL U. ils. 475p. F. M4. $15.00

PEASE, William D. *Playing the Dozens.* 1990. Viking. 1st. author's 1st book. F/F. H11. $25.00

PEAT, Fern Bisel. *Round the Mulberry Bush.* 1933. Saalfield. 1st. ils. VG+. B27. $150.00

PEAT, Frank Edwin. *Christmas Carols.* 1937. Saalfield. ils FB Peat. 46p. G. B18. $17.50

PEATTIE, D.C. *Almanac for Moderns.* 1928. LEC. 1/1500. sm 4to. 338p. gr cloth. F/NF case. B20. $125.00

PEATTIE, D.C. *Natural History of Western Trees.* 1953. Houghton Mifflin. ils Landacre. 751p. cloth. VG/dj. M12. $27.50

PEATTIE, D.C. *Rainbow Book of Nature.* 1957. World. 1st. ils Rudolf Freund. VG/G. P2. $25.00

PEATTIE, R. *Great Smokies & Blue Ridge: Story of Southern Appalachians.* 1943. NY. photos/map. F/fair. M4. $20.00

PECK, Annie S. *Flying Over South America.* 1932. Houghton Mifflin. 1st. photos/map ep. 255p. F3. $25.00

PECK, Dale. *Martin & John.* 1993. FSG. 1st. F/NF. C9. $42.00

PECK, Harry Thurston. *Harper's Dictionary of Classical Literature...* 1963. NY. Cooper Square. 2nd. ils 1701p. dj. D2. $95.00

PECK, J. *Armies With Wings.* 1940. 1st. ils/diagrams. xl. VG. E6. $20.00

PECK, J.M. *Forty Years of Pioneer Life: Memoir of John Mason Peck.* 1965. S IL U. rpt. F/dj. M4. $25.00

PECK, Paula. *Art of Fine Baking.* 1966. S&S. later prt. ils. F/NF. A16. $12.00

PECK, Robert Newton. *King of Kazoo.* 1976. NY. Knopf. 1st. 82p. VG+. D4. $30.00

PECK, Robert Newton. *Last Sunday.* 1977. Doubleday. 1st. VG/dj. P8. $12.50

PECK, T. Whitmore. *William Withering of Birmingham.* 1950. London. 1st. 239p. A13. $50.00

PECKHAM, Howard H. *Narrative of Colonial America.* 1971. Lakeside Classic. 1st thus. teg. dk bl cloth. F/sans. T11. $25.00

PECKHAM, Howard H. *Sources of American Independence.* 1978. Chicago U. 2 vol. 1st. M10. $32.50

PECKHAM, John M. *Fighting Fire With Fire.* 1972. Walter Haessner. 1st. photos. 231p. F/VG clip. T11. $40.00

PEDEN, Rachel. *Land, People: Testament by Author of Rural Free...* 1966. Knopf. stated 1st/Family Bookself. 332p. VG/dj. P12. $10.00

PEDRAZAS, Alan. *Harry Chronicles.* 1995. St Martin. 1st. F/dj. M15. $45.00

PEEL, Colin D. *Hell Seed.* 1979. St Martin 1st Am. NF/dj. M21. $15.00

PEER, F.S. *Soiling, Summer & Winter.* 1882. Rochester. Smith. 153p. cloth. VG. A10. $35.00

PEERY, Janet. *Alligator Dance.* 1993. Dallas. SMU. 1st. sgn. author's 1st book. F/dj. A24. $65.00

PEERY, Janet. *Alligator Dance.* 1993. TX, SMU. 1st. 1/2000. author's 1st book. F/dj. D10. $40.00

PEET, Bill. *Ant & the Elephant.* (1972). Houghton Mifflin. Weekly Reader BC. ils. 46p. G+. T5. $25.00

PEET, Louis Harman. *Trees & Shrubs of Prospect Park.* 1902. NY. 237p. xl. B26. $37.50

PEGLER, Martin M. *Stores of the Year.* 1989. NY. Retail Reporting Corp. 253p. VG. H6. $54.00

PEIRCE, Benjamin. *Idealty in the Physical Sciences.* 1881. Boston. 211p. A13. $60.00

PEIRSON, Erma. *Mojave River & Its Valley.* 1970. AH Clark. 1st. ils/notes/index. 223p. NF/NF. B19. $30.00

PEITGEN & RICHTER. *Beauty of Fractals: Images of Complex Dynamical Systems.* 1986. NY. Springer. NF. B9. $15.00

PEITHMANN, Irvin. *Unconquered Seminole Indians.* 1957. St Pete. Great Outdoors. 4to. 95p. VG/wrp. B11. $15.00

PEIXOTTO, Ernest. *Out Hispanic Southwest.* 1916. Scribner. 1st. ils. 245p. VG. B19. $35.00

PEIXOTTO, Ernest. *Pacific Shores From Panama.* 1913. Scribner. 1st. 24 pl. 284p. teg. cloth. F3. $35.00

PELECANOS, George P. *Down the River Where the Dead Men Go.* 1995. St Martin. 1st. F/dj. M15. $50.00

PELECANOS, George P. *Nick's Trip.* 1993. St Martin. 1st. F/dj. M15. $350.00

PELECANOS, George P. *Sweet Forever.* 1998. Tucson. McMillan. 1st. 1/400. sgn. F/dj/case. M15. $125.00

PELLAPRAT, Henri-Paul. *Modern French Culinary Art.* 1966. World. photos. VG/dj. M17. $20.00

PELLEGRENO, A.H. *World Flight: The Earhart Trail.* 1971. Ames. 1st. sgn. VG/dj. B5. $30.00

PELLEPRAT, H. *Modern French Culinary Art.* 1961. 1st. 752p. VG/VG. E6. $30.00

PELLICIARI, Bartolommeo. *Avertimenti in Fattioni di Gverra.* 1619. Venice. Farri. 4to. title device/3 fld tables. quarter vellum. R12. $150.00

PELLOWE, William. *Royal Road to Mexico: A Travel Log...* 1937. Detroit. 1st. sgn. 168p. F3. $15.00

PELLY, Lewis. *Report on Journey to Riyadh in Central Arabia, 1865.* nd (1977). Cambridge. Oleander. ils/map. 100p. pict brd. VG. Q2. $20.00

PELTZ, Mary Ellis. *Magic of the Opera.* 1960. NY. Praeger. 172p. G/dj. C5. $12.50

PELZER, Louis. *Cattlemen's Frontier: A Record of Trans-Mississippi Cattle.* 1936. Arthur H Clark. ftspc. 351p. teg. cloth. D11. $150.00

PEMBERTON, Max. *Lady Evelyn.* 1906. NY. Authors & Newspaper Assn. 1st. ils AW Brn. 317p. G. G11. $20.00

PENA, Amado. *Pena on Pena.* 1995. Waco. WRS Pub. 1st. ils. F/dj. T10. $30.00

PENCE, Mary Lou. *Boswell: Story of a Frontier Lawman.* 1978. High Plains. photos. VG. J2. $75.00

PENDERGAST, David. *Palenque: Walker-Caddy Expedition to Ancient Maya City...* 1967. Norman, OK. 1st. 213p. dj. F3. $35.00

PENDLEBURY, B.J. *Art of the Rhyme.* 1971. NY. VG/dj. M17. $15.00

PENDLEBURY, J.D.S. *Archaeology of Crete, an Introduction.* (1939). London. Methuen. ils/pl/maps. 400p. gilt gr cloth. K1. $85.00

PENDLETON, Philip E. *Oley Valley Heritage: Colonial Years 1700-1775.* 1994. PA German Soc. 1st. inscr. F/dj. R8. $50.00

PENFIELD, Wilder. *Second Career With Other Essays & Addresses.* 1963. Little Brn. inscr/dtd 1964. 189p. dj. G7. $65.00

PENFIELD, Wilder. *Torch.* 1960. Boston. 1st. 370p. A13. $50.00

PENFIELD & ROBERTS. *Speech & Brain-Mechanisms.* 1959. Princeton. ils. 286p. maroon cloth. VG/dj. G1. $75.00

PENINGTON, Isaac. *Letters of Isaac Penington.* 1796. London. James Phillips. 1st. 132p. V3. $95.00

PENINGTON, Isaac. *Letters of Isaac Penington: Eminent Minister...* nd. Phil Friends Book Store. 12mo. 283p. Obadian Brown bstp. V3. $35.00

PENINGTON, Isaac. *Selections From Works of..., To Which Are Added Selections.* 1818. New Bedford. Abraham Shearman. 12mo. 308p. leather. V3. $120.00

PENINGTON, Isaac. *Works of Long-Mournful & Sorely-Distressed Isaac Penington.* 1761. London. 2 vol. 2nd. 4to. 711+680p. worn leather. V3. $235.00

PENMAN, Sharon Kay. *Falls the Shadow.* 1988. Holt. 1st. VG+/dj. A14. $17.50

PENMAN, Sharon Kay. *Here Be Dragons.* 1985. NY. HRW. 1st. NF/clip. A14. $35.00

PENMAN, Sharon Kay. *Sunne in Splendour.* 1982. HRW. 1st. NF/dj. A14. $28.00

PENMAN, Sharon Kay. *Sunne in Splendour.* 1982. HRW. 1st. VG/dj. S13. $18.00

PENN, Irving. *Flowers.* 1980. Harmony. 1st. 4to. NF/dj. S9. $100.00

PENN, Irving. *Moments Preserved.* 1960. S&S. 1st. folio. F/lacks dj/VG case. S9. $200.00

PENN, William. *Fruits of Solitude in Reflections & Maxims...* nd. Phil. Friends Book Store. 24mo. 192p. G. V3. $15.00

PENN, William. *No Cross, No Crown: Discourse Showing Nature & Discipline...* 1845. NY. Collins. 12mo. 323p. V3. $35.00

PENN, William. *Rise & Progress of People Called Quakers...* nd. Phil. Friends Book Store. 16mo. 86+40p. xl. G. V3. $17.50

**PENN, William.** *Select Works With a Journal of His Life.* 1771. London. Royal Folio. 862p. worn leather. V3. $325.00

**PENN, William.** *Some Fruits of Solitude.* 1900. NY. Truslove Hanson Comba. 24mo. 170p. V3. $16.00

**PENN, William.** *Some of Doctrines of the Christian Religion...* 1886. Phil. Friends Book Store. 12mo. 32p. V3. $10.00

**PENN, William.** *Time.* 1965. Berkeley. Peacock. mini. 1/500. lt gray prt wrp. B24. $40.00

**PENNANT, Thomas.** *Tour in Scotland/Voyage to the Hebrides.* 1776. London. Benj White. 3 vol. 2nd. tall 4to. gilt speckled calf. H13. $1,095.00

**PENNELL, Elizabeth Robins.** *Mary Wollstonecraft Godwin.* 1885. London. Allen. 8vo. gilt cloth. R12. $125.00

**PENNYPACKER, Morton.** *Two Spies.* 1930. Houghton Mifflin. 1st ltd. 1/750. NF. T11. $75.00

**PENTECOST, Hugh.** *Copycat Killers.* 1983. Dodd Mead. 1st. F/dj. M19. $17.50

**PENTECOST, Hugh.** *Judas Freak.* 1974. Dodd Mead. 1st. VG/G. G8. $25.00

**PENTECOST, Hugh.** *Kingdom of Death.* 1960. Dodd Mead. 1st. VG/dj. G8. $25.00

**PENTECOST, Hugh.** *Plague of Violence.* 1970. Dodd Mead. 1st. F/VG. M19. $17.50

**PENZER, N.M.** *Harem: Account of the Institution as It Existed...* 1966. London. Spring. 2nd. sm 4to. 277p. VG. W1. $25.00

**PENZLER, Otto.** *Great Detectives.* 1978. Little Brn. 1st. VG/dj. P3. $25.00

**PEPIN, Jacques.** *Everyday Cooking With...* 1982. Harper. VG/wrp. A16. $9.00

**PEPITONE, Joe.** *Joe, You Coulda Made Us Proud.* 1975. Playboy. 1st. photos. F/VG. P8. $35.00

**PEPITONE & STADIEM.** *Marilyn Monroe Confidential: Intimate Personal Account.* 1979. S&S. 1st. rem mk. NF/dj. A14. $14.00

**PEPLER, H.D.C.** *Letter From Sussex by HDC Pepler About His Friend...* 1950. Chicago. Cherryburn. sm 8vo. 10p. NF/stiff wrp/dj. C6. $65.00

**PEPPE, Rodney.** *House That Jack Built.* (1970). Delacorte. 1st thus. obl 12mo. gilt cloth. T5. $30.00

**PEPPER, Claude.** *Florida Centennial Library of Congress, March 3, 1945.* 1946. Lib Congress. 1st. maps/pl. 36p. VG. M8. $35.00

**PEPPER, James.** *Letters. Raymond Chandler & James M Fox.* 1978. Santa Barbara. Neville+Yellin. 1/26. sgn Fox. F. w/photo. R3. $225.00

**PEPPER, John.** *American Negro Problems.* 1928. NY. Workers Lib. 1st. NF/wrp. B2. $100.00

**PEPPER, John.** *General Strike & General Betrayal.* 1926. Chicago. Daily Worker Pub for Workers. VG+/wrp. B2. $100.00

**PEPPER, O.H. Perry.** *Old Doc.* 1957. Phil. 1st. 247p. A13. $25.00

**PEPPER, William.** *System of Practical Medicine by American Authors.* 1885-1886. Phil. Lea. 5 vol. sheep. G7. $295.00

**PEPPER, William.** *Text-Book of Theory & Practice of Medicine.* 1894. Phil. Saunder. ils/pl. gr cloth/leather labels. G7. $150.00

**PEPPER & PEPPER.** *Straight Life: Story of Art Pepper.* 1979. NY. Schirmer. 1st. F/dj. B2. $65.00

**PEPPER & PEPPER.** *Straight Life: Story of Art Pepper.* 1979. NY. Schirmer. 1st. F/NF clip. O11. $50.00

**PERARD, Victor.** *Hands & Their Construction.* 1940. Pitnam. 1st. 8vo. VG. M5. $65.00

**PERCIVAL, MacIver.** *Fan Book.* 1920. London. Fisher Unwin. 1st. 8vo. 344p. gr cloth. VG. B20. $100.00

**PERCY, Alfred.** *Amherst County Story: A Virginia Saga.* 1961. Madison Hgts, VA. inscr. 126p. VG. B10. $45.00

**PERCY, Bishop Thomas.** *Reliques of Ancient English Poetry...* 1839. London. Lewis. 3 vol. tall 8vo. pebbled cloth. H13. $395.00

**PERCY, John R.** *Study of Variable Stars Using Small Telescopes.* 1986. Cambridge. sm 4to. 265p. VG. K5. $35.00

**PERCY, Walker.** *Lancelot.* 1977. FSG. 1st. F/F. B3. $45.00

**PERCY, Walker.** *Lancelot.* 1977. FSG. 1st. NF/dj. R14. $35.00

**PERCY, Walker.** *Lost in the Cosmos: Last Self-Help Book.* 1983. FSG. 1st. F/NF. B3. $35.00

**PERCY, Walker.** *Love in the Ruins.* 1971. FSG. 1st. F/dj. A23. $50.00

**PERCY, Walker.** *Movie-Goer.* 1961. Knopf. 1st. 8vo. 242p. F/VG+. B20. $1,750.00

**PERCY, Walker.** *Second Coming.* 1980. FSG. 1st/unltd/nonprivate prt. 8vo. 360p. F/dj. W2. $40.00

**PERCY, Walker.** *Thanatos Syndrome.* 1987. FSG. 1st. VG/dj. B30. $30.00

**PEREIRA, Jader U.** *Les Extra-Terrestries.* 1974 (1970). Paris. 2nd. French text. ils/charts. 72p. K5. $18.00

**PEREZ DE LUXAN.** *Expedition Into New Mexico Made by Antonio deEspejo...* 1929. Quivira Soc. 1/500. ils/fld maps. 161p. VG. A4. $350.00

**PEREZ-REVERTE, Arturo.** *Dumas Club.* 1996. London. Harvill. 1st Eng (precedes Am). F/dj. M15. $125.00

**PEREZ-REVERTE, Arturo.** *Flanders Panel.* 1994. Harcourt Brace. 1st Am. F/dj. A24. $40.00

**PERINI, Jimo.** *To Marci With Love.* 1981. Photo Art Masters. 1st. ils. 118p. F/VG. S14. $12.00

**PERKINS, Lucy Fitch.** *Robin Hood: His Deeds & Adventures...* nd. np. 1st. ils. 115p. VG. B18. $45.00

**PERKS, Micah.** *We Are Gathered Here.* 1996. St Martin. 1st. F/dj. S13. $15.00

**PERL, Lila.** *Candles, Cakes, & Donkey Tails.* 1984. Clarion. 1st. ils Victoria deLarrea. 71p. F/NF. T5. $25.00

**PERLE, Richard.** *Hard Line.* 1992. Random. 1st. author's 1st novel. NF/F. H11. $15.00

**PERLMAN, Barbara H.** *Allan Houser (Ha-o-Zous).* 1992. Glenn Green Galleries. 2nd. ils/index. 263p. F/F. B19. $50.00

**PEROWNE, Stewart.** *One Remains: Report From Jerusalem.* 1954. London. Hodder Stoughton. 8vo. ils/pl. 192p. cloth. VG/dj. Q2. $18.00

**PERRAULT, Charles.** *Les Hommes Illustres Qui Ont Paru en France...* 1696 & 1700. Paris. Dezallier. 2 vol. folio. 103 full-p engraved portrits. contemporary bdg. R12. $3,500.00

**PERRAULT, Charles.** *Sleeping Beauty.* 1919. London. Heinemann. 1st. 1/625 total. ils/sgn Rackham. wht brd/vellum. VG/case. D1. $1,500.00

**PERRAULT, Charles.** *Tales of Passed Times by Mother Goose & Morals...* 1796. London. Thomas Boosey. 7th. 12mo. 8 pl. 237p. brn leather/leather label. R5. $1,400.00

**PERRAULT, Giles.** *Red Orchestra.* 1969. S&S. 1st. F/F. H11. $25.00

**PERRIN, William Henry.** *History of Summit County.* 1881. Chicago. 1st. 1050p. VG. B18. $150.00

**PERRY, Anne.** *Belgrave Square.* 1992. Fawcett Columbine. 1st. inscr. F/dj. A23. $42.00

**PERRY, Anne.** *Cardington Crescent.* 1987. St Martin. 1st. F/dj. B2. $65.00

**PERRY, Anne.** *Dangerous Mourning.* 1991. Fawcett Columbine. 1st. F/NF. A23. $25.00

**PERRY, Anne.** *Defend & Betray.* 1992. Fawcett Columbine. 1st. F/dj. A23. $30.00

**PERRY, Anne.** *Farrier's Lane.* 1993. Fawcett Columbine. 1st. sgn. F/dj. A23. $42.00

**PERRY, Anne.** *Highgate Rise.* 1991. Fawcett Columbine. 1st. inscr. F/dj. A23. $42.00

**PERRY, Anne.** *Sleeping Dogs.* 1992. NY. Random. 1st. F/dj. A23. $34.00

**PERRY, Anne.** *Sudden Fearful Death.* 1993. Fawcett Columbine. 1st. sgn. F/dj. A23. $42.00

**PERRY, Anne.** *Traitor's Gate.* 1995. Fawcett Columbine. 1st. F/dj. A23/H11. $25.00

**PERRY, Anne.** *Traitor's Gate.* 1995. NY. Fawcett Columbine. 1st. sgn. F/dj. T2. $35.00

**PERRY, Anne.** *Weighted in the Balance.* 1996. Fawcett. 1st. F/dj. A23. $32.00

**PERRY, Bliss.** *Pools & Ripples: Fishing Essays.* 1927. Boston. 1st. ils. 102p. G. A17. $22.50

**PERRY, Charles.** *Brief Exposition & Vindication of Some...Doctrines...* 1885. Cambridge. Riverside. 1st. 43p. V3. $30.00

**PERRY, J.** *Around the World Making Cookies.* 1940. 5th. VG/VG. E6. $22.00

**PERRY, Jesse P.** *Pines of Mexico & Central America.* 1991. Portland. 231p. AN/dj. B26. $36.00

**PERRY, Ralph Barton.** *Thought & Character of Wm James...* 1935. Little Brn. 2 vol. gr cloth/leather labels. VG/case. G1. $100.00

**PERRY, Thomas.** *Vanishing Act.* 1995. Random. 1st. F/dj. M15. $45.00

**PERRY, Vincent G.** *Boston Terrier.* 1959. Judy Pub Co. 4th. NF/dj. A21. $30.00

**PERSE, St.-John.** *On Poetry.* 1961. NY. Bollingen. 1st. 1/2500. trans WH Auden. F/lt gr wrp. M24. $45.00

**PERSHING, M.W.** *Life of General John Tipton & Early Indiana History.* nd (1900s). Tipton, IN. Literary & Suffrage Club. ils/map. 56p. wrp. B18. $17.50

**PERUCHO, Joan.** *Natural History.* 1988. Knopf. 1st Am. VG/dj. L1. $30.00

**PESCETTI, Orlando.** *Proverbi Italiani...* (1603). Verona. Aspiranti. 12mo. 286p. aeg. full red crushed morocco. K1. $750.00

**PESCI, David.** *Amistad.* 1997. NY. Marlowe. 1st. sgn. F/dj. T11. $55.00

**PESKINS, Allan.** *Volunteers: Mexican War Journals of Pvt Richard Coulter.* 1991. Kent State. 1st. maps/portraits. F/dj. M4. $30.00

**PESKINS, Allan.** *Volunteers: Mexican War Journals of Pvt Richard Coulter...* 1991. Kent State. 1st. maps. 342p. VG/dj. F3. $25.00

**PESMAN, M. Walter.** *Meet Flora Mexicana.* 1962. Globe, AZ. ils/fld map. 278p. vinyl cloth. F. B26. $38.00

**PETER, Harry T.** *Just Hunting.* 1935. Scribner. 1st. ils Betty Babcock. VG. A21. $75.00

**PETER, Laurence.** *Peter's People.* 1979. Morrow. 1st. F/dj. L4. $12.00

**PETERKIN, Mike.** *Global Warning.* 1991. S&S. 1st. 4to. pupups/engineer Ruth Mawdsley. F. B17. $12.50

**PETERKIN, Mike.** *Land Life, a Nature Pop-Up.* 1990. Ideals. popup/engineer Paul Wilgress. F. B17. $10.00

**PETERKIN & ULLMANN.** *Roll, Jordan, Roll.* 1935. NY. RO Ballou. 1st. folio. sgns. quarter wht linen. case. B4. $12,500.00

**PETERS, Elizabeth;** see Mertz, Barbara Gross.

**PETERS, Ellis;** see Pargeter, Edith Mary.

**PETERS, G.W.H.** *Bedfordshire 7 Hertfordshire...Famous Regiment Series.* 1970. London. Leo Cooper. 1st. photos. 120p. VG/dj. S16. $25.00

**PETERS, Margot.** *Mary Sarton: A Biography.* 1997. Knopf. 1st. F/dj. P3. $30.00

**PETERS & SMITH.** *Ann-Margaret: A Photo Extravaganza & Memoir.* 1981. NY. Putnam. 1st. photos. F/NF. C9. $90.00

**PETERS.** *Congreve: The Drama & the Printed Word.* 1990. Stanford. ils. 304p. F/F. A4. $35.00

**PETERSEN, D.** *Racks: Natural History of Antlers & Animals That Wear Them.* 1991. Santa Barbara. ils/maps. NF/wrp. M12. $15.00

**PETERSEN, William J.** *Steamboating on the Upper Mississippi.* 1968. Iowa City. G/dj. A19. $50.00

**PETERSEN, William.** *Hippocratic Wisdom: Modern Appreciation of Ancient Medical.* 1946. Springfield. 1st. 263p. A13. $50.00

**PETERSEN.** *Iowa History Reference Guide.* 1952. 192p. VG. A4. $35.00

**PETERSHAM & PETERSHAM.** *Albanian Wonder Tales.* 1936. Garden City. Jr Books/ Doran. 1st. 8vo. 282p. mc dj. R5. $125.00

**PETERSHAM & PETERSHAM.** *America's Stamps.* 1947. NY. Macmillan. 1st. 4to. blk lettered aqua cloth/pict label. dj. R5. $150.00

**PETERSHAM & PETERSHAM.** *American ABC.* 1941. Macmillan. 1st. 4to. gilt bl cloth. pict dj. R5. $250.00

**PETERSHAM & PETERSHAM.** *Boy Who Had No Heart.* 1955. Macmillan. 1st. unp. red cloth. VG. T5. $45.00

**PETERSHAM & PETERSHAM.** *David.* 1938. Chicago. John Winston. ils. dk bl paper brd. VG. M7. $15.00

**PETERSHAM & PETERSHAM.** *Joseph & His Brothers.* 1938. John Winston. ils. unp. gilt dk bl paper brd. VG. M7. $25.00

**PETERSHAM & PETERSHAM.** *Story Book of Cotton.* nd (c 1939). Phil. Winston. probable 1st. unp. VG. C14. $17.00

**PETERSHAM & PETERSHAM.** *Story Book of Food.* nd (c 1933). Winston. probable 1st. sq 12mo. unp. G+. C14. $14.00

**PETERSHAM & PETERSHAM.** *Story Book of Wheels, Ships, Trains & Aircraft.* 1935. Winston. 8vo. VG. B17. $15.00

**PETERSON, Arthur G.** *Glass Salt Shakers: 1,000 Patterns.* (1970). Wallace Homestead. photos. 196p. F/fair. H1. $45.00

**PETERSON, Charles S.** *Take Up Your Mission: Mormon Colonizing...1870-1900.* 1973. Tucson. U AZ. 8vo. ils/photos. 390p. brn cloth. VG+/dj. F7. $35.00

**PETERSON, Eugene H.** *Under the Unpredictable Plant: An Exploration...* 1992. Eerdmans. 197p. F/dj. B29. $8.00

**PETERSON, Harold L.** *Remington Historical Treasury of American Guns.* 1966. Thomas Nelson. 1st. F/NF. T11. $15.00

**PETERSON, Keith;** see Klavan, Andrew.

**PETERSON, Levi S.** *Juanita Brooks: Mormon Woman Historian.* 1988. UT U. 1st. ils. 505p. F/F. B19. $40.00

**PETERSON, M. Jeanne.** *Medical Profession in Mid-Victorian London.* 1978. Berkeley. 1st. 406p. dj. A13. $30.00

**PETERSON, Michael.** *Time of War.* 1990. Pocket. 1st. NF/dj. R11. $16.00

**PETERSON, Robert.** *Leaving Taos.* (1981). Harper Row. 1st. F/dj. A18. $20.00

**PETERSON.** *Magazines in the Twentieth Century.* 1956. Urbana, IL. VG. P13. $40.00

**PETERSON.** *Magazines in the Twentieth Century.* 1964. Urbana, IL. revised. VG. P13. $40.00

**PETIEVICH, Gerald.** *Money Men & One-Shot Deal.* 1981. Harcourt. 1st. F/F. C15. $35.00

**PETIT-DUTAILLIS, Charles.** *Studies & Notes Supplementary to Stubbs' Constitutional Hist.* 1911. Manchester. blk cloth. worn. M11. $75.00

**PETITUS, Samuel.** *Leges Atticae. Collegit, Digessit, et Libro Commentario...* 1742. Ludguni Batavorum. 1st 18th-C ed. contemporary calf. M11. $450.00

**PETO, S. Morton.** *Resources & Prospects of America, Ascertained During Visit.* 1865. London. Strahan. 1st. 8vo. 428p. contemporary half calf. O1. $90.00

**PETRAN, Tabitha.** *Syria.* 1972. London. Benn. ils/pl. 284p. cloth. VG/dj. Q2. $24.00

**PETRARCH.** *Sonnets of Petrarch.* 1965. NY. LEC at Stamperia Valdonega in Verona. 1/1500. F/dj/case. H5. $200.00

**PETRIE, C.** *Modern British Monarchy.* 1961. London. 1st. F. M4. $10.00

**PETRIE, Chuck.** *Corey Ford Sporting Treasury.* 1987. Minoqua. rpt. F/dj. A17. $15.00

**PETRIE, Sidney.** *Martinis & Whipped Cream.* 1966. NY. Parker. G/dj. A16. $10.00

**PETRINA, John.** *Art Work: How Produced, How Reproduced.* 1930. London. Pitman. 1st. sm folio. 122p. bl cloth. VG+. B20 $85.00

**PETRO, Sylvester.** *Kohler Strike, Union Violence & Administrative Law.* 1961. Chicago. Regnery. G/dj. M11. $35.00

**PETROSKI, Henry.** *Pencil: History of Design & Circumstance.* 1990. NY. ils. VG/dj. M17. $15.00

**PETROVA & WATSON.** *Death of Hitler: The Full Story.* 1995. NY. 1st. dj. T9. $12.00

**PETRY, Ann.** *Country Place.* 1947. Boston. Houghton Mifflin. 1st. VG/dj. B5. $75.00

**PETTENGILL, George W. Jr.** *Story of the Florida Railroads 1834-1903.* 1952. Boston. Railway & Locomotive Hist Soc. 1st. sgn. 133p. VG/wrp. M8. $85.00

**PETTERSSEN, Sverre.** *Introduction to Meteorology.* 1958 (1941). McGraw Hill. 2nd. 327p. VG/dj. K5. $21.00

**PETTIFER & TURNER.** *Automania: Man & the Motor Car.* 1984. Boston/Toronto. 1st. ils. VG/dj. M17. $30.00

**PETTIGREW, Eileen.** *Silent Enemy: Canada & Deadly Flue of 1918.* 1983. Saskatoon. Prairie Books. 1st. F/VG. A26. $15.00

**PETTIGREW, Thomas Joseph.** *Medical Portrait Gallery.* 1840s. London. 4 vol in 2. portraits. half morocco. VG. B14. $250.00

**PETTIT, Arthur G.** *Mark Twain & the South.* 1974. Lexington. U KY. 1st. gilt brick cloth. F/NF. M24. $50.00

**PETTITT, Michael.** *American Light.* 1984. Athens, GA. 1st. sgn. author's 1st book. F/dj. L3. $35.00

**PETZAL, David.** *Expert's Book of Big-Game Hunting in North America.* 1976. S&S. 1st. 223p. F/dj. A17. $12.50

**PEYREFITTE, Roger.** *Manouche.* 1973. London. 1st. trans Coleman. dj. T9. $10.00

**PEYSER, Arnold.** *Squirrelcage.* 1985. DIF. 1st. F/F. H11. $25.00

**PEYTON, Jim.** *Zions Cause.* Chapel Hill, NC. Algonquin. 1st. F/dj. A23. $32.00

**PEYTON, K.M.** *Flambards Divided.* 1982. NY. Philomel. 1st Am. VG/dj. O3. $40.00

**PEYTON, K.M.** *Flambards.* nd. NY. Philomel. VG/dj. O3. $35.00

**PFANZ, Harry W.** *Gettysburg: The Second Day.* 1987. U NC. 1st. F/dj. A14. $28.00

**PFEFFER, Richard M.** *No More Vietnams? War & Future of American Foreign Policy.* 1968. Harper Row. 1st. 299p. VG/clip. R11. $25.00

**PFEIFFER, John.** *Thinking Machine.* 1962. Lippincott. stated 1st. F/dj. P12. $15.00

**PFITZER, Gregory M.** *Samuel Eliot Morison's Historical World...* 1991. Boston. ils. VG/dj. M17. $20.00

**PHAM, Huan.** *Nhung Uat Han Trong Trachien Mat Nuoc 1975.* 1988. San Jose. Pham. 1st. Vietnamese text/photos/map. gilt gr cloth. VG+. R11. $25.00

**PHELAN, James.** *Howard Hughes: The Hidden Years.* nd. Random. 2nd. VG/dj. P3. $10.00

**PHELPS, Alanson Hosmer.** *Genealogy & Short Historical Narrative...Family Geo Phelps.* 1897. Phil. 1st. inscr. 192p. G+. B18. $50.00

**PHELPS, Elizabeth Stuart.** *Hedged In.* 1870. Boston. Fields Osgood. 295p. G. G11. $8.00

**PHELPS, William Lyon.** *Favorite Poems of James Whitcomb Riley.* 1940. Triangle. 4th prt. 8vo. 267p. VG. W2. $55.00

**PHELPS, Willian Lyon.** *City of the Great King & Other Places in Holy Land.* 1926. Cosmopolitan. sm folio. 12 full-p pl. 116p. gr cloth. K1. $175.00

**PHILADELPHIA YEARLY MEETING.** *Faith & Practice of Religious Society of Friends of Phil...* 1935. Phil. Friends Book Store. 12mo. 140p. worn wrp. V3. $10.00

**PHILADELPHIA YEARLY MEETING.** *Rules of Discipline of Yearly Meeting of Friends...* 1869. Phil. Representative Comm. 12mo. 138p. leather. V3. $15.00

**PHILBROOK, Clem.** *Magic Bat.* 1954. Macmillan. 1st. VG. P8. $25.00

**PHILBROOK, Clem.** *Ollie's Team Plays Biddy Baseball.* 1970. Hastings. 1st. F/VG. P8. $25.00

**PHILBY, H. Saint-John.** *Queen of Sheba.* 1981. London. Quartet. ils/pl. 141p. VG. Q2. $24.00

**PHILIP, Peter.** *Antiques: A Popular Guide to Antiques for Everyone.* 1973. Octopus. 1st. ils. 144p. NF/VG. S14. $12.00

**PHILIPS, Shine.** *Big Spring: Casual Biography of a Prairie Town.* 1942. Prentice Hall. 1st. ils. 231p. NF/G. B19. $20.00

**PHILIPS & THOMAS.** *Travelers' Book of Color Photography.* 1966. Crown. VG. S5. $12.00

**PHILLIPS, C.** *New American Dictator, Containing a Number of Useful...* ca 1827. NY. Pub for Proprietor. only ed. 8vo. uncut. plain bl wrp. O1. $150.00

**PHILLIPS, Caryl.** *Crossing the River.* 1994. Knopf. 1st. sgn. F/dj. B20. $20.00

**PHILLIPS, Conrad.** *Dolls With Sad Faces.* 1957. London. Barker. 1st. F/dj. M15. $45.00

**PHILLIPS, Everett Franklin.** *Beekeeping: Discussion of Life of the Honeybee...* 1928. Macmillan. revised. ils/index. 490p. G. H10. $25.00

**PHILLIPS, Henry.** *New Designs for Old Mexico.* 1939. Nat Travel Club. 1st. 336p. dj. F3. $15.00

**PHILLIPS, J.B.** *Four Prophets.* 1963. Macmillan. 161p. VG/torn. B29. $9.50

**PHILLIPS, J.C.** *Natural History of the Ducks.* (1986). NY. Dover. facs (1922-26 1st eds). ils/118 distribution maps. F. M12. $75.00

**PHILLIPS, Jayne Anne.** *Fast Lanes.* 1987. London. Faber. 1st. F/NF. B2. $35.00

**PHILLIPS, Jayne Anne.** *Machine Dreams.* 1984. Dutton. 1st. author's 1st novel. NF/dj. H11/R11. $15.00

**PHILLIPS, Jayne Anne.** *Shelter.* 1994. Houghton Mifflin. 1st. F/dj. R14. $25.00

**PHILLIPS, Jill M.** *Walfords Oak.* 1990. Citadel. 1st. F/dj. M21. $25.00

**PHILLIPS, P.L.** *List of Geographical Atlases in Lib of Congress.* nd. Vol 1-4. 1/100. rpt. notes for 5423 atlases. F. A4. $325.00

**PHILLIPS, P.L.** *Notes on Life & Works of Bernard Romans.* 1975. FL U. Bicentennial series. 12 lg fld facs. F. M4. $45.00

**PHILLIPS, Paul Chrisler.** *Fur Trade.* 1961. U OK. 2 vol. VG/case. J2. $525.00

**PHILLIPS, Philip.** *Round the World With Philip Phillips, Singing Pilgrim.* 1887. NY. Phillips. 1st. 4to. ils. cloth. VG. W1. $24.00

**PHILLIPS, Robert.** *Delmore Schwartz & James Laughlin: Selected Letters.* 1993. NY. Norton. 1st. F/dj. G10. $12.00

**PHILLIPS, W. Glasgow.** *Tuscaloosa.* 1994. NY. Morrow. 1st. sgn. F/dj. O11. $45.00

**PHILLIPS, Wendell.** *Speeches, Lectures & Letters.* 1864. Boston. Walker Wise. 7th thousand. 8vo. 562p. teg. gilt gr cloth. VG. H7. $27.50

**PHILLIPS & WILLIAMS.** *Wisden Book of Cricket Memorabilia.* 1990. Oxford. 4to. 328p. F/F. A4. $50.00

**PHILPOTTS, Eden.** *Nancy Owlett.* 1933. Macmillan. 1st. ils CE Brock. VG/G. P2. $40.00

**PHIPSON, Joan.** *Threat to the Barkers.* 1965. HBW. stated 1st. bl cloth. VG. B36. $12.00

**PHYPPS, Hyacinthe.** *Recently Deflowered Girl: Right Thing to Say...* nd (c 1965). Chelsea House. probable 1st. 47p. VG+/sans. C14. $22.00

**PIAGET, Jean.** *Child's Conception of Physical Causality.* 1930. Kegan Paul/Harcourt Brace. 1st Eng-language. 309p. G1. $100.00

**PIAGET, Jean.** *Construction du Reel Chez l'Enfant.* 1937. Paris. Delachaux Niestle. 398p. prt yel wrp. G1. $100.00

**PIAGET, Jean.** *La Formation du Symbole Chez l'Enfant...* 1945. Paris. Delachaux Niestle. 312p. prt yel wrp. G1. $75.00

**PIAGET, Jean.** *La Genese du Monbre Chez l'Enfant...* 1941. Neuchatel. Delachaux Niestle. 308p. prt buff wrp. G1. $100.00

**PIAGET, Jean.** *La Representation du Monde Chez l'Enfant.* 1926. Paris. Libraire Felix. 424p. prt gray wrp. G1. $175.00

**PIAGET, Jean.** *Moral Judgement of the Child.* 1932. London. Kegan Paul. 1st Eng-language/ later issue. 418p. gr cloth. VG. G1. $75.00

**PIATTI, Celestino.** *Celestino Piatti's Animal ABC.* 1966. NY. Atheneum. 1st Am. 26p. F/NF. D4. $65.00

**PICASSO.** *Fifty-Five Years of His Graphic Work.* 1955. Abrams. 1st. 4to. ils/bibliography. NF/clear acetate wrp. C15. $50.00

**PICHOIS, Claude.** *Baudelaire.* 1987. London. 1st. trans G Robb. T9. $12.00

**PICKENS, T. Boone.** *Boone.* 1987. Houghton Mifflin. 1st. NF/dj. W2. $20.00

**PICKERING, Samuel F.** *Let It Ride.* 1991. Columbia, MO. 1st. F/dj. M23. $15.00

**PICKERING, Timothy.** *Instructions to Envoys Extraordinary & Ministers...* 1798. Phil. Ross. tall 8vo. quarter calf/orig wrp bdg in. R12. $150.00

**PICKERING, William Russell.** *Don't Forget to Smell the Flowers Along the Way.* 1977. Near Eastern Research. 1/1200. 1st. 160p. VG. W1. $55.00

**PICKNEY, Darryl.** *High Cotton.* 1992. FSG. 1st. sgn. author's 1st novel. F/dj. O11. $50.00

**PICKWELL, Gayle.** *Birds.* 1939. NY. ils. 252p. VG. A17. $25.00

**PICOT, Emile.** *Catalogue des Livres Composant la Bibliotheque...Rothschild.* 1965. NY. Burt Franklin. 5 vol. gilt red cloth. F. M24. $200.00

**PIENKOWSKI, Jan.** *ABC Dinosaurs.* 1993. Heinemann. 1st. 4to. F. B17. $15.00

**PIENKOWSKI, Jan.** *Robot.* 1981. Dell. 1st Am. 4to. 7 moveables. F. B17. $15.00

**PIEPER, Josef.** *Fortitude & Temperance.* 1954. Pantheon. 1st Am. 128p. VG/G. H10. $20.00

**PIER, Arthur Stanwood.** *Captain.* 1929. Penn. 1st. VG. P8. $60.00

**PIERCE, David M.** *Write Me a Letter.* 1993. Mysterious. 1st. F/F. H11. $20.00

**PIERCE, Frank C.** *Brief History of the Lower Rio Grande Valley.* 1917. Menasha. Geo Banta. 200p. cloth. D11. $50.00

**PIERCY, Marge.** *Breaking Camp.* 1968. Wesleyan U. 1st. author's 1st book. F/NF. L3. $100.00

**PIERCY, Marge.** *High Cost of Living.* 1978. Harper Row. 1st. F/dj. M25. $25.00

**PIERSOL, George.** *Gateway of Honor: American College of Physicians 1915-59.* 1962. Phil. 1st. 646p. A13. $35.00

**PIERSON, Donald.** *Negroes in Brazil: A Study of Race...* 1942. Chicago. 1st. 392p. VG/wrp. B20. $20.00

**PIESSEL, M.** *Lost World of Quintana Roo.* 1963. NY. photos/map. VG/fair. M4. $15.00

**PIGOTT, Charles.** *Treachery No Crime; or, System of Courts...* 1793. London. Ridgeway. 8vo. brd. R12. $85.00

**PIGOTT, William.** *Scenario, Technique, Continuity & Model Photo-Play.* 1916. LA. Custer-Pigott. ils/ads. prt brd. D11. $100.00

**PIKE, James A.** *Roman Catholic in the White House.* 1960. Doubleday. 1st. VG/dj. N2. $10.00

**PIKE, Robert H.** *Home of the Champions.* 1994. Lambkin. VG/dj. R8. $15.00

**PIKE, Stephen.** *Complete Key to the Teachers Assistant; or, System...* 1837. Phil. 250p. full calf. VG. H3. $50.00

**PILCHER, Rosamunde.** *Flowers in the Rain & Other Stories.* 1991. NY. SMP. 1st. F/F. H11. $30.00

**PILCHIK, Ely E.** *Maimonides on Giving. The Philosophy of Philanthropy.* 1985. Evanston. Schori. mini. gr leather. B24. $95.00

**PILCHIK, Ely E.** *Psalm of David.* 1967. Evanston, IL. Schori. mini. 1/200. 31p/frenchfold. red leather. B24. $95.00

**PILEGGI, Nicolas.** *Casino, Love & Honor in Las Vegas.* 1995. S&S. 1st. VG/dj. C9. $25.00

**PILLER, E.A.** *Time Bomb.* 1945. NY. Arco. 1st. 8vo. VG/dj. A2. $15.00

**PILLSBURY, Walter Bowers.** *Attention.* 1908. Sonnenschein/Macmillan. 1st Eng-language. 346p. panelled crimson cloth. G1. $75.00

**PILLSBURY.** *New Pillsbury Family Cookbook.* 1973. Minnesota. looseleaf. VG. A16. $10.00

**PILLSBURY.** *Pillsbury Kitchen's Cookbook.* 1979. Minnesota. looseleaf. VG. A16. $9.00

**PINART, Alphons.** *Journey to Arizona in 1876.* 1962. Zamorano Club. 1st in Eng. 1/500. 47p. NF/sans. B19. $50.00

**PINE, George W.** *Beyond the West: Containing Account of 2 Year's Travel...* 1871. Utica, NY. 2nd enlarged. 483p. decor cloth. VG. B18. $125.00

**PINEDA, Cecile.** *Face.* 1985. Viking. 1st. author's 1st book. F/G. T12. $25.00

**PINEROS CORPAS, Joaquin.** *El Libro Del Nuevo Reino. Vision de Colombia.* 1966. Bogota. 1st. 179p. F3. $15.00

**PINKERTON, Frank.** *Jim Cummings; or, Great Adams Express Robbery.* 1887. Chicago. Laird Lee. G. A19. $65.00

**PINKNEY, Jerry.** *Sam & the Tigers, an Adaptation to Little Black Sambo.* 1996. Dial. 1st. sgn bookplate. F/dj. B17. $30.00

**PINKUS, Philip.** *Grub Steet Stripped Bare.* 1968. Archon. F/dj. H13. $45.00

**PINNEY, R.** *Animals in the Bible: Identity & Natural History...* 1964. Phil. Chilton. ils. 227p. VG/dj. M12. $25.00

**PINTER, Harold.** *Dwarfs: A Novel.* 1990. London. 1st. dj. T9. $12.00

**PINTER, Harold.** *Tea Party & Other Plays.* 1967. London. Methuen. 1st. VG/dj. A24. $45.00

**PIOTROWSKI, Roman.** *Cartels & Trusts: Their Origin & Historical Development...* 1933. London. Allen Unwin. bl cloth. M11. $65.00

**PIOZZI, Hester Lynch.** *Anecdotes of the Late Samuel Johnson, LLD.* 1786. London. Cadell. 1st. sm 8vo. 306p. H13. $595.00

**PIOZZI, Hester Lynch.** *Anecdotes of the Late Samuel Johnson, LLD...* 1925. Cambridge. sm 8vo. VG. H13. $95.00

**PIOZZI, Hester Lynch.** *Observations & Reflections.* 1967. Ann Arbor. 1st. edit Herbert Barrows. dj. H13. $45.00

**PIPER, Ralph E.** *Point of No Return, an Aviator's Story.* (1990). IA State. 1st. ils. 206p. F/dj. B18. $15.00

**PIPER, Ruth.** *Sudy & Prill.* 1949. Doubleday. stated 1st. ils Brinton Turkle. VG. B36. $20.00

**PIPER, Watty.** *Children of Other Lands.* 1943. NY. ils Holling/Holling. VG. M17. $20.00

**PIPER, Watty.** *Children of Other Lands.* 1956. Platt Munk. 1st thus. 4to. NF/dj. S13. $30.00

**PIPER, Watty.** *Eight Nursery Tales.* nd. Platt Munk. ils (w/Little Blk Sambo). VG. M17. $50.00

**PIRAINO, Maria Teresa.** *Antigono Dosone re di Macedonia.* 1954. Palermo. Italian text. 73p. VG. Q2. $20.00

**PISSARRO, Lucien.** *Notes on the Eragny Press...* 1957. Cambridge. private prt. 1st. 1/500. ils. decor brd. F. M24. $375.00

**PISTONE & WOODLEY.** *Donnie Brasco: My Undercover Life in the Mafia.* 1987. NAL. 1st. F/dj. B4. $100.00

**PITCHFORD, Denys.** *Brendon Chase, by BB.* 1945. NY. Scribner. 1st. VG/fair. O3. $25.00

**PITKIN, T.M.** *Captain Departs: Ulysses S Grant's Last Campaign.* 1973. S IL U. photos. 164p. F/dj. M4. $20.00

**PITKIN, Timothy.** *Statistical View of Commerce of the United States.* 1992. Paragon. rpt. 446p. VG. S5. $15.00

**PITT, George.** *Mystic Religion: Described by a Quaker.* 1905. Croydon. Jesse Ward. 2nd. 16mo. 111p. aeg. G. V3. $22.00

**PITTENGER, Peggy Jett.** *Back Yard Horse.* 1964. NY. Barnes. 1st. VG/VG. O3. $25.00

**PITTMAN & SIMONSEN.** *North Shore Chinook, Lake Huron Salmon on Light Tackle.* 1993. Troy, MI. 164p. wrp. A17. $17.00

**PITZ & WARWICK.** *Early American Costume.* 1929. NY. Century. 1st. 64 pl. 319p. gilt emb bl cloth. F. B14. $55.00

**PIZER, Vernon.** *Rockets, Missiles & Space.* 1962. Lippincott. ils. 160p. dj. K5. $30.00

**PLACE, Marian.** *Cariboo Gold.* 1970. HRW. ils Deane Cate. F/dj. D4. $25.00

**PLAGEMANN, Catherine.** *Fine Preserving: Jams & Jellies, Pickles & Relishes...* 1967. 1st. VG/dj. M17. $17.50

**PLAIDY, Jean;** see Hibbert, Eleanor Alice.

**PLANCK, Willy.** *Lazy Teddy Bear.* 1930. NY. Longman Gr. 1st Am. trans Joseph Auslander. cloth/pict label. dj. R5. $200.00

**PLANTE, David.** *Woods.* 1982. Atheneum. 1st. F/NF. M19. $15.00

**PLATE, Erich J.** *Aerodynamic Characteristics of Atmospheric Boundary Layers.* 1971. Oak Ridge. US Atomic Energy Commission. 190p. xl. K5. $20.00

**PLATH, Sylvia.** *Bell Jar.* 1971. Harper Row. 1st Am. VG/VG. R14. $30.00

**PLATH, Sylvia.** *Letters Home: Correspondence 1950-1963.* 1975. Harper Row. 1st. NF/F. R14. $25.00

**PLATO.** *Trial & Death of Socrates.* 1962. Verona. LEC at Stamperia Valdo Nega. 1/1500. sgns. dj/case. K1. $150.00

**PLATT, Colin.** *Medieval England: Social History & Archaeology...* 1978. Scribner. 1st. NF/dj. P3. $30.00

**PLATT, David.** *Celluloid Power.* 1992. Metuchen. Scarecrow. 632p. VG/dj. C5. $20.00

**PLATT, Kin.** *Body Beautiful Murder.* 1976. Random. 1st. NF/dj. M19. $17.50

**PLATTS, Harvey.** *Knife Makers Who Went West.* 1978. Longmont. 1st. photos. 201p. VG/dj. S16. $95.00

**PLEASANTS, William J.** *Twice Across the Plains in 1849 & 1856.* 1981. Ye Galleon. 1st. F/dj. O4. $15.00

**PLENN, J.H.** *Mexico Marches.* 1939. Bobbs Merrill. 1st. 386p. F3. $10.00

**PLESKE, T.** *Birds of the Eurasian Tundra.* 1928. Boston. 22 pl. 374p. NF. C12. $275.00

**PLETCHER, D.M.** *Diplomacy of Annexation.* 1975. MO U. 656p. F/dj. M4. $25.00

**PLIMPTON, George.** *Curious Case of Sidd Finch.* 1987. Macmillan. 1st. sgn. F/dj. P8. $85.00

**PLIMPTON, Ruth.** *Mary Dyer: Biography of a Rebel Quaker.* 1994. Boston. Branden. 247p. VG/dj. V3. $15.00

**PLOMER, Henry R.** *English Printers' Ornaments.* 1968. NY. Burt Franklin. rpt. gilt maroon cloth. F. M24. $50.00

**PLOWDEN, Gene.** *Those Amazing Ringlings & Their Circus.* 1967. Bonanza. 301p. VG/dj. S5. $15.00

**PLUM, Jennifer;** see Kurland, Michael.

**PLUNKETT, Horace.** *Rural Life Problem of the US.* 1911. Macmillan. cloth. VG. A10. $18.00

**PLUTARCH.** *Plutarch's Lives of Themistocles, Pericles, Aristides...* 1968. Harvard Classics. 61st. VG. P3. $20.00

**PODESCHI, John B.** *Books on the Horse & Horsemanship.* 1981. Paul Mellon Collection. Tate Gallery. NF/dj. A21. $200.00

**PODMORE, Frank.** *Studies in Psychical Research.* 1897. Putnam. 1st Am/prt Am sheets. 458p. gr cloth. G1. $75.00

**PODOLSKY, Edward.** *Management of Addictions.* 1955. NY. Philosophical Lib. 1st. VG/dj. N2. $10.00

**PODOLSKY, Edward.** *Medicine Marches On.* 1934. NY. 1st. 343p. A13. $25.00

**POE, Edgar Allan.** *Bells & Other Poems.* nd (1912). Hodder Stoughton. 1/750. Ed deLuxe. sgn Dulac. Riviere bdg. F/case. H5. $3,000.00

**POE, Edgar Allan.** *Book of Poe.* 1929. Doubleday Doran. 1st. 8vo. 519p. G. H1. $18.00

**POE, Edgar Allan.** *Cask of Amontillado.* 1981. Boston. Bromer. mini. 1/115. prt/ils/sgn Gentry. silver-stp violet brd. B24. $110.00

**POE, Edgar Allan.** *Letters Till Now Unpublished in the Valentine Museum...* 1925. Lippincott. 1/1550. ils. 327p. B10. $100.00

**POE, Edgar Allan.** *Murders in the Rue Morgue.* nd. JH Sears. VG. P3. $20.00

**POE, Edgar Allan.** *Raven.* 1980. Chelonidae. 1/125. ils/sgn AJ Robinson. w/extra suite pts. F/chemise/box. B24. $3,000.00

**POE, Edgar Allan.** *Raven.* 1986. Easthampton, MA. Chelonidae. New ed. 1/225. Artists Proof w/extra pl. H5. $375.00

**POE, Edgar Allan.** *Tales of Mystery & Imagination.* 1971. London. Minerva. ils Harry Clarke. teg. gilt red cloth. F/dj. R3. $45.00

**POE, Edgar Allan.** *Two Poems, by Edgar Allan Poe.* 1984. Utrecht. Catharijne. mini. 1/100. ftspc/sgn Johan deZoete. blk morocco. B24. $200.00

**POESCH, Jessie.** *Art of the Old South: Painting, Sculpture...* 1983. Knopf. ils. 384p. F. D2. $40.00

**POGANY, Willy.** *Willy Pogany's Mother Goose.* ca 1928. London. Nelson. 1st Eng. 4to. gilt bl cloth. dj. R5. $750.00

**POGUE, Forrest C.** *George C Marshall: Organizer of Victory (1943-1945).* 1973. Viking. 1st. sm 4to. 683p. NF/F. W2. $50.00

**POHANKA, Brian.** *Nelson A Miles: Documentary Biography of Military Career...* 1985. Clark. ils. F. J2. $95.00

**POHL, Frederick.** *Case Against Tomorrow.* 1957. Ballantine. 1st. VG. P8. $20.00

**POHL, Frederik.** *Gateway Trip: Tales & Vignettes of the Heechee.* 1990. Ballantine. 1st. AN/dj. M21. $15.00

**POIGNANT, Axel.** *Piccaninny Walkabout: A Story of Aboriginal Children.* 1961 (1957). Sydney. Angus Robertson. rpt. sm 4to. 49p. G/torn. T5. $30.00

**POINTER, Pricilla.** *Lord's Prayer.* 1963. McLoughlin. VG/dj. R8. $20.00

**POITIER, Sidney.** *This Life.* 1980. Knopf. 2nd. photos. 374p. G/dj. P12. $10.00

**POLACK & SIMPSON.** *Jesus in the Background of History.* (1957). NY. McBride. 1st Am. 160p. VG/dj. H10. $15.00

**POLAND, Marguerite.** *Wood-Ash Stars.* 1984. Johannesburg. David Philip. 2nd. sm 4to. ils Shanne Alsthuler. VG+. C14. $12.00

**POLEY & VERLENDEN.** *Friendly Anecdotes.* 1950. Harper. 1st. 12mo. 128p. VG/dj. V3. $15.00

**POLING, James.** *Esquire's World of Jazz.* 1962. NY. Esquire/Grosset. 1st. lg 4to. F/NF. B2. $100.00

**POLING-KEMPES, Lesley.** *Harvey Girls: Women Who Opened the West.* 1989. Paragon. 2nd. ils/map ep. 252p. NF/NF. B19. $30.00

**POLITI, Leo.** *Boat for Peppe.* 1950. Scribner. 1st. 4to. bl cloth. mc pict dj. R5. $125.00

**POLITI, Leo.** *Mieko.* 1969. San Carlos. Golden Gate Jr Books. 1st. ils. pict brd. D11. $50.00

**POLITI, Leo.** *Song of the Swallows.* 1949. Scribner. 1st. cloth. dj. D11. $60.00

**POLLACK, Rachel.** *Temporary Agency.* 1994. St Martin. 1st. sgn. F/dj. M23. $40.00

**POLLAND, Madeleine.** *Queen's Blessings.* 1964. HRW. 1st. xl. VG/G. B36. $10.00

**POLLARD, A.W.** *Italian Book-Illustrations & Early Printing...* 1994. Austin. WT Taylor. rpt. gray linen/paper label. M24. $150.00

**POLLARD, A.W.** *Modern Fine Printing in England & Mr Bruce Rogers.* 1916. Newark, NJ. Cateret BC. 1/275. tan brd/paper spine label. K1. $150.00

**POLLARD, Henry Robinson.** *Memoirs & Sketches of the Life of Henry Robinson Pollard.* 1923. Lewis Pub. 443p. VG. B10. $85.00

**POLLARD, Hugh B.C.** *Hard Up on Pegasus.* 1931. Houghton Mifflin. 1st. ils Gilbert Holiday. VG/dj. A21. $95.00

**POLLARD, J.H.** *Numerical & Statistical Techniques.* 1979. Cambridge. 1st. VG/wrp. B27. $20.00

**POLLARD, William.** *Old-Fashioned Quakerism: Its Origins, Results & Future.* 1889. Phil. Longstreth. 12mo. 122p. wrp. V3. $10.00

**POLLOCK, J.C.** *Centrifuge.* 1984. NY. Crown. 1st. Nf/dj. R11. $17.00

**POLMAR, Norman.** *Strategic Air Command: People, Aircraft & Missiles.* 1979. Nautical/Aviation Pub. 1st. VG/dj. M20. $20.00

**POLSKY, Thomas.** *Curtains for the Editors.* 1939. NY. 1st. 284p. VG/dj. B18. $22.50

**POMA DE AYALA, Don Felipe H.** *Letter to a King: Peruvian Chief's Account of Life...* 1978. NY. Dutton. 1st. 248p. dj. F3. $25.00

**POMERANZ, Gary.** *Out at Home.* 1985. Houghton Mifflin. 1st. F/VG. P8. $15.00

**POMEROY, John Norton.** *Introduction to Municipal Law.* 1864. NY. Appleton. brn pebbled cloth. M11. $450.00

**POMFRET, J.E.** *California Gold Rush Voyages 1848-1849.* 1954. Huntington Lib. 1st. NF/VG. O4. $20.00

**POMFRET, J.E.** *Colonial New Jersey: A History.* 1973. NY. 1st. 327p. F/dj. M4. $30.00

**POMMAUX, Yvan.** *Une Nuit, un Chat...* 1994. Paris. ils. French text. VG. M17. $15.00

**POMPADOUR.** *Memoires.* 1772. np. 2 vol in 1. 8vo. calf. R12. $225.00

**POND, Alonzo W.** *Desert World.* 1962. NY. Thos Nelson. 1st. ils. 342p. VG/dj. W1. $18.00

**PONSOT, Marie.** *Russian Fairy Tales.* 1960. Golden. 1st. ils Benvenuti. VG+. M5. $32.00

**PONTIN, Magnus.** *De Cordis Polypo Pars Prima Theoretica Caus Illustrata.* 1806. Upsaliae. 4to. 1 engraved pl. 18p. G7. $50.00

**POOL, J. Lawrence.** *Neurosurgical Treatment of Traumatic Paraplegia.* 1951. Springfield. Thomas. 107p. stiff morocco. NF. G7. $65.00

**POOL, Raymond J.** *Flowers & Flowering Plants...* 1941. NY. McGraw Hill. 2nd. ils/biblio/index. 428p. VG. H10/S5. $15.00

**POOL & POOL.** *Izaak Walton: Complete Angler & His Turbulent Times.* 1976. Stinehour. 1st. maps. 134p. F/dj. A17. $30.00

**POOLE, Ernest.** *His Family.* 1917. Macmillan. 1st. F/NF. B2. $200.00

**POORTVLIET, Rien.** *Journey to the Ice Age, Mammoths & Other Animals of Wild.* 1994. Abrams. 1st. obl 4to. ils. F/dj. B17. $30.00

**POPE, C.H.** *Reptile World: Natural History of the Snakes, Lizards...* 1974. Knopf. ils/photos/pl. gilt cloth. NF/VG. M12. $22.50

**POPE, Dudley.** *Black Ship.* 1964. Lippincott. 1st. VG/dj. T11. $50.00

**POPE, Dudley.** *Galleon.* 1986. NY. 1st. VG/dj. M17. $22.50

**POPE, Dudley.** *Governor Ramage, RN.* 1973. London. Alison/Secker Warburg. 1st. VG+/clip. A14. $63.00

**POPE, Dudley.** *Governor Ramage, RN.* 1973. NY. S&S. 1st Am. NF/F. T11. $60.00

**POPE, Dudley.** *Ramage & the Dido.* 1989. London. 1st. VG/dj. M17. $35.00

**POPE, Dudley.** *Ramage & the Drum Beat.* 1967. London. Weidenfeld Nicolson. 1st Eng. Ramage #2. NF/VG. T11. $150.00

**POPE, Dudley.** *Ramage & the Rebels.* 1978. London. Secker Warburg. 1st. Ramage #9. F/NF clip. T11. $85.00

**POPE, Dudley.** *Ramage at Trafalger.* 1986. London. Secker Warburg. 1st. Ramage #16. F/NF clip. T11. $85.00

**POPE, Dudley.** *Ramage.* 1965. Lippincott. 1st Am. NF/dj. T11. $150.00

**POPE, Dudley.** *Ramage.* 1965. Weidenfeld Nicolson. 1st. VG+/dj. A14. $70.00

**POPULAR SCIENCE.** *Boy Mechanic.* c 1940. Chicago. 220p. H6. $38.00

**PORGES, Irwin.** *Edgar Rice Burroughs: Man Who Created Tarzan.* 1975. Provo, UT. BYU Pr. 2nd. folio. 819p. F/dj. B20. $75.00

**PORTA, Antonio.** *King of the Storeroom.* 1992. Hanover. Wesleyan U. 1st. F/dj. G10. $17.50

**PORTA, Giovanni Battista.** *Fisionomia Naturale di Gio...* 1626, 1627. Per Pietro Paolo Tozzi. 2nd. 8vo. polished antique calf. G1. $600.00

**PORTE, Barbara Ann.** *Ruthann & Her Pig.* 1989. NY. Orchard. 1st. 8vo. 84p. F/dj. T5. $25.00

**PORTE, Joel.** *Representative Man: Ralph Waldo Emerson in His Time.* 1979. OUP. VG/dj. M17. $22.50

**PORTER, Anna.** *Mortal Sins.* 1988. NAL. 1st thus. F/NF. A23. $25.00

**PORTER, C.L.** *Taxonomy of Flowering Plants.* 1967 (1959). SF. 2nd. 472p. VG+. B26. $26.00

**PORTER, Charles W.** *Adventures to a New World: Roanoke Colony 1585-87.* 1972. Nat Park Service. ils 56p. VG. B10. $6.00

**PORTER, Claude L.** *Cuckoo Over Vienna.* (1989). Traverse City, MI. 1st. ils. 266p. VG/dj. B18. $45.00

**PORTER, David L.** *Biographical Dictionary of American Sports-Baseball.* 1987. Greenwood. 1st. F/sans. P8. $60.00

**PORTER, Eleanor H.** *Oh, Money! Money!* 1918. Houghton Mifflin. 1st. 321p. G. G11. $8.00

**PORTER, Eleanor H.** *Pollyanna Grows Up.* 1915. Boston. LC Page. 1st/1st prt. gilt emb gr silk w/fleur-de-lis. F. w/ad. M24. $165.00

**PORTER, Eleanor H.** *Road to Understanding.* 1917. Houghton Mifflin. 1st. ils Mary Greene Blumenschein. G11. $6.00

**PORTER, Eliot.** *Appalachian Wilderness: Great Smoky Mountains.* 1970. NY. folio. 44 full-p mc photos. F/dj. M4. $40.00

**PORTER, Eliot.** *Forever Wild: Adirondacks.* 1966. Harper Row. 1st. NF/NF. B3. $60.00

**PORTER, Eliot.** *Place No One Knew: Glen Canyon on the Colorado.* 1963. Sierra Club. 1st. photos. F/VG. M4. $80.00

**PORTER, Eliot.** *Place No One Knew: Glen Canyon on the Colorado.* 1968. Sierra Club/Ballantine. abridged. 8vo. 75 mc pl. VG/stiff glossy wrp. F7. $22.50

**PORTER, Gene Stratton.** *Harvester.* 1911. Doubleday Page. 1st. ils WL Jaco. tan cloth. VG. B27. $55.00

**PORTER, Gene Stratton.** *Magic Garden.* 1927. Doubleday Page. 1st. ils Lee Thayer. 271p. VG. P12. $75.00

**PORTER, John Roger.** *Bacterial Chemistry & Physiology.* 1946. Wiley. 1073p. xl. VG. S5. $20.00

**PORTER, Joseph C.** *Paper Medicine Man: John Gregory Bourke & His Am West.* 1986. U OK. 1st. 362p. F/dj. E1. $40.00

**PORTER, Joyce.** *Dover & the Claret Tappers.* 1976. Foul Play. 1st Am. NF/dj. G8. $20.00

**PORTER, Katherine Anne.** *Christmas Story.* 1958. NY. Mademoiselle. 1st. prt brd. F. M24. $45.00

**PORTER, Katherine Anne.** *Christmas Story.* 1967. Delacorte. 1st. 1/500. ils/sgn Ben Shahn. F. M24. $85.00

**PORTER, Katherine Anne.** *Collected Stories of Katherine Anne Porter.* 1965. Harcourt Brace. ARC/1st. RS. F/dj. Q1. $200.00

**PORTER, Katherine Anne.** *Flowering Judas.* 1930. Harcourt Brace. 1st. 1/600. gilt brn quarter cloth. VG. M24. $100.00

**PORTER, Katherine Anne.** *Flowering of Judas.* 1930. Portland, ME. Hound & Horn. 1st. prt wrp. M24. $30.00

**PORTER, Katherine Anne.** *French Song Book.* 1933. Harrison of Paris. 1st. 1/595 on VanGelder. sgn. maroon cloth. F/dj. J3. $250.00

**PORTER, Katherine Anne.** *Katherine Anne Porter & Texas.* 1990. TX A&M. 1st. F/dj. A24. $50.00

**PORTER, Katherine Anne.** *Ship of Fools.* 1962. Atlantic/Little Brn. 1st. F/NF. H11. $60.00

**PORTER, Katherine Anne.** *Ship of Fools.* 1962. Atlantic/Little Brn. 1st. sgn. VG/dj. B30. $125.00

**PORTER, Mark.** *Win Hadley: Winning Pitcher (#1).* 1960. S&S. 1st. VG/dj. P8. $25.00

**PORTER, Noah.** *Human Intellect With Introduction Upon Psychology & Soul.* 1868. Scribner. thick 8vo. ES.VG. G1. $150.00

**PORTER, Theodore.** *Rise of Statistical Thinking, 1820-1900.* 1986. Princeton. 1st. 333p. A13. $35.00

**PORTER, Willard H.** *How to Enjoy the Quarter Horse.* 1973. S Brunswick. 1st. VG/dj. O3. $25.00

**PORTER & PORTER.** *Patient's Progress: Doctors & Doctoring in 18th-C England.* 1989. Stanford, CA. 1st Am. 305p. A13. $25.00

**PORTER & REED.** *Matt Field on the Santa Fe Trail.* 1960. Norman, OK. 1st. 322p. cloth. dj. D11. $60.00

**PORTER & ROBERTS.** *Drinking Cups & Their Customs.* 1869. 2nd. 62p. w/2-letter. E6. $100.00

**PORTER.** *Miss Porter's New Southern Cookery Book.* 1973 (1871). rpt. VG. E6. $15.00

**PORTEUS, S.D.** *Calabashes & Kings.* 1954. London. ils. 284p. VG/poor. M4. $10.00

**PORTIS, Charles.** *True Grit.* 1968. S&S. 1st. F/VG. T11. $30.00

**PORZIO, Domenico.** *Lithography: 200 Years of Art, History & Technique.* 1983. NY. Abrams. 1st Eng-language. 280p. cloth. F/dj. O10. $75.00

**POSEY, Jake.** *Last of the 40-Horse Drivers.* 1959. NY. Vantage. 1st. VG/dj. O3. $65.00

**POSEY, Minnie H.** *Poems of Alexander Lawrence Posey.* 1910. Topeka, KS. Crane & Co Prt. G. A19. $85.00

**POSKA, Valentine J.** *Armadillo.* 1983. Austin. Amistad. mini/frenchfold. ils/poem. half cloth/pict brd. F. B24. $100.00

**POSNER & TA-SHEMA.** *Hebrew Book: Historical Survey.* 1975. NY. Amiel. 1st. 320p. cloth. F/dj. O10. $45.00

**POST, C.J.** *Little War of Private Post.* 1960. Boston. 1st. ils 340p. G/poor. M4. $15.00

**POST, J.B.** *Atlas of Fantasy: Worlds of Tolkien, Burroughs...* 1979 (1973). Ballantine. 1st revised. 100 fantasy maps. VG. B27. $35.00

**POST, John.** *Last Great Subsistence Crisis in Western World.* 1977. Baltimore. 1st. 240p. A13. $35.00

**POST, Lydia.** *Soldiers' Letters From Camp, Battlefield & Prison.* 1865. US Sanitary Comm. 472p. VG. E6. $125.00

**POSTGATE, Raymond.** *Conversations of Dr Johnson.* 1970 (1930). Taplinger. rpt. dj. H13. $45.00

**POSTGATE, Raymond.** *Ledger Is Kept.* 1953. London. Michael Joseph. 1st. F/dj. M15. $65.00

**POSTMAN, Neil.** *Disappearance of Childhood.* 1982. Delacorte. 1st. NF/dj. S13. $25.00

**POTOK, Chaim.** *In the Beginning.* 1975. NY. Viking. 1st. inscr/dtd 1995. VG/dj. R14. $45.00

**POTOK, Chaim.** *Promise.* 1969. Knopf. 1st. NF/dj. S13. $12.00

**POTT, Percival.** *Chirurgical Works.* 1985. Birmingham. facs 1778 Dublin. 2 vol in 1. full leather. A13. $85.00

**POTTER, Beatrix.** *Appley Dapply's Nursery Rhymes.* (1917). London. Warne. 1st. 16mo. lg gr brd/pict label. R5. $585.00

**POTTER, Beatrix.** *Fairy Caravan.* 1953 (1929). London. Warne. rpt. 8vo. 225p. gr cloth. T5. $55.00

**POTTER, Beatrix.** *Ginger & Pickles.* 1909. London. Warne. 1st. sm 4to. 51p. F. H5. $1,100.00

**POTTER, Beatrix.** *Ginger & Pickles.* 1909. Warne. 1st Am. ils. VG. M5. $295.00

**POTTER, Beatrix.** *Rolly-Polly Pudding.* 1908. Warne. 1st Am. sq 8o. VG. D1. $400.00

**POTTER, Beatrix.** *Tale of Jemima Puddle-Duck.* 1995. Warne. 100th Anniversary ed. F/F box. B17. $20.00

**POTTER, Beatrix.** *Tale of Peter Rabbit.* 1903 (1902). London. Warne. 1st w/pict ep (5th overall). 85p. wht lettered gray brd. R5. $800.00

**POTTER, Beatrix.** *Tale of Timmy Tiptoes.* 1911. London. Warne. 1st. 12mo. 84p. F. H5. $850.00

**POTTER, Beatrix.** *Tale of Tom Kitten.* (1907). London. Warne. later ed. sgn/dtd. 16mo. wht lettered tan brd. R5. $1,400.00

**POTTER, Beatrix.** *Tales of Peter Rabbit & His Friends.* 1984. NY. Chatham. 5th. F/dj. T12. $15.00

**POTTER, Beatrix.** *Wag-By-Wall.* 1944. Boston. Horn Book. 1st. ils JJ Lankes. 12mo. wheat buckram/pict label. R5. $175.00

**POTTER, Israel R.** *Life & Remarkable Adventures of Israel R Potter.* 1924. Providence. Henry Trumbull. lacks ftspc/rear ep. G. M17. $30.00

**POTTER, Jack.** *Cattle Trails of the Old West.* 1939. Laura Krehbiel. lg fld map. VG. J2. $155.00

**POTTER, Jerry O.** *Sultana Tragedy: America's Greatest Maritime Disaster.* 1992. Pelican. 1st. F/dj. A14. $25.00

**POTTER, Margaret Horton.** *Castle of Twilight.* 1903. Chicago. McClurg. 1st. ils Chas Weber. 429p. G. G11. $8.00

**POTTER, Stephen.** *Golfmanship.* 1968. NY. 1st. ils Frank Wilson. VG/dj. M17. $20.00

**POTTER & ROSENBLUM.** *Liberators: Fighting on Two Fronts in World War II.* 1992. HBJ. 1st. lg 8vo. ils. F/dj. R11. $15.00

**POTTLE, Frederick A.** *Boswell in Holland, 1763-1764, Including Correspondence...* 1952. London. Heinemann. 1/1050. ils. linen brd/vellum spine. H13. $95.00

**POTTLE, Frederick A.** *James Boswell, the Earlier Years 1740-1769.* 1985. McGraw Hill. 1st. lg 8vo. VG/dj. H13. $65.00

**POTTLE, Frederick A.** *Pride & Negligence: History of the Boswell Papers.* 1982. McGraw Hill. 1st. 8vo. 290p. linen spine/gray brd. F/dj. H13. $85.00

**POTTLE & WIMSATT.** *Boswell for the Defense, 1769-1744.* 1959. McGraw Hill. 1st. fld map/ils. NF. H13. $85.00

**POTTS, William D.** *Freeman's Guide to Polls & Solemn Appeal...* 1864. NY. self pub. 1st. 125p. NF/self wrp. M8. $250.00

**POUCHELLE, Marie.** *Body & Surgery in the Middle Ages.* 1990. New Brunswick, NJ. 1st. 277p. dj. A13. $35.00

**POUGET, Marcel.** *Franco-American Professional Cookbook.* 1962. Exposition. G/dj. A16. $12.50

**POUND, Arthur.** *Turning Wheel: Story of General Motors...1908-1933.* 1934. Doubleday Doran. 1st. NF/dj. B20. $45.00

**POUND, Ezra.** *Exile, No 2.* Autumn 1927. Chicago. Pascal Covici. NF/orange wrp. B9. $50.00

**POUND, Ezra.** *Ezra Pound's Cavalcanti Poems.* 1966. London. Faber. 1/190. sgn. 105p. quarter vellum/yel Roman paper brd. F. H5. $1,750.00

**POUND, Ezra.** *Ta Hio, the Great Learning.* 1936. London. Stanley Nott. 1st Eng. 1/300. yel prt brd. F/NF. M24. $200.00

**POUND, Ezra.** *Ta Hio, the Great Learning.* 1939. New Directions. rpt. F/gr wrp. M24. $20.00

**POUND, Reginald.** *Harley Street.* 1967. London. 1st. 198p. dj. A13. $25.00

**POURADE, Richard.** *Anza Conquers the Desert: Anza Expeditions...* 1971. San Diego. Copley. special ed. sgn author/pub. cloth. D11. $75.00

**POURADE, Richard.** *Silver Dons. Volume Three. History of San Diego.* 1963. San Diego. Union-Tribune. Special ed. sgn. case. w/ephemera. P4. $60.00

**POURELLE, Jerry.** *King David's Spaceship.* 1980. S&S. 1st thus. rem mk. F/NF. G10. $17.00

**POWELL, Anthony.** *O, How the Wheel Becomes It!* 1983. NY. 1st Am. VG/dj. M17. $15.00

**POWELL, Anthony.** *Soldier's Art.* 1966. Little Brn. 1st Am. F/dj. Q1. $40.00

**POWELL, Dawn.** *Locusts Have No King.* 1948. Scribner. 1st. NF/VG-. B4. $250.00

**POWELL, Dawn.** *She Walks in Beauty.* 1928. Brentano. 1st. F/NF. B4. $1,750.00

**POWELL, Edward Alexander.** *By Camel & Car to the Peacock Throne.* 1923. NY. Century. 1st. sm 8vo. 392p. VG+. M7. $35.00

**POWELL, El Sea.** *Sea as Seen by El Sea Powell.* 1962. Malibu. Dawson/Cheney. mini. 1/200. sgn. 8p. Bela Blau bdg. F/dj. B24. $85.00

**POWELL, Hickman.** *Lucky Luciano.* 1975. Secaucus. Citadel. 1st. VG/dj. B5. $15.00

**POWELL, Ivor.** *This... I Believe: Essential Truths of Christianity.* 1961. Zondervan. 222p. VG/dj. B29. $7.50

**POWELL, J.W.** *Exploration of Colorado River of West & Its Tributaries...* 1875. GPO. 4to. orig map. ils (many Thomas Moran). 291p. new ep. rstr cloth. VG. F7. $395.00

**POWELL, J.W.** *Report on Lands of the Arid Region of the US...Lands of UT.* 1879. GPO. 2nd. 4to. 3 maps. rb orig brd/spine. new ep. VG. F7. $225.00

**POWELL, J.W.** *Report on Methods of Surveying in Public Domain...* 1878. GPO. 8vo. 16p. VG/tan wrp. F7. $130.00

**POWELL, J.W.** *Selected Prose of John Wesley Powell.* 1970. Boston. Godine. 1/1500. 8vo. photos. 122p. gr cloth. VG/dj. F7. $45.00

**POWELL, Lawrence Clark.** *Philosopher Pickett: Life & Writings of Chas E Pickett...* 1942. U CA. 1st. 178p. F/VG. B19. $55.00

**POWELL, Lawrence Clark.** *Southwest of the Bookman: Essays...* 1959. UCLA. 1st. 60p. NF/wrp. B19. $35.00

**POWELL, Lawrence Clark.** *Southwestern Book Trails: A Reader's Guide...* 1982. NM. Wm Gannon. unabridged rpt. 91p. brn leatherette. VG+. F7. $25.00

**POWELL, Lawrence Clark.** *Southwestern Century.* 1958. Van Nuys. JE Reynolds. 1st. 1/500. sgn Tom Lea/LC Powell. maroon cloth. F/dj. M24. $200.00

**POWELL, Padgett.** *Woman Named Drown.* 1987. FSG. 1st. F/F. H11. $30.00

**POWERS, Alfred.** *Poems of the Covered Wagon.* 1947. Portland. Pacific Pub. 1st. ils/70+ poems. F. A18. $60.00

**POWERS, Edwin.** *Crime & Punishment in Early Massachusetts 1620-1692.* 1966. Boston. VG/dj. M17. $30.00

**POWERS, R.** *Far From Home: Life & Loss in Two American Towns.* 1991. NY. 1st. F/dj. M4. $15.00

**POWERS, Richard.** *Gold Bug Variations.* 1991. NY. Morrow. 1st. F/dj. Q1. $200.00

**POWERS, Richard.** *Prisoner's Dilemma.* 1988. Morrow. 1st. author's 2nd book. F/VG. B3. $75.00

**POWERS, Richard.** *Prisoner's Dilemma.* 1988. NY. Beech Tree/Morrow. 1st. author's 2nd book. F/F. Q1. $150.00

**POWERS, Richard.** *Three Farmers on Their Way to a Dance.* 1985. NY. Beech Tree. 1st. F/dj. D10. $150.00

**POWERS, Ron.** *Toot Toot Tootsie Goodbye.* 1981. Delacorte. 1st. F/dj. P8. $15.00

**POWERS, Susan.** *Grass Dancer.* 1994. Putnam. 1st. sgn. author's 1st book. F/dj. A24. $35.00

**POWERS, T.** *Expiration Date.* 1996. NY. Tor. 1st. F/NF. G10. $22.00

**POWERS, Tim.** *Anubis Gates.* 1989. Shingletown. Ziesing. 1st Am. sgn. 1984 Philip K Dick award. F/dj. T2. $45.00

**POWERS, Tim.** *Dinner at Deviant's Palace.* 1985. NY. Ace. 1st hc. sgn. 1986 Philip K Dick award. F/dj. T2. $25.00

POWERS, Tim. *Where They Are Hid.* 1995. Lynbrook. Charnel House. 1st. 1/350. ils/sgn Tim Powers. F/sans/case. T2. $125.00

POYER, David. *Winter in the Heart.* 1993. Tor. 1st. F/dj. S18. $20.00

PRAED, Winthrop M. *Poems of...* 1865. NY. Widdleton. 2 vol. 3-quarter tan leather. S17. $50.00

PRATHER, Richard S. *Pattern for Panic.* 1954. Abelard. 1st. VG/G+. G8. $25.00

PRATT, Kristin Joy. *Walk in the Rain Forest.* 1992. CA. Dawn Pub. 1st. 30p. NF/dj. T5. $30.00

PRATT, O.S. *Horse's Friend: Only Practical Method of Educating Horse...* 1876. Buffalo. later prt. ils. 535p. B18. $35.00

PRAWER, J. *Latin Kingdom of Jerusalem. European Colonialism...* 1972. Weidenfeld Nicolson. ils/16 pl/3 maps. 587p. cloth. VG/dj. Q2. $30.00

PRAWER, J. *World of the Crusaders.* 1972. Weidenfeld Nicolson. ils/3 maps. gilt cloth. VG. Q2. $18.00

PREBBLE, John. *Buffalo Soldiers.* 1959. NY. Harcourt Brace. 1st. F/dj. T11. $65.00

PREISS, Byron. *Ultimate Dracula.* 1991. NY. Dell. BC. F/dj. G10. $20.00

PREIST, Christopher. *Anticipations.* 1978. London. Faber. 1st. AN/dj. M21. $20.00

PREJEAN, Helen. *Dead Man Walking: An Eyewitness Account...* 1993. Random. 1st. rem mk. F/dj. B4. $85.00

PRELUTSKY, Jack. *Beneath a Blue Umbrella.* 1990. NY. Greenwillow. 1st. ils. F/dj. D4. $30.00

PRELUTSKY, Jack. *Something Big Has Been Here.* nd (1990). Greenwillow. 1st/3rd prt. sq 8vo. 159p. F/dj. C14. $14.00

PRESCOTT, H.F.M. *Jerusalem Journey.* 1954. Eyre Spottiswode. 8vo. ils/2 fld pl. 242p. cloth. VG. Q2. $12.50

PRESCOTT, H.F.M. *Lost Fight.* 1956. NY. VG/dj. M17. $15.00

PRESCOTT, Samuel. *When MIT Was Boston Tech 1861-1916.* 1954. Cambridge. 1st. 350p. VG/G. B5. $25.00

PRESCOTT, William H. *Conquest of Mexico.* 1981. McKay. 3 vol. rpt. 12mo. gr cloth. G. S17. $7.50

PRESCOTT, William H. *History of Conquest of Mexico.* 1843. NY. Harper. 3 vol. 1st/1st prt. fld maps. gilt gr cloth. M24. $650.00

PRESCOTT, William H. *History of the Conquest of Mexico &...of Peru.* 1980. Random. 4 vol in 1. F/dj. A19. $30.00

PRESNIAKOV, A.E. *Formation of the Great Russian State: A Study...* 1970. Quadrangle. 1st. VG/clip. A2. $20.00

PRESSER & ZAINALDIN. *Law & American History, Cases & Materials.* 1980. St Paul. West Pub. M11. $35.00

PRESTON, Chloe. *Peek-a-Boos.* nd. Hodder Stoughton. 1st Am. ils C Preston. VG. D1. $500.00

PRESTON, J.H. *Gentleman Rebel: Mad Anthony Wayne.* 1930. Garden City. ils. 370p. G. M4. $20.00

PRESTON, Jennifer. *Queen Bess: Unauthorized Biography of Bess Myerson.* 1990. Contemporary Books. 1st. F/dj. W2. $30.00

PRESTON, Richard J. *Rocky Mountain Trees.* 1947 (1940). Ames. 2nd. ils/maps. 285p. VG. B26. $17.50

PRESTON, Richard. *American Steel: Hot Metal & Resurrection of Rust Belt.* 1991. Prentice Hall. 1st. 278p. VG/clip. R11. $12.00

PRESZNICK, Rose M. *Carnival & Iridescent Glass Price Guide.* 1962. self pub. 1st. sgn. ils. 96p. sbdg. G+. H1. $40.00

PREUSS, Edward. *Justification of the Sinner Before God.* nd. Concordia. 135p. VG. B29. $9.50

PREVIN, Dory. *Bog-Trotter: An Autobiography With Lyrics.* 1980. London. Weidenfeld Nicolson. 1st. inscr. ils Joby Baker. F/dj. S9. $65.00

PREVOST, Antoine-Francois. *Histoire du Chevalier Des Grieux...* 1753. Amsterdam. Compagnie. 2 vol. 8vo. calf. R12. $150.00

PRIBRAM, Karl H. *Brain & Behaviour: Selected Readings.* 1969. Penguin. 4 vol. sc. xl. G1. $75.00

PRIBRAM, Karl H. *Languages of the Brain: Experimental Paradoxes & Principles.* 1971. Prentice Hall. 2nd. 432p. prt bl cloth. VG/dj. G1. $40.00

PRICE, A. Grenfell. *Explorations of Capt James Cook in the Pacific...* 1957. Griffin. 1/1500. 4to. 308p. F/NF case. A4. $165.00

PRICE, Alfred. *Battle of Britain.* 1980. Scribner. BC. 12mo. photos. 246p. VG/dj. M7. $15.00

PRICE, Anthony. *Memory Trap.* 1989. London. Gollancz. 1st. F/dj. M15. $45.00

PRICE, Benjamin F. *Centennial Celebration of Springfield, OH...1901.* 1901. Springfield. 1st. 296p. G. B18. $47.50

PRICE, Bruce Deitrick. *Too Easy.* 1994. S&S. 1st. F/F. H11. $20.00

PRICE, Byron. *Cowboys of the American West.* 1996. Thunder Bay. 205p. VG. J2. $65.00

PRICE, Christine. *Happy Days: A UNICEF Book of Birthdays, Name Days...* nd (c 1969). US Comm for UNICEF. 1st. 8vo. 128p. VG/clip. C14. $14.00

PRICE, D.J. *Equatorie of the Planetis...* 1955. Cambridge. 4to. pl. 214p. dj. K5. $65.00

PRICE, Eugenia. *Beauty From the Ashes.* 1995. Doubleday. 1st. F/dj. B30. $24.00

PRICE, George F. *Across the Continent With the Fifth Cavalry.* 1959. Antiquarian. 1/750. 706p. NF. B19. $35.00

PRICE, Harry. *Short-Title Catalogue of Works on Psychical Research... 1929-1935.* London. ils. mc ftspc. NF. $195.00

PRICE, Jack. *News Pictures.* 1937. Round Table. 1st. NF/VG. B20. $40.00

PRICE, Marjorie Yates. *Daughter of the Gold Camp & Legends of the Western Indian.* 1962. Rapid City, SD. ESPE Prt Co. F/dj. A19. $35.00

PRICE, Miles O. *Effective Legal Research, a Practical Manual of Law Books...* 1953. NY. Little Brn. maroon cloth. G. M11. $65.00

PRICE, Reynolds. *Blue Calhoun.* 1992. Atheneum. 1st. sgn/dtd 1993. F/dj. R14. $45.00

PRICE, Reynolds. *Clear Pictures.* 1989. Atheneum. 1st. inscr. F/dj. B4. $85.00

PRICE, Reynolds. *Good Hearts.* 1988. Atheneum. 1st. F/F. B3. $25.00

PRICE, Reynolds. *Kate Vaiden.* 1986. Atheneum. 1st. F/NF. B3. $75.00

PRICE, Reynolds. *Three Gospels: Good News According to Mark...John...* 1996. Scribner. 1st. VG+/dj. B30. $20.00

PRICE, Reynolds. *Tongues of Angels.* 1990. Atheneum. 1st. NF/F. R14. $25.00

PRICE, Richard. *Bloodbrothers.* 1976. Houghton Mifflin. 1st. sgn/dtd 1995. author's 2nd book. VG/dj. R14. $55.00

PRICE, Richard. *Bloodbrothers.* 1976. Houghton Mifflin. 1st. VG/VG. H11. $35.00

PRICE, Richard. *Clockers.* 1992. Houghton Mifflin. 1st. F/NF. H11. $35.00

PRICE, Richard. *Wanderers.* 1974. Houghton Mifflin. 1st. author's 1st book. F/dj. A24. $100.00

PRICE, Richard. *Wanderers.* 1974. Houghton Mifflin. 1st. author's 1st book. NF/dj. R14. $60.00

**PRICE, Willard.** *Amazing Amazon.* 1952. John Day. 1st. 306p. dj. F3. $20.00

**PRIDGEN, T.** *Courage: Story of Modern Cockfighting.* 1938. Boston. 1st. 263p. VG. M4. $100.00

**PRIDHAM, B.R.** *Arab Gulf & the Arab World.* 1988. London/NY/Sydney. 1st. 8vo. 302p. VG/dj. W1. $22.00

**PRIEST, John Michael.** *Captain James Wren's Diary: From New Bern to Fredricksburg.* 1990. Wht Mane Pub. 1st. F/dj. A14. $25.00

**PRIESTLEY, Herbert Ingram.** *Franciscan Explorations in California.* 1946. Arthur H Clark. 189p. teg. cloth. D11. $100.00

**PRIESTLEY, Herbert Ingram.** *Tristan de Luna Conquistador of the Old South.* 1936. Glendale. AH Clark. 1st/ltd. 1/500. 8vo. gilt maroon cloth. VG. B11. $175.00

**PRIESTLEY, Herman Ingram.** *Colorado River Campaign, 1781-1782. Diary of Pedro Fages.* 1913. U CA. 1st. F/prt wrp. P4. $68.00

**PRIESTLEY, J.B.** *Three Men in New Suits.* 1945. London. Heinemann. 1st. NF/dj. A24. $30.00

**PRIHARA, Maria.** *Cossack Holota: Stories Based on Ancient Ukrainian Ballads.* 1985. Biev. ils Heorhiy Yakutovich. trans Mary Skrypnyk. VG. M17. $20.00

**PRINCE, Morton.** *Clinical & Experimental Studies in Personality.* 1929. Cambridge. Sci-Art. thick 8vo. 559p. prt panelled crimson cloth. G1. $85.00

**PRINCE, Morton.** *Dissociation of a Personality: Biographical Study...* 1992. NY. Classics of Psychiatry & Behavioral Sciences Lib. F. G1. $75.00

**PRINCE, Morton.** *Nature of Mind & Human Automatism.* 1885. Lippincott. 12mo. bevelled brn cloth. xl. G1. $250.00

**PRINGLE, David.** *Ultimate Guide to Science Fiction.* 1990. NY. Pharos. 1st thus. F/wrp. G10. $15.00

**PRINGLE, Terry.** *Tycoon.* 1990. Chapel Hill. Algonquin. F/F. H11. $25.00

**PRIOR & PRIOR.** *Stud-Book Lore.* 1951. Bletchley. FM Prior. 1st. G. O3. $95.00

**PRITCHARD, Alan.** *Alchemy: Bibliography of English-Language Writings.* 1980. London. 1st. 439p. dj. A13. $150.00

**PRITCHARD, James.** *Archaology & the Old Testament.* 1958. princeton. 263p. VG/dj. B29. $17.00

**PROBERT, William.** *Ancient Laws of Cambria...* 1823. London. 1st Eng trans. lacks ffe. later crimson cloth. M11. $450.00

**PROCTER, Gil.** *People of the Moonlight.* 1958. Kitchen Mus. 1st. ils/map. 116p. NF/VG. B19. $35.00

**PROCTER, Gil.** *Tucson, Tubac, Tumacacori, to Hell.* 1956. AZ Silhouettes. 1st. 1/950. ils. 110p. dj. B19. $50.00

**PROCTOR, Mary.** *Romance of the Planets.* 1929. NY. Harper. 8vo. 272p. VG/dj. K5. $30.00

**PROCTOR, Richard A.** *Half Hours With the Telescope.* 1889 (1868). London. WH Allen. 10th. ils. 109p. gilt cloth. K5. $70.00

**PROCTOR, Richard A.** *Saturn & Its System.* 1879 (1865). London. Longman Gr. later prt of 1st. 14 pl. 252p. gilt cloth. K5. $250.00

**PROCTOR, Richard A.** *Spectroscope & Its Work.* 1877. London. 128p. cloth. VG. K5. $45.00

**PROCTOR, Roscoe.** *Black Workers & the Class Struggle.* 1972. New Outlook. 2nd. 37p. wrp. R11. $10.00

**PROFFITT, N.** *Gardens of Stone.* 1983. Carroll Graf. 1st. author's 1st book. NF/VG. H11. $15.00

**PROFFITT, N.** *Gardens of Stone.* 1983. NY. Carroll Graf. 2nd. VG/dj. R11. $15.00

**PROGOFF, Ira.** *Death & Rebirth of Psychology.* 1956. NY. Julian. 1st. 8vo. 275p. VG/dj. B11. $25.00

**PROKSCH, J.K.** *Geschichte der Geschlechtskrankheiten.* 1910. Vienna. 1st. 140p. A13. $50.00

**PRONZINI, Bill.** *Breakdown.* 1991. Delacorte. 1st. AN/dj. S18. $27.00

**PRONZINI, Bill.** *Breakdown.* 1991. Delacorte. 1st. F/NF. G8. $20.00

**PRONZINI, Bill.** *Great Tales of Horror/ Supernatural.* Galahad. 1st. F/dj. S18. $8.50

**PRONZINI, Bill.** *Gun in Cheek.* 1982. CMG. 1st. NF/VG clip. P3. $30.00

**PRONZINI, Bill.** *Hangings.* 1989. NY. Walker. 1st. F/F. B3. $25.00

**PRONZINI, Bill.** *Hardcase.* 1995. Delacorte. 1st. NF/VG. G8. $20.00

**PRONZINI, Bill.** *Jade Figurine.* 1972. Bobbs Merrill. 1st. author's 1st book (as by Jack Foxx). NF/dj. M25. $35.00

**PRONZINI, Bill.** *Masques.* 1981. NY. Arbor. 1st. VG/dj. L1. $35.00

**PRONZINI, Bill.** *Midnight Specialist.* 1977. Bobbs Merrill. 1st. xl. G/VG. S18. $5.00

**PRONZINI, Bill.** *Mummy.* 1980. NY. Arbor. 1st. VG/dj. L1. $45.00

**PRONZINI, Bill.** *Scattershot.* 1982. St Martin. 1st. F/F. B3. $45.00

**PRONZINI, Bill.** *Starvation Camp.* 1984. Doubleday. 1st. F/dj. M15. $75.00

**PRONZINI, Bill.** *Starvation Camp.* 1984. Doubleday. 1st. VG/dj. M21. $40.00

**PRONZINI, Bill.** *Voodoo.* 1980. NY. Arbor. 1st. VG/dj. L1. $50.00

**PRONZINI, Bill.** *Werewolf.* 1979. NY. Arbor. 1st. VG/dj. L1. $55.00

**PROSE, Francine.** *Peaceable Kingdom.* 1993. FSG. 1st. F/dj. R14. $30.00

**PROSEK, James.** *Trout.* 1996. Knopf. 1st. 1/15000. sgn. ils. F/dj. T11. $250.00

**PROSKOURIAKOFF, Tatiana.** *Album of Maya Architecture.* 1958. Mexico. Maya Found. 1/1100. obl folio. 36 pl/ils. 72p. F3. $150.00

**PROSSER, C. Ladd.** *Molecular Mechanisms of Temperature Adaptation.* 1967. AAAS. 390p. xl. VG. S5. $15.00

**PROTESTANT EPISCOPAL CHURCH.** *Journal of Proceeding of 75th Annual Council...1864.* 1864. Columbia. Steam-Power Pr of Evans/Cogswell. 1st. 82p. wrp. M8. $375.00

**PROTHEROE, E.** *Handy Natural History.* nd. London. 32 full-p pl/100 engravings. 462p. VG. M12. $17.50

**PROULX, E. Annie.** *Complete Dairy Foods Cookbook: How to Make Everything...* 1982. Emmaus, PA. Rodale. 1st. pict paper brd. F/dj. Q1. $275.00

**PROULX, E. Annie.** *Postcards.* 1992. Scribner. 1st. F/clip. D10. $350.00

**PROULX, E. Annie.** *Shipping News.* 1993. NY. Scribner. 1st. sgn. F/dj. B4. $450.00

**PROUST, Marcel.** *Cities of the Plain.* 1929. London. 2 vol. 1st. trans CK Scott Moncrieff. T9. $60.00

**PROUST, Marcel.** *Selected Letters, Vol 2 1904-09.* 1989. NY. 1st. trans T Kilmartin. edit P Kolb. dj. T9. $15.00

**PROUT, Ebenezer.** *Instrumentation.* nd. Boston. Oliver Ditson. 143p. G. C5. $12.50

**PROVENSEN & PROVENSEN.** *Glorious Flight.* (1983). NY. Viking. 1st. obl 4to. 1984 Caldecott. pict brd. mc pict dj. R5. $150.00

**PROVENSEN & PROVENSEN.** *My Little Hen.* 1973. Random. 32p. VG+. D4/T5. $30.00

**PROVENSEN & PROVENSEN.** *Peaceable Kingdom.* 1978. NY. Viking. 1st. ils. F/NF. D4. $45.00

**PROVENSEN & PROVENSEN.** *Shaker Lane.* 1987. Viking. 1st. obl 4to. F/dj. B17. $25.00

**PROWELL, Sandra West.** *When Wallflowers Die.* 1996. NY. Walker. 1st. sgn. F/dj. A23. $44.00

**PROYSEN, Alf.** *Mrs Pepperpot Again.* 1960. Obolensky. 1st. ils Bjorn Berg. VG/G. P2. $18.00

**PRUDDEN, T. Mitchell.** *On the Great American Plateau: Wanderings Among Canyons...* 1906. Putnam. 12mo. ils Edward Learning/fld map/index. 243p. xl. G. F7. $15.00

**PRUDDEN & SUSSMAN.** *Suzy Prudden's Spot Reducing Program.* 1979. Workman. 1st. sm 4to. 222p. F/NF. W2. $25.00

**PRUDHOMME, Paul.** *Chef Paul Prudhomme's Louisiana Kitchen.* 1884. photos. F/F. E6. $12.00

**PRUETTE, Lorine G.** *Stanley Hall: Biography of a Mind.* 1926. Appleton. pres. sm 8vo. 266p. prt blk cloth. VG/dj. G1. $60.00

**PRUYSER, Paul W.** *Dynamic Psychology of Religion.* 1968. Harper. 1st. 367p. VG/dj. B29. $12.00

**PRYOR, L.D.** *Trees in Canberra.* 1968 (1962). Canberra. 2nd. ils. 199p. VG/dj. B26. $21.00

**PRYOR, Mrs. Roger A.** *Mother of Washington & Her Times.* 1907 (1903). Grosset Dunlap. ils. xl. B10. $8.00

**PSALMANAAZAAR, George.** *Native of the Island of Formosa: A Description of Formosa.* 1926. London. Holden. 1/750. facs of orig. 8vo. 288p. H13. $85.00

**PTACEK, Kathryn.** *Women of Darkness.* 1988. Tor. 1st. F/dj. N4. $25.00

**PUDDEFOOT & RANKIN.** *Hewers of Wood: Story of Michigan Pine Forests.* 1903. Pilgrim. 1st. ils. 352p. gilt cloth. VG. A17. $25.00

**PUHARICH, Andrija.** *Sacred Mushroom: Key to the Door of Eternity.* 1959. Garden City. 1st. 262p. A13. $20.00

**PUHARICH, Andrija.** *Uri: A Journal of the Mystery of Uri Geller.* 1974. NY. Anchor. 1st. NF/dj. H11. $20.00

**PUIG, Manuel.** *Eternal Curse on the Reader of These Pages.* 1992. Random. 1st. VG/dj. B30. $22.50

**PULLEN, H.F.** *Atlantic Schooners.* 1967. Brunswick. 1st Canadian. F/sans. T12. $15.00

**PULLIAM, Nina.** *I Traveled a Lonely Land.* 1955. Bobbs Merrill. 1st. photos. 400p. VG/dj. S14. $22.50

**PULSFORD, Petronella.** *Lee's Ghost.* 1990. London. Constable. 1st. F/dj. G10. $22.00

**PULSZKY, Francis.** *Tricolor on the Atlas; or, Algeria & the French Conquest.* 1855. NY. Thos Nelson. 1st. sm 8vo. 2 fld pl. 402p. rb. VG. H7/W1. $85.00

**PUMPELLY, Raphael.** *Across America & Asia: Notes of 5 Years' Journey...* 1870. Leypoldt & Holt. 2nd. ils. 454p. VG. B19. $75.00

**PUNER, Helen Walker.** *Sitter Who Didn't Sit.* 1949. Lee Shepard. 1st. sq 4to. mc pict brd. dj. R5. $85.00

**PUPIN, Michael.** *Romance of the Machine.* 1930. Scribner. 1st. inscr. 8vo. 111p. dj. K5. $12.00

**PURDON, Eric.** *Black Company.* 1972. WA-NY. 1st. ils. xl. VG/dj. B18. $22.50

**PURDY, James.** *Color of Darkness.* 1957. New Directions. 1st. sgn. VG/dj. R14. $50.00

**PURDY, James.** *Day After the Fair.* 1977. NY. Note of Hand. 1st. sgn. F/NF. R14. $40.00

**PURI, A.N.** *Soils: Their Physics & Chemistry.* 1949. Reinhold. 550p. xl. G. S5. $12.00

**PURINA, Ralston.** *Purina Poultry Guide.* 1933. St Louis. Purina. 1st. 104p. cloth. VG. A10. $12.00

**PUSEY, Merlo J.** *Charles Evans Hughes. Two Volumes.* 1951. Macmillan. G/box. M11. $50.00

**PUSEY, William.** *History & Epidemiology of Syphilis.* 1933. Springfield. 1st. 113p. A13. $140.00

**PUTNAM, Charles E.** *Elephant Pipes.* 1886. Davenport, IA. Glass Axtman. ils. VG. A19. $65.00

**PUTNAM, George.** *Death Valley Handbook.* 1947. DSP. 1st. map ep. 47p. NF/VG. B19. $25.00

**PUTNAM, George.** *Prisoner of War in Virginia 1864-1865.* 1912. 2nd. Sturgis prison statistics. xl. VG. E6. $45.00

**PUTNAM, George.** *Southland of North America.* 1914 (1913). NY. Putnam. 2nd. 425p. pocket map. pict cloth. F3. $30.00

**PUTNAM, R.** *Natural History of Deer.* 1988. Comstock. ils/photos/figures/tables. F/dj. M12. $20.00

**PUZO, Mario.** *Fools Die.* 1978. Putnam. 1st. NF/dj. L4. $30.00

**PUZO, Mario.** *Fools Die.* 1978. Putnam. 1st. sgn. NF/dj. R14. $60.00

**PUZO, Mario.** *Godfather Papers & Other Confessions.* 1972. Putnam. BC. ils. VG/dj. C9. $30.00

**PUZO, Mario.** *Godfather.* 1969. Putnam. 1st. F/NF clip. B4. $850.00

**PUZO, Mario.** *Last Don.* 1996. Random. 1st. F/dj. R14. $45.00

**PUZO, Mario.** *Sicilian.* 1984. NY. Linden. 1st. NF/F. H11. $20.00

**PYLE, A.M.** *Murder Moves In.* 1986. Walker. 1st. NF/dj. G8. $22.50

**PYLE, Howard.** *Book of Pirates.* ltd. ils Pyle. VG/dj. M17. $17.50

**PYLE, Howard.** *Howard Pyle's Book of Pirates.* 1921. NY. Harper. later issue. folio. 36 pl. 246p. teg. F. H5. $500.00

**PYLE, Howard.** *Otto of the Silver Hand.* 1888. Scribner. 1st. lg 8vo. new leather spine. VG. M5. $245.00

**PYLE, Robert Michael.** *Audubon Society Handbook for Butterfly Watchers.* 1984. NY. 1st. ils. VG/dj. M17. $15.00

**PYLE, Robert Michael.** *Thunder Tree: Lessons From an Urban Wildland.* 1993. Houghton Mifflin. 1st. 220p. S15. $9.00

**PYNCHON, Thomas.** *Crying of Lot 49.* 1965. Lippincott. 1st. F/NF. B4. $600.00

**PYNCHON, Thomas.** *Gravity's Rainbow.* nd. BC. NF/dj. S18. $15.00

**PYNCHON, Thomas.** *Gravity's Rainbow.* 1973. Viking. 1st. author's 3rd book. F/dj. B4. $1,000.00

**PYNCHON, Thomas.** *Mindful Pleasures: Essays on Thomas Pynchon.* 1976. Little Brn. 1st. 8vo. F/dj. S9. $50.00

**PYNCHON, Thomas.** *Small Rain.* nd (1982). London. Aloes Books. 1st/1st separate appearance. F/stapled pict wrp. Q1. $50.00

**PYNCHON, Thomas.** *Vineland.* 1990. Little Brn. 1st. F/dj. S18. $23.00

**PYNE, Stephen J.** *Fire on the Rim: Firefighter's Season at the Grand Canyon.* 1989. NY. Weidenfeld Nicolson. 1st. 8vo. map ep. 323p. brn brd. VG+. F7. $35.00

**QUACKENBOS, John D.** *Geological Ancestors of the Brook Trout...* 1916. NY Anglers Club. 1st. inscr. 10 pl. 50 p. lacks spine. H10. $225.00

**QUACKENBUSH, Robert.** *Sherlock Chick's First Case.* 1986. Parents Magazine. 1st. 8vo. ils. F. M5. $10.00

**QUADFLIEG, Roswitha.** *Traumalphabet. Ein Schrift-Bilder-Buch das Dreizehn...* 1986. Hamburg. Raamin-Presse. 1/195. sgn. 4to. frenchfold. Zwang bdg. F/case. B24. $3,500.00

**QUAIFE, Milo.** *Absolom Grimes: Confederate Mail Runner.* 1926. Yale. 1st. xl. VG. E6. $30.00

**QUAIFE, Milo.** *Chicago's Highways Old & New.* 1923. Chicago. DF Keller. 1st. ils/fld map. 278p. G. B18. $25.00

**QUAIFE, Milo.** *Development of Chicago, 1674-1914.* 1916. Caxton Club. 1/175. ils. 290p. NF. A4. $450.00

**QUAIFE, Milo.** *Far Hunters in the Far West.* 1924. Lakeside Classic. VG. J2. $165.00

**QUAIFE, Milo.** *Pictures of Gold Rush California.* 1949. Lakeside Classic. 1st thus. teg. dk red cloth. VG/sans. T11. $35.00

**QUAIFE, Milo.** *Wau-Bun, the Early Days in the North West.* 1932. Lakeside Classic. 609p. VG. J2. $65.00

**QUAMMEN, David.** *Song of the Dodo: Island Biogreography in Age Extinctions.* 1996. Scribner. 702p. xl. VG. S5. $20.00

**QUAMMEN, David.** *Soul of Victor Tronko.* 1987. NY. Doubleday. 1st. sgn. F/NF. B3. $40.00

**QUAMMEN, David.** *To Walk the Line.* 1970. NY. Knopf. 1st. 1/225. sgn. author's 1st book. F/F. B3. $100.00

**QUANDT, William B.** *Saudi Arabia in the 1980s. Foreign Policy, Security & Oil.* 1981. WA, DC. Brookings Inst. 1st. dbl-p map. 190p. VG/wrp. W1. $6.00

**QUARLES, E.A.** *American Pheasant Breeding & Shooting.* 1916. Willmington, DE. Hercules Powder. 1st. ils. 132+8P. G/wrp. H7. $17.50

**QUARLES, Garland R.** *Some Worthy Lives: Mini-Biographies...* 1988. Winchester-Frederick Co Hist Soc. 280p. AN. B10. $25.00

**QUARRINGTON, Paul.** *Home Game.* 1983. Canada. Doubleday. 1st. VG/dj. P8. $30.00

**QUASHA, George.** *Somapoetics.* 1973. Fremont. Sumac. 1st. 1/1000. inscr. NF. L3. $35.00

**QUAYLE, Dan.** *Standing Firm.* 1994. Harper Collins. 8vo. 402p. F. W2. $40.00

**QUAYLE, Eric.** *Collector's Book of Books.* 1971. NY. Clarkson Potter. 1st Am. 144p. cloth. F/dj. O10. $40.00

**QUAYLE, Eric.** *Collector's Book of Detective Fiction.* 1972. London. Studio Vista. 1st. inscr. F/dj. M15. $150.00

**QUAYLE, Eric.** *Little People's Pageant of Cornish Legends.* 1986. S&S. 1st Am. ils Michael Foreman. 108p. F/dj. D4. $35.00

**QUAYLE, Eric.** *Magic Ointment & Other Cornish Legends.* 1986. London. Andersen. 1st. 108p. F/sans. D4. $30.00

**QUAYLE, Eric.** *Shining Princess.* 1989. Arcade. 1st. 8vo. ils Michael Forman. VG/dj. B17. $15.00

**QUEEN, Ellery.** *Double, Double.* 1950. Little Brn. 1st. F/NF. M15. $100.00

**QUEEN, Ellery.** *Ellery Queen's Aces of Mystery.* 1975. NY. Dial. 1st 8vo. cloth. F/dj. O10. $17.50

**QUEEN, Ellery.** *Ellery Queen's Champions of Mystery.* 1977. Dial. 1st. F/dj. N4. $25.00

**QUEEN, Ellery.** *French Powder Mystery.* 1941. Triangle. rpt. VG. N4. $15.00

**QUEEN, Ellery.** *Misadventures of Sherlock Holmes.* 1944. Little Brn. 1st/Dinner Club ed. 1/125. 8vo. 363p. blk cloth. VG/dj. J3. $1,800.00

**QUEEN, Ellery.** *Queen's Bureau of Investigation.* 1954. Little Brn. 1st. VG/dj. M20. $65.00

**QUEEN ELIZABETH II.** *Coronation of Her Majesty Queen Elizabeth II.* 1953. Worcester. St Onge. mini. 1/2000. aeg. Sangorski/Sutcliffe bdg. B24. $175.00

**QUEENY, E.M.** *Cheechako: Story of an Alaskan Bear Hunt.* 1941. NY. 1/1250. intro Nash Buckingham. F. M4. $135.00

**QUEENY, E.M.** *Prairie Wings: Pen & Camera Flight Studies...* 1946. NY. Ducks Unlimited. 1st. 4to. 256p. G. H10. $125.00

**QUENNELL, Peter.** *Mayhew's Characters.* nd. London. Spring Books. M20. $17.00

**QUENNELL, Peter.** *Prodical Rake: Memoirs of William Hickey.* 1962. Dutton. 1st/3rd prt. 8vo. 452p. VG. W2. $12.00

**QUENNELL, Peter.** *Samuel Johnson: His Friends & Enemies.* 1973. McGraw Hill. 1st Am. 8vo. 272p. gilt brn cloth. F/dj. H13. $45.00

**QUENTIN, Patrick.** *Man in the Net.* 1956. S&S. 1st. F/clip. M15. $45.00

**QUENTIN, Patrick.** *Puzzle for Fiends.* 1946. NY. S&S. 1st. F/NF. M15. $45.00

**QUENTIN, Patrick.** *Puzzle for Players.* 1938. S&S. 1st. F/VG clip. M15. $135.00

**QUENZEL, Carrol H.** *Belmont.* 1960. Mary WA College. VG. B10. $5.00

**QUERLE, Anthony James.** *Allah il Allah!* ca 1930s. Sampson Low. 1st? 255p. Vg/wrp. M7. $25.00

**QUERRY, Ronald B.** *Growing Old at Willie Nelson's Picnic.* 1983. TX A&M. 1st. sgn. F/F. B3. $75.00

**QUICK, Dorothy.** *Fifth Dagger.* 1947. Scribner. 1st. VG/G. G8. $40.00

**QUICK, Herbert.** *Brown Mouse.* 1915. Bobbs Merrill. 1st. ils JA Coughlin. 310p. G. G11. $12.00

**QUICK, Herbert.** *Virginia of the Air Lanes.* 1909. Bobbs Merrill. 1st. ils Wm R Leigh. 424p. G. G11. $10.00

**QUICK, Jim.** *Fishing the Nymph.* 1960. Ronald. G. A19. $25.00

**QUIGG, Jane.** *Miss Brimble's Happy Birthday.* 1955. Oxford. 1st. 95p. VG/G. C14. $10.00

**QUIGLEY, Martin.** *Magic Shadows: Story of the Origin of Motion Pictures.* 1948. WA, DC. Georgetown U. 1st. ils. VG/dj. C9. $90.00

**QUIGLEY, Martin.** *Original Colored House of David.* 1981. Houghton Mifflin. 1st. F/VG. P8. $30.00

**QUIGLEY, Martin.** *Today's Game.* 1956. Viking. 1st. F/VG. P8. $27.50

**QUILLER-COUCH, Arthur.** *New Oxford Book of English Verse.* 1961. OUP. new ed. sm 8vo. 1166p. F/VG. W2. $360.00

**QUILLER-COUCH, Arthur.** *Sleeping Beauty & Other Fairy Tales.* 1910. Hodder Stoughton. 1st. ils Edmund Dulac. aeg. 129p. rb morocco/raised bands. F. D1. $750.00

**QUINBY & STEVENSON.** *Catalogue of Botanical Books in Collection RMM Hunt.* nd. 3 vol in 2. 1/400. ils. F. A4. $150.00

**QUINCY, Josiah.** *Essays on the Soiling of Cattle.* 1866. Boston. Williams. 121p. cloth. A10. $35.00

**QUINCY, Josiah.** *Memoir of the Life of John Quincy Adams.* 1858. Boston. Philips Sampson. 429p. VG. B14. $99.00

**QUINCY, Josiah.** *Speeches Delivered in Congress of the United States...* 1874. Little Brn. 8vo. pres from edit. 412p. gilt gr cloth. VG. O1. $75.00

**QUINE, C.R.** *Old Portage & the Portage Path.* 1953. np. 35p. VG/wrp. B18. $25.00

**QUINE, Judith Balaban.** *Bridesmaids: Grace Kelly, Princess of Monaco...* 1989. NY. Weidenfeld Nicholson. 1st. F/dj. T12. $25.00

**QUINLAN, Maurice.** *Samuel Johnson: A Layman's Religion.* 1967. Madison, WI. 1st. dj. H13. $65.00

**QUINN, Dan;** see Lewis, Alfred Henry.

**QUINN, David Beers.** *Roanoke Voyages 1584-1590.* 1955. London. Hakluyt Soc. 2 vol. 8vo. 12 maps/pl. cloth. F. O1. $135.00

**QUINN, Elizabeth.** *Stars sur la Passerelle (Stars on the Boarding Stairs).* 1989. Zoom/Zao. 1st. French/Eng text. VG/dj. C9. $90.00

**QUINN, Gerald V.** *Getting the Most Out of Your Video Gear.* 1986. TAB Books. 1st. VG. S5. $10.00

**QUINN, H.L.** *Arthur Campbell: Pioneer & Patriot of the Old Southwest.* 1990. Jefferson. map. 199p. F. M4. $20.00

**QUINN, Vincent.** *Hart Crane.* 1963. Twayne. VG/rpr. M20. $15.00

**QUINN & STEBBINS.** *Weston's Westons: California & the West.* 1994. Boston. Mus Fine Arts/Bullfinch. 1st. rem mk. F/dj. P4. $50.00

**QUINTERO, Jose.** *If You Don't Dance, They Beat You.* 1974. Little Brn. 1st. F/VG. T12. $50.00

**QUIRK, Lawrence J.** *Fasten Your Seatbelts: Passionate Life of Bette Davis.* 1990. Morrow. 1st. F/dj. T12. $30.00

**QUIRK, Lawrence J.** *Films of Warren Beatty.* 1979. NJ. Citadel. 1st. VG/wrp. C9. $25.00

**QUOGAN, Anthony.** *Fine Art of Murder.* 1988. St Martin. 1st. F/dj. T12. $25.00

RABAN, Jonathan. *Arabia: Journey Through the Labyrinth.* 1979. S&S. 1st. 8vo. 344p. NF/dj. W1. $18.00

RABAN, Jonathan. *Coasting.* 1986. London. Collins Harvill. 1st. NF/dj. A14. $28.00

RABAN, Jonathan. *Coasting.* 1987. London. 1st thus. VG/dj. T9. $15.00

RABB, Kate Milner. *Tour Through Indiana in 1840: Diary of John Parsons...* 1920. NY. McBride. 1st. 391p. VG. H7. $20.00

RABBITT, Mary C. *Colorado River Region & John Wesley Powell.* 1969. GPO. 1st. ils. NF. B19. $50.00

RABELAIS, Francis. *Works...* 1849. London. 2 vol. trans Thomas Urquhart/Motteux. 3-quarter leather. VG. M17. $45.00

RABIN, Chaim. *Ancient West-Arabian.* 1951. London. 19 maps. 226p. gr cloth. G+. Q2. $58.00

RABKIN, Eric S. *Fantastic Worlds.* 1979. Oxford. 1st. VG/dj. P3. $20.00

RACE, Jeffrey. *War Comes to Lon An, Revolutionary Conflict Vietnamese...* 1972. Berkeley. 1st. ils. 299p. G/dj. B18. $35.00

RACHLEFF, Owen S. *Rembrandt's Life of Christ.* nd. Abradale. VG. B9. $65.00

RACKHAM, Arthur. *Cinderella. Retold by CS Evans & Ils by Arthur Rackham.* 1919. London. Heinemann. 1st. 1/300 (850). inscr/dtd 1919. teg. Zaehnsdorf bdg. B24. $1,500.00

RACKHAM, Arthur. *Little Brother & Little Sister & Other Tales...* 1917. London. Constable. 1st. 1/525. sgn. w/extra sgn pl. teg. F/envelope. B24. $2,850.00

RACKHAM, Arthur. *Peter Pan Portfolio.* 1912. London. Hodder Stoughton. 1/500. sgns. 12 mtd pl. half vellum/gr cloth. F. B24. $8,500.00

RACKHAM, Arthur. *Siegfried & the Twilight of the Gods.* 1911. London. Heinemann. 1st. 4to. top edge tinted. gilt brn cloth. R5. $350.00

RACKHAM, Arthur. *Vicar of Wakefield.* 1929. London. Harrap. 1st. 12 mc pl. VG/dj. B5. $150.00

RACKHAM, Bernard. *Guide to Collections of Stained Glass...Victoria/Albert Mus.* 1936. London. 62 pl. bl cloth. VG. B14. $95.00

RACY, John. *Psychiatry in the Arab East.* 1970. Copenhagen. 1st. inscr. 171p. A13. $45.00

RADBILL, Samuel X. *Bibliography of Medical Ex-Libris Literature.* 1951. Los Angeles. Hilprand. 440p. NF. G7. $85.00

RADCLIFFE, Walter. *Secret Instrument: Birth of Midwifery Forceps.* 1947. London. 1st. 83p. A13. $100.00

RADER, Dotson. *Tennessee: Cry of the Heart.* 1985. Doubleday. 1st. VG/dj. M20. $15.00

RADER, Jesse L. *South of Forty From the Mississippi to the Rio Grande...* 1947. Norman, OK. 1st. 1/1000. 336p. cloth. NF. M8. $125.00

RADESTOCK, Paul. *Schlaf und Traum: Eine Physiologisch-Psychologische...* 1879. Leipzig. Breitkopf Hartel. 330p. contemporary bdg. G1. $185.00

RADFORD, William A. *Steel Square & Its Uses.* 1907. Chicago. Am Pub. 2 vol. ils/plans. VG. H7. $35.00

RADIN, Max. *Day of Reckoning.* 1943. Knopf. VG/dj. M11. $75.00

RADIN, Paul. *Story of the American Indian.* 1937. Garden City. 383p. F3. $15.00

RADISSON, Pierre Esprit. *Explorations of Pierre Esprit Radisson.* 1961. Ross Haines. 1st. NF/dj. M20. $42.00

RADL, Emanuel. *History of Biological Theories.* 1930. Oxford. 408p. xl. VG. S5. $45.00

RADOFF, Morris L. *Buildings of the State of Maryland at Annapolis.* 1954. Hall of Records Comm. ils/plans. 173p. VG. B10. $45.00

RAE, Hugh C. *Harkfast: Making of a King.* 1976. St Martin. 1st. NF/dj. M21. $35.00

RAE, Simon. *Faber Book of Murder.* 1994. London. Faber. 1st. F/dj. G10. $17.50

RAE, W. Fraser. *Newfoundland to Manitoba Through Canada's Maritime...* 1881. NY. Putnam. 1st Am. ils/3 fld maps. VG. H7. $100.00

RAEPER, William. *George MacDonald.* (1987). Lion. 1st Eng. photos/notes. AN/dj. A27. $27.00

RAFFELOCK, David. *Echo Anthology of Verse.* (1927). Denver. Echo. 1st. 1/350. fancy brd. VG. A18. $20.00

RAFIZADEH, Mansur. *Witness: From the Shah to the Secret Arms Deal...* 1987. NY. Morrow. 1st. ils. 396p. NF/dj. W1. $18.00

RAGAN, W.H. *Transactions of the Indiana Horticultural Society for 1891.* 1892. Indianapolis. Burford. 239p. cloth. VG. A10. $25.00

RAHEB, Barbara. *Chansons de Noel.* 1984. np. mini. ltd. 12 carols/intl Raheb. label/red leather/filigee clasp. B24. $275.00

RAHEB, Barbara. *Russian Fairy Tales.* 1982. Pennyweight. mini. 2 vol. 1/100. sgn. pict label/full blk morocco. B24. $450.00

RAINES, C.W. *Bibliography of Texas: Being Descriptive List of Books...* 1955. Houston. rpt. 268p. cloth. NF/case. M8. $125.00

RAISOR, Gary. *Obsessions.* 1991. Dark Harvest. 1/500. sgn by 32 contributors. AN/box. T12. $115.00

RAISOR, Gary. *Obsessions.* 1991. Dark Harvest. 1st. F/dj. S18. $35.00

RAITHBY, John. *Study & Practice of Law, Considered in Various Relations...* 1806. Portland. Thos Wait. 1st/only Am. contemporary sheep. M11. $450.00

RAJNEESH, Bhagwan Shree. *Let Go! Darshan Diary.* 1980. Poona, India. Rajneesh Found. 1st. VG/dj. N2. $10.00

RAKOSI, Carl. *Collected Prose of Carl Rakosi.* 1983. Orono. Nat Poetry Found. 1st. inscr. F/wrp. L3. $75.00

RAKOVAC, Milan. *Croatia.* 1987. photos. VG/dj. M17. $20.00

RALEIGH, Walter. *Discoveries of Guiana/Discoveries of the World.* 1966. Cleveland. World. facs. 250p. full vellum/ties/clamshell box/pamphlet. F3. $95.00

RALEIGH, Walter. *Johnson on Shakespeare: Essays & Notes...* 1908. OUP. sm 8vo. gilt blk cloth. H13. $25.00

RALEIGH, Walter. *Samuel Johnson, the Leslie Stephen Lecture at Cambridge...* 1907. Clarendon. 1st. 27p. gray wrp. H13. $65.00

RALLI, Paul. *Nevada Lawyer: Story of Life & Love in Las Vegas.* 1949. Murry Gee. 2nd. inscr. 320p. VG/G. B19. $35.00

RALPHSON, G. Harvey. *Boy Scouts Beyond the Arctic Circle...* c 1913. Chicago. Donahue. 255p. VG. P4. $45.00

RAMBOVA, N. *Mythological Papyri.* 1957. Pantheon. Bolligen series. 2 vol. cloth. F/cloth case. D2. $300.00

RAMPLING, Anne; see Rice, Anne.

RAMSAY, Jay; see Campbell, Ramsey.

RAMSAYE, Terry. *Million & One Nights: History of Motion Picture.* 1926. NY. S&S. 2 vol. 1st. 8vo. photos. teg. NF. H5. $450.00

RAMSEY, Frederic. *Guide to Longplay Jazz Records.* 1954. NY. Long Player Prod. 1st. NF/VG. B2. $40.00

RAMSEY, Frederic. *Where the Music Started.* 1970. New Brunswick. Rutgers Inst Jazz Studies. F/wrp. B2. $45.00

RAMSEY, G.C. *Agatha Christie: Mistress of Mystery.* nd. Dodd Mead. 2nd. VG/clip. P3. $18.00

RAMSEY & RAMSEY. *This Was Mission Country: Orange County, California.* 1973. Laguna Beach, CA. self pub. 1st. sgns. NF/dj. O4. $25.00

**RAMSLAND, Katherine.** *Prism of the Night.* 1991. Dutton. 1st. F/dj. P3. $23.00

**RAND, A.L.** *Handbook of New Guinea Birds.* 1968. NY. Am Mus Nat Hist. ils/figures. 628p. cloth. NF/dj. C12. $260.00

**RAND, Addison.** *Southpaw Fly Hawk.* 1952. Jr Literary Guild. BC. VG/G. P8. $15.00

**RAND, Ayn.** *Anthem.* 1953. Caxton. 1st hc. F/VG. M19. $250.00

**RAND, Paul.** *Paul Rand: A Designer's Art.* 1985. Yale. 1st. ils. F/NF. C9. $150.00

**RANDALL, Bob.** *Calling.* 1981. S&S. 1st. VG/dj. S18. $5.00

**RANDALL, David A.** *Duckdome Large Enough.* 1960. Random. 1st. 8vo. 368p. cloth. F/dj. O10. $45.00

**RANDALL, E.O.** *History of the Zoar Society.* 1904. Columbus. 3rd. ils/fld map. 105p. B18. $35.00

**RANDALL, E.O.** *Ohio Centennial Anniversary Celebration at Chillicothe...* 1903. Columbus. ils. 730p. G. B18. $22.50

**RANDALL, E.O.** *Serpent Mound Adams County, Ohio.* 1993. Adams County, OH. rpt of 1907. 56p. wrp. B18. $8.50

**RANDALL, Ruth Painter.** *Lincoln's Sons.* 1956. Boston. 2nd. ils. VG/dj. M17. $20.00

**RANDISI, Robert J.** *Eyes Have It: First Private Eye Writers of Am Anthology.* (1984). Mysterious. 1/250. sgn all contributors. 8vo. gilt blk cloth. F/box. R3. $75.00

**RANDISI, Robert J.** *Eyes Still Have It.* 1995. Dutton. 1st. NF/dj. G8. $20.00

**RANDISI, Robert J.** *Full Contact.* 1984. St Martin. 1st. sgn. F/NF. A24. $30.00

**RANDISI, Robert J.** *Separate Cases.* 1990. Walker. 1st. NF/dj. N4. $15.00

**RANDOLPH, Clare.** *Nautical Ned.* 1948. Hollow Tree. 1st. ils Leslie Crandall. VG/G. P2. $10.00

**RANDOLPH, Edmund.** *Hell Among the Yearlings.* 1978. Lakeside Classic. 1st thus. teg. brn cloth. F. T11. $22.00

**RANDOLPH, Helen.** *Mystery of Carlitos (#1).* 1936. AL Burt. lists 3 titles. VG/dj. M20. $40.00

**RANDOLPH, L.F.** *Garden Irises.* 1959. St Louis. photos/drawings. 575p. VG/dj. B26. $37.50

**RANDOLPH, Mary.** *Virginia Housewife; or, Methodical Cook-Method...* c 1828. Baltimore. 176p. worn leather/rb cloth. fair. E6. $150.00

**RANKIN, Ian.** *Good Hanging & Other Stories.* 1992. London. Century. 1st. F/dj. M15. $75.00

**RANKIN, Ian.** *Herbert in Motion.* 1997. London. Revolver. 1st. 1/200. sgn. F. M15. $100.00

**RANKIN, Ian.** *Watchman.* 1988. London. Bodley Head. UP/1st. F/wrp. M15. $85.00

**RANKIN, Ian.** *Wolfman.* 1992. London. Century. 1st. F/dj. M15. $85.00

**RANKIN, James.** *Sixteen Years' Experience in Artificial Poultry Raising.* 1889. Springfield, MA. Homestead. 65p. wrp. A10. $25.00

**RANKIN, John.** *Letters on American Slavery...* 1833. Boston. Garrison Knapp. 1st. 12mo. 118p. cloth/paper label. O1. $125.00

**RANKIN, Robert H.** *Small Arms of the Sea Services: A History of Firearms...* 1972. New Milford. Flayderman. 1st. ils/index. 227p. VG/dj. S16. $50.00

**RANSOM, Elmer.** *Last Trumpeters & Other Stories.* 1941. Athens, GA. 1st. 8vo. 228p. VG/dj. B11. $25.00

**RANSOM, Harry.** *Conscience of the University & Other Essays.* 1982. Austin. U TX. 1st. 1/300. edit/sgn/drawing Ransom. quarter morocco. box. M24. $45.00

**RANSOM, Henry.** *Memoirs of a Moviegoer.* 1975. SF. Editorial Service Bureau. 144p. VG/dj. C5. $12.50

**RANSOM, Howard.** *Man Against Pain: Epic of Anesthesia.* 1945. NY. 1st. 337p. A13. $40.00

**RANSOM, John Crowe.** *Chills & Fever: Poems.* 1924. Knopf. 1st. G/dj. Q1. $200.00

**RANSOM, Will.** *Private Presses & Their Books.* 1929. NY. RR Bowker. 1st. 1/1200. 193p. F/NF. O10. $225.00

**RANSOME, Arthur.** *Bohemia in London.* 1907. London. Chapman Hall. 1st. ils Fred Taylor. VG. Q1. $150.00

**RANSOME, Arthur.** *Picts & Martyrs; or, Not Welcome at All.* 1943. London. Cape. 1st. 8vo. 302p. gr cloth. sm stp ffe. T5. $20.00

**RANSOME, Arthur.** *Swallows & Amazons.* 1947 (1930). London. Cape. 24th. 8vo. 375p. gr cloth. T5. $25.00

**RAO, N.S.S.** *Biological Nitrogen Fixation. Recent Developments.* 1988. Gordon/Breach. 8vo. ils. 337p. F/dj. B1. $50.00

**RAPAPORT, David.** *Organization & Pathology of Thought.* 1951. Columbia. thick 8vo. 786p. bl cloth. VG/dj. G1. $65.00

**RAPHAEL, Arthur Michael.** *Great Jug.* 1936. Reilly Lee. ils Clifford Benton. VG/ragged edged dj. M20. $27.00

**RAPHAEL, Frederic.** *Latin Lover & Other Stories.* 1994. London. Orion. 1st. NF/dj. A14. $21.00

**RAPHAEL, Ray.** *Edges: Human Ecology of the Backcountry.* 1986. U NE. 233p. F/wrp. S15. $4.50

**RAPHAEL TUCK & SONS.** *All But One Told by the Flowers.* ca 1895. London. Raphael Tuck. 4to. cloth backed mc pict brd. pict dj. R5. $450.00

**RAPHAEL TUCK & SONS.** *Dolly in Town.* ca 1895. NY. 14p. doll-shaped covers. 14½x7½". R5. $150.00

**RAPPLEYE, Willard.** *Graduate Medical Education.* 1940. Chicago. 1st. 304p. A13. $40.00

**RASCHOVICH, Mark.** *Bedford Incident.* 1963. Atheneum. 1st. F/dj. T12. $50.00

**RASCOE, Burton.** *Belle Starr, the Bandit Queen: True & Sometimes Gory Facts.* 1941. NY. 1st. ils/index. 340p. VG/dj. S16. $45.00

**RASCOVICH, Mark.** *Bedford Incident.* 1963. Atheneum. 1st. author's 2nd book. F/dj. B4. $125.00

**RASHKE, Richard.** *Escape From Sobibor: Heroic Escape of Jews...* 1982. Boston. ils. VG/dj. M17. $15.00

**RASWAN, Carl R.** *Black Tents of Arabia.* nd. London. Hurst Blackett. 8vo. ils/pl/tables. 256p. cloth. VG. Q2. $36.50

**RATCHFORD, Fannie E.** *Letters of Thomas J Wise to John Henry Wrenn...* 1944. Knopf. 1st. 8vo. 591p. F/dj. O10. $85.00

**RATEL, Simonne.** *Weathercock.* 1939. NY. 1st Am. ils Gertrude Mittlemann. VG/dj. B18. $37.50

**RATHBONE, Basil.** *In & Out of Character.* 1962. Doubleday. ils. 278p. VG/dj. B5. $60.00

**RATHBONE, Hannah Mary.** *Letters of Richard Reynolds With a Memoir...* 1855. Phil. Longstreth. 12mo. 285p. G. V3. $20.00

**RATHBUN & RICHARDSON.** *Crustaceans: Harriman Alaska Series, Volume X.* 1910. Smithsonian. 26 pl. 337p. NF/dj. P4. $150.00

**RATHE, G.** *Wreck of the Bark Stafano Off the Northwest Cape Australia.* 1992. Edinburgh. 1st. ils. F/dj. M4. $15.00

**RATIGAN, William.** *Great Lakes Shipwrecks & Survivals.* 1960. Grand Rapids. Eerdmans. 1st. 298p. VG/dj. B18. $42.50

**RATTAN, Volney.** *Popular California Flora; or, Manual of Botany...* 1883. SF. 5th revised. ils/index. 138p. decor cloth. B26. $20.00

**RATTIGAN, Terence.** *French Without Tears: A Play in Three Acts.* nd. London. 1st. VG/wrp. M17. $20.00

**RAUCH, Frederick Augustus.** *Psychology; or, View of Human Soul...* 1841. NY. MW Dodd/Cowperthwait. 2nd revised. 401p. emb Victorian cloth. VG. G1. $200.00

**RAUCHER, Herman.** *Summer of '42.* 1971. Putnam. 1st. author's 2nd novel. F/dj. B4. $150.00

**RAVEN, Charles E.** *Teilhard de Chardin: Scientist & Seer.* 1962. NY. Harper Row. 1st. VG/dj. M20. $15.00

**RAVEN, Charles P.** *Oogenesis: Storage of Developmental Information.* 1961. Pergamon. 274p. xl. VG. S5. $12.00

**RAVEN, Simon.** *Before the Cock Crow: First-Born of Egypt, Vol III.* 1986. London. Muller Blond & Wht. 1st. NF/dj. A14. $28.00

**RAVEN, Simon.** *English Gentleman: Essay in Attitudes.* 1961. London. 1st. dj. T9. $30.00

**RAVIER, Henri-Victor.** *De L'Influence Du Coer Sur Le Cerveau.* 1821. Paris. Didot Le Jeune. 4to. 60p. new stiff wrp. G7. $125.00

**RAWLINGS, James S.** *Virginia's Colonial Churches: An Architectural Guide...* 1963. Garret Massie. 286p. VG/G+. B10. $50.00

**RAWLINGS, Marjorie Kinnan.** *Cross Creek Cookery.* 1942. Scribner. 1st/1ssue (pict cloth). VG+/VG. B30. $100.00

**RAWLINGS, Marjorie Kinnan.** *Cross Creek.* 1942. Scribner. 1st. 8vo. VG/dj. B17. $35.00

**RAWLINGS, Marjorie Kinnan.** *When the Whippoorwill.* 1940. Scribner. 1st. NF/VG+. B4. $350.00

**RAWLINGS, Marjorie Kinnan.** *Yearling.* 1938. NY. Scribner. 1st. NF. T12. $200.00

**RAWLINGS, Marjorie Kinnan.** *Yearling.* 1938. Scribner. 1st. G. A19. $125.00

**RAWLINGS, Marjorie Kinnan.** *Yearling.* 1939. Scribner. Pulitzer Prize ed. ils NC Wyeth. oatmeal buckram. dj. R5. $200.00

**RAWLINSON, George.** *Herodotus: The Persian Wars.* 1947. Modern Lib. 1st. VG/clip. S13. $12.00

**RAWSON, Clayton.** *Golden Book of Magic: Amazing Tricks for Young Magicians...* nd (c 1964). Golden. possible 1st. 104p. VG. C14. $14.00

**RAWSON, W.W.** *Success in Market Gardening: A New Vegetable Grower's...* 1892. Boston. 7th. ils. VG. M17. $25.00

**RAY, Cyril.** *Lancashire Fusiliers: 20th Regiment of Foot...* 1971. Leo Cooper. 1st. photos/chronology. 135p. VG/dj. S16. $30.00

**RAY, G. Whitfield.** *Through Five Republics on Horseback.* nd (ca 1921). Cleveland. Evangelical. 25th revised. 305p. F3. $15.00

**RAY, G.E.** *Early Oklahoma Newspapers. History & Description...* 1928. OK U. ils. 119p. VG. M4. $60.00

**RAY, Man.** *1929.* 1993. Paris. Editions Allia. 1st facs. French text. F/dj. S9. $150.00

**RAY, Michelle.** *Two Shores of Hell: A French Journalist's Life...* 1968. McKay. trans Elizabeth Abbott. VG/G+. R11. $24.00

**RAY, Ophelia.** *Daughter of the Tejas.* 1965. NYGS. 1st. Larry McMurtry ghostwriter? F/dj. D10. $165.00

**RAYMO, Chet.** *Honey From a Stone: A Naturalist's Search for God.* 1987. NY. 1st. ils Bob O'Cathail. VG/dj. M17. $15.00

**RAYMOND, Derek.** *I Was Dora Suarez.* 1990. London. Scribner. 1st. F/dj. M15. $45.00

**RAYMOND, Rossiter W.** *Mineral Resources of the States & Territories.* 1869. GPO. ils. 256p. B18. $37.50

**RAYNAL, Maurice.** *History of Modern Painting From Baudelaire to Bonnard.* 1949. Geneva. ils. VG. M17. $40.00

**RAYNER, John.** *Wood Engravings by Thomas Beswick.* 1947. London/NY. King Penguin. VG. M20. $20.00

**RAZZI, Girolamo.** *Vite di Qvattro Huomini Illustri.* 1580. Florence. Giunti. 8vo. Medici title device. half vellum. R12. $375.00

**REA, John.** *Layman's Commentary on the Holy Spirit.* 1974. Logos. 281p. VG. B29. $8.00

**READ, Daisy I.** *New London: Today & Yesterday.* 1950. JP Bell. 1st. photos. 129p. G/G. B10. $45.00

**READ, Daniel.** *American Singing Book; or, New & Easy Guide to Art...* 1785. New Haven. Prt & Sold for Author. 1st. obl 8vo. 72p. O1. $850.00

**READ, J. Marion.** *History of the California Academy of Medicine, 1870-1930.* 1930. SF. CA Academy Medicine. 1/957. ils/photos. red cloth/blk calf label. K1. $60.00

**READ, J. Marion.** *History of the California Academy of Medicine, 1930-1960.* 1962. SF. CA Academy of Medicine. 89p. gray cloth. NF. P4. $60.00

**READ, Kenneth E.** *High Valley.* (1965). Scribner. not 1st. sm 4to. 266p. F/VG. H1. $12.00

**READ, Miss;** see Saint, Dora Jessie.

**READ, Opie.** *Harkriders.* 1903. Laird Lee. 1st. ils. VG. M19. $45.00

**READ, Piers Paul.** *On the Third Day.* 1990. NY. 1st. dj. T9. $10.00

**READ, Piers Paul.** *Season in the West.* 1988. NY. 1st. dj. T9. $15.00

**READ, Robert W.** *Genus Thrinax.* 1975. WA, DC. photos. 98p. VG. B26. $20.00

**READ.** *Bibliography of British History, Tudor Period, 1485-1603.* 1959. Oxford. 2nd revised. 6543 entries. bstp. VG. A4. $95.00

**READE, Aleyn Lyell.** *Johnsonian Gleanings.* 1968. NY. Octagon. 11 vol in 10. lg 8vo. red cloth. F. H13. $395.00

**READING, Joseph H.** *Ogowe Band: Narrative of African Travel.* 1890. Phil. Reading. 1st. ils/map. 278p. G. H7. $30.00

**READING, Joseph H.** *Voyage Along the Western Coast of Newest Africa...* 1901. Phil. Reading. 1st. photos. 211+2p. floral ep. VG. H7. $90.00

**REAGAN, John Henninger.** *Speech of Hon John H Reagan, of Texas, In House...1860.* 1860. WA, DC. Thos McGill. 1st. 13p. VG/wrp. M8. $75.00

**REAGAN, Michael.** *On the Outside Looking In.* 1988. Zebra. 1st. sm 4to. 286p. F/dj. W2. $25.00

**REAGAN, Nancy.** *My Turn.* 1989. Random. 1st. sm 4to. 384p. F/dj. W2. $75.00

**REAGAN, Ronald W.** *American Life.* 1990. S&S. 1st. inscr/sgn. 748p. F/dj. W2. $150.00

**REAVES, Michael.** *Street Magic.* 1991. NY. Tor. 1st. F/NF. G10. $15.00

**REBOLD, Emmanuel.** *General History of Free-Masonry in Europe.* 1868. Cincinnati. Am Freemason's Magazine. 432p. H6. $88.00

**REBOUX, Paul.** *Food for the Rich.* 1958. London. ils Margaret Costa. VG. M17. $20.00

**RECHNITZER, F.E.** *Bonny's Boy.* 1947. John Winston. 2nd. ils M Kirmse. VG. A21. $35.00

**RECHY, John.** *City of Night.* 1963. NY. Grove. 1st. sgn. author's 1st book. NF/VG. R14. $85.00

**RECHY, John.** *Rushes.* 1979. Grove Weidenfeld. 1st. F/F. H11. $25.00

**RECORD, Paul.** *Tropical Frontier.* 1969. Knopf. 1st. 325p. dj. F3. $15.00

**RECTOR, Carolyn K.** *How to Grow African Violets.* 1951. SF. ils. 94p. sc. B26. $15.00

**REDD, Louise.** *Playing the Bones.* 1996. Little Brn. 1st. F/dj. M23. $20.00

**REDDICK, Allen.** *Making of Johnson's Dictionary, 1746-1773.* 1993. Cambridge. F. H13. $85.00

**REDDING, David.** *Miracles of Christ.* 1964. Revell. 186p. VG/dj. B29. $10.50

**REDDING, Saunders.** *Lonesome Road: Story of Negro's Part in America.* 1958. Doubleday. Mainstream of Am series. 355p. pict ep. VG/dj. B18. $22.50

**REDESDALE, Lord.** *Tales of Old Japan.* 1919. London. ils. 302p. VG. B14. $35.00

**REDFIELD, James.** *Celestine Prophecy.* 1994. Warner. 1st thus. F/F. B30/H11. $45.00

**REDFIELD, James.** *Celestine Prophecy.* 1994. Warner. 1st. 8vo. 246p. NF. W2. $20.00

**REDFIELD, Robert.** *Folk Culture of Yucatan.* 1959. Chicago. 7th. 416p. F3. $20.00

**REDFORD, Robert.** *Outlaw Trail: Journey Through Time.* 1978. NY. Grosset Dunlap. sc. VG. A19. $25.00

**REDFORD.** *Letters of Samuel Johnson, 1731-1784.* 1992-1994. Princeton. 5 vol. ils. F/F. A4. $175.00

**REDMAN, C.L.** *People of the Tonto Rim: Archaeological Discovery...* 1993. WA. ils/maps. 214p. F/dj. M4. $20.00

**REDMAN, Scott.** *Real Men Don't Cook Quiche.* 1982. Pocket. ils Lorenz. 95p. VG. P12. $5.00

**REDMOND, Christopher.** *Canadian Holmes: First Twenty-Five Years.* 1997. Ashcroft. Calabash. 1st. F/dj. T2. $40.00

**REDMOND, Juanita.** *I Served on Bataan.* 1943. Lippincott. 10th imp. 12mo. 167p. VG/G clip. M7. $20.00

**REDON, Joel.** *If Not on Earth, Then in Heaven.* 1991. St Martin. 1st. F/dj. T12. $15.00

**REDPATH, James.** *Echoes of Harper's Ferry.* 1860. Boston. Thayer Eldridge. 1st. gilt brn cloth. M24. $225.00

**REED, Ann.** *Ladies Who Lunch.* 1972. Scribner. VG/dj. A16. $6.50

**REED, David.** *Up Front in Vietnam.* 1967. Funk Wagnall. 217p. stp mk Property of US Navy on top edge. R11. $25.00

**REED, Frank A.** *Lumberjack Sky Pilot.* 1965. Old Forge, NY. N Country Books. 2nd. sgn. VG/dj. A2. $12.50

**REED, Ishmael.** *Japanese by Spring.* 1993. Atheneum. 1st. sgn. F/dj. D10. $45.00

**REED, Ishmael.** *Last Days of Louisiana Red.* 1974. Random. 1st. F/dj. D10. $50.00

**REED, Ishmael.** *Writin' Is Fightin'.* 1988. Atheneum. 1st. sgn. F/dj. R14. $40.00

**REED, Marjorie.** *Butterfield Overland Stage Across Arizona.* 1981. Old Adobe Gallery. 4th. ils. F/sans. B19. $20.00

**REED, Myrtle.** *Weaver of Dreams.* 1911. Putnam. 1st. 8vo. 374p. decor lavender cloth. NF/dj. J3. $95.00

**REED, Rex.** *Big Screen Little Screen.* 1971 (1968). Macmillan. 433p. VG/dj. C5. $12.50

**REED, Robert.** *Exaltation of Larks.* 1995. NY. Tor. 1st. F/dj. G10. $17.00

**REED, Ronald.** *Nature & Making of Parchment.* 1975. Leeds. Elmete. 1st. 1/450. teg. gilt quarter vellum/label. F. M24. $225.00

**REED, Thomas B.** *Modern Eloquence: Library of After-Dinner Speeches...* 1900. Phil. 10 vol. half red leather/marbled brd. VG. B30. $175.00

**REED, TRUEBLOOD & WONG.** *Before Columbus Foundation Fiction Anthology.* 1992. NY. Norton. 1st. sgn Reed/Wong+3 contributors. F/dj. O11. $70.00

**REED, Walt.** *Harold Von Schmidt Draws the Old West.* 1972. AZ. 1st. 230p. F/dj. E1. $75.00

**REEDER, Red.** *Heroes & Leaders of West Point.* 1970. NY. Nelson. 1st. ils. 192p. cloth. F/dj. D4. $25.00

**REEDER, Red.** *Sheridan: General Who Wasn't Afraid to Take a Chance.* 1962. DSP. 1st. 238p. VG/fair. S17. $6.00

**REEDSTROM, Ernest L.** *Bugles, Banners & War Bonnets From Ft Riley...* Bonanza. rpt. ils/photos. 362p. E1. $35.00

**REEDSTROM, Ernest L.** *Scrapbook of the American West.* 1991. Caxton. ils/index. 259p. NF/wrp. B19. $10.00

**REEMAN, Douglas.** *Badge of Glory.* 1984. NY. Morrow. 1st Am. NF/VG clip. T11. $30.00

**REEMAN, Douglas.** *Deep Silence.* 1968. NY. Putnam. 1st Am. NF/clip. T11. $35.00

**REEMAN, Douglas.** *Go in & Sink!* 1973. London. Hutchinson. 1st. sgn on title. VG/clip. A14. $52.50

**REEMAN, Douglas.** *Greatest Enemy.* 1971. NY. Putnam. 1st Am. NF/VG. T11. $60.00

**REEMAN, Douglas.** *His Majesty's U-Boat.* 1973. NY. Putnam. 1st. sgn on title. VG/dj. A14. $35.00

**REEMAN, Douglas.** *Pride & the Anguish.* 1968. London. Hutchinson. 1st. F/NF. T11. $65.00

**REEMAN, Douglas.** *Rendezvous: South Atlantic.* 1972. London. Hutchinson. 1st. sgn. VG/dj. A14. $63.00

**REEMAN, Douglas.** *Surface With Daring.* 1977. NY. Putnam. 1st Am. NF/dj. T11. $45.00

**REEMAN, Douglas.** *To Risks Unknown.* 1970. NY. Putnam. 1st Am. sgn. VG/dj. A14. $35.00

**REEMAN, Douglas.** *Torpedo Run.* 1981. London. Hutchinson. 1st Eng. F/dj. T11. $50.00

**REES, John Rawlings.** *Shaping of Psychiatry by War.* 1945. Norton. 1st. 8vo. 158p. VG/dj. C14. $15.00

**REES, Ronald.** *New & Naked Land: Making the Prairies Home.* 1988. Saskatoon. Western Producer Prairie Books. 1st. AN/dj. A26. $20.00

**REES-MOGG.** *How to Buy Rare Books: A Practical Guide...* 1988. Oxford. 4to. ils. 160p. F/F. A4. $65.00

**REESE, H.H.** *Breeding Morgan Horses.* 1926. WA. phtos. 19p. VG. O3. $45.00

**REESE, W.S.** *Melvin J Nichols Collection of Custeriana...* 1975. Frontier Am Corp. 1/100. ils/map ep. AN/case. J2. $475.00

**REEVES, James.** *Blackbird in the Lilac.* 1959. EP Dutton. 1st Am. 8vo. blk-lettered lilac cloth. R5. $100.00

**REEVES, Robert.** *Doubting Thomas.* 1985. NY. Arbor. 1st. author's 1st novel. F/NF. H11. $25.00

**REEVES & ROBINSON.** *Classic Lines: Gallery of Great Thoroughbreds.* 1975. Birmingham. Oxmoor. 1/25000. sgn Robinson. obl folio. VG/dj. O1. $395.00

**REGAN, Phil.** *Phil Regan.* 1968. Zondervan. 1st. photos. VG/dj. P8. $50.00

**REGIS, Ed.** *Who Got Einstein's Office.* 1987. Reading, MA. Addison-Wesley. 8vo. 316p. F/dj. K5. $20.00

**REGLI, Adolph.** *Mayos: Pioneers in Medicine.* 1942. NY. 248p. A13. $35.00

**REHDER, Alfred.** *Manual of Cultivated Trees & Shrubs in North America.* 1940. Macmillan. 2nd. 996p. G. H10. $37.50

**REICH, Warren.** *Encyclopedia of Bioethics.* 1978. NY. 1st. A13. $250.00

**REICHARD, F.H.** *American Volunteer: History of Fourth Regiment, PA...1898...* 1989. Allentown, PA. 1st. ils. 192p. cloth. VG. M8. $85.00

**REICHEL-DOLMATOFF, Gerado.** *Colombia.* 1965. NY. Praeger. 1st. 231p. xl. dj. F3. $10.00

**REICHEL-DOLMATOFF, Gerado.** *People of Aritama.* 1961. London. Routledge. 1st. ils/index. 483p. dj. F3. $20.00

**REICHLER, Joseph.** *30 Years of Baseball's Great Moments.* 1974. Crown. 1st. photos. F/VG. P8. $15.00

**REID, Alastair.** *To Be Alive.* 1966. Macmillan. 1st. VG/dj. C9. $60.00

**REID, Ed.** *Mafia.* 1957. NY. Random. 1st. VG/dj. B5. $15.00

**REID, Jamie.** *Easy Money.* 1985. NY. Walker. 1st. xl. VG/dj. O3. $15.00

**REID, John Philip.** *Concept of Representation in the Age of American Revolution.* 1989. Chicago. 251p. VG+/dj. M10. $27.50

**REID, Robin Anne.** *Arthur C Clarke: A Critical Companion.* 1997. Greenwood. decor brd. F. P3. $30.00

**REID, Samuel C.** *Scouting Expeditions of McCulloch's Texas Rangers...* 1890. Phil. Keystone. 8vo. 251p. decor cloth. F. O1. $85.00

**REID, T.W.** *Book of the Cheese, Being Traits & Stories of Olde Cheshire.* 1901. London. Fisher Unwin. sm 8vo. 196p+12p ads. gilt brn cloth. H13. $65.00

**REIGER, Barbara.** *Zane Grey Cookbook.* 1976. Prentice Hall. xl. G/dj. A16. $15.00

**REILLY, R.** *British at the Gates: New Orleans Campaign...* 1976. London. 1st. 379p. F/dj. M4. $30.00

**REILLY, S.** *Britain's Master Spy: Adventures of Sidney Reilly.* 1933 (1932). VG/G. E6. $30.00

**REINHART, Theodore R.** *Archeology of Shirley Plantation.* (1984). U VA. ils/charts/maps. 226p. VG. B10. $65.00

**REINHOLD, Karl Leonhard.** *Versuch Einer Neuen Theorie des Menschlichen Vorstellungs...* 1789. Prag und Jena. C Widtmann/IM Mauke. contemporary bdg. G1. $750.00

**REINIKKA, Merle A.** *History of the Orchid.* 1995 (1972). Portland. ils. 344p. AN/dj. B26. $30.00

**REISCHAUER, Edwin O.** *My Life Between Japan & America.* 1986. Harper Row. 1st. F/dj. B9. $12.50

**REISER, Stanley.** *Medicine & the Region of Technology.* 1978. Cambridge. 1st. 317p. A13. $50.00

**REISNER, Robert George.** *Jazz Titans, Including Parlance of Hip.* 1960. Doubleday. 1st. NF/wrp. B2. $40.00

**REIT, Sy.** *Canvas Confidential.* 1963. Dial. 1st. ils Kelly Freas. G+. P3. $30.00

**REJALI, Darius M.** *Torture & Modernity: Self, Society & State in Modern Iran.* 1994. Boulder, CO. Westview. 1st. 8vo. 289p. VG. W1. $22.00

**REMARQUE, Erich Maria.** *All Quiet on the Western Front.* 1929. Little Brn. VG+. S13. $15.00

**REMBAR, Charles.** *End of Obscenity: Trials of Lady Chatterley...* 1968. Random. M11. $25.00

**REMICK, Grace M.** *Jane Stuart's Chum (#2).* 1914. Phil. Penn. 1st. ils AC Williamson. gr cloth/oval label. VG. M20. $17.00

**REMINGTON, Frederic.** *Crooked Trails.* 1898. NY/London. Harper. 1st. 8vo. 49 pl. 151p. VG. O1. $200.00

**REMINGTON, Frederic.** *Cuba in War Time.* 1897. NY. Russell. 1st. 23 pl/ftspc. tan brd. NF/dj. J3. $1,200.00

**REMINGTON, Frederic.** *Done in the Open: Drawings by...* 1902. Colliers. 1st/2nd state. unp. G. H7. $95.00

**REMINGTON, Frederic.** *Frederic Remington Memorial Collection.* 1954. Knoedler Gallery. 1st. ils. F/sans. T11. $60.00

**REMINGTON, Frederic.** *Frederic Remington's Own West.* 1960. NY. ils. F/NF. E1. $50.00

**REMINGTON, Frederic.** *Frederic Remington's Own West.* 1960. NY. Dial. 1st collected. 1/167. sgn. 8vo. 254p. NF/case. H5. $500.00

**REMINGTON, Frederic.** *How the Law Got to the Chaparral...* 1987. Austin, TX. Jenkins. 1st thus. edit JH Jenkins. VG/wrp. M8. $38.00

**REMINGTON, Frederic.** *Remington's Frontier Sketches.* 1898. Akron. 15 pl/letter press tissue guards. unp (18). pict cloth. B18. $550.00

**REMINGTON, Frederic.** *Remington's Frontier Sketches.* 1898. Chicago. Werner. 1st. obl 4to. 15 pl. prt buff brd/rpr spine. O1. $400.00

**REMINGTON & SCHORK.** *Statistics With Applications to Biological & Health...* 1970. Prentice Hall. 418p. xl. VG. S5. $12.00

**RENARD, Jules.** *Impressions.* 1928. Sunset. 1st. inscr. F/NF. M19. $45.00

**RENAULT, Mary.** *Fire From Heaven.* 1969. Pantheon. 1st. F/VG. M19. $17.50

**RENDELL, Ruth.** *Best Man to Die.* 1970. Doubleday. 1st. NF/NF. H11. $60.00

**RENDELL, Ruth.** *Bridesmaid.* 1989. London. Hutchinson. 1st. F/dj. M15. $50.00

**RENDELL, Ruth.** *Bridesmaid.* 1989. London. Hutchinson. 1st. sgn. F/NF. B3. $70.00

**RENDELL, Ruth.** *Dark-Adapted Eye.* 1986. London. Viking. 1st. NF/NF. B3. $75.00

**RENDELL, Ruth.** *Fatal Inversion.* 1987. Bantam. 1st. F/VG. B30. $22.50

**RENDELL, Ruth.** *Fever Tree.* 1983. Pantheon. 1st Am. F/NF. N4. $40.00

**RENDELL, Ruth.** *Gallowglass.* 1990. London. Viking. 1st. sgn. F/F. B3. $60.00

**RENDELL, Ruth.** *Heartstones.* 1987. London. Hutchinson. 1st. sgn. F/F. B3. $50.00

**RENDELL, Ruth.** *Lake of Darkness.* 1980. Doubleday. 1st. NF/VG. S18. $20.00

**RENDELL, Ruth.** *Speaker of Mandarin.* 1983. NY. Pantheon. 1st. sgn. F/F. B3. $50.00

**RENDELL, Ruth.** *Unkindness of Ravens.* 1985. London. Hutchinson. 1st. sgn. NF/F. B3. $60.00

**RENICK, Marion.** *Dooley's Play Ball.* 1949. Scribner. 1st. G. P8. $10.00

**RENNER, Clayton L.** *Ragersville Centennial History...* 1930. 32p. G/wrp. B18. $25.00

**RENNER, Frederic G.** *Charles M Russell: Paintings, Drawings & Sculpture...* 1966. U TX. 1st. ils/pl. blk cloth. F/VG+. T11. $70.00

**RENSCH, Bernhard.** *Biophilosophy.* 1971. Columbia. 377p. xl. VG. S5. $30.00

**RENWICK, W.L.** *English Literature 1789-1815.* 1963. Clarendon. 1st. NF/dj. O4. $20.00

**RENZI, Thomas C.** *HG Wells: Six Scientific Romances Adapted for Film.* 1992. Metuchen. Scarecrow. 238p. VG. C5. $15.00

**REPS, Paul.** *Letters to a Friend: Writings & Drawings 1939-1980.* 1981. Stillgate. 1st. ils/2 fld ils. VG/dj. M17. $60.00

**REPTON, Humphrey.** *Art of Landscape Gardening.* 1907. Boston. 22 pl. 253p. brd. B26. $76.00

**RESTON, James.** *Collision at Home Plate.* 1991. Burlingame. 1st. VG/dj. P8. $25.00

**REUBEN, Shelly.** *Origin & Cause.* 1994. Scribner. 1st. F/NF. A23. $30.00

**REUSS, Frederick.** *Horace Afoot.* 1997. Denver. MacMuray Beck. 1st. sgn. author's 1st novel. F/dj. R14. $40.00

**REUTTER, Winifred.** *Early Dakota Days.* 1962. Stickney, SD. Argus. A19. $40.00

**REVESZ, Geza.** *Die Menschliche Hand: Eine Psychologische.* 1944. Basel. Von S Karger. ils. 122p. prt gray cloth. G1. $25.00

**REVESZ, Geza.** *Psychology of a Musical Prodigy.* 1925. London. Kegan Paul. 1st/Am issue. 180p. gr cloth. VG. G1. $50.00

**REVI, Albert Christian.** *American Art Nouveau.* 1981. Schiffer. 5th. 476p. F/dj. H1. $85.00

**REVI, Albert Christian.** *American Cut & Engraved Glass.* (1965). Thos Nelson. 7th. 4to. 497p. VG/dj. H1. $75.00

**REVI, Albert Christian.** *American Pressed Glass & Figural Bottles.* 1967. Thos Nelson. 2nd. 4to. 446p. AN/dj. H1. $65.00

**REXROTH, Kenneth.** *American Poetry in the Twentieth Century.* (1971). NY. Herder. 1st. F/clip. A18. $30.00

**REXROTH, Kenneth.** *Autobiographical Novel.* 1966. Doubleday. 1st. F/dj. L3. $35.00

**REXROTH, Kenneth.** *Morning Star.* (1979). New Directions. 1st. F/dj. A18. $30.00

**REY, H.A.** *Curious George.* 1941. Houghton Mifflin. 1st. 4to. orange cloth. R5. $250.00

**REY, H.A.** *Where's My Baby.* 1943. Houghton Mifflin. 1st. moveable flaps show baby animals. G+/wrp. D1. $50.00

**REYNOLDS, Abram David.** *Recollections of Major...1847-1925.* 1978. Reynolds House. 1st separate. map. 39p. VG. B10. $25.00

**REYNOLDS, Barbara Leonard.** *Hamlet & Brownswiggle.* 1954. Scribner. ils. tan cloth. VG. B36. $20.00

**REYNOLDS, Barbara.** *Dorothy L Sayers: Her Life & Soul.* (1993). St Martin. 1st Am. photos/notes. AN/dj. A27. $26.00

**REYNOLDS, Chang.** *Pioneer Circuses of the West.* 1966. LA. Westernlore. ils. 212p. cloth. dj. D11. $40.00

**REYNOLDS, Clark.** *Fast Carriers: Forging of an Air Navy.* 1992. Annapolis. ils/photos/index. VG/dj. S16. $25.00

**REYNOLDS, James.** *Ghosts in American Houses.* 1955. NY. FSC. 1st. VG/dj. M20. $30.00

**REYNOLDS, Joshua.** *Discourses...His Letters to Johnson's Idler.* 1907. London. OUP. F. H13. $25.00

**REYNOLDS, Mack.** *Compounded Interests.* 1983. Cambridge. NEFSA. 1st. RS. F/dj. G10. $24.00

**REYNOLDS, Michael.** *Young Hemingway.* 1986. Basil Blackwell. photos. VG/dj. M17. $25.00

**REYNOLDS, Philip.** *Banana: Its History, Cultivation & Place Among Staple Foods.* 1927. Houghton Mifflin. 181p. G+. A10. $25.00

**REYNOLDS, Quentin.** *Fiction Factory: From Pulp Row to Quality Street.* 1955. Random. 1st. VG/dj. P3. $100.00

**REYNOLDS, Stephen.** *Voyage of the New Hazzard to the Northwest Coast, Hawaii...* 1938. Salem. 1st. ils. gilt bl cloth. P4. $135.00

**REYNOLDS, William.** *Theory of the Law of Evidence...* 1883. Chicago. Callaghan. cloth. M11. $125.00

**REZNIK, Charles.** *Testimony Volume II: United States (1885-1915) Recitative.* 1979. Blk Sparrow. 1/100. w/orig typescript correction p. F/mylar. B9. $75.00

**RHEINHARDT, E.A.** *Josephine: Wife of Napoleon.* 1934. Knopf. 3rd. 8vo. VG/G. A2. $16.00

**RHINE, Joseph Banks.** *Extra-Sensory Perception.* 1935. Soc Psychical Research. 1st/1st issue. inscr. 169p. panelled red cloth. G1. $85.00

**RHINE, Joseph Banks.** *New Frontiers of the Mind: Story of Duke Experiments.* 1937. Farrar Rinehart. inscr/dtd 1948. photos. 275p. VG/dj. G1. $65.00

**RHINEHART, Mary Roberts.** *Dangerous Days.* 1919. NY. Doran. 1st. 400p. G. G11. $10.00

**RHODE, John.** *Last Suspect.* 1952. Dodd Mead. ARC/1st. RS. NF/dj. J3. $150.00

**RHODE, John.** *Three Cousins Die.* 1960. Dodd Mead. 1st. F/NF. N4. $35.00

**RHODE, John.** *Venner Crime.* 1933. London. Odhams. 1st. NF/dj. M15. $75.00

**RHODES, Dennis.** *Bookbindings & Other Bibliography.* 1994. Verona. Valdonega. 1st. decor cloth. F. w/pub flyer. M24. $125.00

**RHODES, Eugene Manlove.** *West Is West.* 1917. HK Fly Co. 304p. VG. J2. $195.00

**RHODES, Jewel Parker.** *Voodoo Dreams.* 1993. St Martin. 1st. author's 1st book. VG/dj. L1. $55.00

**RHODES, Robert Hunt.** *All for Union: Civil War Diary & Letters of Elisha H Rhodes.* 1991. NY. Orion/Crown. reissue (1985 Mowbray 1st). F/dj. A14. $21.00

**RHODES, S.A.** *Gerard deNerval, 1808-1855: Poet, Traveler, Dreamer.* 1951. NY Philosophical Lib. 1st Am. 8vo. G/dj. A2. $14.00

**RHODES, Susie.** *Economy Administration Cookbook.* 1912. VG. E6. $35.00

**RHYS, Grace.** *In Wheel About & Cock Along.* 1919. London. Harrap. 1st. NF. T12. $60.00

**RIALA, John L.** *Flowering Crabapples: Genus Malus.* 1995. Portland. photos. 272p. AN/dj. B26. $50.00

**RIBOT, Theodule Armand.** *Die Experimentelle Psychologie de Gengenwart in Deutschland.* 1881. Braunschweig. Druck/Friedrich Vieweg. 1st German-language. 324p. G1. $85.00

**RIBOT, Theodule Armand.** *Diseases of Memory.* 1882. Appleton. 1st Am. 12mo. 209p. decor red cloth. VG. G1. $75.00

**RIBOT, Theodule Armand.** *Essays on Creative Imagination.* 1906 (1900). Chicago. Open Court. 1st Eng-language. 370p+catalog. bl cloth. G1. $75.00

**RIBOT, Theodule Armand.** *Heredity: Psychological Study of Its Phenomena, Laws...* 1875. London. Henry S King. 1st Eng-language. 383p. emb prt gr cloth. VG. G1. $85.00

**RIBOT, Theodule Armand.** *L'Evolution des Idees Generales.* 1897. Paris. Bailliere. 260p. later thatched gray cloth. VG. G1. $75.00

**RIBOT, Theodule Armand.** *La Logique des Sentiments.* 1905. Paris. Felix Alcan. 200p. early marbled brd. G1. $75.00

**RICARD, Robert.** *La Conquete Spirituelle du Mexique.* 1933. Paris Inst d'Ethnologie. 1st in French. 404p. F3. $65.00

**RICCIUTI, Edward R.** *Wildlife of the Mountains.* 1979. Abrams. 232p. VG/box. A17. $17.50

**RICE, Anne.** *Belinda.* 1986. NY. 1st. VG/dj. L1. $75.00

**RICE, Anne.** *Claiming of Sleeping Beauty.* 1983. Dutton. 1st. NF/dj. B30. $75.00

**RICE, Anne.** *Cry to Heaven.* 1982. Knopf. 1st. F/NF. B2. $85.00

**RICE, Anne.** *Cry to Heaven.* 1982. Knopf. 1st. inscr/dtd 1995. NF/dj. R14. $100.00

**RICE, Anne.** *Cry to Heaven.* 1982. Knopf. 1st. VG+/VG. A14. $35.00

**RICE, Anne.** *Exit to Eden.* 1985. Arbor. 1st. VG+/dj. A14. $70.00

**RICE, Anne.** *Exit to Eden.* 1985. Arbor. 1st. VG/dj. P3. $65.00

**RICE, Anne.** *Feast of All Saints.* 1979. S&S. 1st. author's 2nd book. G/dj. L1. $100.00

**RICE, Anne.** *Feast of All Saints.* 1979. S&S. 1st. author's 2nd book. rem mk. F/dj. T10. $175.00

**RICE, Anne.** *Interview With the Vampire.* 1976. Knopf. 1st. author's 1st book. VG+/VG+. A14. $525.00

**RICE, Anne.** *Interview With the Vampire.* 1976. Knopf. 1st. VG/clip gold foil dj. B11. $550.00

**RICE, Anne.** *Lasher.* 1993. Knopf. 1st. NF/F. B30. $35.00

**RICE, Anne.** *Lasher.* 1993. Knopf. 1st. sgn. VG/dj. L1. $85.00

**RICE, Anne.** *Memnoch the Devil.* 1995. Knopf. 1st. F/dj. L4. $22.00

**RICE, Anne.** *Queen of the Damned.* 1988. Knopf. 1st. NF/NF. H11. $35.00

**RICE, Anne.** *Queen of the Damned.* 1988. Knopf. 1st. sgn. F/dj. D10. $75.00

**RICE, Anne.** *Queen of the Damned.* 1988. Knopf. 1st. VG/dj. P3. $25.00

**RICE, Anne.** *Servant of the Bones.* 1996. Knopf. 1st. sgn. VG/dj. L1. $65.00

**RICE, Anne.** *Servant of the Bones.* 1996. Toronto. Knopf. 1st Canadian. F/NF. T12. $40.00

**RICE, Anne.** *Tale of the Body Thief.* 1992. Knopf. 1st. AN/dj. S18. $35.00

**RICE, Anne.** *Tale of the Body Thief.* 1992. Knopf. 1st. sgn. F/dj. D10. $60.00

**RICE, Anne.** *Taltos.* 1994. Knopf. 1st. F/dj. M21. $20.00

**RICE, Anne.** *Vampire Chronicles.* 1990. Knopf. 3 vol. special reissue. sgn. blk cloth. NF/box. A14. $210.00

**RICE, Anne.** *Vampire Lestat.* 1985. NY. Knopf. 1st. rem mk. F/NF. B2. $150.00

**RICE, Anne.** *Violin.* 1997. Knopf. 1st Am. sgn Mayfair House bookplate. F/dj. R14. $35.00

**RICE, Anne.** *Witching Hour.* 1990. Knopf. 1st. F/dj. L4. $35.00

**RICE, Anne.** *Witching Hour.* 1990. Knopf. 1st. sgn. VG/dj. L1. $125.00

**RICE, Craig.** *Fourth Postman.* 1948. S&S. 1st. F/NF. M15. $85.00

**RICE, Damon.** *Seasons Past.* 1976. Praeger. 1st. F/VG. P8. $30.00

**RICE, E.W.** *Orientalisms in Bible Lands.* 1912. Phil. 8vo. ils/pl. 300p. pict cloth. G. Q2. $30.00

**RICE, Josiah M.** *Cannoneer in Navajo Country.* 1970. Denver. Old West Pub. ils. F/dj. A19. $35.00

**RICE, Lawrence D.** *Negro in Texas, 1874-1900.* 1971. LSU. 1st. rem mk. F/NF. B2. $25.00

**RICE, Luanne.** *Stone Heart.* 1991. London. Michael Joseph. 1st. F/F. B3. $15.00

**RICE, Merton S.** *My Father's World.* 1943. Abingdon-Cokesbury. 1st. ils. 103p. G/dj. S14. $9.00

**RICE, Scott.** *Son of 'It Was a Dark & Stormy Night': More...* 1986. Penguin. 1st. NF/ils wrp. A14. $6.00

**RICE, Tamara Talbot.** *Icons.* 1960. London. Batchworth. revised. 192p. VG. M10. $150.00

**RICE & RICE.** *Popular Studies of California Wild Flowers.* 1920. SF. ils/photos. 127p. lacks ffe. B26. $15.00

**RICE & STOUDT.** *Shenandoah Pottery.* 1929. Strasburg, VA. 1st. VG. B5. $90.00

**RICE & TALBOT.** *Icons & Their History.* 1974. NY. Overlook. ils. 191p. cloth. VG/dj. Q2. $63.00

**RICE & VERNAM.** *They Saddled the West.* 1975. Cornell Maritime. ils/photos. 190p. VG. J2. $375.00

**RICH, Andrienne.** *Of Woman Born: Motherhood as Experience & Institution.* 1976. Norton. 2nd. 318p. VG/clip. A25. $15.00

**RICH, Daniel Catton.** *Seurat: Paintings & Drawings.* 1958. Chicago Art Inst. ils. 192p. VG. M10. $4.50

**RICH, Doris.** *Amelia Earhart: A Biography.* 1990. London/WA. Smithsonian. ils/notes. 321p. AN/dj. P4. $22.50

**RICH, L.D.** *Coast of Maine: Informal History.* 1962. NY. revised. 340p. F/dj. M4. $20.00

**RICHARD, Adrienne.** *Accomplice.* 1973. Little Brn. 1st. 174p. F/VG. C14. $14.00

**RICHARD, Caroline Cowles.** *Village Life in America, 1852-1872.* 1913. NY. 1st. 225p. B18. $25.00

**RICHARD, James Robert.** *Snow King: The Lippizan (sic) Horse.* 1957. NY. Lee Shepard. VG/dj. O3. $20.00

**RICHARD, Lionel.** *Concise Encyclopedia of Expressionism.* 1978. Chartwell. ils. VG/dj. M17. $17.50

**RICHARD, Mark.** *Fishboy: A Ghost's Story.* 1993. Doubleday. 1st. F/VG. B30. $22.50

**RICHARD, Mark.** *Ice at the Bottom of the World.* 1989. NY. Knopf. 1st. author's 1st book. F/F. B3. $100.00

**RICHARDS, Carmen.** *Minnesota Writers.* 1961. MN. Denison. sgn. 425p. cloth. F/dj. D4. $40.00

**RICHARDS, Eugene.** *Knife & Gun Club: Scenes From an Emergency Room.* 1989. Altantic Monthly. 1st. VG/dj. S5. $30.00

**RICHARDS, H.S.** *All About Horse Brasses: Collectors' Complete Guide.* 1972. Birmingham. Derverlea. ils. 52p. G. O3. $22.00

**RICHARDS, I.D.** *Story of a River Town: Little Rock in 19th Century.* 1969. Little Rock. photos/maps. 144p. F/dj. M4. $15.00

**RICHARDS, Laura E.** *Captain January.* Dana Estes. 3rd. 78p. VG. B36. $10.00

**RICHARDS, Laura E.** *Isla Heron.* (1896). Boston. Estes Lauriat. 5th thousand. 8vo. 109p. VG. M7. $15.00

**RICHARDS, Lawrence O.** *Practical Theology of Spirituality.* 1987. Zondervan. 253p. VG/dj. B29. $9.50

**RICHARDS, Lockie.** *Dressage: Begin the Right Way.* 1975. Newton Abbot. 1st. VG/dj. O3. $25.00

**RICHARDS, Paul I.** *Manual of Mathematical Physics.* 1959. Pergamon. 1st. bl cloth. VG. B27. $60.00

**RICHARDS, R.** *Best Recipes for Creole Cuisine & Famous Drinks...* 1938. self pub. wrp. VG. E6. $25.00

**RICHARDS, A. Madeley.** *Choirtrainer's Art.* 1914. NY. Schirmer. 8v0o. 196p. VG. A2. $20.00

**RICHARDSON, A.E.** *Old Inns of England.* 1934. Scribner. 1st. ils Brian cook. VG/dj. T10. $25.00

**RICHARDSON, Alan.** *Bible in the Age of Science.* 1961. Westminster. 192p. VG/dj. B29. $8.50

**RICHARDSON, Benjamin.** *Ministry of Health & Other Addresses.* 1879. London. 1st. 354p. A13. $75.00

**RICHARDSON, Bobby.** *Bobby Richardson Story.* 1965. Revell. 1st. sgn. photos. VG/G. P8. $50.00

**RICHARDSON, Edward.** *Standards & Colors of the American Revolution.* 1982. U PA. 1st. 341p. VG/dj. S16. $40.00

**RICHARDSON, J.** *Health & Longevity.* 1911. lg 8vo. ils. VG. E6. $60.00

**RICHARDSON, Robert S.** *Mars.* 1964. HBW. inscr/sgn. ils Chesley Bonestell. 151p. VG/G. K5. $150.00

**RICHARDSON, Robert.** *Book of the Dead.* 1989. London. Vollancz. 1st. sgn. F/dj. M15. $75.00

**RICHARDSON, Robert.** *Murder in Waiting.* 1991. St Martin. 1st Am. NF/dj. G8. $15.00

**RICHARDSON, Robert.** *Scalpel & the Heart.* 1970. NY. 323p. A13. $35.00

**RICHARDSON, Robert.** *Sleeping in the Blood.* 1991. Bristol. Scorpion. 1st. 1/75. sgn. F/dj. T2. $125.00

**RICHARDSON, Rupert Norval.** *Frontier of Northwest Texas.* 1963. Arthur H Clark. 332p. cloth. D11. $100.00

**RICHET, Charles.** *Recherches Experimentals et Cliniques sur la Sensibilite.* 1877. Paris. Masson. 341p. quarter sheep/marbled brd/new rb. G7. $395.00

**RICHLER, Mordecai.** *Incomparable Atuk.* 1963. Toronto. McClelland Stewart. 1st. NF/dj. M25. $45.00

**RICHLER, Mordecai.** *Joshua Then & Now.* 1980. Knopf. 1st. VG/dj. C9. $25.00

**RICHMOND, Al.** *Cowboys, Miners, Presidents & Kings.* 1989. Flagstaff. Northland. revised. 8vo. ils/photos. brn cloth. VG/dj. F7. $35.00

**RICHTER, Conrad.** *Aristocrat.* 1968. Knopf. 1st. F/clip. A24. $18.00

**RICHTER, Conrad.** *Tacey Cromwell.* 1942. Knopf. 1st. 208p. VG/G. B19. $20.00

**RICHTER, Daniel K.** *Ordeal of the Longhouse: Peoples of the Iroquois...* 1992. Williamsburg, VA. Inst Early Am Hist. ils. 436p. NF. M10. $16.50

**RICKER, William S.** *Jefferson Lives.* 1957. Jefferson Standard Life Insurance Co. 63p. B10. $12.00

**RICKETT, Harold William.** *Wild Flowers of the United States: Northeastern States.* 1966. NY. 2 vol. 1st. ils. gr cloth. F/rpr case. S15. $145.00

**RICKETTS, Charles.** *Defence of the Revival of Printing.* 1899. London. Vale. 1st. 1/250. lt bl brd/label/rb. M24. $200.00

**RICKETTS, R.L.** *First Class Polo.* 1928. Aldershot. Gale & Polden. 1st. VG. O3. $85.00

**RICKEY, Don.** *War in the West: Indian Campaigns.* 1956. Ft Collins, CO. 1st. 37p. F/stiff wrp. E1. $20.00

**RIDDELL, James.** *In the Forests of the Night.* 1946. NY. 1st. 228p. VG. A17. $15.00

**RIDDLE, Maxwell.** *Your Show Dog.* 1968. Doubleday. VG/dj. A21. $30.00

**RIDEAL, Samuel.** *Disinfection & Disinfectants...* 1895. London. ils/lg fld plan. red cloth. VG. B14. $125.00

**RIDGAWAY, Henry B.** *Lord's Land: Narrative of Travels in Sinai, Arabia Petraea.* 1876. NY. Nelson Phillips. 1st. ils. 744p. cloth. VG. W1. $65.00

**RIDGE, Alan D.** *Diaries of Bishop Vital Grandin, 1875-1877: Vol I.* (1989). Edmonton. Hist Soc of Alberta. 1st. NF/wrp. A26. $10.00

**RIDGWAY, John.** *Road to Osambre: A Daring Adventure in High Country of Peru.* 1987. Viking. 1st Am. 8vo. F/dj. W2. $30.00

**RIDLON, Marci.** *That Was Summer.* 1969. Chicago. Follett. 1st. 80p. cloth. F/dj. D4. $25.00

**RIDPATH, Ian.** *Stars & Planets.* 1979 (1978). London. Hamlyn. 2nd. 4to. 96p. VG/dj. K5. $12.00

**RIE & RIE.** *Handbook of Minimal Brain Dysfunctions...* 1980. John Wiley. heavy 8vo. 744p. prt bl cloth. VG/dj. G1. $65.00

**RIEFE, Barbara.** *Women Who Fell From the Sky.* 1992. Forge. 1st. NF/dj. S13. $10.00

**RIEFSTAHL, Rudolf M.** *Turkish Architecture in Southwestern Anatolia.* 1931. Cambridge. 186 ils/112 pl. quarger cloth/gray brd. VG. Q2. $290.00

**RIESBECK, E.W.** *Air Conditioning (With Ozone Facts).* 1934. Chicago. Goodheart-Willcox. VG/dj. B9. $30.00

**RIESE, Randall.** *All About Bette.* 1993. Chicago. Contemporary Books. 504p. VG/dj. C5. $15.00

**RIESEN, Rene.** *Jungle Mission.* 1957. NY. 1st. 204p. VG/dj. B5. $30.00

**RIGBY & RIGBY.** *Lock, Stock & Barrel: Story of Collecting.* 1944. Lippincott. 1st. 8vo. 570p. VG. S14. $13.00

**RIGER & KERMIT THE FROG.** *One Frog Can Make a Difference.* 1993. Pocket. 1st. F/dj. M23. $20.00

**RIGG, Robert B.** *How to Stay Alive in Vietnam.* 1966. Stackpole. 95p. ils brd. NF. R11. $50.00

**RIGGE, Ambrose.** *Brief & Serious Warning to Such as Are Concerned...* 1771. London. Mary Hinde. 12mo. 20p. disboudn. G. V3. $85.00

**RIGGIO, Anita.** *Wake Up, William!* 1987. Atheneum. 1st. 8vo. F/dj. M5. $30.00

**RIGGS, A.R.** *Nine Lives of Arthur Lee, Virginia Patriot.* (1976). Bicentennial Comm. ils. 84p. VG. B10. $15.00

**RIGGS, S.R.** *Dakota ABC Wowapi.* 1870. Am Tract Soc. A19. $225.00

**RIGGS, S.R.** *Mary & I: Forty Years With the Sioux.* 1969. Minneapolis, MN. Ross & Haines. rpt. VG/dj. A19. $40.00

**RIGGS, T.F.** *Log House Was Home.* 1961. Exposition. sgn. G/dj. A19. $50.00

**RIGNEY & SMITH.** *Real Bohemia.* 1961. NY. Basic Books. 1st. F/dj. B2. $35.00

**RIGOLEY DE JUVIGNY.** *Les Bibliotheques Francoises de la Croix du Maine.* 1772-1773. Paris. Saillant & Nyon. 6 vol. 4to. mottled calf. R12. $1,250.00

**RIIS, Jacob A.** *Nibsy's Christmas.* 1893. Scribner. 1st. lacks ep. VG. S13. $10.00

**RIIS, Jacob A.** *Old Town.* 1909. Macmillan. 1st. VG. B2. $75.00

**RIIS, Jacob A.** *Theodore Roosevelt, the Citizen.* 1904. NY. Outlook. 1st. F. B2. $65.00

**RILEY, Dick.** *New Bedside, Bathtub & Armchair Companion Agatha Christie.* nd. BC. VG/dj. P3. $10.00

**RILEY, James A.** *Biographical Encyclopedia of the Negro Baseball Leagues.* 1994. Carroll Graf. 1st. ils. F/VG. A2. $25.00

**RILEY, James Whitcomb.** *Home Folks.* (1900). Bowen Merrill. sm 8vo. ftspc. sgn w/6-line poem/dtd 1905. fld/case. K1. $250.00

**RILEY, James Whitcomb.** *Old Sweetheart of Mine.* 1902. Bobbs Merrill. ils HC Christy. VG. M17. $25.00

**RILEY, James Whitcomb.** *Rhymes of Childhood.* 1891. Bowen Merrill. 1st. inscr/orig drawing on ftspc. 186p. Zaehnsdorf bdg. H5. $450.00

**RILEY, James Whitcomb.** *While the Heart Beats Young.* 1906. Bobbs Merrill. 8vo. 110p. VG. D1. $75.00

**RILEY, James.** *Birch Bark Souvenir Views.* ca 1870-80. Portland. Chas Holbrook. mini. 8 engravings on birch bark. B24. $125.00

**RILEY, Pat.** *Show Time.* 1988. Warner. 1st. sm 4to. 259p. F/dj. W2. $50.00

**RILEY & SHUMACKER.** *Sheens: Martin, Charlie & Emilio Estevez.* 1989. St Martin. 1st. VG/dj. C9. $20.00

**RILING, Joseph R.** *Baron von Steuben & His Regulations.* 1966. Phil. 1st. 154p. F/case. B18. $45.00

**RILKE, Rainer Maria.** *Selected Poems of...* 1981. LEC. 1/120 (2000 total). ils/Robert Kipniss. w/suite 10 sgn lithos. F/case/box. B24. $750.00

**RIMMER, Harry.** *Evidences of Immortality.* 1946. Eerdmans. 119p. G/torn. B29. $8.00

**RINALDI & TYNDALO.** *Complete Book of Mushrooms.* 1974. NY. 300 mc pl. 332p. dj. B26. $22.00

**RINEHART, Mary Roberts.** *Out Trail.* 1932. NY. McBride. 8vo. 246p. red cloth. VG. F7. $25.00

RING, Douglas; see Prather, Richard.

RING, Ray. *Telluride Smile.* 1988. Dodd Mead. 1st. author's 1st book. F/NF. H11. $65.00

RINK, Paul. *To Steer by the Stars: Story of Nathaniel Bowditch.* 1969. NY. Doubleday. 8vo. 189p. VG/dj. K5. $14.00

RINTOUL, William. *Drilling Ahead: Tapping California's Richest Oil Fields.* 1981. Santa Cruz. Valley Pub. 289p. cloth. dj. D11. $30.00

RINTOUL, William. *Spudding In: Recollections of Pioneer Days...* 1978. Fresno. Valley Pub. 2nd. 240p. cloth. dj. D11. $40.00

RINZLER, Carol Eisen. *Girl Who Got All the Breaks.* 1980. NY. Putnam. ARC/1st. 191p. F/dj. O10. $20.00

RIOS, Eduardo Enrique. *Life of Fray Antonio Margil, OFM.* 1959. Academy of Am Franciscan Hist. 1st. 159p. NF/sans. B19. $30.00

RIPLEY, Edward Hastings. *Capture & Occupation of Richmond, April 3rd 1865.* 1907. Putnam. 1st. 31p. cloth. M8. $175.00

RIPLEY, W.L. *Dreamsicle.* 1993. Little Brn. 1st. F/F. H11. $30.00

RISENHOOVER, C.C. *White Heat.* 1992. Baskerville. 1st. F/VG. P8. $25.00

RISSE, Guenter. *Hospital Life in Enlightenment Scotland: Care & Teaching...* 1986. London. 1st. 450p. A13. $45.00

RISTER, C.C. *Fort Griffin on the Texas Frontier.* 1969. OK U. ils. 216p. F/dj. M4. $30.00

RISTER, C.C. *Southwestern Frontier, 1865-1881.* 1928. Arthur H Clark. ils/map. 336p. cloth. D11. $175.00

RITCHIE, Carson I. *Shell Carving: History & Techniques.* 1974. S Brunswick/NY. Barnes. 1st. F/dj. T10. $37.50

RITCHIE, Rita. *Pirates of Samarkand.* 1967. Norton. 1st. sm 8vo. 158p. VG. C14. $13.00

RITCHIE, Rita. *Year of the Horse.* 1957. Dutton. 1st. ils LF Bjorklund. VG/G. O3. $25.00

RITTENHOUSE, Jack. *American Horse-Drawn Vehicles.* 1958. Bonanza. VG/dj. A21. $45.00

RITTER, E.A. *Shaka Zulu: Rise of the Zulu Empire.* 1955. London. Longman Gr. 1st. 8vo. 383p. VG/G. M7. $45.00

RITTER, Ema I. *Life at the Amphibian Airport: Beautiful, Peaceful.* 1970. Santa Anta, CA. Pioneer. 1st. NF. O4. $30.00

RITTER, Gerhard. *Luther: His Life & Work.* 1963. Harper Row. 256p. VG/dj. H10. $15.00

RITTER, L. *Glory of Their Times.* 1966. Macmillan. 1st. sgn Harry Hooper. VG/dj. P8. $150.00

RITTER, L. *Lost Ballparks.* 1992. NY. Viking/Studio. 1st. ils/drawings. VG. B27. $45.00

RITTER, W.E. *California Woodpecker & I.* 1938. Berkeley. ils. 340p. xl. VG. C12. $25.00

RITZ, David. *Man Who Brought the Dodgers Back to Brooklyn.* 1981. S&S. 1st. F/VG. P8. $20.00

RIVERA, Diego. *Weekend With Diego Rivera by Barbara Braaun.* 1994. NY. Rizzoli. 1st. F/dj. S9. $45.00

RIVERS, William Halse. *Psychology & Politics & Other Essays.* 1923. Harcourt Brace. 180p. gr cloth. G1. $85.00

RIX, Martyn. *Art of the Plant World: Great Botanical Illustrators...* nd. Woodstock, NY. Overlook. stated 1st. ils. 224p. F/VG. H7. $60.00

RIZK, Salom. *Syrian Yankee.* 1949. Doubleday. sgn Eng/Arabic. 8vo. 317p. cloth. VG. W1. $18.00

ROACH & STEARN. *Hooker's Finest Fruits.* 1989. NY. 1st Am. 96 full-p pl. 222p. F/dj. B26. $34.00

ROBACK, Abraham Aaron. *Behaviorism & Psychology.* 1923. Cambridge. 12mo. 284p+fld chart. crimson cloth. VG. G1. $65.00

ROBACK, Abraham Aaron. *Behaviorism at Twenty-Five.* 1937. Cambridge. Sci-Art Pub. 12mo. 256p. xl. VG/dj. G1. $60.00

ROBACK, Abraham Aaron. *IL Peretz: Psychologist of Literature.* 1935. Cambridge. Sci-Art Pub. pres. 457p. gr cloth. G1. $75.00

ROBACKER, Earl F. *Old Stuff in Up Country Pennsylvania.* 1973. Barnes. 1st. VG/G. R8. $25.00

ROBACKER, Earl F. *Touch of the Dutchland.* 1965. London. Yoseloff/Barnes. 1st. 100+ photos. 240p. F/dj. H1. $22.50

ROBARD, Terry. *California Wine Label Album: 270 Wines to Taste, Collect...* 1986. 4to. mc pict brd. VG. E6. $15.00

ROBB, Bernard. *Welcum Hinges.* 1942. Dutton. 1st. ils Woodi Ishmael. dj. B10. $25.00

ROBB, Candace. *King's Bishop.* 1995. St Martin. 1st. sgn. F/dj. O11. $20.00

ROBB, Candace. *Nun's Tale.* 1995. St Martin. 1st. sgn. F/dj. O11. $20.00

ROBB, Mary Cooper. *William Faulkner: Estimate of His Contribution to Am Novel.* (1961). Pittsburgh. 3rd. tall 8vo. VG/wrp. H4. $35.00

ROBBINS, Clifton. *Mystery of Mr Cross.* 1933. Appleton. VG. N4. $20.00

ROBBINS, Harold. *Dream Merchants.* 1949. Knopf. 1st. VG+/dj. S13. $15.00

ROBBINS, Harold. *Memories of Another Day.* 1979. S&S. 1st. F/dj. T12. $25.00

ROBBINS, Jhan. *Bess & Harry.* 1980. NY. Putnam. 1st. F/VG+. M23. $10.00

ROBBINS, Maria P. *Puss in Books: A Collection of Great Cat Quotations.* 1994. ils. 270p. F/F. A4. $25.00

ROBBINS, Tom. *Another Roadside Attraction.* 1971. Doubleday. 1st. author's 1st book. NF/dj. D10. $450.00

ROBBINS, Tom. *Guy Anderson.* 1977. Seattle Art Mus. 1st. sgn. 36p. F/ils wrp. O11. $100.00

ROBBINS, Tom. *Jitterbug Perfume.* 1984. Bantam. 1st. sgn. F/NF. O11. $50.00

ROBBINS, Tom. *Skinny Legs & All.* 1990. Bantam. 1st. NF/F. R14. $35.00

ROBBINS, Tom. *Skinny Legs & All.* 1990. Bantam. 1st. sgn. F/dj. O11. $50.00

ROBBINS, Tom. *Still Life With Woodpecker.* 1980. Bantam. 1st. VG/G. M19. $45.00

ROBERT, J.C. *Tobacco Kingdom: Plantation, Market & Factory...* 1965 (1938). Gloucester. rpt. 286p. F. M4. $15.00

ROBERTE THE DEUYLL. *Metrical Romance, From Ancient Illuminated Manuscript.* 1798. London. Herbert. sm 4to. 13 pl. quarter morocco. R12. $275.00

ROBERTS, B.H. *Mormon Battalion: Its History & Achievements.* 1919. Salt Lake City. ils. 96p. gilt cloth. D11. $75.00

ROBERTS, Barrie. *Sherlock Holmes & the Devil's Grail.* 1995. London. Constable. 1st. F/dj. T2. $25.00

ROBERTS, Daniel. *Some Account of the Persecutions & Sufferings of People...* 1832. NY. Daniel Cooledge. 24mo. 256p. cloth. V3. $45.00

ROBERTS, Daniel. *Some Memoirs of the Life of John Roberts.* nd. Phil. Friends Book Store. 16mo. 86p. VG. V3. $15.00

ROBERTS, David. *Practical Home Veterinarian.* 1913. Waukesha, WI. 12th. 184p. cloth. A10. $15.00

ROBERTS, James A. *New York in the Revolution as Colony & State.* 1897. Albany. Weed Parsons. 1st ed. ils/fld map. 261p. VG. B18. $125.00

**ROBERTS, Keith.** *Furies.* 1966. London. Hart Davis. 1st. author's 1st book. VG/dj. M21. $200.00

**ROBERTS, Kenneth.** *Black Magic.* 1924. Bobbs Merrill. 1st. VG. T11. $135.00

**ROBERTS, Kenneth.** *Captain Caution.* 1934. Doubleday Doran. 1st. NF/VG+. T11. $120.00

**ROBERTS, Kenneth.** *Europe's Morning After.* 1921. NY. Harper. 1st. 1/1300 sold. author's 1st book. VG. T11. $300.00

**ROBERTS, Kenneth.** *Kenneth Roberts Reader.* 1945. Doubleday. 1st. VG/clip. S13. $10.00

**ROBERTS, Kenneth.** *Lively Lady.* 1931. Doubleday Doran. 1st. 1/5560. VG. T11. $45.00

**ROBERTS, Kenneth.** *Northwest Passage.* 1937. Doubleday Doran. 2 vol. 1st. 1/1050. sgn. teg. F/dj/case. H5. $350.00

**ROBERTS, Kenneth.** *Sun Hunting.* 1922. Bobbs Merrill. 1st. 1/47900. gilt gr cloth. NF/G+. T11. $400.00

**ROBERTS, Kenneth.** *Water Unlimited.* 1957. Doubleday. 1st. NF/dj. T11. $70.00

**ROBERTS, Kenneth.** *Why Europe Leaves Home.* 1922. Bobbs Merrill. 1st. 1/2011. NF/VG. T11. $700.00

**ROBERTS, L.** *MacKenzie.* 1949. NY. Rivers of Am. 1st. ils. F/dj. M4. $25.00

**ROBERTS, Les.** *Infinite Number on Monkeys.* 1987. St Martin. 1st. author's 1st novel. F/NF. A24. $37.50

**ROBERTS, S.C.** *Story of Dr Johnson, Being an Intro to Boswell's Life.* 1919. Cambridge. ils/portrait pl. brn brd/linen spine. H13. $25.00

**ROBERTS, S.C.** *18th-Century Gentleman & Other Essays.* 1930. Cambridge. 1st. 8vo. H13. $35.00

**ROBERTS, T.S.** *Bird Portraits in Color: 295 North American Species.* 1934. U MN. ils. VG/G. M17. $25.00

**ROBERTS, T.S.** *Birds of Minnesota.* 1936 (1932). Minneapolis. 2nd/revised. 92 mc pl. 1568p. NF. C12. $145.00

**ROBERTS, V.C.** *With Their Own Blood: Saga of Southwestern Pioneers.* 1992. TX Christian U. 1st. photos/maps. 286p. F/dj. M4. $25.00

**ROBERTS, W.** *Account of First Discoveries & Natural History of Florida.* 1976. FL U. 102p. F. M4. $35.00

**ROBERTS & ROBERTS.** *Joreau de St Mery's American Journey 1793-1798.* 1947. Doubleday. 1st. 8vo. 394p. tan cloth. G+/fair. M7. $25.00

**ROBERTSON, A.T.** *Word Pictures in the New Testament.* 1930. Broadman. 6 vol. B29. $60.00

**ROBERTSON, Don.** *Ideal Genuine Man.* 1987. Bangor, ME. Philtrum. 1st. intro Stephen King. F/NF. G10. $25.00

**ROBERTSON, Don.** *Prisoners of Twilight: A Novel.* 1989. NY. Crown. 1st. NF/dj. A14. $17.50

**ROBERTSON, George Croom.** *Philosophical Remains of George Croom Robertson.* 1894. London. Wms Norgate. heavy 8vo. 481p. ruled dk bl cloth. G1. $85.00

**ROBERTSON, James Alexander.** *Louisiana Under the Rule of Spain, France & United States...* 1911. Cleveland. AH Clark. 2 vol. 1st. 8vo. maps/plans. gilt maroon cloth. F. B11. $600.00

**ROBERTSON, James I.** *Stonewall Brigade.* (1963). LSU. 1st. ils. VG/VG. B10. $75.00

**ROBERTSON, John.** *Rusty Staub of the Expos.* 1971. Prentice Hall. 1st. photos. F/VG+. P8. $85.00

**ROBERTSON, R.B.** *Of Whales & Men.* 1954. Knopf. ils. gilt bl cloth. VG. P12. $15.00

**ROBERTSON, Terrence.** *Dieppe: Shame & the Glory.* 1962. Little Brn. 1st. 432p. VG/dj. S16. $22.00

**ROBERTSON, W. Graham.** *Blake Collection of W Graham Robertson.* 1952. London. Faber for Wm Blake Trust. ils. 327p. VG/G. A4. $85.00

**ROBERTSON, Wyndham.** *Pocahontas & Her Descendants...Ils Historical Notes.* 1956 (1887). Southern Book Co. rpt of 1887 Randolph. ils. 84p. VG. B10. $35.00

**ROBERTSON & ROBERTSON.** *Cowman's Country: 50 Frontier Ranches in TX Panhandle...* 1981. Paramont. 184p. AN. J2. $90.00

**ROBESON, Kenneth;** see Goulart, Ron.

**ROBIN, Robert.** *Above the Law.* 1992. Pocket. 1st. VG/dj. A28. $8.00

**ROBINETTE, Gary O.** *Guide to Estimating Landscape Costs.* 1983. NY. 200+charts/diagrams/lists/tables. 229p. AN/dj. B26. $27.50

**ROBINSON, Alan James.** *Trout: Brook, Brown & Rainbow.* 1986. Chelonidae. 1/15 (50). w/extra suite. Gray Parrot bdg. AN/chemise/box. B24. $3,500.00

**ROBINSON, Bill.** *Islands.* 1985. NY. photos. VG/dj. M17. $15.00

**ROBINSON, C.** *View From Chapultepec: Mexican Writers on Mexican War.* 1989. U AZ. 1st. 223p. F/dj. M4. $25.00

**ROBINSON, Chandler A.** *J Evetts Haley & the Passing of the Old West.* 1978. Jenkins. 239p. VG. J2. $95.00

**ROBINSON, D.** *History of the Dakota or Sioux Indians.* 1956. Minneapolis, MN. Ross & Haines. F/dj. A19. $65.00

**ROBINSON, Edwin Arlington.** *Sonnets 1889-1927.* 1928. Macmillan. 1st collected. paper brd/cloth spine. F/NF. T10. $50.00

**ROBINSON, Frank.** *Frank: The First Year.* 1976. Holt Rinehart. 1st. sgn. VG/dj. P8. $150.00

**ROBINSON, Gertrude Ina.** *Floral Faries, the Little Miss Hollys.* 1912 (1907). Floral Fairy Pub Co. 1st thus? obl 4to. ils FA Carter/8 full-p pl. VG. M5. $95.00

**ROBINSON, Heath.** *Inventions.* 1973. Duckworth. 1st. ils Robinson. 147p. VG/dj. D1. $30.00

**ROBINSON, Jackie.** *Breakthrough to the Big League.* 1965. Harper Row. 1st. VG/dj. P8. $45.00

**ROBINSON, Jacob S.** *Journal of the Santa Fe Expedition Under Colonel Doniphan.* 1932. Princeton. 96p. gilt cloth. D11. $35.00

**ROBINSON, James M.** *New Quest of the Historical Jesus.* 1966. SCM. 128p. VG/wrp. B29. $11.00

**ROBINSON, Jeffers.** *Californians.* 1916. Macmillan. 1st. F. A18. $250.00

**ROBINSON, Jeffers.** *Such Counsels You Gave to Me.* (1937). Random. 1st. NF. A18. $40.00

**ROBINSON, Jeffers.** *Thurso's Landing & Other Poems.* (1932). NY. Liveright. 1st. NF. A18. $60.00

**ROBINSON, John W.** *Southern California's First Railroad: Los Angeles...* 1978. Dawson's Book Shop. 1/300. photos. prt brd. D11. $50.00

**ROBINSON, Kathleen.** *When Debbie Dared.* 1963. Whitman. 216p. VG. B36. $7.50

**ROBINSON, Kim Stanley.** *Blue Mars.* 1996. London. Harper Collins. 1st. sgn. F/dj. M23. $100.00

**ROBINSON, Kim Stanley.** *Green Mars.* 1994. NY. Bantam. 1st. Hugo Award. F/dj. M23. $125.00

**ROBINSON, Kim Stanley.** *Remaking History.* 1991. NY. Tor. 1st. F/NF. G10. $27.00

**ROBINSON, Lynda S.** *Murder at the God's Gate.* 1995. NY. Walker. 1st. F/dj. M23. $40.00

**ROBINSON, Mabel L.** *Blue Ribbon Stories: Best Current Stories...* 1932. Macmillan. 1st. ils. cloth. VG. B27. $55.00

**ROBINSON, Mabel L.** *Little Lucia's Island Camp.* 1926 (1924). Dutton. 3rd. sm 8vo. 117p. gr cloth. G+. T5. $15.00

ROOSEVELT, Theodore. *Stories of the Great West.* 1913. Century. sm 8vo. 254p. G. H1. $20.00

ROOSEVELT, Theodore. *Wilderness Hunter: Account of Big Game of the US...* (1893). NY. Putnam. ils AB Frost/ Remington/Beard/others. 472p. buckram. VG. B14. $150.00

ROOSEVELT, Theodore. *Winning of the West. Vol 1-4.* 1896. NY. Putnam. 4 vol. Presidential Ed. fld maps. NF. M4. $85.00

ROOSEVELT, Wyn. *Frontier Boys in the Grand Canyon; or, Search for Treasure.* 1908. Cleveland. Arthur Westbrook. 12mo. VG/stiff wrp. F7. $35.00

ROOSEVELT & VAN DYKE. *Deer Family.* 1903. London. macmillan. ils. 333p. teg. G. B18. $38.00

ROOT, A.I. *ABC & XYZ of Bee Culture.* 1974. Medina. Root. 35th. 712p. gilt leatherette. F. A17. $15.00

ROOT, Elihu. *United States & the War, Mission to Russia...* 1918. Cambridge. Harvard. VG. M11. $50.00

ROOT, Ralph Rodney. *Contourscaping.* 1941. Chicago. Seymour. 246p. VG/dj. A10. $85.00

ROPER, Robert. *Royo Country.* 1973. Wm Morrow. 1st. F/dj. A23. $32.00

ROPES, A.R. *Lady Mary Wortley Montague: Select Passages...* 1892. London. Seeley. 8vo. 308p. gilt cloth. xl. VG. Q2. $20.00

ROQUELAURE, A.N.; see Rice, Anne.

ROREM, Ned. *Other Entertainment.* 1996. S&S. 1st. F/F. H11. $30.00

RORER, Sarah Tyson. *Mrs Rorer's Philadelphia Cookbook: Manual of Home Economics.* 1886. 1st. 589p. E6. $50.00

RORER, Sarah Tyson. *My Best 250 Recipes.* (1907). Phil. 162p. G. B18. $15.00

ROSA, Guido. *Mexico Speaks.* 1944. John Day. 1st. 250p. dj. F3. $15.00

ROSA, Joseph. *West of Wild Bill Hickok.* 1982. U OK. 223p. VG/dj. J2. $195.00

ROSA, Joseph. *Wild Bill Hickok: Man & His Myth.* photos. 272p. AN/dj. E1. $25.00

ROSBOTHAM, Lyle. *Jamestown Island.* (1976). self pub. photos. unp. VG. B10. $10.00

ROSCOE, Theodore. *Web of Conspiracy: Complete Story Men Who Murdered Lincoln.* 1960. Englewood Cliffs. 2nd. 562p. VG/dj. B18. $22.50

ROSCOE, Will. *Zuni Man-Woman.* 1991. NM U. 1st. photos/ils. 302p. VG/dj. A25. $18.00

ROSCOE, William. *Butterfly's Ball & the Grasshopper's Feast.* 1977. Boston. Bromer. mini. 1/25 (150 total). ils sgn. w/extra suite pl. F. B24. $850.00

ROSE, Alec. *My Lively Lady.* 1968. Lymington. Nautical Pub. 1st/2nd imp. F/VG clip. M7. $28.50

ROSE, Barbara. *Alexander Liberman.* 1981. NY. Abbeville. rem mk. VG. H4. $75.00

ROSE, Ernie. *Utahs of the Rocky Mountains 1833-1935.* 1968. Montrose Daily. sgn. G. A19. $25.00

ROSE, Jasper. *Lucy Boston.* 1966. NY. Walck. 1st Am. sm 8vo. 71p. VG/dj. T5. $25.00

ROSE, Lois. *Shattered Ring.* 1970. John Knox. 1st. NF/dj. P3. $30.00

ROSE, Pete. *Pete Rose Story.* 1970. World. 1st. VG/dj. P8. $45.00

ROSE, Ralph E. *Diary of..., a View of Virginia...* 1977. McClure. 1st. inscr/edit Ralph Fall. 400p. dj. B10. $65.00

ROSE, Robert T. *Advocates & Adversaries.* 1977. Lakeside Classics. 1st thus. teg. dk bl cloth. F. T11. $30.00

ROSE, William Ganson. *Cleveland, the Making of a City.* 1950. Cleveland. 1272p. VG/dj. B18. $35.00

ROSE & SOUCHON. *New Orleans Jazz: A Family Album.* 1967. Baton Rouge. 1st. F/NF. B2. $60.00

ROSEBERY, Lord. *Napoleon: Last Phase.* 1900. NY/London. Harper. 1st. 8vo. 283p. cloth. VG. W1. $25.00

ROSEN, George. *Preventive Medicine in the United States 1900-1975...* 1977. NY. 1st. 94p. wrp. A13. $25.00

ROSEN, Kenneth. *Man to Send Rain Clouds.* 1974. Viking. F/dj. A19. $25.00

ROSEN, Richard. *Fadeaway.* 1986. Harper Row. 1st. F/F. H11. $30.00

ROSENBAUM, David. *Zaddick.* 1993. Mysterious. 1st. F/NF. H11. $25.00

ROSENBERG, David. *Hidden Holmes: His Theory of Torts in History.* 1995. Harvard. M11. $45.00

ROSENBERG, David. *Movie That Changed My Life.* 1991. Viking. 304p. VG/dj. C5. $15.00

ROSENBERG, Nancy Taylor. *Mitigating Circumstances.* 1993. Dutton. 1st. rem mk. F/F. H11. $25.00

ROSENBERG, Neil V. *Bill Monroe & His Blue Grass Boys.* 1974. self pub/Country Music. 1st. F/wrp. B2. $40.00

ROSENBERG, Philip. *Tygers of Wrath.* 1991. St Martin. 1st. F/dj. S18. $25.00

ROSENBERG, Robert. *Cutting Room.* 1993. S&S. 1st. sgn bookplate. F/dj. T2. $35.00

ROSENBERG, Samuel. *Naked Is the Best Disguise.* 1974. Bobbs Merrill. 1st. VG/dj. P3. $30.00

ROSENBERGER, Francis Coleman. *Jefferson Reader: A Treasury of Writings...* 1953. Dutton. 1st. ils. 349p. VG/dj. B10. $35.00

ROSENFELD, Albert. *Second Genesis: Coming Control of Life.* 1969. Prentice Hall. 327p. xl. VG. S5. $12.00

ROSENHOLTZ, Joseph L. *Elements of Ferrous Metallury.* 1930. Wiley. 1st. cloth. VG. B27. $25.00

ROSENTHAL, Irving. *Sheeper.* 1967. Grove. 1st. 304p. VG/dj. R11. $50.00

ROSENTHAL, Jacques. *Bibliotheca Magica et Pneumatica.* nd. 1/150. rpt. 680p. F. A4. $75.00

ROSETTI, Christina. *Goblin Market.* 1933. London. Harrap. 1/410. ils Rackham. wht vellum. case/pict label. R5. $800.00

ROSEVEAR, John. *Pot: Handbook of Marihuana.* 1967. U Books. VG/dj. R8. $30.00

ROSKE & VAN DOREN. *Lincoln's Commando: Biography of Wm B Cushing.* 1957. Harper. 1st. VG/clip. A14. $25.00

ROSKILL, Stephen. *Churchill & the Admirals.* 1978. NY. Morrow. 1st. 351p. VG/dj. S16. $22.00

ROSS, Alexander. *Fur Trade Hunters of Far West.* 1924. Lakeside Classic. 317p. VG. J2. $135.00

ROSS, Alfred. *Register of Erotic Books.* 1965. NY. Brussell. 2 vol. 1st. VG. N2. $75.00

ROSS, Courtney. *Listen Up: Lives of Quincy Jones.* 1990. NY. Warner. photos. F/wrp. C9. $36.00

ROSS, David William. *Beyond the Stars.* 1990. NY. S&S. 1st. author's 1st book. quarter ivory cloth. F/dj. T11. $20.00

ROSS, David. *Ils Treasury of Poetry for Children.* nd (c 1970). Grosset Dunlap. 338p. F/F case. C14. $26.00

ROSS, E. Denison. *Polyglot List of Birds in Turki, Manchu & Chinese.* 1909. Calcutta. lg 4to. 112p. G/new wrp (orig wrp bound in). C12. $35.00

**ROSS, Edward Alsworth.** *Sin & Society: Analysis of Latter-Day Iniquity.* Nov 1907. Riverside. 1st. 167p. red cloth. F. B14. $45.00

**ROSS, Edward Alsworth.** *Sin & Society: Analysis of Latter-Day Iniquity.* 1907. Houghton Mifflin. 1st. VG. N2. $15.00

**ROSS, Herbert H.** *Synthesis of Evolutionary Theory.* 1962. Prentice Hall. 387p. xl. VG. S5. $20.00

**ROSS, J.K.M.** *Boots & Saddles: Story of Fabulous Ross Stable...* 1956. Dutton. 1st. 272p. G. M10. $18.50

**ROSS, Kate.** *Devil in Music.* 1997. NY. Viking. 1st. sgn. F/dj. T2. $35.00

**ROSS, Kate.** *Whom the Gods Love.* 1995. Viking. 1st. F/dj. G8. $25.00

**ROSS, Kate.** *Whom the Gods Love.* 1995. Viking. 1st. VG/dj. R8. $10.00

**ROSS, Norman.** *Epic of Man.* 1961. NY. Time. 1st. folio. 307p. dj. F3. $10.00

**ROSS, Patricia.** *In Mexico They Say.* 1946. Knopf. 3rd. 211p. dj. F3. $15.00

**ROSS, Paul.** *4 Corners on Main Street.* 1990. Toronto. 1st. F/NF. T12. $15.00

**ROSS, Philip.** *True Lies.* 1988. Tor. 1st. F/F. H11. $20.00

**ROSS, R.** *51st in France.* 1918. ils. VG. E6. $25.00

**ROSS, Robert H.** *Georgian Revolt 1910-22.* 1967. London. 1st. dj. T9. $18.00

**ROSS, W.G.** *Arctic Whalers, Icy Seas. Narratives of Davis Strait...* 1985. Toronto. 1st. sq 4to. ils. 263p. F/dj. A17/M4. $25.00

**ROSS, Z.H.** *Three Down Vulnerable.* 1946. Bobbs Merrill. 1st. F/VG. M15. $50.00

**ROSS & ROSS.** *Long Road South.* 1968. Mitchell. 1st. ils/pl/map. 168p. dj. F3. $15.00

**ROSSETTI, Christina.** *Goblin Market.* 1933. London. Harrap. 1/410. ils/sgn Rackham. 42p. full limp vellum. F/case. H5. $1,500.00

**ROSSETTI, Christina.** *Verses.* 1906. London. Eragny. 1/175 on Arches. 8vo. 75p. NF. H5. $1,500.00

**ROSSETTI, D.G.** *Ballads & Sonnets.* 1881. London. Ellis/White. 2st. gilt dk bl cloth. M24. $150.00

**ROSSETTI, D.G.** *Poems.* 1870. London. FS Ellis. 1st. gilt dk bl cloth. NF. M24. $300.00

**ROSSETTI, D.G.** *Poetical Works of Dante Gabriel Rossetti.* 1900. London. Ellis Elvey. new ed in 1 vol. 8vo. 380+4p ads. teg. NF. H5. $750.00

**ROSSI, Alice S.** *Feminist Papers: From Adams to deBeauvoir.* 1973. Columbia. VG. M17. $20.00

**ROSSI, Paolo.** *Dark Abyss of Time: History of Earth & History of Nations...* 1984. Chicago. 1st. 275p. dj. A13. $30.00

**ROSSMAN, Douglas A.** *Garter Snakes: Evolution & Ecology.* 1996. U OK. ils/maps. 332p. AN/dj. S15. $40.00

**ROSSNER, Judith.** *Emmeline.* 1980. S&S. 1st. F/F. H11. $20.00

**ROSSNER, Judith.** *Looking for Mr Goodbar.* 1975. S&S. 1st. NF/F. S18. $35.00

**ROSTAND, Edmund.** *Story of Chanticleer.* 1913. Stokes. 1st. ils JA Shepard. VG. M5. $60.00

**ROSTEN, Leo.** *Treasury of Jewish Quotations.* 1972. NY. 1st. 716p. VG/dj. B5. $25.00

**ROSTENBERG, Leona.** *Library of Robert Hooke: Scientific Book Trade...* 1989. Santa Monica. Modoc. 8vo. wrp. R12. $30.00

**ROSTENBERG, Leona.** *Minority Press & the English Crown: A Study...* 1971. Nieuwkoop. De Graaf. 4to. ils. cloth. R12. $75.00

**ROSTENBERG & STERN.** *Forty Years in the Book Business.* 1988. Santa Monica. Modoc. ils. 8vo. wrp. R12. $20.00

**ROSTENBERG & STERN.** *Old Books in the Old World.* 1996. New Castle. Oak Knoll. ltd. sgn. ils. case. R12. $45.00

**ROSTOV, Mara.** *Careless Feast.* 1985. Putnam. 1st. F/F. H11. $30.00

**ROSTOVTZEFF, M.** *Caravan Cities.* 1932. Oxford. Clarendon. 4to. 77 ils/35 pl/5 map. 323p. cloth. VG. Q2. $96.00

**ROSTRON, Richard.** *Sorcerer's Apprentice.* 1941. NY. Morrow. 1st thus. 41p. VG. D4. $25.00

**ROTH, Dieter.** *96 Piccadillies.* 1977. Eaton/Mayer. 96 pl/photos/chronology/ exhibit list. F/case. D2. $275.00

**ROTH, Ernst.** *Business of Music: Reflections of a Music Publisher.* 1969. London. Cassell. 1st. VG/dj. N2. $10.00

**ROTH, Philip.** *Anatomy Lesson.* 1983. FSG. 1st. NF/NF. H11. $30.00

**ROTH, Philip.** *Goodbye, Columbus.* 1959. Houghton Mifflin. 1st. NF/clip. B4. $750.00

**ROTH, Philip.** *Great American Novel.* 1973. HRW. 1st. F/VG. P8. $22.50

**ROTH, Philip.** *Operation Shylock: A Confession.* 1993. NY. S&S. 1st. F/NF. G10. $12.00

**ROTH, Philip.** *Our Gang.* 1971. NY. Random. 1st. author's 5th book. NF/NF. H11. $30.00

**ROTH, Philip.** *Sabbath's Theater.* 1995. Houghton Mifflin. ARC. sgn. Nat Book Award. F/wrp. R14. $60.00

**ROTH, Philip.** *Sabbath's Theater.* 1995. Houghton Mifflin. 1st. F/VG+. B30. $25.00

**ROTH, Susan.** *Weekend Garden Guide.* 1991. Emmaus. Rodale. 358p. VG. A10. $18.00

**ROTH.** *Encyclopedia Judaica.* 1972. Jerusalem/NY. 16 vol. 4to. ils/mc pl. VG. A4. $1,250.00

**ROTHENBERG, Jerome.** *Poems 1964-1967.* 1967. Blk Sparrow. 1st. 1/125. sgn/#d. F/dj. L3. $50.00

**ROTHENBERG, Jerome.** *Seneca Journal.* 1978. New Directions. 1st. inscr/dtd 1979. F/wrp. L3. $65.00

**ROTHENBERG, Jerome.** *Shaking the Pumpkin.* 1972. Doubleday. F/dj. A19. $35.00

**ROTHERT, Otto A.** *Outlaws of Cave-in-Rock.* 1924. Cleveland. AH Clark. 1st. ils. 364p. maroon cloth. B11. $450.00

**ROTHERY, Agnes.** *Central American Roundabout.* 1944. Dodd Mead. 1st. 248p. dj. F3. $15.00

**ROTHMAN.** *Mr Rothman's New Guide to London.* 1965. London. Pall Mall. 2nd. F. T12. $30.00

**ROTHSCHILD, Lord.** *Fertilization.* 1956. Metheun. 170p. xl. VG. S5. $12.00

**ROTHSCHILD, Michael.** *Wonder Monger.* 1990. NY. Viking. 1st. F/dj. A23. $32.00

**ROUGHGARDEN, Jonathan.** *Anolis Lizards of the Caribbean: Ecology, Evolution...* 1995. OUP. 200p. AN/wrp. S15. $8.50

**ROUGHHEAD, William.** *Trial of Oscar Slater.* 1925. Edinburgh. Wm Hodge. 3rd. M11. $75.00

**ROUGHLEY, T.C.** *Wonders of the Great Barrier Reef.* 1936. 1st. 52 mc photos. VG. M19. $25.00

**ROURKE, Constance.** *Audubon.* 1936. NY. 342p. F/dj. A17. $15.00

**ROURKE, Constance.** *Troupers of the Gold Coast; or, Rise of Lotta Crabtree.* 1928. Harcourt Brace. 1st. G+. O4. $20.00

**ROURKE, John P.** *Proteas of Southern Africa.* 1980. Cape Town. 236p. VG+/dj. B26. $90.00

**ROURKE, Thomas.** *Gomez: Tyrant of the Andes.* 1936. Morrow. 1st. 320p. dj. F3. $15.00

**ROURREY, Rene.** *Cure D'Ars: Pictorial Biography.* 1959. NY. photos. VG. M17. $20.00

**ROUS, George.** *Thoughts on Government: Occasioned by Mr Burke's Reflection.* 1790. London. 8vo. brd. R12. $125.00

**ROUSCH, Lester Le Roy.** *History of the Rousch Family in America.* 1928. Shenandoah. 747p. G. S5. $60.00

**ROUSE, John.** *Criollo: Spanish Cattle in the Americas.* 1977. Norman, OK. 303p. AN/dj. A10. $40.00

**ROUSSEAU, Jean-Jacques.** *Censure de la Faculte de Theologie de Paris, Contre...* 1762. Paris. Le Prieur. 8vo. calf. R12. $475.00

**ROUSSEAU, Jean-Jacques.** *Confessions of...* 1938. London. Nonesuch. 2 vol. 1/800. 8vo. ils Reynolds Stone. F/case. H5. $300.00

**ROUSSEAU, Jean-Jacques.** *Oeuvres Diveres de Mr Rousseau.* 1927. London. Tonson Watts. 2 vol. ftspc by Cheron. full leather. G. M10. $175.00

**ROUTH, Jonathan.** *Secret Life of Queen Victoria...* 1980. NY. 1st. ils. VG/dj. M17. $15.00

**ROVIN, Jeff.** *Adventure Heroes.* 1994. Facts on File. 314p. VG/dj. C5. $20.00

**ROWE, Dorothy Snowden.** *It Was Fun.* 1972. Indian Hill, OH. self pub. 1st. inscr. 104p. VG+. A25. $25.00

**ROWE, Joseph Andrew.** *California's Pioneer Circus.* (1926). SF. Albert Dressler. 1/1250. 98p. pict bl cloth. K1. $50.00

**ROWLAND, Jon Thomas.** *Faint Praise & Civil Leer.* 1995. Newark. U DE. 1st. gilt blk linen. AN/dj. H13. $35.00

**ROWLAND, Laura Joh.** *Shinju.* 1994. Random. 1st. author's 1st book. store stp on bottom edges. F/F. H11. $20.00

**ROWLAND, Peter.** *Disappearance of Edwin Drood.* 1992. St Martin. 1st Am. F/NF. N4. $25.00

**ROWLEY, H.H.** *Faith of Israel: Aspects of Old Testament Thought.* 1956. Westminster. 220p. G/torn dj. B29. $9.00

**ROWLEY, John.** *Taxidermy & Museum Exhibition.* 1925. NY. 1st. 331p. gilt cloth. G. A17. $40.00

**ROWSE, A.L.** *Cornish Childhood: Autobiography of a Cornishman.* 1979 (1942). NY. Potter. 8vo. rpt. F/dj. A2. $12.00

**ROWSE, A.L.** *Elizabethians & America.* 1959. London. 1st. ils. 221p. VG/dj. M10. $22.50

**ROWSE, A.L.** *Oxford in the History of England.* 1975. Putnam. 1st Am. ils. VG/dj. T10. $35.00

**ROWSE, A.L.** *Poet Auden: A Personal Memoir.* 1988. NY. 1st. dj. T9. $15.00

**ROWSE, A.L.** *Shakespeare's Southampton: Patron of Virginia.* 1965. London. Macmillan. 1st. 8vo. F/dj. A2. $18.00

**ROWSE, A.L.** *Windsor Castle in the History of England.* 1974. Putnam. 1st Am. VG/dj. A2. $17.50

**ROY, Arundhali.** *God of Small Things.* 1997. Random. 1st Canadian. AN/as issued. T12. $70.00

**ROY, Arundhati.** *God of Small Things.* 1997. Random. 1st Am. F/dj. M23. $55.00

**ROYAL SOCIETY.** *Philosophical Transactions of the Royal Society of London.* 1809. London. Baldwin. 18 vol. abridged. 4to. ils/266 pl. K1. $2,500.00

**ROYCE, Sarah.** *Frontier Lady: Recollections of the Gold Rush...* 1932. OUP. 1st. 8vo. 144p. cloth. VG. O1. $70.00

**ROYSTER, C.** *Light-Horse Harry Lee & Legacy of American Revolution.* 1981. NY. 1st. 301p. F/dj. M4. $25.00

**ROZAN, S.J.** *Concourse.* 1995. St Martin. 1st. F/NF. M15. $65.00

**ROZAN, S.J.** *Mandarin Plaid.* 1996. St Martin. 1st. sgn. F/dj. M15. $45.00

**ROZAN, S.J.** *No Colder Place.* 1997. St Martin. 1st. sgn. F/dj. M15. $35.00

**RUARK, Robert.** *Old Man's Boy Grows Older.* 1961. NY. 1st. ils. NF. A17. $25.00

**RUARK, Robert.** *Use Enough Gun, On Hunting Big Game.* 1966. NAL. 333p. NF/NF. A4. $35.00

**RUARK, Robert.** *Use Enough Gun...* 1966. NAL. 1st. ils. F/dj. H10. $65.00

**RUBENSTEIN, S.L.** *Prinzipien und Wege der Entwicklund der Psychologie.* 1963. Berlin. Akademie-Verlag. 1st German. 296p. tan cloth. VG/dj. G1. $65.00

**RUBIE, Peter.** *Werewolf.* 1991. Longmeadow. 1st. author's 2nd book. VG/dj. L1. $50.00

**RUBIN, Barry.** *Cauldron of Turmoil: America in Middle East.* 1992. HBJ. 1st. 306p. NF. W1. $18.00

**RUBIN, Cynthia.** *ABC of Americana From the National Gallery of Art.* 1989. HBJ. 1st. 8vo. xl. VG/dj. B17. $6.50

**RUBIN, Cynthia.** *Shaker Herbs. An Essay by Cynthia Elyce Rubin.* 1984. Northampton. Catawba. mini. 1/155. Blumenthal bdg. w/4 labels. B24. $140.00

**RUBIN, Martin.** *Showstoppers.* 1993. Columbia. 249p. VG/dj. C5. $15.00

**RUBIN, Robert.** *Ty Cobb: The Greatest.* 1978. Putnam. 1st. VG/dj. P8. $85.00

**RUBIN, Ruth.** *Treasury of Jewish Folksongs.* 1950. Schocken. 1st. VG/fair. P2. $30.00

**RUBIN, Wallace.** *Electronystagmorgraphy: What Is ENG?* 1974. Chas Thomas. 1st. 8vo. 105p. F/NF. C14. $10.00

**RUBIN, William.** *Frank Stella.* 1970. MOMA. 1st. 176p. F/VG+. T11. $30.00

**RUBIN & WILLIAMS.** *Larger Than Life: American Tall-Tale Postcard 1905-1915.* 1990. Abbeville. 1st. ils. 132p. F/F. B19. $25.00

**RUBINSTEIN, Arthur.** *My Many Years.* 1980. Knopf. 1st. photos. VG/dj. P12. $20.00

**RUBINSTEIN, Eli A.** *Research in Psychotherapy, Vol I.* 1959. WA, DC. 1st. 8vo. 293p. VG+. C14. $20.00

**RUBOVITS, Norma.** *Marbled Vignettes. Including Muir Dawson & Norman Rubovits.* 1992. Dawson's Book Shop. 1/35 (135). sgn. 5 matted vignettes. w/prospectus. box. B24. $750.00

**RUBULIS, Aleksis.** *Baltic Literature.* 1970. Notre Dame. 1st. F/clip. O4. $15.00

**RUCKER, Wilbur.** *History of the Opthalmoscope.* 1971. Rochester. 1st. sgn. 127p. A13. $125.00

**RUCKHABER, Erich.** *Des Daseins und Denkens Mechanik & Metamechanik.* 1910. Heinrich Springer. inscr. 626p. prt panelled bl-gray cloth. G. G1. $125.00

**RUDD, Niall.** *Johnson's Juvenal: London & Vanity of Human Wishes.* 1981. Birstol. Classical. notes/lists of names. 106p. F/wrp. H13. $35.00

**RUDD, W.H.** *Orrocco Poultry Farm.* 1893. Boston. Rudd. 64p. wrp. A10. $35.00

**RUDNICKI, K.S.** *Last of the War-Horses.* 1974. London. Bachman Turner. 1st. VG/dj. O3. $25.00

**RUDORFF, Raymond.** *Dracula Archives.* 1971. Arbor. 1st. G/dj. L1. $65.00

**RUE, Leonard Lee.** *Game Birds of North America.* 1973. Outdoor Life. ils Doug Allen. 490p. F/dj. A17. $20.00

**RUE, Leonard Lee.** *Sportsman's Guide to Game Animals.* 1973. Harper Row. 10th. photos. 655p. VG/G. P12. $15.00

**RUE, Leonard Lee.** *World of the White-Tailed Deer.* 1962. Lippincott. ils. 134p. NF/VG. S15. $14.00

**RUESCH, Hans.** *South of the Heart: Novel of Modern Arabia.* 1957. Coward-McCann. 1st. 8vo. 316p. VG/torn dj. W1. $18.00

**RUFFNER, Budge.** *All Hell Needs Is Water.* 1972. Tucson, AZ. 1st. sgn. 96p. NF/VG+. B19. $35.00

**RUFFNER, Melissa.** *Prescott: Pictorial History.* 1981. Primrose. sgn. ils/biblio/index. 208p. F/wrp. B19. $35.00

**RUGE, Friedrich.** *Der Gestfrieg: Germany, Navy's Story.* 1957. Annapolis. 1st. 440p. VG/G. B5. $60.00

**RUGGIERI, Guido.** *Secrets of the Sky.* 1969 (1967). London. Hamlyn. trans DD Bayliss. 174p. VG/dj. K5. $15.00

**RUHL, Arthur.** *Central Americans: Adventures & Impressions...* 1928. Scribner. 1st. 284p. F3. $20.00

**RULE, Ann.** *Dead by Sunset: Perfect Husband, Perfect Killer?* 1995. S&S. 1st. ils. 429p. VG/dj. S14. $11.00

**RULE, Roger.** *Rifleman's Rifle: Winchester's Model 70, 1936-1963.* 1982. Northridge, CA. Alliance Books. ltd/sgn. leather. F/box. A19. $300.00

**RULHIERE, Claude.** *History; or, Anecdotes of Revolution in Russia in 1762.* 1798. Boston. Nancrede. 12mo. Catherine II of Russia ftspc. calf. R12. $225.00

**RUMAKER, Michael.** *Gringoes & Other Stories.* 1991. Rocky Mtn. reissue. 1/200 (1800 total). sgn. F/sans. R14. $75.00

**RUMELHART, David E.** *Parrel Distributed Processing: Explorations...* 1988 (1986). MIT. 2 vol. 7th. bl or brn cloth. VG/dj. G1. $65.00

**RUMMER, Thomas A.** *Wagon Trains of '44...* 1990. Clark. 273p. VG/dj. J2. $75.00

**RUNBECK, Margaret Lee.** *Time for Miss Boo.* 1949. Appleton Century Crofts. ils Peggy Bacon. 451p. tan bdg. P12. $12.00

**RUNDELL, M.A.** *New System of Domestic Cookery...* 1807. London. new ed. rb. G+. E6. $150.00

**RUNNER, Meredith N.** *Changing Syntheses in Development.* 1970. Academic. 272p. xl. VG. S5. $15.00

**RUNTE, Alfred.** *Yosemite: Embattled Wilderness.* 1990. U NE. 1st. ils. F/NF. O4. $30.00

**RUNYAN, Damon.** *Guys & Dolls.* 1931. STokes. 1st. blk-lettered red cloth. VG. C15. $100.00

**RUNYAN, Harry.** *Faulkner Glossary.* (1954). NY. Citadel. stated 1st. 8vo. 210p. H4. $25.00

**RUSCHA, Ed.** *Colored People.* 1972. np. self pub. 1st. sgn. ils. F/yel prt wrp. S9. $325.00

**RUSCHA, Ed.** *Crackers.* 1969. Hollywood. Heavy Industry Pub. 1st. 8vo. F/stiff wrp/prt dj. S9. $225.00

**RUSH, George Herman.** *Babe Ruth's Own Book of Baseball.* 1928. Putnam. 1st. photos. G+. P8. $85.00

**RUSH, James.** *Brief Outline of Analysis of Human Intellect.* 1865. Lippincott. 2 vol. emb crimson cloth. VG/NF. G1. $150.00

**RUSH, Norman.** *Mating.* 1991. Knopf. 1st. F/NF. M25. $45.00

**RUSHDIE, Salman.** *Grimus.* 1979. Woodstock, NY. Overlook. 1st Am. author's 1st book. NF/clip. A14. $140.00

**RUSHDIE, Salman.** *Haroun & the Sea of Stories.* 1990. London. Granta. 1st. F/F. B3. $50.00

**RUSHDIE, Salman.** *Is Nothing Sacred?* 1990. NY. Granta. 1st Am (no hc issue). F/wrp. R14. $30.00

**RUSHDIE, Salman.** *Midnight's Children.* 1981. Random. stated 1st Am. F/F. D10. $325.00

**RUSHDIE, Salman.** *Moor's Last Sigh.* 1995. London. Cape. 1st sgn on title. F/dj. A14. $140.00

**RUSHDIE, Salman.** *Moor's Last Sigh.* 1995. Pantheon. 1st Am. sgn. F/dj. D10. $85.00

**RUSHDIE, Salman.** *Moor's Last Sigh: A Novel.* 1995. Pantheon. ARC/1st Am. inscr. pict wrp. Q1. $100.00

**RUSHDIE, Salman.** *Satanic Verses.* 1988. Viking. 1st. F/dj. S18. $50.00

**RUSHDIE, Salman.** *Satanic Verses.* 1989. Viking. 1st. assn/sgn Rushdie's wife. F/dj. D10. $85.00

**RUSHDIE, Salman.** *Shame.* 1983. London. Cape. 1st. author's 3rd novel. F/F. B3. $75.00

**RUSHDY, Rashad.** *Selected Stories & Essays.* 1964. Cairo. Anglo-Egyptian Bookshop. 1st. 8vo. VG/wrp. W1. $5.00

**RUSHER, William A.** *Making of the New Majority Party.* 1975. Sheed Ward. 1st. 8vo. VG/dj. A2. $12.00

**RUSHING, Lilith.** *Cake Cookbook.* 1964. Chilton. 1st. G/dj. A16. $45.00

**RUSKIN, John.** *Dame Wiggins of Lee & Her Seven Wonderful Cats.* 1980. NY. Crowell. 1t. sm 8vo. 29p. F/dj. W2. $20.00

**RUSS, Joanna.** *Zanzibar Cat.* 1983. Arkham. 1st. G+/VG. B30. $45.00

**RUSSELL, Alan K.** *Rivals of Sherlock Holmes.* 1978. Seacaucus, NJ. Castle Books. thick 8vo. ils. bl brd. F/dj. R3. $15.00

**RUSSELL, Andy.** *Andy Russell's Adventures With Wild Animals.* 1978. NY. Knopf. F/dj. A19. $25.00

**RUSSELL, Andy.** *Life of a River.* 1987. Toronto. McClelland Stewart. F/dj. A26. $25.00

**RUSSELL, Bertrand.** *Impact of Science on Society.* 1953. NY. 1st. 115p. A13. $25.00

**RUSSELL, Carl.** *Firearms, Traps & Tools of the Mountain Men.* 1967. Knopf. 448p. VG/dj. J2. $225.00

**RUSSELL, Charles Edward.** *A-Rafting on the Mississippi.* 1928. NY. Century. 1st. fld map. VG+. B2. $35.00

**RUSSELL, Charles M.** *Trails Plowed Under.* 1951. Doubleday. rpt. VG. A19. $30.00

**RUSSELL, D.** *Campaigning With King: Charles King...* 1991. NE U. 187p. F/dj. M4. $20.00

**RUSSELL, Edmund.** *Readings From California Poets.* 1893. SF. Wm Doxey. Sunset Series #2. VG/wrp. A18. $25.00

**RUSSELL, Edward J.** *Soil Conditions & Plant Growth.* 1917. Longman Gr. 243p. xl. VG. S5. $12.50

**RUSSELL, Eric Frank.** *Men, Martians & Machines: Classics of Modern SF Vol I.* 1984. NY. Crown. 1st thus. F/dj. G10. $14.00

**RUSSELL, Franklin.** *Secret Islands.* 1966. Hodder Stoughton. 1st. F/VG. A26. $20.00

**RUSSELL, George.** *Hoofprints in Time.* 1966. S Brunswick. 1st. 4to. G. O3. $55.00

**RUSSELL, Jacqueline.** *If You Like Horses.* 1932. Houghton Mifflin. 1st. 12mo. ils. VG. O3. $25.00

**RUSSELL, James William.** *Stranger in the Mirror.* 1968. Harper Row. 1st. VG/dj. P3. $15.00

**RUSSELL, K.F.** *Bibliography of Anatomical Books Published in English...* 1949. wrp. A13. $17.50

**RUSSELL, Maria.** *Beer Makes It Better Cookbook.* 1971. S&S. G/dj. A16. $15.00

**RUSSELL, Phillips.** *Benjamin Franklin: First Civilized American.* 1926. Brentano. 1st/4th prt. 8vo. 332p. gilt bl cloth. VG. S17. $15.00

**RUSSELL, Randy.** *Caught Looking.* 1992. Doubleday. 1st. F/dj. P8. $20.00

**RUSSELL, Rosalind.** *Life Is a Banquet.* 1977. NY. Random. 259p. VG/dj. C5. $12.50

**RUSSELL, Thomas.** *Egyptian Service, 1902-1946.* 1949. London. Murray. ils/pl/maps. 294p. VG. Q2. $27.00

**RUSSELL, William Howard.** *Diary in East During Tour of Prince & Princess of Wales.* 1869. London. Routledge. 1st. ils. 650+6p ads. morocco-grained cloth. VG. Q2. $200.00

**RUSSELL, William.** *Bolivar Countries.* 1949. McCann. xl. 308p. F3. $10.00

**RUSSELL, William.** *Russell on Scientific Horseshoeing.* 1907. Cincinnati. CJ Krehbiel. 1st. G. O3. $75.00

**RUSSO, Richard.** *Mohawk.* 1986. NY. Vintage. 1st. sgn. rem mk. NF. B3. $40.00

**RUSSO, Richard.** *Nobody's Fool.* 1993. London. 1st Eng. F/dj. M19. $17.50

**RUSSO, Richard.** *Nobody's Fool.* 1993. NY. Random. 1st. F/dj. A23. $45.00

**RUSSO, Richard.** *Nobody's Fool.* 1993. Random. 1st. sgn. F/dj. O11. $65.00

**RUSSO, Richard.** *Straight Man.* 1997. Random. 1st. sgn/dtd 1997. F/dj. R14. $45.00

**RUSSO & SULLIVAN.** *Bibliographical Studies of Seven Authors of Crawfordsville.* 1952. IN Hist Soc. 486p. teg. maroon/tan cloth. F. F1. $35.00

**RUSSO & SULLIVAN.** *Bibliography of Booth Tarkington, 1869-1946.* 1949. 322p. F. A4. $135.00

**RUST, Brian.** *American Record Label Book.* 1978. New Rochelle. Arlington. 1st. F/dj. B2. $85.00

**RUST, Eric C.** *Towards a Theological Understanding of History.* 1963. Oxford. 287p. VG/dj. B29. $11.00

**RUSTEN, Philip.** *On the Growing Edge.* 1981. Tecumseh. sgn pres. 96p. NF/dj. A17. $15.00

**RUSTOW, Dankwart A.** *Oil & Turmoil: America Faces OPEC & Middle East.* 1982. Norton. 1st Am. 8vo. F/VG. A2. $15.00

**RUTH, Babe.** *Home Run King.* 1920. AL Burt. rpt? G+. P8. $70.00

**RUTH, Kent.** *Great Day in the West: Forts, Posts & Rendezvous...* 1963. U OK. ils. VG/dj. J2. $95.00

**RUTHERFORD, William.** *65 Days: 25th Division Luzon.* nd. folio. ils. G+. E6. $60.00

**RUTHERFURD, Edward.** *Russka: Novel of Russia.* 1991. NY. sgn. VG/dj. M17. $20.00

**RUTLEDGE, Archibald.** *Home by the River.* (1944). Bobbs Merrill. photos Noble Bretzman. 175p. VG/G. B10. $15.00

**RUTLEDGE & RUTLEDGE.** *In the Presence of Mine Enemies: Seven Years a POW...* 1973. Fleming Revell. 124p. NF/dj. R11. $35.00

**RUTSTEIN, David.** *Blueprints for Medical Care.* 1974. Cambridge. 284p. A13. $20.00

**RYAN, Alan.** *Night Visions 1: All Original Stories.* 1984. Niles. Dark Harvest. 1st. F/dj. G10. $115.00

**RYAN, Alan.** *Reader's Companion to Mexico.* 1995. Harcourt Brace. 1st. 372p. wrp. F3. $15.00

**RYAN, Ed.** *Me & the Black Hills.* 1950. Rapid City, SD. Holmgrens. sc. G. A19. $25.00

**RYAN, Frank.** *Sweet Summer.* 1987. Quartet. 1st. VG/dj. G8. $7.50

**RYAN, J.C.** *Custer Fell First.* 1966. San Antonio, TX. VG/dj. A19. $30.00

**RYAN, James A.** *Town of Milan.* 1974. Columbus. ils/photos/maps. VG/wrp. B18. $17.50

**RYAN, Lewis Cass.** *Grandpa's Hired Man.* 1933. LA. John Murray. 4to. ils/woodcuts. 44p. bl cloth. K1. $100.00

**RYAN, Marah Ellis.** *That Girl Montana.* 1901. Chicago. Rand McNally. 1st. 357p. G. G11. $12.00

**RYDBERG, P.A.** *Flora of Colorado.* 1906. Ft Collins. Experiment Sta. G. A19. $50.00

**RYDER, Joanne.** *Incredible Space Machines: All About Rocket Ships...* 1982. NY. Random/Children's Television Workshop. 1st. 48p. K5. $20.00

**RYDER, John.** *Six on the Black Art.* nd. London. Wynkyn de Worde Soc. 1/250. sgn. F/box. M24. $60.00

**RYDER, Jonathan;** see Ludlum, Robert.

**RYDER, Lilian.** *Child's Story of Jesus in Living Pictures.* nd. London. World. ne. 4 dbl-p popups. NF. T12. $55.00

**RYDER, Tom.** *High Stepper.* 1979. London/NY. Allen. VG/G. O3. $25.00

**RYDER, Tom.** *On the Box Seat: Manual of Driving.* 1969. Gawsworth. 1st. VG/dj. O3. $75.00

**RYLAND, Elizabeth Hawes.** *King William County, Virginia...* 1955. Dietz. photos. 137p. B10. $55.00

**RYLANT, Cynthia.** *Blue-Eyed Daisy.* 1985. NY. Bradbury. 1st. sgn. 99p. F/dj. D4. $40.00

**RYLE, Gilbert.** *Concept of Mind.* 1949. London. Hutchinson. 334p. bl cloth. VG/dj. G1. $100.00

**RYMAN, Geoff.** *Child Garden.* 1989. London. Unwin Hyman. 1st. sgn. F/dj. M21. $60.00

**RYNNING, Thomas H.** *Gun Notches: Saga of Frontier Lawman Capt Thomas Rynning...* 1971. Frontier Heritage. rpt of 1931. F/NF. B19. $15.00

**RYS, Steven L.** *US Military Power.* 1983. GAllery. 1st. 4to. ils. 224p. F/dj. M7. $20.00

**RYSER, F.A.** *Birds of the Great Basin: A Natural History.* 1985. Reno, NV. 8vo. ils. 604p. VG+. M12. $25.00

SABATIER, Paul. *Modernism.* 1908. NY. 1st. 351p. VG. H10. $25.00

SABATINI, Rafael. *Gamester.* 1949. Houghton Mifflin. 1st. F/VG. T11. $85.00

SABATINI, Rafael. *Urbinian: Tale of Italy in Time of Cesare Borgia.* 1924. Houghton Mifflin. 1st. VG/dj. T11. $40.00

SABERHAGEN, Fred. *Seance for a Vampire.* 1994. NY. Tor. 1st. NF/dj. M21. $17.50

SABIN, Alvah H. *Red-lead & How to Use It in Paint.* 1920. NY. Wiley. 3rd. 139p. cloth. A10. $35.00

SABIN, Edwin. *Wild Men of the Wild West.* 1929. Crowell. ils. VG. J2. $110.00

SABIN. *Dictionary of Books Relating to America.* nd. 29 vol in 2 miniprint. obl 4to. 100,000+ entries. F. A4. $275.00

SABUDA, Robert. *Knight's Castle.* 1994. Artists Writers Guild. 1st. 6 popups. F. B17. $8.50

SACCO, Luigi. *Trattato di Vaccinazione con Osservazioni...* 1809. Milano. Dalla Tipografia Mussi. 4 hand-colored fld pl. 223p. G7. $595.00

SACHAR, Abram Leon. *History of the Jews.* 1966. Knopf. 5th. 478p. VG. P12. $10.00

SACHS, Ernest. *Care of the Neurosurgical Patient: Before, During...* 1945. St Louis. CV Mosby. 1st. 8vo. 268p. NF. C14. $45.00

SACHS, Wulf. *Black Anger.* 1947. Little Brn. 1st. VG/dj. H11. $25.00

SACK, John. *Man-Eating Machine.* 1973. FSG. 1st. VG/dj. R11. $25.00

SACKHEIM & SHAHN. *Blue Line: Collection of Blues Lyrics.* 1969. Tokyo/NY. Mushinsha/ Grossman. 1st. F/NF. B2. $150.00

SACKS, Oliver. *Migraine: Understanding a Common Disorder.* 1985. Berkeley. U CA. revised. F/clip. C9. $25.00

SACKVILLE-WEST, Vita. *Grand Canyon, a Novel.* 1942. Doubleday Doran. 1st. 8vo. 304p. wht cloth. VG/dj. F7. $80.00

SACKVILLE-WEST, Vita. *Sackville-West's Garden Book.* 1983 (1968). NY. photos/index. 250p. sc. F. B26. $15.00

SACKVILLE-WEST, Vita. *Saint Joan of Arc.* 1936. NY. Literary Guild. 1st thus. photos. 395p. VG/dj. A25. $15.00

SADLEIR, Michael. *XIX Century Fiction: A Bibliographic Record.* 1992. Cambridge, MA. 2 vol. facs. 1/350. gilt cloth. M24. $200.00

SADLER, Mark; see Lynds, Dennis.

SAFER, Morley. *Flashbacks: On Returning to Vietnam.* 1990. Random. 1st. F/NF. R11. $15.00

SAFIRE, William. *Freedom: Novel of Abraham Lincoln & Civil War.* 1987. NY. Doubleday. 1st. NF/clip. A14. $17.50

SAGAN, Carl. *Broca's Brain.* 1979. Random. 1st. NF/dj. A24. $30.00

SAGAN, Carl. *Murmurs of Earth...* 1978. Random. ils. 273p. dj. K5. $20.00

SAGAN, Francoise. *Heart Keeper.* 1968. London. John Murray. 1st. VG/VG. B3. $15.00

SAGAN, Francoise. *Those Without Shadows.* 1957. Dutton. 1st. NF/NF. H11. $25.00

SAGAN & SHKLOVSKII. *Intelligent Life in the Universe.* 1966. SF. Holden Day. 1st. F/NF. B4. $350.00

SAGE, Dean. *Salmon & Trout.* 1902. 72186 1st. ils AB Frost. 417p. G. H10. $35.00

SAGE, Lee. *Last Rustler: Autobiography of Lee Sage.* 1930. Little Brn. 1st. 303p. cloth. D11. $50.00

SAGER, Floyd. *Col Sager, Practioner.* 1980. Lexington. The Blood-Horse. 1st. VG. O3. $25.00

SAGGS, H.W.F. *Civilization Before Greece & Rome.* 1989. London. Batsford. ils/3 maps/ map ep. 322p. VG/dj. Q2. $27.00

SAHADI, Lou. *Pirates.* 1980. Times. 1st. F/VG+. P8. $30.00

SAHM, J.A. *Through South America's Southland: With an Account...* 1916. Appleton. 1st. ils. cloth. G. A2. $40.00

SAHN, Timothy. *Dark Force Rising.* 1992. NY. Bantam. 1st. F/dj. M23. $30.00

SAHN, Timothy. *Last Command.* 1993. Bantam. 1st. F/dj. M23. $20.00

SAINSBURY, Noel. *Cracker Stanton.* 1934. Cupples Leon. 1st. VG/dj. P8. $20.00

SAINSBURY, Noel. *Gridiron Grit.* 1934. NY. Cupples. 1st. VG. T12. $15.00

SAINT, Dora Jessie. *Farther Afield.* 1975. Boston. ils John Goodall. VG/dj. M17. $15.00

SAINT, Dora Jessie. *Miss Read's Christmas Book.* 1992. London. Michael Joseph. 1st. ils Tracey Williamson. F/dj. A14. $28.00

SAINT, Dora Jessie. *School of Thrush Green.* 1987. London. Michael Joseph. 1st. F/dj. A14. $28.00

SAINT, H.F. *Memoirs of an Invisible Man.* 1987. Atheneum. 1st. F/F. H11. $35.00

SAINT-GAUDENS, Augusta. *Augustua Saint-Gaudens.* 1948. NY. Am Sculptors #8. photos. VG. M17. $25.00

SAINT-GAUDENS, Homer. *American Artist & His Times.* 1941. Dodd Mead. 1st. 332p. cloth. VG. D2. $25.00

SAINT-JOHN, Bayle. *Montaigne, the Essayist: A Biography.* 1858. London. 2 vol. 3-quarter gr leather/marbled brd. VG. M17. $60.00

SAINT-JOHN, Christopher. *Ellen Terry & Bernard Shaw.* 1932. Putnam. 334p. VG. C5. $12.50

SAINT-JOHN, John. *Britain's Railways Today.* 1954. Naldrett. 1st. VG/dj. M20. $22.00

SAINTINE, X.B. *Picciola: Prisoner of Fenestrella; or, Captivity Captive.* 1893. Appleton. 1st. 8vo. 221+6p ads. VG. B11. $35.00

SAINTSBURY, George. *Notes on a Cellar-Book.* 1933. Macmillan. 1st. F/NF. M19. $25.00

SAITO & WADA. *Magic of Trees & Stones: Secrets of Japanese Gardening.* 1965. NY. Japan Pub. 2nd. 282p. VG/dj. A10. $35.00

SAJOUS, C. *Diseases of the Nose & Throat.* 1888 (1885). ils/pl. 439p. xl. VG. E6. $65.00

SALA, George. *Thorough Good Cook: Series of Chats on Culinary Art...* 1896. 1st. lg sq 8vo. 490p. VG. E6. $75.00

SALAZAR, Adolfo. *Music in Our Time in Music Since the Romantic Era.* 1946. Norton. 1st. 367p. G. C5. $12.50

SALE, Edith Tunis. *Interiors of Virginia Houses of Colonial Times.* 1927. Wm Byrd. 1st. 503p. VG. B10. $65.00

SALINGER, J.D. *Complete Uncollected Short Stories, Vols 1 & 2.* nd. np. 2 vol. 2nd. pict bdg. F. B2. $175.00

SALINGER, J.D. *Franny & Zooey.* 1961. Little Brn. 1st. F/NF. B4. $500.00

SALINGER, J.D. *Raise High the Roofbeam, Carpenters & Seymour.* 1963. Little Brn. 3rd. VG/dj. R14. $30.00

SALINGER, Pierre. *America Held Hostage. The Secret Negotiations.* 1981. Doubleday. 1st. 8vo. ils. 349p. VG/dj. W1. $18.00

SALISBURY, Harrison E. *Behind the Lines: Hanoi, December 23, 1966-January 7, 1967.* 1967. Harper Row. stated 1st. 243p. NF/dj. R11. $30.00

SALISBURY, Harrison E. *Russia in Revolution 1900-1930.* 1978. Holt Rinehart. 1st. F/torn. P12. $20.00

**SALLIS, James.** *Long-Legged Fly.* 1992. Carroll Graf. 1st. author's 1st book. F/dj. A24. $45.00

**SALMON, George.** *Infallibility of the Church.* 1959. Baker. 497p. VG/dj. B29. $14.50

**SALMON, J.B.** *Wealthy Cornith: A History of the City to 338 BC.* 1986 (1984). Clarendon. ils/figures. 464p. VG/dj. Q2. $22.00

**SALSBURY, Cora B.** *Forty Years in Desert: History of Ganado Mission 1901-41.* 1948. np. 8vo. 63p. VG/heavy pict wrp. F7. $35.00

**SALSBURY & SALSBURY.** *Two Captains West: Story in Picture & Text...* 1950. Superior. photos/maps. 235p. VG/dj. J2. $175.00

**SALT, A.E.W.** *Imperial Air Routes.* 1930. London. Murray. 1st. 280p. VG. B18. $75.00

**SALT & WILK.** *Birds of Alberta.* 1958. Edmonton. 1st. ils/maps. 511p. F/NF. C12. $40.00

**SALTA, Romeo.** *Pleasures of Italian Cooking.* 1967 (1962). VG/VG. E6. $15.00

**SALTEN, Felix.** *Bambi.* 1923. Berlin. Ullstein. 1st. 8vo. 186p+4p ads. NF/gr morocco clamshell case. H5. $2,250.00

**SALTEN, Felix.** *Bambi.* 1942. Grosset Dunlap. 1st. ils Disney. pict brd. VG/dj. D1. $85.00

**SALTER, James.** *Dusk & Other Stories.* 1988. Northpoint. 1st. F/F. B3. $75.00

**SALTER, Lord.** *Development of Iraq: A Plan of Action.* 1955. Iraq Development Brd. 2 fld plans. 252p. VG. Q2. $30.00

**SALVATOR, Ludwig Louis.** *Eine Blume aus dem Goldenen Lande, Oder Los Angeles.* 1878. Prag. Heinrich Mercy. 1st. 12 woodcuts. 258p. D11. $350.00

**SALZMANN, Theodor.** *Die Lieder des Zupfgeigenhansl.* 1931. Hofmeister. 186p. G. C5. $12.50

**SAMISH, R.M.** *Recent Advances in Plant Nutrition.* 1971. Gordon Breach. 2 vol. xl. VG. S5. $100.00

**SAMPSON, Anthony.** *Seven Sisters: Great Oil Companies & World They Made.* 1975. NY. Viking. 1st. 8vo. 334p. NF/dj. W1. $25.00

**SAMS, Ferrol.** *Whisper of the River.* 1984. Peachtree. 1st. ils Wm Cawthorne. VG/VG. B30. $25.00

**SAMUEL, C.** *Chilkat Dancing Blanket.* 1990. OK U. ils. 234p. VG. M4. $15.00

**SAMUEL, Edmund.** *Order: In Life.* 1972. Prentice Hall. 403p. xl. VG. S5. $15.00

**SAMUELS, E.A.** *Our Northern & Eastern Birds.* 1883. NY. 1st. ils. 600p. pict cloth. VG. C12. $35.00

**SAMUELS, S.** *Diagnosis & Treatment of Diseases of Peripheral Arteries.* 1936. Oxford. Medical Pub. VG. E6. $15.00

**SAN LAZZARO.** *Homage to Henri Matisse.* 1970. 182 ils. 126p. F/F. A4. $55.00

**SANCHEZ, Thomas.** *Rabbit Boss.* 1973. Knopf. 1st. inscr. F/dj. M25. $60.00

**SANCHEZ-MAZAS, Miguel.** *Spain in Chains.* 1959. NY. VALB. 32p. F/self wrp. B2. $25.00

**SAND, Algo.** *Senor Bum in the Jungle.* 1932. NY. Nat Travel Club. Ils Robert Rotter. 319p. F3. $15.00

**SANDBURG, Carl.** *Abe Lincoln Grows Up.* 1959 (1954). HBW. sm 8vo. 180p. VG. T5. $15.00

**SANDBURG, Carl.** *Abraham Lincoln: War Years.* 1939. Harcourt Brace. 4 vol. photos. gilt bl cloth. VG. S17. $40.00

**SANDBURG, Carl.** *Address of...Before Joint Session of Congress.* 1959. Harcourt Brace. 1st. 1/750 on rag paper. gr cloth. F. M24. $50.00

**SANDBURG, Carl.** *Address...at Ceremony Opening Centennial Exhibition...* 1961. WA. Lib of Congress. 1st. 1/1000. rust cloth. F. M24. $25.00

**SANDBURG, Carl.** *Early Moon.* 1930. Harcourt Brace. 1st. 137p. cloth. VG. D4. $50.00

**SANDBURG, Carl.** *Lincoln Preface.* 1953. Harcourt Brace. 1st. 1/2850. prt decor brd. F. M24. $25.00

**SANDBURG, Carl.** *Remembrance Rock.* 1948. Harcourt Brace. 1st trade. 1067p. G/dj. G11. $20.00

**SANDBURG, Carl.** *Rootabaga Stories.* 1989. HBJ. 1st. 4to. F/dj. B17. $30.00

**SANDBURG, Carl.** *Slabs of the Sunburnt West.* 1922. Harcourt Brace. 1st. NF/dj. Q1. $250.00

**SANDBURG, Carl.** *Storm Over the Land: Profile of the Civil War.* 1942. Harcourt Brace. 1st. 8vo. 440p. G/dj. S14. $22.50

**SANDBURG, Carl.** *Teddy Bear, Teddy Bear.* 1993. Morrow. 1st. 4to. ils/sgn Hague. F/dj. B17. $35.00

**SANDBURG, Helga.** *Sweet Music.* 1963. NY. Dial. 180p. G/dj. C5. $12.50

**SANDEMAN, Christopher.** *Wanderer in Inca Land.* 1949. Scribner. 1st. ils/fld map. 192p. F3. $25.00

**SANDER, Ellen.** *Trips: Rock Life in the Sixties.* 1973. NY. Scribner. 1st. F/NF. B4. $85.00

**SANDERS, Bruce.** *Blonde Blackmail.* (1945). London. Jenkins. 1st. F/NF. M15. $50.00

**SANDERS, Ed.** *Family: Story of Charles Manson's Dune Buggy Attack...* 1971. Dutton. 1st. VG/dj. B30. $25.00

**SANDERS, Lawrence.** *Dream Lover.* 1988. Severn House. 1st. rem mk. NF/dj. S18. $25.00

**SANDERS, Lawrence.** *Fourth Deadly Sin.* 1985. Putnam. 1st. VG/dj. G8. $10.00

**SANDERS, Lawrence.** *McNally's Luck.* 1992. Putnam. 1st. F/dj. N4. $20.00

**SANDERS, Lawrence.** *Rules of Prey.* 1989. Putnam. 1st. NF/NF. H11. $65.00

**SANDERS, Lawrence.** *Tenth Commandment.* 1980. Putnam. 1st. F/F. H11. $25.00

**SANDERS, Lawrence.** *Timothy Files.* 1987. Putnam. 1st. F/dj. T12. $25.00

**SANDERSON, Dwight.** *Rural Community.* 1932. Boston. Ginn. 723p. cloth. VG. A10. $20.00

**SANDERSON, Ivan.** *Animal Treasure.* 1937. Viking. 8vo. 325p. VG/VG. B11. $15.00

**SANDERSON, Ivan.** *Continent We Live On.* 1967. Random. 235 photos. F/dj. A19. $25.00

**SANDERSON, Ivan.** *Follow the Whale.* 1956. Little Brn. 1st. 8vo. 423p. VG/G. B11. $25.00

**SANDERSON, Ivan.** *History of Whaling.* 1993. NY. ils/charts. 423p. F/dj. M4. $25.00

**SANDERSON, Ivan.** *Living Mammals of the World.* 1955. NY. photos. 303p. VG. A17. $20.00

**SANDERSON, Ivan.** *Monkey Kingdom.* 1957. Garden City. ils. 200p. VG. S15. $20.00

**SANDERSON, Ruth.** *Story of the First Christmas.* 1994. Carousel. 1st. popup. F. B17. $15.00

**SANDFORD, John.** *Fool's Run.* 1989. Holt. 1st. F/F. H11. $55.00

**SANDFORD, John.** *Rules of Prey.* 1989. NY. Putnam. 1st. sgn. author's 1st book under this name. F/F. B3. $100.00

**SANDIFORD, Peter.** *Educational Psychology: Objective Study.* 1928. Longman Gr. 406p. VG. G1. $35.00

**SANDISH, Burt L.** *Lefty O' the Big League.* 1914. Barse Hopkins. 1st/1st issue (ils on glossy paper). F/VG+. B4. $300.00

**SANDLER, Irving.** *Triumph of American Painting.* 1970. NY. Praeger. 1st. 4to. F/VG. B11. $25.00

**SANDLIN, Tim.** *Sex & Sunset.* 1987. NY. Holt. 1st. sgn/dtd 1997. F/dj. R14. $75.00

**SANDLIN, Tim.** *Skipped Parts.* 1991. Holt. 1st. sgn. F/dj. O11. $25.00

**SANDLIN, Tim.** *Sorrow Floats.* 1992. NY. Holt. 1st. sgn. F/dj. R14. $40.00

**SANDLIN, Tim.** *Western Swing.* 1988. NY. Holt. 1st. F/dj. O11. $25.00

**SANDLIN, Tim.** *Western Swing.* 1988. NY. Holt. 1st. sgn. NF/NF. B3. $55.00

**SANDNER, David.** *Fantastic Sublime.* 1996. Greenwood. 1st. F. P3. $50.00

**SANDNER, Werner.** *Satellites of the Solar System.* nd. London. Scientific BC. ils/pl. 151p. VG. K5. $20.00

**SANDO, Joe S.** *Pueblo Nations: Eight Centuries of Pueblo Indian History.* 1992. Clear Light. 1st. ils. 282p. F/F. B19. $25.00

**SANDOR, Marjorie.** *Night of Music.* 1989. NY. Ecco. 1st. author's 1st book. F/F. H11. $25.00

**SANDOZ, Mari.** *Son of the Gamblin' Man.* 1960. NY. Clarkson Potter. 1st. sgn. F/NF. O11. $100.00

**SANDROF, Ivan.** *Massachusetts Town & More Massachusetts Towns.* 1963 & 1965. Barre, MA. 2 vol. 1st. sq 8vo. ils. VG. B11. $40.00

**SANDWEISS, M.A.** *Eyewitness to War: Prints & Daguerreotypes of Mexican War.* 1989. WA. 1st. ils/photos/maps. 368p. F/dj. M4. $65.00

**SANDYS, George.** *Anglorum Speculum; or, Worthies of England...* 1684. London. Passinger. 947p. 19th-C calf/red morocco spine label. K1. $250.00

**SANDYS & VAN DYKE.** *Upland Game Birds.* 1902. NY. Macmillan. 1st. Am Sportsman Lib. 429p. G. H10. $30.00

**SANE, Polly.** *Jack Sprat Cookbook.* 1973. Harper Row. VG/dj. M20. $15.00

**SANFORD, John.** *View From This Wilderness: American Literature as History.* 1977. Capra. VG/dj. M17. $20.00

**SANGER, George.** *70 Years a Showman.* 1926. NY. 1st. 249p. VG. B5. $30.00

**SANGER, Margaret.** *What Every Girl Should Know.* nd (1919). Girard, KS. 1st. Little Blue Book 14. 94p. VG/self wrp. A25. $12.00

**SANGER, Marjory Bartlett.** *World of the Great White Heron: Saga of Florida Keys.* 1967. Devin Adair. 1st. 8vo. ils. 147p. VG/G. B11. $25.00

**SANGER, Richard H.** *Arabian Peninsula.* 1954. Ithaca, NY. Cornell. 1st. ils/maps. 295p. VG/dj. W1. $35.00

**SANGER, William W.** *History of Prostitution: Its Extent, Causes & Effects...* 1858. NY. Harper. 1st. 8vo. 685p. O1. $425.00

**SANGSTER, Margaret.** *Women of the Bible: A Portrait Gallery.* 1911. NY. Christian Herald. F. w/sgn letter. V4. $100.00

**SANSON, Joseph.** *Sketches of Lower Canada, Historical & Descriptive...* 1817. NY. Kirk Mercein. 1st. 12mo. 301p. orig brd/later cloth rb/new ep. O1. $250.00

**SANSOVINO, Francesco.** *Concetti Politici.* 1578. Venice. Bertano. 4to. prt device on title. calf. R12. $450.00

**SANTAYANA, George.** *My Host the World.* 1953. London. Cresset. 1st. VG/dj. M10. $9.50

**SANTEE, Ross.** *Bubbling Spring.* 1949. Scribner. 1st. NF/VG. T11. $45.00

**SANTEE, Ross.** *Dog Days.* 1955. Scribner. 1st. ils. 244p. olive cloth. dj. w/2 sgn drawings. K1. $350.00

**SANTINI, Piero.** *Forward Impulse.* 1951. London. Country Life. 2nd. VG/G. O3. $35.00

**SANTMYER, Helen Hooven.** *...And Ladies of the Club.* 1984. NY. Putnam. ARC/1st. F/wrp. Q1. $45.00

**SANTOLI, Al.** *New Americans: An Oral History: Immigrants & Refugees...* 1988. Viking. 1st. VG/dj. N2. $10.00

**SANTOS-DUMONT, A.** *My Air-Ships.* 1904. Century. 1st. photos. 356p. cloth. B18. $195.00

**SAPPELLETTI, Mauro.** *Italian Legal System, an Introduction.* 1967. Stanford. M11. $45.00

**SAPPHIRE.** *Push.* 1996. Knopf. 1st. sgn/dtd 1996. AN/dj. B30. $40.00

**SARA, Dorothy.** *Sewing Made Easy.* 1977. Doubleday. 4th. 428p. H6. $18.00

**SARAVIA, Atanasio.** *Los Missioneros Muertos en el Norte de Nueva Espana.* 1943. Mexico. 2nd. 253p. wrp. F3. $15.00

**SARDI, V.** *Curtain Up at Sardi's.* 1957. 1st. VG/G+. E6. $15.00

**SARETT, Lews.** *Slow Smoke.* (1925). NY. Henry Holt. 1st. inscr/sgn. F. A18. $20.00

**SARF.** *Little Bighorn Campaign, March-Sept 1876.* 1993. photos/maps. 312p. F/F. A4. $35.00

**SARGANT, William.** *Battle for Mind: Physiology of Conversion & Brain Washing.* 1971. Perennial. 367p. VG/wrp. B29. $7.50

**SARGANT, William.** *Battle for the Mind.* 1957. Doubleday. 1st. 8vo. 263p. F/VG. H1. $20.00

**SARGENT, Charles Sprague.** *Manual of the Trees of North America.* 1933 (1905). Boston. 2nd. ils Chas Faxon/Mary Gill. VG/dj. B26. $32.50

**SARNOFF, Paul.** *Russell Sage: Money King, Man Who Banked the Tycoons.* 1965. NY. 1st. ils. VG/dj. M17. $15.00

**SAROS, Theodore.** *Christmas Lighting & Decorating.* 1954. Van Nostrand. 155p. VG. A10. $25.00

**SAROYAN, Aram.** *Genesis Angels: Saga of Lew Welch & the Geat Generation.* 1979. NY. Morrow. 1st. photos. rem mk. NF/wrp. R11. $10.00

**SAROYAN, William.** *Daring Young Man on the Flying Trapeze & Other Stories.* 1984. Yolla Bolly. 1/25 (200 total). sgn Prochnow w/extra suite pl. F/box. B24. $750.00

**SAROYAN, William.** *Human Comedy.* 1943. Harcourt Brace. 1st. NF/G. M19. $45.00

**SAROYAN, William.** *My Name Is Aram.* 1940. Harcourt Brace. 4th. 8vo. 220p. VG. W1. $14.00

**SAROYAN, William.** *Short Drive, Sweet Chariot.* 1966. NY. Phaedra. 1st. sm 8vo. 130p. VG/dj. W1. $22.00

**SARRE, Friedrich.** *Die Kunst des Alten Persiens.* 1923. Berlin. Cassirer. sm 4to. ils. 152 pl. cloth. xl. G. W1. $25.00

**SARTON, George.** *History of Science & New Humanism.* 1937. Cambridge. 1st. 196p. A13. $30.00

**SARTON, May.** *At Seventy: A Journal.* 1984. Norton. 1st. inscr/dtd 1984. 334p. dk gr cloth. NF/dj. J3. $85.00

**SARTON, May.** *Crucial Conversations.* 1975. Norton. 1st. F/F. B3. $45.00

**SARTON, May.** *Fur Person.* 1957. NY. Rhinehart. 1st. ils Barbara Knox. NF/NF. B3. $125.00

**SARTON, May.** *Joanna & Ulysses.* 1963. Norton. 1st. 8vo. 127p. NF/clip. J3. $55.00

**SARTON, May.** *Joanna & Ulysses.* 1963. NY. Norton. 1st. VG/dj. A24. $35.00

**SARTON, May.** *Journal of a Solitude.* 1973. Norton. 1st. VG/G. B30. $27.50

**SARTON, May.** *Magnificent Spinster.* 1985. Norton. 1st. NF/clip. S13. $10.00

**SARTON, May.** *Recovering: A Journal.* 1980. NY. Norton. 1st. NF/NF. B3. $30.00

**SARTON, May.** *Single Hound.* 1938. Houghton Mifflin. 1st. F/VG. B4. $500.00

**SARTRE, Jean-Paul.** *Between Existentialism & Marxism.* 1974. Pantheon. 1st. VG/G+. B30. $25.00

**SARTRE, Jean-Paul.** *Devil & the Good Lord.* 1960. Knopf. 1st Am. VG/dj. B30. $30.00

**SARTRE, Jean-Paul.** *In the Mesh.* 1954. Hunt Barnard. 1st. F/VG. B30. $50.00

**SARTRE, Jean-Paul.** *Iron in the Soul.* 1950. Hamish Hamilton. 1st. F/NF. B2. $65.00

**SARTRE, Jean-Paul.** *No Exit & the Flies.* 1947. Knopf. 1st Am. trans Stuart Gilbert. NF/dj. Q1. $150.00

**SARTRE, Jean-Paul.** *Saint Genet.* 1963. NY. 1st. VG/dj. B30. $40.00

**SARTRE, Jean-Paul.** *Search for Method.* 1963. Knopf. 1st Am. VG/dj. B30. $25.00

**SASSIENE, Paul.** *Comic Book: One Essential Guide for Comic Book Fans...* 1994. Chartwell. ils. VG/dj. M17. $20.00

**SASSON, Jean P.** *Princess: True Story of Life Behind Veil in Saudi Arabia.* 1992. Morrow. 1st. 8vo. ils. VG/dj. W1. $20.00

**SASSOON, Philip.** *Third Route.* 1929. Doubleday. 1st. 8vo. ils/map. 279p. VG/dj. W1. $45.00

**SASSOON, Siegfried.** *Heart's Journey.* 1927. London. Crosby Gaige/Heinemann. 1/591. sgn. NF. B2. $275.00

**SASSOON, Siegfried.** *Memoirs of a Fox Hunting Man.* 1929. Coward McCann. G. A21. $45.00

**SASSOON, Siegfried.** *Sassoon's Long Journey.* 1983. London. 1st. edit P Fussell. dj. T9. $20.00

**SATER, John E.** *Arctic Basin.* 1969. WA. Arctic Inst of N Am. 8vo. 337p. bl cloth. P4. $45.00

**SATTERTHWAIT, Walter.** *Sleight of Hand: Conversations With...* 1993. U NM. 1st. F/NF. P3. $25.00

**SATTERTHWAIT, Walter.** *Wilde West.* 1991. St Martin. 1st. sgn. F/dj. A24. $45.00

**SATURDAY EVENING POST EDITORS.** *Face of America.* 1957. Curtis. VG/tattered. S5. $10.00

**SATURDAY EVENING POST EDITORS.** *I Can Cook Children's Cookbook...* 1980. 1st. 4to. VG/dj. E6. $20.00

**SAUL, John.** *Homing.* 1994. Fawcett Columbine. 1st. F/dj. R8. $10.00

**SAUL, John.** *Shadows.* 1992. Bantam. 1st. NF/dj. L4. $20.00

**SAUNDERS, Blanche.** *Training You to Train Your Dog.* 1965. NY. revised. ils. 299p. VG/dj. A17. $8.50

**SAUNDERS, George.** *Civil War Land in Bad Decline.* 1996. Random. 1st. F/dj. B30. $30.00

**SAUNDERS, Hilary St. George.** *Per Ardua: Rise of British Air Power, 1911-1939.* 1945. London. 1st. ils. 355p. G. B18. $25.00

**SAUNDERS, Richard.** *Carolina Quest.* (1951). U Toronto. ARC. RS. VG/dj. A26. $40.00

**SAUNDERS, Thomas.** *Red River of the North & Other Poems of Manitoba.* 1969. Winnipeg, Manitoba. Peguis. 8vo. 59p. blk cloth. B11. $18.00

**SAVAGE, Henry.** *River of the Carolinas: The Santee.* 1956. NY. 1st. ils Lamar Dodd. 435p. VG/dj. B18. $35.00

**SAVAGE, Richard.** *Works of Richard Savage, Esq, Son of the Earl of Rivers...* 1777. London. T Evans. 2 vol. 8vo. contemporary flame calf/leather labels. H13. $295.00

**SAVAGE, Tom.** *Precipice.* 1994. Little Brn. 1st. author's 1st book. F/F. H11. $35.00

**SAVAGE, William W.** *Indian Life: Transforming an American Myth.* 1977. Norman, OK. F/dj. A19. $30.00

**SAVAGE-LANDOR, Henry.** *Across Unknown South America.* 1913. Boston. Little Brn. 1st Am. 439+377p. gilt bl cloth. H7. $150.00

**SAVARY, Jacques.** *Le Parfait Negociant, ou Instruction Generale...* 1752. Geneva. Gramer Philibert. Nouvelle ed. 2 vol. copper pl. modern calf. F. K1. $1,000.00

**SAVATER, Fernando.** *Childhood Regained: Art of the Storyteller.* 1979. Columbia. ils. VG/dj. M17. $20.00

**SAVILE, Lynn.** *Horses in the Circus Ring.* 1989. Dutton. 1st. obl rto. photos. VG/dj. O3. $15.00

**SAVILLE, Marshall H.** *Narrative of Some Things of New Spain..Temestitan, Mexico.* 1917. NY. Cortes Soc. 1/250. 93p. brd/cloth spine. D11. $100.00

**SAVINIO, Alberto.** *Childhood of Nivasio Dolcemare.* 1987. Eridanos. trans Richard Pevear/intro Dore Ashton. VG/dj. M17. $25.00

**SAVITT, Sam.** *America's Horses.* 1966. Doubleday. obl 4to. VG/G. O3. $25.00

**SAVITT, Todd.** *Medicine & Slavery: Diseases & Health Care of Blacks...* 1978. Urbana, IL. 1st. 168p. A13. $50.00

**SAVOY, Gene.** *On the Trail of the Feathered Serpent.* 1974. Bobbs Merrill. 1st. ils. 217p. dj. F3. $20.00

**SAWATZKY, Harry.** *They Sought a Country: Mennonite Colonization in Mexico.* 1971. Berkeley. 1st. 387p. dj. F3. $25.00

**SAWYER, Charles.** *BB King: Authorized Biography.* 1982. London. Quartet. 1st. NF/ils wrp. A14. $14.00

**SAWYER, Jesse.** *Studies in American Indian Languages.* 1971. U CA. charts. 217p. NF/sans. B19. $20.00

**SAWYER, Josephine Caroline.** *All's Fair in Love.* 1904. NY. Dodd Mead. ils CB Falls. xl. G. G11. $7.00

**SAWYER, Ruth.** *Journey Cake, Ho!* 1953. Viking. 1st. ils McCloskey. mc pict dj. R5. $300.00

**SAWYER, Ruth.** *Least One.* 1941. NY. Viking. 1st. tall 8vo. decor orange cloth. NF/dj. F1. $40.00

**SAWYER, Ruth.** *Maggie Rose, Her Birthday Christmas.* 1952. Harper. 1st. ils Sendak. VG+/$2.00 price dj. M5. $275.00

**SAWYER, Ruth.** *Roller Skates.* 1936. Viking. 1st. 8vo. 1937 Newbery. tan pict cloth. F/mc pict dj. R5. $200.00

**SAWYER, Ruth.** *Roller Skates.* 1936. Viking. 1st. 8vo. ils Valenti Angelo. 1937 Newbery Honor. VG/G. T5. $95.00

**SAXE, Stephen O.** *American Iron Hand Presses.* 1992. New Castle, DE. Oak Knoll. 1st. 8vo. cloth. F/dj. O10. $35.00

**SAXON & SUYDAM.** *Fabulous New Orleans.* 1952. New Orleans. Robert L Crager. F/VG. B11. $30.00

**SAYEGH, Fayez A.** *Discrimination in Education Against Arabs in Israel.* 1966. Beirut. Research Center Palestine Liberation Org. 16mo. VG/wrp. M7. $22.00

**SAYERS, Dorothy L.** *Creed or Chaos?* 1949. Harcourt Brace. 1st Am. VG/G. H10. $20.00

**SAYERS, Frances Clarke.** *Anne Carol Moore: A Biography.* 1972. Atheneum. 1st. 8vo. 303p. xl. VG/dj. C14. $14.00

**SAYERS, Nesta.** *Biological Glossary.* 1951. London. 1st. 168p. A13. $15.00

**SAYERS, Valerie.** *Brain Fever.* 1996. Doubleday. 1st. F/dj. R14. $25.00

**SAYLES, E.B. 'Ted.'** *Fantasies of Gold: Legends of Treasures...* 1968. Tucson, AZ. sgn. ils/notes/index. 136p. F/NF. B19. $35.00

**SAYLES, John.** *Bride of the Bimbos.* 1975. Little Brn. 1st. VG/dj. P8. $150.00

**SAYLES, John.** *Los Gusanos.* 1991. Harper Collins. ARC. sgn. F. O11. $35.00

**SAYLES, John.** *Los Gusanos.* 1991. Harper Collins. 1st. sgn. F/dj. O11. $35.00

**SAYLES, John.** *Union Dues.* 1979. Little Brn. 1st. 8vo. F/dj. S9. $100.00

**SAYLOR, Steven.** *Arms of Nemesis.* 1993. St Martin. 1st. sgn. F/dj. A23. $44.00

**SAYLOR, Steven.** *Murder on the Appian Way.* 1996. St Martin. 1st. sgn. F/dj. A23. $40.00

**SAYLOR, Steven.** *Roman Blood.* 1991. St Martin. 1st. sgn. author's 1st novel. F/NF. T2. $750.00

**SAYRE, Nora.** *Running Time: Films of the Cold War.* 1982. NY. Dial. 1st. F/VG. C9. $30.00

**SCADRON, Arlene.** *On Their Own: Widows & Widowhood in Am Southwest 1848-1939.* 1988. Urbana/Chicago. 1st. 324p. rust cloth. AN/dj. P4. $30.00

**SCADUTO, T.** *Mick Jagger: Everybody's Lucifer.* 1974. NY. 1st. VG/dj. B5. $17.50

**SCAMEHORN, Howard L.** *Buckeye Rovers in the Gold Rush.* 1965. Athens, OH. OH U. 1st. VG/dj. M20. $30.00

**SCAMMON, Charles.** *Marine Mammals of the Northwestern Coast of North America.* 1968 (1874). Dover. rpt. 319p. VG. S15. $12.00

**SCANLAND, John Milton.** *Life of Pat F Garrett & Taming of Border Outlaw.* nd. later prt. 42p. VG/wrp. B28. $22.50

**SCARBOROUGH, Elizabeth Ann.** *Godmother.* 1994. NY. Ace. 1st. F/NF. G10. $14.00

**SCARBOROUGH, Elizabeth Ann.** *Healer's War.* 1988. Doubleday. 1st. F/dj. M23. $40.00

**SCARBOROUGH, Elizabeth Ann.** *Healer's War.* 1988. Doubleday. 1st. sgn. F/dj. R11. $45.00

**SCARLETT, Roger.** *Black Bay Murders.* 1930. Doubleday Crime Club. 1s. inscr. F/dj. M15. $135.00

**SCARRY, Richard.** *Animals Merry Christmas.* 1950. Golden. VG. B17. $20.00

**SCAVULLO, Francesco.** *Scavullo on Men.* 1977. Random. VG. S5. $15.00

**SCAYLEA, Josef.** *Scaylea on Photography. How He Does It.* nd. Seattle. Superior. VG/dj. S5. $10.00

**SCHAAFSMA, Polly.** *Kachinas in the Pueblo World.* 1994. NM U. 1st. ils/biblio/index. 200p. F/F. B19. $20.00

**SCHACHNER, Nathan.** *Thomas Jefferson: A Biography.* (1957). Yoseloff. 2 vol. 5th. 1070. VG/fair. B10. $45.00

**SCHACHT, Al.** *Clowning Through Baseball.* 1941. Barnes. later prt. inscr. G+. P8. $40.00

**SCHAEFER, Jack.** *Heroes Without Glory: Some Goodmen of the Old West.* 1966. Andre Deutsch. 1st. sgn. 323p. NF/NF. B19. $100.00

**SCHAEFFER, Edith.** *L'Abri.* 1969. Tyndale. 1st Am. 228p. VG. B29. $13.00

**SCHAEFFER, Emil.** *Van Dyck: Des Meisters Gemaelde.* 1909. Stuttgart/Leipzig. Deutsche Verlags-Anstalt. 559p. teg. gilt red cloth. VG. D2. $45.00

**SCHAEFFER, Susan Fromberg.** *Anya.* 1974. Macmillan. 1st. sgn. F/dj. Q1. $40.00

**SCHAEFFER, Victor.** *Year of the Seal.* 1970. NY. Scribner. 1st. 205p. cloth. F/dj. D4. $25.00

**SCHAEFFER & SCHAEFFER.** *Everybody Can Know.* 1973. Tyndale. 403p. VG/dj. B29. $10.00

**SCHAFER, Michael.** *Language of the Horse: Habits & Forms of Expression.* nd. London/NY. Kaye & Ward/Arco. 1st Am. VG. O3. $22.00

**SCHAFF, Morris.** *Jefferson Davis: His Life & Personality.* 1922. John Luce. 277p. VG. S16. $35.00

**SCHAFF, Philip.** *Creeds of Christendom With History & Critical Notes.* 1919. Harper. 966p. G. B29. $20.00

**SCHAFFNER, Franklin J.** *Worthington Minor.* 1985. Metuchen. Scarecrow. 296p. VG. C5. $15.00

**SCHAFFNER, Val.** *Algonquin Cat.* 1981 (1980). Delacorte. 2nd. 8vo. F/NF. C14. $17.00

**SCHALLER, George B.** *Mountain Gorilla.* 1988. U Chicago. ils. 429p. NF/wrp. S15. $10.00

**SCHALLER, George B.** *Year of the Gorilla.* 1964. Chicago. 260p. xl. VG. S5. $8.00

**SCHALLER, Julius.** *Das Seelenleben des Menschen.* 1860. Weimar. Hermann Bochlau. 476p. VG. G1. $100.00

**SCHAMA, Simon.** *Citizens: A Chronicle of the French Revolution.* 1989. Knopf. 1st. gilt wht cloth. VG/dj. P12. $20.00

**SCHAPIRO, Meyer.** *Cezanne.* 1965. Abrams. 3rd. 127p. F/VG+. T11. $25.00

**SCHATZ, Howard.** *Newborn.* 1996. Chronicle. 1st. VG/dj. S5. $10.00

**SCHATZ, Letta.** *Bola & the Oba's Drummers.* 1967. McGraw Hill. 1st. 156p. F/dj. D4. $30.00

**SCHAU.** *JC Leyendecker.* 1974. NY. F/dj. P13. $125.00

**SCHAUFFLER, Robert Haven.** *Florestan: Life & Work of Robert Schumann.* 1945. Holt. 574p. G. C5. $12.50

**SCHAW, Jane.** *Journal of a Lady of Quality: Being the Narrative...* 1923. Yale. 3rd. maps. 341p. VG. B10. $45.00

**SCHECHTMAN, Joseph B.** *Mufti & the Fuehrer: Rise & Fall of Haj Amin El-Husseini.* 1965. NY/London. Yoseloff. 8vo. ils. VG/dj. W1. $30.00

**SCHECTER, Ben.** *Game for Demons.* 1972. NY. Harper Row. 1st. VG/dj. L1. $20.00

**SCHEIBER, Harry N.** *Ohio Canal Era: Case Study of Government & Economy.* 1969. Athens, OH. 1st. map. 430p. VG/dj. B18. $45.00

**SCHEIBERT, H.** *Die 6 Panzer-Division 1937-1945, Bewaffnung, Einsatze...* 1975. Friedberg/Dorheim. 1st. ils/maps. 160p. VG/G. S16. $75.00

**SCHEICK, William J.** *Critical Response to HG Wells.* 1995. Greenwood. F. P3. $55.00

**SCHEIDT, Duncan.** *Jazz State of Indiana.* 1977. Pittsboro. 1st. F/wrp. w/TLS. B2. $40.00

**SCHELL, Jonathan.** *Military Half: Account of Destruction of Quang Ngai...* 1968. Knopf. 1st. NF/dj. R11. $25.00

**SCHELLIE, Don.** *Maybe Next Summer.* 1980. NY. Four Winds. 1st. 244p. F/dj. D4. $25.00

**SCHETKY, Ethel Jane.** *Dye Plants & Dyeing: A Handbook.* 1968 (1964). Brooklyn. ils. 101p. sc. B26. $12.50

**SCHEURL, Christoph.** *Libellus: De Sacerdotum...Presentia...Sacerdotu Defensoriu.* 1513. Nuremberg. Weyssenburger. 4to. modern wrp. R12. $750.00

**SCHEVILL, F.** *History of the Balkan Peninsula From Earliest Times...* 1971. NY. rpt (1922). 14+1 fld map. 558p. VG. Q2. $25.00

**SCHIENCK, Hilbert.** *Chronosequence.* 1988. Tor. 1st. AN/dj. M21. $15.00

**SCHIFF, Stuart David.** *Whispers III.* 1981. Doubleday. 1st. rem mk. NF/dj. G10. $14.00

**SCHIFF & YA'ARI.** *Israel's Lebanon War.* 1985. London/Sydney. Allen Unwin. 1st. ils. 320p. NF/dj. W1. $18.00

**SCHILDT, Goran.** *In the Wake of Ulysses.* 1953. Dodd Mead. 1st Am. 8vo. ils. F/VG. A2. $12.00

**SCHILLEBEECKX, Edward.** *Christ: The Experience of Jesus as Lord.* 1983. Crossroad. 925p. VG/wrp. B29. $10.50

**SCHILLER, Francis.** *Paul Broca Founder of French Anthropology Explorer of Brain.* 1979. UC Pr. ils. 359p. AN/dj. G7. $75.00

**SCHILLINGS, C.G.** *Flashlights in the Jungle.* ca 1906. Doubleday Page. lg 8vo. 782p. gr cloth. K1. $50.00

**SCHIMMEL & WHITE.** *Bert Geer Phillips & the Taos Art Colony.* 1994. NM U. 1st. ils. 352p. F/F. B19. $25.00

**SCHINDLER, Harold.** *Orrin Porter Rockwell: Man of God/Sun of Thunder.* 1966. Salt Lake City. U UT. 1st. 399p. brn cloth. VG/dj. F7. $65.00

**SCHINE, Cathleen.** *Rameau's Niece.* 1993. Ticknor. 1st. F/F. H11. $30.00

**SCHINE, Cathleen.** *To the Birdhouse.* 1990. FSG. 1st. F/F. H11. $40.00

**SCHINTO, Jeanne.** *Children of Men.* 1991. NY. Persea. 1st. F/dj. R14. $35.00

**SCHLEE, Ann.** *Proprietor.* 1983. NY. 1st. VG/dj. M17. $15.00

**SCHLEE, Susan.** *Edge of the Unfamiliar Place: History of Oceanography.* 1973. NY. 398p. F/dj. S15. $12.50

**SCHLEIN, Miriam.** *Puppy's House.* 1955. Chicago. Whitman. ils Katherine Evans. cloth/pict label. F/dj. D4. $35.00

**SCHLESINGER, Arthur M.** *Bitter Heritage: Vietnam & American Democracy 1941-1966.* 1967. Houghton Mifflin. 1st. VG/clip. R11. $20.00

**SCHLESINGER, Arthur M.** *Crisis of the Old Order.* 1956. Houghton Mifflin. 8th. 8vo. 557p. VG/F. W2. $25.00

**SCHLESINGER, Arthur M.** *Robert Kennedy & His Times.* 1978. Houghton Mifflin. 1st. sgn. G/dj. B30. $30.00

**SCHLESINGER, Benjamin.** *Jewish Family: A Survey & Annotated Bibliography.* 1971. Toronto. 187p. F/VG. A4. $25.00

**SCHLINDLER, Valentin.** *Lexicon Pentaglotton, Herbraicum, Chaldaicum, Syriacum...* 1637. London. Guilielmus Jones. 2 parts in 1. folio. contemporary calf/brass clasps. K1. $1,000.00

**SCHLOSSBERG, Herberg.** *Idols for Destruction.* 1983. Thos Nelson. 335p. VG/wrp. B29. $8.00

**SCHLOTTER & SVENDSEN.** *Experiment in Recreation With Mentally Retarded...* 1951. IL Dept Public Welfare. revised. 8vo. 142p. cloth. VG/dj. C14. $18.00

**SCHMIDT, John.** *Johns Hopkins: Portrait of the University.* 1986. Baltimore. 1st. 251p. dj. A13. $25.00

**SCHMIDT, Robert.** *Early European Porcelain as Collected by Otto Blohm.* (1953). Munich. Bruckmann. 4to. 284p. pict brd. dj. K1. $100.00

**SCHMIDTT, Martin F.** *Fighting Indians of the West.* 1948. NY. 1st. 270 photos. E1. $75.00

**SCHMITZ, James H.** *Tale of Two Clocks.* 1962. Torquil/Dodd Mead. 1st trade. VG/dj. M21. $75.00

**SCHNABEL, James.** *Policy & Direction: First Year US Army in Korean War.* 1973. WA. fld maps/photos/index. VG. S16. $25.00

**SCHNEIDER, James G.** *Navy V-12 Program: Leadership for a Lifetime.* 1987. Boston. 1st. photos. VG/dj. M17. $20.00

**SCHNEIDER, Linda H.** *Psychobiology of Human Eating Disorders: Preclinical...* 1989. NY Academy of Sciences. thick 8vo. 626p. prt stiff wht wrp. G1. $65.00

**SCHNEIDMAN, Edwin S.** *Psychology of Suicide.* 1970. Sci House. 1st. 8vo. 719p. NF. C14. $20.00

**SCHNELL, Donald E.** *Carnivorous Plants of the US & Canada.* 1972. Winston-Salem. ils. 125p. F/dj. S15. $10.00

**SCHNELL, Donald E.** *Carnivorous Plants of the US & Canada.* 1976. Winston-Salem. photos/range maps/drawings. 125p. F/dj. B26. $25.00

**SCHOEN, Max.** *Art & Beauty.* 1932. Macmillan. 230p. panelled thatched gr cloth/painted label. G1. $45.00

**SCHOENBERG, Robert.** *Mr Capone.* 1992. NY. Morrow. 1st. VG/dj. B5. $15.00

**SCHOENER, A.** *Harlem on My Mind. Cultural Capital of Blk America 1900-68.* 1968. Random. 1st. F/NF. B2. $85.00

**SCHOENHERR, Allan A.** *Natural History of California.* 1992. U CA. ils. 772p. F/dj. S15. $32.00

**SCHOFIELD, Donald F.** *Indians, Cattle, Ships & Oil: Story of WMD Lee.* 1985. U TX. 1st. ils. 205p. F/NF. P12. $10.00

**SCHOLEFIELD, Edmund O.** *Maerick on the Mound.* 1968. World. 1st. VG/dj. P8. $30.00

**SCHOLZ, Jackson.** *Batter Up.* 1946. Morrow. later prt. VG/G. P8. $45.00

**SCHOLZ, Jackson.** *Center Field Jinx.* 1961. Morrow. 1st. VG/G. P8. $55.00

**SCHOLZ, Jackson.** *Fielder From Nowhere.* 1948. Morrow. 1st. VG/dj. P8. $60.00

**SCHOOR, Gene.** *Billy Martin.* 1980. Doubleday. 1st. VG/dj. P8. $20.00

**SCHOOR, Gene.** *Joe DiMaggio.* 1980. Doubleday. 1st. F/VG+. P8. $75.00

**SCHOPEN, Bernard A.** *Ross MacDonald.* 1990. Boston. Twayne. 1st. F/dj. M15. $35.00

**SCHORI, Ward.** *Christmas Carols.* 1966. Evanston. mini. 1/196. 12 carols. aeg. gilt gr morocco. B24. $125.00

**SCHORR, Mark.** *Bully!* 1985. St Martin. 1st. xl. G/dj. L1. $10.00

**SCHORR, Mark.** *Diamond Rock.* 1985. St Martin. 1st. F/NF. G8. $20.00

**SCHOW, David J.** *Black Leather Required.* 1994. Ziesing. 1/300. sgn twice/drawing. ils/sgn A Fenner. F/case. S18. $70.00

**SCHOW, David J.** *Kill Riff.* 1988. Tor. 1st. author's 1st novel. F/dj. G10/M21. $15.00

**SCHOW, David J.** *Silver Scream.* Dark Harvest. 1/500. sgn by 21 contributors. AN/box. T12. $90.00

**SCHREIBER, J.** *Treatment by Massage & Muscle Exercise.* 1887. 1st Am. ils. VG. E6. $15.00

**SCHREINER, Samuel A.** *Place Called Princeton.* 1984. Arbor. 1st. ils. F/dj. A2. $15.00

**SCHRODER, John.** *Catalogue of Books & Manuscripts.* 1970. Cambridge. 1/450. dj. T9. $50.00

**SCHROEDER, Doris.** *Annette: Desert Inn Mystery.* 1961. Whitman. ils. 210p. VG. B36. $8.00

**SCHUBERT CLUB OF LOS ANGELES.** *Towers in the Sun.* 1941. Hollywood, CA. Oxford. poems by members of Poetry Division. F. A2. $8.50

**SCHUCHHARDT, C.** *Schliemann's Excavations: Archaeological & Historical Study.* 1891. London. Macmillan. ils. 361p. xl. M10. $35.00

**SCHUELER, Donald.** *Temple of the Jaguar.* 1993. Sierra Club. 1st. 253p. dj. F3. $25.00

**SCHULBERG, Budd.** *Harder They Fall.* 1947. Random. 1st. inscr/dtd 1993. VG/dj. R14. $50.00

**SCHULER, Stanley.** *Gardening in the East.* 1969. Macmillan. 407p. VG/dj. A10. $20.00

**SCHULIAN & SOMMER.** *Catalogue of Incunbula & Manuscripts in Army Medical Lib.* 1948. NY. ils. 361p. G7. $75.00

**SCHULLERY, Paul.** *Bear Hunter's Century: Profiles From the Golden Age...* 1988. Stackpole. 252p. F/dj. A19. $15.00

**SCHULLERY, Paul.** *Grand Canyon: Early Impressions.* 1981. Boulder. CO Assoc U Pr. 1st. 8vo. 195p. orange cloth. VG/dj. F7. $32.50

**SCHULMAN, Audrey.** *Cage.* 1994. Algonquin. 1st. author's 1st book. F/F. H11. $45.00

**SCHULTES, Richard.** *Hallucinogenic Plants: A Golden Guide.* 1976. Racine. Western/Golden. F/wrp. B2. $65.00

**SCHULTZ, James Willard.** *Indian Winter; or, With the Indians in the Rockies.* 1913. Houghton Mifflin. 228p. VG. H6. $35.00

**SCHULTZ, James Willard.** *My Life as an Indian.* 1983. NY. Beaufort. AN/dj. A19. $25.00

**SCHULTZ, James Willard.** *Sinopah the Indian Boy.* 1913. Houghton Mifflin. 1st. 4 pl. B14. $75.00

**SCHULTZ, Joy.** *West Still Lives: Book Based on Paintings & Sculpture...* 1970. Heritage. 1st. 132p. VG/dj. J2. $95.00

**SCHULTZ, Ken.** *Complete Book of Sport Fishing.* 1989. Mallard. 1st. 191p. NF/dj. T11. $35.00

**SCHULTZ, Philip.** *Like Wings.* 1978. Viking. 1st. inscr. F/NF. L3. $50.00

**SCHULZ, Charles.** *Sandlot Peanuts.* 1977. HRW. 1st. F/VG. P8. $35.00

**SCHULZ, H.C.** *Monograph on the Italian Choir Book.* 1941. SF. David Magee. 1/75. folio. w/vellum leaf from 16th-C Gradual. F. B24. $1,350.00

**SCHULZ & SMITH.** *Guidebook for Field Conference F: Central & South Central...* 1965. NE Academy Sciences. ils/maps. 141p. F/wrp. P4. $17.50

**SCHUMANN, Elka.** *Dream of the Dirty Woman: A Play in One Act...* 1980. Newark, VT. Janus. 1/85. sm 4to. 8p fld to panorama w/2 LP records. F/box. B24. $500.00

**SCHUMANN, Peter.** *St Francis Preaches to the Birds.* 1978. Newark, VT. Janus. 1/100. 28p panorama w/26 mc masonite relief prts. F. B24. $600.00

**SCHUTT, Arthur.** *This Flying Business: A Life of Arthur Schutt.* 1976. Melbourne. Nelson. 1st. inscr. ils/map ep. F/dj. T10. $35.00

**SCHUTZ & SCHULZ.** *Endangered Species in 5-D Stereograms.* July 1994. Bl Mtn Pr. 1st. ils. 32p. F/dj. B27. $45.00

**SCHUYLER, Montgomery.** *Westward the Course of Empire...* 1906. NY. Putnam. ils. 198p. cloth. dj. D11. $45.00

**SCHWANITZ, Franz.** *Origin of Cultivated Plants.* 1966. Cambridge. ils/biblio/index. 175p. VG/dj. B26. $22.50

**SCHWANTES, Carlos A.** *Bisbee: Urban Outpost on the Frontier.* 1992. Tucson, AZ. 1st. ils/notes/index. 143p. F/F. B19. $25.00

**SCHWARKOPF, Chet.** *Heart of the Wild: Animal Stories of California...* 1969. Caxton. enlarged ed. ils. cloth. VG. B27. $45.00

**SCHWARTZ, B.D.** *Pasolini Requiem.* 1992. NY. 1st. dj. T9. $20.00

**SCHWARTZ, Delmore.** *I Am Cherry Alive, the Little Girl Sang.* 1979. Harper Row. 1st thus. sgn pres. ils Barbara Cooney. pict brd. R5. $85.00

**SCHWARTZ, Delmore.** *Summer Knowledge: New & Selected Poems: 1938-1958.* 1959. Doubleday. 1st. F/NF. O11. $175.00

**SCHWARTZ, Delmore.** *Vaudeville for a Princess: And Other Poems.* 1950. New Directions. 1st. yel cloth. F/clip. Q1. $200.00

**SCHWARTZ, Douglas W.** *On the Edge of Splendor: Exploring Grand Canyon...* nd. School Am Research. 4to. 80p. F/stiff wrp. F7. $15.00

**SCHWARTZ, Jeffrey.** *Red Ape.* 1987. London. ils. 337p. F/dj. S15. $12.00

**SCHWARTZ, Leonhard.** *Die Neurosen und die Dynamischen Psychologie Pierre Janet.* 1951. Basel. Benno Schwabe. 465p. prt blk cloth. VG/dj. G1. $75.00

**SCHWARTZ, Lynn Sharon.** *Fatigue Artist.* 1995. Scribner. 1st. F/dj. R14. $25.00

**SCHWARTZ, Richard.** *Boswell's Johnson, a Preface to the Life.* 1978. Madison, WI. 1st. H13. $35.00

**SCHWARTZ, Richard.** *Samuel Johnson & the New Science.* 1971. Madison, WI. 1st. H13. $35.00

**SCHWARTZ.** *Latin American Films, 1932-1994.* 1997. 303p. NF. A4. $65.00

**SCHWARTZOTT, Carol.** *King Zada's Song.* 1995. Niagara Falls. mini. 1/95. sgn. french-fold. pk brd/prt label. B24. $75.00

**SCHWARZ, Jordan A.** *Interregnum of Despair: Hoover, Congress & the Depression.* 1970. Urbana, IL. 1st. F/dj. A2. $20.00

**SCHWARZ-BART, Andre.** *Last of the Just.* nd. NY. MJF Books. 1st hus. F/dj. G10. $20.00

**SCHWATKA, Frederick.** *Report of Military Reconnaissance in Alaska...1883.* 1885. GPO. 1st. 20 fld maps. 121p. xl. B14. $50.00

**SCHWEIGGER, C.** *Handbook of Ophthalmology.* 1878. Lippincott. 1st Am. 555+12p. gilt blk bdg. VG. H7. $35.00

**SCHWEIGHARDT, Joan.** *Island.1* 1992. Sag Harbor. Permanent. 1st. author's 1st book. F/dj. R14. $25.00

**SCHWEITZER, Albert.** *Paul & His Interpreters.* 1948. Black. 252p. G. B29. $22.50

**SCHWEITZER, Darrell.** *Discovering Stephen King.* 1985. Starmont. 1st. AN/sans. T12. $18.00

**SCHWERDT.** *Hunting, Hawking, Shooting... A Catalogue.* nd. 4 vol in 2. 1/150. rpt. 3000 entries. 1135p. F. A4. $150.00

**SCIOLINO, Elaine.** *Outlaw State: Saddam Hussein's Quest for Power...* 1991. NY. Wiley. 1st. 8vo. ils/dbl-p map. NF/dj. W1. $18.00

**SCIPIO, Rudolf.** *Aus Fernen Zonen Orei Erzahlu.* German text. G. A19. $25.00

**SCOGGIE, W. Graham.** *Psalms.* nd. Harper. 2 vol. VG/dj. B29. $25.00

**SCOTT, Ann Herbert.** *On Mother's Lap.* (1972). McGraw Hill. ils Glo Coalson. unp. VG+/G+. T5. $30.00

**SCOTT, Anna M.** *Year With the Fairies.* 1914. Chicago. Volland. 1st. ils MT Ross. VG. D1. $275.00

**SCOTT, Arthur L.** *Mark Twain, Selected Criticism.* 1955. Dallas. SMU. 1st. gilt bl cloth. F/dj. M24. $45.00

**SCOTT, Bernard Brandon.** *Hollywood Dreams & Biblical Stories.* 1993. Fortress. 297p. VG/wrp. B29. $12.00

**SCOTT, Everett.** *Third Base Thatcher.* ca 1925. Grosset Dunlap. rpt. G+. P8. $35.00

**SCOTT, Genio C.** *Fishing in American Waters: 1888.* 1989. Castle. facs of 1888? ils. 539p. F/dj. A17. $15.00

**SCOTT, Geoffrey.** *Portrait of Zelide.* 1925. Scribner. 1st. bl brd/blk linen spine. VG. H13. $65.00

**SCOTT, Geoffrey.** *Portrait of Zelide.* 1934. London. Constable. ils. VG/dj. H13. $35.00

**SCOTT, George D.** *Inmate: Casebook Revelations of Canadian...* 1972. Montreal. Optimum. 1st. F/dj. A26. $15.00

**SCOTT, H.A.** *Blue & White Devils: Third Infantry Division.* 1984. Tenn. 1st. ils/maps. 173p. VG/dj. S16. $28.50

**SCOTT, Jack Denton.** *Spargo.* 1917. Cleveland. World. 1st. F/F. H11. $20.00

**SCOTT, Joanna.** *Arrogance.* 1990. NY. Linden. 1st. F/dj. A24. $25.00

**SCOTT, Justin.** *Hardscape.* 1994. Viking. 1st. sgn. Ben Abbott mystery. F/dj. T2. $35.00

**SCOTT, Justin.** *Rampage.* 1986. S&S. 1st. NF/F. S18. $20.00

**SCOTT, Justin.** *Shipkiller.* 1978. NY. Dial/James Wade. 1st. NF/dj. A14. $28.00

**SCOTT, Justin.** *Stone Dust.* 1995. NY. Viking. 1st. Ben Abbott mystery. F/dj. T2. $20.00

**SCOTT, Kathryn Leigh.** *My Scrapbook: Memories of Dark Shadows.* 1986. LA. Pomgranite. 1st. VG/dj. L1. $55.00

**SCOTT, Melissa.** *Trouble & Her Friends.* 1994. NY. Tor. 1st. F/NF. G10. $14.00

**SCOTT, Morgan.** *New Boys at Oakdale.* ca 1913. AL Burt. rpt. VG. P8. $17.50

**SCOTT, Morgan.** *Rival Pitchers of Oakdale.* 1911. Hurst. 1st. G+. P8. $25.00

**SCOTT, Natalie.** *Gourmet's Guide to New Orleans.* 1939. New Orleans. Stafford. G/wrp. A16. $15.00

**SCOTT, Paul.** *Division of the Spoils.* 1975. Morrow. 1st Am. F/dj. Q1. $45.00

**SCOTT, Paul.** *Jewel in the Crown.* 1955. London. 1st. dj. T9. $75.00

**SCOTT, Robert L.** *God Is My Co-Pilot.* 1943 (1943). Scribner. early prt. 8vo. 277p. VG/fair. M7. $25.00

**SCOTT, Walter.** *Ivanhoe: A Romance.* 1918. Chicago. ils Milo Winter. 637p. pict label. VG. B18. $25.00

**SCOTT, Walter.** *Waverley; or, 'Tis Sixty Years Since.* 1814. Edingurgh. Ballantyne for Constable. 3 vol. 1st. 12mo. VG/case. H5. $1,500.00

**SCOTT, Winifred Townley.** *Mr Whittier & Other Poems.* 1948. Macmillan. 1st. F. A18. $15.00

**SCOTTI, R.A.** *Hammer's Eye.* 1988. DIF. 1st. F/dj. T12. $25.00

**SCRIPTURE, Edward Wheeler.** *Thinking, Feeling, Doing: An Intro to Mental Science.* 1907 (1895). Putnam/Knickerbocker. 2nd revised. 12mo. 261p. prt brn cloth. VG. G1. $30.00

**SCRIVENER, Leslie.** *Terry Fox: His Story.* 1981. McClelland Stewart. 3rd. NF/dj. P3. $15.00

**SCUDAMORE, Frank.** *Sheaf of Memories.* ca 1925. Dutton. 1st. 8vo. 299p. cloth. VG. W1. $45.00

**SCULL, Andrew.** *Social Disorder/Mental Disorder: Anglo-American Psychiatry.* 1989. Berkeley. 1st. 360p. A13. $30.00

**SCULL, Florence.** *Bear Teeth for Courage.* 1964. Van Nostrand. 1st. author's 1st book. 163p. lib bdg (not xl). F. D4. $20.00

**SCULLY, Vincent.** *Architecture: Natural & Manmade.* 1991. St Martin. 1st. 388p. VG/wrp. S14. $17.50

**SCULLY, Vincent.** *Pueblo Mountain, Village, Dance.* 1972. Viking. sgn. VG/dj. A19. $60.00

**SCULLY & SCULLY.** *Official Motorists' Guide to Mexico.* 1937. Dallas. Turner. 238p. dj. F3. $15.00

**SEABURY, Samuel.** *Letters of a Westchester Farmer, 1774-1775...* 1930. Wht Plains, NY. Westchester Co Hist Soc. 162p. VG. M10. $37.50

**SEAGER, R.** *And Tyler Too.* 1963. NY. 1st. sgn pres. VG/dj. B5. $50.00

**SEAL, Basil;** see Barnes, Julian.

**SEALE, Bobby.** *Seize the Time.* 1970. Random. 1st. F/NF. B2. $40.00

**SEAMAN, Louise.** *Mr Peck's Pets.* 1947. Macmillan. 1st. 8vo. 96p. G. C14. $10.00

**SEAMON & WILSON.** *Encyclopedia of Modern Murder.* Arlington. 1st. F/dj. L4. $20.00

**SEARGEANT, Helen H.** *House by the Buckeye Road.* 1960. Naylor. sgn. 8vo. photos. 210p. gr cloth. VG. F7. $40.00

**SEARIGHT, James A.** *Record of Searight Family...* 1893. Uniontown, PA. 1st. 228p. deluxe morocco. NF. M8. $125.00

**SEARIGHT, Sarah.** *British in the Middle East.* 1969. Weidenfeld Nicolson. ils/96 pl/4 map. 215p. cloth. VG/dj. Q2. $36.50

**SEARLE, Ronald.** *Big Fat Cat Book.* 1982. Little Brn. 1st Am. NF. A24. $30.00

**SEARLE, Ronald.** *Searle in the Sixties.* 1964. Eng. Penguin. 1st. NF/wrp. Q1. $35.00

**SEARLS, Hank.** *Blood Song.* 1984. Villard. 1st. F/F. H11. $30.00

**SEARLS, Hank.** *Kataki.* 1987. McGraw. 1st. F/F. H11. $25.00

**SEARS, Alfred Byron.** *Thomas Worthington: Father of Ohio Statehood.* 1958. Columbus, OH. OH State. 1st. 260p. VG/dj. V3. $20.00

**SEARS, Clara Endicott.** *Gleanings From Old Shaker Journals.* 1916. Boston. photos. VG. M17. $45.00

**SEARS, Fred C.** *Productive Orcharding.* 1920 (1914). Phil. 2nd revised. ils. 315p. brn cloth. B26. $16.00

**SEARS, Stephen W.** *Civil War: Best of American Heritage.* 1991. Houghton Mifflin. 1st. F/clip. A14. $14.00

**SEARS, Stephen W.** *For Country, Cause & Leader: Civil War Journal...* 1993. 388p. F/F. A4. $55.00

**SEARS, Stephen W.** *To the Gates of Richmond: Peninsula Campaign.* 1992. NY. photos. VG/dj. M17. $20.00

**SEAVER, James E.** *Life of Mary Jemison: Deh-He-Wa-His: White Woman...* 1856. NY. Miller Orton Mulligan. 4th. 312p. cloth. H7. $90.00

**SEAVER, James E.** *Narrative of Life of Mary Jemison...* 1932. NY. later ed. ils. 459p. teg. B18. $45.00

**SEBASTIAN, Tim.** *Spy Shadow.* 1990. Delacorte. 1st. F/F. H11. $20.00

**SEDELMAYR, Jacobo.** *Jacobo Sedelmayr: Missionary, Frontiersman, Explorer...* 1955. AZ Pioneer Hist Soc. 1/600. fld map. 82p. dj. D11. $40.00

**SEE, Carolyn.** *Golden Days.* 1976. 1st. VG/dj. M17. $15.00

**SEEGER, Alan.** *Letters & Diary of Alan Seeger.* 1917. Scribner. 1st. sm 8vo. 218p. gilt cloth. G+. M7. $55.00

**SEEGMILLER & VAN SICKLE.** *Riverside Readers Primer.* 1911. Houghton Mifflin. ne. 128p. NF. W2. $25.00

**SEELY, L.** *Mrs Seely's Cookbook: A Manual of French & American...* 1908 (1902). 50 photos. 432p. VG. E6. $125.00

**SEFERIS (SEFERIADES), George.** *On the Greek Style.* 1966. Little Brn. 1st Eng-language. 8vo. yel cloth. NF/dj. J3. $55.00

**SEGNIT & SEGNIT.** *Ugly Ducking.* 1993. Aladdin. 1st. popup. F. B17. $12.50

**SEGUIN, Edouard C.** *Idiocy: And Its Treatment by the Physiological Method.* 1994. NY. Classics of Psychiatry & Behavioral Sciences Lib. 457p. G1. $75.00

**SEGUIN, Jean-Pierre.** *Le Jeu de Carte.* 1968. Paris. Hermann. ils/bibliography. decor brd. NF. D2. $150.00

**SEILER, C.** *Diseases of the Throat, Nose & Naso-Pharynx.* 1883. 2nd enlarged. 77 text ils. VG+. E6. $60.00

**SEITZ, Don C.** *Tryal of William Penn & William Mead for Causing Tumult...* 1919. Boston. Marshall Jones. reissue of 1719 ed. M11. $85.00

**SELBY, John.** *Beyond Civil Rights.* 1966. Cleveland. 1st. 216p. VG/dj. B18. $25.00

**SELBY, John.** *Eagle & the Serpent.* 1977. Hippocrene. 1st. 163p. dj. F3. $15.00

**SELDEN, George.** *Chester Cricket's Pigeon Ride.* 1981. Farrar Strauss. 1st. 4to. F/dj. B17. $25.00

**SELDEN, George.** *Harry Cat's Pet Puppy.* 1974. FSG. 1st. 8vo. 168p. VG/G. T5. $45.00

**SELDES, George.** *Can These Things Be!* 1931. NY. VG. M17. $15.00

**SELF, Margaret Cabell.** *Happy Year.* 1963. Manhasset. Channel Pr. 1st. G/dj. O3. $18.00

**SELF, Margaret Cabell.** *Nature of the Horse.* 1977. Arco. VG/dj. O3. $18.00

**SELF, Will.** *Cock & Bull.* 1992. London. Bloomsbury. 1st. pict brd. F/sans. A24. $30.00

**SELF, Will.** *Cock & Bull.* 1992. London. Bloomsbury. 1st. sgn. F/dj. O11. $65.00

**SELF, Will.** *Cock & Bull.* 1993. Atlantic Monthly. 1st Am. sgn. F/dj. O11. $40.00

**SELF, Will.** *Gray Area & Other Stories.* 1994. London. Bloomsbury. 1st. sgn. sbdg. F. O11. $55.00

**SELF, Will.** *Junk Mail.* 1995. London. Bloomsbury. 1st. F/sans. O11. $30.00

**SELF, Will.** *My Idea of Fun.* 1994. Atlantic Monthly. 1st Am. sgn. F/dj. O11. $35.00

**SELF, Will.** *Quanity Theory of Insanity.* 1995. Atlantic Monthly. 1st Am. sgn. F/dj. O11. $25.00

**SELINKO, Annemarie.** *Disiree.* 1953. Morrow. 1st Am. 8vo. 594p. VG. W2. $30.00

**SELL, Frances E.** *Small Game Hunting.* 1955. Stackpole. photos. 158p. VG. A17. $8.50

**SELL & WEYBRIGHT.** *Buffalo Bill & the Wild West.* 1955. NY. OUP. VG/G. O3. $40.00

**SELLECK, George A.** *Quakers in Boston 1656-1964: Three Centuries...* 1976. Friends Meeting at Cambridge. 349p. wrp. V3. $12.00

**SELLEW, Catherine.** *Adventures With Heroes.* 1954. Little Brn. 1st. ils Steele Savage. G/dj. P2. $10.00

**SELLEY, L.B.** *Mrs Thrale: Afterwards Mrs Piozzi...* 1891. NY. Scribner. 1st. ils. gilt bl cloth. H13. $75.00

**SELOUS, F.C.** *Hunter's Wanderings in Africa.* 1925. London. Macmillan. ils/index. 504p. VG. B5. $90.00

**SELOUS, F.C.** *Sport & Travel: East & West.* 1988. Prescott. facs of 1900. 1/1000. leatherette. F. A17. $20.00

**SELTMAN, Charles.** *Greek Coins.* 1933. London. Methuen. ils/64 pl. 311p. xl. G. Q2. $25.00

**SELTZER, Richard.** *Mortal Lessons: Notes on the Art of Surgery.* 1976. NY. 1st. 219p. A13. $15.00

**SELVADURAI, A.P.S.** *Mechanics of Porelastic Media.* 1996. Boston. Kluwer. 1st. rem mk. F/sans. G10. $60.00

**SELZ, Peter.** *Work of Jean Dubuffet.* 1962. MOMA. ils+12p checklist. VG/wrp/dj. C9. $30.00

**SELZER, Richard.** *Confessions of a Knife.* 1979. NY. 1st. VG/dj. M17. $15.00

**SELZNICK, Irene Mayer.** *Private View.* 1983. Knopf. 1st. VG/dj. B11. $15.00

**SEMPLE, Robert.** *Memoirs on Diptheria From Writings of Bretonneau...* 1859. London. 1st. 407p. A13. $75.00

**SEN GUPTA & SUDIPTA.** *Catalogue of Meteorite Collection...Calcutta.* 1982. Calcutta. Geol Survey of India. Catalogue Series #1. 101p. K5. $27.00

**SENAULT, Jean Francois.** *Le Monarqve, ov Les Devoirs dv Sovverain.* 1664. Paris. sm 8vo. calf. R12. $350.00

**SENDAK, Maurice.** *Big Book for Peace.* 1990. Dutton. 1st. 120p. F/dj. w/poster. D4. $30.00

**SENDAK, Maurice.** *Birthday Party.* 1957. NY. Harper. 1st. obl 12mo. mc pict clip dj. R5. $175.00

**SENDAK, Maurice.** *Chicken Soup With Rice (Huhnersuppe Mit Reis).* 1977. Zurich. Diogenes. 1st German. sgn/orig drawing. F/wrp. D4. $225.00

**SENDAK, Maurice.** *In the Night Kitchen.* 1970. Harper Row. 1st. 4to. unp. VG/$4.95 dj. D1. $395.00

**SENDAK, Maurice.** *Little Bear.* 1957. Harper Row. 1st. inscr. NF. T11. $85.00

**SENDAK, Maurice.** *Outside Over There.* 1981. NY. Harper Row. 1st. 140p. F/dj. D4. $75.00

**SENDAK, Maurice.** *Ten Little Rabbits/A Counting Book.* 1970. Rosenbach Found. 1st. 32mo. NF/wrp. D1. $40.00

**SENDAK, Maurice.** *Where the Wild Things Are.* 1963. Harper. 1st. Caldecott Medal. F/1st issue. B4. $650.00

**SENIOR, Evan.** *Concert Goer's Annual No 2.* 1958. London. John Calder. 155p. G. C5. $12.50

**SENN, H. Recherche.** *Luncheon & Dinner Sweets.* 1911. London. 2nd. 174p. VG. E6. $35.00

**SENN, Nicholas.** *Around the World Via India: A Medical Tour.* 1905. Chicago. 1st. 347p. red buckram. xl. A13. $60.00

**SENNETT, Richard.** *Evening of Brahms.* 1984. London. Faber. 1st. NF/dj. A14. $21.00

**SENNETT, Ted.** *Laughing in the Dark.* 1992. St Martin. 341p. VG/dj. C5. $15.00

**SENTER, O.S.** *Health & Pleasure-Seeker's Guide...From Philadelphia...* 1873. Phil. Rogers. 1st. ils. 149p. G+. H7. $80.00

**SENZEL, Howard.** *Baseball: The Early Years.* 1960. Oxford. 1st. VG/dj. P8. $85.00

**SERANELLA, Barbara.** *No Human Involved.* 1997. St Martin. 1st. sgn. F/dj. M15. $100.00

**SERANNE, Ann.** *Complete Book of Desserts.* 1963. Doubleday. G/dj. A16. $10.00

**SERANNE, Ann.** *1,001 Ideas for Parties, Fairs & Suppers.* 1964. Doubleday. G/dj. A16. $10.00

**SEREDY, Kate.** *Chestry Oak.* 1948. NY. 1st. ils. VG/clip. B18. $45.00

**SERETTE, David W.** *Pig Tracks.* 1983. Sebasco. mini. 1/150. sgn. 30p+1¢ stp ftspc. pict wrp. B24. $95.00

**SERLING, Carol.** *Journeys to the Twilight Zone.* nd. NY. MJF Books. 1st thus. NF/dj. G10. $16.50

**SERRANO, Andres.** *Body & Soul.* 1995. NY. Takarajima. 1st. sgn. F/dj. O11. $125.00

**SERVEN, James.** *Cold Firearms From 1836.* 1981. Harrisburg. 401p. VG/dj. S16. $60.00

**SERVER, Lee.** *Over My Dead Body.* 1994. Chronicle. 1st. F/dj. P3. $30.00

**SERVICE, Robert W.** *Rhymes of a Red Cross Man.* (1916). Barse Hopkins. 1st Am. gilt gr cloth. NF. A18. $30.00

**SERVICE, Robert W.** *Spell of the Yukon & Other Verses.* 1915. NY. Barse Hopkins. ils. G. A19. $25.00

**SERVIES, James A.** *Siege of Pensacola, 1781: A Bibliography.* 1981. Pensacola. 1st. 42p. NF/prt wrp. M8. $38.00

**SERVISS, Garrett P.** *Astronomy With an Opera-Glass...* 1888. NY. Appleton. 1st. 8vo. 154p. gilt cloth. K5. $30.00

**SERVISS, Garrett P.** *Round the Year With the Stars.* 1910. NY. Harper. 1st. 10 charts. 147p. gilt cloth. K5. $25.00

**SETH, Vikram.** *Golden Gate.* 1986. Random. ARC. NF/NF. w/promo material & assn TLS. R14. $60.00

**SETH, Vikram.** *Golden Gate.* 1986. Random. 1st. author's 1st novel. F/NF. L3. $45.00

**SETH-SMITH, Michael.** *International Stallions & Studs.* 1974. NY. Dial. 1st Am. VG/dj. O3. $35.00

**SETO, Judith Roberts.** *Young Actors's Workbook.* 1979. Doubleday. 339p. VG/dj. C5. $12.50

**SETON, Ernest Thompson.** *Boy Scouts of America: A Handbook...* 1910. Doubleday Page. ils. 192p. F. A4. $395.00

**SETON, Ernest Thompson.** *Monarch, the Big Bear of Tallac.* 1904. Morang. 1st. ils. 214p. VG+. B19. $20.00

**SETON, Ernest Thompson.** *Sign Talk: Universal Signal Code, Without Apparatus...* 1918. Doubleday Page. 1st. ils. cloth. VG. B27. $295.00

**SETON, Ernest Thompson.** *Two Little Savages: Being Adventures of Two Boys.* 1922 (1911). Doubleday Page. 8vo. ils. 552p. G. T5. $15.00

**SETTLE, Mary Lee.** *Charley Bland.* 1989. NY. FSG. 1st. F/dj. M23. $18.00

**SETTLE, Mary Lee.** *O Beulah Land.* 1956. Viking. 1st. F/dj. B2. $40.00

**SETTLE, William.** *Jesse James Was His Name.* 1967. Columbia, MO. 2nd. VG. B5. $25.00

**SEUSS, Dr.;** see Geisel, Theodore Seuss.

**SEVERIN, T.** *Explorers of the Mississippi.* 1968. NY. 1st. ils. 294p. NF. M4. $20.00

**SEVERIN, T.** *In Search of Genghis Khan.* 1991. London. 1st. 276p. F/dj. M4. $18.00

**SEVERIN, T.** *Sinbad Voyage.* 1983. NY. Putnam. 1st Am. ils. NF/dj. W1. $22.00

**SEVERN, David.** *Cruise of the Maiden Castle.* 1949. Macmillan. 1st. NF/VG. P2. $25.00

**SEVERN, J. Millott.** *Life Story & Experiences of a Phrenologist.* 1929. London. private prt. 1st. ils. 505+4p. VG. H7. $50.00

**SEWALL, Richard B.** *Life of Emily Dickinson.* 1974. FSG. 2 vol. 1st. VG. M10. $60.00

**SEWARD, William H.** *Life & Public Services of John Quincy Adams...* 1849. Auburn. Derby. 1st. 8vo. 404p. VG. B14. $350.00

**SEWARD & SEWARD.** *Current Psychological Issues: Essays in Honor RS Woodworth.* 1958. NY. Holt. sgn. 360p. prt beige cloth. G1. $40.00

**SEWART, Alan.** *Educating of Quinton Quinn.* 1984. Robert Hale. 1st Eng. NF/dj. G8. $10.00

**SEWELL, Anna.** *Black Beauty.* ca 1953. London. Blackie. ne. G. T12. $18.00

**SEWELL, Anna.** *Black Beauty.* nd. Barse Hopkins. ils Hugo VonHofsten. G. A21. $20.00

**SEWELL, Anna.** *Black Beauty.* 1986. Random. 1st. F/dj. M25. $35.00

**SEWELL, Anna.** *Black Beauty.* 1986. Stamford, CT. Longmeadow. ils LK Welch. VG. O3. $16.00

**SEWELL, Anna.** *Black Beauty: Autobiography of a Horse.* ca 1912. London. Jarrold. 26 pl/ils Stokes & Wright. VG. M19. $45.00

**SEWELL, Anna.** *Black Beauty: Autobiography of a Horse.* 1879 (1877). Phil. Altemus. G. T12. $75.00

**SEWELL, Helen.** *ABC for Everyday.* 1930. Macmillan. 1st. 4to. pict brd. mc pict dj. R5. $275.00

**SEWELL, Henry.** *Letter to Lord Worsley on Burthens Affecting Real Property.* 1846. London. Butterworth. pres. modern wrp. M11. $275.00

**SEWELL, William.** *History of Rise, Increase & Progress of Christian People...* 1823. Phil. Kite. 2 vol. worn leather. V3. $55.00

**SEXTUS, F.** *Hypnotism: Its Facts, Theories & Related Phenomena.* 1893. 1st. ils. E6. $45.00

**SEYBOLD, David.** *Fathers & Sons: An Anthology.* 1992. Grove Weidenfeld. 1st. sgn 5 contributors. F/dj. O11. $75.00

**SEYDOR, Paul.** *Peckinpah: Western Films.* 1980. Urbana. U IL. 5-line inscr. ils. 302p. blk cloth. K1. $35.00

**SEYMOUR, Alta Halverson.** *Grandma for Christmas.* 1946. Phil. Westminster. 1st. sm 8vo. VG/dj. M21. $45.00

**SEYMOUR, Catryna Ten Eyck.** *Enjoying the Southwest.* 1973. Lippincott. 1st. 8vo. brn brd. VG/dj. F7. $17.50

**SEYMOUR, Frank C.** *Flora of New England.* 1969. Rutland. 1st. 596p. VG/dj. B26. $42.50

**SEYMOUR, Frederick.** *Wild Animals I Have Met.* 1901. np. Neil. ils/photos. 544p. G. A17. $20.00

**SEYMOUR, Harold.** *Baseball: The Early Years (and) Baseball: The Golden Years.* 1960 & 1971. NY. Oxford. 2 vol. F/NF case. B2. $85.00

**SEYMOUR, Horatio.** *Union, the Constitution & the Laws.* 1863. NY. Comstock Cassidy. 1st. 11p. self wrp. M8. $85.00

**SEYMOUR, W.** *Price of Folly: British Blunders in War...* 1995. London. 1st. ils/maps/plans. NF/rpr. M4. $30.00

**SEYMOUR-SMITH.** *Who's Who in 20th-Century Literature.* 1976. 414p. F/F. A4. $35.00

**SHAARA, Jeff.** *Gods & Generals.* 1996. NY. Ballantine. 1st. F/dj. T11. $35.00

**SHAARA, Michael.** *Killer Angels.* 1974. NY. McKay. 1st. F/dj. B4. $1,250.00

**SHABERMAN, Raphel B.** *George MacDonald: A Bibliographical Study.* 1990. Omnigraphics. 1st ltd. 1/500. sgn. AN/dj. A27. $40.00

**SHACKLETON, E.H.** *Heart of the Antarctic Being Story of British...1907-1909.* 1909. Lippincott. 2 vol. 1st Am. pocket maps. VG. B11. $850.00

**SHACOCHIS, Bob.** *Easy in the Islands.* 1985. Crown. 1st. sgn. F/dj. D10. $110.00

**SHACOCHIS, Bob.** *Next New World.* 1989. Crown. 1st. sgn. F/dj. D10. $50.00

**SHACOCHIS, Bob.** *Next New World.* 1989. NY. Crown. 1st. author's 2nd book. F/dj. A24. $30.00

**SHAFFER, E.T.H.** *Carolina Gardens.* 1939. Chapel Hill. 326p. cloth. A10. $40.00

**SHAFFER, Peter.** *Black Comedy & White Lies.* 1967. NY. Stein Day. 123p. VG/dj. C5. $12.50

**SHAFFER, Peter.** *Collected Plays.* 1982. NY. 1st. VG/dj. M17. $40.00

**SHAGAN, Steve.** *Vendetta.* 1986. Perigord. 1st. F/F. H11. $25.00

**SHAH, Diane K.** *Dying Cheek to Cheek.* 1992. Doubleday. 1st. F/F. H11. $20.00

**SHAHN, Ben.** *For the Sake of a Single Verse...* 1968. NY. Shahn Trust. 1/950. sgn. w/23 lithos. loose. portfolio/box. B24. $2,500.00

**SHAHN, Ben.** *Photographic Eye of Ben Shahn.* 1975. Cambridge. 1st. 100+ photos. F/dj. S9. $85.00

**SHAINSBERG, Lawrence.** *Ambivalent Zen: A Memoir.* 1995. NY. Pantheon. 1st. VG/dj. N2. $10.00

**SHAKERY, Karin.** *Ortho's Complete Guide to Successful Houseplants.* 1984. Ortho. 1st. ils. 320p. VG. S14. $10.00

**SHAKESPEARE, Nicholas.** *Vision of Elena Silves.* 1990. Knopf. 1st Am. F/dj. A24. $25.00

**SHAKESPEARE, William.** *Complete Works of Shakespeare.* 1936. Doubleday Doran. 2 vol. 1/750. ils/sgn Kent. bl brd. VG. B11. $550.00

**SHAKESPEARE, William.** *Dramatic Works of William Shakespeare.* 1823. Cheswick. Whittingham. 12mo. dbl-column text/wood engravings. contemporary bdg. H5. $950.00

**SHAKESPEARE, William.** *Mercury Shakespeare, Twelfth Night.* 1939. Harper. edit Orson Welles/Roger Hill. VG+/sans. C9. $90.00

**SHAKESPEARE, William.** *Orthello.* 1973. Gehenna. 1/400. binder's copy. ils/sgn Baskin. deluxe blk morocco. box. B24. $1,500.00

**SHAKESPEARE, William.** *Romeo & Juliet.* 1884. London. Cassell. lg 4to. 53p. lg gr gilt cloth. VG. H5. $450.00

**SHAKESPEARE, William.** *Shakespeare: A Review & a Preview.* ca 1939. LEC. unp. VG. B18. $20.00

**SHAKESPEARE, William.** *Shall I Die? Shall I Fly?* 1986. Boston. Bromer. mini. 1/35 (160 total). hand illuminated Suzanne Moore. case. B24. $325.00

**SHAKESPEARE, William.** *Songs of Shakespeare.* 1903. London. Anthony Traherne. mini. Waistcoat Pocket Classic. 72p. blk stp red cloth. B24. $110.00

**SHAKESPEARE, William.** *Titus Andronicus.* 1973. Gehenna. 1/400. binder's copy. ils/sgn Baskin. gilt morocco. F/box. B24. $1,500.00

**SHAKESPEARE, William.** *Tragedie of Hamlet Prince of Denmarke.* 1930. Cranach. 1/300 on Maillol handmade. folio. teg. F/box. B24. $6,500.00

**SHAKESPEARE, William.** *Works of...* 1929-1933. Random. 7 vol. 1/500 (of 1600 total). teg. NF. H5. $2,500.00

**SHALE, Richard.** *Academy Awards Index.* 1993. Westport. Greenwood. 785p. VG. C5. $35.00

**SHALER, N.S.** *American Highways: A Popular Account of Conditions...* 1896. Century. 1st. 293p. ES. G+. B18. $47.50

**SHAMBAUGH, Bertha M.** *Amana: Community of True Inspiration.* 1908. Iowa City. State Hist Soc. VG+. B2. $75.00

**SHAMES, Laurence.** *Florida Straits.* 1992. S&S. 1st. author's 1st novel. F/F. H11. $40.00

**SHAMES, Laurence.** *Scavenger Reef.* 1994. S&S. 1st. F/dj. M15. $45.00

**SHAMES, Laurence.** *Sunburn: A Thriller.* 1996. NY. Hyperion. ARC/1st. F/dj. w/promo material. S9. $20.00

**SHANGE, Ntozake.** *Ridin' the Moon in Texas.* 1987. St Martin. 1st. NF/NF. R14. $30.00

**SHANK, Robert.** *Life in the Son: A Study of Doctrine of Perseverance.* 1962. Westcott. 380p. G/dj. B29. $11.00

**SHANKMAN, Sarah.** *He Was Her Man.* 1993. Pocket. 1st. F/dj. R8. $10.00

**SHANKMAN, Sarah.** *Keeping Secrets.* 1988. S&S. 1st. author's 2nd book. NF/dj. A24. $25.00

**SHANKMAN, Sarah.** *Now Let's Talk of Graves.* 1990. Pocket. 1st. VG/dj. R8. $15.00

**SHANKS, David C.** *Management of the American Soldier.* 1918. np. 1st. 80p. VG/wrp. M8. $25.00

**SHANKS, Elsie.** *Novae Narrationes. Completed With a Legal Introduction...* 1963. London. Bernard Quaritch. bl buckram. M11. $65.00

**SHANN, Renee.** *Air Force Girl.* 1943. Phil. Triangle/Blakiston. 1st thus. 275p. VG. A25. $10.00

**SHANNON, David A.** *Decline of American Communism.* 1959. Harcourt Brace. 1st. 8vo. VG/G. A2. $15.00

**SHANNON, Dell.** *Root of All Evil.* 1964. Morrow. 1st. VG/dj. G8. $12.50

**SHANNON, Fred A.** *Farmer's Last Frontier: Agriculture, 1860-1897.* 1945. Farrar Rhinehart. 1st. 8vo. VG/G. A2. $20.00

**SHANNON, George.** *Bean Boy.* 1984. Greenwillow. 1st. sm 8vo. unp. NF/VG. T5. $25.00

**SHANNON, Mike.** *Day Satchel Paige & Pittsburgh Crawfords...* 1992. McFarland. F. P8. $20.00

**SHANNON, Monica.** *California Fairy Tales.* 1957 (1926). NY. Stephen Day. rpt. xl. lib bdg. G+. T5. $22.00

**SHAPIRO, Irwin.** *Uncle Sam's 200th-Birthday Party.* 1974. NY. Golden. slim 4to. 45p. VG. B11. $15.00

**SHAPIRO, Laura.** *Perfection Salad: Women & Cooking...* 1986. 1st Am. VG/dj. M17. $15.00

**SHAPIRO, Mary J.** *How They Built the Statue of Liberty.* 1985. NY. ils Huck Scarry. VG/G. M17. $15.00

**SHAPIRO, Milton.** *Gil Hodges.* 1960. Messner. 1st. photos. F/VG. P8. $125.00

**SHAPIRO, Mitchell E.** *Television Network Weekend Programming 1959-1990.* 1992. McFarland. 464p. VG. C5. $12.50

**SHAPLEN, Robert.** *Forest of Tigers.* 1956. Knopf. 1st. F/NF. H11. $40.00

**SHARIFF, Omar.** *Eternal Male: Omar Shariff, My Own Story.* 1977. Doubleday. 1st. sgn pres. trans from French. 184p. VG/dj. w/mc photo. W1. $30.00

**SHARP, Ann Pearsall.** *Little Garden People & What They Do.* 1938. Akron. Saalfield. 1st. ils. pict brd. F/NF. T10. $125.00

**SHARP, Dallas Lore.** *When Rolls the Oregon.* 1914. Houghton Mifflin. 1st. sm 8vo. 251p. VG. S14. $35.00

**SHARP, Margery.** *Miss Bianco in the Orient.* (1970). Boston. Little Brn. 1st. ils Erik Blegvad. gilt red cloth. pict dj. R5. $50.00

**SHARP.** *Sources of Modern Architecture, a Critical Bibliography.* 1981. revised ed. 192p. F/F. A4. $35.00

**SHARPE, Philip B.** *Complete Guide to Handloading.* 1953. NY. Funk Wagnall. 3rd. ils/index. H10. $40.00

**SHARPE, Philip B.** *Rifle in America.* (1947). NY. 2nd/best. ils/pl. 782p. cloth. VG. M8. $125.00

**SHARPE, Philip B.** *Rifle in America.* 1938. NY. Morrow. 641p. xl. leatherette. fair. H10. $22.50

**SHARPLES, A.** *Scorpion's Tail.* 1975. Taplinger. 1st. VG/dj. O4. $15.00

**SHATNER, William.** *Star Trek Memories.* 1993. Harper Collins. 1st. F/dj. P3. $22.00

**SHATNER, William.** *Teklab.* 1991. Ace/Putnam. 1st. F/F. B3. $15.00

**SHATRAW, Milton.** *Thrashin' Time, Memories of a Montana Boyhood.* 1970. Am West. VG/dj. J2. $55.00

**SHAW, Albert.** *Abraham Lincoln: His Path to the Presidency. Vol II.* 1929. NY. Review of Reviews Corp. 2 vol. 4to. red cloth. case. K1. $85.00

**SHAW, Andrew;** see Block, Lawrence.

**SHAW, Anna Howard.** *Story of a Pioneer.* 1915. Harper. 337p. VG. B18. $22.50

**SHAW, Annie DeWitt.** *Will, Annie & I: Travellers in Many Lands.* 1898. NY. Skinner. 1st. 8vo. ils. 363p. VG. W1. $45.00

**SHAW, Archer H.** *Plain Dealer: One Hundred Years in Cleveland.* 1942. Knopf. 1st. ils. cloth. F/dj. O10. $35.00

**SHAW, Bob.** *Fugitive Worlds.* 1989. London. Gollancz. 1st. F/NF. G10. $20.00

**SHAW, Bob.** *Ragged Astronauts.* 1986. NY. baen. 1st Am. F/NF. G10. $14.00

**SHAW, Bob.** *Wreath of Stars.* 1976. London. Gollancz. 1st. sgn. AN/dj. M21. $35.00

**SHAW, Edward.** *Modern Architect; or, Every Man His Own Master...* 1859. Boston. Wentworth Hewes. ils/engravings. 128p. full leather. B5. $250.00

**SHAW, George Bernard.** *Back to Methuselah: A Metabiological Pentateuch.* 1921. London. Constable. 1st. gilt olive cloth. NF/VG. A24. $95.00

**SHAW, George Bernard.** *Flyleaves.* 1977. Austin. WT Taylor. 1st. 1/350. terra-cotta buckram/prt label. F. M24. $125.00

SHAW, George Bernard. *Quintessence of Bernard Shaw.* 1920. London. Allen Unwin. 1st. VG/dj. A24. $45.00

SHAW, George Russell. *Pines of Mexico.* 1961 (1909). Jamaica Plain. 22 pl/map. AN/wrp. B26. $45.00

SHAW, Irwin. *Beggarman, Thief.* 1977. Franklin Lib. ltd. aeg. bl leather. F. B11. $40.00

SHAW, Irwin. *Mixed Company: Collected Stories.* 1950. Random. 1st. VG/G. B30. $25.00

SHAW, Irwin. *Nightwork.* 1975. Delacorte. 1st. NF/NF. H11. $25.00

SHAW, Irwin. *Top of the Hill.* 1979. Weidenfeld Nicholson. 1st. F/dj. T12. $30.00

SHAW, Irwin. *Young Lions.* Modern Lib/Random. F/NF. L4. $70.00

SHAW, Marlow A. *Happy Islands: Stories & Sketches of the Georgian Bay.* 1926. Toronto. 1st. 12mo. VG. A2. $25.00

SHAW, Reuben Cole. *Across the Plains in Forty-Nine.* 1948. Lakeside Classic. 1st thus. teg. w/pub card. NF. T11. $40.00

SHAW, Richard J. *Field Guide to Vascular Plants of Grand Teton Nat Park...* 1976. Logan. ils/map, 301p. VG/dj. B26. $21.00

SHAW, Robert H. *Ground Level Climatology.* 1967. AAAS. 395p. xl. VG. S5. $40.00

SHAW, Robert K. *Noel: Christmas Echoes Down the Ages, Recaptured by...* 1935. Worcester. St Onge. mini. 1/278. aeg. full dk red leather w/gilt title. B24. $1,750.00

SHAW, Sam. *Marilyn Among Friends.* 1987. Bloomsbury. VG/dj. P3. $20.00

SHAW, Thomas. *Soiling Crops & the Silo.* 1906. NY. Orange Judd. 366p. VG. A10. $22.00

SHAW(N), Frank S.; see Goulart, Ron.

SHAYNE, Mike; see Halliday, Brett.

SHEARER, F.E. *Pacific Tourist.* 1886. NY. ils. 372p. G. B18. $95.00

SHECKLEY, Robert. *Crompton Divided.* 1978. HRW. 1st. NF/dj. G10. $20.00

SHECTAR, Ben. *Hester the Jester.* 1977. Harper Row. I Can Read Book. 1st. 8vo. VG. M5. $15.00

SHECTER, L. *Once Upon the Polo Grounds.* 1970. NY. 1st. VG/dj. B5. $17.50

SHEDD, Margaret. *Inherit the Earth.* 1944. Harper. 1st. VG/clip. S18. $15.00

SHEEHAN, Donald. *This Was Publishing.* 1952. Bloomington. 1st. 288p. VG. B18. $17.50

SHEEHY, Gail. *Love Sounds.* 1970. Random. 1st. author's 1st book. F/dj. A24. $35.00

SHEEHY. *Guide to Reference Books, 9th Edition.* 1976. Am Lib Assn. 4to. 1033p. NF. A4. $75.00

SHEEN, Fulton J. *This Is the Holy Land.* 1961 (1960). Hawthorn. 1st. VG/dj. S5. $15.00

SHEFFIELD, Charles. *Cold as Ice.* 1992. NY. Tor. 1st. F/dj. G10. $14.00

SHELDON, Charles. *Wilderness of Denali: Explorations of a Hunter-Naturalist.* 1960. NY. new ed. index. 412p. F/G. A17. $40.00

SHELDON, Gerard P. *Gentle Ways in Japan.* 1989. SF. Saville Photo Arts. photos. VG/dj. S5. $20.00

SHELDON, Harold P. *Tranquility Revisited.* 1989. Derrydale. 1/2500. 130p. gilt leather. F. A17. $35.00

SHELDON, Sidney. *Other Side of Midnight.* 1974. Morrow. 1st. F/NF. H11. $35.00

SHELDON, Sidney. *Stars Shine Down.* 1992. Morrow. 1st. F/F. H11. $20.00

SHELDON, W. *27th: A Regimental History.* VG. E6. $150.00

SHELFORD, Victor E. *Ecology of North America.* 1978 (1963). U IL. 610p. sc. G. S5. $20.00

SHELFORD, Victor E. *Laboratory & Field Ecology.* 1930. Williams Wilkins. 608p. xl. VG. S5. $15.00

SHELLABARGER, Samuel. *Lord Chesterfield & His World.* 1951. Little Brn. 1st. gilt red cloth. H13. $35.00

SHELLEY, Mary Wollstonecraft. *Frankenstein Annotated.* 1977. Clarkson Potter, NY. 1st. VG/G. L1. $125.00

SHELLEY, Mary Wollstonecraft. *Frankenstein; or, Modern Prometheus.* 1930. NY. Grosset Dunlap. 1st photoplay. 8vo. 240p. Sangorski bdg. F. H5. $950.00

SHELLEY, Mary Wollstonecraft. *Frankenstein; or, Modern Prometheus.* 1983. Pennyroyal. 1/5 (350). sgn Moser/52 initialed pl. Kelm bdg. extra suite. box. B24. $5,000.00

SHELLEY, Percy Bysshe. *Complete Poetical Works of...* 1892. Boston. 4 vol. half leather/marbled brd. F. B30. $225.00

SHELLEY, Percy Bysshe. *Shelley's Complete Poetical Works.* 1901. Boston. teg. half brn leather/marbled brd. F. B30. $40.00

SHELTON, Louise. *Seasons in a Flower Garden.* 1915. Scribner. 2nd. 117p. VG. A10. $40.00

SHENKER, Israel. *In the Footsteps of Johnson & Boswell.* 1982. Houghton Mifflin. 1st. map frontis. dj. H13. $35.00

SHENSTONE, William. *Poetical Works.* 1771. Edinburgh. Prt for C Elliot. sm 8vo. 244p. contemporary sheep. VG. S17. $75.00

SHEPARD, Alan. *Moon Shot.* 1994. Atlanta. Turner. 1st. F/dj. M23. $30.00

SHEPARD, Ernest H. *Drawn From Memory.* 1957. Phil. Lippincott. 1st Am. 8vo. VG/dj. J3. $40.00

SHEPARD, Leslie. *Dracula Book of Great Vampire Stories.* 1977. Citadel. BC. VG/G. L1. $15.00

SHEPARD, Lucius. *Barnical Bill the Spacer & Other Stories.* 1997. London. Orion. 1st. sgn. F/dj. G10. $125.00

SHEPARD, Lucius. *Father of Stones.* 1988. SF Assn. 1/500. sgn Shepard/ils JK Potter. F/F box. B30. $60.00

SHEPARD, Lucius. *Jaguar Hunter.* 1987. Arkham. 1st. author's 1st hc pub. F/dj. B30. $75.00

SHEPARD, Lucius. *Life During Wartime.* 1991. Bantam. 1st. sgn. NF/wrp. R11. $15.00

SHEPARD, Sam. *Cruising Paradise.* 1996. Knopf. 1st. sgn. F/dj. M25. $50.00

SHEPARD, Sam. *Unseen Hand & Other Plays.* 1972. Bobbs Merrill. 1st. F/NF. B2. $40.00

SHEPARD. *Encyclopedia of Occultism & Parapsychology...* 1984. 3 vol. 1628p. F. A4. $250.00

SHEPERD, John. *History of the Liverpool Medical Institution.* 1979. Liverpool. 1st. 319p. A13. $35.00

SHEPHERD, Anthony. *Arabian Adventure.* 1961. London. Collins. 10 pl/map. cloth. G. Q2. $47.00

SHEPHERD, Michael; see Ludlum, Robert.

SHEPHERD, William R. *Guide to Materials for History of US in Spanish Archives.* 1907. WA, DC. 1st. 107p. VG/prt wrp. M8. $75.00

SHERBO, Arthur. *Samuel Johnson's Critical Opinions.* 1995. Newark. U DE. 1st. gilt blk linen. AN/dj. H13. $35.00

SHERIDAN, Richard Brinsley. *Works...* 1821. London. John Murray. 2 vol. 1st collected. tall 8vo. uncut. H13. $225.00

SHERLOCK, C. *Modern Farm Hen.* 1922. Des Moines. Homestead. 236p. cloth. VG. A10. $20.00

**SHERLOCK, Patti.** *Four of a Kind.* 1991. NY. Holiday House. 1st. F/dj. O3. $20.00

**SHERMAN, E. Helene.** *Pearls of Wisdom.* 1965. RE Massmann. mini. frenchfold. hand-bdg faux vellum. B24. $400.00

**SHERMAN, E. Helene.** *Sukie's ABC.* nd. New Britain. mini. 1/300. hand-colored ils. 34p. prt wrp/paper sleeve. B24. $65.00

**SHERMAN, Harold M.** *Hit & Run.* 1929. Grosset Dunlap. 1st. VG/dj. P8. $25.00

**SHERMAN, Harold M.** *Hit by Pitcher.* 1928. Grosset Dunlap. 1st. G/VG. P8. $25.00

**SHERMAN, Kay Lynne.** *Findhorn Family Cookbook.* 1981. Shambhala. G/wrp. A16. $8.00

**SHERRARAD, Philip.** *Marble Threshing Floor.* 1956. London. Vallentine Mitchel. 1st. VG/clip. O4. $15.00

**SHERRINGTON, Charles.** *Integrative Action of the Nervous System.* 1990. Birmingham. Classics of Psychiatry & Behavioral Sciences Lib. G1. $100.00

**SHERRINGTON, Charles.** *On the Spinal Animal Being the Marshall Hall Prize Address.* 1800. London. Royal Medical/Chirurgical Soc. 5 pl. 31p. prt wrp. G7. $295.00

**SHERRY, Edna.** *Tears for Jessie Hewitt.* 1958. Dodd Mead. 1st. xl. VG/dj. G8. $15.00

**SHERRY, Norman.** *Life of Graham Greene Volume One: 1904-1939.* 1989. Lester/Orphen Dennys. 1st. NF/VG. P3. $30.00

**SHERWMAKE, Oscar L.** *Honorable George Wythe: Teacher, Lawyer, Jurist, Statesman.* 1954. Wm & Mary. 2nd. 48p. VG. B10. $25.00

**SHERWOOD, Elmer.** *Buffalo Bill: The Boys' Friend.* 1917. Racine. Whitman. 1st. VG. M21. $12.50

**SHERWOOD, Morgan B.** *Alaska & Its History.* 1967. Seattle. U WA. 8vo. 475p. map ep. half cloth. VG/dj. P4. $30.00

**SHERWOOD, Morgan B.** *Exploration of Alaska 1865-1900.* 1965. New Haven/London. Yale. 1st. ils. 207p. VG/dj. P4. $50.00

**SHERWOOD, N.B.** *Watch & Chronometer Jewelling.* 1892. Chicago. 3rd. 120p. VG/prt gr wrp. B14. $65.00

**SHERZER, Joel.** *Kuna Way of Speaking.* 1990. Austin. 1st wrp ed. 260p. F3. $15.00

**SHEWEN, William.** *True Christian's Faith & Experience Briefly Declared...* 1830. Phil. MTC Gould. 136p. disbound. V3. $35.00

**SHIBLEY, Ronald E.** *Fredericksburg.* (1977). Fredericksburg Found. 1st. photos. 64p. VG/dj. B10. $35.00

**SHIELDS, Carol.** *Various Miracles.* 1985. Stoddard. 1st Canadian. F/sans. T12. $45.00

**SHIELDS, Carol.** *Various Miracles.* 1994. London. Fourth Estate. 1st. F/dj. O11. $40.00

**SHILLING, Arthur.** *Ojibway Dream.* 1986. Montreal. Tundra Books. 1st. 48p. yel-beige cloth. AN/dj. P4. $30.00

**SHILTS, Randy.** *And the Band Played On: Politics, People & Aids Epidemic.* 1987. St Martin. 4th. 630p. VG/dj. A25. $12.00

**SHIMER, J.A.** *Sculptured Earth: Landscape of America.* 1959. Columbia. photos. 255p. VG/torn. M4. $25.00

**SHIMER, R.H.** *Squaw Point.* 1972. Harper Row. 1st. Edgar Award. NF/dj. A24. $30.00

**SHIMURA, Asao.** *Iroha-gami: A Paper Alphabet.* 1980. Tokyo. Bunseido. mini. 26p+48 samples. Oriental-style sewn wrp. B24. $150.00

**SHINER, Lewis.** *Deserted Cities of the Heart.* 1988. Doubleday. 1st. author's 2nd novel. F/dj. S18. $30.00

**SHIPLEY, Joseph T.** *Trends in Literature.* 1949. Philosophical Lib. 1st. NF/VG. O4. $15.00

**SHIPPEY, Lee.** *Folks Ushud Know.* 1930. Sierra Madre, CA. 1st. ils AL Ewing. VG. O4. $20.00

**SHIPPEY, Lee.** *It's an Old California Custom.* 1948. Vanguard. 1st. Am Customs series. NF/VG. T11. $20.00

**SHIRAKAWA, Yoshikazu.** *Eternal America.* 1975. Kodansha Internat. 1st. VG/dj. S5. $50.00

**SHIRAKAWA, Yoshikazu.** *Himalyays.* 1976. Abrams. VG/dj. S5. $18.00

**SHIRAS, George.** *Hunting Wild Life With Camera & Flashlight.* 1935. NGS. 2 vol. ils. G. A17. $35.00

**SHIRER, William L.** *Collapse of the Third Republic.* 1969. S&S. sm 4to. 1082p. NF/dj. W2. $40.00

**SHIRER, William L.** *Rise & Fall of the Third Reich.* 1960. S&S. BC. 1st/13th prt. 584p. F/NF. W2. $35.00

**SHIRLEY, Dame.** *California in 1851: Letters of Dame Shirley.* 1933. SF. Grabhorn. 8vo. P4. $120.00

**SHIRLEY, Glenn.** *Buckskin Joe: Being Unique & Vivid Memoirs of EJ Hoyt...* 1966. NE U. 1st. ils. 194p. NF/VG. B19. $25.00

**SHIRLEY, Glenn.** *Frontier Marshal.* 1963. Phil. Chilton. ils. 231p. VG/G. B5. $25.00

**SHIRLEY, Glenn.** *Heck Thomas, Frontier Marshal.* 1981. OK U. 1st. F/dj. M4. $35.00

**SHIRLEY, Glenn.** *Heck Thomas: Frontier Marshal.* 1962. Chilton. VG/dj. A19. $50.00

**SHIRLEY & STARR.** *Last of the Real Bad Men.* 1965. David McKay. 1st. 208p. VG/dj. B5. $25.00

**SHIRMAN, Li.** *Nosy Friday.* 1964. Abelard Schuman. 1st. 127p. F/dj. D4. $25.00

**SHIVERS, Louise.** *Here to Get My Baby Out of Jail.* 1983. Random. 1st. F/dj. M23. $80.00

**SHLAIN, Bruce.** *Baseball Inside Out.* 1992. Viking. 1st. photos. F/dj. C15. $10.00

**SHLES, Larry.** *Moths & Mothers, Feathers & Fathers: Story About Tiny Owl...* 1984. Houghton Mifflin. inscr/sgn. F/wrp. S15. $8.00

**SHOCK, Nathan.** *Classified Bibliography of Gerontology & Geriatrics.* 1951. Stanford. 1st. 599p. A13. $125.00

**SHOEMAKER, Bill.** *Stalking Horse.* 1994. Fawcett. 1st. F/F. H11. $20.00

**SHOPTON, Clifford K.** *New England Life in the 18th Century.* 1995. Harvard. 626p. NF. M10. $20.00

**SHORT, Bobby.** *Bobby Short: Life & Times of a Saloon Singer.* 1995. Clarkson Porter. 1st. inscr. F/dj. O11. $35.00

**SHORT, Christopher.** *Blue-Eyed Boy.* 1966. Dodd Mead. 1st. VG/G. G8. $10.00

**SHORT, Vaughn.** *Raging River, Lonely Trail.* 1978. Tucson. Two Horses. 1st. sgn. sm 8vo. 159p. NF/stiff wrp. F7. $10.00

**SHORTER, Alfred H.** *Paper Making in the British Isles...* 1972. NY. Barnes Noble. 1st Am. ils. 272p. cloth. F/dj. O10. $45.00

**SHOUMATOFF, Alex.** *Rivers Amazon.* 1978. Sierra Club. 1st. 240p. map ep. F3. $20.00

**SHRADY, M.L.** *In the Spirit of Wonder: A Christmas Anthology for Our Age.* 1961. Pantheon. 1st. ils Johannes Troyer. VG. B27. $20.00

**SHRAKE, Bud.** *Night Never Falls.* 1987. Random. 1st. F/NF. R11. $17.00

**SHREWSBURY, J.F.D.** *History of Bubonic Plague in the British Isles.* 1970. Cambridge. 1st. 661p. A13. $100.00

**SHRIVER, Pam.** *Passing Shots.* 1987. McGraw Hill. VG/dj. R8. $10.00

**SHUKAIRY, Ahmad.** *Territorial & Historical Waters in International Law.* nd. Beirut. PLO Research Center. 1st. 16mo. NF/wrp. M7. $62.00

SHERLOCK, Patti. *Four of a Kind*. 1991. NY. Holiday House. 1st. F/dj. O3. $20.00

SHERMAN, E. Helene. *Pearls of Wisdom*. 1965. RE Massmann. mini. frenchfold. hand-bdg faux vellum. B24. $400.00

SHERMAN, E. Helene. *Sukie's ABC*. nd. New Britain. mini. 1/300. hand-colored ils. 34p. prt wrp/paper sleeve. B24. $65.00

SHERMAN, Harold M. *Hit & Run*. 1929. Grosset Dunlap. 1st. VG/dj. P8. $25.00

SHERMAN, Harold M. *Hit by Pitcher*. 1928. Grosset Dunlap. 1st. G/VG. P8. $25.00

SHERMAN, Kay Lynne. *Findhorn Family Cookbook*. 1981. Shambhala. G/wrp. A16. $8.00

SHERRARAD, Philip. *Marble Threshing Floor*. 1956. London. Vallentine Mitchel. 1st. VG/clip. O4. $15.00

SHERRINGTON, Charles. *Integrative Action of the Nervous System*. 1990. Birmingham. Classics of Psychiatry & Behavioral Sciences Lib. G1. $100.00

SHERRINGTON, Charles. *On the Spinal Animal Being the Marshall Hall Prize Address*. 1800. London. Royal Medical/Chirurgical Soc. 5 pl. 31p. prt wrp. G7. $295.00

SHERRY, Edna. *Tears for Jessie Hewitt*. 1958. Dodd Mead. 1st. xl. VG/dj. G8. $15.00

SHERRY, Norman. *Life of Graham Greene Volume One: 1904-1939*. 1989. Lester/Orphen Dennys. 1st. NF/VG. P3. $30.00

SHERWMAKE, Oscar L. *Honorable George Wythe: Teacher, Lawyer, Jurist, Statesman*. 1954. Wm & Mary. 2nd. 48p. VG. B10. $25.00

SHERWOOD, Elmer. *Buffalo Bill: The Boys' Friend*. 1917. Racine. Whitman. 1st. VG. M21. $12.50

SHERWOOD, Morgan B. *Alaska & Its History*. 1967. Seattle. U WA. 8vo. 475p. map ep. half cloth. VG/dj. P4. $30.00

SHERWOOD, Morgan B. *Exploration of Alaska 1865-1900*. 1965. New Haven/London. Yale. 1st. ils. 207p. VG/dj. P4. $50.00

SHERWOOD, N.B. *Watch & Chronometer Jewelling*. 1892. Chicago. 3rd. 120p. VG/prt gr wrp. B14. $65.00

SHERZER, Joel. *Kuna Way of Speaking*. 1990. Austin. 1st wrp ed. 260p. F3. $15.00

SHEWEN, William. *True Christian's Faith & Experience Briefly Declared...* 1830. Phil. MTC Gould. 136p. disbound. V3. $35.00

SHIBLEY, Ronald E. *Fredericksburg*. (1977). Fredericksburg Found. 1st. photos. 64p. VG/dj. B10. $35.00

SHIELDS, Carol. *Various Miracles*. 1985. Stoddard. 1st Canadian. F/sans. T12. $45.00

SHIELDS, Carol. *Various Miracles*. 1994. London. Fourth Estate. 1st. F/dj. O11. $40.00

SHILLING, Arthur. *Ojibway Dream*. 1986. Montreal. Tundra Books. 1st. 48p. yel-beige cloth. AN/dj. P4. $30.00

SHILTS, Randy. *And the Band Played On: Politics, People & Aids Epidemic*. 1987. St Martin. 4th. 630p. VG/dj. A25. $12.00

SHIMER, J.A. *Sculptured Earth: Landscape of America*. 1959. Columbia. photos. 255p. VG/torn. M4. $25.00

SHIMER, R.H. *Squaw Point*. 1972. Harper Row. 1st. Edgar Award. NF/dj. A24. $30.00

SHIMURA, Asao. *Iroha-gami: A Paper Alphabet*. 1980. Tokyo. Bunseido. mini. 26p+48 samples. Oriental-style sewn wrp. B24. $150.00

SHINER, Lewis. *Deserted Cities of the Heart*. 1988. Doubleday. 1st. author's 2nd novel. F/dj. S18. $30.00

SHIPLEY, Joseph T. *Trends in Literature*. 1949. Philosophical Lib. 1st. NF/VG. O4. $15.00

SHIPPEY, Lee. *Folks Ushud Know*. 1930. Sierra Madre, CA. 1st. ils AL Ewing. VG. O4. $20.00

SHIPPEY, Lee. *It's an Old California Custom*. 1948. Vanguard. 1st. Am Customs series. NF/VG. T11. $20.00

SHIRAKAWA, Yoshikazu. *Eternal America*. 1975. Kodansha Internat. 1st. VG/dj. S5. $50.00

SHIRAKAWA, Yoshikazu. *Himalyays*. 1976. Abrams. VG/dj. S5. $18.00

SHIRAS, George. *Hunting Wild Life With Camera & Flashlight*. 1935. NGS. 2 vol. ils. G. A17. $35.00

SHIRER, William L. *Collapse of the Third Republic*. 1969. S&S. 1st. 4to. 1082p. NF/dj. W2. $40.00

SHIRER, William L. *Rise & Fall of the Third Reich*. 1960. S&S. BC. 1st/13th prt. 584p. F/NF. W2. $35.00

SHIRLEY, Dame. *California in 1851: Letters of Dame Shirley*. 1933. SF. Grabhorn. 8vo. P4. $120.00

SHIRLEY, Glenn. *Buckskin Joe: Being Unique & Vivid Memoirs of EJ Hoyt...* 1966. NE U. 1st. ils. 194p. NF/VG. B19. $25.00

SHIRLEY, Glenn. *Frontier Marshal*. 1963. Phil. Chilton. ils. 231p. VG/G. B5. $25.00

SHIRLEY, Glenn. *Heck Thomas, Frontier Marshal*. 1981. OK U. 1st. F/dj. M4. $35.00

SHIRLEY, Glenn. *Heck Thomas: Frontier Marshal*. 1962. Chilton. VG/dj. A19. $50.00

SHIRLEY & STARR. *Last of the Real Bad Men*. 1965. David McKay. 1st. 208p. VG/dj. B5. $25.00

SHIRMAN, Li. *Nosy Friday*. 1964. Abelard Schuman. 1st. 127p. F/dj. D4. $25.00

SHIVERS, Louise. *Here to Get My Baby Out of Jail*. 1983. Random. 1st. F/dj. M23. $80.00

SHLAIN, Bruce. *Baseball Inside Out*. 1992. Viking. 1st. photos. F/dj. C15. $10.00

SHLES, Larry. *Moths & Mothers, Feathers & Fathers: Story About Tiny Owl...* 1984. Houghton Mifflin. inscr/sgn. F/wrp. S15. $8.00

SHOCK, Nathan. *Classified Bibliography of Gerontology & Geriatrics*. 1951. Stanford. 1st. 599p. A13. $125.00

SHOEMAKER, Bill. *Stalking Horse*. 1994. Fawcett. 1st. F/F. H11. $20.00

SHOPTON, Clifford K. *New England Life in the 18th Century*. 1995. Harvard. 626p. NF. M10. $20.00

SHORT, Bobby. *Bobby Short: Life & Times of a Saloon Singer*. 1995. Clarkson Porter. 1st. inscr. F/dj. O11. $35.00

SHORT, Christopher. *Blue-Eyed Boy*. 1966. Dodd Mead. 1st. VG/G. G8. $10.00

SHORT, Vaughn. *Raging River, Lonely Trail*. 1978. Tucson. Two Horses. 1st. sgn. sm 8vo. 159p. NF/stiff wrp. F7. $10.00

SHORTER, Alfred H. *Paper Making in the British Isles...* 1972. NY. Barnes Noble. 1st Am. ils. 272p. cloth. F/dj. O10. $45.00

SHOUMATOFF, Alex. *Rivers Amazon*. 1978. Sierra Club. 1st. 240p. map ep. F3. $20.00

SHRADY, M.L. *In the Spirit of Wonder: A Christmas Anthology for Our Age*. 1961. Pantheon. 1st. ils Johannes Troyer. VG. B27. $20.00

SHRAKE, Bud. *Night Never Falls*. 1987. Random. 1st. F/NF. R11. $17.00

SHREWSBURY, J.F.D. *History of Bubonic Plague in the British Isles*. 1970. Cambridge. 1st. 661p. A13. $100.00

SHRIVER, Pam. *Passing Shots*. 1987. McGraw Hill. VG/dj. R8. $10.00

SHUKAIRY, Ahmad. *Territorial & Historical Waters in International Law*. nd. Beirut. PLO Research Center. 1st. 16mo. NF/wrp. M7. $62.00

SETON, Ernest Thompson. *Boy Scouts of America: A Handbook...* 1910. Doubleday Page. ils. 192p. F. A4. $395.00

SETON, Ernest Thompson. *Monarch, the Big Bear of Tallac*. 1904. Morang. 1st. ils. 214p. VG+. B19. $20.00

SETON, Ernest Thompson. *Sign Talk: Universal Signal Code, Without Apparatus...* 1918. Doubleday Page. 1st. ils. cloth. VG. B27. $295.00

SETON, Ernest Thompson. *Two Little Savages: Being Adventures of Two Boys*. 1922 (1911). Doubleday Page. 8vo. ils. 552p. G. T5. $15.00

SETTLE, Mary Lee. *Charley Bland*. 1989. NY. FSG. 1st. F/dj. M23. $18.00

SETTLE, Mary Lee. *O Beulah Land*. 1956. Viking. 1st. F/dj. B2. $40.00

SETTLE, William. *Jesse James Was His Name*. 1967. Columbia, MO. 2nd. VG. B5. $25.00

SEUSS, Dr.; see Geisel, Theodore Seuss.

SEVERIN, T. *Explorers of the Mississippi*. 1968. NY. 1st. ils. 294p. NF. M4. $20.00

SEVERIN, T. *In Search of Genghis Khan*. 1991. London. 1st. 276p. F/dj. M4. $18.00

SEVERIN, T. *Sinbad Voyage*. 1983. NY. Putnam. 1st Am. ils. NF/dj. W1. $22.00

SEVERN, David. *Cruise of the Maiden Castle*. 1949. Macmillan. 1st. NF/VG. P2. $25.00

SEVERN, J. Millott. *Life Story & Experiences of a Phrenologist*. 1929. London. private prt. 1st. ils. 505+4p. VG. H7. $50.00

SEWALL, Richard B. *Life of Emily Dickinson*. 1974. FSG. 2 vol. 1st. VG. M10. $60.00

SEWARD, William H. *Life & Public Services of John Quincy Adams...* 1849. Auburn. Derby. 1st. 8vo. 404p. VG. B14. $350.00

SEWARD & SEWARD. *Current Psychological Issues: Essays in Honor RS Woodworth*. 1958. NY. Holt. sgn. 360p. prt beige cloth. G1. $40.00

SEWART, Alan. *Educating of Quinton Quinn*. 1984. Robert Hale. 1st Eng. NF/dj. G8. $10.00

SEWELL, Anna. *Black Beauty*. ca 1953. London. Blackie. ne. G. T12. $18.00

SEWELL, Anna. *Black Beauty*. nd. Barse Hopkins. ils Hugo VonHofsten. G. A21. $20.00

SEWELL, Anna. *Black Beauty*. 1986. Random. 1st. F/dj. M25. $35.00

SEWELL, Anna. *Black Beauty*. 1986. Stamford, CT. Longmeadow. ils LK Welch. VG. O3. $16.00

SEWELL, Anna. *Black Beauty: Autobiography of a Horse*. ca 1912. London. Jarrold. 26 pl/ils Stokes & Wright. VG. M19. $45.00

SEWELL, Anna. *Black Beauty: Autobiography of a Horse*. 1879 (1877). Phil. Altemus. G. T12. $75.00

SEWELL, Helen. *ABC for Everyday*. 1930. Macmillan. 1st. 4to. pict brd. mc pict dj. R5. $275.00

SEWELL, Henry. *Letter to Lord Worsley on Burthens Affecting Real Property*. 1846. London. Butterworth. pres. modern wrp. M11. $275.00

SEWELL, William. *History of Rise, Increase & Progress of Christian People...* 1823. Phil. Kite. 2 vol. worn leather. V3. $55.00

SEXTUS, F. *Hypnotism: Its Facts, Theories & Related Phenomena*. 1893. 1st. ils. E6. $45.00

SEYBOLD, David. *Fathers & Sons: An Anthology*. 1992. Grove Weidenfeld. 1st. sgn 5 contributors. F/dj. O11. $75.00

SEYDOR, Paul. *Peckinpah: Western Films*. 1980. Urbana. U IL. 5-line inscr. ils. 302p. blk cloth. K1. $35.00

SEYMOUR, Alta Halverson. *Grandma for Christmas*. 1946. Phil. Westminster. 1st. sm 8vo. VG/dj. M21. $45.00

SEYMOUR, Catryna Ten Eyck. *Enjoying the Southwest*. 1973. Lippincott. 1st. 8vo. brn brd. VG/dj. F7. $17.50

SEYMOUR, Frank C. *Flora of New England*. 1969. Rutland. 1st. 596p. VG/dj. B26. $42.50

SEYMOUR, Frederick. *Wild Animals I Have Met*. 1901. np. Neil. ils/photos. 544p. G. A17. $20.00

SEYMOUR, Harold. *Baseball: The Early Years (and) Baseball: The Golden Years*. 1960 & 1971. NY. Oxford. 2 vol. F/NF case. B2. $85.00

SEYMOUR, Horatio. *Union, the Constitution & the Laws*. 1863. NY. Comstock Cassidy. 1st. 11p. self wrp. M8. $85.00

SEYMOUR, W. *Price of Folly: British Blunders in War...* 1995. London. 1st. ils/maps/plans. NF/rpr. M4. $30.00

SEYMOUR-SMITH. *Who's Who in 20th-Century Literature*. 1976. 414p. F/F. A4. $35.00

SHAARA, Jeff. *Gods & Generals*. 1996. NY. Ballantine. 1st. F/dj. T11. $35.00

SHAARA, Michael. *Killer Angels*. 1974. NY. McKay. 1st. F/dj. B4. $1,250.00

SHABERMAN, Raphel B. *George MacDonald: A Bibliographical Study*. 1990. Omnigraphics. 1st ltd. 1/500. sgn. AN/dj. A27. $40.00

SHACKLETON, E.H. *Heart of the Antarctic Being Story of British...1907-1909*. 1909. Lippincott. 2 vol. 1st Am. pocket maps. VG. B11. $850.00

SHACOCHIS, Bob. *Easy in the Islands*. 1985. Crown. 1st. sgn. F/dj. D10. $110.00

SHACOCHIS, Bob. *Next New World*. 1989. Crown. 1st. sgn. F/dj. D10. $50.00

SHACOCHIS, Bob. *Next New World*. 1989. NY. Crown. 1st. author's 2nd book. F/dj. A24. $30.00

SHAFFER, E.T.H. *Carolina Gardens*. 1939. Chapel Hill. 326p. cloth. A10. $40.00

SHAFFER, Peter. *Black Comedy & White Lies*. 1967. NY. Stein Day. 123p. VG/dj. C5. $12.50

SHAFFER, Peter. *Collected Plays*. 1982. NY. 1st. VG/dj. M17. $40.00

SHAGAN, Steve. *Vendetta*. 1986. Perigord. 1st. F/F. H11. $25.00

SHAH, Diane K. *Dying Cheek to Cheek*. 1992. Doubleday. 1st. F/F. H11. $20.00

SHAHN, Ben. *For the Sake of a Single Verse...* 1968. NY. Shahn Trust. 1/950. sgn. w/23 lithos. loose. portfolio/box. B24. $2,500.00

SHAHN, Ben. *Photographic Eye of Ben Shahn*. 1975. Cambridge. 1st. 100+ photos. F/dj. S9. $85.00

SHAINSBERG, Lawrence. *Ambivalent Zen: A Memoir*. 1995. NY. Pantheon. 1st. VG/dj. N2. $10.00

SHAKERY, Karin. *Ortho's Complete Guide to Successful Houseplants*. 1984. Ortho. 1st. ils. 320p. VG. S14. $10.00

SHAKESPEARE, Nicholas. *Vision of Elena Silves*. 1990. Knopf. 1st Am. F/dj. A24. $25.00

SHAKESPEARE, William. *Complete Works of Shakespeare*. 1936. Doubleday Doran. 2 vol. 1/750. ils/sgn Kent. bl brd. VG. B11. $550.00

SHAKESPEARE, William. *Dramatic Works of William Shakespeare*. 1823. Cheswick. Whittingham. 12mo. dbl-column text/wood engravings. contemporary bdg. H5. $950.00

SHAKESPEARE, William. *Mercury Shakespeare, Twelfth Night*. 1939. Harper. edit Orson Welles/Roger Hill. VG+/sans. C9. $90.00

SHAKESPEARE, William. *Orthello*. 1973. Gehenna. 1/400. binder's copy. ils/sgn Baskin. deluxe blk morocco. box. B24. $1,500.00

**SHAKESPEARE, William.** *Romeo & Juliet.* 1884. London. Cassell. lg 4to. 53p. lg gr gilt cloth. VG. H5. $450.00

**SHAKESPEARE, William.** *Shakespeare: A Review & a Preview.* ca 1939. LEC. unp. VG. B18. $20.00

**SHAKESPEARE, William.** *Shall I Die? Shall I Fly?* 1986. Boston. Bromer. mini. 1/35 (160 total). hand illuminated Suzanne Moore. case. B24. $325.00

**SHAKESPEARE, William.** *Songs of Shakespeare.* 1903. London. Anthony Traherne. mini. Waistcoat Pocket Classic. 72p. blk stp red cloth. B24. $110.00

**SHAKESPEARE, William.** *Titus Andronicus.* 1973. Gehenna. 1/400. binder's copy. ils/sgn Baskin. gilt morocco. F/box. B24. $1,500.00

**SHAKESPEARE, William.** *Tragedie of Hamlet Prince of Denmarke.* 1930. Cranach. 1/300 on Maillol handmade. folio. teg. F/box. B24. $6,500.00

**SHAKESPEARE, William.** *Works of...* 1929-1933. Random. 7 vol. 1/500 (of 1600 total). teg. NF. H5. $2,500.00

**SHALE, Richard.** *Academy Awards Index.* 1993. Westport. Greenwood. 785p. VG. C5. $35.00

**SHALER, N.S.** *American Highways: A Popular Account of Conditions...* 1896. Century. 1st. 293p. ES. G+. B18. $47.50

**SHAMBAUGH, Bertha M.** *Amana: Community of True Inspiration.* 1908. Iowa City. State Hist Soc. VG+. B2. $75.00

**SHAMES, Laurence.** *Florida Straits.* 1992. S&S. 1st. author's 1st novel. F/F. H11. $40.00

**SHAMES, Laurence.** *Scavenger Reef.* 1994. S&S. 1st. F/dj. M15. $45.00

**SHAMES, Laurence.** *Sunburn: A Thriller.* 1996. NY. Hyperion. ARC/1st. F/dj. w/promo material. S9. $20.00

**SHANGE, Ntozake.** *Ridin' the Moon in Texas.* 1987. St Martin. 1st. NF/NF. R14. $30.00

**SHANK, Robert.** *Life in the Son: A Study of Doctrine of Perseverance.* 1962. Westcott. 380p. G/dj. B29. $11.00

**SHANKMAN, Sarah.** *He Was Her Man.* 1993. Pocket. 1st. F/dj. R8. $10.00

**SHANKMAN, Sarah.** *Keeping Secrets.* 1988. S&S. 1st. author's 2nd book. NF/dj. A24. $25.00

**SHANKMAN, Sarah.** *Now Let's Talk of Graves.* 1990. Pocket. 1st. VG/dj. R8. $15.00

**SHANKS, David C.** *Management of the American Soldier.* 1918. np. 1st. 80p. VG/wrp. M8. $25.00

**SHANKS, Elsie.** *Novae Narrationes. Completed With a Legal Introduction...* 1963. London. Bernard Quaritch. bl buckram. M11. $65.00

**SHANN, Renee.** *Air Force Girl.* 1943. Phil. Triangle/Blakiston. 1st thus. 275p. VG. A25. $10.00

**SHANNON, David A.** *Decline of American Communism.* 1959. Harcourt Brace. 1st. 8vo. VG/G. A2. $15.00

**SHANNON, Dell.** *Root of All Evil.* 1964. Morrow. 1st. VG/dj. G8. $12.50

**SHANNON, Fred A.** *Farmer's Last Frontier: Agriculture, 1860-1897.* 1945. Farrar Rhinehart. 1st. 8vo. VG/G. A2. $20.00

**SHANNON, George.** *Bean Boy.* 1984. Greenwillow. 1st. sm 8vo. unp. NF/VG. T5. $25.00

**SHANNON, Mike.** *Day Satchel Paige & Pittsburgh Crawfords...* 1992. McFarland. F. P8. $20.00

**SHANNON, Monica.** *California Fairy Tales.* 1957 (1926). NY. Stephen Day. rpt. xl. lib bdg. G+. T5. $22.00

**SHAPIRO, Irwin.** *Uncle Sam's 200th-Birthday Party.* 1974. NY. Golden. slim 4to. 45p. VG. B11. $15.00

**SHAPIRO, Laura.** *Perfection Salad: Women & Cooking...* 1986. 1st Am. VG/dj. M17. $15.00

**SHAPIRO, Mary J.** *How They Built the Statue of Liberty.* 1985. NY. ils Huck Scarry. VG/G. M17. $15.00

**SHAPIRO, Milton.** *Gil Hodges.* 1960. Messner. 1st. photos. F/VG. P8. $125.00

**SHAPIRO, Mitchell E.** *Television Network Weekend Programming 1959-1990.* 1992. McFarland. 464p. VG. C5. $12.50

**SHAPLEN, Robert.** *Forest of Tigers.* 1956. Knopf. 1st. F/NF. H11. $40.00

**SHARIFF, Omar.** *Eternal Male: Omar Shariff, My Own Story.* 1977. Doubleday. 1st. sgn pres. trans from French. 184p. VG/dj. w/mc photo. W1. $30.00

**SHARP, Ann Pearsall.** *Little Garden People & What They Do.* 1938. Akron. Saalfield. 1st. ils. pict brd. F/NF. T10. $125.00

**SHARP, Dallas Lore.** *When Rolls the Oregon.* 1914. Houghton Mifflin. 1st. sm 8vo. 251p. VG. S14. $35.00

**SHARP, Margery.** *Miss Bianco in the Orient.* (1970). Boston. Little Brn. 1st. ils Erik Blegvad. gilt red cloth. pict dj. R5. $50.00

**SHARP.** *Sources of Modern Architecture, a Critical Bibliography.* 1981. revised ed. 192p. F/F. A4. $35.00

**SHARPE, Philip B.** *Complete Guide to Handloading.* 1953. NY. Funk Wagnall. 3rd. ils/index. H10. $40.00

**SHARPE, Philip B.** *Rifle in America.* (1947). NY. 2nd/best. ils/pl. 782p. cloth. VG. M8. $125.00

**SHARPE, Philip B.** *Rifle in America.* 1938. NY. Morrow. 641p. xl. leatherette. fair. H10. $22.50

**SHARPLES, A.** *Scorpion's Tail.* 1975. Taplinger. 1st. VG/dj. O4. $15.00

**SHATNER, William.** *Star Trek Memories.* 1993. Harper Collins. 1st. F/dj. P3. $22.00

**SHATNER, William.** *Teklab.* 1991. Ace/Putnam. 1st. F/F. B3. $15.00

**SHATRAW, Milton.** *Thrashin' Time, Memories of a Montana Boyhood.* 1970. Am West. VG/dj. J2. $55.00

**SHAW, Albert.** *Abraham Lincoln: His Path to the Presidency. Vol II.* 1929. NY. Review of Reviews Corp. 2 vol. 4to. red cloth. case. K1. $85.00

**SHAW, Andrew;** see Block, Lawrence.

**SHAW, Anna Howard.** *Story of a Pioneer.* 1915. Harper. 337p. VG. B18. $22.50

**SHAW, Annie DeWitt.** *Will, Annie & I: Travellers in Many Lands.* 1898. NY. Skinner. 1st. 8vo. ils. 363p. VG. W1. $45.00

**SHAW, Archer H.** *Plain Dealer: One Hundred Years in Cleveland.* 1942. Knopf. 1st. ils. cloth. F/dj. O10. $35.00

**SHAW, Bob.** *Fugitive Worlds.* 1989. London. Gollancz. 1st. F/NF. G10. $20.00

**SHAW, Bob.** *Ragged Astronauts.* 1986. NY. baen. 1st Am. F/NF. G10. $14.00

**SHAW, Bob.** *Wreath of Stars.* 1976. London. Gollancz. 1st. sgn. AN/dj. M21. $35.00

**SHAW, Edward.** *Modern Architect; or, Every Man His Own Master...* 1859. Boston. Wentworth Hewes. ils/engravings. 128p. full leather. B5. $250.00

**SHAW, George Bernard.** *Back to Methuselah: A Metabiological Pentateuch.* 1921. London. Constable. 1st. gilt olive cloth. NF/VG. A24. $95.00

**SHAW, George Bernard.** *Flyleaves.* 1977. Austin. WT Taylor. 1st. 1/350. terra-cotta buckram/prt label. F. M24. $125.00

**SHAW, George Bernard.** *Quintessence of Bernard Shaw.* 1920. London. Allen Unwin. 1st. VG/dj. A24. $45.00

**SHAW, George Russell.** *Pines of Mexico.* 1961 (1909). Jamaica Plain. 22 pl/map. AN/wrp. B26. $45.00

**SHAW, Irwin.** *Beggarman, Thief.* 1977. Franklin Lib. ltd. aeg. bl leather. F. B11. $40.00

**SHAW, Irwin.** *Mixed Company: Collected Stories.* 1950. Random. 1st. VG/G. B30. $25.00

**SHAW, Irwin.** *Nightwork.* 1975. Delacorte. 1st. NF/NF. H11. $25.00

**SHAW, Irwin.** *Top of the Hill.* 1979. Weidenfeld Nicholson. 1st. F/dj. T12. $30.00

**SHAW, Irwin.** *Young Lions.* Modern Lib/Random. F/NF. L4. $70.00

**SHAW, Marlow A.** *Happy Islands: Stories & Sketches of the Georgian Bay.* 1926. Toronto. 1st. 12mo. VG. A2. $25.00

**SHAW, Reuben Cole.** *Across the Plains in Forty-Nine.* 1948. Lakeside Classic. 1st thus. teg. w/pub card. NF. T11. $40.00

**SHAW, Richard J.** *Field Guide to Vascular Plants of Grand Teton Nat Park...* 1976. Logan. ils/map. 301p. VG/dj. B26. $21.00

**SHAW, Robert H.** *Ground Level Climatology.* 1967. AAAS. 395p. xl. VG. S5. $40.00

**SHAW, Robert K.** *Noel: Christmas Echoes Down the Ages, Recaptured by...* 1935. Worcester. St Onge. mini. 1/278. aeg. full dk red leather w/gilt title. B24. $1,750.00

**SHAW, Sam.** *Marilyn Among Friends.* 1987. Bloomsbury. VG/dj. P3. $20.00

**SHAW, Thomas.** *Soiling Crops & the Silo.* 1906. NY. Orange Judd. 366p. VG. A10. $22.00

**SHAW(N), Frank S.;** see Goulart, Ron.

**SHAYNE, Mike;** see Halliday, Brett.

**SHEARER, F.E.** *Pacific Tourist.* 1886. NY. ils. 372p. G. B18. $95.00

**SHECKLEY, Robert.** *Crompton Divided.* 1978. HRW. 1st. NF/dj. G10. $20.00

**SHECTAR, Ben.** *Hester the Jester.* 1977. Harper Row. I Can Read Book. 1st. 8vo. VG. M5. $15.00

**SHECTER, L.** *Once Upon the Polo Grounds.* 1970. NY. 1st. VG/dj. B5. $17.50

**SHEDD, Margaret.** *Inherit the Earth.* 1944. Harper. 1st. VG/clip. S18. $15.00

**SHEEHAN, Donald.** *This Was Publishing.* 1952. Bloomington. 1st. 288p. VG. B18. $17.50

**SHEEHY, Gail.** *Love Sounds.* 1970. Random. 1st. author's 1st book. F/dj. A24. $35.00

**SHEEHY.** *Guide to Reference Books, 9th Edition.* 1976. Am Lib Assn. 4to. 1033p. NF. A4. $75.00

**SHEEN, Fulton J.** *This Is the Holy Land.* 1961 (1960). Hawthorn. 1st. VG/dj. S5. $15.00

**SHEFFIELD, Charles.** *Cold as Ice.* 1992. NY. Tor. 1st. F/dj. G10. $14.00

**SHELDON, Charles.** *Wilderness of Denali: Explorations of a Hunter-Naturalist.* 1960. NY. new ed. index. 412p. F/G. A17. $40.00

**SHELDON, Gerard P.** *Gentle Ways in Japan.* 1989. SF. Saville Photo Arts. photos. VG/dj. S5. $20.00

**SHELDON, Harold P.** *Tranquility Revisited.* 1989. Derrydale. 1/2500. 130p. gilt leather. F. A17. $35.00

**SHELDON, Sidney.** *Other Side of Midnight.* 1974. Morrow. 1st. F/NF. H11. $35.00

**SHELDON, Sidney.** *Stars Shine Down.* 1992. Morrow. 1st. F/F. H11. $20.00

**SHELDON, W.** *27th: A Regimental History.* VG. E6. $150.00

**SHELFORD, Victor E.** *Ecology of North America.* 1978 (1963). U IL. 610p. sc. G. S5. $20.00

**SHELFORD, Victor E.** *Laboratory & Field Ecology.* 1930. Williams Wilkins. 608p. xl. VG. S5. $15.00

**SHELLABARGER, Samuel.** *Lord Chesterfield & His World.* 1951. Little Brn. 1st. gilt red cloth. H13. $35.00

**SHELLEY, Mary Wollstonecraft.** *Frankenstein Annotated.* 1977. Clarkson Potter, NY. 1st. VG/G. L1. $125.00

**SHELLEY, Mary Wollstonecraft.** *Frankenstein; or, Modern Prometheus.* 1930. NY. Grosset Dunlap. 1st photoplay. 8vo. 240p. Sangorski bdg. F. H5. $950.00

**SHELLEY, Mary Wollstonecraft.** *Frankenstein; or, Modern Prometheus.* 1983. Pennyroyal. 1/5 (350). sgn Moser/52 initialed pl. Kelm bdg. extra suite. box. B24. $5,000.00

**SHELLEY, Percy Bysshe.** *Complete Poetical Works of...* 1892. Boston. 4 vol. half leather/marbled brd. F. B30. $225.00

**SHELLEY, Percy Bysshe.** *Shelley's Complete Poetical Works.* 1901. Boston. teg. half brn leather/marbled brd. F. B30. $40.00

**SHELTON, Louise.** *Seasons in a Flower Garden.* 1915. Scribner. 2nd. 117p. VG. A10. $40.00

**SHENKER, Israel.** *In the Footsteps of John & Boswell.* 1982. Houghton Mifflin. 1st. ... frontis. dj. H13. $35.00

**SHENSTONE, William.** *Poetical Wo...* 1771. Edinburgh. Prt for C Elliot. sm ... 244p. contemporary sheep. VG. S17. $75...

**SHEPARD, Alan.** *Moon Shot.* 1994. Atla... Turner. 1st. F/dj. M23. $30.00

**SHEPARD, Ernest H.** *Drawn From Men...* 1957. Phil. Lippincott. 1st Am. 8vo. VG ... J3. $40.00

**SHEPARD, Leslie.** *Dracula Book of ...* Vampire Stories. 1977. Citadel. BC. V... L1. $15.00

**SHEPARD, Lucius.** *Barnical Bill the Spa... Other Stories.* 1997. London. Orion. 1st... F/dj. G10. $125.00

**SHEPARD, Lucius.** *Father of Stones.* 198... Assn. 1/500. sgn Shepard/ils JK Potter... box. B30. $60.00

**SHEPARD, Lucius.** *Jaguar Hunter.* ... Arkham. 1st. author's 1st hc pub. ... B30. $75.00

**SHEPARD, Lucius.** *Life During Wa...* 1991. Bantam. 1st. sgn. NF/wrp. R11. $...

**SHEPARD, Sam.** *Cruising Paradise.* ... Knopf. 1st. sgn. F/dj. M25. $50.00

**SHEPARD, Sam.** *Unseen Hand & Other ...* 1972. Bobbs Merrill. 1st. F/NF. B2. $40.0...

**SHEPARD.** *Encyclopedia of Occultis... Parapsychology...* 1984. 3 vol. 1628p. F. A4. $2...

**SHEPERD, John.** *History of the Live... Medical Institution.* 1979. Liverpool... 319p. A13. $35.00

**SHEPHERD, Anthony.** *Arabian Adve...* 1961. London. Collins. 10 pl/map. clot... Q2. $47.00

**SHEPHERD, Michael;** see Ludlum, Ro...

**SHEPHERD, William R.** *Guide to Mat... for History of US in Spanish Archives.* ... WA, DC. 1st. 107p. VG/prt wrp. M8. $...

**SHERBO, Arthur.** *Samuel Johnson's C... Opinions.* 1995. Newark. U DE. 1st. gil... linen. AN/dj. H13. $35.00

**SHERIDAN, Richard Brinsley.** *Wo...* 1821. London. John Murray. 2 vol. 1st ... lected. tall 8vo. uncut. H13. $225.00

**SHERLOCK, C.** *Modern Farm Hen.* ... Des Moines. Homestead. 236p. cloth... A10. $20.00

**SHULMAN, Max.** *Rally Round the Flag, Boys!* 1957 (1954). Doubleday. 278p. G. C5. $12.50

**SHUMAN, M.K.** *Caesar Clue.* 1990. St Martin. 1st. VG/dj. R8. $10.00

**SHUMWAY, Larry V.** *Frontier Fiddler: Life of N Arizona Pioneer KC Kartchner.* 1990. Tucson, AZ. 1st. ils/music/index. 280p. AN. B19. $10.00

**SHUPTRINE, Hubert.** *Jericho. The South Beheld.* 1974. Birmingham. Oxmoor. 1st. VG/dj. B5. $45.00

**SHURTLEFF, Bertrand.** *Short Leash.* 1945. Bobbs Merrill. 1st. ils Diana Thorne. VG/dj. A21. $35.00

**SHUTE, Henry A.** *Brite & Fair.* 1968. Noone House. rpt. 8vo. ils. VG/G. B17. $45.00

**SHUTE, Nevil.** *Old Captivity.* 1940. NY. 1st Am. 333p. VG/dj. B18. $25.00

**SHUTE, Nevil.** *On the Beach.* 1957. Heinneman. 1st. VG+/dj. S13. $25.00

**SHUTE, Nevil.** *Trustee From the Toolroom.* 1960. NY. Morrow. 1st. VG+/NF. T11. $40.00

**SIAS, Beverlee.** *Skier's Cookbook.* 1971. AS Barnes. G/dj. A16. $10.00

**SIBBALD, John.** *Career Makers.* 1992. Harper Business. 1st. sm 4to. 408p. F/dj. W2. $30.00

**SIBLEY, Brian.** *Land of Narnia: Brian Sibley Explores World of CS Lewis.* (199). Harper Row. 1st Am. ils Pauline Baynes. AN/dj. A27. $20.00

**SIBLEY, Celestine.** *Christmas in Georgia.* 1964. Doubleday. 1st. sgn. 95p. F/dj. D4. $45.00

**SIBLEY, Celestine.** *Especially at Christmas.* 1969. Doubleday. 1st. VG/dj. M21. $7.50

**SIBSON, Alfred.** *Agricultural Chemistry.* 1858. London. Routledge. 239p. cloth. A10. $20.00

**SICK, Helmut.** *Tukani.* 1960. Eriksson-Taplinger. 1st Am. 240p. map ep. dj. F3. $20.00

**SICKELS, Evelyn Ray.** *Pet Parade.* 1935. Scribner. 1st. inscr. ils Edna Potter. pict brd. VG. B18. $25.00

**SIDDONS, Ann Rivers.** *House Next Door.* nd. BC. F/NF. S18. $5.00

**SIDDONS, Anne Rivers.** *King's Oak.* 1990. Harper Collins. 1st Canadian. F/F. T12. $25.00

**SIDDONS, Anne Rivers.** *King's Oak.* 1990. Harper Collins. 1st. F/NF. H11. $20.00

**SIDDONS, Anne Rivers.** *Outer Banks.* 1991. NY. Harper. 1st. NF/dj. S13. $10.00

**SIDDONS, Anne Rivers.** *Peachtree Road.* 1988. Harper Row. 1st. NF/dj. M23. $15.00

**SIDDONS, Dan.** *Children of the Night.* 1992. Putnam. 1st. sgn. AN/dj. S18. $35.00

**SIDDONS, Dan.** *Fires of Eden.* 1994. Putnam. 1st. sgn. AN/dj. S18. $30.00

**SIDDONS, Dan.** *Hollow Man.* 1993. Bantam. 1st. sgn. AN/dj. S18. $40.00

**SIDDONS, Dan.** *Love Death.* 1993. Warner. 1st. sgn. AN/dj. S18. $30.00

**SIDIS, Boris.** *Psychopathological Researches: Studies...* 1902. NY. Stechert. tall 8vo. 10 fld pl. 330p. panelled ochre buckram. xl. G1. $125.00

**SIDNEY, Margaret.** *Five Little Peppers & How They Grew.* 1909. Lee Shepard. 410p. G. P12. $10.00

**SIDNEY, Margaret.** *Five Little Peppers & How They Grew.* 1948. Grosset Dunlap. ils. 275p. VG. B36. $8.50

**SIDNEY, Margaret.** *Five Little Peppers Grow Up.* 1893. D Lothrop Co. ils. 527p+ads. gilt gr cloth. VG. B36. $45.00

**SIDNEY, William.** *Good Tidings.* 1950. NY. Farrar. 1st. NF/VG. H11. $25.00

**SIEBERT, Diane.** *Heartland.* 1989. Crowell. 1st. ils Wendell Minor. F/dj. B17. $20.00

**SIEVLING, Earle.** *Earle Sievling's NY Cuisine.* 1985. 1st. mc photos. F/F. E6. $13.00

**SIGAUD, Louis A.** *Belle Boyd: Confederate Spy.* (1944). Dietz. 2nd. 254p. VG/poor. B10. $30.00

**SIGERIST, Henry.** *Medicine & Human Welfare.* 1947. New Haven. 148p. A13. $60.00

**SIGERIST, Henry.** *University at the Crossroads.* 1946. NY. 1st. 162p. A13. $40.00

**SIGNORELLI, Olga.** *Eleonora Duse.* 1959. Milano. Silvana Editoriale D'Arte. VG/dj. B9. $60.00

**SIGUENZA Y GONGORA.** *Mercurio Volante of Don Carlos de Siguenza y Gongora...* 1932. Quivira Soc. 1/665. fld map/12 pl. 148p. NF. A4. $250.00

**SIKES, L.N.** *Using the American Quarter Horse.* 1974. Dayton, TX. Saddlerock. VG/fair. O3. $18.00

**SIKOV, Ed.** *Laughing Hysterically.* 1994. NY. Columbia. 282p. VG/dj. C5. $15.00

**SILKE, James R.** *Here's Looking at You, Kid.* 1976. Little Brn. 1st. 317p. VG. C5. $15.00

**SILL, Edward Rowland.** *Around the Horn, a Journal, Dec 10, 1861 to March 25, 1862.* 1944. New Haven. 79p. quarter cloth. B18. $37.50

**SILLER, Van.** *One Alone.* 1946. Crime Club. 1st. NF/VG. M19. $25.00

**SILLITOE, Alan.** *Loneliness of the Long Distance Runner.* 1959. Knopf. 1st Am. NF/VG. R14. $50.00

**SILLITOE, Alan.** *Rats & Other Poems.* 1960. London. WH Allen. 1st. F/NF. L3. $40.00

**SILLMAN, Leonard.** *Here Lies Leonard Sillman.* 1959. Citadel. 1st. inscr. F/NF. B2. $50.00

**SILLOWAY, P.M.** *Summer Birds of Flathead Lake.* 1901. Missoula, MT. Bull U MT #3. 15 photos. 83p. VG. C12. $38.00

**SILLS, Beverly.** *Bubbles: A Self Portrait.* 1976. Bobbs Merrill. 1st. sgn. VG/dj. B30. $40.00

**SILONE, Ignazio.** *Seed Beneath the Snow.* 1965. Atheneum. 1st. VG/dj. B11. $15.00

**SILTZER.** *Story of British Sporting Prints.* 1929. London. 1/1000. 4to. 413p. VG. A4. $265.00

**SILVER, George.** *Spy in the House of Medicine.* 1976. Germantown, MD. 1st. 308p. A13. $20.00

**SILVER, Rollo G.** *American Printer 1787-1825.* 1967. Charlottesville. 1st. ils. 189p. gilt blk cloth. F. F1. $25.00

**SILVER, Rollo G.** *Typefounding in America, 1787-1825.* 1965. Charlottesville, VA. 1st. ils. brd/cloth spine. VG. M8. $45.00

**SILVER & URSINI.** *Vampire Film.* 1975. AS Barnes. 1st. VG/dj. L1. $50.00

**SILVERBERG, Robert.** *Empires in the Dust: Ancient Civilizations Brought to Light.* 1966. Phil/NY. Chilton. 2nd. 8vo. ils. 247p. VG. W1. $18.00

**SILVERBERG, Robert.** *Ghost Towns of the American West.* 1968. Crowell. 1st. sgn. ils Bjorklund. VG. O4. $35.00

**SILVERBERG, Robert.** *Lord of Darkness.* 1983. Arbor House. 1st. VG/G. L1. $30.00

**SILVERBERG, Robert.** *Parsecs & Parables: Ten Science Fiction Stories.* 1970. NY. Doubleday. 1st. F/NF. G10. $20.00

**SILVERBERG, Robert.** *Star of Gypsies.* 1986. DIF. 1st. NF/dj. M21. $15.00

**SILVERBERG, Robert.** *Tom O'Bedlam.* 1985. DIF. 1st. sgn. F/NF. S18. $40.00

**SILVERMAN, Mel.** *Good-For-Nothing Burro.* 1958. Cleveland. World. 1st. 8vo. red cloth. G. T5. $10.00

**SILVERMAN, Stephen M.** *Fox That Got Away...* 1988. Lyle Stuart. 1st. VG/NF. S14. $10.00

**SILVIS, Randall.** *Dead Man Falling.* 1996. NY. Carroll Graf. 1st. sgn. F/dj. T2. $30.00

**SILVIS, Randall.** *Occasional Hell.* 1993. Sag Harbor. Permanent. 1st. sgn. F/dj. T2. $35.00

**SIM, K.** *Desert Traveller: Life of Jean Louis Burckhardt.* 1969. London. ils. 447p. maps. NF. M4. $35.00

**SIMENON, Georges.** *Blue Room & the Accomplices.* 1964. HBW. 1st. NF/NF. H11. $15.00

**SIMENON, Georges.** *Girl With a Squint.* 1951. HBJ. 1st Am. NF/dj. G8. $15.00

**SIMENON, Georges.** *Intimate Memoirs.* 1984. HBJ. 1st. VG/dj. G8. $15.00

**SIMENON, Georges.** *Maigret & the Apparition.* 1976. HBJ. 1st Am. G+/dj. G8. $10.00

**SIMENON, Georges.** *Maigret & the Spinster.* 1977. HBJ. 1st Am. NF/dj. G8. $25.00

**SIMENON, Georges.** *Maigret & the Spinster.* 1977. London. Hamish Hamilton. 1st. F/dj. M15. $45.00

**SIMENON, Georges.** *Maigret Goes Home.* 1940. HBJ. 1st Am. NF/dj. G8. $20.00

**SIMENON, Georges.** *Maigret Has Doubts.* 1968. London. Hamish Hamilton. 1st. F/clip. M15. $45.00

**SIMENON, Georges.** *Maigret in Society.* 1962. London. Hamish Hamilton. 1st. F/clip. M15. $45.00

**SIMENON, Georges.** *Rich Man.* 1971. HBJ. 1st AM. F/NF. G8. $25.00

**SIMENON, Georges.** *When I Was Old.* 1971. HBJ. 1st. NF/dj. P3. $25.00

**SIMENON, Georges.** *Window Over the Way.* 1951. London. Routledge/Kegan Paul. 1st. F/NF. M15. $85.00

**SIMIC, Charles.** *Dime-Store Alchemy.* 1992. Hopewell. Ecco. 1st. sgn/dtd 1994. F/dj. R14. $45.00

**SIMIC, Charles.** *Return to a Place Lit by a Glass of Milk.* 1974. Braziller. 1st. F/F. B3. $50.00

**SIMIC, Charles.** *Shaving at Night.* 1982. SF. Meadow. 1/200. sgn. ils/sgn Siegl. F/sans. O11. $110.00

**SIMIC, Charles.** *Unending Blues.* 1986. HBJ. 1st. F/dj. O11. $20.00

**SIMKINS, W.S.** *Federal Equity Suit, 2nd Edition.* 1911. Rochester. buckram. xl. M11. $65.00

**SIMMIE, Lois.** *Secret Lives of Sgt John Wilson: True Story...* 1995. Vancouver. Douglas & McIntyre. 1st. F/dj. A26. $15.00

**SIMMONS, Adelma G.** *Herb Gardening in Five Seasons.* 1965. Van Nostrand. BC. 353p. VG/dj. A10. $20.00

**SIMMONS, Adelma G.** *Herb Gardens of Delight.* 1974. Hawthorn. 190p. VG. A10. $10.00

**SIMMONS, Dan.** *Children of Night.* 1992. Putnam. 1st trade. F/dj. M21. $25.00

**SIMMONS, Dan.** *Lovedeath.* 1993. Warner. 1st. AN/dj. B30. $25.00

**SIMMONS, Herbert A.** *Man Walking on Eggshells.* 1962. 1st. NF/VG. M19. $35.00

**SIMMONS.** *Chekhov, a Biography.* 1962. 21 photos. 692p. VG/VG. A4. $35.00

**SIMMS, E.** *Natural History of British Birds.* 1983. London. Dent. ils/maps. F/dj. M12. $37.50

**SIMMS, Gilmore.** *John Smith & Pocohantas.* 1867. John E Potter. 7th. 8vo. 379p. G. S17. $12.50

**SIMON, C.** *Clinical Diagnosis by Microscope & Chemical Methods.* 1897. 2nd. ils/pl. 563p. VG. E6. $25.00

**SIMON, Hilda.** *Splendor of Iridescence.* 1971. NY. lg 8vo. 140 mc ils. NF/VG. S15. $32.00

**SIMON, Merrill.** *God, Allah, & the Great Land Grab.* 1989. NY. Jonathan David. 1st. 8vo. VG/dj. W1. $18.00

**SIMON, Neil.** *Jake's Women.* 1994. Random. 1st. F/dj. A24. $25.00

**SIMON, Neil.** *They're Playing Our Songs.* 1980. Random. 1st. VG/dj. C9. $36.00

**SIMON, Oliver.** *Printer & Playground: An Autobiography.* 1956. London. Faber. 1st. 156p. cloth. F/dj. O10. $40.00

**SIMON, Philip J.** *Log of the Mayflower.* 1957. Chicago. Priam. 208p. VG/G. M10. $12.50

**SIMON, S. Sylvan.** *Let's Make Movies.* 1940. NY. Samuel French. 1st. VG/dj. C9. $72.00

**SIMONDS, John Ormsbee.** *Landscape Architecture.* 1961. McGraw Hill. 244p. VG/dj. A10. $18.00

**SIMONDS, John Ormsbee.** *Landscape Architecture: Shaping...* 1973. NY. Am Elsevier. ils/index. 305p. VG. H10. $30.00

**SIMOSKO & TEPPERMAN.** *Eric Dolphy: A Musical Biography & Discography.* 1974. Smithsonian. 1st. F/NF. B2. $50.00

**SIMPSON, C.H.** *Wild Life in the Far West; or, Detective's Thrilling...* 1905. Chicago. ils. 264p. cheap paper. G. A17. $25.00

**SIMPSON, John E.** *Crossed Wires.* 1992. Carroll Graf. 1st. author's 1st book. F/F. H11. $30.00

**SIMPSON, Lesley.** *Enomienda in New Spain: Beginning of Spanish Mexico.* 1982 (1960). Berkeley. rpt. index/biblio/maps. 263p. F3. $25.00

**SIMPSON, Louis.** *Adventures in the Letter I.* 1971. London. Oxford. 1st. sgn. F/wrp (no cloth issue). R14. $35.00

**SIMPSON, Louis.** *Searching for the Ox.* 1976. Morrow. 1st. inscr/dtd 1976. F/dj. L3. $50.00

**SIMPSON, Louis.** *Selected Poems.* 1965. HBW. 1st. sgn. F/dj. L3. $75.00

**SIMPSON, Louis.** *Selected Prose.* 1989. NY. VG/dj. M17. $15.00

**SIMPSON, Marc.** *Winslow Homer Paintings of the Civil War.* 1988. SF. Fine Arts Mus. ils. VG/dj. M17. $45.00

**SIMPSON, Michael A.** *Dying, Death & Grief: A Critical Bibliography.* 1987. Pittsburgh. 1st. 8vo. F. A2. $20.00

**SIMPSON, Mona.** *Lost Father.* 1992. Knopf. 1st. F/F. H11. $25.00

**SIMPSON, Mona.** *Lost Father.* 1992. Knopf. 1st. sgn. author's 2nd book. NF/dj. S18. $30.00

**SIMPSON, Thomas.** *This Way Madness Lies.* 1992. NY. Warner. 1st. author's 1st book. F/NF. H11. $35.00

**SIMPSON & SIMPSON.** *Torn Land.* (1970). Bell. 2nd. sgns. photos/map. VG/dj. B10. $65.00

**SIMPSON.** *Dying, Death & Grief: Critical Bibliography.* 1987. Pittsburgh. 1700 entries. 276p. F. A4. $45.00

**SIMS, George;** see Cain, Paul.

**SIMS, John.** *Dissertatio Medica Inauguralis, Quaedam de Cerebri...* 1818. Edinburgh. Stewart. 44p. gilt morocco. F. G7. $295.00

**SIMSON, Alfred.** *Garden Mosaics, Philosophical, Moral & Horticultural.* 1903. NY. Appleton. 219p. VG. A10. $20.00

**SINATRA, Tina.** *Man & His Art (Frank Sinatra).* 1991. NY. Random. ARC/1st. 118p. F/dj. w/3 photos+pub slip. S9. $125.00

**SINCLAIR, Andrew.** *Facts in the Case of EA Poe...* 1979. HRW. 1st. sm 8vo. F/dj. O10. $15.00

**SINCLAIR, Andrew.** *Spiegel: Man Behind the Pictures.* 1987. Little Brn. 1st. F/clip. M7. $30.00

**SINCLAIR, April.** *Ain't Gonna Be the Same Fool Twice.* 1996. Hyperion. ARC. F/wrp. R14. $35.00

**SINCLAIR, April.** *Coffee Will Make You Black.* 1994. NY. Hyperion. UP. F/wrp. R14. $45.00

**SINCLAIR, Caroline Baytop.** *Kidnapped Child: A Biographical Novel...* (1983). McClure. 232p. VG/G. B10. $15.00

**SINCLAIR, Carolyn Baytop.** *Stories of Old Gloucester.* (1974). McClure. ils EL Noland. 66p. VG/dj. B10. $15.00

**SINCLAIR, H.M.** *Work of Sir Robert McCarrison.* 1953. London. 1st. 327p. A13. $75.00

**SINCLAIR, Upton.** *Gnomobile: Gnice Gnew Gnarrative With Gnonsense...* 1936. Farrar Rinehart. 1st. ils John O'Hara. brn cloth. VG. B36. $22.00

**SINCLAIR, Upton.** *It Happend to Didymus.* 1958. Sagamore. 1st. NF/NF. H11. $25.00

**SINCLAIR, Upton.** *Jungle.* 1906. Jungle Pub. 1st/sustainer's ed. VG+. B2. $175.00

**SINCLAIR, Upton.** *Jungle.* 1906. NY. 1st. ils gr cloth. VG. B14. $100.00

**SINCLAIR, Walton B.** *Orange: Its Biochemistry & Physiology.* 1961. Berkeley. ils/tables. 475p. blk cloth. VG. B26. $27.50

**SINDELAR, Joseph C.** *Nixie Bunny in Manners-Land.* 1912. Chicago. ils Helen Geraldine Hodge. 144p. pict cloth. VG. B18. $17.50

**SINGER, Charles.** *Short History of Scientific Ideas to 1900.* 1959. London. 1st. 525p. A13/K5. $30.00

**SINGER, Isaac Bashevis.** *Enemies: A Love Story.* 1972. FSG. 1st. F/NF. B4. $75.00

**SINGER, Isaac Bashevis.** *In My Father's Court: A Memoir.* 1966. NY. 1st. VG/dj. M17. $15.00

**SINGER, Isaac Bashevis.** *Naftali, the Storyteller & His Horse.* 1976. FSG. 1st. ils Margot Zemach. VG/dj. B17. $17.50

**SINGER, Isaac Bashevis.** *Naftali, the Storyteller & His Horse.* 1976. FSG. 1st. 129p. F/NF. D4. $50.00

**SINGER, Isaac Bashevis.** *Passions.* 1975. FSG. 1st. NF/clip. R14. $35.00

**SINGER, Isaac Bashevis.** *Penitent.* 1983. Franklin Lib. special bdg ltd 1st. sgn. aeg. gilt leather. F. B2. $125.00

**SINGER, Isaac Bashevis.** *Shosha.* 1978. NY. Farrar. 1st. sgn. NF/dj. B2. $85.00

**SINGER, Isaac Bashevis.** *Yentl the Yeshiva Boy.* 1983. FSG. 1st separate. sgn. ils Antonio Frasconi. F/dj. B4. $275.00

**SINGER, Isaac Bashevis.** *Yentl the Yeshiva Boy.* 1983. FSG. 1st. ils Antoio Frasconi. VG/dj. B17. $20.00

**SINGER, Isaac Bashevis.** *Zlateh the Goat.* 1966. Harper Row. 1st. VG/G. P2. $75.00

**SINGER, Kurt.** *Laughton Story.* 1954. Winston. 1st. VG/dj. P3. $15.00

**SINGER, Marilyn.** *Horsemaster.* 1985. Atheneum. 1st. VG/dj. O3. $25.00

**SINGLETON, Ralph S.** *Film Scheduling.* 1984. Lone Eagle. 1st. VG/lg wrp. C9. $20.00

**SINIGAGLIA, Leone.** *Climbing Reminiscences of the Dolomites.* 1896. London. Fisher Unwin. 1st. ils/fld map. 223p. teg. xl. VG. W1. $75.00

**SINNOTT, Edmund W.** *Meeting House & Church in Early New England.* 1963. NY. McGraw Hill. 1st. 243p. VG/dj. B18. $17.50

**SINSSER, Hans.** *Rats, Lice & History: Life History of Typhus Fever.* 1935. Boston. 1st. 301p. A13. $45.00

**SINYARD, Neil.** *Marilyn.* 1989. Bison Group. 1st. VG. P3. $20.00

**SIODMAK, Curt.** *Donovan's Brain.* Feb 1944. Triangle. 1st thus. G/dj. L1. $100.00

**SIRINGO, Charles A.** *Riata & Spurs: Story of a Lifetime...* 1931. Houghton Mifflin. later prt. 261p. gilt cloth. VG. B18. $37.50

**SIRINGO, Charles A.** *Texas Cowboy; or, Fifteen Years on Hurricane Deck...* 1980. Time-Life. rpt of 1885. aeg. NF/sans. B19. $20.00

**SIRKS & ZIRKLE.** *Evolution of Biology.* 1964. NY. 376p. A13. $25.00

**SISLER, George.** *Sisler on Baseball.* 1954. McKay. 1st. VG/G+. P8. $30.00

**SISLEY, Nick.** *Deer Hunting Across North America.* 1975. Freshet. photos. 281p. AN/dj. A17. $15.00

**SISSON, Rosemary Anne.** *Adventures of Ambrose.* 1952. Dutton. 1st Am. ils Astrid Walford. G/dj. P2. $25.00

**SISSON & WALKER.** *Fiction of Jack London.* 1972. ils. 55p. NF. A4. $35.00

**SITCHEN, Zecharia.** *Lost Realms.* 1990. Santa Fe. Bear & Co. 1st. ils/maps/biblio. 298p. F3. $10.00

**SITGREAVES, L.** *Report of Expedition Down the Zuni & CO Rivers in 1851.* 1854. Chicago. Rio Grande. maps/sketches/ils/index/fld map. 198p. brn cloth. VG. F7. $550.00

**SITGREAVES, L.** *Report of Expedition Down the Zuni & CO Rivers in 1851.* 1962 (1853). facs. VG+. F7. $65.00

**SITWELL, Edith.** *Shadow of Cain.* 1947. London. Lehmann. 1st. 1/3000. gr prt brd. F/dj. M24. $25.00

**SITWELL, Osbert.** *Scarlet Tree.* 1946. Little Brn. 1st. NF/VG. B9. $50.00

**SITWELL, Sacheverell.** *Arabesque & Honeycomb.* 1957. London. Hale. ils/pl. 224p. VG/torn. Q2. $37.00

**SITWELL, Sacheverell.** *Arabesque & Honeycomb.* 1958. Random. 1st. photos. 224p. VG/G. S14. $15.00

**SITWELL, Sacheverell.** *Fine Bird Books 1700-1900.* 1990. Atlantic Monthly. 1st. 180p. F/dj. A17. $50.00

**SITWELL, Sacheverell.** *Great Flower Books 1700-1900...* 1990. Atlantic Monthly. 1st. 50 full-p pl. 189p. F/dj. A17. $50.00

**SITWELL, Sacheverell.** *Great Flower Books 1700-1900...* 1990. NY. fwd Dillon Ripley. VG/dj. M17. $40.00

**SITWELL & SMITH.** *Fish & Game Laws of Maine.* 1880. Portland. Fox. 16mo. wrp. A10. $25.00

**SJOWALL & WAHLOO.** *Abominable Man.* 1972. NY. Pantheon. 1st Am. F/clip. M15. $45.00

**SJOWALL & WAHLOO.** *Cop Killer.* 1975. NY. Pantheon. 1st Am. F/dj. M15. $45.00

**SKAAR, Grace.** *Little Red House.* 1955. NY. Young Scott. obl 8vo. mc pict cloth/dj. R5. $185.00

**SKAL, David J.** *Hollywood Gothic.* 1990. Norton. 1st. VG/dj. L1. $85.00

**SKAL, David J.** *Monster Show.* 1993. Norton. 1st. VG/dj. L1. $75.00

**SKALLERUP.** *Books Afloat & Ashore: A History of Books...* 1974. 289p. F/VG. A4. $55.00

**SKEAPING, John.** *Big Tree of Mexico.* 1953. Bloomington, IN. IU. 1st. 234p. dj. F3. $15.00

**SKELTON, R.A.** *Charts & Views Drawn by Cook & His Officers...* 1955. Hakluyt Soc. folio. fld maps/charts. F. A4. $395.00

**SKELTON, R.A.** *Vinland Map...* 1995. Yale. 19 pl/fld maps. 357p. F/F. A4. $45.00

**SKELTON, Robin.** *Writings of JJ Synge.* 1971. Bobbs Merrill. 1st. F/clip. O4. $15.00

**SKEYHILL, Tom.** *Sergeant York: His Own Life Story & War Diary.* 1928. Doubleday Doran. 1st. sgn. VG/dj. S16. $450.00

**SKINNER, B.F.** *About Behaviorism.* 1974. Knopf. BC. 272p. G+/VG. P12. $10.00

**SKINNER, B.F.** *Science & Human Behavior.* 1992. NY. Classics of Psychiatry & Behavioral Sciences Lib. F. G1. $65.00

**SKINNER, B.F.** *Verbal Behavior.* 1972 (1957). Appleton Century Crofts. Century Psychology series. 6th. 478p. olive cloth. G1. $85.00

**SKINNER, B.F.** *Walden Two.* 1948. Macmillan. sm 8vo. 266p. blk cloth. VG. G1. $75.00

**SKINNER, B.F.** *Walden Two.* 1948. Macmillan. 1st. F/VG. B2. $175.00

**SKINNER, H.** *American Book of Cookery Containing More Than 500 Receipts.* 1850. Boston. 1st. 110p. G. E6. $65.00

**SKINNER, John S.** *Treatise on Milch Cows.* 1866. NY. Orange Judd. 88p. cloth. A10. $20.00

**SKIRKA & SWANK.** *African Antelope.* 1971. Winchester. 1st. F/box. R8. $150.00

**SKLEPOWICH, Edward.** *Death in a Serene City.* 1990. Morrow. 1st. F/F. H11. $25.00

**SKLEPOWICH, Edward.** *Farewell to the Flesh.* 1991. Morrow. 1st. F/F. H11. $20.00

**SKOLLE, John.** *Azalai.* 1956. NY. Harper. 1st. 8vo. 16 pl/3 maps. VG/dj. W1. $10.00

**SKOLNICK, Jerome H.** *Justice Without Trial, Law Enforcement...* 1966. NY. cloth. M11. $25.00

**SKREBITSKI, G.A.** *Forest Echo.* 1967. Braziller. 1st Am. 8vo. 72p. VG. C14. $8.00

**SKVORESKY, Josef.** *Sins for Father Knox.* 1989. London. Faber. 1st. sgn. F/NF. B3. $50.00

**SLACK, Henry J.** *Marvels of Pond-Life; or, Year's Microscopic Recreations...* 1861. London. Groombridge. 8vo. 197p. cloth. G. K5. $75.00

**SLADE, Michael.** *Headhunter.* 1984. Morrow. 1st. VG/dj. L1. $30.00

**SLADEK, John.** *Bugs.* 1989. London. Macmillan. 1st. sgn. F/dj. M21. $25.00

**SLATER, Philip.** *How I Saved the World.* 1985. Dutton. 1st. NF/dj. S18. $30.00

**SLATTA, Richard W.** *Cowboys of the Americas.* 1990. Yale. ils/notes/glossary. 305p. F/F. B19. $25.00

**SLATTERY, Marty.** *Diamonds Are Trumps.* 1990. St Lukes. 1st. F/dj. P8. $10.00

**SLAUGHTER, Carolyn.** *Banquet.* 1984. Ticknor Fields. 1st Am. F/clip. A14. $21.00

**SLAUGHTER, Frank G.** *David: Warrior & King.* nd. World. 2nd. VG/dj. P3. $15.00

**SLAUGHTER, Frank G.** *Golden Isle.* 1947. Doubleday. 1st. G. G11. $5.00

**SLAUGHTER, Frank G.** *Road to Bythinia.* 1951. Peoples. 1st. RS. NF/VG. S18. $17.00

**SLAVITT, David.** *Big Nose.* 1983. Baton Rouge. LSU. 1st. sgn. F/dj. R14. $45.00

**SLAVITT, David.** *King of Hearts.* 1976. NY. Arbor. 1st. NF/clip. A14. $21.00

**SLAYMAKER, S.R.** *Captive's Mansion.* 1973. Harper. 1st. sgn. 220p. VG/dj. B11. $35.00

**SLEIGH, M.A.** *Biology of Cilia & Flagella.* 1962. Pergamon. 242p. xl. VG. S5. $20.00

**SLETTEN, H.M.** *Growing Up on Bald Hill Creek.* 1977. IA U. 1st. photos. 161p. F/dj. M4. $15.00

**SLOAN, Irving J.** *Youth & the Law.* 1981. Dobbs Ferry. Oceana Pub. 4th. M11. $25.00

**SLOAN, James Park.** *War Games.* 1971. Houghton Mifflin. 1st. F/NF. R11. $45.00

**SLOAN, Stephen.** *Pablo Morillo & Venezuela, 1815-1820.* 1974. Columbus, OH. 1st. 249p. dj. F3. $10.00

**SLOAN, William E.** *Letters From Abroad.* 1925. private prt. photos. 182p. VG. H7. $25.00

**SLOANE, Eric.** *ABC, Book of Early Americana.* 1995. Wings Books. rpt. 4to. ils. VG/dj. B17. $12.50

**SLOANE, Eric.** *Diary of an Early American Boy.* 1962. Funk Wagnall. probable 1st. ils. VG/G. P2. $20.00

**SLOANE, Eric.** *Eric Sloane's America.* 1986. NY. ils. F/dj. M4. $35.00

**SLOANE, Eric.** *I Remember America.* 1971. Funk Wagnall. 1st. ils. 184p. VG. B18. $35.00

**SLOANE, Eric.** *Museum of Early American Tools.* 1974. NY. ils. 108p. VG/wrp. M4. $10.00

**SLOANE, Eric.** *Our Vanishing Landscape.* 1974. NY. ils. 107p. VG/wrp. M4. $10.00

**SLOANE, Eric.** *Recollections in Black & White: Enlarged Portfolio Edition.* 1978. NY. 1st. obl 4to. F/dj. M4. $45.00

**SLOANE, Eric.** *Reverence for Wood.* 1973. NY. ils. 111p. NF. M4. $10.00

**SLOANE, Eric.** *Seasons of America Past.* 1988. NY. 4 mc pl. F/dj. M4. $25.00

**SLOANE, Eric.** *Sketches of America's Past.* 1986. NY. ils. 3 books in 1. 336p. F/dj. M4. $35.00

**SLOANE, T. O'Conor.** *Motion Picture Projection.* 1922. NY. Faulk. 1st. VG/dj. C9. $102.00

**SLOCHOWER, Harry.** *No Voice Is Wholly Lost: Writers & Thinkers in War & Peace.* 1946. London. Dennis Dobson. 1st. 324p. VG. N2. $10.00

**SLOVO, Gillian.** *Death Comes Staccato.* 1987. Crime Club. 1st Am. NF/dj. G8. $12.50

**SLUNG, Michelle.** *I Shudder at Your Touch.* nd. BC. VG/F. S18. $5.00

**SLUNG, Michelle.** *I Shudder at Your Touch.* 1991. NY. NAL/Penguin. 1st. AN/dj. T12. $30.00

**SMALL, Abner Ralph.** *Road to Richmond: Civil War Memoirs of...* 1939. Berkeley. U CA. 1st. ils. 314p. cloth. VG. M8. $125.00

**SMALL, David.** *Almost Famous.* 1982. Norton. later prt. VG/F. P8. $20.00

**SMALL, John Kunkel.** *Ferns of the Vicinity of New York.* 1935. Lancaster, PA. fld map. VG/dj. B26. $32.50

**SMALLEY, George H.** *My Adventures in Arizona.* 1966. AZ Pioneer Hist Soc. ils/notes/index. 154p. NF/VG. B19. $35.00

**SMALLEY, George H.** *My Adventures in Arizona.* 1966. Tucson. AZ Pioneers Hist Soc. inscr/sgn/edit YS Moore. VG. F7. $30.00

**SMARIDGE, Norah.** *Raggedy Ann. Big Golden Book.* 1971. NY. Golden. 5th. slim 4to. B11. $18.00

**SMART, R.E.** *Proceedings of the Second International Symposium...* 1988. Auckland, NZ. 365p. sc. B26. $32.50

**SMARTO, Don.** *Setting the Captives Free!* 1993. Baker. 222p. F/wrp. B29. $9.50

**SMATH, Jerry.** *Leon's Prize.* 1987. Parents Magazine. 1st. 8vo. ils. VG. M5. $7.00

**SMEDLEY, Agnes.** *China's Red Army Marches.* 1934. NY. 311p. VG/poor. B5. $35.00

**SMEDLEY, John.** *Home Pork Production.* 1946. NY. Orange Judd. 134p. cloth. A10. $22.00

**SMEE, Alfred.** *Instinct & Reason: Deduced From Electro-Biology.* 1850. London. Reeve Benham. 10 pl/65 text woodcuts. 320p. emb ochre cloth. G1. $250.00

**SMELLIE, William.** *Philosophy of Natural History, With Introduction...* (1829). Boston. Hilliard. 3rd. 327p. VG. M12. $60.00

**SMELLIE, William.** *Philosophy of Natural History.* 1790 & 1799. Edinburgh. Prt for Heirs Chas Elliot. 2 vol. 4to. G1. $750.00

**SMILEY, Jane.** *Catskill Crafts: Artisans of the Catskill Mountains.* 1988. Crown. 1st. sgn. NF/dj. B30. $80.00

**SMILEY, Jane.** *Duplicate Keys.* 1984. Knopf. 1st. VG+/dj. B30. $200.00

**SMILEY, Jane.** *Greenlanders.* 1988. 1st. F/dj. w/promo card. M19. $25.00

**SMILEY, Jane.** *Greenlanders.* 1988. Knopf. 1st. sgn. F/dj. w/pub card. O11. $45.00

**SMILEY, Jane.** *Moo.* 1995. Knopf. 1st. sgn. F/dj. A23. $40.00

**SMILEY, Jane.** *Ordinary Love & Good Will.* 1989. Knopf. 1st. F/F. B3. $75.00

**SMILEY, Jane.** *Thousand Acres.* 1991. Knopf. 1st. F/dj. B30. $80.00

**SMILEY, Jane.** *Thousand Acres.* 1991. Knopf. 1st. sgn. F/dj. O11. $100.00

**SMITH, A.W.** *Gardener's Book of Plant Names: A Handbook...* 1963. NY. 1st. VG/dj. M17. $25.00

**SMITH, Alan.** *Virginia, 1584-1607.* 1957. London. Brun. 1st. 117p. xl. G. M10. $16.50

**SMITH, Alex.** *Mushroom Hunter's Field Guide.* 1969. Ann Arbor. 5th prt. 264p. VG. A17. $15.00

**SMITH, Alice Upham.** *Trees in a Winter Landscape.* 1969. NY. ils. 207p. dj. B26. $26.00

**SMITH, Anne M.** *Ute Tales.* 1992. UT U. 1st. ils. 175p. F/F. B19. $10.00

**SMITH, Anthony.** *Explorers of Amazon.* 1990. Viking. 1st. 344p. dj. F3. $20.00

**SMITH, April.** *North to Montana.* 1994. Knopf. 1st. F/F. H11. $25.00

**SMITH, Arthur.** *Planetary Exploration: 30 Years of Unmanned Space Probes.* 1988. Wellingborough, UK. Patrick Stephens. 8vo. 160p. glossy wrp. K5. $15.00

**SMITH, Audrey.** *Current Trends in Cryobiology.* 1970. Plenum. 252p. xl. VG. S5. $10.00

**SMITH, Bruce.** *Costly Performances, Tennessee Williams: Last Stage.* 1990. Paragon. 1st. sm 4to. 262p. F/dj. W2. $25.00

**SMITH, C.E.** *Jazz Record Book.* 1942. NY. 1st. 514p. VG. B5. $40.00

**SMITH, C.H.** *Natural History of Dogs, Canidae or Genus Canis...* 1840. Edinburgh. Lizars. 31 hand-colored pl/ils. cloth. VG. M12. $137.50

**SMITH, Cam.** *Buckminster Fuller to Children Earth.* 1972. Doubleday. 1st. photos. NF. S13. $5.00

**SMITH, Carter.** *Country Antiques & Collectibles.* 1981. Oxmoor. 1st. photos. 223p. NF/VG. S14. $12.00

**SMITH, Charles H.J.** *Landscape Gardening; or, Parks & Pleasure Grounds...* 1853. NY. Saxton. 1st. 367p. cloth. H10. $145.00

**SMITH, Charlie.** *Canaan.* 1984. S&S. 1st. sgn. rem mk. F/dj. D10. $85.00

**SMITH, Charlie.** *Cheap Ticket to Heaven.* 1996. NY. Holt. 1st. F/dj. R14. $25.00

**SMITH, Charlie.** *Crystal River.* 1991. NY. Linden. 1st. F/F. B3. $40.00

**SMITH, Charlie.** *Crystal River.* 1991. S&S. 1st. F/dj. R14. $30.00

**SMITH, Charlie.** *Lives of the Dead.* 1990. NY. Linden. 1st. F/F. H11. $35.00

**SMITH, Charlie.** *Lives of the Dead.* 1990. NY. Linden. 1st. sgn. F/dj. R14. $40.00

**SMITH, Charlie.** *Shine Hawk.* 1988. NY. Paris Review. 1st. sgn. F/dj. D10. $75.00

**SMITH, Charlotte.** *Book Interlude.* 1983. Newton. Tamazunchale. mini. 1/250. sgn. 46p. aeg. gilt maroon leather. B24. $95.00

**SMITH, Cornelius C.** *Don't Settle for Second: Life & Times of...* 1977. Presidio. 1st. ils. 229p. NF/VG. B19. $35.00

**SMITH, Cornelius C.** *Don't Settle for Second: Life & Times of...* 1977. San Rafael. 1st. 229p. VG. E1. $30.00

**SMITH, Cornelius C.** *Emilio Kosterlitzky: Eagle of Sonora & Southwest Border.* 1970. Clark. 1st. ils/index. 344p. NF. B19. $50.00

**SMITH, Cornelius C.** *Ft Huachuca: Story of a Frontier Post.* 1977. Ft Huachuca. 1st? ils/maps/chronology. 417p. VG/wrp. B19. $75.00

**SMITH, Cornelius C.** *William Sanders Oury: History-Maker of the Southwest.* 1967. Tucson, AZ. 1st. ils/index. 298p. F/F. B19. $75.00

**SMITH, Dama Margaret.** *Hopi Girl.* 1931. Stanford. 8vo. 273p. yel cloth. VG/pict dj. F7. $65.00

**SMITH, Dean.** *Brothers Five: The Babbitts of Arizona.* 1989. Tempe. AZ Hist Foundation. 8vo. 270p. VG+. F7. $27.50

**SMITH, Dennis.** *Report From Engine Co 82.* 1972. Saturday Review. 7th. inscr. red cloth. F/VG+. T11. $30.00

**SMITH, Dwight L.** *Above Timberline: Wildlife Biologist's Rocky Mtn Journal.* 1981. Knopf. 1st. VG/dj. N2. $10.00

**SMITH, Dwight L.** *John D Young & the Colorado Gold Rush.* 1969. RR Donnelley. Lakeside Classic #67. bl bdg. F. B18. $20.00

**SMITH, E. Boyd.** *Country Book.* 1924. Stokes. 1st. obl 4to. gr cloth/pict label. R5. $300.00

**SMITH, E. Boyd.** *Story of Our Country.* 1920. Putnam. G. V4. $160.00

**SMITH, E. Boyd.** *Story of Pocahontas & Capt John Smith.* 1906. Houghton Mifflin. 1st. obl 4to. 26 full-p pl. lt bl cloth. R5. $300.00

**SMITH, E. Newbold.** *Down Denmark Strait.* 1980. Boston. Little Brn. 1st. 212p. VG/dj. P4. $30.00

**SMITH, Edmund Reuel.** *Araucanians; or, Notes of Tour Among Indian Tribes...* 1855. NY. Harper. 1st. 8vo. 335p. cloth. O1. $225.00

**SMITH, Edmund Ware.** *One-Eyed Poacher of Privilege.* 1991. Derrydale. 187p. gilt leather. F. A17. $22.50

**SMITH, Ella Williams.** *Tears & Laughter in Virginia & Elsewhere.* 1972. McClure. 148p. VG/dj. B10. $15.00

**SMITH, Erroll A.** *Checker Classics.* 1924. NY. VG. M17. $15.00

**SMITH, F. Berkeley.** *How Paris Amuses Itself.* 1903. NY. 1st. ils. VG+. M5. $55.00

**SMITH, F. Hopkinson.** *Arm-Chair at the Inn.* 1912. NY. Scribner. 1st. 357p. G. G11. $6.00

**SMITH, F. Hopkinson.** *Colonel Carter's Christmas.* 1903. NY. Scribner. 1st. 1/500. sgn. 12 pl/tissue guard. teg. H5. $150.00

**SMITH, F. Hopkinson.** *Day at Laguerre's & Other Days.* 1892. Houghton Mifflin. 1st. gray cloth. M24. $125.00

**SMITH, F. Hopkinson.** *Felix O'Day.* 1915. Scribner. 1st. G. G11. $6.00

**SMITH, Fay Jackson.** *Father Kino in Arizona.* 1966. AZ Hist Found. 1st. maps. 142p. F/sans. B19. $50.00

**SMITH, Frederika Shumway.** *Old Put: Story of Maj-Gen Israel Putnam.* 1967. Rand McNally. 1st. ils. 296p. VG/dj. M10. $27.50

**SMITH, Gary.** *Happy Hours.* 1987. NY. Harmony. 1st. author's 1st book. F/dj. H11. $40.00

**SMITH, Gary.** *Windsinger.* 1976. Sierra Club. 8vo. photos. 175p. bl cloth. VG/dj. F7. $25.00

**SMITH, Gene.** *Lee & Grant: Dual Biography.* 1984. McGraw Hill. 1st. NF/clip. A14. $21.00

**SMITH, George.** *Assyrian Discoveries: Account of Explorations...1873 & 1874.* 1875. Sambson Low. ils/fld map. 461+40p ads. cloth. G. Q2. $58.00

**SMITH, H. Allen.** *Complete Practical Joker.* 1953. NY. 1st. VG/dj. B5. $22.50

**SMITH, H. Allen.** *Desert Island Decameron.* 1945. Doubleday. 406p. G. C5. $12.50

**SMITH, H. Allen.** *Lo, the Former Egyptian!* 1947. Doubleday. 1st. VG/VG. H11. $15.00

**SMITH, H. Allen.** *Rhubarb.* 1946. Doubleday. 1st. VG/G. P8. $25.00

**SMITH, Herndon.** *Centralia: First Fifty Years 1845-1900.* 1942. Centralia, WA. 1st. VG/dj. N2. $50.00

**SMITH, J.L. Dampier.** *Who's Who in Boswell?* 1970. NY. Russell. rpt (1935 London). H13. $65.00

**SMITH, J.M. Powis.** *Prophets & Their Times.* 1941. Chicago. 341p. VG. B29. $7.50

**SMITH, J.T.** *Nollekens & His Times.* 1949. London. Turnstile. 1st thus. 8vo. 275p. map ep. cloth. H13. $85.00

**SMITH, James P.** *Vascular Plant Families.* 1977. Eureka, CA. 321p. sc. AN. B26. $20.00

**SMITH, Jane S.** *Elsie deWolfe: Life in High Style.* 1982. NY. 3rd. photos. VG/dj. M17. $30.00

**SMITH, Jeffery A.** *Printers & Press Freedom: Ideology of Early Am Journalism.* 1988. OUP. 1st. 233p. cloth. F/dj. O10. $45.00

**SMITH, Jeffery A.** *Printers & Press Freedom: Ideology of Early Am Journalism.* 1988. OUP. 233p. VG. M10. $15.00

**SMITH, Jessie Wilcox.** *Evangeline by Henry Wadsworth Longfellow.* 1897. Houghton Mifflin. 1st. her 1st book. teg. gilt red cloth. R5. $450.00

**SMITH, Joan.** *Full Stop.* 1996. Fawcett. 1st. F/dj. G8. $17.50

**SMITH, Joan.** *Masculine Ending.* 1988. Scribner. 1st. author's 1st book. NF/F. H11. $20.00

**SMITH, Joan.** *Why Aren't They Screaming?* 1989. Scribner. 1st Am. VG/dj. R8. $10.00

**SMITH, John.** *Arts Betrayed.* 1978. London. Herbert. 1st. VG/dj. N2. $10.00

**SMITH, Joseph.** *Book of Mormon.* 1985 (1830). Latter-Day Saints. 12mo. 779p. F. W2. $25.00

**SMITH, Julie.** *Axeman's Jazz.* 1991. St Martin. 1st. sgn. NF/G. M19. $17.50

**SMITH, Julie.** *Huckleberry Fiend.* 1987. Mysterious. 1st. rem mk. F/dj. B2. $30.00

**SMITH, Ken.** *Willie Mays Story.* 1954. Greenberg. 1st. photos. VG+/wrp. P8. $135.00

**SMITH, Kenneth M.** *Biology of Viruses.* 1965. OUP. 142p. xl. VG. S5. $7.50

**SMITH, L.** *And Miles to Go.* 1967. Boston. 1st. VG/dj. B5. $25.00

**SMITH, Larry.** *Human Anatomy: Three Fictions.* (1993). Huron, OH. Bottom Dog. Contemporary Midwest Writers series. 1st. F/wrp. H4. $20.00

**SMITH, Lee.** *Black Mountain Breakdown.* 1980. Putnam. 1st. author's 4th book. F/F. B3. $125.00

**SMITH, Lee.** *Cakewalk.* 1981. Putnam. 1st. sgn. NF/dj. R14. $65.00

**SMITH, Lee.** *Fair & Tender Ladies.* 1989. London. Macmillan. 1st. F/F. B3. $35.00

**SMITH, Lee.** *Me & My Baby View the Eclipse.* 1990. Putnam. 1st. NF/F. H11. $20.00

**SMITH, Lee.** *Me & My Baby View the Eclipse.* 1990. Putnam. 1st. sgn/dtd 1990. rem mk. F/NF. R14. $35.00

**SMITH, Lee.** *Saving Grace.* 1995. NY. Putnam. 1st. sgn. F/dj. M23. $40.00

**SMITH, Lendon.** *Foods for Healthy Kids.* 1981. McGraw Hill. 1st. NF/dj. S13. $10.00

**SMITH, Louisa H.** *Bermuda's Oldest Inhabitants.* 1934. Sevenoaks, Kent. 1st. ils. B26. $22.50

**SMITH, M. Josephine.** *Llewellyn's Tower.* 1938. NY. 1st. ils H Woodward. VG. M17. $15.00

**SMITH, Marie.** *Entertaining in the White House.* 1967. Acropolis. 1st. sm 4to. 320p. F/G. H1. $12.00

**SMITH, Martin Cruz.** *Gorky Park.* 1981. NY. Random. 1st. F/NF. A24. $35.00

**SMITH, Martin Cruz.** *Stallion Gate.* 1986. Random. 1st. sgn. NF/NF. B3. $30.00

**SMITH, Maurice.** *Short History of Dentistry.* 1958. London. 120p. dj. A13. $30.00

**SMITH, Michael.** *Stone City.* nd. BC. F/NF. S18. $8.00

**SMITH, Mitchell.** *Daydreams.* 1987. McGraw Hill. 1st. F/F. H11. $30.00

**SMITH, Mitchell.** *Due North.* 1992. S&S. 1st. F/F. H11. $20.00

**SMITH, Moses.** *Koussevitzky.* 1947. NY. Allen Towne Heath. 400p. xl. G. C5. $15.00

**SMITH, Mrs. White Mountain.** *Indian Tribes of the Southwest.* 1933. Stanford. 1st. ils. 146p. VG. B19. $25.00

**SMITH, Neil C.** *Men of Beersheba.* 1993. Melbourne. 1st thus. 8vo. F/dj. M7. $50.00

**SMITH, Nicholas.** *Songs From the Hearts of Women.* 1903. Chicago. McClurg. 1st. xl. G. G11. $6.00

**SMITH, Nicol.** *Bush Master: Into the Jungles of Dutch Guiana.* 1941. Bobbs Merrill. 1st. 315p. dj. F3. $20.00

**SMITH, O.W.** *Book of the Pike.* 1922. Cincinnati. Kidd. 1st. ils. 197p. gilt cloth. VG/dj. A17. $45.00

**SMITH, P.** *Early Maps of Carolina & Adjoining Regions...* ca 1930. 1st. ils. 47p. NF/wrp. M8. $85.00

**SMITH, Page.** *New Age Begins: A People's History...* 1976. McGraw Hill. 2 vol. 1st. NF/dj. M10. $16.50

**SMITH, Patricia.** *Modern Collector's Dolls.* 1973. Collector Books. 1st. 1000+ photos. 310p. heavy cloth. F/NF. D4. $35.00

**SMITH, Philip.** *Amphibians & Reptiles in Illinois.* 1961. Natural Hist Survey. ils. 298p. F. S15. $18.50

**SMITH, Philip.** *Brinco: Story of Churchill Falls.* 1975. McClelland Sewart. 1st. AN/case. A26. $50.00

**SMITH, Richard P.** *Deer Hunting.* 1978. Stackpole. 256p. F/dj. A17. $12.50

**SMITH, Robert.** *Babe Ruth's America.* 1974. Crowell. 1st. photos. VG/dj. P8. $40.00

**SMITH, Rosamond;** Oates, Joyce Carol.

**SMITH, Samuel Stanhope.** *Essay on Causes of Variety of Complexion & Figure...* 1810. New Brunswick/NY. Simpson/Wms Whiting. 2nd revised/enlarged. modern bdg. G1. $225.00

**SMITH, Scott.** *Simple Plan.* 1993. Knopf. 1st. author's 1st book. AN/dj. S18. $44.00

**SMITH, Scott.** *Simple Plan.* 1993. Knopf. 1st. author's 1st book. F/F. H11. $30.00

**SMITH, Scott.** *Simple Plan.* 1993. Knopf. 1st. sm 4to. 335p. NF/dj. S14. $10.00

**SMITH, SMITH & WEBER.** *How to Know the Non-Gilled Mushrooms.* 1981. Dubuque. 2nd. 324p. sbdg. A17. $15.00

**SMITH, Sol.** *Theatrical Management in the West & South for 30 Years.* 1868. NY. Harper. 276p. prt wrp/custom gr linen fld/case. K1. $150.00

**SMITH, Steve.** *Hunting Upland Gamebirds.* 1987. Stackpole. 176p. F/dj. A17. $12.50

**SMITH, Steve.** *Me Again: Uncollected Writings of Steve Smith.* 1981. Farrar. 1st Am. NF/VG+. S13. $12.00

SMITH, Thomas L. *Elements of the Laws; or, Outlines of the System...* 1878. Lippincott. gr cloth. M11. $125.00

SMITH, Thomas. *De Republica Anglorum, Libri Tres...* 1630. Leyden. Elzeviriana. 16mo. 404p. contemporary vellum. K1. $175.00

SMITH, U.C.M. *Problem of Life: Essay in Origins of Biological Thought.* 1976. NY. 1st. 343p. A13. $20.00

SMITH, W.H.B. *Book of Rifles.* 1965. Stackpole. G/dj. A19. $30.00

SMITH, W.H.B. *Small Arms of the World.* 1969. Stackpole. 9th. 768p. NF/dj. A17. $35.00

SMITH, Walker O. *Polar Oceanography. Part A: Physical Science.* 1990. Academic. 406p. F. S15. $35.00

SMITH, Wallace. *Little Tigress: Tales Out of the Dust of Mexico.* 1923. Putnam. 1st. ils/pl. 209p. decor cloth. F3. $15.00

SMITH, Watkins C. *Prominent Women of Fauguier County, 1979-1981.* 1982. Democrat. 170p. G. B10. $6.00

SMITH, Wilbur M. *Atomic Age & the Word of God.* 1948. Wilde. 359p. VG. B29. $10.00

SMITH, Wilbur M. *Great Sermons on the Birth of Christ.* 1963. Wilde. 236p. VG/dj. B29. $11.00

SMITH, William W. *Pork Production.* 1937. Macmillan. revised. 575p. cloth. VG. A10. $22.00

SMITH & SMITH. *650 More Individual Open Salts Illustrated.* (1973). Country House/self pub. sgns. ils. unp. VG. H1. $24.00

SMITH & WIGGIN. *Arabian Nights: Their Best-Known Tales.* 1937. Scribner. ils Maxfield Parrish. VG. M17. $65.00

SMITH & WU. *Physics of the Space Environment.* 1972. WA, DC. NASA. ils. 171p. xl. K5. $15.00

SMITH & ZURCHER. *Dictionary of American Politics.* 1947 (1944). Barnes Noble. revised. 8vo. VG. A2. $12.50

SMITH. *Georges Cuvier: Annotated Bibliography of Published Works.* 1993. Smithsonian. ils. 271p. NF. A4. $48.00

SMOLLA, Rodney A. *Jerry Falwell Vs Larry Flint.* 1988. St Martin. 1st. 8vo. F/dj. A2. $12.50

SMOLLETT, T.S. *Adventures of Gil Blas of Santillane.* 1836. London. 2 vol. lg 8vo. 3-quarter leather/marbled brd. VG. S17. $100.00

SMYSER, Steven W. *Encyclopedia of Organic Gardening.* 1978. Rodale. 1st. sm 4to. 1236p. F/NF. W2. $50.00

SMYTH, Iain. *Mystery of the Russian Ruby, a Pop-Up Whodunit.* 1994. Dutton. 1st Am. rem mk. F. B17. $15.00

SMYTHE, H. *Atomic Energy for Military Purposes.* 1945. Princeton. 1st hc. VG. E6. $45.00

SMYTHE, Pat. *Jump for Joy.* 1955. Dutton. 1st. VG/G. O3. $18.00

SMYTHIES, B.E. *Birds of Burma.* 1986. Hauts, UK. Liss. 3rd/final. lg 4to. ils/distribution map. 432p. F. C12. $85.00

SNEATH, E. Hershey. *Evolution of Ethics.* 1927. Yale. 370p. VG. B29. $8.50

SNEDIGAR, Robert. *Our Small Native Animals: Their Habits & Care.* 1963. Dover. enlarged revised. 248p. VG. S15. $8.50

SNELL, David. *Lights, Camera...Murder.* 1979. NY. SMP. 1st. F/F. H11. $25.00

SNELL, Roy J. *Sally Scott of the Waves.* 1943. Whitman. ils HJ Meixner. 248p. VG/poor. B36. $13.00

SNELL, T.L. *Wild Shores: America's Beginnings.* 1974. NGS. ils. 203p. F/G. M4. $20.00

SNELLGROVE, D.L. *Himalayan Pilgramage: Study of Tibetan Religion...* 1989. Boston. photos. 304p. F/wrp. M4. $10.00

SNIDER, D. *America 10 Years War, 1855-1965.* VG. E6. $30.00

SNIDER, Duke. *Duke of Flatbush.* 1988. Zebra. later prt. sgn. photos. F/dj. P8. $65.00

SNIVELY & SNIVELY. *Pottery.* 1940. Stephen Daye. 1st. ils. 86p. VG. S14. $5.00

SNODGRASS, R.E. *Insect Metamorphosis.* 1954. Smithsonian. ils. 154p. VG. S15. $8.00

SNOW, C.P. *Coat of Varnish.* 1979. NY. Scribner. 1st. NF/F. H11. $15.00

SNOW, C.P. *In Their Wisdom.* 1974. NY. 1st. VG. T9. $5.00

SNOW, D.W. *Status of Birds in Britain & Ireland.* nd. Blackwell. 333p. xl. VG. S5. $15.00

SNOW, Edward Rowe. *Legends, Maps & Stories.* 1965. Quincy, MA. sgn. photos. VG/wrp. M17. $50.00

SNOW, Edward Rowe. *Romance of Boston Bay.* 1944. Boston. 1st. 319p. G. S17. $8.00

SNOW, Jack. *Magical Mimics in Oz.* 1950s. Reilly Lee. later prt. NF. B9. $100.00

SNOW, Jack. *Shaggy Man of Oz.* 1949. Reilly Lee. 1st. ils Frank Kramer. 32p. NF/dj. D1. $300.00

SNOW, Jack. *Shaggy Man of Oz.* 1950s. Reilly Lee. later prt. NF. B9. $175.00

SNOW, William Parker. *Southern Generals: Their Lives & Campaigns.* 1866. Chas Richardson. 500p. cloth. B10. $100.00

SNOWDEN, Nicholas. *Memoirs of a Spy: Adventures Along Eastern Front...* 1934 (1933). gilt bdg. VG. E6. $30.00

SNOWDEN, Richard. *American Revolution.* 1815. Clinton, OH. 170p. cloth. B18. $250.00

SNYDER, Don. *Veteran's Park.* 1987. Watts. 1st. F/VG. P8. $25.00

SNYDER, Gary. *Earth House Hold.* 1969. New Directions. 1st. F/dj. O11. $150.00

SNYDER, Gary. *Old Ways.* 1977. City Lights. 1st. sgn. F. O11. $55.00

SNYDER, Gary. *Regarding Wave.* 1970. New Directions. 1st. F/dj. O11. $140.00

SNYDER, Gary. *Six Sections From Mountains & Rivers Without End.* 1965. SF. Four Seasons. 1st/ltd. 1/100. sgn. F/dj. L3. $285.00

SNYDER, Gary. *Songs for Gaia.* 1979. Port Townsend, WA. Kai Tai Alliance/Copper Canyon. 1/300. sgn. F/sans. O11. $125.00

SNYDER, Gary. *Sours of the Hills.* (1969). np. Samuel Charters. 1/300. sgn. F. O11. $160.00

SNYDER, Henry M. *Ma-Jung Manual.* 1923. VG. S1. $10.00

SOAMES, Mary. *Clementine Churchill: Biography of a Marriage.* 1979. Houghton Mifflin. 4th. 8vo. 732p. F. W2. $50.00

SOANE, E.B. *To Mesopotamia & Kurdistan in Disguise.* 1926. London. Murray. 2nd. ils/fld map. 421p. cloth. Q2. $125.00

SOBEL, Dava. *Longitude.* 1995. NY. Walker. 1st. F/dj. M23. $40.00

SOBEL, Robert. *They Satisfy: The Cigarette in American Life.* 1978. Anchor/Doubleday. 1st. 255p. F/dj. H6. $38.00

SOBOL, Donald J. *Encyclopedia Brown & the Case of the Secret Pitch.* 1965. Elsevier/Nelson. 1st. VG+. P8. $12.50

SOBY, James Thrall. *Arp.* 1958. MOMA. 1st. photos. 126p. VG/dj. T11. $15.00

SOCHEN, June. *New Woman in Greenwich Village, 1910-20.* 1972. Quadrangle. 1st. sc. 175p. VG. A25. $10.00

SODOWSKY, Roland. *Interim in the Desert.* 1990. TX Christian U. 269p. F/F. B19. $10.00

**SOHN, Monte.** *Elsie & the Looking Club.* (1946). Sandusky, OH. Am Crayon Co. ils Walter Early. mc pict brd. R5. $110.00

**SOHN, Monte.** *Elsie the Cow.* 1942. Dodd Mead. 1st. 8vo. ils Walter Early. orange cloth. dj. R5. $110.00

**SOKOL'SKII, V.N.** *Russian Solid-Fuel Rockets.* 1967. Jerusalem. Israel program Sci Trans. 236p. K5. $40.00

**SOKOLOFF, Alexander.** *Genetics of Tribolium & Related Species.* 1966. Academic. 212p. xl. VG. S5. $25.00

**SOLBRIG, Otto T.** *Principles & Methods of Plant Biosystematics.* 1970. NY. ils. 226p. VG. B26. $26.00

**SOLERI, Paolo.** *Fragments: Selection From Sketchbooks of...* 1981. Harper Row. 1st. ils. 211p. F/clip. B19. $35.00

**SOLOMON, Charmaine.** *Chinese Cookbook.* 1973. Australia. Paul Ahamlyn Pty Ltd. G/dj. A16. $9.00

**SOLTOW & WERY.** *American Women & the Labor Movement, 1825-1974.* 1976. 255p. F. A4. $75.00

**SOLZHENITSYN, Alexander.** *Cancer Ward.* 1968. London. 1st. trans Bethell/Burg. rpr dj. T9. $18.00

**SOLZHENITSYN, Alexander.** *Gulag Archipelago 1918-1956.* 1974. Harper Row. 1st. NF/dj. M25. $25.00

**SOLZHENITSYN, Alexander.** *Noble Lecture.* 1972. Farrar Straus. Bilingual/1st. gr cloth. F. B14. $55.00

**SOLZHENITSYN, Alexander.** *One Day in the Life of Ivan Denisovich.* 1963. NY. 1st. F/dj. B2. $65.00

**SOLZHENITSYN, Alexander.** *One Day in the Life of Ivan Denisovich.* 1963. NY. 1st. trans Hayward/Hingley. VG/dj. T9. $45.00

**SOMES, Joseph Henry V.** *Old Vincennes: History of Famous Old Town & Glorious Past.* 1962. NY. Graphic Books. sgn. ils. 256p. Vg/dj. B18. $22.50

**SONAKUL, S.** *Everyday Siamese Dishes.* 1952. Bangkok. 1st. 92p. VG. E6. $20.00

**SONNICHSEN, C.L.** *Alias Billy the Kid.* 1955. Albuquerque, NM. 1st. ils. 136p. VG/dj. B5. $40.00

**SONNICHSEN, C.L.** *Ambidextrous Historian: Historical Writers & Writing...* 1980. OK U. 1st. 120p. NF/NF. B19. $20.00

**SONNICHSEN, C.L.** *El Paso Salt War.* 1962. El Paso. ils Jose Cisneros. design Carl Hertzog. F/wrp. M4. $40.00

**SONNICHSEN, C.L.** *Roy Bean: Law West of the Pecos.* 1943. Macmillan. fair. A19. $30.00

**SONNICHSEN, C.L.** *Southwest in Life & Literature.* 1962. Devin Adair. 1st. 554p. VG+. B19. $25.00

**SONNICHSEN, C.L.** *Tucson, the Life & Times of an American City.* 1982. OK U. 1st. ils. 369p. F/F. B19. $45.00

**SOOS, Troy.** *Murder at Ebbets Field.* 1995. NY. Kensington. 1st. F/NF. M17. $50.00

**SOPHOCLES, S.M.** *History of Greece.* 1961. Thessalonike. 382p. VG/torn. Q2. $30.00

**SORENSON, John R.J.** *Biology of Copper Complexes.* nd. Humana. 598p. VG. S5. $20.00

**SORRELL, Alan.** *Roman London.* 1959. NY. Arco. 1st. photos. F/dj. T10. $25.00

**SORRENTINO, Gilbert.** *Mulligan Stew.* 1979. Grove. later prt. F/VG. P8. $20.00

**SORRENTINO, Gilbert.** *Red the Fiend.* 1995. NY. Fromm Internat. 1st Am. F/dj. G10. $14.00

**SOULE, Jean Conder.** *Never Tease a Weasel.* (1964). Parents Magazine. probable 1st. sm 4to. ils Denman Hampson. VG. T5. $30.00

**SOUREK, Grace.** *Wildflower.* 1938. Akron. 1st. inscr. 173p. VG. B18. $35.00

**SOUSTELLE, Jacques.** *Mexico.* 1967. Cleveland. World. 1st. 285p. dj. F3. $30.00

**SOUSTELLE, Jacques.** *Olmecs: Oldest Civilization in Mexico.* 1984. Doubleday. 1st. 214p. dj. F3. $30.00

**SOUTH, Frank E.** *Hibernation & Hypothermia: Perspectives & Challenges.* 1972. Elsevier. 743p. xl. VG. S5. $35.00

**SOUTHALL, James P.C.** *In the Days of My Youth...University of Virginia 1888-93.* 1947. UNC. inscr. 197p. VG/G. B10. $20.00

**SOUTHGATE, H.** *Things a Lady Would Like to Know Concerning Domestic...* 1874. London. lg 8vo. aeg. full leather. E6. $135.00

**SOUTHWORTH, Gertrude.** *Our South American Neighbors.* 1924. NY. Iroquois. 1st. ils/maps. 206p. F3. $20.00

**SOUTHWORTH, John vanDyn.** *American History in Verse.* 1976. Valkyrie. 1st. ils Rondla D Reams. 120p. VG/G. B11. $18.00

**SOWERBY, E. Millicent.** *Catalogue of the Library of Thomas Jefferson.* 1952 & 1953. Lib Congress. Vol 1 & 2 only (of 5). ils. VG. A4. $250.00

**SOWERBY, E. Millicent.** *Catalogue of the Library of Thomas Jefferson.* 1983. 5 vol. 1/400. rpt. NF. A4. $225.00

**SOYER, Alexis.** *Modern Housewife; or, Menagere Comprising 1,000 Recipes.* 1849. London. 2nd. 4 pl/2 text ils. E6. $150.00

**SOYER, Alexis.** *Pantropheon; or, A History of Food...* 1977 (1853). NY. rpt. ils. VG/dj. M17. $25.00

**SOYINKA, Wolfe.** *Interpreters.* 1972. NY. Africana. 1st Am hc. F/dj. A24. $30.00

**SPADA & ZENO.** *Monroe: Her Life in Pictures.* 1982. Doubleday. 1st. ils. F/wrp. C9. $60.00

**SPAGNOLI, Madeline.** *Poetry of My Life.* 1995. Winston Derek. 1st. 137p. F. W2. $15.00

**SPALLHOLZ, J.E.** *Selenium in Biology & Medicine.* 1981. Westport. AVI Pub. 8vo. ils/graphs/tables. 573p. cloth. F. B1. $68.00

**SPAMER, Earle.** *Bibliography of Grand Canyon & Lower CO River From 1540.* 1981. Grand Canyon. GCNHA. 1st. 4to. VG. F7. $20.00

**SPANGLER, Edward W.** *Annals of Families of Casper, Henry, Baltzer & Spengler.* 1896. York. np. 605p. G+. B18. $75.00

**SPANNER, D.C.** *Introduction to Thermodynamics.* 1964. Academic. 278p. VG. S5. $10.00

**SPANTON, A.I.** *Fifty Years of Buchtel 1870-1920.* 1922. Akron. 8vo. ils. 446p. VG. B11. $18.00

**SPARK, Muriel.** *Abbess of Crewe.* 1974. London. Macmillan. 1st. NF/dj. A14. $28.00

**SPARK, Muriel.** *Driver's Seat.* 1970. London. Macmillan. 1st. NF/VG. A14. $28.00

**SPARK, Muriel.** *Far Cry From Kensington.* 1988. Toronto. Viking Penguin. 1st Canadian. NF/dj. A14. $21.00

**SPARK, Muriel.** *Not to Disturb.* 1971. London. Macmillan. 1st. NF/VG. A14. $35.00

**SPARK, Muriel.** *Public Image.* 1968. Knopf. 1st. 144p. xl. G/dj. S14. $6.00

**SPARKS, Jared.** *Works of Benjamin Franklin.* 1856. Boston. 10 vol. VG. A15. $100.00

**SPARKS, Jared.** *Writings of George Washington: Being His Correspondence.* (1837). Harper. 12 vol. full leather. G+. B10. $300.00

**SPARKS, Jared.** *Writings of George Washington: Being His Correspondence...* 1837. Boston. Am Stationer's. 12 vol. full leather. VG. B10. $300.00

**SPARKS, Nicholas.** *Notebook.* 1996. Warner. 1st. VG/dj. B30. $25.00

**SPARROW, Archie.** *Twister.* 1983. NY. Walker. 1st. inscr. F/NF. T10. $35.00

**SPARROW, Walter Shaw.** *British Sporting Artists.* 1922. Scribner. 1st. VG. A21. $250.00

**SPAULDING, Edward Selden.** *Venison — And a Breath of Sage: Tales of San Juan Ranch.* 1967. Santa Barbara, CA. 1st. F/dj. O4. $20.00

**SPAULDING, Karen.** *Huarochiri: Andean Society Under Inca & Spanish Rule.* 1984. Stanford. 1st. 364p. dj. F3. $25.00

**SPAYTHE, Jacob A.** *History of Hancock County, Ohio.* 1903. Toledo. ils/rosters/biographies. 312p. VG. B18. $70.00

**SPEAKMAN, Thomas H.** *Divisions in the Society of Friends.* 1893. Lippincott. 2nd/enlarged. 12mo. 112p. V3. $15.00

**SPEARMAN, Arthur Dunning.** *Five Franciscan Churches of Mission Santa Clara, 1777-1825.* 1963. Palo Alto. National Pr. 1st. ils/facs maps/charts/documents. F/dj. T10. $75.00

**SPEARMAN, Charles Edward.** *Psychology Down the Ages.* 1937. Macmillan. 2 vol. bl cloth. VG. G1. $85.00

**SPEARS, John R.** *Story of the New England Whalers.* 1908. NY. 418p. VG. S15. $20.00

**SPECHT, Robert.** *Story of a Young Teacher in Alaska Wilderness.* c 1976. NY. St Martin. 8vo. 358p. VG/dj. P4. $30.00

**SPECTOR, Benjamin.** *One Hour of Medical History.* 1931. Boston. 1st. 88p. A13. $20.00

**SPECTORSKY, A.C.** *Book of the Mountains.* 1955. Appleton Century Crofts. 1st. 8vo. F/dj. A2. $20.00

**SPECTORSKY, A.C.** *Book of the Mountains.* 1955. Appleton Century Crofts. 1st. 8vo. VG. A2. $13.00

**SPEECHLY, William.** *Treatise on Culture of the Vine...* 1790. York. Prt for Author by G Peacock. ils. 224p. gilt calf. G7. $1,250.00

**SPEER, Albert.** *Inside the Third Reich.* 1970. Macmillan. BC. 1st trans from Erinnerungen. 705p. NF/dj. W2. $45.00

**SPEISER, E.A.** *Anchor Bible: Genesis.* 1964. Doubleday. 1st. 8vo. VG/dj. A2. $15.00

**SPELL, Lota M.** *Pioneer Printer, Samuel Bangs in Mexico & Texas.* 1963. Austin, U TX. 1st. gilt maroon cloth. F. M24. $25.00

**SPENCE, Lewis.** *Illustrated Guide to Native American Myth.* 1993. Longmeadow. ils. G/dj. A19. $35.00

**SPENCE, Ruth S.** *Biography of Birmingham, Alabama 1872-1972.* 1973. Birmingham, AL. 1st. 136p. VG/prt wrp. M8. $45.00

**SPENCER, Claire.** *Gallows Orchard.* 1930. NY. Cape Smith. 1st. F/dj. M15. $75.00

**SPENCER, Darrell.** *Our Secret's Out.* 1993. U MO. 1st. F/dj. M23. $20.00

**SPENCER, Edwin Rollin.** *Just Weeds.* 1957. Scribner. BC. 333p. VG/dj. A10. $20.00

**SPENCER, Herbert.** *Principles of Psychology.* 1855. Longman Gr. 620p. emb panelled brn cloth. G1. $550.00

**SPENCER, Herbert.** *Principles of Psychology.* 1870. London. Wms Norgate. 2 vol. 2nd revised/enlarged. thick 8vo. mauve cloth. VG. G1. $250.00

**SPENCER, Paula Underwood.** *Who Speaks for Wolf.* 1983. Austin, TX. Tribe of 2 Pr. AN. A19. $25.00

**SPENCER, Scott.** *Endless Love.* 1979. Knopf. 1st. VG/clip. B30. $25.00

**SPENCER, Scott.** *Endless Love.* 1979. NY. Knopf. 1st. F/dj. R14. $35.00

**SPENCER, Scott.** *Men in Black.* 1995. Knopf. 1st. F/dj. R14. $25.00

**SPENCER, Scott.** *Waking the Dead.* 1986. Knopf. 1st. F/dj. R14. $30.00

**SPENDER, Brenda E.** *On'y Tony: Adventures of Three Ponies & a Little Boy.* 1935. London. Country Life. 1st. 8vo. 96p. VG+. C14. $16.00

**SPENDER, Stephen.** *Journals 1939-83.* 1985. London. 1/150. sgn. edit Goldsmith. case. T9. $150.00

**SPENDER, Stephen.** *Letters to Christopher.* 1980. Blk Sparrow. ltd. sgn/#d. F/mylar. B9. $60.00

**SPENDER, Stephen.** *World Within World, Autobiography.* 1951. London. 1st. dj. T9. $35.00

**SPENSER, Edmund.** *Saint George & the Dragon.* 1963. Houghton Mifflin. 1st. VG/dj. P2. $25.00

**SPERBER, Perry.** *Drugs, Demons, Doctors & Disease.* 1973. St Louis. 1st. 294p. A13. $25.00

**SPERRY, Armstrong.** *Call It Courage.* 1940. Macmillan. 1st. sgn. 1941 Newbery. 95p. pict dj. R5. $350.00

**SPERRY, Margaret.** *Scandinavian Stories.* (1971). Franklin Watts. inscr/sgn. sm 4to. 288p. red cloth. T5. $45.00

**SPEWACK & SPEWACK.** *My 3 Angels.* 1953. Random. 1st. VG/dj. A24. $35.00

**SPICER, Michael.** *Cotswold Moles: A Lady Jane Hildreth Mystery.* 1993. St Martin. 1st. F/dj. R8. $10.00

**SPICER & THOMPSON.** *Plural Society in the Southwest.* 1972. Weatherhead Found. 1st. 367p. NF/G. B19. $35.00

**SPIELMAN, Jean E.** *Stool Pigeon & the Open Shop Movement.* 1923. Minneapolis. Am Pub. 240p. F/wrp. B2. $75.00

**SPIER, Peter.** *Noah's Ark.* 1977. Doubleday. 1st. 1978 Caldecott. mc ils brd. mc pict dj. R5. $175.00

**SPIER, Peter.** *People.* 1980. NY. later prt. ils Spier. VG/G. M17. $20.00

**SPIER, Peter.** *Star-Spangled Banner.* 1973. Doubleday. 1st. ils. VG/dj. M5. $35.00

**SPIES, Joseph R.** *Wild Ponies of Chincoteague.* 1977. Cambridge, MD. Tidewater. 1st. ils. VG/G. O3. $45.00

**SPIES, Werner.** *Lindner.* 1979. Paris. Maeght. 100 ils. 142p. F/NF. H4. $30.00

**SPILLANE, Mickey.** *Black Alley.* 1996. NY. Dutton. 1st. inscr. F/dj. R14. $75.00

**SPILLANE, Mickey.** *Killing Man.* 1989. Dutton. 1st. VG/dj. T12. $25.00

**SPILLANE, Mickey.** *Last Cop Out.* 1973. NY. Dutton. 1st. F/dj. M15. $100.00

**SPILLANE, Mickey.** *Twisted Thing.* 1966. Dutton. 1st. F/NF. M15. $75.00

**SPILLER, Burton L.** *More Grouse Feathers.* 1972. NY. 1/750. sgn. 238p. leatherette. F/dj. A17. $45.00

**SPILLMAN, Louis.** *So This Is South America.* 1962. VA. 1st. inscr. 140p. dj. F3. $15.00

**SPINDEN, Herbert Joseph.** *Maya Art & Civilization.* (1957). Falcon's Wing. lg 8vo. ils/photos/mc ftspc. 432p. blk cloth/brn brd. dj. K1. $150.00

**SPINDLER, Will H.** *Badlands Trails.* 1948. Mitchell, SD. Educator Supply. sgn. sc. G. A19. $45.00

**SPIRES, Robert C.** *Post-Totalitarian Spanish Fiction.* 1996. U MO. 1st. F/dj. S13. $14.00

**SPIRO, Rand J.** *Theoretical Issues in Reading Comprehension...* 1980. Lawrence Earlbaum. 586p. bl cloth. G1. $60.00

**SPITTLER, Russell.** *Perspectives on the New Pentecostalism.* 1976. Baker. 268p. VG/dj. B29. $17.50

**SPITZ, Carl.** *Training Your Dog.* nd. Boston. photos. fwd Clark Gable. VG. M17. $25.00

**SPIVACK, Charlotte.** *Company of Camelot.* 1994. Greewnwood. F. P3. $45.00

**SPLAN, John.** *Life With the Trotters.* 1889. Chicago. HT White. 450p. bstp cloth. VG. B18. $65.00

**SPLETE, Allen P.** *Frederick Remington: Selected Letters.* 1988. Abbeville. VG/dj. A19. $35.00

**SPOCK, Benjamin.** *Dr Spock's Baby & Child Care.* 1985. Dutton. 1st thus/anniversary ed. NF/dj. S13. $10.00

**SPOCK, Benjamin.** *Spock on Spock.* 1989. Pantheon. 1st. F/dj. T11. $8.00

**SPOEHR, Herman A.** *Essays on Science: A Selection From...* 1956. Stanford. 220p. VG/dj. A10. $40.00

**SPOHN, David.** *Home Field.* 1993. Lee Shepard. 1st. F/dj. P8. $15.00

**SPOHR, Louis.** *Musical Journeys.* 1961. OK U. ils. VG/dj. M17. $17.50

**SPOSA, Louis A.** *Television Primer of Production & Direction.* 1947. NY. McGraw Hill. 237p. VG. H6. $36.00

**SPOTO, Donald.** *A Life.* 1989. Boston. 1st. dj. T9. $10.00

**SPOTO, Donald.** *Dark Side of Genius: Life of Alf.* 1983. Little Brn. 1st. VG/dj. P3. $20.00

**SPOTO, Donald.** *Laurence Olivier: A Biography.* 1992. Harper Collins. 1st. photos. 460p. F/dj. S14. $11.00

**SPOTO, Donald.** *Marilyn Monroe: Biography.* 1993. Harper Collins. 1st. F/dj. P3. $30.00

**SPRAGUE, Robert S.** *Ghosts of Palo Duro Canyon.* 1973. Lawton, OK. self pub. F/dj. A19. $25.00

**SPRAGUE, Robert S.** *Grass Money: Lawton's Own Story.* 1970. Lawton, OK. self pub. inscr. VG/dj. A19. $45.00

**SPRATT, G.** *Obstetric Tables: Comprising Graphic Illustrations...* 1847. Phil. Wagner & M'Guigan. 20 pl w/moveable flaps. cloth. G7. $795.00

**SPRIGGE, S. Squire.** *Physic & Fiction.* 1921. london. 1st. 307p. A13. $40.00

**SPRING, Agnes Wright.** *Cheyenne & Black Hills Stage & Express Routes.* 1949. Glendale, CA. Arthur H Clark. F/dj. A19. $200.00

**SPRING, Agnes Wright.** *Cow Country Legacies.* 1976. Lowell. 1st. ils. 122p. B19. $25.00

**SPRING, Gardiner.** *Essays on Distinguishing Traits of Christian Character.* 1813. NY. Dodge Sayre. 1st. 230p. gilt leather. VG. H10. $45.00

**SPRING & SPRING.** *Alaska.* c 1965. Seattle. Superior. 1st. photos. 157p. P4. $30.00

**SPRINGER, Nancy.** *Chains of Gold.* 1987. London. Macdonald. 1st. F/dj. M21. $25.00

**SPRINGS, Eliott White.** *Above the Bright Blue Sky.* 1928. Doubleday Doran. 1st. 275p. VG/dj. B18. $125.00

**SPROUL, R.C.** *Mystery of the Holy Spirit.* 1990. Tyndale. 191p. VG/dj. B29. $9.50

**SPRUNT, A.** *Florida Bird Life.* 1954. Nat Audubon Soc. 1st. 56 mc pl. 527p. NF. C12. $42.00

**SPUHLER, Friedrich.** *Oriental Carpets of the Museum of Islamic Art, Berlin.* 1988. London/Boston. Faber. 1st. 4to. 208 pl. 332p. NF/dj/box-sleeve. W1. $65.00

**SPURR, R.A.** *Glorious Way to Die.* 1981. 1st. G+/G. E6. $12.00

**SPURZHEIM, Emile.** *De la Repartition du Sang Circulant...* 1883. Brussels. inscr pres. 8vo. orig wrp/lacks backstrip/fld case. G7. $150.00

**SPURZHEIM, George.** *View of Elementary Principles of Education...* 1836. Boston. Marsh Capen Lyon. 318+5p ads. linen cloth/paper label. G7. $145.00

**SPURZHEIM, J.** *Phrenology; or, Doctrine of Mental Phenomena.* 1832. vol 1 of 2 only. 14 pl. E6. $50.00

**SPYRI, Johanna.** *Cornelli.* nd. Grosset Dunlap. xl. G. B36. $10.50

**SPYRI, Johanna.** *Cornelli: Story of the Swiss Alps.* 1921. Lippincott. ils ML Kirk. VG. B17. $45.00

**SPYRI, Johanna.** *Erick & Sally.* 1921. Boston. 1st. 8vo. gilt bdg. M5. $35.00

**SPYRI, Johanna.** *Gritli's Children.* 1924. Lippincott. 1st thus. ils M Kirk. 265p. VG. D1. $65.00

**SPYRI, Johanna.** *Heidi.* c 1902 & 1913. Crowell. trans HS White. 433p. teg. dk bl cloth. VG-. B36. $24.50

**SPYRI, Johanna.** *Heidi.* 1922. Phil. McKay. 1st/mixed issue. ils JW Smith. slate bl cloth. pict dj. R5. $300.00

**SPYRI, Johanna.** *Heidi.* 1923. McKay. rpt. NF/dj. S18. $20.00

**SQUIRE, J.C.** *Grub Street Nights Entertainments.* 1924. London. Hodder Stoughton. 1st. NF/dj. M15. $200.00

**ST. CLAIR, Philip R.** *Frederic Remington, the American West.* 1978. Kent, OH. Volair Ltd. 1st. 1/10,000. 329p. fld box. B18. $75.00

**STABLEFORD, Brian.** *Angel of Pain.* 1993. Carroll Graf. 1st Am. F/dj. G10. $20.00

**STABLEFORD, Brian.** *Empire of Fear.* 1990. London. Pan. 1st UK trade paper ed. sgn. F. G10. $35.00

**STACEY, Susannah.** *Knife at the Opera.* 1988. Summit. 1st. F/VG+. N4. $15.00

**STACK, Frederic W.** *Wild Flowers Every Child Should Know.* 1909. NY. ils/photo ep. decor cloth. B26. $26.00

**STACKPOLE, Edward J.** *Chancellorsville: Lee's Greatest Battle.* 1958. Stackpole. 1st. NF/VG. A14. $25.00

**STACKPOLE, Edward J.** *Fredericksburg Campaign: Drama on the Rappahannock.* 1957. Harrisburg, PA. Military Service Pub. 1st. VG/G clip. A14. $21.00

**STACKPOLE, Renny A.** *American Whaling in Hudson Bay 1861-1919.* 1969. Mystic. Marine Hist Assn. map/appenices. stapled wrp. P4. $48.50

**STACTON, David.** *Segaki.* 1959. Pantheon. 1st. VG/clip. N2. $10.00

**STADDEN, Charles.** *Life Guards: Dress & Appointments 1660-1914.* 1971. Almark. 1st. ils/pl. 68p. VG/stiff wrp. S16. $22.50

**STAFFORD, Harry.** *Early Inhabitants of the Americas.* 1959. Vantage. VG/dj. A19. $30.00

**STAFFORD, Jean.** *Mother in History.* 1966. FSG. 2nd. 121p. VG/G. P12. $15.00

**STAFFORD, William.** *Even in Quiet Place.* (1996). Lewiston, ID. Confluence. 1st. AN/dj. A18. $20.00

**STAFFORD, William.** *Fin, Feather, Fur.* 1989. Rexburg. Honeybrook. 1/274. sgn. F/wrp. R14. $55.00

**STAFFORD, William.** *Someday, Maybe.* (1973). Harper Row. 1st. F/dj. A18. $50.00

**STAFFORD, William.** *Stories That Could Be True: New & Collected Poems.* (1977). Harper. 1st. inscr/sgn. F/clip. A18. $150.00

**STAFLEU, F.A.** *Taxomonic Literature.* 1967. Utrecht. 8vo. 556p. cloth. VG. B1. $65.00

**STAGG & ZIENKIEWICZ.** *Rock Mechanics in Engineering Practice.* 1968. Wiley. 1st. cloth. G. B27. $25.00

**STALLARD, Patricia Y.** *Glittering Misery: Dependents of the Indian Fighting Army.* 1978. Presidio. 60+photos. 159p. VG. E1. $55.00

**STALLINGS, Laurence.** *Doughboys: Story of the AEF, 1917-1918.* 1963. Harper Row. 1st. lg 8vo. red cloth. VG/dj. M7. $35.00

**STAMM, Douglas R.** *Underwater: Northern Lakes.* 1977. WI U. 116p. VG/dj. A17. $10.00

**STAMP, Terence.** *Night.* 1993. London. Phoenix. 1st. author's 1st novel. NF/dj. A14. $25.00

**STANARD, Mary Newton.** *Dreamer: Romantic Rendering of Life Story of...Poe.* 1925. Lippincott. 2nd. 389p. VG. B10. $15.00

**STANARD, William G.** *Notes on Journey on James Together With a Guide...* 1929. Whittet Shepperson. new ed. 45p. VG. B10. $10.00

**STANDARD, Stella.** *Cook Book.* 1965. Bonanza. G/dj. A16. $15.00

**STANDIFORD, Les.** *Spill.* 1991. Atlantic. 1st. author's 1st book. F/F. H11. $40.00

**STANDING BEAR, Chief.** *My People the Sioux.* 1928. Houghton Mifflin. ils/photos. 288p. VG/G. B5. $45.00

**STANDISH, Burt L.** *Lefty of Big League: Brick-King, Backstop (#5).* 1914. Barse Hopkins. later prt. VG. P8. $20.00

**STANDISH, Burt L.** *Lefty of Big League: Covering the Look in Corner (#8).* 1915. Barse. later prt. VG. P8. $15.00

**STANDISH, Burt L.** *Lefty of Big League: Crossed Signals (#16).* 1928. Barse. 1st. final of series. VG. P8. $200.00

**STANDISH, Burt L.** *Lefty of Big League: Guarding the Keystone Sack(#10).* 1917. Barse. 1st. VG. P8. $25.00

**STANDISH, Burt L.** *Lefty of Big League: Lefty Locke Wins Out (#15).* 1926. Barse Hopkins. probable 1st. VG/G later issue. P8. $125.00

**STANDISH, Burt L.** *Lefty of Big League: Lefty O' the Blue Stockings (#3).* 1914. Barse Hopkins. 1st. G. P8. $15.00

**STANDLEY, Paul C.** *Type Localities of Plants First Described From New Mexico...* 1910. WA, DC. ils. 119p. wrp/clear plastic dj. B26. $25.00

**STANDRING, Lesley.** *Doctor Who Illustrated A-Z.* 1985. London. WH Allen. 1st. 121p. NF. M21. $15.00

**STANEK, V.J.** *Pictorial Encyclopedia of the Animal Kingdom.* 1971. London. 7th. 614p. dj. A17. $15.00

**STANFORD, J.K.** *Last Chukker.* 1954. Devin Adair. 1st. VG/G. O3. $45.00

**STANFORTH, Deirdre.** *New Orleans Restaurant Cookbook: Colorful History...* 1967. Doubleday. VG. A16. $17.50

**STANGER, Frank M.** *South From San Francisco: San Mateo County, California...* 1963. San Mateo. 1st. photos. 214p. F. S14. $70.00

**STANGER, Margaret A.** *That Quail, Robert.* nd. NY. Buccaneer. ils Cathy Baldwin. rem mk. F/sans. G10. $12.50

**STANIER, Sylvia.** *Mrs Houblon's Side-Saddle.* 1986. London. Allen. VG/dj. O3. $25.00

**STANLEY, Arthur Penrhyn.** *Lectures on History of the Jewish Church.* 1896 & 1899. Scribner. 3 vol. VG. B29. $32.00

**STANLEY, Henry.** *Story of Emin's Rescue...* 1890. Harper. 1st. ils/dbl-p map. 176p. red cloth. VG. B27. $125.00

**STANLEY, Hiram M.** *Studies in Evolutionary Psychology of Feeling.* 1895. Sonnenschein/ Macmillan. inscr. 392p. ruled thatched brn cloth. NF. G1. $75.00

**STANLEY & VENNEMA.** *Bard of Avon.* 1992. Morrow. 1st. inscr. F/dj. W2. $35.00

**STANNARD, David E.** *Putitan Way of Death: A Study of Religion...* 1977. OUP. photos. VG/dj. M17. $30.00

**STANSBERRY, Domenic.** *Spoiler.* 1987. Atlantic Monthly. 1st. F/dj. P8. $20.00

**STANSBERRY, Domenic.** *Spoiler.* 1987. Atlantic Monthly. 1st. sgn. author's 1st novel. F/dj. T2. $40.00

**STANSBURY, Howard.** *Exploration & Survey of the Valley of the Great Salt Lake...* 1852. Phil. Lippincott Grambo. 1st. 8vo. 487p. cloth. O1. $300.00

**STANTON, Robert Brewster.** *Colorado River Controversies.* 1932. Dodd Mead. 8vo. ils. 232p. red cloth. VG/facs dj. F7. $600.00

**STANTON, Robert Brewster.** *Down the Colorado.* 1965. U OK. 1st. intro/edit DL Smith. 237p. VG/dj. F7. $75.00

**STANTON, Shelby L.** *Green Berets: US Army Special Forces in Southeast Asia...* 1985. Novato. Presidio. photos/maps. 360p. VG/dj. R11. $18.00

**STANWICK, Michael.** *Iron Dragon's Daughter.* 1994. NY. Morrow AvoNova. 1st Am. F/NF. G10. $16.50

**STANWOOD, Brooks.** *Glow.* 1979. McGraw Hill. 1st. F/F. H11. $20.00

**STAPP, William.** *Prisoners of Perote.* 1977. Austin. 1st thus/rpt (1845). 226p. dj. F3. $20.00

**STARBUCK, Alexander.** *History of the American Whale Fishery.* 1989. Seucacus. rpt. ils/index. 768p. VG/dj. A17. $15.00

**STARBUCK, Alma J.** *Complete Irish Wolfhound.* 1973. Howell. 3rd. 128p. VG. A17. $15.00

**STARK, Freya.** *Alexander's Path From Caria to Cilicia.* 1958. London. Murray. 1st. 8vo. ils/64 pl/5 map. cloth. VG/dj. Q2. $27.00

**STARK, J.H.** *Antique Views of Boston.* 1967. Boston. revised. ils/full-p engravings. 240p. NF/dj. M4. $50.00

**STARK, Richard;** see Westlake, Donald E.

**STARK, Sharon Sheehe.** *Dealers' Yard & Other Stories.* 1985. Morrow. 1st. author's 1st book. F/F. H11. $40.00

**STARK, Sharon Sheehe.** *Wrestling Season.* 1987. Morrow. 1st. sgn/dtd 1988. NF/NF. R14. $40.00

**STARKE, Ann Cornwell.** *Grandpa's Shadow: Stories for Young & Grown-Up Children.* (1972). Dorrance. ils. 77p. VG/G. B10. $12.00

**STARKELL, Don.** *Paddle to the Amazon.* 1989. CA. Prima Pub. 1st. 319p. dj. F3. $15.00

**STARKEY, Marion.** *Devil in Massachusetts: A Modern Inquiry...* 1950. Borzoi. VG/G. P12. $12.50

**STARKEY, Marion.** *Lace Cuffs & Leather Aprons: Popular Struggles...* 1972. Knopf. 1st. 291p. NF/dj. M10. $18.50

**STARMORE, Alice.** *Celtic Needlepoint.* 1994. N Pomfret, VT. Traflager. 1st. F/dj. T10. $30.00

**STAROBINSKI, Jean.** *History of Medicine.* 1964. NY. 1st. 114p. A13. $15.00

**STARR, Frederick.** *Physical Characters of Indians of Southern Mexico.* 1902. Chicago. 1st separate. ils/mc chart. 59p. wrp. F3. $75.00

**STARR, Henry.** *Thrilling Events: Life of Henry Starr by Himself.* 1982. Creative. rpt. ils/index. 95p. aeg. leather. F. E1. $20.00

**STARR, Jimmy.** *Three Short Biers.* 1946. Hollywood. Murray Gee. 1st. NF/rpr. M15. $125.00

**STARR, Louis.** *American Text-Book of Diseases of Children...* 1896. Phil. Saunders. tall 8vo. 1190p. gr cloth/ leather label. G7. $150.00

**STARRETT, Vincent.** *Bookman's Holiday.* 1943. Random. 1st. inscr. red cloth. VG/dj. J3. $150.00

**STARRETT, Vincent.** *Private Life of Sherlock Holmes.* 1933. Macmillan. 1st. VG. P3. $50.00

**STARZL, Thomas E.** *Puzzle People: Memoirs of a Transplant Surgeon.* 1992. Pittsburgh. ARC. 8vo. 364p. F/NF. C14. $20.00

**STAUFFER, Jay R.** *Potential & Realized Influences of Temperature on...Fishes.* 1976. VA Wildlife Soc. Wildlife Monograph #50. 40p. VG/wrp. S15. $5.00

**STAUNFORD, William.** *Exposition of the Kinges Praerogative Collected...* 1590. London. Richard Totthil. moden calf. M11. $1,500.00

**STAUNTON.** *Chess-Player's Handbook.* 1915. London. revised/edit EH Bermingham. VG. M17. $17.50

**STAUTON, Howard.** *Complete Illustrated Shakespeare.* 1989. NY. Gallery. 813p. VG. C5. $25.00

**STAVELEY, Gaylord.** *Broken Waters Sing: Rediscovering Two Great Rivers of West.* 1971. Boston. 1st. sgn. ils/index. 283p. gr/wht bdg. VG. F7. $22.50

**STAVRIDI, Margaret.** *Hugh Evelyn History of Costume Part 1: 19th Century.* 1966. London. ils Faith Jacques. VG. M17. $25.00

**STCHUR, John.** *Down on the Farm.* 1987. NY. SMP. 1st. F/F. H11. $30.00

**STEADMAN, Melvin Lee.** *Falls Church by Fence & Fireside.* 1964. Falls Church. 1st. ils/map ep. 552p. VG/dj. B10. $50.00

**STEARN, William T.** *English Florilegium.* 1987. London. Thames Hudson. ils after Mary Grierson. 240p. F/dj. A17. $95.00

**STEARNS, Sharon.** *Children's Book of Prayers & Hymns.* 1944. Samuel Lowe. ils. VG. R8. $10.00

**STEBBINS, G. Ledyard.** *Flowering Plants: Evolution Above Species Level.* 1974. Cambridge. 399p. VG/dj. A10. $30.00

**STEBBINS, Henry M.** *Small Game & Varmit Rifles.* 1947. NY. 234p. xl. rb buckram. F. A17. $15.00

**STEBBINS, William C.** *Acoustic Sense of Animals.* 1983. Harvard. 163p. F/dj. S15. $10.00

**STEBEL, S.L.** *Collaborator.* 1968. Random. 1st. NF/VG+. S13. $12.00

**STECK, Francis Borgia.** *Motolina's History of the Indians of New Spain.* 1951. Academy Franciscan Hist. ils 358p. cloth. dj. D11. $30.00

**STEDMAN, J.G.** *Narrative of Five Years' Expedition...1772 to 1777.* 1972. Amherst. U MA. 80 engravings. 480p. beige cloth. VG/dj. P4. $95.00

**STEDMAN, Ray C.** *Spiritual Warfare.* 1976. Word. 145p. VG/dj. B29. $7.00

**STEED, Judy.** *Ed Broadbent: Pursuit of Power.* 1988. Canada. Viking. 2nd. F/dj. P3. $18.00

**STEED, Neville.** *Tinplate.* 1986. London. Weidenfeld Nicolson. 1st. F/NF. B2. $50.00

**STEEL, R.** *Living Dragons: Natural History of World's Monitor Lizards.* 1996. London. Blands. 4to. ils. 160p. F/dj. M12. $30.00

**STEELE, Adison;** see Lupoff, Richard.

**STEELE, C. Frank.** *Prairie Editor: Life & Times of Buchannan of Lethbridge.* 1961. Toronto. Ryerson. 1st. F/dj. A26. $50.00

**STEELE, Danielle.** *Message From Nam.* 1990. Delacorte. 1st. F/dj. R11. $25.00

**STEELE, Harold C.** *Departmental Laboratory Assistant in Biological Science.* 1966. Dorrance. 213p. xl. G. S5. $12.00

**STEELE, I.K.** *Betrayals: Ft William Henry & the Massacre.* 1990. OUP. 1st. ils. 250p. F/dj. M4. $25.00

**STEELE, Philip.** *Last Cherokee Warriors.* 1974. Gretna, LA. Pelican Pub. sc. G. A19. $25.00

**STEELE, Valerie.** *Fetish, Fashion, Sex & Power.* 1996. OUP. 1st. F/dj. C9. $60.00

**STEERE, Douglas V.** *Time to Spare.* 1949. Harper. 12mo. 187p. V#. $10.00

**STEERE, William C.** *Liverworts of Southern Michigan.* 1940. Bloomfield Hills, MI. ils. 97p. bl binder's buckram. B26. $15.00

**STEFAN, Paul.** *Arturo Toscanini.* 1936. Viking. 1st/2nd prt. ils. 126p. G. W2. $45.00

**STEFANSSON, Evelyn.** *Here Is Alaska.* 1943. Scribner. 1st. ils. 157p. map ep. cloth. NF/VG. H7. $12.50

**STEFANSSON, Vilhjalmur.** *Hunters of the Great North.* 1922. NY. 301p. VG. A17. $35.00

**STEFANSSON, Vilhjalmur.** *My Life With the Eskimo.* 1921. NY. Macmillan. later prt. sgn. photos/2 fld map. 538p. NF/dj. P4. $250.00

**STEFFEN, Mart R.** *Special Cattle Therapy.* 1915. Chicago. Am Journal Vet Medicine. 157p. VG. A10. $18.00

**STEFFERUD, Alfred.** *Birds in Our Lives.* 1966. WA. 1st. 561p. F/dj. A17. $25.00

**STEFFERUD, Alfred.** *Crops in Peace & War: Yearbook of Agriculture 1950-51.* 1951. GPO. 942p. cloth. A10. $18.00

**STEGNER, Wallace.** *Beyond the Hundredth Meridian: John Wesley Powell...* 1954. Houghton Mifflin. 1st. map/index/map ep. brn cloth. VG/dj. F7. $200.00

**STEGNER, Wallace.** *Collected Stories of Wallace Stegner.* 1990. Random. 1st. F/dj. R14. $90.00

**STEGNER, Wallace.** *Crossing to Safety.* 1987. NY. stated 1st/2nd prt. VG/dj. M17. $25.00

**STEGNER, Wallace.** *Crossing to Safety.* 1987. Random. 1st. F/NF. B3. $50.00

**STEGNER, Wallace.** *Gathering of Zion: Story of the Mormon Trail.* (1964). NY. later prt. ils/maps. F/dj. M4. $25.00

**STEGNER, Wallace.** *Gathering of Zion: Story of the Mormon Trail.* 1964. McGraw Hill. 1st. ils. cloth. clip dj. D11. $75.00

**STEGNER, Wallace.** *Letters of Bernard deVoto.* 1975. Doubleday. 1st. VG/dj. T11. $25.00

**STEGNER, Wallace.** *Letters of Bernard deVoto.* 1975. Doubleday. 1st. 8vo. rem mk. NF/VG. S9. $35.00

**STEGNER, Wallace.** *Mormon Country.* 1942. NY. DSP. 1st. 8vo. 362p. map ep. VG. F7. $55.00

**STEGNER, Wallace.** *This Is Dinosaur: Echo Park Country & Its Magic Rivers.* 1955. NY. Knopf. 1st. 8vo. 97p. VG/G. F7. $160.00

**STEGNER & STEGNER.** *American Places: Eliot Porter.* 1983. Greenwich. ils. 224p. NF/NF. B19. $25.00

**STEIG, William.** *Dominic.* (1972). FSG. 8vo. ils. 146p. red cloth. VG. T5. $15.00

**STEIG, William.** *Rotten Island.* 1984 (1969). Eng. Viking Kestrel. 1st Eng. 4to. unp. NF. T5. $25.00

**STEIN, Andre.** *Broken Silence.* 1984. Lester/Orpen Dennys. 1st Canadian. VG/dj. P3. $15.00

**STEIN, Charles Francis.** *Origin & History of Howard County, Maryland.* 1972. Baltimore. ils/map ep. 383p. VG/dj. B18. $45.00

**STEIN, Eugene.** *Straitjacket & Tie.* 1994. Ticknor. 1st. author's 1st book. F/F. H11. $15.00

**STEIN, Evaleen.** *Little Shepard of Provence.* 1910. LC Page. 1st. 8vo. ils. VG+. M5. $20.00

**STEIN, Gertrude.** *Autobiography of Alice B Toklas.* 1933. Harcourt Brace. 1st. NF/VG. B4. $450.00

**STEIN, Gertrude.** *Have They Attacked Mary. He Giggled.* 1917. W Chester, PA. Horace F Temple. 1st. 1/200. NF/red prt wrp. M24. $850.00

**STEIN, Gertrude.** *Lectures in America.* 1953. Random. 1st/1st state. 8vo. 246p. NF/dj. J3. $225.00

**STEIN, Gertrude.** *Money.* 1973. Blk Sparrow. 1st. 1/126. gr brd ($1 bill as label). acetate dj. M24. $200.00

STEIN, Gertrude. *Wars I Have Seen*. 1945. 1st. NF/VG. M19. $45.00

STEIN, Gertrude. *When This You See Remember Me*. 1948. Rinehart. early prt. blk cloth. VG+. S13. $20.00

STEIN, Harry. *Hoopla*. 1983. Knopf. 1st. sgn. F/VG. P8. $85.00

STEIN, Jean. *Edie: An American Biography*. 1982. Knopf. BC. ils. 455p. VG/G. P12. $8.00

STEIN, Leonard. *Balfour Declaration*. 1961. S&S. 8vo. 681p. gilt bl cloth. NF/dj. M7. $40.00

STEIN, S.G. III. *Steins of Muscatine: A Family Chronicle*. 1962. np. 53p. VG. S5. $25.00

STEIN & TOKLAS. *Dear Sammy: Letters From Gertrude Stein & Alice B Toklas*. 1977. Boston. 1st. photos. VG/dj. M17. $17.50

STEINBECK, John. *East of Eden*. 1952. NY. Viking. 1st. F/F. L3. $750.00

STEINBECK, John. *Fabulous Redmen*. 1951. Harrisburg. 1st. VG/dj. B5. $35.00

STEINBECK, John. *Grapes of Wrath*. 1939. Viking. 1st. 8vo. 619p. beige cloth. NF/dj. H5. $1,850.00

STEINBECK, John. *Journal of a Novel*. 1969. NY. 1st. F/F. B5. $60.00

STEINBECK, John. *Positano*. 1954. Salemo. Edizioni Saturnia. NF/wrp. B4. $400.00

STEINBECK, John. *Red Pony*. ca 1959. Viking. 120p. NF. C14. $8.00

STEINBECK, John. *Red Pony*. 1945. Viking. 1st. ils Wesley Dennis. VG/worn case. S13. $16.00

STEINBECK, John. *Red Pony*. 1989. Viking. ils Wesley Dennis. NF/dj. A21. $30.00

STEINBECK, John. *Short Reign of Pippin IV*. 1957. Viking. 1st. VG/dj. S13. $25.00

STEINBECK, John. *Sweet Thursday*. 1954. Viking. 1st. F/dj. Q1. $175.00

STEINBECK, John. *Sweet Thursday*. 1954. Viking. 1st. 8vo. VG/clip. S9. $50.00

STEINBECK, John. *Working Days: Journals of Grapes of Wrath*. 1989. NY. Viking. 1st. edit DeMott. NF/F. R14. $35.00

STEINBERG, Alan. *Cry of the Leopard*. 1997. St Martin. 1st. author's 3rd book. VG/dj. L1. $45.00

STEINBERG. *Five Hundred Years of Printing*. 1961. ils. 396p. VG. A4. $25.00

STEINBRUNNER, Chris. *Detectionary*. 1972. Lock Haven. Hammermill Paper Co. ltd ed. F/stiff wrp. M15. $100.00

STEINE, Buena Vista. *Loud With Laughter*. 1943. Los Angeles. 1st. inscr to Sen & Mrs Harry Truman/sgn Truman. VG. S16. $250.00

STEINEL, Alvin. *History of Agriculture in Colorado*. 1926. Ft Collins. 659p. cloth. VG. A10. $92.00

STEINER, Gary A. *People Look at Television: A Study of Audience Attitudes*. 1963. Knopf. 1st. 8vo. F/VG. A2. $30.00

STEINER, Nancy Hunter. *Closer Look at Ariel: Memory of Sylvia Plath*. 1973. Harpers Magazine. 1st. VG/dj. C9. $25.00

STEINER, Robert. *Passion*. 1980. Lincoln, MA. Penmaen. 1/1000. ils Bertha Golahny. gilt wheat cloth. F1. $30.00

STEINHARDT, Jakob. *Woodcuts of Jakob Steinhardt*. (1959). SF. Genuart Co. 1/1250. inscr. folio. ils. gilt purple cloth. dj. K1. $50.00

STEINKE, Darcy. *Suicide Blonde*. 1992. Atlantic Monthly. 1st. sgn. F/dj. D10. $40.00

STEINKE, Darcy. *Up Through the Water*. 1989. Doubleday. 1st. sgn. F/NF. D10. $45.00

STELLE, J.P. *Gunsmith's Manual: Handbook for the American Gunsmith*. 1945. Plantersville, SC. Thomas G Samworth. G. A19. $25.00

STEMP, Jane. *Waterbound*. 1996. Dial. 1st Am. F/dj. T12. $25.00

STENDAHL. *Memoirs of a Tourist*. 1962 (1961). Northwestern. 1st thus. 8vo. G/dj. A2. $10.00

STENHOUSE, Mrs. T.B.H. *Tell It All: Story of a Life's Experience in Mormonism*. 1875 (1874). Hartford. Worthington. 27 pl. 624p. gr cloth. K1. $40.00

STEPANEK, O. *Birds of Heath & Marshland*. 1966. London. 4th. 134p. F/dj. A17. $20.00

STEPANSKY, Paul E. *Memoirs of Margaret Mahler*. 1988. Free Pr. 1st. 8vo. 179p. F/NF. C14. $14.00

STEPHAN, Leslie. *Reprise*. 1988.. SMP. 1st. F/F. H11. $20.00

STEPHEN, Leslie. *Samuel Johnson*. 1878. Harper. 1st Am. brn cloth. H13. $35.00

STEPHENS, Dan V. *Cottonwood Yarns...Mostly Stories Told to Children...* 1935. Fremont. 1st. ils/drawings. G. A17. $25.00

STEPHENS, James. *Crock of Gold*. 1926. Macmillan. 1st. 227p. G. M10. $75.00

STEPHENS, John W. *Leather Manufacture*. 1890. Chicago. Shoe & Leather. hc. VG. B9. $75.00

STEPHENS, M.G. *Season at Coole*. 1972. Dutton. ARC/1st. inscr/dtd 1977. F/NF. L3. $45.00

STEPHENSON, George M. *Puritan Heritage*. 1952. Macmillan. 282p. G/dj. B29. $7.00

STEPHENSON, Neal. *Diamond Age*. 1995. Bantam. 1st. sgn. F/dj. O11. $75.00

STEPHENSON, Neal. *Zodiac*. 1988. Atlantic Monthly. 1st. author's 2nd novel. F/wrp. A24. $45.00

STEPHENSON, Terry E. *Don Bernardo Yorba*. 1963. Glen Dawson. 2nd. 115p. NF. B19. $20.00

STEPHENSON, Terry E. *Don Bernardo Yorba*. 1963. LA. Glen Dawson. 1/600. 115p. gilt cloth. D11. $75.00

STERLING, Bruce. *Holy Fire*. 1996. Norwalk, CT. Easton. 1st. sgn. red leather. F. M23. $60.00

STERLING, George. *Sonnets to Craig*. 1928. NY. Boni. 1st. F. A18. $25.00

STERLING, Stewart. *Fire on Fear Street*. 1958. Lippincott. 1st. VG/dj. G8. $20.00

STERLING, Stewart. *Nightmare at Noon*. 1951. Dutton. 1st. VG/dj. G8. $20.00

STERN, G.B. *Long Lost Father*. 1933. Knopf. 1st Am. F/NF. B4. $100.00

STERN, Louis William. *Psychologie der Fruhen Kindheit bis zum Sechsten...* 1914. Leipzig. Quelle & Meyer. 372p. prt cream cloth. G1. $125.00

STERN, Louis William. *Psychology of Early Childhood Up to Sixth Year of Age*. 1924. London. Allen Unwin. 1st Eng-language. 557p. panelled bl cloth. VG. G1. $65.00

STERN, Madeleine B. *Behind a Mask: Unknown Thrillers of Louisa May Alcott*. 1995. Morrow. 1st. ils. cloth/brd. dj. R12. $25.00

STERN, Madeleine B. *Louisa May Alcott*. 1996. Random. 8vo. ils. wrp. R12. $18.00

STERN, Madeleine B. *Louisa May Alcott: From Blood & Thunder to Health & Home*. 1998. Boston. Northwestern U. 4to. cloth. R12. $47.50

STERN, Philip Van Doren. *Robert E Lee: Man & the Soldier*. 1963. McGraw Hill. 1st. 256p. F/dj. H1. $40.00

STERN, Steve. *Harry Kaplan's Adventures Underground*. 1991. Ticknor Fields. 1st. sgn. AN/dj. B30. $25.00

**STERN, Steve.** *Lazar Malkin Enters Heaven.* 1986. Viking. 1st. sgn. F/dj. B30. $25.00

**STERNBERG & WILSON.** *Landscaping With Native Trees.* 1995. Shelburne, VT. photos. 288p. sc. B26. $22.50

**STERNE, Laurence.** *Sentimental Journey Through France & Italy.* nd. Brentano. 12mo. 210p. VG. B11. $15.00

**STERNE, Laurence.** *Sentimental Journey Through France & Italy.* 1941. NY. Heritage. lg 8vo. gilt red/wht/bl cloth. F/case. M7. $40.00

**STERNE, Laurence.** *Tristram Shandy & a Sentimental Journey.* 1941. Modern Lib. 1st. VG+/dj. S13. $12.00

**STERNE, Laurence.** *Tristram Shandy.* 1895. Stone Kimball. 2 vol. 1st thus. teg. gilt brn cloth. VG+. S13. $75.00

**STETSON, Charlotte Perkins.** *Women & Economics: A Study...* 1898. Sm Maynard. 1st. sgn/dtd 1898. Lib Congress duplicate stp. B4. $5,000.00

**STEVENS, Brooke.** *Circus of the Earth & Air.* 1994. NY. Harcourt. 1st. F/F. H11. $25.00

**STEVENS, David.** *Garden Design Sourcebook.* 1995. London. ils/250 photos. AN/dj. B26. $30.00

**STEVENS, F.L.** *Plant Disease Fungi.* 1954. Macmillan. 469p. xl. VG. S5. $12.00

**STEVENS, Garfield Reeves.** *Dark Matter.* 1990. Doubleday. 1st. NF/dj. S18. $24.00

**STEVENS, Harry R.** *Early Jackson Party in Ohio.* 1957. Durham. Duke. 187p. VG. B18. $25.00

**STEVENS, James.** *Gates of New Life.* 1964. T&T Clark. 251p. VG. B29. $10.50

**STEVENS, Joseph E.** *Hoover Dam: An American Adventure.* 1988. Norman. U OK. 1st. 8vo. blk cloth. VG/dj. F7. $32.50

**STEVENS, Patricia.** *God Save Ireland!* 1974. Macmillan. 1st. 200p. F/dj. D4. $30.00

**STEVENS, Richard M.** *Zipper the Zany: Little Cat Who Tried to Write a Book.* 1945. NY. Penn. 1st. sq 8vo. dj. R5. $100.00

**STEVENS, Shane.** *Anvil Chorus.* 1985. Delacorte. 1st. F/dj. M15. $45.00

**STEVENS, Shane.** *By Reason of Insanity.* 1979. S&S. 1st. F/NF. M19. $17.50

**STEVENS, Sheppard.** *In the Eagle's Talon.* 1902. Boston. Little Brn. 1st. 475p. G. G11. $6.00

**STEVENS, Wallace.** *Poems.* 1985. SF. Arion. 1/326. ils/sgn Jasper Johns. w/prospectus. AN. B24. $2,500.00

**STEVENS, William Chase.** *Kansas Wild Flowers.* 1948. U KS. 463p. xl. VG. S5. $35.00

**STEVENS & WISEBY.** *Gottfried von Strassbourg & Medieval Tristan Legend.* 1990. Cambridge. Brewer. 1st. ils/index. F/dj. T10. $75.00

**STEVENS-ARROYO, Antonio.** *Cave of the Jagua: Mythological World of Tainos.* 1988. U NM. 1st. 282p. F3. $25.00

**STEVENSON, D.E.** *Fletcher's End.* 1973. Thorpe. 1st lg prt. 8vo. 540p. NF/dj. W2. $25.00

**STEVENSON, Elizabeth.** *Park Maker: Life of Frederick Law Olmsted.* 1977. NY. 484p. VG/dj. B26. $26.00

**STEVENSON, G.H.** *Roman Provincial Administration Till Age of Antonines.* 1939. Oxford. Blackwell. 8vo. fld map. cloth/rpr. Q2. $27.00

**STEVENSON, R. Randolph.** *Southern Side; or, Andersonville Prison...* 1995. New Market. 488p. VG/dj. S16. $30.00

**STEVENSON, Robert Louis.** *Amateur Emigrant With Some First Impressions of America.* 1976. Ashland. Lewis Osborne. 1/600. ils/fld map. 96p. beige linen. dj. K1. $50.00

**STEVENSON, Robert Louis.** *Black Arrow.* 1888. Cassell. 1st. red cloth. G. S13. $15.00

**STEVENSON, Robert Louis.** *Black Arrow.* 1926. Saalfield. ne. sm 8vo. 254p. G. W2. $250.00

**STEVENSON, Robert Louis.** *Child's Garden of Verses.* (1900). NY. RH Russell. 1st thus. ils E Mars/MH Squire. dk sea-bl pict brd. R5. $285.00

**STEVENSON, Robert Louis.** *Child's Garden of Verses.* nd (1957). Grosset Dunlap. gift inscr dtd 1969. 104p. F/VG+. C14. $20.00

**STEVENSON, Robert Louis.** *Child's Garden of Verses.* 1900. NY. RH Russell. ils E Mars/MH Squires. 117p. bl brd. F1. $300.00

**STEVENSON, Robert Louis.** *Child's Garden of Verses.* 1905. NY. 1st thus. ils BC Pease. VG. M17. $100.00

**STEVENSON, Robert Louis.** *Child's Garden of Verses.* 1981. Rand McNally. School/Lib ed. ils Tasha Tudor. not xl. F. M5. $45.00

**STEVENSON, Robert Louis.** *Kidnapped.* (1948). Grosset Dunlap. 1st. ils/assn/sgn pres Lynd Ward. prt plastic dj. R5. $150.00

**STEVENSON, Robert Louis.** *Kidnapped.* 1908. McLoughlin. lg 8vo. ils. 139p. G. M7. $25.00

**STEVENSON, Robert Louis.** *Kidnapped.* 1913. NY. Scribner. 1st. ils NC Wyeth. 14p+fld map. teg. blk cloth/label. R5. $285.00

**STEVENSON, Robert Louis.** *Kidnapped.* 1932. Garden City. ils. 322p. G. P12. $12.00

**STEVENSON, Robert Louis.** *Land of Nod.* 1988. Holt. 1st. ils Hague. F. B17. $20.00

**STEVENSON, Robert Louis.** *Prayers Written at Vailima.* 1973. LA. Dawson/Plantin. mini. 1/500. engravings Mary Kuper. w/prospectus. B24. $95.00

**STEVENSON, Robert Louis.** *Strange Case of Dr Jeckyll & Mr Hyde.* 1952. Heritage. lg 8vo. gilt blk cloth. F. M7. $18.00

**STEVENSON, Robert Louis.** *Treasure Island.* 1884. Boston. Roberts Bros. 1st Am. gilt turquoise cloth. VG. M24. $1,000.00

**STEVENSON, Robert Louis.** *Treasure Island.* 1911. Scribner. 1st. ils NC Wyeth. 273p. navy morocco. F. H5. $600.00

**STEVENSON, Robert Louis.** *Treasure Island.* 1953 (1948). London. JM Dent. sm 8vo. ils S VanAbbe. NF/VG. C14. $10.00

**STEVENSON, Violet.** *Successful Flower Marketing.* 1952. London. Collingridge. 164p. VG/dj. A10. $22.00

**STEWARD, Albert.** *Manual of Vascular Plants of Lower Yangtze Valley China.* 1958. Corvallis. OR State. 621p. cloth. xl. VG. A10. $60.00

**STEWARD, Julian H.** *Comparative Ethnology of South American Indians. Vol 5.* 1949. GPO. 8vo. ils/pl/22 maps. 818p. olive cloth. VG. P4. $66.00

**STEWARD, Julian H.** *Notes on Hiller's Photographs of Paiute & Ute Indians...* 1939. Smithsonian. 8vo. 31 pl. 23p. VG/tan wrp. F7. $175.00

**STEWART, A.T.Q.** *Deeper Silence: Hidden Origins of the United Irishmen.* 1993. London. Faber. 1st. 8vo. F/dj. A2. $20.00

**STEWART, Cecil.** *Byzantine Legacy.* 1959. Allen Unwin. 2 maps. 202p. cloth. VG. Q2. $24.00

**STEWART, Charles.** *Treatise on the Law of Scotland Relating to...Fishing...* 1869. Edinburgh. T&T Clark. 1st modern gr cloth. M11. $225.00

**STEWART, Desmond.** *Orphan With a Hoop: Life of Emile Bustani.* 1967. London. Chapman Hall. 8vo. ils. 218p. cloth. VG/dj. Q2. $25.00

**STEWART, Dugald.** *Elements of Philosophy of the Human Mind.* 1818. NY. James Eastburn. 420p. G. G1. $75.00

**STEWART, E.W.** *Prize Essays on Cooked & Cooking Food Domestic Animals...* 1869. NY. Prindle. 64p. VG/wrp. A10. $20.00

STEWART, Edgar I. *Penny-an-Acre Empire in the West.* 1968. Norman, OK. 1st. 268p. E1. $35.00

STEWART, Elihu. *Down the Mackenzie & Up the Yukon in 1906.* 1913. London. John Lane. 2nd. 30 photo pl/fld map. 270p. red cloth. VG. P4. $125.00

STEWART, Elliott. *Feeding Animals: Practical Work Upon Laws of Growths...* 1883. Lake View, NY. self pub. 1st. 523+9p. VG. H7. $30.00

STEWART, Fred Mustard. *Ellis Island.* 1983. Morrow. 1st. VG/dj. S18. $8.00

STEWART, Fred Mustard. *Pomp & Circumstance.* 1991. Dutton. 1st. F/dj. T12. $20.00

STEWART, George R. *Fire.* 1948. Random. 1st. F/VG. M19. $17.50

STEWART, George R. *North-South Continental Highway Looking South.* 1957. Houghton Mifflin. 1st. ils. 230p. dj. F3. $15.00

STEWART, George R. *Pickett's Charge: A Microhistory of Final Attack...* 1959. Houghton Mifflin. 1st. ils/maps. 354p. VG/VG. B10. $75.00

STEWART, Herbert Leslie. *Sir Winston Churchill as Writer & Speaker.* 1954. London. Sidgwick Jackson. 1st. 161p. VG/dj. M10. $22.50

STEWART, Jane L. *Campfire Girls' Adventure in the Mountains.* 1914. Saalfield. 8vo. 245p. G. W2. $20.00

STEWART, Lynette. *Palms for the Home & Garden.* 1987. Ryde, NSW. ils. 72p. sc. VG. B26. $16.00

STEWART, Mary. *Gabriel Hounds.* 1967. Morrow. 1st. NF/dj. S18. $35.00

STEWART, Mary. *Little Broomstick.* 1972. NY. Morrow. 1st Am. F/clip. A24. $45.00

STEWART, Mary. *Walk in Wolf Wood.* 1980. London. 1st Eng. ils Doreen Caldwell. VG/dj. M17. $27.50

STEWART, Michael. *Monkey Shines.* 1983. Freundlich. 1st. F/F. H11. $30.00

STEWART, Oliver. *First Flights.* 1957. London. Routledge. F/VG. B9. $15.00

STEWART, P. *Vintner in the Kitchen: Wine & Cookery in the West.* 1974. ils. easel stand format. VG. E6. $12.00

STEWART, R.J. *Book of Merlin.* 1987. Blandford. 1st. F/dj. P3. $25.00

STEWART, Robert A. *Broken Lives: Personal View of Bosnian Conflict.* 1993. Harper Collins. 1st. photos. F/dj. A2. $20.00

STEWART, Robert. *Sam Steele: Lion of the Frontier.* 1979. Toronto. Doubleday. UP. NF/wrp. A26. $50.00

STEWART, Watt. *Keith & Costa Rica.* 1964. Albuquerque. 1st. 210p. dj. F3. $25.00

STEWART, William Henry. *Description of Battle of Crater, Recollections...* 1876. Norfolk, VA. landmark Office. 1st. 16p. prt wrp. M8. $850.00

STEWART, William Henry. *Pair of Blankets: War-Time History in Letters...* (1911). Broadway Pub. 1st. 2 pl. 217p. cloth. VG. M8. $650.00

STEWART. *Book Collecting.* 1973. ils. 312p. F/NF. A4. $40.00

STICCO, Maria. *Peace of St Francis.* 1961. NY. ils. VG/dj. M17. $15.00

STIDGER, William L. *Edwin Markham.* (1933). NY. Abingdon. 1st. ftspc/index. NF. A18. $15.00

STIEB, Dave. *Tomorrow, I'll Be Perfect.* 1986. Canada. Doubleday. 1st. F/dj. P8. $30.00

STIGAND, C.H. *Hunting the Elephant in Africa.* 1986. NY. photos. 379p. F/dj. S15. $12.00

STILES, Ezra. *History of 3 Judges of King Charles I...Who...Fled to Am...* 1794. Hartford. Elisha Babcock. 1st. 12mo. 3-quarter leather. ES. H7. $50.00

STILES, Jessie Vernan. *Family of Jonathan Stiles of Guernsey Co, OH...* 1957. np. 398p. G. S5. $35.00

STILL, Steven M. *Manual of Herbaceous Ornamental Plants.* 1994 (1980). Champaign. 4th expanded. photos. 814p. VG. B26. $35.00

STILLINGFLEET, Edward. *Unreasonableness of Separation...* 1681. London. Mortlock. 2nd corrected. 4to. 449p. aeg. restoration bdg. box. B24. $3,500.00

STILLMAN, Jacob D.B. *Around the Horn to California in 1849.* 1967. Lewis Osbourne. 1st. 1/1150. F/sans. O4. $25.00

STILLSON, Henry Leonard. *Official History & Literature of Odd Fellowship...* 1897. Boston. Fraternity Pub Co. 896p. VG. H6. $46.00

STILLWELL, Benjamin. *Early Memoirs of the Stillwell Family.* 1878. NY. dk gr half leather/marbled brd. VG. B30. $45.00

STILLWELL, John E. *Genealogy of the Stillwell Family, Vol 2, 3 & 4.* 1930. NY. 3 vol. brn cloth. VG. B30. $75.00

STILLWELL, John E. *Historical & Genealogical Miscellany: Data Relating...* 1903. NY. Vol 1 only. dk gr cloth. G+. B30. $35.00

STINCHFIELD, Sara M. *Psychology of Speech.* 1928. Boston. Expression Co. 331p. prt panelled crimson sloth. VG. G1. $40.00

STINEMAN, Esther Lanigan. *Mary Austin: Song of the Maverick.* 1989. New Haven/London. 1st. 8vo. 269p. AN/dj. P4. $35.00

STINETORF, L. *La Cina Problana.* 1960. Bobbs Merrill. 1st. 256p. dj. F3. $15.00

STINETORF, Louisa A. *White Witch Doctor.* 1950. Phil. Westminster. BC. 276p. VG/dj. A25. $15.00

STIRLING, William. *Some Apostles of Physiology...* 1902. London. Waterlow. inscr pres. ils/portraits. 129p. parchment brd. G7. $250.00

STIRLING-MAXWELL, William. *Annals of the Artists of Spain.* 1891. London. 4 vol. ils. xl. VG. M10. $50.00

STIRNIMANN, F. *Psychologie des Neugeborenen Kindes.* 1940. Zurich/Leipzig. Rascher. 12mo. 108p. prt gray linen. xl. G1. $25.00

STITT, Irene. *Japanese Ceramics of the Last 100 Years.* 1974. Crown. 1st. 214p. VG/fair. S14. $40.00

STOCKARD, Henry Jerome. *Study in Southern Poetry for Use in Schools...* 1911. Neale Pub. 1st. 346p. pict cloth. VG. M8. $75.00

STOCKDELL, Helen. *Speech Made Beautiful.* 1930. NY. Abingdon. 111p. xl. G. C5. $12.50

STOCKING, George. *Victorian Anthropology.* 1987. NY. 1st. 429p. A13. $30.00

STOCKTON, Frank R. *Bee-Man of Orn.* (1964). HRW. 1st. ils Sendak. dk gr bdg/pict label. mc dj. R5. $275.00

STOCKTON, Frank R. *Pomona's Travels.* 1894. Scribner. 1st. ils AB Frost. F. M19. $45.00

STOCKTON, Frank R. *Pomona's Travels.* 1894. Scribner. 1st. ils AB Frost. gilt gr cloth. VG+. S13. $20.00

STODDARD, Edward. *First Book of Magic.* 1953. Franklin Watts. 1st. ils Robin King. F/VG. P2. $20.00

STODDARD, John L. *Comprehensive Story of Ventura County, California.* 1979. Oxnard, CA. M&N Prt Co. 1st. F/sans. O4. $15.00

STODOLA, Frank H. *Chemical Transformations by Micro-organisms.* 1958. Wiley. xl. VG. S5. $9.00

STOEVER, William. *Faire & Easie Way to Heaven: Covenant Theology...* 1978. Weslyan U. 251p. NF. M10. $15.00

**STOKER, Bram.** *Dracula.* nd. Grosset Dunlap. MTI. ils. VG. L1. $40.00

**STOKER, Bram.** *Dracula.* 1965. Heritage. 1st thus. VG/dj. L1. $50.00

**STOKES, Frances K.** *My Father, Owen Wister.* 1952. Laramie, WY. sc. F. A19. $25.00

**STOKES, Terry.** *Crimes of Passion.* 1973. Knopf. ARC/1st. inscr. F/dj. L3. $75.00

**STOKES, William.** *Honduras.* 1950. Madison, WI. 1st. 315p. dj. F3. $20.00

**STOKES.** *Iconography of Manhattan Island.* nd. 6 vol. rpt. several hundred full-p pl (many fold). F. A4. $750.00

**STOKOWSKI, Leopold.** *Music for All of Us.* 1943. S&S. 340p. G. C5. $12.50

**STOLTZFUS, Louise.** *Amish Women: Lives & Stories.* 1994. Good Books. F/dj. R8. $8.00

**STOLZ, Mary.** *Wait for Me, Michael.* 1961. Harper Row. xl. VG/dj. B36. $11.00

**STOMMEL, H.** *Lost Islands: Story of Islands That Have Vanished...* 1984. British Columbia U. 4to. ils/25 maps. F/dj. M4. $30.00

**STOMMELL, Henry.** *View of the Sea.* 1987. Princeton. 165p. F/dj. A17. $12.50

**STONE, George Cameron.** *Glossary of Construction, Decoration & Use of Arms...* 1961. NY. Jack Brussel. ils/biblio. 694p. G/fair. H10. $45.00

**STONE, Irving.** *Depths of Glory: Biographical Novel of Camille Pisarro.* 1985. Doubleday. 1st. sgn. NF/dj. B30. $30.00

**STONE, Irving.** *Greek Treasure.* 1975. Doubleday. 1st. sgn. VG/G. B30. $45.00

**STONE, Irving.** *I, Michelangelo, Sculptor.* 1962. Doubleday. 1st. F/dj. A24. $35.00

**STONE, Irving.** *Men to Watch My Mountains. Opening of Far West 1840-1900.* 1956. Doubleday. 1st. 8vo. 459p. VG. B11. $15.00

**STONE, Irving.** *Passions of the Mind: Biographical Novel of Freud.* 1971. Doubleday. 1st trade. inscr. F/dj. M25. $45.00

**STONE, Irving.** *They Also Ran: Story of Men Who Were Defeated...* 1943. Doubleday Doran. 1st. 8vo. VG/dj. w/promo material+ephemera. S9. $100.00

**STONE, Julius F.** *Canyon Country: Romance of Drop of Water & Grain of Sand.* 1932. Putnam. 1st. 442p. blk cloth. VG/G. F7. $165.00

**STONE, Lee Alexander.** *Power of a Symbol.* 1925. Chicago. Pascal Covici. ltd. G. B9. $40.00

**STONE, Martha.** *At the Sign of Midnight.* 1975. Tucson. 1st. photos. 262p. F3. $20.00

**STONE, Michael.** *Armenian Inscriptions From the Sinai.* 1982. Harvard. ils. 250p. cloth. VG+. Q2. $24.00

**STONE, Raymond.** *Donald Dare, the Champion Pitcher.* 1914. Graham. 1st. ils. G+. P8. $200.00

**STONE, Raymond.** *Tommy Piptop & His Baseball Nine.* 1912. Graham Matlack. 1st. G+. P8. $200.00

**STONE, Reynolds.** *AVC.* 1974. London. Warren Eds. mini. 1/250. prt orange wrp. B24. $150.00

**STONE, Reynolds.** *Note on Wood Engraving by Reynolds Stone 1909-1979...* 1982. London. 1st. paper wrp. T9. $25.00

**STONE, Robert.** *Bear & His Daughter.* 1997. Houghton Mifflin. 1st. sgn. F/dj. R14. $45.00

**STONE, Robert.** *Children of Light.* 1986. Knopf. 1st Am. F/dj. Q1. $50.00

**STONE, Robert.** *Damascus Gate.* 1998. Houghton Mifflin. 1st. sgn. F/dj. R14. $45.00

**STONE, Robert.** *Dog Soldiers.* 1974. Houghton Mifflin. 1st. G/NF. B3. $125.00

**STONE, Robert.** *Flag for Sunrise.* 1981. Knopf. 1st. F/dj. B2. $45.00

**STONE, Robert.** *Flag for Sunrise.* 1981. Knopf. 1st. sgn. VG/dj. B30. $45.00

**STONE, Robert.** *Outerbridge Reach.* 1992. NY. Ticknor. 1st. F/F. H11. $30.00

**STONE, William L.** *Life & Times of Sa-Go-Ye-Wat-Ha or Red Jacket.* 1841. NY. 1/550. ils/5 pl. 484p. gilt cloth. B18. $250.00

**STONE, William L.** *Life & Times of Sir William Johnson, Bart.* 1965. Albany. Munsell. 2 vol. 555/544p. B18. $55.00

**STONELY, Jack.** *Scruffy.* 1979. Random. 1st (stated). 8vo. 156p. brd/cloth spine. VG/dj. T5. $30.00

**STONERIDGE, M.A.** *Horse of your Own.* 1968. NY. revised. photos. 508p. VG/dj. A17. $10.00

**STONG, Phil.** *Horses & Americans.* 1946. Garden City. deluxe ed. ils Kurt Wiese. 333p. NF. A17. $22.50

**STOOKEY, Lorena Laura.** *Robin Cook: A Critical Companion.* 1996. Greenwood. 1st. F. P3. $30.00

**STOPPARD, Tom.** *Lord Malquist & Mr Moon.* 1966. London. Anthony Blond. 1st. author's 1st book. F/NF. A24. $175.00

**STORER & USINGER.** *Sierra Nevada Natural History: Illustrated Handbook.* 1964. U CA. ils. 374p. cloth. VG/fair. M12. $20.00

**STOREY, Gail Donohue.** *Lord's Motel.* 1992. NY. Persea. 1st. author's 1st book. F/dj. R14. $35.00

**STORM, Margaret.** *Dessert Lover's Cookbook.* 1970. LA. Nash. G/dj. A16. $7.00

**STORM, Robert.** *Animal Orientation & Navigation.* 1967. OR State U. 134p. xl. G. S5. $15.00

**STORRING, Gustav.** *Mental Pathology in Its Relation to Normal Psychology.* 1907. Sonnenschein. 1st Eng-language. 298p. tan cloth. G1. $65.00

**STORY, Alfred T.** *Story of Photography.* 1909. NY. McClure. ils. half morocco/cloth. B14. $100.00

**STORY, Joseph.** *Power of Solitude: A Poem. In Two Parts.* 1804. Salem. Macanulty. contemporary tree sheep. M11. $350.00

**STORY, Thomas.** *Doctrines of Society of Friends as Set Forth...* nd. Phil. Assn Friends Diffusion Religious. 16mo. 195p. VG. V3. $15.00

**STORY, Thomas.** *Journal of Life of Thomas Story...* 1747. Newcastle Upon Tyne. Isaac Thompson. folio. 768+8p index. fair. V3. $155.00

**STOTT & SCOTT.** *Chrysanthemums for Pleasure.* 1953 (1950). self pub. 2nd. 318p. G. S14. $7.00

**STOUDT, John Joseph.** *Early Pennsylvania Art & Crafts.* (1964). London. Yoseloff/ Barnes. 3rd. ils. 364p. F/dj. H1. $30.00

**STOUDT, John Joseph.** *Sunbonnets & Shoefly Pie.* 1973. Barnes. 1st. VG/dj. R8. $30.00

**STOUGHTON, John.** *Worthies of Science.* ca 1880. London. Religious Tract Soc. 342p. gilt cloth. K5. $40.00

**STOURZH, Gerald.** *Benjamin Franklin & American Foreign Policy.* 1954. Chicago. 335p. G/VG. M10. $15.00

**STOUT, A.B.** *Daylilies.* 1934. Hemerocallis, NY. 1st. ils/pl. 119p. VG/dj. B26. $50.00

**STOUT, George Frederick.** *Analytic Psychology.* 1896. London. Sonnenschein/ Macmillan. 2 vol. 1st/British issue. VG. G1. $85.00

**STOUT, Joseph Allen.** *Liberators: Filibustering Expeditions Into Mexico, 1848-62.* 1973. Westernlore. 1st. ils/biblio/index. 202p. F/F. B19. $30.00

**STOUT, Neil.** *Perfect Crisis: Beginning of the Revolutionary War.* 1976. NY. ils/notes/ index. VG/dj. S16. $24.00

**STOUT, Rex.** *Alphabet Hicks.* 1941. Farrar Rinehart. 1st. F/NF. M15. $500.00

**STOUT, Rex.** *Corsage.* 1977. Bloomington. JA Rock. 1st. 1/1500. F. M15. $150.00

**STOUT, Rex.** *Father Hunt.* 1968. NY. Viking. 1st. F/dj. M15. $75.00

**STOUT, Rex.** *Father Hunt.* 1968. Viking. 1st. rem mk. NF/G. M19. $25.00

**STOUT, Rex.** *Final Deduction.* 1961. Viking. 1st. NF. T12. $60.00

**STOUT, Rex.** *Justice Ends at Home & Other Stories.* 1977. Viking. 1st. VG/dj. G8. $30.00

**STOUT, Rex.** *Might as Well Be Dead.* 1956. NY. Viking. 1st. inscr. w/2 inscr notes. F/VG. M15. $750.00

**STOUT, Rex.** *Nero Wolfe Cookbook.* 1973. Viking. 1st. VG/dj. B5. $55.00

**STOUT, Rex.** *Three Men Out.* 1953. Viking. 1st. F/VG. P8. $150.00

**STOUT, Rex.** *Trio for Blunt Instruments.* 1964. Viking. 1st. F/VG. M15. $70.00

**STOUT, Sandra McPhee.** *Complete Book of McKee Glass.* 1972. Trojan. 1st. 1/2500. 456p. F/dj. H1. $125.00

**STOUT, Sandra McPhee.** *Depression Glass No 2.* 1971. Wallace Homestead. 1st. ils. cbdg. VG. H1. $24.00

**STOWE, Harriet Beecher.** *Our Charley.* 1858. Boston. Phillips Sampson. 1st. gilt bl cloth. F. M24. $200.00

**STOWE, Harriet Beecher.** *Uncle Tom's Cabin; or, Life Among the Lowly.* 1852. London. Cassell. 1st ils Eng (from 13 weekly parts). modern bdg. M24. $350.00

**STOWE, Harriet Beecher.** *Uncle Tom's Cabin; or, Life Among the Lowly.* 1891. Houghton Mifflin. New ed. inscr/sgn Stowe. 12mo. gilt gr cloth. B11. $2,250.00

**STOWERS, Carlton.** *Innocence Lost.* 1990. Pocket. 1st. ils. 291p. NF/dj. S14. $10.00

**STRAHORN, Carrie Adell.** *Fifteen Thousand Miles by Stage.* 1911. NY/London. Putnam. 1st. 8vo. 673p. VG/case. B11. $550.00

**STRAIGHT, Susan.** *Blacker Than a Thousand Midnights.* 1994. NY. Hyperion. 1st. F/dj. w/pub card. R14. $40.00

**STRALEY, John.** *Music of What Happens.* 1996. Bantam. 1st. sgn. F/dj. R14. $45.00

**STRALEY, John.** *Woman Who Married a Bear.* 1992. NY. Soho. 1st. F/dj. A24. $40.00

**STRAND, Mark.** *Mr & Mrs Baby & Other Stories.* 1985. NY. Knopf. 1st. rem mk. F/dj. G10. $22.50

**STRAND, Paul.** *Time in New England.* 1980. Aperture. photos Strand. edit Nancy Newhall. VG/dj. M17. $50.00

**STRASBERG, Susan.** *Marilyn & Me: Sisters, Rivals, Friends.* 1992. Warner. 1st. F/NF. P3. $22.00

**STRATER, Henry.** *Henry Strater: American Artist.* 1962. Ogunquit, ME. 1/3000. ils. VG. M17. $30.00

**STRATMAN.** *Bibliography of Medieval Drama.* 1972. 2 vol. 2nd/revised. 91000 entries. F/VG. A4. $125.00

**STRATON & TREMAINE.** *Bibliography of Canadiana, Relating to Early History...* 1959. Toronto. 2 vol. ils. VG. A4. $350.00

**STRATTON, Charlotte Kimball.** *Rug Hooking Made Easy.* 1955. NY. ils. VG/dj. M17. $17.50

**STRATTON, Clarence.** *Swords & Statues.* 1937. Winston. 1st. ils Robert Lawson. VG/G. P2. $25.00

**STRATTON, F.J.M.** *Astronomical Physics.* 1924. Dutton. 8vo. 213p. cloth. VG. K5. $40.00

**STRATTON, George Malcolm.** *Psychology of Religious Life.* 1911. London. Geo Allen. 376p+ads. ruled red cloth. G1. $30.00

**STRATTON, Joanna L.** *Pioneer Women: Voices From the Kansas Frontier.* 1981. S&S. 1st. photos. 319p. VG/clip. A25. $20.00

**STRATTON, Owen Tully.** *Medicine Man.* 1989. OK U. 1st. ils/glossary/index. 251p. AN. B19. $10.00

**STRAUB, Peter.** *Blue Rose.* 1985. Underwood Miller. 1/600. sgn. AN/box. T12. $60.00

**STRAUB, Peter.** *Floating Dragon.* 1982. Underwood Miller. 1st. 1/500. VG/dj. L1. $100.00

**STRAUB, Peter.** *Floating Dragon.* 1983. Putnam. 1st. NF/dj. N4/S18. $40.00

**STRAUB, Peter.** *General's Wife.* 1982. Donald Grant. 1st. sgn. VG/sans. L1. $85.00

**STRAUB, Peter.** *Ghost Story.* 1979. Coward. 1st. F/NF. H11. $45.00

**STRAUB, Peter.** *Ghost Story.* 1979. London. Cape. 1st (precedes 1st Am). VG+/dj. A14. $52.50

**STRAUB, Peter.** *Houses Without Doors.* 1990. Dutton. ARC. inscr/sgn. F/dj. A23. $40.00

**STRAUB, Peter.** *Houses Without Doors.* 1990. Dutton. 1st. F/dj. L4. $20.00

**STRAUB, Peter.** *Houses Without Doors.* 1990. NY. Dutton. 1st Am. rem mk. F/F. G10. $12.50

**STRAUB, Peter.** *If You Could See Me Now.* 1977. CMG. 1st Am. VG/dj. M25. $75.00

**STRAUB, Peter.** *If You Could See Me Now.* 1977. London. Cape. 1st. VG+/clip. A14. $70.00

**STRAUB, Peter.** *Julia.* 1976. London. Cape. 1st Eng. NF/clip. A14. $87.50

**STRAUB, Peter.** *Koko.* 1988. Dutton. 1st. F/F. H11. $30.00

**STRAUB, Peter.** *Mystery.* 1990. Dutton. 1st. F/dj. S18. $30.00

**STRAUB, Peter.** *Mystery.* 1990. Dutton. 1st. NF/F. H11. $20.00

**STRAUB, Peter.** *Shadow Land.* 1980. CMG. 1st. inscr/sgn. F/dj. A23. $46.00

**STRAUB, Peter.** *Shadow Land.* 1980. London. Collins. 1st Eng. VG+/dj. A14. $25.00

**STRAUB, Peter.** *Throat.* 1993. Dutton. 1st. F/dj. S18. $20.00

**STRAUSS, Ralph.** *Whip for the Woman: Being...Impartial Account...* 1932. Farrar Rinehart. 1st Am. 243p. cloth. F/NF. O10. $30.00

**STRAVINSKY, Igor.** *Rake's Progress.* 1953. NY. Boosey Hawkes. 1st Am. NF/self wrp. M24. $150.00

**STREET, Frederick.** *Azaleas.* 1959. London. 1st. 278p. VG. B26. $26.00

**STREET, J.** *Goodbye My Lady.* 1954. Phil. Lippincott. 1st. VG/G. B5. $30.00

**STREET, J.C.** *Hidden Way Across the Threshold; or, Mystery...* 1887. Boston. Lee Shepard. G. V4. $150.00

**STREETER, Brunett Hillman.** *Primitive Church Studied With Special Reference...* 1929. NY. Macmillan. 1st. index/map. 323p. VG. H10. $27.50

**STREETER, Thomas W.** *Bibliography of Texas 1795-1845.* 1996. Stoors-Mansfield, CT. Maurizio Martino. 5 vol. rpt. 1/150. cloth. AN. M8. $175.00

**STREHL, Dan.** *One Hundred Books on California Food & Wine.* 1990. LA. Book Collectors. 1/300. 45p. patterned wrp w/flaps. D11. $40.00

**STRICKLAND, W.P.** *Pioneer Bishop; or, Life & Times of Francis Asbury.* 1858. NY. Phillips Hunt. 496p. VG. B18. $50.00

**STRIEBER, Whitley.** *Black Magic.* 1982. NY. Morrow. 1st. sgn. F/dj. T2. $45.00

**STRIEBER, Whitley.** *Hunger.* 1981. Morrow. 1st. author's 2nd book. NF/dj. S18. $45.00

**STRIEBER, Whitley.** *Hunger.* 1981. NY. Morrow. 1st. sgn. F/dj. T2. $60.00

**STRIEBER, Whitley.** *Night Church.* 1983. S&S. 1st. xl. VG/dj. S18. $7.00

**STRIEBER, Whitley.** *Transformation.* 1988. Morrow. 1st. F/dj. S18. $25.00

**STRIEBER, Whitley.** *Unholy Fire.* 1992. NY. Dutton. 1st. sgn. F/dj. T2. $25.00

**STRIEBER, Whitley.** *Wolfen.* 1978. Morrow. 1st. author's 1st book. VG/G. M19. $17.50

**STRIEBER, Whitley.** *Wolfen.* 1978. Morrow. 1st. NF/dj. N4. $55.00

**STRIKER, Fran.** *Lone Ranger & the Mystery Ranch.* 1938. Grosset Dunlap. F/VG. M19. $35.00

**STRIKER, Fran.** *Lone Ranger & the Mystery Ranch.* 1938. Grosset Dunlap. 1st. VG. T12. $25.00

**STRINGER, Arthur.** *Phantom Wires.* 1907. Boston. Little Brn. 1st. bl brd/pict label. F. M15. $75.00

**STRINGER, Arthur.** *Shadow.* 1913. NY. Century. 1st. NF/fragment. M15. $75.00

**STRINGER, Arthur.** *Wire Tappers.* 1906. Little Brn. 1st. NF. M15. $75.00

**STRINGER, George Alfred.** *Leisure Moments in Gough Square...* 1886. Buffalo. Ulbrich Kingsley. 1st. 1/300. lg 8vo. inscr. cloth. H13. $125.00

**STRINGFELLOW & TOWNE.** *Death & Life of Bishop Pike.* 1976. Doubleday. 1st. 443p. VG/dj. S14. $9.00

**STRODE, Hudson.** *Now in Mexico.* 1946. NY. Harcourt. 1st. photos. 368p. dj. F3. $20.00

**STROHM, John.** *Ford Farm-Ranch-Home Almanac.* 1955-59. S&S. A10. $50.00

**STRONG, Charles Agustus.** *Essays on the Natural Origin of the Mind.* 1930. London. Macmillan. 304p. blk cloth. dj. G1. $65.00

**STRONG, Charles Agustus.** *Why the Mind Has a Body.* 1903. Macmillan. 355p. blk cloth. VG. G1. $65.00

**STRONG, Ezra.** *Lives & Exploits of the Most Noted Highwaymen.* 1843. Hartford, CT. leather. G. A19. $250.00

**STRONG, John.** *Concepts of Classical Optics.* 1958. SF. WH Freeman. lg 8vo. 692p. cloth. VG. K5. $40.00

**STRONG, Phil.** *Horses & Americans.* 1939. Stokes. ltd. sgn. A21. $75.00

**STROTHER, David Hunter.** *Virginia Yankee in the Civil War: Diaries of...* (1961). UNC. ils. 294p. VG/VG. B10. $50.00

**STROUD, Carsten.** *Lizard Skin.* 1992. Random. 1st. F/F. H11. $25.00

**STROUD, Patricia Tyson.** *Thomas Say: New World Naturalist.* 1992. U PA. 340p. F/dj. S15. $12.50

**STROUSE, Jean.** *Women & Analysis: Dialogues on Psychoanalytic Views...* 1974. Grossman. 1st. 8vo. 375p. NF/VG. C14. $16.00

**STROUSE, Norman H.** *Cobden-Sanderson the Master Craftsman.* 1969. Harper Woods. Adagio. 1/12 (331 total). w/booklet, prospectus & photo. F. B24. $2,750.00

**STROUSE, Norman H.** *How to Build a Poor Man's Morgan Library.* 1959. Detroit BC. 1st. 1/250. sgn. quarter cloth/paper label. F/dj. M24. $150.00

**STRUBBERG, Friedreich Armand.** *Backwoodsman; or, Life on the Indian Frontier.* ca 1864. London. later prt. 428p. half leather. B18. $125.00

**STRUGHOLD, Hubertus.** *Green & Red Planet...* 1954. London. Sidgwick Jackson. ils. 96p. G/dj. K5. $40.00

**STRUIK, Dirk.** *Yankee Science in the Making.* 1948. Little Brn. 430p. VG. A10. $20.00

**STRUM, Shirley C.** *Almost Human: Journey Into World of Baboons.* 1987. NY. photos. 294p. F/VG. S15. $15.00

**STRUNG, Norman.** *Misty Mornings & Moonless Nights: Waterfowler's Guide.* 1974. NY. 1st. reading list. 253p. F. A17. $15.00

**STRUPP, Hans H.** *Research in Psychotherapy.* 1962. WA. Am Psychological Assn. 1st. 8vo. 342p. F. C14. $18.00

**STRUVE, Otto.** *Stellar Evolution: An Exploration From the Observatory.* 1950. Princeton. 8vo. 266p. VG/dj. K5. $35.00

**STRYKER & WOOD.** *In This Proud Land: America 1935-1943...* 1973. NY. Galahad. photos. VG/dj. M17. $50.00

**STUART, Alexander.** *War Zone.* 1989. Doubleday. 1st. F/dj. A23. $32.00

**STUART, Anna Maude.** *Bread Plates & Platters.* (1965). self pub. 163p. sbdg. VG. H1. $65.00

**STUART, Dora Jessie.** *Miss Clare Remembers.* 1963. Houghton Mifflin. 1st Am. VG/dj. R8. $20.00

**STUART, Dora Jessie.** *Over the Gate.* 1965. Houghton Mifflin. 1st Am. VG/dj. R8. $25.00

**STUART, Ian.** *Satan Bug.* 1962. NY. Scribner. rpt. VG/dj. B11. $25.00

**STUART, Jesse.** *Come Back to the Farm.* 1971. McGraw Hill. 1st. VG/dj. B30. $40.00

**STUART, Jesse.** *Thread That Runs So True.* 1950. 293p. NF/VG. A4. $65.00

**STUART, Ruth McEnery.** *In Simpkinsville: Character Tales.* 1897. NY/London. Harper. 1st. inscr. 16mo. 244p. trade bdg. J3. $150.00

**STUART & STUART.** *Lost Kingdoms of the Mayas.* 1993. NGS. 1st. 248p. dj. F3. $35.00

**STUBBING, Richard A.** *Defense Game: Insider Explores...* 1986. Harper Row. 1st. 8vo. F/dj. A2. $15.00

**STUCK, G.** *Annie McCune: Shreveport Madame.* 1981. Baton Rouge. sgn. photos. 114p. F/dj. M4. $15.00

**STUMP, Al.** *Cobb.* 1994. Algonquin. 1st. F/VG+. P8. $25.00

**STUMPF, Carl.** *Tonpsychologie.* 1883. Leipzig. S Hirzel. 2 vol. orig prt buff wrp. G1. $425.00

**STURGIS, William Bayard.** *Fly-Tying.* 1940. Scribner. ils. G. A19. $30.00

**STUSSMAN, Morton.** *Follow Thru 60th Infantry Regiment.* 1945. Stuttgart, Germany. 1st. ils/maps. 127p. VG. S16. $30.00

**STUTZ, Bruce.** *Natural Lives, Modern Times.* 1992. Crown. 1st. ils. F/dj. R14. $35.00

**STYRON, William.** *As He Lay Dead, a Bitter Grief.* 1981. NY. Atheneum. 1st. 1/300. sgn. F/saddle-stiched wrp. B4. $175.00

**STYRON, William.** *Confessions of Nat Turner.* 1967. NY. Random. 1st. sgn. VG/dj. R14. $125.00

**STYRON, William.** *Confessions of Nat Turner.* 1967. Random. 1st. sgn. F/NF clip. D10. $125.00

**STYRON, William.** *Darkness Visible.* 1990. Random. UP. sgn. F/wrp. D10. $85.00

**STYRON, William.** *Darkness Visible.* 1991. Random. 1st lg prt. sgn. F/dj. R14. $45.00

**STYRON, William.** *Darkness Visible: A Memoir of Madness.* 1990. Random. 1st. F/dj. M23. $30.00

**STYRON, William.** *In the Clap Shack.* 1973. Random. 1st. sgn. F/clip. D10. $110.00

**STYRON, William.** *Inheritance of Night.* 1993. Durham. Duke. 1/250 (1776 total). F/sans. R14. $200.00

**STYRON, William.** *Lie Down in Darkness.* 1951. Bobbs Merrill. 1st. sgn. VG+/dj. D10. $240.00

**STYRON, William.** *Set This House on Fire.* 1960. Random. 1st. sgn. F/NF. D10. $110.00

**STYRON, William.** *Sophie's Choice.* 1979. Random. 1st trade. thick 8vo. bl cloth. F/wrp. R3. $50.00

**STYRON, William.** *Sophie's Choice.* 1979. Random. UP. author's 5th novel. inscr. F. L3. $375.00

**STYRON, William.** *This Quiet Dust & Other Writings.* 1982. Random. 1st. sgn. NF/dj. R14. $85.00

**STYRON, William.** *Tidewater Morning.* 1993. Random. 1st. sgn. F/dj. D10. $50.00

**SUAREZ, Benjamin D.** *7 Steps to Freedom II: How to Escape American Rat Race.* 1994. Hanford. 2nd. sm 4to. 669p. F/dj. W2. $40.00

**SUDELL, Richard.** *Landscape Gardening.* 1948 (1933). London. 480p. B26. $25.00

**SUDHALTER, R.** *Bix. Man & Legend.* 1974. New Rochelle. 1st. VG/dj. B5. $65.00

**SUDHOFF, Kark.** *Essays in the History of Medicine.* 1926. NY. Medical Life. 387p. VG. G7. $125.00

**SUGGS, G.G.** *Water Mills of the Missouri Ozarks.* 1990. OK U. 1st. ils JK Wells. 204p. F/dj. M4. $25.00

**SULLIVAN, Albert J.** *Personality in Peptic Ulcer.* 1950. Chas Thomas. 1st. 8vo. 100p. fabricoid. F/G. C14. $20.00

**SULLIVAN, C.W. III.** *Dark Fantastic.* 1997. Greenwood. F. P3. $65.00

**SULLIVAN, Edmund J.** *Lavengro the Scholar, the Gypsy, the Priest.* 1926. London. Peter Davies. 1st thus. 655p. VG/dj. C6. $30.00

**SULLIVAN, J.W.N.** *Beethoven: His Spiritual Development.* 1972. Bonzoi. 262p. VG/dj. P12. $7.00

**SULLIVAN, M.W.** *Programmed Method for Learning to Play Chess.* 1973. NY. Times. 1st. VG+/stiff wrp. S13. $25.00

**SULLIVAN, Walter.** *What Have They Done to My Game?* 1988. Vantage. 1st. F/VG+. P8. $35.00

**SULLIVAN, William H.** *Mission to Iran: By Last US Ambassador.* 1981. NY. Norton. 1st. 8vo. ils/map. 296p. NF/dj. W1. $18.00

**SULLIVAN, William.** *Secret of the Incas.* 1996. NY. Crown. 1st. 8vo. 413p. half cloth. F/dj. P4. $35.00

**SULLIVAN, Winona.** *Sudden Death at the Norfolk Cafe.* 1993. St Martin. 1st. AN/dj. N4. $25.00

**SULLY, James.** *Human Mind: A Text-Book of Psychology.* 1892. Longman Gr. 2 vol. panelled brn cloth. G1. $150.00

**SULLY, Langdon.** *No Tears for the General.* 1974. Palo Alto, CA. 1st. ils/index. 255p. E1. $35.00

**SUMMERHAYES, Martha.** *Vanished Arizona: Recollections of My Army Life.* 1981. Time Life. rpt. ils. 270p. aeg. emb leather. E1. $35.00

**SUMMERHAYS, Reginald.** *Arabian Horse: Breed in Britain.* 1972. S Brunswick. Barnes. 2nd. VG/dj. O3. $20.00

**SUMMERS, Anthony.** *Goddess: Secret Lives of Marilyn Monroe.* 1985. Gollancz. 1st. F/dj. P3. $30.00

**SUMMERS, Anthony.** *Goddess: Secret Lives of Marilyn Monroe.* 1985. London. Gollancz. 1st. NF/dj. A14. $25.00

**SUMMERS, Montague.** *Supernatural Omnibus.* Nov 1974. Causeway. 1st thus. VG/dj. L1. $65.00

**SUMMERS, Montague.** *Vampire: His Kith & Kin.* 1960. U Books. 1st. VG/G. L1. $75.00

**SUMMERS, Richard.** *Ball Shy Pitcher.* 1970. Steck Vaughn. 1st. F/dj. P8. $30.00

**SUMNER, Cid Ricketts.** *Traveler in the Wilderness.* 1957. Harper. 8vo. map ep. 248p. VG/dj. F7. $40.00

**SUMPTON, Lois.** *Cookies & More Cookies.* 1948. IL. Bennet. G/dj. A16. $10.00

**SUNDERLAND, LaRoy.** *Book of Human Nature: Ils the Philosophy of Instinct...* 1853.. NY. Garnett. later prt. 12mo. 432p. panelled Victorian cloth. G1. $85.00

**SUNNUCKS, Anne.** *Encyclopedia of Chess.* 1970. St Martin. 1st. ils. NF/VG. O4. $30.00

**SUPPLE, Elizabeth.** *Sampler Story Book.* 1934. Saalfield. 1st. lg 4to. ils Corinne Ringel Bailey. pict brd/dj. R5. $100.00

**SUR, A.K.** *Sex & Marriage in India: Ethohistorical Survey.* 1973. India. Allied Pub. 1st. 194p. VG/clip. N2. $10.00

**SURFACE, Bill.** *Roundup at the Double Diamond: American Cowboy Today.* 1974. Houghton Mifflin. 237p. VG. J2. $70.00

**SURMELIAN, Leon Z.** *I Ask You, Ladies & Gentlemen.* 1945. NY. Dutton. 3rd. 8vo. 316p. VG. W1. $18.00

**SURREY & WARREN.** *Federal Income Taxation, Cases & Materials...* 1950. Brooklyn. M11. $25.00

**SUSKIND, Patrick.** *Das Parfum.* 1985. Zurich. Diogenes Verlag AG. true 1st. F/dj. D10. $185.00

**SUSKIND, Patrick.** *Perfume.* 1986. Knopf. 1st. author's 1st novel. F/dj. A24/M21. $40.00

**SUSSMAN, George.** *Selling Mothers' Milk: Wet-Nursing Business in France 1715.* 1982. Urbana, IL. 1st. 210p. A13. $30.00

**SUSSMAN, Maurice.** *Developmental Biology: Its Cellular & Molecular Foundations.* 1973. Prentice Hall. 397p. xl. VG. S5. $12.00

**SUTCLIFF, Rosemary.** *Flame-Colored Taffeta.* 1986. NY. FSG. 1st Am. 130p. F/dj. D4. $35.00

**SUTCLIFF, Rosemary.** *Little Dog Like You.* 1990. S&S. 1st Am. 16mo. 46p. bl cloth/pict label. NF. T5. $25.00

**SUTCLIFF, Rosemary.** *Tristan & Iseult.* 1971. Dutton. 1st. VG/dj. M17. $25.00

**SUTCLIFFE, Joseph.** *Sermons of the Late Rev James Saurin.* 1822. Wheeling. Davis McCarty. full leather. B18. $75.00

**SUTHERLAND, L.W.** *Aces & Kings.* nd (1936). London. John Hamilton. 1st. 276p. VG/facs dj. M7. $185.00

**SUTHREN, Victor.** *Black Cockade.* 1977. Toronto. Collins. 1st ed. F/NF. T11. $65.00

**SUTHREN, Victor.** *Black Cockade.* 1977. Toronto. Collins. 1st. sgn. author's 1st book. VG+/VG. A14. $42.00

**SUTHREN, Victor.** *Golden Galleon.* 1989. NY. 1st. VG/dj. M17. $17.50

**SUTHREN, Victor.** *In Perilous Seas.* 1983. St Martin. 1st Am. Paul Gallant #3. F/NF. T11. $50.00

**SUTHREN, Victor.** *King's Ransom.* 1980. Toronto. Collins. 1st. sgn. VG+/dj. A14. $35.00

**SUTHREN, Victor.** *Royal Yankee.* 1987. Hodder Stoughton. 1st. sgn. NF/dj. A14. $32.00

**SUTHREN, Victor.** *Royal Yankee.* 1987. NY. 1st. VG/dj. M17. $20.00

**SUTHREN, Victor.** *Royal Yankee.* 1987. St Martin. 1st. F/dj. T11. $30.00

**SUTIN, Lawrence.** *In Pursuit of Valis: Selections From the Exegesis.* 1991. Underwood Miller. 1st. 1/250. sgn. F/dj/case. P3. $40.00

**SUTTON, Felix.** *Herman Melville's Moby Dick.* 1976 (1956). Grosset Dunlap. ils HB Vestal. 71p. F. C14. $17.00

**SUTTON, George Miksch.** *At the Bend in a Mexican River.* 1972. NY. Paul Eriksson. 1st. 184p. dj. F3. $45.00

**SUTTON, George Miksch.** *Eskimo Year: Naturalist's Adventures in the Far North.* 1934. Macmillan. 1st. sgn pres. 321p. VG/fair. H1. $42.50

**SUTTON, George P.** *Rocket Propulsion Elements: An Introduction...* 1963. John Wiley. 3rd. 464p. F/dj. H1. $20.00

**SUTTON, O.G.** *Challenge of the Atmosphere: Science of Meteorology.* 1962. London. Hutchinson. 8vo. 227p. xl. K5. $12.00

**SUTTON, Silvia B.** *Crossroads in Psychiatry: A History of McLean Hospital.* 1986. WA. Am Psychiatric. 1st. 8vo. 372p. F/F. C14. $25.00

**SUTTON & SUTTON.** *Appalachian Trail.* 1967. Lippincott. 5th. photos/biblio/index. F/dj. A17. $15.00

**SUYKER, Betty.** *Death Scene.* 1981. St Martin. 1st. author's 1st novel. F/dj. N4. $15.00

**SVENNAS, Elsie.** *Advanced Quilting.* 1980. Scribner. 1st. ils. 144p. F/VG. S14. $10.00

**SVENSRUD, A.** *Readings in Forest Economics: On Selected Topics...* 1969. Oslo. Universiteforlaget. 8vo. F/VG. A2. $40.00

**SWAIM, Douglas.** *Cabins & Castles: History & Architecture of Buncombe...* 1981. NC Dep Cultural Resource. 2nd. photos. 225p. VG. B10. $25.00

**SWAIN, T.** *Comparative Phytochemistry.* 1966. Academic. 360p. xl. VG. S5. $15.00

**SWALLOW, Alan.** *Nameless Sight: Poems 1937-1956.* 1963. Swallow. 1st. 74p. VG+. A18. $15.00

**SWAN, Joseph.** *Delinations of the Brain in Relation to Voluntary Motion.* 1864. London. Bradbury Evans. 18 pl. 65p. later quarter cloth/marbled brd. G7. $595.00

**SWAN, Michael.** *Marches of El Dorado.* 1958. Venezuela. 1st. 304p. dj. F3. $20.00

**SWAN, Walter.** *Adventure Stories: Collection Original Children's Stories.* 1991. Swan Ent. ils. 252p. F/F. B10. $10.00

**SWANBERG, W.A.** *Luce & His Empire.* 1972. NY. Scribner. 1st. 529p. F/dj. O10. $12.50

**SWANN, H.K.** *Synopsis of the Accipitres (Diurnal Birds of Prey).* 1922 (1920). London. revised/2nd. ils. 233p. red ribbed cloth. VG. C12. $135.00

**SWANN, Peter C.** *Chinese Painting.* (1958). Universe Books. photos/pl. VG/G. M17. $25.00

**SWANN, Thomas Burnett.** *Alas, in Lilliput, by Thomas Burnett Swann.* 1964. Worcester. St Onge. mini. 1/500. aeg. gilt bl leather. B24. $150.00

**SWANSON, C.E.** *Predators & Prizes: American Privateering...* 1991. SC U. 1st. ils. 299p. F/dj. M4. $20.00

**SWANSON, Gloria.** *Swanson on Swanson.* 1980. Random. 535p. VG/dj. C5. $12.50

**SWANSON, Logan;** see Matheson, Richard.

**SWANSON, Nellie R.** *Pioneer Women Teachers of North Dakota.* 1965. Minot, ND. sc. G. A19. $25.00

**SWANTON, J.R.** *Social Conditions, Beliefs & Linguistic Relationships...* 1908. BAE 26th Report. removed. pls. NF/later wrp. M4. $20.00

**SWANWICK, Michael.** *Gravity's Angels.* 1991. Saulk City. 1st. 13 stories. F/dj. T2. $25.00

**SWANWICK, Michael.** *Griffin's Egg.* 1990. London. Century/Legend. 1st. F/dj. T2. $20.00

**SWARTH, H.S.** *Avifauna of the Galapagos Islands.* 1931. SF. 299p. rear pocket map. F/wrp. C12. $55.00

**SWARTHOUT, Glendon.** *They Came to Cordura.* 1958. NY. Random. 1st. F/dj. Q1. $60.00

**SWARTZ, David.** *Magnificent Obsession: Seeing First the Kingdom of God.* 1990. Navpress. 235p. G/wrp. B29. $4.50

**SWEDENBORG, Emmanuel.** *Soul or Rational Psychology.* 1887 (1849). NY. New Church Brd of Pub. 1st Eng-language. 388p. VG. G1. $65.00

**SWEENEY, Ed.** *Poorhouse Sweeney: Life in Country Poorhouse.* 1927. NY. Boni. 1st. ils. intro Dreiser. VG+. B2. $65.00

**SWEENEY, Lenora Higginbotham.** *Amherst County, Virginia, in the Revolution...1773-82.* (1951). Bell. 212p. VG. B10. $85.00

**SWEET, Melissa.** *Garden Companion.* 1984. Boston. Bromer. mini. 1/30. ils/hand-lettered Sweet. aeg. Werner bdg/box. B24. $750.00

**SWEET, William Warren.** *Religion in Development of American Culture 1765-1840.* 1952. Scribner. 1st. 338p. VG. H10. $25.00

**SWEETSER, M.F.** *Guide to the White Mountains.* 1918. Houghton Mifflin. 1st thus. 7 fld panoramas. 387p. cloth. VG. H7. $75.00

**SWEETSER, Wesley D.** *Arthur Machen.* 1964. Twayne. VG. P3. $20.00

**SWETE, Henry B.** *Introduction to the Old Testament in Greek.* 1968. KTAV. 626p. VG. B29. $29.00

**SWETTENHAM, John.** *Canada's Atlantic War.* 1979. Canada. Samuel Stevens. 1st. F/dj. T12. $40.00

**SWIFT, Charles F.** *Cape Cod: Right Arm of Massachusetts: Historical Narrative.* 1897. Yarmouth. Register Pub. 1st. worn/lacks backstrip. V3. $40.00

**SWIFT, Graham.** *Ever After.* 1992. Knopf. 1st Am. sgn. F/dj. M25. $35.00

**SWIFT, Graham.** *Ever After.* 1992. London. Picador. 1st. F/dj. M23. $30.00

**SWIFT, Graham.** *Learning to Swim.* 1985. London. Picador. 1st hc. F/dj. A24. $40.00

**SWIFT, Graham.** *Out of This World.* 1988. Poseidon. 1st Am. rem mk. NF/dj. R14. $25.00

**SWIFT, Graham.** *Waterland.* 1984. Poseidon. 1st. sgn. rem mk. F/dj. D10. $55.00

**SWIFT, Jonathan.** *Gulliver's Travels Into Several Remote Regions of World.* nd (1880s). London. ils T Morten. G. M17. $25.00

**SWIFT, Lloyd H.** *Botanical Classifications: A Comparison of 8 Systems...* 1974. Hamden, CT. ils. 374p. F/dj. B26. $50.00

**SWIGGETT, Howard.** *Rebel Raider: Life of John Hunt Morgan.* 1937 (1934). Garden City. map. 341p. fair. B10. $25.00

**SWINBURNE, Algernon Charles.** *Midsummer Holiday & Other Poems.* 1884. London. Chatto Windus. 8vo. 189p. gilt brd edges/turn-ins. teg. F. H5. $1,750.00

**SWINBURNE, Algernon Charles.** *Poems of...* 1904. Harper. 1/149. 6 vol. paper brd/cloth spine. VG. S17. $70.00

**SWINDEN, P.** *Images of India.* 1980. NY. 1st. dj. T9. $8.00

**SWINDOLL, Charles R.** *Growing Strong in the Seasons of Life.* 1983. Multnomah. 414p. VG/dj. B29. $7.00

**SWINDOLL, Charles R.** *Quest of Character.* 1987. Multnomah. 216p. F/dj. B29. $7.50

**SWINNERTON, Jimmy.** *Hosteen Crotchetty; or, How a Good Heart Was Born.* 1965. Best-West Pub. 4to. ils. 40p. tan cloth. F/NF. F7. $175.00

**SWINTON, W.** *Campaigns of the Army of the Potomac.* 1871 (1865). xl. VG. E6. $40.00

**SWISHER, Carl Brent.** *Motivation & Political Technique in CA Constitutional...* 1930. Claremont. Pomona. 132p. prt wrp. D11. $35.00

**SWISHER, Carl Brent.** *Stephen J Field: Craftsman of the Law.* 1930. WA. Brookings Inst. 473p. cloth. dj. D11. $75.00

**SWISHER, Doug.** *Selective Trout.* 1972. Crown. F. A19. $35.00

**SWITKIN, Abraham.** *Hand Lettering Today.* 1976. Harper Row. 1st. 212p. cloth. F/dj. O10. $35.00

**SYDNOR, Charles.** *Gentlemen Freeholders: Policy Practices...* (1952). UNC. 180p. VG/fair. B10. $15.00

**SYKES, Arthur.** *Mysterious Britain.* 1993. London. Weidenfeld Nicolson. 1st. ils/map. F/dj. T10. $25.00

**SYKES, Godfrey.** *Westerly Trend: Being Veracious Chronicle...* 1944. AZ Pioneers Hist Soc. 8vo. 325p. brn cloth. NF/VG. F7. $40.00

**SYKES, John.** *Mountain Arabs: Window in the Middle East.* 1968. Chicago. 1st. 8vo. 229p. NF/dj. W1. $16.00

**SYLVERSTER, Edward J.** *Healing Blade: A Tale of Neurosurgery.* 1993. S&S. 1st. tall 8vo. 240p. F/NF. C14. $20.00

**SYLVESTER, Charles H.** *Journeys Through Bookland: New & Original Plan for Reading.* 1911. Chicago. 11 vol. red cloth. VG. B30. $75.00

**SYLVESTER, Natalie G.** *Home-Baking Cookbook.* 1973. Grosset Dunlap. 1st. G/dj. A16. $25.00

**SYMONDS, Craig L.** *Battlefield Atlas of the American Revolution.* 1986. 41 maps. F. M4. $25.00

**SYMONDS, Craig L.** *Joseph E Johnston: Civil War Biography.* 1992. NY. Norton. 1st. F/dj. A14. $25.00

**SYMONDS, Craig L.** *Naval Institute Historical Atlas of US Navy.* 1995. Annapolis, MD. stated 1st. ils. VG/dj. M17. $25.00

**SYMONDS, John.** *Hurt Runner.* 1968. London. Baker. 1st. NF/dj. A14. $21.00

**SYMONDS, John.** *With a View of the Palace.* 1966. London. 1st. inscr. dj. T9. $28.00

**SYMONS, Julian.** *Charles Dickens.* 1951. Arthur Baker. 1st. VG/G. P3. $20.00

**SYMONS, Julian.** *Conan Doyle: Portrait of an Artist.* 1979. Mysterious. 1st Am. F/dj. G8. $30.00

**SYMONS, Julian.** *Crime & Detection Quiz.* 1983. Weidenfeld Nicolson. 1st. F/sans. M15. $45.00

**SYMONS, Julian.** *Critical Occassions.* 1966. London. 1st. dj. T9. $18.00

**SYMONS, Julian.** *Great Detectives: Seven Original Investigations.* 1981. Abrams. 1st. ils Tom Adams. F/dj. O4. $30.00

**SYMONS, Julian.** *Horatio Bottomley.* 1955. Cresset. 1st. VG. P3. $15.00

**SYMONS, Julian.** *Man Who Killed Himself.* 1967. Harper Row. 1st Am. VG/dj. G8. $15.00

**SYMONS, Julian.** *Man Who Killed Himself.* 1967. Harper Row. 1st. F/dj. M23. $35.00

**SYMONS, R.D.** *Where the Wagon Led: One Man's Memories of Cowboy's Life...* 1973. Toronto. Doubleday. 1st. NF/dj. A26. $15.00

**SYNDER, Charles.** *Massachusetts Eye & Ear Infirmary: Studies on Its History.* 1984. Boston. 1st. 8vo. bl cloth. F. C14. $22.00

**SYSIN, Alexander.** *Training Horses Over Fences.* 1939. Hollywood. private prt. 1st. 1/500. G. O3. $25.00

**SZASZ, Thomas S.** *Law, Liberty & Psychiatry: An Inquiry...* 1963. Macmillan. M11. $35.00

**SZATHMARY, Louis.** *Chef's Secret Cook Book.* 1971. Chicago. Quadrangle. VG/dj. A16. $10.00

**SZILAGYI, Steve.** *Photographing Fairies.* 1992. NY. 1st. VG/dj. M17. $20.00

**SZYK, Arthur.** *New Order.* 1941. NY. Putnam. sm 4to. gray cloth. VG. B14. $125.00

T'SERSTEVENS, A. *Mexico: Three-Storyed Land.* 1959. London. Hutchinson. 1st. photos. 368p. F3. $15.00

TABER, Gladys. *Especially Spaniels.* nd. Phil. photos. VG. M17. $15.00

TAFT, Robert. *Artists & Ils of the Old West, 1850-1900.* 1953. Scribner. 1st. ils. 400p. VG. B19. $45.00

TAFUR, Pero. *Pero Tafur: Travels & Adventures, 1435-1439.* 1926. London. Routledge. 8vo. ils. 261+4p ads. cloth. VG/dj. Q2. $58.00

TAFURI, Nancy. *Who's Counting?* 1986. NY. Greenwillow. 1st. 24p. F/dj. D4. $30.00

TAGGARD, Genevieve. *Circumference: Varieties of Metaphysical Verse 1456-1928.* 1929. Covici Friede. 1st. 1/1050. sgn/#d. F/dj. A18. $50.00

TAGGARD, Genevieve. *Travelling Standing Still.* 1928. Knopf. 1st. F. A18. $20.00

TAGGARD, Genevieve. *Words for the Chisel.* 1926. Knopf. 1st. NF. A18. $20.00

TAGGART, John Q. *Horse: Its Diseases & Treatment.* 1869. Lancaster, PA. 1st. 75p+13p ads. G. O3. $85.00

TAIBO II, Paco Ignacio. *Leonardo's Bicycle.* 1995. NY. Mysterious/Warner. 1st Am. F/dj. G10. $14.00

TAINE, H.A. *History of English Literature.* 1873. Edmonston/Edinburgh. 4 vol. G. S17. $10.00

TAINE, Hippolyte Adolph. *De l'Intelligence.* 1870. Paris. Hachette. 2 vol. contemporary cloth. G1. $225.00

TALBERT, C.G. *Benjamin Logan, Kentucky Frontiersman.* 1962. KY U. F. M4. $35.00

TALBOT, Daniel. *Film: An Anthology.* 1959. S&S. 649p. VG/dj. C5. $15.00

TALBOT, Godfrey. *Queen Elizabeth: Queen Mother 1900-1980.* 1973. London. Jarrolds. 1st. F/dj. T12. $30.00

TALBOT, S.J. *Francis: Saint Among Savages: Life of Isaac Jogues.* 1935. NY. Harper. 1st. NF/VG. T11. $35.00

TALBOT-PONSONBY, J.A. *Art of Show Jumping.* 1960. NY. Barnes. 1st Am. 4to. ils. VG/G. O3. $15.00

TALESE, Gay. *Unto the Sons.* 1992. Knopf. 1st sm 4to. 635p. F/dj. W2. $45.00

TALIAFERRO. *Cartographic Sources in the Rosenberg Library.* 1988. TX A&M. ils 247p. F/F. A4. $45.00

TALLACK, William. *Peter Bedford, the Spilalfields Philanthropist.* 1865. London. SW Partridge. 1st. 12mo. 147p. xl. V3. $12.00

TALLEUR, Richard W. *Fly Tyer's Primer.* 1986. NY. Lyons Burford. AN. A19. $25.00

TALOUMIS, George. *Winterize Your Yard & Garden.* 1976. Lippincott. BC. 288p. VG/dj. A10. $12.00

TAMAR, Henry. *Principles of Sensory Physiology.* 1972. Thomas. 396p. xl. VG. S5. $20.00

TAMAVO, Francisco. *Arboles en Flor de Venezuela.* 1959. Venezuela. ils. 67p. photo brd. VG. B26. $50.00

TAN, Amy. *Kitchen God's Wife.* 1991. NY. Putnam. 1st. F/NF. M23. $25.00

TAN, Amy. *Kitchen God's Wife.* 1991. Putnam. 1st. inscr/sgn. F/F. T11. $55.00

TAN, Amy. *Kitchen God's Wife.* 1991. Putnam. 1st. sgn. dj ils/sgn Gretchen Shields. F/dj. O11. $65.00

TAN, Amy. *Kitchen God's Wife.* 1991. Putnam. 1st. sgn. F/dj. D10. $45.00

TAN, Amy. *Kitchen God's Wife.* 1991. Putnam. 1st. sm 4to. 415p. F/dj. W2. $40.00

TAN, Amy. *Moon Lady.* 1992. Macmillan. 1st. sgn. F/wrp. A24. $30.00

TANAY, Emanuel. *Murders.* 1976. Indianapolis. 1st. F/F. H11. $20.00

TANITCH, Robert. *Brando.* 1994. NY. Studio Vista. 192p. VG/dj. C5. $15.00

TANITCH, Robert. *Guiness.* 1989. Applause. photos. VG/dj. M17. $20.00

TANNEN, Mary. *Easy Keeper.* 1992. FSG. 1st. F/dj. R14. $25.00

TANNENBAUM, Frank. *Slave & Citizen: Negro in Americas.* 1963. NY. Vintage. 1st. 128p. VG/stiff wrp. W1. $5.00

TANNENBAUM, Samuel A. *Handwriting of the Renaissance Being Development...* 1967. NY. Ungar. rpt. 210p. cloth. dj. O10. $45.00

TANNER, Clara Lee. *Indian Baskets of the Southwest.* 1989. Tucson. ils. VG/dj. A19. $45.00

TANNER, Fred Wilbur. *Microbiology of Foods.* 1944. Garrard. 1196p. xl. G. S5. $20.00

TANNER, Lawrence E. *History of the Coronation.* 1952. London. 1st. F/G. T12. $45.00

TANNER, William. *Memoir of..., Compiled Chiefly From Autobiographical...* 1868. London. F Bowyer Kitto. 12mo. 257p. ES. xl. V3. $18.00

TANSILL, Charles Callan. *America Goes to War.* 1938. Little Brn. 1st. ils. 731p. NF. E1. $35.00

TAPLY, H.G. *Fly Tyer's Handbook.* 1949. Durrell. 1st. ils. NF/dj. A17. $30.00

TAPPLY, William. *Dead Winter.* 1989. Delacorte. 1st. F/dj. A23. $30.00

TAPPLY, William. *Follow the Sharks.* 1985. Scribner. 1st. sgn. F/dj. P8. $125.00

TARAVAL, Sigismundo. *Indian uprising in Lower California, 1734-1737.* 1931. Quivira Soc. 1/665. 9 pl. 319p. A4/D11. $250.00

TARBELL, Dean Arthur Wilson. *Story of Carnegie Tech...* 1937. Pittsburgh. Carnegie Inst. 1st. sgn bookplate. 270p. buckram. B18. $17.50

TARDE, Gabriel. *L'Opinion et la Foule.* 1901. Paris. Bailliere. 226p. prt gr wrp. G1. $65.00

TARG, William. *American Books & Their Prices.* 1941-1942. Chicago. Blk Archer. 2 vol. 1/500. 12mo. ils. bl cloth. K1. $85.00

TARKENTON, Fran. *Murder at the Super Bowl.* 1986. Morrow. 1st. F/NF. H11. $30.00

TARKINGTON, Booth. *Beautiful Lady.* 1905. McClure. 1st. red cloth. VG. S13. $18.00

TARKINGTON, Booth. *Claire Ambler.* 1928. Doubleday Doran. 1st. 1/500 on Japan vellum. F/glassine. H5. $200.00

TARKINGTON, Booth. *Gentleman From Indiana.* 1900. NY. Doubleday McClure. trade of author's 1st book. 384p. gr cloth. G. G11. $20.00

TARKINGTON, Booth. *Images of Josephine.* 1945. Doulbeday Doran. 1st. 375p. G. G11. $8.00

TARKINGTON, Booth. *Penrod & Sam.* 1916. Doubleday Page. 1st/1st state (spine lettered in blk). ils W Brehm. VG. M19. $125.00

TARKINGTON, Booth. *Rumbin Galleries.* 1937. Doubleday Doran. 1st. NF/VG. A24. $30.00

TARKINGTON, Booth. *Seventeen.* 1916. Harper. 1st. F. V4. $150.00

TARN, Nathaniel. *Pablo Neruda: Four Odes One Song.* 1990. Honolulu. Labrinth. 1/50 (100 total). sgn Bigus/Tarn. complete. AN/box. B24. $750.00

TARN, W.W. *Treasure of the Isle of Mist.* 1934. Putnam. ils Robert Lawson. 8vo. 184p. yel cloth. pict dj. R5. $100.00

TARR, Judith. *Lord of the Two Lands.* 1993. Tor. 1st. F/dj. M21. $15.00

**TARR, R.L.** *Thomas Carlyle, a Descriptive Bibliography.* 1989. U Pittsburgh. 543p. gilt bl cloth. F. F1. $55.00

**TARTT, Donna.** *Secret History.* 1992. Knopf. 1st. F/dj. A23. $50.00

**TARTT, Donna.** *Secret History.* 1992. Knopf. 1st. inscr. VG/G. B30. $65.00

**TASSIN, Myron.** *For Love! And Money.* 1986. Baton Rouge. Claitor. 1st. VG/dj. O3. $20.00

**TASSIN, Ray.** *Stanley Vestal: Champion of the Old West.* 1973. Arthur Clark. ils. 1st. 299p. NF/VG. B19. $25.00

**TASSIN, Ray.** *Stanley Vestal: Champion of the Old West.* 1973. Arthur Clark. 1st. photos. 299p. F/NF clip. T11. $35.00

**TATE, Allen.** *Poetry Reviews of Allen Tate, 1924-1944.* 1983. LSU. 1st. F/dj. L3. $35.00

**TATE, Donald.** *Bravo Burning.* 1986. Scribner. 1st. F/dj. R11. $30.00

**TATE, Thad W.** *Negro in 18th-Century Williamsburg.* 1994 (1965). Williamsburg. 7th. 143p. VG. B10. $15.00

**TATHAM, David.** *Robert Frost's White Mountains.* 1974. Worcester. St Onge. mini. 1/500. 36p+10¢ Frost commemorative stp. aeg. leather. B24. $85.00

**TATON, R.** *Reason & Chance in Scientific Discovery.* 1957. London. 171p. A13. $30.00

**TATTERSFIELD, D.** *Orbits, for Amateurs With a Microcomputer.* 1984. NY. John Wiley. 2 vol. lg 8vo. VG/dj. K5. $45.00

**TATUM, Arlo.** *Handbook for Conscientious Objectors.* 1968. Central Comm for Conscientious Objectors. 10th. VG/wrp. C9. $25.00

**TAUSSIG, F.W.** *Explorations in Economics: Notes & Essays...* 1967 (1936). Augustus Kelley. rpt. 539p. VG. S5. $15.00

**TAUSSIG, Frederick Joseph.** *Diseases of the Vulva.* 1923. Appleton. 1st. 223p. gilt bl cloth. VG. H7. $35.00

**TAX, Sol.** *Civilizations of Ancient America.* 1951. Chicago. 1st. 328p. wrp. F3. $35.00

**TAX, Sol.** *Evolution After Darwin.* 1960. Chicago. 3 vol. ils/photos. VG/dj. B26. $65.00

**TAYLER, R.J.** *Stars: Their Structure & Evolution.* 1970. London. Wykeman. ils. 207p. G. K5. $15.00

**TAYLOE, Roberta Love.** *Return to Powhatan; Growing Up in Old Virginia.* nd. self pub. ils/photos/charts. 200p. VG. B10. $45.00

**TAYLOR, Alan R.** *Prelude to Israel.* 1970. Beirut. Inst for Palestine Studies. Rpt Series #5. VG. M7. $50.00

**TAYLOR, Albert Pierce.** *Under Hawaiian Skies: A Narrative...* 1926. Honolulu. Advertiser Pub. 2nd. inscr. 607p. G. B18. $19.50

**TAYLOR, Alice.** *Focus on the Middle East.* 1971. London. Praeger. 1st. 8vo. ils. 224p. VG/dj. W1. $18.00

**TAYLOR, Andrew.** *Blood Relation.* 1990. London. Gollancz. 1st. sgn. F/dj. M15. $50.00

**TAYLOR, Andrew.** *Caroline Minuscule.* 1982. London. Gollancz. 1st. F/dj. M15. $175.00

**TAYLOR, Andrew.** *Freelance Death.* 1987. London. Gollancz. ARC/1st. RS. F/dj. M15. $65.00

**TAYLOR, Andrew.** *Sleeping Policeman.* 1992. London. Gollancz. 1st. sgn. F/dj. M15. $50.00

**TAYLOR, Anna.** *Drustan the Wanderer.* 1971. London. Longman. 1st. F/dj. T10. $50.00

**TAYLOR, Archer.** *Book Catalogues: Their Varieties & Uses.* 1987. NY/Winchester. Beil/St Paul's Bibliographies. 2nd. 284p. F/dj. O10. $45.00

**TAYLOR, Art.** *Occult & Scientific Correlations of Religion, Art & Science.* 1968. NY. 1st. 306p. A13. $40.00

**TAYLOR, Arthur.** *Mr Squem.* 1933 (1918). York, PA. Kings Arms. ils WJ Duncan. 8vo. 47p. VG. C5. $15.00

**TAYLOR, Barry.** *Shadow Tiger.* (1989). NY. Walker. 1st. F/dj. A23. $36.00

**TAYLOR, Bayard.** *Eldorado.* 1850. Putnam. 2 vol. rebound. G. A19. $250.00

**TAYLOR, Bayard.** *Travels in Greece & Russia With Excursion to Crete.* 1859. Putnam. 8vo. 426p. xl. W1. $40.00

**TAYLOR, C.B.** *Universal History of the US of America...* 1831. NY. ils. 494p. full leather. B18. $37.50

**TAYLOR, Charles E.** *Island of the Sea: Descriptive of Past & Present St Thomas.* 1896. St Thomas, DWL. Taylor's Book-Store by Author. 2nd. 8vo. aeg. O1. $120.00

**TAYLOR, Charles M.** *Why My Photographs Are Bad.* 1902. Phil. Jacobs. 1st. 173p. VG. H7. $35.00

**TAYLOR, Clyde.** *Vietnam & Black America: An Anthology...* 1973. Garden City. Amherst. 1st. xl. lib bdg. reading copy. R11. $25.00

**TAYLOR, Daniel.** *Myth of Certainty: Reflective Christian & Risk Commitment.* 1986. Jarrell. 154p. VG/dj. B29. $9.00

**TAYLOR, David.** *Nature's Creatures of the Dark.* 1993. Dial. 1st. 4to. 6 popups. VG. B17. $14.50

**TAYLOR, Eleanor Ross.** *New & Selected Poems.* 1983. Stuart Wright. 1/50. sgn/#d. F/sans. B30. $50.00

**TAYLOR, Eleanor Ross.** *Welcome Eumenides.* 1972. Braziller. ARC/1st. inscr. F/F. L3. $50.00

**TAYLOR, Erika.** *Sun Maiden.* 1991. Atheneum. 1st. author's 1st novel. 247p. NF/F. W2. $30.00

**TAYLOR, F.S.** *Conquest of Bacteria.* 1942. NY. 1st. 178p. A13. $25.00

**TAYLOR, Francis Henry.** *Taste of Angels: History of Art Collecting From Ramses...* 1948. Boston. 3rd. ils. VG/dj. M17. $20.00

**TAYLOR, Frank H.** *Philadelpha in the Civil War, 1861-1865.* 1913. Phil. ils. 360p. G. B18. $65.00

**TAYLOR, Fred.** *Saga of Sugar.* 1944. UT-ID Sugar Co. sgn. 234p. VG. A10. $18.00

**TAYLOR, G. Jeffrey.** *Volcanoes in Our Solar System.* 1983. Dodd Mead. ARC. 8vo. 95p. VG/dj. K5. $15.00

**TAYLOR, Henry Osborn.** *Mediaeval Mind: A History of Development of Thought...* 1971. Harvard. 2 vol. 4th/10th prt. cloth. NF/dj. D2. $40.00

**TAYLOR, Ida A.** *Revolutionary Types.* 1904. London. Duckworth. 1st. VG. M10. $15.00

**TAYLOR, Isaac Taylor.** *European Tour of Tarryat-Home Travellers.* 1997. Lilliput. mini. 1/150. pub/sgn Tim Sheppard. teg. gilt brn morocco. B24. $275.00

**TAYLOR, J.E.** *Underground.* 1884. London. ils. 256p. K5. $20.00

**TAYLOR, J.M.** *Witchcraft Delusion: Story of Witchcraft Persecutions...* 1995. NY. 1st. F/dj. M4. $15.00

**TAYLOR, Jeffrey.** *Pru-Bache Murder.* 1994. Harper Collins. 1st. F/dj. A23. $32.00

**TAYLOR, John Russell.** *Hitch: Life & Work of Alfred Hitchcock.* 1978. Pantheon. 1st. VG/dj. P3. $20.00

**TAYLOR, John.** *Pondoro: Last of the Ivory Hunters.* 1955. S&S. F. A19. $100.00

**TAYLOR, Joshua C.** *America as Art.* 1976. Smithsonian. ils. VG/dj. M17. $25.00

**TAYLOR, Joshua C.** *Futurism.* 1961. MOMA. ils. VG/dj. C9. $30.00

**TAYLOR, Joshua C.** *Futurism.* 1961. MOMA. 1st. photos. 154p. NF. T11. $15.00

**TAYLOR, Kathleen.** *Lands & Peoples of the USSR.* 1961. London. Blk. F/clip. B9. $25.00

**TAYLOR, Louis.** *Horse America Made: Story of American Saddle Horse.* 1961. NY. Harper. 1st trade. VG/G. O3. $25.00

**TAYLOR, Lucy.** *Close to the Bone.* 1993. Woodinville. Silver Salamander. 1st. 1/300. sgn. F/dj. T2. $50.00

**TAYLOR, Peter.** *Happy Families Are All Alike.* 1959. McDowell/Obolensky. 1st. VG/dj. B30. $125.00

**TAYLOR, Peter.** *In the Tennessee Country.* 1994. Knopf. 1st. 8vo. F/dj. S9. $40.00

**TAYLOR, Peter.** *Long Fourth & Other Stories.* 1948. Harcourt Brace. 1st. author's 1st book. F/dj. B30. $300.00

**TAYLOR, Peter.** *Miss Leonora When Last Seen.* 1963. NY. Obolensky. 1st. VG/dj. B30. $175.00

**TAYLOR, Peter.** *Old Forest & Other Stories.* 1985. Dial. 1st. VG/G clip. B30. $225.00

**TAYLOR, Peter.** *Oracle at Soneleigh Court.* 1993. Knopf. 1st. AN/dj. B30. $40.00

**TAYLOR, Peter.** *Stand in the Mountains.* (1985). NY. Frederic Beil. 1st. 1/1000. F/sans. Q1. $40.00

**TAYLOR, Peter.** *Summons to Memphis.* 1986. Knopf. 1st. F/dj. D10. $60.00

**TAYLOR, Peter.** *Widows of Thornton.* 1954. Harcourt Brace. 1st. VG/dj. B30. $225.00

**TAYLOR, Philip M.** *Steven Spielberg.* 1992. NY. Continuum. 176p. VG/dj. C5. $12.50

**TAYLOR, R.G.** *Men, Medicine & Water: Building of Los Angeles Aqueduct...* 1982. LA. 1/1000. photos/map. 202p. F. M4. $50.00

**TAYLOR, Robert L.** *Vessel of Wrath.* 1966. NAL. 1st. inscr. quarter blk cloth. F/clip. T11. $45.00

**TAYLOR, Robert L.** *WC Fields: His Follies & Fortunes.* 1949. Doubleday. 1st. NF/VG clip. T11. $45.00

**TAYLOR, Robert Lewis.** *Winston Churchill: Informal Study of Greatness.* 1952. Doubleday. BC. gilt bl cloth. VG/dj. M7. $5.00

**TAYLOR, Robert W.** *Clinical Atlas of Veneral & Skin Diseases...* 1889. Phil. Lea. 2 vol. ils/58 pl. 3-quarter morocco/cloth. G7. $595.00

**TAYLOR, Robert.** *Saranac: America's Magic Mountain.* 1986. Houghton Mifflin. 1st. 8vo. 308p. F/dj. C14. $20.00

**TAYLOR, Telford.** *March of Conquest: German Victories in Western Europe 1940.* 1959. London. Edward Hulton. 460p. VG/dj. S16. $25.00

**TAYLOR, Telford.** *Nuremburg & Vietnam: An American Tragedy.* 1970. Chicago. Quadrangle. 12mo. 224p. NF/VG. R11. $40.00

**TAYLOR, Theodore.** *Thackeray: Humorist & the Man of Letters.* 1864. NY. Appleton. 1st Am. purple-brn pebbled cloth. NF. M24. $275.00

**TAYLOR, Thomas.** *Memoirs of John Howard...* 1836. London. Hatchard. gr morocco. M11. $150.00

**TAYLOR, W.R.** *Marine Algae of the Northeastern Coast of North America.* 1962. Ann Arbor. 2nd revised. 509p. cloth. F. B1. $55.00

**TAYLOR, William.** *Our South American Cousins.* 1878. NY. Nelson Phillips. 1st. 12mo. 318p. cloth. F3. $30.00

**TAYLOR, William.** *With Custer on the Little Bighorn.* 1996. Viking. sq 8vo. ils. 220p. F/F. A4. $28.00

**TAYLOR, Zack.** *Successful Waterfowling.* 1989. Stackpole. 2nd. index/photos/ils. 275p. F/dj. A17. $17.50

**TAYLOR, Zada.** *Time for Cooking.* 1963. Houghton Mifflin. G/dj. A16. $7.00

**TAZEWELL, Charles.** *Littlest Angel.* 1946. Children's Pr. 1st. ils Katherine Evans. NF/dj. P2. $60.00

**TCHAIKOVSKY, P.I.** *Swan Lake.* 1970. Japan. Gakken. ils Shigeru Hatsuyama. F/VG+. D4. $35.00

**TEAL, Louise.** *Breaking Into the Current: Boatwomen of the Grand Canyon.* 1994. Tucson, AZ. ils. 178p. F/F. B19. $20.00

**TEALE, Edwin Way.** *Autumn Across America.* 1950. Dodd Mead. VG/dj. A19. $25.00

**TEALL, Edward N.** *Books & Folks: A Volume of Friendly & Informal Counsel...* 1921. NY. Putnam. 1st. 8vo. 209p. NF/dj. O10. $30.00

**TEASDALE, Sara.** *Stars To-Night.* 1981. Buffalo. Hillside. mini. 1/300. ils D Lathrop. 44p. gilt cream cloth. B24. $125.00

**TEBBEL, John.** *American Indian Wars.* 1960. Harper. VG/dj. A19. $25.00

**TEIWES, Helga.** *Kachina Dolls: Art of Hopi Carvers.* 1991. Tucson. 1st. mc pl/glossary/index. 159p. AN/dj. P4. $30.00

**TEL TODESCO, Charles.** *Havana Cigar: Cuba's Finest.* 1997. Abbeville. 1st Eng-language/2nd prt. AN/dj. A28. $40.00

**TELLER, W.M.** *Search for Captain Slocum.* 1956. NY. 1st. VG/dj. B5/M17. $17.50

**TELLINGTON, Wentworth.** *Endurance & Competetive Trail Riding Manual.* 1967. Badger, CA. Pacific Coast Equestrian Research Farm. 1st. O3. $65.00

**TEMKIN, Owsei.** *Double Face of Janus & Other Essays in History of Medicine.* 1977. Baltimore. 543p. dj. A13. $60.00

**TEMKIN, Owsei.** *Galenism: Rise & Decline of a Medical Philosophy.* 1973. Ithaca. 1st. 240p. A13. $75.00

**TEMPEST, Margaret.** *Curly Cobbler & the Cuckoo Clock.* (1950). London. Collins. 1st. 24mo. 32p. cloth. R5. $100.00

**TEMPEST, Margaret.** *Pinkie Mouse & the Elves.* (1944). London. Collins. 1st. 24mo. cloth/pict brd. R5. $85.00

**TEMPLE, Richard.** *Early Christian & Byzantine Art.* 1990. London. Temple Gallery. ils. 120p. VG. Q2. $20.00

**TEMPLE, William.** *Doctrine in the Church of England.* 1938. NY. Macmillan. 1st Am. 242p. G. H10. $15.00

**TEMPLEMAN, Eleanor Lee.** *Virginia Homes of the Lees.* 1975. self pub. 2nd. unp. VG. B10. $6.00

**TEMPLETON, Charles.** *Succeeding.* 1989. Stoddart. 1st. F/dj. P3. $25.00

**TENEICK, Virginia Elliott.** *History of Hollywood.* 1966. Hollywood, F. xl. G. A19. $50.00

**TENNYSON, Alfred Lord.** *Collection of Poems by...* 1972. Doubleday. BC. 8vo. NF/dj. W2. $300.00

**TENNYSON, Alfred Lord.** *In Memoriam, by Alfred Lord Tennyson.* ca 1905. Glasgow. Bryce. mini. thin India paper. ils. gilt red leather. rpr dj. B24. $250.00

**TENNYSON, Alfred Lord.** *Maud: A Monodrama.* 1893. Hammersmith. Kelmscott. 1st. 1/500. gilt limp vellum/gr silk ties. NF/box. M24. $800.00

**TENNYSON, Alfred Lord.** *Princess & Other Poems.* 1890. NY. Stokes. Vignette ed. 3-quarter tan leather/marbled brd. S17. $35.00

**TENNYSON, John R.** *Singleness of Purpose: Story of Ducks Unlimited.* 1977. Chicago. 127p. F/dj. A17. $25.00

**TEPPER, Marvin.** *Fundamentals of Radio Telemetry.* 1959. NY. Rider. 8vo. 116p. K5. $20.00

**TEPPER, Sheri S.** *Grass.* 1989. NY. Foundation. 1st. F/F. B3. $20.00

**TEPPER, Sheri S.** *Northshore.* 1987. NY. Tor. 1st. author's 1st book. Awakeners #1. F/dj. A24. $25.00

**TEPPER, Sheri S.** *Raising the Stones.* 1990. NY. Doubleday. 1st. F/dj. G10. $16.50

**TERBOUGH, John.** *Diversity & the Tropical Rain Forest.* 1992. Scientific American. photos. 242p. AN/dj. S15. $10.00

**TERENCE.** *Brothers, by Terence. With 27 Drawings by Albrecht Durer.* 1968. Kentfield, CA. Allen. 1/140. 4to. 68p. decor cloth. F/case. w/prospectus. B24. $400.00

**TERHUNE, A.P.** *Dog Names Chips.* 1931. Grosset Dunlap. VG. A21. $24.00

**TERHUNE, A.P.** *Heart of a Dog.* 1924. Garden City. ils Kirmse. VG. A21. $45.00

**TERHUNE, A.P.** *Real Tales of Real Dogs.* nd (c 1935). Akron. Saalfield. possible 1st. 4to. 92p. VG. C14. $25.00

**TERHUNE, A.P.** *Wolf.* 1925. Grosset Dunlap. VG. A21. $20.00

**TERHUNE, David.** *Harp Seal.* 1973. Toronto. photos. VG/G. M17. $17.50

**TERMAN, Douglas.** *First Strike.* 1979. NY. Scribner. 1st. NF/dj. R11. $30.00

**TERRELL, Carroll E.** *Stephen King: Man & Artist.* 1990. Northern Lights. 1/75. sgn. AN/sans. T12. $225.00

**TERRELL, Isaac Long.** *Old Houses in Rockingham County 1750 to 1850.* (1970). McClure. ils/floor plans. 116p. VG/G. B10. $45.00

**TERRELL, John Upton.** *Apache Chronicle: Story of a People.* 1972. 1st. photos. VG/dj. M17. $20.00

**TERRELL, John Upton.** *War for the Colorado River.* 1965. Arthur H Clark. 1st. 2 vol. brn cloth. PT Reilly bstp. VG/dj. F7. $100.00

**TERRELL & WILSON.** *Binary Stars: A Pictorial Atlas.* 1992. Malabar, FL. Krieger. ils. 383p. VG/wrp. K5. $42.00

**TERRES, John K.** *Audubon Society of North American Birds.* 1980. NY. Knopf. 1st. 4to. 1109p. VG/dj. M10. $22.50

**TERRES, John K.** *Discovery: Great Moments in Lives of Outstanding Naturalist.* 1961. Lippincott. 1st. ils Thomas Nason. cloth. VG. B27. $25.00

**TERRY, M.** *Ultimate Evil.* 1987. Doubleday. 1st. VG/dj. B5. $15.00

**TERRY, T. Philip.** *Terry's Guide to Mexico.* 1947. Hingham, MA. revised. 932p. F3. $20.00

**TERRY, Walter.** *Ballet in Action.* 1954. NY. Putnam. unp. G. C5. $12.50

**TERTZ, Abram.** *Fantastic Stories.* 1963. Pantheon. 1st Am. F/VG. M21. $20.00

**TERZAKIS, Angelos.** *Homage to the Tragic Muse.* 1978. Houghton Mifflin. 1st Am. F/dj. A2. $16.00

**TESSIER, Thomas.** *Nightwalker.* 1980. Atheneum. 1st Am. VG/dj. L1. $75.00

**TESTA, Randy-Michael.** *After the Fire: Destruciton of Lancaster County.* 1992. U Pr of New Eng. F/dj. R8. $15.00

**TETU, Randeane.** *Merle's & Marilyn's Milk Ranch.* 1991. Papier Mache pr. 1st. inscr. NF/dj. S13. $25.00

**TEVIS, Walter.** *Hustler.* 1959. Harper. 1st. NF/VG+. B4. $950.00

**TEY, Josephine.** *Franchise Affair.* 1949. NY. Macmillan. 1st Am. F/NF. M15. $75.00

**TEY, Josephine.** *Miss Pym Disposes.* 1947. Macmillan. 1st Am. F/dj. M15. $75.00

**TEY, Josephine.** *Singing Sands.* 1953. Macmillan. 1st Am. F/clip. M15. $65.00

**THACKERAY, A.D.** *Astronomical Spectroscopy.* 1961. NY. Macmillan. ils. 256p. VG/dj. K5. $25.00

**THACKERAY, Anne Isabella.** *Village on the Cliff.* 1869. Boston. Fields Osgood. 277p. G. G11. $7.00

**THACKERAY, William Makepeace.** *Bachelor's Own Book: Being Progress of Mr Lambkin...* nd. Glascow. Bryce. 1st thus. 24 pl/Cruikchank. gilt bl cloth. VG. S13. $75.00

**THACKERAY, William Makepeace.** *English Humorists of the 18th Century: A Series...* 1853. London. Smith Elder. 1st. sgn Riviere. full crimson crushed morocco. M24. $200.00

**THACKERAY, William Makepeace.** *English Humorists of the 18th Century: A Series...* 1853. London. Smith Elder. 1st. 322p. full leather. VG. M10. $250.00

**THACKERAY, William Makepeace.** *Fatal Boots & Cox's Diary.* 1856. London. Bradley Evans. sc. A19. $35.00

**THACKERAY, William Makepeace.** *Pendennis: History of...* 1849. Leipzig. 3 vol. 1st. Am. 24mo. 3-quarter blk leather/marbled brd. VG. S17. $100.00

**THACKERAY, William Makepeace.** *Rose & the Ring; or, History of Prince Giglio...* 1937. Macmillan. 16mo. 212p. VG. C14. $15.00

**THACKERAY, William Makepeace.** *Vanity Fair.* 1848. London. Bradbury Evans. 1st/early issue. 8vo. 40 pl. 624p. Sangorski bdg. case. H5. $3,000.00

**THACKSTON, W.M.** *Century of Princes: Sources on Timurid History & Art.* 1989. Cambridge. Aga Khan Progam for Islamic Architecture. 1st. VG/wrp. W1. $24.00

**THANE, Elswyth.** *Fighting Quaker: Nathanael Greene.* 1972. Hawthorn. 1st. 304p. G/dj. V3. $16.00

**THANE, Elswyth.** *Fighting Quaker: Nathanael Greene.* 1972. NY. 1st. ils. 304p. F/dj. M4. $35.00

**THANE, Elswyth.** *Tryst.* 1939. NY. 5th. VG/dj. B5. $20.00

**THANET, Octave.** *Lion's Share.* 1907. Indianapolis. Bobbs Merrill. 1st. gilt red cloth. NF. M15. $100.00

**THANET, Octave.** *Man of the Hour.* 1905. Bobbs Merrill. ils Lucius Wolcott Hitchcock. 477p. G. G11. $7.00

**THATCHER, Margaret.** *Downing Street Years.* 1993. Harper Collins. 1st/3rd prt. sm 4to. inscr. 914p. F/dj. W2. $175.00

**THATCHER & WILLIAMSON.** *Fantastic Fairy Tale Pop-Up Book.* 1992. Random. 2nd. 4 popups. F. B17. $10.00

**THAW, Harry K.** *Traitor: Being Untampered With, Unrevised Account...* (1926). Phil. Dorrance. 1st. 271p. G+/dj. B18. $35.00

**THAYER, Bert Clark.** *Horses in the Blue Grass.* 1947. DSP. revised/1st prt. ils. NF/dj. A21. $65.00

**THAYER, Charles W.** *Checkpoint.* 1964. Harper Row. 1st. F/NF. H11. $25.00

**THAYER, Ernest Lawrence.** *Casey at the Bat.* 1964. Prentice Hall. 1st. F. P8. $25.00

**THAYER, Lee.** *Dusty Death.* 1966. Dodd Mead. 1st. VG/dj. G8. $20.00

**THAYER, Lee.** *Last Trump.* 1973. Otto Penzler. 1st Am. VG/dj. G8. $25.00

**THAYER, Ruth Hubley.** *Mr Wizard's Junior Science Show.* 1957. Chicago. Rand McNally. 1st. ils Robert Bonfils. VG+. A25. $15.00

**THAYER, T.** *Nathaniel Greene, Strategist of American Revolution.* 1960. NY. 1st. F/VG. M4. $35.00

**THAYER, William M.** *Marvels of the New West.* 1887. Henry Bill. ils/maps. 714p. G. B19. $45.00

THAYER, William Sidney. *Osler & Other Papers*. 1969. Freeport, NY. Books for Lib Pr. rpt. 8vo. 386p. brd. xl. C14. $8.00

THEOCRITUS & THEOCRITUS. *Idyllia*. 1760. London. Hitch Hawes. 1st. Greek/Latin ed. lg 8vo. 494p. contemporary vellum. K1. $275.00

THEODOR, O. *Fauna Palaestina. Insecta I...* 1975. Jerusalem. tall 8vo. 168p. NF. B1. $40.00

THEROUX, Alexander. *Master Snickup's Cloak*. 1979. Harper Row. 1st. 4to. ils Brian Froud. VG/dj. B17. $27.50

THEROUX, Alexander. *Primary Colors: Three Essays*. 1994. NY. Holt. UP. sgn. F/wrp. B4. $100.00

THEROUX, Paul. *Chicago Loop*. 1990. NY. Random. 1st. 8vo. 196p. VG/dj. P4. $20.00

THEROUX, Paul. *Chicago Loop*. 1990. Random. 1st. F/F. H11. $30.00

THEROUX, Paul. *Consul's File*. 1977. London. Hamish Hamilton. sgn. F/clip. R14. $75.00

THEROUX, Paul. *Doctor Slaughter*. 1984. London. 1st. F/NF. B3. $40.00

THEROUX, Paul. *Family Arsenal*. 1976. Hamish Hamilton. 1st. F/F. B3. $75.00

THEROUX, Paul. *Family Arsenal*. 1976. Houghton Mifflin. 1st Am. NF/dj. G10. $16.50

THEROUX, Paul. *Happy Isles of Oceana*. 1992. NY. 1st. dj. T9. $15.00

THEROUX, Paul. *Kingdom by the Sea*. 1983. Houghton Mifflin. 1st Am. F/VG. R14. $25.00

THEROUX, Paul. *Kingdom by the Sea: A Journey Around Great Britain*. 1983. Houghton Mifflin. 1st. sgn. VG/G. B30. $45.00

THEROUX, Paul. *London Embassy*. 1983. Houghton Mifflin. 1st Am. F/dj. M25. $25.00

THEROUX, Paul. *Mosquito Coast*. 1981. London. Hamish Hamilton. 1st. VG/dj. T9. $45.00

THEROUX, Paul. *Mosquito Coast*. 1982. Houghton Mifflin. 1st. NF/dj. H11. $30.00

THEROUX, Paul. *My Secret History*. 1984. London. Hamish Hamilton. 1st. F/VG. B3. $30.00

THEROUX, Paul. *My Secret History*. 1989. NY. Putnam. 1st Am. F/NF. R14. $25.00

THEROUX, Paul. *Old Patagonian Express*. 1979. Houghton Mifflin. 1st. F/dj. Q1. $75.00

THEROUX, Paul. *Sailing Through China*. 1983. Salisbury. 1st. ils P Procktor. dj. T9. $32.00

THESIGER, Wilfred. *Arabian Sands*. 1959. Dutton. 1st. 326p. NF/dj. W1. $30.00

THEVET, Andre. *Andre Thevet's North America*. 1986. Kingston, Canada. McMill-Queens. 1st Eng trans. 18 maps. F/dj. T10. $35.00

THEWLIS, Malford W. *Geriatrics: A Treatise on Senile Conditions, Diseases...* 1919. St Louis. Mosby. 1st. photos. 250p. VG. B14. $60.00

THIBAULT. *Bibliographia Canadiana*. 1973. 4to. 861p. F/NF case. A4. $225.00

THIELE, Colin. *Fire in the Stone*. 1974. Harper Row. 305p. F/dj. D4. $25.00

THIELICKE, Helmut. *Death & Life*. 1970. Fortress. 230p. VG/dj. B29. $10.00

THIELICKE, Helmut. *Evangelical Faith*. 1977. Eerdmans. 2 vol (broken set). VG. B29. $36.00

THOM, Helen. *Johns Hopkins: A Silhouette*. 1929. Baltimore. 1st. 125p. A13. $30.00

THOMA, Kurt H. *Oral Diagnosis & Treatment Planning*. 1937. Phil. Saunders. 1st. 8vo. 379p. cloth. VG. C14. $38.00

THOMAS, Alan G. *Fine Books, Pleasures & Treasures*. 1967. NY. Putnam. 1st. ils/pl. cloth. F/dj. O10. $15.00

THOMAS, Alan G. *Great Books & Book Collectors*. 1975. Putnam. 1st Am. 280p. cloth. F/dj. O10. $45.00

THOMAS, Alfred Barnaby. *Forgotten Frontiers: A Study of Spanish Indian Policy...* 1969. OK U. 1st. fld maps. 420p. F/dj. B19. $35.00

THOMAS, Alice Payne. *Descendants of Margaret Couch Payne & Micajah Payne*. nd. np. 95p. sc. G. S5. $12.00

THOMAS, B. *Island: Natural History of America's Coastal Islands*. 1980. NY. Norton. ils/photos. 208p. F/VG+. M12. $20.00

THOMAS, Bill. *Talking With the Animals*. 1985. Morrow. 1st. VG/dj. R8. $10.00

THOMAS, D.H. *Southwestern Indian Detours*. 1978. Hunter Pub. 1st. ils/maps. 327p. NF/clip. B19. $35.00

THOMAS, D.H. *Southwestern Indian Detours: Story of Fred Harvey...* 1978. Phoenix. Hunter Pub. sgn. 8vo. 327p. yel cloth. VG/dj. F7. $35.00

THOMAS, D.M. *Flute Player*. 1979. Dutton. 1st Am. NF/dj. R14. $25.00

THOMAS, David. *Teen Age Stories of the Diamond*. 1950. Grosset Dunlap. rpt. VG. P8. $4.00

THOMAS, Deborah A. *Dickens & the Short Story*. 1982. Phil. 1st. F/dj. A2. $15.00

THOMAS, Dylan. *Child's Christmas in Wales*. 1955. New Directions. 1st separate. sm 8vo. 31p. NF/dj. H5. $250.00

THOMAS, Dylan. *Child's Christmas in Wales*. 1969. New Directions. 1/100. ils/sgn Fritz Eichenberg. w/extra suite. F/portfolio. B24. $1,250.00

THOMAS, Dylan. *Letters to Vernon Watkins*. 1957. London. Dent/Faber. 1st. NF/dj. A24. $35.00

THOMAS, Dylan. *Me & My Bike*. 1965. London. Triton. 1st trade. 1/500. thin folio. F/NF. B4. $125.00

THOMAS, Edward. *Four Letters to Frederick Evans*. 1978. Edingurgh. Tragara. 1/150. sewn wrp. T9. $95.00

THOMAS, Frank A. *Wines, Cocktails & Other Drinks*. 1936. Harcourt Brace. 1st. 8vo. 228p. VG/dj. H1. $15.00

THOMAS, Frank J. *Mission Cattle Brands*. (1967). LA. Tenfingers. mini. 1/100 on Japanese Kozo. ils cattle brands. vellum brd. B24. $200.00

THOMAS, Frank J. *Myths of California Isle*. (1966). Tenfingers. mini. 1/200. map ftspc. 50p. linen-backed brd. B24. $150.00

THOMAS, Frank. *Sherlock Holmes: Bridge Detective Returns*. 1975. LA. Frank Thomas. 1st. inscr. F/stiff wrp. M15. $50.00

THOMAS, G.L. *Garden Pools, Water-Lilies & Goldfish*. 1958. Princeton. ils/pl. 222p. VG/dj. B26. $16.00

THOMAS, Herbert. *Classical Contributions to Obstetrics & Gynecology*. 1935. Springfield. 265p. xl. G7. $35.00

THOMAS, Isaiah. *History of Printing in America With Biography...* 1970. NY. Weathervane. rpt of 1810 ed. 650p. cloth. F/dj. D2. $35.00

THOMAS, J.J. *Illustrated Annual Register of Rural Affairs Vol II*. 1860. Albany. Tucker. 1st. 332p. cloth. VG. A10. $75.00

THOMAS, John Hunter. *Flora of the Santa Cruz Mountains of California*. 1991 (1961). Stanford. 434p. sc. AN. B26. $18.00

THOMAS, John J. *American Fruit Culturist...* 1885. NY. Wm Wood. ils. 593p. gilt cloth. VG. H7. $45.00

THOMAS, John P. *Notes on the Origin & Use of Book-Plates...* 1907. Columbia, SC. 1st. ils. VG/wrp. M8. $45.00

**THOMAS, John.** *True Story of Lawrence of Arabia.* 1964. Chicago. Childrens Pr. 1st/2nd imp. 143p. VG+. M7. $35.00

**THOMAS, Joseph B.** *Hounds & Hunting Through the Ages.* 1937. Garden City. 233p. VG/dj. A17. $30.00

**THOMAS, Lamont D.** *Rise to Be a People: Biography of Paul Cuffe.* 1986. Urbana/ Chicago. U IL. 1st. 187p. AN/dj. V3. $14.00

**THOMAS, Leslie.** *Onward Virgin Soldiers.* 1972. NAL. 1st. VG/clip. R11. $25.00

**THOMAS, Lowell.** *Good Evening Everybody From Cripple Creek to Samarkand.* 1976. Morrow. 1st. sgn. VG+/dj. B30. $30.00

**THOMAS, Lowell.** *Hero of Vincennes.* 1929. Houghton Mifflin. 1st. ils FC Yohn. VG+/dj. B27. $55.00

**THOMAS, Lowell.** *Rolling Stone: Life & Adventure of Arthur Radclyffe Dugmore.* 1933. Doubleday Doran. 1st. ils. VG/torn. W1. $20.00

**THOMAS, Lowell.** *With Lawrence in Arabia.* 1924. NY/London. Century. 1st. 8vo. 408p. cloth. VG. W1. $14.00

**THOMAS, Marlo.** *Free to Be a Family: A Book About All Kinds of Belonging.* 1987. NY. Bantam. 1st. ils. VG/dj. M17. $15.00

**THOMAS, Piri.** *Down These Mean Streets.* 1967. Knopf. 1st. inscr. NF/dj. T11. $125.00

**THOMAS, Richard H.** *Penelve or Among the Quakers.* 1898. London. Headley. 12mo. 366p. V3. $6.00

**THOMAS, Ross.** *Brass Go-Between.* 1969. Morrow. 1st. F/dj. M15. $250.00

**THOMAS, Ross.** *Briarpatch.* 1984. S&S. 1st. F/dj. N4. $40.00

**THOMAS, Ross.** *Chinaman's Chance.* 1978. S&S. 1st. F/dj. M15. $125.00

**THOMAS, Ross.** *Fools in Town Are On Our Side.* 1971. NY. Morrow. 1st. F/dj. M15. $250.00

**THOMAS, Ross.** *Fourth Durango.* 1989. Mysterious. 1st. F/dj. N4. $20.00

**THOMAS, Ross.** *If You Can't Be Good.* 1973. Morrow. 1st. F/dj. M15. $150.00

**THOMAS, Ross.** *Money Harvest.* 1975. NY. Morrow. 1st. F/dj. M15. $100.00

**THOMAS, Ross.** *Out on the Rim.* 1987. Mysterious. 1st. F/F. H11. $25.00

**THOMAS, Ross.** *Seersucker Whipsaw.* 1967. NY. Morrow. 1st. 8vo. F/NF clip. S9. $600.00

**THOMAS, Ross.** *Singapore Wink.* 1969. Morrow. 1st. F/dj. M15. $250.00

**THOMAS, Tay.** *Follow the North Star.* 1960. Doubleday. inscr. map ep. half cloth. VG/dj. P4. $25.00

**THOMAS, Theodore Gillard.** *Practical Treatise on Diseases of Women.* 1880. Phil. Henry C Lea's Son. 5th. 8vo. 806p. calf. C14. $55.00

**THOMAS, Tony.** *Films of the Forties.* 1975. Citadel. 4th. NF/wrp. C9. $30.00

**THOMAS, William H.B.** *Gordonsville, Virginia; Historic Crossroads Town.* 1971. Green Pub. 2nd. sgn. 156p. VG/VG. B10. $25.00

**THOMAS, William H.B.** *Orange, Virginia: Story of a Courthouse Town.* (1972). McClure. ils. VG. B10. $20.00

**THOMAS, William H.B.** *Patriots of the Upcountry: Orange County, Virginia...* 1976. OC Bicentennial Comm. 166p. VG/dj. B10. $20.00

**THOMAS A KEMPIS, Saint.** *Dell'Imitazione di Cristo...* 1750. Venice. Simone Occhi. sm 12mo. 374p. contemporary vellum. K1. $125.00

**THOMASON, John W.** *Jeb Stuart.* 1930. Scribner. 1st. ils/maps. 512p. VG. B10. $40.00

**THOMASON, John W.** *Lone Star Preacher.* 1941. NY. 1st. VG. B5. $35.00

**THOMASON, Joseph.** *Travels in the Atlas & Southern Morocco...* 1889. NY. Longman Gr. 1st. ils/fld maps. 488p. xl. VG. W1. $65.00

**THOMPSON, C.J.S.** *Lure & Romance of Alchemy.* 1990. NY. facs of 1932. dj. A13. $25.00

**THOMPSON, Edward.** *Crusader's Coast.* 1929. London. Benn. ils. cloth. G+. Q2. $30.00

**THOMPSON, Ernest.** *Lives of the Hunted.* 1901. NY. 1st Am. ils. VG. M17. $25.00

**THOMPSON, Gene.** *Lupe.* 1977. Random. 1st. F/dj. M25. $15.00

**THOMPSON, Hunter S.** *Fear & Loathing: On the Campaign Trail '72.* 1973. SF. Straight Arrow. 1st. 8vo. F/clip. S9. $150.00

**THOMPSON, Hunter S.** *Screwjack.* 1991. Santa Barbara. Neville. 1/300. sgn. F/sans. from $175 to $250.00

**THOMPSON, J. Eric.** *Maya Archaeologist.* 1963. Norman. 1st. 248p. dj. F3. $35.00

**THOMPSON, J. Eric.** *Maya History & Religion.* 1976. Norman. 3rd. 415p. dj. F3. $25.00

**THOMPSON, J. Eric.** *Mexico Before Cortez.* 1933. Scribner. 1st. 298p. F3. $45.00

**THOMPSON, Jerry.** *Sabers on the Rio Grande.* 1974. Austin. Presidial. 1/500. ils. 235p. cloth. D11. $100.00

**THOMPSON, Jim.** *King Blood.* 1973. Otto Penzler. 1st Am. VG/dj. G8. $25.00

**THOMPSON, Jim.** *Now & on Earth.* 1986. Belen. Denis McMillan. ltd. 1/400. F/dj. T2. $125.00

**THOMPSON, John Cargill.** *Boys' Dumas, GA Henty: Aspects of Victorian Publishing.* 1975. Cheadle. Carcanet Pr. 114p. NF. A4. $150.00

**THOMPSON, Josia.** *Six Seconds in Dallas.* 1967. NY. 1st. VG/G. B5. $60.00

**THOMPSON, Kay.** *Eloise at Christmastime.* (1958). NY. Random. 1st. lg 4to. ils Hilary Knight. F/dj. R5. $385.00

**THOMPSON, Kay.** *Eloise in Moscow.* 1959. S&S. 1st. ils H Knight. unp. orange cloth. VG/dj. D1. $225.00

**THOMPSON, Kay.** *Eloise in Paris.* 1957. NY. 4th. VG/dj. B5. $75.00

**THOMPSON, Kay.** *Eloise.* 1955. S&S. 1st prt. lg 4to. wht cloth. pict dj. R5. $585.00

**THOMPSON, Kay.** *Miss Pooky Pekingaugh: And Her Secret Private Boyfriends...* 1970. Harper Row. 1st. unp. NF/dj. C14. $20.00

**THOMPSON, Paul.** *Nature of Work: Introduction to Debates on Labour Process.* 1983. London. Macmillan. 1st. 8vo. F/dj. R11. $25.00

**THOMPSON, Robert.** *Royal Flying Corps: Per Ardua & Astra...* 1968. London. Hamish Hamilton. 1st. photos. 151p. VG/dj. S16. $25.00

**THOMPSON, Ruth Plumly.** *Captain Salt in Oz.* 1936. Reilly Lee. 1st. ils John R Neill. 306p. F1. $300.00

**THOMPSON, Ruth Plumly.** *Giant Horse of Oz.* ca 1935. Reilly Lee. later prt. ils. brick-red cloth. G+. M21. $35.00

**THOMPSON, Ruth Plumly.** *Giant Horse of Oz.* 1928. Reilly Lee. ils John Neill. VG. A21. $260.00

**THOMPSON, Ruth Plumly.** *Gnome King of Oz.* 1927. Reilly Lee. ils John R Neill. lt gr bdg. VG. A21. $300.00

**THOMPSON, Ruth Plumly.** *Handy Mandy in Oz.* 1937. Chicago. Reilly Lee. 1st. 4to. bl-gr cloth/pict label. dj. R5. $600.00

**THOMPSON, Ruth Plumly.** *Kabumpo in Oz.* 1950s. Reilly Lee. later prt. VG/clip. B9. $125.00

THOMPSON, Ruth Plumly. *Lost King of Oz.* 1925. Reilly Lee. 1st. VG+. B9. $250.00

THOMPSON, Ruth Plumly. *Ozoplaning With the Wizard of Oz.* 1939. Reilly Lee. 1st. VG+/G clip. B9. $350.00

THOMPSON, Ruth Plumly. *Pirates in Oz.* 1931. Chicago. Reilly Lee. 1st/1st state. 4to. label/cloth. F. R5. $485.00

THOMPSON, Ruth Plumly. *Pirates in Oz.* 1931. Reilly Lee. 1st. VG. R8. $260.00

THOMPSON, Ruth Plumly. *Princess of Cozytown.* 1922. Volland. 1st ils Janet Laura Scott. VG. M5. $105.00

THOMPSON, Ruth Plumly. *Speedy in Oz.* 1934. Reilly Lee. 1st. VG. R8. $300.00

THOMPSON, Susan Otis. *American Book Design & William Morris.* 1977. NY. RR Bowker. 1st. ils. 258p. F/dj. O10. $95.00

THOMPSON, Susan Otis. *American Book Design & William Morris.* 1996. New Castle, DE/London. Oak KNoll. rpt. 4to. ils. cloth. F/dj. O10. $50.00

THOMPSON, Thomas Payne. *Index to Collection of Americana...* 1912. New Orleans. 1st. pres. 203p. xl. VG. M8. $45.00

THOMPSON, Wallace. *Rainbow Countries of Central America.* 1927 (1926). NY. Chautauqua. 284p. map ep. F3. $20.00

THOMSON, Arthur J. *Scientific Riddles.* 1938. London. BC. 8vo. 384p. K5. $13.00

THOMSON, Bobby. *Giants Win the Pennant! Giants Win the Pennant!* 1991. Zebra. 1st. photos. F/dj. P8. $17.50

THOMSON, Frank. *Ninety-Six Years in the Black Hills.* 1974. Detroit, MI. Harlo. sgn. F/dj. A19. $30.00

THOMSON, J.A.K. *Classical Background of English Literature.* 1948. Macmillan. 1st. VG/sans. O4. $15.00

THOMSON, James. *Poetical Works of...* 1830. London. Pickering. 2 vol. 12mo. full polished tan leather/raised bands. S17. $75.00

THOMSON, James. *Poetical Works.* 1794. London. C Cooke. Pocket ed. 12mo. ils/fore-edge painting. NF/case. H5. $2,500.00

THOMSON, John A.F. *Towns & Townspeople in the Fifteenth Century.* 1988. Gloucester, Eng. Alan Sutton. 1st. 8vo. ils. F/dj. A2. $15.00

THOMSON, June. *Holmes & Watson: Study in Friendship.* 1995. London. Constable. 1st. F/dj. M15. $50.00

THOMSON, Rupert. *Insult.* 1996. Knopf. 1st. F/dj. M23. $20.00

THOMSON, S. *Health Resorts of Britain & How to Profit by Them.* 1860. fld map/ils. VG. B10. $50.00

THON, Melanie Rae. *First Body.* 1997. Boston. Houghton Mifflin. 1/100. sgn. F/dj. R14. $90.00

THON, Melanie Rae. *Girls in the Grass.* 1991. Random. 1st. sgn. rem mk. NF/dj. R14. $45.00

THON, Melanie Rae. *Meteors in August.* 1990. NY. Random. ARC. F/dj. B4. $85.00

THON, Melanie Rae. *Meteors in August.* 1991. Viking. 1st. author's 1st book. F/dj. O11. $30.00

THORBURN, Archibald. *Birtish Birds.* 1925-26. Longman Gr. 4 vol. ils. red cloth/pict label. F. T10. $400.00

THORBURN, Archibald. *British Birds.* 1925-26. London. 4 vol. 5th/revised/final. 192 mc pl. 628p. VG. C12. $220.00

THOREAU, Henry David. *Familiar Letters.* 1894. Houghton Mifflin. 1st. gilt gr cloth. VG. M24. $165.00

THOREAU, Henry David. *Thoreau's Bird-Lore: Being Notes on New England Birds.* 1925. Houghton Mifflin. 1st/1st prt/2nd issue. gilt gr cloth. F. M24. $85.00

THOREAU, Henry David. *Thoreau's Complex Weave.* 1986. U VA. 1st. 8vo. F/dj. S9. $30.00

THOREAU, Henry David. *Walden.* 1966. Peter Pauper. abridges. sm 8vo. 62p. NF. W2. $20.00

THOREAU, Henry David. *Walden; or, Life in the Woods.* 1936. Boston. LEC. 1/1500. sgn/photos Edward Steichen. 290p. blk morocco. xl. NF. H5. $750.00

THOREAU, Henry David. *Week on the Concord & Merrimac Rivers.* (1890). NY. Hurst. 355p. G. M10. $9.50

THOREAU, Henry David. *Winged Life: Poetic Voice of Henry David Thoreau.* 1986. Yolla Bolly. 1/15 (100 total). sgn Bly/McCurdy. w/extra suite. B24. $950.00

THORN, John. *Relief Pitcher.* 1979. Dutton. 1st. F/VG. P8. $20.00

THORNDIKE, Augustus. *Athletic Injuries: Prevention, Diagnosis & Treatment.* 1938. Phil. Lea Febiger. 1st. ils. 208p. red cloth. H7. $75.00

THORNDIKE, Edward Lee. *Animal Intelligence: Experimental Study...* 1898. NY. np. 109p. prt bl wrp. G1. $600.00

THORNDIKE, Edward Lee. *Mental Work & Fatigue & Individual Differences... Vol 3.* 1914. NY. Teachers College. 408p. gilt panelled bl cloth. G1. $40.00

THORNDIKE, Edward Lee. *Notes on Child Study.* 1903. NY/Berlin. Macmillan/Mayer Muller. 2nd enlarged. 181p. prt wrp. G1. $75.00

THORNDIKE, Joseph J. *Very Rich: History of Wealth.* 1976. VG/dj. M17. $25.00

THORNDIKE, Rachel Sherman. *Sherman Letters: Correspondence...1837-1891.* 1969 (1894). NY. Da Capo. reissue. NF/dj. A14. $25.00

THORNDYKE, Helen Louise. *Honey Bunch: Her First Little Circus.* 1936. NY. Grosset Dunlap. F/dj. B14. $40.00

THORNDYKE, Helen Louise. *Honey Bunch: Her First Trip to the Ocean.* 1927. Grosset Dunlap. 12mo. 184p+ads. VG/dj. M7. $25.00

THORNE, Diana. *Drawing Dogs.* 1955. The Studio. 10th. VG/dj. A21. $45.00

THORNE, T.G. *Navigation Systems for Aircraft & Space Vehicles.* 1962. Macmillan. sm 4to. 550p. xl. K5. $50.00

THORNTON, John. *Advanced Physiography.* 1890. Longman Gr. ils/6 maps. 342p. G. B14. $75.00

THORNTON, Lawrence. *Ghost Woman.* 1992. Ticknor Fields. ARC/1st. F/wrp. L3. $50.00

THORNTON, Lawrence. *Imagining Argentina.* 1987. Doubleday. 1st. F/dj. T12. $60.00

THORNTON, Lawrence. *Under the Gypsy Moon.* 1990. Doubleday. 1st. sgn. F/dj. M25. $35.00

THORNTON, Michael. *Royal Feud: Dark Side of the Love Story of the Century.* nd. BC. VG/dj. P3. $10.00

THORP, John. *Letters of Late John Thorp, of Manchester, a Minister...* 1820. Liverpool. Smith. 1st. 199p. cloth. xl. V3. $28.00

THORP, N. Howard. *Story of the Southwestern Cowboy...* 1945. Caxton. 1st. 309p. VG/dj. B18. $37.50

THORP, Roderick. *Rainbow Drive.* 1986. Summit. 1st. F/dj. T12. $35.00

THORPE, Edward. *History of Chemistry.* 1909. London. 2 vol. 1st. A13. $25.00

THORPE, W.G. *Still Life of the Middle Temple...* 1892. London. Bentley. xl. M11. $35.00

**THORWALD, Jugen.** *Century of the Surgeon.* 1957. NY. 331p. A13. $40.00

**THRUSTONE, Louis Leon.** *Multiple-Factor Analysis: A Development & Expansion...* 1947. Chicago. 535p. maroon cloth. G1. $50.00

**THURBER, James.** *Beast in Me & Other Animals: A New Collection of Pieces...* 1948. Harcourt. 1st. VG/dj. B14. $45.00

**THURBER, James.** *My Life & Hard Times.* 1933. Harper. 1st. author's 3rd book. NF. Q1. $175.00

**THURBER, James.** *Thurber Album.* 1952. S&S. 1st. F/VG clip. M19. $25.00

**THURBER, James.** *Thurber Country.* 1953. 1st. ils. VG/dj. M17. $15.00

**THURBER, James.** *White Deer.* 1945. Harcourt Brace. 1st. F/VG+/ A24. $60.00

**THURBER, James.** *13 Clocks.* 1990. NY. ils Marc Simont. VG/dj. M17. $15.00

**THURBER & WEEKS.** *Selected Letters of James Thurber.* 1981. Little Brn. 1st trade. 274p. NF/dj. W2. $55.00

**THURBER & WHITE.** *Is Sex Necessary? Or, Why You Feel the Way You Do.* 1929. NY. Harper. 1st. 8vo. 197p. Raviere bdg. NF. H5. $250.00

**THURMAN, A.R.** *Money Pitcher.* 1952. McKay. 1st. VG. P8. $15.00

**THURMAN, Howard.** *Deep River: Reflections on Relgiious Insight...* 1955. Harper. 8vo. 4-line inscr. ils EO Jones. 96p. AN/dj. B14. $50.00

**THURMAN, Howard.** *Growing Edge.* 1956. Harper. 4-line inscr. 181p. F/dj. B14. $55.00

**THURNER, Frederick W.** *Machine Shop Work.* 1916. Chicago. Am Correspondence School. 2 vol. VG. B9. $15.00

**THURNHAM, Sophie.** *Great Donkey Trek: Journey on Foot Through Spain...* 1991. London. Headline. 1st. VG/dj. O3. $18.00

**THURSTON, Clara Bell.** *Jingle of the Jap.* (1908). Boston. unp. VG. B18. $45.00

**THURSTON, Robert.** *Alicia II.* 1978. Berkley Putnam. 1st. NF/dj. G10. $12.50

**THWAITE, Ann.** *Day of the Duke.* 1969. World. 1st Am. ils George Him. lib bdg. NF/VG. P2. $20.00

**THWAITE, Anthony.** *Beyond the Inhabited World: Roman Britain.* 1976. London. Andre Deutsch. 1st. ils. F/clip. T10. $45.00

**THWAITES, Reuben Gold.** *Original Journals of the Lewis & Clark Expedition, 1804...* (1969). np. Arno. 8 vol (includes atlas vol). gilt stp cloth. AN/box. D11. $250.00

**TIBAWI, AL.L.** *Jerusalem: Its Place in Islam & Arab History.* 1969. Beirut. Inst Palestine Studies. VG/wrp. M7. $30.00

**TIBBLES, Thomas Henry.** *Buckskin & Blanket Days.* 1985. Lakeside Classic. 1st thus. teg. brn cloth. F. T11. $30.00

**TICHENER, Edward Bradford.** *Experimental Psychology: A Manual of Laboratory Practice.* 1901. Macmillan. ils. 214p. panelled brn cloth. G. G1. $85.00

**TICHENER, Edward Bradford.** *Text-Book of Psychology.* 1993 (1909). NY. Gryphon. facs (3rd revised). 12mo. 558p. tooled dk brn leather. G1. $65.00

**TICHI, Cecelia.** *Shifting Gears: Technology, Literature.* 1987. U NC. photos. VG/dj. M17. $20.00

**TICKNER, John.** *Tickner's Show Piece.* 1958. London. Putnam. 93p. G/dj. C5. $12.50

**TIDY, GORDON.** *Little About Leech.* 1931. london. ils. VG. M17. $30.00

**TIEDE, Tom.** *Calley: Soldier or Killer?* 1971. NY. Pinnacle. 158p. F/wrp. R11. $25.00

**TIEDEMAN, Frederic.** *Anatomy of the Foetal Brain...* 1826. Edinburgh. Carfrae. 14 engraved pl. 324p. rb half cloth/marbled brd. xl. G7. $250.00

**TIEMANN, Robert.** *Dodger Classics.* 1983. Baseball Histories. 1st. VG. P8. $30.00

**TIERNEY, Patrick.** *Highest Altar: Story of Human Sacrifice.* 1989. Viking. 1st. 480p. F3. $15.00

**TILDEN, Freeman.** *National Parks.* 1955. Knopf. VG/dj. A19. $25.00

**TILDEN, William A.** *Chemical Discoveries & Inventions in Twentieth Century.* 1919 (1917). London. Routledge. 3rd. ils. VG. A2. $25.00

**TILGHMAN, Christopher.** *In a Father's Place.* 1990. FSG. ARC. F/dj. D10. $50.00

**TILLER, Veronica E. Velarde.** *Jicarilla Apache Tribe: A History 1846-1970.* 1983. NE U. 1st. 365p. F/NF. B19. $45.00

**TILLEY, Patrick.** *Mission.* 1981. Little Brn. 1st. VG/dj. S18. $15.00

**TILLICH, Paul.** *Essential Tillich.* 1987. Macmillan. edit F Forrester Church. 281p. VG/dj. B29. $10.50

**TILLMAN, Lynne.** *Haunted Houses.* 1987. Poseidon. 1st. sgn. F/dj. D10. $75.00

**TILTON, George Fred.** *Cap'n George Fred.* 1928. NY. ils. VG. M17. $32.50

**TIMBS, John.** *London & Westminster: City & Suburb.* 1868. London. 2 vol. 3-quarter tan leather/marbled brd/raised band. VG. S17. $90.00

**TIME-LIFE EDITORS.** *American Indians: People of the Lakes.* 1994. Alexandria. 1st. ils. F. M4. $20.00

**TIMMONS, Wilbreth H.** *Morelos: Priest, Soldier, Statesman of Mexico.* 1963. El Paso. TX Western College. 1/500. 184p. cloth. dj. D11. $125.00

**TIMNER, W.E.** *Ellingtonia: Recorded Music of Duke Ellington.* 1988. Metuchen. Inst Jazz Studies/Scarecrow. 1st. 4to. F/sans. B2. $70.00

**TINKELMAN, David G.** *Childhood Asthma: Pathophysiology & Treatment.* nd (1987). Marcel Dekker. 2nd. 8vo. 385p. F/dj. C14. $25.00

**TINKER, Cauncey Brewster.** *Letters of James Boswell.* 1924. London. OUP. 2 vol. 1st. G. M10. $25.00

**TINKER, Chauncey Brewster.** *Dr Johnson & Fanny Burney.* 1970. Westport. Greenwood. rpt. F. H13. $45.00

**TINKER, Chauncey Brewster.** *Young Boswell.* 1922?. London. Putnam. 1st. ils. H13. $65.00

**TINKER, George H.** *Northern Arizona & Flagstaff in 1887.* 1969 (1887). Arthur Clark. 8vo. 62p. yel cloth. VG. F7. $45.00

**TINLEY, F.C.** *Fables of La Fontaine.* ca 1890. Dutton. ils Tinley. NF. M19. $35.00

**TIPTREE, James;** see Sheldon, Alice Bradley.

**TIRUCHELVAM, Neelan.** *Ideology of Popular Justice in Sri Lanka...* 1984. New Delhi. Vikas. M11. $35.00

**TITHERINGTON, Jeanne.** *Place for Ben.* 1987. Morrow. 1st/2nd prt. obl 4to. VG+/dj. M5. $12.00

**TITLE, Elise.** *Romeo.* 1996. Bantam. 1st. author's 1st book. NF/F. H11. $15.00

**TITMARSH, M.A.;** see Thackery, William Makepeace.

**TITMUSS, Richard.** *Gift Relationship: From Human Blood to Social Policy.* 1971. NY. 1st. 339p. A13. $30.00

**TITUS, Harry.** *Scientific Feeding of Chickens.* 1949. Danville. Interstate. 253p. cloth. VG. A10. $15.00

**TLILI, Mustapha.** *Lion Mountain, a Novel.* 1990. Arcade/Little Brn. 1st. 180p. NF/dj. W1. $18.00

**TOBIAS, Robert.** *Communist Christian Encounter in East Europe.* 1956. School of Religion. 567p. VG/dj. B29. $8.00

**TOBYNS, Gwen.** *Wimbledon: The Hidden Drama.* 1974. Drake. 1st Am. F/NF. C15. $10.00

**TODD, Edwin M.** *Reflections Through a Murky Crystal.* 1986. Pasadena. 126p. 1/1000. G7. $45.00

**TODD, Frederick.** *American Military Equipage 1851-1872: Vol II, State Forces.* 1983. NY. ils. 739p. VG/dj. S16. $60.00

**TODD, Marilyn.** *I, Claudia.* 1995. London. Macmillan. 1st. author's 1st novel. F/dj. M15. $65.00

**TODD, Mark.** *Charisma.* 1989. London. Theshold. 1st. 4to. VG. O3. $20.00

**TODD, William B.** *New Adventures Among Old Books.* 1958. Lawrence, KS. Lib series $. VG/wrp. H13. $15.00

**TODD, William.** *Prospect of Society: Reconstructed From Earliest Version...* 1956. Charlottesville. 1/150. thin 8vo. 31p. gilt blk linen spine. H13. $95.00

**TODOROV, Nikolai.** *Balkan City, 1400-1900.* 1983. Seattle/London. U WA. 1st. ils/tables. 641p. NF/dj. W1. $35.00

**TOEPFER, Ray.** *Scarlet Guidon: A Novel of War Between the States.* 1958. Coward McCann. 1st. VG/dj. A14. $21.00

**TOFFLER, Alvin.** *Power Shift.* 1990. Bantam. 1st. NF/dj. P3. $23.00

**TOGAWA, Masako.** *Kiss of Fire.* 1988. Dodd Mead. 1st Am. NF/dj. G8. $15.00

**TOGAWA, Masako.** *Lady Killer.* 1986. Dodd Mead. 1st Am. F/dj. N4. $27.50

**TOGAWA, Masako.** *Master Key.* 1985. Dodd Mead. 1st. author's 1st book. F/F. H11. $35.00

**TOIBIN, Colm.** *New Writing From Ireland.* 1994. Winchester, MA. Faber. 1st Am. sgn 3 contributors. F. O11. $65.00

**TOLAND, John.** *Adolf Hitler.* 1976. Doubleday. 1st. sgn. VG/fair. B30. $40.00

**TOLAND, John.** *Dillinger Days.* 1963. NY. 1st. VG/dj. B5. $20.00

**TOLD, Thomas D.** *History of Clarke County Virginia...* 1914. Berryville, VA. 1st. 8vo. ils. 337p. bl cloth. VG. C6. $750.00

**TOLISCHUS, Otto D.** *Through Japanese Eyes: Truth About Japan's Master Race...* 1945. NY. VG/dj. M17. $15.00

**TOLKIEN, J.R.R.** *Book of Lost Tales, Part Two: History of Middle-Earth.* 1984. Allen Unwin. 1st. NF/dj. A14. $32.00

**TOLKIEN, J.R.R.** *Book of Lost Tales 1.* 1983. Allen Unwin. 1st. F/NF. B3. $45.00

**TOLKIEN, J.R.R.** *Hobbit.* 1974. Houghton Mifflin. Collector ed. AN/dj. A27. $35.00

**TOLKIEN, J.R.R.** *Hobbit.* 1984. Houghton Mifflin. rpt. ils/sgn Hague. F/wrp. B17. $20.00

**TOLKIEN, J.R.R.** *Letters of JRR Tolkien.* 1981. Allen Unwin. 1st. F/F. B3. $40.00

**TOLKIEN, J.R.R.** *Lord of the Rings.* (1974). Houghton Mifflin. 3 vol. Collector Ed. AN/dj. A27. $75.00

**TOLKIEN, J.R.R.** *Pictures by JR Tolkein.* 1979. Houghton Mifflin. 1st Am. ils. gilt brn cloth. F/case. B27. $125.00

**TOLKIEN, J.R.R.** *Road Goes Ever On.* 1967. Houghton Mifflin. 1st. NF/dj. M21. $75.00

**TOLKIEN, J.R.R.** *Sagan Om Rigen.* 1959. Uppsala. Gebers. 1st Swedish. inscr. VG/wrp. L3. $850.00

**TOLKIEN, J.R.R.** *Silmarillion.* 1977. Houghton Mifflin. 1st. G/VG. B30. $30.00

**TOLKIEN, J.R.R.** *Silmarillion.* 1977. London. Allen Unwin. 1st/Export ed. VG+/midnight bl dj (no price). A14. $21.00

**TOLKIEN, J.R.R.** *Simarillion.* 1977. Allen Unwin. 1st. F/F. B3. $75.00

**TOLKIEN, J.R.R.** *Simarillion.* 1977. London. Allen Unwin. 1st. fld map. 365p. VG+. M10. $45.00

**TOLKIEN, J.R.R.** *Smith of Wootton Major.* 1967. Houghton Mifflin. 1st Am. 16mo. F/NF. A24. $45.00

**TOLKIEN, J.R.R.** *Tolkien's World: Paintings of Middle-Earth.* (1992). Harper Collins. 60 ils. AN/wrp. A27. $20.00

**TOLKIEN, J.R.R.** *Unfinished Tales of Numenor & Middle-Earth.* 1980. London. Allen Unwin. 1st. ils/index/maps by Christopher Tolkien. VG+/dj. A14. $25.00

**TOLKIEN, J.R.R.** *War of the Jewels: Later Silmarillion Part Two.* 1994. Houghton Mifflin. F/dj. G10. $16.00

**TOLKIN, Michael.** *Player.* 1988. Atlantic Monthly. 1st. author's 1st book. NF/dj. R14. $35.00

**TOLMAN, Edward Chance.** *Purposive Behavior in Animals & Men.* 1931. NY. Century. 463p. emb blk cloth. NF/dj. G1. $275.00

**TOLSON, Berneita.** *Beer Cookbook.* 1968. Hawthorn. G/dj. A16. $7.00

**TOLSON, Jay.** *Pilgrim in the Ruins: Life of Walker Percy.* 1992. S&S. 1st. sgn. cloth. F/dj. M24. $25.00

**TOLSTOY, Leo.** *Anna Karenina. Vol I & Vol II.* 1923 & 1926. OUP/Humphrey Mifford. World Classics. 2 vol. G+. M7. $32.50

**TOLSTOY, Leo.** *Resurrection: A Novel in Three Parts.* nd (c 1963). Heritage. 403p. F/F case. C14. $22.00

**TOLSTOY, Leo.** *Work While Ye Have Light.* 1891. London. Heinemann. 1st Eng. intro Edmund Gosse. pk cloth. M24. $85.00

**TOMAIN, Joseph P.** *Nuclear Power Transformation.* 1987. Bloomington, IN. IU. M11. $35.00

**TOMKINS, Silvan.** *Affect Imagery Consciousness.* 1991-92. NY. Springer. 4 vol. cloth. NF/dj. G1. $200.00

**TOMLINSON, H.M.** *All Our Yesterdays.* 1930. London. 1/1025. T9. $65.00

**TOMLINSON, H.M.** *South to Cadiz.* 1934. Heinemann. 1st. VG/dj. S13. $20.00

**TOMPERT, Ann.** *Sue Patch & the Crazy Clocks.* 1989. NY. Dial. 1st. 8vo. 48p. F/NF. M7. $15.00

**TOMPKINS, Ptolemy.** *This Tree Grows Out of Hell.* 1990. NY. Harper. 1st. 189p. dj. F3. $20.00

**TOMPKINS, Walter A.** *It Happened in Old Santa Barbara.* 1976. Santa Barbara Nat Bank. 1st. ils. F/NF. T10. $25.00

**TOMPKINS, Walter A.** *Little Giant of Signal Hill: An Adventure...* 1964. Prentice Hall. 1st. NF/dj. O4. $15.00

**TOOKE, William.** *Accounts & Extracts of Manuscripts in Lib King of France.* 1789. London. Faulder Egerton Williams. 2 vol. thick 8vo. modern wrp. R12. $250.00

**TOOKER, Richard.** *Day of the Brown Horde.* 1929. NY. Clarke. 1st. 12mo. VG/dj. M21. $75.00

**TOOLE, K. Ross.** *Probing the American West: Papers From Santa Fe Conference.* 1962. NM U. 1st. 216p. B19. $25.00

**TOOLEY.** *Mapping of America.* 1988. London. 4to. 179 pl. 529p. F/F. A4. $125.00

**TOOMER, Jean.** *Essentials.* 1931. Chicago. Private Ed. 1st thus. F/dj. L3. $1,000.00

**TOOMER, Jean.** *Flavor of Man.* 1949. Phil. Young Friends Movement Phil Yearly Meeting. 12mo. 32p. V3. $250.00

**TOON, Peter.** *Meditating as a Christian: Waiting Upon God.* 1991. Collins. 187p. F. B29. $6.50

**TOOR, Frances.** *Guide to Mexico.* 1940. McBride. revised. 270p. F3. $15.00

**TORJESEN, Elizabeth Fraser.** *Captain Ramsey's Daughter.* 1953. Lee Shepard. 1st. 223p. Nf/G. C14. $18.00

**TORKILDSEN, Arne.** *Ventriculocisternostom: A Palliative Operation...* 1947. Oslo. Johan Grundt Tanum Forlap. pres. 2 fld tables. 240p. G7. $495.00

**TORME, Mel.** *My Singing Teachers.* 1994. OUP. 228p. G/dj. C5. $12.50

**TORREY, Bradford.** *Field-Days in California.* 1913. Cambridge/Boston/NY. Houghton Mifflin/Riverside. sm 8vo. 234p. gr cloth. G+. F7. $22.50

**TORREY, Volta.** *Wind Catchers: American Windmills of Yesterday & Tomorrow.* 1976. Brattleboro, VT. Stephen Greene. sc. A19. $25.00

**TOSCHES, Nick.** *Trinities.* 1994. Doubleday. 1st. sgn. F/dj. w/promo card. O11. $25.00

**TOULOUSE, Betty.** *Pueblo Pottery of the New Mexico Indians...* 1977. Mus of NM. 6th. ils/map. 88p. AN. B19. $7.50

**TOULOUSE, Julian Harrison.** *Bottle Makers & Their Marks.* 1972. Thos Nelson. 2nd. 900+ older w/300+ modern marks. 624p. F/dj. H1. $95.00

**TOURNEY, Leonard.** *Bartholomew Fair Murders.* 1987. London. Quartet. 1st. F/dj. T2. $20.00

**TOURNEY, Leonard.** *Familiar Spirits.* 1985. London. Quartet. 1st Eng. F/dj. T2. $20.00

**TOURNIER, Michel.** *Friday & Robinson: Life on Speranza Island.* 1972. Knopf. 1st. sm 4to. 118p. xl. G/dj. S14. $5.00

**TOURNIER, Michel.** *La Jeune Fille et la Mort.* 1986. Helsinki. Eurographica. 1/350. sgn. French text. AN/stiff wrp. B4. $150.00

**TOURNIER, Paul.** *Meaning of Gifts.* 1970. John Knox. 62p. VG/dj. B29. $7.50

**TOURTELLOT, Arthur B.** *Charles (River).* 1941. NY. 1st. 356p. VG/dj. A17. $25.00

**TOUT, Otis B.** *Silt: Paula Helps Build Boulder Dam.* 1928. San Diego. Hillcrest. 8vo. sm 8vo. 359p. red cloth. VG. F7. $32.50

**TOUT, W.** *Lincoln County Birds, Lincoln County, Nebraska.* 1947. North Platte. 8vo. 191p. NF. C12. $45.00

**TOWER, Charlemagne.** *Marquis de Lafayette in American Revolution...* 1970. NY. Da Capo. 2 vol. rpt. NF. M10. $55.00

**TOWERS, Deirdre.** *Dance, Film & Video Guide.* 1991. Princeton. 233p. VG/wrp. C5. $12.50

**TOWLE, M.A.** *Ethnobotany of Pre-Columbian Peru.* 1961. NY. photos. 180p. NF/stiff wrp. C12. $50.00

**TOWLE, Tony.** *North.* 1970. Columbia. 1st. inscr/dtd 1975. F/NF. L3. $45.00

**TOWN, Harold.** *Tom Thomson: Silence & the Storm.* 1977. McClelland Stewart. 1st. F/dj. A26. $100.00

**TOWNE, Morgan.** *Treasures in Truck & Trash.* 1949. Doubleday. 205p. xl. H6. $32.00

**TOWNE, Robert D.** *Little Johnny & the Teddy Bears.* 1907. Chicago. Reilly Britton. obl 4to. cloth-backed stiff paper wrp. R5. $400.00

**TOWNE, Robert D.** *Teddy Bears Go Fishing.* 1907. Reilly Britton. 1st. ils JR Bray. ils brd. fair. B27. $35.00

**TOWNE, Robert.** *Chinatown.* 1983. Santa Barbara. Neville. 1st. 1/350. sgn. F/sans. M15. $175.00

**TOWNSEND, Ann A.** *Memoir of Elizabeth Newport.* 1878. Phil. Friends Book Assn. 16mo. 310p. G. V3. $18.00

**TOWNSEND, Doris McFerran.** *Cook's Companion.* 1978. NY. Crown. 1st. VG/dj. A16. $15.00

**TOWNSEND, Grace.** *Imperial Cookbook: Monitor for Am Housewife...* 1897 (1884). sm 4to. 525p. rb. G+. E6. $75.00

**TOWNSEND, John K.** *Narrative of a Journey Across the Rocky Mountains...* 1839. Phil. Henry Perkins. 1st. 8vo. 352p. brn brd. B11. $750.00

**TOWNSEND, Reginald T.** *Book of Building & Interior Design.* 1923. Doubleday Page. ils/photos. 104p. gr bdg. VG+. F1. $85.00

**TOWNSEND, Virginia F.** *Mostly Marjoire Day.* 1892. Lee Shepard. 383p. VG. P12. $7.00

**TOWNSEND, W.H.** *Lincoln & His Wife's Hometown.* 1929. Indianapolis. 1st. VG/dj. B5. $50.00

**TOYE, Randall.** *Agatha Christie Who's Who.* 1980. HRW. 1st. F/clip. M25. $25.00

**TOYNBEE, Arnold J.** *Acquaintances.* 1967. OUP. 1st. photos. 312p. NF/VG. M7. $50.00

**TOYNBEE, Arnold J.** *Study of History.* 1947. OUP. 3-quarter red leather/raised bands. VG. M17. $30.00

**TOYNBEE, Philip.** *Friends Apart: A Memoir.* 1954. London. 1st. fair dj. T9. $25.00

**TOYNBEE, Philip.** *Garden to the Sea.* 1953. London. 1st. inscr. T9. $50.00

**TRACHESEL, Myrtle.** *Mistress Jennifer & Master Jeremiah.* 1937. Dodd Mead. 1st. 8vo. 217p. cloth. VG. D4. $25.00

**TRACHSEL, Herman H.** *Government & Administration of Wyoming.* 1953. NY, NY. inscr. F/dj. A19. $30.00

**TRACHTMAN, P.** *Gunfighters.* 1974. Time-Life Old West. 1st. ils. 238p. F. M4. $20.00

**TRACTMAN, Paula.** *Disturb Not the Dream.* 1981. NY. Crown. 1st. VG/dj. L1. $45.00

**TRACY, Clarence.** *Life of a Savage.* 1971. Oxford. 1st. F/dj. H13. $65.00

**TRACY, Clarence.** *Lives of the Poets.* 1929. OUP. 2 vol. 12mo. gilt bl Oxford bdg. H13. $45.00

**TRACY, David F.** *Psychologist at Bat.* 1951. Sterling. 1st. VG/G. P8. $50.00

**TRACY, Don.** *On the Midnight Tide: A Novel...* 1957. NY. Dial. 1st. NF/dj. A14. $25.00

**TRACY, Jack.** *Subcutaneously, My Dear Watson: Sherlock Holmes...* 1978. Bloomington. James A Rock. 1st. sgn/#d. F/dj. T2. $50.00

**TRACY, Louis.** *Black Cat.* 1925. Clode. 1st. VG/G. G8. $25.00

**TRACY, Marian.** *Picnic Book.* 1957. Scribner. G/dj. A16. $7.50

**TRACY, T.H.** *Book of the Poodle.* 1958. NY. 4th. ils/photos. 136p. VG/dj. A17. $15.00

**TRALINS, Bob.** *Green Murder.* 1990. London. MacDonald. 1st. F/dj. M15. $45.00

**TRANSEAU, E.N.** *Textbook of Botany.* 1953. Harper. revised. xl. G. S5. $15.00

**TRANTER, Nigel.** *Drug on the Market.* 1962. Hodder Stoughton. 1st. VG+/clip. A14. $35.00

**TRANTER, Nigel.** *Enduring Flame.* 1957. Hodder Stoughton. 1st. VG+/dj. A14. $70.00

**TRANTER, Nigel.** *Gold for Prince Charlie.* 1962. Hodder Stoughton. 1st. VG+/dj. A14. $35.00

**TRASKO, Mary.** *Heavenly Soles.* 1989. Abbeville. 1st. ils. VG/dj. C9. $60.00

**TRAUBEL, Horace.** *Good Bye & Hail, Walt Whitman/At the Graveside of Whitman.* 1892. Phil. private prt. 1st. 1/750. gray wrp. M24. $165.00

**TRAUTMANN, F.** *Travels on the Lower Mississippi 1879-1880.* 1990. MO U. 1st. 261p. F/dj. M4. $20.00

**TRAVEN, B.** *Bridge in the Jungle.* 1938. Knopf. 1st Am. NF/VG clip. B4. $400.00

**TRAVEN, B.** *Death Ship.* 1934. Knopf. 1st Am. author's 1st book. F/G. B4. $650.00

**TRAVEN, Von B.** *Der Schatz der Sierra Madre (Treasure of Sierra Madre).* 1927. Berlin. Gutenberg. author's 2nd novel. 8vo. top edge bl. orange cloth. NF. R3. $900.00

**TRAVER, Robert.** *Laughing Whitefish.* 1965. NY. 1st. NF/dj. A17. $50.00

**TRAVER, Robert.** *Trout Madness: Being a Dissertation on Symptoms...* 1960. St Martin. 1st. F/dj. Q1. $75.00

**TRAVER, Robert.** *Trout Magic.* 1974. NY. 1st. 216p. ils. F/dj. A17. $50.00

**TRAVERS, Jeannette.** *Starting From Scratch: Our Islands for Ocelots.* 1975. NY. 150p. NF/dj. S15. $13.50

**TRAVERS, P.L.** *Fox at the Manger.* 1962. Norton. 1st Am. ils. cloth. VG. B27. $45.00

**TRAVERS, P.L.** *Friend Monkey.* 1971. HBJ. 1st. cloth. VG. B27. $55.00

**TRAVERS, P.L.** *Mary Poppins & Mary Poppins Comes Back.* 1939 (1937). Reynal Hitchcock. 1st/2nd prt. ils Mary Shepard. VG. B27. $65.00

**TRAVERS, P.L.** *Mary Poppins in the Park.* 1952. Harcourt Brace. 1st. ils Mary Shepard. VG/dj. M5. $45.00

**TRAVIS, Tristan Jr.** *Lamia.* 1982. Dutton. 1st. F/F. H11. $25.00

**TREADWAY, Jessica.** *Absent Without Leave & Other Stories.* 1992. NY. Delphinium. 1st. sgn. author's 1st book. F/dj. B4. $45.00

**TREAT, Lawrence.** *Big Shot.* 1951. Harper. 1st. inscr/sgn. VG/dj. L3. $25.00

**TREAT, Roger.** *Walter Johnson.* 1948. Messner. 1st. ils Robert Robison. VG/G. P8. $200.00

**TREDGOLD, Thomas.** *Elementary Principles of Carpentry.* 1875. London. 48 pl. B14. $125.00

**TREE, ISabella.** *Ruling Passion of John Gould.* 1992. Grove Weidenfeld. 1st Am. 8vo. VG/dj. B11. $20.00

**TREECE, Henry.** *Great Captains: A Novel of Early Britain.* 1956. NY. VG/dj. M17. $25.00

**TREECE, Henry.** *Jason.* 1961. Random. 1st. 383p. F/dj. D4. $35.00

**TREFOUSSE, H.L.** *Andrew Johnson: A Biography.* 1989. NY. 1st. ils. 463p. NF/dj. M4. $25.00

**TREHERNE, John.** *Strange History of Bonnie & Clyde.* 1984. Stein Day. 1st. VG/dj. B5. $15.00

**TREIBER, Hannelore.** *Studien zur Katunserie der Pariser Mayahandschrift.* 1987. Berlin. Von Flemming. facs pl of Paris Codex/German text. 99p. wrp. F3. $65.00

**TREITEL, Jonathan.** *Red Cabbage Cafe.* 1990. Pantheon. 1st. author's 1st book. F/F. H11. $25.00

**TREND, J.B.** *Bolivar & the Independence of Spanish America.* 1951. Clinton, MA. Bolivarian Soc of Venezuela. 242p. F3. $10.00

**TRENNERT, Robert A.** *Indian Traders on the Middle Border.* 1981. U NE. 1st. F/dj. T10. $25.00

**TRENT, Paul.** *Those Fabulous Movie Years: The '30s.* 1975. NY. Crown. 192p. VG/dj. C5. $15.00

**TRESHNIKOV, A.F.** *Problems of the Arctic & Antarctic.* 1973. New Delhi, India. Amerind. 1st thus? 8vo. ils. VG/dj. A2. $15.00

**TRESS, Arthur.** *Teapot Opera.* 1988. NY. 1st. VG/dj. M17. $27.50

**TREVANIAN.** *Summer of Katya.* 1983. Crown. 1st. F/dj. N4. $25.00

**TREVELYAN, George Otto.** *American Revolution Condensed by Richard B Morris.* 1964. McKay. 580p. VG. M10. $12.50

**TREVELYAN, Humphrey.** *Middle East in Revolution.* 1970. Boston. Gambit. 1st. 8vo. map ep. VG/dj. W1. $18.00

**TREVES, Frederick.** *Land That Is Desolate. Account of Tour in Palestine.* 1912. London. Smith Elder. 8vo. ils/39 pl/fld map. teg. cloth. VG. Q2. $27.00

**TREVINO, Lee.** *They Call Me Super Mex.* 1982. Random. 1st. VG/dj. P12. $12.50

**TREVOR, Elleston.** *Tango Briefing.* nd. BC. VG/dj. P3. $8.00

**TREVOR, Elleston.** *9th Directive.* 1966. Heinemann. 1st. NF/VG. P3. $40.00

**TREVOR, William.** *After Rain.* 1996. Viking. 1st. F/F. H11. $30.00

**TREVOR, William.** *Excursions in the Real World.* 1993. London. Hutchinson. 1st. sgn. F/dj. O11. $75.00

**TREVOR, William.** *Family Sins.* 1990. Toronto. Dennys. 1st Canadian. F/F. B3. $30.00

**TREVOR, William.** *Mrs Eckdorf in O'Neill's Hotel.* 1969. London. Bodley Head. 1st. F/NF. O11. $75.00

**TREW, Anthony.** *Kleber's Convoy.* 1973. St martin. 1st Am. F/NF. T11. $25.00

**TREW, Anthony.** *Two Hours to Darkness.* 1963. London. Collins. 1st. F/VG+. T11. $50.00

**TRICE, James E.** *Butter Molds: Identification & Value Guide.* 1980. Collector Books. 1st. 8vo. 176p. VG/glossy wrp. H1. $35.00

**TRIGAUT, Nicolas.** *Regni Chinensis Descriptio ex Varius Authoribus.* 1639. Leyden. Elzeviriana. sm 12mo. 365p. contemporary vellum. K1. $250.00

**TRILLIN, Calvin.** *Alice, Let's Eat.* 1978. Random. G/dj. A16. $7.00

**TRILLIN, Calvin.** *American Stories.* 1991. Ticknor Fields. 1st. F/dj. R14. $25.00

**TRIMBLE, Stephen.** *Words From the Land.* 1988. Salt Lake City. Smith. 303p. AN/dj. A10. $22.00

**TRIMBLE, Vance H.** *Sam Walton.* 1990. Dutton. 1st. F/dj. W2. $30.00

**TRIMMER.** *National Book Awards for Fiction: An Index...* 1978. 345p. VG. A4. $85.00

**TRIMPEY, Alice.** *Story of My Dolls.* 1935. Whitman. 1st. sgn. ils JL Scott. 76p. VG. D4. $65.00

**TRIPLEIT, Frank.** *Life, Times & Treacherous Death of Jesse James.* 1970. Chicago. Sage Swallow. 1st. VG/dj. B5. $30.00

**TRIPP, Alonzo.** *Crests From the Ocean World.* 1860. Whittemore. Niles Hall. 408p. VG. S17. $10.00

**TRISTRAM, E.W.** *English Medieval Wall Painting.* 1944. Humphrey Milford/OUP. lg 4to. 105 pl/ftspc. 164p. rust buckram. K1. $300.00

**TRISTRAM, W. Outram.** *Coaching Days & Coaching Ways.* 1967. Arno. VG/dj. A21. $65.00

**TROCHECK, Kathy Hogan.** *Every Crooked Nanny.* 1992. Harper Collins. 1st. sgn on title. F/dj. G10. $200.00

**TROCHECK, Kathy Hogan.** *Every Crooked Nanny.* 1992. Harper Collins. 1st. sgn. author's 1st book. F/dj. T2. $125.00

**TROFIMENKOFF, S.M.** *Twenties in Western Canada.* 1972. Ottawa. Nat Mus of Man. Mercury series. VG/wrp. A26. $20.00

**TROLLEY, Jack.** *Balboa Firefly.* 1994. Carroll Graf. 1st. F/F. H11. $25.00

**TROLLOPE, Anthony.** *Belton Estate.* 1866. Phil. Lippincott. 1st authorized Am. bl-gr cloth. lacks ffe o/w G. M24. $125.00

**TROLLOPE, Anthony.** *Hunting Sketches.* 1929. ils Ned King. VG/dj. A21. $24.00

**TROLLOPE, Frances.** *Domestic Manners of the Americans.* 1949. NY. ils. VG/dj. M17. $22.50

**TROLLOPE, Joanna.** *Rector's Wife.* 1991. NY. stated 1st Am. VG/dj. M17. $15.00

**TROTT, Susan.** *Sightings.* 1987. S&S. 1st. F/NF. R15. $25.00

**TROTZKY, Leon.** *Bolsheviki & World Peace.* 1918. NY. Boni Liveright. VG+. B2. $65.00

**TROUPE, Quincy.** *Watts Poets: A Book of New Poetry & Essays.* 1968. CA house of Respect. 1st. VG/wrp. C9. $90.00

**TROW, M.J.** *Lestrade & the Gift of the Prince.* 1991. London. Constable. 1st. F/dj. T2. $25.00

**TROWBRIDGE, J.T.** *Cudjo's Cave: Story of the Civil War.* nd. NY. AL Burt. 308p. V3. $12.00

**TROWBRIDGE, J.T.** *Darius Green & His Flying Machine.* 1910. Houghton Mifflin. 1st. NF. T11. $40.00

**TROWBRIDGE, Lydia Jones.** *Frances Willard of Evanston.* 1938. Chicago. Willett Clark. 1st. pres. photos. 207p. VG. A25. $25.00

**TROY, Judy.** *Mourning Doves.* 1993. NY. Scribner. 1st. F/F. H11. $40.00

**TRUBIANO, Ernie.** *California Cup: 50 Years of Steeplechasing & Socializing.* 1982. Columbia, SC. 104p. VG. O3. $30.00

**TRUDEAU, Noah Andre.** *Last Citadel: Petersburg, VA, June 1864-April 1865.* 1991. Little Brn. 1st. NF/ils wrp. A14. $21.00

**TRUITT, Charles J.** *Breadbasket of the Revolution.* 1975. Historical Books. Bicentennial ed. sgn. F/dj. T11. $35.00

**TRUMAN, Margaret.** *Murder at the Kennedy Center.* 1989. Random. 1st. VG/dj. R8. $9.00

**TRUMAN, Margaret.** *Murder in Georgetown.* 1986. Arbor. 1st. VG/dj. G8. $20.00

**TRUMAN, Margaret.** *Murder in the White House.* 1980. Arbor. 1st. VG/dj. S13. $10.00

**TRUMBELL, James H.** *Natick Dictionary.* 1903. WA. Smithsonian. 3-quarter leather/ gr cloth/marbled edges. VG. S17. $100.00

**TRUMP, Donald J.** *Art of the Deal.* 1987. Random. 1st. F/dj. W2. $30.00

**TRUMP, Ivana.** *For Love Alone.* 1992. Pocket. 1st. F/dj. W2. $35.00

**TRUSKY, Tom.** *Women Poets of the West: An Anthology, 1850-1950.* (1988). Boise. Ahsahta. 5th/revised. sgn. wrp. A18. $10.00

**TRUSS, Lynne.** *Making the Cat Laugh: One Woman's Journal...* 1995. London. 1st. sgn. VG/dj. M17. $17.50

**TRUSS, Lynne.** *Tennyson's Gift.* 1996. London. 1st. sgn. VG/dj. M17. $17.50

**TRUSS, Seldon.** *Truth About Claire Veryan.* 1957. Crime Club. F/NF. M19. $17.50

**TRUSSELL, Arleen.** *Science, Medicine & the State in Germany...* 1993. NY. 1st. 200p. A13. $40.00

**TRYON, Thomas.** *Adventures of Opal & Cupid.* 1992. NY. Viking. 1st. rem mk. F/NF. G10. $15.00

**TRYON, Thomas.** *Other.* 1971. Knopf. 1st. author's 1st novel. NF/dj. M21. $45.00

**TRYON, Tom.** *Night Magic.* 1995. S&S. 1st. F/dj. S13. $10.00

**TRYON, Warren S.** *Mirror for Americans: Life & Manners in US 1790-1870...* 1952. Chicago. Part 1 only. ils. VG. M17. $20.00

**TSAFRIR, Jenni Soussi.** *Light-Eyed Negroes & the Klein-Waardenburg Syndrome.* 1974. Macmillan. 1st. F/clip. N2. $12.50

**TSANOFF, Radoslav A.** *Worlds to Know: Philosophy of Cosmic Perspectives.* 1962. Humanities. 1st. VG/clip. N2. $10.00

**TSCHIFFELY, A.F.** *Tale of Two Horses.* 1935. S&S. 1st. VG. O3. $22.00

**TSELEMENTES, N.** *Greek Cookery.* 1954 (1952). VG. E6. $12.00

**TSUCHIYA, Yukio.** *Faithful Elephants.* 1988. Houghton Mifflin. 1st. ils/sgn Ted Lewin. 32p. F/dj. D4. $45.00

**TSUJI, A.** *Hornbills: Masters of the Tropical Forests.* 1996. Bangkok. 1st. 154 mc photos. 93p. F. C12. $35.00

**TU, A.T.** *Marine Toxins & Venoms. Handbook...Vol 3.* 1988. NY. Marcel Dekker. lg 8vo. 587p. NF. B1. $125.00

**TUCHMAN, Barbara W.** *Practicing History: Selected Essays.* 1981. Knopf. 1st. sm 4to. 306p. G/dj. S14. $9.00

**TUCK, Jim.** *Pancho Villa & John Reed.* 1984. Tucson. 1st. photo. 252p. dj. F3. $20.00

**TUCK, L.M.** *Murres: Their Distribution, Populations & Biology...* 1960. Ottawa. Canadian Wildlife series. ils/tables. 260p. VG. C12. $30.00

**TUCKER, Charlotte Maria.** *ALOE's Picture Story Book.* 1872. London. Thos Nelson. 1st. 10 full-p ils. G. B27. $300.00

**TUCKER, David M.** *Lt Lee of Beale St.* 1971. Vanderbilt U. VG/dj. B30. $40.00

**TUCKER, E.F.J.** *Intruder Into Eden...* 1984. Columbia. Camden. M11. $45.00

**TUCKER, George.** *Federal Penal Code in Force Jan 1, 1910.* 1910. Little Brn. buckram. M11. $50.00

**TUCKER, Glenn.** *High Tide at Gettysburg: Campaign in Pennsylvania.* 1995. Gettysburg. rpt. 462p. VG. S16. $15.00

**TUCKER, Glenn.** *Mad Anthony Wayne: Story of Washington's Front-Line General.* 1973. Harrisburg. 1st. F/NF. M4. $40.00

**TUCKER, Glenn.** *Zeb Vance: Champion of Personal Freedom.* 1965. Bobbs Merrill. 1st. 564p. VG/torn. S16. $35.00

**TUCKER, James.** *Novels of Anthony Powell.* 1976. Columbia U. VG/dj. M17. $25.00

**TUCKER, Louis Leonard.** *Clio's Consort: Jeremy Belknap & Founding of MA Hist Soc.* 1990. Boston. ils. VG/dj. M17. $20.00

**TUCKER, Nicholas.** *Suitable for Children? Controversies...* 1976. Berkeley. U CA. 1st. VG/dj. O4. $15.00

**TUCKER, Robert.** *Palms of Subequatorial Queenland.* 1988. Milton, Queensland. ils/maps. 94p. AN. B26. $25.00

**TUCKER, Sophie.** *Some of These Days.* 1945. inscr. VG/dj. M19. $15.00

**TUCKEY, H.B.** *Dwarfed Fruit Trees.* 1964. Macmillan. lg 8vo. 562p. dj. B1. $50.00

**TUDOR, Bethany.** *Drawn From New England.* 1979. Philomel. rpt. ils Tasha Tudor. F/dj. B17. $45.00

**TUDOR, Bethany.** *Samuel's Tree House.* 1979. NY. Collins. 1st. sgn. sq 12mo. mc pict brd/pict dj. R5. $185.00

**TUDOR, Tasha.** *A Is for Anna Belle.* 1954. Walck. rpt. obl 8vo. VG/G. B17. $65.00

**TUDOR, Tasha.** *Alexander the Gander.* (1939). NY. OUP. 4th. 16mo. gilt gr cloth/pict label. dj. R5. $225.00

**TUDOR, Tasha.** *All for Love.* 1984. Philomel. 1st. 8vo. F/dj. B17. $65.00

**TUDOR, Tasha.** *Amy's Goose.* 1977. Crowell. 2nd. 8vo. VG/dj. B17. $65.00

**TUDOR, Tasha.** *Becky's Birthday.* (1960). NY. Viking. 1st. 4to. red lettered yel cloth. mc pict dj. R5. $385.00

**TUDOR, Tasha.** *Becky's Birthday.* 1992 (1960). Jenny Wren. rpt. sgn. VG/dj. B17. $55.00

**TUDOR, Tasha.** *Christmas Cat.* 1976. Harper Collins. rpt. sgn. F/dj. B17. $110.00

**TUDOR, Tasha.** *Corgiville Fair.* (1971). NY. Crowell. 1st. obl 4to. aqua-gr cloth. mc pict dj. R5. $250.00

**TUDOR, Tasha.** *Dolls' Christmas.* 1950. OUP. sq 12mo. red cloth/pict label. mc pict dj. R5. $375.00

**TUDOR, Tasha.** *Dolls' Christmas.* 1994. Jenny Wren. 1/150. sgn/#d bookplate. leather. F/dj. B17. $90.00

**TUDOR, Tasha.** *Fairy Tales From Hans Christian Andersen.* 1945. NY. OUP. 1st. sgn. 8vo. silvered bl cloth. pict dj. R5. $300.00

**TUDOR, Tasha.** *Family of Man.* 1955. MOMA. rpt. VG/dj. B17. $30.00

**TUDOR, Tasha.** *Favorite Stories.* 1965. Lippincott. 2nd. 4to. VG/G. B17. $50.00

**TUDOR, Tasha.** *First Delights, a Book About the Five Senses.* 1991. Platt Munk. 8vo. F/dj. B17. $50.00

**TUDOR, Tasha.** *First Graces.* 1991. Lutterworth. rpt. 16mo. F/dj. B17. $25.00

**TUDOR, Tasha.** *First Poems of Childhood.* 1988. Platt Munk. rpt. 8vo. F/dj. B17. $55.00

**TUDOR, Tasha.** *Give Us This Day: The Lord's Prayer.* 1987. Philomel. rpt/lg format. 8vo. F/dj. B17. $25.00

**TUDOR, Tasha.** *Lord Is My Shepherd.* 1989. Philomel. rpt of mini ed. less than 16mo. F/dj. B17. $7.00

**TUDOR, Tasha.** *Mother Goose.* nd. Random. rpt. sgn. F/dj. B17. $60.00

**TUDOR, Tasha.** *Mother Goose.* nd. Walck. rpt. VG/dj. B17. $50.00

**TUDOR, Tasha.** *Night Before Christmas in Japanese.* 1980. Kaisei-Sha. lg format. 4to. F/dj. B17. $75.00

**TUDOR, Tasha.** *Night Before Christmas.* nd (1962). Achille J St Onge. mini ed/less than 16mo. aeg. red polished calf. F/dj. B17. $50.00

**TUDOR, Tasha.** *Night Before Christmas.* 1975. Rand McNally. early rpt. 4to. VG. B17. $55.00

**TUDOR, Tasha.** *Real Diary of a Real Boy.* 1967. Noone House. rpt. 8vo. ils. VG/dj. B17. $65.00

**TUDOR, Tasha.** *Rosemary for Remembrance, a Keepsake Book.* 1981. Philomel. rpt. obl 8vo. rem mk. VG. B17. $55.00

**TUDOR, Tasha.** *Secret Garden.* 1962. Lippincott. early rpt. VG/dj. B17. $35.00

**TUDOR, Tasha.** *Tale for Easter.* 1989. Random. 16mo. ils. F/sans. B17. $25.00

**TUDOR, Tasha.** *Tasha Tudor Bedtime Book.* 1977. Platt Munk. rpt. folio. VG. B17. $45.00

**TUDOR, Tasha.** *Tasha Tudor Book of Fairy Tales.* 1961. Platt Munk. early ed. G+. B17. $45.00

**TUDOR, Tasha.** *Tasha Tudor Sketchbook.* 1989. Jenny Wren. 1st. obl 4to. VG. B17. $85.00

**TUDOR, Tasha.** *Treasury of First Books.* 1990s. Lutterworth. 4 vol. VG/box. B17. $65.00

**TUDOR, Tasha.** *Twenty Third Psalm.* 1965. Achille J St Onge. mini ed/less than 16mo. aeg. gr polished calf. F/dj. B17. $50.00

**TUDOR, Tasha.** *Wings From the Wind. An Anthology of Poems...* (1964). Phil. Lippincott. 1st. 4to. gold cloth/gr brd. mc pict dj. R5. $150.00

**TUDOR, Tasha.** *1 Is One.* 1956. OUP. 1st. obl 4to. gray lettered pk cloth. mc pict dj. R5. $300.00

**TUDOR, Williams.** *Letters on the Eastern States.* 1821. Boston. Wells Lily. 2nd/corrected/revised. inscr. 423p. O1. $200.00

**TUDORAN, Radu.** *Schicksal aus Deiner Hand.* 1968. Germany. Fackelverlag. sm 8vo. 563p. NF. W2. $30.00

**TUER, Andrew W.** *History of the Horn Book.* 1979. NY. Arno. rpt. 8vo. cloth. F/NF. O10. $30.00

**TUFTS, Jay Franklin.** *Tufts Family History: A True Account & History...1617-1963.* 1963. Cleveland. 280p. G. S5. $65.00

**TULLY, Jim.** *Shanty Irish.* 1929. London. Knopf. 1st. F/dj. B2. $45.00

**TUNIS, E.** *Colonial Living.* 1957. Cleveland. special ed. 1/975. 157p. F/acetate. M4. $55.00

**TUNIS, Edwin.** *Wheels, a Pictorial History.* 1955. World. VG/dj. A21. $45.00

**TUNIS, John R.** *American Girl.* 1930. NY. Brewer Warren. 1st. author's 1st novel. F/NF. B4. $350.00

**TUNIS, John R.** *Iron Duke.* 1938. Harcourt Brace. later prt. VG/dj. P8. $25.00

**TUNIS, John R.** *Keystone Kids.* 1943. Harcourt. 1st. VG/G. P8. $35.00

**TUNIS, John R.** *Kid Comes Back.* 1946. Morrow. 1st. VG/G. P8. $45.00

**TUNIS, John R.** *Measure of Independence.* 1964. Atheneum. 1st. VG/dj. P8. $65.00

**TUNIS, John R.** *Rookie of the Year.* 1944. Harcourt Brace. 1st. VG/dj. P8. $50.00

**TUNIS, John R.** *Schoolboy Johnson.* 1958. Morrow. 1st. G/dj. P8. $30.00

**TUNIS, John R.** *This Writing Game: Selections...* 1941. NY. Barnes. 1st. NF/fair. B4. $125.00

**TUNIS, John R.** *Two by Tunis.* 1972. Morrow. 1st. G. P8. $20.00

**TUNIS, John R.** *World Series.* 1945. Harcourt Brace. 1st. VG/dj. P8. $45.00

**TURBERVILLE, A.S.** *English Men & Manners in 18th Century.* 1926. Clarendon. 1st. thick 8vo. 531p. blk cloth. VG. H13. $165.00

**TURBERVILLE, A.S.** *Johnson's England: An Account of Life & Manners of His Age.* 1965. Oxford. Clarendon. 2 vol. tall 8vo. ils/150+ pl. gilt bl cloth. NF. H13. $195.00

**TURBOTT, E.G.** *Buller's Birds of New Zealand.* 1967. New Zealand. ils JG Keulemans. 261p. F/dj/case. C12. $95.00

**TURCOTTE, Patricia.** *New England Herb Gardener.* 1990. Woodstock. ils. 254p. sc. AN. B26. $10.00

**TUREK, Leslie.** *Noreascon Proceedings Sept 3-6, 1971.* 1976. NESFA. 1st. F/dj. P3. $75.00

**TURGENEV, Ivan.** *Fathers & Sons.* 1941. Heritage. ils Fritz Eichenberg. VG/case. B11. $15.00

**TURK, H.C.** *Black Body.* 1989. NY. Villard. 1st. F/F. H11. $25.00

**TURKUS, Burton.** *Murder INc.* 1951. Farrar Straus. 1st. VG/dj. B5. $35.00

**TURLEY, R.E.** *Victims: LDS Church & Mark Hoffmann Case.* 1992. IL U. 1st. 519p. F/dj. M4. $20.00

**TURNER, A.E.** *Earps Talk.* 1980. College Sta, TX. Creative. 1st. sgn. ils/index. F/NF. T10. $75.00

**TURNER, Adrian.** *Making of David Lean's Lawrence of Arabia.* 1994. Eng. Dragon World Ltd. 1st. 183p. F/clip. M7. $85.00

**TURNER, Ann.** *Dakota Dugout.* 1985. Macmillan. 1st. ils Ronald Himler. brd/cloth spine. F/NF. T5. $30.00

**TURNER, C.C.** *Old Flying Days.* 1927. London. photos. 347p. G-. B18. $250.00

**TURNER, Carlton.** *Cocaine: An Annotated Bibliography.* 1988. Jackson, MS. 2 vol. B2. $75.00

**TURNER, Dennis C.** *Vampire Bat: A Field Study in Behavior & Ecology.* 1975. Johns Hopkins. 148p. VG/torn. S5. $20.00

**TURNER, Frederick Jackson.** *Frontier in American History.* 1921. Holt. G. A19. $65.00

**TURNER, Frederick.** *Double Shadow.* 1978. Berkeley. 1st. NF/dj. S18. $30.00

**TURNER, George.** *Beloved Son.* 1978. London. Faber. 1st. F/dj. M25. $25.00

**TURNER, George.** *Samoa: A Hundred Years Ago & Long Before...* 1884. London. 8vo. 7 full-p ils/3 maps. 395p. red cloth. VG. B14. $125.00

**TURNER, George.** *Yesterday's Men.* 1983. London. Faber. 1st. F/dj. M25. $25.00

**TURNER, L.W.** *Ninth State: New Hampshire's Formative Years.* 1983. NC U. 1st. 21 maps. 479p. F/dj. M4. $30.00

**TURNER, Mary M.** *Forgotten Leading Ladies of the American Theatre.* 1990. McFarland. 170p. VG. C5. $12.50

**TURNER, Michael.** *King Bear.* 1968. NY. Golden. ils Robert Franenberg. 176p. lib bdg (not xl). VG. D4. $20.00

**TURNER, Philip.** *Sea Peril.* 1968. World. 1st Am. 223p. gold cloth. VG/dj. B36. $13.00

**TURNER, Steven.** *Measure of Dust.* 1970. S&S. 1st. NF/F. T12. $45.00

**TURNER, W.R.** *Old Homes & Families in Nottoway.* 1950. Blackstone. Nottoway. 2nd. 196p. VG. B10. $45.00

**TURNILL, Reginald.** *Jane's Spaceflight Directory, 1987.* 1987. London. Jane's Pub. 3rd. xl. K5. $80.00

**TUROLLA, Pina.** *Beyond the Andes.* 1980. NY. Harper. 1st. 364p. F3. $15.00

**TUROW, Scott.** *Burden of Proof.* 1990. FSG. 1st. NF/dj. A23. $32.00

**TUROW, Scott.** *Laws of Our Fathers.* 1996. FSG. 1st trade. F/dj. W2. $45.00

**TUROW, Scott.** *Pleading Guilty.* 1993. FSG. 1st. F/dj. A23/H11. $25.00

**TUROW, Scott.** *Presumed Innocent.* 1987. FSG. 1st. author's 1st novel. VG/dj. N4. $35.00

**TUROW, Scott.** *Presumed Innocent.* 1987. FSG. 1st. NF/F. H11. $40.00

**TUSTIN, Frances.** *Autism & Childhood Psychosis.* 1972. np. Sci House. 1st. 8vo. 200p. cloth. F/NF. C14. $22.00

**TUTE, George.** *Fleece Press Guide to Art of Wood Engraving.* 1986. Fleece. mini. 1/40 (255 total). w/extra prt. full leather/case. B24. $275.00

**TUTTLE, Dennis.** *Juan Gonzales.* 1995. Chelsea. 1st. sgn Gonzales. F/sans. P8. $85.00

**TUTUOLA, Amos.** *Palm-Wine Drunkard.* 1953. NY. Grove. 1st. NF/dj. Q1. $100.00

**TWEEDDALE.** *Ornithological Works of Arthur, 9th Marquis of Tweeddale.* 1881. London. sm folio. edit/revised RCW Ramsey. 760p. early red cloth. VG. C12. $225.00

**TWEEDIE, W.** *Arabian Horse: His Country & People.* 1961. Los Angeles. Borden. rpt. 4to. 411p. VG/G. O3. $95.00

**TWITCHELL, K.S.** *Saudi Arabia: With Account of Development Natural Resources.* 1953. Princeton. 2nd. ils/48 pl/3 maps. 231p. cloth. VG/dj. Q2. $40.00

**TWITCHELL, Ralph Emerson.** *Old Santa Fe: Story of New Mexico's Ancient Capital.* (1925). Santa Fe Mexican Pub. 1/1000. 488p. gilt fabricoid. D11. $100.00

**TWOMBY, George F.** *All-American Dropout.* 1967. self pub. 1st. VG/dj. P8. $30.00

**TYLER, Ann.** *Celestial Navigations.* 1974. Knopf. 1st. VG/NF. S18. $75.00

**TYLER, Anne.** *Accidental Tourist.* 1985. Chatto Windus. 1st Eng. F/dj. Q1. $50.00

**TYLER, Anne.** *Accidental Tourist.* 1985. Knopf. 1st. F/dj. T10. $65.00

**TYLER, Anne.** *Accidental Tourist.* 1985. NY. Knopf. 1st. inscr to WP Kinsella/dtd 1990. VG/wrp/box. L3. $1,250.00

**TYLER, Anne.** *Breathing Lessons.* 1988. Franklin. 1st. sgn. aeg. emb gr leather. F/swrp. D10. $185.00

**TYLER, Anne.** *Breathing Lessons.* 1988. NY. Knopf. 1st. inscr. F/dj. R14. $125.00

**TYLER, Anne.** *Ladder of Years.* 1995. Knopf. 1st trade. sgn. F/dj. R14. $100.00

**TYLER, Anne.** *Ladder of Years.* 1995. Knopf. 1st. sgn bpl. F/dj. B30. $60.00

**TYLER, Anne.** *Morgan's Passing.* Knopf. 1st. F/clip. M19. $45.00

**TYLER, Anne.** *Saint Maybe.* 1991. Knopf. 1st. sgn tipped-in. F/dj. D10. $85.00

**TYLER, Anne.** *Saint Maybe.* 1991. Knopf. 1st. sgn. F/dj. B30. $60.00

**TYLER, Anne.** *Saint Maybe.* 1991. NY. Random. 1st lg prt. sgn. F/dj. R14. $90.00

**TYLER, Anne.** *Slipping-Down Life.* 1970. Knopf. 1st. F/NF. B2. $250.00

**TYLER, Anne.** *Tumble Tower.* 1993. Orchard Books. 1st. ils Modarressi. F/dj. T11. $40.00

**TYLER, Anne.** *Tumble Tower.* 1993. Orchard Books. 1st. unp. F/dj. C14. $25.00

**TYLER, Anne.** *Visit With Eudora Welty.* 1980. Chicago. Pressworks. 1st. 1/100. F/wrp. Q1. $250.00

**TYLER, Gus.** *Scarcity: A Critque of the American Economy.* 1976. NY. Times. 1st. sgn. VG/dj. S13. $12.00

**TYLER, Homer C.** *Browning .22 Caliber Rifles 1914-1984.* 1985. np. inscr. AN. A19. $65.00

**TYLER, M.C.** *Literary History of the American Revolution.* 1957 (1897). NY. 2 vol. F/dj. M4. $70.00

**TYLER, Parker.** *Classics of the Foreign Film.* 1962. Citadel. 253p. VG. C5. $15.00

**TYRE, Peg.** *Strangers in the Night.* 1994. Crown. 1st. F/dj. G8. $20.00

**TYRON, Thomas.** *Crowned Heads.* 1976. Knopf. 1st. 8vo. 399p. F/NF. W2. $35.00

**TYRON, Thomas.** *Harvest Home.* 1973. Knopf. 1st/3rd prt. 401p. F/dj. W2. $40.00

**TYSON, J.** *Guide to Practical Examination of Urine.* 1888. 6th. ils. VG. E6. $100.00

**TYSON, W.A.** *Revival.* 1925. Cokesbury. 287p. VG. B29. $8.00

**TYTLER, Alex Fraser.** *Elements of General History, Ancient & Modern.* 1818. NY. F Nichols. 8vo. 3 fld maps. 250p. recent full calf. VG. W1. $125.00

U

UBBELOHDE, A.R. *Man & Energy.* 1955. Brazillier. 1st Am. 8vo. VG/dj. A2. $10.00

UCHIDA, Yoshiko. *Hisako's Mysteries.* 1969. Scribner. 1st. 112p. F/dj. D4. $35.00

UCKO, P.J. *Domestication & Exploitation of Plants & Animals.* 1969. London. Duckworth. ils/maps. 581p. VG/wrp. Q2. $20.00

UDALL, Stewart L. *Quiet Crisis.* 1963. HRW. 1st. intro JF Kennedy. 209p. bl cloth. VG/dj. F7. $37.50

UDRY, Janice. *Danny's Pig.* 1960. NY. Lee Shepard. ils Mariana. 32p. cloth. F/NF. D4. $35.00

UEBERHORST, Karl. *Das Wirklich-Komische: Ein Beitrag zur Psychologie...* 1896. Leipzig. Georg Wigand. 562p. contemporary bdg. VG. G1. $125.00

UEBERROTH, Peter. *Made in America.* 1985. Morrow. 1st. NF/dj. W2. $25.00

UHLAN, Edward. *Rogue of Publisher's Row, Confessions of a Publisher.* 1956. NY. Exposition. rpt. 248p. F/VG. O10. $15.00

UHLHORN, Gerhard. *Conflict of Christianity With Heathenism.* 1912. Scribner. 508p. VG. B29. $12.50

ULANOV, Barry. *Duke Ellington.* 1946. Creative Age. 1st. F/NF. B2. $125.00

ULKER, Muhittin. *Torakas Hastaliklari ve Cerrahi Tedavileri.* 1954. Turkey. pres to ils Frank Netter. 396p. worn. G7. $295.00

ULLMAN, J.R. *Age of Mountaineering.* 1954. Phil. 352p. VG. M4. $18.00

ULLMAN, J.R. *Day of Fire.* 1958. World. 1st. NF/dj. M19. $17.50

ULLMAN, James Michael. *Neon Haystack.* 1963. NY. S&S. 1st. F/dj. M15. $45.00

ULLMAN, James Michael. *Venus Trap.* 1966. S&S. 1st. inscr. F/dj. M15. $45.00

ULLMANN, Alex. *Afganistan.* 1991. Ticknor. 1st. author's 1st book. F/F. H11. $20.00

ULLMANN, L. *Changing.* 1977. Knopf. BC. inscr. F/dj. C9. $36.00

ULLRICH & WELCH. *Political Life of American Jewish Women.* 1984. Fresh Meadows. Biblio. 1st. 85p. VG+. A25. $12.00

ULMANN, Doris. *Portrait Gallery of American Editors...* 1925. NY. Wm Rudge. 1/375. prt on watermarked BFK paper. teg. cloth spine/brd. D2. $850.00

ULMANN, Liv. *Changing.* 1977. Knopf. BC. 244p. G/dj. P12. $6.00

ULYANOV, V.I. *Lenin.* 1939. Ogiz, Soviet Union. State Pub House of Political Literature. VG. V4. $125.00

ULYATT, Kenneth. *Longhorn Trail.* 1968. Prentice Hall. 1st. F/NF. M19. $17.50

UMBLE, Diane Zimmerman. *Holding the Line: Telephone in Old Order Mennonite & Amish.* 1996. Johns Hopkins. 1st. F/dj. R8. $20.00

UMFREVILLE, Edward. *Present State of Hudson's Bay...Full Description...* 1770. London. Stalker. 1st. 8vo. 230p. later 3-quarter bl morocco. O1. $1,500.00

UNBEGAUN, B.O. *Selected Papers on Russian & Slavonic Philology.* 1969. Oxford. Clarendon. 8vo. 341p. VG. Q2. $37.00

UNDERHILL, Francis T. *Driving for Pleasure; or, Harness Stable & Its Appointments.* 1987. Appleton. 124 full-p pl. 158p. VG. H10. $185.00

UNDERHILL, Liz. *Lucky Coin.* 1989. Stewart Tabori Chang. 1st. 4to. VG. B17. $13.00

UNDERHILL, Reuben L. *From Cowhides to Golden Fleece: Narrative of California...* 1939. Stanford. 1st. photos. 273p. VG. S14. $50.00

UNDERHILL, Ruth. *Navajos.* 1956. U OK. 1st. 8vo. photos/maps/biblio/index. 299p. brn cloth. VG/dj. F7. $55.00

UNDERHILL, Ruth. *Pueblo Crafts.* 1979. Palmer Lake. Filter Pr. rpt. 139p. yel wrp. P4. $25.00

UNDERWOOD, Larry D. *Custer Fight & Other Tales of the Old West.* 1989. Lincoln, NE. 1st. ils/photos/index. 180p. F/wrp. E1. $25.00

UNDERWOOD, Lucien M. *Our Native Ferns & Their Allies...* 1888. NY. Holt. 1st. 8vo. ils. 156p. VG. H7. $20.00

UNDERWOOD, Michael. *Trout in the Milk.* 1971. Walker. 1st. VG/dj. M20. $15.00

UNDERWOOD, Peter. *Karloff.* 1972. Drake. G+/dj. P3. $25.00

UNDERWOOD, Peter. *Vampire's Bedside Companion.* 1975. London. Leslie Fewin. 1st. VG/dj. L1. $45.00

UNDERWOOD, Tim. *Bare Bones.* 1988. McGraw Hill. 1st. F/NF. P3. $20.00

UNDERWOOD, Tim. *Feast of Fear: Conversations With Stephen King.* 1989. Underwood Miller. 1st. 1/24 pres (600 total). F/dj/case. P3. $150.00

UNDERWOOD, Tim. *Kingdom of Fear.* 1986. Underwood Miller. 1st trade. VG/dj. L1. $55.00

UNDERWOOD & WILLIAMS. *Fishing the Big Three.* 1982. S&S. 1st. photos. VG/dj. P8. $40.00

UNESCO. *Scientific Problems of Humid Tropical Zone Deltas...* 1966. Paris. 422p. VG/dj. A10. $25.00

UNGER, Douglas. *Turkey War.* 1988. Harper Row. 1st. F/NF. R14. $25.00

UNGERER, Miriam. *Too Hot to Cook Book.* 1966. NY. Walker. G/dj. A16. $7.00

UNITED STATES BUREAU OF MINES. *Mineral Facts & Problems.* 1970. WA. Dept Interior. 1291p. cloth. VG. A10. $35.00

UNRUCH, John D. *Plains Across: Overland Emigrants...1840-1860.* 1979. U IL. 565p. VG/dj. J2. $95.00

UNSCHULD, Paul. *Medicine in China: History of Pharmaceutics.* 1986. Berkeley. 1st. 367p. A13. $65.00

UNTERBRINK, Mary. *Jazz Women at the Keyboard.* 1983. Jefferson. McFarland. 1st. NF/wrp. B2. $45.00

UNTERMEYER, Louis. *And Other Poets.* 1916. NY. Holt. 1st. NF/dj. Q1. $150.00

UNTERMEYER, Louis. *Pocket Book of Story Poems.* 1945. NY. Pocket. VG/wrp. M20. $15.00

UNTERMEYER, Louis. *Wonderful Adventures of Paul Bunyan.* 1980. Easton. 8vo. ils. aeg. brn leather. F. B11. $30.00

UNZER, John Augustus. *Principles of Physiology.* 1851. London. Sydenham Soc. 1st Eng-language. 463p. emb gr cloth. VG. G1. $375.00

UPDIKE, John. *Bech Is Back.* 1982. NY. Knopf. 1st. F/dj. Q1. $35.00

UPDIKE, John. *Bech: A Book.* 1970. Knopf. 1st. F/dj. R14. $75.00

UPDIKE, John. *Bech: A Book.* 1970. Knopf. 1st. F/VG+. B30. $50.00

UPDIKE, John. *Brazil.* 1994. Knopf. 1st. rem mk. F/dj. S18. $30.00

UPDIKE, John. *Buchanan Dying.* 1974. Knopf. 1st. author's only play. VG/dj. B30. $40.00

UPDIKE, John. *Carpentered Hen.* 1958. Harper. 1st. 1/2000. author's 1st book. NF/1st issue. L3. $875.00

UPDIKE, John. *Centaur.* 1963. Knopf. 1st. VG/G. B30. $30.00

UPDIKE, John. *Centaur.* 1963. NY. Knopf. 1st. sgn. NF/VG. R14. $250.00

UPDIKE, John. *Child's Calendar.* nd. Knopf. 12 poems. NF. C14. $14.00

**UPDIKE, John.** *Child's Calendar.* 1965. NY. Knopf. 1st. ils Nancy Ekholm Burkert. NF/VG+. S9. $300.00

**UPDIKE, John.** *Collected Poems 1953-1993.* 1993. Knopf. 1st. sgn. F/dj. M25. $50.00

**UPDIKE, John.** *Hugging the Shore.* 1983. NY. Knopf. 1st. NF/dj. R14. $35.00

**UPDIKE, John.** *Just Looking.* 1989. London. Deutsch. 1st Eng. F/dj. R14. $35.00

**UPDIKE, John.** *Marry Me.* 1976. Knopf. 1st. F/F. H11. $25.00

**UPDIKE, John.** *Memories of the Ford Administration.* 1992. Knopf. BC. F/dj. R14. $25.00

**UPDIKE, John.** *Midpoint & Other Poems.* 1969. Knopf. 1st. ils. F/dj. R14. $90.00

**UPDIKE, John.** *Month of Sundays.* 1975. Knopf. 1st. NF/VG clip. R14. $25.00

**UPDIKE, John.** *Museums & Women & Other Stories.* 1972. Knopf. 1st. rem mk. VG/dj. S13. $12.00

**UPDIKE, John.** *Odd Jobs.* 1991. NY. Knopf. 1st. sgn. F/dj. A24. $40.00

**UPDIKE, John.** *On the Farm.* 1965. Knopf. 1st. F/NF. S9. $85.00

**UPDIKE, John.** *Problems & Other Stories.* 1979. Knopf. 1st. sgn. F/NF. R14. $90.00

**UPDIKE, John.** *Rabbit Redux.* 1971. Knopf. 1st. F/NF. H11. $40.00

**UPDIKE, John.** *S.* 1988. Knopf. 1st. F/F. R14. $30.00

**UPDIKE, John.** *S.* 1988. Knopf. 1st. NF/F. H11. $20.00

**UPDIKE, John.** *S.* 1988. London. Deutch. 1st. F/NF. B3. $25.00

**UPDIKE, John.** *Self-Consciousness: Memoirs by John Updike.* 1989. Knopf. 1st. F/F. R14. $30.00

**UPDIKE, John.** *Self-Consciousness: Memoirs by John Updike.* 1989. Knopf. BC. 257p. VG/dj. P12. $10.00

**UPDIKE, John.** *Self-Consciousness: Memoirs by John Updike.* 1989. London. Deutch. 1st. F/NF. B3. $20.00

**UPDIKE, John.** *Six Poems.* 1973. Aloe. 1st. 1/100. sgn. F. L3. $350.00

**UPDIKE, John.** *Telephone Poles & Other Poems.* 1963. NY. Knopf. 1st. NF/VG clip. L3. $50.00

**UPDIKE, John.** *Trust Me.* 1987. Knopf. 1st. sgn. F/dj. M25. $45.00

**UPDIKE, John.** *Witches of Eastwick.* 1984. Knopf. 1st trade. NF/NF. M21. $25.00

**UPDIKE, John.** *Witches of Eastwick.* 1984. Knopf. 1st trade. 307p. NF. W2. $15.00

**UPDIKE, John.** *Witches of Eastwick.* 1984. NY. Knopf. 1st. NF/F. H11. $30.00

**UPFIELD, Arthur.** *Bony & the Black Virgin.* 1959. London. Heinemann. 1st. F/clip. M15. $65.00

**UPFIELD, Arthur.** *Gripped by Drought.* 1990. Missoula. McMillan. 1st Am. F/dj. M15. $65.00

**UPHAM, Elizabeth.** *Little Brown Bear & His Friends.* (1952). NY. Platt Munk. 4to. blk lettered gr cloth. mc pict dj. R5. $85.00

**UPHAM, Thomas C.** *Elements of Intellectual Philosophy.* 1827. Portland, ME. 504p. early patterned mauve cloth. G1. $450.00

**UPHAM, Thomas C.** *Elements of Intellectual Philosophy.* 1828. Portland, ME. Shirley Hyde. 2nd. 576p. contemporary calf. G1. $125.00

**UPHAM, Thomas C.** *Elements of Mental Philosophy.* 1831. Portland, ME. Wm Hyde. 2 vol. cloth-backed brd/paper spine. G1. $325.00

**UPHAM, Thomas C.** *Philosophical & Practical Treatise on the Will.* 1834. Portland, ME. 400p. contemporary quarter leather/ marbled brd. G1. $250.00

**UPHOF, J.C.** *Dictionary of Economic Plants.* 1968. NY. Cramer. 2nd. 591p. xl. A10. $45.00

**UPSHUR, John Andrew.** *Upshur Family in Virginia.* 1955. Dietz. 1st. photos/fld map/charts. 221p. B10. $75.00

**UPSON, William Hazlett.** *Original Letters of Alexander Botts.* 1963. Middlebury, VT. sgn. unp. thick wrp. H7. $30.00

**UPTON, Bertha.** *Adventures of Two Dutch Dolls.* 1898. Longman Gr. 1st. 29 mc pl. pict brd/cloth spine. VG. D1. $350.00

**UPTON, Emory.** *Armies of Asia & Europe: Embracing Offical Reports...* 1878. NY. Appleton. 1st. 8vo. 446p. cloth. W1. $175.00

**UPTON, Harriet Taylor.** *History of the Western Reserve.* 1910. Chicago. 1st. 3 vol. 1874p. rb buckram. VG. B18. $225.00

**UPTON, W.T.** *Art Song in America.* 1930. Boston. 1st. VG/G. B5. $30.00

**URBAN, J.** *Battlefield & Prison Pen: A Prisoner in Rebel Dungeons.* 1882. 1st. VG. E6. $50.00

**URBAN, Martin.** *Emil Nolde Landscapes.* 1970. Praeger. 1st Am. ils/pl. NF/clip. T11. $145.00

**URIS, Leon.** *Battle Cry.* 1953. London. Wingate. 1st. author's 1st book. VG+/dj. A24. $95.00

**URIS, Leon.** *Battle Cry.* 1953. Putnam. 1st/2nd prt. NF/VG. M19. $75.00

**URIS, Leon.** *Haj.* 1984. Franklin Center. ltd 1st. sgn. full leather. F. Q1. $75.00

**URIS, Leon.** *Mitla Pass.* 1988. NY. Doubleday. 1st. F/dj. T12. $40.00

**URIS, Leon.** *Trinity.* 1976. Doubleday. 1st. F/dj. M25. $25.00

**URIS, Leon.** *Trinity.* 1976. Doubleday. 1st. VG/dj. S13. $18.00

**URNESS, Carol.** *Naturalist in Russia: Letters From Peter Pallas...* 1967. U MN. 189p. xl. VG. S5. $15.00

**URQUHART, Beryl Leslie.** *Camelias.* ca 1956. Princeton. ils. VG/dj. B26. $20.00

**URQUHART, Jane.** *Changing Heaven.* 1990. Toronto. McClelland Stewart. 1st. F/F. B3. $35.00

**URQUHART, Jane.** *Whirlpool.* 1989. S&S. 1st. sgn. F/F. B3. $60.00

**URREA, Luis Alberto.** *In Search of Snow.* 1994. Harper Collins. 1st. author's 1st novel. rem mk. F/F. H11. $25.00

**URTON, Gary.** *At the Crossroads of the Earth & the Sky.* 1981. Austin. 8vo. 248p. VG/dj. K5. $30.00

**URWICK, W.** *India Illustrated With Pen & Pencil.* 1891. NY. Hurst. 198p. aeg. VG. H7. $45.00

**URWIN, Greogory J.W.** *Custer Victorious: Civil War Battles...* 1983. East, NJ. 1st. ils. 308p. F/dj. E1. $45.00

**US POSTAL SERVICE.** *Birds & Flowers of the Fifty States: A Collection...* 1982. WA. obl 4to. 60p. F/dj. M4. $35.00

**USHER, Ethel.** *Food for Gourmets.* 1940. New Orleans. 1/1000. VG. E6. $75.00

**UTAMARO.** *Songs of the Garden.* 1984. Metropolitan Mus Art. ils. VG/box. R8. $50.00

**UTLEY, Robert M.** *Billy the Kid: Short & Violent Life.* 1989. NE U. 1st. VG/dj. M20. $40.00

**UTLEY, Robert M.** *Fort Union & the Santa Fe Trail.* 1989. El Passo, TX. TX Western U. VG. A19. $30.00

**UTLEY, Robert M.** *Indian Frontier of the American West 1846-1890.* 1984. NM. 1st. 325p. E1. $55.00

**UTTLEY, Alison.** *Little Grey Rabbit & the Snow Baby.* 1973. London. Collins. 8vo. ils Katherine Wiggleworth. VG. B36. $25.00

**UYTTENBROECK, F.** *Past & Present of Radical Surgery & Gynaecological...* 1987. Leuven. 529p. A13. $30.00

VACHSS, Andrew. *Batman: The Ultimate Evil.* 1995. Warner. 1st. sgn. AN/dj. S18. $40.00

VACHSS, Andrew. *Blossom.* 1990. Knopf. 1st. NF/dj. N4. $25.00

VACHSS, Andrew. *Blossom.* 1990. Knopf. 1st. sgn. rem mk. F/dj. S18. $45.00

VACHSS, Andrew. *Blossom.* 1990. Knopf. 1st. VG/VG. P3. $18.00

VACHSS, Andrew. *Blue Belle.* 1988. Knopf. 1st. F/dj. M21. $20.00

VACHSS, Andrew. *Blue Belle.* 1988. Knopf. 1st. VG/dj. G8. $15.00

VACHSS, Andrew. *Flood.* 1985. DIF. 1st. author's 1st book. F/NF. H11. $45.00

VACHSS, Andrew. *Flood.* 1985. DIF. 1st. author's 1st book. F/VG. M19. $25.00

VACHSS, Andrew. *Footsteps of the Hawk.* 1995. Knopf. 1st. sgn. F/dj. S18. $35.00

VACHSS, Andrew. *Hard Candy.* 1989. Knopf. 1st. F/dj. R14. $45.00

VACHSS, Andrew. *Strega.* 1987. Knopf. 1st. author's 2nd book. F/F. H11. $40.00

VACHSS, Andrew. *Strega.* 1987. Knopf. 1st. rem mk. F/dj. M19. $17.50

VACHSS, Andrew. *Strega.* 1987. Knopf. 1st. sgn. author's 2nd novel. NF/VG. S18. $45.00

VACHSS, Andrew. *Strega.* 1987. Knopf. 1st. author's 2nd book. VG/VG. B3. $15.00

VAKA, D. *Unveiled Ladies of Stamboul.* 1971 (1923). NY. 23 pl. 261p. cloth. VG. Q2. $24.00

VALE, Robert B. *Wings, Fur & Shot: Grass-Roots Guide to American Hunting.* 1936. NY. Stackpole. ils/mc ftspc. lacks ffe. G. H10. $12.50

VALENTINE, A. *Lord North.* 1967. OK U. 2 vol. 1st. F/case. M4. $55.00

VALIN, Jonathan. *Natural Causes.* 1983. Congdon. 1st. NF/dj. G8. $30.00

VALIN, Jonathan. *Second Chance.* 1991. Delacorte. 1st. F/F. H11. $20.00

VALK, Francis. *Lectures on Errors of Refraction & Their Correction...* 1893. NY. Putnam. 3rd. 257p. VG. H7. $22.50

VALLANCE, Aymer. *William Morris: His Art, His Writings & His Public Life.* 1986. London. The Studio. 4to. ils. 462p. NF/dj. M10. $35.00

VALLDEJUKI, C. *Puerto Rican Cookery.* 1981 (1975). self pub. F/VG. E6. $15.00

VALLEE, Rudy. *My Time Is Your Time: Rudy Vallee Story.* 1962. NY. ils. VG/dj. M17. $20.00

VALLEJO & VALLEJO. *Ladies Retold Tales of Goddesses & Heroines.* 1992. Penguin. Nf/dj. A28. $25.00

VALSECCHI, Ambrogio. *Controversy: Birth Control Debate 1968.* 1968. WA. 1st Eng trans. 235p. A13. $25.00

VAN ALLSBURG, Chris. *Ben's Dream.* 1982. Houghton Mifflin. 1st. F/clip. B4. $350.00

VAN ALLSBURG, Chris. *Just a Dream.* 1990. Houghton Mifflin. 1st. sgn pres. tall 4to. cloth backed brd/mc pict dj. R5. $100.00

VAN ALLSBURG, Chris. *Just a Dream.* 1990. Houghton Mifflin. 1st. 48p. F/VG. P2. $45.00

VAN ALLSBURG, Chris. *Polar Express.* 1985. Houghton Mifflin. 1st. obl 4to. wine-red cloth. mc pict dj. R5. $500.00

VAN ALLSBURG, Chris. *Stranger.* 1986. Houghton Mifflin. 1st. ils. 32p. cloth. F/NF. D4. $95.00

VAN ALLSBURG, Chris. *Stranger.* 1986. Houghton MIfflin. 1st. sgn. dk bl cloth. mc pict dj. R5. $175.00

VAN ALLSBURG, Chris. *Two Bad Ants.* 1988. Houghton Mifflin. rpt. folio. ils. VG/dj. B17. $11.00

VAN ALLSBURG, Chris. *Z Was Zapped.* 1987. Houghton Mifflin. 1st. ils. F/dj. D1. $85.00

VAN ALLSBURG, Chris. *Z Was Zapped.* 1987. Houghton Mifflin. 1st. 56p. F/NF. D4. $40.00

VAN ANGLEN, K.P. *New England's Milton: Literary Reception & Cultural...* 1993. PA State. 255p. NF/dj. M10. $15.00

VAN ASH, Cay. *Fires of Fu Manchu.* 1987. Harper Row. 1st. F/F. H11. $30.00

VAN AVER, Philip. *Mother Goose. Twenty Nursery Rhymes...* 1970. Grabhorn-Hoyem. 1/300. 4to. ils. teg. Courtland Benson bdg. F/box. B24. $3,000.00

VAN BIBBER, Jack. *Fast Feasts: A Cookbook for Huried Gourmets.* 1964. Avenel. VG/dj. M20. $14.00

VAN BRUGGEN, Theodore. *Vascular Plants of South Dakota.* 1985. Ames. 2nd. maps/photos. 476p. sc. F. B26. $22.00

VAN CLEVE, Charlotte O. *Three Score Years & Ten: Long-Life Memories of Ft Snelling.* (1888). Minneapolis. 1st. 176p. F. E1. $100.00

VAN DAAL, Gert. *Marmerpapier (Marbled Papers).* 1980. Buren, Netherlands. Frits Knuf. 1/55. sgn. folio. 72p. F/case. B24. $1,000.00

VAN DE BOE, Louis. *Planning & Planting Your Own Place.* 1947 (1938). NY. 290p. B26. $15.00

VAN DE KAMP & VYSSOTSKY. *Study of Proper Motions of 18,000 Stars...* 1937. Charlottesville. 246p. G. K5. $40.00

VAN DE POLL, Willem. *Surinam: Country & Its People.* 1951. Hague, Netherlands. 1st. ils/map ep. 199p. F3. $15.00

VAN DE WATER, Frederic F. *Glory-Hunter: Life of General Custer.* (1934). Indianapolis. 1st. 394p. cloth. VG. M8. $85.00

VAN DE WATER, Frederic F. *Glory-Hunter: Life of General Custer.* 1934. Bobbs Merrill. xl. G. A19. $75.00

VAN DE WETERING, Janwillem. *Butterfly Hunter.* 1982. Houghton Mifflin. 1st. NF/F. H11. $20.00

VAN DE WETERING, Janwillem. *Just a Corpse at Twilight.* 1994. Soho. 1st. F/dj. R8. $15.00

VAN DE WETERING, Janwillem. *Mangrove Mama.* 1995. Tucson. McMillan. 1st. F/dj. M15. $30.00

VAN DE WETERING, Janwillem. *Outsider in Amsterdam.* 1975. Houghton Mifflin. 1st. VG/dj. A24. $55.00

VAN DEN HOEK, C. *Revision of the European Species of Cladophora.* 1963. Leiden. Brill. 55 pl. 248p. xl. VG. A10. $25.00

VAN DER KROGT. *Old Globes in the Netherlands: A Catalogue...* 1984. 4to. 290p. F/F. A4. $95.00

VAN DER MEER, Ron. *Brain Pack.* nd. Running Pr. 4to. popups. F. B17. $15.00

VAN DER MEER, Ron. *Majesty in Flight, Nature's Birds of Prey.* 1984. Abbeville. 1st. 4to. popups/ils Ivan Lapper. VG. B17. $20.00

VAN DER MEER, Ron. *3-D Tour Through Math.* 1994. Scribner. 1st. folio. F. B17. $35.00

VAN DER MEULEN, D. *Wells of Ibn Sa'ud.* 1957. London. Murray. ils. cloth. VG/dj. Q2. $47.00

VAN DER SPUY, Uha. *Ornamental Shrubs & Trees for Gardens in Southern Africa.* 1971 (1954). Cape Town. 2nd. ils. 254p. B26. $24.00

VAN DEURS, George. *Anchors in the Sky.* 1978. San Rafael. 1st. ils. 246p. Vg/dj. B18. $15.00

VAN DEUSEN, Elizabeth K. *Tales of Borinquen (Porto Rico).* 1928. NY. photos. VG. M17. $25.00

VAN DIEMERBROECK, Ysbrand. *Opera Omnia Anatomica et Medica.* 1685. Utrecht. 1st collected. 16 fld pl/lacks ftspc. full vellum. G7. $995.00

**VAN DINE, S.S.** *Bishop Murder Case: A Philo Vance Story.* 1929. Scribner. 1st. 8vo. blk cloth. R3. $125.00

**VAN DINE, S.S.** *Canary Murder Case: A Philo Vance Story.* 1927. Scribner. 1st. author's 2nd book. gr-lettered blk cloth. F/dj. R3. $375.00

**VAN DINE, S.S.** *Garden Murder Case.* 1935. Scribner. 1st. VG/G. B5. $70.00

**VAN DOLSEN, Nancy.** *Cumberland County, an Architectural Survey.* 1990. Cumberland Hist Soc. 1st. F/dj. R8. $40.00

**VAN DOREN, Carl.** *Secret History of the American Revolution.* 1941. Garden City. 533p. VG. M4. $18.00

**VAN DOREN, Carl.** *Secret History of the American Revolution.* 1941. Viking. 1st trade. NF/VG clip. T11. $45.00

**VAN DOREN, Carl.** *Secret History of the American Revolution.* 1941. Viking. 1st trade. sgn. VG/dj. M20. $50.00

**VAN DOREN, Mark.** *Noble Voice: A Study of Ten Great Poems.* nd. Holt. 1st. VG/dj. O4. $15.00

**VAN DRUTEN, John.** *I Am a Camera.* 1952. Random. 1st. VG/dj. A24. $35.00

**VAN DUSEN, A.E.** *Connecticut.* 1961. NY. 1st. ils. 470p. F/dj. M4. $35.00

**VAN DUYN, Mona.** *If It Be Not I: Collected Poems 1959-1982.* 1993. Knopf. 1st. sgn. F/dj. R14. $45.00

**VAN DYK, Jere.** *In Afghanistan: American Odyssey.* 1983. NY. Coward McCann. 1st. 8vo. ils. NF/dj. W1. $20.00

**VAN DYKE, Henry.** *Grand Canyon & Other Poems.* 1914. Scribner. 1st. gilt bdg. NF. B14. $99.00

**VAN DYKE, Henry.** *Grand Canyon & Other Poems.* 1914. Scribner. 1st. 8vo. teg. 78p. gilt gr cloth. VG. F7. $35.00

**VAN DYKE, Henry.** *Little Rivers: Book of Essays in Profitable Idleness.* 1920. Scribner. 2 vol. 1st trade. ftspc ils NC Wyeth. teg. bl cloth. R3. $75.00

**VAN DYKE, Henry.** *Lost Boy.* 1914. Harper. 1st. thin 8vo. ils. emb stp ffe. gr cloth. R3. $100.00

**VAN DYKE, Henry.** *Mansion.* 1911. NY. Harper. ils Elizabeth Shippen Green. 61p. G. G11. $8.00

**VAN DYKE, Henry.** *Out-of-Doors in Holy Land, Unknown Quantity/Ruling Passion.* 1927. Scribner. Syvanora ed. 3 vol. G. B29. $26.00

**VAN DYKE, Henry.** *Out-of-Doors in the Holy Land: Impressions of Travel...* 1909. Scribner. 3rd. 325p. teg. cloth. VG. W1. $10.00

**VAN DYKE, Henry.** *Story of the Other Wise Man.* 1906. Harper. 1st thus. teg. cream cloth. VG-. A24. $20.00

**VAN DYKE, Henry.** *Works of...* 1920. Scribner. 18 vol. 1/504. Autograph Ed. sgn author/pub. NF. R3. $385.00

**VAN DYKE, Theodore S.** *Southern California: Its Valleys, Hills & Streams...* 1886. NY. Fords Howard Hulbert. 1st. 8vo. VG. H7. $60.00

**VAN DYNE, Edith.** *Aunt Jane's Nieces on the Ranch.* 1913. Reilly Britton. 1st. 8vo. 376p. G. H7. $20.00

**VAN DYNE, Edith.** *Flying Girl.* 1911. Chicago. Reilly Britton. 1st. ils. 232p. G. B5. $125.00

**VAN DYNE, George M.** *Ecosystem Concept in Natural Resource Management.* 1969. Academic. 383p. xl. VG. S5. $22.50

**VAN EPPS, Margaret T.** *Nancy Pembroke, Senior (#7).* 1931. NY. AL Burt. 1st. lists to this title. VG/dj. M20. $40.00

**VAN ESS, John.** *Meet the Arab.* 1947. London. Mus Pr. ils. 228p. cloth. G. Q2. $30.00

**VAN EVERY, D.** *Forth to the Wilderness: First American Frontier...* 1977. NY. 369p. F. M4. $25.00

**VAN GIESON, Judith.** *Lies That Bind.* 1993. Harper Row. 1st. F/dj. G8. $30.00

**VAN GIESON, Judith.** *Parrot Blues.* 1995. Harper Collins. 1st. F/F. H11. $25.00

**VAN GIESON, Judith.** *Wolf Path.* 1992. Harper Collins. 1st. sgn. rem mk. F/dj. R14. $45.00

**VAN GULIK, Robert.** *Chinese Maze Murders.* 1962. London. Michael Joseph. 1st. VG/dj. M15. $65.00

**VAN GULIK, Robert.** *Given Day.* 1984. San Antonio. McMillan. 1st Am. 1/300. sgn. F/dj. M15. $75.00

**VAN GULIK, Robert.** *Monkey & the Tiger.* 1965. London. Heinemann. 1st Eng. F/NF. M15. $150.00

**VAN GULIK, Robert.** *Poets & Murder.* 1968. Scribner. 1st. NF/dj. N4. $65.00

**VAN HORNE, John C.** *Correspondence of William Nelson...Governor of VA 1770-71.* 1975. U VA. 176p. VG. B10. $35.00

**VAN HOSEN, W.H.** *Early Taverns & Stagecoach Days in New Jersey.* 1976. Cranbury. 184p. F/dj. M4. $20.00

**VAN LAER, A.J.F.** *Van Rensselaer Bowler Manuscripts...1630-1643.* 1908. Albany. NY State Lib Vol 2. 909p. G. B18. $37.50

**VAN LAWICK, Hugh.** *Solo.* 1974. Boston. ils. 159p. NF. S15. $10.00

**VAN LOAN, Charles.** *Score by Innings.* 1919. Doran. VG/G. P8. $60.00

**VAN LOAN, Sharon.** *Thyme & the River Too.* 1993. Graphic Arts Center. 1st. sm 4to. recipes. F/dj. S14. $26.00

**VAN LOON, Hendirk Willem.** *Thomas Jefferson.* 1943. Dodd Mead. 1st. 106p. xl. G+/fair. B10. $15.00

**VAN LOON, Hendrik Willem.** *Last of the Troubadours.* 1939. S&S. 96p. G/dj. C5. $15.00

**VAN LOON, Hendrik Willem.** *Tolerence.* 1925. NY. 3rd. VG. M17. $15.00

**VAN LUSTBADER, Eric.** *Miko.* 1984. Villard. 1st. NF/dj. M21. $15.00

**VAN LUSTBADER, Eric.** *Sunset Warrior.* 1990. Wallington, UK. Severn. 1st. NF/dj. M21. $20.00

**VAN NIMMEN, Jane.** *NASA Historical Data Book.* NASA. 3 vol. cloth. xl. K5. $150.00

**VAN NORMAN, Richard W.** *Experimental Biology.* 1971. Prentice Hall. 269p. xl. VG. S5. $10.00

**VAN RAKOCZI, Basil.** *Foreseeing the Future.* 1973. NY. Castle. 128p. VG/dj. B11. $15.00

**VAN RENSSELAER, Stephen.** *Checklist of Early American Bottles & Flasks.* 1921. NY. 109p+18 blank pages. G+/wrp. B18. $35.00

**VAN RIPER, Gurnsey.** *Behind the Plate: Three Great Catchers.* 1973. Garrard. 1st. ils Jack Hearne. F. P8. $25.00

**VAN ROYEN, P.** *Podostemaceae of the New World.* 1951. Bergen. Harte. 16 pl. 151p. A10. $55.00

**VAN SLINGELAND, Peter.** *Something Terrible Has Happened.* c 1966. Harper Row. 8vo. ils/map ep. blk cloth. VG/dj. P4. $30.00

**VAN STOCKUM, Hilda.** *Friendly Gables.* 1960. Viking. 1st. 8vo. 186p. VG/dj. T5. $25.00

**VAN TYNE, C.H.** *Loyalists in the American Revolution.* 1970 (1929). NY. rpt. 360p. F. M4. $15.00

**VAN VECHTEN, Carl.** *Red: Papers on Musical Subjects.* 1925. NY. VG. M17. $20.00

**VAN VEEN, Ted.** *Rhodendrons in America.* 1969. Portland. 1st. sgn. 176p. dj. B26. $25.00

**VAN VORST, Marie.** *His Love Story.* 1913. Bobbs Merrill. 1st. ils Howard Chandler Christy. 285p. G. G11. $8.00

**VAN WORMER, Joe.** *World of the Black Bear.* 1966. Phil. 163p. F/dj. A19. $15.00

**VAN WORMER, Laura.** *Jury Duty.* 1996. Mira. sgn. VG/dj. R8. $10.00

**VANCE, Jack.** *Araminta Station.* 1988. London. NEL. 1st. F/dj. T2. $25.00

**VANCE, Jack.** *Big Planet.* 1978. Underwood Miller. 1st hc. F/dj. T2. $30.00

**VANCE, Jack.** *Brave Free Men.* 1983. Underwood Miller. 1st hc. F/dj. T2. $25.00

**VANCE, Jack.** *Cugel's Saga.* 1984. Underwood Miller. 1/500. sgn. F/dj/case. T2. $75.00

**VANCE, Jack.** *Face.* 1980. Underwood Miller. 1st. AN/sans. M21. $30.00

**VANCE, Jack.** *Five Gold Bands.* 1993. Underwood Miller. rpt of The Space Pirate. F/NF. G10. $24.00

**VANCE, Jack.** *Killing Machine.* 1978. NY. Daw. VG/wrp. M20. $15.00

**VANCE, Jack.** *Maske: Thaery.* 1976. Berkley Putnam. 1st. sgn. F/dj. T2. $35.00

**VANCE, Laurence M.** *Outer Side of Calvinism.* 1991. Vance. 475p. AN/wrp. B29. $12.75

**VANCE, William.** *Homicide Lost.* 1956. NY. Graphic. VG/wrp. M20. $15.00

**VANCOUVER, George.** *Voyage of Discovery to North Pacific Ocean & Round World...* 1984. London. Hakluyt Soc. 1st annotated. 8vo. fld ils/10 maps. bl cloth. F. O1. $175.00

**VANDEN BERGH, Leonard John.** *On the Trail of the Pigmies: Anthropological Exploration...* 1921. NY. James McCann. sgn pres. 264p. gilt gr cloth. VG. H7. $50.00

**VANDERBILT, Harold S.** *Enterprise: Story of Defense of America's Cup in 1930.* 1931. NY. 1st. ils. 230p. VG. B5. $100.00

**VANDERBUILT, Gloria.** *Once Upon a Time: A True Story.* 1985. Knopf. 1st. 301p. VG/dj. P12. $10.00

**VANDERCOOK, Margaret.** *Campfire Girls on the Edge of the Desert (#7).* 1917. Phil. Winston. lists to #14. VG/dj. M20. $25.00

**VANDERCOOK, Margaret.** *Ranch Girls' Pot of Gold (#2).* 1912. Phil. Winston. lists 3 titles. VG/dj. M20. $22.00

**VANDERHAEGHE, Guy.** *Homesick.* 1989. Toronto. McClelland Stewart. 1st Canadian. F/NF. B3. $40.00

**VANDERWALKER, F.N.** *Mixing of Colors & Plants.* 1939. Frederick Drake. 1st. ils. VG/dj. B27. $55.00

**VANDERWOOD, Paul.** *Border Fury.* 1988. Albuquerque. 1st. obl 4to. 293p. dj. F3. $20.00

**VANDIVEER, Clarence A.** *Fur-Trade & Early Western Exploration.* 1971. Coopers Sq Pub. 1st. ils. AN. J2. $92.00

**VANDIVER, Frank E.** *Their Tattered Flags: Epic of the Confederacy.* 1970. Harper Row. 1st. NF/dj. A14. $28.00

**VANSITTART, Peter.** *In the Fifties.* 1995. London. 1st. dj. T9. $15.00

**VANTIUS, Sebastian.** *Tractatus de Nullitatibus Processuum ac Sententiarum...* 1588. Cologne. Joannem Gymnicum. 8vo. contemporary vellum. K1. $375.00

**VARCHI, Benedetto.** *La Prima Parte Delle Lezzioni di M Benedetto Varchi.* 1560-1561. Florence. Apresso I Giuti. 2 vol in 1. early vellum. K1. $600.00

**VARGA.** *Esquire Years.* 1987. NY. F/VG. P13. $50.00

**VARGAS LLOSA, Mario.** *Time of the Hero.* 1967. London. 1st. trans L Kemp. dj. T9. $42.00

**VASARINSH, P.** *Clinical Dermatology: Diagnosis & Therapy of Common Skin...* nd (1982). Boston. Butterworths. 8vo. 744p. leatherette. NF/VG. C14. $22.00

**VASEY, George.** *Grasses of the Southwest.* 1891. GPO. USDA. ils. xl. A10. $75.00

**VASILIEV, A.A.** *Histoire de l'Empire Byzantin.* 1932. Paris. Picard. 2 vol. 8vo. ils/pl/tables. quarter morocco. G. Q2. $125.00

**VASSOS, John.** *Dogs Are Like That.* 1941. NY. 1st. photos. G. A17. $10.00

**VAUGHAN, Beatrice.** *Ladies Aid Cookbook.* 1971. VG/VG. E6. $13.00

**VAUGHAN, Beatrice.** *Old Cook's Almanac.* 1966. Gramercy. G/dj. A16. $17.50

**VAUGHAN, H.W.** *Types & Market Classes of Livestock.* 1937. Columbus. Adams. 574p. cloth. VG. A10. $20.00.

**VAUGHAN, Henry.** *Sacred Poems.* 1847. London. Pickering. bl polished calf/raised bands/red labels. VG. S17. $45.00

**VAUGHAN-THOMAS, W.** *Anzio: Massacre at the Beachhead.* 1961. NY. 1st. 243p. VG/torn. S16. $20.00

**VAUGHN, Elizabeth Dewberry.** *Many Things Have Happened Since He Died.* 1990. Doubleday. 1st. sgn. F/NF. M23. $40.00

**VAUGHT, L.A.** *Vaught's Practical Character Reader.* 1907 (1902). Chicago. Vaught-Racine Pub. 258p. H6. $58.00

**VAURIE, C.** *Tibet & Its Birds.* 1972. London. Witherby. 1st. F/dj. C12. $200.00

**VAVRA, Robert.** *Lion & Blue.* 1974. Morrow. 1st. VG+/clip. C14. $20.00

**VAZQUEZ, Pedro Ramirez.** *National Museum of Anthropology, Mexico.* 1968. Abrams. ils/pl. 257p. gilt wht cloth. F/VG. F1. $30.00

**VECSEY, George.** *Joy in Mudville.* 1970. McCall. BC. VG/G. P8. $15.00

**VELAZQUEZ DE VELASCO, Luis J.** *Ensayo Sobre Los Alphabetes de Las Lettras Desconocidas...* 1752. Madrid. Antonio Sanz. 1st. 4to. 20 copper pl. mottled calf. K1. $500.00

**VENABLES, Bernard.** *Baleia. Baleia.* 1969. NY. 204p. VG. S15. $10.00

**VENABLES, Hubert.** *Frankenstein Diaries.* 1980. NY. Viking. 1st. VG/dj. L1. $50.00

**VENABLES, Hubert.** *Frankenstein Diaries.* 1980. Viking. 1st. 8vo. 120p. VG/clip. C14. $28.00

**VERBRUGGE, Martha.** *Able-Bodied Womanhood: Personal Health & Social Change...* 1988. NY. 1st. 297p. A13. $27.50

**VERDELLE, A.J.** *Good Negress.* 1995. Algonquin. 1st. F/dj. M23. $40.00

**VERDELLE, A.J.** *Good Negress.* 1995. Chapel Hill. 1st. sgn. author's 1st novel. F/dj. A24. $60.00

**VERGARA, Ismael Valdes.** *El Cuerpo de Bomberos de Santiago 1863-1900.* 1900. Valparasio. 8vo. ils. 692p. 3-quarter leather. B11. $100.00

**VERKAMP, Margaret M.** *History of Grand Canyon National Park.* 1993. Flagstaff. Grand Canyon Pioneers Soc. 1st. 57p. AN/stiff wrp. F7. $8.00

**VERKLER & ZEMPEL.** *First Editions: A Guide to Identification Statements...* 1984. Peoria. 1st. 231p. NF/VG. M8. $30.00

**VERMANDEL, Janet Gregory.** *Dine With the Devil.* 1970. Dodd Mead. 1st. F/F. H11. $25.00

**VERNBERG & VERNBERG.** *Animal & Environment.* 1970. HRW. 398p. xl. VG. S5. $12.00

**VERNBERG & VERNBERG.** *Environmental Physiology of Marine Animals.* 1972. Springer. 346p. xl. VG. S5. $20.00

**VERNE, Henry.** *Bob Moran & the Sunken Gallery.* nd. Roy Pub. lists to Bucaneer's Hoard. 159p. xl. VG. B36. $10.00

**VERNE, Jules.** *American Gun Club.* 1874. Scribner. 1st. ils. 142p. burnt orange bdg. B18. $150.00

**VERNE, Jules.** *From the Earth to the Moon.* 1918. Scribner. 8vo. 323p. ils cloth. K5. $35.00

**VERNE, Jules.** *Journey to the North Pole.* 1875. London. Routledge. 1st. ils Riou. G+. M20. $55.00

**VERNE, Jules.** *Lighthouse at the End of the World.* 1924. NY. G Howard Watt. 1st Am. 248p. rem bdg w/G&D imp. VG/fair G&D. H1. $27.50

**VERNE, Jules.** *Robur the Conqueror.* 1951. Didier. intro DeSeversky. VG/G. M17. $40.00

**VERNE, Jules.** *Twenty-Thousand Leagues Under the Sea.* 1956. NY. Heritage. 1st thus. quarter cloth. F/sans/F case. T11. $30.00

**VERNON, Arthur.** *History & Romance of the Horse.* 1930. Boston. 1st. ils/index. 525p. NF/dj. A17. $20.00

**VERRIER, E.** *Practical Manual of Obstetrics.* 1884. NY. Wm Wood. 1st Am. ils. 395p. VG+. H7. $30.00

**VERRILL, A. Hyatt.** *My Jungle Trails: Narrative of Adventures in Jungles...* 1937. Boston. Page. 1st. photos. 329p. F3. $45.00

**VERRILL, A. Hyatt.** *Old Civilizations of the New World.* 1943. NY. Home Lib. 393p. dj. F3. $15.00

**VERRILL & VERRILL.** *America's Ancient Civilizations.* 1953. Putnam. 334p. F3. $15.00

**VESEY, Elizabeth.** *Conversations of the Bas Bleu.* 1977. Harvard/Stinehour. 1/250. tall 4to. 75p. F/acetate. H13. $95.00

**VESS, David.** *Medical Revolution in France 1789-96.* 1975. Gainesville. F. 216p. A13. $30.00

**VESTAL, Stanley.** *Kit Carson: Happy Warrior of the Old West.* 1928. Houghton Mifflin. G/dj. A19. $50.00

**VESTAL, Stanley.** *Missouri.* 1945. NY. Rivers of Am. ils. G. M4. $25.00

**VESTER, Bertha Spafford.** *Flowers of the Holy Land.* 1962. Hallmark. 1st. ils. 63p. VG/torn. W1. $14.00

**VESTER, Bertha Spafford.** *Our Jerusalem: An American Family in Holy City 1881-1949.* 1951. London. Evans. 8vo. 366p. cloth. VG. Q2. $55.00

**VETH, Anne Cornelis.** *Comic Art in England.* ca 1930. np (Menno Hertzberger). folio. ils/56 pl. 206p. bl cloth. K1. $125.00

**VETSCH, Earnest.** *New Story of Little Black Sambo.* 1926. Whitman. 16mo. ils Clara Bell Thurston. bl-gray brd. pict dj. R5. $285.00

**VETTER, Charles Edmund.** *Sherman: Merchant of Terror, Advocate of Peace.* 1992. Pelican. 1st. NF/dj. A14. $21.00

**VEXLER, R.I.** *Chronology & Documentary Handbook of State of New Hampshire.* 1979. Dobbs Ferry. 148p. F. M4. $12.00

**VICKERS, Hugo.** *Cecil Beaton.* 1985. Little Brn. 1st. photos. 656p. F/dj. S14. $20.00

**VICKERS, Hugo.** *Vivien Leigh.* 1988. London. Hamish. 1st. F/dj. T12. $40.00

**VICKERS, Roy.** *Maid to Murder.* 1950. Mill. 1st. F/NF. M19. $17.50

**VICKERS, Roy.** *Seven Chose Murder.* 1959. London. Faber. 1st. F/dj. M15. $100.00

**VICKERS, Roy.** *Sole Survivor & the Kynsard Affair.* 1952. London. Gollancz. 1st. F/dj. N15. $75.00

**VICKERY, Oliver.** *Harbor Heritage.* 1979. Mt View. Morgan. sgn. F/NF. B9. $35.00

**VICTOR, Mel.** *Marina Polvay's Best International Recipes.* 1979. Miami. Argo. G. A16. $10.00

**VICTORIUS, Petrus the Elder.** *Variarum l Ectionum Libri XXV.* 1553. Florence. Laurentius Torrentinus. 1st. folio. 140p. later ep. K1. $500.00

**VIDAL, Gore.** *An Evening With Richard Nixon.* 1972. Random. 1st. NF/dj. B30. $30.00

**VIDAL, Gore.** *At Home, Essays 1982-88.* 1988. NY. 1st. dj. T9. $10.00

**VIDAL, Gore.** *Creation.* 1981. NY. 1st. VG/dj. T9. $15.00

**VIDAL, Gore.** *Creation.* 1981. Random. 1st. F/dj. M23. $25.00

**VIDAL, Gore.** *Hollywood.* 1990. Random. 1st. F/F. B3. $25.00

**VIDAL, Gore.** *Julian.* 1964. Little Brn. 1st. VG/dj. R14. $25.00

**VIDAL, Gore.** *Lincoln.* 1984. Random. 1st. F/F. B30. $25.00

**VIDAL, Gore.** *Messiah.* 1980. Gregg. 1st. VG/dj. B30. $27.50

**VIDAL, Gore.** *Palimpsest: A Memoir.* 1995. Random. 1st. F/F. T12. $40.00

**VIDAL, Gore.** *Thirsty Evil.* 1981. SF. Gay Sunshine. 1/100. sgn. F/acetate dj. R14. $125.00

**VIDAL, Gore.** *Williwaw.* 1946. Dutton. 1st. author's 1st book. VG/dj. A24. $300.00

**VIDOR, Charles M.** *Vielles Chansons et Rondes Pour les Petits Enfants.* ca 1931. Paris. Librarie Plon. 48p. gilt/blk-lettered cloth. VG. D4. $95.00

**VIELE, Egbert L.** *Hand-Book for Active Service, Containing Practical...* 1861. NY. Van Nostrand. 1st. 8vo. 10 full-p pl. 252p. O1. $125.00

**VIELLOT, L.J.P.** *Songbirds of the Torrid Zone.* 1979. Kent. 1/1500. 70 full-p pl. 291p. aeg. marbled ep. full leather. F. C12. $300.00

**VIEUCHANGE, Michel.** *Smara: Reiseaufzeichnugen von Michel Vieuchange...* ca 1932. Leipzig. Rentsch. 1st. 8vo. ils/fld map. VG. W1. $20.00

**VIGELAND, Carl A.** *In Concert: Offstage With Boston Symphony Orchestra.* 1989. NY. Morrow. 1st. F/dj. A2. $13.50

**VIGTEL, Gudmund.** *100 Years of Painting in Georgia.* (1992). Alston & Bird. ils. 109p. F/F. B10. $25.00

**VIGUERIE, Richard A.** *Establishment Vs the People.* 1983. Chicago. Regnery. 1st. inscr. F/dj. A2. $20.00

**VILDRAC, Charles.** *Rose Island.* 1957. NY. ils Edy LeGrand. VG+. D4. $30.00

**VILLAGRA.** *Hist of NM by Gaspar Perex deVillagra, Alcala, 1610.* 1933. 1/665. 12 pl. 320p. NF. A4. $250.00

**VILLIARD, O.G.** *John Brown: Biography 1800-1859.* 1929. Garden City. ils. 738p. VG. M4. $40.00

**VILLIERS, A.J.** *Falmouth for Orders.* 1929. Holt. VG/poor. M20. $32.00

**VILLIERS, Alan.** *Cruise of the Conrad...* 1937. NY. 1st. photos. VG. M17. $45.00

**VILLIERS, Alan.** *Quest of the Schooner Argus.* 1951. Hodder Stoughton. VG/dj. M20. $70.00

**VINCE, John.** *Old Farms, an Illustrated Guide.* 1986. Bramhall. 160p. VG/G. H10. $15.00

**VINCE, Joseph.** *Fensing.* 1940. NY. 12th. 62p. VG/dj. A17. $8.50

**VINCE, S.** *Complete System of Astronomy.* 1814. London. 3 vol. 2nd/corrected. half leather/marbled brd. xl. K5. $650.00

**VINCE, S.** *Elements of Astronomy: Designed for Use of Students...* 1811. Phil. Kimber Conrad. 1st Am. rb. G. K5. $90.00

**VINCENT, Boyd.** *Our Family of Vincents.* nd. Kidd Co. G. S5. $35.00

**VINCENT, Frank.** *Around & About South America.* 1891. Appleton. 4th. 473p. F3. $45.00

**VINCENT, Frank.** *Through & Through the Tropics: 30,000 Miles of Travel...* 1882. NY. 2nd. 304p. VG. A17. $25.00

**VINCENT, Marvin R.** *Word Studies in the New Testament.* 1965. Eerdmans. 4 vol. VG/dj. B29. $35.00

**VINDING, Erasmus Paul.** *Regia Academia Hauniensis in Regibus.* 1665. Copenhagen. thick 8vo. calf. R12. $875.00

**VINE, Barbara;** see Rendell, Ruth.

**VINGE, Joan D.** *Catspaw.* 1988. Warner. 1st. AN/dj. M21. $15.00

**VINGE, Joan D.** *World's End: Snow Queen Cycle Vol 2.* 1984. NY. Bluejay. 1st. F/dj. G10. $15.00

**VINGE, Vernor.** *Peace War.* 1984. Bluejay. 1st. F/NF. G10. $18.50

**VINING, Elizabeth Gray.** *Taken Girl.* 1972. Viking. 1st. 190p. VG/dj. V3. $16.50

**VIOLA, Herman J.** *Exploring the West.* 1987. Smithsonian. ils. 256p. brn cloth. F/dj. F7. $35.00

**VIOLA, Herman.** *Exploring the West.* 1987. Abrams. 1st. photos/maps. VG/dj. J2. $65.00

**VIOLLET-LE-DUC, E.E.** *City of Carassone.* 1988. Manchester Center, VT. 1/110. sgn. half cloth. B24. $225.00

**VIORST, Judith.** *When I Stop Being 20 & Other Injustices.* 1987. S&S. 1st. F/dj. T12. $50.00

**VISCONTI, Luchino.** *Three Screenplays: White Nights/Rocco.../The Job.* 1970. NY. Orion. F/wrp. C9. $30.00

**VISCOUNT MONTGOMERY, Bernard.** *Memoirs of Field-Marshal, the Viscount, Monggomery...* 1958. World. 1st. 508p. xl. VG/NF. W2. $275.00

**VISHER, Stephen Sargent.** *Climate of Indiana.* 1944. Bloomington. IU. ils. 511p. cloth. K5. $55.00

**VITA-FINZI, Claudio.** *Archaeological Sites in Their Setting.* 1978. London. ils. 176p. VG/dj. Q2. $12.00

**VITTORINI, Elio.** *In Sicily.* 1949. New Directions. ARC. intro Hemingway. RS. NF/dj. S9. $150.00

**VIVIAN, Alfred.** *First Principles of Soil Fertility.* 1921. Orange Judd. 265p. gilt bdg. VG. H7. $12.50

**VIZETELLY, Henry.** *Christmas With the Poets.* 1851. London. David Bogue. 1st. aeg. full gr morocco/raised bands. M24. $850.00

**VOGT, Gregory.** *Twenty-Fifth Anniversary Album of NASA.* 1983. Franklin Watts. 4to. 90p. xl. K5. $14.00

**VOGT, Per.** *Fridtsof Nansen: Explorer, Scientist, Humanitarian.* 1961. Oslo. ils/map. 202p. VG/worn box. B5. $50.00

**VOIGHT, David Quentin.** *American Baseball.* 1955. Norman, OK. 1st. 8vo. 336p. F/VG. B11. $35.00

**VOINOVICH, Vladimir.** *Fur Hat.* 1989. HBJ. 1st. NF/dj. G10. $12.50

**VOLK, Toni.** *Maybe in Missoula.* 1994. NY. Soho. 1st. F/NF. G10. $10.00

**VOLKMAN, A.G.** *Thoreau on Man & Nature.* 1960. Peter Pauper. 1st. 12mo. 61p. F/clip. M7. $25.00

**VOLLMANN, William T.** *Fathers & Crows.* 1992. NY. Viking. 1st. sgn. rem mk. F/dj. R14. $90.00

**VOLLMANN, William T.** *Ice-Shirt.* 1990. London. Deutsch. 1st. NF/dj. A14. $140.00

**VOLLMANN, William T.** *Ice-Shirt.* 1990. Viking. 1st. rem mk. F/F. M19. $25.00

**VOLLMANN, William T.** *Rainbow Stories.* 1989. Atheneum. ARC/1st Am. sgn. F/dj. D10. $110.00

**VOLLMANN, William T.** *Rainbow Stories.* 1989. London. Deutsch. 1st. VG+/clip. A14. $175.00

**VOLLMANN, William T.** *Thirteen Stories & Thirteen Epitaphs.* 1991. London. Deutsch. 1st. NF/dj. A14. $140.00

**VOLLMANN, William T.** *You Bright & Risen Angels.* 1987. Atheneum. 1st Am. sgn. F/dj. D10. $125.00

**VOLLMANN, William T.** *You Bright & Risen Angels.* 1987. London. Deutsch. 1st. sgn. F/F. B3. $250.00

**VOLNEY, Constantin-Francois.** *View of the Soil & Climate of the United States of America.* 1804. Phil. Conrad. thick 8vo. 2 fld pl/2 fld maps. calf. R12. $600.00

**VOLTAIRE, Francois Marie A.** *Philosophical Dictionary.* 1824. London. J & HL Hunt. 6 vol. 12mo. contemporary bdg. F. H5. $850.00

**VOLTAIRE.** *Candide.* 1929. Random. 1st trade/special ltd. ils Rockwell Kent. purple cloth. B14. $75.00

**VOLTAIRE.** *Elemens de la Philosophie de Neuton...* 1738. Amsterdam. Etienne Ledet. ils/6 pl/1 fld table. 400p. K1. $750.00

**VOLTAIRE.** *Irene Tragedie.* 1779. Paris. 4to. calf. R12. $125.00

**VOLTAIRE.** *La Morte de Cesar, Tragedie.* 1736. Paris. Josse. 8vo. wrp. R12. $140.00

**VOLTAIRE.** *Treatise on Toleration; Ignorant Philospher...* 1779. London. Fielding Walker. 3 parts in 1. 8vo. calf. R12. $450.00

**VOLZ, Emil.** *Home Flower Growing.* 1931. Macmillan. 342p. cloth. VG. A10. $20.00

**VON ABELE, R.** *Alexander H Stephens: A Biography.* 1946. NY. 1st. ils. 337p. F/dj. M4. $30.00

**VON BALTHARAR.** *Von Balthasar Reader.* 1982. Crossroad. 437p. VG/dj. B29. $7.50

**VON BASSEWITZ, Gert.** *Peterchiens Mondfahrt.* ca 1920s. Berlin. Hermann Kelemme. 14 stories/16 pl. 126p. VG. D1. $75.00

**VON BORRIS, Philip.** *Legends of Louisville.* 1993. Altwerger Manel. photos. wrp. P8. $17.50

**VON BOTHMER, Dietrich.** *Antiquities From Collection of Christos G Bastis...* 1987. Mainz. Philipp vonZabern. 352p. F/dj. D2. $150.00

**VON BRAUN, Wernher.** *Bemannte Raumfahrt.* 1969. Frankfurt. Fischer. trans Werner Budeler. cloth. K5. $50.00

**VON BRAUN, Wernher.** *First Men to the Moon.* 1960. HRW. lg 8vo. 96p. w/TLS. K5. $450.00

**VON BRAUN, Wernher.** *History of Rocketry & Space Travel.* 1969 (1966). NY. Crowell. revised. sgn. 276p. VG/dj. K5. $75.00

**VON CAMPENHAUSEN, Axel.** *Staatskirchenrecht, ein Leitfaden Durch Rechtsbeziehungen...* 1973. Munchen. Wilhelm Goldmann. prt wrp. M11. $20.00

**VON ESCHENMAYER, Carl Adloph.** *Psychologie in Drei Theilen als Empirische...* 1817. Buchhandlung. German text. sm 8vo. 567p. later bdg. G1. $200.00

**VON ESCHENMAYER, Carl Adloph.** *Psychologie in Drei Theilen...* 1822. Stuttgart. Cotta. 2nd. German text. sm 8vo. 537p. contemporary bdg. G1. $175.00

**VON HAGEN, Victor.** *Ancient Sun Kingdoms of the Americas: Aztec, Maya, Inca.* 1961. NY. World. 1st. 618p. dj. F3. $25.00

**VON HAGEN, Victor.** *Frederick Catherwood, Architect...* 1950. OUP. 1st. 8vo. 177p. VG/dj. W1. $25.00

**VON HAGEN, Victor.** *Frederick Catherwood.* 1950. NY. Oxford. 2nd. 177p. dj. F3. $30.00

**VON HAGEN, Victor.** *Golden Man: Quest for El Dorado.* 1974. London. BC. 1st Am. 346p. dj. F3. $20.00

**VON HAGEN, Victor.** *Highway of the Sun.* 1955. NY. DSP. 1st. 320p. dj. F3. $25.00

**VON HAGEN, Victor.** *Search for the Maya: Story of Stephens & Catherwood.* 1973. England. 1st. ils. 365p. F/dj. M4. $30.00

**VON HAGEN, Victor.** *Treasure of the Tortoise Islands.* 1940. Harcourt Brace. 1st. inscr. 202p. F/VG. D4. $45.00

**VON HALLER, Albrecht.** *Icones Anatomicae Corporis Humani. A Facsmile Portfolio.* 1982. New Haven. lg folio. 8 pl. A13. $50.00

**VON HARTSEN, Frederik Anthony.** *Untersuchungen uber Psychologie.* 1869. Leipzig. Theodor Thomas. 124p. prt buff wrp. VG. G1. $75.00

**VON HUGEL, Friedrich.** *Spiritual Counsel & Letters of Baron Friedrich Von Hugel.* 1964. Harper Row. 184p. G/dj. V3. $30.00

**VON HUMBOLDT, Fredrich A.** *Ensayo Politico Sobre la Nueva Espana.* 1827. Paris. Renouard. 5 vol. 2 maps. contemporary Spanish mottled calf. D11. $1,000.00

**VON KRAFFT-EBING, R.** *Psychopathia Sexuals.* 1925. NY. Physicians & Surgeons Book Co. sm 4to. 617p. G+. H1. $15.00

**VON LANGSDORFF, George H.** *Voyages & Travels in Various Parts of the World...* 1968. Amsterdam/NY. facs 1813 London. 2 vol. F. P4. $125.00

**VON MELLENTHIN, F.** *Panzer Battles: Employment of Armor in WWII.* 1956. U OK. 1st Am/3rd prt. photos/maps. VG/dj. E6. $30.00

**VON MENGERSHAUSEN, Cornelia.** *K'ehgosone.* 1975. Del Mar, CA. Ettan. 1/45. 4to. sgn/#d. 8 pl. loose w/record. wht suede box. B24. $2,500.00

**VON PARSEVAL, August.** *Graf Zeppelin und die Deutsche Luftfahrt.* 1925. Berlin. 1st. ils. 147p. VG. B18. $250.00

**VON RAD, GERHARD.** *Old Testament Theology.* 1962. Harper Row. 2 vol. VG/dj. B29. $30.00

**VON REZZORI, Gregor.** *Memoirs of an Anti-Semite.* 1981. Viking. 1st. NF/clip. S13. $10.00

**VON SACHS, Julius.** *History of Botany.* 1967. NY. Russell. 2 vol. A10. $65.00

**VON SANDERS, Liman.** *Five Years in Turkey.* 1927. Annapolis. 1st. ils/fld map. 326p. G. B5. $35.00

**VON SIMSON, Otto.** *Gothic Cathedral.* 1974. Princeton. 275p. VG. B29. $8.50

**VON WEIZACKER, Viktor.** *Le Cycle de la Structure (der Gestaltkreis).* 1958. Paris. Desclee De Brouwer. 1st French. 230p. prt gr-gray wrp. G1. $125.00

**VON WOLFF, Christian.** *Psychologia Rationalis Methodo Scientifica Pertractata...* 1734. Regeneriana. 4to. 680p. modern leather. G1. $850.00

**VON WOLFF, Christian.** *Psychologica Empirica Methodo Scientifica Pertracta...* 1779 (1732). Vernona. Apud Haeredes Marci Moroni. sm folio. 19th-C bdg. G1. $285.00

**VONNEGUT, Kurt.** *Bluebeard.* 1987. Delacorte. 1st trade. F/dj. O11. $25.00

**VONNEGUT, Kurt.** *Bluebeard.* 1987. Delacorte. 1st. sgn/dtd 1995. F/dj. R14. $100.00

**VONNEGUT, Kurt.** *Breakfast of Champions.* 1973. Delacorte. 1st. NF/dj. A14. $63.00

**VONNEGUT, Kurt.** *Deadeye Dick.* 1982. Delacorte/Lawrence. 1st trade. F/dj. O11. $30.00

**VONNEGUT, Kurt.** *Deadeye Dick.* 1983. London. Cape. 1st. F/NF. B3. $45.00

**VONNEGUT, Kurt.** *Fates Worse Than Death.* 1991. Putnam. 1st. 1/200. sgn. F/case. R14. $175.00

**VONNEGUT, Kurt.** *Galapagos.* 1985. Delacorte. 1st. F/dj. Q1. $50.00

**VONNEGUT, Kurt.** *Galapagos.* 1985. Delacorte. 1st. sgn/dtd 1995. rem mk. NF/clip. R14. $65.00

**VONNEGUT, Kurt.** *Galapagos.* 1985. Franklin Center, PA. Franklin Pr. 1st. sgn. aeg. tan leather. F. O11. $85.00

**VONNEGUT, Kurt.** *Hocus Pocus.* 1990. Putnam. 1st. NF/NF. H11. $15.00

**VONNEGUT, Kurt.** *Jailbird.* 1979. Delacorte/Lawrence. 1st trade. F/dj. O11. $30.00

**VONNEGUT, Kurt.** *Palm Sunday.* 1981. Delacorte. 1st. rem mk. NF/dj. B3. $35.00

**VONNEGUT, Kurt.** *Palm Sunday.* 1981. NY. 1st. 330p. F/clip. H3. $30.00

**VONNEGUT, Kurt.** *Player Piano.* 1952. NY. Scribner. BC (A on copyright/no pub seal). VG/clip. A14. $21.00

**VONNEGUT, Kurt.** *Slapstick or Lonesome No More.* 1976. London. Cape. 1st. VG+/dj. A14. $32.00

**VONNEGUT, Kurt.** *Slapstick.* 1976. Delacorte. 1st. NF/NF. B3. $35.00

**VONNEGUT, Kurt.** *Slapstick.* 1976. Delacorte/Lawrence. 1st. F/dj. O11. $40.00

**VONNEGUT, Kurt.** *Timequake.* 1997. Putnam. UP. F. R14. $55.00

**VONNEGUT, Kurt.** *Wampeters Foma & Granfallons.* 1974. Delacorte. 1st. F/dj. Q1. $75.00

**VONNEGUT, Kurt.** *Wampeters Foma & Granfallons.* 1974. Delacorte. 1st. NF/dj. A14. $52.50

**VONNEGUT, Kurt.** *Welcome to the Monkey House.* 1968. Delacorte/Lawrence. 1st. sgn. NF/dj. O11. $650.00

**VORHEES, Oscar.** *History of Phi Beta Kappa.* 1945. NY. 372p. A13. $30.00

**VORPAHL, Ben Merchant.** *Frederic Remington & the West.* 1972. Austin, TX. 1st. 294p. F/dj. E1. $30.00

**VOYNICH, E.L.** *Gadfly.* 1897. Holt. 1st Am. VG/dj. N2. $15.00

**VYSHINSKY, Andrei Y.** *Law of the Soviet State.* 1948. Macmillan. cloth. dj. M11. $45.00

# W

WABER, Bernard. *Lyle, Lyle, Crocodile.* (1965). Houghton Mifflin. 11th. 48p. yel cloth. NF/VG. T5. $20.00

WADDELL, Joseph. *Annals of Augusta County, From 1726 to 1871.* 1986 (1902). CJ Carrier. rpt. 545p. VG. B10. $35.00

WADDINGTON, C.H. *New Patterns in Genetics & Development.* 1964 (1962). Columbia. 271p. xl. VG. S5. $22.50

WADE, Brent. *Company Man.* 1992. Algonquin. 1st. author's 1st book. F/dj. H11. $30.00

WADE, Don. *And Then Arnie Told Chi Chi: More Than 200...Golf Stories...* 1993. Contemporary Books. 1st. 244p. NF/dj. P12. $20.00

WADE, Jonathan. *Running Sand.* 1963. Random. 1st. NF/NF. H11. $15.00

WADE, Robert. *Knave of Eagles.* 1969. Random. F/VG. P8. $65.00

WADE-GAYLES, Gloria. *Pushed Back to Strength.* 1993. Boston. Beacon. 1st. F/dj. A24. $25.00

WAGAR, W. Warren. *Good Tidings: Belief in Progress From Darwin to Marcuse.* 1972. np. 1st. 398p. A13. $25.00

WAGENHEIM, Kal. *Clemente.* 1973. Praeger. 1st. F/VG. P8. $45.00

WAGENKNECHT, Edward. *Mark Twain, the Man & His Work.* 1935. New Haven. Yale. 1st. gilt red cloth. F/dj. M24. $100.00

WAGENKNECHT, Edward. *Mark Twain, the Man & His Work.* 1961. Norman, OK. new/revised/1st prt. gilt red cloth. F/dj. M24. $40.00

WAGER, Walter. *Camp Century: City Under the Ice.* 1962. Phil. Chilton. 1st. 143p. F/NF. H7. $20.00

WAGMAN, John. *Civil War Front Pages: A Collection...* 1989. NY. VG. M17. $15.00

WAGNER, C. Peter. *Spiritual Power & Church Growth.* 1986. Strang. 160p. VG/wrp. B29. $6.50

WAGNER, F. *Submarine Fighter of the American Revolution.* 1963. NY. 1st. ils. 145p. F/dj. M4. $25.00

WAGNER, Frederick. *Robert Morris.* 1976. Dodd Mead. 1st. NF/dj. W2. $20.00

WAGNER, Henry R. *Irish Economics: 1700-1783.* 1907. London. J Davy. 95p. D11. $150.00

WAGNER, Henry R. *Letters of Captain Don Pedro Fages...* 1936. Grabhorn. 1/110. VG/wrp. M19. $45.00

WAGNER, Henry R. *Manuscript Atlases of Battista Agnese.* 1931. np. Rpt From Papers of Biblio Soc of Am. 110+p. prt wrp. D11. $100.00

WAGNER, Henry R. *Sir Francis Drake's Voyage Around the World, Its Aims...* 1926. SF. John Howell. 1st. pub sgn. 63 maps/pl/charts. maroon cloth. B11. $600.00

WAGNER, Henry R. *Spanish Southwest, 1542-1794.* nd (1997). Staten Island. rpt 2 vol in 1. 553p. AN/sans. P4. $75.00

WAGNER, Henry R. *Spanish Southwest 1542-1794...* nd. Quivira. 2 vol in 1. 1/150. rpt. F. A4. $75.00

WAGNER, Jane. *Search for Signs of Intelligent Life in the Universe.* 1985. Harper Row. 1st. sgn Wagner/Lily Tomlin. F/dj. B30. $45.00

WAGNER, Ray. *American Combat Planes.* 1968. Garden City. 442p. VG/dj. B18. $15.00

WAGNER, Richard. *Environment & Man.* 1969. Norton. 491p. xl. VG. S5. $12.50

WAGNER, Richard. *Siegfried & the Twilight of the Gods.* 1911. Doubleday. 1st. 4to. ils Rackham. VG. B17. $185.00

WAGNER, Richard. *Wagner on Music & Drama...* 1964. NY. 1st. VG/dj. M17. $27.50

WAGNER, William. *Continental! Its Motors & Its People.* 1983. Fallbrook, CA. Aero. 1st. xl. dj. H6. $48.00

WAGONER, Jay J. *Arizona Territory, 1863-1912: A Political History.* 1970. Tucson, AZ. 1st. ils/index. 587p. VG/dj. B19. $35.00

WAHLENBERG, W.G. *Loblolly Pine: Its Use, Ecology, Regeneration...* 1960. Durham. ils/tables. 603p. VG/dj. B26. $46.00

WAIN, John. *Samuel Johnson, a Biography.* 1975. Viking. VG/dj. H13. $25.00

WAIN, Louis. *Dumpty Cats Painting Book.* ca 1910. London. Raphael Tuck. unrecorded. 4to. pict paper wrp/mc label. R5. $1,650.00

WAIN & WRIGHTMAN. *Chemistry & Mode of Action of Plant Growth Substances.* 1956. Butterworths Pub. 312p. G. S5. $20.00

WAINGROW, Marshall. *Research Edition of The Life of Johnson.* 1994. Edinburgh/Yale. 1st. tall 8vo. 518p. bl linen. AN/dj. H13. $195.00

WAINWRIGHT, John. *All Through the Night.* 1985. St Martin. 1st Am. F/VG. N4. $15.00

WAINWRIGHT, Nicholas B. *History of the Philadelphia Electric Company 1881-1961.* 1961. NY. PECO. 1st. ils. 416p. VG+/VG+. A25. $25.00

WAITE, Arthur Edward. *Holy Grail, Galahad Quest Arthurian Literature.* 1961. NY. U Books. 1st. NF/dj. T10. $125.00

WAITLEY, D. *Roads of Destiny: Trails That Shaped a Nation.* 1970. WA. ils. 319p. VG/torn. M4. $20.00

WAITT, Alden H. *Gas Warfare: Chemical Weapon, Its Use...* 1942. DSP. 1st. sgn pres. 327p. cloth. F. H1. $35.00

WAKEFIELD, H.R. *Clock Strikes Twelve.* 1946. Arkham. 1st. VG/dj. N2. $45.00

WAKEFIELD, H.R. *Old Man's Beard.* 1996. Ashtree. reissue/1st thus. 15 stories. F/dj. T2. $45.00

WAKEFIELD, Pris. *Family Tour Through British Empire.* 1810. London. 4th/improved. weak hinges. A15. $60.00

WAKEFIELD, Robert. *Schwiering & the West.* 1973. Aberdeen, SD. AN/dj. A19. $75.00

WAKEMAN, Frederic. *Hucksters.* 1946. Rinehart. 1st. VG/G. M21. $15.00

WAKOSKI, Diane. *Four Young Lady Poets.* 1962. NY. Totem. 1st. F/pict wrp. M24. $85.00

WAKOSKI, Diane. *Lament of the Lady Bank Dick.* 1969. Sans Souci. 1st. 1/99. sgn on colophon/title. F/tattered. L3. $175.00

WAKOSKI, Diane. *Rings of Saturn.* 1986. Santa Rosa. Blk Sparrow. 1/200. sgn/#d. B9. $50.00

WAKOSKI, Diane. *Trophies.* 1979. Blk Sparrow. 1/60. sgn/#d. F/mylar. B9. $75.00

WAKSMAN, Selman A. *Soil Microbiology.* 1952. John Wiley. 1st. 356p. VG. H1. $12.50

WALBRIDGE, Earle. *Literary Characters Drawn from Life...* 1936. NY. HW Wilson. 1st thus. 192p. cloth. F/NF. O10. $40.00

WALCOTT, Derek. *Antilles: Fragments of Epic Memory.* 1992. NY. FSG. 1st. F/dj. Q1. $35.00

WALCOTT, Derek. *Antilles: Nobel Lecture.* 1993. FSG. 1st. F/dj. R14. $30.00

WALCOTT, Derek. *Caribbean Poetry of Derek Walcott & Art of Romare Bearden.* 1983. LEC. 1/2000. sgn Walcott/Bearden. F/NF cb case. w/lithograph. B4. $550.00

WALCOTT, Derek. *Joker of Seville & O Babylon!* 1978. FSG. 1st. sgn. F/dj. L3. $150.00

WALCOTT, Derek. *Omeros.* 1990. FSG. 1st. F/dj. D10. $40.00

WALCOTT, Derek. *Three Plays.* 1986. FSG. 1st. sgn. F/dj. D10. $65.00

**WALCOTT, Earle Ashley.** *Blindfolded.* 1906. Bobbs Merrill. ils Alice Barber Stephens. 400p. G. G11. $6.00

**WALCOTT, Mary V.** *Illustrations of North Americ'n Pitcher Plants.* 1935. WA, DC. ils/10 distribution maps. F/NF portfolio. C12. $275.00

**WALD, Robert M.** *Space, Time & Gravity: Theory of Big Bang & Black Holes.* 1977. Chicago. NF/VG. B9. $15.00

**WALDECK, Jo Besse McElveen.** *Little Jungle Village.* 1940. NY. Viking. 1st. VG/G. B11. $18.00

**WALDEN, Hillary.** *Ice Cream.* 1985. S&S. G/dj. A16. $10.00

**WALDEN, Howard T.** *Familiar Fresh-Water Fishes of America.* 1964. NY. 1st. 324p. F/dj. A17. $15.00

**WALDMAN, Anne.** *Journals & Dreams.* 1976. NY. Stonehill. ARC/1st. inscr/dtd 1976. F/dj. L3. $65.00

**WALDMAN, C.** *Atlas of the North American Indian.* 1985. NY. ils. 276p. F/wrp. M4. $20.00

**WALDO, Arthur L.** *True Heroes of Jamestown.* 1977. Miami. Am Inst Polish Culture. 1st. VG/dj. N2. $17.50

**WALDROP, Howard.** *Night of the Cooters.* 1990. Kansas City, MO. 1st. 1/374. sgn. AN/case. M21. $45.00

**WALDROP & WALDROP.** *Until Volume One.* 1973. Providence. Burning Deck. 1st. 1/500. sgns. F/wrp/dj. L3. $30.00

**WALDSTEIN, Charles.** *Essays on the Art of Pheidias.* 1885. Cambridge. lg 8vo. ils/pl. 432p. teg. dk bl cloth. K1. $85.00

**WALFORD, Lionel A.** *Marine Game Fishes of the Pacific Coast From AK to Equator.* 1974 (1937). Smithsonian. rpt. 4to. F/sans. A2. $25.00

**WALKER, Alexander.** *Garbo.* 1980. NY. Macmillan. 191p. VG/dj. C5. $15.00

**WALKER, Alexander.** *Stardom.* 1970. Stein Day. 392p. VG/dj. C5. $12.50

**WALKER, Alice.** *Finding the Greenstone.* 1991. HBJ. ARC/1st. F/dj. D4. $30.00

**WALKER, Alice.** *Meridian.* 1976. HBJ. 1st. sgn. F/dj. D10. $275.00

**WALKER, Alice.** *Possessing the Secret of Joy.* 1992. HBJ. 1st. F/dj. R14. $30.00

**WALKER, Alice.** *Temple of My Familiar.* 1989. HBJ. 1st. sgn. NF/dj. B3. $75.00

**WALKER, Alice.** *Temple of My Familiar.* 1989. HBJ. 1st. sgn/dtd. rem mk. NF/dj. O4. $45.00

**WALKER, Alice.** *Third Life of Grange Copeland.* 1970. HBJ. 1st. author's 1st novel/2nd book. F/NF. A24. $320.00

**WALKER, Alice.** *You Can't Keep a Good Woman Down.* 1981. HBJ. 1st. sgn. F/dj. D10. $195.00

**WALKER, Ardis M.** *Rough & the Righteous.* 1970. Paisano. 1st. inscr. decor gold cloth. F/sans. O4. $20.00

**WALKER, Benjamin.** *Encyclopedia of Metaphysical Medicine.* 1978. London. 323p. A13. $50.00

**WALKER, Cora.** *Cuatemo: Last of the Aztec Emperors.* 1934. NY. Dayton. 1st. ils/maps. 348p. F3. $25.00

**WALKER, Dale L.** *Death Was the Black Horse: A Story of Rough Rider...* 1975. Madrona. 1st. ils. 200p. NF/dj. B19. $35.00

**WALKER, Dale L.** *Jack London & Conan Doyle: A Literary Kinship.* 1981. Gaslight. 1st thus. F/sans. T2. $15.00

**WALKER, Daniel S.** *Oriental Rugs of the Hajji Babas.* 1982. NY. Asia Soc/Abrams. 1st. 50 mc pl. 32p. NF/dj. W1. $30.00

**WALKER, David.** *Black Dougal.* 1974. Houghton Mifflin. VG/dj. R8. $12.50

**WALKER, David.** *Fixed in His Folly.* 1995. St Martin. 1st. F/NF. M23. $20.00

**WALKER, Ernest P.** *Mammals of the World.* 1968. Johns Hopkins. 2nd. 644p. xl. VG. S5. $45.00

**WALKER, Ernest P.** *Mammals of the World. Vol III.* 1964. Johns Hopkins. 769p. xl. VG. S5. $35.00

**WALKER, Frances Moorman.** *Early Episcopal Church in the Amherst-Nelson Area...* (1964). VA Book Co. photos. 122p. VG. B10. $20.00

**WALKER, Fred.** *Destination Unknown.* 1935. Lippincott. 1st. 285p. dj. F3. $15.00

**WALKER, H.** *Tennessee Tales.* 1970. Nashville. sgn. ils. 221p. F/dj. M4. $22.00

**WALKER, Henry Pickering.** *Wagonmasters: High Plains Freighting...* 1966. Norman, OK. 1st. VG/dj. O3. $65.00

**WALKER, Holly Beth.** *Meg & the Disappearing Diamonds.* 1969. Whitman. VG. M20. $15.00

**WALKER, J.J.** *Natural History of the Oxford District.* 1926. London. OUP. 12mo. 336p. VG/wrp. M12. $25.00

**WALKER, Judson Elliott.** *Campaigns of General Custer.* 1966. Promontory. G/dj. A19. $25.00

**WALKER, Kenneth.** *Story of Medicine.* 1955. NY. 1st Am. 343p. xl. A13. $27.50

**WALKER, Mary Willis.** *Red Scream.* 1994. Doubleday. 1st. F/dj. M25. $75.00

**WALKER, Mary Willis.** *Red Scream.* 1994. Doubleday. 1st. sgn. F/dj. T2. $100.00

**WALKER, Mary Willis.** *Under the Beetle's Cellar.* 1995. Doubleday. 1st. F/F. H11/S18. $25.00

**WALKER, Robert Harris (Hub).** *Cincinnati & the Big Red Machine.* 1988. IU. 1st. photos. F/dj. P8. $30.00

**WALKER, Sam.** *Up the Slot.* 1984. OK City. 282p. VG. S16. $75.00

**WALKER, Theodore J.** *Red Salmon, Brown Bear: Story of an Alasakan Lake.* 1971. World. 1st. ils. 226p. F/VG. S14. $20.00

**WALKINSHAW, Lawrence H.** *Sandhill Cranes.* 1949. Cranbrook. 202p. xl. VG. S5. $15.00

**WALKINSHAW, Robert.** *On Puget Sound.* 1929. Putnam. 1st. tall 8vo. ils. 294p. F/VG. H7. $30.00

**WALL, John F.** *Famous Running Horses.* 1949. Washington. 1st. ils. 313p. VG/dj. B18. $37.50

**WALLACE, David Foster.** *Broom of the System.* 1987. NY. Viking Penguin. 1st. author's 1st book. F/wrp. A24. $80.00

**WALLACE, David Foster.** *Girl With Curious Hair.* 1989. Norton. 1st. author's 2nd book. F/dj. from $50 to $60.00

**WALLACE, David Foster.** *Girl With Curious Hair.* 1989. Norton. 1st. sgn. F/dj. O11. $75.00

**WALLACE, Diagnosis of Mineral** *Deficiences in Plants by Visual Symptoms.* 1944. HMSO. xl. G. S5. $15.00

**WALLACE, Edgar.** *Down & Under Donovan.* 1929. London. Ward Lock. G. T12. $15.00

**WALLACE, Edgar.** *On the Spot.* 1931. Doubleday Doran Crime Club. 1st. VG. S13. $18.00

**WALLACE, Edgar.** *Sanders of the River.* 1930. Doubleday Doran. 1st Am. F/dj. M15. $100.00

**WALLACE, Edgar.** *White Face.* 1931. Doubleday Crime Club. 1st Am. F/dj. M15. $125.00

**WALLACE, Frederick William.** *Wooden Ships & Iron Men: Story of Square-Rigged Merchant...* ca 1915. NY. Geo Sully. 1st Am. 337+3p. VG. H7. $35.00

WALLACE, Ian. *Sparrow's Song.* 1986. Penguin. 1st. ils. F/dj. M5. $22.00

WALLACE, Irving. *Fan Club.* 1974. S&S. 1st. 8vo. G/VG. B11. $25.00

WALLACE, Irving. *Mexico Today.* 1936. Boston. Meador. 1st. 364p. F3. $20.00

WALLACE, Irving. *Three Sirens.* 1963. S&S. 1st. F/F. H11. $35.00

WALLACE, Irving. *Word.* 1972. S&S. 1st. F/F. H11. $40.00

WALLACE, Lew. *Ben-Hur: Tale of the Christ.* 1959. Random. unp. VG. C5. $12.50

WALLACE, Lew. *Fair God.* 1898. Houghton. 2 vol. 1st thus. ils Eric Pape. dk red cloth. VG+. S13. $75.00

WALLACE, Lew. *Fair God; or, Last of 'Tzins: A Tale of Conquest Mexico.* 1894 (1873). Houghton Mifflin. 586p. gilt pict cloth. F3. $20.00

WALLACE, Lew. *Wooing of Malkatoon/Commodus.* 1898. Harper. 1st. ils DuMond/Weguelin. NF. M19. $17.50

WALLACE, Marcia. *Barefoot in the Kitchen.* 1971. St Martin. G/dj. A16. $10.00

WALLACE, Paul A. *Muhlenbergs of Pennsylvania.* 1950. Phil. 1st. ils. 358p. VG/dj. B18. $20.00

WALLACE, Willard M. *East to Bagaduce.* 1963. Chicago. Regnery. 1st. off-wht linen. NF/VG+. T11. $35.00

WALLACE, Willard M. *Jonathan Dearborn.* 1967. Little Brn. 1st. NF/VG. T11. $25.00

WALLACE, Willard M. *Raiders.* 1970. Little Brn. 1st. NF/clip. T11. $35.00

WALLACE, Willard M. *Raiders: A Novel of the Civil War at Sea.* 1970. Little Brn. 1st. NF/dj. A14. $25.00

WALLACH, Ira. *Muscle Beach.* 1959. Little Brn. 1st. F/NF clip. B4. $125.00

WALLACH & WALLACH. *New Palestinians: Emerging Generations of Leaders.* 1992. Rocklin, CA. Prima. 8vo. map ep. 351p. NF/dj. W1. $18.00

WALLACK, L.R. *American Rifle Design & Performance.* 1977. Winchester. VG/dj. A19. $25.00

WALLER, J. Flint. *West of Suez.* (1970). McClure. photos. 162p. VG. B10. $12.00

WALLER, John H. *Beyond the Khyber Pass: Road to British Disaster...* 1990. NY. ils. VG/dj. M17. $15.00

WALLER, Robert James. *Bridges of Madison County.* 1992. Warner. 1st. F/VG+. B30. $125.00

WALLER, Robert James. *Old Songs in a New Cafe.* 1994. Warner. 1st. 8vo. 172p. F/dj. W2. $45.00

WALLER, Robert James. *Slow Waltz in Cedar Bend.* 1993. Warner. 1st Canadian. F/dj. T12. $35.00

WALLER, Robert James. *Slow Waltz in Cedar Bend.* 1993. Warner. 1st. 8vo. 197p. F/dj. W2. $40.00

WALLIS, Charles L. *Autobiography of Peter Cartwright.* 1956. NY. Abington. 349p. VG/dj. B18. $22.50

WALLON, Henri. *Les Origines du Caractere Chez l'Enfant...* 1934. Paris. Boivin. sq 8vo. 267p. prt gr wrp. G1. $35.00

WALLOP, Douglas. *Year the Yankees Lost the Pennant.* 1954. NY. 1st. author's 1st novel. NF. T12. $100.00

WALLS, Ian. *Tomato Growing Today.* 1977. Newton Abbot. 239p. Vg/dj. A10. $25.00

WALPOLE, Frederick. *Four Years in the Pacific in Her Majesty's Ship Collingwood.* 1850. London. Richard Bentley. 2 vol. ils. cloth. D11. $325.00

WALPOLE, Hugh. *Captain Nicholas: Comedy of Modern Buccaneer.* 1934. 1st. VG/dj. M19. $35.00

WALPOLE, Hugh. *Dark Forest.* 1916. Doran. 1st. 320p. G. G11. $7.00

WALSDORF, John J. *Printers on Morris.* 1981. Beaverton, OR. Beaverdam. mini. 1/26 (326 total). w/extra sgn Moser ftspc. F. B24. $450.00

WALSH, Edmund A. *Total Empire: Roots & Progress of World Communism.* 1952. Milwaukee. Bruce. 2nd. 8vo. VG. A2. $12.50

WALSH, J.H. *Horse in the Stable & the Field...His Varieties...* 1899. London. ils. G. M17. $25.00

WALSH, J.H. *Horse.* 1907. Dutton. G. A21. $45.00

WALSH, Jill Paton. *Wyndham Case.* 1993. NY. St Martin. ARC/1st Am. F/dj. w/promo materials. T2. $20.00

WALSH, John. *Poe the Detective: Curious Circumstances...* 1968. Rutgers. 1st. VG/dj. N4. $30.00

WALSH, Richard. *Adventures of Marco Polo.* 1948. John Day. 1st thus. ils. 208p. G+/dj. D4. $45.00

WALSH, William S. *Around the World in Eighty Minutes...* 1894. Altemus. 1st. 8vo. 223p. VG. W1. $18.00

WALSHAM. *Surgery: Its Theory & Practice.* 1887. 655p. VG. A4. $35.00

WALT, Lewis W. *Strange War, Strange Strategy: A General's Report...* 1970. Funk Wagnall. inscr. G/dj. A19. $30.00

WALTERS, Alice. *Fanny at Chez Panisse.* 1992. Harper Collins. 1st. ils Ann Arnold. 131p. F/dj. D1. $25.00

WALTERS, Helen B. *Wernher Von Braun: Rocket Engineer.* 1965 (1964). Macmillan. 3rd. 187p. xl. K5. $25.00

WALTERS, Minette. *Dark Room.* 1995. London. Macmillan. 1st. F/dj. M15. $55.00

WALTERS, Minette. *Scold's Bridle.* 1994. Bristol. Scorpion. 1st. 1/75. sgn. quarter leather/marbled brd. F/acetate. M15. $200.00

WALTERS, Minette. *Scold's Bridle.* 1994. London. Macmillan. 1st. sgn. F/dj. M15. $80.00

WALTERS, Minette. *Scold's Bridle.* 1994. St Martin. 1st Am. F/dj. N4. $30.00

WALTERS, Minette. *Sculptress.* Oct 1993. St Martin. 1st Am. sgn. author's 2nd book. Edgar Allen Poe Award. VG/dj. L1. $250.00

WALTERS, Minette. *Sculptress.* 1993. St Martin. 1st Am. VG/dj. G8. $22.50

WALTERS, Minette. *Sculptress.* 1993. St Martin. 1st. NF/F. H11. $50.00

WALTHER, C.F.W. *Proper Distinction Between Law & the Gospel.* 1986. Concordia. 426p. VG. B29. $17.50

WALTON, George. *Sentinel of the Plains: Fort Leavenworth & American West.* 1973. Englewood Cliffs. 1st. 210p. NF. E1. $35.00

WALTON, George. *Sentinel of the Plains: Fort Leavenworth & the Am West.* 1973. Englewood Cliffs. 1st. ils. 210p. NF/dj. E1. $50.00

WALTON, Isaak. *Compleat Angler.* 1992. UK. ils Rackham. VG/dj. M17. $30.00

WALTON, Richard J. *Swarthmore College, an Informal History.* 1986. Swarthmore. probable 1st. ils. F/dj. P12. $20.00

WALWORTH, Clarence E. *Oxford Movement in America.* 1974. NY. US Catholic Hist Soc. 175p. VG. H10. $27.50

WALZ & WALZ. *Undiscovered Country.* 1958. DSP. 8vo. 390p. VG/dj. P4. $35.00

WAMBAUGH, Joseph. *Blooding.* 1989. NY. Morrow. 1st. F/dj. T12. $30.00

**WAMBAUGH, Joseph.** *Choirboys.* 1975. Delacorte. 1st. F/NF. H11. $25.00

**WAMBAUGH, Joseph.** *Glitter Dome.* 1981. Morrow. 1st. VG/dj. N4. $25.00

**WAMBAUGH, Joseph.** *New Centurions.* 1970. Atlantic/Little Brn. 1st. author's 1st novel. VG/dj. S18. $20.00

**WAMBAUGH, Joseph.** *New Centurions.* 1970. Atlantic/Little Brn. 1st. F/NF. N4. $40.00

**WAMPLER, Joseph.** *Havasu Canyon: Gem of the Grand Canyon.* 1959. Berkeley. 1st. VG. F7. $22.50

**WAMSLEY, James S.** *Idols, Victims, Pioneers: Virginia's Women From 1607.* (1976). VA Chamber of Commerce. ils. 307p. VG/G. B10. $35.00

**WANGER, E.D.** *Arts & Decoration Book of Successful Houses.* 1940. McBride. 112p. cloth. VG. A10. $25.00

**WAPSHOTT, Nicholas.** *Carol Reed: A Biography.* 1994. NY. 1st Am. photos. VG/dj. M17. $17.50

**WARBURG, James P.** *It's Up to Us.* 1934. NY. Knopf. inscr/sgn. F. B14. $45.00

**WARBURTON, Eliot.** *Crescent & the Cross; or, Travels in Egypt & Holy Land.* 1888. Phil. Hubbard. Edgewood ed. ils. stp olive cloth. VG. H1. $16.00

**WARD, Albert E.** *Limited Activity & Occupation Sites.* 1978. Albuquerque. sc. G. A19. $30.00

**WARD, Charles Willis.** *American Carnation: How to Grow It.* 1903 (1902). NY. ils. 296p. cloth. B26. $45.00

**WARD, Geoffrey C.** *First Class Temperment: Emergence of Franklin Roosevelt.* 1989. NY. Harper Row. BC. VG. M10. $9.50

**WARD, Grace.** *In the Miz.* 1904. Little Brn. 1st. ils/pl. 159p. brd/pict label. NF. D4. $135.00

**WARD, Harry F.** *In Place of Profit: Social Incentives in Soviet Union.* 1933. Scribner. ils Lynd Ward. VG/dj. V4. $150.00

**WARD, James.** *Naturalism & Agnosticism.* 1899. London. Adam/Chas Blk. 2 vol. 8vo. gr cloth. G. G1. $65.00

**WARD, Lynd.** *Biggest Bear.* 1952. Houghton Mifflin. 1st. sgn. 1953 Caldecott. red lettered gray cloth. dj. R5. $450.00

**WARD, Lynd.** *Gods' Man.* 1929. Cape Smith. 1st. ils brd/blk cloth backstrip. VG. C15. $75.00

**WARD, Lynd.** *Story of Siegfried.* (1931). NY. Cape Smith. 1st. 4to. dk bl cloth/bstp vignette. mc dj. R5. $150.00

**WARD, Mary Jane.** *Little Night Music.* 1951. Random. 1st. VG/dj. S13. $12.00

**WARD, Mrs. Humphrey.** *Testing of Diana Mallory.* 1908. NY. Harper. ils W Hatherell. 549p. G. G11. $7.00

**WARD, Nanda.** *Wellington & the Witch.* 1959. Hastings. 1st. xl. VG/G. P2. $20.00

**WARD, Nathaniel.** *Simple Cobbler of Aggawam in America.* 1843. Boston. Monroe. rpt (1657 London). 8vo. 96p. gilt bstp cloth. NF. O1. $40.00

**WARDEN, Carl John.** *Animal Motivation: Experimental Studies on Albino Rat.* 1931. Columbia U. 502p. panelled straight-grain bl cloth. NF. G1. $65.00

**WARDEN, Herbert W.** *In Praise of Sailors: A Nautical Anthology of Art...* 1978. NY. Abrams. 1st. 4to. 299p. F/G. B11. $50.00

**WARE, J.D.** *George Gauld: Surveyor & Cartographer of Gulf Coast.* 1982. FL U. 1st. 13 facs charts. F/dj. M4. $30.00

**WARFIELD, Don.** *Roaring Redhead.* 1987. Diamond Comm. 1st. photos. F/dj. P8. $25.00

**WARGA, Wayne.** *Hardcover.* 1985. Arbor. 1st. NF/F. H11. $30.00

**WARHOL, Andy.** *America.* 1st. sgn twice. sc. O8. $385.00

**WARHOL, Andy.** *Philosophy of Andy Warhol From A to B & Back Again.* 1975. HBJ. 1st. NF/F. T12. $80.00

**WARHOL, Andy.** *Philosophy of Andy Warhol.* 1975. HBJ. 1st trade. VG/dj. T10. $50.00

**WARING, George.** *Draining for Profit & Draining for Health.* 1867. NY. Orange Judd. 244p. cloth. VG. A10. $15.00

**WARINGTON, R.** *Chemistry of the Farm.* 1881. London. Bradbury. 128p. xl. VG. A10. $25.00

**WARKANY, Josef.** *Congenital Malformations: Notes & Comments.* 1971. Chicago. Year Book. 1309p. cloth. G7. $395.00

**WARMAN, Edwin G.** *Milk Glass Addenda.* 1959. Warman. 2nd/enlarged/revised. unp. NF. H1. $97.50

**WARNER, Charles.** *Road to Revolution.* 1961. Garrett Massie. 1st. VG/dj. R8. $20.00

**WARNER, Francis.** *Nervous System of the Child...* 1900. Macmillan. 1st Am. 233p. pebbled gr buckram. G1. $65.00

**WARNER, Francis.** *Physical Expression: Its Modes & Principles.* 1886. Appleton. 1st Am. 12mo. 51 woodcuts. 372p. red cloth. G1. $75.00

**WARNER, Geoffrey.** *Iraq & Syria, 1914.* nd. London. BC. Politics/Strategy 2nd World War series. 180p. cloth. dj. Q2. $15.00

**WARNER, James A.** *Darker Brother.* 1974. Dutton. 1st. sm 4to. photos. VG/dj. R11. $25.00

**WARNER, Oliver.** *Chatto & Windus: A Brief Account of Firm's History...* 1973. London. Chatto Windus. 1st. sm 8vo. cloth. dj. O10. $25.00

**WARNER, Sylvia Townsend.** *Lolly Willowes & Mr Fortunes Maggot.* 1966. Viking. 40th Anniversary ed. G/dj. L1. $35.00

**WARNER & WHITE.** *Chesapeake: Portrait of the Bay Country.* 1982. Creative Resource. sgns. VG/G. R8. $100.00

**WARREN, Edward.** *Doctor's Experiences in Three Continents...* 1885. Baltimore. Cushings Bailey. 1st. 619p. ES. M8. $350.00

**WARREN, Frank A.** *Liberals & Communism: Red Decade Revisited.* 1966. Bloomington, IN. 1st. 8vo. VG/dj. A2. $20.00

**WARREN, G.F.** *Farm Management.* 1916. Macmillan. 590p. cloth. A10. $20.00

**WARREN, H.G.** *Paraguay: Informal History.* 1949. OK U. 1st. ils/maps. 393p. F/dj. M4. $20.00

**WARREN, J. Russell.** *Murder From Three Angels.* 1939. Lee Furman. 1st Am. VG/dj. M15. $45.00

**WARREN, John C.** *Comparative View of Sensoral & Nervous System of Man...* 1822. Boston. Ingraham. 6 engravings. 159p. sugar brd/rb. G7. $595.00

**WARREN, Mary Bowers.** *Little Journeys Abroad.* 1895. Boston. Knight. 1st. ils. xl. VG. W1. $22.00

**WARREN, Raymond.** *Prairie President.* 1930. Chicago. Reilly Lee. 8vo. 427p. brn cloth. G. S17. $5.00

**WARREN, Robert Penn.** *All the King's Men.* 1946. Harcourt Brace. 1st. maroon cloth. F/1st state. M24. $1,350.00

**WARREN, Robert Penn.** *Chief Joseph of the Nez Perce.* (1983). Random. 1st. F/dj. A18. $40.00

**WARREN, Robert Penn.** *How Texas Won Her Freedom.* 1959. Santa Jacinto Monument. Mus of History. 1st. 1/512. inscr/design Gerry Doyle. F. L3. $550.00

**WARREN, Robert Penn.** *Incarnations: Poems 1966-1968.* 1968. Random. 1/250. sgn. F/dj/case. O11. $150.00

**WARREN, Robert Penn.** *Place to Come to.* 1977. Random. 1st. F/dj. A23. $40.00

**WARREN, Robert Penn.** *Promises: Poems 1954-1956.* 1957. Random. 1st. 84p. F/dj. H1. $35.00

**WARREN, Robert Penn.** *Remember the Alamo!* 1958. Random. 3rd. ils Wm Moyers. 182p. VG/dj. B36. $11.00

**WARREN, Robert Penn.** *Who Speaks for the Negro?* 1965. Random. 1st. NF/VG. Q1. $60.00

**WARREN, S. Edward.** *Stereotomy: Problems in Stone Cutting.* 1888. NY. Wiley. 10 fld pl. 126p. fair. H10. $25.00

**WARRINER, Doreen.** *Land Reform & Development in Middle East: A Study...* 1957. London. 8vo. 197p. cloth. VG/dj. Q2. $30.00

**WASHBURN, Robert Collyer.** *Jury of Death.* 1930. Crime Club. 1st. G+. G8. $15.00

**WASHBURN, Wilcomb E.** *Red Man's Land/White Man's Law.* 1971. Scribner. 1st. VG. N2. $10.00

**WASHINGTON, Booker T.** *Up From Slavery: An Autobiography of...* 1901. AL Burt. inscr/dtd 1937. VG/worn. V4. $125.00

**WASHINGTON, George.** *Writings of George Washington...* 1745-1799. GPO. 39 vol. ils. gilt bl cloth. K1. $1,250.00

**WASON, Betty.** *Encyclopedia of Cheese & Cheese Cookery.* 1966. NY. Galahad. G/dj. A16. $10.00

**WASSON, David Atwood.** *Beyond Concord: Selected Writings of David Atwood Wasson.* 1965. Bloomington. 1st. VG+/G+. N2. $10.00

**WASSON, R. Gordon.** *Soma: Divine Mushroom of Immortality.* 1968. NY. 1st. 381p. A13. $40.00

**WATERHOUSE, Francis A.** *Bloodspots in the Sand.* 1930s. London. Sampson Low. 8vo. 248p. VG. M7. $45.00

**WATERHOUSE, Francis A.** *Bun Running Into the Red Sea.* 1930s. London. Sampson Low. 1st? 8vo. 244p. red cloth. G. M7. $40.00

**WATERMAN, Charles F.** *Fisherman's World.* 1971. NY. 1st. biblio/index. 250p. F/dj. A17. $18.50

**WATERMAN, Charles F.** *Hunter's World.* nd. NY. biblio/index. 250p. F/dj. A17. $17.50

**WATERMAN, Charles F.** *Hunter's World.* 1976. Ridge/Random. 1st. ils. NF/dj. B27. $35.00

**WATERMAN, George.** *Practical Stock Doctor...300 Tried & Tested Remedies...* 1912. Detroit. enlarged. 840p. G. A17. $20.00

**WATERMAN, Thomas Tileston.** *Mansions of Virginia 1706-1776.* (1945). UNC. 7th. photos/plans. 456p. B10. $50.00

**WATERS, Alice.** *Fanny at Chez Panisse.* 1992. Harper Collins. rpt. 4to. F/dj. B17. $15.00

**WATERS, Frank.** *Earp Brothers of Tombstone.* 1962. London. Spearman. F. A19. $35.00

**WATERS, Frank.** *Mexico Mystique: Coming 6th World of Consciousness.* 1975. Chicago. Swallow. 2nd. 326p. dj. F3. $20.00

**WATERS, Frank.** *To Possess the Land.* 1973. Sage. 1st. F/VG. T11. $45.00

**WATERS, Frank.** *Yogi of Cockroach Court.* 1947. NY. Rinehart. 1st. inscr. NF. L3. $375.00

**WATERS, Howard J.** *Jack Teagarden's Music.* 1960. Stanhope. WC Allen. 1st. NF/wrp. B2. $75.00

**WATERTON, Charles.** *Wanderings in South America.* 1909. NY. Sturgis Walton. ils CL Bull/16 mc pl. 338p. F3. $45.00

**WATKINS, C. Malcolm.** *Cultural History of Marlborough, VA.* 1968. Smithsonian. 224p. xl. B10. $35.00

**WATKINS, Paul.** *Calm at Sunset, Calm at Dawn.* 1989. Houghton Mifflin. 1st. author's 2nd book. F/F. H11. $45.00

**WATKINS, Paul.** *Calm at Sunset, Calm at Dawn.* 1989. Houghton Mifflin. 1st. author's 2nd book. F/NF. B3. $40.00

**WATKINS, Paul.** *In the Blue Light of African Dreams.* 1990. Houghton Mifflin. 1st. F/NF. H11. $40.00

**WATKINS, Paul.** *In the Blue Light of African Dreams.* 1990. Houghton Mifflin. 1st. sgn/dtd 1994. NF/F. R14. $65.00

**WATKINS, Paul.** *Night Over Day Over Night.* 1988. Knopf. 1st Am. author's 1st book. sgn. F/dj. Q1. $100.00

**WATKINS, Paul.** *Night Over Day Over Night.* 1988. NY. Knopf. 1st. author's 1st book. rem mk. NF/dj. B3. $60.00

**WATKINS, Paul.** *Story of My Disappearance.* 1997. London. Faber. 1st. sgn. F/dj. R14. $75.00

**WATKINS, Ron.** *Sinner Takes All.* 1979. London. Hale. 1st. F/dj. M15. $40.00

**WATKINS, S.C.G.** *Reminiscences of Montclair.* 1929. NY. Barnes. inscr. G. A19. $60.00

**WATKINS, T.H.** *Great Depression: America in the 1930s.* 1993. Boston. 1st. ils. 375p. F/dj. M4. $15.00

**WATKINS, T.H.** *On the Shore of the Sundown Sea.* 1972. Sierra Club. 1st. natural linen. F/NF. O4. $20.00

**WATKINS, T.H.** *Vanishing Arctic: Alaska's National Wildlife Refuge.* 1988. Aperture. 88p. dj. A17. $17.50

**WATKINS & WATKINS.** *West: A Treasury of Art & Literature.* 1994. Hugh Lauter Levin Assoc. 1st. ils/index. 384p. F/F. B19. $50.00

**WATKINSON, Ray.** *William Morris as Designer.* 1990. London. Trefoil. ils/pl. 84p. gilt cream cloth. F/NF. F1. $15.00

**WATSON, Aldren A.** *Hand Bookbinding: A Manual of Instruction.* 1986. NY. 1st. VG/dj. T9. $18.00

**WATSON, Aldren A.** *Hand Bookbinding: A Manual of Instruction.* 1986. NY. Macmillan. 1st. F/dj. O10. $30.00

**WATSON, Elizabeth.** *Guests of My Life.* 1996. Friends General Conference. 1996. VG/wrp. V3. $9.00

**WATSON, Elmo Scott.** *Professor Goes West (JW Powell).* 1954. Bloomington, IL. 1st. 138p. gilt gr cloth. NF. F7. $40.00

**WATSON, G.R.** *Roman Soldier.* 1981 (1969). London. rpt. ils. 256p. cloth. VG/dj. Q2. $30.00

**WATSON, Ian.** *Gardens of Delight.* 1980. London. Gollancz. 1st. AN/dj. M21. $20.00

**WATSON, Ian.** *Lucy's Harvest: First Book of Mana.* 1993. London. Gollancz. 1st. F/dj. G10. $27.50

**WATSON, J.N.P.** *Book of Foxhunting.* 1978. Arco. 1st Am. VG/dj. O3. $18.00

**WATSON, J.N.P.** *Horse & Carriage: Pageant of Hyde Park.* 1990. London. Sportsmans Pr. 1st. F/dj. O3. $25.00

**WATSON, James B.** *New Guinea: Central Highlands.* 1964. Am Anthropoligical Assn. 329p. VG/wrp. S15. $12.00

**WATSON, John Broadus.** *Behaviorism.* 1924. NY. People's Inst Pub Inc. 1st/1st issue. 238p. G1. $200.00

**WATSON, John Broadus.** *Behaviorism.* 1925. People's Inst Pub Co Inc. 1st prt in book form. 251p. blk cloth/paper labels. G1. $75.00

**WATSON, John H.** *Sherlock Holmes Vs Dracula.* 1978. Doubleday. 1st. VG/G. L1. $100.00

**WATSON, John.** *Real Virginian: Saga of Edwin Burnham Trafton.* 1989. Westernlore. 1st. ils/index. 209p. AN. B19. $15.00

**WATSON, Larry.** *Justice.* 1995. Minneapolis. Milkweed. 1st. sgn. F/dj. O11. $25.00

**WATSON, Peter.** *Biography of Rudolf Nureyev.* 1994. London. 1st. dj. T9. $25.00

**WATSON, Peter.** *Crusade.* 1987. London. Hutchinson. 1st. F/dj. T12. $20.00

WATSON, Peter. *Sotheby's: The Inside Story.* 1997. NY. Random. 1st Am. sgn. F/dj. T2. $25.00

WATSON, Sidney. *Mark of the Beast.* 1945. Loizeaux. 245p. G. B29. $8.00

WATSON, Thomas. *Story of France.* 1899. Macmillan. 2 vol. G. S17. $12.50

WATSON, Virginia. *With Cortes the Conquerer.* 1917. Penn. 1st. ils. F. M5. $75.00

WATSON, W.C. *Men & Times of the Revolution; or, Memoirs...* 1856. NY. 1st. 460p. VG. M4. $90.00

WATT, George. *Essay on Dental Surgery for Popular Reading.* 1856. Cincinnati. 72p. new brd/orig label. xl. G7. $145.00

WATT, Henry Jackson. *Common Sense of Dreams.* 1929. Worcester, MA. Clark U. Internat U Series Psychology Vol 6. 212p. G1. $35.00

WATT, Henry Jackson. *Foundations of Music.* 1919. Cambridge. ARC. 239p. panelled red cloth. VG. G1. $65.00

WATT, Montgomery. *Faith & Practice of Al-Ghazali.* 1953. London. Allen Unwin. 155+5p ads. decor cloth. G+/dj. Q2. $17.00

WATTERS, Mary. *History of Mary Baldwin College, 1842-1942.* 1942. The College. ils. 629p. VG. B10. $75.00

WATTERSON, Henry. *History of the Spanish-American War.* (1898). Akron. Werner. 1st. ils. 474p. VG. B18. $25.00

WATTS, Alan W. *Wisdom of Insecurity.* 1954. London. Rider. 1st. F/rpr. B2. $35.00

WATTS, Isaac. *Doctrine of Passions Explained & Improved...* 1795. NY. Shepard Kollock/Robert Hodge. 1st Am. 32mo. 210p. G1. $200.00

WATTS, Mabel. *Dozens of Cousins.* 1950. Whittlesey. 1st. ils Roger Duvoisin. VG/G. M5. $12.00

WATTS, Mabel. *Story of Zachary Sween.* 1967. Parents Magazine. 1st? ils Marylin Haffner. VG. M5. $8.00

WATTS, May Theilgaard. *Reading the Landscape: An Adventure in Ecology.* 1963. Macmillan. 4th. 230p. VG/dj. A10. $30.00

WATTS, Ralph. *Vegetable Gardening.* 1931. Orange Judd. revised. 511p. cloth. VG. A10. $22.00

WATTS, Timothy. *Steal Away.* (1996). NY. Soho. 1st. F/dj. A23. $46.00

WATTS, W.W. *Shropshire: Geography of the Country.* 1919. Shrewsbury. Wilding & Son. pres. 254p. xl. F. B14. $55.00

WAUGH, Alec. *In Praise of Wine & Certain Noble Spirits.* 1959. Wm Sloane. 1st. F/G. M19. $17.50

WAUGH, Alec. *Most Women...* 1931. Farrar Rhinehart. 1st. ils Lynd Ward. VG. S13. $12.00

WAUGH, Auberon. *Bed of Flowers.* 1972. London. Michael Joseph. 1st. VG/clip. R14. $25.00

WAUGH, Dorothy. *Emily Dickinson's Beloved, a Surmise...* 1976. NY. Vanguard. 1st. 75p. VG. M10. $20.00

WAUGH, E.A. *American Peach Orchard: A Sketch of Practice...* 1915. NY/London. ils. 236p. brn cloth. VG. H3. $50.00

WAUGH, Evelyn. *Brideshead Revisited.* 1946. Little Brn. 1st Am trade (precedes ltd). NF/VG. B4. $200.00

WAUGH, Evelyn. *Handful of Dust.* 1934. Farrar Rhinehart. 1st Am. NF/dj. Q1. $450.00

WAUGH, Evelyn. *Helena.* 1950. London. Chapman Hall. 1st. inscr. NF/dj. L3. $1,500.00

WAUGH, Evelyn. *Letters.* 1992. NY. 1st. edit Artemis Cooper. VG/dj. M17. $20.00

WAUGH, Evelyn. *Men at Arms.* 1952. Chapman Hall. 1st. NF/dj. M25. $75.00

WAUGH, Evelyn. *Officers & Gentlemen.* 1955. Little Brn. 1st. VG/dj. S13. $18.00

WAUGH, Evelyn. *Tourist in Africa.* 1960. London. 1st. dj. T9. $50.00

WAUGH, Julia. *Silver Cradle.* 1955. Austin. 1st. 160p. dj. F3. $15.00

WAUGH, T. *Travels of Marco Polo.* 1984. NY. ils. 218p. F/dj. M4. $20.00

WAUGH & WAUGH. *South Builds: New Architecture in the Old South.* (1960). UNC. photos. 173p. F/G. B10. $25.00

WAVELL, Archibald P. *Allenby in Egypt.* 1943. London. Harrap. 1st. 156p. VG/dj. M7. $50.00

WAVELL, Archibald P. *Palestine Campaigns.* 1938. London. Constable. 3rd/8th imp. red cloth. VG/G. M7. $75.00

WAY, Thomas E. *Summary of Travel to Grand Canyon.* 1980. Prescott Graphics. sgn. 14p. VG/stiff yel wrp. F7. $18.00

WAYLAND, John W. *Historic Homes of Northern Virginia & Eastern Panhandle...* 1937. McClure. photos/maps. 625p. VG. B10. $500.00

WAYMOUTH, Charity. *Growth Requirements of Vertebrate Cells in Vitro.* 1981. Cambridge. 541p. xl. VG. S5. $45.00

WAYRE, Philip. *River People.* 1976. London. photos. 189p. F/VG. S15. $11.00

WEADCOCK, Jack. *Dust of the Desert: Plain Tales of the Desert & Border.* 1936. Appleton Century. 1st. ils. 306p. G. B19. $50.00

WEARIN, Otha. *Ellsworth: Artist of the Old West.* 1967. World. 1st. 1/750. sgn. AN. J2. $225.00

WEATHERBY, W.J. *Jackie Gleason: Intimate Portrait of 'The Great One.'* 1992. Pharos. 1st. 8vo. 253p. F/dj. W2. $30.00

WEATHERHEAD, Leslie. *Key Next Door & Other London City Temple Sermons.* 1960. Abingdon. 255p. G/dj. B29. $7.00

WEATHERLY, Frederick Edward. *Rhymes & Roses.* (1888). London. Hildescheimer Falukner. 1st. 4to. 32p. F. H5. $300.00

WEATHERLY, Frederick Edward. *Sunbeams.* (1892). London. Hildescheimer Faulkner. 1st. 16 full-p pl. F. H5. $175.00

WEATHERMAN, Hazel Marie. *Colored Glassware of the Depression Era, Book 1.* 1970. self pub. 1st/2nd prt. 8vo. 239p. F/NF. H1. $38.00

WEATHERMAN, Hazel Marie. *Colored Glassware of the Depression Era, Book 2.* (1974). self pub. 1st. 401p. ils brd. VG. H1. $85.00

WEATHERMAN, Hazel Marie. *Fostoria: Its First 50 Years.* 1972. self pub. 1st. ils. 320p. VG/prt Mylar dj. H1. $150.00

WEATHERS, Lee B. *Living Past of Cleveland County: A History.* (1956). Shelby, NC. Star. photos/map ep. 269p. VG. B10. $35.00

WEAVER, Earl. *Winning!* 1972. Morrow. later prt. sgn. F/VG. P8. $50.00

WEAVER, George. *Beginnings of Medical Education in & Near Chicago...* 1925. Chicago. 1st. 132p. xl. A13. $50.00

WEAVER, J.E. *Native Vegetation of Nebraska.* 1965. U KE. ils. 185p. F/dj. S15. $10.00

WEAVER, John D. *Wind Before Rain.* 1942. Macmillan. 1st. author's 1st book. beige cloth. NF/dj. C6. $35.00

WEAVER, John V.A. *Turning Point.* 1930. Knopf. 1st. 12mo. 69p. NF. M7. $25.00

WEAVER, Louise. *When Sue Began to Cook, With Bettina's Best Recipes...* 1924. AL Burt. ils. E6. $50.00

WEAVER. *Catalogue of Wheeler Gift of Books, Pamphlets...* 1909. 2 vol. 7000 entries. VG. A4. $450.00

WEBB, Beatrice. *My Apprenticeship.* 1926. Longman Gr. 1st. photos. xl. VG. A25. $15.00

**WEBB, Cecil S.** *Odyssey of an Animal Collector.* 1954. Longman Gr. G. A19. $30.00

**WEBB, Charles.** *Graduate.* 1963. NAL. 1st. F/VG. B4. $175.00

**WEBB, George Ernest.** *Three Rings & Telescopes.* 1983. Tucson. U AZ. 1st. VG/dj. O4. $15.00

**WEBB, Jack.** *Make My Bed Soon.* 1963. HRW. 1st. F/NF. T12. $25.00

**WEBB, James Josiah.** *Adventures in the Santa Fe Trade, 1844-1847.* 1931. Arthur H Clark. 301p. D11. $125.00

**WEBB, Joe.** *Care & Training of the Tennesse Walking Horse.* 1962. Searcy, AZ. private prt. 1st. sgn. VG. O3. $45.00

**WEBB, Kenneth.** *As Sparks Fly Upward: Rationale of Farm & Wilderness Camp.* 1973. Canaan. Phoenix. sgn. ils. 196p. VG/clip. R11. $20.00

**WEBB, Lance.** *Conquering the Seven Deadly Sins.* 1955. Abingdon. 224p. VG. B29. $9.50

**WEBB, Mary.** *Armor Wherein He Trusted, a Novel & Some Stories.* (1929). London. Cape. 1st. facs sgn. 8vo. gilt gr cloth. NF/dj. R3. $40.00

**WEBB, Roy.** *If We Had a Boat: Green River Explorers, Adventurers...* 1986. U UT. 8vo. ils. 194p. G+/stiff wrp. F7. $18.50

**WEBB, Sharon.** *Half Life.* 1989. NY. Tor. 1st. F/NF. G10. $12.00

**WEBB, T.W.** *Celestial Objects for Common Telescopes.* 1881 (1859). Longman Gr. 4th. ils/pl. 493p. cloth. K5. $150.00

**WEBB, Walter Freeman.** *Handbook for Shell Collectors.* 1948. Lee. revised. ils. NF/dj. S15. $12.00

**WEBB, Walter Freeman.** *Handbook for Shell Collectors...* 1935. self pub. 2nd. 129p+index. VG. S5. $15.00

**WEBB, Walter Prescott.** *Great Plains.* 1931. Boston, MA. Ginn. G. A19. $35.00

**WEBBER, A.R.** *Early History of Elyria & Her People.* 1930. Elyria. inscr. ils. 326p. G+. B18. $45.00

**WEBBER, Charles W.** *Adventure in the Comanche Country, in Search of Gold Mine.* 1848. Glasgow. Griffin. 2nd. 296p. cloth. D11. $60.00

**WEBBER, Robert.** *Evangelicals on the Canterbury Trail...* 1985. Jarrell. 174p. VG/dj. B29. $8.50

**WEBER, D.J.** *Spanish Frontier in North America.* 1992. Yale. 1st. ils/maps. 579p. F/dj. M4. $45.00

**WEBER, Elizabeth Anne.** *Duk-Duks.* 1929. Chicago. 1st. NF/dj. T10. $75.00

**WEBER, Eugene.** *Hollow Years: France in the 1930s.* 1994. NY. 1st. dj. T9. $15.00

**WEBER, Francis J.** *California on US Postage Stamps.* 1975. Achille St Onge. 1/150. mini. ils+tipped-in stamp. aeg. B27. $45.00

**WEBER, Francis J.** *California on US Postage Stamps.* 1975. Worcester. St Onge. mini. 1/1500+US postage stp. aeg. gilt bl leather. B24. $85.00

**WEBER, Francis J.** *Catholica on American Stamps.* 1976. Tilton, NH. Hillside. mini. 1/250. pub/sgn Frank Irwin. gr cloth brd. F. B24. $200.00

**WEBER, Francis J.** *Christmas in Pastoral California.* 1971. Los Angeles. Blau, Bela. mini. 28p. gr/red prt. gilt gr leather. B24. $45.00

**WEBER, Francis J.** *Letter of Junipero Serra to Rev Father Fray Fermin...* (1984). Pr in Hugus Alley. mini. 1/25. prt wrp/orig envelope. B24. $125.00

**WEBER, Francis J.** *Up to 65 Years in Larchmont.* 1970. Los Angeles. Bela Blau. mini. gilt maroon leather. F. B24. $45.00

**WEBER, Francis.** *Dohenys of Los Angeles.* 1974. Dawson's Book Shop. ils. 49p. cloth. D11. $75.00

**WEBER, Joseph.** *Mayor of Indianapolis, by Father Joseph Weber.* 1975. Worcester. St Onge. mini. 1/300. 26p. aeg. gilt blk leather. B24. $175.00

**WEBER, Lenora Mattingly.** *Leave It to Beany!* (1950). Thos Crowell. 8vo. ils. 239p. gr cloth. VG. T5. $40.00

**WEBER, Otto.** *Die Kunst der Hethiter.* nd. Berlin. Wasmuth. ils. 19p. brd. G. Q2. $20.00

**WEBER, William A.** *Colorado Flora: Eastern Slope.* 1990. Niwot. ils. 526p. AN/dj. B26. $37.50

**WEBSTER, A.L.** *Improved Housewife; or, Book of Receipts...* 1844 (1843). Hartford. 214p. fair. E6. $50.00

**WEBSTER, Daniel.** *On the Powers of Government Assigned to It by Constitution.* (1952). Worcester. St Onge. mini. 1/1000. red cloth brd. B24. $185.00

**WEBSTER, John.** *Introduction to Fungi.* 1970. Cambridge. 424p. xl. VG. S5. $25.00

**WECHSER, Lorainne.** *Encyclopedia of Graffiti.* 1974. Galahad. rpt. F/NF. S18. $10.00

**WECHSLER, David.** *Measurement & Appraisal of Adult Intelligence.* 1958 (1939). Baltimore. Wms Wilkins. 4th/1st prt. sgn. 297p. red cloth. G1. $35.00

**WECHSLER, James A.** *In the Darkness.* 1972. Norton. 12mo. VG/dj. A2. $12.00

**WEDDLE, A.E.** *Techniques of Landscape Architecture.* 1969. Elsevier. 2nd. 226p. VG/dj. A10. $30.00

**WEDDLE, Dennis R.** *I Would Have Gave My Life...But I Don't Think My Parents...* 1978. np. ils/photos. unp. VG/dj. R11. $75.00

**WEDEMEYER, Albert C.** *Wedemeyer Reports: An Objective, Dispassionate Examination.* 1958. Henry Holt. 1st. 497p. VG/torn. S16. $35.00

**WEEDEN, Robert B.** *Alaska: Promises to Keep.* 1978. Boston. Houghton Mifflin. 1st. 8vo. 254p. blk cloth. NF. P4. $25.00

**WEEDON, L.L.** *Child Characters From Dickens.* nd. Nister. ils Arthur Dixon. fair. A21. $50.00

**WEEDON, L.L.** *Child Characters of Dickens.* nd (1905). London. Nister. 1st. 8vo. aeg. 320p. bl pict cloth. NF/dj. H5. $350.00

**WEEDON, L.L.** *Fairy Tales in Wonderland.* ca 1900. London. Nister. 3 popups/ils E Stuart Hardy/others. pict brd. R5. $1,500.00

**WEEDON, L.L.** *My Picture Puzzle Book.* ca 1910. London. Nister. 4to. 6 moveables. pict brd. R5. $2,000.00

**WEEGEE.** *Weegee's Creative Camera.* 1959. Garden City. 1st. 128p. VG/dj. S9. $175.00

**WEEGEE.** *Weegee: An Autobiography.* 1961. Ziff-Davis. 1st. 8vo. 224p. NF/dj. S9. $150.00

**WEEKS, Stephen B.** *Bibliography of Historical Literature of North Carolina.* 1895. Cambridge. 1st. 79p. VG/wrp. M8. $45.00

**WEELAN, Robert J.** *Ecology of Fire.* 1977 (1995). Cambridge Studies Ecology. 346p. rem mk. F. S15. $13.50

**WEEMS, Mason L.** *Life of George Washington.* 1809. M Carey. 9th. ils. 228p. fair. B10. $100.00

**WEHLE, Robert.** *Wing & Shot.* 1971. Country Pr. 4th. NF/dj. A21. $40.00

**WEHR, Julian.** *Animated Antics in Playland.* 1946. Saalfield. obl 4to. mc ils. sbdg. pict dj. R5. $150.00

**WEHR, Julian.** *Puss in Boots.* 1944. NY. Duenwald. 8vo. 6 tab-activated moveables. pict sbdg. dj. R5. $175.00

**WEIGEL, George.** *Tranquillitas Ordinis: Present Failure & Future Promise.* 1987. OUP. 1st. VG/dj. N2. $10.00

**WEIGHT WATCHERS.** *365-Day Menu Cookbook.* 1981. Weight Watchers Inst. G/dj. A16. $10.00

**WEIL, Danielle.** *Baseball: The Perfect Game.* 1992. Rizzoli. 1st. photos. VG/dj. P8. $22.50

**WEIL, Ernst.** *Collected Catalogs of Dr Ernst Weil, Bookseller.* 1/300. 237p index. F. A4. $165.00

**WEIL, Gordon L.** *Sears, Roebuck, USA: Great American Catalog Store...* 1977. Stein Day. 1st. ils/index. F/NF. H6. $38.00

**WEINBERG, Larry.** *Star Wars: Making of the Movie.* 1980. Random. 1st. 8vo. 69p. NF. C14. $10.00

**WEINBERG, Robert.** *Weird Vampire Tales.* 1992. Gramercy. 1st thus. VG/dj. L1. $45.00

**WEINER, Michael.** *Earth Medicine-Earth Food.* 1980. NY. Collier. 230p. VG. A10. $12.00

**WEINER, Norbert.** *Cybernetics; or, Control & Communication...* 1948. NY/Paris. 10th. 194p. red/blk cloth. F. B14. $35.00

**WEINER, Norbert.** *Cybernetics; or Control & Communication in Animal & Machine.* 1948. NY. Technology Pr. 1st. 194p. prt red cloth/prt labels. VG/dj. G1. $350.00

**WEINERT, Richard P.** *Confederate Regular Army.* 1991. Wht Mane Pub. 1st. F/dj. A14. $25.00

**WEINGREEN, J.** *Practical Grammar for Classical Hebrew.* 1959. London. Oxford. 316p. VG. M10. $8.50

**WEINSTEIN, Sol.** *Loxfinger.* 1965. NY. Pocket Books. 1st. F. M15. $45.00

**WEINSTEIN, Sol.** *On the Secret Service of His Majesty, the Queen.* 1966. NY. Pocket. 1st. F. M15. $45.00

**WEINTRAUB, Stanley.** *London Yankees.* 1979. HBJ. 1st. NF/dj. O4. $15.00

**WEINTRAUB, Stanley.** *Whistler: A Biography.* 1974. Weybright Talley. 1st. inscr. 495p. hospital xl. NF/VG+. C15. $20.00

**WEINTZ, Walter H.** *Solid Gold Mailbox.* 1987. Wiley. 1st. NF/clip. P3. $25.00

**WEIR, Ruth Hirsch.** *Language in the Crib.* 1962. The Hague. Moulton. Janua Linguarum Series Major XIV. lg 8vo. 216p. cloth. G1. $65.00

**WEISEL, Elie.** *Legends of Our Time.* 1968. HRW. 1st. inscr. NF/dj. R14. $50.00

**WEISER, C.Z.** *Life of (John) Conrad Weiser.* 1876. Reading. Daniel Miller. 1st. 449p. B18. $45.00

**WEISER, Francis X.** *Christmas Book.* 1952. Harcourt Brace. 1st. inscr. 8vo. 188p. gr cloth. NF/dj. J3. $75.00

**WEISMAN, Abner I.** *Spermatozoa & Sterility: A Clinical Manual.* 1941. Paul Hoeber. 1st. ils. NF. B27. $45.00

**WEISMAN, Alan.** *La Frontera.* 1986. NY. Harcourt. 1st. 200p. dj. F3. $20.00

**WEISS, Dianne.** *Carrousel.* nd. Figment. mini. 1/100. sgn. w/10-animal carousel popup/music box cover. F. B24. $325.00

**WEISS, Dianne.** *Little Bear Who...* nd. Figment. mini. 1/150. sgn. w/Smokey Bear postage stp. prt brd. B24. $135.00

**WEISS, Paul A.** *Science of Life.* 1973. Futura. 137p. xl. VG. S5. $7.50

**WEISS, Peter.** *Exile.* 1968. Delacorte. 1st Am. F/dj. B2. $25.00

**WEIZMAN, Ezer.** *Battle for Peace.* 1981. Bantam. 1st. photos. VG/clip. S14. $9.00

**WELCH, Denton.** *Journals.* 1952. London. 1st. intro Jocelyn Brooke. VG/G. M17. $32.50

**WELCH, Galbraith.** *Unveiling of Timbuctoo: Astounding Adventures of Caillie.* 1939. NY. Morrow. 1st. sm 8vo. ils/map. 351p. xl. VG. W1. $20.00

**WELCH, James.** *Fools Crow.* 1986. Viking. 1st. sgn. F/dj. O11. $115.00

**WELCH, James.** *Indian Lawyer.* 1990. NY. Norton. 1st. sgn. F/F. B3/R14. $60.00

**WELCH, James.** *Riding the Earthboy 40.* 1971. NY. World. 1st. author's 1st book. F/dj. L3/O11. $150.00

**WELCH, James.** *Riding the Earthboy 40.* 1971. World. 1st. sgn. author's 1st book. F/NF. B3. $275.00

**WELCH, James.** *Winter in the Blood.* 1974. NY/London. Harper Row. 1st. F/dj. Q1. $125.00

**WELCH, Paul S.** *Limnology.* 1952. NY. 2nd. 538p. VG. A17. $15.00

**WELCH, Stuart Cary.** *Room for Wonder: Indian Painting During British Period...* 1978. NY. Am Federation Arts. 191p. VG. D2. $15.00

**WELCH, William.** *Pathology & Preventive Medicine.* 1920. Baltimore. 1st. 678p. xl. A13. $100.00

**WELCOME, John.** *Cheltenham Gold Cup: Story of Great Steeplechase.* 1957. London. Constable. 1st. VG. O3. $25.00

**WELDON, Fay.** *And the Wife Ran Away.* 1968. McKay. 1st Am. VG/dj. M25. $60.00

**WELDON, Fay.** *Cloning of Joanna May.* 1990. NY. Viking. 1st Am. F/NF. G10. $14.00

**WELDON, Fay.** *Hearts & Lives of Men.* 1988. NY. Viking. 1st. sgn. F/NF. B3. $20.00

**WELDON, Fay.** *Life & Loves of a She-Devil.* 1983. Pantheon. 1st. rem mk. F/NF. H11. $15.00

**WELDON, Fay.** *Life Force.* 1992. London. Harper Collins. 1st. rem mk. F/dj. G10. $18.50

**WELK, Lawrence.** *Musical Family Album.* 1977. Prentice Hall. unp. G/dj. C5. $12.50

**WELKER & WELKER.** *Pressed Glass in America Encyclopedia of 1st Hundred Years.* 1985. Antique Acres. self pub. ltd 1st ed. 1/1500. ils. 495p. AN/dj. H1. $125.00

**WELLARD, James.** *Great Sahara.* 1965. Dutton. 1st. ils/map ep. 350p. NF/dj. W1. $16.00

**WELLER, Jac.** *Fire & Movement: Bargain-Basement Warfare in Far East.* 1967. NY. Crowell. photos/maps. 268p. VG/dj. R11. $30.00

**WELLER, Philip.** *Life & Times of Sherlock Holmes.* 1992. Crescent. F/dj. P3. $20.00

**WELLES, Orson.** *Mr Arkadin.* 1987. London. WH Allen. 1st. F/dj. C9. $48.00

**WELLMAN, Manly Wade.** *School of Darkness.* 1985. Doubleday. 1st. F/dj. G10. $30.00

**WELLMAN, Manly Wade.** *Took Their Stand: Founders of the Confederacy.* (1959). Putnam. 258p. VG/G. B10. $30.00

**WELLMAN, Paul I.** *Death on Horseback: 70 Years of War for the American West.* 1947. Phil. 3rd. ils/index. 484p. G. E1. $25.00

**WELLS, Anna Mary.** *Miss Marks & Miss Woolley.* 1978. Houghton Mifflin. 1st. 286p. VG/VG. A25. $20.00

**WELLS, Carveth.** *Panmexico!.* 1937. NY. Nat Travel Club. 1st. photo/map ep. dj. F3. $15.00

**WELLS, David A.** *How Much Carriage Building Is Helped by Present Tariff.* 1884. Wilmington, DE. 8p. VG/wrp. O3. $25.00

**WELLS, David A.** *Recent Economic Changes: Their Effects on Production...* 1891 (1880). Appleton. 493p. VG. S5. $20.00

**WELLS, David A.** *Well's Natural Philosophy: For Use of Schools, Academies...* 1897. NY. Ivison Blakeman Taylor. new ed. ils. 206p. VG. A25. $20.00

**WELLS, David W.** *Psychology Applied to Medicine.* 1907. Phil. Davis. 1st. 12mo. 141p. VG+. C14. $22.00

**WELLS, Edward.** *Historic Geography of the New Testament: In Two Parts...* 1708. London. Botham/Knapton. 2 parts in 1. ils/16 copper pl/2 fld maps. K1. $300.00

**WELLS, H.G.** *Autocracy of Mr Parham.* 1930. Doubleday Doran. 1st. 328p. G. G11. $10.00

**WELLS, H.G.** *Critical Edition of the War of the Worlds...* 1993. Bloomington. IU. 1st. F/dj. G10. $27.50

**WELLS, H.G.** *Croquet Player.* 1937. Viking. 1st. VG/$1.25 dj price. S13. $22.00

**WELLS, H.G.** *Experiement in Autobiography.* 1934. Canada. Macmillan. 1st. VG. P3. $35.00

**WELLS, H.G.** *First & Last Things, a Confession of Faith & Rule of Life.* 1908. Putnam. 1st Am. gilt gr cloth. F/dj. M24. $450.00

**WELLS, H.G.** *Joan & Peter.* 1918. Macmillan. 1st. 594p. G. G11. $12.00

**WELLS, H.G.** *Mr Blettsworthy on Rampole Island.* 1928. London. Ernest Benn. 288p. G11. $10.00

**WELLS, H.G.** *Mr Britling Sees It Through.* 1916. NY. Macmillan. 1st. 443p. G. G11. $20.00

**WELLS, H.G.** *Outline of History.* 1921. Macmillan. 2 vol. gilt red cloth. VG. S17. $10.00

**WELLS, H.G.** *Outline of History.* 1949. Garden City. 2 vol. VG. P3. $20.00

**WELLS, H.G.** *Outline of History: Being a Plain History of Life & Mankind.* 1920. Macmillan. 2 vol. 1st Am. VG. M19. $35.00

**WELLS, H.G.** *Star Begotten.* 1937. Chatto Windus. 1st. VG. A24. $50.00

**WELLS, H.G.** *World of William Clissold.* 1926. London. Benn. 3 vol. 1st. 1/198. sgn. quarter vellum/gr cloth. NF/case. H5. $500.00

**WELLS, Helen.** *Cherry Ames, Camp Nurse.* 1957. Grosset Dunlap. lists to title. 182p. VG/dj. B36. $10.00

**WELLS, Helen.** *Cherry Ames, Flight Nurse.* 1945. Grosset Dunlap. 1st. VG/dj. R8. $15.00

**WELLS, James S.** *Plant Propagation Practices.* 1955. Macmillan. ils/index. 344p. G. H10. $15.00

**WELLS, Rosemary.** *My Very First Mother Goose.* 1996. Candlewick. 1st. folio. VG/dj. B17. $17.50

**WELLS, Rosemary.** *Peabody.* 1983. Dial. 1st. ils. F/VG. M5. $24.00

**WELLS, Rosemary.** *Shy Charles.* 1988. Dial. Books for Young Readers. ils/inscr. NF/dj. T5. $35.00

**WELSH, Doris V.** *America Known Before Columbus Discovered It.* 1955. Chicago. Petit Oiseau. mini. 1/100. 32p. cloth. F. B24. $110.00

**WELSH, Doris V.** *Indian & White Man.* 1954. Chicago. Petit Oiseau. mini. 1/100. vignettes. 3-quarter cloth/pict brd. B24. $150.00

**WELSH, Doris V.** *Mayflower Compact.* 1954. Chicago. Welsh. mini. 1/100. 7p. navy cloth. B24. $150.00

**WELSH, Doris V.** *Mecklenburg Declaration of Independence: May 20, 1775.* 1954. Chicago. Petit Oiseau. mini. 1/100. 8p. 3-quarter blk cloth. F. B24. $110.00

**WELTY, Eudora.** *Collected Stories of...* 1980. HBJ. 1st. 1/500. sgn. F/NF case. L3. $450.00

**WELTY, Eudora.** *Delta Wedding.* 1946. Knopf. 1st. 8vo. NF/VG. S9. $275.00

**WELTY, Eudora.** *Eye of the Story.* 1977. Random. 1st. F/dj. B30. $60.00

**WELTY, Eudora.** *Little Store.* 1985. Newton, IA. Tamazunchale. mini. 1/250. aeg. gilt gr leather. B24. $95.00

**WELTY, Eudora.** *Losing Battles.* 1970. Random. 1st. NF/F clip. H11. $35.00

**WELTY, Eudora.** *Photographs.* 1989. Jackson, MS. U MS. 1st. 1/52. sgn. full leather. F/purple silk fld case. B4. $1,000.00

**WELTY, Eudora.** *Photographs.* 1989. Jackson. U MS. 1st trade. 4to. maroon cloth. M24. $125.00

**WELTY, Eudora.** *Ponder Heart.* 1954. Harcourt Brace. 1st. inscr. NF/VG. R14. $225.00

**WELTY, Eudora.** *Ponder Heart.* 1954. Harcourt Brace. 1st. sgn. VG/dj. B30. $200.00

**WELTY, Eudora.** *Robber Bridegroom.* 1942. Doubleday Doran. 1st. author's 2nd book. F/VG. B4. $450.00

**WELTY, Eudora.** *Robber Bridegroom.* 1987. Harcourt Brace. 1st. sgn Welty/Moser. VG+/dj. B30. $160.00

**WELTY, Eudora.** *Short Stories.* 1949. Harcourt Brace. 1st. 1/1500. apricot prt brd. NF. M24. $125.00

**WENDT, Edmund.** *Treatise on Asiatic Cholera.* 1885. NY. 1st. 403p. A13. $65.00

**WENDT, Lloyd.** *Wall Street Journal.* 1982. Rand McNally. 1st. photos. 448p. NF/VG. S14. $10.00

**WENGER, M.A.** *Studies in Infant Behavior III.* 1936. Geo Stoddard. 206p. cloth. G1. $28.00

**WENKER, Mary Albert.** *Art of Serving Food Attractively.* 1951. Doubleday. G/dj. A16. $7.00

**WENTWORTH, Edward Norris.** *America's Sheep Trails, History, Personalities.* 1948. Ames. IA State College. 667p. tan cloth. VG/rpr. P4. $135.00

**WENTWORTH, Lady.** *Arab Horse Nonsense.* 1988. Oxford. Richmond Books. rpt. F/dj. O3. $22.00

**WENTWORTH, Patricia.** *Girl in the Cellar.* 1961. Hodder Stoughton. 1st. F/NF. M15. $45.00

**WENTWORTH, Patricia.** *Queen Ann Is Dead.* 1915. London. Andrew Melrose. 1st. red/gilt bl cloth. F. M15. $200.00

**WENTWORTH, Patricia.** *She Came Back.* 1945. Lippincott. 1st. VG/G. R8. $30.00

**WENTZ, Richard E.** *Pennsylvania Dutch Folk Spirituality.* 1993. Paulist. 1st. VG/dj. R8. $15.00

**WERFEL, Franz.** *Star of the Unborn.* 1946. Viking. 1st Am. VG/dj. M21. $20.00

**WERNER, A.W.** *Manufacture of Fibre Boxes: Story of Corrugated...* 1954 (1941). Chicago Brd Products. 3rd. 4to. VG. A2. $35.00

**WERNER, Fred H.** *Faintly Sounds the War-Cry: Story of Battle Butte...* 1983. Greeley, CO. 1st. sgn. 66p. F/stiff wrp. E1. $25.00

**WERNER, Herbert A.** *Iron Covvins.* (1969). HRW. BC. 8vo. 364p. NF/dj. M7. $22.50

**WERRELL, Kenneth P.** *Evolution of the Cruise Missile.* 1985. Maxwell Air Force Base. sm 4to. 289p. VG/wrp. K5. $25.00

**WERT, Jeffry D.** *Mosby's Rangers: From High Tide of Confederacy...* 1990. S&S. 1st. F/dj. A14. $17.50

**WERTENBAKER, Thomas J.** *Give Me Liberty: Struggle for Self-Government in Virginia.* 1958. AM Phil Soc. ils. 275p. VG. B10. $15.00

**WERTENBAKER, Thomas J.** *Shaping of Colonial Virginia.* (1958). Russell. 816p. G/G. B10. $25.00

**WESCHEKE, C.** *Overcoming Sleeplessness.* 1935. 32nd. xl. VG. E6. $15.00

**WESCOTT, Glenway.** *Apple of the Eye.* 1924. NY. MacVeagh/Dial. 1st. NF/dj. Q1. $100.00

**WESCOTT, Glenway.** *Goodbye Wisconsin.* 1928. NY. Harper. 1st. 1/250. sgn. quarter linen/label. M24. $150.00

**WESLEY, John.** *Primitive Physic; or, Essay & Natural Method of Curing...* 1858 (1858). 24th. G+. E6. $75.00

**WESLEY, Mary.** *Jumping the Queue.* 1983. London. Macmillan. 1st. F/VG. B3. $85.00

**WESLEY, Mary.** *Not That Sort of Girl.* 1987. London. Macmillan. 1st. NF/F. B3. $30.00

**WESLEY, Mary.** *Second Fiddle.* 1988. Viking. 1st. NF/F. B3. $20.00

**WEST, Charles.** *Rat's Nest.* 1990. Walker. 1st. F/dj. S13. $10.00

WEST, Edwin; see Westlake, Donald E.

WEST, Jessamyn. *Except for Me & Thee.* 1969. HBJ. 1st. sgn. NF/dj. M19. $45.00

WEST, Jessamyn. *Friendly Persuasion.* 1945. Harcourt Brace. MTI. F/VG+. B4. $85.00

WEST, Jessamyn. *Friendly Persuasion.* 1945. Harcourt Brace. 1st. author's 1st book. 214p. gray cloth. VG+/dj. J3. $100.00

WEST, Jessamyn. *Hide & Seek: A Continuing Journey.* 1973. HBJ. 1st. 310p. VG/G. V3. $11.00

WEST, Jessamyn. *Massacre at Fall Creek.* 1975. HBJ. 1st. NF/dj. T11. $15.00

WEST, Jessamyn. *State of Stony Lonesome.* 1984. HBJ. 1st. F/F. B3. $20.00

WEST, Lenon. *Making an Etching.* 1932. NY. Studio. 1st. ils. 79p. VG. B5. $27.50

WEST, Morris L. *Clowns of God.* 1981. NY. 1st. VG/dj. T9. $8.00

WEST, Morris L. *Vatican Trilogy.* 1993. Wings. 1st. sm 4to. 721p. F/dj. W2. $50.00

WEST, Nigel. *Faber Book of Espionage.* 1993. London. 1st. dj. T9. $20.00

WEST, Owen; see Koontz, Dean R.

WEST, Paul. *Lord Byron's Doctor.* 1989. NY. 1st. 277p. A13. $20.00

WEST, Paul. *Sheer Fiction.* 1987. New Paltz. McPherson. 1st. F/F. B3. $25.00

WEST, Paul. *Women of Whitechapel & Jack the Ripper.* 1991. Random. 1st. F/dj. R14. $25.00

WEST, Ray. *Kingdom of the Saints: Story of Brigham Young...* 1957. Viking. 389p. VG/dj. J2. $75.00

WEST, Richard S. *Mr Lincoln's Navy.* 1957. NY. 1st. 328p. VG/dj. E1. $30.00

WEST, Thomas Reed. *Flesh & Steel: Literature & Machine in American Culture.* 1967. Vanderbilt. 1st. VG/dj. N2. $10.00

WESTALL, Robert. *Haunting of Charles McGill.* 1983. Greenwillow. 1st Am. F/NF. T12. $25.00

WESTBROOK, Robert. *Rich Kids.* 1992. NY. Birch Lane. 1st. NF/F. H11. $15.00

WESTCOTT, Cynthia. *Anyone Can Grow Roses.* 1952. Van Nostrand. 1st. inscr. 147p. VG/VG. A25. $20.00

WESTERMAN, Gayl. *Juridical Bay.* 1987. OUP. 1st. VG/dj. M17. $25.00

WESTFAHL, Gary. *Cosmic Engineers: A Study of Hard Science Fiction.* 1996. Greenwood. 1st. F. P3. $50.00

WESTLAKE, Donald E. *Ax.* (1997). Mysterious. 1st/ARC. F/dj. A23. $25.00

WESTLAKE, Donald E. *Deadly Edge.* 1971. Random. 1st. F/dj. M15. $100.00

WESTLAKE, Donald E. *Gangway.* 1973. Evans. 1st. F/NF. M19. $25.00

WESTLAKE, Donald E. *Likely Story.* 1984. Penzler Books. 1/250. sgn. 8vo. beige cloth. F/box. R3. $50.00

WESTLAKE, Donald E. *Pity Him Afterwards.* 1964. Random. 1st. NF/VG. C15. $75.00

WESTLAKE, Donald E. *Tomorrow's Crimes.* 1989. NY. Mysterious. 1st. F/dj. G10. $16.50

WESTLAKE, Donald E. *What's the Worst That Can Happen?* 1996. Mysterious. ARC/1st. F/dj. A23. $25.00

WESTLAKE, Donald E. *361.* 1962. Random. 1st. NF/VG. C15. $95.00

WESTLAKE, Dondald E. *High Adventure.* 1985. Mysterious. 1st. F/dj. A23. $40.00

WESTMORELAND, Billy. *Them Ol' Brown Fish.* 1976. Nashville. 1st. photos. F/dj. A17. $15.00

WESTMORELAND, Saly Boner. *Common Herd.* 1955. self pub. 1st. 187p. G. S14. $10.00

WESTON, Mildred. *Vachel Lindsay: Poet in Exile.* (1987). Ye Galleon. 1st. ils. AN. A18. $17.50

WESTON, Rich. *Diamond Greats.* 1988. Meckler. 1st. F/dj. P8. $35.00

WESTOVER, Clyde C. *Dragon's Daughter.* 1912. NY. Neale. 1st. NF/dj. M15. $85.00

WETTSTEIN, Richard. *Tratado de Botanica Sistematica.* 1944 (1901). Barcelona. 4th. ils. 1039p. wht cloth. B26. $95.00

WETZEL, Charles M. *American Fishing Books, a Bibliography...to 1948...* nd. 1/75. ils. 235p. F. A4. $55.00

WEYER, Diane. *Assassin & the Deer.* 1989. Norton. 1st. F/F. H11. $30.00

WEYER, Edward. *Primitive Peoples Today.* 1958. Doubleday. 4to. 288p. dj. F3. $20.00

WEYGAND, James Lamar. *Papyrus Weygand.* 1980. Maestro Books. mini. 1/about 45. brd. B24. $150.00

WEYGAND, James Lamar. *Voyage Aboard the Jupiter: Contemporary Account...* 1967. Nappanee. Pr of IN Kid. mini. 1/100. leather/marbled brd. B24. $125.00

WEYGAND, Phil. *First Battle of Bull Run, an Eye Witness Account.* 1967. Dundee, MI. mini. 1/125. fld ftspc/facs letter. 36p. yel pict brd. B24. $125.00

WHALE, J.S. *Christian Doctrine.* 1956. Cambridge. VG/worn. B29. $3.50

WHALE, J.S. *Protestant Tradition: An Essay in Interpretation.* 1955. Cambridge. 360p. VG. B29. $13.50

WHARTON, Edith. *Age of Innocence.* 1920. NY. Appleton. 1st/1st prt (1 at end of text). red brd. VG. M24. $300.00

WHARTON, Edith. *Artemis to Actaeon.* 1909. London. Macmillan. 1st Eng (from Am sheets). inscr. cloth. VG. B4. $5,000.00

WHARTON, Edith. *Certain People.* 1930. NY. Appleton. 1st. NF/VG. B4. $375.00

WHARTON, Edith. *Crucial Instances.* 1901. Scribner. 1st/2nd prt (Merrymount imp). teg. gray brd. NF. M24. $125.00

WHARTON, Edith. *Descent of Man: And Other Stories.* 1904. Scribner. 1st. teg. VG. Q1. $200.00

WHARTON, Edith. *Glimpses of the Moon.* 1922. NY. Appleton. 1st/1st prt. 12mo. 364p. gilt bl cloth. VG/dj. J3. $675.00

WHARTON, Edith. *In the Custom of the Country.* 1913. Scribner. 1st. F. Q1. $200.00

WHARTON, Edith. *Marriage Playground.* 1928. Grosset Dunlap. MTI. VG/dj. B4. $200.00

WHARTON, Edith. *Mother's Recompense.* 1925. Appleton. 1st. 12mo. 342p. gilt maroon cloth. NF/dj. J3. $500.00

WHARTON, Edith. *Ring of Conspirators: Henry James & His Literary Circle...* 1989. Houghton Mifflin. 1st Am. 283p. gilt bdg. NF/dj. J3. $25.00

WHARTON, Francis. *Treatise on Criminal Law. Eleventh Edition...* 1912. SF. Bancroft Whitney. 3 vol. later ed. buckram. M11. $125.00

WHARTON, William. *Birdy.* 1978. London. Cape. 1st. F/clip. B3. $50.00

WHARTON, William. *Dad.* 1981. Knopf. 1st. author's 2nd novel. NF/VG. A24. $25.00

WHARTON, William. *Last Lovers.* 1991. FSG. 1st. NF/F. H11. $15.00

WHARTON, William. *Pride.* 1985. Knopf. 1st. F/F. B3. $30.00

WHEAT, Carl. *Mapping the Transmississippi West.* 1995. 5 vol in 6. 1/350. rpt. 1300 maps. F. A4. $595.00

**WHEAT, Marvin T.** *Travels of the Western Slope of Mexican Cordillera...* 1857. SF. Whitton Towne. 1st. 438p. marbled brd/leather spine. D11. $250.00

**WHEATLEY, Dennis.** *Desperate Measures.* 1974. London. Hutchinson. 1st. F/dj. M19. $17.50

**WHEATON, J.M.** *Report on the Birds of Ohio.* 1882. Columbus, OH. 440p. F. C12. $65.00

**WHEELER, Daniel.** *Extracts From Letters of Journal of Daniel Wheeler...* 1840. Phil. Joseph Rakestraw. 1st Am. 342p. V3. $140.00

**WHEELER, Daniel.** *Memoir of Daniel Wheeler With Account of His Gospel Labours.* 1859. Phil. Ass Friends for Diffusion. 24mo. 259p. V3. $40.00

**WHEELER, Daniel.** *Memoirs of Life & Gospel Labours of..., Minister...* nd. Phil. Friends Book Store. 600p. xl. V3. $65.00

**WHEELER, George M.** *Progress-Report Upon Geographic & Geological Explorations...* 1874. GPO. maps/4 full-p lithos. 56p. wrp. D11. $175.00

**WHEELER, Homer W.** *Buffalo Days: 40 Years in the Old West...* (1925). AL Burt. rpt. 369p. F/dj. E1. $50.00

**WHEELER, Homer W.** *Buffalo Days: 40 Years in the Old West...* 1925. Indianapolis. 1st. ils. 369p. E1. $85.00

**WHEELER, Homer W.** *Frontier Trial; or, From Cowboy to Colonel...* 1923. Times-Mirror. 334p. VG. J2. $165.00

**WHEELER, John Archibald.** *Journey Into Gravity & Spacetime.* 1990. NY. Scientific Am Lib. 1st. ils. Vg/dj. K5. $25.00

**WHEELER, Keith.** *Railroaders.* nd. Time Life. ils. VG. J2. $45.00

**WHEELER, Lonnie.** *Bleachers: A Summer in Wrigley Field.* 1988. Contemporary. 1st. F/VG+. P8. $30.00

**WHEELER, Richard.** *Children of Darkness.* 1973. Arlington. 189p. VG/dj. B29. $9.50

**WHEELER, Richard.** *Lee's Terrible Swift Sword: From Antietam...* 1992. Harper Collins. 1st. F/dj. A14. $25.00

**WHEELER, Richard.** *Siege of Vicksburg: Seven-Month Battle...* 1978. NY. Crowell. 1st. NF/dj. A14. $25.00

**WHEELER, W.M.** *Demons of the Dust: Study of Insect Behavior.* 1930. NY. 1st. 378p. VG/dj. B5. $45.00

**WHEELHOUSE, M.V.** *Holly House & Ridges Row: A Tale of London...* 1908. Chambers. 1st. thick 8vo. ils MV Wheelhouse. aeg. VG+. M5. $70.00

**WHEELWRIGHT, T.** *Farmers Almanac Cook Book.* 1969. Freeport. 1st. VG/dj. B5. $30.00

**WHELAN, Michael.** *Works of Wonder.* 1987. Del Rey/Ballantine. 1st. NF/VG. A28. $30.00

**WHIPPLE, A.B.C.** *To the Shores of Tripoli.* 1991. Morrow. 1st. 8vo. 357p. VG/dj. S17. $6.50

**WHIPPLE, A.B.C.** *To the Shores of Tripoli.* 1991. NY. Morrow. 1st. 357p. F/VG. M7. $35.00

**WHIPPLE, Allen.** *Evolution of Surgery in the United States.* 1963. Springfield. 1st. 180p. A13. $75.00

**WHIPPLE, Fred L.** *Orbiting the Sun: Planets & Satellites of the Solar System.* 1981. Cambridge. new/enlarged. 338p. VG. K5. $10.00

**WHIPPLE, Guy Montrose.** *Manual of Mental & Physical Tests: Part I...* 1914 & 1915. Baltimore. Warwick York. 2 vol. 2nd revised. ils/tables. panelled red cloth. G1. $65.00

**WHISTLER, J.M.** *Mr Whistler's Ten O'Clock.* 1888. London. Chatto Windus. 1st trade. VG/prt brn wrp. M24. $200.00

**WHISTLER, W. Arthur.** *Coastal Flowers of the Tropical Pacific.* 1980. Lawai. photos. 82p. wrp. VG. B26. $20.00

**WHISTLER, W. Arthur.** *Ethnobotany of Tonga: Plants, Their Tongan Names & Uses.* 1991. Honolulu. Bishop Mus. 8vo. checklist. 155p. F/wrp. B1. $35.00

**WHISTLER, W. Arthur.** *Polynesian Herbal Medicine.* 1992. Lawai, Kauai. ils/photos. 237p. sc. AN. B26 $33.00

**WHITAKER, Alma.** *Trousers & Skirts.* 1923. LA. Times-Mirror. 1st. sm 8vo. 245p. VG/G. M7. $22.00

**WHITAKER, Edmund.** *From Euclid to Eddington: A Study...* 1949. Cambridge. VG. K5. $35.00

**WHITAKER, John O.** *Keys to Vertebrates of Eastern USA Excluding Birds.* 1968. Burgess. 256p. xl. VG. S5. $20.00

**WHITAKER, John.** *Americas to the South.* 1941. Macmillan. 300p. F3. $10.00

**WHITAKER, Muriel.** *Great Canadian Adventure Stories.* 1979. Edmonton. Hurtig. 1st. F/F. A26. $25.00

**WHITAKER & WHITAKER.** *Potter's Mexico.* 1978. NM U. 1st. ils. 136p. NF/dj. B19. $35.00

**WHITCOMB, Adah F.** *Old Mother Goose in a New Dress.* 1932. Chicago. Laidlaw. 1st. obl 4to. yel-orange pict cloth. R5. $125.00

**WHITE, Allan G.** *Nashi: Asian Pear in New Zealand.* 1990. Wellington. ils. sc. B26. $20.00

**WHITE, Anne Terry.** *First Men in the World.* 1953. Random. 5th. ils Aldren Watson. 178p. VG/dj. B36. $14.00

**WHITE, Claire Nicolas.** *River Boy.* 1988. Typographeum. 1/150. sgn. dj. T9. $30.00

**WHITE, Dale.** *John Wesley Powell, Geologist-Explorer.* 1962. Julian Messner. 2nd. 8vo. 192p. VG+. F7. $22.50

**WHITE, David.** *Flora of the Hermit Shale, Grand Canyon, Arizona.* 1929. Carnegie Inst. 8vo. 52p. 221p. xl. VG/stiff wrp. F7. $70.00

**WHITE, E.B.** *Charlotte's Web.* 1952. Harper Row. 1st. ils Garth Williams. VG+. D1. $650.00

**WHITE, E.B.** *Geese.* 1985. Newton, IA. Tamazunchale. mini. 1/250. 46p. gilt gray morocco. B24. $95.00

**WHITE, E.B.** *Letters of EB White.* 1976. Harper. 1st. inscr. NF/VG+. B4. $450.00

**WHITE, E.B.** *Poems & Sketches of EB White.* 1981. NY. Harper. 1st. NF/dj. L3. $35.00

**WHITE, E.B.** *Stuart Little in the Schoolroom.* 1962. Harper. 1st separate. red pict brd. F. M24. $50.00

**WHITE, E.B.** *Stuart Little.* (1945). NY. Harper. 1st. ils Garth Williams. tan cloth. pict dj. R5. $485.00

**WHITE, E.B.** *Stuart Little.* nd (c 1945). Harper Row. K-N prt. sm 8vo. 131p. VG/dj. C14. $15.00

**WHITE, E.B.** *Stuart Little.* 1945. Harper. 1st. ils Garth Williams. G/dj. M5. $60.00

**WHITE, E.B.** *Trumpet of the Swan.* nd (c 1970). Harper Collins. early prt (0670 on dj). 210p. G+/VG. C14. $18.00

**WHITE, Edmund.** *Caracole.* 1985. Dutton. 1st. sgn. F/dj. O11. $45.00

**WHITE, Edmund.** *Carocole.* 1985. Dutton. 1st. F/F. T12. $20.00

**WHITE, Edmund.** *Genet: A Biography.* 1993. NY. Knopf. 1st Am. sgn. F/dj. O11. $50.00

**WHITE, Edmund.** *Our Paris: Sketches From Memory.* 1995. NY. 1st. dj. T9. $12.00

**WHITE, Edmund.** *Skinned Alive.* 1995. Knopf. 1st. sgn. F/dj. B4. $50.00

**WHITE, Edmund.** *States of Desire...* 1980. Dutton. 1st. NF/dj. C9. $60.00

**WHITE, Ethel Lina.** *Man Who Was Not There.* nd. Grosset Dunlap. rpt. VG/G. G8. $15.00

**WHITE, G.** *Natural History & Antiquities of Selbourne.* 1994. Folio Soc. 384p. F/case. M4. $30.00

**WHITE, G. Edward.** *Creating the National Pastime.* 1996. Princeton. UP. photos. P8. $12.50

**WHITE, Grace.** *Family Circle's What's for Dinner?* 1963. Family Circle. G. A16. $5.00

**WHITE, I. Andrew.** *Mr Whittle Invents the Airplane.* 1938. Lee Shepard. 1st. ils Alexander. VG/G. P2. $25.00

**WHITE, J. Todd.** *Fighters for Independence: A Guide to Sources...* 1977. Chicago. 1st. 112. NF/dj. M10. $27.50

**WHITE, Leslie A.** *Pueblo of Sia, New Mexico.* 1962. GPO. 1st. ils/maps. 336p. NF. B19. $65.00

**WHITE, Leslie Turner.** *Me, Detective.* 1936. Harcourt Brace. 1st. VG. P3. $30.00

**WHITE, Lionel.** *Invitation to Violence.* 1958. Dutton. 1st. VG/dj. G8. $8.00

**WHITE, Lionel.** *To Kill a Killer.* 1954. Dutton. 1st. VG/G. G8. $20.00

**WHITE, M.J.D.** *Animal Cytology & Evolution.* 1954. Cambridge. 2nd. 454p. xl. VG. S5. $25.00

**WHITE, Mary.** *Book of a Hundred Games.* 1896. NY. Scribner. 171p. tan cloth. G. B14. $25.00

**WHITE, Owen P.** *Lead & Likker.* 1932. NY. Minton Balch. VG/worn. B5. $25.00

**WHITE, Owen P.** *Them Was the Days: From El Paso to Prohibition.* 1925. Minton Balch. 235p. VG/dj. J2. $245.00

**WHITE, Patrick.** *Burnt Ones.* 1964. Viking. 1st Am. VG/dj. A14. $35.00

**WHITE, Patrick.** *Cockatoos.* 1974. London. Cape. 1st. F/dj. A14. $52.50

**WHITE, Patrick.** *Fringe of Leaves.* 1977. Viking. 1st Am. NF/VG clip. A14. $21.00

**WHITE, Paul Dudley.** *Clues in the Diagnosis & Treatment of Heart Disease.* (1955). Chas Thomas. 2nd. 190p. F. C14. $15.00

**WHITE, Paul Dudley.** *My Life in Medicine: An Autobiographical Memoir.* 1971. Boston. Gambit. 1st. 8vo. 269p. VG. C14. $12.00

**WHITE, Ramy Allison.** *Sunny Boys at the Seashore.* Barse Hopkins. ils Chas Wrenn. F/VG. M19. $17.50

**WHITE, Randy Wayne.** *Captiva.* 1996. Putnam. UP/1st. F/wrp. M15. $75.00

**WHITE, Randy Wayne.** *Captiva.* 1996. Putnam. 1st. NF/dj. G8. $22.50

**WHITE, Randy Wayne.** *Captiva.* 1996. Putnam. 1st. rem mk. NF/dj. A14. $17.50

**WHITE, Randy Wayne.** *Cuban Death-Lift.* 1981. NY. NAL. 1st. sgn. F/wrp. M15. $85.00

**WHITE, Randy Wayne.** *Heat Islands.* 1992. NY. St Martin. 1st. F/NF. M15. $150.00

**WHITE, Randy Wayne.** *Man Who Invented Florida.* 1993. St Martin. 1st. NF/dj. A14. $87.50

**WHITE, Randy Wayne.** *North of Havana.* 1997. Putnam. 1st. sgn. F/dj. M15. $40.00

**WHITE, Ray Lewis.** *Index to Best American Short Stories/O Henry Prize Stories.* 1988. 191p. F. A4. $45.00

**WHITE, Richard.** *It's Your Misfortune & None of My Own.* 1991. Norman, OK. 1st. ils. 644p. F/F. B19. $50.00

**WHITE, Robert W.** *Personality of Joe Kidd.* (1943). np. rpt. 8vo. stapled wrp. C14. $18.00

**WHITE, Simon.** *Clear for Action!* 1978. St Martin. 1st Am. Penhaligon #2. F/NF. T11. $65.00

**WHITE, Simon.** *His Magesty's Frigate.* 1979. St Martin. 1st Am. Penhaligon #3. F/dj. T11. $65.00

**WHITE, Stewart Edward.** *Camp & Trail.* (1907). Toronto. Musson. 1st Canadian. 8vo. 2-tone bl cloth. NF. R3. $20.00

**WHITE, Stewart Edward.** *Daniel Boone: Wilderness Scout.* 1957. NY. Jr Deluxe Eds. 254p. VG/clip. V3. $12.00

**WHITE, Stewart Edward.** *Riverman.* 1909. NY. McClure. 1st. ils NC Wyeth/Clarence F Underwood. 368p. G11. $15.00

**WHITE, T.H.** *Letters to a Friend.* 1982. NY. edit/intro Francois Gallix. VG. M17. $17.50

**WHITE, T.H.** *Scandal Monger.* 1952. London. Cape. 1st. ils. NF/clip. S9. $100.00

**WHITE, Ted.** *Phoenix Time: Quest of the Wolf Vol I.* 1982. VA. Donning Starblaze. 1st thus. ils Tom Yeates. F/wrp. G10. $12.00

**WHITE, Theodore H.** *Breach of Faith: Fall of Richard Nixon.* 1975. Atheneum. 1st. sgn. VG/dj. B30. $35.00

**WHITE, Tom.** *Buffalo Soldiers.* 1996. Tom Doherty. 1st. F/dj. T11. $40.00

**WHITE, W.L.** *They Were Expendable.* 1942. BC. 209p. gl cloth. VG/dj. M7. $16.50

**WHITE, William Alanson.** *Outlines of Psychiatry.* 1926. WA, DC. Nervous & Mental Disease Pub. 11th. 8vo. VG. C14. $15.00

**WHITE, William Alanson.** *William Alanson White: Autobiography of a Purpose.* 1938. Doubleday Doran. 1st. 8vo. VG/G. A2. $25.00

**WHITE, William Allen.** *In the Heart of a Fool.* 1918. NY. Macmillan. 1st. 615p. G. G11. $10.00

**WHITE, William Allen.** *Masks in a Pageant.* 1928. Macmillan. 1st. 8vo. 507p. xl. S14. $9.00

**WHITE, William Allen.** *Woodrow Wilson: Man, His Times & His Task.* 1924. Houghton Mifflin. photos. 527p. VG. B10. $18.00

**WHITE, Wirt.** *Enemy.* 1951. Houghton Mifflin. rpt. gray cloth. F/G+. T11. $15.00

**WHITECLOUD, Tom.** *Indian Prayer.* 1964. Berkeley. Peacock. mini. 1/600. brn/gr prt. yel prt wrp. B24. $40.00

**WHITECOTTON, Joseph.** *Zapotecs: Princes, Priests & Peasants.* 1977. Norman. 1st. 338p. F3. $35.00

**WHITEHEAD, Don.** *FBI Story: A Report to the People.* 1956. Random. inscr. F/dj. A19. $35.00

**WHITEHEAD, George.** *Christian Progress of That Ancient Servant & Minister...* 1725. London. Sowle. 1st. 712p. worn leather. G. V3. $195.00

**WHITEHEAD, George.** *Memoirs of George Whitehead...Being Substance of Account...* 1832. Phil. Kite. 2 vol. From 6th London. 12mo. mismatched bdg. V3. $65.00

**WHITEHEAD, J.** *Chicago Herald Cooking School: Professional Cook's Book...* 1883 (1882). lg 8vo. ads. G+. E6. $65.00

**WHITEHEAD, J.** *Steward's Handbook & Guide to Party Catering in 5 Parts...* 1889. 1st. lg 8vo. 500 dbl-column p. VG. E6. $65.00

**WHITEHOUSE, Arch.** *Legion of the Lafayette.* 1962. Doubleday. 1st. 338p. VG/dj. M7. $35.00

**WHITEHURST, G. William.** *Diary of a Congressman: Abscam & Beyond.* (1985). Donning. photos. 327p. dj. B10. $8.00

**WHITELAW, Ralph T.** *Virginia's Eastern Shore: History of Northampton...* 1951. VHS. 2 vol. VG. B10. $300.00

**WHITELEY, Peter M.** *Deliberate Acts: Changing Hopi Culture...* 1988. Tucson, AZ. ils/notes/biblio. 373p. B19. $40.00

**WHITFIELD, Irene Therese.** *Louisiana French Folk Songs.* 1939. LSU. 1st. brn cloth/brn leather labels. F. B2. $85.00

**WHITFIELD, Philip.** *Hunters...Predators... Anatomy, Architecture & Behavior.* 1978. NY. ils. 160p. F/dj. A17. $17.50

WHITFIELD, Shelby. *Kiss It Goodbye.* 1973. Abelard Schuman. 1st. F/VG+. P8. $35.00

WHITFIELD, Theodore M. *Slavery Agitation in Virginia, 1829-1832.* 1969 (1930). Negro U. rpt. 162p. VG. B10. $25.00

WHITFORD, David. *Extra Innings.* 1991. Burlingham. 1st. F/dj. P8. $20.00

WHITING, F. *Modern Mastoid Operation.* 1905. 4to. 25 halftone pl. half leather. VG. E6. $50.00

WHITING, John. *Treasury of American Gardening.* 1955. Garden City. Flower Grower/ Doubleday. BC. VG/dj. A10. $10.00

WHITLEY, William T. *Artists & Their Friends in England 1700-1799.* 1928. London. Medici Soc. 2 vol. lg 8vo. 23 pl. H13. $185.00

WHITLOCK, Brand. *Turn of the Balance.* 1907. Bobbs Merrill. ils Jay Hambridge. 622p. G. G11. $10.00

WHITLOCK, Herbert P. *Story of the Gems.* 1946. Emerson Books. 8vo. 206p. F/dj. H1. $12.00

WHITMAN, Alden. *Labor Parties 1827-1834.* 1943. NY. Internat. 1st. F/wrp. B2. $30.00

WHITMAN, Sarah Helen. *Edgar Poe & His Critics.* 1860. NY. Rudd Carleton. 1st/1st prt/B bdg. gilt purple cloth/tan ep. F. M24. $150.00

WHITMAN, Walt. *Death of Abraham Lincoln.* 1962. Chicago. Blk Cat. mini. 1/300. ils/marbled ep. aeg. gilt blk leather. F. B24. $150.00

WHITMER, Peter O. *Aquarius Revisited.* 1987. Macmillan. 1st. inscr. F/dj. B9. $25.00

WHITNEY, A.D. *Just How: A Key to the Cook Books...* ca 1880. 311p. VG. E6. $60.00

WHITNEY, Casper. *Guns, Ammunition & Tackle...* 1912. Macmillan. 3 mc pl. 440p. H10. $25.00

WHITNEY, David C. *People of the Revolution: Colonial Spirit of '76.* 1974. Chicago. Ferguson. F. A19. $40.00

WHITNEY, David C. *People of the Revolution: Colonial Spirit of '76.* 1974. Chicago. Ferguson. 4to. ils. 440p. VG. M10. $20.00

WHITNEY, George H. *Hand-Book of Bible Geography.* NY. Nelson Phillips. rpt. gilt maroon cloth. G+. M21. $20.00

WHITNEY, George H. *Hand-Book of Bible Geography.* 1877. NY. Nelson Phillips. 1st. sm 8vo. 14 mc maps. 495p. VG. W1. $65.00

WHITNEY, Janet. *Abigail Adams.* 1949. London. Harrap. 1st. ils. 333p. VG/dj. M10. $12.50

WHITNEY, P.A. *Mystery of the Golden Horn.* 1962. Westminster Pr. ils Helmes. xl. VG. B36. $12.75

WHITNEY, R.M. *Reds in America.* 1924. Beckwith. 1st. F/worn. B2. $75.00

WHITTELSEY, Charles B. *Ancestry & Descendants of John Pratt of Hartford, CT.* 1900. Hartford. 204p. bstp cloth. G+. B18. $65.00

WHITTEMORE, C.P. *General of the American Revolution: John Sullivan...* 1961. Columbia. 1st. ils. 317p. F/dj. M4. $35.00

WHITTEMORE, Reed. *Fascination of the Abomination Poems, Stories & Essays.* 1963. Macmillan. 1st. VG/dj. N2. $12.50

WHITTICK, Arnold. *Symbols, Signs & Their Meaning.* 1960. Newton, MA. 1st. ils. 408p. VG. B5. $50.00

WHITTIER, John Greenleaf. *Boston Book: Being Specimens of Metropolitan Literature.* 1837. Boston. Light Stearns. 1st. emb gr cloth. M24. $150.00

WHITTIER, John Greenleaf. *In War Time, And Other Poems.* 1864. Boston. Ticknor Fields. 1st/earliest ads. teg. gilt bl-gr diamond grain cloth. M24. $85.00

WHITTIER, John Greenleaf. *Poetical Works of...* 1892. Boston. half leather/marbled brd. F. B30. $275.00

WHITTLE, D.W. *Memoirs of Philip P Bliss.* 1878. AS Barnes. intro DL Moody. maroon cloth. VG. S17. $15.00

WHITTLE, Jenny. *Beetle Assembly.* 1985. Lilliput. mini. 1st. 1/250. prt/sgn Armstrong. silk ep/bl morocco. B24. $175.00

WHITTLESEY, Charles. *Early History of Cleveland, Ohio.* 1867. Cleveland. 1st. ils. 487p. VG. B10. $225.00

WHITTLESEY, Charles. *Fugitive Essays.* 1852. Hudson, OH. 1st. 397p. G. B18. $225.00

WHITTON, Blair. *Paper Toys of the World.* 1986. Hobby House. obl 8vo. F/dj. B17. $25.00

WHYMPER, Edward. *Scrambles Amongst the Alps in the Years 1860-1869.* 1893. London. John Murray. 4th. 5 fld maps/ils. teg. Q1. $125.00

WHYTE, Jack. *Eagles' Brood: Dream of Eagles. Volume Three.* 1994. Viking Penguin. 1st. sgn. VG+/ils wrp/French flaps. A14. $21.00

WHYTE, Jack. *Skytone: Camulod Chronicles. Volume One.* 1996. NY. Forge/Tor. 1st Am/1st hc. NF/dj. A14. $25.00

WIATER, Stanley. *After the Darkness.* 1993. Maclay. 1st. sgn all 18 contributors. F/case. S18. $45.00

WIATER, Stanley. *Night Visions 7.* 1989. Dark Harvest. 1st. F/dj. G10. $25.00

WIBBERLY, Leonard. *Little League Family.* 1978. Doubleday. F/VG. P8. $30.00

WICKENDEN, James. *Claim in the Hills.* 1957. Rinehart. 1st. 275p. dj. F3. $15.00

WICKENDEN, Leonard. *Gardening With Nature.* 1956. London. Faber. 317p. VG/dj. A10. $28.00

WICKENDEN, Leonard. *Make Friends With Your Land.* 1949. NY. Devin-Adair. 132p. cloth. VG. A10. $20.00

WICKER, Tom. *Time to Die.* 1975. Quadrangle/NY Times. 1st. ils. 342p. VG/dj. S14. $10.00

WICKERSHAM, James. *Old Yukon Tales, Trails, Trials.* 1973. St Paul. 514p. F. A17. $30.00

WIDDENMER, Margaret. *Golden Friends I Had: Unrevised Memories of...* 1964. Doubleday. 1st. 340p. VG/VG. A25. $20.00

WIDDER, William J. *Fiction of L Ron Hubbard.* 1994. Bridge. 1st. F. P3. $50.00

WIDDIFIELD, Hannah. *Widdifield's New Cookbook, Practical Recipes...* 1856. Phil. 410p. VG. E6. $95.00

WIDEMAN, John Edgar. *Cattle Killing.* 1996. Houghton Mifflin. 1st. sgn. F/dj. R14. $45.00

WIDEMAN, John Edgar. *Fatheralong.* 1994. Pantheon. 1st. F/dj. R14. $25.00

WIDEMAN, John Edgar. *Fever.* 1989. NY. Holt. 1st. sgn. F/dj. O11. $30.00

WIDEMAN, John Edgar. *Hiding Place.* 1984. London. Allison Busby. 1st/1st hc. sgn. F/dj. O11. $40.00

WIDEMAN, John Edgar. *Lynchers.* 1973. HBJ. 1st. Nf/dj. A24. $40.00

WIDEMAN, John Edgar. *Philadelphia Fire.* 1990. NY. Holt. 1st. sgn. F/dj. O11. $30.00

WIDEMAN, John Edgar. *Reuben.* 1987. NY. Holt. 1st. sgn. F/dj. O11. $25.00

WIDEMAN, John Edgar. *Sent for You Yesterday.* 1984. London. Allison Busby. 1st/1st hc. sgn. F/dj. O11. $40.00

WIDEMAN, John Edgar. *Something About a Soldier.* 1986. Random. 1st. F/NF. A24. $40.00

WIDEMAN, John Edgar. *Stories of John Edgar Wideman.* 1992. NY. Pantheon. 1st. F/dj. R14. $25.00

**WIDEMAN, John Edgar.** *Stories of John Edgar Wideman.* 1992. Pantheon. 1st. sgn. F/dj. O11. $30.00

**WIDLENSTEIN, Daniel.** *Gauguin.* 1974. Doubleday. 1st. ils. 95p. VG. T11. $20.00

**WIDMANN, Karl.** *Paramos Venezolanos.* 1980. Caracas. Fundacion Polar. 1st. VG/dj. B26. $30.00

**WIDMER, Jack.** *American Quarter Horse.* 1959. NY. Scribner. VG/fair. O3. $25.00

**WIDMER, Jack.** *American Quarter Horse.* 1959. Scribner. 1st. NF/dj. A21. $45.00

**WIENER, Louis.** *Hand-Made Jewelry, a Comprehensive Handbook...* 1948. Van Nostrand. 1st. ils. VG/worn. M5. $12.00

**WIENPAHL, Robert W.** *Gold Rush Voyage on the Bark Orino...* 1978. Arthur H Clark. 1st. dj. O4. $35.00

**WIER, Albert E.** *Macmillan Encyclopedia of Music & Musicians.* 1938. Macmillan. 1 vol issue. 2088p. G. C5. $25.00

**WIER, Allen.** *Place for Outlaws.* 1989. Harper. 1st. F/NF. S18. $15.00

**WIESE, Kurt.** *You Can Write Chinese.* 1945. NY. Viking. 1st. 1st. obl 4to. 1946 Caldecott. pict dj. R5. $175.00

**WIESEL, Elie.** *Beggar in Jerusalem.* 1970. Random. 1st. NF/dj. S13. $10.00

**WIESEL, Elie.** *Fifth Son.* 1985. Franklin Lib. 1st. sgn. full leather. F. Q1. $30.00

**WIESEL, Elie.** *From the Kingdom of Memory.* 1990. NY. Summit. 1st. F/F. H11. $25.00

**WIESEL, Elie.** *Legends of Our Time.* 1968. Holt. 1st. VG+/dj. B2. $30.00

**WIESEL, Elie.** *Night.* 1960. NY. 1st Am. 116p. VG. B18. $65.00

**WIESEL, Elie.** *Oath.* 1973. Random. 1st. F/NF. H11. $30.00

**WIFFEN, Edwin Thomas.** *Outing Lore.* 1928. NY. 1st. 185p. gilt cloth. VG. A17. $20.00

**WIGGIN, Kate Douglas.** *Affair at the Inn.* 1904. Houghton Mifflin. 1st. ils Martin Justice. G11. $12.00

**WIGGIN, Kate Douglas.** *Birds' Christmas Carol.* 1912. Boston/NY. ils KR Wireman. VG. M17. $15.00

**WIGGIN, Kate Douglas.** *My Garden of Memory: An Autobiography.* 1926. Houghton Mifflin. 10th. sm 8vo. 465p. reading copy. C14. $7.00

**WIGGIN, Kate Douglas.** *New Chronicles of Rebecca.* 1907. Houghton Mifflin. 1st. 278p. VG. D4. $45.00

**WIGGIN, Kate Douglas.** *Rebecca of Sunnybrook Farm.* 1903. Grosset Dunlap. possible 1st. G. A19. $50.00

**WIGGIN, Kate Douglas.** *Rose O'The River.* 1905. Houghton Mifflin. 1st. 177p+3 ads. G. C14. $15.00

**WIGGIN, Kate Douglas.** *Story of Waitstill Baxter.* 1913. Houghton Mifflin. 1st. ils HM Brett. 373p. G. G11. $15.00

**WIGGINS, Walt.** *Alfred Morang: A Neglected Master.* 1979. NM. Pintores. AN/dj. A19. $45.00

**WIGHAM, Eliza.** *Anti-Slavery Cause in America & Its Martyrs.* 1863. London. BEnnett. 8vo. bl cloth. R12. $225.00

**WIGHT, Richard.** *Story of Goochland.* 1935. Richmond. 1st. inscr/dtd. ils. 51p. VG. B10. $85.00

**WIGHTMAN, A.J.** *No Friend for Travellers.* 1959. London. hale. 1st. 8vo. F/VG. A2. $25.00

**WILBER, Cynthia.** *For the Love of the Game.* 1992. Morrow. 1st. F/VG. P8. $25.00

**WILBER, Donald N.** *Iran: Past & Present.* 1958. Princeton. 5th. 312p. VG. W1. $20.00

**WILBERT, James.** *Little Big Horn Diary: Chronicle of 1876 Indian War.* 1977. La Mirada, CA. 1st. 1/500. sgn. E1. $250.00

**WILBUR, Donald N.** *Afghanistan: Its People, Its Society, Its Culture.* 1962. New Haven. ils. 320p. cloth. VG/dj. Q2. $30.00

**WILBUR, Richard.** *Ceremony.* 1950. Harcourt Brace. 1st. F/NF. L3. $125.00

**WILBUR, Richard.** *More Opposites.* 1991. HBJ. 1st. inscr/dtd 1996. F/dj. R14. $30.00

**WILCHER, Talmage S.** *King of Assateague.* 1964. Vantage. 1st. photos. 64p. VG. O3. $15.00

**WILCOX, Barbara.** *Bunty Brown: Probationer.* 1940. Oxford. 1st. ils. VG/clip. A25. $22.00

**WILCOX, James.** *North Gladiola.* 1985. Harper Row. 1st. author's 2nd book. NF/dj. R14. $35.00

**WILCOX, L.A.** *Mr Pepy's Navy.* 1966. Barnes. 1st Am. NF/VG. T11. $35.00

**WILDE, Oscar.** *Ballad of Reading Gaol.* 1910. Duffield. 1st thus. 12mo. gilt bl cloth. VG. M5. $75.00

**WILDE, Oscar.** *Ballad of Reading Gaol.* 1937. NY. Heritage. NF/case. B9. $20.00

**WILDE, Oscar.** *Birthday of the Infanta & Other Tales.* 1982. Atheneum. 1st Am. 73p. F/dj. C14/M5. $15.00

**WILDE, Oscar.** *Birthday of the Infanta.* 1929. Macmillan. 1st. ils Pamela Bianco. 58p. VG/dj. D1. $85.00

**WILDE, Oscar.** *House of Pomegranates.* nd. NY. Brentano. 1st Am. ils Jessie M King/16 mtd pl. 162p. red cloth. VG. D1. $750.00

**WILDE, Oscar.** *Phases & Philosophies for Use of the Young.* 1920-6?. London? private prt. pirated ed. prt wrp. M24. $100.00

**WILDE, Oscar.** *Salome.* 1904. London. Melmoth. 1st pirated. ils Beardsley. 1/250. gilt bl cloth. M24. $125.00

**WILDE, Oscar.** *Salome.* 1911. Portland, ME. Thos Mosher. 1/50 on Japan vellum. sm 4to. F/dj/case. H5. $250.00

**WILDE, Oscar.** *Salome: Tragedy in One Act.* 1927. Dutton. 1/500. ils/sgn Beardsley. F/tattered box. B9. $200.00

**WILDE, Oscar.** *Sixteen Letters From Oscar Wilde.* 1930. Coward McCann. 1st Am. 1/515. gilr red cloth. F. Q1. $125.00

**WILDE, Oscar.** *Teacher of Wisdom.* 1994. Petrarch. 1st. 1/50 (200 total). sgn. F/sewn magenta prt wrp. M24. $100.00

**WILDE, Percival.** *P Moran, Operative.* 1947. Random. 1st. F/dj. M15. $50.00

**WILDENSTEIN, Daniel.** *Monet's Years at Giverny: Beyond Impressionism.* 1978. MOMA. ils. VG/dj. M17. $27.50

**WILDER, F.L.** *English Sporting Prints.* 1974. London. Thames Hudson. 4to. VG. O3. $35.00

**WILDER, Gerrit P.** *Flora of Rarotonga.* 1931. Honolulu. 113p. VG/wrp. B26. $35.00

**WILDER, Laura Ingalls.** *By the Shores of Silver Lake.* 1953. Harper. ils Garth Williams. pk/beige cloth. VG. B11. $25.00

**WILDER, Laura Ingalls.** *Farmer Boy.* 1953. Harper. Newly ils uniform ed. ils Garth Williams. B11. $25.00

**WILDER, Laura Ingalls.** *On the Banks of Plum Creek.* 1965. Harper Row. ils Garth Williams. xl. VG. B36. $10.00

**WILDER, Laura Ingalls.** *These Happy Golden Years.* (1943). NY. Harper. 1st. ils Helen Sewell/Mildred Boyle. tan pict cloth. R5. $285.00

**WILDER, Louise Beebe.** *Pleasures & Problems of a Rock Garden.* 1937 (1928). Garden City. 294p. dj. B26. $32.50

**WILDER, Lucy.** *Mayo Clinic.* 1936. Rochester. 1st. 82p. A13. $30.00

**WILDER, Robert.** *Sounds of Drums & Cymbals.* 1974. Putnam. 1st. NF/dj. T12. $100.00

**WILDER, Thornton.** *Cabala.* 1926. NY. Boni. 1st/1st issue. inscr. author's 1st book. F/dj. B24. $650.00

**WILDER, Thornton.** *Eighth Day.* 1967. Harper Row. 1/500. sgn. Nat Book Award. F/sans. R14. $125.00

**WILDER, Thornton.** *James Joyce.* 1944. Aurora, NY. Hammer. 1st. 1/150. decor brd. w/3 prospecuts. M24. $450.00

**WILDES, Harry Emerson.** *Delaware.* 1940. Farrar Rinehart. rpt. Rivers of Am series. 8vo. cloth. F/NF. O10. $25.00

**WILDING-WHITE, T.M.** *Jane's Pocket Book of Space Exploration.* 1978 (1976). NY. Collier. 2nd thus. 238p. wrp. K5. $16.00

**WILDMANN.** *Der Deutsche Buchhandel in Urkenden und Quellen.* 1965. Hamburg. 2 vol. NF. A4. $150.00

**WILENSKI, R.H.** *Modern Movement in Art.* 1926. NY. Stokes. ARC/1st. ils. 237p. gilt red ribbed cloth. F/dj. F1. $60.00

**WILEY, Bell Irvin.** *Life of Johnny Reb: Common Soldier of the Confederacy.* 1952. Bobbs Merrill. 8vo. 444p. VG. B11. $32.00

**WILHELM, Hans.** *Tales From Land Under My Table.* 1983. Random. 1st. ils. NF. M5. $20.00

**WILHELM, Kate.** *More Bitter Than Death.* 1963. S&S. 1st. xl. G. N4. $35.00

**WILHELM, Peter.** *Nobel Prize.* 1983. Stockholm. 4to. ils. gilt bl cloth. F/dj. R3. $20.00

**WILKIN, Eloise.** *Eloise Wilkin Treasury.* 1985. Western. 1st. lg 4to. 70p. G. P2. $20.00

**WILKIN, Eloise.** *Singing Every Day.* 1950. Ginn. rpt. 8vo. VG. B17. $15.00

**WILKINS, Harold.** *Mysteries of Ancient South America.* 1956. Citadel. 1st Am. 216p. dj. F3. $25.00

**WILKINS, T.** *Clarence King: A Biography.* 1988. NM U. revised/enlarged. 524p. F/dj. M4. $25.00

**WILKINS, Thurman.** *Cherokee Tragedy.* 1970. Macmillan. dj. A19. $35.00

**WILKINSON, Alec.** *Big Sugar: Seasons in the Cane Fields of Florida.* 1989. Knopf. 1st. F/dj. T10. $25.00

**WILKINSON, Anne.** *Lions in the Way: Discursive History of the Oslers.* 1956. Toronto. 1st. 274p. A13. $45.00

**WILKINSON, Brenda.** *Ludell.* 1975. Harper. 1st. F/dj. B2. $35.00

**WILKINSON, D. Marion.** *Not Between Brothers.* 1996. Albany. Boaz. 1st. sgn. F/F. A23. $42.00

**WILKINSON, Doug.** *Arctic Fever: Search for the Northwest Passage.* 1971. Toronto. Clarke Irwin. 1st. F/NF. A26. $20.00

**WILKINSON, E.S.** *Shanghai Bird Year: Calendar of Bird Life...* 1935. Shanghai. 4 photos. 219p. gilt decor cloth. NF/dj. C12. $175.00

**WILKINSON, Frederick.** *Militaria.* 1969. London. Ward Lock. ltd. F. A19. $30.00

**WILKINSON, John.** *Jerusalem Pilgrims Before the Crusades.* 1977. Warminster. Avis Phillips. ils/47 maps/map ep. 225p. cloth. VG/dj. Q2. $92.00

**WILKINSON, Norman.** *El duPont: Botanist, Beginning of a Tradition.* 1972. Charlottesville. 139p. VG. A10. $25.00

**WILLAN, Anne.** *Entertaining Menus.* 1974. NY. CMG. G/dj. A16. $6.00

**WILLARD, Frances E.** *Classic Town: Story of Evanston.* 1891. Chicago. Womens Temperance Pub Assn. 1st. aeg. brn cloth. VG. M24. $125.00

**WILLARD, Frances E.** *Glimpses of Fifty Years.* 1889. Chicago. Woman's Temperance Pub. ils. emb gr cloth. F. P4. $60.00

**WILLARD, James F.** *Union Colony at Greeley, Colorado, Vol 1.* 1918. Denver, CO. Robinson Prt. G. A19. $60.00

**WILLARD, Joseph.** *Address to Members of the Bar of Worcester County...* 1830. Lancaster. Carter Andrews. modern quarter calf. G. M11. $350.00

**WILLARD, Mrs. Eugene S.** *Kin-da-Shon's Wife.* 1892. NY. Fleming Revell. 281p. G. G11. $8.00

**WILLARD, Nancy.** *Ballad of Biddy Early.* 1989. Knopf. 1st. sgn. F/dj. B3. $45.00

**WILLARD, Nancy.** *Highest Hits.* 1978. HBJ. VG/dj. P8. $12.50

**WILLARD, Nancy.** *Nancy Willard Reader.* 1991. Hanover. Middlebury College. 1st. rem mk. NF/NF. B3. $20.00

**WILLARD, Nancy.** *Pish, Posh, Said Hieronymus Bosch.* 1991. NY/London. 1st. ils Dillons. VG/dj. M17. $25.00

**WILLARD, Nancy.** *Sister Water.* 1993. NY. Knopf. 1st. rem mk. F/dj. G10. $12.00

**WILLARD, W.** *Leathernecks Come Through.* c 1944. 5th. VG/dj. E6. $13.00

**WILLCOCK, Colin.** *Enormous Zoo.* 1965. NY. photos. 210p. VG/dj. S15. $15.00

**WILLEFORD, Charles.** *Cockfighter Journal: Story of a Shooting.* 1989. Santa Barbara. Neville. 1st. 1/300. sgn/intro James Lee Burke. F/sans. T2. $100.00

**WILLEFORD, Charles.** *Cockfighter.* 1972. NY. Crown. 1st. F/VG. B4. $375.00

**WILLEFORD, Charles.** *Everybody's Metamorphosis.* 1988. Missoula. McMillan. 1st. 1/400. sgn. F/dj. M15. $150.00

**WILLEFORD, Charles.** *Honey Gal.* 1958. Beacon. 1st. VG+. M21. $150.00

**WILLEFORD, Charles.** *I Was Looking for a Street.* 1988. Countryman. 1st. NF/dj. M21. $25.00

**WILLEFORD, Charles.** *Kiss Your Ass Good-Bye.* 1989. London. Gollancz. 1st. F/dj. T2. $35.00

**WILLEFORD, Charles.** *Machine in Ward Eleven.* 1963. NY. Belmont. 1st. F/wrp. M15. $120.00

**WILLEFORD, Charles.** *New Hope For the Dead.* 1985. St Martin. 1st. F/dj. M15. $225.00

**WILLEFORD, Charles.** *Off the Wall.* 1980. Montclair. Pegasus Rex. 1st. F/dj. M15. $200.00

**WILLEFORD, Charles.** *Shark-Infested Custard.* 1993. Underwood Miller. 1st. F/dj. M15. $45.00

**WILLEFORD, Charles.** *Sideswipe.* 1987. St Martin. 1st. Hoke Moseley novel. F/dj. T2. $25.00

**WILLEFORD, Charles.** *Something About a Soldier.* 1986. Random. 1st. F/dj. T2. $40.00

**WILLEFORD, Charles.** *Something About a Soldier.* 1986. Random. 1st. photo. NF/F. R14. $35.00

**WILLEFORD, Charles.** *Way We Die Now.* 1988. Random. 1st. F/dj. T2. $30.00

**WILLETT, John.** *Art & Politics in Weimar Period: The New Sobriety 1917-33.* 1978. NY. 1st. ils. VG/dj. M17. $30.00

**WILLEY, Basil.** *18th Century Background.* 1941. Columbia. 1st Am. F. H13. $65.00

**WILLIAM, Richard Pardee Jr.** *High School: History of the Episcopal High School in VA...* 1964. Vincent-Curtis. 225p. VG. B10. $15.00

**WILLIAMS, A. Susan.** *Lifted Veil.* 1992. Carroll Graf. 1st Am. F/NF. M21. $30.00

**WILLIAMS, A.B.** *Game Trails in British Columbia.* 1925. NY. Scribner. ils/index. 360p. G. B5. $45.00

**WILLIAMS, A.D.** *Spanish Colonial Furniture.* 1941. Bruce. 1st. ils. 136p. NF/dj. B19. $75.00

**WILLIAMS, Ben Ames.** *Happy End.* 1991. Derrydale. ils Ettinger. gilt leather. F. A17. $22.50

**WILLIAMS, C.K.** *Selected Poems.* 1994. FSG. F/NF. G10. $10.00

**WILLIAMS, Charles.** *Letters to Lalage: Letters of C Williams to Lois Lang-Sims.* (1989). Kent State. 1st Am. intro Glen Cavaliero. AN/wrp. A27. $12.00

**WILLIAMS, D.** *Georgia Gold Rush: Twenty-Niners, Cherokees & Gold Fever.* 1993. SC U. 1st. ils/maps. F/dj. M4. $25.00

**WILLIAMS, David A.** *David C Broderick: A Political Portrait.* 1969. San Marino. Huntington Lib. 8vo. 274p. AN/dj. P4. $20.00

**WILLIAMS, David.** *Lessons to a Young Prince, by an Old Statesman...* 1790. London. Simmons. 8vo. calf/brd. R12. $175.00

**WILLIAMS, E.T.** *Niagara, Queen of Wonders: A Graphic History...* 1916. Boston. Chapple. 1st. sgn. 188p. NF. H7. $30.00

**WILLIAMS, Elsie.** *Popular Fox Terrier.* 1965. Popular Dogs. 1st. NF/dj. A21. $35.00

**WILLIAMS, Frances Leigh.** *They Faced the Future: Sage of Growth.* 1951. Whittet Shepperson. ils. 105p. Vg/box. B10. $12.00

**WILLIAMS, Garth.** *My Bedtime Book.* 1973. Golden. 4th. unp. VG. C14. $12.00

**WILLIAMS, Gladys.** *Semolina Silkpaws Comes to Catstown.* 1967. Hart. 1st. ils Ronald Ferns. F/VG+. M5. $20.00

**WILLIAMS, Hank Jr.** *Living Proof.* 1979. NY. 1st. VG/dj. B5. $17.50

**WILLIAMS, J.D.** *History of the Name O'Kelly.* 1983. History House. 64p. G. S5. $5.00

**WILLIAMS, J.H.** *Great & Shining Road: Epic Story of Transcontinental...* 1988. NY. 1st. 341p. F/dj. M4. $25.00

**WILLIAMS, J.L.** *Territory of Florida or Sketches of Topography...* 1962. FL U. facs rpt. lg fld map. 304p. NF. M4. $45.00

**WILLIAMS, Jack.** *Legion of Time.* 1952. Fantasy. 1st. F/dj. M25. $25.00

**WILLIAMS, Jay P.** *Alaskan Adventure.* 1952. Harrisburg. Stackpole. ils. 299p. map ep. bl cloth. VG. P4. $30.00

**WILLIAMS, Joan.** *County Woman.* 1982. Little Brn. 1st. inscr. VG/dj. B30. $30.00

**WILLIAMS, Joan.** *Pariah & Other Stories.* 1983. Atlantic Monthly. 1st. sgn. VG/dj. B30. $20.00

**WILLIAMS, John A.** *Love.* 1988. Derry, NH/Ridgwood, NJ. Babcock Koontz. 1st. 1/200. sgn. F/sewn wrp. Q1. $75.00

**WILLIAMS, John G.** *Field Guide to the National Parks of East Africa.* 1968. Boston. Houghton Mifflin. 1st Am. F/dj. A17. $15.00

**WILLIAMS, John.** *Atlas of Weapons & War.* 1976. London. 1st. 128p. F/dj. E1. $40.00

**WILLIAMS, Jonathan.** *Magpie's Bagpipe.* 1982. Northpoint. 1st. sgn author/edit Thos Meyer. F/wrp/dj. L3. $35.00

**WILLIAMS, Joseph J.** *Psychic Phenomena of Jamaica.* 1934. Dial. 1st. F/NF. B2. $125.00

**WILLIAMS, Joseph.** *Narrative of Tour From State of Indiana to Oregon Territory.* 1921. NY. Eberstadt. 1/250. 95p. gilt cloth. D11. $150.00

**WILLIAMS, Marion L.** *My Tour in Viet Nam: A Burlesque Shocker.* 1970. NY. Vantage. 1st. 8vo. NF/dj. R11. $140.00

**WILLIAMS, Marjorie.** *Bucks Camp Log, 1916-1928.* 1974. Wautoma, WI. Willow Creek. rpt. 105p. F. A17. $15.00

**WILLIAMS, Martin.** *Where's the Melody?* 1966. Pantheon. 1st. F/dj. B2. $50.00

**WILLIAMS, O.W.** *Pioneer Surveyor, Frontier Lawyer: Personal Narrative...* 1966. El Paso. TX Western College. 350p. cloth. dj. D11. $50.00

**WILLIAMS, Paul.** *US Lawn Tennis Assn & World War.* 1921. NY. 1st. photos. 293p. VG. B5. $100.00

**WILLIAMS, Philip Lee.** *All the Western Stars.* 1988. Peachtree. 1st. author's 2nd book. F/dj. S13. $10.00

**WILLIAMS, Robert Chadwell.** *Klaus Emil Julius Fuchs Atom Spy.* 1987. Harvard. 1st. sm 4to. 267p. F/NF. W2. $30.00

**WILLIAMS, Roger D.** *National Foxhunters' Association Studbook 1904 Vol II.* Lexington, KY. F. O3. $65.00

**WILLIAMS, Roger.** *Resurrection Men.* 1985. London. Hale. 1st. F/dj. M15. $40.00

**WILLIAMS, Samuel H.** *Voodoo Roads.* 1939. Vienna. Jugen Volk. English text. F/dj. B2. $50.00

**WILLIAMS, Stephen.** *Invisible Darkness.* 1996. Little Brn. 1st Canadian. F/dj. T12. $60.00

**WILLIAMS, T. Harry.** *Hayes of the Twenty-Third, the Civil War Volunteer Officer.* 1965. Knopf. 1st. 324p. VG. H1. $35.00

**WILLIAMS, T. St. John.** *Judy O'Grady & the Colonel's Lady...* 1988. London. 1st. ils. 269p. F/dj. B18. $35.00

**WILLIAMS, Tad.** *Stone of Farewell.* 1990. NY. Daw. Special ABA ed sticker. sgn. F. G10. $30.00

**WILLIAMS, Tennessee.** *Baby Doll.* 1956. New Directions. 1st. sgn. NF/clip. L3. $400.00

**WILLIAMS, Tennessee.** *Five O'Clock Angel: Letters of Tennessee Williams...* 1990. Knopf. 1st. F/dj. C9. $30.00

**WILLIAMS, Tennessee.** *Kingdom of Earth.* 1968. New Directions. 1st. 8vo. F/dj. S9. $100.00

**WILLIAMS, Tennessee.** *Memoirs.* 1975. Doubleday. 1st. 1/400. sgn. F/NF case. B4. $400.00

**WILLIAMS, Tennessee.** *Moise & the World of Reason.* 1976. London. Allen. 1st. F/F. B3. $20.00

**WILLIAMS, Tennessee.** *World of Tennesee Williams.* 1978. Putnam. 1/250. sgn. F/case. R14. $325.00

**WILLIAMS, Terry Tempest.** *Refuge.* 1991. NY. Pantheon. 1st. sgn. F/F. B3. $80.00

**WILLIAMS, Valentine.** *Clock Ticks On.* 1933. London. Hodder Stoughton. 1st. F/dj. M15. $150.00

**WILLIAMS, W.** *American Nation.* 1888. Cleveland. Williams. 3 vol. 3-quarter leather. G. S17. $50.00

**WILLIAMS, W.** *Chemistry of Cooking.* 1892 (1885). gilt red brd. VG. E6. $40.00

**WILLIAMS, W.K.** *American Farmer's Business Guide.* 1902. Columbus. Rural Pub. 101p. VG. A10. $10.00

**WILLIAMS, W.W.** *History of the Fire Lands.* 1973. Evansville, IN. Unigraphic. rpt of 1879. 524p. B18. $75.00

**WILLIAMS, Walter Jon.** *Metropolitan.* 1995. NY. Harper Prism. 1st. F/dj. M23. $25.00

**WILLIAMS, William.** *Journal of Life, Travels & Gospel Labours of...* 1828. Cincinnati. Lodge l'Hommedieu Hammond. 12mo. 272p. leather. V3. $135.00

**WILLIAMS, William Carlos.** *Tempers.* 1913. London. Elkin Mathews. 1st. 1/100. author's 2nd book. gilt lt yel brd. NF. B24. $1,250.00

**WILLIAMS & WILLIAMS.** *Modernizing Old Houses.* 1948. Doubleday. 269p. VG/dj. M10. $15.00

**WILLIAMS & WILLIAMS.** *Treasury of Great American Houses.* 1970. Putnam. 1st. ils. F/NF clip. B9. $20.00

**WILLIAMS-CAMMACK, L.M.** *Life & Works of Amos Kenworthy.* 1918. Richmond, IN. Nicholson. 12mo. 292p. G. V3. $12.00

**WILLIAMSON, Chet.** *McKain's Dilemma.* 1988. Tor. 1st. sgn. AN/dj. S18. $40.00

**WILLIAMSON, Harold F.** *Winchester: Gun That Won the West.* 1952. Combat Forces. 1st. NF/dj. T11. $125.00

**WILLIAMSON, Hugh Ross.** *Enigmas of History.* 1957. Michael Joseph. 1st. VG/G+. P3. $20.00

**WILLIAMSON, J.N.** *Book of Websters.* 1993. Longmeadow. 1st. AN/dj. S18. $30.00

**WILLIAMSON, J.N.** *Masques II.* 1987. Maclay. 1st ltd. 1/300. AN/sans. S18. $40.00

**WILLIAMSON, J.N.** *Masques III.* 1989. Maclay. 1st. AN/dj. S18. $40.00

**WILLIAMSON, J.N.** *Masques IV.* 1991. Baltimore. Maclay. 1st. 1/750. sgn by 26 of 27 contributors. F/dj/case. G10. $55.00

**WILLIAMSON, J.N.** *Masques.* 1984. Maclay. 1st. sgn. F/dj. S18. $30.00

**WILLIAMSON, James A.** *Cabot Voyages & Bristol Discovery Under Henry VII...* 1962. Cambridge. Hakluyt Soc. 8vo. 13 maps. 332p. F/dj. O1. $70.00

**WILLIAMSON, Ray A.** *Living the Sky: Cosmos of the American Indian.* 1984. Houghton Mifflin. ils. 366p. VG/dj. K5. $40.00

**WILLIS, Connie.** *Lincoln's Dreams.* 1987. NY. Bantam. 1st. F/NF. G10. $70.00

**WILLIS, H.** *Charleston (SC): Stage in the 18th Century.* 1924. Columbia. 1st. ils. 483p. VG/dj. B5. $50.00

**WILLIS, J.C.** *Dictionary of Flowering Plants & Ferns.* 1982 (1973). Dehra Dun. 8th/rpt. 1245p. AN. B26. $40.00

**WILLIUS, F.A.** *Aphorisms of Dr Charles Horace Mayo & Dr William J Mayo.* 1988. Rochester. 109p. A13. $25.00

**WILLKIE, Wendell.** *One World.* 1943. S&S. 1st/2nd prt. inscr. VG. B30. $45.00

**WILLMAN, Paul.** *Dynasty of Western Outlaws.* 1961. Doubleday. 1st. VG/dj. B5. $30.00

**WILLOCKS, Tim.** *Green River Rising.* 1994. London. Cape. 1st. F/dj. O11. $35.00

**WILLOCKS, Tim.** *Green River Rising.* 1994. Morrow. 1st. author's 1st novel. AN/dj. S18. $40.00

**WILLOCKS, William.** *Sixty Years in the East.* 1935. Edinburgh/London. 8vo. 338p. cloth. Q2. $47.00

**WILLS, Maury.** *How to Steal a Pennant.* 1976. Putnam. 1st. VG+/G. P8. $15.00

**WILLS, Royal Barry.** *Houses for Good Living.* 1940. NY. Architectural Book Pub. 104p. gilt gr cloth. G. F1. $45.00

**WILLSON & PRICE.** *Life & Adventures in California of Don Agustin Janssens...* 1953. San Marino, CA. Huntington Lib. 1st. F/dj. O4. $15.00

**WILLYS, Rufus Kay.** *Pioneer Padre: Life & Times of Eusebio Francisco Kino.* (1935). Dallas. Southwest Pr. 1st. inscr assn to HE Bolton. 230p. cloth. dj. D11. $75.00

**WILMERDING, John.** *American Views: Essays on American Art.* 1991. Princeton. ils/29 pl/notes/index. cloth. F/dj. D2. $50.00

**WILMERDING, John.** *Important Information Inside: Art of John F Peto...* 1983. WA. Nat Gallery of Art. 1st. ils. VG/dj. M17. $40.00

**WILSIE, Carroll.** *Crop Adaptation & Distribution.* 1962. SF. Freeman. 448p. cloth. VG. A10. $22.00

**WILSON, A.E.** *King Planto: Story of Pantomime.* 1935. Dutton. 1st. ils. NF/VG. O4. $30.00

**WILSON, A.E.** *Penny Plain, Two Pence Coloured: History of Juvenile Drama.* ca 1932. Macmillan. 1st Am. 4to. cloth. F/NF. O10. $125.00

**WILSON, A.J.** *Motorcycles & How to Manage Them.* 1901. London. 4th. 125p. VG. B18. $50.00

**WILSON, A.N.** *Daughters of Albion.* 1992. Viking. UP/1st Am. F. R14. $25.00

**WILSON, A.N.** *Love Unknown.* 1986. London. 1st. dj. T9. $25.00

**WILSON, A.N.** *Penfriends From Porlock: Essays & Reviews 1977-1986.* 1989. NY. 1st. VG/dj. M17. $15.00

**WILSON, A.N.** *Rise & Fall of the House of Windsor.* 1993. NY. 1st. dj. T9. $12.00

**WILSON, Adrian.** *Design of Books.* 1967. Reinhold. 1st. 4to. 160p. F/dj. O10. $65.00

**WILSON, Adrian.** *Printing for Theater.* 1957. SF. 1/250. author's 1st book. folio. 57p. cloth. F. B24. $975.00

**WILSON, Adrian.** *Work & Play of Adrian Wilson.* 1983. Austin. W Thomas Taylor. 1/325. folio. 160p. w/samples & prospectus. F. B24. $550.00

**WILSON, Andrew.** *Modern Physician: Being a Complete Guide...* (1900). London. Caxton. 5 vol. ils. G. M10. $30.00

**WILSON, Angus.** *Reflections in a Writer's Eye, Travel Pieces.* 1986. NY. 1st. dj. T9. $14.00

**WILSON, Ann.** *Familiar Letters of Ann Wilson.* 1850. Phil. Parrish. 12mo. 270p. G+. V3. $20.00

**WILSON, August.** *Seven Guitars.* 1996. Dutton. 1st. sgn. F/dj. O11. $25.00

**WILSON, Barbara.** *Noel Streatfield, a Walck Monograph.* 1964. NY. Walck. 1st Am. 61p. F/dj. D4. $25.00

**WILSON, Charles.** *Middle America.* 1944. Norton. 1st. 317p. F3. $15.00

**WILSON, Charles.** *New Crops for the New World.* 1945. Macmillan. 295p. VG/dj. A10. $18.00

**WILSON, Colin.** *Space Vampires.* 1976. Random. 1st. F/dj. A24. $60.00

**WILSON, Colin.** *Space Vampires.* 1976. Random. 1st. NF/dj. N4. $45.00

**WILSON, Colin.** *Violent World of Hugh Greene.* 1963. Houghton Mifflin. 1st. VG. Q1. $50.00

**WILSON, Derek.** *Dresden Text.* 1994. London. Headline. 1st. Tim Lacy Artworld mystery. F/dj. T2. $20.00

**WILSON, Derek.** *Triarchs.* 1994. London. Headline. 1st. Tim Lacy Artworld #1. F/dj. T2. $35.00

**WILSON, Dorothy Clarke.** *Big-Little World of Doc Pritham.* 1971. 1st. photos. VG/dj. M17. $17.50

**WILSON, Earl.** *Hot Times: True Tales of Hollywood & Broadway.* 1984. Chicago. Contemporary Books. 1st. VG/dj. C9. $25.00

**WILSON, Edmond.** *Letters on Literature & Politics 1912-1972.* 1977. NY. edit Elena Wilson. VG/dj. M17. $17.50

**WILSON, Edmund.** *American Earthquake.* 1958. Doubleday. 1st. F/dj. M25. $30.00

**WILSON, Edmund.** *Patriotic Gore: Studies in Literature of American Civil War.* 1962. Oxford. 1st. 816p. dj. B10. $25.00

**WILSON, Edmund.** *Scrolls From the Dead Sea.* 1956. OUP. 121p. VG. H10. $15.00

**WILSON, Edward O.** *Naturalist.* 1994. WA, DC. Island. NF/dj. B9. $15.00

**WILSON, Ernest.** *China: Mother of Gardens.* 1929. Boston. Stratford. 1st. 408p. G+. B5. $150.00

**WILSON, F. Paul.** *Keep.* 1981. Morrow. 1st. VG/NF. M21. $30.00

**WILSON, Gary L.** *Equine Athlete.* 1982. Princeton Junction. Veterinary Learning Systems. 1st. 79p. VG. O3. $15.00

WILSON, George. *Entries or Pleadings in Many of Cases Reported...* 1785. Dublin. Prt by Elizabeth Lynch. contemporary calf. M11. $450.00

WILSON, Helen Van Pelt. *Geraniums for Windows & Gardens.* 1946. NY. 1st. photos/ils. VG/G. M17. $17.50

WILSON, Helen Van Pelt. *Own Garden & Landscape Book.* 1973. Garden City. ils/photos. 238p. VG/dj. B26. $15.00

WILSON, Laura. *Good Morning, Mexico.* 1937. Suttonhouse. 1st. 75p. F3. $10.00

WILSON, Lord. *Eight Years Overseas 1939-1947.* nd. London. Hutchinson. 3rd. 8vo. ils/maps. 285p. VG/dj. Q2. $27.00

WILSON, M.L. *Soil Erosion: A Critical Problem in American Agriculture.* 1935. GPO. 112p. rb buckram. A10. $25.00

WILSON, Mary. *Dream Girl: My Life as a Supreme.* 1986. St Martin. 1st. G/F. W2. $30.00

WILSON, Mary. *Supreme Faith: Someday We'll Be Together.* 1990. Harper Collins. 1st. sgn. F/dj. O11. $35.00

WILSON, Pearl Cleveland. *Living Socrates: Man Who Dared to Question...* 1975. Owings Mills, MD. 1st. ils. VG/dj. M17. $17.50

WILSON, R. McNair. *British Medicine.* 1950. NY. 1st. 48p. dj. A13. $20.00

WILSON, R.L. *Cold: An American Legend.* nd. Abbeville. 1st. obl 8vo. 406p. F/dj. T11. $65.00

WILSON, R.L. *Colt Heritage.* nd. S&S. G/dj. A19. $95.00

WILSON, R.L. *Peacemakers.* 1992. Random. ils. 391p. AN. J2. $95.00

WILSON, Ralph Pinder. *Islamic Art.* 1957. Macmillan. 100 pl. gilt gr cloth. NF/VG. F1. $50.00

WILSON, Richard. *Tarbuck on Showbiz.* 1985. London. Willow. 120p. VG/dj. C5. $12.50

WILSON, Robert A. *Auden's Library.* 1975. NY. Phoenix Bookshop. 1st. 1/300. F/prt wrp. M24. $20.00

WILSON, Robert A. *Modern Book Collecting.* 1980. Knopf. 1st. 270p. F/dj. O10. $30.00

WILSON, Robert C. *Crooked Tree.* 1980. Putnam. 1st. NF/VG. M21. $20.00

WILSON, Robert C. *Gypsies.* 1989. Doubleday. 1st. F/dj. M23/M25. $25.00

WILSON, Robert C. *Icefire.* 1984. Putnam. 1st. F/F. H11. $20.00

WILSON, Robert Thomas. *History of the British Expedition to Egypt...* 1802. London. C Roworth. 4to. ils/3 tables. 354p. modern brn calf/label. K1. $450.00

WILSON, Robley. *Victim's Daughter.* 1991. S&S. 1st. sgn/dtd 1996. NF/F. R14. $30.00

WILSON, Rufus Rockwell. *Out of the West.* 1933. Pr of Pioneers. 1st. ils. 452p. VG. B19. $75.00

WILSON, Rufus Rockwell. *Out of the West.* 1933. Pr of Pioneers. 1st. VG/dj. J2. $135.00

WILSON, Ruth. *Here Is Haiti.* 1957. NY. Philosophical Lib. 1st. inscr. 204p. dj. F3. $20.00

WILSON, T.P. Cameron. *Magpies in Picardy.* 1919. London. Poetry Bookshop. 1st. G. Q1. $75.00

WILSON, T.P. Cameron. *Violent World of Hugh Greene.* 1963. Houghton Mifflin. 1st. VG/dj. Q1. $50.00

WILSON, Theodora. *New Testament Story Told For Children.* ca 1920. NY/Neward, NJ. Barse. ils Arthur Dixon. unp. VG. W1. $8.00

WILSON, Thomas. *Journals of Lives, Travels & Gospel Labours of...* 1847. London. Gilpin. 12mo. 217p. xl. V3. $35.00

WILSON, Tom. *Ziggy's Sunday Funnies: Best of the Seventies.* 1981. Andrew McMeel. unp. G. C5. $12.50

WILSON, Wayne. *Loose Jam.* 1990. Delacorte. 1st. author's 1st book. F/dj. R14. $35.00

WILSON, William. *Duties on Wool & Woolen Goods.* 1892. WA. House. 16p. A10. $15.00

WILSON, Woodrow. *George Washington.* 1897. NY. Harper. 1st. ils Howard Pyle. gilt cloth. VG. S17. $30.00

WILSON, Woodrow. *When a Man Comes to Himself.* 1915 (1901). 36p. G. B10. $10.00

WILSON & WILSON. *How to Grow Fine Flowers.* 1929. Omaha. Ralph. 211p. cloth. A10. $25.00

WILSTACH, Paul. *Correspondence of John Adams & Thomas Jefferson.* (1925). Bobbs Merrill. 196p. G. B10. $35.00

WILSTACH, Paul. *Tidewater Maryland.* 1945 (1931). Tudor. photos. 383p. VG/dj. B10. $15.00

WILTSE, David. *Bone Deep.* 1995. Putnam. 1st. F/dj. R8. $12.00

WILTSE, David. *Close to the Bone.* 1992. Putnam. 1st. NF/dj. G8. $22.50

WILTSEE, Ernest A. *Truth About Fremont: An Inquiry.* 1936. SF. John Nash. 54p. half cloth. F/dj. P4. $95.00

WIMPRESS, R.N. *Internal Ballistics of Solid-Fuel Rockets...* 1950. McGraw Hill. 1st. 214p. G. K5. $75.00

WINCHELL, A. *First Biennial Report, Geological Survey of Michigan...* 1861. Lansing. 339p. VG. A17. $75.00

WINCHESTER, Alice. *Antiques Book.* 1950. NY. AA Wyn. 1st. ils. F/torn. T10. $35.00

WIND, Herbert Warren. *World of PG Wodehouse.* 1972. Praeger. 1st. NF/dj. G8. $30.00

WINDISCH-GRAETZ, Mathilde. *Spanish Riding School.* 1956. AS Barnes. VG/dj. A21. $45.00

WINEAPPLE, Brenda. *Genet: Biography of Janet Flanner.* 1989. Ticknor Fields. 1st. ils. 361p. NF/VG. S14. $10.00

WINEGARDNER, Mark. *Prophet of the Sandlots.* 1990. Atlantic Monthly. 1st. F/dj. P8. $6.00

WINEGARDNER, Mark. *Veracruz Blues.* 1996. NY. Viking. 1st. sgn. F/dj. M23. $45.00

WINES, Frederic. *Liquor Problem in Its Legislative Aspects.* 1897. Boston. 1st. 342p. A13. $75.00

WINFIELD, Arthur M. *Rover Boys at Big Bear Lake.* nd. Grosset Dunlap. later ed/4th format. 310p. G+. H1. $12.00

WINFIELD, Arthur M. *Rover Boys at Big Horn Ranch.* nd. Grosset Dunlap. 4th format. 312p. brn cloth. G. H1. $8.00

WINFIELD, Arthur M. *Rover Boys on a Hunt.* 1920. Grosset Dunlap. 1st/4th format. 310p. brn cloth. G. H1. $8.00

WINFIELD, Arthur M. *Rover Boys on Sunset Trail.* 1925. Grosset Dunlap. 1st/4th format. 304p. brn cloth. VG/dj. H1. $18.00

WINFIELD, Arthur M. *Rover Boys Shipwrecked.* 1924. Grosset Dunlap. 1st/4th format. 306p. G/dj. H1. $15.00

WINFIELD, Charles H. *Block-House by Bull's Ferry.* 1904. NY. Wm Abbatt. 1/200. ils. 61p. VG. B18. $75.00

WINFIELD, Dave. *Winfield: A Player's Life.* 1988. Norton. 1st. F/dj. T12. $35.00

WINFREY, Laurie Platt. *Unforgettable Elephant.* 1980. NY. 96p. F/dj. A17. $12.50

WING, Joseph. *Alfalfa in America.* 1909. Chicago. Sanders. 480p. VG. A10. $30.00

**WINGATE, Anne.** *Buzzards Must Be Fed.* 1991. NY. Walker. 1st. VG/dj. N2. $10.00

**WINGFIELD, Marshall.** *General AP Stewart: His Life & Letters.* 1954. Memphis. inscr. VG/dj. B30. $100.00

**WINGFIELD, Marshall.** *History of Caroline County, Virginia...1724 to 1924.* 1969 (1924). Regional Pub. rpt. ils. 528p. VG. B10. $45.00

**WINGROVE, David.** *Broken Wheel.* 1991. Delacorte. 1st. F/F. H11. $25.00

**WINGROVE, David.** *Chung Kuo.* 1990. Delacorte. 1st. F/NF. H11. $30.00

**WINGROVE, David.** *White Mountain.* 1992. Delacorte. 1st. F/NF. H11. $25.00

**WINGS, Mary.** *She Came by the Book.* 1996. NY. Berkley Pub. 1st. F/dj. C9. $25.00

**WINKELMANN, Friedhelm.** *Studien zu Konstantin dem Grossen und zur Byzantinischen...* 1993. Birmingham. 250p. VG. Q2. $24.00

**WINKLER.** *Greatest of Greatness: Life & Work of Chas C Williamson.* 1992. 10 photos. 370p. F. A4. $30.00

**WINKLER.** *History of Books & Printing: A Guide...* 1979. 776 entries. 225p. F. A4. $95.00

**WINKS, Robin W.** *Modus Operandi.* 1982. Godine. 1st. NF/dj. G8. $25.00

**WINOKUR, Jon.** *Fathers.* 1993. Dutton. 1st. author's 9th book. F/dj. T11. $15.00

**WINSHIP, A.E.** *Jukes-Edwards: Study in Education & Heredity.* 1900. Harrisburg. RL Myers. 12mo. 88p. prt gr cloth. xl. VG. G1. $65.00

**WINSHIP, G.P.** *John Gutenberg: A Lecture...* 1940. Lakeside. 1st. 1/650. F/bl waste-paper wrp over flexible brd. M24. $20.00

**WINSHIP, George Parker.** *Journey of Coronado, 1540-1542, From City of Mexico...* 1922. Allerton Book Co. 12mo. 251p. teg. VG. F7. $27.50

**WINSHIP, George Parker.** *Journey of Coronado, 1540-1542.* 1900. Fulcrum. rpt. ils. 233p. F/F. B19. $25.00

**WINSLOW, Don.** *Death & Life of Bobby Z.* 1997. Knopf. 1st. inscr. AN/dj. S18. $35.00

**WINSLOW, Don.** *Death & Life of Bobby Z.* 1997. Knopf. 1st. NF/F. G8. $30.00

**WINSLOW, Don.** *Long Walk Up the Water Slide.* 1994. St Martin. 1st. F/dj. M15. $50.00

**WINSLOW, Don.** *While Drowning in the Desert.* 1996. St Martin. 1st. sgn. F/dj. G8. $27.50

**WINSOR, Justin.** *Mississippi Basin: Struggle in America...* 1895. Houghton Mifflin. 1st. 484p. teg. quarter leather. B18. $45.00

**WINSWORTH, William.** *Works of...* nd. London. 16 vol. ils Cruikshank. half leather/marbled brd. F. B30. $425.00

**WINTER, Douglas E.** *Black Wine.* 1986. Dark Harvest. 1st trade. AN/dj. T12. $40.00

**WINTER, Douglas E.** *Night Visions 5.* nd. Dark Harvest. 1st trade. AN/swp. M21. $40.00

**WINTER, Douglas E.** *Prime Evil.* 1988. NAL. 1st trade. NF/dj. M21. $20.00

**WINTER, Douglas E.** *Prime Evil.* 1988. NAL. 1st. F/dj. N4/S18. $25.00

**WINTER, Douglas E.** *Stephen King: Art of Darkness.* 1984. NAL. 1st. F/dj. P3. $20.00

**WINTER, George Simon.** *Pferde-Arzt...* 1841. Northampton Co, PA. Herausgegeben VonKleckner/Nolf und Williams. leather. G. O3. $295.00

**WINTERNITZ, Helen.** *Season of Stones: Living in Palestinian Village.* 1991. Atlantic Monthly. 1st. 8vo. 303p. NF/dj. W1. $18.00

**WINTERS, Shelley.** *Shelley II: Middle of My Century.* 189. S&S. 1st. F/NF. W2. $25.00

**WINTERS, Yvor.** *Collected Poems of Yvor Winters.* (1978). Chicago. Swallow. 1st. intro Donald Davie. F/clip. A18. $25.00

**WINTERSON, Jeanette.** *Art & Lies.* 1994. London. Cape. 1st. 206p. F/dj. O11. $35.00

**WINTERSON, Jeanette.** *Art & Lies.* 1995. Knopf. 1st Am. sgn. F/dj. O11. $50.00

**WINTERSON, Jeanette.** *Art Objects.* 1995. London. Cape. 1st. F/dj. O11. $35.00

**WINTERSON, Jeanette.** *Oranges Are Not the Only Fruit.* 1985. London. Pandora. true 1st. sgn. F/pict wrp. D10. $650.00

**WINTERSON, Jeanette.** *Written on the Body.* 1993. Knopf. 1st Am. F/dj. R14. $25.00

**WINTERSON, Jeanette.** *Written on the Body.* 1993. Knopf. 1st Am. sgn. F/dj. O11. $50.00

**WINTHER, Oscar.** *Transportation Frontier.* 1964. HRW. VG. A19. $30.00

**WINTHROP, Elizabeth.** *Belinda's Hurricane.* 1984. Dutton. 1st. 8vo. 54p. NF. C14. $14.00

**WINTHROP, Robert C.** *Life & Letters of John Winthrop...* 1867. Boston. xl. VG. M17. $45.00

**WINTLE, E.D.** *Birds of Montreal.* 1896. Montreal. 1st. lists of 254 species/5 pl. 281p. 2-tone cloth. G. C12. $78.00

**WINTLE, Justin.** *Paradise for Hire.* 1984. London. Secker Warburg. 1st. author's 1st book. rem mk. NF/dj. A14. $25.00

**WINTON, John.** *Fighting Temeraire.* 1971. Coward McCann. 1st. NF/VG. T11. $30.00

**WINTON, John.** *Sir Walter Raleigh.* 1975. CMG. 1st. ils. 352p. VG/dj. M10. $28.50

**WINTON, Tim.** *Minimum of Two.* 1988. Weidenfeld Nicolson. 1st Eng. sgn. F/dj. R14. $50.00

**WINTON, Tim.** *Minimum of Two.* 1988. Weidenfeld Nicolson. 1st. sgn. F/dj. B3. $45.00

**WIRT, Mildred A.** *Dan Carter & Cub Honor.* 1953. Cupples Leon. likely 1st. 12mo. VG/G. A2. $10.00

**WIRT, Mildred A.** *Dan Carter & Cub Honor.* 1953. Cupples Leon. 1st. 12mo. F/VG. A2. $12.00

**WIRT, William.** *Life & Character of Patrick Henry.* nd (late 1800s) Phil. Porter Coates. 468p. VG. B18. $19.50

**WIRT, William.** *Life & Character of Patrick Henry.* nd (1880s). Porter Coates. 468p. poor. B10. $12.00

**WIRTH, A.C.** *Launsberry's Legacy to the World.* nd. Baltimore. mini. 1/50. gilt red cloth. B24. $125.00

**WIRTH, Don.** *Adventures of Harry 'n' Charlie: 2 Vols.* 1981. Montgomery. BASS. 144/144p. F. A17. $25.00

**WIRTH, Zdenek.** *Castles & Mansions (Bohemia & Moravia).* 1955. Prague. Artia. 1st. 272p. 307p. gilt tan cloth. VG/dj. F1. $75.00

**WISE, Henry A.** *Yesteryears on the Eastern Shore & Some Other Things.* 1968. Eastern Shore News. 1st. 105p. VG/VG. B10. $15.00

**WISE, John S.** *End of an Era.* (1899). Houghton Mifflin. 18th imp. 474p. VG. B10. $30.00

**WISE, John.** *System of Aeronautics, Comprehending...* 1850. Phil. Joseph Speel. 1st. sgn. 12 pl+ftspc. 310p. ES. emb gilt bdg. B11. $1,950.00

**WISEMAN, John A.** *Democracy in Black Africa: Survival & Revival.* 1990. Paragon. 1st. 8vo. F/dj. A2. $15.00

**WISEMAN, Robert E.** *Complete Horseshoeing Guide.* 1973. Norman, OK. 2nd. VG/G. O3. $15.00

**WISER, William.** *Disappearances.* 1980. Atheneum. 1st. F/F. H11. $35.00

**WISHNIA, K.J.A.** *Flat Rate & Other Tales.* 1997. E Setauket. Imaginary. 1st. sgn. F. M15. $30.00

**WISNER, Benjamin B.** *History of the Old South Church in Boston...* 1830. Boston. Crocker Brewster. 8vo. lg fld plan. 122p. self wrp. O1. $40.00

**WISSINGER, Joanna.** *Best Kit Homes Save Time & Money...* 1987. Emmaus. 1st. ils. VG/dj. M8. $25.00

**WISSLER, Clark.** *Indians of the United States.* 1940. Doubleday Doran. G. A19. $45.00

**WISTER, Fammy Kemble.** *Owen Wister Out West: His Journals & Letters.* nd. U Chicago. 269p. VG/dj. J2. $50.00

**WISTER, Isaac Jones.** *Autobiography of..., 1827-1905: Half a Century...* 1937. Phil. Wistar Inst. 4to. 528p. G. V3. $50.00

**WISTER, Owen.** *Journey in Search of Christmas.* 1904. NY. Harper. 1st. 8vo. 92p. teg. VG. H5. $100.00

**WISTER, Owen.** *Lady Baltimore.* 1906. NY. Macmillan. 1st. 406p. G. G11. $17.00

**WISTER, Owen.** *Padre Ignacio; or, Song of Temptation.* 1925. Harper. 8vo. ils Zack Hogg (NC Weyth?). blk cloth. NF. R3. $75.00

**WISTER, Owen.** *Virginian: Horseman on the Plains.* 1902. Macmillan. ils. 504p. worn. B19. $10.00

**WITHAM, G.F.** *Shiloh, Shells & Artillery Units.* 1980. Memphis. 1/990. sgn. F. M4. $70.00

**WITHER, George.** *Love Song.* 1903. Concord, MA. Sign of the Vine. woodcut title. lt bl brd. F. F1. $65.00

**WITHNER, Carl L.** *Orchids: A Scientific Survey.* 1959. Ronald. 648p. xl. VG. S5. $40.00

**WITHROW, Robert B.** *Photoperiodism & Related Phonomena in Plants & Animals.* 1959. AAAS. 903p. xl. VG. S5. $25.00

**WITKIN, Joel-Peter.** *Masterpieces of Medical Photography.* 1987. Pasadena. Twelvetrees. 1st. 4to. 40 pl. F/NF. S9. $150.00

**WITKIN, Lee.** *Ten Year Salute.* 1979. Addison House. 1st. NF/VG. P2. $35.00

**WITTEN, Barbara Yager.** *Isle of Fire Murder.* 1987. Walker. 1st. F/dj. N4. $15.00

**WITTIG, Monique.** *Opoponax.* 1966. S&S. 1st Am. F/NF. M25. $25.00

**WITTLIN, Thaddeus.** *Modigliani: Prince of Montparnasse.* 1964. Bobbs Merrill. 1st. VG/dj. S13. $10.00

**WITTMER, Margaret.** *Floreana: Woman's Pilgrimage to Galapagos.* 1990. NY. Moyer Bell. 1st. 240p. wrp. F3. $10.00

**WITTNER, Ruth.** *Chirp, a Little Clown in a Big Circus.* 1942. Am Book Co. 1st. inscr. ils Ottlie Foy. VG. M5. $10.00

**WODEHOUSE, P.G.** *Divots.* 1927. NY. 1st. VG. B5. $100.00

**WODEHOUSE, P.G.** *Fish Preferred.* 1929. Doubleday Doran. 1st. xl. G+. M21. $15.00

**WODEHOUSE, P.G.** *Full Moon.* 1947. Doubleday. 1st. VG. M21. $15.00

**WODEHOUSE, P.G.** *Girl in Blue.* 1971. S&S. 1st. VG/dj. M21. $35.00

**WODEHOUSE, P.G.** *William Tell Told Again.* 1904. London. Blk. 1st. 8vo. 105+2p ads. teg. VG. H5. $1,250.00

**WOIWODE, Larry.** *Born Brothers.* 1988. FSG. 1st. F/NF. R14. $25.00

**WOIWODE, Larry.** *Even Tide.* 1977. FSG. 1st trade. F/dj. L3. $35.00

**WOIWODE, Larry.** *Pappa John.* 1981. FSG. 1st. sgn/dtd 1996. NF/dj. R14. $45.00

**WOIWODE, Larry.** *Poppa John.* 1981. NY. FSG. 1st. F/F. B3. $30.00

**WOLCOT, John.** *Works of Peter Pindar, Esq...* 1812. London. Walker. 5 vol. new/revised/corrected. tall 8vo. tan polished calf. H13. $395.00

**WOLCOTT, R.H.** *Proceedings of the Nebraska Ornithologist's Union Vol 1-6.* 1900-1914. Neligh/Lincoln. 6 vol. ils. 8vo. 450+p. F. C12. $45.00

**WOLDERING, Irmgard.** *Art of Egypt.* 1963. NY. 1st Am. 8vo. 256p. VG. B11. $15.00

**WOLF, Johann.** *Lectionum Memorabilium et Reconditarum Centenarii XVI.* 1600. Lauingen. Leohard Rheinmichel. 2 vol. 1st. folio. ils. K1. $2,250.00

**WOLF, Leonard.** *Annotated Dracula.* 1975. Clarkson Potter. 1st. VG/dj. L1. $150.00

**WOLF, Leonard.** *Dream of Dracula: In Search of the Living Dead.* 1972. Little Brn. 1st. VG/G. L1. $75.00

**WOLF & WOLF.** *Fungi.* 1947. NY. 2 vol. ils. F/dj. B26. $40.00

**WOLFE, Aaron;** see Koontz, Dean R.

**WOLFE, Gene.** *Citadel of the Autarch.* 1983. NY. Tor. 1st. F/NF. M21. $25.00

**WOLFE, Gene.** *Claw of the Conciliator.* 1981. NY. Timescape. 1st. F/dj. M21. $65.00

**WOLFE, Gene.** *Lake of the Long Sun.* 1994. NY. Tor. 1st. F/NF. G10. $12.00

**WOLFE, Gene.** *Shadow of the Torturer.* 1980. S&S. 1st. F/dj. M21. $120.00

**WOLFE, Gene.** *There Are Doors.* 1988. NY. Tor. 1st. F/dj. A24. $25.00

**WOLFE, Humbert.** *Cursory Rhymes.* 1927. London. Ernest Benn. 1st. 124p. VG. M10. $35.00

**WOLFE, T.** *Western Journal.* 1951. Pittsburgh. 1st. VG. B5. $35.00

**WOLFE, Thomas.** *Letters to His Mother.* 1943. Scribner. 1st. 368p. xl. G. G11. $35.00

**WOLFE, Thomas.** *Of Time & the River.* 1935. Scribner. 1st/1st prt. gilt blk cloth. F/NF. M24. $200.00

**WOLFE, Thomas.** *Story of a Novel.* 1936. Scribner. 1st. gilt apricot cloth. F/NF. M24. $150.00

**WOLFE, Tom.** *Bonfire of the Vanities.* 1987. FSG. 1st. F/F. H11. $40.00

**WOLFE, Tom.** *Bonfire of the Vanities.* 1987. FSG. 1st. sgn. NF/dj. Q1. $125.00

**WOLFE, Tom.** *Kandy-Kolored Tangerine-Flake Streamline Baby.* 1965. FSG. 1st. author's 1st book. F/F. A4. $250.00

**WOLFE, Tom.** *Right Stuff.* 1979. FSG. 1st. VG/G. B30. $30.00

**WOLFENSTINE, Manfred R.** *Manual of Brands & Marks...* 1970. Norman, OK. 1st. VG. O3. $65.00

**WOLFF, Geoffrey.** *Bad Debts.* 1969. S&S. 1st. sgn. NF/VG. R14. $85.00

**WOLFF, Geoffrey.** *Inklings.* 1977. Random. 1st. sgn/dtd 1994. NF/dj. R14. $50.00

**WOLFF, Larry.** *Postcards From the End of the World.* 1988. Atheneum. 1st. NF/dj. w/review material. S13. $15.00

**WOLFF, Michael.** *White Kids.* 1979. NY. Summit. 1st. F/dj. R11. $20.00

**WOLFF, Perry S.** *History of the 334th Infantry, 84th Division.* (1945). Mannheim. 1st. photos/fld map. 230p. VG. B18. $65.00

**WOLFF, Perry.** *Tour of the White House With Mrs John F Kennedy.* 1962. NY. 1st. ils. VG/dj. M17. $17.50

**WOLFF, Rick.** *What's a Nice Harvard Boy Like You Doing in Bushes?* 1975. Prentice Hall. 1st. F/VG. P8. $35.00

**WOLFF, Tobias.** *Back in the World.* 1985. Boston. Houghton Mifflin. 1st. sgn. F/F. w/pub postcard. D10. $60.00

**WOLFF, Tobias.** *Back in the World.* 1986. London. Cape. 1st. sgn. F/dj. O11. $55.00

**WOLFF, Tobias.** *In Pharoah's Army: Memories of the Lost War.* 1994. Knopf. 1st. F/F. B4. $45.00

**WOLFF, Tobias.** *Night in Question.* 1996. Knopf. 1st. sgn. F/dj. O11. $50.00

**WOLFF, Tobias.** *Night in Question.* 1996. Knopf. 1st thus. 1/1500. sgn. F/sealed pict wrp. Q1. $60.00

**WOLFF, Tobias.** *This Boy's Life: A Memoir.* 1989. NY. 1st. VG/dj. M17. $40.00

**WOLFF, Tobias.** *Two Boys & a Girl.* 1996. London. Bloomsbury. Chapbook. sgn. F. R14. $35.00

**WOLFF, Werner.** *Island of Death: A New Key to Easter Island's Culture...* 1948. NY. JJ Augustin. 4to. 20 pl. 228p. blk cloth. VG/dj. G1. $65.00

**WOLLASTON, Nicholas.** *Red Rumba.* 1964. London. Readers Union. 192p. dj. F3. $15.00

**WOLLHEIM, Donald A.** *Daw Science Fiction Reader.* 1976. Daw. VG/wrp. M20. $15.00

**WOLMAN, Benjamin B.** *Handbook of Development of Mental Disorders...* 1978. Prentice Hall. heavy 4to. 475p. VG/dj. G1. $65.00

**WOLMAN, Benjamin B.** *Psychological Aspects of Obesity: A Handbook.* 1982. Van Nostrand Reinhold. 1st. 8vo. 318p. F/dj. C14. $25.00

**WOLRAB, Johann Jacob.** *Military Exercises: 1730.* (1962). Ontario. West Hill. rpt. ils. F. E1. $45.00

**WOLSELEY, Garnet.** *American Civil War: An English View.* 1964. U VA. 1st. 230p. F/VG. B10. $35.00

**WOMACK, Bob.** *Echo of Hoofbeats.* 1973. Walking Horse. VG/dj. A21. $95.00

**WOMACK, Jack.** *Ambient.* 1987. Weidenfeld Nicolson. 1st. author's 1st novel. NF/dj. N4. $25.00

**WOMACK, Jack.** *Ambient.* 1987. Weidenfeld Nicolson. 1st. sgn. author's 1st book. F/dj. O11. $65.00

**WOMACK, Jack.** *Elvissey.* 1993. NY. Tor. 1st. sgn. F. O11. $25.00

**WOMEN'S DAY.** *Women's Day Encyclopedia of Cookery.* 1965. Fawcett. 12 vol. 1st. 4to. VG. H1. $42.00

**WOOD, Dennis W.** *Principles of Animal Physiology.* 1974. Am Elsevier. ils. 342p. NF/VG. S15. $13.00

**WOOD, Elena.** *Compadrazgo en Apas.* 1982. Mexico. 1st. 89p. wrp. F3. $10.00

**WOOD, Frank B.** *Photoelectric Astronomy for Amateurs.* 1963. NY. Macmillan. 1st. 8vo. 223p. dj. K5. $30.00

**WOOD, Henry.** *New Old Healing.* 1908. Lee Shepard. 304p. teg. gr cloth. VG. S17. $5.00

**WOOD, James.** *Interpretation of the Bible.* 1958. Duckworth. 179p. VG/dj. B29. $8.00

**WOOD, James.** *Voyage Into Nowhere.* 1966. NY. Vanguard. 1st. F/VG clip. T11. $20.00

**WOOD, John Sumner.** *Virginia Bishop: Yankee Hero of the Confederacy.* 1961. Garret Massie. 187p. VG/dj. B10. $25.00

**WOOD, Kerry.** *Birds & Animals in the Rockies.* ca 1950. Saskatoon. 1st. ils Beebe. VG. A17. $20.00

**WOOD, Lawson.** *Lawson Wood Nursery Rhyme Book.* ca 1920. London. Nelson. lg 4to. cloth backed mc pict brd. R5. $200.00

**WOOD, Lawson.** *Lawson Wood's Fun Fair.* 1931. London. Arundel Prts. 4to. cloth backed brd/mc label. R5. $175.00

**WOOD, Lawson.** *Marking Time With Gran'Pop.* ca 1950. St Paul. Brn Bigelow. sbdg. R5. $100.00

**WOOD, Morrison.** *More Recipes With a Jug of Wine.* 1968. FSG. 11th. 8vo. 400p. NF/dj. W2. $25.00

**WOOD, Morrison.** *With a Jug of Wine.* 1949. FSC. G/dj. A16. $10.00

**WOOD, N.A.** *Birds of Michigan.* 1951. Ann Arbor. 559p. gilt bl cloth. F. C12. $50.00

**WOOD, Nancy.** *Taos Pueblo.* 1989. Knopf. 1st. ils. 162p. F/NF. B19. $55.00

**WOOD, Richard G.** *Stephen Harriman Long, 1784-1864.* 1966. Glendale. AH Clark. ils. 292p. F. F1. $45.00

**WOOD, Robert Lee.** *Nineteenth-Century Fiction: A Bibliographical Catalogue.* 1981-1986. NY/London. 5 vol. gilt gr cloth. F. F1. $550.00

**WOOD, Robert.** *Day Trips to Archaeological Mexico.* 1991. Hastings. revised/updated. ils. 174p. wrp. F3. $10.00

**WOOD, Robin.** *Hitchcock's Films.* 1965. Zwemmer/Barnes. 1st. VG/wrp. C9. $48.00

**WOOD, T.** *Natural History of Mammals.* 1886. London/NY. Nister/Dutton. ils. 244p. VG. M12. $37.50

**WOOD, Ted.** *Flashback.* 1992. Scribner. 1st Am. NF/dj. G8. $20.00

**WOOD, Tom.** *Bright Side of Billy Wilder, Primarily.* 1970. Doubleday. 1st. F/G. T12. $25.00

**WOODARD, Lt., M.D.** see Silverberg, Robert.

**WOODBERRY, George Edward.** *Complete Poetical Works of Percy Bysshe Shelley.* 1892. Cambridge, MA. Riverside. 8vo. lg paper ed. 1/250. VG. S17. $75.00

**WOODBURN, James A.** *American Republic & Its Government.* 1916 (1903). Putnam. 2nd. 8vo. VG. A2. $15.00

**WOODBURY, David O.** *Around the World in 90 Minutes...* 1958. Harcourt Brace. ils. 248p. dj. K5. $25.00

**WOODBURY, David O.** *Colorado Conquest.* 1941. Dodd Mead. 1st. 8vo. tan cloth. VG. F7. $45.00

**WOODFORD, M.H.** *Manual of Falconry.* 1960. London. 1st. NF. C12. $45.00

**WOODHOUSE, Henry.** *Textbook of Naval Aeronautics.* 1918. NY. 2nd. 288p. cloth. VG. M8. $250.00

**WOODHOUSE, Robert.** *Elementary Treatise on Astronomy.* 1812. Cambridge. 8vo. 471p. VG. K5. $150.00

**WOODING, F.H.** *Angler's Book of Canadian Fishes.* 1959. Ontario. 1st. ils. 303p. F/G. A17. $20.00

**WOODMAN, John.** *Journal of Life, Gospel Labours & Christian Experiences...* 1837. Phil. TE Chapman. 12mo. 396p. G+. V3. $60.00

**WOODMAN, Richard.** *Baltic Mission.* 1986. NY. Walker. 1st Am. F/NF. T11. $50.00

**WOODMAN, Richard.** *Bob Vessel.* 1986. NY. Walker. 1st Am. VG+/dj. A14. $28.00

**WOODMAN, Richard.** *Brig of War.* 1983. London. Murray. 1st. NF/dj. A14. $87.50

**WOODMAN, Richard.** *Brig of War.* 1983. London. Murray. 1st. VG+/clip. A14. $70.00

**WOODMAN, Richard.** *Private Revenge.* 1989. NY. 1st. VG/dj. M17. $22.50

**WOODMAN, Richard.** *Private Revenge.* 1989. St Martin. 1st Am. F/dj. T11. $35.00

**WOODRELL, Daniel.** *Muscle for the Wing.* 1988. NY. Holt. 1st. author's 3rd book. F/F. B3. $45.00

**WOODRELL, Daniel.** *Under the Bright Lights.* 1986. Holt. 1st. author's 1st book. F/NF. B3. $75.00

**WOODRESS, James.** *Willa Cather: A Literary Life.* 1987. U NE. VG/dj. P3. $35.00

**WOODRIDGE, C.W.** *Perfecting the Earth, a Piece of Possible History.* 1902. Cleveland. Utopia Pub. NF. B2. $125.00

**WOODS, G.K.** *Personal Impressions of the Grand Canyon of Colorado...* 1899. SF. ils. aeg. 164p. red cloth. VG. F7. $395.00

**WOODS, Margaret.** *Extracts From Journal of Late Margaret Woods...1771-1821.* 1850. Phil. Longstreth. 3rd. 378p. poor. V3. $35.00

**WOODS, Sara.** *Knives Have Edges.* 1968. Collins Crime Club. 1st. F/dj. C15. $25.00

**WOODS, Stuart.** *Dead Eyes.* 1994. Harper Collins. 1st. 1/150. F/dj. M15. $85.00

**WOODS, Stuart.** *Under the Lake.* 1987. NY. S&S. 1st. F/clip. A14. $21.00

**WOODS, William Crawford.** *Killing Zone.* 1970. NY. Harper. 1st. NF/dj. R11. $35.00

**WOODS & WOODWARD.** *Urban Disease & Mortality in 19th-Century England.* 1984. nY. 1st. 255p. A13. $25.00

**WOODSON, R. Dodge.** *Home Plumbing Repair & Replacement.* 1992. Betterway Books. 1st. 224p. F. W2. $50.00

**WOODSTONE, Norma Sue.** *Up Against the War: A Personal Introduction...* 1970. NY. Tower. 187p. NF/wrp. R11. $50.00

**WOODWARD, Arthur.** *Feud on the Colorado.* 1955. Westernlore. 1st. sgn. 8vo. 165p. red cloth. VG/dj. F7. $100.00

**WOODWARD, Bob.** *Commanders.* 1991. S&S. 1st. sm 4to. 398p. F/dj. W2. $35.00

**WOODWARD, Ian.** *Glenda Jackson: Study in Fire & Ice.* 1985. St Martin. 1st. F/dj. T12. $25.00

**WOODWARD, J.J.** *Medical & Surgical History of the War of the Rebellion.* 1870-1888. WA, DC. 6 vol. 4to. mixed issue/bdg/some xl. G7. $1,500.00

**WOODWARD, W.E.** *Meet General Grant.* 1928. Garden City. 1st. photos. VG/dj. S13. $12.00

**WOODWARD, Walter C.** *Timothy Nicolson, Master Quaker.* 1927. Richmond, IN. Nicholson. 252p. xl. V3. $21.00

**WOODWARD & WOODWARD.** *Woodward's Country Homes.* 1865. NY. Woodward. 1st. ils. 166p. VG. H10. $95.00

**WOODWORTH, Robert Sessions.** *Adjustment & Mastery: Problems in Psychology.* 1933. Wms Wilkins. 12mo. orange cloth. VG/tattered. G1. $32.50

**WOODWORTH, Robert Sessions.** *Contemporary Schools of Psychology.* 1948. Ronald Pr. revised/1st prt. sgn. 8vo. 279p. ruled red cloth. G. G1. $35.00

**WOODWORTH, Robert Sessions.** *Experimental Psychology.* 1938. Holt. inscr/sgn. 889p. gray cloth/painted labels. VG/dj. G1. $250.00

**WOODWORTH, Robert Sessions.** *Le Mouvement.* 1903. Paris. Octave Doin. 12mo. 421p. prt gray wrp. G1. $75.00

**WOODWORTH, Robert Sessions.** *Psychology.* 1929. Holt. 2nd revised. inscr/sgn. 12mo. 590p. panelled thatched gr cloth. G1. $50.00

**WOODWORTH, Steven E.** *Jefferson Davis & His Generals...* 1990. BC. ils. VG/dj. M17. $15.00

**WOODWORTH, Steven E.** *Jefferson Davis & His Generals: Failure of Confederate...* 1990. Lawrence, KS. 1st. F/dj. A14. $25.00

**WOODY, Allen.** *Side Effects.* 1980. Random. 1st. F/dj. O4. $20.00

**WOODY, Robert Henley.** *Encyclopedia of Clinical Assessment.* 1980. San Francisco. Jossey-Bass. 2 vol. gr cloth. VG/dj. G1. $65.00

**WOOFTER, T.J.** *Landlord & Tenant on the Cotton Plantation.* 1936. WPA. Div Social Research. ils/charts. 287p. VG. B10. $75.00

**WOOLEN, William Watson.** *Inside Passage to Alaska 1793-1920.* 1924. Cleveland. AH Clark. 2 vol. 1st. ils/map. gilt gr cloth. B11. $650.00

**WOOLF, Virginia.** *Hours in a Library.* 1957. Harcourt Brace. 1st. 1/1800. F/tissue dj. Q1. $125.00

**WOOLF, Virginia.** *Letter to a Young Poet.* 1932. London. Hogarth. Hogarth Letters #8. 28p. NF/wrp. O11. $75.00

**WOOLF, Virginia.** *Pargiters.* 1978. London. Hogarth. 1st. F/dj. A24. $60.00

**WOOLF, Virginia.** *Three Guineas.* 1938. London. Hogarth. 1st. sm crown 8vo. 329p. lemon-yel brd. VG/dj. J3. $600.00

**WOOLHOUSE, H.W.** *Dormacy & Survival.* 1969. Academic. 598p. xl. VG. S5. $30.00

**WOOLLEY, C. Leonard.** *Digging Up the Past.* 1931. NY. 1st. photos. VG. M17. $20.00

**WOOLLEY, C. Leonard.** *Sumerians.* 1995. Barnes Noble. ils. 198p. NF/dj. W1. $18.00

**WOOLMAN, John.** *Serious Considerations on Various Subjects of Importance...* 1773. London. Mary Hinde. 12mo. 137p. worn leather. V3. $55.00

**WOOLMAN, John.** *Works of..., in Two Parts.* 1775. Phil. Crukshank. 2nd. sm 8vo. 432p. worn leather. V3. $150.00

**WOOLNER, Frank.** *Grouse & Grouse Hunting.* 1970. NY. 192p. F/dj. A17. $30.00

**WOOLNER, Frank.** *Timberdoodle!... Woodcock & Woodcock Hunting.* 1974. NY. 168p. F/dj. A17. $25.00

**WOOLRICH, Cornell.** *After-Dinner Story.* 1944. Lippincott. 1st. VG/dj/clamshell box. L3. $950.00

**WOOLRICH, Cornell.** *Best of William Irish.* 1960. Lippincott. Omnibus. F/NF. M15. $175.00

**WOOLRICH, Cornell.** *Dead Man Blues.* 1948. Lippincott. 1st. VG/dj. C15. $85.00

**WOOLRICH, Cornell.** *Six Nights of Mystery.* 1950. NY. Popular Lib. 1st. F/wrp. M15. $150.00

**WOOLRICH, Cornell.** *Times Square.* 1929. Liveright. 1st. VG. C15. $100.00

**WOOLRICH, Cornell.** *4 by Cornell Woolrich.* 1983. London. Zomba. Omnibus. F/dj. M15. $85.00

**WOOS, Prince.** *Open-Air Poultry Houses for All Climates.* 1912. Chicago. Am Poultry Journal. 86p. cloth. A10. $28.00

**WOOSTER, Ralph A.** *Politicans, Planters & Plain Folk: Courthouse & Statehouse.* 1975. Knoxville, TN. U TN. 1st. 8vo. F/dj. A2. $15.00

**WOOSTER, Robert.** *Nelson A Miles & the Twilight of the Frontier Army.* 1993. U NE. ils. VG/dj. M17. $20.00

**WOOTTERS, John.** *Hunting Trophy Deer.* 1977. Winchester. index/photos. 251p. F/dj. A17. $15.00

**WORBY, John.** *Other Half.* 1937. NY. Lee Furman. 1st. F/NF. B2. $60.00

**WORCESTER, Donald E.** *Forked Tongues & Broken Treaties.* 1975. Caldwell, ID. VG/dj. A19. $30.00

**WORDSWORTH, William.** *Decade of Years.* 1911. Hammersmith. Doves. 1/200 (212 total). sm 4to. 230p. NF/case. H5. $850.00

**WORMINGTON, H.S.** *Prehistoric Indians of the Southwest.* 1947. Denver. 8vo. 191p. VG/dj. F7. $40.00

**WORMSER, Richard.** *Kidnapped Circus.* 1968. Morrow. 1st. VG/G. O3. $22.00

**WORTH, C. Brooke.** *Naturalist in Trinidad.* 1967. Lippincott. 1st. ils Don Eckelberry. 291p. F/VG+. S15. $20.00

**WORTLEY, Emmeline Stuart.** *Travels in the United States, Etc, During 1849-1850.* 1855. NY. Harper. early ed. 8vo. 463p. H7. $35.00

**WORZEL, J.L.** *Pendulum Gravity Measurements at Sea 1936-1959.* 1965. Wiley. 1st. ils. cloth. VG. B27. $45.00

**WOUK, Herman.** *Glory.* 1994. Little Brn. 1/200. sgn. F/sans/F case. R14. $125.00

**WOUK, Herman.** *War & Remembrance.* 1978. Boston. 1st. dj. T9. $15.00

**WPA WRITERS PROGRAM.** *Alabama Historical Records Survey.* 1939. Birmingham. 1st. 159p. VG/prt wrp. M8. $75.00

**WPA WRITERS PROGRAM.** *Hands That Built New Hampshire.* 1940. Brattleboro. 1st. 288p. F/dj. M4. $65.00

**WPA WRITERS PROGRAM.** *Jefferson's Albermarle: A Guide to Albemarle County...* (1941). Jarman's. ils. 157p. G+. B10. $35.00

**WPA WRITERS PROGRAM.** *Mississippi: Guide to the Magnolia State.* 1943. NY. 1st. ils. 545p. VG. B18. $65.00

**WPA WRITERS PROGRAM.** *New Orleans City Guide.* 1938. Boston. 1st. ils. 430p. VG. B18. $65.00

**WPA WRITERS PROJECT.** *American Imprints Inventory Number 31...Imprints 1833-55.* 1942. SF. 109p. lib buckram w/orig wrp bdg in. D11. $50.00

**WRANGHAM, Richard.** *Demonic Males: Apes & Origins of Human Violence.* 1996. Houghton Mifflin. 1st. 8vo. 350p. F/dj. C14. $18.00

**WREN, Daniel A.** *White Collar Hobo: Travels of Whiting Williams.* 1987. IA State. 1st. 8vo. F/dj. A2. $15.00

**WRIGHT, B.** *Road to Tokyo.* Nov 1947. 2nd. sq 4to. 254p. VG. E6. $60.00

**WRIGHT, Bruce.** *High Tide & an East Wind: Story of the Black Duck.* 1954. Stackpole. 1st. ils/index. 162p. F/G. A17. $25.00

**WRIGHT, Dare.** *Edith & Midnight.* 1978. Doubleday. 1st. folio. xl. VG/dj. B17. $35.00

**WRIGHT, Dare.** *Lonely Doll Learns a Lesson.* nd (c 1961). Random. apparent 2nd. 4to. unp. VG. C14. $45.00

**WRIGHT, Denis.** *English Amongst the Persians During Qajar Period 1787-1921.* 1977. London. Heinemann. ils/dbl-p map. 218p. VG/dj. Q2. $20.00

**WRIGHT, Edmond.** *History of the World.* 1985. Bonanza. VG/dj. M20. $20.00

**WRIGHT, Eric.** *Death by Degrees.* 1993. Toronto. Doubleday. 1st. sgn. F/dj. M25. $35.00

**WRIGHT, Frank Lloyd.** *Future of Architecture.* 1953. NY. 1st. photos/diagrams. VG/G. M17. $60.00

**WRIGHT, Frank Lloyd.** *Living City.* 1958. NY. 1st. photos/diagrams/fld plan for Broadacre City. VG/dj. M17. $120.00

**WRIGHT, Frank Lloyd.** *Testament.* 1957. NY. 1st. photos. VG/G. M17. $90.00

**WRIGHT, H.** *Headaches: Their Causes & Cure.* 1856. 1st. VG. E6. $50.00

**WRIGHT, Harold Bell.** *Calling of Dan Matthews.* 1909. Chicago Book Supply. 1st. VG. N2. $15.00

**WRIGHT, Harold Bell.** *Eyes of the World.* 1914. Chicago. Book Supply. 1st. 464p. VG. G11. $22.00

**WRIGHT, Harold Bell.** *Helen of the Old House.* 1921. NY. Appleton. 1st. 372p. G. G11. $10.00

**WRIGHT, Harold Bell.** *Re-Creation of Brian Kent.* 1919. Chicago. Book Supply. 1st. ils J Allen St John. G+. G11. $17.50

**WRIGHT, Harold Bell.** *Their Yesterdays.* 1912. Book Supply. 1st. 310p. F. H1. $12.00

**WRIGHT, Harold Bell.** *When a Man's a Man.* 1916. Chicago. Book Supply. 1st (#245223). G+. G11. $15.00

**WRIGHT, Irene A.** *Spanish Documents Concerning English Voyages to Caribbean...* 1929. London. Hakluyt Soc. 8vo. 2 maps/1 facs. 167p. cloth. F. O1. $55.00

**WRIGHT, J.** *Lectures on Diseases of the Rectum.* 1884. Birmingham Medical Lib. 1st. VG. E6. $60.00

**WRIGHT, James.** *Secret Field.* 1985. Durango. Logbridge-Rhodes. F/wrp. R14. $25.00

**WRIGHT, Jim.** *Saskatchewan: History of a Province.* 1955. McClelland Stewart. 1st/Golden Jubilee. F/VG. A26. $55.00

**WRIGHT, John.** *Trout on a Stick: A Mountain Cookbook.* 1991. Minocqua. 1st. 143p. VG/wrp. A17. $10.00

**WRIGHT, L.R.** *Love in the Temperate Zone.* 1988. Viking. 1st. F/dj. H11. $20.00

**WRIGHT, L.R.** *Touch of Panic.* 1994. Scribner. 1st. sgn. NF/dj. G8. $30.00

**WRIGHT, Lyle H.** *American Fiction 1774-1900: A Contribution...* 1969. San Marino, CA. Huntington Lib. 3 vol. 2nd revised. F/VG. H7. $75.00

**WRIGHT, Lyle M.** *American Fiction 1774-1875.* 1948-1957. San Marino, CA. 2 vol. revised. cloth. NF/VG. M8. $85.00

**WRIGHT, Marcus J.** *Official & Illustrated (Civil) War Record.* 1898. WA, DC. folio. ils Thos Nast/others. reading copy. H1. $30.00

**WRIGHT, Michael.** *Complete Indoor Gardener.* 1980. London. Pan. 4to. 256p. NF. M10. $12.50

**WRIGHT, Norman.** *Mexican Kaleidoscope.* 1948. London. ils/index. F3. $10.00

**WRIGHT, Richard.** *Native Son.* 1940. Harper. 1st. 359p. gilt bl cloth. G/fair 2nd state. H1. $12.00

**WRIGHT, Richardson.** *Story of Gardening.* 1934. Dodd Mead. 475p. VG. A10. $30.00

**WRIGHT, Sewell Peaslee.** *Half Wolf Wright.* 1951. Phil. Westminster Pr. 253p. VG/dj. B36. $26.00

**WRIGHT, Stephen.** *Going Native.* 1995. FSG. 1st. F/dj. R14. $25.00

**WRIGHT, Thomas.** *Caricature History of the Georges.* 1898. Chatto Windus. 8vo. 629p. gilt bl cloth. VG. H13. $85.00

**WRIGHT, Thomas.** *History of Domestic Manners & Sentiments in England...* 1862. London. 1st. sq 8vo. full blk leather. E6. $75.00

**WRIGHT, Thomas.** *Some Habits & Customs of the Working Classes...* 1967 (1867). Augustus Kelley. rpt. 276p. VG. S5. $15.00

**WRIGHT, Thomas.** *Womankind in Western Europe From Earliest Times to 17th C.* 1869. London. Groombridge. ils. 340p. rb. VG. M10. $125.00

**WRIGHT, W.** *Grammar of the Arabic Language. Translated From the German.* 1955. Cambridge. reissue (1896-98 3rd ed). 2 vol. cloth. VG/dj. Q2. $75.00

**WRIGHT, W.J.** *Greenhouses: Their Construction & Equipment.* (1917). Orange Judd. revised. 269p. F/G. H1. $18.00

**WRIGHT, Winifred G.** *Wild Flowers of Southern Africa.* 1963. Johannesburg. 168p. VG/dj. B26. $25.00

**WRIGHT & WRIGHT.** *Diary of Humphrey Wanley 1715-1726.* 1966. London. Bibliographical Soc. 2 vol. 8vo. bl cloth. VG. F1. $65.00

**WRIGHT.** *American Fiction, 1774-(1900)...* 1966-1978. 3 vol. 12,600+ entries. VG/dj. A4. $100.00

**WROTH, Lawrence.** *Early Cartography of the Pacific.* 1944. Bibliographical Soc. 22 fld pl. 210p. VG. A4. $275.00

**WU, William F.** *Hong on the Range.* 1989. NY. Millennium Walker. 1st. F/dj. G10. $14.50

**WUENNELL, Peter.** *Prodigal Rake: Memoirs of William Hickey.* 1962. Dutton. 1st/3rd. 452p. VG. W2. $12.00

**WUNDER, John R.** *At Home on the Range.* 1985. Greenwood. 213p. AN/dj. A10. $20.00

**WUNDT, Wilhelm Max.** *Einleitung in die Philosophie.* 1901. Leipzig. Wilhelm Engelmann. 466p. bl cloth. G1. $100.00

**WUNDT, Wilhelm Max.** *Elements of Folk Psychology: Outlines...* 1994. NY. Classics of Psychiatry & Behavioral Sciences Lib. F. G1. $65.00

**WUNDT, Wilhelm Max.** *Ethical Systems. Ethics: An Investigation of Facts...* 1897. Sonnenschein/Macmillan. 1st Eng-language /British issue. brn cloth. G1. $75.00

**WUNDT, Wilhelm Max.** *Ethics: An Investigation of Facts of the Moral Life.* 1901, 1902 & 1906. Sonnenschein/Macmillan. 3 vol. 2nd Eng-language. G1. $250.00

**WUNDT, Wilhelm Max.** *Grundzuge der Physiologischen Psychologie.* 1874. Leipzig. Wilhelm Engelmann. 870p. contemporary bdg. F. G1. $2,250.00

**WUNDT, Wilhelm Max.** *Handbuch der Medicinischen Physik.* 1867. Erlangen. Ferdinand Enke in Stuttgart. thick 8vo. 556p. rare. G1. $375.00

**WUNDT, Wilhelm Max.** *Untersuchungen zur Mechanik der Nerven & Nervencentren.* 1876. Stuttgart. Ferdinand Enke. 71 woodcuts. 144p. prt yel wrp. G1. $375.00

**WURDEMANN, Audrey.** *Bright Ambush.* (1934). NY. John Day. 1st author's 1st book. NF/chip. A18. $25.00

**WURTMAN, Richard.** *Pineal.* 1968. NY. Academic. 1st. 8vo. 199p. F/VG. C14. $28.00

**WURTS, Janny.** *Way Lies Camelot.* 1994. NY. Harper Prism. 1st Am. F/NF. G10. $13.50

**WYATT, Joan.** *Middle Earth Album.* 1979. NY. S&S. 1st. ils. NF/wrp. G10. $18.00

**WYCKOFF, Ralph W.G.** *World of the Electron Microscope.* 1958. Yale. 164p. xl. G. S5. $20.00

**WYETH, Betsy James.** *Wyeth at Kuerners.* 1976. Houghton Mifflin. 1st. obl folio. pl. F/VG clip. T11. $65.00

**WYETH, John Allan.** *Life of General Nathan Bedford Forrest.* 1904 (1899). Harper. ils. 655p. G. B10. $125.00

**WYETH, N.C.** *American Vision: Three Generations of Wyeth Art.* 1987. Boston. 1st. ils. VG/dj. M17. $40.00

**WYETH, N.C.** *American Vision: Three Generations of Wyeth Art.* 1987. NYGS. 1st. photos. gilt brn cloth. F/NF. T11. $75.00

**WYETH, N.C.** *Pike County Ballads.* 1912. Boston. 1st. VG. B5. $90.00

**WYETH, N.C.** *Robin Hood.* 1917. Phil. McKay. 1st. VG. B5. $90.00

**WYKES, Alan.** *Circus!* 1977. London. Jupiter. 1st. sm 4to. ils. VG/G. O3. $25.00

**WYLER, Seymour B.** *Book of Old Silver.* 1937. Crown. G/dj. A19. $50.00

**WYLIE, Phillip.** *Disappearance.* 1951. Rinehart. 1st. VG/G. B5. $30.00

**WYMAN, Donald.** *Dwarf Shrubs.* 1974. BC. 137p. VG/dj. B26. $12.00

**WYMAN, Leland C.** *Blessingway: With Three Versions of the Myth...* 1970. Tucson, AZ. 1st. ils. 660p. NF/VG. B19. $75.00

**WYMAN, Leland C.** *Windways of the Navaho.* 1962. Taylor Mus. 1st. ils. VG/wrp. B19. $75.00

**WYMAN, Max.** *Royal Winnipeg Ballet: First Forty Years.* 1978. Toronto. Doubleday. 1st. NF/VG. A26. $20.00

**WYNDHAM, Francis.** *Other Garden.* 1988. Mt Kisco, NY. Moyar Bell. UP/1st ed. F/pk wrp/dj. M25. $25.00

**WYNDHAM, John.** *Jizzle.* 1954. London. Dennis Dobson. 1st. author's 1st collection short stories. VG/dj. M21. $75.00

**WYNDHAM, Lee.** *On Your Toes Susie.* 1958. Scholastic. 4th. ils Jane Miller. 115p. VG. P12. $10.00

**WYNESS, Fenton.** *City by the Gray North Sea.* 1972. Aberdeen. Impulse. 2nd. 8vo. 324p. NF. W2. $25.00

**WYNTER, A.** *Borderlands of Insanity.* 1875. xl. VG+. E6. $65.00

**WYOMING WRITERS.** *This Is Wyoming: Listen.* 1977. Big Horn Books. sgn. F/dj. A19. $25.00

**WYSE, Lois.** *Grandmothers Are to Love.* 1967. Parents Magazine. probable 1st. 12mo. unp. gr cloth. T5. $20.00

**X, Doctor.** *Abortionist.* 1962. Doubleday. 1st. 8vo. VG/dj. B11. $15.00

**XIA XIA.** *How the Monkeys Fished for the Moon.* 1981. Beijing. 4th/2nd prt. VG. T12. $10.00

**XIMENZA, Fray Francisco.** *Historia de la Provincia de San Vicente de Chiapa...* 1929-1931. Sociedad Geografia Historia Guatemala. 3 vol. F3. $100.00

**YACOWAR, Maurice.** *Tennessee Williams & Film.* 1977. NY. Ungar. 1st. F/wrp. C9. $25.00

**YAKOVLEVA, W.K.** *Language of Ioruba (Western Africa).* 1963. Moscow. Eastern Literature. sm 8vo. map. 152p. VG. W1. $12.00

**YALE, William.** *Near East: A Modern History.* 1958. U MI. 4th. tall 8vo. 486p. cloth. VG/dj. W1. $22.00

**YAM, Lim Bian.** *Exotic Flower Arrangements.* 1969. Funk Wagnall. 1st Am. VG/dj. M20. $22.00

**YAN, Mo.** *Garlic Ballads.* 1995. NY. Viking. 1st Am. trans Howard Goldblatt. F/NF. G10. $11.50

**YAN, Mo.** *Red Sorghum.* 1993. NY. Viking. 1st Am. VG/dj. C9. $25.00

**YANDELL, Elizabeth.** *Henry.* 1976. St Martin. 1st Am. sm 8vo. 136p. NF/VG. C14. $12.00

**YANG, Belle.** *Baba: A Return to China Upon My Father's Shoulders.* (1994). Harcourt Brace. stated 1st. sq 4to. 211p. H4. $15.00

**YAPKO, Michael D.** *Brief Therapy Approaches to Treating Anxiety & Depression.* 1989. Brunner/Malzel. 1st. 8vo. 357p. F/VG. C14. $20.00

**YAPP, M.E.** *Near East Since the First World War.* 1991. London. Longman. ils/map. 526p. F/wrp. Q2. $20.00

**YARBOROUGH, Tom.** *Da Nang Diary: Forward Air Controller's Year of Combat...* 1990. St Martin. 1st. 8vo. 280p. F/NF. S14. $10.00

**YARBRO, Chelsea Quinn.** *Better in the Dark.* Dec 1993. NY. Tor. 1st. sgn. VG/dj. L1. $45.00

**YARBRO, Chelsea Quinn.** *Blood Games.* 1979. St Martin. 1st. sgn. author's 3rd book. VG/G. L1. $60.00

**YARBRO, Chelsea Quinn.** *Crusader's Torch.* Oct 1988. NY. Tor. 1st. sgn. VG/G. L1. $50.00

**YARBRO, Chelsea Quinn.** *Flame of Byzantium.* 1987. NY. Tor. 1st. VG/dj. L1. $60.00

**YARBRO, Chelsea Quinn.** *Hotel Transylvania.* 1978. St Martin. BC. sgn. author's 1st book. VG/dj. L1. $65.00

**YARBRO, Chelsea Quinn.** *Palace.* 1978. St Martin. 1st. Count St Germain #2. VG/dj. L1. $85.00

**YARBRO, Chelsea Quinn.** *Time of the Fourth Horseman.* 1976. Doubleday. 1st. sgn. VG/G. L1. $55.00

**YARBROUGH, Tinsley E.** *Passion for Justice: J Waties Waring & Civil Rights.* 1987. OUP. VG/dj. M17. $15.00

**YARDLEY, Herbert.** *Chinese Black Chamber.* 1983. Houghton Mifflin. 1st. VG/dj. B5. $30.00

**YARNALL, Agnes.** *Circus World.* 1982. NY. Dorrance. 91p. VG/dj. C5. $15.00

**YASTRZEMSKI, Carl.** *Batting.* 1972. Viking. 1st. VG/dj. P8. $30.00

**YATES, Dornford.** *Red in the Morning.* 1946. Ward Locke. 1st Eng. VG/dj. G8. $40.00

**YATES, Elizabeth.** *Amos Fortune, Free Man.* 1950. NY. 2nd. ils Nora S Unwin. VG. M17. $17.50

**YATES, Elizabeth.** *Howard Thurman: Portrait of a Practical Dreamer.* 1964. NY. John Day. 8vo. 249p. dj. V3. $12.50

**YATES, Elizabeth.** *My Widening World: Continuing Diary of...* 1983. Phil. Westminster. 1st. 192p. VG/dj. V3. $12.00

**YATES, Elizabeth.** *One Writer's Way: Creative Years.* 1984. Phil. Westminster. 1st. 192p. VG/dj. V3. $12.00

**YATES, Richard.** *Easter Parade.* 1978. London. Methuen. 1st Eng. F/dj. Q1. $40.00

**YATES, Richard.** *Eleven Kinds of Loneliness.* 1962. Atlantic/Little Brn. 1st. F/NF. B4. $150.00

**YATES, Richard.** *Lie Down in Darkness.* 1985. Ploughshares. 1st. VG/dj. C9. $90.00

**YATES, Richard.** *Revolution Road.* 1961. Toronto/Boston. Little Brn. 1st. author's 1st book. F/dj. Q1. $125.00

**YATES, Richard.** *Special Providence.* 1969. Knopf. 1st. 8vo. F/VG. S9. $45.00

**YAZZIE, Ethelou.** *Navajo History: Volume 1.* 1971. Navajo Community College. 1st. ils. 100p. F/F. B19. $35.00

**YBARRA, T.R.** *Young Man of Caracas.* 1941. Ives Washburne. 1st. 324p. dj. F3. $10.00

**YEAGER, Chuck.** *Press On.* 1988. NY. Bantam. 1st. F/dj. T12. $20.00

**YEAGER, Chuck.** *Press On! Futher Adventures in the Good Life.* 1988. Bantam. 1st. VG/dj. P3. $18.00

**YEAGER, Chuck.** *Yeager: Autobiography.* 1985. Bantam. 1st. F/dj. W2. $35.00

**YEALLAND, L.** *Hysterical Disorders of Warfare.* 1918. London. xl. VG. E6. $20.00

**YEARSLEY, Walter A.** *Practical Self-Cure of Stammering & Stuttering.* 1909. Accington. private prt. 1st. ils. 214+2p. VG. H7. $15.00

**YEATES, G.K.** *Bird Photography.* 1946. London. Faber. 1st. cloth. VG. B27. $25.00

**YEATS, John Butler.** *Further Letters of John Butler Yeats.* 1920. Churchtown, Dundrum, Ireland. Cuala. 1/400. VG. B18. $95.00

**YEATS, William Butler.** *Collected Poems of WB Yeats.* 1951. Macmillan. 2nd (later poems/1st thus). 8vo. 490p. F/VG. H4. $25.00

**YEATS, William Butler.** *Discoveries: A Volume of Essays.* 1907. Dundrum. Dun Emer. 1st. 1/200. 43p. bl brd. NF. B24. $450.00

**YEATS, William Butler.** *Essays & Introductions.* (1965). Macmillan. 1st Am. F/G. H4. $25.00

**YEATS, William Butler.** *In the Seven Woods: Being Poems Chiefly of Irish Heroic Age.* 1903. Macmillan. 1st Am. 12mo. 87p. teg. gilt bl cloth. VG. H4. $120.00

**YEATS, William Butler.** *King's Threshold.* 1904. NY. Prt for Private Circulation. 1st. 1/100. sgn. F/dj/case. B24. $3,000.00

**YEATS, William Butler.** *Per Amica Silentia Lunae.* 1918. London. Macmillan. 1st. F/dj. B24. $450.00

**YEATS, William Butler.** *Stories of Red Hanrahan.* 1904. Dundrum. Dun Emer. 1st. 1/500. F. B24. $400.00

**YEATS, William Butler.** *Tables of the Law; And Adoration of the Magi.* 1914. Shakespeare Head. 1st. 1/510. VG. L3. $75.00

**YEATS, William Butler.** *Tower.* 1928. Macmillan. 1st Am. gilt gr cloth. F. M24. $100.00

**YEATS, William Butler.** *Winding Stair & Other Poems.* 1933. NY. Macmillan. 1st trade. dk bl cloth. M24. $75.00

**YEE, Chiang.** *Silent Traveller in Paris.* nd. NY. 1st. sgn. ils. VG/dj. M17. $37.50

**YEE, Chiang.** *Silent Traveller in San Francisco.* 1964. NY. Norton. 1st. NF/VG. O4. $25.00

**YELVERTON, Therese.** *Zanita: A Tale of the Yo-Semite.* 1872. NY. Hurd Houghton. 296p. cloth. D11. $300.00

**YEO, Margaret.** *Greates of the Borgias.* 1936. NY. ils. VG/G. M17. $17.50

**YEOMAN, R.C.** *Rural Efficiency Guide, Vol 2, Engineering.* 1918. Cleveland. People's. 363p. cloth. VG. A10. $18.00

**YEP, Laurence.** *Star Fisher.* 1991. NY. Morrow. 1st. sgn/orig drawing. 150p. F/dj. D4. $40.00

**YERBY, Frank.** *Fairoaks.* 1957. Dial. 1st. VG/dj. R14. $50.00

**YERBY, Frank.** *Goat Song.* 1967. NY. Dial. 1st. VG/dj. R14. $25.00

**YERBY, Frank.** *Serpent & the Staff.* 1958. NY. Dial. 1st. NF/VG. A24. $30.00

**YERBY, Frank.** *Tobias & the Angel.* 1975. NY. Dial. 1st. NF/dj. A24. $25.00

**YERKES, Robert Mearns.** *Almost Human.* 1925. NY. Century. 2m 8vo. 63 pl. 278p. pict olive cloth. G1. $75.00

**YERKES, Robert Mearns.** *Dancing Mouse: Study in Animal Behavior.* 1907. Macmillan. sm 8vo. 290p. prt thatched brn cloth. VG. G1. $85.00

**YEVTUSHENKO, Yevgeny.** *Divided Twins: Alaska & Siberia.* 1988. Viking. 1st Am. 4to. VG/F. A2. $22.00

**YEVTUSHENKO, Yevgeny.** *From Desire to Desire.* 1976. Doubleday. stated 1st. 8vo. 126p. F/dj. H4. $20.00

**YGESIAS, Rafael.** *Fearless.* 1993. Warner. 1st. F/dj. C9. $25.00

**YING, Mildred.** *New Good Housekeeping Cookbook.* 1986. BC. ils. 825p. VG/dj. S14. $12.00

**YOAKEM, Lola Goelet.** *TV & Screen Writing.* 1958. U CA. 1st. VG/dj. C9. $36.00

**YODER, Paton.** *Tradition & Transition: Amish Mennonites & Older Order...* 1991. Herald. 1st. VG/G. R8. $15.00

**YODER, Paton.** *Traverns & Travelers: Inns of the Early West.* 1969. Bloomington. 1st. 246p. F/dj. E1. $30.00

**YODER, Samuel A.** *Middle-East Sojourn.* 1951. Scottsdale, PA. Herald. sm 8vo. ils. 310p. VG/tattered. W1. $20.00

**YOLEN, Jane.** *Dream Weaver.* 1979. Collins. 1st. ils Michael Hague. F/VG+. M5. $42.00

**YOLEN, Jane.** *Piggins.* 1987. HBJ. 1st. ils. VG/dj. M20. $25.00

**YOLEN, Jane.** *Simple Prince.* 1978. Parents Magazine. 1st. ils Jack Kent. VG+. M5. $10.00

**YOLEN, Jane.** *White Jenna.* 1989. NY. Tor. 1st. F/NF. G10. $13.50

**YOLEN, Jane.** *World on a String.* 1968. Cleveland. World. 143p. reinforced cloth. F/dj. D4. $25.00

**YORINKS, Arthur.** *Hey.* 1986. NY. FSG. 1st. sgn. ils/sgn Richard Egielski. bl cloth. mc dj. R5. $175.00

**YORINKS, Arthur.** *Miami Giant.* 1995. NY. DiCapua/Harper Collins. 1st. ils Sendak. AN/dj. H4. $20.00

**YORK, Carol Beach.** *Revenge of the Dolls.* 1979. NY. Elsevier/Nelson. 1st. 103p. F/dj. D4. $25.00

**YORKE, Margaret.** *Almost the Truth.* 1995. Mysterious. 1st Am. F/dj. G8. $15.00

**YORKE, Margaret.** *Evidence to Destroy.* 1987. Viking. 1st Am. F/NF. G8. $10.00

**YORKE, Margaret.** *Speak for the Dead.* 1988. Viking. 1st. rem mk. F/dj. H11. $20.00

**YOSHIMOTO, Banana.** *Kitchen.* 1993. NY. Grove. 1st Eng-language. F/dj. C9. $30.00

**YOUATT.** *History, Treatment & Diseases of the Horse.* 1883. Lippincott. rpt. 470p. VG. A10. $45.00

**YOUMANS, Eliza.** *Lessons in Cookery, Handbook of Nat Training School...* 1879 (1878). NY. 382p. VG. E6. $30.00

**YOUMANS, N.O.** *Best Seller: Story of a Young Man Who Came to New York...* 1930. Bobbs Merrill. 1st. 8vo. 314p. cloth. F/dj. O10. $15.00

**YOUNG, A.S.** *Great Negro Baseball Stars.* 1953. Barnes. 1st. photos. VG/dj. P8. $325.00

**YOUNG, Agatha.** *Women & the Crisis.* 1959. NY. 1st. ils. 389p. dj. B18. $35.00

**YOUNG, Andrew W.** *First Lessons in Civil Government.* 1846. MC Younglove. G. M20. $15.00

**YOUNG, Andrew W.** *Introduction to Science of Government & Compend...* 1854. Miller Orton Mulligan. not 1st. 362+2p. 3-quarter blk leather/buckram. H7. $10.00

**YOUNG, Andrew.** *Easy Burden: Civil Rights Movement & Transformation of Am.* 1996. Harper Collins. 1st. F/dj. B30. $30.00

**YOUNG, Arthur Henry.** *Hell Up to Date: Reckless Journey of R Palasco-Drant...* (1893). Chicago. Schulte. 8vo. 85p. red cloth. VG. H4. $175.00

**YOUNG, Arthur P.** *Books for Sammies: American Library Association & WWI.* 1981. Beta Phi Mu. 1st. F/sans. N2. $10.00

**YOUNG, Arthur.** *Travels in France...1787-1789.* 1950. Cambridge. 1st/2nd prt. 8vo. 428p. gilt blk cloth. VG. H13. $65.00

**YOUNG, B.A.** *Rattigan Version.* 1986. London. Hamish Hamilton. 1st. 8vo. 228p. F/dj. M7. $40.00

**YOUNG, Brigham.** *Diary of Brigham Young, 1857.* 1980. UT U. 1st. edit EL Cooley. ils/index. 106p. F/VG. B19. $20.00

**YOUNG, Charles.** *Manual of Astronomy: A Text-Book.* 1902. Boston. Ginn. ils. 611p. cloth. G. K5. $18.00

**YOUNG, Clarence.** *Motor Boys in the Clouds.* 1910. Cupples Leon. G. M20. $15.00

**YOUNG, Collier;** see Bloch, Robert.

**YOUNG, Delbert A.** *According to Hakluyt: Tales of Adventure & Exploration.* 1973. Toronto. Clarke Irwin. 1st. rem mk. F/dj. A2. $15.00

**YOUNG, Dick.** *Roy Campanella.* 1952. Barnes. 1st. photos. VG. P8. $60.00

**YOUNG, Doris B.** *Kim's Cookbook for Young People.* 1971. Red Farm Studio. 1st. ils Ellen Nelson. VG. M5. $15.00

**YOUNG, Edward W.** *Germany Awakes: Growing, Fight & Victory of the NSDAP.* 1977. private prt. ils. 153p. F/sans. S16. $75.00

**YOUNG, Edward.** *Brothers, a Tragedy...* 1777. London. Bell. sm 8vo. 63p. recent marbled wrp. VG. H13. $175.00

**YOUNG, Ella.** *Unicorn With Silver Shoes.* 1932. NY. 1st. inscr. 214p. VG. B18. $75.00

**YOUNG, Ernie W.D.** *Alpha & Omega: Ethics at Frontiers of Life & Death.* 1989. Addison-Wesley. ARC. 8vo. 209p. F/NF. C14. $18.00

**YOUNG, Harry.** *Hard Knocks: Life Story of the Vanishing West.* (1915). Portland. Wells. ils. 242p. marbled brd/cloth spine. D11. $50.00

**YOUNG, Harry.** *Hard Knocks: Life Story of the Vanishing West.* 1915. Laird Lee. ils. 242p. VG. J2. $125.00

**YOUNG, J. Russell.** *Around the World With General Grant.* 1879. NY. Am News. 2 vol. 1st. VG. H4. $75.00

**YOUNG, J.P.** *Standard History of Memphis.* 1912. Knoxville. full leather (rpr hinges). G. B30. $300.00

**YOUNG, James C.** *School Days & Schoolmates of Harvey S Firestone.* 1929. np. photos. 58p. G+. B18. $47.50

**YOUNG, James.** *Million Chameleons.* 1990. Little Brn. 1st Am. sm 8vo. F/NF. C14. $15.00

YOUNG, Joanne. *Shirley Plantation: Personal Adventure for Generations.* 1981. Shirley. ils. 64p. VG. B10. $8.00

YOUNG, Joanne. *Washington's Mount Vernon.* 1972. HRW. 1st. photos. unp. F/VG. B10. $10.00

YOUNG, John. *Physical Geography.* (1873). Putnam. 368p. xl. VG. B14. $95.00

YOUNG, Louise B. *Mystery of Matter.* 1965. NY. Oxford. 8vo. 712p. xl. VG. H4. $10.00

YOUNG, M. Jane. *Signs From the Ancestors: Zuni Cultural Symbolism...* 1988. NM U. 1st. ils/index. 308p. NF/dj. B19. $20.00

YOUNG, Mike. *Adventures of Super Ted in Outer Space.* 1985. Random. 1st. ils. VG. P12. $10.00

YOUNG, Otis. *West of Philip St George Cooke, 1809-1895.* 1955. Arthur Clark. ils/maps. VG. J2. $295.00

YOUNG, Paul E. *Back Trail of an Old Cowboy.* 1983. NE U. 1st. 229p. F/F. B19. $25.00

YOUNG, Percy M. *Handel.* 1966. NY. White. 1st. F/VG. T12. $20.00

YOUNG, Peter. *Bedouin Command With Arab Legion 1953-1956.* 1956. London. Wm Kimber. ils/map/plan of Jerusalem ep. 203p. cloth. VG/dj. Q2. $30.00

YOUNG, Peter. *Bedouin Command With the Arab Legion 1953-1956.* 1956. London. Wm Kimber. 1st. photos/map ep. 203+5p. VG. H7. $15.00

YOUNG, Rida Johnson. *Little Old New York.* 1923. Grosset Dunlap. early rpt. ils. VG/G. H7. $17.50

YOUNG, Roland. *Actors & Others.* 1925. Covici. 1st/ltd. sgn. VG. C9. $60.00

YOUNG, Roland. *Not for Children: Pictures & Verse.* (1930). Doubleday. ils. intro Ring Lardner. F. H4. $20.00

YOUNG, S. Hall. *Alaska Days With John Muir.* (1915). NY. Fleming Revell. 1st. 226p. G. H4. $25.00

YOUNG, Scott. *Gordon Sinclair: A Life...And Then Some.* 1987. Macmillan. 1st. F/dj. T12. $20.00

YOUNG, Scott. *Murder in a Cold Climate.* 1989. NY. Viking. 1st Am. author's 1st mystery novel. F/dj. T2. $25.00

YOUNG, Scott. *Shaman's Knife.* 1993. NY. Viking. 1st. F/dj. T2. $20.00

YOUNG, Stark. *Encaustics.* 1926. NY. New Republic. 1st. 8vo. 274p/cream wrp. H4. $50.00

YOUNG, Vernon. *Cinema Borealis: Ingmar Bergman & Swedish Ethics.* 1971. David Lewis. 1st. VG/dj. C9. $60.00

YOUNG, Vernon. *On Film: Unpopular Essays on a Popular Art.* 1972. Chicago. VG/dj. M17. $25.00

YOUNGBLOOD, Charles L. *Mighty Hunter.* 1890. Rand McNally. 1st. 8vo. 360p. prt on poor wood pulp. H4. $135.00

YOUNGBLOOD, Gene Fuller. *Expanded Cinema.* 1970. Dutton. 1st. VG/dj. C9. $48.00

YOUNGER, Edward. *Inside the Confederate Government: Diary of RGH Kean.* 1957. OUP. special ed. sgn. 8vo. 241p. F/dj. H4. $45.00

YOUNGKEN, Heber W. *Textbook of Pharmacognosy.* 1946 (1921). Phil. 5th. 1038p. VG. B26. $72.50

YOUNGSON, A.J. *Scientific Revolution in Victorian Medicine.* 1979. London. 1st. 237p. dj. A13. $22.50

YOURCENAR, Marguerite. *Memoirs of Hadrian.* 1954. London. Secker Warburg. 1st Eng. 8vo. map ep. 320p. cloth. VG. Q2. $20.00

YOWELL, Claude Lindsay. *History of Madison County Virginia.* 1974 (1926). VA Book Co. facs. 203p. VG. B10. $35.00

YUILL, P.B. *Hazel Plays Solomon.* 1974. NY. Walker. 1st. VG/dj. M20. $15.00

YUNGBLUT, John R. *Gentle Art of Spiritual Guidance.* 1991. Rockport, MA. Element. 12mo. 148p. wrp. V3. $9.00

YUNGJOHANN, John. *White Gold: Diary of a Rubber Cutter in the Amazon.* 1989. Synergetic. 1st. 103p. wrp. F3. $15.00

YUNIS, Jorge J. *Human Chromosome Methodology.* 1965. Academic. 258p. xl. VG. S5. $20.00

ZABOR, Rafi. *Bear Comes Home.* 1997. Norton. 1st. author's 1st novel. PEN/Faulkner Award. F/dj. A24. $60.00

ZACHARIAN, O. *Travel in South Africa.* 1927. Johannesburg. 3rd. 8vo. photos/2p map. 331p. VG. H7. $12.50

ZACK, Bill. *Tomahawked.* 1993. S&S. 1st. photos. F/dj. P8. $15.00

ZACOUR, N.P. *Impact of Crusades on Near East.* 1985. Madison, WI. U WI. History of Crusades #5. ils/maps. VG+. Q2. $37.00

ZADAN, Craig. *Sondheim & Company.* 1974. Macmillan. 1st. VG/dj. C9. $48.00

ZAGORDK, I.E. *Teacher's Manual: Novels of Stephen King.* 1981. NAL. 1st. AN/sans. T12. $30.00

ZAHER, Ameen. *Arabian Horse Breeding & the Arabians of America.* 1961. Cairo. 2nd/revised. VG. O3. $275.00

ZAHL, Paul. *Coro-Coro: World of the Scarlet Ibis.* 1954. Bobbs Merrill. 1st. 264p. dj. F3. $30.00

ZAHM, J.A. *From Berlin to Bagdad & Babylon.* 1922. NY. Appleton. 427p. cloth. G. Q2. $43.00

ZAHN, Timothy. *Heir to the Empire: Star Wars Volume 1.* 1991. NY. Bantam. 1st. NF/dj. G10. $20.00

ZAJDLER, Zoe. *Fairy Tales: Polish.* 1959. Follett. 1st. 8vo. VG/dj. B17. $15.00

ZAMORANO CLUB. *Zamorano Club: First Half Century, 1928-78.* 1978. LA. Zamorano Club. 1/200. 99p. patterned brd. D11. $125.00

ZANDMAN, Felix. *Never the Last Journey.* 1996. NY. 1st. F/dj. T12. $15.00

ZANELLI, Leo. *Home Winemaking From A to Z.* 1972. Barnes. 1st. 8vo. F/NF. W2. $20.00

ZANGER, Jack. *Baseball Spark Plub.* 1963. Doubleday. F/G. P8. $15.00

ZANGER, Jack. *Brooks Robinson Story.* 1967. Messner. 1st. VG/G. P8. $65.00

ZANGWILL I. *Dreamers of the Ghetto.* 1899. NY/London. Harper. detached title/lacks ffe. H4. $15.00

ZANUCK, Darryl F. *Tunis Expedition.* 1943. Random. 1st. 160p. map ep. VG/dj. R11. $20.00

ZAREM, Lewis. *New Dimensions of Flight.* 1959. Dutton. sm 4to. photos. 256p. cloth. xl. K5. $12.00

ZARING, Jane. *Return of the Dragon.* 1981. Houghton Mifflin. 1st. inscr/dtd 1981. NF/VG. M21. $75.00

ZARIT, Steven H. *Aging & Mental Disorders: Psychological Approaches...* 1980. Free Pr. 1st. 8vo. 454p. F/VG. C14. $17.00

ZASLAVSKI, Victor A. *Insect Development.* 1988. Springer-Verlag. trans from Russian. ils. 187p. F. S15. $30.00

ZATARAIN, Michael. *David Duke: Evolution of a Klansman.* 1990. Pelican. 1st. sm 4to. 304p. xl. VG/dj. S14. $8.00

ZECK & ZECK. *Mississippi Sternwheelers.* 1982. Minneapolis. photos. VG/dj. M17. $15.00

ZEHMER, John G. *Early Domestic Architecture of Dinwiddie County, Virginia.* 1970. U VA. Master of Architectural Hist. 213p. VG. B10. $65.00

**ZELAZNY, Roger.** *Blood of Amber.* 1986. NY. Arbor. 2nd. 8vo. 215p. F/NF. H4. $15.00

**ZELAZNY, Roger.** *Changing Land.* 1981. Underwood Miller. 1st hc. F/dj. T2. $30.00

**ZELAZNY, Roger.** *Courts of Chaos.* 1978. Doubleday. 1st. sgn. F/dj. M21. $50.00

**ZELAZNY, Roger.** *Eye of Cat.* 1982. Timescape. 1st. F/NF. A24. $30.00

**ZELAZNY, Roger.** *Knight of Shadows.* 1989. Morrow. 1st. F/dj. M21. $30.00

**ZELAZNY, Roger.** *Night in the Lonesome October.* 1993. NY. Morrow AvoNova. 1st. F/dj. G10. $24.00

**ZELAZNY, Roger.** *Prince of Chaos.* 1991. NY. Morrow. 1st. F/NF. B3. $20.00

**ZELAZNY, Roger.** *Sign of Chaos.* 1987. NY. Arbor. 1st. NF/dj. G10. $13.50

**ZELAZNY, Roger.** *Timescape.* 1982. 1st. sgn. rem mk. G/dj. B30. $30.00

**ZELAZNY, Roger.** *To Spin Is Miracle Cat.* 1981. Underwood Miller. 1st. 1/200. sgn/#d. F/dj. A24. $60.00

**ZELIGS, Meyer A.** *Friendship & Fratricide: An Analysis...* 1067. Viking. 1st. 8vo. VG/dj. A2. $20.00

**ZEMACH, Harve.** *Awake & Dreaming.* 1970. FSG. 1st. ils Zemach. bl brd. F/dj. D1/D4. $45.00

**ZEMACH, Margot.** *Duffy & the Devil: A Cornish Tale.* (1973). NY. FSG. 1st. lg 4to. 1974 Caldecott. gilt gr cloth. mc pict dj. R5. $135.00

**ZEMACH, Margot.** *Jake & Honeybunch Go to Heaven.* 1982. FSG. 1st. 32p. F/dj. D4. $45.00

**ZEMACH & ZEMACH.** *Princess & Froggie.* 1975. NY. FSG. 1st. unp. F/NF. D4. $45.00

**ZEMJANIS, R.** *Diagnostic Therapeutic Techniques in Animal Reproduction.* 1962. Baltimore. Williams Wilkins. 1st. VG. O3. $20.00

**ZEMKE, Hub.** *Zemke's Wolf Pack: Story of Hub Zemke & 56th Fighter...* 1988. NY. 1st. ils/index. 256p. VG/dj. S16. $20.00

**ZENKER, John J.** *Cookie Cookery.* 1965. Evans. BC. G/dj. A16. $8.00

**ZERBI, Gabriele.** *Gerontocomia: On Care of Aged & Maximanius...* 1988. Phil. 1st. trans LR Lind. 346p. A13. $40.00

**ZERN, Ed.** *How to Tell Fish From Fishermen.* 1947. Appleton Century. G/dj. A19. $25.00

**ZERN, Ed.** *To Hell With Fishing.* 1945. Appleton Century Crofts. F/dj. H4. $15.00

**ZETA.** *Diagnosis of the Acute Abdomen in Rhyme.* 1955. London. 3rd. 96p. A13. $50.00

**ZETTERLING, Mai.** *Night Games.* 1966. Coward McCann. 1st. F/dj. C9. $25.00

**ZETTNER, Pat.** *Shadow Warrior.* 1990. Atheneum. 1st. author's 1st book. F/F. H11. $20.00

**ZEY, Michael G.** *Seizing the Future.* 1994. S&S. 1st. sm 4to. 414p. F/dj. W2. $30.00

**ZIADEH, N.A.** *Damascus Under the Mamluks.* 1964. Norman, OK. map. 140p. cloth. VG/dj. Q2. $13.50

**ZIADEH, N.A.** *Syria & Lebanon.* 1957. London. Benn. 5 maps. 312p. VG/dj. Q2. $30.00

**ZICH, Arthur.** *Rising Sun.* 1978. Alexandria, VA. Time Life. 2nd. ils. F. M7. $10.00

**ZIEFERT, Harriet.** *Lewis the Firefighter.* 1986. Random. 1st. 8vo. VG+. M5. $12.00

**ZIEGENFUSS.** *Law, Medicine & Health Care: A Bibliography.* 1984. 274p. VG. A4. $35.00

**ZIEGLER, Philip.** *King Edward VIII.* 1991. Knopf. 1st Am. photos. 552p. VG/dj. P12. $15.00

**ZIEHEN, Theodor.** *Die Psycholigie Grosser Heerfuhrer/Der Krieg Gedanken...* 1916. Leipzig. Johann Ambrosius Barth. 94p. VG. G1. $50.00

**ZIEHEN, Theodor.** *Leitfaden in der Physiologischen Psychologie 15 Vorlesungen.* 1908. Jena. Gustav Fischer. 8th revised. 290p. xl. VG. G1. $40.00

**ZIEL, Ron.** *Twilight of World Steam.* 1976. Grosset Dunlap. VG/dj. R8. $15.00

**ZIELINSKI, David.** *Genuine Monster.* 1990. NY. Atlantic Monthly. 1st. F/dj. G10. $20.00

**ZIEROLD, Norman.** *Little Charley Ross: America's 1st Kidnapping for Random.* 1967. Boston. later prt. 301p. brd. VG/dj. B18. $9.50

**ZIEROLD, Norman.** *Moguls.* (1969). Coward McCann. 8vo. photos. 354p. NF/VG. H4. $10.00

**ZIGAL, Thomas.** *Hardrock Stuff.* 1996. Delcorte. 1st. sgn. F/dj. T2. $20.00

**ZIGAL, Thomas.** *Into Thin Air.* 1995. Delacorte. 1st. sgn. author's 1st novel. F/dj. T2. $25.00

**ZIGLAR, Zig.** *Confessions of a Happy Christian.* 1980. Pelican. 199p. VG. B29. $6.50

**ZIGLER, Edward.** *Developmental Approach to Adult Psychopathology.* 1986. NY. Wiley-Interscience. pres. 334p. prt bl cloth. VG/dj. G1. $40.00

**ZIGMOND, M.L.** *Kawaiisu Ethnobotany.* 1981. U UT. rto. 102p. F/wrp. B1. $37.00

**ZIGROSSER, Carl.** *Guide to the Collecting & Care of Original Prints.* 1966. NY. Crown. later prt. 8vo. 120p. F/dj. O10. $25.00

**ZIGROSSER, Carl.** *Misch Kohn.* (1961). NY. Am Federation Arts. ils. 28p. F/dj. H4. $15.00

**ZILAHY, Lajos.** *Dukays.* (1949). NY. Prentice Hall. 1/1500. sgn/trans John Pauker. VG+/VG. H4. $50.00

**ZILBOORG, Gregory.** *Mind, Medicine & Man.* 1943. Harcourt Brace. 1st. 8vo. 344p. VG/dj. C14. $14.00

**ZIMANSKY, Curt.** *English Literature.* 1972. Princeton. 4to. 1293p. H4. $25.00

**ZIMMER, Norma.** *Norma.* 1976. Tyndale. stated 1st. 8vo. 368p. F/F. H4. $8.50

**ZIMMERMAN, Arthur.** *Francisco de Toledo: 5th Viceroy of Peru 1569-1581.* 1938. Caxton. 1st. 307p. F3. $15.00

**ZIMMERMAN, Paul.** *Los Angeles Dodgers.* 1960. Coward McCann. 1st. VG/G. P8. $50.00

**ZIMMERN, Alfred.** *Greek Commonwealth.* 1956. Random/Modern Lib. 1st. 12mo. 487p. F/dj. H1. $10.00

**ZINBERG, Israel.** *History of Jewish Literature.* 1975. Cincinnati/NY. Hebrew Union College/KTAV. 1st. 8vo. 403p. F/NF. H4. $25.00

**ZINDEL, Paul.** *Begonia for Miss Applebaum.* 1989. Harper Row. 1st. 8vo. 180p. NF/VG clip. C14. $20.00

**ZINGG, Paul.** *Harry Hooper: American Baseball Life.* 1993. U IL. 1st. photos. F/dj. P8. $25.00

**ZINKIN, N.I.** *Mechanisms of Speech.* 1968. The Hague. Mouton. 1st Eng. lg 8vo. 463p. bl cloth. VG/dj. G1. $65.00

**ZINMAN, David.** *50 Classic Motion Pictures: Stuff Dreams Are Made Of.* 1971. NY. Crown. 3rd. ils. VG/dj. C9. $36.00

**ZINSSER, William.** *Spring Training.* 1989. Harper. 1st. F/dj. C15. $10.00

**ZIOLKOWSKI, Theodore.** *Fictional Transfigurations of Jesus.* (1972). Princeton. 8vo. 315p. F/dj. H4. $30.00

**ZIRKLE, Raymond.** *Effects of External Beta Radiation.* 1951. McGraw Hill. 242p. VG. S5. $20.00

**ZOLA, Emile.** *Lourdes.* 1897. NY. 2 vol. revised/corrected. VG. M17. $20.00

**ZOLA, Emile.** *Nana.* 1922. Knopf. 1st Am. 1/3000. VG. M20. $22.00

**ZOLBROD, Paul G.** *Dine Bahane: Navajo Creation Story.* 1985. U NM. 2nd. VG/dj. M17. $17.50

**ZOLL, Donald A.** *Reason & Rebellion: Informal History of Political Ideas.* 1963. Prentice Hall. 1st. 8vo. F/VG. A2. $20.00

**ZOLLA, ELEMIRE Xavier.** *Writer & Shaman: Morphology of the American Indian.* (1973). HBJ. stated 1st. 8vo. 312p. F/dj. H4. $30.00

**ZOLLER, Joseph.** *Conceptus Chronographicus de Concepta Sacra Deipara...* 1712. Augsburg. Johannis Michaelis Labhart. folio. 353p. 100 copper pl. K1. $2,500.00

**ZOLLINGER.** *Elliott Carr Cutler & Cloning of Surgeons.* 1988. 246p. F. A4. $35.00

**ZOLOTOW, Charlotte.** *Bunny Who Found Easter.* 1959. CA. Parnassus. ARC/1st. 34p. VG/dj. D4. $45.00

**ZOLOTOW, Charlotte.** *Do You Know What I'll Do?* (1958). Harper. 1st. ils Garth Williams. pict brd. dj. R5. $125.00

**ZOLOTOW, Charlotte.** *I Have a Horse of My Own.* 1980. NY. Crowell. 1st. ils. F/dj. D4. $25.00

**ZOLOTOW, Charlotte.** *My Grandson Lew.* nd (c 1974). NY. Harper Row. 12mo. 32p. xl. VG. C14. $14.00

**ZOLOTOW, Charlotte.** *Song.* 1982. Greenwillow. 1st. ils nancy Tafuri. VG/dj. M20. $25.00

**ZOLOTOW, Maurice.** *Marilyn Monroe.* 1960. Harcourt Brace. 1st. ils. VG/dj. C9. $90.00

**ZOMLEFER, Wendy B.** *Guide to Flowering Plant Families.* 1994. Chapel Hill. 430p. AN. B26. $55.00

**ZON, R.** *Eucalypts in Florida.* 1911. WA, DC. ils. wrp. B26. $25.00

**ZONARAS, Johannes.** *La Prima (-Terza) Parte dell'Historie di Giovanni Zonara...* 1570. Venice. Gabriel Giolito di Ferrarii. 3 parts in 1. 4to. vellum. K1. $750.00

**ZOSS, Joel.** *Pictorial History of Baseball.* 1986. Gallery. 1st. photos. F/VG+. P8. $20.00

**ZUBRO, Mark Richard.** *Simple Suburban Murder.* 1989. St Martin. 1st. inscr. F/dj. N4. $40.00

**ZUCKERMAN, George.** *Last Flapper.* 1969. Little Brn. 1st. F/VG+. H11. $25.00

**ZUCKERMAN, Harriet.** *Scientific Elite: Novel Laureates in the United States.* 1977. Free Pr/Macmillan. 1st. 335p. F/VG. H4. $15.00

**ZUCKERMAN, Nathan.** *Wine of Violence: Anthology of Anti-Semitism.* 1947. NY. Assn pr. 1st. F/VG. B2. $35.00

**ZUCKERMAN, Solly.** *Functional Affinities of Man, Monkeys & Apes...* 1933. London. Kegan paul. 1st. 11 halftones. 357p. bl-gr cloth. G1. $65.00

**ZUCKERMAN, Solly.** *Social Life of Monkeys & Apes.* 1932. London. Kegan Paul. 24 pl. 357p. bl-gr cloth. G1. $65.00

**ZUELKE, Ruth.** *Horse in Art.* 1964. Minneapolis. 1st. sm 4to. 64p. VG. O3. $25.00

**ZUKAV, Gary.** *Dancing Wu Li Masters: Overview of New Physics.* 1979. Morrow. 8vo. 352p. F/dj. H4. $16.00

**ZUKOFSKY, Louis.** *Little.* 1970. Grossman. VG/dj. C9. $25.00

**ZUKOR, Adolph.** *Public Is Never Wrong: My 50 Years in Motion Pictures.* (1953). Putnam. 1st. sgn. NF/dj. H4. $85.00

**ZURIER, Rebecca.** *American Firehouse: Architectural & Socal History.* 1982. Abbeville. 1st. 286p. F/NF. T11. $75.00

**ZVERINA, Silvia.** *And They Shall Have Music: History of Cleveland Music...* 1988. Cleveland. Cobham Hatherton. 1/1500. sgn. 185p. VG. H4. $15.00

**ZWEIFEL, R.G.** *Results of the Puritan-American Museum of Natural History...* 1960. NY Am Mus. ils/maps. 128p. VG/dj. M12. $20.00

**ZWEIG, Arnold.** *Playthings of Time.* 1935. Viking. 1st. VG/dj. H4. $38.50

**ZWEIG, Stefan.** *Balzac.* nd. BOMC. VG/dj. P3. $8.00

**ZWEIG, Stefan.** *Mental Healers: Franz Anton Mesmer, Mary Baker Eddy...* 1932. NY. Garden City. trans Eden & Cedar Paul. 363p. VG/dj. B14. $35.00

**ZWINGER, Ann.** *John Xantus: Ft Tejon Letters 1857-1859.* 1986. AZ U. 1st. ils/biblio/map. 255p. F/dj. A17. $12.50

**ZWINGER, Ann.** *Wind in the Rock.* 1978. Harper Row. 1st. F/G. B3. $20.00

**ZWINGER, Ann.** *Xantus: Letters of John Xantus to Spencer Fullerton Baird...* 1986. Dawson's Book Shop. 422p. VG/sans. B19. $55.00

**ZYSK, Kenneth.** *Asceticism & Healing in Ancient India...* 1991. NY. 1st. 200p. A13. $30.00

**ZYSK, Kenneth.** *Religous Medicine: History & Evolution...* 1993. New Brunswick. 1st. 311p. A13. $60.00

# PSEUDONYMS

Listed below are pseudonyms of many paperback and hardcover authors. This information was shared with us by some of our many contributors, and we offer it here as a reference for our readers. This section is organized alphabetically by the author's actual name (given in bold) followed by the pseudonyms he or she has been known to use. (It is interesting to note that 'house names' were common with more than one author using the same name for a particular magazine or publishing house.)

If you have additional information (or corrections), please let us hear from you so we can expand this section in future editions.

**Edward S. Aarons**
Paul Ayres
Edward Ronns

**Marvin H. Albert**
Albert Conroy
Stuart Jason
Nick Quarry
Anthony Rome

**William (Thomas) Ard**
Ben Kerr
Jonas Ward (some)
Thomas Willis

**Paul Auster**
Paul Benjamin

**Mike Avallone**
Nick Carter (a few)
Troy Conway (a few)
Priscilla Dalton
Stuart Jason
Edwina Noone
Sidney Stuart
Max Walker

**W.T. Ballard**
D'Allard Hunter
Neil MacNeil
John Shepherd

**Bill Ballinger**
B.X. Sanborn

**Robert Barnard**
Bernard Bastable

**Julian Barnes**
Dan Kavanagh
Basil Seal

**Roger Blake**
Mark Sade

**Lurton Blassingame**
Peter Duncan

**Charles Beaumont**
Keith Grantland

**Robert Beck**
Slim Iceberg

**H. Bedford-Jones**
Paul Feval
L. Pemjion

**James Blish**
William Atheling

**Robert Bloch**
Collier Young

**Lawrence Block**
William Ard
Jill Emerson
Chip Harrison
Sheldon Lord
Benjamin Morse, M.D.
Andrew Shaw

**Marion Zimmer Bradley**
Lee Chapman
John Dexter (some)
Miriam Gardner
Valerie Graves
Morgan Ives

**John Brunner**
Keith Woodcott

**Kenneth Bulmer**
Adam Hardy
Manning Norvil
Dray Prescot

**W.R. Burnett**
John Monachan
James Updyke

**William S. Burroughs**
William Lee

**Stuart Byrne**
John Bloodstone

**Paul Cain**
George Sims

**Ramsey Campbell**
Carl Dreadstone
Jay Ramsay

**John Dickson Carr**
Carter Dickson
Roger Fairbairn

**Basil Cooper**
Lee Falk

**Clarence Cooper**
Robert Chestnut

**John Creasey**
Gordon Ashe
Harry Carmichael
Norman Deane
Robert Caine Frazier
Patrick Gill
Michael Holliday
Brian Hope
Colin Hughes
Kyle Hunt
J.J. Marric
Jeremy York

**Michael Crichton**
John Lange

**David Cross**
George B. Chesbro

**Norman Daniels**
Dorothy Daniels
David Wade

**Avram Davidson**
Ellery Queen
(about 2 titles only)

**August Derleth**
Stephen Grendon

**Thomas B. Dewey**
Tom Brandt
Cord Wainer

**Thomas Disch**
Thomas Demijohn
Knye Cassandra (both with
John Sladek)

**James Duffy**
Haughton Murphy

**Peter Beresford Ellis**
Peter Tremayne

**Harlan Ellison**
Paul Merchant

**Dennis Etchison**
Jack Martin

**Frederick S. Faust**
Max Brand
George Owen Baxter

**Paul Fairman**
F.W. Paul

**Lionel Fanthorpe**
John E. Muller

**Philip Jose Farmer**
William Norfolk
Kilgore Trout

**John Russell Fearn**
Aston Del Martia

**Alan Dean Foster**
George Lucas

**Gardner F. Fox**
Glen Chase
Jefferson Cooper
Jeffrey Gardner
Matt Gardner
James Kendricks Gray
Dean Jennings
Simon Majors
Kevin Matthews
John Medford Morgan
Rod Morgan
Bart Summers

**Erle Stanley Gardner**
A.A. Fair
Carleton Kendrake
Charles Kinney

**Randall Garrett**
Walter Bupp
David Gordon
½ of Mark Phillips and
Robert Randall

**Richard Geis**
Robert Owen
Peggy Swenson

**Theodor Seuss Geisel**
Dr. Seuss

**Walter B. Gibson**
Douglas Brown
Maxwell Grant

**Ron Goulart**
Lee Falk
Josephine Kains
Julian Kearney
Kenneth Robeson
Frank S. Shaw(n)
Joseph Silva

**Charles L. Grant**
Felicia Andrew
Deborah Lewis

**Ben Haas**
Richard Meade

**Joe Haldeman**
Robert Graham

**Oakley Hall**
O.M. Hall

**Brett Halliday**
Mike Shayne

**Joseph Hansen**
Rose Brock
James Colton

**Terry Harknett**
Joseph Hedges
Thomas H. Stone

**Timothy Harris**
Harris Hyde

**Eleanor Alice Burford
Hibbert**
Philippa Carr
Victoria Holt
Jean Plaidy

**Carolyn G. Heilbrun**
Amanda Cross

**Jamake Highwater**
J. Marks
J. Marks-Highwater

**Hochstein, Peter**
Jack Short

**C. Hodder-Williams**
James Brogan

**John Robert Holt**
Elizabeth Giles
Raymond Giles

**Cornell Hoppley-Woolrich**
George Hopley
William Irish
Cornell Woolrich

**E. Howard Hunt**
David St.John

**Evan Hunter**
Curt Cannon
Hunt Collins
Ezra Hannon
Richard Marsten
Ed McBain

**J. Denis Jackson**
Julian Moreau

**Oliver Jacks**
Kenneth R. Gandley

**John Jakes**
William Ard
Alan Payne
Jay Scotland
J.X. Williams

**Will F. Jenkins**
Murray Leinster

**H. Bedford Jones**
Lucien Pemjean

**Frank Kane**
Frank Boyd

**Henry Kane**
Anthony McCall

**Hal Kent**
Ron Davis

**Stephen King**
Richard Bachman

**Philip K. Klass**
William Tenn

**Andrew Klavan**
Keith Peterson

**William Knowles**
Clyde Allison
Clyde Ames

**Dean R. Koontz**
David Axton
Brian Coffey
Deanna Dwyer
K.R. Dwyer
John Hill
Leigh Nichols
Anthony North
Richard Paige
Owen West
Aaron Wolfe

**Cyril Kornbluth**
Simon Eisner
Jordan Park

**Jerzy Kosinski**
Joseph Novak
Jane Somers

**P. Kubis**
Casey Scott

**Michael Kurland**
Jennifer Plum

**Louis L'Amour**
Tex Burns
Jim Mayo

**Lawrence Lariar**
Adam Knight

**Keith Laumer**
Anthony LeBaron

**Milton Lesser**
Stephen Marlowe

**Doris Lessing**
Jane Somers

**Alfred Henry Lewis**
Dan Quinn

**Paul Linebarger**
Cordwainer Smith

**Frank Belknap Long**
Lyda Belknap Long

**Peter Lovesey**
Peter Lear

**Mark Lucas**
Drew Palmer

**Robert Ludlum**
Jonathan Ryder
Michael Shepherd

**Richard Lupoff**
Adison Steele

**Dennis Lynds**
Michael Collins
John Crowe
Maxwell Grant (some)
Mark Sadler

**Barry Malzberg**
Mike Berry
Claudine Dumas
Mel Johnson
M.L. Johnson
Barrett O'Donnell
K.M. O'Donnell

**Frederick Manfred**
Feike Feikema

**Marshall, Mel**
Zack Tayler

**Robert Martin**
Lee Roberts

**Van Wyck Mason**
Geoffrey Coffin

**Graham Masterton**
Thomas Luke

**Richard Matheson**
Swanson, Logan

**Dudley McGaughy**
Dean Owen

**Marijane Meaker**
Ann Aldrich
Vin Packer

**H.L. Menken**
Owen Hatteras

**Barbara Gross Mertz**
Barbara Michael
Elizabeth Peters

**Kenneth Millar**
Ross MacDonald
John Ross MacDonald

**Michael Moorcock**
Bill Barclay
Edward P. Bradbury

**Brian Moore**
Bernard Mara
Bryan Michael

**James Morris**
Jan Morris (after sex change)

**Petroleum Nasby**
David R. Locke

**Alan E. Nourse**
Doctor X

**Andre Alice Norton**
Andrew North
Alice Norton
Andre Norton

**Charles Nuetzel**
Albert Jr. Augustus
John Davidson
Charles English
Alec Rivere

**Joyce Carol Oates**
Rosamond Smith

**Andrew Offutt**
John Cleve
Baxter Giles
J.X. Williams (some)

**Henry Patterson**
Martin Fallon
James Graham
Jack Higgins
Harry Patterson
Hugh Marlowe

**James Atlee Philips**
Philip Atlee

**Dennis Phillips**
Peter Chambers
Peter Chester

**Judson Phillips**
Hugh Pentecost

**Richard Posner**
Iris Foster
Beatrice Murray
Paul Todd

**Edith Mary Pargeter**
Ellis Peter

**Richard Prather**
David Knight
Douglas Ring

**R.L. Radford**
Ford, Marcia

**Bill Pronzini**
Jack Foxx

**Peter Rabe**
J.T. MacCargo

**Clayton Rawson**
Stuart Towne

**Ruth Rendell**
Barbara Vine

**Mack Reynolds**
Bob Belmont
Todd Harding
Maxine Reynolds

**Anne Rice**
Anne Rampling
A.N. Roquelaure

**Robert Rosenblum**
Robert Maxxe

**W.E.D. Ross**
Rose Dana
Jan Daniels
Clarissa Ross
Dan Ross
Dana Ross
Marilyn Ross

**Jean-Baptiste Rossi**
Sebastien Japrisot

**John Sandford**
John Camp

**Sandra Scoppetone**
Jack Early

**Con Sellers**
Della Bannion

**Alice Bradley Sheldon**
Alice Bradley
Raccoona Sheldon
James Tiptree

**Robert Silverberg**
Loren Beauchamp
W.R. Burnett (some only)
Walter Drummond
Don Elliott (some)
Hilary Ford
Franklin Hamilton
Calvin Knox
Lt. Woodard, M.D.

**George H. Smith**
J.M. Deer
Jan Hudson
Jerry Jason
M.E. Knerr
Diana Summers

**David Stacton**
Bud Clifton

**Theodore Sturgeon**
Frederick R. Ewing
Ellery Queen (1 book only)

**Ross Thomas**
Oliver Bleeck

**Don Tracy**
Roger Fuller

**Bob Tralins**
Keith Miles
Sean O'Shea

**E.C. Tubb**
Gregory Kern

**Jack Vance**
Peter Held
Ellery Queen (some/few)

**Luther Vidal**
Edgar Box
Cameron Kay
Gore Vidal

**Walter Wager**
John Tiger
Max Walker

**Harold Ward**
Zorro

**Jack Webb**
John Farr

**Joe Weiss**
Ray Anatole
Claude Dauphine
Ken Mirbeau

**Donald E. Westlake**
John B. Allan
Curt Clark
Timothy Culver
J. Morgan Cunningham
Samuel Holt
Alan Marshall
Richard Stark
Edwin West

**Gordon Williams**
P.B Yuill

**Harry Whittington**
Whit Harrison
Shep Shepherd

**Jack Williamson**
Will Stewart

**Don Wollheim**
David Grinnell

**George F. Worts**
Loring Brent

# BOOKBUYERS

In this section of the book we have listed buyers of books and related material. When you correspond with these dealers, be sure to enclose a self-addressed stamped envelope if you want a reply. Do not send lists of books for appraisal. If you wish to sell your books, quote the price you want or send a list and ask if there are any on the list they might be interested in and the price they would be willing to pay. If you want the list back, be sure to send a SASE large enough for the listing to be returned. When you list your books, do so by author, full title, publisher and place, date, edition, and condition, noting any defects on cover or contents.

## Adventure
The Silver Door
P.O. Box 3208
Redondo Beach, CA 90277
310-379-6005

## African-American
Children's Book Adoption Agency
P.O. Box 643
Kensington, MD 20895-0643
310-565-2834 or fax 301-585-3091
KIDS_BKS@interloc.com

Fran's Bookhouse
6601 Greene St.
Philadelphia, PA 19119
215-438-2729 or fax 215-438-8997

Monroe Stahr Books
4420 Ventura Canyon, #2
Sherman Oaks, CA 91423
818-784-0870 or fax 818-995-0866
MStahrBks@aol.com

Recollection Books
4519 University Way NE
Seattle, WA 98105
206-548-1346
recall@eskimo.com

## Alaska
Artis Books
201 N Second Ave.
P.O. Box 822
Alpena, MI 49707
517-354-3401
artis@freeway.net

## Albania
W.B. O'Neill-Old & Rare Books
11609 Hunters Green Ct.
Reston, VA 22091
703-860-0782 or fax 703-620-0153

## Alcoholics Anonymous
The Book Baron
1236 S Magnolia Ave.
Anaheim, CA 92804
714-527-7022 or fax 714-527-5634
bkbaron1@pacbell.net or
bkbaron3@qte.net

## American Southwest
*Arizona, Northern & New Mexcico*
Books West Southwest
W. David Laird
Box 6149, University Station
Irvine, CA 92616-6149
714-509-7670 or fax 714-854-5102
wdlbks@home.com

## Americana
Amaranth Books
P.O. Box 421
Wilmette, IL 60091-0421
708-328-2939

Aplan Antiques & Art
James & Peg Aplan
21424 Clover Pl.
Piedmont, SD 57769-9403
605-347-5016
alpanpeg@rapid.net.com

The Bookseller, Inc.
174 W Exchange St.
Akron, OH 44302
330-762-3101 or fax 330-762-4413
Booklein@Interloc.com or
booklein@apk.net

Bowie & Co. Booksellers, Inc.
314 First Ave. S
Seattle, WA 98104
206-624-4100 or fax 206-223-0966
bowiebks@isomedia.com

Woodbridge B. Brown
P.O. Box 445
Turners Falls, MA 01376
413-772-2509 or 413-773-5710

The Captain's Bookshelf, Inc.
31 Page Ave.
Asheville, NC 28801
828-253-6631 or fax 828-253-4917
captsbooks@aol.com

Chapel Hill Rare Books
P.O. Box 456
Carrboro, NC 27510
919-929-8351

Duck Creek Books
Jim & Shirley Richards
P.O. Box 203
Caldwell, OH 43724
614-732-4856 (10 am to 10 pm)

Terry Harper, Bookseller
P.O. Box 312
Vergennes, VT 05491-0312
802-877-9262
bookvend@together.net

Susan Heller, Pages for Sages
22611 Halburton Rd.
Beachwood, OH 44122-3939
216-283-2665
hellersu@cyberdrive.net

## Jim Hodgson Books
908 S Manlius St.
Fayetteville, NY 13066
315-637-6264
jimhbooks@aol.com

M & S Rare Books, Inc.
P.O. Box 2594, E Side Sta.
Providence, RI 02906
401-421-1050 or fax 401-272-0831
(attention M & S)
dsiegel@msrarebooks.com

Parmer Books
7644 Forrestal Rd.
San Diego, CA 92120-2203
619-287-0693 or fax 619-287-6135
ParmerBook@aol.com

Randall House
Pia Oliver
835 Laguna St.
Santa Barbara, CA 93101
805-963-1909 or fax 805-963-1650
pia@piasworld.com

Thorn Books
P.O. Box 1244
Moorpark, CA 93020
805-529-3647 or fax 805-529-0022
thornbooks@earthlink.net

Yesterday's Books
229 Riverview Dr.
Parchment, MI 49004
616-345-1011
yesbooks@aol.com

## Anarchism
Nutmeg Books
354 New Litchfield St. (Rte. 202)
Torrington, CT 06790
203-482-9696
nutmeg@compsol.net

## Angling
Book & Tackle Shop
29 Old Colony Rd.
P.O. Box 114
Chestnut Hill, MA 02467
phone/fax 617-965-0459 (winter)
phone/fax 401-596-0700 (summer)

## Anthropology
The King's Market Bookshops
P.O. Box 709
Boulder, CO 80306-0709
303-232-3321

## Anthologies
*Cartoonists from 1890-1960*
Craig Ehlenberger
Abalone Cove Rare Books
7 Fruit Tree Rd.
Portuguese Bend, CA 90275

## Antiquarian
A.B.A.C.U.S.®
Phillip E. Miller
343 S Chesterfield St.
Aiken, SC 29801
803-648-4632

*Fine, hard-to-find books*
Arnold's of Michigan
218 S Water
Marine City, MI 48039
810-765-1350 or fax 810-765-7914

The Book Baron
1236 S Magnolia Ave.
Anaheim, CA 92804
714-527-7022 or fax 714-527-5634
bkbaron1@pacbell.net or
bkbaron3@qte.net

Bowie & Co. Booksellers, Inc.
314 First Ave. S
Seattle, WA 98104
206-624-4100 or fax 206-223-0966
bowiebks@isomedia.com

Children's Book Adoption Agency
P.O. Box 643
Kensington, MD 20895-0643
310-565-2834 or fax 301-585-3091
KIDS_BKS@interloc.com

James Tait Goodrich
Antiquarian Books & Manuscripts
135 Tweed Blvd.
Grandview-on-Hudson, NY 10960
914-359-0242 or fax 914-359-0142
jtg.jamestgoodrich.com

Terry Harper, Bookseller
P.O. Box 312
Vergennes, VT 05491-0312
802-877-9262
bookvend@together.net

Murray Hudson
Antiquarian Books & Maps
109 S Church St.
P.O. Box 163
Halls, TN 38040
901-836-9057 or 800-748-9946
fax 901-836-9017
mapman@usit.net

The Old Map Gallery
Paul F. Mahoney
1746 Blake St.
Denver, CO 80202
303-296-7725 or fax 303-296-7936
oldmapgallery@denver.net

Jeffrey Lee Pressman, Bookseller
3246 Ettie St.
Oakland, CA 94608
510-652-6232

Robert Mueller Rare Books
8124 W 26th St.
N Riverside, IL 60546
708-447-6441

Scribe Company
Attn: Bonnie Smith
427 Hidden Forest S
Longview, TX 75605
903-663-6873

*Also Agriculture, Biographies, Law,
Travel, Turn-of-the-Century Fiction &
Philosophy*
David R. Smith
30 Nelson Cir.
Jaffrey, NH 03452
603-532-8666
Bookinc@Cheshire.net

## Antiques, Collectibles & Reference
*Antique & Collectors Reproduction News*
Mark Chervenka, Editor
Box 12130-OB
Des Moines, IA 50312-9403
515-270-8994 or fax 515-255-4530

Collector's Companion
Perry Franks
P.O. Box 24333
Richmond, VA 23224

Galerie De Boicourt
251 E Merrill St.
Birmingham, MI 48009
248-723-5680
Tues - Sat: 10 a.m. to 5 p.m.

Henry H. Hain III
Antiques & Collectibles
2623 N Second St.
Harrisburg, PA 17110
717-238-0534
antcolbks@ezonline.com

## Appraisals
J. Sampson Antiques & Books
107 S Main
Harrodsburg, KY 40330
606-734-7829

Lee & Mike Temares
50 Hts. Rd.
Plandome, NY 11030
516-627-8688
tembooks@aol.com

## Arabian Horses; Arabian Nights
Worldwide Antiquarian
P.O. Box 410391
Cambridge, MA 02141-0004
617-876-6220 or fax 617-876-0839
mbalwan@aol.com

## Archaelogy
Flo Silver Books
8442 Oakwood Ct. N
Indianapolis, IN 46260
phone/fax 317-255-5118
Flosilver@aol.com

## Architecture
Cover to Cover
Mark Shuman
P.O. Box 687
Chapel Hill, NC 27514
919-967-1032

## Arctic
Artis Books
201 N Second Ave.
P.O. Box 822
Alpena, MI 49707
517-354-3401
artis@freeway.net

Parmer Books
7644 Forrestal Rd.
San Diego, CA 92120-2203
619-287-0693 or fax 619-287-6135
ParmerBook@aol.com

## Armenia
W.B. O'Neill-Old & Rare Books
11609 Hunters Green Ct.
Reston, VA 22091
703-860-0782 or fax 703-620-0153

## Art
AL-PAC
Lamar Kelley Antiquarian Books
2625 E Southern Ave., C-120
Tempe, AZ 85282
602-831-3121 or fax 602-831-3193
alpac2625@aol.com

Book & Tackle Shop
29 Old Colony Rd.
P.O. Box 114
Chestnut Hill, MA 02467
phone/fax 617-965-0459 (winter)
phone/fax 401-596-0700 (summer)

Books West Southwest
W. David Laird
Box 6149, University Station
Irvine, CA 92616-6149
714-509-7670 or fax 714-854-5102
wdlbks@home.com

The Captain's Bookshelf, Inc.
31 Page Ave.
Asheville, NC 28801
828-253-6631 or fax 828-253-4917
captsbooks@aol.com

*Fine, applied*
L. Clarice Davis Art Books
P.O. Box 56054
Sherman Oaks, CA 91413-1054
818-787-1322 or fax 818-780-3281
davislc@earthlink.net

Galerie De Boicourt
251 E Merrill St.
Birmingham, MI 48009
248-723-5680
Tues. – Sat..: 10 a.m. to 5 p.m.

Edison Hall Books
5 Ventnor Dr.
Edison, NJ 08820
908-548-4455

Heritage Book Shop, Inc.
8540 Melrose Ave.
Los Angeles, CA 90069
310-659-3674 or fax 310-659-4872
HBSINCLA@aol.com

David Holloway, Bookseller
7430 Grace St.
Springfield, VA 22150
703-659-1798

Significant Books
3053 Madison Rd.
P.O. Box 9248
Cincinnati, OH 45209
513-321-7567

Lee & Mike Temares
50 Hts. Rd.
Plandome, NY 11030
516-627-8688 or fax 516-627-7822
tembooks@aol.com

Xanadu Records, Ltd.
3242 Irwin Ave.
Kingsbridge, NY 10463
212-549-3655

**Arthurian**
Camelot Books
Charles E. Wyatt
P.O. Box 2883
Vista, CA 92083
619-940-9472

**Astronomy**
Knollwood Books
Lee & Peggy Price
P.O. Box 197
Oregon, WI 53575-0197
608-835-8861 or fax 608-835-8421
books@tdsnet.com

**Atlases**
Murray Hudson
Antiquarian Books & Maps
109 S Church St.
P.O. Box 163
Halls, TN 38040
901-836-9057 or 800-748-9946
fax 901-836-9017
mapman@usit.net

The Old Map Gallery
Paul F. Mahoney
1746 Blake St.
Denver, CO 80202
303-296-7725 or fax 303-296-7936
oldmapgallery@denver.net

**Atomic Bomb**
Key Books
P.O. Box 58097
St. Petersburg, FL 33715
813-867-2931

**Autobiographies**
Herb Sauermann
21660 School Rd.
Manton, CA 96059

Warren's Collector Books
For Sale Now
112 Royal Ct.
Friendswood, TX 77546
281-482-7947

Wellerdt's Books
3700 S Osprey Ave. #214
Sarasota, FL 34239
813-365-1318

**Autographs**
Ads Autographs
P.O. Box 8006
Webster, NY 14580-8006
716-671-2651 or fax 716-671-5727

The American Dust Co.
47 Park Ct.
Staten Island, NY 10301
phone/fax 718-442-8253

Michael Gerlicher
1375 Rest Point Rd.
Orono, MN 55364

Susan Heller, Pages for Sages
22611 Halburton Rd.
Beachwood, OH 44122-3939
216-283-2665
hellersu@cyberdrive.net

Heritage Book Shop, Inc.
8540 Melrose Ave.
Los Angeles, CA 90069
310-659-3674 or fax 310-659-4872
HBSINCLA@aol.com

Key Books
P.O. Box 58097
St. Petersburg, FL 33715
813-867-2931

McGowan Book Co.
P.O. Box 4226
Chapel Hill, NC 27515
919-968-1121 or fax 919-968-1644
mcgowanbooks@mindspring.com

Randall House
Pia Oliver
835 Laguna St.
Santa Barbara, CA 93101
805-963-1909 or fax 805-963-1650
pia@piasworld.com

**Aviation**
The Book Corner
Michael Tennero
728 W Lumsden Rd.
Brandon, FL 33511
813-684-1133
bookcrnr@worldnet.att.net

The Bookseller, Inc.
174 W Exchange St.
Akron, OH 44302
330-762-3101 or fax 330-762-4413
Booklein@Interloc.com or
booklein@apk.net

Cover to Cover
Mark Shuman
P.O. Box 687
Chapel Hill, NC 27514
919-967-1032

**Baedeker Handbooks**
W.B. O'Neill-Old & Rare Books
11609 Hunters Green Ct.
Reston, VA 22091
703-860-0782 or fax 703-620-0153

**Barbie**
Glo's Books & Collectibles
Gloria Stobbes
906 Shadywood
Southlake, TX 76092
817-481-1438

**Baseball**
The American Dust Co.
47 Park Ct.
Staten Island, NY 10301
phone/fax 718-442-8253

R. Plapinger, Baseball Books
P.O. Box 1062
Ashland, OR 87520
503-488-1200

**L. Frank Baum**
Alcott Books
Barbara Ruppert
5909 Darnell
Houston, TX 77074-7719
713-774-2202
BRuppert@webtv.net

**Beat Generation**
Twice Read Books & Comics
42 S Main St.
Chambersburg, PA 17201
717-261-8449

**Bibliographies**
About Books
6 Sand Hill Ct.
P.O. Box 5717
Parsippany, NJ 07054
973-515-4591

Books West Southwest
W. David Laird
Box 6149, University Sta.
Irvine, CA 92616-6149
714-509-7670 or fax 714-854-5102
wdlbks@home.com

Oak Knoll Books
310 Delaware St.
New Castle, DE 19720
800-996-2556 or 302-328-7232
fax 302-328-7274
oakknoll@oakknoll.com

**Big Little Books**
Jay's House of Collectibles
75 Pky. Dr.
Syosset, NY 11791

## Biographies
Third Time Around Books
Norman Todd
R.R. #1
Mar., Ontario
Canada N0H 1XO
519-534-1382

Herb Sauermann
21660 School Rd.
Manton, CA 96059

Warren's Collector Books
For Sale Now
112 Royal Ct.
Friendswood, TX 77546
281-482-7947

## Black Americana
*Especially Little Black Sambo*
Glo's Books & Collectibles
Gloria Stobbes
906 Shadywood
Southlake, TX 76092
817-481-1438

*History & literature; general literature*
Thomas L. Coffman, Bookseller
TLC Books
9 N College Ave.
Salem, VA 24153
540-389-3555

*History & literature*
David Holloway, Bookseller
7430 Grace St.
Springfield, VA 22150
703-569-1798

Mason's Bookstore, Rare Books &
Record Albums East
115 S Main St.
Chambersburg, PA 17201
717-261-0541

## Black Fiction & Literature
Almark & Co.-Booksellers
P.O. Box 7
Thornhill, Ontario
Canada L3T 3N1
905-764-2665 or fax 905-764-5771
al@almarkco.com or
mark@almarkco.com

The American Dust Co.
47 Park Ct.
Staten Island, NY 10301
phone/fax 718-442-8253

## Black Studies
Recollection Books
4519 University Way NE
Seattle, WA 98105
206-548-1346
recall@eskimo.com

## Black Hills
James F. Taylor
515 Sixth St.
Rapid City, SD 57701
605-341-3224

## Book Search Service
Authors of the West
191 Dogwood Dr.
Dundee, OR 97115
503-538-8132
Lnash@georgefox.edu

Ackley Books & Collectibles
Bryant & Suzanne Pitner
912 Hidden Cove Way
Suisun City, CA 94585-3511
phone/fax 707-421-9032
abcbooks@webcom.com
(mail order only)

Avonlea Books
P.O. Box 74, Main Station
White Plains, NY 10602-0074
914-946-5923 or fax 914-761-3119
avonlea@bushkin.com

Bookingham Palace
Rosan Van Wagenen & Eileen Layman
52 North 2500 East
Teton, ID 83451
209-458-4431

Heritage Book Shop, Inc.
8540 Melrose Ave.
Los Angeles, CA 90069
310-659-3674 or fax 310-659-4872
HBSINCL@aol.com

Hilda's Book Search
Hilda Gruskin
199 Rollins Ave.
Rockville, MD 20852
301-948-3181

Lost n' Found Books
Linda Lengerich
3214 Columbine Ct.
Indianapolis, IN 46224
phone/fax 317-298-9077

Passaic Book Center
594 Main Ave.
Passaic, NJ 07055
201-778-6646 or fax 201-778-6738

Recollection Used Books
David Brown
4519 University Way NE
Seattle, WA 98105
206-548-1346

The Silver Door
P.O. Box 3208
Redondo Beach, CA 90277
310-379-6005

*Especially children's out-of-print books*
Treasures from the Castle
Connie Castle
1720 N Livernois
Rochester, MI 48306
248-651-7317
treasure23@juno.com

## Book Sets
AL-PAC
Lamar Kelley Antiquarian Books
2625 E Southern Ave., C-120
Tempe, AZ 85282
602-831-3121 or fax 602-831-3193
alpac2625@aol.com

## Books About Books
About Books
6 Sand Hill Ct.
P.O. Box 5717
Parsippany, NJ 07054
973-515-4591

Books West Southwest
W. David Laird
Box 6149, University Station
Irvine, CA 92616-6149
714-509-7670 or fax 714-854-5102
wdlbks@home.com

Bowie & Co. Booksellers, Inc.
314 First Ave. S
Seattle, WA 98104
206-624-4100 or fax 206-223-0966
bowiebks@isomedia.com

First Folio
1206 Brentwood
Paris, TN 38242
phone/fax 901-644-9940
firstfol@aeneas.net

Susan Heller, Pages for Sages
22611 Halburton Rd.
Beachwood, OH 44122-3939
216-283-2665
hellersu@cyberdrive.net

Key Books
P.O. Box 58097
St. Petersburg, FL 33715
813-867-2931

Oak Knoll Books
310 Delaware St.
New Castle, DE 19720
800-996-2556 or 302-328-7232
fax 302-328-7274
oakknoll@oakknoll.com

Randall House
Pia Oliver
835 Laguna St.
Santa Barbara, CA 93101
805-963-1909 or fax 805-963-1650
pia@piasworld.com

George H. Tweney
16660 Marine View Dr. SW
Seattle, WA 98166
206-243-8243

## Botany
Brooks Books
P.O. Box 21473
Concord, CA 94521
510-672-4566 or fax 510-672-3338
brooksbk@interloc.com

*Also gardening, horiticulture, etc.*
Agave Books
P.O. Box 31495
Mesa, AZ 85275-1495
602-649-9097
agavebks@interloc.com

**Charles Bukowski**
Ed Smith Books
20 Paget Rd.
Madison, WI 53704-5929
608-241-3707 or
fax 608-241-3459
ed@edsbooks.com

**Edgar Rice Burroughs**
W.J. Leveridge
W & L Trading Company
2301 Carova Rd.
Carova Beach, Corolla, NC 27927
252-453-3408

**C.S. Lewis & Friends**
Aslan Books
191 Dogwood Dr.
Dundee, OR 97115
503-538-8132
Lnash@georgefox.edu

**California**
W. David Laird
Books West Southwest
Box 6149, University Station
Irvine, CA 92616-6149
714-509-7670 or fax 714-854-5102
wdlbks@home.com

Thorn Books
P.O. Box 1244
Moorpark, CA 93020
805-529-3647 or fax 805-529-0022
thornbooks@earthlink.net

**Canadiana**
David Armstrong, Bookseller
Box 551
Letherbridge, Alberta
Canada T1J 3Z4
403-381-3270
dabooks@telusplanet.net

Third Time Around Books
Norman Todd
R.R. #1
Mar., Ontario
Canada N0H 1XO
519-534-1382

**Cartography**
Overlee Farm Books
P.O. Box 1155
Stockbridge, MA 01262
413-637-2277

**Cartoon Art**
Jay's House of Collectibles
75 Pky. Dr.
Syosset, NY 11791

**Catalogs**
*Glass, pottery, furniture, doll, toy, jewelry, general merchandise, fishing tackle*
Bill Schroeder
P.O. Box 3009
Paducah, KY 42002-3009

*Antiques or other collectibles*
*Antique & Collectors Reproduction News*
Mark Chervenka, Editor
Box 12130-OB
Des Moines, IA 50312-9403
515-270-8994 or fax 515-255-4530

Hillcrest Books
961 Deep Draw Rd.
Crossville, TN 38555-9547
phone/fax 615-484-7680

**Celtic**
Camelot Books
Charles E. Wyatt
P.O. Box 2883
Vista, CA 92083
619-940-9472

**Central America**
Flo Silver Books
8442 Oakwood Ct. N
Indianapolis, IN 46260
phone/fax 317-255-5118
Flosilver@aol.com

**Marc Chagall**
Paul Melzer Fine Books
12 E Vine St.
P.O. Box 1143
Redlands, CA 92373
909-792-7299 or fax 909-792-7218
pmbooks@eee.org

**Children's Illustrated**
Noreen Abbot Books
2666 44th Ave.
San Francisco, CA 94116
415-664-9464

Alcott Books
Barbara Ruppert
5909 Darnell
Houston, TX 77074-7719
713-774-2202
BRuppert@webtv.net

Book & Tackle Shop
29 Old Colony Rd.
P.O. Box 114
Chestnut Hill, MA 02467
phone/fax 617-965-0459 (winter)
phone/fax 401-596-0700 (summer)

Books of the Ages
Gary J. Overmann
Maple Ridge Manor
4764 Silverwood Dr.
Batavia, OH 45103-9740
phone/fax 513-732-3456
e-overman@ix.netcom.com

*Including Dick & Jane readers, Little Golden Books, older Weekly Reader*
Bookcase Books
P. Gayle Hendrington
R.R. 1 Box 242
Newport, NH 03773
603-863-9517
books@bookcasebooks.com

Bromer Booksellers
607 Boylston St.
Boston, MA 02116
617-247-2818 or fax 617-247-2975
books@bromer.com

*Non-series or published after 1925*
Cattermole
20th-Century Children's Books
9880 Fairmount Rd.
Newbury, OH 44065
440-338-3253 or fax 440-338-1675
books@cattermole.com

*19th & 20th Century*
Children's Book Adoption Agency
P.O. Box 643
Kensington, MD 20895-0643
301-565-2834 or fax 301-585-3091
KIDS_BKS@interloc.com

*Free search service*
Steven Cieluch
15 Walbridge St., Suite #10
Allston, MA 02134-3808
617-734-7778
scieluch@channel1.com

Ursula Davidson
Children's & Illustrated Books
134 Linden Ln.
San Rafael, CA 94901
414-454-3939 or fax 415-454-1087
davidson_u@compuserve.com

Drusilla's Books
817 N Howard St.
Baltimore, MD 21201-4696
401-225-0277 or fax 401-321-4955
Tues-Sat: 12 a.m. to 5 p.m.
or by appointment
drusilla@mindspring.com

Edison Hall Books
5 Ventnor Dr.
Edison, NJ 08820
908-548-4455

*Circa 1850s through 1970s*
Encino Books
Diane Yaspan
5063 Gaviota Ave
Encino, CA 91436
818-905-711 or fax 818-501-7711

First Folio
1206 Brentwood
Paris, TN 38242
phone/fax 901-644-9940
firstfol@aeneas.net

Fran's Bookhouse
6601 Greene St.
Phil., PA 19119
215-438-2729 or fax 215-438-8997

*Madeline, Eloise, Raggedy Ann & Andy,*
  *Uncle Wiggly, Wizard of Oz*
Glo's Books & Collectibles
Gloria Stobbes
906 Shadywood
Southlake, TX 76092
817-481-1438

Susan Heller, Pages for Sages
22611 Halburton Rd.
Beachwood, OH 44122-3939
216-283-2665
hellersu@cyberdrive.net

Ilene Kayne
1308 S Charles St.
Baltimore, MD 21230-4219
410-347-7570
kayne@clark.net

Bob Lakin Books
P.O. Box 186
Chatfield, TX 75105
972-247-3291

Marvelous Books
P.O. Box 1510
Ballwin, MO 63022
314-458-3301 or fax 314-273-5452
marvbooks@aol.com

Much Ado
Seven Pleasant St.
Marblehead, MA 01945
781-639-0400 or fax 781-639-0840
muchado@shore.net

Nerman's Books
410-63 Albert St.
Winnipeg, Manitoba
Canada R3B 1G4
204-956-1214 or 204-475-1050
fax 204-947-0753
nerman@escape.ca

Page Books
Margaret E. Page
HCR 65, Box 233
Kingston, AR 72742
870-861-5831
pagebook@eritter.net

Jo Ann Reisler, Ltd.
360 Glyndon St., NE
Vienna, VA 22180
703-938-2967 or
fax 703-938-9057
Reisler@Clark.net

Scribe Company
Attn: Bonnie Smith
427 Hidden Forest S
Longview, TX 75605
903-663-6873

Barbara Smith Books
P.O. Box 1185
Northampton, MA 01061
413-586-1453

Yesterday's Books
229 Riverview Dr.
Parchment, MI 49004
616-345-1011
yesbooks@aol.com

Treasures from the Castle
Connie Castle
1720 N Livernois
Rochester, MI 48306
248-651-7317
treasure23@juno.com

**Children's Series**
Children's Book Adoption Agency
P.O. Box 643
Kensington, MD 20895-0643
301-565-2834 or fax 301-585-3091
KIDS_BKS@interloc.com

*Circa 1900s through 1970s*
Encino Books
Diane Yaspan
5063 Gaviota Ave
Encino, CA 91436
818-905-711 or fax 818-501-7711

*Judy Bolton, Nancy Drew, Rick Brant,*
  *Cherry Ames, etc.; also Dick & Jane*
Glo's Books & Collectibles
Gloria Stobbes
906 Shadywood
Southlake, TX 76092
817-481-1438

Ilene Kayne
1308 S Charles St.
Baltimore, MD 21230-4219
410-347-7570
kayne@clark.net

Bob Lakin Books
P.O. Box 186
Chatfield, TX 75105
972-247-3291

Nerman's Books
410-63 Albert St.
Winnipeg, Manitoba
Canada R3B 1G4
204-956-1214 or 204-475-1050
fax 204-947-0753
nerman@escape.ca

Scribe Company
Attn: Bonnie Smith
427 Hidden Forest S
Longview, TX 75605
903-663-6873

Lee & Mike Temares
50 Hts. Rd.
Plandome, NY 11030
516-627-8688 or fax 516-627-7822
tembooks@aol.com

Yesterday's Books
229 Riverview Dr.
Parchment, MI 49004
616-345-1011
yesbooks@aol.com

**Christian Faith**
Books Now & Then
Dennis & Jan Patrick
P.O. Box 337
Stanley, ND 58784
phone/fax 701-628-2084
bnt@stanley.ndak.net

**Christmas**
*Especially illustrated antiquarian*
Drusilla's Books
817 N Howard St.
Baltimore, MD 21201-4696
410-225-0277 or fax 410-321-4955
Tues-Sat: 12a.m. to 5p.m.
or by appointment
drusilla@mindspring.com

**Sir W.S. Churchill**
Chartwell Booksellers
55 E 52nd St.
New York, NY 10055
212-308-0643

Robert L. Merriam
Rare, Used & Old Books
Newhall Rd.
Conway, MA 01341-9709
413-369-4052
rmerriam@interloc.com

**Cinema, Theatre & Films**
Cinemage Books
105 W 27th St.
New York, NY 10001
212-243-4919
irajoel@aol.com

The American Dust Co.
47 Park Ct.
Staten Island, NY 10301
phone/fax 718-442-8253

Xanadu Records, Ltd.
3242 Irwin Ave.
Kingsbridge, NY 10463
212-549-3655

**Civil War**
Chapel Hill Rare Books
P.O. Box 456
Carrboro, NC 27510
919-929-8351

Stan Clark Military Books
915 Fairview Ave.
Gettysburg, PA 17325
717-337-1728 or 717-337-0581
scmg@mail.wideopen.net

*Also the South*
Elder's Book Store
2115 Elliston Pl.
Nashville, TN 37203
615-327-1867

Rick Harmon
Military Books & Relics
910 Sullivan Dr.
Belvidere, IL 61008
815-547-7580

Jim Hodgson Books
908 S Manlius St.
Fayetteville, NY 13066
315-637-6264
jimhbooks@aol.com

Mason's Bookstore, Rare Books &
    Record Albums East
115 S Main St.
Chambersburg, PA 17201
717-261-0541

K.C. & Jean Owings
Box 389
Whitman, MA 02382
781-447-7850 or fax 781-447-3435

**Cobb, Irvin S.**
*Always paying $3.00 each plus shipping.*
    *Send for immediate payment:*
Bill Schroeder
5801 KY Dam Rd.
Paducah, KY 42003

**Collectibles, Antiques & Reference**
*Antique & Collectors Reproduction News*
Mark Chervenka, Editor
Box 12130-OB
Des Moines, IA 50312-9403
515-270-8994 or fax 515-255-4530

Galerie De Boicourt
251 E Merrill St.
Birmingham, MI 48009
248-723-5680
Tues. – Sat: 10 a.m. to 5 p.m.

Henry H. Hain III
Antiques & Collectibles
2623 N Second St.
Harrisburg, PA 17110
717-238-0534
antcolbks@ezonline.com

**Color Plate Books**
Bowie & Co. Booksellers, Inc.
314 First Ave. S
Seattle, WA 98104
206-624-4100 or fax 206-223-0966
bowiebks@isomedia.com

Drusilla's Books
817 N Howard St.
Baltimore, MD 21201-4696
410-225-0277 or fax 410-321-4955
Tues – Sat: 12 a.m. to 5 p.m.
or by appointment
drusilla@mindspring.com

Worldwide Antiquarian
P.O. Box 410391
Cambridge, MA 02141-0004
617-876-6220 or fax 617-876-0839
mbalwan@aol.com

**Comics**
Passaic Book Center
594 Main Ave.
Passaic, NJ 07055
201-778-6646 or fax 201-778-6738

**Cookery & Cookbooks**
Arnold's of Michigan
218 S Water
Marine City, MI 48039
810-765-1350 or fax 810-765-7914

Book & Tackle Shop
29 Old Colony Rd.
P.O. Box 114
Chestnut Hill, MA 02467
phone/fax 617-965-0459 (winter)
phone/fax 401-596-0700 (summer)

Book Broker
114 Bollingwood Rd.
Charlottesville, VA 22902
804-296-2194 or fax 804-296-1566
bookbrk@cfw.com
mail order or appointment only

RAC Books
P.O. Box 296 RD 2
Seven Valleys, PA 17360
717-428-3776
racbooks@cyberia.com

Barbara Smith Books
P.O. Box 1185
Northampton, MA 01061
413-586-1453

Warren's Collector Books
    For Sale Now
112 Royal Ct.
Friendswood, TX 77546
281-482-7947

**Crime**
The Silver Door
P.O. Box 3208
Redondo Beach, CA 90277
310-379-6005

**Cuba & Panama**
The Book Corner
Mike Tennero
728 W Lumsden Rd.
Brandon, FL 33511
813-684-1133
bookcrnr@worldnet.att.net

**Cyprus**
W.B. O'Neill-Old & Rare Books
11609 Hunters Green Ct.
Reston, VA 22091
703-860-0782 or fax 703-620-0153

**Decorative Arts**
Robert L. Merriam
Rare, Used & Old Books
Newhall Rd.
Conway, MA 01341-9709
413-369-4052
rmerriam@interloc.com

**Detective**
*First editions*
Karl M. Armens
740 Juniper Dr.
Iowa City, IA 52245

Monroe Stahr Books
4420 Ventura Canyon, #2
Sherman Oaks, CA 91423
818-784-0870 or fax 818-995-0866
MStahrBks@aol.com

Mordida Books
P.O. Box 79322
Houston, TX 77279
713-467-4280 or fax 713-467-4182
mordida@swbell.net

Thomas Books
P.O. Box 14036
Phoenix, AZ 85063
602-247-9289 or fax 602-945-1023
sales@thomasbooks.com

The Silver Door
P.O. Box 3208
Redondo Beach, CA 90277
310-379-6005

**Disney**
Cohen Books & Collectibles
Joel J. Cohen
P.O. Box 810310
Boca Raton, FL 33481-0310
561-487-7888

Jay's House of Collectibles
75 Pky. Dr.
Syosset, NY 11791

**Documents**
McGowan Book Co.
P.O. Box 4226
Chapel Hill, NC 27515
919-968-1121 or fax 919-968-1644
mcgowanbooks@mindspring.com

**Dogs**
Kathleen Rais & Co.
211 Carolina Ave.
Phoenixville, PA 19460
610-933-1388

**Earth Science**
*Used, out-of-print, rare*
Patricia L. Daniel, Bookseller
13 English Ave.
Wichita, KS 62707-1005
316-683-2079 or fax 316-683-5448
pldaniel@Southwind.net

**Emily Dickinson**
Robert L. Merriam
Rare, Used & Old Books
Newhall Rd.
Conway, MA 01341-9709
413-369-4052
rmerriam@interloc.com

**Thomas Edison**
Edison Hall Books
5 Ventnor Dr.
Edison, NJ 08820
908-548-4455

**Ephemera**
*Antique valentines*
Kingsbury Productions
Katherine & David Kreider
4555 N Pershing Ave., Suite 33-138
Stockton, CA 95207
209-467-8438

The Mulberry Cat
Yvonne Davis
Jan Davis Martel
P.O. Box 3573
Boone, NC 28607
704-963-7693

**Equestrine**
*Books, antiques, art*
Artiques, Ltd.
Veronica Jochens
P.O. Box 67
Lonedell, MO 63060
314-629-1374
veronica @nightowl.net

**Espionage**
The Silver Door
P.O. Box 3208
Redondo Beach, CA 92077
310-379-6005

**Estate Libraries**
The Book Collector
2347 University Blvd.
Houston, TX 77005
713-661-2665

**Exhibition Catalogs**
L. Clarice Davis Art Books
P.O. Box 56054
Sherman Oaks, CA 91413-1054
818-787-1322 or fax 818-780-3281
davislc@earthlink.net

**Exploration**
*Western*
Terry Harper, Bookseller
P.O. Box 312
Vergennes, VT 05491-0312
802-877-9262
bookvend@together.net

Heritage Book Shop, Inc.
8540 Melrose Ave.
Los Angeles, CA 90069
310-659-3674 or fax 310-659-4872
HBSINCLA@aol.com

Key Books
P.O. Box 58097
St. Petersburg, FL 33715
813-867-2931

Flo Silver Books
8442 Oakwood Ct. N
Indianapolis, IN 46260
phone/fax 317-255-5118
Flosilver@aol.com

**Fantasy**
The Book Baron
1236 S Magnolia Ave.
Anaheim, CA 92804
714-527-7022 or fax 714-527-5634
bkbaron1@pacbell.net or
bkbaron3@qte.net

Camelot Books
Charles E. Wyatt
P.O. Box 2883
Vista, CA 92083
619-940-9472

*Science fiction, horror or supernatural*
Xanadu Records Ltd.
3242 Irwin Ave.
Kingsbridge, NY 01463
718-549-3655

**Farming**
*First editions*
Karl M. Armens
740 Juniper Dr.
Iowa City, IA 52245

*Also gardening*
Hurley Books/Celtic Cross Books
1753 Rt. 12
Westmoreland, NH 03467-4724
603-399-4342 or fax 603-399-8326
hurleybook@adam.cheshire.net

Henry Lindeman
4769 Bavarian Dr.
Jackson, MI 49201
517-764-5728

**Fiction**
*American, European, detective or crime*
The American Dust Co.
47 Park Ct.
Staten Island, NY 10301
phone/fax 718-442-8253

McGee's First Varieties
330 Franklin Rd., Suite 135A-134
Brentwood, TN 37027
615-373-5318 or fax 615-661-4047
TMcGee@BellSouth.net

*Southern*
Alice Robbins, Bookseller
3002 Round Hill Rd.
Greensboro, NC 27408
910-282-1964

Third Time Around Books
Norman Todd
R.R. #1
Mar., Ontario
Canada N0H 1XO
519-534-1382

Warren's Collector Books
For Sale Now
112 Royal Ct.
Friendswood, TX 77546
281-482-7947

*American, European, detective or crime*
Ace Zerblonski Books
Malcolm McCollum, Proprietor
1419 North Royer
Colorado Springs, CO 80907
719-634-3941

Bob Lakin Books
P.O. Box 186
Chatfield, TX 75105
972-247-3291
*19th & 20th-C American*

Mason's Bookstore, Rare Books
& Record Albums East
115 S Main St.
Chambersburg, PA 17201
717-261-0541

**Financial**
Warren's Collector Books
For Sale Now
112 Royal Ct.
Friendswood, TX 77546
281-482-7947

**Fine Bindings & Books**
The Book Collector
2347 University Blvd.
Houston, TX 77005
713-661-2665

Bromer Booksellers
607 Boylston St.
Boston, MA 02116
617-247-2818 or fax 617-247-2975
books@bromer.com

Dad's Old Bookstore
Green Hills Ct.
4004 Hillsboro Rd.
Nashville, TN 37215
615-298-5880

Heritage Book Shop, Inc.
8540 Melrose Ave.
Los Angeles, CA 90069
310-659-3674 or fax 310-659-4872
HBSINCL@aol.com

Terry Harper, Bookseller
P.O. Box 312
Vergennes, VT 05491-0312
802-877-9262
bookvend@together.net

George Robert Kane Fine Books
252 Third Ave.
Santa Cruz, CA 95062
phone/fax 408-426-4133
qkanebks@cruzio.com

Kenneth Karmiole, Bookseller, Inc.
509 Wilshire Blvd.
Santa Monica, CA 94001
310-451-4342 or 310-458-5930
karmbooks@aol.com

Mason's Bookstore, Rare Books &
    Record Albums East
115 S Main St.
Chambersburg, PA 17201
717-261-0541

Paul Melzer Fine Books
12 E Vine St.
P.O. Box 1143
Redlands, CA 92373
909-792-7299 or fax 909-793-7218
pmbooks@eee.org

*Also sets*
Randall House
Pia Oliver
835 Laguna St.
Santa Barbara, CA 93101
805-963-1909 or fax 805-963-1650
pia@piasworld.com

David R. Smith
30 Nelson Cir.
Jaffrey, NH 03452
603-532-8666
Bookinc@Cheshire.net

**Fine Press**
Susan Heller, Pages for Sages
22611 Halburton Rd.
Beachwood, OH 44122-3939
216-283-2665
hellersu@cyberdrive.net

Heritage Book Shop, Inc.
8540 Melrose Ave.
Los Angeles, CA 90069
310-659-3674 or fax 310-659-4872
HBSINCL@aol.com

Randall House
Pia Oliver
835 Laguna St.
Santa Barbara, CA 93101
805-963-1909 or fax 805-963-1650
pia@piasworld.com

**Firearms**
Melvin Marcher, Bookseller
6204 N Vermont
Oklahoma City, OK 73112

**First Editions**
A Tale of Two Sisters
2509 Stone Hollow Dr.
Bedford, TX 76021
fax 817-540-2204
sistwo@flash.net

*After 1937*
A.B.A.C.U.S.®
Phillip E. Miller
343 S Chesterfield St.
Aiken, SC 29801
803-648-4632

*Hyper-modern*
Almark & Co.-Booksellers
P.O. Box 7
Thornhill, Ontario
Canada L3T 3N1
905-764-2665 or fax 905-764-5771
al@almarkco.com or
mark@almarkco.com

*Modern or signed*
AL-PAC
Lamar Kelley Antiquarian Books
2625 E Southern Ave., C-120
Tempe, AZ 85282
602-831-3121 or fax 602-831-3193
alpac2625@aol.com

*Modern or signed*
Alcott Books
Barbara Ruppert
5909 Darnell
Houston, TX 77074-7719
713-774-2202
BRuppert@webtv.net

Amaranth Books
P.O. Box 421
Wilmette, IL 60091-0421
708-328-2939

*Modern or signed*
The American Dust Co.
47 Park Ct.
Staten Island, NY 10301
phone/fax 718-442-8253

Karl M. Armens
740 Juniper Dr.
Iowa City, IA 52245

*Modern*
Bela Luna Books
P.O. Box 260425
Highlands Ranch, CO 80163-0425
800-497-4717 or fax 303-791-7342
Bellalun@aol.com

Between the Covers
35 W Maple Ave.
Merchantville, NJ 08109
609-665-2284 or fax 609-665-3639
mail@betweenthecovers.com

The Book Baron
1236 S Magnolia Ave.
Anaheim, CA 92804
714-527-7022 or fax 714-527-5634
bkbaron1@pacbell.net or
bkbaron3@qte.net

*Modern or signed*
Burke's Bookstore
1719 Poplar Ave.
Memphis, TN 38104-6447
901-278-7484 or fax 901-272-2340
burkes@netten.net

*Modern*
Chapel Hill Rare Books
P.O. Box 456
Carrboro, NC 27510
919-929-8351

*Modern*
Tom Davidson, Bookseller
3703 Ave. L
Brooklyn, NY 11210
718-338-8428 or fax 718-338-8430
tdbooks@att.net

*Modern*
Bernard E. Goodman, Bookseller
7421 SW 147 Ct.
Miami, FL 33193
305-385-8526
BCBooks@bellsouth.net

Edison Hall Books
5 Ventnor Dr.
Edison, NJ 08820
908-548-4455

*Modern*
Susan Heller, Pages for Sages
22611 Halburton Rd.
Beachwood, OH 44122-3939
216-283-2665
hellersu@cyberdrive.net

*Modern*
David Holloway, Bookseller
7430 Grace St.
Springfield, VA 22150
703-569-1798

Ruth Heindel Associates
First Editions, Rare & Used Books
660 Boas St., Suite 1618
Harrisburg, PA 17110
717-213-9010

Heritage Book Shop, Inc.
8540 Melrose Ave.
Los Angeles, CA 90069
310-659-3674 or fax 310-659-4872
HBSINCLA@aol.com

*Modern*
Ken Lopez, Bookseller
51 Huntington Rd.
Hadley, MA 01035
413-584-4827 or fax 413-584-2045
mail@lopezbooks.com

*Also presentation or association copies*
MacDonnell Rare Books
9307 Glenlake Dr.
Austin, TX 78730
512-345-4139

*Modern*
McGee's First Varieties
330 Franklin Rd., Suite 135A-134
Brentwood, TN 37027
615-373-5318 or fax 615-661-4047
TMcGee@BellSouth.net

Monroe Stahr Books
4420 Ventura Canyon, #2
Sherman Oaks, CA 91423
818-784-0870 or fax 818-995-0866
MStahrBks@aol.com

Much Ado
Seven Pleasant St.
Marblehead, MA 01945
781-639-0400 or fax 781-639-0840
muchado@shore.net

Robert Mueller Rare Books
8124 W 26th St.
N Riverside, IL 60546
708-447-6441

Jeffrey Lee Pressman, Bookseller
3246 Ettie St.
Oakland, CA 94608
510-652-6232

*American & British*
Quill & Brush
1137 Sugarloaf Mtn. Rd.
Dickerson, MD 20842
301-874-3200 or fax 301-874-0824
Firsts@qb.com

Alice Robbins, Bookseller
3002 Round Hill Rd.
Greensboro, NC 27408
910-282-1964

*Especially fiction, cookery, children's, business, sports & illustrated*
Eileen Serxner
Box 2544
Bala Cynwyd, PA 19004
610-664-7960
serxner@erols.com

*Modern*
Ed Smith Books
20 Paget Rd.
Madison, WI 53704-5929
608-241-3707 or fax 608-241-3459
ed@edsbooks.com

EScribe Company
Attn: Bonnie Smith
427 Hidden Forest S
Longview, TX 75605
903-663-6873

Spellbound Books
M. Tyree
3818 Vickie Ct. #B
Prescott Valley, AZ 86314
520-759-2625

*20th-century authors of nature, natural history, 20th-century Americana, historical & nautical fiction*
Town's End Books
John D. & Judy A. Townsend
132 Hemlock Dr.
Deep River, CT 06417
860-526-3896
john@townsendbooks.com

*Modern; especially British & European literature*
The Typographeum Bookshop
246 Bennington Rd.
Francestown, NH 03043
603-547-2425

*Modern*
The Early West/Whodunit Books
P.O. Box 9292
College Station, TX 77842
409-775-6047 or fax 409-764-7758
EarlyWest@aol.com

**Harrison Fisher**
Parnassus Books
218 N 9th St.
Boise, ID 83702

**Fishing**
Artis Books
201 N Second Ave.
P.O. Box 208
Alpena, MI 49707
517-354-3401
artis@freeway.net

Edison Hall Books
5 Ventnor Dr.
Edison, NJ 08820
908-548-4455

Jim Hodgson Books
908 S Manlius St.
Fayetteville, NY 13066
315-637-6264
jimhbooks@aol.com

Melvin Marcher, Bookseller
6204 N Vermont
Oklahoma City, OK 73112

Mason's Bookstore, Rare Books & Record Albums East
115 S Main
Chambersburg, PA 17201
717-261-0541

Yesterday's Books
229 Riverview Dr.
Parchment, MI 49004
616-345-1011
yesbooks@aol.com

**Florida**
The Book Corner
Michael Tennero
728 W Lumsden Rd.
Brandon, FL 33511
813-684-1133
bookcrnr@worldnet.att.net

**Fore-Edge Painted Books**
Susan Heller, Pages for Sages
22611 Halburton Rd.
Beachwood, OH 44122-3939
216-283-2665
hellersu@cyberdrive.net

George Robert Kane Fine Books
252 Third Ave.
Santa Cruz, CA 95062
phone/fax 408-426-4133
qkanebks@cruzio.com

**Freemasonry**
Mason's Bookstore, Rare Books & Record Albums East
115 S Main St.
Chambersburg, PA 17201
717-261-0541

**Gambling & Gaming**
Gambler's Book Shop
630 S Eleventh St.
Las Vegas, NV 89101
800-634-6243

**Games**
*Card or board; Whist & Bridge*
Bill & Mimi Sachen
927 Grand Ave.
Waukegan, IL 60085
847-662-7204
FutileWill@aol.com

**Gardening**
The American Botanist Booksellers
P.O. Box 532
Chillicothe, IL 61523
309-274-5254

Brooks Books
P.O. Box 21473
Concord, CA 94521
510-672-4566 or fax 510-672-3338
brooksbk@interloc.com

The Captain's Bookshelf, Inc.
31 Page Ave.
Asheville, NC 28801
828-253-6631 or fax 828-253-4917
captsbooks@aol.com

**Gazetteers**
Murray Hudson
Antiquarian Books & Maps
109 S Church St.
P.O. Box 163
Halls, TN 38040
901-836-9057 or 800-748-9946
fax 901-836-9017
mapman@usit.net

**Genealogy**
Elder's Book Store
2115 Elliston Pl.
Nashville, TN 37203
615-327-1867

**General Out-of-Print**
Best-Read Books
122 State St.
Sedro-Wooley, WA 98284
206-855-2179

Bicentennial Book Shop
820 S Westnedge Ave.
Kalamazoo, MI 49008
616-345-5987
ztkh10a@prodigy.com

The Book Baron
1236 S Magnolia Ave.
Anaheim, CA 92804
714-527-7022 or fax 714-527-5634
bkbaron1@pacbell.net or
bkbaron3@qte.net

Book Den South
2249 First St.
Ft. Myers, FL 33901
813-332-2333

*Pulp fiction & modern first editions*
Bookcase Books
P. Gayle Hendrington
R.R. 1 Box 242
Newport, NH 03773
603-863-9517
books@bookcasebooks.com

The Bookseller, Inc.
174 W Exchange St.
Akron, OH 44302
330-762-3101 or fax 330-762-4413
Booklein@Interloc.com or
booklein@apk.com

Cinemage Books
105 W 27th St.
New York, NY 10001

*Antiquarian*
Eastside Books & Paper
P.O. Box 1581, Gracie Station
New York, NY 10028-0013
212-759-6299

Edison Hall Books
5 Ventnor Dr.
Edison, NJ 08820
908-548-4455

Fran's Bookhouse
6601 Greene St.
Phil., PA 19119
215-438-2729 or fax 215-438-8997

Grave Matters
P.O. Box 32192-08
Cincinnati, OH 45232
513-242-7527 or fax 513-242-5115
books@gravematters.com

George Robert Kane Fine Books
252 Third Ave.
Santa Cruz, CA 95062
phone/fax 408-426-4133
qkanebks@cruzio.com

McGowan Book Co.
P.O. Box 4226
Chapel Hill, NC 27515
919-968-1121 or fax 919-968-1644
mcgowanbooks@mindspring.com

Robert L. Merriam
Rare, Used & Old Books
New Hall Rd.
Conway, MA 01341-9709
413-369-4052
rmerriam@interloc.com

The Mulberry Cat
Yvonne Davis
Jan Davis Martel
P.O. Box 3573
Boone, NC 28607
704-963-7693

Passaic Book Center
594 Main Ave.
Passaic, NJ 07055
201-778-6646 or fax 201-778-6738

RAC Books
P.O. Box 296 RD 2
Seven Valleys, PA 17360
717-428-3776
racbooks@cyberia.com

J. Sampson Antiques & Books
107 S Main
Harrodsburg, KY 40330
606-734-7829

Significant Books
3053 Madison Rd.
P.O. Box 9248
Cincinnati, OH 45209
513-321-7567

A.A. Vespa
P.O. Box 637
Park Ridge, IL 60068
708-692-4210

**Genetics**
The King's Market Bookshops
P.O. Box 709
Boulder, CO 80306-0709
303-232-3321

**Geographies**
Murray Hudson
Antiquarian Books & Maps
109 S Church St.
P.O. Box 163
Halls, TN 38040
901-836-9057 or 800-748-9946
fax 901-836-9017
mapman@usit.net

The Old Map Gallery
Paul F. Mahoney
1746 Blake St.
Denver, CO 80202
303-296-7725 or fax 303-296-7936
oldmapgallery@denver.net

Overlee Farm Books
P.O. Box 1155
Stockbridge, MA 01262
413-637-2277

**Sue Grafton**
Glo's Books & Collectibles
Gloria Stobbes
906 Shadywood
Southlake, TX 76092
817-481-1438

Thomas Books
P.O. Box 14036
Phoenix, AZ 85063
602-247-9289 or fax 602-945-1023
sales@thomasbooks.com

**Grand Canyon & Colorado River**
Five Quail Books — West
P.O. Box 9870
Phoenix, AZ 85068-9870
602-861-0548
5quail@grandcanyonbooks.com

**The Great Lakes**
Artis Books
201 N Second Ave.
P.O. Box 822
Alpena, MI 49707
517-354-3401
artis@freeway.net

**Greece**
W.B. O'Neill-Old & Rare Books
11609 Hunters Green Ct.
Reston, VA 22091
703-860-0782 or fax 703-620-0153

**Zane Grey**
British Stamp Exchange
12 Fairlawn Ave.
N Weymouth, MA 02191
871-335-3075

**Health**
Warren's Collector Books
    For Sale Now
112 Royal Court
Friendship, TX 77546
281-482-7947

**Herbals**
The American Botanist Booksellers
P.O. Box 352
Chillicothe, IL 61523
309-274-5254

Brooks Books
P.O. Box 21473
Concord, CA 94521
510-672-4566 or fax 510-672-3338
brooksbk@interloc.com

**Heritage Press**
Lee & Mike Temares
50 Hts. Rd.
Plandome, NY 11030
516-627-8688 or fax 516-627-7822
tembooks@aol.com

**History**
*American & natural*
Ace Zerblonski Books
Malcolm McCollum, Proprietor
1419 North Royer
Colorado Springs, CO 80907
719-634-3941

*Science & medicine*
Amaranth Books
P.O. Box 421
Wilmette, IL 60091-0421
708-328-2939

*Especially US military, US Marine Corps
    & American Civil War*
Stan Clark Military Books
915 Fairview Ave.
Gettysburg, PA 17325
717-337-1728 or 717-337-0581
scmg@mail.wideopen.net

Camelot Books
Charles E. Wyatt
P.O. Box 2883
Vista, CA 92083
619-940-9472

*Early American & Indian*
Duck Creek Books
Jim & Shirley Richards
P.O. Box 203
Caldwell, OH 43724
614-732-4856 (10 am to 10 pm)

*Postal & postal artifacts*
McGowan Book Co.
P.O. Box 4226
Chapel Hill, NC 27515
919-968-1121 or fax 919-968-1644
mcgowanbooks@mindspring.com

*Local & regional*
Significant Books
3053 Madison Rd.
P.O. Box 9248
Cincinnati, OH 45209
513-321-7567

*General, Civil & Revolutionary Wars*
David R. Smith
30 Nelson Cir.
Jaffrey, NH 03452
603-532-8666
Bookinc@Cheshire.net

Twice Read Books & Comics
42 S Main St.
Chambersburg, PA 17201
717-261-8449

**Hollywood**
Cinemage Books
105 W 27th St.
New York, NY 10001
212-243-4919
irajoel@aol.com

**Horror**
The Book Baron
1236 S Magnolia Ave.
Anaheim, CA 92804
714-527-7022 or fax 714-527-5634
bkbaron1@pacbell.net or
bkbaron3@qte.net

Kai Nygaard
19421 Eighth Pl.
Escondido, CA 92029
619-746-9039

Pandora's Books, Ltd.
P.O. Box 54
Neche, ND 58265
204-324-8548 or fax 204-324-1628
jgthiess@MTS.Net

**Horse Books**
October Farm
2609 Branch Rd.
Raleigh, NC 27610
919-772-0482 or fax 919-779-6265
octoberfarm@bellsouth.net

**Horticulture**
The American Botanist Booksellers
P.O. Box 532
Chillicothe, IL 61523
309-274-5254

*Ornamental*
Brooks Books
P.O. Box 21473
Concord, CA 94521
510-672-4566 or fax 510-672-3338
brooksbk@interloc.com

Woodbridge B. Brown
P.O. Box 445
Turners Falls, MA 01376
413-772-2509 or 413-773-5710

**L. Ron Hubbard**
AL-PAC
Lamar Kelley Antiquarian Books
2625 E Southern Ave., C-120
Tempe, AZ 85282
602-831-3121 or fax 602-831-3193
alpac2625@aol.com

**Humanities**
*Reprint editions*
Dover Publications
Dept. A 214
E Second St.
Mineola, NY 11501

**Hunting**
Artis Books
201 N Second Ave.
P.O. Box 822
Alpena, MI 49707
517-354-3401
artis@freeway.net

Edison Hall Books
5 Ventnor Dr.
Edison, NJ 08820
908-548-4455

Jim Hodgson Books
908 S Manlius St.
Fayetteville, NY 13066
315-637-6264
jimhbooks@aol.com

Melvin Marcher, Bookseller
6204 N Vermont
Oklahoma City, OK 73112

Yesterday's Books
229 Riverview Dr.
Parchment, MI 49004
616-345-1011
yesbooks@aol.com

**Idaho**
Parnassus Books
218 N 9th St.
Boise, ID 83702

**Illustrated**
Noreen Abbot Books
2666 44th Ave.
San Francisco, CA 94116
415-664-9464

The American Dust Co.
47 Park Ct.
Staten Island, NY 10301
phone/fax 718-442-8253

Bowie & Co. Booksellers, Inc.
314 First Ave. S
Seattle, WA 98104
206-624-4100 or fax 206-223-0966
bowiebks@isomedia.com

Books of the Ages
Gary J. Overmann
Maple Ridge Manor
4764 Silverwood Dr.
Batavia, OH 45103-9740
phone/fax 513-732-3456
e-overman@ix.netcom.com

Bromer Booksellers
607 Boylston St.
Boston, MA 02116
617-247-2818 or fax 617-247-2975
books@bromer.com

George Robert Kane Fine Books
252 Third Ave.
Santa Cruz, CA 95062
phone/fax 408-426-4133
qkanebks@cruzio.com
*Old or new; many subjects*

Gary R. Smith
517 Laurel Ave.
Modesto, CA 95351

Barbara Smith Books
P.O. Box 1185
Northampton, MA 01061
413-586-1453

Randall House
Pia Oliver
835 Laguna St.
Santa Barbara, CA 93101
805-963-1909 or fax 805-963-1650
pia@piasworld.com

**Irvin S. Cobb**
*Always paying $3.00 each plus shipping.*
  *Send for immediate payment to:*
Bill Schroeder
5801 KY Dam Rd.
Paducah, KY 42003

**Indians**
*Wars*
K.C. & Jean Owings
Box 389
Whitman, MA 02382
781-447-7850 or fax 781-447-3435

*Plains, Black Hills, etc.*
Flo Silver Books
8442 Oakwood Ct. N
Indianapolis, IN 46260
phone/fax 317-255-5118
Flosilver@aol.com

**Iowa**
Karl M. Armens
740 Juniper Dr.
Iowa City, IA 52245

**Will James**
British Stamp Exchange
12 Fairlawn Ave.
N Weymouth, MA 02191
871-335-3075

**Jazz**
Chartwell Booksellers
55 E 52nd St.
New York, NY 10055
212-308-0643

**John Deere**
Henry Lindeman
4769 Bavarian Dr.
Jackson, MI 49201
517-764-5728

**Judaica**
Stanley Schwartz
1934 Pentuckett Ave.
San Diego, CA 92104-5732
619-232-5888 or fax 619-233-5833
Schwartz@cts.com

**Juvenile**
Cover to Cover
Mark Shuman
P.O. Box 687
Chapel Hill, NC 27514
919-967-1032

Edison Hall Books
5 Ventnor Dr.
Edison, NJ 08820
908-548-4455

Susan Heller, Pages for Sages
22611 Halburton Rd.
Beachwood, OH 44122-3939
216-283-2665
hellersu@cyberdrive.net

Page Books
Margaret E. Page
HRC 65, Box 233
Kingston, AR 72742
870-861-5831
pagebook@eritter.net

Jo Ann Reisler, Ltd.
360 Glyndon St., NE
Vienna, VA 22180
703-938-2967 or fax 703-938-9057
Reisler@Clark.net

Lee & Mike Temares
50 Hts. Rd.
Plandome, NY 11030
516-627-8688 or fax 516-627-7822
tembooks@aol.com

**John F. Kennedy**
British Stamp Exchange
12 Fairlawn Ave.
N Weymouth, MA 02191
871-335-3075

**Kentucky Authors**
Bill Schroeder
P.O. Box 3009
Paducah, KY 42002-3009

**Kentucky History**
Bill Schroeder
P.O. Box 3009
Paducah, KY 42002-3009

**King Arthur**
*Also early Britain*
Thorn Books
P.O. Box 1244
Moorpark, CA 93020
805-529-3647 or fax 805-529-0022
thornbooks@earthlink.net

**Stephen King**
Fostoria Trading Post
Amelia Painter
14 Hwy. Ave. SW
P.O. Box 28
Fostoria, IA 51340
712-262-5936
books@ncn.net

**Labor**
A\K\A Fine Used Books
4124 Brooklyn Ave. NE
Seattle, WA 98107

Volume I Books
One Union St.
Hillsdale, MI 49242
517-437-2228 or fax 517-437-7923
volume1Books@dmci.net

**Lakeside Classics**
Linda Holycross
109 N Sterling Ave.
Veedersburg, IN 47987
fax 765-793-2249

**Landscape Architecture**
The American Botanist Booksellers
P.O. Box 532
Chillicothe, IL 61523
309-274-5254

Brooks Books
P.O. Box 21473
Concord, CA 94521
510-672-4566 or fax 510-672-3338
brooksbk@interloc.com

**Latin American Literature**
Almark & Co.-Booksellers
P.O. Box 7
Thornhill, Ontario
Canada L3T 3N1
905-764-2665 or fax 905-764-5771
al@almarkco.com or
mark@almarkco.com

Flo Silver Books
8442 Oakwood Ct. N
Indianapolis, IN 46260
phone/fax 317-255-5118
Flosilver@aol.com

**Law & Crime**
Meyer Boswell Books, Inc.
2141 Mission St.
San Francisco, CA 94110
415-255-6400 or fax 415-255-6499
rarelaw@myerbos.com

**T.E. Lawrence**
Denis McDonnell, Bookseller
653 Park St.
Honesdale, PA 18431
717-253-6706 or fax 717-253-6786
dmd@ptd.net

**Lawrence of Arabia**
Denis McDonnell, Bookseller
653 Park St.
Honesdale, PA 18431
717-253-6706 or fax 717-253-6786
dmd@ptd.net

**Lebanon**
W.B. O'Neill-Old & Rare Books
11609 Hunters Green Ct.
Reston, VA 22091
703-860-0782 or fax 703-620-0153

**Lewis & Clark Expedition**
George H. Tweney
16660 Marine View Dr. SW
Seattle, WA 98166
206-243-8243

**Literature**
Amaranth Books
P.O. Box 421
Wilmette, IL 60091-0421
708-328-2939

*In translation*
Almark & Co.-Booksellers
P.O. Box 7
Thornhill, Ontario
Canada L3T 3N1
905-764-2665 or fax 905-764-5771
al@almarkco.com or
mark@almarkco.com

*First editions*
Karl M. Armens
740 Juniper Dr.
Iowa City, IA 52245

Bromer Booksellers
607 Boylston St.
Boston, MA 02116
617-247-2818 or fax 617-247-2975
books@bromer.com

*18th & 19th-C English*
The Book Collector
2347 University Blvd.
Houston, TX 77005
713-661-2665

*African-American*
Between the Covers
35 W Maple Ave.
Merchantville, NJ 08109
609-665-2284 or fax 609-665-3639
mail@betweenthecovers.com

The Captain's Bookshelf, Inc.
31 Page Ave.
Asheville, NC 22801
828-253-6631 or fax 828-253-4917
captsbooks@aol.com

Chapel Hill Rare Books
P.O. Box 456
Carrboro, NC 27510
919-929-8351

*Southern*
Elder's Book Store
2115 Elliston Pl.
Nashville, TN 37203
615-327-1867

*18th century*
Hartfield Rare Books
Ruth Inglehart
117 Dixboro Rd.
Ann Arbor, MI 48105
phone/fax 313-662-6035

Susan Heller, Pages for Sages
22611 Halburton Rd.
Beachwood, OH 44122-3939
216-283-2665
hellersu@cyberdrive.net

Ken Lopez, Bookseller
51 Huntington Rd.
Hadley, MA 01035
413-584-4827 or fax 413-584-2045
mail@lopezbooks.com

Mason's Bookstore, Rare Books
    & Record Albums East
115 S Main St.
Chambersburg, PA 17201
717-261-0541

Much Ado
Seven Pleasant St.
Marblehead, MA 01945
781-639-0400 or fax 781-639-0840
muchado@shore.net

*Also records and out-of-print comics*
Twice Read Books & Comics
42 S. Main St.
Chambersburg, PA 17201
717-261-8449

## Magazines
*Mystery only*
Grave Matters
P.O. Box 32192-08
Cincinnati, OH 45232
513-242-7527 or fax 513-242-5115
books@gravematters.com

Robert A. Madle
4406 Bestor Dr.
Rockville, MD 20853
301-460-4712

*Relating to decorative arts*
Mordida Books
P.O. Box 79322
Houston, TX 77279
713-467-4280 or fax 713-467-4182
mordida@swbell.net

Passaic Book Center
594 Main Ave.
Passaic, NJ 07055
201-778-6646 or fax 201-778-6738

## Manuscripts
Susan Heller, Pages for Sages
P.O. Box 2219
Beachwood, OH 44122-3939
216-283-2665
hellersu@cyberdrive.net

Heritage Book Shop, Inc.
8540 Melrose Ave.
Los Angeles, CA 90069
310-659-3674 or fax 310-659-4872
HBSINCL@aol.com

Key Books
P.O. Box 58097
St. Petersburg, FL 33715
813-867-2931

*Asiatic languages*
Worldwide Antiquarian
P.O. Box 410391
Cambridge, MA 02141-0004
617-876-6220 or fax 617-876-0839
mbalwan@aol.com

Randall House
Pia Oliver
835 Laguna St.
Santa Barbara, CA 93101
805-963-1909 or fax 805-963-1650
pia@piasworld.com

## Maps
*State, pocket-type, ca 1800s*
The Bookseller, Inc.
174 W Exchange St.
Akron, OH 44302
330-762-3101 or fax 330-762-4413
Booklein@Interloc.com
booklein@apk.com

Bowie & Co. Booksellers, Inc.
314 First Ave. S
Seattle, WA 98104
206-624-4100 or fax 206-223-0966
bowiebks@isomedia.com

Elegant Book & Map Company
815 Harrison Ave.
P.O. Box 1302
Cambridge, OH 43725
614-432-4068

## Maritime
*Including pirates, treasure, shipwrecks, the*
    *Caribbean, Cuba & Panama*
The Book Corner
Michael Tennero
728 W Lumsden Rd.
Brandon, FL 33511
813-684-1133
bookcrnr@worldnet.att.net

Book & Tackle Shop
29 Old Colony Rd.
P.O. Box 114
Chestnut Hill, MA 02467
phone/fax 617-965-0459 (winter)
phone/fax 401-596-0700 (summer)

Overlee Farm Books
P.O. Box 1155
Stockbridge, MA 01262
413-637-2277

J. Tuttle Maritime Books
1806 Laurel Crest
Madison, WI 53705
608-238-SAIL (7245)
fax 608-238-7249

## Martial Arts
Nutmeg Books
354 New Litchfield St. (Rte. 202)
Torrington, CT 06790
203-482-9696
nutmeg@compsol.net

## Masonic History
Mason's Bookstore, Rare Books
    & Record Albums East
115 S Main St.
Chambersburg, PA 17201
717-261-0541

## Mathematics
Significant Books
3053 Madison Rd.
P.O. Box 9248
Cincinnati, OH 45209
513-321-7567

## Cormac McCarthy
Alice Robbins, Bookseller
3002 Round Hill Rd.
Greensboro, NC 27408
910-282-1964

## Medicine
Amaranth Books
P.O. Box 421
Wilmette, IL 60091-0421
708-328-2939

*Antiquarian*
Book & Tackle
29 Old Colony Rd.
P.O. Box 114
Chestnut Hill, MA 02467
phone/fax 617-965-0459 (winter)
phone/fax 401-596-0700 (summer)

W. Bruce Fye
1607 N Wood Ave.
Marshfield, WI 54449-1298
715-384-8128 or fax 715-389-2990
byfe@tznet.com

*Procedures before 1915*
Ron Gibson, The Bookshop
110 Windsor Cir.
Burlington, IA 52601-1477
319-752-4588

Key Books
P.O. Box 58097
St. Petersburg, FL 33715
813-867-2931

M&S Rare Books, Inc.
P.O. Box 2594, E Side Station
Providence, RI 02906
401-421-1050 or fax 401-272-0831
(attention M & S)
dsiegel@msrarebooks.com

**Medieval**
Camelot Books
Charles E. Wyatt
P.O. Box 2883
Vista, CA 92083
619-940-9472

**Metaphysics**
AL-PAC
Lamar Kelley Antiquarian Books
2625 E Southern Ave., C-120
Tempe, AZ 85282
602-831-3121 or fax 602-831-3193
alpac2625@aol.com

**Meteorology**
Knollwood Books
Lee & Peggy Price
P.O. Box 197
Oregon, WI 53575-0197
608-835-8861 or fax 608-835-8421
books@tdsnet.com

**Mexico**
Flo Silver Books
8442 Oakwood Ct. N
Indianapolis, IN 46260
phone/fax 317-255-5118
Flosilver@aol.com

**Michigan**
Artis Books
201 N Second Ave.
P.O. Box 822
Alpena, MI 49707
517-354-3401
artis@freeway.net

Yesterday's Books
229 Riverview Dr.
Parchment, MI 49004
616-345-1011
yesbooks@aol.com

**Middle Eastern Countries**
Denis McDonnell, Bookseller
653 Park St.
Honesdale, PA 18431
717-253-6706 or fax 717-253-6786
dmd@ptd.net

**Levant countries: travel, archaeology,
    history; Byzantine studies**
Quest Books
Peter & Veronica Burridge
Harmer Hill
Millington
York YO42 1TX UK
Quesbks@aol.com

Worldwide Antiquarian
P.O. Box 410391
Cambridge, MA 02141-0004
617-876-6220 or fax 617-876-0839
mbalwan@aol.com

**Militaria**
The Bookseller, Inc.
174 W Exchange St.
Akron, OH 44302
330-762-3101 or fax 330-762-4413
Booklein@Interloc.com or
booklein@apk.com

Edison Hall Books
5 Ventnor Dr.
Edison, NJ 08820
908-548-4455

Rick Harmon
Military Books & Relics
910 Sullivan Dr.
Belvidere, IL 61008
815-547-7580

Robert L. Merriam
Rare, Used & Old Books
Newhall Rd.
Conway, MA 01341-9709
413-369-4052
rmerriam@interloc.com

Significant Books
3053 Madison Rd.
P.O Box 9248
Cincinnati, OH 45209
513-321-7567

*Histories Before 1900*
Tryon County Bookshop
2071 State Hwy. 29
Johnstown, NY 12905
518-762-1060

Volume I Books
One Union St.
Hillsdale, MI 49242
517-437-2228 or fax 517-437-7923
volume1Books@dmci.net

**Miniature Books**
Bromer Booksellers
607 Boylston St.
Boston, MA 02116
617-247-2818 or fax 617-247-2975
books@bromer.com

*Foreign atlases*
Murray Hudson
Antiquarian Books & Maps
109 S Church St.
P.O. Box 163
Halls, TN 38040
901-836-9057 or 800-748-9946
fax 901-836-9017
mapman@usit.net

Hurley Books/Celtic Cross Books
1753 Rt. 12
Westmoreland, NH 03467-4724
603-399-4342 or fax 603-399-8326
hurleybook@adam.cheshire.net

Gary R. Smith
517 Laurel Ave.
Modesto, CA 95351

**Movies**
Cinemage Books
105 W 27th St.
New York, NY 10001
212-243-4919
irajoel@aol.com

The American Dust Co.
47 Park Ct.
Staten Island, NY 10301
phone/fax 718-442-8253

**Mysteries**
Alcott Books
Barbara Ruppert
5909 Darnell
Houston, TX 77074-7719
713-774-2202
BRuppert@webtv.net

The American Dust Co.
47 Park Ct.
Staten Island, NY 10301
phone/fax 718-442-8253

Karl M. Armens
740 Juniper Dr.
Iowa City, IA 52245

*First editions*
Island Books
P.O. Box 19
Old Westbury, NY 11568
516-759-0233

McGee's First Varieties
330 Franklin Rd., Suite 135A-134
Brentwood, TN 37027
615-373-5318 or fax 615-661-4047
TMcGee@BellSouth.net

Mordida Books
P.O. Box 79322
Houston, TX 77279
713-467-4280 or fax 713-467-4182
mordida@swbell.net

*mail order; primarily first editions*
Norris Books
2491 San Ramon Vly. Blvd.
Suite #1-201
San Ramon, CA 94583
phone/fax 510-867-1218
norrisbooks@slip.net

Pandora's Books, Ltd.
P.O. Box 54
Neche, ND 48265
204-324-8548 or fax 204-324-1628
jgthiess@MTS.Net

RAC Books
P.O. Box 296 RD 2
Seven Valleys, PA 17360
717-428-3776
racbooks@cyberia.com

The Silver Door
P.O. Box 3208
Redondo Beach, CA 90277
310-379-6005

W.J. Leveridge
W & L Trading Company
2301 Carova Rd.
Carova Beach, Corolla, NC 27927
252-453-3408

**Napoleonic Memorabilia**
The Book Collector
2347 University Blvd.
Houston, TX 7005
713-661-2665

**Narcotics**
Nutmeg Books
354 New Litchfield St. (Rte. 202)
Torrington, CT 06790
203-482-9696
nutmeg@compsol.net

**Natural History**
Agave Books
P.O. Box 31495
Mesa, AZ 85275-1495
602-649-9097
agavebks@interloc.com

Thomas C. Bayer
85 Reading Ave.
Hillsdale, MI 49242
517-439-4134 or fax 517-439-5661
bayerbooks@dmci.net

Woodbridge B. Brown
P.O. Box 445
Turners Falls, MA 01376
413-772-2509 or 413-773-5710

Noriko I. Ciochon
Natural History Books
1025 Keokut St.
Iowa City, IA 52240
319-354-9088 or fax 319-354-0844
nathist@avalon.net

Melvin Marcher, Bookseller
6204 N Vermont
Oklahoma City, OK 73112

Snowy Egret Books
1237 Carroll Ave.
St. Paul, MN 55104
612-641-0917
snowy@mr.net

**Nautical**
Much Ado
Seven Pleasant St.
Marblehead, MA 01945
781-639-0400 or fax 781-639-0840
muchado@shore.net

Overlee Farm Books
P.O. Box 1155
Stockbridge, MA 01262
413-637-2277

**Needlework**
Galerie De Boicourt
251 E Merrill St.
Birmingham, MI 48009
248-723-5680

Stanley Schwartz
1934 Pentuckett Ave.
San Diego, CA 92104-5732
619-232-5888 or fax 619-233-5833
Schwartz@cts.com

**Neuroscience**
John Gach Books
5620 Waterloo Rd.
Columbia, MD 21045
410-465-9023 or fax 410-465-0649
inquiry@gach.com

**New England**
Book & Tackle
29 Old Colony Rd.
P.O. Box 114
Chestnut Hill, MA 02467
phone/fax 617-965-0459 (winter)
phone/fax 401-596-0700 (summer)

**Newspapers & Periodicals**
*Significant & unusual American*
Periodyssey
151 Crescent St.
Northampton, MA 01060
413-527-1900 or fax 413-527-1930
periodyssey@the-spa.com

Randall House
Pia Oliver
835 Laguna St.
Santa Barbara, CA 93101
805-963-1909 or fax 805-963-1650
pia@piasworld.com

Thorn Books
P.O. Box 1244
Moorpark, CA 93020
805-529-3647 or fax 805-529-0022
thornbooks@earthlink.net

Wellerdt's Books
3700 S Osprey Ave. #214
Sarasota, FL 34239
813-365-1318

Xanadu Records, Ltd.
3242 Irwin Ave.
Kingsbridge, NY 10463
212-549-3655

**Nonfiction**
Warren's Collector Books
    For Sale Now
112 Royal Court
Friendship, TX 77546
281-482-7947

**Novels**
The Silver Door
P.O. Box 3208
Redondo Beach, CA 90277
310-379-6005

**Occult & Mystics**
AL-PAC
Lamar Kelley Antiquarian Books
2625 E Southern Ave., C-120
Tempe, AZ 85282
602-831-3121 or fax 602-831-3193
alpac2625@aol.com

British Stamp Exchange
12 Fairlawn Ave.
N Weymouth, MA 02191
871-335-3075

**Ohio**
The Bookseller, Inc.
174 W Exchange St.
Akron, OH 44302
330-762-3101 or fax 330-762-4413
Booklein@Interloc.com or
booklein@apk.com

**Omar Khayyam**
Worldwide Antiquarian
P.O. Box 410391
Cambridge, MA 02141-0004
617-876-6220 or fax 617-876-0839
mbalwan@aol.com

**Oriental Books & Art**
Ruth Woods Oriental Books
266 Arch Rd.
Englewood, NJ 07631
201-567-0149 or fax 201-567-1419

**Original Art**
*By children's illustrators*
Kendra Krienke
230 Central Park W
New York, NY 10024
201-930-9709 or 201-930-9765

**Paperbacks**
Michael Gerlicher
1375 Rest Point Rd.
Orono, MN 55364

Bernard E. Goodman, Bookseller
7421 SW 147 Ct.
Miami, FL 33193
305-385-8526
BCBooks@bellsouth.net

*Vintage*
Grave Matters
P.O. Box 32192
Cincinnati, OH 45232
513-242-7527 or fax 513-242-5115
books@gravematters.com

*Also pulp magazines*
Modern Age Books
P.O. Box 325
E Lansing, MI 48826
517-487-9313

*Originals*
Mordida Books
P.O. Box 79322
Houston, TX 77279
713-467-4280 or fax 713-467-4182
mordida@swbell.net

Olde Current Books
Daniel P. Shay
356 Putnam Ave.
Ormond Beach, FL 32174
904-672-8998
peakmyster@aol.com

Pandora's Books, Ltd.
P.O. Box 54
Neche, ND 58265
204-324-8548 or fax 204-324-1628
jgthiess@MTS.Net

*Also trades; want lists welcomed*
Roger Reus
9412 Huron Ave.
Richmond, VA 23294
Mail order only

Tom Rolls
230 S Oakland Ave.
Indianapolis, IN 46201

Andrew Zimmerli
5001 General Branch Ct.
Sharpsburg, MD 21781
301-432-7476

**Robert B. Parker**
Thomas Books
P.O. Box 14036
Phoenix, AZ 85063
602-247-9289 or fax 602-945-1023
sales@thomasbooks.com

**Pennsylvania**
Mason's Bookstore, Rare Books
　& Record Albums East
115 S Main
Chambersburg, PA 17201
717-261-0541

**Performing Arts**
Bowie & Co. Booksellers, Inc.
314 First Ave. S
Seattle, WA 98104
206-624-4100

**Philosophy**
John Gach Books
5620 Waterloo Rd.
Columbia, MD 21045
410-465-9023 or fax 410-465-0649
inquiry@gach.com

**Photography**
The Captain's Bookshelf, Inc.
31 Page Ave.
Asheville, NC 28801
828-253-6631 or fax 828-253-4917
captsbooks@aol.com

Significant Books
3053 Madison Rd.
P.O. Box 9248
Cincinnati, OH 45209
513-321-7567

*19th-C Middle & Far East Countries*
Worldwide Antiquarian
P.O. Box 410391
Cambridge, MA 02141-0004
617-876-6220 or fax 617-876-0839
mbalwan@aol.com

Xanadu Records Ltd.
3242 Irwin Ave.
Kingsbridge, NY 10463
718-549-3655

**Playing Cards**
Bill & Mimi Sachen
927 Grand Ave.
Waukegan, IL 60085
847-662-7204
FutileWill@aol.com

**Poetry**
The American Dust Co.
47 Park Ct.
Staten Island, NY 10301
phone/fax 718-442-8253

Edison Hall Books
5 Ventnor Dr.
Edison, NJ 08820
908-548-4455

Ed Smith Books
20 Paget Rd.
Madison, WI 53704-5929
608-241-3707 or fax 608-241-3459
ed@edsbooks.com

David R. Smith
30 Nelson Cir.
Jaffrey, NH 03452
603-532-8666
Bookinc@Cheshire.net

VERSEtility Books
P.O. Box 1133
Farmington, CT 06034-1133
860-677-0606
versebks@tiac.net

**Polar Explorations & Ephemera**
Alaskan Heritage Bookshop
174 S Franklin, P.O. 22165
Juneau, AK 99802

Parmer Books
7644 Forrestal Rd.
San Diego, CA 92120-2203
619-287-0693 or fax 619-287-6135
ParmerBook@aol.com

**Political**
Realm of Colorado
P.O. Box 24
Parker, CO 80134

*Radical*
Volume I Books
One Union St.
Hillsdale, MI 49242
517-437-2228 or fax 517-437-7923
volume1Books@dmci.net

**Postcards**
Book & Tackle Shop
29 Old Colony Rd.
P.O. Box 114
Chestnut Hill, MA 02467
phone/fax 617-965-0459 (winter)
phone/fax 401-596-0700 (summer)

**Posters**
The Mulberry Cat
Yvonne Davis
Jan Davis Martel
P.O. Box 3573
Boone, NC 28607
704-963-7693

**Pre-Colombian Art**
Flo Silver Books
8442 Oakwood Ct. N
Indianapolis, IN 46260
phone/fax 317-255-5118
Flosilver@aol.com

**Press Books**
Heritage Book Shop, Inc.
8540 Melrose Ave.
Los Angeles, CA 90069
310-659-3674 or fax 310-659-4872
HBSINCLA@aol.com

Randall House
Pia Oliver
835 Laguna St.
Santa Barbara, CA 93101
805-963-1909 or fax 805-963-1650
pia@piasworld.com

**Prints**
The Mulberry Cat
Yvonne Davis
Jan Davis Martel
P.O. Box 3573
Boone, NC 28607
704-963-7693

**Private Presses**
First Folio
1206 Brentwood
Paris, TN 34842
phone/fax 901-644-9940
firstfol@aeneas.net

Susan Heller, Pages for Sages
22611 Halburton Rd.
Beachwood, OH 44122-3939
216-283-2665
hellersu@cyberdrive.net

**Promoters of Paper, Ephemera &
　Book Fairs**
Kingsbury Productions
Katherine and David Kreider
4555 N Pershing Ave., Suite 33-138
Stockton, CA 95207
209-467-8438

**Psychedelia**
Nutmeg Books
354 New Litchfield St. (Rte. 202)
Torrington, CT 06790
203-482-9696
nutmeg@compsol.net

**Psychiatry**
John Gach Books
5620 Waterloo Rd.
Columbia, MD 21045
410-465-9023 or fax 410-465-0649
inquiry@gach.com

**Psychoanalysis**
*Also related subjects*
John Gach Books
5620 Waterloo Rd.
Columbia, MD 21045
410-465-9023 or fax 410-465-0649
inquiry@gach.com

## Psychology
John Gach Books
5620 Waterloo Rd.
Columbia, MD 21045
410-465-9023 or fax 410-465-0649
inquiry@gach.com

The King's Market Bookshops
P.O. Box 709
Boulder, CO 80306-0709
303-232-3321

## Pulps
*Science fiction & fantasy before 1945*
Robert A. Madle
4406 Bestor Dr.
Rockville, MD 20853
301-460-4712

## Quaker
Vintage Books
181 Hayden Rowe St.
Hopkinton, MA 01748
508-435-3499
vintage@gis.net

*Also Shakers, Christians & Collectivists*
Duck Creek Books
Jim & Shirley Richards
P.O. Box 203
Caldwell, OH 43724
614-732-4856 (10 am to 10 pm)

## Quilt Books
Bill Schroeder
P.O. Box 3009
Paducah, KY 42002-3009

Galerie De Boicourt
251 E Merrill St.
Birmingham, MI 48009
248-723-5680

## R.R. Donnelley Christmas Books
Linda Holycross
109 N Sterling Ave.
Veedersburg, IN 47987
fax 765-793-2249

## Arthur Rackham
Books of the Ages
Gary J. Overmann
Maple Ridge Manor
4764 Silverwood Dr.
Batavia, OH 45103-9740
phone/fax 513-732-3456
e-overman@ix.netcom.com

## Railroading
Mason's Bookstore, Rare Books
   & Record Albums
115 S Main St.
Chambersburg, PA 17201
717-261-0541

## Rare & Unusual Books
Chapel Hill Rare Books
P.O. Box 456
Carrboro, NC 27510
919-929-8351 or fax 929-967-2532
rarebooks@mindspring.com

First Folio
1206 Brentwood
Paris, TN 38242
phone/fax 901-644-9940
firstfol@aeneas.net

Susan Heller, Pages for Sages
22611 Halburton Rd.
Beachwood, OH 44122-3939
216-283-2665
hellersu@cyberdrive.net

Kenneth Karmiole, Bookseller, Inc.
509 Wilshire Blvd.
Santa Monica, CA 94001
310-451-4342 or 310-458-5930
karmbooks@aol.com

*Reprint editions*
Dover Publications
Dept. A 214
E Second St.
Mineola, NY 11501

Terry Harper, Bookseller
P.O. Box 312
Vergennes, VT 05491-0312
802-877-9262
bookvend@together.net

Heritage Book Shop, Inc.
8540 Melrose Ave.
Los Angeles, CA 90069
310-659-3674 or fax 310-659-4872
HBSINCLA@aol.com

M & S Rare Books, Inc.
P.O. Box 2594, E Side Station
Providence, RI 02906
401-421-1050 or fax 401-272-0831
(attention M & S)
dsiegel@msrarebooks.com

MacDonnell Rare Books
Kevin MacDonnell
9307 Glenlake Dr.
Austin, TX 78730
512-345-4139
macbooks@interloc.com

Paul Melzer Fine Books
12 E Vine St.
P.O. Box 1143
Redlands, CA 92373
909-792-7299 or fax 909-793-7218
pmbooks@eee.org

The Old London Bookshop
Michael & Marlys Schon
P.O. Box 922
Bellingham, WA 98227-0922
360-733-7273 or fax 360-647-8946
OldLondon@aol.com

Richard C. Ramer
Old & Rare Books
225 E 70th St.
New York, NY 10021
212-737-0222 or 212-737-0223
fax 212-288-4169
5222386@mcimail.com

Revere Books
P.O. Box 420
Revere, PA 18953
610-847-2709 or fax 610-847-1910

Leona Rostenberg
   & Madeleine Stern
Rare Books
40 E 88th St.
NY, NY 10128
212-831-6628 or fax 212-831-1961

Thorn Books
P.O. Box 1244
Moorpark, CA 93020
805-529-3647 or fax 805-529-0022
thornbooks@earthlink.net

## Reference
About Books
6 Sand Hill Ct.
P.O. Box 5717
Parsippany, NY 07054
973-515-4591

## Religion
Books Now & Then
Dennis & Jan Patrick
P.O. Box 337
Stanley, ND 58784
phone/fax 701-628-2084
bnt@stanley.ndak.net

Chimney Sweep Books
419 Cedar St.
Santa Cruz, CA 94060-4304
phone/fax 408-458-1044
chimney@cruzio.com

David R. Smith
30 Nelson Cir.
Jaffrey, NH 03452
603-532-8666
Bookinc@Cheshire.net

## Reptiles
Mason's Bookstore, Rare Books
   & Record Albums East
115 S Main St.
Chambersburg, PA 17201
717-261-0541

## Revolutionary War
K.C. & Jean Owings
Box 389
Whitman, MA 02382
781-447-7850 or fax 781-447-3435

## Scholarly Books
*Reprint editions*
Dover Publications
Dept. A 214
E Second St.
Mineola, NY 11501

## Science & Technology
Thomas C. Bayer
85 Reading Ave.
Hillsdale, MI 49242
517-439-4134 or fax 517-439-5661
bayerbooks@dmci.net

Book & Tackle Shop
29 Old Colony Rd.
P.O. Box 114
Chestnut Hill, MA 02467
phone/fax 617-965-0459 (winter)
phone/fax 401-596-0700 (summer)

Thomas L. Coffman, Bookseller
TLC Books
9 N College Ave.
Salem, VA 24153
540-389-3555

Key Books
P.O. Box 58097
St. Petersburg, FL 33715
813-867-2931

M & S Rare Books, Inc.
P.O. Box 2594, E Side Station
Providence, RI 02906
401-272-0831 or fax 401-272-0831
(attention M & S)
dsiegel@msrarebooks.com

## Science Fiction
AL-PAC
Lamar Kelley Antiquarian Books
2625 E Southern Ave., C-120
Tempe, AZ 85282
602-831-3121 or fax 602-831-3193
alpac2625@aol.com

*Also Fantasy*
Ackley Books & Collectibles
Bryant & Suzanne Pitner
912 Hidden Cove Way
Suisun City, CA 94585-3511
707-421-9032
abcbooks@webcom.com
(mail order only)

The American Dust Co.
47 Park Ct.
Staten Island, NY 10301
phone/fax 718-442-8253

Karl M. Armens
740 Juniper Dr.
Iowa City, IA 52245

Bernard E. Goodman, Bookseller
7421 SW 147 Ct.
Miami, FL 33193
305-385-8526
BCBooks@bellsouth.net

*First editions*
Island Books
P.O. Box 19
Old Westbury, NY 11568
516-759-0233

*Horror & Occult*
Bob Lakin Books
P.O. Box 186
Chatfield, TX 75105
972-247-3291

Robert A. Madle
4406 Bestor Dr.
Rockville, MD 20853
301-460-4712

McGee's First Varieties
330 Franklin Rd., Suite 135A-134
Brentwood, TN 37027
615-373-5318 or fax 615-661-4047
TMcGee@BellSouth.net

*Also fantasy*
Kai Nygaard
19421 Eighth Pl.
Escondido, CA 92029
619-746-9039

Pandora's Books, Ltd.
P.O. Box 54
Neche, ND 58265
204-324-8548 or fax 204-324-1628
jgthiess@MTS.Net

*Also fantasy*
Xanadu Records, Ltd.
3242 Irwin Ave.
Kingsbridge, NY 10463
212-549-3655

## Sciences
Cover to Cover
P.O. Box 687
Chapel Hill, NC 27514

*Reprint editions*
Dover Publications
E Second St.
Mineola, NY 11501

Significant Books
P.O. Box 9248
3053 Madison Rd.
Cincinnati, OH 45209
513-321-7567

## Series Books
Glo's Children's Series Books
Gloria Stobbes
906 Shadywood
Southlake, TX 76092
817-481-1438

## Set Editions
AL-PAC
Lamar Kelley Antiquarian Books
2625 E Southern Ave., C-120
Tempe, AZ 85282
602-831-3121 or fax 602-831-3193
alpac2625@aol.com

Bowie & Weatherford, Inc.
314 First Ave. S
Seattle, WA 98104
206-624-4100

## Sherlockiana
The Silver Door
P.O. Box 3208
Redondo Beach, CA 90277
310-379-6005

## Ships & Sea
Book & Tackle Shop
29 Old Colony Rd.
P.O. Box 114
Chestnut Hill, MA 02467
phone/fax 617-965-0459 (winter)
phone/fax 401-596-0700 (summer)

Parmer Books
7644 Forrestal Rd.
San Diego, CA 92120-2203
619-287-0693 or fax 619-287-6135
ParmerBook@aol.com

J. Tuttle Maritme Books
1806 Laurel Crest
Madison, WI 53705
608-238-SAIL (7245)
fax 608-238-7249

## Signed Editions
Chapel Hill Rare Books
P.O. Box 456
Carrboro, NC 27510
919-929-8351

## Dan Simmons
Thomas Books
P.O. Box 14036
Phoenix, AZ 85063
602-247-9289 or fax 602-945-1023
sales@thomasbooks.com

## Socialism
Volume I Books
One Union St.
Hillsdale, MI 49242
517-437-2228 or fax 517-437-7923
volume1Books@dmci.net

## South America
Flo Silver Books
8442 Oakwood Ct. N
Indianapolis, IN 46260
phone/fax 317-255-5118
Flosilver@aol.com

## South Dakota
*Also any pre-1970 Western-related books*
James F. Taylor
515 Sixth St.
Rapid City, SD 57701
605-341-3224

## Space Exploration
Knollwood Books
Lee & Peggy Price
P.O. Box 197
Oregon, WI 53575-0197
608-835-8861 or fax 608-835-8421
books@tdsnet.com

## Speciality Publishers
*Arkham House, Gnome, Fantasy, etc.*
Robert A. Madle
4406 Bestor Dr.
Rockville, MD 20853
301-460-4712

## Sports
*Baseball or boxing*
Ace Zerblonski Books
Malcolm McCollum, Proprietor
1419 North Royer
Colorado Springs, CO 80907
719-634-3941

Adelson Sports
13610 N Scottsdale Rd. #10
Scottsdale, AZ 85254
602-596-1913 or fax 602-598-1914

Thomas L. Coffman, Bookseller
TLC Books
9 N College Ave.
Salem, VA 24153
540-389-3555

*Rare & out-of-print baseball; general*
R. Plapinger, Baseball Books
P.O. Box 1062
Ashland, OR 97520
541-488-1220

Randall House
Pia Oliver
835 Laguna St.
Santa Barbara, CA 93101
805-963-1909 or fax 805-963-1650
pia@piasworld.com

## Statue of Liberty
Mike Brooks
7335 Skyline
Oakland, CA 94611

## Surveying
*Also tools, instruments & ephemera*
David & Nancy Garcelon
10 Hastings Ave.
Millbury, MA 01527-4314
508-754-2667

## Technology
Thomas C. Bayer
85 Reading Ave.
Hillsdale, MI 49242
517-439-4134 or fax 517-439-5661
bayerbooks@dmci.net

Cover to Cover
P.O. Box 687
Chapel Hill, NC 27514

Significant Books
3053 Madison Rd.
P.O. Box 9248
Cincinnati, OH 45209
513-321-7567

## Tennessee History
Elder's Book Store
2115 Elliston Pl.
Nashville, TN 37203
615-327-1867

## Texana Fiction & Authors
Alcott Books
Barbara Ruppert
5909 Darnell
Houston, TX 77074-7719
713-774-2202
BRuppert@webtv.net

Bob Lakin Books
P.O. Box 186
Chatfield, TX 75105
972-247-3291

## Textiles
Galerie De Boicourt
251 E Merrill St.
Birmingham, MI 48009
248-723-5680

Stanley Schwartz
1934 Pentuckett Ave.
San Diego, CA 92104-5732
619-232-5888 or fax 619-233-5833
Schwartz@cts.com

## Theology
Books Now & Then
Dennis & Jan Patrick
P.O. Box 337
Stanley, ND 58784
phone/fax 701-628-2084
bnt@stanley.ndak.net

Chimney Sweep Books
419 Cedar St.
Santa Cruz, CA 94060-4304
phone/fax 408-458-1044
chimney@cruzio.com

Hurley Books/Celtic Cross Books
1753 Rt. 12
Westmoreland, NH 03467-4724
603-399-4342 or fax 603-399-8326
hurleybook@adam.cheshire.net

## Trade Catalogs
Eastside Books & Paper
P.O. Box 1581, Gracie Station
New York, NY 10028-0013
212-759-6299

## Trades & Crafts
*19th Century*
Cover to Cover
P.O. Box 687
Chapel Hill, NC 27514

Hillcrest Books
961 Deep Draw Rd.
Crossville, TN 38555-9547
phone/fax 615-484-7680

## Travel
*19th-century travel & adventure*
The Book Corner
Michael Tennero
728 W Lumsden Rd.
Brandon, FL 33511
813-684-1133
bookcrnr@worldnet.att.net

*Also exploration*
Duck Creek Books
Jim & Shirley Richards
P.O. Box 203
Caldwell, OH 43724
614-732-4856 (10 am to 10 pm)

Terry Harper, Bookseller
P.O. Box 312
Vergennes, VT 05491-0312
802-877-9262
bookvend@together.net

Heritage Book Shop, Inc.
8540 Melrose Ave.
Los Angeles, CA 90069
310-659-3674 or fax 310-659-4872
HBSINCLA@aol.com

Jim Hodgson Books
908 S Manlius St.
Fayetteville, NY 13066
315-637-6264
jimhbooks@aol.com

Flo Silver Books
8442 Oakwood Ct. N
Indianapolis, IN 46260
phone/fax 317-255-5118
Flosilver@aol.com

## Tasha Tudor
Books of the Ages
Gary J. Overmann
Maple Ridge Manor
4764 Silverwood Dr.
Batavia, OH 45103-9740
phone/fax 513-732-3456
e-overman@ix.netcom.com

## Turkey
W.B. O'Neill-Old & Rare Books
11609 Hunters Green Ct.
Reston, VA 22091
703-860-0782 or fax 703-620-0153

## UFO
AL-PAC
Lamar Kelley Antiquarian Books
2625 E Southern Ave., C-120
Tempe, AZ 85282
602-831-3121 or fax 602-831-3193
alpac2625@aol.com

## Vargas
Parnassus Books
218 N 9th St.
Boise, ID 83702

## Vietnam War
A\K\A Fine Used Books
4124 Brooklyn Ave. NE
Seattle, WA 98107
206-632-5870

Thomas L. Coffman, Bookseller
TLC Books
9 N College Ave.
Salem, VA 24153
540-389-3555

Rick Harmon
Military Books & Relics
910 Sullivan Dr.
Belvidere, IL 61008
815-547-7580

**Voyages, Exploration & Travel**
Chapel Hill Rare Books
P.O. Box 456
Carrboro, NC 27510
919-929-8351

Terry Harper, Bookseller
P.O. Box 312
Vergennes, VT 05491-0312
802-877-9262
bookvend@together.net

Heritage Book Shop, Inc.
8540 Melrose Ave.
Los Angeles, CA 90069
310-659-3674 or fax 310-659-4872
HBSINCLA@aol.com

Jim Hodgson Books
908 S Manlius St.
Fayetteville, NY 13066
315-637-6264
jimhbooks@aol.com

Key Books
P.O. Box 58097
St. Petersburg, FL 33715
813-867-2931

Overlee Farm Books
P.O. Box 1155
Stockbridge, MA 01262
413-627-2277

George H. Tweney
16660 Marine View Dr. SW
Seattle, WA 98166
206-243-8243

**Weapons**
*All edged types*
Knife Readables
115 Longfellow Blvd.
Lakeland, FL 33810
813-666-1133

**Western Americana**
Bowie & Co. Booksellers, Inc.
314 First Ave. S
Seattle, WA 98104
206-624-4100

Dawson's Book Shop
535 N Larchmont Blvd.
Los Angeles, CA 90004
213-469-2186 or fax 213-469-9553
dawsonbk@ix.netcom.com

Terry Harper, Bookseller
P.O. Box 312
Vergennes, VT 05491-0312
802-877-9262
bookvend@together.net

*Rare & historical ephemera*
Jordon Gallery
1349 Sheridan Ave.
Cody, WY 82414
307-587-6689 or fax 307-527-4944

K.C. & Jean Owings
Box 389
Whitman, MA 02382
781-447-7850 or fax 781-447-3435

Thorn Books
P.O. Box 1244
Moorpark, CA 93020
805-529-3647 or fax 805-529-0022
thornbooks@earthlink.net

George H. Tweney
16660 Marine View Dr. SW
Seattle, WA 98166
206-243-8243

*Nonfiction 19th-C outlaws, lawmen, etc.*
The Early West/Whodunit Books
P.O. Box 9292
College Sta., TX 77842
409-775-6047 or fax 409-764-7758
EarlyWest@aol.com

**Wine**
Second Harvest Books
Warren R. Johnson
P.O. Box 3306
Florence, OR 97439
phone/fax 541-902-0215
2harvest@presys.com

Warren's Collector Books
    For Sale Now
112 Royal Ct.
Friendswood, TX 77546
281-482-7947

**Women Authors**
Alice Robbins, Bookseller
3002 Round Hill Rd.
Greensboro, NC 27408
910-282-1964

**Women's History**
*Also related areas of everyday life*
An Uncommon Vision
1425 Greywall Ln.
Wynnewood, PA 19096-3811
610-658-0953 or fax 610-658-0961
Uncommvisn@aol.com

Volume I Books
One Union St.
Hillsdale, MI 49242
517-437-2228 or fax 517-437-7923
volume1Books@dmci.net

**World War I**
Denis McDonnell, Bookseller
653 Park St.
Honesdale, PA 18431
717-253-6706 or fax 717-253-6786
dmd@ptd.net

**World War II**
Cover to Cover
P.O. Box 687
Chapel Hill, NC 27514

# BOOKSELLERS

This section of the book lists names and addresses of used book dealers who have contributed the retail listings contained in this edition of *Huxford's Old Book Value Guide*. The code (A1, S7, etc.) located before the price in our listings refers to the dealer offering that particular book for sale. (When more than one dealer has the same book listing codes are given alphabetically before the price.) Given below are the dealer names and their codes.

Many book dealers issue printed catalogs, list catalogs on the internet, have open shops, are mail order only, or may be a combination of these forms of business. When seeking a book from a particular dealer, it would be best to first write (enclose SASE), e-mail, or call to see what type of business is operated (open shop or mail order).

**A1**
A-Book-A-Brac Shop
6760 Collins Ave.
Miami Beach, FL 33141
305-865-0092

**A2**
Aard Books
31 Russell Ave.
Troy, NH 03465
603-242-3638
aardbooks@cheshire.net

**A3**
Noreen Abbot Books
2666 44th Ave.
San Francisco, CA 94116-2635
415-664-9464

**A4**
About Books
6 Sand Hill Ct.
P.O. Box 5717
Parsippany, NJ 07054
973-515-4591

**A5**
Adelson Sports
13610 N Scottsdale Rd. #10
Scottsdale, AZ 85254
602-596-1913 or fax 602-596-1914

**A6**
Ads Autographs
P.O. Box 8006
Webster, NY 14580-8006
716-671-2651 or fax 716-671-5727

**A7**
Avonlea Books Search Service
P.O. Box 74, Main Station
White Plains, NY 10602-0074
914-946-5923 or fax 914-761-3119
avonlea@bushkin.com

**A8**
AL-PAC
Lamar Kelley Antiquarian Books
2625 E Southern Ave., C-120
Tempe, AZ 85282
602-831-3121 or fax 602-831-3193
alpac2625@aol.com

**A9**
Amaranth Books
P.O. Box 421
Wilmette, IL 60091-0421
708-328-2939

**A10**
The American Botanist
P.O. Box 532
Chillicothe, IL 61523
309-274-5254

**A11**
The American Dust Co.
47 Park Ct.
Staten Island, NY 10301
phone/fax 718-442-8253

**A13**
Antiquarian Medical Books
W. Bruce Fye
1607 N Wood Ave.
Marshfield, WI 54449-1298
715-384-8128 or fax 715-389-2990
bfye@tznet.com

**A14**
Almark & Co.-Booksellers
P.O. Box 7
Thornhill, Ontario
Canada L3T 3N1
905-764-2665 or fax 905-764-5771
al@almarkco.com or
mark@almarkco.com

**A15**
Karl M. Armens
740 Juniper Dr.
Iowa City, IA 52245
319-337-7755

**A16**
Arnold's of Michigan
Judith A. Herba
218 S Water St.
Marine City, MI 48039
810-765-1350 or fax 810-765-7914
800-276-3092
arnodlbk@ees.eesc.com

**A17**
Artis Books
201 N Second Ave.
P.O. Box 822
Alpena, MI 49707-0822
517-354-3401
artis@freeway.net

**A18**
Authors of the West
191 Dogwood Dr.
Dundee, OR 97115
503-538-8132
Lnash@georgefox.edu

**A19**
Aplan Antiques & Art
James & Peg Aplan
21424 Clover Pl.
Piedmont, SD 57769-9403
605-347-5016
alpanpeg@rapidnet.com

**A20**
Ace Zerblonski Books
Malcolm McCollum, Proprietor
1419 North Royer
Colorado Springs, CO 80907
719-634-3941

**A21**
Artiques Ltd.
Veronica Jochens
P.O. Box 67
Lonedell, MO 60360
phone/fax 314-629-1374
veronica@nightowl.net

**A22**
Agave Books
P.O. Box 31495
Mesa, AZ 85275-1495
602-649-9097
agavebks@interloc.com

**A23**
Alcott Books
5909 Darnell
Houston, TX 77074-7719
713-774-2202
BRuppert@webtv.net or
bruppert@worldnet.att.net

**A24**
A Tale of Two Sisters
2509 Stone Hollow Dr.
Bedford, TX 76021
fax 817-540-2204
sistwo@flash.net

**A25**
An Uncommon Vision
1425 Greywall Ln.
Wynnewood, PA 19096-3811
610-658-0953 or fax 610-658-0961
Uncommvisn@aol.com

**A26**
David Armstrong, Bookseller
Box 551
Lethbridge, Alberta
Canada T1J 3Z4
403-381-3270
dabooks@telusplanet.net

**A27**
Aslan Books
191 Dogwood Dr.
Dundee, OR 97115
503-538-8132
Lnash@georgefox.edu

**A28**
Ackley Books & Collectibles
Bryant & Suzanne Pitner
912 Hidden Cove Way
Suisun City, CA 94585-3511
phone/fax 707-421-9032
abcbooks@webcom.com
(mail order only)

**B1**
Thomas C. Bayer
85 Reading Ave.
Hillsdale, MI 49242-1941
517-439-4134 or fax 517-439-5661
bayerbooks@dmci.net

**B2**
Beasley Books
Paul & Beth Garon
1533 W Oakdale, 2nd Floor
Chicago, IL 60657
312-472-4528 or fax 312-472-7857
beasley@mcs.com

**B3**
Bela Luna Books
P.O. Box 260425
Highlands Ranch, CO 80163-0425
800-497-4717 or fax 303-791-7342
Bellalun@aol.com

**B4**
Between the Covers
35 W Maple Ave.
Merchantville, NJ 08109
609-665-2284 or fax 609-665-3639
mail@betweenthecovers.com

**B5**
Bicentennial Book Shop
820 S Westnedge Ave.
Kalamazoo, MI 49008
616-345-5987
ztkh10a@prodigy.com

**B6**
Bibliography of the Dog
The New House
216 Covey Hill Rd.
Havelock, Quebec
Canada J0S 2C0
514-827-2717 or fax 514-827-2091

**B7**
Best-Read Books
122 State St.
Sedro-Woolley, WA 98284
206-855-2179

**B9**
The Book Baron
1236 S Magnolia Ave.
Anaheim, CA 92804
714-527-7022 or fax 714-527-5634
bkbaron1@pacbell.net or
bkbaron3@qte.net

**B10**
Book Broker
114 Bollingwood Rd.
Charlottesville, VA 22902
804-296-2194 or fax 804-296-1566
bookbrk@cfw.com
mail order or appointment only

**B11**
The Book Corner
Michael Tennero
728 W Lumsden Rd.
Brandon, FL 33511
813-684-1133
bookcrnr@worldnet.att.net

**B14**
Book & Tackle Shop
Bernard L. Gordon
29 Old Colony Rd.
P.O. Box 114
Chestnut Hill, MA 02467
phone/fax 617-965-0459 (winter)
phone/fax 401-596-0700 (summer)

**B15**
Book Treasures
P.O. Box 121
E Norwich, NY 11732

**B16**
The Book Den South
Nancy Costello
2249 First St.
Ft. Myers, FL 33901
813-332-2333

**B17**
Books of the Ages
Gary J. Overmann
Maple Ridge Manor
4764 Silverwood Dr.
Batavia, OH 45103-9740
phone/fax 513-732-3456
e-overman@ix.netcom.com

**B18**
The Bookseller, Inc.
174 W Exchange St.
Akron, OH 44302
330-762-3101 or fax 330-762-4413
Booklein@Interloc.com or
booklein@apk.net

**B19**
Books West Southwest
W. David Laird
Box 6149, University Station
Irvine, CA 92616-6149
714-509-7670 or fax 714-854-5102
wdlbks@home.com

**B20**
Bowie & Co. Booksellers, Inc.
314 First Ave. S
Seattle, WA 98104
206-624-4100 or fax 206-223-0966
bowiebks@isomedia.com

**B22**
Bridgman Books
906 Roosevelt Ave.
Rome, NY 13440
315-337-7252

**B23**
British Stamp Exchange
12 Fairlawn Ave.
N Weymouth, MA 02191
871-335-3075

**B24**
Bromer Booksellers
607 Boylston St.
Boston, MA 02116
617-247-2818 or fax 617-247-2975

**B25**
Mike Brooks
7335 Skyline
Oakland, CA 94611

**B26**
Brooks Books
Phil & Marty Nesty
1343 New Hampshire Dr.
P.O. Box 21473
Concord, CA 94521
510-672-4566 or fax 510-672-3338
brooksbk@interloc.com

**B27**
The Bookstall
570 Sutter St.
San Francisco, CA 94102
fax 415-362-1503
bstallsf@best.com

**B28**
Woodbridge B. Brown
312 Main St.
P.O. Box 445
Turner Falls, MA 01376
413-772-2509 or 413-773-5710

**B29**
Books Now & Then
Dennis & Jan Patrick
P.O. Box 337
Stanley, ND 58784
phone/fax 701-628-2084
bnt@stanley.ndak.net

**B30**
Burke's Bookstore
1719 Poplar Ave.
Memphis, TN 38104-6447
901-278-7484 or fax 901-272-2340
burkes@netten.net

**B35**
Brillance Books
Morton Brillant, Bookseller
313 Meeting St. #21
Charleston, SC 29401
803-722-6643
brillbooks@aol.com

**B36**
Bookcase Books
P. Gayle Hendrington
R.R. 1 Box 242
Newport, NH 03773
603-863-9517
books@bookcasebooks.com

**C1**
Camelot Books
Charles E. Wyatt
P.O. Box 2883
Vista, CA 92083
619-940-9472

**C2**
The Captain's Bookshelf, Inc.
Chandler W. Gordon
31 Page Ave.
Asheville, NC 22801
828-253-6631 or fax 828-253-4917
captsbooks@aol.com

**C3**
Cattermole
20th-C Children's Books
9880 Fairmount Rd.
Newbury, OH 44065
440-338-3253 or fax 440-338-1675
books@cattermole.com

**C4**
Bev Chaney, Jr. Books
73 Croton Ave.
Ossining, NY 10562
914-941-1002

**C5**
Chimney Sweep Books
Lillian Smith Kaiser
419 Cedar St.
Santa Cruz, CA 95060-4304
phone/fax 408-458-1044
chimney@cruzio.com

**C6**
Chapel Hill Rare Books
P.O. Box 456
Carrboro, NC 27510
919-929-8351 or fax 929-967-2532
rarebooks@mindspring.com

**C7**
Chartwell Booksellers
55 E 52nd St.
New York, NY 10055
212-308-0643

**C8**
Children's Book Adoption Agency
P.O. Box 643
Kensington, MD 20895-0643
301-565-2834 or fax 301-585-3091
KIDS_BKS@interloc.com

**C9**
Cinemage Books
105 W 27th St.
New York, NY 10001
212-243-4919
irajoel@aol.com

**C10**
Cohen Books & Collectibles
Joel J. Cohen
P.O. Box 810310
Boca Raton, FL 33481-0310
561-487-7888

**C11**
Cover to Cover
Mark Shuman
P.O. Box 687
Chapel Hill, NC 27514
919-967-1032

**C12**
Noriko I. Ciochon
Natural History Books
1025 Keokut St.
Iowa City, IA 52240
319-354-9088 or fax 319-354-0844
nathist@avalon.net

**C14**
Steven Cieluch
15 Walbridge St. Ste. #10
Allston, MA 02134-3808
617-734-7778
scieluch@channel1.com

**C15**
Thomas L. Coffman
TLC Books
9 N College Ave.
Salem, VA 24153
540-389-3555

**C16**
Cover to Cover
Meta Fouts
5499 Belfast Rd.
Batavia, OH 45103
513-625-2628 or fax 513-625-2683
METAFOUTS@aol.com

**D1**
Ursula Davidson
Children's & Illustrated Books
134 Linden Ln.
San Rafael, CA 94901
415-454-3939 or fax 415-454-1087
davidson_u@compuserve.com

**D2**
L. Clarice Davis
Fine & Applied Art Books
P.O. Box 56054
Sherman Oaks, CA 91413-1054
818-787-1322 or fax 818-780-3281
davislc@earthlink.net

**D4**
Carol Docheff, Bookseller
1390 Reliez Vly. Rd.
Lafayette, CA 94549
925-935-9595 or fax 925-256-8569
docheffc@inreach.com

**D5**
Dover Publications
Dept. A 214
E Second St.
Mineola, NY 11501

**D6**
Drusilla's Books
817 N Howard St.
Baltimore, MD 21201-4696
410-225-0277 or fax 410-321-4955
Tues-Sat: 12 to 5; or by appointment
drusilla@mindspring.com

**D7**
Duck Creek Books
Jim & Shirley Richards
P.O. Box 203
Caldwell, OH 43724
614-732-4856

**D8**
Patricia L. Daniel, Bookseller
13 English Ave.
Wichita, KS 62707-1005
316-683-2079 or fax 316-683-5448
pldaniel@Southwind.net

**D9**
Dad's Old Bookstore
Green Hills Ct.
4004 Hillsboro Rd.
Nashville, TN 37215
615-298-5880

**D10**
Tom Davidson, Bookseller
3703 Ave. L
Brooklyn, NY 11210
718-338-8428 or fax 718-338-8430
tdbooks@att.net

**D11**
Dawson's Book Shop
535 N Larchmont Blvd.
Los Angeles, CA 90004
213-469-2186 or fax 213-469-9553
dawsonbk@ix.netcom.com

**E1**
The Early West/Whodunit Books
P.O. Box 9292
College Sta., TX 77842
409-775-6047 or fax 409-764-7758
EarlyWest@aol.com

**E2**
Edison Hall Books
5 Ventnor Dr.
Edison, NJ 08820
908-548-4455

**E4**
Elder's Book Store
2115 Elliston Pl.
Nashville, TN 37203
615-327-1867

**E5**
Elegant Book & Map Company
815 Harrison Ave.
P.O. Box 1302
Cambridge, OH 43725
614-432-4068

**E6**
Eastside Books & Paper
P.O. Box 1581, Gracie Station
New York, NY 10028-0013
212-759-6299

**F1**
First Folio
Dennis R. Melhouse
1206 Brentwood
Paris, TN 38242-3804
phone/fax 910-944-9940
firstfol@aeneas.net

**F2**
Fisher Books & Antiques
345 Pine St.
Williamsport, PA 17701

**F3**
Flo Silver Books
8442 Oakwood Ct. N
Indianapolis, IN 46260
phone/fax 317-255-5118
Flosilver@aolcom

**F5**
Fran's Bookhouse
6601 Greene St.
Phil., PA 19119
215-438-2729 or fax 215-438-8997

**F6**
Fostoria Trading Post
Amelia Painter
14 Hwy. Ave. SW
P.O. Box 28
Fostoria, IA 51340
712-262-5936
books@ncn.net

**F7**
Five Quail Books — West
P.O. Box 9870
Phoenix, AZ 85068-9870
602-861-0548
5quail@grandcanyonbooks.com

**G1**
John Gach Fine & Rare Books
5620 Waterloo Rd.
Columbia, MD 21045
410-465-9023 or fax 410-465-0649
inquiry@gach.com

**G2**
Galerie De Boicourt
Eva M. Boicourt
251 E Merrill St.
Birmingham, MI 48009
248-723-5680
Tues-Sat: 10:00 am to 5:00 pm

**G3**
Gambler's Book Shop
630 S Eleventh St.
Las Vegas, NV 89101
800-634-6243

**G4**
David & Nancy Garcelon
10 Hastings Ave.
Millbury, MA 01527-4314

**G5**
Michael Gerlicher
1375 Rest Point Rd.
Orono, MN 55364

**G6**
Glo's Children's Series Books
Gloria Stobbes
906 Shadywood
Southlake, TX 76092
817-481-1438

**G7**
James Tait Goodrich
Antiquarian Books & Manuscripts
135 Tweed Blvd.
Grandview-on-Hudson, NY 10960-4913
914-359-0242 or fax 914-359-0142
jtg.jamestgoodrich.com

**G8**
Grave Matters
P.O. Box 32192-08
Cincinnati, OH 45232
513-242-7527 or fax 513-242-5115
books@gravematters.com

**G10**
Bernard E. Goodman, Bookseller
7421 SW 147 Ct.
Miami, FL 33193
305-385-8526
BCBooks@bellsouth.net

**G11**
Ron Gibson, The Bookshop
110 Windsor Cir.
Burlington, IA 52601-1477
319-752-4588

**H1**
Henry F. Hain III
Antiques & Collectibles
2623 N Second St.
Harrisburg, PA 17110
717-238-0534
antcolbks@ezonline.com

**H2**
Rick Harmon
Military Books & Relics
910 Sullivan Dr.
Belvidere, IL 61008
815-547-7580

**H3**
Terry Harper, Bookseller
P.O. Box 312
Vergennes, VT 05491-0312
802-877-9262
bookvend@together.net

**H4**
Susan Heller, Pages for Sages
22611 Halburton Rd.
Beachwood, OH 44122-3939
216-283-2665
hellersu@cyberdrive.net

**H5**
Heritage Book Shop, Inc.
8540 Melrose Ave.
Los Angeles, CA 90069
310-659-3674 or fax 310-659-4872
HBSINCLA@aol.com

**H6**
Hillcrest Books
961 Deep Draw Rd.
Crossville, TN 38555-9547
phone/fax 615-484-7680

**H7**
Jim Hodgson Books
908 S Manlius St.
Fayetteville, NY 13066
315-637-6264
jimhbooks@aol.com

**H9**
Murray Hudson
Antiquarian Books & Maps
109 S Church St.
P.O. Box 163
Halls, TN 38040
901-836-9057 or 800-748-9946
fax 901-836-9017
mapman@usit.net

**H10**
Hurley Books/Celtic Cross Books
1753 Rt. 12
Westmoreland, NH 03467-4742
603-399-4342 or fax 603-399-8326
hurleybook@adam.cheshire.net

**H11**
Ken Hebenstreit, Bookseller
813 N Washington Ave.
Royal Oak, MI 48067
phone/fax 810-548-5460
KHBooks@ibm.net

**H13**
Hartfield Rare Books
Ruth Inglehart
117 Dixboro Rd.
Ann Arbor, MI 48105
phone/fax 313-662-6035

**H14**
Ruth Heindel Associates
First Editions, Rare & Used Books
660 Boas St., Ste. 1618
Harrisburg, PA 17110
717-213-9010

**I1**
Island Books
P.O. Box 19
Old Westbury, NY 11586
516-759-0233

**J1**
Jay's House of Collectibles
75 Pky. Dr.
Syosset, NY 11791

**J2**
Jordan Gallery
1349 Sheridan Ave.
Cody, WY 82414
307-587-6689 or fax 307-527-4944
jjordan@trib.com

**J3**
Pricilla Juvelis, Inc.
1166 Massachusetts Ave.
Cambridge, MA 02138
617-497-7570 or fax 617-497-9343
pjbooks@tiac.com

**K1**
Kenneth Karmiole, Bookseller, Inc.
509 Wilshire Blvd.
Santa Monica, CA 90401
310-451-4342 or fax 310-458-5930
karmbooks@aol.com

**K2**
Ilene Kayne
1308 S Charles St.
Baltimore, MD 21230-4219
410-347-7570
kayne@clark.net

**K3**
Key Books
P.O. Box 58097
St. Petersburg, FL 33715-8097
813-867-2931

**K4**
The King's Market Bookshop
P.O. Box 709
Boulder, CO 80306-0709
303-232-3321

**K5**
Knollwood Books
Lee & Peggy Price
P.O. Box 197
Oregon, WI 53575-0197
608-835-8861 or fax 608-835-8421
books@tdsnet.com

**K6**
Kendra Krienke
230 Central Park West
New York, NY 10024
201-930-9709 or 201-930-9765

**K7**
George Robert Kane Fine Books
252 Third Ave.
Santa Cruz, CA 95062
phone/fax 408-426-4133
qkanebks@cruzio.com

**L1**
Bob Lakin Books
P.O. Box 186
Chatfield, TX 75105
972-247-3291

**L2**
Henry Lindeman
4769 Bavarian Dr.
Jackson, MI 49201
517-764-5728

**L3**
Ken Lopez, Bookseller
51 Huntington Rd.
Hadley, MA 01035
413-584-4827 or fax 413-584-2045
mail@lopezbooks.com

**L4**
W.J. Leveridge
W & L Trading Company
2301 Carova Rd.
Carova Beach, Corolla, NC 27927
252-453-3408

**M1**
M & S Rare Books, Inc.
P.O. Box 2594, E Side Station
Providence, RI 02906
401-421-1050 or fax 401-272-0831
(attention M & S)
dsiegel@msrarebooks.com

**M2**
Robert A. Madle
4406 Bestor Dr.
Rockville, MD 20853
301-460-4712

**M4**
Melvin Marcher, Bookseller
6204 N Vermont
Oklahoma City, OK 73112
405-946-6270
(12 pm to 7 pm **only**)

**M5**
Marvelous Books
Dorothy (Dede) Kern
P.O. Box 1510
Ballwin, MO 63022
314-458-3301 or fax 314-273-5452
marvbooks@aol.com

**M6**
Mason's Bookstore, Rare Books
& Record Albums East
115 S Main St.
Chambersburg, PA 17201
717-261-0541

**M7**
Denis McDonnell, Bookseller
653 Park St.
Honesdale, PA 18431
717-253-6706 or fax 717-253-6786
dmd@ptd.net

**M8**
McGowan Book Co.
P.O. Box 4226
Chapel Hill, NC 27515
919-968-1121 or fax 919-968-1644
mcgowanbooks@mindspring.com

**M9**
Paul Melzer Fine & Rare Books
12 E Vine St.
P.O. Box 1143
Redlands, CA 92373
909-792-7299 or fax 909-792-7218
pmbooks@eee.org

**M10**
Robert L. Merriam
Rare & Used Books
39 Newhall Rd.
Conway, MA 01341-9709
413-369-4052
rmerriam@interloc.com

**M11**
Meyer Boswell Books, Inc.
2141 Mission St.
San Francisco, CA 94110
415-255-6400 or fax 415-255-6499
rarelaw@myerbos.com

**M12**
Frank Mikesh
1356 Walden Rd.
Walnut Creek, CA 94596
925-934-9243 or fax 925-947-6113
natscribooks@netvista.net

**M13**
Ken Mitchell
710 Conacher Dr.
Willowdale, Ontario
Canada M2M 3N6
416-222-5808

**M14**
Modern Age Books
Jeff Canja
P.O. Box 325
E Lansing, MI 48826
517-487-9313

**M15**
Mordida Books
P.O. Box 79322
Houston, TX 77279
713-467-4280 or fax 713-467-4182
mordida@swbell.net

**M16**
The Mulberry Cat
Yvonne Davis
Jan Davis Martel
P.O. Box 3573
Boone, NC 28607
704-963-7693

**M17**
Much Ado
Seven Pleasant St.
Marblehead, MA 01945
781-639-0400 or fax 781-639-0840
muchado@shore.net

**M19**
My Book Heaven
2212 Broadway
Oakland, CA 94612
510-893-7273 or 510-521-1683
MBHR@ix.netcom.com

**M20**
My Bookhouse
27 S Sandusky St.
Tiffin, OH 44883
419-447-9842
mybooks@bright.net

**M21**
Brian McMillan, Books
1429 L Ave.
Traer, IA 50675
319-478-2360
(Mon – Sat: 9 am to 9pm)
Brianbks@netins.net

**M22**
M/S Books
53 Curtiss Rd.
New Preston, CT 06777
860-868-0627 or fax 860-868-0504

**M23**
McGee's First Varieties
330 Franklin Rd., Ste. 135A-134
Brentwood, TN 37027
615-373-5318 or fax 615-661-4047
TMcGee@BellSouth.net

**M24**
MacDonnell Rare Books
Kevin MacDonnell
9307 Glenlake Dr.
Austin, TX 78730
512-345-4139
macbooks@interloc.com

**M25**
Monroe Stahr Books
4420 Ventura Canyon, #2
Sherman Oaks, CA 91423
818-784-0870 or fax 818-995-0866
MStahrBks@aol.com

**N1**
Nerman's Books
Gary Nerman
410-63 Albert St.
Winnipeg, Manitoba
Canada R3B 1G4
204-956-1214 or 204-475-1050
fax 204-947-0753
nerman@escape.ca

**N2**
Nutmeg Books
354 New Litchfield St. (Rte. 202)
Torrington, CT 06790
203-482-9696
nutmeg@compsol.net

**N3**
Kai Nygaard
19421 Eighth Pl.
Escondido, CA 92029
619-749-9039

**N4**
Norris Books
Charles Chavdarian, Owner
2491 San Ramon Vly. Blvd.
Ste. #1-201
San Ramon, CA 94583
phone/fax 510-867-1218
norrisbooks@slip.net

**O1**
David L. O'Neal, Antiquarian
   Bookseller
234 Clarendon St.
Boston, MA 02116
617-266-5790 or fax 617-266-1089
staff@onealbooks.com

**O2**
W.B. O'Neill
Old & Rare Books
11609 Hunters Green Ct.
Reston, VA 22091
703-860-0782 or fax 703-620-0153

**O3**
October Farm
2609 Branch Rd.
Raleigh, NC 27610
919-772-0482 or fax 919-779-6265
octoberfarm@bellsouth.net

**O4**
The Old London Bookshop
Michael & Marlys Schon
P.O. Box 922
Bellingham, WA 98227-0922
360-733-7273 or fax 360-647-8946
OldLondon@aol.com

**O5**
The Old Map Gallery
Paul F. Mahoney
1746 Blake St.
Denver, CO 80202
303-296-7725 or fax 303-296-7936
oldmapgallery@denver.net

**O6**
Old Paint Lick School Antique Mall
Raymond P. Mixon
11000 Hwy. 52 West
Paint Lick, KY 40461
606-925-3000 or 606-792-3000

**O7**
Overlee Farm Books
P.O. Box 1155
Stockbridge, MA 01262
413-637-2277

**O8**
K.C. & Jean C. Owings
Box 389
Whitman, MA 02382
781-447-7850 or fax 781-447-3435

**O9**
Olde Current Books
Daniel P. Shay
356 Putnam Ave.
Ormond Beach, FL 32174
904-672-8998
peakmyster@aol.com

**O10**
Oak Knoll Books
310 Delaware St.
New Castle, DE 19720
800-996-2556 or 302-328-7232
fax 302-328-7274
oakknoll@oakknoll.com

**O11**
Orpheus Books
Don Stutheit/Barbara Wight
11522 NE 20th At.
Bellevue, WA 98004-3005
425-451-8343

**P1**
Pacific Rim Books
Michael Onorato
P.O. Box 30575
Bellingham, WA 98228-2575
206-676-0256
PACRIMBKS@AOL.COM

**P2**
Margaret E. Page
Page Books
HCR 65, Box 233
Kingston, AR 72742
870-861-5831
pagebook@eritter.net

**P3**
Pandora's Books Ltd.
P.O. Box 54
Neche, ND 58265
204-324-8548 or fax 204-324-1628
jgthiess@MTS.Net

**P4**
Parmer Books
7644 Forrestal Rd.
San Diego, CA 92120-2203
619-287-0693 or fax 619-287-6135
ParmerBook@aol.com

**P5**
Parnassus Books
218 N 9th St.
Boise, ID 83702

**P6**
Passaic Book Center
594 Main Ave.
Passaic, NJ 07055
201-778-6646 or fax 201-778-6738

**P7**
Pauper's Books
206 N Main St.
Bowling Green, OH 43402-2420
419-352-2163

**P8**
R. Plapinger, Baseball Books
P.O. Box 1062
Ashland, OR 97520
541-488-1220

**P9**
Prometheus Books
59 John Glenn Dr.
Buffalo, NY 14228-2197
716-691-0133 or fax 716-691-0137

**P11**
Pelanor Books
7 Gaskill Ave.
Albany, NY 12203

**P12**
Popek's Pages Past
Pete & Connie Popek
3870 S Hwy 23
Oneonta, NY 13820
607-432-0836
popeks@magnum.wpe.com

**P13**
Periodyssey
151 Crescent St.
Northampton, MA 01060
413-527-1900 or fax 413-527-1930
periodyssey@the-spa.com

**Q1**
Quill & Brush
Patricia & Allen Ahearn
1137 Sugarloaf Mtn. Rd.
Dickerson, MD 20842
301-874-3200 or fax 301-874-0824
Firsts@qb.com

**Q2**
Quest Books
Peter & Veronica Burridge
Harmer Hill
Millington
York YO42 1TX UK
Quesbks@aol.com

**R1**
Raintree Books
432 N Eustis St.
Eustis, FL 32726
904-357-7145

**R2**
Kathleen Rais & Co.
Rais Place Cottage
211 Carolina Ave.
Phoenixville, PA 19460
610-933-1388

**R3**
Randall House
Pia Oliver
835 Laguna St.
Santa Barbara, CA 93101
805-963-1909 or fax 805-963-1650
pia@piasworld.com

**R5**
Jo Ann Reisler, Ltd.
360 Glyndon St., NE
Vienna, VA 22180
703-938-2967 or fax 703-938-9057
Reisler@Clark.net.

**R6**
Wallace Robinson Books
RD #6, Box 574
Meadville, PA 16335
800-653-3280 or 813-823-3280
814-724-7670 or 814-333-9652

**R7**
Tom Rolls
230 S Oakland Ave.
Indianapolis, IN 46201

**R8**
RAC Books
P.O. Box 296 RD 2
Seven Valleys, PA 17360
717-428-3776
racbooks@cyberia.com

**R9**
Realm of Colorado
P.O. Box 24
Parker, CO 80134

**R10**
Roger Reus
9412 Huron Ave.
Richmond, VA 23294
(mail order only)

**R11**
Recollection Books
4519 University Way NE
Seattle, WA 98105
206-548-1346
recall@eskimo.com

**R12**
Leona Rostenberg
   & Madeleine Stern
Rare Books
40 E 88th St.
NY, NY 10128
212-831-6628 or fax 212-831-1961

**R13**
Alice Robbins, Bookseller
3002 Round Hill Rd.
Greensboro, NC 27408
910-282-1964

**R14**
Revere Books
P.O. Box 420
Revere, PA 18953-0420
610-847-2709 or fax 610-847-1910

**R15**
Richard C. Ramer
Old & Rare Books
225 E 70th St.
New York, NY 10021
212-737-0222 or 212-737-0223
fax 212-288-4169
5222386@mcimail.com

**S1**
Bill & Mimi Sachen
927 Grand Ave.
Waukegan, IL 60085-3709
847-662-7204
FutileWill@aol.com

**S2**
J. Sampson Antiques & Books
107 S Main
Harrodsburg, KY 40330
606-734-7829

**S3**
Stanley Schwartz
1934 Pentuckett Ave.
San Diego, CA 92104-5732
619-232-5888 or fax 619-233-5833
Schwartz@cts.com

**S4**
Scribe Company
Attn: Bonnie Smith
427 Hidden Forest S
Longview, TX 75605
903-663-6873

**S5**
Significant Books
3053 Madison Rd.
P.O. Box 9248
Cincinnati, OH 45209
513-321-7567

**S6**
The Silver Door
P.O. Box 3208
Redondo Beach, CA 90277
310-379-6005

**S7**
K.B. Slocum Books
P.O. Box 10998 #620
Austin, TX 78766
800-521-4451 or fax 512-258-8041

**S8**
Barbara Smith Books
P.O. Box 1185
Northampton, MA 01061
413-586-1453

**S9**
Ed Smith Books
20 Paget Rd.
Madision, WI 53704-5929
608-241-3707 or fax 608-241-3459
ed@edsbooks.com

**S12**
Sweet Memories
Sharyn Laymon
400 Mulberry St.
Loudon, TN 37774
615-458-5044

**S13**
Eileen Serxner
Box 2544
Bala Cynwyd, PA 19004
610-664-7960 or fax 610-664-1940
serxner@erols.com

**S14**
Second Harvest Books
Warren R. Johnson
P.O. Box 3306
Florence, OR 97439
phone/fax 541-902-0215
2harvest@presys.com

**S15**
Snowy Egret Books
1237 Carroll Ave.
St. Paul, MN 55104
612-641-0917
snowy@mr.net

**S16**
Stan Clark Military Books
915 Fairview Ave.
Gettysburg, PA 17325
717-337-0581
scmg@mail.wideopen.net

**S17**
David R. Smith
30 Nelson Circle
Jaffrey, NH 03452
603-532-8666
Bookinc@Cheshire.net

**S18**
Spellbound Books
M. Tyree
3818 Vickie Ct. #B
Prescott Valley, AZ 86314
520-759-2625

**T1**
Lee & Mike Temares
50 Hts. Rd.
Plandome, NY 11030
516-627-8688 or fax 516-627-7822
tembooks@aol.com

**T2**
Thomas Books
P.O. Box 14036
Phoenix, AZ 85063
602-247-9289 or fax 602-945-1023
sales@thomasbooks.com

**T4**
Trackside Books
8819 Mobud Dr.
Houston, TX 77036
713-772-8107

**T5**
Treasures From the Castle
Connie Castle
1720 N Livernois
Rochester, MI 48306
248-651-7317
treasure23@juno.com

**T6**
H.E. Turlington Books
P.O. Box 190
Carrboro, NC 27510

**T7**
J. Tuttle Maritime Books
1806 Laurel Crest
Madison, WI 53705
608-238-SAIL (7245)
fax 608-238-7249

**T8**
George H. Tweney
16660 Marine View Dr. SW
Seattle, WA 98166
206-243-8243

**T9**
Typographeum Bookshop
246 Bennington Rd.
Francestown, NH 03043
603-547-2425

**T10**
Thorn Books
P.O. Box 1244
Moorpark, CA 93020
805-529-36647 or fax 805-529-0022
thornbooks@earthlink.net

**T11**
Town's End Books
John D. & Judy A. Townsend
132 Hemlock Dr.
Deep River, CT 06417
860-526-3896
john@townsendbooks.com

**T12**
Third Time Around Books
Norman Todd
R.R. #1
Mar., Ontario
Canada N0H 1XO
519-534-1382

**T13**
Twice Read Books & Comics
42 S Main St.
Chambersburg, PA 17201
717-261-8449

**T14**
Trade Winds
John Singer
201 W 17th St.
Cheyenne, WY 82001
307-638-3400 or fax 307-638-3400

**V1**
VERSEtility Books
P.O. Box 1133
Farmington, CT 06034-1133
860-677-0606
versebks@tiac.net

**V2**
A.A. Vespa
P.O. Box 637
Park Ridge, IL 60068
708-692-4210

**V3**
Vintage Books
Nancy & David Haines
181 Hayden Rowe St.
Hopkinton, MA 01748
508-435-3499
vintage@gis.net

**V4**
Volume I Books
One Union St.
Hillsdale, MI 49242
517-437-2228 or fax 517-437-7923
volume1book@dmci.net

**W1**
Worldwide Antiquarian
P.O. Box 410391
Cambridge, MA 02141-0004
617-876-6220 or fax 617-876-0839
mbalwan@aol.com

**W2**
Warren's Collector Books
    For Sale Now
Warren Gillespie, Jr.
112 Royal Ct.
Friendswood, TX 77546
281-482-7947

**W3**
Ruth Woods Oriental Books & Art
266 Arch Rd.
Englewood, NJ 07631
201-567-0149 or fax 201-567-1419
rwoodsorientbook@mindspring.com

**W4**
Glenn Wiese
5078 Lynwood Ave.
Blasdell, NY 14219
716-821-0972

**Y1**
Yesterday's Books
229 Riverview Dr.
Parchment, MI 49004
616-345-1011
yesbooks@aol.com

**X1**
Xanadu Records, Ltd.
3242 Irwin Ave.
Kingsbridge, NY 10463
718-549-3655

# Schroeder's ANTIQUES Price Guide

. . . is the #1 best-selling antiques & collectibles value guide on the market today, and here's why . . .

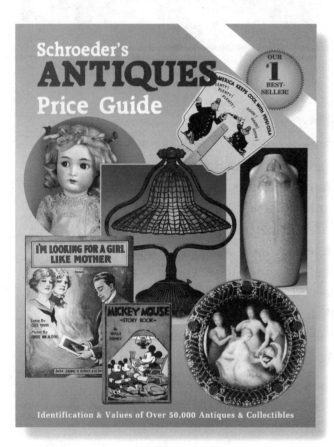

**8½ x 11, 612 Pages, $12.95**

• More than 450 advisors, well-known dealers, and top-notch collectors work together with our editors to bring you accurate information regarding pricing and identification.

• More than 45,000 items in almost 550 categories are listed along with hundreds of sharp original photos that illustrate not only the rare and unusual, but the common, popular collectibles as well.

• Each large close-up shot shows important details clearly. Every subject is represented with histories and background information, a feature not found in any of our competitors' publications.

• Our editors keep abreast of newly developing trends, often adding several new categories a year as the need arises.

If it merits the interest of today's collector, you'll find it in *Schroeder's*. And you can feel confident that the information we publish is up to date and accurate. Our advisors thoroughly check each category to spot inconsistencies, listings that may not be entirely reflective of market dealings, and lines too vague to be of merit. Only the best of the lot remains for publication.

Without doubt, you'll find
**SCHROEDER'S ANTIQUES PRICE GUIDE**
the only one to buy for
reliable information and values.

**COLLECTOR BOOKS**
*A Division of Schroeder Publishing Co., Inc.*